Michael P. Conzen
University of Chicago

Advisory Editor for Cartography

America's History

Some of the earliest known paintings of California are the works of the English journalist and artist Francis Marryat. Marryat first sailed to California in 1849 to chronicle the gold rush. He painted this view of San Francisco in 1851, less than a year after a devastating fire had leveled the city.

Marryat's view, looking east toward the Contra Costa area, shows the growing port at sunrise. People in various national costumes, including Mexicans and Chinese, reflect the international population of the settlement.

THIRD EDITION

America's History

James A. Henretta
University of Maryland

W. Elliot Brownlee
University of California, Santa Barbara

David Brody
University of California, Davis

Susan Ware

Marilynn S. Johnson
Boston College

Worth Publishers

America's History, *Third Edition*

Copyright © 1997 by Worth Publishers, Inc.

All rights reserved.

Manufactured in the United States of America

Library of Congress Catalog Card Number: 96-060600

ISBN: 1–57259–139–0

Printing: 2 3 4 5 — 01 00 99 98 97

Executive editor: Paul Shensa

Development editor: Jennifer E. Sutherland

Design: Malcolm Grear Designers

Art director: George Touloumes

Production editor: Laura Rubin

Production supervisor: Stacey B. Alexander

Layout: Fernando Quinones

Picture editor: Deborah Bull/Photosearch

Picture researcher: Joanne Polster/Photosearch

Line art: Demetrios Zangos

Cartography: Mapping Specialists, Ltd.

Composition and separations: TSI Graphics

Printing and binding: R.R. Donnelley & Sons Company

Cover: *San Francisco, July 1, 1851*, Francis Samuel
Marryat. Chromolithograph, Lithographer: M. and N. Hanhart.
Miriam & Ira D. Wallach Division of Art, Prints, and Photographs.
The New York Public Library, Astor, Lenox, and Tilden Foundations
(detail).

Illustration credits and copyright notices begin on page IC-1, and
constitute an extension of the copyright page.

Worth Publishers
33 Irving Place
New York, NY 10003

For our families

Contents in Brief

Contents

*   *   *

★   ★   ★

Chapter Features

★ ★ ★

FIGURES

Preface

★　　　　★　　　　★

We live in troubled intellectual times. Political turmoil in the academic world and in the wider culture has forced close scrutiny of established beliefs and methods. These "culture wars," as they have been called, have had a direct impact on the interpretation and teaching of history. The debate over the *National Standards for History* provided a forceful reminder that historians assume a great social responsibility when they define the content, structure, and meaning of the nation's past.

We welcome this challenge. From the very inception of *America's History*, we set out to write a *democratic* history, one that would convey the experiences of ordinary people even as it recorded the accomplishments of the great and powerful. We focused not only on the rich diversity of peoples who have become Americans but also on the institutions—political, economic, and social—that forged a common national identity. And we presented political and social history in an integrated way, using each perspective to make better sense of the other. The recent debates over the purposes and meaning of history have confirmed our belief that this is the right approach, and we have therefore continued and improved upon it.

The Third Edition of *America's History* remains committed to presenting a balanced and comprehensive narrative of our nation's past. In our discussion of government and politics, diplomacy and war, we show how they affected—and were affected by—ethnic groups and economic conditions, intellectual beliefs and social changes, and the religious and moral values of the times. Just as important, we place the American experience in a global context. We trace aspects of American society to their origins in European and African cultures, consider the American Industrial Revolution from the perspective of the world economy, and plot the foreign relations of the United States as part of an ever-shifting international system of imperial expansion, financial exchange, and diplomatic alliances.

Organization

As historians explore ever more diverse aspects of the American experience, the need to organize this disparate material for the student becomes more and more imperative. We have therefore given *America's History* a clear chronology and a strong conceptual framework. Each half of the nation's history is divided into three Parts, with each Part corresponding to a distinct phase of development. Each Part begins at a crucial turning point, such as the American Revolution or the Cold War, and emphasizes the dynamic forces that it unleashed and that symbolized the era. To aid student comprehension, each Part begins with a two-page overview: first, a **Thematic Timeline** highlights the key developments in government, the economy, society, culture, and foreign affairs; then these themes are summarized in a brief **Part essay**. Each Part essay focuses on the crucial engines of historical change—in some eras primarily economic, in others political or diplomatic—that created new conditions of life and transformed social relations. The essays and the Part organization help students understand the major themes and periods of American history, to see that bits and pieces of historical data acquire significance as part of a larger pattern of development.

In telling this complex story, we give equal attention to historical actors and to historical institutions, customs, and forces—writing what the historian Lawrence Stone has called "the new narrative history." At the center of our narrative are the actions of individual Americans: we show how people of all classes and groups make their own history. But we also make clear how people's choices are influenced and constrained by circumstances: the customs and institutions inherited from the past and the distribution of power in the present. Such a presentation not only conveys the diversity of the American experience but also helps students un-

derstand their own potential for purposeful action as responsible citizens.

Changes in the Third Edition

Those acquainted with the Second Edition will find much that is familiar and many changes as well. The most important change is the addition of a new author, Professor Marilynn S. Johnson of Boston College. The author of the prize-winning monograph, *The Second Gold Rush: Oakland and the East Bay in World War II*, Dr. Johnson now shares with Susan Ware the major responsibility for twentieth-century America and has used her specialized knowledge to augment our treatment of California and the western United States.

Other changes have resulted from the extraordinarily helpful suggestions of instructors who have used *America's History*. Responding to their concerns, we have made major changes in many chapters. Chapters 13 and 14, on antebellum society and politics, have been significantly reorganized to provide a much stronger chronological emphasis. Chapter 17 has been extensively revised to show more clearly the differing patterns of settlement on the Great Plains and in the Far West. The three chapters devoted to the pivotal 1960–1980 period have been substantially rewritten and reorganized. Chapter 30, "The Ascent of Liberalism," integrates the stories of the civil rights movement and domestic politics in the 1960s. Chapter 31, "The Vietnam Experience," brings together the entire history of the war in a single chapter. Chapter 32, "The Lean Years," presents the social and economic changes and national politics of the 1970s. In addition, Chapter 33 has been significantly revised and updated to provide an integrated analysis of domestic and global changes and trends in the 1980s and 1990s.

Reflecting newly published scholarship, we have significantly revised many sections of the text. We have expanded our treatment of African and native American peoples in the seventeenth and eighteenth centuries and of free African-Americans in the nineteenth century. Reflecting recent work on gender, we have sharpened our analysis of men's as well as women's lives. We have drawn on the new western history to enrich the coverage of Spanish- and English-speaking settlers in Texas and the Southwest in the nineteenth century. We tell the story of cultural interaction in the West from the perspective of all participants—the resident native Americans as well as incoming groups: Mormons, miners, ranchers, and farm families. Our analysis of late nineteenth-century politics incorporates recent scholarship on the New South, while the chapter on the city includes new materials on popular culture and sexuality.

In the twentieth century we have included additional coverage of Mexican-American workers during the Great Depression, new insights on the cold war era based on Soviet archives, and an expanded discussion of cultural dissent in the United States during those years. Drawing on yet another emergent field of scholarship, the Third Edition of *America's History* incorporates more material on the role of the state throughout American history, including recent challenges by Christian groups and New Right activists to the system of national government created during and after the New Deal.

Features

The Third Edition of *America's History* contains a wealth of special features, all closely tied to the main text. We have expanded our much-hailed **American Lives** feature so that every chapter now includes an incisive biography of an important individual or group. Among the new Lives are studies of the seventeenth-century Powhatan chief Opechancanough, social reformer Dorothea Dix, Civil War general William T. Sherman, newspaper mogul William Randolph Hearst, rock music idol Elvis Presley, environmental activist Lois Marie Gibbs, and Bill Gates, the founder of Microsoft.

We have also expanded our coverage of the lives of ordinary Americans and, to make their presence more vivid in the historical record, we have refined our **American Voices** feature. Each chapter contains two or three contemporary first-person accounts from the letters, diaries, autobiographies, and public testimony of ordinary Americans that paint a vivid portrait of the social or political life of the time. Finally, recognizing the challenge of technological change in the present, we have deepened our discussion of **New Technology** in the past; major essays focus on the technical aspects of innovations and how they affected everyday life. Taken together, these documents and essays provide instructors with a range of teaching materials and assist students to enter the life of the past and see it from within.

At the beginning of each chapter, we have added a brief **outline** to provide students with an overview of the main themes. Then, at the end of the chapter, we reiterate the themes in an analytic **Summary** and remind students of important events in an expanded **Timeline**. The annotated **Bibliography** that follows every chapter now begins with a general section containing two or three books of general interest or particular importance.

We have improved and expanded our illustration program. Professor Michael R. Conzen, our advisory editor for cartography, has prepared a dozen entirely new maps, including detailed treatments of Africa during the

era of the Atlantic slave trade, New Spain's northern borderland empire in the late eighteenth century, and the military-industrial complex in Los Angeles during the Cold War. In addition, each chapter includes around fifteen photographs, carefully selected to enhance a particular aspect of the text. To help students understand and remember complicated sequences of events we have added new tables listing, for example, the key legislation of the Reconstruction Era and the major initiatives of President Johnson's Great Society program.

Supplements

Student Guide

by Stephen J. Kneeshaw (College of the Ozarks), Timothy R. Mahoney (University of Nebraska, Lincoln), Linda Moore (Eastern New Mexico University), Thomas R. Frazier (Baruch College, emeritus), and Barbara M. Posadas (Northern Illinois University)

The *Student Guide* is designed to help students improve their performance in the course. Not only will their comprehension of the textbook and their confidence in their abilities be advanced through its conscientious use, but they will develop better learning skills and study habits. The guide begins with an introduction by Gerald J. Goodwin (University of Houston) on how to study history. Each chapter includes a summary of the essential facts and ideas of the text chapter, with fill-in questions; the timeline from the textbook with short explanations of the significance of each event; a glossary; skill-building exercises based on a map, table, or figure from the textbook; exercises for the American Voices documents and the American Lives and New Technology essays; and a self-test.

Instructor's Resource Manual

by Timothy R. Mahoney (University of Nebraska, Lincoln), Linda Moore (Eastern New Mexico University), Thomas R. Frazier (Baruch College, emeritus), and Stephen J. Kneeshaw (College of the Ozarks)

The *Instructor's Resource Manual* contains an abundance of materials to aid instructors in planning the course and enhancing student involvement. For each chapter of the textbook the resources include chapter themes, a brief summary, the timeline from the textbook with additional details, lecture suggestions, class discussions starters, topics for writing assignments, and topics for research. In addition, the manual includes fifteen his-

toriographic essays on a variety of topics by outstanding scholars in these fields. For courses with a topical focus, special documents sets (modules) are provided for constitutional, southern, and diplomatic history, as well as the history of African-Americans, Latinos, native Americans, and women. The *Instructors Resource Manual* also includes a guide to writing about history by Gerald J. Goodwin, a guide to the use of computers and the Internet in teaching history by James B. M. Schick (Pittsburg State University), and a film and video guide by Stephen J. Kneeshaw.

Test Bank

by Thomas L. Altherr and Adolph Grundman (Metropolitan State College of Denver), and James Miller

The test bank provides 120 to 150 questions for each chapter, including multiple-choice questions, fill-ins, map questions, and short and long essay questions. Computerized test-generation systems are also available for IBM-compatible and Macintosh platforms.

Documents Collection

by Cathy Matson (University of Delaware), John K. Alexander (University of Cincinnati), Louis S. Gerteis (University of Missouri, St. Louis), Douglas Bukowski, and Stephen J. Kneeshaw (College of the Ozarks)

The *Documents Collection*, containing approximately 330 key documents, is packaged with the textbook (if required) or available separately. Each document is preceded by a brief introduction and followed by questions to help students understand its context and significance.

Transparencies

A set of 110 full-color acetate transparencies reproduces maps, figures, and fine art from the textbook, along with teaching suggestions.

Lecture Presentation CD-ROM Archive

New for the Third Edition, the presentation CD-ROM software will make it easy for instructors to include multimedia in classroom lectures. The disk, available in Mac and Windows formats, includes electronic lecture outlines and digital images of maps, figures, and fine art from the textbook.

Acknowledgments

We are extremely grateful to the many scholars and teachers who reported on their experiences with the Second Edition or reviewed manuscript chapters of the Third Edition. Their comments often challenged us to rethink or justify our interpretations and always provided a check on accuracy down to the smallest detail.

John K. Alexander, University of Cincinnati

Paula Baker, University of Pittsburgh

Richard Baquera, El Paso Community College

Michael C. Batinski, Southern Illinois University

Roger Biles, East Carolina University

Frederick Blue, Youngstown State University

Nancy H. Bowen, Del Mar College

Dickson D. Bruce, Jr., University of California, Irvine

Jane Turner Censer, George Mason University

Jonathan M. Chu, University of Massachusetts–Boston

Doug Clark, Linn-Benton Community College

Cheryl Ann Cody, Houston Community College

Martin B. Cohen, George Mason University

Richard S. Cramer, San Jose State University

George Daniels, University of South Alabama

Ronald L. F. Davis, California State University, Northridge

William Deverell, California Institute of Technology

Thomas Dublin, Binghamton University

Melvyn Dubofsky, Binghamton University

Keith Edgerton, Montana State University–Billings

Aaron S. Fogelman, University of South Alabama

Dr. Patrick Foley, Editor, *Catholic Southwest: A Journal of History and Culture*

Mario T. Garcia, University of California, Santa Barbara

Louis S. Gerteis, University of Missouri–St. Louis

Paul A. Gilje, University of Oklahoma

Thavolia Glymph, Pennsylvania State University

Esther S. Goldberg, Las Positas College–Livermore

Janettte Thomas Greenwood, Clark University

Adolph H. Grundman, Metropolitan State College of Denver

Linda Dudik Guerrero, Palomar College

Stephen Haar, Texas Technical University

Leslie Harris, Emory University

Robert L. Harris, Jr., Africana Studies and Research Center, Cornell University

Benjamin T. Harrison, University of Louisville

Herman M. Hattaway, University of Missouri–Kansas City

Colette A. Hyman, Winona State University

Joy E. Ingram, Pellissippi State Technical Community College

Frederic Cople Jaher, University of Illinois, Champaign-Urbana

Elizabeth Jameson, University of New Mexico

John Jameson, Kent State University

Robert David Johnson, Williams College

Howard Jones, University of Alabama

K. Austin Kerr, Ohio State University

Tracy K'Meyer, University of Louisville

Thomas J. Knock, Southern Methodist University

William J. Gilmore-Lehne, Richard Stockton College

Cathy Matson, University of Delaware

George S. McCowen, Williamette University

Dr. Lee Augustus McGriggs

Robert C. McMath, Jr., Georgia Institute of Technology

Samuel T. McSeveney, Vanderbilt University

María E. Montoya, University of Michigan

Linda Ann Moore, Eastern New Mexico University

John S. Nader, State University of New York at Delhi

Benjamin H. Newcomb, Texas Technical University

Rich Newman, State University of New York at Buffalo

Margaret E. Newell, Ohio State University

Gregory H. Nobles, Georgia Institute of Technology

David M. Pletcher, Indiana University

Leonard Riforgiato, Pennsylvania State University, Shenango Campus

Glenda Riley, Ball State University

Leanne Sander, University of Colorado

David F. Schmitz, Whitman College

Bruce J. Schulman, Boston University

Nancy Shoemaker, University of Wisconsin–Eau Claire

Barbara Warnick Silberman, Germantown
Historical Society

Kathryn Kish Sklar, Binghamton University

Melvin Small, Wayne State University

Judith M. Stanley, California State University,
Hayward

Marshall F. Stevenson, Jr., Ohio State University

Melvin I. Urofsky, Virginia Commonwealth
University

Susan Williams, Fitchburg State College

Laga Van Beek, Brigham Young University

Robert M. Weir, University of South Carolina

Laura Matysek Wood, Tarrant County Junior
College, Northwest

Randall Bennett Woods, University of Arkansas

Peter M. Wright, Oklahoma City Community
College

Mitch Yamasaki, Chaminade University of
Honolulu

As the authors of *America's History*, we know better
than anyone else just how much of this book is the
work of other hands and minds. We are grateful to R.
Jackson Wilson, who conceived the intellectual scaf-
folding of the project, and to David Follmer, who in
various guises as our editor, publisher, and agent, has
helped us to create it. We are equally appreciative of the
assistance provided by three very special people at
Worth Publishers: Bob Worth gave us the resources and
the incentive to develop the full potential of *America's
History*. Paul Shensa provided us with constant stimulation and extraordinarily helpful advice. And Jennifer
Sutherland held us to the highest scholarly standards as
she masterfully edited our text.

Special thanks are also due to many other individuals: Deborah Bull and the staff of Photosearch; the fine
assistant editors who worked closely with us on the
Third Edition—Jeannine Ciliotta, Phyllis Fisher, Barbara Gerr, and Debra Osnowitz; our project editor,
Laura Rubin; and the Worth production and editorial
staffs: Stacey Alexander, George Touloumes, Demetrios
Zangos, Brad A. Fox, and Yuna Lee.

We also want to express our thanks for the valuable
research assistance provided by Andrew Laas, University of Maryland, Amy Richter of New York University,
and Beverly Bastian and Michael Adamson of the University of California, Santa Barbara.

From the very beginning we have considered this
book as a joint intellectual venture and with each edition our collaborative effort has grown. We are proud
to acknowledge our collective authorship of *America's
History*.

James A. Henretta
W. Elliot Brownlee
David Brody
Susan Ware
Marilynn S. Johnson

About the Authors

★   ★   ★

James A. Henretta is Priscilla Alden Burke Professor of American History at the University of Maryland, College Park. He received his undergraduate education at Swarthmore College and his Ph.D. from Harvard University. He has taught at the University of Sussex, England; Princeton University; UCLA; Boston University; as a Fulbright lecturer in Australia at the University of New England; and in 1991–92 at Oxford University as the Harmsworth Professor of American History. His publications include *The Evolution of American Society, 1700– 1815: An Interdisciplinary Analysis*; *"Salutary Neglect": Colonial Administration under the Duke of Newcastle*; *Evolution and Revolution: American Society, 1600–1820*; *The Origins of American Capitalism*; and important articles in early American and social history. He recently completed a fellowship at the Woodrow Wilson Center working on a study of *The Transformation of the Liberal State in America, 1800–1970*.

W. Elliot Brownlee is Professor of History at the University of California, Santa Barbara. He is a graduate of Harvard University, received his Ph.D. from the University of Wisconsin, Madison, and specializes in U.S. economic history. He has been awarded fellowships by the Charles Warren Center, Harvard University, and the Woodrow Wilson International Center for Scholars. He has been a visiting professor at Princeton and was Bicentennial Lecturer at the U.S. Department of the Treasury. His published works include *Dynamics of Ascent: A History of the American Economy*; *Progressivism and Economic Growth: The Wisconsin Income Tax, 1911–1929*; *Women in the American Economy: A Documentary History, 1675–1929* (with Mary M. Brownlee); *The Essentials of American History* (with Richard N. Current, T. Harry Williams, and Frank Freidel); *Funding the Modern American State: The Rise and Fall of the Era of Easy Finance, 1945–1995*; and *Federal Taxation in America: A Short History*.

David Brody is Professor Emeritus of History at the University of California, Davis. He received his B.A., M.A., and Ph.D. from Harvard University. He has taught at the University of Warwick in England, at Moscow State University in the former Soviet Union, and at Sydney University in Australia. He is the author of *Steelworkers in America*; *Workers in Industrial America: Essays on the 20th Century Struggle*; and *In Labor's Cause: Main Themes on the History of the American Worker*. He has been awarded fellowships from the Social Science Research Council, the Guggenheim Foundation, and the National Endowment for the Humanities. He is past president (1991–92) of the Pacific Coast Branch of the American Historical Association. His current research is on industrial labor during the Great Depression.

Susan Ware specializes in twentieth-century U.S. history and the history of American women. From 1986 to 1995 she taught at New York University and is now an independent scholar based in Cambridge, Massachusetts. She received her undergraduate degree from Wellesley College and her Ph.D. from Harvard University. Ware is the author of *Beyond Suffrage: Women in the New Deal*; *Holding Their Own: American Women in the 1930s*; *Partner and I: Molly Dewson, Feminism, and New Deal Politics*; *Modern American Women: A Documentary History*; and *Still Missing: Amelia Earhart and the Search for Modern Feminism*. She serves on the national advisory boards of the Franklin and Eleanor Roosevelt Institute and the Schlesinger Library of Radcliffe College and has been a historical consultant to numerous documentary film projects.

Marilynn S. Johnson is Assistant Professor of History at Boston College, where she teaches American urban and social history. She received her B.A. degree from Stanford University and her M.A. and Ph.D. from New York University. She is the author of *The Second Gold Rush: Oakland and the East Bay in World War II* and is currently working on a study of urban police violence in the late nineteenth and twentieth centuries. Her articles and reviews have appeared in *Pacific Historical Review, Journal of American History, Journal of Urban History*, and *Labor History*. She recently served on the editorial board of *Pacific Historical Review*.

America's History

P A R T *1*

The Creation of American Society

1450–1775

THEMATIC TIMELINE

	Economy	Society	Government	Religion	Culture
	From Staple Crops to Internal Growth	**Ethnic, Racial, and Class Divisions**	**From Monarchy to Republic**	**From Hierarchy to Pluralism**	**The Creation of American Identity**
1450	Native American subsistence economy Europeans fish off North American coast	Sporadic warfare among Indian peoples Spanish conquest of Mexico, 1519–21	Rise of monarchical nation-states in Europe	Protestant Reformation, 1517	
1600	First staple crops: furs and tobacco	English-Indian warfare African servitude begins in Virginia, 1619	James I rules by "divine right" Virginia House of Burgesses, 1619	Persecuted English Puritans and Catholics migrate to America	Puritans implant Calvinism, education, and freehold ideal
1640	New England trade with sugar islands Mercantilist regulations: first Navigation Act, 1651	White indentured servitude in Chesapeake Indians retreat inland	Puritan Revolution Stuart restoration, 1660 Bacon's rebellion, 1675	Religious liberty in Rhode Island	Aristocratic aspirations in Chesapeake
1680	Tobacco trade stagnates Rice cultivation expands	Indian slavery in Carolinas Ethnic rebellion in New York, 1689	Dominion of New England, 1686–89 Glorious Revolution	Rise of toleration	Emergence of African-American language and culture
1720	Mature subsistence economy in North Imports from Britain increase	Scots-Irish and German migration Growing rural inequality	Rise of the assembly Challenge to "deferential" policies	German and Scots-Irish Pietists in mid-Atlantic region Great Awakening	Expansion of colleges, newspapers, and magazines Franklin and the American Enlightenment
1760	Trade boycotts encourage domestic manufacturing	Uprisings by tenants and backcountry farmers Artisan protests	Ideas of popular sovereignty Battles of Lexington and Concord, 1775	Evangelical Baptists Quebec Act allows Catholicism, 1774	Sense of "American" identity Innovations in political theory

Societies are made, not born. They are the creation of decades, even centuries, of human endeavor and experience. America is no exception to this rule. The first Americans were hunting and gathering peoples who migrated to the Western Hemisphere from Asia many centuries ago. Over many generations these migrants—the native Americans—came to live in a wide variety of societies. In much of North America they developed kin-based cultures that relied on farming and hunting. But in the lower Mississippi region a hierarchical society that was influenced by the great Indian civilizations of Mesoamerica emerged and then slowly declined. The coming of Europeans tore the fabric of native American life into shreds. Native Americans increasingly confronted a *new* American society, one dominated by men and women of European origin.

The Europeans who settled America sought to transplant their traditional societies to the New World—their farming practices, their social hierarchies, their culture, and their religious ideas. But in learning to live in the new land, the Europeans who came to England's North American colonies created distinctly new societies.

First, many settlers compiled an impressive record of economic achievement. Traditional Europe was made up of poor and unequal societies racked by periodic famine. But in the bountiful natural environment of North America, plenty replaced poverty, and the settlers created a bustling economy and prosperous communities of independent farm families. Indeed, the northern mainland colonies became the "best poor man's country" for migrants from the British Isles and Germany.

Second, the new society became a place of oppressive captivity for Africans. Tens of thousands of Africans, from many peoples, were transported to America in chains to labor as slaves on tobacco and rice plantations. Slowly and with great effort, they and their descendants created an African-American culture within a social order dominated by Europeans.

Third, whites in the emerging American societies created an increasingly free and competitive political system. The first English settlers transplanted authoritarian institutions, and the English government sought to manage their lives. But after 1689 traditional controls gradually gave way to governments based in part on representative assemblies. Eventually, the growth of self-rule led to demands for political independence and government based on the sovereignty of the people.

Fourth, the American experience profoundly changed religious institutions and values. Many migrants came to America in search of the right to practice their religion, and the society they created became increasingly religious, especially after 1740. But many Americans rejected the harshest Calvinist beliefs, while others embraced the rationalist view of the European Enlightenment. As a result, American Protestant Christianity became increasingly tolerant, democratic, and optimistic.

Fifth, the new American society was marked by change in the family and the local community. The first English settlers lived in patriarchal families in which the father exercised supreme authority. Their close-knit communities were strictly ruled by religious leaders or men of high status. By 1750, however, many American fathers no longer tightly controlled their children's lives and lived in more diverse and open communities. Many men—and some women—began to enjoy greater personal independence.

Sixth, the new American society was increasingly pluralistic, composed of migrants from varied backgrounds: English, Scots, Scots-Irish, Dutch, Germans, and West Africans as well as many native American peoples. Regional cultures developed in New England, the mid-Atlantic colonies, and the Chesapeake and Carolina areas. An American identity—based on the English language, British legal and political institutions, and shared experiences—emerged only slowly.

The story of the colonial experience is thus both tragic and exciting. The settlers created a new American world but one that warred with native Americans and condemned most African-Americans to bondage even as it offered Europeans rich opportunities for economic security, political freedom, and spiritual fulfillment.

An Indian View of the Spanish Conquest

Spear-throwing Aztec warriors confront armored Spanish soldiers during the battle for Tenochtitlán.

CHAPTER 1

Worlds Collide: Europe and America

1450–1630

★   ★   ★

The United States had its origins in two great historical events—first, the settlement of the Western Hemisphere over thousands of years by various native American peoples and, second, the emergence of a dynamic commercial sector in the traditional agricultural society of Western Europe. Beginning in 1492, these stories fused into a single historical drama that changed the course of world history. The subsequent arrival in the Western Hemisphere of enslaved Africans—in Brazil and the West Indies after 1550 and in North America after 1600—added another dimension to the unfolding drama (see Chapter 3).

Originally migrants from northern Asia, the native Americans were isolated from the rest of the human race for over 12,000 years. Over the course of 400 generations their numbers grew from tens of thousands to tens of millions, and they divided into scores of language groups and hundreds of distinct societies, each with its own culture. By A.D. 1450 some native American peoples were living under vast empires, but many more resided in smaller agricultural societies in which kinship and community formed the primary bonds of government.

Across the Atlantic Ocean, most people in Europe lived in agricultural communities. A small class of armed aristocrats, the feudal nobility, ruled over a mass of illiterate peasants. Except for the city-states of Italy, which had established themselves as centers of trade, European society had little potential for sustained economic growth or expansion into foreign lands. During this period it was the Muslim peoples of the Mediterranean region who controlled the trade among Europe, Asia, and Africa and who led the world in scholarship.

By 1630 all this had changed, in no small measure because of the penetration of Portuguese and Dutch merchants into the trade of Asia and that of Spanish adventurers into the lands of the Western Hemisphere.

The Age of Exploration fueled economic activity in Europe and created prosperity for the upper and middling classes.

For native Americans, European expansion proved to be a tragedy. At first they had to confront military adventurers who came to plunder their wealth and exploit their natural resources. Later, as the pace of change quickened in Europe, as peasants were forced off their land and religious dissenters were persecuted, Indian peoples had to face thousands of Europeans migrating to the Western Hemisphere. The contest was never an equal one, primarily because of the devastating impact of European diseases, so many native American peoples found that their very existence was at risk.

How did Europeans come to replace Arabs as the leaders in world trade and extend their influence across the Atlantic? What made native Americans vulnerable to conquest by Spanish adventurers? How did England, a small and insignificant nation in 1492, acquire the political will and economic resources to establish colonies in the Western Hemisphere? And what led to the transatlantic trade in enslaved Africans? In the answers to these questions lie the origins of the United States.

Native American Worlds

When the Europeans arrived, at least 40 million native Americans were living in the Western Hemisphere in environments as cold as the Arctic and as lush as the tropics. Many North American Indians lived in decentralized hunter-gatherer or kinship-based agricultural societies, but some lived in richer and more complex communities. And in Mesoamerica (present-day Mexico and Guatemala) and Peru some of them had created brilliant civilizations whose art, religion, social structure, and economic practices were as complex as those of Europe and the Mediterranean.

The First Americans

The first people to live in the Western Hemisphere were large family-based groups of hunter-gatherers who migrated from northeastern Asia during the last great Ice Age, which began about 30,000 B.C. and ended about 12,000 B.C. They traveled from Siberia to Alaska, both of which consisted of ice-free tundra, across a land bridge formed when glaciation lowered the sea level and exposed dry land at the Bering Strait. These first "migrants" were not consciously migrating at all but were following herds of caribou and other wild game. Archeological evidence suggests that this haphazard peopling of the American continents continued in successive waves for thousands of years, until the glaciers melted

and the rising ocean waters submerged the land bridge. The people of the Western Hemisphere were then cut off from the rest of the world and would remain so for 400 generations.

Following wild herds and looking for edible plants and fresh water, some of the earliest Americans moved eastward. Crossing the northern Rocky Mountains, they probably traversed an ice-free corridor along the eastern side of the mountains from present-day Alaska to Montana, a land where game animals, nuts, berries, and nutritious grasses were abundant. Over the generations in which the corridor remained free of glaciers, they moved south and then spread out in all directions. By 8000 B.C., when the glaciers finally retreated, groups of hunter-gatherers were already established throughout the hemisphere, from the tip of South America to the Atlantic coast of North America. For another 3,000 years these first Americans subsisted as foragers, living off the wildlife and vegetation they found.

About 5000 B.C. some native American peoples began to develop horticulture—most notably in present-day Mexico. They planted avocado, chili peppers, and cotton; most important, they discovered how to breed maize, or Indian corn, either from a wild grass (teocentli) or from a now-extinct wild maize, creating an ear of grain about the size of an acorn. Over the next 3,000 years they bred this grain into Indian corn, a much larger, extremely nutritious plant that was a good deal hardier than wheat or barley, the staple cereals of Europe and Asia, and had more varieties and a higher

Gold Piece from Peru
Skilled Inca artisans created gold jewelry of striking beauty. Note the intricate detail on the headdress and the stylized treatment of the face.

yield per acre. They also learned to cultivate beans and squash and to plant them together with corn. Since the beans preserved the fertility of the soil by restoring its nitrogen, this trio of vegetables allowed intensive farming and high yields; equally important, it provided a balanced diet rich in calories and essential amino acids. Cultivation of these crops thus provided an agricultural surplus, laying the economic foundation for a settled society and a complex civilization with a population of many millions.

The Maya and the Aztecs

By 100 B.C. the people of Teotihuacán in the central highland valley of present-day Mexico and the Maya in the Yucatan Peninsula and the rain forests of Guatemala had begun to develop sophisticated cultures that would remain vital for a thousand years. Both of these civilizations drew on the culture of the earlier Olmec peoples, who beginning about 1200 B.C. created substantial ceremonial centers in the lowland tropical forests along the Gulf of Mexico. These centers contained colossal stone heads, probably portraits of Olmec rulers, and intricate jade carvings, probably representing their deities, especially the *were-jaguar*, which merged the features of a snarling jaguar and those of a crying human infant.

Around A.D. 300, the Maya began building large religious centers in the rain forests where the flat Yucatan Peninsula rises gradually to the highlands of present-day Guatemala. These were urban communities with elaborate systems of water storage and irrigation. Tikal, one of the largest, had at least 20,000 inhabitants, mostly farmers who worked nearby fields and whose labor was used to build huge stone temples. An elite class that claimed descent from the gods ruled Mayan society, living in splendor on goods and taxes extracted from peasant families. Skilled artisans decorated temples and palaces with magnificent friezes and paintings that often depicted warrior gods and complex rituals. Mayan astronomers developed a complex and precise calendar that recorded historical events and predicted eclipses of the sun and the moon with remarkable accuracy centuries in advance of their occurrence. Most fascinating of all, perhaps, was Mayan hieroglyphic writing, which recorded the royal lineage of the various city-states and noteworthy events, including warfare conducted primarily for taking captives of high status.

Beginning around A.D. 800, Mayan civilization fell into decline for reasons that are still debated. Recent research suggests that a two-century-long dry period caused a significant decline in the population. Faced with ever-increasing burdens imposed on them by the ruling elite, the remaining farmers probably deserted the temple cities and set up small agricultural communi-

Chacmool Statue
Striking statues of a reclining man, called Chacmools, were prominent features of many Mayan temples. Priests placed sacrifices and gifts to the gods on the Chacmools' flat stomachs.

ties in the countryside. Whatever the cause, by A.D. 900 many cities had been abandoned and ritually desecrated, with their monuments mutilated, and had begun to revert to tropical forest.

Teotihuacán and Tula. The other major native American civilization developed in the highlands, centered on the city of Teotihuacán in the central Valley of Mexico. The city, a center of trade between the highland and lowland regions, spread over 8 square miles. At its zenith about A.D. 500, it had more than 100 temples, at least 4,000 apartment buildings, and a population of at least 100,000. It also boasted the Pyramid of the Sun, a huge religious monument that was as large at its base as the great pyramid of Cheops in Egypt.

The Teotihuacán people were headed by an elite of religious leaders, bureaucrats, and military officials who ruled over a vast assemblage of farmers and a variety of artisans. The farmers were agricultural innovators, developing a cultivation system known as *chinampas*— small, intensively cultivated islands that were constructed on a network of natural and artificial lakes. Teotihuacán artisans were no less inventive, working in stone, pottery, cloth, leather, and especially obsidian (hard volcanic glass used for sharp-edged weapons and tools). Teotihuacán had declined by A.D. 700, probably because of a long-term drop in rainfall and persistent invasions by seminomadic peoples, who burned and destroyed many parts of the city. Eventually the militant Toltecs from the deserts of northern Mexico took control of the region, absorbed its culture, and created a

great empire. The Toltecs built their capital at the ancient religious site of Tula, northwest of Teotihuacán, and adopted Quetzalcoatl, the feathered serpent, as their major deity. Tula in its turn was captured in A.D. 1168 by other warrior tribes.

The Aztecs. The last great expression of the Teotihuacán civilization was the Aztec empire. The Aztecs entered the Valley of Mexico from the north toward the end of the twelfth century and attempted to settle among the surviving Toltecs. After being rebuffed, they finally found an unoccupied island in the middle of Lake Texcoco. There, about A.D. 1325, they built a new capital, Tenochtitlán (present-day Mexico City), just 30 miles south of Teotihuacán. Like the Toltecs before them, they learned the settled ways of the resident peoples and mastered their complex irrigation systems. However, they remained an aggressive tribe. Inspired by the sun god, Huitzilopochtli, who was also their god of war, they eventually subjugated the entire central Valley of Mexico.

The Aztecs established a hierarchical society dominated by a celibate priesthood and a warrior noble caste whose members married exclusively among themselves. The priests incorporated the were-jaguar god of the earlier Olmec culture into their religion, along with Quetzalcoatl from the Toltecs. Nobles and priests ruled over twenty clans of free commoners, who farmed communally owned land, as well as huge numbers of slaves and serfs, who worked the private estates of the nobility. Aztec merchants, organized in a hereditary guild (*pochteca*), created trading routes throughout the highland regions and imported furs, gold, textiles, food, and obsidian, while Aztec warriors used brute military force to extend the bounds of the empire. Aztec rulers demanded both economic and human tribute from scores of subject tribes, gruesomely sacrificing untold thousands of men and women to Huitzilopochtli; they feared that without these human sacrifices the sun would cease its daily journey across the sky. By A.D. 1500 Tenochtitlán had grown into a great metropolis with splendid palaces and temples and over 200,000 inhabitants, a monument to centuries of agricultural ingenuity and to the skills of its Aztec rulers.

The Indians of North America

In A.D. 1500, as many as 10 million native Americans were living north of the Rio Grande, in habitats as diverse as the dry lands of the Southwest and the heavily forested lands east of the Mississippi River (see Map 1.1). Like the Mesoamericans, these peoples were descendants of the hunter-gatherers who had crossed the land bridge from Asia—an epic journey that was kept alive from one generation to the next in stories and leg-

ends. A tale of the Tuscarora Indians, who occupied the area of present-day North Carolina, tells of a famine in the old world and a journey over ice toward where "the sun rises," a long trek that finally brought their ancestors to a lush forest with abundant food and game, where they settled.

The Hopewell Culture. Over the centuries, some peoples who lived in the eastern woodlands of North America developed more complex cultures as they domesticated various wild plants, increasing the food supply and promoting the growth of a larger, more sedentary population (see New Technology, page 8). Cultivating small gourds, sunflowers, and small grains and constructing numerous burial mounds, the Adena peoples flourished in southern Ohio and the neighboring regions by 700 B.C. Around A.D. 100 an even more vigorous Hopewell culture spread its influence through trade over the entire Mississippi Valley from Wisconsin to Louisiana. The Hopewell people built large burial mounds that were 30 feet high and 90 feet across at the base, often surrounding them with extensive circular, rectangular, or octagonal earthworks up to 1,500 feet in diameter. They buried their dead with elaborate artifacts: copper beaten into elaborate designs, crystals of quartz, mica cut into the shape of serpents and human hands, and stone pipes carved in the images of frogs, hawks, bears, and other animals. For unknown reasons, the elaborate Hopewell trading network, which stretched from Wyoming to Ontario to the Gulf coast, gradually collapsed around A.D. 400.

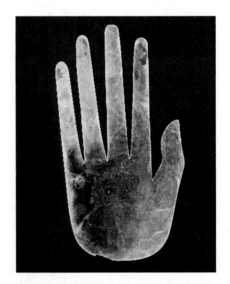

Hopewell Art
The Hopewell people had a rich artistic tradition. Carved objects, such as this elegant (and strikingly modern) mica hand, were commonly placed in burial mounds as gifts to the spirits of the dead.

MAP 1.1

Native American Peoples, 1492

Native Americans populated the entire Western Hemisphere at the time of Columbus's arrival, having learned how to live in many environments. They created diverse cultures that ranged from the centralized agriculture-based empires of the Maya and the Aztecs to seminomadic tribes of hunter-gatherers. The sheer diversity among Indians—of culture, language, tribal identity—inhibited united resistance to the European invaders.

New Mexico and California. As the Hopewell culture declined in the East, three important native American cultures developed along the river valleys of the Southwest. By A.D. 600 farmers of the Hohokam culture in present-day Arizona were using irrigation to grow two crops a year, fashioning pottery with red-on-buff designs and, under Mesoamerican influence, building ball courts and low platform mounds. To the east, in the Mimbres Valley of New Mexico, the Mogollon peoples developed a distinctive black-on-white pottery and, after A.D. 1000, large multiroom stone structures. The

Anasazi of northern Arizona and New Mexico fully developed this architecture, building elaborate residential-ceremonial villages in steep cliffs as well as devising an elaborate ceremonial road system and various astronomical devices. All three peoples, however, fell into decline after A.D. 1250 as long periods of drought and invasions by the Navajo and the Apache disrupted their precarious system of food production. But the descendants of these Pueblo peoples—including the Zuni and the Hopi—were able to sustain their vigorous village societies.

Indian Women and Agriculture

Corn was the dietary staple of most native Americans, and its cultivation shaped their vision of the natural world. The Agawam Indians of Massachusetts began their year with the month of Squannikesas, a word that meant "when they set Indian corn," and subsequent months had names that referred to the weeding, hilling, and ripening of corn. To appease the spirit forces in nature and ensure a bountiful harvest, the Seneca Indians of New York held a corn-planting ceremony. They asked the Thunderers, "our grandfathers," to water their crops and beseeched the sun, "our older brother," not to burn them.

Among the eastern woodland tribes, growing corn was women's work. Indian women prepared the ground with wooden hoes tipped with bone, flint, or clamshells. According to a Dutch traveler, they made "heaps like molehills, each about two and a half feet from the others" and planted "in each heap five or six grains." As the tall slender plants appeared, the women piled on more dirt to support the roots. They also "put in each hill three or four Brazilian [kidney] beans. When they grow up, they interlace with the corn, which reaches to a height of from five to six feet; and they keep the ground free of weeds."

The planting of corn and beans together represented a major technological advance, for it dramatically increased total yields. The beans fixed nitrogen in the soil, preserving fertility, and conserved moisture, preventing erosion. Beans and corn provided a diet rich in vegetable proteins. By cultivating 2 acres, an Indian woman typically harvested 60 bushels of shelled corn—half the calories required by five persons for a year.

This economic contribution enhanced the political influence of women in some tribes, especially those in which names and inheritance rights passed through women (matrilinealism). Thus, among the matrilineal Seneca and the other Iroquois nations, women chose the clan leaders. To preserve their status, women jealously guarded their productive role. A Quaker missionary reported as late as 1809 that "if a man took hold of a hoe to use it, the Women would get down his gun by way of derision & laugh and say such a Warrior is a timid woman."

In seventeenth-century America, English farmers appropriated Indian corn technology and made it part of their own culture. Protestant ministers as well as Indian spiritual leaders prayed for a bountiful harvest of corn. But among European settlers men planted, tended, and harvested the crop—and they worked with horses and plows, not hoes. After clearing their fields of tree stumps, English farmers plowed furrows at 3-foot intervals from north to south. Then they cut east-west furrows, heaping up the soil into Indian-style cornhills at the intersecting points. English planting methods were less labor-intensive than Indian techniques and far less productive, averaging from 10 to 15 bushels per acre, not 30. And, in combination with patrilineal naming and inheritance practices, that meant that women played a subordinate role in the productive life of the society.

Nevertheless, corn became the premier American food crop, and with good reason. As a Welsh migrant to Pennsylvania noted, corn "produced more increase than any other Graine whatsoever." Pigs and chickens ate its kernels, and cows munched its stalks and leaves. Ground into flour and made into bread, cakes, or porridge, corn became the dietary staple of poor people in the northern English colonies and of white tenant farmers and enslaved blacks in the South and the West Indies.

The horticultural work of native American women underlay the political and artistic achievements of the Hopewell and Mississippian cultures and the military strength of the Iroquois and other Indian peoples. Moreover, their presence in the fields constantly reminded English settlers that their own division of labor between the sexes was neither universal nor necessarily the most efficient method of production.

Timucuan women in Florida plant beans and maize while men break up the soil.

Casas Grandes Pot
The artistically and architecturally talented Mogollon and Anasazi peoples of Arizona and New Mexico took utilitarian objects—such as this ordinary pot—and decorated them with black-on-white designs. Their cultures flourished from 1000 to 1250, after which they slowly declined.

In California, distinct environmental zones helped produce a complex pattern of native American life as more than 500 small tribes with diverse forms of speech, religion, and economic life appeared by A.D. 500. The various peoples traded surplus foodstuffs and artifacts—finely woven baskets, carved stone bowls, and sturdy canoes—with one another, allowing a relatively dense population. Political authority was vested in the hands of local big men who presided over kin-based societies.

Mississippian Society. A new burst of creative energy transformed the culture of the Mississippi Valley beginning about A.D. 800. One stimulus was the spread of technology from Mesoamerica. For example, new strains of maize and beans were cultivated that, when eaten together, provided all the amino acids required for a protein-rich diet and, when planted on productive river bottomland, could support a population of ten persons per square mile—about ten times the population density of hunter-gatherers. The resulting agricultural surpluses laid the foundation for a culture based on small fortified temple cities and a ranked social system. The largest city, at Cahokia (present-day East St. Louis, Missouri), probably had a population of 10,000 at its peak around A.D. 1150 and boasted more than

100 temple mounds, including the immense Monks Mound, which was 90 feet high and 900 feet at the base. These fortified temple cities were governed, as in Mesoamerica, by chiefs and in some cases by a privileged class of nobles and priests. This elite was supported in comfort by the handiwork of skilled artisans and the agricultural surplus paid in tribute by a caste of peasant cultivators in the surrounding countryside.

By A.D. 1350 the largest centers of Mississippian civilization were in rapid decline, most likely because of the combined impact of high mortality—from malnourishment stemming from iron deficiency and from urban diseases such as tuberculosis—and warfare prompted by competition for fertile bottomlands. Still, the values and institutions of this civilization lingered for centuries and accounted for the fierce resistance by the Indians of this region to Spanish and French invaders beginning in the 1540s.

The Natchez people of Mississippi maintained elements of the old temple mound culture into modern times. French traders and priests who encountered the Natchez around A.D. 1700 found a rigidly stratified four-class society (see American Voices, page 10). There was the highest caste of Suns, the hereditary leaders of the chiefdom; two intermediate groups of Nobles and Honored People; and a bottom class of peasants, called Stinkards, who cultivated the land. Descent was matrilineal, so that a Great Sun was succeeded not by his own son but by the son of his sister. Undoubtedly influenced by Mesoamerican rituals, the Natchez practiced human sacrifice; the death of a Great Sun called for the sacrifice of his wives and an enlargement of a ceremonial mound to bury their remains. Other Mesoamerican practices persisted among some tribes in Florida and also among the Choctaw, who regarded a mound in present-day Winston County, Mississippi, as *ishki chito*, the "great mother." There, according to a Choctaw legend, "the Great Spirit created the first Choctaws, and through a hole or cave, they crawled forth into the light of day." Class divisions also marked some Muskhogean peoples: the Creek, the Chickasaw, and the Iroquoian-speaking Cherokee. Because of their hierarchical social order and cultural achievements, eighteenth-century British settlers called them the Civilized Tribes.

For the rest of North America, the most important legacy of the Mississippian civilization was its agricultural practices, including the use of flint hoes and superior strains of corn, beans, and squash. This new horticultural technology produced a more reliable and abundant food supply, permitting the tribes of the eastern region to enjoy a more fixed and stable way of life after A.D. 1000. As better nutrition improved health and lengthened the life span, communities grew in size and developed more complex cultures.

Father le Petite

The Customs of the Natchez

Traditional beliefs and institutions from the earlier Mississippian culture (A.D. 1000–1450) served to fortify the Natchez in their resistance to French Jesuit missionaries. In this letter, written about 1730, a missionary accurately describes many Indian customs but misinteprets the rules governing the succession of the chief, which simply followed the normal practice of descent and inheritance in a matrilineal society.

My Reverend Father, The peace of Our Lord.

This Nation of Savages inhabits one of the most beautiful and fertile countries in the World, and is the only one on this continent which appears to have any regular worship. Their Religion in certain points is very similar to that of the ancient Romans. They have a Temple filled with Idols, which are different figures of men and of animals, and for which they have the most profound veneration. Their Temple in shape resembles an earthen oven, a hundred feet in circumference. They enter it by a little door about four feet high, and not more than three in breadth. Above on the outside are three figures of eagles made of wood, and painted red, yellow, and white. Before the door is a kind of shed with folding-doors, where the Guardian of the Temple is lodged; all around it runs a circle of palisades, on which are seen exposed the skulls of all the heads which their Warriors had brought back from the battles in which they had been engaged with the enemies of their Nation. . . .

The Sun is the principal object of veneration to these people; as they cannot conceive of anything which can be above this heavenly body, nothing else appears to them more worthy of their homage. It is for the same reason that the great Chief of this Nation, who knows nothing on the earth more dignified than himself, takes the title of brother of the Sun, and the credulity of the people maintains him in the despotic authority which he claims. To enable them better to converse together, they raise a mound of artificial soil, on which they build his cabin, which is of the same construction as the Temple.

The old men prescribe the Laws for the rest of the people, and one of their principles is . . . the immortality of the soul, and when they leave this world they go, they say, to live in another, there to be recompensed or punished.

This Government is hereditary; it is not, however, the son of the reigning Chief who succeeds his father, but the son of his sister, or the first Princess of the blood. This policy is founded on the knowledge they have of the licentiousness of their women. They are not sure, they say, that the children of the chief's wife may be of the blood Royal, whereas the son of the sister of the great Chief must be, at least on the side of the mother.

In former times the Nation of the *Natchez* was very large. It counted sixty Villages and eight hundred Suns or Princes; now it is reduced to six little Villages and eleven Suns.

Source: The Jesuit Relations and Allied Documents, ed. by Reuben Gold Thwaites (Cleveland: The Murrow Brothers, 1900), vol. 68, pp. 121–135.

The Woodland Indians. On the eve of European contact, most Indian peoples in the eastern woodlands of North America lived in self-governing tribes composed of clans. A *clan* was a group of related families that had a common identity and a real or legendary common ancestor. Clan elders' power came from their ties to this ancestor, and they led ceremonies and regulated personal life in the interests of the tribe as a whole. For example, elders prevented marriage between members of the same clan, a rule that helped prevent genetic inbreeding; they also granted families use rights over certain planting grounds or hunting areas, since the concept of private ownership of land was virtually unknown in Indian culture. Clan leaders also resolved personal feuds, disciplined individuals who violated customs, and decided whether to go to war against their neighbors. However, their power was far less than that of Mayan or Aztec rulers, because their kinship-based system of government worked by consensus, not by coercion.

The peoples of eastern North America spoke at least sixty-eight mutually unintelligible languages that fell into five separate families. Most of the Indians who lived between the St. Lawrence River and Chesapeake Bay, such as the Pequot and the Delaware, spoke Algonquin dialects. The Five Nations of the Iroquois, who dominated the region between the Hudson River and the Great Lakes—the Mohawk, Oneida, Onondaga, Cayuga, and Seneca—spoke Iroquoian languages. The tribes in the territory between the southern Atlantic coast and the Mississippi River, such as the Creek and

the Choctaw, were primarily Muskhogean and Sioux speakers, whereas most of the tribes living in Florida used varieties of the Timucuan and Calusan tongues.

Each people claimed its own territory, but most Indians did not live in permanent settlements. Instead, bands of people moved about, using different parts of their domain on a seasonal basis. Throughout much of eastern North America women and children gathered berries and seeds year-round, while men hunted and fished. In the summer, villages were established near arable lands, where women, using hoes, planted native grasses or, increasingly after A.D. 1000, corn, squashes, and beans that had been carried northward from Mesoamerica. Prospering tribes built semipermanent villages of domed wigwams (or, among the Iroquois, longhouses) near their cornfields and lived there from April to October, celebrating the yearly agricultural cycle with religious ceremonies such as the Iroquois green corn and strawberry festivals. Among the Iroquois, who had made slash-and-burn maize-based agriculture their dominant means of support, women's central role in food production probably enhanced their authority, which was already considerable because of the Iroquois' matrilineal-based clan and inheritance system. Use rights to land and other property passed from mother to daughter, and the senior women of each clan chose the (male) clan chief.

After the harvest, clans often broke into groups consisting of three or four families, with the men hunting together for large game. Given this subsistence economy—a combination of hunting, gathering, and simple hoe agriculture—the woodland peoples lived harsh and rather limited material lives; they did not make intensive use of the environment, and their populations did not grow rapidly. Consequently, these peoples, unlike the native Americans in Mesoamerica, did not live in densely populated communities with elaborate religious sites or trade extensively with other peoples. Instead, each group's economic life depended primarily on the climate and natural resources of its territory. For example, the short growing season along the St. Lawrence River diminished the importance of horticulture for northern Algonquians, such as the Abenaki and Passamaquoddy of present-day Maine, who lived by hunting wild animals, fishing, and gathering wild grasses, nuts, and berries. By contrast, the more southerly Algonquins, such as the Delaware and the Powhatan, depended on farming by women for most of their food. In many cases, foraging peoples traded furs for the foodstuffs grown by the farming groups. Even before the arrival of the Europeans, a long-distance trade in corn, *wampum* (shell money), and furs linked the distant communities of Long Island and Maine. Whatever their economic base, by A.D. 1500 most of the Indian peoples had been living a relatively settled existence on their lands for generations.

Traditional European Society in 1450

Europeans came to America from a predominantly agricultural society. Before 1450 most Europeans were peasants who farmed the soil and were at the mercy of forces beyond their control—from kings and aristocrats who imposed high taxes and rents to bandits, predatory armies, droughts, and plagues that threatened the safety of their families and the livelihood of their communities. Amid these dangers, the main comfort was the Christian religion, which offered the hope of eternal salvation.

The Peasantry

There were only a few large cities in Western Europe before 1450—Rome, Paris, Amsterdam, London, Madrid, the city-states of northern Italy—home to merchants and artisans. More than 90 percent of the population lived in small, relatively isolated rural communities separated from each other by rolling hills or dense forests. A settlement typically consisted of a compact village surrounded by extensive fields. Each peasant family owned or leased a small dwelling in the village and had the right to farm several strips of land in the fields. These fields were "open"—that is, not divided by fences or hedges—making cooperative farming a necessity. Each year the male householders decided which crops to plant and how many cows and sheep each family could graze on the commonly owned meadows.

The open-field system of land tenure produced a strong sense of community that was reinforced by the confiningly primitive state of transportation. Villages were linked only by rough dirt roads and ox-drawn carts. Travel was slow and cumbersome at best and nearly impossible in heavy rain or deep snow. Since there were few merchants, most peasant families exchanged surplus grain or meat with their relatives and neighbors and bartered their produce for the services of local artisans: millers, weavers, blacksmiths, roof thatchers.

Village life was tightly restrictive. Although by 1450 peasants in Western Europe were no longer serfs legally bound to the land, their mobility was limited by geographical isolation and a lack of work outside agriculture. A man might seek a job (or a wife) in a nearby village or be forced to fight as a foot soldier in a distant war. A woman might leave her village to marry, work as a domestic servant, or sell homespun textiles at a regional fair. If she was really lucky, she would make a pilgrimage to a famous shrine or cathedral, such as Canterbury or Chartres. But these events were extraordinary. Most men and women lived hard, unvarying lives in the towns or regions of their birth.

An Idealized Medieval World
In this illustration from a medieval manuscript, well-dressed peasants labor effortlessly in front of a beautiful palace. Only the fortifications hint at the warfare of the era and the nobility's power over the lives of ordinary men and women.

The Seasonal Cycle. As among native Americans, nearly all aspects of European peasant life followed a seasonal pattern. The agricultural year began in March, when the ground thawed and dried, allowing villagers to plow and plant. In England the farming season formally began on Lady Day, March 25, the day in the Christian calendar on which the church celebrated the Annunciation to the Virgin Mary of the impending birth of Jesus Christ. Accordingly, in ceremonies that probably derived from pagan fertility rites, pious peasants prayed to the Virgin for a bountiful crop. With less enthusiasm, they paid the first quarterly installment of rent to their landlords.

Once the agricultural year was under way, the pace of life quickened. Peasants sowed their fields in April and May and cut the first crop of hay in June, storing it as winter fodder for their livestock. During these busy spring months, men sheared the thick winter wool of their sheep, which the women then washed and spun into yarn. After the exhausting work of spring planting and haymaking, life became more relaxed. Families took to mending their fences or repairing their barns and houses. Then, following the strenuous fall harvest, they celebrated with riotous bouts of merrymaking. As winter approached, peasants slaughtered excess live-

stock and salted or smoked the meat. During the cold months, they completed the time-consuming tasks of threshing grain and weaving textiles and had more leisure time to visit friends or relatives in nearby villages. Just before the cycle began again in the spring, rural folk held carnivals to celebrate with drink and dance the end of the long winter night.

Death also followed a seasonal pattern (see Figure 1.1). Many rural folk died in January and February, victims of the cold and viral diseases. August and September were even worse, as infants and old people succumbed to epidemics of fly-borne dysentery. More mysteriously, births also followed a seasonal rhythm. In European villages (and later in rural British America), the greatest numbers of babies were born in February and March, with a smaller peak in September and October. The precise causes of this pattern are unknown. Religious practices—for example, abstention from sexual intercourse by devout Christians during Lent—might have affected the number of conceptions. Even more likely, fluctuations in the food supply or in female work patterns from month to month might have altered a woman's ability to carry a child to full term. One thing is certain. This seasonal pattern of births does not exist in modern urban societies, so it must have been a reflection of traditional rural life.

Over the generations, this pattern of exhausting effort during the spring and summer alternating with exuberant play during the fall and winter became a custom, one that European migrants would bring with them to America. A German who settled in Pennsylvania refused to move farther south because, a traveler reported, he loved his winter leisure. Without cold and snow, "people must work year in, year out, and that was not his fancy; winter, with a warm stove and sluggish days being indispensable to his happiness."

The Peasant's Lot. Most peasants wanted to be *yeomen*, owning enough land to support a family in comfort, but relatively few achieved this goal. For most peasants, a difficult, unpredictable life and an early, arbitrary death were the natural conditions of existence. Mere survival required heavy labor. Other than water- or wind-powered mills for grinding grain, raw muscle was the major source of energy. While horses and oxen strained to break the soil with primitive wooden plows, men staggered as they guided them from behind. At harvesttime, workers cut hay, wheat, rye, and barley with hand sickles, but even when fine weather brought a good harvest, output was at most 10 bushels of grain per acre—one-tenth of a modern yield.

The margin of existence was thin, and it corroded family relations. Before 1650 about half of those born in Europe died before the age of twenty-one. Malnourished mothers fed their babies sparingly, calling them "greedy and gluttonous" little beasts, and many new-

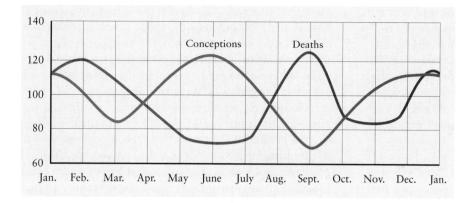

FIGURE 1.1

The Yearly Rhythm of Rural Life
The annual cycle of nature profoundly affected life in the traditional world. Deaths were about 20 percent above normal in February and September. Summer was the healthiest season, with the fewest deaths and the greatest number of successful conceptions (as measured by births nine months later).

An Artisan Family
Work was slow and difficult in a world dependent on simple tools and hand labor, and survival required the efforts of all family members. Here a fifteenth-century French woodworker planes a panel of wood as his wife twists flax fibers into linen yarn for the family's clothes and their son fashions a basket out of reeds.

born girls were "helped to die" so that their older brothers would have enough to eat. To relieve overcrowding at home and instill discipline, English parents commonly sent eight-year-old children to live as servants in other households, where they were often mistreated. Those who survived the rigors of infancy and childhood found hunger, disease, and violence to be constant companions. "I have seen the latest epoch of misery," a French doctor reported as famine and plague struck. "The inhabitants . . . lie down in a meadow to eat grass, and share the food of wild beasts."

Often destitute, usually exploited and dominated by landlords and aristocrats, many peasants simply accepted their condition. Others did not. It would be the deprived rural classes of England and Western Europe, hoping for a better life for themselves and their children, who would supply the majority of white migrants to the Western Hemisphere.

Hierarchy and Authority

In the traditional European social order, as in the Aztec and Mayan empires, authority came from above. Aristocrats, priests, and government officials intruded into the affairs of peasants, and the peasants organized their families and communities in a hierarchical manner. Nearly everywhere the individual submitted to the discipline of superiors or to the consensus of the village community. In such a society dependent relationships were the accepted social norm; few men—and even fewer women—had much personal freedom or developed a strong sense of individual identity. Most people's behavior was shaped by powerful social institutions—family, community, and nobility.

The Family. Social discipline began at home. The man was the head of the house, a patriarch who made all the important decisions. His power was justified by the teachings of the Christian Church. As one English pastor put it, "The woman is a weak creature not embued with

like strength and constancy of mind"; law and custom consequently "subjected her to the power of man." Upon marriage, an English woman not only assumed the family name of her husband and usually moved to his village but also was required under the threat of legally sanctioned physical "correction" to submit to her husband's orders—be they for service or for sexual favors. Moreover, she surrendered to her husband all her property, including her clothes. In her new legal state of *coverture*, a married woman was allowed only the "use" of her personal possessions; upon her husband's death, she received only a dower—usually the use during her lifetime of one-third of the family's land and goods.

Fathers controlled the lives of children in an equally encompassing and authoritarian way. Landowning peasants in Western Europe normally retained legal control of farms until their physical strength ebbed. Only then, after age fifty, did they provide land to sons and dowries (usually livestock or furnishings) to daughters, permitting their children to marry. Consequently, most young men and women worked for their fathers until their middle or late twenties, enduring years of emotional domination and sexual deprivation. When they finally did marry, it was often to someone not of their liking, since most marriages were arranged, with parents choosing partners of comparable wealth and status to protect the family's economic position.

Within the family, children were not born equal: their social position depended on their sex and birth order. In many regions cultural rules dictated that a father bestow most of his land on his oldest son (primogeniture). That son became the new patriarch, responsible for the welfare of his siblings. Custom called for landless brothers and sisters to work on their brother's farm in return for food and shelter, but the small size of most peasant holdings forced many younger children to join the ranks of the roaming poor, condemned to desperate lives on the edge of respectable society.

The Community. In a world of scarcity, the price of survival was unremitting social discipline. Village authorities strictly regulated individual behavior for the common good; for example, in Germany they granted marriage licenses only to couples with sufficient property to support a family. Officials also imposed limits on what could be charged for the staff of life: a loaf of bread, a sack of flour or grain. Fearful of change, they made tradition the measure of all existence. "After a thing had been practiced for so long that it becomes a Custom," an English clergyman proclaimed, "that Custom is Law."

Monarchs and Manorial Lords. The monarchs of Western Europe owned vast tracts of land and, like Aztec and Mayan rulers, lived in splendor off the labor of the masses of peasants. Gradually, the European rulers extended their power, levying royal taxes, creating law courts, and conscripting men for military service. Yet they were far from supreme, given the power of the nobility, who played a major role in the affairs of the villages and kingdoms of Western Europe.

Collectively, these noblemen often challenged the authority of princes and kings. They had their own legislative institutions, such as the French *parlements* and the English House of Lords, and enjoyed special legal privileges, such as the right to a trial before a jury composed of their own (noble) peers. And because nobles had direct control over the peasantry, monarchs had little choice but to appoint them as local judges and militia officers.

Such legacies of the medieval feudal order, when most kings were dependent on the nobility, worked against the formation of strong centralized states. Other privileged groups whose wealth and status limited the rulers' power were the clergy and the merchants. In the Beauvais region of France the Catholic Church and the aristocracy controlled nearly half the land, leaving individual peasants and village communities, who made up more than 95 percent of the population, to divide the rest.

Hierarchy and authority reigned supreme in the traditional European social order both because of the power of established institutions and because, in a harsh and unpredictable world, they offered ordinary people a measure of security and certainty. These values, which migrants carried with them to America, would shape the character of family life and the social order there well into the eighteenth century.

The Power of Religion

The Catholic Church served as one of the great unifying forces in Western European society. By A.D. 1000 Christianity had converted virtually all of pagan Europe, extending its spiritual jurisdiction over Latins, Germans, Celts, Anglo-Saxons, and western Slavs. The pope, as head of the Catholic Church, directed a vast hierarchy of cardinals, bishops, and priests. Latin, the language of scholarship, was preserved by Catholic priests and monks, and Catholic dogma provided a common understanding of God, the world, and human history. Equally important, the church provided another bulwark of authority and discipline in society.

Religion in Daily Life. Christian doctrine penetrated deeply into the everyday lives of peasants. Over the centuries, the church adopted a calendar that accommodated the agricultural cycle and incorporated various pagan festivals, such as the winter solstice, which

Christ's Crucifixion
This graphic portrayal of Christ's death on the cross, by the German painter Grünewald, sought to remind believers of the reality of death and the need for repentance. (Central panel of closed Isenheim Altarpiece, Colmar, Musée Unterlinden)

marked the return of the sun and the victory of light over darkness. The Christian celebration of the birth of Jesus Christ on December 25, a few days later, grafted a new religious meaning onto the solstice, encouraging pagan conversions.

In the spring, when the warmth of the sun revived the earth, the church celebrated Christ's resurrection from the dead on Easter Sunday. This holy day absorbed pagan spring fertility festivals and gave them a distinctively Christian meaning. Christian and pagan traditions blended again in the autumn months as ancient harvest festivals gradually evolved into holy days of thanksgiving.

This merging of the sacred and the agricultural cycles endowed all worldly events with meaning. Few Christians believed that events occurred by chance; they must be the result of God's will. If crops rotted in the ground or withered under a hot sun, the Lord must be displeased with his people. According to the Bible, "The earth is defiled under its inhabitants' feet, for they have transgressed the law" (Isaiah 24:5). To avert calamities, peasants turned to priests for spiritual guidance and to confess their transgressions of God's commands and the church's laws. Every village had a church, and holy shrines dotted the map of Europe, tangible points of contact between the material and spiritual worlds. By

offering prayers to Christ and the saints, whose statues stood in the shrines and churches, Christians hoped to stave off worldly disasters.

God's presence in the world was continually renewed through the Mass and the sacrament of Holy Communion. According to Catholic doctrine, priests had the power to change sacramental bread and wine into the body and blood of Christ. In this way, peasants—along with priests and aristocrats—could partake in the divine.

There was another supernatural force at large in the world: Satan. Satan challenged the majesty of God by tempting people into evil. If prophets spread unusual doctrines, they were surely the tools of Satan. If a devout Christian fell mysteriously ill, the sickness might be the result of an evil spell cast by a witch in league with Satan. Fear of Satan's wiles justified periodic purges of heretics—men and women who questioned the church's doctrine and practices.

The Crusades. As the Catholic Church consolidated its power in Europe, popes and priests urged their followers to crush all those who held other religious beliefs. Muslims became a prime target. After the death of the prophet Muhammad in A.D. 632, the newly united peoples of Arabia set out to convert and conquer the world. They spread the Muslim faith and Arab civilization far beyond its homeland—into sub-Saharan Africa, India, and Indonesia and deep into southern Europe. Between A.D. 1095 and 1272 successive armies of Christians, led by the flower of the nobility, embarked on a series of great Crusades against Muslim "infidels." They halted Arab advances into southern Europe and invaded Palestine, seeking to expel Muslims from the Holy Land where Christ had lived.

The Crusades had some success in their military mission, gaining control of much of Palestine for nearly 200 years, but their spiritual impact on Europe was more profound, strengthening the Christian identity of its population. The resulting religious fervor also contributed to the renewed persecution of Jews in many European countries. England expelled most of its Jewish population in 1290, and France did the same in 1306. Jewish refugees went mostly to Germany, the great center of European Jewry, only to be driven farther east, to Poland, over the next century. At the same time, the Crusades broadened the intellectual and economic horizons of the privileged classes of Western Europe, bringing them into contact with the advanced civilizations of the Middle East and Asia. A fresh wind blew through Europe, resulting in marked changes in that continent's commercial interests and military power—changes that in turn would cause slower but equally significant alterations in its traditional agricultural society.

The Spice Trade
This French manuscript illustration (circa 1380) shows workers in Malabar (near Calicut on the western coast of India) harvesting pepper for the spice trade. The white-skinned man is meant to be Marco Polo, one of the few Europeans to visit India or China before the Portuguese voyages.

Europe and the World, 1450–1550

Europe changed dramatically after 1450. First, a major revival of learning, the Renaissance, expanded the horizons of the commercial and political classes. Second, Portuguese merchants found new trade routes to India and China and became leaders in world commerce. Finally, Spanish adventurers found and invaded the Western Hemisphere, conquering the wealthiest native American empires and, through the spread of European diseases, devastating their peoples. For the first time since the Roman Empire, Europeans became major actors in world history.

Renaissance Beginnings

Beginning about A.D. 1300, first Italy and then the countries of northern Europe experienced a rebirth of learning and cultural life. The main stimulus came from the Crusaders' exposure to the highly developed civilization of the Arab world. Arab traders had access to the fabulous treasures of the East: luxurious Chinese silks, brilliant Indian cottons, precious stones, and exotic spices, including pepper, nutmeg, ginger, and cloves. Arab inventors had developed magnetic compasses, water-powered mills, and mechanical clocks, and from their trading contacts in China, they had learned the properties and uses of gunpowder. In great cultural centers such as Alexandria and Cairo in Egypt, Arab scholars carried on the legacy of Christian Byzantine civilization, which had preserved the great achievements of the Greeks and Romans in religion, medicine, philosophy, mathematics, astronomy, and geography.

At the same time, from Toledo and other cities in Moorish Spain, Arab learning gradually filtered into Europe. The Moors were Arabs who had invaded the Iberian Peninsula centuries before and still controlled its southern region. Moorish scholars had translated Aristotle, Ptolemy, and other ancient writers into Latin, reacquainting the peoples of Europe with their classical heritage.

Astronomers at Istanbul, 1581
Arab and Turkish scholars transmitted ancient texts and learning to Europeans in the Middle Ages and, during the age of discovery, contributed to the expansion of geographical and astronomical knowledge.

The Italian Renaissance. During the Crusades, merchants from the Italian city-states of Venice, Genoa, and Pisa had wrested away a share of the Arab trade with the East. Dispatching ships to Alexandria, Beirut, and other eastern Mediterranean ports, these merchants purchased goods that originally had come from China, India, Persia, and Arabia and sold them throughout Europe. The enormous profits from this commerce created a new class of merchants, bankers, and textile manufacturers who conducted trade, lent vast sums of money, and spurred technological innovation in silk and woolen production. This moneyed elite ruled the republican city-states of Italy, and in *The Discourses*, Niccolò Machiavelli articulated its political culture of *civic humanism*—an ideology that celebrated public virtue and service to the state and that would profoundly influence European and American conceptions of government.

In what was to become the fashion of the age, wealthy Italian families became patrons of the arts and sciences, subsidizing a remarkable array of artistic and intellectual projects. Perhaps no other age in European history has produced such a flowering of artistic genius. Michelangelo, Andrea Palladio, and Filippo Brunelleschi designed and built great architectural masterpieces, while Leonardo da Vinci and Raphael produced magnificent religious paintings, creating styles and setting standards that have endured into the modern era.

Humanism. The Renaissance did not directly affect the average European peasant, but it had a profound impact on the upper classes. The artists and intellectuals of the Renaissance were optimistic in their view of human nature—they were humanists who celebrated individual potential. Whereas traditional paintings had depicted, often grimly, religious themes and symbols, Renaissance works of art and literature showed real men (and a few women) with complex personalities and creative talents. Those who embraced the psychology of the Renaissance saw themselves not as prisoners of blind fate or victims of the forces of nature but as many-sided individuals with the capacity to change the world.

Renaissance Architecture
The columned buildings of the Renaissance recalled the classical world of Greece and Rome, and the symmetrical design reflected the impulse to create a world of ordered beauty.

Renaissance Princes. The idea that the world could be shaped by human ingenuity was particularly appealing to Renaissance rulers, who were eager to shape it to their own benefit. In *The Prince* (1513), Machiavelli provided unsentimental advice on how monarchs could increase their political power. Machiavelli's hero in this treatise was the Italian ruler Cesare Borgia, but he was inspired by the state-building activities of the ambitious monarchs of France and Western Europe.

These monarchs—among them France's Louis XI (1461–1483), England's Henry VII (1485–1509), and Spain's Ferdinand (1479–1516) and Isabella (1474–1504)—created royal law courts and bureaucracies to reduce the power of the landed classes and formed alliances with commercial interests to build strong and prosperous national states. They allowed merchants to trade throughout their realms and granted privileges to artisan guilds, thus encouraging both foreign trade and domestic manufacturing. In return, they extracted taxes from towns and loans from merchants to support their armies and officials. The alliance of monarchs, merchants, and royal bureaucrats challenged the primacy of the agrarian nobility. Indeed, the increasing wealth and power of the monarchical nation-state propelled Europe into its first age of expansion.

Portugal Penetrates Africa and Asia

In 1450 Western Europe was a collection of poor agricultural societies lying isolated and unimportant at the far edge of the Eurasian land mass. Strangely, it was Portugal, a small Atlantic country of only 1.5 million people, that led the way in the great surge of exploration. Portugal boasted political stability, a tradition of seafaring, and a fleet of merchant ships. It also had a prince, Henry the Navigator, who was determined to contest the dominant position of Muslim and Italian merchants by finding a new ocean route to the wealth of Asia.

Henry the Navigator. Prince Henry (1394–1460) was the younger brother of King Edward I of Portugal. Henry was a complex, many-sided individual, at once a Christian warrior and a Renaissance humanist. As a knight of the Order of Christ, Henry had fought against the Arabs in North Africa, an experience that reinforced his desire to extend Portuguese power and the bounds of Christendom. As a humanist, Henry patronized Renaissance thinkers who drew inspiration from classical Greek and Roman (rather than Christian) sources, and he relied on Arab and Italian geographers for the latest knowledge about the shape and size of the continents. In the activist spirit of the Renaissance, Henry sought to fulfill the predictions of his horoscope: "to engage in great and noble conquests and to attempt the discovery of things hidden from other men."

African Slavery. In the 1420s, Prince Henry established a center for exploration and ocean mapping and from there sent out ships to sail the African coast and probe the Atlantic. His seamen soon discovered and settled Madeira and the Azores. By 1435 Portuguese sea captains were regularly roaming the coast of West Africa, seeking ivory and gold in exchange for salt, wine, and fish. By the 1440s they were trading in humans as well, the first Europeans to engage in African slavery. For centuries Arab merchants had conducted a brisk overland trade in slaves, buying sub-Saharan Africans captured during local ethnic conflicts and selling them throughout the Mediterranean region. The Portuguese extended this commerce, at first transporting West Africans from Senegambia to sugar estates in Madeira and the Azores. Eventually they would bring hundreds of thousands of slaves across the Atlantic to toil on the sugar plantations of Brazil and the West Indies (see Chapter 3).

The Portuguese Maritime Empire. After Henry's death in 1460, Portuguese navigators and adventurers continued their explorations, looking for a direct ocean route to Asia. In 1488 Bartholomew Diaz rounded the Cape of Good Hope, the southern tip of Africa. Ten years later Vasco da Gama sailed all the way to India. The Arab, Indian, and Jewish merchants and traders on India's Malabar Coast shunned da Gama as a dangerous commercial rival, but he returned to Portugal with a valuable cargo of cinnamon and pepper, the latter being in such great demand for flavoring and preserving meat that the voyage realized a profit of 6,000 percent. Da Gama returned to India in 1502 with twenty-one fighting vessels and immediately attacked his rivals in a naked challenge for commercial dominance. Square-rigged Portuguese caravels outmaneuvered and outgunned Arab fleets, while on land plunder-hungry Portuguese adventurers burned cities and seized the property of rival traders.

The Portuguese government set up fortified trading posts for its merchants at key points around the Indian Ocean—at Goa in India, Hormuz in Arabia, and Malacca in Malaysia—and soon opened trade routes from Africa to Indonesia and up the coast of Asia to China and Japan. Portuguese merchants easily undersold Arab traders, for their ships held more and traveled faster than overland caravans. In a momentous transition, Portuguese Christians replaced Arab Muslims as the leaders in world commerce and in the trade in African slaves (see Map 1.2).

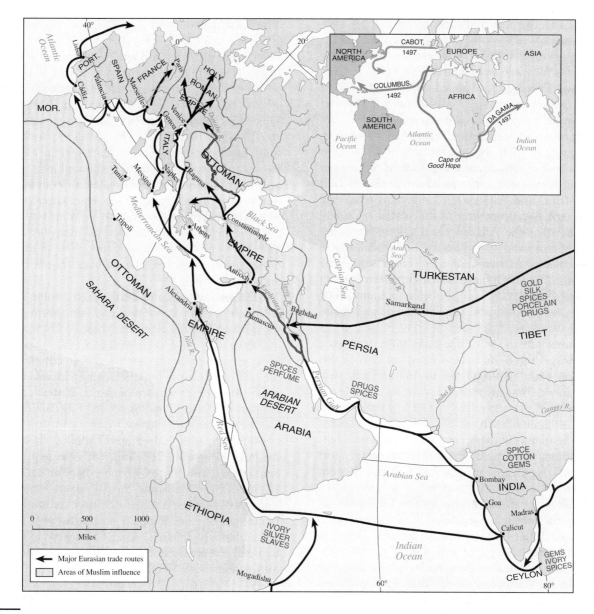

MAP 1.2

Europeans Seek Control of World Trade
For centuries the Mediterranean Sea was the meeting point for the commerce of
Europe, northern Africa, and southern Asia. Beginning in the 1490s, Portuguese, Spanish, and Dutch adventurers and merchants opened up new trade routes, challenging
the primacy of the Muslim-dominated Mediterranean.

Spain and America

Spain quickly followed Portugal's example. As Renaissance rulers, King Ferdinand of Aragon and Queen Isabella of Castile saw national unity and commerce as
the keys to prosperity and power. Married in their teens
in an arranged match, the young rulers had combined

their kingdoms. They devoted their energies and resources to the *reconquista*, the centuries-long campaign
to oust the Moors from Spanish soil. In 1492 their
armies finally reconquered Granada, the last outpost of
Islam in Western Europe. Continuing their effort to use
religion to build a sense of "Spanishness," Ferdinand
and Isabella launched a brutal Inquisition against sus-

pected Christian heretics and expelled (or forcibly converted) thousands of Jews. Then they turned their attention to expansion, looking across the seas for new opportunities for trade and empire.

Because Portugal controlled the southern, or African, approach to Asia, Isabella and Ferdinand sought a western route and soon were giving a hearing to a Genoese sea captain, Christopher Columbus. Columbus was familiar with the findings of Italian geographers who had rediscovered the maps of the ancient Greeks and had reached the mistaken conclusion that Europe, Africa, and Asia covered more than half the earth's surface. Accepting these miscalculations, Columbus believed that the Atlantic Ocean, long feared by Arab sailors as an endless "green sea of darkness," was little more than a narrow channel of water separating Europe from Asia. With financial backing from Spanish merchants, Ferdinand and Isabella commissioned Columbus "to discover and acquire islands and mainland in the Ocean Sea."

Columbus set sail with three small ships on August 3, 1492. An ambitious man, he wanted not only to discover a new route to China but to find and rule new lands, receiving from his monarch-patrons the titles of viceroy and governor as well as that of admiral. On October 12, 1492, after a voyage of 3,000 miles, he landed at one of the islands of the present-day Bahamas. Whatever his original intentions, the Italian adventurer had "discovered" for Europeans the lands of the Western Hemisphere.

Columbus set about exploring the Caribbean islands, claiming them for Spain and demanding gold from the local Carib and Arawak peoples. Believing that he had reached Asia, or "the Indies" in fifteenth-century parlance, he called these native inhabitants "Indians," and the Caribbean islands thus became known as the West Indies. Buoyed by the natives' stories of rivers of gold lying "to the west," Columbus left forty men on the island of Hispaniola and returned triumphantly with several Caribs to display to Queen Isabella and King Ferdinand.

Those monarchs were sufficiently impressed by Columbus's discovery that over the next twelve years they supported three more voyages. During those expeditions Columbus began the transatlantic trade in slaves, carrying a few hundred Indians to slavery in Europe and importing black slaves from Africa to work as artisans and farmers in the Spanish settlements, but he failed to find great kingdoms or valuable goods; his death in 1506 went virtually unrecognized. In one of the more curious ironies of history, the two continents that Columbus revealed to Europe were named by a German geographer after the Florentine merchant Amerigo Vespucci, who had traveled in South America around 1500 and had called it a *nuevo mundo*, a New World.

The Conquest

The Spaniards who followed Columbus, settling on Cuba, Hispaniola, and other Caribbean islands, were hardened men. Many were soldiers, veterans of the *reconquista* and of subsequent wars in North Africa. They were eager to spread the Christian faith and equally eager to get rich. The Spanish Crown licensed some of them as *adelantados* (entrepreneurs or proprietors), and this entitled them to land, plunder, the management of conquered territory, and titles of nobility; in return they pushed forward the boundaries of the empire. After subduing the Arawak and Caribs and wiping out, through disease and war, as many as a million Tainos on the island of Hispaniola, these military chieftains quickly penetrated the mainland in search of gold and other booty.

Disappointment and death greeted some adventurers, such as Juan Ponce de León, who went searching for gold and slaves along the coast of Florida in 1513 and gave the peninsula its name; in 1521 his attempt to conquer and settle the new land was cut short by an arrow from a Calusa Indian. Other Spaniards won fame rather than fortune: Vasco Núñez de Balboa crossed the Isthmus of Darien (Panama) in 1513, becoming the first European to see the Pacific Ocean.

Some Spanish adventurers fulfilled their fondest dreams. Between 1519 and 1535 a few thousand Spaniards seized control of the powerful Aztec empire in the Mexican highlands, the Mayan settlements in the Yucatan Peninsula, and the rich Inca civilization in the mountains of Peru. Within a generation these adventurers and their monarch, King Charles I (1516–1556), had become masters of the wealthiest and most populous regions of the Western Hemisphere.

The Fall of the Aztecs. In 1519, Hernando Cortés, the first of the great Spanish *conquistadors* (conquerors), landed on the Mexican coast near Veracruz, leading a Spanish force of 600 men. Drawn by rumors of the golden splendor of the Aztec empire, Cortés and his men marched inland. Within two years they had conquered the entire Aztec empire (see Map 1.3). This impressive feat was partly the result of a startling coincidence. Cortés arrived in the very year in which Aztec mythology had predicted the return of the god Quetzalcoatl to his earthly kingdom. Believing that Cortés was indeed that god, Moctezuma, the Aztec ruler, received him with great ceremony and initially allowed him free rein.

European technology was also an important factor in Cortés's triumph, both as a sign of Cortés's divinity and as an instrument of warfare. The sight of the Spaniards in full armor, with cannon that shook the heavens, made a deep impression on the Aztecs. The Aztecs had learned how to purify gold and fashion it

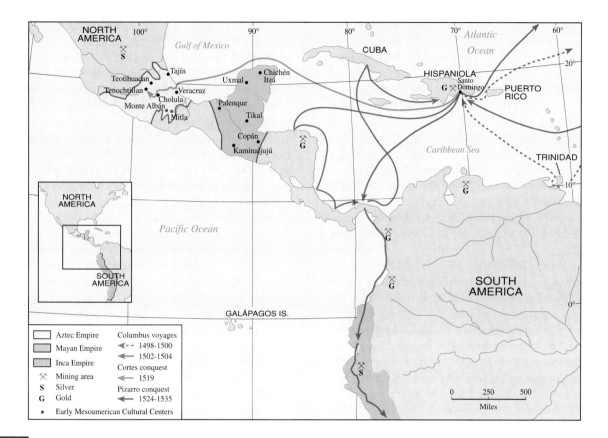

MAP 1.3

The Spanish Conquest

The Spanish first invaded the islands of the Caribbean. Rumors of a magnificent golden civilization led to Cortés's invasion of the Aztec empire in 1519. By 1535 other Spanish conquistadors had conquered the Mayan temple cities and the Inca empire in Peru, completing one of the great conquests in world history.

into ornate religious objects, but they did not produce iron for tools or weapons. Moreover, they had no wheeled carts or cavalry, for horses, once abundant in the Western Hemisphere, had died out thousands of years before. Consequently, Aztec warriors, fighting on foot with flint- or obsidian-tipped spears and arrows, were no match in small-group combat for Spanish conquistadors seated high on their horses, protected by heavy armor, and wielding steel swords.

Still, the peoples of the Aztec empire, who numbered in the millions, could have crushed the European invaders if they had presented a united front. But Cortés deftly exploited existing conflicts within Indian society. The various tribes and nations dominated by the Aztecs had long resented their cruel and oppressive rulers, who had seized their finest goods and sacrificed vast numbers of their people to the Aztec gods. To rid themselves of their overlords, many of these subject peoples rebelled, providing Cortés with supplies, information, and thousands of soldiers. Moctezuma had been killed early in the struggle (probably by followers upset by his weak military policies), and after a three-month siege the

main city of Tenochtitlán fell and the Aztec empire collapsed, the victim not only of superior Spanish military technology but of the rebellion by its subject Indian peoples.

Events then took an unexpected turn, thwarting the hopes of the subject Indian peoples and allowing the conquistadors to take over the centralized Aztec political system. The Western Hemisphere had been isolated from the viral illnesses of Europe and Asia for thousands of years, so native Americans lacked resistance to ordinary European diseases such as smallpox, influenza, and measles. A savage smallpox epidemic devastated the Aztec capital of Tenochtitlán even as the Spanish attacked, and new epidemics were swiftly spread throughout the region by Indian traders and Spanish explorers. Diseases struck down tens of thousands of native Americans, depriving the Indian peoples of leaders and warriors and sapping the morale of the survivors. Cortés quickly extended Spanish rule over the entire Valley of Mexico, and his lieutenants subdued the rest of the highland peoples and then moved against the Maya in the Yucatan, quickly conquering them as well.

The Incas. In the 1520s Francisco Pizarro, another conquistador, embarked on an expedition to the mountains of Peru, home of the rich and powerful Inca empire. Starting around A.D. 1440 as a small chiefdom centered on the Andean valley of Cuzco, some 9,000 feet above sea level, the Inca state quickly extended its control over lands stretching 2,000 miles along the Pacific coast of South America. Some 24,000 miles of roads and carefully placed administrative centers linked the far-flung empire, which boasted cities constructed of finely crafted stone. A semidivine Inca king ruled the empire, assisted by a hierarchical bureaucracy staffed by noblemen, many of whom were his relatives. By the time Pizarro reached Peru, half the population had already died from European diseases. Weakened militarily and emotionally by this abrupt loss of people and fighting among themselves over succession to the throne, the Inca nobility was easy prey for Pizarro and his army.

The Northern Frontier. Even as Pizarro conquered the Incas, other Spanish adventurers sought wealth in North America, establishing a short-lived settlement in present-day Georgia in 1526. Cortés himself dispatched expeditions along the Pacific coast; in 1533, one of his pilots, Fortún Jiménez, discovered the peninsula of Baja California and, drawing on a popular tale of chivalry that described a mythical island of California, named the region after it. A decade later Juan Rodríguez Cabrillo, a veteran of the conquest of Tenochtitlán, became the first European to reach the Pacific coast of the present-day United States. His expedition explored the California coast as far north as Oregon.

Meanwhile, the Viceroy of New Spain, Antonio de Mendoza, commissioned Francisco Vázquez de Coronado to penetrate into the heart of North America in search of the fabled seven cities of Cíbola, said by previous Spanish explorers to lie north of present-day Albuquerque and to be capped with golden towers. Coronado's expedition of 1540–1542 included 300 Spanish adventurers (including at least 3 women), 6 Franciscan missionaries, 1,000 Indian allies, and 1,500 pack horses. Traveling over well-worn Indian trails, Coronado reached and captured the alleged Cíbola, which turned out to be a poor Zuni pueblo of 100 families. Refusing to abandon his quest, Coronado dispatched expeditions that discovered the Grand Canyon in Arizona and explored much of the Rio Grande Valley in New Mexico, where they encountered the Pueblo people for the first time. Coronado himself drove eastward, pursuing more empty rumors, eventually reaching the grasslands of central Kansas (see Map 2.1, page 39).

Simultaneously, Hernando de Soto, driven by visions of gold and glory and subsidized by Genoese merchants based in Seville, embarked from Florida on a *adelantado* mission of conquest and plunder. De Soto's force of 600 adventurers cut a bloody swath across the densely populated Southeast, enslaving native peoples and doing battle with the chiefdoms of the once-powerful Mississippian culture: the Apalachee of northern Florida, the Cofitachequi of South Carolina, and the Coosa of northern Alabama. In 1541 he crossed the Mississippi, going into Arkansas and parts of Texas, but to no avail. De Soto found caches of freshwater pearls but, like Coronado in the west, no gold, with the result that until the activities of Pedro Menéndez de Avilés in the 1560s (see American Lives, pages 24–25), Spain largely ignored North America.

The Legacy of the Conquest. The Spanish invasion forever changed life throughout the Western Hemisphere, first and foremost through its devastation of the native population. Although estimates vary, it seems likely that as many as 25 million Indians were living in present-day Mexico and Guatemala at the time of the Spanish invasion of 1519. Disastrous epidemics in 1521, 1545, and 1575 took millions of lives; by 1650, only 3 million native Americans were left. In Peru, the population plummeted from 9 million in 1533 to fewer than one-half million a century later. The Pueblo peoples of the Southwest and the Mississippian chiefdoms of Florida and the Southeast may have suffered declines of an equal magnitude as a result of European diseases.

Warfare and economic exploitation hastened the decline of the population. As Bartolomé de Las Casas argued, the Indians derived few material benefits from Spanish rule (see American Voices, page 23). Spanish overlords expelled native Americans from their agricultural lands, which had provided corn, squash, and beans for human consumption, and used their labor on vast new plantations, raising wheat and livestock for export to Europe. Spanish priests suppressed their traditional gods and converted them to Catholicism; Spanish bureaucrats imposed taxes and supervised their lives; and 500,000 Spanish migrants eventually settled on their lands.

The change was profound on both sides of the Atlantic. The coming of the Spanish altered the character of the American environment as imported grains and grasses supplanted native flora. Horses, which were first brought over by Cortés, began to spread throughout the Western Hemisphere and in the following centuries would change the way of life of hundreds of Indian communities, especially on the Great Plains of the United States. The food products of the Western Hemisphere—maize, tomatoes, manioc—had an equally great impact on Europe and Africa, increasing agricultural yields and stimulating the growth of populations. Nor was that all. The gold and silver that had honored Aztec gods now flowed into the counting houses of Spanish mine owners and merchants and the treasury of the Spanish kings, making that nation the most powerful in Europe until 1650.

Bartolomé de Las Casas

The Spanish Conquest Condemned

In 1542 Bartolomé de Las Casas, Dominican friar and Bishop of Chiapas (in present-day Mexico), wrote to the Spanish king to condemn the brutal treatment of native Americans by the conquistadors. Las Casas's books were widely read throughout Europe, creating the Black Legend, a picture of Spain as a vicious and cruel nation, determined at all costs to impose Catholicism on Indians—and on Protestant Europeans.

Now to come to the continent, we dare affirm of our own knowledge that there were ten kingdoms as large as the kingdom of Spain. . . . Of all this the inhumane and abominable villainies of the Spanish have made a wilderness, for though it was formerly occupied by vast and infinite numbers of men, it has been stripped of all people . . . over twelve million souls innocently perished, women and children being included in the sad and fatal list. . . .

As for those that came out of Spain, boasting themselves to be Christians, they had two ways of extirpating the Indian nation from the face of the earth: the first was by making bloody, unjust, and cruel wars against them; the second was by killing all those that so much as sought to recover their liberty, as some of the braver sort did. And as for the women and children that were left alive, the Spaniards let so heavy and grievous a yoke of servitude upon them that the condition of beasts was much more tolerable. . . .

What led the Spanish to these unsanctified impieties was the desire for gold to make themselves suddenly rich, in order to obtain dignities and honors that were in no way fit for them. . . . The Spanish so despised the Indians (I now speak what I have seen without the least untruth) that they used them not like beasts, for that would have been tolerable, but looked upon them as if they had been the dung and filth of the earth, and so little did they regard the health of their souls that they permitted the great multitude to die without the least light of religion. . . .

From which time forward the Indians began to think of ways that they might take to expel the Spaniards from their country. And when the Spanish saw this they came with their horsemen well armed with swords and lances, making a cruel havoc and slaughter among them, overrunning cities and towns and sparing neither sex nor age. Nor did their cruelty take pity on women with children, whose bellies they ripped up, taking out the infants to hew them to pieces. They

Bartolomé de Las Casas

would often lay wagers as to who could cleave or cut a man through the middle with the most dexterity, or who could cut off his head at one blow. The children they would take by the feet and dash their innocent heads against the rocks. . . . They erected a kind of gallows broad and low enough so that the tormented creatures might touch the ground with their feet, and upon each one of these they strung thirteen persons, blasphemously affirming that they did it in honor of our Redeemer and his apostles.

Source: Bartolomé de Las Casas, *The Tears of the Indians, Being an Historical and True Account of the Cruel Massacres and Slaughters of above Twenty Millions of Innocent People*, trans. John Phillips (London, 1656), 4–9.

By that time, the once magnificent civilizations of Mexico and Peru lay in ruins, and the surviving native Americans had lost much of their identity as separate peoples. Most Spanish settlers were men and many married Indian women, so their descendants eventually formed a predominant *mestizo* population with a mixed cultural heritage. As early as 1531 an Indian convert to Christianity began this process of cultural blending, reporting a vision of a dark-skinned Virgin Mary. Known as the Virgin of Guadalupe, this new Christian symbol became the object of great devotion and eventually of Mexican cultural nationalism. Resisting such assimi-

lation, small groups of Maya and other peoples left their lands and retreated into the mountains and preserved their traditional agricultural practices and values. In the centuries to come, their descendants, unlike the inhabitants of Africa and India, would never have the numbers or the power to oust the Europeans and so remained dependent peoples. Today only a single Indian tongue, Guarani in Paraguay, is a recognized national language, and no native American state sits in the United Nations. For the original Americans, the consequences of the Spanish intrusion in 1492 were tragic and irreversible.

Luis de Velasco/Opechancanough/ Massatamohtnock: Multiple Identities

Long before the Chesapeake Bay took its present name, it was known as the Bahía de Santa María (the Bay of Saint Mary), claimed by Spain and part of the giant colony of Florida that stretched from present-day Texas to Newfoundland. And long before the first English adventurers set foot in the colony they called Virginia, Spanish Jesuits established a mission there (in 1571) at Ajacán, the name they imposed on the land near the bay; they came to convert the local Algonquian inhabitants, the Powhatan people, to the Catholic faith.

For eighty years, from the 1560s to the 1640s, this land would be contested ground, as Spanish conquistadors and English adventurers and native chiefs vied with each other for control of the land and its people. The life of one man spanned this eighty-year struggle for power. The Spanish knew him as Don Luis de Velasco, a young Indian *cacique* (or chief) who had lived in Spain and become a pious convert to the Catholic faith. A generation later the English encountered him as Opechancanough, a local chief, "the King of the Pamaunches" (Pamunkey), who was also the elder brother of the Powhatan of the region and an astute negotiator who seemed to be a force for interracial peace. Finally, when he succeeded his brother as the main chief in 1621, at the age of seventy-seven, this man assumed a new name, Massatamohtnock, and a new role: a diplomat-warrior who led two Indian uprisings.

Spanish Catholic convert, pacific leader and diplomat, zealous native American patriot: Was this a case of multiple identities? A confused response to contradictory cultural pressures? Or simple deception?

This puzzle has its origins in 1561, when two vessels commanded by the famous Spanish mariner and adventurer Pedro Menéndez des Avilés sailed into the Bahía de Santa María. Like other conquistadors, Menéndez came looking for gold and plunder, but he also sought good harbors for naval garrisons that would protect Spanish treasure ships from pirates. Menéndez went away without riches but with a plan to return as an *adelantado*, the conqueror-proprietor of the entire east coast of North America. He also took with him the seventeen-year-old son of a local chief, an Indian youth "of fine presence and bearing," whom he promised to take to Europe "that the King of Spain, his lord, might see him." King Philip II was equally impressed by the imposing stature of the young *cacique*, who must have stood more than six feet tall, and by his intelligence, for he granted him an allowance and had Dominican friars teach him the Spanish language and the principles of the Catholic faith.

Three years later, the young man was in Mexico, where he acquired a new patron, Don Luis de Velasco, the Viceroy of New Spain, who became his godfather and gave the Indian his own name. Anxious to return to his people, in 1566 the Indian Don Luis accompanied a expedition to the Bahía de Santa María that was blown off course, and he found himself once again in Spain. Now taught by Jesuits, a contemporary chronicler noted, "he was made ready and they gave him the holy sacraments of the altar and Confirmation." For his part, Don Luis convinced the Jesuit Father Juan Baptista de Segura of his "plan and determination . . . of converting his parents, relatives, and countrymen to the faith of Jesus Christ, and baptizing them and making them Christians as he was."

Thus it was that the young Christian convert and eight Jesuit missionaries landed in 1570 in Ajacán, 5 miles from the later site of Jamestown. Once restored to the land of his childhood, Don Luis readopted its customs, taking a number of wives. When he was publicly chastised for adultery by Father Segura, he returned to his native village. When three missionaries came to fetch him, Don Luis had them killed with a "shower of arrows"; then, according to one account, he murdered Father Segura and the rest of the Jesuits with his own hand. This massacre brought quick retribution. In 1572 Menéndez personally led a punitive expedition that killed dozens of Indians, but his onetime protégé escaped his wrath. Renouncing his Spanish identity, the young *cacique* took a new name, Opechancanough, "He whose soul is white," and joined his younger brother, the Powhatan, in building the strongest chiefdom in the region.

As Spanish dreams of an eastern North American empire faded in the face of fierce native American resistance, England dispatched its own adventurers to search

for gold and propagate "the Christian religion to such People as yet live in Darkness." Opechancanough first confronted the new invaders in December 1607, when he captured Captain John Smith but spared his life. Two years later, when Smith grabbed the chief "by the long lock of his head; and with my pistol at his breast . . . made him fill our bark with twenty tuns of corn," Opechancanough did not seek revenge. Instead, for the next decade, the Pamunkey chief pursued a complicated diplomatic strategy: he "stood aloof" from the English and "would not be drawn to any Treaty," strongly resisting proposals to take Indian children from their parents so that they might be "brought upp in Christianytie." At the same time, he served the cause of interracial peace by acquiescing in the marriage of his niece Pocahontas to John Rolfe and by arranging a treaty between the Chickahominy and the English. Opechancanough stood between the two peoples, an Algonquin in culture and purpose but one whose was soul was still "white."

Then, once again, the chief assumed a new identity, taking the name Massatamohtnock in 1621 when he succeeded his younger brother as the Powhatan. The number of English migrants had increased significantly, leading many Algonquins to believe that the English would take up "all their lands and would drive them out the country." To prevent this, the aging Massatamohtnock played a double game. While assuring Governor Wyatt that "the Skye should sooner falle than Peace be broken, on his parte," he secretly mobilized the Pamunkey and more than two dozen other Indian peoples for a surprise attack that took the lives of 347 English men, women, and children (see Chapter 2). Urging the chief of the Potomacks to continue the onslaught, Massatamohtnock declared his goal: "before the end of two Moons there should not be an Englishman in all their Countries."

Finally defeated in the late 1620s by English scorched-earth warfare, the old chief reappeared in 1644, orchestrating a surprise assault that took the lives of "near five hundred Christians." Now a hundred years old, "so decrepit that he was not able to walk alone but was carried about by his men," Massatamohtnock was captured by the English and taken to Jamestown, where an ordinary soldier "basely shot him through the back . . . of which wound he died."

The absence of Algonquin sources makes it unlikely that we will ever know the complete history or the real motives of this remarkable man called Opechancanough for most of his life. But the violent treatment Don Luis meted out to Father Segura and the resistance Massatamohtnock unleashed in 1622 and 1644 suggest that ultimately he defined himself as an Indian patriot, a resolute enemy of the European invaders and their Christian religion.

The murder of Father Segura by the Indian Don Luis de Velasco at Ajacán in 1571, as depicted in a European engraving.

The Protestant Reformation and the Rise of England, 1500–1630

While Spain was conquering the indigenous societies of the New World, traditional European society was under siege from within. In 1517 a major schism divided the Catholic Church, plunging Europe into religious wars that lasted for decades. Simultaneously, gold and silver from America set off a great inflation, which altered traditional European society. England in particular was reshaped by these forces. Inflation, along with the enclosure of open fields, disrupted the lives of the peasantry, laying the foundation for a vast transatlantic migration. At the same time, English monarchs, seeking greater wealth, assisted the expansion of shipping and trade, creating the maritime resources required to establish overseas colonies. Finally, these rulers, trying to impose a single national Protestant church, persecuted Calvinist Protestants and Roman Catholics, prompting thousands to seek refuge in America.

The Protestant Movement

For more than a millennium the peoples of Western and Central Europe had been united in a common faith and their allegiance to the pope in Rome. The Protestant Reformation, which began in 1517, ushered in an era of war and social turmoil that lasted more than a century, forever shattering that unity.

At first, reformers wanted only to cleanse the church of corruption and abuses. Over the centuries the Catholic Church, through gifts, fees, and taxes, had become a large and wealthy institution, owning vast estates throughout Europe. Some bishops and cardinals, the princes of the church, used the income from church lands to live well, often luxuriously. Corruption became all too common. Pope Leo X (1513–1521), a member of the powerful Italian Medici family, received half a million ducats a year from the sale of religious offices, a practice known as *simony*. In England, Cardinal Thomas Wolsey set an equally poor example by giving church positions to his relatives. Ordinary priests and monks extracted their share of the spoils, using their authority to obtain economic or sexual favors. These abuses ignited a smoldering anticlericalism. One reformer proclaimed that the clergy were a "gang of scoundrels" who should be "rid of their vices or stripped of their authority." But until 1517 those raising their voices in protest had been either ignored or condemned as heretics and executed.

Martin Luther. In 1517, Martin Luther, a German monk and a professor at the university in Wittenberg, publicly challenged church leaders by nailing his famous Ninety-five Theses to the door of the town cathedral. This document, which was widely reprinted, condemned the church's pervasive and highly lucrative practice of selling *indulgences*—official dispensations that promised the purchasing sinner release from punishments in the afterlife. Luther argued that indulgences were worthless; redemption could come only from God through grace, not from the church, for a fee. When Luther refused to recant his views, he was excommunicated by Pope Leo X and threatened with punishment by King Charles I of Spain, who was also head of the Holy Roman Empire (see Table 1.1). The sentiment for reform was particularly strong in the German states, and northern German princes embraced Luther's doctrines and protected him from arrest. Soon Europe was at war as Charles dispatched armies to restore his authority, and Catholicism, throughout the Holy Roman Empire.

Luther broadened his attack, lashing out at church dogma and ritual not explicitly based on Scripture. His beliefs differed from Roman Catholic doctrine in four major respects. First, Luther rejected the doctrine of St.

TABLE 1.1

Spanish Monarchs, 1474–1598

Monarch	Dates of Reign	Achievements
Ferdinand and Isabella	1474–1516	Expelled Moors
Charles I	1516–1556	Dispatched Columbus; also Holy Roman Emperor, 1519–1556
Philip II	1566–1598	Attacked Protestantism; mounted Spanish Armada

Thomas Aquinas, the great medieval philosopher, that Christians could win salvation by their faith and good deeds (what Luther called "justification by works"). Stressing God's power and human weakness, Luther argued that people could be saved only by faith ("justification by faith") and that faith—and salvation—came as a gift of grace from God, not as a result of human action.

Second, Lutherans—and all Protestants—rejected the spiritual authority of the pope, partly because of corruption in the Italian-controlled papacy and partly because of political developments. As the Reformation gathered force, the rulers in many Protestant states declared themselves to be the official head of the churches within their realms, gaining the power to appoint bishops and control the church's property. Third, Luther downplayed the role of priests as mediators between God and the people, denying, for example, that priests had the power to grant absolution for sins. Instead he proclaimed the priesthood of all believers: "Our baptism consecrates us all without exception and makes us all priests." Fourth, Protestants considered the Bible the sole authority in matters of faith, raising the prospect of a multitude of individual interpretations. So that everyone could read the Bible, it was translated from Latin into the languages of the common people: German, French, and English. Luther himself did the German translation.

Social Revolution. Luther's attacks on existing authority encouraged the proliferation of radical religious doctrines and, in 1524, popular revolt against manorial landlords by the oppressed peasantry in Germany. The revolt was ruthlessly suppressed (a response that was applauded by Luther), but dissenting ideas continued to simmer below the surface. Ten years later a group of Anabaptists, religious radicals who rejected the doctrine of infant baptism, seized control of the city of Münster. They placed political power in the hands of "Saints"— those who felt God had saved them through grace—and their new government promptly abolished most rights to private property.

Fearing such social revolutions, most rulers in southern Europe did not contest the authority of the pope. Luther also affirmed the need for social discipline, arguing that whereas spiritual liberty was a private matter, Christians owed complete obedience to established political authorities. In the Peace of Augsburg in 1555, which ended a generation of religious wars, princes in the old Holy Roman Empire won the right to decide whether their subjects were to be Catholic or Protestant. Northern German princes made Lutheranism the official state religion, to which all members of the realm had to conform.

The Teachings of John Calvin. A more rigorous version of Protestantism appeared in Geneva, Switzerland, under the leadership of the great French theologian John Calvin. Even more than Luther, Calvin stressed the omnipotence of God and the corruption of human nature caused by Adam's sin. His masterly *Institutes of the Christian Religion* (1536) depicted God as an awesome and absolute sovereign, governing the "wills of men so as to move precisely to that end directed by him." Relentlessly pursuing this train of thought to its ultimate conclusion, Calvin enunciated the doctrine of *predestination*, the idea that God had "predestined" certain women and men for salvation even before they were born, condemning the rest to the eternal misery and torture of hell.

In Geneva, Calvin set up a model Christian community. He eliminated bishops altogether and placed spiritual power in the hands of ministers chosen by the members of each congregation. In the eyes of Calvinists, the state was an instrument of the church; its duty was to remake society into a disciplined religious community. Accordingly, ministers and pious laymen ruled the city, prohibiting all frivolity and luxury and banishing those who resisted.

Calvinism won converts all over Europe despite persecution by princes determined to suppress religious minorities in the name of national unity. Calvinism was the creed proclaimed by French Huguenots, by Protestants in Belgium and Holland, by Presbyterians in Scotland, and by Puritans in England and, eventually, America (see Map 1.4, page 28).

Spain's Rise and Decline

Luther's challenge to Catholicism in 1517 came just two years before Cortés conquered the Aztec empire, and the two sets of events remained linked. Gold and silver from rich mines in Mexico and Peru poured into Spain at the rate of 3 million ducats per year between 1550 and 1575 and averaged about 9 million ducats annually for the rest of the century, making Spain the wealthiest nation in Europe. Twenty percent of this immense treasure—the Royal Fifth—went directly to the Spanish monarch, helping Philip II (1556–1598), the great-grandson of Ferdinand and Isabella, become the most powerful ruler in Europe. From the Escorial, a massive monastery-palace that he built outside Madrid, Philip presided over a vast empire that included the wealthiest states of Italy, the commercial and manufacturing provinces of the Spanish Netherlands (Holland and Belgium), and, after 1580, Portugal and all its possessions in America, Africa, and the East Indies.

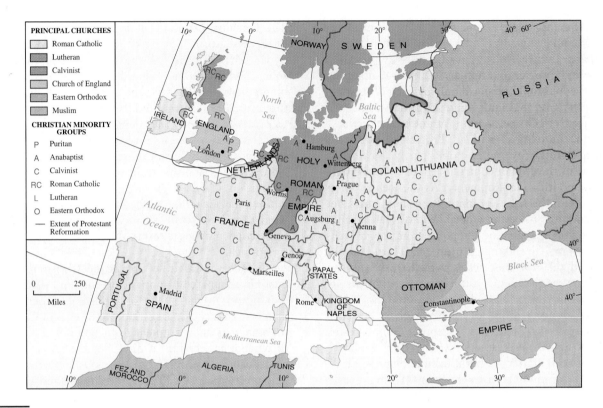

MAP 1.4

Religious Diversity in Europe

By 1600 Europe was permanently divided. Catholicism remained dominant in the south, but Lutheran princes and monarchs ruled northern Europe, and Calvinism had strongholds in Switzerland, Holland, and Scotland. Radical sects were persecuted by legally established Protestant churches as well as by Catholic clergy and monarchs. These religious conflicts encouraged the migration of minority sects to America.

The Dutch Revolt. Philip was an ardent Catholic and used his American wealth in a decades-long struggle against Protestantism in the Netherlands. Calvinism had taken strong root in these Dutch- and Flemish-speaking provinces, which had become wealthy from deep-sea fishing, commercial ties with the Portuguese empire, and the manufacture of woolen and linen fabrics. Their inhabitants feared that Philip would extend the Spanish Inquisition to wipe out their faith and take away their traditional political liberties. A popular anti-Catholic and anti-Spanish uprising in 1566 brought fierce repression by Philip's armies, but the revolt continued nonetheless.

Led by William of Orange in the province of Holland, the seven northern provinces declared their independence from Spain in 1581, becoming the Dutch Republic (or the Netherlands). To support the new Protestant state, Queen Elizabeth of England dispatched 6,000 troops to the Continent in 1585. In response, Philip assembled the Spanish Armada, and in 1588 he sent this impressive fleet of 130 ships (with 30,000 men and 2,400 pieces of artillery) to attack England. To Philip, this was the start of a holy crusade, for

he intended to conquer England, reimpose Catholicism there, and then wipe out Calvinism in Holland. But the Armada failed utterly, as English ships and a fierce storm destroyed the Spanish fleet and Philip's dream of a Catholic Europe along with it.

The Dutch were the big gainers. In 1609 Philip's successor tacitly accepted Dutch independence, and Amsterdam quickly emerged as the financial and commercial capital of northern Europe. After the formation of the Dutch East India Company, the Netherlands replaced Portugal as the dominant European power in Asia and coastal Africa. The Dutch also looked across the Atlantic, investing in sugar plantations in Brazil and the Caribbean and establishing fur-trading posts in North America (see Chapter 2).

As the Netherlands prospered, Spain faltered. Philip had spent much of his American bullion outside Spain, contributing to a long-term decline of the Spanish economy. Seeking greater opportunities, hundreds of thousands of Spaniards migrated to the new empire in America. Philip's massive expenditure of bullion also doubled the money supply of Europe, contributing to a runaway inflation that historians now refer to as the

A Dutch Merchant Family
This painting captures the serious Calvinist ethos—and the prosperity—of Holland in
the sixteenth century and also the character of the patriarchal family, with its rigid hierarchy of gender and age.

price revolution of the sixteenth century. The price of a
bushel of wheat, for example, rose by 300 percent between 1530 and 1600 because more money was "chasing" the limited supply of food and handmade goods
and because a sharp rise in Europe's population was increasing the demand for them (see Figure 1.2). The chief
beneficiaries of the price revolution were the Netherlands, France, and England. Stimulated by the influx of
Spanish gold and silver, their economies boomed, enabling them to seize the initiative in commerce, manufacturing, and diplomacy. At Philip's death in 1598,
Spain was in serious decline, exhausted financially and
psychologically by war and inflation.

Social Change and Migration from England

England's rise came slowly. As early as 1497, John
Cabot had explored the coasts of Newfoundland and
Nova Scotia, establishing an English claim to the region, but for the next half century England was too
weak in numbers, wealth, and military power to do
more than send fishing fleets across the Atlantic. Then a
decline in the death rate (because of fewer plagues and
epidemics) prompted a sustained rise in the population
from 3 million to 5 million between 1500 and 1630. A
larger population created more wealth but also caused
shortages of food, clothes, and housing. With goods in

FIGURE 1.2

Inflation and Living Standards
The influx of Spanish bullion was the
main cause of the great inflation in grain
prices, but increased demand (from a
constantly growing population) also
played a role. Higher prices cut real
wages, resulting in lower living
standards.

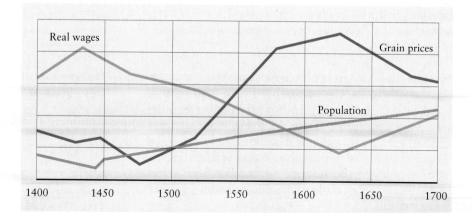

short supply and bullion plentiful, prices spiraled upward, bringing economic changes that profoundly altered the traditional class structure and, beginning in the 1550s, encouraged commercial expansion and overseas settlement.

Aristocracy, Gentry, Yeomanry. Most profoundly affected by the price revolution were the nobility, who had customarily rented out their estates on long leases for fixed rents. In the past, such arrangements had provided them with a secure income and plenty of leisure. As one English nobleman put it, "We eat and drink and rise up to play and this is to live like a gentleman." Then inflation struck. In the space of two generations, prices tripled on virtually everything, but the nobility's income from the rents on its farmlands remained virtually the same. Consequently, the wealth and status of the aristocracy declined both in local communities and in the nation as a whole.

Two other social groups benefited from the price revolution: the yeomen and the gentry. The *gentry* were substantial landholders who lacked the titles and legal privileges of the aristocracy. The gentry's estates were usually smaller than those of the nobility but they managed them more efficiently. For instance, the gentry rented their lands on short leases so they could raise rents to keep pace with inflation. Some yeomen also benefited from rising prices. Described by a European traveler as "middle people of a condition between gentlemen and peasants," *yeomen* owned some land, which they worked with family help. Since their labor costs remained constant, the yeomen's sale of grain brought increasing profits, which the more affluent among them used to build substantial houses and provide land for their children.

As aristocrats lost wealth, their branch of Parliament, the House of Lords, declined in influence. At the same time, members of the rising gentry, supported by the votes of other rural property owners, entered the House of Commons, the political voice of the propertied classes. The gentry demanded new rights and powers for the Commons, such as control of taxation. Thus the price revolution encouraged the rise of governing institutions in which property owners had a voice, a development with profound consequences for American political history.

Peasants and Enclosures. Peasants and farm laborers made up three-fourths of the population of England, and their lives, too, were transformed by the great inflation. As in the rest of Western Europe, many of these rural folk lived in open-field settlements, owning or leasing a house plot in the village center and holding the right to farm strips of the large surrounding fields. After 1500, rising prices and a growing demand for wool disrupted this communal agricultural system. Profit-

minded landlords and wool merchants used their influence in Parliament to pass *Enclosure* acts, which allowed owners to fence in the open fields and put sheep to graze on them, pushing villagers off their lands.

Thus dispossessed, families moved to small cottages in the countryside, creating a new class of landless laborers known as *cotters*. Constantly on the brink of poverty, cotters spun and wove the wool of the sheep that had taken their place on the land or worked as wage laborers on large estates owned by merchants or the gentry. Wealthy men had "taken farms into their hands," a critical observer noted in 1600, "and rent them to those that will give most, whereby the peasantry of England is decayed and become servants to gentlemen." English agriculture thus became increasingly capitalistic, with a few families owning the land and many other families working for them (see Figure 1.3).

These changes in English rural life precipitated a substantial migration to North America after 1600. As the population grew and land prices rose, thousands of yeoman farm families migrated to the English colonies to maintain their status as landowners. The enclosure

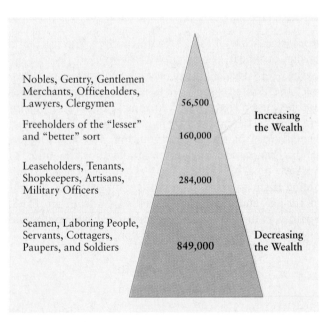

FIGURE 1.3

The Structure of English Society: 1688

This famous table of the structure of English society, devised by Gregory King in the 1680s, shows the result of centuries of aristocratic rule and of the enclosure movement. The majority of English families (some 849,000, according to King) lacked land or other productive resources and therefore, he thought, were "Decreasing the Wealth of the Kingdom." In fact, the labor of the propertyless produced a good deal of the wealth owned by those 500,500 families at the middle and top of the social scale.

movement created even greater numbers of dispossessed and impoverished peasants, many of whom crossed the Atlantic as humble indentured servants in hopes of a better life in the New World.

Mercantilist Expansion

The migration of so many English men and women would not have been possible without a vigorous and expanding merchant community. Beginning about 1350, English merchants began to sell high-quality English wool to manufacturers in France and the Netherlands. After 1500, English merchants themselves became textile manufacturers, creating a new *outwork* system of rural household production that was an early form of capitalist industry. In this system the merchants bought wool from landowners and provided it to landless cotters, who spun and wove the wool into cloth. The merchants then sold the finished product in English and foreign markets.

The Crown helped merchant capitalists expand the putting-out system and export goods to foreign markets. In 1563, the Statute of Artificers (artisan workers) gave justices of the peace the authority to fix wages, preventing cotters from demanding higher pay for their work. A new Poor Law in 1601 further ensured manufacturers a pool of cheap labor by making it more difficult for poor people to receive public assistance or private charity. Under the Tudor monarchs, especially Elizabeth I (1558–1603), special monetary bonuses were awarded to manufacturers who exported goods. Moreover, the government negotiated commercial treaties with foreign states and gave special privileges to merchant groups. In 1555, the Crown gave a royal charter to the Muscovy Company, providing it with a monopoly on the export of English cloth to Russia. Similar charters were granted to the Levant Company (Turkey) in 1581, the Guinea Company (Africa) in 1588, and the East India Company in 1600.

Mercantilism. The sixteenth-century system of state-supported manufacturing and trade became known in later centuries as *mercantilism*. English monarchs, like the rulers of many European states, pursued mercantilist policies to increase national power and wealth. By encouraging merchants to invest in domestic manufacturing, the Crown reduced the importation of foreign-made goods and boosted exports, a strategy designed to give England a favorable balance of trade. Gold and silver flowed into the country in payment for English manufactures, stimulating further economic expansion and enriching the merchant community. Increased trade meant higher revenues from import duties, which swelled the royal treasury and enhanced the power of the national government.

The success of these mercantilist policies made overseas colonization possible. The first attempts to establish a permanent English presence in America were small-scale efforts backed by individual aristocrats. All of them failed. In the 1580s, Sir Humphrey Gilbert's settlement in Newfoundland collapsed for lack of sufficient financial backing. Sir Ferdinando Gorges's colony along the coast of Maine also failed because of inadequate supplies and the harsh climate. Sir Walter Raleigh's three expeditions to North Carolina ended in failure, with one, the famous "lost" colony of Roanoke, completely vanishing, its 100 men, women, and children gone without a trace or any apparent cause.

What finally made English colonization possible was the banding together of successful merchants in *joint-stock companies*, which sold shares of stock to many investors, thus raising substantial amounts of money for commercial enterprises. It was a royally chartered joint-stock venture, the Virginia Company of London, that founded the first permanent English settle-

Sir Walter Raleigh and His Son
Raleigh was one of the great figures of his age. A distinguished courtier (as this portrait suggests), he was also a man of action—as a conquering soldier in Ireland, an explorer in South America, and the organizer of England's first colonial ventures.

ment in America at Jamestown (Virginia) in 1607. The investors hoped, like the Spanish, to grow rich by finding gold and by trading with the natives or exploiting their labor.

The English Reformation and the Puritan Exodus

While English merchants sought wealth in Virginia, thousands of other English men and women migrated to Massachusetts and Maryland to escape religious conflict and persecution. King Henry VIII (1509–1547) had initially opposed the spread of Protestantism in his kingdom. Then he petitioned the papacy for a divorce from Catherine of Aragon, an aunt of Charles V, the Holy Roman Emperor. When his request was denied, Henry broke with Rome, established a national Church of England (which granted his divorce), and declared himself supreme head of that church with complete control over ecclesiastical appointments. This break from Rome set in motion a series of religious conflicts that ended in a massive migration to America and civil war in England.

The Church of England. Henry VIII made few changes in traditional religious dogma, organization, or ritual. Priests, sacraments, and elaborate ceremonies remained important, and spiritual authority still flowed downward in a hierarchical and authoritarian fashion—from king to bishops to priests. Indeed, except for its emphasis on the authority of the Bible and its recognition of justification by faith, the Church of England under Henry was barely Protestant. But Henry's severance of the link with Rome was crucial. When his elder daughter, Queen Mary (1553–1558), briefly restored Catholicism as the state religion, her action was deeply resented, and her execution of 300 Protestant clergymen further inflamed anti-Catholic sentiment.

By the time Henry's younger daughter, Elizabeth I (1558–1603), ascended the throne, pressure for Protestant reform was irresistible, and the new queen was quick to respond by approving a Protestant confession of faith. The Thirty-nine Articles were carefully crafted to appeal to as many English Christians as possible. They incorporated both the Lutheran doctrine of justification by faith and the Calvinist belief in predestination but retained the clerical hierarchy of bishops and archbishops as well as traditional religious services—now conducted in English rather than Latin.

Elizabeth I (1558–1603)
Attired in richly decorated clothes, Queen Elizabeth I celebrates the destruction of the Spanish Armada (pictured in background) and proclaims her nation's imperial ambitions. The Queen's hand rests on a globe, asserting England's claims in the Western Hemisphere.

Presbyterianism. In an age of passionate religious controversy, Elizabeth's compromise was bound to be challenged. Many English Protestants condemned the power of bishops as "anti-Christian and devilish and contrary to the Scriptures" and called for a more radical change in church organization. Some reformers took inspiration from Calvin's Geneva, where the laity of each church controlled all of its affairs. Others preferred the presbyterian system devised by John Knox for the Calvinist Church of Scotland; there, local congregations elected lay elders (presbyters), who assisted ministers in running the church. By 1600, 500 ministers in the Church of England wanted to eliminate bishops and install a presbyterian form of church government.

The Puritans. Other reform-minded English Protestants focused their attention on religious practice. Calling themselves "unspotted lambs of the Lord" or (embracing a term used to insult them) "Puritans," they sought to purify the church of "false" teachings and practices. Although Puritans differed among themselves, they were generally united on three basic principles of ritual and doctrine. First, they wanted the authority over spiritual and financial matters to rest primarily with the lay members in each local congregation, not with bishops or even Presbyterian synods. Second, Puritans asserted the priesthood of each individual, maintaining that all Christians, not only ministers, could understand and interpret the Bible. Third, they condemned most traditional religious rites as magical or idolatrous. Puritans were offended by elaborately robed priests and by gaudy churches filled with statues and fragrant with incense; they denied that the sacraments of Baptism and Communion had miraculous powers.

As part of their attack on what they saw as magical religion, Puritans denied that God spoke to people through the *senses*. True spirituality and genuine religious knowledge, they argued, came through the *mind*. Consequently, they taught their children the importance of reading the Bible (which produced a highly literate population). The centerpiece of their religious service was the sermon—a finely wrought argument on dogma and ethics.

Religious Persecution. King James I (1603–1625), a Scot who was the first Stuart to rule England, continued Elizabeth's policy of resisting radical religious reform. He remarked bitterly that presbyterians favoring representative institutions of church government "agreeth as well with a monarchy as God with the Devil." James endorsed the absolute power of kings, not shared power with Parliament. In *The True Laws of Free Monarchy*, he maintained that kings drew their authority directly from God and thus had a *divine right* to rule. As for the congregationalist-minded Puritans, James threatened to "harry them out of the land, or else do worse."

Radical Protestants took the king at his word and fled England to avoid persecution. To preserve their "pure" Christian faith, some sects separated completely from the Church of England (and hence were called "Separatists"). One such group was the Pilgrims, who left England and settled among like-minded Dutch Calvinists at Leiden in Holland. Fearing the loss of their English way of life, some Pilgrims decided to migrate to America to preserve both their religious freedom and their sense of national identity. Led by William Bradford, thirty-five Pilgrims, joined by sixty migrants from England, founded the Plymouth colony in 1620.

During the next two decades, the repressive policies of James I and Charles I (1625–1649) drove thousands of Puritans across the Atlantic to establish settlements in the West Indies and at Massachusetts Bay. Like the Pilgrims, the Puritans envisioned a reformed Christian society, a genuinely "new" England. However, rather than break with the Church of England, they hoped to reform it; hence, they were "non-Separatist" congregationalists. They were strict Calvinists nonetheless, and the colonies they founded embodied some of the most radical thought of the Protestant Reformation.

Religious intolerance drove English Catholics to America as well. Persecuted by the dominant Church of England for their religious beliefs and their allegiance to the pope, they began settling in America in 1634, establishing the colony of Maryland. Thousands of other settlers accompanied the Catholics and Puritans, fleeing poverty or hoping for greater prosperity in the new settlements.

The English Legacy to America. The economic and religious transformation of England during the sixteenth century greatly influenced the character of its North American settlements. Since the aristocracy was on the decline and played a small role in colonization, the American settlements were not dominated by a legally privileged nobility. Conversely, the rise of English merchants enhanced their role in overseas expansion and resulted in the rapid creation of a transatlantic trading economy. Moreover, the social upheaval produced by enclosure and agricultural capitalism in England prompted the migration of thousands of yeomen and peasant families seeking land to farm. Finally, as a result of the influence of Calvinism on English Protestantism, many of these migrants carried radical forms of Christianity to North America.

The legacy was rich and complex. As products of traditional Europe, the settlers brought with them age-old principles of authority and a hierarchical social organization. Yet the old European order had already been partially overturned: the English colonies in America were founded by a nation in the midst of violent economic, political, and religious transformation. Their character and their fate were unpredictable.

Summary

The first inhabitants of the Western Hemisphere were hunter-gatherers from Asia who migrated across a land bridge during the last Ice Age. Their descendants settled throughout North and South America, establishing a great variety of cultures. In Mesoamerica, the Mayan and Aztec peoples developed densely populated agricultural societies with highly sophisticated systems of art, religion, and politics. In North America, the peoples of the Hopewell and Mississippian cultures created elaborate ceremonial and urban sites, as did the Pueblo peoples of the Southwest. Most North American Indians, however, lived in small-scale, self-governing communities of foragers, hunters, and horticulturalists.

The Europeans who invaded America came from an agricultural society in which an elite ruled a mass of peasants. The Christian religion gave emotional richness and meaning to life. Church and state endorsed values of hierarchy and authority, demanding strict discipline as the price of survival in a world of scarcity.

Europeans gradually acquired the skills and power required to colonize the Western Hemisphere. The Crusades opened their eyes to the learning of the Arab Muslim world, while the Italian Renaissance and the emergence of strong monarchical nation-states began to transform Europe from a static to a dynamic society. Portugal broke the Arab monopoly of trade with Asia by dispatching merchants around the African continent. After completing the *reconquista*, Spain sent the Italian sea captain Christopher Columbus to find a westerly route across the Atlantic. Instead of Asia, Columbus found a "new world." Within a generation, Spanish conquistadors had pillaged the wealthy civilizations of Peru and Mexico, but they failed to find gold and empire north of the Rio Grande. The coming of Europeans—and their diseases, government, and religion—brought death to millions of native Americans and changed forever the lives of those who survived.

Gold and silver from America changed European society as well, triggering a price revolution that disrupted traditional society, which was already reeling from the Protestant Reformation. These twin forces—inflation and religious dissent—undermined Spain's dominant position in Europe while encouraging the maritime expansion of Holland, France, and England. In England, monarchs used mercantilist policies to promote manufacturing, foreign trade, and colonization. The enclosure movement and religious conflicts likewise prompted a mass migration to America. Coming from a society in flux, the migrants carried both traditional and modern ideas and institutions across the Atlantic.

TIMELINE

30,000–10,000 B.C.	Settlement of eastern North America
3000–2000 B.C.	Cultivation of crops begins in Mesoamerica
1200 B.C.	Olmec culture appears
A.D. 100–400	Hopewell culture in Mississippi Valley
300	Rise of Mayan civilization
500	Zenith of Teotihuacán civilization
600	Emergence of Pueblo cultures
700–1100	Spread of Arab Muslim civilization
800–1350	Mississippian culture
1096–1291	Crusades bring Europeans into contact with Islamic civilization
1212–1492	Spanish *reconquista*
1300–1450	Italian Renaissance
1325	Aztecs establish their capital at Tenochtitlán
1415–1500	Portuguese establish maritime empire
1440s	Portugal enters trade in African slaves
1492	Christopher Columbus's first voyage to America
1513	Juan Ponce de Leon explores Florida
1517	Martin Luther starts Protestant Reformation
1521	Hernando Cortés leads Spanish conquest of Mexico
1534	Henry VIII establishes Church of England
1536	John Calvin's *Institutes of Christian Religion*
1539–1543	Hernando de Soto invades southeastern region of America
1540–1542	Francisco Vázquez de Coronado searches for Cíbola
1550–1630	Price revolution / English mercantilism / Enclosure movement
1556	Philip II becomes king of Spain
1558–1603	Elizabeth I, queen of England
1560s	English Puritan movement begins
1560s	Pedro Menéndez de Avilés plans North American empire
1603–1625	James I, first Stuart king of England

★   ★   ★

BIBLIOGRAPHY

One of the few works that covers the history of the various European and native American peoples is Eric Wolf, *Europe and the People without History*. See also Alfred W. Crosby, Jr., *Ecological Imperialism: The Biological Expansion of Europe, 900–1900* (1986); Robert R. Reynolds, *Europe Emerges: Transition toward an Industrial World-Wide Society, 600–1750* (1961); and G. V. Scammell, *The World Encompassed: The First European Maritime Empires* (1981).

Native American Worlds

Brian M. Fagan, *The Great Journey; The People of Ancient America* (1987), synthesizes recent scholarship on prehistoric American Indians, while his *Kingdoms of Gold, Kingdoms of Jade: The Americas before Columbus* (1991) does the same for the Mesoamerican peoples. See also Stuart J. Fiedel, *Prehistory of the Americas* (1992); Inga Clendinnen, *Aztecs: An Interpretation* (1991); John S. Henderson, *The World of the Maya* (1981); David Carrasco, *Quetzalcoatl and the Irony of Empire* (1982); R. C. Padden, *The Hummingbird and the Hawk* (1962); and R. Tom Zuidema, *Inca Civilization in Cuzco* (1992). Two fine supplements are Michael Coe et al., *Atlas of Ancient America* (1986), and Manuel Lucena Salmoral, *America in 1492* (1991), a photographic survey of dress, artifacts, and architecture.

Alfred W. Crosby, Jr., *The Columbian Exchange: Biological and Cultural Consequences of 1492* (1972), traces the impact of European diseases. See also Henry F. Dobyns, *Their Numbers Became Thinned: Native American Population Dynamics in Eastern North America* (1983), and William M. Denevan, *The Native Population of the Americas in 1492* (1992).

On North America, consult Alvin M. Josephy, Jr., ed., *America in 1492* (1993); Linda S. Cordell, *Ancient Pueblo Peoples* (1994); Bruce D. Smith, ed., *The Mississippian Emergence* (1990); Carl Waldman and Molly Braun, *Atlas of the North American Indian* (1985); and Robert Silverberg, *Mound Builders of Ancient America: The Archaeology of a Myth* (1968). Roger Kennedy, *Hidden Cities* (1994), surveys the early Indian civilizations of the Mississippi Valley.

Traditional European Society

Barbara W. Tuchman, *A Distant Mirror: The Calamitous Fourteenth Century* (1978), and Johan Huizinga, *The Waning of the Middle Ages*, present vivid portraits of the late medieval world. Two wide-ranging studies of subsequent developments are George Huppert, *After the Black Death: A Social History of Modern Europe* (1986), and Henry Kamen, *European Society, 1500–1700* (1984). Illuminating specialized studies include Peter Burke, *Popular Culture in Early Modern Europe* (1978); Pierre Goubert, *The French Peasantry in the Seventeenth Century* (1986); Philippe Ariès, *Centuries of Childhood* (1962); B. H. Slicher Van Bath, *The Agrarian History of Western Europe, A.D. 500–1850* (1963); and Emanuel Le Roy Ladurie, *The Peasants of Languedoc* (1974). See also Joel Mokyr, *The Lever of Riches: Technological Creativity and Economic Progress* (1990), and E. P. Thompson, *Customs in Common: Studies in Traditional Popular Culture* (1991).

Europe and the World

The preconditions for European expansion are treated in James D. Tracy, ed., *Rise of Merchant Empires: Long Distance Trade in the Early Modern World, 1350–1750* (1990). For the southern European background, read selectively in Fernand Braudel's massive and stimulating *The Mediterranean and the Mediterranean World in the Age of Philip II* (1949).

Paul H. Chapman, *The Norse Discovery of America* (1981), and Boies Penrose, *Travel and Discovery in the Renaissance, 1420–1620* (1952), illuminate the growth of geographical knowledge. For the expansion of the Iberian peoples see Bailey W. Diffie and George Winius, *Foundations of the Portuguese Empire, 1415–1580* (1977), and Henry Kamen, *Crisis and Change in Early Modern Spain* (1993). A good short biography of Columbus and his times is Felipe Fernández-Armesto, *Columbus* (1991).

For the Spanish and Portuguese colonial empires, see Charles R. Boxer, *The Portuguese Seaborne Empire* (1969), and James Lockhard and Stuart B. Schwartz, *Early Latin America: Colonial Spanish America and Brazil* (1984). Fine accounts of the Spanish conquest include the memorable firsthand report by Bernal Diaz del Castillo, *The Discovery and Conquest of Mexico* (ed. by I. A. Leonard, 1956); Leon Portilla, *Broken Spears: The Aztec Account of the Conquest of Mexico* (1962); and Hugh Thomas, *Conquest: Montezuma, Cortés and the Fall of Old Mexico* (1994). The impact on native society in New Spain is portrayed in Daniel T. Reff, *Disease, Depopulation, and Culture Change in Northwestern New Spain, 1518–1764* (1991); for the story north of the Rio Grande, see David J. Weber, *The Spanish Frontier in North America* (1992), and Ramon Gutiérrez, *When Jesus Came, the Corn Mothers Went Away: Marriage, Sexuality, and Power in New Mexico, 1500–1846* (1991).

The Protestant Reformation and the Rise of England

On the European Reformation, consult William J. Bouwsma, *John Calvin* (1987), and De Lamar Jensen, *Reformation Europe: Age of Reform and Revolution* (1981). For England, see Patrick Collinson, *The Religion of the Protestants: The Church in English Society, 1559–1625* (1982), and Susan Doran and Christopher Durston, *Princes, Pastors, and People: The Church and Religion in England, 1529–1689* (1991).

On the decline of Spain, consult Henry Kamen, *Spain: A Society in Conflict, 1479–1714*, 2d ed. (1991), and John Lynch, *The Hispanic World in Crisis and Change, 1598–1700* (1992), which also traces the growing economic independence of New Spain. For a general analysis of economic change in Europe, see T. S. Ashton, ed., *The Brenner Debate* (1987).

A brilliant and forceful portrait of English preindustrial society is offered by Peter Laslett, *The World We Have Lost*, 3d ed. (1984). Other important works are Keith Wrightson, *English Society, 1580–1680* (1982), and two books by Lawrence Stone, *The Crisis of the Aristocracy* (1965), and *Family, Sex, and Marriage in England, 1500–1800* (1977). On the movement of people, see Ida Altman and James Horn, eds., *"To Make America": European Emigration in the Early Modern Period* (1991).

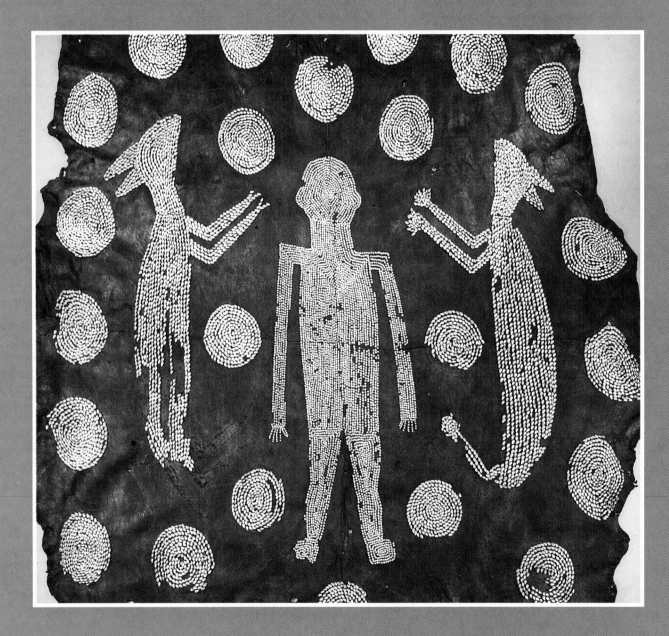

Cloak Worn by Powhatan

This deerskin, decorated with shells, is believed to be one of
the ceremonial cloaks worn by Powhatan, the leading chief
of the Indians of eastern Virginia. It was taken to England in
1614, a few years after the English first settled at Jamestown.

CHAPTER 2

Invasion and Settlement
1565–1675

★   ★   ★

By 1565 Spain had established a permanent settlement in North America, and France, Holland, and England would soon claim shares of the continent. For the next century those four nations battled for control of North America. In the process, they established very distinct colonial systems, focused either on religious conversion, the fur trade, or the settlement of European colonists. Spanish priests and a few Spanish colonists spread their religion and culture into Florida and New Mexico; French peasants farmed the St. Lawrence valley while French and Dutch merchants negotiated with Indian peoples over the fur trade; and English settlers along the Atlantic seaboard slowly moved westward.

English expansion began slowly. By 1625 England had established only two tiny colonies on the mainland: Jamestown and Plymouth, both in eastern North America. Then, between 1625 and 1675, tens of thousands of English men and women migrated to America, buying or seizing land from the Indian peoples, first in the Chesapeake Bay region and then in New England. These colonists came from markedly different backgrounds, and life in America pushed them in fresh directions. The Chesapeake was invaded primarily by adventurers seeking wealth and power, and it developed as an export-oriented plantation society in which life for most people was short, hard, and so oppressive that it sparked a violent civil war.

By contrast, New England evolved in an orderly fashion. Its settlement was directed by a purposeful group of leaders who had strong religious and communal values. Many settlers arrived in families, bolstering social cohesion, and joined Puritan churches, which enforced strict moral standards. Consequently, New England developed as a tightly governed society with a relatively egalitarian and self-sufficient yeoman economy.

This first century of European settlement prefigured the course of North American history. The triumphs of the invaders—as missionaries, fur traders, or settlers—came largely at the expense of the various Indian peoples, who gradually—through European diseases, sporadic wars, and religious conversions—lost their lives, lands, and cultural values.

Spanish, French, and Dutch Goals

Largely ignored before 1600, North America became the object of European diplomatic and religious rivalries. Spanish and French missionaries encouraged native Americans to renounce their ancestral religions and become Catholics. French and Dutch merchants sought to control the fur trade, often by setting one Indian people against another. To the Indians, these strangers had to be treated with great care, for they might be either benefactors or dangerous enemies. Wherever Europeans went as missionaries or fur traders rather than as settlers, the white population remained small, and the Indians had a much better chance of retaining their traditional lands and identities. But nearly everywhere the native peoples eventually rose in revolt.

Imperial Rivalries and American Settlements

By the 1560s few Spaniards still dreamed of finding rich Indian empires in North America. However, officials in New Spain wanted to reinforce their claims to the continent and protect the treasure fleets that skirted its eastern coast on their way to Spain. The danger was real, for Spanish gold was a powerful lure to English adventurers. In the 1560s Sir John Hawkins and other "sea dogs" plundered Spanish possessions in the Caribbean.

The Contest for Florida. France was also on the move. As far back as the 1530s Jacques Cartier had sailed into the Gulf of St. Lawrence in search of a northwestern passage to Asia and had laid France's claim to all the adjacent lands. Then, in the late 1550s, French corsairs systematically attacked Spanish treasure ships, cutting the Spanish Crown's revenue in half. French Protestants settled in Brazil in 1555, and in 1564 they moved into the Florida peninsula, land long claimed by Spain, constructing a fort on the St. John River.

King Philip II acted quickly, appointing Pedro Menéndez de Avilés as *adelantado* of the province of Florida, directing him to find the encroaching Frenchmen and "cast them out by the best means." Menéndez carried out his orders with a vengeance, massacring about 300 members of the "evil Lutheran sect." In 1565 Menéndez established a Spanish fort at St. Augustine, the first permanent European settlement in the future United States, and six other bases, the most important at Saint Elena on Port Royal Sound in present-day South Carolina. From there he sent expeditions into the interior and to the Bahía de Santa María (Chesapeake Bay), where in 1571 Spanish Jesuits founded a short-lived mission (see American Lives, Chapter 1). However, attacks by the Calusa and Timucuan peoples soon destroyed most of the Spanish settlements, causing Menéndez to condemn them as an "infamous people, Sodomites, sacrificers to the devil . . . [who should be] given as slaves."

New Mexico and California. The Spanish Crown adopted a more pacific policy toward native Americans. The Comprehensive Orders for New Discoveries, issued in 1573, placed the "pacification" of new lands primarily in the hands of missionaries, excluding adventurers such as Menéndez. In the 1580s Franciscan friars rediscovered the Pueblo world visited by Coronado two generations before, naming the area San Felipe del Nuevo México and establishing missions among the Indian settlements (see Map 2.1). But in 1598, the *adelantado* Juan de Oñate led an expedition of 500 soldiers and settlers into New Mexico to establish a military *presidio* (fort) and a trading villa. As their supplies dwindled, Oñate's men seized corn and clothing from the Pueblo peoples and murdered and raped those who resisted. Indians of the pueblo of Acoma struck back, killing 11 Spanish soldiers and prompting the remaining Spanish troops to destroy the pueblo, killing 500 men and 300 women and children. Faced by now-hostile Indian peoples, most of the settlers withdrew to New Spain.

English Ventures. Meanwhile, English adventurers stepped up their attacks on the Spanish empire. In 1577 Sir Francis Drake sailed around the tip of South America and attacked a Spanish bullion fleet in the Pacific. After landing in California, which he claimed for England, Drake sailed west to Asia. Circumnavigating the globe, he returned home with £600,000 in bullion (equal to about $30 million in 1995), twenty times the annual income of the wealthiest aristocrat. A decade later, in 1586, Drake sacked the treasure port of Cartagena (in present-day Colombia) and then razed St. Augustine, nearly wiping out the fledgling garrison-colony.

These attacks, along with Raleigh's expeditions to North Carolina, alarmed Spanish officials. They grew more concerned as the Virginia Company's settlement at Jamestown in 1607 and the founding of French Quebec in 1608 challenged Spain's monopoly over North America. This rivalry with France and England prompted Spain to maintain a token presence north of the Rio Grande, as did the continuing desire to convert the Indian peoples. In 1608 the Spanish Crown decided to maintain the garrison in St. Augustine and authorized Franciscans to remain in New Mexico. However, Spanish officials decided that an outpost in California

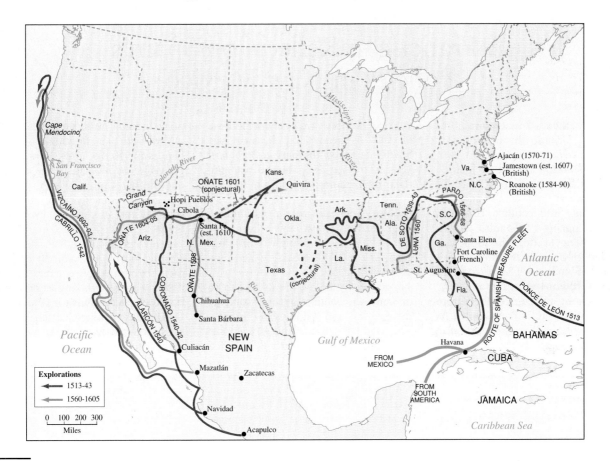

MAP 2.1

New Spain Looks North, 1513–1610

The quest for gold drew Spanish adventurers deep into North America. Hernando de Soto and Francisco Vázquez de Coronado led wide-ranging expeditions in the 1540s, but the first permanent settlement to the north of New Spain came only in 1565, at St. Augustine in present-day Florida. A generation later, following the explorations of Juan de Oñate, the Spanish founded Santa Fe in New Mexico.

would not be worth the cost, delaying permanent European occupation of that area until 1769.

New Spain: Territory and Missions

The Catholic Church was the primary force in colonizing New Spain north of the Rio Grande. Throughout the seventeenth century, Franciscan friars established missions among the Pueblo peoples of New Mexico and the Muskhogean-speaking villagers of Georgia and the north Florida peninsula, baptizing tens of thousands. Personal zeal accounted in part for the Franciscans' success; disdaining personal comfort, the friars built their missions and churches near existing pueblos and villages and often learned Indian languages. But government support in the form of supplies and soldiers also played a role in their success. Protected by soldiers, friars smashed the religious idols of the native Americans and, to win their allegiance to Christ and the concepts

of sin and heaven and hell—all new ideas for the Indians—dazzled them with rich vestments, gold crosses, and silver chalices (see American Voices, page 40).

For the Franciscans, religious conversion and cultural assimilation went hand in hand. The missionaries introduced European agricultural practices, with men instead of women growing most of the crops, and imposed Spanish language and customs, encouraging the Indians to farm, cook, eat, dress and walk like Spaniards. Those who committed sexual sins or worshiped traditional spirits were punished, usually by whipping.

For most native Americans, the missions were coercive institutions. They tolerated the Franciscans out of fear of military reprisals or in hopes of gaining access to their spiritual secrets. When prayers to Jesus and the Christian saints failed to prevent European diseases and rapacious soldiers and settlers from devastating their communities, many Indians turned back to their traditional deities.

A Franciscan Reflects on Spain's Policies in New Mexico

New Spain extended its empire north of the Rio Grande through military force and religious conversion. But Spanish *adelantados* such as Juan de Oñate and Franciscan friars had differing interests and goals and frequently came into conflict. However, these two agents of Spanish expansionism often needed to cooperate. The friars frequently called on troops stationed in military *presidios* to induce local Indians to settle (and stay) at the missions and protect them from attacks by nomadic Indian peoples. As a close reading will suggest, this plea from a Franciscan to the Viceroy of New Spain endorses the limited use of military force even as it condemns past excesses.

The first and foremost difficulty, from which have sprung all the evils and the ruin of this land, is the fact that this conquest was entrusted to a man of such limited resources as Don Juan de Oñate. The result was that soon after he entered the land, his people began to perpetrate many offenses against the natives and to plunder their pueblos of the corn they had gathered for their own sustenance; here corn is God, for they have nothing else with which to support themselves. Because of this situation and because the Spaniards asked the natives for blankets as tribute, even before teaching them the meaning of God, the Indians began to get restless, abandon their pueblos, and take to the mountains. Your lordship must not believe that the Indians part willingly with their corn, or the blankets with which they cover themselves; on the contrary, this extortion is done by threats and force of arms, the soldiers burning some of the houses and killing the Indians. This was the cause of the Acoma war [of 1598], as I have clearly established after questioning friars, captains, and soldiers. And the war which was recently waged against the Jumanas started the same way. In these conflicts, more than eight hundred men, women, and children were killed, and three pueblos burned.

I do not hesitate to say that his majesty could have discovered this land with fifty well-armed Christian men, giving them the necessary things for this purpose, and that what these fifty men might discover could be placed under the royal crown and the conquest effected in a Christian manner without outraging or killing these poor Indians, who think that we are all evil and that the king who sent us here is ineffective and a tyrant. By so doing we would satisfy the wishes of our mother church, which, not without long consideration and forethought and illuminated by the Holy Spirit, entrusted these conquests and the conversions of souls to the kings of Castile, our lords, acknowledging in them the means, Christianity, and holiness for an undertaking as heroic as is that of winning souls for God.

Because of these matters (and others that I am not telling), we cannot preach the gospel now, for it is despised by these people on account of our great offenses and the harm we have done them. At the same time it is not desirable to abandon this land, either for the service of God or the conscience of his majesty since many souls have already been baptized. Besides, this place where we are now established is a good stepping stone and site from which to explore this whole land.

Source: G. P. Hammond and Agapito Rey, *Don Juan de Oñate, Colonizer of New Mexico, 1595–1628* (Albuquerque: University of New Mexico Press, 1953), Part II, pp. 692-695.

And well they might, for the resident Spaniards systematically exploited their labor. Franciscans ran their missions with Indian workers, who grew their crops and carried them to market, often on their backs. Spanish settlers, some of them privileged citizens, or *encomenderos*, collected tribute from the natives, usually in goods but often through a system of forced labor known as *repartimiento*. Still other native Americans, often women and children captured by nomadic Indian peoples, were ransomed by Spanish settlers and forced to work as slaves. Elaborate codes of Spanish law meant to regulate or prohibit the exploitation of Indian labor were rarely enforced in frontier regions.

Native peoples tried to save themselves, sometimes rising in disorganized revolts. By 1680 years of forced tribute, drought, and raids by nomadic Navajos and Apaches combined to threaten many Pueblos with extinction. Led by Popé, an Indian shaman (priest) accused of sorcery by the Spanish, the peoples of two dozen pueblos mounted a carefully coordinated rebellion. They killed over 400 Spaniards and forced the remaining 2,000 colonists to flee 300 miles down the Rio Grande to El Paso. Overtly rejecting Christianity, the Pueblo peoples desecrated churches and tortured and killed twenty-one missionaries. Reconquered a decade later by Diego de Vargas, the Indians rebelled again in 1696,

Conversion in New Mexico
Franciscan friars introduced Catholicism to the Indian peoples north of the Rio Grande, assisted by nuns of various religious orders. This 1631 engraving shows La V. M. María de Jesús de Agreda preaching to a nomadic people (*los chichimecos*) in New Mexico.

only to be subdued. Exhausted by war but now able to practice their own religion and avoid forced labor, for the next century the Pueblo peoples accepted their dependent position, joining with the Spanish to defend their lands against attacks by nomadic Indian peoples.

New France: Furs and Souls

The French came late to North America, and even after the founding of Quebec in 1608, they came only in small numbers. Therefore, in 1627 the French Crown chartered the Company of New France to encourage migration to the settlement. The company recruited few women (only about 12 percent of the total), and the men were mostly young peasants who had fled rural poverty and ended up in the cities of western France. And most of them, probably 70 percent of the 67,000

migrants to Quebec between 1608 and 1763, eventually returned to France, their hopes for prosperity dashed by the realities of life in the northern colony with its long, bitter winters.

Nor did conditions in France encourage migration. Many French peasants held strong legal rights to their village lands, and few had been displaced by the enclosure of common fields. Moreover, the French government discouraged migration in order to ensure an ample supply of farm laborers and military recruits—and thus preserve French power in Western Europe. Finally, the Catholic monarchs of France barred Huguenots (French Protestants) from seeking refuge in the colony, where the Crown feared they might undermine state interests. Consequently, New France proved a failure as a settler colony: in 1698 its European population was only 15,200, a much lower number than the 100,000 settlers then residing in the English colonies.

Instead, French Canada became a vast fur-trading enterprise as explorers traveled deep into the continent seeking new suppliers and claiming new lands for France (see Map 2.2). In 1673 Jacques Marquette, a priest of the Society of Jesus (Jesuits), journeyed west from Quebec with the fur trader Louis Joliet, eventually reaching the Mississippi River and traveling down it from present-day Wisconsin to Arkansas. René Robert Cavelier, Sieur de La Salle, completed the exploration of the majestic river in 1681, asserting French sovereignty over the entire Mississippi Valley while seeking a personal fortune. As a French priest noted with disgust, La Salle's party hoped "to buy all the Furs and Skins of the remotest Savages, who, as they thought, did not know their Value; and so enrich themselves in one single voyage." La Salle named the region Louisiana in honor of Louis XIV, the Sun King. By the early eighteenth century, despite Spain's renewed claims to Texas and the lower Mississippi Valley, New France included a thriving port at New Orleans, on the Gulf of Mexico.

The intrusion of French traders and explorers had a catastrophic impact on native Americans living near the Great Lakes. The *coureurs de bois* (runners of the woods) introduced deadly European diseases that killed anywhere from 25 to 90 percent of the native population. Moreover, as they exchanged European manufactures such as blankets and steel knives for partially tanned deerskins and beaver pelts, they set in motion a devastating series of Indian wars.

The Iroquois of New York had been organized since 1550 in large towns of 500 to 2,000 persons and were united in a great "longhouse" confederation, the Five Nations. In the 1640s they embarked on a decades-long war to seize control of the lucrative trade in furs from their neighbors. Becoming what one historian has called an "engine of destruction," the Five Nations virtually destroyed two western Iroquois tribes, the Eries and the Neutrals; forced the Iroquois-speaking Huron

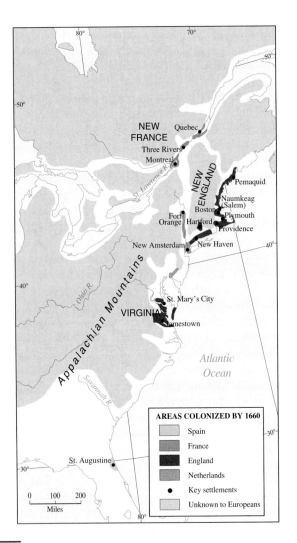

MAP 2.2

Eastern North America in 1660
Four European nations had permanent settlements
in eastern North America by 1660 but only England
had substantial numbers of settlers—some 25,000 in
New England and another 15,000 in the Chesapeake. Even so, the English settlements hugged the
coastline, leaving most of the land in the hands of
native American peoples.

French priests sought to expand the fur trade
among the Huron and pacify the Iroquois by converting
the native peoples to Catholicism. Between 1625 and
1763 hundreds of Jesuit priests lived among the Indians,
sharing their hardships and, to a greater extent than the
Spanish friars, coming to understand their values. One
Jesuit reported a belief among the Huron that "our
souls have desires which are inborn and concealed, yet
are made known by means of dreams" and used it to
explain the Christian doctrines of immortality and salvation. Indians responded in an equally pragmatic way,
at first welcoming the Black Robes as *manitou*, powerful spiritual beings who held magical secrets, such as the
way to forge iron. Gradually they demoted the missionaries to the status of ordinary men when prayers to the
Christian God (the "Great Manitou") did not protect
them from disease, famine, or enemy attack. "His fables
are good only in his own country," charged a leading
Peoria chief; "we have our own, which do not make us
die as his do."

However, unlike the Spanish Franciscans, the
French missionaries did not use Indians for forced labor,
and they protected the native Americans by preventing
brandy from becoming a bargaining item in the French
fur trade (even as rum fueled the English trade in pelts).
Moreover, the Jesuits won converts by advancing Christian doctrines that addressed the needs of some Indians.
In the 1690s young women among the Illinois embraced
the cult of the Virgin Mary in part because they could
use its emphasis on chastity to assert the common Algonquin belief that unmarried women were "masters of
their own body." Yet most native Americans who had
the choice found it more satisfying to hold on to their
traditional religion and culture. It was primarily Indians
who had been subdued by force and confined to praying
towns or reservations who adopted European religious
beliefs.

New Netherland: Commerce

Unlike the French and Spanish, the first Dutch settlers
in North America had little interest in religious conversion. Instead, commerce was their overriding concern.
Like France and England's New World colonies, New
Netherland was sponsored by private companies. The
Dutch Republic had become the commercial hub of Europe after it had wrested independence from Spain (see
Chapter 1), and its American settlements were part of
its worldwide empire. Henry Hudson, an Englishman in
the service of the Dutch East India Company, found and
named the Hudson River in 1609, and a few years later
the Dutch established fur-trading posts on Manhattan
Island and at Fort Nassau (present-day Albany). In
1621 the Dutch government chartered the West India
Company, giving it a trade monopoly in West Africa

to move north of the Great Lakes; and pushed a dozen
Algonquian-speaking peoples—Ottawas, Fox, Sauks,
Kickapoos, Miamis, Illinois—out of their traditional
lands north of the Ohio River. The Algonquian refugees
crowded into a newly formed multitribal region west of
Lake Michigan (present-day Wisconsin) and, to protect
themselves against the powerful Iroquois, allied themselves in the 1670s with the French, who also feared the
Five Nations. By 1701 Algonquin-French attacks had so
weakened the Iroquois that they agreed to the Grand
Settlement, promising neutrality in French-British warfare and abandoning efforts to dominate the western Indian nations.

and the exclusive authority to establish settlements in America. The new company took over the trading post at Fort Nassau (which it renamed Fort Orange) and set up new posts in Connecticut, New Jersey, Delaware, and Pennsylvania. In 1624 the director of the company, Peter Minuit, "purchased" all of Manhattan Island from the Indians and founded the town of New Amsterdam as the capital of the New Netherland colony (see Map 2.1).

These wilderness outposts attracted few settlers because New Netherland did not have a surplus agricultural population, and their small size made them vulnerable to invasion from New England or New France. To encourage migration, the West India Company granted huge estates along the Hudson River to wealthy Dutchmen, stipulating that each proprietor, or *patroon*, settle fifty tenants on his land within four years or the estate would revert to the company. Among all the patroons, only Kiliaen Van Rensselaer, a diamond merchant, brought over enough peasant-tenants to retain his vast American holding, the manor of Rensselaerswyck. By 1646 the population in Dutch North America had reached only 1,500.

Although New Netherland failed as a settler colony, it flourished briefly as a fur-trading enterprise, albeit a bloody one. In the 1640s Governor William Kieft embarked on an expansionist policy, dispatching armed Dutch bands to seize prime farming land from the neighboring Algonquian peoples and take over their trading network, in which corn and wampum from Long Island were exchanged for furs from Maine. Threatened by the Dutch guns supplied to their traditional Iroquois enemies, the Algonquians responded with force. By the end of "Kieft's War" (1643–1646), more than two hundred Dutch residents and a thousand Indians had been killed, many in brutal massacres of women, children, and elderly men. In the wake of this disaster, the Dutch West India Company largely ignored its crippled North American settlement, concentrating instead on the profitable importation of African slaves to its sugar plantations in Brazil.

Local Dutch officials ruled as they thought best. Continuing Kieft's expansionist policies, Governor Peter Stuyvesant ordered the conquest in 1655 of New Sweden, a small fur-trading rival on the Delaware River. Stuyvesant also rejected the demands of English settlers on Long Island for a representative system of government, alienating the colony's increasingly diverse population of Dutch, English, and Swedes. Consequently, in 1664, during one of a series of Anglo-Dutch wars, the population of New Amsterdam offered little resistance to English invaders and generally accepted English rule. For the rest of the century the renamed towns of New York and Albany remained small fur-trading centers, Dutch-English outposts in a region still dominated by native Americans.

Social Conflict in the Chesapeake

The English came to the Chesapeake Bay region of present-day Virginia and Maryland seeking gold, furs, and trading opportunities. Quite unexpectedly, they developed a settler society with a booming tobacco economy based on the exploitation of native American lands and the labor of white indentured servants. The Chesapeake settlements were an economic success but a social and moral failure. Settlers fought with Indians to acquire land, and prominent families used wealth, deceit, and force of arms to rule the society.

The English Invasion

Like New Netherland, the first English settlement in North America was a corporate colony, an enterprise of ambitious merchants. In 1606 the merchant stockholders of the Virginia Company of London received a charter from James I that granted them the right to exploit the riches of North America from present-day North Carolina to southern New York. The company's directors had chosen the name Virginia both to honor Elizabeth I, the "Virgin Queen" who had died in 1603, and to enhance their chances of obtaining a charter. As an additional inducement, they promised to "propagate the *Christian* religion" among "infidels and Savages." Charter in hand, the company's directors were able to raise funds from no fewer than 56 London commercial firms and 659 individual investors. Their goal was to find and exploit rich and populous Indian peoples.

In 1607 the company dispatched an expedition to Virginia to found a trading outpost, not a settler colony. Only men and boys—not families—were aboard the three small ships—*Sarah Constant, Goodspeed*, and *Discovery*—that set sail from London. The company retained ownership of all the land in Virginia and appointed a governor and a small council to direct the migrants, who were its employees or "servants." The company expected them to procure their own food and ship anything of value—gold, exotic crops, or Indian merchandise—back to England.

The migrants were unprepared for the challenges they faced. Some were young gentlemen with financial or personal ties to the shareholders of the Virginia Company but no experience in living off the land—a bunch of "unruly Sparks, packed off by their Friends to escape worse Destinies at home," as one observer put it. The rest were cynical adventurers, men bent on conquering the Indians for their gold or turning a quick profit from trade. Like the company's directors, they expected to find established towns with ample supplies of food and labor and Indians with gold to trade for English cloth and tinware.

The "Starving Time." They were soon disappointed. Arriving in the spring, after a hazardous voyage of four months, the newcomers laid out the settlement of Jamestown on a swampy peninsula on the James River (both named after the new king) and explored the region. They found forty Algonquian-speaking Indian peoples, among them the Monacan and the Chickahominy, who willingly exchanged corn for English goods but had little else to offer and no interest in working for the traders. And the traders were not much interested in working for themselves, at least not in planting crops and raising food. All they wanted, one of them noted, was to "dig gold, refine gold, load gold." But there was no gold.

Of the 120 Englishmen who embarked on the expedition, only 38 were still alive after nine months in America, the rest having fallen victim to malnutrition and disease. Only the determination of Governor John Smith, a soldier of fortune who ran the infant colony like a dictator, saved the enterprise from total collapse, and when Smith left, starvation loomed. As of 1611, the Virginia Company had sent 1,200 settlers to Jamestown, but fewer than half had survived. "Our men were destroyed with cruell diseases, as Swellings, Fluxes, Burning Fevers, and by warres," one of the leaders reported, "but for the most part they died of meere famine." Desperate for food, survivors raided Indian villages, provoking hostility. The new governor, Thomas West, imposed military discipline on the migrants and demanded that the native Americans acknowledge the sovereignty of James I.

The Powhatan, the leading chief of a loose confederation of some two dozen tribes, was prepared to extend privileges to the English traders if they would support him against his Indian rivals. But faced with food seizures and West's haughty demands, the chief accused the English of coming "not to trade but to invade my people and possess my country." Nevertheless, Powhatan, whom Smith described as a "grave majestical man," accepted the presence of the English, giving his daughter Pocahontas in marriage to the adventurer John Rolfe in 1614.

Rolfe had come to Virginia in 1610, and he would play a leading role in the colony until his death in 1622. Soon after his arrival Rolfe imported tobacco seeds from the West Indies and began to cultivate the crop. Tobacco was already popular in England as a result of imports from Spanish America. Within a few years Virginia was exporting tobacco to London; and the colony's leading men wanted more workers to grow it, so they imported hundreds of poor white men from England. And, Rolfe noted in 1619, "a Dutch man of warre . . . sold us twenty Negars." These black laborers, who probably worked as servants rather than slaves,

Carolina Indians, 1585
John White was one of the first English settlers in Sir Walter Raleigh's colony on Roanoke Island, and his watercolors provide a rich visual record of native American life. The shallow waters inside the Outer Banks (Albemarle Sound in present-day North Carolina) provided Indian peoples with a protein-rich diet of fish. (© British Museum)

were the first Africans in British North America and, in a sense, the first African-Americans.

As hopes for the Indian trade declined and the prospect of exporting tobacco rose, the Virginia Company instituted a new and far-reaching set of policies. In 1617 it allowed individual settlers to own land, granting 100 acres of land to every freeman in Virginia, and it established a *headright* system, by which every incoming head of a household had a right to 50 acres of land and 50 additional acres for every adult family member or servant. The company also approved a new "charter of privileges, orders, and Lawes" that provided for a system of representative government. The House of Burgesses (so called because its election procedures followed those of the English boroughs, or "burgs") was

first convened by Governor George Yeardley in Jamestown in 1619. This body had the authority to make laws and levy taxes, although its legislative acts could be vetoed by the governor or nullified by the company. Together, these two incentives—land ownership and local self-government—achieved the desired result: between 1617 and 1622, about 4,500 new recruits set sail from England. Virginia was about to become a settler colony.

The Indian Uprising of 1622. The sudden influx of settlers sparked all-out war with the resident Indians. The new migrants were farmers who wanted land that the Indians had long since cleared and were using for their own crops. The Englishmen's demands alarmed Opechancanough, Powhatan's brother and his successor as the leading chief of the region (see American Lives, Chapter 1). Forming an alliance with other Chesapeake tribes, the chief launched a surprise attack, killing nearly a third of the white population and vowing to drive the rest back across the ocean. The English retaliated by burning the Indians' cornfields, depriving them of food, a strategy that secured the safety of the colony by the late 1620s.

The cost of the war was high. The Indians killed many settlers and burned a lot of property, but their own losses were even worse. Moreover, the time of coexistence was past; as one English militiaman put it, "[we now felt we could] by right of Warre, and law of Nations, invade the Country, and destroy them who sought to destroy us; whereby wee shall enjoy their cultivated places, turning the labourious Mattock [hoe] into the victorious Sword (wherein there is more ease, benefit, and glory) and possessing the fruits of others' labour."

Royal Government. Two years after the Indian uprising of 1622, James I dissolved the Virginia Company, accusing its directors of mismanaging the increasingly valuable tobacco colony. Thereafter, Virginia became a *royal colony*, the first in English history. A governor and the members of a small advisory council were appointed by the king. The House of Burgesses was retained, but any legislation it enacted required ratification by the king's Privy Council. James also legally established the Church of England in Virginia; this meant that all property owners had to pay taxes to support the clergy. These institutions—a royal governor, an elected assembly, and an established Anglican church—became the model for royal colonies throughout America.

The Founding of Maryland. The neighboring settlement of Maryland also became a tobacco-growing colony, but it was founded on a completely different political and religious basis. Maryland was a *proprietary colony*, meaning that it was owned by a "proprietor." In 1632 Charles I (1625–1649), James's successor, gave Cecilius Calvert, Lord Baltimore, a charter that made him the proprietor of the territory between the Potomac River and the Delaware Bay. Lord Baltimore owned all the land in his colony and could sell it, lease it, or give it away as he wished. He also had the authority to appoint the governor and all public officials and could found churches and appoint ministers.

A Catholic, Baltimore wanted Maryland to become a refuge for his coreligionists, such as the Brent family (see American Lives, pages 46–47), who were being persecuted in England. He therefore devised a policy of religious toleration to minimize confrontations between Catholics and Protestants. He instructed the governor (his brother, Leonard Calvert) to allow "no scandall nor offence to be given to any of the Protestants" and to "cause All Acts of Romane Catholicque Religion to be done as privately as may be."

The settlement of Maryland began in 1634. Twenty gentlemen (mostly Catholics) and 200 artisans and laborers (mostly Protestants) established St. Mary's City high on a bluff overlooking the mouth of the Potomac River. The population grew quickly, for the Calvert family carefully planned and supervised the colony's development, hiring skilled artisans and offering ample grants of land to wealthy migrants. Since Maryland's soil proved almost as suitable for the cultivation of tobacco as Virginia's, the booming European market for the new crop helped ensure the success of the colony.

The main problems were political. Baltimore's charter specified that the proprietor had to govern with the "Advice, Assent, and Approbation" of the freemen of the colony. However, Governor Leonard Calvert tried to ignore that stipulation. Beginning in 1638, a representative assembly elected by the freemen insisted on the right to initiate legislation, which Baltimore grudgingly granted. After an armed uprising by Protestants, in 1649 the assembly enacted a Toleration Act that granted religious freedom to all Christians, thus protecting the Catholic settlers, who remained a minority of the population. By 1650 Baltimore had accepted the separation of the legislature into an upper house consisting of an appointed council and a lower house filled with leading men elected by propertied freeholders. As in Virginia, local self-government was balanced by limits on the settlers' autonomy; all laws passed by the assembly and the council and approved by the proprietor had to be consistent with those of England. But the fluid conditions of life in America—notably the absence of traditional authoritarian institutions—enhanced the political power of ordinary people and their ambitious leaders.

Margaret Brent:
A Woman of Property

In 1647 the new Maryland colony was in crisis. Protestants had revolted against the Catholic government and seized control of the colony. To preserve Maryland as a refuge for Catholics and safeguard his family's interests, Governor Leonard Calvert hired mercenary soldiers from Virginia. Lacking hard currency to pay them, he pledged his estate and that of his brother, Cecilius Calvert (Lord Baltimore, the proprietor of Maryland), as security for their wages. But just as his soldiers put down the revolt, Governor Calvert died, plunging the government into disarray, without authority or funds to pay the restless mercenaries. On his deathbed Leonard Calvert named Thomas Green to succeed him as governor but entrusted his personal estate to a prominent landowner, Margaret Brent. Telling her "I make you my sole Exequtrix. Take all, pay all," he left the resolution of the crisis in her hands.

The woman who accepted this challenge was born around 1601 in Gloucestershire, England, into a substantial gentry family. But as Catholics, the Brents' religious freedom and fortune were increasingly precarious. Since the death of Queen Mary in 1557, English Catholics had endured almost continuous religious persecution, and the growing power of militant Puritans

A nineteenth-century painting depicts Margaret Brent asking for voting rights in the Maryland assembly.

during the 1630s promised new hardships for the Brents and other Catholics. The family faced a troubled financial future as well. With thirteen children, Margaret Brent's parents had done their utmost to propagate their Catholic faith, but their fruitfulness threatened the next generation with economic decline. In migrating to Maryland, the Brent children hoped to use the modest funds provided by their parents and their ties with the Calverts to maintain their gentry status.

Margaret Brent, her sister Mary, and their brothers Giles and Fulke arrived in Maryland in 1638. They carried a letter from their coreligionist Lord Baltimore recommending that they be granted land on favorable terms, and the grant was made. Margaret and Mary took up the "Sisters Freehold" of 70 acres in St. Mary's City, the capital of the colony. Four years later Margaret acquired another 1,000 acres on Kent Island from her brother Giles. Margaret soon won the trust and favor of Governor Calvert, sharing with him the guardianship of Mary Kitomaquund, the daughter of a Piscataway chief, who was being educated among the English.

The governor's death during the 1647 crisis threatened the Brents' ambitions, which depended on Catholic rule and access to the governing family and its allies in the assembly. To preserve her family's religious freedom—and its wealth and influence—Margaret Brent would have to save the colony from the mutinous soldiers. Now a mature woman of forty-six, Brent was unusually well qualified for this task. Like many women of gentle birth, she had received some preparation for public affairs; she had enjoyed a basic education in England and had watched her father conduct the business of his estate. But, almost unheard of for a woman, she also had considerable experience in the public arena. As a single woman of property in Maryland, she had appeared frequently before the Provincial Court to file suits against her debtors. In addition, she had occasionally acted as an attorney, pleading the cases of her brother Giles and various women before the court.

Brent did not hesitate to use the power and authority Calvert had assigned to her. First, since food was in short supply and the soldiers camped in St. Mary's City were demanding bread, she arranged for corn to be imported from Virginia. Then, to pay the soldiers, she spent all of Leonard Calvert's personal estate. When that proved inadequate, she adroitly exploited her position as the governor's legal executor to draw on the resources of the Lord Proprietor. Using the power of attorney Governor Calvert had held as Baltimore's representative, Brent sold the proprietor's cattle to pay the troops. Once paid, the soldiers promptly dispersed— some becoming settlers—allowing Governor Green to

restore order to the increasingly Protestant colony. To preserve Maryland as a refuge for Catholics, Lord Baltimore had the assembly pass a Toleration Act (1649), which allowed the free exercise of religion by all Christians.

Margaret Brent's vigorous advocacy of the interests of her family and the Calverts did not go unchallenged. In January 1648 she demanded two votes in the assembly, one for herself as a freeholder and one in her role as the proprietor's attorney. For reasons that do not appear on the record, the Provincial Court opposed her claim: it "denyed that the said Mrs. Brent should have any vote in the house." From England, Lord Baltimore launched a "bitter invective" against Brent, protesting against the sale of his cattle and accusing her of wasting his estate. Baltimore's attack was partly designed to convince the Puritan Parliament, which had just defeated the king in the English Civil War, that he did not favor Catholics. He also hoped to recover some of his property, which he suspected had fallen into the hands of the Brent family. Although the Maryland assembly declined to grant Margaret Brent a vote, it did defend her stewardship of Baltimore's estate, advising him that it "was better for the Collonys safety at that time in her hands than in any mans . . . for the Soldiers would never have treated any others with that Civility and respect. . . ."

No longer assured of the proprietor's favor, the Brents turned to new strategies to advance their interests. Giles Brent married Mary Kitomaquund, the Piscataway Indian, perhaps hoping to gain land or power from her influential father, and moved with her to Virginia in 1650. The next year Margaret and Mary Brent also took up lands in Virginia, on the Northern Neck, gradually settling their estate with migrants from England. Margaret Brent never married, making her one of the very few English women in the early Chesapeake not to do so. She died on her Virginia plantation, named "Peace," in 1671, bequeathing extensive property in Virginia and Maryland, mostly to her brother Giles and his children.

Margaret Brent is often hailed as an early feminist and woman lawyer, but viewed in the context of the time, her actions and achievements were essentially those of an "adventurer" and an assertive woman of property. Born into privileged circumstances and determined to maintain that status, she had struck out on her own—settling in the wilderness of Maryland, defending her interests before the Provincial Court, asserting her rights as a property owner in the assembly, and helping to save the colony—and her family's fragile stake in America—in a time of crisis.

Tobacco and Disease

Tobacco and disease shaped the early history of Maryland and Virginia. Indians in North America and the West Indies had long cultivated the tobacco plant, using its leaves as a medicine and a stimulant. By the 1620s tobacco was popular in England as well, as men and women of the upper and middling classes developed a craving for it and the nicotine it contained. They found many ways to use tobacco: smoking, chewing, or snorting it in its powdered form, snuff. Initially King James I was not impressed. He condemned the use of this "vile Weed" and warned that its "black stinking fumes" were "baleful to the nose, harmful to the brain, and dangerous to the lungs." But his attitude changed as the "vile weed" proved to be a valuable crop. In 1619 he imposed a duty (an import tax) on tobacco, and the revenues filled the royal coffers.

The demand for tobacco in Europe set off a forty-year economic boom in the Chesapeake. The exotic crop commanded such high prices that thousands of profit-hungry migrants flocked to the region, where tobacco thrived in the warm, humid climate. "All our riches for the present do consist in tobacco," a happy planter remarked in 1630. The Chesapeake colonies exported about 3 million pounds of the plant in 1640 and 10 million pounds in 1660. The tobacco leaf became the symbol of the new colonies of Virginia and Maryland, and the tobacco plantation became a characteristic form of settlement. Planters moved up the river valleys, establishing large farms at a considerable distance from one another but easy to reach by water (see Map 2.3). Few towns grew up in the Chesapeake colonies, and there

was a much weaker sense of community there than in the open-field villages of rural England.

Unfortunately, tobacco was not the only thing that flourished in the mild Chesapeake climate. Mosquitoes bred quickly and spread malaria through their bites. Malaria made people weak to the point where they were unable to resist other diseases. It struck pregnant women especially hard; many died after bearing their first or second child, and so settler families were small. Malaria and other sicknesses—smallpox, fevers, dysentery—took such a high toll that although more than 15,000 settlers arrived in Virginia between 1622 and 1640, the population rose only from 2,000 to 8,000.

For most of the seventeenth century life in the Chesapeake colonies remained harsh and short (see Figure 2.1). Most men never married because there were few women settlers. The marriages that did take place often ended abruptly with an early death, destroying the normal bonds of family, friendship, and community. Rarely did both parents survive to see their children grow to adulthood. Unmarried young men and orphaned children accounted for a substantial portion of the population.

The precarious state of family life altered the traditional male system of authority in the household. Because men could expect their male relatives to die young, many Chesapeake husbands deviated from custom and named their wives as the executors of their wills. Those wills enhanced the position of widows (in relation to child-heirs) by giving them the use of more of the family property than was strictly required by law. Frequently a man's will permitted his widow to retain an ample legacy even if she remarried, as most women

MAP 2.3

River Plantations in Virginia
The first migrants settled in widely dispersed plantations along the James River. The growth of the tobacco economy continued this pattern as wealthy planter-merchants traded with English ship captains from their riverfront plantations. Consequently, few substantial towns or trading centers developed in the Chesapeake region.

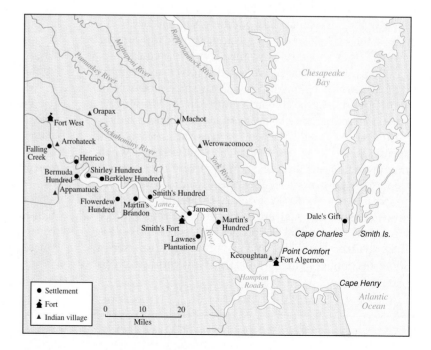

FIGURE 2.1

Average Life Expectancy at Age Twenty in Virginia and New England, 1640–1700

Malaria and other diseases brought early death to English migrants in the Chesapeake region, producing a society filled with orphaned children. Settlers in New England lived into their sixties, often transmitting their customs and values to their grandchildren.

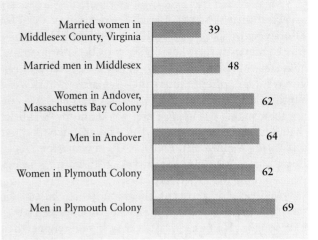

Married women in Middlesex County, Virginia	39
Married men in Middlesex	48
Women in Andover, Massachusetts Bay Colony	62
Men in Andover	64
Women in Plymouth Colony	62
Men in Plymouth Colony	69

The Tobacco Economy

Most poor farmers raised tobacco, for it grew well in small fields and was easy to process. But larger plantations, such as the one pictured above, used the labor of indentured servants and slaves. The workers cured the tobacco stalks by hanging them for several months in a well-ventilated shed; then they stripped the leaves and packed them tighly into large barrels, or "hogsheads," for shipment to Europe.

did. In fact, women who survived the rigors of life in the Chesapeake often improved their social position and legal privileges through inheritance and remarriage.

Indentured Servitude

Despite the dangers, the lure of land ownership and tobacco wealth was so strong that between 1640 and 1700 over 80,000 English settlers moved to Virginia and at least 20,000 more sought their fortunes in Maryland. Shipping registers from the port of Bristol provide a glimpse of the lives of 5,000 people among these English emigrants. As was the case among migrants to New France, three-quarters of them were men, and most were under twenty-five years old; many had traveled hundreds of miles to Bristol, some intent on embarking for Virginia and others simply looking for work. Taking full advantage of their plight, merchants and sea captains concluded labor contracts called *indentures* with these youths. Indentures bound them to work in return for room and board for a period of four or five years (or, in the case of younger servants, until the age of twenty-one). Upon reaching Virginia or Maryland, the merchants assigned the contracts to local planters in return for cash or tobacco.

Indentured servitude was very profitable for those who owned the contracts. For merchants servants were valuable cargo, because they fetched high prices in the labor-starved Chesapeake. For plantation owners, they were an incredible bargain. In return for providing food, clothing, and shelter for their indentured workers, the planters received all the profits of their servants' labor for four or five years. With the price of tobacco at six pence a pound, a male indentured servant could produce five times his purchase price in a single year. Furthermore, indentured servants were counted as household members, so planters in Virginia received 50 acres of land for every servant they acquired.

Masters had the legal right to regulate nearly every aspect of their servants' lives. They could beat them for disobeying or slacking off; they could withhold permission to marry. If servants ran away or became pregnant, a master could go to court to increase their term of service. Planters often abused their female servants. As a Virginia law of 1692 put it, "dissolute masters have gotten their maids with child; and yet claim the benefit of their service." Planters could get rid of uncooperative servants by selling their contracts to new masters. As an Englishman in Virginia remarked in disgust, "servants were sold up and down like horses."

And so, for most of these migrants, indentured servitude did not provide the escape from poverty they had sought. Half the men died before receiving their freedom, and another quarter remained poor. The remaining quarter got some benefit from their ordeal, acquiring property and respectability. If they survived, women servants generally fared better, prospering because men in the Chesapeake had grown "very sensible of the Misfortune of Wanting Wives." Some married their masters or other men with substantial incomes. By migrating to America, these few—and very fortunate—men and women escaped a life of landless poverty in England.

The Seeds of Revolt

During the boom years of the 1620s tobacco sold for twenty-four pence or more a pound; forty years later it was fetching only a few pence per pound—barely one-tenth as much. Overproduction in the Chesapeake was the prime cause of the bust in the tobacco market, but political decisions made in England also played a role.

The Navigation Acts. In 1651, in an effort to exclude Dutch ships and merchants from England's overseas possessions, Parliament passed an *Act of Trade and Navigation.* As revised and extended in 1660 and 1663, the Navigation Acts permitted only English or colonial-owned ships to enter American ports. They also required the colonists to ship certain "enumerated articles," including tobacco, only to England. Chesapeake planters could thus no longer legally trade with Dutch merchants, who traditionally paid the highest prices for tobacco.

Moreover, the English monarchs continually raised the duty on tobacco in order to increase royal revenues. Those duties, by keeping the price of imported tobacco high, stifled the growth of the market, and planters received only one penny a pound for their crop by the 1670s. Yet as living conditions improved and more children were born and survived to adulthood, the number of planters in Virginia and Maryland grew each year, as did tobacco exports—from about 20 million pounds

annually in the 1670s to 41 million pounds between 1690 and 1720, more than the slowly expanding market could absorb. Profit margins were very thin, and few planters prospered.

Poor Tenants, Rich Planters. Economic stagnation after 1660 meant that the Chesapeake ceased to be a land of upward social mobility. Yeomen families earned just enough to scrape by. Each year a typical small freeholder family grew about 1,800 pounds of marketable tobacco. Taxes (often paid in tobacco) amounted to 200 pounds of the crop and clothes accounted for another 800, leaving only about 800 pounds to be sold or bartered for supplies and equipment. Many freeholders fell into debt and had to sell their land.

Even harder hit were newly freed indentured servants, who found it nearly impossible to save the money required to become property owners. Under the headright system, freed servants could *patent* (be granted) 50 acres of uncleared land, provided that they could afford to pay the fees for surveying the land and recording the deed. Then, to become planters, they had to buy tools, seed, and livestock. Few succeeded, and most had to sell their labor once again—as wage laborers, tenant farmers, or even servants.

Established planters weathered the decline in tobacco prices with greater success. Many had accumulated large landholdings; now they leased small plots to the growing army of tenant farmers. They also lent money at high rates of interest to hard-pressed yeomen families. Some well-to-do planters became commercial middlemen, setting up small retail stores or charging a commission for storing the tobacco of their poorer neighbors or selling it to English merchants.

Gradually the economic life of the Chesapeake colonies came to be dominated by an elite of planter-merchants. In Virginia those men were able to accumulate nearly half the patented land by using their political power to extract huge land grants from the royal governor and in some cases by claiming headright shares for fictitious migrants. In Maryland wealthy planters controlled labor with equal success; in Charles County they owned about 40 percent of the work force through the indenture system. As aggressive entrepreneurs confronted a growing number of young, landless laborers, social divisions intensified.

Governor William Berkeley. Tensions in Chesapeake society reached a breaking point during the corrupt regime of Governor William Berkeley. Berkeley, who served as governor of Virginia between 1642 and 1652, had won fame in 1644 by repulsing a second Indian uprising led by Opechancanough and concluding a peace treaty that, by guaranteeing certain lands to the Indians, preserved peace for a generation. When he became governor again in 1660, he made large land grants to him-

Green Spring
Governor Berkeley ran Virginia from his country estate at Green Spring, with its large but architecturally undistinguished residence. The wooden outbuildings housed equipment and the indentured servants who worked as farm laborers.

self and members of his council. Berkeley's Green Spring faction, named after his country estate, soon became a corrupt oligarchy. Council members exempted their own lands from taxation and appointed friends as county judges and local magistrates. Berkeley suppressed dissent in the House of Burgesses through the lavish use of patronage, assigning land grants to friendly legislators and appointing their relatives to the profitable posts of sheriff, tax collector, and justice of the peace.

Berkeley staved off every challenge to his rule for fifteen years. Once his favorites were in the House of Burgesses, he refused to call new elections. When the demand for elections could no longer be ignored, the corrupt Burgesses changed the voting system to exclude landless freemen, who constituted half the population of the adult white men. Property-holding yeomen retained the vote, but they were unhappy about falling tobacco prices, rising taxes, and political corruption. The Virginia elite—unlike the English aristocracy and gentry—was too newly formed and too crudely ambitious to command the respect of the lower orders. Social and political unrest began to reach the boiling point.

Bacon's Rebellion

Conflict with the Indians. In 1675 there were 40,000 whites in Virginia, and their views of frontier issues were based largely on class and geography. Most of the wealthy planters lived in the coastal districts and opposed a policy of armed expansion into Indian territory, as did the planter-merchants who traded with the native Americans for furs. However, poor freeholders and aspiring tenant farmers who had settled farther inland, seeking cheap land, insisted that the Indians be expelled or exterminated.

The Indians in Virginia were few and weak, their numbers having dwindled from about 30,000 in 1607 to 2,000 in 1675. Most lived on lands guaranteed by treaty—lands now coveted by the frontier settlers. But the Susquehannock people had migrated into the region

from the north, settling on the upper reaches of the Potomac River, and actively encouraged the other Indians to resist white expansion.

War broke out in the summer of 1675, when Virginia militiamen crossed the Potomac River into Maryland and without provocation murdered thirty Indians. Defying orders from Governor Berkeley, a larger force of 1,000 militiamen then surrounded a fortified Susquehannock village. Under a flag of truce, they lured four chiefs out of the stockade and killed them on the spot. The outraged Susquehannock retaliated by killing eighty whites in raids on outlying plantations.

Berkeley did not want war, which would disrupt the fur trade, and proposed a defensive military policy, asking the House of Burgesses in March 1676 to raise money to build a series of forts to protect the frontier plantations. Western settlers dismissed this strategy as useless against roving Indian bands and an excuse to levy high taxes. Berkeley's plan, one freeholder argued, was a plot by the coastal planters and the political elite—the "grandees," as he called them—to break the freeholders financially and take "all our tobacco into their own hands."

Nathaniel Bacon. Nathaniel Bacon emerged as the leader of the western settlers. A wealthy young man, he had recently arrived from England and settled on a frontier estate. Although he was only twenty-eight, Bacon commanded the respect of his neighbors in part because of his high status, for Berkeley had made him a member of the governor's council, but more because of his personality. Bacon was forceful and bold, confident of his goals and purposeful in pursuing them. When Berkeley refused to grant Bacon a military commission, the young man marched his frontiersmen against the Indians anyway, slaughtering members of the peaceful Doeg people.

The massacre triggered a political upheaval that completely overshadowed the Indian question. Condemning Bacon's men as "rebels and mutineers," Berkeley expelled Bacon from the council and placed him under arrest. Then, realizing that the rebel leader com-

manded a large military force, the governor reinstated Bacon, gave in to the demand for legislative elections, and accepted the far-reaching political reforms enacted by the new House. The Burgesses, who now included influential supporters of Bacon, curbed the powers of the governor and the council to grant lands and allow tax exemptions. And to cut the patronage powers of the Green Spring faction, the Burgesses converted many local offices into elected posts, giving yeomen freeholders more control over the government. The legislature also restored voting rights to landless freemen.

These much-needed reforms did not end the rebellion, however. Bacon, who was well connected in England, was bitter at having been treated by the governor as a young upstart; the men in his army, resentful of exploitation by the "grandees," were eager to flaunt their newly won power. Backed by 400 armed men, Bacon forced the governor and the Burgesses to commission him "General of Virginia." Then he toppled Berkeley and seized control of the colony.

Popular Rebellion. In August 1676 Bacon announced his goals in an uncompromising "Manifesto and Declaration of the People." It demanded the death or removal of all native Americans and an end to the rule of wealthy "parasites." "The poverty of the country," Bacon proclaimed, "is such that all the power and sway is got into the hands of the rich, who by extorious advantages, having the common people in their debt, have always curbed and oppressed them in all manner of ways."

Bacon's coup brought civil war to Virginia. Berkeley led 500 armed supporters in a successful attack on Jamestown, after which Bacon's army promptly recaptured the capital, burned it to the ground, and plundered the plantations of Berkeley's allies. Only Bacon's sudden death from dysentery in October gave Berkeley the upper hand. The governor dispersed Bacon's army of frontiersmen and servants and then took his revenge, seizing the estates of well-to-do rebels and hanging twenty-three men.

Bacon's rebellion was a pivotal event in the history of the Chesapeake region. Planter-merchants continued to dominate the colony, but they realized that it was dangerous to let a governor and a corrupt oligarchy rule unchecked. In the future they would limit the governor's authority and find public positions for substantial property owners who, like Bacon, had political ambitions. The planter-merchant elite also learned how to contain the fury of the lower social orders, supporting an expansionist military policy that won the votes of tenants and poor yeomen by promising them access to Indian lands.

The uprising also contributed to the emergence of a new labor system: African slavery. Slavery in the Chesapeake had already grown for economic reasons, such as the scarcity of English indentured servants and a surge in the transatlantic trade in African captives (see Chapter 3). Now its expansion was fueled by the Chesapeake elite's desire to forestall another rebellion by freed white servants. In All Hallows Parish in Maryland, permanently enslaved Africans made up 10 percent of the population in 1675; by 1700 they accounted for 35 percent. Thus, to maintain their privileged class position, the leaders of Virginia and Maryland committed themselves and their descendants to a social system based on the exploitation of enslaved blacks.

Puritan New England

Adopting the Puritans' view of themselves, many historians depict the Puritan exodus to America as a heroic effort to preserve the "pure" Christian faith. Yet many Puritans migrated for economic reasons, and their desire for land to provide food and farmsteads for their growing families was only slightly less intense than that of the openly profit-minded adventurers in Virginia. Puritan magistrates found biblical justification for seizing lands from the native Americans, imposed strict religious orthodoxy on their own followers, and condemned dozens of women to death for the crime of "witchcraft." However, the Puritan story does have impressive qualities. These religious migrants created a stable society of independent farm families in New England and gave a moral dimension to American history.

The Puritan Migration

The Pilgrims at Plymouth. The histories of New England and Virginia differed from the beginning. Jamestown was settled by unruly male adventurers; Plymouth, the first permanent community in New England, was filled with pious Protestant families—English Pilgrims who had settled in Holland and other religious dissenters who wished, as they put it, to advance the true "gospell of the Kingdome of Christ in those remote parts of the world."

Before sailing to America aboard the *Mayflower* in September 1620, the Pilgrims had organized themselves into a joint-stock corporation to secure financial backing from sympathetic Puritan merchants. Their stated intention was to settle in the territory granted to the Virginia Company, but either by accident or, more likely, by design they landed far to the north, on the rocky coast of New England. There, outside the jurisdiction of Virginia and lacking a charter from King James I, they created their own covenant of govern-

ment, the Mayflower Compact, to "combine ourselves together into a civill body politick." This document, which was signed by forty-one adult men, was the first "constitution" adopted in North America. It translated into political terms the Pilgrims' long-standing belief in the autonomy of the religious congregation and, while recognizing the sovereignty of the king, produced a system of self-government based on the rule of law.

That first winter in America tested the Pilgrims' spiritual mettle. In Plymouth, as in Jamestown, hunger and disease took a heavy toll: of the 100 migrants who arrived in November, only half survived until the spring. Thereafter the Plymouth colony—unlike Virginia—became a healthy and thriving community because of the cold climate, which inhibited the spread of mosquito-borne diseases, and the religious discipline of the determined settlers. Unlike the gold-hungry adventurers in Virginia, the Pilgrims set about building small, solid houses and planting ample crops of grain and vegetables. The settlement grew quickly through natural increase and migration and had a population of 3,000 by 1640. Aided by epidemics that killed off the Indians, the settlers spread across the landscape and established ten new towns with extensive powers of self-government.

New England Domestic Architecture
Well-to-do Puritans affirmed their commitment to America by building well-constructed dwellings. Most late-seventeenth-century houses were built of wood and had plain symmetrical facades and substantial central chimneys—to preserve heat during the cold New England winters.

In 1636 they adopted a legal code that provided for a colonywide system of representative government and contained a rudimentary bill of rights.

The Pilgrims were devout Christians and tried to live according to the laws and ethics of the Bible, which in their view required limiting the power of the state over religion. As "Separatists," they had cut themselves off from the Church of England and believed that each congregation should be self-governing, free from control by either a religious or a political hierarchy. In that limited sense, they anticipated the "separation of church and state."

Religious Conflict in England. Meanwhile, England was plunging deeper into religious turmoil. King Charles I, James I's successor, reaffirmed his father's support for the Church of England and its traditional liturgy and ecclesiastical hierarchy. But Charles personally repudiated some of the Calvinist doctrines of the Anglican creed, such as justification by faith. The Puritans, who had gained many seats in Parliament, directly challenged the king, accusing him of "popery."

Charles's response was to dissolve Parliament in 1629. For the next decade he ruled by "divine right," raising money on his own authority through royal edicts, higher customs duties, and the sale of monopolies. The king's arbitrary rule struck at the dignity of the landed gentry, who expected to exercise authority through the House of Commons. The merchant community, another stronghold of Puritanism, was also displeased as higher tariffs ate away at their profits.

Religious strife intensified when the king chose William Laud to be bishop of London in 1628. Laud loathed Puritans and, when he became archbishop of Canterbury in 1633, banished hundreds of Puritan ministers from their pulpits, forcing Anglican rituals on their congregations. Tens of thousands of ordinary men and women felt the impact of arbitrary rule. However, their faith in the Puritan creed remained unshaken: they conducted services in secret, and some of them went further, planning to seek refuge in America.

The Massachusetts Bay Colony. In 1630, 900 Puritans boarded eleven ships and sailed across the Atlantic under the leadership of John Winthrop, a well-educated, highly regarded country squire. Having obtained a charter from Charles I, the Puritans established a new settlement, the Massachusetts Bay colony, in the area around Boston. Even more than the Pilgrims, the Puritans saw themselves as central actors in a great historical drama. They were a "saving remnant" chosen by God to preserve the true faith in America. The Lord "has sifted a whole nation," a Puritan minister declared, "that he might send choice grain over into this Wilderness."

Governor John Winthrop
This portrait captures the gravity and intensity of Winthrop, whose policies of religious orthodoxy and elite rule shaped the early history of the Massachusetts Bay colony.

Winthrop decided to go to America for economic as well as religious reasons. Believing England to be corrupt in morals and "overburdened with people," he sought land and opportunity for his children. But he also saw a chance to preserve the true Christian church and set an example for all Europe to follow. "We must consider that we shall be as a City upon a Hill," Winthrop told his fellow passengers aboard the ship *Arbella* in 1630. "The eyes of all people are upon us." Though the Puritan experiment has long since vanished, Winthrop's words still evoke in Americans a vision of their destiny as a people and a nation.

Once they arrived in America, Winthrop and his associates transformed their joint-stock business corporation, the General Court of shareholders, into a legislature that was empowered to enact laws for the new colony. Over the next decade about 10,000 Puritans migrated to the Massachusetts Bay colony, along with 10,000 others—yeomen and artisan families, along with their servants—fleeing from hard times in England (see Map 2.4). To ensure rule by the godly, the Puritans enacted a law limiting the right to vote and hold office to men who were members of an approved Puritan church.

By the mid-1630s the General Court had become a representative assembly elected by the members of Puritan congregations in the various towns. With John Winthrop as governor (he served for fifteen years), the General Court sought to create a religious common-

wealth, establishing Puritanism as the official state-supported religion and barring members of other faiths from conducting services. The Bible was the basis for some of the laws enacted by the Massachusetts Bay government. For example, the Puritans followed a biblical rule by dividing inheritances among all heirs, with a double portion going to the oldest son, thus rejecting the custom of many English families of giving all the land to the eldest son (primogeniture). "Where there is no Law," the court advised local magistrates, they should rule "as near the law of God as they can."

Puritans and Pequots

The Puritans' conception of themselves as God's chosen people shaped their relations with native Americans. Initially they felt obliged to justify their intrusion into the Indians' domain. "By what right or warrant can we enter into the land of the Savages," they asked themselves while still in England, "and take away their rightfull inheritance from them and plant ourselves in their places?" An answer to this question was provided by John Winthrop, who suggested that a disastrous smallpox epidemic that killed hundreds of Indians in 1633 was in fact a mark of divine favor. "If God were not pleased with our inheriting these parts," he asked, "Why doth he still make roome for us by diminishing them as we increase?"

For a second justification the Puritans turned to the Book of Genesis, which instructed them to "be fruitful, and multiply, and replenish the earth, and subdue it." From this, the magistrates of Massachusetts Bay argued that because the Indians had not "subdued" most of their land by plowing or fencing it, they had no "just right" to it.

Bolstered by these religious beliefs, the Puritans often treated native Americans with a brutality equal to that of Spanish conquistadors and Nathaniel Bacon's frontiersmen. A vivid instance of this occurred in 1637, when Pequot warriors attacked Puritan farmers who had begun to intrude onto their fertile lands in the Connecticut River Valley. As sporadic violence escalated into war, Puritan militiamen and their Indian allies led a surprise attack on a Pequot village and massacred about 500 men, women, and children. "God laughed at the Enemies of his People," one soldier boasted, "filling the Place with Dead Bodies." Puritan forces ruthlessly tracked down the survivors, selling many into slavery in the Caribbean. In the end, the Pequot people were virtually exterminated.

Like most Europeans, the English invaders viewed the Indians as "savages," culturally inferior people who did not deserve civilized treatment. Indeed, to some Puritans the Indians were latter-day "Philistines," a biblical people that had been justly slain by the Jews, God's

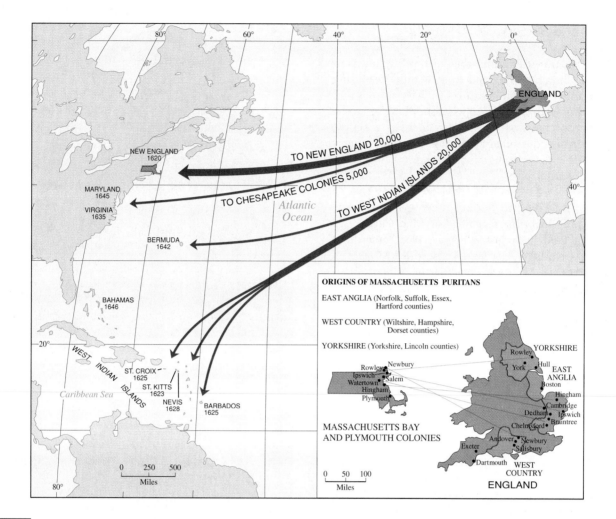

MAP 2.4

The Puritan Migration to America

Nearly 50,000 Puritans left England between 1620 and 1640. In New England, migrants from the three major areas of English Puritanism—Yorkshire, East Anglia, and the West Country—commonly settled among those from their own region. They named American communities after their English towns of origin and transplanted regional customs, such as the open-field agriculture practiced in Rowley in Yorkshire and Rowley in Massachusetts Bay.

original chosen people. Yet the Puritans were not racist as the term is understood today. To them, native Americans were not genetically inferior and indeed were not even members of a different race—they were white people with sun-darkened skins. Not race but sin accounted for the Indians' "degenerate" condition. "Probably the devil" delivered these "miserable savages" to America, wrote the Puritan minister Cotton Mather, "in hopes that the gospel of the Lord Jesus Christ would never come here to destroy or disturb his absolute empire over them."

This interpretation of Indian history inspired attempts at conversion. John Eliot, a Puritan minister, translated the Bible into Algonquian and undertook missions to Indians outside Boston and on Cape Cod. Because Puritans demanded that the Indians conform to

English customs and master Puritan theology, only a few native Americans became full members of Puritan congregations. However, the Puritans achieved what the Spanish Franciscans had only hoped for in New Mexico: a controlled Indian population. Within a generation there were more than a thousand "praying Indians" living under Puritan supervision in fourteen special mission towns. Their numbers severely diminished by European diseases and English arms, their traditional kinship and communal institutions in shreds, these "survivors" placed themselves under Puritan political and religious control. Thus, a combination of European diseases, military force, and Christianization pacified most of the seaboard Algonquian peoples, guaranteeing, at least temporarily, the safety of new white inhabitants of New England.

Religion and Society, 1630–1670

Unlike the Separatist Pilgrims, the Puritans' wish was to reform the Church of England from within. Disposing of ostentatious "Catholic" features such as bishops and elaborate rituals, they followed what they believed to be the practice of the first Christians, devising a simple church structure controlled by the laity, or the ordinary members of the congregation. Hence their name, *Congregationalists.*

The Elect. According to Puritan theology, which was derived mainly from the teachings of John Calvin (see Chapter 1), God had chosen a few "elect" men and women for salvation—they were predestined for heaven even before they were born. The doctrine of predestination was a harsh one, for it seemed to deny people any control over their salvation. Moreover, it led to a sharp division between church members, the Elect or Saints, as they were called, and the rest of the population, who constituted a majority of the adult population of New England. The Saints set extraordinarily high standards for church membership. Many people did not even bother to apply; those who did were subjected to a rigorous oral examination of their morals and beliefs. Even the Saints lived in great anxiety, for they could never be sure that they were really among the elect. Consequently, Puritan deathbeds were scenes of agony and doubt. "I have seen Persons Quaking on their Death Beds, and their very beds therewith Shaking under them," Cotton Mather reported, with their deathbed utterances testifying to their terror: "O! The wrath of a Dreadful God, Makes me Tremble; I Tremble, I Tremble, at that wrath."

Puritans dealt with the uncertaities of divine election in three ways. Some congregations pointed to the transforming effect of the conversion experience: as God infused the sinner's soul with grace, he or she was "born again" and *knew* that salvation was at hand

Changing Images of Death

Death—sudden and arbitrary—was a constant presence in the preindustrial world. Pre-1700 New England gravestones often depicted death as a frightening skull, warning sinners to repent of their sins. After 1700 a smiling cherub adorned many gravestones, suggesting a more optimistic view of the afterlife.

A Puritan Meetinghouse

Puritan churches were plain but handsome buildings. Inside, the most prominent feature was the pulpit, symbolizing the importance of the sermon and the Word of God. Outside, most meetinghouses were painted in bright colors (not white, as they are today).

John Dane

The Life Story of a Puritan Tailor

The conscience of a Puritan was always active, always seeing God's hand in ordinary events and prompting self-examination and self-control in an unending battle against the temptations of the world. John Dane migrated to Massachusetts Bay in the 1630s and, after surviving a near suicide, lived in Ipswich until his death in 1684.

I first settled in Berkhampstead [England]. . . .On a night when most folks was abed, a maid came into the shop and sat with me, and we jested together, but at the last she carried it so, and put herself in such a posture, as that I made as if I had some special occasion abroad and went out, for I feared if I had not [left] I should have committed folly with her. But I often thought that it was the prayers of my parents that prevailed with God to keep me.

[Subsequently, at Hereford:] There was, whether fly, wasp, or hornet I cannot tell, but it struck my finger, and water and blood came out of it and pained me much. I went up to a house and showed it [to the people there], but they knew not what a sting I had

at my heart. Now I thought of my mother's words, that God would find me out. . . . The pain and swelling increased and swelled up to my shoulder. I prayed earnestly to God that He would pardon my sin and heal my arm. I went to a surgeon and asked him what it was. He said it was "take." I asked him what he meant. He said it was taken by the providence of God. This knocked home on my heart what my mother said, "God will find you out." Now I made great promise that if God would hear me this time I would reform.

I then bent myself to come to New England, thinking that I should be more free here than there from temptations, but I find here a devil to tempt, and a corrupt heart to deceive. . . . Many troubles I passed through, and I found in my heart that I could not serve God as I should. . . . [At that time] with my gun on my shoulder charged, in the mile brook path beyond Deacon Goodhewe's, I had several thoughts [which] came blocking into my mind that I had better make away [with] myself than to live longer. I walked discoursing with such thoughts

[for] the best part of an hour, as I judged it. At length I thought [that] I ought of two evils to choose the least, and that it was a greater evil to live and to sin against God than to kill myself—with many other satanical thoughts. I cocked my gun, and set it on the ground, and put the muzzle under my throat, and took up my foot to let it off. And then there came many things into my head, one [was] that I should not do evil that good might come of it. . . . I was then much lost in my spirit, and, as I remember, the next day Mr. Rogers preached, expressing himself that those were blessed that feared God and hoped in His mercy. Then I thought that blessedness might belong to me, and it much supported my spirit. . . . Thus God hath all along preserved and kept me all my days. Although I have many times lost His special presence, yet He hath returned to me in mercy again.

Source: John Dane, "A Declaration of Remarkable Providences in the Course of My Life." *New England Historical and Genealogical Register*, VIII (1854), 149–156.

(see American Voices, above). Other Puritans stressed "preparation," the confidence that came from years of spiritual guidance and church discipline. Many of these "preparationists" followed the Dutch Protestant theologian Jacob Arminius in conceiving of God as a more reasonable and merciful deity than the one portrayed by Calvin. If a person expressed "the merest desire to be saved," declared one Arminian-influenced Puritan, God would bestow His saving grace. Still other New England Puritans reassured themselves by embracing a collective interpretation of their destiny. They believed that God had entered into a *covenant*, or contract, with the Puritans, promising to treat them as a divinely "chosen people" as long as they ordered their lives in accordance with His laws.

Roger Williams and Rhode Island. To remain in God's favor, Puritan magistrates purged their society of religious dissidents. One target was Roger Williams, who had become the minister of the Puritan church in Salem in 1634. Williams applauded the Pilgrims' separation of church and state and condemned the legal establishment of Congregationalism in Massachusetts Bay. He taught that political magistrates should have authority only over the "bodies, goods, and outward estates of men," not over their spiritual lives. Moreover, the outspoken Salem preacher questioned the moral and legal justification for seizing (rather than buying) Indian lands. When Williams refused to end his criticism, the Puritan magistrates banished him from Massachusetts Bay in 1635.

Williams and his followers resettled in Rhode Island in 1636, founding the town of Providence on land acquired from the Narragansett Indians. Other religious dissidents joined him in nearby Portsmouth and Newport. In 1644 these towns obtained a corporate charter from the English Parliament, which was controlled by Puritans, granting them full authority "to rule themselves." Rhode Islanders used their new political freedom to ensure religious liberty. In Rhode Island there was no legally established church; every congregation was autonomous, and individual men and women could worship God as they pleased.

The Heresy of Anne Hutchinson. Puritan magistrates detected another threat to their holy commonwealth in the person of Anne Hutchinson, a middle-aged woman, the wife of a merchant and the mother of seven, who worked as a midwife. Hutchinson held weekly prayer meetings in her house—often attended by as many as sixty women—in which she questioned the teachings of certain Boston clergymen, saying that they placed undue emphasis on church laws and good behavior. In words that recalled Martin Luther's rejection of indulgences (see Chapter 1), Hutchinson argued that salvation was not something that people could earn; there was no "covenant of works." Rather, salvation was bestowed by God through the "covenant of grace." Hutchinson stressed the importance of revelation: the direct communication of truth by God to the individual believer. Since this doctrine diminished the role of ministers and, indeed, of all established authority, Puritan magistrates found it threatening.

The magistrates also resented Hutchinson because of her sex. Like other Christians, Puritans believed in the equality of souls—both men and women could be saved; they also believed that the soul had a feminine nature. When it came to practical matters regarding the governance of church and state, however, women were seen as being clearly inferior to men. As the Pilgrim minister John Robinson put it, women "are debarred by their sex from ordinary prophesying, and from any other dealing in the church wherein they take authority over the man." Puritan women could never be ministers, lay preachers, or even voting members of the church.

In 1637 the Massachusetts Bay magistrates put Hutchinson on trial for heresy as an *antinomian*, a person who looks inward for grace or truth and asserts freedom from the rules of the church. Hutchinson defended her beliefs with great skill and tenacity, and even Winthrop admitted that she was "a woman of fierce and haughty courage." But the odds were against her. The judges not only found her guilty of heresy for claiming a direct relationship with God but also condemned her for exceeding her proper station in life. In Winthrop's words, she should have "attended her household affairs, and such things as belong to women."

The General Court banished Hutchinson from the Massachusetts Bay colony. Her merchant allies, affluent men who also resented the power of the clergy, were unable to protect her. Defeated, she followed Roger Williams into exile in Rhode Island, where she and a small group of supporters founded Portsmouth. Later Hutchinson moved to Westchester County, New York, where she was killed in an Indian raid. Puritan magistrates noted Hutchinson's death with grim satisfaction, interpreting it as a sign of God's approval of their enforcement of religious orthodoxy.

The Connecticut Colony. The banishing of dissidents prompted some devout Puritans, among them the Reverend Thomas Hooker of Newtown (Cambridge), to flee from the authority of the Massachusetts Bay magistrates. In 1636 Hooker led a hundred settlers to the Connecticut River Valley, where they established the town of Hartford. Other Bay colony residents followed, settling along the river at Wethersfield and Windsor. In 1639 the Connecticut Puritans adopted the Fundamental Orders, a plan of government that included a representative assembly and a popularly elected governor. A royal charter from King Charles II in 1662 bestowed self-government on these Connecticut towns, whose population had grown to almost 5,000, and joined them to another Puritan settlement at New Haven. Connecticut was patterned after Massachusetts Bay, with a firm union of church and state and a congregational system of church government, but voting rights were extended to most property-owning men—not just church members (see Table 2.1).

The Cambridge Platform. In Massachusetts Bay leading magistrates and ministers gave up their efforts to impose a single definition of orthodoxy. In the Cambridge Platform of 1648, the laity won a written guarantee that each church would be independent and equal. Although the platform specified that "consociations" of clergy might meet to discuss church dogma and discipline, most Puritan congregations could act as they pleased, deciding matters of doctrine, choosing and dismissing ministers, and admitting new members. In religion as in politics, hierarchy gave way to local self-rule.

The Puritan Revolution. Many migrants had expected that the settlement of New England would be the beginning of the *millennium*, the thousand-year rule of Christ on earth predicted in the Book of Revelation. At first, events in England appeared to bear them out. In 1637 Archbishop Laud imposed a new prayer book on Presbyterian Scotland and threatened to send bishops to impose religious discipline. Popular riots against Laud's edicts led to armed resistance. In 1639 a Scottish Presbyterian army invaded England, forcing Charles to call Parliament into session to vote funds for the war. The

TABLE 2.1

European Colonies in North America before 1660

	Date	First Settlement	Type	Religion	Chief Export or Economic Activity
New France	1608	Quebec	Royal	Catholic	Furs
New Netherland	1613	New Amsterdam	Corporate	Dutch Reformed	Furs
New Sweden	1628	Fort Christina	Corporate	Lutheran	Furs; farming
English Colonies					
Virginia	1607	Jamestown	Corporate (Merchant)	Anglican	Tobacco
Plymouth	1602	Plymouth	Corporate (Religious)	Separatist Puritan	Mixed farming; livestock
Massachusetts Bay	1629	Boston	Corporate (Religious)	Puritan	Mixed farming
Maryland	1634	St. Mary's	Proprietary	Catholic	Tobacco; grain
Connecticut	1635	Hartford	Corporate (Religious)	Puritan	Mixed farming; livestock
Rhode Island	1636	Providence	Corporate (Religious)	Separatist Puritan	Mixed farming; livestock

Puritan-dominated House of Commons seized the chance to demand an end to arbitrary measures. When Charles resisted, the nation divided into Royalist and Parliamentary factions. In 1642 thousands of English Puritans—and scores of Puritans who had returned from America—took up arms against the king. After four years of civil war, the Parliamentary forces led by Oliver Cromwell were victorious. In 1649 Parliament executed Charles, proclaimed a republican commonwealth, and imposed Presbyterianism on the Church of England. God's rule on earth seemed imminent.

But the Puritan experiment in England lasted just a decade. Popular support for saintly rule quickly declined, especially when Cromwell took dictatorial control of the government in 1653. After Cromwell's death a repentant Parliament summoned Charles I's son, Charles II, back to the throne. In 1660 the monarchy was restored, and bishops reclaimed their authority in the Church of England. For many steadfast Puritans the Restoration represented the victory of the Antichrist—a false church preaching false Christian doctrines.

The Halfway Covenant. The outlook in New England seemed equally grim. Puritans in America were experiencing grave doubts about their religious "errand into the wilderness," for the second generation had not sustained the intense religious spirit of the original migrants. Many younger Puritans had been baptized as infants but, perhaps intimidated by the religious zeal of their parents, had not experienced conversion and become full church members. Their "deadness of soul" threatened to end the Puritan experiment, since the un-

Richard Mather (1596–1669)
Mather migrated to New England in 1635 after Archbishop Laud stripped him of his pulpit. His son Increase Mather was a leading Boston clergyman, as was his grandson Cotton Mather, the author of *Magnalia Christi Americana*, an epic of the Puritan adventure in New England.

converted could not present their own children for baptism. Never more than a bare majority, the Saints had imposed their religious vision out of determination, not numbers. If Puritans became a small minority, they might well lose control of the colony.

To keep the churches vigorous, Puritan ministers devised the Halfway Covenant in 1662. This covenant altered Calvinist theology by making salvation more predictable, indeed almost hereditary. Under its terms, the children of all baptized Puritans could be presented for baptism and thus become "halfway" members. Not conversion but birth became the key to Puritan identity. For example, the First Church of Milford, Connecticut, had 962 members in the period 1639–1770. No fewer than 693 of these Puritan Saints (72 percent) were members of the thirty-six families who had established the original congregation.

The Halfway Covenant began a new phase of the Puritan experiment. Puritans had come to America to preserve the "pure" Christian church; many of them half expected to return in triumph to a Europe ready to receive the true Gospel. In the course of events, that sacred mission had been dashed, and so Puritan ministers instead exhorted their congregations to create in the American wilderness a new society based on high moral and intellectual principles.

The Puritan Imagination and Witchcraft

Like the native Americans they encountered in New England, the Puritans (and other seventeenth-century Europeans) thought that the physical world was full of supernatural forces. This belief in "spirits" was not completely inconsistent with their Christian heritage, since Catholics believed in supernatural miracles and Protestants hoped that "grace" would infuse their hearts. However, it stemmed primarily from the system of pagan beliefs that were still current in Christian Europe, among both ordinary people and highly educated individuals.

The diary of Samuel Sewall provides a glimpse into the Puritan imagination. Sewall was born in England in 1652 and educated at Harvard College, which had been founded by Massachusetts Bay Puritans in 1635. He enjoyed a long and distinguished life as a Boston merchant, politician, and judge. Sewall was a devout Puritan: the Bible shaped his consciousness and provided him with clues to the meaning of events. Thus, he applauded a proposal to establish a French Protestant colony in territory claimed by Catholic Spain, interpreting it as part of God's plan to pull down "the throne of Antichrist, as is so designed in the [Book of] Revelation."

Sewell constantly sought a supernatural design in natural events. For example, he spent an evening with Cotton Mather, an influential minister, discussing why "more Ministers' Houses than others proportionably had been smitten with Lightning; inquiring what the meaning of God should be in it." At times this belief in supernatural forces led Sewall into pagan practices. For example, before occupying a new addition to his house, he drove a metal pin into the floor to fend off evil spirits.

Devout Protestants such as Sewall thought they received many celestial signs or warnings from God in the form of blazing stars, deformed births, and rainstorms of blood. They also followed pagan astrological charts printed in farmers' almanacs. Those charts, along with diagrams and pictures, correlated the movements of the planets and stars with the signs of the zodiac. By deciphering the charts, farmers determined the best times to plant crops, marry off their children, and make other important decisions.

Zealous Protestant ministers attacked such beliefs and practices and condemned "cunning" individuals who claimed to have special powers as healers or prophets. Many ordinary Christians looked on folk doctors or conjurers as "wizards" or "witches" who acted at the command of Satan. Between 1647 and 1662, civil authorities in Massachusetts and Connecticut hanged fourteen people for witchcraft. Most of the victims were older women, who, their accusers claimed, were "double-tongued," "had an unruly spirit," or in some way challenged prevailing customs.

The most dramatic episode of witch-hunting took place in Salem, Massachusetts, in 1692. The causes are complex and not easily discovered, but they seem to have involved group rivalries and blatant deception. Poor and resentful Puritan farmers in rural Salem village apparently sought revenge against certain wealthier church members, who lived near the seaport of Salem town, by bringing charges of witchcraft against their families and friends. This community conflict got out of hand, in part because judges allowed the introduction of dubious evidence; Massachusetts authorities arrested 175 people and executed 22 of them—again mostly women. Fear and suspicion spread into the neighboring village of Andover. Its people "were much addicted to sorcery," claimed one observer, and "there were forty men in it that could raise the Devil as well as any astrologer."

The Salem episode, in concert with the imposition of royal government in Massachusetts (see Chapter 3), marked a major turning point in the history of New England. The intense government-supported religiousness of the first two generations of Puritans was dealt one blow by popular revulsion against the hysteria—and the mass executions—at Salem; there would be no more legal prosecutions for witchcraft. The European Enlightenment (see Chapter 4), which began around 1675, delivered a second blow by propagating a more rational understanding of the natural world. Increasingly people explained events such as an unforeseen accident or a sudden death as being caused by natural

forces, not by God or Satan or the movements of the stars or a witch's spell. Unlike Sewall and Cotton Mather, well-read men of the next generation, such as Benjamin Franklin, would conceive of lightning not as a supernatural sign but as a natural phenomenon.

A Freeholding Society

Essential to the Puritans' God-fearing "just society" was the freeholder ideal. In creating New England communities, they consciously avoided the worst features of the traditional agricultural regime of Europe. They did not wish to live in a society where a few wealthy landowners dominated a large population of poor landless families or in a state where a strong central government levied oppressive taxes. The Puritans wanted a world of independent communities and churches made up of landowning, socially responsible families.

Local Government. New England governments used land-grant policies to fashion a new social order. The General Courts of Massachusetts Bay and Connecticut did not adopt the Chesapeake headright system, which enabled wealthy planters to accumulate land patents. Nor did they normally give thousands of acres of land to favored individuals. Instead, they bestowed the title to a township—usually measuring about 6 miles by 10 miles—on a group of settlers. These settlers, or *proprietors*, then distributed the land among themselves, giving the largest amounts to men of high social status, who often became the political leaders of the town. However, all male heads of families had a voice in the town meeting, the main institution of local government. Each year the town meeting chose *selectmen* to manage town affairs. It also levied taxes; enacted ordinances regarding fencing, lot sizes, and road building; and regulated the common fields used for grazing livestock and cutting firewood. These communities had much more power over taxes and local affairs than was the case in most peasant villages in Europe.

The political power of the towns determined the structure of colonywide government. Beginning in 1634, each town in the Massachusetts Bay colony elected its own representatives to the General Court. As the number of towns increased, the Court gained authority at the expense of the governor and magistrates in Boston.

Town autonomy encouraged diversity in social and cultural practices. For instance, most of the settlers of Rowley, Massachusetts, came from the East Riding region of Yorkshire in northern England and brought with them many Yorkshire manorial customs, such as communally regulated open-field agriculture. In contrast, the proprietors of Watertown, who came primarily from the East Anglia region northeast of London, quickly duplicated that area's system of enclosed fields and separate family farmsteads.

Land and Social Authority. Whatever their county of origin, Puritans were careful not to transplant feudal land customs. New England governments granted land to town proprietors or to individuals in *fee simple*. This form of title meant that the holders owned the land outright, free from manorial obligations or feudal dues; they could sell, lease, or rent it as they pleased. Moreover, fee simple owners did not have to pay the government (or an aristocrat) an annual *quitrent*, a token sum of money that symbolized the authority of the state or the lord. Puritan leaders wanted a society of independent freeholders (see Map 2.5).

Widespread ownership of land did not imply equality of wealth or status. Like most Europeans of the time, Puritans accepted—indeed, embraced—a social and economic hierarchy that provided order and security in an uncertain world. "God had Ordained different degrees and orders of men," proclaimed the wealthy Boston merchant John Saffin, "some to be Masters and Commanders, others to be Subjects, and to be commanded." Otherwise, Saffin noted with disdain, "there would be a meer parity among men."

An Affluent Puritan Woman
This well-known painting of Elizabeth Freake and her daughter, Mary, is perhaps the finest portrait of a seventeenth-century American and suggests the growing prosperity of the Boston merchant community. (*Mrs. Elizabeth Freake and Baby*, circa 1671–1674)

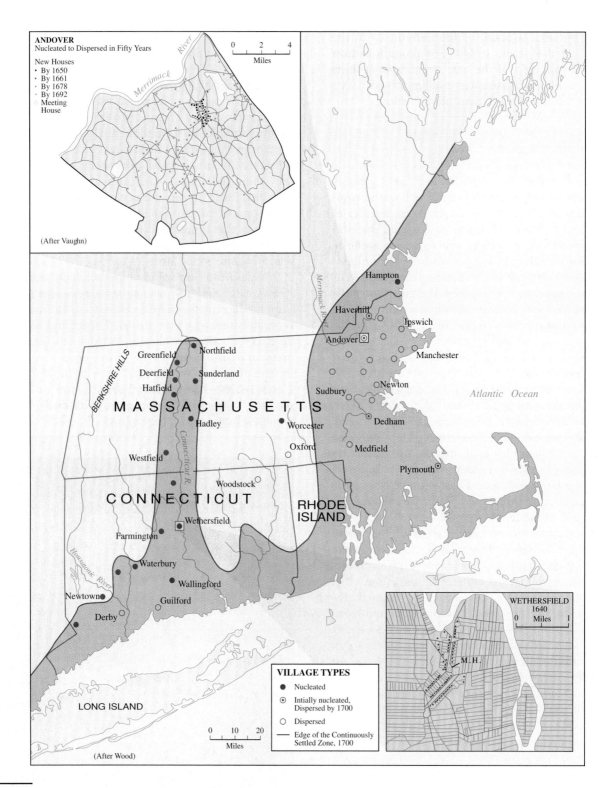

MAP 2.5

Settlement Patterns in New England

Initially, most Puritan towns were compact; families lived close to one another in the
"nucleated" village center and traveled daily to the surrounding fields. In 1640 this
pattern was apparent in Wethersfield, which was situated on the broad plains of the
Connecticut River Valley. The rugged geography of eastern Massachusetts encouraged
a more dispersed form of settlement. By 1692 many residents of Andover lived outside the village center—on their own farms.

Migrants from privileged backgrounds in England used their high social status to reap immediate material benefits in America. For example, Edward Johnson came to New England from Kent, where he had been a man of "rank and quality." Johnson became well known on both sides of the Atlantic as the author of the *Wonder-Working Providence of Zion's Saviour*, a prophetic tract published in 1650, but he prospered in Massachusetts Bay primarily because, as a gentleman, he was able to claim a large land grant in Woburn. The most influential proprietors received the lion's share of land in many other towns. In Windsor, Connecticut, for example, the upper tenth received 40 percent of the land, and the lowest fifth of the settlers only 4 percent.

Occasionally the General Court did make large grants to individuals. John Pynchon was given thousands of acres along the Connecticut River at Springfield, Massachusetts, as a reward for his exploits as an Indian fighter. More than most important migrants, Pynchon was able to live like a landed English gentleman, presiding over dozens of tenants. In 1685 Pynchon rented land or housing to 49 of the 120 male adults in Springfield. Thanks to his wealth and status, he dominated the political life of the town.

The rough economic equality among New England farm families would soon be challenged. Initially, the larger proprietors owned sizable farms, ranging in area from 200 to 600 acres—enough land to divide among all their sons, usually three or four. Smallholders were less fortunate and usually could provide land for only some of their sons. Nonproprietors were the least well off, for they had to buy land or work as tenants or laborers. By 1702, in Windsor, Connecticut, about 30 percent of adult male taxpayers were landless. It would take years of saving, or migration to a new town, for these men and their families to become freeholders.

Despite these inequalities, nearly all New England settlers had a real opportunity to acquire property, and even those at the bottom of the social scale enjoyed some economic security. When he died in the 1690s, Nathaniel Fish was one of the poorest men in Barnstable, Massachusetts, yet he owned a two-room cottage, 8 acres of land, an ox, and a cow. For him and thousands of other settlers, New England had proved to be the promised land, a new world of opportunity.

The Indians' New World

Native Americans, whose ancestors had lived on the American continents for millennia, found that they too were living in a new world, but for them it was a bleak, dangerous, and conflict-ridden place, rendered deadly by European diseases and thousands of armed settlers.

They responded in a variety of ways: banding together in new tribes, retreating to mountainous areas to preserve their culture, and on occasion doing battle with the invading Europeans.

Metacom's War

By the 1670s the white population of New England had grown to 55,000. The Indian population of southern New England continued to decline: from 120,000 in 1570, to 70,000 in 1620, to barely 16,000 in 1670. Like Opechancanough in Virginia and Popé in New Mexico, Metacom, leader of the Wampanoag tribe, concluded that only united resistance could stop the relentless advance of the Puritans, whose towns now stretched along the Massachusetts coast and deep into the Connecticut River Valley (see Map 2.2).

Metacom (King Philip), Chief of the Wampanoag
The Indian uprising of 1675 left an indelible mark on the historical memory of New England. This painting of 1850 was used by traveling performers to tell the story of King Philip's War and was done on semitransparent cloth so that it could be lit from behind for dramatic effect. (Shelburne Museum)

Mary Rowlandson

A Captivity Narrative

Mary Rowlandson, a minister's wife in Lancaster, Massachusetts, was one of many settlers taken captive by the Indians during Metacom's War. Some young captives remained with the Indians for their entire lives, gradually becoming Indians in manner and outlook, but most captives were ransomed. Mrs. Rowlandson spent eleven weeks and five days in captivity, traveling constantly, until her family ransomed her for £20. Her account of this adventure, published in 1682, became one of the most popular prose works of its time.

On the tenth of February 1675, came the Indians with great numbers upon Lancaster: their first coming was about sunrising; hearing the noise of some guns, we looked out; several houses were burning, and the smoke ascending to heaven. . . . [T]he Indians laid hold of us, pulling me one way, and the children another, and said, "Come go along with us"; I told them they would kill me: they answered, if I were willing to go along with them, they would not hurt me. . . .

The first week of my being among them I hardly ate any thing; the second week I found my stomach grow very faint for want of something; and yet it was very hard to get down their filthy trash; but the third week . . . they were sweet and savory to my taste. I was at this time knitting a pair of white cotton stockings for my [Indian] mistress; and had not yet wrought upon a sabbath day. When the sabbath came they bade me go to work. I told them it was the sabbath-day, and desired them to let me rest, and told them I would do as much more tomorrow; to which they answered me they would break my face. . . .

Then I went to see King Philip. He bade me come in and sit down, and asked me whether I would smoke . . . but this no way suited me. For though I had formerly used tobacco, yet I had left it ever since I was first taken. It seems to be a bait the devil lays to make men lose their precious time. . . .

. . . During my abode in this place, Philip spake to me to make a shirt for his boy, which I did, for which he gave me a shilling. I offered the money to my master, but he bade me keep it; and with it I bought a piece of horse flesh. Afterwards he asked me to make a cap for his boy, for which he invited me to dinner. I went, and he gave me a pancake, about as big as two fingers. It was made of parched wheat, beaten, and fried in bear's grease, but I thought I never tasted pleasanter meat in my life. . . .

Hearing that my son was come to this place, I went to see him. . . . He told me also, that awhile before, his master (together with other Indians) were going to the French for powder; but by the way the Mohawks met with them, and killed four of their company, which made the rest turn back again, for which I desire that myself and he may bless the Lord; for it might have been worse with him, had he been sold to the French, than it proved to be in his remaining with the Indians. . . .

My master had three squaws, living sometimes with one, and sometimes with another one. . . . [It] was Weetamoo with whom I had lived and served all this while. A severe and proud dame she was, bestowing every day in dressing herself near as much time as any of the gentry of the land: powdering her hair, and painting her face, going with necklaces, with jewels in her ears, and bracelets upon her hands. When she had dressed herself, her work was to make girdles of wampom and beads. . . .

About that time there came an Indian to me and bid me come to his wigwam at night, and he would give me some pork and ground-nuts. Which I did, and as I was eating, another Indian said to me, he seems to be your friend, but he killed two Englishmen at Sudbury, and there lie their cloaths behind you. I looked behind me, and there I saw bloody cloaths, with bullet-holes in them. Yet the lord suffered not this wretch to do me any hurt. . . .

On Tuesday morning they called their general court (as they call it) to consult and determine, whether I should go home or no. And they all as one man did seemingly consent to it, that I should go home. . . .

Source: C.H.Lincoln, ed., Original Narratives of Early American History, Narratives of Indian Wars, 1675–1699, vol. 14 (New York: Barnes and Noble, 1952).

Forging a military alliance with the Narragansett and Nipmuck peoples in 1675, Metacom, whom the Puritans called King Philip, attacked white settlements throughout New England. Bitter fighting continued into 1676, ending only when Metacom was killed. By the end of the war the Indians had burned 20 percent of the English towns in Massachusetts and Rhode Island and had killed 5 percent of the adult white population (see American Voices, above). But the Indians' losses—from war, famine, and disease—were even higher: 4,000 native Americans, or 25 percent of an already severely diminished population. Many of the survivors were sold into slavery, including Metacom's wife and nine-year-old son.

The outcome of Metacom's revolt was typical. By 1700 the English invaders had conquered many of the native peoples along the Atlantic coast. Small remnants of those groups, stripped of their lands and traditions, survived on the margins of white society and live on into the present. But they had suffered a double tragedy, failing both to repel the English and to maintain the integrity of their traditional cultures.

The Fur Trade and the Inland Peoples

For the time being the Indian peoples in the interior of North America were able to maintain their identity, independence, and, with more difficulty, traditional way of life. Traders brought European diseases as well as brandy and rum, so that epidemics and drunkenness sapped the vitality of some peoples. Moreover, as native Americans exchanged furs for iron utensils and cloth blankets, they made fewer flint hoes, clay pots, and skin garments. After two or three generations, some eastern Indians had come to rely on European manufacturers for many basic goods. Among Indian peoples to the west of the Appalachians and the Great Lakes, however, imported goods were in short supply, in part because canoes carried small cargoes, and traditional subsistence activities remained strong.

Everywhere competition for beaver and deer pelts led to conflict among native Americans. Families or villages within a tribe would claim exclusive hunting and trapping rights over an area, undermining clan unity. Conflict between Indian peoples also increased as the population of fur-bearing animals dwindled and rival bands of hunter-warriors competed for new trapping areas. After subduing the Huron and Erie peoples, the Iroquois extended their dominion southward to include the Delaware and the Susquehannock. As in all societies, a commitment to warfare increased the influence of those who made war, so the balance of power shifted from elders to headstrong young warriors.

The fur trade also transformed the Indians' relationship with the natural world. Native Americans were animists in religion, believing that everything in nature—animals, trees, rocks—had a living spirit that demanded respect. The members of each clan in a tribe venerated an animal as its *totem*, or symbol, often considering themselves actual descendants of that animal. Tribesmen could hunt those totem animals—fox, deer, beavers—only if they followed certain customs. As they skinned beavers or butchered deer for their food and clothing, they thanked the spirits of the animals and a principal guardian spirit, a "master of the animals," by offering prayers or burning tobacco. They also respectfully buried the carcasses and the entrails. To throw the bones into a fire or a river was taboo, an act that might bring misfortune.

In bringing about the deaths of millions of beaver, the European fur trade altered the ecology of eastern North America, for their dams no longer controlled the flow of creeks and streams. It brought spiritual upheaval to the Indians as well. Warriors now hunted ceaselessly in order to trade with the French in Quebec and the English in New York. As they killed more and more deer and beaver, the Indians sensed the displeasure of the spirits in nature. The epidemics that swept their communities confirmed their fears: the spirits of the animals were taking their revenge. The warriors of the Micmac of Nova Scotia confessed that they no longer knew "whether the beavers are among our friends or our enemies." No less than military conquest and religious conversion, the fur trade drastically altered the character of Indian society.

America had become a new world for Indians as well as for Europeans. All the invaders—Dutch and French fur traders no less than Spanish conquistadors and English settlers—destroyed traditional native American societies, forcing their members to fashion new ways of life.

Ætatis suæ 21. Aº. 1616.

An English View of Pocahontas
By depicting the Indian princess Pocahontas as a well-dressed European woman, the artist implicitly casts her as a symbol of peaceful assimilation to English culture. In actuality, marriages between white men (often fur traders) and Indian women usually created a bilingual hybrid culture that existed uneasily between the two societies.

Summary

Beginning in 1575, first Spain and then England, France, and Holland established permanent settlements in North America. Spain claimed most of the continent, but its empire consisted primarily of a few military garrisons and Franciscan missions in Florida and New Mexico. Both soldiers and friars exploited the labor of the native peoples and threatened their culture, prompting Indian revolts that expelled most Spaniards by 1700. Far to the northeast, the fur trade became the lifeblood of New France and New Netherland. French fur traders and Jesuit priests extended France's influence among the native peoples of the Mississippi Valley. The English came primarily as settlers, and their relentless quest for land brought war with the Indian peoples.

The English created two very different types of colonies in North America. Settlers in the Chesapeake region overcame a disease-ridden environment to create a plantation society that raised tobacco for export to Europe. Wealthy planters controlled Chesapeake society, dominating a population of freeholding farm families, propertyless freemen, and white indentured servants. The pursuit of self-interest by Governor Berkeley and his faction in Virginia and the end of the tobacco boom prompted Nathaniel Bacon's unsuccessful rebellion of 1675–1676. Subsequently, planters made some concessions to white freeholders and turned increasingly to slave labor from Africa.

The English migrants who settled amid the rocky soil and harsh climate of New England grew rapidly in numbers and raised crops mostly for their own consumption. Reacting against the religious hierarchy and economic hardships they had experienced in England, Puritan settlers consciously created a society based on widespread ownership of land and self-governing churches and towns. At first Puritan magistrates enforced religious orthodoxy, banishing Roger Williams, Anne Hutchinson, and other religious dissidents, but eventually they conceded extensive power to local Congregational churches, ensuring political stability.

Wherever Europeans intruded, the native peoples died from new epidemic diseases and went to war to defend their lands. The Pueblo peoples rose in major revolts in 1598 and 1680, the Chesapeake Indians nearly wiped out the Virginia colony in 1622, and Metacom's forces dealt New England a devastating blow in 1675–1676. By 1700, however, many native American peoples along the Atlantic seaboard had been nearly annihilated by disease and warfare, and the lives of most Indians east of the Mississippi River had been transformed by the fur trade.

TIMELINE

1560s	English and French attack Spanish treasure ships
1565	Spain establishes St. Augustine, Florida
1573	Spanish Comprehensive Orders for New Discoveries
1580s	Failure of Roanoke and other English colonies
1598	Acoma War in New Mexico
1600	Franciscans in Florida and New Mexico
1603–1625	King James I of England
1607	English adventurers settle Jamestown, Virginia
1608	Samuel de Champlain founds Quebec
1613	Dutch fur traders on Manhattan Island
1619	First Africans arrive in Chesapeake Virginia House of Burgesses convened
1620	Pilgrims found Plymouth colony
1620–1660	Tobacco boom in Chesapeake colonies
1621	Dutch West India Company chartered
1622	Opechancanough's uprising
1624	Virginia becomes a royal colony
1625	Jesuits undertake missionary work in Canada
1625–1649	King Charles I of England
1627	Company of New France urges migration to Quebec
1630	Puritans found Massachusetts Bay colony
1634	Maryland settled
1635–1637	Pequot War Roger Williams, banished, settles in Rhode Island Anne Hutchinson expelled from Massachusetts Bay
1640s	Five Iroquois Nations go to war over fur trade
1649–1660	Puritan Commonwealth in England
1651	First Navigation Act passed
1660	William Berkeley Governor of Virginia until 1678
1660–1720	Poor tobacco market
1662	Connecticut receives royal charter Halfway Covenant revises Puritan theology
1664	English conquer New Netherland
1670s	Indentured servitude declines
1673	Marquette and Joliet explore Mississippi
1675–1676	Bacon's rebellion Metacom's uprising Expansion of African slavery in the Chesapeake
1680	Popé's rebellion in New Mexico
1681	La Salle claims Louisiana for France
1692	Salem witchcraft trials

★   ★   ★

BIBLIOGRAPHY

David Weber, *The Spanish Frontier in North America* (1992), and Richard White, *The Middle Ground: Indians, Empires, and Republics in the Great Lakes Region, 1650–1815* (1991), are magisterial studies, while Bernard Bailyn, *The Peopling of British North America* (1986), offers a useful overview of the early English colonies.

Spanish, French, and Dutch Goals

For Spain's northern empire see, in addition to Weber, Ramón Gutiérrez, *When Jesus Came, the Corn Mothers Went Away: Marriage, Sexuality, and Power in New Mexico, 1500–1846* (1991). The French threat to its domain is traced by Robert S. Weddle, *The French Thorn: Rival Explorers in the Spanish Sea, 1682–1762* (1991), and Daniel H. Usner, Jr., *Indians, Settlers, and Slaves in a Frontier Exchange Economy: The Lower Mississippi Valley Before 1783* (1991).

The best general studies of French Canada are by W. J. Eccles, *The Canadian Frontier, 1534–1760* (1983) and *France in America*, rev. ed. (1990). French interaction with native Americans is covered by Bruce G. Trigger, *The Children of Aataentsic: A History of the Huron People to 1660* (1976); Daniel K. Richter, *The Ordeal of the Long House: The Peoples of the Iroquois League in the Era of European Colonization* (1992); and Patricia O. Dickason, *Canada's First Nations: A History of the Founding Peoples from Earliest Times* (1992).

For English expansion, see Kenneth Andrews, *Trade, Plunder, and Settlement: Maritime Enterprise and the Genesis of the British Empire, 1480–1630* (1984); Nicholas Canny, *Kingdom and Colony: Ireland in the Atlantic World, 1560–1800* (1988); A. L. Rowse, *Sir Walter Raleigh* (1962); David B. Quinn, *England and the Discovery of America, 1481–1620* (1974); and Karen O. Kupperman, *Roanoke* (1984). The interaction of the English and Dutch with native Americans can be followed in Gary B. Nash, *Red, White, and Black: The Peoples of Early America* (1982); Francis Jennings, *The Invasion of America* (1975); and two works by James Axtell, *The European and the Indian* (1981) and *The Invasion Within: The Contest of Cultures in Colonial North America* (1985).

Social Conflict in the Chesapeake

Alden Vaughan, *American Genesis: Captain John Smith and the Founding of Virginia* (1975), covers the earliest years, while Edmund S. Morgan, *American Slavery, American Freedom: The Ordeal of Colonial Virginia* (1975), provides a brilliant analysis of the rest of the colonial period. Important essays appear in Thad W. Tate and David L. Ammerman, eds., *The Chesapeake in the Seventeenth Century* (1979), and Lois Green Carr, Philip D. Morgan, and Jean B. Russo, *Colonial Chesapeake Society* (1989). Significant community studies include Carville Earle, *The Evolution of a Tidewater Settlement Pattern: All Hallows Parish, Maryland, 1650–1783* (1975), and Lois Green Carr et al., *Robert Cole's World: Agriculture and Society in Early Maryland* (1991).

For a discussion of political institutions, see W. F. Craven, *The Southern Colonies in the Seventeenth Century, 1607–1689* (1949), and David W. Jordan, *Foundations of Representative Government in Maryland, 1632–1715* (1988).

Contrasting accounts of Bacon's rebellion can be found in T. J. Wertenbaker, *Torchbearer of the Revolution* (1940), and Wilcomb B. Washburn, *The Governor and the Rebel* (1958).

Puritan New England

For the Puritan migration, see Edmund Morgan, *The Puritan Dilemma: The Story of John Winthrop* (1955); Sumner Chilton Powell, *Puritan Village: The Formation of a New England Town* (1963); David Grayson Allen, *In English Ways: The Movement of Societies and the Transferral of English Local Law and Custom to Massachusetts Bay in the Seventeenth Century* (1981); and David Cressy, *Coming Over: Migration and Communication between England and New England in the Seventeenth Century* (1987).

Puritanism as an intellectual movement is best explored in the works of Perry Miller; see especially *The New England Mind: The Seventeenth Century* (1939). Charles Hambrick-Stowe, *The Practice of Piety: Puritan Devotional Disciplines* (1982), discusses the emotional dimension of Puritanism, while David D. Hall, *World of Wonder, Days of Judgment: Popular Religious Belief in Early New England* (1989), explores its nonrational aspects. See also Andrew Delbanco, *The Puritan Ordeal* (1989).

For a discussion of dissent in early New England, consult Philip Gura, *A Glimpse of Sion's Glory: Puritan Radicalism in New England, 1620–1660* (1984); Edwin S. Gaustad, *Liberty of Conscience: Roger Williams in America* (1991); Amy Schrager Lang, *Prophetic Woman: Anne Hutchinson and the Problem of Dissent in the Literature of New England* (1987); Paul Boyer and Steven Nissenbaum, *Salem Possessed: The Social Origins of Witchcraft* (1974); Carol F. Karlsen, *The Devil in the Shape of a Woman: Witchcraft in New England* (1987); and David D. Hall, ed., *Witch Hunting in Seventeenth-Century New England: A Documentary History, 1632–1691* (1991).

Community studies that reveal the lives of ordinary New England men and women include John Demos, *The Little Commonwealth: Family Life in Plymouth Colony* (1971), and Kenneth A. Lockridge, *A New England Town . . . Dedham, Massachusetts, 1636–1736* (1970). See also John Demos, *The Unredeemed Captive: A Family Story from Early America* (1994).

The Indians' New World

James H. Merrell, *The Indians' New World: Catawbas and Their Neighbors from European Contact through the Era of Removal* (1989), is a pathbreaking study. Douglas Leach, *Flinthawk and Tomahawk: New England in King Philip's War* (1958), is the standard treatment of the conflict. See also Karen Ordahl Kupperman, *Settling with the Indians: The Meeting of English and Indian Cultures in America, 1580–1640* (1981); Bernard Sheehan, *Savagism and Civility: Indians and Englishmen in Colonial Virginia* (1980); and Daniel K. Richter and James H. Merrell, *Beyond the Covenant Chain: The Iroquois and Their Neighbors in Indian North America* (1987). Two illuminating ecological studies are Calvin Martin, *Keepers of the Game: Indian-Animal Relations and the Fur Trade* (1978), and William Cronon, *Changes in the Land: Indians, Colonists, and the Ecology of New England* (1983).

Bristol Docks and Quay (detail)

The bustle and prosperity of the English port of Bristol is well conveyed in this eighteenth-century painting. Thousands of migrants embarked for America from Bristol, which became a hub of the triangular trade with Africa, the West Indies, and the mainland colonies.

CHAPTER 3

The British Empire in America

1660–1750

★   ★   ★

By 1660 English traders and settlers had pushed aside native American peoples and founded two clusters of colonies along the eastern coast of North America. The English government used mercantilist policies to profit from the products and commerce of those colonies, creating an empire based on trade. To protect their increasingly valuable colonies from European rivals in the West Indies and on the Continent—the Dutch in New Netherland, the French in Quebec, and the Spanish in Florida—English officials expanded the navy and repeatedly went to war.

The West Indian sugar islands were England's most prized overseas possessions. Sugar produced with enslaved labor from Africa brought wealth to English planters and merchants and would soon make England a world power. Settler colonies from New England to the Carolinas bolstered this economic empire by providing crucial supplies to the sugar islands and shipping tobacco and rice to European markets.

England's dominion in America rested on a combination of force and consent. English planters used brute force to control the tens of thousands of African slaves who labored on the plantations, while English governors and bureaucrats won the voluntary support of white settlers by granting power to their representative assemblies. The result, as defined by a British imperialist in 1745, "was a magnificent superstructure of American commerce and British naval power on an African foundation."

The Politics of Empire, 1660–1713

By 1660 England had thriving colonies in America but lacked a firm, uniform policy for governing them. Over

the next twenty-five years England tightened its control, first by imposing strict trade regulations and then by centralizing colonial government. Accustomed to running their own affairs, the colonists resisted those efforts, sometimes through open rebellion. Then upheaval in England brought to power new political leaders who consented to a measure of American self-government.

The Restoration Colonies

In 1660 Charles II (1660–1685) returned from exile and restored the Stuart monarchy. Like the earlier Stuarts, Charles supported the Anglican Church and believed in the divine right of kings. A robust and vigorous man, Charles offended many of his subjects by marrying a Portuguese Catholic princess and presiding over a sexually permissive royal entourage. His generosity and extravagance kept him in debt—a fact of considerable importance for American affairs.

On ascending the throne, Charles rewarded the aristocrats who supported the Restoration by giving them millions of acres of land in America. In 1663 he gave the Carolinas, which included much of Spanish Florida, to eight aristocrats, including Sir George Carteret, Lord John Berkeley, and his brother Sir William Berkeley, the governor of Virginia. In 1664 the king granted the territory between the Delaware and Connecticut rivers to his brother James, the duke of York. Later that year James also took possession of the newly captured Dutch colony of New Netherland, renaming it New York after his title. Because he wished to concentrate on governing New York, James gave ownership of New Jersey to two of the Carolina proprietors, Sir George Carteret and Lord John Berkeley. And so, in just two years, vast tracts of land fell into the hands of a few English noblemen.

The new colonies were proprietorships in which all the land belonged to the proprietors to do with as they pleased. As in Maryland, their charters required only that their laws conform broadly to those of England. These generous provisions allowed the proprietors to shape the character of their possessions. Most proprietors sought to create a traditional social order, presided over by a gentry class and a legally established Church of England (see Table 3.1).

The Carolinas. The Carolina proprietors were especially determined to build a traditional rural society. They instructed John Locke, who would later become the political theorist of propertied individualism and popular government, to devise a scheme of government for the new colony. The result, the Fundamental Constitutions of Carolina (1669), prescribed a manorial sys-

A King in Waiting, circa 1655
While Oliver Cromwell imposed stern Puritan rule on England, the future Charles II (1660–1685) danced his way across Europe. As king, Charles presided over a court known for its extravagance and debauchery.

TABLE 3.1

English Colonies in North America, 1660–1750

	Date	Type	Religion	Status in 1775	Chief Export or Economic Activity
Carolina	1663	Proprietary	Church of England	Royal	Mixed farming; naval stores
North	1691				
South	1691				Rice; indigo
New Jersey	1664	Proprietary	Church of England	Royal	Wheat
New York	1664	Proprietary	Church of England	Royal	Wheat
Pennsylvania	1681	Proprietary	No established church	Proprietary	Wheat
Georgia	1732	Trustees	Church of England	Royal	Rice
New Hampshire (separated from Massachusetts)	1739	Royal	Congregationalist	Royal	Mixed farming; lumber; naval stores
Nova Scotia	1749	Royal	Church of England	Royal	Fishing; mixed farming; naval stores

tem in which land was equated with political power and social rank: noble "landgraves" were to preside over baronies populated both by free families and by "leet men"—serfs bound to the land.

This aristocratic fantasy bore no relation to reality. The first settlers in North Carolina, poor families from Virginia, refused to work on large manors and lived instead on modest farms, raising grain and tobacco. Ignoring this repudiation of their manorial plans, the proprietors continued to grant deeds that required the payment of an annual quitrent. Farmers in Albemarle County, angered by the cost of this claim of lordship and by taxes on tobacco exports, rebelled in 1677. Led by John Culpepper, they deposed the governor and forced the proprietors to abandon most of their legal claims.

The settlement of South Carolina was equally unsuccessful for the landed proprietors. The colonists, many of whom had come from Barbados, by then an overcrowded sugar island, refused to accept the Fundamental Constitutions or the proprietors' demands for quitrents. The Barbadians introduced racial slavery, using a small number of African slaves to raise cattle and food crops for export to the West Indies. They also opened a lucrative trade with native Americans, exchanging English manufactured goods for furs and Indian slaves. This commerce encouraged slave-raiding attacks on Franciscan missions in Florida, which could have led to war with Spain, and in 1715 prompted a violent war with the resident Yamasee people. These struggles made South Carolina an ill-governed, violence-ridden frontier settlement until the 1720s.

William Penn and Pennsylvania. In stark contrast to the Carolinas, the proprietary colony of Pennsylvania devel-

oped into a peaceful and prosperous settlement. In 1681 Charles II bestowed this land on William Penn, primarily in payment of a large debt the king owed to Penn's father, the admiral Sir William Penn. The younger Penn was an enigmatic man. Born to wealth, he seemed destined for renown as a friend and servant of kings but in his early twenties he converted to the Society of Friends (Quakers), a radical Protestant sect, and became one of its ardent supporters. His pamphlet *No Cross, No Crown* offered an articulate defense of the Quakers' belief in religious liberty, and he used his prestige to spread their influence. Pennsylvania, his greatest achievement, was designed as a refuge for Quakers, who were persecuted in England because they refused to serve in the army or pay taxes to support the Church of England.

Like the Puritan migrants to New England, Quakers wanted to restore to religion the simplicity and spirituality of early Christianity. But Quakers were not Calvinists, who restricted salvation to a small elect. Rather, Quakers followed the teachings of their founders, the English visionary George Fox and his associate Margaret Fell, who argued that all women and men could be saved because God had imbued each person with an inner "light" of grace or understanding. The principal Quaker religious institution—the weekly meeting for worship—was designed to help members to discover this inner light. The meetings were not led by a minister and did not center on a sermon. Instead, Friends encouraged anyone, man or woman, who felt the promptings of the inner light to speak. "Nearest the front by the wall are two benches," a traveler reported after a visit to a Philadelphia meetinghouse. "In these pews sit those of both sexes who either are already accustomed to preach or expect to be inspired by the Holy Ghost."

Penn's Frame of Government, which he drew up in 1681, guaranteed political liberty and religious freedom: it prohibited an established church and religious taxes and allowed Christians of all faiths to vote and hold office. During the 1680s thousands of Quakers, primarily from the middling classes of northwestern England, came to Pennsylvania. Most settled along the Delaware River, in or near the city of Philadelphia, which Penn himself planned. To attract more settlers, the proprietor sold land at low prices—and in fee simple, without quitrents or other obligations—and had his *Brief Account of the Province of Pennsylvania* translated into Dutch and German. In 1683 migrants from Krefeld in Saxony founded Germantown just outside Philadelphia, and thousands of other Germans soon joined them.

In 1682 James, duke of York, gave Penn another colony, Delaware, originally a Swedish settlement that had been conquered first by the Dutch and then, in 1664, by the English. The Quaker leader incorporated the Delaware settlements into Pennsylvania as the Lower Counties, and after 1703 he allowed the inhabitants to select their own representative assembly. Religious liberty and ethnic diversity made Pennsylvania and the Lower Counties the most open and democratic of all the Restoration colonies.

The New Mercantilism

Although Charles II was generous with land, giving away vast domains to pay his political and financial debts, he kept a tight grip on colonial trade by enacting new mercantilist legislation. His policies were meant to channel the trade of the empire through England and raise royal revenues from custom duties.

Before 1650 the English government followed traditional mercantilist thinking, encouraging exports while restricting imports. These policies were designed to give England a favorable balance of trade with European countries, forcing those countries to pay the difference in gold or silver. After 1650, as the economic potential of the colonies became apparent, the government devised new mercantilist policies to regulate their trade. The initial phase of this policy, expressed in the Navigation Act of 1651, was aimed expressly at Dutch merchants who were supplying the English colonies with European manufactures and carrying their sugar and tobacco directly to European markets. To help English traders and secure shipping fees for English merchants, the act required that all goods imported into England or the colonies be carried on ships registered in England, Ireland, or the colonies.

Upon ascending the throne in 1660, Charles II endorsed the Navigation Act. He also created a new committee of the Privy Council, the Lords of Trade and Plantations, to formulate colonial policy. The king had Parliament pass a new Navigation Act (1660) that strengthened the ban on foreign shipping and stipulated that sugar, tobacco, and indigo could be shipped only to other English possessions. In 1663 the Staple Act required that these crops be sent directly to England, from which they could be reexported to other countries at a great profit. The Staple Act also stipulated that European exports to America be shipped through England, inflating the prices of those goods and thus increasing the sale of English manufactures.

To enforce these laws and raise money, Parliament passed the Revenue Act of 1673; it imposed a special "plantation duty" on certain American exports and created, for the first time, a staff of customs officials to col-

TABLE 3.2

Navigation Acts, 1651–1751

	Date	Purpose	Result
Act of 1651	1651	Cut Dutch trade	Mostly ignored
Act of 1660	1660	Ban foreign shipping; enumerated goods only to England	Partially obeyed
Act of 1663	1663	European imports only through England	Partially obeyed
Staple Act	1663	Enumerated goods and European imports pass through England	Mostly obeyed
Revenue Act	1673	Impose "plantation duty"; create customs system	Mostly obeyed
Act of 1696	1696	Prevent frauds; create Vice-Admiralty Courts	Mostly obeyed
Woolen Act	1699	Prevent export or intercolonial sale of textiles	Partially obeyed
Hat Act	1732	Prevent export or intercolonial sale of hats	Partially obeyed
Molasses Act	1733	Cut American imports of molasses from French West Indies	Extensively violated
Iron Act	1750	Prevent manufacture of finished iron products	Extensively violated
Currency Act	1751	End use of paper currency as legal tender in New England	Mostly obeyed

lect the levy in American ports. In 1696 another Navigation Act required American governors to enforce trade regulations and increased the legal powers of customs agents. This act replaced the Lords of Trade with a new administrative body, the Board of Trade, composed of politicians and officials with knowledge of colonial affairs. During the following decades the board proposed new laws to regulate specific American industries (see Table 3.2).

The English government backed its mercantilist policy with force. "What we want," declared the duke of Albemarle, "is more of the trade the Dutch now have." In three commercial wars between 1652 and 1674 the English navy broke Dutch supremacy in world trade, driving the Dutch from New Netherland, their only base in North America, and ending their dominance of the West African slave trade. Meanwhile, English merchants expanded their fleets and established a dominant position in Atlantic commerce.

The Dominion of New England

For England, the new mercantilism was a spectacular success. In America, however, Charles II's policies were resented as an economic burden and an intrusion into the colonies' internal affairs, so most of the colonies initially resisted the new measures. In Massachusetts, a customs official named Edward Randolph reported that the Puritan government took "no notice of the laws of trade," welcoming Dutch merchants as usual and importing goods directly from the French sugar islands. Indeed, Puritan leaders claimed that their original royal charter exempted them from most of the regulations. Outraged, Randolph called on his superiors to use English troops to "reduce Massachusetts to obedience."

At Randolph's urging, the Lords of Trade and Plantations decided to assert their authority over the Puritan colonies. In 1679 they denied the claim the Massachusetts Bay colony had laid to the adjoining frontier province of New Hampshire and created a separate colony with a royal governor. Then, in 1684, the Lords of Trade persuaded the English Court of Chancery to annul the charter of Massachusetts Bay on the grounds that the Puritan government had virtually outlawed the Church of England and violated the Navigation Acts.

The accession of James, duke of York, to the throne as James II (1685–1688) gave the Lords of Trade an opportunity to increase royal authority. James was an admirer of Louis XIV, the despotic king of France, and was bent on curbing the power of Parliament at home and that of representative institutions in America. With James's support, in 1686 the Lords revoked the corporate charters of Connecticut and Rhode Island and merged them with the Massachusetts Bay and Plymouth colonies to form a new royal

province, the Dominion of New England (see Map 3.1). Two years later the Lords added New York and New Jersey to the dominion, creating a single colony stretching from the Delaware River to Maine.

The Dominion of New England represented a new authoritarian model of colonial administration. As the name implied, New England was to be the king's own "dominion." James named Sir Edmund Andros, a military officer and former governor of New York, to rule the new entity. Dispatched to Boston with orders to abolish the existing legislative assemblies, Andros ruled Massachusetts Bay by administrative fiat, attacking all the major institutions of Puritan society. He advocated public worship in the Church of England, offending Puritan Congregationalists. He banned town meetings and so undermined the local autonomy of settlers in scores of rural villages. And he levied arbitrary taxes and challenged the validity of all land titles granted under the original Massachusetts charter. While Andros offered to provide new deeds, they were not in fee simple; title holders were required to pay an annual quitrent. The Puritans protested vigorously against the new regime, but James refused to restore the old charter.

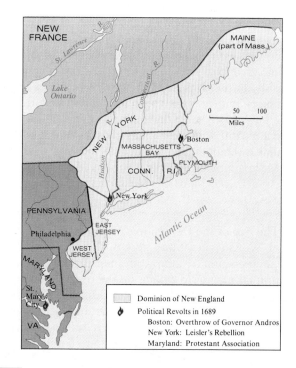

MAP 3.1

The Dominion of New England 1688–1689
The Dominion created a vast new royal colony stretching nearly 500 miles along the Atlantic coast. After the Glorious Revolution in England, revolts in Boston and New York City ousted royal officials, effectively ending the Dominion. In Maryland a Protestant Association mounted a third revolt, deposing the Catholic proprietary governor.

The Glorious Revolution of 1688

Fortunately for the colonists, James made as many enemies at home as Andros made in the colonies. The new monarch angered political leaders by revoking the charters of many English towns and corporate bodies and rejecting the advice of Parliament. He also offended many English people by openly practicing Roman Catholicism and prosecuting Anglican bishops when they questioned his authority over church appointments.

Dissent reached a crisis in 1688, when James's second wife, a Spanish Catholic princess, gave birth to a son. The prospect of a Catholic heir to the throne ignited a quick and bloodless coup known as the Glorious Revolution. Backed by popular protests and the army, Protestant parliamentary leaders forced James into exile and enthroned Mary, his Protestant daughter (by his first wife), and her Dutch husband, William of Orange. Queen Mary II (1689–1694) and King William III (1689–1701) agreed to rule as constitutional monarchs, forgoing the Stuarts' claim to a "divine right," and accepted a Declaration of Rights. This document limited the powers of the monarch and enhanced both the liberties of subjects and the powers of Parliament.

The political philosopher John Locke tried to justify the Glorious Revolution. In his *Two Treatises on Government* of 1690, Locke argued that individuals are endowed with inalienable natural rights to life, liberty, and property and that the legitimacy of government rests on the consent of the governed. Locke's views on liberty and popular sovereignty—and his advocacy of representative government—had a lasting influence on many Americans, especially those who sat in the colonial assemblies and wanted to increase their powers. More immediately, the Glorious Revolution sparked popular rebellions in Massachusetts, Maryland, and New York.

The Fall of the Dominion. When news of the accession of William and Mary reached Boston in April 1689, Congregational ministers immediately circulated a printed manifesto calling on the townspeople to "seize the vile persons who oppressed us." The town militia took Governor Andros prisoner, and a hastily formed Committee of Safety forced him to return to England. In London the eminent American Puritan minister Increase Mather petitioned the new monarchs for restoration of the old charter of 1629.

William and Mary agreed to break up the Dominion of New England, which many English Parliamentary leaders viewed as a symbol of Stuart despotism. They insisted, however, on retaining close supervision of the dominant northern colony of Massachusetts Bay. In 1691 a new charter combined Massachusetts Bay, Plymouth, and Maine into the new royal colony of Massachusetts. The Crown would appoint the governor

The Target of the Glorious Revolution
The stance and facial expression of James II (1685–1688) suggest his forceful, arrogant personality. His arbitrary measures and Catholic sympathies prompted rebellions in England and America and cost him the throne.

(and naval officers to supervise the ports), while the townspeople would elect delegates to the assembly, the House of Representatives. The charter broadened the franchise to include property owners who were not members of Puritan congregations and guaranteed religious freedom to members of the Church of England. This new charter, which gave Massachusetts considerable political autonomy while increasing royal control over trade and military defense, worked well for the next seventy years.

Uprising in Maryland. In Maryland the result of James II's overthrow was bitter religious conflict. A Protestant Association led by John Coode quickly removed the officials appointed by the Catholic proprietor, Lord Baltimore, accusing them of "Popish Idolatry and Superstition." Coode's rebellion reflected the long-standing conflict between Protestants, who constituted the majority of the residents, and Catholics, who held most of the wealth and political offices. But economic problems were also important in Maryland. The stagnant tobacco market had struck hard at the finances of

smallholders, tenant farmers, and former indentured servants. Like Nathaniel Bacon's followers in Virginia, they were suffering not only from falling prices but also from rising taxes and the high fees imposed by proprietary officials.

To quiet the Protestant rebels, the Lords of Trade suspended Lord Baltimore's proprietorship, imposed royal government, and established the Church of England as the colony's official church. This settlement lasted until 1715, when Benedict Calvert, the fourth Lord Baltimore, converted to the Anglican faith and the Crown restored the proprietorship to the Calvert family (which held it until the American Revolution). With the government firmly in Protestant hands and with Catholics forced to practice their faith in private, political conflict diminished, and a united governing class emerged. As in Virginia, the main lines of social division in Maryland now involved class and race, with a planter elite controlling a population of servants, slaves, and tenants. In Maryland, the uprisings of 1689 had eliminated Catholicism as a major political force.

Ethnic Rebellion in New York. In New York the Glorious Revolution produced even more ethnic and religious strife, class tension, and political instability. After England conquered New Netherland in 1664, James II (as duke of York) imposed strict authoritarian rule, prohibiting representative institutions. However, he did not expel or persecute the Dutch residents; indeed, he allowed the Rensselaers and other Dutch manorial lords to retain their large land holdings, and most of the Dutch inhabitants remained in the colony. Thirty years later nearly 60 percent of the taxpayers in New York City were Dutch artisans and shopkeepers. As proud Protestants from Holland, they welcomed the accession of Mary and her Dutch husband to the English throne.

In 1689, a month after the uprising in Boston, the New York militia ousted Colonel Francis Nicholson, who, under Sir Edmund Andros, was lieutenant governor of New York and New Jersey. Dutch artisans in New York City joined with Puritan farmers on Long Island in this attack on Nicholson, an alleged Catholic

sympathizer, and other "Popish Doggs & Divells" appointed by James II. They replaced Nicholson with Jacob Leisler, a migrant German soldier who had married into a prominent Dutch merchant family. At first Leisler had the support of all classes and ethnic groups, but when he freed debtors from prison and urged the creation of a more democratic, town-meeting form of government, this solidarity disintegrated.

In the political struggle that followed, Dutch artisans in New York City sided with Leisler, taking control of the ten-member Board of Aldermen, while wealthy merchants, who had traditionally controlled the city government, attacked the legitimacy of Leisler's seizure of power. Class animosity suffused a pamphlet written by a merchant, Nicholas Bayard, who accused Leisler of being like a "Masaniello," the peasant fishmonger who in 1647 had led a popular revolt in Naples, Italy. Leisler held on to power until 1691, when he was forced to surrender to Henry Sloughter, the new royal governor. Influenced by Bayard and his wealthy merchant friends, Sloughter had Leisler and seven of his associates indicted for treason. An English jury convicted Leisler and Jacob Milburne, his son-in-law, and the two men were hanged and then decapitated—treatment reserved for those found guilty of the most heinous crimes. A new Board of Aldermen, dominated again by merchants, passed ordinances reducing artisans' wages. These measures broke the power of the Dutch artisans, but political conflict between the Leislerian and anti-Leislerian factions continued until the 1710s.

The Glorious Revolution of 1688–1689 began a new phase in English imperial history. In America, the uprisings in Boston and New York toppled the authoritarian institutions of the Dominion of New England and restored internal self-government. In England, a new constitutional monarchy gave effective control of the affairs of state to representatives of the propertied classes. These men promoted an empire based on commerce by curbing royal monopolies (such as the East India and Royal African companies), giving free rein to enterprising merchants and financiers, and developing the American colonies as a source of trade.

A Prosperous Dutch Farmstead
Many Dutch farmers in the Hudson River Valley prospered, because of easy access to markets and their exploitation of black slaves. To record his success, Martin Van Bergen of Leeds, New York, had this mural painted over his mantelpiece.

The Empire in 1713

To preserve its growing power in Europe, England fought two great wars at the end of the seventeenth century, the first against France—the War of the League of Augsburg (1689–1697)—and the second against France and Spain—the War of the Spanish Succession (1702–1713). In both conflicts England's prime goal was to prevent Louis XIV (the "Sun King") from extending France's boundaries and gaining dominance in Europe, but the fighting spilled over into the three nations' empires in North America. There Britain fought to save its foothold along the eastern coast, while France extended its dominion over the lower Mississippi Valley. Spain assumed a defensive posture, viewing its North American colonies as marginal and dispensable (see Table 3.3).

War in America. During the War of the League of Augsburg (known in America as King William's War), New England troops and their Iroquois allies fought against French troops and their Algonquin allies, mostly in Indian territory. French and Indian forces destroyed the frontier town of Schenectady, New York, in 1690, while Massachusetts troops captured Port Royal, the capital of Acadia. The Treaty of Ryswick, which ended the war in 1697, returned all captured territory in North America but confirmed French control of the western half of the rich sugar island of Santo Domingo, present-day Haiti.

Two years later France broke Spain's exclusive control of the Gulf coast of North America, establishing a fort at the mouth of the Mississippi River. In 1702, however, France and Spain became allies during the War of the Spanish Succession when the grandson of Louis XIV of France ascended to the Spanish throne. In that conflict, called Queen Anne's War in America, English forces from South Carolina burned the Spanish town of St. Augustine but failed to capture the fort.

Then, in 1704, the Carolinians mobilized a force of thousands of Creek warriors (won over by the promise of rum, guns, plunder, and trade goods) and rebel mission Indians (who resented the forced-labor system). This army destroyed the remaining Franciscan missions in northern Florida, attacked the Spanish settlement at Pensacola, and massacred those Apalachee who remained loyal to the Spaniards. A joint Spanish-French force twice assaulted Charleston but failed to capture it.

Far to the northeast, Abenaki warriors joined with the French to destroy English settlements in Maine, and in 1704 a force of Abenaki and Mohawk attacked the western Massachusetts town of Deerfield, killing 48 residents and making captives of 112 more. The New York frontier remained quiet because the Iroquois had been forced by a French-Algonquin alliance to accept a general settlement in 1701 and because no one wanted to disrupt the lucrative fur trade. In 1710 British troops, augmented by New England volunteers who feared French Catholicism, again seized Port Royal, but a major expedition against the French stronghold at Quebec in 1711 failed miserably despite the presence of twelve British men-of-war and more than 5,000 troops.

Although there were few major battles, the stakes in these American confrontations were high: for Britain and France, nothing less than the future control of the continent was at issue; for Spain, the defense of its empire in Mesoamerica and the Caribbean. To preserve control of Florida and protect Havana in nearby Cuba, the Spanish reinforced St. Augustine. And to safeguard the rich silver mines in northern New Spain from attack by the new French colony of Louisiana, the Spanish established permanent settlements in Texas, beginning at San Antonio in 1718. Four years later there were 250 Spanish soldiers and 10 Franciscan missions in the infant frontier colony.

Native Americans, caught in the middle of these European-bred conflicts, maneuvered to protect their interests. The prosperous town-dwelling Caddo peo-

TABLE 3.3

English Wars, 1650–1750

	Date	Purpose	Result
Anglo-Dutch	1652–1654	Commercial markets	Stalemate
Anglo-Dutch	1664	Markets—conquest	England takes New Amsterdam
Anglo-Dutch	1673	Commercial markets	England makes maritime gains
King William's	1689–1697	Maintain European balance of power	Stalemate in North America
Queen Anne's	1702–1713	Maintain European balance of power	British get Hudson Bay and Nova Scotia
Jenkins' Ear	1739	Expand markets in Spanish America	Stalemate
King George's	1740–1748	Maintain European balance of power	Capture and return of Louisbourg

ples, one of whose confederacies, the "Kingdom of Tejas," would give Texas its name, expelled the first Spanish Franciscan missionaries in 1693, blaming them for a fatal smallpox epidemic. A generation later the Tejas refused baptism (believing "that the [holy] water kills them") and successfully resisted Spanish control by turning to the French for firearms and trade goods.

In New York, the Five Iroquois peoples—the Mohawk, Oneida, Onondaga, Cayuga, and Seneca—had long lived in a strong political confederation. Now, by means of astute diplomacy, the Iroquois created a "covenant chain" of treaties with tribes in Pennsylvania and the Ohio River Valley and adopted a policy of "aggressive neutrality," exploiting their central geographical location by trading with the English and the French but refusing to fight for either. The Delaware leader Teedyuscung explained this strategy by showing his people a pictorial message from the Iroquois: "You see a Square in the Middle, meaning the Lands of the Indians; and at one End, the Figure of a Man, indicating the English; and at the other End, another, meaning the French. Let us join together to defend our land against both."

In 1713 the Treaty of Utrecht ended this series of wars and provided Britain with major territorial and commercial gains (see Map 3.2). From France, Britain obtained Newfoundland, Acadia (Nova Scotia), the Hudson Bay region of northern Canada, and, most important, suzerainty over the Iroquois and access to the western Indian trade. As a result, Albany and Oswego in New York soon rivaled Montreal as commercial centers of the fur trade. From Spain, Britain acquired commercial privileges in Spanish America and the strategic fortress of Gibraltar at the entrance to the Mediterranean. These gains solidified Britain's commercial supremacy and brought peace to North America for the next generation.

Limited Administrative Reform. The wars focused attention on the English empire in America, which had developed in a haphazard fashion. Some colonies produced crops for export and were commercially tied to England; others were settlements of religious dissidents who wanted to be left alone. Some colonies had corporate charters, others were proprietary ventures, and still others had royal governors.

In 1696 Parliament sought to establish a uniform system by creating a new Board of Trade and filling it with rising politicians and experienced bureaucrats, who drew upon the thinking of leading economist theorists—such as John Locke. The Board sought to install royal governors in all the American settlements but lacked the political influence to do so. Colonists and proprietors resisted reforms, as did English political leaders: Parliament had just overthrown a power-hungry monarch at home and was unwilling to increase royal power in America.

MAP 3.2

Britain's American Empire, 1713

Britain's West Indian possessions were small—mere dots on the Caribbean Sea. However, in 1713 they were by far the most valuable parts of the empire. Their sugar crops brought wealth to English merchants, trade to the northern colonies, and a brutal life (and early death) to African workers.

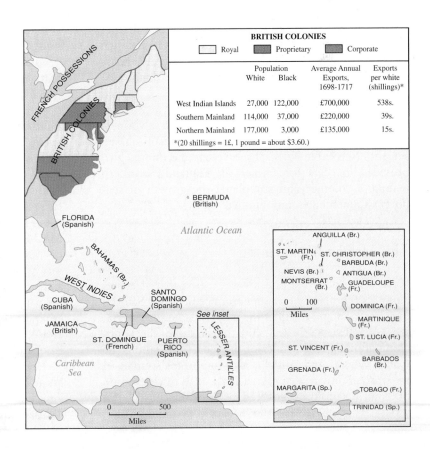

BRITISH COLONIES		
☐ Royal	▨ Proprietary	▨ Corporate

	Population White	Population Black	Average Annual Exports, 1698-1717	Exports per white (shillings)*
West Indian Islands	27,000	122,000	£700,000	538s.
Southern Mainland	114,000	37,000	£220,000	39s.
Northern Mainland	177,000	3,000	£135,000	15s.

*(20 shillings = 1£, 1 pound = about $3.60.)

Consequently, the empire retained a diverse set of governing institutions. New York continued as a royal province; the separate settlements of East and West New Jersey came under royal control in 1702. As in other royal colonies, a governor was appointed by the Crown and an assembly was elected by the people. Connecticut and Rhode Island, as corporate colonies, had greater political autonomy. Like all colonies, they were bound by the Navigation Acts and their laws were subject to review by the Privy Council in London, but they elected their governors and all other local officials. The proprietors retained uneasy control of Carolina, which was formally divided into two colonies in 1713. In Maryland and Pennsylvania, the Calvert and Penn families retained their land rights and political authority. In 1713, as in 1660, the English settlements in North America resembled a patchwork quilt, its colors and textures representing corporate, proprietary, and royal colonies. Those colonies, however, were no longer mere religious outposts or baronial fantasies. They were parts of a thriving commercial empire.

The Imperial Slave Economy

Between 1550 and 1700 European merchants and migrants created a new type of agricultural system. Using land seized from native Americans and the labor of enslaved Africans, the migrants created plantations in Brazil and the West Indies that raised sugar, tobacco, and other valuable crops, which the merchants then brought to markets in Europe. This transoceanic trade in American products, known as the South Atlantic system, changed the history of four continents. It sapped the human resources of West Africa, set off a commercial revolution in Europe, and populated North America and South America with a score of racially mixed societies (see Table 3.4). This slave-based economy also provided markets for farmers in England's northern mainland colonies and stimulated the growth of seaports and merchant communities.

The African Background

West Africa is a vast and diverse region that stretches along 2,000 miles of coastline from present-day Senegal to Cameroon and includes the modern states of Liberia, the Ivory Coast, Ghana, and Nigeria. To the south along another 1,200 miles of that coast lie Gabon, the Congo, Zaire, and Angola, also important sources of the transatlantic trade in slaves. In 1500 a thick expanse of tropical rain forest covered much of the coast, but a series of great rivers—the Senegal, Gambia, Volta,

TABLE 3.4

Slave Destinations, 1520–1810

Destination	Number of Africans Exported
South America	
Brazil	3,650,000
Dutch America	500,000
West Indies	
British	1,660,000
French	1,660,000
Central America	
Spanish	1,500,000
North America	
British colonies	500,000
Europe	175,000
Total	9,645,000

Niger, and Congo—provided relatively easy access to the woodlands, plains, and savanna of the interior.

Most residents were farmers who lived in extended families in small villages and cultivated plots of 6 to 8 acres. Normally, men cleared the land and women planted and harvested the crops. On the plains of the savanna, millet, cotton, and livestock were the prime products, while the forest peoples grew yams, which they ate in the form of porridge or dough, and harvested palm nuts for oil. Forest dwellers exchanged kola nuts, a mild stimulant, for the textiles and leather goods produced by savanna dwellers. Salt produced along the seacoast was also traded, often for iron or gold mined in the hills of the interior.

Political and Social Organization. Most West Africans spoke related Congo-Kordofanian languages, but they were divided into hundreds of distinct cultural and political groups. A majority of the people in both the savanna and the forest lived in hierarchical, socially stratified societies ruled by princes. For example, the Akan peoples organized themselves into complex states ruled by kings whose powers were limited by a council of ministers. The Wolof kings of Senegambia were much more powerful. Warrior-rulers with an army of soldier-slaves, they appointed local chiefs and grew rich from tax revenues and from levies on merchants and conquered peoples. Women of the royal Wolof clans exercised considerable power as well, collecting tribute from various villages and judging cases of adultery.

Many other West Africans resided in stateless societies organized by family and lineage, much as the Woodland Indians of North America did (see Chapter 1). The Tiv people along the Niger River, for example, created a

relatively egalitarian society in which land was available to all; chiefs and elders administered justice but could neither impose taxes and rents nor control individual laborers. Other West Africans lived in communities managed by a village council.

Both women and men had secret societies, corporate bodies that unified society by cutting across lineage and clan loyalties in stateless cultures and by checking the powers of rulers in princely states. The most important societies were the *Poro* for men and the *Sande* for women; they provided sexual education for the young, conducted adult initiation ceremonies, and, by shaming individuals or officials, enforced a code of public conduct and private morality.

Supernatural beliefs underlay the power of the *Poro* and the *Sande*. Although some West Africans had been converted to the Muslim faith and believed in a single god, most recognized a variety of deities ranging from a remote creator-god who seldom interfered in human affairs to numerous spirits that lived in the earth, animals, and plants. Male blacksmiths (who had mastered the secrets of iron making) and female potters (who had

transformed the basic elements of earth, water, and fire) captured these spiritual powers in amulets, "power generators" that protected those who wore them. Africans also paid homage to their ancestors, the "living dead," who were believed to inhabit a spiritual world from which they could intercede on behalf of their descendants. Royal families paid elaborate homage to their ancestors, endowing themselves with an aura of divinity.

European Traders and African Society. At first European traders had a positive impact on life in West Africa by introducing new plants and animals. Portuguese merchants carried coconuts from East Africa, oranges and lemons from the Mediterranean, and pigs from Western Europe. From the New World traders brought sweet potatoes, peanuts, papaya, pineapples, and tobacco. The most important plants were American maize and cassava (manioc), which gradually displaced millet and yams as the staple foods in the West African diet; indeed, their higher yields per acre prompted growth of the population in many areas.

Early Portuguese merchants also expanded existing trade networks, stimulating the domestic economy. European iron bars and metal products joined kola nuts and salt moving inland, whereas grain, gold, ivory, and cotton textiles flowed to the coast to provision and stock European ships heading for Asia and other regions of West Africa. This inland trade remained in the hands of Africans, in part because of disease: Europeans were quickly stricken by yellow fever, malaria, and dysentery, and their death rate was more than 50 percent a year.

Europeans also joined in the trade in human laborers. Unfree status had existed for many centuries in West Africa. Some people were held in bondage as security for debts; others were sold into servitude by their kin, often in return for food in times of famine; still others were enslaved war captives. Although treated as property and exploited as agricultural laborers, these slaves usually were considered members of the society that had enslaved them and often were treated as kin. Most retained the right to marry, and their children were often free.

A small proportion of unfree West Africans were "trade slaves," sold from one kingdom to another or carried overland to the Mediterranean region, mostly by Arab Muslim traders. The first Portuguese in Senegambia found that the Wolof king, the Buurba Jolof,

An African King
This striking bronze plaque, circa 1550–1680, from Benin, an important kingdom in West Central Africa, depicts a mounted king, his attendants, and (probably) his children.

supports himself by raids which result in many slaves from his own as well as neighboring countries. He employs these slaves in cultivating the land allotted to him: but he also sells many to the Azanaghi merchants in return for horses and other goods, and also to the Christians, since they have begun to trade with these blacks.

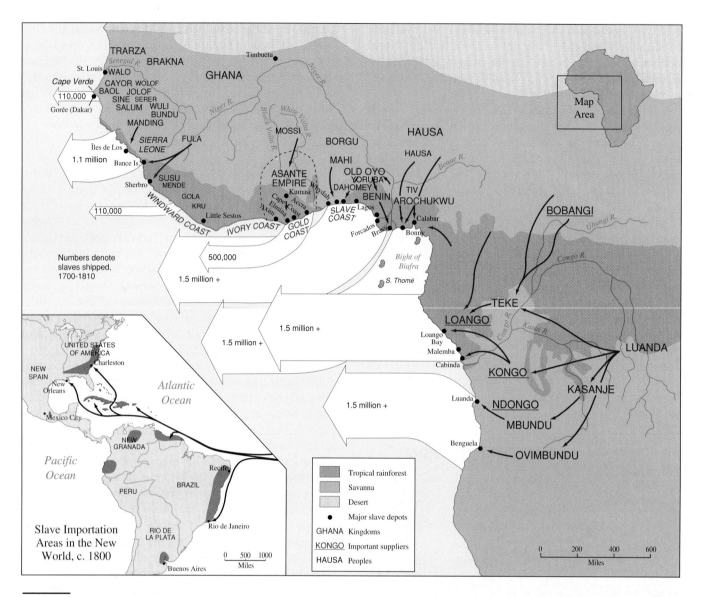

MAP 3.3

Africa in the Eighteenth Century
The tropical rain forest region of West Africa was home to scores of peoples and dozens of kingdoms. Some, such as Dahomey, became aggressive slavers, taking tens of thousands of war captives and funneling them to the seacoast, where they were purchased by European traders. About 15 percent of enslaved Africans died on the transatlantic voyage, the feared "middle passage"; most of the survivors labored on sugar plantations in Brazil and the British and French West Indies (see Table 3.4).

tuguese and then Dutch merchants annually transported about 10,000 Africans across the Atlantic to Brazil and the Caribbean. After England's triumph in the Anglo-Dutch wars, English and French merchants took over this trade in humans, developing African-run slave-catching systems that extended far into the interior. Between 1700 and 1810 they carried over 6 million Africans—800,000 in the 1780s alone—to toil and die in the Americas, primarily on sugar estates in the West Indies.

The South Atlantic System

The demand for labor in Europe's New World plantations gradually transformed the scale and nature of African slavery (see Map 3.3). Between 1440 and 1550 Portuguese traders carried a few thousand Africans each year to labor on sugar plantations in Madeira and the Canary Islands. Then, between 1550 and 1700, Por-

Sugar from Brazil and the West Indies was the cornerstone of the South Atlantic system. Before 1500 Europeans had few sources of sweetness—primarily honey and fruit juices. The cultivation of sugarcane and later the sugar beet changed the diet of Europe and the world. Once people had tasted sweetness, they craved

it. They added sugar to tea and coffee, pies and cakes, and ate it straight in the form of candy. (By 1900 sugar accounted for 20 percent of the calories consumed by people throughout the world.)

Like other European nations, England met the demand for sugar by expanding its plantations. Beginning about 1650, English merchants developed Barbados as a sugar colony. Around 1700 they invested heavily in the Leeward Islands and then turned to Jamaica; by 1750 Jamaica had 700 large sugar plantations worked by more than 105,000 African slaves.

Sugar and the English Economy. Sugar production was complex and expensive. It required fertile land on which to grow the cane, labor to plant and cut it, and heavy equipment to process it into raw sugar and molasses. Because only wealthy merchants or landowners had the capital to outfit a plantation, a planter-merchant elite developed in the sugar industry. Successful planters earned 8 to 10 percent annually on their investment, double the rate of return on government bonds. Their enrichment led the Scottish economist Adam Smith to declare in *The Wealth of Nations* (1776) that sugar was the most profitable crop in either Europe or America.

The South Atlantic system made England a wealthy nation, stimulating its economy in four ways. First, it absorbed the direct profits of sugar production because most West Indian planters lived in England as "absentees." Second, the Navigation Acts, by requiring that American staple crops be exported through England, raised the level of English trade; by 1750 reexports of sugar and tobacco accounted for half of all British exports. Third, English merchants enjoyed a bonanza; for example, in the 1680s the Royal African Company sold male slaves in the West Indies for five times what it had paid for them. Such profits made England the leading maritime power in Europe. Its shipyards built hundreds of vessels to transport slaves, machinery, and settlers to the Western Hemisphere. Commercial expansion also provided England with a supply of experienced sailors, helping to make the Royal Navy the most powerful fleet in Europe. Fourth, transatlantic commerce expanded the domestic economy of England (and Scotland), creating thousands of jobs as men built the port facilities, warehouses, and dwellings of Liverpool, London, and Glasgow—the cities that became the centers of the trade in slaves, sugar, and tobacco. More men and women worked as sugar or tobacco refiners, rum distillers, and manufacturers of textiles and iron products for the growing markets in Africa and America.

Thanks to the South Atlantic system, England was no longer dependent for its prosperity on the raw wool trade. Transatlantic commerce and the mercantilist policies of the Navigation Acts advanced the development of capitalist institutions, making England a wealthy and powerful nation.

The Impact on Africa. Whatever the benefits for Europeans, the South Atlantic system was a tragedy for West Africa and certain parts of East Africa, such as Madagascar. Between 1550 and 1870, the Atlantic slave trade uprooted about 15 million Africans, draining the resources of the continent and provoking untold human misery. Overall, the iron, tinware, rum, and cloth that entered the African economy in exchange for slaves was worth from one-tenth (in the 1680s) to one-third (by the 1780s) as much as the goods those slaves produced. Thus Atlantic slavery enhanced the prosperity of Europe even as it diminished the wealth and population of Africa.

The spiritual and political cost of the slave trade cannot be calculated. The European demand for slaves made kidnapping common in much of West Africa, disrupting the lives of millions of African families (see American Voices, page 82). More significantly, it encouraged violence among peoples; an observer noted in 1739 that "whenever the King of Barsally wants Goods or Brandy . . . , the King goes and ransacks some of his enemies' towns, seizing the people and selling them." Indeed, slaving became a way of life in Dahomey, where the royal house made the sale of slaves a state monopoly between 1730 and 1800 and used the resulting access to European guns to create a centralized military despotism. Dahomey's army, which included a contingent of 5,000 women, became a war-making machine that systematically raided the interior for captives, exporting thousands of slaves each year. The Asante kings also used the firearms and wealth acquired through the Atlantic trade to create a bureaucratic empire of 3 million to 5 million people. Yet active slaving remained a choice, not a necessity. The old and still powerful Kingdom of Benin, famous for its output of superb cast bronzes and carved ivory, resolutely opposed the slave trade, prohibiting the export of men for over a century.

Nonetheless, the South Atlantic slave trade transformed West African life by encouraging powerful centralized states to conquer egalitarian stateless societies. Class divisions also hardened as people of noble birth sold those of lesser status. Law courts became vindictive, selling into slavery even those people who had committed minor crimes. Women's lives changed as well, for more men (about 65 percent of the total) than women were consigned to the transatlantic slave trade, both because European planters preferred male laborers and because African traders withheld female captives for the domestic slave trade market. Thus more African men took several wives, from whom they extracted agricultural labor as well as marital pleasures. Most important, harsh forms of slavery that denied marriage rights or were hereditary gradually became a characteristic institution in Africa, eroding the dignity of human life there as well as on the plantations of the Western Hemisphere.

Olaudah Equiano

The Brutal "Middle Passage"

Olaudah Equiano, also known as Gustavus Vasa, experienced domestic slavery in Africa and plantation slavery in Barbados and Virginia. After buying his freedom in 1766, he fled to London, where twenty years later he published a memoir of his life.

My father, besides many slaves, had a numerous family of which seven lived to grow up, including myself and a sister who was the only daughter. . . . I was trained up from my earliest years in the art of war, my daily exercise was shooting and throwing javelins, and my mother adorned me with emblems after the manner of our greatest warriors. One day, when all our people were gone out to their works as usual and only I and my dear sister were left to mind the house, two men and a woman got over our walls, and in a moment seized us both, and without giving us time to cry out or make resistance they stopped our mouths and ran off with us into the nearest wood. I was left in a state of distraction not to be described. I cried and grieved continually, and for several days I did not eat anything but what they forced into my mouth. At length, after many days' travelling, during which I had often changed masters, I got into the hands of a chieftain in a very pleasant country. This man had two wives and some children, and they . . . could to comfort me, particularly the first wife, who was something like my mother. Although I was a great many days' journey from my father's house, yet these people spoke exactly the same language with us. This first master of

Olaudah Equiano

mine, as I may call him, was a smith, and my principal employment was working his bellows.

I was again sold and carried through a number of places till . . . at the end of six or seven months after I had been kidnapped I arrived at the sea coast.

The first object which saluted my eyes when I arrived on the coast was the sea, and a slave ship which was then riding at anchor and waiting for its cargo. I now saw myself deprived of all chance of returning to my native country . . . ; and I even wished for my former slavery in preference to my present situation, which was filled with horrors of every kind. . . . I was soon

put down under the decks, and there I received such a salutation in my nostrils as I had never experienced in my life; so that with the loathsomeness of the stench and crying together, I became so sick and low that I was not able to eat, nor had I the least desire to taste any thing. I now wished for the last friend, death, to relieve me; but soon, to my grief, two of the white men offered me eatables, and on my refusing to eat, one of them held me fast by the hands and laid me across I think the windlass, and tied my feet while the other flogged me severely. I had never experienced anything of this kind before, and although, not being used to the water, I naturally feared that element the first time I saw it, yet nevertheless could I have got over the nettings, I would have jumped over the side, but I could not. . . .

At last we came in sight of the island of Barbados; the white people got some old slaves from the land to pacify us. They told us we were not to be eaten but to work, and were soon to go on land where we should see many of our country people. This report eased us much; and sure enough soon after we were landed there came to us Africans of all languages.

Source: The Interesting Narrative of the Life of Olaudah Equiano, or Gustavus Vasa, the African, Written By Himself (London, 1789).

Slavery and Society in the Chesapeake

Africans first arrived in Virginia in 1619, but for the next forty years their numbers remained small, and they were not legally enslaved. English common law acknowledged varying degrees of bondage, such as indentured servitude, but not the concept of *chattel*

slavery—the ownership of one human being by another. If legalized slavery was to exist in the English colonies, the settlers would have to create it.

Virginia's Decision for Slavery. The decision in favor of slavery was easy for some migrants. The English in the West Indies and those who migrated from there to

South Carolina simply imitated the labor system used by the Spanish, Portuguese, and Dutch sugar planters and soon gave it legal form. In the tobacco colonies of Maryland and Virginia slavery developed more slowly. Three or four hundred Africans lived in the Chesapeake colonies in 1649, making up about 2 percent of the population; by 1670 the proportion of blacks was still only 5 percent. These Africans were forced to work hard and were ill fed and ill clothed, but so too were most English indentured servants in this exploitative tobacco economy. And a significant number of black workers (one-third in one Maryland community) received their freedom by completing the term of service or converting to Christianity. Some African Christian freemen even purchased slaves or bought the labor contracts of English servants. In this raw and unformed society there were few set rules.

The success of these Africans suggests that religion and personal initiative were initially as important as race in determining social status. The English in the Chesapeake had always seen Africans as "different," sometimes referring in personal letters and official documents to skin color or language but focusing primarily on religion. To the colonists, Africans were first and foremost pagans or Muslims. Thus, by becoming a Christian and a planter, an enterprising African could aspire to near equality with the English settlers.

Beginning in the 1660s, however, new laws gradually lowered the status of all Africans. The reason for this change is not clear. Perhaps the English elite grew more conscious of race as the number of Africans increased, or perhaps the end of the tobacco boom prompted greater social control over blacks as well as over white servants and poor farmers. In any event, new legislation in Virginia forbade Africans to own guns or join the militia. Between 1667 and 1671 the House of Burgesses abridged the property rights of Africans, barring them—"tho baptized and enjoying their own Freedom"—from buying the labor contracts of white servants and specifying that conversion to Christianity did not qualify Africans for eventual freedom. Being black was becoming a mark of inferior legal and social status.

After Bacon's rebellion of 1675–1676, planters imported thousands of Africans, primarily because it had become cheaper to buy blacks than to import white servants and also because slaves had few legal rights and could be disciplined more strictly. A law of 1692 prohibiting sexual intercourse between English and Africans was intended to separate the two laboring groups and create a racially divided society. Blacks found that their servitude was permanent and hereditary, binding their children as well as themselves. Finally, in 1705, a Virginia statute explicitly defined virtually all resident Africans as slaves: "All servants imported or brought into this country by sea or land who were not Christians in their native country shall be accounted and be slaves." The English elite in the Chesapeake colonies had chosen to create a society based on slave labor.

The New Chesapeake Social Order. The social order in the Chesapeake changed significantly after 1700. As settlement moved inland, away from swampy lowlands, disease took fewer lives, and English migrants lived long enough to form stable families and communities. Men reassumed control of family property, no longer naming their wives as executors of their estates and legal guardians of their children (as they did when death rates were high) but bestowing those powers on their male kin. Reaffirming the primacy of male heirs, they also restricted widows' estates to the customary one-third share.

The reappearance of strict patriarchy within the family mirrored larger social developments. As the planter elite consolidated its authority, it created a rural social hierarchy that reflected European traditions, with a few gentry families on the top, a small yeoman class, a much larger group of white tenant farmers, and an army of dependent black laborers. Thousands of African slaves grew their masters' food as well as their export tobacco; built houses, wagons, and tobacco casks; and made shoes, clothes, and other necessities. Their increased self-sufficiency helped wealthy Chesapeake planters weather the depressed tobacco market between 1680 and 1720. Small-scale planters fared less well, falling deeper into debt to their creditors among the elite.

To prevent another rebellion like Bacon's, the Virginia gentry reduced taxes on these middling and poor whites. The annual poll tax paid by every free man fell from 45 pounds of tobacco in 1675 to only 5 pounds a year by 1750. When Royal Governor Alexander Spotswood tried to raise the property requirement for voting, the gentry strongly opposed him. Their strategy was to curry the favor of voters at election time, bribing them with rum, food, and money; once in office, they enacted laws that favored small-scale farmers. In return, yeomen planters elected their wealthy neighbors to political office and deferred to their authority. By creating solidarity among whites, this political compromise prevented a black uprising; by enhancing the power of the planter elite, it limited the authority of the royal governor.

This political compromise worked because most Chesapeake white men shared a common culture. The gentry was still a boisterous, aggressive class, and poor and wealthy planters enjoyed many of the same amusements, from hunting, hard drinking, and gambling on horse races and cockfights to sharing tales of their manly prowess in seducing female servants and slaves. As time passed, however, affluent Chesapeake planters

took on the trappings of wealth, modeling themselves after the English aristocracy (see American Lives, pages 86–87). Between 1720 and 1750 they replaced their modest wooden houses with mansions of brick and mortar. Increasingly, planters—and their wives—sought elegance and refinement, avidly reading English newspapers and pamphlets, importing English clothes, and dining in the English fashion, with an elaborate afternoon tea. They hired English tutors to teach etiquette to their daughters and sent their sons to London to pass a few years at the Inns of Court (the training ground for English lawyers) and to be educated as gentlemen. Most of these young men returned to America, married young ladies (preferably charming and rich ones), and took up the life of slave owning planters, managing plantations and participating in politics. Gentry women now lived in less raucous and more genteel households, their identities increasingly shaped by the conventions of domesticity: deferring to their husbands' authority, rearing pious children, and maintaining elaborate social networks. Committed to life in America, the planter-merchants of the Chesapeake used the profits from the South Atlantic system to form a stable ruling class that was increasingly well educated and refined.

The Expansion of Slavery

The wealth of the white elite came from the labor of black slaves. By 1770 slaves numbered about 500,000 and made up about a third of the southern population. Yet black slavery became an institution not because it was "necessary"—whites grew most of the tobacco and could have cultivated rice and sugar—but because it meant less work and greater profits for those who owned slaves. African labor not only supported a wealthy elite of planter-merchants—such as the Carters, Lees, Burwells, and Randolphs in the Chesapeake and the Bulls, Pinckneys, and Gadsdens in South Carolina—but also raised the living standards of many other white southerners: 60 percent of farm families owned at least one slave by the 1770s.

In contrast to the comfortable lives it provided for planters, eighteenth-century slavery was a brutal experience for Africans. Torn from their villages, they were marched in chains to coastal ports. From there they made the infamous "middle passage"—the perilous voyage to the New World in disease-ridden ships so overcrowded that there was barely room to move. Some Africans jumped overboard, choosing to drown rather

Two Views of the Middle Passage
As the slave trade boomed, ship designers packed in more and more human cargo (below), treating enslaved Africans with no more respect than hogsheads of sugar or tobacco. By contrast, the watercolor, painted by a naval officer, captures their humanity and dignity.

than endure more suffering. Others—about 15 percent of the total and no fewer than 750,000 during the eighteenth century—died aboard ship from sickness or disease, mostly dysentery, smallpox, or scurvy. The survivors, headed mostly for Brazil or the West Indies, faced a degrading life of backbreaking labor.

The Sugar Islands. The waste of human life in the West Indies was staggering. Disease was rampant; thousands of Africans died in epidemics of yellow fever, smallpox, and measles. Thousands more were killed by inadequate food, oppressive work, and inhuman living conditions. Planting and harvesting the sugarcane required intense labor under a subtropical sun, with a pace often set by the overseer's whip. Some planters were little more than killers; with sugar prices high and the cost of slaves low, they worked slaves to death and then imported more. In fact, the mortality rate was so high that although British sugar planters on Barbados imported about 85,000 Africans between 1708 and 1735, the black population of the island increased by only 4,000 (from 42,000 to 46,000).

Initially, because West Indian planters purchased four men for every woman, most slaves could not marry. But women survived at a much higher rate, possibly because they were whipped less often, and gradually female slaves formed half the work force. These women bore few children, because planters forced pregnant women to work in the fields up to the time of birth and miscarriages were frequent. In the sugar colonies, the African population did not increase through reproduction until after slavery was abolished.

The Chesapeake. In Maryland and Virginia living conditions for slaves were less severe, and many lived relatively long lives. Producing tobacco was less physically demanding than growing sugar, and because plantations in the Chesapeake were small and dispersed, epidemic diseases did not spread easily. Moreover, since tobacco planting was only modestly profitable, planters could not constantly buy new slaves and therefore treated those they had less harshly.

Tobacco planters sought to increase their work force through reproduction, purchasing higher numbers of female slaves and encouraging Africans to have large families. In 1720 women made up about a third of the African population of Maryland, and the black population had begun to increase through reproduction. One absentee owner instructed his plantation agent "to be kind and indulgent to the breeding wenches, and not to force them when with child upon any service or hardship that will be injurious to them." And, he added, "the children are to be well looked after." Planters imported Africans again when tobacco prices rose after 1720, but by midcentury American-born slaves formed a majority among Chesapeake blacks. The tobacco

economy, with its relatively healthful plantations and modest profit margin, permitted the emergence of a large African-American population.

South Carolina. In South Carolina, which was settled by land-hungry whites from Barbados in the 1680s, slaves lived under a more demanding regime. The colony grew slowly until Africans from rice-growing cultures, who knew how to plant, harvest, and process that nutritious grain, turned rice into a profitable export crop (see New Technology, page 88). By 1730 Charleston merchants were shipping about 17 million pounds of rice a year to southern Europe, where it was in demand; by 1775 annual rice exports had reached 75 million pounds.

To expand production of their lucrative crop, white planters and merchants imported tens of thousands of Africans (see Figure 3.1). As early as the 1710s Africans made up a majority of the population of South Carolina and about 80 percent of those living in the rice-growing lowlands, but most met an early death. Mosquito-borne epidemic diseases flourished in the hot swampy lowlands of coastal Carolina and took the lives of thousands of slaves. Overwork killed many other Africans, for moving tons of dirt to construct irrigation works was brutally hard work. As in the West Indies, there were many deaths and few births.

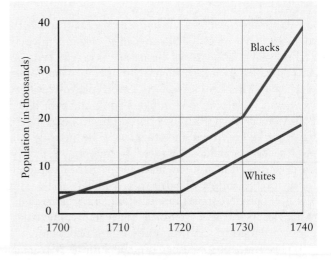

FIGURE 3.1

The Growth of Slavery in South Carolina
To grow more rice, white planters imported thousands of African slaves, giving South Carolina a black majority and prompting the development of a strong Afro-centric language and culture.

William Byrd II and the Maturation of the Virginia Gentry

William Byrd aimed high. In 1692, a mere stripling of eighteen, he sought a post with the Lords of Trade, the body charged with administering England's colonial empire. Nearly two decades later, like his father before him a member of the Virginia Council, Byrd again sought preferment from imperial authorities, trying to become governor of Virginia. He renewed this unsuccessful quest in 1714 and again in 1722.

His father's ambition explained much. The son of a goldsmith and a London tradesman turned Virginia Indian trader and planter-merchant, the older William Byrd had high hopes for his son, shipping him across the Atlantic at age seven to be educated as an English gentleman at the Felsted School. The goal was elusive. Apparently ostracized as a "colonial" by his status-conscious classmates, the young Byrd nonetheless embraced his father's vision: Living in England for the next twenty-four years, he consciously practiced the precepts of self-control and courtesy laid down in a well-known manual of etiquette, Richard Brathwait's *The Perfect Gentleman*. He became a learned man who read Hebrew, Greek, Latin, French, and Italian, and he wrote witty (and minor) poetry and prose.

All to little avail. While living in London from 1692 to 1705, Byrd practiced the arts of a young gentleman and man-about-town, but he never mastered them. As he confessed in a revealing self-portrait, "Inamorato L'Oiseaux" (the Enamored Bird, a word play on his family name), "He wou'd look like a fool, and talk like a Philosopher, when both his eyes and his Tongue shou'd have sparked with wit and waggery." The failure might have been personal, for despite his attempt at gallantry, Byrd was essentially a shy man. Or perhaps it was cultural, for the stigma of birth to a colonial family with few aristocratic connections was difficult to overcome. Whatever the cause, Byrd failed utterly in his almost desperate attempts to secure a rich post or a rich wife.

The death of his father brought him back to reality—in Virginia, a "lonely . . . silent country" that sometimes seemed like "being buried alive." Indeed, Virginia was not only culturally isolated but also medically dangerous, still beset by epidemic disease and early death. But Byrd survived his provincial exile and there, between 1705 and 1714, gradually assumed a coherent identity. As a merchant, slaveowning planter, and receiver of royal revenues, the young Virginian commanded a handsome annual income of some 1,500 English pounds sterling. And after taking as a wife Lucy Parke, the daughter of the colonial-born governor of the Leeward Islands, he succeeded his father as the proprietor of Westover, a tobacco estate on the James River, and as a local and provincial magnate. The parish vestry awarded him "the best pew in the church"; he was appointed commander in chief of the militia in Henrico and Charles City counties; and, the biggest prize of all, the king's ministers named him a member of the Council, the advisory body to the governor and the highest court in the colony. By 1710, at age thirty-six, Byrd had risen about as high as a Virginia-born gentleman could go.

It was not enough. Driven—perhaps by his father's ambition or by his own compulsions, perhaps by the allure of imperial prestige or English high society—Byrd embarked on a decade-long quest for power and wealth. The result was nearly calamitous for Byrd, even as it reveals the inner dynamics of the politics and culture of his time.

Byrd's first goal was political power: the governorship of Virginia, the most prestigious imperial post on the mainland. From his long stay in England he had aristocratic friends, including Sir John Perceval, the earl of Egmont, and Sir John Campbell, the duke of Argyll, who had influence in high places, such as the Board of Trade. But these patronage connections were frail. The great duke of Marlborough, whose army would best that of France's King Louis XIV, curtly dismissed Byrd's petition, stating that "no one but soldiers should have the government of a plantation." Marlborough needed lucrative offices for his retired generals, and he wanted governors with military expertise in the event of an attack from New France or New Spain. Rather than Byrd, he named Sir Alexander Spotswood to govern Virginia.

Rebuffed politically, the ambitious young man sought greater wealth. To inherit the Virginia estate of his wife's deceased father, Byrd agreed in 1712 to "pay all Colonel Parke's debts," a financial miscalculation

William Byrd in the pose of an English aristocrat, London, circa 1702. (Colonial Williamsburg Foundation)

that cost him dearly. Unknown to his son-in-law, Parke had incurred debts in England of £3,000, a burden that would weigh down Byrd for the next thirty years. Like most wealthy eighteenth-century Virginia planters (who fell into debt because of extravagant life-styles), he found himself in a position of humiliating dependence on the credit of London merchant houses.

In 1714 Byrd returned to England to deal with Parke's debts and to undermine Governor Spotswood, whose policies threatened the power of the Council and Byrd's business in the Indian trade. Two years later Lucy Parke Byrd joined him, only to succumb to smallpox: "Gracious God what pains did she take to make a voyage hither to seek a grave," Byrd lamented. In premodern England as in early Virginia, death struck quickly and arbitrarily, without regard to age or social status.

The next years were unhappy ones for Byrd, who was unable to dislodge Spotswood from the governorship, pay off Parke's debts, or marry a rich woman. As he avidly (and awkwardly) pursued an heiress twenty years younger than himself with flowery letters addressed to "Sabina" from "Veramour" (True Lover), Byrd satisfied his sexual desires with a string of prostitutes, recording the encounters and his daily routine in the "Secret Diaries," which he wrote in code during most of his adult life:

> [January 26, 1719] I rose about 8 o'clock, having taken my asses' milk, and read a chapter in Hebrew and some Greek in Lucian. I said my prayers and had milk porridge for breakfast. About 10 o'clock came Annie Wilkinson and I rogered her. . . .

Once again Byrd's colonial origins defeated him: his Virginia estate of 43,000 acres and 200 black slaves failed to impress Sabina's father: "an Estate out of this Island appears to him little better than an Estate in the moon." Rejected as a suitor, Byrd vented his hostility against Sabina in verse:

> *Let Age with double speed oretake her;*
> *Let Love the room of Pride supply;*
> *And when the Fellows all forsake her*
> *Let her gnaw the sheets & dy.*

Byrd once again faced the prospect of a living death in Virginia. In 1719 the Board of Trade ordered him to return to the colony (and threatened to remove him as a councillor if he did not comply), but Byrd stayed in Virginia for only eighteen months before returning to London, where he lived for another five years.

Only in 1726, at age fifty-two and driven by financial necessity, did Byrd finally renounce his quest to be an English gentleman or imperial governor. He returned to Virginia with a young wife (who brought only a small dowry and bore him four children), at last prepared emotionally to accept a lesser destiny as a member of the Virginia gentry. Finally giving up his "rooms" in London in 1728, he built an elegant two-story brick mansion on the family's estate at Westover. From there, he led the Virginia gentry in an unsuccessful effort to prevent Parliamentary approval of the Colonial Debts Act (1732), which allowed English creditors to seize American lands and slaves to pay off debts. And there, during the 1730s, he wrote an unpublished "History of the Dividing Line" between Virginia and North Carolina, an ironic yet celebratory portrait of America and its people.

The personal odyssey of William Byrd II mirrored that of the Virginia gentry as a whole. They had come to America to get rich and return to England in triumph, only to discover that they were bound to Virginia by the curse of their inferior colonial birth. It was a hard and bitter lesson but far from a tragic one, for they remained members of a privileged slaveowning provincial gentry. As Byrd put it after his return to America: "Like one of the patriarchs, I have my flocks and my herds, my bond-men and bond-women, and every soart of trade amongst my servants, so that I live in a kind of independance on every one, but Providence."

Rice: Riches and Wretchedness

Technology always has cultural significance, for its use reveals the systems of value and power in a society. Occasionally, as in the case of the introduction of rice to America, the relation between culture and technology is particularly dramatic. Rice was not grown in England, and the first white settlers in South Carolina failed to plant it successfully during the 1670s and 1680s. As a planter later recalled, "The people being unacquainted with the manner of cultivating rice, many difficulties attended to the first planting and preparing it, as a vendable commodity."

Unlike Europeans, many West Africans had a thorough knowledge of rice. Along the Windward Coast of Africa, an English traveler noted, rice "forms the chief part of the African's sustenance." As he explained, "The rice fields or *lugars* are prepared during the dry season, and the seed sown in the tornado season, requiring about four or five months to bring it to perfection." Enslaved blacks brought these skills to South Carolina. As early as 1690 an Englishman named John Steward was actively promoting rice production both as a potential export and as a cheap food for his slaves. For their part, Africans welcomed the cultivation of a familiar food, and their knowledge was crucial to its success.

English settlers had been unable to master not only the planting and harvesting of rice but also its hulling. At first they tried to come up with a machine—a "rice mill"—to separate the tough husk of the rice seed from the nutritious grain inside. Thus, in 1691 the government awarded Peter Jacob Guerard a two-year patent on a "Pendulum Engine, which doeth much better, and in lesser time and labour, huske rice." Machines did not prove equal to the task, however, and English planters turned to African technology. In 1700 a royal official informed the English Board of Trade that the settlers had "found out the true way of raising and husking rice" by having slave women use traditional mortar and pestle methods to process it. The women placed the grain in large wooden mortars hollowed from the trunks of pine or cypress trees and then pounded it with long wooden pestles, quickly removing the husks and whitening the grains. Their labor was prodigious. By the 1770s slaves were annually processing 75 million tons of rice for export and millions more for their own consumption.

African labor and technology brought both wealth and wretchedness to South Carolina. The planter-

In this early twentieth-century photograph, the descendants of enslaved women use African technology to hull rice in South Carolina.

merchant aristocracy that controlled the rice industry became immensely wealthy; for example, nine of the ten richest Americans who died around 1770 came from South Carolina and had grown rich from rice. The tens of thousands of enslaved Africans who labored in the rice swamps and plantations lived hard and short lives; many died of disease, and until the late eighteenth century, those slaves who survived had little to show—in material comforts or a stable family life—for their years of labor. Although the technology of rice production was not inherently elitist, in America it became part of a slave-based plantation society with immense racial and economic divisions.

The Creation of an African-American Community

Chesapeake planters imported slaves from many regions of West Africa, but about 60 percent of the Africans landing along the York River in Virginia in the 1720s came from Calabar and other lands near the Bight of Biafra. South Carolina slave owners preferred laborers from the Gold Coast and Gambia, but because the slave trade shifted to the south after 1730, they got more than 30 percent of their work force from Angola. In no colony, however, did any African people or language group become dominant, primarily because white planters consciously attempted to ensure security through cultural diversity. "The safety of the Plantations," declared a widely read English pamphlet, "depends upon having Negroes from all parts of Guiny, who do not understand each other's languages and Customs and cannot agree to Rebel."

The slaves regarded each other not as "Africans" but as members of specific peoples or language groups. Gradually, however, enslaved Africans found it in their interest to transcend their diverse identities. In the low-lands of South Carolina, which were populated largely by African-born blacks, they created a new language, the Gullah dialect, which incorporated English and African words in an African grammatical structure and so was widely understood. In the Chesapeake, with more American-born blacks and a less concentrated slave population, many Africans gave up their native tongues for English. "All the blacks spoke very good English," a European visitor to Virginia in the mid-eighteenth century noted with surprise.

The acquisition of a common language, whether Gullah or English, was a prerequisite for the creation of an African-American community. The growth of stable family and kin networks was another requirement. In South Carolina a high death rate prevented long-term family formation, but after 1725 Chesapeake blacks created strong nuclear families and extended kin relationships. These "African-Americans" gradually developed a culture of their own, passing on family names, traditions, and knowledge to the next generation.

In this newly formed ethnic community, aspects of the slaves' African heritage could be seen in wood carvings, the giant wooden mortars and pestles used for hulling rice, and the design of shacks, which often had

African Culture in South Carolina
The dance and the musical instruments are of Yoruba origin, the contribution of Africans from the Niger River–Gold Coast region (the homeland of the Yoruba), an area that accounted for one-sixth of the slaves imported into South Carolina.

rooms arranged from front to back in a distinctive "I" pattern (not side by side, as was common in English houses). Many African-Americans retained their traditional religious beliefs, observing Muslim religious practices or relying on the spiritual powers of conjurers. But others adopted Protestant Christianity, reshaping its doctrines, ethics, and rituals to fit their needs. For their part, whites were influenced by African musical rhythms. Virginians have "what I call everlasting jigs," reported Nicholas Creswell, an Englishman. "A Couple gets up and begins to dance a jig (to some Negro tune)."

Yet slavery drastically limited African-American creativity. Slaves had few opportunities for education and self-expression because most blacks worked as farm laborers and accumulated few material goods. "We entered the huts of the Blacks," commented a well-traveled European who visited Virginia in the late eighteenth century:

> They are more miserable than the most miserable of the cottages of our peasants. The husband and wife sleep on a mean pallet, the children on the ground; a very bad fireplace, some utensils for cooking. . . . They work all week, not having a single day for themselves except for holidays.

He concluded that without question, "the condition of our peasants is infinitely happier." The comparison between slaves and peasants was apt. Both African-American slaves and European peasants were peoples who, because of their poverty and dependence, had only limited ways to express their identity. Consequently, they bequeathed to posterity not great works of art or literature but distinctive cultures based on language, family, community, and religion.

Moreover, African-American society was still in the process of formation. The parents or grandparents of eighteenth-century slaves had come to the American mainland in chains and as strangers to one another. Yet unlike their fellow Africans in the West Indies, they not only had survived but also had developed family networks, a common language, and a culture of their own. The power of that culture is conveyed by a story told by a traveler in the southern backcountry. He came upon

Slave Dwellings at Mulberry Plantation
Most plantation scenes depict the imposing mansions of the slave owners. This view of Mulberry plantation in South Carolina, however, steals a look behind the big house to the meager dwellings of the slaves, whose labor produced the wealth of the plantation.

an African-American who had been taken prisoner and adopted by Indians, who had given him "a wife, a mother, and plenty of land to cultivate if he chose it, and the liberty of doing everything but making his escape." But the black man rejected this freedom, rendering "himself up a voluntary slave to his former master, that he might there once more embrace those friends and relatives from whom he had been so long separated." To this African-American, family and cultural identity were worth more than greater freedom in an alien society.

Oppression and Resistance

Returning to slavery was an act of great courage: slave owners were not a forgiving group. They came from a culture in which the poor were systematically oppressed, religious heresy ended in bloodshed, and minor crimes were punishable by death. Masters did not hesitate to impose harsh discipline on white indentured servants, whipping them without mercy or doubling their time of service for running away, and because African slaves were an alien people, all moral restraints vanished. In the West Indies English planters routinely branded troublesome slaves with hot irons. To keep their slaves in submission, Chesapeake planters resorted to castration, nose slitting, and the amputation of fingers, toes, and ears. Declaring the chronic runaway Ballazore an "incorrigeble rogue," Robert "King" Carter of Virginia ordered his toes cut off: "nothing less than dismembering will reclaim him." The worst aspects of human nature and of the harsh traditions of early modern Europe found expression in a slave-based society.

Terror and Control. White violence was related to the size and density of the slave population. On the malaria-ridden lowland plantations of South Carolina a few whites generally had charge of twenty-five to a hundred slaves and they could maintain authority only by inspiring fear. Black workers were forbidden to leave the plantation without special passes, and rural patrols enforced those regulations. Slaves who disobeyed, refused to work, or ran away were punished brutally. Even in the Chesapeake, where slaves constituted a minority of the population, planters often resorted to the whip.

Whites who grew up in this society learned to use terror to maintain their superior position. No one knew this better than Thomas Jefferson, who witnessed brutality on his father's plantation in the mid-eighteenth century. Each generation of whites, he noted, was "nursed, educated, and daily exercised in tyranny," for the relationship "between master and slave is a perpetual exercise of the most unremitting despotism on the one part, and degrading submission on the other. Our children see this and learn to imitate it."

Iron Shackles and a Silver Service
Colonial metalworkers fashioned shackles for enslaved Africans as well as elaborate silver urns and cups for wealthy slave owners. The juxtaposition of these objects of beauty and oppression confronts the vast disparity of life in a slave society.

Slaves dealt with their plight in a variety of ways. Some cooperated with their owners, agreeing to do extra work in return for better food or clothes. Others resisted by working slowly or carelessly or by stealing from their masters. Still others attacked their owners or overseers, taking a small measure of revenge, though it was punishable by mutilation or death.

A successful rebellion was nearly impossible on the mainland, because whites were both numerous and armed. Full-fledged slave revolts occurred mostly on densely settled sugar plantations, and then only in areas where nearby mountains offered a secure refuge, such as Jamaica. But some newly arrived slaves without ties to African-American culture escaped to the frontier, where they tried to establish African villages (for example, near Lexington, Virginia, in 1728) or, more often, married into Indian tribes. Others, especially those who were fluent in English, fled to towns, where they tried to pass as free blacks.

The Stono Rebellion. Imperial rivalries sparked a major slave revolt in British North America. In the late 1730s the governor of Spanish Florida promised freedom and land to slaves who fled from South Carolina.

By February 1739 at least sixty-nine slaves had reportedly escaped to St. Augustine, and rumors circulated "that a Conspiracy was formed by Negroes in Carolina to rise and make their way out of the province." When war between England and Spain broke out later that year, the conspirators acted. Banding together near the Stono River, seventy-five Africans, some of them Portuguese-speaking Christians from the African Kingdom of Kongo, killed a number of whites, stole guns and ammunition, and marched south toward Florida "with Colours displayed and two Drums beating." Unrest swept the countryside, but the white militia killed many of the Stono rebels and dispersed the rest, preventing a general uprising.

The Stono rebellion frightened whites throughout the mainland. South Carolina planters tightened plantation discipline and bought fewer new Africans. Elsewhere slaveholders acted vigorously to quell discontent. After several unexplained fires and burglaries in New York City in 1741, the authorities alleged a plot among slaves, who formed almost 20 percent of the population and were owned by over 40 percent of the city's white households. After a judicial inquisition, they hanged or burned to death twenty blacks and four whites—alleged accomplices in the conspiracy—and transported eighty slaves to the West Indies. For Africans, the price of active resistance was high.

The Northern Economy

The West Indies Trade. Not only New York City but the entire northern mainland economy participated in the South Atlantic system. The sugar islands provided a ready market for American bread, lumber, fish, and meat. As a West Indian explained as early as 1647, planters in the islands "had rather buy food at very dear rates than produce it by labour, so infinite is the profit of sugar works." By 1700 the economic systems of the West Indies and New England were tightly interwoven. After 1720 farmers and merchants in New York, New Jersey, and Pennsylvania entered this trade, shipping wheat, corn, and bread to the West Indies.

This commerce tied the empire together economically. In return for sugar exports to England, West Indian planters received bills of exchange—basically credit slips—from London merchant houses. The planters then used those bills to pay slave traders for newly arrived Africans and to reimburse mainland merchants for the agricultural goods produced by northern farmers. The merchants in turn exchanged their bills for British manufactures, thus completing the cycle.

The West Indian trade created the first American merchant fortunes and major urban industries. New England merchants built factories in Boston, Newport, and Providence to process raw sugar, imported from the islands, into refined sugar, which previously had been imported from England. They also invested in distilleries to turn West Indian molasses into rum for domestic and foreign consumption. By the 1740s Boston distillers were exporting more than half a million gallons of rum annually.

Seaport Cities. As a result of this mercantile activity, American port cities grew rapidly. By 1750 Newport, Rhode Island, and Charleston, South Carolina, had nearly 10,000 residents apiece; Boston had 15,000, and New York had almost 18,000. The largest port, Philadelphia, whose population would reach 30,000 by 1776, was the size of most European provincial cities and formed the center of a sprawling regional economy.

Trade was the lifeblood of these cities. Merchants in Boston and Philadelphia, along with those in New York, handled most of the mainland's imports from Britain and managed exports to the West Indies. A bustling export trade in wheat transformed Baltimore from a sleepy village to a major port in the two decades after 1740. Charleston, the only major southern seaport, shipped deerskins, indigo, and rice to European markets. In addition, New England merchants, operating out of Boston, Salem, Marblehead, and smaller ports, built a major fishing industry, providing mackerel and cod to feed the slaves of the sugar islands and to export to southern Europe. By 1750 the New England fishing fleet numbered more than 600 ships and provided employment for over 4,000 men.

Coastal towns were centers of the shipbuilding and lumber industries. By the 1740s seventy sawmills dotted the Piscataqua River in New Hampshire, providing low-cost wood for homes, warehouses, and especially shipbuilding. Scores of shipwrights turned out oceangoing vessels, while hundreds of other artisans made ropes, sails, and metal fittings for the new fleet. Shipyards in Boston and Philadelphia launched about 15,000 tons of oceangoing vessels annually, augmenting English shipbuilding so successfully that colonial-built ships eventually made up about a third of the British merchant fleet.

Interior Towns. The impact of the South Atlantic system extended far into the interior of North America, because of an intricate transportation network. For instance, a small fleet of trading vessels sailed back and forth between Philadelphia and the villages along the Delaware Bay, exchanging cargoes of European goods for barrels of flour and wheat. Land-based transport in Maryland, meanwhile, was handled by hundreds of professional teamsters who by the 1750s annually moved to market 370,000 bushels of wheat and corn and 16,000 barrels of flour, representing 10,000 wagon trips. To accommodate this traffic, entrepreneurs and artisans set up taverns, livery stables, and barrel-making

shops in small towns along the wagon roads, providing additional jobs.

Prosperous towns attracted a wide variety of artisans; for example, Lancaster, Pennsylvania, had more than 200 German and English artisans. The South Atlantic system thus provided not only markets for farmers, by far the largest group of northern residents, but also opportunities for merchants, artisans, and workers in country towns and seaport cities.

Seaport Society

American Merchants. A small group of wealthy merchants stood at the top of urban society. The Apthorp, Bowdoin, Faneuil, and Oliver families in Boston; the Beekmans, Crugers, Waltons, and Roosevelts in New York; and the Norris and Pemberton clans in Philadelphia were among the first great American entrepreneurs, and their ventures in West Indian and European

trade reaped handsome profits (see Map 3.4). By 1750 about 150 merchants controlled 70 percent of Philadelphia's trade. Their taxable assets averaged £3,000, a huge sum at the time.

Like the Chesapeake gentry, wealthy northern merchants imitated the British upper classes in their cultural tastes. Guided by imported design books from England, merchants built mansions in the new Georgian architectural style—grand houses that, with their large windows symmetrically flanking elaborate columned porticoes, conveyed the wealth of their owners. Their wives created a genteel culture, decorating their houses with the best furniture and entertaining guests at elegant dinners.

Artisans. Artisans and shopkeepers, along with their families, constituted nearly half the seaport population and provided the residents with food, housing, and clothing. Their ranks included innkeepers, butchers, seamstresses, shoemakers, weavers, bakers, carpenters,

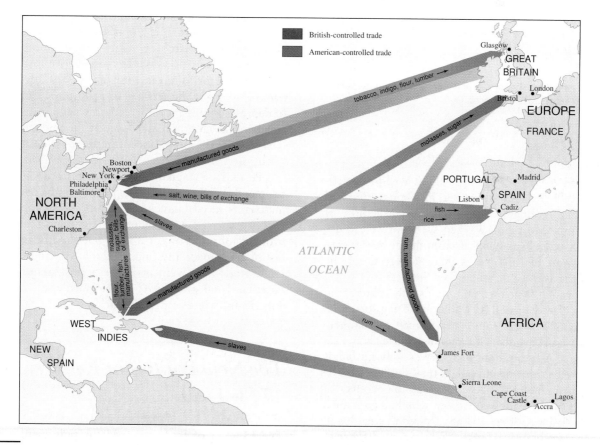

MAP 3.4

The Rise of the American Merchant, circa 1750
In accordance with mercantilist doctrine, British merchants controlled most of the transatlantic trade in manufactures, sugar, tobacco, and slaves. However, merchants in Boston, New York, and Philadelphia seized control of the West Indian trade, while Newport traders imported slaves from Africa, and Boston and Charleston merchants carried fish and rice to southern Europe.

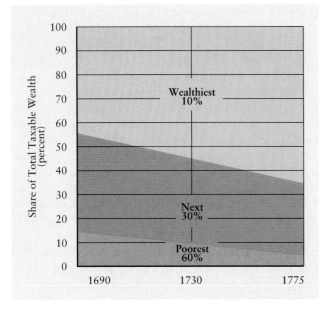

FIGURE 3.2

Wealth Inequality in the Northern Cities

As commerce expanded, the wealth of merchants grew much faster than did that of artisans and laborers. By the 1770s the poorest 60 percent of the taxable inhabitants of Boston, New York, and Philadelphia owned less than 5 percent of the taxable wealth, whereas the top 10 percent—the merchant elite and its allies—controlled 65 percent.

masons, and dozens of other specialists. Well-to-do artisans owned their own tools, shops, and houses and had taxable assets averaging about £300, a tenth those of the merchants. Most craft workers were not well-to-do, however. A tailor was lucky to accumulate £30 worth of property in his lifetime, a mere 1 percent of the wealth of the average merchant (see Figure 3.2).

Artisans had their own culture, usually centered on their particular craft and its traditions. They socialized among themselves and sometimes formed mutual-help societies to assist members in times of need, such as a serious illness or a business loss. Wives and husbands often worked as a team and taught the "mysteries of the craft" to their children. Indeed, a discernible number of shops were run by widowed women who had continued the family business. Some artisans aspired to wealth and status, an entrepreneurial ethic that prompted them to hire apprentices and expand production. But the goal of most artisans was a "competency"—an income sufficient to maintain the family in modest comfort and dignity.

Laborers and Slaves. Laboring men and women formed the lower ranks of the urban social order. Hundreds of

well-muscled men worked as stevedores on the docks of Boston, Philadelphia, and New York, transferring tons of manufactured goods and molasses from inbound ships to warehouses and then loading the ships with barrels of wheat, fish, and rice for export. Hundreds of other men worked for wages in a variety of semiskilled jobs, while poor women—whether single, married, or widowed—eked out a living washing clothes, spinning wool, or working as servants. Black slaves and white indentured servants performed many of the most menial and demanding jobs. In Philadelphia, African-American slaves and indentured German migrants made up about 20 percent of the city's residents but held nearly half the laboring jobs.

Whether enslaved, indentured, or merely poor, wage workers and merchant seamen were indispensable to the economy of every port city. Yet they owned little property. Most lived in small rented houses or tenements in the back alleys of the crowded waterfront districts, scraping by on household budgets that left no margin for sickness, accidents, or unemployment. To make ends meet, women took in washing and sewing and children were sent out to work as soon as they were able. In good economic times such personal sacrifices brought security or, for many sailors and laborers, enough money to drink cheap New England rum in waterfront taverns, often in the company of adventurous or poor women who worked as prostitutes. But periods of depressed trade meant irregular work, hunger, dependence on the charity handed out by the town-appointed overseers of the poor, and—for the most desperate—a life of petty thievery.

Periods of stagnant commerce affected all townspeople, the rich as well as the poor. Even the most astute merchants faced financial hardship and possible bankruptcy when prices plunged. Commerce not only brought jobs and opportunities but also the uncertainties of a complex and unpredictable system of transatlantic trade. Involvement in the South Atlantic system between 1660 and 1750 transformed the lives of all Americans, white as well as black.

The New Politics of Empire, 1713–1750

The triumph of trade changed the politics of empire. The British government, pleased with the prosperous commerce in staple crops, ruled its colonies with a gentle hand. This policy of "salutary neglect" gave the colonists a significant degree of self-government and economic autonomy and ultimately allowed Americans to challenge the rules of the British mercantilist system.

The Rise of the Assembly

Before 1689 political affairs in most colonies were dominated by royal governors or authoritarian elites. The duke of York ran New York by fiat, Puritan magistrates suppressed dissent in New England, and Governor Berkeley and his Green Spring faction ruled Virginia with an iron hand. These oligarchs denounced critics of their policies as traitors and condemned opposition groups as illegitimate "factions." Such arrogance reflected a widespread belief that power came from above, not from below. In the words of Robert Filmer, a royalist political philosopher in England, "Authority should Descend from *Kings* and *Fathers* to *Sons* and *Servants*."

As the American settlements became mature provinces after 1700, they developed a more representative system of politics. The seeds of this change were planted during the Glorious Revolution in England, when the political faction known as the Whigs led the fight for a constitutional monarchy that limited the authority of the Crown. The English Whig ideal was a "mixed government," one that divided power among the three social orders: the monarchy, the aristocracy, and the commons. Whigs did not advocate democracy, but they did believe that property owners (the "commons") should have some political power, especially with regard to the levying of taxes. When Whig politicians forced William and Mary to accept a Declaration of Rights in 1689, they strengthened the powers of the House of Commons at the expense of the Crown.

Emulating the English Whigs, the leaders of the American representative assemblies established the same committees that existed in the House of Commons, such as those on rights and privileges. They insisted on the assemblies' authority to levy taxes and demanded a position of constitutional equality with the royal or proprietary governor. Gradually, colonial leaders won partial control of patronage and the budget, angering imperial bureaucrats and absentee proprietors. "The people in power in America," complained the proprietor William Penn during a struggle with the Pennsylvania Assembly, "think nothing taller than themselves but the Trees."

The American political system remained more elitist than democratic. Although most property-owning white adult men had the right to vote after 1700, in some colonies—Virginia and South Carolina, for example—only men of considerable wealth and status stood for election. By the 1750s seven members of the Lee family, representing five counties, sat in the Virginia House of Burgesses and—along with members of other powerful Virginia families, such as the Byrds, Randolphs, and Carters—dominated its major committees.

Similar family dynasties and alliances appeared in the northern colonies (see Figure 3.3). In New England,

the children and grandchildren of the original Puritans had intermarried and formed a core of political leaders. "Go into every village in New England," John Adams said in 1765, "and you will find that the office of justice of the peace, and even the place of representative, have generally descended from generation to generation, in three or four families at most." Marriage ties created powerful political networks. A European traveler noted that the political leaders in New Brunswick, New Jersey, were "General White, Colonel Bayard, and Judge Patterson—all these families are related and live in close contact."

Although the royal governors remained powerful, dispensing patronage and land grants, political authority came increasingly to reside in local leaders and the assemblies in which they sat. Most assemblymen had first been elected to office as town selectmen, county justices of the peace, or officers in the militia and could count on local support to resist governors or royal bureaucrats. These self-confident American politicians used the "power of the purse"—their control of taxation and revenue—to prevent the implementation of unpopular imperial policies. In Massachusetts during the 1720s, for example, the assembly refused repeatedly to obey the king's instructions to provide a permanent salary for the royal governor and, adding insult to injury, refused to pay even a yearly stipend to Governor Shute as long as he continued to press the issue.

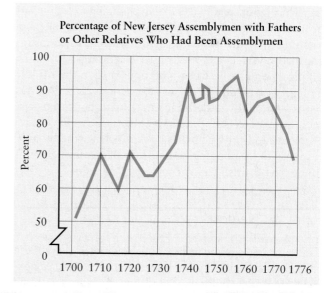

FIGURE 3.3

Family Connections and Political Power

By the 1750s nearly every member of the New Jersey assembly came from a family with a history of political leadership, clear testimony to the emergence of an experienced governing elite in the colonies.

Like Shute, most royal governors lacked the political clout to impose controversial policies on the powerful assemblies. And neither governors nor assemblies had the power to impose unpopular edicts on the people. The crowd actions that overthrew the Dominion of New England in 1689 were a regular part of political life in both England and America and were used to achieve social and economic aims. To uphold community values, for example, a mob in New York closed houses of prostitution, and one in Salem, Massachusetts, ran people with infectious diseases out of town. In Boston during Queen Anne's War (1702–1713), hungry artisans and laborers rioted to prevent merchants from exporting much-needed grain. A generation later in New Jersey, farmers closed down the law courts to prevent proprietary claimants from seizing disputed lands. In New England, lumbermen attacked the king's Surveyors of the Woods when they sought to reserve certain tall pine trees as masts for the British navy.

Crowds were often outmaneuvered by astute officials who waited for their passion to subside, or they were outlasted by entrepreneurs or land speculators who had money and often law on their side. But mobs were forces to be reckoned with. When officials in Boston sought to restrict the sale of farm produce to a designated public marketplace, a crowd destroyed the building and defied the authorities to arrest them. "If you touch One you shall touch All," an anonymous letter warned Sheriff Edward Winslow, "and we will show you a Hundred Men where you can show one."

This letter made clear the changing relations of power. The expression of popular opinion—in the give-and-take of New England town meetings, in the rum-warmed conviviality of Virginia electioneering, in the political contests between ambitious men in the Middle Colonies, and ultimately in the actions of rebellious mobs—gradually undermined the old authoritarian system. In its place stood political institutions—local governments and provincial assemblies—that were broadly responsive to popular pressure and increasingly immune from British control.

Salutary Neglect

Contributing significantly, though unwittingly, to the rise of American self-government were the policies pursued by British politicians and bureaucrats (see Table 3.5). During the reigns of George I (1714–1727) and George II (1727–1760), royal bureaucrats relaxed their supervision of internal colonial affairs, focusing instead on defense and trade. Two generations later the eminent British political philosopher Edmund Burke would praise this strategy of mild rule as one of "salutary neglect," a mercantilist strategy that Burke believed had

contributed to the colonies' wealth and population growth.

Sir Robert Walpole. Salutary neglect was a by-product of the political system developed by Sir Robert Walpole, leader of the Whigs in the House of Commons, who served as the king's chief minister between 1720 and 1742. By strategically dispensing appointments, pensions, and gifts, Walpole won parliamentary support for his policies, transforming the formerly antagonistic relationship between king and Parliament into one of harmonious cooperation. In effect, he governed in the monarch's name but with Parliament's consent.

Walpole's tactics offended some members of Parliament. His chief opponents, who called themselves Real Whigs, argued that by using patronage and bribery to create a strong *Court* (or *Crown*) *party,* he had betrayed the constitutional monarchy established by the Glorious Revolution of 1688. Other critics, organized in a loose *Country party* of landed gentlemen, celebrated the independence of the individual members of Parliament. They condemned Walpole's close ties with merchants and financial institutions such as the Bank of England and his creation of a large national debt, warning that high taxes, a bloated royal bureaucracy, and a standing army threatened the liberties of the people.

American Real Whigs. The arguments of the Real Whigs and the Country party appealed to Americans who wanted to preserve the hard-won powers of the provincial assemblies. In their eyes, the royal governors in America still had too much arbitrary power: they could veto legislation and use land grants and political appointments to influence voting in the assemblies. "By increasing the number of officers dependent on the Crown," a writer in the Boston *Weekly Newsletter*

TABLE 3.5		
English Monarchs, 1660–1760		
	Dates of Reign	Family/Dynasty of Origin
Charles II	1660–1685	Stuart
James II	1685–1688	Stuart
Mary II and	1689–1694	Stuart
William III	1689–1702	House of Orange
Anne	1702–1714	Stuart
George I	1714–1727	House of Hanover
George II	1727–1760	House of Hanover

Sir Robert Walpole, the King's Minister
Walpole (left) offers advice to the Speaker of the House of
Commons. A brilliant tactical politician, Walpole used patronage to command a majority in the Commons. By looking
out for the financial interests of George I and George II—the
German-speaking monarchs from the duchy of Hanover—he
won their support as well. Walpole's personal motto, "let
sleeping dogs lie," helps to explain his colonial policy of salutary neglect. (© National Trust Photographic Library/John
Hammond)

charged, the royal governor sought to destroy "the liberties of the people." Such rhetoric was excessive. Few
governors could actually wield despotic power, but the
accusation nevertheless stirred public anxiety.

Even as Walpole's political tactics were alarming
Americans, his patronage policies were undermining the
royal bureaucracy in America. His ministers filled colonial posts with mediocre officials who had good political connections and whose main goal was not to
advance imperial policies but to enrich themselves. In
New York, for example, William Cosby became governor during the 1730s primarily because his wife was related to Lord Halifax, an influential aristocrat. Cosby
was hungry for money, and his salary demands and selling of offices threw the province into political chaos for
a decade. His successor, George Clinton, appointed

through a family connection with the duke of Newcastle (Walpole's chief political manager), lacked the will or
political acumen to uphold imperial interests. In 1744,
for example, he cautioned his superiors against imposing a stamp tax, warning that "the people in North
America are quite strangers to any Duty but such as
they raise themselves." Rather than challenging this
outlook, Clinton simply accepted it as a fact of political
life (see American Voices, page 98).

Patronage also weakened the Board of Trade as
Walpole and Newcastle packed it with their supporters
in Parliament. These mediocre *placemen* (so called because they did little work but merely occupied a
"place") weakened the morale of capable imperial officials. Governor Gabriel Johnson went to North Carolina in the 1730s as a potential reformer determined to
"make a mighty change in the face of affairs" by curbing the power of the assembly, but he soon became discouraged by the lack of support at home. Like other
imperial officials during the era of salutary neglect, he
became a cautious governor, deciding "to do nothing
which can be reasonably blamed, and leave the rest to
time, and a new set of inhabitants."

Thus Walpole's political strategy weakened imperial
rule in America in three different ways. First, his support
for a merchant-run empire based on trade inhibited
forceful imperial rule, allowing the "rise of the assembly" in America. Second, his corrupt domestic policies
persuaded American Real Whigs that British rule posed
a threat to their political liberties, weakening respect for
royal governors. Third—and most directly—his patronage system weakened the royal bureaucracy in America.
Salutary neglect did not "cause" Americans to seek independence; in fact, in the short run mild rule actually
strengthened the colonists' allegiance to Britain (as did
the increasing popularity of British goods and culture).
But the legislative autonomy allowed by salutary neglect
did encourage Americans to expect a position of political equality within the empire and eventually to claim it.

Consolidating the Mercantile System

Beginning in the 1730s Walpole's ministry did act decisively in protecting British commercial interests in
America, both from foreign military threats and American economic competition. One major initiative was to
provide a subsidy for the new colony of Georgia.

The Founding of Georgia. In the early 1730s General
James Oglethorpe and a group of social reformers influenced by the Enlightenment (see Chapter 4) successfully
petitioned King George II for land south of the Carolinas. They named the new colony Georgia (in honor of
the king) and planned it as a refuge for Britain's poor.

Governor George Clinton

The Waning of British Authority

Authority has to be exercised firmly to command respect. Lax administration in London and weak officials in America opened the way for colonial assemblies to defy imperial policy. In a letter to the Lords of Trade written in 1742, Governor Clinton confesses his inability to control the provincial New York Assembly.

My Lords,

I have in my former letters inform'd Your Lordships what Incroachments the Assemblys of this province have from time to time made on His Majesty's Prerogative & Authority in this Province in drawing an absolute dependence of all the Officers upon them for their Saleries & Reward of their services, & by their taking in effect the Nomination to all Officers. . . .

1stly, That the Assembly refuse to admit of any amendment to any money bill, in any part of the Bill; so that the Bill must pass as it comes from the Assembly, or all the Supplies granted for the support of Government, & the most urgent services must be lost.

2ndly, It appears that they take the Payment of the [military] Forces, passing of Muster Rolls into their own hands by naming the Commissaries for those purposes in the Act.

3rdly, They by granting the Saleries to the Officers personally by name & not to the Officer for the time being, intimate that if any person be appointed to any Office his Salery must depend upon their approbation of the Appointment . . . .

I must now refer it to Your Lordships' consideration whether it be not high time to put a stop to these usurpations of the Assembly on His Majesty's Authority in this Province and for that purpose may it not be proper that His Majesty signify his Disallowance of the Act at least for the payment of Saleries.

Source: E. B. O'Callaghan, ed., *Documents Relative to the Colonial History of the State of New York* (Albany, 1860–).

Envisioning a society of small farms worked by independent landowners and white indentured servants, the trustees of Georgia limited most land grants to 500 acres and, unlike all other British colonies, outlawed slavery.

Walpole provided Georgia with a subsidy from Parliament, not because he shared the founders' vision, but because he wished to protect the increasingly valuable rice colony of South Carolina from attack from Spanish Florida. Spain had long resented the British presence in Carolina and was outraged by the expansion into Georgia, where Spanish Jesuits and Franciscans had established Indian missions. Responding to Spanish threats, Walpole dispatched a regiment of troops to Georgia in 1737 and appointed Oglethorpe commander in chief of all military forces in Georgia and South Carolina. Simultaneously, merchant interests in Parliament formed an alliance with the Georgia trustees to push for an aggressive anti-Spanish policy. After the Treaty of Utrecht in 1713 British merchants had steadily increased their trade in slaves and manufactured goods to Spain's American colonies, eventually controlling two-thirds of their overseas trade. Spanish officials began to resist this commercial imperialism, much of it illegal, so the merchants wanted their government to go to war.

War with Spain. In 1739 Spanish naval forces sparked the so-called War of Jenkins' Ear by physically mutilating Robert Jenkins, an English sea captain who was trading illegally with the Spanish West Indies. Britain used this provocation to begin the first significant military conflict in America in a generation. In 1740 British regulars commanded by Governor Oglethorpe, together with provincial troops from South Carolina and Georgia and some Indian allies, launched an unsuccessful expedition against St. Augustine, which was defended by Spanish soldiers and escaped African slaves. Later that year the governors of the other mainland colonies raised 2,500 volunteers, who joined a British naval force in an assault on the Spanish seaport of Cartagena in present-day Colombia. The attack failed, and instead of enriching themselves with Spanish booty, hundreds of colonial troops died of tropical diseases.

The War of Jenkins' Ear became part of a general European conflict, the War of the Austrian Succession (1740–1748). This struggle pitted Britain and its traditional ally, Austria, against Spain, France, and Prussia. Although the British and French navies clashed in the West Indies, the long frontier between the British colonies and French Canada remained calm. Then, in 1745, more than 3,000 New England militiamen, supported by a British naval squadron, captured the powerful French naval fortress of Louisbourg on Cape Breton Island near the mouth of the St. Lawrence River; the fort surrendered without a fight.

The Treaty of Aix-la-Chapelle, which ended the war in 1748, mandated the return of all captured territory in

North America, and this bitterly disappointed the New England provinces. Yet the war secured the territorial integrity of Georgia by reaffirming British military superiority in the region. British merchants continued to expand their commerce within the Spanish empire.

The Politics of Mercantilism. The expansion of British commerce that had opened the way to the era of salutary neglect ultimately brought it to a close. As American economic growth threatened various British interests, pressure mounted in England to assert greater administrative control over the colonies. In general, mercantilist policy called for colonies to produce only agricultural goods and raw materials, reserving the more profitable provision of manufactured goods and commercial services for artisans and merchants in the home country. Parliament implemented this policy by enacting the Woolens Act of 1699 and the Hat Act of 1732, which prohibited the intercolonial sale of American-produced textiles and hats, and the Iron Act of 1750, which allowed the export of pig iron to England but banned new iron-working forges and mills in the colonies.

The Navigation Acts, however, had a major loophole. By allowing Americans to own ships and transport goods, they enabled colonial merchants to gain control of 95 percent of the commerce between the mainland and the West Indies. American merchant houses also carried three-quarters of the manufactures shipped across the Atlantic from London and Bristol. Quite unexpectedly, British mercantilism had created a dynamic and wealthy community of colonial merchants.

The Molasses Act. American enterprise eventually clashed with the powerful British interests. By the 1720s the rapidly growing mainland settlements were producing more flour, fish, and barrels than the British sugar islands had use for, and so colonial merchants began to sell them in the French West Indies. These inexpensive foodstuffs and supplies helped French planters produce low-cost sugar and control the competitive European market. American rum distillers imported cheap French molasses, cutting off another market for British sugar products. By the 1730s the British sugar industry was on the verge of collapse.

British sugar producers petitioned Parliament for help and won passage of the Molasses Act of 1733. This act permitted the mainland colonies to export fish and farm products to the French islands but placed a high tariff (6 pennies per gallon) on molasses imported from non-British colonies. Parliament expected the act to benefit British planters by making their prices competitive.

American merchants and public officials strongly protested the Molasses Act, arguing not only that it would cut farm exports and cripple their distilling industry but also that the resulting loss of revenues would make it more difficult for colonists to purchase British goods. When Parliament ignored their protests, American merchants simply refused to obey the act, importing French molasses and bribing customs officials to ignore the new tax. Fortunately for the Americans, sugar prices rose in the mid-1730s, quieting the concerns of the British planters, so that the act was never enforced and the Royal Customs Service collected only a pittance. But the act foreshadowed a new era of imperial control.

Currency and Trade. The financial policies of the provincial assemblies also troubled imperial officials. Because American merchants sent most of the bullion and bills of exchange from the West Indian trade to Britain to pay for manufactures, the colonists lacked an adequate amount of currency. To create a domestic money supply, the assemblies of ten colonies established land banks, which lent money. Farmers gave the banks a mortgage on their land (hence the term *land bank*) and received loans in the form of paper currency. This creative system of finance stimulated both trade and investment by providing ordinary people with a medium of exchange and landowners with money to invest in equipment.

In some colonies the misuse of paper currency created conflicts with merchants, both British and American. The Rhode Island assembly paid its expenses not by levying taxes but by printing paper money (not backed by land mortgages), producing a severely depreciated currency. Eventually a Rhode Island bill with a face value of £10 would buy only £5 worth of goods. Creditors, many of them British merchants, rightly complained that they were being financially harmed because Rhode Islanders could pay off old debts with new, depreciated currency.

Because Rhode Island was a small colony and did not have a royal governor, British officials tolerated this fiscal abuse. But when Massachusetts tried to issue paper currency in 1740, the British government intervened, strongly supporting Governor Belcher's veto, even though the currency would be backed by a land bank. Then, in 1751, Parliament passed a broad Currency Act that prevented all the New England colonies from establishing new land banks and, with Rhode Island in mind, prohibited the use of public bills of credit to pay private debts. Many British merchants thought such decisive action was long overdue.

Imperial officials were equally distressed by the growing power of the provincial assemblies and seized on the currency issue as a case in point. Charles Townshend of the Board of Trade charged that American assemblies had assumed many of the "ancient and established prerogatives wisely preserved in the Crown." By 1750 many British political and financial leaders were determined to replace salutary neglect with a more rigorous system of imperial control.

Summary

When Charles II was restored to the English throne in 1660, he paid his political and personal debts by bestowing land in America as proprietary colonies. The Carolina colony was given to a group of aristocrats. New York, conquered from the Dutch in 1664, fell to Charles's brother James, duke of York. Pennsylvania was awarded to William Penn. However, Charles adopted new mercantilist policies, securing the enactment of Navigation Acts, which tightly regulated colonial exports and imports. In 1685, the new king, James II, tried to impose tighter political controls as well, abolishing the existing charters of the northern mainland colonies and creating the Dominion of New England. The Glorious Revolution of 1688 cost James his throne, and revolts in Boston, New York, and Maryland helped secure the restoration of the colonists' traditional rights and institutions.

The South Atlantic system, based on the West Indian sugar trade, laid the foundation for England's wealth and power. To work the sugar plantations of the West Indies and Brazil, millions of Africans were forced into slavery and premature death. In Virginia, where Africans mainly raised tobacco and the conditions of servitude were less severe, the number of black laborers grew dramatically through importation and natural increase. In North America, the South Atlantic system brought great profits to white planters, the creation of African-American communities, and prosperity for northern seaports, merchants, and farmers.

The Treaty of Utrecht (1713) ushered in a generation of peace among the European powers in North America, leaving the British colonies free to develop their social and political institutions. Aided by the unofficial British policy of salutary neglect, American political leaders strengthened the power of the provincial assemblies, which were controlled by the elite but responsive to the views of ordinary people. After 1730 pressure from British interests prompted greater imperial control of American affairs.

In 1733, alarmed by the decline of the British sugar industry because of colonial trade with the French West Indies, the British passed the Molasses Act, again tightening mercantilist controls on colonial trade. Additional legislation restricting manufacturing in the colonies and regulating their financial policies signaled that by 1750 the era of salutary neglect was rapidly coming to an end.

TIMELINE

1651	First Navigation Act Barbados becomes sugar island
1660	Restoration of Charles II
1660s	Virginia moves toward slave system New Navigation Acts
1663	Carolina proprietorship granted
1664	New Netherland captured; becomes New York
1669	Fundamental Constitution of Carolina
1681	William Penn founds Pennsylvania
1685	James II becomes king of England
1685–1689	Dominion of New England
1688	Glorious Revolution
1689	Rebellions in Massachusetts, Maryland, and New York
1689–1702	Mary II and William III govern England
1689–1713	Intermittent war in Europe and America
1696	Board of Trade created
1699	Woolens Act
1705	Virginia statute defines slavery
1713	Treaty of Utrecht
1714–1750	British policy of "salutary neglect" Rise of American assemblies British "reexport" trade in sugar and tobacco Dahomey becomes "slaving" state
1718	Spanish missions and garrison in Texas
1720–1742	Sir Robert Walpole chief minister
1720–1750	Black natural increase in Chesapeake African-American society created Rice exports from Carolina soar Africans in Carolina create Gullah language Planter aristocracy in southern colonies Expansion of seaport cities on mainland
1732–1733	Georgia colony chartered; Spain protests Hat Act and Molasses Act
1739	Florida governor encourages slave desertions Stono rebellion War of Jenkins' Ear
1740	Veto of Massachusetts land bank
1740–1748	War of the Austrian Succession
1750	Iron Act
1751	Currency Act

BIBLIOGRAPHY

The best short overview of England's empire is Michael Kammen, *Empire and Interest: The American Colonies and the Politics of Mercantilism* (1970), but see also Alison Olson, *Making the Empire Work: London and American Interest Groups, 1690–1790*. On Africa, see Paul Bohannan and Philip Curtin, *Africa and the Africans*, 3d ed. (1988). For the mingling of cultures in Virginia, read Mechel Sobel, *The World They Made Together* (1987).

The Politics of Empire

Robert Bliss, *Revolution and Empire: English Politics and the American Colonies in the Seventeenth Century* (1990), explores the impact of the Puritan Revolution, whereas Jack M. Sosin, *English America and the Restoration Monarchy of Charles II: Transatlantic Politics, Commerce, and Kinship* (1980), does the same for the restored king. See also Stephen S. Webb, *1676: The End of American Independence* (1984). For the events of 1688–1689 see David S. Lovejoy, *The Glorious Revolution in America* (1972). More specific studies include Jack M. Sosin, *English America and the Revolution of 1688: Royal Administration and the Structure of Provincial Government* (1982), and Lois Green Carr and David W. Jordan, *Maryland's Revolution of Government, 1689–1692* (1974). Ethnic tension in New York can be traced in Robert C. Ritchie, *The Duke's Province: Politics and Society in New York, 1660–1691* (1977); Thomas J. Archdeacon, *New York City, 1664–1710: Conquest and Change* (1976); Donna Merwick, *Possessing Albany, 1630–1710: The Dutch and English Experiences* (1990); and Joyce Goodfriend, *Before the Melting Pot: Society and Culture in Colonial New York City, 1664–1730* (1992). Jack M. Sosin, *English America and Imperial Inconstancy: The Rise of Provincial Autonomy, 1696–1715* (1985), outlines the new imperial system.

The Imperial Slave Economy

For the African background, see John Thornton, *Africa and Africans in the Making of the Atlantic World, 1400–1680* (1992), and Richard Olaniyan, *African History and Culture* (1982). Specialized studies of forced African migration include Philip Curtin, *The Atlantic Slave Trade: A Census* (1969); Paul Lovejoy, ed., *Africans in Bondage: Studies in Slavery and the Slave Trade* (1986); James A. Rawley, *The Transatlantic Slave Trade* (1981); Joseph E. Inikori and Stanley L. Engerman, eds., *The Atlantic Slave Trade* (1992), and Barbara L. Solow, ed., *Slavery and the Rise of the Atlantic System* (1991).

Richard S. Dunn, *Sugar and Slaves: The Rise of the Planter Class in the English West Indies, 1624–1713* (1972), provides a graphic portrait of the brutal slave-based economy, whereas Sidney W. Mintz, *Sweetness and Power: The Place of Sugar in Modern History* (1985), explores the impact of its major crop. Winthrop D. Jordan, *White over Black, 1550–1812* (1968), remains the best account of Virginia's decision for slavery. T. H. Breen and Stephen Innes, *"Myne Owne Ground": Race and Freedom on Virginia's Eastern Shore, 1640–1676* (1980), closely examines the lives of the first slaves and free blacks. For the creation of African-American society see Allan Kulikoff, *Tobacco and Slaves: Southern Cultures in the Chesapeake, 1680–1800* (1986); Daniel C. Littlefield, *Rice and Slaves: Ethnicity and the Slave Trade in Colonial South Carolina* (1981); and Peter H. Wood, *Black Majority: Negroes in Colonial South Carolina through the Stono Rebellion* (1974). See also Orlando Patterson, *Slavery and Social Death: A Comparative Study* (1982); Richard Price, ed., *Maroon Societies: Rebel Slave Communities in the Americas* (1973); and Ira Berlin and Philip D. Morgan, eds., *Cultivation and Culture: Labor and the Shaping of Slave Life in the Americas* (1992).

On white society in the South, see Daniel Blake Smith, *Inside the Great House: Planter Family Life in Eighteenth-Century Chesapeake Society* (1980); Rhys Isaac, *The Transformation of Virginia, 1740–1790* (1982); Timothy H. Breen, *Tobacco Culture* (1985); and the fine older study by Charles Sydnor, *American Revolutionaries in the Making: Political Practices in Washington's Virginia* (1952). Urban society and trade are explored in Gary B. Nash, *The Urban Crucible* (1979); Gary M. Walton and James F. Shephard, *The Economic Rise of Early America* (1979); and Christine L. Heyrman, *Commerce and Culture: The Maritime Communities of Colonial Massachusetts, 1690–1750* (1984). See also Marcus Rediker, *Between the Devil and the Deep Blue Sea: Merchant Seamen, Pirates, and the Anglo-American Maritime World, 1700–1750* (1987).

The New Politics of Empire

The appearance of a distinctive American polity is traced in Jack P. Greene, *The Quest for Power: The Lower Houses of Assembly in the Southern Royal Colonies, 1689–1776* (1963); Bernard Bailyn, *The Origins of American Politics* (1968); Patricia U. Bonomi, *A Factious People: Politics and Society in Colonial New York* (1971); A. Roger Ekirch, *"Poor Carolina": Politics and Society in Colonial North Carolina, 1729–1776* (1981); and Richard Bushman, *King and People in Provincial Massachusetts* (1985). John Schutz, *William Shirley* (1961), shows how a competent colonial governor wielded power, whereas Thomas C. Barrow, *Trade and Empire: The British Customs Service in Colonial America, 1660–1775* (1967), and Alison G. Olson, *Anglo-American Politics, 1660–1775* (1973), explore various aspects of British mercantilism.

Douglas E. Leach, *Roots of Conflict: British Armed Forces and Colonial Americans, 1677–1763* (1986), and Howard H. Peckham, *The Colonial Wars, 1689–1762* (1964), cover the diplomatic and military conflicts of the period, but these Anglo-American perspectives should be balanced by David J. Weber, *The Spanish Frontier in North America* (1992).

An English Country House

Imported English books and art, such as this painting of the
English gentry at play, defined cultural standards for many
upper-class Americans. (Colonial Williamsburg Foundation)

CHAPTER 4

Growth and Crisis in American Society

1720–1765

★   ★   ★

Britain's North American settlements grew spectacularly, from about 400,000 residents in 1720 to nearly 2 million by 1765. Widespread ownership of land made American farming communities very different from peasant villages in Europe, but throughout British North America old family values remained intact: men owned most of the property, and women were accorded an inferior legal and social position.

Regional differences among the northern colonies grew more pronounced. New England continued to be dominated by Puritans and freeholding farm families. A population explosion and economic hardship in Europe prompted a massive migration of Germans and Scots-Irish to the mid-Atlantic colonies, giving them greater ethnic and religious diversity than was the case in New England and, indeed, any society in Western Europe. The resulting cultural and religious tensions were offset, at least to a degree, by economic prosperity, resulting from a growing international trade in wheat.

Before 1720 most Americans lived much simpler lives than Europeans, because they were unable to recreate the cultural sophistication of their homelands. After 1720 mainland settlers began participating in the intellectual and religious movements of the larger world. Many educated Americans embraced the ideas of the European Enlightenment, or Age of Reason. Far more residents, of African as well as European ancestry, were swept up in a new wave of religious enthusiasm that derived from European Pietism.

Americans also were swept up in the Great War for Empire, known in the colonies as the French and Indian War, which gave Britain control of all of eastern North America, and in the great expansion of trade sparked by the early stages of the British Industrial Revolution. The colonists sent huge quantities of tobacco, rice, and wheat to European markets and, after 1750, consumed 15 to 20 percent of all British exports. Now larger, with

a more diverse population, the British possessions found themselves increasingly divided internally along the lines of wealth, geographical residence, and ethnic identity.

Freehold Society in New England

Even though their religious vision faltered after a century in America, the Puritans achieved many of their social goals. In 1720 New England remained a predominantly rural society in which most men owned their own land, farming it with the aid of their dependent wives and children. By 1750, however, the population threatened to outstrip the supply of arable land and pastureland, posing a severe challenge to the freehold ideal.

Farm Families: Women's Place

In America as in Europe, law and custom elevated men over women. Men claimed not only political power in the state but also, particularly in New England, domestic authority within the family. As the Reverend Benjamin Wadsworth of Boston advised women in his pamphlet *The Well-Ordered Family* (1712), it made no difference if they were richer, more intelligent, or of higher social status than their husbands: "Since he is thy Husband, God has made him the head and set him above thee." Therefore, Wadsworth concluded, it is "thy duty to love and reverence him."

All through their lives women had it impressed on them that theirs was a subordinate role. Small girls watched their mothers defer to their fathers. As they grew to adulthood, they learned that their marriage portions would be different from and smaller than those of their brothers: they would receive not land but money, livestock, or household goods. In a typical will, Ebenezer Chittendon of Guilford, Connecticut, left all his land to his sons, decreeing that "Each Daughter have half so much as Each Son, one half in money and the other half in Cattle."

In rural New England—indeed, throughout the colonies—a woman's place was as a dutiful daughter to her father and a helpmeet (helpmate) to her husband,

The Character of Family Life: The Cheneys
Life in a large early American family was very different from that in a small modern one. Mrs. Cheney's face shows the rigors of having borne ten children, a task that occupied her entire adult life. Her children grew up with many older (or younger) siblings, which blurred differences between the generations.

who tilled the land and represented the family in the community. Some farmwives fulfilled these roles in an exemplary fashion. They spun thread and yarn from flax or wool and wove it into shirts and gowns; knitted sweaters and stockings; made candles and soap; learned the difficult arts of turning milk into butter and cheese, brewing malt into beer, and preserving meats; and mastered dozens of other productive household tasks.

The community lavished praise on these "notable" women, setting them up as models. "I have a great longing desire to be very notable," one woman wrote upon her marriage. Women who lacked skills felt their shortcomings keenly, although their labor was no less crucial to the rural household economy. As Abigail Hyde, a New England farmwife, confessed in a letter, "The conviction of my deficiencies as a mother is overwhelming."

Bearing and raising children was not an easy task. Most women in the northern colonies married in their early twenties and bore five to seven children before the onset of menopause in their early forties. There were no drugs to ease the pain of labor and no antibacterial medications to prevent infections. Yet most women survived numerous childbirths, helped by midwives—women who prepared them emotionally for the experience of giving birth, stayed with them during labor, and attended to the needs of the newborn and the mother. A large family sapped a woman's emotional strength and kept her energies focused on domestic activities. For about twenty of her most active years a woman was either pregnant or breast-feeding. Sarah Ripley Stearns, a Massachusetts farmwife, explained that she had no time for religious activities because "the care of my Babes takes up so large a portion of my time and attention."

Over time, the shrinking size of farms prompted many couples to choose to have fewer children. After 1750 families in long-settled communities such as Andover, Massachusetts, had an average of only four children. Smaller families meant that women had fewer mouths to feed, fewer clothes to wash and mend, and more time to pursue other tasks. Susan Huntington of Boston, who had the good fortune to be rich, spent more time in "the care & culture of children, and the perusal of necessary books, including the scriptures." With fewer children, ordinary farm women could make extra yarn, cloth, or cheese to exchange with their neighbors or sell to shopkeepers, thus enhancing the family's standard of living. (After 1770 some would become wage workers in a new merchant-run putting-out system, stitching the soft upper parts of women's shoes.)

But women's participation in the daily affairs of life was limited by cultural rules. For example, Puritan men were reluctant to have their wives work in the fields. "Women in New England," Timothy Dwight reported approvingly, "are employed only in and about the house and in the proper business of the sex." Yet strong-

Tavern Culture
By the eighteenth century, many taverns were run by women, such as this "Charming Patroness," who needed all her charm to deal with her raucous clientele. It was in taverns, declared puritanical John Adams, that "diseases, vicious habits, bastards, and legislators are frequently begotten."

minded wives often defied their husbands and assumed authority in the household or over their own lives.

One such woman was Hannah Heaton of North Haven, Connecticut, a devout Puritan wife who reproved her husband's family for "wicked practices" and left his church. Like other Puritan women, Heaton had taken advantage of the Protestant emphasis on reading the Bible and had learned to read and write. She chafed under the restrictions in most Congregational churches that denied women the opportunity of voting or even speaking. Like Anne Hutchinson (see Chapter 2), Heaton questioned the authority of her minister, thinking him unconverted and a "blind guide." Eventually she joined an evangelical congregation that, like more radical Protestant churches, gave women an active role

in religious matters. For example, Quakers believed "that women can be called to the ministry as well as men," as a French visitor noted, and Baptists in Rhode Island permitted women to vote on church affairs. Yet these differences among churches were only variations on the general theme of female subordination. Despite their increasing freedom from child-rearing most women—not only in New England but also in other regions of British America—remained in an inferior position, their lives tightly bound by a web of laws, cultural expectations, and religious restrictions.

Farm Property: Inheritance

By contrast white American men had escaped many traditional constraints. Whereas in England the nobility and the gentry owned 75 percent of the arable land and had it farmed by servants, tenants, and wage laborers, in the northern mainland colonies 70 percent of the settled land was owned by yeomen freeholders. "The hope of having land of their own & becoming independent of Landlords is what chiefly induces people into America," an official reported in the 1730s.

Not that it was easy to get hold of even a small farm in the colonies. Children from poor families often began their working lives as indentured servants. Their parents, unable to provide them with work or food, bound them out to farmers who could. Young men ended their indentures at age eighteen or twenty-one with many farming skills but without land. For ten or twenty years they struggled as wage-earning farm laborers or tenants to save enough to buy a few acres of their own. And if they failed to acquire enough property to leave a landed estate, their children would have to repeat the slow climb up the agricultural ladder: from servant, to laborer, to tenant, to freeholder.

Having learned the importance of a landed inheritance from bitter experience in Europe, most yeomen farmers assumed responsibility for the economic fate of their children. As their sons and daughters reached marriageable age—usually twenty-three to twenty-five—these farmers provided them with a *marriage portion* consisting of land, livestock, and sometimes farm equipment. The marriage portion repaid children for their labor on the parents' farm and ensured their future loyalty. Parents knew they would need help in their old age (there were no pension or social security systems). To guarantee that they would not be left helpless, some farmers kept legal title to the land until they died.

Because parents began to transfer their hard-earned land and goods to their children upon marriage, a family's future prosperity depended on a wise choice of marriage partners. Yeomen parents usually decided whom their children would marry. Normally, children had the right to refuse an unacceptable match, but they did not have the luxury of "falling in love" with whomever they pleased.

Once married, a woman had fewer property rights than did her husband and children. A new bride gave legal ownership of all her personal property to her husband. Any land a woman might possess fell under the

Lady Undressing for a Bath, circa 1730–1740
This delightful painting attributed to Gerardus Duyckinck captures a moment of intimacy between an unknown but obviously well-to-do American couple. Many marriages were "arranged" but grew into love matches. Others began with strong emotional bonds that withered over time. One affluent Philadelphia woman found herself in a perfect romantic match, writing to her husband: "Our Hearts have been united from the first, in so firm, so strong, so sweet an affection, that words are incapable of setting it forth."

control of her husband. English and colonial law compensated married women for this loss of property by giving them *dower rights*. When a woman's husband died, she had the right to use a third of the family's estate during her lifetime. If she remarried, however, she forfeited this right. And she could not sell her one-third interest, for it legally belonged to her children; her rights were restricted to use. The wife's property rights were subordinated to those of the family "line," which stretched, through the children, across the generations.

To preserve the ideal of a freehold society based on family property, American farmers followed a number of strategies. Some fathers used the traditional English legal device of *entail* by willing the farm to a male child and specifying that it remain undivided and in the family forever. For example, Ebenezer Perry of Barnstable, Massachusetts, willed his land to his son, Ebenezer, Jr., stipulating that it devolve in turn on the younger Ebenezer's "eldest son surviving and so on to the male heirs of his body lawfully begotten forever."

Other farm parents in New England used a *stem family* system to preserve a freehold estate. They chose a married son or son-in-law to work the farm with them and he became the "stem," or center, of the entire family, inheriting the farm after the father's death. Still other parents wrote wills that gave the family farm to the oldest son but required that he pay money or goods to the younger children. All these devices—entail, the stem system, and legally binding wills—favored one son to keep the family farm intact across the generations. Most parents, however, provided their other children with money, apprenticeship contracts, or frontier tracts to enable them to become freeholders in other communities.

Farmers in New England who wished to give land to all their male children divided their farms, a pattern common among 90 percent of the fathers in Chebacco, Massachusetts. Division could be a risky strategy, because many sons ended up with too little land to provide a comfortable living. A better solution, chosen by other equality-minded farmers, was to move their young families to frontier regions, where life was hard but land was cheap and abundant. "The Squire's House stands on the Bank of the Susquehannah," a traveler named Philip Fithian reported from the Pennsylvania backcountry in the late colonial period. "He tells me that he will be able to settle all his sons and his fair Daughter Betsy on the Fat of the Earth."

The historic accomplishment of New England farmers was the creation of communities composed of independent property owners. A French visitor remarked that the sense of personal worth and dignity in this rural world contrasted sharply with European peasant life. In America he found "men and women whose features are not marked by poverty, by lifelong deprivation of the necessities of life, or by a feeling that they are insignificant subjects and subservient members of society."

The Crisis of Freehold Society

Yet the threat of deprivation was increasing because the number of residents doubled with each generation, mostly as a result of natural increase. The Puritan colonies had about 100,000 people in 1700, 200,000 in 1725, and almost 400,000 by 1750. In long-settled areas, lands that had been ample for the original migrant families had been divided and then subdivided until many parents could no longer provide land for their children. The Reverend Samuel Chandler of Andover, Massachusetts, noted in the 1740s that he had "been much distressed for land for his children," seven of whom were boys. Dispersing the land among so many heirs usually meant a decline in living standards (see Table 4.1). In

TABLE 4.1

Diminishing Property in the Fuller Family, Kent, Connecticut

	Date of Birth	Highest Assessment on Tax List
First Generation		
Joseph Fuller	1699	203 pounds
Second Generation		
Joseph Jr.	1723	42
Zachariah	1725	103
Jeremiah	1728	147
Nathaniel	?	67
Adijah	?	46
Simeon	?	49
Abraham	1737	136
Jacob	1738	59
Isaac	1741	7
	Average:	72 pounds
Third Generation		
Abel	?	40
Abraham, Jr.	?	50
Oliver	1747	50
Daniel	1749	65
Howard	1750	28
Benejah	1757	32
Ephraim	1760	100
John	1760	?
Asahel	1770	48
James	1770	40
Revilo	1770	35
Samuel	?	14
	Average:	42 pounds

Concord, Massachusetts, by the 1750s, about 60 percent of farmers owned less land than their fathers had.

Because parents had less to give their children, they had less control over their children's lives. The system of arranged marriages broke down. Young people moved to newly settled regions or had premarital sex and used pregnancy to win permission to marry. The number of firstborn children conceived before marriage rose spectacularly throughout New England, from about 10 percent in the 1710s to 30 percent in the 1740s and, in some communities, to 40 percent by the 1760s. If these young people had it to do over, they "would do the same again," an Anglican minister observed, "because otherwise they could not obtain their parents' consent to marry."

On the eve of the American Revolution, farm communities in New England responded to the threat to their freehold ideal in three basic ways. First, many towns petitioned the provincial government for assistance. In 1740 Massachusetts farmers unsuccessfully demanded a land bank that, by issuing paper currency, would provide them with loans and stimulate trade. With greater success, they sought new land grants along the frontier. Settlers continually moved inland—into New Hampshire and the future Vermont—hacking new farms out of the virgin forest and creating new communities of freehold farmers.

Second, settlers who remained on the original farmsteads planted different crops. Even before 1750 they had replaced the traditional English crops of wheat and barley (for bread and beer) with a grazing economy based on corn, cattle, and hogs. Corn offered a hardy food for humans, and its abundant leaves furnished feed for cattle and pigs, which provided milk and meat. The physician William Douglass observed in the 1720s that poor people in New England subsisted on "salt pork and Indian beans, with bread of Indian corn meal, and pottage of this meal with milk for breakfast and supper." After 1750 New England farmers raised the output of this mixed-crop grazing economy by planting potatoes, whose high yield offset the disadvantage of smaller farms. Farmers also introduced nutritious English grasses, such as red clover and timothy, to provide forage for their livestock and nitrogen for the depleted soil (though they didn't know the chemistry). These innovative measures not only averted a food shortage but also generated a surplus for export. New England became the major supplier of salted and pickled meat to the West Indies; in 1770 preserved meat accounted for about 5 percent of the value of all exports from the mainland colonies.

Third, to compensate for the reduced size and limited resources of their properties, farm families not only had fewer children but also increased productivity by helping one another. Men lent each other tools, draft animals, and grazing land. Women and children joined other families in spinning yarn, sewing quilts, and shucking corn. Farmers plowed the fields of artisans, who in turn fixed the pots, plows, and furniture brought to them for repair. By sharing labor and goods, every farm—and the entire economy—was able to achieve maximum output at the minimum cost.

This system of economy and exchange—the "household mode of production," as one historian has called it—worked well because New England was a homogeneous, close-knit society. Typically, no money changed hands between relatives or neighbors. Instead, farmers, artisans, and shopkeepers recorded debts and credits in personal account books, and every few years the accounts were "balanced" through the transfer of small amounts of cash. Thus, New England farmers averted a social crisis and preserved their freehold society well into the nineteenth century.

The Mid-Atlantic: Toward a New Society, 1720–1765

The middle colonies—New York, New Jersey, and Pennsylvania—lacked the cultural uniformity of New England, containing instead a mixture of settlers from many European countries with diverse traditions and religions (see Map 4.1). Yet these settlements had more order and purpose than one might think. Strong ethnic ties bound German settlers to one another, as did deep religious loyalties among the members of various churches: Scots-Irish Presbyterians, English and Welsh Quakers, German Lutherans, and Dutch Reformed Protestants. These religious and ethnic ties generated conflicts among cultural groups, as did increasing economic inequality.

MAP 4.1

Ethnic and Racial Diversity, 1775
In 1700 most colonists were English, but by 1775 those of English descent constituted a minority. African-Americans accounted for one-third of the population of the South, while the presence of Germans and Scots-Irish created ethnic and religious diversity in the middle colonies and southern backcountry.

FIGURE 4.1

*Population Growth, Wheat Prices, and English Imports
in the Middle Colonies*
Wheat prices soared in Philadelphia because of demand in the
West Indies and Europe. Exports of grain and flour paid for
English manufactures, which were imported in large quanti-
ties after 1750.

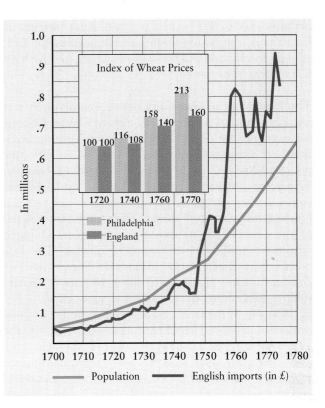

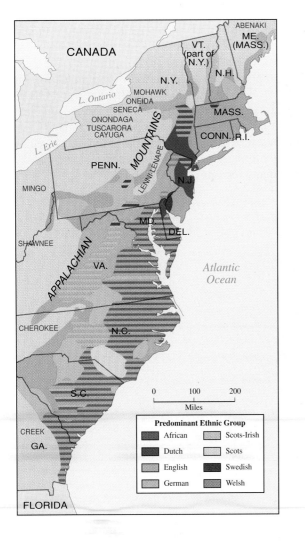

Opportunity and Equality

Pennsylvania, New York, and New Jersey attracted
huge numbers of migrants in the eighteenth century,
with the combined population rising from 50,000 in
1700 to 120,000 in 1720 and to 350,000 by 1765. An
ample supply of fertile land and a long frost-free growing season of about 180 days attracted migrants, who
prospered because the population explosion in Western
Europe had created a huge demand for wheat, which
they were able to supply. Wheat prices doubled in the
Atlantic world between 1720 and 1770, and profits
from wheat financed the settlement of the region. By
1770 the value of the wheat, corn, flour, and bread
shipped from the middle colonies amounted to over 15
percent of all mainland exports (see Figure 4.1).

Many farm families prospered from growing grain,
but few became large-scale producers, because preindustrial technology greatly limited output. A worker
with a hand sickle could reap only half an acre a day,
and if ripe grain was not cut promptly, it sprouted, rendering it useless. The *cradle*, a long-handled scythe
with wooden fingers that arranged the wheat for easy
collection and binding, was introduced during the
1750s and doubled or tripled the amount a worker
could cut. Even so, a family with two adult workers
could not easily harvest more than about 15 acres of
wheat in a growing season, from which it could thresh

perhaps 150 to 180 bushels of grain. After meeting its own needs, the family might sell the surplus for £15, enough to buy salt and sugar, tools, cloth, and perhaps a few acres of new land.

The Emergence of Inequality. Rural Pennsylvania was initially a land of economic equality. In Chester County, for example, the original migrants came with approximately the same resources (see Figure 4.2). In 1693, the poorest 30 percent of the taxpayers owned a substantial 17 percent of the assessed wealth and the top 10 percent controlled only 23 percent. Most families lived in small houses with one or two rooms. Their furniture consisted of a few benches or stools and a bed in a loft. Only the wealthiest families ate off pewter or ceramic plates imported from England or Holland. The great majority consumed their simple fare from wooden *trenchers* (platters) and drank from wooden *noggins* (cups).

The rise of the wheat trade—and the influx of poor settlers—introduced marked social divisions. By the 1760s some farmers had grown wealthy by hiring the poor and using their labor to raise large quantities of wheat for market sale. Others had become successful entrepreneurs, providing newly arrived settlers with land, equipment, goods, and services. These large-scale farmers, rural landlords, speculators, storekeepers, and gristmill operators gradually formed a new class of wealthy agricultural *capitalists*—the owners of productive property. The estate inventories of this economic elite include mahogany tables, four-poster beds, table linen, couches, and imported Dutch dinnerware—all of which testify to growing economic inequality. In the 1760s the richest 10 percent of the Chester County's property-owning families controlled 30 percent of their communities' assets, while the poorest 30 percent held a mere 6 percent.

Moreover, a new landless class, one with no taxable property, had appeared at the bottom of the social order. In five agricultural towns in New Jersey in the 1760s, half the white men aged eighteen to twenty-five were without land, while in Chester County, Pennsylvania, nearly half of *all* white men were propertyless. Some landless men were the sons of property owners and would eventually inherit at least a part of the family estate. But just as many were Scots-Irish *inmates*, single men or families "such as live in small cottages and have no taxable property, except a cow," as the tax assessor in the Scots-Irish township of Londonderry explained. There was also an "abundance of Poor people" in the predominantly German settlement of Lancaster, Pennsylvania. A merchant noted that they "maintain their Families with great difficulty by day Labour."

These landless Scots-Irish and German migrants hoped to improve their lot by becoming tenants and then landowners, but such goals were either unrealistic or very hard to achieve. Land prices had risen sharply in settled areas with good transportation, and the acquisition of a farmstead was the work of a lifetime. Merchants and artisans took advantage of the ample supply of labor by organizing a putting-out system: they bought wool or flax from some farm families and paid others to spin it into yarn or weave it into cloth. An English traveler reported in the 1760s that hundreds of Pennsylvanians had turned "to manufacture, and live upon a small farm, as in many parts of England." By that time eastern areas of the middle colonies, as well as New England, had become as crowded and socially divided as many regions of rural England.

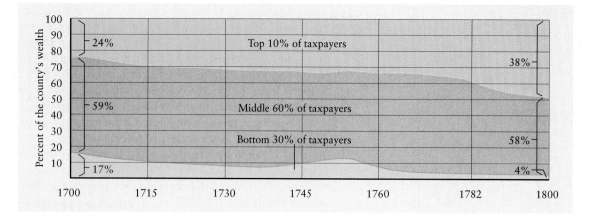

FIGURE 4.2

Increasing Social Inequality in Chester County, Pennsylvania
By renting land and selling goods to a growing population, the county's landed and commercial elite grew rich. Eventually the top tenth of the taxpayers commanded nearly 40 percent of the wealth, far above the paltry 4 percent owned by the poorest 30 percent.

Tenancy on the Hudson Manors. Migrants to New York faced an even more arduous road to land ownership. Long-established Dutch families—the Rensselaers, the Van Cortlandts, the Philipses—still presided over the patroonships created by the Dutch West India Company in the fertile Hudson River Valley (see Map 4.2). The first English governors of New York augmented the ranks of this landowning class by bestowing huge tracts of land on the Livingston, Morris, and Heathcote families. These clans had a stranglehold on the best land and refused to sell an acre of it. They wanted to live like European aristocrats, masters of scores of tenant families.

For that reason, many migrants refused to settle in the Hudson River Valley. In 1714 the manor of Rensselaerswyck had only 82 tenants on hundreds of thousands of acres. But gradually population growth caused a scarcity of freehold land in eastern New York, and more families were forced to accept tenancy leases. To attract tenants, the lords of the manors began to grant long leases and the right to sell (to the next tenant) any improvements made to the property. Thus, Rensselaerswyck had 345 tenants in 1752 and nearly 700 by 1765. With determination, luck, and wheat profits, some tenants saved enough to buy freehold property, but the Hudson River Valley remained primarily a region of tenant farmers, distinct from the predominantly freehold communities in Pennsylvania, New Jersey, and New England.

Even communities of yeomen farm families were increasingly divided by economic interests and class position. In Pennsylvania, gentlemen farmers and commercial middlemen had grown rich whereas German and Scots-Irish inmates still struggled for subsistence. In New England, which lacked a major export crop, many small-scale freeholders had fallen into debt; even the most creative farmers could generate only a limited surplus. Throughout the mainland colonies, smallholding farm families worried about finding enough land to give their children and feared—with good reason—a return to the exploited status of the European peasantry.

Ethnic Diversity

When the Swedish traveler Peter Kalm visited Philadelphia in 1748, he found no fewer than twelve religious denominations, including Anglicans, Quakers, Swedish and German Lutherans, Scots-Irish Presbyterians, and even Roman Catholics. Large communities of German sectarians, such as the Moravians in the Pennsylvania towns of Bethlehem and Nazareth, added to this religious diversity.

The Quaker Experiment. Members of the Society of Friends (Quakers) were the dominant social group in

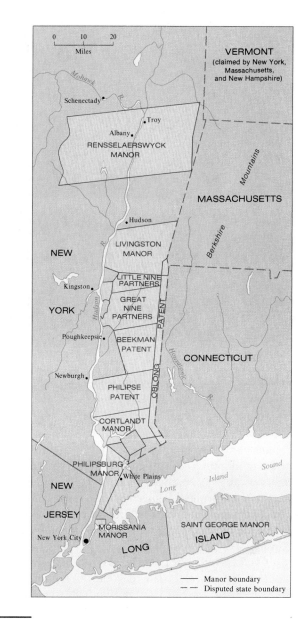

MAP 4.2

The Hudson River Manors

Dutch and English manorial lords dominated the fertile eastern shores of the Hudson River Valley—leasing small farms to German tenant families and refusing to sell land to migrants from overcrowded New England. From this powerful elite emerged Patriot leaders, such as Gouverneur Morris (see *American Lives,* pages 204–205), and influential American families, such as the Roosevelts.

A Quaker Meeting for Worship
Quakers dressed plainly and met in plain, unadorned buildings. They sat in silence, speaking only when inspired by the "inner light." Women spoke frequently and were listened to with respect, an experience that prepared Quaker women to take a leading part in the nineteenth-century women's rights movement. This British work, entitled *Quaker Meeting*, shows an elder (his hat placed temporarily on a peg above his head) exhorting the congregation.

Pennsylvania, at first because they outnumbered the others and later because, despite a huge influx of new migrants after 1720, they retained wealth and influence. Quakers controlled Pennsylvania's representative assembly (established by the proprietor William Penn's Frame of Government) until the 1750s and exercised considerable power in New Jersey.

Quakers had a distinct social ethic. They wore plain clothes without elaborate decoration and refused to defer to their "superiors" by removing their hats. In talking among themselves and with strangers, they used the familiar "thee" and "thou" rather than the more formal "you." Friends refused to use law courts to settle disputes among themselves, relying instead on arbitrators to judge what was "right," not simply what was "legal." Around 1750 some Quakers extended these egalitarian values to their relations with blacks, freeing their own slaves. Indeed, some Quaker meetings not only condemned the institution of slavery but also expelled any members who continued to keep slaves, making Quakers the first religious group to advocate the abolition of slavery.

Quakers were pacifists, and so they avoided war with native Americans. Penn negotiated the first treaty with the Delaware Indians in 1682, and the Pennsylvania government purchased Indian land rather than seizing it by force. These conciliatory policies enabled Pennsylvania to avoid a major Indian war until the 1750s, a record unmatched elsewhere in the British colonies. In diplomacy as in religious matters, the Quakers' radical social experiment was largely successful and attracted thousands of migrants from eighteenth-century Europe.

The Pennsylvania Germans. Germans came to the middle colonies in a series of waves, fleeing their homeland because of war, religious persecution, and poverty. First to arrive, in 1683, was a group of Mennonites attracted by Penn's pamphlet promising religious freedom. Beginning in 1709, boatloads of impoverished peasants from the Palatine region of western Germany, an area devastated by religious warfare, settled as tenants on Hudson River manors. Then, in the 1720s, continuing religious upheaval and population growth in southwestern Germany and Switzerland stimulated another wave of migrants. "Wages were far better than here," Heinrich Schneebeli reported to his friends in Zurich after an exploratory trip to Pennsylvania, and "one also enjoyed there a free unhindered exercise of religion." Thirty citizens of Zurich immediately asked the authorities for permission to emigrate. Many Germans and Swiss had the resources to pay their own way; they migrated to provide better opportunities for their children. Others signed on as *redemptioners,* a kind of indentured servant, to get to Pennsylvania (see American Voices, page 113).

In 1749, after the War of the Austrian Succession, thousands of Germans and Swiss fled their overcrowded and war-torn homeland for the middle colonies. By 1754, when the outbreak of the Seven Years War (the European component of the Great War

Gottlieb Mittelberger

The Perils of Migration

The lure of ample land and a better life prompted thousands of Germans to endure the hardships of migration, which were described in a book published by Gottlieb Mittelberger in 1750. A Lutheran minister who returned to Germany, Mittelberger viewed America with a critical eye, warning his readers of the difficulties of life in a competitive, pluralistic society.

[The journey from Germany to Pennsylvania via Holland and England] lasts from the beginning of May to the end of October, fully half a year, amid such hardships as no one is able to describe adequately with their misery. Both in Rotterdam and in Amsterdam the people are packed densely, like herrings so to say, in the large sea-vessels. One person receives a place of scarcely 2 feet width and 6 feet length in the bedstead, while many a ship carries four to six hundred souls. . . .

During the journey the ship is full of pitiful signs of distress—smells, fumes, horrors, vomiting, various kinds of sea sickness, fever, dysentery, headaches, heat, constipation, boils, scurvy, cancer, mouth-rot, and similar afflictions, all of them caused by the age and the highly-salted state of the food, especially of the meat, as well as by the very bad and filthy water, which brings about the miserable destruction and death of many. . . . All this misery reaches its climax when in addition to everything else one must also suffer through two to three days and nights of storm with everyone convinced that the ship with all aboard is bound to sink. In such misery all the people on board pray and cry pitifully together.

Children between the ages of one and seven seldom survive the sea voyage; and parents must often watch their offspring suffer miserably, die, and be thrown into the ocean, from want, hunger, thirst, and the like. I myself, alas, saw such a pitiful fate overtake thirty-two children on board our vessel, all of whom were finally thrown into the sea. Their parents grieve all the more, since their children do not find repose in the earth, but are devoured by the predatory fish of the ocean. It is also worth noting that children who have not had either measles or smallpox usually get them on board the ship and for the most part perish as a result.

When the ships finally arrive in Philadelphia after the long voyage only those are let off who can pay their sea freight or can give good security. The others, who lack the money to pay, have to remain on board until they are purchased and until their purchasers can thus pry them loose from the ship. In this whole process the sick are the worst off, for the healthy are preferred and are more readily paid for. The miserable people who are ill must often still remain at sea and in sight of the city for another two or three weeks—which in many cases means death. Yet many of them, were they able to pay their debts and to leave the ships at once, might escape with their lives.

Thus let him who wants to earn his piece of bread honestly and in a Christian manner and who can only do this by manual labor in his native country stay *there* rather than come to America.

But the fact that so many still go to America and especially to Pennsylvania is to be blamed on the swindles and persuasions practiced by so-called Newlanders. These thieves of human beings tell their lies to people of various classes and professions, among whom may be found many soldiers, scholars, artists, and artisans. They abduct people from their Princes and Lords and ship them to Rotterdam or Amsterdam for sale. There they get three florins, or one ducat, from the merchant, for each person ten years or older. On the other hand the merchants get from sixty to seventy or eighty florins for such a person in Philadelphia, depending on the debts that said person has incurred on the voyage. . . .

Source: Gottlieb Mittelberger, *Journey to Pennsylvania* (1756), ed. and trans., Oscar Handlin and John Clive (Cambridge, Mass.: Harvard University Press, 1960).

for Empire) abruptly halted migration, 37,000 new settlers (of a pre-1776 total of 102,000) had landed in Philadelphia. German settlements soon dominated certain areas of the rich Lancaster plain in Pennsylvania. Other groups moved down the Shenandoah Valley into the western districts of Maryland, Virginia, and the Carolinas. Most of them managed to improve their lives. As the German minister Gottlieb Mittelberger reported from Pennsylvania in the 1750s, "Even in the humblest or poorest houses, no one eats bread without butter or cheese."

These migrants did not seek to create an all-German colony but were content to live in a British-defined political community. This decision reflected their class origins and religious ideology; few came from politically active segments of German society, and many

German Artisanry
German artisans in Pennsylvania, carrying on the traditions of the old country, frequently decorated their furniture with abstract designs and simple folk motifs, such as the rectangular patterns and angels on this chest of drawers.

religious sectarians explicitly rejected political activism. They slid easily into the status of loyal subjects of the German (and German-speaking) Hanoverian king of England, engaging in politics only to protect their religious liberty and property rights. Most Germans, however, sought to guard their linguistic and cultural heritage. A minister in North Carolina admonished his congregation "not to contract any marriages with the English or Irish," explaining that "we owe it to our native country to do our part that German blood and the German language be preserved in America." In fact, most American-born Germans took marriage partners of their own ancestry, spoke to each other and read newspapers in German, and attended church services conducted in German. They also continued German agricultural practices: English visitors to the middle colonies remarked that German women were "always in the fields, meadows, stables, etc. and do not dislike any work whatsoever."

The Scots-Irish. The Scots-Irish made up the largest group of new migrants to British North America, with some 150,000 arriving between 1720 and 1776. They settled throughout the mainland but primarily in the middle colonies and the southern backcountry. These migrants were Presbyterians, the descendants of Scots

who had been sent to northern Ireland to bolster English control there in the mid-seventeenth century. In Ireland the Scots had faced discrimination and economic regulation from the dominant English. For example, the Test Act of 1704 excluded both Scottish Presbyterians and Irish Catholics from holding public office in Ireland, reserving this privilege for members of the Church of England. English mercantilist regulations placed heavy import duties on the woolen goods produced by Scots-Irish farmers and weavers.

Rising taxes and poor harvests stimulated a major Scots-Irish migration to America during the 1720s. "Read this letter, Rev. Baptist Boyd," a New York settler wrote back to his minister, "and tell all the poor folk of ye place that God has opened a door for their deliverance. . . . all that a man works for is his own; there are no revenue hounds [tax collectors] to take it from us here." Lured by such reports, thousands of Scots-Irish sailed for Philadelphia and spread out across the mid-Atlantic region and southward down the Shenandoah Valley. Like the Germans, the Scots-Irish were determined to keep the culture of their homelands alive. They held to their Presbyterian faith and encouraged marriages within the church.

The middle colonies were not a "melting pot"; the diverse European cultures did not blend together to produce a homogeneous "American" outlook but kept their separate identities. Thus, defying New York law, many Dutch families maintained inheritance practices that favored wives over children. The major exception to cultural separatism was the Huguenots, French Calvinists who were expelled from France and settled in New York and various seacoast cities; they intermarried with other Protestants during the eighteenth century. More typical was the experience of Welsh Quakers; 70 percent of the children of the original migrants to Chester County, Pennsylvania, married other Welsh Quakers, as did 60 percent of the third generation. By marrying within their own groups, these and other European settlers created a pluralistic society of diverse nationalities, cultures, and religions in the middle colonies.

A Pluralistic Society

In their religious and ethnic diversity, the mid-Atlantic colonies constituted a society distinct from Europe (see Map 4.3). In Western Europe pluralism in religion was an untried experiment, and even in America most European-trained ministers remained committed to religious uniformity enforced by an established church backed by the government. "Throughout Pennsylvania the preachers do not have the power to punish anyone, or to force anyone to go to church," Gottlieb Mittelberger complained. As a result, "Sunday is very badly kept.

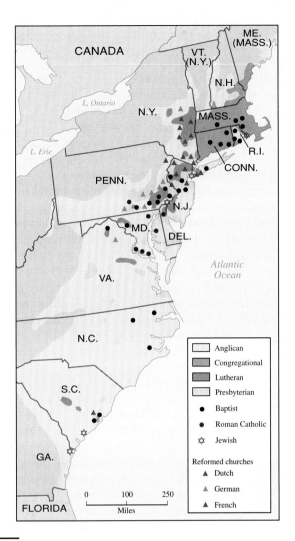

MAP 4.3

Religious Diversity in 1750
By 1750 religious diversity was on the rise. Baptists had grown in numbers in New England—long the stronghold of Congregationalism—and would later dominate Virginia. Already there were pockets of Presbyterians and Lutherans in the South, where Anglicanism was the established religion.

Many people plough, reap, thresh, hew or split wood and the like." He concluded that "Liberty in Pennsylvania does more harm than good to many people, both in soul and body."

Mittelberger failed to appreciate the power of communal self-discipline. The various religious sects in Pennsylvania enforced moral behavior among their members. Each Quaker family, for example, regularly attended a weekly meeting for worship and a monthly meeting that handled discipline. A committee met with each family four times a year and made certain that its

children received proper religious instruction. The committee also reported on the moral behavior of adults. In Chester County the men acted on such a report by disciplining one of their members "to reclaim him from drinking to excess and keeping vain company."

Communal sanctions also effectively sustained a self-contained and prosperous Quaker community. Permission to marry was granted only to couples with sufficient land, livestock, and equipment to support themselves and their future children. Marriage with non-Quakers usually was prohibited, and those who disobeyed were treated as outcasts. In Chester County about two-thirds of the young men and women who married outside the faith were barred from Quaker meetings. Over the generations this strict system shaped the character of the Quaker community. The children of well-to-do Friends had ample marriage portions and usually married within the sect. Those who lacked the resources remained unmarried or left the Society. Thus the Quakers created a prosperous religious community of urban merchants and rural freeholders. Clearly, a single established church was not necessary to avoid social chaos.

Yet Pennsylvania did not escape the tensions inherent in a society composed of distinct ethnic groups. By the 1750s Pennsylvania politics was sharply divided along cultural and religious lines. Scots-Irish Presbyterians on the frontier were challenging the pacifism of the Quaker-dominated assembly and demanding a more aggressive policy toward the Indians. Newer German migrants, many of whom belonged to Lutheran and Reformed churches, also opposed the Quakers; they wanted laws that respected their inheritance customs (which gave the community some say in the disposition of a family's property) and representation in the provincial assembly in proportion to their numbers. Other Germans, particularly the Mennonites, supported the Quakers because of their pacifism. Religious outlook increasingly determined political allegiance. As one observer noted, Scots-Irish Presbyterians, German Baptists, and German Lutherans had begun to form "a general confederacy" against the "ruling party" of Quakers in Pennsylvania, but this alliance was fragile. A foreign visitor remarked during the 1750s that these groups had "a mutual jealousy, for religious zeal is secretly burning." Latent religious and ethnic passions would break out during the following decade and again during the War for Independence, nearly destroying the new republican government of Pennsylvania.

Yet this experiment in freedom and diversity, which would survive the revolutionary era, offered a glimpse of the future. Cultural pluralism and an open religious and political order subject to passionate ethnic and social conflicts would characterize much of American society in the nineteenth and twentieth centuries.

The Enlightenment and the Great Awakening, 1740–1765

Two great European cultural movements swept across the Atlantic to America between the 1730s and the 1760s: the Enlightenment and Pietism. The *Enlightenment* emphasized the power of human reason to shape the world; it appealed especially to better-educated men and women, mostly from merchant or planter families, and to urban artisans. *Pietism* was an emotional, evangelical religious movement that stressed people's dependence on God. Although Pietism attracted all social groups, it was most successful among farmers, urban laborers, and slaves. Both the Enlightenment and Pietism promoted independent thinking, but in different ways. Together they transformed American intellectual and cultural life.

The Enlightenment in America

Americans of European ancestry came from a Christian culture, and some believed they had been sent to the New World on a religious mission. Many others found formal religion less persuasive than superstitions and folk wisdom. They saw the world in animistic terms: spirits and powers were everywhere and could be used for good or evil. Swedish settlers in Pennsylvania ascribed magical powers to the great white mullein, a common wild plant. When they had a fever, a traveler reported, they would "tie the leaves around their feet and arms." Even educated people believed that events occurred for reasons that today would be called magical. When a measles epidemic struck Boston in the 1710s, the Puritan minister Cotton Mather sought to contain its spread by "getting the Blood of the Great Passover sprinkled on our Houses." Like most Christians of the time, Mather believed that the earth stood at the center of the entire universe and that God intervened directly in human affairs.

The New Learning. The Scientific Revolution of the seventeenth century challenged these traditional world views, altering the outlook of the educated elite. The observation of the sixteenth-century astronomer Copernicus that the earth travels around the sun, not vice versa, had offered a new and more modest view of humankind's place in the universe. Other scholars conducted experiments using empirical methods—actual observed experience—to discover more about natural phenomena such as earthquakes and lightning. These intellectual innovations convinced many educated Europeans that human beings could analyze—and ultimately understand and improve—the world in which they lived.

The European Enlightenment began around 1675, coinciding with discoveries of the laws that governed the natural world. The Enlightenment was a complex intellectual movement, but it was based on four fundamental principles: the lawlike order of the natural world; the power of human reason; the natural rights of individuals, including the right to self-government; and the progressive improvement of society.

The English scientist Isaac Newton did more than anyone else to advance this "new learning." His *Principia Mathematica* (1687) used mathematics to explain the orderly movement of the planets around the sun. Although Newton retained a belief in magical forces (seeking through alchemy to change lead into gold), his laws of motion and his concept of gravity described how the universe could operate without the constant intervention of a god, thus challenging traditional Christian explanations of the cosmos.

Other Enlightenment thinkers applied critical, rational modes of thought to human society in an effort to define its natural laws. In his *Essay Concerning Human Understanding* (1690), John Locke rejected the belief that human beings are born with God-given "innate" ideas. On the contrary, Locke argued that the infant's mind was a *tabula rasa,* a "blank slate" that was gradually filled with information conveyed by the senses and arranged by reason. By emphasizing the impact of environment, experience, and reason on human behavior, Locke proposed that the character of people and societies could be changed through education and purposeful action. Indeed, in his *Two Treatises on Government* (1690) justifying the Glorious Revolution of 1688, Locke advanced a revolutionary theory of government: political authority was not divinely ordained but sprang from "*social compacts*" that people made to preserve their "natural" rights to life, liberty, and property. Not princes but people conferred political legitimacy, so that governments might change through the decision of a majority.

The Enlightment in the Colonies. The Enlightenment ideas of Locke and others came to America with books and travelers and quickly affected the colonists' conceptions of religion and science. As early as the 1710s the Reverend John Wise of Ipswich, Massachusetts, combined Locke's political principles and Calvinist theology to defend the decision of Congregational churches to vest power in their lay members. Wise argued that just as the "social compact" formed the basis of political society, the religious covenant made the congregation—not bishops or monarchs, as in the Church of England—the interpreter of spiritual authority. Simi-

larly, Enlightenment science influenced Cotton Mather when a smallpox epidemic threatened Boston in the 1720s. Mather sought a scientific remedy, joining with Zabdiel Boylston, a prominent Boston physician, in supporting the new technique of inoculation (with a less virulent strain of the smallpox virus) against the disease.

By midcentury Enlightenment ideas had become second nature to many educated Americans. Elizabeth Smith, an upper-class mother, invoked Lockean principles when, in a letter to a friend, she wrote about her newborn child: "The Infant Mind is a blank that easily receives my impression." Some upper-class colonists— Virginia planters and New York merchants—as well as urban artisans became *deists*. Influenced by Enlightenment science, deists believed that God had created the world but allowed it to operate according to the laws of nature. Their God was a rational being, a divine "watchmaker" who did not intervene directly in history or in people's lives. Rejecting the authority of the Bible and established churches, deists relied on people's "natural reason" to define a moral code, adherence to which would be punished or rewarded after death.

Franklin and the American Enlightenment. Benjamin Franklin was the epitome of an Enlightenment thinker in America. Born into the family of a devout Calvinist candlemaker in Boston in 1706, Franklin had little formal schooling. He was self-taught, having acquired a taste for knowledge as a printer's apprentice, and he mastered a wide variety of political and scientific works. Franklin's imagination was shaped by Enlightenment literature, not by the Christian Bible. In fact, as he explained in his *Autobiography*, "from the different books

I read, I began to doubt of Revelation itself." Franklin became a deist.

As a tradesman, printer, and journalist in Philadelphia, Franklin formed "a club of mutual improvement," which met every Friday evening to discuss "Morals, Politics, or Natural Philosophy." Although personally somewhat of a skeptic, Franklin propagated the outlook of the rational Enlightenment—optimistic, secular, and materialistic—in *Poor Richard's Almanac*, which was read by thousands of farmers. In 1743 he helped found the American Philosophical Society, an institution devoted to "the promotion of useful knowledge." He came up with an improved stove (the Franklin stove) and invented bifocal lenses for eyeglasses and the lightning rod. His research in the infant science of electricity won international acclaim. In fact, the English scientist Joseph Priestley praised Franklin's book on electricity, first published in England in 1751, as the greatest contribution to science since the work of Newton.

Franklin's Philadelphia became the showplace of the American Enlightenment. It boasted a circulating library filled with the latest scientific treatises from Europe. The first American medical school was founded there in 1765. Quaker and Anglican merchants built a Hospital for the Sick Poor in 1751 and then, in 1767, added a Bettering House to shelter the aged and disabled and offer employment to the poor. These philanthropists were acting as much from economic self-interest as from moral conviction, for they hoped these institutions would reduce the taxes they paid for relief of the poor. Nonetheless, the hospital and the bettering house were expressions of the Enlightenment belief that purposeful human action could improve society.

Enlightenment Philanthropy: The Philadelphia Hospital

This imposing structure, built in 1753 with public funds and private donations, embodied two Enlightenment principles—that purposeful action could improve society and that the world should express reason and order (exhibited here by the symmetrical facade). Etchings such as this one, *A Southeast Prospect of the Pennsylvania Hospital*, circa 1761 by John Streeper and Henry Dawkins, bolstered Philadelphia's reputation as the center of the American Enlightenment.

The life of the mind came of age in British North America as educated men founded clubs, schools, and publications. The first American newspapers had appeared in Boston in 1704 and Philadelphia in 1719, but their numbers increased dramatically after 1740; by 1765 nearly every colony had a regularly published newspaper. Ambitious printers produced magazines aimed at wealthy gentlemen, including the *New York*, the *Massachusetts*, and Franklin's *General*. Although most of them were failures—local newspapers and books from Europe filled the needs of the reading public—they were the first significant nonreligious publications (apart from newspapers) to appear in the colonies. The European Enlightenment had added a secular dimension to colonial intellectual life, preparing the way for the great American contributions to republican political theory during the Revolutionary Era.

Pietism in America

While American deists challenged old religious views, many other Americans embraced the new European devotional movement known as *Pietism*. Pietism paid little attention to theological dogma, emphasizing instead moral behavior, emotional church services, and a mystical union with God. Pietist preachers appealed to the hearts, not the minds, of their followers. They exhorted people to be devout—that is, "pious"—Christians; hence the name. Their teachings were particularly popular among the lower orders of European society, and peasants, artisans, and laborers joined pietistic churches by the thousands.

Pietism came to America with German migrants in the 1720s and led to a religious revival in the middle colonies. In Pennsylvania and New Jersey the Dutch minister Theodore Jacob Frelinghuysen moved from church to church, preaching to German settlers and arousing them with vigorous, emotional sermons. Frelinghuysen then harnessed their enthusiasm, organizing private prayer meetings and encouraging lay members of the congregation to preach a message of spiritual urgency to growing congregations. William Tennent and his son Gilbert were Presbyterian clergymen who copied Frelinghuysen's approach and during the 1730s led a series of revivals among Scots-Irish migrants in New Jersey and Pennsylvania.

Simultaneously, an American pietistic movement was born in Puritan New England. Puritanism had been part of an upsurge of piety in sixteenth-century England, but over the years many Puritan congregations had lost their religious zeal. During the 1730s Jonathan Edwards sought to restore spiritual commitment to the Congregational churches of the Connecticut River Val-

ley, urging people—especially young men and women—to commit themselves to a life of piety and prayer (see American Lives, pages 120–121).

George Whitefield and the Great Awakening

Religious revival was carried to new heights in the 1740s by George Whitefield, a young English evangelist. Whitefield had experienced conversion in England after reading German pietistic tracts. He became a disciple of John Wesley, the founder of Methodism, who himself had been inspired by German Moravian Pietists during a stay in Georgia. Wesley combined enthusiastic preaching with disciplined "methods" of worship. Soon he had persuaded thousands of Anglicans and scores of ministers to become pietistic Methodists within the Church of England.

Whitefield preached with equal success in America, where, outside of New England, he found a society with few ministers and a weak churchgoing tradition. Whitefield established an orphanage in Georgia in 1738 and then returned to preach throughout the colonies from 1739 to 1741. Huge crowds of "enthusiasts" greeted the young preacher wherever he went, from Georgia to Massachusetts. "Religion is become the Subject of most Conversations," the Pennsylvania *Gazette* reported. "No books are in Request but those of Piety and Devotion." The usually skeptical and restrained Benjamin Franklin was so impressed by Whitefield's oratory that when the preacher asked for contributions, Franklin emptied his pockets "wholly into the collector's dish, gold and all." By the time the evangelist reached Boston, the Reverend Benjamin Colman reported that the people were "ready to receive him as an angel of God."

Whitefield owed his appeal partly to his compelling personal presence. "He looked almost Angelical—a young, slim, slender youth," according to one Connecticut farmer. And he spoke magnificently and with great force, impressing on his audience that they all had sinned and must seek salvation. Like most evangelical preachers, Whitefield did not read his sermons but spoke from memory, as if inspired, raising his voice for dramatic effect, gesturing eloquently, and making striking use of biblical metaphors. The young preacher evoked a deep emotional response. Hundreds of men and women suddenly felt the "new light" of God's grace within them; strengthened and self-confident, these New Lights were prepared to follow in Whitefield's footsteps. The evangelist's eloquence transformed the local revivals in the Connecticut Valley and the middle colonies into a genuine Great Awakening that spanned the mainland settlements, spreading a set of shared religious values.

Religious Upheaval in the North

Old Lights versus New Lights. Like all cultural explosions, the revival was controversial. Conservative ministers such as Charles Chauncy of Boston condemned the "cryings out, faintings and convulsions" produced by emotional preaching. These "Old Lights," as they were called by the awakeners, feared—with good reason—that revivalism would destroy the established churches. Inspired by Whitefield's example, dozens of farmers, women, and artisans roamed the countryside, preaching that the Old Lights were "unconverted" sinners.

To silence the revivalists, the Old Lights in Connecticut persuaded the legislative assembly to prohibit traveling preachers from speaking to established congregations without the ministers' permission. Thus, when Whitefield returned to Connecticut in 1744, he found many pulpits closed to him. But the New Lights stoutly resisted attempts by civil authorities to silence them. "I shall bring glory to God in my bonds," a dissident preacher wrote from a Massachusetts jail. The New Lights won repeal of the Connecticut law in 1750, but the battle was far from over.

The Awakening's Significance. The Great Awakening gradually altered American perceptions of the proper religious order. One major confrontation involved the issue of religious taxes and, beyond that, the legitimacy of an established church. As outsiders, many New Lights and Baptists questioned government involvement in religion and favored a greater separation between church and state. According to the Baptist preacher Isaac Backus, "God never allowed any civil state upon earth to impose religious taxes." In New England many New Lights simply left the established Congregational Church; by 1754 they had founded 125 "separatist" churches. Other dissidents joined growing Baptist congregations (see Figure 4.3). In New York and New Jersey, the Dutch Reformed Church split into two factions as New Lights resisted the conservative church authorities in the Netherlands. After the Great Awakening, established churches lost their aura of authority; many people reluctantly paid taxes to the established minister but joined other congregations. State-supported religion was no longer an unquestioned norm.

The Awakening also challenged the authority of the ministry. Traditionally, preachers had commanded respect because of their education in theology and knowledge of the Bible. But Gilbert Tennent questioned these criteria in his influential pamphlet *The Dangers of an Unconverted Ministry* (1740). Tennent maintained that what qualified ministers to hold office was not theological training but conversion—the experience through which a person came to know the grace of God. Thus, anyone who was saved could speak with ministerial authority. Traditional churches—formal, hierarchical, doctrine-bound—began to lose members to denominations, such as the Baptists, that emphasized piety rather than theology, emotions rather than dogma, lay preaching rather than clerical wisdom. By reasserting Luther's commitment to "the priesthood of all believers," Pietists created a more democratic religious community.

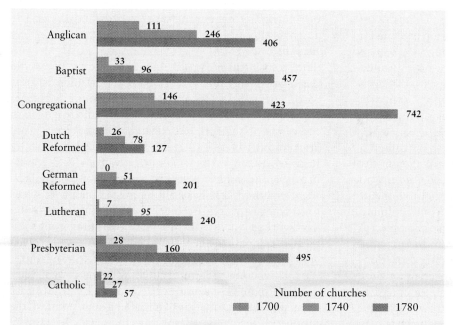

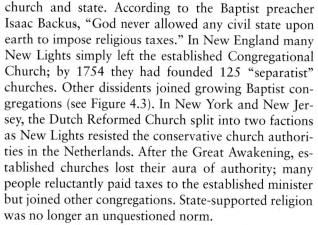

FIGURE 4.3

Church Growth by Denomination, 1700–1780

Some churches, such as the Dutch Reformed, grew only from the natural increase of their members. After 1740, the fastest-growing denominations were immigrant churches—the German Reformed and Lutheran—and those with an evangelical message, such as the Baptists.

Jonathan Edwards:
Preacher, Philosopher, Pastor

Jonathan Edwards did not mince words. Echoing the harsh theology of John Calvin, Edwards preached that men and women were helpless creatures completely dependent on God: "There is Hell's wide gaping mouth open; and you have nothing to stand upon, nor any thing to take hold of: there is nothing between you and Hell but the air; 'tis only the power and mere pleasure of God that holds you up."

Edwards spoke (a listener noted) with great "inward fervor, without much noise of external emotion," and without a single gesture. His controlled demeanor underlined the torments that awaited those who fell into the eternal flames:

> How dismal will it be . . . to know assuredly that you never, never shall be delivered from them; . . . after you shall have endured these torments millions of ages . . . your bodies, which shall have been burning and roasting all this while in these glowing flames, yet shall not have been consumed, but will remain to roast through an eternity yet.

Such was the terrible—and inevitable—fate that Edwards the preacher promised to complacent Christians in his most famous sermon, *Sinners in the Hands of an Angry God* (1742). But Edwards the pastor preached a more hopeful message of personal repentance and spiritual rebirth, telling congregations that this fate awaited only those who "never passed under a great change of heart, by the mighty power of the spirit of God upon your souls; all that were never born again, and made new creatures."

With such impassioned words, Edwards inspired a religious revival in the Connecticut River Valley in the mid-1730s and helped George Whitefield stir up an even greater one in the 1740s. But this minister, one of the leading revivalists of his age, was also a profound and original philosopher, perhaps the most intellectually brilliant colonial American.

Jonathan Edwards was born in East Windsor, Connecticut, in 1703, the fifth child and only son among the eleven children of Timothy and Esther Stoddard Edwards. The parents' identities shaped their son. The father came from a wealthy family but ended up a poorly paid rural minister who fought constantly with his congregation over his salary and authority, battles that Jonathan would also fight with his church. The mother was the daughter of Solomon Stoddard, a great revivalist and the most famous churchman in Connecticut, a family legacy that would both help and haunt Jonathan Edwards throughout his life.

As a child Jonathan embraced his grandfather Stoddard's theology, rejecting the Calvinist belief in God's omnipotence over people's lives and labeling it "a horrible doctrine." But as a preacher, he became a committed Calvinist, explaining in a *Personal Narrative* written later in life that at age seventeen he experienced "a *delightful* conviction" of the Almighty's absolute sovereignty, an "inward sweetness . . . [of] sweetly conversing with Christ, and wrapt and swallowed up in God." In fact, Edwards found his Calvinist God only with great difficulty. He came to adopt a Calvinist outlook only after many years of personal torment as a young adult and a series of physical and emotional collapses.

The Enlightenment came more easily to Edwards. While studying for the ministry at Yale College, he read the works of Isaac Newton, John Locke, and other Enlightenment thinkers, starting a lifetime of philosophical inquiry into the meaning of words and things. He accepted Locke's argument in the *Essay Concerning Human Understanding* (1690) that our ideas are not innate from birth but are the product of experience and the senses—our ability to see, hear, feel, and taste the world around us. A person who has never *tasted* a pineapple, said Locke, will never have "the true idea of the relish of that celebrated and delicious fruit." But Locke's theory was less successful in explaining *abstract* ideas—God, man, angel, love, salvation—and it was here that Edwards made his contribution. Locke had suggested that such ideas resulted when the mind mixed together various sense experiences, but Edwards—who had worked out his theological doctrines through intense personal torment—argued that they involved emotional apprehension as well—since, for example, "love" (whether of God or a fellow human) was "felt" and not merely understood. It followed that abstract ideas were emotional as well as rational entities, the product of the passions as well as the senses.

Edwards used his theory of knowledge to justify his

This portrait, painted by Joseph Badger in 1720, suggests that even as a young man Edwards was grave and dignified.

style of preaching, arguing that vivid words promoted conversions by conveying abstract ideas in their full emotional intensity. As he put it in *A Treatise Concerning Religious Affections* (1746), "true religion, in great part, consists in holy affection," an emotional state created by words that evoked the terrors of eternal damnation and the necessity of repentance. It was reasonable, Edwards declared, "to endeavor to fright persons away from Hell." In the end the philosopher was at one with the preacher.

Edwards put these ideas into practice as pastor of the Congregational church in Northampton, Massachusetts, taking over that position from his grandfather, Solomon Stoddard, in 1729. He worked hard, spending thirteen hours a day composing sermons and treatises, and more than matched his grandfather's success as a revivalist, especially among young people. Beginning in 1734, Edwards reported, "the number of true saints multiplied . . . the town seemed to be full of the presence of God: it never was so full of love, nor so full of joy; and yet so full of distress as it was then." News of the Northampton revival stimulated religious fervor up and down the Connecticut River Valley "till there was a general awakening."

Edwards interpreted his success as "a remarkable Testimony of God's Approbation of the Doctrine . . . that we are justified only by faith in Christ, and not by any manner of virtue or goodness of our own." He maintained that uncompromising Calvinist position during the widespread revivals of the 1740s. Also seeking to restore an older communal order, he took issue with New Lights who asserted "the absolute Necessity for every Person to act singly . . . as if there was not another human Creature upon earth." Repudiating that spirit of individualism, Edwards insisted that aspiring Saints should heed their pastors, who were "skilful guides," and then make a "credible Relation of their inward Experience" to the congregation, thus strengthening the covenant bonds that knit members together in a visible church. Edwards extended his critique of individualism to economic affairs, speaking out against "a narrow, private spirit" among merchants and landlords, those men who "are not ashamed to hit and bite others [and] grind the faces of the poor. . . ."

Edwards's rigorous standards and assault on religious and economic individualism deeply offended the wealthiest and most influential members of his congregation. Continuing struggles over his salary and disciplinary authority culminated in a final battle in 1750, when Edwards repudiated Stoddard's practice of admitting almost all churchgoers to Communion and thus full church membership, adhering instead to the Calvinist doctrine that God bestowed grace only on chosen Saints. By a vote of 200 to 20, the Northampton congregation dismissed the great preacher and philosopher from his pastorate. Impoverished and with a family of ten children to support, Edwards moved to Stockbridge, Massachusetts, a small frontier outpost. There he ministered, without great success, to the Housatonic Indians and wrote an impressive philosophical work, *Freedom of the Will*. Just as he was about to take up the presidency of the College of New Jersey (Princeton) in 1757, Edwards was inoculated against smallpox, took the inoculation badly, and died. He left a pair of spectacles, two wigs, three black coats, and some 300 books, including 22 written by himself—but not much else in the way of earthly goods.

As he lay dying, this turn of fate puzzled America's first great philosopher. Why had God called him to Princeton only to give him no time to undertake his duties? As a preacher and pastor Edwards had always responded to such questions by stressing God's arbitrary power and the "insufficiency of reason" to understand God's purpose. Now he himself had to accept that grim and emotionally unsatisfying answer, showing through his personal experience why Calvinism was such a hard faith by which to live . . . or die.

By reinforcing the strong community values of ordinary farmers and rural people, some pietistic revivals also questioned the morality of economic competition and growing disparities in wealth. Many rural Pietists were suspicious of merchants and land speculators, fearing that the mercenary values of the marketplace had eroded traditional moral principles. Jonathan Edwards spoke for many rural Americans when he said that a "private niggardly spirit" was more suitable "for wolves and other beasts of prey, than for human beings." By joining and participating in religious revivals, many farm families reaffirmed their commitment to the cooperative ethic of rural life. "In any truly Christian society," Gilbert Tennent explained, "mutual *Love* is the *Band and Cement*."

The Awakening also injected new vigor into education and intellectual pursuits, especially religious learning, as the various churches founded new colleges to educate the youth and train ministers (see Table 4.2). New Light Presbyterians established the College of New Jersey (Princeton) in 1746, and New York Anglicans founded King's College (Columbia) in 1754. Baptists set up the College of Rhode Island (Brown); the Dutch Reformed Church subsidized Queen's College (Rutgers) in New Jersey. The true intellectual legacy of the revival was not education for the few, however, but a new sense of spiritual power and independence among the many. The Baptist preacher Isaac Backus captured the democratic thrust of the Awakening when he noted that "the common people now claim as good a right to judge and act in matters of religion as civil rulers or the learned clergy."

Social and Religious Conflict in the South

In the southern colonies religious conflict took an intensely social form, especially in Virginia. The Church of England, the established church, was supported by public taxes, yet it had never ministered to most Virginians. About 40 percent of the population was made up of African-Americans, who generally were excluded from membership. Whites were required by law to attend services, but many landless families—another 20 percent of the population—came irregularly. Middling white freeholders, who made up 35 percent of the population, formed the core of most Anglican congregations, but it was the remaining 5 percent, the prominent planters, who held power in the church. They controlled the parish vestries, the lay organizations that helped ministers manage church affairs. Indeed, these vestrymen used their control of parish finances to keep Anglican ministers under control. One clergyman complained that vestrymen dismissed any minister who "had the courage to preach against any Vices taken into favor by the leading Men of his Parish."

New Light Presbyterians. The vestry's power could not inhibit the new religious fervor. In 1743 a bricklayer named Samuel Morris, who had been inspired by reading George Whitefield's sermons, led a group of Virginia Anglicans out of the established church to seek a more vital religious experience. Morris and his followers invited New Light Presbyterian ministers from Scots-Irish settlements along the Virginia frontier to lead prayer meetings. Soon local revivals spread across the back-

---

TABLE 4.2

Colonial Colleges

	Date of Founding	Colony	Religious Affiliation
Harvard	1636	Massachusetts	Puritan
William and Mary	1693	Virginia	Church of England
Yale	1701	Connecticut	Puritan
College of New Jersey (Princeton)	1746	New Jersey	Presbyterian
King's (Columbia)	1754	New York	Church of England
College of Philadelphia (University of Pennsylvania)	1755	Pennsylvania	None
College of Rhode Island (Brown)	1764	Rhode Island	Baptist
Queen's (Rutgers)	1766	New Jersey	Dutch Reformed
Dartmouth	1769	New Hampshire	Congregationalist

country and into the so-called Tidewater region along the Atlantic coast.

The political leaders of Virginia feared that a full-scale Presbyterian pietistic revival would undermine their authority. It was their custom to attend Church of England services with their families and display their fine clothes, well-bred horses, and elaborate carriages to the assembled community. Some vestrymen flaunted their power by marching in a body to their seats in the front rows. These opportunities for a show of their authority would vanish if freeholders joined the New Light Presbyterians, and religious pluralism might threaten the gentry's ability to tax the masses to support the Church of England. The fate of the established church seemed to hang in the balance.

To restrain the New Light Presbyterians, Governor William Gooch denounced their "false teachings." Anglican justices of the peace closed down Presbyterian meetinghouses and harassed Samuel Davies, a popular New Light preacher. These actions kept most white yeomen within the Church of England, as did the elitist outlook of most Presbyterians. Presbyterian ministers—even New Lights such as Davies—were highly educated and sought converts among skilled workers and propertied farmers, seldom preaching to poor whites and enslaved blacks.

Baptist Revivals and Black Protestantism. Baptists succeeded where Presbyterians failed. Like the Quakers, Baptists were a radical offshoot of the Protestant Reformation, direct descendants of the Anabaptists (see Chapter 1). Condemned or outlawed by the authorities throughout Europe, Baptists drew their congregations from among the poor, developing emotionally charged rituals—such as baptizing adults by full immersion—that offered solace and hope in a world of trouble. During the 1760s thousands of yeomen and tenant farm families in Virginia flocked to revivalist meetings, drawn by the enthusiasm and democratic ways of Baptist preachers.

Slaves were welcome at Baptist revivals. As early as 1740 George Whitefield had openly condemned the brutality of slaveholders and urged that Africans be brought into the Christian fold. A handful of New Light planters took up this challenge in South Carolina and Georgia, but with limited success. The hostility of the white population and the commitment of many Africans to their ancestral religions kept the number of converts low. The first significant conversion of slaves took place two decades later among second- or third-generation African-Americans in Virginia. Hundreds of those slaves, who knew English and English ways, joined Baptist churches run by ministers who taught that all men and women were equal in God's eyes.

The ruling gentry reacted violently to this courting of blacks and poor whites. Anglican sheriffs and justices of the peace organized armed bands of planters who broke up Baptist services by force. In Caroline County, Virginia, an Anglican posse attacked one Brother Waller. Waller was attempting to pray when, a fellow Baptist reported, "he was violently jerked off the stage; they caught him by the back part of his neck, beat his head against the ground, and a gentleman gave him twenty lashes with his horsewhip."

The intensity of the gentry's response reflected class antagonism, loyalty to the Anglican church, and fear: the Baptists posed a threat to their traditional culture. Baptist ministers condemned as vices such customary pleasures of Chesapeake men as gambling, drinking, whoring, and cockfighting and proposed to replace those boisterous habits with puritanical, cooperative Christian living. Baptist preachers urged their followers to work hard and lead virtuous lives. They emphasized equality by calling one another "brother" and "sister."

Their central ritual, of course, was baptism. In contrast to most other Christian churches, in which people were baptized as infants, Baptists received this sacrament as adults, often by complete immersion in water. Once men and women had experienced the infusion of grace—had been "born again"—they were baptized in an emotional public ceremony that was a celebration of shared fellowship. One Sunday "about 2,000 people came together," a Baptist minister noted:

> We went to a field and making a circle in the center, there laid hands on the persons baptized. The multitude stood around weeping, but when we sang *Come we that love the lord* they lifted up their hands and faces toward heaven and discovered such cheerful countenances in the midst of flowing tears as I have never seen before.

The appeal of Baptist preaching and ritual was overwhelming. Despite fierce resistance from the gentry, by 1775 about 20 percent of Virginia's whites and hundreds of enslaved blacks belonged to Baptist churches.

Anglican slaveholders retained their economic and political power, but the revival threatened their control and privileged position. For one thing, it spread democratic principles of church organization among white yeomen and tenant farmers. Also, belief in a living God gave meaning to the lives of poor families and better prepared them to assert their social values and economic interests. Finally, as Baptist—and, later, Methodist—ministers spread Christianity among the slaves, the cultural gulf between blacks and whites shrank, undermining one justification for slavery and giving blacks a new sense of spiritual identity. Within a generation African-Americans would develop their own version of Protestant Christianity.

The Midcentury Challenge: War, Trade, and Land

Between 1740 and 1765 colonial life was transformed not only by Pietism and the Enlightenment but also by war, economic change, and frontier violence. First, Britain embarked on a major war in America, the so-called French and Indian War, which became a world-wide conflict and redefined the British empire. Second, the expansion of transatlantic trade increased colonial prosperity but put Americans into debt to British creditors. Third, Britain's ouster of the French from North America in 1763 stimulated a great westward migration that led to new battles with the Indians, armed conflicts between settlers and landowners, and frontier rebellions against eastern governments.

The French and Indian War

In the aftermath of the War of Jenkins' Ear, British officials began to appreciate the economic and military potential of their colonial empire. Governor William Shirley of Massachusetts predicted that within a century the population of the mainland colonies would equal that of France and "lay a foundation for a Superiority of British power upon the continent of Europe."

Population and Diplomacy. Before the middle of the eighteenth century few Europeans had settled in the vast Mississippi Valley. The main French settlements, including the fur-trading centers of Montreal and Quebec, were along the St. Lawrence River, with only forts and fur-trading posts dotting the interior of the North American continent. British settlers had not moved across the Appalachians because there were few natural transportation routes. Moreover, the territory was a stronghold of the Iroquois, who were still allied with western native Americans in a covenant chain. For a generation the Iroquois and the western Algonquin had extorted guns and subsidies from English and French officials and traded with merchants for blankets and metal goods, holding off white settlements with threats of war. In the late 1740s this "play-off" system broke down for three interrelated reasons: both the British and the French refused to pay the rising cost of "gifts" to native Americans; Delaware and Shawnee Indians along the Ohio River declared their autonomy, disrupting the Iroquois' covenant chain; and a land shortage in New England and the influx of European migrants into the middle colonies increased Anglo-American migration on to Indian lands. During the 1750s William Johnson, the Indian agent for the British government in New York, bestowed manufac-

tured goods on the Mohawk nation to win its permission to settle Scottish migrants west of Albany but earned only distrust.

In the South land-hungry settlers and speculators were also on the march. In 1749 Governor Robert Dinwiddie of Virginia and a group of prominent planters organized the Ohio Company, which enlisted the support of John Hanbury and other London merchants with political connections and obtained a royal land grant of 200,000 acres along the upper Ohio River and the promise of 300,000 more acres (see Map 4.4). These initiatives infuriated the Iroquois, who told the British in 1753: "We don't know what you Christians, English and French intend; we are so hemmed in by both, that we have hardly a hunting place left."

The Road to War. To secure British claims to the Ohio region, Governor Dinwiddie sent Colonel George Washington—a young planter eager to speculate in western lands—to ward off the French with a force of the Virginia militia. This initiative raised the prospect of war. French officials and merchants wanted to reestablish their influence among the newly strident Delaware and Shawnee and viewed Washington's expedition as a threat to France's claim of sovereignty over the entire Mississippi Valley. To deter Indian rebellions and British incursions, they ordered the construction of Fort Duquesne at the point where the Monongahela and Allegheny rivers join to form the Ohio (present-day Pittsburgh). In July 1754 French troops repulsed the Virginia force and captured Washington and the garrison at Fort Necessity (a hastily built military redoubt 60 miles south of Fort Duquesne). Virginia was at war with France in the American backcountry, and the Ohio Indians, like the Iroquois, regarded themselves as potential victims of a European military contest.

MAP 4.4

European Spheres of Influence, 1754

France and Spain laid claim to vast areas of North America and sought to use Indian allies to combat the numerical advantage of British settlers. For their part, native Americans played off one European power against another. As a British official observed: "To preserve the Ballance between us and the French is the great ruling Principle of Modern Indian Politics." By expelling the French from North America, the Great War for Empire disrupted this balance, leaving Indian peoples on their own to resist encroaching Anglo-American settlers.

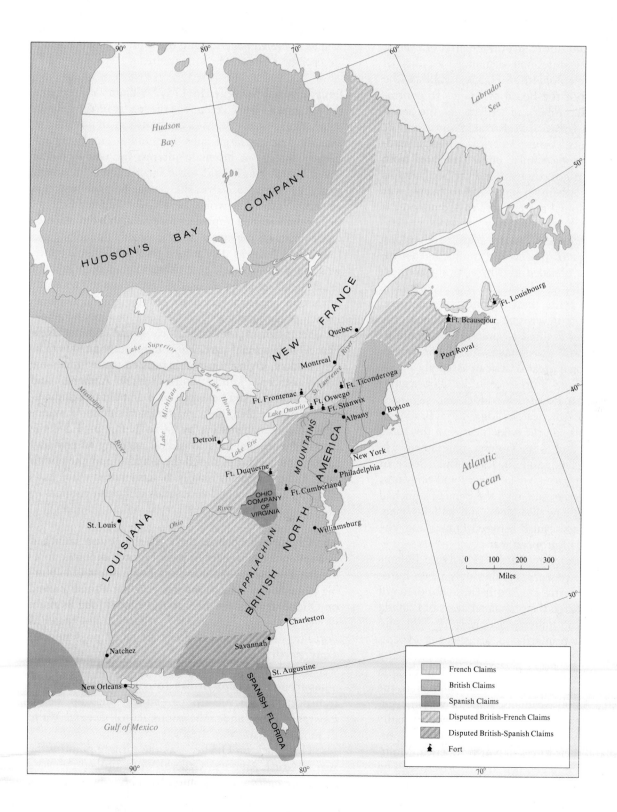

The British government had no desire to see this fighting continue. Its coffers were still empty from the long and expensive war with France that had ended in 1748. Wars required new taxes, which were strongly opposed in Parliament, as Prime Minister Henry Pelham knew: "There is such a load of debt, and such heavy taxes already laid upon the people, that nothing but an absolute necessity can justifie our engaging in a new War."

But Pelham could not control the march of events. William Pitt, a rising statesman, demanded a policy of expansionism in the colonies, as did Lord Halifax, the energetic new head of the Board of Trade. To coordinate the efforts of the American settlements, the board proposed a "union between ye Royal, Proprietary, & Charter Governments." Some American political leaders were thinking along similar lines. Delegates from most of the northern governments and the Six Iroquois Nations had met at Albany in June 1754 to discuss war policies, and the colonial representatives had adopted a Plan of Union, which was primarily the work of Benjamin Franklin. Under the Albany plan, each colony would send delegates to an American continental assembly, which would be presided over by a royal governor-general. This assembly would assume responsibility for all western affairs: trade, Indian policy, and defense. The proposed union never materialized because the provincial assemblies wanted to preserve their autonomy and the imperial government feared the consequences of convening a great American assembly.

To counter the French presence in the Ohio region, Britain dispatched Sir Edward Braddock and two regiments of troops to America. In May 1755 Braddock started marching through the wilderness with this force of 1,400 regulars and 450 Virginia militiamen. He never reached Fort Duquesne. In July a small force of French and a larger group of Delaware and Shawnee, who had now decided to side with the French, launched a surprise attack, killing Braddock and half his men. With this battle, the skirmish between France and Virginia escalated into a European war.

Initially there were few battles. The Ohio Indians adopted a defensive posture, fighting only when Europeans entered their territory. And because hundreds of miles of forest separated the populated areas of Canada and British America, military action by Britain and France was limited primarily to water-borne expeditions. In June 1755 British and New England naval and military forces captured Fort Beauséjour in Nova Scotia (Acadia). To eliminate the French from this region, the British deported 6,000 Acadians, some of whom eventually settled in Louisiana. Just before war was formally declared in 1756, the French sent the Marquis de Montcalm to command their forces in North America. Montcalm promptly captured and destroyed Fort Oswego on Lake Ontario.

The Great War for Empire

Two years of fighting in America precipitated the Seven Years' War in Europe. In 1756, France made a pact with Austria, Britain's longtime continental ally, and French and Austrian armies threatened Hanover, the homeland of King George II of England, as well as Prussia, the territory of Britain's new ally, Frederick the Great. When armed conflicts broke out in India and West Africa as well as in North America and the West Indies, the struggle became a Great War for Empire.

Pitt's Imperial Strategy. In 1757 William Pitt replaced the irresolute Henry Pelham as the leader of the government. Pitt honored Britain's commitment to its Prussian ally by sending large subsidies and a small expeditionary force, but his main interest lay overseas. The Seven Years' War would not be just another in a long string of European dynastic struggles with colonial episodes. Instead, it would be a Great War for Empire. Britain had reaped unprecedented wealth from its trading empire in the West Indies, North America, and India, and Pitt was determined to crush France, which was the main obstacle to further expansion. Pitt used the British fleet to bottle up the French navy in its home ports and began a systematic attack against overseas French possessions.

Pitt planned the critical campaign against New France with special care. He sought out vigorous military leaders, giving top commands to three impressive young officers: James Wolfe, Jeffrey Amherst, and William Howe. And he exploited a demographic advantage: Britain's 2 million mainland residents outnumbered the French settlers by 14 to 1. Pitt provided the colonies with generous subsidies, agreeing to pay half the cost of the troops raised there and supply them with arms and equipment. Finally, he committed main units of the British navy and thousands of British regulars to the American conflict.

The Capture of Quebec. In 1758 the British launched attacks on the perimeter of New France's defenses, forcing the French to abandon Fort Duquesne and capturing Louisbourg. The following year the British moved on Quebec from three directions. Colonel John Stanwix moved to the northeast from Fort Duquesne—renamed Fort Pitt—and General Amherst led an Anglo-American army northward from New York. These expeditions were designed to distract French forces and their Indian allies from the major British force—50 warships, 200 transports, and 8,500 troops—which sailed up the St. Lawrence River under the command of General Wolfe in June 1759 (see Map 4.5).

The attack on Quebec was the turning point of the war in North America. General Wolfe probed the city's strong defenses for three months. Then one day, in the

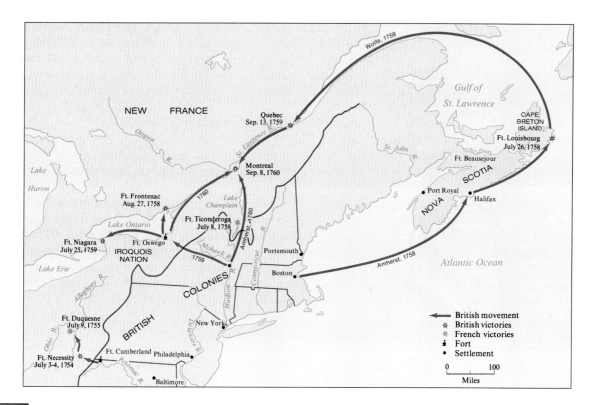

MAP. 4.5

The Anglo-American Conquest of New France
After years of preparation, British and American forces attacked the heartland of
New France, capturing Quebec in 1759. The conquest both united and divided the
allies. Colonists celebrated the great victory—"The Illuminations and Fireworks
exceeded any that had been exhibited before," reported the South Carolina *Gazette*—
but British officers viewed provincial soldiers with disdain: "the dirtiest, most con-
temptible, cowardly dogs you can conceive."

hours before dawn, 4,000 British troops scaled the 200-
foot cliffs behind the city and took up positions on the
high plains. French troops led by Montcalm advanced
against Wolfe's army but were overwhelmed by British
discipline and firepower. Quebec fell. The Royal Navy
prevented French reinforcements from crossing the Atlantic, and when British forces captured Montreal in
1760, the conquest of Canada was complete.

Pontiac's Uprising. The war in America had one more
scene to play. Early in 1763 the Ottawa chief Pontiac
led a group of loosely linked uprisings by tribes from
New York to Michigan. During the war the tribes had
been defrauded by rum-peddling British traders, and
they resented the British military occupation of the old
French forts as well as General Amherst's decision to
curtail "gifts" and supplies of gunpowder. Fearing the
influx of Anglo-American settlers, Pontiac hoped to re-

store the old French alliance, declaring, "I am French,
and I want to die French." Other Indians were inspired
by Neolin, a Delaware prophet who, blending Christian
doctrine with native American beliefs, urged the repudiation of all Europeans—along with their tools and
clothes—and a return to traditional customs.

Acknowledging this separatist pan-Indian outlook,
Pontiac astutely directed it against the British, capturing
nearly every British garrison west of Fort Niagara. The
uprising ended ultimately with the British in control:
the Indians returned British prisoners, surrendered
some of their leaders for punishment, and accepted the
British as their new political "fathers." For their part,
the British evinced somewhat greater respect for native
Americans, bargaining with them and, in the Proclamation Line of 1763, which temporarily forbade settlement west of the Appalachians, safeguarding their
territory from land-hungry settlers.

Pontiac
This portrait depicts Pontiac both as an Indian, symbolized by the necklace of bear claws, and as a European-style ruler with a regal demeanor and a flowing robe. Pontiac did indeed partake of two worlds, absorbing French culture as he asserted his Indian identity.

The Treaty of Paris. On the other battlefronts around the world, the British went from success to success. The East India Company captured French commercial outposts and took control of trade in large sections of India. British forces seized French Senegal in West Africa, the French sugar islands of Martinique and Guadeloupe, and the Spanish colonies of Cuba and the Philippine Islands. When the war ended, Pitt was no longer in office, but his maritime strategy had extended British power all over the world. The first British empire was at the height of its power.

The Treaty of Paris of 1763 confirmed the triumph of British arms. Britain gained sovereignty over half the continent of North America, including French Canada, all French territory east of the Mississippi River, and Spanish Florida. As recompense, Spain received all of Louisiana west of the Mississippi River, which it ruled for the next forty years, along with the restoration of

Cuba and the Philippines. The French empire in North America was reduced to a handful of valuable sugar islands in the West Indies and two rocky islands off the coast of Newfoundland.

British Economic Growth

Britain owed its triumph in large part to its unprecedented economic resources. Ever since it had wrested control of many oceanic trade routes from the Dutch at the end of the seventeenth century, Britain had been the dominant commercial power. Now, in the middle of the eighteenth century, it was becoming the first country to undergo the Industrial Revolution. Its new technology and work discipline made Britain the first—and for over a century the most powerful—industrial nation in the world.

The Industrial Revolution and the Expansion of Trade. By 1750 British artisans had designed and built water- and steam-driven machines that powered lathes for shaping wood, jennies and looms for making textiles, and hammers for forging iron. The new machines produced goods far faster than human labor could. Furthermore, the entrepreneurs who ran the new factories drove their employees hard, forcing them to labor long hours and keep pace with the machines. This new work discipline made it possible for the British to produce more wool and linen textiles, iron tools, paper, chinaware, and glass than ever before—and sell those goods at lower prices.

English and Scottish merchants launched aggressive campaigns to market their products in the rapidly growing mainland colonies. They extended a full year's credit, instead of the traditional six months, to American traders. Colonial shopkeepers and merchants took advantage of these liberal terms to expand their inventories and increase their sales to distant backcountry farmers. Americans increased their consumption and soon accounted for 20 percent of all British exports (see Figure 4.4). The settlers bought equipment for their farms and all kinds of household goods—cloth, blankets, china, and cooking utensils. This first "consumer revolution," as some historians have called it, raised the living standard of many Americans.

American Exports. To pay for these imports, Americans increased their agricultural exports. Tobacco from the Chesapeake remained the most important export, accounting for about 25 percent of the total. Planters sent 52 million pounds of tobacco abroad in 1740 and more than 75 million pounds in 1765. Entrepreneurs in Scotland financed this expansion by subsidizing Virginia planters and Scots-Irish migrants who moved into

A Philadelphia Merchant
James Tulley stands well-dressed and proud in his counting-house, his ships in the background preparing for the next voyage. Merchants like Tulley were the first great American entrepreneurs, organizing trade between the mainland, the West Indies, and Britain.

the Piedmont, a region of plains and rolling hills inland from the Tidewater counties. Scottish-run stores granted ample credit to these white settlers—to purchase land, slaves, and equipment—and took part of their tobacco crop in payment. By the 1760s Scottish merchants were buying nearly half the annual Chesapeake tobacco crop and reexporting most of it to expanding markets in France and central Europe.

Agricultural exports also supported the luxurious life-style of the white slaveowners of South Carolina. The British government subsidized the cultivation of indigo, and by the 1760s planters were annually sending indigo valued at £117,000 to English textile factories while carrying on an expanding export trade in rice to Holland and markets in southern Europe, selling about 65 million pounds of rice a year.

A booming export trade in wheat and flour permitted residents of the mid-Atlantic region to participate in the consumer revolution. With Europe in the throes of a population explosion, Continental merchants were buying wheat from America—at first only in poor harvest years, then regularly. Wheat prices in Philadelphia jumped almost 50 percent between 1740 and 1765, bringing high profits to farmers and merchants. New York, Pennsylvania, Maryland, and Virginia became the breadbasket of the Atlantic world.

But even this boom in exports could not defray the cost of the consumer frenzy. During the 1750s and 1760s exports paid for only 80 percent of imported British goods. The remaining 20 percent—millions of pounds—was financed by British merchants who extended credit. The first American spending binge, like most subsequent splurges, landed many consumers in debt.

FIGURE 4.4

Population, British Imports, and the American Trade Deficit
Around 1750 the rate of growth of British imports into the American colonies outpaced their rate of population growth, indicating that consumption per capita was increasing. The colonists then went into debt to pay for these goods, running an annual deficit with their British suppliers.

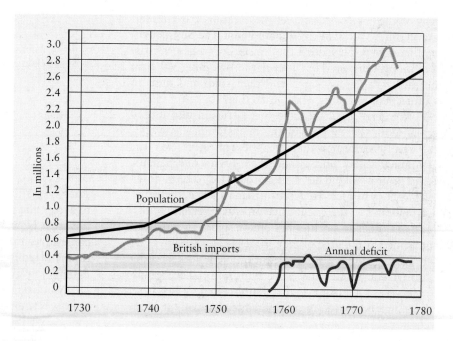

The return of peace after the Great War for Empire brought an end to boom times. Britain slashed its troop levels and military expenditures in America, and the loss of military markets, contracts, and cash subsidies made it more difficult for Americans to purchase British goods. Merchants looked anxiously at their overstocked warehouses and feared bankruptcy. "I think we have a gloomy prospect before us," a Philadelphian noted in 1765, "as there are of late some Persons failed, who were in no way suspected." The increase in transatlantic trade had raised living standards but also had made Americans more dependent on overseas creditors and the world economy.

Land Conflicts

In times of prosperity and in times of stagnating trade, the colonial population continued to grow. By 1750 the shortage of arable land in long-settled areas had become so acute that political conflicts broke out over land rights (see Map 4.6). With each new generation the problem got worse. In 1738, for example, men and women who traced their American ancestry back four generations founded the new town of Kent in western Connecticut. Their families had been moving slowly to the north and west for a century, and Kent was at the generally accepted western boundary of the colony. The next generation would have to find somewhere else to go.

Migration out of New England. In the 1750s Connecticut farmers formed the Susquehannah Company and petitioned the Connecticut legislature to help them claim lands in the West. According to the colony's seventeenth-century charter, its boundaries stretched all the way to the Pacific Ocean, yet those claims crossed land granted by Charles II to William Penn. The Susquehannah Company persuaded the legislature to assert jurisdiction over disputed territory in the Wyoming Valley in northeastern Pennsylvania and then sold land titles to Connecticut migrants who settled there.

The Penn family resisted this intrusion into its domain. With the support of the Pennsylvania assembly, the Penns reaffirmed their proprietary rights over the Wyoming Valley and issued their own land patents. Rival groups of land claimants proceeded to burn down each other's houses. To avert further violence, the Pennsylvania and Connecticut governments referred the dispute to British authorities in London, where it remained undecided at the time of independence.

Land disputes also broke out on New York's border with Massachusetts and New Hampshire. The boundaries were not precise, and hundreds of families from New England moved into disputed territory in the Hud-

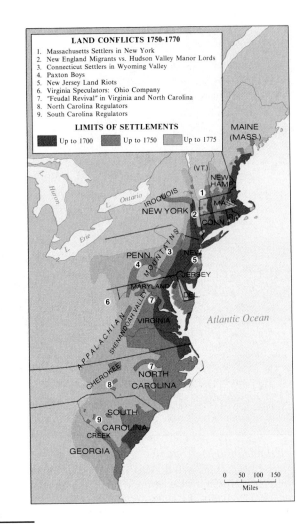

MAP 4.6

Westward Expansion and Armed Conflict
Between 1750 and 1775 the mainland population doubled—from 1.2 million to 2.5 million—sparking legal battles over land, which became increasingly valuable. Violence broke out in newly settled regions as backcountry settlers fought with Indians, rival claimants, and eastern-dominated governments.

son River Valley. New England yeomen farmers refused to accept the tenancy leaseholds that were customary on the great New York manorial estates. Instead, they purchased freehold titles from Massachusetts land speculators and roused the long-settled Dutch and German tenants to repudiate their manorial leases.

Manorial lords enforced their claims in New York courts, setting off a rebellion. In 1766 New England mi-

grants and tenant farmers in Westchester, Dutchess, and Albany counties refused to pay rent and used the threat of mob violence to close the courts. At the behest of the royal governor, General Thomas Gage led two British regiments to assist local sheriffs and manorial bailiffs in suppressing the tenant uprising and evicting New England squatters.

Proprietary Power. Other large landowners also won legal and political battles. In New Jersey and throughout the southern colonies, resident landowners and English aristocrats revived old land grants from the time of Charles II (1660–1685), and judges supported their claims to quitrents in regions settled by yeomen farmers and to vast tracts of undeveloped land. Lord Granville, an heir of one of the original Carolina proprietors, collected quitrents in the Granville district of North Carolina, and a legal suit gave Lord Fairfax ownership of the entire northern neck of Virginia along the Potomac.

Long-established proprietary families profited anew from the increased demand for land. Many farmers in settled regions could not afford "improved" freehold properties with cultivated fields, orchards, and fenced grazing land. Reluctantly, they turned to proprietors for tenancy leases on manorial estates or for undeveloped land. By the 1760s the Maryland proprietor, Lord Baltimore, was one of the richest men in England because of his American real estate. The Penn family reaped great profits from land sales and rents in Pennsylvania.

This revival of proprietary power underscored the growing strength of the landed gentry and the increasing resemblance between rural societies in Europe and America. High-quality land east of the Appalachians was getting more expensive, and much of it was controlled by English aristocrats, manorial landlords, and wealthy speculators. Unless something changed, tenants and even yeomen farmers might soon be reduced to the status of European peasants.

Uprisings in the West

As farmers moved west in search of land, they found themselves in the middle of new political and economic conflicts over Indian policy, political representation, and bankruptcy. Events erupted in violence on the frontiers of Pennsylvania and North and South Carolina.

The Paxton Boys. In Pennsylvania the white community came to blows over Indian policy. As long as Quakers had dominated Pennsylvania politics, relations with native American tribes had remained peaceful. After 1740, however, when large numbers of Scots-Irish migrants settled along the frontier, they wanted to push the Indians off the land. When the Quakers refused to help them, the frontiersmen reacted with violence. In 1763 the Paxton Boys, a band of Scots-Irish farmers, massacred twenty members of the Conestoga tribe, which included the last remnants of the once numerous Susquehannock people. When Governor John Penn attempted to protect the tribe and bring the murderers to justice, about 250 armed Scots-Irish advanced on Philadelphia, forcing the governor to mobilize the militia to defend the city. Benjamin Franklin intercepted the angry mob at Lancaster to seek a compromise, and a battle outside Philadelphia was narrowly averted (see American Voices, page 133).

Ultimately, the prosecution of the accused men failed for lack of witnesses, and the Scots-Irish dropped their demands for the expulsion of the Indians. But the episode left a legacy of racial and ethnic hatred and political resentment. During the independence crisis the Scots-Irish would take their revenge against both Indians in the West and the Quaker and Anglican elite in the East.

The South Carolina Regulators. During the French and Indian War there had been brutal warfare between land-seeking whites and the Cherokee in the backcountry of South Carolina. After the war outlaw bands of whites continued to roam the countryside, unchallenged by government authority. To subdue the outlaw bands and restore order, slaveowning planters and yeomen farmers banded together in an armed vigilante group called the Regulators. They took it upon themselves to impose moral discipline on the "low people"—the hunters, squatters, and landless laborers who lived on the fringes of society—by whipping people suspected of poaching or stealing goods.

The Regulators also struggled for western rights, presenting a list of demands to the eastern authorities: they wanted more local courts, fairer taxes, and greater representation in the provincial assembly. The South Carolina government accepted Regulator rule in the west despite its illegal character. Both the royal governor and the members of the provincial assembly were afraid to send troops to the backcountry because they feared slave revolts on the lowland rice plantations if the militia was away. They therefore compromised with backcountry insurgents, creating locally controlled courts in the west in 1767 and reducing the fees for legal documents. Lowland planter-merchants kept a firm grip on political power, however, refusing to reapportion the legislature to give western settlers representation proportionate to their growing numbers. The assembly also continued to tax the thin soil of the upland region at the same rate as the fertile lands of the low country.

A Backcountry Road
The first settlers in interior valleys lived in small, crude log cabins that were strung
out along the road. Loneliness and desolation, suggested here by a solitary rider, were
overcome by concerted efforts to build social communities, often through church-
centered activities. (Collection of The New-York Historical Society)

Because many western residents resisted their arbitrary assumption of power, the Regulators could not continue the struggle. Vowing to end Regulator rule, men
who had previously served as justices of the peace in the
backcountry organized a Moderator movement. In
March 1769, 600 armed supporters of each faction met
near the Saluda River and exchanged angry words, then
gunshots. Only an agreement to restore authority to the
provincial government averted wholesale violence. Like
the Paxton Boys in Pennsylvania, the Regulators attracted
attention to western interests but failed to alter the balance of power. Eastern interests remained dominant.

The North Carolina Regulators. In North Carolina the
key issue dividing east and west was commercial credit.
By the 1760s the transatlantic market system extended
far into the backcountry. At small stores owned by Scottish merchants, farmers and planters exchanged tobacco, wheat, and hides for manufactured goods and
bought land and slaves on credit. The more ambitious
among them created small-scale slave plantations, so
that the number of blacks rose. In Orange County, North
Carolina, the number of enslaved African-Americans
jumped from 45 in 1754 to 729 by 1767.

But tobacco prices plummeted after the Great War
for Empire, and many farmers found themselves deeply
in debt. In one three-year period, merchants in
Granville County brought 350 debt suits to local courts.
Judges directed sheriffs to seize the property of bankrupt farmers and sell it at auction to pay creditors and
court costs. Backcountry farmers resented this recourse
to the courts both because it generated high fees for
lawyers and court officials and because it violated local
customs. As in rural communities in New England,
loans among neighbors were based on trust and often
ran for years.

To save their farms, North Carolina debtors created
their own Regulator movement. At first the Regulators
intimidated judges, closed courts by force, and broke
into jails to free their leaders. Then they sought to elect
planters and farmers to the legislature. Their leader, a
migrant from Maryland named Herman Husband, told
his followers not to vote for "any Clerk, Lawyer, or
Scotch merchant. We must make these men subject to
the laws or they will enslave the whole community."
The Regulators demanded a law allowing them to pay
their taxes in the "produce of the country" rather than
in cash; they also wanted legal fees reduced, and—like
the South Carolina Regulators—they asked for fairer
taxes and greater legislative representation.

The North Carolina Regulators developed the most
broad-based and democratic program of all the back-

Henry Melchior Muhlenberg

The Paxton Boys March on Philadelphia

Racial conflict on the frontier sparked ethnic and religious confrontation in Pennsylvania as armed Scots-Irish Presbyterians marched on Philadelphia. Lutheran Germans opposed many of the policies of the politically dominant (and usually pacifist) Quakers and their German Moravian allies. This journal entry by the leading Lutheran minister Henry Melchior Muhlenberg mocks the hypocrisy of the Quakers and, in the process, reveals the extent of ethnic antagonism in Pennsylvania.

February 5. Toward evening the rumor sprang up that a corps of backwoods settlers—Englishmen, Irishmen, and Germans—were on the march toward Philadelphia to kill the Bethlehem Indians at the barracks outside the city. Some reported that they numbered seven hundred, others said fifteen hundred, etc. The Friends, or so-called Quakers, and the Moravians ran furiously back and forth to the barracks, and there was a great to-do over constructing several small fortresses or ramparts near the barracks. Cannons were also set up. Some remarked concerning all this that it seemed strange that such preparations should be made against one's own fellow citizens and Christians, whereas no one ever took so much trouble to protect from the Indians His Majesty's subjects and citizens on the frontier.

As far as I can learn, the opinion and sentiment of various ones of our German citizens is as follows:

That the Quakers and Bethlehemites had only used some of the aforesaid Indians as spies and that they had in view only their own selfish interests . . . which explained why the Quakers, etc. in Philadelphia did not exhibit the least evidence of human sympathy, etc. when Germans and other settlers on the frontiers were massacred and destroyed in the most inhuman manner by the Indians.

After two o'clock at night the watchmen began to cry, "Fire!" I asked our watchman, who is a member of our congregation, where the fire was. He said there was no fire, but that the watchmen had orders to cry out, "Fire," because the above-mentioned backwoodsmen were approaching. Thereupon all the alarm bells began to ring at once and a drum was sounded to summon the inhabitants of the city to the town hall plaza. The ringing sounded dreadful in the night.

A whole *troup* of small boys followed a prominent Quaker down the street shouting in amazement, "Look, look! a Quaker carrying a musket on his shoulder!" Indeed, the older folks also looked upon it as a miraculous portent to see so many old and young Quakers arming themselves with flintlocks and daggers, or so-called murderous weapons! What heightened their amazement was this: that these pious sheep, who had such a tender conscience during the long Spanish, French, and Indian War, and would rather have died than lift a hand for defense against the most dangerous enemies, were now all of a sudden willing to put on horns of iron like Zedekiah, the son of Chenaanah (I Kings 22), and shoot and smite a small group of their poor, oppressed, driven, and suffering fellow inhabitants and citizens from the frontier!

Source: Theodore G. Tappert and John W. Doberstein, eds., *The Notebook of a Colonial Clergyman* (Philadelphia, 1959).

---

country movements. In Anson County, for example, they argued that each person should pay taxes "in proportion to the profits arising from his estate." But the North Carolina insurgents were no more successful than were the other western protesters. In 1771 Governor William Tryon mobilized the militia and defeated a large Regulator force at the Alamance River; seven insurgent leaders were summarily executed. Not since Leisler's 1689 revolt in New York had political conflict in America resulted in so much bloodshed.

In 1771 as in 1689, colonial conflicts became intertwined with imperial politics. In far-off Connecticut, the Reverend Ezra Stiles defended the Regulators. "What shall an injured & oppressed people do," he asked, when they are faced with "Oppression and tyranny (under the name of Government)?" Stiles saw himself as an American patriot, and his condemnation of Governor Tryon in 1771 reflected American resistance to British imperial control. But Stiles's remarks also served as a commentary on developments in the mainland colonies between 1720 and 1765. These were years of crisis—agricultural, religious, ethnic, and military—but also of transformation. In 1765 America was still a dependent society closely tied to Britain by trade, culture, and politics, but it was also an increasingly complex society with the potential for an independent existence. British policies would determine the direction the maturing colonies would take.

Summary

By 1720 a freeholding yeoman society had developed in New England. Its families were controlled by men, who assumed ownership of their wives' property and provided inheritances for the children. When rapid population growth began to threaten the freehold ideal, New England farmers averted a crisis by planting higher-yielding crops, sharing their labor and goods with each other, and moving farther to the west.

In the mid-Atlantic colonies the rising European demand for wheat, their principal crop, brought prosperity to many farmers. A great influx of German and Scots-Irish migrants created an ethnically diverse society where religious groups held to their own beliefs but tolerated the traditions of others. Ethnic conflict did break out, especially over the Quakers' pacifist Indian policy, and the emergence of stark economic inequality created new tensions. While some gentlemen farmers and entrepreneurs grew wealthy, a new landless class began to appear at the bottom of the social order.

As the American colonies became more integrated into the world economy, they also participated more fully in the intellectual life of Europe. Enlightenment rationalism influenced educated Americans such as Benjamin Franklin, and pietistic religion reinvigorated colonial churches. The preaching of George Whitefield prompted a Great Awakening in the early 1740s that brought spiritual renewal to thousands of Americans, but not without sparking conflict. In the northern colonies enthusiastic New Lights condemned traditional Old Lights, and in Virginia evangelical Baptists converted white tenant farmers and enslaved blacks, challenging the religious and social dominance of the Anglican elite.

Beginning in the 1740s, the mainland colonies experienced a series of upheavals. Manorial lords in New York suppressed tenant uprisings, and proprietors in many colonies successfully asserted their economic and legal rights. Yeomen families who had migrated into the backcountry of the Carolinas fought with native Americans and other settlers over land and challenged the authority of eastern political leaders. And British and American soldiers fought a major war against the French, conquering Quebec and driving the French out of North America. These conflicts, along with the expansion of transatlantic trade, testified to the growing involvement of the colonies in the diplomacy, commerce, and intellectual life of Europe. Britain's North American provinces were growing—in economic complexity, political vitality, and military potential.

TIMELINE

1700	Freehold ideal in rural communities
	Household mode of production
	Arranged marriages common
	Woman's "place" as subordinate helpmate
	Female literacy in New England expands
1700–1714	New Hudson River manors created
1720s	German migrants settle in middle colonies
	Scots-Irish migration grows
	Enlightenment ideas spread to America
	Frelinghuysen holds revivals
1730s	Tennents lead Presbyterian revivals
	Jonathan Edwards preaches in New England
1739	George Whitefield and the Great Awakening
	War of Jenkins' Ear
1740–1760s	Population pressure in New England
	Smaller family size; more premarital pregnancies
	Women active in religion and market activities
	Ethnic pluralism in middle colonies
	Rising grain and tobacco prices
	Increasing rural inequality
1740s	Old Lights versus New Lights
	Religious establishment questioned
	New colleges founded
	Newspapers increase
	Enlightenment ideas (Locke, Newton) spread
1743	Franklin founds American Philosophical Society
1749	Ohio Company formed
	Susquehannah Company in Connecticut
1750s	Proprietary resurgence
	Industrial Revolution begins in England
	Consumer "revolution" raises American debt
	Indian "play-off" system breaks down
1754	French and Indian War begins
	Albany Congress
1755	French Acadians deported
1759	Fall of Quebec
1760s	New York and New England border conflicts
	Regulator movements in the Carolinas
	Evangelical Baptists in Virginia
1762	Treaty of Fontainebleau gives Louisiana to Spain
1763	Treaty of Paris ends Great War for Empire
	Florida and Canada ceded to Britain
	Postwar colonial recession
	Pontiac leads Indian uprising
	Paxton Boys in Pennsylvania

★   ★   ★

BIBLIOGRAPHY

A fine collection of important articles can be found in Stanley Katz, John Murrin, and Douglas Greenberg, eds., *Colonial America: Essays in Politics and Social Development*, 4th ed. (1993). John J. McCusker and Russell R. Menard, *The Economy of British America, 1607–1783* (1985), survey economic change, whereas Jon Butler, *Awash in a Sea of Faith: Christianizing the American People* (1990), covers religious developments. Jack P. Greene, *Pursuits of Happiness* (1988), offers a provocative comparative analysis of regional social evolution.

Freehold Society in New England

A good local study is Daniel Vickers, *Farmers & Fishermen: Two Centuries of Work in Essex County Massachusetts, 1630–1830* (1994), whereas Bruce C. Daniels, *The Fragmentation of New England: Comparative Perspectives on Economic, Political, and Social Divisions in the Eighteenth Century* (1988), and Allan Kulikoff, *The Agrarian Origins of American Capitalism* (1992), offer a wider view. See also Robert Gross, *The Minutemen and Their World* (1976), and Richard Bushman, *From Puritan to Yankee: Character and the Social Order in Connecticut, 1690–1765* (1967). On women's lives, see Laurel Thatcher Ulrich, *Good Wives: Image and Reality in the Lives of Women of Northern New England, 1650–1750* (1982), and Marylynn Salmon, *Women and the Law of Property in Early America* (1986). For studies of material culture that reveal the character of society, see Robert B. St. George, ed., *Material Life In America, 1600–1860* (1988).

The Mid-Atlantic: Toward a New Society

On Pennyslvania, consult Michael Zuckerman, ed., *Friends and Neighbors: Group Life in America's First Plural Society* (1982); Allan Tully, *William Penn's Legacy: Pennsylvania, 1726–1755* (1978); and Barry J. Levy, *Quakers and the American Family* (1988). James T. Lemon, *The Best Poor Man's Country* (1972), pays some attention to ethnicity, as does Marilyn J. Westerkamp, *Triumph of the Laity: Scots-Irish Piety and the Great Awakening, 1625–1760* (1988). On white indentured servants and ethnic migration, see the classic study by Abbot E. Smith, *Colonists in Bondage* (1947); R. Greg Roeber, *Palantines, Liberty, and Property: German Lutherans in Colonial British America* (1993); R. J. Dickson, *Ulster Immigration to Colonial America, 1718–1775* (1966); Jon Butler, *The Huguenots in America* (1983); Ned Landsman, *Scotland and Its First American Colony, 1683–1775* (1985); and A. Roger Ekirch, *Bound for America: The Transportation of British Convicts to the Colonies, 1718–1775* (1987). Other important studies include Patricia U. Bonomi, *A Factious People: Politics and Society in Colonial New York* (1971), and Thomas L. Purvis, *Proprietors, Patronage, and Money: New Jersey, 1703–1776* (1986).

The Enlightenment and the Great Awakening

Henry F. May, *The Enlightenment in America* (1976), is still the standard treatment, but see also Paul Merrill Spurlin, *The French Enlightenment in America* (1984), and Herbert Leventhal, *In the Shadow of the Enlightenment: Occultism and Renaissance Science in Eighteenth-Century America* (1976). For medical knowledge see Richard Shryock, *Medicine and Society in America, 1660–1860* (1960). Brooke Hindle, *The Pursuit of Science in Revolutionary America, 1735–1789* (1956), and John C. Greene, *American Science in the Age of Jefferson* (1984), are also relevant.

Good studies of the Great Awakening include David S. Lovejoy, *Religious Enthusiasm in the New World: Heresy to Revolution* (1985); Patricia U. Bonomi, *Under the Cope of Heaven: Religion, Society, and Politics in Colonial America* (1986); and Harry S. Stout, *The New England Soul: Preaching and Religious Culture in Colonial New England* (1986). Three good biographies of New England revivalists are Patricia Tracy, *Jonathan Edwards, Pastor* (1979); W. G. McLoughlin, *Isaac Backus and American Pietistic Tradition* (1957); and Christopher Jedrey, *The World of John Cleaveland* (1979). Richard Bushman, ed., *The Great Awakening* (1970), and Rhys Isaac, *The Transformation of Virginia, 1740–1790* (1982), capture the emotions of ordinary participants.

Bernard Bailyn, *Education in the Forming of American Society* (1960), is a stimulating introduction, while Lawrence A. Cremin, *American Education: The Colonial Experience, 1607–1783* (1970), offers a comprehensive treatment. William L. Joyce et al., eds., *Printing and Society in Early America* (1983), assesses the impact of books, pamphlets, and newspapers on the American mind.

The Midcentury Challenge: War, Trade, and Land

Douglas E. Leach, *Roots of Conflict: British Armed Forces and Colonial Americans, 1677–1763* (1986), sets the Great War for Empire in a larger context. See also Edward P. Hamilton, *The French and Indian Wars* (1962); Guy Fregault, *Canada: The War of the Conquest* (1969); George F. G. Stanley, *New France: The Last Phase, 1744–1760* (1968); and Fred Anderson, *A People's Army: Massachusetts Soldiers and Society in the Seven Years' War* (1984). Richard White, *The Middle Ground* (1991), and Francis Jennings, *Empire of Fortune: Crown, Colonies, and Tribes in the Seven Years' War* (1988), describe the crucial role played by Indians in the conflict. See also Richard Aquila, *The Iroquois Restoration: Iroquois Diplomacy on the Colonial Frontier, 1701–1754* (1983), and David H. Corkran, *The Cherokee Frontier: Conflict and Survival, 1740–1762* (1966).

Gary M. Walton and James F. Shepherd, *The Economic Rise of Early America* (1979), trace the growing importance of commerce. See also Paul G. E. Clemens, *The Atlantic Economy and Colonial Maryland's Eastern Shore: From Tobacco to Grain* (1980), and Jacob M. Price, *Capital and Credit in British Overseas Trade: The View from the Chesapeake, 1700–1776* (1980).

Backcountry political agitation forms the focus of Richard D. Brown, *The South Carolina Regulators* (1963), and some of the essays in Alfred Young, ed., *The American Revolution: Essays in the History of American Radicalism* (1976). See also W. Stitt Robinson, *The Southern Colonial Frontier, 1607–1763* (1979); Charles E. Clark, *The Eastern Frontier: The Settlement of Northern New England, 1610–1763* (1970); and Richard Beeman, *The Evolution of the Southern Backcountry* (1984).

Occupation of Concord by the British (detail)

The British marched to Lexington and Concord in force and searched houses in the town center for arms and munitions. Hearing of the skirmishes, the New England portraitist Ralph Earl visited the sites, creating this and other paintings of the campaign.

CHAPTER 5

Toward Independence: Years of Decision

1763–1775

★ ★ ★

At the end of the Great War for Empire the American colonists were loyal subjects of Great Britain. Twelve years later the colonies stood on the brink of civil war—angry, armed, and resistant to British authority. How had it happened, asked the president of King's College in New York, that such a "happily situated" people should decide to "hazard their Fortunes, their Lives, and their Souls, in such a Rebellion"?

This rapid and unexpected change had two broad sets of causes. First, the character of the American political and social system fostered dreams of autonomy. Unlike most colonial peoples, Americans lived in a prosperous, stable society with a strong tradition of representative government. This unique historical experience created vigorous, experienced leaders and a self-confident populace capable of supporting an independence movement. Still, most Americans had been content for generations under British rule. What sparked them to rebel—the second, and immediate, cause of the independence movement—was Britain's attempt to reform the imperial system.

The story of the rebellion unfolded in four distinct phases. First, a British reform initiative began during the war and culminated in the Stamp Act of 1765. This tax legislation led to the second phase, an angry protest against new economic burdens and the constitutional principles on which they were based. A political compromise provided only a temporary respite; between 1767 and 1770 the third phase of the confrontation witnessed the imposition of new British taxes, the revival of American resistance, and a second compromise. Then a final crisis precipitated by a tax on tea unleashed the deep passions stirred up by a decade of reform and resistance, producing a civil war within the British empire.

The Reform Movement, 1763–1765

Military power made Britain the dominant nation in Europe after the Great War for Empire. France had been checked on the Continent, and Britannia ruled the waves for the next century and a half. By driving the French out of Canada, Britain had also achieved dominance over eastern North America (see Map 5.1). The way was clear for Britain to impose central control on its American colonies.

Tensions in the Imperial System

The Great War for Empire strained the imperial political system and brought to light deep-seated differences between Britain and its colonies. Before 1754 only royal governors and a few merchants and naval officers had experienced life in the American provinces. During the conflict, however, hundreds of British army officers and middle-level bureaucrats came to the mainland colonies, and they did not like what they saw. Provincial soldiers were drawn from the dregs of society, General James Wolfe told a friend. "There is no depending on them in

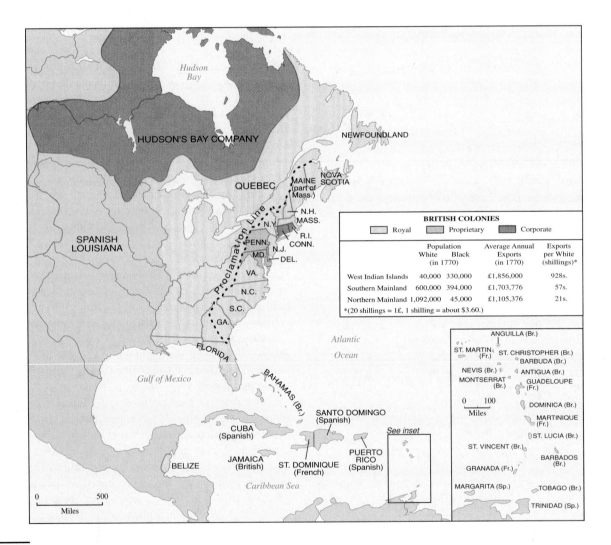

BRITISH COLONIES

	Royal		Proprietary		Corporate

	Population (in 1770) White	Black	Average Annual Exports (in 1770)	Exports per White (shillings)*
West Indian Islands	40,000	330,000	£1,856,000	928s.
Southern Mainland	600,000	394,000	£1,703,776	57s.
Northern Mainland	1,092,000	45,000	£1,105,376	21s.

*(20 shillings = 1£, 1 shilling = about $3.60.)

MAP 5.1

Britain's American Empire in 1763
In 1763 Britain was dominant in the West Indies and controlled all of eastern North America. British ministers dispatched troops to the conquered colonies of Florida and Quebec and, with the Proclamation Line of 1763, sought to prevent Anglo-American settlement west of the Appalachian Mountains.

action." For their part, Americans were shocked by the arrogance of upper-crust British officers and by the rigors of military discipline. British troops, a Massachusetts militiaman wrote in his diary, "are but little better than slaves to their officers."

Disputes over Taxes and Trade. The war also exposed the weakness of British administrative control, especially as it was wielded by the royal governors. In theory, governors had extensive political powers, including command of the provincial militia. In reality, they had to share power with the colonial assemblies, which refused to support the war effort with taxes and troops unless the governor relinquished control over military appointments and operations. Britain's Board of Trade complained that in Massachusetts "almost every act of executive and legislative power is ordered and directed by votes and resolves of the General Court."

In Virginia the assembly refused to levy additional taxes to pay for the war. The Burgesses resorted instead to deficit financing, printing paper currency in amounts sufficient to pay the province's bills. As the colony's government bought military supplies and paid troops, the purchasing power of the currency fell nearly 20 percent. Yet Virginia law required merchants and other creditors to accept the currency as legal tender, at face value. British merchants in the colony refused to accept payment in depreciated currency and applied to Parliament for relief. Parliament had helped before, passing a Currency Act in 1751 that had placed strict regulations on the issuing of government bills of credit by the New England colonies and had prohibited their use as legal tender to pay private debts. Now the British legislature passed another Currency Act (1764), banning the use of paper money as legal tender in Virginia and all the colonies. Americans would have to pay their debts to merchants with British currency, foreign coins, or bills of exchange. Equally important, Parliament had seized control of the colonial monetary system from the American assemblies.

Imperial authorities also began to enforce the Navigation Acts, regulating colonial trade more strictly. Before the war American merchants had routinely bribed colonial customs officials to circumvent the Molasses Act of 1733. To curb such corruption, in 1762 Parliament passed a Revenue Act, which prohibited officeholders in the customs department from leasing offices to deputies, who had often accepted bribes to support themselves while paying the absentee officeholders. Moreover, the Royal Navy was instructed to block all trade with the French islands. Royal officials had been shocked to find that during the war with France colonial merchants had continued to ship food and supplies to the French islands. It was absurd, declared an outraged British politician, that French armies attempting

"to Destroy one English province, are actually supported by Bread raised in another." Such commerce, the British ministry charged, allowed the French "to sustain and protract this long and expensive war."

British Troops in America. The most striking evidence of Britain's determination to protect and control its colonies was the decision in 1763 to station a large peacetime army—fifteen regiments of infantry, about 10,000 men—in North America. There were three reasons for this move. First, because most French settlers, some 60,000 in number, chose to remain in Canada, Britain needed troops to discourage rebellion in the newly captured province of Quebec. British troops also occupied Florida, which Spain wanted back but whose Spanish residents had mostly fled to Havana.

Second, officials in London feared another Indian war. The rebellion begun by the Ottawa chief Pontiac in May 1763 was still raging (see Chapter 4) and seemed to confirm the wisdom of maintaining substantial garrisons in the forts taken from the French. Pontiac's rebellion had also taught the British that what the Indians most feared was white settlement. In October, as an additional step to prevent trouble in the Ohio River Valley, King George III issued the Proclamation of 1763, which prohibited white settlement west of the crest of the Appalachians and regulated the fur trade with the Indian peoples. The Proclamation angered American land speculators, whose drive for expansion in the Ohio River Valley had started the war with France in the first place, and was ignored by thousands of land-hungry white settlers. As many as 50,000 whites—"too Lawless and Licentious ever to be restrained," according to one British official—may have lived west of the Appalachians by 1775.

The third reason for deploying the troops was the apprehension on the part of some British politicians of an American independence movement, a fear that had been growing since the late 1740s. "I have been publickly told," the Swedish traveler Peter Kalm reported from America in 1748, "that within thirty or fifty years, the English colonies may constitute a separate state, wholly independent of England." Only the danger of a French invasion from Canada, Kalm thought, deterred colonists from demanding greater autonomy. For that reason, some British officials argued during the peace negotiations of 1763 that it would be prudent to return Canada to France while keeping the West Indian sugar islands of Guadeloupe and Martinique. Given the decision to keep Canada, officials such as Henry Knox, a former treasury official in Georgia, recommended a strong British military presence in the mainland colonies. Indeed, Knox wrote in a memorandum to policy makers, "The main purpose of Stationing a large Body of Troops in America is to secure the Dependence of the Colonys on Great Britain."

Of course, the presence of British troops would not necessarily stop Americans from demanding political autonomy. In the 1740s, when land riots had broken out in New Jersey, Governor Jonathan Belcher had advised royal authorities that simply stationing British troops in the colony would not "drive Assemblies or people from their Obstinate ways of Thinking, into reasonable measures." Belcher knew that to be effective, military power had to be used to impose royal edicts or curb the power of local officeholders. In establishing a large military presence in America, the British ministry showed that it might be prepared to use force to preserve and extend imperial rule.

The Financial Legacy of the War

Britain paid a substantial price at home for its military successes abroad. During the Great War for Empire the British East India Company had routed the French in India, opening up the rich subcontinent to British commerce and eventual conquest, but the conflict had drained the company. Its well-connected officials looked to the British government for new subsidies and privileges, but the Treasury was empty. The government had borrowed heavily from British and Dutch bankers to finance the war, and the national debt had almost doubled, from £75 million in 1754 to £133 million in 1763.

This huge war debt placed a new financial burden on the British prime minister, Lord Bute, the lackluster favorite of George III who had replaced William Pitt in 1761. As the war came to a close, Bute's ministry had to find funds to pay the interest on the debt as well as the normal expenses of government. Treasury officials advised against raising the land tax, which was already at an all-time high and was paid by the propertied classes, whose support the government needed. The ministry therefore imposed higher import duties on tobacco and sugar, which manufacturers passed on to consumers in the form of higher prices. The government also increased *excise levies*—sales taxes—on goods such as salt and beer and distilled spirits, once again passing along the costs of the war to ordinary people.

To collect these taxes and duties, the British government had to expand its bureaucracy (see Figure 5.1). Between 1750 and 1775 the number of royal officials in Britain jumped from about 5,000 to more than 11,000. Parliament gave the new bureaucrats increased administrative and legal powers. Customs agents and informers patrolled the coasts of southern Britain, arresting smugglers and seizing tons of goods—such as French wines and Flemish textiles—on which import duties had not been paid. Convicted smugglers faced heavy penalties, including death or "transportation" to America as indentured servants.

The legacy of the war was therefore a paradoxical mix. Along with immense military power and increased national pride for Britain came huge debts, tighter governmental control, and rising domestic dissent. Beginning with the ascendancy of Sir Robert Walpole in the 1730s, radical Real Whigs and conservative Country party landlords had emphasized the dangers of unlimited government, and now their worst fears seemed to have come to pass. The Treasury was at the mercy of the "monied interest"—the banks and financiers who had paid for the war and were reaping millions of

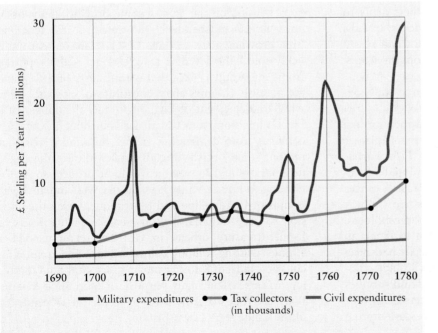

1690   1700   1710   1720   1730   1740   1750   1760   1770   1780

— Military expenditures   ●—● Tax collectors (in thousands)   — Civil expenditures

£ Sterling per Year (in millions)

FIGURE 5.1

The Growing Power of the British State

As Britain built a great navy and subsidized the armies of its European allies, the government's military expenditures soared, as did the number of tax collectors. The tax bureaucracy doubled in size between 1700 and 1735 and doubled again between 1750 and 1780.

Britain Triumphant
This painting celebrates the Great War for Empire by praising two of its heroes, Prime Minister William Pitt and General James Wolfe, who was killed during the battle of Quebec. It also conveys a political message with Real Whig overtones, warning the king against "Evil and Corrupt Ministers."

pounds in interest from government bonds. And with the number of royal officers skyrocketing, the evils of patronage and administrative abuse became more apparent. Warning that a corrupt Parliament filled with "worthless *pensioners* and *placemen*" had embarked on a systematic plan to extinguish British liberty, reformers demanded that Parliament be made more representative. In 1763, for example, the Radical Whig John Wilkes demanded an end to *rotten boroughs*—tiny districts whose voters were controlled by wealthy aristocrats and merchants. The price of empire abroad was debt and dissent at home.

British Reform Strategy

The Great War for Empire brought a decisive end to the era of salutary neglect. During the war a new generation of British political leaders had come to power, determined not only to defeat France but also to reform the imperial system. Charles Townshend of the Board of Trade and Prime Minister William Pitt had a broad vision. They agreed with Thomas Pownall, the former governor of Massachusetts, that "the spirit of *commerce* will become the predominant power, which will rule the powers of Europe" and that the American colonies were the key to commercial success. In their eyes, the mainland settlers had systematically evaded their responsibilities, defying the Navigation Acts by smuggling, trading with the French during wartime, and refusing to pay a fair share of the cost of their military defense. The continued growth of British trade and national power depended on the reform of imperial administration and taxation.

At first political instability in Britain hampered the quest for reform. When George III came to the throne in 1760, he reasserted the power of the monarchy, disrupting Walpole's system of cooperation between the king and Parliament. In particular, George insisted in 1761 on installing Lord Bute, his favorite, as prime minister even though Bute did not control a majority in the House of Commons. Bute successfully negotiated the Treaty of Paris, ending the war, but resigned in 1763, unable to resolve the growing financial crisis. The king then turned reluctantly to George Grenville, who enjoyed strong support in Parliament.

The Sugar Act. Grenville, an astute politician, embraced the cause of imperial reform. Shortly after becoming prime minister, he introduced the Sugar Act of 1764. This new Navigation Act, a revision of the Molasses Act of 1733, resulted from a wide-ranging review of the West Indian trade system by Treasury officials Thomas Whatley and Charles Jenkinson. Whatley and Jenkinson had long been governmental contacts for colonial agents—resident Americans or English merchants who represented the interests of the colonial assemblies in London. They knew that the mainland settlers had to sell their wheat, fish, and lumber in the French islands. Without the molasses, sugar, and bills of exchange that those sales brought, the colonists would lack the funds to buy British manufactured goods. The Treasury officials therefore resisted demands from British sugar planters to cut off this trade by enforcing the Molasses Act's high duty of 6 pence per gallon on molasses imported from the French West Indies. Instead, they instituted a smaller duty of 3 pence per gallon, arguing that this levy would allow British molasses to compete with the cheaper

French product without destroying the mainland's export trade or distilling industry.

But American merchants and manufacturers refused to accept this compromise. Many New England traders, such as John Hancock of Boston, had made their fortunes by smuggling huge quantities of French molasses without paying any duty. Their profits—illegally gained in the first place—would be severely cut by the new regulations. The merchants, joined by New England distillers who feared higher costs, orchestrated a petition campaign against the Sugar Act. Publicly, they protested that the tax called for in the Sugar Act would wipe out trade with the French islands. Privately, they vowed to evade the duty by smuggling or by bribing officials.

Imperial reform had legal and political as well as economic consequences as merchants and their allies raised constitutional objections to the Sugar Act. Thomas Cushing, speaker of the Massachusetts House of Representatives, argued that the duties constituted a "tax," so that the Sugar Act was "contrary to a fundamental Principall of our Constitution: That all Taxes ought to originate with the people." A House committee went further, declaring that such parliamentary acts "have a tendency to deprive the colonies of some of their most essential Rights as British subjects." Whatley and Jenkinson's attempt to balance the interests of British sugar planters and those of mainland settlers had become a bitterly contested constitutional issue. The terms of debate had shifted, and fatefully so.

Vice-Admiralty Courts and the "Rights of Englishmen."
In addition to levying duties, the Sugar Act of 1764 extended the jurisdiction of *vice-admiralty courts*—maritime tribunals that operated without the procedures and protections of English common law. There was no trial by jury in those courts. Rather, a judge—usually one with British sympathies—heard arguments and decided cases solely on the basis of Parliamentary legislation.

For half a century colonial legislatures had vigorously opposed vice-admiralty courts, which had been introduced to put teeth in the Navigation Acts. To limit the power of these courts, which had long been opposed in Britain not only by smugglers but also by principled opponents of royal power, the assemblies extended the jurisdiction of their own courts over all customs offenses occurring in American seaports or coastal waters. Thus merchants charged with violating the Navigation Acts often were acquitted by well-disposed common-law juries or American-born judges. By extending the jurisdiction of vice-admiralty courts to all customs offenses wherever they occurred, the Sugar Act closed this loophole.

The powers given to the vice-admiralty courts thus revived old American fears and raised new constitu-

tional objections. Richard Bland, an influential Virginia planter, charged that the courts illegally discriminated against British subjects living in America; the colonists "were not sent out to be the Slaves but to be the Equals of those that remained behind," Bland asserted. John Adams, a young Massachusetts lawyer who defended John Hancock on a charge of smuggling, took a similar position:

> Here is the contrast that stares us in the face. The Parliament in one Clause guarding the People of the Realm, and securing to them the benefit of a Tryal by the Law of the Land, and by the next Clause, depriving all Americans of that Privilege. What shall we say to this Distinction? Is there not in this Clause a Brand of Infamy, or Degradation, and Disgrace, fixed upon every American? Is he not degraded below the rank of an Englishman?

The logic of Adams and Bland was compelling, though they had some of the facts wrong. Vice-admiralty courts had long played a major role in Britain. Adams and Bland were unaware of this or, caught up in the debate over imperial reform and American rights, were deliberately misleading their fellow colonists. In any case, the new vice-admiralty legislation did not discriminate against Americans. Instead, it extended British legal practices—albeit unpopular ones—to America.

The real issue was not the suppression of traditional American liberties but the growing authority of the British state both at home and abroad. The expanded royal bureaucracy was determined to root out smuggling and to raise revenues in Britain and North America. The colonists' righteous anger reflected their past experience; raised under a policy of salutary neglect, they instinctively resisted the new rules and procedures.

Yet in a larger sense, knowledgeable Americans such as Bland and Adams were right when they claimed that British policy challenged the existing constitutional structure of the empire. After the war many British officials denied that the colonists had the right to claim either the privileges inscribed in their royal charters or the traditional "rights of Englishmen." For example, when Royal Governor Francis Bernard of Massachusetts heard that the Massachusetts assembly had objected to the Sugar Act, claiming no taxation without representation, he asserted that the people in America did not have that constitutional right. "The rule that a *British* subject shall not be bound by laws or liable to taxes, but what he has consented to by his representatives," Bernard argued, "must be confined to the inhabitants of Great Britain only." In Bernard's eyes and those of many British political leaders, Americans were second-class subjects of the king, their rights limited by the Navigation Acts and the national interests of the British state as determined by Parliament.

The Stamp Act

The issue of taxation brought about the first great imperial crisis. When Grenville introduced the Sugar Act in Parliament in 1764, he also announced his intention to seek a colonial stamp tax the following year. He hoped that part of the £200,000 per year needed to clothe, house, feed, and pay the 10,000 soldiers the ministry planned to station in America would be covered by this new measure, which would require tax stamps on court documents, land titles, contracts, playing cards, newspapers, and other printed items. A similar English tax levied since 1694 had yielded an annual revenue of £290,000, and Grenville hoped the American levy would raise at least £60,000 (about $5 million today). The prime minister knew that some Americans would object to the tax on constitutional grounds, so he asked explicitly if any member of the House of Commons doubted "the power and sovereignty of Parliament over every part of the British dominions, for the purpose of raising or collecting any tax." No one rose to object.

Grenville informed the American assemblies that unless they could "raise a sum adequate to their defence,"

George Grenville, *Architect of the Stamp Act*
As prime minister from 1764 to 1766, Grenville assumed leadership of the movement for imperial reform and taxation. But most British politicians believed that the colonies should be better regulated and share the cost of the empire.

a stamp tax would be voted in 1765. This challenge threw the London agents of the colonial legislatures into confusion. They all agreed that the assemblies could not apportion the defense budget among themselves; the colonies had met together only on a single occasion, the Albany Congress of 1756, and not a single assembly had accepted its proposals. Agent Richard Jackson, an English merchant, advised the assemblies to accept the stamp tax because he believed that their long-standing claim to the sole right of taxation lacked a firm constitutional basis and that the tax would be imposed on them whether they liked it or not.

Benjamin Franklin, representing the Pennsylvania assembly, countered with a proposal for American representation in Parliament. "If you chuse to tax us," he suggested to a British friend, "give us Members in your Legislature, and let us be one People." But with the exception of William Pitt, who prepared a draft proposal for American representation in Parliament, British politicians rejected this radical idea. They argued that the colonists were "virtually" represented by the merchants who sat in Parliament and by other members with interests in America. Even colonial leaders were skeptical of Franklin's plan; they were "situate at a great Distance from their Mother Country," the Connecticut assembly declared in a printed pamphlet dispatched to London and therefore "cannot participate in the general Legislature of the Nation." Influential Philadelphia merchants, worried that a handful of colonial delegates would be powerless in Parliament, warned Franklin "to beware of any measure that might extend to us seats in the Commons."

But American leaders had no alternative to the plan proposed by Grenville, who was determined to assert the constitutional supremacy of Parliament. The Stamp Act was "the great measure of the Sessions," Grenville's chief assistant observed, "on account of the important point it establishes, the Right of Parliament to lay an internal Tax upon the Colonies." The ministry's plan worked smoothly. The House of Commons refused to accept American petitions opposing the new legislation, which it passed by an overwhelming vote of 205 to 49. Parliament also approved Grenville's proposal that violations of the Stamp Act be tried in vice-admiralty courts so that the colonists would have no hope of acquittal by friendly juries in local common-law courts.

Finally, at the request of General Thomas Gage, commander of British military forces in America, Parliament passed a Quartering Act that directed colonial governments to provide barracks and food for the British troops stationed there. During the French and Indian War the assemblies of Massachusetts and New York had refused to accept this financial burden, and the ministry was determined to force the colonists into compliance.

Grenville's design was complete. He had firmly declared the supremacy of the British Parliament and pushed forward the movement for imperial reform. But he also provoked a constitutional confrontation with the American assemblies not only on the crucial issue of taxes but also on the right to a trial by a local jury and on the support of a standing army. The intentions of the imperial authorities had become clear.

The Dynamics of Rebellion, 1765–1766

With the Sugar and Stamp acts, Grenville had thrown down the gauntlet to the American colonists. Would they resist this curtailment of the political autonomy achieved during the decades of salutary neglect? If they did, what were their chances of success? Settlers in various colonies had opposed unpopular laws or arbitrary governors, but they had never before faced a reform-minded ministry and Parliament. Some Patriots—as the defenders of American rights came to be called—resisted the new British measures forcefully by organizing resistance committees, rioting in the streets, or delivering speeches that bordered on treason. Many other Americans, moved by anti-imperial sentiments, economic self-interest, and religious and constitutional principles, rallied to the Patriot side. Still others, perhaps a majority, remained loyal to the king even as they questioned the wisdom of his ministers' policies.

The Crowd Rebels

The American response to the Stamp Act was more drastic than Grenville had predicted. Disciplined mobs led by men who called themselves the Sons of Liberty demanded the resignation of newly appointed stamp-tax collectors, most of whom were native-born colonists. One of the first incidents took place in Boston in August 1765, when the Boston Sons of Liberty made an effigy of the collector Andrew Oliver, which they beheaded and burned before destroying a new brick building that he owned. Boston merchants who opposed the Stamp Act advised Oliver to resign; otherwise "his House would be immediately destroyed and his Life in Continual Danger." Two weeks later Bostonians attacked the house of Lieutenant Governor Thomas Hutchinson. As a defender of social privilege and imperial authority, Hutchinson had many enemies. Now, in the heat of crisis, the common people took their revenge by destroying his house and burning his library.

In nearly every colony similar crowds of angry but purposeful people—the "rabble," as their American and

A British View of American Mobs
The artist depicts the Sons of Liberty as sadists, subjecting a British excise officer to physical abuse, and as wanton destroyers of property, dumping tea into the harbor. The Liberty Tree in the background raises the question: Does Liberty mean Anarchy?

British detractors called them—intimidated royal officials. Near Wethersfield, Connecticut, 500 farmers and artisans confronted the tax collector Jared Ingersoll. Ingersoll had been born into a prominent Connecticut family and had served as the assembly's agent in London. He had worked actively against the Stamp Act, but once it passed, he sought to profit from it by becoming a tax collector. Confronted by the fruits of that decision, Ingersoll debated with the leaders of the crowd for hours, but they refused to be swayed by his previous service to the colony or his high social status. An observer heard one rioter shout that he "lookt upon this as the Cause of the People" and would not "take Directions about it from any Body." Ingersoll finally capitulated. At the behest of the mob, he gave three cheers for "Liberty and Property," tossed his hat into the air, and, humbled, resigned from his office.

Motives of the Crowds. The strength of the Liberty mobs was surprising, but such crowd actions were a fact of political life in both Britain and America. For example, Protestant mobs burned the pope in effigy every November 5 to celebrate the failure of Guy Fawkes, a Catholic, to overturn the English government in 1605. Colonial mobs regularly destroyed houses used as brothels and often expressed anti-imperial sentiments. In 1747 Boston crowds rioted for three days to protest the impressment of merchant seamen for service in the Royal Navy. The crowds protesting the Stamp Act were simply acting according to tradition—beheading an effigy of Oliver reenacted the ritual killing of the pope on Guy Fawkes Day, and destroying Hutchinson's dwelling recalled attacks on houses of prostitution (see American Voices, page 146).

The social composition of the rioters was as traditional as their behavior, for premodern mobs usually represented a cross section of the middle and lower orders of society. Most Sons of Liberty were property-owning artisans who had previously known each other in jobs, churches, or neighborhoods. For example, of the thirty-six young men who formed the Sons of Liberty of Albany, New York, in 1765, twenty belonged to the same firefighter's club and twelve sat together in the balcony of the Dutch Reformed Church. The crowds themselves—which usually numbered in the hundreds and occasionally reached a few thousand—were more diverse. Seeking adventure and excitement, young apprentices and journeymen marched with their artisan masters, as did day laborers and unemployed sailors, the "rabble" of the port cities.

What distinguished the Stamp Act rioters were the motives of many of the participants. Some urban artisans joined the Liberty mobs out of economic self-interest. Imports of low-priced British shoes and other products were threatening their livelihood, and they feared that the stamp tax would lower their standard of living further—for the benefit of a rich governing class in Britain and America. Unlike "the Common people of England," a well-traveled colonist observed, "the people of America . . . never would submitt to be taxed that a few may be loaded with palaces and Pensions and riot in Luxury and Excess, while they themselves cannot support themselves and their needy offspring with Bread."

The religious passions aroused by the Great Awakening were another source of popular resistance. Some skilled workers were evangelical Protestants who led disciplined, hardworking lives, and they resented the arrogance and immorality of many British officers and the corrupt behavior of many royal bureaucrats. The image of the greedy British official seeking only the "gratification of his private Passions" loomed large in the pages of the *Independent Reflector*, a Real Whig newspaper published in New York during the 1750s.

Still other artisans had carried over from Britain the antimonarchical sentiments of the seventeenth-century Puritan revolution. A letter sent to a Boston newspaper promising to save "all the Freeborn Sons of America" from "tyrannical ministers" was signed "Oliver Cromwell." Other letters and handbills signed "O.C." threatened British officials and sympathizers with violence. The cry of "Liberty and Property" forced on Jared Ingersoll echoed ideological resistance to the taxes imposed by the Stuart kings. Thus, traditional fears of tyrannical power merged with economic self-interest and religious passion to create a potent anti-imperial outlook among the artisans and workers of the colonial cities.

Growing Popular Resistance. When the Stamp Act went into effect on November 1, 1765, most influential Americans advocated nonviolent resistance. In New York City, 200 merchants announced a boycott, vowing not to import British goods. Traders in Boston and Philadelphia quickly followed their example, but popular resentment against British policy was not easily contained. In New York less prosperous merchants such as Isaac Sears mobilized shopkeepers, tradesmen, artisans, laborers, and seamen in a mass protest meeting. They marched through the streets, breaking streetlamps and windows and crying "Liberty!" On November 2 nearly 3,000 New Yorkers joined a mob that plundered the house of an unpopular British officer and surrounded Fort George, where the tax stamps were stored, threatening to seize and destroy them.

On Guy Fawkes Day, November 5, Lieutenant Governor Cadwallader Colden feared an open assault on the fort and called on General Gage to use his small military force against the crowd. But the British commander refused. "Fire from the Fort might disperse the Mob, but it would not quell them," he told Colden, "and the consequence would in all appearances be an Insurrection, the Commencement of Civil War." Colden had to surrender the tax stamps.

Popular resistance nullified the Stamp Act throughout the colonies. Frightened collectors distributed few stamps to angry Americans, and royal officials and judges were at a loss. Slow communications across the Atlantic meant that the ministry's response to the riots would not be known until the following spring. In the meantime officials had to accept legal documents without the stamps.

The popular revolt of 1765 not only repudiated British authority but also gave a democratic cast to the emerging sense of American political identity. "Nothing is wanting but your own Resolution," a New York Son of Liberty declared during the upheaval, "for great is the Authority and Power of the People." Royal officials could no longer count on the deferential behavior that had ensured political stability for three generations. "What can a Governor do without the assistance of the

William Almy

A Stamp Act Riot, 1765

The Sons of Liberty attacked stamp-tax collectors in many cities, including Newport, Rhode Island. This letter describes the rituals observed by the Newport mob and the political awareness of its leaders (the devil-infested "Boot" is a satiric reference to Lord Bute, the prime minister from 1761 to 1763). It also suggests the high emotional and material price paid by those who opposed the Patriots by speaking and writing in defense of the Stamp Act.

In the morning of the 27th Inst. between five and six a Mob Assembled and Erected a Gallows near the Town House and then Dispers'd, and about Ten A Clock Reassembled and took

The Effigys of the Above Men and the Stamp Master and Carted them up Thames Street, then up King Street to the said Gallows where they was hung up by the Neck and Suspended near 15 feet in the Air, And on the Breast of the Stamp Master, was this Inscription THE STAMP MAN . . . and upon the Breast of the Doct'r was write, THAT INFAMOUS, MISCREATED, LEERING JACOBITE DOCT'R MURFY. . . . And about five A Clock in the Afternoon they made a Fire under the Gallows which Consum'd the Effigy's, Gallows and all, to Ashes. I forgot to tell you that a Boot hung over the Doctor's Shoulder with the Devil Peeping out of it. . . .

We thought it was all over. But last Night about Dusk they all Muster'd Again, and first they went to Martin Howard's, and Broke Every Window in his house, Frames and all, likewise Chairs Tables, Pictures and every thing they cou'd come across. . . .

This Moment I'v Rec'd a Peace of News which Effects me so Much that I Cant write any More, which is the Demolition of your worthy Daddy's house and Furniture etc. But I must just let you know that the Stamp Master has Resign'd. . . .

Source: William Almy to Dr. Elisha Story, *Proceedings of the Massachusetts Historical Society*, vol. 55 (1921-1922), pp. 235–236.

Governed?" the Philadelphia customs collector lamented. The Stamp Act crisis of 1765 eroded the emotional foundations of power and left the British government on the defensive in America.

Ideological Roots of Resistance

Merchants and Lawyers Take the Lead. The American resistance movement began in the seaport cities, and for good reason. Urban residents—artisans, merchants, and lawyers—were directly affected by British policies. The Stamp Act taxed city-based products and services, such as newspapers and legal documents. The Sugar Act and the accompanying customs reform raised the cost of molasses to urban merchants and distillers, while the Currency Act complicated their trade and financial transactions. To make matters worse, beginning in the early 1750s, British firms had begun to sell goods directly to colonial shopkeepers at special auction sales, bypassing American mercantile houses and cutting their profits. The combination of British governmental regulation and business competition undermined the merchants' loyalty to the empire. As an official in Rhode Island reported in 1765, the interests of Britain and the colonies were increasingly "deemed

by the People almost altogether incompatible in a Commercial View."

American lawyers were prominent in mobilizing public opinion against the British. In part, the lawyers reflected the views of the merchants who hired them to prevent seizure of their ships by zealous customs officials or vice-admiralty judges. But their own professional values also prompted lawyers to contest the legality of various imperial measures. When the Board of Trade changed the terms of appointment for colonial judges from "during good behavior" to "at the pleasure" of the royal governor, lawyers protested that the new procedure compromised the independence of the judiciary. American lawyers also opposed the extension of vice-admiralty courts; as men trained in English common law, they favored trial by jury. A deep respect for established institutions ultimately led many older lawyers to remain loyal to the Crown, but young lawyers embraced the revolutionary cause; of the fifty-six men who signed the Declaration of Independence in 1776, twenty-five were lawyers.

As merchants and lawyers debated political and constitutional issues in taverns and coffeehouses, on street corners, and in public meetings, they broadened the terms of debate. Initially they argued for particularistic "liberties and privileges" embodied in colonial

charters or political traditions. But they also drew on the works of seventeenth-century English philosophers such as Thomas Hobbes, James Harrington, and John Locke, who had advanced the concept of natural rights; the French theorists Montesquieu and Voltaire, who argued against the arbitrary exercise of political power; and the Scottish Enlightenment thinkers David Hume and Frances Hutcheson, who advocated skeptical philosophical inquiry.

Influenced by an emerging Enlightenment tradition, the arguments of the American urban elite took on a more universal cast. Liberty became more an abstract ideal than a set of historical privileges. Pamphlets of remarkable political sophistication circulated throughout the colonies, providing the resistance movement with an intellectual rationale and a political agenda. This urban-based political agitation swayed the outlook of men from rural communities, who dominated the American assemblies numerically, and encouraged them to make a principled defense of American rights.

Intellectual Traditions. Educated colonists drew on three intellectual traditions to build their arguments. The first was English common law, the centuries-old body of legal rules and procedures that protected the king's subjects against arbitrary acts by other subjects or by the government. As early as 1761 James Otis of Boston had cited English legal precedents in the famous Writs of Assistance case, disputing the constitutionality of a general search warrant that permitted customs officials to inspect the property and possessions of any person. Similarly, when John Hancock, an influential Boston merchant, was accused of smuggling, his young lawyer, John Adams, used common-law principles to demand a jury trial. "This 29th Chap. of Magna Charta" respecting jury trials, Adams argued in a legal treatise of 1765, "has for many Centuries been esteemed by Englishmen, as one of the noblest Monuments, one of the firmest Bulwarks of their Liberties." An essential argument of Otis, Adams, and other New England lawyers was that customary or common-law rights could not be abridged by parliamentary statutes. The Georgia assembly took a similar position. Although there were only twenty-nine British soldiers in the colony, it refused on principle to comply with the Quartering Act to prevent establishing "a precedent they by no means think justifiable." Because the colonists' "essential rights as British subjects" were being violated, such resistance was imperative.

A second major intellectual resource for educated Americans was the rationalism cultivated during the Enlightenment. Unlike common-law attorneys, who valued precedent and venerated the ways of the past, Enlightenment philosophers questioned the past and appealed to reason to discover and correct the ills of so-

Sam Adams, Boston Agitator
This painting by John Singleton Copley, *Samuel Adams* (circa 1772), shows the radical Patriot pointing to the Massachusetts Charter of 1692, suggesting that "charter rights" accounted for Adams's opposition to British policies. But Adams also was influenced by the natural rights tradition.

ciety. Most Enlightenment thinkers followed John Locke in believing that all individuals possessed certain "natural rights"—such as life, liberty, and property—and that it was the responsibility of government to protect those rights. For many educated colonists this belief provided an intellectual justification for resistance to British authority. Samuel Adams, John's cousin and a radical Patriot, asked rhetorically if it was "lawful to resist the Supreme Magistrate, if the Commonwealth cannot be otherwise preserved" and used arguments based on the individual's natural rights to justify the Stamp Act uprising.

English political tradition provided a third ideological basis for the American Patriot movement. Some Americans, particularly those in Puritan New England, venerated the Commonwealth era, the brief period between 1649 and 1660 when England was a republic. These republicans joined with members of the provincial assemblies in applauding the Glorious Revolution of 1688 and the various constitutional restrictions placed on the monarchy by the English Whigs, such as the ban on royally imposed taxes. Subsequently, many educated

Americans absorbed the arguments of Real Whig spokesmen such as John Trenchard and Thomas Gordon (the authors of *Cato's Letters*), who attacked the power of government financiers and condemned the idea of standing armies. Well-informed colonists also joined in criticizing Walpole and his successors as politically corrupt. "Bribery is so common," John Dickinson of Pennsylvania noted during a visit to London in the 1750s, "that there is not a borough in England where it is not practiced." This critical Real Whig view of British politics predisposed many Americans to distrust any attempt at imperial reform. Joseph Warren, a Boston physician and Patriot, reported that many townspeople thought the Stamp Act was intended "to force the colonies into rebellion," after which the ministry would use "military power to reduce them to servitude."

The rhetoric was exaggerated, but the charges had a basis in fact. British administrative reform threatened the interests of many Americans. The Proclamation Line of 1763, for example, protected Indian peoples by curbing the activities of white land speculators, fur traders, and westward migrants. In 1764 the Sugar Act extended the jurisdiction of the vice-admiralty courts, and in 1765 the Stamp Act imposed British taxes directly on Americans. Finally, Britain's growing economic presence threatened the colonists' sense of control over their financial lives. It seemed to one pamphleteer that Americans were being compelled to give the British "our money, as oft and in what quantity they please to demand it."

Many Americans viewed these events narrow-mindedly as threats to their self-interest, but common-law attorneys, natural-rights theorists, and Real Whig critics of ministerial policy stated their objections in broad philosophical terms. Their ideological statements endowed colonial opposition to British control with high moral significance, turning a series of particularistic tax protests into a broad resistance movement.

The Informal Compromise of 1766

While mobs protested in the streets, opposition-minded politicians sharpened their arguments in the assemblies. In May 1765 the eloquent young Virginian Patrick Henry urged the House of Burgesses to condemn the Stamp Act. Conservative Burgesses silenced Henry when the young orator compared George III to Charles I and seemed to call for a new Oliver Cromwell to seize power in Britain. However, the Burgesses endorsed many of his resolutions, declaring that any attempt to tax the colonists without their consent "has a manifest Tendency to Destroy AMERICAN FREEDOM." More significantly, the Stamp Act provoked the first effort by the colonial assemblies to speak with one voice. Even before the Burgesses' resolutions reached Boston, the

Patrick Henry, A Great Orator
Henry drew on evangelical Protestantism to create a new mode of political oratory. "His figures of speech . . . were often borrowed from the Scriptures," a contemporary noted, while his style and speech conveyed "the earnestness depicted in his own features."

Massachusetts House of Representatives had called for a meeting of the colonies in New York in October to consider a "loyal and humble representation" to the king and Parliament "to implore Relief."

Nine colonial assemblies sent delegates to the Stamp Act Congress. As politicians trained in the art of compromise, the twenty-eight delegates did not threaten to rebel but devised a set of Stamp Act Resolves that contested the constitutionality of the Stamp and Sugar acts. The Resolves declared that only the colonists' elected representatives could impose taxes on them and that because of their distance from Britain and their distinct interests, Americans could not be represented in the House of Commons. The delegates protested strongly against the loss of American "rights and liberties," especially trial by jury. Then, assuring Parliament that Americans "glory in being subjects of the best of Kings having been born under the most perfect form of government," the delegates humbly petitioned for repeal of the Stamp Act.

TABLE 5.1

Ministerial Instability in Britain

Leading Minister	Dates of Ministry	American Policy
Lord Bute	1760–1763	Mildly reformist
George Grenville	1763–1765	Ardently reformist
Lord Rockingham	1765–1766	Accommodationist
William Pitt/ Charles Townshend	1766–1770	Ardently reformist
Lord North	1770–1782	Coercive

The Stamp Act Resolves were received by a Parliament in turmoil. George III had lost confidence in Grenville (because of issues unrelated to the Stamp Act) and had replaced him as prime minister with Lord Rockingham (see Table 5.1). For Americans, Rockingham was an ideal prime minister. Young, inexperienced, and open to persuasion, he led a party of Old Whigs hostile to Grenville's American policies. Indeed, the Rockingham Whigs stood for the earlier policy of salutary neglect, believing that America was important as a source of "flourishing and increasing trade" that added to the national wealth, not as a source of tax revenue. Some Old Whigs even agreed with the colonists that the new tax was unconstitutional. Lord Camden, chief justice of the Court of Common Pleas, told his Parliamentary colleagues that "taxation and representation are inseparably united" and concluded, "I can never give my assent to any bill for taxing the American colonies while they remain unrepresented."

British merchants also favored the colonists' cause. The decision by most American traders not to import British goods had caused a drastic fall in sales, and Britain had large inventories of goods on hand. "The Avenues of Trade are all shut up," a Bristol merchant complained. "We have no Remittances and are at our Witts End for want of Money to fulfill our Engagements with our Tradesmen." In January 1766 the leading commercial centers of London, Liverpool, Bristol, and Glasgow deluged Parliament with petitions, arguing that as a result of the colonial boycott, the Stamp Act threatened British prosperity.

Neither this argument nor those of the Old Whigs persuaded the members of Parliament who were outraged by the popular rebellion in America. These hard-liners demanded that substantial numbers of British soldiers be sent to the seaport cities to suppress the riots and that Americans submit to the constitutional supremacy of Parliament. "The British legislature," declared Chief Justice Sir James Mansfield, "has authority to bind every part and every subject, whether such subjects have a right to vote or not." He insisted that the ministry discipline the upstart colonists, warning that "when the supreme power abdicates, the government is dissolved."

William Pitt, pro-American in sentiment yet firmly committed to British national power, devised yet a third, more ambiguous, response to the American resistance movement. Stating that Parliament had no right to tax the colonies, Pitt demanded that "the Stamp Act be repealed absolutely, totally, and immediately," but at the same time he acknowledged that British authority over America was "sovereign and supreme, in every circumstance of government and legislation whatsoever."

Rockingham tried to reconcile these conflicting opinions and factions. First, to mollify colonial opinion and assist British merchants, he secured the repeal of the Stamp Act. He also instructed army commanders in the colonies not to use troops against the crowds, and he refused to send additional troops to the seaport cities. Next, Rockingham fashioned a compromise to change the Sugar Act: he reduced the duty on French molasses from 3 pence to 1 penny a gallon, but he risked another constitutional confrontation by applying the duty to imports of British molasses as well. Thus, the revised Sugar Act not only regulated foreign trade, which most American politicians accepted, but also raised revenue through a tax on a British product, which some colonists challenged as unconstitutional. Rockingham sharpened the constitutional debate—and pacified imperial reformers and hard-liners—with the Declaratory Act of 1766, which explicitly reaffirmed

Mixing Business and Politics, 1766
Hurt by the colonists' trade boycott, British manufacturers campaigned for repeal of the Stamp Act. To celebrate the repeal—and expand the market for its teapots in America—the Cockpit Hill factory in Derby quickly produced a commemorative design.

Eliza Lucas Pinckney

The Wedding of George III, 1762

As a young woman, Eliza Lucas (1722–1793) won acclaim for producing indigo dye in South Carolina. In 1744 she married Charles Pinckney (1699–1758), an influential Charleston lawyer and politician, and from 1753 to 1758 she lived with him in London, where she left her two sons to continue their education. A member of the Anglo-American elite, Mrs. Pinckney in 1762 expressed a natural loyalty to Britain and great curiosity about "my Sovereign and his Consort," King George III and his bride, Charlotte Sophia of Mecklenburg. And she acknowledged the great tax burdens assumed by her British friends. Beginning in the late 1760s her allegiance to the empire slowly waned. By 1775 Mrs. Pinckney supported Patriot calls for independence, and her sons became leaders of the rebellion.

How, dear Madam, could you think of this remote spott in the midsts of the splendour of Royal Weddings, Coronations, Gay Courts and the attendant cheerfulness that must follow in their train long after. . . .

You cant think how many people you have gratified by your obliging me with so particular a discription of the Queen. We had no picture of her Majesty nor discription that could be depended upon till I received your favour. . . . If, Madam, you have ever been witness to the impatience of the people of England about a hundred mile from London to be made acquainted with what passes there, you may guess a little at what our impatience is here when I inform you that the curiosity increases with the distance from the Center of affairs; and our impatience is not to be equaled with any peoples within four thousand mile.

In half an hour after I was favoured with a vizet from our new Gov., Mr. B[oone], lately arrived here from his former Government in the Jerseys, who I found (tho' he has an extensive good acquaintance in England) knew as little of the New Queen as we did here. I had the pleasure to read him also the discription. . . . On the whole I am a very Loyal Subject and had my share of Joy in the agreeable account of my Sovereign and his Consort.

When, my Dear Madam, shall we have peace? Till then I have little prospect of seeing my Children and friends in England; and a Spanish warr we are told is unavoidable. We are pretty quiet here just now, but 'tis much feared it will continue no longer than the winter. We never was so taxed in our lives, but what is our taxes to yours [?]. However, we are a young Colony and our Seas does not throw up sands of gold, as surely the British does to enable you to bear such prodigious Expences.

Source: The *Letterbook of Eliza Lucas Pinckney, 1739–1762*, edited by Elise Pinckney (University of North Carolina Press, 1972), 174–176.

---

the "full power and authority" of the British Parliament to "bind the colonies and people of America in all cases whatsoever."

Despite these strong words, the Stamp Act crisis ended in an informal compromise. The Americans had won an important victory. Their riots, boycott, and petitions had secured repeal of the hated tax. Yet Grenville and other advocates of imperial reform also triumphed. In a showdown with the provincial assemblies they had obtained a statement of Parliamentary supremacy. Rockingham's compromise gave each side just enough to claim victory. And because the confrontation had ended quickly, it seemed possible that it might be forgotten even more quickly. The constitutional status of the American provinces remained uncertain, but political positions had not yet hardened. Leaders of goodwill could still hope to work out an imperial relationship acceptable to both sides (see American Voices, above).

The Growing Confrontation, 1767–1770

The compromise of 1766 was short-lived. Within a year political rivalries in Britain sparked a new and more prolonged struggle with the American provinces over taxes. Economic self-interest and ideological rigidity on both sides of the Atlantic aggravated the conflict. Only after a lengthy commercial boycott and the threat of military action was a second compromise finally achieved.

The Townshend Initiatives

Often the course of history is changed by a small event—a leader's illness, a personal grudge, a chance re-

mark. So it was in 1767, when Rockingham's Old Whig ministry collapsed and George III named William Pitt to head a new ministry. Pitt, the master strategist of the Great War for Empire, now sat in the House of Lords as the earl of Chatham, but he was chronically ill with gout. Because of Chatham's frequent absences from cabinet meetings and Parliamentary debates, Chancellor of the Exchequer Charles Townshend assumed command. Chatham was sympathetic toward America; Townshend was not. Since his service on the Board of Trade in the 1750s, Townshend had favored imperial reform; now he had the power to push it through.

What prompted Townshend to act was a chance confrontation with his longtime political rival George Grenville. As the chancellor presented the military budget to Parliament in 1767, Grenville rose from his seat to demand that the colonists pay for the British troops in America. Grenville's challenge put Townshend on the defensive, and he made an unplanned, fateful policy decision. Convinced of the necessity of imperial reform and eager to reduce the English land tax, Townshend promised that he would find a new source of revenue in America.

The new tax legislation, known as the Townshend Act of 1767, imposed duties on paper, paint, glass, and tea imported into the colonies. The tax was expected to raise between £35,000 and £40,000 a year—a small sum but one that Townshend was determined to use shrewdly. To mollify Grenville, he allocated part of the revenue for military expenses, but he reserved the major part "to defray the costs of Civil Government"—that is, to pay the salaries of governors, judges, and other imperial officials.

Townshend's initiative was intended to change the political balance of power in the colonies. He wanted to free royal officials from financial dependence on the American legislatures, enabling them to enforce Parliamentary laws and royal directives and depriving the colonial assemblies of much of their political leverage. To enhance the power of the royal bureaucracy, Townshend devised the Revenue Act of 1767, reorganizing the Customs Service. The new act created a Board of American Customs Commissioners in Boston and four vice-admiralty courts, in Halifax, Boston, Philadelphia, and Charleston. These administrative innovations were far-reaching and posed a greater threat to American autonomy than did the small sums raised by the import duties.

In fact, Townshend's overriding concern was to diminish the powers of the American representative assemblies, and events in New York gave him a chance. As in Georgia, the New York assembly had refused to comply with the Quartering Act of 1765, which required the lodging of British troops. Fearing an unlimited drain on its treasury, the New York legislature initially denied General Gage's requests for barracks and supplies and later limited its assistance to the housing of two infantry battalions and one artillery company. The struggle intensified when the ministry instructed the New Yorkers to assume complete financial responsibility for defense against Indian attacks. If the New York assembly refused, some members of Parliament were ready to impose an extra port duty on New York imports and exports to raise the needed funds.

The secretary of state, William Petty, earl of Shelburne, came up with a stronger, more coercive set of policies. He suggested a military governor for New York, with authority to seize funds from the colony's treasury to quarter the troops and "to act with Force or Gentleness as circumstances might make necessary." Ultimately, Townshend decided on a less provocative measure, pushing through Parliament the so-called Restraining Act of 1767, which suspended the New York assembly until it submitted to the Quartering Act. Faced with the loss of self-government, the New Yorkers finally gave in. They appropriated funds to support the resident military garrison and defend themselves against Indian attacks.

The Restraining Act was an important innovation. The British Privy Council had always supervised the colonial assemblies, over the decades invalidating about 5 percent of all colonial laws—such as those establishing land banks or vesting new powers in the assemblies—as contrary to British laws or policy. The Restraining Act was a much more powerful administrative weapon because it threatened not just particular laws but the existence of the lawmaking body itself. Townshend, like his critic Grenville, was determined to tax the colonists and subordinate their representative political institutions to Parliamentary authority.

America Again Resists

The debate on the Townshend duties, which most American public officials condemned as unconstitutional, hinged superficially on a distinction between "internal" and "external" taxes. In response to the Stamp Act, Daniel Dulany, a conservative Maryland lawyer, had suggested that Americans would accept external duties on trade even as they opposed internal taxes. Benjamin Franklin had made essentially the same argument to the House of Commons in seeking repeal of the Stamp Act. Colonists would more readily accept higher prices for molasses and rum arising from duties on imported goods, he argued, than they would agree to the directly collected taxes of the Stamp Act. Townshend thought that this distinction between internal and external taxes amounted to "perfect nonsense," but he told Parliament that "since Americans were pleased to make that distinction, he was willing to indulge them [and] . . . to confine himself to regulations of Trade."

In reality, only a few colonial leaders saw any difference between internal taxes and external duties; the majority agreed with John Dickinson, author of *Letters from a Farmer in Pennsylvania* (1768), that the real issue was the intention or goal of the legislation. Because the Townshend duties were not designed to regulate trade but to bring revenue to the imperial government, they amounted to taxes imposed without consent. As Dickinson sarcastically declared, "I think it evident that we *must* use paper and glass; that what we use *must* be *British*; and that we *must* pay the duties imposed, unless those who sell these articles are so generous as to make us presents of the duties they pay."

The Massachusetts House of Representatives took the lead in opposing the new duties. In February 1768 it sent a letter to other assemblies condemning the Townshend Act for infringing on the colonists' "natural & constitutional Rights." This initiative received a lukewarm response, primarily because the American merchant community was divided. To pressure Parliament to repeal the legislation, Boston merchants began a new boycott of British imports in April 1768; New York traders followed suit in August. Philadelphia merchants, however, refused to join the boycott because they were more heavily involved in direct trade with Britain and believed that they had too much to lose. Philadelphia's sailors and dockworkers supported this decision, for they also feared that a lengthy boycott would ruin them financially. In Pennsylvania, therefore, protests were confined to words, with residents encouraging the assembly to petition the king for repeal of the Townshend duties.

Nonimportation. In 1768, unlike 1765, many Americans questioned the wisdom of a nonimportation strategy. Nonetheless, public support for the boycott gradually spread from Boston and New York to smaller port cities, such as Salem, Newport, and Baltimore, and into the countryside. In Puritan New England ministers and public officials supported nonimportation by condemning "luxury and dissipation" and decrying the use of "foreign superfluities." They discouraged reliance on imported goods and promoted the domestic manufacture of necessities such as cloth and paper.

American women, especially religious women, added their support to the nonimportation movement. Ordinarily women were excluded from prominent roles in public affairs; in times of religious and social upheaval, such as the Great Awakening or a severe shortage of food, a few women would emerge as prophets or preachers or would lead a mob, demanding that shopkeepers provide reasonably priced grain. But the boycotts prompted a more sustained involvement by women in the public world. During the crisis over the Stamp Act groups of young women with ties to Patriot leaders declared their support for the American cause.

For example, in Providence, Rhode Island, in March 1766, "eighteen daughters of liberty, young ladies of good reputation," met to spin yarn, declaring that they would not purchase British manufactures. The contest over the Townshend duties elicited support from a much broader group, religious women in New England, who organized spinning matches, bees, and demonstrations at the homes of their ministers. Some gatherings were openly patriotic, such as that at Berwick, Maine, where the spinners, "as true Daughters of Liberty," celebrated American goods, "drinking rye coffee and dining on bear venison." But many more combined support for nonimportation with the fulfillment of social obligations and charitable work by gathering to spin flax and wool, which they donated to their ministers and needy members of the community. Just as the tradition of crowd actions influenced men's response to the imperial crisis, so women's concerns with the well-being of their communities guided their efforts.

Ultimately, the efforts of patriotic young ladies and religious women prompted thousands of other women to redouble their efforts at the spinning wheel and the loom and won broad public support. Newspapers celebrated these patriotic heroines, whose production of "homespun" cloth made America less dependent on British textile imports, which totaled about 10 million yards a year. It was a newsworthy event when the women of the Freeman, Smith, and Heard families of Woodbridge, New Jersey, announced that they had attained an annual household output of 500 yards. Town-wide production was also a source of pride. One Massachusetts town claimed an annual output of 30,000 yards of cloth; East Hartford, Connecticut, reported 17,000 yards.

The men of Boston and New York had other methods of promoting nonimportation. The Sons of Liberty published the names of merchants who refused to comply with the boycott, broke their store windows, and harassed their employees. In Charleston, South Carolina, the merchant Christopher Gadsden joined the Liberty Boys and helped persuade his fellow traders to support the boycott. But in many seaports merchants deeply resented the crowd's attacks on their reputations and property. Fearing mob rule, they condemned nonimportation and stood by the royal governors.

Despite this split between radical Patriots and future Loyalists, the boycott gathered momentum, uniting thousands of Americans in a common political movement. In March 1769, responding to public pressure, most Philadelphia merchants finally stopped importing British goods. Two months later the members of the Virginia House of Burgesses agreed not to buy dutied articles, British luxuries, or slaves. "The whole continent from New England to Georgia seems firmly fixed," the Massachusetts *Gazette* proudly announced; "like a strong, well-constructed arch, the more weight there is

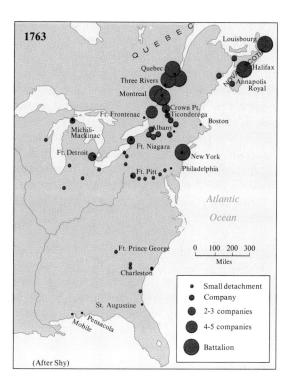

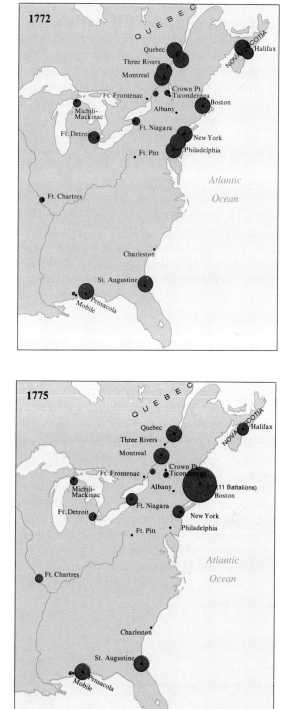

laid upon it, the firmer it stands; and thus with America, the more we are loaded, the more we are united." Reflecting colonial self-confidence, Benjamin Franklin called for a return to the pre-1763 imperial system. "It is easy to propose a plan of conciliation," Franklin declared: "*repeal* the laws, *renounce* the right, *recall* the troops, *refund* the money, and *return* to the old method of requisition."

Britain Responds. The home authorities had something very different in mind. The boycott and crowd violence had exhausted their patience. When a copy of the Massachusetts House's letter opposing the Townshend duties reached London in mid-1768, Lord Hillsborough, the secretary of state for American affairs, branded it as "unjustifiable opposition to the constitutional authority of Parliament." He told Governor Francis Bernard to dissolve the House if it refused to rescind its action. Hillsborough backed up his words by dispatching four regiments of troops to Boston to strengthen the "Hand of Government," particularly the hand of the customs commissioners, who had been forced by a mob of furious Bostonians protesting the seizure of John Hancock's ship *Liberty* on a smuggling charge to take refuge on the British warship *Romney*. Hillsborough's main goal was not to prevent smuggling along the seacoast but to prepare for an armed showdown with the radical Boston Patriots.

By the end of 1768 a thousand British regulars were encamped in Boston, and military coercion was a very real prospect (see Map 5.2). General Gage accused Massachusetts public leaders of "Treasonable and des-

MAP 5.2

British Troop Deployments, 1763–1775

As the imperial crisis deepened, British military priorities changed. In 1763 most British battalions (the large circles represent 350 men) were stationed in Canada to deter Indian attacks and French-Canadian revolts. After the Stamp Act riots of 1765, the British established larger garrisons in New York and Philadelphia. By 1775 eleven battalions of British regulars occupied Boston, the center of the American Patriot movement.

perate Resolves" and advised the ministry to "Quash this Spirit at a Blow." Parliament threatened to appoint a special commission to hear evidence of treason. King George supported Hillsborough's plan to repeal the Townshend duties in all the colonies except Massachusetts, thus isolating the agitators, and then use the British army to bring the rebellious New Englanders to their knees.

The stakes had risen. In 1765, American resistance to taxation had provoked an argument in Parliament; in 1768, it produced a plan for military coercion.

The Second Compromise

At this critical moment the British ministry's resolve faltered. Britain was having domestic problems. Poor harvests caused a food shortage in 1768, and riots swept the countryside. Mobs protested against high prices and raided supplies of grain and bread. In the highly publicized "Massacre of Saint George Fields," troops killed seven demonstrators. Opposition politicians exploited the situation and called for a new ministry. Supported by associations composed of merchants, tradesmen, and artisans (who resented corrupt aristocratic government) the Radical Whig John Wilkes stepped up his attacks on government corruption and won election to Parliament. American Patriots identified with Wilkes, drank toasts in his honor, and purchased thousands of teapots and drinking mugs that carried his picture. They followed events apprehensively as on four occasions the ministry denied Wilkes his seat when the popular leader was elected, and reelected, to Parliament in 1768 and 1769. Riots in Ireland over the growing military budget there added to the ministry's difficulties.

The American trade boycott also began to hurt. Normally the mainland colonies had an annual deficit of £500,000 in their trade with Great Britain, but in 1768 they imported far fewer goods, cutting the deficit to £230,000. In 1769 the boycott had a major impact on the British economy (see Figure 5.2). By continuing to export tobacco, rice, fish, and other goods to Britain while refusing to buy its manufactured goods, Americans accumulated a huge trade surplus of £816,000. To revive their flagging fortunes, British merchants and industrialists petitioned Parliament for repeal of the Townshend duties. The decline in manufacturing and trade also bit deeply into government revenues, since no less than 68 percent came from excise taxes and duties on exports and imports.

The Crisis Resolved. By late 1769 the threat of military coercion seemed to have passed. Merchants' petitions had persuaded some ministers that the Townshend duties were a mistake, and the king no longer supported Hillsborough's plan to punish the Massachusetts Patriots. Early in 1770 Lord North became prime minister, and he pointed out that it was "contrary to the true principles of commerce" for Britain to tax its own exports to America, because the goal of mercantilism was to encourage the consumption of British products in the colonies. North arranged a compromise by which Parliament repealed the Townshend Act's duties on glass, paper, paint, and other manufactured items but retained the tax on tea as a symbol of Parliament's supremacy. This stratagem worked. In a spirit of goodwill (and to restore their own flagging fortunes), merchants in New York and Philadelphia rejected pleas from Patriots in Boston to continue the boycott. Most Americans did not insist on strict adherence to their constitutional principles, contesting neither the duty on British molasses required by the Sugar Act of 1766 nor the symbolic tax on tea. They simply avoided paying those taxes by smuggling and bribing customs agents.

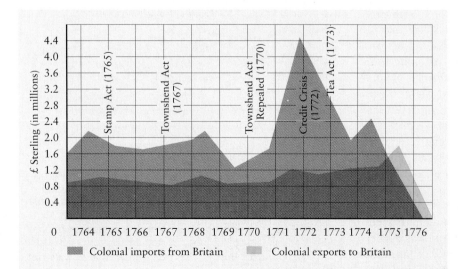

FIGURE 5.2

Trade as a Political Weapon, 1763–1776

Political upheaval did not affect the mainland colonies' exports to Britain, which rose slightly over the period, but imports fluctuated greatly. The American boycott of 1768–1769 brought a sharp fall in the importation of British manufactures, which then soared after the repeal of the Townshend duties.

John Wilkes, British Radical
Wilkes won fame as the author of *North Briton, Number 45*, a pamphlet that called for political reform in Britain. At a dinner in Boston, Radical Whigs raised their glasses to Wilkes—toasting him 45 times!

Not even a new outbreak of violence in New York City and Boston in 1770 could disrupt the spirit of compromise. During the boycott New York artisans and workers had taunted British regulars in the resident garrison, mostly with words but occasionally with stones and fists. In January 1770 the troops responded by tearing down a Liberty Pole in front of a tavern, setting off a week of sporadic street fighting—the Golden Hill riots—in which both sides suffered only minor injuries. In Boston, where a much larger group of British soldiers competed with townsmen for the favor of local women and for part-time jobs, tensions came to a head in the "Boston Massacre" of March 1770. A mob of laborers and seamen attacked a group of soldiers, who fired into the crowd, killing five men, including one of the leaders—Crispus Attucks, a mulatto who had escaped from slavery in Massachusetts in 1750 and worked as a seaman. Seeking to uphold the honor of Boston while condemning British policy, Patriot leaders played a double game. No less a Patriot than John Adams defended the soldiers in a Boston court, blaming the incident on "a motley rabble of saucy boys, negroes and mulattoes,

Irish teagues and outlandish jack tarrs," and won their acquittal. Simultaneously, another Patriot, James Bowdoin, wrote *A Short Narrative of the Horrid Massacre in Boston*, accusing the British of deliberately planning the killing. This pamphlet circulated widely in the colonies and inflamed public opinion against the imperial authorities.

Sovereignty Debated. Most Americans still remained loyal to the empire, but five years of conflict over taxes and constitutional principles had built ill will on both sides of the Atlantic. Even Lord Chatham thought the American merchants and assemblies had carried "their notions of freedom too far" and were unwilling, on a number of crucial issues, to "be subject to the laws of this country." Benjamin Franklin recognized that the colonies had repudiated the power of Parliament to impose taxes and had questioned other aspects of its authority as well. He wanted to redefine the imperial relationship, giving America political equality within the empire. Perhaps thinking of various European "composite monarchies" (in which kings ruled far-distant and semiautonomous provinces acquired by inheritance or conquest), Franklin suggested that the colonies were now "distinct and separate states" but ones that had "the same Head, or Sovereign, the King."

Thomas Hutchinson, the American-born royal governor of Massachusetts, was horrified at Franklin's proposal, rejecting the idea of "two independent legislatures in one and the same state." For Hutchinson, the British empire was a single entity, and sovereignty was indivisible—all or nothing. "I know of no line," he told the Massachusetts House of Representatives, "that can be drawn between the supreme authority of Parliament and the total independence of the colonies." But a House committee disagreed, adopting Franklin's position: if Britain and its American colonies were united by the king as their "one head and common sovereign," they could "live happily in that connection." (More than a century and a half later this idea would come to fruition in the British Commonwealth of Nations.)

The second crisis—and compromise—had significantly altered the terms of the debate. In 1765 American public leaders had accepted Parliament's authority. The Stamp Act Resolves had opposed only certain "unconstitutional" legislation. By 1770 the most outspoken Patriots—including Franklin, Patrick Henry of Virginia, and Samuel Adams and his followers in the Massachusetts House—had repudiated Parliament and claimed equality for their assemblies under the king. Nor did they flinch when reminded that George III condemned their agitation. As the Massachusetts House told Hutchinson, "There is more reason to dread the consequences of absolute uncontrolled supreme power, whether of a nation or a monarch, than those of total independence."

There the matter rested. The British had twice tried to impose taxes on the colonies, and American Patriots had twice forced them to retreat. It was now clear that if Parliament insisted on exercising its claim to sovereignty, at least some Americans would have to be subdued by force. Fearful of civil war, the ministry hesitated to take the final fateful step.

The Road to War, 1771–1775

The repeal of most of the Townshend duties in 1770 restored harmony to the British empire, and for the next three years most disputes were resolved peacefully or were confined to individual colonies. The continued existence of the empire seemed assured. Yet history moves in unpredictable ways, and below the surface lay strong fears and passions—and mutual distrust. Suddenly, in 1773, those undercurrents erupted, overwhelming any hope for compromise. In less than two years the Americans and the British stood on the brink of war.

The Tea Act

Parliament's repeal of the Townshend duties did not satisfy radical Patriots, who now wanted American independence. They kept the Boston Massacre vivid in public memory and exploited events—such as a British credit crisis in 1772, which caused economic distress in the colonies—to warn Americans about the dangers of imperial domination. In November 1772 Samuel Adams persuaded the Boston town meeting to establish a Committee of Correspondence "to state the Rights of the Colonists of this Province." Within a few months eighty Massachusetts towns had set up similar committees. This movement spread to other colonies when, in January 1773, the British government set up a royal commission to investigate an incident involving the *Gaspée*, a British customs vessel Rhode Island Patriots had burned in June 1772 to protest the diligence of its captain in enforcing the Navigation Acts. The royal commission's powers, particularly its authority to send Americans to Britain for trial, aroused Patriot sentiment. In Virginia the House of Burgesses created a Committee of Correspondence "to communicate with the other colonies" about the situation in Rhode Island. By July 1773 similar committees had sprung up in Connecticut, New Hampshire, and South Carolina.

The Compromise Overturned. However, the first link in the chain of events that led directly to war was Parliament's passage of a Tea Act in May 1773. The purpose of the act was to provide financial relief to the British East India Company, a royally chartered firm that was deeply in debt both because of mismanagement and because of the cost of military expeditions that extended British trade in India. The Tea Act provided a government loan to the company and, more important, eliminated the customs duties on the tea that it brought to Britain and then reexported to America. This provision cut costs for the East India Company, allowing it to undersell other British merchants, who had to pay the customs levies, and giving it a virtual monopoly of the provincial market.

Lord North knew that the Tea Act would be unpopular in America but failed to gauge just how unpopular it would be. Since 1768, when the Townshend Act had placed a duty of 3 pence a pound on tea, American traders had boycotted the British product, buying illegally imported tea from the Dutch instead. By the 1770s about 90 percent of the tea consumed in America was contraband. But the Tea Act would make East India Company tea cheaper than the smuggled Dutch tea, and American merchants and consumers in those circumstances might choose to buy the British tea and pay the 3-pence duty. Colonial opponents of the act charged that the ministry was bribing Americans to give up their principles; as an anonymous woman put it in the *Massachusetts Spy*, "the use of tea is considered not as a *private* but as a *public* evil . . . a handle to introduce a variety of . . . oppressions amongst us." This was exactly what North wanted. Like Grenville and Townshend before him, he was not content to declare Parliament's authority to tax the colonies—he wanted to demonstrate it.

North's insensitivity to the fragile state of the colonial relationship cost the empire dearly, for it revived American resistance. The East India Company decided to distribute the tea directly to shopkeepers in major American cities, a tactic that shocked colonial merchants. The Tea Act would not only eliminate the illegal Dutch trade but also cut American merchants out of the British tea business. "The fear of an Introduction of a Monopoly in this Country," General Haldimand reported from New York, "has induced the mercantile part of the Inhabitants to be very industrious in opposing this Step and added Strength to a Spirit of Independence already too prevalent."

The Committees of Correspondence took the lead in organizing resistance to the Tea Act. All along the seaboard the Sons of Liberty prevented East India Company ships from landing tea, forced the captains to return it to Britain or store it in public warehouses, and held public bonfires at which they persuaded their fellow citizens (sometimes gently, sometimes not) to consign their tea to the flames. By these means, Patriots effectively nullified the Tea Act.

The Boston Tea Party. In Boston events took a more ominous turn. For decades Massachusetts had stead-

fastly resisted British authority, and in the 1760s had assumed leadership of the anti-imperial movement. Boston lawyers James Otis and John Adams had raised the first constitutional objections to legislation enforcing imperial reform, Boston mobs were the first to oppose the Stamp Act, and Boston merchants such as John Hancock had led colonial opposition to the Townshend duties. As early as 1768 Bostonians had condemned the tax on tea as a devious plot by "the politicians who planned our ruin," and it was they who provoked the Boston Massacre two years later. Boston was destined to spark the final conflagration with Great Britain.

Chance also figured in this outcome. The governor of Massachusetts, Thomas Hutchinson, bitterly opposed the Patriots, and with good reason. Stamp Act rioters had looted his house; Benjamin Franklin and Boston Patriots had smeared his reputation by stealing and publishing his private correspondence; and the Massachusetts House had condemned his defense of Parliamentary power. A combination of personal grudges and constitutional principles made Hutchinson determined to uphold the Tea Act.

The governor had a scheme to collect the tax and land the tea. Several of the agents chosen by the East India Company to handle the tea in Boston were Hutchinson's sons. When the tea arrived on the *Dartmouth*, the governor had his sons pass the ship through customs. Once this legal entry had been achieved, the *Dartmouth* could not depart without paying the duties on its cargo. Hutchinson had time on his side. If the tea duty was not paid within twenty days, customs officials could seize the cargo, land it with the help of the British army, and sell the tea at auction.

The Massachusetts Patriots met the governor's challenge. The Boston Committee of Correspondence sent Paul Revere, William Molineaux, and Thomas Young to lead a group of Patriots, most of whom were artisans, aboard the *Dartmouth*. On a cold night in December 1773 they boarded the ship while disguised as Indians, broke open the 342 chests of tea (valued at about £10,000, or about $800,000 today), and threw them into the harbor. "This destruction of the Tea is so bold and it must have so important Consequences," John Adams wrote in his diary, "that I cannot but consider it as an Epoch in History" (see American Lives, pages 158–159).

The Coercive Acts. Adams was not exaggerating. The British Privy Council was outraged, as was the king. There would be no more compromises. "Concessions have made matters worse," George III declared. "The time has come for compulsion." Parliament decisively rejected a proposal to repeal the duty on American tea. Instead, in the spring of 1774 it enacted four Coercive Acts to force Massachusetts into submission. A Port Bill closed Boston Harbor until the East India Company received payment for the destroyed tea. A Government Act annulled the Massachusetts charter and prohibited most local town meetings. A new Quartering Act required the colony to build barracks or put soldiers into private houses. And an Administration of Justice Act allowed royal officials accused of capital crimes to be tried in other colonies or in Britain.

Hillsborough had proposed a similar "divide-and-rule" strategy in 1769 when he had suggested isolating Massachusetts from the other mainland colonies. By 1774, however, the boycott against the Townshend duties and the activities of the Committees of Correspondence had created a firm sense of unity among the colonies. In far-off Georgia, a Patriot warned the "Freemen of the Province" that "every privilege you at present claim as a birthright, may be wrested from you by the same authority that blockades the town of Boston." "The cause of Boston," George Washington declared from Virginia, "now is and ever will be considered as the cause of America."

Religion and Rebellion

Many American Protestants hated bishops and the ecclesiastical power they represented. This cartoon warns that the Quebec Bill of 1774, which allowed the practice of Catholicism in Canada, was part of a plot by the hierarchy of the Church of England to impose bishops on the American colonies.

George R. T. Hewes and the Meaning of the Revolution

George Hewes, 1835
This portrait of George Hewes was painted by Joseph Cole.

George Robert Twelves Hewes was born in Boston in 1742. He was named George after his father, Robert after a paternal uncle, and Twelves after his maternal grandmother, whose maiden name was Twelves. Apart from his long name, Hewes received little from his parents—not size, for he was unusually short at five feet, one inch; not wealth, for his father, a failed tanner, died a poor soap boiler when Hewes was seven; not even love, for Hewes spoke of his mother only as someone who whipped him for disobedience. When he was fourteen she apprenticed him to a shoemaker, one of the lower trades.

This harsh upbringing shaped Hewes's personality. As an adult he spoke out against all brutality, even the tar and feathering of a Loyalist who had almost killed him. And throughout his life he was extremely sensitive about his class status. He was "neither a rascal nor a vagabond," Hewes retorted to a Boston gentleman who pulled rank on him, "and though a poor man was in as good credit in town as he was."

The occupation of Boston by 4,000 British soldiers in 1768 drew the twenty-six-year-old Hewes into the resistance movement. At first his concerns were personal: he took offense when British sentries challenged him and when a soldier refused to pay for a pair of shoes. Then they became political: Hewes grew angry when some of the poorly paid British soldiers moonlighted, taking jobs away from Bostonians, and even angrier when a Loyalist merchant fired into a crowd of apprentices who were picketing his shop, killing one of them. And so on March 5, 1770, when British soldiers came out in force to clear the streets of rowdy civilians, Hewes joined his fellow townspeople: "They were in the king's highway, and had as good a right to be there" as the British troops, he said.

Fate—and his growing political consciousness—had placed Hewes in the middle of the Boston Massacre. Not only did he know four of the five workingmen shot down that night by British troops, but one of them, James Caldwell, was standing by his side, and Hewes caught him as he fell. Outraged, Hewes armed himself with a cane, only to be confronted by Sergeant Chambers of the 29th British Regiment and eight or nine soldiers, "all with very large clubs or cutlasses." Chambers seized his cane, but as Hewes stated in a legal deposition, "I told him I had as good a right to carry a cane as they had to carry clubs." This deposition, which went on to tell of the soldiers' threats to kill more civilians, was included in *A Short Narrative of the Horrid Massacre in Boston* published by a group of Boston Patriots.

Hewes had chosen sides, and his political radicalism did not go unpunished. His outspokenness roused the ire of one of his creditors, a Loyalist merchant tailor. Hewes had never really made a go of it as a shoemaker and constantly struggled on the brink of poverty. Unable to make good on a two-year-old debt of £6. 8s. 3p. (about $300 today) for "a sappled coat & breeches of fine cloth," he landed in debtor's prison in September 1770. Such extravagance of dress on Hewes's part was rare; his purchase of the suit had been the desperate ploy of a propertyless artisan to win the hand of Sally Summer, the daughter of the sexton of the First Baptist Church, whom Hewes had married in 1768. Prison did not blunt Hewes's enthusiasm for the Patriot cause. On the night of December 16, 1773, he turned up as a volunteer at the Tea Party organized by the radical Patriot leaders of Boston. He "daubed his face and hands with coal dust in the shop of a blacksmith" and then found, somewhat to his surprise, that "the commander of the division to which I belonged, as soon as we were on board the ship, appointed me boatswain, and ordered me to go to the captain and demand of him the keys to the hatches."

Hewes had been singled out and made a minor

leader, and he must have played the part well. Thompson Maxwell, a volunteer sent to the Tea Party by John Hancock, recalled that "I went accordingly, joined the band under one Captain Hewes; we mounted the ships and made tea in a trice." In the heat of conflict the small man with the large name had been elevated from a poor shoemaker to "Captain Hewes."

A man of greater ability or ambition might have seized the moment, using his reputation as a Patriot to win fame or fortune, but that was not Hewes's destiny. During the War of Independence he fought as an ordinary sailor and soldier, shipping out twice on privateering voyages and enlisting at least four times in the militia, about twenty months of military service in all. He did not win riches as a privateer (although, with four children to support, that was his hope) or find glory, or even adequate pay in battle: "we received nothing of the government but paper money, of very little value, and continually depreciating." Indeed, the war cost Hewes the small stake he had in society: "The shop which I had built in Boston, I lost"; it was pulled down and burned by British troops.

In material terms, the American Revolution did about as much for Hewes as his parents had. When a journalist found the shoemaker in New York State in the 1830s, he was still "pressed down by the iron hand of poverty." The spiritual reward was greater. As his biographer, Alfred Young, put it: "He was a nobody who briefly became a somebody in the Revolution and, for a moment near the end of his life, a hero." Because Americans had begun to celebrate the memory of the Revolution, Hewes was brought back to Boston in 1835 in triumph as one of the last surviving participants in the Tea Party—the guest of honor on Independence Day.

But a more fundamental spiritual reward had come to Hewes when he became a revolutionary, casting off the deferential status of "subject" in a monarchy and becoming a proud and equal "citizen" in a republic. What this meant to Hewes, and to thousands of other poor and obscure Patriots, appeared in his relationship—both real and fictitious—with John Hancock. As a young man Hewes had sat tongue-tied and deferential in the rich merchant's presence. But in his story of the Tea Party Hewes made Hancock his equal, placing him at the scene (which was almost certainly not the case) and claiming that he "was himself at one time engaged with him in the demolition of the same chest of tea." In this lessening of social distance—this declaration of *equality*—lay one of the profound meanings of the American Revolution.

The Boston "Tea Party"
Led by radical Patriots disguised as Mohawk Indians, Bostonians dump taxed British tea into the harbor. The rioters underlined their political motives by punishing those who sought personal gain; a man who stole some of the tea was "stripped of his booty and his clothes together, and sent home naked."

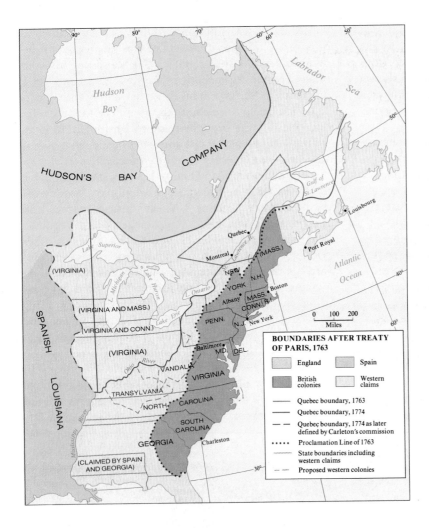

MAP 5.3

British Western Policy, 1763–1774
The Proclamation Line of 1763 restricted white settlement west of the Appalachian Mountains. Nevertheless, colonial land speculators planned the new colonies of Vandalia and Transylvania. However, the Quebec Act of 1774 designated these western lands as Indian reserves and, by vastly increasing the boundaries of Quebec, eliminated the sea-to-sea land claims of many eastern colonies. The act angered many Americans: settlers and land speculators who wanted easy access to the west, New England Protestants who had long feared Catholicism in French Canada, and colonial political leaders who condemned its failure to provide a representative assembly in Quebec.

In 1774 Parliament passed the Quebec Act, heightening the Americans' sense of common danger. This law extended the boundaries of Quebec into the Ohio River Valley, thus threatening to restrict the western land boundaries of Virginia and other seaboard colonies (see Map 5.3). It also gave legal recognition to Roman Catholicism, a concession to the French residents of Canada that aroused old religious hatred, especially in New England, where Puritans detested Catholicism and associated it with arbitrary royal government. The ministry had not intended the Quebec Act as a coercive measure, but many colonial leaders saw it as another demonstration of Parliament's power to intervene in American domestic affairs.

The Continental Congress Responds

To respond to the new British measures, American leaders called for a new all-colony assembly, the Continental Congress. The newer colonies—Florida, Quebec, Nova Scotia, and Newfoundland—did not attend, but delegates from all the other mainland provinces (except

Georgia, whose assembly was effectively controlled by a royal governor) met in Philadelphia in September 1774.

New England delegates to the First Continental Congress advocated political union and immediate military preparations. Southern leaders, fearing a British plot "to overturn the constitution and introduce a system of arbitrary government," also favored resistance. Many delegates from the middle colonies held out for a political compromise. Led by Joseph Galloway of Pennsylvania, these men of "loyal principles" outlined a scheme for a new imperial system resembling the Albany Plan of Union of 1754. Under Galloway's proposal, America would have a legislative council selected by the colonial assemblies and a president-general appointed by the king, with the new government having veto power over Parliamentary legislation affecting America. Despite this feature, the delegates refused to endorse Galloway's plan; with British troops "occupying" Boston, it was thought to be too conciliatory.

Instead, the First Continental Congress passed a Declaration of Rights and Grievances that condemned the Coercive Acts and demanded their repeal. The Congress also repudiated the Declaratory Act of 1766,

which had proclaimed Parliament's supremacy over the colonies, and demanded that Britain restrict its supervision of American affairs to matters of external trade. Finally, the Congress began a program of economic retaliation. It decreed that new nonimportation and nonconsumption agreements would come into effect in December 1774, and if Parliament did not repeal the "Intolerable Acts," as the Patriots called them, by September 1775, all colonial exports to Britain, Ireland, and the West Indies would be cut off. Ten years of constitutional conflict had ended in all-out commercial warfare.

Even at this late date a few British leaders continued to hope for a compromise. In January 1775 the earl of Chatham (William Pitt) proposed the removal of British troops from Boston and asked Parliament to give up its claim to tax the colonies and to recognize the Continental Congress as a lawful body. In return for these and other concessions, he proposed that the Congress acknowledge Parliamentary supremacy and grant a continuing revenue to cover part of the British national debt.

Chatham's dramatic intervention, like Galloway's in the colonies, was doomed to failure. The British ministry was unyielding. Twice it had backed down; a third retreat was impossible. The honor of the nation was at stake. The ministry rejected Chatham's plan, branding the Continental Congress an illegal assembly, and also rejected a proposal by Lord Dartmouth, the colonial secretary, to send commissioners to America to negotiate a settlement.

Instead, Lord North set stringent terms: Americans must pay for their own defense and administration and must acknowledge Parliament's authority to tax them. To give teeth to these demands, North imposed a naval blockade on American trade with foreign nations and ordered General Gage to suppress dissent in Massachusetts. Former Governor Thomas Hutchinson, now living in exile in London, reported that the British prime minister had told him, "Now the case seemed desperate. Parliament would not—could not—concede. For aught he could see it must come to violence."

The Rising of the Countryside

Although the Patriot movement began in the seaport cities, its success depended on the support of the predominantly rural population. Most farmers initially had little interest in imperial issues. Their lives were deeply rooted in the soil, and their prime allegiance was to their families and communities. Then the French and Indian War took their sons away from home and nibbled at their income. In the community of Newtown on Long Island, for example, farmers had paid an average of 10 shillings (about $20 today) in taxes before 1754;

WILLIAMM PITT.

"IL FAUT DECLARER LA GUERRE A LA FRANCE."

William Pitt

Hobbled by gout and age, William Pitt (Lord Chatham) addresses the House of Lords on the American question. By 1775 Pitt's eloquence could not soothe the mutual suspicion and anger created by a decade of conflict. (Metropolitan Museum of Art)

by 1756 taxes had jumped to 30 shillings to cover New York's military expenses. Peace brought only slight relief; the Quartering Act cost each Newtown resident 20 shillings in taxes in 1771. Many rural Americans found these exactions onerous, although in fact they paid much less in taxes than did most Britons (see Table 5.2).

The Patriots. Political as well as economic issues infiltrated from the cities into the countryside. Rural Patriots rallied to support the nonimportation movements of 1765 and 1769, and the Daughters of Liberty in hundreds of small towns and villages spun and wove wool into homemade cloth to support American resistance. It was this outburst of rural patriotism that encouraged the Continental Congress to declare a new economic boycott of British goods in 1774 and to create a network of local Committees of Safety and Inspection to enforce it. The Congress identified ways of supporting the boycott. For example, it condemned Americans who wore expensive imported clothes at funerals, approving only "a black crape or ribbon on the arm or hat for gentlemen, and a black ribbon and necklace for ladies."

These symbolic affirmations of traditional rural thriftiness reflected harsh economic realities for many

TABLE 5.2

Patriot Resistance, 1762–1775

British Action	Date	Patriot Response
Revenue Act	1762	Merchants complain privately
Proclamation Line	1763	Land speculators voice discontent
Sugar Act	1764	Protests by merchants and Massachusetts House
Stamp Act	1765	Riots by Sons of Liberty Stamp Act Congress First nonimportation movement
Quartering Act	1765	New York Assembly refuses to implement until 1767
Townshend Duties	1767	Second nonimportation movement Harassment of pro-British merchants
Troops occupy Boston	1768	Boston Massacre of 1770
Gaspée affair	1772	Committees of Correspondence created
Tea Act	1773	Widespread resistance Boston Tea Party
Coercive Acts and Quebec Act	1774	First Continental Congress Third nonimportation movement
British raids on Lexington and Concord	1775	Armed resistance by Minutemen Second Continental Congress

smallholders. The yeoman tradition of agricultural independence was everywhere under attack. In long-settled regions arable land was scarce and expensive, while in many new communities merchants were seizing farmsteads for delinquent debts. In New York manorial landlords were demanding higher rents, and entrepreneurial speculators controlled large frontier tracts. The new demands of the British government would further drain "this People of the Fruits of their Toil," complained the town meeting of rural Petersham, Massachusetts. "The duty on tea," added a Patriot pamphlet, "was only a prelude to a window-tax, hearth-tax, land-tax, and poll-tax, and these were only paving the way for reducing the country to lordships." By the 1770s many northern yeomen felt personally threatened by British policies.

Chesapeake slaveowners had similar fears despite their much higher standard of living. Beginning in the 1750s, many planters had sunk into debt. A Virginia planter observed in 1766 that a debt of £1,000 had once been considered excessive, but "ten times that sum is now spoke of with indifference and thought no great burthen on Some Estates." High living had led to economic anxiety. Slaveowners, accustomed to being masters on their plantations, resented their financial dependence on British merchants. Moreover, the Coercive Acts raised the threat of political dependence in the minds of many planters. They worried that once Parliament had subdued Massachusetts, it might seize control of Virginia's county courts and House of Burgesses. This prospect moved many planters to action. "The spark of liberty is not yet extinct among our people," one planter declared, "and if properly fanned by the Gentlemen of influence will, I make no doubt, burst out again into a flame."

The Loyalists. Support for the Patriot cause, however, was far from unanimous. As early as 1765 various groups of Americans had worried that resistance to Britain would destroy respect for all political institutions and end in mob rule. This fear was particularly strong among propertied families—large landowners, substantial slaveowners, and wealthy merchants—and their fears increased as the Sons of Liberty used violence to enforce nonimportation. One well-to-do New Yorker complained, "No man can be in a more abject state of bondage than he whose Reputation, Property and Life are exposed to the discretionary violence . . . of the community."

Thousands of ordinary colonists became Loyalists, for a variety of reasons. Class antagonism was one factor. Many Hudson Valley tenant farmers turned to Loyalism when their landlords embraced the Patriot cause. Similar social divisions prompted backcountry Regulators in North Carolina and Maryland farmers on the eastern shore of the Chesapeake Bay to oppose the policies advocated by the Patriot gentry. Ethnicity and religion also played a role, as many Quakers and Germans in Pennsylvania, Dutch and Germans in New York and New Jersey, and Scots in the Carolinas supported the king both because of conflicts with their Patriot neighbors and because they feared political change.

Beginning in 1774, these conservative Americans of "loyal principles" began joining together to denounce Patriot schemes of independence. Royal governors—such as Thomas Hutchinson of Massachusetts, Benning Wentworth of New Hampshire, and Lord Dunmore of Virginia—stood at the head of the Loyalists. They mobilized royal officials, merchants with military contracts, clergy of the Church of England, and well-established lawyers into a small but wealthy and articulate pro-British party. Clergymen such as Jonathan Boucher of Virginia denounced Patriot agitators from their pulpits, while Loyalist landlords and merchants used the threat of economic retaliation to

at which the people were advised to close the royal courts of justice and transfer their political allegiance to the popularly elected House of Representatives. Crowds of armed men prevented the Court of General Sessions from meeting, and rural Patriots harassed supporters of the royal regime.

General Thomas Gage, now governor of Massachusetts as well, tried desperately to maintain imperial power. In September 1774 he ordered British troops to march out of Boston and seize Patriot armories and storehouses at Charlestown and Cambridge. Far from subduing the Patriots, this action only created more support for their cause. Twenty thousand colonial militiamen mobilized to safeguard depots of military supplies at Concord and Worcester. The Concord town meeting voted to raise two companies of troops to "Stand at a minutes warning in Case of alarm," thus creating the famous Minutemen. Eighty percent of male heads of families and a number of single women in Concord signed a Solemn League and Covenant vowing support for nonimportation, and other rural towns also expressed allegiance to the rebellious Patriot government. Gage's authority was increasingly limited to Boston, where it rested primarily on the bayonets of his 3,500 troops.

This stalemate lasted for six months. Gage, unwilling to undertake new raids that might precipitate an armed conflict, waited for orders from Britain. In the meantime, the Massachusetts House met on its own authority. It issued regulations for the collection of taxes, assumed the responsibilities of government, and strengthened the militia. Even before the news of Massachusetts's defiance reached London, the Colonial Secretary, Lord Dartmouth, declared Massachusetts to be in a state of "open rebellion." He told Gage that "force should be repelled by force" and sent orders to the governor to march quickly against the "rude rabble."

On the night of April 18 Gage followed his orders and dispatched troops to capture colonial leaders and supplies at Concord. Paul Revere and two other Bostonians warned the Patriots, however, and at dawn on April 19 local militiamen met the British at Lexington. Shots rang out, and a British volley killed 8 Americans and wounded several others. Pressing on to Concord, the 700 British soldiers confronted 400 Patriots. This time the British took the heavier losses: 3 dead and 12 wounded. The worst was yet to come. As the British retreated along the narrow, winding roads to Boston, they were repeatedly ambushed by 1,000 militiamen from neighboring towns. By the end of the day, 73 British soldiers lay dead, 174 were wounded, and 26 were missing. British fire had killed 49 American militiamen and wounded 39.

Too much blood had been spilled to allow a peaceful compromise. Twelve years of economic conflict and constitutional debate had ended in civil war.

Political Propaganda: The Empire Strikes Back
A British cartoon attacks the women of Edenton, North Carolina, for supporting the boycott of British trade, hinting at their sexual lasciviousness and—by showing an enslaved black woman among these supposed advocates of liberty—their moral hypocrisy.

persuade indebted tenants and workers to oppose radical demands. But in most areas there were too few Loyalists, and they were too poorly organized to affect the course of events in 1774 and 1775. A Tory Association started by Governor Wentworth in New Hampshire had only fifty-nine members, fourteen of whom were Wentworth's relatives. At this crucial point Americans who favored resistance to British rule commanded the allegiance—or at least the acquiescence—of the majority of white Americans.

The Failure of Compromise

When the Continental Congress met in September 1774, New England already stood in open defiance of British authority. In August 150 delegates from neighboring towns had gathered in Concord, Massachusetts, for a Middlesex County Congress, an illegal convention

Summary

The Great War for Empire brought a decisive end to the era of salutary neglect and began an era of imperial reform. The war had exposed the weakness of Britain's control over its American colonies and had left that nation with a crushing load of debt. When George Grenville became prime minister in 1763, he embraced the cause of reform. To raise money—and reassert British authority—he enacted the Sugar Act, which extended the jurisdiction of vice-admiralty courts, and the Stamp Act, which imposed a direct tax for the first time.

The colonists resisted reform, protesting against the stamp duty through mob violence, a trade boycott, and an extralegal Stamp Act Congress. Educated colonists based their arguments for American rights on English common law, Enlightenment thought, and the writings of Real Whigs, whereas the Sons and Daughters of Liberty drew inspiration from evangelical Protestantism and the English republican tradition. To assist British merchants and manufacturers, Parliament repealed the Stamp Act in 1766, but it explicitly reaffirmed its complete authority over the colonies.

In 1767 Charles Townshend undermined this first informal compromise by imposing a new tax on trade. Americans responded with a second nonimportation movement and new constitutional arguments proclaiming the authority of their assemblies over provincial affairs. While the British ministry nearly adopted a plan to crush American resistance by force, domestic problems prompted it to repeal most of the Townshend duties by 1770.

Lord North disrupted this second compromise by passing the Tea Act in 1773. When Bostonians resisted the new law, the British used coercion in Massachusetts to try to destroy the Patriot resistance movement. In 1774 American political leaders met in the First Continental Congress, which challenged British authority and devised a new program of economic warfare. The Congress had the support of a majority of American farmers and planters, who were now prepared to resist British rule. The failure to find a new compromise resulted in bloodshed at Lexington and Concord in April 1775 and then in civil war.

TIMELINE

1754–1763	Salutary neglect ends British national debt doubles
1760	George III becomes king
1761	Lord Bute becomes prime minister
1762	Revenue Act reforms customs service Royal Navy stops trade with French islands
1763	Treaty of Paris ends Great War for Empire Spanish evacuate Florida Proclamation Line restricts western settlement Peacetime army in America Grenville becomes prime minister John Wilkes demands reform of Parliament
1764	Currency Act Sugar Act Colonists oppose vice-admiralty courts Franklin proposes American representation in Parliament
1765	Stamp Act Quartering Act Patrick Henry and Virginia Resolves Stamp Act Congress Riots by Sons of Liberty
1765–1766	First nonimportation movement
1766	First Compromise: Rockingham repeals Stamp Act and enacts Declaratory Act
1767	Townshend duties "Restraining Act" in New York Second nonimportation movement begins Daughters of Liberty make homespun cloth Increased illegal imports of Dutch tea
1768	British army occupies Boston Support for boycott grows
1770	Second Compromise: North repeals most Townshend duties Golden Hill riots in New York Boston Massacre
1772	*Gaspée* burned in Rhode Island Colonial Committees of Correspondence
1773	Tea Act Boston Tea Party
1774	Coercive Acts punish Massachusetts Quebec Act First Continental Congress Third nonimportation movement Loyalists organize
1775	British ministry orders Gage to suppress rebellion Battles of Lexington and Concord

★   ★   ★

BIBLIOGRAPHY

Jack P. Greene and J. R. Pole, eds., *The Blackwell Encyclopedia of the American Revolution* (1991), illuminates both obscure and well-known aspects of the Revolutionary Era. A good interpretive synthesis is Edward Countryman, *The American Revolution* (1985).

The Reform Movement

For the state of the empire in 1763, see Alison Gilbert Olson, *Making the Empire Work: London and the American Interest Groups, 1690–1790* (1992), and Jack P. Greene, *Peripheries and Center: Constitutional Development . . . 1607–1788* (1986). The impact of the Seven Years' War is traced in the classic study by Lawrence H. Gipson, *The Coming of the Revolution, 1763–1775* (1954), and the following works: Richard Middleton, *The Bells of Victory: The Pitt-Newcastle Ministry and the Conduct of the Seven Years' War, 1757–1762* (1985); Alan Rogers, *Empire and Liberty: American Resistance to British Authority, 1755–1763* (1974); Howard H. Peckham, *Pontiac and the Indian Uprising* (1947); and Joseph A. Ernst, *Money and Politics in America, 1755–1775* (1973). Marc Egnal, *A Mighty Empire: The Origins of the Revolution* (1988), attempts an interpretive synthesis.

British politics and imperial reform can be traced in John Brewer, *Party Ideology and Popular Politics at the Accession of George III* (1976); P. D. G. Thomas, *British Politics and the Stamp Act Crisis: The First Phase of the American Revolution, 1763–1767* (1975); Thomas C. Barrow, *Trade and Empire: The British Customs Service in Colonial America, 1660–1775* (1967); John L. Bullion, *A Great and Necessary Measure: George Grenville and the Genesis of the Stamp Act, 1763–1765* (1982); Carl Ubbelohde, *The Vice-Admiralty Courts and the American Revolution* (1960); and Philip Lawson, *George Grenville: A Political Life* (1984).

The Dynamics of Rebellion

For the American response to the British reform laws, see Edmund S. Morgan and Helen M. Morgan, *The Stamp Act Crisis: Prologue to Revolution* (1963); Pauline Maier, *From Resistance to Revolution: Colonial Radicals and the Development of American Opposition to Britain, 1765–1776* (1972); and Gary B. Nash, *The Urban Crucible: Social Change, Political Consciousness, and the Origins of the American Revolution* (1979). Merrill Jensen, *The Founding of a Nation: A History of the American Revolution, 1763–1776* (1968), and Robert Middlekauff, *The Glorious Cause: The American Revolution, 1763–1789* (1982), provide detailed narratives.

Studies of individual colonies capture the spirit of the resistance movement. See Paul A. Gilje, *The Road to Mobocracy: Popular Disorder in New York City, 1763–1834* (1986); David Lovejoy, *Rhode Island Politics and the American Revolution* (1958); and Ronald Hoffman, *A Spirit of Dissension: Economics, Politics, and the Revolution in Maryland* (1973). The motives of Patriots are best addressed through biographies. See Leo J. Lemay, ed., *Reappraising Benjamin Franklin: A Bicentennial Perspective* (1993); Pauline Maier, *The Old Revolutionaries: Political Lives in the Age of Samuel Adams* (1980); Library of Congress Symposium, *The Development of a Revolutionary Mentality* (1972); Milton E. Flower, *John Dickinson, Conservative Revolutionary* (1983); Richard R. Beeman, *Patrick Henry: A Biography* (1974); John R. Alden, *George Washington: A Biography* (1984); and Helen Hill Miller, *George Mason: Gentleman Revolutionary* (1975).

The most important single study of Patriot ideology is Bernard Bailyn, *The Ideological Origins of the American Revolution* (1967), but see Robert M. Calhoon, *Dominion and Liberty: Ideology in Anglo-American Political Thought, 1660–1801* (1994). Other works include Caroline Robbins, *The Eighteenth-Century Commonwealthman* (1959); Morton White, *The Philosophy of the American Revolution* (1978); Garry Wills, *Inventing America: Jefferson's Declaration of Independence* (1978); and H. T. Dickinson, *Liberty and Property: Political Ideology in Eighteenth-Century Britain* (1978). For a discussion of the legal tradition, see Charles H. McIlwain, *The American Revolution: A Constitutional Interpretation* (1923), and John Phillip Reid, *Constitutional History of the American Revolution: The Authority of Rights* (1986).

The Growing Confrontation

Peter D. G. Thomas, *The Townshend Duties Crisis: The Second Phase of the American Revolution, 1767–1773* (1987), is the most comprehensive treatment, but see Colin Bonwick, *English Radicals and the American Revolution* (1977), and Ian R. Christie and Benjamin W. Labaree, *Empire or Independence, 1760–1776* (1976). On American resistance, consult Richard Alan Ryerson, *The Revolution Is Now Begun: The Radical Committees of Philadelphia, 1765–1776* (1978); Peter Shaw, *American Patriots and the Rituals of Revolution* (1981); and Stanley Godbold, Jr., and Robert W. Woody, *Christopher Gadsden* (1982). The confrontation between Patriots and British authority is covered in John Shy, *Toward Lexington: The Role of the British Army in the Coming of the American Revolution* (1965), and Hiller B. Zobel, *The Boston Massacre* (1970).

The Road to War

Benjamin Labaree, *The Boston Tea Party* (1964), is comprehensive and stimulating and can be supplemented by Peter D. G. Thomas, *Tea Party to Independence: The Third Phase of the American Revolution* (1991); Bernard Donoughue, *British Politics and the American Revolution: The Path to War, 1773–75* (1972); and David Ammerman, *In the Common Cause: American Response to the Coercive Acts of 1774* (1968). A fine study of the resistance movement is Edward F. Countryman, *A People in Revolution: The American Revolution and Political Society in New York* (1983). On prewar Loyalism, see Bernard Bailyn, *The Ordeal of Thomas Hutchinson* (1974), and Janice Potter, *The Liberty We Seek: Loyalist Ideology in Colonial New York and Massachusetts* (1983). For the rising of the countryside, see David Hackett Fischer, *Paul Revere's Ride* (1994); Gregory H. Nobles, *Divisions throughout the Whole: Politics and Society in Hampshire County, Massachusetts, 1740–1775* (1983); Jere R. Daniell, *Experiment in Republicanism: New Hampshire Politics and the Revolution, 1741–1790* (1970); and Richard Bushman, *King and People in Provincial Massachusetts* (1985). The transfer of authority is described in Jerrilyn Greene Marston, *King and Congress: The Transfer of Political Legitimacy, 1774–1776* (1987).

P A R T **2**

The New Republic
1775–1820

	Government	Diplomacy	Economy	Society	Culture
	Creating Republican Institutions	**European Entanglements**	**Expansion of Commerce and Manufacturing**	**Defining Liberty and Equality**	**Pluralism and National Identity**
1775	State constitutions written	Independence declared (1776) French alliance (1778)	Wartime expansion of manufacturing	Slavery emancipation in the North Murray, "On the Equality of the Sexes" (1779)	Paine's *Common Sense* calls for a republic
1780	Articles of Confederation ratified (1781) Legislative supremacy in states Philadelphia convention drafts U.S. Constitution (1787)	Treaty of Paris (1783) British trade restrictions in West Indies	Bank of North America (1781) Commercial recession (1783–89) Western land speculation	Virginia Statute of Religious Freedom (1786) Idea of republican motherhood	Land ordinances create a national domain in the West German settlers preserve own language Webster defines American English
1790	Bill of Rights (1791) First national parties: Federalists and Republicans	Wars of the French Revolution Jay's and Pinckney's treaties (1795) Undeclared war with French (1798)	First Bank of the United States (1792–1812) States charter business corporations Outwork system expands	Sedation Act limits freedom of the press (1798)	Indians form Western Confederation Sectional divisions emerge between South and North
1800	Revolution of 1800 Activist state legislatures Chief Justice Marshall asserts judicial power	Napoleonic wars (1802–15) Louisiana Purchase (1803) Embargo of 1807	Cotton expands into Old Southwest Farm productivity improves Embargo encourages domestic manufacturing	Youth-run marriage system New Jersey ends woman suffrage (1807) Atlantic slave trade legally ended (1808)	African-Americans absorb Protestant Christianity Tecumseh develops Indian identity
1810	Triumph of Republican party State constitutions democratized	War of 1812 Treaty of Ghent (1816) Monroe Doctrine (1823)	Second Bank of the United States (1816–36) Supreme Court protects contracts and corporations Emergence of a national economy	Expansion of suffrage for white men New England abolishes established church (1820s)	War of 1812 tests national unity Second Great Awakening shapes American identity

The American war is over, the Philadelphia Patriot Benjamin Rush declared in 1787, "but this is far from being the case with the *American revolution*. On the contrary, nothing but the first act of the great drama is closed. It remains yet to establish and perfect our new forms of government." The job was even greater than Rush imagined, for the republican revolution of 1776 challenged the values and institutions of the colonial social order, forcing changes in many spheres of life—economic, religious, cultural.

The first and most fundamental task was to devise a republican system of government. In 1775 no one in America knew what powers the central and state governments should have or how they should be organized. It took time and experience to find out. The states wrote constitutions by 1780, but their legislatures pursued prodebtor policies that were controversial and socially divisive. It took another decade for Americans to reach agreement on a national government, and even longer to assimilate a new institution, the political party, into the workings of government. These years of experiment and party strife witnessed the success not only of popular sovereignty—government of the people—but also the rise of activist state legislatures—government for the people—and a slow but steady movement toward political democracy—government by the people.

Second, to create and preserve their new republic, Americans had to fight two wars against Great Britain, an undeclared war against France, and many battles with Indian peoples and confederations. The wars against Britain divided the country into bitter factions—Patriots versus Loyalists in 1776, and prowar Republicans against antiwar Federalists in 1812—and expended much blood and treasure. Tragically, the extension of American sovereignty over the trans-Appalachian West brought about the demise of many Indian peoples—their lives taken by European diseases, their lands seized by white settlers. Yet by 1820 the United States was a strong independent state, free at last from a half-century of entanglement in the wars and diplomacy of Europe.

Third, by this time the expansion of the market system had laid the foundations for a strong national economy. Merchants financed a banking system and devised extensive outwork industries. State governments used charters and legal incentives to spur improvements in transportation, finance, and manufacturing. Southern planters carried slavery west to Alabama and Mississippi and grew rich by exporting a new crop—cotton—to markets in Europe and the North. Vast numbers of farm families settled new lands in the West or undertook additional labor as handicraft workers in the Northeast. By 1820 the new American republic had begun to achieve economic as well as political independence.

Fourth, Americans tried to define the nature of their republican society, but found themselves divided along lines of gender, race, religion, and class. Then as now, Americans disagreed on fundamental issues—legal equality for women, the future status of slavery, the meaning of free speech and religious liberty, and the extent of public responsibility for social inequality. These years saw the triumph of liberty of conscience and, except in New England, the end of established churches. The northern states gradually emancipated their slaves, but social equality—not only for blacks, but for women and many white men—remained elusive. In 1820, as in 1775, authority in the family and society remained firmly in the hands of men of property.

The fifth and final task Americans set themselves—creating a distinct culture and identity—was very hard to achieve. The United States remained a land of diverse peoples and distinct regions. Native Americans still lived in their own clans and nations, while black Americans, one-fifth of the enumerated population, were developing a new, African-American culture. The white inhabitants, divided among those of English, Scots-Irish, German, and Dutch ancestry, also preserved many aspects of their traditional cultures. Nevertheless, political institutions united Americans, as did their engagement in the market economy and their increasing participation in evangelical Protestant churches. By 1820, to be an American meant, for the dominant white population, being a republican, a Protestant, and an enterprising individual in a capitalist-run market system.

***The Attack on Bunker Hill with the Burning of
Charles Town*** (detail)

The British attacked Patriot militiamen, who were dug in on
Breed's Hill and Bunker Hill, on June 17, 1775. Before
dislodging the rebel troops, the British suffered heavy losses.

CHAPTER 6

War and Revolution

1775–1783

★   ★   ★

With the battles at Lexington and Concord in April 1775, the American Patriots became rebels, willing to use military force to achieve their political ends. Only a minority of Patriots demanded independence at that point, but the outbreak of fighting gave the advantage to the most intrepid, perhaps even the most foolhardy. During the last months of 1775 these radical Patriots began to dominate local meetings, provincial assemblies, and the Continental Congress, urging a complete break from British rule.

On July 4, 1776 the Patriots formally became rebels by agreeing to a Declaration of Independence that severed their ties to Great Britain. More momentously, they became revolutionaries, for the insurgents followed the advice of the Continental Congress and created new republican state governments. Repudiating aristocratic and monarchical rule, the Patriots vested sovereignty in the people as a whole, only to argue among themselves over what that meant in practice. Thus began the age of the democratic revolutions.

To defend their state governments, Patriot men and women went to war against an invading British army. Initially, most of the battles took place in the North, devastating dozens of communities between New York and Philadelphia. Simultaneously, the cost of fighting the war devastated the fiscal resources of the Continental Congress and the state governments. Only a miraculous victory at Saratoga and an alliance with France saved the fledgling rebellion.

Thereafter the fighting shifted to the South, where British forces again initially gained the upper hand. Gradually, a bitter war of attrition sapped the strength of the British army, while political unrest at home undermined the resolve of the British ministry. In a stunning diplomatic triumph, the rebel Patriot statesmen won independence largely on their own terms.

Nonetheless, the War of Independence had lasted six years, taken thousands of lives, and required vast expenditures of scarce resources. By the time it ended, the war had sharpened social divisions among the American people, had nearly destroyed their new financial institutions, and had tested their commitment to republican ideals.

Toward Independence, 1775–1776

The Battle of Concord was fought on April 19, 1775, but another fourteen months would elapse before the rebels made a final break with Britain. In the intervening time, the most vocal Patriots decided that preserving the "rights of Englishmen" wasn't enough: they wanted independence. In one colony after another Patriot legislators threw out the royal governors and created the two essentials for independence: a government and an army. Loyalists protested in vain against the rebellious fervor sweeping the colonies.

Civil War

The Second Continental Congress. The outbreak of fighting in Massachusetts lent great urgency to the Second Continental Congress, which met in Philadelphia in May 1775. With John Adams exhorting its members to rise to "the defense of American liberty," radical Patriots pressed for a Continental army. They wanted George Washington of Virginia to take command of the New England forces that had surrounded the British in Boston, and they wanted to call for new volunteers. More cautious delegates and those with Loyalist sympathies opposed these measures, warning that they would lead to more violence and commit the colonists irretrievably to rebellion. After bitter debate, Congress approved the proposals—but, as Adams lamented, only "by bare majorities."

While Congress deliberated in Philadelphia, hostilities continued to rage in Massachusetts. On June 17 more than 3,000 British troops attacked new American fortifications on Breed's Hill and Bunker Hill, which overlooked Boston. It took three assaults, during which 1,000 British soldiers were killed or wounded, to dislodge the Patriot militiamen. Despite the bloodshed, a majority in Congress still hoped for reconciliation with Britain. Led by John Dickinson of Pennsylvania, a moderate Patriot, they passed an Olive Branch petition, expressing loyalty to George III and asking him to repeal oppressive parliamentary legislation. Zealous Patriots in the Congress, such as Samuel Adams of Massachusetts and Patrick Henry of Virginia, countered by winning passage of a somewhat contradictory Declaration

of the Causes and Necessities of Taking Up Arms, asserting that Americans dreaded the "calamities of civil war" but were "resolved to die Freemen rather than to live [as] slaves."

King George did not exploit these divisions among the Patriots. He refused even to receive the Olive Branch petition, which the Loyalist Richard Penn brought to London in August. Instead, he issued a Proclamation for Suppressing Rebellion and Sedition, expressing his determination to crush the American revolt. By that time his intemperate words were perhaps justified, for Congress had decided at the end of June to invade Canada, hoping to unleash a popular uprising and add a fourteenth colony to the rebellion. Patriot forces easily took Montreal, but in December 1775 they failed to capture Quebec.

Meanwhile, Patriot merchants resorted to financial warfare, implementing Congress's resolution to cut off all exports to Britain and its West Indian possessions. By disrupting the tobacco trade and sugar production, they hoped to undermine the British economy. Parliament retaliated in December 1775 with a Prohibitory Act outlawing all trade with its rebellious colonies.

Rebellion in the South. In the meantime, the fighting in Massachusetts had sparked skirmishes between Patriots and Loyalists in the southern colonies. In June 1775 the Patriot-dominated House of Burgesses seized authority in Virginia, forcing the royal governor, Lord Dunmore, to take refuge on a British warship in Chesapeake Bay. From there Dunmore organized two military forces: one of whites, the Queen's Own Loyal Virginians, and one of blacks, the Ethiopian Regiment. Citing the king's proclamation, Dunmore branded the Patriots "traitors" and declared martial law. Then, in November, the governor issued a controversial proclamation of his own, offering freedom to slaves and indentured servants who belonged to rebels but joined the Loyalist cause. Patriot slaveowners now faced the possibility of black uprisings as well as military attack. Alarmed by Dunmore's proclamation, many planters threatened runaway slaves with death and called for a final break with Britain.

In the Carolinas, too, demands for independence grew more insistent in response to British military threats. Early in 1776 North Carolina's royal governor, Josiah Martin, tried to reestablish his authority with a force of 1,500 Scottish Highlanders from the Carolina backcountry. The Patriot militia quickly mobilized, and in February they defeated Martin's army in the Battle of Moore's Creek Bridge, capturing more than 800 of his troops. In Charleston, South Carolina, in June 1776 a group of armed artisans joined three Continental regiments and repelled a British naval assault.

As the violence escalated, radical Patriots seized control and moved toward independence. Early in 1776 the rebels transformed the North Carolina assembly into

an independent Provincial Congress; in April that body instructed its representatives "to concur with the Delegates of other Colonies in declaring Independency, and forming foreign alliances." Virginia followed suit. Led by George Mason, James Madison, Edmund Pendleton, and Patrick Henry, Patriots called a special convention in May at which they resolved unanimously "to declare the United Colonies free and independent states."

Common Sense

The break with Britain did not come easily. It was not difficult for Patriots to repudiate Parliament—the author of the hated tax laws—but most Americans retained a deep loyalty to the Crown. Joyous crowds had toasted the health of King George III after the repeal of the Stamp Act, and even as the imperial crisis worsened, Benjamin Franklin proposed that the king rule over autonomous American assemblies. Americans condemned the legislation enacted by Parliament, not the king or the institution of monarchy.

The roots of this loyalty ran deep in the structure of American society. Like most men and women in the early modern world, Americans used metaphors of age and family to describe the system of social authority and imperial rule. Colonists often pictured their society as the dependent offspring—the child—of Britain, the "mother country." They respected "elders" in town meetings and church congregations. In their minds, the family was a "little commonwealth" ruled by its male head and the king was the "father" of his people. Denial of the legiti-

macy of the monarchy threatened paternal authority and the hierarchical order of society. Yet events had prepared Americans to reject their political father. Economic and religious changes had lessened the power and authority of fathers and traditional leaders. And by 1775 zealous Patriots were accusing George III of supporting ministers who passed oppressive legislation and of ordering the use of military force against them.

Agitation against the king became especially intense in Philadelphia, the largest American city but not previously a bastion of Patriot sentiment because of the Loyalist sympathies of many of its merchants. Now artisans took the initiative. Constituting about half the city's population, artisans owned nearly 40 percent of its wealth but feared for their future prosperity. Many felt that British imports threatened their small-scale manufacturing enterprises and that Parliament was bent on eliminating their "just Rights and Privileges." After the outbreak of fighting in Massachusetts the artisans, now organized into a Mechanics Association, became a powerful force in the Patriot movement. By February 1776 forty artisans were sitting alongside forty-seven merchants on the Philadelphia Committee of Resistance, the extralegal body that enforced the latest trade boycott.

More than economic self-interest was at work here. Some artisans and more of the city's laborers were Scots-Irish Presbyterians who had migrated to Pennsylvania to escape oppressive British rule in northern Ireland, and many adhered to the doctrine of religious equality propounded by Gilbert Tennent and other New Light ministers. As pastor of Philadelphia's Second Presbyterian Church, Tennent had told his congregation

The Royal Family
George III strikes a regal pose, surrounded by his queen and numerous offspring, all brilliantly attired. Patriots repudiated not only monarchy but also the fancy dress and aristocratic manners of the *ancien régime,* championing a society of republican simplicity.

that all men and women are equal before God. Translating religious equality into political terms, New Light Presbyterians shouted in street demonstrations that they had "no king but King Jesus." In addition, republican ideas derived from the European Enlightenment circulated freely in Pennsylvania. Well-educated scientists and statesmen—such as Benjamin Franklin, David Rittenhouse, Charles Thomson, and Benjamin Rush—joined artisans in questioning not only the wisdom of George III but also the legitimacy of the monarchy.

At this pivotal moment, with popular sentiment in a state of flux, a single pamphlet tipped the balance. In January 1776 Thomas Paine published *Common Sense,* a call for independence and republicanism. Paine, a corset maker and minor bureaucrat in Britain, had been fired from the English Customs Service for agitating for higher wages. He migrated to Philadelphia in 1774, armed with a letter of introduction from Benjamin Franklin. There he met Benjamin Rush and others who shared his republican sentiments. "Monarchy and hereditary succession have laid the world in blood and ashes," Paine proclaimed in *Common Sense,* leveling a personal attack against the king, "the hard hearted sullen Pharaoh of England." Mixing insults with biblical quotations, Paine blasted the British system of "mixed government," which yielded only "monarchical tyranny in the person of the King and aristocratical tyranny in the persons of the peers."

Paine presented the case for independence in a way that the general public could understand and respond to, suggesting the absurdity of an island ruling or conquering a continent. *Common Sense* went through twenty-five editions and reached hundreds of thousands of homes. Its message was clear: reject the arbitrary powers of king and Parliament and create independent republican states. "A government of our own is our natural right," Paine concluded. "'TIS TIME TO PART."

Independence Declared

Fired by Paine's arguments and the escalating military conflict with Loyalists, the American call for a break with Britain sounded with increasing urgency in Patriot conventions throughout the colonies. In June 1776 these disparate demands were given a single voice in the Continental Congress when Richard Henry Lee presented the Virginia Convention's resolution: "That these United Colonies are, and of right ought to be, free and independent states . . . absolved from all allegiance to the British Crown." Faced with certain defeat, staunch Loyalists and anti-independence moderates withdrew from the Congress, leaving committed Patriots to take the fateful step. On July 4, 1776, the Congress approved the Declaration of Independence.

The main author of the Declaration was Thomas

Affirming the Declaration of Independence
The mood in the room is solemn as Congress formally declares independence from Great Britain. The delegates were now traitors to their country and king, their fortunes and even their lives hinging on the success of Patriot arms.

Jefferson, a young Virginia planter and legislative leader whose pamphlet *A Summary View of the Rights of British America* had mobilized resistance to the Coercive Acts. In composing the Declaration, Jefferson primarily wanted to justify Congress's action both to domestic critics and to foreign observers by putting the blame for the rupture on the king. To this end, he enumerated the acts of the imperial government that had oppressed Americans, suggesting that powerful centralized governments are inherently dangerous to liberty. Simultaneously, he provided a detailed indictment of the king's conduct, discrediting monarchical rule. Through the power of his prose, Jefferson sought to convince his fellow Americans of the perfidy of George III: "He has plundered our seas, ravaged our coasts, burned our towns, and destroyed the lives of our people. . . . A prince, whose character is thus marked by every act which may define a tyrant, is unfit to be the ruler of a free people."

In ringing phrases Jefferson proclaimed a series of "self-evident" truths: "that all men are created equal"; that they possess the "unalienable rights" of "life, liberty, and the pursuit of happiness"; that government derives its "just powers from the consent of the governed" and can rightly be overthrown if it "becomes destructive of these ends." His prose, steeped in the ideas and rhetoric of the European Enlightenment and the Glorious Revolution of 1688, celebrated the doctrines of individual liberty and popular sovereignty. All Americans are heirs of this revolutionary republican tradition.

For Jefferson, as for Paine, the pen was mightier than the sword. Almost overnight many halfhearted Americans were radicalized into republican revolution-

aries. In rural hamlets and seaport cities, crowds celebrated the Declaration by burning George III in effigy; in New York City, they toppled a huge statue of the king. With these acts of destruction, Patriots broke their psychological ties to the mother country and the father monarch. Americans were now ready to create republics, state governments that derived their authority from the people.

The Perils of War and Finance, 1776–1778

The Declaration of Independence brought an end to the minor skirmishing of a civil war. For the next two years Britain mounted large-scale offensives against the Continental army commanded by George Washington, defeating the rebel forces in nearly every battle. A few inspiring American victories kept the rebellion alive, but in late 1776 and again during the winter of 1777–1778, at Valley Forge, the fate of the Patriot cause hung in the balance.

War in the North

Early in 1776 the British ministry decided to use overwhelming military force to crush the American revolt. The task looked easy. Great Britain had a population of 11 million, compared with about 2.5 million in the thirteen rebel colonies, nearly 20 percent of whom were African-American slaves. The British enjoyed a great economic advantage because of the immense profits of the South Atlantic system and the newly emerging Industrial Revolution. Militarily, Britain enjoyed clear superiority: it had a standing army of 48,000 men (and the financial resources to hire or raise thousands more) and the most powerful navy in the world. The imperial government also expected support from the tens of thousands of Loyalists in America and from various Indian tribes hostile to white expansion.

In contrast, the rebellious Americans looked weak. They had no navy, and their small Continental army consisted mostly of militiamen whose enlistments would expire at the end of 1776. True, the Patriots could field thousands of militiamen, but only for short periods and only near their own farms or towns. Assessing the two antagonists in 1776, few observers would have given the rebels a chance for victory.

Lord North, who was still the prime minister, moved quickly to put down the rebellion. Alarmed by the American invasion of Canada in 1775, he ordered an ambitious military mobilization and replaced the ineffective General Gage with a new commander, General William Howe. Howe had served in the colonies during the French and Indian War and had distinguished himself in Wolfe's siege of Quebec. North ordered him to capture New York City and seize control of the Hudson River, isolating the radical Patriots in New England from the rest of the colonies.

Howe proceeded with dispatch. In March 1776 he transferred the British forces in Boston to a new military headquarters in Halifax, Nova Scotia, where they were joined by dozens of new regiments. By the summer he was ready to move. While the Continental Congress was declaring independence in Philadelphia, Howe was landing 10,000 troops—British regulars and German mercenaries—outside New York City. By August the

The Evacuation of Boston
Surrounded by American militiamen and facing bombardment by Patriot artillery, General Howe directs the withdrawal of British troops from Boston in March 1776. Four months later he launched a major offensive against Washington's army near New York City.

British army had swollen to 32,000 soldiers, supported by a fleet of thirty warships and 10,000 sailors. This formidable force faced, on the American side, General Washington's newly formed, poorly trained army of about 18,000 troops, nearly half of whom were short-term militiamen hastily recruited by the state governments of Virginia and New England. Many American officers were capable men who had served in the French and Indian War, but even the most experienced had never commanded a large force or faced a disciplined army capable of the intricate maneuvers of European warfare. The advantage of the British forces was overwhelming; their officers had been tested in combat, and their soldiers were well armed.

British superiority was immediately apparent. On August 27, 1776, Howe attacked the Americans in the Battle of Long Island and forced them to retreat to Manhattan Island. There Howe outflanked Washington's troops, nearly trapping them on several occasions. Outgunned and outmaneuvered, the Continental army again retreated, first to Harlem Heights, then to White Plains, and finally across the Hudson River to New Jersey. Howe pursued the Americans cautiously, seeking to envelop Washington's main force in a pincer movement. By December the British army had pushed the Continental troops out of New Jersey and across the Delaware River into Pennsylvania, and Congress was forced to flee from Philadelphia to Baltimore.

From the Patriots' perspective, winter came just in time, for it was customary in the eighteenth century to halt military campaigns during cold and snowy weather. Moreover, the overconfident British let down their guard, allowing the Americans to score a few triumphs. On Christmas night in 1776 Washington crossed the Delaware River and staged a surprise attack on Trenton, New Jersey. About a thousand Hessians, German mercenaries who had long fought for the British army, were forced to surrender. Then, on January 3, 1777, the Continental army won a small engagement at nearby Princeton. These victories raised sagging Patriot morale and prompted the British to evacuate New Jersey, a withdrawal that allowed the Continental Congress to return to Philadelphia and worried potential Loyalists throughout America. Bright stars in a dark night, the American triumphs could not mask British military superiority. These are the times, wrote Tom Paine, that "try men's souls."

Armies and Strategies

British superiority did not break the will of the Continental army, and the rebellion continued. Howe himself was partly responsible for prolonging the conflict. While in Britain he had opposed the Coercive Acts, and as the British military commander he still hoped for a compro-

mise—indeed, he had authority from Lord North to negotiate with the rebels. Consequently, instead of following up his early victories with a ruthless pursuit of the retreating American army, Howe was content to show his superior power and tactics, hoping to convince the Continental Congress that resistance was futile.

Howe's cautiousness reflected the conventions of eighteenth-century warfare, in which generals sought to outmaneuver the opposing forces and win their surrender rather than destroy them. Of course, he was also aware that his troops were 3,000 miles from supplies and reinforcements; in case of a major defeat, it would take six months to replenish his forces, especially since neither the ministry nor the royal governors had encouraged Loyalists to join or supply the army. However understandable Howe's tactics were, they cost the British the opportunity to nip the rebellion in the bud. Instead, Howe allowed the American army to survive to fight another day and to claim victories at Trenton and Princeton.

Howe's failure to win a decisive victory was paralleled by Washington's success in avoiding a spectacular defeat. He, too, was cautious, challenging Howe's army on selected occasions but retreating in the face of superior strength. As Washington told Congress, "On our

Washington at the Battle of Trenton
Washington told Congress that "on our Side the War should be defensive," but his bold attack across the Delaware on Christmas night, 1776, gave Americans their first military victory.

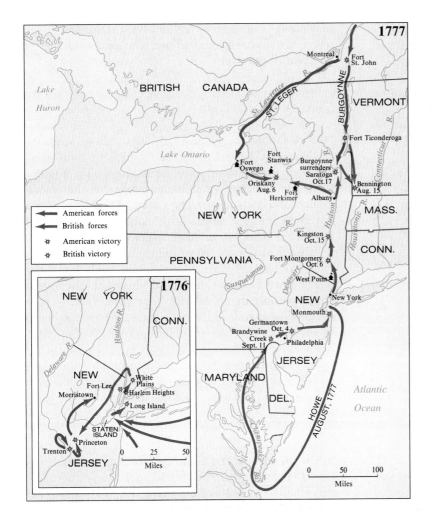

MAP 6.1

The War in the North

In 1776 the British army drove Washington's forces across New Jersey into Pennsylvania. The Americans counterattacked at Trenton and Princeton, setting up winter headquarters at Morristown. In 1777 General Howe captured Philadelphia from the south, while General Burgoyne and Colonel St. Leger launched invasions from Canada. Aided by thousands of New England militia, troops commanded by General Horatio Gates defeated Burgoyne at Bennington and then at Saratoga, the military turning point of the war.

Side the War should be defensive." The American general's strategy was to draw the British away from the seacoast to extend their lines of supply and sap their morale. His primary goal was to keep the Continental army intact as a symbol and instrument of American resistance (see Map 6.1).

In achieving this goal, Washington had more to contend with than Howe. Congress vowed to field a regular force of 75,000 men, but the Continental army never reached half that number; at its peak Washington's main force had only 18,000 men, few of whom were experienced soldiers. Yeomen farmers and trained militiamen preferred to serve in local units near their fields and families and refrained from joining the Continental forces. Consequently, the American army drew its recruits from the lower ranks of society. For example, the soldiers in the Continental units commanded by General William Smallwood of Maryland were either poor American-born youths or older foreign-born men—British ex-convicts and former indentured servants. They enlisted not to express their patriotic fervor but to make their way in the world, enlisting for three years in return for a bonus of $20 in cash (about $200 today) and the promise of 100 acres of land. Even so,

the declining purchasing power of Continental currency hurt the soldiers and their families financially, undermining their morale. Moreover, it took time to mold these men into a fighting force. In the face of a British artillery bombardment or a flank attack, many recruits panicked; hundreds of others deserted, unwilling to submit to the discipline and danger of military life. They also resented the contemptuous way Washington and other American officers treated the camp followers—the women who came along with the recruits and took care of their material and emotional needs.

Such support was crucial, for the Continental army did not receive much encouragement from the public. Radical Whig Patriots had long viewed a peacetime standing army as a threat to liberty and even in wartime hesitated to create a professional force. They placed their hopes in the militia, men organized in local units and supplied and aided by their families and communities. The Continental army went begging, without adequate goods from the populace or money from the Congress. General Philip Schuyler of New York complained that his troops were "weak in numbers, dispirited, naked, destitute of provisions, without camp equipage, with little ammunition, and not a single piece

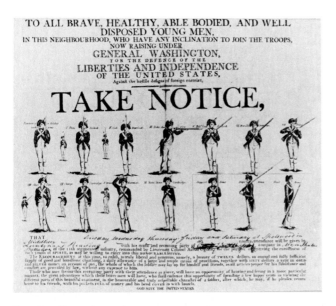

Patriots Recruit an Army

Some Americans became soldiers because of the glamour of bearing arms, but the citizens of Peacham, New Hampshire, were motivated by Real Whig fears of British tyranny: "Although we . . . had but six or eight men in the town, we sent two of them . . . for we feared if the British were not going to be stopped, we shall all be ruined."

Joseph Brant

The Mohawk chief Thayendanegea, known to the whites as Joseph Brant, secured the support of four of the Six Iroquois Nations for the British. In 1778 and 1779 he led Iroquois warriors and Tory Rangers in attacks on American settlements throughout western New York. This portrait by Charles Willson Peale was painted in 1797.

of cannon." Given this situation, Washington was fortunate not to have suffered an overwhelming defeat in the first year of the war.

Victory at Saratoga

Howe's failure to achieve a decisive victory surprised and dismayed Lord North and his ministers, who came to realize that restoration of the empire would require a long-term military commitment similar to that in the French and Indian War. Accepting the challenge, the government increased the British land tax to finance the war and prepared to mount a major campaign in 1777.

The isolation of New England remained the primary British goal. To accomplish this, the colonial secretary, Lord George Germain, devised a three-pronged attack converging on Albany, New York. General John Burgoyne was to lead the main force, a large contingent of British regulars, from Quebec down the St. John's River, across Lake Champlain, and then down the upper Hudson River to Albany. A second, smaller force under Lieutenant Colonel Barry St. Leger would attack Albany from the west, moving through the Mohawk River Valley. Leger's troops were mostly Iroquois warriors from central New York. The Iroquois had allied themselves with the British to protect their land from American settlers, and Germain was confident that they would cut down the rebels all along the New York frontier. Finally, to reinforce Burgoyne from the south, Germain ordered Howe to dispatch a contingent from his army northward from New York City.

Howe had a plan of his own. He proposed to attack Philadelphia, the home of the Continental Congress, hoping to force Washington into a fixed battle and end the rebellion with a single major victory. With Germain's apparent approval, Howe set his forces in motion—but very slowly. Rather than march overland through New Jersey, the troops sailed south from New York and then up Chesapeake Bay to approach Philadelphia from the southwest. Once on the ground, however, the British army showed its tactical skill. Howe's troops easily outflanked the American positions along Brandywine Creek, forcing Washington to withdraw. The British marched triumphantly into Philadelphia on September 26, half assuming that the capture of the rebels' capital would end the uprising. However, the Continental Congress fled into the interior, first to Lancaster and then to York, and would hear no words of surrender.

The British paid a high price for this victory. Howe's leisurely advance against Philadelphia exposed Burgoyne to defeat in the north. Initially, Burgoyne's troops had sped across Lake Champlain, overwhelming the American defenses at Fort Ticonderoga and driving onward toward the upper reaches of the Hudson River.

Moses Hall

Partisan Warfare in the South

The British campaign in the South unleashed a bitter struggle between resident Patriots and Loyalists, many of whom had old grudges to settle. Patriots labelled British Lieutenant Colonel Banastre Tarleton "Bloodly Tarleton" because of his wanton disregard for the rules of warfare; but the Patriots responded in kind, and the war in the southern backcountry left a trail of brutality.

Our troops and this body of Tories and Colonel Tarleton['s Tories] all being in the same neighborhood, our troops on the march met said body of Tories at a place called the Race Paths, and [the Tories], mistaking our troops for Tarleton's, Colonel Lee and Officers kept up the deception and Colonel Lee and his light horse marching in one column or line, and Major or Colonel Dixon's command in another, some interval apart, the Tories passed into this interval between our lines. . . .

They frequently uttered salutations of a friendly kind, believing us to be British. Colonel Lee knew what he was about and so did Major Dixon. . . . In a few minutes or less time, and at the instant they, the Tories, were completely covered by our lines upon both flanks, or front and rear as the case may have been, the bugle sounded to attack, and the slaughter began, the Tories crying out, "Your own men, your own men, as good subjects of His Majesty as in America." It was said that upwards of two hundred of these Tories were slain on the ground.

The evening after our battle with the Tories, we having a considerable number of prisoners, I recollect a scene which made a lasting impression upon my mind. I was invited by some of my comrades to go and see some of the prisoners. We went to where six were standing together. Some discussion taking place, I heard some of our men cry out, "Remember Buford" [a slaughter of Virginian troops by Tarleton's Tories], and the prisoners were immediately hewed to pieces with broadswords. At first I bore the scene without any emotion, but upon a moment's reflection, I felt such horror as I never did before nor have since, and, returning to my quarters and throwing myself upon my blanket, I contemplated the cruelties of war until overcome and unmanned by a distressing gloom from which I was not relieved until commencing our march next morning before day by moonlight. I came to Tarleton's camp, which he had just abandoned leaving lively rail fires. Being on the left of the road as we marched along, I discovered lying upon the ground something with appearance of a man. Upon approaching him, he proved to be a youth about sixteen who, having come out to view the British through curiosity, for fear he might give information to our troops, they had run him through with a bayonet and left him for dead. Though able to speak, he was mortally wounded. The sight of this unoffending boy, butchered, . . . relieved me of my distressful feelings for the slaughter of the Tories, and I desired nothing so much as the opportunity of participating in their destruction.

Source: Hall's Pension application, Record Group 15 of the Records of the Veterans Administration, National Archives. Available in John C. Dann, ed., *The Revolution Remembered: Eyewitness Accounts of the War for Independence* (Chicago: University of Chicago Press, 1980), 201–204 *passim.*

Then they stalled, for Burgoyne—"Gentleman Johnny," as he was called—fought with style, not speed. His heavy baggage train moved slowly, weighed down with comfortable tents and ample stocks of food and wine (see American Voices, above). Its progress was further impeded by the Continental forces of General Horatio Gates, who felled trees across the crude wagon trail and raided the long, thinly stretched supply lines to Canada. By the end of the summer Burgoyne's army—6,000 regulars (half of them German mercenaries) and 600 Loyalists and Indians—was in trouble, bogged down in the wilderness near Saratoga, New York.

The Patriot militia delivered the final blow. On August 16 at a military depot at Bennington, Vermont, 2,000 militiamen left their farms to fight a bitter pitched battle that deprived British raiders of much-needed supplies of food, horses, and oxen. Burgoyne then received more bad news: Patriot militiamen in the Mohawk Valley had forced St. Leger's troops to retreat. And to meet Howe's request for additional troops to occupy Philadelphia, the British commander in New York City had to recall the relief force he had sent toward Albany. While Burgoyne waited in vain for help, thousands of Patriot militiamen from Massachusetts, New Hampshire, and New York joined Gates's forces. They "swarmed around the army like birds of prey," an English sergeant wrote in his journal, and on October 17, 1777, forced Burgoyne to surrender.

The battle of Saratoga proved to be the turning point of the war. The Americans captured 5,000 British troops and their equipment—a price in men and materiel that far outweighed Howe's capture of Philadel-

phia. More important, the victory virtually assured the success of American diplomats in Paris, who were seeking a military alliance with France. Patriots on the home front were equally delighted, though their joy was muted by an awareness of the difficulties that lay ahead.

Wartime Trials

In the twentieth century two world wars disrupted the lives of millions of ordinary women and men, conscripting them into war industries, destroying their property, turning them into refugees, taking their lives. On a much smaller scale, the American War of Independence exposed tens of thousands of civilians to deprivation, displacement, and death. "An army, even a friendly one, are a dreadful scourge to any people," a Connecticut soldier wrote home from Pennsylvania. "You cannot imagine what devastation and distress mark their steps." New Jersey was particularly hard hit by the fighting as British and American armies marched back and forth across the state. Those with reputations as Patriots or Loyalists fled from their homes to escape arrest—or worse. Soldiers and partisans looted farms, seeking food or political revenge. Drunk and disorderly troops harassed or raped women and girls. Wherever the armies went, families lived in fear.

People learned to fear their neighbors as well, for the War of Independence was in many respects a civil war. Mobs of Patriot farmers in New England beat suspected Tories or destroyed their property. "Every Body submitted to our Sovereign Lord the Mob," a Loyalist preacher lamented. "Now we are reduced to a State of Anarchy." Patriots in most communities quickly organized a new institution of local government called a Committee of Safety. Those committees collected taxes, sent food and clothing to the Continental army, and imposed fines or jail sentences on those who failed to support the Patriot cause. "There is no such thing as remaining neutral," declared the Committee of Safety of Farmington, Connecticut.

Financial Crisis. Wars are not won by guns alone. Armies have to be fed, clothed, and paid. Victory often goes to the side that has the most money or is prepared to make the greatest financial sacrifices. When the War of Independence began, the new American governments were neither wealthy nor politically secure. Since opposition to taxes had fueled the independence movement in the first place, Patriot officials were reluctant to increase taxes for fear of undermining their fragile authority. To finance the war, the state governments first borrowed money, in gold or silver or British currency, from wealthy individuals. Those funds quickly ran out, so the states created a new monetary system based on the dollar (not the English pound) and issued $260 million in

currency and transferable bonds, using the new money to pay soldiers and purchase supplies. Theoretically the new notes could be redeemed at a stated time in gold or silver. But since they were printed in huge quantities and were not backed by tax revenues or mortgages on land, many Americans questioned their worth and refused to accept them at the face value. Indeed, North Carolina's paper money came to be worth so little that the state government refused to accept it. Many state governments teetered on the brink of bankruptcy.

The monetary system created by the Continental Congress collapsed as well, despite the best efforts of the Philadelphia merchant Robert Morris, the "financier of the Revolution." Until 1781 the Congress was essentially an ad hoc coalition of independent state governments without legal authority of its own and completely dependent on funds requisitioned from the member states, which frequently paid late or not at all. To raise money, Congress depended on loans, but with no funds of its own, the government could not assure creditors that they would be repaid. Congress therefore borrowed $6 million from France and pledged it as security; wealthy Americans promptly purchased $27 million in Continental loan certificates, essentially gambling on the Patriot cause. When those funds and other French and Dutch loans were exhausted, Congress followed the lead of the states and financed the war by printing money. Between 1775 and 1779 it issued $191 million in currency. By 1780 tax revenues from the states had retired only $3 million of those bills

A Flood of Paper Currency
The Continental Congress issued this bill in 1776, declaring it to be worth "SIX Spanish Milled DOLLARS" or the equivalent in gold or silver, but by 1780 most Americans no longer had confidence in the currency and its value collapsed to virtually nothing—giving rise to the phrase "not worth a continental."

from circulation, so the value of the remaining bills continued to fall.

Indeed, the enormous increase in the volume of paper currency created the worst inflation in American history. The amount of goods available for purchase—both domestic foodstuffs and foreign manufactures—had shrunk significantly because of the fighting and the British naval blockade, even as the amount of currency had multiplied. Inevitably, consumers "bid up" the prices of goods. In Maryland, for example, a bag of salt that had cost $1 in 1776 was valued at $3,900 a few years later. This soaring inflation forced nearly every family to look out for its own interests. Unwilling to accept worthless currency, hard-pressed farmers refused to sell their crops, even to the American army. To supply their own needs, farmers resorted to barter—trading wheat for tools or clothes—or sold goods only to those who could pay in gold or silver. In towns, women led mobs that seized overpriced sugar, tea, and bread from storekeepers. With civilian morale and social cohesion crumbling despite the victory at Saratoga, some Patriot leaders began to doubt that the rebellion could succeed.

Valley Forge. Fears reached their peak during the winter of 1777–1778. After the capture of Philadelphia, Howe established winter quarters there, and he and his officers partook of the finest wines, foods, and entertainment the city could offer. Washington's army retreated into the Pennsylvania countryside, establishing its base for the winter some 20 miles to the west, in Valley Forge. About 12,000 soldiers, accompanied by hundreds of camp followers, arrived at the camp in December. Everyone suffered horribly. "The army . . . now begins to grow sickly," a surgeon confided to his diary. "Poor food—hard lodging—cold weather—fatigue—nasty clothes—nasty cookery. . . . Why are we sent here to starve and freeze?" Many soldiers deserted, unable to endure the harsh conditions; by spring over a thousand men had vanished into the countryside. Another 3,000 soldiers and scores of camp followers died from malnutrition and disease. One winter at Valley Forge took as many American lives as had two years of fighting against General Howe.

Precarious public backing for the rebellion also threatened the army, which could not depend on farmers for support. Ethnic and religious divisions among Americans who lived near Valley Forge directly affected military operations. For example, most New Light members of the Dutch Reformed Church in nearby New Jersey actively supported the American cause, joining the militia and raiding British encampments, but many Old Lights were Loyalists and fed information and supplies to the British. A number of Quakers and German sectarians in Pennsylvania were pacifists, unwilling to support either side.

Self-interest also contributed to the deprivation of Washington's army at Valley Forge. Many farmers hoarded their grain over the winter, hoping to profit from high prices in the spring. Others bullied their way through Patriot roadblocks to Philadelphia, where British quartermasters paid in gold and silver. Even farmers who supported the rebellion could not afford to supply the American army when their labors were rewarded with rapidly depreciating Continental Congress dollars. "Such a dearth of public spirit, and want of public virtue," Washington complained—but to no effect. The suffering at Valley Forge continued, graphic testimony to divided loyalties among the public and the inability of the Congress to raise sufficient revenue.

In this dark hour Baron von Steuben, a former Prussian military officer, raised the morale and self-respect of both officers and enlisted men by instituting a standardized system of drill and maneuver at Valley Forge. Von Steuben was one of a handful of foreigners who had volunteered their services to the American cause. His efforts encouraged officers to become more professional in their demeanor and behavior and instilled greater order and discipline in the ranks. Thanks to von Steuben, the smaller Continental army that emerged from Valley Forge in the spring was a much tougher and better disciplined force with a renewed sense of purpose.

The Path to Victory, 1778–1783

The Patriots' prospects improved dramatically in 1778, when the United States formed a military alliance with France, the most powerful nation on the European continent. The alliance not only brought the Americans money, troops, and supplies but also changed the conflict from a colonial rebellion to an international war.

The French Alliance

Negotiating the Treaty. In 1777 Benjamin Franklin and two other diplomats, Arthur Lee and Silas Deane, had begun negotiations for a commercial and military treaty with France. Since 1763 France had been seeking revenge for its defeat in the French and Indian War and its loss of Canada. The French foreign minister, the comte de Vergennes, was a determined opponent of Britain and an early supporter of American independence. In 1776 he persuaded King Louis XVI to extend a secret loan to the rebellious colonies and supply them with gunpowder. When news of the American victory at Saratoga reached Paris in December 1777, Vergennes urged the king to approve a formal alliance with the Continental Congress.

Franklin and his associates craftily exploited the ri-

valry between France and Britain. They used the threat of a negotiated settlement with Britain to win an explicit French commitment to American independence. The Treaty of Alliance of February 6, 1778 specified that after France entered the war against Great Britain, neither partner would sign a separate peace before the "liberty, sovereignty, and independence" of the United States was assured. In return, the American diplomats pledged that their government would recognize any French conquests in the West Indies.

France and America were unlikely partners. France was Catholic and a monarchy; the United States was largely Protestant and a federation of republics. The two peoples had been on opposite sides in wars from 1689 to 1763. But now they were united against a common enemy. After two years of armed resistance, the fledgling American federation had earned the respect of the nations of Europe and had come to figure in the international balance of power. The Franco-American alliance isolated Britain diplomatically and placed it militarily on the defensive: British forces not only confronted the Patriots in North America but had to defend Gibraltar against Spain, and the West Indies, India, and Britain itself against France.

The British Response. The war became increasingly unpopular in Britain. Radical agitators and republican-minded artisans supported American demands for greater rights and campaigned for political reforms at home—such as broadening the right to vote and eliminating electoral corruption. The landed gentry and urban merchants protested against rising taxes. To meet the military budget, the government had already increased the land tax and the stamp duty and imposed new levies on carriages, wine, and imported goods. "It seemed we were to be taxed and stamped ourselves instead of inflicting taxes and stamps on others," a British politician complained. Yet George III continued to demand that the rebellion be crushed at any cost. If America won independence, he warned Lord North, "the West Indies must follow them. Ireland would soon follow the same plan and be a separate state, then this island would be reduced to itself, and soon would be a poor island indeed."

Lord North took a more pragmatic position. To forestall a Franco-American alliance and keep the colonies in the British empire, North announced his intention in February 1778 to seek a negotiated constitutional settlement. At his bidding, Parliament repealed the Tea and Prohibitory acts and, in an amazing concession, renounced its right to tax the American colonies. The prime minister then appointed a commission, headed by Lord Carlisle, to negotiate with the Continental Congress and offer a return to the constitutional relationship that had existed in 1763, before the Sugar and Stamp acts. But it was too late. By early 1778, not

only had the military pact with France been signed but a majority of Americans had embraced independence and republicanism.

The Impact of the Alliance. The alliance with France infused new life into the Patriots' cause. With access to military supplies and European loans, the American army soon improved and hopes soared. "There has been a great change in this state since the news from France," a Patriot soldier reported from Pennsylvania; farmers—"mercenary wretches," he called them— "were as eager for Continental Money now as they were a few weeks ago for British gold."

The Congress also showed renewed energy and purpose, finally addressing the demands of the officer corps for pensions. Most officers came from the upper ranks of society and used their own funds to equip not only themselves but sometimes their men as well; in return they demanded pensions for life at half pay. Although John Adams condemned the petitioners as "Mastiffs, scrambling for rank and pay like apes for nuts," Congress agreed to give the officers half pay after the end of the war, though only for seven years. General Washington had urged Congress to make this concession, warning the lawmakers that "the salvation of the cause depends upon it."

War in the South

The French alliance expanded the war without bringing it to a rapid conclusion. When France entered the conflict in June 1778, it had other goals besides a quick victory over the British forces in North America. Hoping to capture a rich sugar island, France concentrated its naval forces in the West Indies. Spain, which entered the war in 1779, also had its own agenda: in return for providing naval assistance to France, it hoped to win back Florida and Gibraltar in the peace settlement. The destiny of the new American republic was enmeshed in a web of European alliances and territorial quarrels.

This diplomatic morass gave Britain one more opportunity to crush the rebellion—or at least limit it. Saratoga had spelled an end to British hopes of recapturing New England and holding all the rebellious mainland colonies. But in many ways New England was the least valuable part of the empire. Far more important to the South Atlantic system were the southern colonies, with their rich crops of rice and tobacco. The British ministry, beset by a war on many fronts, settled on a more modest strategy in America. It would use its army to recapture Virginia, the Carolinas, and Georgia and then rely on Loyalists to hold and administer the reconquered territory.

Until that time the British had made little use of Americans who remained loyal to the king. They knew,

however, that recent migrants with little sympathy for the rebel cause made up a sizable portion of the population of the southern backcountry. Some, such as the Scottish Highlanders in North Carolina, retained an especially strong allegiance to the Crown. The British hoped to recruit other Loyalists from the ranks of the Regulators, who had opposed the political dominance of low-country planters. They also hoped to take advantage of racial divisions in the South. Over 1,000 Virginia slaves had fought for Lord Dunmore in 1776 under the banner "Liberty to Slaves!" and thousands more might support a new British offensive. At the least, racial divisions would undermine the Patriots' military efforts. Blacks formed 30 to 50 percent of the population, yet whites were afraid to arm them. Many planters refused to allow their sons or white overseers to join the Continental forces, keeping them home to prevent slave revolts.

Implementing this southern strategy became the responsibility of Sir Henry Clinton, who had replaced the discredited Howe early in 1778. In June 1778 Clinton ordered the main British army to evacuate Philadelphia and move to more secure quarters in New York. In De-

cember he finally launched his southern campaign, landing a force of 3,500 men near Savannah, Georgia. The British army took the city, mobilized hundreds of blacks to build barricades and unload military supplies, and then moved inland, capturing Augusta early in 1779. By the end of the year the British had reconquered Georgia and had 10,000 troops poised for an assault on South Carolina. To counter this threat, the Continental Congress suggested that South Carolina raise 3,000 black troops, but the state assembly overwhelmingly rejected the proposal.

During most of 1780 British forces moved from one victory to another. In April Clinton laid siege to Charleston, South Carolina, which surrendered six weeks later. He captured General Benjamin Lincoln and his 5,000 troops in the single largest American surrender of the war. After this success Lord Cornwallis assumed control of the British forces and sent out expeditions to secure the countryside. In August Cornwallis routed an American force commanded by General Horatio Gates, the hero of Saratoga, at Camden in the heart of the Carolina pine barrens, giving the British control of South Carolina (see Map 6.2).

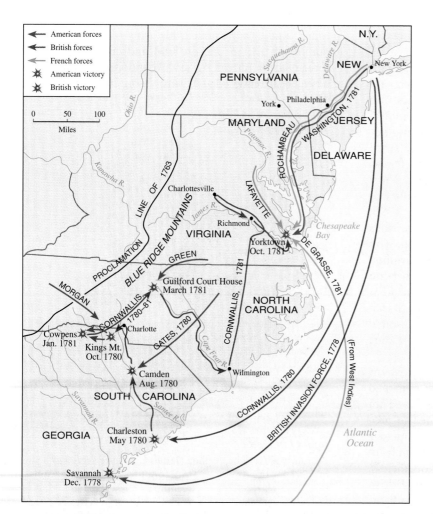

MAP 6.2

The Campaign in the South

The British ministry's southern strategy started well. British forces captured Savannah in December 1778 and Charleston in May 1779. Brutal warfare raged in the interior over the next eighteen months, fought more by small bands of irregulars than by disciplined armies. When Cornwallis carried the battle into Virginia in late 1781, a Franco-American army led by Washington and Lafayette surrounded his forces at Yorktown, aided by the French fleet under Admiral de Grasse.

This victory seemed to confirm the wisdom of the southern strategy. After the British attack, hundreds of blacks fled to Florida and hundreds more sought protection behind British lines, providing labor for the invading army. Moreover, southern Loyalists rallied to the support of the Crown, forming military units and providing supplies and information to British forces as they moved through Georgia and South Carolina. In contrast, the local Patriots were of little use to General Gates's army. Only about 1,200 militiamen joined Gates at the battle of Camden—a fifth of the number of local Patriots at Saratoga—and many of them panicked and fled without firing a shot.

Then the tide of battle turned. Far off in Europe, the Dutch declared war against Britain, making its diplomatic isolation complete; of more immediate importance, France dispatched troops to America. The French decision was partly the work of the marquis de Lafayette, a republican-minded French aristocrat who had offered his services to the American cause long before the alliance of 1778. Lafayette had returned to France early in 1780 to persuade Louis XVI to change French military priorities and prosecute the war against Britain in North America more vigorously. In July 1780 a French army of 5,500 men commanded by General comte de Rochambeau arrived in Newport, Rhode Island, where it posed a threat to the British forces in New York.

In the South, Washington replaced Gates with Nathanael Greene as the American commander, and Greene immediately devised new military tactics and strategies. To make the best use of the Patriot militiamen, many of whom were "without discipline and addicted to plundering," Greene divided them into small groups under strong leaders and used them to harass the larger but less mobile British forces. A militia force of Patriot farmers defeated a regiment of Loyalists at King's Mountain, North Carolina, in October 1780, taking about a thousand prisoners. American guerrillas led by the "Swamp Fox," General Francis Marion, won a series of small but fierce battles in South Carolina, while General Daniel Morgan led another American force to a bloody victory over a British regiment at Cowpens, North Carolina, in January 1781. On March 15 General Greene's force fought Cornwallis's seasoned army to a draw at North Carolina's Guilford Court House.

Patriot forces had broken the back of the British offensive, but Loyalist garrisons and militia remained powerful, and the well-organized Cherokee posed an additional threat to Patriot forces. Determined to protect their lands, the Cherokee attacked American settlers in the southern backcountry, preventing them from joining the battle against the British. Nonetheless, Greene's army slowly began to wear down the British and reconquer the Carolinas and Georgia. "We fight, get beaten, and fight again," General Greene declared.

In the spring of 1781 Cornwallis made the crucial decision to concede the southernmost states to Greene and seek a decisive victory in Virginia. Aided by reinforcements from Clinton in New York, Cornwallis moved through eastern North Carolina and into Virginia's Tidewater region. His forces, led by Benedict Arnold, the infamous traitor to the Patriot cause (see American Lives, pages 184–185), ranged up and down the James River, meeting only slight resistance from a small American force commanded by Lafayette. Then, in May 1781, as the armies of Lafayette and Cornwallis sparred near the York Peninsula in Virginia, the French monarch ordered the large fleet in the West Indies commanded by Admiral François de Grasse to sail to North America.

Emboldened by the ample forces at his disposal, Washington launched a well-coordinated attack. To keep Clinton's troops in the North, he feinted an assault on New York City and secretly had General Rochambeau's army march from Rhode Island to Virginia, where it joined Washington's troops. Simultaneously, Admiral de Grasse positioned his fleet off the coast of Virginia, where, in combination with a smaller French naval force from Rhode Island, it established control of Chesapeake Bay. By the time the British discovered Washington's audacious plan, it was too late. Cornwallis found himself surrounded, his army of 9,500 men outnumbered two to one on land and cut off from reinforcement or retreat by sea. Abandoned by the British navy, he surrendered at Yorktown on October 19, 1781.

James Lafayette
Born into slavery in Virginia, James Lafayette served as a spy in 1781 for the American army commanded by the marquis de Lafayette, receiving his freedom as a reward and taking Lafayette's surname as his own. The two Lafayettes met again in 1824, when the Frenchman visited the United States.

American Soldiers at Yorktown, 1781
A French observer captured the diversity of the American army: a black infantryman from Rhode Island, a French-Canadian volunteer, a buckskin-clad rifleman from Virginia, and (holding the gunnery torch) an artilleryman from the Continental army.

The Franco-American victory at Yorktown broke the resolve of the British government. "Oh God! It is all over!" Lord North exclaimed when he heard the news. His ministry lacked the will or resources to raise a new army to fight a long war of attrition in America, and Britain's European rivals posed an immediate threat. The combined fleets of France and Spain were menacing the British sugar islands, Dutch merchants were recapturing American and European markets from English and Scottish traders, and a newly formed group of European states—the League of Armed Neutrality—was threatening to use force to break Britain's commercial blockade of France. Isolated diplomatically in Europe, stymied militarily in America, and—perhaps most important—lacking public support at home, the British ministry gave up active prosecution of the war. Only isolated attacks by Loyalists and Indians reminded Americans that their country was still at war.

The Patriot Advantage

Angry members of Parliament demanded an explanation for this stinging military defeat. How could mighty Britain, victorious in the Great War for Empire, with its formidable financial and military resources, be defeated by a motley group of upstart colonists? The ministry blamed the military leadership, pointing with some justification to a series of blunders made by British generals. Why had Howe not been more ruthless in his pursuit of Washington's army in 1776? How could Germain have failed to coordinate the movements of Howe's and Burgoyne's armies in 1777? Why had Cornwallis been allowed to march deep into the powerful rebel state of Virginia in 1781?

Historians have been equally critical of the military command, but they also have pointed out the high odds against British success, given the broad-based support for the rebel cause. While only a third of the white population consisted of "true Patriots," deeply committed to the rebellion, another third was supportive enough to pay the taxes imposed by the state governments. Unlike most revolutionaries, the Patriots had assumed control of well-established institutions, and their leaders were experienced politicians who could command public support and manage governments. And while the Continental army had to be built from scratch and was never very large, it was fighting on its own territory with the assistance of thousands of militiamen. Even the substantial number of Loyalists and Indian allies—more than 55,000 Tories fought as regular soldiers or militiamen during the war, and thousands of native Americans served as auxiliary troops—could not offset these advantages.

The odds changed over time. Once the rebels had the military, diplomatic, and financial support of France, they could reasonably hope for victory. Britain now faced an expanding conflict, requiring more resources. A charismatic leader such as William Pitt or a great general might have rallied British political opinion to the cause, suppressed the American rebellion, and restored imperial authority. But ordinary politicians and mediocre generals were destined to fail.

Americans, by contrast, were extremely lucky to have George Washington as commander of the Continental army, for his leadership was inspired. The American general deferred to the civil authorities, winning respect—and political and financial support—from the Congress and the state governments alike. He exercised firm control over his subordinates yet supported their just complaints. Confident of his own abilities, he recruited outstanding men such as Baron von Steuben to instill discipline into the ranks of the fledgling Continental army and turn it into a respectable fighting force. Washington also came to understand that warfare in a lightly governed agricultural society required the deft use of rural militia units.

The Enigma of Benedict Arnold

Benedict Arnold was different: a military hero for both sides in the same war. He began his career as an American Patriot in May 1775, when he and Ethan Allen led the brigade that captured Fort Ticonderoga on Lake Champlain. Arnold's heroics continued in September, when he led an expedition of 1,150 riflemen against Quebec, the capital of British Canada. The American commander drove his men hard through the Maine wilderness, overcoming leaky boats, spoiled provisions, treacherous rivers, and near starvation to arrive at Quebec in November, his force reduced to 650 men. These losses did not deter Arnold. Joined by General Richard Montgomery, who had arrived with 300 troops after capturing Montreal, Arnold's forces attacked the strongly fortified city, only to have the assault end in disaster. A hundred Americans were killed, including

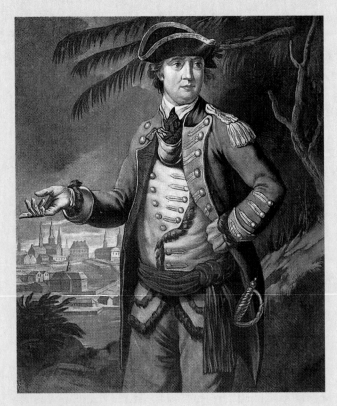

Benedict Arnold

Montgomery; 400 were captured; and many were wounded, including Arnold, who fell as he stormed over a barricade, a ball through his leg.

Quebec was only the beginning. For the next five years Arnold served the Patriot side with distinction in one battle after another, including a dangerous assault against the center of the British line at Saratoga, where he was again wounded in the leg. No general was more imaginative than Arnold, no field officer more daring, no soldier more courageous.

Yet Arnold has gone down in history not as a hero but as a villain, a military traitor who, as commander of the American fort at West Point, New York, in 1780, schemed to hand it over to the British. Of his role in this conspiracy there is no doubt. His British contact, Major John André, was caught with incriminating documents in Arnold's handwriting, including routes of access to the fort. Arnold, fleeing down the Hudson River on a British ship, defended his treason in a letter to Washington, stating that "love to my country actuates my present conduct, however it may appear inconsistent to the world, who very seldom judge right of any man's actions."

But judge we must. Why did Arnold desert the cause for which he had fought so gallantly and twice been wounded? Was there any justification for his conduct?

When the fighting began at Lexington and Concord in April 1775, Arnold was thirty-four, an apothecary and minor merchant in New Haven, Connecticut—but also a militia captain and ardent Patriot. "Good God," he had exclaimed at the time of the Boston Massacre, "are the Americans all asleep and tamely giving up their Liberties?" Eager to support the rebellion, Arnold coerced the town's selectmen into supplying powder and ball to his men and promptly marched them to Boston, which was under siege by the New England militia. On the way Arnold thought up the attack on Fort Ticonderoga (realizing that the fort's cannon could be used to force the British out of Boston) and persuaded the Massachusetts Committee of Safety to approve his plan and make him a colonel. That done, he raced to New York to take command so that the glory would be his. The victory achieved, Arnold submitted an inflated

Major John André Executed as a British Spy
Unable to catch the traitor Benedict Arnold, the American army executed his British accomplice, whose elegance, intelligence, and dignity won the hearts of his captors: "He died universally esteemed and universally regretted," noted Alexander Hamilton.

claim for expenses (£1,060 in Massachusetts currency, or about $60,000 today) and protested vehemently when legislators closely examined each item.

These events illuminated Arnold's great strengths and fatal flaws and were prophetic of his ultimate fate. He was bold and creative, a man who sized up a situation and acted quickly. He was ambitious and extravagant, an egocentric man who craved power and the financial rewards that came with it. He was intrepid and ruthless, willing to risk his life—and the lives of others—to get what he wanted.

Such men often are resented as much as they are admired, and so it was with Arnold. At Quebec some New England officers accused him of arrogance and tried to withdraw from his command, but Congress rewarded the intrepid colonel by making him a brigadier general. When Arnold again distinguished himself in battle in early 1777—having his horse shot out from under him—Congress promoted him to major general and gave him a new horse "as a token of their admiration of his gallant conduct." But then, in the middle of the struggle at Saratoga, General Horatio Gates, the American commander, relieved Arnold of his command, partly for insubordination and partly because Gates considered him a "pompous little fellow." Washington rewarded Arnold nonetheless, appointing him commandant at Philadelphia in July 1778, after the British evacuation of the city.

By then Arnold was an embittered man, disdainful of his fellow officers and resentful toward Congress for not promoting him more quickly and to even higher rank. A widower, he threw himself into the social life of the city, holding grand parties, courting and marrying Margaret Shippen—a talented young woman of good family, who, at nineteen, was half his age—and falling deeply into debt. Arnold's extravagance drew him into shady financial schemes and into disrepute with Congress, which investigated his accounts and recommended a court-martial. "Having . . . become a cripple in the service of my country, I little expected to meet [such] ungrateful returns," he complained to Washington.

Faced with financial ruin, uncertain of future promotion, and disgusted with congressional politics, Arnold made a fateful decision: he would seek fortune and fame in the service of Great Britain. With cool calculation, he initiated correspondence with Sir Henry Clinton, the British commander, promising to deliver West Point and its 3,000 defenders for £20,000 sterling (about $1 million today), a momentous act that he hoped would spark the collapse of the American cause. Persuading Washington to place the fort under his command, Arnold moved in September 1780 to execute his audacious plan, only to see it fail when André was captured. As André was executed as a spy, Arnold received £6,000 from the British government and appointment as a brigadier general.

Arnold served George III with the same skill and daring he had shown in the Patriot cause. In 1781 he led devastating strikes on Patriot supply depots: in Virginia he looted Richmond and destroyed munitions and grain intended for the American army opposing Lord Cornwallis; in Connecticut he burned ships, warehouses, and much of the town of New London, a major port for Patriot privateers.

In the end, Benedict Arnold's moral failure lay not in his disenchantment with the American cause—for many other officers returned to civilian life disgusted with the decline in republican virtue and angry over their failure to win a guaranteed pension from Congress. Nor did his infamy stem from his transfer of allegiance to the British side—for other Patriots chose to become Loyalists, sometimes out of principle but just as often for personal gain. Arnold's perfidy lay in the abuse of his position of authority and trust: he would betray West Point and its garrison—and if necessary the entire American war effort—to secure his own success. His treason was not that of a principled man but that of a selfish one, and he never lived that down. Hated in America as a consort of "Beelzebub . . . the Devil," Arnold was treated with coldness and even contempt in Britain. He died as he lived—a man without a country.

Finally, Washington had a greater margin for error than did the British generals who opposed him. He needed only to maintain an army in the field to keep the cause alive, given the fact that for every active Loyalist there were two Patriots and that the rebels usually controlled the local governments. Though they often wavered in their support, these ordinary citizens mobilized the economic resources required to fight a long war and came through at crucial moments in the military campaigns. Patriot partisans deprived the British troops of safe camps and local supplies. Thousands of militiamen besieged General Gage in Boston in 1775, surrounded Burgoyne at Saratoga in 1778, and forced Cornwallis to relinquish the Carolinas in 1781.

In the end, the allegiance of the American people decided the outcome of the conflict. Preferring Patriot rule, the majority of farmers and artisans refused to support Loyalist forces or accept imperial control in areas occupied by the British army. Consequently, though the British won many military victories, they achieved little, whereas their two major defeats—at Saratoga and Yorktown—proved catastrophic.

Diplomatic Triumph

After Yorktown it took the diplomats two years to conclude the war. Peace talks began in Paris in April 1782, but the French and Spanish stalled for time, hoping for a major naval victory or territorial conquest. Their delaying tactics infuriated the American diplomats—Benjamin Franklin, John Adams, and John Jay—who feared that drawn-out negotiations would tempt France to sacrifice American interests. Consequently, the Americans negotiated secretly with the British; if necessary, they were prepared to cut their ties to France and sign a separate peace. The British ministry was also eager to obtain a quick settlement, because many members of Parliament no longer supported the war, and ministers feared the loss of a rich sugar island in the West Indies or the creation of a new French empire in North America.

Astutely exploiting the rivalry between Britain and France, Franklin and his colleagues won a major victory at the bargaining table. The Treaty of Paris, signed in the French capital on September 3, 1783, formally recognized the independence of the United States. Britain retained Canada, but only the part north and west of the Great Lakes. All the land between the Appalachian Mountains and the Mississippi River that Britain had wrested from France twenty years before was ceded to the new American republic. This was still the domain of undefeated native American peoples, but Britain made no attempt to secure the land rights of its Indian allies. Instead, it promised to withdraw its garrisons across the trans-Appalachian West "with all convenient speed," leaving native Americans to their fate. As an Indian of the Wea people complained, "In endeavouring to assist you it seems we have wrought our own ruin."

Other provisions granted Americans fishing rights off Newfoundland and Nova Scotia, forbade the British from "carrying away any negroes or other property of the American inhabitants," and guaranteed freedom of navigation on the Mississippi to British subjects and American citizens "forever." In its only concession, the American government promised "earnestly" to recommend to the state legislatures that they return Loyalist property seized in the war and treat Loyalists as free and equal citizens.

In the Treaty of Versailles, signed at the same time as the Treaty of Paris, Britain made peace with France

Making Peace
Benjamin West's uncompleted painting of 1783, *American Commission of the Preliminary Peace Negotiation with Great Britain* (detail), portrays the American negotiators, including Benjamin Franklin, John Jay, and John Adams. The Americans bargained hard with the British during the fall of 1782 and signed the preliminary treaty on November 30. A Patriot diplomatic triumph, the treaty acknowledged the independence of the United States and extended its boundaries to the Mississippi River.

and Spain. France had diminished the size and wealth of the British empire, but its only territorial gain was the Caribbean island of Tobago. More significant for the future, by joining the war of American independence France had quadrupled its national debt, and in six years cries for tax relief and for political liberty at home would spark the French Revolution. Spain failed in its main objective of retaking Gibraltar, but it did reacquire Florida from Britain. Americans welcomed this diplomatic outcome, for Spain was a far weaker power than Britain or France.

However, the two treaties were vague in defining the boundaries between the United States and its British and Spanish neighbors, so that territorial disputes would mar relations for another thirty years. But the peace settlement opened the interior of the continent to American expansion and made possible the development of a large and powerful nation.

Republicanism Defined and Challenged

From the moment of its creation, Americans began to define the character of their new republican society. In the Declaration of Independence Thomas Jefferson proclaimed that all individuals have the right to "life, liberty, and the pursuit of happiness." Jefferson drew his list from the writings of John Locke, but he substituted the word *happiness* for Locke's *property*. Jefferson's choice reflected the idealism of many Patriots and their commitment to *republican virtue*, an enlightened quest for the public interest. But it also suggested that many Americans considered the private ownership of property a prerequisite for happiness. The tension between self-interest and the public interest—between individual property rights and the welfare of the community—would shape the history of the new nation.

Republican Ideals and Wartime Pressures

The Republican Ideal. In the simplest terms, a republic is a state without a monarch. For many Americans, republicanism was much more—not simply a political system but a social philosophy. "The word *republic*," wrote Thomas Paine, "means the *public good*, or the good of the whole" (from the Latin *republica*: thing, *res*; of the people, *publica*). It followed that the members of a republic assumed important social responsibilities. "Every man in a republic is public property," asserted the Philadelphia Patriot Benjamin Rush (who eventually extended this notion to include women as well). "His time and talents—his youth—his manhood—his old age—nay more, life, all belong to his country."

Wartime fears allowed this collectivist vision to find ample expression, often at the cost of individual choice. When a local Patriot Committee of Safety suppressed a dissenting Loyalist or demanded that a merchant lower prices, its members saw themselves as acting in the public interest, according to the maxim of ancient Rome: "Take care that the commonwealth should receive no damage." Similarly, when General Howe occupied Philadelphia in 1777, the Pennsylvania legislature invoked republican principles to justify the extreme steps it took to safeguard the state. It required loyalty oaths of all citizens, expelled suspected Tories, and executed two Quakers on charges of treason. Ultimately the assembly, dominated by Scots-Irish Presbyterians, went further, invoking evangelical Protestant values in a controversial campaign to outlaw gambling, horse racing, theatrical shows, and all "evil practices which tend to debauch the minds and corrupt the morals of the subjects of the Commonwealth."

The Ideal Tested in the Military. Because republicanism lauded public virtue, the Continental Congress praised the self-sacrifice of the militiamen who fought and fell at Lexington and Concord, Saratoga, and Camden. In contrast, its members deprecated the Continental officer corps's demand for lifetime pensions as a "total loss of virtue," as Henry Laurens of South Carolina put it. Having been raised as gentlemen, officers were supposed to be the prime exemplars of the ideal of republican virtue—far from demanding recompense, they should give freely to the republic.

As the war continued, the zeal for self-sacrifice diminished. Continental troops stationed at Morristown, New Jersey, mutinied during the winters of 1779 and 1780, unable or unwilling to endure the harsh conditions. To restore authority, Washington ordered the execution of several leaders of the mutiny, and despite its precarious finances, Congress used monetary incentives—back pay and new clothing—to pacify the rest of the recruits. Unrest among higher-ranking military men lurked below the surface throughout the war, erupting finally at Newburgh, New York, in 1783, when Washington had to use his personal authority to thwart a potentially dangerous challenge to Congress's policies by a group of disgruntled officers.

Republican Virtue versus Self-Interest in the Marketplace. Civilians also found it difficult to sustain their virtue as economic hardship brought the war closer to home. The British naval blockade nearly eliminated the New England fishing industry along the Atlantic coast and cut off the supply of European manufactured goods to American consumers. Domestic trade and production declined as well. The British occupation of Boston, New York, and Philadelphia put thousands of people out of work. Unemployed shipwrights, dock laborers, masons,

coopers, and bakers left the cities and drifted into the countryside; the population of New York City declined from 21,000 in 1774 to less than half that at the war's end. In the Chesapeake the British blockade deprived tobacco planters of markets in Europe, forcing them to turn to the cultivation of wheat, corn, and other food-stuffs. All across the land the pace of commercial activity slackened as farmers and artisans adapted to a war economy.

The scarcity of imported goods brought a sharp rise in prices and widespread appeals for government regulation. Consumers decried merchants and traders as "enemies, extortioners, and monopolizers." In 1777 a convention of New England states restricted increases in the price of domestic commodities and imported goods to 75 percent above their prewar level; to enforce this directive, the Massachusetts legislature passed an "Act to prevent Monopoly and Oppression." Many farmers and artisans refused to sell goods at the established prices. Some wanted to pass along their own rising costs, but others were determined to profit from wartime shortages. In the end consumers had to pay the market price, a government official admitted, "or submit to starving."

Personal distress prompted many Americans to re-examine the meaning of republican virtue. Philadelphia, where severe food shortages and soaring prices followed the British withdrawal in 1778, saw the most spirited debate. In May 1779 a crowd of artisans and laborers, having caught a merchant illegally exporting flour, called a town meeting and created a Committee on Prices that set wholesale and retail rates for thirty-two commodities. The artisan-led committee justified these restraints by invoking the traditional concept of the "just price," reflecting their fear of exploitation by well-to-do merchants and calculating storekeepers.

Led by the influential Patriot financier Robert Morris, Philadelphia merchants argued against price controls and articulated a "classical liberal" ideology of free trade and enlightened self-interest. They pointed out that regulation would only cause farmers to store their crops, whereas allowing prices to rise would bring goods to market and relieve scarcity. Morris's arguments found favor among farmers, who wanted to sell their goods at the highest prices, and members of the Continental Congress, including Benjamin Franklin, who condemned price controls as "contrary to the nature of commerce."

But most Philadelphians were skeptical. At a town meeting in August 1779, 2,115 voters endorsed government regulation of the market and only 281 opposed it. Most craft workers and laborers wanted fair trade (rather than free trade) and supported republican community controls—at least in *principle*. In practice, many artisan-republicans—shoemakers, tanners, and bakers—found that they could not support their families on

fixed prices and so refused to abide by them. In civilian life as in the military, self-interest tended to triumph over republican virtue.

Women and Household Production. Faced with a shortage of goods and with constantly rising prices, government officials found it nearly impossible to purchase supplies for the troops. They met this challenge by requisitioning goods directly from the people. For example, in 1776 Connecticut officials called on the citizens of Hartford to provide 1,000 coats and 1,600 shirts and assessed smaller towns on a proportionate basis. In 1777 officials again pressed the citizenry to provide shirts, stockings, and shoes for the men from their communities serving in the Continental army. Soldiers added their own pleas to these exhortations. During the Battle of Long Island, for example, Captain

War Mobilization

A few American women actually fought in the war (see *American Lives,* Chapter 9) and many thousands more traveled with the Continental army, providing the troops with food and support. This 1779 woodcut (which accompanied a poem by Molly Guttridge, a "Daughter of Liberty") symbolizes the contributions of the Patriot women of war-torn Marblehead, Massachusetts. (Collection of The New-York Historical Society)

Edward Rogers lost "all the shirts except the one on my back," he wrote to his wife. "The making of cloath . . . must go on. . . . I must have shirts and stockings & a jacket sent me as soon as possible & a blankit."

Patriot women seized this opportunity to contribute to the war effort, increasing their production of home-spun cloth. One Massachusetts town claimed an annual output of 30,000 yards of cloth, while women in Elizabeth, New Jersey, promised "upwards of 100,000 yards of linnen and woolen cloth."

With their husbands and sons away, many women assumed the burden of farm production. Some went into the fields themselves, plowing or cutting and loading grain. Others supervised hired laborers or slaves, acquiring a taste for decision making in the process. "We have sow'd our oats as you desired," Sarah Cobb Paine wrote to her absent husband; "had I been master I should have planted it to Corn." Taught from childhood to act selflessly—to value the welfare of their fathers, brothers, and husbands above their own—most Patriot women did not experience the conflict between republican virtue and self-interest that plagued men. The production of cloth, meat, and grain boosted their self-esteem as contributors to the war effort and prompted some women to claim greater rights in the new republican society; and it began the process of increasing productivity within farm households that pushed forward the American transition to a capitalist economy (see Chapters 7 and 9).

Fiscal Crisis. Nearly all Americans—women as well as men—found that they could maintain their standard of living only by carefully calculating every economic transaction. The cost of the war was the main culprit, since it was paid for primarily by printing money, which steadily depreciated in value. By 1778 so much currency had been printed that it took $7 in Continental bills to buy goods worth $1 in gold or silver. And things only got worse, with the ratio increasing to 42 to 1 in 1779 and 100 to 1 in 1780. When the rate of exchange between Continental currency and specie reached 146 to 1 in 1781, not even the most virtuous Patriots would accept paper money.

Congress tried to halt the spiraling inflation by redeeming its currency and removing it from circulation. In 1780 it asked the states to assess taxes that could be paid in Continental currency at the rate of 40 paper dollars for every silver dollar owed by a taxpayer. This initiative resulted in the redemption of $120 million in Continental bills and yielded a substantial profit to astute speculators, who had seen a future value in the currency. They had bought Continental bills from thousands of ordinary citizens at rates of 80, 100, or 120 to 1, and they now used those bills to pay their taxes, receiving credits worth double or triple their investment. At the end of the war speculators still held

$71 million in Continental notes; they hoped that the currency eventually would be redeemed at its face value, giving them an even greater profit.

In this financial game there were more losers than winners. The big losers were farmers and artisans who had received Continental bills for supplies and soldiers who had taken them as military pay. As soon as they received the currency, it lost purchasing power, literally depreciating in their pockets. Individually these losses were small, amounting to a tiny "tax" every time an ordinary citizen received a paper dollar, kept it for a week, and then spent it. But collectively these "currency taxes" paid the huge cost of the war. It was these personal sacrifices, willing or not, made by hundreds of thousands of American citizens that financed the struggle for independence.

The experience was a sobering one. "Private Interest seemed to predominate over the public weal," a leading Patriot complained as the war came to an end, and "avaricious and ambitious men" seemed to be everywhere. Was this the society for which Americans had fought and died? "Let us have patience," Benjamin Rush replied to such questions. He admitted that self-interest might be in the ascendancy, but he had faith that "our republican forms of government will in time beget republican opinions and manners. All will end well." Events would not completely bear this out, but for Rush and many other Patriots, public virtue remained the preeminent principle of the new American republics.

The Loyalist Exodus

As the war turned in favor of the Patriots, Loyalists faced disaster. Fearing for their lives, more than 100,000 Tories emigrated to Canada, the West Indies, or Britain. This exodus disrupted the established social order, for some of the Loyalists were wealthy and politically powerful merchants, lawyers, and landowners. Some of those who migrated to Canada—where they became known as the United Empire Loyalists—assumed the leadership of the English-speaking colonies of Nova Scotia, New Brunswick, and Ontario.

The land, buildings, and goods left behind by the Loyalists raised the touchy issue of the sanctity of property rights. Some Patriots wanted to confiscate the property of "traitors," and the passions of war lent urgency to their arguments. Initially, the government of North Carolina rented out Loyalists' estates, but when the British army invaded the South, the Patriot-dominated assembly confiscated the estates outright. Officials in New York also seized Loyalists' lands and goods, claiming the "sovereignty of the people of this state in respect to all property."

Many public officials opposed the seizure of Loyal-

ist property as contrary to Patriot principles. Following the classical liberal thought of John Locke as well as the dictates of common law, the Massachusetts Constitution of 1780 declared that every citizen should be protected "in the enjoyment of his life, liberty, and property, according to the standing laws," and state officials extended these rights to Loyalists. Most Tory property in Massachusetts was handled by the court system under the Act to Provide for the Payment of Debts. The courts mandated the seizure of land and goods needed to reimburse creditors, but the remaining property reverted to the agents of departed Loyalists.

Thus, there was no government-led social revolution. Respect for property rights and the states' need to raise revenue meant that most states seized only a limited amount of property—that owned by notorious Loyalists—and they generally sold it to the highest bidder, which usually meant a wealthy Patriot rather than a poor yeoman or foot soldier. For example, Georgia seized 128,000 acres of land from 166 Tories but sold it to only 188 Patriots. In a few cases the sale of Loyalist property produced a more democratic result. In North Carolina about half the new owners of Loyalist lands were small-scale farmers. And on the former Philipsburg manor in New York, Patriot tenants successfully converted their leases into fee-simple ownership. But unlike France after 1789 or Russia after 1917, the revolutionary upheaval did not drastically alter the structure of rural society.

Social turmoil was greater in the cities as upwardly mobile Patriot merchants replaced Tories at the top of the economic ladder. In Massachusetts, the Lowell, Higginson, Jackson, and Cabot families moved their trading enterprises to Boston to fill the vacuum created by the departure of the Hutchinsons and Apthorps and their friends. Small-scale traders in Philadelphia and its environs stepped into the vacancies created by the collapse of Anglican and Quaker mercantile firms during the war. In the countinghouses as on the battlefield, Patriots emerged triumphant. The War of Independence drove out thousands of Loyalist merchants and shopkeepers, replacing a tradition-oriented economic elite—one that invested primarily in foreign trade and urban real estate—with a group of entrepreneurial-minded republican merchants.

The Problem of Slavery

The American Revolution generated intense debate over the institution of slavery, in part because of the active role played by African-Americans on both sides of the struggle. Thousands of slaves in the South sought freedom by taking refuge behind British lines. Two neighbors of Richard Henry Lee, the Virginia Patriot, lost "every slave they had in the world" during the war.

Fifty-three blacks, including eight mothers and their children, fled from another Virginia plantation, subsequently winning their freedom by working or fighting for the king. When the British army evacuated Charleston, more than 6,000 former slaves went with the troops; another 4,000 left Savannah with the British. Hundreds of black Loyalists settled permanently in Canada, but over 1,000 others, poorly treated and settled on inferior land in Nova Scotia, sought a better life in the abolitionist settlement in Sierra Leone in West Africa.

Just as many African-Americans served the Patriot cause. Free blacks from New England enrolled in Patriot units such as the First Rhode Island Company and the Massachusetts "Bucks." In Maryland, Patriots recruited a large number of slaves for military duty and later freed them in return for their service, a policy that was rejected by other southern states. In those states many slaves struck informal bargains with their Patriot masters, trading loyalty in wartime for a promise of liberty. The Virginia assembly passed an act allowing *manumission* (literally, "letting go from the hand") in 1782, and planters freed 10,000 slaves within a decade.

These events revealed a contradiction in the Patriots' republican ideology. "How is it that we hear the loudest *yelps* for liberty among the drivers of Negroes?" the British author Samuel Johnson chided, and some white Patriots took his point to heart. "I wish most sincerely there was not a Slave in the province," Abigail Adams wrote to her husband, John, as Massachusetts went to war. "It always appeared a most iniquitous Scheme to me—to fight ourselves for what we are daily robbing and plundering from those who have as good a right to freedom as we have."

Gradual Emancipation in the North. This intense questioning of slavery was fairly new. In the prerevolutionary world inequality of condition and status was accepted as the norm for all people, part of God's design for the world. Racial slavery was only the most extreme form of natural inequality. Significantly, it was the Quakers, whose belief in religious equality had made them sharp critics of many inequities in social life, who took the lead in condemning slavery. Beginning in the 1750s, the evangelist John Woolman and a few other Quakers had urged their coreligionists to free their slaves. The outbreak of the war led many North Carolina Quakers to "clear their hands" of the institution by manumitting their slaves. Other rapidly growing pietistic groups, notably the Methodists and the Baptists, advocated emancipation and admitted both enslaved and free blacks into their congregations. In 1784 a conference of Virginia Methodists declared that slavery was "contrary to the Golden Law of God on which hang all the Law and Prophets."

Enlightenment principles of knowledge also played a role in the debate over slavery. John Locke had argued that ideas were not innate but stemmed from impressions and experience. Accordingly, Enlightenment thinkers pointed out that the oppressive conditions of slavery accounted for the debased situation of Africans in the Western Hemisphere; the slaves were not an inherently inferior people. "A state of slavery has a mighty tendency to shrink and contract the minds of men," an American observer noted. Anthony Benezet, a Quaker philanthropist who funded a school for blacks in Philadelphia, contradicted popular belief by declaring that African-Americans were "as capable of improvement as White People."

These religious and secular arguments placed slavery on the defensive, especially in the North, where there were relatively few African-Americans. By 1784, Massachusetts had abolished slavery outright and three other states—Pennsylvania, Connecticut, and Rhode Island—had provided for its gradual end. Within another two decades every state north of Delaware endorsed gradual emancipation, which meant that liberty came slowly to northern blacks. For example, the New York Emancipation Edict of 1799 granted freedom only to the *children* of slaves, and only when they reached the age of twenty-five. As late as 1810, 30,000 slaves in the northern states—nearly a fourth of their African-American populations—still served masters.

Emancipation came slowly for several reasons. Many whites feared that black freedom would mean competition for jobs and housing and, even more threatening, a melding of the races. Consequently, in 1786 Massachusetts reenacted a colonial-era law that prohibited whites from marrying blacks, Indians, or mulattoes. Moreover, state lawmakers wanted to protect property rights, and gradual emancipation was a means of providing compensation to slaveowners in the form of a few more years of enforced African-American labor. Even in the North the whites' right to property had priority over the blacks' right to liberty.

Emancipation in the Chesapeake Region. The tension between the republican values of liberty and property was greatest in the South. Slaves made up 30 to 60 percent of the population and represented a huge financial investment. Most political leaders were slaveholders, and they used state power to preserve slavery. In 1776 the North Carolina legislature condemned Quaker manumissions as "highly criminal and reprehensible" and passed a number of laws ordering the enslavement of freed blacks or their expulsion from the state (see American Voices, page 192). Yet many Chesapeake slaveholders, moved by religious principles or oversupplied with workers on their declining tobacco plantations, allowed blacks to buy their freedom through paid work as artisans or laborers. By 1810 manumission and self-purchase had raised the number of freed blacks in Maryland to about a third of the African-American population. In Delaware freed blacks outnumbered slaves three to one.

But these forces were not strong enough to overthrow slavery in the Chesapeake. Most whites did not want a society filled with freed blacks. The Virginia legislature discussed emancipation but in 1792 imposed financial conditions that made it more difficult for whites to free their slaves. Following the lead of Thomas Jefferson, who owned more than a hundred slaves, many Chesapeake planters argued that slavery was a "necessary evil" required to maintain white supremacy and their luxurious life-styles.

And so, within a decade after the end of the Revolution, the tide had turned against emancipation in the Chesapeake. (It was never seriously considered by the expansionist-minded, rice-planting gentry of South Carolina and Georgia.) Its fate was sealed in 1800 when Virginia authorities discovered and prevented a slave uprising planned by Gabriel Prosser and then hanged him and about thirty of his followers. "Liberty and equality have brought the evil upon us," a letter to the *Virginia Herald* proclaimed in the aftermath of the abortive rebellion, for such doctrines are "dangerous and extremely wicked in this country, where every white man is a master, and every black man is a slave." Throughout the South, most whites reaffirmed their commitment to slavery and white property rights, whatever the cost to republican principles.

Symbols of Slavery—and Freedom
The scar on the forehead of this black woman, widely known as "Mumbet," underlined the cruelty of slavery. Winning emancipation through a legal suit, she chose a name befitting her new status: Elizabeth Freeman.

African-American Freemen from North Carolina Petition Congress

To safeguard the institution of slavery, the North Carolina legislature enacted a law in 1788 that allowed whites to reenslave African-Americans who had been manumitted by their owners. To escape this fate, these former slaves fled the state, and in 1797 they petitioned the national legislature to protect their rights as free citizens. At the insistence of southern representatives, Congress refused to accept their petition.

That, being of African descent, late inhabitants and natives of North Carolina, to you only, under God, can we apply with any hope of effect, for redress of our grievances, having been compelled to leave the State wherein we had a right of residence, as freemen liberated under the hand and seal of humane and conscientious masters, the validity of which act of justice in restoring us to our native right of freedom, was confirmed by judgment of the Superior Court of North Carolina, wherein it was brought to trial; yet, not long after this decision, a law of that State was enacted, under which men of cruel disposition, and void of just principle, received countenance and authority in violently seizing, imprisoning, and selling into slavery, such as had been so emancipated.

I, Jacob Nicholson, also of North Carolina, being set free by my master, Joseph Nicholson, but continuing to live with him till, being pursued day and night, I was obliged to leave my abode, sleep in the woods, and stacks in the fields, &c., to escape the hands of violent men who, induced by the profit afforded them by law, followed this course as a business; at length, by night, I made my escape, leaving a mother, one child, and two brothers, to see whom I dare not return.

I, Job Albert, manumitted by Benjamin Albertson, who was my careful guardian to protect me from being afterwards taken and sold, providing me with a house to accommodate me and my wife, who was liberated by William Robertson; but we were night and day hunted by men armed with guns, swords, and pistols, accompanied with mastiff dogs; . . . I was discovered and seized by Alexander Stafford, William Stafford, and Thomas Creesy, who were armed with guns and clubs. After binding me with my hands behind me, and a rope round my arms and body, they took me about four miles to Hartford prison, where I lay four weeks, suffering much for want of provision; from thence, with the assistance of a fellow-prisoner, (a white man,) I made my escape, and for three dollars was

conveyed, with my wife, by a humane person, in a covered wagon by night, to Virginia, where, in the neighborhood of Portsmouth, I continued unmolested about four years, being chiefly engaged in sawing boards and planting.

I, Thomas Pritchet, was set free by my master Thomas Pritchet, who furnished me with land to raise provisions for my use, where I built myself a house, cleared a sufficient spot of woodland to produce ten bushels of corn; the second year about fifteen, and the third, had as much planted as I suppose would have produced thirty bushels; this I was obliged to leave about one month before it was fit for gathering, being threatened by Holland Lockwood, who married my said master's widow, that if I would not come and serve him, he would apprehend me, and send me to the West Indies.

We beseech your impartial attention to our hard condition, . . . both for our relief as a people, and towards the removal of obstructions to public order and well-being. . . .

JACOB NICHOLSON,
JOB ALBERT, his mark,
THOMAS PRITCHET, his mark.

Source: Annals of Congress, Fourth Congress, Second Session (Washington, D.C., 1855), 2015–2017.

A Republican Religious Order

Before 1776 only the Quaker- and Baptist-controlled colonies of Pennsylvania and Rhode Island had repudiated the idea of an established church and celebrated religious liberty of conscience. Political revolution, however, had broadened the appeal of these libertarian principles, forcing Patriot lawmakers to devise new and distinct relationships between churches and state governments.

Separation of Church and State. The most dramatic change in the religious situation came in Virginia, where the Church of England was the established church. To preserve their legally privileged position, most Anglicans quickly renounced allegiance to the king, the head of the Church of England, and reorganized themselves as the Protestant Episcopal Church of America. Moreover, the Anglican gentry stopped harassing New Light Presbyterians and Baptists in order to win their support for the military effort. Finally, leading Virginia Patriots who embraced the Enlightenment questioned the wisdom of an established church. In 1776 James Madison and George Mason persuaded the Virginia convention to issue a Declaration of Rights that guaranteed the "free exercise of religion" to all Christians. Later that year the Virginia legislature passed an act exempting dissenters from paying taxes to support the Anglican Church.

The debate over state support for religion continued after the war. In general, Baptists in all the states opposed the use of taxes to support religion. Their political influence in Virginia prompted lawmakers to reject a bill supported by George Washington and Patrick Henry that would have imposed a general assessment tax to provide funds for all Christian churches. Instead, in 1786 the Virginia legislature enacted Thomas Jefferson's Bill for Establishing Religious Freedom, which made all churches equal before the law and granted direct financial support to none. A similar result obtained in New York and New Jersey, where the sheer number of churches—Episcopalian, Presbyterian, Dutch Reformed, Lutheran, and Quaker, among others—prevented legislative agreement on an established church or compulsory religious taxes.

Yet many Americans still clung to traditional European principles, arguing that a firm union of church and state promoted morality and respect for authority. "Pure religion and civil liberty are inseparable companions," a group of North Carolinians advised their minister. "It is your particular duty to enlighten mankind with the unerring principles of truth and justice, the main props of all civil government."

Thus the separation of church and state came slowly, especially in New England, where Congregationalist ministers had strongly supported the independence movement and would use their prestige to maintain a legally established church until the 1830s. Now, however, New England Congregationalists no longer attempted to suppress Baptist and Methodist churches and allowed them to use religious taxes to support their own ministers. After the Revolution, the primacy of a single established church was no longer the norm.

Freedom of Conscience. Nonetheless, the extent of religious freedom remained the subject of debate. In Virginia, Jefferson's Bill for Establishing Religious Freedom endorsed the principle of liberty of conscience and outlawed religious requirements for political and civil posts. Many states, however, continued to offer tax exemptions on church property, enforce religious criteria for voting and officeholding, and penalize individuals who questioned the doctrines of Protestant Christianity. For example, the North Carolina constitution of 1776 disqualified from public office any citizen "who shall deny the being of God, or the Truth of the Protestant Religion, or the Divine Authority of the Old or New Testament." New Hampshire had a similar provision in its constitution until 1868.

Such restrictive doctrines commanded widespread support both among the public at large and in courts of law. In one celebrated case Chancellor James Kent of the New York Supreme Court flouted the principle of religious liberty by upholding the conviction of Timothy Ruggles for blasphemy (publicly and disrespectfully shouting the name of Christ). Kent overruled Ruggles's contention that the charge infringed his liberty of conscience under the New York constitution of 1777, which guaranteed "the free, equal and undisturbed enjoyment of religious opinion." Kent declared that "the people of this State profess the general doctrines of Christianity," and for Ruggles to slander Christ was "to strike at the root of moral obligation and weaken the security of social ties." For Kent, religion underpinned the authority of the republic and had a higher priority than the individual's right of free speech.

Americans who were influenced by Enlightenment values condemned interference in matters of conscience whether by courts or by churches. Thomas Paine attacked religious institutions as "no other than human inventions set up to terrify and enslave mankind, and monopolize power and profit." Rationalist thinkers extended republican principles to religion, arguing that God had given human beings the power of reason so that they could determine moral truths for themselves. Ethan Allen of Vermont, whose Green Mountain Boys had captured Fort Ticonderoga in 1775, wrote a widely circulated pamphlet called *Reason: The Only Oracle of Man* (1784).

Allen was a deist, as were many of the leading American Patriots, such as Thomas Jefferson and Benjamin Franklin. They thought God had created the world the way a watchmaker builds a clock; once set in motion, it ran according to its own laws. "God Almighty is himself a Mechanic," proclaimed Thomas Cooper, president of the College of South Carolina. Philip Freneau, an ardent Patriot poet and deist, wrote that in "Nature" one could

> see, with most exact design,
> The world revolve, the planets shine.
> The nicest order, all things meet,
> A structure in itself complete.

To protect society from what they called "ecclesiastical tyranny," most deists demanded complete freedom of expression.

Many evangelical-minded American Protestants also favored freedom of conscience, but their goal was to protect themselves and their churches from state control. Isaac Backus warned New England Baptists not to incorporate their churches or accept tax funds under the general assessment laws of Massachusetts. Instead, Backus favored voluntary church support. In Connecticut a devout Congregationalist layman approved of voluntarism because it undermined the clerical hierarchy and thus furthered "the spirit of toleration" and "the principles of republicanism." In the aftermath of the Revolution, for a variety of causes, American Protestant Christianity became increasingly republican in structure and spirit.

Summary

Beginning in April 1775, civil war disrupted the British empire. Small-scale battles between Loyalist and Patriot militias brought more bloodshed and made compromise difficult, as did George III's determination to crush the rebellion. Thomas Paine's *Common Sense* attacked the monarchical system and persuaded many Americans to support republicanism and independence, which was declared by the Continental Congress on July 4, 1776.

British troops under General Howe defeated Washington's Continental army in a series of battles during 1776, but Patriot triumphs at Trenton and Princeton revived American morale. Howe captured Philadelphia, the Patriots' capital, in the summer of 1777, but because of poor British planning, the rebels won a major victory at Saratoga in October. The Patriots nearly lost their main army to cold and hunger at Valley Forge during the winter of 1777–1778. Simultaneously, a severe inflation caused by the excessive distribution of paper money by the Continental Congress and the states undermined Patriot morale and nearly destroyed public support for the new republican governments.

The tide turned in February 1778, when an alliance with France aided the Patriot cause financially, militarily, and diplomatically. Congress rejected British overtures for a negotiated settlement, and Lord North embarked on a southern military strategy. British troops won major victories in Georgia and the Carolinas during 1779 and 1780, but Patriot troops and guerrillas finally forced General Cornwallis into Virginia, where he suffered a major defeat at Yorktown in October 1781, the last great battle of the war. The Treaty of Paris in 1783 acknowledged the independence of the United States and defined its western boundary at the Mississippi River, opening the trans-Appalachian West to white settlement.

During the war idealistic Americans attempted to define the social and economic values of republicanism as pursuit of the common good and stressed the citizen's responsibility to the community. Some Americans embraced a Lockean liberal outlook that celebrated the pursuit of individual achievement and self-interest. Moreover, most Americans suffered financially during the war because of inflation—a hidden tax that paid for the Patriots' military effort—making it necessary for many soldiers and civilians to give the highest priority to the economic security of their families. Even so, independence and republicanism initiated significant changes in American society and public values, bringing about the immediate departure of thousands of Loyalists, the gradual abolition of slavery in the North, and a growing commitment to freedom of religious worship and separation of church and state.

TIMELINE

1775	Second Continental Congress
	Battle of Bunker Hill
	Olive Branch petition
	Lord Dunmore's proclamation to slaves
	American invasion of Canada
	British Prohibitory Act
1776	Patriots skirmish with Loyalists in South
	Thomas Paine's *Common Sense*
	Declaration of Independence (July 4)
	Howe defeats Washington in New York
	Virginia Declaration of Rights
	American victories at Trenton (December 26) and Princeton (January 3, 1777)
1777	Patriot women assist war economy
	Howe occupies Philadelphia
	Horatio Gates defeats Burgoyne at Saratoga
	Continental army suffers at Valley Forge
	Patriot paper currency creates inflation
1778	Franco-American alliance (February 6)
	Lord North seeks negotiated settlement
	Congress grants officers half-pay pension
	British begin "southern" strategy by capturing Savannah
1779	Confrontation in Philadelphia over price regulation
	Seizure and sale of Loyalist property begins
1780	General Clinton captures Charleston
	French army lands in Rhode Island
	Patriots prevail at King's Mountain
	Greene's forces harass Cornwallis's army
	Continental currency continues to depreciate
1780s	Debate over religious establishment: general assessment laws and freedom of conscience
1781	Cornwallis invades Virginia; surrenders at Yorktown
	Large-scale Loyalist emigration to Canada and Britain
	Partial redemption of Continental currency
	Escaped slaves depart with British
1782	Slave manumission act in Virginia (reversed in 1792)
1783	American officers at Newburgh, New York, plot against Congress
	Treaty of Paris (September 3)
1784	Ethan Allen publishes *Reason: The Only Oracle of Man*
1786	Virginia Bill for Establishing Religious Freedom
1799	New York enacts Gradual Emancipation Act
1800	Gabriel Prosser's rebellion in Virginia

★   ★   ★

BIBLIOGRAPHY

Gordon Wood, *The Radicalism of the American Revolution* (1992), offers a fine overview of the Revolutionary Era; for a contrasting interpretation, see the essays in Alfred F. Young, ed., *Beyond the American Revolution: Explorations in the History of American Radicalism* (1993).

Toward Independence

Jerrilyn Green Marston, *King and Congress: The Transfer of Political Legitimacy, 1774–1776* (1987), and Jack N. Rakove, *The Beginnings of National Politics: An Interpretative History of the Continental Congress* (1979), discuss the movement toward independence. See also Eric Foner, *Tom Paine and Revolutionary America* (1976), and Garry Wills, *Inventing America: Jefferson's Declaration of Independence* (1978). On Loyalism, read William N. Nelson, *The American Tory* (1961), and Robert M. Calhoon et al., *The Loyalist Perception* (1989).

The Perils of War and Finance

The military history of the war is covered in James L. Stokesbury, *A Short History of the American Revolution* (1991), and Piers Mackesy, *The War for America, 1775–1783* (1964). Don Higginbotham, *George Washington and the American Military Tradition* (1985), and Ronald Hoffman and Peter Albert, eds., *Arms and Independence: The Military Character of the American Revolution* (1984), offer a more analytic perspective. The war in the North can be followed in Ira D. Gruber, *The Howe Brothers and the American Revolution* (1972), and Richard J. Hargrove, Jr., *General John Burgoyne* (1983).

Studies of the soldiers who fought the war include Rodney Attwood, *The Hessians* (1980); Sylvia R. Frey, *The British Soldier in America* (1981); Robert K. Wright, Jr., *The Continental Army* (1983); and John C. Dann, ed., *The Revolution Remembered: Eyewitness Accounts of the War for Independence* (1980). For the importance of the military bureaucracy, see R. Arthur Bowler, *Logistics and the Failure of the British Army in America, 1775–1783* (1975), and E. Wayne Carp, *To Starve the Army at Pleasure: Continental Army Administration and American Political Culture, 1775–1783* (1984).

Local studies include Jean Butenhoff Lee, *The Price of Nationhood: The American Revolution in Charles County* (1994); Robert A. Gross, *The Minutemen and Their World* (1976); Richard Buel, Jr., *Dear Liberty: Connecticut's Mobilization for the Revolutionary War* (1980); and Donald Wallace White, *A Village at War: Chatham, New Jersey, and the American Revolution* (1979).

African-American participation in the war is discussed by Gary A. Puckrein, *The Black Regiment in the American Revolution* (1978), and Sidney Kaplan, *The Black Presence in the Era of the American Revolution* (rev. ed., 1989). The native American response is described in Barbara Graymont, *The Iroquois in the American Revolution* (1972); Isabel T. Kelsey, *Joseph Brant, 1743–1807* (1984); and James H. O'Donnell III, *Southern Indians in the American Revolution* (1973).

Two classic discussions of the fiscal problems created by the war are E. James Ferguson, *The Power of the Purse: A History of American Public Finance: 1776–1790* (1961), and

Clarence L. Ver Steeg, *Robert Morris, Revolutionary Financier* (1954). A more recent study is William G. Anderson, *The Price of Liberty: The Public Debt of the American Revolution* (1983).

The Path to Victory

Bradford Perkins, *The Creation of a Republican Empire, 1776–1865* (1993), and Jonathan R. Dull, *A Diplomatic History of the American Revolution* (1985), provide good overviews of this topic. More specialized studies include James H. Hutson, *John Adams and the Diplomacy of the American Revolution* (1980); Richard B. Morris, *The Peacemakers: The Great Powers and American Independence* (1965); and Ronald Hoffman and Peter Albert, eds., *Peace and the Peacemakers: The Treaty of 1783* (1986).

For the southern campaign, consult W. Robert Higgins, ed., *The Revolutionary War in the South* (1979); Ronald Hoffman, Thad W. Tate, and Peter J. Albert, eds., *An Uncivil War: The Southern Backcountry during the American Revolution* (1985); and Jeffrey J. Crow and Larry E. Tise, eds., *The Southern Experience in the American Revolution* (1978). Studies of military action include Hugh F. Rankin, *Francis Marion: The Swamp Fox* (1973), and John S. Pancake, *The Destructive War, 1780–1782* (1985).

Republicanism Defined and Challenged

Milton M. Klein et al., *The Republican Synthesis Revisited* (1992), is a good historiographical introduction. Charles Royster, *A Revolutionary People at War: The Continental Army and American Character, 1775–1783* (1979), explores the fate of republican ideals. On women's lives during the war, see Ronald Hoffman and Peter J. Albert, eds., *Women in the Age of the American Revolution* (1989); Mary Beth Norton, *Liberty's Daughters: The Revolutionary Experience of American Women, 1750–1800* (1980); Lynn Withey, *Dearest Friend: A Life of Abigail Adams* (1980); and Joy Day Buel and Richard Buel, Jr., *The Way of Duty: A Woman and Her Family in Revolutionary America* (1984).

On the black experience, consult Sylvia R. Frey, *Water from the Rock: Black Resistance in a Revolutionary Age* (1991); Ira Berlin and Ronald Hoffman, eds., *Slavery and Freedom in the Age of the American Revolution* (1983); Gary B. Nash, *Forging Freedom: The Formation of Philadelphia's Black Community, 1720–1840* (1988); and David Brion Davis, *The Problem of Slavery in the Age of Revolution, 1770–1823* (1975). See also James W. St. G. Walker, *The Black Loyalists: The Search for a Promised Land in Nova Scotia and Sierra Leone, 1783–1870* (1976), and Shane White, *Somewhat More Independent: The End of Slavery in New York City, 1770-1810* (1991).

On changes in American religion, see Ronald Hoffman and Peter J. Albert, eds., *Religion in a Revolutionary Age* (1994); Rhys Isaac, *The Transformation of Virginia, 1740–1790* (1982); Fred Hood, *Reformed America 1783–1837* (1980); and Nathan O. Hatch, *The Democratization of American Christianity* (1989). The spiritual roots of a new secular religion are traced by Catharine Albanese, *Sons of the Fathers: The Civil Religion of the American Revolution* (1976), and Ruth Bloch, *Visionary Republic: Millennial Themes in American Thought* (1985).

The American Star

The portraits of kings and queens had traditionally served as icons or symbols of their monarchical nations. This idealized portrait of Washington by Frederick Kemmelmeyer celebrates his prowess and seeks a symbolic way of depicting a republic.

The New Political Order

1776–1800

★ ★ ★

Many wars for national independence end in political chaos or military rule, but the United States escaped those unhappy fates. The departure of the Loyalists, who would have formed a reactionary monarchist opposition, eliminated a potential political threat to the new republic. The attitude of General Washington, who firmly supported civilian rule and refused to consider becoming king, lessened the danger of a military coup d'état. Authority remained firmly in the hands of the leaders of the Patriot resistance movement, who wished to establish governments based on popular sovereignty and republican principles.

Beginning in 1776, state officials undertook the daunting task of devising new constitutions acceptable to the people. The Continental Congress also sought a constitutional mandate for its rule to enable it to address the vexing issues of war finance, inflation, the disposition of western lands, and social unrest—all of which were made more difficult by a postwar economic recession. These problems prompted a movement for a stronger national government, which found expression in the Philadelphia constitution of 1787. A controversial document, the new constitution was hotly debated and was ratified only by narrow majorities in key states.

Political life remained conflict-ridden during the 1790s. Alexander Hamilton's system of public finance and the ideological passions of the French Revolution divided Americans into warring camps and led to the rise of organized political parties. Before the election of President Thomas Jefferson ended the political crisis of the 1790s, the national government had curtailed the rights of citizens and had almost gone to war with France.

Despite these conflicts—and in part *because* of them—the period between 1776 and 1800 was the most creative era in American political and constitutional development. It was one of the most successful periods as

well. Everywhere people with democratic views saw the United States as the exemplar of political liberty, and, as Tom Paine had put it, "the last best hope of mankind."

Creating New Institutions, 1776–1787

The Revolution of 1776 was both a struggle for home rule (independence) and, in the words of the historian Carl Becker, a conflict over "who should rule at home." The first conflict ended with a military victory over Britain. The second, a struggle over the character of state constitutions and governments, was less easily resolved and involved both a debate over centuries-old issues of political theory and practical politics. Who would control the new republican institutions, the traditional elites or ordinary citizens?

The State Constitutions: How Much Democracy?

Patriot leaders acted swiftly and decisively to establish the legitimacy of their rule. On May 10, 1776, Congress urged Patriots to suppress royal authority and establish institutions based on popular rule. Most states readily complied. By the end of 1776, Virginia, Maryland, North Carolina, New Jersey, Delaware, and Pennsylvania had written new constitutions; Connecticut and Rhode Island had transformed their colonial charters, which provided for extensive self-government, into republican charters by deleting all references to the king.

The Dilemma of Popular Sovereignty. The Declaration of Independence stated the principle of popular sovereignty—governments derive "their just powers from the consent of the governed"—but left unclear exactly what that meant in practice. In 1776 the Virginia constitutional convention adopted a comprehensive "declaration of rights" as the "foundation of government," and the Delaware constitution of that year linked popular sovereignty with political power: "the Right of the People to participate in the Legislature, is the Foundation of Liberty and of all free government."

But which people? During the colonial period, most political offices were occupied by the rich and wellborn, and ordinary Americans deferred to their "social betters." Even after the Revolution leading Patriots employed a narrow definition of the political nation: voting and office holding were the province of propertied white men; women, blacks, native Americans, and propertyless whites were excluded. Conservative Patriots went further, denying that popular sovereignty

meant political rights for those who owned only a little property. Thus Jeremy Belknap of New Hampshire insisted that "the people be taught . . . that they are not able to govern themselves."

Radical Patriots turned this argument on its head. In the heat of revolution they frankly embraced a democratic outlook: every citizen who supported the rebellion—property owner or not—had "an equal claim to all privileges, liberties and immunities," declared an article in the Maryland *Gazette*. The backcountry farmers of Mecklenburg County, North Carolina, instructed their representatives to the state's constitutional convention of 1776 to "oppose everything that leans to aristocracy or power in the hands of the rich and chief men exercised to the oppression of the poor." Voters in Virginia felt the same way, electing a new assembly that, an observer remarked, "was composed of men not quite so well dressed, nor so politely educated, nor so highly born. . . . They are the People's men."

Democratic-republicanism received its fullest expression in Pennsylvania, where a coalition of Scots-Irish farmers, Philadelphia artisans, and Enlightenment-influenced intellectuals took control of state politics and formulated a constitution that created the most democratic institutions of government in America or Europe. The Pennsylvania constitution of 1776 abolished property owning as a qualification for political participation, giving all men who paid taxes the right to vote and hold office. It also rejected the system of mixed government and created a *unicameral* (one-house) assembly that had complete legislative power. No council or upper house was reserved for the wealthy, and no governor exercised executive authority. Other clauses mandated an extensive system of elementary education, protected citizens from imprisonment for debt, and called for a society of economically independent freemen.

Pennsylvania's radical constitution alarmed leading Patriots in other states, most of whom did not believe in democracy. Conservatives feared that popular rule would lead to the tyranny of legislative majorities, with ordinary citizens using their numerical advantage to tax the rich. In Philadelphia, prosperous Anglican merchants founded a Republican Society to lobby for repeal of the constitution. In Boston, John Adams denounced Pennsylvania's unicameral legislature as "so democratical that it must produce confusion and every evil work."

To thwart the spread of democratic institutions, Adams dispatched copies of his *Thoughts on Government* to friends at constitutional conventions in other states. In this political treatise Adams adapted the theory of mixed government devised by English Whigs (a system with a monarch, a house of lords, and a house of commons) to a republican society. Instead of dividing state power along social lines, he assigned each function—lawmaking, administering, and judging—to a distinct branch of government. Adams argued that his scheme

was republican because the people would elect the chief executive and the members of a two-house *(bicameral)* legislature. It would also preserve liberty because the various branches would check and balance each other: men of property in the upper house could check the excesses of popular majorities in the lower house, and an appointed—not elected—judiciary would review legislation. As a further curb on democracy, an elected governor would have the power to veto laws.

Leading Patriots in most states preferred Adams's mixed and balanced government, in part because it was less democratic than Pennsylvania's system and in part because it was more familiar. Most colonies had an elected assembly, an appointed council (upper house), and a royal governor. Adapting existing institutions seemed easier than beginning anew. Consequently, the framers of most state constitutions retained the existing bicameral legislature but made both houses elective. Reacting against royal governors, they reduced the powers of the executive; only three constitutions gave veto power to the governor. One of those states was New York, which was dominated by a conservative Patriot elite. The New York constitution of 1777, written chiefly by John Jay (with a copy of Adams's *Thoughts on Government* by his side), provided for a bicameral legislature with seats in the lower house apportioned by population, a governor with veto power, an appointed judiciary, and suffrage limited by property qualifications so that only 40 percent of white men were eligible to vote for the governor and the upper house.

The most flagrant use of property qualifications to maintain elite power occurred in South Carolina. That state's constitution of 1778 required candidates for governor to have a debt-free estate of £10,000 (about $450,000), senators to be worth £2,000, and assemblymen to have property valued at £1,000. These provisions ruled out office holding for about 90 percent of the white adult population; high property qualifications similarly restricted voting to a minority of South Carolina's white men.

Toward a Democratic Polity. Nonetheless, the character of American politics became more democratic for two reasons. First, the state constitutions apportioned seats in the lower houses of the legislatures on the basis of population, giving yeomen farmers in western areas the representation they had long demanded. Second, the Revolution had raised the political consciousness of ordinary Americans. During the war Patriot militiamen had claimed the right to elect their officers, "for annual election is so essentially necessary to the Liberty of Freemen." Subsequently, many veterans, whether or not they had property, demanded the right to vote and no longer automatically elected their social betters; rather, one observer noted, they chose men of "middling circumstances" who knew "the wants of the poor."

These democratic tendencies changed the composition of American legislatures (see Figure 7.1). Before the war, 85 percent of the assemblymen in the six colonies of New York, New Hampshire, New Jersey, Maryland, Virginia, and South Carolina were wealthy men with estates averaging in excess of £2,000. By 1784, however, middling farmers and artisans controlled the lower houses of the three northern states and formed a sizable minority in those of the three southern states. Flexing their new political muscles, these middling citizens successfully opposed the collection of back taxes and other measures that tended "toward the oppression of the people." In most states, backcountry residents were able to transfer the state capital from merchant-dominated seaports (such as New York City and Philadelphia) to inland cities (Albany and Harrisburg); even conservative South Carolina moved its seat of government inland from Charleston to Columbia.

The political legacy of the Revolution was complex. Conservative Patriots such as John Adams had blunted the edge of the democratic movement in that the structure of most political institutions remained conservative. Only in Pennsylvania—and Vermont, which copied Pennsylvania's constitution—were radical Patriots able to take power and create new democratic-republican insti-

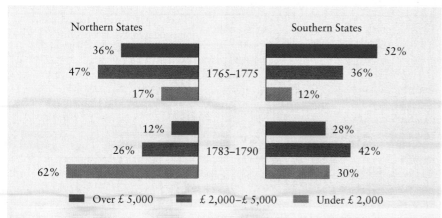

Northern States   Southern States

36%   52%
47%   1765–1775   36%
17%   12%

12%   28%
26%   1783–1790   42%
62%   30%

■ Over £ 5,000   ■ £ 2,000–£ 5,000   ■ Under £ 2,000

FIGURE 7.1

Change in the Wealth of Elected Officials, 1765–1790

Before the Revolution men of wealth and property predominated in the colonial assemblies. In the new republic the proportion of less prosperous men in state legislatures increased dramatically, especially in the North.

Source: Adapted from Jackson T. Main, "Government by the People: The American Revolution and the Democratization of the Legislatures," *William and Mary Quarterly,* 3d ser., vol. 23 (1966).

tutions. Yet political life—day-to-day electioneering and interest-group bargaining—had become more responsive to a broader segment of white men who owned property.

The Political Status of Women. Although debate continued over property requirements for voting, custom dictated that only men could engage in political discourse, just as the army, the militia, legislatures, juries, and other public institutions were limited to men. The extraordinary excitement of the Revolutionary Era, however, tested this division of the social order by gender. Upper-class women entered into political debate, filling their letters and diaries (and undoubtedly their conversations) with opinions on public issues. "The men say we have no business [with politics]," Eliza Wilkinson of South Carolina complained in 1783, "but I won't have it thought that because we are the weaker sex as to bodily strength we are capable of nothing more than domestic concerns. They won't even allow us liberty of thought, and that is all I want."

On the surface, Wilkinson was not asking for much. Like other wealthy, well-educated, politically aware American women, she did not demand complete equality with men by seeking voting rights or membership in public bodies such as juries. But Wilkinson's demands and those of other women were potentially revolutionary, for they challenged long-established customs and legal rules. A case in point was the proposal by Abigail Adams that Patriots create a republican *legal* order that would give women greater autonomy. Under American common law, marriage saddled a woman with the subordinate status mandated by the English feudal "law of baron and feme" ("lord and woman"); her civic and economic identity was subsumed under that of her "lord" (see Chapter 1). Thus, a married women could not own property or enter into contracts or make legal decisions by herself. If they continued to hold such power over women, "men would be tyrants," Abigail Adams chided her husband, John, in a famous exchange of letters. Even as her husband and other Patriots were busy "emancipating all nations" from monarchical despotism, she astutely pointed out, "you insist upon retaining absolute power over Wives."

Male leaders paid some attention to women's requests for greater social and legal rights. In Pennsylvania a new law in 1785 allowed women to seek either an absolute divorce or a separation with discretionary alimony, enhancing their legal position somewhat. In Massachusetts the state attorney general persuaded a jury that girls had equal rights to schooling under the state's constitution. Over time, these changes promoted gender equality. With greater access to public elementary schools as well as new female academies, many young women became literate and knowledgeable, intellectually prepared to play a larger role in the public world. By the mid-nineteenth century in the northeastern states, the percentage of women who could read and write would be nearly the same as that of men. Women authors would command a large readership among men as well as women, and literate women would again challenge their subordinate legal and political status.

But for two generations after the Revolution politics remained a male preserve. The new state constitutions either explicitly restricted suffrage to men or imposed property qualifications for voting that effectively excluded married women. An exception was New Jersey. Its constitution of 1776 granted suffrage to all free adult inhabitants worth £50, ambiguous phrasing that—apparently intentionally—permitted widows and unmarried women with property to vote. Few women exercised this option until the late 1790s, when a series

John and Abigail Adams
Both Adamses had strong personalities. In 1794 John fondly accused his wife of being a "Disciple of Wollstonecraft," but Abigail's commitment to legal equality for women long predated Wollstonecraft's *A Vindication of the Rights of Woman* (1792).

for the admission of the states carved out of the territory as soon as their populations equaled that of the smallest state. The Land Ordinance of 1785 established a rectangular grid system for surveying land (see Map 8.2) and a set of legal rules that spurred the creation of a full-fledged capitalist economy. These rules specified that western lands be surveyed before settlement to deter squatters, transferred in fee simple without quitrents or other dues to encourage an active land market, and sold mostly in large blocs to favor large-scale investors and land speculators.

The Northwest Ordinance of 1787 applied these general principles by providing for the creation of three to five territories in the Old Northwest—the national domain north of the Ohio River—eventually comprising the states of Ohio, Indiana, Illinois, Michigan, and Wisconsin. Reflecting the antislavery sentiments of Jefferson and many other Patriots, the ordinance prohibited slavery in those territories. It encouraged education, directing that funds from the sale of certain lands go toward the support of schools. It specified that

initially each new territory would be ruled by a governor and judges appointed by Congress. Once the number of free adult men reached 5,000, the settlers could elect their own legislature. When the population grew to 60,000, the residents could write a republican constitution and apply to join the Union. Once admitted, a new state would enjoy all the rights and privileges of the existing states.

The ordinances of the 1780s were a great and enduring achievement. They provided for the orderly settlement of the West while reducing the prospect of secessionist movements and preventing the emergence of dependent "colonies." Moreover, the ordinances added a new dimension to the national identity, providing both a source of revenue for the central government and a new vision for the young nation. Whatever the continuing problems in the West—native American land claims, illegal British forts, threats from Spanish officials—the United States was no longer confined to thirteen governments on the eastern seaboard. It had the potential to become a dynamic, expanding society.

MAP 7.1

The Confederation and Western Land Claims

The Confederation Congress resolved the conflicting land claims of the states by creating a "national domain" to the west of the Appalachian Mountains. From 1781 to 1802 all the seaboard states with western land claims ceded them to the national government. The Confederation Congress established territories with democratic political institutions in this domain and declared that all of those territories were to be open to settlement by citizens from every state.

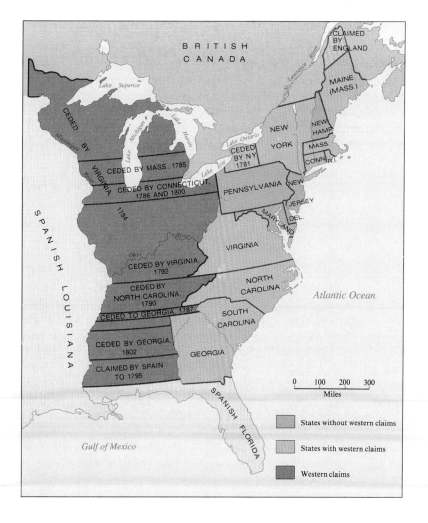

Gouverneur Morris:
An Aristocratic Liberal
in a Republican Age

The American Revolution had many meanings, and the life of Gouverneur Morris reveals one of them. Born into the New York aristocracy, Morris had an acute understanding of the dangers to his class posed by a "democratic" revolution supported by social nobodies such as Robert Twelves Hewes (see American Lives, Chapter 5). In 1774, at the tender age of twenty-two, Morris advised the New York elite "to seek for reunion with the parent state." Otherwise, "I see, and I see it with fear and trembling, that . . . we shall be under the worst of all possible dominions . . . the domination of a riotous mob." "The mob begin to think and reason," he warned again in 1775 after watching a debate between radical tradesmen and conservative Patriot merchants. "Poor reptiles! it is with them a vernal [spring] morning, . . . they bask in the sunshine, and ere noon they will bite, depend on it."

Family background had a lot to do with Morris's disdain of ordinary men and women. His grandfather, Lewis Morris, was the first lord of Morrisania, a 1900-acre manor in Westchester County, New York, and from 1738 to 1746 served as the king's governor of New Jersey. His father, Lewis Jr., was judge of the vice-admiralty court of New York and on his deathbed provided that Gouverneur, a younger son, should have "the best Education that is to be had in Europe or America": study at the Academy of Philadelphia and King's College in New York followed by an apprenticeship with the eminent lawyer William Smith, Jr. But since he lacked inherited wealth, the young Morris's choices were stark. He could either live in genteel poverty or exploit his social connections and personal talents—a fine mind, sophisticated manners, and great personal charm—to make his own fortune.

For all his aristocratic beliefs, Morris became a Patriot, refusing to follow his mother, many relatives, and his legal mentor, Smith, into Loyalism. In 1775 he won election to the Patriot Provincial Congress of New York and soon sought to shape the course of the revolutionary struggle. At the Provincial Convention that drafted New York's relatively conservative constitution of 1777, Morris argued strenuously for maintaining the

Gouverneur Morris, Federalist Statesman

old aristocratic method of voting by public declaration but more republican-minded members mandated voting by ballot. Still, the convention heeded Morris's ultra-conservative voice by imposing a property qualification for voting: ownership of a freehold worth 20 pounds.

Morris was equally active at the national level. As one of New York's delegates to the Continental Congress, he was shocked by the financial weakness of the Confederation and tried to enhance its authority. As early as 1778 Morris proposed the elimination of state currencies, the creation of a national domain in the West, and national tariffs to pay off the growing war debt. Three years later he happily enlisted as the assistant to the new superintendent of finance, the merchant

Robert Morris. Together the Morrises (who were not related) devised measures to restore the government's credit. In 1781 they won approval for the Bank of North America; the following year they issued a "Report on Public Credit," which called for the Confederation government to assume the entire national debt, issue new interest-bearing debt certificates, and impose tariffs and internal taxes to pay the interest costs. Here in outline was the fiscal program implemented a decade later by Alexander Hamilton.

Like Hamilton, Gouverneur Morris was a man of "spirit and nerve" who never doubted his own judgment and rarely respected that of others. George Washington chastised Morris for displaying his "brilliant imagination" too quickly and recklessly, whereas a French aristocrat observed that "his [air of] superiority, which he has taken no pains to conceal, will prevent his ever occupying an important place" in republican America. Never humbled, not even by an accident in 1780 that left him with a wooden leg, Morris used charm and brilliance to compensate for these flaws in his character. He played a prominent role at the Philadelphia convention in 1787, insisting that "property was the sole or primary object of Government & Society." To protect property rights, Morris argued for an aristocratic-type Senate whose members would serve without pay and for life, a national freehold property qualification for voting, and a strong president with the power of the veto.

Significantly, Morris did not defend aristocratic property. In debates in 1777 over the New York constitution, Morris had argued for "abolishing all quit rents within this State." He also called for the end of "domestic slavery . . . so that in future ages, every human being who breathes the air of the State, shall enjoy the privileges of a freeman," a proposition he reiterated with great force at the Philadelphia convention.

Morris's defense of freedom—of individuals, of the alienation of land, of commerce and legal contracts—aligned him with those Patriots who gave a "classical liberal" definition to the American Revolution. Valuing individual liberty higher than majority rule, liberal Patriots such as Morris hoped the new Constitution would protect property rights from popularly elected state legislatures and encourage economic growth. Indeed, Morris's outlook—and increasingly his life—reflected the emergent principles of laissez-faire capitalism. After serving as Robert Morris's assistant, Gouverneur became his business partner. The two men invested jointly in land in New York and Pennsylvania, in a maritime venture in Massachusetts, and in supplying tobacco to the French tobacco monopoly. Even as such speculations landed Robert Morris in debtor's prison, they made Gouverneur Morris a rich man, finally able to live in the aristocratic style to which he had been bred.

Beginning in 1788, Morris resided in Europe for ten years, first as a speculating merchant, then as the American minister to France (1792–1794), and finally as a cultured man of independent wealth. Fluent in French, polished in manners, confident of his talents, Morris fit easily into Parisian high society, taking as a mistress the young wife of an aging aristocrat, forming a lifelong friendship with the formidable Madame de Staël, and sharing the hopes and the fears of the endangered *ancien régime*. While disparaging the French nobility for "Hugging the Privileges of Centuries long elapsed," Morris refused to support the republican reforms proposed by Lafayette and others, declaring that he was "opposed to the Democracy from Regard to Liberty." Indeed, as republicans took control of France in 1792, Morris joined an unsuccessful aristocratic plot to smuggle King Louis XVI out of Paris.

In the end Gouverneur Morris stands forth as an aristocratic liberal, an American precursor of Alexis de Tocqueville (see Chapter 10). Aristocratic in manners and fearing mob rule, Morris wanted to limit the new republican polity to men of property and status even as he celebrated classical liberal principles of personal freedom, economic enterprise, and equal opportunity.

The Postwar Crisis

Success was far from assured, however, and the 1780s were a critical decade for the new nation. Peace did not bring a return to prewar prosperity. The war had destroyed many American merchant ships and disrupted trade; exports—especially of Chesapeake tobacco—declined because of the loss of long-established ties with British merchant houses. Deprived of a subsidy from the British government, South Carolina's lucrative indigo industry nearly vanished. The British Navigation Acts, which had contributed to the expansion of colonial commerce, now worked against the United States as American-owned ships were barred from trading with the sugar islands in the British West Indies.

Economic Hard Times. The postwar recession lowered the American standard of living. The population of the United States continued to grow—from 2.4 million to 3.6 million between 1775 and 1787—but exports increased only slightly, from $10.7 million to $11.6 million. As a result, individual Americans had less income to spend on imported manufactures. Nevertheless, low-priced British goods flooded urban markets, driving many artisans and war-created textile firms out of business. Responding to protests by artisans, New York, Rhode Island, Pennsylvania, and Massachusetts imposed tariffs on imported manufactures.

The financial legacy of the war compounded these problems. Most state governments emerged from the conflict with worthless currencies and big debts. North Carolina owed its creditors $1.7 million, while Virginia was liable for $2.7 million in war bonds. Speculators—wealthy merchants and landowners—had purchased many state debt certificates for far less than their face value. Now these shrewd and influential men advocated high taxes so the states could redeem the bonds quickly and at full value.

As economic recession and high taxes pressed hard on debtors, they sought political solutions to their financial problems. In South Carolina farmers won the passage of a law that prevented sheriffs from selling seized farms to repay debts; instead, creditors had to accept installment payments over a three-year period. South Carolina legislators also assisted debtors by increasing the supply of paper currency. But these prodebtor measures were controversial. David Ramsay, a physician and the future author of the well-known *History of the American Revolution* (1789), assailed the South Carolina legislature for undermining "the just rights of creditors." To avert similar prodebtor legislation and preserve elite rule in Maryland, Charles Carroll of Carrollton persuaded wealthy Maryland landowners to adopt conciliatory economic policies toward yeomen and tenant farmers. Accordingly, the Maryland legislature replaced the customary poll tax, which bore hard on the poor, with a graduated property tax. When the Maryland House of Delegates enacted profarmer and prodebtor measures in 1785 and 1786, they were rejected by the more conservative state senate.

As James Madison of Virginia pointed out, these political struggles were not primarily between "the Class with, and Class without, property." The real battle was between wealthy merchants and landowners on the one hand and a larger coalition of middling farm owners, small-scale traders, artisans, and tenant farmers on the other. Creditors might be angered by legislation favoring farmers and artisans, but prodebtor laws eased the financial strain and probably prevented a major social upheaval.

Shays's Rebellion. The absence of debtor-relief legislation in Massachusetts provoked the first armed uprising in the new nation. When the war ended, merchants and creditors in eastern Massachusetts lobbied successfully for high taxes and against paper money. These procreditor policies facilitated rapid repayment of the state's war debt but undermined the fragile finances of farmers in newly settled areas. Creditors and sheriffs hauled delinquent farmers into court, saddled them with high legal fees, and threatened to imprison them for debt or repossess their property. In 1786 residents of western counties called extralegal meetings and protested against high taxes and aggressive eastern creditors. Meanwhile, bands of angry farmers closed the courts by force and freed debtors and fellow protesters from jail. Resistance gradually grew into a full-scale revolt. Ignored by the state legislature, hundreds of farmers in western and central Massachusetts organized an army under the leadership of Daniel Shays, a former Continental army captain, and prepared to use force to resist state authority.

Shays's Rebellion, a struggle against high taxes and nonlocal political control, resembled the American resistance movements between 1763 and 1775. "The people have turned against their teachers the doctrines which were inculcated to effect the late revolution," complained the conservative Massachusetts political leader Fisher Ames. Radical Patriots were no less troubled by popular conventions and crowd actions. As Samuel Adams put it, "those Men, who . . . would lessen the Weight of Government lawfully exercised must be Enemies to our happy Revolution and Common Liberty."

To preserve its authority, the Massachusetts legislature passed a Riot Act outlawing illegal assemblies. With the financial support of nervous eastern merchants, Governor James Bowdoin equipped a strong fighting force to put down the rebellion and called on the Confederation Congress to supply an additional 1,300 soldiers. A national army was not needed. Shays's army dwindled during the winter of 1786–1787, falling victim to freezing weather and inadequate supplies.

"Gen. *Daniel Shays*, Col. *Job Shattuck*."
This woodcut was published in *Bickerstaff's Boston Almanack* for 1787 by Friends of Government who attacked the rebel leaders as upstarts and demagogues. "Liberty is still the object I have in view," a Shaysite declared in reply, but the former radical Sam Adams would have none of it: "The man who dares to rebel against the laws of a republic ought to suffer death." Shattuck was sentenced to death for treason but then pardoned; Shays fled to New York State, where he died in 1821, still a poor farmer.

Bowdoin's military force easily dispersed the rebels, and state authority was restored.

Though the rebellion collapsed, the discontent that caused it was not so easily suppressed. Massachusetts voters turned Governor Bowdoin out of office, and farmers in New York, northern Pennsylvania, Connecticut, New Hampshire, and Vermont (a separate republic until 1791, when it was admitted to the Union over the protests of New York land speculators) closed courthouses and demanded economic assistance. British officials in Canada predicted the imminent demise of the United States, and many Americans feared for the success of their republican experiment. Indeed, Shays's Rebellion was important primarily for its political impact. It prompted leaders with a national perspective to redouble their efforts to create a stronger central government.

The Constitution of 1787

From the moment of its creation, the Constitution was a complex and controversial document. Written in a time of crisis, it embodied the values and interests of men with a personal stake in its outcome. But, reflecting the intellectual talents of the framers and intense debates over political principles, the Constitution was also a principled and innovative statement of republican political theory. Beyond that, it addressed the pressing issue of the distribution of power between the states and the central government.

The Rise of a Nationalist Faction

Prominent among the Patriots who favored a stronger central government were military officers, diplomats, and officials who had served in the Continental Congress. Their experiences during the war of independence had made their political outlook national rather than state or local. General Washington, the financier Robert Morris, and the diplomats Benjamin Franklin, John Jay, and John Adams were all advocates of giving the national government the power to control foreign commerce and impose tariffs.

Americans were well acquainted with restrictions on commerce in the form of the Navigation Acts, and after independence key commercial states in the North—New York, Massachusetts, Pennsylvania—devised their own trade policies, providing subsidies to merchants and imposing protective tariffs. But the nationalists' proposals to place trade in the hands of Congress ran afoul of regional interests: southern planters wanted free trade with Europe, whereas northern merchants, artisans, and manufacturers called for protective tariffs and preferential treatment for American ships.

Tax policy was another divisive issue. Nationalist leaders were particularly troubled by the poverty of the Confederation government. The refusal by Rhode Island and New York to levy a national import duty and the decision by other states to assume and discharge some of the national debt had undermined Robert Morris's scheme to prop up the Confederation. Without tax revenue or state contributions, Congress was unable to pay even the interest on the foreign debt. To many nationalists, the American republic seemed on the verge of collapse. "I am really more distressed by the posture of our public affairs, than I ever was by the most gloomy appearances during the war," confessed William Livingston of New Jersey. The "stubborn Dignity" of the states, another nationalist complained, "will never permit a federal Government to exist."

By 1786 nationalists had yet another reason for concern: the fiscal policies of the states. Legislatures in Virginia and other southern states were granting tax relief to various groups of citizens, thus diminishing public revenue and delaying redemption of government debts. Public creditors feared that their government-issued bonds would become worthless; as Charles Lee of Virginia lamented, taxpayers were being led to believe "they will never be compelled to pay." State governments also jeopardized the sanctity of private debts by providing relief to debtors—staying the collection of private debts or exempting personal property from seizure. Four states had gone much further, forcing merchants and creditors to accept depreciated paper currency in payment for debts. "The debtor interest . . . operates in all the forms of injustice & oppression," a South Carolina creditor complained. "While men are

madly accumulating enormous debts, their legislators are making provisions for their nonpayment."

Adding these concerns to their agenda, the nationalists took the initiative in 1786. Madison persuaded the Virginia legislature to call a commercial convention in Annapolis, Maryland, to discuss tariff and taxation policies. After this discussion (by twelve delegates from only five states), the nationalists called for another meeting, in Philadelphia, to undertake a broad review of the responsibilities and powers of the Confederation. Shays's Rebellion raised the prospect of social revolution and underscored the need for action. In January 1787 nationalists in Congress won the passage of a resolution supporting a revision of the Articles of Confederation to make them "adequate to the exigencies of government and the preservation of the Union." To many nationalists the Philadelphia meeting seemed the last opportunity to save the republic. "Nothing but the adoption of some efficient plan from the Convention," a fellow Virginian wrote to James Madison, "can prevent anarchy first & civil convulsions afterwards."

The Philadelphia Convention

The Philadelphia convention began in May 1787. Fifty-five delegates attended, representing every state except Rhode Island, whose legislature opposed any increase in central authority. Some members, such as Benjamin Franklin of Pennsylvania, had been leaders of the independence movement. Others, including George Washington and Robert Morris, had come to prominence during the war. Most were merchants, slaveholding planters, or "monied men"; there were no artisans, backcountry settlers, or tenants and only a solitary yeoman farmer.

Several of the most famous Patriots missed the convention. John Adams and Thomas Jefferson were in Europe, serving as the American ministers to Britain and France. Thomas Paine was also in Europe, and his fellow radical Samuel Adams was not chosen as a delegate by the Massachusetts legislature. The Virginia firebrand Patrick Henry was selected but refused to attend because he favored a limited national government. Their places were taken by capable younger men such as James Madison and Alexander Hamilton. Both were nationalists, committed to the creation of a central government that, as Hamilton put it, would protect the republic from "the imprudence of democracy" in the state legislatures.

Hamilton's views were extreme, but most of the delegates shared his procreditor and nationalist outlook. The Philadelphia convention was filled with men who supported creditor factions in their own states and wanted to protect property rights. They believed in a stronger central government that would curb what

Madison, in an important memorandum of 1787, would call the "Vices of the Political System" of the various states. They differed only on the means by which to accomplish this goal.

The Virginia Plan. The delegates began the convention by electing Washington as the presiding officer and deciding to deliberate behind closed doors to forestall popular opposition. (In fact, Americans knew little about the proceedings of the convention until the 1840s, when Madison's notebooks were published.) They agreed that each state would have one vote at the convention, as in the Confederation, and that a majority would decide an issue. Then the delegates exceeded their mandate to revise the Articles of Confederation by agreeing to consider the Virginia Plan, a scheme devised by James Madison that called for a different constitutional framework: a truly national government.

Madison arrived in Philadelphia determined to fashion a new political order. He was a graduate of Princeton,

Portrait of James Madison, 1805–1807, by Gilbert Stuart
An intellectual, Madison was also a successful politician, especially in the decade after 1785—when he helped enact the Virginia Statute of Religious Liberty, write and ratify the Constitution of 1787, win passage of the Bill of Rights, and found the Democratic-Republican party.

where he had read classical and modern political theory, and had served in both the Confederation Congress and the Virginia assembly. His experience in Virginia convinced him of the "narrow ambition" of many state political leaders and their lack of public virtue. He wanted to design a national government that would curb factional disputes and ensure the rule of men of high character.

The Virginia Plan differed from the Articles of Confederation in three crucial respects. First, it rejected state sovereignty in favor of the "supremacy of national authority." In Madison's scheme the central government had the power "to legislate in all cases to which the separate States are incompetent" and to overturn state laws. Second, it called for a *national* republic that drew its authority directly from all the people of the United States and would have direct power over them. As Madison explained, the new central government would bypass the states and operate directly "on the individuals composing them." Third, the Virginia Plan would create a three-part national government structured like many state governments. It called for a lower house elected by the voters, an upper house elected by the lower house, and an executive and judiciary chosen by the entire legislature.

From a political perspective, Madison's plan contained a fatal flaw: because it assigned great authority to the lower house and based its composition on population, the plan would dramatically increase the power of the larger states. Consequently, delegates from the less populous states rejected this plan out of hand. Their states had enjoyed equal representation in both the Continental Congress and the Confederation Congress. They feared that, as a Delaware delegate proclaimed, the populous states would "crush the small ones whenever they stand in the way of their ambitious or interested views."

To protect their interests, delegates from small states rallied behind a plan devised by William Paterson of New Jersey. The New Jersey Plan had many nationalist aspects: it would transform the Confederation by giving the central government the power to raise revenue, control commerce, and make binding requisitions on the states. But it would preserve equality among the states by limiting each state to one vote in a unicameral legislature, as in the Articles of Confederation. Of course, this provision made the New Jersey Plan unacceptable to delegates from the larger states. After a month of debate a bare majority of the states voted to accept the Virginia Plan as the basis for further discussion.

This decision changed the course of American history, for it raised the prospect of a new constitutional structure. Although two New York delegates walked out in protest, the rest redoubled their efforts. They met six days a week during the hot, humid summer of 1787, debating high principles and working through a multitude of technical details. As experienced and realistic politicians, the delegates knew that their plan had to be acceptable to existing political factions and powerful social groups. Pierce Butler of South Carolina expressed this dilemma by invoking a classical Greek precedent: "We must follow the example of Solon, who gave the Athenians not the best government he could devise but the best they would receive."

The Great Compromise. Representation remained the central problem. To satisfy all the states, large and small, the Connecticut delegates suggested changing the Virginia Plan so that the upper house, the Senate, would have two members from each state regardless of a state's size. In the lower chamber, the House of Representatives, seats would be apportioned on the basis of population, which would be determined every ten years by a national census. Delegates from the large states accepted the Great Compromise, but only after bitter debate; it seemed to them less a compromise than a victory for the smaller states.

Having resolved this major issue, the delegates quickly settled other matters that involved the interests of the existing state governments. One delegate objected to a proposal to extend the national judiciary into the states, declaring that "the states will revolt at such encroachments." The convention therefore defined the judicial power of the United States in broad terms and vested it "in one supreme Court," leaving to the new national legislature the thorny issue of establishing lower national courts in the states. The convention also decided against imposing a uniform freehold property qualification for voting in national elections. "Eight or nine states have extended the right of suffrage beyond the freeholders," George Mason of Virginia pointed out. "What will people there say if they should be disfranchised?"

Ultimately, the delegates devised ingenious ways to give the states a prominent role in the new constitutional structure. For example, they placed the selection of the president, the chief executive official, in the hands of an *electoral college* that would be chosen on a state-by-state basis. The delegates also specified that state legislatures, not the voters at large, would elect the members of the Senate. By giving state governments an important role in the new system, the delegates hoped those governments would accept the reduction of their sovereign power.

Compromise over Slavery. Although the conflict between the large and small states dominated the convention's debates, another kind of conflict—a regional division between the North and the South on the slavery issue—also began to emerge. While no one proposed the abolition of slavery, Gouverneur Morris of New York condemned it as "a nefarious institution" and George Mason of Virginia argued eloquently for national laws

against the slave trade. Delegates from the Carolinas and Georgia insisted that the trade continue. As John Rutledge of South Carolina warned his colleagues, "the true question at present is whether the Southern states shall or shall not be parties to the Union."

To maintain a national union, the delegates treated slavery as a political question, not a moral issue. Compromise was the watchword. Thus, the Constitution contained a "fugitive" clause enabling masters to reclaim slaves or servants who had taken refuge in other states. This provision appealed to the white planters who controlled Georgia and the Carolinas, as did a clause that denied Congress the power to regulate the importation of slaves for twenty years after ratification. To mollify antislavery sentiment in the northern states, the delegates agreed that the slave trade could thereafter be abolished by legislative action.

Another compromise resolved the slavery-related issues of taxation and representation. Southern delegates wanted to include slaves in a state's population for the purpose of determining representation in Congress. Northerners objected, arguing that propertyless slaves, lacking the vote, were not full members of the republic and should not be counted at all. The convention finally agreed that for the purposes of representation and taxation a slave (slaves were carefully referred to in the Constitution as "all other Persons") would be counted as three-fifths of a free person.

National Power. Having allayed the concerns of small states and slave states, the delegates proceeded to fulfill their goal of creating a powerful, procreditor national government. The finished document declared that the Constitution and all national legislation and treaties made under its authority were to be the supreme law of the land. It gave the national government broad powers over taxation, military defense, and external commerce as well as the authority to make all laws "necessary and proper" to implement those and other provisions. To establish the fiscal credit of the central government, the Constitution mandated that the United States honor the existing national debt.

As the Constitution enhanced national authority, it restricted that of the states. State governments could no longer issue money to assist debtors in paying their bills. Prodebtor legislatures were also forbidden to enact any "Law impairing the Obligation of Contracts," thus prohibiting debtor-relief legislation.

The proposed Constitution was not a "perfect production," Benjamin Franklin admitted on September 17, 1787, as he urged the forty-one delegates still present to sign it. Yet the great diplomat confessed his astonishment "to find this system approaching so near to perfection as it does." His colleagues apparently agreed; all but three signed the document. Their handiwork would now be judged by their fellow Americans.

The Debate over Ratification

The procedures for ratifying the new Constitution were controversial. The convention hesitated to submit its nationalist scheme to the state legislatures for their unanimous consent, as required by the Articles of Confederation, because it undoubtedly would be rejected by Rhode Island and possibly a few other states. The delegates therefore specified a different procedure: the Constitution would go into effect upon ratification by special conventions in at least nine of the thirteen states. Because of its nationalist sympathies, the Confederation Congress winked at this extralegal procedure and sent the new Constitution to the states. Surprisingly, the state legislatures complied, calling for the election of delegates to state ratification conventions.

A great national debate began almost immediately. The nationalists seized the initiative with two bold moves. First, they called themselves "Federalists," a term that suggested a loose, decentralized system of government and thus partially obscured their goal of establishing a strong central authority. Second, they undertook a coordinated political campaign, publishing dozens of pamphlets and newspaper articles. In this literature they argued that the proposed Constitution would remedy the acknowledged defects of the Articles of Confederation and create a strong and prosperous Union.

The Antifederalists. The opponents of the Constitution became known as the Antifederalists. They came from diverse backgrounds and were less organized than the Federalists. Some, like Governor George Clinton of New York, enjoyed great power and patronage in their states and feared losing it. Others were agrarian democrats who had long opposed merchants and creditors. "These lawyers and men of learning and monied men expect to be managers of this Constitution," argued a biblically minded Massachusetts farmer, "and get all the power and all the money into their own hands and then they will swallow up all of us little folks . . . just as the whale swallowed up Jonah."

Highly educated Americans with a "traditional" republican outlook provided ideological leadership for the Antifederalist cause. Following the argument of the French political philosopher Montesquieu, they believed that republican institutions were suitable only for cities or small states. "No extensive empire can be governed on republican principles," James Winthrop of Massachusetts declared. Like most Antifederalists, Winthrop worried that a strong national administration would restore the worst features of British rule—high taxes, an oppressive bureaucracy, and a standing army controlled by a tyrant—thus ending the republican experiment in popular government. George Mason of Virginia, one of the three delegates who refused to sign the

Constitution, argued that the new charter was "totally subversive of every principle which has hitherto governed us. This power is calculated to annihilate totally the state governments." Because they were committed to keeping government "close to the people," Antifederalists maintained that keeping the old Articles was preferable to adopting a new document with such obvious defects.

Many Antifederalists stressed the danger of tyranny and elite rule. Melancton Smith of New York warned that the Constitution's provision for creating large electoral districts would inevitably lead to the concentration of power in the hands of a few wealthy upper-class men, since only such men would be prominent enough to be elected. Yet it was well known, Smith maintained, that "a representative body, composed principally of respectable yeomanry, is the best possible security to liberty." Patrick Henry of Virginia called attention to the immense taxing power of the central government. "A great and mighty President" would "be supported in extravagant munificence," he predicted; "the whole of our property may be taken by this American government, by laying what taxes they please, and suspending our laws at their pleasure." Henry and other Antifederalists envisioned the new nation as a collection of small sovereign republics tied together only for trade and defense—not the "United States" but the "States United."

The Federalist. In New York, where ratification was hotly contested, James Madison, John Jay, and Alexander Hamilton countered these arguments in a series of newspaper articles called *The Federalist.* These ardent nationalists stressed the need for a strong government to conduct foreign affairs and insisted—also invoking Montesquieu—that central authority would not foster domestic tyranny. In his *Thoughts on Government* John Adams had adapted Montesquieu's well-known analysis of British institutions, *The Spirit of the Laws* (1748), to fit American conditions, suggesting that a "separation of powers" within the government would preserve the liberty of citizens. The authors of *The Federalist* expanded this argument, pointing out that authority in the national government would be divided among a president, a bicameral legislature, and a judiciary. Each branch of government would "check and balance" the others, thus preserving liberty.

James Madison went further, denying that republicanism was suited only to small states. Indeed, in *The Federalist,* No. 10, he maintained that the sheer size of the national republic would be the greatest deterrent to tyranny. It was "sown in the nature of man," Madison wrote, that individuals would seek power and form factions to advance their own interests. Indeed, "a landed interest, a manufacturing interest, a mercantile interest, a moneyed interest, with many lesser interests, grow up of necessity in civilized nations." The task of govern-

ment in a free society, the young Virginian continued with true brilliance, was not to suppress those groups but to prevent any single faction from becoming dominant. This end could best be achieved not in a small republic, as Montesquieu and James Winthrop had maintained, but in a large one. "Extend the sphere," Madison concluded, "and you take in a greater variety of parties and interests; you make it less probable that a majority of the whole will have a common motive to invade the rights of other citizens."

Madison's hardheaded realism—his classical liberal emphasis on self-interest as the source of human conduct—was tempered by a traditional republican belief in public virtue. "I go by this great republican principle," Madison told the Virginia ratifying convention, "that the people have virtue and intelligence to select men of virtue and wisdom"—and, he undoubtedly hoped, to ratify the new Constitution.

The Ratification Conventions. Madison's hopes were tested in the ratifying conventions, which met in twelve states between December 1787 and June 1788. (Rhode Island again was the exception; it ratified only in 1790.) Unlike the men at the Philadelphia convention, the delegates to the state caucuses represented a wide spectrum of Americans: untutored farmers and middling artisans as well as educated gentlemen. In general, delegates from the backcountry were Antifederalists whereas those from the seacoast strongly supported the Federal-

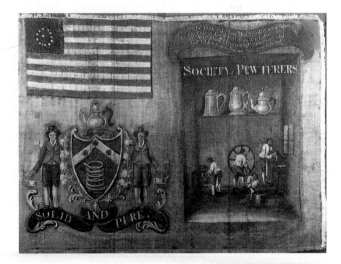

Artisans Support the Constitution
Seeking tariff protection from lower-priced British tinware, New York's Society of Pewterers supported ratification of the Philadelphia constitution. Their call for "Sons Joined in One Social Band" conveyed the ideal of an artisan republican community, and in its call for brotherhood, anticipated the French Revolutionary slogan of "Liberty, Equality, and Fraternity." (Collection of The New-York Historical Society)

ists. Thus, in Pennsylvania a coalition of merchants, artisans, and commercial farmers from Philadelphia and its vicinity spearheaded an easy Federalist victory. Other early Federalist successes came in the less populous states of Delaware, New Jersey, Georgia, and Connecticut. In each case the delegates hoped that a stronger national government would offset the power of their large neighbors.

The Constitution's first real test came in January 1788 in Massachusetts, one of the most populous states and a hotbed of Antifederalist sentiment (see Map 7.2). Influential Patriots—including Samuel Adams and Governor John Hancock—publicly opposed the new charter, as did Shaysite sympathizers in the west. But astute Federalist politicians won over wavering delegates by warning of political chaos, and Boston artisans, who hoped for tariff protection from British imports, supported ratification. By a close vote of 187 to 168, the Federalists carried the day (see American Voices, page 213).

Spring brought Federalist victories in Maryland and South Carolina. When New Hampshire ratified in June (by 57 votes to 47), the required nine states had approved the Constitution. But the outcome was still in doubt, for the powerful states of Virginia and New

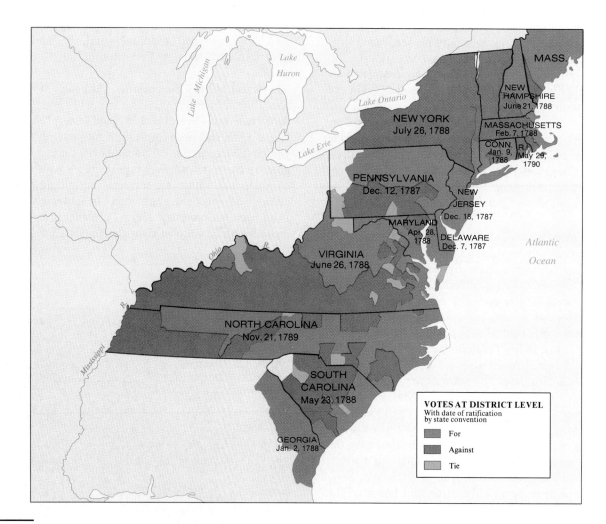

MAP 7.2

Ratifying the Constitution

In 1907 the geographer Owen Libby plotted the votes of the state ratification conventions on a map. He noted that most delegates from seaboard or commercial farming districts favored the Constitution whereas those from backcountry areas opposed it. Subsequent research has confirmed Libby's socioeconomic interpretation in North and South Carolina and Massachusetts; however, other factors influenced delegates in some states with frontier districts, such as Georgia, where the Constitution was ratified unanimously.

Jonathan Smith

A Farmer Praises the Constitution

Scores of ordinary men—middling farmers, shopkeepers, artisans—sat alongside their social betters in the state ratifying conventions; their opinions and votes were often crucial to the outcome. Here a farmer explains his support of the constitution to the Massachusetts convention in language that is plain but effective, punctuated with phrases taken from the Bible and analogies drawn from personal experience.

Mr. President, I am a plain man, and get my living by the plough. I am not used to speak in public. . . . I have lived in a part of the country where I have known the worth of good government by the want of it. There was a black cloud [Shays's Rebellion] that rose in the east last winter, and spread over the west. It brought on a state of anarchy that led to tyranny. . . . People, I say, took up arms, and then, if you went to speak to them, you had the musket of death presented to your breast. They would rob you of your property, threaten to burn your houses. . . .

When I saw this Constitution, I found that it was a cure for these disorders. I got a copy of it and read it over and over. I had been a member of the convention to form our own state constitution, and had learnt something of the checks and balances of power; and I found them all here. . . .

I don't think the worse of the Constitution because lawyers, and men of learning, and moneyed men are fond of it. [They] are all embarked in the same cause with us, and we must all swim or sink together. Suppose two or three of you had been at the pains to break up a piece of rough land, and sow it with wheat—would you let it lie waste because you could not agree what sort of fence to make? There is a time to sow and a time to reap. We sowed our seed when we sent men to the federal convention. Now is the harvest; now is the time to reap the fruit of our labor. And if we won't do it now, I am afraid we never shall have another opportunity.

Source: Jonathan Elliot, ed., *The Debates. . .on the Adoption of the Federal Constitution* (Washington, D.C.: 1830), II, pp. 101–102.

York had not yet acted. Now Madison, Jay, and Hamilton, writing in *The Federalist*, used their superb rhetorical skills to win over delegates in those key states. In addition, leading Federalists promised that the Constitution would be amended to include a Bill of Rights. This promise addressed the most powerful argument of the Antifederalists, that the new national Constitution, unlike most state constitutions, failed to protect basic individual rights, such as liberty of conscience in religious matters and the right to a jury trial. In the end, the Federalists won a narrow victory in Virginia, 89 votes to 79, and this success carried them to victory in New York by the even smaller margin of 30 votes to 27.

Few Federalists had expected a more resounding victory in light of the resistance during the 1780s to a strong central government. Working against great odds, they had created a national republic, a triumph that had profound ideological and social implications. The United States Constitution of 1787 represented the resurgence of the traditional political elite and the decline of the yeomanry. At least temporarily, creditors and merchants were in the ascendancy. The Revolutionary Era had come to an end.

The Constitution Implemented

The Constitution gave American political life a new, national dimension. Voters had long chosen local and state officials; now they elected national officeholders as well. A single political system was beginning to tie together the interests and concerns of Georgia planters, Pennsylvania artisans, Massachusetts merchants, and scores of other social groups.

Devising the New Government. The Federalists who had written the Constitution swept the election of 1788. No fewer than forty-four of the ninety-one members of the first United States Congress, which met in 1789, had helped write or ratify the Constitution. Only eight Antifederalists were elected to the House of Representatives, and they never formed a cohesive political faction. The Constitution specified that "electors" chosen by voters in the various states would select the president and vice-president. As expected, the electors chose George Washington of Virginia as president; John Adams of Massachusetts received the second highest number of electoral votes and became vice-president. The newly

elected officials took up their posts in New York City, the temporary home of the national government.

Washington, the military savior of his country, now became its political father, establishing many enduring institutions and practices. At fifty-seven years of age, he was a man of great personal dignity and influence. Instinctively cautious, the new president followed many administrative practices of the Confederation government. Washington asked Congress to reestablish existing executive departments—Foreign Affairs (State), Finance (Treasury), and War—but demanded that the president have administrative control of the bureaucracy. The chief executive also had the power to appoint major officials with the consent of the Senate, and Washington insisted on his authority to remove them at will. To head the Department of State, Washington chose Thomas Jefferson, a fellow Virginian and an experienced diplomat. For secretary of the treasury he turned to Alexander Hamilton, a lawyer and a wartime military aide. Washington designated Jefferson, Hamilton, and Secretary of War Henry Knox as his *cabinet,* or body of advisers.

Congress also set about implementing the Constitution. The new national charter created a Supreme Court but left it to Congress to establish the number and jurisdiction of the lower courts. In law as in politics, Federalists wanted national institutions to supersede state institutions and act directly on individual citizens. Consequently, in the Judiciary Act of 1789 they created a comprehensive and hierarchical federal system with thirteen district courts, one for each state, and three circuit courts to hear appeals from the district tribunals. As the Constitution specified, the Supreme Court had the final say. Moreover, the Judiciary Act permitted appeals to the Supreme Court on state court decisions that involved matters specified in the Constitution, ensuring that national judges would have the final say.

The Bill of Rights. The Federalists kept their promise to amend the Constitution to protect the liberties of citizens. Drawing on lists of rights in state constitutions, James Madison, now a member of the House of Representatives, submitted nineteen amendments to the first Congress after carefully weeding out most of those that would have weakened the national government. Ten amendments received legislative approval and were ratified by the states, eventually becoming known as the Bill of Rights. Most of these amendments guaranteed legal procedures such as the right to a jury trial and freedom from arbitrary arrest; others safeguarded sacred political rights such as freedom of speech and freedom of assembly. The Second Amendment guaranteed citizens the right to bear arms so that they might protect themselves, serve in the militia, and defend their liberties. The Tenth Amendment limited the potential authority of the national government by reserving nondelegated powers to the states or the people.

As a political maneuver, the Bill of Rights yielded immediate results, quieting the fears of many Antifederalists and enhancing the legitimacy of the Constitution of 1787. As a constitutional safeguard, the amendments have had a complex history. Like all constitutional clauses and ordinary laws, they have been subject to interpretation, which has changed with time and circumstance. Moreover, in 1833 the Supreme Court (in the case of *Barron v. Baltimore*) declared that the amendments safeguarded rights only from infringement by the national government; for protection from state authorities, citizens would have to rely on the state constitutions. Nearly a century later, in the 1920s, the national courts began to use the Fourteenth Amendment (1868) to protect the rights enumerated in the first ten amendments against violation by governments at every level—national, state, and local.

The ratification of the Bill of Rights completed the implementation of the Constitution. The president and the Congress had given definite form to the executive, legislative, and judicial departments, creating the intricate mechanism of "balanced" government envisioned by the Philadelphia convention. The Bill of Rights demanded by the Antifederalists ensured broad political support for the new national government.

The Political Crisis of the 1790s

Although the new Constitution was in place by 1790, the final decade of the century brought fresh political crises. The Federalists split into two irreconcilable factions in regard to financial policy, and the French Revolution caused rifts over political ideology. The wars sparked by the revolution in France (1793–1801) expanded American trade, bringing substantial profits to farmers and spectacular fortunes to merchants, but also divided American public opinion between pro-British Federalists and pro-French Republicans. Political conflict culminated in an undeclared naval war against France in the Atlantic and the repression of free speech at home.

Hamilton's Program

One of George Washington's most important decisions was his choice of Alexander Hamilton to be secretary of the treasury. Hamilton was an ambitious self-made man, the son of a Scottish merchant in the West Indies; he was raised by his mother, Rachel Faucett, after his father abandoned the family. The precocious child learned the ways of trade from his mother, who ran a small store, and was soon apprenticed to a prominent import-export firm. Hamilton moved to the mainland in 1772

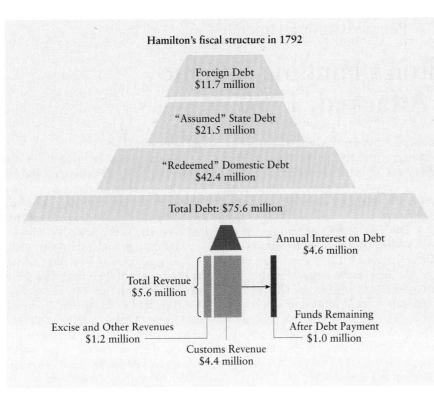

Hamilton's fiscal structure in 1792

Foreign Debt
$11.7 million

"Assumed" State Debt
$21.5 million

"Redeemed" Domestic Debt
$42.4 million

Total Debt: $75.6 million

Annual Interest on Debt
$4.6 million

Total Revenue
$5.6 million

Excise and Other Revenues
$1.2 million

Customs Revenue
$4.4 million

Funds Remaining
After Debt Payment
$1.0 million

FIGURE 7.2

Hamilton's Fiscal Structure, 1792
Hamilton used the revenue from excise taxes and customs duties to defray the annual interest on the national debt. Hamilton did not pay off the debt because he wanted to tie wealthy American bondholders to the new national government.

and enrolled at King's College in New York. His military abilities and personal charm impressed Washington, who chose him as a personal aide during the war. In the 1780s Hamilton married Elizabeth Schuyler, the daughter of a wealthy Hudson River landowner, and established close connections with the mercantile community, becoming one of the leading lawyers in New York City. At the Philadelphia convention he condemned the "amazing violence and turbulence of the democratic spirit" and called for an authoritarian government headed by a president with nearly monarchical powers. Although he left the convention early, Hamilton championed the new Constitution in *The Federalist*.

As treasury secretary, Hamilton devised innovative financial policies to overcome the fiscal problems that had bedeviled the Confederation (see Figure 7.2). Not surprisingly, his ambitious program favored men of his immediate acquaintance: financiers and seaport merchants. His recommendations took form in three major reports to Congress: on public credit (January 1790), on a national bank (December 1790), and on manufactures (December 1791).

Public Credit. The financial and social implications of Hamilton's "Report on the Public Credit" made it instantly controversial. The report asked Congress to redeem at face value the millions of dollars in securities issued by the Confederation government. Redeeming the debt in full would bolster the credit of the national

treasury but would also provide a windfall to speculators who had invested heavily in depreciated securities. For example, in one transaction the Burrell & Burrell merchant house of Boston had paid about $600 for Confederation notes with a face value of $2,500. If those notes were paid off in full, the firm would reap an enormous profit. Hamilton hoped that such windfalls, together with the strong credit of the new government, would induce financiers to continue in their role as public creditors. He proposed to redeem the old notes with new government securities, which would pay interest at about 4 percent. Creating a permanent debt would tie the interests of wealthy Americans to the new national government.

Hamilton's scheme reawakened fears of British monopolies and governmental corruption. Republican ideology warned that wealth—and the luxury that went with it—undermined public virtue, a particular concern among leaders in the southern agricultural states. "Money in a state of civilization is power," argued John Taylor of Virginia, who was wary of the rising wealth and power of the northern commercial elite. His thought might have been finished by Patrick Henry, who proclaimed on behalf of the Virginia assembly that "to erect, and concentrate, and perpetuate a large monied interest, must prove fatal to the existence of American liberty."

But Hamilton ignored those objections and advanced a second proposal that favored wealthy credi-

A Pennsylvania Farmer

Hamilton's Funding Scheme Attacked, 1790

Hamilton's plan to redeem at full value the remaining war debt of the Continental Congress roused widespread anger, for most of the money—which would be raised by import duties on goods like tea and sugar—would go to speculators, not to the soldiers and farmers who originally held the certificates.

In a former letter I took notice of the injuries which the proposed funding system will do the soldiers and other original holders of certificates, by compelling them to pay taxes in order to increase the value of certificates in the hands of quartermasters, speculators, and foreigners. The Secretary of the Treasury has declared that these people sold their certificates from choice. This I believe is true only in a few in-

stances. A hungry creditor, a distressed family, or perhaps, in some instances, the want of a meals victuals, drove most of them to the brokers' offices, or compelled them to surrender up their certificates. . . .

This case I shall mention is of a sick soldier, who sold his certificates of £69.7.0 for £3.0.11 to a rich speculator. He went to this speculator after he recovered, and offered to redeem his certificate—but he refused to give it up. Now, can it be right that this poor soldier, every time he sips his bohea tea, or tastes a particle of sugar, should pay a tax to raise £3.0.11 to £67.7.0 in the hands of this speculator?

Thus we see public credit (that much hackneyed and prostituted phrase) must be established at the expense of national justice, gratitude,

and humanity. . . .

Would it not be proper for the farmers to unite immediately, and remonstrate against all these evils? They never were in half the danger of being ruined by the British government that they now are by their own.

Had any person told them in the beginning of the war that, after paying the yearly rent of their farms for seven years to carry on this war, at the close of it their farms would only be worth one-fourth of their original cost and value, in consequence of a funding system—is there a farmer that would have embarked in the war? No, there is not. Why then should we be deceived, duped, defrauded, and ruined by our new rulers?

Source: Pennsylvania Gazette, February 3, 1790.

---

tors. He devised an *assumption* plan in which the national government would take on all the outstanding war debts of the states (see American Voices, above). This proposal unleashed a flurry of financial speculation and even an episode of governmental corruption. Before Hamilton announced the plan, Assistant Secretary of the Treasury William Duer used insider knowledge to buy up the depreciated bonds of the southern states. By the end of 1790 Duer and other northern speculators owned more than half the war bonds of Virginia and the Carolinas, selling them as their value rose.

Secretary of State Jefferson and other southern leaders condemned such shady dealings and the "corrupt squadron of paper dealers" who arranged them. Concerned members of Congress pointed out that some states, such as Virginia and Maryland, had already levied high taxes to pay off their war debts; now they would be taxed to pay the debts of other states as well, mostly for the benefit of rich northern speculators. To win support for assumption, Hamilton proposed to repay those states and struck a deal with members of Congress from Maryland and Virginia. He agreed to support their plan to locate the national capital (which

the Constitution specified would consist of a special "district") along the banks of the Potomac. In return, they gave him the votes he needed to secure passage of his assumption plan in the House of Representatives.

This bargain only sharpened fears of Hamilton's plans. James Madison had questioned the morality of Hamilton's redemption and assumption proposals, since the financial rewards would go to the present holders of Confederation securities, not to the original owners—the thousands of shopkeepers, farmers, and soldiers who had accepted government certificates during the dark days of the war. Now Madison presented Congress with legislation that would give present holders only "the highest price which has prevailed in the market," with the remaining funds going to the original owners. His scheme, Madison argued, "will do more real justice . . . than any other expedient."

Madison's proposal was impractical because of the difficulty of identifying the original owners. Furthermore, nearly half the members of the House of Representatives were owners of Continental or Confederation securities and stood to profit from Hamilton's plans. Melding practicality with self-interest, the House de-

feated Madison's proposal by a solid margin of 36 to 13. Madison became an avowed opponent of Hamilton's economic program—and he was not alone. By way of protest, an angry citizen composed an ode, "On the Rejection of Mr. Madison's Motion":

A soldier's pay are rags and fame,
A wooden leg—a deathless name.
To specs, both in and out of Cong.
The four and six per cents belong.

The Bank of the United States. Hamilton outraged Madison again by asking Congress to charter a national financial institution, the Bank of the United States. The bank's stock would be owned by both private investors and the national government. The bank would make loans to merchants, handle government funds, and issue financial notes, thus providing a respected medium of exchange for the specie-starved American economy. These considerable benefits persuaded a majority of both houses to enact the bank bill and send it to President Washington for approval.

At this critical juncture Secretary of State Thomas Jefferson joined ranks with Madison against Hamilton. Jefferson believed that Hamilton's scheme for a national bank was unconstitutional. "The incorporation of a Bank," Jefferson told President Washington, was not "delegated to the United States by the Constitution." Adopting a *strict* interpretation of the national charter, Jefferson maintained that the central government had only the limited powers explicitly assigned to it in the document.

In response, Hamilton articulated a *loose* interpretation of the Constitution, noting that Article I, Section 8, empowered Congress to make "all Laws which shall be necessary and proper" to carry out the Constitution. In Hamilton's view, "if the *end* be clearly comprehended within any of the specified powers, and if the measure is not forbidden by any particular provision of the Constitution, it may safely be deemed to come within the compass of national authority." Washington agreed with Hamilton and signed the legislation creating the bank, which was to have its headquarters in Philadelphia.

The Report on Manufactures. As an advocate of an economically powerful nation, Hamilton had a vision of America as self-sufficient in manufactures. In 1790 he appointed Tench Coxe, the secretary of the Pennsylvania Manufacturing Society, as an assistant secretary of the treasury. With Coxe's aid, Hamilton prepared a "Report on Manufactures," which provided the first comprehensive survey of American manufacturing and, more important, presented a coherent rationale for an American mercantilist system. In the report Hamilton took issue with the view put forth by the Scottish economist Adam Smith in his influential treatise *The Wealth*

of Nations, which had been published the same year as the Declaration of Independence. Smith had condemned traditional state-directed mercantilist regulations, arguing that they subsidized inefficient producers and inhibited personal enterprise. Instead he had advocated a *laissez-faire* (leave alone) economy in which the demand for goods would determine their production and price. Following this logic, Smith suggested that the United States raise farm products—which it could do more cheaply than could European countries—and exchange them for foreign manufactures, which were less expensive than American products.

Hamilton disputed Smith's reasoning, pointing out that manufacturing costs were not fixed but could be lowered by technological innovation or public policy. If American manufacturers were given tariff protection or direct subsidies—what Hamilton called "the patronage of government"—they could compete with European producers. Yet Hamilton hesitated to impose high tariffs; instead, he joined with Coxe to create a private Society for Establishing Useful Manufactures, a venture that met with little success. Effective national support for manufacturing came only in the 1810s, with a new generation of politicians.

Factions and Taxes. As Washington began his second four-year term as president in 1793, Hamilton's financial measures split the national legislature into irreconcilable factions. Hamilton had formed political alliances in Congress to support his program; now Madison, joined by Jefferson, who resigned as secretary of state at the end of 1793, organized the opposition. "Mr. Madison, co-operating with Mr. Jefferson," Hamilton complained, "is at the head of a faction decidedly hostile to me . . . and subversive of good government." At first these groups divided along North-South lines. For example, northern congressmen had supported the Bank of the United States by a margin of 33 to 1, while southern representatives had opposed it by 19 to 6. By the elections of 1794 the factions had a more diverse makeup and had acquired names—Federalists supported Hamilton; Democratic-Republicans followed Madison and Jefferson.

Meanwhile, Hamilton pushed for the enactment of the final element of his financial system: a national revenue that would be used to pay interest charges on the permanent debt. At Hamilton's insistence, Congress imposed a variety of domestic excise taxes, including a duty on spirits, such as whiskey, distilled in the United States. It also revised the schedule of tariffs. In 1789 Congress had imposed a tax of 50 cents a ton on foreign ships entering American ports and a duty of 5 to 15 percent on the value of imported goods. Hamilton did not propose drastic increases—high "protective" tariffs that would exclude foreign goods—because that would have hurt his merchant allies and cut government revenues.

Technology and Republican Values

In 1805 the young American scientist Benjamin Silliman visited the industrial city of Manchester, England. Silliman was impressed by the great factories, "the wonder of the world and the pride of England," but disturbed by the condition of the workers—"at best an imbecile people," degraded by the conditions in which they lived and worked. "Heaps of dung, rubble from buildings, putrid, stagnant pools are found here and there among the houses, and a sort of black smoke covers the city," another visitor reported. "Under this half daylight 300,000 human beings are ceaselessly at work . . . the crunching wheels of machinery, the shriek of steam from boilers, the regular beat of the looms, the heavy rumble of the carts, these are the noises from which you can never escape."

Silliman contrasted this dismal scene of early industrialization with a peaceful image of rural America: "fields and forests, in which pure air . . . and simple manners, give vigour to the limbs, and a healthful aspect to the face." Were the wonders of British technology, he asked, worth "the physical and . . . moral evils which they produce?"

No American struggled harder with this question than Thomas Jefferson. "Those who labour in the earth are the chosen people of God," Jefferson wrote in his *Notes on the State of Virginia* (1785), and he remained committed to the moral superiority of a society of yeomen farm families. Yet Jefferson knew that "a people who are *entirely* dependent upon foreigners for food or clothes, must always be subject to them." Even before the Embargo of 1807 and the War of 1812 convinced him of the necessity of American manufacturing, Jefferson advocated the use of advanced technology. He introduced cast-iron plows and improved threshing machines on his plantation near Monticello, Virginia, and rotated crops in accordance with the latest scientific theory.

The household as factory

Jefferson championed manufacturing on the plantation as well. As early as 1796 he bought an iron-cutting machine to make nails and, by employing a dozen slave men, made 10,000 nails a day. By 1812 Jefferson had built two water-powered mills at another plantation and had equipped his Monticello slaves to manufacture textiles. He and other Americans, the former president boasted to a European friend, "have reduced the large and expensive machinery for most things to the compass of a private family. . . . I need 2,000 yards of linen, cotton and woolen yearly, to cloth my family [of slaves], which this machinery, costing $150 only, and worked by two women and two girls, will more than furnish."

Here, then, was Jefferson's way of avoiding the "dark Satanic mills" of Manchester. Each American household would become a small factory, using the labor

---

But he won Congressional approval for a modest increase in customs duties. As a result, customs revenue rose steadily, providing about 90 percent of the national government's income from 1790 to 1820 and ensuring the financial success of Hamilton's redemption and assumption programs.

Hamilton's design was now complete. His bold, if controversial, policies created a fiscally strong national government, protected the financial investments and commercial interests of the merchant class, and laid out a program for national economic development.

Jefferson's Vision

Few southern planters and western farmers shared Hamilton's view of the American future, and Thomas Jefferson spoke for them. A man of great learning as well as a politician and diplomat, Jefferson was well read in architecture, natural history, scientific farming, and political theory. Embracing the optimistic spirit of the Enlightenment, he declared his firm conviction in the "improvability of the human race." But progress was not inevitable, and Jefferson deplored both financial

of "women, children, and invalids" to enhance the prosperity and independence of American freehold farmers. For Jefferson, the key was democratic ownership of the means of agricultural and industrial production.

Jefferson's dream was noble and not at all unrealistic. The United States did become a nation of household producers between 1790 and 1820 (see Chapter 9). Hundreds of rural men made nails as a wintertime employment, thousands of farm women made butter and cheese for market sale, and tens of thousands of families worked in their homes manufacturing shoes, textiles, and other goods for merchant entrepreneurs. Particularly in the Northeast, the American countryside became a vast workshop.

Yet Jefferson's vision concealed important aspects of American rural life and was flawed by internal contradictions. Many families in the Northeast were driven to home manufacture by the threat of poverty; their subdivided farms yielded only a bare subsistence. The situation in the southern states was even more problematic. Was the enslaved labor that made Jefferson's nails and textiles more consonant with republican moral and economic principles than was the wage labor in Manchester factories? And over the long run, could household producers compete successfully with the water- and steam-driven factories owned by wealthy capitalists?

A candid observer must answer no to these questions. With his customary skill, Jefferson had identified the crucial issues: how the means of production should be owned and organized and who should benefit financially from the new technology. He was unable, however, to show how the technological advances and social conditions of his age could be made compatible with the republican value of liberty and the democratic ideal of equality. That question remains unresolved to this day.

An iron works, one of the "dark Satanic mills" of industrial England.

speculation and an urban industrial society. He had visited the manufacturing regions of Britain and had seen the masses of propertyless laborers there. He concluded that those workers, poor and dependent on wages, lacked the economic independence required to sustain a republican polity (see New Technology, above).

Jefferson's vision of the American future was more agrarian and more democratic. Although he had grown up as a privileged and well-educated slaveowner among the Virginia elite, he understood the values and needs of yeomen farmers and other ordinary white Americans.

In the Declaration of Independence Jefferson had proclaimed the primacy of "life, liberty, and the pursuit of happiness," and he gave form and substance to this vision in his Notes on the State of Virginia (1785). "Those who labor in the earth are the chosen people of God," he declared; independent yeomen farmers formed the very soul of the republic. When Jefferson drafted the Ordinance of 1784, he pictured a West settled by families who would produce bountiful harvests. Their grain and meat would feed European nations, who "would manufacture and send us in exchange our clothes and

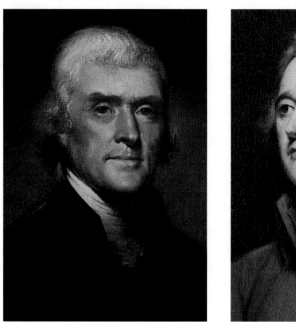

other comforts." Jefferson hoped that westward expansion and foreign commerce would remedy two of the worst features of eighteenth-century agriculture—widespread tenancy in the South and subdivided farms in New England—while preserving its best features. He wanted to ban slavery from the territories (though he did not advocate abolishing it in the South) so that the American West would become a vigorous, incorruptible society of independent white yeomen farm families.

War and Politics

Events in Europe created opportunities for both Jeffersonian farmers and Hamiltonian merchants, pulling the United States out of the economic doldrums of the 1780s. The French Revolution began in 1789; four years later, the French republican government went to war against a British-led coalition of monarchical states. With the war disrupting European farming, wheat prices in Europe leapt from 5 to 8 shillings a bushel and remained at that level for twenty years. Farmers in the Chesapeake and the Middle Atlantic states capitalized on the situation, increasing their grain exports and reaping substantial profits.

Simultaneously, a boom in cotton exports revived the southern economy. Americans had expanded cotton production during the War of Independence so that they could make their own textiles. Subsequently, the mechanization of cloth production in Britain created a huge market for raw cotton. During the 1790s the invention of gins—machines that combed seeds from cotton fibers—cut costs dramatically (see Chapter 8). Soon the annual value of American cotton exports outstripped that of to-

bacco, the traditional southern export crop. As Jefferson had hoped, European markets brought high prices and prosperity to many American planters and farmers.

American merchants profited even more handsomely from the European war. President Washington issued a Proclamation of Neutrality enabling U.S. citizens to trade legally with the belligerents on both sides. As neutral carriers able to pass through the British naval blockade of the French coastline, American merchant ships took over the lucrative trade between France and its West Indian sugar islands. The American merchant fleet became one of the largest in the world, increasing from 355,000 tons in 1790 to more than 1.1 million tons in 1808. Commercial earnings rose spectacularly, averaging $20 million annually in the 1790s—twice the value of cotton and tobacco exports.

After two decades of stagnation American ports came alive. Shipowners invested part of their rising profits in new vessels, providing work for thousands of shipwrights, sail makers, laborers, and seamen. Hundreds of carpenters, masons, and cabinetmakers found work building warehouses and elegant Federal-style town houses for newly affluent merchants. New buildings went up in Philadelphia, a European visitor reported, "chiefly of red brick, and in general three stories high. A great number of private houses have marble steps to the street door, and in other respects are finished in a style of elegance." Real estate values jumped, reflecting the growth in population and wealth. During the 1790s the assessed value of property in New York City soared from $5.8 million to $20.7 million.

The French Revolution and America. Commerce with Europe engaged Americans with the differing political

Federalist Gentry

A prominent New England Federalist, Oliver Ellsworth served as Chief Justice of the United States (1796–1800); his wife, Abigail Wolcott Ellsworth, was the daughter of a Connecticut governor. In 1792 the artist Ralph Earl captured the aspirations of the Ellsworths by giving them an aristocratic demeanor and prominently displaying their mansion (in the window).

Urban Affluence

New York merchants built large town houses and furnished them with fine pieces of furniture. John Rubens Smith's painting *The Shop and Warehouse of Duncan Phyfe* illustrates the success of America's most skilled artisan entrepreneur. (Metropolitan Museum of Art)

ideologies and naval policies of the belligerents. Many Americans had welcomed the French Revolution of 1789 because it abolished the last vestiges of feudalism and established a constitutional monarchy. Yet the creation of the more democratic French republic in 1792 and the execution of King Louis XVI the next year divided public opinion in the United States.

On one side many American artisans praised the egalitarianism of the French republicans. In New York, they had King Street renamed Liberty Street; in Boston, Royal Alley became Equality Lane. More important, artisans founded Democratic-Republican clubs modeled on the radical Jacobin clubs in Paris. In Philadelphia Democratic-Republicans had a dinner to celebrate the beheading of Louis XVI; there, an observer reported, "the head of a roasted pig was severed from its body, and being recognized as an emblem of the murdered King of France, was carried round to the guests. Each one placing the cap of liberty on its head, pronounced the word 'tyrant'." Adopting French republican practice, many Americans began addressing each other as "citizen," a symbol of equality; some condemned Hamilton's economic policies as "aristocratic."

On the other side of this ideological controversy were men and women of wealth, conservative religious convictions, or Hamiltonian sympathies. They denounced the Terror—the executions of Louis XVI and his aristocratic supporters—and condemned the new French regime for abandoning Christianity in favor of a

Peter Porcupine (William Cobbett)

A Federalist Attacks French Republicanism

American Democratic-Republicans declared that "he who is an enemy to the French Revolution, cannot be a firm republican." In reply, William Cobbett, a British journalist who settled in Philadelphia and supported the Federalist party in caustic and very effective pamphlets, invokes the horrors of the Terror in France, during which hundreds of aristocrats and ordinary citizens were executed, warning Americans of the dangers of radical republicanism.

France is a *republic*, and the decrees of the Legislators were necessary to maintain it a republic. This *word* outweighs, in the estimation of some persons (I wish I could say they were few in number), all the horrors that have been and that can be committed in that country. One of these modern republicans will tell you that he does not deny that hundreds of thousands of innocent persons have been murdered in France; that the people have neither religion nor morals; that all the ties of nature are rent asunder; . . . that its riches, along with millions of the best of the people, are gone to enrich and aggrandize its enemies; that its commerce, its manufactures, its sciences,

its arts, and its honour, are no more; but at the end of all this, he will tell you that it must be happy, because it is a *republic*. I have heard more than one of these republican zealots declare, that he would sooner see the last of the French exterminated, than see them adopt any other form of government. Such a sentiment is characteristic of a mind locked up in a savage ignorance.

Shall we say that these things never can take place among us? . . . We are not what we were before the French revolution. Political projectors from every corner of Europe, troublers of society of every description, from the whining philosophical hypocrite to the daring rebel, and more daring blasphemer, have taken shelter in these States.

We have seen the *guillotine* toasted to three times three cheers. . . . And what would the reader say, were I to tell him of a Member of Congress, who wished to see one of these murderous machines employed for lopping off the heads of the French, permanent in the State-house yard of the city of Philadelphia?

If these men of blood had succeeded in plunging us into a war; if

they had once got the sword into their hands, they would have mowed us down like stubble. The word *Aristocrat* would have been employed to as good account here, as ever it had been in France. We might, ere this, have seen our places of worship turned into stables; we might have seen the banks of the Delaware, like those of the Loire, covered with human carcasses, and its waters tinged with blood: ere this we might have seen our parents butchered, and even the head of our admired and beloved President rolling on a scaffold.

I know the reader will start back with horror. His heart will tell him that it is impossible. But, once more, let him look at the example before us. The attacks on the character and conduct of the aged *Washington*, have been as bold, if not bolder, than those which led to the downfall of the unfortunate French Monarch. Can it then be imagined, that, had they possessed the power, they wanted the will to dip their hands in his blood?

Source: William Cobbett, *Peter Porcupine in America*, ed. by David A. Wilson (Ithaca: Cornell University Press, 1994), 150–154.

new religion of reason (see American Voices, above). American politics was soon dominated by the passions of the French Revolution, with admirers of the French republic toasting the diplomat Edmond Genêt and advocating war against Britain. Federalists accused Genêt of violating Washington's Proclamation of Neutrality and persuaded the president to demand his recall. In 1794 the Federalist-dominated Congress passed a Neutrality Act that prohibited American citizens from fighting in the war and barred the belligerents' naval vessels from American ports.

The Whiskey Rebellion. Meanwhile, a domestic issue sparked violence in western Pennsylvania. In 1792 farmers began protesting against Hamilton's excise tax on spirits. The tax had raised the price—and thus cut

the demand—for the corn whiskey the farmers sold locally and bartered for eastern manufactures. As resistance grew, an extralegal assembly in Pittsburgh challenged the constitutionality of the tax. Like the Patriots of 1765 and the Shaysites of 1785, the Whiskey rebels attacked tax collectors and challenged the authority of a distant government. Only now they waved banners proclaiming the French revolutionary slogan "Liberty, Equality, and Fraternity!"

The ideology of the French Revolution had sharpened the debate over Hamilton's economic policies and helped justify domestic rebellion. To uphold national authority (and deter secessionist movements along the frontier, where he owned extensive property), President Washington raised an army of 15,000 troops and suppressed the rebels.

GENERAL GEORGE WASHINGTON.
Reviewing the Western army at Fort Cumberland the 18ᵗʰ of October 1794

Washington Puts Down the Whiskey Rebels
Because of his speculations in western lands, President Washington took a personal interest in the suppression of the Whiskey Rebellion. He raised a sizable army and traveled to Fort Cumberland to review it.

Jay's Treaty. Britain's maritime strategy widened the growing political divisions in the United States. In November 1793 the Royal Navy began seizing American ships bound for France from the West Indies. In six months the British took more than 250 vessels and confiscated their cargoes of sugar as contraband, invoking the so-called Rule of 1756. (This British legal doctrine restricted the commerce of neutral states during wartime to the amount conducted during peacetime.) Federalist merchants denied that the rule was an accepted principle of international law, but their claims usually were rejected by British admiralty courts. Yet the merchants did not demand retaliation, fearing that a war against Great Britain would throw the United States into the arms of radical French republicans, destroy the American merchant fleet, and undermine Hamilton's system of public finance.

To avert war, President Washington sent John Jay to negotiate with Britain. Jay returned with a comprehensive treaty that addressed the maritime issues as well as territorial and financial disputes dating back to the War of Independence. Jay's Treaty required the United States to make "full and complete compensation" to British merchants for all prewar debts owed by American citizens. It also acknowledged Britain's right to remove French property from neutral ships, thus relinquishing the American merchants' claim that "free ships make free goods." In return, the treaty allowed American merchants to submit claims of illegal seizures to an arbitration tribunal, ended British aid to western Indians,

and mandated the withdrawal of British military garrisons from six forts in the American Northwest.

Jefferson and his Democratic-Republican followers denounced Jay's Treaty as too conciliatory and tried to prevent its ratification. The Senate did ratify the treaty in June 1795, but only by a vote of 20 to 10, barely winning the two-thirds majority required by the Constitution. This outcome reaffirmed the government's diplomatic position. As long as Hamilton and his Federalist allies were in power, the United States would have a pro-British foreign policy.

The Rise of Parties

Political conflicts over foreign affairs, taxes and tariffs, and fiscal policy spurred the appearance of rival political parties during the presidential election of 1796. Indeed, the election marked a new stage in American politics as candidates for local, state, and national office were elected not as individuals but as representatives of parties that stood for political principles. To prepare for the election, the Federalists and Democratic-Republicans (who were now known simply as Republicans) called legislative caucuses in Congress and in the states. The members of those informal conventions discussed policies, nominated candidates, and mobilized support among the voters.

Parties were a new phenomenon. Colonial legislatures had often divided into factions based on family al-

liances, ethnicity, or regional concerns, but those groups were poorly organized and usually temporary. The new state and national constitutions made no provision for parties because their authors assumed that representative institutions adequately expressed the will of the people. As president, Washington had tried to stand above parties, but his continuing support for Hamilton's policies exposed him to partisan attack and influenced his decision not to seek a third term. Jefferson too believed that parties were unnecessary and dangerous. Only Madison accepted the inevitability of political parties, and even he assumed that they would be temporary coalitions that would form around a specific issue and then disappear.

Born into a world of deferential politics, these leaders underestimated the impact of the revolutionary ideology of popular sovereignty. A politically active citizenry laid the basis for a competitive party system. Once political parties appeared, they attracted the long-term allegiance of regional or occupational groups. Merchants and creditors in the northeastern states supported the Federalist party, as did wheat-exporting slaveholders in the Tidewater districts of the Chesapeake states. The Republican coalition was more diverse. By the mid-1790s it included mechanics and artisans in seaport cities, southern tobacco planters, German and Scots-Irish settlers, and subsistence farmers throughout the country. Republican policies appealed to a wider range of social groups, but the Federalists' prestige, wealth, and experience made them a potent political force.

In 1796, in an election dominated by conflict over ideology and foreign policy, Federalist candidates triumphed, winning a majority in Congress and in the electoral college. The electors chose John Adams as president. When some Federalist electors refused to vote for Adams's choice for vice-president, Thomas Pinckney of South Carolina (offended by a treaty he had negotiated with Spain), Thomas Jefferson, the Republican candidate for president, won the second highest number of electoral votes and, as stipulated in the Constitution, became vice-president. Thus the nation had a divided administration.

As chief executive, John Adams upheld the Federalists' pro-British foreign policy. He condemned French seizures of American merchant ships and accused France of meddling in the American domestic affairs. When three agents of Prince Talleyrand, the French foreign minister, solicited a loan and a bribe from American diplomats, Adams urged Congress to prepare for war. To overcome Republican objections, he charged that Talleyrand's agents, whom he dubbed X, Y, and Z, had insulted the honor of the United States. The Federalist-controlled Congress cut off trade with France and authorized American privateers to seize French ships. Between 1798 and 1800 the United States became an unofficial ally of Great Britain—a monarchy and its recent enemy—and fought an undeclared war against France, a republic and its major supporter during the War of Independence.

The Crisis of 1798–1800

The Alien and Sedition Acts. For the first—but not the last—time in American history, a controversial foreign war prompted domestic protest and governmental repression. Pro-French immigrants from Ireland viciously attacked Adams's foreign policy in newspapers and pamphlets. To silence them, in 1798 the administration enacted an Alien Act that authorized the deportation of foreigners. A few Federalist supporters favored even harsher treatment. "Were I president, I would hang them for otherwise they would murder me," declared a Philadelphia pamphleteer. To allay such exaggerated concerns, the administration passed a Naturalization Act, which increased the residence requirement for citizenship from five to fourteen years. Also in 1798, the Federalist Congress enacted a harsh Sedition Act, prohibiting the publication of ungrounded or malicious attacks against the president or Congress. "He that is not for us is against us," thundered the Federalist *Gazette of*

An Anti-French Cartoon
A five-headed monster, representing the leaders of France under the Directory, demands a bribe ("Money, Money, Money") from American diplomats. Federalists used the incident, named the XYZ affair for the three anonymous French agents who asked for the bribe, to whip up anti-French sentiment in the United States and launch an undeclared naval war.

the United States. Using the legal powers of the new act, Federalist prosecutors arrested more than twenty Republican newspaper editors and politicians, charged them with sedition, and sent some of them to prison.

Republicans assailed the Sedition Act as contrary to the Bill of Rights. Because the First Amendment to the Constitution prohibits the national government from "abridging the freedom of speech, or of the press," the Sedition Act was probably unconstitutional. But Republican leaders did not turn to the Supreme Court for redress. The Court's powers were still vague, particularly with regard to the "judicial review" of Congressional legislation. Besides, the Court was an appointed body packed with Federalists, who would probably have upheld the Sedition Act.

Madison and Jefferson instead took the fight to elected bodies—the state legislatures not dominated by Federalists. In November 1798 the legislature of Kentucky—the first western territory to become a state, in 1792—passed a resolution declaring the Alien and Sedition Acts to be "unauthoritative, void, and of no force." More important, the resolution asserted that the national government owed its existence to a compact among the states, which meant that "each party has an equal right to judge by itself." The Virginia resolution similarly claimed that the states had the right to refuse to enforce federal laws that exceeded the powers granted by the Constitution. The Kentucky and Virginia resolutions thus laid the theoretical basis for subsequent "states' rights" interpretations of the Constitution.

In 1798, as in the ratification conventions in 1788, Federalist assertions of national authority provoked a debate over the nature of the Union. Even Madison—the architect of the Constitution—had second thoughts and argued that the national government had resulted from a compact among the states. In the heat of partisan conflict Jefferson also experienced ideological conversion; once opposed in principle to political parties, he now endorsed them as valuable "to watch and relate to the people" the activities of the government.

The Election of 1800. The debate over the Sedition Act set the stage for the election of 1800. Republicans supported Jefferson's bid for the presidency by pointing to the wrongful imprisonment of newspaper editors and championing the rights of the states. President Adams responded to these attacks by reevaluating his foreign policy. Adams was a complicated man, often vain, easily offended, dogmatic, but possessed of great personal strength and determination. He showed his quality as a statesman by rejecting the advice of Hamilton and other Federalist leaders to intensify the undeclared war with France and benefit politically from nationalistic fervor. Instead, he entered into diplomatic negotiations that brought the war to an end.

Federalists attempted to win the election by depicting Jefferson as an irresponsible pro-French radical—"the archapostle of irreligion and free thought"—but they were unsuccessful. The Republicans won a resounding victory. Voters had registered their protest against a foreign war—and a special national tax on land and houses levied in 1798 to pay for it—by giving Republicans a majority in both houses of Congress and a narrow edge in the electoral college. The electors, however, gave Jefferson and Aaron Burr of New York (Jefferson's choice for vice-president) the same number of votes for the office of president. In the event of such a tie, the Constitution specified that the House of Representatives would select the president, with each state having one vote to cast. (The Twelfth Amendment, ratified in 1804, remedied this constitutional defect by requiring the electors to cast separate ballots for president and vice-president.)

Alexander Hamilton played a crucial role in the drama that followed. For thirty-five ballots Federalists in the House of Representatives blocked Jefferson's election. Then the former treasury secretary intervened. Calling Burr an "embryo Caesar" and the "most unfit man in the United States for the office of president," Hamilton persuaded key Federalists to permit the selection of Jefferson, his longtime rival. The Federalists' concern for political stability also played a role. As Senator James Bayard of Delaware explained, "It was admitted on all hands that we must risk the Constitution and a Civil War or take Mr. Jefferson."

Jefferson called the election the "Revolution of 1800," and so it was. It signaled the twilight of Federalism and its aristocratic outlook and the dawn of a more democratic era. The election also testified to the strength of the American experiment in self-government. Federalists had attacked Republicans as social radicals, traitors, and atheists for nearly a decade, with all sincerity, yet they peacefully relinquished power to their enemies. This bloodless transfer of power was genuinely revolutionary. It demonstrated that governments elected by the people could be changed by the people in an orderly, civilized way even in times of bitter partisan conflict. In his inaugural address in 1801 Jefferson referred to this achievement, declaring: "We are all Republicans, we are all Federalists." He called on Americans to temper the "will of the majority" with respect for the rights of those in the minority, "which equal laws must protect, and to violate would be oppression."

Over the course of a quarter century Jefferson had remained true to his principles. In 1801, as in the Declaration of Independence of 1776, he defined the American republic as a government based on both majority rule and minority rights, with laws that treated citizens equally and respected their liberty.

Summary

The state constitutions of 1776–1780 created new institutions of republican government. Most had property qualifications for voting and a separation of powers that inhibited popular rule. The Pennsylvania and Vermont constitutions were more democratic, with broad voting rights for men and a powerful one-house legislature. For a time New Jersey permitted women with property to vote, but most women continued to be excluded from the political sphere. A few women asserted claims of intellectual and social equality and sought greater legal rights, mostly without success. On the national level the government created by the Articles of Confederation began the orderly settlement of the trans-Appalachian West, but it lacked the authority to regulate foreign trade or raise enough revenue to pay off wartime debts. Power remained with the states, where clashes over financial policy culminated in Shays's Rebellion, an uprising of indebted farmers in western Massachusetts.

The perceived weaknesses of the Confederation led nationalists and creditors to convene a constitutional convention in Philadelphia in 1787. The delegates devised a new constitution that derived its authority not from the states but directly from the people, who were represented in the lower house of the legislature. They also created a strong national government with the power to levy taxes, issue money, and control trade. Its legislation was to be the supreme law of the land. In several important states the Constitution was ratified by only narrow margins because it diminished the sovereignty of the states and seemed to provide for a potentially oppressive central government immune from popular control.

George Washington was elected as the first president under the new government and, along with the first Congress, established the executive and judicial departments. The economic policies of Washington's secretary of the treasury, Alexander Hamilton, favored northern merchants and financiers. To oppose them, Thomas Jefferson and James Madison organized farmers, planters, and artisans into the Democratic-Republican party. The French Revolution and naval warfare led to bitter ideological struggles and, during an undeclared war with France, to political repression in the form of the Alien and Sedition Acts of 1798. The peaceful transfer of power to Jefferson and the Democratic-Republicans in 1800 ended a decade of political strife.

TIMELINE

1776	Declaration of Independence Pennsylvania's democratic constitution John Adams, *Thoughts on Government*
1777	Articles of Confederation (ratified 1781) New York's conservative constitution
1779	Judith Sargent Murray, "On the Equality of the Sexes"
1780	Postwar commercial recession Burdensome debts and creditor-debtor conflicts in states
1781	Robert Morris superintendent of finance Bank of North America Rhode Island vetoes national import duty
1784	Ordinance outlines policy for new states
1785	Land Ordinance sets up survey system Jefferson's *Notes on the State of Virginia*
1786	Annapolis commercial convention Shays's Rebellion
1787	Northwest Ordinance Philadelphia convention Madison's "nationalist" Virginia Plan
1788–1789	Ratification conventions *The Federalist* (Jay, Madison, Hamilton)
1789	George Washington becomes first president Judiciary Act establishes federal court system Outbreak of French Revolution National tariff; aid to American shipping
1790s	Boom in wheat and cotton exports Expansion of American commerce
1790	Alexander Hamilton's program: redemption and assumption
1791	Bill of Rights ratified
1792	Debate over Bank of United States Mary Wollstonecraft, *A Vindication of the Rights of Woman* First French Republic declared; Louis XVI executed (1793)
1793	Democratic-Republican party founded War between Britain and France Washington's Proclamation of Neutrality
1794	Whiskey Rebellion
1795	Jay's Treaty
1796	John Adams elected president
1797	XYZ Affair
1798	Undeclared war against France Alien, Sedition, and Naturalization acts Kentucky and Virginia resolutions
1800	Jefferson elected in "Revolution of 1800"

★   ★   ★

BIBLIOGRAPHY

Richard B. Bernstein and Kym S. Rice, *Are We to Be a Nation? The Making of the Constitution* (1987), provides a general discussion of constitution making, whereas Stanley Elkins and Eric McKitrick, *The Age of Federalism: The Early Republic, 1788–1800* (1993), offers a comprehensive assessment.

Creating New Institutions

Elisha P. Douglass, *Rebels and Democrats* (1965), documents the struggle for equal political rights. See also Jackson T. Main, *The Sovereign States, 1775–1783* (1973), and Ronald L. Hoffman and Peter Albert, eds., *Sovereign States in an Age of Uncertainty* (1981). Important studies of state constitutions include Willi Paul Adams, *The First American Constitutions* (1980); Edward Countryman, *A People in Revolution: The American Revolution and Political Society in New York, 1760–1790* (1981); and Donald Lutz, *Popular Consent and Popular Control: Whig Political Theory in the Early State Constitutions* (1980).

On women and republicanism, see Linda K. Kerber, *Women of the Republic: Intellect and Ideology in Revolutionary America* (1980), and Ronald Hoffman and Peter Albert, eds., *Women in the Age of the American Revolution* (1989). Fine in-depth studies include Rosemarie Zagarri, *A Woman's Dilemma: Mercy Otis Warren and the American Revolution* (1995); Judith Sargent Murray, *The Gleaner*, ed. by Nina Baym (1992); and Edith B. Gelles, *Portia: The World of Abigail Adams* (1992).

Gordon Wood, *The Creation of the American Republic, 1776–1790* (1965), links state and national constitutional development. It should be supplemented by Merrill Jensen's two classic studies, *The Articles of Confederation, 1774–1781* (1940) and *The New Nation, 1781–1789* (1950). Other important works on the 1780s include Peter S. Onuf, *The Origins of the Federal Republic: Jurisdictional Controversies in the United States, 1775–1787* (1983); Roger H. Brown, *Redeeming the Republic: Federalists, Taxation, and the Origins of the Constitution* (1993); Richard B. Morris, *The Forging of the Union, 1781–1789* (1987); and Robert A. Gross, ed., *In Debt to Shays: The Bicentennial of an Agrarian Rebellion* (1993).

The Constitution of 1787

In 1913 two studies initiated the modern analysis of the Constitution: Charles A. Beard, *An Economic Interpretation of the Constitution of the United States*, and Max Farrand, *The Framing of the Constitution*. For critiques of Beard's work, see Leonard Levy, ed., *Essays on the Making of the Constitution* (rev. ed., 1987); a recent narrative similar to that of Farrand is Christopher Collier and James L. Collier, *Decision in Philadelphia* (1987).

Other important works include Forrest McDonald, *Novus Ordo Seculorum: The Intellectual Origins of the Constitution* (1985); Edmund S. Morgan, *Inventing the People: The Rise of Popular Sovereignty in England and America* (1988); and Michael Kammen, *A Machine That Would Go by Itself: The Constitution in American Culture* (1986). Three fine collections of essays are Richard R. Beeman et al., eds., *Beyond Confederation: Origins of the Constitution and*

American National Identity (1987); Ellen Frankel Paul and Howard Dickman, eds., *Liberty, Property and the Foundations of the American Constitution* (1989); and Herman Belz et al., eds., *To Form a More Perfect Union: The Critical Ideas of the Constitution* (1992).

On the Antifederalists and ratification, see Patrick T. Conley and John P. Kaminski, eds., *The Constitution and the States* (1988); Stephen L. Schechter, *The Reluctant Pillar: New York and the Adoption of the Federal Constitution* (1985); and Herbert Storing, *The Antifederalists* (1985). Two recent studies of the Federalist papers are David F. Epstein, *The Political Theory of "The Federalist"* (1984), and Charles R. Kesler, ed., *Saving the Revolution: "The Federalist Papers" and the American Founding* (1987).

R. A. Rutland, *The Birth of the Bill of Rights, 1776–1791* (rev. ed., 1983), offers the basic narrative; more analytic treatments include Michael J. Lacey and Knud Haakonssen, *A Culture of Rights* (1991); David J. Bodenhemer and James W. Ely, Jr., *The Bill of Rights in Modern America* (1993); and Joyce Lee Malcolm, *To Keep and Bear Arms: The Origins of an Anglo-American Right* (1993).

The Political Crisis of the 1790s

A good synthesis is James Rogers Sharp, *American Politics in the Early Republic: The New Nation in Crisis* (1993). Studies of important statesmen include Forrest McDonald, *Alexander Hamilton: A Biography* (1979), and James T. Flexner, *George Washington and the New Nation, 1783–1793* (1970) and *George Washington: Anguish and Farewell, 1793–1799* (1972). For Jeffersonian ideology, see Joyce Appleby, *Capitalism and a New Social Order: The Republican Vision of the 1790s* (1984); Drew McCoy, *The Elusive Republic: Political Economy in Jeffersonian America* (1982); and Lance Banning, *The Jeffersonian Persuasion: The Evolution of a Party Ideology* (1978).

Richard Hofstadter, *The Idea of a Party System: The Rise of Legitimate Opposition in the United States, 1790–1840* (1969), offers an overview of the subject; also see William Nisbet Chambers, *Political Parties in the New Nation: The American Experience* (1963), and John F. Hoadley, *Origins of American Political Parties, 1789–1803* (1986). More detailed studies are Thomas P. Slaughter, *The Whiskey Rebellion* (1986), and Richard J. Twomey, *Jacobins and Jeffersonians* (1989). On diplomatic and military history, consult Henry Ammon, *The Genêt Mission* (1973); Jerald A. Combs, *The Jay Treaty* (1970); Richard H. Kohn, *Eagle and Sword: The Federalists and the Creation of the Military Establishment in America, 1783–1802* (1975); and Lawrence D. Cress, *Citizens in Arms: The Army and the Military to the War of 1812* (1982).

On Adams's administration, see Ralph Brown Adams, *The Presidency of John Adams* (1975), and Stephen G. Kurtz, *The Presidency of John Adams: The Collapse of Federalism, 1795–1800* (1957). More specialized studies are William Sinchcombe, *The XYZ Affair* (1980), and Leonard Levy, *The Emergence of a Free Press* (1985).

Good state histories include Patricia Watlington, *The Partisan Spirit: Kentucky Politics, 1779–1792* (1972); Richard R. Beeman, *The Old Dominion and the New Nation, 1788–1801* (1972); and Mary K. Bonsteel Tachau, *Federal Courts in the Early Republic: Kentucky, 1789–1816* (1978).

Settlers Move West through Pennsylvania (detail)

Thomas Birch captured the spirit of families moving to
the West to clear and farm the land in his 1816 painting
Conestoga Wagon on the Pennsylvania Turnpike.

Toward a Continental Nation

1790–1820

★ ★ ★

When they declared independence in 1776, the thirteen colonies were confined to a narrow strip of land along the Atlantic seaboard. But in 1783 Britain surrendered its claim not only to those settled areas but also to vast stretches of the North American interior, more than tripling the size of the new United States. The land beyond the Appalachians was mostly forested, dotted with French and British forts and fur-trading posts and peopled by tens of thousands of native Americans. Yet within fifty years all this would change. White Americans would drive the Indians toward the Mississippi River, found new communities in the trans-Appalachian region, and build turnpikes and canals to tie them to eastern markets.

Even before this process was well begun, President Thomas Jefferson doubled the size of the nation. The Louisiana Purchase added most of the lands between the Mississippi River and the Rocky Mountains. To assert control over the western lands and resolve maritime conflicts, the United States embarked on a new war with Britain. Before the War of 1812 was over, Indians in the trans-Appalachian region rose in revolt and eastern Federalists threatened secession from the Union. Only a surprising victory at the Battle of New Orleans preserved the honor of the United States.

Regional differences within the new nation determined the course of the war and of subsequent cultural developments. Traditional institutions shaped life in the various seaboard societies, and westward-moving migrants transplanted many customs, re-creating a yeoman farm society in the Old Northwest and a plantation economy based on slave-produced cotton in the Old Southwest. Migration to the West had a particularly disruptive impact on African-Americans, destroying well-established communities and kinship groups, and on native Americans, forcing tens of thousands of

Indians from their ancestral lands. It also ignited new diplomatic conflicts with Spain, which was trying to create a North American empire stretching from Florida to California. With the settlement of the trans-Appalachian West and the exploration of the trans-Mississippi region, a new "continental" phase of American history had begun.

Westward Expansion

Between 1776 and 1790 the combined white and black population of the United States had grown from 2.5 million to 3.9 million people, but only 200,000 Americans lived west of the Appalachian Mountains. During the next thirty years the geographical dimensions of the United States multiplied along with the population. By 1820 there were 9.6 million white and black Americans, and 2 million of them—a number almost as high as the total population in 1776—inhabited nine new states and three territories west of the Appalachians.

Native American Resistance

The American War of Independence was an unmitigated disaster for most native American peoples. Although most Indians had fought on the Loyalist side, British negotiators failed to protect their lands or independence at the Paris peace conference. As one British statesman put it, the Indian nations were "remitted to the care of their neighbours." That care was far from benevolent. The new American republic asserted its ownership of all Indian lands west of the Appalachians both by right of conquest and by the terms of the Paris treaty of 1783. Native Americans refused to honor this claim, pointing out that they had not signed the treaty and had never been conquered.

The Confederation Congress brushed aside those arguments. In 1784 it dispatched commissioners to meet with representatives of the four pro-British Iroquois tribes—the Mohawk, Onondaga, Cayuga, and Seneca—and insist that they accept the treaty. The commissioners got their way by threatening to use military force. In the second Treaty of Fort Stanwix, signed in October 1784, the Iroquois relinquished most Seneca land in Pennsylvania and western New York and gave away territories they claimed in Ohio but hadn't controlled for a generation. That was just a taste of what was to follow. Pennsylvania officials coerced the Iroquois into surrendering more territory, as did Governor George Clinton of New York. Freely dispensing liquor, manufactured goods, and bribes, New York officials and land speculators secured new treaties that gave them title to millions of acres of Indian land in central

Treaty Negotiations at Greenville
In 1785 the Shawnee, Chippewyan, Ottawa, Miami, and other tribes formed the Western Confederacy to stop white settlement at the Ohio River. The American victory at the Battle of Fallen Timbers (1794) opened up the region, but the Treaty of Greenville (1795) recognized many Indian rights.

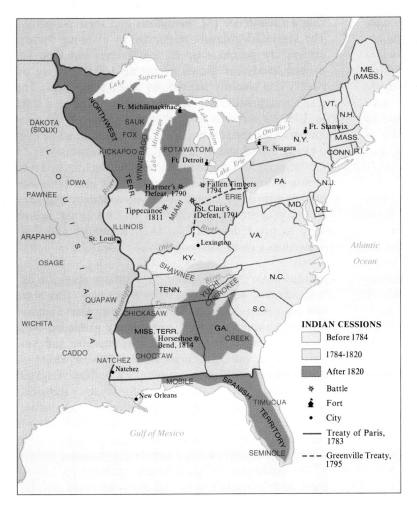

MAP 8.1

Expansion: Military and Diplomatic
The United States claimed sovereignty over the entire trans-Appalachian West by right of conquest of Britain. When the tribes of the Western Confederacy contested this claim, the American government upheld it by force, sending armies into the West during the 1790s and the War of 1812. During the 1820s and 1830s this armed diplomacy forced native American peoples to cede by treaty most of their lands east of the Mississippi River.

and western New York. By 1800 the once-powerful Iroquois peoples were confined to relatively small reservations. Even the Oneida and Tuscarora, who had supported the Patriot cause, lost most of their lands.

The American commissioners used similar tactics to extract agreements from tribes farther to the west. In 1785 the Chipewyan, Delaware, Ottawa, and Wyandot signed away most of the future state of Ohio, but they later repudiated the agreements, claiming—justifiably—that the treaties had been signed under duress. Soon those peoples, along with the Miami, Shawnee, and Potawatomi, formed a Western Confederacy to defend their lands and lives from aggressive settlers from Kentucky. Led by Little Turtle, they defeated an American expeditionary force commanded by General Josiah Hamar in 1790 and in 1791 crushed General Arthur St. Clair's army, killing 600 soldiers at the cost of only twenty-one Indian lives.

The American government's aggressive stance toward the Indians divided political opinion. Eastern critics charged that using force against native Americans

was immoral and warned that a "standing" army also could be used to suppress domestic political dissent. Westerners worried that an army would not only fight Indians but also impose national authority over settlers and squatters. Yet a majority in Congress feared an alliance between the Western Confederacy and the British in Canada and therefore supported President Washington's decision to double the army to 5,000 men. Washington chose General "Mad Anthony" Wayne to lead the western army. In August 1794 Wayne defeated the Indian allies in the Battle of Fallen Timbers (near what is present-day Toledo, Ohio).

Despite Wayne's victory, the Western Confederacy remained strong, forcing the American negotiators to compromise (see Map 8.1). In the Treaty of Greenville (Ohio) in 1795, the United States acknowledged Indian ownership of the trans-Appalachian West, renouncing a claim to the land that had been based on the right of conquest. The treaty, however, required native Americans to cede the southeastern corner of the Northwest Territory as well as certain strategic areas on the Great

Lakes, including Detroit and the future site of Chicago, and to acknowledge American sovereignty over the entire region. The Indians agreed to place themselves "under the protection of the United States, and no other Power whatever." This agreement had great diplomatic significance, for it prevented an Indian alliance with Britain and increased the likelihood that Britain would comply with its obligation (reaffirmed in Jay's Treaty of 1795) to withdraw its military garrisons from American territory in the West.

As the fighting ended, white families moved westward. Ohio entered the Union in 1803 and two years later had more than 100,000 residents, many of them clamoring for fertile Indian lands. Thousands more migrants moved into Indiana and Illinois, sparking conflicts with the native peoples over hunting rights. As the Delaware put it, "The Elks are our horses, the buffaloes are our cows, the deer are our sheep, & the whites shan't have them." To meet the Americans' land hunger, William Henry Harrison, governor of the Indiana Territory, used threats, bribes, and deceit to purchase millions of acres. State officials and land speculators in Georgia, Tennessee, and the Mississippi Territory made similar deals with other Indian nations. All along the western frontier the remorseless advance of white settlement threatened native Americans with eviction from their ancestral lands.

Settlers and Speculators

From the North and the South, migrants poured across the Appalachians. Settlers heading for Kentucky and Tennessee came from the Chesapeake region; they were primarily white tenant farmers, poor yeomen, and young couples. Fleeing the depleted soils and planter elite of the Tidewater region, these migrants—no fewer than 225,000 between 1790 and 1810—sought freedom and fertile land. Landlords tried to stop this massive loss of farm labor. A worried planter warned readers of the Maryland *Gazette* that "boundless settlements open a door for our citizens to run off and leave us, depreciating all our landed property and disabling us from paying taxes." But the exodus continued.

Land Conflict in Kentucky. Having defied their planter landlords, migrants who moved through the Cumberland Gap into the Kentucky territory had to battle Virginia authorities and land speculators. Basing their claims on "the ancient cultivation law" governing frontier tracts, an assembly of migrants asked the Virginia government, which administered the territory, to confirm their "Preoccupancy" (squatter's) titles. They invoked the argument of Hermon Husband, leader of the North Carolina Regulators (see Chapter 4), that the poor had a customary right "from time out of Mind" to occupy "back waste vacant Lands" sufficient "to pro-

vide a subsistence for themselves and their posterity." The Virginia legislature responded by allowing "actual settlers" to purchase up to 1,400 acres but then bestowed handsome grants averaging 100,000 acres on twenty-one wealthy individuals and partnerships. The result was predictable. When Kentucky became a state in 1792, a handful of speculators held title to one-fourth of the entire state, while half the adult white men owned no land and lived as squatters or tenants.

Nonetheless, thousands of new settlers flocked into Kentucky and along the Knoxville Road into Tennessee (which joined the Union in 1796), confident that they would prosper by growing cotton and hemp, which were in great demand. By 1820 Kentucky and Tennessee had a combined population of nearly a million.

Exodus from New England. A northern wave of migrants flowed out of New England into New York State and beyond, seeking to plant new yeomen farm communities. The quest for land had already propelled New England farmers north into New Hampshire and Vermont and east along the coast of Maine. Now, after two centuries of population growth, many New England communities were crowded with small subdivided farms, their rocky soils on the verge of exhaustion. Many parents were unable to provide farmsteads for the four or five children who survived to adulthood. In 1796, for example, Kent, Connecticut (founded only in 1738), contained 103 farmsteads inhabited by 100 fathers and 109 adult sons. All the other sons and the daughters who had not married local men had moved away, mostly to the West.

The lands of New York beckoned. In 1796 ten Kent families moved toward the Hudson River to Amenia, New York. By selling their small but well-established farms in Kent for $20 to $30 per acre, they were able to buy enough uncultivated land—at $2 to $3 per acre—to provide farmsteads for all their children. Hundreds and then thousands of farm families followed their example. They hitched their oxen and horses to wagons and carried tools, plows, and household goods into the plains and rolling hills of upstate New York. By 1820, 800,000 migrants were living in a string of settlements stretching from Albany to Buffalo. Thousands more New Englanders traveled on to Ohio.

This vast migration was carefully organized not by joint-stock companies or governments but by the people themselves. To lighten the economic and emotional burdens of migration, many settlers moved in large family groups. As a traveler reported from central New York: "The town of Herkimer is entirely populated by families come from Connecticut. We stayed at Mr. Snow's who came from New London with about ten male and female cousins." Members of Congregational churches often migrated together, transplanting the strong religious and cultural traditions of New England directly into western communities.

A Roadside Inn
Dozens of inns dotted the roads of the new republic, providing food and accommodation for settlers moving west and for cattle drovers and teamsters taking western produce to eastern markets.

As in Kentucky, much land fell initially into the hands of politically well-connected speculators. In the 1780s the financier Robert Morris acquired 1.3 million acres in the Genesee region of central New York for $75,000—about 6 cents an acre. Morris took a quick profit by selling the land to a group of British investors headed by Sir William Pulteney. Those investors made their profits over the long run; by 1829 Pulteney's agents in New York had received $1.2 million from sales to migrant farmers. Elsewhere in New York the Dutch-owned Holland Land Company acquired and gradually sold millions of acres of land.

Because speculators drove up the price of farms, many aspiring yeomen could not realize their dream of landed independence. In New York's Genesee region the Wadsworth family bought thousands of acres of prime land and created leasehold estates similar to the manors of the Hudson River Valley. To attract tenants, the Wadsworths leased farms rent-free for the first seven years, after which they charged rents. Seeking freehold ownership, many New England yeomen shunned these terms. They preferred to sign lease-purchase agreements with the Holland Land Company so that they would have a claim to the land while saving the money to buy it. In fact, high interest rates and the difficulty of transporting goods to market put many farmers in debt and forced them to remain tenants indefinitely. Soon the combined debt of farmers in the counties west of the Genesee River amounted to $5 million, and tenants far outnumbered freeholders. These American farmers had fled declining prospects in the East only to find themselves at the bottom of a new economic hierarchy in the West.

Eastern Agricultural Change. The massive exodus to the West left eastern towns drained of labor and capital, and many eastern farmers compensated by planting different crops and improving their methods of cultivation. In New England more farmers turned to potatoes, a high-yielding nutritious crop. In the wheat-growing Middle Atlantic states enterprising farmers replaced metal-tipped wooden plows with cast-iron models, which dug a deeper furrow and required a single yoke of oxen instead of two or three. By reducing the cost of livestock and labor, cast-iron plows enabled small-scale farmers to keep up production even though their sons and daughters had gone west.

Wealthier eastern farmers prospered by adopting the progressive farming methods advocated by British agricultural reformers. They rotated their crops to maintain the fertility of the soil, ordering their workers or tenants to plant nitrogen-rich clover and follow it with wheat, corn, wheat, and then clover again. In

The "Onion Maidens" of Wethersfield, Connecticut
Founded in 1634 and densely settled by 1750, Wethersfield
remained prosperous through agricultural innovation, turning
after 1790 to market gardening. Women assumed a dominant
role in this intensive horticulture and made Wethersfield the
"onion capital" of the United States.

Pennsylvania and the Chesapeake region crop rotation
doubled the average wheat yield from 12 to 25 bushels
per acre.

Yeomen also adopted crop rotation to increase the
variety of what they produced. In the fall they planted
winter wheat to sell as a market crop and provide bread
for their families. In the spring they sheared flocks of
sheep, selling the wool to expanding textile manufacturers, and planted corn to feed milk cows during the winter. Women and girls milked the cows and developed a
major new industry, making butter and cheese for market sale in the growing towns and cities.

Rural families now worked harder, laboring all
twelve months of the year, but whether they were hacking fields out of western forests or carting manure to replenish eastern soils, their labor was rewarded by higher
output and income. Westward migration thus boosted
the entire American economy and improved the quality
of rural life.

The Transportation Bottleneck

The geography of the American continent threatened to
cut short this economic advance. In both Europe and
America the pattern of settlement and trade had long
been determined by water routes. Chesapeake planters
and Hudson River manor lords relied on river transportation—which was convenient and cost only 5 or 6
cents a ton-mile—to get their crops to market. Farmers
without access to rivers had to haul their crops by ox-
cart over narrow dirt trails that turned into mudholes
during wet seasons. Even in dry weather, ox-drawn
carts moved slowly and carried only small loads. They
were expensive, too, costing farmers 30 cents a ton-mile.
Incredibly, Pennsylvania farmers paid as much to send
their wheat and corn 30 miles overland to Philadelphia
as they spent to ship it from Philadelphia to London
by sea. Without improved transportation, settlers in
most interior regions—especially those west of the Appalachian Mountains—could not afford to send goods
to eastern markets.

The enhancement of inland travel and trade therefore became a high priority of the new state governments, which actively encouraged transportation
ventures. The Pennsylvania legislature granted corporate charters to fifty-five private turnpike companies between 1793 and 1812; Massachusetts chartered over a
hundred similar enterprises. The turnpike companies
charged tolls for the use of the level, graveled roads they
built, but the roads cut travel time significantly. State
governments and private entrepreneurs also undertook
the construction of inland waterways, which were even
more cost-efficient. They dredged rivers to make them
navigable and constructed canals, mostly to bypass wa-
terfalls or rapids. In 1816 the United States had about
100 miles of canals, but only three canals were more
than 2 miles long and none breached the great Appalachian barrier (see the physical features map at the
front of the book).

The great rivers of the interior represented the hope
of the West. Western settlers paid premium prices for
land along navigable streams, and speculators bought
up likely sites for towns along the Ohio, Tennessee, and
Mississippi rivers. To take cotton and surplus grain and
meat to market, western farmers and merchants built
shallow barges and floated them down this interconnected river system to the port of New Orleans. By
1815 the southern port was shipping about $5 million
in agricultural products yearly.

The tens of thousands of migrants in the interior of
New York faced a bigger transportation problem, for
no rivers connected their settlements to the East. As one
pioneer recalled:

> In the early years, there was none but a home market
> and that was mostly barter—it was so many bushels of

The River Town of Cincinnati
Thanks to its location on the Ohio
River, Cincinnati became one of the
great market cities of the trans-
Appalachian West. By the 1820s,
passenger steamboats as well as freight
barges connected the city with Pittsburgh
and the ocean port of New Orleans.
(M. and M. Karolik Collection. Courtesy Museum of Fine Arts, Boston)

wheat for a cow; so many bushels for a yoke of oxen.
The price of a common pair of cowhide boots would
be $7, payable in wheat at 62 cents per bushel.

Only in 1819, when the first section of the Erie
Canal connected the central counties of New York with
the Hudson River, could farmers ship their crops to
eastern markets (see Chapter 10).

Despite these transportation bottlenecks, white
Americans continued to move westward. They knew
that it would take the labor of a generation to clear
land; build houses, barns, and roads; and plant orchards. Even if markets remained elusive, they were
confident that their sacrifices would yield future security—a farmstead that would provide an independent
livelihood for themselves and their children. The humble achievements of thousands of yeomen and tenant
farm families transformed the landscape of the trans-
Appalachian West, turning forests into farms and beginning the conquest of the interior of the North American
continent.

Republican Policy and Diplomacy

Between 1801 and 1825 three Republicans from Virginia—Thomas Jefferson, James Madison, and James
Monroe—each served two terms as president. Supported by strong majorities in Congress, this Virginia
Dynasty reversed many Federalist policies, completing
what Jefferson called the Revolution of 1800. The West
played a prominent role in Republican policy and, together with maritime disputes with Great Britain, precipitated the War of 1812.

The Jeffersonian Presidency

Thomas Jefferson was a brilliant man, perhaps the most
accomplished and versatile statesman in American history. A seasoned diplomat and an insightful political
philosopher, he was also a superb politician. On becoming president in 1801, Jefferson moved quickly to win
over his Federalist opponents. Reserving the crucial post
of secretary of state for his Virginia ally James Madison,
he appointed three men from Federalist New England to
major government posts: Levi Lincoln as attorney general, Henry Dearborn as secretary of war, and Gideon
Granger as postmaster general. To prepare for new electoral battles, Jefferson used patronage appointments to
bolster the Republican party in New England.

Politics and Courts. Jefferson was the first chief executive to be inaugurated in the District of Columbia, the
new national capital. But he did not begin with a clean
slate, for after a dozen years of Federalist presidents, he
inherited a government filled with his political opponents. In addition to the bureaucracy that managed the
day-to-day operations of the small national government, the judiciary was packed with Federalists. Among
these men the most important was John Marshall of
Virginia, who had been appointed chief justice of the
United States by John Adams in January 1801 (he
would serve until 1835). Most frustrating of all for Jefferson, the outgoing Federalist-controlled Congress had
passed a Judiciary Act in 1801, creating sixteen new
judgeships, six additional circuit courts, and a variety of
posts for marshals and court clerks. Adams filled those
positions in a series of "midnight appointments" just
before he left office. The Federalists "have retired into

the judiciary as a stronghold," Jefferson complained, ". . . and from that battery all the works of Republicanism are to be beaten down and destroyed."

The Republicans fought back. The new Congress repealed the controversial Judiciary Act, dismissing the midnight judges as superfluous. It also used constitutional provisions to punish Federalist judges for their political partisanship on the bench. The Constitution empowered the House of Representatives to bring impeachment charges against officials for "high crimes and misdemeanors"; the accused was then brought to trial before the Senate. First the House impeached a mentally unstable Federalist judge, John Pickering of New Hampshire, and won his removal from office. Then House Republicans brought impeachment charges against Supreme Court Justice Samuel Chase in retaliation for his overzealous enforcement of the Sedition Act. But enough senators balked at this obviously political move to allow Chase to escape removal by a narrow vote.

Jefferson pursued a more conciliatory policy. He supported repeal of the recent Judiciary Act but judged Federalist bureaucrats on the basis of ability, not party loyalty. During eight years as chief executive he removed only 109 of 433 Federalist officeholders, 40 of whom had been midnight appointees of Adams.

The "Revolution of 1800." Jefferson was determined to change the character of the national government. The Federalists, he charged, had swollen its size and power; Republicans would shrink it back to its constitutional size and shape. When the Alien and Sedition Acts expired in 1801, Congress did not reenact them, charging that they were politically motivated and unconstitutional. The Naturalization Act was amended to permit resident aliens to become citizens after five years.

For his part, Jefferson modified many Federalist policies. During the 1790s Federalist administrations had paid tribute to the Barbary States of North Africa— that is, bribed them to spare American merchant ships from attack in the Mediterranean Sea. Jefferson stopped the payments in 1801, and when the city-states of Tunis, Morocco, Tripoli, and Algiers renewed their assaults, he ordered U.S. naval and marine units to retaliate. But Jefferson knew that an extended campaign would require a buildup of the army and navy, which would increase taxes and the national debt. He therefore accepted a diplomatic solution, reviving the Federalist tribute system but, by threatening new military action, at a much lower cost.

In domestic affairs, too, Jefferson set his own course—moderate but clearly Republican. He abolished all internal taxes, including the excise tax that had sparked the Whiskey Rebellion of 1794. Addressing his party's fears of a military takeover of the government, Jefferson reduced the size of the permanent army. He came to accept the Bank of the United States, which he

had condemned as unconstitutional in 1791, because of its importance to the nation's economy, but he was still opposed to a large public debt. One of his most important appointments was that of Albert Gallatin, a brilliant Swiss-born Republican, as secretary of the treasury. Gallatin was a fiscal conservative who believed that the national debt was "an evil of the first magnitude." By carefully controlling government expenditures and using customs revenues to redeem government bonds, he reduced the debt from $83 million in 1801 to $45 million in 1808. After the "Revolution of 1800" Jefferson and Gallatin saw to it that the nation was no longer run in the interests of northeastern creditors and merchants.

Jefferson and the West

The main objective of the Jefferson administration was to help the yeomen farm families who were settling the West. Long before his presidency Jefferson had championed western prosperity. He had celebrated the pioneer farmer in *Notes on the State of Virginia* (1785), helped compose the Confederation's land ordinances, and strongly supported Pinckney's Treaty of 1795, which allowed westerners to ship crops down the Mississippi for export through Spanish-held New Orleans. Now he had the opportunity to shape the nation's land policy.

The Northwest Territory. The settlement of the Old Northwest had been carefully planned by the Confederation Congress. The ordinances of 1785 and 1787, which had created the Northwest Territory, had divided it into uniform sections or townships. Townships were about the same size as New England communities, 6 miles square, and were divided into thirty-six sections of 1 square mile, or 640 acres, surveyed in a grid pattern (see Map 8.2).

Despite Jefferson's efforts, the ordinance of 1785 had a class bias, favoring speculators over yeomen. It specified a minimum price of $1 per acre and required that half the townships be sold in single blocks of 23,040 acres each, making direct purchase impossible for all but the wealthy. The other half of the townships were divided into parcels of 640 acres. But even this was too expensive for many migrants; only well-to-do farmers could afford the $640 cash price for an ordinary farmstead, not to mention the considerably higher amount needed to buy high-quality or well-placed land. Poorer migrants demanded better terms, but the Federalist-dominated Congresses of the 1790s turned a deaf ear. Many Federalist politicians were eastern landlords and had no desire to lose their tenants to cheap land in the West. In fact, the Federalist Land Act of 1796 doubled the minimum price to $2 per acre. Much of the best land fell into the hands of speculators, such as those in the Ohio and Scioto land companies, as the authors of the ordinances had intended.

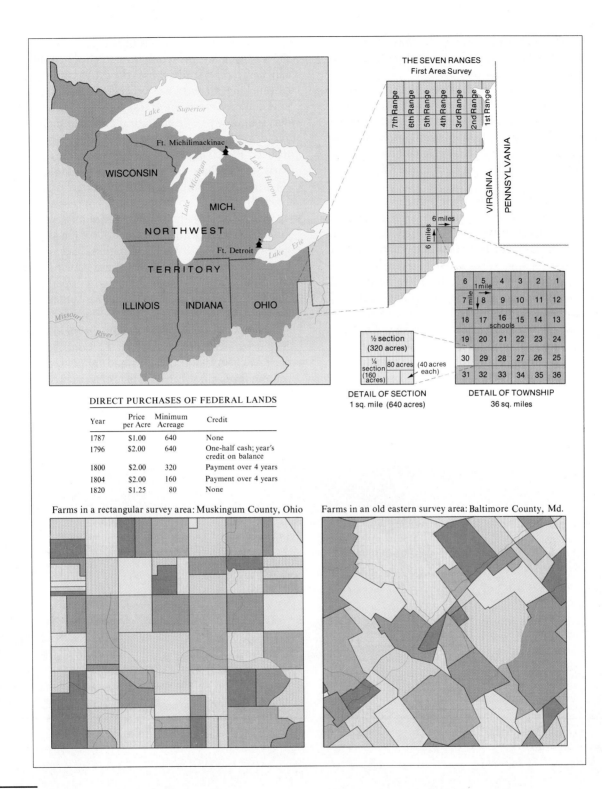

DIRECT PURCHASES OF FEDERAL LANDS

Year	Price per Acre	Minimum Acreage	Credit
1787	$1.00	640	None
1796	$2.00	640	One-half cash; year's credit on balance
1800	$2.00	320	Payment over 4 years
1804	$2.00	160	Payment over 4 years
1820	$1.25	80	None

Farms in a rectangular survey area: Muskingum County, Ohio

Farms in an old eastern survey area: Baltimore County, Md.

MAP 8.2

Land Divisions in the Northwest Territory

Throughout the Northwest Territory, surveyors imposed a rectangular grid on the landscape in advance of settlement, so that farmers bought neatly defined properties. Thus the right-angled property lines in Muskingum County, Ohio (lower left), contrasted sharply with those in Baltimore County, Maryland (lower right), where—as in most eastern states—boundaries followed the contours of the land.

Because Jefferson wanted to see the West populated with yeomen farm families, his Republican colleagues in Congress passed legislation that assisted cash-poor migrants. New laws in 1800 and 1804 reduced the minimum allotment to 320 and then 160 acres, and allowed payment in installments over four years. Eventually, the Land Act of 1820 reduced the minimum purchase to 80 acres and the price to $1.25 per acre, enabling a farmer with only $100 in cash to buy a farm in the West.

The Louisiana Purchase. It was not only the Federalists who jeopardized Jefferson's dream. In 1799 Napoleon Bonaparte, a daring thirty-year-old general, seized power in revolution-torn France and immediately began an ambitious campaign to establish a French empire both in Europe and in America. In 1800 he coerced Spain into signing a secret treaty that returned Louisiana to France; two years later Spanish officials began restricting American access to New Orleans. Meanwhile, Napoleon mobilized an expeditionary force to restore French rule in Haiti, the rich sugar island then called Saint-Domingue, which was under the control of rebellious blacks led by Toussaint L'Ouverture.

Napoleon's actions prompted Jefferson to question the traditional pro-French foreign policy of the Republican party. The trade down the Mississippi guaranteed by Pinckney's Treaty was crucial to the West; any nation that denied Americans access to New Orleans, Jefferson declared, must be "our natural and habitual enemy." To avoid crossing swords with Napoleon, he instructed Robert R. Livingston, the United States minister in Paris, to purchase New Orleans. Simultaneously Jefferson sent James Monroe, a former congressman and governor of Virginia, to Britain to seek its assistance in case of war. "The day that France takes possession of New Orleans," the president warned, "we must marry ourselves to the British fleet and nation." Secretary of State James Madison took the first step toward war by encouraging American merchants to cooperate with the black government of Haiti in its resistance against the French.

Jefferson's determined diplomacy yielded a magnificent prize—the entire territory of Louisiana. By 1802 the French invasion of Haiti had faltered, the victim of yellow fever and spirited black resistance. Napoleon hesitated to send reinforcements because a new war

The American Eagle over New Orleans
Jefferson's purchase of Louisiana made New Orleans an American city, but the architecture (note the steeply pitched roofs on the right) and culture of the French settlers (Creoles) remained strong for decades. A traveler noted that "the great enmity existing between the Creoles . . . & the Americans results in fights and Challenges—there are some of both sides in jail."

with Britain threatened in Europe and he feared that American troops would invade Louisiana. Acting with characteristic decisiveness, Napoleon gave up his dream of an empire in America, and in April 1803 he offered to sell not only New Orleans but the entire territory of Louisiana as well. For about $15 million ($180 million today), Livingston and Monroe, who had joined him in Paris, concluded what became known as the Louisiana Purchase (see Map 8.3). "We have lived long," Livingston remarked to Monroe, "but this is the noblest work of our lives." The Republican statesmen had acquired the vast region between the Mississippi River and the Rocky Mountains, doubling the size of the nation.

The magnitude of the Louisiana Purchase overwhelmed the president's reservations. Jefferson had always advocated a strict construction of the Constitution, arguing that it limited action by the national government to "expressly" delegated powers. Yet the Constitution contained no provision for adding new territory. Given his dreams for the West, Jefferson was pragmatic and used the treaty-making powers in the Constitution to complete the deal with France. Federalists roundly criticized Jefferson's inconsistency but

The Continent Described

Meriwether Lewis and William Clark fulfilled Jefferson's injunction to explore the trans-Mississippi West, filling their journals with drawings and descriptions of its topography, plants, and animals, such as this detailed report on the white salmon trout.

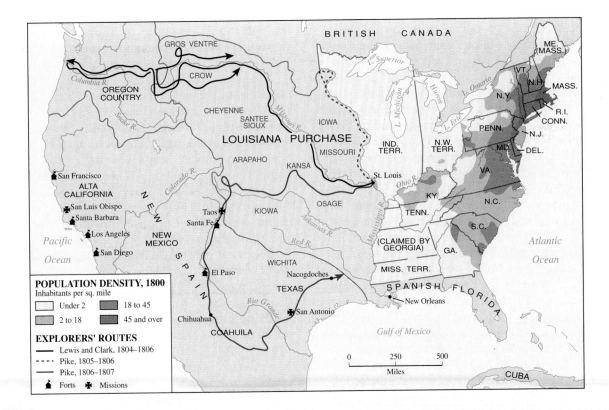

MAP 8.3

The Louisiana Purchase, 1803

The Louisiana Purchase ended France's quest for a North American empire. It doubled the size of the United States, prompting Jefferson to predict that the vast Mississippi Valley "from its fertility . . . will ere long yield half of our whole produce, and contain half of our whole population." Now only Spain stood in the way of an American continental empire.

largely approved his diplomatic triumph, with the Senate ratifying the treaty by a vote of 26 to 6.

A scientist as well as a statesman, Jefferson wanted detailed information about the physical features of the Louisiana Territory and its plant and animal life. He sent out his personal secretary, Meriwether Lewis, to explore the region. Aided by Indian guides, Lewis and William Clark, an army officer, traveled up the Missouri River, across the Rocky Mountains, and down the Columbia River to the Pacific Ocean. After two years the explorers returned with the first maps of this immense wilderness and vivid accounts of its natural resources and native American inhabitants.

Threats to Union. The Louisiana Purchase had been a magnificent acquisition, but it brought a threat to the American Union. New England Federalists had long feared that western expansion would diminish their region's political power. Now some Federalists, including the Massachusetts congressman Timothy Pickering and the geographer Jedidiah Morse, talked openly of the secession of the northeastern states. They approached Alexander Hamilton, but the great New York Federalist refused to support their plan for a separate Northern Confederacy—a scheme that they continued to advocate until the Hartford convention of 1814.

The secessionists then turned to Aaron Burr, the ambitious Republican vice-president. When Burr accepted the support of secessionist Federalists in his campaign for the governorship of New York in 1804, Hamilton accused him of plotting to dismember the Union. In reply Burr challenged his longtime enemy to a duel, the preferred aristocratic method for settling personal disputes. The illegal duel took place in New Jersey in July 1804. Hamilton died from a gunshot wound, and Burr was indicted for murder by state courts in New York and New Jersey.

This tragic event led Burr to yet another secessionist scheme. He completed his term as vice-president early in 1805 and then moved west to avoid prosecution. There he conspired with General James Wilkinson, the American military governor of the Louisiana Territory, although their plan remains a mystery. It involved capturing Spanish territory in Mexico or leading a rebellion to establish Louisiana as a separate nation headed by Burr. In any event, Wilkinson got cold feet and betrayed his ally, arresting him on a charge of treason as the former vice-president led an armed force down the Ohio River. Chief Justice Marshall presided over Burr's trial, which was both a political and a legal contest. Jefferson tried to get Burr convicted by giving a loose construction to the definition of treason in the Constitution. But Marshall repeatedly intervened from the bench, insisting, for a change, on a strict reading of the Constitution. Burr was acquitted.

The decision in Burr's trial was less important than the dangers to national unity that it revealed. The Republicans' expansionist policies had increased sectional tension and party conflict, giving new life to states' rights sentiments and secessionist schemes.

Crisis at Sea

The outbreak of the Napoleonic Wars in Europe (1802–1815) distracted attention from the West and, despite American efforts to avoid involvement, enmeshed the new nation in European political conflicts. Great Britain and France, the major belligerent powers, refused to respect American neutrality, claiming the right to board its merchant ships and confiscate their cargoes, just as they had in the wars of the 1790s.

Naval Blockades. This economic warfare intensified in 1805 when Admiral Horatio Nelson resoundingly defeated the French navy in the Battle of Trafalgar, enabling Britain to tighten its naval blockade of the Continent. The British promptly seized the American freighter *Essex* for carrying sugar and molasses from the West Indies to France and refused to classify those products as American reexports, even though the *Essex* had intentionally stopped at a U.S. port in order to make that claim. This action threatened the profits of American merchants and revived anti-British sentiment.

Napoleon replied to the British blockade with a blockade of his own. The Berlin (1806) and Milan (1807) decrees, known collectively as the Continental System, banned British ships—and neutral vessels that stopped in Britain—from European ports under French control. To counter Napoleon's strategy to destroy its export trade, Britain required neutral shippers to obtain a special license—and carry British goods—to pass through its naval blockade of Europe. American merchants were trapped. If their ships stopped at a British port to pick up a license or cargo, they faced seizure by France; but if they refused to carry British permits, their cargoes might be seized by the British as contraband. American traders were more afraid of the Royal Navy than of French customs officials, so they carried British goods to Europe, thus undermining Napoleon's Continental System.

Impressment. Both Federalists and Republicans resented British high-handedness. They railed against the British policy of stopping American merchant ships to search for sailors who had deserted from the Royal Navy and *impress* them (force them back into military service). During the wars of the 1790s British warships had seized about 2,400 sailors from American ships; but between 1802 and 1811 they had impressed nearly

8,000. Some of the men seized were British subjects carrying forged identity papers; others were Americans impressed by accident—or, more and more frequently, by design.

Long-simmering American resentment erupted in 1807 when the British warship *Leopard* attacked the U.S. frigate *Chesapeake*, killing or wounding twenty-one men and seizing four alleged deserters. "Never since the battle of Lexington have I seen this country in such a state of exasperation as at present," Jefferson declared. But instead of retaliating, Jefferson demanded monetary reparations and an end to impressment. To demonstrate his resolve, he barred British warships from entering American ports for resupply. The astute British government apologized and promised eventual compensation, but continued its blockade and impressment policies.

The Road to War

The Embargo of 1807. To protect American interests while avoiding war, Jefferson adopted a policy of *peaceful coercion*. Working closely with Secretary of State Madison, the president devised the Embargo Act of 1807. As passed by Congress, this legislation prohibited American ships from leaving their home ports until Britain and France repealed their restrictions on U.S. trade. The embargo was imaginative—an economic weapon similar to the nonimportation movements between 1765 and 1775—but naive. Jefferson and Madison overestimated the dependence of Britain and France on American shipping and underestimated the determination of both countries to continue the war despite the economic cost. The Republican leaders also underestimated the cunning of Federalist merchants, who subverted the Embargo Act by ordering their captains to steer clear of American harbors and sail between foreign ports until the embargo was lifted. Trade was the merchants' lifeblood; they were prepared to take their chances with the British navy and Napoleon's officials rather than pass up wartime profits.

However, the embargo did cripple the trade in American exports, which plunged from $108 million in 1806 to $22 million in 1808, and Federalists who represented the interests of New England merchants in Congress attacked Jefferson and Madison for jeopardizing the nation's economy. Federalists grew more alarmed when the Republican Congress passed a Force Act to prevent smuggling across the border between New England and Canada. The act gave customs officials extraordinary legal powers, reviving fears of government tyranny. "Would to God," exclaimed one Federalist, "that the Embargo had done as little evil to ourselves as it has done to foreign nations."

Madison as President. Despite public discontent with the embargo, the voters elected one of its authors, James Madison, to the presidency in 1808, giving him 122 electoral votes to 47 for the Federalist Charles C. Pinckney. As the main architect of the Constitution, an advocate of the Bill of Rights, and a congressman and party leader, Madison had served the nation well. But he was not a diplomat. He had performed poorly as secretary of state, and he lacked administrative skills. As John Beckley, a loyal Republican activist, observed in 1806, "Madison is deemed by many too timid and indecisive as a statesman." Thus, at a crucial juncture in foreign affairs, a man with little understanding of the devious, cutthroat world of international politics became president.

Madison did try to find an effective diplomatic policy. In 1809 he acknowledged the failure of the embargo, secured its repeal, and replaced it with the Nonintercourse Act. This legislation benefited merchants by permitting trade with all nations except France and Britain and offered the two belligerents the promise of normal commerce if they respected America's neutral rights. When Britain and France ignored

I Josiah the first do by this my Royal Proclamation announce myself King of New England, Nova Scotia and Passamaquoddy. Grand Master of the noble order of the Two Cod Fishes.

Poking Fun at the Federalists
A Republican cartoon of 1812 shows the Federalist Josiah Quincy—whose wealth came from the fish trade—as Grand Master of the Cod Fishes and gives him the face of a fish, mocking the Federalists' claim of social superiority.

this overture, Madison bowed to pressure from Congress and accepted a legislative act called Macon's Bill No. 2, named after Congressman Nathaniel Macon. The act reopened legal trade with Britain and France in 1810 but authorized new sanctions if either nation interfered with American commerce. The British ministry refused to alter its policies, daring the United States to cut off trade. Napoleon exploited this ill-conceived legislation more astutely. Publicly he exempted American commerce from the Berlin and Milan decrees, but privately he instructed customs officials to enforce them. "The Devil himself could not tell which government, England or France, is the most wicked," the exasperated Macon declared.

Tecumseh's Challenge. Other Republicans were pretty sure it was Britain. In 1809 eastern party leaders such as George Clinton of New York, Madison's vice-president, began to take a stand against British maritime policies. The following year Republican congressmen from the West—the future War Hawks of 1812—accused Britain of arming the Indian tribes in the trans-Appalachian region. Governor-General James Craig of Canada had in fact quietly renewed military assistance to native Americans in the Ohio River Valley, hoping that the Indians could defend their territory and continue to trade with the British. The Shawnee chief Tecumseh, assisted by his brother, the Prophet Tenskwatawa, revived the Western Confederacy of the 1790s and extended it to the southern tribes. To prevent further cessions, they revived the old doctrine of common tribal ownership of the territory north of the Ohio River and vowed to exclude white settlers.

Tecumseh and Tenskwatawa constructed a new ideology that blended ancestral religious values and various Christian teachings. Like Indian leaders before them, they called for a ban on liquor, less dependence on European goods, and an end to the cohabitation of Indian women with white men. The Shawnee leaders exploited pride in Indian ways to encourage military alliances among the western tribes, and Tenskwatawa prophesied that Indian warriors would emerge from battle unscathed. To symbolize the religious roots of Indian resistance, Tecumseh centered his confederacy at a sacred town at the junction of the Tippecanoe and Wabash rivers. He also traveled widely among southern tribes to win their allegiance, raising the prospect of war along the entire frontier.

The Decision for War. The presence of thousands of white settlers in the West began to affect American foreign policy. Expansionists in Congress condemned British support for the Western Confederacy and threatened to retaliate by seizing Florida from Spain, Britain's ally. Urged on by such talk, some Americans invaded the western (panhandle) region of Florida and sought to

Tenskwatawa, "The Prophet," 1836
Tenskwatawa added a spiritual dimension to native American resistance, urging a holy war against the invading whites. His religious message transcended differences among Indian peoples, helping to create a formidable political and military alliance.

annex it to the United States. Southern planters campaigned for the conquest of eastern Florida to prevent slaves from taking refuge among the Seminole Indians.

Meanwhile, Republican politicians claimed that it would be just as easy to conquer British Canada. Henry Clay, an avowed War Hawk from Kentucky and the new Speaker of the House of Representatives, pushed Madison toward war with Great Britain, as did John C. Calhoun, a rising young congressman from South Carolina. The outbreak of fighting with the Shawnee and their allies in the Indiana Territory might have decided the issue. In 1811 Governor William Henry Harrison defeated the Shawnee in the Battle of Tippecanoe and burned their sacred town (see American Voices, page 243).

With fighting along the frontier, influential Republicans in Congress pressing for war, and national elections quickly approaching, Madison abandoned the strategy of economic coercion. He demanded that the British respect American territorial sovereignty in the West and neutral rights in the Atlantic. When the British failed to respond quickly, Madison asked Congress to declare war. In June 1812 a sharply divided Senate voted 19 to 13 for war; the House of Representatives concurred, 79 to 49.

Chief Shabonee

The Battle of Tippecanoe

His mind sharpened by defeat, the Potawatomi chief Shabonee offers a penetrating view of reality: the unfaithfulness of allies, the confidence and impulsiveness of youth, and the false promises of war leaders.

It was fully believed among the Indians that we should defeat General Harrison, and that we should hold the line of the Wabash and dictate terms to the whites. The great cause of our failure, was the Miamies, whose principal country was south of the river, and they wanted to treat with the whites so as to retain their land, and they played false to their red brethren and yet lost all. They are now surrounded and will be crushed. The whites will shortly have all their lands and they will be driven away. . . .

Our young men said: We are ten to their one. If they stay upon the other side, we will let them alone. If they cross the Wabash, we will take their scalps or drive them into the river. They cannot swim. Their powder will be wet. The fish will eat their bodies. The bones of the white men will lie upon every sand bar. Their flesh will fatten buzzards. These white soldiers are not warriors. Their hands are soft. Their faces are white. One half of them are calico peddlers. The other half can only shoot squirrels. They cannot stand before men. They will all run when we make a noise in the night like wild cats fighting for their young. . . .

Such were the opinions and arguments of our warriors. They did not appreciate the great strength of the white men. I knew their great war chief, and some of his young men. He was a good man, very soft in his words to his red children, as he called us; and that made some of our men with hot heads mad. I listened to his soft words, but I looked into his eyes. They were full of fire. I knew that they would be among his men like coals of fire in the dry grass. The first wind would raise a great flame. I feared for the red men that might be sleeping in its way. . . .

Our women and children were in the town only a mile from the battlefield waiting for victory and its spoils. They wanted white prisoners. The Prophet had promised that every squaw of any note should have one of the white warriors to use as her slave, or to treat as she pleased. Oh how these women were disappointed! Instead of slaves and spoils of the white men coming into town with the rising sun, their town was in flames and women and children were hunted like wolves and killed by hundreds or driven into the river and swamps to hide. With the smoke of that town and the loss of that battle I lost all hope of the red men being able to stop the whites.

Source: David J. Rothman and Sheila Rothman, eds., *Sources of the American Social Tradition* (New York: Basic Books, 1975).

The causes of the War of 1812 have been much debated. Officially, the United States went to war because of violations of its neutral rights—the seizure of its ships and the impressment of its sailors. But Congressional voting and the results of the election of 1812 suggest that the War of 1812 was "a western war with eastern labels," that is, a war fought for land rather than maritime rights. The war was opposed by Federalist merchants and seamen as well as by a majority of voters in the maritime states. The Federalist candidate for president, De Witt Clinton of New York, received 89 electoral votes, primarily from New England and the Middle Atlantic states.

In contrast, Madison amassed 128 electoral votes, mostly from the South and West—regions whose congressmen had heeded the demands of their constituents and voted for war. Western farmers were angry because the British blockade had cut the price of their crops, while settlers in frontier districts demanded war against the Indians and their British allies. War Hawks in Congress not only had their eye on expansion into Florida and Canada but saw political advantage in a war. It might discredit the Federalists and drive home once and for all America's independence from Britain.

Whatever their motives, the Republicans translated them into elevated moral principles, claiming that the pride of the nation was at stake. As President Madison declared in his second inaugural address on March 1813, when the fighting was already under way, "National honor is national property of the highest value."

The War of 1812

The War of 1812 was a near disaster for the United States, both militarily and politically. Republican congressmen had predicted an easy military victory in Canada, but when General William Hull, governor of the Michigan Territory, invaded western Canada in the summer of 1812, he had to retreat almost immediately because of attacks from Indians under Tecumseh and lack of reinforcements. American forces, however, en-

joyed naval superiority on the Great Lakes as Commodore Oliver Hazard Perry defeated a small British flotilla on Lake Erie, and so the United States remained on the offensive. General William Henry Harrison launched a land attack on British and Indian forces near Detroit, forcing the British to withdraw and killing Tecumseh, who had become a British general, at the Battle of the Thames in October 1813. Another American force captured and burned the Upper Canadian capital of York (now Toronto) but, short of men and supplies, immediately withdrew.

A second major invasion of Canada was impossible because of political divisions in the United States. New England governors opposed the war effort and prohibited their states' militiamen from fighting outside the nation. Boston merchants and banks declined to lend money to the national government—some actually invested in British funds instead—making it difficult to finance the war. In Congress, Daniel Webster, a dynamic young representative from New Hampshire, led Federalist opposition to higher taxes and tariffs. To force a negotiated peace, he also discouraged army enlistments and prevented the conscription of state militiamen into the American army. Having led a divided nation into war, Madison and the Republicans were unable to strike the British in Canada—their weakest point.

The American navy was no more successful in the Atlantic Ocean. The British lost scores of merchant vessels to American privateers in the first months of the war, but thereafter the powerful Royal Navy redeployed its fleet and British commerce moved in relative safety. By 1813 Britain had taken the initiative at sea. A flotilla of British warships moved up and down the American coastline, interfering with shipping and threatening seaport cities. In 1814 the fleet sailed up Chesapeake Bay, and British army units stormed ashore. They attacked the District of Columbia and set government buildings on fire in retaliation for the burning of York. The British then advanced on Baltimore but were repulsed by courageous resistance at Fort McHenry. After two years of sporadic warfare the United States was stalemated in Canada and on the defensive along the Atlantic coast, its new capital city in ruins.

Sectional political opposition to the war became even stronger in 1814. The Massachusetts legislature called for a convention "to lay the foundation for a radical reform in the National Compact," and Federalists from all the New England states gathered in Hartford, Connecticut, in December. Some delegates to the Hartford convention proposed secession from the Union, but the majority moderately called for a revision of the Constitution. Their object was to reverse the declining role of the Federalist party—and of New England—in the expanding nation. To end the Virginia Dynasty, delegates proposed a constitutional amendment limiting the presidency to one four-year term and rotating the office

among citizens from different states. Other Federalists suggested amendments restricting commercial embargoes to sixty days and requiring a two-thirds majority in Congress to declare war, prohibit trade, or admit a new state into the Union. A minority in the nation and divided among themselves, the Federalists could not hope to prevail unless the war continued to go badly.

That was a very real prospect. In the late summer of 1814 a major British invasion of the Hudson River Valley had been narrowly averted by an American naval victory at the Battle of Lake Champlain. In December British transports landed thousands of seasoned veterans at New Orleans, threatening to cut off the West's access to the sea. The United States was now under siege from both the north and the south. The only hopeful sign was that Britain had finally defeated Napoleon in Europe and was interested in securing peace with the United States to lower taxes at home and reestablish trade with America.

The British began negotiations with an American delegation at Ghent, Belgium, late in 1814. The American commissioners—John Quincy Adams, Albert Gallatin, and Henry Clay—initially demanded territory in Canada and Florida. British diplomats insisted on a buffer state between the United States and Canada to serve as a refuge for their native American allies. In the end, both sides realized that the small concessions that might be won at the bargaining table were not worth the cost of protracting the war. The Treaty of Ghent, signed on Christmas Eve, 1814, restored the prewar borders and referred unresolved disputes to future negotiations.

Andrew Jackson and the Battle of New Orleans. These results hardly justified three years of fighting and a sharply divided nation. Indeed, the outcome confirmed the view of contemporary critics (and later historians) that the War of 1812 was unnecessary and was undertaken primarily for partisan reasons. But a final victory in combat lifted American morale and, for many citizens, justified the fighting. Before news of the Treaty of Ghent reached the United States, newspaper headlines proclaimed "ALMOST INCREDIBLE VICTORY!! GLORIOUS NEWS." On January 8, 1815, troops commanded by General Andrew Jackson crushed the British forces attacking New Orleans.

The victory at New Orleans brought a very different kind of leader onto the American national scene. A son of the West, Jackson was a rugged slaveowning planter from Tennessee. He first came to public attention as an Indian-fighter after leading a troop of militia in a series of battles against the Creek in 1813 and 1814. After winning the Battle of Horseshoe Bend, he forced the Indian chiefs to sign a treaty ceding 23 million acres of land. These actions earned Jackson a reputation as a ruthless man determined to remove the Indians from the path of white settlement.

The Battle of New Orleans (detail)
As shown in Jean Hyacinthe de Laclotte's painting, British troops attacked the center and the right flank of the American defenses. Secure behind their battlements, Jackson's troops repelled the assaults and took thousands of prisoners.

Jackson's victory at New Orleans made him a national hero and a symbol of the emerging West, the land of frontier fighters. Yet Jackson won the contest at New Orleans not with Kentucky sharpshooters in coonskin caps but with a traditional deployment of regular troops, including a contingent of French-speaking black Americans, the Corps d'Afrique. The Americans fought from carefully constructed breastworks and were amply supplied with cannon, which rained "grapeshot and cannister bombs," on the massed British formations. "The slaughter must have been great," remarked one American witness. Indeed it was. The British lost thousands of their finest troops, with 700 dead and 10,000 wounded or taken prisoner. American casualties totaled only 13 dead and 58 wounded.

For Americans, the Battle of New Orleans was the most significant event of the war, testifying, as one headline put it, to the "RISING GLORY OF THE AMERI-CAN REPUBLIC!" It redeemed the nation's battered pride and, along with the coming of peace, undercut the Hartford convention's demands for a revision of the Constitution. The political institutions of the new nation had survived a war and a generation of sectional strife.

The tumultuous era of the early republic had come to an end. Peace in Europe had ended two decades of conflict over foreign policy, and the continuing success of the Republicans brought about the demise of the Federalists, whose eastern-oriented policies and elitist outlook received little support in an expanding, increasingly democratic nation. "No Federal character can run with success," Gouverneur Morris of New York lamented, and the election results of 1818 bore out his pessimism. After the voting, Republicans outnumbered Federalists in the Senate by 37 to 7 and in the House of Representatives by 156 to 27.

The decline of the Federalists prompted contemporary observers to call the two terms of President James Monroe, from 1817 to 1825, the Era of Good Feeling. Actually, national political harmony was more apparent than real, for the dominant Republican party—now home to many former Federalists—split into factions that struggled over power and patronage, and, after 1820, economic policy.

Regional Diversity and National Identity

The political divisions manifested during the War of 1812 showed that regional differences were stronger than ever. There were four American cultures—New England, Middle Atlantic, Chesapeake, and Lower South—each with distinctive values and political interests (see Map 8.4). As migrants transplanted those cultures to the Old Northwest and Old Southwest, American life became even more diverse, divided be-

tween complex seaboard societies and frontier farming regions. To unify this increasingly fragmented society, politicians and statesmen defined a new national goal: a continental American empire.

Northern Seaboard Societies

Generations of observers had contrasted the race- and class-divided societies of the Chesapeake with the freehold farming regions of the North, particularly New England. Popular speech reflected some of these differences: "Yankee," a foreign traveler learned, was "a name given derisively, or merely jestingly," to the residents of New England because of their shrewd bargaining habits. "The name of 'Buckskin' is given to the inhabitants of Virginia," he went on to observe, "because their ancestors were hunters and sold buck, or rather deer skins."

European visitors saw genuine cultural differences in the popular stereotypes. In 1800 a British observer detected religious "fanaticism" in New England as well

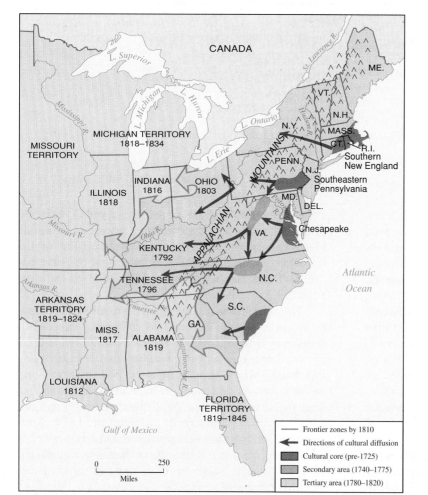

MAP 8.4

Regional Cultures Move West, 1720–1820
By 1720 four distinct "core" cultures had developed along the Atlantic seaboard. By 1775 settlers from the mid-Atlantic and Chesapeake regions had carried their customs and institutions into the southern backcountry. Then, between 1780 and 1820, settlers from New England and the Lower South transplanted their regional cultures into other parts of the trans-Appalachian West. Extensive cultural intermixture—and conflict—occurred only in certain regions, such as southern Ohio, Kentucky, and Tennessee.

as "a great strain of industry among all ranks of people." He thought that "the lower orders of citizens have a better education, are more intelligent, and better informed" than those he met in the southern states. Visitors to the Chesapeake commented on the rude manners and heavy drinking of white tenant farmers and small freeholders. They had a "passion for gaming at the billiard table, a cock-fight or cards."

New Englanders did indeed set a higher store by education than did residents of the Chesapeake. The Puritan legacy included strong traditions of primary schooling and Bible reading. As a result, most of the men and more than half the women in New England in 1790 could read and write. In Virginia, most white women and a third of adult white men could not even write their names; they signed legal documents such as wills and marriage licenses with an "X" or another mark. This disparity in the literacy rate reflected different social and fiscal priorities. The slaveholding elite that ruled southern society refused to provide services or schooling for ordinary white families. In 1800 the 4,000 free inhabitants of Essex County in Virginia spent about $1,000 for local government, including schooling. The same year the 900 residents of Acton, Massachusetts, spent $950 for public purposes—four times as much per capita as in Essex County—$550 on education alone.

Regional differences were also apparent in the observance of holidays. In Virginia, South Carolina, and other states with an Anglican heritage, Christmas was an occasion for feasting and celebration. Not so in New England, where Puritans condemned such celebrations as profane. Most New England churches did not celebrate Christmas until the 1850s; for them, Thanksgiving Day, commemorating the trials and triumphs of the first Pilgrim and Puritan settlers, was the focus of celebration. During the War of Independence New England customs had become political symbols as Congress frequently declared days of fasting and thanksgiving.

Regional identity was especially intense in New England because of ethnic and religious uniformity. By the 1820s most men and women in the region could trace their American roots back six or seven generations. No fewer than 281 members of the Newhall family resided in Lynn, Massachusetts, along with 259 Breeds, 195 Alleys, and 162 Johnsons. A list of only twelve family names encompassed 1,660 persons, or 27 percent of the town's population. In a very real sense New England was a "big family" composed of large, interrelated groups.

The culture of the Middle Atlantic region was more diverse, because the people came from different ethnic backgrounds. In Pennsylvania and New Jersey, Quakers, Germans, and Scots-Irish married largely within their own ethnic groups, and to a lesser extent so did the Dutch. Germans held on to their language as well as

Puritan Culture Persists
Like good Puritans, this prosperous New England couple wear plainly cut clothes and hold the symbols of piety and literacy—a book and a pen. The artist shows his stepmother looking directly at him (and us), suggesting that he enjoyed a better relationship with her than with his stern-faced father, a traditional New England patriarch.

their customs, especially in the small agricultural villages of Pennsylvania and the isolated backcountry districts of Maryland, Virginia, and North Carolina. A visitor to Hanover, Maryland, noted around 1820, "The inhabitants are all German. Habits, speech, newspapers, cooking—all German." In nearby Frederick Town the Lutheran church kept all its records and held Sunday-school classes in German.

This diversity among and within the various regions inhibited the establishment of an American national identity. Until the growth of interregional commerce created a national economy (see Chapter 9), only certain political events—such as the War of 1812—reminded people that they were citizens of the United States. For example, the term "Uncle Sam" came into use during the War of 1812. "This cant name for our government has got almost as common as John Bull [for the British]," a newspaper in Troy, New York, reported: "The letters U.S. on government waggons &c are supposed to have given rise to it." The immediate popular-

German Dress and Manners in America
A gentleman in traditional dress strolls among giant tulips, a familiar motif in Pennsylvania German folk art. The lace cuffs, white stockings, and walking stick suggest his high social status, as does the genteel way he holds his pipe.

ity of "The Star Spangled Banner," written by Francis Scott Key during the battle at Fort McHenry, also testified to the role of the war in promoting an American national identity.

Newspapers played an increasingly important role in fostering national identity and common cultural values. By 1820 the cities of the United States boasted thirty daily newspapers. Another thousand newspapers, mostly four-page weeklies, provided national news, market information, and advertisements to people in small towns and rural areas. Political parties subsidized some of these newspapers, creating a national debate on various legislative issues. The influential *Niles Weekly Register,* established in Baltimore in 1811, and the *North American Review,* founded in Boston in 1815, carried news from Europe and the East to every region. But only members of certain elites—merchants, politicians, lawyers—participated fully in this national culture. Most Americans lived out their lives within the regional culture into which they had been born.

The Old Northwest

When Jedidiah Morse published *American Geography* in 1793, he listed three "grand divisions of the United States": northern, middle, and southern. In the edition of 1819 he added a new section: "Western States and Territories." Some seventy years later, in an essay called "The Significance of the Frontier in American History" (1893), the historian Frederick Jackson Turner placed the West at the center of the American experience. Turner argued that an identifiable national character first developed in the West because that area was controlled by the national government. He also maintained that the western frontier experience itself—the life-or-death struggle with nature—created a character and a system of values that were distinctly American: individualistic, optimistic, pragmatic, and democratic.

Turner's theories provoked a generation of scholarly research and debate, but historians no longer accept many of his views. For instance, Turner underestimated the force of cultural tradition. Most migrants to the West, like most Europeans who came to America, sought to preserve their old values and customs. Thus, when 176 residents of Granville, Massachusetts, decided to move to Ohio, they carefully chose a site whose "peculiar blending of hill and valley" resembled the landscape of their New England community. They transplanted their Congregational church to Ohio whole, complete with ministers and elders, along with their system of freehold agriculture. So it was throughout the trans-Appalachian West: in many respects "new" communities were not new—they were old communities that had moved inland.

Yet Turner was right about the self-sufficiency of the majority of frontier communities. Cut off from most trade with outside markets, settlers made their own clothes, repaired old tools, and lived in a local barter economy, exchanging goods or labor with their neighbors. "A noble field of Indian corn stretched away into the forest on one side," an English visitor to an Ohio farm in the 1820s noted, waxing romantic,

> and immediately before the house was a small potato garden, with a few peach and apple trees. The woman told me that they spun and wove all the cotton and woollen garments of the family, and knit all the stockings; her husband, though not a shoemaker by trade, made all the shoes. She manufactured all the soap and candles they use. All she wanted with money, she said, was to buy coffee, tea, and whiskey, and she could "get enough any day by sending a batch of butter and chickens to market."

A low standard of living prevailed for this and other farm families for more than a generation. As late as 1840, per capita income in the Old Northwest was only 70 percent of the national average.

Apart from its relative poverty, the distinctiveness of the region lay in the conflict among competing cultural traditions. In Indiana, education-conscious migrants from New England set up a system of public primary schools, but only after a twenty-year battle with tax-shy yeomen from the southern states. Although the New England influence was strong, the states of the Old Northwest developed largely along the model of the Middle Atlantic states—Pennsylvania, New Jersey, and New York—with their diverse cultural traditions and ethnic political factions.

Slavery Moves into the Old Southwest

As poor whites fled from the Chesapeake states to Kentucky and Tennessee, wealthy planters and up-and-coming young men from the Chesapeake and the Lower South set up new slave plantations in the Old Southwest—the future states of Alabama, Mississippi, and Louisiana. Consequently, the southwestern frontier became a stronghold not of Turner's individualism and democracy but of slavery.

Indeed, slavery expanded in newly settled areas. As planters from the Lower South states of Georgia and South Carolina moved into the backcountry, they imported new slaves from Africa. They had used their influence at the Philadelphia convention of 1787 to protect this trade from national regulation for twenty years, and when the time limit expired in 1808, Congress responded to antislavery settlement in the North by banning American participation in the transatlantic slave trade. But by that time 250,000 new slaves had entered the United States, a number equal to that of all slaves imported during the colonial period. The black population had also grown through reproduction, increasing from half a million in 1775 to 1.8 million in 1820.

Many of these Africans and African-Americans still toiled on tobacco and rice plantations. When soil exhaustion caused tobacco production to stagnate in the Tidewater region of the Chesapeake, white planters took the crop into the Virginia Piedmont, North Carolina, Kentucky, and Tennessee. The rice industry of South Carolina and Georgia expanded until the 1820s, when many of its overseas markets were lost to cheaper rice imports from Asia. By that time white planters in Louisiana—some of them refugees from black-controlled Haiti—had established a booming economy based on sugar. Slaves in Louisiana, like those on the sugar plantations of the West Indies, were brutally exploited and died quickly from disease and overwork.

The Coming of Cotton. However, it was a new crop—cotton—that provided the impetus for the expansion of slavery. For centuries most Europeans had worn clothing made from wool or flax; cotton textiles imported from India were only for the rich. Cotton spinning and weaving had been taken up in England but had remained a minor industry. Then, after 1750, the European population explosion increased the demand for woolen and cotton cloth just as the technological breakthroughs of the Industrial Revolution were boosting production and lowering prices. Soon consumer demand and the newly invented water-powered spinning jennies and weaving mules generated a seemingly insatiable demand for raw cotton.

Beginning in the 1780s, American planters responded to this demand by importing a rot-resistant, smooth-seed, long-fiber variety of cotton from the West Indies and planting it on sea islands along the southern Atlantic coast. Then, in the 1790s, a number of inventors—including Connecticut-born Eli Whitney—developed machines to separate the seeds from the fiber of short-staple cotton, which grew well in many regions of the South.

The combination of British demand and American innovation created a new agricultural industry and a massive demand for land and labor. Thousands of white planters moved into the interior of South Carolina and Georgia to grow cotton. After the War of 1812, production spread into Alabama and Mississippi, which entered the Union in 1817 and 1819, respectively. In a single year a government land office in Huntsville, Alabama, sold $7 million of uncleared land. The expression "doing a land-office business"—a metaphor for rapid commercial expansion—dates from this time.

Cotton's Impact on African-Americans. For enslaved blacks the coming of cotton meant social upheaval. Entire black communities were uprooted from the Chesapeake and Lower South and forced to move west with their owners; even more wrenchingly, thousands of young women and men were taken away from their families through a new domestic slave trade. By 1820 whites had displaced more than 250,000 African-Americans from their birthplaces to new tobacco regions and the booming cotton states.

The history of the Tayloe family's Mount Airy plantation in Virginia illustrates the impact of cotton on the lives of blacks. In 1747 John Tayloe owned 167 slaves at Mount Airy. Over the next sixty years twice as many slaves were born as died on this plantation, creating a large, interrelated African-American community—and, from the Tayloes' point of view, a "surplus" of workers. Hence, in 1792 John Tayloe III advertised a sale of 200 slaves, at least 50 of whom were from Mount Airy. Between 1828 and 1860 Tayloe and his sons would move 180 Mount Airy slaves to their new cotton plantations in Alabama.

These sales and forced migrations brought great wealth to a few white families and untold misery to blacks. Torn from their loved ones, African-Americans

Arise! Arise! and weep no more dry up your tears, we shall part no more. Come rise we go to Tennessee, that happy Shore. To old virginia never — never — return. —

The Internal Slave Trade

Mounted whites escort a convoy of slaves from Virginia to Tennessee in Louis Miller's *Slave Trader, Sold to Tennessee*. The trade was a lucrative one for whites, pumping money into the declining Chesapeake economy and valuable workers into the plantations of the cotton belt. For blacks it was a traumatic journey, a second Middle Passage that broke up families and communities.

had to rebuild their lives, laboring "from day clean to first dark" on frontier plantations in Alabama and Mississippi. "I am Sold to a man by the name of Peterson a trader," lamented one Georgia slave. "My Dear wife for you and my Children my pen cannot Express the griffe I feel to be parted from you all."

Antislavery Efforts and the Missouri Compromise. The expansion of slavery into the Old Southwest dashed the hopes of those who thought slavery would "die a natural death" after the decline of the tobacco economy and the end of the Atlantic slave trade. Some antislavery advocates had worked to prevent the illegal importation of enslaved Africans. Others had persuaded the legislatures of northern states to pass *personal liberty laws* protecting free blacks from kidnapping or seizure under the terms of the Fugitive Slave Act of 1793.

More important, reformers had opposed the expansion of slavery into the western territories. Despite their efforts, Louisiana, Mississippi, and Alabama joined the Union with state constitutions permitting slavery. When

Missouri applied for admission on a similar basis in 1819, the antislavery forces rallied. Congressman James Tallmadge of New York proposed a ban on the importation of slaves into Missouri and the gradual emancipation of its black inhabitants. When Missouri whites rejected those conditions, the northern majority in the House of Representatives blocked the territory's admission to the Union. In response, southerners used their power in the Senate, which was equally divided between eleven free and eleven slave states, to withhold statehood from Maine, which was seeking to separate itself from Massachusetts. Tempers flared in the heat of debate. Senator Thomas W. Cobb of Georgia accused Tallmadge of kindling "a fire which all the waters of the ocean cannot put out and which seas of blood can only extinguish."

Controversy raged for two years before Congress resolved the stalemate. Representative Henry Clay of Kentucky and other skilled politicians put together a series of agreements known collectively as the Missouri Compromise, by which Maine entered the Union as a

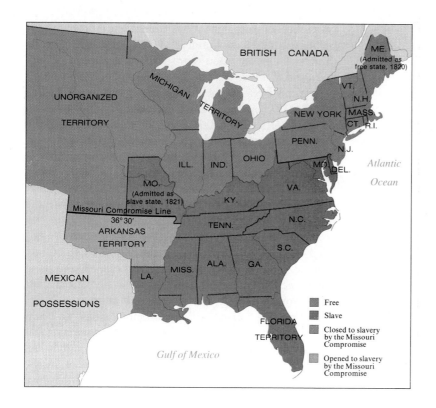

MAP 8.5

The Missouri Compromise, 1820

The Missouri Compromise resolved for a generation the issue of slavery in the lands of the Louisiana Purchase. Slavery was forbidden north of the Missouri Compromise line (36° 30' north latitude), with the exception of the state of Missouri. To maintain an equal number of free and slave states in the U.S. Senate, the compromise provided for the nearly simultaneous admission of Maine and Missouri.

free state in 1820 and Missouri was admitted as a slave state the following year (see Map 8.5). This bargain preserved the existing sectional balance in the Senate and set a precedent for the future admission of states in pairs—one free and one slave. To mollify antislavery sentiment in the House of Representatives, southern congressmen accepted the restriction of slavery in the rest of the Louisiana Territory north of latitude 36° 30', the southern boundary of Missouri.

The tradition of political compromise on the issue of slavery thus continued. In 1821 as in 1787, the white leaders of the North and the South gave priority to the Union, finding complex but workable ways to reconcile the interests of their regions. But the task had become more difficult. The Philadelphia delegates had resolved their sectional differences in two months; Congress took two years to work out the Missouri Compromise, and there was no guarantee that it would work. The fates of the West, the Union, and the black race had become inextricably intertwined, raising the prospect of civil war. As Thomas Jefferson exclaimed at the time of the Missouri controversy, "This momentous question, like a fire-bell in the night, awakened and filled me with terror."

African-American Society and Culture

After 1800 a more unified African-American culture began to develop in the United States for three reasons. First, the end of the transatlantic slave trade in 1808

eliminated the need to assimilate newly arrived Africans. Even in South Carolina, only about 20 percent of the enslaved population in 1820 had been born in Africa. Second, the movement of slavery into the Old Southwest reduced differences among slaves; for example, the black Gullah dialect of the Carolinas disappeared on the cotton plantations of Alabama and Mississippi because slaves from the Chesapeake had adopted English. Third, free blacks, especially in northern cities, consciously began to foster a sense of a distinct African-American culture.

Many African elements persisted in the new African-American culture. About half the slaves who entered the United States between 1800 and 1808 came from the Congo and Angola, making those regions important sources of African influences. As the traveler Isaac Holmes reported in 1821:

> In Louisiana, and the state of Mississippi, the slaves . . . dance for several hours during Sunday afternoon. The general movement is in what they call the Congo dance; their music often consists of nothing more than an excavated piece of wood . . . one end of which is a piece of parchment.

Similar descriptions of blacks who "danced the Congo and sang a purely African song to the accompaniment of . . . a drum made by stretching a skin over a flour barrell" appeared as late as 1890.

Marriage and Family Life. African-Americans also maintained some of the social rules of their West

African-American Banjos
In 1794 an Englishman in Virginia watched slaves dancing to the music of an African-style banjo "made of a gourd something in the imitation of a Guitar, with only four strings and played with the fingers in the same manner."

African homeland, such as rigid incest taboos. Unlike the white elite of South Carolina, which practiced cousin marriage to keep property in the family and maintain an intermarried ruling group, enslaved blacks shunned marriages between cousins even on relatively self-contained plantations. For example, on the Good Hope plantation in South Carolina about 175 slave children were born between 1800 and 1857, and no fewer than 40 percent of those children were related by blood to three slaves from Africa. Within this elaborate tangle of kinship, only one marriage between cousins took place.

Masters and slaves also had different ideas about the sanctity of marriage. Whites insisted on legally binding marriage contracts among themselves both to regulate sexual behavior and to establish the ownership of property. But slaveowners forbade legal marriage be-

tween blacks so that they could sell their slaves without breaking a marriage bond. Enslaved African-Americans therefore devised their own marriage rituals. Young men and women first asked their parents' consent to marry and then sought their owner's permission to live together in their own cabin. Following African custom, many couples signified their union in a public ceremony by jumping over a broomstick together. Christian blacks often had a religious service performed by a white or black preacher, but these rites never ended with the customary phrase "until death do you part." Everyone knew that black marriages could end with the sale of one or both of the spouses.

Many married slaves who were not separated by sale lived in stable unions. Among the slaves on the Good Hope plantation in South Carolina, about 70 percent of the women had all their children by the same man. Most other women had their first child (with an enslaved man) before marriage in what the community called an "outside" birth and bore the rest of their children within a stable union. On plantations in Louisiana black family ties were much more fragile, in part because labor in the sugar fields killed many men. Thirty percent of the slave women on one Louisiana plantation lived alone with their children, who were fathered by a succession of men.

Thus, the oppressive conditions of slavery only partially undermined blacks' efforts to create solid family bonds. To maintain their identity, many recently imported slaves in South Carolina and Georgia bestowed African names on their children; males born on Friday were often called Cuffee—the name of that day in several West African languages. Most Chesapeake slaves chose names of British origin and bound one generation to another by naming sons after fathers, uncles, or grandfathers; daughters were often named after grandmothers. Names had great social importance, for they acknowledged the biological ties of kinship (see Table 8.1). Like incest rules and marriage rituals, naming patterns created order in a harsh and arbitrary world.

As an African-American cultural community developed, the quality of slave life gradually improved. During the eighteenth century a lack of social organization among African-born slaves resulting from their diverse origins had made it easy for white men to take advantage of blacks. They had raped women and punished defiant men in horrible ways, branding them, or cutting off their fingers or ears, or even castrating them. Such abuses did not stop after 1800, but they were questioned more often. White politicians condemned rape as an aristocratic vice that was ill suited to life in a republican society. The spread of evangelical Christianity encouraged many masters to treat their slaves more humanely. African-Americans also put themselves in a position to resist the worst forms of oppression by forming stable families and strong communities. They insisted that work gangs be sold "in families" and de-

TABLE 8.1

African-American Naming Patterns

Good Hope Plantation Slaves, Orangebury, South Carolina

Date of Birth	Baby's Name	Parents' Names	Source of Baby's Name
1793	Hector	Bess, Hector	Father
1806	Clarinda	Patty, Primus	Mother's mother
1811	Sambo	Affy, Jacob	Mother's father
1813	Primus	Patty, Primus	Father
1824	Sarah	Phoebe, Jack	Mother's mother
1828	Major	Clarinda, Abram	Father's father

fied their owners when they were not. Faced with transport to Mississippi and separation from his wife, one Maryland slave, his owner reported, "neither yields consent to accompany my people, or to be exchanged or sold." Masters ignored such resistance at their risk. They now faced the prospect that a slave's relatives might retaliate for violence or arbitrary sale with arson, poison, or destruction of crops or equipment.

Work and Community. Blacks in the rice-growing lowlands of South Carolina were particularly successful in gaining control over their work lives. By the Revolutionary Era those slaves had won the right to labor by the *task*. Each day a worker had to complete a precisely defined task—turn up a quarter acre of rice land, hoe a half acre, or pound seven mortars of rice. Many slaves finished their task "by one or two o'clock in the afternoon," a Methodist preacher reported. They had "the rest of the day for themselves, which they spend in working their own private fields, consisting of 5 or 6 acres of ground . . . planting rice, corn, potatoes, tobacco &c. for their own use and profit." African-Americans extended these customary rights during the War of Independence, as black drivers took over the management of many plantations, and jealously guarded them afterward. "Should any owner increase the work beyond what is customary," a South Carolina rice planter warned around 1800, "he subjects himself . . . to such discontent amongst his slaves as to make them of little use to him."

Still, white masters had virtually unlimited power—both legal and physical—over their slaves. In upland cotton-growing regions of South Carolina and Georgia and in Alabama and Mississippi, owners forced workers to labor in supervised "gangs." They sold those who were recalcitrant and punished those they viewed as lazy. Particularly on newly settled plantations, profit-conscious masters used the lash to extract labor.

Enslaved blacks found ways to resist the tyranny of slavery. Some, such as Gabriel Prosser of Virginia, plot-

ted mass uprisings and murders. Denmark Vesey, a free black married to a slave woman, planned a rebellion in Charleston, South Carolina, in 1822, but, like Prosser's, it was discovered and crushed at the last moment. Most blacks knew that a successful revolt was highly unlikely because of white strength in numbers and military superiority. Flight was also perilous. The northern and western states were hotbeds of racial prejudice, and masters could use the Fugitive Slave Law (1793) to carry them back to bondage. Yet hundreds of Chesapeake slaves fled to the free states, and thousands more threatened to do so, forcing their masters to treat them better.

Enslaved blacks in the Lower South and Old Southwest had fewer options. One avenue of escape—to Spanish Florida—was cut off in 1819 when the United States annexed Florida. Slaves had no option but to build the best possible lives for themselves where they were. As the black abolitionist Frederick Douglass would observe, these slave communities were "pegged down to a single spot" and "must take root there or nowhere." Enslaved blacks developed a culture similar to that of European peasants. They worked as dependent agricultural laborers and built close-knit communities based on family, kinship, and religion.

Meanwhile, the relatively small population of free African-Americans (about 5 percent of the total by 1820) explored the dimensions of its newfound liberty. The great majority lived on low wages from menial jobs as farm workers or city laborers and laundresses, and their lives were circumscribed by racial prejudice. But a few blacks were able to make full use of their talents and achieved great distinction. The mathematician and surveyor Benjamin Bannaker published an almanac and helped lay out the new national capital; Phyllis Wheatley won praise for her poetry, as did Joshua Johnston for his portraiture; and Robert Sheridan acquired a small fortune from his mercantile enterprises. But even more impressive and enduring were the institutions created by this first generation of free African-Americans (see American Lives, pages 254–255). Hundreds of

Richard Allen and African-American Identity

Richard Allen was a success. Born into slavery in Philadelphia in 1760, he died in 1831 not only free but influential, a founder of the African Methodist Episcopal Church and its first bishop. Allen's rise has much of the classic American success story about it, but he bears a larger significance: Allen, as one of the first African-Americans to be emancipated during the Revolutionary Era, had to forge an identity for his people as well as for himself.

Sold as a child along with his family to a farmer in Delaware, Allen began his ascent in 1777, when he was converted to Methodism by Freeborn Garretson, an itinerant preacher. Garretson also converted Allen's master and convinced him that on Judgment Day slaveholders would be "weighted in the balance, and . . . found wanting." Allowed by his repentant owner to buy his freedom, Allen earned a living sawing cordwood and driving a wagon during the Revolutionary War. After the war he furthered the Methodist cause by becoming a "licensed exhorter," preaching to blacks and whites from New York to South Carolina. His efforts attracted the attention of Methodist leaders, including Francis Asbury, the first American bishop of the Methodist Church. In 1786 Allen was appointed as an assistant minister in Philadelphia, serving the racially mixed congregation of St. George's Methodist Church. The following year he and Absalom Jones, another black preacher, joined other ex-slaves and Quaker philanthropists to form the Free African Society, a quasireligious benevolent organization that offered fellowship and mutual aid to "free Africans and their descendants."

Allen remained a staunch Methodist throughout his life. In 1789, when the Free African Society adopted various Quaker practices, such as having fifteen minutes of silence at its meetings, Allen led a withdrawal of those who preferred more enthusiastic Methodist practices. In 1794 he rejected an offer to become the pastor of the church the Free African Society had built, St. Thomas's African Episcopal Church, a position ultimately accepted by Absalom Jones. A large majority of the society had chosen to affiliate with the white Episcopal (formerly Anglican) Church because much of the city's black community had been Anglican since the 1740s. "I informed them that I could not be anything else but a Methodist, as I was born and awakened under them," Allen recalled.

To reconcile his faith and his African-American identity, Allen decided to form his own congregation. He gathered a group of ten black Methodists and took over a blacksmith's shop in the increasingly black southern section of the city, converting it to the Bethel African Methodist Episcopal Church. Although the Bethel Church opened in a ceremony led by Bishop Francis Asbury in July 1794, its tiny congregation worshiped "separate from our white brethren."

Allen's decision to found a black congregation was partly a response to white racism. Although most white Methodists in the 1790s favored emancipation, they did not treat free blacks as equals. They refused to allow African-Americans to be buried in the congregation's cemetery and, in a famous incident in 1792, segregated them into a newly built gallery of St. George's Methodist Church. But Allen's action also reflected a desire among African-Americans to control their religious lives, to have the power, for example, "to call any brother that appears to us adequate to the task to preach or exhort as a local preacher, without the interference of the Conference." By 1795 the congregation of Allen's Bethel Church numbered 121; a decade later it had grown to 457, and by 1813 it had reached 1,272.

Bethel's rapid expansion reflected the growth of Philadelphia's black population, which numbered nearly 10,000 by 1810, and the appeal of Methodist practices. Newly freed blacks welcomed "love feasts," which allowed the full expression of emotions repressed under slavery. They were attracted as well by the church's strict system of discipline—its communal sanctions against drinking, gambling, and infidelity—which helped them bring order to their lives. Allen's preaching also played a role; the excellence of his sermons was recognized in 1799, when Bishop Asbury ordained him as the first black deacon of the Methodist Church.

The Mount Bethel African Methodist Episcopal Church, Philadelphia

But over the years Allen and other blacks grew dissatisfied with Methodism, as white ministers retreated from their antislavery principles and attempted to curb the autonomy of African-American congregations. In 1807 the Bethel Church added an "African Supplement" to its articles of incorporation; in 1816 it won legal recognition as an independent church. In the same year Allen and representatives from four other black Methodist congregations (in Baltimore; Wilmington, Delaware; Salem, New Jersey; and Attleboro, Pennsylvania) met at the Bethel Church to organize a new denomination, the African Methodist Episcopal Church. Allen was chosen as the first bishop of the church, the first fully independent black denomination in America. He had succeeded in charting a separate religious identity for African-Americans.

Allen also recognized the importance of education to the future of the African-American community. In 1795 he opened a day school for sixty children and in 1804 founded the "Society of Free People of Colour for Promoting the Instruction and School Education of Children of African Descent." By 1811 there were no fewer than eleven black schools in the city.

But where did Allen think "free people of colour" should look for their future? This question had arisen in Philadelphia in 1787, when William Thornton had promoted a plan devised by antislavery groups in London to settle free American blacks (and emancipated slaves from the West Indies) in Sierra Leone, an independent state they had founded on the west coast of Africa.

Many blacks in Boston and Newport had endorsed this scheme, but the members of Philadelphia's Free African Society had rejected it. They preferred to seek advancement in America, but on their own cultural terms. The process took place on two levels: as a social group, Philadelphia blacks embraced their ancestral heritage by forming "African" churches and benevolent societies. As individuals, however, they affirmed their American identity by taking English names (although virtually never those of their former owners). This dual strategy brought pride but not significant gains in wealth and status. Nonetheless, Philadelphia's African-Americans rejected colonization; when the issue was raised again just after 1800, only four people signed up for emigration to Sierra Leone.

Instead, the city's black community petitioned the state and national governments to end slavery and the slave trade and repeal the Fugitive Slave Act of 1793, which allowed slaveowners to seize blacks without a warrant. As if to underline the importance of these political initiatives, Allen was temporarily seized in 1806 as a fugitive slave, showing that even the most prominent northern blacks could not be sure of their freedom. This experience may account for Allen's initial support for the American Colonization Society, a predominantly white organization founded in 1817 to promote the settlement of free blacks in Africa. This scheme was immediately condemned at a mass meeting of nearly 3,000 Philadelphia blacks, who set forth a different vision of the African-American future: "Whereas our ancestors (not of choice) were the first successful cultivators of the wilds of America, we their descendants feel ourselves entitled to participate in the blessings of her luxuriant soil."

Philadelphia's black community, including Allen, was more favorably inclined toward the Haitian Emigration Society, which was founded in 1824 to help African-Americans settle in that island republic. But when that venture failed, Allen forcefully urged blacks to remain in the United States. In November 1827 he made a compelling argument in *Freedom's Journal*, the nation's first black newspaper: "This land which we have watered with our *tears* and our *blood* is now our *mother country*."

Born a slave of African ancestry, Allen learned to live as a free man in white America, rejecting emigration and preserving his cultural identity by creating separate African-American institutions. But it meant that he cast his lot, and that of his descendants, with a society pervaded by racism. It was a brave decision, both characteristic of the man who made it and indicative of the limited choices available to those freed from the bonds of slavery.

them joined together to found black schools, mutual-benefit and fellowship societies, antislavery organizations, and religious denominations. Over the years these institutions helped create a sense of cultural autonomy among African-Americans and gave public expression to their lives and values.

African-American Religion. After the family, the religious community played the most important role in lives of enslaved African-Americans. Many blacks maintained African practices, invoking traditional spirits in time of need. In Louisiana, some slaves from Haiti practiced the folk religion of voodoo, a blend of African and Catholic customs. Many enslaved African-Americans in the Chesapeake became Christians, absorbing and adapting the religious views of white Baptists and Methodists. As black ministers preached or founded churches (which often met in secret to avoid repression), they advanced their own interpretation of Christian doctrines. Black theology generally ignored the issues of original sin and predestination. It also downplayed biblical passages in which the church is viewed as lawgiver and symbol of authority. Black Christians preferred to envision God as a warrior who had liberated his chosen people. "Their cause was similar to the Israelites'," Martin Prosser (Gabriel's brother) told his fellow slave conspirators during the thwarted rebellion in Virginia in 1800. "I have read in my Bible where God says, if we worship him, we should have peace in all our land and five of you shall conquer a hundred and a hundred of you a hundred thousand of our enemies."

The Christian message valued spiritual endurance as well as physical resistance. Some slaves identified with the persecuted Christ, who had suffered and died so that his followers might find peace and justice in the next world. Amid the manifest injustice of their lives, these African-Americans used Christian principles to affirm their equality with whites in the eyes of God. They took the language and religion of their masters but adapted them for their own ends. Trapped in a bicultural world, these African-Americans learned from whites but lived as blacks.

The Fate of Native Americans

"Next to the case of the black race within our bosom," James Madison remarked as he left the presidency in 1817, "that of the red race on our borders is the problem most baffling to the policy of our country." Most American political leaders had fewer misgivings than Madison did. They wanted to open lands in the trans-Appalachian West, regardless of the cost to the native American inhabitants. "Cut up every Indian Cornfield and burn every Indian town," proclaimed William Henry Drayton of South Carolina, so that their "nation be extirpated and the lands become the property of the public." For many educated whites the conquest of the interior and its aboriginal inhabitants represented the historical progress of humanity in which primitive life would be replaced by higher cultural forms. As a congressional committee put it in 1818, "Those sons of the forest should be moralized or exterminated."

Cultural Assimilation, circa 1805
Merchant Benjamin Hawkins points to a plow, encouraging Creek Indians to adopt European farming techniques. By this time the Creeks were bartering corn and other crops (as well as furs) for manufactured goods.

Red Jacket

A Seneca Chief's Understanding of Religion

The Seneca chief Red Jacket (c. 1758–1830) acquired his name during the Revolutionary War, when he fought for the British "redcoats." Reconciling himself to American rule, he joined an Indian delegation that met George Washington. He rejected Christianity, however, and in 1805 he explained why to a group of missionaries, whom he addresses as "Brother."

Brother: Continue to listen. You say that you are sent to instruct us how to worship the Great Spirit agreeably to his mind; and, if we do not take hold of the religion which you white people teach, we shall be unhappy hereafter. You say that you are right, and we are lost. How do we know this to be true? We understand that your religion is written in a book. If it was intended for us as well as you, why has not the Great Spirit given to us, and not only to us, but why did He not give to our forefathers, the knowledge of the book, with the means of understanding it rightly?

Brother: The Great Spirit has made us all, but he has made a great difference between his white and red children. He has given us different complexions and different customs. To you He has given the arts [i.e., manufacturing]. To these He has not opened our eyes. We know these things to be true. Since He has made a great difference between us in other things, why may we not conclude that He has given us different religion according to our understanding? The Great Spirit does right. He knows what is best for his children; we are satisfied.

Source: David J. Rothman and Sheila Rothman, eds., *Sources of the American Social Tradition* (New York: Basic Books, 1975).

Attempts at Assimilation. In the name of "civilization," government officials sought to destroy the traditional cultural practices of native Americans. Henry Knox, Washington's first secretary of war, had advocated breaking up commonly owned tribal lands and distributing farming plots to individual Indian families as private property, a concept alien to the Indians, who did not own wealth as individuals but circulated goods to fulfill social obligations. Thomas Jefferson was also an assimilationist, hoping that Americans would "form one people" as Indians would "mix with us by marriage." To this end, white leaders demanded that Indians abandon tribal governments and submit to the authority of the state and the nation. Public officials also encouraged the efforts of missionaries to change the Indians' religious beliefs. The object, as one Kentucky minister put it, was to make the Indian "a farmer, a citizen of the United States, and a Christian."

Many native Americans actively resisted such attempts to redefine their identity. "Born free and independent," an observer noted, Indians were "struck with horror at whatever has the shadow of despotic power." Many tribes drove out white missionaries and forced Christian converts to participate in traditional Indian rites. To justify their ancestral values, native American leaders devised theories of cultural and religious dualism (see American Voices, above). They argued that the Great Spirit had made the two races different; as a

Munsee prophet put it, "there are two ways to God, one for the whites and one for the Indians."

Nevertheless, under pressure from white missionaries, many tribes broke into hostile religious factions. Among the Seneca of New York, for example, the prophet Handsome Lake promoted traditional agricultural ceremonies—the green corn dance, the strawberry festival, and the false-face pageant—that gave ritual thanks to the earth, plants, animals, water, and sun. But Handsome Lake also adopted some Christian precepts, such as belief in heaven and hell, and used them to discourage his followers from drinking alcohol, gambling, and practicing witchcraft. More conservative people among the Seneca clung to the old ways, believed in witchcraft, and resisted the influence of white missionaries.

Strong ancestral values prompted Indians to reject European agricultural methods. Handsome Lake's political enemy, Red Jacket, led the Seneca in opposing innovations such as having men work in the fields. Traditionally, Indian women were responsible for providing much of the food supply—growing corn, squash, beans, and other basic foods—and because of matrilineal customs they often controlled the inheritance of cultivation rights on certain lands. Unlike white farm women, they enjoyed authority over property rights, and among most Eastern Woodland peoples, women's economic importance led to political responsibility. For

example, the Shawnee chose female "war" and "civil" chiefs; the latter could prevent the dispatch of war parties and save captives from being tortured. Consequently, Indian women insisted on retaining their role as cultivators, and few Indian men wished to assume traditional female responsibilities, preferring the roles of hunter and warrior.

Even Christian Indians would not give up their social identity. They viewed themselves not as individuals but as members of a clan, all descendants of the same person. Most clans adopted an animal—a deer, turtle, fox, or bear—as their *totem*, or designation, often because of a vision of their original ancestor. Indians also superimposed new Christian identities onto familiar clan spirits. To accept European views of the individual or the family would be to repudiate clan identity and the essence of Indian life.

The Cherokee. Native Americans assimilated European ways only under special circumstances and for specific purposes. Beginning in the late eighteenth century, the Cherokee of Georgia and the Carolinas organized an unusually centralized political system to resist the advancing white settlers who wanted their lands for growing cotton. A Cherokee national council headed by two respected chiefs oversaw all 13,000 members of the tribe with respect to certain activities—maintaining a mounted police force, abolishing clan revenge for murder, and establishing a limited *patrilineal* inheritance system.

These innovations were implemented by a small faction of Christian Cherokee mixed-bloods. Most mixed-bloods were the offspring of white fur traders and Indian women. Growing up in a bicultural world, they learned the language and political ways of white people. A few were quite prosperous and dressed and behaved like white planters. James Vann, a Georgia Cherokee, owned more than twenty black slaves, two trading posts, and a gristmill. Forty other Cherokee mixed-blood families owned a total of more than 1,000 slaves. When whites attempted to oust the Cherokee from their ancestral land, first in 1806 and again in 1817, the mixed-bloods attempted to forge a strong national identity among their people. Sequoyah, a mixed-blood, developed a system of writing for the Cherokee language, and the tribe published a newspaper. In 1827 the Cherokee introduced a new charter of government modeled directly on the U.S. Constitution.

Mixed-blood Christians were caught between two cultures and accepted by neither. Whites treated them as Indians, to be pushed ever westward, and full-blooded Cherokee condemned their white values. During the 1820s full-bloods seized power in the Great Smoky Mountains and, because of their numbers, gradually took control of the national council, which then resisted both cultural assimilation and forced removal. Like

Divisions among the Cherokee
In 1821 Sequoyah, a mixed-blood, devised a written script for the Cherokee language, and the tribe published a newspaper printed in both English and Cherokee. Few full-blooded Cherokee could read either language; they maintained the traditional oral culture.

most native Americans, the Indians of the Old Southwest wanted to practice their traditional culture on ancestral lands. "We would not receive money for land in which our fathers and friends are buried," a Creek chief declared. "We love our land; it is our mother."

Continental Empire: Spain and the United States

As the United States challenged Indian control of the Old Southwest, Spain reasserted its claims to the lands stretching from Texas to California. Before the 1760s Spain had suffered one setback after another in North America, losing control of the Carolinas and Georgia to British settlers and Louisiana to French fur traders. A further blow came in 1763, at the end of the French and Indian War, when the Spanish monarchy was forced to cede Florida to Britain.

Yet Spain also profited from the peace settlement of 1763. When France ceded Canada to Britain, it withdrew completely from North America, ceding Louisiana to its Spanish ally. Once again Spain held title to all lands west of the Mississippi River (see Map 8.6). Title

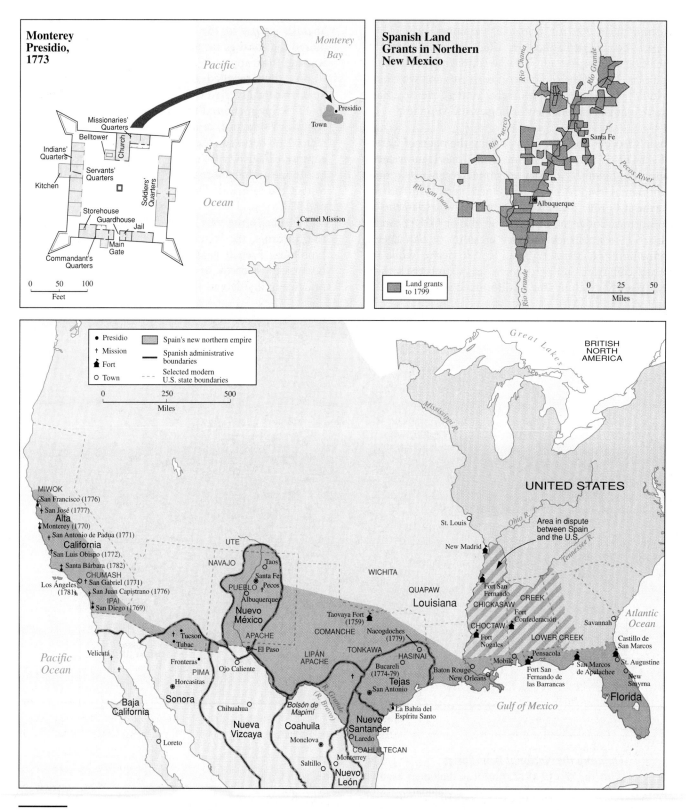

MAP 8.6

New Spain's Northern Empire in the Late Eighteenth Century

Following its acquisition of Louisiana in 1763, Spain tried to create a great northern empire. It established missions and forts in California (such as that at Monterey), expanded Spanish settlements in New Mexico, and by joining in the American War of Independence, reclaimed Florida from Britain. By 1800, this dream had been shattered by Indian uprisings in California and Texas, Napoleon's seizure of Louisiana, and American threats to Florida.

did not mean control. Louisiana remained primarily a French colony, inhabited in 1763 by 4,000 French-speaking whites and 5,000 enslaved blacks, while much of Texas, New Mexico, and southern Arizona was dominated by Apache peoples, who raided the scattered small Spanish settlements for horses and supplies.

Spain's Borderlands Empire. During the reign of Carlos III (1759–1788), a dynamic and American-oriented monarch, Spanish officials attempted to create a grand continental empire by uniting these territories on the northern border of New Spain with new settlements in California. Under the direction of José de Gálvez, Spanish troops established military presidios at San Diego, Santa Barbara, Monterey, and San Francisco while the Franciscan friar Junípero Serra set up missions there and elsewhere along the California coast. To protect

Spanish claims to the region, a naval expedition explored the coast as far north as Alaska, seeking to expel Russian fur trappers.

As they repelled Russian advances in the west, Spanish officials tried to dislodge the British in the east. In 1779 Spain entered the War of Independence on the American side and, in a series of daring campaigns directed by Bernardo de Gálvez (the nephew of José), captured British forts along the Mississippi River and at Mobile and Pensacola. Those victories enabled Spain to win the return of Florida in the Paris peace accords of 1783.

To pacify the vast borderland region from Florida to California, the Spanish devised a new Indian policy. Emulating French practice, Bernardo de Gálvez, who became the viceroy of New Spain in 1785, pursued a practice of divide and rule. His *Instructions of 1786* or-

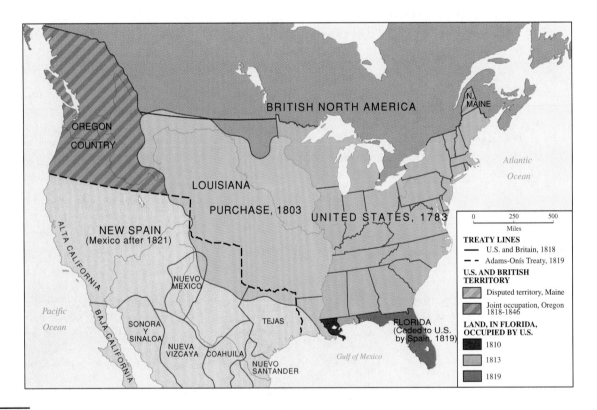

MAP 8.7

Defining the National Boundaries

After the War of 1812, American diplomats negotiated treaties with Great Britain and Spain that defined the boundaries with Canada in the north and New Spain (which in 1821 became the independent nation of Mexico) in the west. These treaties eliminated the threat of war until the 1840s, providing the United States with a much-needed period of peace and security.

dered local commanders to contain or exterminate the warlike Apache, if possible by fomenting disputes between them and other Indian peoples so that they would "destroy one another." More cooperative peoples would be offered treaties and gifts—especially arms and alcohol—to make them dependent on Spanish trade.

These treaties and trade brought peace to New Spain's northern frontier by the late eighteenth century and allowed the movement of Spanish ranchers and farmers from Mexico into Texas, New Mexico, and Arizona. In California, however, Spanish policy led to rebellion as troops raped native women and drafted labor for work at the missions. Also, as the missionaries converted the Indians to Christianity and a more settled life, European diseases cut the native population along the coast nearly in half, from 60,000 in 1769 to 35,000 in 1800.

After only a few decades of restored vigor the Spanish Borderlands Empire came under pressure from the newly independent and highly aggressive American republic. To deter American settlement west of the Appalachians, Spanish authorities restricted American trade on the Mississippi River in 1784 and entered into an alliance with the Creek peoples, who also feared American frontiersmen. But American threats and military setbacks in Europe forced Spain to accept Pinckney's Treaty of 1795, which gave Americans free access to the great river and voided Spanish land claims in the Ohio River Valley and along the Mississippi. To curry favor with Napoleon and prevent further American expansion, Spain ceded Louisiana to France in 1800 and reacted strongly when the Louisiana Purchase undermined this strategy. Spanish diplomats argued that Louisiana was limited to lands along the Mississippi River (the present-day states of Louisiana, Arkansas, and Missouri). In contrast, Thomas Jefferson claimed that the territory extended to the Rio Grande and the Rocky Mountains, which would place all of Texas and half of New Mexico under American control. This issue remained unresolved at the end of the War of 1812, as did the status of West Florida, which had been occupied by American troops during the war. American adventurers also had their eye on East Florida and mounted insurrections against Spanish authorities there (see Map 8.7).

John Quincy Adams and the West. All the disputes between Spain and the United States were resolved by John Quincy Adams. Although he was the son of John Adams, the Federalist president, John Quincy joined the Republican party before the War of 1812. As secretary of state under President Monroe, the younger Adams pursued an expansionist western policy that would have astounded his father. In 1817, when General Andrew Jackson led an expedition into East Florida, seized two Spanish forts, and executed two British subjects, accusing them of encouraging Seminole raids into the United States, Adams defended the general despite strong reservations about his conduct.

Indeed, Adams used the diplomatic crisis created by Jackson's attack to put Spain on the defensive. Threatening to invade Florida, he secured the Adams-Onís Treaty of 1819, in which East Florida was annexed to the United States. In return, the American government accepted responsibility for the financial claims of American citizens against Spain, renounced its dubious claim to Spanish Texas, and agreed on a compromise boundary between New Spain and the Louisiana Territory.

Adams also negotiated important agreements with Great Britain. The Rush-Bagot Treaty of 1817 eliminated a long-standing source of conflict by limiting British and U.S. naval forces on the Great Lakes. More important, in 1818 the two countries agreed to establish the border between the Louisiana Territory and British Canada at the 49th parallel. As a result of Adams's diplomatic efforts, the United States gained undisputed possession of nearly all of the land south of the 49th parallel and between the Great Lakes and the Rocky Mountains.

The Monroe Doctrine. Secretary Adams and President Monroe had this continental empire in mind when they outlined a new foreign policy that, thirty years later, became known as the Monroe Doctrine. In an address to Congress in 1823, Monroe, at Adams's behest, warned Spain and other European powers to stay out of the Western Hemisphere. During and after the Napoleonic Wars, patriots in Mexico and other Spanish colonies had revolted and established independent republics. The United States had extended diplomatic recognition to the new republics, and now Monroe warned Spain not to try to subdue them. The president, hoping to prevent the Russians from extending their fishing camps and fur-trading posts south of Alaska, declared that the American continents were not "subject for further colonization" by the nations of Europe. In return, Monroe reiterated that it was the policy of the United States "not to interfere in the internal concerns" of European nations. Monroe and Adams had turned their backs on Europe. They now looked purposefully westward, envisioning an American empire that would stretch from the Atlantic to the Pacific.

Summary

With the acquisition of Louisiana and white settlement of the trans-Appalachian West, the United States became a continental nation. The pace of white advance was slowed by native Americans fighting to defend their lands, the difficulties of transport and trade across the mountains, and the high price of land sold by both the U.S. government and speculators. Nonetheless, by 1820, 2 million Americans, white and black, were living west of the Appalachians.

Led by Thomas Jefferson, who favored westward expansion, the Republicans wrested political power from the Federalists. While retaining the Bank of the United States and many Federalist bureaucrats, Jefferson eliminated excise taxes, reduced the national debt, cut the size of the army, and lowered the price of national lands in the West. Faced with British and French seizures of American ships and sailors, he devised the Embargo of 1807, but it failed to change the belligerents' policies. Eventually, Indian uprisings and expansionist demands by western Republicans led President Madison into the War of 1812. The war split the nation, prompting a secessionist movement in New England, but a negotiated peace ended the war, and Jackson's victory at New Orleans preserved American honor.

The war strengthened American national identity, but regional customs remained strong. Migrants from New England carried their way of life to the Old Northwest whereas southern planters grew cotton and created a slave-based society in the Old Southwest. Enslaved blacks adopted English and some white religious practices but, along with free blacks in northern cities, also forged a distinct African-American culture. American society was increasingly divided by region and race, creating a sectional confrontation over slavery that the Missouri Compromise of 1820 did not resolve. The Cherokee and other native American peoples in the West sought to preserve their culture and territory from both Christian missionaries and land-hungry settlers from New Spain and the United States. Spanish officials tried to create a vast Borderlands Empire stretching from Florida to California but failed because of Indian resistance, European diplomatic setbacks, and pressure from the expansion-minded American government. The diplomacy of John Quincy Adams led to the annexation of Florida and the settlement of boundaries with British Canada and Spanish Texas.

TIMELINE

1784	Treaty of Fort Stanwix
1787	Northwest Ordinance
1790s	Western (Indian) Confederacy White settlers move into Northwest Territory Cotton production expands Agricultural "improvement" in East Turnpikes and short canals built
1790–1791	Little Turtle defeats American armies
1792	Kentucky joins Union; Tennessee follows (1796)
1794	General Wayne wins Battle of Fallen Timbers
1795	Treaty of Greenville Jay's Treaty Pinckney's Treaty
1800s	Chesapeake blacks adopt Protestant beliefs Handsome Lake revival among Iroquois
1800	Gabriel Prosser's rebellion in Virginia Political "Revolution of 1800"
1801	Judiciary Act passed and repealed Spain restores Louisiana to France
1801–1807	Presidency of Thomas Jefferson Gallatin reduces national debt Naval war with Barbary States Price of federal land reduced
1802–1815	Napoleonic Wars in Europe Seizures of American ships and sailors
1803	Louisiana Purchase
1804–1805	Lewis and Clark expedition Aaron Burr and western secession
1807	Embargo
1808	Tecumseh and Tenskwatawa mobilize Indians Congress bans importation of slaves
1810s	Expansion of slavery into Old Southwest Cherokee resist white advance Decline of Federalist party
1811	War Hawks call for expansion Battle of Tippecanoe
1812	War of 1812
1814	Hartford convention
1815	Andrew Jackson wins Battle of New Orleans Treaty of Ghent ratified
1817	Rush-Bagot Treaty Alabama joins Union; Mississippi follows (1819)
1817–1825	Era of Good Feeling
1819	Adams-Onís Treaty: Florida annexed, and Texas boundary defined
1820	Missouri Compromise
1823	Monroe Doctrine

★   ★   ★

BIBLIOGRAPHY

Gregory Evans Dowd, *A Spirited Resistance: The North American Indian Struggle for Unity, 1745–1815* (1992), offers a fine comparative analysis of the Indian peoples, and Donald R. Wright, *African Americans in the Early Republic, 1789–1831* (1993), provides a good overview. Donald R. Hickey, *The War of 1812: A Forgotten Conflict* (1989), puts the war in an economic and diplomatic context.

Westward Expansion

For studies of white policy toward native Americans see Bernard Sheehan, *Seeds of Extinction: Jeffersonian Philanthropy and the American Indian* (1973); Reginald Horsman, *Expansion and American Indian Policy, 1783–1812* (1967); Dorothy Jones, *License for Empire: Colonialism by Treaty in Early America* (1982); and Richard Slotkin, *Regeneration through Violence: The Mythology of the American Frontier* (1973). Works dealing with the impact of Christian missions on native American culture include Henry Warner Bowden, *American Indians and Christian Missions: Studies in Cultural Conflict* (1981); William W. Fitzhugh, ed., *Cultures in Contact* (1985); William G. McLoughlin, *Cherokees and Missionaries, 1789–1839* (1984); and Earl P. Olmstead, *Blackcoats among the Delaware* (1991). Other analyses of cultural interaction include William G. McLoughlin, *Cherokee Renascence in the New Republic* (1986), and J. Leitch Wright, Jr., *Creeks and Seminoles: The Destruction and Regeneration of the Muscogulge People* (1986).

A fine account of settlers and speculators is Alan Taylor, *Liberty Men and Great Proprietors: The Revolutionary Settlement on the Maine Frontier, 1760–1820* (1990). For developments west of the mountains, see Malcolm J. Rohrbough, *The Transappalachian Frontier: Peoples, Societies, and Institutions, 1775–1850* (1978), and John Mack Faragher, *Sugar Creek: Life on the Illinois Prairie* (1986).

Republican Policy and Diplomacy

Two good general accounts are Marshall Smelser, *The Democratic Republic, 1801–1815* (1968), and Ralph Ketcham, *Presidents above Party: The First American Presidency, 1789–1829* (1984). Detailed studies of Jefferson's presidency include Daniel Sisson, *The Revolution of 1800* (1974); Dumas Malone, *Jefferson the President* (2 vols., 1970 and 1974); Richard E. Ellis, *The Jeffersonian Crisis: Courts and Politics in the New Republic* (1971); and Noel Cunningham, *The Process of Government under Jefferson* (1978). For the Louisiana Purchase, see Alexander DeConde, *This Affair of Louisiana* (1976); Donald Jackson, *The Letters of the Lewis and Clark Expedition* (1963); and James P. Ronda, *Lewis and Clark among the Indians* (1984).

The activities of Aaron Burr are covered in Milton Lomask, *Aaron Burr* (1979), whereas the Federalists are discussed in David Hackett Fischer, *The Revolution of American Conservatism: The Federalist Party in the Age of Jeffersonian Democracy* (1965); Linda K. Kerber, *Federalists in Dissent: Imagery and Ideology in Jeffersonian America* (1970); and James Banner, *To the Hartford Convention: The Federalists and the Origins of Party Politics in the Early Republic, 1789–1815* (1970).

American attempts to avoid involvement in the Napoleonic Wars are traced in Lawrence Kaplan, *"Entangling Alliances with None": American Foreign Policy in the Age of Jefferson* (1987), and Bradford Perkins, *The First Rapprochement: England and the United States, 1795–1805* (1967) and *Prologue to War: England and the United States, 1805–1812* (1961). See also Clifford L. Egan, *Neither Peace nor War: Franco-American Relations, 1803–1812* (1983), and Doron S. Ben-Atar, *The Origins of Jeffersonian Commercial Policy and Diplomacy* (1993). On Madison, see Robert A. Rutland, *The Presidency of James Madison* (1990); J. C. A. Stagg, *Mr. Madison's War: Politics, Diplomacy, and Warfare in the Early Republic, 1783–1830* (1983); and Drew McCoy, *The Last of the Fathers: James Madison and the Republican Legacy* (1989). Native American involvement in the war is discussed in R. David Edmunds, *The Shawnee Prophet* (1983) and *Tecumseh and the Quest for Indian Leadership* (1984), as well as H. S. Halbert and T. H. Ball, *The Creek War of 1813 and 1814* (1970).

Regional Diversity and National Identity

For life in the northern seaboard states, see Benjamin W. Labaree, *The Merchants of Newburyport, 1764–1815* (1962), and Sean Wilentz, *Chants Democratic: New York City and the Rise of the American Working Class, 1788–1850* (1984). The essays in R. A. Burchell, ed., *The End of Anglo-America* (1991), document various shifts in cultural identity.

F. S. Philbrick, *The Rise of the West, 1754–1830* (1964), provides an overview of life in the Old Northwest; a more sophisticated analysis is Andrew R. L. Cayton and Peter S. Onuf, *The Midwest and the Nation* (1990). More detailed studies include Richard C. Wade, *The Urban Frontier: The Rise of Western Cities, 1790–1840* (1973), and Andrew Cayton, *The Frontier Republic: Ideology and Politics in the Ohio Country, 1789–1812* (1986).

Peter Kolchin, *American Slavery, 1619–1877* (1993), provides a fine overview. On the expansion of slavery, see Ira Berlin and Ronald Hoffman, eds., *Slavery and Freedom in the Age of the American Revolution* (1983); Donald L. Robinson, *Slavery in the Structure of American Politics, 1765–1820* (1971); and Albert Raboteau, *Slave Religion* (1968). Also see Ira Berlin and Philip D. Morgan, eds., *Cultivation and Culture: Labor and the Shaping of Slave Life* (1993), and Dena J. Epstein, *Sinful Tunes and Spirituals: Black Folk Music to the Civil War* (1977). Two good studies of the Carolina region are Joyce E. Chaplin, *Agricultural Innovation and Modernity in the Lower South, 1730–1815* (1993), and Peter A. Coclanis, *The Shadow of a Dream: Economic Life and Death in the South Carolina Low Country, 1670–1920* (1988).

For blacks in the northern states, see Gary B. Nash, *Forging Freedom: Philadelphia's Black Community, 1720–1840* (1988). Glover Moore, *The Missouri Compromise* (1953), provides a detailed analysis of that crisis. See also Merton L. Dillon, *Slavery Attacked: Southern Slaves and their Allies, 1619–1865* (1990).

Spain's quest for empire is covered in David Weber, *The Spanish Frontier in North America* (1992), whereas American initiatives are the subject of Walter LaFeber, ed., *John Quincy Adams and American Continental Empire* (1965), and Ernest May, *The Making of the Monroe Doctrine* (1976).

Launching of Fame, *Essex, Massachusetts, 1802* (detail)

The work of twenty shipwrights in Becket's yard, *Fame* was
destined for the East India trade, carrying American goods
and furs to China and returning with ceramics and tea.

CHAPTER 9

Toward a Capitalist Protestant Republic

1790–1820

★   ★   ★

On the fiftieth anniversary of the founding of the United States white Americans had cause for celebration. They lived free of an arbitrary government that imposed high taxes and an established church that enforced rigid dogma. They also had cause for mourning. On July 4, 1826, within a few hours of each other, John Adams and Thomas Jefferson died. The deaths of two former presidents on Independence Day seemed to many Americans to be a sign that God looked with favor on their experiment in self-government. Two of the greatest Founders had died, but the republic lived on.

Indeed, the years between 1790 and 1820 marked the maturation of the republican economic and social order begun during the American Revolution. That society had a number of distinct characteristics. First, it boasted a new system of political economy intended to enhance the welfare of the American people by increasing the "common-wealth." To that end, state legislatures embarked on ambitious programs of economic development, investing public resources in some projects and encouraging private investors to sponsor others. For the first but not the last time in American history, the state became an active force in economic life. Governmental initiatives pushed forward an already dynamic economy. In 1820 nearly 10 percent of the population resided in cities or small towns, and more people were sending crops and manufactured products into the market, expanding the commercial sector of the agricultural system.

A second prominent feature of the new society was its increasingly republican culture. Beginning in 1776, leading Americans developed a political system based on the republican principle of "ordered liberty" and gradually expanded suffrage to include most adult white men. They also applied republican ideals to reorganize traditional social institutions such as families and schools and reevaluated customary rights and du-

ties. As a result, many individuals—women as well as men—gained more freedom to choose their marriage partners and social values.

Third, Americans reassessed women's place in the social order. Even as political and religious leaders advocated a separate sphere of domestic concerns, white women assumed a public role in American life by joining the Second Great Awakening and organizing new religious associations. Together with evangelical preachers and male laymen, they pushed forward a continuous wave of religious revivals that made Protestant Christianity one of the defining features of the national character of the United States.

This new capitalist, republican, Protestant society had its flaws, but for the white population it balanced private freedom with public responsibility. Reflecting the patriotism and self-confidence of the age, its proponents hailed the new social order as a model for all peoples. "The temperate zone of North America," a Kentucky judge declared in a Fourth of July speech, "already exhibits many signs that it is the promised land of civil liberty, and of institutions designed to liberate and exalt the human race."

Political Economy: The Capitalist Commonwealth

The nation that declared its independence in 1776 was overwhelmingly agrarian and dependent on Great Britain for markets, credit, and manufactured goods. Over the next fifty years the United States achieved a measure of economic independence, as rural Americans became manufacturers, bankers supplied credit to expand industry and trade, merchants developed regional market economies, and state governments took an active role in encouraging economic development. This emerging economy was capitalist not only because it was based on private property and market exchanges but also because capitalists—moneyed men—shaped its political and economic policies. Yet the new economy was also shaped by the ideology of the republican commonwealth and therefore was governed in part by policies that emphasized the common good.

A Capitalist Society

American Merchants. Merchants had dominated the economic life of port cities in colonial times, and with the departure of the British they began to set the social and cultural tone as well. "It is a Nation of Merchants," a British visitor reported from Philadelphia in 1798, "always alive to their interests; and keen in the pursuit of wealth in all the various modes of acquiring it."

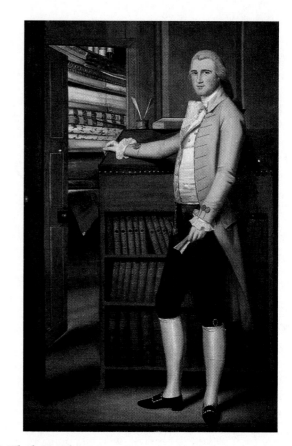

A Cloth Merchant
Elijah Boardman and other American merchants annually imported millions of yards of cloth from Britain. When war cut off trade, some merchants financed the domestic production of textiles, first in rural households and then in factories.

After the economic contraction that followed independence, European wars from 1792 to 1815 brought rising profits to established merchant houses and fortunes to daring entrepreneurs. Among the many success stories were those of two immigrants, Robert Oliver and John Jacob Astor, who prospered phenomenally. Oliver arrived in Baltimore in 1783 as the American agent for Irish merchants who sold linens in the United States and foodstuffs in the West Indies. Two years later he began his own business—a mercantile partnership—and watched his investment of £2,000 grow slowly to £3,300 during the recession of the 1780s. Then, during the wartime shipping boom, his firm's assets soared to £110,000. Caught up in a restless pursuit of wealth, Oliver began to trade on his own, reaping enormous profits from the West Indian coffee trade and speculating in gold and silver from Spanish America. By 1807 he was a millionaire.

John Jacob Astor, who migrated from Germany to New York City in 1784, became wealthy by exploiting the fur trade in the Pacific Northwest. Soon Astor emerged as the leading New York merchant trading

with China. Investing his profits in real estate, he became the largest landowner in the rapidly growing port of New York. Astor's success was unusual only in its extent; the wartime commercial boom brought prosperity to the mercantile elite in all the seacoast cities and fostered the emergence of a distinct "business class" (see Chapter 10).

Banking and Credit. To finance the expansion of mercantile enterprise, Americans had to devise an entirely new banking system. Before 1776 the colonists had found it difficult to secure loans. Farmers had relied on government-sponsored land banks, pledging their land as security, while merchants such as Oliver arranged partnerships, borrowed funds from other merchants, or relied on British suppliers to extend credit. Then, in 1781, several Philadelphia merchants, Robert Morris among them, persuaded the Confederation Congress to charter the Bank of North America to provide short-term commercial loans. Traders in Boston and New York founded similar banks in 1784. These institutions provided merchants with the credit they needed to finance their transactions. "Our monied capital has so much increased from the Introduction of Banks, & the Circulation of the Funds," the Philadelphia merchant William Bingham noted as early as 1791, "that the Necessity of Soliciting Credits from England will no longer exist, & the Means will be provided for putting in Motion every Specie of Industry."

In 1791 Congress chartered the Bank of the United States as part of Alexander Hamilton's plan to centralize the expanding American financial system. The bank had the power to issue notes and make commercial loans, and by threatening to demand payment in specie, it restrained state banks from issuing too many notes. Although the bank's managers used their lending powers cautiously, limiting loans to three times the value of the bank's holdings in gold and silver, profits still averaged a handsome 8 percent annually. By 1805, in response to the continuing demand for commercial credit, the managers had set up branches in eight major cities.

Nonetheless, for political reasons, the First Bank of the United States did not survive. Jeffersonians had long condemned a national bank, warning that it would produce "a consolidated, energetic government supported by public creditors, speculators, and other insidious men lacking in public spirit of any kind." Consequently, when the bank's twenty-year charter expired in 1811, President Madison did not seek its renewal, forcing merchants, artisans, and farmers to turn to state legislatures to support banking. New York chartered the Mechanics' and Farmers' Bank of Albany in 1811, and other states followed suit. By the time Madison chartered the Second Bank of the United States in 1816, also for twenty years, there were 246 state-chartered banks. Unfortunately, many state banks issued notes without

adequate reserves of specie, causing the notes to fall in value and inhibiting commercial growth.

Poorly managed state banks were one cause of the Panic of 1819, a credit crisis sparked by a sharp drop in world agricultural prices. Their income suddenly cut by a third, many American farmers were unable to pay their creditors, setting in motion the successive bankruptcies of local storekeepers, wholesale merchants, and scores of overextended state banks. Economic recession continued for two years as many Americans got their first taste of the "business cycle" of a capitalist market. Nonetheless, the American economy had entered a new phase. With the rapid emergence of the banking system, the United States was no longer completely dependent on British credit. The new nation had its own financial institutions that promoted foreign trade and domestic development.

Rural Manufacturing. Since colonial times American artisans had handcrafted furniture, tools, wagons, shoes, saddles, clothing, and dozens of other items. Especially in New England and the Middle Atlantic states, many artisans enjoyed a modest but comfortable life from their labor, selling or exchanging their goods mostly within the local community. For example, during the 1780s John Hoff of Lancaster, Pennsylvania, sold his fine wooden-cased clocks locally or bartered them with his neighbors for such things as a dining table, a bedstead, shoes, pine boards, and labor on his small farm.

Some artisans—especially those who worked in large, specialized groups—had their eyes on more distant markets. Shipbuilders in seacoast towns, iron smelters in Pennsylvania and Maryland, and shoemakers in Lynn, Massachusetts, all sold their products to customers outside their regions. During the Revolutionary War merchants financed the expansion of various enterprises, encouraging rural men and women to make cheese, textiles, paper, and gunpowder. After the war national pride prompted calls for the expansion of *all* domestic handicrafts. "Until we manufacture more," the Boston *Gazette* declared in 1788, "it is absurd to celebrate the Fourth of July as the birthday of our independence."

With peace restored, many merchants ignored pleas to invest in domestic manufacturing; it was more profitable to sell low-priced British goods. Still, some entrepreneurs continued to develop wider markets for American rural manufactures. For instance, merchants sold goods made on Massachusetts farms not only in Boston but also in the other seaport towns of New England. As a Polish traveler in central Massachusetts reported in 1798, "Along the whole road from Boston, we saw women engaged in making cheese."

Some inland merchants were not content with marketing farm-produced goods and handicrafts and devel-

American Country Furniture
Country artisans, such as the unknown maker of this high chest of drawers from Norwich, Vermont (circa 1780), simplified high-style English designs. Using common woods, such as birch and pine, these rural manufacturers built furniture that was both useful and elegant. (Shelburne Museum)

oped their own version of the European *outwork* or *putting-out* system (see Chapter 1, page 31). These capitalist entrepreneurs actively recruited and organized households in rural communities to manufacture specific goods. The experience of Berlin, New Hampshire, was typical. For many years Berlin artisans had made tinware—baking pans, cups, eating utensils, lanterns—and carried it to local farmers with "a horse and two baskets." After the Revolutionary War, merchants in Berlin paid artisans to increase their output and hired young men, whom they furnished "with a horse and a cart covered with a box or with a wagon," to market the tinware in the South, a market long dominated by British imports. Soon these traders blanketed areas of the South, acquiring the dubious reputation of crafty, hard-bargaining "Yankees." Their commercial success extended the size of the capitalist sector of the American domestic economy.

The greatest success of the putting-out system occurred in the shoe and boot trade, which also found markets in the South, especially on slave plantations. In the 1780s merchants and master craftsmen in Lynn, Massachusetts, began buying large quantities of leather, thread, and awls and soon put thousands of families in the New England countryside to work. Farm women and children stitched together the thin leather and canvas uppers of the shoes, and the half-finished shoes were taken by wagon to Lynn for assembly by journeymen shoemakers. When the Embargo of 1807 cut off competition from British-made shoes, merchants in Lynn and over thirty other Massachusetts towns expanded their output and produced millions of shoes. By the 1820s these entrepreneurs had mobilized an enormous work force in the New England countryside and had begun to create a *national* market.

Their success stemmed primarily from innovations in organization and marketing, not in technology. Even as their markets expanded, tinworkers, shoemakers, and other artisans continued to use their traditional *preindustrial* handcraft technology. The use of power-driven machines—the product of the Industrial Revolution in Britain—came slowly to America, beginning with the textile industry. In the 1780s merchants built hundreds of small mills along the creeks and rivers of New England and the Middle Atlantic states. They installed water-powered machines and hired workers to card and comb wool—and later cotton—into long strands. For several decades the next steps in the manufacturing process were accomplished under the outwork system. Farm women and children spun the strands into yarn, receiving wages for their work, while men, usually in other households, wove the yarn into cloth. In his *Letter on Manufactures* (1810), Secretary of the Treasury Albert Gallatin reported that there were about 2,500 outwork weavers in New England. A decade later more than 12,000 household workers in that region were weaving woolen cloth, which was then taken to water-powered fulling mills, where it was pounded flat and given a smooth finish. Thus, even before textile production was centralized in factories, the nation had a profitable and expanding outwork system of manufacturing.

From a Market Economy to a Capitalist Economy. With these advances in rural manufacturing, the United States took yet another step toward a capitalist economy. At the center of this developing system stood a dynamic group of merchant-entrepreneurs who organized production; at the periphery were hundreds of thousands of farm families who supplied the labor. When a French traveler visited central Massachusetts in 1795, he found "almost all these houses . . . inhabited by men who are both cultivators and artisans; one is a tanner, another a shoemaker, another sells goods, but all are farmers." As these families made cheese, yarn, shoes, nails, and dozens of other products for market sale, they looked for better ways of making goods and then patented their inventions. The American countryside emerged as a center not only of production but also of invention and technical change.

Indeed, the rise of rural manufacturing transformed the local agricultural economy. To supply merchants and artisans with raw materials, ambitious farm families switched from mixed-crop agriculture to raising livestock. The shoe business consumed thousands of beef hides each year, the new cheese industry required large herds of dairy cows, and textile producers purchased the wool from tens of thousands of sheep. High prices for these raw materials brought prosperity and new businesses to many farming towns. In 1792 Concord, Massachusetts, had one slaughterhouse and five small tanneries; a decade later there were eleven slaughterhouses and six large tanneries in the town. Foul odors from the stockyards and tanning pits drifted over Concord, but its people were able to purchase more goods.

The emergence of a full-fledged cash-based market economy took decades, as the experience of the book-manufacturing firm of Ebenezer and Daniel Merriam of Brookfield, Massachusetts, demonstrates. When the Merriams began selling books to publishing houses in New York City, Philadelphia, and Boston during the 1810s, they received neither cash nor credit in return but other *books*—which they had to barter with local storekeepers to get supplies for their business. The Merriams paid their own workers on a barter basis as well; a journeyman printer received the use of a small house, credits to his accounts at local stores, and no less than one-third of his "wages" in books, which he had to peddle for himself if he wanted more than a literary profit from his labors.

Yet gradually a cash economy replaced this complex barter-exchange system. As farm families joined the outwork system, they stopped producing all their own food and making their own clothing and bedding. Instead of bartering their surplus crops for household necessities, they supplied merchants with specialized goods in return for cash or store credit. "Straw hats and Bonnets are manufactured by many families," a Maine official commented in the Census of Manufacturing of 1820, while another observer noted that "probably 8,000 females" in the vicinity of Foxborough, Massachusetts, braided rye straw into hats for market sale. These women used the income from the sale of their labor to shop in local stores.

The new capitalist-run market economy had its drawbacks. Rural parents—and their children—worked longer and harder, making shoes or hats or cloth during the winter as well as planting, weeding, and harvesting crops during the warmer seasons. Perhaps more important, they lost some of their economic independence. Instead of working completely for themselves as yeomen farm families, they toiled as part-time wage laborers for merchants and manufacturers. Thus the new market system decreased the self-sufficiency of both individual families and whole communities even as it made them more productive.

Increased output boosted the income of farm families and the collective wealth of the United States. Beginning around 1800, the per capita income of Americans increased at a rate of more than 1 percent per year—more than 30 percent in each generation. By the 1820s the extraordinary increase in output, artisan skills, and merchant capital had laid the foundation for the American Industrial Revolution (see Chapter 10). After a half century of political independence, the nation was beginning to achieve economic independence from Britain.

State Mercantilism: The "Commonwealth" System

Throughout the nineteenth century state governments were the most important political institutions in the United States. State legislatures took the lead in regulating social life, for example, abolishing slavery in the North and retaining it in the South. State governments enacted laws governing criminal and civil affairs, set voting requirements, established the taxation system, and oversaw county, city, and town officials. Beginning in the late 1810s, many states rewrote their constitutions in order to make them more democratic, decreasing property requirements for voting, reapportioning legislatures, and increasing the number of elected (rather than appointed) officials. Consequently, state governments—particularly state legislatures—had a much greater impact on the day-to-day lives of Americans than did the national government.

Beginning in the 1790s, many state legislatures sought to enhance prosperity by devising a new, American system of mercantilism known as the "commonwealth" system. Just as the British Parliament had promoted the imperial economy by passing Acts of Trade, state legislatures enacted measures to stimulate commerce and economic development in America. In particular, state governments granted hundreds of *corporate charters* to private businesses that were intended to be, as the act establishing the Massachusetts Bank put it, "of great public utility." Chartered companies were not new, of course—English investors had used them to establish the first American colonies. Under English law, however, colonial governments were discouraged from creating corporations, so merchants had financed mills, shipyards, and trading ventures through private partnerships, which lacked the legal and economic advantages of government-chartered corporations.

Private partnerships also lacked the funds required to build the large-scale transportation projects—the economic infrastructure—that had become a high priority for many state governments. State legislatures therefore issued numerous charters of incorporation to promote investment in roads, bridges, and canals. For example, after receiving a monopoly charter from the

Pennsylvania assembly, the Lancaster Turnpike Company opened a graded gravel road between Lancaster and Philadelphia in 1794. Its success set off a boom in turnpike construction. Soon improved roads connected dozens of inland market centers to seaport cities, but it would take a generation to build an integrated system of all-weather roads.

By 1800 state governments had granted more than 300 corporate charters. Legal incorporation enhanced the status of private companies in two ways. First, some charters protected investors through *limited liability*: in the event of business failure, the shareholders' personal assets could not be used to pay the debts of the corporation. Second, most transportation charters included the power of *eminent domain*, a legal provision that allowed turnpike, bridge, and canal corporations to force the sale of land along their routes. This power—previously available only to the government—permitted private corporations to take lands from property owners for a reasonable price even if the owners did not want to sell. By infringing on private property rights, eminent domain promoted economic development for the good of the commonwealth.

Such uses of state power by private companies were controversial and, in the eyes of some critics, contrary to republicanism, "which does not admit of granting peculiar privileges to any body of men." Charters not only violated the "equal rights" of all citizens, opponents argued, but also infringed on the sovereignty of the state. As a Pennsylvanian put it, "whatever power is given to a corporation, is just so much power taken from the State, in derogation of the original power of the mass of the community."

Nonetheless, state courts consistently upheld the validity of corporate charters. Judges routinely approved grants of eminent domain to private corporations even when they infringed on the property rights of citizens, arguing that economic development was in the public interest. "The opening of good and easy internal communications is one of the highest duties of government," a New Jersey court declared.

State mercantilism soon encompassed much more than transportation. After the Embargo of 1807, which cut off goods and credit from Europe, the New England state governments awarded charters to 200 iron-mining, textile-manufacturing, and banking firms. Over the next few decades the Pennsylvania legislature was even more active, chartering more than 1,100 corporations and authorizing them to hold over $150 million in capital. Corporations—in the form of incorporated towns and cities, incorporated charitable institutions, and chartered private business organizations—were becoming a central institution in American society. As one contemporary put it, "the whole political system" was "made up of concatenations of various corporations, political, civil, religious, social and economical."

Thus, by 1820, the innovative policies of the state governments had created a new political economy: the commonwealth system. This system elevated the good of the public—the common-wealth—above that of private individuals, but because it used private corporations for public purposes, it also enhanced the economic and political power of capitalist entrepreneurs. This instrumental use of state legislation to improve the general welfare would continue for another generation. In 1820 Missouri lawmakers incorporated this outlook into that state's first constitution, specifying that "internal improvements shall forever be encouraged by the government of this state."

Law and the "Commonwealth": Republicans versus Federalists

Both Federalists and Republicans endorsed commonwealth ideology, but in different ways. Federalists looked to the national government for economic leadership. Most Federalists supported Hamilton's program of *national* mercantilism, in which the central government encouraged economic development through tariff and banking policies. Jeffersonian Republicans generally opposed such schemes, relying instead on the state legislatures. After the War of 1812, however, some Republicans, led by Henry Clay of Kentucky, began to support national economic initiatives. As Speaker of the House of Representatives, Clay supported the creation of the Second Bank of the United States in 1816. The following year he won passage of the Bonus Bill, sponsored by Representative John C. Calhoun of South Carolina, which would have established a national fund for roads and other internal improvements. But most Republicans still opposed national mercantilist policies; they agreed with President Madison, who vetoed the Bonus Bill because he felt it exceeded the powers delegated to the national government by the Constitution. This fundamental disagreement over the role of the national government would become a major issue of political debate for the next thirty years (see Chapter 11).

Common Law and Statute Law. Differing conceptions of law also separated Federalists and Republicans. From the earliest colonial times American jurisprudence had been shaped by English common law. In deciding cases, judges relied on *precedents*—decisions in similar earlier cases—and they assumed, as a Maryland lawyer put it, that "the Common Law takes in the Law of Nature, the Law of Reason and the Revealed Law of God." In this view, held by many Federalists, law was a venerable and unchanging entity.

The revolutionary republican doctrine of popular sovereignty undermined the intellectual foundations of this old legal order. As Americans debated constitu-

tional principles, many of them recognized that law was a human invention—the product of politics—and not a sacred body of timeless truths. In fact, during the 1790s Thomas Jefferson and other leaders of the Republican party directly attacked the common-law system. They maintained that law made by judges following common-law precedents was inferior to the statute ("positive") law enacted by the representatives of the people. As a Republican jurist put it, a magistrate "should be governed himself by *positive* law, and executes and enforces the will of the supreme power, which is the will of THE PEOPLE."

Federalist judges and politicians warned that popular sovereignty had to be curbed. Without safeguards, Federalists feared, representative government would result in the "tyranny of the majority"—the passage of statutes that would infringe on the existing property rights of individual citizens. To keep property rights from being overridden by state legislatures, Federalist lawyers asserted that judges had the power to void laws that violated traditional common-law principles or were contrary to "natural law" or "natural rights" (see Chapter 4).

Common Law versus Economic Development. Because common-law precedents had evolved in a relatively static agricultural economy, they often discouraged new modes of enterprise, such as manufacturing. For example, capitalist entrepreneurs who erected dams to operate flour or textile mills often flooded adjacent farmlands; outraged farmers sued, arguing that the dams not only infringed on their property rights but also were a "nuisance" to the public and should be pulled down. At first the farmers won most of these cases. In 1795, for example, a New Jersey court used common-law precedents in ruling that it was illegal to interfere with the natural flow of a river for nonfarming purposes "without the consent of all who have an interest in it."

Such decisions threatened to stifle economic development. Consequently, republican-minded state legislatures enacted statutes that overrode the common law by limiting the legal recourse available to landowners. In Massachusetts, the Mill Dam Act of 1795 allowed mill proprietors to flood adjacent farmlands and prevented farmers from blocking the construction of dams or seeking damages, forcing them to accept "fair compensation" for their lost acreage. This prodevelopment legislation justified the taking of private property by asserting the superior rights of individuals who made a dynamic, rather than a static, use of their property.

State judges with Republican leanings accepted the doctrines of popular sovereignty and legislative power and therefore usually upheld mill acts, just as they supported legislative statutes that granted eminent domain to private turnpike and canal corporations. To these

judges, *social utility*—the greatest good for the greatest number—justified the government's intrusion into the property rights of individual citizens. Such rulings shocked Daniel Webster, the great Federalist lawyer and politician, who considered them no less than a "revolution against the foundations on which property rests." Both parties favored economic development, but they prescribed different political and legal paths to that goal. Federalists favored national mercantilism, common law, and a static theory of property rights; Republicans advocated state activism, statute law, and a dynamic concept of property.

Federalist Law: John Marshall

Upon becoming president in 1801, Thomas Jefferson warned that his Federalist opponents were retreating into the judiciary, and from that fortress "all the works of Republicanism are to be beaten down and erased." The legal career of John Marshall confirmed Jefferson's prediction. Appointed chief justice of the Supreme Court by John Adams in 1801, Marshall upheld Federalist principles until his death in 1835. His success stemmed not from a mastery of legal principles and doctrines—indeed, his opinions usually cited very few precedents—but from the power of his logic and the

Chief Justice John Marshall
Marshall had a commanding personal presence and made over the United States Supreme Court in his image, elevating it from a minor department into a major institution in American legal and political life.

force of his personality. Until 1821 Marshall dominated his colleagues on the Supreme Court, and they largely accepted his definition of its powers and interpretation of the law.

Three principles shaped Marshall's Federalist jurisprudence: a commitment to judicial power, the supremacy of national over state legislation, and a traditional, static view of property rights.

Judicial Power: *Marbury v. Madison*. The celebrated case of *Marbury v. Madison* (1803) demonstrated Marshall's commitment to the preeminent authority of the judiciary. The case arose from the controversial "midnight" appointments of President John Adams in 1801 (see Chapter 8). As Jefferson's secretary of state, James Madison had refused to deliver a commission appointing William Marbury as a justice of the peace. When Marbury asked the Supreme Court to intervene by issuing a legal writ directing his appointment, Marshall ruled that while Marbury had a right to his commission, that right was not enforceable by the Court. This was so, Marshall declared, because the section of the Judiciary Act of 1789 that gave the Supreme Court the power to issue writs in such cases was unconstitutional. Marshall's decision was politically astute, condemning Madison's actions while avoiding a direct confrontation with the Republican administration.

More important, this decision marked the first time the Supreme Court had overturned a national law. Five years earlier, during the dispute over the Alien and Sedition Acts, the Republican-dominated Kentucky and Virginia legislatures had asserted the authority of state legislatures to determine the constitutionality of national laws. But the Constitution implied that the Supreme Court had this power of *judicial review*, and now Marshall claimed it explicitly: "It is emphatically the province and duty of the judicial department to say what the law is." The doctrine of judicial review evolved slowly. During the first half of the nineteenth century the Supreme Court and the state courts used it to overturn *state* laws that conflicted with constitutional principles, but not until the *Dred Scott* decision of 1857 would the Supreme Court void another national law. After the Civil War, however, the Court frequently invoked judicial review to overturn Congressional as well as state legislation.

Nationalism: *McCulloch v. Maryland*. Marshall's nationalism was most eloquently expressed in the controversial case of *McCulloch v. Maryland* (1819). When Congress created the Second Bank of the United States in 1816, the bank was given the authority to handle the notes of the state banks, a power that it used to monitor their financial reserves and create a national system of credit.

Many state governments resented the dominant position of the new national bank. The Maryland legislature imposed an annual tax of $15,000 on notes issued by the Baltimore branch of the Second Bank and, to preserve the independence and competitive position of its own state-chartered banks, limited the Second Bank's powers. The national bank contested the constitutionality of Maryland's action, claiming that it infringed on the powers of the national government. In response, lawyers for the state of Maryland adopted Jefferson's argument against the First Bank of the United States, maintaining that Congress lacked the constitutional authority to charter a national bank. Even if such a bank could be created, the lawyers argued, Maryland had a right to tax its activities within the state.

Marshall firmly rejected both arguments. He declared that the Second Bank was constitutional because its existence was "necessary and proper," given the national responsibility to control currency and credit. Like Alexander Hamilton and other Federalists, Marshall preferred a loose construction of the Constitution: "Let the end be legitimate, let it be within the scope of the Constitution and all means which are appropriate, which [are consistent] . . . with the letter and the spirit of the constitution, are constitutional."

As for Maryland's right to tax all institutions within its borders, the chief justice embraced the nationalist position advanced by Daniel Webster, a fellow Federalist and legal counsel to the Second Bank. "The power to tax involves the power to destroy," Marshall observed, suggesting that Maryland's tax would render the national government "dependent on the states"—a situation that "was not intended by the American people" when their representatives ratified the Constitution. With this decision, Marshall asserted the dominance of national statutes over state legislation and, by outlining a broad interpretation of the Constitution, laid the legal foundation for the subsequent expansion of national authority.

Two years later Marshall declared the supremacy of national courts of law over state tribunals. In the case of *Cohens v. Virginia* (1821) he proclaimed that the Constitution had diminished the sovereignty of the states. State courts did not have the last say on issues that fell within the purview of the national Constitution, and their decisions could be appealed to the federal judiciary.

Property Rights: *Fletcher v. Peck*. Marshall found in the national Constitution the basis for legal guarantees that protected property rights against claims by governments and by developers. With respect to governments, Marshall noted that the *contract clause* of the Constitution (Article I, Section 10) prohibits the states from passing any law "impairing the obligation of contracts." The delegates had included this clause primarily

to assist merchants and other creditors by voiding state laws that protected debtors. Marshall, however, used the contract clause to defend other property rights against legislative challenge. For example, the case of *Fletcher v. Peck* (1810) involved a large grant of land made by the Georgia legislature to the Yazoo Land Company. A newly elected state legislature later canceled the grant, alleging that it had been obtained through fraud and bribery, and speculators in other states who had purchased Yazoo lands appealed to the Supreme Court. Speaking for the Court, Marshall ruled that the purchasers had valid contracts whose obligations could not be impaired by the state of Georgia. This decision was far-reaching. It not only gave constitutional protection against subsequent state legislation to those who purchased state-owned lands but also, by upholding the rights of out-of-state speculators, encouraged the development of a national capitalist economy.

The case of *Dartmouth College v. Woodward* (1819) gave property owners even greater protection against state interference. Dartmouth was a private institution established by a charter granted by King George III in 1769. In 1816 the Republican-dominated legislature of New Hampshire tried to convert the college into a public university so that it could educate more students and enhance the common-wealth of the state. The Dartmouth trustees resisted the plan and engaged Daniel Webster to plead their case before the Supreme Court. Webster based his argument squarely on the Court's decision in *Fletcher v. Peck*. The royal charter had bestowed "corporate rights and privileges" on the college, Webster maintained; therefore, the charter constituted a contract and could not be tampered with by the New Hampshire legislature. Dartmouth College was in effect private property.

Marshall had difficulty persuading his colleagues to accept Webster's argument. Although he was still the dominant member of the Court, by 1819 five Supreme Court justices had been appointed by the Republican presidents Jefferson, Madison, and Monroe. Some of those justices favored the commonwealth system and believed that a public university would better serve the common good. Others hesitated to restrict the powers of the state legislatures or endorse the broad legal protection of property rights set forth in *Fletcher v. Peck*. Only after months of deliberation—and the preparation of a precedent-filled decision by Associate Justice Joseph Story, a New England jurist with strong Federalist leanings—did the justices follow Marshall and rule in favor of the college. *Dartmouth v. Woodward* not only endorsed a static, or "vested," conception of property rights (repudiating the dynamic, commonwealth-oriented view of the New Hampshire legislature) but extended those rights from individuals to business corporations. Thereafter, corporations would claim that their state-granted charters were "contracts" that protected them—forever—from regulation or control by the governments that had created them.

Marshall's triumph seemed complete. In the decisions handed down between 1819 and 1821—*Dartmouth, McCulloch,* and *Cohens*—he had incorporated Federalist principles into the law of the land, championing judicial review, nationalism, and a static conception of property rights. Many of Marshall's legal principles, such as judicial review and corporate rights, became central fixtures of the American legal order. But even before the chief justice's death in 1835, states' rights–minded jurists qualified his nationalist vision, and republican-minded state legislators used commonwealth ideology to justify the taking of private property for public purposes. Yet this legal conflict was primarily over means, not ends. Both Marshall and his Republican opponents strongly supported the private ownership of property and the expansion of a market economy. Together they laid the legal and political foundations for the American Industrial Revolution (see Chapter 10).

Visions of a Republican Social Order

After independence, Americans tried to become "republicans" in their political outlook, social behavior, and cultural values. American men applied the doctrines of legal equality and social mobility to gain the right to vote and improve their social status. Some young people sought more egalitarian marriages and more affectionate ways of raising and educating their children. Many more members of the rising generation condemned the aristocratic pretensions of old-style political leaders and the cold formality of conservative lawyers and judges. The pursuit of republican ideals was complex and conflict-ridden, but it gradually changed the character of American society.

Mobility and Democracy for Men

Between 1780 and 1820 hundreds of well-educated Europeans visited the United States to acquire firsthand knowledge of life in a republican society. These visitors came from countries characterized by political hierarchy, religious orthodoxy, patriarchal families, and profound social inequality. They wondered—as successive generations of historians have wondered—whether America represented a more just social order. The French-born essayist Crèvecoeur had no doubts. Com-

A Country Tavern
The stylishly dressed dancers command the attention of the onlookers, but the scene suggests the social cohesion and equality in rural communities and the spontaneous character of leisure-time activities.

paring the Old World and the New in his famous *Letters from an American Farmer* (1782), Crèvecoeur wrote that European society was composed "of great lords who possess everything, and of a herd of people who have nothing." In America, by contrast, there "are no aristocratical families, no courts, no kings, no bishops." Reflecting these conditions, many Americans maintained—as a letter to a newspaper put it—that people should be valued not for their "wealth, titles, or connections" but for their "talents, integrity, and virtue."

Social Mobility. To many Europeans, America was distinctive in regard to the availability of economic opportunity—it was the "best poor man's country," at least for whites. As an Englishman explained, "A consciousness of independence forms the character of the American because the means of subsistence being so easy in this country, and their dependence on each other consequently so trifling, the spirit of servility to those above them so prevalent in European manners is wholly unknown to them" (see American Voices, page 275).

Republican ideology emphasized legal equality for all free men and thus further undermined traditional hierarchical authority. "The law is the same for everyone both as it protects and as it punishes," one European noted. "In the course of daily life everyone is on the most perfect footing of equality." Foreign visitors were well aware that class divisions existed in the United States but saw them as different from those in Europe. The American colonies had never had—and the republican state and national constitutions had in fact prohibited—a legally defined, privileged nobility. The absence of an aristocracy of birth encouraged enterprising American men to seek upward social mobility and jus-

tify class divisions based on achievement. "In Europe to say of someone that he rose from nothing is a disgrace and a reproach," an aristocratic Polish visitor explained. "It is the opposite here. To be the architect of your own fortune is honorable. It is the highest recommendation."

Only a few disagreed. American men who owed their position to inherited wealth and social status questioned the moral legitimacy of a social order determined by personal effort or financial success. "The aristocracy of Kingston [New York] is more one of money than any village I have ever seen," complained Nathaniel Booth in 1825. Booth's ancestors had once ruled Kingston but had later lost predominance in the rapidly growing Hudson River town. "Man is estimated by dollars," he lamented; "what he is worth determines his character and his position at once." But Booth spoke for a minority. For most white American men republicanism meant the opportunity to advance their interests and those of their families.

Extending the Franchise. By the 1820s republicanism had also come to mean voting rights for free white men. Political democracy reflected the decline of class as the foundation of citizenship. In repudiating the hierarchical ideal of Federalists such as Samuel Stone, who called for "a *speaking* aristocracy in the face of a *silent* democracy," Americans rejected the "deferential" political practices of the eighteenth century. They refused to vote for Federalist politicians who flaunted their high social status, with their hair in "powder and queues" and their "top boots, breeches, and shoe buckles"; instead, they elected Republican politicians who dressed simply and advocated an extension of the franchise.

Charles W. Janson

Manners in the New Republic

Most European immigrants were from the poorer classes and welcomed the absence of strong class barriers in the United States, but many upper-class visitors took offense at American presumptions of social equality. This account by an English traveler also shows that the dignity felt by some whites came at the expense of blacks.

Let me suppose, like myself, you had fallen in with an American innkeeper who at the moment would condescend to take the trouble to procure you refreshment. . . . He will sit by your side, and enter in the most familiar manner into conversation; which is prefaced, of course, with a demand of your business, and so forth. He will then start a political question (for here every individual is a politician), force you to answer, contradict, deny, and, finally, be ripe for a quarrel, should you not acquiesce in all his opinions. . . .

If you arrive at the dinner hour, you are seated with "mine hostess" and her dirty children, with whom you have often to scramble for a plate. This is esteemed wit, and consequently provokes a laugh, at the expense of those who are paying for the board. . . .

The arrogance of servants in this land of republican liberty and equality is particularly calculated to excite the astonishment of strangers. To call persons of this description servants, or to speak of their master or mistress, is a grievous affront.

Having called one day at the house of a gentleman of my acquaintance, on knocking at the door, it was opened by a servant-maid, whom I had never before seen, as she had not been long in his family. The following is the dialogue, word for word, which took place on this occasion:
"Is your master at home?"
"I have no master."
"Don't you live here?"
"I stay here."
"And who are you then?"
"Why, I am Mr. ——— 's help. I'd have you to know, man, that I am no sarvant. None but negers are sarvants."

Source: C. W. Janson, *The Stranger in America, 1793–1806* (1807), 85–88.

Concurrently, legislators redefined political citizenship on the basis of gender and race, raising the status of middling and poor white men by elevating them above white women and free black men. A number of states, such as Pennsylvania and New York, denied the franchise to free African-Americans or subjected them to high property qualifications for voting. Because women traditionally had been banned from public life, they were routinely excluded from the franchise either by custom or by state constitutional fiat. The New Jer-

The Old House of Representatives, 1822

Representative government is the essence of republicanism. By highlighting the august red draperies and golden candlelight, this painting by Samuel F. B. Morse (who would later invent the telegraph) celebrates the deliberations of the popularly elected national legislature.

sey constitution of 1776, however, granted suffrage to all propertyholders, and beginning in the 1790s, propertied women became active participants in electoral battles between Federalists and Republicans. In 1807 a Republican-dominated legislature in New Jersey abolished property-holding requirements for voting and consciously defined full citizenship as an attribute of men, excluding women from suffrage. To justify this exclusion of women, legislators invoked traditional biological and social arguments. As one letter to a newspaper put it, "Women, generally, are neither by nature, nor habit, nor education, nor by their necessary condition in society fitted to perform this duty with credit to themselves or advantage to the public."

Other states also moved toward political democracy for men. Maryland extended the vote to all adult men in 1810, and the constitutions of the new states of Indiana (1816), Illinois (1818), and Alabama (1819) prescribed a broad male franchise. By the end of the 1820s only a few states—North Carolina, Virginia, Rhode Island—required the ownership of freehold property for voting.

Others, such as Ohio and Louisiana, limited suffrage to men who paid taxes or served in the militia, but a majority of the states had instituted universal white manhood suffrage (see Map 9.1).

Popular pressure brought other constitutional changes as well. Between 1818 and 1821 reform-minded politicians in Connecticut, Massachusetts, and New York pushed through important revisions in their state constitutions, reapportioning their legislatures on the basis of population and instituting more democratic forms of local government—such as the election rather than the appointment of judges and justices of the peace. If such "democratic doctrines" had been advanced ten years earlier, Chancellor James Kent of New York protested, they "should have struck the public mind with astonishment and terror."

The Legal Profession. A similar democratic revolution took place in the legal profession. During the Revolutionary Era, American attorneys had raised the standards of their profession by establishing bar

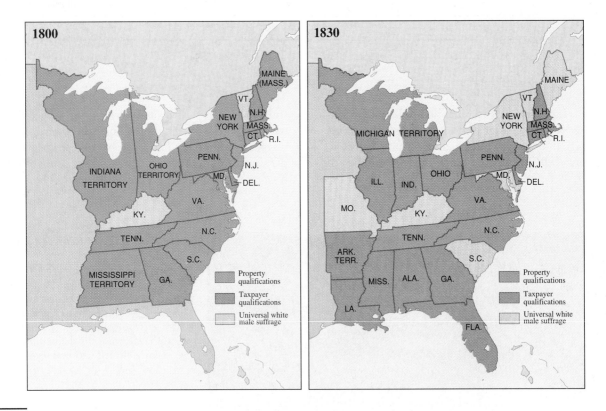

MAP 9.1

The Expansion of Voting Rights for White Men
Between 1800 and 1830 the United States moved steadily toward political democracy for white men. Many existing states revised their constitutions, replacing property ownership with taxpaying or militia service as a qualification for voting. Some new states in the West extended the franchise to all adult white men. As parties sought votes from a broader electorate, the tone of politics became more open and competitive—swayed by the interests and values of ordinary people.

TABLE 9.1

Number of Lawyers in Three Selected States, to 1820

	Number of Lawyers	Lawyers per 10,000 Population
Massachusetts (including Maine)		
1740	15	10
1775	71	24
1780	34	11
1785	92	24
1790	112	24
1800	200	35
1810	492	70
1820	710	87
Connecticut		
1790	129	54
1800	169	67
1820	248	90
South Carolina		
1771	24	19
1820	200	40

Source: George Dargo, *Law in the New Republic: Private Law and the Public Estate* (New York: Knopf, 1983), 49. Reprinted by permission of McGraw-Hill, Inc.

Judge Tapping Reeve
The founder of Litchfield Law School, Reeve sits in his study surrounded by volumes of reports of English and American cases. Published reports enhanced the authority of judges, who cited them as precedents for their rulings.

associations and winning legislation that prevented untrained lawyers—whom they called "pettifoggers"—from practicing law. By 1800 most of the sixteen states required lawyers to have three to seven years of formal schooling or apprenticeship training. Harvard, Columbia, and William and Mary colleges all offered lectures on legal issues, and in 1784 Judge Tapping Reeve founded the famous Litchfield, Connecticut, law school. By the 1820s Litchfield had graduated more than a thousand lawyers, including three future Supreme Court justices and two vice-presidents (Aaron Burr of New York and John C. Calhoun of South Carolina).

As legal rules became a more central part of American life, the legal profession grew in importance. In many states (as Table 9.1 suggests) the number of lawyers grew faster than did the population. Lawyers gained in prestige, impressing the voters with their eloquence in local courtrooms, and increasingly won election to public office. As early as 1820, 15 percent of the members of the Massachusetts assembly and 35 percent of those in the Senate were lawyers, though men of the law constituted only 1 percent of the state's adult male population. Thoroughly conversant with law as a system of power, lawyers pushed forward the activism of state legislatures, which enacted hundreds of statutes affecting many aspects of life.

The growing power of the legal profession inspired calls for its reform. Republican-minded critics attacked what they called the "professional aristocracy" of lawyers, demanding the regulation of attorneys' fees and the creation of small-claims courts in which ordinary citizens could represent themselves. Both reforms made the legal system more accessible to those without means. Reformers also succeeded in obtaining more relaxed standards for admission to the bar. By the 1820s only eleven of the twenty-six states required a fixed period of legal instruction. These reforms lowered the intellectual quality of the legal profession but made it more democratic in composition and spirit.

Republican Families

Republicanism was a potent ideology that, as John Adams lamented, "spread where it was not intended," deep into the heart of the social order. For example, the republican emphasis on equality and independence directly challenged the traditional concept of family life,

which was patriarchal and constricting. In Europe and in British North America husbands had dominated their wives and maintained legal control over the family's property. Now, in the eyes of some women who wanted to control an inheritance or speak out on public matters, their subordination to men seemed arbitrary, at odds with a belief in equal natural rights. Patriarchy was no longer seen as "natural"; it could be justified only on pragmatic grounds, "for the sake of order in families," as Mercy Otis Warren put it.

Economic and cultural changes also contributed to the erosion of customary family relations. Traditionally, parents arranged marriages to ensure the economic well-being of both their children and themselves during old age. As land holdings shrank in long-settled rural communities, however, parents could no longer bequeath substantial farms to their children and so lost the economic incentives by which they had controlled their children's lives. Increasingly, sons and daughters chose their own partners.

Sentimentalism. In making these choices, many young Americans were influenced by the new cultural attitude of *sentimentalism*. Originating in Europe during the so-called Romantic movement of the late eighteenth century, sentimentalism celebrated the importance of "feeling"—that is, an emotional understanding of life's experiences. People that were influenced by sentimentalism sought a physical, sensuous appreciation of God, nature, and other human beings. By 1820 sentimentalism had touched all classes of American society. It dripped from the pages of German and English literary works read in educated circles. It fell from the lips of actors in tear-jerking melodramas, which soon became the most popular theatrical entertainments in the United States. And it infused the rhetoric of revivalist preachers, who appealed to the passions of the heart rather than the cool logic of the mind.

Sentimentalism encouraged couples to marry for love. Parents had always taken physical attraction and emotional compatibility into account in arranging marriages for their children, but romance did not have a high cultural value. Most parents were realists, influenced mostly by the character and financial resources of a prospective son- or daughter-in-law. One skeptical Virginia mother argued that young women should remain single "till they were old enough to form a proper *judgement* of mankind" and not be deceived by their emotions. Wealthy fathers were equally concerned; after the Revolution they tended to bequeath more resources to their children (often at the expense of their widowed wives) and often placed funds in legal trusts so that their daughters would not be completely dependent on their husbands. As a Virginia planter wrote to his

lawyer, "I rely on you to see the property settlement properly drawn before the *marriage*, for I by no means consent that Polly shall be left to the Vicissitudes of Life." By such means parents became paternalists, protecting the interests of those who married for love.

Republican Marriages. Republicanism made marriage, rather than parenthood, the fundamental family relationship, and the new youth-run marriage system gave young adults greater freedom. Magazines promoted marriages "contracted from motives of affection, rather than of interest," encouraging a young person to seek a spouse who was, as Eliza Southgate of Maine put it, "calculated to promote my happiness" (see American Voices, page 279). Yet many young adults lacked the maturity and experience to choose wisely. Many were disappointed when their spouses failed as financial providers or faithful companions. Divorce petitions reflected their fate. Before 1800 the few people who petitioned for divorce had charged their spouses with neglect, abandonment, or adultery—serious offenses against the moral order of society. Now emotional complaints dominated divorce petitions. One woman complained that her husband had "ceased to cherish her," and a male petitioner lamented that his wife had "almost broke his heart." Reflecting these changed cultural values, some states expanded the legal grounds for divorce to include personal cruelty and drunkenness and made divorces available through judicial decree, rather than, as in the past, only through a special act of the legislature.

Still, most unions, happy or not, lasted until death and, especially among urban Americans of middling status, were affected by the republican ideal of a "companionate" marriage. This noble ideal, in which husbands and wives had "true equality, both of rank and fortune," sharing responsibility for decisions and treating each other with respect, foundered in the face of deeply ingrained cultural habits that favored men and legal rules that placed all property in their hands. Moreover, since the new marriage system discouraged parents from playing an active role in their children's lives, young wives could no longer rely on their parents for emotional or financial support and became more dependent on their husbands.

Consequently, the net effect of republican marriage patterns was to diminish the control of parents over children but not the power of husbands over wives. The marriage contract "is so much more important in its consequences to females than to males," a young man at the Litchfield Law School noted astutely in 1820, "for besides leaving everything else to unite themselves to one man, they subject themselves to his authority. He is their all—their only relative—their only hope."

Eliza Southgate

The Dilemmas of Womanhood

Eliza Southgate was born into a wealthy Maine family in 1783. At school in Boston, she discovered both radical doctrines of sexual equality and the reality of female subordination. In this letter to a male cousin, written in 1801, she tries to resolve these contradictory messages and define her own stance toward the world of men.

But every being who has contemplated human nature on a large scale will certainly justify me when I declare that the inequality of privilege between the sexes is sensibly felt by us females, and in no instance is it greater than in the liberty of choosing a partner in marriage; true, we have the liberty of refusing those we don't like, but not of selecting those we do. This is undoubtedly as it should be. . . .

I never was of opinion that the pursuits of the sexes ought to be the same; on the contrary, I believe it would be destructive to happiness, there would be a degree of rivalry incompatible with the harmony we wish to establish. I have ever thought it necessary that each should have a separate sphere of action—in such a case there could be no clashing unless one or the other should leap their respective bounds. Yet to cultivate the qualities with which we are endowed can never be called infringing the prerogatives of man. . . .

The cultivation of the power we possess, I have ever thought a privilege (or I may say duty) that belonged to the human species, and not man's exclusive prerogative. Far from destroying the harmony that ought to subsist, it would fix it on a foundation that would not totter at every jar. Women would be under the same degree of subordination that they now are; enlighten and expand their minds, and they would perceive the necessity of such a regulation to preserve the order and happiness of society. . . .

It does not follow (O what pen!) that every female who vindicates the capacity of the sex is a disciple of Mary Wolstoncraft. Though I allow her to have said many things which I cannot approve, I confess I admire many of her sentiments.

Source: David J. Rothman and Sheila Rothman, eds., *Sources of the American Social Tradition* (New York: Basic Books, 1975).

Raising and Educating Republican Children

In all societies, marriage has many purposes: it channels sexuality, facilitates the inheritance of property, and by creating strong family and kinship ties, eases the raising of children. In the United States the triumph of republican values altered assumptions not only about marriage but also about inheritance and child-rearing. Republican-minded state legislators provided for the equal distribution of estates among child-heirs when the property owner died without a will. In conjunction with longer-term social changes, republican ideology also altered the size and values of many American families.

Fewer Children. In long-settled regions of the United States the creation of a republican society coincided with a dramatic fall in the birth rate. For example, in the farm village of Sturbridge, Massachusetts, women who had married around 1750 bore an average of 8.8 children whereas women who married around 1810 had only about 6 children. The decline was even greater in the urban areas of Massachusetts, where by the 1820s native-born white women bore an average of 4 children. This urban birth rate barely sufficed to maintain the population, for one-third of all children in the cities died from measles, diphtheria, or smallpox.

The United States was one of the first countries in the world to experience this sharp decline in the birth rate, which is known as the *demographic transition*. The causes were several. The migration of thousands of young men to the trans-Appalachian West left many women without marriage partners and delayed the marriages of many more. Women who married later—say, at age 26 rather than age 20—had fewer children because they were married for fewer of their most fertile years. More important, thousands of white American couples deliberately limited the size of their families. After having four or five children, they used birth control or abstained from sexual intercourse to avoid conception. Farms were shrinking in size, and parents wanted to provide each of their children with an adequate inheritance.

The New Conjugal Family
Grace and Philip Schuyler pose informally with their daughters and encourage their musical and literary talents. The affectionate mood of this early nineteenth-century scene stands in sharp contrast to the hierarchy and discipline seen in the family portraits painted in earlier eras (see pages 29 and 104). (Collection of The New-York Historical Society)

Rearing the Young. At the same time, many American parents raised their children in new ways. Child-rearing practices are difficult to document, not being matters of public record, but reports from foreign visitors suggest that white Americans indulged their children and failed to discipline them. "Mr. Schuyler's second son is a spoiled little child, as are all American children, very willful, mischievous, and likeable," the Marquis de Chastelleux observed in 1780.

Visitors attributed this behavior, at least in part, to republican ideology. Because of the "general ideas of Liberty and Equality engraved on their hearts," a Polish aristocrat suggested, American children had "scant respect" for their parents. A British traveler was dumbfounded when an American father excused his son's "resolute disobedience" with a smile and the remark "A sturdy republican, sir." Foreigners guessed that parents encouraged such independence to enable young people to "go their own way" in the world.

The child-rearing literature of the period gives some support to this interpretation. Ministers, who wrote most of the pamphlets and books giving advice on raising children, were divided into two camps. Religious writers influenced by John Locke and the Enlightenment argued that children were "rational creatures" who should be encouraged to act correctly by means of praise, advice, and reasoned restraint. Those who held to Calvinist principles taught that infants were "full of the stains and pollution of sin" and needed strict discipline.

These two approaches—the authoritarian Calvinist and the affectionate rationalist—appealed to different social and religious groups in the United States. Edu-

cated or wealthy Americans, who were often members of Episcopal or Presbyterian churches, usually treated their children kindly. Since foreign commentators usually mixed with these well-to-do Americans, they reported this set of customs as the social norm. Actually, most yeomen and tenant farmers were much stricter and more authoritarian in their dealings with children, especially in families that belonged to Baptist or Calvinist-oriented Congregational churches.

Republican ideals affected this outlook. Evangelical Baptists and Methodists in the early nineteenth century still insisted on the need to instill humility in children and teach them to subordinate their desires to God's will. Fear was a "useful and necessary principle in family government," the minister John Abbott advised parents; a child "should submit to your authority, not to your arguments or persuasions." Yet even Abbott cautioned that it was wrong "exclusively to control him by this motive."

Rationalist writers placed more and more emphasis on children's capacity for education. They suggested that training should be focused on developing children's consciences so that young people would learn to police their own behavior. To that end, affectionate parents read their children stories that stressed self-discipline and neatness. They encouraged children to accept the burdens of independence: they must think and act for themselves. Foreigners observed that American children had greater freedom than did their counterparts in Europe, being allowed to participate in conversations among adults and venture into public without a chaperon. What passed unnoticed was the responsibility

these young Americans had to assume for their own lives. In private life as in public, republicanism balanced rights with duties.

Education Debated. Some Americans were well aware of the fragility of their republican experiment and sought to buttress its principles through education. Before independence, formal education had played a minor role in the lives of most American youth. In New England locally funded public schools provided most children with basic instruction in reading and writing. In other regions fewer children were given an education: about a quarter of the boys and perhaps 10 percent of the girls attended privately funded schools or had personal tutors. Even in New England, only a small fraction of the men—and almost no women—went on to grammar (high) school, and only 1 percent of men graduated from college.

After independence, Caleb Bingham, an influential textbook author from Boston, called for "an equal distribution of knowledge to make us emphatically a 'republic of letters.'" Thomas Jefferson and Benjamin Rush, the Philadelphia physician, separately proposed ambitious schemes for educational reform. Both mapped out plans for a comprehensive system of primary and secondary schooling, followed by colleges to educate young men (but not women) in the liberal arts—classical literature, history, and philosophy. They also proposed the establishment of a university where distinguished scholars would lecture on law, medicine, theology, and political economy.

These ideas fell on deaf ears. To ordinary citizens such elaborate schemes smacked of elitism. Farmers, artisans, and laborers looked to schools for basic instruction in the "three R's": reading, 'riting, and 'rithmetic. They supported public funding for primary schools but not for secondary schools or colleges, which were of no use to their teenage children, who already labored as apprentices, domestic servants, or farm workers. "Let anybody show what advantage the poor man receives from colleges," an anonymous "Old Soldier" wrote to the Maryland *Gazette*. "Why should they support them, unless it is to serve those who are in affluent circumstances, whose children can be spared from labor, and receive the benefits?" New or revised state constitutions responded to the wishes of the majority by calling for the legislatures to fund a broad system of primary education.

Even plans for basic education made little headway before 1820, when a new generation of reformers campaigned successfully for the improvement of public elementary schools. Led by merchants and manufacturers, they raised standards by certifying qualified teachers and appointing state superintendents of education. Self-interest as well as public virtue motivated these gentlemen reformers, many of whom were old Federalists

suspicious of the popular will. They wanted schools to instill the virtues of self-discipline and individual enterprise. Consequently, textbooks praised honesty and hard work while condemning gambling, drinking, and laziness. Gentlemen reformers also demanded that students be required to study American history, for they thought patriotic instruction would foster shared cultural ideals. The experience of Thomas Low, a New Hampshire schoolboy of the 1820s, would have satisfied their fondest hopes:

> We were taught every day and in every way that ours was the freest, the happiest, and soon to be the greatest and most powerful country of the world. This is the religious faith of every American. He learns it in his infancy and can never forget it.

The task of educators had been to transmit widely accepted knowledge and values from one generation to the next. In the new republican society they were also entrusted with instilling patriotism.

Literary Independence. Patriotism—the sense of an American identity—appeared again in the quest for a distinctive republican literature. Before the Revolution most American writers were ministers who published sermons, moral tracts, and commentaries on religious experience. Many books imported from Europe were religious in character: the Bible, commentaries on Scripture, moral advice, and the like. Most of the political treatises and literary works read in America were also by European writers. With respect to literary matters, the British mainland colonists were a dependent people.

As early as the 1780s Noah Webster had asserted that "America must be as independent in *literature* as she is in politics." Webster's contribution, in his *Dissertation on the English Language* (1789), was to standardize the American spelling of various words (such as *labor* for the British *labour*). His "blue-backed speller," first published in 1783, sold 60 million copies over the next half century and helped give Americans of all backgrounds a common vocabulary and grammar. "None of us was 'lowed to see a book," an enslaved black recalled, "but we gits hold of that Webster's old blue-back speller and we . . . studies that spelling book." Webster blended instruction in grammar and pronunciation with moral principles: "Vir-tue ex-alt-eth a na-tion, but sin is a re-proach to a-ny peo-ple" was a typical example. In other works Webster called on his fellow republican citizens to detach themselves "from the dependence on foreign opinions and manners, which is fatal to the efforts of genius in this country."

Echoing Webster's plea, Joel Barlow, a Yale graduate and an ardent Jeffersonian Republican, called for an epic literature that would celebrate America. To that end he offered his own epic poem, *The Columbiad* (1807), an ambitious but undistinguished work that

The Genius of Washington Irving
In fashioning his stories, Irving drew upon the history and folk traditions of the early Dutch settlers of New York. Ichabod Crane (shown here with the "Headless Horseman") was one of his most popular characters.

had Columbus predict the future glory of North America. Charles Brockden Brown of Philadelphia, the first American novelist, wrote six psychologically informed gothic novels between 1798 and 1801, but they all attracted few readers. Mercy Otis Warren's *History of the American Revolution* (1805) contained stirring portraits of leading American patriots, as did the best-selling *Life of George Washington* written around 1800 by "Parson" Mason Weems, an Episcopal minister. Neither work had much literary or historical merit; still, they won acclaim as contributions to popular culture and patriotism.

The most accomplished and successful writer in the new republic was Washington Irving, a Federalist in politics and outlook. His essays and histories, including *Salmagundi* (1807), *Diedrich Knickerbocker's History of New York* (1809), and *The Sketch Book* (1819), had substantial American sales and won fame abroad because Europeans were fascinated by his tales of Dutch-American life. Irving lived in Europe for seventeen years, drawn by its aristocratic manners and intense intellectual life.

Apart from Irving, no American author was well known in Europe, partly because most American writers had their primary careers as planters, merchants, or lawyers. "Literature is not yet a distinct profession with us," Thomas Jefferson told an English friend, explaining the dearth of intellectual life in the United States. "Now and then a strong mind arises, and at its intervals from business emits a flash of light. But the first object of young societies is bread and covering." Not until Emerson and the Transcendentalists would native-born authors make a real contribution to the great literature of the Western world (see Chapter 12).

Protestant Christianity and Women's Lives

Religion had always been a significant aspect of American life, but in the decades between 1790 and 1820 a series of revivals planted the values of Protestant Christianity deep in the American national character. In the process, religious revivalism created new public roles for women, initially by enlarging the dimensions of women's sphere.

The Second Great Awakening

The revivals that began around 1790 were much more complex than those of the First Great Awakening. In the 1740s most revivals occurred in existing congregations; fifty years later they also took place in camp meetings and often involved the creation of new churches and denominations. Even more strikingly, the Second Great Awakening spawned a wide variety of organizations dedicated to the cause of social and political reform.

Evangelical Churches. The churches that prospered in the new nation were typically well suited to a republican society. Because of its hierarchical structure, for example, the Roman Catholic Church attracted few converts either among Protestants, who embraced Luther's doctrine of the priesthood of all believers, or among the unchurched, who feared priestly power. Few ordinary Americans joined the Episcopal Church; not only was it dominated by the wealthy and snobbish, but power flowed downward—from bishops to ministers

and then to the congregations. In contrast, the Presbyterian Church was more popular, in part because it was more "republican": ordinary members elected laymen to the synods (congresses) where doctrine and practice were formulated.

Methodism attracted even more adherents. It retained a religious hierarchy, as bishops took the lead on theological issues and enforced order in the church, but the evangelical fervor of early Methodism fostered lay preaching, emotional worship, and communal singing, creating an egalitarian religious culture. The most democratic forms of church government belonged to Quakers, Baptists, and Congregationalists. No bishops or governing bodies stood above the local congregations, and most church decisions—on matters of theology as well as administration—rested with church members. Partly because of their democratic features, Methodist and Baptist churches grew spectacularly, and by the early nineteenth century they had become the largest religious denominations in the United States (see Map 9.2).

Revivalism. Between 1790 and 1830 every decade brought another upsurge of Protestantism somewhere in the new nation. Baptists and Shakers evangelized the New England backcountry. Then a new sect of Universalists, who repudiated the Calvinist doctrine of predestination and taught that salvation was universal, attracted thousands of converts in northern New England.

After 1800 enthusiastic camp meeting revivals swept across the frontier regions of South Carolina, Kentucky, Tennessee, and Ohio. James McGready, a Scots-Irish Presbyterian preacher, "could so array hell before the wicked," an eyewitness reported, "that they would tremble and Quake, imagining a lake of fire and brimstone yawning to overwhelm them." When frontier preachers got together at a revival meeting, they were electrifying. As a young man of twenty, James Finley attended the Cane Ridge, Kentucky, revival of 1802 and was so moved that he became a Methodist minister:

> The noise was like the roar of Niagara. The vast sea of human beings seemed to be agitated as if by a storm. I counted seven ministers, all preaching at one time, some on stumps, others on wagons. . . . Some of the people were singing, others praying, some crying for mercy. A peculiarly strange sensation came over me. My heart beat tumultuously, my knees trembled, my lips quivered, and I felt as though I must fall to the ground.

Through such revivals, Baptist and Methodist preachers reshaped the spiritual landscape of the South and the Old Southwest. They won over most of the white population and, with the assistance of black ministers, began to implant evangelical Protestant Christianity among African-Americans as well.

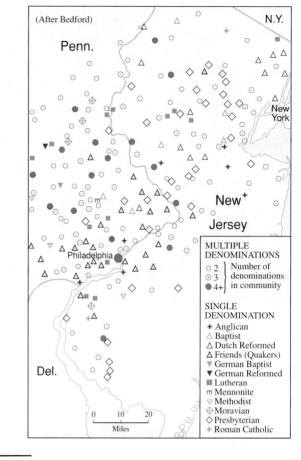

MAP 9.2

Ethnicity and Religion in Eastern Pennsylvania and New Jersey, circa 1780
Long-established churches, founded by English Quakers and Dutch Reformed Protestants, nested side by side with those established by new ethnic groups, such as German Lutherans and Scots-Irish Presbyterians. Many communities had churches from two or three different denominations, a situation that fostered religious toleration and undermined the idea of a legally established church.

Unlike the First Great Awakening, which in the 1740s had split many churches into hostile New Light and Old Light factions, the Second Awakening brought friendly competition among Protestant churches, each seeking new members among the unconverted and new methods of spreading the faith. In New England and the Middle Atlantic states pious women supplemented the work of preachers and lay elders, doubling the amount of organized spiritual energy. In the South and West, Baptist and Methodist preachers traveled constantly. Instead of settling in a congregation, a Methodist cleric followed a circuit, "riding a hardy pony or horse . . . with his Bible, hymn-book, and Discipline." Wherever they went, these "circuit riders" established new

Women in the Awakening
The preacher is a man, but women fill the audience. The Awakening was one of the most far-reaching influences on women's lives in American history, mobilizing women for action not only in religion but also in education and social reform. (Collection of The New-York Historical Society)

churches by searching out devout families, bringing them together for worship, and then appointing lay elders to lead the congregation and enforce moral discipline until they returned.

Evangelical ministers copied the techniques of George Whitefield and other eighteenth-century revivalists, codifying their intuitive genius in manuals on "practical preaching." To attract converts, preachers were cautioned to emphasize piety as opposed to theology and learning and were told that extemporaneous speech was more powerful than a written sermon. "Preach without papers," advised one minister, "seem earnest & serious; & you will be listened to with Patience, & Wonder; both of your hands will be seized, & almost shook off as soon as you are out of the Church." Vigorous preaching imparted enthusiasm and a sense of purpose to hundreds of local revivals.

These missionary innovations shifted the denominational base of American religion toward the Baptists, Methodists, and other evangelical churches, which grew rapidly because they actively sought converts. The leading churches of the Revolutionary Era—the Congregationalists, Episcopalians, and Quakers—declined in relative membership. Their leaders and members were content for the most part to maintain existing congregations or grow slowly through natural increase.

New Religious Thought and Institutions. The Second Great Awakening changed the character of American thought—and social action—in dramatic ways. Before the Awakening, a Calvinist preoccupation with human depravity and weakness had shaped the thinking of many writers, teachers, and statesmen. Then, in the early nineteenth century, ministers—whether or not they were revivalists—began placing greater stress on human ability and individual free will. This view imparted a new optimism to the intellectual culture of the United States.

In New England, the primary source of the new theology, many educated and economically well-off Congregationalists became Unitarians. Rejecting the concept of the Trinity—God the Father, Son, and Holy Spirit—Unitarians believed in an indivisible and "united" God (hence the name Unitarians). Reacting against the emotionalism of Methodist and Baptist services, Unitarians stressed the power of human reason. "The ultimate reliance of a human being is, and must be, on his own mind," argued the famous Unitarian minister William Ellery Channing, "for the idea of God is the idea of our own spiritual nature, purified and enlarged to infinity." This emphasis on a believer's reason, a legacy of the Enlightenment, gave Unitarianism a humanistic and individualistic thrust.

Optimistic ideas affected mainstream Congregational churches as well. Lyman Beecher, the leading New England clergyman of the first half of the nineteenth century, accepted the anti-Calvinist idea of universal salvation. Although Beecher insisted that humans had a natural tendency to sin, he repudiated the doctrine of predestination, declaring that all men and women had the capacity to choose God. In Beecher's sermons, redemption referred to a self-induced spiritual awakening, not an arbitrary summons from a stern God. By emphasizing choice—the free will of the believer—he testified to the growing confidence in the power of human action.

Samuel Hopkins—a disciple of the great philosopher of the First Awakening, Jonathan Edwards—linked individual salvation with social reform through the concept of religious *benevolence*. Benevolence was the practice of disinterested virtue, to be undertaken by those who had received God's sanctifying grace. Those people "are thereby constituted his *Almoners*," suggested the New York Presbyterian minister John Rodgers, with a duty "to dole out his charity to their poorer brothers and sisters." Inspired by such arguments, merchants and philanthropists founded the New York Humane Society and the New York Dispensary to unite "the different classes of the community." Similar charitable organizations appeared in most cities and towns, marking the beginning of the Benevolent Empire (see Chapter 10). By the 1820s some conservative church leaders complained that through their benevolence lay men and women were devoting themselves to secular reforms—such as antislavery and the prevention of pauperism—and neglecting spiritual goals.

These new religious ideas spread quickly as a result of the founding of theological seminaries such as the Congregationalist institutions of Andover in Massachusetts and Lane in Ohio. Even more than the older divinity schools at Harvard, Yale, Princeton, and other colleges, these institutions fostered cooperation among the clergy, creating loyalty to nationwide denominations. As individual clergymen cooperated with one another, American Protestant churches became less dogmatic in their teachings. Many congregations abandoned books and pamphlets such as the orthodox *Watts Hymnal*, which took controversial stances on old theological debates over predestination and the efficacy of the sacraments, replacing them, a layman explained, with publications that would not give "offense to the serious Christians of any denomination."

Indeed, five interdenominational societies were founded between 1815 and 1826: the American Education Society (1815), the American Bible Society (1816), the American Sunday School Union (1824), the American Tract Society (1824), and the American Home Missionary Society (1826). The new organizations were based in New York, Boston, and Philadelphia but ministered to a national—and eventually an international—congregation. Each year they dispatched hundreds of missionaries to frontier regions and foreign lands—Africa, India, China—and distributed tens of thousands of religious pamphlets.

Organization on this scale gave momentum and power to the Second Great Awakening. National institutions united the individual energies of thousands of church members in a great collective undertaking, unleashing their ambitions and freeing their imaginations. "I want to see our state evangelized," declared one pious New York layman:

Suppose the great State of New York in all its physical, political, moral, commercial, and pecuniary resources should come over to the Lord's side. Why it would turn the scale and could convert the world. I shall have no rest until it is done.

For the first time in America, men and women in small villages scattered across the landscape saw themselves as part of a large religious movement, one that could change the course of history.

As a result of the Second Awakening, religion had become too important a force in American society to be kept separate from secular affairs. On July 4, 1827, the Reverend Ezra Stiles Ely called on the members of the Seventh Presbyterian Church in Philadelphia to begin a "Christian party in politics." In the sermon "The Duty of Christian Freemen to Elect Christian Rulers," Ely set out a new goal for the American republic—a religious goal that Thomas Jefferson and John Adams would have found strange, if not troubling. The two presidents, who had died the year before, believed that America's mission was to spread political republicanism. Ely urged the United States to become an evangelical Christian nation dedicated to religious conversion at home and abroad. As Ely put it, "All our rulers ought in their official capacity to serve the Lord Jesus Christ." The Second Great Awakening had added an intense religious dimension to American politics and the emerging national identity.

Women and Religion

Republican ideology raised the question of women's rights and, along with changes in social and economic life, had created new opportunities for American women. During and after the Revolutionary Era, a few women proclaimed the goal of complete equality with men, and many young women took advantage of new educational possibilities. Still other women took a more direct role in the market, producing farm goods for sale or working in expanding outwork industries. And an increasing number of women embraced the new ideal of companionate marriage, which raised the prospect of a more equal division of authority within the family. Despite these changes, deeply ingrained cultural patterns of male dominance remained intact. Indeed, the early nineteenth century brought a new ideology that limited women's sphere to domestic responsibilities. Only in American religious life did women achieve a significant public presence.

Women's Sphere. Traditionally, most American women had focused their lives on domestic duties: the bearing and raising of children and work in the home or on the

Separate Spheres
Art often reveals cultural values—here the new emphasis on child-rearing and women's domestic authority. The mother sits in the center of the room, controlling the household domain. The father enters from the outside, his prime concerns lying elsewhere, in the world of business.

farm. As the changing political order challenged long-standing relations of authority, a few upper-class women sought a public voice, but most women—and certainly most men—did not assume that the egalitarian logic of republican ideology would affect their customary gender roles. Few demanded or even supported a substantial public role for women in American society. Instead, many clergymen and political leaders promoted the notion of a separate women's sphere. Women had special domestic skills and responsibilities, they argued, and should devote themselves to the running of the home and family life.

Women's enhanced domestic role stemmed in part from changes in Christian thought. Traditionally, most religious writers had viewed women as morally inferior to men, as sexual temptresses or witches. By 1800 the clergy had revised this image, and religious teaching held men responsible for sexual misconduct. Indeed, moralists claimed that modesty and purity were inherent in the nature of women, giving them a unique ability to educate the spirit. The sustaining of virtue became part of women's sphere.

Political leaders also called on women to ensure the future of the new American republic. In his *Thoughts on Female Education* (1787), Benjamin Rush argued that a young woman should be given intellectual training so that she would be a fit republican wife, "an agreeable companion for a sensible man" who would, as another moralist put it, "excite his perseverance in the paths of rectitude." Rush and other men of affairs welcomed the emergence of loyal "republican mothers"

who would instruct "their sons in the principles of liberty and government." As a list of "Maxims for Republics" put it, "Some of the first patriots of ancient times were formed by their mothers."

Ministers embraced the idea of republican motherhood and devised new roles for women in moral and religious education. "Preserving virtue and instructing the young are not the fancied, but the real 'Rights of Women,'" the Reverend Thomas Bernard told the Female Charitable Society of Salem, Massachusetts, in 1803. He urged his audience to forget about the public roles advocated by Mary Wollstonecraft and other feminists. Instead, women should remain content to care for their children, because this gave them "an extensive power over the fortunes of man in every generation." Bernard wanted women to remain in their traditional domestic sphere while insisting that its value should be enhanced.

Many American women from the middling classes accepted this limited revision of their social identity. As a young New England woman wrote in 1803, "She is still *woman*, with duties prescribed her by the God of Nature essentially different from those of *man*." Some educated upper-class women, however, insisted on equality of the separate male and female worlds. "I will never consent to have our sex considered in an inferior point of light," Abigail Adams, the wife of President John Adams, proclaimed in 1799. And some ministers envisioned a public role for women's domestic virtues. As Thomas Grimké, a South Carolina minister, said, "Give me a host of educated pious mothers and sisters and I will revolutionize a country, in moral and religious taste."

Public Women. Taking advantage of their enhanced moral status, women in Britain and America undertook new religious initiatives in the late eighteenth century. Mother Ann Lee founded the Shaker sect in Britain and migrated in 1774 to America, where she and a handful of followers attracted numerous recruits. The Shakers were a controversial sect; their enthusiasm, clannishness, celibacy, and commitment to female equality set them apart. By the 1820s Shaker communities dotted the countryside from New Hampshire to Kentucky and Indiana (see Chapter 12). In Rhode Island, Jemima Wilkinson, a female revivalist, won hundreds of converts to her sect (see American Lives, pages 288–289). Women in mainstream churches also became more active. In New Hampshire women managed more than fifty local "cent" societies that raised funds for the Society for Promoting Christian Knowledge; evangelical women in New York City founded a charitable institution, the Society for the Relief of Poor Widows; and young Quaker women in Philadelphia ran the Society for the Free Instruction of African Females.

Women became active in religion and charitable

work partly because they were excluded from other spheres of public life and partly because they formed a substantial majority in many denominations. For example, after 1800 about 70 percent of the members of New England Congregational churches were women. Ministers acknowledged this female presence by changing their religious practices. In many Protestant faiths men and women traditionally sat on opposite sides of the church during regular Sunday services, and ministers often conducted separate prayer meetings for each sex. Now evangelical Methodist and Baptist preachers encouraged mixed praying, which critics condemned as "promiscuous." But Presbyterian and Congregational churches in frontier areas adopted this innovation with impressive results. "Our prayer meetings have been one of the greatest means of the conversion of souls," a minister in central New York reported in the 1820s, "especially those in which brothers and sisters have prayed together."

As women's involvement in religion began to challenge traditional gender roles, their activities and organizations became controversial. Many laymen resented the emphasis on women's moral superiority and the religious and social activism that sprang from it. "Women have a different *calling*," one man argued. "They are neither required nor permitted to be exhorters or leaders in public assemblies. . . . That they *be chaste, keepers at home* is the Apostle's direction." But many ministers continued to encourage the creation of women's organizations, and women became increasingly conscious of their new social power. By the 1820s mothers throughout the United States had founded local maternal associations to encourage Christian childrearing. Newsletters such as *Mother's Magazine* were widely read in hundreds of small towns and villages, giving women a sense of shared purpose and identity.

In their capacity as moral paragons, women had an immediate and direct impact on social behavior. Imbibing the principle of female virtue, many young women and the men who courted them postponed sexual intercourse until after marriage—a form of self-restraint that had not been common in the eighteenth century. In Hingham, Massachusetts, and many other New England towns about 30 percent of the women who married between 1750 and 1800 had borne a child within eight months of their wedding day; by the 1820s the proportion had dropped to 15 percent.

Women's Education. Female religious activism pushed forward the education of women. Churches established scores of seminaries and academies where girls—primarily from the middling classes—were given sound intellectual training as well as moral instruction. Emma Willard, the first American to advocate higher education for women, opened the Middlebury Female Seminary in Vermont in 1814 and later founded schools for girls in Waterford and Troy, New York.

Women educated in female seminaries and academies gradually displaced men from their traditional roles as teachers in locally supported public schools. By the 1820s women were teaching the summer session in many schools; in the following decade they would work the more demanding winter term as well. Women took over teaching in primary schools because they had few other job opportunities and because school authorities could pay them less than they paid men. Women earned $12 to $14 per month as schoolteachers, with room and board—less than a farm laborer. But they were also beneficiaries of the higher moral status now accorded to women and the imperatives of republican motherhood; they would instruct the young not only at home but also in school. As schoolteachers, these women had an acknowledged place in public life that had been beyond their reach in the colonial and Revolutionary periods. Through their active presence in the Second Great Awakening, thousands of American women had enhanced their personal identity and won for their sex a public role in the life of the American republic.

A Young Ladies Seminary, circa 1810–1820
Female academies equipped young women from middling and elite families with cultural skills and knowledge of the world. In this miniature panorama, two students master the intricacies of geography while another girl sharpens her musical talents.

Unruly Women: Jemima Wilkinson and Deborah Sampson Gannett

1776 was a year of new beginnings: In July the thirteen colonies repudiated 150 years of monarchical rule and declared themselves independent republics—the United States of America. In October Jemima Wilkinson of Cumberland, Rhode Island, became ill with a fever and had a vision in which she died and her body was now inhabited by the "Spirit of Light"; repudiating her birth name, Wilkinson declared herself the founder of a new religion—the Publick Universal Friend. And, beginning in 1776, Deborah Sampson, a tall and strong sixteen-year-old indentured servant in Middleborough, Massachusetts, first realized that "my mind became agitated with the enquiry—why a nation, separated from us by an ocean . . . [should] enforce on us plans of subjugation." Sampson's resolution "to become one of the severest avengers of the wrong" led her in 1782 to join the army—a cross-dressing American soldier.

George Whitefield had a hand in all these new beginnings. Since 1739 the great English evangelist had inspired Americans to turn to God and question established authority. By the 1760s New Light Presbyterians in Philadelphia and elsewhere had declared they had "no king but King Jesus" and had joined the Patriot movement. At about the same time—around 1768, when she was sixteen—Jemima Wilkinson discovered Whitefield by reading his sermons; two years later she joined the religious revival that followed his final visit to New England. By 1776 she had forsaken Quakerism, the faith of four generations of Rhode Island Wilkinsons, and joined the New Light Baptists.

In 1780 Deborah Sampson also became a Baptist, though she was expelled two years later for behaving in a "verry loose and unchristian" fashion. Accused of "dressing in men's clothes, and enlisting as a Soldier in the Army," Sampson had resisted the admonitions of her brethren to give "Christian satisfaction" for her conduct. Nor was this the end of the tale. Compressing her breasts with cotton cloth and enlisting again, Sampson served in the Light Infantry 4th Massachusetts Regiment of the Continental army for seventeen months and, while scouting the enemy in war-torn Westchester County, New York, was wounded in an engagement with the Tory militia. Like Whitefield's preaching, Sampson's adventure had "turned the world up-side down."

Sampson and Wilkinson were "disorderly women,"

Jemima Wilkinson, the "Universal Friend"

as contemporaries put it, examples of what the historian Natalie Zemon Davis has called the "woman-on-top." Both in Europe and in America, such audacious women challenged the social conventions that bound their sex, sometimes acting in "unwomanly" ways by leading food riots or political protests, sometimes donning the garb of men in symbolic protests against women's inferior status. "I burst the tyrant bands, which held my sex in awe," Sampson would proclaim in her public lectures in 1802.

Jemima Wilkinson was no less daring. A tall and graceful woman with dark hair and dark eyes, she had a magnetic personality and a powerful preaching style that created fervent disciples. Judge William Potter of Rhode Island was so moved by the Universal Friend that he gave up a promising political career, freed his slaves, and built a fourteen-room addition to his mansion for Wilkinson to use. Another wealthy farmer provided her with a home in Pennsylvania, and supporters built churches in three New England towns. Wilkinson's success—and notoriety—stemmed in part from her religious message, which blended the Calvinist warning of "a lost and guilty, gossiping, dying World" with a Quaker-inspired social gospel that advocated plain dress, pacifism, and the emancipation of slaves. But even more it reflected her revolutionary persona. Like

Mother Ann Lee, the founder of the Shakers, Wilkinson preached celibacy and never married. More controversial still, she dressed like a man, wearing a black robe similar to a clergyman's gown, and—emphasizing the ambiguity of her gender—told her followers to address her not as "she" or "her" but as "the Friend."

This radicalism—of social doctrine and personal identity—alienated more people than it attracted. Although she was touted by some of her disciples as a messiah, Wilkinson's attempts at faith healing and prophesying scandalized even the tolerant Quakers and Baptists of Rhode Island and Pennsylvania, where she was attacked by a stone-throwing mob. Forsaking evangelism, she gave up preaching to the "wicked world" and turned to utopianism, in 1790 establishing the community of Jerusalem in the wilderness of western New York; ten years later the settlement had 260 inhabitants. But few new recruits joined the sect, and its purpose and energy gradually drained away. Within two decades of Wilkinson's death in 1819 her sect had disappeared. Its only legacy is a short doctrinal pamphlet, *The Universal Friend's Advice to Those of the Same Religious Society* (1794).

Deborah Sampson left a slightly deeper imprint on American history, in part because she participated in the nation's founding war and in part because her personal radicalism was less extreme. Returning to Massachusetts after the war, she married Benjamin Gannett, a poor farmer with whom she had three children. To alleviate the family's poverty, Deborah Gannett showed the same "enterprise" that had sent her off to war. She cooperated with the author of her memoir in 1797 and, to win support for her petition for a soldier's pension, undertook a speaking tour throughout New England and New York in 1802.

In her lecture to curious audiences attracted by her military exploits and cross-dressing, Gannett conveyed a mixed message. On the one hand, she celebrated her decision in 1782 to throw off "the soft habiliment of my sex" and reaffirmed her culturally revolutionary act by performing a military drill, "Equipt in complete uniform." On the other hand, Gannett confessed her "error and presumption" in swerving "from the accustomed flowery path of female delicacy." By asking forgiveness from her "respectable" listeners for this "unnatural, unwise and indelicate" behavior, she affirmed women's traditional roles, which had been redefined as those of the proper "republican wife" and the pious "republican mother." Her performance was a study in ambiguity, at once dangerously assertive and socially reassuring.

In the broad sweep of history, the contributions of figures such as Deborah Sampson Gannett and Jemima Wilkinson are often ignored. Neither had won a major battle or devised an enduring religious doctrine. Yet their lives are important for what they reveal about the age in which they lived. Wilkinson attacked slavery, as did many others in the North, bringing about its gradual demise there. She called for a more enthusiastic religion and, along with other inspired preachers, sparked the Second Great Awakening. She showed that women could take an active part in religious affairs, and thousands of American women made the same choice, gradually changing the composition, practice, and outlook of many Protestant churches. First as a soldier and then more prominently a speaker, Deborah Sampson Gannett also claimed a public presence for women. Her long and ultimately successful public campaign for a Revolutionary War pension bridged differences of gender in asserting the sense of entitlement felt by all the veterans who had fought for their country.

But the most enduring legacy of Gannett and Wilkinson was their remarkable efforts—partly instinctive, partly conscious—to transcend the cultural limits of their time. Their lives challenged the increasingly influential ideology of "separate spheres," which divided the world into a masculine domain of public affairs and a feminine world of domestic concerns. This challenge was revolutionary even in an age of revolution and remains controversial two centuries later.

Deborah Sampson, Soldier and Speaker

Summary

By the 1820s a distinct national character had emerged in the United States, reflecting three long-term historical developments that shaped the lives of most white Americans. First, as a result of their increasing involvement in an ever shifting capitalist market economy, Americans became a competitive and "calculating" people. Between 1780 and 1820 merchant capitalists sought profits by creating a flourishing outwork system of rural manufacturing, and state governments devised a commonwealth system of political economy—awarding corporate charters and subsidies to assist transportation companies, manufacturers, and banks. Republican-minded state legislatures enacted statutes that encouraged economic development by redefining common-law property rights. Led by John Marshall, the Supreme Court protected the traditional rights of property owners and the charter privileges of business corporations. Entrepreneurs took advantage of state legislation and judicial protection to create new business enterprises, strong regional economies, and the beginnings of a national market system.

Second, republican precepts of liberty and equality created a citizenry that was suspicious—if not hostile—toward anyone with aristocratic pretensions. Taking advantage of legal and commercial equality, ambitious men sought to rise in the world. In contrast, political and religious leaders promoted the notion of a separate "women's sphere" consisting of domestic responsibilities. Republicanism—in concert with sentimentalism—influenced the private lives of many Americans, encouraging young people to marry for love as well as for economic security and prompting parents to raise their children using reason as well as authority.

Third, the Second Great Awakening made Americans a fervently Protestant people and dramatically increased the influence of evangelical Baptist and Methodist churches. Religious revivalism also enhanced the status of women, whose moral activism broadened the dimensions of their "sphere" to encompass teaching in public schools and the creation of female-run charitable groups and religious societies. Developing religious institutions thus gave women a new and growing presence in the public life of the United States.

The shared historical experiences of hundreds of thousands of white Americans between the 1770s and the 1820s—fervent Protestantism, entrepreneurial capitalism, and social republicanism—formed the core of an emerging national identity. Within this new framework of life and thought, Americans struggled to work out their individual destinies.

TIMELINE

1780s	Rural outwork system, especially shoes and textiles
1781	Philadelphia merchants found Bank of North America
1782	St. Jean de Crèvecoeur, *Letters from an American Farmer*
1783	Noah Webster's *American Spelling Book* ("the blue-backed speller")
1787	Benjamin Rush, *Thoughts on Female Education*
1790s	State mercantilism encourages economic development Parents limit family size Second Great Awakening Republican motherhood defined
1791	First Bank of the United States founded; dissolved in 1811
1794	Lancaster Turnpike Company
1795	Massachusetts Mill Dam Act
1800s	State-chartered banks proliferate Legal profession democratized Rise of sentimentalism and republican marriage system Women's religious activism Spread of evangelical Baptists and Methodists Beginnings of Benevolent Empire
1801	John Marshall becomes chief justice
1803	*Marbury v. Madison* states theory of judicial review
1805	Mercy Otis Warren, *History of the American Revolution*
1807	New Jersey excludes propertied women from suffrage
1809	Washington Irving, *Diedrich Knickerbocker's History of New York*
1810s	Expansion of suffrage for men Lawyers important in politics
1810	Albert Gallatin, *Report on Manufactures* *Fletcher v. Peck* expands contract clause
1816	Second Bank of the United States chartered
1817	Bonus Bill vetoed by Madison
1819	*McCulloch v. Maryland* enhances power of national government *Dartmouth College v. Woodward* protects corporate property rights
1818–1821	Democratic revision of state constitutions
1820s	Expansion of public primary school system Women become schoolteachers Growth of cash-based market economy
1821	*Cohens v. Virginia* declares supremacy of national courts

★   ★   ★

BIBLIOGRAPHY

Two penetrating local studies, Christopher Clark, *The Roots of Rural Capitalism* (1990), and Laurel Thatcher Ulrich, *A Midwife's Tale: The Life of Martha Ballard* (1990), capture the texture of life in the early republic. Nathan O. Hatch, *The Democratization of American Christianity* (1987), offers an interpretation of religious change.

Political Economy: The Capitalist Commonwealth

Thomas Doerflinger, *A Vigorous Spirit of Enterprise: Merchants and Economic Development in Revolutionary Philadelphia* (1986); John Denis Haeger, *John Jacob Astor* (1991); and Stuart Bruchey, *Robert Oliver: Merchant of Baltimore* (1956), are fine studies of merchant enterprise. The standard history is Curtis R. Nettels, *The Emergence of a National Economy, 1775–1815* (1965). See also Diane Lindstrom, *Economic Development in the Philadelphia Region, 1810–1860* (1983); Ronald Hoffman, John J. McCusker, and Peter Albert, eds., *The Economy of Revolutionary America* (1987); and Daniel P. Jones, *The Economic and Social Transformation of Rhode Island, 1780–1850* (1992).

On banking, see Bray Hammond, *Banks and Politics in America* (1957), and Richard H. Timberlake, *Monetary Policy in the United States* (1992). Studies of manufacturing are Thomas C. Cochran, *Frontiers of Change: Early Industrialism in America* (1981); David Jeremy, *Transatlantic Industrial Revolution: The Diffusion of Textile Technology between Britain and America, 1790–1830* (1981); and Judith A. McGaw, *Early American Technology* (1994).

The classic studies of state mercantilism are Oscar and Mary Handlin, *Commonwealth: A Study of the Role of Government in the American Economy: Massachusetts, 1774–1861* (1947), and Louis Hartz, *Economic Policy and Democratic Thought: Pennsylvania, 1776–1860* (1948). State support for transportation can be traced in Carter Goodrich, *Government Promotion of American Canals and Railroads* (1960); Erik F. Hiates et al., *Western River Transportation: The Era of Early Internal Development, 1810–1860* (1975); Philip Jordan, *The National Road* (1948); and Harry N. Scheiber, *Ohio Canal Era: A Case Study of Government and the Economy* (1969).

Two good introductions to legal issues are George Dargo, *Law in the Early Republic* (1982), and Jamil S. Zainaldin, *Law in Antebellum Society* (1983). The legal implications of commonwealth ideology are analyzed by Leonard Levy, *The Law of the Commonwealth and Chief Justice Shaw* (1955), and Morton Horwitz, *The Transformation of American Law, 1790–1860* (1976). R. Kent Newmyer, *The Supreme Court under Marshall and Taney* (1968), offers a concise treatment. See also Robert K. Faulkner, *The Jurisprudence of John Marshall* (1968); Francis N. Stites, *John Marshall: Defender of the Constitution* (1981); and Thomas C. Shevory, ed., *John Marshall's Achievement* (1989). A fine case study is C. Peter McGrath, *Yazoo: Law and Politics in the New Republic* (1966).

Visions of a Republican Social Order

Warren S. Tryon, *A Mirror for Americans: Life and Manners in the United States, 1790–1870, as Recorded by European Travelers* (3 vols., 1952), suggests the distinctive features of republican society. Michael Grossberg, *Governing the Hearth* (1985), discusses changing marriage rules. Catherine M. Scholten, *Childrearing in American Society, 1650–1850* (1985), should be supplemented by Philip Greven's pathbreaking analysis, *The Protestant Temperament: Patterns of Childrearing, Religious Experience, and the Self in Early America* (1977). Other important works include Daniel Blake Smith, *Inside the Great House: Planter Family Life in Eighteenth-Century Chesapeake Society* (1980); Bernard Wishy, *The Child and the Republic* (1970); and Jan Lewis, *The Pursuit of Happiness: Family and Values in Jefferson's Virginia* (1983).

On education, see Lawrence Cremin, *American Education: The National Experience, 1783–1861* (1981), and Carl F. Kaestle, *Pillars of the Republic: Common Schools and American Society, 1780–1860* (1983). Russell B. Nye, *The Cultural Life of the New Nation, 1776–1830* (1960), is comprehensive; a recent penetrating analysis is Richard Bushman, *The Refinement of America* (1992). Important studies of American literature include Cathy N. Davidson, *Revolution and the Word: The Rise of the Novel in America* (1986), and Jay Fliegelman, *Prodigals and Pilgrims: The American Revolution against Patriarchal Authority, 1750–1800* (1982). See also William L. Hedges, *Washington Irving: An American Study, 1802–1832* (1965).

Clement Eaton, *Henry Clay and the Art of American Politics* (1957), perceptively describes the coming of political democracy. More detailed studies are Ronald Formisano, *The Transformation of Political Culture: Massachusetts Parties, 1790s–1840s* (1983), and Chilton Williamson, *American Suffrage from Property to Democracy* (1960).

Protestant Christianity and Women's Lives

For women's lives see Harriet B. Applewhite and Darline G. Levy, eds., *Women and Politics in the Age of Democratic Revolution* (1990), and Linda Kerber, *Women of the Republic: Intellect and Ideology in Revolutionary America* (1980). Specialized studies include Joan M. Jensen, *Loosening the Bonds: Mid-Atlantic Farm Women, 1750–1850* (1986); Nancy F. Cott, *The Bonds of Womanhood: "Women's Sphere" in New England, 1780–1835* (1977); Jeanne Boydston, *Home and Work* (1990); and Susan Juster, *Disorderly Women: Sexual Politics and Evangelicalism in Revolutionary New England* (1994).

Women's religious initiatives are discussed in Mary P. Ryan, *Cradle of the Middle Class* (1981); Barbara Epstein, *The Politics of Domesticity: Women, Evangelism, and Temperance* (1978); and Keith Melder, *Beginnings of Sisterhood: The American Women's Rights Movement, 1800–1850* (1977), which also traces the growth of female academies.

Perry Miller, *The Life of the Mind in America* (1966), offers a good overview of the Second Great Awakening. For revivalism see Stephen A. Marini, *Radical Sects of Revolutionary New England* (1982); Bernard A. Weisberger, *They Gathered at the River* (1958); Jon Butler, *Awash in a Sea of Faith* (1989); and P. Jeffrey Potash, *Vermont's Burned Over District* (1991). The course of religious thought in New England is traced in D. P. Edgell, *William Ellery Channing* (1955), and Daniel Walker Howe, *The Unitarian Conscience* (1970).

P A R T *3*

Early Industrialization and the Sectional Crisis
1820–1877

	Economy	Society	Culture	Politics and Government	Sectionalism
	The Industrial Revolution Begins	**The Emergence of a New Class Structure**	**Reform and Reaction to Reform**	**Democratization and Western Expansion**	**From Compromise to Civil War and Reconstruction**
1820	Waltham textile factory (1814) Erie Canal (1825)	Business class emerges Rural women and girls recruited as factory workers	The Benevolent Empire dominates reform Charles Finney leads revivals	Most adult white men gain the vote The rise of Jackson and the Democratic party	Missouri Compromise (1820) South becomes world's largest cotton producer
1830	American textile manufacturers achieve competitive superiority over British Panic of 1837	Mechanics form craft unions Depression shatters labor movement	Joseph Smith founds Mormon church (1830) Garrison abolitionism (1831)	Indian Removal Act (1830) Whig party formed (1834); Second Party System emerges	Nullification crisis (1832) Compromise Tariff (1833) Texas Republic
1840	Stationary steam engines used to power factories Modern factories built in East Coast cities	Working-class districts emerge in cities Irish immigration accelerates	Brook Farm (1841) Seneca Falls convention (1848)	Manifest Destiny (1845) Mexican War (1846–47) Free Soil party (1848)	South attempts to win guarantees for slavery
1850	Railroad trunk lines Panic of 1857	Settlement of Oregon and California	*Uncle Tom's Cabin* (1852)	Whig party disintegrates; Third Party System emerges *Dred Scott* (1857)	Compromise of 1850 Kansas-Nebraska Act (1854) John Brown's raid
1860	War industries thrive in the North Republicans enact economic program	Emancipation Proclamation (1863) Free blacks struggle for control of land	Thirteenth Amendment abolishes slavery (1866)	Lincoln elected (1860) Civil War (1861–65) Reconstruction	South Carolina secedes (1860) Confederate States of America (1861–65)
1870	Panic of 1873	Rise of debt peonage in the South	Fifteenth Amendment (1870) Free black communities	Compromise of 1877	Southern states readmitted to Union

In 1820 America was still a predominantly agricultural society; by 1877 it had become one of the world's most powerful industrial economies. This profound transformation began slowly in the Northeast and then, during the 1840s and 1850s, accelerated and spread throughout the northern states. During this half century the Industrial Revolution had an impact on virtually every aspect of American life.

First, technological and organizational innovations transformed the economy. High-speed machines and a new system of factory labor boosted production while canals and railroads created a vast national market. The industrial sector produced an ever increasing share of the country's wealth—from a negligible proportion in 1820 to a third in 1877.

Second, industrialization spurred the creation of a society divided by new social classes. Many Americans—middle-class people as well as the very wealthy—benefited from the new economic opportunities. An ambitious and powerful business class emerged and sought to assert its leadership, often enlisting religion to justify the new economic order and promote its reformist agenda. Many other Americans, however, lost wealth or status. Especially threatened were artisans whose skills were made redundant by technological advances. By 1840, half the nation's free workers labored for wages, and income and wealth had increasingly become more concentrated in the hands of relatively fewer families.

Third, industrialization increased pressures to democratize political life. Most important, rival social groups organized to advance their interests and at times even to challenge the power of the business class. Farmers turned to political action to address problems involving land, credit, and monopoly power. Some workers proposed the reform of industrial society through the workingmen's parties of the 1820s and 1830s. And immigrant groups arriving from Ireland, Germany, and Canada during the 1840s and 1850s espoused social and religious values that often differed from those of the business class. Under the leadership of Andrew Jackson, the Democratic party became the major vehicle for advancing the interests of those groups. To compete with the Democratic party, the parties of the business class, first the Whigs and then the Republicans, embraced tactics that encouraged wider participation in politics.

Fourth, many Americans became profoundly troubled by the changes sweeping the country. Some sought radical reform—equal rights for women and the abolition of slavery. Abolitionists at first condemned slavery as a sinful expression of arbitrary personal power, but during the 1840s many shifted their ground, attacking a "Slave Power" that seemed to threaten free labor and the economic foundations of the republic.

Fifth, industrialization sharpened sectional divisions. The North was developing an urban industrial economy whereas the South remained a predominantly rural slave-holding society. During the 1840s and 1850s each section tried to impose its distinctive labor system on the West. The defeat of the South in this competition and the fear that it could no longer protect its vital interests led to the secession movement. The secession of a large number of southern states, met by the resolve of Abraham Lincoln's Republican government to preserve the Union, produced the Civil War.

Each side believed that it was fighting to preserve its fundamental institutions and values. Each side fought to preserve a democratic republic and a labor system regarded as essential to democracy. Eventually the North declared its intention to smash slavery. The war became a total war—a war between two societies as well as two armies—and with industrial technology at their disposal, the two sides endured unprecedented casualties and costs.

The war lasted long enough for the North to build the most potent military machine in the world. The fruits of victory were substantial. During Reconstruction, the North imposed its interpretation of the Constitution on the nation, built an enduring base of power for the Republican party, eradicated slavery, and began to extend the benefits of democracy to African-Americans. But the North lacked the will to complete its work—to undertake the economic restructuring that was required to enable freed slaves to participate with full equality in American society.

Lockport on the Erie Canal (detail)

This 1852 watercolor by Mary Keys portrays Lockport, New York, a town that grew up around the locks of the Erie Canal near Buffalo.

The Industrial Revolution
1820–1840

★   ★   ★

In 1831–1832 Alexis de Tocqueville, a French aristocrat, visited the United States; in 1835 he wrote a famous treatise, *Democracy in America*, which described for a European audience the character of republican society in America. Tocqueville observed Americans at work and remarked, "What most astonishes me . . . is not so much the marvelous grandeur of some undertakings, as the innumerable magnitude of small ones." Tocqueville astutely identified a key feature of the Industrial Revolution in America: it was the product of thousands of small innovations—and thousands of small innovators.

In the late eighteenth century those innovators began the transformation of America from a predominantly agricultural society to what would become, a century later, the world's most powerful industrial economy. The 1820s and 1830s were crucial decades in this process, for they saw the most dramatic acceleration of the innovations in manufacturing that had begun so tentatively and in a piecemeal fashion during the 1790s. And even though most Americans remained farmers and most manufacturing was done by craftsmen in traditional shops until after the Civil War, the era of early industrialization was quite distinct from the preindustrial period.

For one thing, by the 1820s the very meaning of the word *manufacturing* had changed. From its original sense of making things by hand, it had come to mean production carried on in factories by workers tending power-driven machinery. More important, industrialization enabled Americans to produce far more goods and services per person. And innovations in pioneering industries such as textiles triggered additional advances—in agriculture, transportation, and other industries—which increased productivity further. Thus the new, more productive era that began in the 1820s provided the basis for a great rise in the living standards for the vast majority of Americans.

Americans sensed that they were living in a new era. Some welcomed it, but many feared the disruption of traditional social relationships. For many, religion provided the glue to keep society—and the new social classes—together.

The Rise of Northeastern Manufacturing

The Industrial Revolution had originated in Great Britain in the middle of the eighteenth century (see Chapter 4). Britain's head start gave it an early advantage that endured for many years. The first factories of the American Industrial Revolution, concentrated in the Northeast, used machines copied from British models and often were supervised by British technicians. But by 1840 Americans had reduced their reliance on British technology and were developing their own machinery and factory organization in order to exploit the nation's main advantage—an abundance of natural resources.

New Organization and New Technology

The first increases in productivity had resulted from the outwork system of rural manufacturing organized by merchants after the Revolutionary War (see Chapter 9). The new ways of organizing workers made manufacturing more efficient even without any technological improvements. As late as 1850 shoe manufacturers running complex outwork systems were the largest employers in Massachusetts but still did not use modern machinery.

Upper Falls of the Genesee River, 1835
Like many early industrial sites, these prosperous flour mills at Rochester, New York, were located to take advantage of natural resources. The Genesee River provided water to irrigate the wheat farms of the Genesee Valley and to transport the grain to mills; its falls powered the mill machinery. (Collection of The New-York Historical Society)

For tasks that were not suited to the outwork system, manufacturers developed a different approach to organizing workers: they brought them all together under one roof. They created the modern *factory*, which concentrated as many of the elements of production as possible in one place and divided the work into specialized tasks. For example, in the 1830s Cincinnati merchants built slaughterhouses that included "disassembly" lines for butchering hogs. A simple system of overhead rails moved the carcasses past workers who were assigned specific tasks: splitting the animals, removing various organs, trimming, weighing, and, finally, hosing down the cleaned carcasses before packers pickled them

and stuffed them in barrels. All these tasks could have been done on any Ohio farm, and the workers were no more skilled than was the typical Ohio farmer. But in the factory the entire butchering and packing process required less than one minute. By the 1840s Cincinnati was disassembling so many hogs that the city had become known as "Porkopolis."

Technological improvements alone could also increase productivity. As early as 1782 the prolific Delaware inventor Oliver Evans had built a highly automated, labor-saving flour mill driven by water power. His machinery lifted the grain to the top of the mill, cleaned the grain as it fell into hoppers, ground it into flour, conveyed the flour back to the top of the mill, and then cooled the flour during its descent into barrels. Evans needed only six men to mill 100,000 bushels of grain a year. His labor-saving techniques spread quickly and became permanent elements in flour milling.

What made industrial development in the United States distinctive during the 1820s and 1830s was the fact that for the first time manufacturers *combined* organizational and technological innovations. By applying technological advances to a factory setting, Americans finally achieved the dramatic productivity gains of the Industrial Revolution. In the United States the first technologically advanced factories were the New England mills that made woolen and cotton cloth.

The Textile Industry

The Industrial Revolution had begun in the textile mills of northern England in the middle of the eighteenth century. After the Revolutionary War their cheap factory-made cloth flooded the American market, threatening the livelihood of hand spinners and weavers. Desperate to recapture the domestic market, American merchants resolved to copy—or steal if necessary—the new British technology.

The earliest practitioners of industrial espionage in America were British *mechanics,* as skilled workers were then called. These workers pursued crafts or what were known as "the mechanical arts." Lured by high wages or offers of partnerships, thousands of British mechanics—who often were machine builders—pirated the detailed and up-to-date information American manufacturers coveted and set sail for the United States. Since British law prohibited the emigration of mechanics as well as the export of textile machinery, many disguised themselves as ordinary laborers or crossed the Atlantic hidden in barrels. In 1812 there were more than 300 British mechanics at work in the Philadelphia area alone.

Samuel Slater. The most important of these mechanics was Samuel Slater, who emigrated from the industrial district of Derbyshire, England, in 1789. He had served as an apprentice to Jedediah Strutt, a partner of Richard Arkwright, the inventor and operator of the most advanced machinery for spinning cotton. Having memorized the design of Arkwright's machinery, the young Slater, disguised by a beard, set sail for New York. There he contacted Moses Brown, a wealthy merchant who had been trying unsuccessfully to duplicate British spinning machinery in his cotton mill in Providence, Rhode Island. Slater took over the management of Brown's mill and replicated the entire set of Arkwright's machines. This was by far the most advanced mill in America, and for that reason the year of its opening—1790—is often considered to mark the beginning of the Industrial Revolution in the United States (see New Technology, page 298).

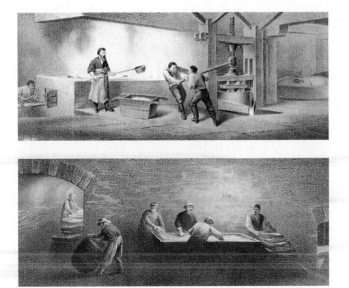

Pork Packing in Cincinnati
This pork-packing plant in Cincinnati used little modern technology except an overhead moving pulley system that carried hog carcasses past the workers. The plant's efficiency was primarily organizational: each worker was assigned a specific task. Such plants pioneered the design of the moving assembly lines that reached a high level of sophistication in the twentieth-century automobile factories of Henry Ford.

Cotton-Spinning Machines

The Industrial Revolution in America began in the textile factories of New England. By 1800 a wide array of machines were being used to card cotton—turning raw cotton into clean fibers—and prepare the fibers for weaving. *Carding machines*, which consisted of two or more cylinders covered with wire pins, combed the fibers into parallel strands. *Roving machines* rolled the carded cotton into a loose roll called a roving.

The real revolution in textile manufacturing came with changes in spinning technology. Rates of production had been severely limited by the slow process of spinning cotton fibers into yarn. As late as the 1760s all yarn was spun by individuals—usually young women—at hand-turned spinning machines. In 1765 the British inventor James Hargreaves invented the *spinning jenny*. (The name likened the machine to a young woman.) The key tool in spinning had always been the spindle, which first elongated and then twisted together strands of fiber to make yarn. Hargreaves's spinning jenny imitated the function of spinning wheels. The operator manually turned a wheel that spun a series of spindles, each of which simultaneously drew out the roving and twisted it into thread.

Jennies saved labor by turning from 24 to more than 100 spindles at once. However, a jenny required a skilled operator. The spinner placed bobbins (spools) with roving on the machine's frame and tied a bit of roving from each bobbin to a spindle, first passing the fibers through a carriage that moved back and forth on the frame. After elongating the roving by moving the carriage, the spinner clamped the rovings to the carriage and then turned the wheel to spin the spindles. When the thread had been given enough twist, the operator moved the carriage forward again while turning the spindles more slowly to wind the thread onto the bobbins. The jenny had to be stopped between the drawing and the twisting and slowed before winding, so it had to be driven by hand. Because of the labor costs involved, relatively few American manufacturers adopted jennies for cotton spinning.

Americans preferred the *spinning frame,* or *water frame* (a *frame* was a common name for a loom). Richard Arkwright patented this loom in Britain in 1769, and Samuel Slater brought it to the United States. Its chief innovation was to separate the functions of drawing and twisting. After two pairs of rollers had elon-

Samuel Slater's Water Frame
Samuel Slater's water frame had two rows of bobbins, twenty-four in each row, on the front and back of the lower portion of the machine.

gated the thread, it was passed down the arm of a flier, a device attached to a spindle. The flier twisted the thread and wound it onto a bobbin attached to the spindle.

The only skill needed to operate a water frame was the ability to knot a broken thread. The machine ran continuously on inexpensive water power. In addition to saving expensive labor, the frame worked much faster than did the jenny. A single water frame produced as much yarn as several hundred spinning wheels working together could. Moreover, the water frame produced yarn that was coarse enough for the rugged cloth used for most clothing in America. Even more significantly, its yarn was strong enough to be used on power looms for the warp, the vertical rows of yarn strung in tension, through which the weft yarn was woven to form the finished cloth.

American inventors quickly made significant improvements in the water frame. By 1830 virtually all the processes involved in the manufacture of cotton cloth had been mechanized in the United States, and most new mills had separate departments for carding, dressing, spinning, and power-loom weaving. The enormous gains in textile productivity and profitability inspired a host of inventors and entrepreneurs to mechanize other industries. The Industrial Revolution had seized the American imagination.

Problems of Competition. Even a mill as advanced as Slater's had difficulty competing with British mills, but Americans had one major advantage: an abundance of natural resources. America's rich agriculture produced a wealth of cotton and wool, and its rivers provided a cheap source of energy. From Maine to Delaware, all along the *fall line*, where the Appalachian foothills drop to the Atlantic coastal plain, the rivers cascade downhill in falls and rapids that can easily be harnessed to run power machinery.

Against this the British had numerous advantages. Falling shipping rates made it cheaper to ship goods across the Atlantic than to transport them within the United States, given its primitive transportation network. British interest rates were lower, so British firms could build factories and market their goods less expensively. And because British companies were better established, they could afford to engage in cutthroat competition, cutting prices briefly but sharply to drive the newer American firms out of business.

The most important British advantage was cheap labor. Britain had a larger population—about 12.6 million in 1810 compared with 7.3 million Americans—and its workers were paid less. Landless agricultural workers and underemployed urban laborers were more than willing to perform simple, repetitive factory jobs, even for low wages. Since unskilled American workers could obtain good pay for farm or construction work, American manufacturers had to offer relatively high wages to attract them to factory jobs.

To make matters worse, the federal government did little to protect the nation's high-wage workers and high-cost industries as they were learning how to meet British competition. Congress did not pass its first major protective *tariff*—a tax on imported goods—until 1824. The measure levied a fairly modest 35 percent tax on imported iron, woolens, cotton, and hemp. But in 1833, under pressure from southern planters and western farmers who wanted to keep down the price of manufactured goods, Congress began to reduce even those tariffs (see Chapter 11).

As a consequence of all these factors, American textile manufacturers often failed. Even those who survived made good profits only when the Embargo of 1807 and the War of 1812 cut off British competition. To overcome their British rivals, American textile manufacturers would have to address the central problem of low-cost British labor.

The Boston Manufacturing Company

In 1811 Francis Cabot Lowell, a wealthy Boston merchant, spent an apparently casual holiday touring British textile mills. A well-educated and charming young man, he flattered his hosts by asking a great many questions, but his easy manner hid a serious purpose. Lowell paid close attention to the answers he received, and later, in his hotel rooms, secretly made detailed drawings of the mills and power machinery he had seen. On returning to the United States, Lowell turned over his drawings to an experienced American mechanic, Paul Moody, who made additional improvements. Lowell then joined with two other merchants, Nathan Appleton and Patrick Tracy Jackson, to raise the staggering sum of $400,000 to form the Boston Manufacturing Company. In 1814 they opened a textile plant in Waltham, Massachusetts, on the Charles River. The Waltham plant was the first in America to perform all the operations of cloth making under one roof. More important, thanks to Moody's improvements, Waltham's innovative power looms operated at even higher speeds

Women Workers in a Textile Mill
This lithograph shows women working in a British cotton factory that closely resembled those in America. They tended spinning machines and looms driven by water power transmitted by a system of belts and wheels. The women here are probably knotting broken threads while the man is most likely adjusting the machinery.

than did those Lowell had seen in Great Britain, making it possible to produce cloth with fewer workers. Improved technology was one part of the answer to Britain's cheaper labor; finding less expensive American workers was the other.

The Waltham Plan. The Boston Manufacturing Company solved the other part of its problem by pioneering a manufacturing system that became known as the Waltham plan. It recruited thousands of farm girls and women as operators of textile machinery, offering them higher wages than they could earn in the outwork system of shoe and broom production or in service as maids or cooks. In addition, manufacturers provided company-run boardinghouses and cultural activities such as evening lectures. The mill owners reassured anxious parents by enforcing strict curfews, prohibiting alcoholic beverages, and requiring regular church attendance. At Lowell (1822), Chicopee (1823), and other sites in Massachusetts and New Hampshire, the Boston company built new cotton factories on the Waltham plan. During the 1820s and 1830s other Boston-owned firms, such as the Hamilton, Suffolk, and Tremont corporations, also adopted the Waltham plan (see Map 10.1).

Some of the young women working under the Waltham plan banked their wages. One worker wrote to a cousin that she wanted to attend Oberlin College (the first coeducational U.S. college, founded in 1833) "because I think it the best way of spending the money I have worked so hard to earn." Others used their wages to help support their families and parents. A girl might help her father to pay off a farm mortgage, a brother to acquire more schooling, or her family to accumulate a dowry for her own marriage. In 1835 eleven-year-old Lucy Larcom of Lowell, Massachusetts, went to work in a textile mill. In 1889 she recalled that she started work "with a light heart" because the work meant that she "was not a trouble or burden or expense" to her widowed mother (see American Voices, page 301). Regardless of what the young women did with their wages, they enjoyed the greater degree of personal independence that their incomes provided. "Don't I feel independent!" another mill worker wrote to her sister in the 1840s. "The thought that I am living on no one is a happy one indeed to me."

Throughout the 1820s and 1830s young women made up a majority of all workers in the cotton-textile industry and nearly half the workers in woolen-textile manufacturing. In the early 1830s more than 40,000 women were working in textile mills. Most of the remaining 20,000 textile workers were children under the age of fourteen, the majority of whom were girls. Men constituted only a small fraction of the textile operatives. The few men in the industry worked primarily in Rhode Island under the Fall River plan, which offered unskilled factory work to entire families. The success of

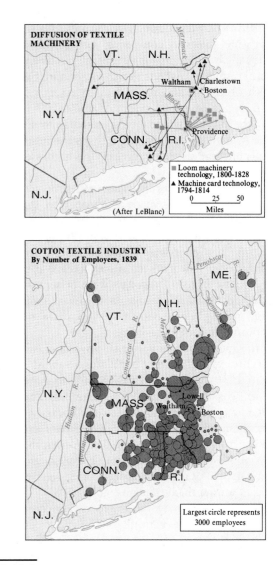

MAP 10.1

Early Industrial Enterprise in New England

As new and improved textile machinery spread across New England, modern textile factories sprang up and became concentrated at locations such as Waltham and Lowell in eastern Massachusetts. On the lower map each circle is placed on a town with one or more textile factories. The size of each circle indicates the relative number of spindles or employees in that town; the data are sufficiently similar for historians to be able to trace and compare the development of the industry over this period.

the Waltham and Fall River plans was due largely to the meager profitability of New England agriculture and the high birth rate among New England farm families, which led most of their young people to seek other opportunities. The region's poorer farms could not hold young people, who quickly turned to factory work even though it meant operating fast-moving machines, doing highly repetitive tasks, and disrupting traditional family life (see Chapter 11).

Lucy Larcom

Early Days at Lowell

Lucy Larcom (1824–1893) went to work in a textile mill in Lowell, Massachusetts, when she was eleven years old. She remained there until 1846, when she moved west to Illinois with her sisters and a great tide of other New Englanders. In later life she became a teacher and a writer; this selection is from her autobiography, *A New England Girlhood*.

I never cared much for machinery. The buzzing and hissing and whizzing of pulleys and rollers and spindles and flyers around me often grew tiresome. I could not see into their complications, or feel interested in them. But in a room below us we were sometimes allowed to peer in through a sort of blind door at the great waterwheel that carried the works of the whole mill. It was so huge we could only watch a few of its spokes at a time, and part of its dripping rim, moving with a slow, measured strength through the darkness that shut it in. It impressed me with something of the awe which comes to us in thinking of the great Power which keeps the mechanism of the universe in motion.

. . . We did not call ourselves ladies. We did not forget that we were working girls, wearing coarse aprons suitable to our work, and that there was some danger of our becoming drudges. I know that sometimes the confinement of the mill became very warisome to me. In the sweet June weather I would lean far out of the window, and try not to hear the unceasing clash of sound inside. Looking away to the hills, my whole stifled being would cry out

Oh, that I had wings!

Still I was there from choice, and

The prison unto which we doom ourselves,
No prison is.

I regard it as one of the privileges of my youth that I was permitted to grow up among these active, interesting girls, whose lives were not mere echoes of other lives, but had principle and purpose distinctly their own. Their vigor of character was a natural development. The New Hampshire girls who came to Lowell were descendants of the sturdy backwoodsmen who settled that State scarcely a hundred years before. Their grandmothers had suffered the hardships of frontier life. . . . Those young women did justice to their inheritance. They were earnest and capable; ready to undertake anything that was worth doing. My dreamy, indolent nature was shamed into activity among them. They gave me a larger, firmer ideal of womanhood. . . .

Country girls were naturally independent, and the feeling that at this new work the few hours they had of every-day leisure were entirely their own was a statisfaction to them. They preferred it to going out as "hired help." It was like a young man's pleasure in entering upon business for himself. Girls had never tried that experiment before, and they liked it. It brought out in them a dormant strength of character which the world did not previously see.

Source: Lucy Larcom, *A New England Girlhood* (Boston: Houghton Mifflen, 1889), 153–155, 181–183, 196–200.

New England's Success. Less than forty years after the founding of Slater's mill, New England companies finally achieved competitive superiority over the British in American markets. In 1825 Thomas Jefferson, who had earlier warned against the dehumanizing perils of industrialization, was moved to express his pride in the American achievement: "Our manufacturers are now very nearly on a footing with those of England. [England] has not a single improvement which we do not possess, and many of them adopted by ourselves to our ordinary use." The Waltham and Fall River plans also gave New England manufacturers a competitive edge over other American textile manufacturers. In New York and Pennsylvania, where agricultural employment was far better paid than in New England, textile producers were slower to adopt the technology of the Industrial Revolution. They concentrated on modifying traditional technology to produce higher-quality cloth than the British and New England mills manufactured. In the South textile entrepreneurs almost always failed because they lacked a cheap supply of labor. Poor whites disdained factory work, and the cost of buying or renting slaves was prohibitive because of the huge profits slaveowners could earn by growing cotton. The southern textile industry languished until after the Civil War.

American Mechanical Genius

Until the 1840s individuals of modest wealth provided most of the capital required to start new manufacturing firms. Only in Massachusetts did wealthy merchant capitalists such as Francis Cabot Lowell invest in modern industry. More typically, it was mechanics and small

merchants who took the risks, pooling their capital and often borrowing from family members and friends to start factories. Some storekeepers, hoping to expand their business, invested in small mills. A mill could increase a storekeeper's ability to purchase supplies for his store and, by generating jobs and income, increase the local market for his goods. Storekeeper-manufacturers commonly tried to pay workers with credit at their stores in order to make certain they spent their wages on store goods.

Rockdale. The early history of industry in Rockdale, Pennsylvania, a small mill village in the Delaware Valley near Philadelphia, illustrates the entrepreneurial role of small manufacturers. In 1825 there were four cloth manufacturers in Rockdale. One was William Martin, a young, modestly wealthy Philadelphia merchant who had purchased his mills at a sheriff's sale (a sale of bankrupted property), using his savings and those of his brother-in-law. He expanded the mills by borrowing from an uncle and mortgaging the property. In 1829, however, cloth prices tumbled and he was forced into bankruptcy. The second manufacturer was John Phillips, the son of a once-prominent Philadelphia merchant who had fallen on hard times. John had married well, and he borrowed from his new brother-in-law to buy mills. Strong family support and prudent management enabled him to survive and, in 1835, to relocate his machinery to a new mill in Philadelphia. The third entrepreneur was John Crozer, a farmer and the owner of a failing sawmill. He bought a textile mill at a sheriff's sale by mortgaging his farm and borrowing from a brother-in-law. With enormous personal energy and sustained family assistance, he built the mill into a thriving business and became one of the wealthiest men in Rockdale. The fourth manufacturer, John Carter, was an immigrant and the only one of the four with experience in textiles, from his years as a mill manager in Britain. Because of his expertise, he was able to borrow extensively from local banks. Nonetheless, largely because he lacked relatives with capital, he suffered a devastating bankruptcy in 1826. The lesson was clear: success was impossible without determination, skill, and family finances.

Mechanics often crossed into the ranks of small manufacturing entrepreneurs by joining them as partners or by starting their own manufacturing firms. Literally thousands of modest mechanics developed the simple inventions that cumulatively revolutionized American manufacturing. Few of these craftsmen had formal education, but they had learned about machinery in small, traditional craft shops and, increasingly, in modern factories.

One such inventor, Richard Garsed, started working in a textile mill in New Hope, Pennsylvania, when he was only eight years old. Ten years later, in 1837,

after his father had purchased a small mill in Rockdale, Garsed experimented with improvements on his father's power looms. In three years he nearly doubled their speed. By 1842 he had invented a cam and harness device (patented in 1846) that allowed elaborately figured fabrics such as damask to be woven by machine.

The Sellars Family and the Franklin Institute. Garsed was only one of the many American mechanics who by the 1820s had replaced British immigrants at the cutting edge of technological innovation, usually basing their success on elaborate ties of family and friendship. In the Delaware Valley the remarkable Sellars family dominated an interrelated group of inventors who transmitted their mechanical knowledge from one generation to the next. Samuel Sellars, Jr., invented a machine for twisting worsted woolen yarn. His son John harnessed water power for the efficient operation of the family's sawmills and gristmills and devised a machine to weave wire sieves. John's sons and grandsons built machine shops that turned out a variety of new products: riveted leather fire hoses, papermaking equipment, and eventually locomotives.

In 1824 members of the Sellars family and other mechanics and small manufacturers founded the Franklin Institute in Philadelphia. Named after Benjamin Franklin, whom the mechanics admired for his scientific accomplishments and idealization of hard work, the institute fostered the mechanics' sense of professional identity. It also underscored the fact that mechanics had become more than traditional craftsmen. Increasingly, mechanics included engineers and inventors at the forefront of the Industrial Revolution. The institute published a journal; provided high school instruction in mechanics, chemistry, mathematics, and mechanical drawing; and organized annual fairs to exhibit the most advanced products and reward their designers. At the 1842 fair the institute's judges awarded a silver medal to Richard Garsed for cotton and worsted damask tablecloths that promised "successful competition with the imported." Craftsmen in Ohio and other states soon established their own mechanics institutes, offering the same kinds of programs that the Franklin Institute had pioneered.

Machine Tools. The most outstanding contribution of American mechanics to the Industrial Revolution was the development of machines capable of making other machines, that is, *machine tools*. In the textile industry mechanics invented devices—lathes, planers, and boring machines—that could make interchangeable textile-machine parts. These machine-tooled parts, which required only a minimum of filing and fitting, made it possible to manufacture textile machinery that was low in price and precise enough in design and construction to operate at higher speeds than British equipment.

Once American craftsmen had perfected machine tools for the textile industry, the Industrial Revolution swept through the rest of American manufacturing. If anything, the impact of machine tools was even greater in industries that produced goods made of iron or steel, such as plows, scythes, and axes. In 1832 the mechanics David Hinman and Elisha K. Root, employed by Samuel W. Collins in his Connecticut ax-making company, built a vastly improved die-forging machine—a device that pressed and hammered hot metal into *dies,* or cutting forms. Using the improved machine, a skilled worker could increase his production of ax heads from 12 to 300 a day.

Some of the most important machine-building innovators worked in the firearms industry. Beginning in the 1790s, the federal government created a demand for muskets that traditional producers, relying almost entirely on skilled workers and the slow crafting of muskets one-by-one, could not meet. Eli Whitney, an inventor and business promotor, was the first to receive a federal contract for muskets so large that it required mass-production techniques to fulfill. The machine tools he and his co-workers designed in his New Haven factory between 1798 and his death in 1825 represented the first major steps toward realizing the idea that interchangeable parts could make possible large-scale, high-speed production (see American Lives, pages 304–305).

After Whitney's death, his work was completed by his partner John H. Hall, an engineer at the federal armory at Harpers Ferry, Virginia. Hall developed all the basic machine tools required to produce modern arms: turret lathes, milling machines, and precision grinders. By 1840 Hall and other American mechanics had created the first modern machine-tool industry in the world. Thereafter, manufacturers could use machine tools to produce complicated machinery at high speed and in great quantity. The direct transmission of information and insight across just two generations of engineers connected the innovations of Whitney and Hall with Henry Ford's introduction of the first fully automated assembly line in 1913.

The Expansion of Markets

During the 1820s and the 1830s the Industrial Revolution stimulated the rapid expansion of the American marketplace. Manufacturers and merchants in the industrializing Northeast developed a national system of markets, stimulated the growth of cities and towns, and promoted the construction of a massive transportation system to link the Northeast and the Old Northwest.

Regional Trade Patterns

In the first forty years after independence Americans relied on the exportation of farm products to Europe. Between 1790 and 1810 as much as 15 percent of the national product was exported—roughly the level that had prevailed in the mid-eighteenth century. However, this changed dramatically during the 1820s. By enhancing the incomes of Americans, the Industrial Revolution enabled Americans to consume a larger share of the production of domestic farmers and manufacturers. American producers in turn sharply reduced their reliance on European markets. By 1830 they were exporting only 6 percent of the national product, a level that remained constant until the mid-twentieth century.

Eli Whitney's Factory and Village
Whitney's Mill Rock armory, which he began building in 1798 near New Haven, Connecticut, produced inexpensive, high-quality guns until his death in 1825. Whitney tried to supervise every detail of his workers' lives in the mill village of Whitneyville.

Eli Whitney: Machine Builder and Promoter

Eli Whitney once described the world as "a Lottery in which many draw blanks." But he was often lucky during a life (1765–1825) that spanned the chaotic years between the American Revolution and the Industrial Revolution. His luck, combined with relentless social ambition and exceptional talents for self-advertisement and mechanical innovation, allowed him to exert a major influence on the course of the Industrial Revolution in the United States.

Whitney was born on a Westborough, Massachusetts, farm in economic circumstances that were typical of many farm families in New England during the late eighteenth century. His family's land was relatively poor, but the farm produced enough for the family to live comfortably, and Eli's father, who served for many years as a justice of the peace, was a respected member of the community.

As a child, Eli found routine farm chores boring and even depressing. As often as he could, he fled to the farm's workshop to fashion and repair household furniture and farm tools. Early on, Eli showed a talent for crafting wood and metal, and he preferred tinkering in the shop to the drudgery of the barns and fields. The young Whitney also found that he enjoyed talking with neighboring townspeople. His sister recalled that as a child he "possessed a great measure of affability." It was probably in those conversations that Whitney sharpened his awareness of how the marginal and overcrowded land in the settled parts of New England constrained economic opportunities for young people.

The death of his mother in 1777 and the nearly simultaneous outbreak of the American Revolution opened new doors for Eli. His father remarried in 1779, but in the interim Eli had the freedom to employ his mechanical and social skills and explore new economic horizons. When he was fourteen, Whitney persuaded his father to install a forge in the workshop so that he could produce nails and knife blades as substitutes for the British imports that were no longer available. His enterprise flourished, as did many like it in New England, and he soon hired a worker to help him meet the demand. Two years later an avalanche of cheap nails from Britain ruined Eli's market. But he demonstrated his exceptional flexibility by shifting his efforts to the production of women's hatpins and men's walking sticks.

Despite his successes in household manufacturing, Whitney knew that the family farm could not provide a living for himself, two younger brothers, and four sisters. In any case, farm life did not appeal to him. Whitney aspired to greater wealth and status and concluded that college would provide the most reliable access to the traditional elites of New England. But he lacked the required college preparation in English grammar, classics, and mathematics. He enrolled at Leicester Academy, a private secondary school, and to finance his studies taught school for six years (1783–1789) in neighboring towns. There he made the connections that would eventually get him into Yale College.

At Yale, Whitney might have studied engineering or science if the college had offered those subjects. But like the other colleges of the day, Yale did not. In any event, Whitney was more interested in the social connections the school provided. At graduation in 1792 the president of Yale and Phineas Miller, a Yale alumnus in Georgia, found Whitney a job as tutor on a plantation.

In traveling south Whitney met Catherine Greene, the young widow of the Revolutionary War general Nathanael Greene. Whitney's tutoring position fell through, and she invited him for an extended visit to her Georgia plantation, Mulberry Grove, which Miller managed. Mrs. Greene found Whitney charming and recognized that his "affability" and Yale-bred manners would make him a social asset. Whitney, for his part, became fascinated by the exclusive world of the planters. He paid close attention to their concerns and discovered a way to employ what he learned as a youth to help them solve an economic problem, win social acceptance, and make a fortune at the same time. With the encouragement of Catherine Greene and Phineas Miller, he set up a rough workshop and applied the technique he had used to produce women's hatpins to fashion the tines for the prototype of the cotton gin, the machine that would revolutionize cotton production.

In 1793 Whitney returned to New Haven and began manufacturing gins in quantity by using special machine tools he had developed. He hoped to maintain a monopoly for his gin, which he had patented in 1794.

Eli Whitney

Eli Whitney posed for this portrait in the 1820s, when he had achieved both prosperity and social standing. His success inspired his admiring portraitist and New Haven neighbor, Samuel F. B. Morse, to shift his energy from painting to industrial technology in the 1830s and 1840s, during which he devised the first successful commercial telegraph.

He proudly reported to his father that "One of the most Respectable Gentlemen in N. Haven [said] that he would rather be the author of the Invention than the prime minister of England."

But the patent did not protect Whitney from the numerous planters who made their own gins or from manufacturers who made slight improvements on his design. A year after he took out his patent, hundreds of southern operators employed gins modeled after Whitney's but paid him no royalties. Over the years Whitney continued to market his own gins but spent much of the profit on largely futile lawsuits to protect his patent rights.

To get out of debt, Whitney turned to manufacturing a product that would have a larger—and guaranteed—market. His Yale network again served him well. In the effort to patent his gin, he had formed a friendship with another Yale alumnus, Oliver Wolcott, who became secretary of the treasury in 1795. In 1798 Whitney persuaded Wolcott that he knew how to mechanize the production of firearms and thus produce them at an unprecedented scale and pace. Whitney's information and timing were superb. The federal government had established two armories, in Springfield, Massachusetts, and Harpers Ferry, Virginia, but their production was dismal. Congress feared war with France and just before Whitney's petition to Wolcott it had authorized the Treasury to contract for arms with private parties. Almost immediately Wolcott offered Whitney a contract to manufacture 10,000 muskets in only twenty-eight months.

Whitney knew little about the details of musket manufacture, but he did understand the potential of machine tools. He was confident that he could design tools that would enable him to produce interchangeable musket parts and thus speed the production of muskets. He assured a doubtful Wolcott that he would "form the tools so that the tools themselves shall fashion the work and give to every part its just proportion—which when once accomplished will give expeditious uniformity, and exactness to the whole." Whitney went on to devise improved forms and jigs to guide the hands of mechanics; he also crafted the first milling machine, which used sharp teeth on a gearlike wheel to cut metal; and he achieved a greater degree of interchangeability of parts than had anyone before him.

Nonetheless, Whitney was unable to develop all the tools he needed to fulfill his original contract on time. It was 1809 before he produced the 10,000 muskets, and even then he had to resort to traditional handicraft. But Wolcott remained loyal, as did the government inspector in New Haven, who was another Yale alumnus. Also helpful was a group of ten prominent citizens of New Haven, including Pierpont Edwards, the wealthy son of Jonathan Edwards. This group, most of whose members were Yale graduates, guaranteed an additional advance of federal money to Whitney. Whitney also won important supporters outside the Yale circle. The most influential was Thomas Jefferson, who had been interested in interchangeability since the 1780s. He had followed Whitney's career from the time Whitney had applied for a patent for the cotton gin, and as president-elect, had witnessed a dramatic public demonstration of interchangeability that Whitney staged in Washington. Jefferson understood what the perfection of Whitney's techniques could do for the productivity of industry.

With Jefferson's encouragement, Whitney continued to develop his techniques. During the War of 1812 and afterward, he won new federal contracts. He also had contracts to supply muskets to the militias of Connecticut and New York. The new work, along with shrewd investment advice from Oliver Wolcott, provided Whitney with the wealth and social position of which he had dreamed. He dined regularly with New Haven's elite, and Yale awarded him an honorary master's degree. In 1817 Whitney joined one of New England's most respected families by marrying Henrietta Edwards, the daughter of Pierpont Edwards.

When Whitney died in 1825, he had still not achieved his goal of complete mass production. But his self-promotion, linked with his promotion of interchangeability and mechanization, did much to ensure that the Industrial Revolution would spread throughout American manufacturing during the next seventy years.

The Yankee Peddler
Even as late as 1830, the approximate date of this painting, most Americans lived too far from town markets to shop there regularly. Farm families, such as this affluent one represented by an unknown artist, purchased most of their tinware, silverware, clocks, yard goods, pins and needles, and notions from peddlers, often New Englanders, who traveled far and wide with their vans.

While exports declined in significance, the domestic trade in agricultural and manufacturing goods flourished. Americans traded with one another in two ways. First, they exchanged goods *within* regions. Philadelphians, for example, traded locally manufactured textiles for farm products grown nearby: flour and corn; dairy products; fruits and vegetables; hay for the horses that pulled carriages, coaches, and omnibuses; and wood for heating and cooking. Second, Americans exchanged products *among* regions. Most important, merchants in the industrializing Northeast exchanged textiles, clothing, boots and shoes, muskets, and farm equipment for wheat, corn, whiskey, and hogs from farms in the Great Lakes Basin and the Ohio Valley. Manufacturers and farmers in the Northeast and the Old Northwest specialized in production for shipment to other regions. Because this interregional trade grew rapidly, they increased their scale of production, became more efficient, and enlarged their profits.

The exception to the trend of increased domestic trade was the South, which continued to produce primarily for international markets. As the Cotton Kingdom expanded across the Old Southwest, the United States became the world's largest cotton producer. Although southern farmers supplied the textile mills of the Northeast, they exported most of their cotton to Britain. And although the flow of manufactured goods from the Northeast to the South increased, southerners continued to import the majority of their manufactured goods from British suppliers. Southerners also obtained most of their financial and marketing services from British import houses. Food did not figure in this trade:

Southerners fed themselves almost entirely from nearly self-sufficient plantations and small farms on the fringe of the cotton economy.

Thus the South's economy remained tied not to other parts of the United States but to Britain. Its plantation economy more closely resembled those of Brazil and Cuba. As in those colonial economies, earnings from exports went largely to Europeans and local planters. Like the landed classes in other plantation societies, southern planters reinvested their profits by expanding their slave labor force and increasing the size of their estates.

The Growth of Cities and Towns

Industrialization and the expansion of interregional trade stimulated the growth of northern cities and towns in the 1820s. For the first time urban places—defined as localities with more than 2,500 inhabitants—began to grow more rapidly than did the population as a whole. There were also more such places: the number of towns and cities with 2,500 to 50,000 people more than doubled in twenty years, from 58 towns in 1820 to 126 in 1840. The total urban population grew fourfold, from 443,000 in 1820 to 1,844,000 in 1840.

Fall-Line Towns. The most rapidly growing urban areas were the new industrial towns. Since early mills used water power to run their machinery, factory towns sprang up all along the fall line. In 1822, for example, the Boston Manufacturing Company decided to build a new complex of mills in East Chelmsford, Massachusetts, on the Merrimack River. Within a few years the sleepy village was transformed into a bustling town, now named Lowell in honor of the company's founder. Hartford, Connecticut; Trenton, New Jersey; and Wilmington, Delaware, also surged as mill owners recruited workers from the surrounding countryside.

Western Cities. Western cities grew almost as rapidly. In 1830 New Orleans, Pittsburgh, Cincinnati, and Louisville accounted for almost three-quarters of the urban population in the West. St. Louis joined the West's largest cities by 1840, its growth stimulated by increased traffic to and from the territory west of the Mississippi. Rochester, Buffalo, Cleveland, Detroit, and Chicago also grew rapidly during the 1830s. The initial expansion of all these cities resulted from their location at points where goods had to be transferred from one mode of transport, such as canal boats or farmers' wagons, to another, such as steamboats or sailing vessels. Merchants and bankers took advantage of the special location of these cities to develop the marketing, provisioning, and financial services that were essential to farmers and small-town merchants in the hinterland.

Despite their commercial dynamism, however, manufacturing in these communities remained mostly traditional in technology and organization. At this time no western city challenged the industrial preeminence of the eastern seaport cities.

The Rise of New York. The old Atlantic seaports—Boston, New York, Philadelphia, and Baltimore—remained the largest American cities, but of the four only New York grew more rapidly than did the population as a whole. New York's growth rate was phenomenal, twice that of the nation as a whole during the 1820s and 1830s. New York overtook Philadelphia as the nation's largest city in 1810 and over the next two decades became the economic center of America (see Map 10.2).

New York boasted the best harbor in the United States. Ocean vessels could sail or steam 150 miles up the Hudson River to Albany; no other Atlantic port provided such deep penetration of the interior. Moreover, ships had unobstructed, yet protected, access to the docks on Manhattan Island. And New York merchants were unusually enterprising. They had made their city the smuggling center of British North America during the eighteenth century and had used their wits to survive British occupation during the Revolution. New York merchants, more so than merchants in Boston or Philadelphia, welcomed outsiders and their money. In 1817 New York merchants founded the New York Stock Exchange, which soon became the nation's chief market for securities.

In their most aggressive stroke, New York merchants persuaded their state government to enact a law that earmarked tax revenues for the construction of a project private investors regarded as too risky—the Erie Canal. It would stretch from Albany to Buffalo and Lake Erie. Opened in 1825, the canal connected New York City and Albany with the vast interior—the burgeoning farming communities of upstate New York and the entire Great Lakes region (see pages 310–311).

New York merchants sought to control foreign commerce as well. In 1818 four Quaker merchants founded the Black Ball Line to carry goods between New York and European ports such as Liverpool, London, and Le Havre. This was the first transatlantic *packet service*. The ships carried cargo, people, and mail on a regular schedule, and their dependability made the

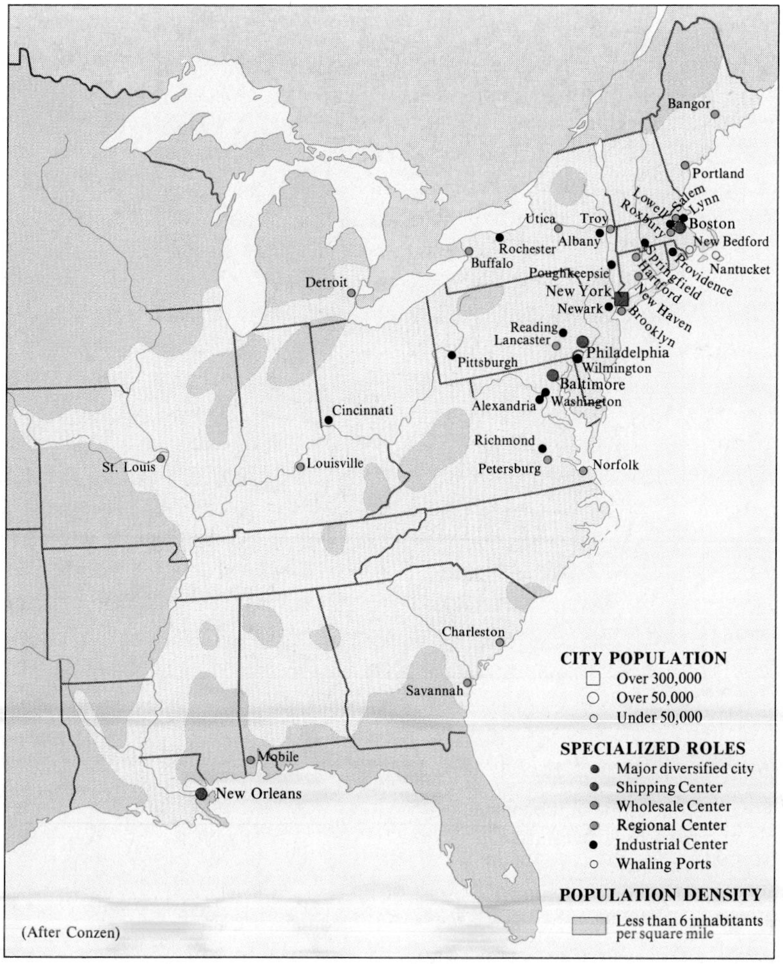

MAP 10.2

The Nation's Major Cities in 1840
By 1840 American cities developed specialized roles—Cincinnati and Pittsburgh became industrial centers, Hartford and Lancaster grew as regional centers for farm communities, and Brooklyn and Buffalo developed as wholesaling centers. The oldest ports on the Atlantic seaboard remained the most diversified and played a critical role in managing and organizing the national economy.

service extremely attractive to international traders. New York merchants also gained an unassailable lead in commerce with the newly independent Latin American nations of Brazil, Peru, and Venezuela. Finally, they controlled a small but growing portion of the cotton trade. Their agents in southern ports offered finance, insurance, and shipping to cotton exporters and won for New York a dominant share of the cotton that passed through northern harbors. By 1840 New York's mercantile community controlled almost two-thirds of the nation's foreign imports and almost half of all foreign trade, both imports and exports.

The West: Farming New Land

The Industrial Revolution affected farming people in the United States in a far different way than it did in Europe. In Europe it forced a massive reduction and relocation of rural populations; in the United States it promoted the rapid occupation of new lands by farmers and a huge increase in the rural population (see Map 10.3). At the same time that the nation's industrial

towns and seaport cities were gaining in size and importance, millions of farming families were still moving west.

Migration Routes. These pioneers migrated in three great streams. In the South, cotton producers continued the migration into the Old Southwest that had begun after the War of 1812. They moved their slaves and the Cotton Kingdom into the new states of Mississippi (admitted to the Union in 1817) and Alabama (1819) and on into Louisiana (1812), Missouri (1821), Arkansas (1836), and Texas (1845). Southerners also pioneered the early settlement of the Old Northwest. Small farmers from the Upper South, especially Virginia and Kentucky, created a second stream as they followed westward routes that had been established as early as the 1790s. They ferried their wagons across the Ohio River and introduced corn and hog farming to the southern parts of Ohio (1803), Indiana (1816), and Illinois (1818).

The third stream of migrants came from the Northeast. This flow had begun during the 1790s when settlers had poured into upstate New York; it reached the

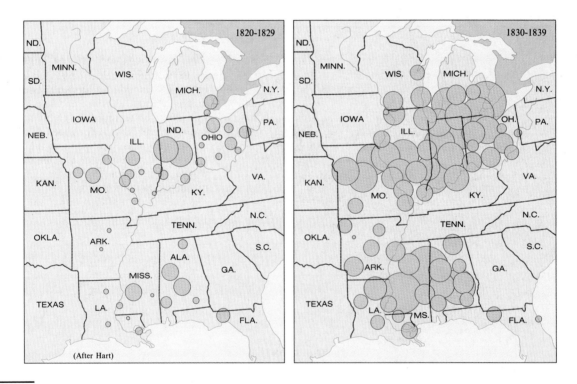

MAP 10.3

Western Land Sales, 1820–1839

Land offices opened up on the frontier to sell government land. Each circle centers on a land office, and the area of each circle represents the relative amount of land sold at that office. The maps show how settlement spread and intensified in the farmland of the Ohio Valley and the cotton plantations of the Old Southwest during the 1820s and the 1830s.

trans-Appalachian West during the 1820s. During that decade and the next, settlers from New England and the Middle Atlantic states, particularly New York, traveled along the Erie Canal to establish wheat farms in the Great Lakes Basin: northern Ohio, northern Illinois, Michigan (1837), and Wisconsin (1848).

Westward migration significantly shifted the population center of American society. In 1830 about 3 million people—more than a fourth of the nation's population—lived west of the Appalachians. By 1840 the figure was over 5 million, more than a third of all Americans. Western growth often entailed the stagnation or decline of eastern communities. Vast numbers of men and women left the seaboard states where they were born, taking with them their savings, personal property, and skills. During the 1820s and 1830s the Carolinas, Vermont, and New Hampshire lost nearly as many people through migration as they gained through the excess of births over deaths. In New England abandoned farms and homes dotted the countryside, their owners gone in search of better lands farther west.

The Incentives. Farmers moved west for complex and various reasons. Some simply wanted to increase their profits, and others wanted to acquire enough land to maintain their children in traditional rural communities. However, all farmers appreciated the economic opportunities offered by the virgin soils of the West. A cotton planter from upland Georgia, a prosperous wheat farmer from the Connecticut Valley, and a hardscrabble subsistence farmer from Vermont might have very different values, but all could recognize the economic advantage of farming on new land. Cotton planters who moved to new lands in the Southwest were glad to leave behind soil depleted by relentless cultivation. Wheat farmers migrating to the prairies of the Old Northwest were relieved of the heavy labor required to clear land of forests and rocks. The settlers soon discovered that the sweat and toil expended on a patch of fresh prairie yielded a much larger crop than could be obtained from a plot of the same size in the East.

The Tools. New and improved tools made farmers even more eager to occupy new lands. During the 1830s farmers throughout the North bought the new cast-iron plow invented in 1819 by Jethro Wood, a farmer in upstate New York. With this device, farmers could cut their plowing time in half and till much larger fields. Wood's plow, which could be repaired with replaceable cast-iron parts, spelled doom for village blacksmiths. Their handmade product could not compete with this low-cost, high-quality product of northeastern foundries. Western farmers purchased many other sturdy, inexpensive mass-produced necessities: shovels and spades, which Alan Wood began fabricating

from rolled iron at his Delaware Iron Works in 1826; axes, which the Collins Company of Connecticut began forging in the same year; and horseshoes, which Henry Burden of Troy, New York, began to make in 1835.

The Land. Cheap land prices made western settlement an even more practical choice. In 1820 Congress reduced the price of federal land from $2.00 an acre to $1.25—just enough to cover the cost of surveying and sale. For $100 a farmer could buy 80 acres, the minimum required under federal law. With the federal government offering huge quantities of public land at that price, the basic market price for all undeveloped land remained low. Purchasing land was well within the reach of most migrating people. During the 1820s and 1830s the average American family could save enough in two years to make the minimum purchase even without raising money from the sale of an old farm.

Effects on Industrialization. Although farms, not factories, dominated the economic life of the West, western settlement did promote industrial development indirectly. Efficient western farms provided eastern manufacturers with low-cost cotton, wool, leather, and other raw materials, thus helping them compete with the British. In addition, these farms supplied abundant and inexpensive grain, meat, vegetables, and fruit that helped maintain the health and strength of factory workers. The growing urban populations of the Northeast increased the demand for, and the prices of, all types of farm goods. Western markets in turn were of growing importance to eastern industry. During the 1830s the production of farm implements—horseshoes, plows, shovels, scythes, hoes, and axes—accounted for fully half the nation's consumption of pig iron. Westward expansion enabled industrializing America to take advantage of cheap land and realize the economic advantages of regional specialization.

The Transportation Revolution

The dramatic expansion of the domestic economy during the Industrial Revolution required a revolution in transportation. The road building that had begun in the 1790s achieved little by 1820. In that year the nation had no true road system, particularly in the West. Spring thaws, rainstorms, and winter conditions often made dirt roads impassable. Western settlers complained to the federal government that they lacked roads to get their goods to market. To correct that problem and integrate large chunks of territory into their buoyant economy, Americans rapidly built a transportation system of unprecedented size, complexity, and cost (see Figure 10.1).

FIGURE 10.1

Inland Freight Rates, 1784–1900
The costs of shipping goods inland on rivers, canals, and railroads fell as new technologies were developed between 1784 and 1900. If a logarithmic scale had not been used for cents per ton-mile, a much larger chart would have been necessary to show the enormous gap between wagon rates and the other rates.

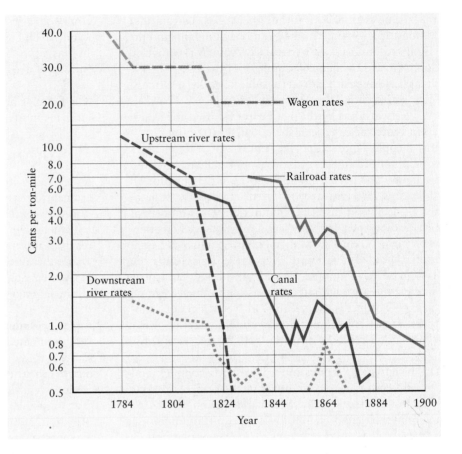

Roads. After 1820 local road building continued, especially in long-settled areas, but the quality of roads did not improve until the introduction of automobiles early in the twentieth century, and no interregional system of roads emerged until the 1830s. Then, in cooperation with state governments, the federal government built interregional roads for pedestrians, horses, herds of livestock, and heavily loaded wagons. The federal government regarded the creation of this vital infrastructure as a legitimate part of its responsibilities. The most significant feat was the National Road, which started in Cumberland, Maryland, passed Wheeling (then in Virginia) in 1818, crossed the Ohio River in 1833, and reached Vandalia, Illinois, in 1850. By that time construction of major interregional roads had ceased, their role taken over by canals and railroads.

Canals. After the War of 1812 Americans began to build canals to connect the inland areas along rivers and lakes with coastal cities and towns, but progress was slow. When the New York legislature began the Erie Canal in 1817, no canal in the United States was longer than 28 miles—a reflection of the huge capital investment required for canals and the lack of engineering expertise. A canal frenzy swept the nation, and canals became the most important part of the transportation revolution.

New Yorkers drove hard to complete the Erie Canal. Three key advantages made the project possible: the vigorous support of New York City merchants; the backing of De Witt Clinton, New York's powerful governor; and the relative gentleness of the terrain. Even amateur surveyors—such as James Geddes and Benjamin Wright, who had been trained as lawyers—were able to design and construct much of the canal.

The Erie Canal was an instant success. The first section, a stretch of 75 miles opened in 1819, immediately generated large revenues for New York State. When the canal was completed in 1825, the 40-foot-wide ribbon of water, complete with locks to raise and lower boats, reached 364 miles from Albany to Buffalo and reduced the journey for passengers traveling from New York City to Buffalo from twenty days to six. The canal also greatly accelerated the flow of goods. On a road in upstate New York, four horses would take an entire day to pull a 1-ton load 12 miles. On the canal, two horses on the towpath could pull a 100-ton load 24 miles in a day.

The Erie Canal fulfilled every promise made by its promoters. It moved settlers from the East to the Old Northwest. It gave the new western farmers of the Great Lakes Basin, as well as those of upstate New York, cheap access to the port of New York. And it placed western communities within easy reach of eastern manufacturers and the merchants of New York City.

Construction of the Erie Canal

Gangs of construction workers on the Erie Canal had to excavate deep cuts through rough land. The artist who sketched this scene, like the canal planners, was more interested in the scale of the project than in the personalities of the faceless workers. Working conditions were even worse in the marshes near Syracuse where, in 1819, a thousand workers fell ill with fever, many of whom died.

After a trip on the Erie Canal in 1830, the novelist Nathaniel Hawthorne wrote:

> Surely the water of this canal must be the most fertilizing of all fluids, for it causes towns with their masses of brick and stone, their churches and theaters, their business and hubbub, their luxury and refinement, their gay dames and polished citizens, to spring up, till in time the wondrous stream may flow between two continuous lines of buildings, through one thronged street, from Buffalo to Albany.

The spectacular benefits and profits brought by the Erie Canal prompted a national canal boom. Civic and business leaders in major cities and towns competed to build their own canals to capture trade with the West. Some promoters took advantage of New York's experience by hiring the young men who had learned canal engineering while building the Erie. Many promoters also copied New York's fiscal innovations. They persuaded their state governments to charter companies, guarantee the companies' credit, and invest directly in them or force mutual savings banks to do so—sometimes even to take over the ownership of such companies. Altogether, state governments provided—often by borrowing from British and Dutch investors—almost three-quarters of the $200 million invested in canals by 1840. By then the new canals had provided three critical transportation links: (1) from the coastal plain to the upcountry of the Atlantic seaboard states, (2) from the seaboard states to the Great Lakes Basin and the Ohio Valley, and (3) from the Great Lakes to the Ohio and Mississippi rivers (see Map 10.4).

The Romance of the Erie Canal

Apart from this artist's romanticized portrayal of life on and along the completed Erie Canal, the canal was a great commercial success. Among the economic benefits to communities along the canal was the demand for skilled carpenters to build and maintain facilities such as wharves and locks. The artist depicted those workers, but not the day laborers who labored in the thousands along the canal. (Collection of the New-York Historical Society)

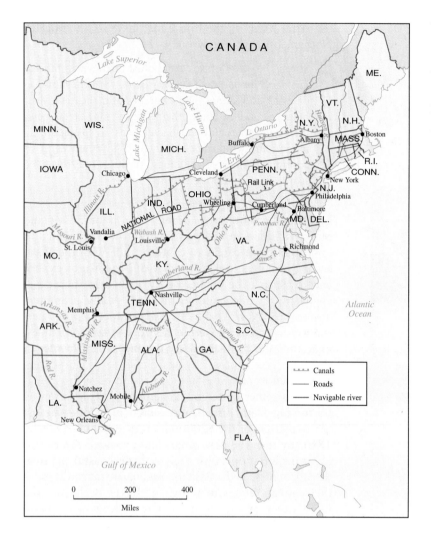

MAP 10.4

The Transportation Revolution: Roads and Canals, 1820–1860
By 1840 the United States had completed a transportation system based on roads, natural waterways, and canals. Even though this system lacked railroads until the 1840s, it was adequate for launching the Industrial Revolution.

Steamboats. The steamboat, another product of the industrial age, ensured the success of America's vast water transportation system. On canals, rivers, and lakes, steamboats traveled faster, met tighter schedules, and carried more cargo than did sailing ships.

The engineer-inventor Robert Fulton built the first American steamboat, the *Clermont*, which he navigated up the Hudson in 1807. But steamboats' large consumption of wood or coal for fuel made them very expensive to run, and they could not navigate shallow western rivers. During the 1820s engineers broadened the hulls of these boats—to increase their cargo capacity and, most important, to give them a shallower draft—and reduced their weight by using lighter wood. Able to navigate in as little as 3 feet of water, the new steamboats could maneuver around tricky snags and sandbars. Moreover, the wider, flat decks speeded the loading and unloading of cargo. During the 1820s alone, the new steamboats cut in half the cost of upstream river transport. By 1830 steamboat travel dominated the major rivers and lakes of the country.

The canals and the new boat technology increased the flow of goods dramatically. In 1835 farmers in the Old Northwest shipped 268,000 barrels of flour on canal boats to eastern markets; just five years later they shipped more than 1 million barrels. Water transport also enabled people to travel more cheaply and sped the exchange of news, technical information, and business advice (see Map 10.5). In 1830 a traveler or a letter from New York could go by water to Boston in a day and a half, to Charleston in five days, and to New Orleans or Detroit in two weeks. Thirty years earlier the same journeys, by road or sail, would have taken twice as long. Businesses and individuals communicated far more efficiently than ever before, and this in turn stimulated business.

The system of long-distance interregional water travel was essentially complete by 1840. But another transportation era was about to dawn: the Baltimore and Ohio Railroad had received a charter in 1828. But railroads were small, unconnected systems in 1840; the great era of railroad building lay in the future.

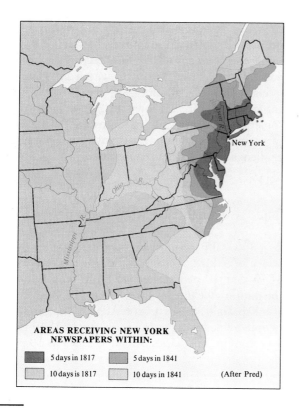

MAP 10.5

The Speed of Business News

The transportation revolution and aggressive entrepreneurs increased the speed of trade and communication between the Atlantic seaboard and the interior. The national circulation of newspapers grew along with trade, and New York's dailies became the most important sources of economic news. This map shows the dramatic improvements in communication between 1817 and 1841.

Within the map:

AREAS RECEIVING NEW YORK NEWSPAPERS WITHIN:

5 days in 1817
5 days in 1841
10 days is 1817
10 days in 1841

(After Pred)

Government and the Business Corporation

State governments had been granting charters to corporations since the 1790s (see Chapter 9). By extending such privileges to transportation companies in the 1820s, the states accelerated the accumulation of the huge amounts of capital needed to build transportation systems and reduced the need to tax the public for that purpose. Banks also incorporated, but few mercantile firms and almost no manufacturers did. Until after the Civil War manufacturers did not need large accumulations of capital and preferred to continue as partnerships or sole proprietorships to remain free from state regulation.

States gradually made the ability to incorporate a right rather than a privilege. During the 1820s states reduced the conditions necessary for incorporation, and in the 1830s legislatures stopped granting corporate charters one by one through the passage of special acts. Instead, they established general incorporation acts that turned over the chartering process to administrators. As more businesses received charters, however, it became difficult to protect the monopoly privileges that corporate charters often guaranteed. Younger entrepreneurs frequently challenged the monopoly privileges of established businesses for being inconsistent with the ideals of a republic. State courts responded to these challenges by weakening the legal definition of corporate privilege and thus promoting more entrepreneurial uses of property.

The Supreme Court under John Marshall also encouraged business enterprise. In the crucial case of *Gibbons v. Ogden* (1824) the Court struck down a monopoly the New York legislature had granted to Aaron Ogden for steamboat passenger service across the Hud-

An Eastern Steamboat

This watercolor by the Russian artist Pavel Petrovich Svinin (1787–1839) portrays deck life on the *Paragon*, which was owned by Robert Fulton and traveled the Hudson River. Designed primarily for passengers, eastern steamboats lacked the great paddle wheels and superstructures that became characteristic of steamboats on western rivers during the 1840s.

son River between Manhattan and Elizabethport, New Jersey. The Court's ruling, however, did not clearly favor an instrumental view of property, that is, a view hostile toward monopolies and favorable to entrepreneurial competition. The Court overturned Ogden's monopoly because the competitor, Thomas Gibbons, had a federal coasting license, and the Court believed that the federal government had paramount authority over the regulation of interstate commerce.

An instrumental view of property triumphed fully only after John Marshall died in 1835. In the landmark case of *Charles River Bridge v. Warren Bridge* (1837) the new chief justice, Roger B. Taney, ruled in favor of the Warren Bridge Company, which in 1828 had received a charter from the Massachusetts legislature to collect tolls for crossing the Charles River. He ruled against the Charles River Bridge Company, which had received an earlier charter that, the company claimed, granted an *exclusive* right to collect bridge tolls on that river. Taney did adhere to Marshall's doctrine that state governments had to respect charters, but he also argued that a legislature could not be *presumed* to have granted an exclusive, monopolistic right. His language affirmed wide access to the benefits of government: "While the rights of private property are sacredly guarded, we must not forget that the community also has rights, and the happiness and well-being of every citizen depends on their faithful preservation." In effect, he claimed that the destruction of monopoly and the consequent stimulation of competition were in the best interests of the community.

The courts thus reconciled government-granted privileges with the ideals of a republican society. State governments could follow both Marshall and Taney: Following Marshall, they could protect the privileges granted in corporate charters; following Taney, they could diffuse those privileges as widely as possible through society. State governments thus could maintain privilege but reduce its significance. Widening access to privilege increased the flow of capital to corporations and promoted the construction of the national transportation system.

Social Structure in an Industrializing Society

The Industrial Revolution transformed the material life of people in the United States. For most Americans the bonanza of factory-produced goods meant an improved standard of living. But industrialization was a socially disruptive process; the new affluence had its costs. The economic system sharpened and widened class distinctions based on the ownership and use of property and stirred animosity between classes. For a small elite—mostly merchants, factory owners, and financiers concentrated in northeastern cities and towns—industrialization meant great wealth. But for wage earners who did not own property, industrialization sometimes meant a loss of status and an uncertain future. Industrialization thus posed an unprecedented challenge to American republican ideals.

The Concentration of Wealth

By 1800, 10 percent of the nation's families owned between one-third and one-half of the nation's wealth. By 1860 that 10 percent owned more than two-thirds of the nation's wealth.

Especially in the major Atlantic seaports, wealthy people owned most of the property. In 1840 the richest 1 percent in those cities owned as much as 10 percent of the population had owned fifty years earlier. This top 1 percent owned more than 40 percent of all *tangible* property—land, ships, buildings, and household furnishings. In New York City the richest 4 percent of the population owned more than three-quarters of the tangible property. Their share of *intangible* property—stocks, bonds, and mortgages—was even greater.

The growing concentration of wealth in the cities had come about primarily as a result of the opportunities created by industrial and commercial expansion. Hence, great concentrations of wealth were less common in smaller towns or agricultural areas. Yet similar trends existed there as well. Even in modest-sized, nonindustrial Massachusetts towns the richest 10 percent of families increased their holdings so that by 1840 they typically owned 50 percent or more of the tangible property.

The new manufacturers, such as Francis Cabot Lowell, increased their fortunes most rapidly. More generally, the Americans whose incomes rose most were those who exploited the innovations of the Industrial Revolution. Since technical advances were concentrated primarily in the textile, machine-tool, and firearm industries, owners and skilled workers in those industries benefited the most. Individuals who designed or adapted the most modern machinery and mobilized and disciplined the labor needed to operate it enjoyed the most rapidly growing profits, salaries, or wages.

The concentration of wealth increased more rapidly than did the pace of technological and organizational change. This occurred partly because the wealthy, often linked by business and family ties, could more easily acquire the best information about new investment opportunities. Moreover, nineteenth-century governments

almost never taxed inheritances or intangible property and usually taxed real estate and personal property (furniture, tools, and machinery, for example) at extremely low rates. Although wealthy Americans paid the largest share of state and local taxes, government was small and taxes were modest. Therefore, wealthy manufacturing and mercantile families could retain their fortunes, and their economic power, into the second or third generation.

But wealthy families often failed to keep their hardearned assets. Foolish investments, poor business sense, imprudent living, or bad luck took their toll. In fact, the Industrial Revolution increased the rate at which fortunes, large and small, were lost. Financial panics drove growing numbers of even the most cautious and calculating investors into bankruptcy. Jeremiah Thompson, New York's largest cotton trader and an organizer of the Black Ball Line, went bankrupt in 1827. Philip Hone, a wealthy merchant and mayor of New York in the 1820s, never recovered from his losses and the bankruptcy of his son during the Panic of 1837, the worst financial crisis before the Civil War.

Middle-Class Property Owners. Far more people, however, improved their economic and social standing than lost ground. The middle class grew rapidly in size and importance. Most mechanics found their skills in high demand and their wages rising. Building contractors, grocers, shopkeepers, and butchers in booming urban areas profited from an abundance of prosperous customers. The growing urban demand for meat, dairy products, and perishables, as well as for staples such as wheat, corn, and cotton, increased farmers' incomes. Most Americans saved about 15 percent of their income, often placing their surplus funds in local banks and new savings institutions. Many eventually bought property with their savings. By 1840 about half of all free American men over the age of thirty had acquired at least moderate wealth—a house, furniture, a little land, and some savings. In agricultural communities an even higher percentage owned some land. The new members of the middle class hoped to pass on to their children the advantages of skills, education, and property ownership.

The New Urban Poor

For many Americans, however, the Industrial Revolution meant a loss of opportunity and a betrayal of republican ideals. By 1840 as many as half the nation's free workers were laboring for wages rather than for their own profit. Among these workers, those who lacked skills, education, or property found that even

though their real wages were rising, the gap between themselves and other Americans was widening. For ordinary laborers social mobility was extremely limited and difficult. They could look forward only to a life of work for others in factories, machine shops, and stores and on construction projects and sanitation crews. No matter how hard they worked or how thrifty they were, most could accumulate only modest savings. And an economic recession or sickness could quickly dash their hopes of rising in the world. They faced a high probability of a lifetime with little chance to buy a home or land, let alone start a business. For wage laborers who acquired no property, hope for upward social mobility rested with their children. But those workers had few resources to pass on. In fact, most could not afford to educate their offspring, apprentice them, or accumulate small dowries so that their daughters could marry men with better prospects. Instead, their children had to work to help support their families.

In Massachusetts in 1825, the daily wage of a common (unskilled) laborer—about 75 cents—was about two-thirds that of a mechanic. By the 1840s, the laborer's wage had increased to about $1 but was now less than half the typical mechanic's earnings. More-

A Chimney Sweep
The low-paid and exceedingly dirty and unhealthy work of cleaning chimneys, which were a major fire hazard in the cities of the Northeast, became largely the work of Irish immigrants and African-Americans. An Italian artist, Nicolino Calyo, painted this portrait in New York City in the early 1840s.

over, the poorest workers in the cities in the 1830s had to spend $2 of every $3 they earned just to feed their families, so they had relatively less money left to take advantage of the rapidly falling prices of manufactured goods. Middle-class families, in contrast, could feed themselves on less than a third of their earnings. Thus during the early years of the Industrial Revolution people who lacked skills or property were even worse off in relative terms than their low wages indicated.

And unskilled work offered little satisfaction. Raised in rural areas, most wage laborers were accustomed to the seasonal and task-oriented work regime of agricultural society. They resented the strict year-round labor schedule of most urban jobs. These workers often did not report to their jobs on time, and they sometimes skipped whole days of work when they were not in dire need of money.

The wage laborers who faced the worst conditions were casual workers—those hired on a short-term basis, often by the day, for the most arduous jobs. Altogether, casual workers accounted for about 10 percent of the labor force. The day laborers who dug out dirt and

stones to build canals, carried lumber and bricks for construction projects, and loaded and unloaded ships and wagons were the most numerous. In 1840 nearly 25,000 day laborers serviced the traffic on the Erie Canal. Among the casual workers the poorest were free African-Americans and Irish immigrants, who began arriving in the cities of the Northeast during the 1830s (see Chapter 14).

Day laborers owned no property except the clothes they wore, and their work did not provide economic security. In depressions they bore the brunt of unemployment, and even in the best of times their jobs were unpredictable, seasonal, and dangerous. Serious injury, which was common, often meant that a worker could no longer support his family. Disease took a toll. Laborers building canals through swamps often contracted malaria or yellow fever. In 1831 the economist Mathew Carey reported that 5 percent of the workers on the Erie Canal returned to their families in the winter with their health broken "by fevers and agues."

Since nothing tied them down, casual laborers were the most geographically mobile workers, and many looked eagerly to the West. Joining casual laborers on the way west were people who had once been prosperous but had suffered economic reversals. Many household weavers, blacksmiths, and harness makers, for example, left eastern towns and cities when their customers turned to cheap goods produced in factories. Some craftsmen were fortunate enough to reestablish their trade farther to the west, where high transportation costs made goods from eastern factories more expensive. But others with traditional skills had to work for wages in the West, even as casual laborers, easing their hardship by maintaining a garden or keeping a few animals to supplement the family diet. This recourse, however, was of only slight assistance during the winter, when food was scarce and storms and frozen rivers and canals could shut down trade. Winter was often a season of appealing for charity and searching continuously, sometimes fruitlessly, for a little work chopping wood or cutting ice.

In cities, most wage laborers and their families lived in conditions that discouraged any hope for the future. By the 1830s factory workers, journeymen, and unskilled casual laborers in northeastern towns and cities lived in well-defined neighborhoods. Certain blocks became dominated by large, crowded boardinghouses where many single men and women lived together in unhealthy conditions. Landlords converted houses, including basements and attics, into apartments and then used the profits from rentals to build more workers' housing. Often the developers squeezed a number of buildings, interspersed with outhouses and connected by foul-smelling courtyards and dark alleys, onto a single lot.

The Hot Corn Seller
Free African-Americans such as this woman, painted (1840–1844) by Nicolino Calyo, persisted in the face of discrimination and harsh economic conditions. She might have been lucky enough to have a garden plot that grew more food than her family needed to survive. The extra produce offered an opportunity to supplement her meager income.

Philip Hone

A Food Riot in New York

Philip Hone (1780–1851) was a carpenter's son who made a fortune in the New York auction business. He entered civic affairs and in 1825 was elected to a one-year term as mayor. He presided over New York's reception of Lafayette and the opening of the Erie Canal. From 1828 until five days before his death he kept a secret diary, which presents a detailed picture of New York life.

Monday, Feb 13 [1837]—*Riots*. This city was disgraced this morning by a mob regularly convened by public notice in the park for the notable purpose of making bread cheaper by destroying the flour in the merchants' warehouses. The following notice was extensively published on Saturday by placards at the corners of the streets:

Bread, Meat, Rent, Fuel—Their Prices Must Come Down.

The Voices of the People Shall be Heard and Will Prevail.

The People will meet in the Park, rain or shine, at four o'clock on Monday afternoon to inquire into the cause of the present unexampled distress, and devise a suitable remedy. All friends of humanity, determined to resist Monopolists and Extortioners, are invited to attend.

Many thousands assembled on this call. The day was bitter cold and the wind blew a hurricane, but there was fire enough in the speeches of Messrs. Windt and Ming to inflame the passions of the populace. These two men . . . did not tell them in so many words to attack the stores of the flour merchants, but stigmatized them as monopolists and extortioners, who enriched themselves at the expense of the laboring poor. They said that Eli Hart & Co. had 50,000 barrles of flour in their store, which they held at an exorbitant price whilst the poor of the city were starving. This was a fire-

brand suddenly thrown into the combustible mass which surrounded the speaker, and away went the mob to Hart's store in Washington near Cortland Street, which they forced open, threw 400 or 500 barrels of flour and large quantities of wheat into the street, and committed all the extravagant acts which usually flow from the unlicensed fury of a mob. The mayor and other magistrates, with the police officers, repaired to the spot, and with the assistance of many well-disposed citizens, succeeded after a time in clearing and getting possession of the store. From thence the mob went to Herrick & Co. in Water Street, and destroyed about fifty barrels of flour. The mayor ordered out a military force, which with the other measures adopted, kept the rioters in check.

Source: Allan Nevins, ed., *The Diary of Philip Hone* (New York: Dodd, Mead, 1936) 241–242.

Under such conditions, the lives of many wage earners deteriorated. Emotional tension and insecurity took hold; they became anxious over the breakdown of the traditional order, their loss of social status, and their worsening working and living conditions (see American Voices, above). To alleviate their distress, many workers turned to the dubious solace of alcohol.

In the eighteenth century liquor had been an integral and accepted fact of American life; it had lubricated ceremonies, celebrations, work breaks, barn raisings, and games. But during the 1820s urban wage earners led Americans to new heights of alcohol consumption. Aiding them were the nation's farmers, who increasingly chose to distill gin and whiskey as a low-cost way to get their grain to market. Falling prices led drinkers to switch from rum to these "spirits." By 1830 per capita consumption of gin and whiskey had risen to more than 5 gallons a year, more than twice the present-day levels of liquor consumption.

Drinking habits changed as well. At work, those workers who were not members of craft unions committed to abstinence began to drink on the job—and not just during the traditional 11 A.M. and 4 P.M. "refreshers." Journeymen used apprentices to smuggle whiskey into shops, and then, as one baker recalled, "One man was stationed at the window to watch, while the rest drank." Grogshops and tippling houses appeared on almost every block in working-class districts, and many workers who frequented these saloons became less interested in casual camaraderie than in solitary and heavy drinking. The saloons became focal points for urban disorder and crime, including assault, burglary, and vandalism. Fueled by unrestrained drinking, a fistfight among young men one night could turn into a brawl the second night and a full-scale riot the third. The urban police forces, consisting of low-paid watchmen and amateur constables, were unable to contain the lawlessness.

The Rise of the Business Class

In 1800 most whites in rural America shared a common culture. Gentlemen farmers talked easily with yeomen about crop yields, livestock breeds, and the unpredictability of the weather. Poor southern whites and aristocratic slaveowners shared the same forms of amusement: gambling, cockfighting, and horse racing. In the North poor and rich Quakers attended the same meetinghouse, as did Presbyterians, Episcopalians, and Congregationalists of different economic groups. "Almost everyone eats, drinks, and dresses in the same way," a European visitor to Hartford, Connecticut, reported in 1798, "and one can see the most obvious inequality only in the dwellings." Social hierarchies existed in these towns and villages, but the various levels of society shared many cultural and religious values.

Origins of the Business Class. The Industrial Revolution shattered this social order. The wealthiest merchants and manufacturers—the new business elite—began the process of fragmentation by setting themselves apart as a social group. They did this first by reorganizing work in ways that separated them from wage earners. With the outwork and factory modes of organization, a new, more impersonal system of wage labor and large-scale production replaced the small, intimate shops where masters, journeymen, and apprentices had worked side by side. This separation of employers and wage earners affected residential patterns. Before the Industrial Revolution most wage earners had lived close to their employers, often in the same homes. By the 1830s, though, most employers in the largest northeastern cities had stopped providing their employees with housing and many had fled to residential communities on the urban fringe, destroying the continuity between household and workplace.

During the 1820s and 1830s another social group emerged: affluent property owners who were, in economic terms, literally a "middle class"—standing between the very wealthy factory owners, merchants, financiers, and landowners at one extreme and the non-propertied wage earners at the other. Middle-class men and women sensed growing differences between themselves and the rapidly increasing numbers of those who owned nothing and had to struggle just to survive. Their education, material well-being, and aspirations led growing numbers of middle-class Americans, especially in the North, to identify with the wealthy families of the business elite. Together, the middle class and the business elite formed a truly new social stratum—the *business class.* There might be an enormous economic gulf between a wealthy factory owner and his clerks, foremen, and mechanics, but they were beginning to share the same moral and religious ideas and, therefore, membership in the business class.

Most members of the business class were the relatives of men who had accumulated enough money to live comfortably. They were the contractors, foremen, and mechanics valued by manufacturers; they were prosperous farmers; they were professional men of modest means; and they were shopkeepers or manufacturers' clerks and agents. They owned small enterprises or worked in large banks, firms, or stores that they did not own. Typically, they had been able to buy a house and perhaps a little land.

Such people dressed well. They could afford a small carriage and a good horse or two. Their wives and daughters were literate and could play the pianos that graced the carefully decorated front parlors of their well-built houses. There were books on the shelves and usually a servant or two in the kitchen and stables. They attended church and sent their sons and daughters to good schools. They were most numerous in New England, but there were business-class families in every American town, even in the agrarian South.

Pennsylvania Family with Servant
Women as well as men worked as day laborers, usually in domestic service. Discrimination limited employment opportunities for free African-Americans and forced them to work in disproportionate numbers as domestic servants, like the woman with this middle-class family painted by an unknown artist in York, Pennsylvania.

Ideology of the Business Class. The members of the business class defined themselves by how they thought about themselves and their relationship to society. They developed their own ideology of work, redefining traditional Christian moral injunctions. The founders of seventeenth-century New England had believed that hard work in an earthly "calling" was a duty that people owed to God. The Puritans had stopped short of believing that God would reward good Christians with worldly riches. In contrast, the business class embraced a secular ideal of work. In the late eighteenth century Benjamin Franklin had expressed this secular ideal in his *Autobiography*, in which he implied that an industrious man would become a rich one. When Franklin's *Autobiography* was finally published in full in 1818, it found a huge audience, mostly young men ready and willing to believe that if they followed Franklin's example—worked hard, saved their money, and were temperate in their habits and honest in their dealings—success would be theirs. The same lessons were taught in countless magazines, children's books, self-help manuals for young men, and novels. The business class made the ideal of the "self-made man" a central part of American popular culture.

Perceptive members of the business class sensed a contradiction between their wealth and their ideology. They urged all Americans to adopt the virtues of industry and rise in the world. At the same time, they recognized that industrialization had widened economic divisions and that many Americans would never improve their status. A yeoman society made up of independent families of farmers and artisans no longer seemed possible. "Entire independence ought not to be wished for," Ithamar A. Beard, the paymaster of the Hamilton Manufacturing Company, told a mechanics association in 1827. "In large manufacturing towns, many more must fill subordinate stations and must be under the immediate direction and control of a master or superintendent, than in the farming towns."

The message was clear. Business-class values were democratic, but the economic system that supported them was not. The clash between the democratic values of the business class and its privileged financial position became a persistent preoccupation for many Americans.

Every day this contradiction was visible in the streets of cities and towns when employers and middle-class property owners brushed up against the new urban poor. Even though neighborhoods were growing more distinct, no class dominated any single section of the city. People across the social spectrum retained a high degree of day-to-day physical proximity even in the largest cities. These were cities where most people lived within walking distance of work, schools, churches, shops, and saloons. Most middle-class housing remained within walking distance of cheap rooming houses and factories. As the horse-drawn bus—too costly for most workers—moved slowly through the late afternoon crowds, the wealthy could not avoid the sight of disorderly, sometimes drunken crowds in the muddy cobblestone streets.

When the wealthy began to ponder this disturbing reality and attempted to resolve conflicts of conscience, they did not seek to halt or reverse the Industrial Revolution. Instead, they worked to eradicate its negative aspects and control the social disorder it had created. They attempted to introduce new forms of discipline, first into their own lives and then into the lives of ordinary working people.

The Benevolent Empire

The leaders of the business class attempted to create a society marked by moral discipline. During the 1820s ministers in Congregational and Presbyterian churches, together with well-established merchants and their wives, launched programs of social regulation. One of the ministers' leading spokesmen, the Presbyterian Lyman Beecher of Boston, proclaimed their purpose: to restore "the moral government of God." Because of this aggressive quest for moral purity and firm belief in charity, historians have labeled the movement the "Benevolent Empire." It was never a formal organization, however, just a collection of reform organizations linked by overlapping membership and shared ideals.

The Benevolent Empire targeted age-old evils such as drunkenness, prostitution, and crime, but its methods were new. Instead of relying on charity, church sermons, and other traditional local initiatives, the reformers set out to institutionalize charity and combat evil systematically. They established large-scale regional and even national organizations, for example, the Prison Discipline Society and the American Society for the Promotion of Temperance. Each organization had a managing staff, a network of volunteers and chapters, and a newspaper. Together the groups set out to "rescue" prostitutes and save the abandoned children of the poor. Some reformers worked to have the insane taken from attics and cellars and put into well-ordered and disciplined asylums. Other reformers labored to change the mission of the criminal justice system from the punishment and humiliation of criminals to their rehabilitation in penitentiaries where moral self-discipline would be emphasized. By removing from their midst individuals whom they viewed as both incompetent and evil, the reformers claimed that they would ensure the vitality and independence of the citizenry and consequently strengthen the republic.

Women played an increasingly active role in reforms inspired by the Benevolent Empire. Since the 1790s upper-class women had sponsored a number of charitable organizations, such as the Society for the Re-

lief of Poor Widows with Small Children founded in New York in 1797 by Isabella Graham, a devout Presbyterian widow. By the 1820s Graham's society was assisting hundreds of widows and their children in New York City. Her daughter, Joanna Bethune, set up other charitable institutions, including the Orphan Asylum Society and the Society for the Promotion of Industry, which gave subsidized employment to hundreds of poor women.

Keeping the Sabbath. The most deeply held conviction of the men and women who ran the Benevolent Empire was that religion provided the answers to social problems. One of the greatest threats they saw to the "moral government of God" was the decline of the traditional Sabbath. The conduction of business on Sunday became increasingly common during the 1820s, especially among merchants and shippers who did not want their goods and equipment to lie idle one day of every seven. Congress had even passed a law in 1810 that allowed mail to be transported—though not delivered—on Sunday. In 1828 Lyman Beecher and other Congregationalist and Presbyterian ministers formed the General Union for Promoting the Observance of the Christian Sabbath. To these reformers, the question of the Sunday mail law was not important in itself. It was a symbolic issue chosen to rally Christians to the task of social purification. The Union spread its chapters—usually with women's auxiliaries—from Maine to the Ohio Valley. It lobbied for local Sabbath regulations, collected funds, published tracts, organized rallies, and circulated petitions. In short, the Union behaved much like a political party.

Although the Benevolent Empire found support in every community, it also met resistance, especially with respect to keeping the Sabbath. Owners of barges on the Erie Canal and proprietors of taverns and hotels refused to close on Sundays. Men who labored twelve or fourteen hours a day six days a week scorned the notion that they ought to spend their one day of recreation in meditation and prayer. Baptist and Methodist clergymen, whose congregations tended to be poorer than those of the Congregationalists and Presbyterians, objected to the patronizing tone of the General Union. And when the Benevolent Empire proposed to teach Christianity to the slaves or send missionaries among the Indians, white southerners were outraged.

Such popular resistance or indifference limited the success of the Benevolent Empire, whose purpose was all too obviously to regulate the behavior of others—by persuasion if possible, but by law if necessary. A different kind of message was required if religious reformers were to do more than preach to the already converted and discipline the already disciplined.

Business-Class Revivalism and Reform

Charles Grandison Finney. Beginning in 1825, the Presbyterian minister Charles Grandison Finney brought a new message to people living along the Erie Canal: evil was avoidable, and *all* sinners could be saved. His ministry accelerated the pace of the Second Great Awakening—the wave of Protestant revivalism that had begun after the Revolution (see Chapter 9). Finney was not part of a traditional religious elite. Born to poor farmers in Connecticut in 1792, he was determined to make himself part of the new middle class as a lawyer. But in 1823 he underwent a highly emotional conversion experience, and he was ordained as a minister after two years of informal religious study.

In strikingly emotional revival meetings Finney preached that God waited to welcome any sinner who

Charles Finney, Evangelist
Finney (1792–1875) had a long and influential career after his New York revivals. In 1835 he established a theology department at the newly founded Oberlin College, where he helped train a generation of ministers. Finney served as president of the college from 1851 to 1866. This daguerreotype was taken in 1850, while Finney and his second wife, Elizabeth Atkinson, were on an evangelistic tour of Great Britain.

truly wanted salvation and that only God's grace, poured into the heart of the believer, made a moral life possible. He rejected an emphasis on original sin and stressed that the exercise of free will—submission to the Holy Spirit—could lead to a Christian conversion. He believed that religious instruction in official church doctrine by a trained minister did not bring—and might even hinder—salvation. What counted, Finney proclaimed, was not a person's belief in the technical doctrines of a church but the will to be saved. His was an emotional faith that rejected the intellectually based faith of many established Protestant churches.

Wherever he preached, Finney won converts among churchgoing Protestants and those who had drifted away from their churches. The conversions were dramatic and often tearful. Although most of Finney's converts were members of the middle class, he became famous for converting wealthy individuals and the poor, who seemed lost to drink, sloth, and misbehavior. Finney used religious conversion to bring everyone, rich and poor, into the same moral community. The pride of the rich (if not their wealth) and the shame of the poor (if not their poverty) would give way to an exultant celebration of a new brotherhood in Christ. Conversion changed not only people's eternal fate but also their moral standing, identifying them spiritually with earnest, pious, middle-class respectability.

The Rochester Revival. Finney's most spectacular triumph came in 1830 when he moved his revivals from small towns to Rochester, New York, a major Erie Canal city, at the invitation of local business and political leaders. For six months he preached every day. He employed a new tactic: group prayer meetings in family homes, in which women played an active role. Finney's wife, Lydia, took a visible part in his ministry. She and other pious middle-class wives visited the homes of the unconverted, often while disapproving husbands were at work. Week after week Rochester was saturated with the evangelical message. Schools and businesses stopped for prayer. Spontaneous religious meetings were held in houses and in the streets.

Finney won over members of the business elite and their wives and soon claimed that he had converted the "great mass of the most influential people" of Rochester, especially the manufacturers and merchants who shipped grain on the Erie Canal. As part of their conversion, those "influential people" often confessed that their lives had been overly governed by money and too little devoted to the moral well-being of their own souls and those of their employees. With this confession came a pledge to reform their lives and those of their workers. They would attend church, drink only water, work steady hours, and encourage their employees to follow suit. In 1831 one of Rochester's Presbyterian churches rewrote its covenant in a way that gave a new meaning to the concept of "business." Every member pledged to "renounce all the ways of sin, and to make it the business of our life to do good and promote the glory of God."

A Family's Morning Devotional

This 1842 illustration from *Godey's Lady's Book*, a leading influence on the tastes of the emerging business class, portrays the kind of family Bible reading and prayer that the Finney revivals encouraged. Here, *Godey's* idealizes an affluent young mother and father who are trying to set a good example for their child and two servants.

And so the business leaders of Rochester set out to reform their city. Their favorite target was alcohol, which seemed to be the most wasteful and damaging social habit of their workers and the most obvious sign of a collapsing social order. But they also tried to meet what they thought were the workers' spiritual needs. In 1832 wealthy businessmen founded a new Free Presbyterian Church—called "free" because members did not have to pay for pew space. This church was specifically designed to serve canal workers, transients, and the settled poor. Soon two similar evangelical churches were founded in the city. To reinforce the work of those churches, Rochester's business elite founded other institutions: a savings bank to encourage thrift, Sunday schools for poor children, and the Female Charitable Society to provide relief for the families of the unemployed.

Within limits, the attempt to create a harmonious community of morally disciplined Christians was effective. During the 1830s many workers, often led by their wives, followed their employer's example and became converts and church members. And employers who had been "saved" often confirmed the respectability of the newly converted with raises, promotions, or bonuses. However, Finney's revival seldom moved poor people. Least responsive to the Protestant evangelists were the Irish-Catholic immigrants who had recently begun arriving in American cities, including Rochester. Skilled workers who belonged to strong craft organizations—bootmakers, carpenters, stonemasons, and boat builders—also resisted the message.

Some even supported newspapers opposing the revival, arguing that workers needed organization, higher wages, and schools more than sermons and prayers (see Chapter 11). But these critics only heightened the converts' zeal for rebuilding society into an evangelically defined Christian order.

The Spread of Business-Class Revivalism. During the 1830s revivals swept through cities and towns from New England to the Ohio Valley. Dozens of younger ministers—Baptist and Methodist as well as Congregationalist and Presbyterian—energetically adopted the evangelical message and its techniques. They succeeded wherever the middle class was large and considerable numbers of workers had reaped benefits from the Industrial Revolution. In New York City, where Finney successfully established himself soon after leaving Rochester, the wealthy silk merchants Arthur and Lewis Tappan founded a magazine, *The Christian Evangelist*, to promote his ideas. With the assistance of manufacturers and merchants, evangelists soon reached sinners the way that most aggressive businessmen reached customers: They standardized and simplified their religious message, aimed it at masses of people, and measured their success in quantitative terms—by the number of converts (see Figure 10.2).

Temperance. The temperance movement proved to be the most effective arena for evangelical reform on a national scale. Evangelicals gained control of the American Temperance Society, which had been organized in

The Ecstasy of a Camp Meeting (detail)

In isolated rural areas, especially those with many Baptists and Methodists, the camp meeting was a more common forum for evangelical revivals than were church and prayer meetings. Such meetings, organized while farm work was slack, attracted families who camped in wagons and tents for as long as a week to join in the intense religious excitement and social life.

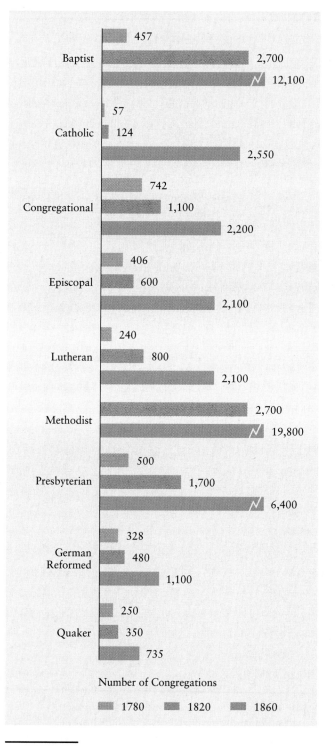

Number of Congregations

■ 1780 ■ 1820 ■ 1860

FIGURE 10.2

Church Growth by Denomination, 1780–1860

Christian congregations increased phenomenally between 1780 and 1860—nearly three times more rapidly than did the population. With the state now removed from religion, all denominations grew but revivialism played an especially important role in Protestant expansion.

1828. By the mid-1830s it had grown to 2,000 chapters with more than 200,000 members. The society adapted the methods that had worked so well in the revivals—group confession and prayer, a focus on the family and the spiritual role of women, and sudden, emotional conversion—and took them into virtually every town and city in the North. These techniques worked best among the families of the business class, for whom drink was becoming a fearful mark of social disrepute. Some business-class wives embraced temperance reform as a way to curb alcoholic husbands. On one day in New York City in 1841, 4,000 people took the temperance "pledge." The average annual consumption of spirits fell from about 5 gallons per person in 1830 to about 2 gallons in 1845.

The Work Ethic. Evangelical reformers also turned their efforts to revising and invigorating the work ethic that had been so important to the American tradition. They put a religious twist on Benjamin Franklin's formula for success. Laziness, drinking, and other wasteful habits could not, they preached, be cured simply by Franklin's patient methods of self-discipline. Instead, people had to undergo a profound change of heart, possible only through religious conversion. With God's grace would come the determination to turn away from drink, sloth, and sin. Then even the poorest family could look forward to a prosperous new life.

Only a minority of the large and diverse communities of laboring men and women joined the evangelical movement. Most of the religious converts were at least moderately prosperous and enjoyed a respectable standing in their communities. Evangelical religion reinforced the sense of common identity within the business class and that group's commitment to the concepts of individual enterprise, success, and moral discipline that constituted the ethic of the Industrial Revolution. Those Americans who joined the business class saw religion as a powerful cement for holding society together in the face of industrialization, which threatened to overwhelm the nation with social disorder and class animosity and conflict. But evangelical reform could not be contained within the Benevolent Empire, and it soon spilled over into the radical and utopian movements discussed in Chapter 12.

Summary

During the 1820s the nation's merchants, mechanics, and small manufacturers brought the Industrial Revolution to America. Through innovations in manufacturing organization and technology, Americans become more efficient producers. The combination of low-cost natural resources, the development of labor-saving innovations, and the recruitment of an industrial labor force consisting largely of women and children enabled textile manufacturers in the Northeast to become economically independent of the British.

Manufacturers and merchants in the Northeast and Northwest developed a vigorous domestic trade in agricultural and manufactured goods. Southerners participated in that trade but remained dependent on the exportation of cotton, the importation of British manufactured goods, and British commercial services. As domestic commerce grew, urbanization accelerated in the Northeast, led by New York City, which became the nation's leading trading center. Industrialization also stimulated the settlement of the West, resulting in increasing agricultural production that helped sustain the nation's economic growth. To integrate the national market, Americans built a transportation system. To encourage the flow of capital into the building of that system, state governments encouraged the use of the corporate form of organization by transportation companies. By 1840 the new national transportation system, based heavily on waterways, was unprecedented in size and complexity. In that year, however, the railroad was only in its infancy. America had launched the Industrial Revolution without the benefits of a modern railroad system.

Economic growth meant that most Americans, especially those who could take advantage of modern technological change, improved their standard of living. But industrialization widened distinctions among classes, disrupted working relations and residential patterns, and offered little opportunity for the large number of Americans who did not acquire skills, education, or property.

Economic growth fostered the development of a new social class: the business class, which consisted of middle-class property owners led by a business elite. Its members publicly acknowledged the disorder that accompanied industrialization and tried to harmonize class interests. They joined revivals led by evangelical clergymen such as Charles Finney, who believed that Christian conversions could mobilize the free will of individuals on behalf of worldly perfection. In Finney's re-

vivals business leaders and middle-class citizens pledged to attend church regularly, respect their families, abstain from alcohol, and urge others to embrace religion. A temperance pledge became an important badge of respectability. Revivalism and reform made the members of the business class even more certain that they were special—united, they believed, not only by material success but also by moral and spiritual superiority.

TIMELINE

1765	James Hargreaves invents spinning jenny
1782	Oliver Evans develops automated flour mill
1790	Samuel Slater's cotton mill opens in Providence, R.I.
1793	Eli Whitney manufactures cotton gins
1807	Robert Fulton launches the *Clermont*
1814	Boston Manufacturing Company builds Waltham cotton mill
1817	New York Stock Exchange founded Erie Canal begun
1818	First transatlantic packet service founded
1819	Cast-iron plow invented
1820	Price of federal land reduced to $1.25 per acre
1824	Franklin Institute founded Passage of a major protective tariff Supreme Court strikes down a monopoly in *Gibbons v. Ogden*
1825	Erie Canal completed Jefferson proclaims U.S. technological independence
1828	Baltimore and Ohio Railroad chartered
1831	Charles Grandison Finney begins Rochester revival
1832	First die-forging machine built
1833	National Road crosses Ohio River
1837	Supreme Court decides *Charles River Bridge v. Warren Bridge*

★   ★   ★

BIBLIOGRAPHY

The Rise of Northeastern Manufacturing

Surveys of the broad economic setting and impact of the Industrial Revolution include W. Elliot Brownlee, *Dynamics of Ascent: A History of the American Economy* (1979); Stuart Bruchey, *Enterprise: The Dynamic Economy of a Free People* (1990); Thomas C. Cochran, *Frontiers of Change: Early Industrialism in America* (1981); and Douglass C. North, *The Economic Growth of the United States, 1790–1860* (1961). Another useful survey is the pioneering work in economic geography, Donald W. Meinig, *The Shaping of America: A Geographical Perspective on 500 Years of History*, Volume 2: *Continental America, 1800–1867* (1993).

Books on the role of technological change include Gary Cross and Rick Szostak, *Technology and American Society: A History* (1995); H. J. Habakkuk, *American and British Technology in the Nineteenth Century: The Search for Labour-Saving Inventions* (1962); David Freeman Hawke, *Nuts and Bolts of the Past: A History of American Technology, 1776–1860* (1988); Brooke Hindle and Steven Lubar, *Engines of Change: The American Industrial Revolution, 1790–1860* (1986); David A. Hounshell, *From the American System to Mass Production, 1800–1932: The Development of Manufacturing Technology in the United States* (1984); Harold C. Livesay, *American Made: Men Who Shaped the American Economy* (1979); Nathan Rosenberg, *Perspectives on Technology* (1976); and Barbara M. Tucker, *Samuel Slater and the Origins of the American Textile Industry* (1984).

Stanley Lebergott, *Manpower in Economic Growth: The United States Record since 1800* (1964), provides a useful survey of the contribution of labor to the Industrial Revolution. An in-depth analysis of a critical group of women workers is Thomas Dublin, *Women at Work: The Transformation of Work and Community in Lowell, Massachusetts, 1826–1860* (1979), and *Transforming Women's Work: New England Lives in the Industrial Revolution* (1994). Regional studies of the early Industrial Revolution include Peter J. Coleman, *The Transformation of Rhode Island* (1963), and Dianne Lindstrom, *Economic Development in the Philadelphia Region, 1810–1850* (1978); and Anthony F.C. Wallace, *Rockdale: The Growth of an American Village in the Early Industrial Revolution* (1978).

The Expansion of Markets

Urban development in this period is best explored in R. G. Albion, *The Rise of New York Port, 1815–1860* (1939); Eric E. Lampard, "The Evolving System of Cities in the United States: Urbanization and Economic Development," in *Issues in Urban Economics* (ed. Harvey S. Perloff and Lowdon Wingo, Jr., 1968); Richard C. Wade, *The Urban Frontier: Pioneer Life in Early Pittsburgh, Cincinnati, Lexington, Louisville, and St. Louis* (1964); and Alan R. Pred, *Urban Growth and the Circulation of Information: The United States System of Cities, 1790–1840* (1973). The best introductions to the agricultural expansion in this period are Paul W. Gates, *The Farmer's Age: Agriculture, 1815–1860* (1960), and Lewis C. Gray, *History of Agriculture in the Southern United States to 1860* (1933). The classic history of the role of transportation is George R. Taylor,

The Transportation Revolution, 1815–1860 (1951). On the role of canals, consult Carter Goodrich et al., *Canals and American Economic Development* (1961), and Ronald E. Shaw, *Canals for a Nation: The Canal Era in the United States, 1790–1860* (1990). On the contribution of the law to early industrialization, see Oscar Handlin and Mary Flug Handlin, *Commonwealth: A Study in the Role of Government in the American Economy, Massachusetts, 1774–1861* (1947); Morton J. Horwitz, *The Transformation of American Law, 1780–1860* (1977); and James Willard Hurst, *Law and the Conditions of Freedom in the Nineteenth-Century United States* (1964).

Social Structure in an Industrializing Society

The following provide a good introduction to the study of the distribution of wealth and income in the early nineteenth century: Frederic C. Jaher, *The Urban Establishment: Upper Strata in Boston, New York, Charleston, Chicago, and Los Angeles* (1982); Edward Pessen, *Riches, Class, and Power Before the Civil War* (1973); and Jeffrey G. Williamson and Peter H. Lindert, *American Inequality: A Macroeconomic History* (1980). These studies should be supplemented with analyses of social mobility such as Robert Doherty, *Society and Power: Five New England Towns, 1800–1860* (1977); Don H. Doyle, *The Social Order of a Frontier Community: Jacksonville, Illinois, 1825–1870* (1978); Peter R. Knights, *The Plain People of Boston, 1830–1860* (1976); and Stanley Lebergott, *The American Economy: Income, Wealth, and Want* (1976). Some of the disruptive effects of mobility on urban life are addressed in Karen Haltunen, *Confidence Men and Painted Women: A Study of Middle-Class Culture in America, 1830–1870* (1982); Alan Dawley, *Class and Community: The Industrial Revolution in Lynn* (1976); Bruce Laurie, *Working People of Philadelphia: The Coming of Industrial Order: Town and Factory Life in Rural Massachusetts* (1983); W. J. Rorabaugh, *The Alcoholic Republic: An American Tradition* (1979); Christine Stansell, *City of Women: Sex and Class in New York, 1789-1806* (1986); and Sam Bass Warner, Jr., *The Private City* (1968). For an innovative discussion of the effects of early industrialization on the countryside, see Christopher Clark, *The Roots of Rural Capitalism: Western Massachusetts, 1789–1860* (1990).

The concept of the business class is developed in Michael Katz et al., *The Social Organization of Early Industrial Capitalism* (1982). Surveys of reform movements closely linked to the Second Great Awakening include Alice F. Tyler, *Freedom's Ferment: Phases of Social History from the Colonial Period to the Outbreak of the Civil War* (1944); and Ronald G. Walters, *American Reformers, 1815–1860* (1978). Studies of the relationship between religious evangelism and reform are particularly abundant for communities in New York State. See Paul E. Johnson, *A Shopkeeper's Millennium: Society and Revivals in Rochester, New York, 1815–1837* (1978), and Mary Ryan, *Cradle of the Middle Class: The Family in Oneida County, New York, 1790–1865* (1981). For more general studies of the religious ferment during the early republic, see John Butler, *Awash in a Sea of Faith: Christianizing the American People* (1990); Nathan O. Hatch, *The Democratization of American Christianity* (1989); and R. Lawrence Moore, *Selling God: American Religion in the Marketplace of Culture* (1994).

President's Levee

Andrew Jackson's chaotic 1829 inauguration, represented in
this painting by Robert Cruikshank as "all Creation going to
the White House," was the first "people's inaugural."

A Democratic Revolution

1820–1844

★   ★   ★

The Industrial Revolution transformed the lives of millions of American men and women. In traditional society, where people lived and worked together in self-sufficient, close-knit communities, their institutions—the family, the village or urban neighborhood, the artisan's shop, the religious congregation, and the town meeting—had functioned well. But the new economy drew people out of those intimate settings and into larger spheres, and even into national and international affairs. The new world was less predictable, less personal, and far more complicated.

The dislocations and disorders caused by the Industrial Revolution had a profound effect on American politics. This turmoil fueled a process of political democratization, and it paved the way for the emergence of Andrew Jackson and his new Democratic party. In the early years of the republic the byword had been *republicanism*. Now the clarion cry was for *democracy*. The movement for democracy even reached beyond politics into American workplaces. Some workers accepted the Industrial Revolution and organized to improve their situations. Others organized to challenge the legitimacy of the business class. Virtually all workers agreed that westward expansion was necessary to preserve economic opportunity for average Americans.

Jackson defined himself as the protector of farmers and workers and made a commitment to advance their liberty by attacking the "special privileges" of the rich and the business class, protecting the Union, and removing native American tribes from the path of westward settlement. Jackson was a product of the democratization movement, and as president he transformed his office and the federal government into potent instruments of democracy.

Jackson's opponents—the Whigs—gradually defined themselves as the party of economic improvement and prosperity; they would create opportunity by using

the federal government to promote business, transportation, and industry. The Whig challenge to Jackson's Democratic party began what historians have called the Second Party System—a system that endured until the rise of the Republican party in the 1850s. This fiercely competitive system of two parties, in which each party claimed to speak for "the people," completed a democratic revolution that in its scope and significance matched the Industrial Revolution.

Democratizing Politics, 1820–1829

The quest for political democracy that began in the 1780s accelerated because of the Industrial Revolution. With the exception of the most traditional elites in seaboard cities and the plantation South, virtually all Americans supported democratization of the republic—especially through the expansion of white male voting—as a way to fulfill the ideals of the American Revolution. But the Industrial Revolution increased the tempo of democratization and took it beyond extension of the franchise—into the development of modern political parties.

Democratic Institutions

Industrialization created a public that was much more complex in its composition, better informed, and more emotionally involved in politics. Rapid economic change created new economic interests and intensified conflict among social and economic groups, thus raising the stakes of politics. Many people saw the possibility of using government to promote their own interests or oppose the interests of others. Through government, they could either promote or resist the forces of industrialization. At the same time, the growing ease of communication made state and national issues more important at the local level. In addition, the accelerating growth of western communities, where enthusiasm for broad participation in political life had always been greatest, increased the pressures for democratization.

The Right to Vote. Expansion of the franchise was the most dramatic expression of the democratic revolution (see Chapter 9). With the removal of property requirements, even the poorest wage laborer could vote. By 1840 the electorate included more than 90 percent of the adult white male population. Most states also established the direct popular election of governors, presidential electors, and some judges. More than half a century after the American Revolution, the idea that all white men had the right to participate fully in the political life of the nation had finally triumphed.

Democracy, however, still excluded more than half the population. Native Americans remained nations to themselves, with no voice in the halls of government where their fate was determined. Every state denied women the franchise and the right to hold office. Almost every state denied the vote to free blacks. And in 1840 nearly 3 million African-Americans—about 17 percent of all Americans—lived in slavery, with no rights at all. But the essence of democracy's appeal was its universality, and when women and blacks launched drives for equal rights in the 1840s and 1850s, they drew heavily on the language of democracy first enunciated in the Declaration of Independence.

Political Parties. In response to the challenge posed by economic and social change, new parties emerged in every state during the 1820s and 1830s. These parties were more democratic than their predecessors, but they were concerned as much with organization and discipline as with increasing participation. Party organization was the crucial ingredient required to shape a wide diversity of interests into workable coalitions that could give the electorate clear choices and produce coherent legislation. In large and diverse states such as New York, party loyalty and discipline were crucial. Party members had to be persuaded to support the party's candidate even if they disagreed with some of his ideas. In return, party members got a chance to participate, influence government, and benefit from patronage. By the 1830s, although unrecognized by the Constitution, political parties had become central elements in American government.

During the 1820s the New York politician Martin Van Buren pioneered in making party discipline an effective tool for governing. Using skills that earned him the nickname the "Little Magician," Van Buren and his associates took over and transformed New York State's Republican party. They introduced collective leadership, strong party loyalty and discipline, and an elaborate apparatus of party organization. Widely circulated party newspapers such as the Albany *Argus* promoted the party line and helped maintain discipline. The focus of party activity was on shaping the actions of legislatures. Party members learned that they could advance their interests in the New York legislature by accepting the majority decisions of a meeting, or *caucus*, of party members. On one crucial occasion, after seventeen Republicans in the state legislature had threatened to vote against the party line, Van Buren pleaded that they "magnanimously sacrifice individual preferences for the general good." They agreed and were rewarded with a banquet where, as one observer wrote, "something approaching divine honors were lavished on the Seventeen."

In a nation as diverse as the United States parties had to embrace *platforms*, or programs of proposed action, that would appeal to a broad coalition of voters.

The party leader most successful in reaching across sectional and class lines to establish a national constituency was Andrew Jackson.

The Election of 1824 and the "Corrupt Bargain"

Whereas state political parties became more vigorous and organized during the early 1820s, the national parties were in disarray. The Federalist party had virtually disappeared, and the Republican party was badly fragmented. In the election of 1824 to succeed Monroe, no fewer than five presidential candidates, all calling themselves Republicans, crowded the field. Three were veterans of Monroe's cabinet: Secretary of State John Quincy Adams, the son of John Adams; Secretary of War John C. Calhoun; and Secretary of the Treasury William H. Crawford. The fourth was Speaker of the House Henry Clay from Kentucky, and the fifth was General Andrew Jackson, at that time a senator from Tennessee.

As a native of Nashville, where he was linked to the most influential families through marriage and his career as an attorney, cotton planter, and slave owner, Jackson spoke most clearly for the voters of the Old Southwest. But virtually all Americans revered Jackson as the hero of the Battle of New Orleans. Tall and rough-hewn—nicknamed "Old Hickory" by the press—he embodied the nationalistic pride that had swelled in the wake of the War of 1812. His rise to prominence from common origins demonstrated republican virtue and even suggested divine favor.

Nominated for the presidency by the Tennessee legislature, Jackson followed tradition and did not campaign actively. But his supporters vigorously promoted him as a man of integrity who would root out corruption and preserve American freedom. They did not dwell on specific issues except to condemn the practice, customary under the First Party System, of having a *Congressional caucus*—a meeting of each party's Congressional members—nominate presidential candidates. They had especially harsh words for the Congressional caucus of 1824, in which less than a third of the Republicans had chosen the "official" presidential candidate, William H. Crawford. Significantly for Jackson, the 1824 election was the first in which the majority of presidential electors were selected by the voters. Only six of the twenty-four states retained the practice of having the state legislature choose the electors.

The result was a complete surprise to political leaders: Jackson won 99 electoral votes, Adams 84, Crawford 41, and Clay only 37. Crawford, paralyzed by a stroke, won only Georgia, his home state, and Virginia, where he had been born. Adams had broader national support, largely because of his prominence as secretary of state, but the public identified him as the candidate of New England. Clay's support was limited largely to the Ohio Valley. (John C. Calhoun had bowed to political realities and switched over to the vice-presidential race, which he won easily with the support of the Jackson forces.)

Since no candidate had received an absolute majority, the House of Representatives had to choose the president from among the three leading contenders. Many established politicians were horrified at the thought of Jackson in the White House. Clay had been particularly derisive during the campaign, scorning Jackson as a mere "military chieftain." Out of the race, Clay resolved to block Jackson's election in the House, where Clay still served as Speaker. By the time the House met on February 9, 1825, Clay had put together a New England–Ohio Valley coalition that threw the election to Adams. Adams showed his gratitude by appointing Clay secretary of state. This was a significant appointment, since it had served the last three presidents as the final stepping-stone to the highest office, but it was a fatal mistake for both men. Jackson's supporters immediately decried the arrangement as a "corrupt bargain" and began almost at once to prepare for the next election.

The Presidency of John Quincy Adams, 1825–1829

As president, Adams presented a bold and sweeping program to promote the nation's economic and social development. He fully embraced the basic features of Clay's American System: (1) a protective tariff to stimulate manufacturing; (2) internal improvements (roads and canals) to stimulate commerce; and (3) a national bank to provide a uniform currency and expand credit. But Adams had an even more expansive view of the federal government's responsibilities. In his first message to Congress in December 1825 he advocated legislation to promote "the cultivation of the mechanic and of the elegant arts, the advancement of literature and the progress of the sciences, ornamental and profound." And he called for the establishment of a national university in Washington, extensive scientific explorations of the Far West, the adoption of a uniform standard of weights and measures, and the building of a national observatory.

Many politicians attacked Adams for showing favoritism to his most loyal supporters, the business class of the Northeast. On his deathbed, Thomas Jefferson argued that Adams was seeking to establish "a single and splendid government of an aristocracy . . . riding and ruling over the plundered ploughman and beggared yeomanry." There were constitutional objections as well. Madison had vetoed Calhoun and Clay's Bonus Bill in 1817 because he felt it would have exceeded the govern-

John Quincy Adams
A famous photograph of John Quincy Adams (1767–1848), taken about 1843 by Philip Haas, suggests the tenacity and moral commitment that contributed to his seventeen-year career as a congressman from Massachusetts. Far more effective in Congress than he had been as president, Adams became a vigorous opponent of slavery.

ment's constitutional powers, and Adams's program was even more ambitious. Adams made matters worse by openly questioning the wisdom of democracy. He warned that America seemed to "proclaim to the world that we are palsied by the will of our constituents."

In the end, all that Adams was able to get from of a hostile Congress was a modest improvement in navigation and a start on extending the National Road from Wheeling, Virginia, into Ohio. He had no success in raising tariffs until the end of his term, and the tariff that was passed then was not of his devising.

In December 1827 the Jacksonians won control of Congress, and they decided to push through their own tariff to bolster their leader's prospects in the next election. The Tariff of 1824 had imposed a protective tax of 35 percent on imported iron, woolens, cotton, and hemp. The new tariff raised the rate on manufactured goods to about 50 percent of their value, providing significantly greater protection to New England cloth manufacturers. To appeal to voters in New York, Pennsylvania, Ohio, and Kentucky, where Jackson was weak, the act also increased tariffs on imported raw materials, including flax, hemp, iron, lead, molasses, and raw wool. Despite his reservations, Adams signed the legislation.

The tariff was bitterly attacked in the South, which relied heavily on trade with Britain. By raising the cost of imports from Britain, the tariff reduced the flow of British goods and made it difficult for the British to pay for the cotton they imported from the South. Southern politicians, especially in South Carolina, denounced it as the "Tariff of Abominations," favoring interests in the West and the North. Southern leaders vowed to overturn it in the future, one way or another.

Adams's problems in the South were aggravated by his apparent support for the rights of native Americans. In 1825 the Creek nation had signed a treaty with United States commissioners, ceding its remaining land in Georgia. Adams concluded that Georgia had obtained the treaty through fraud and ordered that another treaty be negotiated. The new treaty, negotiated and ratified in 1826, delayed the removal of the native Americans, but when Georgia's governor, a backwoodsman named George M. Troup, heard about the new terms, he angrily defied Adams and threatened to take control of the Creek lands. Adams declared that it was the president's duty to uphold federal jurisdiction "by all the force committed for that purpose to his charge." But Adams was helpless before Georgia's determined resistance and finally urged the Creek to leave quickly, which almost all of them did between 1827 and 1829.

Adams the patrician viewed the presidency as being above politics. He ignored his waning popularity and disregarded the need to build support within his party. He failed to use presidential patronage to reward his supporters. He retained even hostile politicians in appointed positions so long as they were competent. When he decided to run for reelection in 1828, he refused to pay any attention to his campaign. He reinforced this aloof, paternalistic image by telling supporters that he would not ask the American people to reelect him. "If my country wants my services," he said, "she must ask for them."

The Election of 1828: The Birth of the Democratic Party

As Adams's problems mounted, Jackson's campaign gathered momentum. Jackson did not campaign personally, but his organization was brilliant. He assembled a broad, seemingly incongruous coalition of political leaders: his close friends in the Old Southwest; the South Carolina supporters of John C. Calhoun, who was again his semiofficial running mate; the Crawford supporters and the Virginians who had inherited power from Jefferson, Madison, and Monroe; the former Pennsylvania Federalists, who lacked a political home; and the skilled, disciplined leaders of Martin Van

Buren's New York organization. The state leaders organized local groups that planned newspaper campaigns, mass meetings, torchlight parades, and barbecues to excite public interest.

The Democrats' Message. Jackson's supporters conveyed the same message as in 1824, but more thoroughly and with greater emotion. The republic, Jacksonians charged, had been corrupted by "special privilege," which Jackson would ruthlessly root out. Though they championed Jefferson as their hero, they emphasized, more than he or the Republicans ever had, the idea that forceful democratic measures, especially majority rule, were necessary to purify the republic. Their evolving party label reflected this new emphasis on democracy. Initially, the Jacksonians had called themselves "Democratic-Republicans," in contrast to other Republicans. But as the campaign wore on, they simplified their name to "Democrats."

Jackson's supporters attacked Adams as the very personification of the corrupt consequences of special privilege. Had he not stolen the presidency through a "corrupt bargain" with Clay? They even made the sensational (but untrue) charge that as minister to Russia, Adams had tried to procure an American girl for the tsar. In contrast, they exalted Jackson's virtue, stressing his frontier origins and his rise to wealth and fame without benefit of formal education or association with a political faction. Jackson was described as a "natural" aristocrat, a man who had achieved success by his own efforts in an environment of liberty. For the Jacksonians, their leader personified the potential of the republic and gave Americans an opportunity to express their nationalism by casting their votes for him.

Jacksonian hostility to special privilege—in particular Jackson's hatred of corrupt bankers—appealed especially to urban workers and artisans in the Northeast who felt threatened by industrialization. But it also appealed to farmers and small property owners who believed that Henry Clay's American System represented unconstitutional favoritism and had narrowed economic opportunity.

In the South the Jacksonians courted planters and small farmers opposed to the American System. On the crucial question of the Tariff of Abominations, as on other issues, Jackson avoided making concrete pledges that might alienate large numbers of voters. Instead, he allowed his supporters to publish a letter in which he declared his preference for an unspecified "judicious" tariff. More important, most white southerners felt that the famed Indian fighter shared their desire to remove the remaining native Americans from the Southeast.

In the West, although Jackson remained vague about how much support government should give to western expansion, his military record during the War of 1812

was crucial (see Chapter 8). It suggested that he would vigorously support the ambitions of westerners and of all Americans for whom the West symbolized opportunity.

The Democrats Triumph. The Jacksonian strategy worked. Whereas only about a fourth of the eligible electorate had voted in 1824, more than half voted in 1828, overwhelmingly for Jackson (see Figure 11.1). There were now only two states, South Carolina and Delaware, where the legislature chose the presidential electors. Jackson and Calhoun received 178 of 261 electoral votes. Jackson and his supporters had fashioned a unified national coalition that included urban workers, western settlers, and southern farmers—planters and yeomen alike. He was the first president to be elected from the West, rather than from Virginia or Massachusetts.

Jackson's only area of weakness was New England, which Adams swept. Jackson's election was unsettling to the northern business elite. After the election Daniel Webster, an old Federalist, predicted to his business friends in Boston that when Jackson came to Washington, he would "bring a breeze with him. Which way it will blow, I cannot tell. . . . My *fear* is stronger than my *hope*." On inauguration day, after watching an unruly crowd clamber over the elegant furniture in the White House to shake the new president's hand, Supreme Court Justice Joseph Story declared, "The reign of King 'Mob' seemed triumphant."

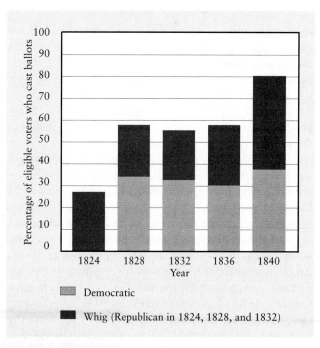

FIGURE 11.1

Changes in Voting Patterns, 1824–1840
With the return of two-party competition, voter participation soared in the critical presidential elections of 1828 and 1840.

The Jacksonian Presidency, 1829–1837

The democratizing of politics—the expansion of the franchise and the emergence of the first modern political party—had carried Andrew Jackson to the presidency. Now he turned his efforts to holding and enlarging his popular support by transforming the basic institutions of government. He expanded the powers of the presidency as an instrument of popular will. In the process, he stripped Congress of control of national politics and transferred that control to the Democratic party. Then, with powers greater than those of any president before him, he set out to smash any obstacles that impeded an independent citizenry intent on opportunity and expansion.

Party Government

To implement the people's will—the will of the majority—through party government, President Jackson reformed federal office holding. He declared that long tenure in federal jobs encouraged officeholders to view their positions as personal fiefdoms. During the election he had promised to introduce rotation in office, so that every four years officials would have to return "to making a living as other people do." He dismissed the argument that rotation would deny the government the service of experienced officials. The duties of public service, Jackson said, were "so plain and simple that men of intelligence may readily qualify themselves for their performance." Other Democrats put it more bluntly. In the words of William L. Marcy, a Jackson supporter from New York, "To the victors belong the spoils." The policy of rotation—the *spoils system*—was a distinctly democratic principle.

The spoils system, as implemented by Jackson, strengthened the federal government. Jackson used the greater power over appointments to build loyalty to the Democratic party. Stronger party loyalty in turn made it possible for Jackson to invoke party discipline in enacting and administering legislation. Rewarding loyal Democrats with public office helped build loyalty to the party. In addition, Jackson used his appointment power carefully, with attention to the quality of government. On the one hand, he dismissed some officials who were guilty of serious abuses of power. On the other hand, he protected some talented bureaucrats despite the fact that they were not Democrats.

Jackson used his highest-level political appointments to consolidate the power of his party. He selected cabinet officers purely for their ability to represent the various Democratic constituencies harmoniously. But Jackson never called cabinet meetings, relying instead

Andrew Jackson

This 1830s painting by Asher Durand captures the striking blend of romance and rugged force of character that were central to Jackson's image as a "natural aristocrat." Durand, who viewed painting as a patriotic art, was a founder of the Hudson River School of landscape art and an illustrator of James Fennimore Cooper's popular Revolutionary War novel, *The Spy*. (Collection of The New-York Historical Society)

on an informal group of advisers whose opinions he valued. Among the participants in this Kitchen Cabinet were several newspaper editors, including Francis Preston Blair of Kentucky, who edited the Washington *Globe;* Roger B. Taney of Maryland, who was to become attorney general and then chief justice of the United States; several Treasury Department officials, including Amos Kendall, also from Kentucky, who collaborated with Jackson on many of his state papers; and, most influential of all, Secretary of State Martin Van Buren.

Jackson versus the Bank

Jackson's most vigorous political offensive was his attack on the Second Bank of the United States, one of the key elements of the American System. Jackson began to dismantle the American System in May 1830, when he vetoed a bill that would extend the National Road from Maysville, Ohio, to Lexington, Kentucky. Jackson worried about the potential for corruption because the bill provided for federal purchase of stock in a Kentucky turnpike company. This issue was even more salient in Jackson's attack on the Second Bank.

The Second Bank of the United States. The Second Bank was a large commercial bank that the federal government had chartered in 1816 and partially owned (to the extent of 20 percent of the bank's stock). Its federal charter would expire in 1836. The Second Bank's most important role was to stabilize the nation's money supply. Most American money consisted of notes—in effect, paper money—that state-chartered commercial banks issued with the promise to redeem the notes with "hard" money—gold or silver coins, also known as *specie*—on demand. The Second Bank played its stabilizing role by regularly collecting these state bank notes at its various branch offices, returning them to the banks that had issued them, and demanding that the banks convert them into gold and silver coin. The intention was that, with the threat of collection hanging over them, the state banks would be conservative about extending credit. The state banks continued to issue more notes than they could redeem at any given time, thereby expanding the money supply. But under the discipline imposed by the Second Bank, they had to do so cautiously. During the prosperous 1820s, under the leadership of its president, Nicholas Biddle, the Second Bank performed especially well, maintaining steady, predictable increases in the money supply. By enhancing investors' confidence in the monetary stability of the developing West, Biddle and the bank increased the supply of capital for economic development. This was a service especially appreciated by bankers and entrepreneurs in Boston, New York, and Philadelphia.

Most Americans did not understand commercial banking, particularly the banks' capacity to enlarge the money supply through the lending of bank notes. Nor did they appreciate the role of the Second Bank in regulating credit. It was easy to believe that banking was a nonproductive, parasitic activity and that bankers earned their profits illegitimately through the exercise of special privileges. Many Americans had specific grievances against bankers. Jackson himself blamed them for financial instability in general and for the large sums he had lost in speculative investments during the 1790s. Wage earners were especially distrustful and hostile because they sometimes received payment in highly depreciated notes issued by unstable state banks. In response, they often advocated an end to all banking in the hope that there would be no money except specie (gold and silver coin). Other groups played on popular prejudices for the purpose of killing the Second Bank. Wealthy New York bankers, including supporters of Martin Van Buren, wanted to see federal monies deposited in their banks instead; some bankers in the smaller cities, including Nashville supporters of Jackson, wanted to be free of the inhibiting supervision of the Second Bank.

The Bank Veto. In 1832 Jackson's opponents in Congress, led by Henry Clay and Daniel Webster, united to embarrass him. They knew that the president opposed the Second Bank. Anticipating that many Democrats in Congress favored the Second Bank, Clay and Webster hoped to lure Jackson into the trap of a divisive and unpopular veto just before the 1832 elections. They persuaded Biddle, who would have preferred to remain neutral, to request an early recharter of the Second Bank, and they engineered the passage of a bill to accomplish that.

Jackson vetoed the bill, and that in itself was highly unusual. Before Jackson, presidents had vetoed legislation only nine times, always on constitutional grounds. But Jackson accompanied his veto with a powerful message that ranged far beyond constitutional issues to focus on the ways in which the bill was "dangerous to the liberties of the people." Using the vocabulary of the Revolution, he made the Second Bank the focus of resentment against the era's unsettling social and economic changes. He denounced the Second Bank as a nest of special privilege and monopoly power that promoted "the advancement of the few at the expense of the many." It damaged the "humbler members of society—the farmers, the mechanics, and laborers—who have neither the time nor the means of securing like favors to themselves." The president singled out the monopolists who had profited from special privileges and inside dealing. By inference, he attacked Webster, a director of the Boston branch of the Second Bank, for drawing on the Second Bank for loans and receiving fees from it for legal services. Finally, Jackson made a connection that was especially damning in the eyes of republican patriots: He emphasized the heavy investment by British aristocrats in the Second Bank.

The Election of 1832. Riding on the popular appeal of his veto message, Jackson and his new running mate, Martin Van Buren, faced Henry Clay, who headed the National Republican ticket, in the presidential election of 1832. Clay attacked Jackson for abusing patronage and the veto power, reproclaimed the American System, and called for rechartering the Second Bank. Clay was a popular campaigner, but Jackson and Van Buren carried a majority of the popular vote and overwhelmed Clay in the electoral vote, 219 to 49.

Jackson's veto and his parading of the veto in the campaign showed that he had a better sense of the public's anticorporate mood than did the champions of the Second Bank. His most fervent support came from a broad spectrum of people who resisted industrialization. But Jackson's position also won favor with some promoters of economic growth. Among them were state bankers who had originally supported the Second Bank but later concluded that its demise would open the way for more speculative investments by their banks. Also supporting Jackson were middle-class people who favored industrialization but wanted their rightful share

of its benefits. Thus Jackson managed to include additional groups in his coalition, even though some held diametrically opposite positions on the value of banking and even that of industrialization.

The Bank War. Immediately after his reelection Jackson launched a new attack on the Second Bank, which became known as the "Bank war." The Second Bank still had four years left on its original charter, but Jackson decided to destroy it immediately by withdrawing the federal government's deposits. After removing two uncooperative secretaries of the treasury, he appointed Roger B. Taney, an enemy of the Second Bank who had helped Jackson with the veto message. He ordered Taney to move the government's cash to state banks—called "pet banks" by Jackson's opponents. This action probably violated the Bank's charter, but Jackson claimed that he had the authority to act because the recent election had given him a mandate to destroy the Second Bank. It was the first time a president had claimed that his electoral victory gave him the power to act independently of Congress.

Congress and the Second Bank retaliated. While the House of Representatives defended Jackson, in March 1834 the Senate passed a resolution that censured him. Henry Clay had drafted it, and he declared: "We are in the midst of a revolution, hitherto bloodless, but rapidly descending towards a total change of the pure republican character of the Government, and the concentration of all power in the hands of one man." For his part Nicholas Biddle contracted the Second Bank's loans sharply, increasing the pressure on other banks to restrict their loans and creating a brief recession in 1834. But Jackson and Taney held firm, and in 1836 the Second Bank became a state bank chartered under the laws of Pennsylvania. Jackson rewarded Taney by appointing him chief justice of the United States in 1836, after the

death of John Marshall. Until his death in 1864, Taney led the Court in giving constitutional legitimacy to Jackson's antimonopoly policies and implementing Jackson's belief that a government under control of the majority could be trusted to promote the common good.

The Tariff and the Nullification Crisis

After the 1832 election, Jackson's eagerness to defend the destiny of the republic led him to attack a state government. The occasion was the South Carolina nullification controversy, which stemmed from the chronic insecurity of that state's slaveholding elite. The only state with a slave majority—56 percent of the population in 1830—South Carolina was more like Haiti, Jamaica, or Barbados than the rest of the South. In the rice-growing districts along the coast the ratio of blacks to whites was more than ten to one. Like their West Indian counterparts, South Carolina planters lived in constant fear of slave rebellions and the power of outside authorities to abolish slavery.

During the 1820s South Carolina planters watched in apprehension as the British Parliament moved toward the abolition of slavery in the West Indies. (Parliament took this action, with compensation for slaveowners, in August 1833.) Might the United States move in the same direction? South Carolina's leaders decided to contest the limits of federal power, choosing the tariff as their target.

They had reason to focus on tariffs. The planters had lost repeatedly on tariff questions, most recently in July 1832, when Congress had passed legislation that retained the high rates of the Tariff of Abominations on manufactured cloth and iron. In effect, northern majorities in Congress had used their votes to redistribute

The Bank War

This political cartoon shows Jackson ordering the withdrawal of federal funds from the Second Bank of the United States. Crushed by the collapse of the Bank are Nicholas Biddle, whom the cartoonist represented as the devil, Biddle's cronies, and the newspapers Biddle supported in the war with Jackson. The man behind Jackson is "Major Jack Downing," the pseudonym for Seba Smith, a pro-Jackson humorist.

Charleston, South Carolina

This painting, by S. Bernard, a South Carolina artist, shows Charleston's Battery, the fashionable harborfront district. In this idealized scene, gentlemen and ladies stroll along the promenade, looking toward Britian, which they are trying to emulate. Beneath the confident exteriors of Charleston's elite residents lurked worries about their future in the only state with a slave majority.

wealth from the South to northern manufacturers, who received an artificially high price for their goods. The economic damage to southern states raised an issue endemic to American federalism: What recourse do states have when the federal government harms interests they regard as vital? (Some southern delegates to the Philadelphia convention in 1787, anticipating the threat tariffs might pose to their states, had proposed that a two-thirds majority of Congress be required to enact tariff legislation.)

Southern opposition to the tariff surged in the months after Jackson signed the bill. Antitariff forces under planter leadership won impressively in South Carolina's election that fall, and on November 24, 1832, a South Carolina state convention took a bold step. It adopted an Ordinance of Nullification, declaring the tariffs of 1828 and 1832 null and void and forbidding the collection of tariff duties in the state after February 1, 1833. Furthermore, should the federal government try to use force, South Carolina would secede.

Calhoun's *Exposition*. South Carolina's act of nullification rested on the constitutional arguments of Jackson's first vice-president, John C. Calhoun, as presented in his anonymous tract *The South Carolina Exposition and Protest* (1828). Calhoun had directly assaulted the Jack-

sonian position that majority rule should be at the heart of republican government. To protect individual liberty, the Constitution had to restrain majority rule. "Constitutional government and the government of a majority are utterly incompatible," Calhoun wrote. "An unchecked majority is a despotism," while "government is free, and will be permanent in proportion to the number, complexity, and efficiency of the checks, by which its powers are controlled."

Calhoun drew on the arguments of Jefferson and Madison in the Kentucky and Virginia resolutions of 1798. He returned to the Antifederalist argument that sovereignty lay not with the American people as a whole but with collections of people acting through their state governments. Only conventions such as those that had ratified the Constitution could determine whether acts of Congress were constitutional. If a state decided that a federal law was unconstitutional, it could "interpose" by declaring that law null and void within its borders. The challenged law would remain nullified unless three-fourths of the other states ratified an amendment assigning Congress the power in question. And if such an amendment was adopted, the dissident state then had the option of seceding from the republic. Calhoun's ideas would form the basis of *states' rights* (or *state rights*) arguments well into the twentieth century.

Calhoun did not immediately admit authorship of the *Exposition,* but he took a public position on the issue of states' rights in 1830 after a long Senate debate between Robert Y. Hayne of South Carolina and Daniel Webster of Massachusetts over the nature of the Union. The debate began in January 1830 when Senator Hayne, protesting a resolution by Samuel A. Foot of Connecticut to restrict western land sales, suggested that the West should join forces with the South to oppose the land and tariff policies of the Northeast. Webster defended his section, turning from economic issues and challenging Hayne to debate the issue of states' rights. Hayne responded with the arguments of the *Exposition,* while Calhoun looked on approvingly. Webster, often speaking directly to Calhoun, replied with a stirring defense of national power in which he concluded: "Liberty *and* Union, now and forever, one and inseparable!" What became known as Webster's "Second Reply to Hayne" circulated more widely than had any previous Congressional speech.

Jackson kept Republicans in suspense about his position until an April 1830 banquet celebrating Jefferson's birthday. Opening the formal toasts, Jackson looked squarely at Calhoun and unequivocally declared: "Our Federal Union—it must be preserved." As vice-president, it was Calhoun's turn to rise next. His glass trembling in his hand, he delivered his toast: "The Union—next to our liberty the most dear! May we all remember that it can only be preserved by respecting the rights of the states and distributing equally the benefits and burdens of the Union."

In 1831 Calhoun finally admitted his authorship of the *Exposition* and elaborated on his views. Jackson—spurred on by Secretary of State Van Buren, who wanted the vice-presidency—dropped Calhoun from the ticket in May 1832.

Jackson Defends the Constitution. Jackson's response to the Ordinance of Nullification was swift and firm. On December 10 he issued a proclamation declaring that "disunion by armed force is *treason.*" Appealing to patriotism, he declared that nullification violated the Constitution and was "unauthorized by its spirit, inconsistent with every principle on which it is founded, and destructive of the great object for which it was formed." Privately, he threatened to hang Calhoun. This was the final straw for Calhoun, who resigned as vice-president in December with three months left of his term. From then on he would defend nullification from the floor of the Senate, to which he was immediately appointed by the South Carolina legislature.

South Carolina refused to relent even when Jackson brandished federal power by reinforcing federal forts in South Carolina and sending a warship and several armed boats to the port of Charleston. Finally, in January 1833, Jackson asked Congress to pass a "force bill"

John C. Calhoun (1782–1850)
This daguerreotype, made close to the time of Calhoun's death, suggests the emotional intensity he brought to bear on the issues of states' rights and slavery.

authorizing him to use the army and navy to compel obedience.

Jackson had firmly established national supremacy, but he wanted Congress to remove a principal source of the conflict: high tariffs. Henry Clay, determined to protect America's fledgling industries for at least a few more years, worked out a compromise. He proposed a new measure that provided for a gradual, annual reduction of the tariff so that by 1842 rates would return to the modest levels set in 1816. On March 1, 1833, Congress passed both the Compromise Tariff and the force bill. Jackson was satisfied. He believed he had established that no state could nullify a law of the United States.

Having saved face on the tariff issue, South Carolina's leaders promptly repealed the nullification ordinance. No other state had joined South Carolina in its confrontation with federal power. Like Jackson, most southerners did not perceive an imminent threat to slavery. They held the Union in high regard and did not believe that restoring low tariffs warranted a challenge either to federal authority or to President Jackson, who was popular in the South. Jackson's aggressive defense of the national interest against the nullifiers won widespread support in the South as well as the North. Still, South Carolinians resented their defeat over nullification, and support for Calhoun's theories remained widespread in the South. The compromise of 1833 was only a truce, not a definitive solution to the conflict over the meaning of the Union.

Andrew Jackson's Legacy for American Government

Jackson left the federal government—in particular the presidency—far stronger than he had found it. While he defended the republican values of Jefferson, he built a far more powerful, dynamic federal government than Jefferson had favored. And the constitutional argument Jackson set forth in his proclamation against nullification would provide the basis for Abraham Lincoln's response to the secession crisis of 1861.

Jackson opposed increased powers for governments only when they fostered special privilege and corruption, as he believed they tended to do when legislatures were too powerful. "The President," Jackson declared in 1834, "is the direct representative of the American people." Acting on this belief, Jackson had freely used the veto power, fired federal officeholders and replaced them with his political supporters, defied the Supreme Court and Congress, and mobilized federal force against a disobedient state. Jackson was convinced that when the people controlled the federal government through their party and their president, the republic had nothing to fear.

Westward Expansion and Conflict

During the 1820s and 1830s Americans of virtually all regions and classes believed in the importance of new opportunities to the west of the Appalachians. They believed that average Americans had to have access to fresh land to preserve the economic and political health of the republic. In their view, democracy could prosper only if average Americans owned productive land. But the massive migration westward during the 1820s and 1830s put Americans into direct conflict with Indian tribes, which still occupied much of the land west of the Appalachians, and posed the threat of future trouble with Mexico. Contests for disputed lands and the likelihood of more such contests in the future made Americans, particularly in the West, appreciate the kind of strong central government forged by Andrew Jackson.

Removal of the Native Americans. By the 1820s most Americans had concluded that the federal government must remove Indian tribes from the path of American expansion. It was not enough to break the resistance of western Indians to white settlement. It was necessary, they believed, to remove all native Americans east of the Mississippi, even those in seaboard states who had adapted to white society and did not threaten their white neighbors. Removal was necessary because the native American tribes possessed land that white farmers coveted. Removal was Andrew Jackson's policy, as he made clear in his first inaugural address. Jackson and

most Americans justified removal with the assertion that Indians were barbaric and could never become part of American society. Some Americans, including Jackson, also rationalized the removal of Indians as a humane way to protect an inferior people from direct competition with a superior race.

The Black Hawk War. By the time Andrew Jackson was elected president, the federal government had nearly broken the back of the resistance of native Americans to removal from the Old Northwest. In 1832 Jackson finished the assault. He sent regular army troops to frontier areas of Illinois in 1832 to remove Chief Black Hawk, a leader of the Sauk and Fox tribes, from rich farmland along the Mississippi in western Illinois (see American Voices, page 338). The troops refused Black Hawk's offer to surrender and pursued him into the Wisconsin Territory. On August 3 the army ended its pursuit with the eight-hour-long Bad Axe Massacre, leaving alive only 150 of the 1,000 warriors who had followed Black Hawk. During the next five years nearly all the other tribes in the Northwest moved or were forced to move west of the Mississippi River.

Black Hawk
This portrait was painted by George Catlin (1796–1872), who visited more tribes of western Indians than did any other artist during the 1830s. He assembled nearly 600 paintings in an "Indian Gallery" and traveled with it throughout America between 1837 and 1851, appealing to intrigued but unsympathetic audiences. (Courtesy of the Gilcrease Institute)

Black Hawk

Prelude to the Black Hawk War

Black Hawk (1767–1838), or Makatai-meshekiakiak in the language of his people, was a chief of the Sauk and Fox Indians. He was born the same year as Andrew Jackson in a Sauk village where present-day Rock Island, Illinois, is located. Also like Jackson, he was a warrior, leading armies of more than 500 by the time he was in his thirties. In 1833 he dictated his life story to a government interpreter, who in turn worked with a young Illinois newspaper editor to publish the narrative. In this passage Black Hawk describes some of the events leading up to the Black Hawk War.

We had about eight hundred acres in cultivation. . . . The land around our village . . . was covered with bluegrass, which made excellent pasture for our horses. . . . The rapids of Rock river furnished us with an abundance of excellent fish, and the land, being good, never failed to produce good crops of corn, beans, pumpkins, and squashes. We always had plenty—our children never cried with hunger, nor our people were never in want. Here our village had stood for more than a hundred years. . . .

Nothing was now [1828] talked of but leaving our village. Ke-o-kuck [the principal chief] had been persuaded to consent to . . . remove to the west side

of the Mississippi. . . . I . . . raised the standard of opposition to Ke-o-kuck, with full determination not to leave my village. . . . I was of the opinion that the white people had plenty of land, and would never take our village from us. . . . During the winter [1828–1829], I received information that three families of whites had arrived at our village, and destroyed some of our lodges, and were making fences and dividing our corn-fields for their own use. . . . I went to my lodge, and saw a family occupying it. . . . The interpreter wrote me a paper, and I went back to the village, and showed it to the intruders, but could not understand their reply. I expected, however, that they would remove, as I requested them.

. . . we came up to our village, and found that the whites had not left it—but that others had come, and that the greater part of our corn-fields had been enclosed . . . the whites appeared displeased because we had come back. We repaired the lodges that had been left standing, and built others. . . .

In consequence of the improvements of the intruders on our fields, we found considerable difficulty to get ground to plant a little corn. Some of the whites permitted us to plant small patches in the fields they had fenced, keeping all the best ground for themselves. . . .

The white people brought whisky into our village, made people drunk, and cheated them out of their homes, guns, and traps!

That fall [1829] I paid a visit to the agent, before we started to our hunting grounds. . . . He said that the land on which our village stood was now ordered to be sold to individuals; and that, when sold, *our right* to remain, by treaty, would be at an end, and that if we returned next spring, we would be *forced* to remove!

I refused . . . to quit my village. It was here, that I was born—and here lie the bones of many friends and relatives. For this spot I felt a sacred reverence, and never could consent to leave it, without being forced therefrom. [1830]

I directed my village crier to proclaim, that my orders were, in the event of the war chief coming to our village to remove us, that not a gun should be fired, not any resistance offered. That if he determined to fight, for them to remain quietly in their lodges, and let them *kill them if he chose*! [Spring, 1831]

Source: David Jackson, ed., *Black Hawk, An Autobiography* (Urbana: University of Illinois Press, 1964), 88–113.

The "Five Civilized Tribes." The Cherokee and Creek in Georgia, Tennessee, and Alabama; the Chickasaw and Choctaw in Mississippi, Alabama, and Tennessee; and the Seminole in Florida—the so-called five civilized tribes—remained in the South, in control of large enclaves. The Cherokee were particularly successful because they had a centralized political system, a thriving agricultural economy, and leaders who worked to gain white sympathy by adopting the trappings of a plantation society (see Chapter 8). Tragically, the five tribes occupied high-quality cotton land that was directly in the path of white settlement.

Jackson's first move was to withdraw the federal troops protecting the tribal enclaves that had been created in the southeastern states after the War of 1812. He realized that this action would leave native Americans subject to state law, which he knew had a sharp anti-Indian edge. In 1828 Georgia declared that the Cherokee were not an Indian nation but a collection of individuals who were tenants on state-owned land. Other states followed Georgia's example. By restricting the tribal rights of native Americans, they opened the way for whites to acquire Indian lands.

Jackson then pushed through the Indian Removal

Act of 1830, which offered southern Indians land west of the Mississippi in exchange for their eastern holdings. When Jackson sent agents to negotiate with the five tribes, he instructed them to tell the Indians "as friends and brothers to listen to their father." In the West, the agents should promise the tribes, "their white brothers will not trouble them, . . . will have no claim to the land," and the Indians "can live upon it, they and all their children, as long as grass grows and water runs." Realizing that the United States was prepared to send federal troops to remove them, tribes in the North and the South negotiated almost a hundred treaties for such exchanges.

Jackson carried out his Indian policy despite two rulings by the Supreme Court that tended to uphold Indian rights. In 1827 the Cherokee had adopted a constitution and proclaimed themselves a separate nation within the United States. After Georgia's 1828 declaration denied their claim to nationhood, the Cherokee appealed to the Supreme Court, arguing that Georgia's denial of their independence as a "foreign nation" violated the U.S. Constitution. In *Cherokee Nation v. Georgia* (1831) Chief Justice John Marshall denied the Cherokee claim of independence and refused to hear their case. But speaking for a majority of the justices, he argued that the Indians were "domestic dependent nations." In another case, *Worcester v. Georgia* (1832), Marshall held that the Indian nations were "distinct political communities, having territorial boundaries,

within which their authority is exclusive . . . which is not only acknowledged, but guaranteed by the United States." Jackson reputedly responded, "John Marshall has made his decision; now let him enforce it." Because of the wide popularity of Jackson's Indian policy, no significant support emerged for the Court, and Jackson took no steps to challenge Georgia.

The Trail of Tears. The Cherokee refused to budge. They repudiated a treaty, forced on them in 1835, that required them to leave by May 23, 1838. By the deadline, only 2,000 of the 17,000 Cherokee had left. During the summer Martin Van Buren, who had assumed the presidency a year earlier, sent General Winfield Scott with an army of 7,000 men to enforce the treaty. Scott rounded up 15,000 Cherokee and concentrated them in government camps, where many died. A few escaped to isolated Cherokee villages in the mountains of North Carolina. In the fall and winter the rest were forced to undertake a 1,200-mile march to the new Indian Territory in present-day Oklahoma—a route they remembered as the Trail of Tears (see Map 11.1). Only 11,000 reached Oklahoma; on the journey as many as 4,000 died of starvation and exposure, victims of racism and the ruthless hunger of whites for land. Only the Seminole remained in the Southeast. Aided by runaway slaves, many of whom had married into the tribe, the Seminole fought a guerrilla war into the 1840s against federal troops and the state militia.

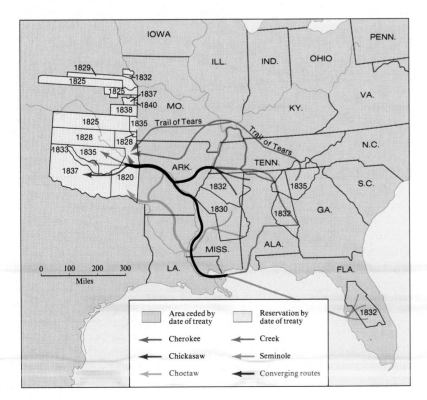

MAP 11.1

The Removal of Native Americans
This map shows the lands of the southeastern tribes before and after their removal during the 1820s and 1830s and the routes of their forced migrations. A comparison of this map with the map of land sales on page 308 shows that the tribal lands ceded in Alabama and Mississippi became those most sought after by white settlers during the 1830s. No white settlers occupied land on the new reservations before the Civil War.

Dreams of Expansion into Texas. During the 1820s, while some Americans moved onto the rich cotton lands that native Americans had once possessed, others dreamed of cultivating cotton even farther west, in Texas, on lands in Mexican territory. As they expanded the geographical reach of the American economy, they planted the seeds for a confrontation between the United States and Mexico.

Spanish, Mexican, and American Settlement. The Spanish had called the northeastern zone of their American empire Tejas or Texas, after the local native American word for "friends," and had employed Texas as a buffer against the French. With the Louisiana Purchase in 1803, Texas became Spain's buffer against the incursion of Anglo-Americans. Adventurers from the United States did arrive, encouraged by officials in the administration of James Madison. But by the time of the 1819 treaty between Spain and the United States, violent conflicts—among Spanish settlers, Spanish troops, Spanish-American republicans rebelling against Spain, and native American tribes whom the Spanish used to discourage foreign settlement—had turned Texas into an impoverished and unattractive place.

After winning independence from Spain in 1821, Mexico began to encourage immigration north of the Rio Grande. Mexican officials recognized that they could not keep illegal immigrants from the United States out of Mexico. They decided to try instead to turn them into loyal citizens and thereby perhaps block American political expansion. During the 1820s Mexico granted Stephen F. Austin and other Americans from the lower Mississippi Valley some of the best land in Texas (see Map 11.2). By 1830 about 7,000 Americans were living in Texas, outnumbering the 3,000 Mexicans there. The Americans, however, did not assimilate. They settled largely in eastern and central Texas, well removed from the largely Mexican settlements of Goliad and San Antonio to the southwest. Looking forward to planting cotton, the American Texans had imported slaves by finding loopholes in Mexico's restrictions against slavery.

The Mexican government, worried about the strength of this American community in Texas, passed laws in 1830 that restricted American immigration and prohibited the importation of slaves. (Mexico had abolished slavery the year before.) These actions and the news that American abolitionists planned to establish a refuge for free blacks in Texas led the American immigrants to begin violent protests. Meanwhile, immigration increased dramatically; by 1835, 27,000 Anglo-Americans and their 3,000 slaves lived in Texas.

One group of Americans, the "peace party," under the leadership of Stephen Austin, worked to win more self-government for Texas within Mexico. Another group, the "war party," demanded independence.

Austin won significant reforms, but before he could achieve statehood for Texas within Mexico, General Antonio López de Santa Anna became president of Mexico, appointed a military commandant for Texas, and centralized power in Mexico City. The leaders of the war party provoked a rebellion that both parties ultimately supported. On March 2, 1836, the two groups joined in proclaiming the independence of Texas and adopting a constitution that legalized slavery.

The Texas Rebellion. At first the tide of battle went against the Texans. Only four days after the declaration of independence, Santa Anna wiped out the garrison, including Davy Crockett and Jim Bowie, that was defending the Alamo in San Antonio. At Goliad he ordered the execution of 371 rebel prisoners, whom he regarded as mercenaries rather than Texans because they had arrived from the United States only recently. By the end of March, Santa Anna thought he had crushed the rebellion.

The defeat at the Alamo, however, captured the attention of New Orleans and New York newspapers,

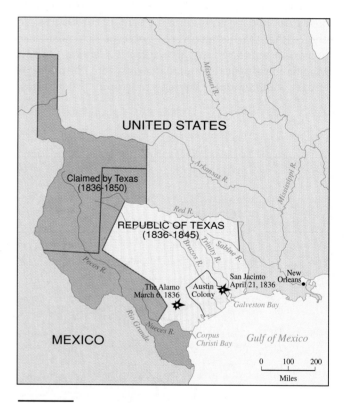

MAP 11.2

The American Settlement of Texas

In 1821 Stephen F. Austin established the first organized Anglo-American settlement in Texas, at the mouth of the Brazos. By the end of 1833, under grants from Mexican authorities, he had issued land titles to over 1,000 families. For the export of cotton, his prosperous colony had access to both Corpus Christi Bay and Galveston Bay.

Juan N. Seguín

A Tejano and the Texas Rebellion

Juan N. Seguín (1806–1890) was the most prominent of the Tejanos (Spanish-speaking inhabitants of Texas) who joined the Anglo-Americans in the 1836 rebellion against Mexico. Those, like Seguín, who fought alongside the rebels soon faced the greed and discrimination of the more recent immigrants to Texas. In 1842, three years before the annexation of Texas, Seguín left Texas for Mexico, and in 1846–1847 he led a company of soldiers in resisting the invading forces of the United States during the Mexican War.

A native of the city of San Antonio de Béxar, I embraced the cause of Texas at the sound of the first cannon which foretold her liberty, filled an honorable role within the ranks of the conquerors of San Jacinto, and was a member of the legislative body of the Republic [1837–1840]. . . .

The tokens of esteem and evidences of trust and confidence repeatedly bestowed upon me by the . . . dignitaries of the Republic, could not fail to arouse a great deal of invidious and malignant feeling against me. The jealousy evinced against me by several officers of the companies recently arrived at San Antonio from the United States soon spread among the straggling American adventurers, who were already beginning to work their dark intrigues against the native families, whose only crime was that they owned large tracts of land and desirable property.

I will also point out the origin of another enmity which, on several occasions, endangered my life. In those evil days, San Antonio swarmed with

Juan N. Seguín
After the Mexican War, Seguín returned to San Antonio where he resumed a career as a popular political leader, serving during the 1850s as a justice of the peace, an election precinct chairman, and a founder of the Democratic party in Bexar County. After his opponents charged him with treason to the Republic of Texas, he wrote his memoirs to defend his record.

adventurers from every quarter of the globe. Many a noble heart grasped the sword in the defense of the liberty of Texas, cheerfully pouring out their blood for our cause, and to them everlasting public gratitude is due. But there were also many bad men, fugitives from their country who found in this land an opportunity for their criminal designs. . . .

San Antonio claimed then, as it claims now [1858], to be the first city of Texas. It was also the receptacle of the scum of society. My political and social situation [as mayor of San Antonio, 1841–1842] brought me into continual contact with that class of people. At every hour of the day and night my countrymen ran to me for protection against the assaults or exactions of those adventurers. Sometimes, by persuasion, I prevailed on them to desist; sometimes, also, force had to be resorted to. How could I have done otherwise? Were not the victims my own countrymen, friends, and associates? Could I leave them defenseless, exposed to the assaults of foreigners who, on the pretext that they were Mexicans, treated them worse than brutes?

. . . I resolved to seek a refuge among my enemies, braving all dangers. But before taking this step, I sent in my resignation as mayor of the city to the municipality of San Antonio, stating to them that, unable any longer to suffer the persecutions of some ungrateful Americans who strove to murder me, I had determined to free my family and friends from their continual misery on my account, and go and live peaceably in Mexico. That for these reasons I resigned my office, with all my privileges and honors as a Texan.

Source: Jesús F. de la Teja, ed., *A Revolution Remembered: The Memoirs and Selected Correspondence of Juan N. Seguín* (Austin: State House Press, 1991), 73–74, 89–90.

whose correspondents romanticized the heroism of the Texans. Using some of the strongest anti-Catholic rhetoric of the day, the newspapers described the Mexicans as tyrannical butchers in the service of the pope. Thousands of adventurers, learning of Texan offers of land bounties, set sail from New York, the Gulf states,

and the Mississippi Valley. Reinforced by the new arrivals and led by General Sam Houston, the Texas rebels routed the Mexicans in the Battle of San Jacinto on April 21, 1836. Although Mexico refused to recognize the new republic, it abandoned efforts to reconquer it (see American Voices, above).

The Issue of Annexation. The Texans immediately voted by plebiscite for annexation by the United States. But Jackson and Martin Van Buren, who succeeded Jackson as president in 1837, took no position on the matter. Jackson was strong-willed and decisive, but he also knew when the best policy was to do nothing. He recognized that adding Texas as a state would disrupt the even balance of free and slave states established by the Missouri Compromise. In addition, he feared that such a step would lead to war with Mexico and a division of the Democratic party into northern and southern factions. Privately, however, Jackson supported annexation and even encouraged the Texans to seize Mexican territory all the way to the Pacific Ocean.

The Early Labor Movement, 1794–1836

The movement for democratization extended beyond politics to the workshops. Some artisans believed that they had gained independence and even prosperity from the Industrial Revolution and saw little reason to challenge the inherently undemocratic nature of the new working conditions. They organized societies, associations, and unions, but only as a way to increase their share of the growing economic pie. Others organized with a more radical purpose: to resist the business class. Many artisans with traditional skills had been hurt by industrialization, and they looked with suspicion on business-class efforts to reform society. To them the political task was not to create harmony between owners and workers but to recognize the inevitable conflict of interest between people who sold their labor and people who bought it.

Artisan Self-Consciousness

The earliest labor unions drew sustenance from the craft identity and social solidarity that had existed for generations among artisans—carpenters, shoemakers, shipbuilders, and other skilled workers. The skilled shoemakers in Philadelphia were representative. They had formed the Federated Society of Journeymen Cordwainers in 1794 to press for a uniform wage for their members. (Shoemakers took the name *cordwainers* from the high-quality cordovan leather they worked.) Their repeated strikes against wage cuts had some success until 1806, when their leaders were convicted of criminal conspiracy under the common law in *Commonwealth v. Pullis*. The idea that a workers' combination was illegal—"a government unto themselves," in the words of the Philadelphia court—hampered the

union movement for many years but did not stop it.

As the Industrial Revolution gathered momentum during the 1820s and 1830s, many artisans developed a new sense of social identity. Their group consciousness did not yet include black or women workers or even the spouses who toiled alongside as "helpmates." It also did not include the growing numbers of unskilled workers, including the vast majority of factory workers. But the vision of the artisans was expanding. They began to see themselves not only as being linked with others skilled in a particular craft but as members of a larger class. During the 1820s and 1830s class-conscious artisans, many of whom had traditional skills still needed in the industrial era, led a union movement.

Workers in the Building Trades

Prominent among the leaders in unionization were workers in the building trades: carpenters, house-painters, stonecutters, masons, nailers, and cabinetmakers. These workers were able to challenge employers in a sustained way because the Industrial Revolution, far from undermining their skills, actually increased the demand for them. Workers in the building trades organized largely with the aim of increasing their remuneration—which they regarded as including leisure time as well as money—and their prospects for independence and security in the new industrial society.

Rapid urbanization during the 1820s and the building of homes, stores, and factories triggered a strong demand for construction skills. The traditional hours of work for virtually all laborers were "sun to sun," but the quickening pace of economic activity was leading many employers to demand a greater intensity of effort. In the building trades, the pressure became most intense during the spring and summer. Not only was construction then at fever pitch, but the regular working day exceeded twelve hours.

As the demand for their skills increased, so did the bargaining position of artisans in the building trades. They attempted to take advantage of this by forming labor unions and demanding a shorter workday. In 1825 about 600 carpenters in Boston struck against their contractor-employers, demanding a ten-hour day, 6 A.M. to 6 P.M., with an hour each for breakfast and dinner. Their effort failed, but this was the first great strike for the ten-hour day. Two years later a group of journeymen carpenters in Philadelphia had greater success. After a brief strike, several hundred workers won the ten-hour day and initiated coordinated action by groups of unions in the city. Their success led the building-trade workers to found the Mechanics' Union of Trade Associations. They reached out to other trades and formed the first effective citywide organization of wage earners in Philadelphia. "The real object . . . of

this association," stated the constitution of the Mechanics' Union, is "to assist in establishing a just balance of power . . . between all the various classes and individuals which constitute society at large."

The building-trade workers went even further. They founded a political party, the Working Men's party, in 1828. The party's platform included equal taxation, the abolition of banks, and universal education. For a time the Working Men held enough seats to control Philadelphia's city council.

A large majority of workers considered the advancement of public education their most important goal. They were convinced that public schools would give their children skills with enduring value and allow them to advance more rapidly into the ranks of the propertied. Therefore, the Working Men's party demanded that the city and state provide all citizens with public education that would combine "one or more mechanical arts" with "literary and scientific instruction." Such training would "place the citizens of this extensive republic on an equality [and] bring the children of the poor and rich to mix together as a band of republican brethren," so that "united in youth in the acquisition of knowledge, they will grow up together, jealous of naught but the republican character of their country." The Working Men's party helped persuade Philadelphia to expand public schooling and the Pennsylvania legislature to authorize, in 1834, universal, free, tax-supported schools.

The members of the building-trade unions maintained their traditional values. They continued to take pride in their occupations and make a comfortable living, and they stressed the importance of the communal solidarity of their respective crafts. In the growing urban economy of the 1820s and 1830s their relative economic position improved, and they expanded their property holdings significantly. They saw little reason to criticize the new industrial order in a fundamental way and considerable reason to promote their own version of social harmony.

The Threatened Artisans

The position of artisans directly threatened by industrialization was less happy. These workers faced declining incomes, unemployment, and loss of status as machines took over their jobs. Hatters, printers, and weavers were among the most threatened workers, and during the 1820s and 1830s they banded together to form craft unions. Their leaders formulated a "producer's" ideology that defined their position in relation to both the business class and unskilled wage earners. They advanced a *labor theory of value*, arguing that the price of a product should reflect the labor required to make it and that most of the income from its sale should go to the person who made it. Artisans condemned the accumulation of wealth by capitalist employers and proclaimed their fear of becoming, as they put it, "slaves to a monied aristocracy."

A key group of threatened workers were the journeymen shoemakers. In the 1820s and 1830s shoe manufacturers began to change the way shoes were made. They hired more journeymen but moved them to large back-room shops where the workers cut leather into soles and "uppers." Then the masters sent out the uppers to shoe binders, usually women who worked at home binding the uppers and sewing in fabric linings. The employers then passed on the uppers and soles to journeymen who assembled entire shoes in small shops ("ten footers") commonly located in their backyards. Finally, the journeymen returned finished shoes to the central shops for inspection and packing. The new system of production made the master into a mere employer, the "shoe boss," and eroded workers' control over the pace and conditions of labor.

In 1830 the journeymen shoemakers of Lynn, Massachusetts, united to form the Mutual Benefit Society of Journeymen Cordwainers to defend their interests as employees and, insofar as possible, to establish their independence from the shoe bosses. "The division of society into the producing and nonproducing classes," they explained, "and the fact of the unequal distribution of value between the two, introduced us at once to another distinction—that of capital and labor. . . . Labor now becomes a commodity, wealth capital, and the natural order of things is entirely reversed." Therefore, "antagonism and opposition is introduced in the community; capital and labor stand opposed." In 1836 the cordwainers and journeymen printers set up national craft unions to coordinate the activities of local unions.

The new unions of cordwainers and printers, along with other artisans in similar situations, quickly turned to politics. Union members supported the Jacksonian movement, which in turn energized the workers' political efforts. Union members formed a small but vocal portion of the Democratic leadership. They became the most radical Democrats, agitating for antimonopoly legislation and antibanking regulations by the states, the adoption of universal suffrage for white men, and the abolition of imprisonment for debt. They also supported new taxes—general property taxes—that would apply to personal property such as stocks, bonds, machinery, and furniture as well as to real estate. In their political campaigns artisans appealed to the spirit of the American Revolution, which had destroyed the monopolies and special privileges created by the king, they said. Now a new revolution was needed to destroy the monopolies created by capital. Only then could individuals regain the dignity and independence befitting free citizens of a republic (see American Lives, pages 344–345).

Frances Wright: Radical Reformer

Frances Wright (1795–1852) arrived in New York City on New Year's Day, 1829, with a radical plan: to persuade the city's workers to assault business-class power. She hoped to win workers' support for a frontal attack on the religious foundations of business-class revivalism. She hoped that from New York her message would "spread far and wide, and invigorate the exertions of good and bold men throughout the land."

Born in Glasgow, Scotland, into the family of a wealthy merchant devoted to the republicanism of Thomas Paine, Wright had discovered America at age sixteen. "From that moment on," she wrote, "my attention became rivetted on this country as upon the theatre where man might first awake to the full knowledge and exercise of his powers." She was one of the many Europeans drawn to American shores by the magnet of the Declaration of Independence.

In 1818 Wright made her first Atlantic crossing. When she returned to Britain in 1821, she published an enthusiastic account of life in America, *Views of Society and Manners in America*. Translated into three languages, the book reached a large international readership.

Among the readers of the book was the French hero of the American Revolution, the Marquis de Lafayette, who became Wright's friend and patron. A few months after initiating a correspondence with Lafayette, she and her sister moved in with him, a sixty-four-year-old widower, on his country estate. Over the objections of his family, Frances stayed on in his household for almost two years. At one point she begged him either to marry her or adopt her as his daughter.

In 1824, Wright accompanied Lafayette on his triumphal return to America. During a six-week stay with Thomas Jefferson at Monticello she revealed a bold plan to set up a utopian community of whites and freed slaves, who would live together in full equality.

Encouraged by Jefferson, Wright founded the community, called Nashoba, in 1825, on 320 acres of western Tennessee wilderness. She gathered support from other young idealists, enlarged Nashoba to nearly 2,000 acres, and purchased about thirty slaves. Her scheme was to allow them to earn emancipation by working on the land. During that time Nashoba would provide their children with an education.

Wright worked alongside the slaves in the arduous clearing and ditching of the marshy land. However, the slaves saw little improvement in their lives, and the summer heat and waves of malarial fevers wore down the enthusiasm of everyone except Wright. Her dreams soared to embrace the ideals of Robert Owen, a Scottish industrialist and philanthropist who had formed his own utopian community in New Harmony, Indiana, in 1824. Following Owen's search for alternatives to private property, organized religion, and marriage, Wright declared that Nashoba would become a society "where affection shall form the only marriage, kind feelings and kind action the only religion, respect for the feelings and liberties of others the only restraint, and reunion of interest the bond of peace and security." But potential recruits were repelled by what the British author Frances Trollope described as the "savage aspect of the scene."

By 1828 Wright concluded that America had become too conservative for an "individual experiment" such as Nashoba to succeed. What was required was to reform the "collective body politic." She left Nashoba and joined forces with Owen's son, Robert Dale Owen, who had become infatuated with her, and launched a lecture campaign that took her to New York.

As a lecturer, Wright was a sensation. Rumors of free love and racial mixing at Nashoba did their part. And she challenged gender stereotypes: she was the first woman to address large mixed audiences in America. Wright would sweep onto a stage with a group of women apostles and throw off her cloak to reveal her revolutionary garb—a tunic of white muslin. Producing a copy of the Declaration of Independence, she would lecture in a resonant, musical voice. The poet Walt Whitman, who heard Wright when he was a young boy, remembered that "we all loved her; fell down before her: her very appearance seemed to enthrall us."

Frances Wright
This 1826 painting shows the thirty-two-year-old Frances Wright at Nashoba. She is wearing the simple, practical costume the New Harmony community adopted for women— a coat reaching to the knees over pantaloons.

Wright announced to her packed audiences that the "laboring class of the community" faced oppression by a "monied aristocracy" and a "professional aristocracy of priests, lawyers, and politicians." She lashed out at evangelical ministers, calling them hypocritical and unrepublican, challenging their claims of divine revelations, and describing the Benevolent Empire as the "would-be Christian Party in politics." She argued that the only path between the extremes of the enslavement of all labor and violent revolution was reform focused on education. She called on Americans to educate all children between the ages of two and sixteen in compulsory boarding schools; this would enforce social equality and insulate children from organized religion. Among the beneficiaries would be women, who would learn to break their "mental chains" and attain equality under the law.

To nurture a radical culture among New York's workers, Wright and Owen took over an abandoned church near the Bowery, in the heart of the workers' neighborhood, and transformed it into a "Hall of Science." There they established a newspaper, *The Free Enquirer*, a printing press for other radical publications, a lecture auditorium, a day school, a deist Sunday school, a reading room, and a free medical dispensary.

Wright won a large following among artisans and journeymen, some of whom turned to politics and energized the Working Men's party. In 1829 twenty men wrote her name on their ballots for the New York assembly. Nonetheless, she failed to convert most of New York's radical workers; they believed that a maldistribution of wealth and opportunities—not religion—was at the heart of their powerlessness.

Disheartened, in 1831 Wright and Owen sold the Hall of Science to a new Methodist congregation. While Owen returned to New Harmony as a Democratic reform politician, Wright transported her freed slaves to Haiti and then sailed for Paris, where she married a French educational reformer and gave birth to a daughter.

Wright never abandoned her dreams, however. Inspired by stories of Jackson's war against the Second Bank, she returned to America in 1835. But her lectures, including speeches for Martin Van Buren, met with indifference or hostility. Newspaper editors called her the "Red Harlot of Infidelity," and pious parents used her name to frighten their children.

Wright settled in Cincinnati, where she lived out her life in oblivion, writing her memoirs, occasionally promoting her old causes, and winning a pioneering suit for divorce. In 1852 she died of complications from a broken hip. In her later years she became pessimistic about America. She felt as if she had "fallen from a strange planet among a race whose sense and perceptions are all different from my own."

During the 1830s, however, the threatened artisans shifted from politics to concentrate on the same economic issues that concerned the building trades. Following the model of the Philadelphia building trades, unions formed citywide coalitions across craft lines. In 1834 federations from Boston to Philadelphia joined to form the National Trades' Union, the first national union of different trades. By 1836 federations from as far south as Washington, D.C., and as far west as Pittsburgh and Cincinnati had joined.

In a series of strikes and boycotts during the 1830s workers across a broad spectrum of crafts successfully used their bargaining power, forcing employers to accept ten hours as the standard workday for most skilled workers in the large cities and for virtually all skilled workers in the building trades. Philadelphia was the scene of the most dramatic victories. In 1835 the Philadelphia city council set a ten-hour day for local public works, and the following year President Jackson, recognizing the importance of the Philadelphia artisans to his party, established a ten-hour day at the Philadelphia navy yard. The ten-hour day victories were significant: American skilled workers were the first in the industrializing world to wrest this concession from their employers.

Buoyed by their victories, the unions turned their energies to winning increases in wages, organizing more than fifty strikes during 1836 and 1837. In most instances the strikers won, often because the trade unions cooperated. For example, when journeymen bookbinders in Philadelphia struck for higher wages in 1836, thirty-seven trade unions from New York to Washington provided financial support that enabled them to hold out for over two months. The grateful journeymen declared that their cause had become "the sacred cause of every skilled laborer in the civilized world."

Factory Workers

The success of the artisans' organizations inspired another group of workers—factory laborers. They were a new group without a history of organization or traditional craft identity and were poorer than the artisans. Nonetheless, they marshaled the strength to resist the growing demands of their employers that they do more work for less pay.

There were about 20,000 cotton-mill operatives by the 1830s, mostly unskilled women and girls. To protest pay cuts or more stringent work rules, many of them engaged in sporadic strikes. In 1828 women mill workers in Dover, New Hampshire, had struck against two new rules. The first levied fines for lateness; the second initiated a system under which workers leaving the mill would receive certificates of regular discharge only if they had been "faithful" employees. The strikers worried that rebellious workers would be fired and then be unable to find jobs because they lacked certificates. The employers prevailed, but in 1834 more than 800 Dover women struck again to protest wage cuts.

In Lowell, Massachusetts, 2,000 women backed up a strike in 1834 by withdrawing their savings from a Lowell bank owned by their employers. The Boston *Transcript* reported that "one of the leaders mounted a pump, and made a flaming . . . speech on the rights of women and the iniquities of the 'monied aristocracy.'" But the 1834 strikes failed. The employers fired the leaders, and the rest of the workers returned to the mills. The Lowell women remained restless and militant, however. Two years later, when the mill owners raised boardinghouse charges, Lowell workers organized again. This time their rallies, marches, and slowdown of production persuaded the owners to reduce or eliminate the increases in board charges.

Victories were rare, however. Strikes of unskilled operatives almost always failed. Overpowered by the employers and viewing factory employment as temporary and peripheral to their lives, women mill workers did not react to defeat by forming strong and permanent unions.

Employers on the Counterattack

Employers had resisted workers' demands since the end of the eighteenth century, but only rarely had they acted together to combat labor. Employers' cooperation had been limited to the regulation of production or the fixing of prices. In response to the waves of strikes in 1836 and 1837, however, employers from Massachusetts to St. Louis dramatically mobilized against the unions. Among the antiunion tactics they developed was the *blacklist.* In 1836 employers in New York City agreed not to hire workers belonging to the Union Trade Society of Journeymen Tailors and circulated a list—a blacklist—of its members. The employers also used the courts. Their lawsuits targeted the *closed shop* agreement, by which employers promised to hire only union members. Most unions secured closed shop agreements when they won wage increases. During the 1830s employers sued the carpet weavers' union in Thompsonville, Connecticut; the shoemakers' unions in Geneva and Hudson, New York; the tailors' union in New York City; the plasterers' union in Philadelphia; and the union of journeymen cordwainers in Boston. Employers charged that closed shop agreements violated the common law or, in New York State, statutes that prohibited such "conspiracies."

The New York Supreme Court ruled against the Geneva shoemakers in 1835. The closed shop, the court held, had caused "an industrious man" to be "driven out of employment" and trade to be restricted. "It is im-

portant to the best interests of society," the court held, "that the price of labor be left to regulate itself." In other words, individual workers were denied the opportunity to organize. Following this precedent, a lower court found the New York tailors guilty of conspiracy.

Unions protested the decision. Twenty-seven thousand workers and their supporters demonstrated outside New York's city hall, and workers intimidated juries hearing similar cases. Later in 1836 juries acquitted the Hudson shoemakers, the Philadelphia plasterers, and the Thompsonville carpet weavers.

The rising power of organized labor was particularly threatening to the business class. Unionization—the increasingly successful effort to democratize the workplace—was only part of the threat. At least as serious was the simultaneous democratization of national politics. It appeared that workers, cooperating with other groups dissatisfied with the effects of the Industrial Revolution, might take control of government and check the power of the business class. In the mid-1830s leaders of the business class themselves attempted to use the new, more democratic political system to win support, even among American workers, for their vision of American society.

Workers Protest, 1836
This poster appealed to workers to protest the conviction of the Geneva shoemakers for conspiracy. At the meeting held in the park fronting New York's city hall, the crowd burned judges in effigy and passed resolutions calling for the creation of a new labor party.

Democrats and Whigs: The Second Party System, 1836–1844

Jackson's party and politics presented the northern business class with the first concerted challenge to its power. To check the growing power of democracy, prominent members of the business class took the lead in organizing a new national political grouping—the Whig party. The two parties that resulted, Democratic and Whig, constituted the Second Party System, which survived until the rise of the Republican party in the mid-1850s. Both political parties competed for support among farmers and urban workers, and in every electoral contest victory went to the party that appealed most successfully to Americans of modest wealth and social status.

The Emergence of the Whigs

As early as Jackson's first term, his opponents in Congress began to form an alliance. They called themselves "Whigs" and referred to Jackson as "King Andrew I." Those names conjured up associations with the pre-Revolutionary American and British parties—also called Whigs—that had opposed the power of King George III. Whigs charged that Jackson had violated the Constitution through tyrannical abuse of executive power and

that Whigs were better defenders of the republic than Democrats. In effect, the Whigs were attempting to turn Jackson's republican rhetoric against him.

Initially, the Congressional Whigs were united only by their opposition to Jackson. They included Senators Webster of Massachusetts, Clay of Kentucky, and Calhoun of South Carolina. Webster and Clay had a bond of common economic interests; Webster spoke on behalf of New England's business elite, and Clay represented the commercial interests of the Ohio and Mississippi valleys. Calhoun, having broken with Jackson over nullification, had little choice but to join the Whigs. However, as a representative of the planter class of the lower South, he had reservations about the economic ideas of his Congressional allies.

Andrew Jackson's victory over Henry Clay in the 1832 presidential election deeply troubled Jackson's Congressional opponents, who regarded his victory as a popular mandate for his position on the Second Bank. Clay and Webster feared that Jackson's election had opened the door to the destruction of all privilege and the undermining of legislative government. In Webster's home state of Massachusetts Whigs listened apprehensively as the Jacksonian George Bancroft told the workingmen of Northampton:

The feud between the capitalist and the laborer, the house of Have and the house of Want, is as old as social union. . . . It is now for the yeomanry and the mechanics to march at the head of civilization. The merchants and the lawyers, that is, the moneyed interest, broke up feudalism. The day for the multitude has now dawned.

To check such democratization, Congressional Whigs began elaborating their own plan for the nation's future. By the 1836 election they had formulated a well-defined alternative to the Democratic vision and had begun to popularize it among the northern middle class.

Whig Ideology. Whigs believed that it was "natural" for a relatively few individuals to acquire a large share of the nation's wealth, represent the people in a republican government, and use government power as they thought necessary for the welfare of all. They attempted to reconcile their elitism with republican ideals in several ways. First, they asserted that American society was really classless because it did not ascribe permanent status to groups and individuals and because its institutions fostered upward mobility. Second, they argued that in a republic it was "natural" for wealthy individuals to represent other citizens. A republican Constitution and the moral influence of religion would compel elites to govern in the best interests of all. Third, pointing to dramatic advances in banking, manufacturing, and transportation, the Whigs claimed that a strong ruling elite promoted economic growth, which strengthened the republic by creating a more prosperous citizenry and unifying labor and capital.

To the Whigs, even the most modern factories were sources of potential social harmony. In 1830 Edward Everett, a congressman from Massachusetts and a leading Whig publicist, told a Fourth of July crowd in Lowell that "the alliance which you have . . . established between labor and capital . . . may truly be called a holy alliance." He proclaimed that factories such as those at Lowell "form a mutually beneficial connection between those who have nothing but their muscular power and those who are able to bring into the partnership . . . property which was itself, originally, the work of men's hands, but has been converted, by accumulation and thrift, from labor into capital." He concluded, "Woe to the land where labor and intelligence are at war! Happy the land whose various interests are united together by the bonds of mutual benefit and kind feeling!"

The Whigs criticized Jackson and the Democrats for underestimating the possibilities for upward mobility, pitting the poor against the rich, and disrupting social harmony. They attacked Jackson's strong presidency, warning against powerful, highly individualistic executives who pandered to the growing masses of vot-

"BORN TO COMMAND."

OF VETO MEMORY.

HAD I BEEN CONSULTED.

KING ANDREW THE FIRST.

A Whig Cartoon
This political cartoon lampooned Andrew Jackson as a monarch decked out with the trappings of royalty and trampling on the Constitution. It emphasized Jackson's contempt for judges and criticized many of his political appointments. It concluded by asking, "Shall he reign over us, or shall the PEOPLE RULE?" (Collection of The New-York Historical Society)

ers. And the Whigs claimed that Democratic economic programs would turn back the clock, impoverishing and weakening the republic.

As an alternative, the Whigs offered legislative rule and a program of governmental intervention in the economy. They wanted a more vigorous national government, and wanted Congress rather than the president to lead it. And the Whigs wanted that government to enact the American System of Henry Clay and John Quincy Adams.

Calhoun's Appeal to Capitalists. The only Congressional opponents of Andrew Jackson who had reservations about the full-blown Whig ideology and program were Calhoun and his southern followers. Calhoun disliked Whig nationalism and Clay's tariff policies, but his

greatest concern was the Whig objection to fixed classes. He argued that the Whig ideal of equal opportunity contradicted the realities of slavery and an industrial society. In 1837 he wrote, "There is and always has been in an advanced stage of wealth and civilization a conflict between labor and capital." He argued that southern slave owners and northern factory owners belonged to the same privileged class and faced the same threat from below. Calhoun therefore urged northern capitalists to join the planters in a defensive alliance. In his view, social harmony could be achieved only through the recognition, acceptance, and reinforcement of the existing sharp distinctions of class. Whigs, he argued, ought to unite around a common defense of privilege and social order.

The other Whig leaders refused to accept Calhoun's antidemocratic analysis. Calhoun's description of "a clear and well-defined line between capital and labor," Daniel Webster agreed, might fit the South or Europe, but in the North "this distinction grows less and less definite as commerce advances." Pointing to Massachusetts, Webster declared, "I do not believe there is on earth, in a highly civilized society, a greater equality in the condition of men than exists there." Webster maintained that Calhoun had neglected the growing importance of the northern middle class. As it turned out, it was the middle class, attracted by the promise of upward mobility, that became the backbone of the Whig, and later the Republican, party.

The Whig Coalition

Led by the Congressional Whigs, a coalition of groups emerged to run candidates at the state and local levels in opposition to the Jacksonian Democrats in the 1834 elections. These groups proved powerful enough to gain control of the House of Representatives. The coalition was strongest in New England, New York, and the new communities along the shores of the Great Lakes. The American System had a great appeal in those areas because they had the highest concentrations of prosperous farmers, small-town merchants, and machinists and other skilled industrial workers who identified with their employers. Whig politicians realized that they had interests in common with business-class enthusiasts for moral reform. Government intervention along Whig lines could be seen as part of a comprehensive program designed to restore social harmony and invigorate the Industrial Revolution. And on a practical level, Whig leaders found that workers and farmers who had been drawn to the perfectionist message of evangelical Protestantism (see Chapter 10) tended also to embrace Whig politics, with its emphasis on individual upward mobility and social improvement.

The Whig message, as publicized by Henry Clay, also won support from people of southern origin in the Ohio and Mississippi valleys. The farmers, bankers, and shopkeepers in the southern tier of the northwestern states differed from northern Whigs in their religious affiliations and culture. But they agreed that positive government action—conscious planning and collective effort—was needed for economic development. They found public investment in internal improvements particularly attractive and supported the ideal of a classless society led by "natural" elites. Consequently, they gradually formed alliances with the business class in the North.

In the South support for the Whig party was less cohesive, resting more on the appeal of specific elements in its program than on the force of the Whigs' social vision. For example, many nonslaveholding whites in the backcountry, especially in western Virginia and the deepest hill country of the other seaboard states, were Whigs because they favored a federal program of banking and internal improvement to break the grip of planter elites. A significant Whig minority also existed among wealthy planters who had invested heavily in railroads, banks, and factories and had maintained close ties to northern markets and New York capitalists. Finally, some states' rights Democrats in Virginia and South Carolina, upset with Jackson's willingness to use force to suppress nullification, joined the Whigs, at least temporarily.

The Election of 1836. In the 1836 presidential election Martin Van Buren, whom Jackson had handpicked to be his successor, was the Democratic candidate. He successfully campaigned on Jackson's record, which included not only the veto of the Second Bank but also the Bank war. The Democrats claimed that they offered Americans "liberty," in contrast with the coercion threatened by the Whigs and the social elites that the Democrats claimed that the Whigs represented. The Whigs ran three presidential candidates, hoping to maximize the opposition votes from the various sections and to force the election into the House of Representatives, which the Whigs controlled. The plan failed to accomplish this goal. The electoral votes collected by the Whigs—73 by William Henry Harrison of Ohio, 26 by Hugh L. White of Tennessee, and 14 by Daniel Webster—fell short of Van Buren's 170 votes. Van Buren's base of support in the populous states of New York, Pennsylvania, and Virginia had proved decisive. Still, the size of the Whig vote showed that the Whig message of social development—economic improvement and moral uplift—had strong appeal not only to middle-class Americans but also to farmers and workers with little or no property. Van Buren had prevailed, but his political problems were just beginning.

The Depression of 1837–1843

The prolonged and steady expansion of the economy from 1820 to 1837 had led many Americans to consider prosperity a permanent feature of life. Few realized that their prosperity still depended heavily on events in Europe. True, American production for export was declining relative to production for domestic consumption and cotton exports were important primarily to the South, but any disruption of foreign credit flowing to the South had a severe ripple effect on the entire economy. Furthermore, American industrialization and territorial expansion depended on large amounts of long-term investment from Europe, primarily from Great Britain, to finance the construction of canals and railroads. Whenever the flow of investment came to a halt, depression was likely to radiate throughout the American economy. Amplifying these problems was the fact that industrialization had made the economy more complex; its parts were more interdependent. Disruptions in any sector had more serious effects on other sectors than had been the case earlier.

The Panic of 1837. The Panic of 1837 began in Britain. In late 1836 the Bank of England, convinced that it was sending too much specie to the United States, curtailed the flow of investment. Partly as a result, British demand for cotton declined sharply, causing the bankruptcy of British and American mercantile firms whose lending was based on the use of cotton as security. These events set off a wave of bankruptcies and restrictions of credit that affected merchants and bankers throughout the United States (see Map 11.3). Without adequate credit, American trade, manufacturing, and farming slid into a depression.

Years of Depression. The depression dragged on until 1843, becoming the most severe American depression until the 1870s. The Bank of England continued to keep credit tight until the early 1840s. At the same time bumper cotton crops in the late 1830s drove down cotton prices, making matters even worse for merchants in international trade. Many states, unable to raise taxes or borrow in depressed conditions, defaulted on the bonds that they had issued to finance canal building and

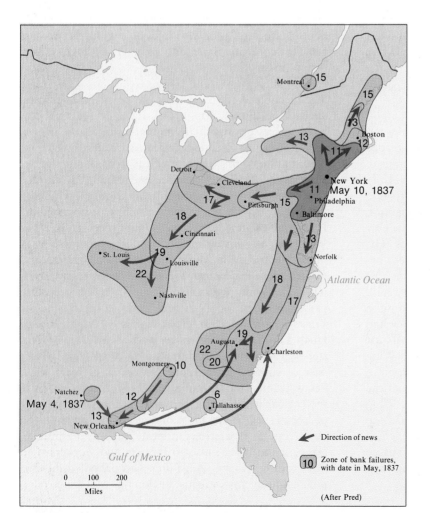

MAP 11.3

Anatomy of a Panic: Bank Suspensions in May 1837
Although the first bank failures occurred in Natchez and Tallahassee, it was the collapse of New York City banks several days later that precipitated a chain reaction of national panic. Rivers, canals, and post roads carried news of the panic from New York to St. Louis in just twelve days. The resulting pattern of bank failures provides a dramatic picture of the economic nerve system of the nation—a nerve system dominated by New York.

The Aftermath of the Panic of 1837
This cartoon pictures the Independence Day celebration in New York in 1837 as being marred by the symptoms of economic depression—unemployed workers, mothers begging and pawning their possessions, goods that cannot be sold, sheriff's sales of property, runs on banks, and alcoholism. A prison and an almshouse are in the background. (Collection of The New-York Historical Society)

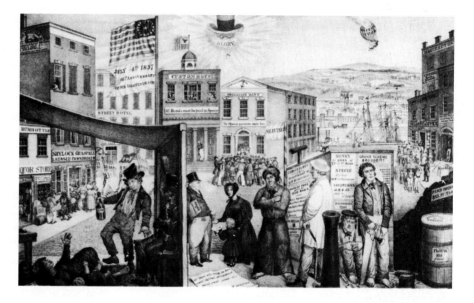

thereby undermined British confidence in American investments. To protect themselves, American banks insisted on holding larger amounts of specie. But this cautious policy reduced the amount of money available to the general public. As a result, overall spending, capital investment, and prices declined even further, deepening the depression.

By 1843, as compared with 1837, prices on average had fallen by almost half and overall investment in the American economy had declined by almost 25 percent, led by a 90 percent drop in canal construction. Investment in railroads and manufacturing also fell dramatically. Slumping investment and production forced workers out of jobs, and in 1838 unemployment rose to an unprecedented level of almost 10 percent; in seaports and industrial centers it approached 20 percent. In concert with the bankruptcies of farms and businesses, this meant that a vast spectrum of Americans were stricken. In the words of the Reverend Henry Ward Beecher:

> The world looked upon a continent of inexhaustible fertility (whose harvest had glutted the markets, and rotted in disuse), filled with lamentation, and its inhabitants wandering like bereaved citizens among the ruins of an earthquake, mourning for children, for houses crushed, and property buried forever.

Economic instability had become a significant aspect of American life. It heightened all the other disruptive forces of the Industrial Revolution, and its effects were particularly harsh on people who lacked property or skills.

Destruction of the Labor Movement. As might be expected, the depression shattered the labor movement. Union successes in the early 1830s had been based on labor shortages. But now, for the first time in fifty years,

there was a surplus of skilled workers. In 1837, 6,000 masons, carpenters, and other building-trade workers were discharged in New York City alone. The dramatic rise in unemployment among skilled workers decimated union membership.

Artisans faced additional dilemmas. Factory competition had already forced large numbers of them to abandon their crafts and consequently their union movement. During the depression increasing numbers of artisans, despairing of the possibility of organizing to oppose the forces of industrialization, dropped out of the labor movement. Consequently, most local unions and workers' assemblies and all the national labor organizations disappeared, along with their newspapers and other publications.

One of the few bright spots for the labor movement came in 1842, when Chief Justice Lemuel Shaw of Massachusetts handed down his ruling in *Commonwealth v. Hunt*. The case had begun in 1840, when the Whig district attorney for the city of Boston had brought members of the Boston Journeymen Bootmakers' Society into municipal court for trying to enforce a closed shop. Shaw overturned earlier precedent by making two critical rulings: (1) A union was a criminal organization only if its *objectives* were criminal, and (2) union members were within their rights in attempting to enforce closed shops, even by striking. This decision discouraged courts from finding that unions were inherently criminal or that the closed shop was socially harmful. But courts, which generally were dominated by unsympathetic Whig judges, usually found other grounds to restrict strikes and boycotts.

Workers, with their unions destroyed and the movement for greater democracy in the workplace faltering, increasingly turned to politics. The Democrats offered a warm welcome. President Van Buren contin-

ued Jackson's effort to court workers and in 1840 signed an executive order establishing the ten-hour day for federal employees. Ironically, this victory, the most dramatic achievement of the early labor movement, came after the unions had lost their power in the marketplace.

The Election of 1840

The election of 1840, held in the middle of the depression, created a political crisis for the Democrats in which, ironically, Andrew Jackson's success proved a liability. In turning the presidency into an agent of the people, Jackson had convinced many Americans that the president could make a difference in terms of maintaining prosperity. Most people did not understand the overwhelming influence of international forces on the business cycle and readily blamed Jackson and Van Buren for their economic troubles. In particular, they decided that Jackson had been wrong to attack the Second Bank and had been responsible for the Panic of 1837.

President Van Buren seemed helpless in the face of the political crisis. The only substantial measures successfully sponsored by his administration were the ten-hour day for federal employees and the Independent Treasury Act. That act confirmed the public's identification of the Democrats as the antibanking party by requiring the federal government to keep its cash in government vaults rather than in banks. Its chief objective was to prevent the government from playing favorites among bankers and from using federal deposits to promote banking and expand the money supply.

William Henry Harrison. The Whigs made the most of their opponents' discomfiture. The depression helped them by discrediting the Democrats, making it less important that the Whigs take clear positions on the issues. In their first national convention the Whigs renominated William Henry Harrison of Ohio, a military hero noted for his victories over native Americans at Tippecanoe and over the British in the Battle of the Thames (Ontario) in the War of 1812. Harrison lacked executive ability and was sixty-eight years old, but that mattered little to the Whig leaders, Clay and Webster. They did not want a strong president; they planned to use Harrison as a rubber stamp for Congressional enactment of the Whig program. Moreover, Harrison's military record, Virginia roots, and strong identification with western interests made him a Whig version of Andrew Jackson. Harrison believed that he matched Jackson's commitment to democracy, although he gave it a Whig twist. He believed that democracy coupled with a robust banking system provided "the only means, under

Heaven, by which a poor industrious man may become a rich man without bowing to colossal wealth."

Economic events stacked the cards against Van Buren. A more charismatic man might have been able to retain the public's favor in spite of the depression. But Van Buren was known primarily as a manipulative professional politician. And he lacked the ties with the Revolutionary generation or the military experience that might have boosted his vote-getting appeal.

The Log-Cabin Campaign. In the 1840 campaign the Whigs concentrated on organizing the electorate and demonstrating their commitment to upward social mobility rather than taking a stand on the issues. As a result, the Harrison campaign was the first in American history to be conducted as an exuberant carnival. The Whigs turned pamphleteering, songfests, parades, and well-orchestrated mass meetings into a new political style that would become the norm for American elections. Colorful Whig spectacles helped persuade participants and observers alike that they were engaged in a fundamentally democratic cause. The Whigs also made the most of the democratic message in their nomination of a popular war hero who had worked himself up from the ranks. When a Democratic newspaper unwisely de-

The Log-Cabin Campaign, 1840
Campaign banners such as this one portrayed Harrison as a simple, generous, and patriotic man of the people. (Collection of The New-York Historical Society)

scribed Harrison as a man who would be happy to retire to a log cabin if he had a pension and an ample supply of hard cider, the Whigs seized on that description to present their candidate as a simple man who loved log cabins and cider. Although Harrison was actually a man of some wealth, the 1840 election became the "log-cabin" campaign, and the candidate demonstrated his common touch by breaking with precedent and joining the campaign celebrations.

The Whigs succeeded in portraying their candidate as a man of the people and blaming the Democrats for the depression. Although their popular victory was a narrow one, the Whigs won an overwhelming electoral victory (including the votes of New York and Pennsylvania) and gained control of Congress. Popular interest in a presidential election had never been greater. Whereas less than 60 percent of the eligible voters had taken part in 1832 and 1836, more than 80 percent voted in 1840.

The Resurgence of the Democratic Party

The election of Harrison seemed to clear the way for the enactment of Henry Clay's economic program. The Whigs had the misfortune, however, of immediately losing the leader on whom they had pinned their hopes when Harrison died of pneumonia one month after his inauguration. Succeeding him was Vice-President John Tyler, a Virginian who was far from a typical southern Whig. Tyler actually opposed the urban commercial interests in his own state and had shared Jackson's hostility to the Second Bank. He had joined the Whig party because of his enthusiasm for states' rights and his disgust with Jackson's nationalism.

John Tyler. As president, Tyler betrayed the Whig party. He took it on himself to block single-handedly the Whig program of economic nationalism. He vetoed two bills sponsored by Senator Henry Clay to reestablish the national bank, and he also blocked major protective tariffs. Clay broke with Tyler in disgust. Then Tyler's cabinet, all of them Whigs, resigned, with the exception of Secretary of State Daniel Webster, who stayed on to influence the course of foreign policy.

Whig successes during the Tyler administration were few and limited: repeal of the independent Treasury in 1841 and a modest increase in tariffs in 1842. The most important legislation of Tyler's administration—the Preemption Act—passed because strong western support for it forced the Whigs to work with the Democrats. The Preemption Act of 1841 gave most American citizens and also immigrants the right to stake a claim to 160 acres of land and purchase it later at the standard price of $1.25 an acre, provided that they built a house on the land and made other "improvements," such as clearing the land. The preemption process recognized that people commonly settled on public land before purchasing it from the government. Its intent was to give an advantage to actual settlers as opposed to land speculators; its effect was to accelerate the pace of westward expansion.

The New Democratic Coalition. Tyler's rejection of Clay's American System gave the Democrats some precious time—time they needed to consolidate their opposition to the Whigs. During the 1840s the Democratic party vigorously recruited supporters from the farming community: poor farmers in the North and planters and small farmers in the South. At the same time the party went after the votes of the urban working class, in part by strongly opposing any economic program that seemed to offer benefits to wealthy members of the business class. Immigrant workers provided a new source of support, in particular Catholic immigrants, who were repelled by the insistent Protestantism of the Whigs and appreciated the Democrats' greater acceptance of religious and economic diversity. In New York City during the 1840s about 95 percent of Irish-Catholic voters supported Democratic candidates.

A Mass-Based Political Culture. For the first time two national parties were competing vigorously for the loyalties of a mass electorate. Each party relied on a network of newspapers to convey its message; virtually every crossroads town had both a Jacksonian and a Whig newspaper. In Washington, D.C., the *Washington Globe* represented the Democrats while the *National Intelligencer* spoke for the Whigs. Each party offered a distinct vision of industrialization and of the social and political order, and they competed on terms that were reasonably equal. The Democrats held an edge in party discipline and mass loyalty. But in organizing popular appeals the Whigs had a major advantage because of their wealth and the cohesiveness of their leadership and support. That support was based on the interests of the business class, yet the Whigs also managed to make powerful inroads among workers and farmers.

The Second Party System was in place, and the new two-party competition invigorated American democracy. Both Democrats and Whigs built coalitions of diverse groups and interests. Each party tried to persuade Americans to use its ideas and rhetoric in approaching every public issue. Each party established a national identity and helped dilute and diffuse sectional disagreements. The parties were managed by professional politicians who worked to create a political "product" that would satisfy as many different kinds of voters as possible. Together, the two parties molded a new political culture.

Summary

The rise of the business class stimulated group consciousness throughout American society. All groups saw politics as the best way to advance their interests (sometimes by blocking the interests of others), and their collective pressure forced a democratization of politics—a democratic revolution—during the 1820s and 1830s. That revolution swept Andrew Jackson into the presidency, and Jackson mobilized the support of large numbers of laborers, farmers, and southern planters for the Democratic party. He was the first president to regard himself as more than just the enforcer of the nation's laws. He saw himself as an instrument of democracy—expressing the will of the majority. In the process of implementing his vision he transformed his party and the presidency into powerful instruments for majority rule. Jackson used those instruments to challenge the power of the Second Bank of the United States, defend the Union against the threat of South Carolina's Ordinance of Nullification, and remove native Americans to the west of the Mississippi. Jackson was capable of caution as well. While he sympathized with the desire of the new republic of Texas to enter the Union, he did not take up that cause lest he fracture the Democratic party into northern and southern wings and put the Union at risk.

Some workers, especially those with traditional skills, sought democracy in their places of work. They challenged the new industrial order and the power of the business class not only through politics but also through a union movement. They tried to reform working conditions by forming labor unions to demand a ten-hour day and establishing political parties to promote a more equitable society. Strikes increased during the 1830s, and the unions made some limited gains.

The democratic revolution, dramatized by Jackson's veto of the rechartering of the Second Bank of the United States, disturbed the emerging business class and stimulated the formation of the Whig party. Its initial goal was to check the power of the mass-based Democratic party. But the new political realities forced the Whigs to design a message that would have broad appeal to the common people. Led by Henry Clay and Daniel Webster, the Whigs invited middle-class Americans to join the business class and designed an ideology and a program to reconcile elitism with republican ideals. Whereas Democrats emphasized liberty, Whigs stressed material improvement and opportunity. This marked the beginning of the Second Party System. The democratic revolution was now carried forward by the intense competition between the Whig and Democratic parties, both of which established coalitions of support that were national in scope.

The depression that followed the Panic of 1837 halted both the labor movement and Jacksonianism and contributed to the election of a Whig president, William Henry Harrison. But the betrayal of the Whigs by Harrison's successor, John Tyler, blocked the enactment of the Whig economic program.

TIMELINE

1821	Mexico encourages immigration to Texas
1825	John Quincy Adams elected president by the House of Representatives
1827	Philadelphia Working Men's party organized
1828	Tariff of Abominations Andrew Jackson elected president *The South Carolina Exposition and Protest*
1830	Jackson's Maysville Road veto Mexico restricts immigration and prohibits the importation of slaves Journeymen cordwainers organize Indian Removal Act
1831	*Cherokee Nation v. Georgia*
1832	Bad Axe Massacre Jackson vetoes renewal of the charter of Second Bank of the United States South Carolina nullifies Tariff of Abominations
1833	Force bill and Compromise Tariff
1834	Peak of the Bank war
1835	Ten-hour day for skilled workers
1836	Texans proclaim independence from Mexico Martin Van Buren elected president
1837	Depression of 1837–1843 begins with the Panic of 1837
1838	Trail of Tears
1840	William Henry Harrison elected president
1841	John Tyler succeeds to presidency Preemption Act
1842	*Commonwealth v. Hunt*

★　　　　★　　　　★

BIBLIOGRAPHY

The most useful surveys of the Jacksonian era are Edward Pessen, *Jacksonian America* (1970); Charles Sellers, *The Market Revolution: Jacksonian America, 1815–1846* (1992); Glydon Van Duesen, *The Jacksonian Era* (1959); and Harry L. Watson, *Liberty and Power: The Politics of Jacksonian America* (1990).

Democratizing Politics and the Jacksonian Presidency

Arthur M. Schlesinger, Jr., *The Age of Jackson* (1945), initiated modern reexamination of Andrew Jackson and his significance. Among the most provocative are other older studies: Lee Benson, *The Concept of Jacksonian Democracy: New York as a Test Case* (1961); Marvin Meyers, *The Jacksonian Persuasion: Politics and Belief* (1957); and John William Ward, *Andrew Jackson; Symbol for an Age* (1962). More recently scholars have studied Jacksonian democracy in the context of democratic political culture and the rise of the Second Party System. For an innovative study of Jackson as an institution builder, see Donald Cole, *The Presidency of Andrew Jackson* (1993). On the politics of the Bank war, see Robert V. Remini, *Andrew Jackson and the Bank War* (1967). On the nullification crises, see William W. Freehling, *Prelude to Civil War* (1966), and Richard E. Ellis, *The Union at Risk* (1987). On the spoils system, see Leonard D. White, *The Jacksonians: A Study in Administrative History, 1828–1861* (1954). Books treating Jackson's Indian policy and the Indians include Ralph S. Cotterill, *The Southern Indians* (1954); Grant Forman, *Indian Removal* (1953); Michael D. Green, *The Politics of Indian Removal* (1982); William G. McLoughlin, *Cherokee Renascence in the New Republic* (1986); Gary E. Moulton, *John Ross: Cherokee Chief* (1978); Francis P. Prucha, *American Indian Policy in the Formative Years* (1962) and *American Indian Treaties: The History of a Political Anomaly* (1994); and Ronald N. Satz, *American Indian Policy in the Jacksonian Era* (1975). On the settlement of Texas and the Texas rebellion, see David J. Weber, *The Spanish Frontier in North America* (1992) and *The Mexican Frontier, 1821–1846: The American Southwest under Mexico* (1982). For biographies of leading figures, see Robert V. Remini, *Andrew Jackson and the Course of American Freedom, 1822–1833* (1977), *Andrew Jackson and the Course of American Democracy, 1833–1845* (1984), and *The Life of Andrew Jackson* (1988). On John Quincy Adams, see Samuel Flagg Bemis, *John Quincy Adams and the Union* (1956), and Leonard L. Richards, *The Life and Times of Congressman John Quincy Adams* (1986). On Martin Van Buren, see John Niven, *Martin Van Buren: The Romantic Age of American Politics* (1983); Robert V. Remini, *Martin Van Buren and the Making of the Democratic Party* (1959); and James C. Curtis, *The Fox at Bay* (1970). The Great Triumvirate has attracted numerous biographers. On John C. Calhoun, see Richard N. Current, *John C. Calhoun* (1963), and Charles M. Wiltse, *John C. Calhoun* (3 vols., 1944–1951); on Daniel Webster, see Irving H. Bartlett, *Daniel Webster* (1978); and on Henry Clay, see Robert V. Remini, *Henry Clay: Statesman for the Union* (1991). For the presidency of John Tyler, see Robert J. Morgan, *A Whig Embattled* (1954).

The Early Labor Movement

An earlier generation of historians of labor emphasized the organization of unions during early industrialization. See Norman Ware, *The Industrial Worker, 1840–1860* (1924), and John R. Commons, *History of Labour in the United States*, Vol. 1 (1918). More recently, historians have carefully explored the political and social context of the labor movement. See Mary H. Blewett, *Men, Women, and Work: Class, Gender, and Protest in the New England Shoe Industry, 1780–1910* (1988); Jeanne Boydston, *Home and Work: Housework, Wages, and the Ideology of Labor in the Early Republic* (1990); Alan Dawley, *Class and Community: The Industrial Revolution in Lynn Massachusetts, 1780–1860* (1981); Paul G. Faler, *Mechanics and Manufacturers in the Early Industrial Revolution: Lynn, Massachusetts* (1981); Paul A. Gilje and Howard B. Rock, eds., *Keepers of the Revolution: New Yorkers at Work in the Early Republic* (1992); Susan E. Hirsch, *Roots of the American Working Class: The Industrialization of Crafts in Newark, 1800–1860* (1978); Bruce Laurie, *Working People of Philadelphia, 1800–1860* (1980); Jonathan Prude, *The Coming of the Industrial Order: Town and Factory Life in Rural Massachusetts, 1810–1860* (1983); Ronald Schultz, *The Republic of Labor: Philadelphia Artisans and the Politics of Class* (1993); and Sean Wilentz, *Chants Democratic, New York City and the Rise of the American Working Class, 1788–1850* (1984).

Democrats and Whigs: The Second Party System

A rich literature describes the emergence of the Whigs and the larger topic—the formation of the Second Party System. Books that deal broadly with the new party structure include John Ashworth, *"Agrarians" & "Aristocrats": Party Political Ideology in the United States, 1837–1846* (1983); Richard Hofstadter, *The Idea of a Party System* (1972); Daniel W. Howe, *The Political Culture of the American Whigs* (1979); Robert Kelley, *The Cultural Pattern in American Politics: The First Century* (1979); Lawrence F. Kohl, *The Politics of Individualism: Parties and the American Character in the Jacksonian Era* (1989); Richard P. McCormick, *The Second American Party System: Party Formation in the Jacksonian Era* (1966); and Joel H. Silbey, *The Partisan Imperative: The Dynamics of American Politics before the Civil War* (1985). Studies that are more specialized include Thomas Brown, *Politics and Statesmanship: Essays on the American Whig Party,* (1985); Ronald P. Formisano, *The Birth of Mass Political Parties: Michigan, 1827–1861* (1971) and *The Transformation of Political Culture: Massachusetts Parties, 1790s–1840s* (1983); William G. Shade, *Banks or No Banks: The Money Issue in Western Politics, 1832–1865* (1972); Harry L. Watson, *Jacksonian Politics and Community Conflict: The Emergence of the Second Party System in Cumberland County, North Carolina* (1981); and Chilton Williamson, *American Suffrage from Property to Democracy, 1760–1860* (1960).

Mormon Treks across the Great Plains

After the successful establishment of Mormon communities in
the valley of the Great Salt Lake, several thousand impoverished
migrants, largely from Britain and Scandinavia, formed "handcart
companies" and hauled their meager possessions across the
Great Plains.

Freedom's Crusaders

1820–1860

★　　　★　　　★

The Industrial Revolution and territorial expansion had contradictory effects on the way Americans thought about themselves as individuals and as a society. Growing economic opportunity seemed to liberate individuals and make men and women believe that each person could become the master of his or her own fate.

But these changes also brought new restraints and obligations. The new economic order demanded social organization and an increasing degree of standardization. For one thing, men and women had to submit to common disciplines of work. And to solve a new array of social and economic problems, they had to accept a greater measure of discipline—working cooperatively, for example, within the Second Party System.

Alexis de Tocqueville observed the contest between the supremacy of the individual and the demands of social responsibility during his 1831–1832 tour of the United States. In *Democracy in America* he described the tendency of Americans to be moved in opposite ways, by self-interest but also by devotion to the interests of the community. Americans, he said, seemed at one time to be "animated by the most selfish cupidity; at another by the most lively patriotism." These opposing passions were so powerful, he thought, that Americans must have them "united and mingled in some part of their character."

It was on account of these conflicting passions that a wave of reform movements washed over America during the Industrial Revolution. The wave was so strong that it spilled out of the conservative channels first carved by business-class reformers—those who had championed regular church attendance, abstinence from alcohol, and evangelical religion—to challenge some of the basic premises of American society. The labor movement offered a sweeping criticism of industrial society but did not win wide support from middle-

class Americans, and labor's power waned after the Panic of 1837. In contrast, the new reform movements won a growing middle-class following despite their radical edge. These radical movements also broke through the barriers erected by national politicians to bring order to American public life and control the debate over social issues. Radical reformers demanded action; they either sought change outside the political system or demanded that the system respond immediately to their ideals.

The effort to abolish slavery was potentially the most disruptive of the radical movements. If abolitionists could win substantial middle-class support in the North, they would pit section against section. But by the early 1840s the popular reaction to abolitionism—in the North as well as the South—was primarily outrage. It remained to be seen whether the abolitionists could mount a successful political crusade. If they did, would the dominant parties address the issue of slavery? And if that happened, could the parties still maintain their national support and the unity of the republic? The answers to all these questions would come during the late 1840s and the 1850s.

Transcendentalists and Utopians

Among the reformers who most vigorously championed individual freedom—the liberation of individuals to act freely on their personal choices—were the transcendentalists, a group of intellectuals who emerged in the New England heartland of the Industrial Revolution. At first they sought primarily to loosen the constraints imposed by the traditional Congregationalist faith, but some became so distressed about the difficulties of individual fulfillment that they rejected industrial society as well. Many of these radical transcendentalists, like other groups of Americans, withdrew into utopian experimental communities. Those communities had numerous and diverse goals, ranging from the establishment of a separate, more rewarding social order for like-minded people to the transformation of American society as a whole.

Ralph Waldo Emerson

The first transcendentalists were young men—often Unitarian ministers—and were generally members of wealthy and privileged New England families. They were American romantics who focused on ideas borrowed from the philosopher Immanuel Kant and from German romanticism, as translated by Harvard professor Edward Everett, who had studied in Germany, and the English poet Samuel Taylor Coleridge. Like the German and English romantics, they believed that behind the concrete world of the senses was another, *ideal* order of reality. This reality "transcended," or went beyond, the usual ways by which people know the world. This ideal reality could be known only by means of mysterious intuitive powers through which, at moments of inspiration, people could travel past the limits of their ordinary experience and gain mystical knowledge of ultimate and eternal things. The intellectual leader of the transcendentalists—and the most popular of all of them—was a second-generation Unitarian minister, Ralph Waldo Emerson.

Emerson resigned his Boston pulpit in 1832, at the age of twenty-nine, after a crisis of conscience that led him to choose individual moral insight over organized religion. He moved to Concord, Massachusetts, and turned to writing essays and lecturing, supported in part by a legacy from his first wife. His message centered on the idea of the radically free individual. "Our age," Emerson's great complaint began, "is retrospective." People were trapped in their inherited institutions and societies. They wore the ideas of people from earlier times—the tenets of New England Calvinism, for example—as a kind of "faded masquerade." They needed to break free of the boundaries of tradition and custom. That could be done only if each individual discovered his or her own "original relation with Nature." Emerson celebrated individuality, self-reliance, dissent, and nonconformity as the only methods by which a person could become free to discover a private harmony with what he called, in an almost mystical fashion, "currents of Universal Being." For Emerson, the ideal setting for such a discovery was nature—solitude under an open sky, among nature's rocks and trees.

Emerson's message reached hundreds of thousands of people, primarily through his lectures. Public lectures had become a spectacularly successful new way of spreading information and fostering discussion among the middle classes, across the boundaries of religious and political institutions. In 1826 an organization known as the American Lyceum was formed to "promote the general diffusion of knowledge." The Lyceum organized lecture tours by speakers of all sorts—poets, preachers, scientists, reformers—and soon took firm hold, especially in the North. In 1839, 137 local Lyceum groups in Massachusetts invited slates of lecturers to their towns during the fall and winter "season" to speak to more than 33,000 subscribers. Among the hundreds of lecturers on the Lyceum circuit, Emerson was the most popular. Between 1833 and 1860 he gave 1,500 lectures in more than 300 different towns in twenty states.

Emerson's celebration of the liberated individual tapped currents of faith that already ran deep among his middle-class audiences. The publication of the autobiography of Benjamin Franklin in 1818 had earlier

given Americans a down-to-earth model of an individual determined to reach "moral perfection" through the solitary cultivation of private virtues. Charles Grandison Finney's account of his own conversion experience in 1823 also pointed in Emersonian directions. Finney, who was the foremost business-class evangelist, pictured his conversion as a mystical union of an individual, alone in the woods, with God (see Chapter 10). In addition, Emerson's notion that a solitary individual could transcend the constraining boundaries of society and discover a new self was a familiar idea to the millions of Americans who read the fiction of Washington Irving and James Fenimore Cooper.

Emerson's romantic individualism, however, was more extreme. His emphasis on nature as the route to finding God—a kind of pantheism—stood outside Christian doctrine, and after he criticized organized religion in an address to the senior class of the Harvard Divinity School in 1838, Harvard refused to invite him back for thirty years. Moreover, Emerson criticized the new industrial society. He observed the lives of New Englanders who had been forced to abandon their farms for factories and sensed "the disproportion between their faculties and the work offered them." And he worried that a preoccupation with the consumption of factory-made goods would drain the moral energy of the more affluent. "Things are in the saddle," Emerson wrote, "and ride mankind."

Emerson's genius lay in his capacity to translate radical but vague ideas into examples that made sense—and were acceptable—to ordinary middle-class Americans. He soft-pedaled some of his more radical ideas in his lectures. Thus, he described his pantheism as the idea that all of nature was saturated with the presence of God. Emerson said that if God was everywhere, then God was present in even the most routine sights of everyday life, such as a bare pasture and a railroad. In the same way Emerson took the edge off his hostility to materialism. He translated the celebration of the possibilities of human achievement into a celebration of common things that philosophers had traditionally ignored or scorned. At times he even celebrated money itself. Rather than being "the root of all evil," it "represents the prose of life. [It] is in its effects and laws, as beautiful as roses."

Emerson's Disciples

Emerson hoped to expand the influence of transcendentalism by revolutionizing literature—by creating a genuinely democratic American literature. In 1837 he had delivered an address at Harvard entitled "The American Scholar," intended as a literary declaration of independence from what he called the "courtly muse" of old Europe. He urged American writers to celebrate democracy and individual freedom and find inspiration in the "familiar, the low . . . the milk in the pan; the ballad in the street; the news of the boat; the glance of the eye; the form and gait of the body."

Henry David Thoreau. Henry David Thoreau heeded Emerson's call. Thoreau, who lived near Emerson in Concord, Massachusetts, decided to take Emerson's notion of solitude in nature literally. He built a cabin at the edge of Walden Pond, near Concord, and lived there from 1845 to 1847. In 1854 he published an account of his experiment in self-reliance, *Walden, Or Life in the Woods*. It was the story of a radical, nonconforming quest—his spiritual search for meanings that went beyond the traps and artificiality of life in a "civilized" society. On the practical side, Thoreau listed his accounts, a profit-and-loss statement that recorded his expenditures for a little sugar or a bit of string, and his income from the little surplus production he managed. He presented this accounting to lead readers to recall the pecuniary calculations of Benjamin Franklin in his *Autobiography*. Thoreau wanted to highlight his record of a "commerce" with the deeper, spiritual meaning of life. It was this kind of venture in self-discovery, rather than hermitlike subsistence farming, that he was promoting:

> I went to the woods because I wished to live deliberately, confront only the essential facts of life, and see if I could not learn what it had to teach, and not, when I came to die, discover that I had not lived.

Although Thoreau's essay had little impact outside transcendentalist circles during his lifetime, *Walden* has become an essential text of American literature and an inspiration to succeeding generations of utopian builders. And its most famous metaphor provides an enduring justification for independent thinking: "If a man does not keep pace with his companions, perhaps it is because he hears a different drummer."

Walt Whitman. Another writer who responded to Emerson's call was the poet Walt Whitman, who said that when he first encountered Emerson, he had been "simmering, simmering." Then Emerson "brought me to a boil." Whitman had been a journalist, an editor of the *Brooklyn Eagle* and other newspapers, but it was poetry that had been the "direction of his dreams." In *Leaves of Grass*, first published in 1855 and constantly revised and expanded for almost four decades afterward, he recorded his attempt to pass a number of "invisible boundaries": between solitude and community, between body and spirit, between prose and poetry, and even between the living and the dead. It was a wild, exuberant poem in both form and content. It self-consciously violated every poetic rule and every canon of respectable taste, daring readers to shut the book in revulsion or accept Whitman's idiosyncratic vision whole.

At the center of *Leaves of Grass* is the figure of the poet, "I, Walt." He begins alone: "I celebrate myself, and sing myself," loafing in nature, "observing a spear of summer grass." But because he has what Emerson calls an "original relation" with nature, the poet claims not solitude but perfect communion with others: "And what I assume you shall assume, / For every atom belonging to me as good belongs to you." Whitman was celebrating democracy as well as himself. He argued militantly that a poet in a democracy could claim a profoundly intimate, mystical relationship with a mass audience. For both Emerson and Thoreau, the individual had a divine spark. For Whitman, however, the individual had expanded to *become* divine—infusing democracy with divinity and making organized religion irrelevant.

Whitman, Thoreau, and Emerson were not naively optimistic. Whitman wrote of human suffering with as much passion as he wrote of everything else. Emerson's accounts of the exhilaration that could come in nature were tinged with anxiety. "I am glad," he said, "to the brink of fear." Thoreau's gloomy judgment of everyday life is well known: "The mass of men lead lives of quiet desperation." Still, such dark murmurings were muted in their work, woven into their triumphant and expansive assertions that nothing was impossible for an individual who could break free from tradition, law, and other social restraints.

Hawthorne and Melville. Emerson's influence also reached two great novelists, Nathaniel Hawthorne and Herman Melville. Hawthorne, who for a time was a member of Emerson's circle, and Melville had more pessimistic visions. They dwelt on the vanity, corruption, and excesses of individualism rather than on its positive potential. Both sounded powerful warnings that unfettered egoism could destroy individuals as well as their social arrangements. They embraced the ideal of individual freedom but at the same time urged the acceptance of an inner discipline.

Hawthorne's most brilliant exploration of this theme of excessive individualism appeared in his novel *The Scarlet Letter* (1850). The two main characters, Hester Prynne and Arthur Dimmesdale, challenge their seventeenth-century New England community in the most blatant way—by committing adultery, producing a child, and refusing to bend to the community's condemnation. The result of their assertion of individual freedom against communal discipline is not exaltation but tragedy. Wracked by guilt and unable to confess, Dimmesdale dies in anguish. Prynne learns from her experience that the way to a truly virtuous life can be found only by a person who is willing to do good within the social order.

Melville, strongly influenced by Hawthorne, explored the same problem in even more extreme and tragic terms and emerged as a scathing critic of tran-

Walt Whitman

Whitman (1819–1892) took dangerous steps for an artist in the nineteenth century by condemning organized religion with its "creeds and priests" and treating sex explicitly. Emerson tried to persuade him to drop those sections from *Leaves of Grass,* but Whitman explained that "if I had cut sex out," the poetry "would have been violated at its most sensitive spot."

Edgar Allan Poe

Born and bred in Virginia, Poe (1809–1849) identified with the South and defended slavery. But he rose above his time and place, never using southern subjects in his work. As an editor and critic in Baltimore, Philadelphia, and New York, he advanced the ideas that art should strive for beauty, not truth, and that writers should calculate their effects on their readers with precision.

Emily Dickinson

Emily Dickinson (1830–1886), born into a well-to-do family in Amherst, was a rebellious student at South Hadley Female Seminary (now Mount Holyoke College) and might have had a brief love affair with a married Philadelphia minister. Though she was a prolific writer—in a single year, 1862, she produced 356 poems—only seven poems were published during her lifetime.

scendentalism. He made his most powerful statement in *Moby Dick* (1851). The novel begins as a whaling captain, Ahab, embarks on an obsessive hunt for a white whale, Moby Dick, that had severed his leg during an earlier expedition. Ahab is a version of Emerson's liberated individual with an intuitive grasp of hidden meanings in nature. He believes that the whale is pure, demonic evil. Ahab's form of "self-reliance" is to hunt the whale down, no matter what the cost. The trouble, as Melville tells the story, is that Ahab can hunt the whale only in a social way. Ahab's ship, the *Pequod*, is an industrial community. In fact, the novel's depiction of whaling is perhaps the most detailed literary description of an actual industry ever written in the United States or Britain. Ahab's transcendental adventure subverts the legitimate purposes of the whaling voyage. As a result, not only Ahab but the crew of workers die. Only one person, Ishmael, is left to tell the tale.

Poe and Dickinson. *Moby Dick* was a commercial failure. The middle-class audience that was the primary target of American publishers was unwilling to follow Melville into the dark, dangerous realms of individualism gone mad. It was also unenthusiastic about the visions of terror and evil that Edgar Allan Poe, a southern-born admirer of Hawthorne, created in "The Raven" (1845) and other poems and short stories. Poe won respect in New York literary circles but could not find a middle-class audience. Emily Dickinson, another poet whose work expressed doubts about individualism, did not even try to find readers. During the 1850s she kept private the poetry she had begun to write in isolation in Amherst, Massachusetts. At the same time, both *Walden* and *Leaves of Grass* also failed to find a large readership. The middle-class audience was unimpressed by Thoreau's extreme and demanding version of transcendentalism and by Whitman's boundless claims for the mystical union between the man of genius and the democratic masses. They emphatically preferred the more modest examinations of individualism offered by Emerson.

Margaret Fuller. One of the writers inspired by Emerson was Margaret Fuller (1810–1850). She edited the leading transcendentalist journal, the *Dial*, and published *Woman in the Nineteenth Century*, which appeared in the *Dial* in 1843 and as a book in 1844. Fuller proclaimed that a "new era" was coming for men and women. Although she knew the writings of Mary Wollstonecraft, her philosophy was based on a transcendental religious vision that women had an independent relationship with God that gave them an identity that had nothing to do with gender. She believed that every woman deserved psychological and social independence—the ability "to grow, as an intellect to discern, as a soul to live freely and unimpeded." She declared, "We would have every arbitrary barrier thrown down" and

Margaret Fuller
Margaret Fuller (1810–1850) learned to read the classics of six languages when she was a child, educated her four siblings, and taught in a girls' school in Providence before she became interested in women's rights and transcendentalism. In 1839 she inaugurated a transcendental "conversation," or discussion group, for elite Boston women.

"every path laid open to Woman as freely as to Man." If societies placed men and women—"the two sides of the great radical dualism" of human nature—on an equal footing, they could end all injustice. Fuller's book never attracted a large middle-class readership, but it made her ideas well known in New York literary circles and, by influencing Emerson, helped spread her message of self-help to middle-class lecture audiences. After 1845 Fuller gained visibility as the New York *Tribune*'s literary critic and as a correspondent in Italy during that country's revolution in 1848. Her friends hoped that she would become a leader in the growing women's movement, but in 1850, returning to the United States at the age of forty, she drowned in a shipwreck (see American Voices, page 362).

Brook Farm

At one time or another virtually all transcendentalists, including Emerson, felt that American society as it existed could not accommodate their aspirations for individual realization and achievement. Many of them acted on that perception by withdrawing into insular communities. Their aim was to reform society by setting an example.

The most important communal experiment of the transcendentalists was Brook Farm, founded in 1841 by a Unitarian minister named George Ripley, in West Roxbury, Massachusetts. Free from the tension and degradation of a competitive society, community mem-

Margaret Fuller

Woman in the Nineteenth Century

Margaret Fuller hoped that her book *Woman in the Nineteenth Century* (1845) would win a larger audience than had the *Dial* article on which it was based. At the suggestion of her editor, Horace Greeley, she dropped the original title, "The Great Lawsuit.— Man *versus* Men; Woman *versus* Women," which she had hoped would convey how "the action of prejudices and passions which attend . . . the growth of the individual, is continually obstructing the holy work that is to make the earth a part of heaven."

. . . We would have every arbitrary barrier thrown down. We would have every path laid open to Woman as freely as to Man. . . .

What Woman needs is not as a woman to act or rule, but as a nature to grow, as an intellect to discern, as a soul to live freely and unimpeded, to unfold such powers as were given her when we left our common home . . . .

Another sign of the times is furnished by the triumphs of Female Authorship. These have been great, and are constantly increasing. Women have taken possession of so many provinces for which men had pronounced them unfit, that, though these still declare there are some inaccessible to them, it is difficult to say just where they must stop. . . .

Male and Female represent the two sides of the great radical dualism. But, in fact, they are perpetually passing into one another. . . . There is no wholly masculine man, no purely feminine woman. . . .

Nature provides exceptions to every rule. She sends women to battle, and sets Hercules spinning; she enables women to bear immense burdens, cold, and frost; she enables the man, who feels maternal love, to nourish his infant like a mother. . . .

The growth of Man is two-fold, masculine and feminine.

So far as these methods can be distinguished, they are so as

Energy and Harmony;

Power and Beauty;

Intellect and Love;

or by some such rude classification; for we have not language primitive and pure enough to express such ideas with precision. . . .

There cannot be a doubt that, if these two developments were in perfect harmony, they would correspond to and fulfill one another, like hemispheres, or the tenor and bass in music. . . .

In families that I know, some little girls like to saw wood, others to use carpenters' tools. Where these tastes are indulged, cheerfulness and good-humor are promoted. Where they are forbidden, because "such things are not proper for girls," they grow sullen and mischievous. . . .

I have no doubt, however, that a large proportion of women would give themselves to the same employments as now, because there are circum-stances that must lead them. Mothers will delight to make the nest soft and warm. Nature would take care of that; no need to clip the wings of any bird that wants to soar and sing, or finds in itself the strength . . . for a migratory flight unusual to its kind. The difference would be that *all* need not be constrained to employments for which *some* are unfit. . . .

I have urged on Woman independence of Man, not that I do not think the sexes mutually needed by one another, but because in Woman this fact has led to an excessive devotion, which has cooled love, degraded marriage, and prevented either sex from being what it should be to itself or the other.

I wish Woman to live, *first* for God's sake. Then she will not make an imperfect man her god, and thus sink to idolatry. Then she will not take what is not fit for her from a sense of weakness and poverty. Then, if she finds what she needs in Man embodied, she will know how to love, and be worthy of being loved.

By being more a soul, she will not be less Woman, for nature is perfected through spirit.

Now there is no woman, only an overgrown child.

Source: Margaret Fuller, "Woman in the Nineteenth Century," in *Woman in the Nineteenth Century and Kindred Papers Relating to the Sphere, Condition, and Duties of Woman* (New York: The Tribune Association, 1869), 13, 37–38, 63, 93, 114–116, 169–170, 174–176.

---

bers hoped to create a harmonious environment for the full development of the mind and soul. In the first few years the community's economy rested primarily on agriculture. The Brook Farmers sold their milk, vegetables, and hay for cash but emphasized the way in which farming allowed them to remain relatively independent from the marketplace and work close to nature. In addition, they acquired revenue by insisting that residents who did not work on the farm make cash payments—in effect, tuition for what was virtually a boarding school.

The intellectual life at Brook Farm was electric. Hawthorne lived there for a time and later used the setting for *The Blithedale Romance* (1852). All the major transcendentalists, including Emerson and Fuller, were residents or frequent visitors. A former member recalled that the transcendentalists "inspired the young with a passion for study, and the middle-aged with deference and admiration, while we all breathed the intellectual grace that pervaded the atmosphere." Music, dancing, games, plays, parties, picnics, and dramatic readings

filled leisure hours. Emerson wrote that Brook Farm meant "education" to most of its residents. It was, he said, "to many the most important period of their life . . . a French Revolution in small."

Brook Farm might have represented moral progress, but it faltered in achieving economic self-sufficiency. Most of its members in the initial years were ministers, teachers, writers, and students. Relatively few families lived at Brook Farm; Ripley's message appealed mostly to young, single people from well-to-do Boston families who were Unitarians and sought alternatives to careers devoted to the acquisition of wealth. Only a few farmers and artisans joined. And for the first three years Ripley and his followers paid little attention to the need to organize their farming and crafts efficiently.

In 1844 the residents began to run Brook Farm in a more disciplined fashion, particularly in arranging housekeeping chores to free women to produce handicrafts. Under their new plan the Brook Farmers attracted some artisans and farmers. Still, the community made only marginal economic gains and did so by imposing regimented routines that depressed many of the original members. One resident wrote that "the joyous spirit of youth was sobered." Finally, after a devastating fire in 1846, the organizers disbanded and sold the farm.

The Decline of Transcendentalism

After the failure of Brook Farm the transcendentalists abandoned their attempts at comprehensive reform. Most became resigned to the structure of American industrial society; its material accomplishments seemed too great to resist. During the 1850s the transcendentalists—as poets, historians, scientists, lawyers, and ministers—became thoroughly integrated into the cultural elite of New England. Their approach to the reform of industrial communities was one of philanthropy, often focused on the education of workers. Some remained radicals on one issue, however—slavery. In the 1840s and 1850s a few aging transcendentalists and a younger generation of their disciples applied their passion for individual freedom to the liberation of slaves.

The Phalanxes

When the Brook Farmers reorganized their community in 1844, they adopted a constitution that embraced the ideas of Charles Fourier, a contemporary French utopian, as interpreted by his idealistic American disciple, Arthur Brisbane. Fourier and Brisbane envisioned

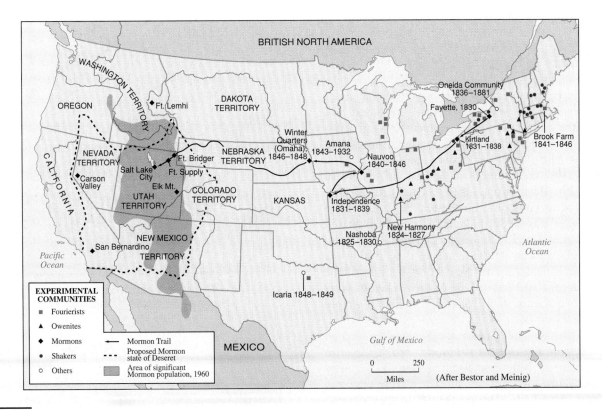

MAP 12.1

Communal Experiments before 1860
Some experimental communities sought out frontier locations, but the vast majority simply looked for secluded areas in well-settled regions. The avoidance of the South by these groups is striking. The most successful experimenters by far were the Mormons, who ultimately sought extreme isolation and built an agrarian empire in Utah.

cooperative work and living units—"phalanxes"—in which those who labored would receive the largest portion of the community's earnings. The members of a phalanx would be its shareholders; they would own all property in common, including stores and a bank as well as a school and a library. Fourier and Brisbane proposed a model for what they hoped would be a practical, more humane alternative to industrial society. "In society as it is now constituted," Brisbane wrote, "monotony, uniformity, intellectual inaction and torpor reign: distrust, isolation, separation, conflict and antagonism are almost universal: very little expansion of the generous affections and feelings obtain. . . . Society is spiritually a desert."

Brisbane skillfully promoted Fourier's ideas through his influential *The Social Destiny of Man* (1840), a regular column in Horace Greeley's New York *Tribune*, and hundreds of lectures, many of them in the towns along the Erie Canal. He inspired educated farmers and craftsmen to start close to 100 cooperative communities from Massachusetts to Michigan, mostly during the 1840s (see Map 12.1). However, almost all, like Brook Farm, were unable to support themselves and quickly died. Some contemporary observers, including the radical minister John Humphrey Noyes, believed that the Fourierists had failed because their communities lacked the strong religious ethic required for sustained altruism and cooperation.

The Shakers

When John Humphrey Noyes criticized the phalanxes, he had in mind, by way of contrast, the oldest and largest of the radical utopian experiments in America—the Shaker communities. Noyes described those communities as "the pioneers of modern Socialism."

The Shaker communities dated back to the era of the American Revolution. In 1770 Ann Lee (Mother Ann), a young cook in Manchester, England, had a vision that she was the second incarnation of Christ and thus the Second Coming. Four years later she led a band of eight followers to America, where they established a new church near Albany, New York. Because of the ecstatic dances that became part of their religious worship, they became known as "Shaking Quakers" or, more simply, "Shakers."

After Mother Ann's death the Shakers decided to withdraw from the evils of the world into strictly run communities of believers. Beginning in 1787, they founded twenty communities, mostly in New England, New York, and Ohio. During the 1820s they entered their most vigorous period of community formation, and during the 1830s they attracted more than 3,000 converts.

Shakers embraced the common ownership of property; accepted the government of the church; pledged to

abstain from alcohol, tobacco, politics, and war; and made a commitment to celibacy. Men and women lived apart in gender-segregated dormitories. Applicants had to declare themselves "sick of sin" and undertake a program of systematic confession that could last for years. To the Shakers, sin was wholly the product of a society that put obstacles in the way of a chaste and self-denying life.

The Shakers' beliefs that God was "a dual person, male and female" and that Mother Ann represented God's female element provided the underpinning for their attempt to give up marriage and banish distinctions between the sexes. In practice, they maintained a traditional division of labor between men and women, but the Shakers vested the authority for governing each community—in both its religious and economic spheres—in women and men alike, the Elders and Eldresses.

New members flowed steadily into the Shaker communities, with women outnumbering men more than two to one. The communities welcomed blacks as well as whites. To Rebecca Cox Jackson, an African-American seamstress from Philadelphia, the Shakers seemed to be

***The Shaker Community at Poland Hill, Maine* (detail)**
This Shaker community in Poland Hill, Maine, painted by Joshua H. Bussell around 1850, had typical Shaker architecture—unadorned buildings and a large central dwelling for communal living.

"loving to live forever." New members were drawn in by the highly structured nature of the community, the opportunity to escape from the stresses of American life, the chance offered to women to assume leadership roles, and the economic success of the communities. Shaker agriculture and crafts, especially furniture making, acquired a reputation for quality that enabled most of the communities to become self-sustaining and even comfortable. However, during the 1840s and 1850s the communities stopped growing, and some began to decline. Because Shakers had no children of their own, they relied on converts to replenish their numbers. During the last part of the nineteenth century most of the communities disappeared, with only a few surviving into the twentieth century.

The celibate Shaker communities could never provide a model for society as a whole; they could serve only as a refuge from industrial society. But their marriageless society highlighted the potent role of marriage and gender roles in defining social relationships in America as a whole.

The Oneida Community

In the 1830s John Humphrey Noyes established a utopian experiment after closely studying Fourierist, Shaker, and other models. He also visited many of them, including Brook Farm. Noyes intended his community to be a model for recasting all of industrial society on the basis of cooperation and Christian ethics.

Noyes and "Perfectionism." Noyes was a well-to-do Dartmouth College graduate who had left the study of law for the ministry after hearing Charles Finney preach in 1831. Noyes's divinity studies led him in radical directions, however, and the Congregationalist Church expelled him from the ministry for his unorthodox teachings. His doctrines, which Noyes promoted through the religious magazines he edited, made him the leader of "perfectionism," an evangelical cult that gathered thousands of followers during the 1830s, primarily among New Englanders who had settled in New York. Perfectionists believed that the Second Coming of Christ had already occurred. Because the Kingdom of Heaven on earth was a reality, people could aspire to perfection—to freedom from sin. To Noyes the major barrier to achieving this ideal state was marriage, which did not exist in heaven. "Exclusiveness, jealousy, quarreling have no place at the marriage supper of the Lamb," Noyes wrote. He sought to reform marriage to liberate individuals from sin, as had the Shakers. But his solution was dramatically different: Noyes and his followers embraced the doctrine of "complex marriage"—all the members of his community were married to one another.

"Complex Marriage." Like the Shakers, Noyes was attempting to gain community control over sexuality. His solution was love, usually expressed in sex without male orgasm, between successive partners, with childbearing strictly regulated by the community. Closely related objectives were to free women from being regarded as the property of their husbands and to free children, who were raised in community nurseries, from being regarded as the property of their parents. Among all the founders of communities organized along socialist lines—with common ownership of property—Noyes presented the most radical alternative to traditional marriage and family life.

In the 1830s Noyes began to collect like-minded followers in his hometown of Putney, Vermont. In 1848 the scandalousness of the doctrine of complex marriage forced Noyes to move his community to Oneida, New York. By the mid-1850s more than 200 people lived in the community, but it remained financially insecure. Its fortunes improved when the inventor of what proved to be a highly successful steel animal trap joined the community. With the profits from the production of traps, Oneida diversified into making other products, notably silverware with the brand name Community Plate. Its quality provided the basis for an economic success that continued long after 1879, when Noyes fled to Canada to avoid prosecution for adultery and the community abandoned complex marriage. In 1881 its members founded a joint-stock company, the Oneida Community, Ltd., which survived into the twentieth century.

In the case of both the Shakers and the Oneida Community, radical efforts to free individuals from sin and from the constraints of industrial society had extended to recasting the meaning of marriage and the family. Thus, in this period, when all kinds of changes seemed possible, some communitarians were willing to tinker with even the most deeply rooted institutions in American society. Neither the Shakers nor the Oneidians aroused fierce hostility to their social experiments. To most outsiders the Shakers seemed pathetic eccentrics, and the followers of Noyes were too few to be worrisome. Business-class evangelism had reinforced the institution of marriage, limiting the scope and appeal of communal experiments and restricting the ability of women to develop a full-fledged feminist ideology.

The Mormon Experience

The most successful of all the insular experiments in attracting followers was that of the Mormons, or the Church of Jesus Christ of Latter-Day Saints. The Mormons emerged from the religious ferment that swirled along the route of the Erie Canal during the 1820s and represented the greatest threat to the values of business-class evangelism.

Joseph Smith. The founder of the Mormon Church was a vigorous, powerful individual, Joseph Smith, who was born in Vermont in 1805. Smith moved at the age of ten with his rather poor farming and shopkeeping family to Palmyra in western New York. His education was rudimentary, but with his mother he heard innumerable sermons and read the Bible constantly. In a series of religious experiences that began in 1820, Smith came to believe that God had singled him out for a special, immediate, and private revelation of divine truth. Smith felt that God had called him to be a prophet with a message for redeeming a sinful society fatally flawed by excessive individualism. Ultimately he chose to stand apart from that society. In 1830 Smith published his revelations as *The Book of Mormon*, which he claimed he had translated from ancient hieroglyphics on gold plates shown to him by an angel named Moroni. The *Book of Mormon* told the story of ancient civilizations from the Middle East that had migrated to the Western Hemisphere and of the visit of Jesus Christ, soon after the Resurrection, to one of them. On a metaphorical level, the book describes the success of societies that follow the Ten Commandments and revelations.

Also in 1830, Smith organized a church in western New York. Smith's theology and leadership of the church addressed the growing tension between the claims of the individual—claims that his career as prophet typified—and the need for social order. He offered as a solution a church that would assert control over all aspects of life. Smith encouraged his followers to adopt the patterns of behavior that were central to the Industrial Revolution: hard work, saving, and risk taking. However, he also emphasized the need for a communal framework that would concentrate power in the church elders, protect the Mormon "New Jerusalem" from outside threats, and create a structure for achieving human perfection.

Nauvoo. Smith struggled to establish a sanctuary for his new community. In the face of persecution at the hands of neighboring communities, Smith and his small congregation trekked from western New York to Kirtland, Ohio, then to Independence, Missouri, and, in 1839, to Nauvoo, Illinois, a town they founded on the Mississippi River. By the early 1840s Smith, his message, and his social organization had become phenomenally successful. Nauvoo was the largest of all the utopian communities, having attracted as many as 30,000 converts, but Illinois ultimately proved to be a hostile environment. The demands of the Mormons' social order, their hostility to other sects, the secrecy with which they conducted their affairs, their block voting in Illinois elections, their great success in attracting converts, and their prosperity all fueled the resentment of their neighbors. And Smith helped turn this resentment into overt hostility when he refused to abide by any Illinois law that he did not approve personally, asked Con-

gress to turn Nauvoo into a federal territory free of state control, and declared himself a candidate for president of the United States in 1844. In addition, Smith had a new revelation that encouraged *polygamy*—taking more than one wife at the same time. This was typical of Smith's innovations: radical reforms designed to preserve a traditional institution, in this case marriage and the family. The revelation did not become public until 1852, but rumors of it, as well as disputes over economic issues, divided the Mormon community from within and encouraged assaults from without. In 1844 Smith was arrested and charged with treason for conspiring with foreign powers to create a Mormon colony in Mexico. In June an anti-Mormon mob led by members of the Illinois militia stormed the Carthage jail where Smith and his brother were being held and murdered them.

Brigham Young and Utah. Now led by Brigham Young, an early convert to the church, the Mormon elders resolved that they could ensure their religious independence only by leaving the United States and seeking a home in the wilderness. In 1846, leaving the antipolygamy minority behind, Young began a phased migration of more than 10,000 people across the Great Plains. (Under the leadership of Smith's son, Joseph Smith III, the group that remained behind formed the Reorganized Church of Jesus Christ of Latter-Day Saints, headquartered in Independence, Missouri.) Young's party reached the Great Salt Lake in what was still Mexican territory. Within a decade he and his theocracy had transformed the alkaline desert landscape by building elaborate irrigation systems. The Mormons used communal labor and developed innovative principles of communal water rights that the federal government and all the states of the semiarid West later adopted. The Mormons quickly spread planned agricultural communities along the base of the Wasatch Range in present-day Utah.

The Mormons versus the Federal Government. During the 1850s the Mormons faced challenges to their isolation, but none of those challenges disrupted their society. Many westward migrants made detours from the Oregon and California trails to purchase supplies from Mormon farmers, but that only contributed to Mormon prosperity. Potentially more serious was the effort of the federal government to assert authority over Utah, which the United States had acquired from Mexico in 1848. Congress rejected a Mormon petition to create a new state, Deseret, stretching all the way to Los Angeles and San Diego. Instead, it set up the much smaller Utah Territory in 1850, with Young as territorial governor. In 1857–1858 Democratic President James Buchanan intervened, submitting to pressure from concerned federal officials in Utah and from his Republican challengers. He removed Young from the governorship and sent a

A Mormon Man and His Wives
Mormon families, such as this one pictured in the late 1840s, achieved a degree of prosperity that was unusual for pioneer farm families, partly because of the labor of multiple wives. This homesteader's cabin, although cramped for such a large family, is well built, with a brick chimney and—a luxury for any pioneer home—a glass window.

small army to Salt Lake City. The "Mormon War," however, proved bloodless. Buchanan decided to negotiate, fearing that an attack on the "domestic institution" of polygamy might be used as a precedent to justify attacks on another "domestic institution," slavery. Ultimately he withdrew the troops and accepted his failure to establish federal control in Utah.

Republicans were more eager than were Buchanan and the Democrats to wipe out polygamy. In their 1856 platform they referred to polygamy and slavery as "relics of barbarism." But preoccupation with the Civil War prevented the administration of Abraham Lincoln from paying much attention to Utah. Consequently, the Mormons found themselves free to build their community. The Mormons did not formally abolish polygamy until 1890, six years before Utah became a state. They had succeeded where other social experiments and utopian communities had failed. They had devised the ideological, organizational, and physical means to make their community prosper and expand into the twentieth century.

The Women's Movement

Women played an instrumental role in the radical reform movements of the Industrial Revolution. They had participated in religious revivals and had joined conservative temperance, moral reform, and educational reform movements. During the 1830s some women went beyond these to movements, such as transcendentalism, that sought to remove limitations on individual freedom. Slavery was among the targets of women reformers, and it was abolitionism that radicalized many of them. Abolitionism encouraged women to develop an ideology that argued that women had social and political rights as free individuals—rights that equaled those of men.

Origins of the Women's Movement

The Industrial Revolution shaped in complex ways the opportunities that were available to women in the home and in public life. On the surface the Industrial Revolution seemed to limit economic opportunities for women and reinforce their confinement to a "separate sphere." The Industrial Revolution sharpened the lines of demarcation between the home and the workplace while accentuating the division of labor within the home. Middle-class women were less involved in the production of goods (for example, in household workshops) and more concerned with providing personal services in the home. Partly because of the influence of revivals, mothers increasingly became the keepers of religion and morality. They were preoccupied with setting a superior moral example and providing solace and support for family members who worked outside the home.

On a psychological level, however, these changes in the role of women in the family created a basis for greater female independence and power. Middle-class women drew on the enhanced esteem attached to their family roles, reinforced each other through intensified community and kinship ties, and found sanctification for their roles in religion. With all this mutual reinforcement, middle-class women built a common identity in "womanhood." They used it to enlarge their influence over decisions in all areas of family life, including the timing of pregnancies and their husbands' choice of work. For most middle-class women greater influence over family life was enough. But some women seized on the logic implicit in the emphasis on the moral role of women to increase their involvement outside the home.

Young middle-class women in New York and New England entered the public arena through the religious revivals of the 1820s and 1830s. The evangelical revivals emphasized the power of individual free will—even for dependents such as wives and daughters—and provided a central role for women in the conversion process. The revivals also involved women more deeply in community life, enhanced their sense of self-esteem, and led them into other reform movements.

Moral reform was the first of their efforts in the public arena. Women reformers attempted to end prostitution, punish those whose sexual behavior violated the Ten Commandments, redeem fallen women, and protect single women from moral corruption. The movement began in 1834 when a group of middle-class women founded the New York Female Moral Reform Society and elected Lydia Finney, the wife of the evangelical minister Charles Finney, as its president. By 1837 the New York society had 15,000 members and 250 chapters.

The American Female Moral Reform Society. In 1840 the New York society organized a national association, the American Female Moral Reform Society, with 555 chapters throughout the North. Employing only women as its agents, bookkeepers, and staff, this society concentrated on the problems of young women who worked and lived away from their families. They focused on the need to provide moral "government" for factory girls, seamstresses, clerks, and servants who lived beyond the direct control of their families and churches. Women reformers even visited brothels, where they sang hymns, offered prayers, searched for runaway daughters, and noted the names of clients. They founded homes of refuge for prostitutes, homeless girls, and migrant women. They petitioned for state laws regulating sexual behavior—including making seduction a crime—and succeeded in arranging the passage of such laws in Massachusetts in 1846 and New York in 1848.

Women with backgrounds in evangelical reform also turned their energies to the reform of social institutions. Almshouses, asylums, hospitals, and jails became targets for improvement in a movement that involved both men and women. Women visited these places, which were growing in number during the 1830s and 1840s, with the aim of easing the condition of the residents. Dorothea Dix in particular succeeded in both reforming and expanding institutions for society's most dependent individuals: the insane and the mentally retarded (see American Lives, pages 370–371).

The energy and public accomplishments of moral reformers such as Dix inspired other women to undertake more radical reforms, including the abolition of slavery and the establishment of women's rights under the law. Dix, however, did not become active in the antislavery movement despite her personal support of it.

(She had denounced slavery and slaveholders as early as 1831.) Instead, she tried to draw other reformers to *her* cause and often succeeded. She won abolitionist support by stressing the parallels between the treatment of slaves and the treatment of the insane.

Abolitionism and Women

Under the influence of ideas and political strategy drawn from the movement to abolish slavery, a few women began to question whether they should continue to accept a restricted role in society. They faced severe opposition, but in contrast to Frances Wright, who had denounced business-class evangelism, they advanced their ideas within a religious context and thus avoided the extreme forms of public outrage Wright had encountered in championing women's rights a decade earlier (see American Lives, Chapter 11, pages 344–345).

The Grimké Sisters. The abolitionist sisters Angelina and Sarah Grimké shaped the ideas of radical women. They had left their father's South Carolina plantation, converted to Quakerism and abolitionism in Philadelphia, and become antislavery lecturers. In 1837, after some Congregationalist clergymen demanded that she cease speaking to mixed male and female audiences, Sarah Grimké responded: "The Lord Jesus defines the duties of his followers in his Sermon on the Mount. . . without any reference to sex or condition. . . . Men and women are CREATED EQUAL! They are both moral and accountable beings and whatever is right for man to do is right for woman." The next year Angelina Grimké declared that gender should not affect the manner in which people shape society:

> It is a woman's right to have a voice in all the laws and regulations by which she is governed, whether in Church or State. . . . The present arrangements of society, on these points are a *violation of human rights, a rank usurpation of power*, a violent seizure and confiscation of what is sacredly and inalienably hers.

By 1840 the Grimkés were asserting that traditional roles amounted to the "domestic slavery" of women.

Not all abolitionist women shared those views. But they all gained experience and confidence outside the home and learned much about the organizational requirements for successful reform. And as their participation in the movement grew, many women demanded equality with men within the abolitionist movement. To these women equality meant representation in antislavery societies equal to their numbers. At the same time, however, their activities, especially the vigorous antislavery lectures by the Grimkés, aroused opposition from abolitionist clergymen who believed that the women's behavior was immoral. They also drew criticism from male abolitionists who feared that such visi-

The Grimké Sisters

Sarah Moore Grimké (1792–1873) and Angelina Emily Grimké (1805–1879) joined the Philadelphia Female Anti-Slavery Society and began abolitionist lecturing in 1836. They drew crowds of thousands—and scathing criticism for having lost, as some Massachusetts clergymen put it, "that modesty and delicacy . . . which constitutes the true influence of women in society." The Grimké sisters responded with powerful statements protesting male domination of women.

ble departures from tradition would damage the political fortunes of the antislavery movement.

However, a leading abolitionist, William Lloyd Garrison, argued that "our object is *universal* emancipation, to redeem women as well as men from a servile to an equal condition." At the convention of the American Anti-Slavery Society in 1840 he insisted on the right of women to participate equally in the organization. The votes of several hundred New England women elected Abby Kelley to the organization's business committee. This event precipitated the split between the supporters of Garrison and those who left the organization to found the American and Foreign Anti-Slavery Society.

A group of women abolitionists led by Abby Kelley, Lucretia Mott, and Elizabeth Cady Stanton remained with Garrison. They recruited new women agents, including Lucy Stone, to address hostile audiences on the common interests of slaves and free women. Stanton admired Frances Wright and kept her works on her library table, but she had learned from Wright's defeats. During the 1840s women abolitionists focused on a pragmatic course of action for expanding the influence of women.

The Program of Seneca Falls

By the 1840s celebration of self—of individual identity and liberation—had become important to women in public life. Nonetheless, during the 1840s and 1850s most critics of "domestic slavery" stopped short of challenging the institution of marriage or even the con-

ventional division of labor within the family. They focused instead on using the American political system to strengthen the position of women under the law, within the existing social order. They wanted women to enter the mainstream of American life rather than separate themselves from it.

The Convention. In 1848 leaders of the nascent women's movement took a critical step by calling a convention in Seneca Falls in upstate New York. Organized by Elizabeth Cady Stanton and Lucretia Mott, who had met at the World's Anti-Slavery Convention in 1840, and joined by a few sympathetic male abolitionists, the convention outlined for the first time a coherent program for women's equality. The delegates at Seneca Falls based their program on republican ideology, adopting resolutions patterned directly on the Declaration of Independence. Among their declared principles was "that all men and women are created equal; that they are endowed by the Creator with certain inalienable rights: that among these are life, liberty and the pursuit of happiness." They asserted, however, that "the history of mankind is a history of repeated injuries and usurpations on the part of man toward woman, having in direct object the establishment of an absolute tyranny over her." To educate the public about this reality, they resolved to "use every instrumentality within our power. . . . We shall employ agents, circulate tracts, petition the State and national legislatures, and endeavor to enlist the pulpit and the press on our behalf."

Elizabeth Cady Stanton

Elizabeth Cady Stanton (1815–1902), daughter of a judge in Johnstown, New York, attended Emma Hart Willard's demanding Troy Female Seminary. In 1840 she married Henry B. Stanton, an abolitionist leader, and traveled to the World Anti-Slavery Convention in London, where she met Lucretia Mott and started down the intellectual path that led to Seneca Falls. (This photograph, with her grandson, was taken after the Civil War.)

Dorothea Dix: Innovative Moral Reformer

Dorothea Dix (1802–1887) once wrote, "I never knew childhood." She was born in Hampden, Maine. Her grandparents, Elijah and Dorothy Dix, were prominent Bostonians, but her father, Joseph Dix, had dropped out of Harvard and married an older woman of whom his family disapproved. He had moved to Maine to manage some of his father's land developments but failed and became an itinerant (and alcoholic) Methodist minister. For Dorothea and her two brothers, family life was one of poverty, frequent moves, and emotional abuse. At age twelve she left to live with her well-to-do grandmother. But her grandmother was rigid and remote, and Dorothea proved to be precocious and willful. After two years she moved in with a great-aunt, where she remained for three years. In 1819 she returned to her grandmother's Boston mansion.

Partly because of her emotionally scarred childhood, Dorothea developed an interest in the education of children and at the age of fourteen opened her first school. In 1821, after intense private instruction and reading in the libraries of Boston, she created a school in the Dix mansion. Like other "dame" or "marm" schools, it offered private instruction to young children, either in preparation for public grammar schools, where discipline was harsh, or as a substitute for those schools. In addition, Dorothea persuaded her grandmother to allow her to open a "charity school" to "rescue some of America's miserable children from vice and guilt." She ran such schools for the next seventeen years, except during periods when illness compelled her to rest.

Dix often wrote when illness left her too weak to teach. In 1824 she published a short book of knowledge, *Conversations on Common Things*, with an emphasis on natural science and moral improvement. It went through sixty editions, the last one appearing in 1869. Between 1825 and 1832 Dix published six more books, establishing herself as a public personality. Substantial royalties, along with an inheritance from her grandmother, gave her financial independence.

Dix also used periods of recuperation to widen her social horizons. During a convalescence William Ellery Channing, the prominent Boston Unitarian minister, invited her to teach his children. She drew on her close friendship with him and incorporated Unitarian ideas

Dorothea Dix

Dorothea Dix (1802–1887) pointed to the need for institutions that would strengthen individuals in the face of the pressures of industrialization. She rhetorically asked the Pennsylvania legislature: "Is it not to the habits, the customs, the temptations of civilized life and society" that America owes the calamity of insanity? Consequently, "Should not society make the compensation which alone can be made for these disastrous fruits of its social organization?" Her call for government intervention into social relations put her on the frontier of reform.

into her work. When her health and spirits broke in 1836, she spent eighteen months on the English estate of William Rathbone, a wealthy Unitarian merchant and philanthropist. There she met British reformers who were interested in pragmatic programs to correct the maladies of industrial society, and they inspired her to look for similar possibilities in America.

Dix was ready for a career in reform when, in March 1841, she taught a Sunday School class for women incarcerated in a Cambridge, Massachusetts, jail. She was outraged to find that insane women had been put into jail along with criminals. She appeared in court to represent the women and mobilized Boston philanthropists to support her cause.

New Jersey State Lunatic Asylum
Built in 1845, this was the first state institution built in response to a memorial by Dorothea Dix, and it was New Jersey's first state mental hospital. As was often the case, Dix deeply involved herself in selecting the site (in Trenton) and designing the buildings for this institution, which she described as her "firstborn child."

Dix felt so strongly about what she had seen in the Cambridge jail that she launched a two-year systematic investigation of the institutionalized treatment of individuals who were insane or mentally retarded. She approved of new asylum-reform programs that lavished love on mental patients. But she complained that those programs served only the families of New England's elite whereas indigent patients typically faced neglect and cruelty.

In 1843 Dix presented her findings in an extensive *Memorial to the Legislature of Massachusetts* on "the condition of the miserable, the desolate, the outcast." She mobilized powerful reformers to aid her cause. The legislature responded by enlarging the state hospital in Worcester so that it could accommodate the indigent.

Dix's success was exhilarating. She proceeded to crusade nationally to establish separate, well-funded state hospitals for the insane. Between 1843 and 1854 she traveled more than 30,000 miles and visited 18 state penitentiaries, 300 county jails and houses of correction, and more than 500 almshouses in addition to innumerable hospitals and houses of refuge. She prepared dozens of reports and memorials to state legislatures and became an exceptional student of the legislative process. Her success in arousing public opinion led many states to create or significantly expand their state hospitals.

Because Dix despaired of state governments ever being able to provide the tax revenues required to support mental hospitals, she began to propose a national responsibility. "The insane poor," she wrote, "through the Providence of God, are wards of the nation." In 1848 she asked Congress to place 5 million acres into a national trust that would fund asylums for the insane. She noted that canal and railroad developers lobbied for public lands and asked, "Why can I not too, go in with this selfish, struggling throng, and plead for God's poor . . . that they shall not be forgotten?"

Dix lobbied relentlessly from a committee room headquarters that her Congressional supporters provided. The House passed her proposal in 1850; the Senate, in 1851. In addition, she charmed Vice-President Millard Fillmore, who formed a close friendship with her. When he became president in 1850, he was ready to sign her bill. Finally, in 1854, Dix persuaded both houses of Congress to pass legislation that would have set aside 12.5 million acres for asylums. But the Democratic president, Franklin Pierce, vetoed it, claiming it was an unconstitutional encroachment on state government. In the face of the growing national crisis over slavery, Pierce and other supporters of the South feared any measure that might create precedents for the federal government to shape social relations.

Dix was depressed but soon resumed her frenetic pace. She returned to her work at the state level, founded an international movement to improve the treatment of the insane, and, when the Civil War began, accepted an appointment by Abraham Lincoln as superintendent of nurses. This job put her in charge of hospital nursing for the Union forces and made her the highest-ranking woman in the federal government. In 1866 Dix, tired and ill, returned to private life. She kept at good works but lacked the energy for new projects. In 1881 she retired to die in the New Jersey state hospital in Trenton that she had helped establish in 1845.

Dix's career illustrates the ability of women reformers to influence American society. Her moral enthusiasm was characteristic of reformers during the mid-nineteenth century, but her tactics were advanced for her time. She studied legislative behavior and, more than any other reformer before the Civil War, relied on the systematic investigation of social problems—an approach that late in the nineteenth century became a hallmark of reform and the expansion of government. It took nearly a century for the federal government to adopt the kind of social policy advocated by Dix—a redistribution of wealth that favored individuals who were unable to participate in an industrial economy.

By powerfully staking out claims for equality for women in public life, the Seneca Falls convention represented a major challenge to the idea that the assignment of separate spheres to men and women was part of the natural order of society.

The Reform Program. The ideals of Seneca Falls inspired women reformers to forge a practical program of action. Throughout the 1850s national women's rights conventions were held annually, as were numerous local and regional meetings. At those conventions women promoted a diverse reform program: establishing the right of married women to control their own property and earnings, guaranteeing mothers custody of children in the event of divorce or the father's death, ensuring women's right to sue or testify in court, revising concepts of female inferiority in established religious theology, and—above all else—winning the vote for women. The 1851 national convention of women resolved that the right of suffrage was "the corner-stone of this enterprise, since we do not seek to protect woman, but rather to place her in a position to protect herself."

Women's Property Rights. The only legislative victories of the women's movement before the Civil War came in the area of property rights. Fourteen states followed New York's pioneering law of 1848 and adopted laws protecting the property of married women after the death or incapacitation of their husbands. Joining the reformers in this effort were upper-class conservative males. Their principal motive was to protect propertied men in the event of bankruptcy (by preserving their spouses' assets intact) and to protect patriarchs with large estates who feared that dissolute or incompetent sons-in-law might lose or ruin their family holdings.

Susan B. Anthony. Despite its dearth of victories before the Civil War, the suffrage effort did advance the organization of the women's movement. Meetings and publicity widened the participation of women in women's causes, and their leaders grew in number and in their mastery of organization, as exemplified by Susan B. Anthony. Whereas many women leaders of the 1830s and 1840s had been gifted lecturers, Anthony's chief talents were organizational. Anthony was a member of a Massachusetts Quaker family that had moved to a farm near Rochester, New York. She had participated in moral reform and in a female antislavery society. She had lectured on antislavery and religion, resigned a teaching position in bitter protest over discrimination against women, and joined the temperance movement as a paid fund-raiser. In 1851, when she was thirty-one, Anthony joined the movement for women's rights and forged an enduring friendship with Elizabeth Cady Stanton. Her experience in the temperance movement had taught her "the great evil of woman's utter dependence on man for the necessary means to aid reform movements."

In promoting reforms during the 1850s Anthony created a network of political "captains," all of them women. Because each New York county had a captain, her group could collect thousands of signatures on petitions in just a few days. Anthony lobbied the state legislature relentlessly. In 1860 her efforts culminated in New York granting women the legal right to collect their own wages (which fathers or husbands previously could insist on collecting and keeping), bring suit in court, and, if widowed, acquire full control of the property they had brought to the marriage.

The organizational and legislative successes of the women's rights movement during the 1850s provided the basis for the more aggressive reform attempts that followed the Civil War (see American Voices, page 373). The political strategy of the radical women had widened their support and won the help of moderate women abolitionists. During the 1850s, however, most Americans, even most abolitionists, did not regard the issues that the women's rights movement had raised to be of great concern. Most stressed a higher immediate priority: the abolition of slavery.

Harriet Beecher Stowe and Sojourner Truth. Women who had never joined an antislavery society could join women's rights leaders in expressing evangelical outrage over slavery. The novelist Harriet Beecher Stowe, for example, did not participate in the organized movement

Susan B. Anthony
As a child, Susan B. Anthony (1820–1906) worked on the Rochester, New York, farm of her father, who had failed in textile manufacturing. She served as "headmistress" of the Female Department at Canajoharie Academy before joining the temperance movement. As she passed "from town to town," she wrote, "I was made to feel the great evil of woman's utter dependence on man for the necessary means to aid reform movements."

Lucy Stone

The Question of Women's Rights

Lucy Stone (1818–1893) graduated from Oberlin College in 1847 and came to the issue of women's rights through abolitionist lecturing. This is an excerpt from a speech she delivered extemporaneously at a national women's rights convention in Cincinnati in 1855.

The last speaker alluded to this movement as being that of a few disappointed women. From the first years to which my memory stretches, I have been a disappointed woman. When, with my brothers, I reached forth after sources of knowledge, I was reproved with "It isn't fit for you; it doesn't belong to women." Then there was but one college in the world where women were admitted, and that was in Brazil. I would have found my way there, but by the time I was prepared to go, one was opened in the young state of Ohio—the first in the United States where women and negroes could enjoy opportunities with white men. I was disappointed when I came to seek a profession worthy of an immortal being—every employment was closed

to me, except that of the teacher, the seamstress, and the housekeeper. In education, in marriage, in religion, in everything, disappointment is the lot of woman. It shall be the business of my life to deepen this disappointment in every woman's heart until she bows down to it no longer. I wish that women, instead of begging of their fathers and brothers the latest and gayest new bonnet, would ask of them their rights.

The question of Women's Rights is a practical one. . . . The flour merchant, the house-builder, and the postman charge us no less on account of our sex; but when we endeavor to earn money to pay all these, then, indeed we find the difference. Man, if he have energy, may hew out for himself a path where no mortal has ever trod, held back by nothing but what is in himself; the world is all before him, where to choose; and we are glad for you, brothers, men, that it is so. But the same society that drives forth the young man, keeps woman at home—a dependent—working little cats on

worsted, and little dogs on punctured paper; but if she goes heartily and bravely to give herself some worthy purpose, she is out of her sphere and she loses caste. . . . I know not what you believe of God, but I believe He gave yearnings and longings to be filled, and that He did not mean all our time should be devoted to feeding and clothing the body. The present condition of woman causes a horrible perversion of the marriage relation. It is asked of a lady, "Has she married well?" "Oh yes, her husband is rich." Woman must marry for a home, and you men are the sufferers by this; for a woman who loathes you may marry you because you have the means to get money which she cannot have. But when woman can enter the lists with you and make money for herself, she will marry you only for deep and earnest affection.

Source: Elizabeth Cady Stanton, Susan B. Anthony, and Matilda Joslyn Gage, *History of Woman Suffrage* (New York, 1881), 1, 165–166.

against slavery but grew angry over slavery and moved other women to share her feelings. Her novel *Uncle Tom's Cabin* delivered an abolitionist message to more homes than any antislavery campaigner ever had. Beecher charged that among the greatest moral failings of slavery was its destruction of the slave family and the degradation of slave women. This charge was substantiated by a former slave, Sojourner Truth, who was one of the many African-American women who lectured to both antislavery and women's rights conventions. Truth hammered home the point that women slaves were denied not only their basic human rights but also the protected separate "sphere" enjoyed by free women. "I have ploughed and planted and gathered into barns, and no man could head me—and ain't I a woman?" she asked in 1851. "I have borne thirteen children, and seen most of 'em sold into slavery, and when I cried out with my mother's grief, none but Jesus heard me—and ain't I a woman?"

The Antislavery Movement, to 1844

Sojourner Truth and other ex-slaves inspired what became the dominant movement to reform American society—the drive to abolish slavery. Beginning in the 1830s, white evangelists joined African-Americans in radical attacks on slavery.

By 1820 opponents of slavery, influenced by republican ideology and British antislavery advocates such as William Wilberforce, had accomplished a good deal. Congress had outlawed the importation of slaves in 1808, the earliest date permitted by the Constitution. Most northern states had already abolished slavery, and the Missouri Compromise had prohibited slavery in most of the Louisiana Purchase. But the most vocal opponents of slavery wanted to go much further. Three dif-

ferent approaches to ending slavery competed between 1820 and 1840: (1) gradual emancipation of the nation's slaves—1.5 million in 1820—and return of the freed slaves to Africa, with compensation paid to their former owners, (2) emancipation through slave flight or rebellion, and (3) emancipation through direct appeals to the conscience of slave owners. Then, during the 1840s and 1850s, most opponents of slavery united as they turned to political tactics and developed a fourth approach to abolition: excluding slavery from the territories.

African Colonization

The American Colonization Society. Proponents of the plan for compensated emancipation and African colonization had founded the American Colonization Society in 1817. For the most part it was led by prominent people from the Upper South who wanted to eradicate slavery in order to foster economic and social development along northern lines. Society members from New England and New York, however, were interested primarily in removing free African-Americans from the North.

Northern colonizationists regarded the North's 250,000 free blacks as "notoriously ignorant, degraded and miserable, mentally diseased, brokenspirited, acted upon by no motive to honourable exertions, scarcely reached in their debasement by the heavenly light," in the words of the American Colonization Society's 1829 report. Colonizationists often played a key role in maintaining disfranchisement and segregation. By 1860 only five northern states (Maine, Massachusetts, New Hampshire, Rhode Island, and Vermont, which together accounted for only 6 percent of the northern black population) had extended suffrage to all adult male African-Americans. New York imposed special property and residence requirements on black voters. Connecticut, New Jersey, and Pennsylvania denied African-Americans the right to vote, as did Ohio, Indiana, Illinois, and every southern state.

Southern supporters of colonization also believed that African-Americans lacked the capacity to succeed in American society. Colonization, they thought, was necessary to prevent a destructive race war, especially because slaves made up almost 40 percent of the southern population in 1820. The Kentuckian Henry Clay, for example, wanted full emancipation but declared that emancipation without colonization "would be followed by instantaneous collisions between the two races, which would break out into a civil war that would end in the extermination or subjugation of the one race or the other." By 1830 the American Colonization Society, with money raised from individuals, state governments, and churches, had succeeded in transport-

ing 1,400 African-Americans to a colony the society called Liberia, on the west coast of Africa. However, only 200 of the colonists had won freedom as a consequence of the society's efforts. In the last analysis the society was far more interested in shoring up slavery by removing free African-Americans from the South than in a program of emancipation.

Liberia. The colonists declared Liberia an independent republic in 1847 and adopted a constitution modeled after that of the United States. The country did not receive American recognition until 1862, after the Confederate states had left the Union. The African-American colonists and their descendants, who remained Protestant and continued to speak English, formed a small ruling class—little more than 10 percent of the population by the mid-twentieth century—that dominated the indigenous tribes. Liberia's economic life remained closely tied to that of the United States, and in the twentieth century American rubber companies, working with the local elite, largely controlled the economy.

A Radical Solution

Most free blacks rejected colonization. In 1817, three thousand met in Philadelphia's Bethel Church and denounced it. They informed "the humane and benevolent inhabitants of the city" that "we have no wish to separate from our present homes for any purpose whatever." They explained that they were "contented with our present situation and condition" and wanted only "the use of those opportunities . . . which the Constitution and the laws allow to all." African-Americans throughout the North seconded these sentiments at conventions and in pamphlets and newspapers. They also called for an end to slavery—through rebellion if necessary.

Walker's *Appeal*. In 1827 John Russwurm and Samuel D. Cornish began the first African-American newspaper, *Freedom's Journal*, in New York. The Boston agent for the newspaper was David Walker, a free African-American from North Carolina who made a living selling secondhand clothes. In 1829 Walker published a stirring pamphlet entitled *Appeal . . . to the Colored Citizens*. It ridiculed the religious pretensions of slaveholders, justified slave rebellion, and warned America that the slaves would revolt if justice was delayed. To white Americans Walker said, "We must and shall be free . . . in spite of you. . . . And woe, woe, will be it to you if we have to obtain our freedom by fighting." He added: "I do declare that one good black man can put to death six white men." Within a year Walker's *Appeal* had gone through three printings and had begun to reach free blacks in the South.

In 1830 Walker and other African-American abolitionists called a national convention in Philadelphia. Walker died under mysterious circumstances later that year, but the convention became an annual event. The delegates never adopted a position as radical as Walker's, but they regularly condemned slavery, colonization, and northern discriminatory legislation. They also urged free blacks to use every legal means to improve the condition of their race and asked for divine assistance in breaking "the shackles of slavery."

Nat Turner's Rebellion. In 1831 the major violence that David Walker had contemplated took concrete form when Nat Turner, a slave in Southampton County, Virginia, staged a bloody revolt. Turner had taught himself to read as a child and had hoped to be emancipated, but a new master forced him into field work and another master separated him from his wife. Turner became deeply spiritual, seeing visions and concluding that he might carry Christ's burden of suffering in a race war. Taking an eclipse of the sun as an omen, Turner plotted with a handful of relatives and close friends to meet the masters' terror with terror of their own. They killed almost sixty slave owners and members of their families, in many cases dismembering and decapitating them. Turner had hoped that an army of slaves would join his liberation force, but he had mustered only sixty men by the time a white militia formed to protect two large plantations and dispersed his poorly armed and exhausted followers. In retaliation, whites killed slaves at random all over the county. One company of cavalry killed forty in two days, putting the heads of fifteen on poles to warn "all those who should undertake a similar plot." Fifty slaves were tried formally, and twenty of them were hanged. After hiding for nearly two months, Turner was captured and hanged, still identifying his mission with that of Christ's.

Evangelical Abolitionism, to 1840

The threat of a bloody racial revolution, coupled with the inspiring example of free African-Americans who sought to eradicate slavery, had a profound effect on some young white opponents of slavery. Many were evangelical ministers and their supporters. They became evangelists against slavery, appealing to the Christian conscience of individual slave owners for immediate emancipation. Gradual change or compromise had no place in their new campaign. The issue was absolute: slave owners and their supporters were sinning by depriving slaves of their God-given status as free moral agents. If the slave owners did not repent, the evangelical abolitionists believed, they inevitably faced the prospect of revolution in this world and damnation in the next.

William Lloyd Garrison. The two most influential leaders of the antislavery movement during the 1830s were William Lloyd Garrison and Theodore Dwight Weld. Garrison was an early antislavery advocate and was less influenced by the evangelical revivals than were Weld and other white abolitionists. A Massachusetts-born printer, Garrison had collaborated in Baltimore during the 1820s with a Quaker, Benjamin Lundy, who published the *Genius of Universal Emancipation*, the leading antislavery newspaper of the decade. In 1830 Garrison went to jail, convicted of libeling a New England merchant engaged in the domestic slave trade. After seven weeks he was released because, through Lundy's intervention, Arthur Tappan, a wealthy New York merchant, paid the fine. Garrison went on to found his own antislavery weekly, *The Liberator*, in Boston in 1831. In the following year he spearheaded the formation of the New England Anti-Slavery Society.

From the outset *The Liberator* deplored gradual or compensated emancipation and demanded the immediate abolition of slavery without any reimbursement for slaveholders. Garrison condemned the American Colonization Society, charging that its real aim was to

William Lloyd Garrison
This daguerreotype captures the moral intensity Garrison displayed in 1854 when he publicly burned the Constitution and declared: "So perish all compromises with tyranny." His self-righteous defiance of proslavery laws was part of a passionate quest to destroy all institutions that prevented individuals from discovering their full potential.

strengthen slavery by removing troublesome African-Americans who were already free. He even attacked the Constitution for its recognition of slavery. It was, he pronounced, "a covenant with death, an agreement with Hell." Nothing was safe from Garrison's criticism. He denounced ministers and even the authenticity of Scripture whenever he felt slavery had been sanctioned. Increasingly, he concluded that slavery was a sign of deep corruption infesting *all* institutions and called for comprehensive reform of American society as a whole.

Garrison's radical position attracted many avid followers, and to them he became a cultural hero on the scale of Emerson or Finney. Like those men, he made thundering assertions of his own identity. In the first number of *The Liberator*, he declared: "I will be harsh as truth and as uncompromising as justice. . . . I am in earnest—I will not equivocate—I will not excuse—I will not retreat a single inch—AND I WILL BE HEARD."

Theodore Dwight Weld. In contrast to Garrison, Theodore Dwight Weld came to abolitionism from the religious revivals of the 1830s. Weld was a more restrained abolitionist. The son of a Congregationalist minister, he made a commitment to reform after hearing Charles Finney preach in Utica, New York. Weld worked within the churches of New York and the Old Northwest and shifted his focus from temperance and educational reform to abolitionism. In these churches, primarily Presbyterian and Congregational, he preached the moral responsibility of all Americans for the denial of liberty to slaves. In 1834 Weld inspired a group of students at Lane Theological Seminary in Cincinnati to form an antislavery society. When Lane's president, Lyman Beecher, tried to repress the society, the "Lane rebels" left, enrolling at Oberlin College and joining Weld in his evangelism. Weld's crusade gathered force, buttressed by the theological arguments he advanced in *The Bible against Slavery* (1837). Collaborating closely with him were two South Carolina abolitionists—Angelina Grimké, whom he married in 1838, and her sister, Sarah.

With the assistance of the Grimké sisters, Weld provided the antislavery movement with a new base of evidence in a massive book, *American Slavery as It Is: Testimony of a Thousand Witnesses* (1839). Weld addressed the reader "as a juror to try a plain case and bring in an honest verdict." The question he posed was: "What is the actual condition of the slaves in the United States?" In answering, Weld presented evidence from southerners themselves, some of it taken from the more than 20,000 editions of southern newspapers he had researched. Among the firsthand accounts he cited were those of Angelina Grimké, who recalled her childhood in Charleston. She told, for example, of a treadmill that

Charleston slave owners used for punishment and of a prominent white woman who sent slaves there regularly: "One poor girl, whom she sent there to be flogged, and who was accordingly stripped naked and whipped, showed me the deep gashes on her back—I might have laid my whole finger in them—*large pieces of flesh had actually been cut out by the torturing lash.*" Weld's book sold over 100,000 copies during its first year alone.

The American Anti-Slavery Society. In 1833 Weld, Garrison, Arthur and Lewis Tappan, and sixty other delegates, black and white, met in Philadelphia to establish the American Anti-Slavery Society. They received financial support from the Tappans and with it aimed to reach the middle-class public. Led by this society, abolitionists developed two approaches: one for the general public and the other aimed at politicians. First they sought to create a moral climate so intense that slave owners would have to accept programs of abolition. They used the tactics of the religious revivalists: public meetings led by stirring speakers, small gatherings sponsored by local antislavery chapters, and home visits by agents of the movement. The abolitionists also used new techniques of mass communication. Garrison's radical individualism did not stand in the way of attempts to reach a mass market. Assisted by the new steam press, the American Anti-Slavery Society was able to distribute more than 100,000 pieces of literature in 1834 and more than 1 million in 1835. Most dramatic was the "great postal campaign" begun in 1835, which flooded the nation, including the South, with abolitionist pamphlets. In July 1835 alone abolitionists mailed more than 175,000 items through the New York City post office.

The abolitionists' second broad strategy was to mobilize public pressure on legislative bodies—in particular, Congress. In 1835 the American Anti-Slavery Society encouraged local chapters and members to bombard Congress with petitions for specific action: abolition of slavery in the District of Columbia, abolition of the domestic slave trade, removal of the "three-fifths compromise" from the Constitution, and denial of the admission of new slave states to the Union. By 1838, nearly 500,000 signed petitions had arrived in Washington.

These activities drew increasing numbers of middle-class men and women to abolitionism. During the 1830s local abolitionist societies grew swiftly, from about 200 in 1835 to more than 500 in 1836 and nearly 2,000 by 1840. Almost 200,000 people joined them. Meanwhile, the leadership of the abolitionist movement broadened beyond the original core of free blacks, Quakers, and evangelical Christians. Some transcenden-

Anti-Slavery Almanac
The heart-wrenching breakup of families by the slave trade was a common theme in abolitionist literature.

talists, for example, felt shattered by the stark contrast between their claims for individual potential and the reality of slavery. Thanks to their literary skills and in some instances their wealth, many became leaders of the movement in New England. Emerson was less interested in the condition of slaves than in the moral failure of a free society that tolerated slavery, but he spoke out frequently against the institution and, as the Civil War neared, condoned abolitionist violence.

Thoreau was eloquently transcendental in his condemnations of slavery and his calls for civil disobedience. In 1846 Thoreau protested the Mexican War and slavery by refusing to pay his taxes and submitting to arrest. Two years later he published anonymously an essay entitled "Civil Disobedience" that outlined how individuals, by resisting governments that sanctioned slavery and through loyalty to a higher moral law, could transcend their complicity in slavery and redeem the state from its crimes. Even if outnumbered, moral individuals could prevail if they were true to their beliefs. "A minority is powerless while it conforms to the majority," Thoreau explained. But it becomes "irresistible when it clogs by its whole weight."

The Role of Women. Women also contributed to the power of the abolitionist movement. African-American women were crucial, and one of them, Maria W. Stewart, was among the first abolitionists, speaking out in

Boston in the early 1830s. Even earlier than the Grimké sisters, she made speeches to mixed audiences of men and women. As the movement grew, thousands of white women throughout the North followed her example. They condemned the immorality of slavery, delivered lectures to audiences of men and women, supplied more than half the signatures on the petitions the American Anti-Slavery Society sent to Congress, and conducted home "visitations" to win converts among other women and their husbands.

Women abolitionists also established their own organizations, including the Philadelphia Female Anti-Slavery Society, founded by Lucretia Mott in 1833; the Boston Female Anti-Slavery Society, founded by Maria Weston Chapman and twelve other women; and the Anti-Slavery Conventions of American Women, formed by a network of local societies during the late 1830s. Among their accomplishments, the women's societies raised money for *The Liberator* and the American Anti-Slavery Society, supported agents and speakers against slavery, distributed literature, and established schools for free blacks.

By the late 1830s the abolitionist movement had mobilized and merged the reform ideas and energies of both religious revivalism and transcendentalism. What remained uncertain was the ability of its leaders to develop practical strategies that would succeed in eradicating slavery.

Hostility to Abolition

In the South the conjunction of Nat Turner's slave rebellion, the imminent abolition of slavery by the British in the West Indies, and the beginnings of Garrison's *Liberator* touched off an intense effort to defend slavery. The final effort to address the slavery problem peacefully came in 1831–1832, after Turner's rebellion, when the Virginia legislature considered a program of gradual emancipation and colonization. When the bill was rejected by a vote of 73 to 58, the possibility that southern states would legislate an end to slavery faded forever. Instead, in the 1830s the southern states toughened their slave codes, limiting the movement of slaves and prohibiting anyone from teaching them to read to prevent them from absorbing abolitionist literature. Southern legislatures banned abolitionism and passed resolutions demanding that northern states follow suit. The Georgia legislature even offered a $5,000 reward to anyone who would kidnap Garrison and bring him to the South to be tried for inciting rebellion. Public meetings routinely offered rewards for the capture of persons distributing abolitionist literature. In Nashville vigilantes whipped a northern college student for distributing abolitionist pamphlets. In 1835 a Charleston mob attacked the post office and destroyed sacks of abolitionist mail from the North. After that southern postmasters generally refused to deliver mail of suspected abolitionist origin.

The New Defense of Slavery. At the same time, southern leaders—politicians, newspaper editors, and clergymen—developed a new intellectual defense of the institution. It was new in that they moved beyond the defense of slavery as a "necessary evil" and developed a "positive good" argument linked to industrial conditions and buttressed with Christian doctrine. They argued that slavery protected slaves against the evils of the industrial system; it promoted "harmony" in relations between the races; it provided for a more efficient and orderly labor supply than was available in the North; and it had a basis in Scripture. The last argument was particularly crucial to southerners who needed a rationalization for enslaving a population that had become overwhelmingly Christian. Defenders of slavery such as Thornton Stringfellow, a Baptist minister from Virginia, claimed that St. Paul had recognized Christian churches that contained both masters and servants. Stringfellow cited Paul's injunction: "Servants, obey your masters."

According to this sharpening self-image of plantation society, only an exceptional person—the planter—deserved genuine freedom. He was seen as being surrounded by people who were incompetent and incapable of freedom. His task was to achieve a "disinterested benevolence" so that he could lead and manage. Only his exceptional willpower, reason, and self-control made society and order possible. Indeed, southern leaders such as John C. Calhoun advised the northern business elite that it could hold northern society together only by asserting the power that flowed from its "natural superiority." Calhoun exhorted northern business leaders to think and act more like southern planters.

Northern Antiabolitionists. The southern arguments won considerable support in the North. Some wealthy northerners sympathized with the South's appeal for unity among social elites and feared that the abolitionist attack on property held as slaves could turn into a general assault on property rights. Traditional elites, as well as many members of the business class, were troubled by the tactics of the abolitionists, who seemed to threaten the stability of the family by encouraging the active participation of women in their movement. The economic self-interest of northerners also prompted hostility to abolitionism. For example, some New York merchants and New England textile producers found it profitable to support the arguments of their southern customers or suppliers. And some wage earners saw abolitionism as a threat to their jobs; they feared that freed slaves, willing to work for subsistence wages, would pour into northern communities. Finally, only a small minority of any class of northerners believed in African-American equality; the rest were sympathetic to the racism of the planters and abhorred the thought of racial mixing, which the abolitionists seemed to advocate indirectly through their attacks on racism and the colonization movement. In the North the extreme tone of the abolitionists was particularly resented in the communities of the Ohio Valley, which southerners had founded and peopled and in which the fear of freed slaves was especially intense.

Northern opponents of abolition could be as violent as those in the South. Mobs, sometimes led by people whom the abolitionists described as "gentlemen of property and standing," intimidated free blacks and abolitionists. They disrupted abolitionist meetings and routinely destroyed abolitionist printing presses. Fifteen hundred New Yorkers, the first antiabolitionist mob, stormed a church in 1833 in a search for William Lloyd Garrison and Arthur Tappan. The next year prominent New Yorkers cheered a mob of casual laborers who vandalized and set fire to Lewis Tappan's house, and a white mob swept through Philadelphia's African-American neighborhoods, clubbing and stoning residents, destroying homes and churches, and forcing crowds of black women and children to flee the city. In 1835 in Utica, New York, a group of lawyers, local politicians, mer-

chants, and bankers broke up an abolitionist convention and beat several delegates. That same year a Boston mob dragged Garrison through the streets, threatening to hang him. And two years later in Alton, Illinois, a mob shot and killed an abolitionist editor, Elijah P. Lovejoy.

The "Gag Rule." President Andrew Jackson, swayed by these demonstrations of northern hostility to abolition, privately approved of South Carolina's censorship of the United States mails. Publicly, in his annual message to Congress in 1835, Jackson called on northern states to suppress abolitionism and asked Congress to restrict the use of the mails by abolitionist groups. Congress did not respond, in part because Calhoun wanted an extreme measure—banning the delivery of abolitionist tracts in any state or territory that prohibited such material. In 1836, however, the House of Representatives did adopt the "gag rule." Under this rule, which remained in force until 1844, antislavery petitions were automatically tabled when they were received so that they could not become the subject of debate in the House. In the same year Connecticut passed a "gag law" in an attempt to suppress abolitionist speakers, but no other northern state followed suit.

The violence and suppression stunned antislavery advocates and shocked many people who had not participated in abolitionism but had joined evangelical revivals. The disorder and violence seemed to be symptoms of a deeply troubled society. Evangelical Protestants redoubled their efforts to find a means to promote social harmony. Some of the abolitionists among them worked to build the Whig party. Others focused their efforts more specifically on slavery as a political question.

The Rise of Political Abolitionism

As assaults on the antislavery movement mounted, most abolitionists dissociated themselves from Garrison's broad attack on American institutions. Many evangelical Protestants, often following the Tappans, continued to work through their churches. Some of them, working with more secular abolitionists, drew on their experience in managing the postal and petition campaigns of the 1830s and turned to practical politics. They wanted to attract moderate Americans—people who neither supported nor opposed abolition—and propose practical political solutions. They were no less radical than Garrison in terms of their commitment to abolition but were more willing to work within the existing political system. Most of these conservative abolitionists felt that American society, while seriously flawed by slavery, was at its core healthy.

Garrison and his supporters, however, became even more insistent that their American Anti-Slavery Society retain a broad platform that included equal participation for women in the society, pacifism, abolition of prisons and asylums, and in 1843 expulsion of slave states from the Union. The attacks on abolitionists had in fact made the Garrisonians even more radical. Then, in 1837, Garrison came under the influence of John Humphrey Noyes and the perfectionists. He began to emphasize his belief that institutions, rather than individuals, were the source of all sin and that virtually all American institutions were corrupt.

This growing rift in the abolitionist movement fractured Garrison's American Anti-Slavery Society in 1840. Some abolitionists left it to join the American and Foreign Anti-Slavery Society, with its leadership in New York and its major financial backing from Lewis Tappan. Others—such as Theodore Weld, who had left the organized movement along with the Grimkés in 1838—avoided both the Garrison and the Tappan camps, although Weld retained an evangelical approach to abolition. Weld tried to avoid factional disputes within the movement and in any case found both camps lacking. He disliked Garrison's dilution of abolitionism in a broad-based reform effort but found distasteful what he described as the "anti-woman" attitude of more conservative abolitionists.

The Liberty Party. In 1840 most of the abolitionist leaders who had split with Garrison began to emphasize electoral politics as a means to eliminate slavery. They established the Liberty party and nominated James G. Birney as its presidential candidate in 1840 and 1844. Birney was a former slave owner who had lived in Alabama and Kentucky; after a Princeton education and conversion by Weld to abolitionism, he had founded an antislavery newspaper in Cincinnati. In contrast with Garrison and his demands for sweeping reform of the nation's institutions, Birney was willing to work within the Constitution, and he recast abolitionism in terms of republican ideals. He and the Liberty party took the position that the Constitution did not recognize slavery, regarding it as a state institution; that the Fifth Amendment, by barring any Congressional deprivation of "life, liberty, or property," prevented the federal government from sanctioning slavery; and that slaves became automatically free when they entered areas of federal authority, such as the District of Columbia and national territories. But even this more moderate stance failed to attract a substantial following; the Liberty party won less than 3 percent of northern votes for its presidential candidate in 1844. Political abolitionism, as well as the more radical Garrisonian approach, appeared to have little future.

Summary

Industrialization challenged Americans to reconcile claims for the supremacy of the individual with society's need for cohesion. Efforts to resolve this conflict produced a widening variety of reform crusades. These crusades were considered more radical than the business-class moral campaigns.

Many of the new reformers came close to rejecting industrial society. Transcendentalists and other groups formed experimental communities that they hoped would reform society by setting an inspiring example. Religious sects such as the Shakers tried to control sin by withdrawing into insular communities. The most successful of these communities were created by the Mormons, who attempted to provide a communal structure to channel destructive individualism.

Some middle-class women who had been involved in moral reform turned to abolitionism and began to develop an ideology that challenged the traditional division of labor in the household. While they developed this challenge, they launched a movement to establish equal rights for women in public life. They did not gain suffrage but made advances in winning property rights for women.

The most dramatic outlet for reform enthusiasm was a new attack on slavery. In the 1830s a group of abolitionists emerged who shared the moral intensity of the business-class evangelists but were far more radical. In attacking slavery, the abolitionists challenged traditional property rights, and some condemned all institutions that seemed to limit human freedom.

In the late 1830s and early 1840s conservative opposition in both the North and the South nearly halted the movement to abolish slavery as well as all radical reform efforts. In response, some abolitionists tried to broaden the appeal of their message by describing slavery as being much more than the denial of freedom to individual slaves or an expression of the unbridled individualism of slaveholders.

In contrast with Garrison's demands for radical reform of all the nation's institutions, they accepted working within the Constitution. The political abolitionists moved away from directly challenging slavery and slave owners in the South. Instead, they focused on areas that were directly under federal authority, like the District of Columbia and the territories, and argued that in such places the federal government could not, under the Constitution, sanction slavery. Such abolitionists managed to form a political party and run presidential candidates in 1840 and 1844, but the political approach to abolitionism appeared to offer little more promise for winning the support of a large middle-class audience in the North than did Garrison's radical abolitionism.

TIMELINE

1817	American Colonization Society founded
1818	Publication of Benjamin Franklin's autobiography
1826	American Lyceum founded
1829	David Walker's *Appeal*
1830	Joseph Smith publishes *The Book of Mormon*
1831	William Lloyd Garrison begins publishing *The Liberator* Nat Turner's rebellion Alexis de Tocqueville begins his tour of America
1832	Ralph Waldo Emerson resigns his pulpit New England Anti-Slavery Society founded
1834	New York Female Moral Reform Society established
1836	House of Representatives adopts "gag rule"
1837	Emerson's lecture "The American Scholar" Mob kills Elijah P. Lovejoy
1839	Mormons found Nauvoo
1840	Liberty party launched with James G. Birney as its candidate
1841	Transcendentalists found Brook Farm Dorothea Dix begins her investigations
1844	Margaret Fuller's *Woman in the Nineteenth Century* Mob kills Joseph Smith James G. Birney runs again for president
1845	Thoreau withdraws to Walden Pond
1846	Mormons begin trek to Salt Lake Brook Farm disbanded
1847	Liberia declared an independent republic
1848	John Humphrey Noyes founds Oneida Community Seneca Falls convention
1850	Publication of Nathaniel Hawthorne's *The Scarlet Letter*
1851	Herman Melville's *Moby Dick* Susan B. Anthony joins movement for women's rights
1852	Harriet Beecher Stowe's *Uncle Tom's Cabin*
1854	Presidential veto of Dorothea Dix's program for national asylums
1855	First publication of Walt Whitman's *Leaves of Grass*
1858	The "Mormon War"

★   ★   ★

BIBLIOGRAPHY

General surveys of antebellum reform movements include Robert H. Abzug, *Cosmos Crumbling: American Reform and the Religious Imagination* (1994); C. S. Griffen, *The Ferment of Reform, 1830–1860* (1967); Alice F. Tyler, *Freedom's Ferment: Phases of Social History from the Colonial Period to the Outbreak of the Civil War* (1944); and Ronald G. Walters, *American Reformers, 1815–1860* (1978).

Transcendentalists and Utopians

The leading study that connects transcendentalism with reform movements is Ann C. Rose, *Transcendentalism as a Social Movement, 1830–1850* (1981). See also Catherine L. Albanese, *Corresponding Motion: Transcendental Religion and the New America* (1977). On communitarian experiments see Arthur Bestor, Jr., *Backwoods Utopias: The Sectarian and Owenite Phases of Communitarian Life in America* (1970); Lawrence Foster, *Religion and Sexuality: Three American Communal Experiments of the Nineteenth Century* (1981); Jean McMahon Humez, ed., *Gifts of Power: The Writings of Rebecca Jackson, Black Visionary, Shaker Eldress* (1981); Louis J. Kern, *An Ordered Love: Sex Roles and Sexuality in Victorian Utopias—The Shakers, the Mormons, and the Oneida Community* (1981); Spencer Klaw, *Without Sin: The Life and Death of the Oneida Community* (1995); Charles Nordhoff, *The Communistic Societies of the United States* (1875, reprinted 1960); and Stephen J. Stein, *The Shaker Experience in America* (1992). On the Mormon experience see James B. Allen and Glen M. Leonard, *The Story of the Latter-Day Saints* (1992); Leonard J. Arrington, *The Mormon Experience: A History of the Latter-Day Saints* (1992); John L. Brooke, *The Refiner's Fire: The Making of Mormon Cosmology, 1644–1844* (1994); Grant Underwood, *The Millenarian World of Early Mormonism* (1993); and Kenneth H. Winn, *Exiles in a Land of Liberty: Mormons in America, 1830–1846* (1989). Recent studies that link literary developments to reform themes and cultural history include Harold Kaplan, *Democratic Humanism and American Literature* (1972); David S. Reynolds, *Beneath the American Renaissance: The Subversive Imagination in the Age of Emerson and Melville* (1988) and *Walt Whitman's America: A Cultural Biography* (1995); R. Jackson Wilson, *Figures of Speech: American Writers and the Literary Marketplace, from Benjamin Franklin to Emily Dickinson* (1989); and Larzar Ziff, *Literary Democracy: The Declaration of Cultural Independence in America* (1981). On the linkages between religion and the utopians, see Paul E. Johnson and Sean Wilentz, *The Kingdom of Matthias: A Story of Sex and Salvation in 19th-Century America* (1995), and Timothy L. Smith, *Revivalism and Social Reform: American Protestantism on the Eve of the Civil War* (1980).

The Women's Movement

The most comprehensive history of women in the United States is Nancy Woloch, *Women and the American Experience* (1984). On the social history of women, see W. Elliot Brownlee and Mary M. Brownlee, *Women in the American Economy: A Documentary History, 1675–1929* (1976); Nancy F. Cott, *The Bonds of Womanhood: "Women's Sphere" in New England, 1780–1835* (1977); Carl N. Degler, *At Odds: Women and the Family in America from the Revolution to the Present* (1980); and Mary P. Ryan, *Cradle of the Middle Class: The Family in Oneida County, New York, 1790–1865* (1981). The most thorough description of the participation of women in benevolence and reform is Keith Melder, *Beginnings of Sisterhood: The American Women's Rights Movement, 1800–1850* (1977). For studies of more specific aspects of women's involvement in reform see Barbara J. Berg, *The Remembered Gate: Origins of American Feminism: The Woman and the City, 1800–1860* (1978); Estelle B. Freedman, *Their Sisters' Keepers: Women's Prison Reform in America, 1830–1860* (1981); Lori D. Ginzberg, *Women and the Work of Benevolence: Morality, Politics, and Class in the Nineteenth-Century United States* (1990); Nancy A. Hewitt, *Women's Activism and Social Change: Rochester, New York, 1822–1872* (1984); and Jean F. Yellin, *Women and Sisters: The Antislavery Feminists in American Culture* (1989). On Dorothea Dix, see David Gollaher, *Voice for the Mad: The Life of Dorothea Dix* (1995), and Charles M. Snyder, *The Lady and the President: The Letters of Dorothea Dix & Millard Fillmore* (1975). The leading histories of feminists and the early women's rights movement include Kathleen Barry, *Susan B. Anthony—A Biography: A Singular Feminist* (1988); Ellen Du Bois, *Feminism and Suffrage: The Emergence of an Independent Women's Movement, 1848–1869* (1978); and Eleanor Flexner, *Century of Struggle: The Woman's Rights Movement in the United States* (1959). On Margaret Fuller, see Paula Blanchard, *Margaret Fuller: From Transcendentalism to Revolution* (1978); Charles Capper, *Margaret Fuller: An American Romantic Life* (1992); and Joan von Mehren, *Minerva and the Muse: A Life of Margaret Fuller* (1994).

The Antislavery Movement

Surveys of reform that focus on antislavery include Robert H. Abzug, *Passionate Liberator: Theodore Dwight Weld and the Dilemma of Reform* (1980); David Brion Davis, *The Problems of Slavery in the Age of Revolution, 1770–1823* (1975); Louis Filler, *The Crusade against Slavery, 1830–1860* (1960); Leon F. Litwack, *North of Slavery: The Negro in the Free States, 1790–1860* (1961); Stephen B. Oates, *To Purge This Land with Blood: A Biography of John Brown* (1970); Lewis Perry, *Childhood, Marriage, and Reform: Henry Clarke Wright, 1797–1870* (1980); Benjamin Quarles, *Black Abolitionists* (1969); James B. Stewart, *Holy Warriors: The Abolitionists and American Slavery* (1976); John L. Thomas, *The Liberator: William Lloyd Garrison* (1963); and Bertram Wyatt-Brown, *Lewis Tappan and the Evangelical War against Slavery* (1959). For the role of women in the antislavery movement, consult Edmund Fuller, *Prudence Crandall: An Incident of Racism in Nineteenth-Century America* (1971); Blanche Hersh, *The Slavery of Sex: Female Abolitionists in Nineteenth-Century America* (1978); Gerda Lerner, *The Grimké Sisters from South Carolina: Pioneers for Women's Rights and Abolition* (1967); and Alma Lutz, *Crusade for Freedom: Women of the Antislavery Movement* (1968). On northern hostility to abolition, see Leonard L. Richards, *"Gentlemen of Property and Standing": Anti-Abolition Mobs in Jacksonian America* (1970).

Plantation Economy in the Old South, circa 1876

Although this detail from a painting by William Aiken Walker idealizes life on a cotton plantation—much as the defenders of slavery did—it suggests the importance of slavery and self-sufficiency to the largest plantations in the South. Small farms in the South outnumbered large plantations, but the plantations established economic and social styles that most white southerners tried to emulate.

Sections and Sectionalism
1840–1860

★ ★ ★

As the antislavery movement gathered force during the 1840s and 1850s, setting North against South, the acceleration of the Industrial Revolution accentuated the distinctiveness of the two sections. While the North grew increasingly industrial, the fortunes of the South became ever more tied to its "peculiar institution," as slavery was sometimes called. Two distinctly different economic and social systems were evolving, with two different ways of thinking about the relationship between the individual and society. And people in the two sections became acutely conscious of their differences. Indeed, they celebrated them—that is to say, *sectionalism* increased in the decades before the Civil War.

Westward expansion further intensified sectionalism. Each society, southern and northern, believed that westward expansion was necessary to preserve its way of life. In the 1840s and 1850s the acceleration of industrialization gave the North a major demographic advantage. Northerners, motivated by the push of the Industrial Revolution and the pull of fresh land, came pouring into the West in vast numbers. Southerners feared the admission of more new free states than slave states and a loss of their ability to protect slavery within the Union.

The Slave South: A Distinctive Society

On a superficial level, southern planters were similar to northern capitalists: both groups did what they considered necessary to protect their investments and maximize their profits. But the key investment for planters lay in human beings and land rather than factories and machines. That reality required a justification of slavery

in which planters deemphasized or denied their economic motivations. As the profits from slave owning mounted during the 1840s and 1850s, so did the efforts at rationalization. Planters increasingly described themselves as superior beings—natural aristocrats who altruistically protected their human property.

The Slave Economy

Between 1840 and 1860 the South's economy grew rapidly and generated high incomes for both slave owners and other whites. Per capita income, even taking the meager incomes of slaves (food, clothing, and shelter) into account, increased more rapidly in the South than in the United States as a whole. In 1860 only the Northeast, Great Britain, and Australia had higher per capita incomes than the South. Southern prosperity was based on the exportation to Europe of tobacco, rice, sugar, and—above all—cotton. By the 1850s, after the Cotton Kingdom had swept across the Mississippi River into Texas, the South was producing more than two-thirds of the world's cotton. In 1860 southern cotton accounted for almost two-thirds of the total value of exports from the United States.

Southern agriculture was highly productive, generating large revenues compared with the investment of labor, capital, and land. But unlike northern farmers, southern planters did not depend on domestic consumers or improvements in farm technology. Their high profits depended on three other factors: British markets, fresh land, and slavery.

The British connection was crucial. The buoyant demand of British textile mills drove up the export price of cotton, and British mercantile houses were the major source of capital for southern planters. And because southern agriculture relied heavily on foreign markets, the region enjoyed a high degree of economic independence from the rest of the United States.

The availability of fresh land was equally significant because cotton ruined the soil more quickly than did most other crops. By 1860 nearly three-fourths of the South's cotton production came from the region's newer plantations—on lands stretching from western Georgia to eastern Texas. In the early 1850s an observer described Georgia's eastern plantation belt as "red old hills stripped of their native growth and virgin soil, and washed with deep gullies, with here and there patches of Bermuda grass, and stunted pine shrubs, struggling for a scanty subsistence on what was one of the richest soils in America." The ravaging of southern land continued into the twentieth century.

Most important, southern planters became increasingly dependent on slave labor. Slavery allowed planters to organize labor into large-scale specialized routines that resembled factory work but were far more demanding, intense, and brutal. While the northern business class relied heavily on the appeal of evangelical

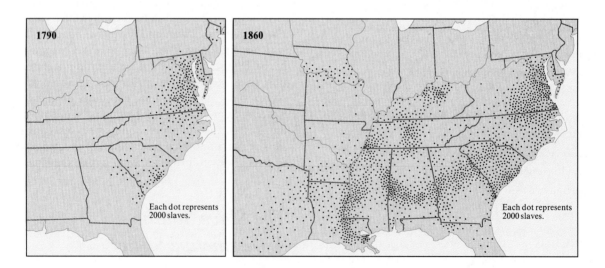

MAP 13.1

The Distribution of the Slave Population, 1790–1860
The cotton boom was largely responsible for the westward shift of the slave population. In 1790 slaves were concentrated most heavily on the tobacco plantations of the Chesapeake and the rice and indigo areas of South Carolina. By 1860 slaves were most heavily concentrated on the cotton and sugar land of the lower Mississippi Valley and along an arc of fertile cotton land—the "black belt"—sweeping from Mississippi through Georgia.

Christianity and the promise of economic rewards to discipline workers, southern planters used coercion, terror, and suppression of open communication to keep slaves in line. Planters could use those tactics as long as they insulated their society from the rest of the nation.

Immigration offered little assistance in building a southern labor force. Most migrants from the North and from Europe avoided the South, and the majority of those who did go there found jobs that did not force them to compete with cheap slave labor. Few immigrants settled there even during the 1850s, when there were growing opportunities for work in southern cities. The South actually *lost* free workers, because a significant portion of its white population, especially in the border states, migrated to the upper Ohio Valley and, during the 1850s, to Oregon and California. Few slaves arrived from Africa after 1808, when Congress banned their importation (and exportation). The high birth rate of the existing slave population provided the labor force needed for the westward expansion of the Cotton Kingdom (see Map 13.1).

The Gang Labor System. Planters who grew cotton or sugar and owned more than twenty slaves forced their slaves into intensely specialized and disciplined work. In 1860 such planters accounted for only about 10 percent of all slaveholders but owned about 50 percent of the slaves.

Those planters or their overseers assigned slaves specific tasks, which varied by season, and organized the hands into disciplined teams, or "gangs," as they were called. The gangs worked in the fields at a feverish and often brutal pace. Overseers, most of whom were white, and drivers, who were themselves slaves, used the threat of the whip to force their gangs into tight, co-ordinated units for plowing, hoeing, and picking. A traveler in Mississippi in 1854 watched an army of slaves return from the fields at the end of a summer day:

> First came, led by an old driver carrying a whip, forty of the largest and strongest women I ever saw together; they were all in a simple uniform dress of a bluish check stuff, the skirts reaching little below the knee; their legs and feet were bare; they carried themselves loftily, each having a hoe over the shoulder, and walking with a free, powerful swing.

Next marched the plow-hands with their mules, "the cavalry, thirty strong, mostly men, but a few of them women." Finally, "a lean and vigilant white overseer, on a brisk pony, brought up the rear." As large-scale cotton and sugar production grew, gang labor became more common than the somewhat less demanding "task" system that prevailed in the cultivation of other crops and had been the most common way of organizing slave labor before 1820.

Plantation owners could not have organized *free* farm workers to labor under the discipline of the gang system. On family farms and farms with only a few slaves, workers, both free and slave, insisted on a degree of independence and on work routines involving a variety of tasks. In the South as well as the North, whenever farm owners tried to organize free workers into gangs, the laborers demanded wages that made their output unprofitable. Or they simply quit, preferring to find employment as sharecroppers, casual workers, or factory hands. There was a great difference between the high wages that free laborers would have demanded from cotton planters and the cost of rearing and maintaining slaves. That saving in labor costs represented the economic gain planters reaped from slavery.

Harvesting Sugarcane
This watercolor by Franz Holzlhuber shows slaves harvesting sugarcane in the late 1850s in southern Louisiana, where American sugar production was concentrated. Sugar plantations, which had been the first to introduce gang labor, were even harder on slaves than were cotton plantations because of the continuous ditching and draining of marshlands and the laborious processing of the cane.

The Economic Impact of Slavery. The gang labor system, the availability of new land, and the enormous demand for cotton all made owning slaves extremely profitable. Planters—all except those with the poorest land—made profits from their investments in slaves that averaged about 10 percent a year in the 1840s and 1850s. Even the most successful New England textile mills rarely produced a higher rate of return.

The high profits from cotton production and slavery created two long-term economic problems. First, southern investors concentrated their resources in cotton and slaves rather than in manufacturing. Consequently, the percentage of people who lived in towns and cities and worked in manufacturing was twice as high in the North as in the South. The only major cities in the South by national standards were the old seaports of Baltimore, Charleston, and New Orleans, which remained predominantly commercial centers. A more tragic liability was slavery's discouragement of investment in human beings. Planters made little or no effort to educate or train their slaves or to provide schooling for poor whites. In fact, laws actually forbade education for slaves. Without large urban and industrial sectors and without a large force of skilled, educated workers, the South faced severe difficulties in long-term economic development.

Realities and Ideals of the Planter Class

The planters made up a tiny minority of southern whites, who by 1860 constituted a majority of the population in most southern states (see Figure 13.1). In 1860 only about 46,000 individuals—little more than 0.5 percent of the white population of the South—owned twenty or more slaves. Only about 8,000 planters owned fifty or more slaves. Small as it was, this minority increased its influence in the 1840s and 1850s and came to dominate southern society more completely than the business elite controlled the North.

The planters were able to increase their power by holding out to the majority of whites the possibility of entering their elite class. Although most planters lived in relatively unpretentious farmhouses, the enormous profits of the 1840s and 1850s enabled the wealthiest planters to build splendid plantations and indulge in displays of conspicuous consumption. In the new cotton lands of the Mississippi Valley many large cotton planters had risen from modest circumstances. Their prosperity whetted the appetites of all slave owners—more than 380,000 individuals belonging to about a fourth of white southern families—and of the small farmers who aspired to own slaves.

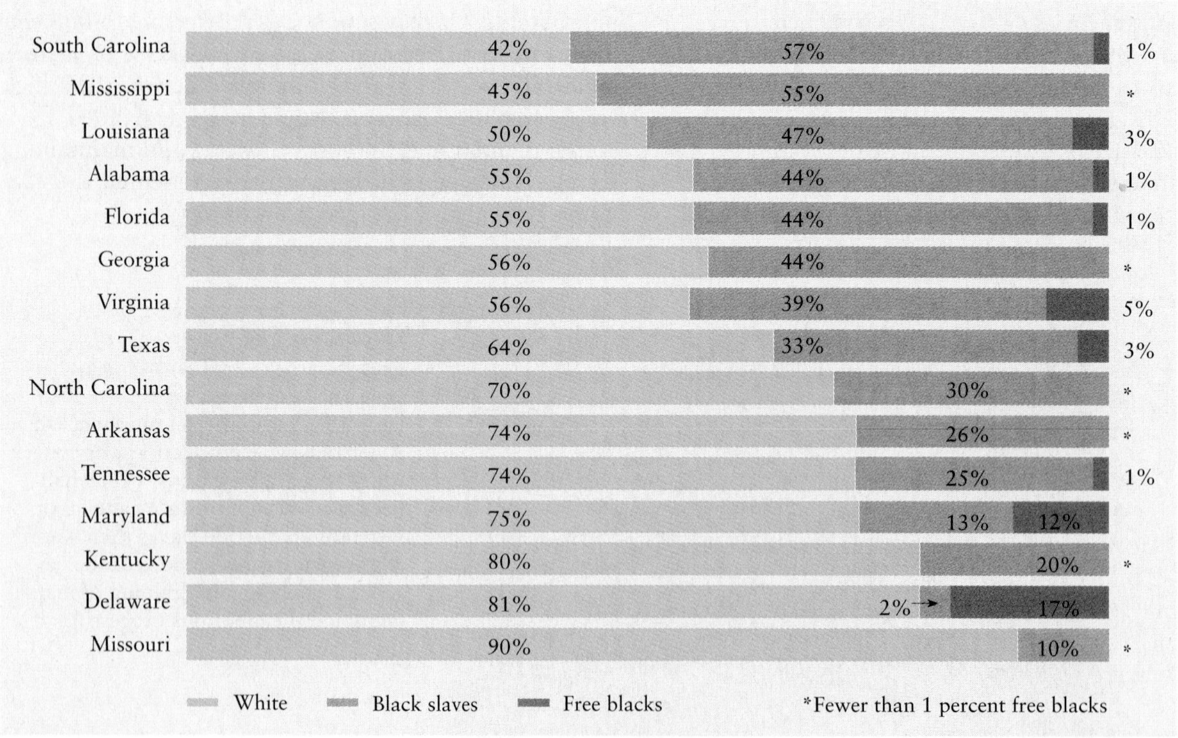

State	White	Black slaves	Free blacks
South Carolina	42%	57%	1%
Mississippi	45%	55%	*
Louisiana	50%	47%	3%
Alabama	55%	44%	1%
Florida	55%	44%	1%
Georgia	56%	44%	*
Virginia	56%	39%	5%
Texas	64%	33%	3%
North Carolina	70%	30%	*
Arkansas	74%	26%	*
Tennessee	74%	25%	1%
Maryland	75%	13%	12%
Kentucky	80%	20%	*
Delaware	81%	2%	17%
Missouri	90%	10%	*

*Fewer than 1 percent free blacks

FIGURE 13.1

Proportion of Blacks and Whites in the South, 1860
Whites were in the minority in only two states of the slave South and constituted more than two-thirds of the population in eight slave states.

Mary Boykin Chesnut

A Slaveholder's Diary

Mary Boykin Chesnut (1823–1886), the wife of the South Carolina senator James Chesnut, lived most of her life on plantations near Camden, South Carolina. She made no secret of her hatred of slavery but believed that blacks were innately inferior. She revealed her views in the extensive diary she kept during the Civil War.

March 18, 1861 . . . I wonder if it be a sin to think slavery a curse to any land. [Massachusetts senator Charles] Sumner said not one word of this hated institution which is not true. Men and women are punished when their masters and mistresses are brutes and not when they do wrong—and then we live surrounded by prostitutes. An abandoned woman is sent out of any decent house elsewhere. Who thinks any worse of a negro or mulatto woman for being a thing we can't name? God forgive us, but ours is a *monstrous* system and wrong and iniquity. Perhaps the resent of the world is as bad—this *only* I see. Like the patriarchs of old our men live all in one house with their wives and their concubines, and the mulattoes one sees in every family exactly resemble the white children—and every lady tells you who is the father of all the mulatto children in everybody's household, but those in her own she seems to think drop from the clouds, or pretends so to think. Good women we have . . . the purest women God ever made. Thank God for my country-women—alas for the men! No worse than men everywhere, but the lower their mistresses, the more degraded they must be.

November 27, 1861 . . . Now what I have seen of my mother's life, my grandmother's, my mother-in-law's:

These people were educated at Northern schools mostly—read the same books as their Northern contemners, the same daily newspapers, the same Bible—have the same ideas of right and wrong—are highbred, lovely, good, pious—doing their duty as they conceive it. They live in negro villages. They do not preach and teach hate as a gospel and the sacred duty of murder and insurrection, but they strive to ameliorate of the condition of these Africans in every particular. . . . These women are more troubled by their duty to negroes, have less chance to live their own lives in peace than if they were African missionaries. They have a swarm of blacks about them as children under their care—not as Mrs. Stowe's fancy paints them, but the hard, unpleasant, unromantic, undeveloped savage Africans. And they hate slavery worse than Mrs. Stowe. . . .

We are human beings of the nineteenth century—and slavery has to go, of course. All that has been gained by it goes to the North and to negroes. The slave-owners, when they are good men and women, are the martyrs. And as far as I have seen, the people here are quite as good as anywhere else. I hate slavery. I even hate the harsh authority I see parents think it their duty to exercise *toward their children.*

Source: C. Vann Woodward, *Mary Chesnut's Civil War* (New Haven: Yale University Press, 1981), 29–30, 245–246.

The "Cavaliers" and Their Wives. The elaborate defense of slavery that began during the 1830s reinforced the message conveyed by the planters' wealth and conspicuous consumption. Planters promoted descriptions of themselves as superior, noble beings whom other whites should admire or at least treat with deference. Sermons, novels, and tracts defending slavery pictured the planter as a born leader who acted with grace and restraint. Planters were Christian patriarchs, it was said, who treated their dependents—slaves, wives, and children—with responsible generosity. They were described as hospitable, courageous, loyal, and—in the spirit of Sir Walter Scott's novels, which were popular in the South—exceptionally chivalrous. In his novel *George Balcombe* (1836) Nathaniel Beverley Tucker described planters as descendants of "the ancient cavaliers of Virginia." They were "men in whom the spirit of freedom was so blended with loyalty as to render them alike incapable of servility and selfishness."

Also idealized was the planter's wife. Defenders of southern culture believed that the planter's wife had the exceptional qualities, such as generosity, graciousness, and charm, required to match those of her spouse. Especially prized was sexual purity—contrasted with what was stereotypically described as the passionate sexuality of black women. Planters' wives became symbols of the moral superiority of whites over blacks.

The reality of plantation life was far more complex. Like northern women in their "separate sphere," most planters' wives educated their children and cared for the sick. In addition, they managed large, complicated households and often entire plantations when their husbands were absent. Southern white men did not object if white women directed the work of black men, but they firmly ruled out sexual intimacy between the two. White men brutally punished any suspected black offenders and insisted that slavery was necessary to protect southern womanhood and prevent the mixing of the races.

This belief and the strength of its appeal partly reflected the guilt of planters who routinely had sex with their female slaves and fathered children by them. As one southern woman put it, "violations of the moral law made mulattoes as common as blackberries." Planters' wives generally kept quiet about this, perhaps doing nothing more than writing in their diaries (see American Voices, page 387).

A Racist Ideology. Planters increasingly relied on a racist ideology to maintain the loyalty of non-slaveholders. Central to this ideology was the claim that blacks were an inferior race permanently unsuited for freedom and requiring rigid social control. Supporters of slavery also argued that slavery had a highly positive result. It provided what the South Carolina senator James H. Hammond described in 1858 as a "mud-sill" class—the foundation on which whites, freed from the most degrading kinds of work, had built "progress, civilization, and refinement." During the 1850s Hammond and other advocates of slavery increasingly saw slavery as guaranteeing equality, freedom, and democracy for whites and thereby protecting the highest values of the republic. As William Yancey of Alabama explained to a northern audience, "Your fathers and my fathers built this government on two ideas; the first is that the white race is the citizen and the master race, and the white man is the equal of every other white man. The second is that the Negro is the inferior race."

The planters faced no significant competition for the loyalty of non-slaveholders, who constituted a majority of the white population. Manufacturers, merchants, lawyers, doctors, editors, and ministers made up a far smaller proportion of the population in the South than they did in the North, and most were closely related to or dependent on wealthy planters. In contrast with the planters, members of the southern middle class generally supported government promotion of banking, transportation, and manufacturing, but they agreed with the planters on the prime importance of defending slavery.

Moreover, new ideas were slow to penetrate the South. Southern cities remained small, and the sparse rural population was widely scattered. The vehicles for disseminating new ideas—schools, lecturers, magazines, newspapers—that were so common in the North reached few southerners beyond the major cities. Before the Civil War no southern state had a statewide public school system, and only Kentucky and North Carolina appropriated a significant share of public revenues for education. Whereas wealthy southerners sent their children to private academies, poor whites typically taught their children at home. Whereas less than half of 1 percent of the white population in New England was illiterate in 1850, nearly 20 percent of white southerners could not read or write. This cultural isolation meant that reform movements in nineteenth-century America were limited largely to the North and that planters were able to exercise great influence over all aspects of life in the South.

Slave Life

The legal status of slaves remained unchanged in the antebellum South. The inhuman, brutal reality at the core of slavery was that slaves, in the eyes of the law, were *chattel*—personal property. They could be disciplined at will and bought and sold as if they were horses. As Thomas Ruffin, a justice of the North Carolina Supreme Court, said in 1829, "The power of the master must be absolute to render the submission of the slave perfect."

The material lives of slaves did improve, however, reflecting the prosperity of the plantation system. Most slaves were somewhat better clothed and housed than were the poorest whites in both the South and the North. The slaves' food—particularly when supplemented by greens from their own garden plots and by game and fish—was probably better than that of unskilled workers in the North. On some large plantations children, the sick, and the elderly received better care than northern society provided for those groups. But the slaves realized that planters gave them material favors primarily to protect their investment and promote a high birth rate, rarely out of benevolent concern.

The working conditions of slaves varied widely. On small farms slaves might work alongside their masters. And on every plantation some slaves were household servants, drivers who helped white overseers in the fields, or skilled workers such as blacksmiths and carpenters. However, roughly half of the slaves lived on farms or plantations that had more than twenty slaves, and they worked in the fields under the gang system.

The most oppressive conditions were found in the Old Southwest. The weather in Alabama, Mississippi, Louisiana, Arkansas, and Texas was hotter, the work routines more demanding, and the planters more harsh than was the case farther east. The slave population in those states increased from about 500,000 in 1840 to more than 1.5 million in 1860. These slaves accounted for about a fifth of the South's 2.4 million slaves in 1840 and more than a third of its 4 million slaves in 1860.

The Domestic Slave Trade. Many African-Americans came to southwestern plantations through the growing domestic slave trade, which broke up families and communities. Masters in the coastal and border states sold slaves "down the river" (the Mississippi) to increase their profits and punish those they regarded as difficult to handle. During the 1840s and 1850s profits in this trade became a major source of income for planters in the Chesapeake region and the older cotton areas of

Slaves on Auction in Richmond
The 1808 prohibition of the international slave trade forced the new cotton planters in the Deep South to import most of their slaves from the older areas of the South. Consequently, planters in those areas could reap huge profits from the slave trade. Upper South markets like this one in Richmond, Virginia, expedited that trade, and planters could use the threat of sale "down the river" to discipline their slaves.

Georgia and South Carolina, which were suffering from soil depletion. By the 1850s slave owners were shipping 25,000 slaves a year from the East to the West, and this trade helped retain the grip of slavery on the older regions of the South.

The Slave Family. In the face of intensified workloads and disrupted lives, slaves nurtured family relationships for protection and support and to foster personal identities independent of their masters. By midcentury slave families had become unusually resilient despite the lack of legal protection. Because slaves could not make contracts, marriages between them could not be legally binding. The North Carolina Supreme Court brushed aside Christian tradition in 1853 when it ruled that

> Our law requires no solemnity or form in regard to the marriage of slaves, and whether they "take up" with each other by express permission of their owners, or from a mere impulse of nature, in obedience to the command "multiply and replenish the earth" cannot, in the contemplation of the law, make any sort of difference.

A Slave Burial, circa 1860
Burials, wakes, and memorials were rituals vital to African-American culture. Slave funerals often carried on West African traditions. They were pageants that brought together friends and relatives who did not routinely see each other. By paying elaborate tribute to the dead, funerals provided a communal celebration of the living.

Frederick Douglass

Slave Songs

In this selection from his autobiography Frederick Douglass describes the singing during the days between Christmas and New Year's, which were typically allowed the slaves as holidays. He always took pains to urge his white audiences to find the hidden meanings in the words and rituals of slaves.

The fiddling, dancing, and "jubilee beating" was carried on in all directions. The latter performance was strictly southern. It supplied the place of violin, or of other musical instruments, and was played so easily that almost every farm had its "Juba" beater. The performer improvised as he beat the instrument, marking the words as he sang so as to have them fall pat with the movement of his hands. Among a mass of nonsense and wild frolic, once in a while a sharp hit was given to the meanness of slaveholders. Take the following example:

We raise de wheat,
Dey gib us de corn;
We bake de bread,
Dey gib us de crust;
We sif de meal,

Dey gib us de huss;
We peel de meat,
Dey gib us de skin;
And dat's de way
Dey take us in;
We skim de pot,
Dey gib us de liquor,
And say dat's good enough
*   for nigger.*
Walk over! Walk over!
Your butter and de fat;
Poor nigger you cant get over
*   dat . . .*

This is not a bad summary of the palpable injustice and fraud of slavery, giving, as it does, to the lazy and the idle the comforts which God designed should be given solely to the honest laborer.

. . . I did not, when a slave, understand the deep meaning of those rude and apparently incoherent sounds [of the slaves' songs]. I was myself within the circle; so that I neither saw nor heard as those without might see and hear. They told a tale of woe which was then altogether beyond my feeble comprehension; they were tones loud, long, and deep; they breathed the prayer and complaint of souls boiling over with the bitterest anguish. Every tone was a testimony against slavery, and a prayer to God for deliverance from chains. The hearing of those wild notes always depressed my spirit, and filled me with ineffable sadness. I have frequently found myself in tears while hearing them. The mere recurrence to those songs, even now, afflicts me; and while I am writing these lines, an expression of feeling has already found its way down my cheek. To those songs I trace my first glimmering conception of the dehumanizing character of slavery, and quicken my sympathies for my brethren in bonds. . . .

I have often been utterly astonished, since I came to the north, to find persons who could speak of the singing, among slaves, as evidence of their contentment and happiness. It is impossible to conceive of a greater mistake. Slaves sing most when they are most unhappy. The songs of the slave represent the sorrows of the heart; and he is relieved by them, only as an aching heart by its tears.

Source: Frederick Douglass, *My Bondage and My Freedom* (New York, 1855), 253–54.

Nevertheless, many slaves married outside the law and lived together throughout their lives. If not broken up by sale, couples usually maintained close nuclear families within plantation communities. Parents helped their children to be as independent as possible from the discipline of the master. Mothers not only worked alongside men but also cooked, kept gardens, and raised children, often nursing babies in the field.

During this period slaves also developed elaborate kinship networks that included distant relations and even individuals who had no blood or marital ties but shared in the life of the family. Elderly slaves, for example, often played the role of community patriarch, conducting religious services and disciplining difficult children. Young slaves learned to address their elders by kin titles such as "Aunt" and "Uncle," preparing them for the day when they might be separated from their parents. Even when parted by sale, members of both nuclear and extended families kept track of one another. Many runaway slaves returned to their home plantations and, after emancipation during the Civil War, thousands tried to reunite their families. When distances were too great to maintain marriages, many slaves started new families in their new locations. When the Union army registered African-American marriages in Mississippi at the end of the Civil War, it was found that the slave trade had separated about a fourth of the men over forty years old from their wives.

Slave Religion. In their quarters, slaves built a community life rich with mutual obligations. They shared insights regarding the world of their masters and news

from the outside world. Religion was central to their culture. The Christianity of the slaves focused on the endurance of the Israelites in Egypt and the caring of Christ for the oppressed. They sometimes had to conduct their services and prayers at night or in the woods in "bush meetings" to keep them secret from their masters. Religion offered a message of hope—of eventual liberation from life's sorrows—and helped most slaves endure their bondage. Organized prayer enabled them to express love for one another and share burdens with others. Confident of their special relationship with God, the slaves prepared themselves spiritually for emancipation, which they regarded as deliverance to the Promised Land (see American Voices, page 390).

Resistance and Rebellion

Slaves resisted the growing inhumanity of bondage with the same tactics of evasion and sabotage that they had employed for generations. Slaves resisted by being deliberately careless with the master's property, losing or breaking tools, or setting fire to houses and barns. They could slow the pace of work, perhaps by feigning illness or incompetence. In the instances of greatest desperation, they could make themselves useless by cutting off their fingers or even committing suicide.

The Underground Railroad. Slave resistance sometimes took the form of flight. Tens of thousands of slaves ran away during the 1840s and 1850s, even though their chances of making it to the North or Canada were slim. In the Deep South white patrols with bloodhounds were constantly on the lookout for runaway slaves. All blacks on public roads or paths were presumed to be runaways unless they carried passes that proved otherwise. The odds for success were best for those who lived near a free state. They might receive aid from the "underground railroad," an informal network of white and, even more important, African-American abolitionists. Many escaped slaves, such as Harriet Tubman, who returned to the South nineteen times to free hundreds of slaves, risked reenslavement or death by working with the "railroad." As Tubman wrote:

> There was one of two things I had a *right* to, liberty, or death; if I could not have one, I would have the other; for no man should take me alive; I should fight for my liberty as long as my strength lasted, and when the time came for me to go, the Lord would let them take me.

Members of the small communities of free African-Americans in cities such as Baltimore, Richmond, Charleston, and New Orleans were the most important source of help. In fact, they were virtually the only free people in the South who aided escapees. In Baltimore, it was a free African-American sailor who lent his identification to Frederick Douglass, who disguised himself, used the papers to escape to New York, and then mailed the papers back to the sailor. Such acts were common despite the consequences for the benefactor if the fugitive was unable to return the papers or was captured. Despite all the obstacles, thousands of slaves escaped to freedom.

Slaves could go beyond everyday sabotage and flight to violent rebellion in which they turned on their masters and killed them. Planters used the fear of such violence to build support for slavery among non-slaveholding whites. The fear of massacre became a binding, cohesive force among whites, who recognized that their power over slaves depended on terror and that slaves might want to repay the terror. Planters could point to many slave rebellions, including the bloody revolution on the island of Santo Domingo that overthrew the French and culminated in the creation of the republic of Haiti in

Harriet Tubman

In 1849 Harriet Tubman (1823–1913, pictured far left with some of the slaves she helped to freedom) escaped from a Maryland plantation. During the next ten years she was a leader of the underground railroad and became a popular abolitionist speaker. She served as a spy for the Union army during the Civil War and then set up schools for ex-slaves in North Carolina. In 1896 she played an active role in founding the National Association of Colored Women.

1803. Within the United States revolts were local disturbances such as that of Denmark Vesey in Charleston, South Carolina, in 1822. Although such revolts were small-scale, they were numerous. As many as 200 of these small uprisings occurred during the first half of the nineteenth century, although some of the reported revolts undoubtedly took place mostly in the imaginations of slave owners. The most dramatic example of the capacity of enslaved African-Americans to fight back was Nat Turner's rebellion of 1831 (see Chapter 12).

But slaves generally recognized, especially after Turner's defeat, how heavily the odds were stacked against successful rebellion. The ratio of blacks to whites in the South was lower than that in any other slave society in the Western Hemisphere. The South was not an island that could be captured and cut off from the outside world. Southern whites were well armed, unified, and militant, and the South had no impenetrable jungles, mountains, and swamps where a guerrilla army could hide out for a long period of time.

Still, few planters were entirely certain about their security, and their anxiety rose during the 1850s. In 1856 William Proctor Gould of Green County, Alabama, warned his slaves not to become involved in an alleged conspiracy. Although they pledged their loyalty, Gould was still uneasy: "What they might have done if there had been an actual outbreak must forever remain unknown to us."

Free Blacks

While 4 million African-Americans lived as slaves in 1860, about 500,000 were free. About half of the free blacks lived in slave states, and of that number, slightly more than 85 percent lived in the Upper South. Most free African-Americans or their parents had obtained freedom before 1800. The number of slaves obtaining freedom legally, through manumission or self-purchase, then dwindled as King Cotton began to make slave owning more profitable, and as southern states restricted manumission, especially during the 1830s. Natural increase and, to a much lesser extent, escaping slaves roughly doubled the size of the free black population between 1820 and 1860, but its rate of increase was still much lower than that of the slave population.

Regardless of where they lived, free blacks were second-class citizens. They could vote only in four New England states and in New York. No state admitted to the Union after Maine in 1820 extended the suffrage to African-Americans. In New York they had to own a certain amount of property, a requirement not imposed on white voters. Every state except Massachusetts prevented them from testifying against whites in court. The federal government did not allow blacks to work for the postal service, claim public lands, or hold a U.S. passport. Congress admitted to the Union states whose constitutions denied the vote to blacks. Virtually all public facilities were segregated throughout America, and most states, including all the southern states, denied free blacks access to public schools.

In the South free blacks faced even greater legal restrictions on their liberty, and the restrictions intensified during the 1840s and 1850s, when states tightened the system of slavery under the threat of abolitionism. Some southern states prohibited teaching slaves to read or write. They also enacted vagrancy and apprenticeship laws that were thinly disguised devices to force free blacks into slavery. Under their criminal laws, southern states subjected free blacks as well as slaves to whippings and judgments without a jury trial. By 1860 every southern state prohibited the entry of free blacks. In those states they had to carry documents establishing their free status, and in some states they needed official permission to travel across county lines. If they could not prove their status, they were subject to enslavement. Even if they had good papers, free blacks had to be careful in both the South and the North; kidnapping and sale into slavery was a constant threat.

Everywhere, free blacks endured severe discrimination when they sought work, and this discrimination intensified during the 1840s and 1850s. Most were confined by custom or law to the most menial kinds of work and to poverty. In rural areas, most were farm laborers or tenant farmers. In towns and cities, most were domestic servants or casual laborers who worked by the day. If free black women wanted to work outside of domestic service, they had almost no options except to peddle on street corners or take in laundry.

The shortage of skilled workers in southern cities, however, created opportunities. Some blacks were able to become carpenters, blacksmiths, barbers, butchers, and shopkeepers. In Charleston, Denmark Vesey, for example, won a lottery, purchased his freedom, and opened a carpentry shop. Some of these skilled workers hired other free blacks and occasionally bought slaves, usually relatives whom they wished to emancipate.

These skilled workers often formed and maintained vibrant communities of free blacks clustered in southern cities. In cities such as Baltimore, Richmond, Charleston, and New Orleans free blacks formed their own benevolent societies and churches, which became the core of their urban communities. The spirituality of the churches coupled with their practical programs of education, recreation, and social welfare provided a degree of social distance from the planter class. By 1860, as a consequence of the magnetism of urban black communities, most free blacks in the Lower South and about one-third of those in the Upper South lived in urban areas.

In some places wealthier free blacks, particularly the children of white masters and black women, felt superior to common laborers and field hands and drew apart from their communities. In New Orleans and Charleston elite free blacks formed especially close ties with the planter class and adopted its trappings of status. In New Orleans they sponsored an opera company and established literary journals. A few owned land and slaves.

Generally, however, free blacks sympathized with slaves and worked to ease their condition and even to abolish slavery. Many had been slaves, were the children of slaves, or had relatives who were slaves. They knew that so long as slavery existed even their minimal freedom was tenuous and that they had little chance to improve their status. As discrimination intensified in the 1840s and 1850s, they identified even more closely with slaves. In the North many free blacks, such as David Walker, Frederick Douglass, and Sojourner Truth, became important abolitionists. The position of free blacks in the South was much weaker, but many welcomed slaves who wanted to participate in their churches and communities. At times churches used the Sunday offering to help members who were slaves buy their freedom. Some free blacks took the risk of sheltering and protecting slaves who had escaped from their masters. A few free blacks, such as Denmark Vesey, became leaders of slave rebellions. Collectively, free blacks, despite their second-class citizenship, helped keep alive the hope of freedom from slavery.

The Northeast and the Midwest: The Industrial Revolution Accelerates

The business class of the Northeast drove industrialization forward at an increasing pace during the 1840s and 1850s and incorporated the Midwest in the expanding industrial economy. As people from the Northeast moved westward, agriculture and industry developed in close conjunction, and the economies of the Northeast and the Midwest became inextricably linked. Moreover, the economy of the Midwest became increasingly industrial in its structure. All the peoples of these two regions—even those of southern origin living in the Ohio Valley—became closely tied to the economic and social life of the North. The economic results were phenomenal. By 1860 the United States was third in the world in manufacturing, behind only Great Britain and France. Northern industrial production already was more than two-thirds that of either of those countries and was increasing even more rapidly.

Factories Triumphant

The acceleration of industrialization during the 1840s and 1850s resulted from the modernizing efforts of northern manufacturers, hundreds of whom built factories that relied on modern technology and large numbers of workers. Factory owners extended the use of power-driven machines and assembly lines from the processing of agricultural produce to the manufacture of guns, watches, sewing machines, and agricultural machinery. Manufacturers flourished not only in the first industrial towns, where falling water powered mills, but also in the older seaports and, with stunning swiftness, in the towns and cities of the Midwest. The industrialization of interior cities such as Chicago and St. Louis helped make that region a functional part of the Northeast.

The most important technological innovation adopted by manufacturers in the 1840s was the stationary steam engine, which was used to power other machines. Steam engines freed manufacturers from dependency on water power and enabled them to locate factories in the nation's largest cities: the great Atlantic seaports and the booming ports on the Great Lakes. During the 1840s manufacturers for the first time took advantage of all the benefits offered by a big-city location: easy access to the cheapest labor, highly developed markets for capital, sophisticated trading services, and urban consumers. Manufacturers in the seaports and the largest western cities, particularly Chicago, broke the near monopoly that the smaller inland cities had held on the most modern industries.

Machine Tools. The manufacturers' growing demand for machinery stimulated the machine-tool industry, which became even more critical to the advancement of industrialization. The same machines that made uniform parts for firearms were used to make parts for sewing machines. By the late 1850s five Connecticut clockmakers were using modern machine tools to make intricate works for half a million clocks a year. Some of the products of modern machine tools remained well known for generations—Colt revolvers, Remington rifles, Singer sewing machines, Waltham watches, Yale locks, and McCormick reapers.

Using the modern machine tools and new sources of power, some manufacturers introduced modern assembly lines in the 1850s. Cyrus McCormick of Chicago developed power-driven conveyor belts to assemble reapers, and Samuel Colt built an assembly-line factory in Hartford, Connecticut, to produce his invention—the "six-shooter," as it became known. By the late 1850s Colt's factory responded to the enormous demand for small arms by turning out 60,000 weapons annually.

McCORMICK'S FIRST REAPER

The McCormick Reaper, 1851
The McCormick reaper was a complex piece of machinery, but it was designed to be operated and repaired by average farmers. Company advertisements indicated that its parts were "numbered and marked with paint, showing the connection of the parts with one another so that they can readily be put together by the farmer."

In 1851, at the Crystal Palace Exhibition in London, the first world's fair in the industrial era, Cyrus McCormick and Samuel Colt displayed their machine-tooled products. The amazement of British manufacturers quickly turned to anxiety when McCormick and Colt built factories in Great Britain that used American machinery and production techniques. Two teams of technicians sent by the British government to investigate American factories reported that many different industries were organized "in large factories, with machinery applied to almost every process, the extreme subdivision of labor, and all reduced to an almost perfect system of manufacture."

The Impact of Factory Workers. The increasing scale and complexity of production, however, made it difficult for manufacturers to estimate the demand for their products. During the 1850s periods of overproduction followed by the layoff and dismissal of workers became common. One such episode coincided with the Panic of 1857—a crisis produced by overexpansion of railroad investment—and a long depression followed. Unemployment remained at about 10 percent until the outbreak of the Civil War in 1861.

Steam power and assembly lines further sharpened the class divisions that had begun to emerge in the 1820s and 1830s. To make the most of their large new investments, manufacturers increased the pace at which their workers toiled, and many workers resisted. For example, in 1845 a group of workers in Lowell, Massachusetts, under the leadership of Sarah G. Bagley, a weaver, formed the Lowell Female Labor Reform Association to protest a speedup. As working conditions became more grueling, most of the young women who had poured into factories left the paid work force to marry and raise families.

Immigration

Manufacturers turned more and more to immigrants—men and women largely from Ireland and the German states. Lacking the economic opportunities available to Americans, immigrants were willing to work for longer periods of time, at lower wages, and with greater intensity. As a result, in the 1840s immigrants began to fill the unskilled labor force.

By 1860 immigrants accounted for more than a fourth of the white adult men in the United States and more than a third of those in the North. Between 1820 and 1860 about 2 million Irish immigrants settled in the United States, along with 1.5 million Germans and 750,000 Britons (see Figure 13.2). Some of the immigrants were skilled workers, but more than two-thirds were peasants, unskilled laborers, and farmers dislocated by industrial and agricultural advances in Europe. Most of the newcomers took low-skilled jobs in factories, construction projects, docks, warehouses, and private homes. No federal legislation restricted immigration, and state immigration laws, which attempted to set minimum health standards and exclude paupers, were ineffective.

The economic situation of immigrants varied greatly by national group. The wealthiest were the British, many of whom were professionals, former landowners, and skilled workers. Many German immigrants were prosperous enough to draw on their own savings to finance travel and buy land in America. The poorest immigrants were the Irish.

The immigration of the Irish had more to do with poverty in their homeland than with economic opportunity in America. Although they arrived in increasing numbers during the 1830s, the Irish began to come in force only in 1847, after a devastating potato famine in

FIGURE 13.2

Immigration to the United States, 1820–1860

Immigration accelerated dramatically in the late 1840s. Fewer immigrants arrived in the middle and late 1850s as economic conditions improved in Ireland and the German states and the United States entered a depression.

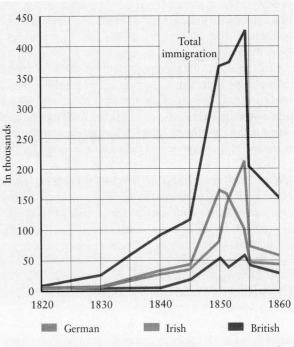

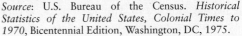

Source: U.S. Bureau of the Census. *Historical Statistics of the United States, Colonial Times to 1970*, Bicentennial Edition, Washington, DC, 1975.

Ireland. They found new homes in the Northeast, especially in the cities of New England. By 1850 the Irish accounted for more than a third of the workers in Boston. Their labor enabled Boston industrialists to compete for the first time with manufacturers in the smaller mill towns of Massachusetts and Rhode Island. By 1860 each of the largest factories producing women's clothing in Boston employed about a hundred young Irishwomen. During the late 1840s and early 1850s the Irish made only a modest contribution to the farm population. Although most had been farmers in Ireland, they were too poor to buy land in the United States.

Living conditions for many Irish immigrants, like those for other unskilled immigrants and native-born day laborers, proved to be only marginally better than the grinding poverty and rampant disease that had filled their lives in the Old World. Per capita consumption of food increased during the Industrial Revolution, and most immigrants were much better nourished than they had been in Europe. Even so, many unskilled laborers could not afford to buy the food they needed to keep up the intense pace of factory work. In addition, the stress and insecurity of work drove many unskilled workers to spend an increasing portion of their income on the entertainment and alcoholic relief found in taverns. Malnutrition increased in the largest cities, resulting in higher rates of miscarriage and death from infectious diseases.

The crowding of immigrants in the old commercial cities of the Northeast threatened public health. Sanitation systems were primitive. Poorly sealed privies drained into drinking wells, and open sewers ran through the streets. Infectious diseases ravaged the weakened, malnourished poor. Epidemics of cholera,

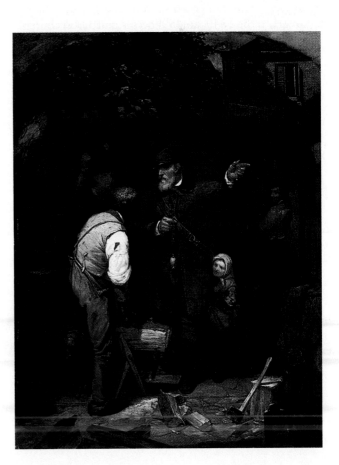

The Status of Immigrants, 1855

The painter Charles F. Blauvelt was one of the rare artists of the period who made immigrants and African-Americans his subject, and he treated both groups with realism and sympathy. In this painting he might have meant to highlight the generosity of African-Americans by portraying a black woodcutter helping lost immigrants even though the new immigrants, solely by virtue of the color of their skin, enjoyed higher status. (North Carolina Museum of Art)

yellow fever, typhoid fever, smallpox, diphtheria, and tuberculosis struck the major cities with increasing frequency. In the summer of 1849 cholera epidemics hit New York, St. Louis, and Cincinnati. More than 5,000 people, mostly immigrants, died in New York, and many entire families succumbed. Wealthy families moved out of the cities during the epidemics, while, as one observer wrote, the immigrants remained crowded "into a few wretched hovels, amidst filth and bad air, suffering from personal neglect and poisoned by eating garbage [at] which a well-bred hog on a western farm would turn up his snout." In 1860 mortality rates in New York, Philadelphia, and Boston reached a level of more than thirty-four deaths per thousand population annually, compared with about fifteen per thousand in rural areas.

Irish Identity and Anti-Catholicism

The Catholic Church. In the 1840s and 1850s the United States remained overwhelmingly Protestant in private allegiance and public culture. But many of the new immigrants—French-Canadians, many Germans, and particularly the Irish—relied on the Catholic Church not only to sustain their spiritual lives but also to reinforce their sense of class and ethnic identity. The Church's expansion closely paralleled the growth of Irish immigration, increasing from 16 dioceses and 700 churches in the 1840s to 45 dioceses and 3,000 churches by 1860. Throughout the areas settled by Irish immigrants, traveling priests were replaced by resident ones. The Irish purchased many church buildings from Protestant congregations that had moved to more spacious quarters. In towns and cities, using the church as a foundation, the Irish also built a network of charitable societies, orphanages, militia companies, parochial schools, newspapers, social clubs, and political organizations. These community institutions supported Irish immigrants in their search for housing, jobs, education, and security.

These new institutions had no equivalent in Ireland. They developed in the United States in response to the desire of Irish immigrants to maintain their native culture, to which existing American institutions were hostile or, at best, indifferent. The church network was important to immigrants in large cities, especially those who worked in factories. It provided community services and a sense of group identity, much as a labor union might have done. The institutions that the Irish created had a great impact on later groups of Catholic immigrants. Because the Irish arrived early and because many spoke English, they built the church structure and the urban political machinery through which most European Catholic immigrants established a place for themselves in American life.

The relative autonomy of Catholic communities disturbed many American Protestants, still the dominant majority in almost all of the United States. During the 1830s, when Irish immigration first started to increase, lurid anti-Catholic propaganda began to circulate. Its authors raised the specter of a sinister, highly organized menace. According to the propaganda, the pope, acting through Catholics over whom he exerted total authority, was plotting to subvert republican institutions.

Samuel F. B. Morse. A leading anti-Catholic propagandist was Samuel F. B. Morse, who would later make the first commercial adaptation of the telegraph. In 1834 Morse published *Foreign Conspiracy against the Liberties of the United States* anonymously. The book came out under his own name in 1835 and was endorsed by Protestant ministers of many denominations. Morse declared that the "past history" of Roman Catholics and "the fact that they everywhere act together, as if guided by one mind, admonish us to be jealous of their influence, and to watch with unremitted care all their movements in relation to our free institutions." He warned in particular of the political facility of Irish Catholics, who "in an especial manner clanned together, and kept alive their foreign feelings, associations, habits and manners." Morse advocated the formation of an "Anti-Popery Union" to resist the perceived Catholic threat.

Millions of young Americans read *Foreign Conspiracy* in Protestant Sunday schools and public libraries and schools. It became a textbook for anti-Catholic crusaders. In 1838 the citizens of Sutton and Millbury, Massachusetts, asked Congress to investigate "whether there are not now those amongst us, who, by their oath of allegiance to a foreign despotic Prince or Power, are solemnly bound to support his interests and accelerate his designs."

Native American Clubs. The anti-Catholic movement became exceptionally intense because of the dislocations associated with industrialization. It appealed especially to mechanics who had lost their jobs or feared that they might lose them as a consequence of the factory system. By attacking Catholics, they could blame cheap immigrant labor for their economic situation and at the same time persuade themselves that they had a superior culture and religion. Threatened workers took the lead in organizing Native American Clubs, which called for an extension of the waiting period before naturalization from five to twenty-one years, the restriction of public offices to native-born Americans, and exclusive use of the (Protestant) Authorized Version of the Bible in public schools.

Even workers who felt secure in their jobs were afraid that their children would face competition from immigrants. They strongly opposed proposals from

Riot in Philadelphia

Philadelphia's anti-Irish rioting climaxed in Southwark on June 7, 1844. Pennsylvania's governor, John Cadwalader, had called out the militia to protect Catholic churches, including one (pictured in background) in which young Irish-Americans had stored muskets for self-defense. The Protestant rioters and the militia exchanged musket fire, and the rioters even fired a cannon into the militia. Militia reinforcements ended the riots, but Philadelphia's politics became focused on ethnic and racial issues.

Catholic clergymen and Democratic legislators in many northeastern states that Catholics' taxes be reserved for parochial (religious) schools—thus weakening the public schools. Another source of anti-Catholic sentiment was the temperance movement as a number of evangelical ministers denounced the abuse of alcohol among Irish immigrants. Such appeals won recruits to the business class among native-born Protestant workers and impeded the development of a labor movement across ethnic and religious lines. Many Protestant laborers became convinced that they had more in common with their employers than with Catholic workers.

In almost every city with a large Catholic immigrant population, the anti-Catholic movement turned to violence. In 1834, in Charlestown, Massachusetts, a quarrel between Catholic laborers in an Ursuline convent and Protestant workers in a neighboring brickyard turned into a full-scale riot. The anti-Catholic mob, convinced that a young Protestant woman was being held against her will, drove out the residents of the convent and burned it to the ground. Urban rioting escalated during the 1840s as the Irish began to acquire political power in eastern cities. In Philadelphia the violence peaked in 1844 after the Catholic bishop persuaded public school officials to use both Protestant and Catholic versions of the Bible. Anti-Irish rioting, provoked by the city's Native American Clubs, lasted for two months and escalated into open warfare between the Protestants and the Pennsylvania militia, causing many casualties.

Business-Class Consumption

In the mid-1850s the annual increase in per capita income approached 2.5 percent, a remarkable rate that the United States has never since matched. The nation achieved this rate despite the great surges of immigration during the 1840s and 1850s, which tended to reduce per capita income.

These phenomenal income gains allowed native-born Americans with property or skills to reap an extraordinary material bonanza. During the 1840s and 1850s industrialization brought a sweeping wave of consumption to middle-class life in the North. New consumer goods served as badges of economic success and membership in the business class. The availability of inexpensive mass-produced goods, many of them new during the 1840s and 1850s, made the trappings of status widely accessible to the middle class. The new material culture reinforced a prideful sense of northern uniqueness that increasingly united affluent and upwardly mobile Americans from New England through the Great Lakes states.

Middle-Class Housing: The Balloon Frame. When they could afford it, middle-class families built their homes of brick and stone. But wooden residences became much more numerous during the 1840s, and they were constructed very differently from log cabins or traditional frame buildings. In the 1830s American carpenters had devised a faster method to construct housing: the *balloon frame*.

Traditional wood construction depended on the careful fitting together of heavy timbers; experienced housewrights fashioned a strong frame with mortise-and-tenon joints, whereas western farmers fitted trimmed logs together. The balloon frame, much lighter in weight (as its name implied) but almost as strong, formed a house with a vertical grid of thin wooden studs joined by nails to cross-pieces at the top and bottom. Once the carpenter had thrown up the frame, he

Constructing a Balloon-Frame House
The fragile-looking balloon frame shown on the left provides a surprisingly strong skeleton for the substantial type of house on the right. Because people of modest means could build balloon-frame houses with the labor of family members, friends, or low-skilled carpenters, they could afford houses that had been available only to the very wealthy before the 1830s.

simply nailed wood sheathing to the studs as walls and then added a layer of clapboard siding. Even an inexperienced carpenter could erect a balloon frame. The process saved enough labor to reduce the cost of housing by 40 percent—and it was quick. The balloon frame made it possible for western cities such as Chicago, where it was first introduced, to spring up almost overnight. The four-room balloon-frame house became the standard residence, replacing the one-or two-room house of preindustrial society.

Architects published self-help manuals with detailed plans of simple houses for carpenters and families building their own homes. In the 1840s and 1850s the manuals featured larger houses with more bedrooms to enhance the privacy of each family member. The leading architectural philosopher of the era was Andrew Jackson Downing, who lauded such designs in his most famous book, *The Architecture of Country Houses* (1850). Downing argued that his new houses would promote a "refinement of manners" and strengthen the life of the family, which was "the best social form." Within the single-family home, he proclaimed, "truthfulness, beauty, and order have the largest dominion." Ample homes, even if more standardized, would provide a medium for the success of republican ideals.

Household Goods. Prosperous urban families furnished their homes with an array of new comforts, decorations, and devices. Furnaces heated both interiors and water. Europeans marveled at them and at the American desire for warmth. One visitor complained that it was impossible to escape hot air: "It meets you the moment the street-door is opened to let you in, rushes after you when you emerge again, half-stewed and parboiled into the wholesome air." In most homes, beds with springs of woven rope or iron wire replaced beds with wooden slats. Homemade featherbeds, mattresses, and down pillows spread rapidly after mass-produced ticking and sheeting became available in stores. Households acquired goods that made traditional chores more efficient. Beginning in the 1850s, some women purchased treadle-operated sewing machines. Most prosperous urban households had stoves with ovens, including broilers and movable grates, instead of open hearths. Women used a variety of pots, pans, and kettles; mechanical equipment such as grinders and presses; and washboards. And these households had iceboxes, which ice-company wagons filled daily. As early as 1825 the Underwood Company of Boston was marketing well-preserved Atlantic salmon in jars. With the introduction of the Mason jar in 1858, households vastly increased their ability to preserve other perishable foods.

The new household furnishings also included mass-produced clocks. Before 1820, townspeople and villagers relied on public clocks or bells, and country folk told time by the sun. By the 1840s, inexpensive clocks and watches manufactured in Connecticut had become the main methods of keeping time. Clocks had revolu-

Advertisement for Stoves, 1856
The broadside advertisement represented an early effort to use the mass media to sell expensive household goods. Manufacturers gave romantic names to the various stove models, such as "Medallion" and "Black Warrior," pictured here, to appeal to prosperous urban families.

tionary effects, allowing people to organize themselves to meet the more intense pace of daily life produced by the Industrial Revolution.

Middle-Class Literature

During the 1840s and 1850s American democracy came to include a "democracy of print." Middle-class Americans provided a virtually insatiable market for books, magazines, and newspapers. By 1850 nine of ten adult white Americans could read, and millions bought books. Libraries were growing in both number and size. By 1860 there were over 50,000 public libraries, containing nearly 13 million volumes. Readers and libraries were, however, concentrated in the North. The books were no doubt the most forceful component of the new material culture of the northern middle class; they fostered a powerful sense of community and reinforced the values of individualism, self-control, and republican virtue.

The Industrial Revolution swept over American publishing, dramatically widening popular access to information. The Napier steam-driven press (1825) and the Hoe rotary press (1847) made it possible to mass-produce cheap books. Publishing houses in New York, Philadelphia, and Boston competed with each other, offering discounts to booksellers, advertising in magazines and newspapers, sending sales agents into the field, and recruiting authors the way manufacturers recruited engineers and designers. Between 1820 and 1850 American book publishers such as Harper Brothers and G. P. Putnam's Sons increased their annual sales from about $2.5 million to $12.5 million. The religious press also contributed to the explosion. Dozens of Bible societies (led by the American Bible Society, founded in 1816) and tract societies published more than 1 million Bibles and 6 million books, pamphlets, and magazines each year.

Irving and Cooper. Fiction constituted a large part of the literary consumption of middle-class Americans. America's first successful writers of fiction were Washington Irving and James Fenimore Cooper. In *The Sketch Book*, Irving painted unforgettable portraits of two characters who became part of American folk culture, Ichabod Crane and Rip Van Winkle. An equally celebrated fictional character was the frontier scout Leatherstocking in the novels of Cooper. Beginning with *The Pioneers* (1823) and *The Last of the Mohicans* (1826) and ending with *The Deerslayer* (1841), Cooper built an enormously popular legend around his hero. The key personality trait of Leatherstocking—or "Hawkeye," "Natty Bumppo," or "Deerslayer," as he was also known—was his solitude in nature. His moral goodness grew directly out of his "original relation" with nature. He was a radically free individual, at odds with law and custom and comfortable only in the forest, a model of American self-reliance and nonconformity. Cooper fashioned his hero to represent the nobility, innocence, and strength of frontier Americans. Preoccupied with defending American democracy to Europeans, Cooper struck a responsive chord in his American readers. Corresponding in popularity to Irving and Cooper among American poets was Henry Wadsworth Longfellow. Poems such as *Hiawatha* (1855) and *The Courtship of Miles Standish* (1858) used the American past and American settings in imaginative ballads infused with the themes of God, nature, and moral improvement. For most nineteenth-century Americans, Longfellow defined poetry.

Currier & Ives
By the 1850s the most popular prints showed idealized images of a prosperous rural life. This verdant scene, one of several entitled *Home, Sweet Home*, dates from 1869. The apparently unscathed Union soldier returns to a perfect home, an orderly oasis in the woods.

The Beecher Family: Cultural Innovators

The evangelical reform movements of the nineteenth century were led by powerful individuals with a highly developed sense of self. Prominent among them were the members of an extraordinary family—the Beechers. No family had a greater influence on business-class reform.

Born in New Haven, Connecticut, Lyman Beecher (1775–1863) studied theology at Yale University and as the pastor of churches in New York and Boston became a central figure in the Benevolent Empire. He published a best-selling book of sermons on temperance and helped found the American Bible Society. Married three times, Lyman had thirteen children, eleven of whom survived into adulthood.

Lyman paid close attention to the spiritual development of his children. He believed in the presence of original sin, and he expected each child to undergo a deep and intense conversion experience. Eventually all his children found Lyman's spiritual code too strict. But Lyman moderated a harsh Calvinist determinism by preaching that individuals were responsible for their own salvation. This approach to personal salvation helped most of his children develop a sense of individuality and self-confidence in their spiritual progress. And, in adulthoods inspired by Lyman's evangelical appeals to individual action, some of them turned from spiritual to worldly matters, embracing the belief that they were responsible for the moral welfare of others. Seven of Lyman's nine sons joined the ministry, and three of his four daughters became influential social reformers.

Lyman's most accomplished son was Henry Ward Beecher (1813–1887). A minister at the Congregationalist Plymouth Church in Brooklyn, Henry held audiences spellbound with sermons of hope and optimism.

The Beecher Family

Taken at the studio of the photographer Mathew Brady around 1859, this Beecher family portrait includes Lyman (center, seated) and nine of his children: his sons, from the left, Thomas, William, Edward, Charles, and Henry Ward, and his daughters, from the left, Isabella, Catharine, Mary, and Harriet.

He became noted during the 1850s for his denunciations of slavery as morally evil. However, his abolitionism was moderate. Although he believed that the system of slavery was sinful, he argued that individual slaveholders were not, and he worked, along with his father, to maintain church unity across sectional lines. Both he and Lyman embraced African colonization and the free-soil movement. Henry's flamboyancy and political influence, particularly within the new Republican party, increased in the 1850s.

None of the other six Beecher sons who became ministers were as influential or prosperous as Henry. They lived out their lives in the genteel poverty that was typical of the Protestant ministry in the nineteenth century.

It was the Beecher daughters who became cultural innovators—even celebrities. While Lyman's sons found legitimate and familiar channels for fulfilling their father's expectations, his daughters had to struggle to define their social roles. They had to innovate, working out their concern for the self-improvement of individuals within the family and for the reform of society. In the process they discovered ways of influencing the public beyond the limits imposed by women's separate sphere. But the Beecher daughters never agreed on a common agenda. The differences among them reflected the difficulties and ambiguities middle-class women generally experienced in finding their special mission.

Lyman's oldest daughter, Catharine (1800–1878), never married or had a home of her own and was often at odds with the rest of her family. Nonetheless, she became the nation's leading advocate on behalf of family life and a separate sphere in which women would draw on their superior moral authority. Her passion for educational reform extended beyond schools to the family. She led in the development of a popular self-help literature designed to inspire middle-class wives and mothers. In manuals and magazines Catharine Beecher taught middle-class women how to make their homes more efficient and more moral. To improve their homes, she argued, women had to first improve themselves with better health practices, physical activity, and diet. Catharine's *Treatise on Domestic Economy* (1841) was reprinted almost every year during the 1840s and 1850s, becoming the standard text on housekeeping, child-rearing, and self-improvement for women.

Harriet Beecher Stowe (1811–1896), after the death of her mother in 1816, was placed under Catharine's care and attended one of her model schools, the Hartford Female Seminary. She found Catharine overbearing and chafed under her surrogate mothering. Harriet broke away from her sister's dominance in 1836 when she married a minister, Calvin Stowe. Despite having five children in the first seven years of marriage, she managed to publish her first article for money in 1838 and her first volume of fiction in 1843. (She had two other children later.) She gradually discovered that she could earn an income that helped relieve the chronic financial problems that stemmed in part from Calvin's ill health. Hiring others to care for their children, she wrote *Uncle Tom's Cabin* in 1852. It brought her worldwide fame and made her one of the wealthiest authors in the world. In 1853 she took over the support of her family, including the management of its money. As her income grew during the 1860s and 1870s, she contributed to the support of her father and his third wife and sustained four of her adult children through a variety of financial difficulties.

In her novels Harriet popularized the same moral ideas that Catharine promoted. Her most successful novel, *Uncle Tom's Cabin*, carried the advancement of American family life into the realm of politics and the sectional crisis. She appealed to women as mothers to recognize how slavery destroyed family life and to use their moral authority to reform the nation.

Isabella Beecher Hooker (1822–1907), the youngest Beecher daughter, was the only one to challenge traditional assumptions of womanhood. Envying Harriet's fame, she became the leading advocate for women's rights in Connecticut, securing the passage of a bill giving property rights to married women in 1877. She joined the more radical New York branch of the suffrage movement and quickly assumed a leadership role. (The more moderate New England suffragists had named her half brother Henry as its president.) But she was ostracized from her family only in 1875, when she defended the editor Victoria Woodhull, a free-love advocate who had published an article charging Henry Ward Beecher with adultery. During the sensational trial that followed, Isabella attacked the double standard that condemned Woodhull but exonerated Henry. Harriet and Catharine insisted on their brother's innocence and felt that Isabella was unfaithful to the family. Isabella was bitter that the family did not appreciate her work for suffrage and women's rights.

Mary Beecher Perkins (1805–1900) was the most traditional of the daughters, remaining aloof from the reform impulses that gripped her three sisters. She particularly disapproved of Isabella but supported all of them by offering her Hartford, Connecticut, home as a refuge. Ironically, it was Mary's granddaughter, Charlotte Perkins Gilman (1860–1935), who spun the family's reform history in a radical direction. During the 1890s Charlotte left her husband and family to lead a liberated life and developed a powerful feminist argument for the economic independence of women.

Women Novelists. A group of women writers were even more popular. They, at least as much as Irving, Cooper, and Longfellow, defined a new American literature—and new American themes. In their writing they reinforced the values promoted by business-class evangelism.

Female writers contributed to a redefinition of the role of women in middle-class life. Women formed growing majorities in most religious congregations, and middle-class women in northern communities played increasingly important roles in reform movements. They were marrying later or not at all. They were having fewer children and employing two or three times as many servants by the 1860s as they had at the end of the Revolution. And they were prodigious readers, constituting a majority of the reading public. In the 1850s, according to the estimate of *Harper's Magazine*, four out of five readers of books or magazines were women. And women were writing many of those books and editing and filling the pages of magazines with stories and poems.

Novels by the leading women writers of the day often sold hundreds of thousands of copies in the North. Catharine Maria Sedgwick won wide popularity in the 1820s, as did Caroline Howard Gilman and Caroline Lee Hentz in the next decade. But the largest audiences were reached by Harriet Beecher Stowe in the 1840s and 1850s, and by Sara Parton, Augusta Evans Wilson, and Susan Warner in the 1850s. Their sentimental melodramas, often punctuated by tearful domestic scenes, shared an assumption that had become increasingly popular in America since the 1790s: women occupied a "separate sphere" with its own morality and possibilities.

The dominant message was that women could achieve their potential only within the sphere of marriage and the family. For women, as Hentz wrote in *Ernest Linwood* (1856), "In the depth of the heart there is a lower deep, which is never sounded save by the hand that wears the *wedding-ring*." In her last novel, *Married or Single* (1857), Sedgwick concluded that "God has appointed marriage" for woman; marriage is "the great circumstance" of a woman's life.

For these writers marriage did not imply a submissive or passive role; they were claiming a superior status for women within the sphere of family life. Women, they suggested, were ultimately responsible for forming the character of their husbands and sons. In *Means and Ends* (1839), Sedgwick wrote, "By an unobtrusive and unseen process, are the characters of men formed, at home, by the mother . . . where the moral basis is fixed."

The most successful woman novelist of the period was Harriet Beecher Stowe. *Uncle Tom's Cabin* (1852), which sold 350,000 copies in its first year, was not merely an antislavery novel but an extended discussion of the role of women and the family. Time after time,

women and even little girls are shown to be morally more sensitive than and superior to the men around them. In Stowe's portrayal of slave society it is women who offer the best hope of eventual freedom for slaves and of salvation for both African-Americans and whites. Home and family held deeply religious meanings for Stowe. In *The Minister's Wooing* (1859) she wrote that home was the "appointed sphere for woman, more holy than cloister, more saintly and pure than church and altar."

The commercial success of women novelists put an ironic twist on their celebration of the private sphere of marriage and family. These writers were actually engaged in a very public—and commercial—enterprise. They often began their careers writing under assumed names—almost always female names—but eventually dropped their anonymity. Bargaining with their publishers, often making their own livings, and even supporting their families, they were among the first successful professional women in the United States. Their success seemed to support Caroline Lee Hentz's judgment that "Mind, we verily believe, is of no sex."

These writers offered a new justification for the independent woman—a justification used by the increasing numbers of women who participated in religious congregations and reform organizations in the North. If talented and energetic women could find a way to give their unusual abilities a *moral* use, the contradiction between "domestic" and "public" life could then be softened. Given such a formula, women writers and their heroines could be seen as female versions of ministers. Stowe told her readers that she would make them feel "as if you had been hearing a sermon." Hentz spoke of her writing career as a legitimate calling, or "vocation . . . for which God has endowed me." These novelists, reaching a wide audience, encouraged northern middle-class women to attempt to improve both family life and society at large.

Education

A hallmark of the northern business class was its investment in young people. Parents who aspired to higher status and income for their children tried to provide them with a healthier environment, better food, basic academic skills, and the personal and social qualities appropriate to urban life. They spent more money educating their children, kept them in school longer, and devoted more attention to their upbringing.

The improvement of schools attracted the support of women. From Maine to Wisconsin women vigorously supported the movement led by Horace Mann to expand and standardize public elementary schools. During the 1840s and 1850s thousands of young middle-class women became teachers. Part of the reason was

economic. Towns wanted to hire teachers at the lowest possible wages and began, especially after the Panic of 1837 had restricted public credit, to fill teaching positions with young women rather than men. School boards recognized both the rise in the number of women with schooling and the degree to which the lack of jobs for them had depressed their wages.

Teaching drew young women into its ranks through its moral appeal as well as its economic reward. The message of Catharine Beecher was the most powerful. Along with other members of her distinguished family, she was a powerful reformer of American culture. Beecher founded academies for young women in Hartford and Cincinnati in the 1820s and 1830s and became the intellectual leader of the thousands of young women who took teaching jobs. Her message to them was that women had a special calling in education. Because "to enlighten the understanding and to gain the affections is a teacher's business," and because "the mind is to be guided chiefly by means of the affections," she asked, "is not *woman* best fitted to accomplish these important objects?" To Beecher, "moral and religious education must be the foundation of national instruction" and education must be carried out by "energetic and benevolent women" (see American Lives, pages 400–401).

Family Planning and Population Growth

Northern families found the time and money to educate their children partly by limiting the size of their families. Families in cities and towns relied on primitive but moderately effective means of birth control: abstinence, coitus interruptus, condoms fashioned from animal skins and intestines, and abortions induced by potent herbs. Business-class families led the movement to restrict family size. They, more than families that owned little property, recognized the value of urban-based skills. More important, they did not feel a pressing need for their children to bring home wages or support them in old age. Rather, they felt pressure to buy new goods and, in order to purchase more goods, to restrict the number of children they had.

Some rural parents in long-settled agricultural areas of the Northeast also limited the size of their families. Farmers wanted to provide their children with ample land, which rising prices made more difficult to buy, or to prepare them for skilled urban employment. In frontier areas fertility rates declined more slowly. There, only the most highly mobile, disrupted families restricted family size. On the frontier, where the price of land remained low, the labor of children retained greater relative value.

As a consequence of the birth control practiced by northern families, the average size of an American family declined from 5.8 to 5.3 members (including adults)

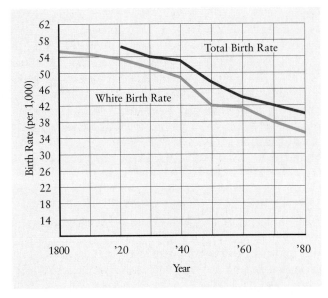

FIGURE 13.3

Birth Rate by Race, 1800–1880
Although American birth rates fell steadily from 1800 to 1880, the sharpest decline took place during the 1840s.

between 1800 and 1860. The national birth rate, however, continued to be high—from forty-five to fifty live births per thousand people per year, compared with thirty per thousand in Europe (see Figure 13.3). The vast majority of American parents, even in the Northeast, remained confident about their ability to provide for a large number of children.

The high birth rate and increasing immigration caused the American population to swell from 17 million in 1840 to over 31 million in 1860. By 1860 the American population exceeded the British in size and was about to overtake both the German and the French. The North dominated this demographic surge; between 1840 and 1860 the northeastern and Great Lakes states accounted for nearly two-thirds of the growth in the nation's population.

The Midwest

Most settlers moving to the West during the 1840s and 1850s migrated from New England and the Middle Atlantic states to the Old Northwest—Ohio, Indiana, Illinois, Michigan, and Wisconsin—and Missouri. Some pushed beyond the Mississippi into the fertile prairies of Iowa and Minnesota (see Map 13.2). This large geographical area became known as the Midwest. Migrants to the Midwest established wheat farms, settled the towns that serviced those farms, and built other, in-

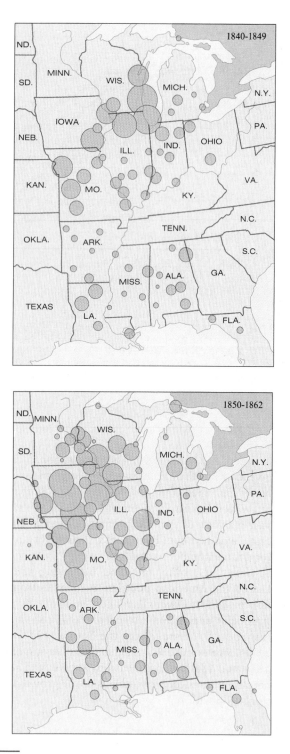

MAP 13.2

Western Land Sales, 1840–1862
Land offices continued to open up on the frontier to sell government land. Each circle centers on a land office, and the size of each circle depends on the relative amount of land sold at that office. During the 1840s and 1850s the tide of settlement shifted to the west and northwest into Indiana, Michigan, Iowa, Wisconsin, and Minnesota.

creasingly industrial towns. The demographic balance in the Midwest shifted dramatically in favor of settlers of northeastern rather than southern origin, and the growth of the Midwest dominated the growth of the West. By 1860 the westward movement had taken about half the nation's 31.4 million people west of the Appalachian Mountains (see Figure 13.4). But the great majority of westerners lived in the states of the Old Northwest (the "East Central North" states) rather than in Texas and the Old Southwest (the "East Central South" states).

Agriculture was buoyant in the Midwest, and it depended increasingly on the Northeast. Farmers relied on northeastern markets and on the products of industrial technology. The availability of low-cost labor-saving machinery quickened settlement, particularly on the fertile grain-producing prairies bordering the Great Lakes. John Deere's steel plow, superior in strength to the cast-iron plow, won widespread acceptance during the 1850s. In 1837, as a blacksmith in Grand Detour, Illinois, Deere had made his first steel plow from old saws; ten years later, in Moline, he opened a factory that used mass-production techniques. In addition, various companies—McCormick, Hussey, Atkins, and Manny—made reapers that grain farmers found invaluable. Previously, one worker with a cradle scythe had cut 2 to 3 acres a day. In the 1850s, with a self-raking reaper, a farmer could cut 12 acres daily. Largely because midwestern farmers had begun to use the products of modern factories in their fields, their productivity and incomes increased more than 20 percent during the 1850s.

The flow of cheap midwestern food stimulated the growth and productivity of northeastern communities. Midwestern wheat and flour enabled people in the Northeast to improve their diets. As a consequence, infants and nursing mothers became healthier and infant mortality declined. This helped keep the rate of population growth high in the Northeast despite the falling birth rate. Unskilled factory workers could not afford to share fully in the new agricultural bounty, but their diets also improved. Consequently, they were better able to endure the long hours of work that factories required. The "breadbasket" of the Midwest became vital to the health and productivity of the Northeast.

The Railroads. It was another product of industrial technology—the railroad—that cemented the union between the Northeast and the Midwest. As late as 1852 canals were still carrying twice as much tonnage as were railroads, but in the next five or six years track mileage increased dramatically. The new railroads included trunk lines that stretched across New York and Pennsylvania to provide through traffic from New York City and Philadelphia to Cleveland and Chicago (see Map 13.3). More convenient and faster than canals, the railroads had become the main carriers of freight by 1859.

FIGURE 13.4

Population by Region, 1820–1860 (as percentages of U.S. total)

Between 1820 and 1860 the most dramatic population growth took place west of the Appalachians. The population of the Northeast and the South Atlantic regions declined from 76 percent of the national total in 1820 to 50 percent in 1860.

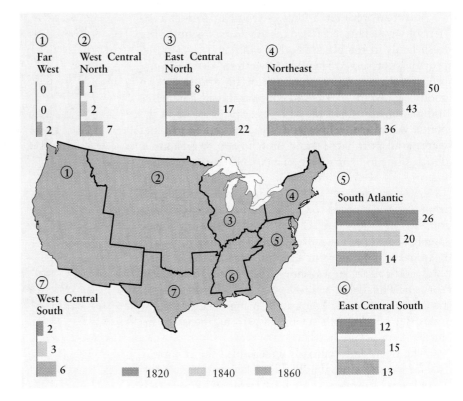

MAP 13.3

Railroads of the North and South, 1850–1860

The decade before the Civil War witnessed explosive growth in the nation's railroad network, but it was geographically uneven. The Northeast and Midwest acquired extensive, dense railroad systems that stimulated economic development. The South built a much simpler system. Numerous highly competitive companies built railroad lines, often using different track gauges that hindered the efficient flow of traffic and made the transshipment of goods slow and expensive. Such problems were frustrating to the military and proved especially severe in the South during the Civil War.

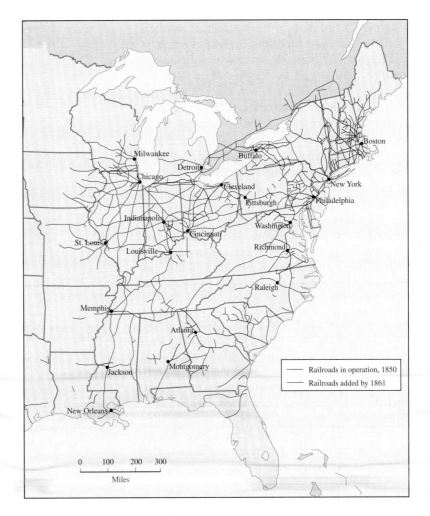

Railroads promoted midwestern prosperity in a variety of ways. They hastened the advance of people onto fresh lands in remote areas that canal and river transport did not serve. They made western farming more profitable by lowering the costs of transporting farm goods (see Map 13.4). And they promoted commerce and manufacturing in the Midwest. Springing up at the points where trunk lines converged or rail routes met water transport were grain storehouses, warehouses, docks, flour mills, packing plants, and farm machinery factories as well as mercantile and financial firms. In 1846 Cyrus McCormick moved his reaper production from western Virginia to Chicago to be closer to his customers. St. Louis and Chicago became boom towns largely because of the railroads. By 1860 they surpassed Boston and Baltimore in size and became the nation's third and fourth largest cities, respectively, after New York and Philadelphia. Taking advantage of the stationary steam engine, St. Louis and Chicago became major industrial centers with strong links to northeastern industrial centers and markets.

The trunk-line railroads undermined the economic base of western cities that had been key regional centers along water routes, especially Cincinnati, Pittsburgh, Buffalo, and Rochester. Thousands of dockworkers, teamsters, and warehouse workers in those cities lost their jobs when the railroads provided efficient through traffic. During the depression of the late 1850s many of those workers roamed the country in search of casual employment or charity.

Railroads also became a force in modernizing the iron industry, a critical component of northeastern manufacturing. This industry responded to the demand of railroads for high-quality iron. By 1860 the rail mills, which were located primarily in and around Philadelphia, were the largest and most technically advanced iron mills in the country. The engineering requirements for train engines had a similar effect on steam engine production. Moreover, to service complex locomotives, the railroads built a large network of machine shops that extended into the Midwest. The spread and expansion of these shops disseminated industrial skills and fostered the development of a skilled labor force.

Links of Culture. The migration of people and capital ensured that cultural links between the Northeast and the Midwest would follow the powerful economic ties despite the high degree of geographical mobility. In migrating westward, people who owned property or had skills faced formidable risks. They knew that in new communities, as in old ones, economic success depended heavily on the quality and strength of personal relationships. In the new communities throughout the Midwest the first residents with property and aspirations created networks among themselves. The first merchants, artisans, and professionals established loyal

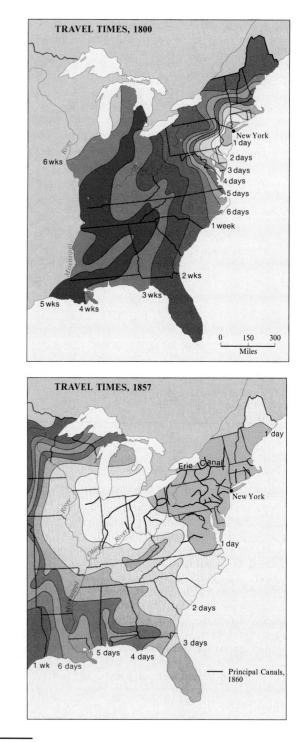

MAP 13.4

The New Mobility of Goods and People, 1800–1857

The transportation revolution dramatically decreased travel times by 1860. In 1800 a traveler from New York required an entire day to reach Philadelphia and a full week to reach Pittsburgh or western New York State. In 1860 a day on the railroad could take a New York traveler as far west as Cleveland. In a week the traveler could reach the Kansas Territory or the uppermost reaches of the Mississippi River.

clienteles, sound reputations, and good credit ratings. From this core came the leaders and prime beneficiaries of the Industrial Revolution. These people celebrated their success, becoming the greatest "boosters" of the new communities.

Later-arriving migrants sought out family members or established friends. Often wives corresponded with sisters, cousins, and old friends to identify communities where their families would find support. As a result, westward migrants usually moved to communities founded by people of similar backgrounds. New Englanders, for example, largely avoided the towns of the Ohio Valley that southerners had established and settled in newer places in northern Ohio, northern Illinois, and Wisconsin. And in their new communities migrants sought out familiar churches, fraternal lodges, crafts, and professions as places to form new friendships.

The first generations of community leaders became patrons of new migrants. They backed ambitious young men who had some education, skill, or family connections and helped them acquire skills or lent them money to start new businesses. Often they supported their daughters' decisions to marry industrious migrants. Many of the young men in turn scouted western opportunities for relatives still living in the East. Conversely, success in the new communities usually required membership in the stable core of local property owners. Through this mechanism the business class of the Midwest established powerful links with its members in the older towns and cities of the Northeast.

Conflict over the Trans-Mississippi West, 1844–1846

In the 1840s American territorial ambitions soared, reaching beyond the area of the Louisiana Purchase to encompass huge new chunks of the continent. Those ambitions meant that the United States could come into conflict with Mexico and Great Britain, the two nations whose territory or claims to territory could block American expansion to the Pacific. At the same time the South and the North came into conflict over the lands west of the Mississippi. Southern leaders recognized that the settlement of northerners in the Old Northwest had become more rapid than that of southerners in the Old Southwest and feared that if that trend extended west of the Mississippi, free states would outnumber slave states. Southern politicians launched a program of acquiring territory to protect slavery on their southern and western boundaries. This policy led the United States toward a war of conquest against Mexico. Ultimately, it put the South on a fateful collision course with the industrializing North.

Manifest Destiny

In the 1840s Americans, both southern and northern, developed a continental vision—captured by the term *Manifest Destiny*. It was coined in 1845 by John L. O'Sullivan, the editor of the *Democratic Review* and the *New York Morning News*, who wrote: "Our manifest destiny is to overspread the continent allotted by Providence for the free development of our yearly multiplying millions." O'Sullivan's vision was shared equally by southern imperialists who wanted to export slavery to new territories and by a northern business class that wanted to expand its dynamic mix of industry and agriculture.

Manifest Destiny expressed the romantic faith of Americans in their special mission to bind together nature, westward settlement, and political freedom. Virtually every aspect of mainstream American culture reinforced the imagery. Artists, for example, gave the message visual form. Thomas Cole (1801–1848) and Asher B. Durand (1796–1886), who started their careers as print engravers, established a national tradition of landscape art. They and their disciples, who were collectively known as the Hudson River School, along with the so-called Rocky Mountain painters, who began working in the 1850s, all viewed painting as a patriotic art—a visual expression of Manifest Destiny. As Philip Hone, one of Cole's patrons, remarked, "Every American is bound to prove his love of country by admiring Cole."

Although other terms had been used to describe the nation's expansionist spirit, Manifest Destiny precisely captured the mood of the 1840s and 1850s and became a permanent part of the American vocabulary. O'Sullivan left the geographical scope of Manifest Destiny vague; America's continental mission might encompass only Oregon, where Britain and the United States had conflicting claims, or it could include parts of Canada and follow the colonization of Texas as a model to reach all of Mexico and even the Caribbean islands.

O'Sullivan meant to imply that the United States had a divinely inspired mission to bring its neighbors, including Mexico, within the American democratic experiment. For behind the rhetoric of Manifest Destiny was cultural arrogance—the assumption of the cultural and even racial superiority of Americans. As "inferior" peoples were brought under American rule, they would be pushed to adopt American forms of government, convert to Protestantism, and learn from American teachers. This arrogance would long shape the nation's relationships with the rest of the world. Also behind the rhetoric of Manifest Destiny were the powerful economic motives that led Boston and New York merchants, southern planters, and small farmers throughout the nation to agree that the United States must expand to the shores of the Pacific.

The Great American Desert and Oregon Fever

By 1840 settlers had pushed westward into Texas, but few other Americans had crossed the 95th meridian. Beyond this north-south line, which lay not far beyond the western boundary of Arkansas and Missouri, stretched what most Americans called the Great American Desert. For fifty years mapmakers had put that label on the Great Plains because they believed the 1820 report of an army explorer, Major Stephen H. Long, who claimed that the entire area between the Missouri River and the Rocky Mountains was "almost wholly unfit for cultivation." This assumption led the federal government to regard the 95th meridian as a permanent frontier between white settlement and the Indian reservations that Andrew Jackson had carved out to the west.

For farmers who poured into the prairies of the Mississippi Valley from New England, New York, and Ohio in the 1840s and 1850s, the 95th meridian was not a meaningful barrier. They had plenty of room to settle in Wisconsin, Iowa, and Minnesota and did not feel overcrowded on the land until after the Civil War. However, for farmers who had filled in the best lands of Louisiana, Arkansas, Missouri, and the Ohio River Valley during the 1830s, the barrier was real. It forced those who sought new land to settle in Texas, which was still alien territory with an uncertain political future; to consider settling among the New Englanders, New Yorkers, and immigrants in the Midwest; or to cast their eyes beyond the Great Plains to the forested valleys of Oregon.

Oregon under Joint Occupation. The United States and Britain both had claims to Oregon. In 1818 a British-American convention had failed to resolve the dispute, establishing the Canadian-American boundary only as far west as the Rocky Mountains. But the convention provided that both British and Americans could settle anywhere in the Oregon Territory, which then stretched from the 42nd parallel in the south (the border with Mexico) to 54° 40' in the north (the border with Russian territory) (see Map 13.5).

Settlement had proceeded without conflict under the joint occupation agreement. The Hudson's Bay Company carried on a lucrative fur trade, while several hundred Americans, including a large group of Methodist missionaries, settled there during the 1830s. Most took up land south of the Columbia River, in the Willamette Valley, which was of little interest to the Hudson's Bay Company. Based on this settlement, the United States established a claim, unchallenged by the British, to the zone between the 42nd parallel and the Columbia River.

In 1842 American interest in Oregon increased dramatically. Navy lieutenant Charles Wilkes published widely circulated reports on his four years of Pacific explorations. He wrote glowingly of the potential harbors

he had found in the Strait of Juan de Fuca, Admiralty Inlet, and Puget Sound, which were of great interest to the New England merchants plying the China trade. Also in 1842 the first large party, over a hundred people, crossed the Oregon Trail, which fur traders and explorers had blazed through the Great Plains and the Rocky Mountains. Their reports told of a mild climate and fertile soil. This publicity and the beginnings of recovery in the rest of the nation from the depression that had followed the Panic of 1837 bred ambitious planning. "Oregon fever" suddenly raged.

The Oregon Trail. The following May a thousand men, women, and children gathered in Independence, Missouri, for the overland trek on what soon became known as the Oregon Trail (see Map 13.6). They were farming and trading families from Missouri, Ohio, Indiana, Illinois, Kentucky, and Tennessee; they had more than 5,000 oxen and cattle and over 100 wagons. With military-style organization and formations, they overcame flooding streams, dust storms, illness and death, insects and snakes, hunger and thirst, bruised feet and ruined clothes, overweight furniture and equipment, dying livestock, and encounters with Indians. (Most of those encounters, however, involved peaceful trade; over the life of the Oregon Trail fewer than 400 travelers died as a result of Indian attacks.) The trail was an ordeal for all, but women found it especially difficult. It

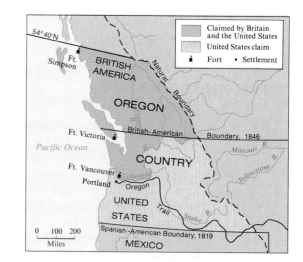

MAP 13.5

Territorial Conflict in Oregon
The American and British governments disputed whether the Oregon Territory should be divided along the Columbia River to include Ft. Vancouver or along the more northerly boundary that eventually divided the two countries. An agreement granting the citizens of each country equal access to Oregon enabled thousands of Americans to pour into the area.

MAP 13.6

Settlement of the Trans-Missouri West, 1840s
In the 1840s several trails carried settlers thousands of miles through unfamiliar and rugged terrain to the trans-Missouri West. Although greed and violence were common on the westward treks, cooperation, trade, and mutual assistance among migrants and with native Americans were more typical.

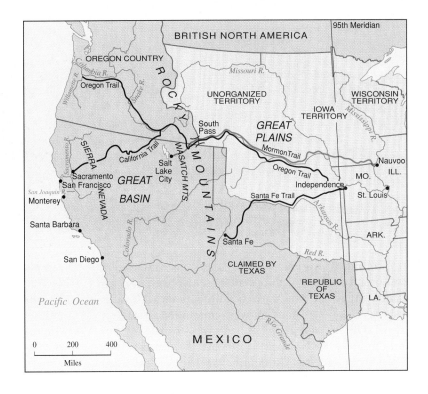

required them to submit to male discipline, add to their traditional chores the strenuous work of driving wagons and animals, and give up domesticity and female friends. After six months on the trail they reached the Willamette Valley—more than 2,000 miles across the continent. During the next two seasons another 5,000 people, still largely from the Ohio Valley, reached Oregon. By the Civil War some 350,000 people had attempted the Oregon Trail, heading for California as well as Oregon; some 34,000 died in the effort—about 17 deaths per mile. The walking migrants wore 3-foot-deep paths, and their wagons carved 5-foot-deep ruts across sandstone formations; the tracks are still visible in southern Wyoming well over a century later.

California. The land-hungry farmers streaming toward Oregon felt more secure settling in areas where the United States had staked out a claim, and they knew more about Oregon than about any other region in the Far West. However, about one in ten of the pioneers traveling the Oregon Trail turned left just past Fort Hall on the Snake River and struggled southward down the California Trail into Mexican territory. Almost all settled in the interior valley of the Sacramento River.

California had been the most remote corner of Spain's American empire, and Spain had been slow to develop its resources. In fact, Spain established a significant foothold there only in the late eighteenth century, when it built a system of missions and *presidios* stretching from San Diego to San Francisco (see Chapter 8). Almost immediately, in the 1780s, New England merchants began trading with the Spanish settlements in

California, largely for sea otter pelts that they carried to China. Their commerce increased after Mexico won its independence from Spain in 1822. At the same time, other American traders carried on a small but lucrative trade in gold, furs, and mules between Independence, Missouri, and Santa Fe, following the Santa Fe Trail.

To promote economic development, the new Mexican government welcomed Yankee traders to California. To the same end, it secularized the missions and promoted large-scale cattle ranching on former mission lands. Secularization also released the mission Indians, who numbered about 21,000 in 1821. Many left coastal communities for interior areas of California, where 200,000 Indians lived, but many others remained to become laborers, often in peonage on large *ranchos*. Some intermarried with the local *mestizos* ("mixed blood" Spanish-Indians). All of this meant prosperity to the New England merchants who brought hides and tallow from California ranchos home to the boot and shoe industry. To handle the business, beginning in the 1820s, New Englanders dispatched dozens of resident agents to the coastal towns of California. More often than not they fell in love with California, married into the families of the elite Mexicans—the *Californios*—became Catholics and Mexican citizens, and adopted the dress and manners of the *Californios*. A crucial exception was Thomas Oliver Larkin, the most successful merchant in Monterey. Larkin established a close working relationship with Mexican authorities and often lent them money but remained an American citizen and plotted for the peaceful annexation of Upper California. In 1843 he became the U.S. consul in California.

The Monterey Colonial House
Thomas O. Larkin's house, completed in
1837, represented the fusing of American and Mexican building traditions
and set architectural fashions during
the early 1840s for the American and
Mexican elite in Monterey. The house
combined eastern features, such as a
symmetrical facade and a timber frame
supporting an upper story, with adobe
construction.

In contrast with most of the Americans who lived in
the coastal towns of California, the settlers in the Sacramento Valley had no desire to assimilate into Mexican
society. Their legal standing was tenuous. Most had received dubious land grants or had simply squatted without any title. They hoped to emulate the Americans in
Texas by colonizing, extinguishing what they regarded
as an inferior culture, and making California another
example of the beneficent workings of Manifest Destiny. Their number grew swiftly, to about 700 in 1845,
while the coastal population of 7,000 Mexicans, an uncounted number of Indians, and roughly 300 Americans
remained stable.

Southern Imperialism

During the 1840s the South aggressively tried to protect
slavery where it existed by extending it to new lands.
Some planters wanted to make sure they did not run out
of fertile land. Southern politicians also realized that
every new free state in the West increased the threat of
abolition by shifting power in Congress toward the
North. Moreover, if the federal government did not protect slavery in the West, it would sanction what white
southerners believed to be a denial of their rights as free
Americans. They feared that if Congress failed to protect southern rights in the territories, it might not respect those rights within the states of the South.

Anxiety about the future of slavery in the West was
nothing new. Southerners had pressed for the acquisition of Louisiana and Florida in order to gain new lands
where slavery could expand. They had also cited the
Monroe Doctrine to warn the British not to interfere
with slavery anywhere in the Western Hemisphere.
When Britain abolished slavery in the West Indies in
1833, southern planters feared that pressures for emancipation would release a wave of slave rebellions like
Nat Turner's. The planters also were afraid that Britain
would actively encourage abolition in the United States
to undermine the American plantation economy and increase the international competitiveness of British plan-

tations in India and Egypt. Calhoun proposed that the
British wished to abolish slavery in the United States
and Brazil to "transfer the production of cotton, rice,
and sugar etc. to her colonial possessions, and . . . consummate the system of commercial monopoly, which
she has been so long and systematically pursuing." The
annexation of Texas, which had declared independence
in 1836, had offered an opportunity to avoid abolitionist containment of slavery, but both Andrew Jackson
and Martin Van Buren had deflected this push in the interest of party and national unity.

During the 1840s the planters' worries intensified.
They noted that in 1839 Britain, along with France, had
intervened in Mexico to force it to pay its debts, and
they heard rumors that Britain wanted California as
payment. They saw evidence that Britain was encouraging Texas to remain independent, was expanding its involvement in Central America, and had designs on
Cuba. It all seemed to add up to a grand scheme by the
British to block American expansion by establishing an
antislavery barrier from the West Indies through Mexican territory—a barrier sweeping from Texas all the
way to California. The result, southerners feared,
would be not only an end to economic opportunity but
increasing pressure for emancipation in the South. A
surrounding ring of free territory could provide bases
for abolitionist raids on plantations and provide havens
for runaway slaves.

The Election of 1844

Oregon fever opened the door for southern leaders who
wanted to protect slavery through a program of territorial expansion. Suddenly, in 1843, northerners as well
as southerners were calling for territorial expansion.
This northern support for expansion finally made it
possible for southern leaders to champion the annexation of Texas without threatening the unity of the Democratic party.

In 1843 Americans throughout the Ohio Valley and
the Great Lakes states called on the federal government

to renounce joint occupation and oust the British from Oregon. Democrats and Whigs jointly organized "Oregon conventions" throughout the Midwest. In July a bipartisan national convention demanded that the United States seize Oregon all the way to 54° 40' north latitude, the southern limit of Russian-controlled Alaska.

Meanwhile, President John Tyler, disowned by the Whigs, had joined the Democratic party in the hope of becoming its nominee in 1844. In 1843 Tyler settled on a program designed to please expansionists among both southern and northern Democrats: the annexation of Texas and the seizure of Oregon to the 54° 40' line.

As a first step toward annexing Texas, Tyler appointed Senator John C. Calhoun of South Carolina as secretary of state in 1844. Calhoun had rejoined the Democratic party because he feared the national economic program and abolitionist tendencies of the Whigs. Convinced that it was necessary to prevent British domination of the West, Tyler and Calhoun submitted an annexation treaty to the Senate in April. In July Calhoun brushed aside an offer from the British, now fearful of American hostility, to settle the Oregon question.

The treaty encountered opposition from two leaders with presidential ambitions in 1844: the Democrat Martin Van Buren and the Whig Henry Clay. Each feared alienating northern voters by supporting the annexation of Texas. At their urging, Whigs and northern Democrats united to defeat the treaty.

The Candidacy of James K. Polk. The economic issues that had dominated the presidential campaign of 1840 gave way to the issues of Texas and Oregon in 1844. The Democrats had great success in unifying their party on Texas. They passed over both Tyler, who had failed to win the trust of his adopted party, and Van Buren, whom southern Democrats despised for failing to sup-

port their position on Texas. Instead, they selected former Governor James K. Polk of Tennessee, a slave owner who was Andrew Jackson's personal favorite. Polk was unimpressive in appearance, but he was a man of iron will and boundless ambition for the nation. He and the Democrats called for the annexation of Texas and the taking of all of Oregon. "Fifty-four forty or fight!" became the war cry of his campaign.

The Whigs were less successful in uniting their party. They nominated Henry Clay, who once again championed his American System of internal improvements, high tariffs, and national banking. Throughout his campaign Clay was defensive about his opposition to the annexation of Texas. He finally suggested, but only hesitantly, that he might support annexation under certain circumstances. His position annoyed many southern Whigs, who were willing to bolt the party, sacrificing its economic program in return for the annexation of Texas. At the same time, Clay disappointed the thousands of northern Whigs who opposed any expansion of slavery. His waffling on Texas led them to support the Liberty party candidate, James G. Birney of Kentucky. Birney won less than 3 percent of the popular vote, but he might have taken enough votes from Clay to deprive Clay of the electoral votes of New York and Michigan, with which he would have won. That was the conclusion of Clay's supporters, who blamed his defeat on the desertion of both proslavery and abolitionist Whigs.

Polk and a Democratic majority in Congress were elected by voters who had accepted the argument of Tyler and Calhoun that the British were determined to block the expansion of the republic into Oregon and Mexico. Many Americans who might have otherwise opposed the extension of slavery had accepted Tyler and Calhoun's linkage of the Texas and Oregon issues and endorsed Polk's territorial ambitions. Thus, the strategy that Tyler and Calhoun devised and Polk implemented of uniting Democrats around expansion in Texas and Oregon had succeeded.

Congress Votes for Texas Annexation. Polk's victory led northern Democrats in Congress to reject Van Buren's leadership, close ranks with southern Democrats, and annex Texas even before Polk's inauguration. In February 1845 proannexation Democrats finessed the opposition of antislavery senators by approving annexation through a joint resolution, which required majority votes in both houses rather than the two-thirds Senate vote needed to ratify a treaty. Mexico challenged the legality of annexation—it had never recognized Texas's independence—and broke diplomatic relations with the United States. The continuing dispute with Mexico would soon give Polk the opportunity he sought to go beyond his party's 1844 platform and acquire New Mexico, Alta (Upper California), and perhaps more Mexican territory (see Chapter 14).

A Polk Political Banner, 1844
The "lone star" outside the group of twenty-six stars represents Texas. The banner was intended to leave no doubt about the importance of the annexation of Texas to Polk's presidential campaign.

Summary

During the 1840s and 1850s southern society became increasingly dependent on slavery. Planters exploited the system of slavery more aggressively as a source of profits and developed an elaborate defense of it in order to control slaves and guarantee the loyalty of non-slaveholding whites. In response to the cruel realities of slavery, which included harsh work routines and trading in human lives, slaves devised elaborate networks of family and community support. Outside the formal system of slavery in the South there was a large community of free African-Americans. They, as well as free blacks in the North, had second-class citizenship but helped keep alive the hope of freedom from slavery.

Meanwhile, industrialization tightened its hold on northeastern society by stimulating economic productivity, middle-class consumption, and business-class culture. Industrialization also promoted immigration, which accelerated during the 1840s and 1850s. Many of the new immigrants, especially those from Ireland, were poor and encountered a virulent anti-Catholic movement. Industrialization accelerated the settlement of the Old Northwest, helping to fill the land of the Great Lakes Basin and the prairies of the Mississippi Valley with people from the Northeast and stimulating the commerce and industry in new midwestern towns and cities. Settlers in the Midwest replicated the links among agriculture, community life, and industry that prevailed in the Northeast. In short, industrialization bound together the Northeast and the Midwest.

Both northerners and southerners agreed on the need for continued westward expansion and on the Manifest Destiny of continental expansion. Consequently, during the 1840s they embarked on great migrations across the Great Plains to British-American Oregon and to the vast territories of Mexican California. These migrations and the nationwide support they received created an opportunity for southern leaders such as John C. Calhoun to develop a program of expansion that promised to relieve anxiety over British and abolitionist threats to slavery. In 1844 James K. Polk won the presidency by promising to implement part of this program: annexing Texas and taking all of Oregon. Temporarily masked by national support for Polk's 1844 platform was the fact that the South's commitment to a slave-labor system had placed the region in direct competition with the North over the future of the West.

TIMELINE

1841	Catharine Beecher's *Treatise on Domestic Economy* James Fenimore Cooper's *The Deerslayer*
1842	Charles Wilkes reports on Pacific explorations Migration to Oregon begins
1843	Calhoun warns of a British conspiracy to block expansion Thomas Oliver Larkin becomes U.S. consul in California Oregon conventions organized
1844	Anti-Catholic rioting in Philadelphia Tyler appoints John C. Calhoun as secretary of state James K. Polk elected president
1845	Lowell Female Labor Reform Association formed Editor John L. O'Sullivan coins the term *Manifest Destiny* Texas admitted to the Union as a slave state
1846	Democratic Congress restores the Independent Treasury Walker Tariff passed Mexican War begins Cyrus McCormick opens Chicago factory
1847	Refugees from Irish potato famine arrive in large numbers Hoe rotary press introduced
1849	Cholera epidemics in cities
1850	A. J. Downing's *The Architecture of Country Houses*
1851	Crystal Palace Exhibition
1852	*Uncle Tom's Cabin*
1857	Economic panic begins depression
1858	Mason jar introduced
1859	Railroads carry more freight than do canals

★   ★   ★

BIBLIOGRAPHY

There are no general surveys of the social history of sections and sectionalism during the 1840s and 1850s; useful books on major aspects of the subject include Stuart M. Blumin, *The Emergence of the Middle Class: Social Experience in the American City, 1760–1900* (1989); Albert Fishlow, *American Railroads and the Transformation of the Ante-Bellum Economy* (1965); Robert W. Fogel, *Without Consent or Contract* (1989); David Alan Johnson, *Founding the Far West: California, Oregon, and Nevada, 1840–1890* (1992); James Oakes, *The Ruling Race: A History of American Slaveholders* (1982); and William R. Taylor, *Cavalier and Yankee: The Old South and American National Character* (1961).

The Slave South

The culture of the planter class and non-slaveholding whites can be explored in O. Vernon Burton, *In My Father's House Are Many Mansions: Family and Community in Edgefield, South Carolina* (1985), and Drew Gilpin Faust, *Southern Stories: Slaveholders in Peace and War* (1992). The best studies of women in southern slave society are Catherine Clinton, *The Plantation Mistress* (1983), and Elizabeth Fox-Genovese, *Within the Plantation Household: Black and White Women of the Old South* (1988). Efforts to connect southern culture with southern politics include George M. Frederickson, *White Supremacy: A Comparative Study in American and South African History* (1981), and J. Mills Thornton III, *Politics and Power in a Slave Society: Alabama, 1800–1860* (1978). On the nature of violence in southern society, see John Hope Franklin, *The Militant South 1800–1861* (1956), and Bertram Wyatt-Brown, *Southern Honor: Ethics and Behavior in the Old South* (1982).

On the role of family life and religion in helping African-Americans cope with the oppression of slavery, the pioneering studies were John W. Blassingame, *The Slave Community: Plantation Life in the Antebellum South* (1979); Eugene D. Genovese, *Roll, Jordan, Roll* (1974); Herbert G. Gutman, *The Black Family in Slavery and Freedom, 1750–1925* (1976); and Lawrence W. Levine, *Black Culture and Black Consciousness* (1977). More recent studies include Jacqueline Jones, *Labor of Love, Labor of Sorrow: Black Women, Work, and the Family from Slavery to the Present* (1986), and Deborah G. White, *Ar'n't I a Woman? Female Slaves in the Plantation South* (1985).

On slave revolts see Herbert Aptheker, *American Negro Slave Revolts* (1943); Stephen B. Oates, *The Fires of Jubilee: Nat Turner's Fierce Rebellion* (1975); Eugene D. Genovese, *From Rebellion to Revolution: Afro-American Slave Revolts in the Making of the Modern World* (1979); and Winthrop D. Jordan, *Tumult and Silence at Second Creek: An Inquiry into a Civil War Slave Conspiracy* (1993). On the ambiguous position of free blacks in slave society, see Ira Berlin, *Slaves without Masters: The Free Negro in the Antebellum South* (1974).

The Northeast and the Midwest

The economic changes in the North during the 1840s and 1850s can be studied in many of the economic history sources listed in Chapter 10.

On the sources and character of European immigration, consult Maldwyn Allen Jones, *American Immigration* (1960), and Philip Taylor, *The Distant Magnet: European Immigration to the U.S.A.* (1971). The most useful introduction to the nature of immigrant communities during the 1840s and 1850s is Oscar Handlin, *Boston's Immigrants: A Study in Acculturation* (1979). See also Kathleen Neils Conzen, *Immigrant Milwaukee, 1836–1860* (1976), and Bruce Laurie, *Working People in Philadelphia, 1800–1850* (1980).

No scholarly book surveys the development of middle-class society culture in the decades before the Civil War. Explorations of the relationship between women's roles and the development of popular literature include Ann Douglas, *The Feminization of American Culture* (1977), and Mary Kelley, *Private Woman, Public Stage: Literary Domesticity in Nineteenth-Century America* (1984). On birth control see Linda Gordon, *Woman's Body, Woman's Rights: A Social History of Birth Control in America* (1976), and James Reed, *From Private Vice to Public Virtue: The Birth Control Movement and American Society since 1830* (1978). On educational reform see Lawrence A. Cremin, *American Education: the National Experience, 1783–1876* (1980); Carl F. Kaestle, *Pillars of the Republic: Common Schools and American Society, 1780–1860* (1983); and Stanley K. Schultz, *The Culture Factory: Boston Public Schools, 1789–1860* (1973). On the Beecher family see Jeanne Boyston et al., eds., *The Limits of Sisterhood: The Beecher Sisters on Women's Rights and Woman's Sphere* (1988); Milton Rugoff, *The Beechers: An American Family in the Nineteenth Century* (1981); and Kathryn Kish Sklar, *Catharine Beecher: A Study in American Domesticity* (1973), which is a definitive biography.

Conflict over the Trans-Mississippi West

Manifest Destiny is treated in Norman Graebner, *Empire on the Pacific: A Study of American Continental Expansion* (1955); Reginald Horsman, *Race and Manifest Destiny: The Origins of American Racial Anglo-Saxonism* (1981); Frederick Merk, *Manifest Destiny and Mission in American History* (1963); and Albert K. Weinberg, *Manifest Destiny: A Study of Nationalist Expansionism in American History* (1935).

In recent years a number of books have opened up exciting new approaches to the history of western America. Leading examples of this scholarship include Patricia Nelson Limerick, *The Legacy of Conquest: The Unbroken Past of the Unbroken West* (1987); Clyde A. Milner II, *The Oxford History of the American West* (1994); Kevin Starr, *Americans and the California Dream, 1850–1915* (1973); David J. Weber, *The Mexican Frontier, 1821–1846* (1982); and Richard White, *"It's Your Misfortune and None of My Own": A History of the American West* (1991). This newer scholarship presents a more complete view of women in the West. See, for example, Susan Armitage and Elizabeth Jameson, eds., *The Women's West* (1987); John Mack Faragher, *Women and Men on the Overland Trail* (1979); Julie R. Jeffrey, *Frontier Women: The Trans-Mississippi West, 1840–1860* (1979); and Joanna L. Stratton, *Pioneer Women: Voices from the Kansas Frontier* (1981).

On the politics of expansion to the Pacific see William J. Cooper, *The South and the Politics of Slavery, 1828–1856* (1978); and Charles G. Sellers, *James K. Polk: Continentalist, 1843–1846* (1966).

John Brown (1800–1859)

Just before his hanging, John Brown wrote out a prophetic message: "I John Brown am now quite *certain* that the crimes of this *guilty land*: will never be purged *away*; but with Blood."

CHAPTER 14

Disrupting the Union

1846–1860

★　　　　★　　　　★

For nearly a generation after the Missouri Compromise in 1820 the two major parties succeeded in preventing the issue of slavery from polarizing the nation. They were able to do this even after the democratization of politics under the Second Party System and after a confrontation between evangelical abolitionism and the proslavery movement. The two parties devised programs that were *national* in appeal and built coalitions of groups and interests that were national in scope. Both parties struggled to avoid the slavery issue because they recognized its potential for fracturing the parties and the nation along sectional lines. In the early 1840s prospects for continuing to blunt the divisive potential of slavery seemed bright because abolitionism was stalled by the antiabolitionist movement and the split between Garrisonians and anti-Garrisonians.

The sectional arrangement of 1820 had survived into the 1840s for another reason as well: northern and southern societies had been able to expand into the West without appearing to threaten each other. But the Mexican War—and the acquisition of immense new territories in the West—changed everything.

After the Mexican War national politicians searched for a formula to resolve the status of slavery in the new lands, but their compromises became increasingly fragile as Americans took matters into their own hands. Abolitionists fought off slave catchers in northern towns, and free-soilers and defenders of slavery attacked each other in "Bleeding Kansas." When the radical abolitionist John Brown attempted to incite a slave rebellion, many southerners became convinced that only secession could protect their "peculiar institution."

The Mexican War and Its Aftermath, 1846–1850

Territorial expansion was the main goal of President James K. Polk, who had been elected on a platform that called for taking all of Oregon and annexing Texas. He and his administration were convinced that they had a national mandate for an even more ambitious and aggressive program of westward expansion. They believed that Americans wanted Polk to go beyond his party's 1844 platform and acquire additional lands—New Mexico, Alta (Upper) California, and perhaps even more of Mexico's territory. The war of conquest that followed brought huge new territories into the United States and doomed the Missouri Compromise as a means of reconciling the interests of the South and the North in the West.

The Mexican War, 1846–1848

Polk's Expansionist Program. Polk took office in March 1845 with the intention of completing the annexation of Texas and acquiring at least California and New Mexico from Mexico. Shortly after his inauguration Polk told his secretary of the navy that he regarded the acquisition of California to be as important as the "Oregon question." He would try diplomacy but was prepared to go to war if that failed. In April he sent a confidential agent to Mexico to see whether Mexico's government was willing to resume diplomatic relations and negotiate a settlement that would resolve differences over Texas and possibly even transfer California to the United States.

On July 4, 1845, Texas formally decided to join the United States but claimed that the Rio Grande was its western and southern boundary, despite the fact that its boundary had never extended beyond the Nueces River under Spanish and Mexican rule and that the Mexican government had rejected the claim. Polk agreed with Texas, and to strengthen his hand in negotiations he ordered Brigadier General Zachary Taylor, an army veteran with almost forty years of service, to lead several thousand troops to occupy the disputed territory south of the Nueces. Taylor camped near the town of Corpus Christi, just south of the Nueces at its mouth (see Map 14.1). By October, Taylor had doubled his force, making it the largest concentration of American troops since the War of 1812.

In November, after learning that Mexico would receive an American minister, Polk dispatched a secret emissary to Mexico City. Polk instructed John Slidell to buy New Mexico and California and secure acceptance of the Rio Grande boundary for as much as $30 million and American assumption of the claims of American citizens against the Mexican government. But Slidell was instructed not to discuss the right of the United States to annex Texas and to make no deal that sacrificed the Rio Grande boundary. Mexico, however, rejected the legality of the American annexation of Texas and refused to see Slidell when he arrived during the first week of December. The central objective of the Mexican government was to maintain national honor and protect valuable lands from an aggressive neighbor. Mexican leaders hoped that the United States would become embroiled in a war with Britain that would divert it from its southwestern ambitions. But Mexico was prepared to fight if necessary.

The same week Slidell arrived in Mexico City, Polk unveiled a new policy toward Britain. In a bellicose State of the Union Message to Congress the president claimed that British intentions in the Pacific Northwest violated the Monroe Doctrine. Polk intended to drive the British from Oregon and discourage them from taking California, which they wanted as compensation for debts owed to them by Mexico.

Meanwhile, Polk advanced his plans to take Alta California. His strategy was to foment a revolution that would lead, as had been the case in Texas, to the creation of an independent republic and a request for annexation. In October 1845 Polk's secretary of state, James Buchanan, advised Thomas O. Larkin, the U.S. consul in the major port of Monterey, that the United States would protect Californians if they sought independence from Mexico. If the Californians "should desire to unite their destiny with ours," Larkin added, Americans would welcome them as "brethren." Larkin began a quiet campaign among leading citizens, including some powerful *Californios*, in the coastal settlements to win support for a peaceful shift of sovereignty. However, Polk also prepared for war. He sent secret orders for John Sloat, the commander of the U.S. naval squadron in the Pacific, to seize San Francisco Bay and California's coastal towns if Mexico declared war on the United States. And Polk followed the activities of a young army officer, Captain John C. Frémont, who, under War Department orders, had struck out from St. Louis and marched deep into Mexican territory in the spring of 1845 with an "exploring" party of heavily armed soldiers. Frémont later wrote that "in arranging this expedition, the eventualities of war were taken into consideration." In December 1845 he reached California's Sacramento Valley and received permission from the Mexican commander in Monterey to winter in California if he stayed away from the coastal communities. In March, however, Frémont engaged in a show of force, even building fortifications near Monterey. But when Mexican authorities threatened to fight and Larkin warned Frémont that conflict would ruin the chances for the peaceful acquisition of California, he withdrew across the Oregon border.

In January 1846, when Polk learned of the failure of Slidell's mission, he increased the military pressure on Mexico. In the disputed territory between the Rio

MAP 14.1

The Mexican War, 1846–1848

This map shows the major military expeditions that seized the northern frontier of Mexico and occupied Mexico City. In the last phase of the war, as Winfield Scott assembled an invasion army off the coast of Mexico, Santa Anna tried to take advantage of the division of American forces by attacking the army of Zachary Taylor. At Buena Vista (February 1847) Taylor's smaller forces repulsed Santa Anna, who had to return to defend Mexico City. Scott's most significant victory in his march on Mexico City came in the mountains, at Cerro Gordo.

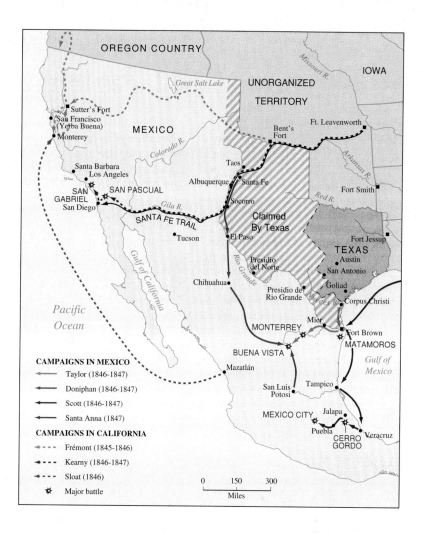

Grande and the Nueces, Polk created an incident designed to insult the Mexicans by sending General Taylor southward to establish a fort near the Rio Grande. As Ulysses S. Grant, a young officer serving with Taylor, said much later, "We were sent to provoke a fight, but it was essential that Mexico should commence it." Also, Secretary of State Buchanan sent secret orders to Frémont, which reached him in Oregon in May. Frémont destroyed the orders, along with a letter from Thomas Hart Benton, an expansionist senator from Missouri who chaired the Committee on Territories. The precise contents of the communications from Washington are unknown, but Frémont marched back to California and established a base near Sacramento. He later described his return as "the first step in the conquest of California."

News of skirmishing between Mexican and American forces near the Rio Grande reached Polk in early May. On May 9 he delivered a war message he had drafted long before, saying that Mexico "has passed the boundary of the United States, has invaded our territory, and shed American blood upon the American soil." Congress declared war four days later, and that action was followed by large, almost hysterical demonstrations of support across the nation. An editorial in the New York *Herald* declared that the war would "lay

the foundation of a new age, a new destiny, affecting both this continent and the old continent of Europe."

Meanwhile, Polk worked to avoid a simultaneous war with Britain, even though that meant betraying his promise to northern Democrats. He recommended that the Senate adopt the British proposal to divide the Oregon country at the 49th parallel. The Senate agreed, ratifying the Oregon Treaty on June 15, 1846. (In 1848 Congress organized the Oregon Territory, and in 1859 it admitted the state of Oregon to the Union.)

The War in California. In June 1846 the Americans in the interior, although unaware of the formal state of war between the United States and Mexico, staged a revolt and captured the town of Sonoma with the support of Frémont's forces. Frémont did not have formal authority to take California, so he prevented the rebelling Americans from flying the Stars and Stripes. The Americans designed a crude flag displaying the strongest animal in California and proclaimed the Bear Flag Republic on July 4. Commander Sloat, knowing that hostilities with Mexico had broken out south of the Nueces, landed 250 marines and seamen in Monterey. He declared that California "henceforward will be a portion of the United States" and raised the American flag.

Captain Franklin Smith

Behind the Lines in the Mexican War

Captain Franklin Smith (1807–?) was the quartermaster for the First Mississippi Regiment of volunteers stationed in Carmargo, Mexico, in 1846 and 1847. Carmargo, just south of the Rio Grande, was a major supply base for Zachary Taylor's army. Smith organized supply trains sent from Carmargo to Monterrey and points farther south; he followed and at times participated in a bitter guerrilla war in northern Mexico between the U.S. Army and the Mexican rancheros. After the war Smith returned to a law practice in Canton, Mississippi. Little is known about his life there except for an unsuccessful effort in 1855 to publish the journal he had kept in Carmargo. He believed his descriptions of "the miseries, the disgraces, the infamies of war" might help persuade Americans to find a way to avoid a civil war.

October 3d, 1846. In the evening Col. Redd commanding [sic] the Georgia Cos. [volunteer companies] called at my tent and took supper with me. He is a young man about 23 gallant and brave as a lion. . . . He thinks now they [the Mexicans] are learning to shoot better and from late indications are united and patriotic, he thinks the fighting has just commenced. He says

it is his intention not to trouble Genl. Patterson with prisoners—but hang all Mexicans who give him battle here to Monterrey or present themselves in hostile array. I told him I thought he ought not to hang but if he killed them that hanging would have a tendency to arouse the spirit of indignation and produce probably a rise en masse.

January 19th, 1847. America was designed to be the defender not the oppressor of man—An asylum for truth, justice, and liberty! And whenever she forgets the old reading and her early teachings and begins a career of conquest and dominion . . . which will end in her overthrow. . . . Our liberties may prove unsafe in our own hands (God grant they may not) but one thing is certain they would be very unsafe in the hands of the Mexicans. We should therefore whip the Mexicans first and then examine the ancient land-marks of our constitution and the principles of our Revolution and see how far we have strayed . . . from the line of Right.

January 29th, 1847. Had these people [the Mexicans] sense they would desire to have the laws of the American Union extended over them to shield them from Robbers, their own government and the Comanches to whose in-

roads in turn they are perpetually exposed. . . . But . . . their hatred to the Americans is deep seated. Those who have joined us will become outcasts—with the great mass hatred to Americans will become an inheritance from father to son. I believe if this war is continued beyond May rivers of blood will flow before it ceases while thousands and tens of thousands of our brave men will perish . . . one thing I am satisfied that the longer the war lasts the more national it will become and the more will disappear the prospect of the two races ever living together in harmony.

January 31st, 1847. The Col. then gave orders to burn the Ranche which consisted of one dwelling-house main ranche, one out house as a kitchen, and one other out house filled with corn shucks, fodder, and wool—This was a proper order. The Ranche was undoubtedly the head quarters of the Robbers. . . . The main building contained lances, escopettes [short muskets], swords, pistols, and all the appliances of war.

Source: Joseph E. Chance, ed., *The Mexican War Journal of Captain Frank Smith* (Jackson: University Press of Mississippi, 1991), 31–32, 157, 179, 196, 199–200.

American forces quickly moved to gain control of New Mexico and all of California. A small army under General Stephen Kearney captured Santa Fe without opposition in August and then marched on to California. By autumn Frémont and Commodore Robert F. Stockton, who had assumed command of the U.S. forces in California, seemed to have subdued the province. But in the southern part of Alta California the Mexicans mounted stiff resistance, driving the Americans from Los Angeles and winning a victory over Kearney's forces at the Battle of San Pascual outside San Diego. Only reinforcements under Stockton turned the tide, allowing Kearney and Stockton to retake Los Angeles in a decisive battle at the San Gabriel River. By mid-January

1847 the combined American forces had also captured San Francisco, Santa Barbara, and San Diego. In his diary, Polk wrote that he would accept no treaty that failed to cede New Mexico and California to the United States.

Across the Rio Grande. On May 1, even before Congress declared war, Zachary Taylor's army moved decisively toward the Rio Grande. After two bloody battles in which the outnumbered American forces displayed their great advantage in artillery, Taylor crossed the Rio Grande and occupied Matamoros. On September 25, 1846, after a fierce six-day battle, Taylor took the interior town of Monterrey (see American Voices, above). In

November a U.S. naval squadron in the Gulf of Mexico seized Tampico, Mexico's second most important port, as a base for an inland assault. In December another force, under Colonel Alfred A. Doniphan, set out on a 600-mile march south from Santa Fe toward Chihuahua, which it took in March 1847. By the end of 1846 the United States controlled a long line across northeastern Mexico.

Polk expected that the Mexicans, having lost large territories and with no chance of winning Britain as an ally, would sue for peace. But he had underrated Mexican national pride and strength. Under the leadership of General Antonio Lopez de Santa Anna, who was elected president in December 1846, Mexico refused to agree to a peace, let alone a cession of territory. Polk, supported by Winfield Scott, the commanding general of the army, decided to strike deep into the heart of Mexico. In November 1846 Polk decided to send Scott to storm the port of Veracruz and advance 260 miles inland to Mexico City. But while Scott gathered his forces, a large Mexican army under Santa Anna attacked the depleted units of Zachary Taylor at Buena Vista on February 22, 1847. The outcome was uncertain and the fighting was intense, but superiority in artillery enabled Taylor to eke out a victory and hold the American line in northeastern Mexico.

In March 1847 Scott captured Veracruz. Leading Scott's 14,000 troops were talented West Point officers who would become famous in the Civil War: Robert E. Lee, George Meade, and P. G. T. Beauregard. Scott then boldly moved his army inland. Well-read soldiers realized that they were following the route of Cortés's Spanish conquerors three centuries earlier and even looked

Mexican War Volunteers, 1846
This daguerreotype by an unknown photographer shows volunteers from Exeter, New Hampshire, preparing for war. When news of Zachary Taylor's victories reached most towns, men scrambled to volunteer before the war was over. In New York, Herman Melville wrote that "people here are all in a state of delirium. . . . Nothing is talked of but the 'Halls of the Montezumas.'"

for the locations of Cortés's battles. Scott's forces persistently outflanked the enemy during a 7,400-foot climb over rugged terrain. At Cerro Gordo his troops crushed Santa Anna's attempt to block their march, although both armies suffered heavy casualties. On August 20, at the Battle of Churubusco, near Mexico City, Santa

Street Fighting in Monterrey, 1846
The taking of Monterrey, which Spain's troops had been unable to capture during Mexico's war for independence, was a bloody affair of house-to-house fighting. Americans, however, immediately romanticized it. This is a typical lithograph of the day, picturing soldiers fighting in what seems to be a medieval setting.

Anna lost more than 4,000 of the 25,000 soldiers in his army while Scott's forces, which casualties and garrison requirements had already reduced to 10,000, sustained 1,000 casualties. Scott finally seized Mexico City on September 14, 1847, and a new Mexican government had no choice but to make peace.

National euphoria had accompanied the early phase of the war, peaking with Taylor's occupation of Matamoros. Many Americans initially viewed the war as a noble struggle to promote republican ideals in the spirit of the American Revolution. A U.S. victory, they believed, would secure American institutions in the West and free Mexico from a corrupt, weak regime that might fall under the influence of ambitious European monarchies. And at the end of the war, whatever they thought about its goals, even more Americans agreed with Polk's judgment that the war had demonstrated that a democratic republic could fight a foreign war "with the vigor" characteristic of "more arbitrary forms of government."

A few Whigs, such as Charles Francis Adams of Massachusetts and Joshua Giddings of Ohio, called "conscience Whigs" because of their antislavery views, had denounced the war from the start as part of a proslavery conspiracy. Most Whigs, however, had participated in or at least tolerated the national enthusiasm for the early phase of the war. But by the time news of Scott's victory in Mexico City reached Washington, the nation was badly divided over its war aims, and Whig opposition had become stronger and bolder.

Whig leaders in the North were ready to move toward antislavery positions partly because their championing of Henry Clay's American System no longer seemed to help them win national elections. In July 1846 Polk and the Congressional Democrats acted on their belief that they had a popular mandate not only to pursue territorial expansion but also to overturn the American System. They restored the Independent Treasury (see Chapter 11) and passed the Walker Tariff, which dramatically reduced tariffs and paid only lip service to the principle of protectionism. The Walker Tariff paralleled Britain's repeal of the Corn Laws (tariffs on imported bread grains) in the same year and seemed to herald the adoption of free trade throughout the Anglo-American world. Trade and tariff revenues were so buoyant that the Polk administration did not have to raise taxes to pay for the war. Existing taxes funded more than 60 percent of the $100 million of wartime costs, and borrowing covered the rest. After the war the continued robustness of customs duties enabled the federal government to pay off nearly all its Mexican War debts by the time of the Civil War. Demoralized by the popularity of the Polk administration's economic programs, Congressional Whigs lost their enthusiasm for campaigning on the American System.

Northern Whigs who were critical of the Mexican War drew confidence from the elections of 1846, which gave their party control of Congress, and increasing numbers of northern Whigs began to agree with the conscience Whigs. Additional slave states in the West might jeopardize the expansion of free agriculture and assure control of the federal government by the Democratic representatives of planters and immigrants. They grew more vocal as the casualties mounted, particularly during the bloody march to Mexico City. Of the 92,000 Americans who bore arms during the war, over 13,000 were killed or died of disease. After Taylor's victory at Buena Vista, the House passed a resolution thanking him—but not until the Whigs had amended it to declare that the war had been "unconstitutionally and unnecessarily begun by the President."

The Wilmot Proviso. It was a Democrat, however, who had devised the most disruptive way of opposing the war. On a warm August evening in 1846, David Wilmot, a congressman who was trying to broaden his base of support in his Pennsylvania district, proposed a simple amendment to a military appropriations bill: slavery would be prohibited in any territory acquired from Mexico. This provision, known as the Wilmot Proviso, quickly became the rallying point for northerners who feared the expansion of slavery into the West.

The Wilmot Proviso gained strong bipartisan support from northern Democrats as well as Whigs, particularly after Scott's costly invasion of Mexico. In the House a minority of Democrats, including key supporters of Martin Van Buren, joined forces with most Whigs to pass it on several occasions, but the predominantly southern, more proslavery Senate killed it each time. The legislatures of fourteen northern states passed resolutions urging their senators to vote for it.

Meanwhile, the most fervent expansionists among the Democrats became even more aggressive. They argued that the rising cost of the war meant that the nation should enlarge its war aims. The national Democratic party leaders—Polk, Secretary of State Buchanan, and senators Stephen A. Douglas of Illinois and Jefferson Davis of Mississippi—all wanted the United States to take at least part of Mexico south of the Rio Grande.

That goal put the Democratic leadership at odds with the vocal antislavery minority of northeastern Democrats and many midwestern Democrats, who were already disappointed that Polk had failed to acquire more of Oregon. Moreover, a few southern Democratic leaders worried that the Mexican people would oppose slavery; that the United States could not absorb the Mexicans, whom they regarded as an "inferior" people; and that prolonging the war dangerously risked augmenting the power of the federal government. This group included John C. Calhoun, who supported the taking of only Alta California and New Mexico, the most sparsely populated areas of Mexico.

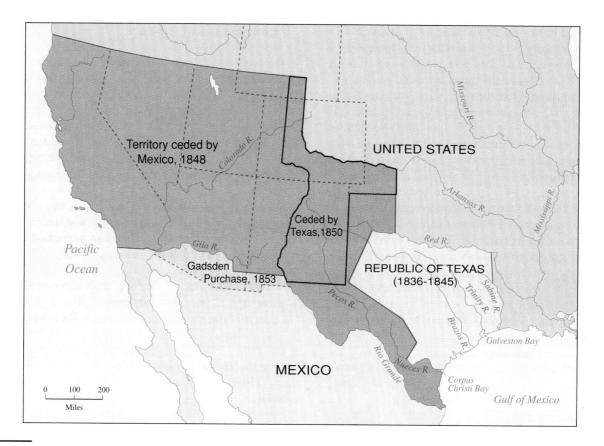

MAP 14.2

The Mexican Cession

The Mexican cession encompassed an area that includes not only California, almost all of New Mexico, and more than half of Texas but also Nevada, Utah, most of Arizona, and parts of Wyoming, Colorado, Kansas, and Oklahoma. After Mexico ratified the Treaty of Guadalupe Hidalgo, Polk told Congress that the new territories "constitute of themselves a country large enough for a great empire, and their acquisition is second in importance only to that of Louisiana in 1803."

Treaty of Guadalupe Hidalgo. Once again, as during the administrations of Jackson and Van Buren, the president put the interests of party unity foremost. He and Buchanan retreated from their early support of "All Mexico" and backed Calhoun's policy. Moreover, Polk wanted to make certain that hostilities were over and achieve a settlement with Mexico well before the elections of 1848. Consequently, Polk endorsed the Treaty of Guadalupe Hidalgo (February 2, 1848), in which the United States promised to pay Mexico $15 million in return for more than one-third of the territory of Mexico: Texas north of the Rio Grande, New Mexico, and Alta California (see Map 14.2). In addition, the United States also agreed to assume all the claims of its citizens, totaling $3.2 million, against the Mexican government. The Senate quickly ratified the treaty in March 1848.

The Polk administration had gained northern Mexico, as well as Texas and Oregon, without sacrificing party unity. But now the nation faced an even more contentious issue: What would be the future of slavery in the newly acquired territory?

The Free-Soil Movement

The Wilmot Proviso energized those abolitionists who had been seeking a political, legislative solution to the problem of slavery. After the defeat of the Liberty party in 1844, its founders had relaxed even further the intensity of their moral demands, deemphasizing the natural rights of slaves. In the Wilmot Proviso the political abolitionists further recast abolitionism, defining the problem of slavery not as an individual sin but as a threat to republican institutions. This new approach had the desired effect: the Wilmot Proviso was the first proposal that attracted broad popular support to the antislavery movement.

Between 1846 and 1848 antislavery leaders redefined their position. They stressed that there was a tyrannical "Slave Power" conspiracy composed of southern planters and those northern business people who depended on them. That conspiracy had produced, they claimed, the Mexican War. The conspiracy was said to draw its strength from an absolute control over human beings that endangered the republic. To defeat the Slave Power it would be necessary to prohibit slavery in the national territories.

The new antislavery program became known as *free soil*, and in 1848 its proponents reorganized the old Liberty party under a new name, the Free Soil party. Its platform promised to keep the West, thought to be the key to the future of the republic, pure of slavery and secure for freedom. The Free Soil party retained an enthusiasm for individual freedom but ultimately expressed a greater interest in protecting the freedom of whites occupying new lands than in championing the freedom of slaves. That shift of emphasis led the radical abolitionist William Lloyd Garrison to denounce the free-soil doctrine as "whitemanism," a racist effort to make the territories white.

Free-Soil Supporters. Although many Americans did not believe that slave owning was sinful or that African-Americans deserved equality, they could be convinced that slavery threatened liberty and economic opportunity for white people in the West. Those conservative supporters dominated the free-soil movement, but there were radical supporters as well. Despite Garrison's hostility, the new political approach won the support of many women abolitionists, who were denied the political rights that white men enjoyed. Women in the American and Foreign Anti-Slavery Society established dozens of new female societies throughout the Great Lakes states to work for free soil.

Frederick Douglass was also a major supporter of free soil. He had emerged during the 1840s as a leading antislavery strategist, the most electrifying of all abolitionist orators, and the foremost African-American abolitionist (see American Lives, pages 424–425). Douglass was unhappy with the Free Soil party's racism and watered-down platform with regard to slavery and free blacks; he urged free-soilers to pay greater attention to emancipation in the South and civil rights for African-Americans in the North. But Douglass and many other radical abolitionists, both black and white, reluctantly decided that supporting the growing free-soil movement was the only sensible political choice. They believed that the terror used to maintain slavery would ultimately require a violent confrontation between slavery and freedom, and they felt that the free-soil movement was the only viable way to provoke it. In short, free soil had radical dimensions in that it threatened both slavery and the Second Party System.

The Election of 1848

The sectional divisions among Democrats that had surfaced during the Mexican War affected the election of 1848. Free-soil and midwestern Democrats unhappy with Polk's Oregon treaty probably would have forced their party to dump Polk in the 1848 election. But before that could happen an exhausted Polk, who had worked from dawn late into the night throughout his presidency, declined to run; he would die three months after leaving office (see Table 14.1). In search of a replacement who could unify the party, the Democrats nominated the dull Senator Lewis Cass of Michigan. Cass was an expansionist who had advocated the purchase of Cuba, the annexation of Mexico's Yucatan Peninsula, and the acquisition of all of Oregon. In an effort to keep both southerners and northerners in the party, the Democrats left their platform deliberately vague on the expansion of slavery. Cass promoted a new policy concept called *popular sovereignty*. Under this policy, each territorial government would have the right to determine the status of slavery in its territory.

The nomination of Cass did not satisfy free-soil Democrats, who demanded unambiguous opposition to the expansion of slavery. Many of them threw their support to the newly formed Free Soil party. To win Democratic votes, the Free Soil party nominated Martin Van Buren for president. Though still a Democrat, he ran out of a combination of idealism and vindictiveness. He had converted to free-soil beliefs and to support of the Wilmot Proviso, but he also wanted to punish southern Democrats for denying him the nomination in 1844. The Free Soil party appealed to Whigs by nominating Charles Francis Adams, the son of John Quincy Adams, for vice-president. Adams had inherited many of the conscience Whig supporters of his father, who died in 1848 after distinguished service as an antislavery congressman from Massachusetts.

The Candidacy of Zachary Taylor. The division among Democrats created an opportunity for the Whigs, who did their best to suppress their own sectional disputes. Whig leaders avoided adopting a specific platform, even though northern Whigs generally supported the Wilmot Proviso. The Whigs nominated General Zachary Taylor. The fact that he came from Louisiana and owned a hundred slaves was less important to northern Whigs than his vagueness on the issue of slavery in the territories and his popularity throughout the nation. Known as "Old Rough and Ready," Taylor possessed a common touch that had won him the affection of his troops and made him the greatest hero of the Mexican War. Numerous biographers described him as a "natural" American leader. "Our Commander on the Rio Grande," wrote Walt Whitman, "emulates the Great Commander of our revolution"—George Washington.

TABLE 14.1

American Presidents and the Sectional Crisis, 1841–1861

	Term in Office	Party	Fate
William Henry Harrison	1841	Whig	Died in office
John Tyler	1841–1845	Whig	Broke with Whig party
James K. Polk	1845–1849	Democrat	Did not seek second term; died three months after leaving office
Zachary Taylor	1849–1850	Whig	Died in office
Millard Fillmore	1850–1853	Whig	1852 Whig nomination won by Winfield Scott
Franklin Pierce	1853–1857	Democrat	1856 Democratic nomination won by James Buchanan
James Buchanan	1857–1861	Democrat	Democratic party split, nominating Stephen Douglas and John Breckinridge

The tactic of running a military hero worked for the Whigs, just as it had when Harrison had run in 1840. Taylor won the election with 47 percent of the popular vote and 163 electoral votes against Cass's 42 percent and 127 electoral votes. Taylor carried seven free states but was stronger in the South, where he won 51 percent of the popular vote and carried eight states, or nearly two-thirds of that region's electoral votes. In the North the Free Soil party of Van Buren and Adams made a strong showing, receiving over 290,000 votes, more than 10 percent of the total. The Free Soil party drew voters away from both Taylor and Cass in the North but hurt the Democrats more than it hurt the Whigs. Van Buren received about 14 percent of the northern vote and might have taken enough votes from Cass in New York to cost Cass the state and the national election.

The swift growth of the Free Soil party and the popularity of the Wilmot Proviso left southerners—both Whigs and Democrats—stunned and fearful. Slave owners became even more aggressive in seeking the expansion of slavery, demanding more explicit commitments from the two major parties. Consequently, in the future the two national parties would have difficulty maintaining ambiguity on the status of slavery in the territories.

Alternatives to the Wilmot Proviso

The election of 1848 persuaded virtually all southern politicians that they could not win support that was national in scope for their territorial ambitions. They also realized that they would have to secure a future for slavery in territory already acquired as well as in new acquisitions from Mexico or Cuba. After the election they concentrated on meeting the challenge of the Wilmot Proviso by trying to establish slavery firmly in the territories taken from Mexico. They advocated three different approaches to achieve that objective.

Calhoun's "Common Property" Doctrine. John C. Calhoun put forward the most extreme position—explicit support for the spread of slavery into federal territories. He held that Congress had no constitutional authority to regulate slavery in the territories and thus could not exclude slavery from a territory prior to admission to statehood. According to Calhoun's common property doctrine, the citizens of any state had the same rights as the citizens of any other state to take their property into areas owned commonly by the states. His argument won support from many Democrats and Whigs in the Deep South but repelled too many northerners in both parties for it ever to win much support in Congress.

Extending the Missouri Compromise Line. Most southern leaders in both parties advocated or were willing to accept a more moderate position: an extension of the Missouri Compromise line through the Mexican cession (the territory purchased from Mexico) to the Pacific coast. This proposal would guarantee slave owners access to at least some western territory, particularly southern California; would remove the antislavery threat from the Deep South's western boundary; and would almost certainly add slave states to the Union. This approach even appealed to some northern Democrats. Buchanan and Douglas, for example, hoped the offer to prohibit slavery in northern territories would prevent free-soil Democrats from bolting the party. But free-soil Democrats and Whigs opposed *any* expansion of slavery as a matter of principle and rejected the plan.

Popular Sovereignty. The third alternative was popular sovereignty, Lewis Cass's position in the 1848 election. Because it relieved Congress of the responsibility of addressing the slavery issue by passing it on to territorial governments, popular sovereignty won support from many northern Democrats who otherwise might have converted to free soil.

Frederick Douglass:
Development of an Abolitionist

Frederick Douglass was born a slave in 1818 on the eastern shore of Maryland. He took his mother's family name of Bailey—derived perhaps from the Muslim *Belali*. He never knew who his father was, although talk in the slave-quarters had pointed toward a man Douglass later described as "his master."

For most of his time in slavery Douglass's master was Thomas Auld, who acquired the young Frederick in 1827 as part of a property settlement and sent him to live with his brother Hugh in Baltimore. There were no other slaves in that home, and Frederick was treated much like the other children. He listened to Sophia Auld read the Bible, learned to read from a spelling book borrowed from the Auld children, figured out the meaning of *abolition* by reading newspapers, and heard about slaves running away to the North. At the age of twelve he purchased a copy of *The Columbian Orator*, a collection of speeches for young boys learning to declaim the virtues of the republic—including its devotion to "the rights of man." Enthralled, Douglass memorized and recited the speeches to his friends, including the free blacks he sought out at Methodist and Baptist churches.

In 1833 Thomas Auld returned Frederick to the sleepy eastern shore town of St. Michaels, perhaps to prevent him from running away or becoming mixed up in antislavery agitation. Frederick hoped that Auld would get religion and free him. When he did not, Frederick became rebellious, organizing a Sabbath school and resisting the routines of work. In 1834 Auld hired Douglass out to Edward Covey, a farmer with a reputation for "breaking" unruly slaves. After six months of disciplined labor and regular beatings Frederick had a brutal fight with Covey. Douglass recalled that the battle "was the turning point in my '*life as a slave*.' . . . I was nothing before; I WAS A MAN NOW." From that point he was determined "to be a FREEMAN."

The next year Auld hired Douglass out to a more lenient master. Douglass again organized a school and, with six other slaves, hatched a plan for an escape up the Chesapeake. Betrayed by a fellow conspirator, he found himself in jail, facing sale into the Deep South. But Auld again intervened, returning Douglass to Balti-

Frederick Douglass
The daguerreotype of Douglass was taken when he was in his twenties. Describing Douglass, an admirer wrote: "He was more than six feet in height, and his majestic form . . . straight as an arrow, muscular, yet lithe and graceful, his flashing eye, and more than all, his voice, that rivaled Webster's in its richness, and in the depth and sonorousness of its cadences, made up such an ideal of an orator as the listeners never forgot."

more with a promise that if Frederick applied himself to a trade, he would free him at the age of twenty-five.

Douglass did apply himself. He became a journeyman caulker in the shipyards and in 1838 struck a deal with Hugh Auld that allowed him to control his living and working arrangements in return for a guaranteed

weekly payment. Douglass plunged into the life of Baltimore's free African-American community, almost 30,000 in number. He courted a free woman, Anna Murray, and joined a group of black caulkers—all free but him—called the East Baltimore Mental Improvement Society. But this life came to an abrupt end when he fell two days behind in his payments to Hugh Auld, who then ordered him to give up his independent earnings, employment, and housing. Unwilling to surrender the small measure of independence he had gained, Douglass decided to run away (see Chapter 13). Less than a month later, in the fall of 1838, he stepped off a ferry in New York City; a few days later he married Anna.

Frederick and Anna settled first in the seaport of New Bedford, Massachusetts, where he took a new name—Douglass—to avoid capture. He found work, made his first antislavery speech to a white audience, and heard William Lloyd Garrison lecture. At a meeting of the Massachusetts Anti-Slavery Society in 1841 he delivered a powerful address that won the admiration of Garrison and other leading abolitionists, who hired him as an agent of the American Anti-Slavery Society. His celebrated lecturing took him to hundreds of communities in the Northeast, where audiences were spellbound by his speeches. Elizabeth Cady Stanton described an 1842 address in Boston's Faneuil Hall:

> Around him sat the great antislavery orators of the day watching the effect of his eloquence on that immense audience, that laughed and wept by turns, completely carried away by the wondrous gifts of his pathos and humor. On this occasion, all the other speakers seemed tame after Frederick Douglass.

In his speeches Douglass denounced both slavery in the South and racial discrimination in the North. He was uncomfortable, however, with Garrison's Perfectionism and in particular with Garrison's insistence on expulsion of the southern states, which Douglass believed would leave the slaves completely at the mercy of their owners. Douglass did not take issue with Garrison's radicalism publicly, for he hoped it would motivate white America to take practical steps—such as abolishing slavery in the District of Columbia—toward the eradication of slavery. His differences with Garrison grew, however, and in 1847 he returned from a British tour determined to chart an independent course. (In an important way his independence was more secure because in 1846 admiring British abolitionists financed the purchase of his freedom from Auld to ensure that he would not be arrested as a fugitive.)

Douglass moved to Rochester, New York, where he founded an antislavery newspaper, the *North Star*, financed heavily by Gerrit Smith, a Liberty party leader.

The next year Douglass attended the Buffalo convention that created the Free Soil party, and the *North Star* extended a cautious endorsement to the party. In that year he also attended the Seneca Falls convention, writing in the *North Star*: "We are free to say that in respect to political rights, we hold woman to be justly entitled to all we claim for men."

In 1851 Douglass publicly defied the American Anti-Slavery Society by defending the Constitution, and in 1852 he delivered what became known as his "Fifth of July" speech, probably the most moving and influential of his career. He denied that the Constitution was proslavery. "In *that* instrument," he declared, "I hold there is no warrant, license, nor sanction of the hateful thing; but, interpreted as it *ought* to be interpreted, the Constitution is a GLORIOUS LIBERTY DOCUMENT."

Douglass's involvement in practical politics deepened during the 1850s. Although he believed that violence would be necessary to abolish slavery, he was cautious in encouraging slave insurrections, declining to join John Brown's raid on Harpers Ferry. Nonetheless, suspicion that he was a key conspirator led Douglass to flee to Canada and Britain. When he resumed speechmaking in America in the summer of 1860, the victory of the Republican party and its program of free soil seemed imminent.

Douglas remained a leader of former abolitionists and African-Americans for the rest of his life. During the Civil War he pressed Abraham Lincoln and the Republicans to embrace abolition of slavery as a war aim and was delighted when Lincoln adopted his view of the Constitution. He also helped the War Department recruit black soldiers. Throughout Reconstruction he spoke and lobbied effectively for equal treatment—including the right to vote—for African-Americans. But his service to the Republican party went virtually unrewarded. Republican presidents appointed him to the minor positions of marshal (1877) and then recorder of deeds for the District of Columbia (1881). It was not until the age of seventy that he finally received a significant appointment as minister to Haiti.

Before his death in 1895 Douglass's optimism finally waned. In 1894 his last major speech warned that the "presence of eight millions of people in any section of this country constituting an aggrieved class, smarting under terrible wrongs, denied the exercise of the commonest rights of humanity . . . is not only a disgrace and scandal to that particular section but a menace to the peace and security of the people of the whole country."

It seemed an inherently fair, democratic approach. Popular sovereignty, however, was a vague and slippery concept. It did not specify at what point the people of a territory could legalize or prohibit slavery; nor did it say how much authority territorial governments could exercise in regulating slavery. If Calhoun's doctrine was correct, the constitutional protection of slavery meant that territorial governments could decide the status of slavery only at the *end* of the territorial process, when they framed a constitution and applied for statehood. Southern Democrats preferred this interpretation, believing that it gave slavery a good chance to become established in the territories. In contrast, Northern Democrats believed that territorial legislatures had the power to exclude slavery and could do so as soon as a territory was organized.

As long as each side left this ambiguity unresolved, popular sovereignty held the greatest possibility for maintaining the unity of the Democratic party—and national unity—on the slavery issue. However, the ability of popular sovereignty to unify was tested far sooner than anyone expected in another major sectional confrontation.

The Compromise of 1850

The "Forty-Niners." In January 1848 workmen building a mill for John A. Sutter discovered flakes of gold in the Sierra Nevada foothills. Sutter was a Swiss immigrant who had arrived in California in 1839, become a Mexican citizen, and established a kind of feudal barony in the Sacramento Valley, well removed from the Mexican authorities. He tried to keep the discovery of gold a secret, but by May Americans from San Francisco were pouring into the foothills (see Map 14.3). In September the news reached the Northeast, but newspaper readers remained skeptical until December, when Polk confirmed the gold discoveries in his annual message to Congress. By January 1849 sixty-one crowded ships had departed from northeastern ports to sail around Cape Horn for San Francisco. By May 12,000 wagons had crossed the Missouri River, headed for the goldfields. In 1849 alone, more than 80,000 migrants—the "forty-niners"—arrived. The pace of growth would remain hectic. In 1852 there would be more than 200,000 Californians, and by 1860 the state's population would reach 380,000.

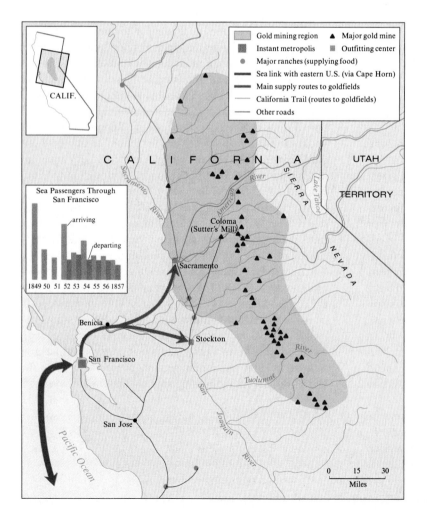

MAP 14.3

The California Gold Rush

Hundreds of thousands of fortune seekers converged on the California goldfields beginning in 1849. Miners traveling by sea landed at San Francisco, which became an instant metropolis. They outfitted for their journey inland at Sacramento and Stockton, which were commercial outposts of San Francisco. The vast population influx put pressure on existing ranches for food and stimulated new farming enterprise in the Sacramento, American, and San Joaquin River valleys.

Gold Prospectors
Working at the head of the Auburn Ravine in about 1850, these prospectors used a primitive technique—panning—to separate gold from sand and gravel. Most of the wage laborers in the early years of the gold rush were Indians or Chinese, who numbered over 25,000 in California by 1852.

Taylor and California Statehood. In California, which was not yet organized into a territory, American settlers—especially the forty-niners, who lived in crowded, chaotic towns and mining camps—demanded effective government. President Zachary Taylor advised the Californians to apply for statehood immediately. Taylor's objectives were simple: to satisfy the forty-niners' demands, to avoid wrestling with the ambiguities of popular sovereignty, and to provide dramatic evidence that the Whigs could promote westward expansion without intensifying the slavery issue. Behind his approach lay his desire to establish the Whigs as the dominant national party. On the one hand, he hoped to draw Free Soil party voters and free-soil Democrats into the Whig party; on the other hand, he hoped to persuade southern Whigs that they could protect slavery in the South without insisting on slavery in the territories.

Taylor made his proposal when he took office in March 1849. By November California voters had ratified a state constitution and applied for statehood. In the swift process of constitution making, the advocates of slavery fared poorly. Few of the many southerners who flocked to the goldfields, San Francisco, and the farms of the Sacramento Valley owned slaves or wanted to own them. Only ranchers in sparsely populated southern California had a strong interest in promoting slavery. Consequently, the California constitutional convention, copying much of the new Iowa state constitution, prohibited slavery. When Congress convened in December 1849, President Taylor urged the admission of California and New Mexico as free states.

Southern defenders of slavery were startled and alarmed by the swift victory of the antislavery forces in California. Popular sovereignty seemed to offer only empty promises of protection. Vast numbers of northerners now seemed likely to overwhelm slavery anywhere that they settled in the new territories, just as they had in California. Popular opposition to slavery in

California was usually racist, as hostile to African-Americans as it was to the institution of slavery, but that provided no comfort to southern slave owners. The farmers from Tennessee and the Irish immigrants from New York were in different wings of California's Democratic party but they shared a hatred of slavery and African-Americans. They agreed that the future of California should resemble that of the free-soil Midwest.

The imminent prospect of California's admission to the Union also disturbed southerners because it threatened the carefully maintained regional balance in the Senate. In 1845 the admission of Texas and Florida had given slavery a temporary edge of fifteen slave states against thirteen free states, but the admission of Iowa in 1846 and Wisconsin in 1848 reestablished the balance. California's admission would give the free states a political advantage in shaping states carved from the Mexican cession and the unorganized areas of the Louisiana Purchase. Moreover, southerners feared that the new state of California would create a base for abolitionists within the territory acquired from Mexico.

Southern leaders were willing to accept California's admission as a free state only if the federal government guaranteed the future of slavery. Southerners were not agreed on what they needed for an adequate guarantee, but they knew it was more than popular sovereignty in the Mexican cession. And so, in passionate debates that lasted for eight months, southern leaders forced Congress to examine all the issues surrounding the current and future status of slavery.

The most extreme southern position was taken by Calhoun, who doubted that the North and the South could arrive at a lasting compromise. In what would be his farewell address, read to Congress on his behalf shortly before he died, Calhoun said the nation could prevent the South's secession and eventual civil war only by guaranteeing slavery in all the territories and adopting a constitutional amendment to establish a per-

William H. Seward

Seward (1801–1872) was a New York State senator (1830–1834) and a Whig governor of New York (1838–1842) before serving two terms (1849–1861) in the U. S. Senate. After failing to win the Republican nomination for president in 1856 and 1860, he entered Lincoln's cabinet as secretary of state, an office he held until 1867. As early as 1835, after a trip through Virginia, he denounced slavery as "incompatible with all . . . the elements of the security, welfare, and greatness of nations."

Salmon P. Chase

Trained as a lawyer, Chase (1808–1873) was drawn to the antislavery movement by his defense of fugitive slaves. He served as U.S. senator (1849–1855), Republican governor of Ohio (1855–1860), secretary of the treasury (1861–1864), and chief justice of the Supreme Court (1864–1873).

manent balance of sectional power. He was thinking of an amendment that would turn the presidency into a dual office, providing executives from both the South and the North and giving each president full veto power.

Antislavery advocates in both parties lent credence to Calhoun's prediction of civil war. Senators Salmon P. Chase, an Ohio free-soiler who had been elected by a Democratic–Free Soil party coalition, and William H. Seward, a New York Whig, urged the government to contain slavery within its existing limits. Their goal was its ultimate extinction. Seward declared that the government had a responsibility to "a higher law than the Constitution, which regulates our authority over the domain . . . the common heritage of mankind."

The issues were finally being clearly drawn, as were the risks to the future of the nation. The clash in Congress tore both national parties along sectional lines and stirred fears that the Union might dissolve.

Forging a Compromise. Having moved to the brink of disaster, senior Whigs and Democrats did their best to back away and reach a compromise. Through a long, complex legislative process the Whig leaders Henry Clay and Daniel Webster and the Democrat Stephen A. Douglas organized a package that, when implemented, consisted of six distinct laws. Those laws were known collectively as the Compromise of 1850. The Compromise, enacted in September, attempted to mollify the South by adopting the Fugitive Slave Act. That act replaced a weak 1793 law with a strong one that put the federal government at the disposal of slave owners chasing runaway slaves. The intent was to remove the free states as havens for runaway slaves and reduce the ability of abolitionists to use free-soil bases to attack slavery. The Compromise tried to satisfy the North by establishing the principle of popular sovereignty in the Mexican cession. The Compromise of 1850 (1) admitted California as a free state, ending the equal balance of free and slave states, (2) organized (by two of the six laws) the rest of the Mexican cession into the territories of New Mexico and Utah on the implied basis of popular sovereignty, (3) resolved a boundary dispute between New Mexico and Texas in favor of New Mexico through federal assumption of the $10 million in unpaid debts of the Republic of Texas, (4) abolished the slave trade, but not slavery, in the District of Columbia, and (5) passed the Fugitive Slave Act.

The Compromise averted a secession crisis in 1850—but only barely. In the end northern Democrats and southern Whigs accounted for most of the votes for the Compromise. Northern Whigs such as Seward and southern Democrats such as Jefferson Davis opposed it. Most southern Democrats objected to admitting California under any terms and regarded the Fugitive Slave Act as an inadequate protector of slavery. Robbed of

their longtime leader by Calhoun's death before the vote, they would soon regroup to become an increasingly potent obstacle to sectional compromise. Northern Whigs opposed both the fugitive slave law and popular sovereignty. Those Whigs held their ground even after Vice-President Millard Fillmore of New York, a northern Whig who supported popular sovereignty, succeeded to the presidency in July 1850. (Taylor had died suddenly of a violent stomach ailment and heat prostration suffered during a Fourth of July celebration.) In other words, most northern Whigs and southern Democrats in Congress were willing to defy the leadership of their parties and risk the Union for the sake of their principles. The Compromise did not augur well for the future.

Sectional Strife and the Third Party System, 1850–1858

The Compromise of 1850 was intended to prevent the slavery issue from disrupting politics and government. Both northern Democratic and southern Whig leaders hoped that the Compromise would be as effective as its predecessor in 1820 had been and that the new compromise—particularly its fugitive slave law and popular sovereignty elements—would enable each party to maintain a national base of support. But any such hopes were quickly dashed as northern hostility to slavery swelled and southern demands for slavery's protection grew more insistent.

The Fugitive Slave Act

The most controversial element of the Compromise proved to be the Fugitive Slave Act. Under its terms, federal judges or special commissioners determined the status of blacks who denied that they were runaways. The accused African-Americans were denied jury trials and the right to testify. A commissioner would receive a $10 fee if an alleged fugitive was found guilty but only $5 if the accused was found innocent—a tremendous incentive to render a guilty verdict. Federal marshals were instructed to support slave catchers and could impose heavy penalties on anyone who helped a slave escape or obstructed the efforts of slaveholders to recover their slaves. Even slaves who had long before fled to freedom were subject to recapture. The law was effectively enforced, and many fugitives were convicted and reenslaved.

Resistance in the North. The plight of the runaways and the appearance of slave catchers in northern communities personalized the message of abolitionism, and

popular hostility to the Fugitive Slave Act grew. Abolitionists organized vigilante groups to block enforcement of the law. Frederick Douglass abandoned pacifism, declaring that "the only way to make the Fugitive Slave Law a dead letter is to make half a dozen or more dead kidnappers." In October 1850 Theodore Parker and other Boston abolitionists defied the law by helping two slaves escape to freedom and driving a Georgia slave catcher out of town. In September 1851, in the Quaker village of Christiana, Pennsylvania, more than twenty African-American men, including two escaped slaves, exchanged gunfire with a group of slave catchers from Maryland; the slave owner was killed, and his son was severely wounded. President Fillmore sent marines and federal marshals to arrest thirty-six blacks and four whites around Christiana and had them indicted for treason. But the jury acquitted one defendant, and a public uproar forced the government to drop charges against the rest. In Syracuse, New York, 2,000 rioters broke into a courthouse and freed a fugitive slave in October 1851.

Some northern legislators and judges openly resisted federal authority. Several state legislatures passed *personal liberty* laws to protect accused fugitive slaves from federal officers. Those laws attempted to exempt state officials from enforcing proslavery laws such as the Fugitive Slave Act. In 1857 the supreme court of Wisconsin, in the case of *Ableman v. Booth*, held that a state court had the power to declare an act of Congress unconstitutional. The Fugitive Slave Act, the court ruled, violated the Constitution and could not be enforced in Wisconsin. In 1859 the case reached the Supreme Court, where Chief Justice Taney ruled against Wisconsin.

Uncle Tom's Cabin. It was in reaction to the Fugitive Slave Act that Harriet Beecher Stowe composed her abolitionist novel *Uncle Tom's Cabin*. Published first in 1851–1852 as a serial in a Washington free-soil newspaper, the *National Era*, the novel tells of a compassionate but weak slaveholder in Kentucky who is forced by debts to sell two slaves, Uncle Tom and a five-year-old boy, to a slave trader. The beautiful Eliza Harris, the boy's mother, refuses to be separated from her son. With the child in her arms, she crosses the Ohio River on cakes of ice just ahead of the vicious slave trader. Eliza escapes to freedom and reaches the house of an Ohio politician who had voted for a fugitive slave law, having set aside his "private feeling." His wife persuades him to trust his heart rather than his head and to help Eliza and her child escape to Canada. Meanwhile, Tom is eventually sold to Simon Legree, a brutal overseer on a southern plantation. Legree beats Tom to death but never conquers the slave's Christian soul.

Uncle Tom's Cabin further intensified northern hostility to the Fugitive Slave Act. When the novel first appeared in book form in 1852, more than 300,000

Uncle Tom's Cabin
In these illustrations from the original 1852 edition of *Uncle Tom's Cabin*, the engraver portrayed Eliza Harris (top) and Tom (bottom panel).

Americans bought copies. Countless families saw an emotionally charged stage version produced by theater companies throughout the North. For most of those people Stowe's novel connected the abstract moral principles of abolitionism with heartrending personal situations to which they could respond with anger or grief.

The Southern Response. To the South's political leaders the Fugitive Slave Act was important because it meant that the government recognized and protected their "property" everywhere. The fierce northern defiance of the act mobilized leading southern politicians, who were already upset by the admission of California, the introduction of popular sovereignty, and the abolition of the slave trade in Washington, D.C. To protect what they called Southern Rights, they organized special conventions in South Carolina, Georgia, Mississippi, and Alabama in 1850 and 1851. The governor of South Carolina declared that there was not "the slightest doubt" that his state would secede from the Union to protect slavery. Although all the conventions considered secession, moderates in Georgia, Mississippi, and Al-

abama defused the crisis by persuading the conventions to support the Compromise of 1850. In return, the moderates agreed to support secession in the future if Congress abolished slavery anywhere, failed to recognize slavery in a new territory, or refused to admit a state into the Union because its proposed constitution permitted slavery. The victorious Georgia Unionists declared in the Georgia Platform that the protection of Southern Rights and the "preservation of our much beloved Union" depended most importantly on "a faithful execution of the Fugitive Slave Law." Moderate arguments carried less weight in South Carolina, where secession failed only because many secessionists doubted that they could go it alone, without the cooperation of other states.

The Election of 1852: A Shift in Party Balance

The northern Whigs, who dominated their party, carried their powerful hostility to the Fugitive Slave Act and popular sovereignty into the 1852 election. They passed over President Fillmore because he had vigorously enforced the act and supported popular sovereignty. Instead they nominated another general from the Mexican War, Winfield Scott, in the hope that a popular general, like Harrison in 1840 and Taylor in 1848, would attract national support. The southern Whigs were not satisfied by the Scott nomination and the offhanded endorsement of the Compromise of 1850 that the northern Whigs and Scott offered to keep southerners in the party. Many southern Whigs, particularly in the Deep South, withheld support from their party; some went so far as to vote for the Democratic ticket.

The Whigs had problems in the North too; whereas their economic program still had supporters, many northern Whigs wanted the party to address slavery and immigration issues in a straightforward, compelling fashion. Also, the deaths of Henry Clay and Daniel Webster in 1852 had robbed the party of its most articulate leaders and most effective voices for national unity.

Franklin Pierce. The Democrats displayed no more vision in 1852 than did the Whigs, but they were more successful in avoiding a division along sectional lines. Some southern Democrats wanted to nominate a candidate who supported Calhoun's radical position that the federal government should protect slavery in all the territories. Most realized, however, that that would ensure defeat for the party in the North. The Democratic convention passed over all the advocates of popular sovereignty, including Lewis Cass, Stephen Douglas, and James Buchanan, none of whom could obtain the neces-

Franklin Pierce
In this engraving (circa 1847), Pierce poses as a brigadier general of volunteers in the Mexican War.

sary two-thirds majority. On the forty-ninth ballot it chose Franklin Pierce of New Hampshire. The public knew Pierce only as a handsome and congenial New Englander with no identifiable enemies, but southern Democrats were assured that he would be sympathetic to the South's interests.

Pierce and the Democrats crushed the Whigs in the 1852 election. The Democrats not only attracted southern Whigs but also won back some of the northern Democrats who had voted for the Free Soil party in 1848. Pleased by the outcome of popular sovereignty in California, those free-soilers were satisfied that the popular sovereignty provisions of the Compromise of 1850 would effectively prevent the expansion of slavery. Even Martin Van Buren, the former candidate of the Free Soil party, supported Pierce. Votes for the Free Soil party and its candidate, John P. Hale of New Hampshire, declined to about 5 percent of the total, only about half the share the party had won four years earlier. Although General Scott attracted more popular votes than Taylor

had in 1848, Scott carried only four of the thirty-one states.

The Whigs never again waged a national campaign. The Compromise of 1850 had driven a wedge between northern and southern Whigs. The task of maintaining the political unity of the nation now fell to the Democrats.

In trying to maintain itself as a *national* party, the Democratic party had some powerful assets. Most Democratic leaders took the broadly appealing stance of supporting popular sovereignty. The Democrats also had a diverse base of voters, including the growing number of immigrant voters in northern cities and the many settlers of southern ancestry in the Ohio Valley. They also appealed to the many voters across the country who thought that preserving the Union was more important than preserving slavery or freeing the slaves.

But the Democratic party also had some important liabilities. Its program of popular sovereignty was unacceptable both to many southerners—those who insisted that slaves be treated as property throughout the Union—and to northerners who wanted the federal government to prohibit slavery in the western territories. The Democratic party was unattractive to those northern voters who resented the recruitment of immigrants, particularly Catholics, into the party and to those who wanted vigorous federal programs to promote economic development.

Pierce's Expansionist Foreign Policy

President Pierce set out to broaden his support and divert attention from sectional disputes with a familiar Democratic strategy: an expansionist foreign policy. Pierce hoped that, like Polk in the early phases of the Mexican War, he could broaden his support among Americans, both northern and southern, who were interested in spreading republican institutions and expanding trade opportunities. Pierce cast his eyes toward Latin America, particularly Mexico, the Caribbean, Central America, and across the Pacific toward Japan.

Unlocking Japan. Pierce inherited a diplomatic opportunity in Japan. American trade with China had declined in the 1840s, and in response some northeastern merchants had scouted new markets in the western Pacific. In 1846 they had persuaded the federal government to send its first mission to Japan. In 1852 President Fillmore followed up by authorizing a naval expedition under Commodore Matthew C. Perry. Pierce continued the support of Perry, and in 1854 Perry's squadron of four "black ships" led Japan to sign a treaty of friendship. President Pierce rejected Perry's desire to acquire Pacific territory, including Formosa, but was unhappy that the treaty fell far short of establishing

full diplomatic and trading relations. In 1854 he sent Townsend Harris, a tough, experienced China trader, to Japan with full authority to negotiate a commercial treaty. Harris played successfully on Japanese fears of Russia and other European powers. In 1858, on an American warship in Edo (later Tokyo) Bay, Japan signed a full commercial treaty with the United States. This was the first such treaty Japan had made with any industrial power.

The Gadsden Purchase. Pierce inherited an array of Mexican-American problems, including a dispute over New Mexico's southern boundary and American acquisition of transit routes across northwestern Mexico. Pierce and his secretary of war, Jefferson Davis, hoped to pressure the Mexican government of Santa Anna, who had just returned to the presidency, to sell land to America as part of a comprehensive settlement. Pierce sent James Gadsden, a South Carolina politician and railroad promoter, to Mexico to negotiate with Santa Anna. Gadsden threatened force if Mexico did not cede a major portion of northern Mexico and Baja (Lower) California. Santa Anna refused but agreed to a settlement that included the sale of about 30,000 square miles south of the Gila River, territory Gadsden wanted for a southern railroad to the Pacific Ocean. Completed in 1854, the Gadsden Purchase, as it became known, represented the last territory acquired from Mexico, but it served to rub salt in Mexico's wounds, reminding it of the power of its northern neighbor.

Cuba. The early expansionist plans of the Polk administration had included purchasing Cuba from Spain. But those schemes had accomplished little despite the vigorous efforts of some southerners and their northern supporters, such as the New York newspaper editor John Louis O'Sullivan. Those expansionists tried to stir up a revolution in Cuba in the hope that widespread republican hostility to the Spanish monarchy would then lead to the admission of Cuba, which they hoped would turn out to be a slave state. The expansionists funded three filibustering expeditions to the island by a Cuban exile, General Narciso López.

President Pierce resumed those efforts in 1853 by covertly supporting another such expedition to Cuba—to be led by John A. Quitman, a former governor of Mississippi. While Quitman built up his forces, the Pierce administration nearly precipitated a war. In February 1854 Spanish officials in Cuba confiscated the cargo of the American ship *Black Warrior*, which had violated port regulations, creating an incident that could provide an excuse for taking Cuba by force. In March Pierce asked Congress for permission "to obtain redress for injuries received, and to vindicate the honor of our flag." Secretary of State William L. Marcy, who hoped that expansionism would win him the presiden-

tial nomination in 1856, instructed Pierce's minister in Spain, Pierre Soulé, a Louisianan who advocated taking Cuba, to demand an apology and a large indemnity for the *Black Warrior*'s losses. The Spanish government stalled, and by May Pierce had learned that northern Democrats in Congress would not support a war to add a new slave state. He accepted the Spanish terms for settling the *Black Warrior* claims and tried to signal Quitman to abandon his expedition by issuing a proclamation that the federal government would prosecute anyone who violated the neutrality laws.

Pierce meanwhile attempted to purchase Cuba. In April Marcy authorized Soulé to offer as much as $130 million for Cuba and, if he failed, to attempt "to detach that island from the Spanish dominion." After Soulé failed to start a revolution in Cuba, Marcy instructed him to meet with James Buchanan, the U.S. minister to Great Britain, and John Y. Mason, the minister to France, to devise an alternative plan. In October the three sent Pierce an inflammatory message that became known as the Ostend Manifesto. In it, they invoked the rhetoric of Manifest Destiny and declared that the United States would be justified "by every law, human and Divine" in "wresting" Cuba from Spain "if we possess the power." In November, within two weeks of the document's arrival in Washington, it had been leaked to the press, triggering a new wave of northern resentment against the South. Pierce halted his own efforts to acquire Cuba and finally persuaded Quitman to give up his filibustering plan, which he had never completely abandoned.

Nicaragua. In 1855 another American, William Walker, led an invasion of Nicaragua. Born and raised in Tennessee, Walker had acquired a taste for Latin American adventures in California, where he had won popularity for his schemes to annex Sonora and Baja California. In 1854 he had led forty-eight followers to La Paz to participate in a rebellion against Mexican rule. After the rebellion failed, he landed in Nicaragua with sixty men and made himself dictator of that country. He announced a grand scheme to create a new nation that would include Central America and Cuba. Most of his followers had the simpler mission of bringing Nicaragua into the Union as a slave state. In 1856 Walker announced the reestablishment of slavery in Nicaragua. His government was recognized by the Pierce administration and won an endorsement in the Democratic party platform, but Walker alienated his Central American neighbors and was driven out of power in 1857. He died before a Honduran firing squad in 1860. The resistance of Latin American nations, coupled with the growing force of free-soil sentiment in the North, meant that foreign policy and plots for taking Manifest Destiny to Latin America could not be the Democrats' key to national cohesion.

Kansas-Nebraska and the Republicans

The Democrats' main hope for sustaining their party as a national institution now depended on the success of popular sovereignty. The doctrine was put to its first test since California in the northern—and largest—portion of the Louisiana Purchase.

The Kansas-Nebraska Act. Because the Missouri Compromise guaranteed free soil in the Louisiana Purchase north of 36° 30', southerners had largely blocked the political organization of that area, allowing only the admission of Iowa to the Union in 1846 and the formation of the Minnesota Territory. Even though most of the unorganized area was in the "Great American Desert," the appetite of people in the Ohio River Valley and the Upper South for new land made them impatient. The same sense of confinement that had sent thousands of them to Oregon led them to demand that the government organize the vast northern region of the Louisiana Purchase into territories and open it for settlement. The Democratic senator Stephen A. Douglas of Illinois became their foremost spokesman. He championed development of the West and wanted Chicago to become the eastern terminus of a transcontinental railroad. He also yearned to be president. In 1854 he introduced a bill to extinguish native American rights and organize a large territory in what he called Nebraska.

Douglas's bill conflicted with the plans of southern senators, who wanted to guarantee slavery in the territories and hoped that New Orleans, Memphis, or St. Louis would be chosen as the eastern railroad terminus. To win southern support Douglas made two major concessions. First, he agreed with southerners that the popular sovereignty principle embraced by the Compromise of 1850 had voided the Missouri Compromise's prohibition of slavery in the northern part of the Louisiana Purchase. Second, he advocated the formation of two new territories, Nebraska and Kansas, rather than one, giving slaveholders a chance to dominate the settlement of Kansas, the more southern territory (see Map 14.4). Douglas believed that the demographic advantage of non-slaveholders in Kansas, coupled with a physical environment that he thought would be hostile to plantation agriculture, would ensure that Kansas, like California earlier, would remain free. Those concessions attracted the support of almost all southerners in Congress, and the Kansas-Nebraska Act passed in May 1854 despite the opposition of northern Whigs and half of Douglas's own northern Democrats, who were less sanguine about the future of free labor in the West.

Throughout the North abolitionists and free-soilers denounced the Kansas-Nebraska Act; Douglas had seriously misread northern opinion. The repeal of the Missouri Compromise seemed to attack freedom in an area that had been secure for more than a generation. Suddenly the idea caught fire that a Slave Power conspiracy had undertaken a dangerous program of aggression. Many free-soilers became convinced that the federal government had been captured by slaveholders and had abandoned sectional neutrality.

Formation of the Republican Party. Many northern Whigs, adrift without a national party, seized the opening Douglas had created. They began to cooperate with "Anti-Nebraska" Democrats. The two groups then joined with supporters of the Free Soil party. In 1854 they began to organize a new party, reviving the Jeffer-

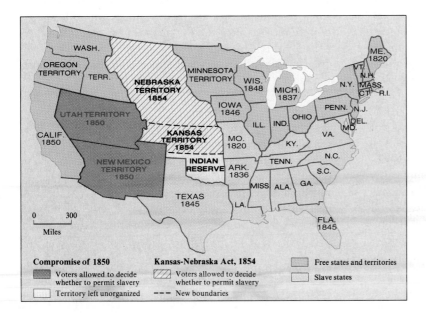

MAP 14.4

The Compromise of 1850 and the Kansas-Nebraska Act, 1854

Vast territories were at stake in the contest over the extension of slavery. The Compromise of 1850 and the Kansas-Nebraska Act provided that the future of slavery in most of the West—in the Kansas, Nebraska, Utah, and New Mexico territories—would be decided by popular sovereignty.

sonian term *Republican* for themselves. The Republicans emphasized absolute opposition to the expansion of slavery into any new territories—generalizing the principle of the Wilmot Proviso—and ran their first candidates in the Congressional elections of that year.

The Know-Nothings. Another party—the "Know-Nothings"—was already attracting support from former Whigs. The party had its origins in the anti-immigrant, anti-Catholic passions that had flared in the 1840s. In 1850 various secret anti-Catholic societies had banded together in the Order of the Star-Spangled Banner; a year later they formed a new political party, the American party. Its members sometimes answered outsiders' questions by saying "I know nothing," which gave the party its nickname. The program of the Know-Nothings, however, was not mysterious. They supported the program of the Native American Clubs and in addition advocated literacy tests for voters, which they thought would disfranchise most recent immigrants. The Know-Nothings attempted to unite northern and southern voters behind a program of nativist opposition to Catholics—both Irish and German—and the "alien menace."

Republicans and Know-Nothings Cooperate. In the 1854 elections in the North, the Republicans cooperated with the better established Know-Nothings. Whereas the Republicans stressed free soil, the Know-Nothings emphasized anti-Catholic nativism. The Republicans and Know-Nothings were wary of each other, uncertain which party had the better formula for long-term political success. But a coalition of the two new parties had much to recommend it. The conspiracy theory of the Know-Nothings—suggesting a threat to republican institutions—paralleled the free-soilers' description of the Slave Power conspiracy and created the ideological basis for the coalition. Many Republicans were uncomfortable with fervent anti-Catholicism but appreciated the fact that outside the South Know-Nothings applauded free-soil policy, regarding its potential antiblack thrust as being consistent with the Know-Nothing program of excluding everyone but white Protestants from America. There were also practical political reasons for a coalition. Neither of the national parties, the Whigs and the Democrats, had supported their programs, and most of the supporters of both the Know-Nothings and the Republicans were former Whigs. In 1854 the Know-Nothings won a number of seats in Congress and temporarily gained control of the state governments of Massachusetts and Pennsylvania. Together, the Republicans and Know-Nothings won a majority in the House of Representatives in 1854. Suddenly the Republican–Know-Nothing coalition seemed a potent alternative to the Democrats and popular sovereignty.

Republican Ideology versus the Defense of Slavery

Like most American political parties, the Republican party was a coalition, and its platform contained proposals designed to appeal to each of the groups that made up its alliance. But the party's ideas and political language were not just the sum of those proposals. Republican ideology was strongly shaped by a perception of the different kinds of human personalities and societies that developed under slavery and freedom.

In the Republican view, slavery produced only two classes of people: masters and slaves. The master class was corrupted by wielding power that knew no limits. In their dealings with slaves—and with their poorer white neighbors—slave masters would inevitably claim limitless privilege and inflict limitless injustice. This kind of excess could only produce habits of subservience, ignorance, and sloth among slaves and poor whites.

In the Republicans' description of a free society no person had unlimited power over another. The ancient division of society into permanent classes was eradicated by freedom and mobility. As Abraham Lincoln, a Whig who became a Republican after the passage of the Kansas-Nebraska Act, put it, in northern society "there is no permanent class of hired laborers among us." Every man had a chance to become an owner and an employer, and "if any continue through life in the condition of the hired laborers, it is not the fault of the system, but because of either a dependent nature which prefers it, or improvidence, folly, or singular misfortune." In the faith of Lincoln and his fellow Republicans the typical men and women of such a society would be proudly independent, creative, ambitious, and energetic. Such people would be disciplined not by authority but by their own free determination to meet their responsibilities to their families, churches, and communities. Thus, the Republicans asserted the values of individualism and republicanism in the face of increasing class divisions and tensions in the industrializing North.

Southerners saw things very differently. They had long defended slavery on racist grounds; black people, they claimed, were inferior, lacked any capacity for freedom, and were dependent on their benevolent masters. Many southerners invoked St. Paul's recognition of unequal stations in life. But in the 1850s, in response to northern attacks on slavery and celebrations of free labor, a new defense of slavery began to take shape. Proslavery novelists, for example, produced more than a dozen books between 1852 and 1854 to counter the searing images of *Uncle Tom's Cabin*. In two books, *Sociology for the South; or, the Failure of Free Society* (1854) and *Canni-*

bals All: or, Slaves without Masters (1857), a Virginia planter, lawyer, and writer, George Fitzhugh, delivered the most elaborate proslavery statement.

In a free-labor system, the new argument ran, labor is simply a commodity whose price is determined by the ruthless laws of the market. In the market, greed is the only morality, supply and demand the only law, and money the only goal. Every member of such a society, rich or poor, becomes grasping and selfish. Anyone too old, too weak, or too young to sell labor in the market is "free" only to be hungry and homeless. In such a world self-interest dominates; no one has a sense of community, civic values, or responsibility for others.

Whereas slavery requires some people to work to enrich others, the argument continued, it produces a master class that differs greatly from the ruling class of a capitalist society. Masters assume lifelong responsibility for their slaves, including the old and the sick. The slave owner, unlike the capitalist employer, is committed to community and civic responsibility. The master class in a slave society—whether in ancient Greece or Rome or in the American South—cultivates the graces and virtues that can thrive only in a frankly aristocratic culture.

Thus, in each section ideologies were taking shape that defined the differences between North and South in ways that utterly precluded political compromise. Each ideology suited the interests and world view of the dominant groups—the planters in the South and the business class in the North. Northerners and southerners argued that slavery and free labor were not simply different labor systems but expressed different social orders and produced irreconcilably different kinds of men and women. Every passing year made it more likely that a majority of the voters in each section would decide that societies as different as the North and the South could no longer be joined in a constitutional union.

"Bleeding Kansas"

The Kansas-Nebraska Act channeled the clash of rival ideologies into the settlement of the newly organized territory. In 1854 thousands of settlers began a rush into Kansas. Many believed they had a mission to defend the fundamental principles of their society, whether northern or southern; they were putting popular sovereignty to the test. On the side of slavery, Senator David R. Atchison of Missouri organized residents of his state to cross into Kansas and intervene in crucial elections (see American Voices, page 436). Opposing him were the agents of the New England Emigrant Aid Society, organized by abolitionists in 1854 to colonize Kansas with free-soilers. The preference of the Pierce administration was clear. In March 1855 the administration recognized a Kansas territorial legislature that had been elected largely by Missourians who had crossed the border simply to cast ballots. The territorial legislature declared that questioning the legitimacy of slavery was a felony and that aiding a fugitive slave was a capital offense. Pierce assisted the legislature with federal troops and proslavery judicial appointees.

Violence peaked in the summer of 1856. A proslavery gang, 700 strong, sacked the free-soil town of Lawrence, destroying two newspaper offices, burning down buildings, and looting stores. While Lawrence

Free-State Battery, 1856
For these free-soil settlers in Topeka, Kansas, there was a very real sense that the Civil War began in 1856 rather than 1861. Their cannon had seen service in the Mexican War.

Hannah Anderson Ropes

Six Months in "Bleeding Kansas"

In September 1855 Hannah Anderson Ropes moved with her two children from Brookline, Massachusetts, to join her husband in Lawrence, Kansas. But in March 1856, terrified by the violence, she returned to Brookline two months before the sack of Lawrence. During her six months in Kansas, Anderson wrote long letters to her mother and kept a diary.

November 21, 1855. Last week . . . a man living about six miles from here upon a claim . . . was shot down by a party of Missourians, without any provocation. The border Missourians are a horseback people; always off somewhere; drink a great deal of whiskey, and are quite reckless of human life. There is no necessity for hard work to those who have long lived in this country, the earth yields so abundantly. They ride fine horses, and are strong, vigorous-looking animals themselves. To shoot a man is not much more than to shoot a buck. After killing this poor Yankee, they stood around him till they saw a man approach, and then rode deliberately away.

My dear mother, this is Saturday evening. . . . How strange it will seem to you to hear that I have loaded pistols and a bowie-knife upon my table at night, three of Sharp's rifles, loaded, standing in the room. . . . All the week every preparation has been made for our defence; and everybody is worn with want of sleep. . . .

The Missourians have taken awful oaths to destroy this Yankee town, and a price is set upon the heads of some of our most honored citizens. Already they have assembled to the number of two hundred at Franklin, a little town south of us, and many more at Douglas, a village farther up the river. They are moving with great secretiveness; but when was a Yankee "caught napping," in the faintest prospect of danger?

To-night everybody is at the hall. My orders are, if fire-arms sound like battle, to place Alice [her daughter] and myself as near the floor as possible, and be well covered with blankets. We already have one bullet in the wall, and, since that, one struck the "shakes" close by the bed's head and glanced off. Now, for the first time, I begin to take an interest in Lawrence, as a city; and, prospectively, her destiny is almost as my own. How well her men bear themselves . . . [is] now so important as a matter of national history. . . .

December 5, 1855. Mother of mine, . . . we now have an armed force of five hundred men, who are under the command of Dr. Robinson, now commander-in-chief, and Col. Lane, both of whom have had experience in actual battle, in Mexico and California. Out of my south window I can see them drilling. . . . Boys there are in the ranks; but the soberness of manhood is upon them, and the determination of "Seventy-six" in their step. The blood warms in my veins as I look. . . .

Undated, December 1855. How we, at the North, have always believed implicitly in the chivalry of the South, and the wide-hearted generosity of the West. It is not till we arrive in Kansas, away from everything dear and familiar . . . that the truth really dawns upon us. Mother, there is no indignity to be mentioned which has not been heaped upon us. By it I feel myself robbed of a large estate—my faith in human nature.

Undated, March 1856. I am not only proud, but thankful, very thankful, that New England is the land of my birth. Her laws and institutions are dearer to us than ever before; and Kansas, without a similar elevating basis of social and moral restraint, would not be worth travelling two thousand miles to secure. . . .

Source: Hannah Anderson Ropes, *Six Months in Kansas by a Lady* (Boston: John P. Jewett and Co., 1856), *passim.*

burned, an abolitionist from New York and Ohio named John Brown, together with his four sons and two helpers, was on his way to Lawrence with a free-state volunteer militia to defend the town. Brown, born in 1800, had started more than twenty business ventures in six states, had gone through bankruptcy, and had often had to defend himself against lawsuits. Nonetheless, he had an intelligence and a moral intensity that won the trust of influential people, including leading abolitionists, whom he sought out beginning in the early 1830s. According to a free-soil minister who sheltered him, Brown believed "that God had raised him up on purpose to break the jaws of the wicked." The day after Brown heard about the sack of Lawrence, he acted with a vengeance. He and his followers, with broadswords honed like razors, murdered and mutilated five proslavery settlers in Kansas. We must "fight fire with fire" and "strike terror in the hearts of the proslavery people," Brown declared. The "Pottawatomie massacre," as the killings became known, provoked reprisals and initiated a guerrilla war that cost about 200 lives.

The violence even reached the civilized halls of Congress. In an inflammatory speech, "The Crime against Kansas," Senator Charles Sumner of Massachusetts denounced the Pierce administration, the South, and Senator Andrew P. Butler of South Carolina, who Sumner said had taken "the harlot slavery" as his mistress. Butler's nephew and protégé, Preston Brooks, a member of the House, took personal offense at Sumner's attack and decided to punish him according to the southern code of chivalry. Brooks accosted Sumner at his desk while the Senate was not in session and beat him on the head with a walking cane. Sumner struggled to his feet, wrenched his desk loose from the screws that held it to the floor, and finally fell, unconscious and bleeding. Sumner did not return to the Senate for two and a half years; Massachusetts kept his seat open for him to honor him, and create a symbol of his martyrdom. The House censured Brooks, but South Carolina voters returned him to Congress with an almost unanimous show of support. Many of them sent him new canes to replace the one he had broken in the attack.

The Election of 1856

The violence in Kansas and the halls of Congress dominated the presidential election of 1856. The Democrats stayed with their policy of popular sovereignty, but with their party's center of gravity now resting in the South, they had to go beyond generalities and explicitly reaffirm the Kansas-Nebraska Act. To strengthen the party in the North in the face of Pierce's close association with Bleeding Kansas, the Democrats turned away from him and nominated James Buchanan of Pennsylvania. A

tall, dignified, white-haired figure of sixty-four years, Buchanan had more than forty years of experience in politics but was an unimaginative, uninspiring, and timid leader. Fortunately for his candidacy, he had been minister to Great Britain during the controversy over the Kansas-Nebraska Act and had no record on that volatile issue.

The Republicans counted on a northern backlash against the Democrats over Bleeding Kansas despite the success of Pierce's third territorial governor, John W. Geary of Pennsylvania, in establishing peace in Kansas in September. The Republican platform denounced the Kansas-Nebraska Act and insisted that the federal government prohibit slavery in all the territories. The platform also called for federal subsidies to transcontinental railroads, reviving the element of the Whig economic program that was most popular among midwestern Democrats. The Republicans nominated John C. Frémont, a celebrated army explorer with a meager political record. He was a genuine free-soiler and was famous throughout the nation for his role in the conquest of California.

The Know-Nothings had appeared to be strong early in 1856, but they proved to be only a minor factor in the election. They had quickly split into warring factions—North and South—over Kansas-Nebraska. The Republicans cleverly maneuvered the northern party—called the North American party—into endorsing Frémont. Meanwhile, the southern fragment of the American party nominated Millard Fillmore. He ran strongly in many southern states, but in the North most Know-Nothings disappeared into the ranks of the Republican party. By incorporating anti-Catholic nativism but emphasizing free soil, the Republican message resonated more closely with the deepest concerns of northern voters.

FORCING SLAVERY DOWN THE THROAT OF A FREESOILER

A Free-Soil Cartoon, 1856
This Republican cartoon, published during the presidential campaign of 1856, proposes that the Democrats and their platform would compel free-soilers in Kansas to accept slavery. Using a black man to symbolize slavery and presenting him in a derogatory fashion suggest the racist aspect of the free-soil message.

For the Republicans the great issue of the election was the expansion of slavery. They grabbed the offensive—and adopted the Slave Power conspiracy theory—charging that the South, through the Democratic party, was seeking to extend slavery throughout the nation. The sense of destiny and impending doom that the election created was captured by the poet Walt Whitman, a former Democrat who campaigned for Republicans in 1856. "No man knows what will happen next," Whitman wrote, "but all know some such things are to happen as mark the greatest moral convulsions of the earth."

Many southern Democrats threatened to press for secession if Frémont won. Fearful of such a cataclysm—and still believing that popular sovereignty could solve the crisis—enough northern Democrats remained loyal to give the election to Buchanan. He drew 1.8 million votes to 1.3 million for Frémont. But the Republican party stunned the nation by running up impressive victories in the free states. Frémont attracted enough former Whigs, Know-Nothings, and free-soil Democrats to carry eleven free states. Buchanan took only five, and the race was very close in two of them—Illinois and Pennsylvania. A small shift of the popular vote to Frémont in those two states would have won him the presidency, even though he received no support in the South. In the slave states the race was simply a contest between Buchanan and Fillmore, who won only Maryland.

The Third Party System. A dramatic restructuring of parties had suddenly taken place: the Third Party System—with Democrats and Republicans replacing Democrats and Whigs—had become a reality. The implications for the sectional crisis were ominous. The Republican party was within striking distance of the presidency after only one campaign despite the fact that it was a sectional party, with no support in the South. And the Democratic party had succeeded in bridging sectional conflicts only by the slenderest of margins. Many Americans, both in the North and the South, sensed that they stood on the brink of a revolution. The future of the Union would depend on the ability of President Buchanan to persuade the North that slavery would not threaten free labor in the West and to convince the South that the federal government would protect slavery.

The Democratic Blunders of 1857–1858

The *Dred Scott* Decision. However attractive to northern voters, the free-soil program of the Republicans had never been subjected to a clear test of its constitutionality. The Supreme Court had never reviewed the free-soil doctrine or the contrary proposition of John C. Calhoun that the Constitution protected slavery in the territories and that the people of a territory could prohibit

Dred Scott

Dred Scott's odyssey began in St. Louis in 1834, when he was sold to John Emerson and taken to Illinois, then to Fort Snelling in Wisconsin Territory, and finally back to Missouri. After Emerson died, Scott sued Emerson's wife for his freedom. Two months after the Supreme Court decision, the former Mrs. Emerson, who had married an antislavery politician from Massachusetts, freed Scott.

slavery *only* at the moment of admission to statehood, not before. Many on both sides of the issue hoped the Court would resolve the question in their favor. In 1857 the Court made an effort.

In 1856 the case of Dred Scott, a slave suing for his freedom, reached the Supreme Court. Scott had lived for a time with his master, an army surgeon, in the free state of Illinois and the Wisconsin Territory, where the Northwest Ordinance (1787) and the Missouri Compromise (1820) prohibited slavery. In his suit, which began in 1846 in the courts of Missouri, Scott claimed that his residence in a free state and a free territory had made him a free man. In March 1857, only two days after Buchanan's inauguration, the Court reached a decision in *Dred Scott v. Sandford*.

There was little consensus among the justices on the issues raised by the case, but seven members of the Court agreed on one critical matter—Scott remained a slave. There was no majority opinion—every justice wrote his

own—but Chief Justice Roger B. Taney's was the most influential. Taney ruled that blacks, free *or* slave, could not be citizens of the United States and that Scott therefore had no right to sue in a federal court. Taney could have stopped there. Instead, he insisted on going further and making two broad points. First, he ruled that the Fifth Amendment's prohibition of taking property without due process of law meant that Congress could not pass a law depriving persons of their slave "property" in the territories. Thus, the Missouri Compromise, voided three years earlier by the Kansas-Nebraska Act, had *always* been unconstitutional, and Scott's residence in the Wisconsin Territory had not freed him. Second, Congress could not extend to territorial governments any powers that Congress itself did not possess. Since Congress had no power to prohibit slavery in a territory, neither did the government of that territory. Thus Taney endorsed Calhoun's interpretation of the constitutional protection of slavery and definition of popular sovereignty.

Five of the seven justices, including the chief justice, who was from Maryland, were southern Democrats. They and President Buchanan—who privately twisted the arm of his fellow Pennsylvanian, Justice Robert C. Grier, to join the five—had a specific political purpose in mind when they arranged the decision. They prayed that it would be accepted by Democrats and Republicans alike out of respect for the Court and for law and order and thus ease the sectional crisis. Buchanan also wanted a decision that would strip Republicans of their free-soil platform.

But the Court's decision did just the opposite of calming the sectional waters. In a single stroke the Democratic Supreme Court had declared the Republicans' antislavery platform unconstitutional. It was a decision the Republicans could not tolerate. Led by Senator William H. Seward of New York, they accused the Supreme Court and President Buchanan of participating in the Slave Power conspiracy. Even many northern Democrats were outraged, including Stephen Douglas, who had labored so hard to protect his party's strength in the North by invoking the popular sovereignty doctrine.

The Lecompton Constitution. President Buchanan then made an even more serious blunder by deciding to support the proslavery forces in Kansas. In early 1858 he recommended the admission of Kansas as a slave state under the so-called Lecompton constitution. Most observers—including Stephen Douglas—believed that that constitution had been obtained by fraud, particularly because the antislavery majority in Kansas had previously rejected the constitution in a referendum. Douglas thought that admitting Kansas under the Lecompton constitution would be a travesty of democracy, a parody of popular sovereignty, and an embarrassment to the party in most of the North. Angered, Douglas broke

with Buchanan and the southern Democrats and mobilized western Democrats and Republicans in the House of Representatives to defeat the Lecompton constitution. (Kansas finally entered the Union as a free state in 1861, after secession was well under way and many southern representatives had left Congress.)

Buchanan's support for the Lecompton constitution meant that he had decided to worry more about the anxieties of the South than about those of the North. It was a catastrophic choice. He failed to organize Kansas on a proslavery basis, fractured the Democratic party, and provided the Republicans with more evidence that an insidious Slave Power was threatening the rights of free labor and, ultimately, the existence of the republic. Buchanan had made it virtually impossible for either the Democratic party or popular sovereignty to provide the basis for preserving national unity.

Abraham Lincoln and the Breaking of Union, 1858–1860

The disintegration of the national Democratic party that had begun over Bleeding Kansas accelerated after the elections of 1856 and the *Dred Scott* decision. Former Democrats and Whigs continued to switch to the new Republican party. During this crisis of Union Abraham Lincoln emerged as the pivotal figure in American politics. His rise to power illustrates how the issue of slavery came to dominate politics and change the way Americans thought about the future of their society.

Lincoln's Early Career

Economic development and the rise of the business class in the small towns of the Ohio River Valley shaped Lincoln's early career. His restless farming family of modest means had moved from Kentucky, where Lincoln was born in 1809, to Indiana and then to Illinois. In 1831 Lincoln set out on his own, settling in New Salem, a small town on the Sangamon River in central Illinois. He rejected the farming life and began working as a store clerk. He had already displayed signs of business entrepreneurship, having twice, in 1828 and 1831, taken flatboats laden with farm produce down the Mississippi River to New Orleans. The profits helped him become a partner in a general store in New Salem.

In New Salem Lincoln was equally at home with the rough, footloose young men of the town and its emerging business class. He excelled in the games, pranks, and fights of a gang of young men who hung

out in a local saloon, and in 1831 they elected him captain of the company of New Salem men who volunteered for the Black Hawk War. He had little formal schooling, but with the help of the local schoolmaster he mastered English grammar and elementary mathematics. Another villager introduced him to Shakespeare. During Lincoln's first winter in town he became a regular participant in the New Salem Debating Society.

Illinois State Legislator. Lincoln's ambition was, as a friend later described it, "a little engine that knew no rest." That ambition ran not to business but to politics. In 1832 Lincoln ran for the state legislature on a business-class program of increased state investment in internal improvements and education. Universal education, he said in his campaign, would give people "the advantages and satisfaction to be derived from all being able to read the scriptures and other works, both of a religious and moral nature, for themselves."

Lincoln lost the 1832 election but won almost all the votes cast in New Salem and rapidly extended his influence. He was appointed postmaster and deputy county surveyor and began to study law with a prominent attorney who was also a state legislator and the foremost Whig in the county. In 1834 Lincoln ran again for the state legislature and won. Admitted to the bar in 1837, he moved to Springfield, the new state capital. There he met Mary Todd, the daughter of a successful Kentucky businessman and politician; they married in 1842. They were a picture in contrasts. Her tastes were aristocratic; his were humble. She was volatile; he was easygoing and deliberate. Bouts of depression, which plagued Lincoln throughout his life, tried her patience. Yet those episodes were integral to the remarkable growth of his personality and mind.

During Lincoln's four terms in the lower house of the Illinois legislature he had a powerful influence on the building of the Whig party. As Whig floor leader and chairman of the finance committee, Lincoln promoted state banking and extensive internal improvements—turnpikes, canals, and railroads—that the Whigs hoped would increase their appeal in the normally Democratic areas of southern and central Illinois. In 1840 he made two long campaign tours on behalf of William Henry Harrison in southern Illinois, and in 1844 he campaigned for his political hero, Henry Clay, in the southern Indiana towns of his boyhood. In 1846 Lincoln drew on his expanded network of Whig friends and supporters to win election to Congress.

Congressman. Until entering Congress in 1847, Lincoln had successfully avoided taking a stand on the contentious issue of slavery. But now the Mexican War and its implications for the future of slavery forced him to state his position.

Lincoln had concluded, perhaps as early as one of his youthful trips to New Orleans, that slavery was unjust. And in 1838 he had spoken out in general terms against the mob violence that was directed at abolitionists and had resulted in the killing of Elijah Lovejoy in nearby Alton. But Lincoln's roots in the Ohio River Valley towns settled largely by migrants from southern states and his desire to build Whig support in those towns worked against any sympathy for abolitionism, which emphasized the sinfulness of slaveholding. He knew, moreover, that abolitionism was a threat to the Whigs. This had come home to him in 1844 when he had watched the Whig abolitionists in New York throw their votes to James G. Birney, the Liberty party candidate, and seemingly deny Henry Clay the presidency. And he did not believe that the federal government had any authority to tamper with slavery where it existed.

Lincoln entered Congress in 1847 with a firm conviction that the Whigs had to abstain from abolitionism yet find a way to hold the allegiance of the growing number of people opposed to slavery. Consequently, he supported the appropriations bills necessary to sustain American forces in Mexico but, at the same time, condemned the Polk administration for its war of aggression, introduced resolutions pressing Polk on the constitutionality of the war, and, most important, voted for the Wilmot Proviso in its various forms. In addition, Lincoln introduced a resolution for the gradual abolition of slavery in the District of Columbia. His bill would have provided compensation to slave owners and required approval by a referendum of the "free white citizens" of the District. It was this kind of moderate program of opposition to slavery's expansion and encouragement of gradual emancipation, coupled with the colonization of freed slaves in Africa and elsewhere, that Lincoln argued was the only practical way to solve the problem of slavery. It was on the basis of this program that he argued in 1848, while campaigning for Zachary Taylor in Massachusetts, Chicago, and even his own district, that antislavery Whigs should remain in the party because Whigs and supporters of the Free Soil party had similar views on the spread of slavery.

Corporate Lawyer. The abolitionists denounced Lincoln's approach. In response to his gradualist proposal for emancipation in the District of Columbia, the abolitionist Wendell Phillips called Lincoln "the slave hound of Illinois." But Lincoln's position, particularly his condemnation of the Mexican War, put him too far out of step with the voters in his district, and he went into a prudent retirement from politics that lasted from 1849 until 1854. While he engaged in an increasingly lucrative legal practice, one in which some of the leading railroads and manufacturers in Illinois became his clients, Lincoln agonized over the disintegration of the Whig party and

Abraham Lincoln

Abraham Lincoln became the most photographed man of his time, yet none of the photographs suggests how striking and sparkling people found him. The photography of that day required subjects to stand absolutely still, their heads against a rack, for long periods, and this caused Lincoln to lapse into a sad and abstracted mood.

The Campaign of 1854. Lincoln's dual quest for the moral high ground on slavery and a way to preserve the Union brought him back into politics in 1854, after the passage of Stephen Douglas's Kansas-Nebraska Act. That act "aroused" him "as he had never been before." The opening of Kansas to popular sovereignty placed freedom and slavery on the same ethical level and at the same time threatened the Union. Moreover, the act created an opportunity for the Whigs to win the allegiance of Democrats who feared that Douglas was betraying them by opening the West to slavery and to blacks. Lincoln made a last, desperate effort to save the Whig party in Illinois. He plunged into the campaigns with an attack on Douglas, support for Whig candidates, and his own campaign for both the Illinois legislature and the U.S. Senate.

Lincoln stated his position in what became known as his Peoria address. He did not want to threaten slavery in areas where it existed. White southerners were, he said, "just what we would be in their situation." He believed that "some system of gradual emancipation might be adopted," but "for their tardiness in this, I will not undertake to judge our brethren of the south." But the Kansas-Nebraska Act had repealed the Missouri Compromise and threatened to expand slavery. Politicians had to face the ethical issue that slavery was founded, he said, "in the selfishness of man's nature," whereas opposition to it was based "in his love of justice." However, the risks to the Union were obvious. Those principles were in "eternal antagonism" and "when brought into collision so fiercely as slavery extension brings them, shocks, and throes, and convulsions must ceaselessly follow."

Lincoln concluded his Peoria address by appealing to supporters of the Free Soil party and abolitionists to join the Whigs in restoring the Missouri Compromise. By joining forces they could both block slavery's extension and uphold the Union. In short, Lincoln expressed what would become key tenets of the Republican party: moral opposition to slavery, assertion of the right of the national government to exclude slavery from the territories, and the conviction that the nation must eventually cut out slavery like a "cancer."

Republican Party Leader. After a handful of Anti-Nebraska Democrats in the state legislature blocked Lincoln's election to the Senate, he decided, finally, to abandon the Whig party. That way, he might win the support of Anti-Nebraska Democrats who could not bring themselves to endorse a Whig. As the violence escalated in Kansas and the Whig party splintered, he worked to unite all the Anti-Nebraska forces—conservative Whigs, members of the Free Soil party, abolitionists, Know-Nothings, and bolting Democrats—in opposition to the Democratic party and to Stephen

the apparent failure of moderate approaches to resolve the sectional crisis. In a speech eulogizing Henry Clay after his death in 1852, Lincoln condemned both the proslavery fanatics who denied the tenet of the Declaration of Independence that "all men are created equal" and the abolitionists, who would "shiver into fragments the Union of these States; tear to tatters its now venerated constitution; and even burn the last copy of the Bible, rather than slavery should continue a single hour."

Douglas and the doctrine of popular sovereignty. In May 1856, in a state convention of all the dissident groups, Lincoln emerged as the most powerful leader in the coalition that formed the Republican party in Illinois, and Illinois Republicans put him forward as their favorite-son candidate for vice-president.

The *Dred Scott* decision in 1857 gave Lincoln new ammunition in his campaign to win over Democrats. He warned that the Supreme Court, in its "next Dred Scott decision," would simply "decide that no State under the Constitution can exclude" slavery. If the followers of Buchanan had their way, "we shall *awake* to the *reality* . . . that the *Supreme* Court has made *Illinois* a *slave* State." The Court now seemed to be a partner in the Slave Power conspiracy. Although Republicans would abide by the Court's decision, they dedicated themselves to reversing it.

By 1858, Lincoln's position in the Illinois Republican party was even stronger, and he again received the party's nomination as the challenger to Stephen Douglas for U.S. senator. In accepting the nomination he delivered the most radical statement of his career. Quoting from the Bible, "A house divided against itself cannot stand," he warned that the nation could not resolve the slavery issue without a crisis. There were only two possible outcomes:

> I believe this government cannot endure permanently half *slave* and half *free*. I do not expect the Union to be dissolved—I do not expect the house to *fall*—but I do expect it will cease to be divided. It will become *all* one thing, or *all* the other.

Thus Lincoln dismissed as insignificant the differences between Douglas and Buchanan on the issue of slavery. Americans had to choose, according to Lincoln, between opposition and advocacy.

Lincoln versus Douglas

Lincoln's challenge to Douglas's bid for reelection as a senator from Illinois proved to be the highlight of the 1858 elections. The political duel attracted national interest because of Douglas's prominence and his break with the Buchanan administration. Adding to the excitement was Lincoln's reputation as a formidable attorney, politician, and stump speaker. To increase his national exposure, Lincoln challenged Douglas to a series of seven debates.

During those debates Lincoln attacked slavery as an institution that subverted equality of opportunity. He expressed doubts about the innate abilities of African-Americans and explicitly rejected formulas that would give them social and political equality, but he declared that blacks were entitled to "all the natural rights enumer-

Stephen Douglas
This photograph, taken in Mathew Brady's New York studio in 1860, suggests why Stephen Douglas (1813–1861) was known as the "Little Giant."

ated in the Declaration of Independence." This meant, Lincoln explained, that "in the right to eat the bread, without leave of anybody else, which his own hand earns," the black was "the equal of every living man."

Lincoln described the master conspiracy he saw at work. The Kansas-Nebraska Act (which Douglas had introduced), the *Dred Scott* decision, and Buchanan's cynical endorsement of the fraudulent Lecompton constitution were part of a master plan to extend slavery throughout the territories. If the South succeeded, it would eventually insist that slavery be legalized throughout the United States. Lincoln then pressed Douglas to explain how he could accept the *Dred Scott* decision and at the same time advocate popular sovereignty.

In a debate in Freeport, Illinois, Douglas responded by elaborating on a reformulation of popular sovereignty that he had been working on since mid-1857. In what became known as the Freeport doctrine, he asserted that settlers could exclude slavery from a territory in practice simply by not adopting local legislation to protect it. In other words, he claimed that even if ter-

ritorial governments followed Taney and did not prohibit slavery, municipalities could still do so by failing to support the "peculiar institution." In effect, this was a legalistic formulation of his view that demography and geography made the victory of slavery in the territories almost impossible. To southerners the Freeport doctrine meant that they could be denied the victory won in the *Dred Scott* decision.

The Republicans made great gains in 1858, including control of the House. Lincoln, however, was not among the victors. Douglas was reelected to the Senate by a narrow margin in the state legislature, but Lincoln had virtually buried popular sovereignty in Illinois. Douglas's victory resulted from the overrepresentation in the legislature of the staunchly Democratic counties in southern Illinois rather than any popularity of the Freeport doctrine, which was too flimsy a basis for rebuilding the Democratic party.

The Election of 1860

The Congressional elections of 1858 made southern Democrats intensely nervous. They knew that the Republicans might win in 1860, so they increased their demands. The more moderate party members, known as Southern Rights Democrats, insisted that the Democratic party and the federal government make specific commitments to protect slavery, such as the enactment of a territorial slave code that would counter the Freeport doctrine. One of their leading spokesmen was Senator Jefferson Davis, a Mississippi planter and Mexican War hero. More radical southern Democrats, such as Robert Barnwell Rhett of South Carolina and William Lowndes Yancey of Alabama, demanded that Douglas and his followers support relegalization of the international slave trade. Called *fire-eaters*, those radicals were secessionists who hoped to drive a wedge between the North and the South. In response, Douglas made it plain that if the Democratic party platform included such proposals in 1860, he would not support it. He had no choice in drawing a hard line. If he did not, he would sacrifice his home base of support.

John Brown's Raid. In the meantime a shocking event further deepened the anxiety of southerners. One night in October 1859, John Brown, leader of the Pottawatomie massacre, led eighteen heavily armed followers, both black and white, in a raid that seized the federal arsenal at Harpers Ferry, Virginia. Brown's explicit purpose was to arm a slave rebellion and create an African-American state in the South. The local militia and U.S. Marines under the command of Colonel Robert E. Lee quickly reclaimed the arsenal; they captured Brown and killed ten of his party.

Republican leaders dismissed Brown as a criminal, but Democrats in both the North and the South called Brown's plot, in the words of Stephen Douglas, "a natural, logical, inevitable result of the doctrines and teachings of the Republican party." Fueling the Democratic charges were letters, discovered near Harpers Ferry and widely published in the press, that incriminated six leading abolitionists, known as the Secret Six, for financing Brown's raid. The group included two Unitarian ministers, Thomas Wentworth Higginson and Theodore Parker. Parker used his home as a station on the underground railroad for escaped slaves, and Higginson had run unsuccessfully as a Free Soil party candidate for Congress in 1850. During the Civil War he would command a regiment of African-American soldiers. Higginson admitted his involvement and declared that Brown's "acquittal or rescue would do half as much good as being executed; so strong is the personal sympathy with him."

Virginia gave the abolitionists the Christian martyr they wanted. The governor charged Brown with trea-

John Brown Pledging Allegiance to the Flag
This is the earliest known photograph of John Brown, probably taken in 1846. In 1847 Frederick Douglass had dinner with Brown and learned that he had a plan to establish abolitionist bases in the Appalachian Mountains and induce slaves to escape to freedom.

Harpers Ferry Armory
The town of Harpers Ferry was strategically situated at the confluence of the Shenandoah and Potomac rivers, at the point where the Baltimore and Ohio Railroad crossed the Potomac. Adding to the town's strategic importance were the federal armory (including the machine shops at the right in the photograph), the federal arsenal (an arms storehouse), and on a nearby island in the Shenandoah, Hall's Rifle Works, where sixty gunsmiths produced firearms for the U.S. Army. At the left is the fire-engine house where Brown and his raiders made their last stand.

son, a state court sentenced him to death, and Brown was hanged. At a church meeting in Concord, Massachusetts, Henry David Thoreau described Brown as "an angel of light," "the bravest and humanest man in all the country." Emerson proclaimed that Brown would "make the gallows as glorious as the cross." Slaveholders were horrified, assuming that those widely publicized utterances revealed the sentiments of the entire North and that abolitionists were organizing new slave rebellions. More than ever slaveholders were convinced that a Republican victory in 1860 would lead to the destruction of slavery.

The Democrats Divide. When the Democratic party convened in Charleston, South Carolina, in April 1860, the southern wing was determined to force the party to embrace the program of Jefferson Davis and his followers: positive protection of slavery in the territories in line with the *Dred Scott* decision. Northern Democrats refused. They wanted only a vague endorsement of popular sovereignty and the suggestion that disputed issues be left to the Supreme Court. When the convention adopted the northern platform, the delegates from eight southern states left the hall. Because Buchanan had lost the confidence of northern Democrats, he was not a contender for the nomination, and Douglas led the balloting for a presidential candidate. However, his determined foes denied him the two-thirds majority that the party rules required for nomination. The party adjourned and then reconvened in Baltimore in June. Most of the southerners reappeared but soon walked

out again. The Baltimore convention then nominated Stephen Douglas. The bolting southerners convened separately in Baltimore and nominated Buchanan's vice-president, John C. Breckinridge of Kentucky. The Democratic party had finally broken into two sectional pieces.

The Republicans Choose Lincoln. The Republicans sensed victory and acted cautiously. They settled on Abraham Lincoln, who had a more moderate position on slavery than the best-known Republicans, Senator William H. Seward of New York and former Governor Salmon P. Chase of Ohio. Lincoln also conveyed a compelling egalitarian image that could appeal to small farmers and workers. And Lincoln's home territory—the Ohio River Valley of Illinois and Indiana—was a crucial "swing" area in the competition between Democrats and Republicans.

The Republican platform also attempted to strike a moderate tone. It adhered to free-soil doctrine but ruled out direct interference with slavery in the South. It denied the right of states to secede. It also endorsed the old Whig program of economic development, which had gained increasing support among Democrats in the Midwest, especially after the onset of depression conditions in 1857.

Douglas campaigned nationally against three competitors, each of whom was, for all practical purposes, a regional candidate. However, in September and October he concentrated his efforts in the South, having concluded that Lincoln would win in the North. Douglas

underscored the seriousness of the sectional crisis by shattering tradition and campaigning personally. He warned Breckinridge supporters about secession, telling them that the North and northern Democrats would not allow them to destroy the Union and arguing that *his* Democratic party provided the only feasible instrument for compromise. Competing with Breckinridge and Douglas in the South and also offering a Unionist message was John Bell, a former Tennessee senator who became the nominee of the Constitutional Union party, a residue of southern Whiggery. The forces of moderation were ebbing in the South. Since the shock of John Brown's raid on Harpers Ferry, waves of hysteria over slave rebellion had swept through the region. Southern panic intensified during the presidential campaign. Fires of unknown origin and the deaths of whites under peculiar circumstances initiated reports of arson and poisoning.

Lincoln's Victory. Lincoln won only a plurality of the popular vote—about 40 percent of the total—but received a majority of the electoral vote (see Map 14.5). His victory in the North was overwhelming: he won every state except New Jersey. Of crucial importance to

Lincoln's election were Pennsylvania, Indiana, and his home state of Illinois, all of which had cast their electoral votes for Buchanan in 1856. In ten of the slave states Lincoln was excluded from the ballot; in the other five slave states he won no electoral votes. Breckinridge won every state in the Deep South as well as Delaware, Maryland, and North Carolina. Bell carried the Upper South states where the Whigs had been strongest: Kentucky, Tennessee, and Virginia. Douglas won electoral votes in only two states—Missouri, which he carried, and New Jersey, where he won three of the state's seven electoral votes—despite winning 21 percent of the popular vote. His broad support was wasted in a winner-take-all system.

The Republicans had united the Northeast, the Midwest, and the Far West behind free soil. They had been able to absorb abolitionism and still unify enough businessmen, workers, and farmers to achieve victory. A political party with support in only one section of the country and a clear mission had finally come to power. To many southerners, it now seemed time to think carefully about the meaning of Lincoln's 1858 words, that the Union must "become all one thing, or all the other."

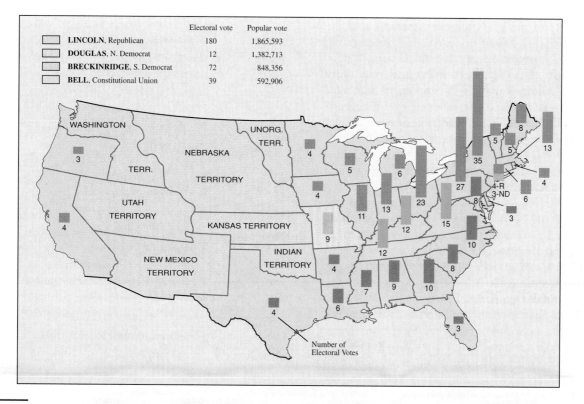

MAP 14.5

The Election of 1860

Four presidential candidates vied for election in 1860. Douglas's few electoral votes are striking in light of his strong showing in the popular vote. In most states Douglas ran second to Lincoln or Breckinridge, who took all of the electoral votes in the states that they won.

Summary

The American experience, so full of material and spiritual promise, took a tragic turn in the 1840s, when the South's ambitions led the United States into a war of conquest against Mexico. President Polk's policy of territorial expansion was successful, but the new territories and continued western expansion doomed the Missouri Compromise as a means of accommodating the interests of the South and the North in the West. The sectional threat to the unity of the two major political parties and to the Union became so great that leaders of both parties joined in framing a settlement, known as the Compromise of 1850. The Compromise temporarily preserved the Second Party System, but most southern Democrats and most northern Whigs did not support it. They stood ready to risk the Union if they could not dominate the West.

The Compromise of 1850 and the Second Party System died in the violence of the 1850s, casualties of the first armed struggles over slavery. Antislavery northerners defied the Fugitive Slave Act, battling southern slave catchers. When northern Whigs opposed the act, southerners deserted the party, killing it as a national organization.

The ability of the U.S. political system to hold the Union together then rested exclusively on the national appeal of the Democratic party and its doctrine of popular sovereignty. But that doctrine brought only more violence—"Bleeding Kansas"—as opponents and supporters of slavery fought a guerrilla war over the meaning of popular sovereignty. Bleeding Kansas pushed North and South farther apart and weakened the Democratic party.

Northern Whigs and supporters of the Free Soil party joined dissident Democrats and Know-Nothings to establish the Republican party, which supported free soil. By 1856 the Second Party System of Democrats and Whigs had given way to the Third Party System of Democrats and Republicans. In 1856 the Republicans united a majority of voters in the Northeast and Northwest around free-soilism.

The national Democratic party finally fractured over the *Dred Scott* decision and President Buchanan's support for the Lecompton constitution. Former Democrats and Whigs continued to switch to the Republican party. In 1859 John Brown, an abolitionist veteran of the Kansas struggle, captured a federal arsenal in Virginia and tried to start a war against slavery. Southerners then demanded more protection for slavery than northern Democrats would provide. Consequently, in the 1860 election the Democrats divided along sectional

lines. At the same time Abraham Lincoln succeeded in uniting northern society around the free-soil vision and won the presidency for the Republican party.

TIMELINE

1845	Polk's inauguration
	Frémont sets out from St. Louis
	Texas accepts admission to the Union
	Polk sends Zachary Taylor south of the Nueces River
	Slidell's mission
	Frémont reaches the Sacramento Valley
1846	Polk sends Taylor south of the Rio Grande
	United States declares war on Mexico
	Oregon treaty ratified
	"Bear Flag Republic" proclaimed; Sloat seizes Monterrey
	Walker Tariff passed
	Wilmot Proviso introduced in Congress
	Taylor's victory at Monterrey
1847	Taylor's victory at Buena Vista
	Scott captures Mexico City
1848	Gold discovered in California
	Treaty of Guadalupe Hidalgo
	Free Soil party organized
	Taylor elected
1849	Taylor proposes immediate admission of California
1850	Compromise of 1850
1851	Christiana riot
	American party formed
1852	*Uncle Tom's Cabin* appears in book form
	Franklin Pierce elected president
1853	Perry's expedition to Japan begins
1854	Kansas-Nebraska Act
	Republican party formed
	Ostend Manifesto
	Know-Nothing movement peaks
1856	"Pottawatomie massacre"
	James Buchanan elected president
1857	*Dred Scott v. Sandford*
	Panic of 1857
1858	Buchanan backs Lecompton constitution
	Lincoln-Douglas debates
1859	John Brown's raid on Harpers Ferry
1860	Abraham Lincoln elected president

★   ★   ★

BIBLIOGRAPHY

Histories that discuss the disruption of the Union between the Mexican War and the onset of the Civil War in a comprehensive fashion are rare. The best is David M. Potter, *The Impending Crisis, 1848–1861* (1976).

The Mexican War and Its Aftermath

Study of expansionism in the 1840s should begin with Frederick Merk, *The Monroe Doctrine and American Expansion, 1843–1849* (1972). On the coming of the Mexican War, consult Paul H. Bergeron, *The Presidency of James K. Polk* (1987); David Pletcher, *The Diplomacy of Annexation: Texas, Oregon, and the Mexican War* (1973); and Charles G. Sellers, *James K. Polk: Continentalist, 1843–1846* (1966). On the fighting of the war, see K. Jack Bauer, *The Mexican War, 1846–1848* (1974), and Otis A. Singletary, *The Mexican War* (1960). For an analysis of the relationship between the war experience and American culture, see Robert W. Johannsen, *To the Halls of the Montezumas: The Mexican War in the American Imagination* (1985), and John H. Schroeder, *Mr. Polk's War: American Opposition and Dissent* (1973). For the Mexican viewpoint see Gene M. Brack, *Mexico Views Manifest Destiny, 1821–1846: An Essay on the Origins of the Mexican War* (1975). On Congressional politics during the 1840s, see Chaplain Morrison, *Democratic Politics and Sectionalism: The Wilmot Proviso Controversy* (1967); Merrill Peterson, *The Great Triumvirate: Webster, Clay, and Calhoun* (1987); and Joel H. Silbey, *The Shrine of Party: Congressional Voting Behavior, 1841–1852* (1967). On the Compromise of 1850, see Holman Hamilton, *Prologue to Conflict: The Crisis and Compromise of 1850* (1964). For an interpretation stressing the contingency of the South's commitment to the Union, consult William W. Freehling, *The Road to Disunion: Secessionists at Bay, 1776–1854* (1991).

Sectional Strife and the Third Party System

General studies of sectional conflict in the 1850s include Avery O. Craven, *The Growth of Southern Nationalism* (1953), and Roy F. Nichols, *The Disruption of American Democracy* (1948). On the Fugitive Slave Act, consult Stanley W. Campbell, *The Slave Catchers* (1970). The best study of the politics of southern expansionism is Robert E. May, *The Southern Dream of a Caribbean Empire, 1854–1861* (1973). The leading studies of Frederick Douglass include Philip S. Foner, *Frederick Douglass: A Biography* (1964); Nathan I. Huggins, *Slave and Citizen: The Life of Frederick Douglass* (1980); William S. McFeely, *Frederick Douglass* (1991); and Benjamin Quarles, *Frederick Douglass* (1948). Essential sources on Douglass include three versions of his autobiography: *The Narrative of the Life of Frederick Douglass, An American Slave* (1845), which he wrote as an antislavery tract; *My Bondage and My Freedom* (1855), which provides an elaborate and highly personal analysis of slavery; and *Life and Times of Frederick Douglass, Written by Himself* (1881).

On the development of the Republican party, see Eric Foner, *Free Soil, Free Labor, Free Men: The Ideology of the Republican Party before the Civil War* (1970); William E. Gienapp, *The Origins of the Republican Party, 1852–1856* (1987); and Michael Holt, *The Political Crisis of the 1850s* (1978). The crisis over Kansas is discussed in James A. Rawley, *Race and Politics: Bleeding Kansas and the Coming of the Civil War* (1969), and Gerald W. Wolff, *The Kansas-Nebraska Bill: Party, Section, and the Coming of the Civil War* (1977). On the Buchanan administration, see Kenneth M. Stampp, *America in 1857: A Nation on the Brink* (1990). On *Dred Scott*, see Don E. Fehrenbacher, *The Dred Scott Case: Its Significance in American Law and Politics* (1978). For a biography of Stephen A. Douglas, see Robert W. Johannsen, *Stephen A. Douglas* (1973). The best biography of John Brown is Stephen Oates, *To Purge this Land with Blood: A Biography of John Brown* (1970).

Abraham Lincoln and the Breaking of Union

Abraham Lincoln has inspired a host of biographies. Classic studies include James G. Randall, *Mr. Lincoln* (1957, distilled by Richard N. Current from Randall's four-volume *Lincoln the President*, with vol. 4 completed by Current); Carl Sandburg, *Abraham Lincoln: The Prairie Years* (1929); and Benjamin Thomas, *Abraham Lincoln: A Biography* (1952). The most recent major biography of Lincoln is David Herbert Donald, *Lincoln* (1995). For a stimulating set of essays, see Richard N. Current, *The Lincoln Nobody Knows* (1958). The most valuable book on Lincoln's formative political years is Don E. Fehrenbacher, *Prelude to Greatness: Lincoln in the 1850s* (1962). For other interpretations, see George B. Forgie, *Patricide and the House Divided* (1979); Stephen Oates, *With Malice toward None: A Life of Abraham Lincoln* (1977); and Garry Wills, *Lincoln at Gettysburg* (1992).

The Seventh Regiment Departing for the War,
April 19, 1861 (detail)

Stunned by the massive demonstrations of support for the
Union after Lincoln's call to arms, a New York woman
wrote, "It seems as if we never were alive till now; never had
a country till now." Thomas Nast evoked that spirit in this
painting done in 1869.

CHAPTER 15

Two Societies at War

1861–1865

★   ★   ★

For the political leaders of the South, the victory of Abraham Lincoln and the Republicans in the fateful election of 1860 presented a clear and immediate danger to the institution of slavery. They knew that Lincoln regarded slavery as morally wrong and had united northern society in opposing the "Slave Power" and the extension of slavery into the territories. Moreover, unlike any preceding president, he owed the South not a single electoral vote. Soon, southern leaders were certain, he would appoint abolitionists and free blacks to federal jobs in the South and reopen the flow of abolitionist literature. The result would be disastrous waves of bloody slave revolts. White southerners believed that no loyal American should have to fear such a cataclysm. They were convinced that the Constitution protected slavery. Moreover, in their view slavery was a bulwark of democracy: by guaranteeing equality and freedom for whites, it protected the highest values of the republic.

Many southerners swiftly concluded that they could save slavery from the Republican threat only through secession: southern states would leave the Union and establish their own nation, in accordance with John C. Calhoun's constitutional theory that sovereignty lay not with the American people as a whole but with collections of people acting through their state governments. If Lincoln would not recognize states' rights, the South would fight.

And so came the Civil War. Called the "War between the States" by Confederates and the "War of the Rebellion" by Unionists, it tested the founding principles of the republic. It resolved once and for all the great dividing issue of slavery. And it cost more lives than all the nation's subsequent wars put together.

Choosing Sides, 1861

The two societies, South and North, were poised for confrontation in 1861. Many southerners were convinced that in defending states' rights and slavery they were being more true in their Americanism and more stalwart in their support of republican ideals than were Republicans in the North. By contrast, Lincoln and his party regarded secession as despicable and treasonous. There was only the slimmest chance that during the early months of 1861 the nation's politicians could emulate the architects of the great compromises of 1820, 1833, and 1850 and once again postpone the sectional confrontation.

The Secession Crisis

The movement toward secession was most rapid in South Carolina—the home of Calhoun and the state with the greatest concentration of slaves. The fire-eaters took the lead in organizing a convention to consider se-

cession, which most of them had been calling for since 1850. On December 20, only six weeks after Lincoln's election, the convention unanimously enacted an ordinance dissolving "the union now subsisting between South Carolina and other States."

During the next six weeks fire-eaters in six other cotton states called conventions. They moved quickly, before southern Unionists could mount an effective opposition. Meanwhile, vigilante groups and military companies organized. They sometimes engaged in strong-arm intimidation of Unionists, who were often willing to secede but usually preferred to wait until Lincoln had shown his hand. In early January, in an atmosphere of public celebration, Mississippi enacted a secession ordinance. In less than a month Florida, Alabama, Georgia, Louisiana, and Texas also left the Union (see Map 15.1). The jubilant secessionists proclaimed a new nation—the Confederate States of America. In early February commissioners from those states, meeting in Montgomery, Alabama, adopted a provisional constitution and named Jefferson Davis provisional president. Secession proceeded so briskly that all this was done before James Buchanan left the White House.

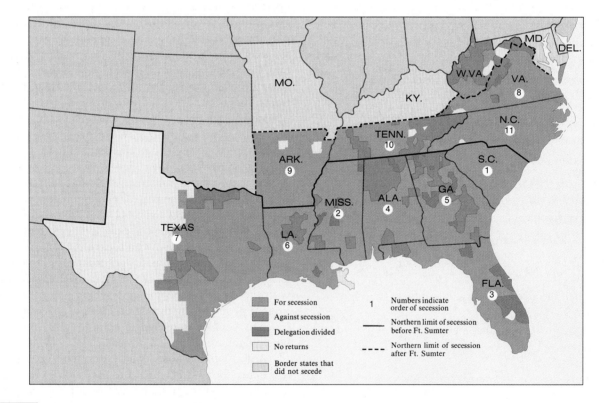

MAP 15.1

The Process of Secession
Comparing the order of secession with the distribution of slaves in Map 13.1 (page 384), it is clear that states with the highest concentrations of slaves led the movement to secede. The secession of the Upper South followed the Confederate firing on Fort Sumter. The map also shows how delegates to the secession conventions or special sessions of legislatures voted. Significant minorities in most states opposed secession.

Panic was less severe in the Upper South, where concentrations of slaves were not as large. Nevertheless, secessionist fervor had been gathering momentum there from the time of Lincoln's election, and many political leaders in the eight Upper South states (Arkansas, Delaware, Kentucky, Maryland, Missouri, North Carolina, Tennessee, and Virginia) defended the right of any state to secede. In January 1861 the Virginia and Tennessee legislatures pledged to resist any federal invasion of the seceded states. But they went no further. Upper South leaders proposed federal guarantees for slavery in the states where it existed, hoping to relieve the anxieties of the seceding states and bring them back into the Union.

While the seceding states acted, the Union government, still under control of the Democrats, floundered. President Buchanan did not support secession, but the southerners in his cabinet persuaded him that if he confronted the seceding states, he would alienate southern Unionists and accelerate the secession drive. In his last message to Congress in December 1860 he declared secession illegal but said that the federal government lacked the authority to force a state to return to the Union. South Carolina responded quickly by claiming that Buchanan's message implied recognition of its independence and by demanding the surrender of Fort Sumter, a federal garrison in Charleston harbor. But even Buchanan was reluctant to turn over federal property; he decided to test cautiously the secessionists' resolve. In January 1861 he ordered an unarmed merchant ship to reinforce Fort Sumter. When South Carolinians fired on the ship as it entered the harbor, Buchanan backed off, declining to send the navy to escort the ship into the harbor.

The Crittenden Plan. As the South Carolina crisis worsened, Buchanan urged Congress to find a compromise. The proposal that received the most support was submitted by Senator John J. Crittenden of Kentucky, an aging follower of Henry Clay. Crittenden proposed amending the Constitution with a set of provisions that could never be changed. Congress would be prohibited from abolishing slavery in the states, and the Missouri Compromise line would be extended westward across the territories as far as the California border. Whereas slavery would be barred north of the line, it would be recognized and protected south of the line, including in any territories "hereafter acquired."

After consulting with President-elect Lincoln, Congressional Republicans rejected Crittenden's plan. Lincoln feared that extending the Missouri Compromise line would encourage the South to embark on an imperialist expansion of slavery into Mexico, the Caribbean, and Latin America. If adopted, Lincoln charged, Crittenden's plan would be "a perpetual covenant of war against every people, tribe, and State owning a foot of land between here and Tierra del Fuego." Lincoln was determined not to repudiate the Republicans' chief plank: free soil in the territories.

Lincoln Takes Command. In his inaugural address on March 4, 1861, Lincoln carefully balanced the possibility of reconciliation with his firm commitment to protect the Union. He promised to welcome back the seceded states after time had allowed passions to cool and repeated his support for guaranteeing slavery in states where it existed. But he continued to stand by free soil, offering no compromise on the future of slavery in the territories. Most important, he stated that secession was illegal and that acts of violence in its support constituted insurrection. He announced equally clearly that he intended to enforce federal law throughout the Union and—of particular relevance to Fort Sumter—hold federal property in the seceded states. If force was necessary to preserve the Union, he promised to use it. The choice would be the South's—return to the Union or face war.

Lincoln had hoped to wait out the Fort Sumter crisis, but the garrison urgently needed supplies. He was reluctant to appear aggressive, but he was also unwilling to abandon the fort, fearing that his efforts to maintain the Union would lose credibility. Consequently, only a month after his inauguration, Lincoln dispatched an armed relief expedition and informed South Carolina of his intentions.

Jefferson Davis and his government received word of Lincoln's action on April 8. They welcomed Lincoln's move, believing that his show of force would set the wavering southern states against the North and win foreign support for the Confederate cause. The next day they resolved to take the fort before Union reinforcements arrived. Jefferson Davis authorized General P. G. T. Beauregard, the Confederate commander in Charleston, to take the fort—by force if necessary. When Major Robert Anderson refused to surrender, the Confederates opened fire. On April 14, after two days of bombardment that destroyed large portions of the fort but killed no one, Anderson surrendered. The next day Lincoln called 75,000 state militiamen into federal service for ninety days. As he put it, they were needed to put down an insurrection "too powerful to be suppressed by the ordinary course of judicial proceedings." War had come.

In the North, Fort Sumter became a symbol of national unity and Major Anderson became a hero. Northern states responded enthusiastically to Lincoln's call to arms. Governor William Dennison of Ohio, when asked to provide thirteen regiments of volunteers, sent twenty. "The lion in us is thoroughly roused," he explained. Many northern Democrats were equally fervent. As Stephen Douglas explained just six weeks before his death: "There are only two sides to the question. Every man must be for the United States or against it. There can be no neutrals in this war, *only patriots—or traitors.*"

The Contest for the Upper South

After the fall of Fort Sumter, Lincoln hoped to hold as many of the eight states of the Upper South as possible. If he could keep them from seceding, he might swiftly restore the Union. In the event of war, the Upper South would be of great strategic value. Those eight states accounted for two-thirds of the South's white population, more than three-fourths of its industrial production, and well over half of its food and fuel. They were home to many of the nation's best military leaders, including Colonel Robert E. Lee of Virginia, a career officer whom General-in-Chief Winfield Scott recommended to Lincoln as field commander of the new Union army. And they offered key geographical advantages. Kentucky, with its 500-mile border on the Ohio River, was essential to the movement of troops and supplies. Maryland was vital to national security because it surrounded the nation's capital on the north. It also contained the major port of Baltimore and adjoined the industrial state of Pennsylvania. Virginia was psychologically strategic as the home of Washington and Jefferson.

Virginia, North Carolina, Tennessee, and Arkansas. Lincoln never had a chance to hold Virginia. His inaugural address, with its implied threat of invasion, had silenced Unionists in eastern Virginia. His call to arms prompted them to embrace secession. After the fall of Fort Sumter, William Poague, a former Unionist lawyer who quickly enlisted in a Virginia artillery unit, explained that "the North was the aggressor. The South resisted her invaders."

On April 17 Virginia's secession convention passed an ordinance of secession by a vote of 88 to 55, an almost direct reversal of the vote taken earlier that month. The dissenting votes came mainly from the mountainous northwestern counties, where whites resented the power of the Tidewater planters and often looked to Ohio and Pennsylvania for trade and leadership. On April 18 General Scott offered Robert E. Lee field command of the Union troops. Despite his description of himself as "one of those dull creatures that cannot see the good of secession," Lee not only declined the offer but resigned from the army. "Save in defense of my native state," Lee told Scott, "I never desire again to draw my sword." At the same time Virginia's militia seized the federal armory and arsenal at Harpers Ferry and the Gosport navy yard at Newport. The Upper South states of North Carolina, Tennessee, and Arkansas promptly joined Virginia in the Confederacy and sent their militias to that state's defense.

Western Virginia, Maryland, Kentucky, and Missouri. Lincoln moved aggressively to hold the rest of the Upper South in the Union. In May he ordered General George B. McClellan, who had assembled a Union force in Ohio, to cross the Ohio River into Virginia. By June McClellan's army had secured the route of the Baltimore and Ohio Railroad, which linked Washington with the Ohio River Valley. In July he established control of northwestern Virginia. In October the voters in fifty western Virginia counties overwhelmingly approved the creation of a new state. West Virginia was admitted to the Union in 1863.

In Maryland southern sympathizers were quite militant, but Lincoln made it clear he would use force to keep the state in the Union. Less than a week after Fort Sumter fell a pro-Confederate mob attacked Massachusetts troops marching between railroad stations in Baltimore and caused the war's first combat deaths: four soldiers and twelve civilians. A few days later Maryland secessionists destroyed railroad bridges and telegraph lines. Without delay Lincoln stationed Union troops along the state's railroad lines and imprisoned many suspected secessionists, including Baltimore's police chief and members of the state legislature. He released them only in November 1861, after the Union party had won a decisive victory in state elections.

In Kentucky secessionist and Unionist sentiments were evenly balanced, and Lincoln at first moved cautiously, trying to avoid pushing it into the Confederacy. He asserted his right to send troops into the state but took no immediate military action. In August, after Unionists had won control of the state legislature, he took steps to shut off Kentucky's thriving export trade in horses, mules, whiskey, and foodstuffs to the Lower South and to the Confederate troops on its borders. Then the Confederacy played into Lincoln's hands by moving troops into Kentucky, seizing Columbus and Bowling Green. Outraged by this aggression, the Kentucky legislature called on the federal government to protect it from invasion. In September, Union troops—Illinois volunteers under the command of the relatively unknown brigadier general Ulysses S. Grant—crossed the Ohio River to drive out the Confederates. Thus the Confederates inadvertently helped keep Kentucky in the Union. Over the course of the war about three-fifths of the white Kentuckians who took up arms did so for the Union.

In Missouri, Lincoln moved promptly to control communications and trade on the upper Mississippi and Missouri rivers. By July a small Union force stationed in St. Louis, composed largely of regiments organized by the city's German-American community, had defeated Confederate sympathizers commanded by Governor Claiborne Jackson. Confederate guerrilla bands led by William Quantrill and Jesse and Frank James—dubbed "bushwhackers" (ambushers) by Unionists—waged campaigns throughout the war. But the Union maintained control of the state, and most Missouri men who fought joined the Union armies—80,000 whites and 8,000 blacks. Of the eight states of the Upper South, Lincoln had kept four (including Delaware) and a portion of a fifth (western Virginia) in the Union.

War Aims and Resources, North and South

Setting Out War Aims. On July 4, 1861, Lincoln made his first major statement of war aims to a special session of Congress: the war was a noble crusade in which the future of democracy throughout the world would be determined. The issue of the war was "whether a constitutional republic, or a democracy—a government of the people, by the same people—can or cannot maintain its territorial integrity against its domestic foes." The war would test "whether discontented individuals, few in number, can arbitrarily break up their government and thus practically put an end to free government upon the face of the earth." Only by crushing the rebellion would the nation survive.

Lincoln did not foresee in 1861 how difficult it would be to crush the rebellion. The Union had to break the will of the southern people, not just smash the Confederate armies. To win, the Union had to fight a *total war*—a war against an entire society, not just its armies. But Lincoln's conception of the Union's war aims, which was well developed even at the war's outset, advanced the great task. His lofty statements of what was at stake helped rally the people of the Union to make a deep and sustained commitment to the war. Like Lincoln, they came to perceive the war as a democratic crusade against southern society.

Confederate leaders also called on their people to fight for democracy. At his inauguration in February 1861, Jefferson Davis identified the Confederate cause with the principles of the American Revolution. He claimed that southerners were fighting, just as their grandfathers had, against tyranny and on behalf of the "sacred right of self-government." A month later, shortly after his election as vice-president of the Confederacy, Alexander Stephens of Georgia defined more explicitly what Confederate democracy meant: the Confederacy's "cornerstone rests upon the great truth that the Negro is not equal to the white man, that slavery—subordination to the superior race—is his natural or normal condition." Slavery made democracy for whites possible, he argued, and the alternative to slavery for blacks was serfdom—dependence on economic elites—for whites.

Davis and other Confederate leaders stressed that their strategy for protecting democracy was defensive: to defend the independence of the Confederacy. As Davis put it in his inaugural, the Confederacy sought "no conquest, no aggrandizement, no concession of any kind from the states with which we were lately confederated; all we ask is to be let alone." This strategy gave Confederate leaders a major advantage. Although they might dream about a battlefield victory that would force formal recognition, they were willing to settle for the Union's abandoning the fight and implicitly accepting Confederate independence. If they could make the cost of the war high enough to induce the North to quit, their cause would be victorious. A draw on the battlefield would be good enough.

Resources, Human and Material. The Union entered the war with some obvious advantages. Lincoln's success in securing the border slave states gave the Union nearly total control over the Ohio River. With nearly two-thirds of the American people, about two-thirds of the nation's railroad mileage, and very nearly 90 percent of American industrial output, the North's economy was far superior to the South's (see Figure 15.1). The North produced all goods in larger quantities and had an especially great advantage in the manufacture of cannon and rifles because of earlier advances in mass-production technology.

But the Confederate position was not as weak as these figures might suggest. Virginia, North Carolina,

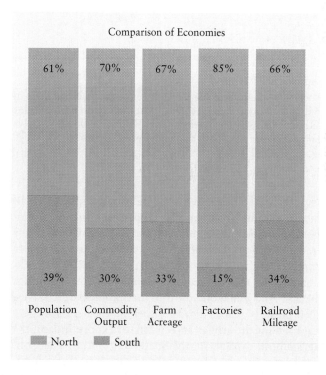

Comparison of Economies

Population	Commodity Output	Farm Acreage	Factories	Railroad Mileage
61%	70%	67%	85%	66%
39%	30%	33%	15%	34%

■ North   ■ South

FIGURE 15.1

Economies, North and South, 1860

The economic advantages of the North were even greater than this chart suggests because the population figures included slaves, commodity output was dominated by farm goods, farm acreage included unimproved acres (greater in the South), and southern factories were, on average, much smaller than northern factories.

Source: Stanley Engerman, "The Economic Impact of the Civil War," in Robert W. Fogel and Stanley L. Engerman, *The Reinterpretation of American Economic History* (New York: Harper & Row, 1971), 371; U.S. Census data.

Industrial Richmond

Located at the falls of the James River, Richmond had flour mills, tobacco factories, railroad and port facilities, and, most important, a profitable and substantial iron industry. In 1861 the Tredegar Iron Works, employing nearly 1,000 workers, was the only facility in the South that could produce large machinery and heavy weapons.

and Tennessee had substantial industrial capacity. Richmond, with its Tredegar Iron Works, was already an important industrial center, and in 1861 the Confederacy transported to Richmond the gun-making machinery captured at the U.S. armory at Harpers Ferry. With 9 million people, the Confederacy could mobilize enormous armies. And while one-third of that number were slaves, their masters expected to keep them in the fields, producing food for the armies and cotton for export. Indeed, the agricultural capacity of the South was crucial. The Confederacy was self-sufficient in food production and dominated world production of cotton—by far America's most lucrative export commodity. "King Cotton" could provide revenue to purchase the clothes, boots, blankets, and weapons that the Confederacy needed but could not produce. Used as a weapon of diplomacy, cotton might induce the British, who depended on imports of southern cotton to supply their textile and clothing factories, to recognize the independence of the Confederacy and supply it with military and economic aid.

The Confederacy thus had sufficient resources to wage an extended and punishing war. It had other assets as well, notably a strong military tradition and a healthy supply of trained military officers. Moreover, it enjoyed important strategic advantages. It would be fighting largely on familiar terrain among local supporters. And even though its railroad system was inferior to the North's, it could move troops and supplies rapidly by interior lines within a defensive perimeter extending from Virginia to Texas. Its long, irregular coastline made it difficult to blockade. Finally, with its defensive stance the South could take full advantage of a new weapon—the rifle-musket (see New Technology, page 455). For the first time in military history well-protected riflemen could repulse cavalry. Britain's Enfield rifles, together with 100,000 captured Union rifles and the production of the Richmond armory, enabled the Confederacy to provide every infantryman with a modern weapon by 1863.

Thus the odds did not necessarily favor the Union, despite its superior resources. The citizens of the Union would have to decide to fight a total war and then learn how to fight such a war on both the battlefield and the home front. The decision and learning were painful and slow in coming. As late as November 1864 the outcome could have gone either way.

== NEW TECHNOLOGY ==

The Rifle-Musket

1861 Springfield Rifle
The rifle-musket strengthened defensive forces by weakening the offensive power of artillery. Civil War artillery pieces had much shorter ranges than did the rifle-muskets, and when armies brought their artillery close enough to be effective as offensive weapons, the defending infantrymen were usually able to pick off the artillerymen.

In 1855 U.S. Secretary of War Jefferson Davis ordered an end to the production of the smooth-bore musket and began equipping American soldiers with rifle-muskets. Most Union infantrymen used the Springfield rifle, a rifle-musket first manufactured by the U.S. armory at Springfield, Massachusetts. Confederate soldiers often used the Enfield rifle, a similar weapon manufactured in Britain. These new weapons accounted for most of the casualties of the war.

Hunting rifles dating back to the eighteenth century had tapered barrels that were *rifled*—lined with spiral grooves—to give the bullet greater speed and accuracy. Unlike the smooth barrels of muskets, however, the grooved rifle barrel quickly accumulated gunpowder and required frequent cleaning, which was inconvenient and dangerous in combat.

In the early 1850s James S. Burton, an American mechanic working at the Harpers Ferry armory, developed a new bullet based on the innovations of Captain Claude E. Minie of the French army. Burton's cylindro-conoidal bullet, radically different from the round bullets of the day, was cast with a cavity at its base. When the rifle hammer exploded powder at the base of the barrel, hot gas expanded the cavity and forced the bullet to engage the grooves of the rifling as it sped through the barrel. The bullet thus cleaned the grooves with each shot.

For the first time infantrymen could be efficient, effective riflemen. Rifle-muskets built to fire the new bullets could hit targets half a mile away, whereas the maximum range of a musket was barely 250 yards. Firing two shots a minute, a veteran with a rifle-musket could kill reliably at 300 yards; his aim with a musket was assured only at 100 yards or less.

The new gun was called a rifle-musket rather than a rifle because it retained certain characteristics of the musket. It fired a single shot, was loaded through the muzzle, and had a long barrel, usually 40 inches. Like the musket, the rifle-musket was cumbersome to load. Before aiming and firing, a soldier had to take out a paper-wrapped cartridge of gunpowder, rip open the cartridge with his teeth, pour the powder down the barrel, insert the bullet into the barrel, jam the bullet and

powder down with a ramrod, half cock the hammer, insert a percussion cap, and finally cock the hammer. Some soldiers could do all this lying on their backs, but most, in order to fire two or three times a minute, had to load from a kneeling or standing position, often exposing themselves to enemy fire.

The rifle-musket was not a modern rifle; it was not breech-loading and did not fire multiple rounds. Although modern rifles were refined during the war and adopted in limited quantities, both sides preferred to stay with the familiar and proven rifle-musket.

The rifle-musket revolutionized warfare and military strategy. Its greater range and accuracy and relatively quick reloading enormously strengthened defensive forces. Defenders could fire on attackers almost continuously and, if the defenders were ensconced in well-protected positions with a broad field of vision, they could usually keep attackers from getting close enough for hand-to-hand combat. (Bayonets accounted for less than 1 percent of all wounds in the Civil War.) If attacking forces did manage to break through defensive lines, they were usually so weakened that they had to retreat or surrender in the face of counterattacks. Elaborate entrenchments strengthened defensive positions even more. Used by both sides in almost every battle by 1863, these trenches, together with the rifle-musket, enabled infantrymen to turn back assaults by forces three to four times their size. The trench warfare that developed around Petersburg, Virginia, in the last weeks of the Civil War presaged the trenches of World War I and the further strengthening of defensive positions by true rifles, automatic rifles, and machine guns.

Infantry commanders, however, were slow to change the tactics that they had inherited from the days of the musket and bayonet. Commanders still attacked in dense close-order formations with thousands of infantrymen, assaulting enemy positions in successive waves. In battle after battle charging infantrymen went down like harvested wheat. The terrible losses at Gettysburg finally forced a reformation of military tactics.

War Machines, North and South

In mobilizing their peoples for war, Abraham Lincoln and Jefferson Davis faced similar challenges: to establish their powers as commanders-in-chief, recruit troops for their armies, suppress dissent, and pay for the enormous costs of the conflict. Lincoln, aided by a strong party and a talented cabinet, quickly consolidated his power and organized a strong central government. Davis was less successful, but his task was more formidable. He had to fight a war while leading eleven states that were deeply suspicious of centralized government.

Mobilizing Armies

At first both Lincoln and Davis mobilized troops by calling for volunteers. But the initial surge of enlistments fell off in 1862 as Americans saw the realities of war—heavy losses to disease and dreadful battle carnage. Thus both presidents faced the necessity of a draft.

The Confederacy, with its relative shortage of military manpower, was the first to act. In April 1862, after the defeat at Shiloh (see page 462), the Confederate Congress imposed the first draft in American history. One law extended all enlistments for the duration of the war; another made all able-bodied men between eighteen and thirty-five subject to serve in the Confederate army for three years. In September a standoff at Antietam prompted the Congress to raise the upper age limit to forty-five. The same law exempted one white man—planter or overseer—for each twenty slaves. Drafted men could hire substitutes, and by 1863 the price for a substitute was $300 in gold—about three times the annual wage of a skilled worker in Richmond. (The substitute law was repealed in 1864.) Impoverished young farmers in the South angrily complained that it was "a rich man's war and a poor man's fight." Conscription proved unenforceable in some parts of the South, and nearly half the eligible nonvolunteers never served.

In midsummer 1862 the Union undertook a quasi-draft. The Militia Act of 1862 used the draft as a threat. When Lincoln's secretary of state, Edwin M. Stanton, announced that any state that failed to meet its quota of volunteers would be subject to the draft, enough volunteers came forward to satisfy Union needs for a year. In 1863, as the scale of hostilities increased, Congress passed the Enrollment Act, which subjected to the draft all able-bodied male citizens and aliens applying for naturalization aged twenty to forty-five. Each Congressional district was assigned a quota, based on its population, which it could meet with either conscripts or volunteers. Districts used cash bounties to compete for volunteers, sometimes bidding against one another to entice recruits. The federal government also offered bounties for enlistment and permitted men to avoid the draft by providing a substitute or paying a $300 commutation, or exemption, fee. The 46,000 draftees and 118,000 substitutes who enlisted under the act amounted to only about 10 percent of the Union soldiers. However, the bounties stimulated the voluntary enlistment or reenlistment of almost a million men.

Meanwhile, the Lincoln administration took steps to suppress any dissent that might impede mobilization. In September 1862 Lincoln proclaimed that during the "insurrection" all persons who discouraged enlistment, resisted the draft, or were guilty of any disloyal practice were subject to martial law. He did this so that they would be tried by military courts rather than local juries. He suspended normal constitutional guarantees, such as the writ of habeas corpus (designed to protect people from arbitrary arrest and detention). By the war's end his administration had imprisoned nearly 15,000 individuals, mostly in the border states, where pro-Confederate political movements were strongest.

The Draft Riots. Lincoln faced the most violent internal challenge of the war after the passage of the Enrollment Act of 1863. Conscription and the high commutation fee—at least half of a worker's annual income—generated resentment among men who were unenthusiastic about the war but could not afford to buy their way out. Democratic opponents of Lincoln exploited this resentment in urban working-class districts by making racist appeals to recent immigrants and wage earners. The Democrats argued that Lincoln was drafting poor whites in order to free the slaves and flood the cities with black workers. Thus the draft became a focal point for preexisting hostility to Republicans and African-Americans.

In July 1863 hostility to the draft spilled onto the streets. After draftees' names were announced in New York City, ferocious rioting broke out among immigrant Irish workers. For five days mob violence ran rampant in what was the most terrible riot in American history. Men and women rioters burned the draft office, sacked the homes of important Republicans, and assaulted the police. The rioters lynched and mutilated at least a dozen African-Americans, drove hundreds of black families from their homes, and burned down the Colored Orphan Asylum. Lincoln's reaction was swift and strong: he rushed in Union troops. The police and soldiers of the Army of the Potomac, who had faced the Confederates at Gettysburg two weeks earlier, killed more than a hundred rioters and suppressed the urban insurrection.

President Davis was never able to match this degree of force. Most Confederate leaders, such as Governors Joseph Brown of Georgia and Zebulon Vance of North Carolina, had powerful states' rights convictions and wanted to avoid creating a national government as centralized and powerful as the one they had left. Because the Confederate constitution vested sovereignty in the

Draft Riots in New York City
The riots—the worst in all of U.S. history—demonstrated that powerful issues of class and race were not far from the surface of American politics. But business-class denunciation of the riots and of Peace Democrats strengthened Lincoln's hand. (This engraving appeared in the *Illustrated London News* on August 8, 1863.)

individual states, state governors could thwart the president's will. Brown and Vance simply ignored Davis's first draft call in early 1862. In parts of the South state judges issued writs of habeas corpus ordering the Confederate government to release draftees. The Confederate Congress was reluctant to impose its authority on the state courts; it granted Davis the authority to suspend the writ of habeas corpus and thus enforce conscription for only two brief periods totaling sixteen months. Its failure to appoint a supreme court contributed to this jurisdictional dilemma.

Nevertheless, Davis's failure to organize an effective draft did not cripple the Confederacy. About four-fifths of the Confederate men eligible for the draft actually served; by contrast, only half the eligible Union men served. Moreover, the Confederate government was able to keep armies in the field by requiring volunteers to extend their enlistments. But as the scale of the fighting grew, as casualties mounted, and as the Union gained control of more Confederate territory, the manpower crisis became severe. By 1864 Confederate generals could not rotate their soldiers to rest areas for relief.

Mobilizing Money

The financial requirements of fighting a total war were enormous. In the Union war costs drove up government spending from less than 2 percent of the gross national product to an average of 15 percent, close to the 20 percent reached in the early 1990s. To finance those expenditures the Republicans had to go beyond their 1860 economic platform and build the kind of revenue system needed to establish a powerful modern state. The financial demands on the Confederacy were even greater, but it avoided using any revenue machinery that required coercion by the central government.

Taxes, almost all of them new, financed about 20 percent of Union war costs. For the first time the government levied an income tax—a graduated tax reaching a maximum rate of 10 percent. The Union placed excise taxes on virtually all consumer goods, license taxes on a wide variety of activities (including every profession except the ministry), special taxes on corporations, stamp taxes on legal documents, and taxes on inheritances. Each wartime Congress also raised tariffs on foreign goods, doubling the average tariff rate by the end of the war.

The Union government financed about two-thirds of its war costs by running deficits and borrowing money through the sale of bonds by the U.S. Treasury. Secretary of the Treasury Salmon P. Chase had no prior financial experience, but he learned quickly from Jay Cooke, a Philadelphia banker. Chase and Cooke adopted four key policies. First, they made interest on the bonds payable in gold, making the bonds financially attractive. Second, they kept income tax rates low, thereby winning support among the wealthy for the bond program. Third, they pioneered techniques for marketing bonds. Although banks and wealthy people in America and Britain bought most of the bonds, Cooke's newspaper advertisements and his 2,500 subagents persuaded nearly a million northerners—a fourth of all ordinary families—to buy them too. Working through a private financier, the Lincoln administration was innovative in developing the propaganda techniques that would become essential to funding all the major wars of the twentieth century.

Fourth, Chase led in creating a national banking system—an important element in every modern centralized government. The National Banking acts of 1863

and 1864 established this system to induce bankers to purchase bonds. The federal government offered state-chartered banks national charters, allowing them to issue national banknotes. The national banks could acquire the notes only with U.S. bonds, which they were required to buy with at least one-third of their capital. But because the national banks were more heavily regulated, state banks did not rush into the new system. So, in 1865 the federal government placed a crippling tax on the notes of state banks. By the end of 1865 the number of national banks had tripled, and their purchases of U.S. bonds had increased nearly four times.

The Union also financed the war by issuing paper money backed by faith in the government rather than by specie. In February 1862 Congress passed the Legal Tender Act, authorizing the issue of $150 million of Treasury notes, which became known as *greenbacks*. Congress required the public to accept those notes as legal tender. Only tariff duties and interest on the national debt still had to be paid in gold or silver coins. This paper money, amounting to nearly $500 million by the end of the war, funded only 13 percent of the war's cost. If the Union government had been weaker—less able to tax its citizens or induce Americans and Europeans to lend it money—it would have had to rely more heavily on the creation of money.

In short, the Union government built the financial foundations of a modern industrial nation-state. Imposing broad-based taxes, borrowing from the middle class as well as the wealthy, and creating a functional money supply mobilized huge sums for the Union cause. In the process, the Union's program of public finance created ties of mutual dependency between the war effort and the millions of Americans who had paid taxes, lent their savings, and accepted paper money.

In sharp contrast with the Union, the Confederacy covered less than 5 percent of its expenditures through taxation. The Confederate Congress fiercely opposed taxes on cotton exports and on the property of planters. It did pass a modest property tax in 1861 but exempted property in the form of slaves and left its collection to the states. Only one state, South Carolina, imposed the tax; the others generally borrowed money or paid the Confederacy with state-issued IOUs. In 1863 the Congress passed a more comprehensive tax law, but it still exempted property in slaves. As a result, the tax burden fell primarily on middle-class citizens and non-slaveholding small farmers, who commonly refused to pay, especially when Confederate armies were far away. An 1864 revision that included a 5 percent property tax on slaves came too late to raise much revenue or restore popular faith in the fairness of the Confederate tax system.

The Confederacy was able to borrow enough money for only 35 percent of its war effort. Although wealthy planters had enough capital to fund a relatively large part of the war, most rebuffed pleas that they buy Con-

federate bonds by pledging their cotton revenues. At first they were unwilling to accept low interest rates; later they began to doubt that the Confederacy would prevail. Europeans came to share those doubts, and the only major loan to the Confederacy came from a French banking house in 1863.

And so the Confederacy was forced to finance about 60 percent of its expenses with unbacked paper money. This created a new problem—soaring inflation, which was compounded by a flood of counterfeit copies of the poorly designed and badly printed Confederate notes. The great battles and sieges created growing numbers of refugees, and this added to inflationary pressures by reducing the food supply and thereby raising food prices even higher. In the early spring of 1863 a wave of riots broke out in southern cities. In more than a dozen towns women ransacked shops and supply depots for food. In Richmond several hundred women broke into bakeries, crying, "Our children are starving while the rich roll in wealth."

The inflation worsened in 1863 as an inflationary psychology—a panic—took hold. Southerners became convinced that inflation would accelerate and rushed to spend their depreciating paper money before it became even less valuable, producing runaway inflation—the only such episode in America since the Revolutionary War. By the spring of 1865 prices had risen to ninety-two times their 1861 levels. A South Carolina judge wrote, "You take your money to the market in the market basket, and bring home what you buy in your pocketbook."

The runaway inflation severely hampered Confederate mobilization. The orderly supply of armies became impossible when farmers refused to accept Confederate money. Confederate supply officers then tried to confiscate what they needed, leaving behind worthless IOUs. Some cavalry units just took what they needed without even pretending to pay. Ironically, partly because it was so fearful of taxation, the Confederacy was forced to resort to great violations of property rights to sustain the war effort.

Economic Programs

Lincoln mobilized men by introducing conscription, used force to suppress war resistance, and taxed the people of the North at unprecedented rates. But economic reforms were also needed to increase the effectiveness of wartime organization and win the support of those who voted, paid taxes, and fought. Consequently, Lincoln and the Republican leadership enacted virtually the entire economic program that they had inherited from Henry Clay and the Whigs.

The many Republicans who had begun their political careers as Whigs had been waiting more than twenty

years for this opportunity. They faced the continued opposition of northern Democrats, but the war had eliminated almost all southern Democrats from Congress while those northern Democrats who had become Republicans relaxed their resistance to national banking and protective tariffs. Most fundamentally, the Republicans won new support from workers and small farmers, arguing that the Republican economic program would help prevent a return to the depression conditions of the late 1850s. And, by celebrating economic opportunity in the North and focusing on the threat that slavery posed to opportunity, the Republicans diverted attention from the failures and limitations of American industrialization. Finally, the southern challenge to northern society helped persuade many farmers and workers to set aside their doubts about the Whig platform and support the nationalizing economic program of the Republican party and the business class in order to win the war.

Each element of the Republican economic program won a substantial following. The tariff received support from manufacturers and those laborers and farmers who feared cheap foreign labor. Capitalists large and small applauded the national banking system. Republican land policy, designed to accelerate free-soil settlement, won the enthusiastic support of almost all farmers. In 1862 Congress passed the Homestead Act, giving heads of families or individuals age twenty-one or older the right to 160 acres of public land after five years of residence and improvement. Although the act contained many loopholes, allowing speculators to put together large blocks of property, numerous small farmers also acquired land. In 1862 Lincoln followed through on the Republican promise to build transcontinental railroads. Congress chartered the Union Pacific and Central Pacific railways and subsidized them lavishly. It gave the railroads twenty sections (20 square miles) of federal land in alternate plots for every mile of track they put down. Congress provided a similar charter and subsidy to the Northern Pacific in 1864.

The Confederate government, however, undertook almost no restructuring of national economic life. True to its states' rights philosophy, the Confederacy left much governmental intervention in the economy in the hands of the state governments operating under their police powers. When the Davis administration did intervene, it did so out of desperation over the inadequacy of the economy for fighting a total war. Consequently, the Confederacy adopted extremely coercive programs. With an economy that was less developed than that of the North, the Confederacy took extraordinary measures: it built and operated its own shipyards, armories, foundries, and textile mills; commandeered food and scarce raw materials such as coal, iron, copper, and lead; requisitioned slaves; and exercised direct control over foreign trade. The unprecedented nature of these encroachments was all the more resented as the war wore

on, because the Confederate government failed to explain its wartime needs or cope with misery on the home front.

Rather than undertaking reforms designed to maintain loyalty and support through economic self-interest, the Confederate leadership relied on a defense of slavery and racial solidarity. Jefferson Davis told whites that they were fighting to be able to expand westward into new territories. Without expansion, he said, "an overgrown black population" would "crowd upon our soil . . . until there will not be room in the country for whites and blacks to subsist in." Containment would destroy slavery "and reduce the whites to the degraded position of the African race."

The Home Front: Civilian Support for the War

In both the Confederacy and the Union, civilians made enormous contributions to the war effort. No civilian effort was more important than relieving the suffering on the battlefield.

The Sanitary Commission. In the North the most important voluntary agency was the United States Sanitary Commission, which prominent New Yorkers established in April 1861 and Lincoln endorsed two months later. Its task was to provide medical services and prevent a repeat of the debacle of the Crimean War between Britain and Russia (1854–1856), in which disease accounted for over three-fourths of the British casualties. Through its network of 7,000 local auxiliaries, the Sanitary Commission gathered supplies; distributed clothing, food, and medicine to the army; improved the sanitary standards of camp life; recruited battlefield nurses; and recruited doctors for the Union Army Medical Bureau, which came to be led by an innovative surgeon general, William A. Hammond. Hammond professionalized the bureau, increasing the number of surgeons, building more hospitals, organizing a trained ambulance corps, and integrating the services of the Sanitary Commission into the war effort.

The results of all this organized medical effort were not readily visible. Diseases—primarily dysentery, typhoid, and malaria but also childhood diseases such as mumps and measles, to which many rural men had not developed an immunity—killed twice as many Union soldiers (about 250,000) as combat did. Surgeons inadvertently took more lives by spreading infection than they saved. Nurses could do little more for the wounded than dress their wounds and comfort them with reminders of home. Still, the rate of mortality from disease and wounds was substantially lower than in other major nineteenth-century wars, partly because of the attention given to sanitation and the quality of food.

The health care available to Union troops surpassed that in the Confederacy. Great numbers of southern women volunteered as nurses, but the Confederate health care and hospital system remained disorganized. Thousands of Confederate soldiers suffered from scurvy because of the lack of vitamin C in their diets, and they died from camp diseases at even higher rates than did Union soldiers.

Women in the War Effort. Most of the Sanitary Commission nurses and workers were women. Organized by Dorothea Dix, the first woman to receive a major federal appointment—as superintendent of female nurses—the nurses overcame prejudice against women treating men and opened a new occupation to women. The nurse Clara Barton, who later founded the American Red Cross, recalled, "At the war's end, woman was at least fifty years in advance of the normal position which continued peace would have assigned her." Barton might have been overly optimistic, but the war effort did open the way for middle-class women to participate not only in nursing but also in government as they either replaced male clerks who went to war or took new jobs in the expanding bureaucracies. This was true not only in the North but also in the South, where women staffed the efficient Confederate postal service.

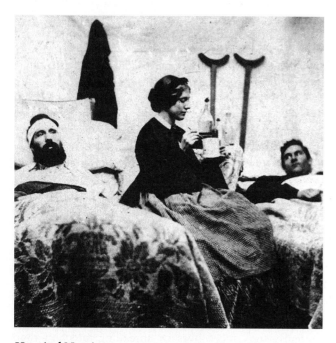

Hospital Nursing
Most Civil War nurses served as unpaid volunteers and spent most of their time cooking and cleaning for their patients. A sense of calm prevailed in this Union hospital in Nashville, well removed from the battlefield. In contrast, conditions at field hospitals were chaotic under the pressure of heavy casualties and shifting battle sites.

While some women assumed new kinds of jobs, far more women in both the North and the South dramatically increased their responsibilities in their households, on their farms, in schools, and in textile, clothing, and shoe factories. They made mobilization possible in both the Union and the Confederacy by substituting their labor for that of men. On plantations some women took over the management of slaves and production. On small farms in both the South and the North women worked with far greater intensity and effort than they had before the war, taking on chores that men had done. Some farm women not only performed demanding chores but took jobs outside the home to make ends meet.

Military Deadlock, 1861–1863

Between 1861 and 1863 the Lincoln administration created a complex war machine and a powerful structure of command and production. Northern government, industry, and finance capital worked in an integrated manner, making the North's advantages in population and material resources available to the Union army. But the Union had not yet fully resolved to fight a total war against southern society. The Confederacy, successfully prosecuting its limited, defensive war, forced the Union into a deadlock on the battlefield.

Early Stalemate, 1861–1862

The First Battle of Bull Run. At the war's beginning Lincoln rejected the military strategy proposed by his general-in-chief, Winfield Scott, who was a Virginia Unionist. This strategy, dubbed the Anaconda (a large constricting snake) Plan by its opponents, involved blockading the South on all sides from the sea and the Mississippi River and then gradually squeezing the Confederacy into submission through psychological pressure and economic sanctions. Instead, Lincoln chose a more aggressive beginning—a swift assault on P. G. T. Beauregard's Confederate force of over 20,000 based at Manassas, a major rail junction in Virginia only 30 miles southwest of Washington. Lincoln, along with many Union commanders with Mexican War experience, believed in vigorous offensives; he recognized that northern public opinion called for a strike toward Richmond, the Confederate capital, and he hoped an early Union victory would discredit the secessionists. Consequently, in mid-July 1861, Lincoln sent Union General Irvin McDowell with an army of more than 30,000 to attack Beauregard's army.

Northern newspapers and southern spies advertised the advance of McDowell's army, so Beauregard had plenty of time to establish his army south of Bull Run, a

small stream north of Manassas. He also brought reinforcements by rail from the Shenandoah Valley, thus seizing the advantage provided by having interior lines. McDowell attacked strongly on July 21, but panic swept through his troops during a Confederate counterattack. For the first time the Union troops, who had fought almost fourteen hours with little water to relieve the Virginia heat, heard the startling scream of the rebel yell. "The peculiar corkscrew sensation that it sends down your backbone under these circumstances can never be told," one Union veteran wrote. "You have to feel it."

McDowell's troops retreated to Washington, scrambling along with the many civilians who had come down from the capital with their Sunday picnic baskets and binoculars to observe the battle. The Confederate troops also dispersed. They were as confused as the beaten Union soliders, and they lacked wagons and supplies to pursue McDowell's army. While Confederate leaders rejoiced in their victory, Lincoln replaced McDowell with General George B. McClellan of Pennsylvania and Ohio. He also signed bills for the enlistment of 100,000 additional men, who would serve for three years in what would soon be named the Army of the Potomac. In November 1861, when Winfield Scott retired, Lincoln made McClellan general-in-chief. Although neither Lincoln nor Davis fully anticipated total war as yet, it was now clear that the war would not be quick or easy.

The War in the West. While eastern armies were fighting to capture the opposing capital or demoralize the enemy's army, Union and Confederate troops in the West struggled to dominate territory—the great interior river valleys. Union control of communications and transportation along those strategic rivers would divide the Confederacy into isolated pieces and reduce its ability to supply and move armies. The Confederacy had already lost the Ohio Valley when Kentucky remained in the Union. Retaining the Tennessee and Mississippi valleys was vital to the South's communications with its vast western territory.

In 1862 the Union launched a series of highly innovative land and water operations designed to seize control of the Tennessee and Mississippi rivers. In February, in a brilliant tactical maneuver, Ulysses S. Grant, still a relatively unknown Union commander, used riverboats clad with iron plates to take Fort Henry on the Tennessee River and Fort Donelson on the Cumberland. Grant then moved south along the Tennessee to take control of critical railroad lines. Meanwhile, as the southern part of a giant pincer movement, Admiral David G. Farragut struck from the sea. In April 1862 he led a Union squadron up the Mississippi from the Gulf of Mexico and took New Orleans. In one naval offensive the Union had captured the South's financial center and largest city, acquired a major base for future operations, and denied the Confederacy an important port (see Map 15.2).

Union Soldiers Camped Near Cumberland Landing, 1862
The Civil War armies required encampments that were huge and intricate. The logistic demands on the Union armies were great because they generally fought in enemy territory and maintained long supply lines. The rule of thumb was that a Union army of 100,000 men consumed 600 tons of supplies a day and required 2,500 supply wagons and at least 35,000 animals.

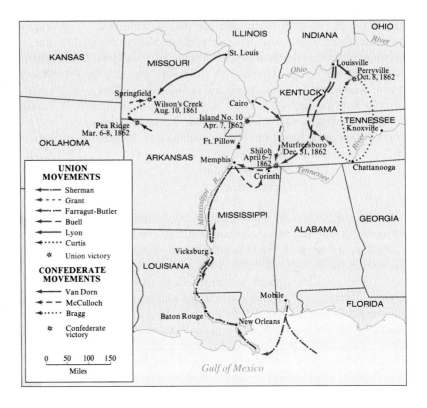

MAP 15.2

The Western Campaigns, 1861–1862
Control of the great valleys of the Ohio, Tennessee, and Mississippi rivers was at stake during the early part of the Civil War. By the end of 1862, Union armies had kept Missouri in the Union and driven the Confederate armies out of Kentucky and half of Tennessee. They also controlled New Orleans and almost all of the Mississippi River, and at Shiloh they had proved that they could not be driven out of the Lower South.

Shiloh. Confederates under Albert Sidney Johnston and P. G. T. Beauregard slowed Grant's advance by catching him by surprise a few miles from the Tennessee River near a small log church named Shiloh. In the ensuing battle on April 6–7, 1862, Grant relentlessly threw troops into the battle and forced a Confederate withdrawal. About 20,000 men were killed or wounded at Shiloh, making it the bloodiest battle to that point. Grant described a large field "so covered with dead that it would have been possible to walk over the clearing in any direction, stepping on dead bodies, without a foot touching the ground."

Grant's victory at Shiloh was a major turning point: it marked the beginning of the end of Confederate power in the Mississippi Valley. By June the Union controlled the Mississippi as far south as Memphis, Tennessee. Also, the ghastly triumph at Shiloh began to transform the Union leaders' strategic thinking. Shiloh persuaded Lincoln and the most foresighted generals that a long, protracted war would be necessary, even in the West. Grant later wrote that after Shiloh he "gave up all idea of saving the Union except by complete conquest."

The Eastern Theater, 1862. After Bull Run both the Union and the Confederacy continued to seek a victory in the East that would end the war. Confederate and Union commanders jockeyed for position around Washington and Richmond. Each tried to outflank the other, place his army between the capital and its defenders,

and, if possible, punish the opposing army. As they maneuvered, the commanders used virtually identical battlefield tactics, since almost all had been taught by the same instructors and had read the same textbooks at West Point.

After meticulously training 150,000 men during the winter of 1861–1862, McClellan moved his troops up the peninsula between the York and James rivers toward Richmond. In a maneuver that required skillful logistics, he transported about 100,000 troops by boat down the Potomac River and Chesapeake Bay and then up the peninsula. But he failed to anticipate some major problems. In May a Confederate army under Thomas J. ("Stonewall") Jackson marched rapidly north up the Shenandoah Valley, threatening the army of Nathaniel P. Banks that was protecting Washington. To head off Jackson, Lincoln diverted 30,000 troops from McClellan's army. Jackson proved himself a brilliant general by defeating three Union armies in five battles in the valley. Then, in June, as McClellan finally moved toward Richmond, Robert E. Lee, the new commander of the Army of Northern Virginia, with a force of 85,000, attacked him ferociously in the Seven Days' battles (June 25–July 1). McClellan's troops inflicted heavy casualties (20,000 to the Union's 10,000), but he was unwilling to renew the offensive unless he received 50,000 fresh troops. Lincoln believed that McClellan would only find another excuse not to attack Lee and the president withdrew the Army of the Potomac from the peninsula. Richmond remained secure.

Lee's First Invasion of the North. Lee then went on the offensive, hoping for victories that would humiliate Lincoln's government. Lee sent Jackson to destroy a Union army under John Pope in northern Virginia before McClellan returned. On August 29–30, only 20 miles from Washington, Jackson's troops, joined by the forces of Lee and General James P. Longstreet, routed Pope's army in the Second Battle of Bull Run. Lee struck north through western Maryland, and Lincoln ordered McClellan to confront Lee's army. Lee almost met with disaster when he divided his force—sending Stonewall Jackson to capture Harpers Ferry—and a copy of his orders to Jackson fell into McClellan's hands. Once again, however, McClellan hesitated, and Lee had time to occupy a strong defensive position behind Antietam Creek, near Sharpsburg, Maryland. Although outnumbered 87,000 to 50,000, Lee repelled McClellan's attacks until Jackson's troops arrived, just as Union regiments were about to overwhelm Lee's right flank (see Map 15.3).

The fighting at Antietam was some of the most savage of the war. A Wisconsin officer described his men as "loading and firing with demoniacal fury and shouting and laughing hysterically." At a critical point in the battle a sunken road, Bloody Lane, filled with Confederate bodies two and three deep, and the attacking Union troops knelt on "this ghastly flooring" to shoot at the retreating Confederates.

McClellan might have defeated Lee with another major effort, but the casualties appalled him and he feared that enemy troops might outnumber his own. He let Lee fall back to Virginia while he buried the dead and set up field hospitals for the wounded. September 17, 1862, at Antietam proved to be the bloodiest single day in U.S. military history. Lee lost somewhat fewer men than did McClellan, but Lee's losses represented one-fourth of his army. Together, the Confederate and Union dead numbered 4,800 and the wounded 18,500, of whom 3,000 soon died. (In comparison, 6,000 Americans were wounded or killed on D-Day in World War II.)

The military setbacks prior to Antietam had begun to erode popular support for the war. To rally public opinion, Lincoln declared Antietam a victory. Privately, he believed that McClellan should have fought Lee to the finish. McClellan was a masterful organizer of men and supplies but had never been willing to risk a major com-

MAP 15.3

The Eastern Campaigns, 1861–1862
The greatest concentration of major Civil War battlefields was in the corridor between Washington and Richmond. There, during the eastern campaigns of 1861 and 1862, the audacity and imagination of Confederate generals Robert J. "Stonewall" Jackson and Robert E. Lee almost produced decisive victories. But, as often in the Civil War, the victors were usually too exhausted to exploit their triumphs.

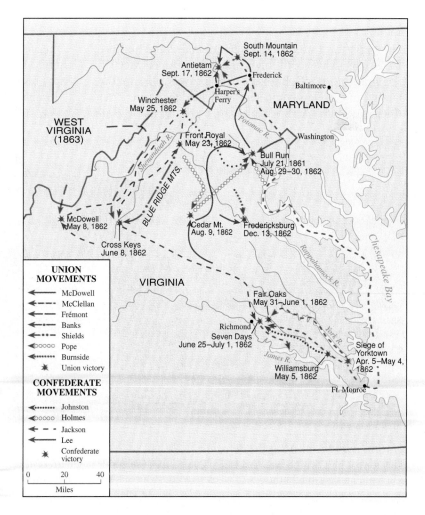

Antietam

This painting, *The Battle of Antietam: The Fight for Burnside's Bridge,* is the work of Captain James Hope of the 2nd Vermont Volunteers, who was a survivor of Antietam. The Rohrbach Bridge, nicknamed "Burnside's Bridge," was the scene of some of the heaviest fighting.

mitment of his forces, perhaps because he could not face the carnage that would follow. Lincoln replaced McClellan with Ambrose E. Burnside, who proved to be a more daring but even less competent battlefield tactician. After losing large parts of the Army of the Potomac in futile at-

tacks against well-entrenched Confederate forces at Fredericksburg, Virginia, on December 13, Burnside offered to resign his command. Lincoln replaced him with Joseph ("Fighting Joe") Hooker. As 1862 ended, the war was still a stalemate.

Lincoln with the Army of the Potomac

This formal photograph records Lincoln's visit to McClellan's headquarters near the Antietam battlefield. On this visit Lincoln vigorously urged McClellan to advance on Richmond. McClellan did not respond and was removed from command a month later.

Emancipation

As the war dragged on during 1861 and 1862, Lincoln, some of his generals, and some Republican leaders began to redefine it as a struggle not only against Confederate armies but also against southern society. In particular, Lincoln and his administration decided that they had to attack the very cornerstone of southern society—the institution of slavery.

At the beginning of the war a few abolitionist leaders had hoped that the South would be allowed to secede so as to rid the Union of the stain of slavery. But other abolitionists tried to persuade the Republican party to make abolition a goal of the war. They argued on grounds not just of morality but of "military necessity": it was the labor of the slaves that enabled the Confederacy to feed and supply its armies. Frederick Douglass wrote that "the very stomach of this rebellion is the Negro in the form of a slave. Arrest that hoe in the hands of the Negro, and you smite the rebellion in the very seat of its life."

"Contrabands." It was the slaves themselves who forced the issue of emancipation. From the very outset of the war, slaves exploited the disorder of wartime to seize their freedom. Over the course of the war tens of thousands escaped from plantations and ran to Union lines.

The first Union officials who dealt with the status of escaped slaves were the commanders in the field. In May 1861 General Benjamin Butler, who had taken military control of Annapolis and Baltimore, was commanding a fort on the Virginia coast. When three slaves escaped to his lines, he refused to return them to their master. He did not declare them free but labeled them "contraband of war." His term stuck, and for the rest of the war slaves found behind Union lines were known as *contrabands*. By August 1861 a thousand contrabands were camping with Butler's army.

The increasingly large number of runaway slaves behind Union lines forced the Union government to establish a policy regularizing their status. In August 1861 Lincoln signed the First Confiscation Act, authorizing the seizure of all property—defined to include slaves—used to support the rebellion. This law applied only to slaves within reach of Union armies and it did not actually emancipate them. The act was designed only to undermine the Confederate war effort, but it did begin the process that would end in abolition.

As early as the summer of 1861 almost all Republicans opposed slavery and were ready for some kind of emancipation. But they divided into three groups over the timing and method. The conservatives, the smallest of the three groups, wanted to end slavery but believed that this should occur slowly as the federal government blocked the extension of slavery into the territories; emancipation in existing states, they believed, should be left to state governments. More numerous were the radicals, who wanted the government to abolish slavery straightaway, wherever it existed. The moderates, the most numerous of all and led by Lincoln, wanted emancipation to proceed more expeditiously than did the conservatives but feared that immediate abolition would cause a dramatic loss of Union support in the border states and stimulate a racist backlash in northern cities.

But as battlefield casualties mounted in 1861 and 1862, so did popular support for punishing slave owners by taking away their slaves; so did support for emancipation as a means of mobilizing slaves against their masters; so did moral enthusiasm for freeing the slaves and thus ennobling the carnage on the battlefield; and so did the influence of the radical Republicans. Their leaders included Salmon P. Chase, Secretary of the Treasury; Charles Sumner, the chairman of the Senate Committee on Foreign Relations; and Thaddeus Stevens, the chairman of the House Ways and Means Committee. Both Sumner and Stevens held stern and uncompromising views on slavery, but Stevens was the more masterful in manipulating Congress, where he served as a representative from Pennsylvania from 1849 to 1853 and from 1859 until his death in 1868. Among all the Republicans in Congress, Stevens was probably the one most completely committed to racial equality.

In the spring of 1862 Lincoln and moderate Republicans in Congress began to move slowly toward abolition. In April 1862 Congress enacted legislation abolishing slavery in the District of Columbia while promising compensation to the former slave owners in the hope of winning their loyalty to the Union. In June Congress took its second step, abolishing slavery in the federal territories. This law affected only a few slaves but represented the fulfillment of the free-soil platform. Congress took a more radical step in July when it passed the Second Confiscation Act, which went beyond the first one by declaring "forever free" all captured and fugitive slaves of rebels. Although it affected only those slaves under the direct control of the Union army, it did for the first time embrace emancipation as an instrument of war. Also in July, Lincoln read a draft of a proclamation to his cabinet, testing out an even more radical conception of emancipation, one that would transform the Union armies into agents of liberation.

The Emancipation Proclamation. Lincoln was pondering how he could use his power to emancipate the slaves not affected by previous actions. Some lived in areas loyal to the Union, but most were in areas controlled by the Confederacy. He was certain that he had to leave the former alone because the Constitution protected slavery within the Union, but he believed he could free the latter under his wartime power to take enemy resources. He worried, however, that if he did that while the war was going badly, he would be seen as cynically trying to

Lincoln and His Cabinet
The painting portrays Lincoln reading the preliminary Emancipation Proclamation to his cabinet on September 21, four days after the Battle of Antietam. Lincoln had first presented a draft proclamation to the cabinet on July 22, but Secretary of State William H. Seward had persuaded him to "postpone its issue until you can give it to the country supported by military success."

divert attention from military defeats. And abolishing slavery while the Union was losing the war would in fact be an empty gesture; if the tide of battle did not go Lincoln's way, he could free no additional slaves. After Antietam, Lincoln decided that the time had come. He declared Antietam a victory and told his cabinet that he took it as "an indication of the Divine Will" that he should "move forward in the cause of emancipation." On September 22, 1862, he issued a preliminary Emancipation Proclamation, declaring that on January 1, 1863, slaves in all states wholly or partly in rebellion would be free. Thus Lincoln gave the rebellious states a hundred days to return to the Union and keep slavery intact. None chose to do so.

The proclamation was politically astute as well as constitutionally correct. Lincoln wanted to keep the loyalty of the border states, where racism was most severe, so he left slavery intact there. He also wanted to win the allegiance of the areas occupied by Union armies— western and middle Tennessee, western Virginia, and southern Louisiana, including New Orleans—so he left slavery untouched there. Thus, the Emancipation Proclamation had no immediate, practical effect on the life

of a single slave. Abolitionists were disappointed, but they were confident that emancipation would have to go further. Wendell Phillips believed Lincoln was "only stopping on the edge of Niagara." Jefferson Davis called the proclamation the "most execrable measure recorded in the history of guilty man." Lincoln predicted that the proclamation would change the nature of the war; it would become a war of "subjugation" in which "the old South is to be destroyed and replaced by new propositions and ideas."

Many Union officers doubted whether they wanted to fight for emancipation and worried that the proclamation would incite slave rebellions. McClellan, who had aspirations for a political career as a Democrat, privately admitted that he "could not make my mind to fight for such an accursed doctrine as that of a servile insurrection." But McClellan reminded his officers that the "remedy for political errors . . . is to be found only in the action of people at the polls."

The Elections of 1862. The Democrats, in fact, made emancipation the primary issue in the elections of 1862. Leading Democrats used emancipation to focus popular

frustration over the seeming futility of the bloody war. They denounced emancipation as unconstitutional; some warned of massive bloodshed in the South and claimed that a "black flood" would sweep away the jobs of white laborers. Horatio Seymour, candidate for governor of New York, declared that if abolition was the purpose of the war, then the South could not—and should not—be conquered. Seymour won his election; other Democrats did well in New York, Pennsylvania, Ohio, and Illinois; and Democrats gained 34 seats in Congress. But this was the smallest loss since 1842 of Congressional seats in an off-year election by the party controlling the presidency. Moreover, Republicans held a 25-seat majority in the House and gained 5 seats in the Senate. They blamed their losses on the inability of soldiers at the front to vote.

Lincoln would have preferred a stronger showing in the elections but saw no reason to retreat. After the election he did not hesitate to remove McClellan, whose views on emancipation were well known, from command of the Army of the Potomac. In December the House endorsed the preliminary proclamation and passed an act requiring West Virginia to abolish slavery as a condition of statehood. In his message to Congress that month Lincoln promised that slaves freed "by the chances of war" would remain free. And on New Year's Day, 1863, Lincoln signed the Emancipation Proclamation. As a gesture to those who feared slave rebellions Lincoln hedged a bit, making it clear that he wanted slaves to "abstain from all violence." But in other ways he went beyond the September proclamation, justifying emancipation as an "act of justice" as well as a military tactic and expressing his intention to accept slaves freed by the proclamation into military service. In one stroke Lincoln had changed the meaning of the war, focusing it on abolition and revolutionizing southern society. "If my name ever goes into history," he said, "it was for this act."

The Thirteenth Amendment. During 1864 and 1865 the pace of legal emancipation accelerated. Maryland and Missouri amended their constitutions to free their slaves, and the three occupied states of Tennessee, Arkansas, and Louisiana followed suit. But what would happen elsewhere in the South after the war was over? Abolitionists worried that the Emancipation Proclamation, based on the president's wartime powers, would lose its force. There was nothing in the Constitution to prevent southern states from reestablishing slavery after the war. To solve that problem, Congress, urged on by Lincoln, began the final step toward the full legal emancipation of slaves. On January 31, 1865, it approved the Thirteenth Amendment, which prohibited slavery altogether. By the end of the year the necessary number of states had ratified the amendment.

Union Gains in 1863

The Fall of Vicksburg. During 1863 the Union made substantial progress in the western theater of the war. This progress began as Grant drove south along the Mississippi to the west of the river and hammered persistently at Confederate defenses around Vicksburg, Mississippi (see American Voices, page 468). Then, in a clever maneuver, he moved his troops across the river, swung them around the city, and attacked from the east. After a six-week siege the exhausted and starving garrison surrendered on July 4, 1863. Five days later Port Hudson, Louisiana, fell to Union forces, and a week later an unarmed merchant ship completed an uneventful trip from St. Louis to New Orleans. The Union now controlled the whole length of the Mississippi. Grant's campaign had split the Confederacy in two, cutting off Louisiana, Arkansas, and Texas from the remaining Confederate states.

Later in 1863 the Union also gained control of eastern Tennessee and the vital railroad hubs of Knoxville and Chattanooga. On September 9, Union forces under William S. Rosecrans occupied Chattanooga, Tennessee, which commanded the gateway to Georgia. Faced by large Confederate forces, Rosecrans was defeated by Braxton Bragg in the Battle of Chickamauga on September 19–20. The Union troops retreated to Chattanooga, where they faced a siege by Bragg. Grant finally charged to the rescue and, in the Battle of Chattanooga on November 24–25, drove the Confederates into Georgia.

Davis and the other civilian leaders of the Confederacy keenly felt the great Union pressure in the West and wanted to throw in reinforcements to defeat Grant in Mississippi or Rosecrans in Tennessee. But Lee, buoyed by a brilliant victory over Hooker at Chancellorsville in May, persuaded them to let him instead invade the North again. He argued that this would relieve the pressure on Vicksburg by drawing Union armies east and enable his army to resupply itself from the rich northern countryside. If he could win a large victory and then go on to capture Washington or another large city, the Union might lose its will to fight, and the setbacks in the West would be irrelevant.

Gettysburg. Lee won approval for his strategy and moved north, determined to win a great victory on northern soil. In June 1863 he maneuvered his army west to the Shenandoah Valley and then north through Maryland into Pennsylvania. The Union army also moved quickly west to stay positioned between Lee and Washington. Then, in the middle of the campaign, Hooker resigned and Lincoln replaced him with George G. Meade. Two days later the two great armies met in an accidental but momentous confrontation at Gettysburg, Pennsylvania. The battle was precipitated by Lee's

Elizabeth Mary Meade Ingraham

A Vicksburg Diary

Elizabeth Mary Meade Ingraham (1806–?) was the sister of Union General George Meade but sided with the Confederacy. In 1831 she and her husband, who had been an agent of the Bank of the United States, moved from Philadelphia to Mississippi, where they lived on Ashwood Plantation, 30 miles from Vicksburg. Her diary, which covers the six weeks between May 2 and June 13, 1863, describes how Grant's Vicksburg campaign changed the relationship between masters and slaves.

May 4. Osterhaus' Division, scum of St. Louis, camped in the big field. All the corn ruined in the field, and nearly all consumed in the granaries. . . . Nancy [a slave] sent me a little. Elsie, faithful and true, and Jack and Emma [all slaves] very attentive.

May 8. The last thing Eddens [a slave] did was to save some meat for me. He slept in the spare room Sunday night, and Monday at noon he had quit our service. . . . Parker, Sol, Mordt, Jim Crow, Isaiah, and Wadloo, have quit us, but the rest are here, and very attentive and willing. . . . I have a few mean ones [slaves] . . . , who tell what they know and implicate the faithful ones, and the servants have had a hard time. They [Union officers] have forced them to work for them. . . .

May 13. Elsy still faithful, feeds us, and does what she can; Rita Jane too; Bowlegs very attentive. Emma beginning to tire of waiting on me, did not come up at noon; Nancy not true.

May 15. Edward's [her son] sash and six pairs of gloves taken out of my wardrobe. I am afraid Emma has done this; don't feel as if I could trust any one but Elsy; she feeds and takes care of me.

May 18. [We] have reason to think the hands will all leave; only a question of time, they are not quite ready; Elsy still true; but Jack doubtful. . . .

May 27. Negro meetings are being held, and the few whites left begin to be very anxious. . . . Powers was burnt out by his own negroes. I fear the blacks more than I do the Yankees. Jack trying to persuade Elsie to leave. . . . She tells him to get her a home and a way of earning a living, and she is ready to go, but [I] told her, if he left here, to move up into the wash-house with her children. I would give her $12, a month and free her four children.

June 3. Our darkeys in great commotion, yesterday, on account of Secesh [secessionists], who, about twenty-five in number, have been going the rounds, and setting the negroes to work; they whipped one fellow . . . and hung another; and we thought last evening all ours but a few meant to go. . . . I wish the Secesh would come. . . .

June 6. Martha with her thee children and Emma, left at midnight Friday . . . and the rest are packing to-day. Hays resolved to go, and I dread lest he take his wife with him, for I can hardly get along as it is, and shall die if I have the cooking to do.

June 10. Fanny, John Smith, and the children, Buck and his family, Dave and his, Kate and hers, making in all thirteen who have gone—Dave intending to come back, but the Yankees would not let him. . . . those who have stayed are utterly demoralized; if they work for you, the job is only half done.

Source: W. Maury Darst, "The Vicksburg Diary of Mrs. Alfred Ingraham," *Journal of Mississippi History* 44 (May 1982), 148–179.

---

awareness that he was on the brink of losing his supply lines to Virginia and Meade's concern that Lee might get control of a major junction of roads at Gettysburg.

On the first day of battle, July 1, Lee was able to bring more troops into action and drove Meade's advance guard to the south of town (see Map 15.4). Meade moved cautiously, waiting for the reinforcements that would give him numerical superiority. He placed his troops in well-defended positions on the hills outside town. Reinforcements for both sides arrived all day and throughout the night. By the morning of the second day Meade outnumbered Lee 90,000 to 75,000. Although aware that he was outnumbered, Lee was bent on victory. He attacked Meade's army on both flanks. The flanking efforts failed. General Richard B. Ewell, assigned to attack the Union right, was unwilling to risk his men in an all-out assault against the forces dug in on Cemetery Hill. Longstreet, assigned the Union left, was unable to attack quickly enough to prevent Meade's forces from strengthening their hold on Little Round Top.

Despite the failures of the previous two days, Lee decided to proceed with a final frontal assault on the center of the Union lines. He had enormous confidence in his troops and mistakenly believed that they faced demoralized Union soldiers stretched out in a thin defensive line. Also, he realized that an attack was the only alternative to a retreat into the South with the loss, perhaps forever, of an opportunity to inflict a crushing psychological defeat on the North.

On the third day, after the heaviest artillery barrage of the war, Lee ordered 14,000 men under General George E. Pickett and two other officers to take Cemetery Ridge. Lee was unaware that Meade had reinforced the center of his line with artillery and his best troops. When Pickett's men charged across a mile of open terrain, they were cut down by massive, withering enemy fire. Once again, artillery and the rifle-musket demonstrated their potency against a traditional infantry assault, but Lee, along with commanders on both sides, had to use the technique because officers could not control troops beyond voice or vision. Thousands of the charging Confederates were killed, wounded, or captured, and the few who managed to charge over the Union fortifications were shot or forced to surrender. When ordered to rally his troops to repel a possible counterattack, Pickett answered, "General Lee, I *have* no division, now."

Gettysburg took more lives than did any other Civil War battle. Meade lost 23,000 killed or wounded; Lee lost 28,000, one-third of the Army of Northern Virginia. Lee could never again invade the North. But he still had a substantial force, thanks largely to Meade,

who was so pleased with his victory and wary of Lee that he allowed the remaining Confederate soldiers to escape. Lincoln believed that Meade could have ended the war at Gettysburg. "As it is," Lincoln brooded, "the war will be prolonged indefinitely." Lincoln's pessimism was justified; the two sides were still deadlocked.

The victory at Gettysburg did, however, increase popular support for the war in the North. During the fall of 1863, in state and local elections in Pennsylvania, Ohio, and New York, Democrats once again tested support for the war by challenging Republicans on the issue of emancipation, accusing them of favoring social equality for blacks. For governor of Ohio, the Democrats nominated Clement L. Vallandigham after Lincoln had banished him from the Union for treasonously denouncing the war as one fought "for the freedom of the blacks and the enslavement of the whites." Republicans benefited from the patriotic pride in the victory at Gettysburg, the heroics of African-American soldiers, and white embarrassment over the New York draft riots that summer. Lincoln intervened in the election, declaring that when the war was won, "there will be some black men who can remember that, with silent tongue,

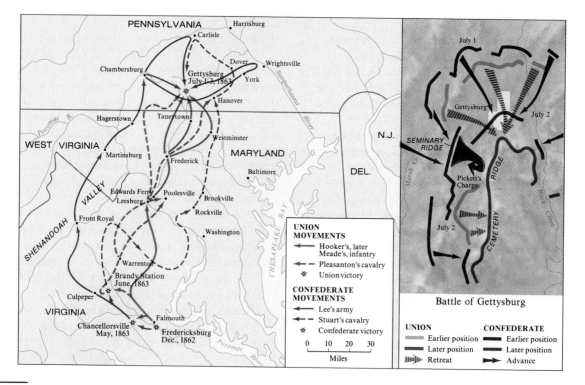

MAP 15.4

The Battle of Gettysburg
Lee's invasion of the North after Confederate victories at Fredericksburg and Chancellorsville was designed to threaten northern cities, persuade Europeans that the Confederacy would win the war, and strengthen the hand of the Peace Democrats. Lee's strategy might have ended the war if he had won at Gettysburg.

and clenched teeth, and steady eye, and well-poised bayonet, they have helped mankind on to this great consummation; while, I fear, there will be some white ones, unable to forget that, with malignant heart, and deceitful speech, they have strove to hinder it." Lincoln made stick the charge that to oppose emancipation was to oppose northern victory. Republicans swept to decisive victories across the three key states, including Ohio, where Vallandigham's opponent won a record share of the vote.

At the same time, the Confederate defeat at Gettysburg contributed to growing war weariness in the South. As a consequence of flagging morale, the Confederate elections of 1863 went sharply against the Jefferson Davis administration. Former secessionists lost ground, and former Whigs gained. As it turned out, the strongest support for Davis was in Union-occupied districts, where regular elections were impossible. Large minorities in the new Confederate Congress were outspokenly hostile to the Davis administration. Some advocated peace negotiations, but more criticized the ineffectiveness of the war effort. The Confederate vice-president, Alexander Stephens, compared Davis to "my poor old blind and deaf dog."

Wartime Diplomacy

Gettysburg also advanced the Union cause by neutralizing the European powers as factors in the outcome of the war. Great Britain in particular had been a key participant as an arms supplier to both the North and the South and as a potential source of economic and additional military aid to the Confederacy.

At the beginning of the war the Confederacy had begun diplomatic efforts to gain foreign recognition of its independence. Because Great Britain depended on the South for four-fifths of its raw cotton, southern leaders hoped that it would offer the Confederacy enough support to cause the Union to give up the fight. Moreover, France's Emperor Napoleon III might be of assistance. He dreamed of an empire in Mexico and by the summer of 1862 had sent thousands of troops to overthrow a republican regime there. In June 1863 the French army, which had grown to 35,000, succeeded, and in 1864 Napoleon installed as emperor of Mexico Archduke Ferdinand Maximilian, the brother of the emperor of Austria. France was bound by a diplomatic agreement to defer to the British in American affairs, but if Britain recognized the independence of the Confederacy, France was virtually certain to follow and might even challenge Union power west of the Mississippi.

Shortly after hostilities began, Great Britain proclaimed its neutrality. This meant that Britain recognized the Confederacy as a belligerent power and therefore re-

garded it as having the right, under international law, to borrow money and purchase weapons in neutral nations. A concerned Lincoln administration protested that the conflict was a domestic insurrection and not a war and that Britain's declaration of neutrality might be taken to imply recognition of the Confederacy as a sovereign state. Lincoln feared that the British might next help break the ever-tightening naval blockade of the southern coast he had established in April 1861.

The dispute with Britain came to a head over two issues. First, in November 1861, a Union sloop seized a British steamer, the *Trent,* on the high seas; two Confederate commissioners, James Mason and John Slidell, who were on their way to Britain and France, were arrested. In response, the British demanded the release of the diplomats and ordered troops to Canada. Then, in the spring of 1862, British shipbuilders agreed to supply cruisers to the Confederacy. That summer a British firm also contracted to build the "Laird rams," two well-armed ironclads designed to break the blockade. The cruisers included the *Alabama,* which sailed from Liverpool in the summer of 1862 and sank or captured more than a hundred Union merchant ships.

Lincoln, Secretary of State William H. Seward, and the minister to Great Britain, Charles Francis Adams, released Mason and Slidell in December 1861 and adroitly avoided provoking Britain into siding with the Confederacy. In the summer of 1863 they even persuaded the British to impound the Laird rams.

"King Cotton" was less powerful than Lincoln had feared. Before the war British manufacturers had stockpiled textile products, and the blockade enabled them to reap extremely high profits from their sale. During the war they were able to buy raw cotton from Egypt and India. British munitions suppliers, who sold to both sides, and British shipowners, who profited from the South's attacks on the North's merchant marine, also had no interest in hastening the end of the war by choosing sides. British consumers had no wish to raise food prices by disrupting imports of grain from the North. In addition, British workers and reformers were enthusiastic champions of abolition, which the Emancipation Proclamation seemed to establish as a Union war aim.

The most important influence on the British, however, was Lee's defeat at Gettysburg, which convinced the British of the military might of the Union. The British did not want to risk their Canadian colonies or their merchant marine by provoking a strong, well-armed United States. Consequently, they decided not to recognize the Confederacy and remain neutral. Napoleon still favored recognition but had no enthusiasm for facing Union forces alone, particularly after Lincoln, to warn France and Mexico, sent General Banks on a successful mission to capture Brownsville, Texas, just north of the Mexican border, late in 1863.

The Union Victorious, 1864–1865

Despite Gettysburg, the outcome of the war remained very much in doubt well into 1864. Even though the Confederacy could no longer mount an invasion of the North, the Union's failure to crush Lee's army at Gettysburg meant that the Confederacy had new chances to erode northern support for the Union cause. If the war went poorly for the Union, the election of 1864 might enable the Democrats to challenge Lincoln's definition of war aims and persuade northern voters that the Union should end hostilities and begin negotiations with the Confederacy. Confederate leaders believed that such an outcome would result in de facto independence of the Confederacy. Two major developments, however, strengthened the ability of the Union to prosecute a total war: the enlistment of African-American soldiers and the discovery of generals capable of fighting a modern war.

African-American Soldiers

From the beginning of the war, both free blacks and fugitive slaves had sought to enlist in the Union army to advance the cause of freedom. Abolitionists and a few Union generals had tried to help. Frederick Douglass embraced the liberating power of military service in the cause of Union: "Once let the black man get upon his person the brass letters, 'U.S.,' let him get an eagle on his buttons and a musket on his shoulder and bullets in his pockets, and there is no power on earth which can deny that he has earned the right to citizenship in the United States." But that was exactly what northern whites feared: enlistment of African-Americans could threaten traditional race relations in the North. And most Union generals doubted that they would fight. Consequently, until the Emancipation Proclamation the Lincoln administration gave little encouragement to black aspirations for military service. Nonetheless, in 1862 several regiments of free and "contraband" blacks formed in South Carolina, Louisiana, and Kansas.

The logic of tying the abolition of slavery to the war effort, combined with the carnage of battle, helped produce a change in popular attitudes and government policy. Increasingly after the Emancipation Proclamation, northern whites concluded that if blacks were to benefit from a Union victory, then they, too, should share in the fighting and dying. In early 1863 the War Department began to authorize the enlistment of free blacks in the North and slaves in the areas of the South occupied by Union armies. During the summer of 1863, when the army's demand for soldiers increased and white resistance to the draft grew as well, the Lincoln administration began to recruit as many African-Americans as it could.

The performance of the first African-American regiments also helped shift policy. One of those regiments was the First South Carolina Volunteers, under the command of Thomas Wentworth Higginson, a white abolitionist. In January 1863 he wrote a glowing news-

Black Soldiers in the Union Army

These are the proud soldiers of a guard detail of the 107th Colored Infantry at Fort Corcoran, near Washington, D.C. In January 1865 their regiment participated in the daring capture of Fort Fisher, which protected Wilmington, North Carolina, the last of the Confederate ports open to blockade runners. Their chaplain declared that in nine battles the regiment "never faltered, gave way, or retreated, unless ordered by the General commanding."

paper account of the fighting of his troops: "No officer in this regiment now doubts that the key to the successful prosecution of the war lies in the unlimited employment of black troops." In July northerners read of the heroic and tragic attack on Fort Wagner, South Carolina, by another black regiment, the 54th Massachusetts Infantry, which was led by Robert Gould Shaw, the son of a prominent abolitionist. These accounts convinced many white northerners, including Union officers, of the value of black soldiers.

By the spring of 1865 there were nearly 200,000 African-Americans, primarily former slaves, serving as soldiers and sailors, constituting about 10 percent of those who served in the Union forces. Their regiments contributed to the Union cause in a number of major battles during 1864–1865, especially in Grant's grinding siege of Petersburg. During the election of 1864 Lincoln claimed that their participation in the war effort was so great that if the Union renounced emancipation and the recruiting of black soldiers, "we would be compelled to abandon the war in three weeks."

Black soldiers knew that they were fighting for freedom and were shifting the military odds in favor of the Union. Moreover, they hoped that victory would not only end slavery but also help them achieve full equality in American society. Nonetheless, the racial attitudes of northern whites did not undergo a fundamental change during the war, and the Union army, while developing more confidence in blacks as fighting soldiers, still held them in a second-class status. The army kept them in segregated regiments, used them primarily for menial labor or for garrisoning forts and guarding supply lines in occupied southern territory, routinely denied them commissions, and paid them less than white soldiers ($7 versus $13 per month) until June 1864, when the protests of black soldiers finally led Congress to equalize pay. In addition, the Lincoln administration did not protect captured African-Americans from Confederate violations of their rights as prisoners of war. The War Department ended exchanges of prisoners of war in 1863 when the Confederacy threatened to execute or enslave black prisoners of war. On the occasions when the Confederates acted on those threats, however, Lincoln was unwilling to take sterner measures. In July 1863 he threatened retaliation—execution of rebel soldiers or their employment at hard labor on public works—but never followed through.

Despite second-class citizenship, black soldiers persisted and endured. They did so because they understood what was at stake. One soldier found himself facing his former master, who had been taken as a prisoner of war. "Hello, Massa," he said, "bottom rail on top dis time." The worst fears of the secessionists had come true; in a real sense, the great slave rebellion had materialized, though not as a slave revolt.

The New Military Strategy

Lincoln and Grant. The successful Vicksburg and Chattanooga campaigns convinced Lincoln that in Ulysses S. Grant he had finally found a military leader who produced results. He realized that Grant understood how to fight a modern war—a war relying on industrial technology and directed at an entire society.

During his cadet days at West Point, Grant had been bored with studying conventional strategies—ones that stressed, for example, the advantages of interior lines of supply. Now new strategies offered a chance to win the war. During what was the first major war fought with railroads, the telegraph, and ironclad ships, Grant emphasized taking advantage of the ability to move troops and supplies rapidly and overcoming the Confederate advantage of interior lines.

Unlike McClellan and Meade, Grant was willing to accept heavy casualties in assaults on strongly defended positions. He was convinced that only by going on the offensive, even when it meant a great loss of life, could the Union end the war swiftly. "To conserve life, in war," Grant wrote, "is to fight unceasingly." Grant's tactics earned him a reputation as a butcher—a reputation enhanced by his persistent efforts to destroy armies in retreat. Grant was certain that the only way to victory was to crush the southern people's will to resist.

Lincoln, frustrated with the stalemate on the battlefield and worried about reelection in 1864, finally implemented his own approach to modern war. In March 1864 he placed Grant in charge of all the Union armies and created a command structure appropriate to the large, complex organization that the Union army had become. From then on, the president would determine general strategy and Grant would decide how best to implement it. Aiding the process was General Henry W. Halleck, the consummate office soldier. He served as chief of staff, channeling communications and lifting administrative burdens from both Lincoln and Grant. Along with the Prussian general staff, the Union's military command structure was the most efficient in the world.

Lincoln, advised by Grant, drew up a new strategy to break the Confederacy's will to resist. Instead of launching campaigns to take specific places, cities, and territory, he planned a simultaneous crushing advance of all the Union armies, mustering the maximum manpower and resources in their support. Grant would seek victories with a will and power that, Lincoln hoped, would overcome any obstacle.

In early May 1864 Grant ordered the 115,000-man Army of the Potomac, commanded by General George Meade, to destroy Lee's remaining 75,000 troops regardless of the cost in Union lives. He ordered General William Tecumseh Sherman, who shared Grant's views

Grant Planning an Attack
On June 2, 1864, the day this photograph was taken, Grant moved his headquarters to the Bethesda church, carried the pews out under the shade of the surrounding trees, and planned the costly attack he would make at Cold Harbor the next day. While Grant leaned over the pew, gesturing at a map, other officers read reports of the war in newspapers that had just arrived from New York City.

on the nature of warfare, to move simultaneously to invade Georgia and take Atlanta. As Sherman prepared, he wrote that "all that has gone before is mere skirmish. The war now begins."

The Wilderness Campaign. In Virginia, Grant advanced toward Richmond, hoping to force Lee's 75,000 troops to fight in open fields where the Union's superior manpower and artillery could prevail. Lee, remembering Gettysburg, maintained strong defensive positions, attacking only when he held a superior position. He twice seized such opportunities, making the Union take 32,000 casualties in return for 18,000 of his men in the battles of the Wilderness on May 5–7 and Spotsylvania Court House on May 8–12. Grant drove toward the railroad junction at Cold Harbor to outflank Lee, who countered and met Grant there, 10 miles from Richmond. Disregarding his earlier losses, Grant attacked Lee on June 1–3, but broke off after losing 7,000 more men in a frontal assault that lasted less than sixty minutes.

During this monthlong Wilderness campaign Grant eroded Lee's forces, which suffered 31,000 casualties, but Grant paid with 55,000 of his own men. A Union captain, Oliver Wendell Holmes, Jr., wrote, "Many a man has gone crazy since this campaign began from the terrible pressure on mind and body." Another Union officer described his men as feeling "a great horror and dread of attacking earthworks again." During 1861–1863, battles

had been relatively brief, typically lasting one to three days with intervals between the bloodlettings. But with the Wilderness campaign the fighting took on a sustained quality. In Virginia, Grant's relentless offensive tactics and Lee's successful defensive tactics had turned the war into one of grueling attrition (see Map 15.5).

The Siege of Petersburg. On June 12, in a surprise maneuver, Grant pulled away from Lee and Richmond, now heavily fortified, and swung south toward Petersburg, a major railroad center. By occupying it, he hoped to force Lee into the final battle of the war. Lee, however, alertly entrenched his troops at Petersburg and denied Grant the advantage of position. In June 1864 Grant laid siege to Petersburg.

Protracted trench warfare, which foreshadowed that of World War I, ensued. The spade had become more important than the sword as soldiers on both sides, including many who had been engineers in civilian life, built complex networks of trenches, tunnels, artillery emplacements, barriers of debris, and clearings designed to be killing zones. The two armies extended the trenches for almost 50 miles around Richmond and Petersburg as Grant inched toward control of Richmond's railroads. An officer described the continuous artillery firing and sniping as "living night and day within the 'valley of the shadow of death.'" The stress was especially great for the Confederate troops because of the

MAP 15.5

The Closing Virginia Campaigns
In 1865 the armies of Grant and Lee were locked in a deadly dance across the Virginia countryside. By threatening Lee's lines of communication, Grant attempted to force him into open battles. Until April 1865, Lee resisted, taking strong defensive positions that forced Grant to accept protracted sieges and steady casualties, which threatened to undermine northern support for the war.

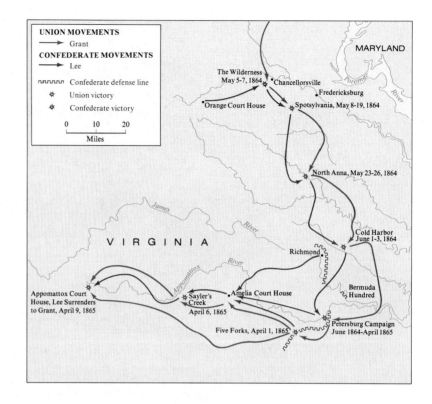

Confederacy's manpower crisis. Some of the Confederate regiments had to spend six months in the muddy, sickening trenches without rotation to the rear.

Lincoln and Grant were confident that their siege would eventually prevail, but time was not on their side. They feared that the enormous casualties and military stalemate might lead to Lincoln's defeat in the November election and, as a consequence, to the abandonment of the Union war effort (see American Voices, page 475).

The Shenandoah Campaign. The daring raids of 15,000 Confederate cavalry and other troops under Jubal Early made matters worse for the Union. Based in the Shenandoah Valley, Early's force crossed the Potomac in early July, passed Union defenses in Maryland only 5 miles north of the White House, and caused Grant to send some of his best troops from Petersburg to chase Early back to the Shenandoah. Before returning, two of Early's brigades invaded Pennsylvania and burned the town of Chambersburg when the city council refused to pay a ransom of $500,000.

The Union struck back with a vengeance. To punish and control the valley, which served as both a refuge for Confederate cavalry and a breadbasket for the Army of Northern Virginia, Grant created a new army, the Army of the Shenandoah, under his favorite cavalry officer, Philip H. Sheridan. Grant ordered Sheridan not only to destroy Early's forces but also to turn the Shenandoah Valley into "a barren waste . . . so that crows flying over it for the balance of this season will have to carry their

provender with them." During the fall Sheridan's troops conducted a scorched-earth campaign in the valley, destroying grain supplies, barns, farming implements, and gristmills, and burning the homes of people suspected of sheltering the "bushwhackers" who had murdered three of Sheridan's officers. The goal was to destroy the valley's economy and break the will of its people to resist the Union. For the first time in the Civil War a major army terrorized civilians.

Guerrillas had conducted terrorist activities against civilians in "Bleeding" Kansas during the 1850s and in the Upper South, particularly in the Shenandoah Valley and Missouri, since the outset of the war. Early's attack on Chambersburg was part of a gradual escalation of such warfare. And soldiers on both sides, frustrated and angered by the indecisiveness of the war, were increasingly tempted to commit acts of vengeance against hostile civilians. But with Sheridan's campaign, terror directed at civilians took on a far more organized form.

The new terrorism was limited for the most part to the destruction of property rather than life, but it nonetheless went beyond the military norms of the day. Conventional generals such as McClellan regarded civilians as innocents whom the military should protect and feared terrorism for the way it could disrupt military discipline. The decision of Lincoln, Grant, and the other Union generals in 1864 to carry the war to Confederate civilians in an organized fashion changed the definition of conventional warfare. The direction of organized terror against civilians was another way in which the Civil War approached the total warfare of the twentieth century.

Elisha Hunt Rhodes

The Diary of a Union Soldier

In June 1861 nineteen-year-old Elisha Hunt Rhodes left his widowed mother and enlisted in the Second Rhode Island Volunteers. Over the next four years he participated in every campaign of the Army of the Potomac. Surviving twenty major battles, he rose from private to lieutenant colonel and commander of the regiment.

April, 1861 [Pawtuxet]

Sunday night after I had retired, my mother came to my room and with a spirit worthy of a Spartan mother of old said, "My son, other mothers must make sacrifices and why should not I? If you feel that it is your duty to enlist, I will give my consent." She showed a patriotic spirit that much inspired my young heart.

July 21, 1861 [Bull Run]

On reaching a clearing . . . we were saluted with a volley of musketry, which, however, was fired so high that all the bullets went over our heads. I remember that my first sensation was one of astonishment at the peculiar whir of the bullets, and that the Regiment immediately laid down without waiting for orders.

As I emerged from the woods I saw a bomb shell strike a man in the breast and literally tear him to pieces. I passed the farm house which had been appropriated for a hospital and the groans of the wounded and dying were horrible. I then descended the hill to the woods which had been occupied by the rebels. . . . The bodies of the dead and dying were actually three and four deep . . . while the trees were spattered with blood.

September 23, 1862 [Antietam]

Sunday morning we found that the enemy had recrossed the river. O, why did we not attack them and drive them into the river? I do not understand these things. But then I am only a boy.

July 3, 1863 [Gettysburg]

Soon the Rebel yell was heard, and . . . the Rebel General Pickett made a charge with his Division and was repulsed after reaching some of our batteries. Our lines of Infantry in front of us rose up and poured in a terrible fire. As we were only a few yards in rear of our lines we saw all the fight. The firing gradually died away, and but for an occasional shot all was still. But what a scene it was. Oh the dead and dying on this bloody field.

December 22, 1864 [entrenchments near Petersburg]

We do not fear the result of an assault by the enemy on our works. . . . The forts and batteries . . . are within range of each other and are connected by curtains or rifle pits. In front of our works are deep ditches now filled with water and in front of this an abatis [barrier] made of limbs and trees driven slanting into the ground and with the points sharpened. Then we have wires stretched about in every direction about six inches or a foot above the ground. And still in front of all this the trees are slashed and are piled up in great confusion. I wish the Rebels would try to take our lines. It would be fun for us.

Source: Robert Hunt Rhodes, ed., All for the Union: The Civil War Diary and Letters of Elisha Hunt Rhodes (New York: Orion, 1991), passim.

Sherman, Atlanta, and the Election of 1864

As the siege at Petersburg dragged on, Lincoln and Grant knew that their hopes of proving to voters that the war could be won rested with Sherman in Georgia. At the beginning of the siege in Virginia, Sherman had penetrated to within about 30 miles of Atlanta, a great railway hub that controlled the heart of the Confederacy. Although his army outnumbered that of General Joseph E. Johnston, 90,000 to 60,000, he declined to attack Johnston directly and decided to pry him out of his defensive positions. Sherman feared that his supply line, extending by rail all the way to Louisville, was overexposed to Confederate cavalry and guerrilla attacks and recognized the advantage to its defenders provided by the rugged terrain of northern Georgia. Johnston, for his part, was unwilling to risk his smaller army and gradually fell back southward toward Atlanta. Finally, on June 27, at Kennesaw Mountain, Sherman engaged Johnston in a set battle but took 3,000 casualties while inflicting only about 600. Sherman seemed to be stalled in his effort to destroy Johnston's army; Confederate morale soared.

In July, Jefferson Davis, tired of Johnston's defensive tactics, replaced him with General John B. Hood. Sherman, however, welcomed the change, which one of his generals remarked was "to have our enemy grasp the hot end of the poker." What followed, as one Union soldier described it, was "a common slaughter of the enemy," out in the open and unprotected by fortifications. By late July, Sherman was laying siege to Atlanta. But the next month brought little gain; both Sherman and Grant seemed to be bogged down in hopeless campaigns.

As Union and Confederate audiences focused on the fate of Atlanta, the 1864 presidential campaign began. In June the Republican party convention endorsed all of Lincoln's war measures, demanded the unconditional surrender of the Confederacy, and called for a constitutional amendment to abolish slavery. To emphasize the need for restoration of the Union and attract Democratic support, the party temporarily renamed itself the National Union party and nominated for vice-president Andrew Johnson, a Tennessee Democrat who had remained loyal and stayed in the Senate until 1862, when Lincoln named him military governor of Tennessee.

By August many Republican leaders thought Lincoln would lose the presidency to General George B. McClellan, the likely Democratic nominee. With the armies of Grant and Sherman stalled, the expanded war effort seemed almost hopeless. Some Republicans talked about calling a new convention and dropping Lincoln from the ticket. The Republican National Committee urged Lincoln to abandon emancipation as a war aim and offer Jefferson Davis peace in return only for "acknowledging the supremacy of the constitution." Lincoln was tempted, but he refused to abandon emancipation even though he had decided he would be beaten "and unless some great change takes place *badly* beaten." Meanwhile, Republicans rushed through the admission of Nevada to the Union, believing that its electoral votes might tip a close election in their favor.

The Democratic national convention met in late August, nominated McClellan, and declared that party's opposition to emancipation—and to Lincoln's harsh treatment of internal dissent. A slight majority—the War Democrats—wanted to continue the war, despite their criticisms of the Lincoln administration. But the rest—the Peace Democrats—wanted to end the fighting. By threatening to bolt the convention, they obtained nearly unanimous agreement on a platform calling for "a cessation of hostilities, with a view to an ultimate convention of the states, or other peaceable means, to the end that, at the earliest practicable moment, peace may be restored on the basis of the Federal Union." McClellan himself was a War Democrat, but he gave private assurances to the Peace Democrats that he would recommend an immediate armistice and a peace convention. Alexander Stephens, the vice-president of the Confederacy, declared that the platform offered "the first ray of real light I have seen since the war began." Stephens believed that if Confederate forces could hold on to Atlanta and Richmond through the election of 1864, Lincoln might well go down to defeat. A Democratic victory would probably mean the "cessation of hostilities," and Stephens sensed that once the fighting had stopped, Union leaders would be unable to get it going again and the Confederacy would, in effect, be independent.

The Fall of Atlanta. Stephens made his remarks before he learned the fateful news: on September 2 Atlanta fell to Sherman. In a stunning move, he had pulled his troops back from the trenches and had swept around the city to destroy its roads and rail links to the rest of the Confederacy. After failing to stop Sherman, Hood abandoned Atlanta, fearing that Sherman would be able to trap and destroy his army. Sherman wired Lincoln: "Atlanta is ours, and fairly won." In her diary Mary Chesnut recorded that she "felt as if all were dead within me, forever." For the first time she despaired of the possibility for a Confederate victory: "We are going to be wiped off the earth."

Amid the 100-gun salutes in northern cities that greeted the news of Sherman's victory, McClellan repudiated the Democratic peace platform, and Republicans abandoned all efforts to dump Lincoln. They campaigned hard, pinning the peace platform to McClellan's campaign and charging, with some accuracy, that groups of Peace Democrats—or Copperheads (poisonous snakes), as the Republican press called them—had hatched or were hatching treasonous plots in the border states and the southern part of the Old Northwest.

Lincoln's Election. Lincoln's victory in November was not a landslide, but it was clear-cut. He won 212 of 233 electoral votes, carrying every state except Delaware, Kentucky, and New Jersey. He increased his percentage of the popular vote in the free and border states from the 48 percent he had received in 1860 to 55 percent. His opposition was concentrated in border districts and the immigrant wards of large cities. Republicans also won 145 of the 185 seats in the House of Representatives and increased their Senate majority to 42 of 52 seats. The margin of victory in many places came from Union soldiers. The soldiers cast absentee ballots or returned home, briefly furloughed by commanders to cast ballots in areas where the Democrats had blocked absentee balloting. More than three-fourths of the Union troops voted for Lincoln. They wanted the war to continue until the Confederacy met every Union demand, including emancipation. As in 1863, the elections of 1864 lent democratic sanction to the Union war effort. Grant wrote a friend that "the overwhelming majority received by Mr. Lincoln and the quiet with which the election went off . . . will be worth more than a victory in the field both in its effect on the Rebels and in its influence abroad."

Sherman's "March to the Sea"

After abandoning Atlanta, Hood moved into northern Georgia to cut Sherman's supply lines but was forced to retreat to Alabama. Once Sherman set out for the sea,

Hood marched north to Tennessee, convinced that his only chance was to lure Sherman into giving chase. But Sherman declined to follow. He decided that rather than wear out his troops or spread them dangerously thin by protecting captured territory, he would simply "cut a swath through to the sea." Lincoln and Grant were dubious, but Sherman prevailed, arguing that if he marched through Georgia, "smashing things" all the way to the Atlantic coast, he would divide the Confederacy and win a major psychological victory. It would be "a demonstration to the world, foreign and domestic, that we have a power Davis cannot resist."

As he marched, Sherman carried out the concept of total war that he and Sheridan had pioneered—destruction of the enemy's economic and psychological resources. "We are not only fighting hostile armies," Sherman wrote, "but a hostile people, and must make old and young, rich and poor, feel the hard hand of war." Union armies "cannot change the hearts of those people of the South but we can make war so terrible . . . that generations would pass away before they would again appeal to it." He promised to "make Georgia howl!"

Sherman left Atlanta in flames. He destroyed Confederate railroads, property, and supplies, terrorizing the civilian population, in a 300-mile march to the sea. A Union veteran wrote that "[we] destroyed all we could not eat, stole their niggers, burned their cotton & gins, spilled their sorghum, burned & twisted their R.Roads and raised Hell generally." A Union officer described the march as "probably the most gigantic pleasure excursion ever planned." Letters from Georgia describing the havoc so demoralized Confederate soldiers at the front that many deserted and fled home to their loved ones. When Sherman reached Savannah, Georgia, in mid-December, the 10,000 Confederate troops defending the city evaporated almost at once. Sherman presented the city to President Lincoln as a Christmas gift (see Map 15.6).

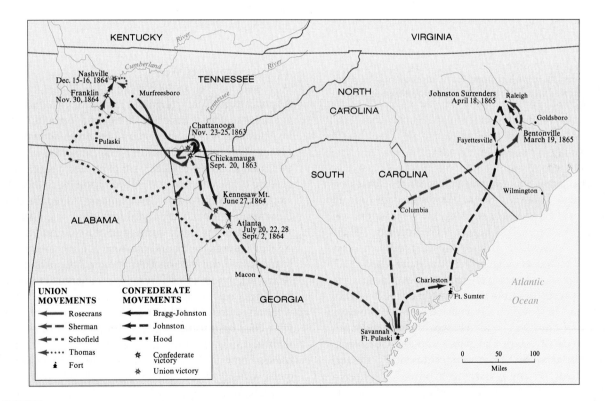

MAP 15.6

Sherman's March through the Confederacy

The Union victory at Chattanooga in November 1863 was almost as critical as those at Gettysburg and Vicksburg. Having already split the Confederacy along the Mississippi, the Union was now in position to split the Confederacy again with a line running from Kentucky through Tennessee and Georgia to the sea. Sherman captured Atlanta and then, largely ignoring John B. Hood's failed invasion of Tennessee, swept to the Atlantic.

Atlanta in Ruins
Not all of the destruction in Atlanta came at the hands of
Sherman's forces. The wreckage seen in this photograph is of
a factory that Hood's retreating troops blew up to avoid having it fall under Sherman's control. But Union troops finished
the work, destroying a Georgia Central roundhouse and car
sheds (on the right).

In February 1865 Sherman turned his forces to
sweep through South Carolina. He planned to link up
with Grant at Petersburg and, along the way, punish the
state where secession had begun. "The truth is," Sherman wrote, "the whole army is burning with an insatiable desire to wreak vengeance upon South Carolina."
His troops cut a comparatively narrow swath across the
state but ravaged the countryside even more thoroughly
than they had in Georgia. On February 17 the business
district, most churches, and the wealthiest residential
neighborhoods of South Carolina's capital, Columbia,
burned to the ground. "*This* disappointment," Jefferson
Davis moaned, "to me is extremely bitter." By March
Sherman had reached North Carolina and was on the
verge of linking up with Grant and crushing Lee's army
(see American Lives, pages 480–481).

Confederate Morale. Sherman's march, together with
Lincoln's victory in 1864, proved that the Union had
both the armies and the willpower to prevail in a total
war. Moreover, the military setbacks that culminated
with Sherman's march to the sea, coupled with the early
"20-Negro Exemption," exposed an internal Confeder-

ate weakness: rising class resentment on the part of poor
whites. Southern men resisted conscription at rates that
increased dramatically; in 1865 desertion became epidemic. In all, over 100,000 Confederates deserted.
Many linked up with draft evaders to form guerrilla
forces that ruled backcountry areas. To add to the
South's troubles, secret societies of Unionists operated
openly in the Appalachian Mountains, the hill country
of Alabama, the Ozarks of Arkansas, parts of Texas,
and all other areas where there were few slaves. These
Unionists aided northern troops and sometimes enlisted
in the Union army when it marched nearby.

By 1865 the Confederacy was experiencing a profound manpower crisis. In March its leaders decided on
an extreme measure: arming its own slaves. Howell
Cobb, a powerful Georgia politician, had pointed out
that "if slaves will make good soldiers our whole theory
of slavery is wrong." Nonetheless, urged on by Lee, the
Confederate Congress voted to enlist black soldiers.
Davis added an executive order granting freedom to all
blacks who served in the Confederate army. The war
ended too soon, however, to reveal whether any slaves
would seek freedom by joining their masters in defense
of the Confederacy.

The End of the War

Appomattox. While Sherman marched, Grant continued
his siege of the entrenched Army of Northern Virginia.
In April 1865 he finally forced Lee into a showdown by
gaining control of a crucial railroad junction near Richmond and cutting off Lee's supplies. Lee abandoned the
defense of the city and turned west, hoping to meet Johnston in North Carolina. While Lincoln visited the ruins of
Richmond, mobbed by joyful former slaves, Grant pursued Lee and his small army of 25,000. Grant swiftly cut
off Lee's escape route, and on April 9, almost exactly four
years after the attack on Fort Sumter, Lee surrendered to
Grant at Appomattox Court House, Virginia. In accepting, Grant set a tone of egalitarianism and generosity. He
wore an unpressed jacket and muddy trousers, in contrast
with Lee's handsome uniform and sword in its gold-inlay
scabbard, and allowed Lee's enlisted men to take their
horses home for spring planting. Afterward, Grant's soldiers willingly shared their ample rations with hungry
Confederates.

Nine days later General Johnston signed an
armistice with Sherman near Durham, North Carolina.
He surrendered later in the month; by May 26 all the
other Confederate generals had also surrendered. There
was no formal conclusion to the hostilities: the Confederate army and government simply dissolved. After fleeing from Richmond, hoping that the South would
continue to resist, Jefferson Davis was captured by
Union cavalry in Georgia.

The armies of the Union had destroyed the Confederacy. During four years of war they had destroyed much of the South's productive capacity. Its factories, warehouses, and railroads were in ruins, as were many of its farms and cities. Almost 260,000 Confederate soldiers—nearly one in three—had paid for secession with their lives. And most significant, the Union armies had destroyed slavery (see Map 15.7).

The Union's victory had been tragically costly. From Fort Sumter to Appomattox, more than 360,000 Union soldiers had died and hundreds of thousands of others had been maimed and crippled. But the hard and bitter war had been won. Americans from the North and South, both blacks and whites, had to turn to the tasks of peace. Lincoln had spoken at Gettysburg of "finishing the work." It was time to decide exactly what that "work" was. Freed slaves faced the question of what freedom would bring. Their former masters began to try to salvage what they could from defeat. People in all parts of the North pondered the meaning of a victory so costly and so complete. They wondered whether the "terrible, swift sword" of the "Battle Hymn of the Republic" should be put away in reconciliation or loosed again in a hard and bitter peace.

Lee's Surrender

Lee surrendered to Grant in the parlor of a modest farmer, Wilmer McLean, who could not escape the war. McLean had fled to Appomattox for peace and quiet after leaving a Manassas home, which Confederate soldiers had used as a headquarters and Union forces had shelled during the first major battle of the war.

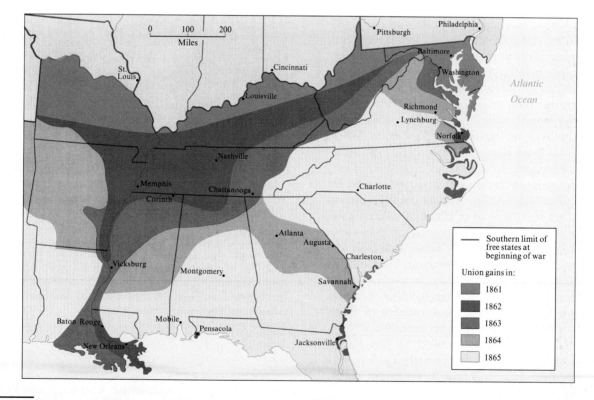

MAP 15.7

The Conquest of the South, 1861–1865

This map reveals how the Union slowly took control of Confederate territory. Nearly half of the territory of the Confederacy held fast until the last year of the war. The Union's victory depended primarily on its ability to control strategic lines of communication and destroy the armies of the Confederacy.

William Tecumseh Sherman: An Architect of Modern War

William Tecumseh Sherman's (1820–1891) obsession with social order motivated the innovations that made him one of the most important architects of modern warfare and a major force in the Union victory in the Civil War.

Sherman's ancestors had long been socially prominent in Connecticut, but after his attorney father, Charles R. Sherman, moved to Lancaster, Ohio, the family fell on hard times. After Charles's death in 1829 his wife could afford to keep only two of their eleven children. At the age of nine, the sixth child, Tecumseh (named after the Indian chief, whom Charles described as "a great warrior"), went to live with Thomas Ewing, a close family friend and a wealthy Lancaster lawyer.

On the one hand, "Cump" (as Tecumseh's own family had nicknamed him) appreciated the privileges provided by Ewing. On the other hand, Cump never got over the embarrassment of his father's financial failure and his family's inability to provide him with a home. His foster mother's insistence that a priest baptize Cump into her Catholic faith and give him a Christian name ("William Tecumseh") only heightened his sense of not belonging. In 1836 he left to enter West Point, where Ewing, who had been elected to the Senate in 1831, had found a place for him.

Sherman adopted the army as a second family. He chafed at cadet discipline but was an excellent student and found that the corps of professional officers gave him a sense of belonging. After his graduation in 1840, assignments in Florida, Alabama, South Carolina, and Georgia appealed to his curiosity about American life and geography.

The Ewings pressured Sherman to leave the army, particularly after their daughter Ellen agreed to marry him, but he refused, fearing greater dependency. Also, Sherman saw opportunity in the Mexican War. But by the time he arrived in California in early 1847 to take up his assignment there was little to do except paperwork.

In 1853 Sherman, depressed by his slow advance, resigned from the army. Unstable financial times, however, ruined his career as head of the San Francisco and

William Tecumseh Sherman
Sherman's severity in this May 1865 photograph might have partly reflected his difficulty in sitting still for Mathew Brady as much as his sense of victory. When he was seated, he crossed and uncrossed his legs incessantly, and a journalist described his fingers as always "twitching his red whiskers—his coat buttons—playing a tattoo on the table—or running through his hair." In the field Sherman smoked cigars and talked continuously.

New York branches of a St. Louis bank, and he became a reluctant business partner of two Ewing foster brothers. In 1860 he rejoined the army as superintendent of the brand-new Louisiana Military Seminary (which would eventually become Louisiana State University).

Sherman's earlier assignments in the South had already made him sympathetic to the planter class. By 1860 he was certain that slavery was necessary for southern social order. But his conviction that the Union was the primary instrument for national stability had deepened during the chaotic 1850s. Sherman's Whig ideology, army loyalties, and personal insecurities combined to give the concept of the Union great symbolic force.

When Louisiana troops seized the U.S. arsenal at Baton Rouge in January 1861 and deposited captured weapons at his academy, Sherman resigned his position. He told his southern friends that secessionists had driven him away. "There can be no *peaceable secession*," he wrote. Secession represented the "tendency to anarchy" and constituted treason. The only way to crush it was to show the secessionists that they could not get away with it. "If war comes, as I fear it surely will," he told the southerners, "I must fight your people whom I best love."

Sherman understood how costly and bloody the war would be. He believed that the Union could smash southern society, but he doubted that the administration of Abraham Lincoln had the will to do so, and Sherman had no desire to associate himself with another failed enterprise. While he hung back, Senator Ewing and one of Sherman's younger brothers, John Sherman, who had just been elected to the Senate from Ohio, persuaded him to become a colonel of a newly formed brigade.

Bull Run, Sherman's first taste of combat, drove him into a depression over the ability of a democracy to wage war. "The want of organization and subordination of our people is a more dangerous enemy than the armies of the South," he wrote. By October 1861 Sherman had risen to the rank of brigadier general and had command of all the Union forces in Kentucky, but he became darkly pessimistic amid the political and military chaos of that border state. Suddenly, in November, the Lincoln administration relieved the seemingly erratic Sherman of his command.

General Henry Halleck continued to support Sherman, however, particularly because he agreed with his warnings about southern strength. Sherman's powerful family also continued to lobby for him. In February 1862 Halleck restored a well-rested Sherman to a command under Ulysses S. Grant in Kentucky. Grant provided just the sense of direction and confidence that Sherman needed. He agreed with Sherman's stress on adequately supplying and disciplining armies and on the swift and decisive deployment of forces. Most important, he was willing to share with Sherman the credit for victories.

Under Grant's leadership, Sherman enjoyed a string of successes. He distinguished himself at Shiloh, and his friends and family in Washington made certain Lincoln immediately promoted him to major general. As military governor of Memphis he pacified a strategic sector of the Mississippi River. Then he served under Grant in the campaign that led to Vicksburg's fall. In Tennessee he began to implement his concept of a war against southern society, employing harsh tactics to deal with anti-Union guerrillas. "When one nation is at war with another, all the people of one are enemies of the other," he wrote. After guerrillas fired on a boat with Unionist passengers and goods near Randolph, Tennessee, he sent a regiment to level the town. He told a Vicksburg citizens' committee that "we are justified in treating all inhabitants as combatants . . ."

In March 1864 Sherman became commander of all military operations in the West. Now only Grant was more powerful, and he consulted closely with Sherman as they drew up a coordinated plan to destroy the Confederacy. Over the next year, Sherman's taking of Atlanta, his "march to the sea," and his sweep through the Carolinas demonstrated his tactical genius and understanding that the Civil War was a war between two societies. He preferred psychological warfare to the bloody, direct confrontations of armies.

After the Union victory Sherman received international acclaim. His former troops revered him, grateful American businessmen made him wealthy, and world leaders honored him. Sherman felt that he had at last established his own identity.

Sherman remained active in public life, but only within the military. He led a war against the Great Plains Indians and then served as commanding general of the army between 1869 and his retirement in 1883. Between 1868 and 1888 politicians, both Democrats and Republicans, regularly approached him to run for the presidency. However, Sherman's distaste for democratic politics had grown even stronger. In fact, Sherman never even voted in a presidential election, except in 1856, when he cast a ballot for Buchanan. In 1883 he ended talk of his candidacy with the often-quoted words "I will not accept if nominated and will not serve if elected." He felt that the honor of having played a central role in preserving the Union was enough. His tombstone epitaph, which he wrote, read simply "Faithful and Honorable."

Summary

The Democrats had divided along sectional lines in the 1860 elections because southerners sought more protection for slavery than northern Democrats would provide. When the Republicans won the presidency, the South concluded that it could no longer both preserve slavery and remain in the Union. The South then seceded and used force to discourage the North from trying to maintain the Union.

The conflict became a total war, one of unsurpassed cost in American lives and resources, because of the great strength of the two regions and because of their conflict over fundamental political and social values. Between 1861 and 1863 the Confederacy several times came close to a decisive victory—at Bull Run, at Antietam, and at Gettysburg. Meanwhile, the Union learned that to win it had to wage total war and smash southern society.

As the Civil War became a war between two peoples, the South and the North each had to address major issues of social unity. For the South, the key questions were: Would slaves work loyally in the fields to sustain their masters and the war effort? And would non-slaveholding whites fight and die in a war if they believed they were simply defending the interests of slave owners? For the North, the central issue of national unity was whether workers and farmers would conclude that they were fighting only to defend the interests of the northern business class and therefore refuse to fight and die.

The year 1864 turned out to be decisive. The North proved to be better organized and more unified. It had acquired the necessary military leadership, resources, and political support to wage total war. Critical to the massive mobilization was the enactment of the Republican economic program, the establishment of emancipation as a war aim, and the enlistment of vast numbers of former slaves.

During 1864 President Lincoln mounted two great offensives. The South resisted vigorously and once again came close to wearing down the will of the North to fight. But the equally stubborn determination of the Union armies, combined with their superior strength and a fortunate victory at Atlanta before the election of 1864, made both offensives successful. The war ended when Sherman's march through Georgia and South Carolina and Grant's relentless pursuit of Lee convinced ordinary southerners that they could not win the war.

TIMELINE

1861	Confederate States of America formed (February 4)
	Abraham Lincoln inaugurated (March 4)
	Confederates fire on Fort Sumter (April 12)
	Virginia convention votes to secede (April 17)
	Lincoln blockades of southern coast
	General Benjamin Butler declares runaway slaves "contraband of war"
	Lincoln states war aims (July 4)
	First Battle of Bull Run (July 21)
	Lincoln signs First Confiscation Act
	Fifty counties in western Virginia vote to form new state (October)
	George B. McClellan made general-in-chief of Union army (November)
1862	Congress passes Legal Tender Act (February)
	Congress passes Second Confiscation Act
	Battle of Shiloh (April 6–7)
	David G. Farragut takes New Orleans (April 25–29)
	Confederacy introduces first draft
	Seven Days' battles (June 25–July 1)
	Second Battle of Bull Run (August 29–30)
	Homestead Act
	Battle of Antietam (September 17)
	Preliminary Emancipation Proclamation (September 22)
	Battle of Fredericksburg (December 13)
1863	Lincoln signs the Emancipation Proclamation (January 1)
	Enrollment Act establishes draft in the North
	Battle of Chancellorsville (May 2–4)
	France sets up Mexican regime
	Battle of Gettysburg (July 1–3)
	Fall of Vicksburg (July 4)
	New York City draft riots
	Britain impounds Laird rams
	Union forces seize Brownsville, Texas
1864	Ulysses S. Grant takes command of all Union armies (March 9)
	Grant's Wilderness campaign
	Siege of Petersburg begins (June 15)
	Jubal Early's raids
	Atlanta falls to William T. Sherman (September 2)
	Shenandoah campaign of Philip H. Sheridan
	Lincoln's reelection
	Sherman's march through Georgia
1865	Congress approves Thirteenth Amendment
	Columbia, South Carolina, burns (February 17)
	Robert E. Lee surrenders
	Ratification of Thirteenth Amendment

★   ★   ★

BIBLIOGRAPHY

The best up-to-date, comprehensive one-volume surveys of the Civil War are James M. McPherson's *Battle Cry of Freedom: The Civil War Era* (1988) and *Ordeal By Fire: The Civil War and Reconstruction* (1993). An excellent brief survey is Charles P. Roland, *An American Iliad: The Story of the Civil War* (1991). Compelling older surveys include Shelby Foote, *The Civil War: A Narrative,* 3 vols. (1958–1974), and Allan Nevins, *War for the Union,* 4 vols. (1959–1971).

Choosing Sides

Classic studies of the secession crisis include Richard N. Current, *Lincoln and the First Shot* (1963); David M. Potter, *Lincoln and His Party in the Secession Crisis, 1860–61* (1950); and Kenneth M. Stampp, *And the War Came: The North and the Secession Crisis, 1860–61* (1950). Histories of the secession of the Deep South include William L. Barney, *The Secessionist Impulse: Alabama and Mississippi in 1860* (1974), and Michael P. Johnson, *Toward a Patriarchal Republic: The Secession of Georgia* (1977). On the Upper South, see Daniel W. Crofts, *Reluctant Confederates: Upper South Unionists in the Secession Crisis* (1989).

War Machines

To study northern society and politics during the war, consult Iver Bernstein, *The New York City Draft Riots* (1990); Gabor S. Boritt, ed., *Lincoln the War President: The Gettysburg Lectures* (1992); Adrian Cook, *The Armies of the Streets: The New York City Draft Riots of 1863* (1974); George M. Fredrickson, *The Inner Civil War: Northern Intellectuals and the Crisis of Union* (second edition, 1993); J. Matthew Gallman, *The North Fights the Civil War: The Home Front* (1994); Mary E. Massey, *Bonnet Brigades: American Women and the Civil War* (1966); William Q. Maxwell, *Lincoln's Fifth Wheel: The Political History of the United States Sanitary Commission* (1956); Mark E. Neely, Jr., *The Fate of Liberty: Abraham Lincoln and Civil Liberties* (1991); Phillip S. Paludan, *The Presidency of Abraham Lincoln* (1994); Susan M. Reverby, *Ordered to Care: The Dilemma of American Nursing, 1850–1945* (1987); Joel Silbey, *A Respectable Minority: The Democratic Party in the Civil War Era* (1977); Hans Trefousse, *The Radical Republicans* (1969); and Garry Wills, *Lincoln at Gettysburg* (1992). Important biographies on Union leaders include Michael Fellman, *Citizen Sherman: A Life of William Tecumseh Sherman* (1995); John F. Marszalek, *Sherman: A Soldier's Passion for Order* (1993); William McFeely, *Grant: A Biography* (1981); Stephen B. Oates, *With Malice towards None: The Life of Abraham Lincoln* (1977); Stephen W. Sears, *George B. McClellan: The Young Napoleon* (1988); and the Abraham Lincoln studied cited in Chapter 14.

Among the best histories of the Confederacy are George C. Rable, *The Confederate Republic: A Revolution against Politics* (1994), and Emory M. Thomas, *The Confederate Nation: 1861–1865* (1979). Important biographies on leading Confederates include William C. Davis, *Jefferson Davis, the Man and His Hour: A Biography* (1991), and Thomas E. Schott, *Alexander H. Stephens of Georgia: A Biography* (1988).

Studies of non-slaveholding whites in the Confederacy include Paul Escott, *After Secession: Jefferson Davis and the Failure of Southern Nationalism* (1978); Drew Gilpin Faust, *The Creation of Confederate Nationalism: Ideology and Identity in the Civil War* (1988); and Philip S. Paludan, *Victims: A True History of the Civil War* (1981).

Studies of wartime emancipation include Herman Belz, *A New Birth of Freedom: The Republican Party and Freedmen's Rights, 1861–1866* (1976); John Hope Franklin, *The Emancipation Proclamation* (1963); Louis S. Gerteis, *From Contraband to Freedom: Federal Policy toward Southern Blacks, 1861–1865* (1973); James M. McPherson, *The Struggle for Equality: Abolitionists and the Negro in the Civil War and Reconstruction* (1964); and Benjamin Quarles, *The Negro in the Civil War* (1953). The best scholarship on the lives of slaves during the war is found in Ira Berlin et al., eds., *Freedom: A Documentary History of Emancipation, 1861–1867,* Series I, Volume I: *The Destruction of Slavery* (1985) and Series I, Volume III: *The Wartime Genesis of Free Labor: The Lower South* (1990). See also Winthrop D. Jordan, *Tumult and Silence at Second Creek: An Inquiry into a Civil War Slave Conspiracy* (1993).

Fighting the Civil War

The most useful introductions to the military aspects of the war are T. Harry Williams, *The History of American Wars* (1981) and *Lincoln and His Generals* (1952). On the experiences of Civil War soldiers, see Albert Castel, *Decision in the West: The Atlanta Campaign* (1992); Gerald F. Linderman, *Embattled Courage: The Experience of Combat in the American Civil War* (1987); James M. McPherson, *What They Fought For, 1861–1865* (1994); Reid Mitchell, *Civil War Soldiers* (1988) and *The Vacant Chair: The Northern Soldier Leaves Home* (1993); and Joseph T. Glatthaar, *The March to the Sea and Beyond: Sherman's Troops in the Savannah and Carolinas Campaign* (1985). On the participation of African-Americans in the war, see Ira Berlin et al., *Freedom: A Documentary History of Emancipation, 1861–1867,* Series II, *The Black Military Experience* (1982), and Joseph T. Glatthaar, *Forged in Battle: The Civil War Alliance of Black Soldiers and White Officers* (1990). On Confederate military tactics, see Grady McWhiney and Perry D. Jamieson, *Attack and Die: Civil War Military Tactics and the Southern Heritage* (1982), and Steven E. Woodworth, *Jefferson Davis and His Generals: The Failure of Confederate Command in the West* (1990). An innovative exploration of the dynamics of violence is found in Charles Royster, *The Destructive War: William Tecumseh Sherman, Stonewall Jackson, and the Americans* (1991). The most graphic account of a single battle is Stephen W. Sears, *Landscape Turned Red: The Battle of Antietam* (1983). On the most violent guerrilla war ever fought in the United States, see Michael Fellman, *Inside War: The Guerrilla Conflict in Missouri during the American Civil War* (1989). On the Civil War in the Far West, consult Alvin M. Josephy, Jr., *The Civil War in the American West* (1991). For insightful analyses of the war's outcome see Richard E. Beringer et al., *Why the South Lost the Civil War* (1986); Joseph T. Glatthaar, *Partners in Command: The Relationships between Leaders in the Civil War* (1993); Herman Hattaway and Archer Jones, *How the North Won: A Military History of the Civil War* (1983); and Archer Jones, *Civil War Command and Strategy: The Process of Victory and Defeat* (1992).

Robert B. Elliott

Robert B. Elliott (1842–1884) was born in Boston and
educated there and in Jamaica and England. After studying
law and serving in the navy during the Civil War, he moved
to Charleston and served in the state legislature (1868–1870),
Congress (1871–1874), and as speaker of the South Carolina
house (1874–1876). This 1874 lithograph, *The Shackle
Broken by the Genius of Freedom*, shows him addressing
state legislators on civil rights. After Reconstruction he left
politics and practiced law in New Orleans.

The Union Reconstructed

1865–1877

★　　　★　　　★

When the Confederacy collapsed in the spring of 1865, President Lincoln hoped that he could achieve a swift reconciliation between the triumphant North and the shattered South. In his second inaugural address Lincoln had spoken of the need to "bind up the nation's wounds." But many questions remained unanswered. Who would control the rebuilding of the Union—the president or Congress? How long should the rebuilding last? How far should it go: should it exclude former Confederates from politics and reward freedmen with land confiscated from their former masters?

At the end of the war most Republican leaders defined the task of rebuilding simply as a matter of *restoration*. These moderates wanted to establish loyal, pro-Union state governments and restore the southern states' representation in Congress. But freedmen, former abolitionists, and some Republican politicians favored a more radical plan—one requiring a degree of *reconstruction* of the South. In their view, steps should be taken to ensure a measure of political and even economic equality for the freed slaves and to prevent the return to power of unrepentant planters. For radicals, the key to reconstructing the South was to make the Republican party dominant there.

When northern Republicans adopted a policy of radical reconstruction in 1867, ex-Confederates and their Democratic sympathizers in the North maintained that their goal should be the *redemption* of the South. They claimed that the Union victory had defeated democracy in the South, depriving southerners of control over their economic, social, and political systems. The Union would be rebuilt, the redeemers claimed, only when white southerners regained power over their states and their own affairs.

The Reconstruction Era—the years from 1865 to 1877—was shaped by continuous struggles among the groups holding these differing views. It was a time of

unparalleled peacetime turmoil and violence. In the struggles, every kind of tactic was brought to bear: the assassination of one president and the impeachment of another; the adoption of three amendments to the Constitution and a welter of new legislation; the use of violence, including nighttime terrorism by robed whites in the South; the creation of new institutions by African-Americans; and conventional compromises and deals by politicians on all sides.

Presidential Restoration

Lincoln and his successor, Andrew Johnson, took the initiative in rebuilding the Union. Both believed that the southern states had never legally left the Union, that rebuilding the nation was simply a process of restoring state governments loyal to the Union, and that this political process could take place quickly, largely under presidential direction. This moderate approach put the presidents on a collision course with those Republicans in Congress who sought a reconstruction of southern society.

Restoration under Lincoln

The process of rebuilding had actually begun during the war as Lincoln tried to subvert the southern war effort. Lincoln thought that a policy of moderation and reconciliation in the portions of the South occupied by federal troops would induce the Confederates to abandon the rebellion. In implementing his restoration plan, Lincoln relied on his power as military commander in chief. He assumed that states could not legally secede and that reorganizing the Union was purely an administrative mat-

ter. (In 1869, in *Texas v. White*, the Supreme Court accepted Lincoln's constitutional interpretation, ruling that secession was impossible under the Constitution.)

Lincoln's Plan. In December 1863 Lincoln announced his restoration plan. He offered a general amnesty to all Confederate citizens except high-ranking civil and military officials. Citizens of states seeking to reconstitute their governments would have to take an oath pledging their *future* loyalty to the Union and accepting the Union's wartime acts and proclamations concerning slavery. When 10 percent of the number of voters in 1860 had taken the loyalty oath, those individuals could organize a new state government.

Lincoln aimed his plan at former southern Whigs, many of whom he had known well as former political allies. Under his plan they would step forward, declare allegiance to the Union, and take charge of southern state governments. That is what happened in three states under military occupation: Louisiana, Arkansas, and Tennessee. The former Whigs who organized loyal governments under Lincoln's supervision often retained their economic power. In Louisiana, for example, Whig sugar planters who declared their loyalty to the Union received help from Generals Benjamin F. Butler and Nathaniel P. Banks, who used their troops to enforce labor discipline, transforming slaves into wage laborers and enabling the former Whigs to save their plantations.

Radical and Moderate Republicans. Many members of his own party, including some of his fellow moderates, disapproved of Lincoln's plan. Their opposition was based in part on a different constitutional interpretation. They argued that the southern states *had* left the Union and were now the equivalent of conquered provinces with territorial status. As such, they were subject to Congressional rule rather than executive authority.

Radical Republicans

Lincoln's readmission plan was harshly criticized by radical Republicans. One of their leaders was Thaddeus Stevens (front row, second from left), pictured here with fellow members of Congress in a photograph by Mathew Brady. Stevens outlined a radical economic plan that called for a redistribution of land in the South. He believed that the former slaves needed more than the vote to control their fate—they needed land. He was unable to muster support for this radical plan.

The most strenuous criticism came from a group of radical Republicans, some of whom had abolitionist backgrounds. Led by Senator Charles Sumner of Massachusetts and Representative Thaddeus Stevens of Pennsylvania, the radicals wanted a harder, slower peace. In Stevens's words, the federal government should "revolutionize Southern institutions, habits, and manners." He declared that "the foundations of their institutions . . . must be broken up and relaid, or all our blood and treasure will have been spent in vain."

Stevens, Indiana Congressman George W. Julian, and African-American leaders, including Frederick Douglass, staked out the most radical definition of what reconstruction should mean. The core of their program was an economic one: confiscation and redistribution of southern plantations to the freed slaves and to white farmers who had been loyal to the Union. The program was meant to fulfill the dreams of the former slaves, whose expectations had been raised by emancipation, and of the poor white farmers of the South. To the former slaves, emancipation and freedom meant control over their lives. But to control their fate in an agricultural economy, they knew they needed to own land. But Stevens and Julian were unable to recruit other members of Congress to support a large-scale redistribution of land in the South. The majority of radical Republicans regarded such a plan as a violation of the Constitution's protection of property rights and a threat to the capitalist order.

The radical Republicans did agree on three key points: (1) The leaders of the Confederacy should not be allowed to return to power in the South, (2) steps should be taken to establish the Republican party as a major, even dominant, force in southern political life, and (3) the federal government should ensure that African-Americans participated in southern society with full *civil* equality by guaranteeing their voting rights. The last point was especially important. As Frederick Douglass declared in May 1865, "Slavery is not abolished until the black man has the ballot."

Moderate Republicans in Congress shared the radicals' view that Lincoln's program was too lenient, and they endorsed the first two points of the radical program. But as a group they hesitated to go further and support black suffrage and civil equality. Like virtually all conservative Republicans and Democrats, some moderates were profoundly racist and believed that African-Americans could never become responsible citizens. Like Lincoln, other moderates had confidence in blacks' abilities. But they wanted to avoid the violent resistance that southern whites might mount in response to drastic changes in the relationship between the races.

The Wade-Davis Bill. In 1864 the radical and moderate Republicans in Congress devised an alternative to Lincoln's program that was based on the two reconstruction principles on which they could agree. In the Wade-Davis bill, passed by Congress on July 2, 1864, they set harsher conditions for former Confederate states to rejoin the Union. A *majority* of a state's adult white men would have to swear an oath of allegiance to the Union. The state could then hold a constitutional convention, but no one could vote in the election for delegates or serve as a delegate unless he swore that he had never carried arms against the Union or aided the Confederacy in any way. Requiring this pledge, which became known as the *ironclad oath*, would exclude most southern whites, therefore leaving the task of constitution making to those white men who had overtly opposed the Confederacy. Finally, the bill required that slavery be prohibited and that Confederate civil and military leaders be permanently disfranchised.

The Wade-Davis bill proposed going further than Lincoln's plan in punishing ex-Confederates, especially those who had led the rebellion. Despite this difference, Lincoln seemed ready to compromise with the Congressional Republicans. Rather than openly challenging Congress by vetoing the Wade-Davis bill, he executed a "pocket" veto by not signing it before Congress adjourned. At the same time he initiated informal talks with members of Congress aimed at producing a compromise solution when the war ended. He even suggested that he might support the radical program of establishing federal control over race relations in the South and guaranteeing the vote to African-Americans there. In the last speech he ever delivered, on April 11, 1865, Lincoln demonstrated that he was moving pragmatically to endorse freedmen's suffrage, beginning with those who had served in the Union army and those who were educated.

The Assassination of Lincoln. Whether Lincoln and his party could have forged a unified approach to reconstruction is one of the great unanswered questions of American history. On April 14, 1865—Good Friday—Lincoln was shot in the head at Ford's Theater in Washington by an unstable actor named John Wilkes Booth. Ironically, Lincoln might have been spared if the war had dragged on longer, for Booth and his Confederate associates had originally plotted to kidnap the president to force a negotiated settlement. After Lee's surrender, Booth became desperate for revenge. In the middle of the play he entered Lincoln's box, shot him at close range, stabbed a member of the president's party, and fled. Booth was hunted down and killed by Union troops. Eight people were eventually convicted as accomplices by military courts, and four of them were hanged.

Lincoln never regained consciousness and died on April 15. The Union—and the hundreds of thousands of African-Americans for whom his name had become synonymous with freedom—went into profound mourning. Even Lincoln's critics suddenly conceded his

greatness. Millions of Americans honored his memory by waiting in silence to watch the train carrying his body back to Illinois for burial.

Lincoln's death dramatically changed the prospects for a moderate reconstruction. At one stroke John Wilkes Booth had sent Lincoln to martyrdom, convinced many northerners that harsher measures against the South were necessary, and forced the presidency into the hands of Vice-President Andrew Johnson.

Restoration under Johnson

Andrew Johnson was a self-made man and former slaveholder from the hills of eastern Tennessee. A Jacksonian Democrat, he saw himself as the champion of ordinary white people. He hated what he called the "bloated, corrupt aristocracy" of the Northeast, and he blamed southern planters for the Civil War. His political career had led from the Tennessee legislature and governorship to the U.S. Senate, where he remained, loyal to the Union, after Tennessee seceded. He served as military governor of his home state after federal forces captured Nashville. In 1864 the Republicans nominated him as vice-president in an effort to promote wartime political unity and to court the support of southern Unionists.

Like Lincoln, Johnson believed that the southern states had retained their constitutional status and that reunification was exclusively an executive matter. During the summer of 1865, when Congress was not in session, Johnson unilaterally executed his own plan for restoration. He insisted only that the states revoke their ordinances of secession and ratify the Thirteenth Amendment, which abolished slavery. He offered amnesty and a return of all property except slaves to almost all southerners if they took an oath of allegiance to the Union. Southerners who were excluded from amnesty—high-ranking Confederate military officers and civil officials and persons with taxable property of more than $20,000—could petition Johnson personally. By December 1865 all the former Confederate states had functioning governments and had met Johnson's requirements for rejoining the Union.

Johnson's plan would not become complete until Congress accepted the senators and representatives from the former Confederacy. Under the Constitution, Congress is "the judge of the elections, returns and qualifications of its own members" (Article I, Section 5), and it would not convene again until December 1865. This step need not have been a problem for Johnson. Whereas most moderate Republicans in Congress hoped to make changes in Johnson's program to bring it closer to the Wade-Davis bill, they supported the basic outline of his program. Perhaps most important, they agreed with Johnson that the federal government should not protect African-American suffrage or civil equality. Even most radicals were optimistic. They liked the stern treatment of Confederate leaders, and they hoped that the new southern governments would respond positively to Johnson's conciliatory attitude and offer the vote at least to African-Americans who were literate and owned property (probably no more than 10 percent of adult black men).

During the summer and fall, however, Johnson lost the support of radical Republicans. They first became angered over a telegram that Johnson had sent in August to the provisional governor of Mississippi, who was presiding over the state's constitutional convention. Johnson urged that the vote be given to literate African-Americans on the grounds that "the radicals, who are wild upon negro franchise, will be completely foiled." The telegram also embarrassed Republican moderates, who had hoped to win the support of the radicals as well as that of Johnson for a compromise program.

In the fall of 1865 news reports of conditions in the South alarmed the moderates and further outraged the radicals. They learned that ex-Confederates were frequently attacking freedmen and white Union supporters, that the new provisional governments were making

Andrew Johnson
The president was not an easy man. This photograph of Andrew Johnson (1808–1875) conveys some of the personal qualities that contributed so centrally to his failure to reach an agreement with Republicans on a program of moderate reconstruction.

no effort to enfranchise African-Americans, and that ex-Confederates had taken control of southern governments. Southern voters elected to Congress nine men who had served in the Confederate Congress, seven former officials of Confederate state governments, four generals and four colonels from the Confederate army, and even the vice-president of the Confederacy, Alexander Stephens. It turned out that Johnson had been exceedingly liberal in pardoning ex-Confederate leaders. He seemed less interested in punishing them than in humbling them by making them submit to his personal power.

As radical Republicans increased their attacks on Johnson, he shifted away from his strongly bipartisan stance. He began to believe he could build a coalition of white southerners, northern Democrats, and conservative Republicans to support the creation of a democracy for white southerners. To avoid embarrassing potentially supportive Republicans or ex-Whigs in the South, his banner would be "National Union." Democrats in both the North and the South praised Johnson as the leader they needed to restore their party on a national basis. As the president warmed to Democratic applause, he granted more and more pardons to wealthy southerners—an average of a hundred a day in September.

The president's movement toward the Democrats further agitated radical Republicans and dismayed the moderates. By December 1865, when Congress convened, the moderates had become convinced that they had to join the radicals in order to protect the Republican party. It would be necessary, they concluded, to take action to guarantee the civil rights of former slaves and establish the Republican party in the South.

The Republican party acted quickly to reject the newly elected southern representatives and proposed that Johnson work with Congress on a new program for reconstructing the South. A House-Senate committee—the Joint Committee on Reconstruction—was formed to develop that program in cooperation with the president.

The Joint Committee conducted public hearings on conditions in the former Confederacy and publicized alarming reports from army officers, federal officials, and white and black southerners. The testimony augmented the newspaper reports by revealing an astonishing level of violence and providing disturbing details on how southern planters and legislatures were attempting to resubjugate the freed slaves. Although most moderates were still not ready to impose black suffrage on the South, almost all of them were shocked by what they regarded as a movement to circumvent the Thirteenth Amendment.

Acting on Freedom: African-Americans in the South

While congressmen discussed conditions in the South, African-Americans were already far advanced in acting on their idea of freedom. They were exultant and hopeful; their main concern was economic independence, which they assumed was necessary for true freedom. During the Civil War they had acted on this assumption throughout the South whenever Union armies drew near. But many officers actively sympathized with the planters, allowing those who expressed loyalty to the Union to retain control of their plantations and their former slaves. Other officers wished to destroy the power of the planters but preserve a class system in the South. In 1863, General Lorenzo Thomas, for example, devised a plan to lease plantations in the Mississippi Valley to loyal northern men who would hire African-American laborers under conditions set by the army.

During the final months of the war, when the Union directed its military operations against civilians, freedmen found greater opportunities to win control of land. Most visibly, General William T. Sherman reserved vast tracts of coastal lands in Georgia and South Carolina—the Sea Islands and the abandoned plantations within 30 miles of the coast—for black settlers and gave them

Schoolhouse, Port Hudson, Louisiana
This was probably the first schoolhouse built for freedmen by Union forces. In front, African-American soldiers from the Port Hudson "Corps d'Afrique" pose with their textbooks. In 1865 and 1866 most new schools in the South were established by blacks forming societies and raising money among themselves.

Eliphalet Whittlesey

Report on the Freedmen's Bureau

In October 1865, Colonel Eliphalet Whittlesey, an assistant commissioner for the Freedmen's Bureau in North Carolina, wrote the following report on the activities of the Bureau. He was later promoted to general and served as a trustee of the national Freedman's Savings Bank in Washington, D.C. He was typical of many Freedmen's Bureau officials in that he saw his role as one of mediating between two worthy groups: former slaves and former masters.

On the 22d of June I arrived at Raleigh with instructions . . . to take the control of all subjects relating to "refugees, freedmen, and the abandoned lands" within this State. I found these subjects in much confusion. Hundreds of white refugees and thousands of blacks were collected about this and other towns, occupying every hovel and shanty, living upon government rations, without employment and without comfort, many dying for want of proper food and medical supplies. A much larger number, both white and black, were crowding into the towns, and literally swarming about every depot of supplies to receive their rations. My first effort was to reduce this class of suffering and idle humanity to order, and to discover how large a proportion of these applicants were really deserving of help. . . .

It was evident at the outset that large numbers were drawing rations who might support themselves. . . . orders were issued that no able-bodied man or woman should receive sup-

plies, except such as were known to be industrious, and to be entirely destitute. . . . The homeless and helpless were gathered in camps, where shelter and food could be furnished, and the sick collected in hospitals, where they could receive proper care. . . .

Suddenly set free [the freedmen] were at first exhilarated by the air of liberty, and committed some excesses. To be sure of their freedom, many thought they must leave the old scenes of oppression and seek new homes. Others regarded the property accumulated by their labor as in part their own, and demanded a share of it. On the other hand, the former masters, suddenly stripped of their wealth, at first looked upon the freedmen with a mixture of hate and fear. In these circumstances some collisions were inevitable. . . .

. . . [M]any freedmen need the presence of some authority to enforce upon them their new duties. . . . The efforts of the bureau to protect the freedmen have done much to restrain violence and injustice. Such efforts must be continued until civil government is fully restored, just laws enacted, or great suffering and serious disturbance will be the result. Contrary to the fears and predictions of many, the great mass of colored people have remained quietly at work upon the plantations of their former masters during the entire summer. . . . In truth, a much larger amount of vagrancy exists among the whites than among the blacks. . . .

The report is confirmed by the fact that out of a colored population of nearly 350,000 in the State, only about 5,000 are now receiving support from the government. . . . Our officers . . . have visited plantations, explained the difference between slave and free labor, the nature and the solemn obligation of contracts. The chief difficulty met with has been a want of confidence between the two parties.

. . . Rev. F. A. Fiske, a Massachusetts teacher, has been appointed superintendent of education, and has devoted himself with energy to his duties. . . . the whole number of schools . . . is 63, the number of teachers 85, and the number of scholars 5,624. A few of the schools are self-supporting, and taught by colored teachers, but the majority are sustained by northern societies and northern teachers. The officers of the bureau have, as far as practicable, assigned buildings for their use, and assisted in making them suitable; but time is nearly past when such facilities can be given. The societies will be obliged hereafter to pay rent for school-rooms and for teachers homes. The teachers are engaged in a noble and self-denying work. They report a surprising thirst for knowledge among the colored people—children giving earnest attention and learning rapidly, and adults, after the day's work is done, devoting the evening to study. . . .

Source: *Report of the Joint Committee on Reconstruction*, 39th Cong., 1st sess. (Washington, D.C.: U.S. Government Printing Office, 1866), II: pp. 186–192.

"possessory titles" to 40-acre tracts. Sherman had little use for radicals and freedmen; he only wanted to relieve the pressure that African-American refugees were placing on his army as it marched across the Lower South. But the freedmen assumed that Sherman's order meant

that the land would be theirs—a reasonable expectation after one of Sherman's generals told a large group of freedmen "that they were to be put in possession of lands, upon which they might locate their families and work out for themselves a living and respectability."

The Freedmen's Bureau. The resettlement of freedmen was organized by the Bureau of Refugees, Freedmen, and Abandoned Lands, which Congress created in March 1865. Known as the Freedmen's Bureau, it was charged with feeding and clothing war refugees of both races, renting confiscated land to "loyal refugees and freedmen," and drafting and enforcing labor contracts between freedmen and planters. The Freedmen's Bureau also worked with the large number of northern voluntary associations that sent missionaries and teachers to the South to establish schools for former slaves (see American Voices, page 490).

By the end of the war the army and the Freedmen's Bureau had resettled about 10,000 families on half a million acres of "Sherman" land in Georgia and South Carolina. Reports of such actions inspired many African-American families to stay on their old plantations in the hope that they would own some of the land after the war. When the South Carolina planter Thomas Pinckney returned home, his freed slaves told him, "We ain't going nowhere. We are going to work right here on the land where we were born and what belongs to us." One Georgia freedman offered to sell to his former master the share of the plantation he expected to receive after the federal redistribution.

Johnson's amnesty plan allowed pardoned Confederates to recover their land if Union troops had confiscated or occupied it. In October, Johnson ordered General Oliver O. Howard, head of the Freedmen's Bureau, to tell Sea Island blacks that they did not hold legal title to the land and that they would have to come to terms with the white landowners. When Howard reluctantly obeyed, the dispossessed farmers protested: "Why do you take away our lands? You take them from us who have always been true, always true to the Government! You give them to our all-time enemies! That is not right!" When some of the Sea Islanders refused to deal with the restored white owners, Union soldiers forced them to leave or work for their old masters.

The former slaves resisted efforts to remove them. Often led by African-American veterans of the Union army, they fought pitched battles with plantation owners and bands of ex-Confederate soldiers. Whenever possible, landowners attempted to disarm and intimidate the returning black soldiers. One soldier wrote from Maryland: "The returned colard Solgers are in Many cases beten, and their guns taken from them, we darcent walk out of an evening. . . . they beat us badly and Sumtime Shoot us." In this warfare federal troops often backed the local whites, who generally prevailed in recapturing their former holdings.

A New Labor System. Throughout the South high postwar prices for cotton prompted returning planters not only to reclaim land but also to establish a labor system that was as close to slavery as they could make it. On paper, emancipation had cost the slave owners about $3 billion—the value of their capital investment in former slaves—a sum that equaled nearly three-fourths of the nation's economic production in 1860. The *real* losses of planters, however, depended on whether they lost control of their former slaves. Planters attempted to reestablish that control and to substitute low wages for the food, clothing, and shelter that their slaves had previously received. They also refused to sell or rent land to blacks, hoping to force them to work for low wages.

The freedmen resisted the new wage system as well as the loss of land. During the growing seasons of 1865 and 1866 thousands of former slaves abandoned their old plantations and farms. Many freedmen sought better lives in the towns and cities of the South. Those who remained in the countryside either refused to work in the cotton fields or tried to reduce the amount of time they worked there. When they could, freedmen developed their own garden plots, guaranteeing themselves a subsistence level of rations during the postwar disruptions. Freedmen who did return to work in white-owned cotton fields refused to submit to the grueling gang system that had been the major tool of economic exploitation under slavery. Now they wanted a pace of work and independence that reflected their new status. What was freedom all about if not to have a bit more leisure time, to work less intensely than they had as slaves, and to work for themselves and their families?

Wage Labor of Ex-Slaves
This photograph, taken in South Carolina shortly after the Civil War, shows former slaves being led from the cotton fields. Although they now worked for wages, they were probably organized into a gang not far removed from the earlier slave gangs. Their plug-hatted crew leader is dressed much as his slave-driving predecessor would have been.

The Black Codes. The efforts of former slaves to control their own lives ran counter to deeply entrenched white attitudes. Emancipation had not destroyed the racist assumptions and fears that the planters had fostered in order to maintain and defend slavery. Former slave owners and many poorer whites who looked to them for leadership attempted to maintain the South's caste system. Beginning in 1865, southern legislatures enacted laws—known as Black Codes—that were designed to keep African-Americans in a condition close to slavery.

The codes varied from state to state, but virtually all required the arrest of blacks for vagrancy if they were found without employment. In most cases they could not pay the fine, and the county court would then hire them out to an employer, who could hold them in slaverylike conditions. Several state codes established specific hours of labor, spelled out the duties expected of laborers, and declared that any laborer who did not meet those standards was a vagrant. The codes usually restricted black employment opportunities outside agriculture by requiring licenses for those who wished to pursue skilled work or even "irregular job work."

The state legislatures went even further, sanctioning the efforts of local governments to circumscribe the lives of blacks. Localities set curfews, required black agricultural workers to obtain passes from their employers, insisted that blacks who wanted to live in town obtain white sponsors, and, in an effort to prevent political gatherings, sharply regulated meetings of blacks, including those held in churches. Fines and forced labor were the penalties for violators.

Congressional Initiatives

Reports of southern repression aroused moderate Republicans in Congress, who decided to provide some guarantees of the civil rights of freedmen. The moderates first drafted a bill to extend the life of the Freedmen's Bureau and enlarge its powers, including the authority to establish courts to protect the freedmen's rights.

The news from the South had not, however, convinced Republicans that they should confiscate land and give it to the freedmen. A large majority of Republicans voted down an amendment to the Freedmen's Bureau bill proposed by Thaddeus Stevens that would have made "forfeited estates of the enemy" available to freedmen. Still, Republicans were now willing to go further in creating opportunities for land ownership. Thus the Freedmen's Bureau bill countermanded Johnson's order to Howard to evict the freedmen from the confiscated lands on the Sea Islands. Also, two days after the bill's passage, the House passed another bill, sponsored by George Julian, that became the Southern Homestead

Act of 1866. It designated about 45 million acres of public land in Alabama, Arkansas, Florida, Louisiana, and Mississippi for 80-acre grants to settlers who cultivated the land for five years. Congress prohibited anyone who had supported the Confederacy from filing a claim until 1867. Although Republicans were unwilling to violate planters' property rights, they offered freedmen the same chance to acquire land that northerners had enjoyed since the passage of the Homestead Act of 1862.

Republicans approved the Freedmen's Bureau bill almost unanimously, but in February 1866 Johnson vetoed it. The bill was unconstitutional, he argued, because the Constitution did not authorize a "system for the support of indigent persons" and because the states most directly affected by its provisions were not yet represented in Congress. His veto, implying that *any* Reconstruction legislation passed without southern representation was unconstitutional, enraged moderate Republicans. They tried to override the veto but failed, just barely, to hold the votes of enough conservative Republicans to collect the necessary two-thirds majority.

Democrats applauded Johnson's firmness. To celebrate the veto and Washington's birthday, a group of Democrats went to the White House to serenade him. The president emerged to deliver an impromptu, impassioned speech that suggested to many listeners that he was drunk. Accusing the radical Republicans of being traitors, he likened Stevens and Sumner to Confederate leaders because they all were "opposed to the fundamental principles of this Government." He mentioned himself two hundred times in the speech and suggested that the radicals were plotting to assassinate him.

The First Civil Rights Bill. Johnson's veto and his Washington's birthday speech pushed the moderate Republicans close to a complete break with him. But they still expected his cooperation on their second major piece of legislation, a civil rights bill. Passed in March 1866, it defined the citizenship rights of freedmen—for example, the rights to own and rent property, make contracts, and have access to the courts. And it authorized federal authorities to bring suit against anyone who violated those rights and guaranteed that appeals in such cases could be heard in federal courts. The moderate Republicans were prepared to expand federal protection of civil rights, though they were still not ready to guarantee black suffrage.

Against the advice of his cabinet, Johnson vetoed the civil rights bill. He restated his constitutional point about absent southern representation and added a new objection, with the votes of Democratic wards in the large cities in mind. The bill, he argued, discriminated against whites by providing immediate citizenship for newly freed slaves. Under federal law, he pointed out, immigrants had to wait five years.

Johnson's veto was the last straw for almost all moderate Republicans. They now agreed with the radicals that Congress must take charge of Reconstruction. In April moderates engineered an override of Johnson's veto, and in July—after watering down the Freedmen's Bureau bill by requiring freedmen to buy the confiscated land on the Sea Islands—they won the votes of enough conservative Republicans to pass the Freedmen's Bureau bill over a second veto.

The Fourteenth Amendment. The central part of the independent plan that moderates and radicals now undertook was to provide freedmen with constitutional as well as legislative protection. In April the Joint Committee on Reconstruction drafted and submitted to Congress a proposal for a fourteenth amendment to the Constitution. It did not provide what the radicals wanted—a guarantee of black suffrage—but it went beyond the Civil Rights Act of 1866.

Section 1 declared that "all persons born or naturalized in the United States" were citizens. No state could abridge "the privileges or immunities of citizens of the United States," deprive "any person of life, liberty, or property, without due process of law," or deny anyone "the equal protection of the laws." The drafters intended these phrases to be vague but hoped that their force would increase over time, especially since Section 5 gave Congress the power to enforce the amendment. Section 2 penalized any state that denied suffrage to any adult male citizen. A state's representation in the House of Representatives would be reduced by the percentage of adult male citizens who were denied the vote.

Rising violence against African-Americans throughout the South clinched the support of moderates for the amendment. Most dramatic were three days of race rioting in Memphis in May. Forty-six blacks and two whites were left dead, and hundreds of black houses, churches, and schools were looted and burned. In June 1866 Congress forwarded the Fourteenth Amendment to the states for ratification.

President Johnson attacked the Fourteenth Amendment. Even its moderate provisions went too far in protecting African-Americans for his taste, and he wanted to create an issue for the 1866 elections. At his urging, ten ex-Confederate states, joined by Delaware and Kentucky, turned it down, denying the amendment the necessary approval of three-fourths of the states. Among the former states of the Confederacy, only Tennessee approved the amendment, and it was formally readmitted to the Union in July 1866.

The Congressional Elections of 1866. Johnson planned to attack the Fourteenth Amendment and advance his National Union movement during the Congressional elections of 1866. In July a National Union Convention met to unite his supporters from around the nation. But

Resistance in the South

The engraving, subtitled "Verdict, 'Hang the D---Yankee and Nigger,'" appeared in *Harper's Weekly* in March 1867. It may have led readers to recall the killing of the Republicans who attended the black suffrage convention in New Orleans the previous summer. There are no reliable estimates of the number of Republicans, white and black, killed by ex-Confederates during Reconstruction.

the Republican and Democratic politicians in attendance were unwilling to share power across party lines, and the convention did not attempt to create a new national party. Another problem for Johnson's movement was a major race riot in the South just two weeks before the convention assembled. A white mob in New Orleans attacked the delegates to a black suffrage convention and, aided by the local police, killed forty people, including thirty-seven blacks. Popular support in the North for radical Reconstruction seemed to grow instantly.

In August and September Johnson tried to win back support in a disastrous "swing around the circle"—a railroad tour from Washington to Chicago and St. Louis and back. It was unprecedented for a president to campaign personally, and Johnson made matters worse by engaging in shouting matches with hecklers and insulting members of the hostile crowds. His message was consistent: Congress had acted illegally by approving the Fourteenth Amendment without the participation of

all the southern states, southerners were now loyal to the Union, and the real traitors were the radical Republicans who were delaying restoration of the Union.

Moderate and radical Republicans responded by escalating their attacks on Democrats. They charged that ex-Confederates wanted to resume the Civil War and, in a practice that became known as "waving the bloody shirt," charged that the Democratic party had caused the Civil War and then sided with the traitors. Indiana's Republican governor, Oliver Morton, described the Democratic party as "a common sewer and loathsome receptacle, into which is emptied every element of treason North and South, every element of inhumanity and barbarism which has dishonored the age."

The 1866 Congressional elections brought a humiliating defeat for the president, who still had two years left to serve. The Republicans won a three-to-one majority in Congress (margins of 42 to 11 in the Senate and 143 to 49 in the House) and gained control of the governorship and legislature in every northern state, as well as West Virginia, Missouri, and Tennessee. The moderate Republicans interpreted the election results as a clear call for radical Reconstruction rather than mere restoration of the South. The most important policy shift was the moderates' acceptance of the radicals' proposition that the federal government must guarantee the vote for black men, at least in the South.

Radical Reconstruction

In the months following the 1866 elections, moderates and radicals in Congress joined together to take control of Reconstruction. They agreed on a more radical program than even the one proposed in the Wade-Davis bill. Congressional Reconstruction began by treating the South as conquered territory. It proceeded to protect the civil rights of former slaves through the Fourteenth Amendment to the Constitution, protect their suffrage through the Fifteenth Amendment, and establish state governments in the South in which former slaves played important roles.

The Congressional Program

In March Congress passed the Reconstruction Act of 1867, designed to implement the radical plan. It organized the South as a conquered land, dividing it (with the exception of Tennessee) into five military districts, each under the command of a Union general. Each commander was ordered to register all adult black men in his district but was given considerable discretion in registering former Confederates. After the registration, the commander was to supervise the election of a convention to write a state constitution and make certain that the constitution included guarantees of black suffrage. Congress would readmit the state to the Union if its voters ratified the new constitution, if that document proved acceptable to Congress, if the new state legislature approved the Fourteenth Amendment, and if enough states had already ratified the Fourteenth Amendment to make it part of the Constitution. Johnson vetoed the act, but Congress overrode the veto. In 1868 six states—North Carolina, South Carolina, Florida, Alabama, Louisiana, and Arkansas—met the requirements and were readmitted to the Union. (See Table 16.1 for a summary of the Reconstruction laws and constitutional amendments.)

Such measures were radical, but a few radical Republicans argued that even more dramatic steps were needed to guarantee racial equality. They pressed for the distribution of land to former slaves, federal support for black schools, and disfranchisement of ex-Confederates. Congressman George Julian warned that "the power of the great landed aristocracy in these regions, if unrestrained by power from without, would inevitably assert itself." But even the most extreme radicals accepted the new Reconstruction policies as all they could get in 1867.

The Tenure of Office Act. Republicans also acted to check the power of President Johnson to undermine their Reconstruction plan. At the same time the Reconstruction Act of 1867 became law, Congress passed the Tenure of Office Act, which required Senate consent for the removal of any official whose appointment had required Senate confirmation. Congress chiefly wanted to protect Secretary of War Edwin M. Stanton, a Lincoln appointee and the only member of Johnson's cabinet who favored radical Reconstruction. In his position Stanton could do much to prevent Johnson from frustrating the goals of Reconstruction. Congress also required the president to issue all orders to the army through its commanding general, Ulysses S. Grant, who was also a supporter of radical Reconstruction. In effect, Congress was attempting to reconstruct the presidency as well as the South.

Johnson appeared to cooperate with Congress at first, appointing generals recommended by Stanton and Grant to command the five military districts in the South. But he was just biding his time. In August 1867, after Congress had adjourned, he "suspended" Stanton until Congress reconvened and replaced him with Grant on a temporary basis, believing that Grant would act like a good soldier and follow orders. Next Johnson replaced four Republican generals who commanded southern districts, including Philip H. Sheridan, Grant's favorite cavalry general.

TABLE 16.1

Primary Reconstruction Laws and Constitutional Amendments

Law (Date of Congressional Passage)	Key Provisions
Thirteenth Amendment (January 1865*)	Prohibited slavery
Civil Rights Act of 1866 (April 1866)	Defined citizenship rights of freedmen Authorized federal authorities to bring suit against those who violated those rights
Fourteenth Amendment (June 1866†)	Established national citizenship for persons born or naturalized in the United States Reduced state representation in House of Representatives by the percentage of adult male citizens denied the vote
Reconstruction Act of 1867 (March 1867‡)	Divided the South into five military districts, each under the command of a Union general Established requirements for readmission of ex-Confederate states to the Union
Tenure of Office Act (March 1867)	Required Senate consent for removal of any federal official whose appointment had required Senate confirmation
Fifteenth Amendment (February 1869)	Forbade states to deny citizens the right to vote on the grounds of race, color, or "previous condition of servitude"
Ku Klux Klan Act (April 1871)	Authorized president to use federal prosecutions and military force to suppress conspiracies to deprive citizens of the right to vote and enjoy the equal protection of the law

*Ratified by three-fourths of all states in December 1868.
†Ratified by three-fourths of all states in July 1868.
‡Ratified by three-fourths of all states in March 1870.

Johnson, however, had misjudged Grant, who wrote a letter protesting the president's thwarting of Congress and then deliberately leaked it to the press. When the Senate reconvened in the fall, it intensified the political drama by overruling Stanton's suspension. Grant increased the pressure on Johnson by resigning so that Stanton could resume his office. Johnson overreacted, publicly protesting Grant's resignation. Grant responded by becoming an open enemy of the president.

The Impeachment of Johnson. Johnson decided to challenge the constitutionality of the Tenure of Office Act. In February 1868 he formally dismissed Stanton. This time Stanton barricaded the door of his office and refused to admit the replacement Johnson had appointed. Three days later, on February 24, the House of Representatives lashed out at Johnson by using the power granted by the Constitution to impeach—to charge federal officials with "Treason, Bribery, or other high Crimes and Misdemeanors." The House overwhelmingly (128 to 47) brought eleven counts of criminal misconduct, nine of which dealt with violations of the Tenure of Office Act, against the president.

The trial in the Senate, which the Constitution empowers to act as a court in impeachment cases, lasted eleven weeks and was presided over by Chief Justice Salmon P. Chase. On May 16 thirty-five senators voted for conviction, one vote short of the two-thirds majority required. Seven moderate Republicans had broken ranks, voting for acquittal along with twelve Democrats. The reluctant moderates were overwhelmed by the drastic nature of impeachment and conviction; Congress had removed federal judges from office, but never before had it seriously considered removing a president. Whereas these moderates agreed that Johnson had broken the law, they felt that the real issue was a disagreement between Congress and the president over a matter of policy. They feared that a conviction based on a policy dispute would establish a dangerous precedent and undermine the presidency. The Civil War had demonstrated to them the need for a strong federal government administered by a powerful executive. These moderates doubted that the nation could preserve internal unity, advance the Republican economic program, and defend itself against foreign enemies without a strong presidency.

The radical Republicans had failed to convict Johnson, but they had defeated him politically. For the remainder of his term Johnson was forced to allow Reconstruction to proceed under Congressional direction.

The Elections of 1868. The impeachment controversy made Grant, already the North's most popular war hero, a hero of Reconstruction as well, and he easily won the Republican presidential nomination. In the fall campaign he supported radical Reconstruction and "waved the bloody shirt," but he also urged reconciliation between the sections. His Democratic opponent was Horatio Seymour, a former governor of New York and a Peace Democrat who almost declined the nomination, certain that Grant would win. In the face of rising violence in the South, Seymour and the Democrats received little support for their claim that the government should let southern state governments reorganize on their own. Grant won about the same share of the northern vote (55 percent) that Lincoln had in 1864, collected a majority of the national popular vote, and received 214 of 294 electoral votes, including those of six of the eight reconstructed states. The Republicans also retained two-thirds majorities in both houses of Congress. The Republicans were convinced they had a strong popular mandate for their program of radical Reconstruction.

The Fifteenth Amendment. The Republicans quickly produced the last major piece of Reconstruction legislation—the Fifteenth Amendment. Intended to guarantee black male suffrage, the amendment forbade states to deny their citizens the right to vote on the grounds of race, color, or "previous condition of servitude."

Some radical Republicans would have preferred more aggressive protection of black citizenship such as prohibiting state governments from using property ownership or literacy tests to disqualify blacks as voters. But Republican moderates did not want to ban tactics that northern and western states might want to employ to deny immigrants the vote. Massachusetts and Connecticut used literacy as a requirement for voting, as did California, which sought to deny the vote to Chinese immigrants. Even though it failed to prohibit such tactics, the Fifteenth Amendment was much more effective than the Fourteenth in promoting African-American suffrage. The amendment was passed in February 1869, and Congress required the unreconstructed states of Virginia, Mississippi, Texas, and Georgia to ratify it before they were readmitted to the Union.

The Issue of Suffrage for Women

Radical Reconstruction could have changed the legal status of women. Instead, by referring to adult "male citizens," the Fourteenth Amendment wrote the term "male" into the Constitution for the first time and, in effect, sanctioned the denial of suffrage for women. Under the Fourteenth Amendment, suffrage limitations based on gender—alone among all the possible restrictions on suffrage—would not reduce a state's representation in Congress.

Former abolitionists such as Elizabeth Cady Stanton and Susan B. Anthony were deeply disappointed. They had organized a massive petition drive that had collected almost 400,000 signatures in support of the Thirteenth Amendment; they believed that their male collaborators would reciprocate by supporting universal suffrage. In fact, many did, but most assumed that the public was not ready for the idea. As Wendell Phillips told women leaders, "One question at a time. This hour belongs to the Negro."

The leaders of the women's movement did not oppose ratification of the Fourteenth Amendment. They accepted defeat at the federal level and focused on the reform of state constitutions. Through a new organization, the American Equal Rights Association—which they formed in 1866 at the first women's rights convention since the Civil War—they launched a campaign to win *universal* suffrage at the state level.

The Fifteenth Amendment wounded those who sought the vote for women even more deeply; it made no reference to gender and thus permitted states to deny

A Woman Suffrage Quilt Made around 1875
Homemade quilts provided funds and a means of persuasion for the temperance and antislavery movements. But woman suffrage quilts, such as this detail from "The Suffragette Quilt" (circa 1860–1880), picturing a women's rights lecturer, were rare. The leaders of the woman suffrage movement usually regarded quilts and needlework as representing the domestic subjugation of women.

suffrage to women. In response, Stanton and Anthony concluded that feminists should develop a program independent of any political party. They broke with Republican abolitionists and refused to support the Fifteenth Amendment unless it was accompanied by a new amendment enfranchising women. Stanton argued that ratification of the Fifteenth Amendment alone would create an "aristocracy of sex." She declared, "All manhood will vote not because of intelligence, patriotism, property or white skin, but because it is male, not female." In promoting a new amendment she made a special appeal to women of the business class:

> American women of wealth, education, virtue and refinement, if you do not wish the lower orders of Chinese, Africans, Germans and Irish, with the low ideas of womanhood to make laws for you and your daughters . . . to dictate not only the civil, but moral codes by which you shall be governed, awake to the danger of your present position and demand that woman, too, shall be represented in the government!

Other advocates of woman suffrage, including Lucy Stone and Frederick Douglass, saw the politics of suffrage differently. The Fifteenth Amendment had opened up a schism in the ranks of the women's movement. In 1868 Stone and Douglass broke with the American Equal Rights Association of Stanton and Anthony and formed a new group, the New England Woman Suffrage Association. Their goal was to maintain an alliance with Republicans and support the Fifteenth Amendment. They believed that this was the best way to enlist Republican support for women's suffrage after Reconstruction issues had been settled.

The differences between the two groups increased in the postwar years. In 1869 the American Equal Rights Association renamed itself the National Woman Suffrage Association and elected Stanton as its first president. It concentrated on mobilizing local suffrage societies in communities around the country. Meanwhile, the New England Woman Suffrage Association reorganized itself as the American Woman Suffrage Association. Its members elected Henry Ward Beecher, a prominent Brooklyn minister, as its president and cultivated strong ties with Republicans and men who had been abolitionists.

For twenty-one years the two national organizations competed for the leadership of the women's movement. The "American" association tended to focus on suffrage, whereas the "National" association developed a more comprehensive reform posture. While the split weakened the movement in the short run, the formation of the "National" association meant that a major part of the women's movement had broken away from abolitionism and Republicanism and was free to develop independent political strategies.

The South during Radical Reconstruction

Between 1868 and 1871 all the southern states met the Congressional stipulations and rejoined the Union. The Reconstruction governments under Republican control remained in power for periods ranging from a few months in Virginia to nine years in South Carolina, Louisiana, and Florida. African-Americans were at the center of forming and maintaining these Republican governments. In Alabama, Florida, South Carolina, Mississippi, and Louisiana they constituted an outright majority of registered voters. They provided the votes for Republican victories there and in Georgia, Virginia, and North Carolina as well, where they accounted for nearly half the registered voters. But the Republican governments were more than African-American regimes; they also drew support from whites who had not owned slaves and from white northerners who had moved south after the war (see Map 16.1).

Democratic ex-Confederates satirized and stereotyped the Republicans who dominated the reconstructed state governments. They mocked and scorned black

The First Vote
This lithograph appeared in *Harper's Weekly* in November 1867. The voters represent elements of African-American political leadership: an artisan with tools, a well-dressed member of the middle class, and a Union soldier.

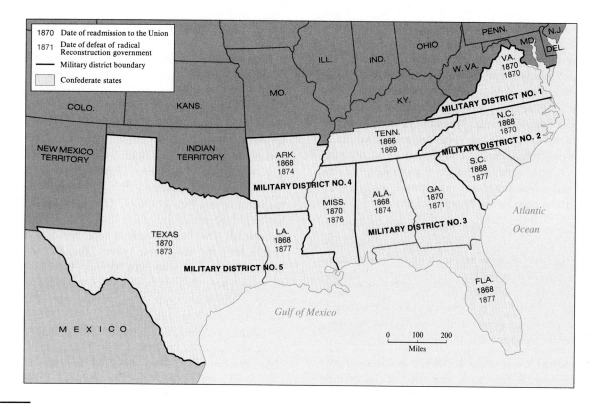

MAP 16.1

Reconstruction

The federal government organized the Confederate states into five military districts during radical Reconstruction. For each state the first date indicates when that state was readmitted to the Union; the second date shows when radical Republicans lost control of the state government. All the ex-Confederate states rejoined the Union from 1868 to 1870, but the periods of radical rule varied widely. Radicals lasted only a few months in Virginia; they held on until the end of Reconstruction in Louisiana, Florida, and South Carolina.

Republicans as ignorant field hands who could only play at politics, and they referred to whites who became Republicans as *scalawags*—an ancient Scots-Irish term for underfed, runty, worthless animals. White settlers who had come from the North were denounced as *carpetbaggers*—transient exploiters who carried all their property in cheap suitcases called carpetbags. Carpetbaggers held more than half the Republican governorships in the South and almost half of the southern seats in Congress.

Actually, few southern Republicans conformed to these stereotypes. Some carpetbaggers had come south to seek personal profit, but they also brought capital and skills to invest in the region's future. Most were former officers of the Union army who had fallen in love with the South—its climate, people, and economic opportunities. Many carpetbaggers were professionals and college graduates. The scalawags were even more diverse. Some were wealthy ex-Whigs and even former slave owners. Some of these groups saw Republicanism as the best way to attract northern capital to southern railroads, mines, and factories. Immigrant workers and

farmers were often found among the Republicans. The largest such group were the Germans in southwest Texas. They sent to Congress Edward Degener, an immigrant and a San Antonio grocer whom Confederate authorities had imprisoned and whose sons had been executed for treason. But most numerous among the scalawags were yeomen farmers from the backcountry districts who wanted to rid the South of its slaveholding aristocracy. Scalawags had generally fought against, or at least refused to support, the Confederacy; they believed that slavery had victimized whites as well as blacks. "Now is the time," a Georgia scalawag wrote, "for every man to come out and speak his principles publickly and vote for liberty as we have been in bondage long enough."

African-American Political Leadership. The Democrats' stereotypes of black political leaders were just as false. Until 1867 most African-American leaders in the South, attracted to the movement for black suffrage, came from the elite that had been free before the Civil War. When Congress began to organize Republican

governments in 1867, this diverse group of ministers, artisans, shopkeepers, and former soldiers reached out to the freedmen. African-American speakers, some financed by the Republican Congressional Committee, fanned out into the old plantation districts and drew ex-slaves into political leadership. Still, few of the new leaders were field hands; most had been preachers or artisans. The literacy of one ex-slave, Thomas Allen, who was a Baptist minister and shoemaker, helped him win election to the Georgia legislature. "In my county," he recalled, "the colored people came to me for instructions, and I gave them the best instructions I could. I took the *New York Tribune* and other papers, and in that way I found out a great deal, and I told them whatever I thought was right."

Many of the African-American leaders who emerged in 1867 had been born in the North or had spent many years there. They moved south when Congressional Reconstruction began to offer the prospect of meaningful freedom. Like white migrants, many were veterans of the Union army. Some had fought in the antislavery crusade, some were employed by the Freedmen's Bureau or northern missionary societies, and a few were from free families and had gone north for an education. Others had escaped from slavery and were returning home. One of these was Blanche K. Bruce, who became one of two black U.S. senators from Mississippi. He had received tutoring on the Virginia plantation of his white father. During the war Bruce escaped to Kansas from Missouri, where his father had moved, and then returned to Missouri, establishing a school for African-Americans in Hannibal. He arrived in Mississippi in 1869 and entered politics; in 1874 he became the second African-American elected to the Senate and the first elected to a full term until 1966.

Although the number of African-Americans who held office during Reconstruction never reflected the black share of the electorate, they held positions of importance throughout most of the South, and their significance increased in every state under Republican rule. Sixteen African-Americans served in the U.S. House of Representatives in the Reconstruction Era. In 1870 Mississippi sent Hiram Revels, a minister born in North Carolina, to the Senate as its first African-American member. In 1868 African-Americans won a majority in one house of the South Carolina legislature; subsequently they won half the state's eight executive offices, elected three members of Congress, and won a seat on the state supreme court. Over the entire course of Reconstruction twenty African-Americans served as governor, lieutenant governor, secretary of state, treasurer, or superintendent of education, and more than six hundred served as state legislators. Almost all the African-Americans who became state executives had been freemen before the Civil War, whereas most of the legislators had been slaves. Because these African-Americans

represented districts that large planters had dominated before the Civil War, they embodied the potential of Reconstruction for revolutionizing class relationships in the South.

The Radical Program. Southern Republicans believed that the South needed to be fundamentally reconstructed. They wanted to end its dependence on cotton agriculture and unskilled labor and create an economy based on manufacturing, capital investment, and skilled labor. Southern Republicans fell far short of making this vision a reality, but they accomplished much more of it than their critics gave them credit for.

Southern Republicans made their societies more democratic. They repealed Black Codes and rejected new proposals for enforcing labor discipline. They modernized state constitutions, extended the right to vote, and made more offices elective. They established hospitals, penitentiaries, and asylums for orphans and the insane. South Carolina purchased medical care for poor people, while Alabama provided them with free legal counsel. Republican governments built roads in areas where roads had never existed. They supervised the rebuilding of the region's railroad network and subsidized investment in manufacturing and transportation. They undertook major public works programs. And they did all this without federal financing. To pay for their ambi-

Hiram R. Revels
In 1870 Hiram R. Revels (1822–1901) was elected to the U.S. Senate from Mississippi to fill Jefferson Davis's former seat. Revels was a free black from North Carolina who had migrated to the North and attended Knox College in Illinois. He recruited blacks for the Union army and as an ordained Methodist minister served as chaplain of a black regiment in Mississippi, where he settled after the war.

tious programs they introduced the taxes that northern states had relied on since the Jacksonian period. These were general property taxes that taxed not only real estate but the trappings of wealth—personal property such as furnishings, machinery, tools, and even cash. The goal was to force planters to pay their fair share of taxes and to force uncultivated land onto the market. In many plantation counties, especially in South Carolina, Louisiana, and Mississippi, former slaves served as tax assessors and collectors, administering the taxation of their onetime owners.

The most important accomplishments of the southern Republicans came in education. Republican state governments viewed schooling as the foundation for a democratic order in the South. Led by both black and white superintendents of education, many of whom had served in the Freedmen's Bureau, the Reconstruction governments built public schools that served more people, black and white, than had ever been reached by free education in the South. African-Americans of all ages rushed to attend the newly established schools, even when they had to pay tuition. An elderly man in Mississippi explained his desire to go to school: "Ole missus used to read the good book [the Bible] to us . . . on Sunday evenin's, but she mostly read dem places where it says, 'Servants obey your masters.' . . . Now we is free, there's heaps of tings in that old book we is just suffering to learn." By 1875 about half of all the children in Florida, Mississippi, and South Carolina were enrolled in school.

Virtually all the new schools were segregated by race; only Louisiana attempted to establish an integrated system. But most African-Americans seemed to agree that segregation was an issue for a later day; most shared Frederick Douglass's judgment that what was most important was the fact that separate schools were "infinitely superior" to no schools at all.

Social Institutions in Freedom. The building of schools was part of a larger effort by African-Americans to fortify the institutions that had sustained their spirit during the days of slavery. Most important, they strengthened family life as the cornerstone of new communities. Families moved away from the slave quarters, usually building homes scattered around or near their old plantations and farms. Sometimes they established entirely new all-black villages. Husbands, wives, and children who had been separated by the slave trade often reunited, sometimes after journeys of hundreds of miles. Couples stepped forward to record marriages that had not been recognized under slavery. As slavery crumbled, mothers rescued their children from the control of planters and overseers. Many women refused to work in the fields. Instead, they insisted on tending gardens, managing households, and bringing education and religion to their children. Wives asserted their independence, opening individual bank accounts, refusing responsibility for their husbands' debts at country stores, and bringing complaints of abuse and lack of child support to the Freedmen's Bureau.

Christianity had played a central role in nineteenth-century slave society, and freed slaves buttressed their new communities by founding their own churches. They rejected participation in biracial congregations, which usually accorded blacks only second-class status, requiring them to worship in segregated balcony pews and denying them rights in church ownership or governance. Instead, they purchased land and built their own churches. These churches joined together to form African-American versions of the Southern Methodist

A Freedmen's School

An 1866 sketch from *Harper's Weekly* of a Vicksburg, Mississippi, school run by the Freedmen's Bureau illustrates the desire for education by ex-slaves of all ages. Because most southern blacks were farmers, schools often offered night classes that left students free for field work during the day.

and Southern Baptist denominations. The largest new denominations were the National Baptist Convention and the Colored Methodist Episcopal Church. The vigorous new churches served not only as places of worship but as schools, social centers, and political meeting halls. The ministers were community leaders and often held political office during Reconstruction. Charles H. Pearce, a Methodist minister in Florida, declared, "A man in this State cannot do his whole duty as a minister except he looks out for the political interests of his people." The religious message of black ministers, who called for a recognition of the brotherhood of man and a special destiny like that of the "Children of Israel," provided a powerful religious bulwark for the Republican politics of their congregations.

The Planters' Counterrevolution

Even if radical Reconstruction had been adopted right at the end of the Civil War, it would have sparked southern resistance to federal power. But coming after Johnson's lenient policy of restoration, which had enabled ex-Confederates to regain control of the South, the reaction was especially intense. Former slave owners were the most bitter opponents of the Republican program, especially the effort to expand political and economic opportunities for African-Americans, because it threatened their vested interest in traditional agriculture and their power and status in southern society. Led by former slave owners, the ex-Confederates staged a massive counterrevolution—one designed to "redeem" the South by regaining control of its state governments.

The former slave owners united under the Democratic banner to oppose the Republicans. In the eight southern states where whites formed a majority of the population—all except Louisiana, Mississippi, and South Carolina—planters sought to return ex-Confederates to the rolls of registered voters. They appealed to racial solidarity and southern patriotism, and they attacked black suffrage as a threat to the social status of whites. Relying primarily on conventional, albeit unsavory, means of political competition, Democrats recovered power in Tennessee in 1869 and Virginia in 1870.

But the Democrats were prepared to go far beyond conventional techniques. Throughout the Deep South and almost everywhere that Republicans and Democrats were nearly equal in number, planters and their supporters engaged in terrorism against people and property. They organized secret societies to frighten blacks and Republican whites from voting or taking other political action.

The Ku Klux Klan. The most widespread of these groups, the Ku Klux Klan, was organized in Tennessee in 1865 and quickly spread throughout the South. The

Klan's first leader was Nathan Bedford Forrest, a former Confederate general. A skilled and ferocious leader, Forrest was notorious in the North for an incident at Fort Pillow, Tennessee, in 1864, when his troops killed African-American soldiers holding the fort after they had surrendered. Forrest based the initial organization of the Klan on Confederate army units and openly threatened to kill Republicans if they tried to suppress the Klan.

By 1870 the Klan was operating almost everywhere in the South as a military force serving the Democratic party. The Klan murdered and whipped Republican politicians, burned black schools and churches, and attacked party gatherings. In October 1870 a group of Klansmen assaulted a Republican rally in Eutaw, Alabama, killing four African-Americans and wounding fifty-four. For three weeks in 1873 Klansmen laid siege to the small town of Colfax, Louisiana, which was defended by black veterans of the Union army who were holding the county seat after a contested election. On Easter Sunday, armed with a small cannon, the whites overpowered the defenders and slaughtered fifty blacks and two whites after they had surrendered under a white flag. Such terrorist tactics enabled the Democrats to seize power in Georgia and North Carolina in 1870 and make substantial gains elsewhere. An African-

Klan Portrait, 1868
Two armed Klansmen from Alabama pose proudly in their disguises. Northern audiences saw a lithograph based on this photograph in *Harper's Weekly* in December 1868.

Harriet Hernandes

The Intimidation of Black Voters

The following testimony was given in 1871 by Harriet Hernandes, a black resident of Spartanburg, South Carolina, to the Joint Congressional Select Committee investigating conditions in the South. The terrorizing of black women through rape and other forms of physical violence was among the means of oppression used by the Ku Klux Klan.

Question: How old are you?

Answer: Going on thirty-four years....

Q: Are you married or single?

A: Married.

Q: Did the Ku-Klux come to your house at any time?

A: Yes, sir; twice....

Q: Go on to the second time....

A: They came in; I was lying in bed. Says he, "Come out here, sir; come out here, sir!" They took me out of bed; they would not let me get out, but they took me up in their arms and toted me out—me and my daughter Lucy. He struck me on the forehead with a pistol, and here is the scar above my eye now. Says he, "Damn you, fall." I fell. Says he, "Damn you, get up." I got up. Says he, "Damn you, get over this fence!" and he kicked me over when I went to get over; and then he went on to a brush pile, and they laid us right down there, both together. They laid us down twenty yards apart, I reckon. They had dragged and beat us along. They struck me right on top of my head, and I thought they had killed me; and I said, "Lord o' mercy, don't, don't kill my child!" He gave me a lick on the head, and it liked to have killed me; I saw stars. He threw my arm over my head so I could not do anything with it for three weeks, and there are great knots on my wrist now.

Q: What did they say this was for?

A: They said, "You can tell your husband that when we see him we are going to kill him...."

Q: Did they say why they wanted to kill him?

A: They said, "He voted the radical ticket [slate of candidates], didn't he?" I said, "Yes," that very way....

Q: When did [your husband] get back home after this whipping? He was not at home, was he?

A: He was lying out; he couldn't stay at home, bless your soul! ...

Q: Has he been afraid for any length of time?

A: He has been afraid ever since last October. He has been lying out. He has not laid in the house ten nights since October.

Q: Is that the situation of the colored people down there to any extent?

A: That is the way they all have to do—men and women both.

Q: What are they afraid of?

A: Of being killed or whipped to death.

Q: What has made them afraid?

A: Because men that voted radical tickets they took the spite out on the women when they could get at them.

Q: How many colored people have been whipped in that neighborhood?

A: It is all of them, mighty near.

Source: Report of the Joint Select Committee to Inquire into the Condition of Affairs in the Late Insurrectionary States, House Reports, 42d Cong., 2d sess. (Washington, D.C.: U.S. Government Printing Office, 1972), Vol. 5, South Carolina, December 19, 1871.

American politician in North Carolina wrote, "Our former masters are fast taking the reins of government" (see American Voices, above).

Congress responded to the Klan-led counterrevolution by passing the Force Acts in 1870 and 1871, which included the Ku Klux Klan Act (1871). The acts authorized the president to use federal prosecutions, military force, and martial law to suppress conspiracies to deprive citizens of the right to vote, hold office, serve on juries, and enjoy equal protection of the law. For the first time, the government had made private criminal acts violations of federal law. Federal agents penetrated the Klan and gathered evidence that provided the basis for thousands of arrests, and federal grand juries indicted more than 3,000 Klansmen. In South Carolina, where the Klan was most deeply entrenched, federal troops occupied nine counties, made hundreds of arrests, and drove as many as 2,000 Klansmen from the state. The U.S. attorney general brought several dozen notorious Klansmen to trial and sent most to jail. Elsewhere, victories were only temporary. Justice Department attorneys usually faced all-white juries, and the department lacked the resources to prosecute effectively. Only about 600 Klansmen were convicted under the Force Acts, and only a small fraction of them served significant prison terms.

The Grant administration's war against the Klan raised the spirits of southern Republicans, but if they

were going to prevail, they required what one carpet-bagger described as *"steady, unswerving power from without."* In particular, to defeat the well-armed paramilitary forces of the ex-Confederates, they needed sustained federal military aid. However, after seeming to defeat the Klan, northern Republicans increasingly lost enthusiasm for fighting—let alone enlarging—what amounted to a guerrilla war. Republican leaders continued to "wave the bloody shirt," but with each election it had less appeal to voters. Northerners grew weary of the financial costs of Reconstruction and the continuing bloodshed it seemed to produce. Moreover, they became preoccupied with the severe economic depression that began in 1873. Conservative and even moderate Republican leaders began to regard southern Republican governments as too radical and to conclude that they had much in common with southern economic elites. Racism played a role as well; many moderate Republicans in the North began to conclude that Republican defeats in the South reflected the incompetence of black politicians. Because of diminishing federal help, Republican governments in the South eventually found themselves overwhelmed by ex-Confederate politicians during the day and by terrorists at night. Democrats overthrew Republican governments in Texas in 1873, in Alabama and Arkansas in 1874, and in Mississippi in 1875.

The defeat in Mississippi demonstrated the crucial role of federal aid. As elections neared in 1875, paramilitary groups such as the Rifle Clubs and Red Shirts operated openly. Often local Democratic clubs paraded armed, as if they were militia companies. They identified black leaders in assassination lists called "dead-books," broke up Republican meetings, provoked rioting that left hundreds of African-Americans dead, and threatened voters, who still lacked the protection of the secret ballot. Mississippi's Republican governor, Adelbert Ames, a Congressional Medal of Honor winner from Maine, appealed to President Grant for federal troops, but Grant refused, fearing damage to Republicans in northern elections and lacking the heart for more bloodshed. Ames then contemplated organizing a state militia but ultimately decided against it, believing that only blacks would join. Rather than escalate the fighting and turn it into a racial war, he conceded victory to the terrorists.

By 1877 Republican governments, along with token U.S. military units, remained in only three states: Louisiana, South Carolina, and Florida. Southern Republicans had done their best to reconstruct southern society, but the ex-Confederates had exhausted northern Republicans. They even won some sympathy from the northern Republicans, who finally abandoned the southern members of their party (see American Lives, pages 504–505).

The Economic Fate of the Former Slaves

The greatest failure of radical Reconstruction lay in not redistributing land, along with the resources required to cultivate it, from planters to former slaves. The only major federal program enabling freedmen to obtain land, the Southern Homestead Act, turned out to provide little assistance. Although the land was free, very few freedmen had the capital to move their families and buy the necessary seeds, tools, and draft animals to get in their first crop. Fewer than 7,000 ex-slaves claimed land, and only about 1,000 eventually qualified for ownership, most of them in sparsely populated areas of Florida. Compounding the problem, state governments rarely had the resources to help freedmen buy and settle land. Alone among the Republican state governments, South Carolina purchased land from planters and resold it to former slaves on long-term credit. Between 1872 and 1876 the South Carolina land commission enabled more than 14,000 African-American families (accounting for about one-seventh of the state's black population) to purchase homesteads.

Without guaranteed economic independence, the content of freedom depended largely on thousands of conflicts between freedmen, acting individually and collectively, and the planter class. Here too the federal government failed to assist the freedmen in a significant way. The vast majority of army officers and federal marshals held the racist assumption that had been behind the Black Codes—that former slaves were suited only for agricultural labor. If these agents of the federal government had different ideas at first, they usually came to support the economic interests of the planters. A Louisiana freedman described the process as follows: "Whenever a new Provost Marshall comes he gives us justice for a fortnight or so; then he becomes acquainted with planters, takes dinners with them, receives presents; and then we no longer have any rights, or very little." In disputes between employers and laborers, federal marshals generally sided with the planters and sustained their authority. Army commanders complied with the requests of planters for help in forcing African-Americans to work. They expelled former plantation workers from towns and cities and punished them for disobedience, theft, vagrancy, and erratic labor.

Even agents of the Freedmen's Bureau often supported the planters. Many Bureau officials interpreted their mandate to promote a transition to free labor as meaning that they should teach former slaves to be industrious, reliable agricultural workers. They preached the gospel of work to African-Americans. To discourage labor violence, they warned that it was better "to suffer wrong than to do wrong." They urged former slaves to vindicate the cause of abolition by staying at home and working even harder than they had under slavery.

Nathan Bedford Forrest: A Violent Defender of Honor

There was much violence in the life of Nathan Bedford Forrest (1821–1877). Most of the violence was focused on the protection of slavery during the Civil War and on the defeat of radical Reconstruction afterward. More than any other white southerner, Forrest was responsible for defeating Reconstruction governments and efforts to extend democracy to African-Americans.

At the age of twenty-four Forrest demonstrated his readiness to use violence when he leapt to the defense of his family's honor. Armed with only a pistol and a bowie knife, he fought off four men who had a grudge against his uncle, a merchant in the hamlet of Hernando, Mississippi. The uncle died from a bullet meant for his nephew, but young Forrest had shown that he could meet violence with violence. He became a local hero and soon used his pistol again, facing down a well-armed planter who had just killed a friend of his. The local citizens rewarded Forrest's courage by making him town constable and county coroner, and a respectable young woman from Hernando agreed to marry him.

Forrest's father had been a yeoman farmer and blacksmith who followed the frontier from North Carolina to Tennessee, where Bedford, the oldest child of eleven, was born. His family moved to northern Mississippi in 1834, but three years later, when he was only sixteen, his father died, leaving Bedford the primary breadwinner. He had no more than six months of schooling but supported the family, working on its small farm and then joining an uncle's horse-trading business. At the age of twenty-one, when his mother remarried, he left home for Hernando.

Recognized and respected in Hernando, the hard-driving young Forrest was able to scratch his way up the social ladder in the booming cotton economy. He took over his uncle's store, ran a stagecoach service between Hernando and Memphis, opened a brickyard, again traded horses and cattle, and then turned to buying and selling slaves. By 1850 he owned three of his own. In 1851 Forrest's ambition took him and his family to nearby Memphis, Tennessee. In that Mississippi River town he became one of the largest interstate slave traders and entered the ranks of the planter class. He

Nathan Bedford Forrest
In his often violent career Forrest was a farmer, slave trader, planter, politician, cavalry general, Grand Wizard of the Ku Klux Klan, and railroad entrepreneur. This portrait was done by Nicola Marshall, circa 1866. (Collection of the Tennessee State Museum)

purchased large land holdings, including a Mississippi plantation of more than 3,000 acres worked by dozens of slaves. He even entered politics, winning election to the Memphis Board of Aldermen in 1857.

The Civil War created new opportunities for Forrest. His reputation for boldness and shrewdness, as

well as his riding and shooting skills, won him an appointment from the governor of Tennessee as a lieutenant colonel. He organized a cavalry regiment and, after distinguishing himself at Shiloh, was promoted to brigadier general in July 1862. In the course of the war he became the premier cavalry officer of the Confederacy, perhaps the best on either side. The Confederate government failed to make the best use of Forrest and his troops, but he almost always carried out his missions with dramatic success, protecting Confederate armies in retreat, raiding Union lines of communications, and attacking Union posts, often deep behind enemy lines.

Forrest's intimate knowledge of the countryside and the people of the Mississippi, Tennessee, and Cumberland river valleys, superb organizational skills, powerful tactical sense of when to use bluff and deception, sobriety, and ability to inspire his troops served him well. He had a ferocious temper and used it to good advantage in combat, turning a zest for fighting into enraged fury whenever his honor or the honor of his troops seemed to be at stake. He counted thirty Union soldiers that he had killed personally—one more than the number of horses shot out from under him. And he was wounded by saber cut or gunfire several times, including once by a junior Confederate officer whom Forrest quickly stabbed to death.

Forrest's code of honor, readiness for violence, racism, and commitment to slavery, all honed and hardened by war, have suggested to many that Forrest played a role in the slaughter of black troops at Fort Pillow, Tennessee, on April 12, 1864. Forrest approached the assault on the fort with a combination of anger and contempt for the garrison there—largely white pro-Union Tennesseans and former slaves. The war in western Tennessee had taken a bitter turn in 1864, involving civilians more directly in combat, and Forrest was outraged at rumors that the garrison had been harassing local whites loyal to the Confederacy. Although Forrest's direct role in the slaughter remains uncertain, it is clear that his troops believed that they were acting as he wished, that they experienced the same fury he usually displayed in battle, and that he accepted the outcome with equanimity.

The war left Forrest exhausted but determined to recreate as much of his old life as possible. That meant adapting to the new economic system and, when necessary, to the reality of Union victory. In 1866, to restore his plantation labor force, he rented his Mississippi land to seven former Union officers and worked closely with the Freedmen's Bureau, writing some of the highest-wage contracts. He drew on some of his old slave-trading skills to bring in workers from as far away as Georgia. At the same time he moved into new enterprises: provisioning the reorganized plantations, selling fire and life insurance, and contracting for paving the streets of Memphis and for laying railroad track. In building the Memphis and Little Rock Railroad, Forrest used labor supplied by the Freedmen's Bureau. Meanwhile, he sought a pardon from President Johnson, which was granted in 1868.

But Forrest was determined to oppose a radical Reconstruction. As conflicts between ex-Confederates and coalitions of former Unionists and freedmen intensified, Forrest's ambition, racism, and loyalty to his comrades—a sense of honor defined by shared wartime experiences—led him to support the effort to restore the social world of 1860. In 1867 he joined secret organizations in Memphis and Nashville that became chapters of the Ku Klux Klan. He soon became the Klan's Grand Wizard and turned the organization into a major force throughout most of the South. Under cover of his insurance business Forrest corresponded with perhaps thousands of Confederate veterans and traveled to neighboring states to confer with other ex-generals.

In 1868 the Republican governor of Tennessee, "Parson" William G. Brownlow, threatened to organize a militia of eastern Tennessee Unionists to root out the Klan. Forrest told his former troops to prepare for civil war, warning a reporter from the Cincinnati *Commercial* that he could "raise 40,000 men in five days, ready for the field." Forrest's intimidation worked, as it had so often in the past. Brownlow resigned early in 1869 to take a seat in the U.S. Senate, and his replacement sought to appease the Democrats and the Klan. Victorious in Tennessee and hoping to reduce pressure from Washington on the Klan, Forrest ordered its members to destroy their regalia and moderate their excesses, such as whippings and jailbreaks. Forrest knew full well that he had no power to implement such an order.

Forrest might have continued a secret life within the Klan, but after his political victory he appeared to devote his full attention to his businesses. He tried to combine northern capital with new sources of cheap labor. Marketing bonds in New York, he established the Selma, Marion, and Memphis Railroad. He promoted Chinese immigration to the South and made extensive use of convict labor on his railroad and plantation crews. But he achieved only modest success in the depression of the 1870s and became embroiled in complicated, massive litigation. In 1877 he died of a debilitating intestinal illness that might have been related to his wartime wounds.

One Bureau official told some freedmen that their former master "is not able to do without you, and you will . . . find him as kind, honest, and liberal as other men" and that "you can be as free and as happy in your old home, for the present, as anywhere else in the world." The agents of the Freedmen's Bureau who did side with African-Americans were stymied by northern racism, lack of funds, understaffing, poor coordination within the Bureau, and uncooperative military authorities.

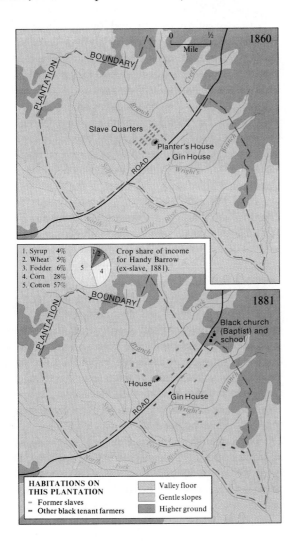

MAP 16.2

The Barrow Plantation

Comparing the 1860 map of this central Georgia plantation with the 1881 map reveals the changing patterns of black residence and farming. In 1860 the slave quarters were clustered near the planter's house, which sat on a small hilltop. The free sharecroppers of 1881 built cabins along the spurs or ridges of land between the streams, scattering their community over the plantation. A black church and school were built by this date. A typical sharecropper on the plantation earned most of his income from growing cotton.

Sharecropping. The Freedmen's Bureau did help change, however, the way planters controlled the labor of their former slaves. It encouraged, even compelled, planters and freedmen to agree on written contracts through a formal bargaining process. The labor contract system was a poor substitute for land ownership, but it assisted the freedmen in attaining something else they greatly desired: the elimination of gang labor.

As early as 1865 written contracts between freedmen and planters provided that the former slaves would work for wages. But the contracts also provided for less supervision, a slower pace of work, and more free time than had been typical under slavery as well as the elimination of drivers and overseers. By 1866 the process of bargaining between planters and freedmen had become more difficult, partly because a shrinking money supply had reduced the amount of cash available to pay wages. To resolve the growing number of conflicts over labor contracts, Freedmen's Bureau agents introduced a form of compensation that was common, though not typical, in northern agriculture: payment of agricultural workers in shares of the crop rather than in wages. This system was known as *sharecropping*. While it came to involve many poor whites in the South, it was far more important for blacks. For them, sharecropping became the dominant mode of agricultural labor (see Map 16.2).

At first freedmen were enthusiastic about sharecropping. It increased their control over working conditions and allowed them to improve their standard of living. Under typical sharecropping contracts, sharecroppers turned over half to two-thirds of their harvested crops to their landlord. The owner's share was not necessarily excessive, because the landlord commonly provided land, seed, fertilizer, tools, and assistance in marketing.

The sharecropping system joined laborers and the owners of land and capital in a common sharing of risks and returns. But it produced little upward mobility. By the end of Reconstruction only a fraction of sharecroppers, no more than one-quarter of the total, had managed to save enough to rent land with cash payments, as most landless whites did. Even though these so-called tenant farmers could take their crops directly to market, they remained impoverished.

Land Ownership. Virtually all African-American farmers struggled long and hard to buy the land they tilled, and some of the cash renters gradually succeeded. They were willing to pay exorbitant prices for land just for the sake of being independent. But the system was stacked against them. African-American renters had far less access to land ownership than did their white counterparts. Planters made agreements among themselves to drive up the price of land to blacks or even refuse to sell to them. Some planters used the Ku Klux Klan to intimi-

Sharecropping
This sharecropping family seems proud of its new cabin and crop of cotton, which it planted in every available bit of ground. But the presence of the white landlord in the background suggests the forces that led families like this one into debt peonage.

date blacks who tried to buy land. Despite the adversity, by 1910 black farmers owned nearly a third of the land they cultivated. But black farm owners usually occupied marginal land—in the coastal swamps of Georgia and South Carolina, for example—and the land usually cost far more than its productivity warranted.

Debt Peonage. The financial condition of all African-American farmers was extremely difficult. Sharecropping, cash renting of land, and land ownership enabled former slaves to raise their incomes but also increased their financial needs. They wanted more food and better clothing than they had received under slavery; they often needed more farm supplies than their landlords were willing to provide; and renters and owners had to purchase all their seed, fertilizer, and equipment. The purchase of major farm supplies almost always required borrowing, but southern banks were reluctant to lend money to black farmers, whom they saw as bad risks, and cash was generally in short supply.

The owners of country stores stepped in. Eager to lend money, they furnished everything black farmers needed and extended credit for the purchases. The country merchants took advantage of the weak bargaining power of the former slaves, especially the sharecroppers, by charging unusually high prices and interest rates. In effect, these storekeepers became rural loan sharks. Once sharecroppers accepted credit from country merchants, high interest rates made it difficult for them to settle their accounts. At best they broke even after paying their debts. Most sharecroppers fell deeper and deeper into debt.

Throughout the South, when Democrats regained

control of state governments, they passed laws that gave force to this economic system by providing merchants with the right to take liens on crops. Merchants could seize crops to settle sharecroppers' debts and seek criminal prosecution of sharecroppers who could not pay the full amount of the interest they owed. Indebted African-American farmers faced imprisonment and forced labor unless they toiled on the land according to the instructions of the merchant-creditor. Increasingly, merchants and landlords cooperated to maintain this lucrative system, and many landlords became merchants. The former slaves had become trapped in the vicious circle of *debt peonage,* which tied them to the land and robbed them of their earnings.

In sum, despite the odds against them, the freedmen won some modest economic gains. But the gains came only within the restrictions of the system of debt peonage that replaced slavery. Thus, most African-Americans and many whites remained mired in an agricultural poverty created by racism and economic forces.

The North during Reconstruction

Although the Republicans in Congress failed to break the hold of the planter elite on the South, they did reconstruct the economy of the North. They enacted nearly all of their nationalizing economic program—national banking, tariff protection, and subsidies for internal improvements—despite resistance from the Democrats. The Republican program promoted unprecedented economic growth and industrial development.

A Dynamic Economy

The Civil War disrupted the nation's economic life, yet by the 1870s Americans had become more productive than ever before. Northeastern industry led the way. Production of iron more than doubled between the end of the Civil War and 1870 and doubled again by 1880. Steel production grew even more rapidly, increasing fivefold between 1865 and 1870 and then nearly twenty times by 1880. The era began an *age of capital*—a period that lasted until World War I and was marked by great increases in investment in factories and railroads. It also began the era of big business, which was characterized by the rise of giant corporations.

The Republican Economic Program. During Reconstruction, Republicans expanded the ambitious economic program they had enacted during the war. The broad support middle-class northerners gave to the program indicated that they now largely shared business-class values.

The scope of the program was vast. Republicans strengthened government regulation of the banking system, winning praise from investors who appreciated a more predictable economic environment. Republican Congresses expanded subsidies to national rail systems and chartered new railroads, expanded the national postal system, and financed major river and harbor development throughout the North. They also funded the cavalry forces that fought the nation's wars against the Indians in the Great Plains (see Chapter 17). In fact, military spending accounted for 60 percent of the federal budget by 1880. Republicans also used the Homestead Act of 1862 to subsidize the settling of the Great Plains.

Revenues raised from the Civil War tax system paid for those programs. Postwar Congresses kept the high tariffs, which had proved lucrative and appealed to average Republicans because they seemed to provide protection against foreign workers. Congress also retained the "emergency" wartime taxes on alcohol and tobacco, which were popular among many Republicans because they taxed "sin."

The tariffs and "sin" taxes not only funded programs but also provided money to pay back Americans who had bought Union bonds during the war. Because the taxes increased the cost of everyday items, average Americans were paying a far higher share of their income for debt repayment than were the wealthy. Moreover, the repayment was going largely to the wealthy, who owned a disproportionate share of Civil War bonds. Republicans were intentionally redistributing wealth from the poor to the rich, who were more likely to save and invest, as a way of increasing the supply of capital and accelerating the rate of economic growth.

The most popular Republican economic program was the Civil War pension program, which the government extended and broadened virtually every year. It provided disabled veterans and the widows and children of Union veterans with generous benefits, which were particularly welcome during the severe depressions of the 1870s and 1890s. At the same time, the pensions solidified the Republican loyalty of the families of men who had served in the Union army.

An ideological shift also contributed to the Republicans' success in enacting their economic program. The Civil War had led many Americans to relax their traditional suspicion of concentrations of power in both business and government. This was particularly true of the men and women who had served in the Union army and the Sanitary Commission. The war had given them their first direct experience of living and working within modern bureaucracies—elaborate hierarchies that imposed a high degree of job specialization and rigorous discipline. Wartime service also had taken them, usually for the first time, far from home and placed them in intimate contact with people who came from distant places but served in the same cause. And the Union had won the war. This disciplined, collective, national—and successful—experience predisposed northerners to accept American business, the Republican party, and the federal government as the central agencies of national economic development.

Republican Foreign Policy

Some Republican leaders were alert to new possibilities for expansion abroad. The most important advocate of expansion was William H. Seward, Lincoln and Johnson's secretary of state. Believing in the importance of foreign commerce to the long-term health of the republic, Seward promoted the acquisition of colonies that could be used as trading bases in the Caribbean and the Pacific. But Seward was ahead of his time. During the Reconstruction Era most Americans wanted to concentrate on developing their own territory.

Seward inherited his most pressing foreign policy issues from the Civil War. In Mexico, Napoleon III's puppet government under Archduke Maximilian was still in power; the threat this European regime posed to American interests in the Southwest was especially great since it might draw die-hard Confederate soldiers to its support. "On to Mexico," Grant only half jokingly told an aide just a day after he accepted Lee's surrender at Appomattox. It was a good guess as to where the next war

might take place. Within a year President Johnson and Seward sent General Philip Sheridan with 50,000 battle-hardened Union veterans to the Mexican border, while Seward negotiated the withdrawal of French troops. The threat of force worked. The French left in 1867, abandoning Maximilian to a Mexican firing squad.

The American government was also troubled by another Civil War issue: Great Britain's allowing the *Alabama* and other Confederate cruisers to sail from British shipyards to raid Union commerce. Seward claimed that Britain had violated international laws of neutrality and owed compensation for damages. Britain, fearing that Americans might build ships for British enemies in a future war, accepted Seward's legal analysis and agreed to submit the *Alabama* claims to arbitration. However, Charles Sumner, chairman of the Senate Foreign Relations Committee, insisted that the compensation cover "indirect" damages. Including lost shipping revenue and the costs of Britain's prolonging the war, his estimates reached more than $2 billion. Sumner was angry over British aid to the Confederacy during the war and wanted to acquire Canada as part of the financial deal with Britain. In 1866 Congress restricted Canadian trade and fishing privileges in an attempt to force Canadians to support annexation. However, with the stakes so high, the British refused to agree to a settlement during Johnson's presidency.

Meanwhile, American expansionist ambitions in the Caribbean and the Pacific met with only mixed success. Supporting the U.S. Navy's demands for a base in the Caribbean, Seward negotiated a treaty with Denmark to purchase the Virgin Islands, but the Senate rejected the $7.5 million price. The Senate also turned down his proposal to annex Santo Domingo (the present-day Dominican Republic), which had won independence from Spain in 1865. Seward did persuade Congress to annex the small Midway Islands west of Hawaii after his effort to acquire the Hawaiian Islands had failed. Most important, in 1867 Seward persuaded the Senate to ratify a treaty to buy Alaska from Russia and to appropriate the $7.2 million for the purchase. Critics referred to Alaska as "Johnson's Polar Bear Garden" and "Seward's Folly," but its acquisition promised to obstruct British ambitions in North America. Also, the price was reasonable when weighed against even the low estimates that Congress made of Alaska's fish, fur, lumber, and mineral resources.

When Ulysses S. Grant became president in 1869, he took up the cause of expansion in the Caribbean. He was influenced by American investors and adventurers in Santo Domingo, including Orville E. Babcock, his former military aide, who became his personal secretary in the White House. Grant proposed a treaty to annex the country as a colony for freed slaves dissatisfied with Reconstruction. The Senate defeated Grant's imperial ambition in 1870. Leading the attack was Charles Sumner, who feared that annexation would threaten the independence of the neighboring black republic of Haiti. "These islands by climate, occupation, and destiny . . . belong to the colored people," he declared.

Grant's secretary of state was the genteel Hamilton Fish, a former Whig who had been governor of New York and a U.S. senator. Fish had less interest than Seward in acquiring new territory and concentrated on settling differences with Britain. Part of his goal was to strengthen the ties of capital and commerce between the two nations. Interest in annexing Canada still remained high, but Fish finally persuaded Grant that the British North America Act of 1867, uniting Canada in a confederation (the Dominion of Canada) and providing for greater self-government, had removed any serious Canadian interest in annexation. Fish then quickly negotiated the Treaty of Washington in 1871, which submitted for arbitration all the outstanding issues between the two countries, including the *Alabama* claims. In 1873 the British government obeyed the ruling of an international tribunal established under the treaty and presented a $15.5 million check to the U.S. government. A period of unprecedented goodwill between America and Britain followed.

The Politics of Corruption and the Grant Administration

During the Grant administration the Democratic party, seeking to reestablish its national base of power, made the Republican economic program its primary target. Since the key elements of Republican policy had wide support, the Democrats avoided attacking specific programs. Instead, they renewed their traditional assault on "special privilege."

Democrats warned that Republican programs were creating islands of privilege, enabling wealthy individuals to buy favors from the federal government and allowing the Republicans to buy support from the people that their programs served. The result, Democrats charged, was an increasing concentration of wealth and power in the hands of the wealthy and a corruption of the republic. By stressing corruption, the Democrats tried to appeal to Americans who valued honesty and still cherished the Jeffersonian ideal of a society composed of independent and virtuous farmers, artisans, and small entrepreneurs. The Democrats claimed they would restore the competitive economy that had been lost during the Industrial Revolution and the Civil War.

"*Grantism*"

Grant was lampooned on both sides of the Atlantic for the scandalous behavior of his administration. The British magazine *Puck* showed Grant only barely defying gravity in protecting corrupt members of his administration. Despite the scandals, the British public welcomed Grant with admiration on his triumphal foreign tour in 1877.

Dissident Republicans. Some Republicans joined the Democratic chorus condemning Grant's policies. The dissidents included radicals on Reconstruction such as Charles Sumner, but most numerous and influential were men such as Charles Francis Adams—wealthy, well-educated members of established northeastern families—who resented the critical role professional politicians had come to play in the party. They attacked Grant for turning the Republican party into a self-serving bureaucracy with too many professional politicians in executive positions, especially cabinet posts. And they faulted their party for requiring government workers to pay a portion of their salaries into the party's treasury.

The dissidents coined the term *Grantism* to describe this new system of party patronage. To counter it they endorsed a program of civil service reform, beginning with a *merit system* to replace the spoils system established under Jackson. A civil service commission would administer competitive examinations as the basis for appointments.

The Liberal Republicans and the Election of 1872. When the dissident Republicans failed to replace Grant as the party's nominee in 1872, they called themselves the Liberal Republicans and formed a new party. The name reflected their commitment to liberty, competition, and limited government. Their platform emphasized civil service reform and—in an appeal for Democratic support—amnesty for all former Confederates and removal of troops from the South. For president they nominated Horace Greeley, the influential editor and publisher of the New York *Tribune*. In an attempt to steal the Liberals' thunder, the Democrats nominated Greeley too, but with little enthusiasm. Although Greeley supported reconciliation with ex-Confederates, he had earlier favored a radical approach to Reconstruction, and he supported high tariffs, which conflicted with the views of the Democrats.

In the election of 1872 Grant won an even larger percentage of the popular vote—56 percent—than he had in 1868. In fact, this was a higher percentage of the popular vote than any candidate had won since Andrew Jackson in 1828. Grant carried every northern state and, because of support for him among African-American voters and the distaste of ex-Confederates for Greeley, Grant also carried all the states of the former Confederacy except Tennessee, Georgia, and Texas.

Crédit Mobilier and the Whiskey Ring. During Grant's second term the issue of corruption in the Republican party erupted again. In 1873 a Congressional committee confirmed newspaper reports of a complicated deal in which high-ranking Republicans appeared to have cheated the taxpayers. The scandal centered on Crédit Mobilier, a construction company that contracted for work on the Union Pacific Railroad. It turned out that Crédit Mobilier was a dummy corporation. Union Pacific stockholders had formed it and made enormous purchases from it, sometimes for services that were never delivered, and paid for those purchases with Union Pacific stock and federal subsidies. In an attempt to prevent a Congressional investigation, the insiders had sold Crédit Mobilier stock at a discount to several members of Congress.

An even more dramatic scandal, which reached into the White House itself, involved the Whiskey Ring, a network of large whiskey distillers and Treasury agents who defrauded the Treasury of millions of dollars of excise taxes on liquor. The ring was organized by a Union general, John A. McDonald, whom Grant had ap-

pointed to the post of supervisor of internal revenue in St. Louis. Grant's private secretary, Orville Babcock, kept a protective eye on McDonald's activities and funneled some of the spoils into the campaign chests of the Republican party. The game was up in 1875 when Benjamin Bristow, an upright and ambitious secretary of the treasury, exposed the ring and brought indictments against more than 350 distillers and government officials. Babcock was later acquitted, but more than a hundred men, including McDonald, went to prison.

The Whiskey Ring scandal ruined Grant's second term and crushed whatever prospects he might have had for a third. Grant had ordered Bristow to "Let no guilty man escape," but Grant protected his good friend Babcock with extraordinary measures, possibly even perjuring himself in a deposition he gave in the presence of Chief Justice Morrison Waite.

The Depression of 1873–1877. These scandals occurred in the midst of the worst depression the nation had ever endured. By 1876 nearly 15 percent of the labor force was unemployed, and thousands of farmers had gone bankrupt. The precipitating event was the Panic of 1873, which involved the bankruptcy of the Northern Pacific Railroad and its major investor, Jay Cooke. Both Cooke's privileged role as a financier of the Civil War and the extensive Republican subsidies to railroads suggested to many suffering Americans that Republican financial manipulations had caused the depression.

To Americans who had suffered economic loss or even ruin, the Grant administration seemed unresponsive. Especially troublesome was the important issue of how much paper money should be in circulation. Rapidly falling prices hurt small farmers and all others who were heavily in debt. Forced to repay debts with dollars that were swiftly increasing in value, they called on the federal government to increase the nation's money supply, an action that they hoped would stop prices from falling. The Grant administration ignored the debtors' pleas for relief and further angered them by insisting that Civil War bondholders be fully repaid in gold, even though they had bought their bonds with greenbacks and had received only the guarantee that the interest on the bonds would be paid in gold. In 1874 the Democrats gained sufficient support from Republicans to push through Congress a bill that would have increased the number of greenbacks in circulation and eased the money pinch. But President Grant vetoed it, fueling Democratic charges that Republicans served only the special interests of capitalists. In the election of 1874 the Democrats rode their criticism of Grant's leadership to gains in both houses of Congress and a majority in the House of Representatives—for the first time since secession.

Before the new Congress met, however, the lame-duck Republicans passed the Specie Resumption Act of 1875. This law provided that the federal government would exchange gold for greenbacks, thus making federal paper money as "good as gold." It put the nation's money supply squarely on the gold standard, a step that increased the confidence of investors in the economy and helped foreign trade. But by increasing the value of greenbacks the act induced wealthy Americans to hoard them, reducing the amount of money in circulation, pushing prices up more sharply, and increasing still more the burden of carrying debts. The severe financial pain felt by many Americans worsened even further the political prospects of the Grant administration.

The Political Crisis of 1877

Republican leaders approached the 1876 presidential campaign with a sense of foreboding. If they were to thwart the Democrats, they had to shake themselves free of the atmosphere of scandal and special privilege that had come to surround President Grant. They turned to the electoral-vote-rich state of Ohio for a candidate—Governor Rutherford B. Hayes, who had won three closely contested races. His scandal-free terms had won him a reputation for honesty, he had a good Civil War record, and he was a supporter of civil service reform. He was a moderate on Reconstruction and a former Whig whose election strategy included an appeal to southern conservatives, especially former southern Whigs.

The Democrats concentrated on the Grant scandals. They nominated Governor Samuel J. Tilden of New York, a well-known fighter of corruption who had helped break the control of the infamous Tweed Ring over New York City politics. Their platform emphasized reform, especially of the civil service, promising to save the nation from "a corrupt centralism which has honeycombed the offices of the Federal government itself with incapacity, waste, and fraud."

The Election of 1876. On election night the outcome seemed clear; headlines announced that Tilden had won. The Democrats celebrated, and the Republicans were plunged into gloom. In Ohio, Hayes went to bed convinced that he had been defeated. Tilden had won a bare majority of the popular vote—51 percent. The Democrats had made deep inroads in the North, carrying New York, New Jersey, Connecticut, and Indiana, and had apparently swept the southern states (see Map 16.3).

But by dawn two or three sleepless politicians at Republican headquarters in New York City had woven a daring strategy. Republicans still controlled election procedures in three southern states: Louisiana, South

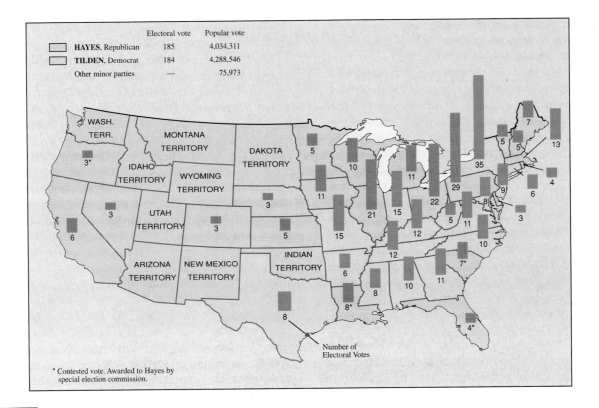

MAP 16.3

The Election of 1876

Tilden made such large inroads in northern states that Hayes could not win without the contested votes of three states in the Deep South. (Hayes also needed to defeat the efforts of the governor of Oregon to replace a Republican elector from that state with a Democrat.)

Carolina, and Florida. If they could argue that Democratic fraud and intimidation had affected the election results in those states, they could certify Republican victories and report Republican electoral votes. Of course, newly elected Democratic officials in the three states would send in electoral votes for Tilden. As a result, there would be two sets of electoral votes from those states when Congress counted them early in 1877. If Congress accepted all the Republican votes, Hayes would have a one-vote electoral majority. The audacious announcement came: Hayes had carried the three southern states and won the election.

The Compromise of 1877. The Constitution had not established a method to resolve this unprecedented dispute over the validity of electoral votes, and the long period of uncertainty between the election in November and the inauguration the following March was filled with rumors: There might be a violent coup by Democrats if the Republicans tried to steal the election; Presi-

dent Grant might use the military to prevent Tilden from taking office; there might be a new election or even a new civil war. The commander of the army, General William T. Sherman, believed that he might be the only person able to preserve the peace, and he deployed four artillery companies in Washington. While the rumors flew, various interests tried to gain advantage from the situation. Railroad promoters jockeyed for new federal subsidies, promising to deliver blocs of support in Congress to the party that made the best promises. Politicians on all sides flirted with the opposition, hoping for rewards.

In the end, political compromise and accident won out. Congress decided to appoint an electoral commission to settle the question. The commission included seven Republicans and seven Democrats. The fifteenth and deciding vote would go to Justice David Davis of the Supreme Court, a man with a reputation for being free of party loyalty. But Davis resigned from the Court at the crucial moment to accept election to the Senate

Beyond the well-populated states bordering the Mississippi, railroads would have to be built mostly in advance of the economic demand for them. In addition to generous land grants along the right-of-way, the federal government offered millions of dollars in public loans to the two companies that undertook the transcontinental project: the Union Pacific and the Central Pacific. Even so, raising private capital proved hard, requiring bonds at very high interest rates and a flood of stock with little underlying value. On top of that, the railroad promoters plundered shamelessly, diverting into their own pockets over half the construction costs.

The Union Pacific, building westward from Omaha, made little headway until the Civil War ended but then advanced rapidly across Indian country, reaching Cheyenne, Wyoming, in November 1867. It took the Central Pacific nearly that long moving eastward from Sacramento to cross the crest of the Sierra Nevada. Both then worked furiously—since the government subsidy was based on miles of track built—until, to great fanfare, the tracks met at Promontory Point, Utah, in 1869. The transcontinental link was actually a pretty rickety affair, capable of moving people but not a lot of freight. It would eventually have to be wholly rebuilt. None of the other land-grant railroads made it as far as the Rockies before the Panic of 1873 hit, throwing them into bankruptcy and bringing work to an abrupt halt.

By then, however, railroad tycoons had changed their minds about the Great Plains. No longer did they see it through the eyes of the Oregon-bound settlers—as a place to be gotten through en route to the Pacific. Rail transportation, they realized, was laying the basis for the economic exploitation of the Great Plains. This calculation spurred the railroad boom that followed economic recovery in 1878. Construction soared. During the 1880s, 40,000 miles of track were laid west of the Mississippi. There were new routes to southern California via the Southern Pacific from New Orleans and the Santa Fe from Kansas City and to Portland, Oregon, via the Northern Pacific from St. Paul, Minnesota, plus feeder lines and regional systems that crisscrossed the interior West.

The Cattle Kingdom. Of all the opportunities beckoning on the Great Plains, the most obvious was cattle raising. All prospective ranchers had to do was to observe the great herds of grazing buffalo to imagine the plains as cow country. And now, just as the ranchers stood poised to move in, those herds disappeared. A small market for buffalo robes had existed for years. Then, in the early 1870s, eastern tanneries discovered how to cure the hides, and a huge demand developed among shoe and harness manufacturers. Parties of professional hunters with high-powered rifles swept across the plains and began a systematic slaughter of the buffalo (see American Lives, pages 524–525). The great

Killing the Buffalo
This woodcut shows passengers shooting buffalo from a Kansas Pacific Railroad train. . . . A small thrill added to the modern convenience of traveling west by rail.

herds, already diminished by disease and shrinking pasturage, almost vanished within ten years. Many people spoke out against this mass killing, but no way existed to stop people bent on making a quick dollar. Besides, as General Philip H. Sheridan pointed out, exterminating the buffalo would starve the Indians into submission and open up the feeding grounds for a more valuable commodity, the Texas longhorn.

Bred from Spanish stock on Mexican ranchos since the eighteenth century, these tough cattle had spread across the Rio Grande and been acquired by Anglo ranchers. About 5 million head roamed south Texas in 1865, hardly worth bothering about because they could not be profitably marketed. That year, however, the Missouri Pacific Railroad reached Sedalia, Missouri. At that terminal, which connected to hungry eastern markets, a $3 longhorn might command $40. With this incentive, Texas ranchers inaugurated the famous Long Drive as cowboys herded the longhorn cattle hundreds of miles north to the railroads that were pushing west across Kansas.

At Abilene, Ellsworth, and, beginning in 1875, Dodge City, ranchers sold their cattle, and trail-weary cowboys went on a binge. These wide-open cattle towns captured the nation's imagination as symbols of the Wild West. The reality was much more ordinary. The cowboys, many of them blacks and Hispanics, were in fact farmhands on horseback, working long hours under harsh conditions for small pay. Colorful though it seemed, the Long Drive was actually a makeshift method of bridging a gap in the developing transportation system. As soon as railroads reached the Texas range country during the 1870s, ranchers abandoned the hazardous and wasteful Long Drive.

Buffalo Bill and the Wild West

Scott County, Iowa, was still frontier country when William F. Cody was born there on February 26, 1846. Kansas, where his family moved in 1854, was even wilder, for it not only was frontier country but was racked by bloody conflict between proslavery and free-soil settlers. Bill's father, Isaac Cody, was active on the free-soil side, serving in the Topeka legislature and frequently in harm's way from neighboring southern sympathizers and marauding border ruffians. One of Bill's first exploits was a wild gallop, with proslavery men in hot pursuit, to warn his father of a trap set for him near the family farm. Isaac Cody was less an idealist, however, than a typical enterprising westerner on the lookout for the main chance. He had been an Indian trader, a farm manager, a stagecoach operator, and, in Kansas, a land speculator around Grasshopper Falls. When he died suddenly in 1857, Cody left the family with a pile of land titles but little money.

Bill, never much for schooling anyway, had to find work. Only eleven, he was taken on by Majors and Waddell, the firm that transported goods from Fort Leavenworth to army posts west of the Missouri River. Bill worked as a messenger boy, livestock herder, and teamster helper on the freight wagons. When his employers (now Russell, Majors, and Waddell) organized the short-lived Pony Express in 1860, Cody became a stocktender and occasional rider in the Colorado-Nebraska division. Most of this was hard and tedious labor, but there were flashes of excitement—scrapes with Indians and bandits (at fifteen, Bill killed one), buffalo stampedes, and brief encounters with Wild Bill Hickock and other tough western characters on whom Bill could model himself. In the early part of the Civil War, Cody was at loose ends. Among other things he engaged in horse thieving disguised as guerrilla activity in Missouri, and he became a heavy drinker. After a stint in the Seventh Kansas Cavalry and a halfhearted effort to settle down after the war (and an unhappy marriage), Cody got his lucky break in 1867.

The Kansas Pacific Railroad was building a line through Indian country to Sheridan, Kansas. To provision the work crews, the contractors hired Cody at

Buffalo Bill Cody

$500 a month—excellent pay—to bring in twelve buffalo a day for the cooks. Cody was a crack shot and an excellent horseman, and he knew buffalo hunting. This assignment was duck soup for him, and the aplomb with which he carried it off soon gave him the name "Buffalo Bill."

The next summer, 1868, Indian war broke out in Kansas, and Cody got his second claim to fame when he was hired as chief scout for the U.S. Fifth Cavalry. Cody knew the Kansas landscape intimately, seemed to have a remarkable instinct for following a trail, and was intrepid in the face of danger. At the height of the fighting in 1868–1869 Cody saw repeated action. In the climactic Battle of Summit Springs, his scouting played a decisive role and he himself shot the Cheyenne chief, Tall Bull. Although the legends later built up around Buffalo Bill (and the claims of others) have inclined scholars to be skeptical, Buffalo Bill was in fact an authentic hero. Perhaps the best testimony was the extra $100 awarded him by the normally tightfisted army "for extraordinarily good services as a trailer and fighter in the pursuit of hostile Indians."

Out of these promising materials there began to emerge a mythic figure. In July 1869 the dime novelist Ned Buntline (Edward Zane Carroll Judson) came through Kansas, met Cody, and, after returning to New York, wrote *Buffalo Bill, the King of the Border Men*—the first of some 1,700 potboilers to feature Cody's name and exploits. Then there were the buffalo-hunting parties of the rich and famous that Cody periodically led, including a royal hunt in 1872 with the Grand Duke Alexis of Russia that had the entire country agog. With his white horse, buckskin suit, crimson shirt, and broad sombrero, Buffalo Bill began to play his part to the hilt. "He realized to perfection the bold hunter and gallant sportsman of the plains," wrote one appreciative participant. In 1872 Cody was persuaded to appear as himself in a play Buntline proposed to put on in New York. Buntline was said to have dashed off *The Scouts of the Prairie* in four hours, and critics pronounced it "execrable." But Buffalo Bill, who mostly ad-libbed, was a great hit, and so was the production. Cody was launched on his career as a showman.

From then on the lines between reality and make-believe began to blur. Not only did Buffalo Bill draw on his past exploits when he went on stage, but he had the stage in mind when he returned to the real world. During the Sioux wars of 1875–1876 Cody was again out in the field as an army scout. (Fortunately, the fighting took place during the theatrical off-seasons in the East.) Shortly after the annihilation of Custer's troops at Little Big Horn, Cody gained a measure of vengeance in a famous skirmish in which he killed and scalped a Sioux chief named Yellow Hand. Cody rode into that engagement wearing his stage *vaquero* outfit—black velvet and scarlet with lace—so that when he reenacted the mayhem on stage, he could say that he was wearing the very clothes in which he had seen action. Over time, with some help from Cody, the fight with Yellow Hand assumed legendary proportions, becoming a formal duel, with a challenge laid down by the Indian chief, and troopers and Indian warriors lined up on opposing sides to watch Buffalo Bill and Yellow Hand fight it out.

The mythic West Cody was creating became full-blown in his Wild West Show. Modeled on the circus and rodeo, it was first staged in 1883. It was an open-air extravaganza with displays of horsemanship, sharp-shooting by Little Annie Oakley, real Indians (in one season Chief Sitting Bull toured with the company), and reenactments of stagecoach robberies and great events such as Custer's Last Stand. The Wild West toured the country every year and was a smashing success in Europe as well.

Buffalo Bill had been keen enough to see the hunger of city people for a legendary West. He traded on his talents as a showman, but he relied as well on his grasp of the authentic world behind the make-believe. When Cody died in 1917, that world had long gone, but his Wild West Show kept it alive in legend, where it still remains in the mythic figures of cowboys and Indians that populate our movies and television screens.

Buffalo Bill's Wild West Show
The Wild West Show had worldwide appeal. This poster celebrates one of Buffalo Bill's European tours. (Buffalo Bill Historical Center)

The Cowboy at Work
Open-range ranching, in which cattle from different ranches grazed together, gave rise to distinctive traditions. At the roundup, cowboys separated the cattle by owner and branded the calves. The cowboy, traditionally a colorful figure, was really a farmhand on horseback, with the skills to work on the range. He earned twenty-five dollars a month, plus meals and a bed in the bunkhouse, in return for long hours of grueling, lonesome work.

Others, meanwhile, introduced longhorns to the northern ranges and found that the cattle could survive the harsh winters. In Texas ranchers owned or leased the land they used, sometimes in huge tracts. But what legal basis did they have for grazing cattle north of Texas? If the land was controlled by Indians, ranchers believed no one owned it. And if it was controlled by the federal government, then it was beyond reach, since government policy reserved the public domain for family-sized farms. So entering cattlemen simply helped themselves, treating the land as a free commodity for anyone who seized it and put it to use. Hopeful ranchers would spot a likely area along a creek and claim as much land as they could qualify for as settlers under federal homesteading laws, plus what could be added through the fraudulent claims made by one or two ranch hands. By a common usage that quickly became established, ranchers had a "range right" to all the adjacent land rising up to the divide—the point where the land sloped down to the next creek.

News of easy money traveled fast: calves at $5, steers at maybe $60 on the Chicago market. Rail connections were in place or coming in, and the grass was free. Profits of 40 percent per annum were a sure thing. The rush was on, drawing from as far away as the East Coast and Europe both the smart money and the romantics (like the recent Harvard graduate Teddy Roosevelt), eager for a taste of the Wild West. By the early 1880s the plains were overflowing with cattle; as many as 7.5 million head were decimating the grass and trampling the water holes.

A cycle of good weather only postponed, and made worse, the inevitable disaster. When it came—a hard winter in 1885, a severe drought the following summer, and then record blizzards and bitter cold—cattle died by the hundreds of thousands. An awful scene of rotting carcasses greeted the cowhands riding out onto the range the following spring. The recent slaughter of buffalo had produced equally ghastly sights, but no one owned the buffalo (and horror at their fate was therefore regarded as "sentimental") whereas every dead steer represented some rancher's investment. On top of that, beef prices collapsed when hard-pressed ranchers dumped the surviving cattle on the market. The boom had turned into a financial disaster, and investors fled, leaving behind a more enduring ecological disaster: the native grasses never recovered from the relentless overgrazing during the drought cycle.

Open-range ranching came to an end. Ranchers fenced their land and planted hay for the winter. No longer would cattle be left to fend for themselves on the open range. The crucial adaptation was to shift from reliance on wild vegetation to the cultivation of feed crops. Elsewhere, Hispanic grazers from New Mexico brought sheep in to feed on the forbs and woody plants that had replaced the native grasses. Sheep raising, previously scorned by ranchers as unmanly and resisted as a threat to cattle, became a major enterprise in the sparser high country after the beef debacle of the mid-1880s. Some ranchers even sold out to the despised "nesters"—those who wanted to farm the Great Plains.

Homesteaders. The movement of farmers onto the plains was not exactly spontaneous. Powerful interests devoted themselves to overcoming the notion of a Great American Desert. Foremost were the railroads, which were eager to sell the public land they had been granted—180 million acres of it—and develop traffic for their routes. They advertised aggressively, offered cut-rate tickets, and sold their land holdings at bargain prices. Land speculators, steamship lines, and the western states and territories did all they could to encourage settlement. And so did the federal government, with its offer under the Homestead Act (1862) of 160 acres of public land to settlers.

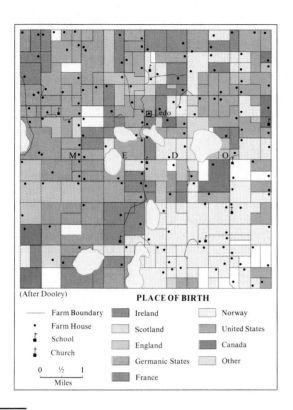

(After Dooley)

PLACE OF BIRTH

— Farm Boundary	Ireland	Norway
• Farm House	Scotland	United States
School	England	Canada
Church	Germanic States	Other
0 ½ 1	France	
Miles		

MAP 17.2

The Rural Ethnic Mosaic: Blue Earth County, Minnesota, 1880

What could have been more natural for emigrants such as Ida Lindgren (see American Voices, page 528) than to settle next to others sharing common ties to a homeland. This map of Medo township reveals that in rural America, no less than in the cities, ethnicity strongly influenced where people lived.

"Why emigrate to Kansas?" asked a testimonial in *Western Trail*, the Rock Island Railroad's gazette. "Because it is the garden spot of the world. Because it will grow anything that any other country will grow, and with less work. Because it rains here more than any other place, and at just the right time." Too boastful, a prospective settler might think, but surely holding a grain of truth. Besides, the climate might improve. "Why may we not suppose that the genial influences of civilization—that extensive cultivation of the earth—might contribute to the multiplication of showers?" asked Josiah Gregg, an early traveler on the plains. Might not "these sterile regions . . . be thus revived and fertilized, and their surface covered one day by flourishing settlements to the Rocky Mountains?" Over time Gregg's vision became an article of faith among boosters of the plains. As if to confirm that optimism, an exceptionally wet cycle occurred between 1878 and 1886. "As the plains are settled up we hear less and less of drouth, hot winds, alkali and other bugbears that used to hold back the adventurous," remarked a Nebraska man. Some settlers attrib-

uted the increased rainfall to soil cultivation and tree planting. Others credited God. As a settler on the southern plains remarked, "The Lord just knowed we needed more land an' He's gone and changed the climate."

No amount of optimism, however, could dispel the pain of migration. "That last separating word *Farewell*! sinks deeply into the heart," one pioneer woman recorded in her diary, thinking of family and friends left behind. Emigrants had always seen parting as a kind of death, with reunion unlikely "on this side of the dark river." But then came the treeless land, an alien and frightening place to a Swedish emigrant such as Ida Lindgren (see Map 17.2 and American Voices, page 528). "Such an air of desolation," wrote another Nebraska-bound woman; and, from the Texas plains, "such a lonely country." One old hand likened these despairing feelings to an illness. "A stranger travelling on the prairie would get his hopes up, expecting to see something different on making the next rise." But all he found was "grass and then more grass—the monotonous, endless prairie! . . . To him the disappointment and monotony were terrible. 'He's got loneliness,' we would say of such a man."

For women, this hard experience had a liberating side to it. Prescribed gender roles broke down as women shouldered men's work on new farms and gained a heightened sense of self-reliance in the face of danger and hardship. When husbands died or got sick, their wives took up the reins and operated farms on their

Buffalo Chips

With no trees around for firewood, settlers on the plains had to make do with dried cow and buffalo droppings. Gathering the "buffalo chips" must have been a regular chore for Ada McColl on her homestead near Lakin, Kansas (1893).

Ida Lindgren

Swedish Emigrant in Frontier Kansas

Like many emigrants, Ida Lindgren did not find it easy to adjust to the harsh new life on the frontier. Her diary entries and letters home show that the adjustment for the first generation was never complete.

May 15, 1870 [Lake Sibley, Nebraska]
What shall I say? Why has the lord brought us here? Oh, I feel so oppressed, so unhappy! Two whole days it took us to get here and they were not the least trying part of our travels. We sat on boards in the work-wagon packed in so tightly that we could not move a foot, and we drove across endless, endless praries, on narrow roads; no, no, not roads, tracks like those in the fields at home when they harvested grain. No forest but only a few trees which grow along the rivers and creeks. And then here and there you see a homestead and pass a little settlement. The Indians are not so far away from here, I can understand, and all the men you see coming by, riding or driving wagons, are armed with revolvers and long carbines, and look like highway robbers.

No date [probably written July 1870]
Claus and his wife lost their youngest child at Lake Sibley and it was very sad in many ways. There was no real cemetery but out on the prairie stood a large, solitary tree, and around it they bury their dead, without tolling of bells, without a pastor, and sometimes without any coffin. A coffin was made here for their child, it was not painted black, but we lined it with flowers and one of the men read the funeral service, and then there was a hymn, and that was all.

August 25, 1874 [Manhattan, Kansas]
It has been a long time since I have written, hasn't it? . . . When one never has anything fun to write about, it is no fun to write. . . . We have not had rain since the beginning of June, and then with this heat and often strong winds as well, you can imagine how everything has dried out. There has also been a general lamentation and fear for the coming year. We are glad we have the oats (for many don't have any and must feed wheat to the stock) and had hoped to have the corn leaves to add to the fodder. But then one fine day there came millions, trillions of grasshoppers in great clouds, hiding the sun, and coming down into the fields, eating up *everything* that was still there, the leaves on the trees, peaches, grapes, cucumbers, onions, cabbage, everything, everything. Only the peach stones still hung on the trees, showing what had once been there.

July 1, 1877 [Manhattan, Kansas]
. . . It seems so strange to me when I think that more than seven years have passed since I have seen you all. . . . I can see so clearly that last glimpse I had of Mamma, standing alone amid all the tracks of Eslov station. Oliva I last saw sitting on her sofa in her red and black dress, holding little Brita, one month old, on her lap. And Wilhelm I last saw in Lund at the station, as he rolled away with the train, waving his last farewell to me. . . .

Source: H. Arnold Barton, ed., *Letters from the Promised Land.* (Minneapolis: University of Minnesota Press, 1975), 143–145, 150–156.

own. Under the Homestead Act widows and single women had as heads of households the same rights as men; according to land-office records, women filed 12 percent of the claims in Colorado and Wyoming. "People afraid of coyotes and work and loneliness had better leave ranching alone," advised one woman homesteader. "At the same time, any woman who can stand her own company . . . and is willing to put in as much time at careful labor as she does at the washtub, will certainly succeed; will have independence, plenty to eat all the time, and a home of her own in the end."

The vision of new land to be farmed drove men and women onto the plains. By the 1870s the midwestern states had filled up, and farmers looked hungrily westward. "Hardly anything else was talked about," recalled the short story writer Hamlin Garland about his Iowa neighbors. "Every man who could sell out had gone west or was going. . . . Farmer after farmer joined the march to Kansas, Nebraska, and Dakota. . . . The movement . . . had . . . become an exodus, a stampede."

The same excitement took hold in northern Europe. Not only Germans came; for the first time Russians, Norwegians, and Swedes arrived in large numbers. At the peak of the "American fever" in 1882, over 105,000 Scandinavians emigrated to the United States. Swedish and Norwegian became the primary languages in parts of Minnesota and the Dakotas. Roughly a third of the farmers on the northern plains were foreign-born (see Map 17.2).

The Exodusters. The motivation for most settlers, American or European, was prosaically economic, but for some southern blacks Kansas briefly represented something more precious—the modern land of Canaan. Blacks from Kentucky and Tennessee had been migrating to Kansas all through the 1870s. Then, in the spring

Exodusters
Driven from their homes by terror raids, these southern blacks camped out on a Mississippi levee on the way to Kansas.

of 1879, with Reconstruction over and federal protection withdrawn, black communities fearful of white vengeance were swept by religious enthusiasm for Kansas. Within a month or so some 6,000 blacks from Mississippi and Louisiana arrived via St. Louis, most of them with nothing more than the clothes on their backs and faith in the Lord. How many of these Exodusters remained is hard to say, but the 1880 census reported 40,000 blacks in Kansas, by far the largest African-American concentration in the West aside from Texas, whose expanding cotton frontier attracted hundreds of thousands of black migrants during the 1870s and 1880s.

No matter where they came from (except perhaps for emigrants from the Russian steppes), homesteaders had seen nothing like the plains before. A cloud of grasshoppers might descend and destroy a crop in a day; a brushfire or hailstorm could do the job in an hour. What forested land had always provided—springs for water, lumber for cabins and fencing, ample firewood—was absent. Water had to be hauled long distances or collected in rain cisterns, fuel came from cow chips and hay twisted into "cats," and shelter took the form of dugouts cut into hillsides and, after a season or two, sod houses built of turf cut from the ground. The absence of trees, on other other hand, meant that far less labor was needed for clearing the land for the first crop. New technology and better seed overcame obstacles once thought insurmountable: steel plows enabled homesteaders to break the tightly matted ground; barbed wire, invented in 1874 by Joseph F. Glidden, an Illinois farmer, provided cheap, effective fencing against roaming cattle; and strains of hard-kernel wheat that could tolerate the extreme temperatures of the plains came in from Europe. The open, level land was ideal for grain crops. Homesteaders had good crops while the wet cycle held and began to anticipate the wood-frame house, deep

well, and full coal bin that might make life tolerable on the plains.

Then, in the later 1880s, the dry years came and silenced those hopeful calculations. "From day to day," reported the budding novelist Stephen Crane from Nebraska, "a wind hot as an oven's fury . . . raged like a pestilence," destroying the crops and leaving farmers "helpless, with no weapon against this terrible and inscrutable wrath of nature. . . . It was as if upon the massive altar of the earth, their homes and their families were being offered in sacrifice to the wrath of some blind and pitiless deity." Recently settled land emptied out, as homesteaders fled in defeat. The Dakotas lost 50,000 settlers between 1885 and 1890, and comparable departures occurred up and down the drought-stricken plains.

Others held on grimly. Stripped of the illusion that rain followed the plow, the survivors came to terms with the semiarid climate prevailing west of the 98th meridian. The Mormons in the area near the Great Salt Lake had demonstrated how irrigation could turn a wasteland into a garden. But the Great Plains mostly lacked the surface water needed for irrigation. The answer lay in dry-farming methods, which involved deep planting to bring subsoil moisture to the roots and quick harrowing after rainfalls to turn over a dry mulch that slowed evaporation. Dry farming produced a low yield per acre, however, and was not suited for the unequipped homesteader. Dry farming developed most fully on the corporate farms that covered up to 100,000 acres in the Red River Valley in North Dakota. But even family farms, which remained the norm elsewhere, could not operate with less than 300 acres of cereal crops and without machinery for plowing, planting, and harvesting. The McCormick reaper, although invented before the Civil War, began to be produced in quantity in response to the demand of western farmers.

By the turn of the century the Great Plains had fully submitted to agricultural development. About half the nation's cattle and sheep, a third of its cereal crops, and nearly three-fifths of its wheat came from the newly settled lands. In this process there was little of the "pioneering" that Americans associated with the westward movement. The railroads came before the settlers, eastern capital financed the ranching bonanza, and agriculture depended on sophisticated dry-farming techniques and modern machinery.

And where was the economic capital of the Great Plains? Far off in Chicago. There, at the hub of the nation's rail system, the wheat pit traded western grain and consigned it to world makets, the great packing houses slaughtered western cattle and supplied the nation with sausage, bacon, and sides of beef. In return, western ranchers and farmers received lumber, barbed wire, McCormick reapers, and Sears Roebuck catalogues. Chicago was truly "nature's metropolis."

The Impact on the Indians

What about the native Americans who had inhabited the Great Plains? Basically, their fate has been told in the foregoing account of western settlement. "The white children have surrounded me and have left me nothing but an island," lamented the great Sioux chief Red Cloud in 1870, the year after the completion of the transcontinental railroad. "When we first had all this land we were strong; now we are all melting like snow on a hillside, while you are grown like spring grass."

No matter that provision for a permanent Indian country had been written into federal law and ratified by treaties with various tribes. By 1860 all the resettled eastern tribes (see Chapter 11), treaties notwithstanding, had been forced to cede their lands and move farther west.

The nomadic tribes presented a more formidable barrier. As incursions into their lands increased from the late 1850s on, the Indians struck back all along the frontier: the Apache in the Southwest, the Cheyenne and Arapaho in Colorado, and the Sioux in the Wyoming and Dakota territories. Fighting ferociously between 1865 and 1867, the Sioux prevented a wagon road from being built through their prized Powder River hunting grounds to the booming mining town of Bozeman, Montana. The Indians hoped that if they resisted stubbornly enough and made the cost high enough, the whites would tire of the struggle and leave them in peace. This seemed not altogether fanciful in the weary aftermath of the Civil War. But the federal government did not give up; instead it formulated a new policy for dealing with the western Indians (see Map 17.3).

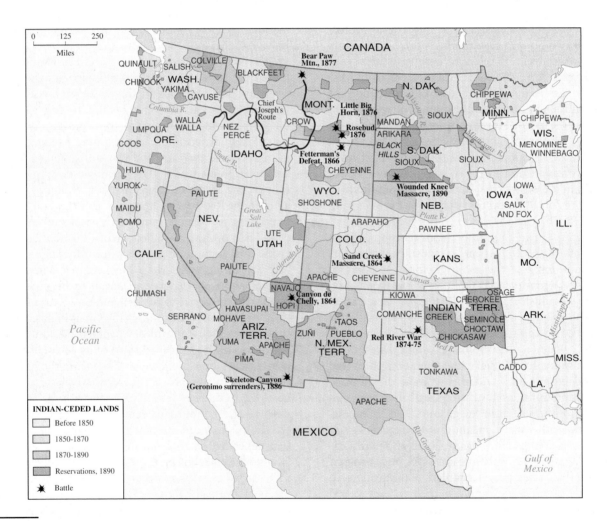

MAP 17.3

The Indian Frontier

As settlement pushed onto the Great Plains after the Civil War, the Indians put up bitter resistance, but ultimately to no avail. Over a period of decades they ceded most of their lands to the federal government, and by 1890 they were confined to scattered reservations where most could expect an impoverished and alien way of life.

The Reservation Solution. Few whites questioned the necessity of moving the native Americans out of the path of settlement and into reservations. This process had already begun, and now it would be pushed to a conclusion. And to it would be linked something new: a planned approach for weaning the Indians from their tribal way of life. Under the guidance of the Office of Indian Affairs, they would be wards of the government until they learned "to walk on the white man's road."

The government set aside two extensive areas for the Indians. It allocated the southwestern quarter of the Dakota Territory—present-day South Dakota west of the Missouri River—to the Teton Sioux tribes. And it assigned what is now Oklahoma to the southern Plains Indians as well as to the Five Civilized Tribes—the Choctaw, Cherokee, Chickasaw, Creek, and Seminole—and other eastern Indians who were already there. Scattered reservations went to the Apache, Navaho, and Ute in the Southwest and to the mountain Indians in the Rockies and beyond.

As in the past, land was transferred through the legal process of treaty making. And, as in the past, the white settlers bribed and tricked the Indian chiefs and in the end forced them to accept what they could not prevent. In 1868 the western Sioux tribes signed a treaty ceding all their land outside the Dakota reservation but explicitly retaining their hunting grounds in the Powder River country. "We have now selected and provided reservations for all, off the great road," concluded the western commanding general in September 1868. "All who cling to their old hunting-grounds are hostile and will remain so till killed off." That they would resist was inevitable. "You might as well expect the rivers to run backward as that any man who was born a free man should be contented when penned up and denied liberty to go where he pleases," said Chief Joseph of the Nez Percé, who, under his leadership, undertook in 1877 a remarkable 1,500-mile march from eastern Oregon almost to Canada trying to escape confinement in a small reservation.

The U.S. Army was thinly spread, having been cut back after the Civil War to a total force of 27,000. But these were veteran troops, including 2,000 black cavalrymen of the Ninth and Tenth regiments, whom Indians called with grim respect "buffalo soldiers." Technology also favored the army. Telegraph communications and railroads enabled the troopers to be quickly concentrated; repeating rifles and Gatling guns increased their firepower. As fighting intensified in the mid-1870s, a reluctant Congress made appropriations to augment the western troopers. Tribal rivalries meant that the army always had Indian allies; for example, the Kiowas and Pawnee could be counted on to fight the Sioux. But the worst disadvantages facing the Indians derived less from a formidable U.S. Army or their own disunity than from the overwhelming impact of white settlement.

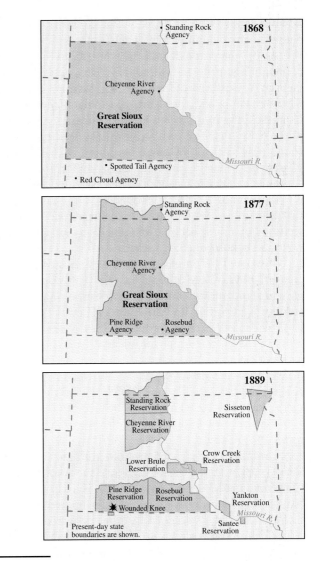

MAP 17.4

The Sioux Reservations in South Dakota, 1868–1890

In 1868, when they bent to the demand that they move onto the reservation, the Sioux thought they had gained secure rights to a substantial part of their ancestral hunting grounds. But as they learned to their sorrow, fixed boundary lines only increased their vulnerability to the land hunger of the whites and sped up the process of expropriation.

Resisting the reservation solution, the Indians fought on for years—in Kansas in 1868–1869, in the Red River Valley of Texas in 1874, and sporadically in New Mexico among the Apache until the capture of Geronimo in 1886. On the northern plains the crisis came in 1875, when the Indian Office—despite the treaty of 1868—ordered the Sioux to vacate their Powder River hunting grounds and withdraw to the reservation.

Led by Sitting Bull, Sioux and Cheyenne warriors gathered on the Little Big Horn River to the west of the

Powder River country. In a typical concentrating maneuver, army columns from widely separated forts converged on the Little Big Horn from three sides. The commanding general, Alfred H. Terry, sent Colonel George A. Custer ahead with a small force to locate the Sioux encampment, with orders to block the Indians from escaping into the Big Horn Mountains before the main army forces arrived. Instead, the reckless Custer sought out battle on his own. On June 25, 1876, he advanced on what he thought was a minor Indian encampment. This turned out to be the main force of 2,500 warriors, who surrounded and annihilated Custer and his 256 men. It was a great native American victory but not a decisive one. The day of reckoning was merely postponed.

Weakened by unrelenting military pressure and increasing physical privation, the Sioux bands one by one gave up and moved onto the reservation. The last to come in were Sitting Bull's followers. They had retreated to Canada, but in 1881, after five hard years, they recrossed the border and surrendered at Fort Buford, Montana.

By then the open plains were no more. Homesick bands of southern Cheyenne learned this bitter truth in 1878 when they escaped from their reservation in the Indian Territory of Oklahoma. Along the route to their native grounds in the Wyoming Territory lay three railroads, numerous telegraph lines, and ranchers and homesteaders eager to report the Cheyenne's movements. The Cheyenne made their way through Kansas and Nebraska, but the army eventually caught up and captured them. The survivors declared that they preferred death to returning to the reservation. The government relented and permitted them to stay on their native land.

It was not Indian resistance but relentless white pressure that wrecked the reservation solution. Prospectors began in the mid-1870s to dig gold in the Black Hills, sacred land to the Sioux and entirely inside their reservation. Unable to hold back the prospectors or buy out the Sioux, the government opened up the Black Hills to gold seekers at their own risk, and in 1877, after Sioux resistance had crumbled, forced the cession of the western third of their Dakota reservation (see Map 17.4).

The Indian Territory of Oklahoma met the same fate. Two million acres in the heart of the territory had not been assigned to any tribe, and white homesteaders coveted that fertile land. The "Boomer" movement, stirred up initially by railroads running across the Indian Territory during the 1880s, agitated tirelessly to open this so-called Oklahoma District to settlers. In 1889 the government gave in and placed the Oklahoma District under the Homestead Act. On April 22, 1889, a horde of claimants rushed in and staked out the entire district within a few hours. Two tent cities—Guthrie with 15,000 people and Oklahoma City with 10,000— were in full swing by nightfall.

Severalty. The completion of the land-grabbing process was hastened, ironically, by the avowed friends of the native Americans. The Indians had never lacked sympathizers, especially in the East. After the Civil War reformers created the Indian Rights Association. The movement got a boost from Helen Hunt Jackson's powerful book *A Century of Dishonor* (1881), which told the story of the unjust treatment of the Indians. The reformers, however, had little sympathy for the tribal way of life. They could think of no future for the Indian other than assimilation into white society.

During the 1870s the Office of Indian Affairs had developed a program to train Indian children for farming and manual work and prepare them for citizenship.

The Cherokee Strip

This photograph captures the wild race into the Cherokee Strip in the northern part of Oklahoma Territory on September 16, 1893, the second such "run" that opened the region to white settlement. The winners staked out their claims under the Homestead Act and looked forward to a prosperous future on some of the richest farmland in America. Those who lost out hoped for better luck as other parts of the territory opened up. The Indians who had lived on the land had nothing to hope for because this process spelled the end of their way of life.

Some attended reservation schools, while the less lucky were sent to boarding schools distant from family and home. The reformers approved of this educational program and favored the efforts by the Indian Office to undercut tribal authority. In particular, they highly esteemed private property as a "civilizing" force.

The resulting policy was called *severalty*—the division of reservation lands into individually owned parcels. Even though private ownership was a concept repugnant to the Indians and earlier experiments with land allotments had failed dismally, the reformers remained unshaken in their faith that private property would transform the native Americans into prudent, hardworking members of white society. With their blessing, the Dawes Severalty Act of 1887 authorized the president to divide tribal lands, giving 160 acres to each family head and smaller parcels to other individuals. The land would be held in trust by the government for twenty-five years, and the recipients would become U.S. citizens. The remaining reservation lands would be sold off, with the proceeds placed in an Indian education fund.

The Last Battle: Wounded Knee.

The Sioux were among the first to feel the full effect of the Dawes Act. According to the proposed allotments, roughly half their Dakota lands would become "surplus" and available for white settlement. The government drew up a plan to divide the Sioux reservation into six smaller ones (see Map 17.4) and again began the familiar process of negotiating assent from the unwilling Indians.

On February 10, 1890, the federal government announced that it had gained the required number of Sioux signatures (three-quarters of the population) and opened the ceded land to white settlement. But no surveys had been made of the reservation boundaries, nor any provision for land allotments for Indians living in the ceded areas. On top of these signs of bad faith, drought wiped out the Indians' crops. It seemed beyond endurance. The Sioux had lost their ancestral lands and faced a future as sedentary farmers that was alien to their traditions. And immediately confronting them was a hard winter of starvation.

But news of salvation had also come. An Indian messiah, a holy man who called himself Wovoka, was preaching a new religion on a Paiute reservation in Nevada. In a vision, Wovoka had gone to heaven and received God's word that the world would be regenerated. The whites would disappear, all the Indians of past generations would return to earth, and life on the Great Plains would go back to the time of the roaming buffalo. All this would come to pass in the spring of 1891. Preparatory to that great day, the Indians should follow Wovoka's commandments and practice the Ghost Dance. That daylong ritual of dancing and praying sent participants into trancelike states during which their spirits rose to heaven.

Wovoka's teachings were nonviolent and not specifically antiwhite, but among Wovoka's Sioux adherents the new religion took a belligerent and increasingly threatening turn against white settlers. As the frenzy of the Ghost Dance swept through some Sioux encampments in the fall of 1890, resident whites became alarmed and called for army intervention.

When Indian police backed by federal troops tried to arrest Sitting Bull on December 14, a gun battle broke out, killing the old chief and at least twelve others. Worse was to come. Within the Minneconjou tribe, the medicine man Yellow Bird had stirred up a fervent Ghost Dance following. But with their chief, Big Foot, desperately sick with pneumonia, the tribe had given up and come in under military escort to an encampment at Wounded Knee Creek on December 28. The next morning, when the soldiers attempted to disarm the Indians, a battle exploded in the encampment. In American Voices (page 534) Black Elk describes what happened. Twenty-five U.S. troopers died, and among the Indians 146 men, women, and children perished, many of them shot down as they fled.

Wounded Knee was the final episode in the long war of suppression of the Plains Indians, but it was not the

The Dead at Wounded Knee

In December 1890 U.S. soldiers massacred about 146 Sioux men, women, and children in the Battle of Wounded Knee in South Dakota. It was the last big fight on the northern plains between the Indians and the whites. Black Elk, a Sioux holy man, related that "after the soldiers marched away from their dirty work, a heavy snow began to fall . . . and it grew very cold." The body of Yellow Bird lay frozen where it had fallen.

AMERICAN VOICES

Black Elk

Wounded Knee: "Something terrible happened . . ."

Black Elk, an Oglala Sioux holy man, was at Wounded Knee when the killing occurred. This is his account, as he recollected the event forty years later.

It was in the evening when we heard that the Big Foots were camped over there with the soldiers. . . . In the morning [December 29, 1890] I went out after my horses, and while I was out I heard shooting off toward the east, and I knew from the sound that it must be wagon guns [cannon] going off. The sounds went right through my body, and I felt that something terrible would happen. . . .

A little way ahead of us, just below the head of the dry gulch, there were some women and children who were huddled under a clay bank, and some cavalrymen were there pointing guns at them. . . .

I had no gun, and when we were charging, I just held the sacred bow out in front of me with my right hand. The bullets did not hit us at all. . . .

After the soldiers marched away, I heard from my friend, Dog Chief, how the trouble started, and he was right there by Yellow Bird when it happened. This is the way it was:

In the morning the soldiers began to take all the guns away from the Big Foots. Soldiers were on the little hill and all around, and there were soldiers across the dry gulch to the south and over east along Wounded Knee Creek too. The people were nearly surrounded, and the wagon-guns were pointing at them.

Some had not yet given up their guns, and so the soldiers were searching all the tepees, throwing things around and poking into everything. There was a man called Yellow Bird, and he and another man were standing in front of the tepee where Big Foot was lying sick. They had white sheets around and over them, with eyeholes to look through, and they had guns under these. An officer came to search them. He took the other man's gun, and then started to take Yellow Bird's. But Yellow Bird would not let go. He wrestled with the officer, and while they were wrestling, the gun went off and killed the officer. As soon as the gun went off, Dog Chief told me, an officer shot and killed Big Foot who was lying sick inside the tepee.

Then suddenly nobody knew what was happening, except that the soldiers were all shooting and the wagon-guns began going off right in among the people.

Many were shot down right there. The women and children ran into the gulch and up west, dropping all the time, for the soldiers shot them as they ran. There were only about a hundred warriors and there were nearly five hundred soldiers. The warriors rushed to where they had piled their guns and knives. They fought soldiers with only their hands until they got their guns. . . .

It was a good winter day when all this happened. The sun was shining. But after the soldiers marched away from their dirty work, a heavy snow began to fall. The wind came up in the night. There was a big blizzard, and it grew very cold. The snow drifted deep in the crooked gulch, and it was one long grave of butchered women and children and babies, who had never done any harm and were only trying to run away.

Source: John G. Neihardt, ed., *Black Elk Speaks: The Legendary "Book of Visions" of an American Indian* (1932; rpt. New York: Washington Square Press, 1971), 216–223.

end of their story. The process of severalty then proceeded without hindrance. On the Dakota lands the Teton Sioux fared relatively well, and many of the younger generation settled down as small farmers and stock grazers. Ironically, the more fortunate tribes were probably those occupying reservation lands that did not attract white settlement and thus were bypassed by the severalty process. The flood of whites into South Dakota and Oklahoma, on the other hand, left the Indians as small minorities in lands that were once wholly theirs—20,000 Sioux in a South Dakotan population of 400,000 in 1900 and 70,000 members of various tribes in a population of a million when Oklahoma became a state in 1907.

Even so, tribal identities survived until, with the restoration of the reservation policy in 1934, they once again rested on a communal territorial basis. All along, native American cultures had been adaptive, some of them, for example, developing written languages during the nineteenth century. This cultural resilience would persist—in religion, in tribal structure, in crafts—but the fostering native American world was gone, swept away, as an Oklahoma editor put it in the year of statehood, by "the onward march of empire."

California and the Far West

On the western edge of the Great Plains, the Rocky Mountains rise up to form a great barrier between the flat eastern two-thirds of the country and the rugged Far West (see Map 17.1). Beyond the Rockies lie two vast plateaus: on the north side the Columbia plateau, extending into eastern Oregon and Washington, and flanking the southern Rockies, the Colorado plateau. Where they break off, the plateaus carve out the desert-like Great Basin that covers eastern Utah and all of Nevada. The Great Basin gives way southeastwardly to plains and mountain ridges that are equally rainless but are drained by the rivers of lower Arizona and New Mexico. Separating this arid interior from the Pacific are two great mountain ranges—the Sierra Nevada and, to the north, the Cascades—beyond which lies a coastal region that is cool and rainy in the upper corner but increasingly dry as one proceeds southward until, in southern California, rainfall becomes almost as sparse as it is in the interior.

What most impressed Americans about this far western country was its sheer inhospitability. "Who are to go there?" asked Senator George McDuffie in 1843 when the nation was preparing to seize this land. "The territory consists of mountains almost inaccessible, and low lands . . . where rain never falls, except during spring; and even on the [part of the territory fit for occupation—the part lying on the seacoast] no rain falls from April to October, and for the remainder of the year there is nothing but rain. Why, sir, sir, of what use will this be for agricultural purposes? I would not, for that purpose, give a pinch of snuff for the whole territory."

Too grim, perhaps, but with enough truth to it to explain why the Far West could not be occupied in standard American fashion—that is, by a multitude of settlers moving westward along a broad front, blanketing the land and bringing it under cultivation homestead by homestead. The wagon trains moving to Oregon's Willamette Valley adopted an entirely different strategy of occupation—the planting of distant oases in a vast, mostly barren landscape. This was the strategy pursued by New Spain ever since it had sent the first wagon trains 700 miles northward from Mexico into the upper Rio Grande Valley in 1598. When the Southwest was taken from Mexico by the United States 250 years later, major Hispanic settlements existed in New Mexico and California, and lesser settlements—some of them, like Tucson, little more than *presidios*, or fortified towns—were scattered along the borderlands into south Texas. At that time, aside from Oregon, the only significant Anglo settlement was around the Salt Lake in Utah, where Mormons had moved to escape persecution and plant a New Zion. Fewer than 100,000 Euro-Americans—roughly

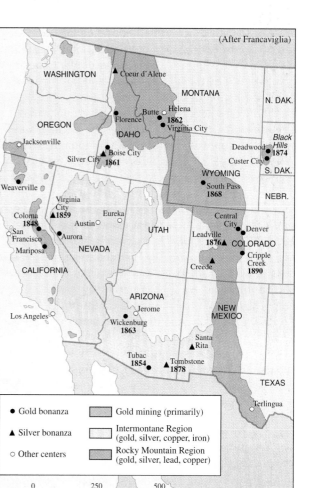

MAP 17.5

The Mining Frontier

The Far West was America's gold country because of its geological history. Veins of gold and silver form when molten material from the earth's core is forced up into fissures caused by the tectonic movements that create mountain ranges, such as the ones that dominate the far western landscape. It was these veins, the product of mountain-forming activity many thousands of years earlier, that prospectors began to discover after 1848 and furiously exploit. Although widely dispersed across the Far West, the lodes that they found followed the mountain ranges, bisecting the region and bypassing the great plateaus not shaped by the ancient tectonic activity.

25,000 of them Anglo and the rest Hispanic—lived in the entire Far West in 1848.

More emigrants would be coming in, certainly, but Senator McDuffie's slight valuation of the nation's newly acquired western territory seemed about right. California was "hilly and mountainous," noted a U.S. naval officer in 1849, too dry for farming and surely not "susceptible of supporting a very large population."

But the naval officer had not taken into account the recent discovery of gold in the Sierra foothills. California would indeed support a very large population, drawn, however, not by the lure of arable land but by dreams of gold. Extraction of mineral wealth became the basis for the Far West's development, and that meant, first of all, explosive growth. By 1860, when the Great Plains was still Indian country, California was a booming state with 300,000 residents. There was also a burst of city building. Overnight San Francisco became a bustling metropolis—it had 57,000 residents by 1860—and was the hub of a mining empire that stretched to the Rockies. For the mining camps on the eastern slope, it was Denver that became the metropolis. In its swift urbanization, the Far West resembled gold-rush Australia much more than it resembled the American Midwest; like San Francisco, Melbourne was a city incongruously grand amid the empty spaces and rough mining camps of the Australian "outback." Finally, the distinctive pattern of nucleated settlement persisted, driven now, however, by a proliferation of mining sites and by people moving not east to west, but coming mainly from California and moving west to east.

The Mining Frontier

By the mid-1850s, as easy pickings in the California gold country rapidly diminished, disappointed prospectors began to pull out of the region and spread across the West in hopes of striking it rich elsewhere. Gold was discovered on the Nevada side of the Sierras, in the Colorado Rockies, and along the Fraser River in British Columbia. New strikes occurred in Montana and Wyoming during the 1860s, in the Black Hills of South Dakota a decade later (an anomalous outcropping du-

plicating on the Great Plains the mineral geology otherwise found only in the mountainous Far West), and in the Coeur d'Alene region of Idaho during the 1880s.

As the news of each gold strike spread, a wild, remote area turned almost overnight into a mob scene of prospectors, traders, gamblers, prostitutes, and saloon keepers. At least 100,000 fortune seekers flocked to the Pike's Peak area of Colorado in the spring of 1859. Trespassers on government or Indian land, the prospectors made their own law. The mining codes devised at community meetings limited the size of a mining claim to what a person could reasonably work. This kind of informal lawmaking also became an instrument for excluding or discriminating against Mexicans, Chinese, and African-Americans in the goldfields. And it turned into hangman's justice for the many outlaws who infested the mining camps.

The heyday of the prospectors was always brief. They were equipped only to skim gold from the surface of the earth and from streambeds. Extracting the metal locked in underground lodes required mine shafts and crushing mills, which took capital, technology, and business organization. The original claim holders quickly sold out after exhausting the surface gold or when a generous bidder came along. At every gold-rush site prospecting soon gave way to entrepreneurial development and large-scale mining. Rough mining camps turned into big towns.

Virginia City. Nevada's Virginia City started out as a bawdy, ramshackle mining camp. But with the opening of the Comstock silver lode in 1859, it soon boasted a stock exchange, five newspapers and, in short order, ostentatious mansions for the mining kings, fancy hotels, opera, even Shakespearean theater. The underlying characteristics of a boomtown persisted, however. Vir-

Virginia City, Nevada

This undated photograph shows a mature Virginia City, taken around the mid-1870s, when the Comstock lode was yielding 500 tons of ore per day. The industrial face of the city can be seen on the upper left, where on the outskirts of town a processing mill crushed the ore and extracted the silver. Virginia City gave the appearance, with its churches and fine public buildings, of a place destined to last forever. But in fact, when the Comstock lode played out in the early 1880s, Virginia City quickly declined and, in a fate all too common in bonanza mining, became a ghost town.

ginia City was a magnet for job seekers of both sexes: men laboring as miners for $4 a day, and many of the working-class women becoming dance-hall entertainers and prostitutes because that was the best chance offered them by the city's bonanza economy. In 1870 the ratio of men to women was two to one, and children made up only 10 percent of the population. There were a hundred saloons, and brothels lined D Street.

When James Galloway arrived from California looking for work on February 4, 1875, however, he brought his family with him, as did many other miners. By 1880 there were as many women and children as men in Virginia City. Galloway's diary describes a family life that was not out of the ordinary—churchgoing, picnics, the purchase of a lot for a small house. But Galloway was infected by Virginia City's pervasive gambling fever: he speculated regularly in mining stock and always lost money. In the end he fell victim to the extraordinary hazards of hard-rock mining. He was killed when his sleeve got caught in the gears of a mine machine. He might have survived if he had permitted rescuers to hack off his arm, but he took a long chance on being cut loose and coming out whole, and lost.

Industrialization of Western Mining. In its final stage the mining frontier passed into the industrial world. At some sites gold and silver proved less important than the more common metals—copper, lead, zinc—for which there was a huge demand in eastern manufacturing. Beginning in the mid-1870s, copper mining thrived in the Butte district of Montana, especially after the opening of the fabulous Anaconda mine, and also flourished in the Globe and Copper Queen fields of New Mexico and Arizona. In the 1890s, after earlier finds at Leadville, Colorado, the Coeur d'Alene silver district became the nation's main source of lead and zinc.

Entrepreneurs raised capital, built rail connections, devised the technology for treating the lower-grade copper deposits, constructed smelting facilities, and recruited a labor force. As elsewhere in American industry, trade-union organization appeared among the miners (see Chapter 18). And as elsewhere in corporate America, the western metal industries went through a process of consolidation. The Anaconda Copper Mining Company and other Montana mining firms came under the control of the Amalgamated Copper Company in 1899. That same year, the American Smelting and Refining Company brought together the bulk of the nation's lead-mining and copper-refining properties. Blackfeet and Crow country in the 1860s, the Butte copper district was a center of industrial capitalism barely thirty years later.

The Pacific Slope. If the Far West had lacked mineral wealth, its history would certainly have been very different. Before the discovery of gold at Sutter's mill, it was Oregon's Willamette Valley, not dry California, that mostly attracted westward-bound settlers. And had it not been for the gold rush, California likely would have remained like the Willamette Valley—an economic back-

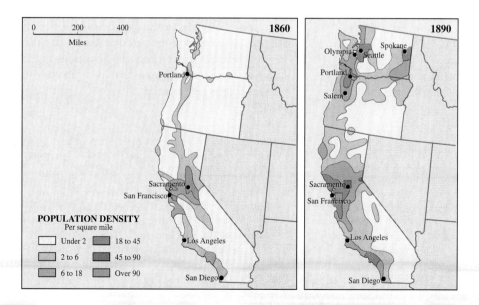

MAP 17.6

The Settlement of the Pacific Slope
In 1860 the settlement of the Pacific slope was remarkably uneven—fully under way in northern California, scarcely begun anywhere else. By 1890 a new pattern had begun to emerge, with the swift growth of southern California already foreshadowed and the settlement of the Pacific Northwest well launched.

water lacking markets for its products and slow to build its population. In 1860, although already a state, Oregon had scarcely 25,000 inhabitants, and its principal city, Portland, was little more than a village. It was booming California (see Map 17.6) and the mining country tributary to it that pulled Oregon from the doldrums by creating a market for the Willamette farms and for the state's fisheries and timber. North of Oregon, territory very thinly settled into the 1870s, the arrival of rail transportation in the early 1880s had an equally tonic effect. The development of Washington on the Pacific side largely duplicated Oregon's experience, but east of the Cascades, on the fertile, semiarid Columbia plateau, a rich grain-producing region also sprang up.

During the 1880s Oregon and Washington (which became a state in 1889) grew prodigiously. Where scarcely a hundred thousand settlers had lived twenty years earlier, by 1890 there were nearly three-quarters of a million. Portland and, even more dramatically, Seattle had blossomed into important commercial centers, both prospering from a robust mixed economy of farming, ranching, logging, and fishing.

California's fertile central valley and forested north coast experienced a comparable development, as did the irrigated valleys of Utah, which by 1890 had over 200,000 people. At a certain point, especially as railroads opened up eastern markets, this diversified growth became self-sustaining. But what had triggered it, what had provided the first markets and underwritten the service infrastructure, was the bonanza mining economy, at the hub of which stood San Francisco, metropolis for the entire Far West.

Hispanics, Chinese, Anglos

The Hispanic Southwest. California was the anchor of two distinct far western regions. First, it joined with Oregon and Washington to form the Pacific slope. Second, by climate and Hispanic heritage, it was linked to the Southwest, which today includes Arizona, New Mexico, and Texas. Here, along a 1,500-mile borderland, settlements had been planted over many years by the viceroys of New Spain and had formed, after the 1821 revolution, the northernmost provinces of Mexico. Most populous and best established were the settlements along the upper Rio Grande Valley in New Mexico; the main town, Santa Fe, over 200 years old, contained 4,635 residents in 1860. Farther down along the Rio Grande was El Paso, nearly as ancient but much smaller, and, as the Rio Grande emptied into the Gulf of Mexico, newer towns such as Laredo. A grazing economy spread up to the Nueces River. Beyond lay San Antonio, which had been founded to establish Spain's claim to central Texas. At the other end, in California, a Hispanic population was spread thinly in presidio towns along the coast and in great ranchos in the countryside.

The economy of this Hispanic crescent was pastoral, consisting primarily of cattle and sheep ranching. In south Texas there were family-run rancheros. Everywhere else the social order was highly stratified. At the top stood an elite, beneficiaries of royal land grants, proudly Spanish, and devoted to the traditional life of a landed aristocracy. Below them, with little in between, was a laboring population of servants, artisans, *vaqueros* (cowboys), and farm workers.

In New Mexico there was a large *mestizo* population, a peasantry of mixed Hispanic and Indian blood. Although Spanish-speaking and faithfully Catholic, in their village life and farming methods these New Mexicans bore the marks of their Pueblo Indian origins more than their Hispanic heritage. The Indian population, although reduced from the golden age of the Pueblo civilization before the arrival of the Spaniards, still occupied much of the Rio Grande Valley, living in the old ways in adobe villages and making the New Mexico countryside

Vaqueros *in a Corral*
On California cattle ranches owners relied on Mexican cowhands—*vaqueros*—whose skills as riders and rope handlers were unexcelled. This striking painting was done in 1877 by James Walker, who came from New York City but had a special enthusiasm for southwestern scenes. (Thomas Gilcrease Institute)

a patchwork of Hispanic and Pueblo settlements. And to the north a vibrant new people, the Navajo, had appeared, warriors like the Apache from which they had sprung but also skilled at crafts and living as sheep-raising pastoralists. New Mexico was one place where European and native American cultures managed a successful, if uneasy, coexistence and where the Indian inhabitants were equipped to hold their own against the Anglo challenge.

In California, by contrast, the Hispanic occupation was harder on the indigenous hunter-gatherer peoples, inevitably undermining their tribal structure, reducing them to coerced labor, and making them easy prey for the aggressive Anglo miners and settlers, who, in short order, nearly wiped out California's once numerous Indian population.

The fate of the Hispanic Southwest after its incorporation into the United States depended on the rate of Anglo immigration. In New Mexico, which remained off the beaten track even after the arrival of railroads in the 1880s, the Santa Fe elite more than held its own, incorporating the Anglo newcomers into Hispanic society through intermarriage and business partnerships. In California, on the other hand, the expropriation of the great ranchos was relentless even though the 1848 peace treaty with Mexico had recognized the property rights of the *californios* and had made them U.S. citizens. The fact that they actually won most of the lawsuits challenging their Mexican land grants did not matter very much. Burdened by huge legal expenses, rising taxes, and the costs of removing squatters, the dons saw their ranchos auctioned off or lost in swindles by Yankees swarming in with business deals. Around San Francisco the rancho system disappeared almost in a puff of smoke. Farther south, where Anglos were slow to arrive, the dons held on longer. By the 1880s just a handful of the original families still retained their Mexican land grants.

The New Mexico peasants found themselves similarly embattled. Crucial to their livelihood were their grazing rights on communal lands. But these were customary rights that could not withstand legal challenge when Anglo ranchers established title and began putting up fences. The peasants responded resiliently. Their subsistence economy relied on a division of labor that gave women a central productive role in the village economy. Women raised much of the family food in small gardens, engaged in the village bartering trade, made the clothes, and plastered the adobe houses. With the loss of the communal lands, the men began to leave the villages seasonally to work on the railroads or in the Colorado mines and sugar-beet fields, earning crucial dollars while leaving the village economy in their wives' hands.

Elsewhere, hard-pressed Hispanics struck back for what they considered rightfully theirs. In El Paso the fighting issue was control over nearby salt beds. Salt was always a precious commodity, sometimes serving in ancient times as money; *sal* is the Latin root of the word *salary*. So El Pasoans rose in revolt when title to their communal salt beds passed into private hands in 1879. When Anglo ranchers began to fence in communal lands in San Miguel County, the New Mexicans long settled there, *los pobres* (the poor ones), organized themselves into masked night-riding raiders and in 1889 and 1890 mounted an effective campaign of harassment against the interlopers. After 1900, when Anglo farmers swarmed into south Texas bent on exploiting new irrigation methods, the displaced *Tejanos* responded with sporadic but persistent night-riding attacks. Much of the raiding by Mexican "bandits" from across the border in the years before World War I was really a civil war fought by embittered *Tejanos* who had lived north of Rio Grande for generations.

But they, like the New Mexico villagers who became seasonal wage laborers, could not avoid being driven into the ranks of a Mexican-American working class as the Anglo economy developed. The same development, however, also began to attract increasing numbers of immigrants from old Mexico.

Mexican Immigrants. All along the southwest borderlands, economic activity was picking up in the late nineteenth century. Railroads were being built, copper mines were opening in Arizona, cotton and vegetable agriculture was being developed in south Texas, and fruit growing was introduced in southern California. There is no way of knowing how many Mexicans migrated to the work thus created, since the borders were open until 1917 and few bothered to register when they entered the United States. In Texas the Hispanic population increased from about 20,000 in 1850 to 165,000 in 1900. Some came as contract workers for railway track gangs and harvest labor; virtually all were relegated to the lowest-paying and most backbreaking work; and everywhere they were discriminated against and reviled by higher-status Anglo workers.

Mostly the Mexicans came as short-term and casual workers, not as permanent settlers, but some remained and swelled the numbers and resources of established Mexican-American communities. In Tucson, a Mexican elite dominated the expanding local economy. But most Mexican urban dwellers were poor laboring people segregated in what was already identifiably the *barrio*—the Mexican ghetto—of the southwest borderland cities.

What stimulated the Mexican migration, of course, was the enormous demand for workers by a region undergoing explosive economic development. Hence the exceptionally high numbers of immigrants in the California population of that era: between 1860 and 1890 roughly one-third were foreign-born, more than twice the level for the country as a whole. Many came from Europe; most numerous were the Irish, followed by the

Germans and British. But there was also another group that was unique to the West—the Chinese.

The Chinese Migration. Attracted first by the California gold rush of 1849, 200,000 Chinese came to the United States over the next three decades. In those years they constituted a considerable minority of California's population—around 9 percent—and because virtually all were actively employed, they represented a much larger proportion of the state's labor force—probably a quarter. Elsewhere in the West, at the crest of mining activity, their presence could surge remarkably, for example, to over 25 percent of Idaho's population in 1870.

The coming of the Chinese to North America was not an isolated event, but part of a worldwide Asian migration that began in the mid-nineteenth century. Driven by poverty from their overpopulated lands, the Chinese went to Australia, Hawaii, and Latin America; Indians moved to Fiji and South Africa; and Javanese immigrated to Dutch colonies in the Caribbean. Most of these Asians migrated under the system of indentured servitude, which in effect made them the property of others. That was not true of the Chinese who came to America. Contrary to the stubborn image of a "coolie trade," they came as free workers, their passage financed by a *credit-ticket system*. Under that system migrants merely borrowed passage money from a broker; unlike indentured servants, they retained their personal freedom and the right to choose their employers.

Once they arrived, however, Chinese immigrants normally entered the orbit of the Six Companies—a powerful confederation of Chinese merchants in San Francisco's Chinatown. Most of the arrivals were unattached males eager to earn a stake and return to their native Cantonese villages. The Six Companies not only acted as an employment agency but provided them with the social and commercial services they needed to survive in an alien world. The few Chinese women—the male/female ratio was thirteen to one—worked mostly as servants and prostitutes, sad victims of the desperate poverty that drove the Chinese to America. Some were sold by impoverished parents; others had been enticed into fraudulent marriages or kidnapped by procurers and transported to America.

Until the early 1860s, when surface mining played out, Chinese men labored mainly in the California goldfields—as prospectors where the white miners permitted it, as laborers and cooks where they did not. Then, when construction began on the transcontinental railroad, the Central Pacific hired Chinese workers. Eventually they constituted four-fifths of the railroad's labor force, doing most of the pick-and-shovel labor laying the railroad tracks across the Sierras. The Central Pacific perfected a system of contract labor for employing the Chinese. Many were recruited directly from around Canton by labor agents and worked in labor gangs

Building the Central Pacific
Chinese laborers at work on the great trestle spanning the canyon at Secrettown in the Sierra Nevada.

under the control of "China bosses," who not only supervised but fed, housed, paid, and often cheated them.

When the transcontinental railroad was completed in 1869, the Chinese scattered. Some continued to work in construction gangs for the railroads, while others labored on swamp-drainage and irrigation projects in the Central Valley and then became agricultural workers and, if they were lucky, small farmers and orchardists. The mining districts of Idaho, Montana, and Colorado also attracted large numbers of Chinese, but according to the 1880 census nearly three-quarters remained in California. In San Francisco many of them became factory workers. The Chinese were excluded from higher-wage trades, but they soon dominated certain industries—such as cigar making—that competed with eastern products and could survive only with cheap labor. "Wherever we put them, we found them good," remarked Charles Crocker, one of the promoters of the Central Pacific. From the standpoint of employers, "their orderly and industrious habits make them a very desirable class of immigrants."

The Anti-Chinese Agitation. White workers, however, did not share this enthusiasm for Chinese labor. Why they should have taken so venomous a view of the Chinese has never been easy to explain. It involved, most certainly, a sense of unfair economic competition that pitted them against "Chinamen's wages" and "Chinamen's living conditions." But the hatred clearly went deeper. In other parts of the country, racism was directed against African-Americans; in California, where there were few blacks, it found a target in the Chinese. They were "an infusible element" who could not be assimilated into American society, wrote the young jour-

nalist Henry George in a famous 1869 letter that made his reputation as a spokesman for California labor. "They practice all the unnameable vices of the East. [They are] utter heathens, treacherous, sensual, cowardly and cruel." Sadly, this vicious racism was intertwined with labor's republican ideals. The Chinese, argued George, would drive out free labor, "make nabobs and princes of our capitalists, and crush our working classes into the dust . . . substitut[ing] . . . a population of serfs and their masters for that population of intelligent freemen who are our glory and our strength."

The anti-Chinese agitation climaxed in San Francisco in the late 1870s when mobs ruled the streets, at one point threatening to burn the docks of the Pacific Mail Steamship Company at which the Chinese arrivals landed. The fiercest agitator, an Irish teamster named Denis Kearney, quickly became a dominant figure in the California labor movement. Under the slogan "The Chinese Must Go!" Kearney led a Workingmen's party that strongly challenged the state's major parties. Democrats and Republicans, however, jumped on the bandwagon, joining together in 1879 to write a new state constitution replete with anti-Chinese provisions and pressuring Washington to take up the issue. Finally, after renegotiating the Burlingame Treaty (1868) that had granted China most-favored-nation trade status, Congress in 1882 passed the Chinese Exclusion Act, which barred the further entry of Chinese laborers into the country.

Chinese immigration effectively came to an end, but not the job opportunities that had attracted the Chinese in the first place. If anything, the West's agricultural development intensified the demand for cheap labor, especially in California, which was shifting from wheat, the state's first great cash crop, to fruits and vegetables.

This intensive agriculture required lots of workers: stoop labor, meagerly paid and mostly seasonal. This was not, as one San Francisco journalist put it, "white men's work." That ugly phrase serves as a touchstone for California agricultural labor as it would thereafter develop—a kind of caste labor system, always drawing some downtrodden, footloose whites into it, yet basically defined along color lines. But if not the Chinese, then who? First, Japanese immigrants, who came in increasing numbers and by the early twentieth century constituted half of the state's agricultural labor force. Then, when anti-Japanese agitation closed off that population flow in 1908, Mexico became the next, essentially permanent, provider of migratory workers for California's booming commercial agriculture.

The irony of the state's social evolution is painful to behold. Here was California, a land of limitless opportunity, boastful of its democratic egalitarianism. Yet simultaneously, and from its very birth, it was a racially torn society, at once exploiting and despising the Hispanic and Asian minorities whose hard labor helped make California the enviable land it was.

The Golden West

The hundreds of thousands of fortune seekers who descended on California changed everything. Mineral wealth poured in, first from the gold country, then from Nevada's Comstock lode, and finally from mining sites up and down the Far West. Railroad building accelerated and agriculture boomed. California counted over a million residents by 1890, fully a quarter of them living in San Francisco.

Life in California contained all that the modern world of 1890 had to offer—a cosmopolitan city, com-

Market Scene, Sansome Street
This exuberant painting by William Hahn captures downtown San Francisco as he saw it in 1872, a veritable boiling pot of races (note the black woman at left and the Chinese group at right) and classes (note, in the middle of the market bustle, the proper lady at far left with her Lord Fauntleroy son). It was its role as metropolis for the entire Far West that gave San Francisco the great vitality conveyed in this painting. (Crocker Art Museum)

fortable travel, a high living standard, colleges and universities, and even resident painters and writers. Yet California was still remote from the rest of America, still a long journey away and, of course, differently and spectacularly endowed by nature. Location, environment, and history all conspired to set California somewhat apart from the American nation. And so, in certain ways, did the Californians.

California Culture. What Californians yearned for was a cultural tradition of their own. Closest to hand was the bonanza era of the Forty-Niners. California had the great good fortune of attracting to its parts one Samuel Clemens. Clemens arrived in the Nevada Territory in 1861, did a bit of prospecting, became a reporter in Nevada City, and adopted the pen name Mark Twain. In 1864 he left for San Francisco, where he became a newspaper columnist writing about what he pronounced "the livest, heartiest community on our continent."

Exiled briefly in 1865 to Angel's Camp in the Sierra foothills because his sharp pen had made him dangerous enemies, Twain listened to the tales of the old miners from the neighborhood. One he jotted in his notebook, as follows:

> Coleman with his jumping frog—bet stranger $50— stranger had no frog, and C. got him one:—in the meantime stranger filled C's frog full of shot and he couldn't jump. The stranger's frog won.

In Twain's hands this fragment was transformed into a tall tale that caught the imagination of the country and made his reputation as a humorist. What "The Celebrated Jumping Frog of Calaveras County" had somehow encapsulated was the entire world of make-or-break optimism in the mining camps.

In short stories such as "The Luck of Roaring Camp" and "The Outcasts of Poker Flat," Twain's fellow San Franciscan Bret Harte developed this theme in a more literary fashion and firmly implanted it in California's memory. Other writers—among them the amateur historian Charles Howard Shinn in his *Mining Camps: A Study in American Frontier Government* (1885)—gave a more serious gloss to California's bonanza origins. Even so, this past was too raw, too suggestive of the tattered beginnings of so many of the state's leading citizens—in short, too disreputable—for an up-and-coming society.

Then, in 1884, Helen Hunt Jackson published her novel *Ramona*. In this story of a half-caste girl caught between two cultures, Jackson intended to advance the cause of the Indians, but she placed her tale in the evocative context of Old California, and that rang a bell. By then the Spanish missions—disestablished by the Mexican government in 1833, long before the influx of Yankees—had fallen into total disrepair and the padres were wholly forgotten, their Indian acolytes scattered and in dire poverty. Now that lost world of "sun, silence and adobe" became all the rage. Sentimental novels and histories appeared in abundance, and there was a movement to restore the missions. The Spanish-Mexican dons of the great ranchos became larger in death than they had ever been in life. Many communities began to stage Spanish fiestas, and the mission style of architecture enjoyed a great vogue among developers.

In its Spanish past California found the cultural traditions it needed. The same kind of discovery was taking place elsewhere in the Southwest, although in the case of Santa Fe and Taos there were live Hispanic roots to celebrate.

Land of Sunshine. All this enthusiasm was of course strongly tinged with commercialism, as was a second distinctive feature of California's development. The southern part of the state was neglected, thinly populated, and too dry for anything but grazing and some chancy wheat growing. What it did have, however, was an abundance of sunshine. At the beginning of the 1880s there burst upon the country amazing news about the charms of southern California. "There is not any malaria, hay fever, loss of appetite, or languor in the air; nor any thunder, lightning, mad dogs . . . or cold snaps." This publicity was mostly the work of the Southern Pacific Railroad, which had reached Los Angeles in 1876 and was eager for business. When the Santa Fe arrived in 1885, a furious rate war broke out and it became possible to travel from Chicago or St. Louis to Los Angeles for $25 or less. Thousands of people, mostly midwesterners, poured in; a dizzying real estate boom developed, along with the frantic building of resort hotels such as San Diego's opulent Hotel del Coronado. Los Angeles County had less than 3 percent of the state's population in 1870; it had 12 percent by 1900. Although the real estate bubble burst at the end of the 1880s, by then southern California had firmly established itself as the land of sunshine and orange groves. It had found a way to translate climate into riches.

The Great Outdoors. That California was specially favored by nature some Californians knew even as the great stands of redwoods and sugar pine were being hacked down, the soil depleted by the relentless cycle of wheat crops, the streams polluted, and the hills torn apart by reckless mining techniques. Back in 1864 influential Americans who had seen it prevailed on Congress to grant to the state of California "the Cleft, or Gorge in the granite peak of the Sierra Nevada Mountain, known as Yosemite Valley," which would be reserved "for public pleasuring, resort, and recreation." When the young naturalist John Muir arrived in California four years later, he headed straight for Yosemite. Its "grandeur . . . comes as an endless revelation," he

Kitty Tatch and Friend on Glacier Point, Yosemite
From the time the Yosemite Valley was set aside in 1864 as a place for "public pleasuring, resort, and recreation," it attracted a stream of tourists eager to experience the grandeur of the American West. As is suggested by this photograph taken sometime in the 1890s, the magic of Yosemite was enough to set even staid young ladies dancing.

wrote. Muir, and others like him, became devoted to studying the High Sierras and protecting them from "despoiling gain-seekers . . . eagerly trying to make everything immediately and selfishly commercial." One result was the creation of California's national parks in 1890—Yosemite, Sequoia, and King's Canyon. Another was the formation in 1892 of the Sierra Club, which became a powerful voice of the defenders of California's wilderness.

They won some and lost some. In particular, there was an uphill battle against the advocates of water-resource development, who insisted that California's irrigated agriculture and thirsty cities could not grow without tapping the abundant snowpack of the Sierras. By the turn of the century, Los Angeles faced a water crisis that threatened its growth. The answer was a 238-mile aqueduct to the Owens River in the southern Sierras. A bitter controversy blew up over this immense project, driven by objections by local residents and

preservationists to the damming up of the beautiful Owens Valley. More painful was the defeat suffered by John Muir and his allies in their battle to save the Hetch Hetchy gorge north of Yosemite National Park. In 1913, after years of controversy, the federal government approved the damming of Hetch Hetchy to serve the water needs of San Francisco.

When the development stakes became high enough, nature lovers like John Muir generally came out on the short end. Even so, something original and distinctive had been added to California's heritage—the linking of a society's well-being with the preservation of its natural environment.

The Agricultural Interest

In certain grain-growing areas, such as California's Central Valley until the 1890s, farmers might be large-scale and even corporate operators. In the South after Reconstruction the typical farmer was a tenant or sharecropper. Elsewhere, and most commonly, farmers were independent freeholders operating family farms. The freeholder tradition was deeply rooted in the Jeffersonian ideal of a country of independent farmers, an ideal enshrined in the national policy of providing land from the public domain for homesteaders. In an age of trusts and corporations, farmers succeeded as did no other group in retaining the *forms* of economic independence. But their *functions* took them far from the self-sufficient yeoman farmer tradition of Jeffersonian America. American farmers had, for better or worse, been fully inducted into the modern economic order.

The Farming Business

With the settlement of the Great Plains, the regional patterns of American agriculture (see Map 17.7) became well defined. The wheat belt lay on the western edge of the Midwest, from North Dakota down to Kansas and into northern Texas. Wheat had always been a virgin crop, the first to be planted when new land opened up. As the frontier moved on, wheat growing moved steadily westward. It settled on the Great Plains, where hardy European strains resisted the harsh climate and produced a bread flour superior to that from the soft-kerneled wheat of milder regions. On the wheat-producing Columbia plateau in the Northwest, Spanish and Australian varieties did best. In the Midwest the main crop was corn—feed for the nation's livestock. North of the corn belt, dairy farming stretched from Minnesota as far east as New York and New England. In California wheat growing gave way to orange groves, fruit orchards, vineyards, and vegetable crops. Cotton

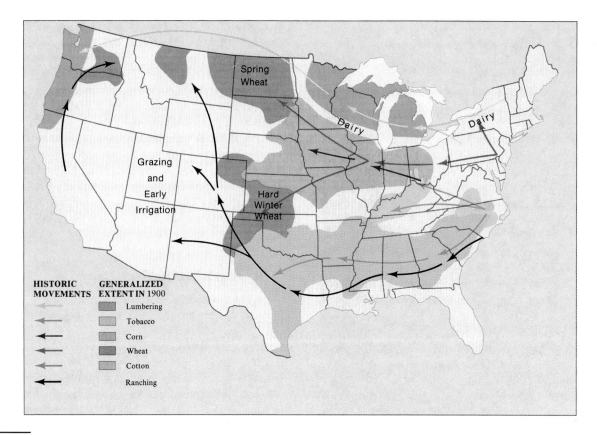

MAP 17.7

Agricultural Regions, 1900
The development of agricultural regions reflected the commercial bent of American agriculture—that is, farmers raised crops for market rather than for home consumption. Regional specialization matched climate and soil to the most suitable crops. The westward movement carried crops westward, of course. Wheat, generally a first crop choice in frontier areas, was concentrated finally on the northern and central plains and in the Northwest. By 1900 the basic pattern of crop specialization was well established in the United States.

dominated southern agriculture, spreading during the last third of the nineteenth century westward from the old Cotton Kingdom into Texas and northward into Oklahoma and Arkansas.

General farming, in which no crop represented as much as 40 percent of a farm's total production, was still common; and so was subsistence farming in areas, such as New England and the southern Appalachians, where the terrain was hilly and infertile. But a cash crop was what farmers wanted, and that preference made for the remarkable regional specialization of American agriculture. "The old rule that a farmer should produce all he required is part of the past," remarked one farm journal. "Agriculture, like all other business, is better for its subdivisions, each one growing that which is best suited for his soil, skill, climate and market, and with its proceeds purchasing his other needs."

Specialization in cash crops was one manifestation of the commercial bent of American farmers. Another was their attitude toward land. Americans had little of

the passionate identification with the soil that tied European peasants to their inherited plots. In 1910 more than half of American farmers had moved within the previous five years. Farmers saw their acreage as a commodity. In frontier areas, where newly developed land appreciated rapidly, they anticipated as much profit, if not more, from the land's value as from the crops it produced. Nor were farmers averse to borrowing money. In boom times they rushed into debt to buy more land and better farm equipment. They relished the innovations of the industrial age, especially the railroad. They happily supported whatever inducements that might be necessary, such as the public purchase of railway bonds, to lure a line to their towns. All these enthusiasms—for cash crops, land speculation, borrowed money, and new technology—bore witness to the conviction that farming was a business, "like all other business."

The bedrock of their commercial identity was the larger economic system in which they were situated: farmers stood at the center of a vast and complex net-

work of trade and industry. A sophisticated array of commodity exchanges determined prices and found buyers throughout the country and beyond. Great processing industries turned wheat into flour, livestock into dressed meat, and fruits and vegetables into canned goods. Entire rail systems, port facilities, and fleets of ships were devoted to moving the products of American farmers. All this activity gave farmers access to the expanding urban markets in the United States and overseas; about 20 percent of American agricultural production went abroad during the late nineteenth century. American farmers were likewise abundantly supplied with modern goods and services. The capital they needed came, via mortgage companies and banks, from distant eastern and European lenders. The McCormick Reaper Company, John Deere, and other manufacturers sold them labor-saving farm machinery that cut production costs for the leading crops by about half between 1850 and 1900.

No one could deny that the result was an agricultural system of amazing abundance; farm output more than tripled between 1860 and 1900. To an Austrian observer reflecting on the scarcity that had always been humankind's lot, the surplus produced by American agriculture seemed "the greatest event of modern times."

Agrarian Distress

Somehow this triumph of American agriculture as a productive system did not translate into good times on the farm. On the contrary, the late nineteenth century was a time of deep agricultural discontent.

Farm Life. The grievances of farmers stemmed partly from the harshness of rural life. No one labored longer or harder. Farmers worked an average of sixty-eight hours a week in 1900, twelve hours longer than industrial workers; in 1850 the difference had been only six hours. Mechanization did not actually reduce the workload on farms, as it generally did in factories. Crop acreage tended to increase in step with more efficient planting and harvesting machinery. Most other chores remained on the farmer's shoulders.

For women, too, farming demanded unrelenting labor. Like other work in America, farm work was sextyped. Except under dire necessity, northern farm women did not labor in the fields after the pioneering days. It was true that substantial numbers of widows and single women ran farms on their own—300,000 were recorded in the 1900 census—but the evidence suggests that these women mostly relied on hired hands for the heavy field work. In the South, especially among poor tenant farmers, it was different; wives, both black and white, commonly went into the fields, making "a full hand at whatever the occasion demands—plowing, hoeing, chopping, putting down fertilizer, picking cotton."

Even without working in the fields, however, farm women contributed crucially to the farm enterprise. Farming could be thought of as a "dual economy" in which men's labor brought in the big payment at season's end while women's labor provisioned the family day by day and produced a steady bit of money for groceries. And if the crop failed, it was women's labor that carried the family through. No wonder rural society placed a high premium on marriage: a mere 2.4 percent of Nebraska women in 1900 had never married. The western farmer was well advised to take a wife for the "pecuniary advantage in the domestic economy of his household."

Throughout rural America, children, as soon as they were old enough, pitched in with the farm chores and field work. "Many a time a shudder has passed through the mother heart of me," said a Missouri woman, "at the sight of some little fellow struggling with the handles of a plow, jerking and stumbling over cloddy ground from daylight till dark. Boys 'making a full hand,' 'helping Pa.'" Farm children in 1900 attended school only two-thirds as many days as did city children, and they left school at an earlier age. In an era of rapidly advancing urban education farm children still attended gloomy, ungraded one-room schools—hardly the little red schoolhouses of popular mythology.

Rural Schooling
In one-room schoolhouses, such as this one, probably in Colorado, farm children got the rudiments of an education. Teaching offered one of the few opportunities for rural women to support themselves and obtain a paying job, albeit for very skimpy wages.

Farm families might have accepted how hard they labored, how the men and women were worn out and the children sacrificed, for the living they wrested from the soil. It was harder to swallow the widening discrepancy in the quality of life between farm and city. Electricity, indoor plumbing, and paved roads had not yet come to the farm. Work in the kitchen remained almost unaffected by appliances that were already commonplace in many urban homes. Laundry was "the most trying" of all household chores, involving long hours spent lugging and boiling water, bent over washtubs and rubbing boards. Even on well-equipped farms, a Michigan woman observed, "the women must still do the work much as their mothers did before." "I have in mind a small, delicate woman," wrote another woman from Pennsylvania, "with a family of small children who does all her own housework, milks four or five cows, cooks for extra help, carries from the spring all the water—no time to read a paper or book. . . . Yet neither [her husband] nor she has any idea they could make her burden easier."

The isolation of homesteading was most severely felt on the Great Plains, with its cruel winters and long, empty distances. Farm life everywhere, however, tended to be lonely and circumscribed. Rural neighborhoods, even in long-settled areas, totaled 3 or 4 square miles where perhaps a dozen families lived. As one writer remarked, "the end of the neighborhood was almost the end of the world." Hamlin Garland and other authors of the late nineteenth century wrote powerfully about the dullness of the countryside and the lure of the city. "I hate farm life," grumbled one of Garland's heroines. "It's nothing but fret, fret and work the whole time, never going any place, never seeing anybody but a lot of neighbors just as big fools as you are. I spend my time fighting flies and washing dishes and churning. I'm sick of it all."

Understandably, when farmers formed organizations they provided for social activity first of all. This was true of the National Grange of the Patrons of Husbandry, whose local granges spread by the thousands across rural America in the early 1870s. The Grange became the social center for farm families through its fraternal ceremonies and its dances, picnics, and lectures. Women and men joined on an equal footing. Oliver H. Kelley, the government clerk who founded the Grange in 1867, hoped that participation by "the young folks of both sexes . . . will have a tendency to instill in their minds a fondness of rural life, and prevent in great measure so many of them flocking to the cities."

Economic Problems. The hunger for social activity cemented organizational ties, but the dynamism of agrarian movements came from economic grievances. The farmers' basic problem was their imperfect participation in the economic transformations of the late nineteenth century. They remained individual operators in a business world that was becoming ever more complex and highly organized. And they were, in certain ways, acutely aware of their predicament. They understood, for example, the disadvantages they faced as individuals dealing with the big businesses that supplied them with machinery, arranged their credit, and marketed their products.

Farmers had first formed cooperatives, mostly stores and creameries, before the Civil War. The Grange took up the cooperative idea in a big way by purchasing in bulk from suppliers and by setting up cooperative banks, insurance companies, grain elevators, and processing plants. The Iowa Grange even started to manufacture farm implements in 1873.

Unfortunately, opposition by private business was too unrelenting, cooperative managers too unskilled, and the pooled resources of the farmers too thin. Most of the Grange cooperatives eventually failed. The cooperative idea, however, was highly resilient and would be revived by every successive farmers' movement. Ultimately, in the twentieth century, rural cooperatives of many kinds—marketing unions, stores, grain elevators, telephone exchanges—would dot the countryside. The farmers' hostility to middlemen also left as a legacy the great mail-order house of Montgomery Ward, which had been founded in 1872 to serve Grange members. As a solution to the organizational weakness of the farmer in the marketplace, however, cooperative movements had to be accounted a failure.

The power of government, however, might be enlisted to do for farmers what they could not do for themselves. The Grange was itself a social-educational organization, but in the early 1870s it encouraged the formation of independent political parties that ran on antimonopoly platforms. The main targets were grain elevator companies and railroads that routinely cheated farmers (so they felt) on storage charges, wheat grading, and freight rates. In a number of prairie states these agrarian parties won control of the legislature and passed so-called Granger laws regulating grain elevators, fixing maximum railroad rates, and prohibiting discriminatory practices against small and short-haul shippers. Constitutional difficulties arose, however, over the question of whether the states were exceeding their police powers when they tried to regulate interstate commerce. In *Wabash v. Illinois* (1886) the Supreme Court decided that they were, voiding an Illinois law that prohibited long- and short-haul rate discrimination and putting all the Granger laws in jeopardy. By then, however, a movement had started for federal regulation of the railroads. The Interstate Commerce Act (1887) created the Inter-

TABLE 17.1

Freight Rates for Transporting Crops

Grand Island to Omaha (150 miles)				Grand Island to Chicago (650 miles)			
Date effective	Corn	Wheat (in cents per hundredweight)	Oats	Date effective	Corn	Wheat (in cents per hundredweight)	Oats
January 1, 1883	18	19½	18	January 7, 1880	32	45	32
April 16, 1883	15	16½	15	September 15, 1882	38	43	38
January 10, 1884	18	19½	18	April 5, 1887	34	39	34
March 1, 1884	17	19½	17	November 1, 1887	25	30	25
August 25, 1884	20	20	20	March 21, 1890	22½	30	25
April 5, 1887	10	16	10	October 22, 1890	22	26	22
November 1, 1887	10	12	10	January 15, 1891	23	28	25

Source: Sigmund Diamond, ed., *The Nation Transformed* (New York: George Braziller, 1963), p. 352.

state Commerce Commission—the first federal regulatory agency—and made railroad regulation a permanent part of national public policy, although not with much practical effect for the next twenty years.

Farmers turned to cooperatives and government regulation out of a deep sense of organizational disadvantage. But that disadvantage, real as it was, did not really account for the unprofitability of farming in these years. Manufacturers and banks lacked the degree of market control ascribed to them by angry farmers. The much-maligned mortgage companies actually could not rig credit markets in the western states; their interest rates matched those in the rest of the country. Nor, for the period 1865–1890, could manufacturers establish a relative price advantage over agriculture. In fact, the wholesale prices of all commodities fell at a slightly faster rate than did farm prices during these years. And on the railroads, freight rates fell steadily and East-West differentials narrowed as improved technology reduced operating costs and the volume of western traffic increased (see Table 17.1).

The Wheat and Cotton Belts. The impact of the general fall in prices, or *deflation*, did have dire consequences for certain kinds of farmers, however. First, there were those whose crops were subject to wider, more unpredictable price swings—namely, cotton and wheat. The second category of farmers at risk in deflationary periods were those in debt, since falling prices forced them to pay back more in real terms than they had borrowed. And who was most deeply in debt? The same two groups: cotton and wheat farmers.

The nature of their indebtedness was different. Tenant farmers growing cotton normally got credit from the local furnishing merchant to carry them through the growing season, with the crop serving as collateral. The debt was short-term but nevertheless painfully hard if they had to repay with earnings reduced by falling cotton prices. For wheat farmers, indebtedness was a more deep-seated and entangling problem because, in the nineteenth century, wheat was characteristically a virgin-land crop. Settling new land meant going into debt to start up—to pay for machinery, fencing, a new house, and so on. So wheat farmers were frequently debtors. And if, as commonly occurred in frontier areas, a speculative spirit took hold and land prices were bid up, the debt burdens of newly mortgaged farmers could become insupportable when prices dropped.

This happened, for example, in Harrison Township, Nebraska, which was first settled in 1872. Land that sold for $8 an acre in 1880 brought $25 and up a few years later. Given wheat prices in the late 1880s, an investigator noted, no one taking out a mortgage to buy land at $25 an acre could hope to meet the payments at 6 percent interest. "One is almost tempted to draw the moral that the would-be purchaser . . . had almost better throw his money away than invest it in farming operations in Nebraska."

In the 1870s the major wheat-growing states had been Illinois, Wisconsin, and Minnesota. Those states had been at the center of the Granger agitation of that decade. By the 1880s wheat had moved on to the Great Plains. Among the indebted wheat farmers of Kansas, Nebraska, and the Dakotas, along with the cotton farmers of the South, the deflationary economy of the 1880s made for stubbornly hard times. All it would take was a sharp drop in world prices for wheat and cotton to bring on a real crisis.

Summary

In 1860 the Great Plains were still the ancestral home of nomadic Indian tribes that had built a vibrant society based on the horse and the buffalo. By 1890 the Indians had been crowded onto reservations and forced to abandon their tribal way of life. With railroads leading the way, cattle ranchers and homesteaders in short order displaced the Indians and domesticated the Great Plains. Beyond the Rockies, a different pattern of settlement occurred. Because so much of this region was arid and uninhabitable, occupation took the form of oases of settlement rather than the progressive occupation along a broad frontier that had prevailed east of the Rockies. And while arable land had been the lure for settlers up to that point, what drove settlement beyond the Rockies was the discovery of mineral wealth. For the entire trans-Mississippi West, the pace of occupation was accelerated by the nation's economic development. Industry needed the West's mineral resources; the cities demanded agricultural products; and, from railroads to barbed wire, the industrial economy provided the means for a swift and decisive conquest of the West.

By population, economy, and strategic position, California was the regional power dominating the Far West in the late nineteenth century. It was the anchor both of a crescent of Hispanic settlement to the southwest and of the Pacific slope region stretching up to the Canadian border. The discovery of gold had set off a huge migration that overwhelmed the thinly spread Hispanic inhabitants and swiftly transformed California into a populous state with a large urban sector. California developed a distinctive culture that capitalized on its rediscovered Hispanic heritage and its climate and natural environment. The treatment of the Chinese, Japanese, and Mexicans who provided the state with cheap labor, however, infused a dark streak of racism into its society.

The settlement of the West completed a national agricultural development characterized by regional crop specialization. American farming became integrated into the modern industrial order. However, that integration was imperfect, in particular because farming remained a family operation in an economy increasingly dominated by large-scale enterprise. Most aggrieved, and most prepared to protest, were the cotton farmers of the South and the wheat farmers of the Great Plains.

TIMELINE

1849	California Gold Rush Chinese migration begins
1862	Homestead Act
1864	Yosemite Valley reserved as public park
1865	Long Drive of Texas longhorns begins
1867	Patrons of Husbandry (the Grange) founded U.S. government adopts reservation policy for Plains Indians
1868	Indian treaty confirms Sioux rights to Powder River hunting grounds
1869	Union Pacific–Central Pacific transcontinental railroad completed
1874	Barbed wire invented
1875	Sioux ordered to vacate Powder River hunting grounds; war breaks out
1876	Battle of Little Big Horn
1877	San Francisco anti-Chinese riots
1879	Exoduster migration to Kansas
1882	Chinese Exclusion Act
1884	Helen Hunt Jackson's novel *Ramona*
1886	Dry cycle begins on the Great Plains *Wabash v. Illinois*
1887	Dawes Severalty Act Interstate Commerce Act
1889	Oklahoma opened to white settlement
1890	Indian massacre at Wounded Knee, South Dakota U.S. census declares end of the frontier

BIBLIOGRAPHY

Western history has become a bitterly contested ground in recent years. The fountainhead of the voluminous traditional scholarship is Frederick Jackson Turner's famous essay "The Significance of the Frontier in American History" (1893), reprinted in Ray A. Billington, ed., *Frontier and Section: Selected Essays of Frederick Jackson Turner* (1961). The most comprehensive recent Turnerian history is Ray A. Billington and Martin Ridge, *Westward Expansion: A History of the American Frontier*, 5th ed. (1982). The "new" western history is critical of Turnerian scholarship for being "Eurocentric"—for seeing this history only through the eyes of frontiersmen and settlers—and for masking the rapacious and environmentally destructive underside of western settlement. Patricia N. Limerick's skillfully argued *The Legacy of Conquest: The Unbroken Past of the American West* (1987) opened the debate. Richard White, *"It's Your Misfortune and None of My Own": A New History of the American West* (1991), provides the fullest synthesis of the new scholarship. For an authoritative, balanced treatment of the main themes of western history, see the essays in Clyde A. Milner II et al., *The Oxford History of the American West* (1994). On women's experience—another primary concern of the new western history—the starting point is Susan Armitage and Elizabeth Jameson, eds., *The Women's West* (1987). There are incisive environmental essays in Donald Worster, *Under Western Skies: Nature and History in the American West* (1992). For the period covered by this chapter, see Rodman Paul, *The Far West and the Great Plains in Transition, 1859–1900* (1988).

The Great Plains

The classic book, stressing the settlers' adaptation to climate and environment, is Walter P. Webb, *The Great Plains* (1931). There is an excellent chapter on the ecological history of the southern plains in Donald Worster, *The Dust Bowl* (1979). Robert M. Utley, *The Indian Frontier of the American West, 1846–1890* (1984), is a good introduction and Robert H. Lowie, *Indians of the Great Plains* (1954), is a classic anthropological study. On the religious life of the Plains Indians, see Howard L. Harrod, *Renewing the World: Plains Indians Religion and Morality* (1987). The best study of white attitudes is Richard Drinnon, *Facing West: The Metaphysics of Indian-Hating and Empire-Building* (1980). On phases of plains settlement see Oscar Winther, *The Transportation Frontier: The Trans-Mississippi West, 1865–1890* (1964); Lewis Atherton, *The Cattle Kings* (1964); Everitt Dick, *Sod-House Frontier* (1954); and Mary W. M. Hargreaves, *Dry-Farming in the Northern Great Plains* (1954). The peopling of the plains can be explored in Craig Miner, *West of Wichita: Settling the High Plains of Kansas 1865–1890* (1986); Frederick C. Luebke, ed., *Ethnicity and the Great Plains* (1980); Nell Irvin Painter, *Exodusters: Black Migration to Kansas after Reconstruction* (1976); Julie Roy Jeffrey, *Frontier Women: The Trans-Mississippi West, 1840–1880* (1979); and Glenda Riley, *The Female Frontier: A Comparative View of the Prairie and the Plains* (1988). On the integration of the plains economy with the wider world, an especially rich book is William Cronon, *Nature's Metropolis: Chicago and the Great West* (1991). Richard Slotkin, *The Fatal Environment: The Myth of the Frontier in the Age of Industrialization, 1800–1890* (1985), deals with the process by which Americans translated the hard realities of conquering the West into a national mythology.

California and the Far West

The best book on western mining is Rodman Paul, *Mining Frontiers of the Far West: 1848–1880s* (1963). An important case study of women in a mining town is Paula Petrik, *Women and Family on the Rocky Mountain Frontier: Helena, Montana, 1865–1900* (1987). On western miners the standard book is Mark Wyman, *Hard Rock Epic: Western Miners and the Industrial Revolution, 1860–1910* (1979). Two valuable regional histories are Carlos A. Schwantes, *The Pacific Northwest: An Interpretive History* (1989), and Donald W. Meinig, *Southwest: Three Peoples in Geographical Change, 1600–1970* (1971). A very imaginative recent treatment of the New Mexico peasantry is Sarah Deutsch, *No Separate Refuge* (1987). On Hispanic Texas an important book is David Montejano, *Anglos and Mexicans in the Making of Texas* (1987). Leonard Pitt, *The Decline of the Californios: A Social History of the Spanish-Speaking Californians, 1846–1890* (1960), offers a narrative history of that subject, with an emphasis on the fate of the large ranchers. Important local studies of laboring Hispanics and their communities are Mario T. Garcia, *Desert Immigrants: The Mexicans of El Paso, 1880–1920* (1981), and Richard Griswold del Castillo, *The Los Angeles Barrio, 1850–1890* (1979). On the Asian migration to America, the best introduction is Ronald Takaki, *Strangers from a Different Shore: A History of Asian Americans* (1989), which can be supplemented with Gunther Barth, *Bitter Strength: A History of the Chinese in the United States, 1850–1870* (1964), and Sucheng Chan, *This Bittersweet Soil: The Chinese in California Agriculture, 1860–1910* (1986). Labor's opposition to the Chinese is skillfully treated in Alexander Saxton, *The Indispensable Enemy: Labor and the Anti-Chinese Movement in California* (1971). Kevin Starr, *California and the American Dream, 1850–1915* (1973), provides a comprehensive account of the emergence of a distinctive California culture. On John Muir and the California wilderness, see Michael L. Smith, *Pacific Visions: California Scientists and the Environment, 1850–1915* (1987).

The Agricultural Interest

The standard works are Fred A. Shannon, *The Farmer's Last Frontier, 1860–1897* (1945); Gilbert Fite, *The Farmer's Frontier, 1865–1900* (1966); and Allan G. Bogue, *From Prairie to Corn Belt: Farming on the Illinois and Iowa Prairies in the Nineteenth Century* (1963). Most helpful on cotton farmers are the relevant chapters in Gavin Wright, *Old South, New South: Revolutions in the Southern Economy since the Civil War* (1986), and Edward L. Ayers, *The Promise of the New South: Life after Reconstruction* (1992). On farm women, see Deborah Fink, *Agrarian Women: Wives and Mothers in Rural Nebraska, 1880–1940* (1992), and Elaine Lindgren, *Land in Her Own Name: Women as Homesteaders in North Dakota* (1991). The flavor of farm life can best be captured in fiction: Hamlin Garland, *Main-Travelled Roads* (1891); Willa Cather, *My Antonia* (1918); and Ole E. Rölvaag, *Giants in the Earth* (1927).

Montgomery Ward & Co.

In 1872 Aaron Montgomery Ward began selling goods to rural customers through mail-order catalogues. Montgomery Ward, along with Sears, Roebuck & Co., represented one part of a revolution in American retailing, which included department stores and chain stores as well as the great mail-order houses.

CHAPTER 18

Capital and Labor in the Age of Enterprise

1877–1900

★ ★ ★

Reconstruction ended in 1877. That year also marked the end of the first great crisis in America's emerging system of industrial capitalism. In 1873, four years earlier, the major banking house Jay Cooke & Co. had failed, triggering a financial panic. In the economic depression that followed, 47,000 firms went under. Wholesale prices fell about 30 percent, railroad building almost ground to a halt, and orders for industrial goods disappeared. And with unemployment running as high as 25 percent, hundreds of thousands of workers lost their jobs. Suffering was widespread. Across the country workers demanded "bread for the needy, clothing for the naked, and houses for the homeless." Before long the foundations of the social order began to shake.

On July 16, 1877, railroad workers in West Virginia went on strike against the Baltimore and Ohio system to protest wage cuts. In railway towns along the B&O tracks crowds cheered as the strikers attacked company property and prevented trains from running. The strike spread quickly to other lines. In Pittsburgh the Pennsylvania Railroad roundhouse went up in flames on July 21, followed by the Union Depot the next day. Rioters and looters roamed freely. For nearly a week violent strikes swept other cities, including San Francisco, St. Louis, Omaha, and Chicago. President Rutherford B. Hayes called up the National Guard, which gradually restored order. On August 15, the president wrote in his diary: "The strikers have been put down *by force*." The Great Strike of 1877 had been crushed, but never had the nation edged so close to social revolution.

And then recovery came. Within months the economy was booming again. The march toward industrial power resumed. The physical output of manufactured goods increased over 150 percent between 1877 and 1890. The vitality of industrial capitalism renewed America's confidence in the future. "Can there be any

doubt that cheapening the cost of necessaries and conveniences of life is the most powerful agent of civilization and progress?" asked a railroad president in 1888. "History and experience demonstrate that . . . material progress must come first and . . . upon it is founded all other progress."

Industrial Capitalism Triumphant

Economic historians speak of the late nineteenth century as the age of the Great Deflation. Prices fell steadily worldwide, including in the United States. Following a brief upturn after 1877, wholesale prices declined by almost 30 percent between 1880 and 1892. Normally, falling prices are a sign of economic stagnation: there is not enough demand for the available goods and services. But that was not America's experience in these years. Because of increasing efficiencies in production and distribution, manufacturers were able both to cut prices *and* to earn profits and invest in better equipment. So that while in England, which was a mature industrial power, the Great Deflation did indeed signal economic decline, in the United States it was associated with dramatic industrial expansion (see Figure 18.1).

Basic Industry

By the 1870s manufacturing already had a long history in America. But the early factories were really appendages of the larger agricultural economy. They processed farm and forest products and, as in preindustrial times, relied on hand labor and water wheels for power. The goods they produced—textiles, boots and shoes, paper and furniture—were primarily consumer goods that replaced existing homemade or artisan-made products. Gradually, however, a different kind of demand developed. This was the result of the surging economic growth of the country. Railroads needed locomotives, new factories needed machinery, and the expanding cities needed vast quantities of building materials for trolley lines, sanitation systems, and commercial buildings. Locomotives, machinery, and construction materials were *capital goods*—that is, goods that themselves added to the productive capacity of the economy. While consumer goods remained very important, it was the manufacture of capital goods that became the core of America's industrial economy.

Iron and Steel. Central to this development was the shift from iron making to the manufacture of steel. An extensive metal-making industry already produced large quantities of wrought iron, whose malleability made it ideally suited for use by country blacksmiths and farmers. But wrought iron was expensive—it was produced in small batches by skilled puddlers and rollers—and did not stand up under heavy use as railway track. In 1856 the British inventor Henry Bessemer perfected a new process for refining iron. Unlike the puddling furnaces that made wrought iron, Bessemer converters produced steel—a harder, more durable metal—and did so in large amounts with little labor (see New Technology, page 553). Others took up this invention, but it was Andrew Carnegie who demonstrated its revolutionary importance.

Carnegie had arrived from Scotland in 1848 at the age of twelve with his poverty-stricken family. He became a telegraph operator and then went to work for the Pennsylvania Railroad and rapidly climbed the managerial ladder. Having become wealthy from a series of successful speculations, Carnegie resigned in 1865 to become an iron manufacturer. His main customers were his former associates in the railroad business.

Keenly aware of the possibilities of the Bessemer converter, Carnegie embarked in 1872 on a venture aimed at the fullest exploitation of the new refining

FIGURE 18.1

Business Activity and Wholesale Prices, 1869–1913
This graph shows the key feature concerning the performance of the late nineteenth-century economy: namely, that while output was booming, the price for goods was falling.

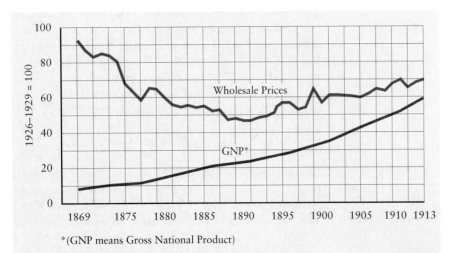

*(GNP means Gross National Product)

Iron and Steel

Iron was not a product new to the nineteenth century in the sense that plastic is new to the twentieth century. Early Europeans made iron tools and weapons at least a thousand years before Christ. Since those remote times the underlying processes have not changed, for these are dictated by the nature of iron metallurgy. What did change were the techniques for carrying out those processes.

The first break from ancient methods came when blast furnaces appeared in Belgium around 1340. Ore was melted in a charcoal-burning furnace to which limestone had been added. A blast of air then set off a combustion process that combined carbon from the charcoal with the molten iron while the impurities combined with the limestone to form a slag. The slag was drawn off from the top while the molten iron was tapped from the bottom into sand forms resembling piglets feeding from a sow—hence the term "pig iron."

By the late eighteenth century Great Britain was running out of wood for charcoal. The substitution of coke, made by superheating coal, saved the industry and gave Britain the competitive edge it needed to launch the Industrial Revolution. Endowed with ample forests, the United States was slow to adopt coke-using furnaces, but by 1860 it had caught up with Britain technologically.

The search for a metal harder and more durable than wrought iron resulted in the invention in 1856 of an entirely different refining process by the Englishman Henry Bessemer. The Bessemer converter was a pear-shaped vessel that was open at the top and had a bottom perforated by many holes. Molten pig iron flowed into the top while the converter was tilted on its side. Air was blasted through the perforated bottom with great force, and the converter then swung back to its upright position. The resulting combustion set off a spectacular display of flame and smoke. Within fifteen minutes, the impurities in the molten iron burned off and the flames died down. The converter was again tilted on its side, and after manganese and other chemicals had been added, the purified iron was emptied into ingot molds. The refined metal, called steel, was ideally suited for use as railroad track.

Bessemer's device, although invented primarily with the aim to gain a more durable metal, also proved vastly more efficient than the hand-operated puddling furnaces that produced wrought iron. The Bessemer converter turned out great quantities of steel with virtually no labor, and this forced changes up and down the line. To feed the converters' appetite for pig iron, blast fur-

The Bessemer Steel Furnace

naces were built larger and, with the introduction of the hot blast, became much faster. To handle the flow of steel from the converters, rolling mills became increasingly mechanized and automatic. The stages of production became integrated, which made the integrated steel plant of 1900—capable of producing 2,500 tons or more a day—a voracious consumer of ore and coal.

The commanding lead the United States had built up by 1900 rested on the world's best reserves of coking coal in western Pennsylvania and the vast ore deposits in Minnesota's Mesabi Range, northern Michigan's older fields, and Alabama.

The geographical face of American industrialism changed as the places best located in relation to raw materials, transportation, and markets—Pittsburgh, the steel towns along the Great Lakes, and Birmingham, Alabama—became the great centers of steel production. American cities relied on steel for the construction of skyscrapers, trolley lines, subways, and the vast underground complexes of pipe that supplied the urban millions with water and gas and carried away their sewage. Without steel, the emerging automobile industry would not have grown, nor would a host of other industries.

It is no wonder that historians have called the last decades of the nineteenth century America's Age of Steel. What was overlooked at the time and for long afterward was the fact that the nation's natural resources were not inexhaustible. It is the exhaustion of the great Mesabi Range that has leveled the playing field among global competitors and helped trigger the recent decline of the American steel industry.

process. He built a massive steel mill outside Pittsburgh that utilized the most advanced equipment of the day. Equally important, the mill integrated all the stages of production—smelting, refining, and rolling—into a single operation that began with iron ore and ended with finished steel rails. Carnegie's mill, which he named the Edgar Thompson Works after his admired former boss at the Pennsylvania Railroad, repaid its investment in a few years and became a model for the modern steel industry.

Large, integrated steel plants swiftly replaced the older blast furnaces and puddling mills. At first steel went mostly into railroad building; rails made up nearly three-quarters of the total output of steel in 1885. But thereafter, as railroad building slowed, the demand became more diversified. More and more steel went into bridges, skyscrapers, machinery, and a host of other industrial uses, such as pipes and tubing, sheet steel and wire, and armor for the nation's new navy.

Expanding the Industrial Base. The production of copper and other nonferrous metals went through a similar development. Before the Civil War, copper had been employed mainly in the manufacture of kettles, pots and pans, and other household products. Now it became a key ingredient in oil-refining equipment, electric generators, and other new products such as telephone cable. Copper output grew at a phenomenal rate, increasing from 14,000 tons in 1870 to 130,000 tons in 1890.

The growth of the metal industries depended on the intensive exploitation of the country's mineral resources. Major discoveries of rich iron ore deposits occurred from the 1850s onward, first in upper Michigan and then in the huge Mesabi Range of Minnesota. The Mesabi ore was shipped down the Great Lakes to the growing steelmaking centers in Pennsylvania, Ohio, and Illinois, giving the nearest lakeshore points, such as South Chicago and Gary, Indiana, a competitive advantage and contributing to the westward shift of the industry (see Map 18.1).

Coal mining, a minor enterprise before 1850, grew rapidly, first in the anthracite region of eastern Pennsylvania and then in the bituminous (soft coal) fields of western Pennsylvania and Ohio. The production of bituminous coal, the primary industrial fuel, doubled every decade after 1870 (see Table 18.1) and exceeded 400 million tons by 1910.

It was the insatiable energy needs of American industrialism that spurred this remarkable expansion in coal mining. Carnegie's blast furnaces and Bessemer converters burned prodigious amounts of coal. Coal-burning steam engines drove locomotives and ships and increasingly became the power source for factories. As much machinery was powered by steam engines as by water wheels by 1880; steam was six times as important twenty years later.

At the Philadelphia Centennial Exhibition of 1876 visitors gazed in wonder at the enormous Corliss reciprocating engine, which had a flywheel 30 feet in diameter and could drive all the other exhibits in Machinery Hall. The reciprocating engine, however, was superseded by the steam turbine in the 1880s. The turbine was an inherently superior design because it utilized continuous rotation rather than the back-and-forth motion of the reciprocating engine. These advances in turn

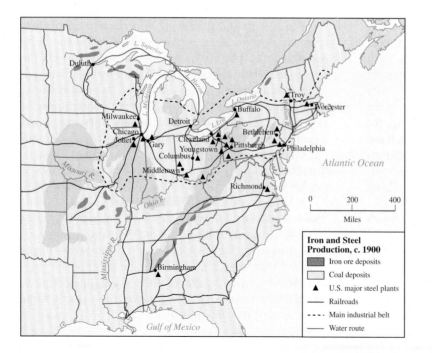

MAP 18.1

The Westward Movement of Iron and Steel Production

Before the Civil War, the iron industry was concentrated in eastern Pennsylvania and northern New Jersey. With the shift to steel and the westward movement of population and industry, production moved first to western Pennsylvania, and then to Ohio, Indiana, and Illinois and southward into Alabama. The specific locations—Pittsburgh, Youngstown, Chicago, Birmingham—were dictated by the rail network, new sources of coal and iron ore, and markets for steel.

TABLE 18.1

Increasing Output of Heavy Industry, 1870–1910

	Bituminous Coal (thousands of tons)	Rolled Iron and Steel (thousands of tons)	Copper (tons)	Industrial Machinery (millions of dollars)
1870	20,471	850*	14,112	110.4†
1880	50,757	3,301	30,240	98.6‡
1890	111,302	6,746	129,882	185.6
1900	212,318	10,626	303,059	347.6
1910	417,111	24,216	544,119	512.4

*Approximate total.
†Data for 1869.
‡Data for 1874.

The Corliss Engine
The symbol of the Philadelphia Centennial in 1876 was the great Corliss engine, which towered over Machinery Hall and powered all the equipment on exhibit there. Yet the Corliss engine also signified the incomplete nature of American industrialism at that time; it soon became obsolete. Westinghouse turbines generating electricity would be the power source for the nation's next great World's Fair in Chicago in 1893.

laid the basis for the next major innovation: the coupling of the steam turbine to the electric generator. After 1900 factories rapidly converted from steam to electric power.

Thus, in the decades after the Civil War the modern metal-producing industries were established, the nation's mineral resources came under intensive exploitation, and energy was harnessed to the manufacturing system. All these basic elements of modern industrialism—steel, coal, and energy output—grew after 1870 at rates far exceeding that of manufacturing production itself.

The Railroads

Much the largest demand for the capital goods mentioned in the previous section came from the railroads. They were the best customers for iron and steel, made the heaviest demands on the nation's machine-building capacity, and consumed a big portion of the coal it produced. Americans never doubted that they wanted railroads. Water transportation had developed impressively before the Civil War. But canal barges and riverboats, while good for carrying bulky raw materials, could not provide the year-round, on-time service demanded by the growing industrial economy.

Railroads had started in the 1830s as feeders linking river and canal traffic to inland towns and cities but quickly grew into a system that rivaled water transportation. By 1860, with a network of tracks already covering the states east of the Mississippi, the railroad clearly was going to be industrial America's mode of transportation (see Map 18.2).

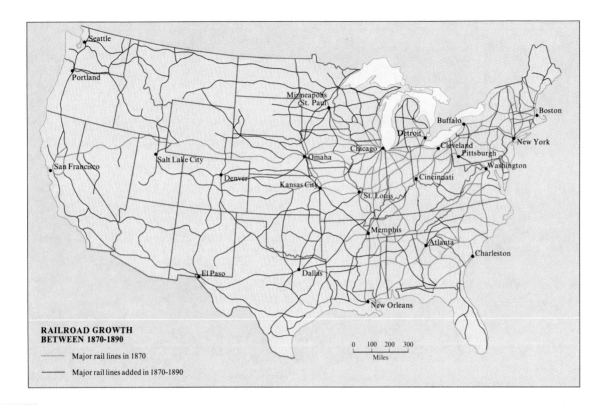

MAP 18.2

The Expansion of the Railroad System, 1870–1890

In 1870, the nation had 53,000 miles of rail track; in 1890, 167,000 miles. That burst of construction essentially completed the nation's rail network, although there would be additional expansion for the next two decades. The main areas of growth were in the South and west of the Mississippi. The Great Plains and the Far West accounted for over 40 percent of all railroad construction in this period.

The question was: Who would pay for railroad development? Two options were available. Railroads could be state enterprises, as the canals had been, supported by public funding as an internal improvement that would benefit the entire community. Or, alternatively, they could be treated as private enterprises financed by investors trying to make money.

The United States—unlike most European countries—chose to leave railroads to private enterprise, but there was no avoiding a big role for the government because of the huge public interest in getting the railroads built. Many towns and cities, for example, offered financial aid, mostly by subscribing for bonds, to attract railroads. States gave similar financial help, especially in the devastated South, where during Reconstruction railroads were seen as essential to economic recovery. States that had public domains, such as Texas and Maine, offered land grants to railroads. And land grants were the principal means by which the federal government encouraged interregional railroads, beginning in 1850 with the Illinois Central, which linked Chicago to the South, and culminating with huge grants to the transcontinental railroads because of the national inter-

est in tying the Far West to the rest of the country. Altogether, some 180 million acres were conveyed to the railroads from the state and federal domains.

The most important boost that government gave the railroads, however, was not money or land but a legal form of organization—the *corporation*—that enabled them to raise private capital in prodigious amounts. Those who bought stock in the railroads— and thus became their legal owners—enjoyed *limited liability*: they risked only the money they had invested; their personal assets could not be seized to pay the corporation's debts. A corporation also could borrow money by issuing interest-bearing bonds. Most of the money raised by the railroads came from bond issues; that is, it was borrowed money. Stock became a debased financial instrument, often given away to sweeten the sale of bonds or used by railroad promoters to gain control of other properties or reward themselves. Much of it represented no underlying value and was considered to be "watered."

The actual responsibility for railroad building generally was given over to a "construction company," which, despite the name, was really another part of the

elaborate financing system. Hiring and compensating the contractors and suppliers—the formal job of the construction company—often involved persuading them to accept the railroad's bonds as payment and, when that failed, wheeling and dealing to raise cash by selling or borrowing on the bonds. Since the promoters of the railroad and the owners of the construction company were one and the same, the opportunities for plunder were enormous. In the case of the most notorious construction company, the Union Pacific's Crédit Mobilier, probably half the building costs ended up in the pockets of the promoters.

Railroad promotion was not for the faint of heart. Most successful were promoters with the best access to capital—their own or that of others. John Murray Forbes, a great Boston merchant in the China trade, recruited New England money to develop the Chicago, Burlington and Quincy Railroad into the preeminent midwestern system. Cornelius Vanderbilt, who left the steamboat business in 1863 to become a railroad tycoon, was essentially a consolidator, tying together previously independent lines up the Hudson River and across New York State to form the New York Central Railroad. Vanderbilt and his son William built the Central into a trunk line to Chicago that was rivaled only by the Pennsylvania Railroad. James J. Hill, who without federal subsidy made the Great Northern into the best of all the transcontinental railroads, was certainly the nation's champion railroad builder. In contrast, Jay Gould, who at one time or another controlled the Erie, Wabash, Union Pacific, and Missouri Pacific systems, always remained a stock-market speculator at heart. Whether he was a *robber baron*—someone who loots commerce and gives nothing in return—can be answered only by closer inspection of his career (see American Lives, pages 558–559).

Railroad development in the United States was often sordid, fiercely competitive, and subject to boom and bust. When the Panic of 1893 hit, a third of the industry (by track mileage) went bankrupt. Yet there was no denying what had been achieved. Vast sums of capital had been raised—well over $10 billion, probably a quarter of it attracted from Europe—and the network that was built exceeded the trackage of the rest of the world combined. By 1900 virtually no corner of the country lacked rail service.

The Railway System. Accompanying this physical growth was the rising efficiency of railway transportation. The early system, built by competing local companies, had been a jumble of discontinuous segments. Gauges of track—the width between the rails—varied widely, and at terminal points railroads were not physically connected. Many rivers lacked railroad bridges. Also, each railroad company reserved the use of its track exclusively for its own equipment. As late as 1880 goods could not be shipped through from Massachu-

setts to South Carolina. Eight times along the way, freight cars had to be emptied, with the contents physically moved and loaded onto new cars across a river or at the other side of a city.

Beginning with the Civil War years, however, pressure increased for integration of the railroads. Track was hastily laid through Philadelphia, Richmond, and other cities to speed the shipment of troops and equipment. The postwar economy, as it grew more complex and interdependent, demanded a better-organized rail system. Much railroad integration took place through the expansion of great trunk lines such as the Pennsylvania, New York Central, and Illinois Central to connect different regions of the country. By the end of the 1880s a standard track gauge (4 feet 8 1/2 inches) had been adopted across the country. In 1883 the railroads rebelled against the jumble of local times that made scheduling a nightmare and, acting on their own, divided the country into the four standard time zones that we still use. Fast-freight firms and standard accounting procedures enabled shippers to use the railroad network as if it were a single unit, moving their goods without breaks in transit, transfers between cars, or the other delays that had once bedeviled them.

At the same time, railroad technology was advancing. With more durable steel rails in place, locomotives became heavier and more powerful, freight cars progressively larger, and freight trains longer. The Consolidation-type locomotive, with four sets of driving wheels, nearly tripled the pulling power of freight trains. To control the great mass and length of the new freight trains, the inventor George Westinghouse perfected the automatic coupler, the air brake, and the friction gear for starting and stopping a long line of cars. Costs per ton-mile fell by 50 percent between 1870 and 1890, resulting in a steady drop in freight rates for shippers.

The railroads brilliantly met the transportation needs of the maturing industrial economy. However, this achievement did not stem from any orderly plan or design; it sprang from the competitive energy of a freewheeling market economy. For the railroads, the costs of unrestrained growth were painfully high. On many routes there were too many railroads, and they fought for the available traffic by cutting rates to the bone. Many were saddled with huge bonded debt from the extravagant construction years; about a fifth of this volume of debt failed to pay interest even in a pretty good year such as 1889. So it was no wonder that when the economy turned bad, as it did in 1893, there were wholesale bankruptcies.

Out of the rubble, however, came a major railroad reorganization that was primarily the handiwork of Wall Street. Investment banking firms such as J. P. Morgan & Co. and Kuhn, Loeb & Co. had sprung up to feed the railroads' insatiable appetite for capital. Investment bankers performed the key middleman's role, taking the stocks and bonds issued by railroads and finding

Jay Gould: Robber Baron?

. . . JAY GOULD was an operator pure and simple, although, in a general way of speaking, he was as far as possible from pure and as far as possible from simple. . . . It would be at least very difficult to show that the Nation as a whole is a dollar richer by the existence of JAY GOULD, while he himself has become the richer . . . from the expansion of the city and the Nation. He has simply absorbed what would have been made in spite of him.

Thus did the *New York Times* bid farewell to Jay Gould at his death on December 3, 1892. There was a name for the kind of businessman the *Times* thought Gould was: a robber baron—in the Middle Ages, the renegade knights who exacted tribute from all who passed by and in Gould's time, capitalists who extracted riches from, while adding nothing to, the economic system. By that definition, was Gould a robber baron? Yes, said historians for many years, following the thesis first advanced by Matthew Josephson in his book *The Robber Barons* (1934). Today, knowing a great more about Gould than Josephson ever did, historians are no longer so sure.

Jay Gould was born on May 27, 1836, in Roxbury, New York, in the mountainous Catskill region. John Gould wanted Jay, his only son, to take over the family farm, but the boy was small and sickly, and he detested farm work. By sheer tenacity Jay got more education than most farm boys, but tenacity could not get him to Yale, which had been his dream. At sixteen he became a surveyor, at nineteen he wrote a flowery history of Delaware County for money, and then at twenty he got a big break. An eccentric but wealthy tanner, Zadock Pratt, befriended Gould, taking him as a partner to set up a tannery in Pennsylvania, where Gould had located a rich new source of tanning bark. The venture succeeded thanks to Pratt's money and Gould's hard work, but after two years there was a falling out, and Pratt proposed terminating the partnership. He would buy Gould's share for $10,000 or sell out to the young man for $60,000. Gould found backers among the leather merchants who marketed the tannery's output and bought out the surprised Pratt. This was a typical Gould maneuver—bold, unexpected, and decisive. The new partnership quickly turned sour, primarily because

Jay Gould

of a collapse of the leather market. The damage to well-reputed merchants discredited Gould in the leather trade. He had made money amid the wreckage of other people's businesses, another Gould trademark. In 1860 he settled in New York, bent on satisfying what had become his obsession: he wanted to be rich.

Enlisting in the Union army probably never occurred to him; the Civil War was too good a chance for turning quick profits; and besides, Gould had no taste for fighting. He married the daughter of a wealthy New York merchant in 1863, sired six children in rapid succession, and became a devoted family man. These were, above all, schooling years for Gould. He learned about the railroads from a controlling interest he gained in a small Vermont road. And—no one knows exactly

how—he developed a consummate mastery of the intricacies of Wall Street finance. Few could have been aware of this when Gould was elected in 1867 to the executive board of the Erie Railroad just as a titanic battle for control of the Erie was taking shape.

The protagonist was Cornelius Vanderbilt, who wanted to ally the Erie with his emerging New York Central system. Vanderbilt began secretly buying up Erie stock, a maneuver that had gained him control of other key railroad properties. This time, however, Erie stock mysteriously kept entering the market even though no more could legally be issued by the Erie. Gould was exploiting a dubious loophole: freshly minted convertible bonds that could be immediately converted to stock. Vanderbilt countered with court injunctions, forcing Gould and his confederates to decamp to New Jersey, and in Albany Vanderbilt lobbied to prevent legalization of the convertible bond gambit. A bidding war began for legislators' votes, which, with the Erie dollars overflowing his satchel, Gould finally won. To settle things, however, Vanderbilt and his allies had to be compensated for their losses, which Gould ingeniously arranged by spending $9 million from the Erie treasury to buy back their stock at inflated prices. The Erie was effectively bankrupted, but it was now firmly in Gould's hands.

Gould proceeded to show how money—lots of it—could be made from control of a large enterprise that was itself unprofitable and badly managed. The trick was to manipulate stock prices, buying and selling with an insider's advance knowledge. For example, Gould announced that he was replacing the United States Express Company, which operated on the Erie line, with a new company that he intended to form. United's stock dropped from 60 to 16, at which point Gould bought, renewed the contract, and sold on the stock's rebound. He walked away with a cool $3 million. Under Gould's rule, the Erie never earned enough to service its debt. Long-suffering European stockholders finally rebelled, forcing him out in March 1872, and charged him with criminal fraud. Resourceful as ever, Gould tied up the suit in the courts, finally persuading the plaintiffs to accept a settlement that was of little account.

Gould was never able to shed the unsavory reputation he acquired during the Erie years. But even in that buccaneering period there was another side to him as a railroad man. Indifferent to day-to-day operations, Gould had a brilliant strategic sense for how railroads should grow. The key, he knew, was integrated development, with trunk line service between major centers. Right off Gould moved to take over the local roads west of Pittsburgh and Buffalo, hoping to make the Erie the dominant system linking the Atlantic seaboard and the Midwest. But he lacked the resources, and the Pennsylvania and the New York Central, spurred by his challenge, beat him out, capturing the key western lines and leaving the Erie a weak secondary system.

Yet the vision had been Gould's, and ten years later he found greener fields for his strategic talents in the area west of St. Louis and southward into Texas. The railroads in this region were a jumble of incomplete, disconnected lines when Gould came on the scene in 1879. He began buying control, finishing the lines, and linking them into a regional system operating more than 5,000 miles of track under his parent company, the Missouri Pacific. He also moved aggressively in other parts of the country, challenging established railroads and cutting rates ruthlessly to take traffic from them. By 1882 he controlled 15 percent of the nation's entire trackage and Western Union and the New York Elevated besides.

The economic boom that fostered this empire building did not last, however, and after 1881 Gould found himself on the wrong side of the stock market, overextended in holdings that were falling in value. On the verge of ruin in early 1884, he managed to get a "corner" on the stock of the Missouri Pacific, forcing up its price and thus saving himself. But Gould was not the same man after that. He lost his iron nerve, and his health began to fail. He swore off speculation. His business dealings, while still far-flung, became more cautious and defensive. But to the end he remained a tough customer, never justifying himself, never cloaking himself in religious piety, not even seeking to make amends by a show of philanthropy. In death he thumbed his nose at the world: his entire fortune—$75 million—went in trust to his family.

A century later, historians can perhaps appreciate better than Gould's obituarists the positive side of Gould's amazing business career. The nation's railroad network bore in some considerable degree Gould's mark by virtue of his own system building and the spur he gave to others. Moreover, his forays into the territory of other railroads broke open monopoly markets and drove shipping prices down. Railroads might have made less money, but shippers and consumers benefited from cheaper transportation costs. Even Gould's purely speculative ventures might have contributed to the nation's economic growth. Economists say that money made in speculation is an especially efficient source of fresh capital, and that is what Gould's winnings were to America's capital-hungry railroads.

Let us suppose that Gould never understood this. Let us suppose further that he was motivated by greed, that his methods were unscrupulous, and that if he had lived at a later time, he probably would have ended up in prison. Are we justified in calling him a robber baron?

buyers among banks, insurance companies, and investors in this country and abroad. And when railroads fell into bankruptcy—or rather, into receivership, because they could not be permitted to stop operating—the investment bankers stepped in to pick up the pieces. They persuaded investors to help out by accepting lower interest rates or putting up more money. Railroads emerged healthier from receivership. Just as important, the competitive pressures on them eased. The investment bankers did this by consolidating rival roads or developing "communities of interest" among them. Through interlocking directorates orchestrated by J. P. Morgan, once-competing railroads ended up effectively sharing a common board of directors. By the early twentieth century, half a dozen great regional systems had emerged, and the nerve center of American railroading had shifted to Wall Street.

The Managerial Revolution

At one time, observed the railroad expert Marshall M. Kirkman in 1896, it had been thought "practically impossible to manage a great railway effectively." On the early railroads "management had been personal and autocratic; the superintendent, a man gifted with energy and clearness of perception, moulded the property to his own will. But as the properties grew, he found himself unable to give his personal attention to everything. Undaunted, he sought to do everything and do it well. He ended by doing nothing."

It is not hard to understand the mistake of the early railroad superintendent. Where in a world of small businesses could he find a model for running an enterprise that was too big for personal and direct control? No problem was harder to grasp, no solution harder to imagine.

As trunk lines moved westward from Baltimore, Philadelphia, and New York before the Civil War, they came up against a managerial crisis that had not troubled shorter railroads. In 1856 the Erie Railroad official Daniel C. McCallum offered a crucial insight into the problem. On a 50-mile railroad the superintendent could attend to every detail personally, "and any system, however imperfect, may prove comparatively successful." But not on 500-mile railroads: "I am fully convinced that in the want of a system lies the true secret of their failure." Thus, McCallum identified the need for a *system*—a formal administrative structure—for the successful operation of large-scale, complex enterprises. He knew he was working in the dark: "We have no precedent or experience upon which we can fully rely."

The railroads were the most complex form of nineteenth-century enterprise. They had to raise huge amounts of capital, and their properties stretched over ever-greater distances. They employed armies of workers—nearly 50,000 on the Pennsylvania system by 1890. And unlike the leisurely traffic on canals, trains had to be precisely scheduled and closely coordinated. Even with the use of telegraphic communication, train accidents took a heavy toll.

Step by step, always under the prod of necessity, the early trunk lines pioneered the main elements of modern business administration. They separated overall management from day-to-day operations and created departments along functional lines—maintenance of way, rolling stock, and traffic. Then they carefully defined the lines of communication from the operating divisions upward to the central office. When Albert Fink perfected his cost-accounting system for the Louisville and Nashville Railroad after the Civil War, managers at last had precise data with which to assess the performance of their railroads. By the end of the 1870s the managerial crisis of the railroads had been resolved.

As industrial enterprises became comparably complex, they confronted the same kind of managerial problems. However, manufacturers benefited from the experience of the railroads. Andrew Carnegie, for example, drew on his early career with the Pennsylvania Railroad. Whether by learning from the railroads or through trial and error, large companies moved toward a modern management structure and solved the problems of administering far-flung business empires.

Mass Markets and Large-Scale Enterprise

The railroads sparked a revolution in the distribution and marketing of goods. Until well into the industrial age, business firms were typically small. Most manufacturers produced goods in limited quantities, mainly for nearby markets, and left the marketing to wholesale merchants and commission agents. Products normally passed through numerous hands on their way from the factory to final sale to the consumer.

Then after the Civil War the scale of economic activity began to grow dramatically. "Combinations of capital on a scale hitherto wholly unprecedented constitute one of the remarkable features of modern business methods," the economist David A. Wells wrote in 1889. He could see "no other way in which the work of production and distribution can be prosecuted." The increasing scale of enterprise seemed "not voluntary on the part of the possessors and controllers of capital, but necessary or even compulsory." What was there about the nation's economic activity that led to Wells's sense of inevitability?

The dynamic features of American growth—availability of capital, receptivity to technology, and the emergence of an industrial base—certainly played a role. But the key to large-scale enterprise lay in the

American market. Immigration and a very high birth rate swelled the population from 40 million in 1870 to over 60 million in 1890. People flocked to the cities, and the railroads brought these dense consuming markets within the reach of distant producers. The telegraph, which was in widespread use by the Civil War, eliminated communication barriers. Unlike Europe, America was not carved up into many national markets; no political frontiers impeded the flow of goods across the continent. Meanwhile, high tariffs protected American industry from foreign competition. Nowhere else did manufacturers have so vast and accessible an internal market for their products.

Gustavus Swift and Vertical Integration. The meatpacking industry was a case in point. Before the Civil War, Cincinnati and Chicago had become great processors of preserved products such as salt pork and smoked beef. But fresh meat remained the province of local butchers and slaughterhouses whose practices had scarcely changed since the preindustrial era. Fresh meat was a luxury item, and the diet of city dwellers, especially the poor, depended heavily on salt pork.

The coming of the railroads brought big changes to the fresh-meat business. Cattle raising shifted to the grazing ranges of the Great Plains and the feedlots of the corn belt. Chicago, the rail terminal for the upper Midwest, became the hub of the American meat trade once the Union Stock Yards opened in 1865. Cattle were shipped by railroad from Chicago to eastern cities, where, as before, they were slaughtered in local "butchertowns." Nothing more was needed for the meat trade to service an exploding urban population indefinitely. In Europe no further development ever did occur.

But Gustavus F. Swift, a shrewd Massachusetts cattle dealer who settled in Chicago in 1875, saw the future differently. Processing fresh meat locally seemed inefficient to him. Livestock in cattle cars deteriorated en route to the East, and local slaughterhouses were too small to utilize waste by-products and cut labor costs. If a way could be found to keep the dressed beef fresh in transit, processing operations could be concentrated in Chicago. Primitive refrigeration already enabled Chicago pork-packing plants to operate year-round. The problem was how to apply this technology to a railroad

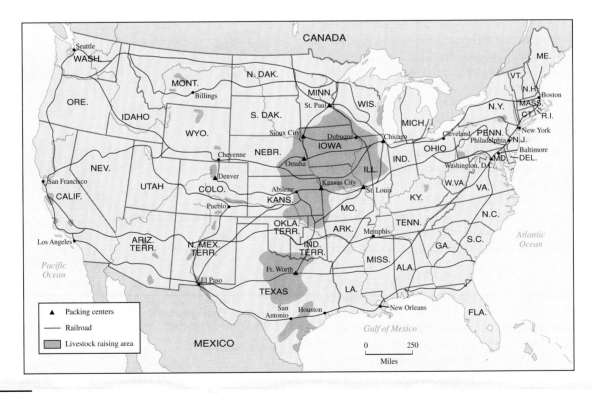

MAP 18.3

The Dressed Meat Industry
The meat-packing industry clearly shows how transportation, supply, and demand combined to foster the growth of the American industrial economy. The main centers of beef production in 1900—Chicago, St. Paul, Kansas City, Fort Worth—were great rail hubs with connections westward to the cattle regions and eastward to the great cities hungry for cheap supplies of meat. Vertically integrated enterprises sprang from these elements, linked together by an efficient and comprehensive railroad network.

freight car. After Swift's engineers figured out an effective system of air circulation, he built a fleet of refrigerator cars and constructed a central beef-processing plant at the Chicago stockyards.

This was only the beginning of Swift's innovations. Since no refrigerated warehouses existed in the cities to which he shipped chilled beef, Swift built his own network of branch houses. Next, he established a fleet of wagons to distribute his products to retail butcher shops. Swift constructed additional facilities to process the fertilizer, chemicals, and other usable by-products from his slaughtering operations. He also added to his line of business other perishable commodities, including dairy products, so that he could fully utilize his refrigerated cars and branch houses. As the demand grew, Swift built more packing houses in other stockyard centers, including Kansas City, Fort Worth, and Omaha.

Step by step, Swift created a new kind of enterprise, the *vertically integrated* firm—that is, a national company capable of handling within its own structure all the functions of an industry. In effect, Swift & Co. replaced a large number of small specialized firms operating in local markets. Several other Chicago companies that had started as preserved pork packers—Armour & Co. was the most prominent—followed Swift's lead. By the end of the 1890s five firms, all of them nationally organized and vertically integrated, produced nearly 90 percent of the meat shipped in interstate commerce. The entire geography of the meat industry had changed (see Map 18.3).

The Birth of Mass Marketing. The development of the refrigerator car had made all this possible in the fresh-meat trade. In most other fields no single event was so decisive. But other manufacturers did share Swift's insight that the essential step was to identify a mass market and then develop a national enterprise capable of serving it. In the petroleum industry John D. Rockefeller built the Standard Oil Company partly by taking over rival firms, but he also developed a national distribution system to reach the enormous market for kerosene to light and heat homes. The Singer Sewing Machine Company formed its own sales organization, using both retail stores and door-to-door salesmen. Through such distribution systems, manufacturers provided technical information, credit, and repair facilities for their products. Like the meat packers, these companies became vertically integrated firms that served a national market.

To gain the benefits of mass distribution, retail business went through comparable changes. Montgomery Ward and Sears, Roebuck developed into national mail-order houses for rural consumers. From Vermont to California farm families selected identical goods from mail-order catalogues and became part of the nation-

wide consumer market. In the cities, mass distribution followed different strategies. Department stores, a form of retailing pioneered by John Wanamaker in Philadelphia, spread to every large city. The most important innovators in this field were Jewish families such as the Strauses of New York, the Lazaruses of Columbus, Ohio, and the Mays of Colorado, most of whose founders had started as peddlers or small dry goods proprietors. An alternative route to urban distribution was provided by the establishment of chain store systems; this was the strategy of the Great Atlantic and Pacific Tea Company (A & P) and the F. W. Woolworth Company.

American society prepared its citizens to be consumers of the standardized goods produced by national manufacturers and sold by mass marketers. The high rate of geographical mobility broke down the local loyalties and regional identities that were so strong in Europe. And social class in America, though by no means absent, was blurred at the edges. Equally important, it did not call for distinguishing ways of dressing. Foreign

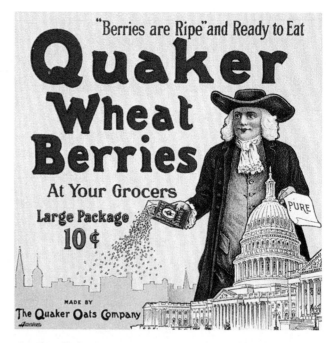

Quaker Oats
Like crackers, sugar, and other nonperishable foods, oatmeal had traditionally been marketed to consumers in bulk from barrels. In 1882 the grain merchant Henry P. Cowell completed the first continuous-process mill for oatmeal, cutting production costs and greatly increasing output. He also hit on the idea of selling oatmeal in boxes of standard size and weight to a national market. Broadsides showing the Quaker Oats man soon appeared in every American town, advertising a product of reliable quality and uniform price. (National Museum of American History, Smithsonian Institution)

visitors often noted that ready-made clothing made it difficult to tell salesgirls from debutantes on city streets.

The American consumer's receptivity to standardized goods should not be exaggerated. Gustavus Swift, for example, encountered great resistance to his Chicago beef: How could it be wholesome weeks later in Boston or Philadelphia? Cheap prices helped, but advertising perhaps had a greater influence. Modern advertising was born during the late nineteenth century, bringing brand names and an urban landscape increasingly cluttered by billboards and signs. By 1900 advertisers were spending more than $90 million a year for space in newspapers and magazines. Advertisements urged readers to bathe with Pears' soap, eat Uneeda biscuits, sew on a Singer machine, and snap pictures with a Kodak camera. The active molding of demand for brand names became a major function of American business.

The New South

"Shall we dethrone our idols?" This was a question that southerners had to ask themselves as they enviously observed the burst of economic activity in the North. For many the answer was a resounding yes. Nostalgia for the glories of the Old South became the chief target of the advocates of southern economic development. The South, they argued, had always given "the places of trust and honor" to "warriors and orators," forgetting that "what it would most need was the practical wisdom of businessmen." Led by Henry W. Grady of the Atlanta *Constitution*, an influential group of publicists made the "practical wisdom of businessmen" the credo of a "New South."

Catching up with the North was no easy task. The plantation economy of the Old South had strongly im-

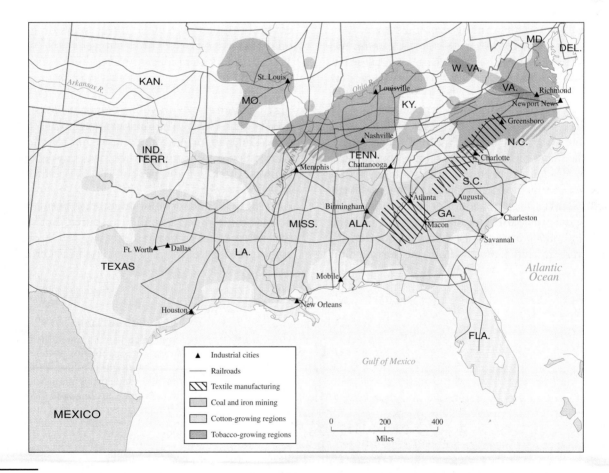

MAP 18.4

The New South, 1900

The economy of the Old South focused on raising staple crops, especially cotton and tobacco. In the New South staple agriculture continued to dominate but there was marked industrial development as well. Industrial regions developed, producing textiles, coal and iron, and wood products. By 1900 the South's industrial pattern was well defined.

peded industrial development. In 1860 railroad building lagged far behind; there were few cities, a primitive distribution system, and not much manufacturing. After the devastation of the Civil War this modest infrastructure was quickly restored. In 1877, with both Reconstruction and economic depression ended, outside capital flowed in and a railroad boom developed. Track mileage doubled in the next decade and, at least by that measure, the South became nearly competitive with the rest of the country (see Map 18.4).

But the South remained overwhelmingly an agrarian society; two of every three persons lived on the land. Farming and poverty are not necessarily linked, but in the South they were. Sharecropping, which required a cash crop (see Chapter 16), committed the South to cotton despite soil depletion and unprofitable prices. With leases on a year-to-year basis, neither tenant nor owner had an incentive to invest in long-term improvements. At a time of rapid advances in northern agriculture, cotton growing remained tied to the mule, the plow, and the hoe.

The result was a stagnant agricultural system. Low productivity and low cotton prices translated into low-wage agriculture. The price for southern farm labor fell steadily, until in South Carolina and Georgia it stood at scarcely half the national average by the 1890s—roughly 75 cents a day without board for a farm laborer.

Southern Industry. This low agricultural wage turned out to be the salvation of the South's hopes for industrialization. Consider, for example, how southern textile mills got started in the Piedmont upcountry of North Carolina, South Carolina, and Georgia in the mid-1870s. Capital was raised locally, subscribed in large amounts and small under a drumbeat of boosterism. Workers were recruited mostly from the surrounding

hill farms, where people struggled to make ends meet. To attract them, mill wages had to be higher than their farm earnings, but not much higher. And since the agricultural wage was so low in the South, the new mills had a great competitive advantage over the long-established New England industry—an estimated 40 percent in labor costs in 1897.

The labor system that evolved likewise reflected southern agrarian society. To begin with, it was a family system. "Papa decided he would come because he didn't have nothing much but girls and they had to get out and work like men," recalled one woman. It was not Papa, in fact, but his girls whom the mills wanted for work as spinners and loom tenders. But they could not be recruited individually: no right-thinking parent would have permitted that. There was, on the other hand, no objection to hiring by families; after all, everyone had been expected to work on the farm. And so the family system of mill labor developed, in which half or more of the operatives were women and the work force was very young. Fully a quarter of all southern textile workers in the 1880s were under fifteen years of age; three-quarters were twenty-four or younger.

The hours were long—twelve hours a day was the norm—but life in the mill villages was, in the words of one historian, "like a family." Employers tended to be highly paternalistic, providing company housing and a variety of services. The mill workers themselves built close-knit, supportive communities, but for whites only. Although they sometimes worked as day laborers and janitors, blacks hardly ever got jobs as operatives in the mills.

Cheap, abundant labor might have been termed the South's most valuable natural resource. But the South was rich in other natural resources as well. From its rich soil came tobacco, the region's second cash crop. When

The Industrial South

No development so raised the hopes of New South proponents as the success of the region's textile industry. After 1877 new mills had sprung up in South Carolina, North Carolina, and Georgia. Investors received a high rate of return—average profits ran at 22 percent in 1882—and publicists boasted that new jobs were being created for "the necessitous masses of poor whites." This 1887 engraving of a "model" mill at Augusta, Georgia, conveys the South's sense of pride in its new industrial prowess.

TABLE 18.2

Comparison of South and Non-South Value Added per Worker, 1910

Type of Industry	South	Non-South
Lumber and timber products	820	1020
Cotton goods	544	764
Cars and general shop construction by steam railroad companies	657	746
Turpentine and resin	516	—
Tobacco manufactures	1615	1394
Foundry and machine-shop products	1075	1307
Printing and publishing	1760	2100
Cottonseed oil and cake	1715	—
Hosiery and knit goods	461	724
Furniture and refrigerators	732	1052
Iron and steel	1182*	1433
Fertilizer	1833	1947

This table reveals the consistency with which northern industries (except tobacco manufactures) controlled the more skilled—and hence, more value-creating—processes of production.

*Partially estimated.

Source: Gavin Wright, *Old South, New South: Revolutions in the Southern Economy since the Civil War* (New York: Basic Books, 1986) 163.

cigarettes became fashionable in the 1880s, the young North Carolina entrepreneur James B. Duke seized the new market by taking advantage of a southern invention—James A. Bonsack's machine for producing cigarettes automatically. Blacks retained the manual tasks of stemming and stripping the leaf that they had always performed, but as in the textile mills, machine tending was restricted to white women.

Lumbering, by contrast, was largely integrated, with a labor force evenly divided between black and white men. The extensive pine forests of the South were rapidly—*heedlessly* is perhaps the better word—exploited in those years. Finally, the rich coal and iron ore deposits of Alabama were vigorously developed from the late 1870s onward, so that by 1890 nearly a million tons of pig iron were being produced in the Birmingham district.

Despite the South's high hopes, this burst of industrial development did not lift the region out of poverty. Industrial output increased more rapidly than in the North but not enough to make much headway against the dominant agricultural sector. In 1900 two-thirds of all southerners made their living from the soil, just as they had in 1870. Moreover, the industries that did develop were usually extractive, such as forestry and mining. Nearly two-thirds of the South's labor force worked in the production of raw materials, compared with hardly one-eighth in the Middle Atlantic and New England states. Processing rarely went beyond coarse, semifinished goods, even in textiles. Industry by industry, the key statistic—the value added by manufacturing—showed the South lagging consistently behind the North (see Table 18.2).

Southerners tended to blame the North: the South was a "colonial" economy controlled by New York and Chicago. There was some truth to this charge. Much of the capital—by no means all—did come from the North, and the integrating processes of the economy did subordinate regional to national interests. When the railway network moved to a standard gauge, it was the southern railroads that were most out of line. In 1886, in one massive effort, the entire South converted to the 4 feet 8 1/2 inch standard of the North. Nor was there a lack of instances in which northern interests used their muscle to maintain the interregional status quo. Railroads, for example, varied freight rates so that it was cheap for southern cotton and timber to flow out and for northern manufactured goods to flow in.

Yet in the end the South's economic backwardness was mostly of its own making. The crowning irony was that the great advantage of the South—its cheap labor—kept it from developing a more technologically advanced economy. First, low wages discouraged employers from replacing workers with machinery. Second, low wages attracted labor-intensive industry, such as textiles. Third, a cheap labor market inhibited investment in education. (In its way, this was a rational choice: better-educated workers would flee to higher-wage markets, and the investment in them would be lost.)

What was special about the southern labor market was that it was *insulated* from the rest of the country: the normal flow of workers back and forth did not occur, and wage differentials did not narrow. So long as this condition persisted, the South would remain a tributary economy, a supplier on unequal terms to the advanced industrial heartland of the North.

The World of Work

In a free enterprise system profit drives the entrepreneur. But the industrial order is not populated only by profit makers. It includes—in vastly larger numbers—wage earners. What is done for profit always acts directly and powerfully on those who work for wages. Never did those actions have more profound consequences for working people than in the late nineteenth century.

Labor Recruits

Wherever in the world industrialism took hold, it set people in motion. Artisans moved into factories, farm folk migrated to manufacturing centers, an industrial labor force emerged. These events took place in all industrializing nations. But the United States built its work force in a distinctive way. Unlike European countries, it could not rely primarily on its own population.

For one thing, the demand for labor was enormous. American industry required nearly three times as many workers in 1900 as it had in 1870 (see Figure 18.2). No less important, except in the South, native-born Americans could no longer be attracted into factories. Rural people, who still accounted for about 75 percent of the population in 1870, were certainly mobile, but the many who went westward remained farmers. About half of all farm migrants did move to cities, but not into the factories. The desirable jobs—those of puddlers, rollers, molders, and machinists—required industrial skills not held by rural Americans. But these people did have a basic education; they could read and calculate, and they understood American institutions and ways of doing things. City-bound white Americans found their opportunities in the multiplying white-collar jobs in offices and retail stores rather than in the nation's factories.

As for rural blacks, even the lowest factory job probably seemed better than sharecropping or day labor on a farm. Modest numbers of blacks began to migrate northward and westward—roughly 80,000 between 1870 and 1890 and another 200,000 from 1890 to 1910. Most of them settled in cities, but they encountered racial barriers as impenetrable as those in the South. The great majority of black men ended up as casual laborers and janitors, and black women worked as

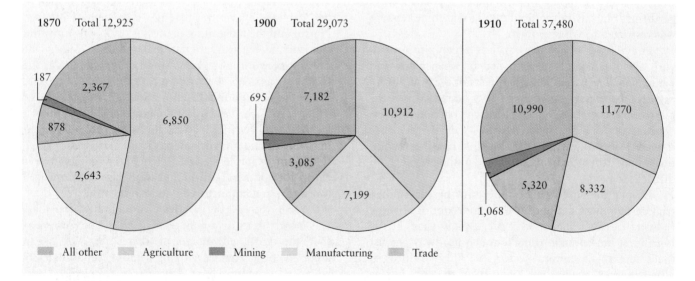

FIGURE 18.2

Changes in the Labor Force, 1870–1910
The numbers represent thousands of people (i.e., 12,925 = 12,925,000 workers).
They reveal both the enormous increase in the labor force between 1870 and 1910
and the dramatic shift from agriculture to industry and other nonagricultural jobs.

Ironworkers—Noontime
The qualities of the nineteenth-century craft worker—dignity, "unselfish brotherhood," a "manly" bearing—shine through this painting by Thomas P. Anschutz. *Ironworkers—Noontime* became a popular painting when it was reproduced as an engraving in *Harpers' Weekly* in 1884.

maids and laundresses. Only 7 percent of African-American men held factory jobs in 1890. Their opportunity had been preempted by another source of cheap labor. Blacks could be excluded because industrial employers had plenty of foreign workers.

Immigrant Labor. The exodus from the Old World had started in the 1840s when over a million Irish peasants fled the potato famine. In the following years, European agriculture became increasingly commercialized while peasant populations grew and outstripped the available land. The erosion of peasant economies struck first in Germany and Scandinavia. Then, later in the nineteenth

century, troubled times spread eastward into Austria-Hungary and Russia and southward into Italy and the Balkans. In the industrial districts of Europe the forces of economic change also cut loose many workers in the declining artisan trades and in obsolete occupations such as hand-loom weaving.

Ethnic origin largely determined the kind of work that the immigrants found in their new country. Seasoned artisans and industrial workers generally sought the same types of jobs that they had held in the Old World. The nineteenth-century occupational structure took on an ethnic character: the Welsh worked as tin-plate workers, the English as miners, the Germans as

Immigrant Workers
Many native-born Americans resented the influx of peasant immigrants from eastern and southern Europe that began in the 1880s. In fact, the newcomers, more than any other group, manned the machines, laid the railroad tracks, and performed the heavy construction labor that built the nation's cities. They were Europe's gift—its most vigorous and hardworking people.

machinists and traditional artisans, the Belgians as glass workers, and the Scandinavians as seamen on Great Lakes boats. For common labor, employers had long counted on the brawn of Irish rural immigrants.

As industrialization advanced, European craft skills became outmoded while the need for unskilled workers increased. As a result, immigration began to shift away from northern Europe during the 1880s (see Figure 18.3). More than 9 million people migrated to America from eastern and southern Europe between 1900 and 1914. Italian and Slavic immigrants without industrial skills flooded into the lowest rungs of American industry. Heavy, low-paid factory labor became the domain of the recent immigrants. Blast-furnace jobs, a job-seeking investigator heard, were "Hunky work," not suitable for him or any other American.

It was not only the skills they had that determined where immigrants ended up in American industry. The newcomers, although generally traveling on their own, moved within well-defined networks. They followed relatives or fellow villagers already in America, joined

their households as family members or boarders, and relied on them to find a job. A high degree of ethnic clustering resulted even within a single factory. At the Jones and Laughlin steel works in Pittsburgh, for example, the carpentry shop was German, the hammer shop Polish, and the blooming mill Serbian. Immigrants also had different job preferences. Men from Italy, for example, liked outdoor work better than factory labor. And, already accustomed to it, they worked in gangs under a *padrone* (boss), much as they had in Italy.

Immigrants entered a modern industrial order, but they saw their surroundings through peasants' eyes. With the disruption of the traditional rural economies of eastern and southern Europe, many lost their lands and fell into the class of dependent, propertyless servants. Peasants could avoid that bitter fate only if they had money to buy property. In Europe job-seeking peasants commonly tried seasonal agricultural labor or temporary work in nearby cities. America represented merely a larger leap, made possible by cheap and speedy steamship transportation across the Atlantic. The peasant immigrants, most of them young and male, came intending to earn enough money to buy land in their native villages. As many as half did return, departing from America in great numbers during depression years. No one knows how many saved enough money to achieve their peasant goals and how many left for lack of work. Their willingness to take the worst jobs and their tendency to leave in bad times clearly made them an ideal labor supply for the new industrial order.

A few fields, such as railroading, employed mostly native-born workers. Overall, however, immigrants manned American industry, constituting well over half the labor force of the nation's principal manufacturing and mining industries after the turn of the century.

Working Women

Between 1870 and 1900 the number of American women grew by half, but the number in wage-earning jobs jumped by almost two-thirds. Women became increasingly important to the industrial economy; by 1900 they made up more than a fourth of the total non-farm labor force. The role that they found as workers was shaped by their gender. Contemporary beliefs about womanhood largely determined which women entered the work force and how they were treated when they became wage earners.

Wives were not supposed to hold jobs. In 1890 fewer than 5 percent of married white women worked outside the home. Black married women had a much higher labor participation rate of over 30 percent. Except in affluent families, young women generally worked until they married. In most working-class

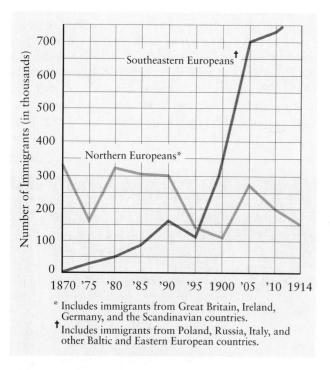

* Includes immigrants from Great Britain, Ireland, Germany, and the Scandinavian countries.
† Includes immigrants from Poland, Russia, Italy, and other Baltic and Eastern European countries.

FIGURE 18.3

American Immigration, 1870–1914
This graph shows the surge of European immigration in the late nineteenth century. While northern Europe continued to send substantial numbers, it was overshadowed after 1895 by southern Europeans pouring into America to work in mines and factories.

Switchboard Operators

Telephone work offers a prime historical example of sex typing in American employment. When the first telephone exchange was set up in Boston in 1878, it was operated by teen-age boys, which followed the practice set in the telegraph industry. During the 1880s, however, young women increasingly replaced the boys, and by 1900 switchboard operation was defined strictly as women's work. In this photograph of a telephone exchange in Columbus, Ohio, in 1907, the older woman at left has risen to the position of supervisor, but it is the two men in the picture who are clearly in charge. The other major occupations in this new industry—telephone installation and line maintenance—were just as strictly male as switchboard operation was female, but of course on a much higher pay scale.

households, in fact, daughters had no choice because their earnings were needed by the family. The bulk of employed women therefore were young: the majority in 1890 were between sixteen and twenty-four years of age. When older women worked, one observer remarked, it "was usually a sign that something had gone wrong"—their husbands had died, deserted them, or stopped working.

Since women were held to be inherently different from men, it followed that they should not be permitted to do "men's work." And regardless of the value of their labor, they could not be paid a man's wage. The dominant view was that a woman did not require a "living wage" because, as one investigator reported, "it is expected that she has men to support her." Moreover, the occupation that served as the baseline for all women's jobs was domestic service, always very poorly paid or, in a woman's own home, not paid at all.

At the turn of the century women workers fell into three roughly equal numerical categories. A third worked as maids or other types of domestic servants. Another third held "female" white-collar jobs in teaching, nursing, sales, and office work. In industry, where the remainder worked, most women were classified as *operatives*—machine tenders and hand workers. They were heavily concentrated in the garment trades and textile mills but could be found throughout industry in "light" occupations—as packers, inspectors, assemblers, or sausage stuffers in packing houses. Few worked as supervisors, fewer in the crafts, and nearly none as day laborers.

Just how jobs came to be defined as male or female—in sociological lingo, the sex typing of occupations—is not easy to explain. Some jobs originally held by men, such as telephone operators and store clerks, had by the 1890s been taken over by women. In each

case, as an occupation became feminized, it was redefined as having female attributes even though very similar or even identical work elsewhere was done by men. Once a job was identified as women's work, it became unsuitable for men. There were no male telephone operators by 1900.

Sex typing of work was legitimized by the sentimental view of women as the weaker sex, but powerful interests also played a role. Craft workers protected their male domain, and employers profited from cut-rate work. Wherever they worked, women earned less than did the least skilled males. At the turn of the century the weekly wage of women factory workers came to roughly $7, $3 less than that of unskilled men and $5 below the average for all industrial employees.

As with male workers, ethnicity and race played a big part in the distribution of women's jobs among particular groups. Exclusion from all but the most menial jobs applied as rigidly to black women as it did to black men. White-collar jobs were reserved for the native-born, although in the cities those people were often the second-generation daughters of immigrants. And as with men, ethnicity created clustering patterns in the jobs held by wage-earning women or, in the case of Italian families, restricted them to subcontracting tasks, such as sewing, that could be done at home.

But if ethnicity mattered in the workplace, gender mattered at least as much. Women's identity gave their work distinctive meaning. Department store clerks, for example, developed a work culture and language just as robust as that of the hard-drinking Danbury hatters described later in this chapter. Most important was the fact that wage-earning women were young and unmarried. For many, the first job was also an escape from family discipline. It represented an opportunity to gain some independence, form friendships with other young women, and experience, however briefly, a fun-loving time of nice clothes, dancing, and other "cheap amusements." Young male workers, by contrast, underwent a process of job socialization presided over by seasoned, older co-workers. Being young mattered to male workers, certainly, but did not define the work experience for them as it did for women.

To some degree, their youthful preoccupations made it easier for working women to overlook or accept the miserable terms under which they labored. But this did not mean that they lacked a sense of group solidarity and self-respect. Fashionable clothes might appear frivolous to the casual observer, but they also conveyed the message that the working girl considered herself to be as good as anyone. And there were occasions, as occurred with the Jewish garment workers of New York and the Irish-American telephone operators of Boston, when the rebellious youth culture united

with feelings of job grievance to produce astonishing strike movements among working women.

The Family Economy. Disapproval of wives working outside the home, although expressed in sentimental and moral terms, was based on solid necessity. From the standpoint of the labor market, the basic economic unit consisted of the individual employee. For workers, however, the family was the economic unit, to which the wife contributed crucially. Cooking, cleaning, and tending the children were not income-producing or reckoned in terms of money. But everyone knew that the family household could not function without the wife's contribution. Therefore, her place was in the home.

Working-class families, however, found the going hard on a single income. Only among highly skilled workers, wrote an investigator of the family budgets of miners and iron workers, "was it possible for the husband unaided to support his family." For most working-class families the hardest period came during the childbearing years, when there were many mouths to feed and only the earnings of the father. Thereafter, the family income began to grow. Not only unmarried sons and daughters but the younger children as well contributed their share. In 1900 one of every five children below the age of sixteen worked, including probably a quarter of a million younger than ten. "When the people own houses," remarked a printer from Fall River, "you will generally find that it is a large family all working together."

By the 1890s all the northern industrial states had passed laws prohibiting child labor and regulating work hours for teenagers. Most of those states also required children under fourteen years of age to attend school for a certain number of weeks each year. Working-class families continued to rely on a second income, but this money came more and more from the wife. After 1890 the proportion of working married women crept steadily upward. About a fifth of the wives of unskilled and semiskilled men in Chicago held jobs in 1920. Wage-earning wives, many with children, were on their way to becoming a primary part of America's labor force.

Autonomous Labor

No one supervised the nineteenth-century coal miner. He was a tonnage worker who was paid for the amount of coal he produced. He provided his own tools, worked at his own pace, and knocked off early when he chose. Such autonomous craft workers—almost all of them men—flourished in many branches of nineteenth-century industry. They were mule spinners in cotton mills; puddlers and rollers in iron works; molders in

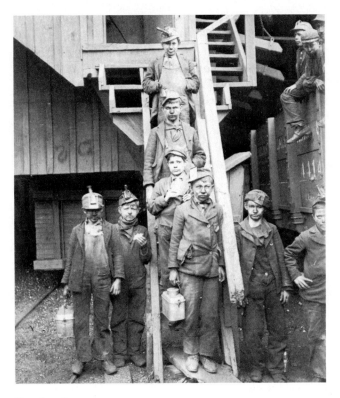

Breaker Boys

In the anthracite districts of eastern Pennsylvania, giant machines called breakers processed the coal as it came out of the mines, crushing it and sorting it by size for sale as domestic fuel. The boys shown in this photograph had the job of picking out the slate and refuse as the processed coal came down the chutes, working long hours in a constant cloud of coal dust for less than a dollar a day. Breaker boy was the first job, often begun before the age of ten, in a lifetime in the mines. The photograph does not show any old men, but sick and disabled miners often ended their careers as breaker boys—hence the saying among coal diggers, "Twice a boy and once a man is the poor miner's life."

stove making; and machinists, glassblowers, and skilled workers of many other types.

In the shop they abided by the *stint*, a limit placed by themselves on the amount that they would produce each day. This informal system of limiting output infuriated efficiency-minded engineers. But to the worker it signified personal dignity and "unselfish brotherhood" with fellow employees. The male craft worker took pride in a "manly" bearing toward both his fellows and the boss. One day a shop in Lowell, Massachusetts, posted regulations requiring all employees to be at their posts in work clothes at the opening bell and remain, with the shop door locked, until the dismissal bell. A

machinist promptly packed his tools and quit, declaring that he had not "been brought up under such a system of slavery."

Underlying this ethical code was a keen sense of craft groups, each of which had its own history and customs. Hat finishers, masters of the art of applying fur felting to top hats and bowlers, had a language of their own. When a hatter was hired, he was "shopped"; if fired, he was "bagged"; when he quit work, he "cried off"; and when he took an apprentice, the boy was "under teach." The hatters, most of whom worked in Danbury, Connecticut, or Orange, New Jersey, formed a distinctive, self-contained community.

The craft worker's skills were crucial to nineteenth-century production. He was also valued for the responsibilities he assumed. He hired his own helpers, supervised their work, and paid them from his earnings. In an era when the scale of production was expanding, autonomous craft workers relieved their employers of the mounting burden of shop-floor management. Many factory managers tried to shift this responsibility to their employees. A system of inside contracting developed in metal-fabricating firms that did precise machining and complex assembling. Contractor-employees hired and paid their own men and supervised them.

The skilled worker was one central figure in nineteenth-century industry; the common laborer was another. Great numbers of laborers had been needed to dig canals, lay railroad tracks, and build cities. They were equally important in heavy industry. Until the last years of the century virtually all hauling of materials was done by hand. In the steel mills, a third or more of the workers shoveled coal and iron ore from freight cars, loaded the furnaces, and handled the tons of hot metal that passed through the mill daily. They worked in gangs, completely under the charge of the foreman or gang boss, who hired them, told them what to do, and disciplined and fired them.

Dispersal of authority was thus characteristic of nineteenth-century industry. The aristocracy of the workers—the craftsmen, inside contractors, and foremen—had a high degree of autonomy. However, their subordinates often paid dearly for that independence. The opportunities for abuse were endless. Any worker who paid his helpers from his own pocket might be tempted to exploit them. In the Pittsburgh area, foremen were known as "pushers," notorious for driving their gangs mercilessly. However, industrial labor in the nineteenth century was still on a human scale. People dealt with each other face to face and often developed cohesive ties within the shop. Striking craft workers commonly received the support of helpers and laborers, and labor gangs sometimes walked out on behalf of a popular foreman.

Systems of Control

As technology advanced and modern management emerged, controls over the work process intensified. Despite fierce resistance, workers increasingly lost the proud independence that had characterized nineteenth-century craft work.

When mine owners introduced undercutting machines in the 1880s, they deprived coal miners of the pick work that was their most prized skill. "Anyone with a weak head and a strong back can load machine coal," grumbled one Kentucky miner. "But a man has to think and study every day like you was studying a book if he is going to get the best of the coal when he uses only a pick." Similar complaints came from many other craft workers as their skills fell victim to machinery—from hand-loom weavers early in the nineteenth century to glassblowers a hundred years later.

The main source of this deskilling process was a new system that became known as *mass production*. The essential feature of this system was that it turned out standardized, high-volume products. Consider, for example, how work changed as a result of the creation of a national market for dressed beef in the 1870s. The huge packing houses that sprang up in Chicago shifted from the traditional reliance on skilled butchers to a highly specialized division of labor. At the Armour plant, workers performed seventy-eight distinct jobs, working efficiently and at high speed as the carcasses moved along, hooked to overhead conveyors. In a ten-hour day a gang of 157 workers could handle 1,050 head of cattle, many more per employee than was the case when one skilled butcher did everything. Machinery did not replace workers; rather, it was the division of labor that increased workers' output.

In most cases, however, the division of labor did lead to mechanization. This occurred because once jobs had been broken down into simple, repetitive tasks, it was generally possible to design machines that could do those tasks. The greatest opportunity came in the manufacture of products assembled from standardized, interchangeable parts, such as agricultural implements, sewing machines, typewriters, bicycles, and, after 1900, automobiles. In all these cases, machine tools that cut, drilled, and ground the metal parts had originally been manned by skilled machinists. But as machine tools became more specialized, they became *dedicated* machines—machines set up to do the same job over and

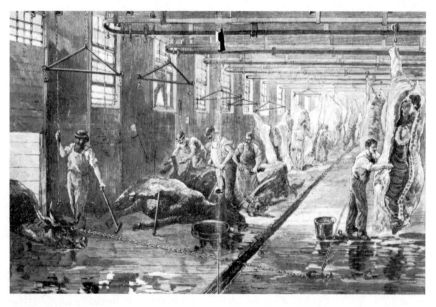

The Killing Floor
To the modern eye, the labor process depicted in this 1882 engraving of a Chicago meat-packing plant seems primitive and inefficient, but it contains the seeds of America's mass-production revolution. At the far left the steer has already been stunned by one specialist, killed by a second, and attached to a chain that will lift it onto the overhead conveyor. The division of labor is already in place (each of the workers on the line does a single repetitive task), and the process is continuous. It would be only a small step from the killing floors of the Chicago packing plants to Henry Ford's assembly line.

John Morison

The Impact of Mechanization

John Morison, a machinist, describes to a Senate investigating committee in 1883 what technological progress has meant to him and his fellow skilled workers.

Q. Is there any difference between the conditions under which machinery is made now and those which existed ten years ago?

A. A great deal of difference. . . . The trade has been subdivided and those subdivisions have been again subdivided, so that a man never learns the machinist's trade now. Ten years ago he learned, not the whole of the trade, but a fair portion of it. Also, there is more machinery used in the business, which again makes machinery. In the case of making the sewing-machine, for instance, you find that the trade is so subdivided that a man is not considered a machinist at all. Hence it is merely laborers' work. . . . Through this system of work, 100 men are able to do now what it took 300 or 400 men to do fifteen years ago.

Q. Have you noticed the effect upon the intellect of this plan of keeping a man at one particular branch?

A. Yes. It has a very demoralizing effect upon the mind throughout. The man . . . has got no chance whatever to learn anything else because he is kept steadily and constantly at that particular thing, and of course his intellect must be narrowed by it.

Q. And does he not finally acquire so much skill in the manipulation of his particular part of the business that he does it without any mental effort?

A. Almost. In fact he becomes almost a part of the machinery. . . . When I first went to learn the trade a machinist considered himself more than the average workingman; in fact he did not like to be called a workingman. He liked to be called a mechanic. . . . Today he recognizes the fact that he is simply the same as any other ordinary laborer, no more and no less.

Q. What is the social air about the ordinary machinist's house? Are there evidences of happiness, and joy, and hilarity, or is the general atmosphere solemn, and somber, and gloomy?

A. To explain that fully, I would state first of all, that machinists have got to work ten hours a day in New York, and that they are compelled to work very hard. In fact the machinists of America are compelled to do about one third more work than the machinists do in England in a day. . . . Of course when a man is dragged out in that way he is naturally cranky, and he makes all around him cranky; so, instead of a pleasant house it is every day expecting to lose his job by competition from his fellow workmen, there being so many out of employment, and no places for them, and his wages being pulled down through their competition, looking at all times to be thrown out of work in that way, and staring starvation in the face makes him feel sad, and the head of the house being sad, of course the whole family is the same, so the house looks like a dull prison instead of a home. . . .

Q. Where do you work?

A. I would rather not have it in print. Perhaps I would have to go Monday morning if I did. We are so situated in the machinist's trade that we daren't let them know much about us. If they know that we open our mouths on the labor question, and try to form organizations, we are quietly told that "business is slack," and we have got to go.

Source: U.S. Senate, Committee on Education and Labor, *Report on the Relations between Labor and Capital* (1885), I, pp. 755–759.

over—and the need for skilled operatives disappeared.

Technology took hold and set the pace of operations. The machine, not the worker, determined how fast production would go. "If you need to turn out a little more," boasted a superintendent at Swift & Co., "you speed up the conveyor a little and the men speed up to keep pace." Workers' frustrations and complaints about speedups were sure signs of the loss of control over their jobs.

"A man never learns the machinist's trade now," John Morison (see American Voices, above) complained in 1883. In the manufacture of sewing machines "the trade is so subdivided that a man is not considered a machinist at all. One man may make just a particular part of a machine and may not know anything whatever about another part of the same machine." Such a worker, noted an observer, "cannot be master of a craft, but only master of a fragment." The horror of what that meant is conveyed by one worker's description of another worker whose job at Western Electric was to cut rubber plates for ten hours a day. "When he talked to me he had to move his hand this way [indicating], as though he would take a piece of rubber plate and put it under the buzz saw. He has become a part of that machine. That machine is the means of his subsistence and that of his family."

Frederick W. Taylor and Scientific Management. The impact of machinery on labor was essentially unintentional. Employers recognized that mechanization would better enable them to discipline their workers, but that was only an incidental benefit of the efficiencies that came from the machinery itself. Gradually, however, employers came to realize that managing workers might itself be a way to reduce the cost of production.

The pioneer in this field was Frederick W. Taylor. Taylor had made a name for himself as an expert on metal-cutting methods. In 1895 he published a landmark essay, "A Piece-Rate System," that proposed a strategy for getting the maximum work from the individual worker. Taylor suggested two basic reforms. The first would eliminate the brain work from manual labor. Managers would assume "the burden of gathering together all of the traditional knowledge which in the past has been possessed by the workmen and then of classifying, tabulating, and reducing this knowledge to rules, laws, and formulae." The second reform, a logical consequence of the first, would deprive workers of the authority they had exercised on the shop floor. Workers would "do what they are told promptly and without asking questions or making suggestions. . . . The duty of enforcing . . . rests with the management alone."

Once they had the knowledge and the power, according to Taylor, managers would put labor on a "scientific" basis. That meant subjecting each task to a *time-and-motion study*, with an engineer analyzing and timing each job with a stopwatch. A personnel office would hire and train the right person for each job. Workers would be paid at a differential rate—that is, a certain amount if they met the stopwatch standard and a higher rate for additional output. Taylor claimed that his techniques would guarantee the optimum level of worker efficiency. His assumption was that only money mattered to workers and that they would automatically respond to the lure of higher earnings.

Taylor called his method *scientific management*. It was not in practice a roaring success. His reforms called for a total restructuring of factory administration. No company ever adopted Taylor's entire system, and the few that tried paid dearly for the effort. His job-analysis method, which was widely used, met with stubborn resistance. "It looks to me like slavery to have a man stand over you with a stopwatch," complained one iron molder. A union leader insisted that "this system is wrong, because we want our heads left on us." Far from solving the labor problem, as Taylor claimed it would, scientific management embittered relations on the shop floor.

Yet Taylor achieved something of fundamental importance. He was a brilliant publicist, and his teachings spread throughout American industry. Taylor's disciples moved beyond his simplistic economic psychology,

creating new professions of personnel administration and industrial psychology that purported to know how to extract more and better labor from workers. A threshold had been crossed into the modern era of labor management.

So the circle closed on American workers. With each advance, the quest for efficiency cut deeper into their cherished autonomy. Mechanization, scientific management, and the growing scale of industrial activity diminished workers and cut them down to fit the production system. The process occurred unevenly. For textile workers the loss had come early, but miners and ironworkers felt it much more slowly. Others, such as craft workers in the building trades, escaped the process almost entirely. But increasing numbers of workers found themselves in an environment that crushed any sense of mastery or even understanding.

The Labor Movement

Wherever industrialization has taken hold, workers have organized and responded collectively. However, the movements they built have varied from one industrial society to another. In the United States, workers were especially uncertain about the path they wanted to take. Only in the 1880s did the American labor movement settle into a fixed course.

Reformers and Unionists

In 1883 a New York wagon driver named Thomas B. McGuire testified before a Senate committee. He had saved $300 from his wages "so that I might become something of a capitalist eventually." But he soon failed. "A man in the express business today owning one or two horses and a wagon cannot even eke out an existence from the business," McGuire complained. "The competition is too great from the Adams Express Company and all those other monopolies." McGuire's prospects seemed no better in the hack (hired carriage) business:

> Corporations usually take that business themselves. They can manage to get men, at starvation wages, and put them on a hack, and put a livery on them with a gold band and brass buttons, to show that they are slaves—I beg pardon; I did not intend to use the word slaves; there are no slaves in this country now—to show that they are merely servants.

Slave or liveried servant, the symbolic meaning was the same to McGuire. He was speaking of the crushed aspirations of the independent American worker.

Labor Reform and the Knights of Labor. What would satisfy the Thomas McGuires of the nineteenth century? Only the restoration of a republican society in which all members were social and political equals and everyone might hope to become independent. Recapturing the republican virtues did not require returning to the agrarian past but, rather, moving beyond the selfishness of the existing industrial order to a future when no distinction would exist between capitalists and workers. All would be "producers" laboring together in what was commonly called the "cooperative commonwealth." This ideal inspired wave after wave of labor-reform movements going back to the workingmen's parties of the 1830s and culminating after the Civil War in the Noble and Holy Order of the Knights of Labor.

The Knights of Labor was founded in 1869 as a secret society of Philadelphia garment cutters. The organization gradually spread to other cities and by 1878 had become a national movement. Led by Grand Master Workman Terence V. Powderly, the Knights boasted an elaborate ritual and ceremony calculated to appeal to the fraternal spirit of nineteenth-century workers. They got from the Knights of Labor a sense of belonging very much like that offered by the Masons or Odd Fellows. For the Knights, however, fraternalism was harnessed to labor-reform advocacy. The goal was to "give voice to that grand undercurrent of mighty thought, which is today [1880] crystallizing in the hearts of men, and urging them on to perfect organization through which to gain the power to make labor emancipation possible."

But how was "emancipation" to be achieved? The Knights tried a number of solutions, including cooperation. Funds would be raised to set up cooperative factories and shops owned and run by the employees. As those cooperatives flourished and spread, American society would be transformed into a cooperative commonwealth. But little was actually done. In reality, the Knights concentrated mainly on "education." Powderly regarded the organization as a vast labor lyceum that almost anyone could join. The cooperative commonwealth would arrive in some mysterious way as more and more "producers" became members and learned the group's message from lectures, discussions, and publications. Social evil would not end in a day but "must await the gradual development of educational enlightenment."

Trade Unionism. The labor-reform movement expressed the higher aspirations of American workers. Another kind of organization—the trade union—tended to their day-to-day needs. Unions had long been central in the lives of craft workers. Apprenticeship rules regulated entry into a trade, and the *closed shop*—by reserving all jobs for union members—kept out lower-wage and incompetent workers. Union rules specified the terms of work, sometimes in minute detail. Above all, trade unionism defended the craft worker's traditional skills and rights.

The union also expressed the social identity of a craft. Hatters took pride in their drinking prowess, an on-the-job privilege that was jealously guarded, and their unions sometimes resembled drinking clubs. More often, however, craft unions had an uplifting character. A Birmingham iron puddler claimed that his union's "main object was to educate mechanics up to a standard of morality and temperance, and good workmanship." Because operating trains was a high-risk occupation, the railroad brotherhoods stressed mutual aid, providing ac-

A Railroad Brotherhood
Locomotive firemen, who fed the boilers on nineteenth-century steam engines, ranked below locomotive engineers but still considered theirs a privileged occupation. This union certificate conveys the respectable values to which locomotive firemen adhered and, as depicted in the scenes on the right-hand side, the need they felt to protect their families (through the affordable insurance provided by their union) in the event of accidents that were so much a part of the dangerous trade they followed.

cident and death benefits and encouraging members to assist one another. On the job and off, the unions played a big part in the lives of craft workers.

The earliest unions were local groups of workers in the same trade. Many of them, especially among German workers, were organized initially along ethnic lines. As expanding markets broke down their insularity, these unions began to form national organizations, starting with the International Typographical Union in 1852. By the 1870s molders, ironworkers, bricklayers, and about thirty other trades had formed national unions.

The protection of job interests might have seemed a far cry from the reform idealism of the Knights of Labor, but both motives arose from a single workers' culture. Seeing no conflict, many workers carried membership cards for both the Knights of Labor and a trade union. The careers of many labor leaders, including Powderly, likewise embraced both kinds of activity. For many years even the functional lines were indistinct. At the local level, little separated a trade assembly of the Knights from a local trade union; both engaged in fraternal and job-oriented activities.

Trade unions generally barred women, and so did the Knights until, in 1881, women shoe workers in Philadelphia struck in support of their male co-workers and won the right to form their own local assembly. By 1886 probably 50,000 women belonged to the Knights of Labor. Their courage on the picket line prompted Powderly's rueful remark that women "are the best men in the Order." For a handful, such as the hosiery worker Leonora M. Barry, the Knights provided a rare chance to take up leadership roles as organizers and officials. For many others the liberation was more modest but very real: "timid young girls—girls who have been overworked from their cradle—stand[ing] up bravely . . . swayed . . . by the wrongs heaped upon their comrades, talk[ing] nobly and beautifully of the hope of redress to be found in organization." Similarly, the Knights of Labor grudgingly expanded the opportunity for black workers to join, because of the need for solidarity and, just as important, in deference to the Order's egalitarian principles. The Knights could rightly boast that their "great work has been to organize labor which was previously unorganized."

The American Federation of Labor

In the early 1880s the Knights began to act increasingly like a trade union. Boycott campaigns against the products of "unfair" employers achieved impressive results. With the economy booming and workers in short supply, the Knights began to win strikes, including a major victory against Jay Gould's Southwestern railway sys-

tem in 1885. Workers flocked into the organization, and its membership jumped from 100,000 to perhaps 700,000 in less than a year. For a brief time the Knights stood poised as a potential industrial-union movement capable of bringing all workers into its fold.

The rapid growth of the Knights of Labor frightened the national trade unions. They tried to keep their local branches away from the Knights, but they met with little success. The unions then began to insist on a clear separation of roles, with the Knights confined to the field of labor reform. This was partly a battle over turf, but it also reflected a deepening divergence of labor philosophies.

This divergence is perhaps best seen in the debate over the shorter workday. For labor reformers, the need for more leisure arose from the duties workers had "to perform as American citizens and members of society." More free time for workers was a precondition for a healthy republican society. Increasingly, however, the issue was seized by trade unionists, who gave the demand for the eight-hour day a more practical bent: it would spread the available jobs among more workers, protect them against overwork, and (like higher wages) give them a better life. "Eight hours for work, eight hours for rest, eight hours for what we will" was the slogan of the trade unions, not the Knights of Labor.

The Haymarket Square Riot. The trade unions set May 1, 1886, as the deadline for achieving the eight-hour day. As that day approached, a wave of strikes and demonstrations broke out. In Chicago a battle on May 3 at the McCormick agricultural implement works resulted in the deaths of four strikers. Chicago was a hotbed of American *anarchism*—the revolutionary advocacy of a stateless society—and local anarchists, most of them German immigrants, called a protest meeting the next evening at Haymarket Square. The meeting went peacefully, but when police moved in at the end to break it up, someone threw a bomb and several policemen were killed or wounded.

The anarchist organizers of the rally were charged wih criminal conspiracy, a legal doctrine so broad that it required no proof of direct involvement in the bombing to justify a verdict of guilt. There was in fact no evidence linking them to the bombing. Four men were executed, one committed suicide, and the others received long prison sentences. They were victims of one of the great miscarriages of American justice.

Seizing on the antiunion hysteria set off by the Haymarket affair, employers took the offensive against the campaign for an eight-hour day. They broke strikes violently, compiled blacklists of strikers, and forced others to sign *yellow-dog contracts* guaranteeing that, as a condition of employment, they would not join a union. If trade unionists needed further confirmation of the

Abraham Bisno

Trade Unionist

Repeated strikes in Chicago caused a government commission to come to that city in 1900 to investigate the reasons for the labor troubles. Bisno, a garment worker and "walking delegate"—a local union agent—gives the trade-union side of the story.

Q. Present occupation.

A. Collecting fares on the loop here for the Union Elevated Railway Company.

Q. Former occupation.

A. I am a cloak maker by trade—made cloaks for some years—and I have had several occupations within the last few years. I have been walking delegate for our union.

Q. What union is that?

A. The Chicago Cloak Makers' Union. . . .

Q. Is the union to which you belong still in existence?

A. It is lately organized again; it was broken up after the defeat of the strike 2 years ago. . . .

Q. Are you a believer in the union of labor?

A. Yes. . . . Unless a firm recognizes the union and agrees to employ nobody except members of the union, the union cannot exist. In my own trade,

when our union was weak, our best men were victimized, and were out of a job most of the time; I mean our most intelligent men—men who do not want to put up with abuse easily. . . . So when these men demand that the union be recognized to the extent of not employing other people except members of their union, this is essential to the very existence of the organization. It is a life-and-death question with them. . . .

Q. You recognize that the strike is a coercive measure—an act of war [and] and an interference with the civil rights of a concern?

A. . . . Yes; but then the reduction in wages, or failing to raise the wages when conditions warrant, are acts of war and interference with my civil rights in a time of peace. It is the same thing. . . .

Q. What are the steps of persuasion brought into use to influence a man who has failed to yield to argument and has gone to work?

A. Well several. For instance, in one case we have alienated a man from the affections of his co-church members.

Q. That you call persuasion?

A. Yes; we went into the church and denounced the fellow as a traitor to

our interests, cutting our throats, sort of sinning against the religious laws, inflicting damage on so many families.

Q. That is one step?

A. That was one of the means; called him scab.

Q. Called him scab?

A. Yes; on the streets.

Q. To his face?

A. Yes. As I told you, it depends upon the temperament of the man. We would go after him in a hundred and one ways, if we can, to drive him out of the community.

Q. That you call persuasion?

A. Within the law; and I think under certain conditions it is right for a person to violate the law and take the consequences. Supposing I am fined for calling a man a scab. I am put into a fine, say, of $10 and have to go to jail for 20 days. The abuse I am suffering may be so great that I would take my medicine. I would tell a man he was a scab, and take my medicine for it and go to jail. . . .

Source: Report of the U.S. Industrial Commission (Washington, D.C.: U.S. Government Printing Office, 1901), VIII, pp. 53–58, 79–82.

tough world in which they lived, they found it in Haymarket and its aftermath.

Samuel Gompers and the AFL. In December 1886, having failed to persuade the Knights of Labor to desist from union activity, the national trade unions formed the American Federation of Labor (AFL). The AFL embodied the belief of the national unions that they constituted a distinctive movement. The Federation in effect locked into place the trade-union structure as it had evolved by the 1880s. Underlying this structure was the conviction that workers had to take the world as it was, not as they dreamed it might be.

The architect of the American Federation of Labor and its president for nearly forty years was Samuel Gompers. Gompers, a cigar maker from New York City, hammered out the philosophical position that would define American "pure and simple" unionism. First, the focus would be on concrete short-term gains. Second, unions would rely on economic power rather than politics. Third, they would limit their membership to workers organized along strictly occupational lines. Finally, the unions strongly rejected the theories and grand schemes that had excited the labor reformers. Gompers developed these views as general propositions, but they were grounded in the hard experience of

Samuel Gompers
This is a photograph of the labor leader in his forties taken when he was visiting striking miners in West Virginia, an area where mine operators resisted unions with special fierceness. The photograph was taken by a company detective.

unionists such as Abraham Bisno (see American Voices, page 577) who tried to organize their fellow workers and bargain collectively with employers. Bisno would have nodded in agreement with Gompers's assertion that "no matter how just . . . unless the cause is backed up with power to enforce it, it is going to be crushed and annihilated."

The steady growth of the trade unions seemed to justify Gompers's confidence that he had found the correct formula for the American labor movement. The Knights of Labor lost momentum. Hard hit by the anti-labor reaction to the Haymarket affair, the organization retreated from the trade-union field and returned to the rhetoric of labor reform. In many localities not yet reached by the AFL, Knights' assemblies for a time met the need for labor organization. But by the late 1890s the Knights of Labor had faded away.

Industrial War

The trade unions were conservative in that they accepted the economic order; all they wanted was a larger share of it for working people. This was, however, reason enough for employers to resist collective bargaining. In the 1890s the trade-union movement came under fierce attack.

The Homestead Strike. Among America's workers, few had more reason to be satisfied with their lives than the skilled steelworkers of Homestead, Pennsylvania. They earned good wages, lived comfortably, and generally owned their own homes. The town was very much their community, with a municipal government elected from their ranks. And in Andrew Carnegie the Homestead workers thought they had a truly sympathetic employer. For had not Good Old Andy said in a famous magazine article that the right of workers to combine was no less sacred than that of capitalists? or that workers held a moral claim on their jobs that forbade the use of strike-breakers by employers?

Carnegie, unfortunately, had other plans. In his view the union had become too expensive. It deprived his steel company of the full benefits of the advanced machinery he was introducing; and with that machinery, the skills of his workers counted for less. Lacking the stomach for the hard battle ahead, Carnegie hid himself in his remote castle in Scotland but left behind a second-in-command eminently qualified for the job at hand. This was Henry Clay Frick, a former coal baron with a fearsome reputation as an enemy of trade unionism.

After some perfunctory bargaining Frick announced that effective July 1, 1892, the company would no longer deal with the Amalgamated Association of Iron and Steel Workers. If the employees wanted to work, they would have to return on an individual basis. Frick's strategy was already clear. Preparations had been made to fortify the plant so that strikebreakers could be brought in to resume operations and defeat the union. At stake now was not just wage cuts but the defense of a way of life. To preserve their "workers' republic," Homesteaders thought they had the right to deny the company access to the plant, and town authorities turned away the county sheriff when he tried to take possession of the plant. The entire community—women no less than men—mobilized in defense of the union.

At dawn on July 6 two bargeloads of Pinkerton guards were seen approaching Homestead up the Monongahela River. Behind hastily erected barricades, the strikers opened fire, and a bloody battle ensued. When the Pinkertons finally surrendered, they were mercilessly pummeled by the enraged women of Homestead as they retreated to the railway station. Frick ap-

pealed to the governor of Pennsylvania, who called out the state militia. Homestead was placed under martial law; strike leaders and town officials were arrested on charges of riot, murder, and treason; and the great steel works was taken over and opened to strikebreakers.

The defeat at Homestead marked the beginning of the end for trade unionism in the iron and steel industry. Ended too were any lingering illusions about the sanctity of workers' communities such as Homestead. "Men talk like anarchists or lunatics when they insist that the workmen of Homestead have done right," asserted one conservative journal. Nothing could be permitted to interfere with private property or threaten law and order.

The Homestead strike ushered in an era of strife in which working people faced not only the formidable power of corporate industry but the even more formidable power of their own government.

The Great Pullman Boycott. The fullest demonstration of that hard reality occurred at a place that seemed an even less likely site for class warfare than Homestead. Pullman, Illinois, was a model factory town, famous for the amenities it offered to workers and the beauty of its landscaping and city plan. The town was named for its creator, George M. Pullman, who had made a fortune as the inventor and manufacturer of the Pullman sleeping cars that brought comfort and luxury to railway travel. Still, when the Panic of 1893 struck, business fell off and the Pullman Company cut wages. But the rents for company housing were not cut, and many workers' take-home pay shrank to a pitiful level.

When a committee finally called on him in May 1894 to present the workers' grievances, Pullman refused to budge. There was no connection between his roles as employer and landlord, he insisted. As for the

The Pullman Strike
Chicago was the hub of the railwork network and the strategic center of the battle between the Pullman boycotters and the trunk line railroads. For the strikers, the crucial thing was to prevent those trains with Pullman cars attached from running; for the railroads, it was to get the trains through at any cost. The arrival of federal troops meant that the trains would move and that the strikers would be defeated.

committee members who approached him, they were fired.

The strike that ensued might have become no more than a footnote in American labor history but for the fact that the Pullman workers belonged to the American Railway Union (ARU), a rapidly growing industrial union of railroad workers recently formed by the labor leader Eugene V. Debs. In response to the strikers' plea, the ARU directed its members not to handle Pullman sleeping cars, which were operated by the railroads but were owned and serviced by the Pullman Company. This was a classic example of a *labor boycott* , in which force is applied at a secondary point (the railroads) to put pressure on the primary target (Pullman).

Railroad officials, already fearful of the growing power of the ARU, saw the Pullman boycott as their chance to break the union. The General Managers' Association, which represented the railroads serving Chicago, insisted on running the Pullman cars. Since ARU members refused to operate trains with Pullman cars, a far-flung strike soon spread across the country and threatened to disrupt the entire economy.

Quite deliberately, the railroad managers maneuvered to bring the federal government into the dispute. Their hook was the U.S. mail cars, which they attached to every train hauling Pullman cars. When strikers tried to stop those trains, the General Managers' Association appealed to President Cleveland to send in troops to protect the U.S. mail and put an end to the growing violence. It so happened that in Attorney-General Richard Olney, a former railroad lawyer, the General Managers' Association had a direct link to the president. Overriding the protests of the liberal Illinois governor, John P. Altgeld, Cleveland sent federal troops. When this tactic failed to quell the popular resistance, Olney got court injunctions prohibiting the ARU leaders from conducting the strike. Debs and his subordinates refused to obey; they were held in contempt of court and jailed. Now leaderless and hopelessly uncoordinated, the strike quickly disintegrated.

No one could doubt why the great Pullman boycott had failed: it had been crushed by the naked use of government power on behalf of the railroad companies.

American Radicalism in the Making

Oppression does not radicalize all of its victims, but for some, it does. And when social injustice is most painfully felt, when the underlying power realities stand most clearly revealed, the process of radicalization speeds up. Such was the case during the depression years of the 1890s. Out of the industrial strife of that decade emerged the main forces of twentieth-century American radicalism.

Eugene Debs and American Socialism. Very little in Eugene Debs's background suggested that he would one day become the nation's preeminent socialist. Born in 1855 to middle-class French-Alsatian parents, Debs grew up believing in the essential goodness of American society as he found it in his hometown of Terre Haute, Indiana, a prosperous midwestern railroad center. Active in the Democratic party and very popular in the community, Debs might have made a career in politics or business. Instead, he returned to the railway yards where he had worked as a boy, got involved in the local labor movement, and in 1880, at the age of twenty-five, was elected national secretary-treasurer of the Brotherhood of Locomotive Firemen.

This was one of the craft unions that represented the skilled operating trades on the railroads. It was highly conservative, opposed to strikes, and indifferent to the well-being of low-paid track and yard laborers. This began to bother Debs, and in 1892 he unexpectedly resigned from his comfortable union post to devote himself to a new organization—the American Railway Union—that would organize all railroad workers irrespective of skill, that is, an *industrial union*.

The Pullman boycott, as it developed into a life-and-death struggle, visibly changed Debs. It had become "a contest between the producing classes and the money power of the country," he declared. Debs was sentenced to six months in the federal penitentiary not for violating any specific law but for refusing to obey court orders he knew to be trumped-up and prejudicial. He came out of jail an avowed radical, committed to a lifelong struggle against a system that enabled employers to enlist the powers of government to enforce their arbitrary rule over working people. Initially Debs identified himself as a Populist, but he quickly gravitated toward the socialist camp.

German refugees had brought the ideas of Karl Marx, the German radical philosopher, to America after the failed 1848 revolutions in Europe. Marx offered a powerful economic critique of capitalism. His prescription for revolution through class struggle inspired the most durable radical movements in the industrial world. Although little noticed in most parts of American society, Marxist socialism struck deep roots in the growing German-American communities of Chicago and New York. In 1877 the Socialist Labor party was

formed, and from that time on Marxist socialism maintained a continuing, if narrowly based, presence in American politics.

When Eugene Debs appeared in their midst in 1897, the socialists were in a state of crisis. Their leader, Daniel De Leon, was a brilliant theorist but a poor political manager. He preferred an ideologically pure party to one that tried to win the popular vote. De Leon's rigid beliefs prompted a revolt within the Socialist Labor party, in which Debs joined. When the rival Socialist Party of America was formed in 1901, it was with the aim of building a broad-based political movement.

A spellbinding campaigner, Debs was a superb spokesman for his party. He had the common touch and attracted a devoted national following. Debs talked about socialism in a popular idiom, making Marxism understandable and persuasive to many ordinary Americans. Under him the new party began to break down ethnic barriers and attract American-born voters. Many trade unionists, disillusioned as Debs had been by the unsettling events of the 1890s, went through the same kind of radical evolution and joined the party in large numbers. In Texas, Oklahoma, and Minnesota socialism exerted a powerful appeal among cotton and wheat farmers. The party was also highly successful at attracting women activists. Inside of a decade, with a national network of branches and state organizations, the Socialist party had become a force to be reckoned with in American politics.

Western Radicalism. In the meantime, a different brand of American radicalism was taking shape in the West. After many years of mostly friendly labor relations, the situation in the western mining camps turned ugly during the 1890s. Powerful new corporations were taking over, and they wanted to get rid of the miners' union, the Western Federation of Miners (WFM). Moreover, silver and copper prices became increasingly unprofitable in the early 1890s, bringing pressure to cut miners' wages. When strikes resulted, they took a particularly violent turn.

In 1892 at Coeur d'Alene, a silver-mining district in northern Idaho, striking miners engaged in gun battles with company guards, sent a car of explosive powder careering into the Frisco Mine, and threatened to blow up processing plants. Martial law was declared, federal troops came in, the strikers were crowded into "bullpens" (enclosed stockades), and the strike was broken. Similarly violent strikes took place at Cripple Creek, Colorado, in 1894; at Leadville, Colorado, in 1896; and again in Coeur d'Alene in 1899.

In those western strikes government intervention was particularly naked and unrestrained. This was partly a reaction to the level of violence, but it stemmed also from the character of politics in the lightly settled western states: either the miners would dominate state politics—as they did in a coalition with the Populists during their successful strike at Cripple Creek in 1894—or, as was increasingly true, the mine owners would dominate, with disastrous consequences for the miners.

The union leaders—Ed Boyce, Charles Moyer, and "Big Bill" Haywood—all served time in the bullpens or on the barricades and drew the appropriately grim conclusions. Initially their radicalism led them, like Debs, into the Socialist party, but they were strongly inclined toward direct action. In 1897, WFM President Boyce called on all union miners to arm themselves with rifles, and his rhetoric—that the wage system was "slavery in its worst form"—had a hard edge. Any lingering faith in the political process died in the Colorado state elections of 1904, after the suppression of bitterly fought strikes across the state in the previous two years. The miners thought they had defeated their archenemy, the Republican governor James H. Peabody, only to have the Colorado Supreme Court overturn the election results and reinstall Peabody (who, by prearrangement, resigned in favor of his lieutenant governor).

In 1905 the Western Federation of Miners led the way in creating a new radical labor movement, the Industrial Workers of the World (IWW). Although the IWW initially had links to the Socialist party, it swiftly repudiated political action and settled on its own radical course. The Wobblies, as IWW members were called, fervently supported the Marxist class struggle—but strictly in the industrial field. Through action at the point of production and an unending struggle against employers—ultimately by means of a general strike—they believed that the workers themselves would bring about a revolution. A workers' society would emerge, run directly by the workers through their industrial unions. The term *syndicalism* describes this brand of workers' radicalism.

In both of its major forms—the politically oriented Socialist party and the syndicalist IWW—American radicalism flourished after the crisis of the 1890s, but only on a limited basis. Socialists and Wobblies lived, in a sense, on the tolerance of society. They would later be crushed without ceremony. Nevertheless, they served a larger purpose. American radicalism, by its sheer vitality, bore witness to what was exploitative and unjust in the new industrial order.

Summary

American industrialism took its modern shape during the last decades of the nineteenth century. Central to this development were the shift from iron making to the manufacture of steel, the great expansion of coal mining, and the technology for generating steam and electric power. These advances made possible the production of the capital goods and energy required by an expanding manufacturing economy. An efficient railway system provided access to national markets. A managerial revolution enabled entrepreneurs to master the complex business organizations they were building. The scale of enterprise grew very large, and the vertically integrated firm became the predominant form of business organization. Only in the South did prevailing conditions—in particular, its insulated, low-wage labor market—retard the growth of an advanced industrial economy.

In the North the enormous demand for labor led to a great influx of immigrants, making ethnic diversity a distinctive feature of the American working class. Gender also defined occupational opportunity. Women joined the labor force in growing numbers, but almost universally they were subjected to a sex-typing process that relegated them to "women's work," always at wage rates below those of men. Mass production—the high-volume output of standardized products—vastly improved the productivity of American manufacturing but also deskilled workers and mechanized their jobs. Scientific management, the brainchild of Frederick W. Taylor, cut further into the traditional autonomy of American workers by systematizing the labor process and shifting control into the hands of supervisors.

The late nineteenth century gave rise to the American labor movement in its modern form. In the Knights of Labor anticapitalist labor reform enjoyed one final surge during the mid 1880s and then succumbed to the "pure and simple" unionism of the American Federation of Labor. The AFL was conservative in that it accepted the economic order, but its insistence on a larger share of the benefits for working people guaranteed that the trade-union movement would be fiercely resisted by employers. The result was a series of bitter strikes: Homestead in 1892, the Pullman boycott of 1894, and, most violently, the series of metal miners' strikes in the Far West. The industrial warfare of the 1890s stirred new radical impulses, leading on the one hand to the political socialism of Eugene Debs and on the other to the industrial radicalism of the IWW.

TIMELINE

1869	Knights of Labor founded in Philadelphia First transcontinental railroad completed
1872	Montgomery Ward, first mail-order house, founded Andrew Carnegie starts construction of Edgar Thompson steel works near Pittsburgh
1873	Panic of 1873 ushers in economic depression
1875	John Wanamaker establishes first department store in Philadelphia
1876	Philadelphia Centennial Exhibition showcases Corliss steam engine
1877	Baltimore and Ohio workers initiate nationwide railroad strike
1878	Gustavus Swift introduces refrigerator car
1879	Jay Gould begins to build Missouri Pacific railway system
1883	Railroads establish national time zones
1886	Haymarket Square bombing in Chicago American Federation of Labor (AFL) founded
1890	U.S. surpasses Britain in producing iron and steel
1892	Homestead steel strike crushed Coeur d'Alene miners' strike inaugurates era of industrial warfare in western mining
1893	Panic of 1893 starts depression of the 1890s Wave of railroad bankruptcies; reorganization by investment bankers begins
1894	President Cleveland sends troops to break Pullman boycott
1895	Frederick W. Taylor explains scientific management in "A Piece-Rate System" Southeastern European immigration exceeds northern European immigration for the first time
1901	Eugene V. Debs helps found Socialist party
1905	Industrial Workers of the World (IWW) launched

★   ★   ★

BIBLIOGRAPHY

The most useful introduction to the economic history of this period is Edward C. Kirkland, *Industry Comes of Age, 1860–1897* (1961). A more sophisticated analysis can be found in W. Elliot Brownlee, *Dynamics of Ascent* (rev. ed., 1979). For essays on many of the topics covered in this chapter, consult Glenn Porter, ed., *Encyclopedia of American Economic History* (3 vols., 1980).

Industrial Capitalism Triumphant

On railroads a convenient introduction is John F. Stover, *American Railroads* (1970). The growth of the railroads as an integrated system has been treated in George R. Taylor and Irene D. Neu, *The American Railway Network, 1861–1890* (1956). Thomas Cochran, *Railroad Leaders, 1845–1890* (1953), is a pioneering study of the industry's entrepreneurs. Julius Grodinsky, *Jay Gould: His Business Career, 1867–1892* (1957), is a complex study that describes the contributions this railroad buccaneer made to the transportation system. Books such as Cochran's and Grodinsky's have gone a long way toward resurrecting Gilded Age businessmen from the debunking tradition first set forth with great power in Matthew Josephson, *Robber Barons: Great American Fortunes* (1934). Peter Temin, *Iron and Steel in the Nineteenth Century* (1964), is the best treatment of that industry. Joseph F. Wall, *Andrew Carnegie* (1970), is the definitive biography of the great steelmaker. Equally definitive in regard to the oil king is Allan Nevins, *A Study in Power: John D. Rockefeller* (2 vols., 1953). On the development of mass production the key book is David A. Hounshell, *From the American System to Mass Production, 1800–1932* (1984). Alfred D. Chandler, *The Visible Hand: The Managerial Revolution in American Business* (1977), is not an easy book but will amply repay the labors of interested students.

On the New South the standard work has long been C. Vann Woodward, *Origins of the New South, 1877–1913* (1951). Equally essential as a modern reconsideration is Edward L. Ayers, *The Promise of the New South: Life after Reconstruction* (1992). A brilliant reinterpretation of the causes of the South's economic retardation is Gavin Wright, *Old South, New South: Revolutions in the Southern Economy since the Civil War* (1986). Jacqueline Jones, *The Dispossessed: America's Underclasses from the Civil War to the Present* (1992), contains an excellent treatment of southern labor.

The World of Work

To understand the impact of industrialism on American workers, three collections of essays make the best starting points: Herbert G. Gutman, *Work, Culture and Society in Industrializing America* (1976); Michael S. Frisch and Daniel J. Walkowitz, eds., *Working-Class America: Essays on Labor, Community, and American Society* (1983); and Leon Fink, *In Search of the Working Class* (1994). On the introduction of Taylorism, the most useful book is Daniel Nelson, *Managers and Workers: Origins of the New Factory System* (1975). The impact of Taylorism on American workers is treated with insight in David Montgomery, *The Fall of the House of Labor: The Workplace, the State, and American Labor Activism, 1865–1925* (1987).

Two valuable collections of essays on immigrant workers are Richard Ehrlich, ed., *Immigrants in Industrial America* (1977), and Dirk Hoerder, ed., *American Labor and Immigration History, 1877–1920: Recent European Research* (1983). David Brody, *Steelworkers in America: The Nonunion Era* (1960), examines workers in a single industry. John Bodnar, *Immigration and Industrialization: Ethnicity in an American Mill Town* (1977), is an important case study of a single community. On women workers the best introduction is Alice Kessler-Harris, *Out to Work* (1982). Ava Baron, ed., *Work Engendered: Toward a New History of American Labor* (1991), is a rich collection of essays that apply gender analysis to the history of working people. On black workers useful introductions are William H. Harris, *The Harder We Run: Black Workers since the Civil War* (1982), and Philip S. Foner, *Organized Labor and the Black Worker* (1974). Walter Licht, *Getting Work: Philadelphia, 1840–1950* (1992), is a pioneering history of a labor market in operation.

The Labor Movement

The standard book on the struggle between labor reform and trade unionism is Gerald N. Grob, *Workers and Utopia, 1865–1900* (1961). For the Knights of Labor, it should be supplemented by Leon Fink, *Workingmen's Democracy: The Knights of Labor and American Politics* (1983), which captures the cultural dimensions of labor reform not seen by earlier historians. The place of labor in the political environment is the subject of David Montgomery, *Citizen Worker* (1993). Paul Krause, *The Battle for Homestead, 1880–1892* (1992), puts the great strike in a larger social context. The most recent survey, incorporating much of the latest scholarship, is Bruce Laurie, *Artisans into Workers: Labor in Nineteenth Century America* (1989).

The founder of the AFL is the subject of a lively brief biography by Harold Livesay, *Samuel Gompers and Organized Labor in America* (1978). Among the many books on individual unions, Robert Christie, *Empire in Wood* (1956), best reveals the way pure-and-simple unionism worked out in practice. On industrial conflict the most vivid book is Robert V. Bruce, *1877: Year of Violence* (1959). Stanley Buder, *Pullman: An Experiment in Industrial Order and Community Planning, 1880–1930* (1967), provides an informed account of the great Pullman strike and places it in its local context. The best book on the IWW is Melvyn Dubofsky, *We Shall Be All* (1969). On socialism, David Shannon, *The Socialist Party of America* (1955), remains the standard account. There is, however, a fine biography of that party's leader that supersedes previous studies: Nick Salvatore, *Eugene V. Debs: Citizen and Socialist* (1982). A dimension of American radicalism long neglected has received sensitive attention in Mari Jo Buhle, *Women and American Socialism, 1870–1920* (1982).

Bandanna, 1888 Election Memorabilia

During the late nineteenth century, politics became a vibrant part of America's culture. Party paraphernalia, such as the bandanna above, flooded the country. (Museum of American Political Life)

CHAPTER *19*

The Politics of Late Nineteenth-Century America

★   ★   ★

Ever since the founding of the republic, foreign visitors had been coming to America to study its political system. Most famous of the early observers was Alexis de Tocqueville, who wrote *Democracy in America* in 1832. When an equally brilliant visitor, the Englishman James Bryce, sat down to write his own account fifty years later, he decided that Tocqueville's great book could not serve as his model. For Tocqueville, Bryce noted "America was primarily a democracy, the ideal democracy, fraught with lessons for Europe." In his book, *The American Commonwealth* (1888), Bryce was much less rhapsodic. Democratic government as it existed in the America of the 1880s seemed to Bryce "a cause not so potent in the moral and social sphere as [Tocqueville] deemed it." The robust democracy celebrated by Tocqueville had devolved half a century later into the dreary machine politics of the Gilded Age.

Bryce was anxious that the European readers for whom he was writing not misunderstand him. His rigorously factual account of American politics contained "much that is sordid, much that will provoke unfavourable comment." Europeans should place those facts not in the context of their own countries, however, but in that of the United States. They needed to be aware of "the existence in the American people of a reserve of force and patriotism more than sufficient to sweep away all the evils now tolerated." Bryce was ultimately an optimist: "A hundred times in writing this book have I been disheartened by the facts I was stating; a hundred times has the recollection of the abounding strength and vitality of the nation chased away these tremours."

Just what it was that Bryce found so disheartening in the practice of American politics is the first subject of this chapter; the chapter will then discuss how the underlying vitality Bryce sensed began to reinvigorate the nation's politics by the start of the twentieth century.

The Politics of the Status Quo, 1877–1893

In times of national ferment, as a rule, public life becomes magnified. Leaders emerge. Electoral campaigns debate great issues. The powers of government expand. That had certainly been true of the Civil War era. During the crises of Union and Reconstruction the nation's public institutions had been tested to the utmost. The final crisis had occurred over the contested presidential election of 1876. In 1877, with the Republican Rutherford B. Hayes safely settled in the White House and the last federal troops withdrawn from the South, the era of sectional strife finally ended.

Political life went on, but it had been drained of its earlier drama. In the 1880s there were no Lincolns and no great national debates. Whereas defenders of the Union had once envisioned a social order and an economic system reshaped by an activist state, in the 1880s the nation's political leaders retreated to a more modest conception of state power. There remained an irreducible core of public functions—from managing the currency to crafting an Indian policy—and even, as on the question of railroad regulation, grudging acceptance of new governmental engagement. But the dominant rhetoric celebrated that government which governed least and as compared with the Civil War era, American government did govern less. In other ways, however, political life remained robust. The parties were highly organized and very active. And politics provided an arena in which the fierce cultural conflicts dividing Americans could be played out. But public policy itself seemed of no great moment; the nation's central concerns lay elsewhere.

The National Scene

There were five presidents from 1877 to 1893: Rutherford B. Hayes (Republican, 1877–1881), James A. Garfield (Republican, 1881), Chester A. Arthur (Republican, 1881–1885), Grover Cleveland (Democrat, 1885–1889), and Benjamin Harrison (Republican, 1889–1893). All were estimable men. Hayes, Garfield, and Harrison boasted distinguished war records. Hayes had served effectively as governor of Ohio for three terms, and Garfield had done well as a Congressional leader. Arthur, despite his reputation as a machine politician, had demonstrated fine administrative skills as head of the New York customs house. Cleveland had made his mark as reform mayor of Buffalo and governor of New York. None was a charismatic leader, and only Cleveland, the lone Democrat, was an assertive public figure. But circumstances more than personal qualities explain why these presidents did not make a larger mark on history.

Grover Cleveland
In the years after Reconstruction, Americans did not look for charismatic personalities or dramatic leadership in their presidents. They preferred men who accepted the limits of executive power, men of "sound conservatism." Grover Cleveland fitted the bill to perfection. For political reformers, Cleveland had the additional virtues of independence and personal integrity. He best represented the late nineteenth-century ideal of the American president.

Their biggest job was to dispense political patronage. Under the spoils system, government appointments were treated as rewards for those who had served the victorious party. Reform of this system became an urgent issue after President Garfield was killed in 1881. His assassin, Charles Guiteau, was a deranged religious fanatic, but advocates of civil-service reform managed to blame Garfield's death on the poisonous atmosphere of the spoils system. The resulting Pendleton Act of 1883 created a list of civil-service jobs to be filled on the basis of examinations administered by the new Civil Service Commission. The list originally included only 10 percent of all federal jobs, however, and patronage remained a preoccupation in the White House. When the Democrats won the presidency in 1884 for the first time in nearly thirty years, the pent-up hunger for jobs by the party faithful nearly overwhelmed Grover Cleveland. He was

known to complain bitterly about the "damned, everlasting clatter for office." The standards of public administration did rise measurably, but there was no American counterpart to the elite professional civil services taking shape in Britain and Germany in these years.

Other than dispensing patronage, presidents did not have a lot to do. As late as 1897 the White House staff consisted of half a dozen assistants plus a few clerks, doorkeepers, and messengers. The president exerted little control over the federal bureaucracy. Budgetary matters were not his province but Congress's, and federal agencies accordingly paid much more heed to Capitol Hill and the key money-dispensing committees than to the White House.

The functions of the executive branch were, in any event, limited in these years. Of the 100,000 federal employees in 1880, fully 56 percent worked for the U.S. Post Office. During the 1880s the important government departments—Treasury, State, War, Navy, Interior—were sleepy places carrying on largely routine duties. Virtually all federal income came from customs duties and the excise tax on liquor and tobacco. These sources produced more money than the government spent. The question of how to reduce the federal *surplus* ranked as one of the most troublesome issues of the 1880s.

As for setting a national agenda, this was—unlike in Lincoln's day or our own—not to be looked for from the White House. "The office of President is essentially executive in nature," Cleveland insisted, not involving policy making. In fact, as a Democratic president facing a hostile Republican Senate, Cleveland did begin to assert himself on policy matters, but in a mostly negative way: in his first term he vetoed a record number of bills.

Congressional Government. On matters of national policy presidents took a back seat to Congress. But Congress was not well set up to do its work. Party discipline was weak, and procedural rules frequently stymied legislative business. Neither party ever stayed in power long enough to push through a coherent legislative program. From 1877 to 1893 neither Democrats nor Republicans controlled both houses for more than a single two-year term. Most of the time, the Democrats controlled the House and the Republicans ran the Senate.

Historically, the two parties represented somewhat different traditions. The Democrats favored states' rights and limited government whereas the Republicans were heirs to the Whig enthusiasm for publicly assisted economic development. After Reconstruction the Republicans backed away from that activist position and, in truth, neither party was eager to translate the remaining differences into well-defined positions. On most of the leading issues of the day—civil-service reform, the currency, and regulation of the railroads—the divisions occurred within the parties, not between them. The laws Congress passed could not be clearly identified as either Democratic or Republican.

Only the tariff retained its potency as a partisan issue. From Lincoln's day onward high duties protected American industry against imported goods. It was an article of Republican faith, as President Harrison said in 1892, that "the protective system . . . has been a mighty instrument for the development of the national wealth." The Democrats, free traders by tradition, regularly attacked Republican protectionism. In practice, however, the tariff was a negotiable issue like any other. Congressmen voted in accordance with their constituents' interests, regardless of party rhetoric. As a result, every tariff bill was a patchwork of bargains among special interests.

In 1887 President Cleveland cast off his reluctance to lead the nation and made the tariff a defining Democratic issue. Ardently opposed to protectionism, Cleveland devoted his entire annual message to Congress to tariff reform and campaigned on that basis for reelection in 1888. His narrow defeat seemed to confirm the political wisdom of evading big issues. "They told me it would hurt the party," he later wrote. "Perhaps I made a mistake from the party standpoint; but damn it, it was right. I had at least that satisfaction."

Campaign Politics. The major parties treated issues gingerly partly because they were so equally balanced. The Democrats, in retreat immediately after the Civil War, quickly regrouped and by the end of Reconstruction stood on virtually equal terms with the Republicans. Every presidential election from 1876 to 1892 was decided by a thin margin, and neither party gained command of Congress. Political caution seemed wise; any false move on national issues might tip the scales to the other side.

The Englishman James Bryce, accustomed to the ideological divisions between Tories and Liberals, grumbled about the indistinctness of American politics. "Neither party has any principles, any distinctive tenets," he wrote. Perhaps Bryce exaggerated when he added, "All has been lost, except office or the hope of it." But electoral success had unquestionably taken precedence over party principle.

This was evident in the way the Republican party treated its Civil War legacy. The major unfinished business after 1877 involved the needs of the former slaves in the South. The Republican agenda called for federal funding to combat illiteracy and, even more threatening to the South, federal protection for black voters in southern Congressional elections. Neither measure managed to make it through Congress, and both died during the Harrison administration. With little left to gain from Reconstruction politics, the Republicans backpedaled on the race issue and gradually abandoned the blacks to their fate.

The Republicans were not so willing to abandon their Civil War identification as saviors of the Union. In every election campaign Republican orators "waved the bloody shirt" against the "treasonous" Democrats. Service in the Union army gave candidates a strong claim to public office. One-third of Republican congressmen in the 1880s had a war record, and veterans' benefits always stood high on the Republican agenda. The Democrats played the same game in the South as the defenders of the Lost Cause. Bryce criticized American politicians for "clinging too long to outworn issues and neglecting the problems . . . which now perplex the country."

Alternatively, campaigns could descend into comedy. In the hard-fought election of 1884, for example, the Democrat Cleveland burst onto the scene as a reformer, fresh from his victories over corrupt machine politics as Buffalo mayor and New York governor. The Kansas editor William Allen White saw Cleveland as the champion of a people "sick with politics" and "nauseated at all politicians." But it turned out that years

earlier Cleveland had fathered an illegitimate child, and throughout the campaign he was dogged by the ditty "Maw, Maw, where's Paw? He's in the White House, haw-haw-haw." His opponent, James G. Blaine, already on the defensive for taking favors from the railroads, got tangled up in the scandalous charge by a too ardent Republican supporter that the Democrats were the party of "Rum, Romanism and Rebellion." In the midst of all the mudslinging, the issues got lost.

The characteristics of public life in the 1880s—the inactivity of the federal government, the evasiveness of the political parties, and the absorption in politics for its own sake—derived ultimately from the conviction that little was at stake in public affairs. In 1887 Cleveland vetoed a small appropriation for drought-stricken Texas farmers with the remark that "though the people support the Government, the Government should not support the people." Governmental activity was itself considered a bad thing. All that the state can do, said Republican Senator Roscoe Conkling, "is to clear the way of impediments and dangers, and leave every class and every individual free and safe in the exertions and pursuits of life." Conkling was expressing the political corollary to the doctrine of *laissez-faire*—the belief that that government was best which governed least.

The Ideology of Individualism

In 1885, when the Knights of Labor were at their peak, the cotton manufacturer Edward Atkinson gave a talk to the textile workers of Providence, Rhode Island. They had, he told them, no cause for discontent: "There is always plenty of room on the front seats in every profession, every trade, every art, every industry. . . . There are men in this audience who will fill some of those seats, but they won't be boosted into them from behind." (There were certainly women as well in the audience—at least half the Rhode Island labor force was female—but, as was characteristic of the times, Atkinson assumed that economic opportunity was of interest only to men.) Every man, Atkinson continued, got what he deserved. For example, Cornelius Vanderbilt had amassed a fortune of $200 million by building the New York Central Railroad. Atkinson made some rapid calculations. Every person in the audience consumed about a barrel of flour a year. In 1865 it had cost $3.45 to ship that barrel from Chicago to Providence. In 1885 the New York Central carried it for 68 cents, taking 14 cents as profit, so that the workingman saved nearly $3. "Wasn't Vanderbilt a cheap man for you to employ as a teamster?" Atkinson asked. "Do you grudge him the fourteen cents?"

Atkinson's homely talk went to the roots of conservative American thought: any man, however humble, could rise as far as his talents would carry him; every

The Plumed Knight

In the fierce party politics of the Gilded Age the political cartoon became a polished art form, and its high priest was Thomas Nast. In this cartoon Nast pillories James G. Blaine, celebrated as the "Plumed Knight" among his Republican supporters but fatally damaged in his ambitions to become president by reports that as Speaker of the House of Representatives he had taken bribes from an Arkansas railroad. Nast depicts the "knight" Blaine jousting in a tournament, with this ironic comment: "The 'Great American' Game of Public Office for Private Gain."

Facing the World

The cover of this Horatio Alger novel (1893) captures the myth of opportunity that Edward Atkinson extolled to his audience of textile workers. Our hero "Harry Vane" is a poor but earnest lad, valise packed, ready to make his way in the world and, despite the many obstacles thrown in his path, sure to succeed. In some 135 books Horatio Alger repeated this story, with minor variations, for an eager reading public that numbered in the millions.

person received his just reward, great or small; and the success of the individual, so encouraged, contributed to the progress of the whole. How persuasive the workers listening to Atkinson found his message we have no way of knowing. But the confidence with which Atkinson presented his case is evidence of the continuing appeal of the ideology of individualism in the age of industrial expansion.

A wide variety of popular writings trumpeted the individualist creed, from the rags-to-riches tales of Horatio Alger to the stream of success manuals with titles such as *Thoughts for the Young Men of America, or a Few Practical Words of Advice to those Born in Poverty and Destined to be Reared in Orphanages* (1871). It was a lesson celebrated in the lives of self-made men such as Andrew Carnegie, whose book *Triumphant Democracy* (1886) paid homage to a nation that had enabled a penniless Scottish child to rise from bobbin boy to steel magnate.

From the pulpit came the assurances of the Episcopal bishop William Lawrence of Massachusetts that "Godliness is in league with riches." Bishop Lawrence

was voicing a tradition in American Protestantism that went back to the Puritans: success in one's earthly calling signified the promise of eternal salvation. It was all too easy for a conservative ministry to make the furious acquisitiveness of industrial America morally reassuring. "To secure wealth is an honorable ambition," intoned the Baptist minister Russell H. Conwell in his lecture "Acres of Diamonds." "Money is power. Every good man and woman ought to strive for power, to do good with it when obtained." This notion of *stewardship*—the idea that wealth carried with it a social obligation—Andrew Carnegie elevated into a formal doctrine that he called "the gospel of wealth." Carnegie argued that it was the responsibility of the rich to put their money to good use. They should not coddle the less privileged but provide the libraries, education, and cultural and scientific institutions by which the worthy poor might prepare themselves for life's challenges.

Social Darwinism. American individualism drew strong intellectual support from the most important scientific theory of the age. In *The Origin of Species* (1859) the British naturalist Charles Darwin had presented a bold hypothesis to explain the evolution of plants and animals. In nature, Darwin wrote, all living things struggle and compete. Individual members of a species are born with characteristics that better enable them to survive in their particular environment: camouflage coloring for a bird, for example, or resistance to thirst in a desert animal. These survival characteristics, since they are heritable, become dominant in future generations, and the species evolves. This process of evolution, which Darwin called *natural selection*, created a revolution in biological science.

Although unintentionally, Darwin's theory made a big impact on the study of human society. Drawing on Darwin, the British philosopher Herbert Spencer developed an elaborate analysis of how society evolved through constant competition and "survival of the fittest." Social Darwinism, as Spencer's ideas became known, was championed in America by William Graham Sumner, a sociology professor at Yale. Competition, said Sumner, is a law of nature that "can no more be done away with than gravitation." Furthermore, "if we do not like the survival of the fittest, we have only one possible alternative, and that is the survival of the unfittest. The former is the law of civilization; the latter is the law of anti-civilization." And who are the fittest? "The millionaires. . . . They may fairly be regarded as the naturally selected agents of society. They get high wages and live in luxury, but the bargain is a good one for society."

Social Darwinists also argued against any interference with social processes. "The great stream of time and earthly things will sweep on just the same in spite of us," Sumner wrote in a famous essay, "The Absurd At-

tempt to Make the World Over" (1894). "That is why it is the greatest folly of which a man can be capable to sit down with a slate and pencil to plan out a new social world." As for the government, it had "at bottom . . . two chief things . . . with which to deal. They are the property of men and the honor of women. These it has to defend against crime." The political meaning of Social Darwinism was clear. As Sumner put it: "Minimize to the utmost the relations of the state and industry."

The Supremacy of the Courts. This antigovernment appeal not only paralyzed political initiative but also shifted power away from the executive and legislative branches. "The task of constitutional government," declared Sumner, "is to devise institutions which shall come into play at critical periods to prevent the abusive control of the powers of a state by the controlling classes in it." Sumner meant the judiciary. From the 1870s onward the courts increasingly accepted the role that he assigned to them, becoming the guardians of the rights of private property against abuse by an intrusive government.

The main targets of the courts were the states rather than the national government. This was the case because, under the federal system as it was understood in the late nineteenth century, the residual powers—those not delegated by the Constitution to the federal government—left to the states primary responsibility for social welfare and economic regulation. The basis for this authority was the *police powers* of the states to ensure the health, safety, and morals of their citizens. How to strike a balance between state responsibility for the general welfare and the liberty of individuals to pursue their private interests was the dominant legal issue of the era. The problem might have been harder except for the fact that most states, caught up in the conservative ethos of the day, were themselves cutting back on expenditures and public services. Even so, there were more than enough state initiatives to alarm vigilant judges. Thus, in the landmark case *In Re Jacobs* (1885), the New York Supreme Court struck down a state law prohibiting cigar making in tenements on the grounds that such regulation exceeded the police powers of the state. The 1880s saw a record number of laws declared unconstitutional by state courts.

Increasingly, however, it was federal judges who took up the battle against state activism. The Supreme Court's crucial weapon in this campaign was the Fourteenth Amendment (1868), which prohibited the states from depriving "any person of life, liberty, or property, without due process of law." The due-process clause had been adopted during Reconstruction to protect the civil rights of the former slaves. But due process protected the property rights and contractual liberty of any "person," and corporations counted as persons. So interpreted, the Fourteenth Amendment became by the turn of the century a powerful means of restraining the states in the use of their police powers.

The Supreme Court erected similar barriers against the federal government through a narrow reading of the Constitution. In 1895 the Court ruled that the federal power to regulate interstate commerce did not cover manufacturing and struck down a federal income tax law. And in areas where federal power was undeniable—such as the regulation of railroads—the Supreme Court reserved for itself the oversight of decisions that invaded property interests, such as how much railroads could charge their customers. The courts in effect were claiming for themselves the power to shape public policy on economic affairs.

The preeminent conservative jurist of the day, Stephen J. Field, made no bones about the dangers he saw in the nation's headlong industrial development: "As population and wealth increase—as the inequalities in the conditions of men become more and more marked and disturbing—as . . . angry menaces against order find vent in loud denunciations—it becomes more and more the imperative duty of the court to enforce with a firm hand every guarantee of the Constitution."

Power conferred status. The law, not politics, attracted the ablest people and held the public's esteem. A Wisconsin judge boasted: "The bench symbolizes on earth the throne of divine justice. . . . Law in its highest sense is the will of God." Judicial supremacy reflected the degree to which the ideology of individualism had become dominant in industrial America; it also testified to the low esteem to which American politics had sunk after Reconstruction.

Cultural Politics

Yet for all the criticism leveled against it, politics figured centrally in the nation's life. Proportionately more voters turned out in presidential elections from 1876 to 1892 than at any other time in American history, and these voters showed the highest commitment to the party of their choice. People voted Democratic or Republican for a lifetime. Many participated actively. Among Republican voters in New York City, a fourth were dues-paying party members. National conventions attracted huge crowds. "The excitement, the mental and physical strains," remarked an Indiana Republican after the 1888 convention, "are surpassed only by prolonged battle in actual warfare, as I have been told by officers of the Civil War who later engaged in convention struggles." The convention he described had nominated the colorless Benjamin Harrison on a routine platform. What was all the excitement about? Why did politics mean so much to late nineteenth-century Americans?

For one thing, politics was a vibrant part of the nation's culture. The journalist George M. Towle told a

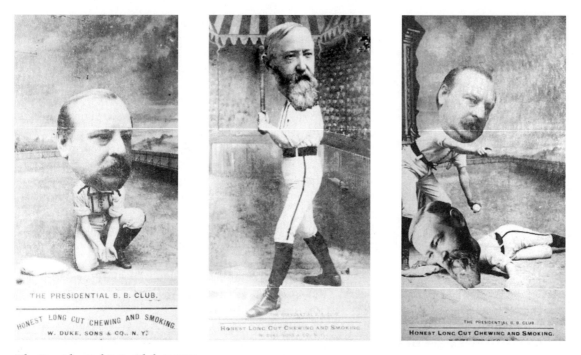

The Presidential B.B. Club (1888)
On the left, Grover Cleveland is the baseman; at center Benjamin Harrison is at bat;
and on the right, Cleveland tags Harrison out—not, alas, the right prediction, since
Harrison won the 1888 election.

British audience that America "is a land of conventions and assemblies, where it is the most natural thing in the world for people to get together in meetings, where almost every event is the occasion for speechmaking." Spellbinding orators such as Herbert G. Ingersoll drew enormous crowds at Republican rallies. During the election season the party faithful marched in impressive torchlight parades. Party paraphernalia flooded the country—handkerchiefs, mugs, posters, and buttons emblazoned with the Democratic donkey or the Republican elephant, symbols that had been adopted in the 1870s. In 1888 the presidential hopefuls were pictured on cards, like baseball players, in packs of Honest Long Cut tobacco. Campaigns had the suspense of baseball pennant races plus the excitement of the circus coming to town. In an age before movies and radio, politics ranked as one of the great American forms of mass entertainment.

Party loyalty was a deadly serious matter, however. Civil War emotions lasted a long time in both the North and the South. The Republican party, recalled the Cleveland reformer Brand Whitlock, was "a synonym for patriotism, another name for the nation. It was inconceivable that any self-respecting person should be a Democrat." In the North, Republicans had higher incomes and prided themselves on being the respectable elements of society. Senator George F. Hoar of Massachusetts described them as the people "who do the work of piety and charity in our churches . . . adminis-

ter the school systems, own and till their own farms . . . perform the skilled labor in the shops."

Ethnocultural Politics. More important than class, however, was religion and ethnic background. The two parties drew voters from different segments of society. Statistically, Democrats outside the South tended to be foreign-born and Catholic, whereas Republicans tended to be native-born and Protestant (see Figure 19.1). Among Protestants, the more pietistic a person's faith was—that is, the more personal and direct the believer's relationship to God—the more likely he or she was to be a Republican and to favor using the powers of the state to legislate public morality and regulate individual behavior. The Democrats, on the other hand, favored "the largest individual liberty consistent with public order."

During the 1880s ethnic tensions began to build in many cities. Education became an arena of bitter conflict. One issue was the place of foreign languages in the schools. Immigrant groups, especially the Germans, wanted their children taught in their own languages. However, native-born Americans passsed laws making English the language of instruction. In St. Louis, a heavily German city, the long-standing policy of teaching German to the entire student body was overturned after an acrimonious campaign.

Religion was an even more explosive educational issue. The use of the King James Version of the Bible in schools angered Catholics, who also fought a losing

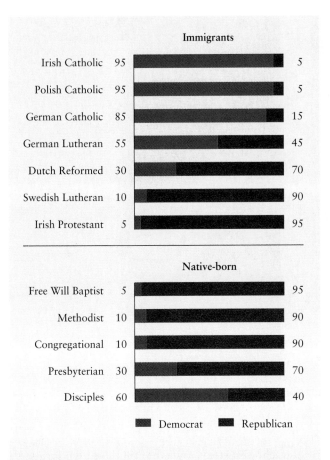

Immigrants

Group	Democrat	Republican
Irish Catholic	95	5
Polish Catholic	95	5
German Catholic	85	15
German Lutheran	55	45
Dutch Reformed	30	70
Swedish Lutheran	10	90
Irish Protestant	5	95

Native-born

Group	Democrat	Republican
Free Will Baptist	5	95
Methodist	10	90
Congregational	10	90
Presbyterian	30	70
Disciples	60	40

■ Democrat ■ Republican

FIGURE 19.1

*Ethnocultural Voting Patterns in the Midwest,
1870–1892*

These figures demonstrate how voting patterns among midwesterners reflected ethnicity and religion in the late nineteenth century. Especially striking is the overwhelming
preference by immigrant Catholics for the Democratic party.
Among Protestants there was an equally strong preference
for the Republican party by certain groups of immigrants
(Swedish Lutherans and Irish Protestants) and native-born
(Free Will Baptists, Methodists, and Congregationalists), but
other Protestant groups were more evenly divided in their
party preferences.

battle over public aid for parochial schools. By 1900
such aid had been prohibited by twenty-three states. In
Boston a furious controversy broke out in 1888 over
the use of an anti-Catholic history textbook. When the
school board withdrew the offending book, angry
Protestants mounted a campaign to throw the moderates off the board and return the text to the curriculum.

Then there was the regulation of public morals. In
many states so-called blue laws restricted activity on
Sundays. When Nebraska banned Sunday baseball, the
state supreme court approved the law as a blow struck
in "the contest between Christianity and wrong." But

German and Irish Catholics, who saw nothing evil in a
bit of fun on Sunday, considered blue laws a violation of
their personal freedom.

The same kind of ethnocultural conflict flared over
the liquor question. In a speech introducing the first
constitutional amendment for national prohibition in
1876, Senator Henry W. Blair of New Hampshire laid
down a challenge to his immigrant critics: "Upon discussion of this issue Irishman and German will in due
time demonstrate that they are Americans." Although
the Blair amendment languished, the antiliquor movement intensified. Many states adopted strict licensing
and local-option laws governing the sale and consumption of alcoholic beverages. Indiana permitted drinking,
but only joylessly in rooms containing "no devices for
amusement or music . . . of any kind."

The hottest issues of the day—education, the liquor
question, and observance of the Sabbath—were contested along ethnic and religious lines. Because they
were also party issues—more so than tariffs, currency,
and civil-service reform—they gave deep significance to
party affiliation. Crusading Methodists thought of Republicans as the party of morality. For embattled Irish
and German Catholics the Democratic party was the
defender of their freedoms. The battles over public education and the liquor question were fought mostly at
the state and local levels of northern politics. (The
South, which received few immigrants, had a cultural
politics driven by race rather than ethnicity.) In the
North ethnocultural issues infused party affairs with a
significance that would scarcely have been apparent to
anyone looking only at the national scene.

Organizational Politics

Political life was also important because of the remarkable organizational activity it generated. By the 1870s
both major parties had evolved a formal, well-organized
structure. At the base lay the precinct or ward, where
meetings could be attended by all party members.
County, state, and national committees ran the ongoing
business of the parties. Conventions determined party
rules, adopted platforms, and selected the party's candidates for public office.

At election time the party's main job was to get out
the vote. Wherever elections were close and hard-fought,
the parties mounted intensive efforts organized down to
the individual voter. In Indiana, for example, the Republicans appointed 10,000 "district men" in 1884, each responsible for turning out a designated group of voters.
The Pennsylvania Republican party maintained a list of
800,000 voters classified by degree of voting reliability.

Only professionals could manage such a highly organized political system. The German sociologist Max
Weber remarked that Americans regarded "politics as a

The Levi P. Morton Association
The top-hatted gentlemen in this photograph constituted the local Republican party organization of Newport, Rhode Island, named in honor of Levi P. Morton, Republican leader and vice-president during the Benjamin Harrison administration (1889–1893). The maleness of party politics leaps from the photograph and asserts more clearly than a thousand words why the suffragist demand for the right to vote was met with ridicule and disbelief.

vocation." This factor, above all else, gave American politics its special character. The distinguishing trait of American politicians, James Bryce observed, was "that their whole time is more frequently given to political work, that most of them draw an income from politics . . . that they . . . are proficient in the arts of popular oratory, of electioneering, and of party management." The party system required professionals, and professionalism created careers. Politics, like professional sports and trade unionism, served as an avenue of upward mobility for the many whose ethnic or class background barred them from the opportunities open to other Americans.

Machine Politics. Party administration seemed, on its face, highly democratic. In theory, all power derived from the party members in the precinct and ward organizations. In practice, however, the professionals ran the parties through unofficial internal organizations called *machines*, which consisted of insiders willing to accept discipline and do work in exchange for getting on the public payroll or pocketing bribes and other forms of "graft." The machines tended toward one-man rule, although the "boss" ruled more through the consent of the secondary leaders than through his own absolute power. Some bosses held public office. For state leaders, the U.S. Senate was preferred because, until the adoption of the Seventeenth Amendment in 1913, senators were chosen by state legislatures rather than by popular election. But public office was not necessary for the boss to run the show.

Absorbed in the tasks of power brokerage, machine bosses tended to see public issues as somewhat irrelevant. And the high stakes of money, jobs, and influence

made for intense factionalism. In New York, Manhattan's Tammany Hall was always at odds with the upstate Demcratic machine run by Senator David B. Hill. At the national level, Republicans fought bitterly among themselves after Ulysses S. Grant left the White House in 1877. For the next six years the party was divided into two warring factions—the Stalwarts, who followed Senator Roscoe Conkling of New York, and the Halfbreeds, who were led by James G. Blaine of Maine. The split was sparked by a personal feud between Conkling and Blaine, and it lasted because of a furious struggle over patronage. The Halfbreeds represented a newer Republican generation that was more inclined to pay lip service to political reform and less committed to the old Civil War issues. But issues had little to do with the war between Stalwarts and Halfbreeds. They were really fighting over the spoils of party politics.

And yet the record was not wholly negative. Machine politics raised the standards of government in certain ways. Disciplined professionals, veterans of machine politics, measurably improved the performance of state legislatures and Congress. More important, party machines filled a void in the nation's public life. They did informally much of what the governmental system left undone, especially in the cities (see Chapter 20).

The Mugwumps. But machine politics never managed to win public legitimacy. The social elite—intellectuals, well-to-do businessmen, and old-line families—deeply resented a politics that excluded people like themselves—the "best men." There was, too, a genuine clash of values. Political reformers called for "disinterested-

ness" and "independence"—the opposite of the self-serving careerism and party regularity fostered by the machine system. Many of them had earned their spurs as Liberal Republicans fighting the reelection of President Grant in 1872.

In 1884 Carl Schurz, Edwin L. Godkin, and Charles Francis Adams, Jr., split from the Republican party again because they could not stomach its presidential candidate, James G. Blaine, whom they associated with corrupt party politics. Mainly from New York and Massachusetts, these Republicans became known as Mugwumps—a derisive bit of contemporary slang, supposedly of Indian origin, referring to pompous or self-important persons. The Mugwumps threw their support to the Democrat Grover Cleveland and might have ensured his victory by giving him the votes by which he narrowly carried New York State. After the 1884 election, something of a national reform movement sprang up, spawning good-government campaigns across the country. Although they won some municipal victories, the Mugwumps achieved more as the nation's opinion molders. They controlled the respectable newspapers and journals and occupied a strategic place in the urban world.

Most of all, the Mugwumps defined the terms of debate over party politics by denouncing the machine system for its violation of American political values. The potency of this attack was most evident in their campaign for the secret ballot, which had been pioneered in Australia. Under this reform citizens would, in the privacy of a voting booth, mark an official ballot listing the candidates of all the parties instead of submitting in public view a party-supplied ticket at the polling place. The Australian ballot, which was adopted throughout the United States in the early 1890s, freed voters from party surveillance as they exercised the right to vote.

The Mugwumps were reformers, but not on behalf of social justice. The problems of working people did not evoke their sympathy, nor did they favor using the powers of the state to alleviate the suffering of the poor. As far as the Mugwumps were concerned, that government was best which governed least. Theirs was the brand of "reform" perfectly in keeping with a politics of the status quo.

Women's Political Culture

The young Theodore Roosevelt, an up-and-coming Republican state politician in 1884, referred to the Mugwumps contemptuously as "man-milliners." The sexual slur was not accidental. In attacking organizational politics, the Mugwumps were challenging one of the bastions of male society of the late nineteenth century. Party meetings and conventions were occasions not only for

carrying on the business of politics but also for performing the satisfying rituals of male sociability amid cigar smoke and whiskey. Moreover, politics was identified with manliness. It was brutally competitive. It dealt in the commerce of power. It was frankly self-aggrandizing. Party politics in short was no place for a woman.

So it was no wonder that the woman suffrage movement met with fierce opposition in those years. Susan B. Anthony succeeded in having a constitutional amendment introduced in 1878, but the cause of woman suffrage made little headway in Congress (see American Voices, page 595). Suffragists mounted campaigns at the state level, but before 1900 women gained the right to vote in only four western states: Wyoming, Idaho, Colorado, and Utah. In other states the most they could win was the right to vote for school boards or on tax issues. "Men are ordained to govern in all forceful and

Carry Nation Under Arrest

Opponents of alcohol had traditionally advocated temperance; that is, self restraint. The Woman's Christian Temperance Union took a more coercive approach. It demanded legal prohibition of alcohol. Some prohibitionists turned to direct action. Carry Nation became famous for her ax-wielding attacks on saloons. She meant to draw attention to the struggle, and so gladly went to jail—where she is headed in this photograph, taken in Enterprise, Kansas, in 1901.

Helen Potter

The Case for Women's Political Rights

In 1883 Helen Potter testified before the Senate Committee on Education and Labor about the sanitary conditions of the poor in New York City. But in the course of her testimony she delivered a powerful indictment of the unequal treatment of women that spoke volumes about the evolving women's political culture of the late nineteenth century.

The Witness. It is really an important question—this of the condition of women in our community. When I was a young girl I had some ambition, and when I heard a good speaker, or when I read something written by a good writer, I had an ambition to do something of that kind myself. I was exceedingly anxious to preach, but the churches would not have me; why, they said that a woman must not be heard. . . .

Q. I suppose you have an idea that women might abolish some of the tricks of the politician's trade?

A. Well, sir, it would take them a long time to learn to dare to do those things that men do in the way of politics—to sell and buy votes. . . .

Q. What would be the effect of conferring suffrage upon women? Would not the effect be injurious to the moral character and high influence of woman, if she should devote herself to the tricks of the politician's trade, which you very properly criticize so severely?

A. . . . I certainly think it would clean our streets, and I think it would purify politics, at least for the next two hundred years. It would take about that time to get women to understand the tricks of politicians as at present practiced. I do not think that women would be injured by it. . . . This Government is based upon the will of the people—women are "people," yet we have not a word to say about the laws. You will hear women in the course of your acquaintance say they wish they were men; I never heard a man say he wished he was a woman. . . .

Q. Why do you think that the suffrage is not extended to women by men— what is the true reason, the radical reason, why men do not give up one half their political power to women?

A. Well, it may arise from a false notion of gallantry. I think most men feel like taking care of, and protecting the ladies. . . . It would be all very well, perhaps, if all women had representatives, and if all had a generous, straightforward honorable man to rep- resent them. But take the case of a good woman who has a drunken husband; how can he represent her? He votes for liquor and for everything he may happen to want, even though it may ruin her and turn her out of doors, and even though it may ruin her children. If the husband is a bad man would it not be better for that woman to represent herself?

Q. What effect do you think the extension of the suffrage to women would have upon their material condition, their wage-earning power and the like?

A. They would get equal pay for equal work of equal value. I do not think a woman ought to be paid the price of an expert, when she is not herself an expert, but I believe there would be a stimulus for a woman to fit herself for the very best work. What stimulus is there for woman to fit herself properly, if she never can attain the highest pay, no matter what sort of work she does? If women had a vote I think larger avenues of livelihood would be opened for them and they would be more respected by the governmental powers.

Source: U.S. Senate, Committee on Education and Labor, *Report upon Relations Between Labor and Capital* II, (1885), pp. 627, 629–632.

material things, *because they are men*," asserted an antisuffrage resolution, "while women, by the same decree of God and nature, are equally fitted to bear rule in a higher and more spiritual realm, where the strong frame and the weighty brain count for less"—that is to say, not in politics. Yet this invocation of the doctrine of "separate spheres"—that men and women had different natures, and that women's nature fitted them for "a higher and more spiritual realm"—did open a channel for women to enter public life.

"Women's place is Home," acknowledged the journalist Retha Childe Dorr. "But Home is not contained within the four walls of an individual house. Home is the community. The city full of people is the Family. . . . And badly do the Home and Family need their mother." So believing, women had engaged in charitable and reform activities since the early nineteenth century. Women's organizations fought prostitution, assisted the poor, agitated for the reform of women's prisons, and tried to improve educational and job opportunities for women. Since many of these goals required state intervention, women's organizations of necessity became politically active, but not, they stressed, out of any desire to participate in partisan politics or gain the ballot. Quite the contrary: women were bent on creating their own political sphere.

Thus, in 1869, Sorosis, a women's professional club in New York City, convened a Women's Parliament in the hope of launching a parallel government responsible for public matters that were of concern to women. Nothing came of the Women's Parliament, but it did indicate the degree to which the women's sphere could take a political form. If not a parallel government, the social activism of women certainly gave rise to a female political culture that made itself felt in the public life of late nineteenth-century America.

The Woman's Christian Temperance Union. No issue joined home and politics more poignantly than did the liquor question. Just before Christmas in 1873 the women of Hillsboro, Ohio, began to hold vigils and prayer meetings in front of the town's saloons, pleading with the owners to close down and end the suffering of families of hard-drinking fathers. Thus began a spontaneous uprising of women that spread across the country and, it was estimated, closed 3,000 saloons. The temperance movement had been inactive for twenty years. Now, from this groundswell of public agitation, came the Woman's Christian Temperance Union (WCTU), which after its formation in 1874 rapidly blossomed into the largest organization of women in the country.

The WCTU had a powerful consciousness-raising effect on its members and, because it excluded men, was the spawning ground for a new generation of women leaders. Under the guidance of Frances Willard, who became president in 1879, the WCTU moved beyond temperance and adopted a "Do-Everything" policy. Alcoholism, women recognized, was not simply a personal failing; it stemmed from larger social evils afflicting men. There was also an institutional reason for adopting a broader social vision. Willard's strategy would attract women who had no particular interest in the liquor question. Local bodies were encouraged to undertake causes that were important in their own communities. By 1889 the WCTU had thirty-nine departments concerned with labor, social purity, health, and international peace as well as temperance.

Most important, the WCTU was drawn to woman suffrage. This was necessary, Willard argued, "because the liquor traffic is entrenched in law, and law grows out of the will of majorities, and majorities of women are against the liquor traffic." Women needed the vote, said Willard, to fulfill their social responsibilities *as women*. This was very different from the claim made by the suffragists—that the ballot was an inherent right of all citizens *as individuals*—and was less threatening to masculine pride.

Not much changed in the short run. The WCTU was internally divided on the suffrage issue and did not become a major participant in the later struggles for women's right to vote. But by linking women's social concerns and women's political participation, the

Frances Willard
This photograph shows Willard at age thirty-three, when she was Dean of the Women's College of Northwestern University. A year later, she became corresponding secretary of the newly formed WCTU and embarked on her life's work as a temperance leader.

WCTU helped lay the groundwork for a fresh, broader-based attack on male electoral politics early in the twentieth century. And in the meantime, even without the vote, the WCTU demonstrated how potent a voice women could find in the public realm and how vibrant a political culture they could build.

The Crisis of American Politics: The 1890s

Ever since the end of Reconstruction in 1877 national politics had been stalemated by two evenly balanced parties. This equilibrium finally began to break down late in the 1880s. Benjamin Harrison's election in 1888 was the last of the cliff-hanger victories: the Democrat Grover Cleveland actually got a larger popular vote. Thereafter, the tide went heavily against the Republicans. In 1890 Democrats took the House of Representatives decisively, capturing 235 seats to the Republicans' 88, and won a number of governorships in normally Republican states. These losses can partly be explained by the lackluster performance of the Harrison administration and the success of the Democrats at tarring the

protectionist McKinley Tariff of 1890 as a giveaway to the vested interests. Less visible but more ominous for the Republicans was an erosion of grass-roots ethnocultural support, with defections on the evangelical right to the Prohibitionist party and gains by the Democrats in local battles over education and public morality. In 1892 Cleveland regained the presidency by the largest margin in 20 years.

Had everything else remained equal, the events of 1890 and 1892 might have inaugurated a long period of Democratic supremacy. But everything else did not remain equal. By the time of Cleveland's inauguration, rising farm foreclosures and railroad bankruptcies signaled economic trouble. On May 3, 1893, the stock market crashed. Before the end of the year 16,000 firms and hundreds of banks had failed. In Chicago 100,000 jobless workers walked the streets; nationwide, the unemployment rate soared to over 20 percent. As always in hard times, suffering and unrest mounted alarmingly.

As the economic crisis of the 1890s set in, which party would prevail and on what platform became an open question. The first challenge arrived from the West and the South in the form of the Populist party.

The Populist Revolt

Farmers were of necessity joiners. They needed organization to overcome their social isolation and to obtain crucial economic services—hence the enormous appeal of the Patrons of Husbandry and, after its decline, of the farmers' alliances that began to spring up among southern and western farmers after 1877. From diffuse organizational beginnings, two dominant organizations emerged. One was the Farmers' Alliance of the Northwest, which was confined mainly to the midwestern states. More dynamic was the movement that originated in Texas. In the mid-1880s the Texas-based National (or Southern) Farmers' Alliance spread rapidly across the Great Plains and eastward into the cotton South as "travelling lecturers" extolled the virtues of cooperative activity and reminded farmers of "their obligation to stand as a great conservative body against the encroachments of monopolies and . . . the growing corruption of wealth and power." While thus recapitulating Granger resentment against railroads and merchants that had fueled earlier third-party movements, the alliances conceived of themselves as agents of social and economic reform rather than as incipient political parties.

How they were drawn into politics may be best seen in the experience of the Texas Alliance, which had established a massive cooperative, the Texas Exchange, that marketed the crops of cotton farmers and provided them with cheap credit. When cotton prices fell sharply in 1891, the Texas Exchange failed. The Texas Alliance then proposed a new scheme: a *subtreasury system* that would enable farmers to store their crops in public warehouses. Farmers would be able to borrow against those crops from a federally supplied fund at low interest rates until prices rose enough so their cotton could be marketed profitably. The subtreasury plan would provide the same credit and marketing functions as had the defunct Texas Exchange, but with a crucial difference: the federal government would play the key role. The subtreasury plan was thus a *political* proposal, and when it was rejected by the Democratic party as being too radical, the Texas Alliance decided to strike out in politics independently.

These events in Texas revealed, with special clarity, a process of politicization that went on throughout the Alliance movement. Rebuffed by the established parties, alliancemen more or less reluctantly abandoned their Democratic and Republican allegiances. Across the South and West, as they grew stronger and more impatient, state alliances began to field independent slates. In 1890 third parties won control of the Nebraska and Kansas legislatures and captured several governorships and eight state legislatures in the South. These successes led to the formation of the national People's (Populist) party. In the 1892 election, with the veteran antimonopoly campaigner James B. Weaver as their presidential

Mary Elizabeth Lease

As a political movement, the Populists were short on cash and organization, but long on rank-and-file zeal and tub-thumping oratory. No one was more rousing on the stump than Mary Elizabeth Lease, who came from a Kansas homestead and pulled no punches. "What you farmers need to do," she proclaimed in her speeches, "is to raise less corn and more *Hell!*"

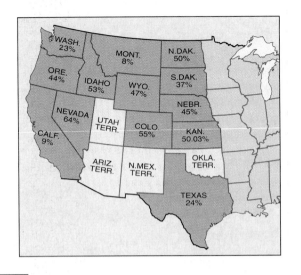

MAP 19.1

The Heyday of Western Populism, 1892
This map shows the percentage of the popular vote won by James B. Weaver, the People's party candidate, in the presidential election of 1892. Except for California and Montana, the Populists won broad support across the West and genuinely threatened the established parties in that region.

candidate, the Populists captured a million votes and carried four western states (see Map 19.1). For the first time agrarian protest truly challenged the national two-party system.

The challenge was driven as much by ideology as by the quest for political power. Populism contained a strong radical bent. The problems afflicting farmers, Populists felt, could stem only from some basic evil. They identified that evil as the control of the "money power" over the levers of the economic system. "There are but two sides," proclaimed a Populist manifesto. "On the one side are the allied hosts of monopolies, the money power, great trusts and railroad corporations. . . . On the other are the farmers, laborers, merchants and all the people who produce wealth. . . . Between these two there is no middle ground."

By this reasoning, farmers and workers formed a single producer class. The Texas-based alliance renamed itself in 1889 the National Farmers' Alliance and Industrial Union. The title was not merely rhetorical. Organized in Knights of Labor assemblies, Texas railroad workers and Colorado miners cooperated with the farmers' alliances, got their support in strikes, and actively participated in forming state Populist parties. The platform of the national party contained strong labor planks, and party leaders earnestly sought the support of the labor movement. In its explicit class appeal—in recognizing that "the irrepressible conflict between capital and labor is upon us"—Populism differed fundamentally from the two mainstream parties.

Populism was also distinguished by the prominent role that women played in the movement. In the established parties the grass-roots organizations—the local political clubs—were for men only. Populism, on the other hand, arose from a network of suballiances that had formed for largely social purposes and welcomed women. "The Alliance has come to redeem woman from her enslaved condition," proclaimed a female member from Texas. "She is admitted into the organization as an equal to her brother" and is free of "the ostracism which has impeded her intellectual progress in the past." Although women participated actively and

En Route to a Populist Rally, Dickinson County, Kansas
Farm people traveled miles to rallies and meetings for the chance to voice their grievances and socialize with like-minded folks. This tradition infused Populism with a special fervor. Gatherings such as the one these Kansans were heading for were a visible sign of what Populism meant—a movement of the "people."

Lorenzo Dow Lewelling

Populist Confessional

In this 1894 speech given before a party gathering, the governor of Kansas, Lorenzo Lewelling, gives witness to the outrage at social injustice that animated the Populists and drove their crusade against the political status quo.

I have been asked why I was a Populist. I want to say to you, friends, that the same principles that made me a Republican in the early days, have today made me a populist, and I'll tell you what they are. I remember when I was a little boy my parents were the old line abolition kind of people that believed in equal rights for all and special privileges to none. God bless them for that sentiment, and don't you say so? Well, I remember . . . a picture of an African slave with his hands uplifted and in chains, and around the rim of the coin a motto "Am I not a man and Brother?" That made a wonderful impression on my mind. I was taught thus in my infancy to stand for . . . the weak against the strong, for God knows the strong can take care of themselves. . . . The working men and women of this country, many of them, are simply in the shackles of industrial slavery.

. . . What is government to me if it does not make it possible for me to live? and to provide for my family! . . . If the Government don't do that, what better is the Government to me than a state of barbarism?

. . . The condition of the farmer is . . . about the same as that of the laborer. His earnings are naught. Add several ciphers together and you will have the sum of his profits this year and last. Take his wheat, which is worth twenty-five cents a bushel, and cost forty cents to raise it. How is he going to come out this year? I will tell you something: did you know that 43 percent of the homes in Kansas have already passed into the hands of landlords, who toil not neither do they spin? . . . We have got in the State of Kansas 10,000 people who are made homeless every year by the foreclosure of mortgages and this has been going on for several years.

Call me calamity howler if you will. I wish I had the voice and pen and reputation of Jeremiah that I might howl Calamity until the people all over this broad land should hear me. It seems to me that the night of despair is really at hand. And I ask you who is to be responsible for our civil government, if you please, by which we are turned into beasts by conditions that the Government can and should prevent?

. . . The People's party has stepped into the breach between the classes to demand justice for the poor as well as to the rich and for every man. . . . I am willing, if you are willing, to place truth against the world. Truth is mighty and it will prevail.

Source: George B. Tindall, ed., *A Populist Reader* (New York, Harper & Row, 1966). pp. 148–159. Copyright George B. Tindall.

served prominently as speakers and lecturers, only a handful achieved high office in the alliances, and their role diminished once the Populist party entered politics. In deference to the southern wing, the Populist platform was silent on woman suffrage. Still, the major parties would scarcely have countenanced a spokeswoman such as the fiery Mary Elizabeth Lease, who became famous for calling on farmers "to raise less corn and more *Hell*." Lease insisted just as strenuously on Populism's "grand and holy mission . . . to place the mothers of this nation on an equality with the fathers."

In an age dominated by laissez-faire doctrine, what most distinguished Populism from the major parties was its positive attitude toward the state. The Populist platform declared: "We believe that the powers of government—in other words, of the people—should be expanded as rapidly and as far as the good sense of an intelligent people and the teachings of experience shall justify, to the end that oppression, injustice and poverty should eventually cease in the land." Populists such as Lorenzo Dow Lewelling (see American Voices, above) considered it to be "the business of the Government to make it possible for me to live and sustain the life of my family."

The Populist program called for nationalization of the railroads and communications; protection of the land, including natural resources, from monopoly and foreign ownership; a graduated income tax; the creation of postal savings banks; the Texas Alliance's subtreasury plan; and the free and unlimited coinage of silver. From this array of issues, it was free silver that emerged as the overriding demand of the Populist party.

Free Silver. Cotton and grain farmers were especially vulnerable to falling commodity prices (see Chapter 17, page 547). In the early 1890s rock-bottom prices wreaked havoc among cotton, wheat, and corn growers and made them the core constituency of Populism. Inflationary solutions strongly attracted them. Increasing the money supply would raise farm prices and, since

farmers would be paying back their loans in cheaper dollars, lighten the burden of farm debt. But how could the money supply be increased? One way was to get the government to issue paper dollars. This was the demand that had made the Greenbackers a robust third party in much of the South and West a decade earlier. And it was a key feature of the subtreasury plan: the funds lent to farmers on the collateral of their stored crops would be new money issued by the federal government.

But free silver—the expansion of the money supply by means of the unlimited coinage of silver—quickly became the more attractive alternative. For one thing, free silver was the simpler course and was more likely to be adopted than was the subtreasury plan. In addition, free silver would bring in hefty contributions to the Populist party from silver-mining interests. The mine operators, scornful though they might be of Populist radicalism, yearned for the day when the government would buy at a premium price all the silver they could produce, and to that end they were prepared to support the Populists.

Urban social democrats such as Henry Demarest Lloyd of Chicago and agrarian radicals such as Georgia's Tom Watson pleaded that free silver not be made the leading Populist issue. It would undercut the broader Populist program, they argued, and alienate wage earners, who had no enthusiasm for inflationary measures. Any chance of a farmer-labor alliance that might transform Populism into an American version of a social democratic party would be doomed. As Lloyd complained, free silver was "the cowbird of reform," stealing in and taking over the nest that others had built.

Although fiercely debated within the party, the outcome was never in doubt. The political appeal of free silver was simply too great. But once Populism made that choice, its capacity to maintain an independent existence was fatally compromised. For free silver was not an issue on which the Populists held a monopoly. Free silver was, on the contrary, a question at the very center of mainstream politics in the 1890s.

Money and Politics

In a rapidly developing economy such as nineteenth-century America's, the money supply is bound to be a big political issue. Money has to increase rapidly enough to meet the economy's needs or growth will be stifled. How fast the money supply should grow, however, is a question that creates sharp divisions. Debtors and victims of low prices want a larger money supply: more money in circulation inflates prices and reduces the real cost of borrowing. The "sound-money" people—creditors, individuals on fixed incomes, those in the slower-growing sectors of the economy—have the opposite interest. Touching people in the pocketbook as it does, the clash of interests can be explosive.

Before the Civil War the main source of the nation's money supply had been the banknotes circulated by several thousand local banks. Although more or less subject to state regulation, those banks issued notes in their private role as providers of credit to their customers. The banknotes they gave borrowers circulated as money until they were presented to the banks for redemption. Economists tell us that the burgeoning economy's need for money was amply met by the state banks, although the goodness of the banknotes—the ability of the issuing banks to stand behind their notes and redeem them at par—was always uncertain. During the Civil War this freewheeling system came to an end. Banknotes still existed, but the National Banking Act of 1863 required that they be backed by U.S. government bonds.

The effects of this action were threefold. First, the money supply became inadequate for the country's needs. Second, the ensuing economic troubles—the deflation of prices and the scarcity of credit—magnified public debate over the money question. Third, since solutions depended so heavily on what the federal government did, the money question became much more politicized.

The constitutional power of the federal government to issue money was in theory unlimited. The Lincoln administration had paid for the Civil War largely by printing paper money—greenbacks, so-called—backed by nothing more than the government's declaration that the greenbacks were legal tender. The prevailing policy, however, going back to the founding years of the republic, was to base the federal currency on the amount of *specie*—gold and silver—held by the U.S. Treasury.

Under the bimetallic standard, silver and gold were fixed in value at a ratio of sixteen to one: 16 ounces of silver equaled 1 ounce of gold. Silver, however, had become scarce relative to gold after mid-century. As silver rose in market price, it became more valuable as metal than as money, and it disappeared from circulation. In 1873 silver was officially dropped as a medium of exchange. Soon afterward great silver discoveries occurred in Nevada, Arizona, and elsewhere in the West. With this new supply, silver prices dropped swiftly. If the government resumed the coinage of silver at a ratio of sixteen to one, silver would flow into the Treasury and greatly expand the volume of currency. This would also, of course, greatly enrich the silver-mining interests.

With so much at stake for so many people, the currency question became one of the staple issues of post-Reconstruction politics. Twice the prosilver coalition in Congress won modest victories. First, under the Bland-Allison Act of 1878, the U.S. Treasury was required to purchase and coin between $2 million and $4 million worth of silver each month. Then, in the more sweeping Sherman Silver Purchase Act of 1890, 4.5 million ounces of silver bullion was to be purchased monthly to serve as the basis for new issues of U.S. Treasury notes.

These legislative battles, although hard-fought, cut across party lines in the characteristic fashion of post-Reconstruction politics.

But in the early 1890s silver suddenly became a defining issue between the parties; in particular, it had a radicalizing effect on the Democratic party.

The Cleveland Administration and the Silver Question.

When the crash of 1893 hit, the Democrats were in power in Washington. The party in office usually gets blamed if the economy falters, but President Cleveland made things worse for the Democrats. When jobless marchers arrived in Washington in 1894 to appeal for federal relief, Cleveland's response was to disperse them forcibly and arrest their leader, Jacob S. Coxey. Cleveland's brutal handling of the Pullman strike further alienated the labor vote. Nor was he able to deliver on his campaign promise to reverse the protectionist McKinley Tariff of 1890. In a signal failure of presidential leadership, Cleveland lost control of the Congressional battle for tariff reform. The resulting Wilson-Gorman Tariff of 1894, which he allowed to pass into law without his signature, caved in to special interests and cut average rates only slightly.

Most disastrous, however, was Cleveland's rigidity on the silver question. Cleveland was a committed sound-money man who had repeatedly denounced "the dangerous and reckless experiment of free, unlimited, and independent silver coinage." Nothing that happened after the depression set in—not collapsing prices, not the suffering of farmers, not the groundswell of support for free silver in his own party—budged Cleveland from that position.

Economic pressures, in fact, soon pushed him in the opposite direction. The problem was a persistent drain on U.S. gold reserves caused partly by transfers of gold overseas due to an unfavorable balance of international payments and partly by redemptions of gold by holders of U.S. Treasury notes. To help stem the gold outflow, Cleveland persuaded Congress in 1893 to repeal the Sherman Silver Purchase Act, effectively sacrificing the country's painfully crafted effort at maintaining a partial bimetallic standard.

As his administration's difficulties deepened, Cleveland turned in 1895 to a syndicate of private bankers led by J. P. Morgan to finance the gold purchases needed to replenish the Treasury's depleted reserves. The administration's secret negotiations with Wall Street, once discovered, enraged Democrats and completed Cleveland's isolation from his party.

William Jennings Bryan and the Election of 1896.

At their national convention in Chicago in 1896, the Democrats repudiated Cleveland and turned left. The leader of the triumphant silver Democrats was William Jennings Bryan of Nebraska. Bryan was a political phenom-

enon. Only thirty-six years old, he had already served two terms in Congress and had become a passionate advocate of free silver. He was a consummate politician and, no less important, an inspiring public speaker. Bryan, remarked the journalist Frederic Howe, was "pre-eminently an evangelist. . . . He was a missionary . . . the *vox ex cathedra* of the Western self-righteous missionary mind." Bryan spoke with a biblical fervor that swept up his audiences, and he did so again when he joined the debate on free silver at the Democratic convention. He had been quietly building up delegate support while distancing himself from convention politicking. Bryan locked up the presidential nomination when he electrified the convention with a stirring attack on the gold standard: "You shall not press down upon the brow of labor this crown of thorns, you shall not crucify mankind on a cross of gold."

Bryan's nomination meant that the Democrats had identified themselves as the party of free silver; his "cross of gold" speech meant that Bryan would turn the money question into a national crusade. No one could be neutral on this defining issue. Silver Republicans bolted their party; gold Democrats went for a splinter Democratic ticket or supported the Republican party; even the Prohibition party split into gold and silver wings. The Populists, meeting after the Democratic convention, accepted Bryan as their candidate. The free silver issue had become so vital that they could not do

William Jennings Bryan

As this ironic portrait of him suggests, Bryan's special genius as a politician was to place himself above politics and link his cause with moral values deep in the American psyche.

otherwise. Although they nominated their own vice-presidential candidate, the Georgian Tom Watson, the Populists found themselves for all practical purposes absorbed into the Democratic silver crusade.

The Republicans took up the challenge. Their key party leader was Mark Hanna, a wealthy Cleveland ironmaker, a brilliant political manager, and an exponent of the new industrial capitalism. He orchestrated an unprecedented money-raising campaign among America's corporate interests. Hanna's candidate, William McKinley of Ohio, personified the virtues of Republicanism, standing solidly for prosperity, high tariffs, and honest money. While Bryan broke with tradition and crisscrossed the country in a furious whistle-stop campaign, the dignified McKinley received delegations at his home in Canton, Ohio. As Bryan orated with passionate moral fervor, McKinley talked of industrial progress and a full dinner pail.

Lawyers March for the Gold Standard
Presidential campaigns of the late nineteenth century were always hard-fought, none more so than the 1896 election. Big issues were at stake: Would the country stay on the gold standard or drastically expand the money supply through the free coinage of silver? Lawyers paraded in the streets of New York City to demonstrate their conviction that the nation's fate hung on sound money and the election of the Republican William McKinley.

Not since 1860 had the United States witnessed such a hard-fought election over such high stakes. The nation's currency had exceptional social resonance in American life. For the middle class, sound money meant the soundness of the social order. With jobless workers tramping the streets and bankrupt farmers up in arms, Bryan's fervent assault on the gold standard struck fear in many hearts. Republicans denounced the Democratic platform as "revolutionary and anarchistic." They called Bryan's supporters "social misfits who have almost nothing in common but opposition to the existing order and institutions."

Although little noticed at the time, ethnocultural issues also figured strongly in the campaign. The Republicans had been the party of morality in the 1880s, appealing to supporters of temperance and Sunday laws but thereby alienating the foreign-born and Catholic vote. The Democrats had capitalized on these tensions in making their bid for electoral dominance in 1890 and 1892. Now, in 1896, the Republicans beat a strategic retreat from the politics of morality. McKinley himself had represented a mixed district in northeastern Ohio in Congress. In appealing to his immigrant and working-class constituents he had learned the art of easy tolerance, as expressed in his phrase "live and let live." Of the two candidates, the prairie orator Bryan, with his biblical rhetoric and moral righteousness, presented the more alien image to traditional Democratic voters in the big cities.

McKinley won handily, with 271 electoral votes to Bryan's 176 (see Map 19.2). He kept the Republican ground that had been regained in the 1894 midterm elections and pushed into Democratic strongholds, especially in the cities. Boston, New York, Chicago, and Minneapolis, all taken by Cleveland in 1892, went for McKinley in 1896. Bryan ran strongly only in the South, in silver-mining states, and in the Populist West. The gains his evangelical style brought in some Republican rural areas did not compensate for his losses in traditionally Democratic urban districts.

The paralyzing equilibrium of American politics ended in 1896. The Republicans prevailed through their skillful handling of both the economic and the cultural challenges. The Republicans persuaded the nation that they were the party of prosperity and reduced the liability of being perceived as the party of moral intolerance. In 1896, too, electoral politics regained its place as an arena for national debate, setting the stage for the reform politics of the Progressive Era after 1900.

The Decline of Agrarian Radicalism. As for Populism, it simply faded away. Fusion with the Democrats in 1896 deprived the People's party of its identity and undermined its organizational structure. After the election, the issue on which Populism had staked its fate—free sil-

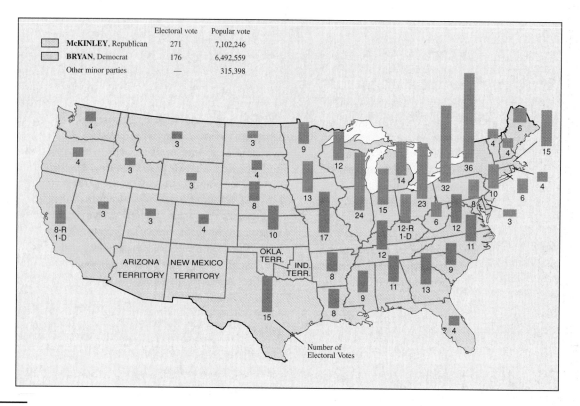

MAP 19.2

The Election of 1896

The 1896 election was one of the truly decisive elections in American history. The Republican party won by its largest margin since 1872. More important, the Republicans established a firm grip on the key midwestern and Middle Atlantic states—especially New York, Indiana, Ohio, and Illinois—that had been the decisive states in every national election since Reconstruction. The 1896 election broke a party stalemate of twenty years' duration and began a period of Republican domination that would last until 1932.

ver—vanished. During the 1890s gold was discovered in South Africa, Colorado, and the Yukon, while the new cyanide refining method greatly increased ore yields. The newly abundant gold supply took the sting out of the lost battle for free silver. At this point, moreover, the world market for agricultural commodities turned favorable. Wheat went from 72 cents a bushel in 1896 to 98 cents in 1909, corn rose from 27 cents to 57 cents, and cotton went from 6 cents to 14 cents a pound. Farm prices rose faster than did the prices of other products, and as a result, so did the real income of farmers. A new spirit of optimism took hold in the "golden age" of American agriculture before World War I.

The farmers' sense of inferiority and deprivation—that they were "rubes" and "hicks" and that life was inherently better in the city—began to subside after 1900. The new prosperity meant that more farmers could afford labor-saving home appliances and farm machinery

to lighten field work. New inventions eased the isolation and monotony of rural life. The telephone became commonplace, not so much because of the spread of commercial service but through the determined efforts of farmers themselves. Telephone cooperatives were the most common type of farm cooperative in the early twentieth century. The automobile, especially the Ford Model T, gave rural Americans a mobility they had never before known. The Country Life Commission, formed in 1908, took an optimistic view of farm society: "There has never been a time when the American farmer was as well off as he is today, when we consider not only his earning powers but the comforts and advantages he may secure."

The farmers' self-conception also changed irreversibly. In an agrarian nation, the distress of farmers could readily be regarded as a disorder of the entire country. Pushed far enough, farmers might mobilize to seize po-

litical power. In short, they could become Populists. But by the opening of the twentieth century farmers no longer constituted a majority of the population. In 1900 scarcely more than a third of the labor force earned a living from the soil; the proportion doing so would shrink in each succeeding census until, in our own time, fewer than 3 percent of the labor force is engaged in agriculture (see Appendix).

There would be times in the twentieth century when distressed farmers would turn again to insurgent politics, but never with the potency generated by the Populist party. It was as an organized interest group, not as a political movement, that farmers in the future would advance their cause.

Agriculture had long been at the heart of American life. In the twentieth century agriculture became just one more economic interest—important but subordinate in the larger scheme of the modern industrial order.

Race and Politics in the South

When Reconstruction ended in 1877, so did the hopes of African-Americans that they would enjoy the equal rights of citizenship promised them by the Fourteenth and Fifteenth amendments. Schools everywhere were strictly segregated. Access to jobs, justice, and social welfare was racially determined and unequal. And in 1883 the Supreme Court struck down the Civil Rights Act of 1875, exempting private citizens—owners of restaurants, theaters, and hotels—from the antidiscriminatory provisions of the Fourteenth Amendment. But southern state laws did not yet *require* that black pa-

trons be segregated in public accommodations, and practices varied a good deal across the South. The status quo was not stable, however, particularly when it came to railroad travel. As this became more common, whites demanded that blacks be excluded from first-class cars. By the late 1880s southern railroads were becoming the first public accommodation subject to segregation laws.

In politics the situation was even more fluid. Blacks had not been driven from politics. On the contrary, although varying from state to state, their turnout at elections was not far from that of whites in the early 1880s. But blacks did not participate on equal terms with whites. In the black belt areas, where African-Americans sometimes outnumbered whites, whites gerrymandered the districts to ensure that while blacks got some electoral representation, political control remained in white hands. Blacks, moreover, were routinely subject to intimidation and fraud at the polls—hence the large numbers whose votes were recorded as Democratic in those years. Even so, an impressive majority remained staunchly Republican, refusing, as the last black congressman from Mississippi told his House colleagues in 1882, "to surrender their honest convictions, even upon the altar of their personal necessities."

Whatever hope blacks entertained for better days, however, faded during the 1880s and then, in the next decade, expired in a terrible burst of racist terrorism. What made this outcome so tragic was that it coincided with a positive effort to overcome racial divisions. Black disfranchisement and rigid segregation stemmed directly from the crisis of the 1890s and, in particular, from a political upheaval that briefly challenged Democratic party rule in the South.

Disfranchisement
This political drawing that appeared in *Judge* magazine on July 30, 1892, shows members of the Ku Klux Klan barring black voters from the polls. By 1892, in fact, this drawing was behind the times. Literacy tests and poll taxes were beginning to disfranchise blacks with less menace and more likelihood of evading the constitutional requirement (note the sign behind the Ku Kluxers) under the Fifteenth Amendment that the right to vote not be denied "on account of race, color, or previous condition of servitude."

The Failure of Biracial Politics

No democratic society can survive if it does not enable competing economic and social interests to be heard. In the United States the two-party system performs that role. The Civil War crisis severely tested the two-party system because in both the North and the South political opposition came to be seen as treasonous. In the victorious North, despite the best efforts of the Republicans, the Democrats shed their disgrace and reclaimed their status as a major party. The South, however, was the defeated section. The scars of war went deep, and Reconstruction cut even deeper. The struggle for "home rule" empowered the Democrats. They had "redeemed" the South from black Republican domination—hence the name southern Democrats adopted: Redeemers. Cloaked in the mantle of the Lost Cause, the Redeemers claimed a monopoly on political legitimacy.

The Republican party did not fold up, however. On the contrary, it soldiered on, sustained by tenacious black loyalty, a hard core of white support, patronage from Republican national administrations, and a key Democratic vulnerability. This was the gap between the universality the Democrats claimed as the party of Redemption and the reality of who in fact controlled the party—a business elite of new entrepreneurs and older plantation owners indifferent to the plight of poor southerners.

Class antagonism, although often muted, was never absent from southern society. There had been long-smoldering differences between hill-country farmers and planters. Fresh sources of conflict now arose from the sharecropping system—which increasingly included whites as well as blacks—and from an emerging industrial working class. Unable to break the grip of the conservative elite, distressed southerners broke with the Democratic party in the early 1880s and mounted independent movements across the South. Most successful were the Readjusters, who briefly gained power in Virginia by opposing full repayment of Reconstruction debts that would enrich bond-holding speculators while leaving the state destitute. But conservative Democrats everywhere faced substantial challenges from disaffected farmers organized in Granges and acting through independent or greenback parties or, as in Tennessee, Louisiana, and Arkansas, by utilizing the Republican party. And then, after subsiding briefly, agrarian discontent revived with a vengeance, welling out of the farmers' alliances that sprang up across the South and spawning the formidable Populist challenge to Democratic rule.

What distinguished the South was not that it experienced intense agrarian protest—so, as we have seen, did the West—but that this agrarian challenge provoked a crisis in the southern party system. Refusing to countenance any opposition as legitimate, the ruling Democrats stuffed ballot boxes, intimidated black voters, murdered opponents, and stirred up racial animosity by shouting "Negro domination!" If opposition was illegitimate, moreover, did it not follow that the incurably disloyal should be excluded from politics altogether? Exclusion had been the purpose behind the cumulative poll tax adopted by Georgia in 1877 and of South Carolina's "eight-box" law (1882), which made voting a nightmare for uneducated voters. It was clear, too, which voters these disfranchising measures mainly targeted: the blacks, whose political participation everywhere insulted southern sensibilities and, in black belt districts, made rule by white Democrats perpetually uneasy.

But Populists were themselves uneasy about black participation. Racism cut through southern white society and, so some thought, most infected the lowest rungs. "The white laboring classes here," wrote an Alabaman in 1886, "are separated from the Negroes, working all day side by side with them, by an innate consciousness of race superiority," which "excites a sentiment of sympathy and equality with the classes above them, and in this way becomes a healthy social leaven." Yet when times got bad enough, hard-pressed whites could also see blacks as fellow victims. "They are in the ditch just like we are," asserted one white Texan. Southern Populists never fully reconciled these contradictory impulses. They never questioned the conventions of social inequality: blacks had not been admitted to the suballiances. Nor were the economic interests of white landowning farmers and black tenants and laborers always in concert. But once agrarian protest turned political, the logic of racial solidarity became hard to deny.

Kept out of the Southern Alliance, black farmers had organized separately into the Colored Farmers' Alliance, giving them a certain amount of leverage with the emerging Populist movement. The Knights of Labor, which was open to blacks, also argued for interracial unity. The realities of partisan politics, once the alliances had taken that step, clinched the argument. In places where the Populists fused with the Republican party, such as North Carolina and Tennessee, they automatically became allies of black leaders and gained a black constituency. In areas where fusion did not happen, the Populists knew they needed to appeal to black voters. "The accident of color can make no difference in the interest of farmers, croppers, and laborers," argued the Populist leader Tom Watson. "You are kept apart that you may be separately fleeced of your earnings." By making this interracial appeal, even if not always wholeheartedly, the Populists put at risk the foundations of conservative southern politics.

The Repudiation of Racial Equality. The Populist challenge was put down, but at a frightful cost to racial justice in the South. In the contest for the black vote the

conservative Democrats had many advantages: money, control of the local power structures, and a paternalistic relationship to the black community. They also played the race card to the hilt. The Democrats paraded as the "white man's party" while excoriating the Populists for courting "Negro rule." When all this did not suffice, mischief at the polls enabled the Democrats to beat back the Populists. Hence the Mississippian Frank Burkitt's bitter attack on the conservatives: they were "a class of corrupt office-seekers" who had "hypocritically raised the howl of white supremacy while they debauched the ballot boxes . . . disregarded the rights of the blacks . . . and actually dominated the will of the white people through the instrumentality of the stolen negro vote."

In the midst of these deadly struggles the Democrats decided to settle matters once and for all. Disfranchising the blacks, hitherto pursued hesitantly, now turned into a potent sectionwide movement. Florida adopted poll tax and multibox laws in 1889, but it was Mississippi's constitutional provision the next year for a literacy test that provided the foolproof device for driving blacks out of politics. The motives behind it were cynical, but the literacy test could be dressed up as a re-

form for Mississippians tired of the fraud and violence it took to maintain political control. "Their children and grandchildren," argued one, should not be left "with shotguns in their hands, a lie in their mouths and perjury on their lips in order to defeat the negroes." Better, a Mississippi journalist wrote, to devise "some legal defensible substitute for the abhorrent and evil methods on which white supremacy lies." This argument even persuaded some weary Populists: Frank Burkitt, for example, argued *for* the Mississippi literacy test in the words quoted in the previous paragraph. Other disfranchising methods—registration laws, property qualifications, the secret ballot (which demanded some basic literacy), and the already familiar poll tax—were also widely enacted during the 1890s, but none matched the literacy test as a flexible and efficient instrument for driving blacks from the polls (see Map 19.3).

The race issue had been instrumental in bringing down the Populists; now it helped reconcile them to defeat. Embittered poor whites, deeply ambivalent all along about interracial cooperation, turned their fury on the blacks. Insofar as disfranchising measures asserted militant white supremacy, poor whites approved. It was important, of course, that their own vulnerabil-

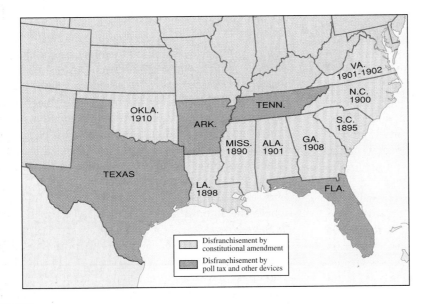

MAP 19.3

Disfranchisement in the South

In the midst of the Populist challenge to Democratic one-party rule in the South, a movement to deprive blacks of the right to vote spread from Mississippi across the South. By 1910 every state in the region except Tennessee, Arkansas, Texas, and Florida had made constitutional changes designed to prevent blacks from voting, and these four states accomplished much the same result through poll taxes and other exclusionary methods. For the next half century the political process in the South would be for whites only.

ity be partially protected by lenient enforcement and exemptions. The literacy test, for instance, was softened by Mississippi's understanding clause, which permitted illiterate voters to explain a constitutional passage that was read to them, and by Louisiana's grandfather clause, which exempted those entitled to vote on January 1, 1867, together with their sons and grandsons, from the test. But poor whites were not protected from property and poll-tax requirements, and many stopped voting. They might have objected more had they not been given a voice within the Democratic party.

From the 1890s onward a new brand of southern politician spoke for the poor whites, appealing not to their class interests but to their racial prejudices. Tom Watson, the fiery Georgia Populist, rebuilt his political career as a brilliant practitioner of race baiting. Starting in the early 1900s, he and other racial demagogues thrived throughout the South.

The Ascendancy of Jim Crow. The Populist struggle, tragically, produced a brand of white supremacy more virulent and impenetrable than anything blacks had faced since Emancipation. The color line, hitherto incomplete, became rigid and comprehensive. Segregated seating in trains, already in force generally since it was first enacted by Florida in 1887, provided a precedent for the legal separation of the races in public accommodations. Such racial legislation, known as Jim Crow laws, soon applied to every type of public facility—restaurants, hotels, streetcars, even cemeteries. In the 1890s the South became for the first time a fully segregated society by law.

The Supreme Court of the United States soon ratified the South's decision. In the case of *Plessy v. Ferguson* (1896) the Court ruled that segregation was not discriminatory—that is, it did not violate black civil rights under the Fourteenth Amendment—provided that blacks had accommodations equal to those of whites. The "separate but equal" doctrine of course had little regard for the realities of southern life: segregated facilities were rarely if ever "equal" in any material sense, and segregation was itself intended to underscore the inferiority of blacks. With a similar disregard for reality, the Supreme Court in *Williams v. Mississippi* (1898) validated the disfranchising devices of the southern states: so long as race was not a specified criterion for disfranchisement, the Fifteenth Amendment was not being violated even though the practical effect was the virtually total exclusion of blacks from politics in the South.

Race hatred became an accepted part of southern life, manifested in a wave of lynchings and race riots and in the public vilification of blacks. For example, Benjamin R. Tillman, governor of South Carolina and after 1895 a senator, excoriated blacks as "an ignorant and debased and debauched race." This ugly racism came from several sources, including intensified competition between whites and blacks during the depression of the 1890s and the reaction of whites against a less submissive black generation born after slavery. Recent scholarship also suggests more deep-seated psychological causes for this unreasoning and often murderous racism: the rage against blacks served as a way of reasserting a traditional sense of southern "manhood" that was under assault by rapid social and economic change. Lynching, moreover, occurred most frequently in transitional areas such as the Gulf plain and the new cotton country where the population was thinly spread, community ties were weak, and blacks and whites were strangers to one another.

But what triggered the antiblack offensive was the crisis over Populism. From then on white supremacy propped up the one-party system that the Redeemers had been fighting for ever since Reconstruction. If the southern elite had to share political power with demagogic poor white leaders such as Tom Watson and James K. Vardaman, this sharing would be on terms agreeable to them—the exclusion from the political arena of any serious challenge to the economic status quo.

The Black Response

Where did this leave blacks? In 1890 African-Americans comprised more than half the population of Grimes County, a cotton-growing area in east Texas. They had kept the local Republican party going after Reconstruction and regularly sent black representatives to the Texas legislature during the 1870s and 1880s. More remarkably, the local Populist party that appeared in 1892 among white farmers proved immune to the Democrats' taunts of "black rule." A Populist-Republican coalition swept the county elections in 1896 and 1898, surviving well after the collapse of the national Populist movement.

In 1899 defeated Democratic office seekers and prominent citizens of Grimes County organized the secret White Man's Union. Armed men prevented blacks from voting in town elections that year. The two most important black county leaders were shot down in cold blood. Night riders terrorized both white Populists and black Republicans. When the Populist sheriff proved incapable of enforcing the law, the game was up. The White Man's Union, now out in the open, became the county Democratic party in a new guise. The Democrats won Grimes County by an overwhelming vote in 1900. The day after the election members of the Union laid siege to the Populist sheriff's office. They killed his brother and a friend and drove the sheriff, badly wounded, out of the county forever.

The White Man's Union ruled Grimes County for the next fifty years. The whole episode was the handiwork of the county's "best citizens," suggesting how respectable the use of terror had become in the service of white supremacy. The Union intended, as one of its leaders said, to "force the African to keep his place." After 1900 blacks could survive in Grimes County only if they tended to their own business and stayed out of trouble with whites.

Like the blacks of Grimes County, southern blacks in many places resisted white oppression as best they could. When Georgia adopted the first Jim Crow law applying to streetcars in 1891, Atlanta blacks declared a boycott, and over the next fifteen years there were boycotts against segregated streetcars in at least twenty-five cities. "Do not trample on our pride by being 'jim crowed,'" the Savannah *Tribune* urged its readers: "Walk!" Ida Wells-Barnett emerged as the most outspoken black crusader against lynching, so enraging the Memphis white community with the editorials in her newspaper *Free Speech* that she was forced to leave the city in 1892. And there were individual blacks, such as Robert Charles (see American Lives, pages 610–611), who, driven beyond endurance, struck back, at the inevitable sacrifice of their own lives.

Like Charles, some were drawn to the back-to-Africa movement. It was a sign of their despair that Africa was again seen as the place of black salvation. But emigration was not a real choice, and like the blacks of Grimes County, African-Americans everywhere had to bend to the raging forces of racism and find a way to survive.

The Atlanta Compromise. Booker T. Washington, the foremost black leader of the South of his day, responded to that grim reality in a famous speech in Atlanta in 1895. Washington marked out a line of retreat from the defiant stand of an older generation of black abolitionists exemplified by Frederick Douglass, who died the same year that the Atlanta speech launched Washington into national prominence. Washington was conciliatory toward the South; it was a society that blacks understood and loved. He considered "the agitation of the question of social equality the extremest folly." Washington accepted segregation, provided that blacks had equal facilities. He accepted educational and property qualifications for the vote, provided that they applied equally to blacks and whites.

Washington's doctrine came to be known as the Atlanta Compromise. His approach was "accommodationist" in the sense that it avoided a direct assault on white supremacy. Despite the humble face he put on be-

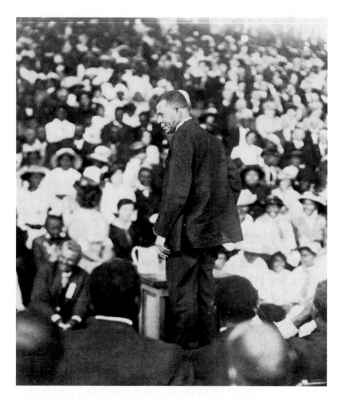

Booker T. Washington

In an age of severe racial oppression, Washington emerged as the acknowledged leader of black people in the United States. He was remarkable both for his ability as spokesman to white Americans and his deep understanding of the aspirations of black Americans. Born a slave, Washington suffered the indignities experienced by all blacks after Emancipation. But having been befriended by several whites as he grew to manhood, he also understood what it took to gain white support—and maneuver around white hostility—in the black struggle for equality.

fore white audiences, however, Washington did not concede the struggle. Behind the scenes he did his best to resist Jim Crow laws and disfranchisement. More important, his Atlanta Compromise, while abandoning the field of political protest, opened up a second front of economic struggle.

Washington sought to capitalize on a particular southern dilemma about the economic role of the black population. Racist dogma dictated that blacks be kept down and that they conform to their image as lazy, shiftless workers. But for the South to prosper it needed an efficient labor force. Washington made this need the target of his efforts. As founder of the Tuskegee Institute in Alabama in 1881, he advocated *industrial educa-*

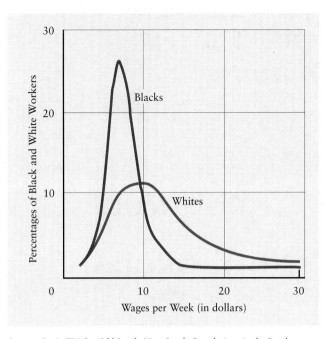

Source: Gavin Wright, *Old South, New South: Revolutions in the Southern Economy since the Civil War* (New York: Basic Books, 1986), p. 184.

FIGURE 19.2

Distributions of Weekly Wages for Black and White Workers in Virginia, 1907

This graph reveals that wages for common labor were nondiscriminatory (otherwise no or few whites would have been bunched at the low end of the wage scale) but that discrimination denied blacks entry into higher-paying southern jobs.

tion—that is, manual and agricultural training. He preached the virtues of thrift, hard work, and property ownership. Washington's industrial education program won generous support from northern philanthropists and businessmen and, following his Atlanta speech, applause from progressive supporters of the New South.

Washington assumed that black economic progress would be the key to winning political and civil rights. He regarded members of the white southern elite as crucial allies, because ultimately only they had the power to act. More important, they could see "the close connection between labor, industry, education, and political institutions." When it was in their economic interest and when they had grown dependent on black labor and black enterprise, white men of business and property would recognize the justice of black rights. As Washington put it, "There is little race prejudice in the American dollar."

Do the facts suggest that Washington was right? Or, to put the question as an economist might: Was it the impersonal market or race prejudice that most determined the economic treatment of blacks? For southern industry the answer seems mixed. Employers did not discriminate very much in wage rates—that is, they did not pay whites higher wages than they paid blacks for the same work. But racial barriers certainly prevented blacks from moving into better-paid and more highly skilled jobs. This hard truth is made graphically clear in the comparative wage distributions of whites and blacks shown in Figure 19.2. In agriculture, too, the picture was mixed. The opportunity for black farmers to advance themselves clearly did exist. The proportion who became landowners inched slowly upward to roughly 25 percent in 1900. But the racial gap remained very wide, with whites almost three times as likely as blacks to be landowners.

To what extent black self-help—hard work, industrial education, the husbanding of small resources—might counterbalance the barriers of race prejudice was the nub of Booker T. Washington's problem. Where the almighty dollar reigned, there was some hope of progress. Elsewhere, as Washington saw it, there was none.

For twenty years after his Atlanta address Washington dominated organized black life in America. In an age of severe racial oppression no black dealt more skillfully than Washington with the leaders of white America or wielded greater political influence. The black community knew him as a hard taskmaster. Intensely protective of his authority, he did not regard opposition kindly. Black politicians, educators, and editors stood up to him at their peril.

Even so, a crack began to appear after 1900, especially among younger educated blacks, who thought Washington was conceding too much. He instilled black pride, but of a narrowly middle-class and utilitarian kind. What about the special genius of blacks that W. E. B. DuBois celebrated in his collection of essays, *The Souls of Black Folk* (1903)? And what of the "talented tenth" of the black population whose promise could only be stifled and restrained by manual education? Blacks also became increasingly impatient with Washington's silence on segregation and lynching. By the time of his death in 1915 Washington's approach had been superseded by a strategy that relied on the courts and political leverage, not on black self-help and accommodation (see Chapter 21).

Robert Charles: Black Militant

The trouble began in an ordinary way. Two black men were sitting quietly on the steps of a house on Dryades Street in New Orleans, between Washington and 6th streets. It was Monday evening, July 24, 1900. One was nineteen-year-old Leonard Pierce; the other was an older man named Robert Charles. They were waiting for a friend of Charles's, Virginia Banks, and her roommate to return from a day at Baton Rouge. Around 11 P.M. three policemen approached Pierce and Charles and began to question them roughly. When Charles stood up, Officer Mora grabbed him. A scuffle followed, and Mora began to beat Charles about the head with his billy club. Charles, a big man, broke away. There was an exchange of gunfire, wounding both in the thigh, Officer Mora more seriously. In a hail of bullets, Charles ran off.

"In any law-abiding community Charles would have been justified in delivering himself up immediately to the properly constituted authorities and asking for a trial by a jury of his peers," wrote the antilynching crusader Ida Wells-Barnett in her pamphlet on what followed. "Charles knew that his arrest in New Orleans, even for defending his life, meant nothing short of a long term in the penitentiary, and still more probable death by lynching at the hands of a cowardly mob." Those must have been Charles's thoughts as he made his way back to the room he shared with Pierce on 4th Street, took down his Winchester rifle, and got ready to fight.

In the meantime Pierce had been brought to the police station, where Charles's name and address were soon "sweated" out of him. Captain John T. Day, a local hero who had rescued fourteen people from a hotel fire, led a squad to bring Charles in. The entrance to Charles's room was along an alley. When the police arrived, Charles swung open the door, shot Day through the heart, then turned and fatally wounded a second officer. The other two policemen cowered along the wall and slipped into another house, where they hid in the dark. The officers on the street refused to enter the unlit alley. When reinforcements arrived at 5 A.M.,

Robert Charles
This is the only known picture of Charles, an engraving done for the cover of Ida Wells-Barnett's pamphlet on Charles's slaying.

Charles had slipped away, and the manhunt commenced.

The New Orleans newspapers labeled Charles a "fiend incarnate." No one who had known him would have said so. Robert Charles was one of thousands of rural blacks who had sought to escape from grinding poverty by migrating to southern cities. Robert Charles was born just after the end of slavery, in 1865 or 1866, in Copiah County, Mississippi. His parents were sharecroppers, and he was one of ten children. He worked as a day laborer on the railroads and, after arriving in New Orleans around 1894, at a variety of odd jobs. In July 1900 he was unemployed. Charles was unmarried and rather stylish in his dress, favoring a brown derby hat. Acquaintances remembered him as quiet and intelligent. He had received little education, but his room contained the well-thumbed books and papers of a studious man. One other thing about Charles: he ardently believed that blacks should return to Africa.

The back-to-Africa movement, which enjoyed a revival in those hard years, reflected the despair that poor blacks like Robert Charles felt about life in America. Africa was their only salvation, preached Bishop Henry M. Turner, the combative leader of the movement: "I see no other shelter from the stormy blast, from the red tide of persecution, from the horrors of American prejudice." Charles was a reader of Bishop Turner's fiery paper, *Voice of Missions*, and in 1899 began to sell subscriptions. He also became a local agent for the International Migration Society, working on commission to sign up members who would secure transportation to Liberia by contributing a dollar a month for forty months.

Recent events fortified Charles's conviction that blacks had no hope in America. He was said to have been infuriated by the most infamous lynching of the era, the burning and dismemberment of Sam Hose in Georgia in 1899. In Louisiana, moreover, blacks had been disfranchised in 1898, and a crisis was brewing in state politics. As the elections of 1900 approached, the Democrats vowed that on no account would they allow the Republicans and Populists to emerge as winners. In Charles's pocket was a newspaper clipping about an opposition leader who had called on his supporters to "*oil up their Winchesters* and prepare to fight" if Democrats tried to steal the election. In *Voice of Missions* there was a similarly desperate message: in one editorial Bishop Turner had urged that "Negroes Get Guns" in self-defense.

Charles, in fact, habitually carried a Colt .38 revolver; it was in his belt when Officer Mora accosted him. There is no knowing what went through his mind when he chose not to submit to the policeman's abuse.

But by drawing his gun Charles had stepped across the line. From then until his inevitable death, he was making a political statement.

That was how the whites of New Orleans saw Charles too: he was challenging the white power structure. As a leader of the mob that gathered in the streets on Wednesday put it:

> The only way you can teach these niggers a lesson and put them in their place is to go out and lynch a few of them as an object lesson. String up a few of them, and the others will trouble you no more. . . . On to the Parish Prison and lynch Pierce!

The mob couldn't get at Pierce, but they took their fury out on any other unfortunate black they encountered as they surged through the city. In the next two days at least six people were killed and dozens of others were brutally beaten. Only late on Thursday did the police and militia restore a semblance of law and order to New Orleans. But Charles remained at large. Then, on Friday afternoon, July 27, the police got a tip that he was hiding in a small house on Saratoga Street.

Springing from a back closet, Charles shot down the two police officers who came to investigate and then made his way up to the second story. A crowd soon surrounded the house, peppering it with bullets. Dodging from window to window, Charles returned the fire for nearly two hours. In grudging admiration, one reporter wrote of his "diabolical coolness" and "wonderful marksmanship [that] never failed him for a moment." More than twenty of his attackers were hit, three fatally. As dusk began to fall, the building was set ablaze, and Charles was forced out. Still defiant, he almost made it across the courtyard when he was stopped by a bullet and went down. The crowd was on him in an instant, firing dozens of shots into him, and stomping on his head. His body was carried off in a police wagon, his battered head hanging grotesquely from the back. Later that night the mob broke loose again, burning buildings and murderously attacking six more blacks.

No New Orleans black would have dared say out loud that Robert Charles had done right. But Ida Wells-Barnett, writing from the safety of Chicago, insisted that he had: "The white people of this country may charge that he was a desperado, but to the people of his own race Robert Charles will always be regarded as the hero of New Orleans." Five weeks after Charles's burial in a potter's field, a neighbor of Fred Clark's on South Ramparts Street came up behind Clark, put a gun to his head and shot him dead. Fred Clark was the black man who had given away Charles's hiding place to the police.

Summary

When Reconstruction ended in 1877, national politics became less issue-oriented and, as a formal process, less important in American life. This situation resulted from weaknesses in governmental institutions, the prevailing philosophy of laissez-faire, and the paralysis of evenly matched political parties. Yet politics in the years after 1877 had great vigor, as can be seen in the high levels of popular participation. For one thing, politics was the arena in which the nation's ethnic and religious conflicts were largely fought out. Equally important, the party machines were powerful and performed crucial functions that properly belonged to, but were still beyond the capacity of, governmental institutions. Finally, despite the slow headway made toward woman suffrage, women's organizations carved out for themselves a broadening public sphere of social reform activity.

During the 1890s national politics again became an important arena. Threatened by the rise of Populism, the Democratic party committed itself to free silver and made the election of 1896 a contest over issues of real significance. The Republicans won decisively, ending a paralyzing party stalemate that had lasted for twenty years and assuring themselves of political dominance for the next thirty years. At the same time, the 1890s saw, in the failure of Populism, the last great challenge to the mainstream two-party system. And in the South the Populist failure turned into a grim reaction that disfranchised African-Americans, completed a rigid segregation system, and let loose a terrible cycle of racial hatred and violence. Blacks resisted but had to bend to overwhelming white power. The accommodationist philosophy of Booker T. Washington seemed to be the best strategy for black survival in an age of extreme racism.

TIMELINE

1874	Woman's Christian Temperance Union (WCTU) founded
1877	Rutherford B. Hayes inaugurated; end of Reconstruction
1881	President James A. Garfield assassinated
1883	Pendleton Civil Service Act Supreme Court strikes down Civil Rights Act of 1875
1884	Mugwump reformers bolt the Republican party to support Grover Cleveland, first Democrat elected president since 1856
1887	Interstate Commerce Act creates the Interstate Commerce Commission to regulate railroads Florida adopts first law segregating railroad travel
1888	James Bryce's *The American Commonwealth*
1890	The McKinley Tariff Democrats sweep Congressional elections, inaugurating brief era of Democratic party dominance Mississippi becomes first state to adopt literacy test to disfranchise blacks
1892	People's (Populist) party founded
1893	Panic of 1893 leads to national depression Repeal of Sherman Silver Purchase Act (1890)
1894	Coxey's army
1895	Booker T. Washington sets out Atlanta Compromise
1896	Election of William McKinley; free silver campaign crushed *Plessy v. Ferguson* upholds constitutionality of "separate-but-equal" facilities
1897	Economic depression ends; era of agricultural prosperity begins

★   ★   ★

BIBLIOGRAPHY

The best introductions to American politics in the late nineteenth century are John A. Garraty, *The New Commonwealth, 1877–1890* (1968), and R. Hal Williams, *Years of Decision: American Politics in the 1890s* (1978). More detailed and comprehensive is Morton Keller, *Affairs of State: Public Life in Late Nineteenth-Century America* (1977).

The Politics of the Status Quo

Various aspects of national politics are discussed in Robert D. Marcus, *Grand Old Party: Political Structure in the Gilded Age* (1971); J. Rogers Hollingsworth, *The Whirligig of Politics: The Democracy of Cleveland and Bryan* (1963); H. Wayne Morgan, *From Hayes to McKinley: National Party Politics, 1877–1896* (1969); and David J. Rothman, *Politics and Power: The Senate, 1869–1901* (1966). On the development of public administration, see Leonard D. White, *The Republican Era, 1869–1901* (1958), and Stephen Skowronek, *Building a New American State: The Expansion of National Administrative Capacities* (1982).

The ideological basis for conservative national politics is fully treated in Sidney Fine, *Laissez Faire and the General Welfare State, 1865–1901* (1956); Robert G. McCloskey, *American Conservatism in the Age of Enterprise* (1951); and the opening section of Morton J. Horwitz, *The Transformation of American Law, 1870–1960* (1992). On the popular sources of political participation, see especially Michael E. McGerr, *The Decline of Popular Politics: The American North, 1865–1928* (1986), and Paul Kleppner, *The Third Electoral Party System, 1853–1892: Parties, Voters, and Political Cultures* (1979). On the Mugwump reformers, see John G. Sproat, *The "Best Men": Liberal Reformers in the Gilded Age* (1965); Gerald W. McFarland, *Mugwumps, Morals and Politics, 1884–1920* (1975); and Ari Hoogenboom, *Outlawing the Spoils: The Civil Service Reform Movement, 1865–1883* (1961). The existence of a women's political culture in the late nineteenth century can be traced in Carl N. Degler, *At Odds: Women and the Family from the Revolution to the Present* (1979). A valuable book setting the stage is Ellen Carol DuBois, *Feminism and Suffrage: The Emergence of an Independent Women's Movement in America, 1848–1869* (1978).

The Crisis of American Politics

The most recent synthesis on Populism is Robert C. McMath, *American Populism* (1993). Richard D. Hofstadter, *The Age of Reform* (1955), stresses the darker side of Populism, in which intolerance and paranoia figure heavily. Hofstadter's thesis, which once dominated debate among historians, has given way to a much more positive assessment. The key book here is Lawrence Goodwyn, *Democratic Promise: The Populist Moment in America* (1976), which argues that Populism was a broadly based radical response to industrial capitalism. Peter H. Argersinger, *The Limits of Agrarian Radicalism: Western Populism and American Politics* (1994), offers a careful assessment of the politics of western Populism. Two stimulating books that follow the history of Populism into the twentieth century are Grant McConnell, *The Decline of Agrarian Democracy* (1953), which focuses on farm organizations, and Michael Kazin, *The Populist Persuasion* (1995), which describes how the language of Populism entered the discourse of mainstream American politics.

The money question is elucidated in Walter Nugent, *Money and American Society, 1865–1880* (1968), and Allan Weinstein, *Prelude to Populism: Origins of the Silver Issue* (1970). On the politics of the 1890s, see especially Robert F. Durden, *Climax of Populism: The Election of 1896* (1965), and Paul W. Glad, *McKinley, Bryan, and the People* (1964).

Race and Politics in the South

On southern politics the seminal book for the post-Reconstruction period is C. Vann Woodward, *Origins of the New South, 1877–1913* (1951), which still defines the terms of discussion among historians. The most far-reaching revision is Edward L. Ayers, *The Promise of the New South* (1992). Complementary books on the social basis of southern politics are Dwight B. Billings, *Planters and the Making of "New South": North Carolina, 1865–1900* (1979), and Paul Escott, *Many Excellent People: Power and Privilege in North Carolina, 1850–1900* (1985).

The classic book on segregation is C. Vann Woodward, *The Strange Career of Jim Crow* (2d ed., 1968), but it should be supplemented by Howard N. Rabinowitz, *Race Relations in the Urban South, 1865–1890* (1978). A powerful analysis of southern racism, stressing its psychosocial roots, is Joel Williamson, *A Rage for Order: Black/White Relations in the American South since Emancipation* (1986). Disfranchisement is treated with great analytic sophistication in J. Morgan Kousser, *The Shaping of Southern Politics: Suffrage Restriction and the Establishment of the One-Party South, 1880–1910* (1974), and as an aspect of progressivism in Jack Temple Kirby, *Darkness at the Dawning: Race and Reform in the Progressive South* (1972). August Meier, *Negro Thought in America, 1880–1915* (1963), is a key analysis of black accommodation and protest. The preeminent exponent of accommodation is the subject of a superb two-volume biography by Louis B. Harlan, *Booker T. Washington: The Making of a Black Leader* (1973) and *Wizard of Tuskegee* (1983); and equally fine on Washington's main critic is David Levering Lewis, *W.E.B. Du Bois: Biography of a Race, 1868–1919* (1993).

Indianapolis in the 1890s

Theodore Groll, a German who had come to America for the
World's Columbian Exposition of 1893, painted this massive
canvas of Indianapolis at dusk. The view is of Washington
Street, with its clanging horsecars, street peddlers, busy
shoppers, and general bustle. In this prosperous medium-
sized city—the novelist Booth Tarkington, a native son, called
it a "typical American" place—urban life seemed less remote
from traditional America than in great metropolises such as
New York or Chicago.

The Rise of the City

★   ★   ★

In 1820, after 200 years of settlement, fewer than 5 percent of Americans lived in cities with a population of 10,000 or more. But after that, decade by decade, the urban population swelled, turning into a flood after midcentury. The same process was happening in Europe, but at a slower pace. During the nineteenth century, the percentage of Europeans living in cities tripled whereas in the United States the increase was sevenfold.

By 1900 one of every five Americans lived in an urban center of 100,000 or more residents. The greatest growth took place in the great metropolitan cities. Nearly a tenth of the nation—6.5 million persons—lived in just three cities: New York, Chicago, and Philadelphia. The late nineteenth century, an economist remarked in 1899, was "not only the age of cities, but the age of great cities."

The growth of the cities had enormous implications for American society. The city was the arena of the nation's vibrant economic life. Here the factories went up, and here the multitudes of working people settled. New immigrants swelled the ranks of the working class. At the turn of the century upwards of 30 percent of the residents of major American cities were foreign-born. Here, too, lived the millionaires and a growing urban middle class of white-collar workers and businessmen. For all these people the city was more than a place to make a living. It provided the setting for an urban culture unlike anything seen before in the United States. City people, although differing vastly among themselves, became distinctively and recognizably urban.

Urbanization

The march to the cities seemed inevitable to nineteenth-century Americans. "The greater part of our population must live in cities—cities much greater than the world has yet known," declared the Congregational minister Josiah Strong in 1898. "In due time we shall be a nation of cities." There was "no resisting the trend," said another writer. Urbanization became inevitable because of its link to another inevitability of American life—industrialization.

The Sources of City Growth

Until the Civil War, cities had been centers of commerce, not industry. Located strategically along transportation routes, they were the places where merchants bought and sold goods for distribution into the interior or shipment out to the world market. Early industrialism, on the other hand, sprang up in the countryside.

Mills and factories needed water power from streams and rivers, access to sources of fuel and raw materials, and workers drawn from the surplus farm population. Only five of the nation's cities in 1860 reported as much as 10 percent of the labor force engaged in manufacturing activity.

After midcentury industry began to abandon the countryside. Once they had access to steam engines, mill operators no longer needed to locate along streams. In the iron industry coal replaced charcoal as the primary fuel, and so iron makers did not have to be near forests. Improved transportation, especially the railroads, gave entrepreneurs a greater choice in selecting the best sites in relation to supplies and markets. The result was a geographical concentration of industry. Iron makers gravitated to Pittsburgh because of its access not only to coal and iron ore but also to markets for iron and steel products. Chicago, ideally located between livestock suppliers and consuming markets, became a great meat-packing center (see Map 20.1).

Many smaller industrial cities depended on a high degree of economic specialization. Youngstown, Ohio,

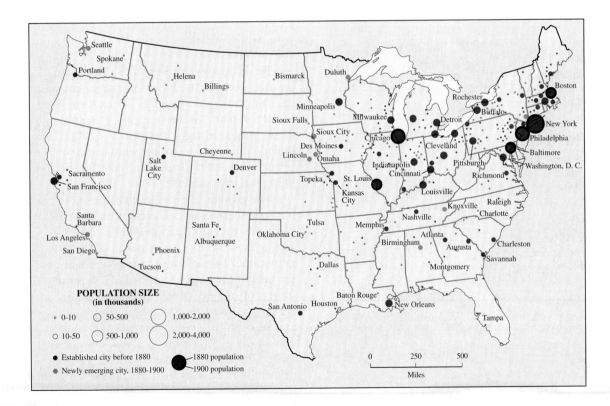

MAP 20.1

The Growth of America's Cities, 1880–1900
The number of Americans living in urban places more than doubled between 1880 and 1900. The most dramatic increases occurred in the largest metropolitan centers. New York grew from 1.2 million to 3.4 million, and Chicago from 500,000 to 1.7 million. Notable among newly emerging cities—places that had been small towns or minor cities in 1880—were Los Angeles, Seattle, Birmingham, Omaha, and Atlanta.

and Johnstown, Pennsylvania, specialized in iron and steel; Brockton and Haverhill, Massachusetts, in boots and shoes; Troy, New York, in collars and cuffs; and East Liverpool, Ohio, in pottery. Other cities processed the raw materials of their regions. Sacramento canned fruits and vegetables, Richmond made cigarettes, Minneapolis milled grain, and Memphis handled lumber and produced cottonseed oil.

This geographical concentration of industry was one source of urban growth in the late nineteenth century. Another was the increasing scale of production that became characteristic of modern industry. A factory that employed thousands of workers instantly created a small city in its vicinity. The result was often a company town—for example, Aliquippa, Pennsylvania, which became body and soul the property of the Jones and Laughlin Steel Company. Many firms set up their plants near a large city so they could draw on its labor supply and transportation facilities. George Pullman located his sleeping-car works and model town southwest of Chicago, and George Westinghouse built his electrical equipment plant just east of Pittsburgh. Sometimes the nearby metropolis spread and absorbed the smaller city, as happened with Pullman, Illinois. Elsewhere, as in northern New Jersey or along the lakeshore south of Chicago, the lines between industrial towns blurred and an extended urban-industrial area emerged. The same process could be seen in Europe, where industrial regions were emerging in northeastern France around Lille and in Germany's Ruhr Valley.

The established commercial cities also grew significantly in this era, benefiting from industry's need for complex marketing and administrative structures. The greatest centers—New York and Chicago—became headquarters for corporations operating across the country. Finance, publishing, distribution, advertising, and fashion were concentrated in the metropolitan centers.

These commercial centers also offered factory sites and economic services that attracted certain kinds of industries. Warehouse districts could readily be converted to small-scale manufacturing; a distribution network and transportation facilities were right at hand. In addition, as gateways for immigrants, port cities offered abundant cheap labor. Boston, Philadelphia, Baltimore, and San Francisco became hives of small-scale, labor-intensive industrial activity. New York's enormous pool of immigrant workers made that city a magnet for the garment trades, cigar making, and diversified light industry. Preeminent as a city of trade and finance, New York also ranked as the nation's largest manufacturing center.

By 1870 a core industrial region had formed from New England down through the Middle Atlantic states to Maryland. In this region the percentage of people living in urban places was twice the national average. Forty years later, in 1910, the original industrial core was nearly three-quarters urbanized. It had also thrust westward to include the Great Lakes states, which became America's industrial heartland. Important new centers for steelmaking, manufacturing, and food processing sprang up in this region. Pittsburgh, Cleveland, Detroit, Milwaukee, Minneapolis—all of them small cities or modest commercial centers in 1870—had by 1910 grown into major industrial cities with 300,000 to well over half a million inhabitants.

TABLE 20.1

Ten Largest Cities by Population, 1870 and 1910

1870		1910	
City	Population	City	Population
1. New York	942,292	New York	4,766,883
2. Philadelphia	674,022	Chicago	2,185,283
3. Brooklyn*	419,921	Philadelphia	1,549,008
4. St. Louis	310,864	St. Louis	687,029
5. Chicago	298,977	Boston	670,585
6. Baltimore	267,354	Cleveland	560,663
7. Boston	250,526	Baltimore	558,485
8. Cincinnati	216,239	Pittsburgh	533,905
9. New Orleans	191,418	Detroit	465,766
10. San Francisco	149,473	Buffalo	423,715

*Brooklyn was consolidated with New York in 1898.
Source: U.S. Census data.

City Building

"The only trouble about this town," wrote Mark Twain on arriving in New York in 1867, "is that it is too large. You cannot accomplish anything in the way of business, you cannot even pay a friendly call, without devoting a whole day to it. . . . The distances are too great." Finding ways of moving nearly a million New Yorkers around was not as hopeless as it might have seemed to Twain, but it did pose a challenge to city builders. The city demanded innovation no less than did industry itself and, in the end, compiled an equally impressive record of technological achievement.

The commercial cities of the early nineteenth century had been compact places, densely settled around a harbor or along a river. As late as 1850, when it had 565,000 people, greater Philadelphia covered only 10 square miles. From the foot of Chestnut Street on the Delaware River a person could walk to almost anywhere in the city within forty-five minutes. Thereafter, however, Philadelphia—and indeed all American cities—tended to spread out as it developed.

A downtown area emerged, usually in what had been the original commercial city. Downtown in turn broke up into shopping, financial, warehousing, manufacturing, hotel and entertainment, and red-light districts. Although somewhat fluid at their edges, all these districts were well-defined areas of specialized activity. Moving out from the center, industrial development tended to follow the arteries of transportation—railroads, canals, and rivers—and, at the city's outskirts, to spread out into complexes of heavy industry. At the same time the middle class moved in large numbers out to new suburban areas.

Urban development was markedly different in continental Europe, where even rapidly growing cities remained physically compact, with boundaries that broke sharply at the surrounding countryside. In America, cities constantly expanded, spilling beyond their formal boundaries and forming what the federal census began to designate in 1910 as metropolitan areas. While American cities were highly congested at the center, their population density was actually much below that of European cities: 22 persons per acre for fifteen American cities in the 1890s, for example, versus 157.6 for a comparable group of German cities. Given this difference, the development of efficient urban transportation had a much higher priority in the United States than in Europe.

Mass Transit. The first innovation, dating back to the 1820s, was the omnibus, an elongated version of the horse-drawn coach. The omnibus was a convenience, but it did not do much to relieve congestion; downtown, people could walk just as fast. Much more effective was the horsecar, which ran on iron tracks. The

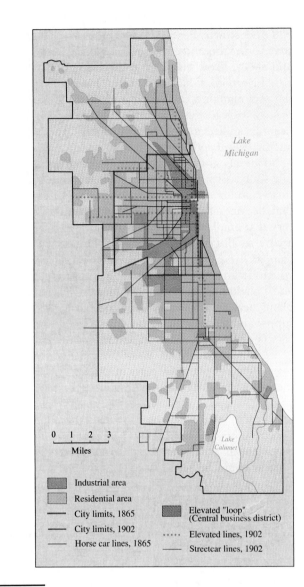

MAP 20.2

The Expansion of Chicago

In 1865 Chicagoans depended on horsecar lines to get around town. By 1900 the city limits had expanded enormously, accompanied by an equally dramatic extension of streetcar service, by then electrified. Elevated trains also helped ease congestion in the urban core. New streetcar lines, some extending beyond the city limits, were important to suburban development in the coming years.

horsecar carried more passengers, moved them at a faster clip through congested city streets, and reached out into residential areas. All this happened because of a modest but crucial refinement in railroad track design in 1852—a grooved rail that was flush with the pavement. For the next forty years horsecars became the mainstay of urban transit across America, accounting for 70 percent of the traffic in 1890.

The horse was less than an ideal source of locomotion. It moved slowly, had limited pulling power, and

Then came the electric trolley car. Its development was primarily the work of Frank J. Sprague, an electrical engineer once employed by the inventor Thomas A. Edison. In 1887 Sprague designed an electricity-driven system for Richmond, Virginia: a "trolley" carriage running along an overhead power line was attached by cable to streetcars equipped with an electric motor—hence the name *trolley car*. After Sprague's success, the electric trolley swiftly displaced the horsecar and by 1900 became the primary means of public transportation in most American cities.

In the great metropolitan centers, however, mounting congestion led to demands that public transit be moved off the streets. The railroad had long been used by affluent suburbanites to commute to the city. The problem was how to harness railway technology to serve the needs of ordinary city dwellers. In 1879 the first elevated lines went into operation on Sixth and Ninth avenues in New York City. Powered at first by steam engines, the "els" converted to electricity following Sprague's success with the trolley. Chicago developed elevated transit most fully (see Map 20.2). New York, on the other hand, turned to the subway. Although Boston opened a short underground line in 1897, the completion in 1904 of a subway running the length of Manhattan demonstrated the full potential of underground rapid transit. Thinly settled areas of northern Manhattan and the Bronx, predicted the *New York Times*, would soon boast "a population of ten millions . . . housed comfortably, healthfully and relatively cheaply." The subway would especially delight "all who travel with the sole purpose of 'getting there' in the least time possible." Mass transit had become *rapid* transit.

Traffic Jam in Downtown Chicago, 1905
The purpose of urban transit systems was to move masses of people rapidly and efficiently through the city. However, better transportation brought more congestion as well, as this scene of gridlock at Randolph and Dearborn streets in Chicago shows.

left piles of manure behind. Among various early improvements was the cable car, which was pulled by an undergound cable set below the tracks and driven by steam engines at a central power house. The first cable cars ran in San Francisco in 1873, and more than twenty other cities used them during the 1880s. But the cable car could run only at a slow, unvarying speed, and systemwide breakdowns occurred frequently.

The Chicago Elevated, 1900
This is Wabash Avenue, looking north from Adams Street. For Americans from farms and small towns, this photograph by William Henry Jackson captured something of the peculiarity of the urban scene. What could be stranger than a railroad suspended above the streets in the midst of people's lives?

Nowhere else in the world was the demand for mass urban transit as acute as it was in U.S. cities. In 1890 the number of passengers carried on American street railways was more than 2 billion per year, over twice that of the rest of the world combined. Berlin, which boasted the best system in Europe, had a per capita usage that was exceeded by twenty-one American cities. In Great Britain the horsecar remained dominant long after it had disappeared from American streets. In Tokyo, the biggest Asian city, the horsecar was not even introduced until 1882, and the electric streetcar appeared for the first time in 1903.

Bridges. Rivers had in earlier times been the city's lifeline of trade; now they became barriers that interrupted rail traffic and hindered urban expansion. Hundreds of iron and steel bridges went up in the second half of the nineteenth century. Some from this great age of bridge construction—among them the Eads Bridge (1873) spanning the Mississippi River at St. Louis and the Brooklyn Bridge (1883) over New York's East River—are still in use. The Brooklyn Bridge, linking Brooklyn and Manhattan, took fifteen years to build. A giant suspension structure, the Brooklyn Bridge was not only an engineering marvel but the symbol of a new kind of functional architecture—"the first product of the age of coal and iron to achieve completeness of expression," wrote the twentieth-century architectural critic Lewis Mumford.

The Skyscraper. If urban transit evolved in response to the geographical expansion of the American city, the need for more space in the downtown business districts drove advances in building construction. New materials made it possible to construct commercial buildings of greater height, interior space, and fire resistance. With the availability by the 1880s of steel girders, mass-produced durable plate glass, and the passenger elevator, a wholly new way of construction developed. A steel skeleton would support the building, and the walls, previously weight-bearing, would serve as curtains enclosing the structure; the sky, so to speak, became the limit.

The first "skyscraper" to be built on this principle was the ten-story Home Insurance Building (1885) in Chicago. Although this pioneering effort was itself conventional in appearance—it looked just like the other commercial buildings in the downtown district—the steel-girdered structure swiftly liberated the aesthetic perceptions of American architects. A Chicago school sprang up, dedicated to the design of buildings whose form expressed, rather than masked, their structure and function. The masterpiece of the Chicago school was Louis Sullivan's Carson, Pirie, Scott and Company department store (1904). Chicago pioneered skyscraper construction, but New York, with its unrelenting need

for prime downtown space, took the lead after the mid-1890s. The climax of New York's construction surge came with the completion in 1913 of the fifty-five-story Woolworth Building. Aptly called the "Cathedral of Commerce," this building towered over its neighbors and marked the beginning of the modern Manhattan skyline.

By contrast, the magnificent rail terminals that graced the great cities tried to mask their function. Reflecting the architectural forms of ages past, the terminals were marvels of structural design in their soaring interiors and use of steel, glass, and stone. New York's Grand Central Station (1913), built in the French baroque style, was completely electrified. It made superb use of underground space and had a loop system that enabled trains to turn around without reversing course. New York's other great terminal, Pennsylvania Station (1910), was modeled after a Roman bath.

The Electric City. For ordinary citizens the electric lights that dispelled the gloom of the city at night probably offered the most dramatic evidence that times had changed. The mainstay of city lighting since the early

Manhattan's First Skyscraper
The Tower Building at 50 Broadway was completed in 1889. To the modern eye, this first New York skyscraper seems modest and old-fashioned. Compared with its squat neighbors, however, it was a revolutionary building based on new principles of slender, soaring architecture.

nineteenth century had been the gaslight—which used illuminating gas produced from coal—but at 12 candle-power, gaslight was too dim to brighten the downtown streets and public spaces of the modern city. When generating technology for electricity became commercially feasible in the 1870s, the first application was for better city lighting. Charles F. Brush's electric arc lamps, installed in the windows of the Wanamaker department store in Philadelphia in 1878, threw a brilliant light and soon replaced gas lamps in stores and hotel lobbies and on city streets across the country. The following year Thomas Edison created the first practical incandescent bulb, which brought electric lighting into American homes. Edison's motto—"Let there be light!"—truly described the experience of the modern city.

Electricity was the source of the quickening tempo of city life. Before it had any significant effect on industry, electricity lifted and lowered elevators and powered streetcars and subway trains. Electric lighting was integral to the designs of the pioneering steel-frame buildings of the Chicago school. Meanwhile, the telephone, patented by Alexander Graham Bell in 1876, speeded up communication beyond anything imagined previously. Twain's complaint of 1867 that it was impossible to carry on business in New York had been answered: all one needed to do was pick up the phone. By 1900, 1.5 million telephones were in use, linking urban activity into a network of instant communication.

The Private City

City building was very much an exercise in private enterprise. The lure of profit spurred the great innovations—the trolley car, electric lighting, the skyscraper, the elevator, the telephone—and drove urban real-estate development. The investment opportunities looked so tempting that new cities sprang up almost overnight from the ruins of the Chicago fire of 1871 and the San Francisco earthquake of 1906. Real-estate interests, eager to develop subdivisions, often were instrumental in pushing streetcar lines outward from the central districts of cities.

Urban transit became big business. In the early 1880s Peter A. B. Widener and William L. Elkins teamed up to unite much of Philadelphia's streetcar system in the Philadelphia Traction Company. They did the same in alliance with Charles T. Yerkes in Chicago and William C. Whitney and Thomas Fortune Ryan in New York. By 1900 their syndicate controlled streetcar systems in more than a hundred cities and had expanded to include utilities supplying gas and electricity to urban customers. The city, like industry, became an arena for enterprise and profit.

Providing city services privately, however, was a matter of choice. Under the law, cities had extensive powers of self-development. In a key decision in 1897, New York state courts authorized New York City to build a municipally owned subway, ruling that cities had to determine their needs and then carry out their responsibilities as they saw fit. Even the use of privately owned land was subject to whatever regulations the city might impose.

But unlike in Europe, American cities generally hesitated to use their broad powers. America produced what the urban historian Sam Bass Warner has called the "private city"—one shaped primarily by the actions of many private individuals. All these persons pursued their own goals and tried to maximize their own profit. The prevailing belief was that the sum of such private activity would far exceed what the community could accomplish through public effort. This meant that the city itself handled only functions that could not be undertaken efficiently or profitably by private enterprise.

Despite that limitation, American cities actually compiled an impressive record of public works in the late nineteenth century. Nowhere in the world were there more massive public projects: water aqueducts, sewage systems, street paving, bridge building, extensive park systems. Though by no means free of the corruption and wastefulness of earlier days, city governments in these years became more centralized, better administered and more professional, and, above all, more expansive in the functions they undertook. How else could they have gathered the resources and built the infrastructure on which the modern industrial city depended?

Massive though it was, however, this public contribution did not undercut the prevailing conception of the city as an arena for private enterprise. The nation paid an enormous price for such unrestricted development. A century later we are still adding up the costs in terms of the quality of American urban life.

The Urban Environment. Some of those costs could be seen right away. In 1879 a British visitor observed the blight that spread along streets on which elevated trains operated:

> The nineteen hours and more of incessant rumbling day and night from the passing trains; the blocking out of a sufficiency of light; the full, close view passengers on the cars can have into rooms on the second and third floors.

Skyscrapers also shut out the light and added to downtown congestion. People regarded such conditions as sad but inevitable costs of progress.

Other consequences were more clearly the result of deliberate choice. Priority was given to projects considered vital to a city's economic development. Thus bridge construction flourished. Grand public buildings, symbols of a city's eminence, enjoyed great popularity. Philadelphia's city hall, said one critic, had been "pro-

jected on a scale of magnificence better suited for the capitol of an empire than the municipal building of a debt-burdened city." On the other hand, the condition of the streets, mainly a matter of convenience for the people, often remained scandalously bad. "Three or four days of warm spring weather," remarked a New York journalist, would turn Manhattan's garbage-strewn, snow-clogged streets into "veritable mud rivers."

A visitor to Pittsburgh noted "the heavy pall of smoke which constantly overhangs her . . . until the very sun looks coppery through the sooty haze." As for the lovely hills rising from the rivers, "they have been leveled down, cut into, sliced off, and ruthlessly marred and mutilated, until not a trace of their original outlines remains." Pittsburgh presented "all that is unsightly and forbidding in appearance, the original beauties of nature having been ruthlessly sacrificed to utility."

These failings resulted not only from the low value placed on the quality of urban life. The city's dynamism confounded efforts to provide adequate services. When it was completed in 1842, New York's Croton aqueduct was hailed as "more akin in magnificence to the ancient and Roman aqueducts [than anything] achieved in our times." Yet less than a decade later water consumption was outstripping the capacity of the aqueduct. In 1885 New York started to build a second and larger aqueduct. That one also failed to meet the city's needs, and so New York built still another aqueduct a hundred miles away in the Catskill Mountains. Each new facility and innovation seemed to fall short, not merely outstripped by the rising demand but also contributing to that demand. This occurred with urban transportation, high-rise building, and modern sanitation systems. They attracted more users, created new needs, and caused additional crowding and shortages.

It was not that America lacked an urban vision. On the contrary, an abiding rural ideal had exerted a powerful influence on American cities for many years and inspired many urban planners. Frederick Law Olmsted, who designed New York's Central Park and many other great parks, wanted cities that exposed people to the beauties of nature. One of Olmsted's projects, the Chicago Columbian Exposition of 1893, gave rise to the influential "City Beautiful" movement. The results included larger park systems, broad boulevards and parkways, and, after the turn of the century, zoning laws and planned suburbs.

But cities usually heeded urban planners too little and far too late. "Fifteen or twenty years ago a plan might have been adopted that would have made this one of the most beautiful cities in the world," Kansas City's park commissioners reported in 1893. At that time "such a policy could not be fully appreciated." Nor, even if Kansas City had foreseen its future, would it have shouldered the "heavy burden" of trying to shape its development. The American city had placed its faith in the dynamics of the marketplace, not the restraints of a planned future.

Housing. Hardest hit by urban growth were the poor. In earlier times low-income city residents had lived in makeshift wooden structures in the alleys and back streets and, increasingly, in the subdivided homes of more prosperous families that had fled to other neighborhoods. When rising land values after the Civil War made this practice unprofitable, speculators began to build housing specifically designed for the urban masses. In New York City, the dreadful result was the "dumbbell" tenement, shaped to utilize nearly all the standard lot of 25 by 100 feet. A five-story building of this type could house twenty families in cramped, airless apartments (see Figure 20.1). In New York's Eleventh Ward an average of 986 persons occupied each acre, a density matched only in Bombay, India. In other cities crowding was not as severe. Chicago, Boston, and St. Louis relied on two- and three-story buildings for low-income housing, whereas Philadelphia and Baltimore made do with dingy row houses.

Civic-minded people everywhere considered these districts to be blights on the city. Here is how one investigator described Chicago's Halsted Street in 1896:

> The filthy and rotten tenements, the dingy courts and tumble-down sheds, the foul stables and dilapidated outhouses, the broken sewer pipes, the piles of garbage fairly alive with diseased odors, and . . . children filling every nook, working and playing in every room, eating and sleeping in every windowsill, pouring in and out of every door, and seeming literally to pave every scrap of "yard."

Reformers recognized the problem but seemed unable to solve it. Some favored model tenements financed by public-spirited citizens willing to accept a limited return on their investment. When private philanthropy failed to make much of a dent in the problem, cities turned to housing codes. The most advanced of these was New York's Tenement House Law of 1901, which required interior courts, indoor toilets, and fire safeguards for new housing but did little to remedy the problems of existing housing stock. Commercial development had pushed up land values in downtown areas. Only high-density, cheaply built housing could earn a sufficient profit for the landlords of the poor. This economic fact defied nineteenth-century solutions.

A Balance Sheet: Chicago and Berlin. In 1902 Chicago and Berlin had virtually equal populations. Their histories were, however, profoundly different. Seventy years earlier, when Chicago was just a muddy frontier outpost, Berlin had 250,000 inhabitants and was the royal seat of the Hohenzollerns of Prussia. With German unification in 1871, the imperial authorities rebuilt Berlin

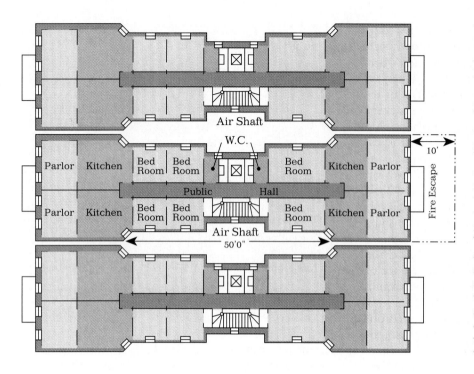

FIGURE 20.1

Floor Plan of a Dumbbell Tenement
In a contest for a design that met an 1879 requirement that every room have a window, the dumbbell tenement won. The interior indentation, which created an airshaft between adjoining buildings, gave the tenement its "dumbbell" shape. What was touted as a "model" tenement demonstrated instead the futility of trying to reconcile maximum land usage with decent housing. Each floor contained four apartments of three or four rooms, the largest only 10 by 11 feet. The two toilets in the hall became filthy or broke down under the daily use of forty or more people. The narrow airshaft provided almost no light for the interior rooms and served mainly as a dumping ground for garbage. So deplorable were these tenements that they became the stimulus for the next wave of New York housing reform.

on a grander scale. "A capital city is essential for the state, to act as a pivot for its culture," proclaimed the Prussian historian Heinrich von Treitschke, and Berlin served that national purpose—"a center where [Germany's] political, intellectual, and material life is concentrated, and its people can feel united." Chicago had no such pretensions. It was strictly a place of business, made great by virtue of its strategic grip on the commerce of America's industrial heartland. Nothing in Chicago evoked the grandeur of Berlin's boulevards or its monumental palaces and public buildings, nor were Chicagoans ever witness to the pomp and ceremony of the imperial parades through the Brandenburg Gate and up broad, tree-lined Unter den Linden to the national cathedral.

Yet as a functioning city Chicago was in many ways superior to Berlin. Chicago's waterworks pumped 500 million gallons of water a day, providing 139 gallons of water per person, whereas Berliners had to make do with 18 gallons. Flush toilets, a rarity in Berlin in 1900, could be found in 60 percent of Chicago's homes. Its streets were lit by electricity whereas Berlin still relied mostly on gaslight. Chicago had a much more extensive streetcar system, twice as much acreage devoted to parks, and a public library containing many more volumes than Berlin's. And Chicago had just completed an amazing sanitation project to protect its water supply in Lake Michigan. By means of the new Sanitary and Ship Canal, the course of the Chicago River had been reversed so that its waters—and the city's sewage—would flow away from the lake and southward down into the Illinois and Mississippi rivers. The giant canal, involv-

ing the excavation of over 30 million cubic yards of dirt, was the greatest earth-moving project in municipal history up to that time.

Giant sanitation projects were one thing; an inspiring urban environment was something else. For well-traveled Americans admiring of things European, the sense of inferiority was palpable. "We are enormously rich," admitted the journalist Edwin L. Godkin, "but . . . what have we got to show? Almost nothing. Ugliness from an artistic point of view is the mark of all our cities." Thus the urban balance sheet: a utilitarian infrastructure that was superb by nineteenth-century standards but "no municipal splendors of any description, nothing but population and hotels."

City People

The city symbolized energy and enterprise with its soaring skyscrapers, rushing subways and jostling traffic, and hum of business activity. When the budding writer Hamlin Garland and his brother arrived in Chicago from rural Iowa in 1881, they knew immediately that they had entered a new world: "Everything interested us. . . . Nothing was commonplace, nothing was ugly to us." In one way or another every city-bound migrant, whether from the American countryside or from a foreign land, experienced something of this exhilaration and wonder.

But with the opportunity and boundless variety came disorder and uncertainty. The urban world was

utterly unlike the rural communities that the newcomers had left. In the countryside every person had been known to his or her neighbors. Mark Twain found New York "a splendid desert, where a stranger is lonely in the midst of a million of his race. A man walks his tedious miles through the same interminable streets every day, yet never seeing a familiar face, and never seeing a strange one the second time. . . . Every man rushes, rushes, rushes, and never has time to be companionable—never has any time at his disposal to fool away on matters which do not involve dollars and duty and business." If rural roles and obligations had been well understood, in the city the only predictable relationships were those dictated by the marketplace.

The newcomers could never re-create in the city the worlds they had left behind. But new ways developed to meet the social needs of urban dwellers—to give them a sense of their place in the community, teach them how to function in an impersonal, heterogeneous environment, and make the complex, dynamic city understandable. An urban culture emerged, and through it there developed a new breed of American who was entirely at home in the modern city.

Immigrants

At the turn of the century upwards of 30 percent of the residents of New York, Chicago, Boston, Cleveland, Minneapolis, and San Francisco were foreign-born. Except in the South, America's cities had attracted large numbers of immigrants for many years. In 1900 the dominant groups still represented mainly the earlier mi-

Italian Bread Peddlers, New York City
Because of crowded conditions in East Side tenements, immigrant life spilled out onto the streets, which offered a bit of fresh air, a chance to socialize with neighbors, and a place to shop for food, including bread.

TABLE 20.2

Foreign-Born Population of Philadelphia, 1870 and 1910

	1870	1910
Irish	96,698	83,196
German	50,746	61,480
Austrian	519	19,860
Italian	516	45,308
Russian	94	90,697
Hungarian	52	12,495
Foreign-born population	183,624	384,707
Total population	674,022	1,549,008

Source: Allen F. Davis and Mark Haller, *The Peoples of Philadelphia* (Philadelphia: Temple University Press, 1973), 205.

gration from northern Europe. The biggest ethnic group in Boston was Irish; in Minneapolis, Swedish; in most other northern cities, German. But by 1910 the influx from southern and Eastern Europe had changed the ethnic complexion of many of these cities. The experience of Philadelphia is shown in Table 20.2. In Chicago, Poles and Russians (mostly Jewish) took the lead; in New York, Italians were second to Russians; and in San Francisco, Italians became the largest foreign-born group.

All these immigrants—old and new—carried experiences and customs from the homeland that shaped their lives in the New World. But for the later arrivals from southern and Eastern Europe there was less intermingling with the older populations than had been possible in the earlier "walking cities." Beginning in the 1880s, observers invariably reported that only foreign-born people lived in the poorer downtown areas of the great eastern and midwestern cities. "One may find for the asking an Italian, a German, a French, African, Spanish, Bohemian, Russian, Scandinavian, Jewish, and Chinese colony," remarked the Danish-American journalist Jacob Riis in his study of New York in 1890. "The one thing you shall vainly ask for in the chief city of America is a distinctively American community."

The foreign-born had little choice about where they lived; they needed to be near their jobs and could not afford better housing. Some, such as Maksymilian Markiewicz (see American Voices, page 626), gravitated to the outlying factory districts; others settled in the congested downtown ghettos. The immigrants did not settle randomly in those districts, however. Even where that seemed to happen, as in Philadelphia, closer study revealed that ethnic groups clustered in certain houses and portions of blocks. More commonly, as Riis discov-

The Economy of the Ghetto

Downtown immigrant neighborhoods would not have struck the casual observer as industrial districts, but tucked away in the tenements were commercial lofts and small workshops. An entire ready-made clothing industry flourished within the ghettos of large cities, drawing especially on the young women of the neighborhood to perform the low-paid sewing tasks.

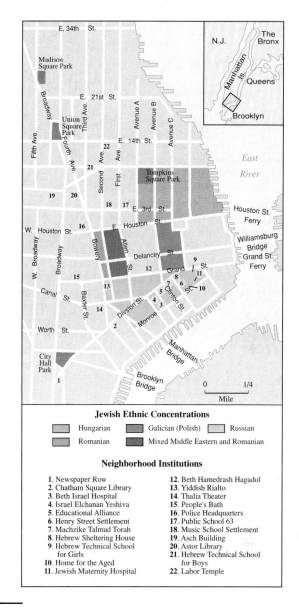

Jewish Ethnic Concentrations

| | Hungarian | | Galician (Polish) | | Russian |
| | Romanian | | Mixed Middle Eastern and Romanian | | |

Neighborhood Institutions

1. Newspaper Row
2. Chatham Square Library
3. Beth Israel Hospital
4. Israel Elchanan Yeshiva
5. Educational Alliance
6. Henry Street Settlement
7. Machzike Talmud Torah
8. Hebrew Sheltering House
9. Hebrew Technical School for Girls
10. Home for the Aged
11. Jewish Maternity Hospital
12. Beth Hamedrash Hagadol
13. Yiddish Rialto
14. Thalia Theater
15. People's Bath
16. Police Headquarters
17. Public School 63
18. Music School Settlement
19. Asch Building
20. Astor Library
21. Hebrew Technical School for Boys
22. Labor Temple

MAP 20.3

The Lower East Side, New York City

As this map shows, the Jewish immigrants dominating Manhattan's Lower East Side preferred living in neighborhoods populated by those from their home regions of Eastern Europe. It was their sense of a common identity, however, that made for a remarkable flowering of educational, cultural, and social institutions on the Jewish East Side.

ered, an ethnic group took over an entire neighborhood. In New York (see Map 20.3), Italians crowded into the Irish neighborhoods west of Broadway, and Russian and Polish Jews pushed the Germans out of the Lower East Side. A dense colony of Hungarians lived around Houston Street, and Bohemians occupied stretches along the Upper East Side between Fiftieth and Seventy-sixth streets.

Within ethnic groups, one could also spot clusterings of people from the same province or even the same village. Among New York Italians, for example, Neapolitans and Calabrians populated the Mulberry Bend district whereas Genoese lived on Baxter Street. Other northern Italians occupied the Eighth and Fifteenth wards west of Broadway. In 1903, along a short stretch of Elizabeth Street, there lived several hundred families from a single Sicilian fishing town, Sciacca, and as in Sicily, Sciacca's patron saint was celebrated every year.

Capitalizing on the fellow feeling that drew ethnic groups together, a variety of institutions sprang up to meet their needs. Wherever substantial numbers of immigrants lived, newspapers appeared. In 1911 the 20,000 Poles in Buffalo, New York, supported two Polish-language daily papers. Immigrants throughout the country avidly read *Il Progresso Italo-Americano* and the Yiddish-language *Jewish Daily Forward*, both published in New York City. Conviviality could always be found on street corners, in barbershops and club rooms, and in saloons. A 1905 survey showed that Chicago had as many saloons as grocery stores, meat markets, and dry-goods stores together. Italians marched in saints' day parades, Bohemians gathered in singing societies, and New York Jews patronized a vibrant Yiddish theater. To provide help in times of sick-

Maksymilian Markiewicz

The Odyssey of a Polish Immigrant

In these letters to his cousin Waclaw (whom he addresses as "brother"), Maksymilian Markiewicz records the life experience of a typical Polish immigrant to urban America.

South Chicago, August 7, 1906

Dear Brother Waclaw: Fortune arranged it so that unexpectedly we both became pilgrims to America. So I feel my brotherly attachment to you, and that it is so, let it be proved by my letter to you. . . . So I inform you that I came to America, i.e., to New York, on February 13, and then I went to my friends in New Kensington [Pennsylvania] . . . . I worked in a glass factory for 8 hours a day. The work was not heavy, but hot. I earned $12.50 to $14.00 a week; it depended on how much glass was made.

I left because the factory closed. . . . I went to Chicago. There I found my acquaintances and my cousin Leonard Król, my mother's uncle's son, with whom I am living up to the present. Since I came to South Chicago, I am working with Polish carpenters 8 hours a day. I am paid 35 cents an hour. And naturally, while it is summer, I am very busy with this

work, but in winter it will surely stop. Then I hope to get into a factory.

Indiana Harbor, April 30, 1908

Dear Brother Waclaw: I inform you that I moved from South Chicago to Indiana Harbor, nearer my work, so that now I can go on foot to the factory and I don't need to pay 15 cents a day for the railway passage. . . .

I got a letter from our country, from mother, father and brother Wiktor. When Wiktor was still in Petersburg I wrote him that I intended to marry in America, and that I would therefore never come back to our country. . . . My mother begs me much, in her first letter to me, to remove these thoughts from my head, to come back to our country. . . . My heart grieves at the words of my beloved mother, and I am ready to satisfy her wish in the future.

As to the question how I look upon religion and socialism, dear brother, I don't bother myself profoundly with either the first or the second. . . . I am not devout, for I have no time to pray, because every Sunday I must work, and—I confess it to you alone—I worked even on Easter from

7 until 2. . . . But nevertheless I desire to remain a Catholic up to my death.

December 14, 1908

Dear Brother: In the factory where I am working very few men have good work—only the engineers and we three carpenters. As to ordinary workers in the mill, may God pity them, so bad is their work. . . . With me everything is good . . . only I am bored here, because in this small town I am as solitary as in a forest. . . . Write me what you think about the Polish National Alliance and the Polish Sokols [gymnastic societies].

October 5, 1909

Dear Brother Waclaw: My old boss told me today that he had much work, so perhaps I knew some carpenters, and if so I should send them to him. . . . I advise you to come, dear brother. . . . We would live in the foreign land together. . . . We could meet in South Chicago and speak about the business while drinking a glass of beer.

Source: William I. Thomas and Florian Znaniecki, *The Polish Peasant in Europe and America* (Urbana: University of Illinois Press, 1984, abridged ed.), 123–133.

---

ness and death, the immigrants organized mutual-aid societies. The Italians in Chicago had sixty-six of these organizations in 1903, composed mainly of people from particular provinces and towns. Immigrants built a rich and functional institutional life in urban America, to an extent unimagined in their native villages.

Urban Blacks. The vast majority of African-Americans—85 percent in 1880—lived in the rural South. In the ensuing years some of them migrated to the modestly growing southern cities. By 1900 blacks constituted roughly a third of the South's urban population, ranging from 20 percent in Louisville and Dallas to absolute majorities in Memphis and Charleston.

The great African-American migration to northern cities was just beginning. The black population of New

York increased by 30,000 between 1900 and 1910, making New York second only to Washington, D.C., as a black urban center, but the 91,000 blacks in New York in 1910 represented fewer than 2 percent of the population, as did Chicago's 45,000 black residents and Cleveland's 6,000.

Despite their relatively small numbers, urban blacks could not escape becoming targets of the fierce racism of the age. In northern cities generally, residential segregation was intensifying, and the scattered black neighborhoods were giving way to concentrated ghettos—Chicago's Black Belt on the south side, for example, or the early outlines of New York's Harlem. Because of race prejudice, job opportunities were likewise narrowing. Whereas 26 percent of Cleveland's blacks had been skilled workers in 1870, only 12 percent were by 1890,

and entire occupations, such as barbering (except for a black clientele), disappeared. Two-thirds of Cleveland's blacks in 1910 worked as domestic and day laborers, with little hope of moving up the job ladder.

In the face of segregation and pervasive discrimination, urban blacks built their own communities. They created a flourishing press, fraternal orders, a vast array of women's organizations, and a middle class of doctors, lawyers, and small entrepreneurs. Above all, there were the black churches—twenty-five in Chicago in 1905, mainly Methodist and Baptist. More than any other institution, remarked one scholar in 1913, it was the church "which the Negro may call his own. . . . A new church may be built . . . and . . . all the machinery set in motion without ever consulting any white person. . . . [It] more than anything else represents the real life of the race." Just as it was in the southern countryside, the church was the central institution for city blacks, and the preacher—"a leader, a politician, an orator, a 'boss', an intriguer, an idealist," so W. E. B. Du Bois described him—was the most important local citizen. Manhattan's Union Baptist Church, housed like many others in a storefront, attracted the "very recent residents of this new, disturbing city" and, ringing with spirituals and fervent prayer, made Christianity come "alive Sunday mornings."

Ward Politics

Race and ethnicity tended to divide newcomers to the city and turn them in on themselves. Politics, on the other hand, acted as a powerful instrument for integrating immigrants and blacks into the larger urban society. The basic unit of city governance was the *ward*, each one entitled to its representative on the city council or board of aldermen. Whether realizing it or not, every migrant to an American city automatically belonged to a ward and, by living on a particular street, immediately acquired a spokesman at city hall.

In earlier days the aldermen had been the dominant figures in urban politics, but that was no longer the case in the late nineteenth century. Power had largely passed to the mayor's office and the various citywide administrative agencies. But the city council still represented the parochial interests of the wards, and immigrants learned very quickly that if they needed anything from city hall, the alderman was the person for them. That was how streets got paved, or water mains were extended, or variances were granted—so that, for example, in 1888 Vito Fortounescere could "place and keep a stand for the sale of fruit, inside the stoop-line, in front of the northeast corner of Twenty-eighth Street and Fourth Avenue" in Manhattan, or that the parishioners of Saint Maria of Mount Carmel could set off fireworks at their Fourth of July picnic.

Interlinked with this formal representation was the pervasive presence of party machines in immigrant and black neighborhoods. Machine control of political parties existed at every level of American politics (see Chapter 19). The system flourished most luxuriantly, however, in the big cities. Most famous was Tammany Hall, the political machine that dominated Manhattan's Democratic party; but the major parties of most large cities—Democratic or Republican—had their versions of Tammany.

The power of urban machines depended on a loyal party constituency. This meant organization down to the grass roots. The wards were divided into election districts of a few blocks, each with a district captain who reported to the ward boss (who might also have been the alderman). It was the main job of these functionaries to be accessible and, as best they could, to serve the needs of the party's constituents.

The machine performed a similar function for the business community. Entrepreneurs of many kinds wanted something from the city. Contractors sought city business; gas companies and streetcar lines wanted licenses and privileges; manufacturers needed services and not-too-nosy inspectors; and the liquor trade and numbers racket relied on a tolerant police force. All of them turned to the machine boss and his lieutenants. In addition to these everyday functions, the machine continuously mediated among conflicting interests and oiled the wheels of city government. The machines filled a void in the public life of the nineteenth-century city, doing informally much of what the municipal system left undone. "Nowhere else in the world," remarked the journalist Henry Jones Ford, "has party organization had to cope with such enormous tasks . . . and its efficiency in dealing with them is the true glory of our political system."

Of course, the machine exacted a price for all these services. The tenement dweller gave his vote. The businessman wrote a check. Those who became the machine's beneficiaries enabled it to function. Corruption permeated this informal system. Some of the money that changed hands inevitably ended up in the pockets of machine politicians. This boodle could take the form of outright corruption: kickbacks by contractors; protection money from gamblers, saloonkeepers, and prostitutes; and payoffs from gas and trolley companies. The Tammany ward boss George Washington Plunkitt, however, insisted that he had no need for kickbacks and bribes. He favored what he called "honest graft," the easy profits that came to savvy insiders. Plunkitt himself made most of his money building wharves on Manhattan's waterfront. Big Tim Sullivan (see American Lives, pages 628–629) used his contacts to build a vaudeville empire. One way or another, legally or otherwise, machine politics rewarded its supporters.

For the young and ambitious this was reason enough to favor the machine system. American society

Big Tim Sullivan: Tammany Politician

Timothy D. Sullivan was born on July 23, 1863, near the Hudson River docks in Lower Manhattan. His parents were Irish immigrants, part of the mass migration of potato famine victims that flooded into New York in the 1840s. Four years later Tim's father died, leaving his young widow, Catherine Connelly Sullivan, with four small children. Soon thereafter Catherine married Lawrence Mulligan, an Irish laborer, and the family moved to the notorious Five Points district on the Lower East Side. There the 1870 census found them, a household of ten (including three boarders) living in an overcrowded tenement at 25 Baxter Street (see Map 20.3 for the urban geography of Sullivan's career).

Tim had a harsh childhood. His stepfather drank heavily and regularly beat his wife and children. To make ends meet, Catherine took in washing and Tim went to work at age seven bundling paper for $1.50 a week on Newspaper Row across from City Hall. Tim got through grammar school, but his family needed his earnings too much for him to go on to high school. "Free as it was," he later remarked, "it was not free enough for me to go there." Instead—Horatio Alger style—he made his way up in the newspaper business and by age eighteen was well established as a wholesale newspaper dealer. He soon became the proprietor of two saloons and, in his early twenties, was ready for politics. Sullivan was a big fellow, over six feet tall, handsome, and quick with his fists. He gained a local reputation by thrashing a tough he had encountered on the street beating up a woman. True or not, the story helped him win the Democratic nomination at age twenty-three for the New York State Assembly from the Second District.

In 1889 Sullivan opposed a bill granting Manhattan's police virtually unlimited powers to detain people with jail records. The champion of the bill was Thomas F. Byrnes, chief inspector of the New York Police Department and the most celebrated detective in the country. Byrnes did not take kindly to opposition from small-time politicians. He raided Sullivan's saloons, arrested two barkeepers for excise tax violations, and denounced Sullivan as a consorter with criminals. Against the advice of friends, Sullivan took the Assembly floor to answer the charge. In tearful tones Sullivan cast him-

Big Tim Sullivan

self as an "honest Bowery boy," describing his impoverished childhood, his saintly mother, and his struggle to rise in the world. "When, at the conclusion [so a reporter recorded], he asked if he had any time or money to spend with thieves, there was a 'No' on nearly every member's lips." It was the making of the obscure assemblyman. Although he gained a notoriety with uptown New Yorkers that would dog him throughout his career, he won the hearts of his constituents, who reveled in the success story of one of their own. They thought "Big Tim" a fine fellow, and so did the Tammany leaders.

The Bowery at Night, 1895
This painting by W. Louis Sonntag, Jr., shows Big Tim's stomping ground, the Bowery, crowded with shoppers and pleasure-seekers. It was during this time that the Bowery gained its raffish reputation.

When the Tammany machine swept into power in the 1892 elections, Boss Richard Croker tapped Sullivan to run the new Third Assembly District centering on the Bowery. Sullivan swiftly consolidated his power. His inner circle was all Irish, but for election district captains he appointed Jews, Italians, and Germans who were well connected in the immigrant communities that populated his fiefdom. Sullivan became famous for his summer "chowders," when he transported his constituents by riverboat to the country for a rowdy day of picnicking. At Christmas there was a fine dinner for all who were in need. And in February Sullivan handed out wool socks and shoes—always with the sentimental tale of how a teacher had given him free shoes one cold winter. Big Tim also attended assiduously to the nitty-gritty business of running a political machine. He got jobs for his supporters, visited the jails regularly to offer bail and other aid to the inmates, and on election day made sure his strong-arm crews patrolled the polling places. Sullivan's district became the best organized in the city, and Tammany hailed him as "the most popular man on the East Side."

In the meantime, Sullivan was making his fortune. His particular form of "honest graft" was commercial entertainment. Big Tim knew instinctively how important a good time was to city people. Besides, the main street of his district, the Bowery, was the gaudy center of low-life entertainment for the entire city, lined with burlesque houses, concert saloons, restaurants, and cheap hotels. In the mid-1890s Sullivan formed a partnership with two theatrical producers and began to invest in vaudeville houses. He contributed not only

money and a shrewd head but the political contacts that assured lax enforcement of building codes and easy access to liquor licenses. Sullivan also became involved in professional boxing, horse racing, and, more illicitly, the gambling dens that dotted his district.

Sullivan was accused of trafficking in East Side prostitution, but this he indignantly denied. "Nobody who knows me well will believe I would take a penny from any woman, much less from the poor creatures who are more to be pitied than any other human beings on earth. I'd be afraid to take a cent from a poor woman of the streets for fear my old mother would see me. I'd a good deal rather break into a bank and rob the safe. That would be a more manly and decent way of getting money."

When Boss Croker resigned in 1902, Sullivan might have succeeded him, but Big Tim preferred his own district and threw his support to Charles F. Murphy, who ruled Tammany for the next twenty-two years. Sullivan served briefly in Congress, made a lot more money investing in the early movie industry and in vaudeville syndicates across the country, and in the final phase of his career became a champion of progressive social legislation in the New York Senate. In 1912 Sullivan suffered a severe mental breakdown, possibly caused by tertiary syphilis. A year later he died under the wheels of a freight train after running off from his brother's house outside New York. His funeral procession down the Bowery was one of the largest in memory and brought out an immense crowd from every stratum of New York society, from statesmen to prizefighters and scrubwomen.

celebrated personal achievement but denied economic opportunity to poor immigrants. Not only did they lack the means to get started in business, remarked Robert A. Woods about the inhabitants of Boston's South End, "but they have to meet strong prejudices of race and religion. Politics, therefore, is for them apparently the easiest way to success in life." In the mid-1870s over half of Chicago's forty aldermen were foreign-born, sixteen of them Irish immigrants. The first Italian was elected to the board in 1885 and the first Pole in 1888, followed in the 1890s by Czechs and Scandinavians. Blacks did not manage to get on Chicago's board of aldermen until after 1900; but in Baltimore an African-American represented the Eleventh Ward from 1890 onward, and Philadelphia had three black aldermen by 1899. As a ladder for social mobility, machine politics (like professional sports, entertainment, and organized crime) was the most democratic of American institutions.

For most tenement dwellers, however, the machine had a more modest value. It acted as a rough-and-ready social service agency, providing jobs for the jobless, a helping hand for a bereaved family, and intercession with an unfeeling city bureaucracy. As a Boston ward boss remarked, "There's got to be in every ward somebody that any bloke can come to—no matter what he's done—and get help. *Help, you understand; none of your law and justice, but help*." The Tammany ward boss Plunkitt had a "regular system" when fires broke out in his district. "Any hour of the day or night, I'm usually there . . . as soon as the fire engines. If a family is burned out I don't ask whether they are Republicans or Democrats, and I don't refer them to the Charity Organization Society. . . . I just get quarters for them . . . and fix them up till they get things runnin' again. It's philanthropy, but it's politics, too—mighty good politics. . . . The poor look up to George W. Plunkitt as a father, come to him when they are in trouble—and don't forget him on election day."

Plunkitt was an Irishman, and so were most of the ward politicians controlling Tammany Hall. But by the 1890s Plunkitt's Fifteenth District was filling up with Italians and Eastern European Jews. In general the New York Irish had no love for these newer immigrants, but Plunkitt played no favorites. On any given day (as recorded in a diary) he might attend an Italian funeral in the afternoon and a Jewish wedding in the evening, and at each he probably paid his respects with a few Italian words or a bit of Yiddish.

"Think what New York is and what the people of New York are," remarked Richard Croker, the powerful head of Tammany during the 1890s, and Plunkitt's boss:

> One half, more than half, are of foreign birth. . . . They do not speak our language, they do not know our laws, they are the raw material from which we have to build up the state. . . . [Tammany] looks after

them for the sake of their vote, grafts them upon the Republic, makes citizens of them, in short. . . . Who else would do it if we did not? . . . There is not a mugwump in the city who would shake hands with the [immigrant voter].

The Mugwump reformer (see page 594) would doubtless have responded that the nation could do without citizens whose notion of politics was only what was in it for them. But Croker spoke a powerful truth. In an era when so many forces acted to isolate ghetto communities, politics served an *integrating* function, cutting across ethnic lines and giving immigrants and blacks a stake in the larger urban order.

Religion and Ethnicity

Among immigrant groups, religion was an abiding concern and was so intertwined with ethnic identity as to be inseparable from the story of how the newcomers adapted to the American city.

Jewish Immigrants. When Jews from Eastern Europe began their mass migration in the 1880s, about 250,000 Jews, mostly of German origin, were living in America. The German Jews, well established and increasingly prosperous, embraced Reform Judaism, abandoning religious practices "not adapted to the views and habits of modern civilization." Anxious to preserve the traditional piety, Yiddish-speaking immigrants founded their own Orthodox synagogues, often in vacant stores and ramshackle buildings. The number of synagogues in the United States jumped from 270 in 1880 to 1,901 in 1916.

Many Jewish immigrants found it difficult, however, to adhere to the traditional forms of their religion. In the isolated villages of Eastern Europe, Judaism stood for not only worship and belief but an entire way of life. Not even the closely confined urban American ghetto could re-create the communal environment essential for strict religious observance. "The very clothes I wore and the very food I ate had a fatal effect on my religious habits," confessed the hero of Abraham Cahan's novel *The Rise of David Levinsky* (1917). "If you . . . attempt to bend your religion to the spirit of your surroundings, it breaks. It falls to pieces." Levinsky shaved off his beard and plunged into the Manhattan clothing business. Orthodox Judaism survived this shattering of faith, but only by sharply reducing its claims on the lives of the faithful.

Catholic Immigrants. Catholics faced much the same problem. The issue, explicitly defined within the Roman Catholic Church as "Americanism," turned on how far Catholicism should respond to American society. Catholics fought out the question on many fronts. Should

Catholic children attend parochial or public schools? Should they intermarry with non-Catholics? Should the traditional education for the clergy be changed? Bishop John Ireland of St. Paul, Minnesota, felt that "the principles of the Church are in harmony with the interests of the Republic." But traditionalists, led by Archbishop Michael A. Corrigan of New York, denied the possibility of such harmony and argued, in effect, for insulating the Church from a hostile environment.

In 1895 Pope Leo XIII announced his support of the traditionalists. America, with its religious pluralism and sharp separation of church and state, did not afford "the most desirable status of the Church." The pope regretted the absence of the benefits that came from state support and urged Catholics "to prefer to associate with Catholics, a course which will be very conducive to the safeguarding of their faith." Because of its hierarchical structure, Catholicism had a better chance than Judaism to resist American influences.

The Church's traditional wing had the support of immigrant Catholics, who wanted to preserve the religion as they had known it in Europe. But the needs of the immigrants extended beyond religious matters; they wanted the Church also to be an expression of their ethnic identities. Newly arrived Catholics wanted their own parishes where they could celebrate their own customs and holidays, speak their own languages, and educate their children in their own parochial schools. When they became numerous enough, they also demanded their own bishops.

The Church had difficulty responding. The demands of its immigrant congregations seemed to challenge the Catholic hierarchy, which was dominated by Irish Catholics, and even the integrity of the Church itself.

The desire for ethnic parishes did more than divide Catholics; it also led to demands for local control of Church property. In addition, if the Church appointed bishops with jurisdiction over specific ethnic groups, that would mean disrupting the diocesan structure that unified the Church.

The severity of the conflict depended partly on the religious traditions of each ethnic group. Italians, for example, harbored strong anticlerical feelings, much strengthened by the papacy's opposition to the unification of Italy. Italian men also had a tradition of religious apathy. On the other hand, the Church played such an important part in the lives of Polish immigrants that they resented any interference by the Catholic hierarchy. In 1907 fifty parishes formed the Polish National Catholic Church of America, which adhered to Catholic ritual without recognizing the pope's authority.

On the whole, however, the Church reconciled its authority with the ethnic needs of the immigrant faithful. It met the demand for representation in the hierarchy by appointing Polish and other immigrant priests as auxiliary bishops within existing dioceses. Before World War I, American Catholics worshiped in more than 2,000 foreign-language churches and in many others that were bilingual. The Catholic Church thus became a central institution for the expression of ethnic identity in urban America.

Urban Protestantism. For the Protestant churches the city posed different but not easier challenges. With each wave of immigration urban populations became increasingly non-Protestant. At the same time, Protestant congregations were abandoning the older residential neighborhoods. Many formerly prosperous churches

Immaculate Heart of Mary Church, 1908

In crowded immigrant neighborhoods the church rose from undistinguished surroundings to assert the centrality of religious belief in the life of the community. This photograph is a view of Immaculate Heart of Mary Church taken from Polish Hill in Pittsburgh in 1908.

Paddy and Friends

Newsboys of New York

City dwellers encountered poverty every day in the form of ragged newsboys hawking papers on the streets. In 1854 the first Newsboys' Lodging House was opened as a shelter for these mostly homeless youngsters. By trial and error, the Lodging House accommodated itself to the fierce independence of the newsboys, who continued to ply their trade and indeed contributed to the upkeep of the Lodging House. Charles Loring Brace, a major Protestant charity figure who was well known to the boys, brought some friends to hear what the boys had to say: "Whom do you choose for your speaker?"

"Paddy, Paddy!" they shouted. "Come out, Paddy, an' show yerself."

Paddy came forward and mounted a stool; a youngster not more than twelve, with little round eyes, a short nose profusely freckled, and a lithe form full of fun.

"Bummers," he began, "Snoozers and citizens, I've come down here among yer to talk to yer a little. Me an' me friend Brace have come to see how yer gittin' along an' to advise yer. You fellers w'at stands at the shops with yer noses over the railin', a smellin' of the roast beef an' hash,— you fellers who's got no home,—think of it, how are we to encourage yer? [Derisive laughter, and various ironical kinds of applause.] I say bummers, for

ye're all bummers, [in a tone of kind patronage] I was a bummer once meself. [Great laughter.] I hate to see yer spending yer money for penny ice-creams an' bad cigars. Why don't yer save yer money? I have hopes fer yer all. . . . I want yer to grow up to be rich men,—citizens, gover'ment men, lawyers, ginerals, an' inflooence men. Well, boys, I'll tell yer a story. Me dad was a hard un. One beautiful day he went on a spree. . . . He clipped me over the head with an iron pot an' knocked me down, an' me mother drapped in on him an' at it they wint. . . . Ye should have seen 'em, an' whilst they were a fightin' I slipped meself out o' the back dure an' away I wint like a scart dog. . . . I ran away, an' here I am. Now, boys, be good, mind yer manners, copy me, an' see what ye'll become."

One solution much touted by reformers was to send homeless boys to the West to live with farm families. No doubt some of the streetwise newsboys suspected that they were wanted only as cheap farm labor. But this speaker on that Sunday evening had higher hopes:

"Do ye want to be newsboys always, an' shoeblacks, an' timber merchants in a small way sellin' matches? If ye do, ye'll stay in New York; but if ye don't, ye'll go out West an' begin to be farm-

City Newsboys

ers, for the beginnings of a farmer, me boys, is the makin' of a Congressman an' a President. Do ye want to be rowdies an' loafers an' shoulder-hitters? . . . I'm booked for the West in the next company from the Lodging-House. I hear they have big school-houses there, an' a place for me in the winter time. I've made up me mind to be somebody, an' you'll find me on a farm in the West . . . I can't say no more at present, boys. Good bye."

Source: Helen Campbell, *Darkness and Daylight: or, Lights and Shadows of New York Life* (Hartford, 1892) reprinted in Sigmund Diamond, ed., *The Nation Transformed* (New York: George Braziller, 1963), 300–301.

found themselves stranded in squalid ghetto neighborhoods. Seventeen Protestant churches moved out of lower Manhattan during the twenty years after 1868 as the area below Fourteenth Street filled up with immigrants.

Nearly every major city retained great downtown churches where wealthy Protestants worshiped. Some of those churches, richly endowed, took pride in nationally prominent pastors, including Henry Ward Beecher of the Plymouth Congregational Church in Brooklyn

and Phillips Brooks of the Trinity Episcopal Church in Boston. The eminence of those churches, with their fashionable congregations and imposing edifices, emphasized the growing remoteness of Protestantism from much of its urban constituency. "Where is the city in which the Sabbath day is not losing ground?" lamented a minister in 1887. The families of businessmen, lawyers, and doctors could be seen in any church on Sunday morning, he noted, "but the workingmen and their families are not there."

To counter this decline, the Protestant churches responded in two ways. They evangelized among the unchurched and indifferent, for example, through the Sunday-school movement. Protestants also made their churches instruments of social uplift. Starting in the 1880s, many city churches provided facilities such as reading rooms, day nurseries, clubhouses, and vocational classes. Sometimes the churches linked evangelism and social uplift. Protestant reformers did charity work of many kinds in the cities, such as the Newsboys' Lodging Houses (see American Voices, page 632). The Salvation Army, which arrived from Great Britain in 1879, spread the gospel of repentance among the urban poor and built an assistance program that ranged from soup kitchens to homes for former prostitutes. When all else failed, the down-and-outers of American cities knew they could count on the Salvation Army.

The Young Men's and Women's Christian Associations attracted large numbers of the young single people who flocked into the cities. Originating in Britain, the two organizations had arrived in the United States before the Civil War and had flourished. By the mid-1880s virtually all large cities had YMCAs equipped with gymnasiums, auditoriums, and dormitories. Housing for single women was an especially important mission of the YWCAs. No other organizations better met the needs of young adults for physical recreation, education, and companionship, or so effectively combined those services with an evangelizing appeal in the form of Bible classes, nondenominational worship, and a religious atmosphere.

The need of many people to unite religion with social uplift could be seen in the enormous popularity of a book called *In His Steps* (1896). The author, the Congregational minister Charles M. Sheldon, told the story of a congregation that resolved to live by Christ's precepts for one year. "If the church members were all doing as Jesus would do," Sheldon asked, "could it remain true that armies of men would walk the streets for jobs, and hundreds of them curse the church, and thousands of them find in the saloon their best friend?"

Urban Revivalism. The most potent form of urban evangelism—revivalism—said little about social uplift. From its beginnings in the eighteenth century, revivalism had steadfastly focused on the individual and had stressed personal redemption. The defeat of earthly problems would follow the conversion of the people to Christ. Beginning in the mid-1870s, revival meetings swept through the cities.

The pioneering figure was Dwight L. Moody, a former Chicago shoe salesman and YMCA official. After preaching in Britain for two years, Moody returned to America in 1875. With his talented chorister and hymn writer, Ira D. Sankey, Moody staged revival meetings that drew thousands. He preached an optimistic, uncomplicated, nondenominational message. Eternal life could be had for the asking, Moody shouted as he held up his Bible. His listeners needed only "to come forward and take, TAKE!"

Many other preachers followed in Moody's path. The most notable was Billy (William Ashley) Sunday, a hard-drinking former outfielder for the Chicago White Stockings who mended his ways and found religion. Like Moody and other city revivalists, Sunday was a farm boy. His ripsnorting cries against "Charlotte-russe Christians" and the "booze traffic" carried the ring of rustic America. By realizing that many people remained villagers at heart, revivalists found the key to bringing city dwellers back into the church.

In a larger sense, however, revivalism was expressive of a more general fundamentalist movement that sought to preserve old-time religion against the increasing complacency and doctrinal liberalism of mainstream Protestantism. Just as Methodism had arisen against the Church of England in the eighteenth century, so now in the late nineteenth century new churches arose against Methodism. The Holiness evangelical movement was at first nondenominational but then began to spawn new denominations such as the Church of the Nazarene (1908). Out of the Holiness Revival came the more radical Pentecostal movement, which by 1914 had brought together many local bodies into the Assemblies of God.

Leisure in the City

City people divided life's activities into separate units, setting workplace apart from home and working time apart from free time. "Going out" became a necessity, demanded not only as relief from a day of hard work but as proof that life was better in the New World than in the old. "He who can enjoy and does not enjoy commits a sin," a Yiddish-language paper told its readers. And enjoyment now meant buying a ticket and being entertained. A realm of public entertainment had emerged, open to all, created by a new class of entrepreneurs who gave the public what it wanted.

Public Entertainment. Amusement parks—Boston's Paragon Park, Philadelphia's Willow Grove, Atlanta's Ponce de Leon Park, Cleveland's Euclid Beach, San Francisco's the Chutes—went up at the end of trolley lines in cities across the country. Most remarkable was Luna Park at New York's Coney Island, "an enchanted, storybook land of trellises, columns, domes, minarets, lagoons, and lofty aerial flights. . . . It was a world removed—shut away from the sordid clatter and turmoil of the streets." In fact, that escape from everyday urban life explains the appeal of amusement parks. The cre-

Luna Park, Coney Island
Luna Park was the Disneyland of the industrial age, but more unbuttoned and casual, intended to lift city dwellers out of their workaday lives for a few hours. The view is down the main thoroughfare looking toward the entrance.

ators of Luna Park intended it to be "a different world—a dream world . . . where all is bizarre and fantastic . . . gayer and more different from the every-day world."

The theater likewise attracted huge audiences. Chicago had six vaudeville houses in 1896 and twenty-two in 1910. Evolving from cheap variety and minstrel shows, vaudeville moved from boisterous beer halls into grand theaters. Vaudeville cleaned up its routines, making them suitable for the entire family, and turned them into thoroughly professional entertainment handled by national booking agencies. With its standard program of nine acts of singing, dancing, and comedy, vaudeville attained enormous popularity just as the movies arrived. The first primitive films, a minute or so of humor or glimpses of famous people, appeared in 1896 in penny arcades and as filler in vaudeville shows. Within a decade millions of city people were watching dramatic films of increasing length and artistry at nickelodeons (named after the five-cent admission charge) across the country.

For young unmarried workers the cheap amusements of the city created a new social space. "I want a good time," a New York clothing operator told an investigator. "And there is no . . . way a girl can get it on $8 a week. I guess if anyone wants to take me to a dance he won't have to ask me twice." Hence the widespread ritual among the urban working class of "treating." The girls spent what money they had dressing up; their beaus were expected to pay for the fun. Parental control over courtship broke down, and amid the bright

lights and lively music of the dance hall and amusement park, working-class youth forged a more easygoing culture of sexual interaction and pleasure-seeking.

The functionally defined geography of the big city carved out ample space for commercialized sex. Prostitution was not new to urban life, but in the late nineteenth century it became less closeted and more intermingled with other forms of public entertainment. In New York the most famous sex district in this period was the Tenderloin, running northward from Twenty-third Street between Fifth and Eighth avenues and eventually up to Times Square and beyond. This was also the locale of the city's fanciest restaurants, the best hotels, and the theater district. On the side streets many of the brownstones, abandoned by their well-to-do owners for the quieter parts of town, were taken over by brothels. The nearby concert saloons—the forerunners of the nightclub—featured not only stage shows and bartenders but also well-dressed prostitutes working the premises.

The Tenderloin and the Bowery were also the sites of a robust gay subculture. The long-held notion that homosexual life was covert, in the closet, in Victorian America appears not to be true, at least not in the country's premier city. Homosexuality was illegal, but as with prostitution, the law was mostly a dead letter. In certain corners of the city a gay world flourished, with a full array of saloons, meeting places, and drag balls, which were widely known and often patronized by uptown "slummers."

Baseball. Of all forms of male diversion none was more specific to the city, nor so spectacularly successful, as professional baseball. The game's promoters decreed that baseball had been created in 1839 by Abner Doubleday in the village of Cooperstown, New York. Actually, baseball was neither of American origin—it developed from the British game of rounders—nor a product of rural life.

Organized play began in the early 1840s in New York City, where a group of gentlemen enthusiasts competed on an empty lot. During the next twenty years the aristocratic tone of baseball disappeared. Clubs sprang up across the country, and intercity competition developed on a scheduled basis. In 1868 baseball became openly professional, following the example of the Cincinnati Red Stockings in signing players to contracts at a negotiated salary for the season.

Big-time commercial baseball came into its own with the launching of the National League in 1876. The team owners were profit-minded businessmen who carefully shaped the sport to please the fans. Wooden grandstands gave way to the concrete and steel stadiums of the early twentieth century, such as Fenway Park in Boston, Forbes Field in Pittsburgh, and Shibe Park in Philadelphia.

The National Pastime

This lithograph celebrates the opening game of the 1889 season, with the Boston Base-Ball Club taking on the New York Base-Ball Club. The National League was then scarcely twelve years old. The fielders played barehanded, but otherwise the game today is much as the artist pictured it a century ago, down to the umpire's characteristic stance.

For the urban multitudes baseball grew into something more than an occasional afternoon at the ballpark. By rooting for the home team, fans found a way of identifying with the city they lived in. Amid the diversity and anonymity of urban life, the common experience and language of baseball acted as a bridge among strangers.

Students of the game have suggested that baseball was peculiarly attuned to city life. It followed strict, precise rules, which indicated an underlying order to the chaotic city. Far from respecting the rules, however, the players tried to get away with whatever they could in order to win. Did this not match the competitive scramble of urban life? The blue-coated umpire, the symbol of authority, was scorned by players and derided by fans. What better substitute for the resentment against the powers-that-be who ruled the lives of city people? Baseball, like many other emerging urban institutions, served as a mechanism for inducting people into the life of the modern city.

Newspapers. The press undertook this task in a clear-eyed, calculated way. Ever since Benjamin H. Day had established the New York *Sun* in 1833, American newspapers had aimed for a broad audience. James Gordon Bennett, founder of the New York *Herald*, wanted "to record the facts . . . for the great masses of the community." Journalism defined the news to be whatever interested city readers. The *Herald* covered crime, scandal, and sensational events. After the Civil War the *Sun's* editor, Charles A. Dana, added the human-interest story, which made news of ordinary, insignificant happenings. Newspapers also targeted specific audiences. A women's page offered recipes and fashion news, separate sections covered sports and high society, and the Sunday supplement helped fill the weekend hours.

Newspaper wars erupted periodically, as when Joseph Pulitzer, the owner of the St. Louis *Post-*

Joseph Pulitzer

Pulitzer (1847–1911) left Hungary at seventeen because he wanted to be a soldier, and his best chance was with the Union army in America. He was the greatest newspaper publisher of the century, extraordinary for his insight into what an urban reading public wanted from a newspaper and because he came to this task as a foreigner, without English as his mother tongue and without roots in American society.

Dispatch, invaded New York in 1883 by buying the *World*. In 1895 William Randolph Hearst, who owned the San Francisco *Examiner*, bought the New York *Journal* and challenged the *World* (see American Lives, Chapter 22). Hearst developed a sensational style of newspaper reporting and writing that became known as *yellow journalism*. The term, linked to the first comic strip to appear in color, "The Yellow Kid" (1895), referred to a type of reporting that treated accuracy as less important than a good story.

"He who is without a newspaper," said the great showman P. T. Barnum, "is cut off from his species." Barnum was speaking of city people and their hunger for information. By meeting this need, newspapers revealed their sensitivity to the public they served.

Upper Class/Middle Class

Wealth, more than anything else, has determined social class and standing in the United States. By that measure, American society was highly stratified during the nineteenth century. The top 1 percent of Americans held roughly a quarter of the country's wealth, and the richest 12 percent of households owned about 86 percent. This concentration of wealth appeared early in America's Industrial Revolution and remained relatively constant throughout the nineteenth century. Income levels were also sharply unequal. In 1890 industrial workers averaged $439 a year, clerical workers in manufacturing made twice that—$848 a year—whereas middle-class people such as doctors, lawyers, editors, and managers earned between $3,000 and $5,000. In the topmost ranks, of course, earnings derived less from salaries and wages than from investments. The top 10 percent of households had a larger income than the bottom 50 percent.

Wealth, of course, needed to be translated into the visible signs of social position. In the compact city of the early nineteenth century, class distinctions had been expressed by the way men and women dressed, the way they behaved, and the deference they demanded from or granted to others. As the industrial city grew, these interpersonal marks of class began to lose their force. In the anonymity of a large city, recognition and deference no longer served as mechanisms for conferring status. Instead, people began to rely on external signs: conspicuous displays of wealth, exclusive association in clubs and similar social organizations, and, above all, the choice of a neighborhood.

People's places of residence had previously depended primarily on the location of their work. For the poor that continued to be true. But for higher-income urbanites, where to live became a matter of personal means and social preference.

The Urban Elite

As early as the 1840s Boston merchants took advantage of the new railway service to move out of the congested central city. Fine rural estates appeared in Milton, Newton, and other outlying towns. By 1848 roughly 20 percent of Boston's businessmen were making the long trip from the countryside to their downtown offices. They traveled on 118 scheduled trains that served stations within 15 miles of the city center. Ferries that plied the harbor between Manhattan and Brooklyn or New Jersey served the same purpose for New Yorkers.

As commercial development engulfed downtown residential areas and as transportation services improved, the exodus from cities by the well-to-do spread across America. In Cincinnati wealthy families settled on the scenic hills rimming the crowded, humid tableland that ran down to the Ohio River. On those hillsides, a traveler noted in 1883, "the homes of Cincinnati's merchant princes and millionaires are found . . . elegant cottages, tasteful villas, and substantial mansions, surrounded by a paradise of grass, gardens, lawns, and tree-shaded roads." Residents of the area, called Hilltop, founded several country clubs, the Cincinnati Riding Club, the New England Society, five downtown gentlemen's clubs, and many other institutions that assured an exclusive social life for Cincinnati's elite.

Despite the temptations of country life, many of the very richest people preferred the heart of the city. Chicago had its Gold Coast; San Francisco, Nob Hill; Denver, Quality Hill; and Manhattan, Fifth Avenue. The New York novelist Edith Wharton recalled how the comfortable midcentury brownstones—"all so much alike that one could understand how easy it would be for a dinner guest to go to the wrong house"—gave way to the "'new' millionaire houses," which then spread northward beyond Fifty-ninth Street and up Fifth Avenue along Central Park. Great mansions, reminiscent of European aristocratic houses and filled with Old World artifacts, lined Fifth Avenue at the turn of the century.

By carving out fashionable areas in the heart of a city, the rich visibly demonstrated their capacity to assert their will over the larger society. But great fortunes did not automatically confer high social standing. An established elite stood astride the social heights even in relatively raw cities such as San Francisco and Denver. It had taken only a generation—and sometimes less—for money made in commerce or real estate to shed its tarnish and become "old" and genteel. In older cities such as Boston wealth passed intact through several generations. A high degree of intermarriage occurred there among the so-called Brahmin families. By withdrawing from trade, and by asserting a high cultural and moral code, the proper Bostonians kept moneyed newcomers at bay. Elsewhere urban elites tended to be

more open, but only to the socially ambitious who were prepared to make visible and energetic use of their money.

New York's Metropolitan Opera was one of the products of this ongoing struggle among the wealthy. The Academy of Music, home to the city's opera since 1854, was controlled by the Livingstons, the Bayards, the Beekmans, and other old New York families. Frustrated in their efforts to purchase boxes at the Academy, the Vanderbilts and their allies decided to sponsor a rival opera house. In 1883, with its glittering opening to the strains of Gounod's *Faust*, the Metropolitan proclaimed its ascendancy in the opera world and in due course won the patronage of even the Beekmans and Bayards. During this battle of the opera houses the Vanderbilt circle achieved social recognition.

"High Society." New York became the home of a national elite as the most successful people gravitated to this preeminent center of American economic and cultural life. Manhattan's extraordinary vitality, in turn, kept the city's high society fluid and relatively open. The tycoon Frank Cowperwood, in Theodore Dreiser's novel *The Titan* (1914), reassured his unhappy wife that if Chicago society would not accept them, "there are other cities. Money will arrange matters in New York—that I know. We can build a real place there, and go in on equal terms, if we have money enough." New York thus came to be a magnet for millionaires. The city attracted them not only because of its importance as a financial center, but also through the opportunities it offered for display and social recognition.

From Manhattan an extravagant life of leisure radiated outward to resort centers such as Saratoga Springs, New York; Palm Beach, Florida; and Newport, Rhode Island. Newport featured a grand array of summer "cottages" crowned by the Vanderbilts' Marble House and the Breakers. To these resorts and elsewhere, the affluent traveled in great comfort by private railway car. A style of living emerged that was incredible for its lavish excess, ranging from yachting and horse racing to huge feasts at luxurious restaurants such as Sherry's and Delmonico's. "Our forefathers would have been staggered at the cost of hospitality these days," remarked one New Yorker.

This infusion of wealth shattered the older elite society of New York. Seeking to be assimilated into the upper class, the flood of moneyed newcomers simply overwhelmed it. There followed a curious process of reconstruction, a deliberate effort to define the rules of conduct and identify those who properly "belonged" in New York society.

The key figure in this process was Ward McAllister, a southern-born lawyer who made a quick fortune in gold-rush San Francisco and then devoted himself to a second career as the arbiter of New York society. In 1888 McAllister compiled the first *Social Register*, which announced that it would serve as a "record of society, comprising an accurate and careful list" of all those deemed acceptable to participate in New York so-

The Breakers
The favorite summering place of the New York elite was the historic colonial port of Newport, Rhode Island. The opulent mansions there were known as "cottages." The Breakers was built in 1892 at a cost of $5 million for Cornelius Vanderbilt II. Designed in the style of an Italian palace, the Breakers had seventy-three rooms, thirty-three of them to house the small army of servants. The ornate dining room is shown in this photograph.

ciety. McAllister instructed the socially ambitious on how to select guests, set a proper table, arrange a ball, and launch a young lady into society. McAllister fostered an ordered social round of assemblies, balls, and dinners that defined the boundaries of an elite society. The key lay in the creation of associations sponsored by established social leaders, "organized social powers, capable of giving a passport of society to all worthy of it." To top things off, McAllister got the idea of "the Four Hundred"—the true cream of New York society. His list corresponded to those invited to Mrs. William Astor's great ball of February 1, 1892.

Social registers, coming-out balls for debutantes, and lesser versions of Ward McAllister soon popped up in cities throughout the country. In this fashion, the socially ambitious struggled to master the fluidity at the height of the social order.

Americans were adept at making money, noted the journalist Edwin L. Godkin in 1896, but they lacked the European traditions for spending it. "Great wealth has not yet entered our manners," Godkin remarked. "No rules have yet been drawn to guide wealthy Americans in their manner of life." In their struggle to find rules and establish standards, the moneyed elite made an indelible mark on urban life. If there was magnificence in the American city, it was mainly their handiwork. And if there was conspicuous waste and vulgarity, it was also their doing. In a democratic society wealth finds no easier outlet than through public display.

The Middle Class

The middle class left a smaller imprint on the public and the cultural faces of urban society. Its members, unlike the rich, preferred privacy and retreated into the domesticity of suburban comfort and family life.

The emerging corporate economy spawned a new middle class. Bureaucratic organizations required managers, accountants, and clerks. Advancing technologies called for engineers, chemists, and technicians. The distribution system sought salesmen, advertising executives, and buyers. These salaried ranks increased sevenfold between 1870 and 1910, growing at a much faster rate than any other occupational group. The traditional business class that had emerged in the first stages of industrialization before the Civil War—independent businessmen and professionals—also grew, but only at a third the rate of salaried personnel. Nearly 9 million people held white-collar jobs in 1910, more than a fourth of all employed Americans.

The middle class, particularly its salaried portions, was an urban population. Some lived within the city, in the row houses of Baltimore or Boston or the comfortable apartment houses of New York and other metropolitan centers. But many more preferred to escape the clamor and congestion of the city. They were attracted by a persisting "rural ideal." They agreed with the landscape architect Andrew Jackson Downing, who thought that "nature and domestic life are better than the society and manners of town." With the extension of rapid transit service from the city center, middle-class Americans followed the wealthy into the countryside. All sought what a Chicago developer promised for his North Shore subdivision in 1875: "qualities of which the city is in a large degree bereft, namely, its pure air, peacefulness, quietude, and natural scenery." And advanced building techniques—mass-produced materials and balloon-frame construction—made suburban housing affordable for the American middle class.

No major American city escaped rapid suburbanization during the last third of the nineteenth century. City limits everywhere expanded rapidly. By 1900 more than half of Boston's people lived in "streetcar suburbs" outside the original city. The U.S. Census of 1910 reported that nationwide about 25 percent of the urban population lived in suburbs outside the city limits.

On the European continent, by contrast, cities remained highly concentrated, and insofar as expansion occurred, it was the poor, not the well-to-do, who inhabited the margins. Unlike their American counterparts, the European middle class was not attracted (except in Britain) to the rural ideal and valued urban life for its own sake. In Europe mass transit developed much more slowly, traditional beam-and-post construction techniques persisted, and there was little of the freewheeling real-estate development that encouraged American suburbanization. Nor, finally, did the culturally homogeneous European cities give rise to the impulse felt by middle-class Americans to escape from the racially and ethnically diverse urban masses who occupied the city centers.

American suburbs were middle-class territory, but the middle class was not monolithic. It ranged from prosperous business proprietors and lawyers to clerks and traveling salesmen who earned no more than did foremen and craft workers. Close in to the city, the suburbs increasingly took on a working-class character.

The geography of the suburbs was truly a map of class structure in America, because where a family lived told where it ranked. The farther the distance from the center of the city, the finer the houses and the larger the lots. The affluent had the leisure and flexible schedules to travel the long distance into town. People closer in wanted direct transit lines convenient to home and office. Lower-income suburbanites were more likely to have more than one wage earner in the family, less secure employment, and jobs requiring movement around the city. They needed easy access to crosstown transit lines, which ran closer in to the city center.

Divisions within suburbs, although always a precise measure of economic ranking, never became rigidly

Cincinnati Suburb
The lives of the people inhabiting these neat homes along this tree-lined street were woven into the dynamic capitalism of a major industrial metropolis, including the children lounging on the corner, who were most certainly being educated for service in the new economic order. Looking at the bucolic setting of this Cincinnati street, no one would have thought so, and that was just the illusion that the suburb was intended to create: that Americans still partook of a rural ideal and could hold at bay the modern industrial order of which they were now a part.

fixed. People in the city center who wanted to better their lives moved to the cheapest suburbs. Those already settled there fled from these newcomers, in turn pushing the next higher group farther out in search of space and greenery.

Suburbanization was the sum of countless individual decisions. Each move represented an advance in living standards—not only more light, air, and quiet but also better housing than the city afforded. Suburban housing had more space and better design as well as indoor toilets, hot water, central heating, and, by the turn of the century, electricity. Even people in the inner suburbs came to regard these amenities as standard comforts. The suburbs also restored a basic opportunity that had seemed sacrificed by rural Americans when they moved to the city: home ownership again became the norm. "A man is not really a true man until he owns his home," propounded the Reverend Russell H. Conwell in his famous sermon on the virtues of making money, "Acres of Diamonds."

The small town of the rural past had fostered community life. Not so with the suburbs. The grid street pattern, while efficient for laying out lots and providing utilities, offered no natural focus for group life. Nor did the stores and services that lay scattered along the trolley-car streets. Not even schools and churches were located where they could become centers of community life. Suburban development conformed to the economics of real estate and transportation, and so did the thinking of middle-class homeseekers entering the suburbs. They wanted a house that gave them good value and convenience to the trolley line.

The need for community had lost some of its force for middle-class Americans. Two other attachments assumed greater importance: work and family.

Middle-Class Families

The family had been the primary productive unit in the preindustrial economy. Farmers, merchants, and artisans had carried on their work within a family setting, and the value of family members could be reckoned by their economic contribution. The family circle included not only blood relatives but all others living and working in the household. As industrialism progressed, production gradually moved out of the household. For the middle class in particular, the family became dissociated from economic activity. The father left the home to earn a living, clothing was bought ready-made, food came increasingly in cans and packages, and children spent more years in school. Middle-class families became smaller, excluding all but nuclear members and consisting in 1900 typically of husband, wife, and three children.

Within this family circle relationships became intense and affectionate. "Home was the most expressive experience in life," recalled the literary critic Henry Seidel Canby of his growing up in the 1890s. "Though the family might quarrel and nag, the home held them all, protecting them against the outside world." In a sense, the family served as a refuge from the competitive, impersonal business world. The suburbs provided a fit setting for such middle-class families. The quiet, tree-lined streets created a domestic world insulated from the hurly-burly of commerce and enterprise.

The Wife's Role. The burdens of this domesticity fell heavily on the wife. It was nearly unheard of for her to seek an outside career; that was her husband's role. She had the job of managing the household. "The woman who could not make a home, like the man who could not support one, was condemned," Canby remembered. But with better household technology, greater reliance on purchased goods, and fewer children, the wife's workload declined. Moreover, servants still played an important part in middle-class households. In 1910 there were about 2 million domestic servants, the largest job category for women.

Middle-Class Domesticity

For middle-class Americans the home was a place of nurture, a refuge from the world of competitive commerce. Perhaps that explains why their residences were so heavily draped and cluttered with bric-a-brac, every space filled with overstuffed furniture. All of it emphasized privacy and pride of possession. The young woman shown playing the piano symbolizes another theme of American domesticity—wives and daughters as ornaments and as bearers of culture and refinement.

As the physical burdens of household work eased, higher-quality homemaking became the new ideal. This was the message of Catharine Beecher's best-selling book *The American Woman's Home* (1869) and of magazines such as the *Ladies' Home Journal* and *Good Housekeeping*, which first appeared during the 1880s. The wife did more than make sure food was on the table, clothes were washed and mended, and the house was kept clean. She had the higher calling of bringing sensibility, beauty, and love to the household. "We owe to women the charm and beauty of life," wrote one educator. "For the love that rests, strengthens and inspires, we look to women." In this idealized view, the wife made the home a refuge for her husband and a place of nurture for their children.

Womanly virtue, even if a happy marriage depended on it, by no means put wives on equal terms with their husbands. Although the legal status of married women—the right to own property, control separate earnings, make contracts and bring suit, and get a divorce—improved markedly during the nineteenth century, sufficient legal discrimination remained to establish their subordinate role within the family. More important, custom dictated a wife's submission to her husband. She relied on his ability as the family breadwinner and, despite her superior virtues and graces, ranked as his inferior in vigor and intellect. Her mind could be employed "but little and in trivial matters," wrote one prominent physician, and her proper place was as "the companion or ornamental appendage to man."

No wonder that bright, independent-minded women rebelled against marriage. The marriage rate in the United States fell to its lowest point during the last forty years of the nineteenth century. More than 10 percent of women of marriageable age remained single, and the rate was much higher among college graduates and professionals. Only half the Mount Holyoke College class of 1902 married. "I know that something perhaps, humanly speaking, supremely precious has passed me by," remarked the writer Vida Scudder. "But . . . how much it would have excluded!" Married life "looks to me often as I watch it terribly impoverished, for women."

The strains of marriage were manifest in the number of middle-class families that broke up. Most of these domestic failures went unrecorded because of the stigma attached to divorce. In a Chicago suburb in the 1880s, at a time when divorce was virtually unknown there, about 10 percent of households had an absent spouse. The annual divorce rate increased from 1.2 per 1,000 marriages in 1860 to 7.7 in 1900. It was more difficult to document the other ways in which women responded to marriages that denied their autonomy and downplayed their sexuality. Middle-class women became the principal victims of neurasthenia, a disorder whose symptoms included depression and general disability. Some unhappy housewives found "silent friends" in opium and alcohol, which often were dispensed in well-laced patent medicines.

A happier release came through the companionship of other women. In an age that defined separate spheres for men and women, close ties commonly formed between schoolmates, cousins, and mothers and daughters. The intimacy and intensity of such attachments can be sensed in the letters of separated friends. Such enduring female ties yielded an emotional gratification not always found in marriage. Husbands, absorbed in busi-

ness, frequently played a secondary and remote role in the lives of their wives. Women's own sphere often filled that emotional vacuum.

Changing Views of Sexuality. In earlier times sexuality and reproduction had been more or less in harmony. A large family was considered a good thing, and the heavy toll of repeated pregnancies on the wife was accepted as God's will. In lower-class families this fatalism persisted, but not among middle-class couples, who increasingly wanted to limit the size of their families. Birth control, however, was not an easy matter. From the 1830s onward information about contraception became widely available, as did an array of commercial devices—condoms, diaphrams, sponges, douches. But the knowledge purveyed was imperfect or, as with advice about the rhythm method, absolutely wrong (doctors thought women were most fertile around the menstrual period). And the devices were for the most part not very effective or, as in the case of the condom, were stigmatized by association with the brothel.

Before these barriers could be surmounted, birth control was swept up in the social-purity campaign championed by Anthony Comstock. From the 1870s onward contraceptive devices and birth-control information were legally classified as obscene, barred from the mails, and criminalized in many states. Abortion, which had long been protected by the common law, became illegal except to save the mother's life. Although the practice of abortion probably remained widespread, it was expensive and dangerous, and shameful besides.

A painful tension existed between sexuality and family planning. The most prudent course would have been to delay marriage and then, except when a child was desired, to practice restraint. Sexual discipline was indeed the official wisdom of the day. Many doctors objected to contraception because they believed that by uncoupling sexuality from procreation, the sexual appetites of men would be released, to the detriment of their health and the moral fiber of society. It is this official writing that has given us the notion of a Victorian age of sexual repression. Letters and diaries suggest that in the privacy of their homes husbands and wives acted otherwise. Yet they must have done so in constant fear of unwanted pregnancy and with anxieties that exacted a heavy toll on middle-class marriage. A fulfilling sexual relationship was not easily squared with the desire to limit and space childbearing.

Around 1890 a change set in. Although the birth rate continued to decline, more young people married, and at an earlier age. These developments reflected the beginnings of a sexual revolution in the American middle-class family. Despite the Comstock laws, contraception became more acceptable and reliable. Experts began to abandon the notion, put forth by one popular medical text, that "the majority of women (happily for society)

are not very much troubled by sexual feeling of any kind." In succeeding editions of his book *Plain Home Talk on Love, Marriage, and Parentage*, the physician Edward Bliss Foote began to favor a healthy sexuality that gave pleasure to both women and men.

During the 1890s the artist Charles Dana Gibson created the image of the "new woman" in his drawings for *Life* magazine. The Gibson girl was tall, spirited, athletic, and chastely sexual. Constrictive clothing such as bustles, hoop skirts, and hourglass corsets gave way to shirtwaists and other natural styles that did not hide or disguise the female form. In the city, moreover, women's sphere began to take on a more public character. Among the new urban institutions catering to women, the most important was the department store, which became a temple for their emerging role as consumers.

The New Woman
John Singer Sargent's painting *Mr. and Mrs. Isaac Newton Phelps Stokes* (1897) captures on canvas the essence of the "new woman" of the 1890s. Nothing about Mrs. Stokes, neither how she is dressed nor how she presents herself, suggests physical weakness or demure passivity. She confidently occupies center stage, a fit partner for her husband, who is relegated to the shadows of the picture.

And the Children. The children of the middle class went through their own revolution. In the past, American children everywhere had been regarded as an economic asset—added hands for the family farm, shop, or countinghouse. That no longer held true for the urban middle class. Parents stopped treating their children as working members of the family. In the old days, Ralph Waldo Emerson remarked in 1880, "children had been repressed and kept in the background; now they were considered, cosseted, and pampered." There was such a thing as "the juvenile mind," lectured Jacob Abbott in his book *Gentle Measures in the Management and Training of the Young* (1871). The family was responsible for providing a nurturing environment in which the young personality could grow and mature.

Preparation for adulthood became increasingly linked to formal education. School enrollment went up 150 percent between 1870 and 1900. High school attendance, while still encompassing only a small percentage of teenagers, increased at the fastest rate. The years between childhood and adulthood began to stretch out, and a new stage of life—adolescence—emerged. Rooted in an extended period of family dependency, adolescence at the same time shifted much of the socializing role from parents to peer group. A youth culture—one of the hallmarks of American life in the twentieth century—was starting to take shape.

The Higher Culture

America's metropolitan centers, repositories of the nation's wealth, became the site for new institutions of higher culture. A hunger for the cultivated life did not of course originate in cities. Before the Civil War the lyceum movement had sent lecturers to the remotest towns, bearing messages of culture and learning. The Chautauqua movement, founded in upstate New York in 1874, carried on this work of cultural dissemination in the last decades of the nineteenth century. However, large cultural institutions such as museums, public libraries, opera companies, and symphony orchestras could flourish only in metropolitan centers.

The first major art museum, the Corcoran Gallery of Art, opened in Washington, D.C., in 1869. New York's Metropolitan Museum of Art started in rented quarters two years later. In 1880 that museum moved to its permanent site in Central Park and launched an ambitious program of art acquisition. J. P. Morgan became chairman of the board in 1905, assuring the Metropolitan's preeminence. The Boston Museum of Fine Arts was founded in 1876, and Chicago's Art Institute in 1879. By 1914 virtually every major city and about three-fifths of all cities with more than a 100,000 people had an art museum.

Top-flight orchestras also appeared, first in New York under the conductors Theodore Thomas and

Leopold Damrosch in the 1870s. Symphonies started in Boston and Chicago during the next decade. National tours by these leading orchestras planted the seeds for orchestral societies in many other cities. Public libraries grew from modest collections (in 1870 only seven had as many as 50,000 books) into major urban institutions. The greatest library benefactor was Andrew Carnegie, who announced in 1881 that he would build a library in any city that was prepared to maintain it. By 1907 Carnegie had spent more than $32.7 million to establish about a thousand libraries throughout the country.

If the late nineteenth century was the great age of moneymaking, it was also the great age of money *giving*. Surplus private wealth flowed in many directions, particularly to universities. These schools included Vanderbilt, Tulane, and Johns Hopkins universities, all named for their chief benefactors, and the University of Chicago, founded by John D. Rockefeller. Urban cultural institutions also received their share, partly as a matter of civic pride. To some extent patronage of the arts also served the need of the newly rich to establish themselves in society, as in the founding of the Metropolitan Opera in New York. But the higher culture was not only a commodity of civic pride and social display; museums and opera houses received support out of a sense of cultural deprivation.

"In America there is no culture," pronounced the English critic G. Lowes Dickinson in 1909. Science and the practical arts, yes, "every possible application of life to purposes and ends," but "no life for life's sake." Such condescending remarks received a respectful hearing in the United States because of a deep sense of cultural inferiority to the Old World. In 1873 Mark Twain and Charles Dudley Warner published a novel, *The Gilded Age*, satirizing America as a land of moneygrubbers and speculators. This enormously popular book touched a nerve in the American psyche. Its title has in fact been appropriated by historians to characterize the late nineteenth century—America's "Gilded Age"—as an age of materialism and cultural shallowness.

Some members of the upper class, including the novelist Henry James, despaired of the country and moved to Europe. Others spent their lives in the kind of perpetual alienation that Henry Adams described in his ironic memoir *The Education of Henry Adams* (1907).

The more common response was to try to raise the nation's cultural level. The newly rich had a hard time of it. They did not have much opportunity to cultivate a taste for art, and a great deal of what they collected was mediocre and garish. On the other hand, George W. Vanderbilt, grandson of the rough-hewn Cornelius Vanderbilt, became a patron of the Art Students League in New York and an early champion of French Impressionism. And the coal and steel baron Henry Clay Frick built a brilliant art collection that remains housed as a public museum in his mansion in New York City. The enthusiasm of moneyed Americans—not always well di-

rected—largely fueled the great cultural institutions that arose in many cities during the Gilded Age.

A deeply conservative idea of culture sustained this generous patronage. The aim was to embellish urban life, not to probe or reveal its meaning. "Art," says the hero of the Reverend Henry Ward Beecher's sentimental novel *Norwood* (1867), "attempts to work out its end solely by the use of the beautiful, and the artist is to select out only such things as are beautiful."

Culture had also become firmly linked to femininity. In America, remarked one observer, culture was "left entirely to women. . . . It is they, as a general rule, who have opinions about music, or drama, or literature, or philosophy. . . . Husbands or sons rarely share in those interests." Men represented the "force principle," said the clergyman Horace Bushnell, and women represented the "beauty principle."

Literature. The treatment of life, an eminent editor wrote, "must be tinged with sufficient idealism to make it all of a truly uplifting character. We cannot admit stories which deal with false or immoral relations. . . . The finer side of things—the idealistic—is the answer for us." The *genteel tradition*, as this literary school came to be called, dominated American cultural agencies such as universities and publishers from the 1860s on.

Rebellion against the genteel tradition sparked the main creative impulses of late nineteenth-century American literature. *Realism* became the rallying cry of a new generation of writers. Their champion, William Dean Howells, resigned in 1881 as editor of the *Atlantic Monthly*, a stronghold of the genteel tradition. He became the editor of *Harper's Monthly* and called for literature that "wishes to know and to tell the truth" and seeks "to picture the daily life in the most exact terms possible." In a series of realistic novels—*A Modern Instance* (1882), *The Rise of Silas Lapham* (1885), and *A Hazard of New Fortunes* (1890)—Howells captured the world of the urban middle class.

Henry James, a greater writer, also treated the novel as "a direct impression of life" and aimed at achieving "an air of reality." He wrote about the world of leisured Americans, and his central concern was the study of moral decay and regeneration. This concern, often set in motion by the confrontation of American innocence with European corruption, appears in *The American* (1877), *The Portrait of a Lady* (1882), and *The Golden Bowl* (1904).

The nostalgia of urbanized Americans for their agrarian past helped sustain a vigorous literature of local color and regionalism. These writings included the mining camp stories of Bret Harte, the Uncle Remus tales of Joel Chandler Harris, the Indiana poetry of James Whitcomb Riley, and the New England fiction of Sarah Orne Jewett. Such literature fit comfortably within the genteel tradition, for it was generally sentimental, reassuring, and morally uplifting.

Mark Twain, on the other hand, was an entirely different kind of regional writer. Starting his career as a western journalist and humorist (see Chapter 17), Twain avoided the influence of the eastern literary establishment. His greatest novel, *The Adventures of Huckleberry Finn* (1884), violated the custom of keeping "low" characters in their proper place for the amused inspection of the culturally superior reader. Huck, an outcast boy, seizes control of the story. The words are his, and so is the innocence with which he questions right and wrong in America. No other novel so fully engaged the themes of racism, injustice, and brutality in nineteenth-century America.

Although not graced with Twain's genius, other novelists did begin to come to grips with the hard realities of city life. Stephen Crane's *Maggie: A Girl of the Streets* (1893), privately printed because no publisher would touch it, unflinchingly described the destruction of a slum girl. In another urban novel, Henry Blake Fuller's *The Cliff-Dwellers* (1893), the city itself occupied the author's imagination. This story traces the fortunes of the occupants—"cliff-dwellers"—of an immense Chicago office building. In *McTeague* (1899) Frank Norris captured the sights, sounds, and, most acutely, smells of the city. Although the novel was set in San Francisco, Norris insisted that it "could have happened in any big city, anywhere."

These *naturalistic* novels stressed the insignificance of the individual and his or her helplessness in the face of urban life and the inexorable logic of Darwin's survival of the fittest. Frank Norris's character McTeague, more animal than man, is the creature of his instincts and his environment and cannot escape coming to a bad end. In Norris's *The Octopus* (1901) the implacable force is the Southern Pacific Railroad; in *The Pit* (1903) it is the Chicago grain market. The city itself, however, most powerfully influenced the naturalistic writers.

The best of those authors, Theodore Dreiser, surmounted the crude determinism of Frank Norris. But the city people as they exist in his great novels *Sister Carrie* (1900), *Jennie Gerhardt* (1911), *The Financier* (1912), and *The Titan* (1914) are no less hostage to an urban world that they cannot understand or control. Dreiser tried to capture this world in all its spectacular detail, "to talk about life as it is, the facts as they exist, the game as it is played."

Visiting his fiancée's Missouri farm home in 1894, Dreiser had been struck by "the spirit of rural America, its idealism, its dreams." But this was an "American tradition in which I, alas!, could not share." Said Dreiser, "I had seen Pittsburgh. I had seen Lithuanians and Hungarians in their 'courts' and hovels. I had seen the girls of the city—walking the streets at night." The city had irrevocably entered the American imagination. By the early 1900s it had become a main theme of American art and literature and an overriding concern of the Progressive Era.

Summary

America, an agrarian society since its birth, became increasingly urbanized after the Civil War. By 1900 about 20 percent of the population was living in cities with 100,000 or more people. City growth stemmed primarily from industrialization—the concentration of industry at key points, the increasingly large scale of production, and the need for commercial and administrative services that were best located in urban centers. A burst of innovation, including mass transit systems, steel-frame buildings, the telephone, and electric lighting, solved the problems arising from the concentration of an extremely large population in a confined area. Although amply endowed with regulatory powers, American cities left decision making as much as possible in the hands of private interests. The result was dramatic growth but not much attention to the impact of growth on the urban environment.

In the cities geography defined the social order of the population. The poor were found in the city centers and the factory districts, the middle class spread out into the suburbs, and the rich lived insulated in exclusive central sections of the cities or beyond the suburbs. A distinctive urban culture emerged, drawing heavily on ethnic social institutions and new leisure activities, enabling city dwellers to accommodate themselves to the world of the city. For the wealthy, an elite society emerged, stressing an opulent life-style and exclusive social organizations. The middle class, on the other hand, withdrew into the private world of the family. For wives, the cult of domesticity reigned, but its more repressive features began to relax as the idea of the "new woman" took hold in the 1890s. Child nurturance persisted, but as the years of dependent childhood lengthened, a new phase of adolescence began to emerge that would draw teenagers out of the family orbit.

The great cities of the United States became the sites of a higher culture, including art museums, opera companies, symphony orchestras, and libraries. A new literature emerged that took the urban world as its subject. From the late nineteenth century on, American life would increasingly be defined by what happened in the nation's cities.

TIMELINE

Year	Event
1869	Corcoran Art Gallery opens in Washington, D.C.
1871	Chicago fire
1873	Mark Twain and Charles Dudley Warner publish *The Gilded Age*
1875	Dwight L. Moody launches urban revivalist movement
1876	Alexander Graham Bell patents the telephone National Baseball League founded
1878	Electric arc-light system installed in Philadelphia
1879	Thomas Edison's incandescent light bulb Salvation Army arrives from Britain
1881	Carnegie offers to build libraries for every American city
1883	New York City's Metropolitan Opera founded Brooklyn Bridge opens Joseph Pulitzer purchases the *New York World*
1885	William Jenney builds first steel-frame structure, Chicago's Home Insurance Building
1888	First electric trolley line constructed in Richmond, Virginia
1892	Rockefeller founds University of Chicago
1893	Chicago Columbian Exposition "City Beautiful" movement
1895	William Randolph Hearst enters New York journalism The comic strip "The Yellow Kid" appears
1897	Boston builds first American subway
1900	Theodore Dreiser publishes *Sister Carrie*
1901	New York Tenement House Reform Law
1904	New York subway system opens
1906	San Francisco earthquake
1913	Woolworth Building, New York City

BIBLIOGRAPHY

Useful introductions to urban history are Charles N. Glaab and A. Theodore Brown, *A History of Urban America* (1967); Arthur M. Schlesinger, *The Rise of the City* (1936), a pioneering study; and Blake McKelvey, *The Urbanization of America, 1860–1915* (1963). A sampling of the innovative scholarship that opened new historical paths can be found in Stephan Thernstrom and Richard Sennett, eds., *Nineteenth-Century Cities: Essays in the New Urban History* (1969).

Urbanization

Allan Pred, *Spatial Dynamics of U.S. Urban Growth, 1800–1914* (1971), traces the patterns in which cities grew. On the revolution in urban transit, see the pioneering book by Sam B. Warner, *Streetcar Suburbs: The Process of Growth in Boston, 1870–1900* (1962). In a subsequent work, *The Private City: Philadelphia in Three Periods* (1968), Warner broadened his analysis to show how private decision-making shaped the character of the American city. Innovations in urban construction are treated in Carl Condit, *American Building Art: Nineteenth Century* (1969) and *Chicago School of Architecture* (1964); Robert C. Twombly, *Louis Sullivan* (1986); Alan Trachtenberg, *The Brooklyn Bridge* (1965); and Harold L. Platt, *The Electric City: Energy and the Growth of the Chicago Area, 1880–1930* (1991). The problems of meeting basic human needs are treated in Jon C. Teaford, *The Unheralded Triumph: City Government in America, 1870–1900* (1984); Eric H. Monkkonen, *Police in Urban America, 1860–1920* (1981); and David B. Tyack, *The One Best System: A History of American Urban Education* (1974). The struggle to reshape the chaotic nineteenth-century city can be explored in John D. Fairchild, *The Mysteries of the Great City: The Politics of Urban Design, 1877–1937* (1993); William H. Wilson, *The City Beautiful Movement in Kansas City* (1964); and David Schuyler, *The New Urban Landscape: The Redefinition of City Form in Nineteenth-Century America* (1986).

City People

Among the leading books on immigrants and the city are Moses Rischin, *The Promised City: New York's Jews, 1870–1914* (1962); Josef Barton, *Peasants and Strangers: Italians, Rumanians, and Slovaks in an American City, 1890–1950* (1975); and Humbert S. Nelli, *The Italians in Chicago, 1860–1920* (1970). On blacks in the city, see Gilbert Osofsky, *Harlem: The Making of a Ghetto, 1890–1930* (1966); Allan H. Spear, *Black Chicago, 1860–1920* (1966); and Kenneth L. Kusmer, *A Ghetto Takes Shape: Black Cleveland, 1870–1930* (1976). David C. Hammack, *Power and Society: Greater New York at the Turn of the Century* (1982), is a sophisticated treatment that places the party machine in the larger context of municipal power politics. Also useful are Zane Miller, *Boss Cox's Cincinnati* (1968), and Bruce M. Stave, ed., *Urban Bosses, Machines, and Progressive Reformers* (1972). The encounter of Protestantism with the city is treated in Henry F. May, *Protestant Churches and Urban America* (1949); Aaron I. Abell, *The Urban Impact on American Protestantism* (1943); and William G. McLoughlin, *Modern Revivalism* (1959). On the Catholic Church see Robert D. Cross, *The Emergence of Liberal Catholicism in America* (1958). Aspects of an emerging city culture are studied in Gunther Barth, *City People: The Rise of Modern City Culture in Nineteenth-Century America* (1982); Susan Porter Benson, *Counter Cultures: Saleswomen, Managers, and Customers in American Department Stores, 1890–1940* (1986); John F. Kasson, *Amusing the Million: Coney Island at the Turn of the Century* (1978); Timothy J. Gilfoyle, *City of Eros: New York City, Prostitution and the Commercialization of Sex, 1790-1920* (1991); Kathy Peiss, *Cheap Amusements: Working Women and Leisure in Turn-of-the-Century New York* (1986); and David Nasaw, *Going Out: The Rise and Fall of Public Amusements* (1993). George Chauncey, *Gay New York: Gender, Urban Culture, and the Making of the Gay New York World, 1890–1940* (1994), reveals a terrain hitherto invisible to the historian.

Upper Class/Middle Class

Urban social mobility is the focus of Stephan Thernstrom, *The Other Bostonians: Poverty and Progress in an American City, 1880–1970* (1973), which also contains a useful summary of mobility research on other cities. On the social elite, see Frederic C. Jaher, *The Urban Establishment: Upper Strata in Boston, New York, Charleston, Chicago, and Los Angeles* (1982). Two recent books greatly advance our understanding of the urban middle class: Stuart S. Blumin, *The Emergence of the Middle Class: Social Experience in the American City, 1760–1900* (1989), and Olivier Zunz, *Making America Corporate, 1870–1920* (1990). Aspects of middle-class life are revealed in Richard Sennett, *Families against the City: Middle-Class Homes of Industrial Chicago, 1872–1890* (1970); Margaret Marsh, *Suburban Lives* (1990); Gwendolyn Wright, *Moralism and the Model Home: Domestic Architecture and Cultural Conflict in Chicago, 1873–1913* (1980); Susan Strasser, *Never Done: A History of American Housework* (1983); John F. Kasson, *Rudeness and Civility: Manners in Nineteenth-Century America* (1990); and, on the entry of immigrants into the middle class, Andrew R. Heinze, *Adapting to Abundance: Jewish Immigrants, Mass Consumption, and the Search for American Identity* (1990). Contemporary notions of sexuality are skillfully captured in John S. Haller and Robin M. Haller, *The Physician and Sexuality in Victorian America* (1980). Whether those views actually applied to the private world of the middle class is strongly questioned in Karen Lystra, *The Searching Heart: Women, Men, and Romantic Love in Nineteenth-Century America* (1989). Control over reproduction is fully explored in Janet Farrell Brodie, *Contraception and Abortion in Nineteenth-Century America* (1994). On the fostering of high culture in the American city, see Daniel M. Fox, *Engines of Culture: Philanthropy and Art Museums* (1963). The best introduction to intellectual currents in the emerging urban society is Alan Trachtenberg, *The Incorporation of America: Culture and Society, 1865–1893* (1983).

The Cliff Dwellers

This 1913 painting by George Bellows shows a poor
tenement neighborhood in New York's Lower East Side.

The Progressive Era

1900–1914

★　　　★　　　★

On the face of it, the political ferment of the 1890s ended after the election of 1896. The bitter struggle over free silver left the victorious Republicans with no stomach for political crusades. The McKinley administration devoted itself to maintaining business confidence: sound money and high tariffs were the order of the day. The main thing, as party chief Mark Hanna said, was to "stand pat and continue Republican prosperity."

Yet beneath the surface a deep uneasiness was taking hold of the country. The depression of the 1890s had unveiled harsh truths not acknowledged in better days. One such discovery was the power of vested economic interests. In Wisconsin, for example, utility and transit companies had raised prices, reduced services, and received special tax relief—all at the expense of the public. This discovery of corporate arrogance launched movements in Wisconsin for tax reform, municipal ownership of utilities, and an end to boss-run party politics.

The labor unrest of the 1890s taught a similar lesson. The Cleveland administration had broken the great Pullman strike of 1894 by plotting with the railroad operators, issuing injunctions against the strike leaders, and sending in troops to get the trains moving. The architect of that policy, Attorney General Richard Olney, took little satisfaction from his success in suppressing the strike. He asked himself what might be done in the future to avoid the need for such one-sided intervention. Olney began to advocate labor legislation—the Erdman Mediation Act of 1898 marked the first step—that would regulate labor relations on the railroads and prevent crippling strikes. In such ways did the crisis of the 1890s turn the nation's thinking to reform.

The problems themselves, however, were of much older origin. For more than half a century Americans had been absorbed in developing their nation. At the beginning of the twentieth century they paused, looked

around, and began to add up the costs. With industrial-ization had come a frightening concentration of corpo-rate economic power and, equally troubling, a restless working class. The cities had spawned widespread mis-ery and corrupt machine politics. The heritage of an earlier America seemed to be succumbing to the de-mands of the new industrial order.

With the crisis of the 1890s over, reform became an absorbing concern of many Americans. It was as if social awareness had reached a critical mass around 1900 and set reform activity going as a major, self-sustaining phe-nomenon. For this reason the years from 1900 to World War I have come to be known as the Progressive Era.

The Course of Reform

Historians have sometimes spoken of a progressive "movement." But progressivism was not a movement in any meaningful sense. There was no single progressive constituency, no agreed-upon agenda, and no unifying organization or leadership. At different times and places, different social groups became active. People who were reformers on one issue might be conservative on another. The term *progressivism* embraces a widespread, many-sided effort after 1900 to build a better society. Progres-sive reformers shared only this objective, plus an intellectual style that can be called "progressive."

The Intellectual Roots of Progressivism

Intellectual climates change. Why they change is usually hard to explain, but it is not so difficult to tell when new ideas are taking hold. Such a change of ideas clearly seemed about to happen as the twentieth century began.

A Sense of Mastery. The Progressive Era was an age of scientific investigation. The federal government con-ducted massive statistical studies of immigration, women's and children's labor, and working conditions in many industries. Vice commissions studied prostitu-tion, gambling, and other moral ills of American cities. Among private investigations the classic was the *Pitts-burgh Survey* (1911–1914). Financed by Margaret Olivia Sage and other New York City philanthropists, a team of investigators recorded in great detail living and working conditions in Pittsburgh's steel district.

The facts were important because they formed the basis for corrective action. When the young journalist Walter Lippmann wrote *Drift and Mastery* (1914), he as-serted the progressive's confidence in people's ability to act purposefully and constructively. This sense of mastery expressed itself in many ways. For example, people had great faith in academic experts. In Wisconsin the state

university became a key resource for Governor Robert M. La Follette's progressive administration. "The close intimacy of the university with public affairs explains the democracy, the thoroughness, and the scientific accuracy of the state in its legislation," boasted one La Follette supporter.

Scientific management exerted a particularly strong attraction on progressives. The original aim of scientific management had been to reorganize and rationalize work in factories (see Chapter 18, page 574). But its founder, Frederick W. Taylor, argued that his basic ap-proach—the "scientific" analysis of human activity—offered solutions to waste and inefficiency in municipal government, schools and hospitals, and even homes and churches. "The fundamental principles of scientific management are applicable to all kinds of human activi-ties," Taylor insisted, and could solve all the social ills that arise "through such of our acts as are blundering, ill-directed, or inefficient."

Attacking Nineteenth-Century Formalism. The essen-tial thing, in the progressive view, was to resist intellec-tual formulations that denied people this sense of mastery. This denial characterized the Social Darwinian writings of the British philosopher Herbert Spencer and his many disciples among American conservative thinkers (see Chapter 19, page 589). Spencer argued that society develops according to fixed laws that can-not be changed. Spencer's intellectual approach was *for-malistic;* that is, its conclusions were based not on factual investigation but on abstract theory.

Critics of Spencer denied that the evolution of soci-ety is guided by absolute and unvarying rules. "It is folly," protested the Harvard philosopher William James, "to speak of the 'laws of history,' as of some-thing inevitable, which science only has to discover, and which any one can then foretell and observe, but do nothing to alter or avert." Man could "shape environ-mental forces to his own advantage," the sociologist Lester F. Ward argued. Society could advance through "rational planning" and "social engineering."

The assault against formalism took place in many academic disciplines. In classical economics, for exam-ple, scholars assumed that markets were perfectly com-petitive and thus perfectly responsive to the laws of supply and demand. Such a system left no room for re-form, which would only disrupt what could not be im-proved. Critics of classical economics—they called themselves "institutional economists"—denied that the market ever operated so perfectly. They conducted field research to determine how institutions and power rela-tionships influenced the operation of the marketplace. In his *Theory of the Leisure Class* (1899) and *The In-stinct of Workmanship* (1914) the economist Thorstein Veblen lampooned the classical economists' abstract image of economic man. In the real world, Veblen con-

tended, people acted not out of pure economic calculation but from complex motives ranging from vanity to pride in their work.

In legal thought, too, formalism had dominated the field. The courts treated legal rights as if they were eternal principles that were not rooted in—or to be tested by—social reality. Thus, in the famous *Lochner v. New York* decision (1905) the Supreme Court invalidated a law limiting the long working hours of bakers in New York State. Such regulation, the Court concluded, violated the contractual freedom of *both* employers and workers. Justice Oliver Wendell Holmes, the leading dissenter, objected; in his view, the *Lochner* decision was based on a fictional equality. If the choice was between working and starving, could it really be said that workers freely accepted jobs requiring that they labor fourteen hours a day, or that limiting their working hours violated their liberty of contract?

Holmes had earlier asserted the essence of the progressive legal critique: "The life of the law has not been logic; it has been experience. The felt necessities of the time, even the prejudices which judges share with their fellow-men, have had a good deal more to do than [logic] in determining the rules by which men shall be governed." "Sociological jurisprudence," as Dean Roscoe Pound of the Harvard Law School termed it, called for "the adjustment of principles and doctrines to the human conditions they are to govern rather than assumed first principles." The law, moreover, should not claim a false neutrality; on the contrary, as Pound's student Felix Frankfurter argued, law should be "a vital agency for human betterment."

In philosophy, it was William James who led the assault on formalism as an intellectual system. James denied the existence of absolute truths. In his philosophy of *pragmatism*, ideas were judged by their consequences; ideas served as guides to action that produced desired results. Philosophy should be concerned with solving problems, not with contemplating ultimate ends.

James's most important disciple was John Dewey. Like James, Dewey had a great interest in psychology, whose insights he applied to education. In his Laboratory School at the University of Chicago, Dewey broke from the rigid curriculum of traditional education and instead stressed problem solving and practical activity as the keys to children's personal growth. Children were encouraged to explore and discover for themselves rather than learn lessons by rote. Nowhere could the intellectual bent of progressivism in action be better seen than in Dewey's experiments, which, fittingly, came to be known as progressive education.

Idealism. Progressive reformers prided themselves on being tough-minded. They had confidence in people's capacity to take purposeful action. But there was another side to the progressive mind. It was deeply infused with idealism. Progressives framed their intentions in terms of high principle. The progressive cause, pronounced Theodore Roosevelt, "is based on the eternal principles of righteousness."

Much of this idealism came from the American past. No American hero loomed larger in the minds of progressives than Abraham Lincoln. For many, such as Jane Addams, the Great Emancipator was a lifelong guide. Lincoln's example, in particular, inspired the battle for political reform. "Go back to the first principles of democracy; go back to the people," Robert La Follette told his audience when he launched his attack on the Republican machine in Wisconsin. Political reformers typically described their work as political restoration. They frequently said that they had converted to reform after discovering how far party politics had drifted from the ideals of representative government.

Progressive idealism also derived from American radical traditions. Many progressives traced their conversion to Henry George's *Progress and Poverty* (1879), which asked why, in the midst of fabulous wealth, so many Americans should be condemned to poverty. George's answer—that private control of land siphoned the community's wealth into the hands of nonproductive landlords—led to a Single Tax movement that served as a school for many budding progressives. Others traced their awakening to Edward Bellamy's novel *Looking Backward* (1888), with its utopian vision of an ordered, affluent American socialism, or to the Chicago social democrat Henry Demarest Lloyd's *Wealth against Commonwealth* (1894), with its powerful indictment of the Standard Oil trust. In later years this radical tradition was transmitted mainly through the Socialist party, which flourished after 1900 under the leadership of Eugene V. Debs. Walter Lippmann and many other young reformers passed through socialism on their way to progressivism, whereas others, such as Charlotte Perkins Gilman, never left the socialist camp.

The most important source of progressive idealism, especially among social reformers, was religion. Protestant churches had long been concerned with the plight of the urban poor (see Chapter 20, page 631). Now that concern blossomed into a major doctrine—the Social Gospel. The Baptist cleric Walter Rauschenbusch, its most influential exponent, had been deeply affected by his ministry near the squalid Hell's Kitchen section of New York City. Shocked by the conditions there, Rauschenbusch fought for more playgrounds and better housing in slum neighborhoods. The churches had to reassert the "social aims of Jesus," he argued. The "Kingdom of God on Earth" would be achieved not by striving for personal salvation but by struggling for social justice. To coordinate that effort, reform-minded clerical leaders formed the Federal Council of Churches in 1908. The council aimed at "promoting the application of the law of Christ in every relation to human life."

Progressive leaders characteristically grew up in families imbued with evangelical piety. Many went through a religious crisis, having sought and failed to experience a conversion, and ultimately settled on a career in social work, education, journalism, or politics, where they could translate inherited religious belief into modern secular action. Jane Addams, for example, had taken up settlement-house work with this intention. She believed that by uplifting the poor in tenement districts, settlement workers would themselves be uplifted: they would experience "the joy of finding Christ" by acting "in fellowship" with the needy.

Progressive thought thus contained a pervading Christian undercurrent. The philosopher John Dewey called democracy "a spiritual fact" and the "means by which the revelation of truth is carried on." Theodore Roosevelt launched his Progressive party in 1912 with the battle cry, "We stand at Armageddon and we battle for the Lord." His supporters at the party's national convention marched around the hall singing "Onward Christian Soldiers."

The Muckrakers. The progressive mode of thought—idealistic in intent and tough-minded in approach—nurtured a new kind of reform journalism. A growing urban audience had created a market during the 1890s for a rash of popular magazines, including *Munsey's,*

McClure's, and *Collier's.* Unlike the highbrow *Atlantic Monthly* or *Harper's,* these journals sold for only 10 cents and catered to a broad audience. Almost by accident—Lincoln Steffens's article "Tweed Days in St. Louis" in the October 1902 issue of *McClure's* is credited with getting things started—magazine editors discovered that what most excited readers was the exposure of evildoing and set investigative reporters such as Charles Edward Russell (see American Voices, page 651) on the trail of evildoers.

In a series of powerful articles Lincoln Steffens wrote about "the shame of the cities"—the corrupt ties between business and political machines. Ida M. Tarbell attacked Standard Oil, and David Graham Phillips told how money controlled the Senate. William Hard exposed industrial accidents in "Making Steel and Killing Men" (1907) and child labor in "De Kid Wot Works at Night" (1908). Others described slum conditions, Wall Street abuses, and the adulteration of food. Hardly a sordid corner of American life escaped the scrutiny of these tireless reporters. They were moralists as well, infusing their factual accounts with a powerful spirit of personal indignation. "The sights I saw," wrote the pioneering slum investigator Jacob Riis, "gripped my heart until I felt I must tell of them, or burst, or turn anarchist."

President Roosevelt, among many others, thought these journalists went too far. In a 1906 speech he com-

Ida Tarbell Takes on Rockefeller

A popular biographer of Napoleon and Lincoln in the 1890s, Ida Tarbell turned her journalistic talents to muckraking. Her first installment of "The History of the Standard Oil Company" appeared in *McClure's Magazine* in November 1902. John D. Rockefeller, she wrote, "was willing to strain every nerve to obtain for himself special and illegal privileges from the railroads which were bound to ruin every man in the oil business not sharing them with him." As Tarbell built her case, criticism rained down on Rockefeller. A more sympathetic cartoon in the magazine *Judge* pleads with Rockefeller's critics: "Boys, don't you think you have bothered the old man just about enough?"

Charles Edward Russell

Muckraking

In this autobiographical account Charles Russell, a newspaperman, describes how he got into muckraking journalism and what he thought it was all about. He never did, by the way, get back to writing music.

All America had been accustomed to laud and bepraise the makers of great fortunes. . . . Money had become the touchstone and perfect measure of worth. . . . Now, of a sudden, men began to discover that these great and adored fortunes had been gathered in ways that not only grazed the prison gate but imposed burdens and disadvantages upon the rest of the community; that vast hoards for one man meant much less for others. In the shock of this discovery, a literature of exposition arose and daily the magazine editors looked for new dark, malodorous corners of money-grabbing upon which the spotlight could be turned.

Pure accident cast me, without the least desire, into the pursuit of this

fashion. I had finally withdrawn from the newspaper business, and having enough money to live modestly I was bent upon carrying out a purpose long cherished in quite a different line. [I had concluded] that what we call the separate arts of music and poetry are really but one, and I now conceived that with a piano, my Swinburne, and some sheets of music paper I could demonstrate this priceless fact to a palpitating world. Upon this task I was intent when the whole business was upset with a single telegram.

One day, Mr. J. W. Midgley, who was a famous expert on railroad rates and conditions . . . let loose a flood of startling facts about the impositions practised by the owners and operators of refrigerator cars. My friend, Mr. Erman J. Ridgway . . . of *Everybody's Magazine* wired asking me to see Mr. Midgley and get him to write for *Everybody's* an article along the lines of his testimony. I conferred accordingly and Mr. Midgley positively refused all offers to become an exposé

writer. [So] Ridgway wire[d] asking me to furnish the article *Everybody's* wanted. I had not the least disposition to do so, except only that Ridgway was my friend. . . . The next thing I knew a muck-rake was put into my hand and I was plunged into the midst of the game. . . .

I wrote two or three articles on the refrigerator car scandal and then went on to write a series on the methods of the Beef Trust and was not in the least astonished to find that I was become an unmitigated scoundrel, a hired assassin of character, a libeller of good men, an enemy of society and of the government, and probably an Anarchist in disguise. . . . We were all up and away, full of the pleasures of the chase . . . and all that business about poetry and music sheets forgotten. It was exhilarating sport, hunting the money octopus.

Source: Charles Edward Russell, *Bare Hands and Stone Walls* (New York, Charles Scribner's Sons, 1933), 135–139.

---

pared them to the man with the muckrake in *Pilgrim's Progress* by the seventeenth-century English preacher John Bunyan. That man was too absorbed with raking the filth on the floor to look up and accept a celestial crown. Thus the term *muckraker* became attached to journalists who exposed the underside of American life. Their efforts were in fact health-giving. More than any other group, the muckrakers called the people to arms.

Political Reformers

Progressives acted out of a deep sense of idealism. And they were confident about the human capacity to take purposeful action. This much all progressives had in common but, in pursuit of reform, they were not all drawn to the same targets. Nor, in making their choices, were progressives indifferent to their own self-interests. In politics especially, the battles for reform reflected mixed motives of self-regard and civic betterment.

Municipal Reform. In many cities the demand for better government came from local businessmen. They complained that the economic burdens of old-fashioned party rule had become too heavy. Taxes went up, but needed services always lagged. There had to be an end, as one manufacturer said, to "the inefficiency, the sloth, the carelessness, the injustice and the graft of city administrations." The solution, argued John Patterson of the National Cash Register Company, lay in putting "municipal affairs on a strict business basis." Cities should be run "not by partisans, either Republican or Democratic, but by men who are skilled in business management and social service."

In 1900 a hurricane devastated Galveston, Texas, drowning 5,000 people and destroying the municipal port. Local businessmen took over and, in the course of rebuilding the city, replaced the mayor and board of aldermen with a five-member commission. The Galveston plan, although widely copied, had a serious flaw: it gave too much power to the individual commissioners. Day-

ton, Ohio, resolved this problem by assigning policy matters to a nonpartisan commission and administrative functions to an appointed city manager. The commission-manager system aimed at running the American city "in exactly the same way as a private business corporation." Municipal political reform was chiefly the work of the business community and overtly a matter of the balance sheet.

It was also a way of grabbing power. Municipal reformers favored citywide elections, nonpartisanship, and professional city administration. All these reforms attacked the ward politics that traditionally had given ethnic and working-class groups access to political power. As a result, municipal control shifted to the urban middle class. In fact, municipal reform contained a decidedly antidemocratic bias. "Ignorance should be excluded from control," said former Mayor Abram Hewitt of New York in 1901. "City business should be carried on by trained experts selected upon some other principle than popular suffrage."

A different kind of urban progressive opposed such elitist reform. Mayor Brand Whitlock of Toledo, Ohio, believed "that the cure for the ills of democracy was not less democracy, as so many people were always preaching, but more democracy." The prototype of this new breed of urban politician was the shoe manufacturer Hazen S. Pingree, who led the Republicans to victory against the Democratic machine in Detroit in 1889. Although drafted by a business coalition, Pingree skillfully appealed for support from trade unions and ethnic groups. His administration not only attacked municipal corruption and inefficiency but also concerned itself with the needs of Detroit's working people. An increasing number of cities came under the leadership of such progressive mayors, including Samuel M. "Golden Rule" Jones in Toledo, Tom Johnson in Cleveland, and Mark Fagan in Jersey City. By combining popular programs and campaign magic, they won over the urban masses and challenged the rule of the machines.

State Politics. The major battles for democratic reform, however, took place at the state level. Preeminent among state progressives was Robert M. La Follette of Wisconsin. La Follette was a seasoned politician. Born in 1855, he had followed a conventional party career as a lawyer, district attorney, and then congressman for three terms before breaking with the Wisconsin Republican machine in 1891, allegedly because of an attempt by the top party boss to bribe him. La Follette became a tireless exponent of political reform. "I was merely expressing a common and widespread, though largely unconscious, spirit of revolt among the people," La Follette said of his fight to unseat the state's Republican old guard. At first it was an uphill battle. But after a decade of unremitting campaigning, La Follette finally gained the Republican nomination and won the governorship in 1900 on a platform of higher taxes for corporations, stricter utility and railroad regulation, and political reform.

La Follette's key proposal was a direct primary law by which party candidates would be chosen through popular election rather than in machine-run conventions. Pushed through in 1903, this democratic reform both expressed La Follette's political ideals and suited his particular political talents. The party regulars opposing him were insiders, more comfortable in the caucus room than out on the hustings. But that was where La Follette excelled. A brilliant campaigner, he aimed at dramatizing the issues and generating grass-roots support. The direct primary gave La Follette the means to control the Republican party in Wisconsin through good times and bad until his death twenty-five years later.

What was true of La Follette was more or less true of all successful progressive politicians. Albert B. Cummins of Iowa, Harold U'Ren of Oregon, and Hiram Johnson of California all espoused democratic ideals and made skillful use of the direct primary to win polit-

Robert M. La Follette
La Follette was transformed into a political reformer when a Wisconsin Republican boss attempted to bribe him in 1891 to influence a judge in a railway case. As he described it in his *Autobiography*, "Out of this awful ordeal came understanding; and out of understanding came resolution. I determined that the power of this corrupt influence . . . should be broken." This photograph captures La Follette at the top of his form, taking his case in 1897 to the people of Cumberland, Wisconsin.

ical power and push through reform programs. If they were newcomers—as Woodrow Wilson was when he left academic life to enter New Jersey politics in 1910—they showed a quick aptitude for politics and gained a solid mastery of the trade. Once in office, they asserted control over their parties and beat the political bosses at their own game. They practiced a new kind of popular politics. In a reform age, it could be a more effective way to power than were the backroom techniques of the old-fashioned machine politicians.

Not even the most radical progressive reforms—the initiative, the referendum, and the recall—lived up to their billing. All three reforms were put forth as mechanisms for returning political power to the people. Under the *initiative*, ordinary citizens could get issues of interest to them placed on the ballot. The *referendum* enabled voters to decide big legislative issues (including propositions arising from the initiative) by popular vote, whereas the *recall* empowered citizens to remove from office politicians who had lost the public's confidence. It soon became clear, however, that direct democracy did not supplant organized politics. Initiative, referendum, and recall campaigns put a premium on organization, money, and expertise, and those were attributes not of the people at large but of well-organized special interests. As with the direct primary, the initiative, referendum, and recall had as much to do with power relations as with democratic idealism.

The Woman Progressive

Reform movements arise through a process of *recruitment*. Why do people enlist in a great cause? Because they are linked in some personal way to an evil crying out for correction. For middle-class women of the Progressive Era, the link was between their domestic identity as wives and mothers and the responsibility this gave them for the social well-being of their communities.

Middle-class women had long borne the burden of humanitarian work in American cities. Characteristically, they did most of the legwork for the charity organization societies that since the 1870s had sprung up to coordinate citywide private relief. As voluntary investigators, women visited needy families, assessed their problems, and referred them to relief agencies.

After many years of dedicated charity work, Josephine Shaw Lowell of New York City concluded that it was not enough to give assistance to the poor. "If the working people had all they ought to have, we should not have the paupers and criminals," she declared. "It is better to save them before they go under, than to spend your life fishing them out afterward." Lowell founded the New York Consumers' League in 1890. Her goal was to improve the wages and working conditions of female clerks in the city's stores. To bring pressure on reluctant merchants, the league issued a "White List"—a very short one at first—of shops that met its standards for a living wage and decent treatment of clerks.

From these modest beginnings, the league became broadly concerned with exploitation in women's occupations, spread to other cities, and blossomed into the National Consumers' League in 1899. By then the women who ran the league had concluded that voluntary action was insufficient and that only state action could rescue poor urban families. Under the crusading leadership of Florence Kelley, formerly a chief factory inspector in Illinois, the Consumers' League became a powerful lobby for protective legislation for women and children.

Among its achievements, none was more important than the *Muller v. Oregon* decision (1908), which upheld an Oregon law limiting to ten hours the workday of women workers. The Consumers' League had pushed that law through the state legislature and recruited the brilliant Boston lawyer Louis D. Brandeis to defend it before the Supreme Court. In his brief, Brandeis devoted only two pages to legal citations on the narrow constitutional issue—whether, under its police powers, Oregon had the right to regulate women's working hours. Instead Brandeis rested his case on a vast amount of data gathered by the Consumers' League showing how long hours damaged women's health and family roles. The *Muller* decision, which accepted Brandeis's reasoning, was a victory for the new "sociological jurisprudence" (see page 671) and cleared the way for a wave of protective laws across the country.

Women's organizations became a strong voice in state legislatures and in Congress on behalf of women and children (see American Lives, pages 654–655). Their victories included the first law providing public assistance for mothers with dependent children, in Illinois in 1911; the first minimum wage law for women, in Massachusetts in 1912; more effective child labor laws in many states; and, at the federal level, the Children's and Women's bureaus in the Labor Department, in 1912 and 1920, respectively. The welfare state, insofar as it arrived in America in those years, was what women progressives had made of it; they had erected a "maternalist" welfare system.

The Settlement Houses. In addition to public advocacy, women's urban activism sought direct engagement with the underprivileged. This was the aim of the settlement-house movement, which began in 1884 when Oxford University students founded Toynbee Hall in the slums of London. Inspired by that example, two young American women, Jane Addams and Ellen Gates Starr, established Hull House on Chicago's West Side in 1889.

Frances Kellor:
Woman Progressive

From the day its doors opened in 1892, the University of Chicago was a major center of American learning. Financed by John D. Rockefeller, the university modeled itself on the great German research universities and, unlike Yale and Harvard, concentrated on graduate education. At Chicago and other American universities modern social science was taking shape, breaking from its nineteenth-century moral foundations and seeking a scientific basis for the study of society. Economics, political science, and sociology demanded a rigorous course of study certified by the granting of the Ph.D. But if the social sciences were becoming professional, their guiding purpose was not yet disinterested research but the improvement of society. The University of Chicago saw the city surrounding it as a great laboratory for social betterment. Its students were being prepared, whether they knew it or not, to be in service to the American progressivism of the next decade. The University of Chicago, moreover, was receptive to the admission of women, and for them in particular, graduate education was a breeding ground for careers as social reformers.

Among the women entering in 1898 was Frances Alice Kellor, a recent graduate of Cornell University. Kellor was born in Columbus, Ohio, in 1873. Her father abandoned the family before she was two, and her mother made a hard living as a domestic and laundress. This was not the kind of privileged background from which most woman progressives sprang, but Kellor's experience came closer to the norm than her threadbare circumstances might have suggested. In 1875 her family moved to Coldwater, Michigan, a former abolitionist center (and station on the underground railroad) and a stronghold of Yankee culture. From the Coldwater community, with its high moral standards and strong educational institutions, Kellor received the reformist values that other budding progressives learned from their families. Kellor, moreover, had a remarkable talent for finding patrons, gaining by her wits the financial means her fellow progressives were born to. Her first patrons were the well-to-do librarians of Coldwater,

Mary and Frances Eddy, who befriended her and took her into their home. Born Alice, Kellor began to call herself "Frances" as a sign that she considered herself adopted by the Eddy sisters. She graduated from high school, became a reporter for the *Coldwater Republican,* and then, with the backing of the Eddys, enrolled at Cornell in 1895. Highly athletic, Kellor made her first mark as a fighter for equal rights on a sports issue: she led the campaign for a women's crew. She got a solid education in the social sciences at Cornell and decided to become a criminologist.

Sociology was an infant discipline when Frances Kellor arrived in Chicago in 1898, with little in the way of systematic theory and an emphasis on high-minded investigations of social problems. Kellor's interest in crime was encouraged by the Chicago faculty. The prevailing theory of the time, advanced by the Italian Cesare Lombroso, was that criminality was an inherited trait. Criminals were born criminal, and this was manifest in their physical features. Skeptical, Kellor conducted a study of the female inmates of five midwestern prisons. Comparing them with a control group of college women, she could find no physical differences. Kellor concluded that it was not heredity, but social environment, economic disadvantage, and poverty, that made for criminality. Kellor also rejected "the prevailing opinion that when women are criminal they are more degraded and more abandoned than men." People thought so only because of "the difference in the standards which we set for the two sexes."

A second project on criminality among southern blacks likewise rejected heredity and stressed environmental factors, but Kellor's conclusions were pessimistic and racially conservative. Centuries of slavery and indolent southern life had left blacks so morally weakened that "the Negro at present has neither the perceptions nor the solidity of character that would enable him to lead his race." She considered the southern restrictions on blacks' legal and politic rights unfortunate but necessary, and she believed that "the free intermingling of the two races is impossible, at least for many generations."

Her first project was a study of unemployment. Kellor rejected the prevailing notion that being jobless was a sign of personal weakness. She was among the first investigators to see that unemployment was an economic problem, the result not primarily of individual shiftlessness or incompetence but the impersonal operations of the labor market. Her book *Out of Work* (1904) was a truly pioneering investigation, paving the way for the modern study of unemployment. Kellor was especially concerned with the plight of jobless women and their exploitation by commercial employment agencies. Representing the Women's Municipal League of New York, Kellor lobbied successfully for state regulation of these agencies. Kellor thus employed her research to bring about social change. The combination of professional investigation and robust political advocacy became the hallmark of Kellor's progressivism. Her next study, on the problems of immigrants in New York, led to the establishment of the New York State Bureau of Industries and Immigration in 1910. Kellor was chosen to be its head, the first woman to hold so high a post in New York's state government.

The high point of Kellor's career came two years later, when Theodore Roosevelt launched the Progressive party. Convinced that social reform required strong government, Kellor was drawn to the New Nationalism. She linked it with her own fervent advocacy of women's political rights. Always a fighter, she was entirely at ease in the rough-and-tumble of partisan politics. After Roosevelt's defeat in 1912, the Progressive party set up the National Progressive Service, a kind of think tank to study social problems and formulate legislative proposals. The idea was mainly Kellor's, and she was tapped to chair the Service. This was truly a pinnacle for a woman in American politics at a time when women in most states could not vote in national elections. Unfortunately, Kellor's emphasis on scientific investigation put her at odds with the practical politicians, and she was forced out in early 1914. Hers was a brief run in national politics, exhilarating while it lasted and unique for a woman of her generation.

Kellor never married. Like many other woman progressives, including Jane Addams, she found personal fulfillment in an enduring relationship with another woman. This was Mary Dreier, one of two wealthy sisters who played leading roles in New York progressivism. From the time Kellor moved into the Dreier home in Brooklyn Heights in 1904 until her death almost fifty years later, she and Mary were constant companions. Kellor's later professional life was devoted to a distinguished career with the American Arbitration Association.

Frances Kellor
This photograph of Kellor was taken in her early twenties, when she was a student at Cornell University.

In drawing these illiberal conclusions, Kellor was echoing the views of her teachers and indeed of most white progressives of her generation.

Despite her precocious record, Kellor left the university in 1902 without a degree. The reasons are not altogether clear but doubtless had something to do with a painful truth of which Kellor must have been aware: the University of Chicago almost never placed its female graduate students in university teaching jobs. To be a professor, it seemed, was still a male prerogative. There was, however, a positive side to Kellor's decision. Like many of her fellow students, she had fallen under the spell of Jane Addams. Kellor lived periodically at Hull House, joined the circle of social reformers that congregated there, and began to see her future out among the disadvantaged rather than in the university. When she left Chicago, it was to do social research for New York's College Settlement Association.

Saving the Children

In the early years at Hull House, Jane Addams recalled, toddlers sometimes arrived for kindergarten tipsy from a breakfast of bread soaked in wine. To settlement-house workers, the answer to such ignorance was in child care education, and so began the program to send visiting nurses into immigrant homes. They taught mothers the proper methods of caring for children—including, as this photograph shows, the daily infant bath, in a dishpan if necessary.

During the next fifteen years scores of settlement houses sprang up in the slum neighborhoods of the nation's cities. The settlement houses served as community centers run by middle-class residents, who acted as amateur social workers for the surrounding immigrant communities. Hull House had meeting rooms, an art gallery, clubs for children and adults, and a kindergarten. Addams herself led battles for garbage removal, playgrounds, better street lighting, and police protection. At the Henry Street Settlement in New York City, Lillian D. Wald made visiting nursing a major service. Mary McDowell, head of the University of Chicago Settlement, installed a bathhouse, a children's playground, and a citizenship school for immigrants.

Beyond the modest good they did in slum neighborhoods, settlement houses served as a breeding ground for social reform. At least half the women residents went on to careers in social service. Settlement houses thus contributed significantly to the emerging profession of social work. To a remarkable degree, the leaders of social reform—both men and women—served apprenticeships in settlement houses.

For the middle-class residents, more deep-seated needs were also being satisfied. In a famous essay Jane Addams spoke of the "subjective necessity" of the settlement house. She meant that it was as much a response to the desire of educated young men and women to serve as it was a response to the needs of slum dwellers. Addams herself was a case in point. She had

grown up in a comfortable Illinois family and had graduated from Rockford College. Then she faced an empty future as an ornamental wife if she married or a sheltered spinster if she did not. Hull House became her salvation. The settlement was "a protest against a restricted view of education," against the genteel schooling that never got her beyond "the always getting ready for life." Now, at Hull House, she could "begin with however small a group to accomplish and to live."

The Revival of the Struggle for Women's Rights. Almost imperceptibly, women activists such as Jane Addams and Florence Kelley breathed new life into the suffrage movement. Why should a woman who was capable of running a settlement house or lobbying for a bill be denied the right to vote? Suffrage, moreover, became firmly linked to social reform. If women had the right to vote, they and their male supporters argued, more enlightened legislation and better government would certainly result. Finally, through their activities among working-class women, women progressives helped broaden the social base of the suffrage movement.

Believing that working women should be encouraged to help themselves, social reformers founded the National Women's Trade Union League in 1903. Financed and led by wealthy supporters, the league organized women workers, played a considerable role in their strikes, and, perhaps most important, helped to develop working-class leaders. For example, Rose

Rose Schneiderman, 1913

In their battles for better conditions, women garment workers produced their own leaders, and none was more devoted to their cause or more fiery on the platform than Rose Schneiderman. The daughter of a widowed immigrant woman, Schneiderman went to work at thirteen, quickly got caught up in union activities, and fashioned for herself a lifetime career as a trade unionist, including becoming president of the National Women's Trade Union League.

Schneiderman became a union organizer among garment workers in New York City, and Agnes Nestor led women glove workers in Illinois; both were also lobbyists for protective legislation. Athough often resenting the patronizing ways of their well-to-do sponsors, such trade-union women identified their cause with the broader struggle for women's rights. When New York State held referenda on woman suffrage in 1915 and 1917, strong support came from the Jewish and Italian precincts inhabited by unionized garment workers.

Suffrage activity began to revive nationwide. Women won the right to vote in the state of Washington in 1910, in California in 1911, and in four more western states during the next three years (see Map 21.1). Women also altered their tactics. In Britain, suffragists had begun to picket Parliament, assault politicians, and go on hunger strikes in jail. This disruptive strategy, which gave the cause of the British suffragists new power, impressed their sisters in the United States.

Most important among the American converts was Alice Paul, a young Quaker who had lived in Britain and knew how to apply the confrontational tactics of the British suffragists. Rejecting the slower route of enfranchisement by the states, Paul advocated a constitutional amendment that in one stroke would give women across the country the right to vote. In 1916 Paul organized the militant National Woman's party. The National Ameri-

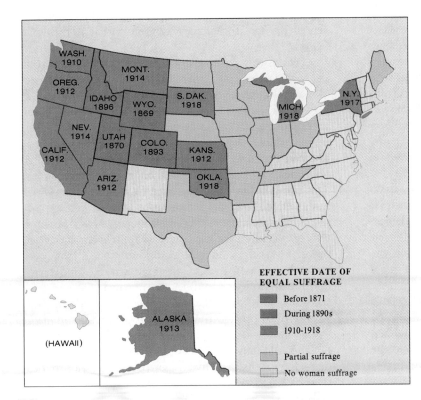

MAP 21.1

Woman Suffrage, 1869–1918

By 1909, after more than sixty years of agitation, only four lightly populated western states had granted women full voting rights. A number of other states offered partial suffrage, limited mostly to voting for school boards and such issues as taxes. Between 1910 and 1918, as the effort shifted to the struggle for a constitutional amendment, eleven states (and Alaska) joined the list granting full suffrage. The most stubborn resistance was in the South.

Suffragists on Parade, 1912
After 1910 the suffrage movement went
into high gear. Suffragist leaders decided
to demand a constitutional amendment
rather than rely on gaining the vote state
by state. In 1912 they served notice on
both parties that they meant business
and, as shown in this suffragist parade
in New York, made their demands a visible part of the presidential campaign.

can Woman Suffrage Association (NAWSA), from which
Paul had split off, was also rejuvenated. Carrie Chap-
man Catt, a skilled political organizer from the New
York movement, took over as national leader in 1915.
Under her guidance, NAWSA brought a broad-based or-
ganization to the campaign for a federal amendment.

Feminism. In the midst of this suffrage struggle something new and more fundamental began to happen. A
new generation of women activists who were college
graduates or experienced trade unionists was arising.
Out in the world and self-supporting, these women
were determined not to be hemmed in by the social constraints of women's "separate sphere." "Breaking into
the Human Race" was the intention they proclaimed at
a mass meeting in New York in 1914. "We intend simply to be ourselves," declared the chair Marie Jenny
Howe, "not just our little female selves, but our whole
big human selves."

The women at this meeting called themselves *feminists,* a term that was just coming into use. In this, its
first incarnation, feminism meant freedom for full personal development. In its specifics this covered many
things—freedom to follow a career, freedom from the
double standard in sexual morality, freedom from social
convention—but in a larger sense it meant freedom from
the stifling stereotypes of women's separate sphere. Thus
did Charlotte Perkins Gilman, famous for her advocacy
of communal kitchens as a means of liberating women
from homemaking, imagine the new woman: "Here she
comes, running, out of prison and off pedestal; chains
off, crown off, halo off, just a live woman."

Feminists were militantly prosuffrage but, unlike
their more traditional suffragist sisters, did not stake
their claim on any presumed uplifting effect of the
women's vote on American politics. Rather, they demanded the right to vote because they considered themselves fully equal to men. At the point that the suffrage
movement was about to triumph, it was overtaken by a
larger revolution that redefined the struggle for women's
rights as a battle against all the constraints that prevented women from achieving their potential as human
beings.

Feminism gave a fresh thrust to social uplift, bringing forth a new and more radical type of woman progressive: Margaret Sanger. As a public health nurse in
New York, Sanger had been repeatedly asked by immigrant women about the "secret" of how to avoid having
more babies. When one of her patients died of a
botched abortion, Sanger decided to devote herself to
teaching poor immigrant women about birth control.
This brought her up against the Comstock laws, which
outlawed contraceptive literature and devices as obscene materials (see Chapter 20, page 641). Whereas it
was easy enough for the educated middle class to evade
those laws, birth control could only reach the poor
through an open campaign of education. Undeterred
by police raids or public disapproval, Sanger gave
speeches, published the pamphlet *Family Limitation,*
and in 1916 opened the first birth control clinic in the
United States. If her ends were not different from those
of Jane Addams—both wanted to uplift the downtrodden—the means used by Sanger posed a more provocative challenge to the status quo.

Urban Liberalism

The evolution of the women's movement—in particular, the recruitment of working-class women to what had been a middle-class struggle—was entirely characteristic of how progressivism evolved more generally.

When Hiram Johnson first ran for governor of California in 1910, he was the candidate of the urban middle class and the farming community. He had made a name as prosecutor of the corrupt San Francisco boss Abe Ruef. Johnson pledged to purify California politics and curb the Southern Pacific Railroad, the dominating power in the state's economic and political life. By his second term Johnson was championing social and labor legislation. His original base in the middle class had eroded and had been replaced by an immigrant working-class vote that kept him in power for years. These events illustrated the most enduring achievement of progressivism: the activation of America's working people as a force in reform politics and the launching of the strain of progressivism that historians have called *urban liberalism*. In New York the starting point for urban liberalism was a tragic fire.

Thirty minutes before quitting time on Saturday afternoon, March 25, 1911, fire broke out at the Triangle Shirtwaist Company in downtown New York City (see American Voices, page 660). The flames trapped the workers, mostly young immigrant women. Forty-seven leapt to their deaths; another ninety-nine never made it to the windows. The tragedy caused a national furor and led two months later to the creation of the New York State Factory Commission.

In the next four years the commission developed a remarkable program of labor reform: fifty-six laws dealing with fire hazards, unsafe machines, homework, and wages and hours for women and children. The chairman of the commission was Robert F. Wagner; the vice-chairman, Alfred E. Smith. Both were Tammany Hall politicians and Democratic party leaders in the state legislature. Wagner and Smith sponsored the resolution establishing the commission, participated fully in its work, and marshaled the party regulars to pass the proposals into law. All this the two men did with the approval of the Tammany machine. The labor code that resulted was the most advanced in the United States.

Tammany's reform role reflected a trend in American cities. Urban political machines increasingly recognized their limitations as social agencies in the modern industrial age: only the state could prevent future Triangle fires or cope with the evils of factory work and city life. Also, a new generation had entered machine politics. Al Smith and Robert Wagner, men of social vision, absorbed the lessons of the Triangle investigation. They formed durable ties with middle-class progressives such as the social worker Frances Perkins, who sat on the commission as the representative of the New York Consumers' League.

For all their organizational muscle, the urban machines could not ignore popular sentiment. In the successes of reform politicians such as Toledo's Sam Jones

The Triangle Shirtwaist Fire

The doors were the problem. Most were locked (to keep the working girls from leaving early); the few that were open became jammed by bodies as the flames spread. When the fire trucks finally came, the ladders were too short. Compared with those caught inside, the girls who leapt to their deaths were the lucky ones. "As I looked up I saw a love affair in the midst of all the horror," a reporter wrote. A young man was helping girls leap from a window. The fourth "put her arms about him and kiss[ed] him. Then he held her out into space and dropped her." He immediately followed. "Thud—dead, Thud—dead . . . I saw his face before they covered it. . . . He was a real man. He had done his best."

Pauline Newman

Working for the Triangle Shirtwaist Company

Pauline Newman was an organizer and educational director for the International Ladies Garment Workers Union until her death in 1986. As a child she had worked at the notorious Triangle Shirtwaist factory in New York.

A cousin of mine worked for the Triangle Shirtwaist Company and she got me on there in October of 1901. It was probably the largest shirtwaist factory in the city of New York then. They had more than two hundred operators, cutters, examiners, finishers. Altogether more than four hundred people on two floors. . . . We started work at seven-thirty in the morning, and during the busy season we worked until nine in the evening. They didn't pay you any overtime and they didn't give you anything for supper money. . . . What I had to do was not really very difficult. It was just monotonous. When the shirtwaists were finished at the machine there were some threads that were left, and all the youngsters—we had a corner on the floor that resembled a kindergarten—we were given little scissors to cut the threads off. It wasn't heavy work, but it was monotonous, because you did the same thing from seven-thirty in the morning until nine at night.

Well, of course, there were [child labor] laws on the books, but no one bothered to enforce them. The employers were always tipped off if there was going to be an inspection. "Quick," they'd say, "into the boxes!" And we children would climb into the big boxes the finished shirts were stored in. Then some shirts were piled on top of us, and when the inspector came—no children. The factory always got an okay from the inspector, and I suppose someone at City Hall got a little something, too.

The employers didn't recognize anyone working for them as a human being. . . . If you went to the toilet and you were there longer than the floor lady thought you should be, you would be laid off for half a day and sent home. And, of course, that meant no pay. You were not allowed to have your lunch on the fire escape in the summertime. The door was locked to keep us in. That's why so many people were trapped when the fire broke out. . . .

I stopped working at the Triangle Factory during the strike in 1909 and I didn't go back. The union sent me out to raise money for the strikers. I apparently was able to articulate my feelings and opinions about the criminal conditions, and they didn't have any-

one else who could do better so they assigned me. . . .

After the 1909 strike I worked with the union, organizing in Philadelphia and Cleveland and other places, so I wasn't at the Triangle Shirtwaist Factory when the fire broke out, but a lot of my friends were. . . . It's very difficult to describe the feeling because I knew the place and I knew so many of the girls. The thing that bothered me was the employers got a lawyer. . . . One hundred and forty-six people were sacrificed, and the judge fined Blank and Harris seventy-five dollars!

Conditions were dreadful in those days. But . . . even when things were terrible, I always had that faith. . . . Only now, I'm a little discouraged sometimes when I see the workers spending their free hours watching television—trash. We fought so hard for those hours and they waste them. We used to read Tolstoy, Dickens, Shelley, by candlelight, and they watch the "Hollywood Squares." Well, they're free to do what they want. That's what we fought for.

Source: Joan Morrison and Charlotte Fox Zabusky, eds., *American Mosaic: The Immigrant Experience in the Words of Those Who Lived It* (New York: E.P. Dutton, 1980), 9–14. Copyright © 1980 by Joan Morrison and Charlotte Fox Zabusky. Reprinted by permission.

---

and Cleveland's Tom Johnson, the machines saw the appeal of progressive programs in working-class wards. There was a threat from the left as well. The Socialist party was making headway in the cities, electing Milwaukee's Victor Berger as the nation's first socialist congressman in 1910 and winning municipal elections in towns and cities across the country. The political universe of the urban machines had changed, and they had to pay more attention to opinion in the precincts.

The Labor Movement. Always highly pragmatic, city machines adopted urban liberalism without much of an

ideological struggle. The same could not be said of trade unions, the other institution that represented American working people. During its early years the American Federation of Labor (AFL) had strongly opposed state interference in labor's affairs. Samuel Gompers preached that workers should not seek from government what they could accomplish through their own initiative and activities. Economic power and self-help, not the state, would be the worker's salvation. *Voluntarism*, as trade unionists called this doctrine, did not die out, but it weakened substantially during the progressive years.

Organized labor enlisted in the cause of urban liberalism partly for defensive reasons. In the early twentieth century the labor movement came under severe attack by antiunion employers who had at their disposal powerful legal weapons. For one thing, they could sue unions under the Sherman Antitrust Act. In the Danbury Hatters case (1908), the Supreme Court found a labor boycott—a call by the Hatters' Union for people not to patronize the antiunion D. E. Loewe & Company—to be a conspiracy in restraint of trade and awarded triple damages to the company. Hundreds of union members stood to lose their homes and life savings until the labor movement raised the money to pay the fines. More harmful to the economic power of the unions was the employers' routine use of the labor *injunction*—a court order prohibiting a union from carrying out a strike or boycott. The justification was to prevent "irreparable damage" to an employer while the legality of a union's acts was being adjudicated, but the effect of this "temporary" measure was to immobilize and defeat the union; this had happened, for example, to the American Railway Union in the great Pullman boycott of 1894 (see Chapter 18, pages 579–580).

Only a political response could blunt these assaults on labor's economic weapons. In its "Bill of Grievances" of 1906 the AFL demanded that Congress grant unions immunity from court attack. Rebuffed, the labor movement decided to become more politically active, adopting a strategy of nonpartisan support for candidates who favored its program. The AFL intended to "reward our friends and punish our enemies." The practical effect of this "nonpartisan" strategy was to draw labor closer to the Democratic party, which was more responsive than the Republican party to labor's pleas for a curb on the courts.

Once into politics, the labor movement had difficulty denying the case for social legislation. The AFL, after all, claimed to speak for the entire working class. When muckrakers exposed exploitation of women and children and middle-class progressives came forward with solutions, how could the labor movement fail to respond? Gompers served on the Triangle factory commission, and if—according to Frances Perkins—he was a less eager student than the Tammanyite members, learn he did. In state after state, organized labor joined the battle for progressive legislation and increasingly became its strongest advocate.

Conservative labor leaders offered the excuse that protective laws were for women and children, who could not defend themselves. In practice, however, trade unions became more flexible about legislative protection for men as well, and on the issue of workers' compensation they lobbied vigorously for new legislation.

Accidents took an awful toll in American factories and mines. Two thousand coal miners were killed every year, dying from cave-ins and explosions at a rate 50 percent higher than that in German mines. Liability laws, which were still governed by common-law principles, so heavily favored the employer that victims of industrial accidents rarely got compensation. Nothing cried out more for reform than the plight of maimed workers and penniless widows. In Germany and Britain, state-funded accident insurance guaranteed compensation regardless of fault. Efforts to provide comparable protections for American workers quickly received the backing of the trade unions. Between 1910 and 1917 workers' compensation for industrial accidents went into effect in all the industrial states.

Social Insurance Deferred. But the United States fell far behind European countries on other fronts. Health insurance and unemployment compensation, although widely accepted in Europe, scarcely made it onto the American political agenda. Old-age pensions, which Britain adopted in 1908, got a serious hearing, only to come up against an odd barrier: the United States already had a pension system of a kind. This was for Civil War veterans, 1 million of whom were drawing benefits in 1900. Thus, the constituency for a pension system was already largely satisfied: as many as half of all native-born white men over sixty-four or their survivors were receiving veterans' pensions in the early twentieth century. It did not help, moreover, that pensions had long been a partisan issue shamelessly exploited by the Republican party; that administration of the program was notoriously corrupt and laced with patronage; or, finally, that easy access to veterans' benefits often reinforced fears of state-induced dependency. Clarence J. Hicks, a famous industrial-relations expert, recalled Civil War pensioners idling away the hours around the wood stove in the grocery store in his Wisconsin town. They had decided "that the country owed them a living," lost their initiative, and "retreat[ed] from the battle of life."

It would take another generation and the ravages of the Great Depression before the country would be ready for social insurance. A secure old age, unemployment compensation, health insurance—these human needs of a modern industrial order were beyond the reach of urban liberals in the Progresive Era.

In Defense of Cultural Pluralism. Urban liberalism was driven not only by the plight of the economically downtrodden but also by a sharpening attack on the cultural values and way of life of immigrants. Old-stock evangelical Protestants had long agitated for laws that would impose their moral and cultural norms on American society. After 1900 those activities gained a new lease on life, forming a strand of progressive reform that conflicted with urban liberalism. The Anti-Saloon League, which called itself "the Protestant church in action," became a formidable force for prohibition in many states. Outlawing the sale of liquor was related to

other reform targets: the saloon made for dirty politics, poverty, and bad labor conditions. Like progressives on other fronts, prohibitionists pronounced their movement a "Revolt of Decent Citizens."

The moral-reform agenda expanded to include a new goal: restricting the immigration of southern and Eastern Europeans into the United States. "The entrance . . . of such vast masses of peasantry, degraded below our utmost concepts, is a matter which no intelligent patriot can look upon without the gravest apprehension and alarm," warned Francis A. Walker, the president of the Massachusetts Institute of Technology. These concerns were shared by many progressive academics, such as by La Follette's close adviser Edward A. Ross of the University of Wisconsin, who denounced the "pigsty mode of life" of immigrants. The danger, respected social scientists argued, was that the nation's Anglo-Saxon population would be "mongrelized" and its civilization swamped by "inferior" Mediterranean and Slavic cultures. Feeding on this fear, the Immigration Restriction League spearheaded a movement to end America's historic open-door policy. Like prohibition, immigration restriction was considered by its proponents to be a progressive reform.

Urban liberals thought otherwise. They bitterly resented demands for prohibition and immigration restriction as attacks on the personal liberty and worthiness of urban immigrants. Prohibition, protested one Catholic academic, was "despotic and hypocritical domination." The Tammany politician Martin McCue accused the Protestant ministry of "seeking to substitute the policeman's nightstick for the Bible."

Urban liberal leaders championed both the economic needs of city dwellers and their right to follow their religious and cultural preferences. In many ways, certainly until the Great Depression of the 1930s, ethnocultural issues provided the stronger basis for urban liberal politics. And because the northern wing of the party cultivated the immigrant vote, the Democrats became the beneficiaries of the rise of urban liberalism. The rapid growth of this city vote destined the Democrats to become the majority party. The shift from Republican domination, although not completed until the 1930s, began during the Progressive Era.

Racism in an Age of Reform

The direct primary was the flagship of progressive politics—the crucial reform, as La Follette said, for defeating the party bosses and returning politics to "the people." The primary electoral system of nominating party candidates originated not in Wisconsin, however, but in the South, and by the time La Follette got his primary law in 1903, it was already operating in seven southern states. As in the North, the southern primary

was celebrated as a democratizing reform, and its adoption frequently brought reform administrations into power.

In the South, however, it was a *white* primary; black voters were excluded. Since the Democratic nomination was tantamount to election, to be excluded from the primary meant in effect to be disfranchised. The direct primary was a reform *intended*, among other things, to drive blacks out of politics. How could democratic reform and white supremacy be thus wedded together?

The answer is to be found in the racist thinking of the age. "A black skin means membership in a race of men which has never of itself succeeded to reason," pronounced Professor John W. Burgess of Columbia University in a 1902 book on Reconstruction; for Congress to have granted blacks the vote after the Civil War was a "monstrous thing." Burgess was a southern-born historian, but he was confident that his northern audience saw the "vast differences in political capacity" between blacks and whites and approved of black disfranchisement in the South. Even the Republican party, once it reconciled itself to relying on "lily white" organizations in the South midway through Roosevelt's administration, had no quarrel with this view. Indeed, as president-elect in 1908, William Howard Taft applauded the southern laws as necessary to "prevent entirely the possibility of domination by . . . an ignorant electorate" and reassured southerners that "the federal government has nothing to do with social equality."

In the North the Progressive Era was marked by growing racial tensions. Over 200,000 blacks migrated from the South between 1900 and 1910. Their arrival in northern cities invariably sparked white resentment. Attacks on blacks became widespread. The worst episode was a bloody race riot in Springfield, Illinois, in 1908. Even more indicative of racist sentiment was the huge success of D. W. Griffith's epic film *Birth of a Nation* (1915), with its crude depiction of Reconstruction as a moral struggle between rampaging blacks and a chivalrous Ku Klux Klan. Woodrow Wilson found the film's history "all so terribly true." His Democratic administration marked a low point for the federal government as the ultimate guarantor of equal rights: during Wilson's tenure, segregation of the U.S. civil service would have gone into effect had there not been an outcry among black leaders and a handful of influential white progressives.

The Revival of the Civil Rights Struggle. In these bleak years a core of young black professionals, mostly northern-born, began to fight back. The key figure was William Monroe Trotter, the pugnacious editor of the Boston *Guardian* and an outspoken critic of Booker T. Washington (see Chapter 19, page 608). "The policy of compromise has failed," Trotter argued. "The policy

of resistance and aggression deserves a trial." In this endeavor, Trotter was joined in 1903 by W. E. B. Du Bois, a Harvard-trained sociologist and preeminent black intellectual of his generation. In 1906 the two of them, having broken with Washington, called a meeting of twenty-nine supporters at Niagara Falls—but in Canada, because no hotel on the U.S. side would admit blacks. The Niagara Movement, which resulted from that meeting, had an impact far beyond the scattering of members and local bodies it organized. The principles it affirmed would define the struggle for the rights of African-Americans: first, encouragement of black pride by all possible means; second, an uncompromising demand for full political and civil equality. Above all, "We refuse to allow the impression to remain that the Negro-American assents to inferiority, is submissive under oppression and apologetic before insults."

The revival of black protest found a small echo within white progressivism. Going against the grain, a handful of reformers were drawn to the plight of African-Americans. Among the most devoted was Mary White Ovington. By upper-class background and social outlook, she very much resembled Jane Addams, except that Ovington came from a family of abolitionists and thought of herself as a socialist. Like Addams, Ovington became a settlement-house worker, but among urban blacks rather than in an immigrant neighborhood. News of the bloody Springfield race riot of 1908 changed her life. Convinced that her duty lay in the struggle for equal rights, Ovington called a meeting of sympathetic white progressives that led to the formation of the National Association for the Advancement of Colored People (NAACP) in 1909.

The Niagara Movement, torn by internal disagreements, was breaking up, and most of the black activists joined the NAACP. Its national leadership was, in the early years, dominated by whites, however. The one exception proved to be of crucial importance. Du Bois became the editor of the NAACP's journal, *The Crisis*. With a passion that only a black voice could provide, Du Bois used that platform to proclaim the demand for black equality.

In the field of social welfare the principal concern during the Progressive Era was to help black migrants arriving in northern cities. In 1911 the National Urban League united the principal organizations that had sprung up for this purpose. Like the NAACP, the Urban League was interracial, including white reformers such as Ovington and black welfare activists such as William Lewis Bulkley, a New York school principal who played the most important role in the founding of the Urban League.

Progressivism was a house of many chambers. Most were infected by the respectable racism of the age, but not all. There was a saving remnant of white progressives who allied themselves with black activists and created, in the NAACP and the Urban League, the national institutions that would dominate the black struggle for a better life over the next half century.

Progressivism and National Politics

The gathering forces of progressivism reached the national scene slowly. Reformers had been activated by immediate concerns—by problems that affected them directly and by evils that were visible to them. Washing-

Editorial Office, The Crisis
In its early years no activity undertaken by the NAACP was more important than the publication of its journal, *The Crisis*, which under the brilliant editorship of W. E. B. Du Bois became the strongest voice for equal rights and black pride in the country. In this photograph of the magazine's editorial office, Du Bois is the balding man at the right rear.

TABLE 21.1

Progressive Legislation and Supreme Court Decisions

State Laws	Federal Laws	Supreme Court Decisions
1903 Wisconsin primary law Oregon ten-hour law for women	1898 Erdman Railway Mediation Act	1895 *U.S. v. E.C. Knight* shelters manufacturing from antitrust law
1910 New York Bureau of Industries and Immigration Washington State adopts women's suffrage	1902 Newlands Reclamation Act 1903 U.S. Bureau of Corporations 1906 Hepburn Railway Act Pure Food and Drug Act	1898 *U.S. v. Trans-Missouri* quashes "rule of reason" in antitrust suits
1911 Illinois law providing aid for mothers with dependent children New York State Factory Commisssion	1909 Payne-Aldrich Tariff Act 1913 Underwood Tariff Act Federal Reserve Act	1904 *U.S. v. Northern Securities* orders dissolution of a company ruled a monopoly under the Sherman Act
1912 Massachusetts minimum wage law for women and children	1914 Federal Trade Commission Act Clayton Antitrust Act	1905 *Lochner v. New York* invalidates a state law limiting hours of bakers
	1916 Seamen's Act	1908 *Muller v. Oregon* approves a state law limiting working hours of women *Loewe v. Lawlor* (Danbury Hatters case) finds a labor boycott to be a conspiracy in restraint of trade
		1911 *U.S. v. Standard Oil* restores rule of reason as guiding principle in antitrust cases

ton seemed remote from the battles that they were waging in their cities and states. But progressivism was bound to come to the capital. In 1906 Robert La Follette moved from the governor's office in Wisconsin to the U.S. Senate. Other seasoned progressives, also ambitious for a wider stage, made the same move. By 1910 a highly vocal progressive bloc was making itself heard in both houses of Congress.

The crucial entry point of progressivism into national politics was not Congress, however, but the presidency. This was partly because the White House was a "bully pulpit," to use Theodore Roosevelt's phrase, for mobilizing opinion and defining national issues. But just as important was the twist of fate that brought Roosevelt—the epitome of the progressive politician—to the White House on September 14, 1901.

The Making of a Progressive President

Except for his aristocratic background, Theodore Roosevelt was cut from much the same cloth as other progressive politicians. Born in 1858, he came from a wealthy old-line New York family, attended Harvard, and might have chosen the life of a leisured literary gentleman. Instead, scarcely out of college, he plunged into

Republican politics, and in 1882 entered the New York state legislature. His reasons matched the high-minded motives of other budding progressives. Like most of them, Roosevelt had received a moralistic, Christian upbringing. A political career would enable him to act constructively on those beliefs. Roosevelt always identified himself—loudly—with the side of righteousness, but he did not scorn power and its uses. He showed contempt for the amateurism of the Mugwumps— "those political and literary hermaphrodites," he called them—and much preferred the professionalism of party politics. Roosevelt rose in the New York party because he skillfully translated his moral fervor into broad popular support and thus forced himself on reluctant state Republican bosses.

After returning from the Spanish-American War as the hero of San Juan Hill (see Chapter 22), Roosevelt won the New York governorship in 1898. During his single term he clearly signaled his reformist inclinations by pushing through civil-service reform and a tax on corporate franchises. He discharged the corrupt superintendent of insurance over the Republican party's objections and asserted his confidence in the government's capacity to improve the life of the people.

Hoping to neutralize him, the party bosses promoted Roosevelt in 1900 to what normally would have been a

dead-end job as William McKinley's vice-president. Roosevelt accepted reluctantly. But on September 6, 1901, an anarchist named Leon F. Czolgosz shot the president. When McKinley died eight days later, Roosevelt became president. It was a sure bet, groaned Republican boss Mark Hanna, that "that damn cowboy" would make trouble in the White House.

Roosevelt in fact moved cautiously. In his first official statement he reassured the nation that he would "continue absolutely unbroken" McKinley's policies. The conservative Republican bloc in Congress greatly limited Roosevelt's freedom of action. He treated the Senate leader, Nelson W. Aldrich of Rhode Island, with kid gloves. Much of Roosevelt's energy was devoted to consolidating his position as he skillfully used the patronage powers of the presidency to gain control of the Republican party. But Roosevelt was also restrained by uncertainty about what reform role the federal government ought to play. At first the new president might have been described as a progressive without a cause.

Even so, Roosevelt gave early evidence of his activist bent. An ardent outdoorsman, he devoted part of his first annual message to Congress to conservation. A national movement had begun late in the nineteenth century to protect the country's natural resources and scenic wonders against reckless exploitation. With the establishment of Yellowstone National Park in 1872, the national park system had been launched, and the Forest Reserve Act of 1891 began the process of withdrawing timberland from unregulated commercial use.

Unlike John Muir (see Chapter 17, page 543), Roosevelt was not a preservationist broadly opposed to exploitation of the nation's wilderness. Rather, he wanted to *conserve* the country's resources. He was not against commercial development as long as it was regulated and mindful of the public interest. Roosevelt added more than 125 million acres to the national forest reserve and brought mineral lands and water power sites into the reserve system. In 1902 he backed the Newlands Reclamation Act, which designated the proceeds from public land sales for irrigation in arid regions. His administration upgraded the management of public lands and, to the chagrin of some Republicans, energetically prosecuted violators of federal land laws. In the cause of conservation Roosevelt demonstrated his enthusiasm for exercising executive authority and his disdain for those who sought profit "by betraying the public."

The same inclinations influenced Roosevelt's handling of the anthracite coal strike of 1902. Hard coal was the main fuel for home heating in those days. As cold weather approached with no settlement in sight, the government faced a national emergency. The United Mine Workers, led by John Mitchell, were willing to submit to arbitration, but the coal operators adamantly opposed recognition of the union. Roosevelt's advisers told him there was no legal basis for federal intervention. Nevertheless, the president called both sides to a conference at the White House on October 1, 1902. When the conference failed, Roosevelt threatened the operators with a government takeover of the mines. He also persuaded the financier J. P. Morgan to use his considerable influence with them. At that point the coal operators caved in. The strike ended with the appointment by Roosevelt of an arbitration commission to rule on the issues, another unprecedented step. Roosevelt did not especially support organized labor, but he became infuriated by the "arrogant stupidity" of the mine owners.

"Of all the forms of tyranny the least attractive and the most vulgar is the tyranny of mere wealth," Roosevelt wrote in his autobiography. He was prepared to deploy all his presidential authority against the "tyranny" of irresponsible business.

The Trust Problem. The economic issue that most concerned Roosevelt was a disturbing assault on the competitive market by big business. The drift toward large-scale enterprise had been under way for many years as entrepreneurs sought the efficiencies of nationwide, vertically integrated firms (see Chapter 18, pages 561–562). But larger business units also could be used to limit competition and control markets. The depression of the 1890s, which had intensified competition and caused staggering business losses, led to a scramble to merge rival firms once economic recovery began in 1897. These mergers—*trusts*, as they were called—greatly increased the degree of business concentration in the economy. Of the seventy-three largest industrial companies in 1900, fifty-three had not existed three years earlier. By 1910, 1 percent of the nation's manufacturers accounted for 44 percent of the total industrial output.

The sheer economic power of the new combines was not their only disturbing feature. Most of them were heavily *watered*; that is, the stocks and bonds they issued greatly exceeded the real value of the properties they controlled. For their underwriting services in launching the new trusts, moreover, investment bankers such as J. P. Morgan charged huge fees. Worse yet, financiers did not relinquish control over the combines they had fathered, for they sat on the boards of directors of the new firms and exerted a backroom influence on the operating executives. Almost overnight a "money power"—a cabal of Wall Street bankers—seemed to have gained a stranglehold on the American economy.

Roosevelt's sense of the nation's uneasiness became evident as early as his first annual message, in which he referred to the "real and grave evils" of economic concentration. But what weapons could the president use in response?

The basic legal principles upholding free competition were already firmly established. Under the common law—the body of judge-made legal precedents that

Jack and the Wall Street Giants
In this vivid cartoon from the humor magazine *Puck*, Jack (Theodore Roosevelt) has come to slay the giants of Wall Street. To the country, trust-busting took on the mythic qualities of the fairy tale—with about the same amount of awe for the fearsome Wall Street giants and hope in the prowess of the intrepid Roosevelt. J. P. Morgan is the giant leering at front right.

America had inherited from Britain—it was illegal for anyone to conspire to restrain or monopolize trade; persons who were economically injured by such actions could sue for damages. These common-law rights had been enacted into statute law in many states during the 1880s and then, because the problem went beyond state jurisdictions, had been incorporated into the Sherman Antitrust Act of 1890 and had become part of federal law.

Neither the Cleveland administration nor the McKinley administration had been much inclined to enforce the Sherman Act, except against organized labor.

Of the eighteen federal suits brought before 1901, half were against trade unions. Nor were the courts any more enthusiastic about attacking business. In *U.S. v. E. C. Knight* (1895) the Supreme Court ruled that manufacturing was not covered by the Constitution's commerce clause and thus was beyond the reach of federal antitrust regulation. This ruling crippled the Sherman Act but did not kill it. The potential of the act rested above all on the fact that it incorporated common-law principles of unimpeachable validity. In the right hands, the Sherman Act could be a strong weapon against the abuse of economic power.

Trust-Busting. Roosevelt made his opening move when he strengthened the government's capacity to administer the law. In 1903, despite considerable opposition, Congress accepted Roosevelt's proposal for a Bureau of Corporations within the newly created Department of Commerce and Labor. Empowered to investigate business practices, the bureau provided the factual record on which the Justice Department could mount antitrust suits. The first suit had been filed in 1902 against the Northern Securities Company, a combination of the railroad systems of the Northwest. In a landmark 1904 decision the Supreme Court ordered Northern Securities dissolved. The next year the Court reversed the *Knight* doctrine by ruling that manufacturing fell under the commerce clause and was therefore subject to federal antitrust law.

In 1904 Roosevelt handily defeated a weak conservative Democratic candidate, Judge Alton B. Parker. Now president in his own right, Roosevelt stepped up the attack on the trusts, taking on forty-five of the nation's giant firms, including Standard Oil, American Tobacco, and DuPont. The president accompanied these actions with a rising crescendo of rhetoric. He became the nation's trustbuster, a crusader against "predatory wealth."

Despite his rhetoric, Roosevelt was not antibusiness; he regarded large-scale enterprise as a natural result of modern industrialism. Only firms that abused their power deserved punishment. But how would those companies be identified? Under the common law and under the Sherman Act as originally intended, it had been up to the courts to decide whether an act in restraint of trade was "unreasonable," that is, actually harmed potential competitors or damaged the public interest. This was a highly flexible arrangement that allowed the courts to evaluate the actions of corporations on a case-by-case basis. In 1897, however, the Supreme Court had repudiated this "rule of reason" in the *Trans-Missouri* case. Now, even if the impact on the market was not harmful, actions that restrained or monopolized trade would automatically put a firm in violation of the Sherman Act.

Little noticed when it was first decided, *Trans-Missouri* placed Roosevelt in an awkward position when he began to enforce the Sherman Act. Roosevelt had no desire to hamstring legitimate business activity, but he could not rely on the courts to distinguish between "good" and "bad" trusts. The only solution was for Roosevelt to assume that responsibility. This the president could do because it was up to him—or his attorney general—to decide whether or not to initiate antitrust prosecutions in the first place.

That Roosevelt would use this discretionary power became clear in November 1904, shortly after the Bureau of Corporations began to investigate the United States Steel Corporation. The company's chairman, Elbert H. Gary, asked for a meeting with Roosevelt. Gary proposed an arrangement: cooperation in exchange for preferential treatment. The company would open its books to the Bureau of Corporations; if the bureau found evidence of wrongdoing, the company would be advised privately and given a chance to set matters right. Roosevelt accepted this "gentlemen's agreement," which was followed by one with International Har-

J. Pierpont Morgan
J. P. Morgan was a giant among American financiers. He had served an apprenticeship in investment banking under his father, a leading Anglo-American banker in London. A gruff man of few words, Morgan had a genius for instilling trust and the strength of will to persuade others to follow his lead and do his bidding—qualities the great photographer Edward Steichen captured in this portrait.

vester the next year. J. P. Morgan controlled both firms, and from his standpoint the arrangement seemed entirely sensible. Two great powers, one political and the other economic, would meet as equals and settle matters between them. For Roosevelt, the gentlemen's agreements solved a serious dilemma: he could accommodate the realities of the modern industrial order while maintaining his public image as the champion against the trusts.

Railroad Regulation. Abuse of economic power by the railroads posed a different kind of problem for Roosevelt. As quasi-public enterprises, the railroads had always been subject to public regulation. Initially, this had been the responsibility of the states, but with the passage of the Interstate Commerce Act of 1887, the federal government had entered the field, establishing in the Interstate Commerce Commission (ICC) the nation's first federal regulatory agency. As with the Sherman Act, however, railroad regulation remained pretty much a dead letter in its early years. Restrained by a hostile Supreme Court, the ICC lapsed into inactivity. Roosevelt was convinced, however, that the railroads needed firm regulation. The Elkins Act of 1903 empowered the ICC to act against discriminatory rebates, that is, reductions on published rates for preferred or powerful customers. Then, with the 1904 election behind him, Roosevelt made his push for a major expansion of railroad regulation.

The central issue was the setting of rates. Roosevelt considered it essential that the ICC have that power. Senator Nelson Aldrich and his conservative bloc opposed it just as firmly. In 1906, after nearly two years of wrangling, Congress passed the Hepburn Railway Act, which empowered the ICC to set maximum rates upon complaint of a shipper and to prescribe uniform methods of bookkeeping. But as a concession to the conservative bloc the courts retained broad powers to review ICC rate decisions.

The Hepburn Act was a triumph of Roosevelt's skills as a political operator. He had maneuvered brilliantly against determined opposition and had come away with the essentials of what he wanted. Despite grumbling by Senate progressives critical of any compromise, Roosevelt was satisfied. He had achieved a landmark expansion of the government's regulatory powers over business.

Consumer Protection. The regulation of consumer products, another hallmark of progressive reform, was very much the handiwork of muckraking journalists. In 1905 Samuel Hopkins Adams published a series of eye-opening articles on the patent-medicine business in *Collier's*. The first paragraph opened with these riveting words:

den lifted from the executive branch, Attorney General George W. Wickersham stepped up the pace of antitrust actions.

The United States Steel Corporation immediately became a prime target. Among the charges against the Steel Trust was that it had violated the antimonopoly provision of the Sherman Act by acquiring the Tennessee Coal and Iron Company (TCI). The purchase had been made in 1907 from a banking house that had fallen into trouble and urgently needed to sell its TCI stock to raise capital. Roosevelt had personally approved the acquisition as a necessary step—as U.S. Steel representatives had explained it to him—to prevent a financial collapse on Wall Street. Taft's suit against U.S. Steel thus amounted to an attack on Roosevelt: he had as president entered into a private agreement with U.S. Steel to circumvent the Sherman Act. Nothing was better calculated to propel Roosevelt into action than an issue that was both an affair of personal honor and a question of broad principle.

The New Nationalism. The country did not have to choose between breaking up big business and submitting to corporate rule, Roosevelt argued. There was a third way. The federal government could be empowered to oversee big business to make sure it acted in the public interest. The tool would be a federal trade commission with powers comparable to those exerted by the Interstate Commerce Commission over the railroads. Industrial corporations would be treated in effect as if they were natural monopolies or public utilities and would be placed under direct public oversight.

In a speech in Osawatomie, Kansas, in August 1910 Roosevelt made his case for what he called the New Nationalism. The central issue, he argued, was human welfare versus property rights. In modern society property had to be controlled "to whatever degree the public welfare may require it." The government would become "the steward of the public welfare."

This formulation removed the restraints from Roosevelt's thinking. Ultimately, he did not stop short of advocating government price-fixing for corporate industry. He took up the cause of social justice, adding to his program a federal child labor law, federal workers' compensation, regulation of labor relations, and a national minimum wage for women. Most radical, perhaps, was Roosevelt's attack on the legal system. Insisting that the courts should not be making social policy, Roosevelt proposed sharp curbs on their powers, even raising the possibility of popular recall of court decisions.

Beyond these specifics, the New Nationalism presented a new political philosophy. The key source was a book by the journalist Herbert Croly, *The Promise of American Life* (1909), which called for a uniting of rival strains in the American political tradition. From Hamilton's federalism Croly drew his emphasis on strong national government; from Jefferson's republicanism came Croly's enthusiasm for democracy and the primacy of the interests of the common citizen. The result, however, was a genuine break from America's political past. The New Nationalism offered a *statist* solution—an enormous expansion of the role of the federal government—to the problem of corporate power.

Early in 1912 Roosevelt announced his candidacy for the presidency and immediately swept the Progressive Republicans into his camp. A bitter and divisive party battle ensued in which Taft proved to be a tenacious opponent. Roosevelt won the states that held primary elections, but Taft controlled the party organizations elsewhere. Dominated by the party regulars, the Republican convention chose Taft.

Roosevelt, considering himself cheated out of the nomination, led his followers into a new Progressive party that was soon nicknamed the "Bull Moose" party. In a crusading campaign Roosevelt offered the New Nationalism to the people.

Woodrow Wilson and the New Freedom

While the Republicans battled among themselves, the Democrats were on the move. The scars caused by the free silver campaign of 1896 had faded, and in the 1908 campaign William Jennings Bryan had established the progressive credentials of the rejuvenated party. The Democrats made dramatic gains in 1910, taking over the House of Representatives for the first time since 1892, winning ten Senate seats, and capturing a number of traditionally Republican governorships. After fourteen years as the party's standard-bearer, Bryan reluctantly made way for a new generation of leaders.

The ablest was Woodrow Wilson of New Jersey. Wilson was an academic, a noted political scientist who, as president of Princeton, had brought it into the front rank of American universities. In 1910, without any experience with public office, he left Princeton to accept the Democratic nomination for governor of New Jersey. Wilson compiled a brilliant record: he cleaned up the boss system and passed a direct primary law, workers' compensation, and stronger regulation of railroads and utilities. With those credentials as a reformer, Wilson went on, in a bruising battle, to win the Democratic presidential nomination in 1912.

Wilson possessed, to a fault, the moral certainty that characterized the progressive politician. He almost instinctively assumed the mantle of righteousness and showed little tolerance for the views of his critics. Only gradually, however, did Wilson hammer out, in reaction to Roosevelt's New Nationalism, a coherent reform program, which he called the New Freedom.

July 13 1912   THE NEW RIDER   Price 10 Cents

On to the White House

At the Democratic convention Woodrow Wilson only narrowly defeated the front-runner, Champ Clark of Missouri. *Harper's Weekly* triumphantly depicted Wilson immediately after his nomination—the scholar turned politician riding off on the Democratic donkey, with his running mate, Thomas R. Marshall, hanging on behind. The magazine's editor, George Harvey, had identified Wilson as presidential timber back in 1906, long before the Princeton president had thought of politics, and had worked on his behalf from then on.

It is important to recognize how much ground Wilson shared with Roosevelt. *"The old time of individual competition is probably gone by,"* Wilson stressed. "We will do business henceforth, when we do it on a great and successful scale, by means of corporations." Like Roosevelt, Wilson opposed not bigness but the abuse of economic power. Nor did Wilson think that the abuse of power could be prevented without a strong federal government. He parted company from Roosevelt over *how* the authority of government should be used to restrain private power.

Roosevelt's advocacy of direct public control over corporations was anathema to Wilson. As he warmed to the debate, Wilson cast the issue in the fundamental terms of slavery and freedom. "This is a struggle for emancipation," he proclaimed in October 1912. "If America is not to have free enterprise, then she can have

freedom of no sort whatever." Wilson also scorned Roosevelt's social program. Welfare might be benevolent, he declared, but it also would be paternalistic and contrary to the traditions of a free people. The New Nationalism represented a future of collectivism, Wilson warned, whereas the New Freedom would preserve the political and economic liberties of the individual.

How, then, did Wilson propose to deal with the problem of corporate power? Court enforcement of the Sherman Act was Wilson's basic answer. His task was to figure out how to make that long-established antitrust approach work better. In this effort Wilson relied heavily on a new adviser, Louis D. Brandeis, famous as the "people's lawyer" for his public service in many progressive causes (including the landmark *Muller* case).

An expert on regulatory matters, Brandeis understood that an all-powerful trade commission was likely to end up not as a defender of the public interest but in a cozy relationship with the industries it was supposed to regulate. Nor did Brandeis believe that bigness meant efficiency. On the contrary, he argued that trusts were wasteful compared with firms that vigorously competed in a free market. The main thing was to prevent the trusts from unfairly using their power to curb free competition. It should be the aim of public policy "so [to] restrict the wrong use of competition that the right use of competition will destroy monopoly."

The 1912 election fell short of being a referendum on the New Nationalism versus the New Freedom. The outcome turned on a more humdrum reality: Wilson was elected because he kept the traditional Democratic vote while the Republicans split between Roosevelt and Taft. Although he won by a landslide in the electoral college (see Map 21.2), Wilson received only 42 percent of the popular vote, 115,000 fewer votes than Bryan had amassed against Taft in 1908.

Moreover, turnout fell substantially, from 65.4 percent of eligible voters in 1908 to 58.8 percent in 1912. If there was a beneficiary of the reform ferment sparked by the presidential campaign, it was not Wilson but the Socialist candidate, Eugene V. Debs, who captured 900,000 votes, 6 percent of the total. At best it could be said that the 1912 election signified that the American public was in the mood for reform: only 23 percent, after all, had voted for the one candidate who stood for the status quo, President Taft. Woodrow Wilson's own reform program, however, had not received a mandate from the people.

Yet anticlimactic as it might have seemed, the 1912 election proved to be a decisive event in the history of national reform. The debate between Roosevelt and Wilson had brought forth, in the New Freedom, a program capable of finally resolving the crisis over corporate power that had gripped the nation for a decade. Just as important, the election created a rare opportu-

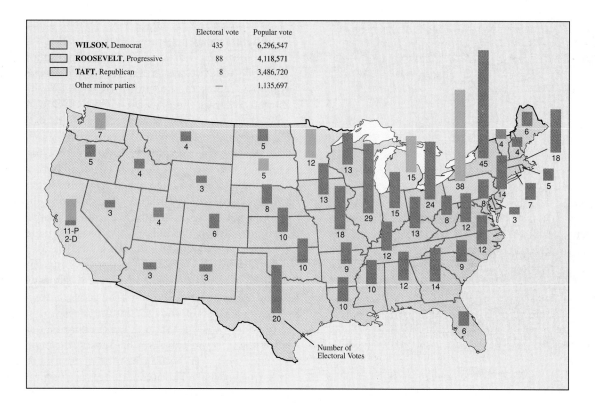

	Electoral vote	Popular vote
WILSON, Democrat	435	6,296,547
ROOSEVELT, Progressive	88	4,118,571
TAFT, Republican	8	3,486,720
Other minor parties	—	1,135,697

Number of
Electoral Votes

MAP 21.2

The Election of 1912

The 1912 election reveals why the two-party system is so strongly rooted in American politics. The Democrats, although a minority party, won an electoral landslide because the Republicans divided their vote between Roosevelt and Taft. This result indicates what is at stake when major parties splinter. The Socialists, despite a record vote of 900,000, got no electoral votes. To vote Socialist in 1912 meant in effect to throw away one's vote.

nity for decisive legislative action in Washington. Wilson became president with the Democrats in firm control of both houses of Congress and united in their eagerness to get on with the New Freedom.

The New Freedom in Action. Upon entering the White House, Wilson chose a flanking attack on the problem of economic power. So long out of office, the Democrats were hungry for tariff reform. From the prevailing average of 40 percent, the Underwood Tariff Act of 1913 pared rates down to an average of 25 percent. Targeting especially the trust-dominated industries, Democrats confidently expected the Underwood Tariff to spur competition and reduce prices for consumers by opening protected American markets to foreign products.

The administration then turned to the nation's banking system, whose key weakness was the absence of a central reserve bank. The main functions of a central bank are to regulate private banks and to back them up in case they cannot meet their obligations to depositors. In practice, this role had been assumed by the great New York banks, which handled the accounts of outlying banks and assisted them when they came under pressure. However, if the New York banks weakened, the entire system could collapse. That had nearly happened in 1907, when the Knickerbocker Trust Company failed and panic swept through the nation's financial markets.

The need for a reserve system became widely accepted, but the form it should take was hotly debated.

Wall Street wanted a centralized system controlled by the bankers. Rural Democrats and their spokesman, Senator Carter Glass of Virginia, preferred a decentralized network of reserve banks. Progressives in both parties agreed that the essential feature should be public control over the reserve system. The bankers, whose practices were already under scrutiny by Congress, were on the defensive in this contest.

President Wilson, who was no expert to begin with, learned quickly and reconciled the reformers and bankers. The monumental Federal Reserve Act of 1913 gave the nation a banking system that was resistant to financial panic. The act delegated reserve functions to twelve district reserve banks, which would be controlled by their member banks. The Federal Reserve Board imposed public regulation on this regional structure. In one stroke the act strengthened the banking system and placed a measure of restraint on the "money trust."

The Clayton Act and the FTC. Having dealt with tariff and banking reform, Wilson turned to the question of corporate power. He wanted to rely on the Sherman Act but was not sure how to make its antitrust principles more effective. Brandeis had already formulated two main approaches. One was to define with precision the prohibited practices: interlocking directorates, discriminatory pricing, and exclusive contracts that shut out competitors. The second approach was to create a new federal trade commission that would aid the executive branch in administering the antitrust laws.

Both approaches contained knotty problems. Was it feasible to make strict definitions of illegal practices? Brandeis finally decided that it was not, and Wilson assented. In the Clayton Antitrust Act of 1914, revising the Sherman Act, the definition of illegal practices was modified by these crucial words: "where the effect may be to substantially lessen competition or tend to create a monopoly in any line of commerce." As for the trade commission, the problem was: How much power and what functions should it have? Wilson was understandably sensitive on this matter, given his principled opposition to Roosevelt's conception of a powerful trade commission overseeing American business. Initially Wilson wanted only an advisory, information-gathering agency. But ultimately, under the 1914 law establishing it, the Federal Trade Commission (FTC) received broader powers to investigate companies and issue "cease and desist" orders against unfair trade practices that violated antitrust law. FTC decisions, however, were subject to court review, so that Wilson's entire program was situated within the original conception of antitrust enforcement. As before, it would ultimately be up to the courts to decide which business practices were illegal.

Despite a good deal of commotion, this arduous legislative process was actually an exercise in consensus building. Wilson himself had opened the debate in a conciliatory way. "The antagonism between business and government is over," he said, and the time was ripe for a program representing the "best business judgment in America." Afterward, Wilson felt he had brought the long controversy over corporate power to a successful conclusion, and in fact he had. Steering a course between Taft's conservatism and Roosevelt's radicalism, Wilson carved out a middle way—what the historian Martin J. Sklar has termed "corporate liberalism." This middle way brought to bear the powers of government without threatening the constitutional order and dealt to some degree with abuse of corporate power without threatening the capitalist system.

Wilson's Social Program. On social policy, too, Wilson carved out a middle way. During the 1912 campaign he had denounced the social program of the New Nationalism as paternalistic. Compared with his accommodation to big business, Wilson was resistant to special legislation for workers and farmers. He accepted cosmetic language in the Clayton Act stating that labor and farm organizations were not illegal combinations, but he rejected exempting them from antitrust prosecution.

The labor vote had grown increasingly important to the Democratic party, however. As his second presidential campaign drew nearer, Wilson lost some of his scruples about prolabor legislation. In 1915 and 1916 he championed a host of bills beneficial to American workers: a model federal workers' compensation law, a federal child labor law, the Adamson eight-hour law for railroad workers, and the landmark Seamen's Act, which eliminated age-old abuses of sailors aboard ship and granted them the individual rights held by other workers. Likewise, after stubborn earlier resistance, Wilson approved in 1916 the Federal Farm Loan Act, providing the low-interest rural credit system long demanded by farmers.

Wilson encountered the same dilemma that confronted all successful progressives: the claims of moral principle versus the unyielding realities of political and economic life. Progressives were high-minded but not radical. They saw evils in the system, but they did not consider the system itself evil. Furthermore, they prided themselves on being realists as well as moralists. So it stood to reason that Wilson, like other progressives who achieved power, would find his place at the center.

Summary

A new chapter in American reform began at the start of the twentieth century. For decades the problems resulting from industrialization and urban growth had been mounting. Now, after 1900, reform activity began to dominate the nation's public life. The unifying element in progressive reform was a common intellectual outlook, highly principled and idealistic as to goals and confident of the human capacity to find the means.

Beyond this shared outlook, progressives broke up into diverse and often conflicting groups. Political reformers included business groups concerned chiefly with improving the efficiency of city government, while other progressives, such as Robert La Follette, opposed privilege and wanted to democratize the political process. Both groups worked to enhance their power at the expense of entrenched party machines.

Social welfare became the province of American women, and that effort reinvigorated the struggle for women's rights. In the cities, working people and immigrants also became reform-minded and set in motion a new political force—urban liberalism. While progressivism was infected by the prevailing racism in American life, there was a reform wing that joined with black activists to forge the major institutions of black protest and uplift of the twentieth century: the National Association for the Advancement of Colored People and the Urban League.

At the national level, progressives focused primarily on controlling the economic power of corporate business. This overriding problem led to Theodore Roosevelt's Square Deal, then to his New Nationalism, and finally to Woodrow Wilson's New Freedom. The role of the federal government expanded dramatically, but in service to a cautious and pragmatic approach to the problems of the country.

TIMELINE

1887	Interstate Commerce Commission established
1889	Jane Addams and Ellen Gates Starr found Hull House
1890	Sherman Antitrust Act
1893	Economic depression (until 1897)
1899	National Consumers' League founded
1900	Robert M. La Follette elected Wisconsin governor
	First commission form of city government in Galveston, Texas
1901	President McKinley assassinated; Theodore Roosevelt succeeds
	United States Steel Corporation formed
1902	President Roosevelt settles national anthracite strike
1903	National Women's Trade Union League
1904	Supreme Court dissolves the Northern Securities Company
1905	*Lochner v. New York* overturns law restricting length of the workday
1906	Hepburn Railway Act
	AFL adopts Bill of Grievances
	Upton Sinclair's *The Jungle*
1908	*Muller v. Oregon* upholds regulation of working hours for women
	Federal Council of Churches founded
	William Howard Taft elected president
1909	NAACP formed
	Herbert Croly's *Promise of American Life*
1910	Roosevelt announces the New Nationalism
	Woman suffrage movement revives; suffrage victory in Washington State
1911	*Standard Oil* decision restores "rule of reason"
	Triangle Shirtwaist fire
1912	Progressive party formed
	Woodrow Wilson elected president
1913	Federal Reserve Act
	Underwood Tariff
1914	Clayton Antitrust Act

★   ★   ★

BIBLIOGRAPHY

The most recent survey of the Progressive Era is John Milton Cooper, *Pivotal Decades: The United States, 1900–1920* (1990). Two older but still serviceable narrative accounts are George E. Mowry, *The Era of Theodore Roosevelt, 1900–1912* (1958), and Arthur S. Link, *Woodrow Wilson and the Progressive Era, 1910–1917* (1954). A highly influential interpretation of progressive reform that is worth reading despite its disputed central arguments, is Richard Hofstadter, *The Age of Reform* (1955). Robert H. Wiebe, *The Search for Order, 1877–1920* (1967), places progressive reform in a broader context of organizational development. On the debate over progressivism as a movement see Daniel Rodgers, "In Search of Progressivism," *Reviews in American History* 10 (1982).

The Course of Reform

The progressive mind has been studied from many different angles. The religious underpinnings are stressed in Robert M. Crunden, *Ministers of Reform: The Progressives' Achievement in American Civilization, 1889–1920* (1982). In *The New Radicalism in America, 1889–1963* (1965), Christopher Lasch sees progressivism as a form of cultural revolt. Samuel Haber traces the influence of Frederick W. Taylor in *Efficiency and Uplift: Scientific Management in the Progressive Era* (1964). On the intellectual basis for progressivism the key book is Morton G. White, *Social Thought in America: The Revolt against Formalism* (1975). Most useful on political thinkers is Charles Forcey, *The Crossroads of Liberalism: Croly, Weyl, Lippmann, and the Progressive Era* (1961). A provocative study set in an international context is James T. Kloppenberg, *Uncertain Victory: Social Democracy and Progressivism in European and American Thought, 1870–1920* (1986). On the journalists see David M. Chalmers, *The Social and Political Ideas of the Muckrakers* (1964), and Harold S. Wilson, *McClure's Magazine and the Muckrakers* (1970).

Political reform has been the subject of a voluminous literature. Wisconsin progressivism can be studied in David P. Thelen, *The New Citizenship: Origins of Progressivism in Wisconsin, 1885–1900* (1972). Important progressives are discussed in Spencer C. Olin, *California's Prodigal Son: Hiram Johnson and the Progressive Movement* (1968), and Richard Lowitt, *George W. Norris: The Making of a Progressive* (1963). On city reform see Bradley R. Rice, *Progressive Cities: The Commission Government Movement* (1972); Jack Tager, *The Intellectual as Urban Reformer: Brand Whitlock and the Progressive Movement* (1968); and Melvin G. Holli, *Reform in Detroit: Hazen S. Pingree and Urban Politics* (1969).

The best treatment of the settlement-house movement is Allen F. Davis, *Spearheads of Reform* (1967). Allen F. Davis, *American Heroine: Jane Addams* (1973); George Martin, *Madame Secretary: Frances Perkins* (1976); and Kathryn Kish Sklar, *Florence Kelley and the Nation's Work: The Rise of Women's Political Culture* (1995), deal with leading woman progressives. The connection to working women is effectively treated in Nancy S. Dye, *As Equals and Sisters: Feminism, the Labor Movement, and the Women's Trade Union League of New York* (1980). Women garment workers, the key labor constituency for women progressives, are studied with great skill and insight in Susan A. Glenn, *Daughters of the Shtetl:*

Life and Labor in the Immigrant Generation (1990). Two pathbreaking books on the origins of American feminism are Rosalind Rosenberg, *Beyond Separate Spheres: The Intellectual Origins of Modern Feminism* (1982), and Nancy F. Cott, *The Grounding of Modern Feminism* (1987). The leading social reformer to spring from feminism is treated in Ellen Chesler, *Woman of Valor: Margaret Sanger and the Birth Control Movement* (1992).

On urban liberalism the standard book is John D. Buenker, *Urban Liberalism and Progressive Reform* (1973). The relationship to organized labor can be followed in Irwin Yellowitz, *Labor and the Progressive Movement in New York State* (1965). Two important recent books by historical sociologists treat the halting progress toward the welfare state: Theda Skocpol, *Protecting Soldiers and Mothers* (1992), and, in a comparison of the United States with Canada and Britain, Ann Shola Orloff, *The Politics of Pensions* (1993). The most comprehensive survey is Morton Keller, *Regulating a New Society: Public Policy and Social Change In America, 1900–1933* (1994). On the South see Dewey Grantham, *Southern Progressivism* (1983), and on the racial conservatism of social progressives see Elizabeth Lasch-Quinn, *Black Neighbors: Race and the Limits of Reform in the American Settlement-House Movement* (1993). The revival of black protest is vigorously described in Stephen R. Fox, *The Guardian of Boston: William Monroe Trotter* (1971), and David Levering Lewis, *W. E. B. Du Bois: Biography of a Race, 1868–1919* (1993).

Progressivism and National Politics

National progressivism is best approached through its leading figures. John Milton Cooper, *The Warrior and the Priest* (1983), is a provocative joint biography of Roosevelt and Wilson that emphasizes their shared world view. Other good biographies include John Morton Blum, *The Republican Roosevelt* (1954); Donald E. Anderson, *William Howard Taft* (1973); John Morton Blum, *Woodrow Wilson and the Politics of Morality* (1956); and Melvin I. Urofsky, *Louis D. Brandeis and the Progressive Tradition* (1981). Lewis S. Gould, *The Presidency of Theodore Roosevelt* (1991), provides a useful synthesis. Aspects of national progressive politics can be followed in James Penick, *Progressive Politics and Conservation: The Ballinger-Pinchot Affair* (1968); James Holt, *Congressional Insurgents and the Party System* (1969); and David Sarasohn, *The Party of Reform: The Democrats in the Progressive Era* (1989). On the socialists, in addition to the books cited in Chapter 18, see Aileen S. Kraditor, *The Radical Persuasion, 1890–1917* (1981), and James Weinstein, *The Decline of American Socialism, 1912–1925* (1967). Naomi Lamoreaux, *The Great Merger Movement in American Business, 1895–1904* (1985), offers a sophisticated modern analysis of trust activity, and Thomas K. McCraw, ed., *Regulation in Perspective* (1981), contains valuable interpretive essays on the problems of trust regulation. Albro Martin, *Enterprise Denied: The Origins of the Decline of American Railroads, 1897–1917* (1971), assesses the impact of railway regulation. A comprehensive rethinking of the progressive struggle to fashion a regulatory policy for big business is offered in Martin J. Sklar, *The Corporate Reconstruction of American Capitalism, 1890–1916: The Market, the Law, and Politics* (1988).

Battle of Santiago de Cuba, 1898

James G. Tyler's dramatic painting of the final sea battle of
the Spanish-American War showcased America's newest
weapon of war, the battleship.

An Emerging World Power

1877–1914

★　　　★　　　★

I n 1881 Great Britain sent a new envoy to Washington. He was Sir Lionel Sackville-West, son of an earl, brother-in-law of the Tory leader Lord Denby, but otherwise distinguished only as the steadfast lover of a celebrated Spanish dancer. His well-connected friends wanted to park Sir Lionel somewhere comfortable and out of harm's way, so they made him minister to the United States.

Twenty years later such an appointment would have been unthinkable. All the major European powers had by then elevated their missions in Washington to embassies and routinely staffed them with top-of-the-line ambassadors. And they treated the United States, without question, as a fellow Great Power.

When Sir Lionel arrived in Washington in 1881, the United States scarcely cast a shadow on world affairs. As a military power the United States was puny, even comical. Its army was smaller than Bulgaria's; its navy ranked thirteenth in the world and was a threat mainly to the crews on its unseaworthy ships. Twenty years later, however, the United States was flexing its muscles. It had just made short work of Spain in a brief but decisive war and acquired for itself an empire that stretched from Puerto Rico to the Philippines. America's standing as a rising naval power was manifest, and so was its aggressive assertion of national interest in the Caribbean and the Pacific.

In practice, the United States still acted as a regional power, but Europeans had become keenly aware of its capacity to cut a wider swath whenever it chose to do so. "Are we to be confronted by an American peril . . . before which the Old World is to go down to irretrievable defeat?" wondered a former French foreign minister. The notion of an "American peril" became a lively topic after 1900 among Europeans surveying the industrial and military potential of the United States. No one could be sure what America's role would be, since the

United States retained its traditional policy of nonalignment in European affairs. But in chanceries across the Continent, the importance of the United States was universally acknowledged and its likely response to every event was carefully assessed.

How the United States emerged onto the world stage in the decades before World War I is the subject of this chapter.

The Roots of Expansionism

In 1880 the United States had a population of 50 million and by that measure ranked with the great European powers. It was the world's leading producer of wheat and cotton. In industrial production the United States was second only to Britain and was rapidly closing the gap. Anyone who doubted the military prowess of Americans needed only to recall the ferocity with which they had fought one another in the Civil War. The great campaigns of Lee, Sherman, and Grant entered the military textbooks and were closely studied by army strategists everywhere. In the encounter between the *Monitor* and the *Merrimack* at Hampton Roads on March 9, 1862, the world had seen the first example of modern naval warfare.

Nor, when its vital interests were at stake, had the United States shown itself to be lacking in diplomatic vigor. Both major crises with European powers arising from the Civil War had been settled to America's satisfaction. In 1867 France abandoned its imperial adventure in Mexico and withdrew its forces. And in 1871 Britain expressed regret for belligerent acts against the Union during the war and agreed to the arbitration of the *Alabama* claims (see Chapter 16, page 509).

Diplomacy in the Gilded Age

In the years that followed, the United States lapsed into diplomatic isolation not out of weakness but for lack of any clear national purpose in world affairs. In this industrializing age George Washington's warning against entangling alliances seemed as pertinent as it had when America had been a thinly populated land of farmers. The business of building the nation's industrial economy absorbed Americans and turned their attention inward. And while the new international telegraphic cables provided the country with swift overseas communication after the 1860s, wide oceans still kept the world at a distance and gave Americans a sense of isolation and security. Nor did European power politics, which centered on Franco-German rivalry and on nationalistic conflict in the Balkans, seem to matter very much. As far as Cleveland's secretary of state, Thomas F. Bayard, was concerned, "we have not the slightest share or interest [in] the small politics and backstage intrigues of Europe . . . upon which we look with impatience and contempt."

As for the empire building in which the European powers were now avidly engaged, this expression of national prowess did not tempt the United States. Even so ardent an American nationalist as the young Theodore Roosevelt saw the folly of overseas expansion. "We want no unwilling citizens to enter our Union," he wrote in 1886. "European nations war for the possession of thickly settled districts which, if conquered, will for centuries remain alien and hostile to the conquerors; we, wiser in our generation, have seized the waste solitudes that lay near us."

In those circumstances, with no external threat to be seen, what was the point of maintaining a big navy? After making certain of the French departure from Mexico in 1867, the American government began to dismantle the Civil War fleet. The ships that remained on duty gradually deteriorated. Of the 125 ships on the navy's active list, only about 25 were seaworthy at any given time. No effort was made to keep up with European advances in weaponry and battleship design; the American fleet consisted mainly of sailing ships and obsolete ironclads.

During the administration of Chester A. Arthur (1881–1885) the navy began a modest upgrading program. New ships were put into service, standards for the officer corps were raised, and the Naval War College was founded. But the fleet remained small, and the squadrons lacked a unified naval command. The mission of the navy remained as before: to maintain coastal defenses and a modest cruising fleet capable of preying on enemy commerce at sea. An expenditure of 1 percent of the gross national product for the entire military establishment seemed entirely adequate in the 1880s.

The conduct of diplomacy was likewise of little account. Appointment to the foreign service was made mostly through the spoils system. American ministers and consular officers were a mixed lot, with many idlers and drunkards among the hardworking and competent. Domestic politics, moreover, made it difficult to develop a coherent program. Although foreign relations was an executive responsibility, the U.S. Senate jealously guarded its right to give "advice and consent" on treaties and diplomatic appointments. Partisan squabbling between Democrats and Republicans left the White House with even less room for maneuver. For its part the State Department tended to be inactive, exerting little control over policy or its missions abroad. It was remarkable how many actions (some of them later repudiated or simply ignored by the State Department) were taken independently by consuls and naval officers

out in the field. In remote parts of the world, the American presence was often primarily religious: the intrepid missionaries bent on Christianizing the native populations of Asia, Africa, and the Pacific islands.

Latin American Diplomacy. In the Caribbean the United States remained the dominant power, but the expansionist enthusiasms of the Civil War era subsided. Nothing came of the grandiose plans of Secretary of State William H. Seward or of President Grant's efforts to purchase Santo Domingo in 1870, and the Senate regularly blocked later moves to acquire bases in Haiti, Cuba, and Venezuela. The long-cherished interest in an interoceanic canal across Central America also faded. Despite pronouncing that no one else should build such a canal, the United States stood by when a French company headed by the builder of the Suez Canal, Ferdinand de Lesseps, started to dig across the Panama isthmus in 1880. That project failed after a decade, but the reason was bankruptcy, not American opposition.

On becoming secretary of state in 1881, James G. Blaine engaged in a flurry of diplomatic activity in Latin America. He got involved in a border dispute between Mexico and Guatemala, tried to settle a war Chile was waging against Peru and Bolivia, and called the first Pan-American conference. Blaine's interventions in Latin American disputes went badly, however, and his successor canceled the Pan-American conference after Blaine left office in late 1881. This was a characteristic instance of Gilded Age diplomacy, driven partly by partisan politics and carried out without any clear sense of national purpose.

Pan-Americanism—the notion of a community of American states—took root, however, and in 1888 Congress asked President Cleveland to call a conference of American states to promote trade and peace in the Western Hemisphere. Blaine, returning in 1889 for a second stint at the State Department under the new Republican administration of Benjamin Harrison, took up the plans that had already been made for a new Pan-American conference. An impressive agenda called for a customs union, improved communications, and arbitration treaties. But the only result was the creation of an agency in Washington that was later named the Pan-American Union. Any Latin American goodwill won by Blaine's efforts was soon blasted by the humiliation the United States visited upon Chile because of a riot against American sailors in the port of Valparaiso in 1891. Threatened with war, Chile was forced to apologize to the United States and pay an indemnity of $75,000.

Pacific Episodes. In the Pacific, American interest centered on Hawaii. American missionaries had long been active among the islanders. With a climate ideal for rais-

Sugar Cane Plantation, Hawaii
Over 300,000 Asians from China, Japan, Korea, and the Philippines came to work in the Hawaiian cane fields between 1850 and 1920. The hardships they endured are reflected in plantation work songs, such as this one by Japanese laborers:

Hawaii, Hawaii
But when I came what I saw was Hell
The boss was Satan
The lunas [overseers] his helpers.

ing sugarcane, Hawaii also attracted American planters and investors. Nominally an independent nation with its own monarchy, Hawaii came increasingly within the American orbit. An 1875 treaty granted Hawaiian sugar duty-free entry to the American market and declared the islands off limits to other powers. A second treaty in 1887 gave the United States naval rights at Pearl Harbor.

Having encouraged the sugar economy in Hawaii, the United States abruptly withdrew Hawaii's trading advantages in the McKinley Tariff of 1890 by removing the duty on all foreign sugar while granting domestic producers a special subsidy to compensate for the drop in sugar prices. Anxious to gain the same benefit, American planters in Hawaii began to plot for annexation to the United States. Aided by the U.S. minister to Hawaii and with American sailors conspicuously present, they revolted in January 1893 against Queen Liliuokalani. Within a month the provisional government that they

installed negotiated a treaty of annexation with the Harrison administration. Before annexation could be approved by the Senate, however, Grover Cleveland returned to the presidency and, after an investigation of the Hawaiian episode, withdrew the treaty. To annex Hawaii, he declared, would violate both America's "honor and morality" and its "unbroken tradition" against acquiring territory far from the nation's shores.

The American presence elsewhere in the Pacific had meanwhile grown stronger. In the northern Pacific this was the result of the 1867 purchase of Alaska from imperial Russia, which gave the United States not only a huge territory with vast natural resources but an unlooked-for presence stretching across the northern Pacific.

Far to the south, with even less forethought, the United States had become involved in the remote Samoan islands. In 1878 the United States secured the right to a coaling station in Pago Pago harbor—a key link on the route to Australia—and in exchange promised local Polynesian leaders to use its good offices in Samoa's relations with other foreign powers. An informal protectorate resulted. In the mid-1880s Germany began to press its claims to the islands, and the United States, stung by German arrogance, responded with equal fervor. In 1889 naval warfare might have broken out but for a fierce hurricane that wrecked the German and American fleets. At that point, agreement on a tripartite protectorate (the third European power was Britain) averted further strife and preserved American rights in Pago Pago.

American diplomacy in these years has been characterized as a series of incidents, not the pursuit of a foreign *policy*. Many things happened, but intermittently and without a plan, driven by individuals and pressure groups, not by any well-founded and coherent conception of national objectives. This was possible because, as the Englishman James Bryce remarked in 1888, America still sailed "upon a summer sea." In the stormier waters that lay ahead, a different kind of American diplomacy would be required.

Economic Sources of Expansionism

"A policy of isolation did well enough when we were an embryo nation," remarked Senator Orville Platt of Connecticut in 1893. "But today things are different. . . . We are 65 million people, the most advanced and powerful on earth, and regard to our future welfare demands an abandonment of the doctrines of isolation."

America's gross national product quadrupled between 1870 and 1900, and industrial output quintupled. But were there sufficient markets to absorb the staggering volume of goods flowing from America's farms and factories? It was true that America itself constituted an enormous market. Over 90 percent of American output in the late nineteenth century was consumed at home. Even so, foreign markets were important. Roughly a fifth of the nation's agricultural output was exported, and for the major staple crops—cotton, wheat, tobacco—the proportion was much higher, up to 80 percent, for example, in the case of cotton.

As the industrial economy expanded, so did factory exports. Between 1880 and 1900, the industrial share of total exports jumped from 15 percent to over 30 percent. Although only 9 percent of manufactured output went overseas in 1900, the export share in key industries was much larger: 57 percent for petroleum products, 50 percent for copper, 25 percent for sewing machines, and 15 percent for iron and steel.

The importance of foreign sales was evident in the efforts of major firms to develop overseas production and marketing facilities. As early as 1868 the pioneering Singer Sewing Machine Company established its first foreign plant in Glasgow, Scotland. The most prominent American firm doing business abroad was Standard Oil. Beginning with the Anglo-American Oil Company in 1888, Rockefeller's firm created affiliates across Europe to operate its tankers, establish bulk stations, and distribute its kerosene to foreign retailers. In Asia, Standard Oil's kerosene cans, converted into utensils and roofing tin, became an infallible index of American market penetration. Brand names such as Kodak

The Singer Sewing Machine

The sewing machine was an American invention that swiftly found markets abroad. The Singer Company, the dominant firm, not only exported large quantities but produced 200,000 machines annually at a Scottish plant that employed 6,000 workers. Singer's advertising rightly boasted of its prowess as an international company and of a product that was "The Universal Machine."

(cameras), McCormick (agricultural equipment), and later Ford (the Model T) became household words around the world.

Foreign trade was important partly for reasons of international finance. As a developing economy, the United States attracted a lot of foreign capital but sent relatively little abroad—scarcely 1 percent of all the money Americans invested in the late nineteenth century. The result was a heavy outflow of dollars from the United States in the form of interest and dividend payments to foreign investors. To balance this account, the United States needed to export more goods than it imported. In fact, a favorable import-export balance was achieved in 1876 (see Figure 22.1). But because of its status as a net importer of capital, America would have to be constantly vigilant about the health of its foreign trade.

Even more important, however, was the relationship that many Americans perceived between foreign markets and the nation's social stability. In hard times, as we have seen, farmers took up radical politics and workers became militant strikers. The problem, many thought, was that the nation's capacity to produce was outrunning its capacity to consume. And when the economy slowed and domestic demand fell, the impact on farmers and workers was devastating, driving down farm prices and wages and causing layoffs and farm foreclosures across the country. The answer was to make sure that there would always be enough buyers for America's surplus products, and this meant, more than anything else, access to foreign markets.

Overseas Trade and Foreign Policy. The nub of the question was how these concerns about foreign markets linked up to America's foreign policy. The bulk of American exports in the late nineteenth century—over 80 percent—went to Europe and Canada (Table 22.1). In those countries the normal instruments of diplomacy

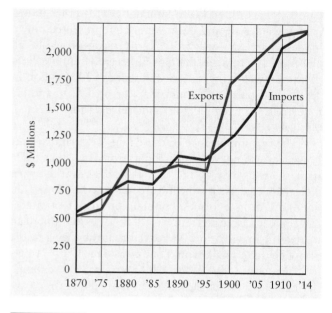

FIGURE 22.1

Balance of U.S. Imports and Exports, 1870–1914
By 1876 the United States had become a net exporting nation. The brief reversal after 1888 aroused fears that the United States was losing its foreign markets and helped fuel the expansionist drive of the 1890s.

suffced. In Europe, for example, a major issue during the 1880s was the restrictions placed on imports of American pork, allegedly on health grounds. The United States protested vigorously, threatened to embargo the imports of countries that discriminated against American meat products, and in 1891 negotiated a satisfactory settlement.

But other foreign markets—Asia, Latin America, and other "backward" regions—seemed to demand a more vigorous kind of American intervention. Here the

TABLE 22.1

Exports to Canada and Europe Compared with Exports to Asia and Latin America

Year	Exports to Canada and Europe ($)	Percentage of Total	Exports to Asia and Latin America ($)	Percentage of Total
1875	494,000,000	86.1	72,000,000	12.5
1885	637,000,000	85.8	87,000,000	11.7
1895	681,000,000	84.3	108,000,000	13.4
1900	1,135,000,000	81.4	200,000,000	14.3

Source: Compiled from information in *Historical Statistics of the United States*, 1960; U.S. Department of Commerce, *Long Term Growth, 1860–1965, 1966*; National Bureau of Economic Research, *Trends in the American Economy in the Nineteenth Century*, 1960.

United States found itself competing with other industrial powers. Asia and Latin America represented only a
modest part of America's export trade—roughly an
eighth of the total in the late nineteenth century. Still,
this trade was growing—it was worth $200 million in
1900—and parts of it mattered a great deal to specific
industries, for example, the China market for American
textiles.

The real importance of these non-Western markets,
however, was not so much the extent of current trade
with them as it was the fact that they, not Europe,
were expected to be the future market for American
goods. With its enormous population of potential customers, China exerted a powerful hold on the American
mercantile imagination. Many felt that the China trade,
although quite small, would one day be the key to American prosperity. Therefore, China and other beckoning
markets must not be closed to the United States.

From the mid-1880s onward, with the surge of European imperialism, the fear of being excluded became
more real. In a burst of modernizing energy Japan transformed itself into a major power and began to challenge
China's claims over Korea. In the Sino-Japanese War of
1894–1895, Japan won an easy victory and started a
scramble among the Great Powers, including Russia, to
carve China up into spheres of influence. In Latin America, United States interests began to be challenged more
aggressively by Britain, France, and Germany. On the
European continent, moreover, the free-trade liberalism
of earlier years gave way after the 1870s to protectionism, threatening established European markets for
American goods just as empire building was closing off
new markets elsewhere.

On top of all this came the Panic of 1893, setting
in motion labor strikes and agrarian protests that
many Americans, such as Cleveland's secretary of state,
Walter Q. Gresham, took to be "symptoms of revolution." With the nation's social stability seemingly at
stake, securing the markets of Latin America and Asia
became an urgent necessity that inspired the expansionist diplomacy of the 1890s.

The Making of an Expansionist Foreign Policy

"Whether they will or no, Americans must now begin
to look outward. The growing production of the country requires it." So wrote Captain Alfred T. Mahan,
America's leading naval strategist, in his book *The Influence of Seapower upon History* (1890). An obscure
naval officer posted to a rickety ship cruising Latin
America, Mahan had spent his spare time reading history. In a library in Lima, Peru, he hit upon the idea that
great empires—first Rome and, in modern times, Great
Britain—had derived their power from control of the

Alfred T. Mahan
Mahan's theory about the influence of sea power on history
came to him while he was killing time on a tour of naval duty
reading Roman history in a library in Lima, Peru, in 1885.
His insight was personal as well as intellectual: embarrassed
by the decrepit ships on which he served, Mahan thought the
United States should have a modern fleet in which officers
like himself could serve with pride (and with some hope of
professional advancement).

seas. From this insight Mahan developed a naval analysis that became the cornerstone of American strategic
thinking.

The United States should no longer regard the
oceans as barriers, Mahan argued, but as "a great highway . . . over which men pass in all directions." Travers-
ing that highway required a robust merchant marine
(America's had fallen on hard times since its heyday in
the 1850s) and a powerful navy to protect American
commerce. "When a question arises of control over distant regions . . . it must ultimately be decided by naval
power," Mahan advised. To sustain its navy and its
commerce, the United States needed strategic overseas
bases. Here technology played a role because, having
converted to steam, navies required coaling stations far
from home. Without such stations, Mahan warned,
warships were "like land birds, unable to fly far from
their own shores."

Mahan called for a canal across Central America to
connect the Atlantic and Pacific oceans. Such a canal
would enable the eastern United States to "compete
with Europe, on equal terms as to distance, for the markets of East Asia." The canal's approaches would need
to be guarded by bases in the Caribbean Sea. And
Hawaii would have to be annexed to extend American
power into the Pacific, a step that Mahan considered
"natural, necessary, irrepressible." This, it should be
noted, was a distinctive and limited form of colonial-

ism—not the rule over large territories and native populations to which European empire builders aspired, but control over strategic bases from which American power could be asserted in areas where Americans wanted to trade.

Mahan was offering the United States a *coherent* foreign policy: first, foreign markets secured for the nation's surplus products; second, of equal importance, the nation's development as a naval power; and third, sustaining both of those goals, an expansionist strategy anchored on an interoceanic canal and bases in the Caribbean and the Pacific.

Mahan's reasoning was eagerly taken up by other exponents of a powerful America, including Whitelaw Reid of the New York *Tribune* and young politicians such as Theodore Roosevelt and Henry Cabot Lodge. The influence of those men, few in number but strategically placed, increased during the 1890s. They pushed steadily for what Lodge called a "large policy." But mainstream politicians also accepted Mahan's underlying logic, and from the inauguration of Benjamin Harrison in 1889 onward, a surprising consistency began to emerge in the conduct of American foreign policy.

Rebuilding the Navy. This consensus was most evident in the rethinking of naval strategy. The crucial thing, Mahan argued, was to drop the reliance on shore defense and lightly armed cruising ships and create instead a battleship fleet capable of roaming the far seas and striking a decisive first blow against an enemy. This was the line that Benjamin F. Tracy, Harrison's secretary of the navy, took in his first annual report. Battleships might be expensive, but they were "the premium paid by the United States for the insurance of its acquired wealth and its growing industries." In 1890 Congress appropriated funds for the first three battleships in the two-ocean

fleet envisioned by Secretary Tracy. The battleship took on a special aura for those, such as the young Roosevelt, who wanted to see the United States flexing its muscles: "Oh, Lord! if only the people who are ignorant about our Navy could see those great warships in all their majesty and beauty, and could realize how [well fitted they are] to uphold the honor of America!"

The incoming Cleveland administration was less spread-eagled and, by canceling Harrison's scheme for annexing Hawaii, established its antiexpansionist credentials. But after a brief period of hesitation the Democrat Cleveland picked up the naval program of his Republican predecessor, pressing Congress just as forcefully for more battleships (five were authorized) and making the same basic argument. The nation's commercial vitality—"free access to all markets," in the words of Cleveland's second secretary of state, Richard Olney—depended on its naval power.

While rejecting the colonialist aspects of Mahan's thinking, Cleveland absorbed the underlying strategic arguments about where America's vital interests lay. This explains the remarkable crisis that suddenly blew up in 1895 with Great Britain over Venezuela.

The Venezuela Crisis. For years a border dispute had simmered between Venezuela and British Guiana. In the past the United States had urged arbitration, only to be told by the haughty British that they did not submit their interests to the judgments of third parties. Now that answer could no longer be accepted. Britain's claims seemed to be part of a larger pattern of European aggressiveness in Latin America, including ominous moves against Nicaragua, Brazil, Trinidad, and Santo Domingo. European empire building was carving up Africa and Asia in this period. How could the United States be sure that Europe did not have similar designs

The Battleship Oregon
The battleship was the centerpiece of naval strategy in the industrial age and the key marker in the naval arms race among the Great Powers. Building a battleship fleet was America's ticket of entry to that race.

on Latin America? Indeed, prompted by President Cleveland, Secretary of State Olney made that point in a bristling note to London on July 25, 1895, demanding that Britain accept arbitration or face the consequences.

Invoking the Monroe Doctrine, Olney warned that the United States could not tolerate any European attempt to intimidate or overthrow nations in the Western Hemisphere. "Today the United States is practically sovereign upon this continent, and its fiat is law upon the subjects to which it confines its interposition," Olney asserted. Olney's words sound bombastic, but they were intended to convey a clear message to Britain and the European powers that the United States would brook no challenge to its vital interests in the Caribbean. (Note that these were America's vital interests, not those of Venezuela, which was not consulted during the entire dispute.)

Because the Venezuela crisis blew up so suddenly, because it seemed so out of proportion to the boundary issue itself, and because it created war hysteria in the United States—for these reasons historians have found it difficult to recognize that the pugnacious stand of the Cleveland administration was not an aberration but a logical step in the new American foreign policy. Once the British realized that Cleveland meant business, they backed off and agreed to arbitration of the boundary dispute. Afterward, Secretary of State Olney remarked with satisfaction that, as a great industrial nation, the United States needed "to accept [its] commanding position" and take its place "among the Powers of the earth." And those countries would have to accommodate the American need for access to "more markets and larger markets for the consumption and products of the industry and inventive genius of the American people."

The Ideology of Expansionism. As policy makers hammered out a new foreign policy, a sustaining body of ideology took shape. One source of expansionist dogma was the Social Darwinist theory that dominated the political thought of this era (see Chapter 19, page 589). If animals and plants evolved through the survival of the fittest, so did nations. "Nothing under the sun is stationary," warned the American social theorist Brooks Adams in *The Law of Civilization and Decay* (1895). "Not to advance is to recede." By this criterion, the United States had no choice; if it wanted to survive, it had to expand.

Linked to Social Darwinism was a spreading belief in the inherent superiority of the Anglo-Saxon "race." On both sides of the Atlantic, Anglo-Saxonism was in vogue. John Fiske, an American philosopher and historian, popularized Social Darwinism and Anglo-Saxonism by lecturing the nation on its future responsibilities. "The work which the English race began when it colonized North America," Fiske declared, "is destined to go on until every land on the earth's surface that is not al-

ready the seat of an old civilization shall become English in its language, in its religion, in its political habits, and to a predominant extent in the blood of its people."

Fiske entitled his lecture "Manifest Destiny." This term had been used half a century earlier to convey the sense of national mission—America's "manifest destiny"—to sweep aside the native American peoples and occupy the continent. In his widely read book *The Winning of the West* (1896) Theodore Roosevelt drew a parallel between expansionism in his own time and the suppression of the Indians. It mattered little what happened to "backward peoples" because their conquest was "for the benefit of civilization and in the interests of mankind. It is indeed a warped, perverse and silly morality which would forbid a course of conquest that has turned whole continents into the seats of mighty and flourishing civilized nations." More than historical parallels, however, linked Manifest Destiny of the past and present.

In 1890 the U.S. Census reported the end of the westward movement: there was no longer a frontier line beyond which land remained to be conquered. The psychological impact of that news on Americans was profound, spawning among other things a new historical interpretation that stressed the importance of the frontier in shaping the nation's character. In his landmark essay setting out this thesis—"The Significance of the Frontier in American History" (1893)—the young historian Frederick Jackson Turner suggested a linkage between the closing of the frontier and overseas expansion. "He would be a rash prophet who should assert that the expansive character of American life has now entirely ceased," Turner wrote. "Movement has been its dominant fact, and, unless this training has no effect upon a people, the American energy will continually demand a wider field for its exercise." As Turner predicted, Manifest Destiny did turn outward.

Thus a strong current of ideas, deeply rooted in American experience and ideology, justified the new diplomacy of expansionism. The United States was eager to step onto the world stage. All it needed was the right occasion.

An American Empire

Ever since Spain had lost its vast empire in South America in the early nineteenth century, Cubans had yearned to join their mainland brothers and sisters in freedom. Movements for independence had sprung up repeatedly, most recently in a rebellion that had lasted from 1868 to 1878. In February 1895, inspired by the poet Jose Martí, Cuban patriots again rebelled against Spanish rule. Although Martí died in an early skirmish and no mass uprising occurred, the rebels built up substantial

fighting forces and mounted a guerrilla war against the Spaniards. A standoff developed; the Spaniards controlled the towns, while insurgents held much of the countryside. In early 1896 the newly appointed Spanish captain general, Valeriano Weyler, adopted a harsh policy of *reconcentration*. The Spaniards forced entire populations into armed camps and treated any Cuban on the outside as a rebel. Because it was not followed by aggressive pursuit, reconcentration only inconvenienced the guerrilla fighters. The toll on civilians, however, was extremely brutal. Out of a population of 1.6 million, as many as 200,000 died of starvation, exposure, or dysentery.

The Cuban Crisis

The rebel leaders shrewdly saw that their best hope was not military but political: they had to draw the United States into their struggle. Some Cubans lived in the country, mostly in Florida, where Cuban cigar makers taxed themselves heavily for the cause of independence. But the nerve center of the United States was New York City, and it was there that a key group of exiles—the *junta*—set up shop to make the case for *Cuba Libre*. By itself, their cause would not have stirred much interest. The Spaniards were not behaving more dishonorably than any other colonial power in similar circumstances; nor were atrocities in short supply elsewhere in the world if Americans cared to know. The Cuban exiles, however, came on the scene at a critical juncture in American sensationalist journalism. William Randolph Hearst had just purchased the nearly moribund *New York Journal* and was in a hurry to build circulation (see American Lives, pages 686–687). Cuba was ideal for his purposes. Locked in a furious circulation war, Hearst's *Journal* and Joseph Pulitzer's *New York World* elevated Cuba's agony into flaming front-page headlines.

Across the country powerful sentiments began to be stirred, mixing humanitarian concern for the Cubans, a superpatriotism that was tagged *jingoism*, and increasing demands that the Cubans be freed. Responding to public opinion, Congress passed resolutions for limited Cuban self-government in 1896 and for complete independence early the next year.

The White House took a cooler view of the situation. Cleveland was still in office when the rebellion broke out. As with Venezuela, his concern was with America's vital interests, which, he told Congress, were "by no means of a wholly sentimental or philanthropic character." First, economic interests were at stake. The rebellion was disrupting the sizable trade between the two countries and destroying profitable American investments, especially in Cuban sugar plantations. Of course, it was the rebels who were burning the crops, but Spain was accountable for not maintaining security.

Then there were strategic considerations. The United States could no longer tolerate instability in the Caribbean and worried that Spain's troubles might draw other European powers into the situation. A chronically unstable Cuba was not compatible with America's increasing strategic interests in the region, especially its plans for an interoceanic canal whose approaches would have to be safeguarded.

If Spain could put down the rebellion, that was fine with Cleveland. But as Spain's impotence became clear, he urged the Spanish government to make reforms and warned that the United States would have to intervene unless there was a speedy resolution of the crisis.

On that central matter there was continuity between Cleveland and the McKinley administration that took office in March 1897. Both were guided by the conception of the United States as the dominant Caribbean power, with vital interests that had to be defended. McKinley, however, was inclined to take a tougher line with the Spaniards. For one thing, he was more appalled by Spain's "uncivilized and inhumane conduct" in Cuba and was not as indifferent as Cleveland to the aspirations of the rebels. In addition, McKinley had to contend with rising jingoism in the Republican party. At the 1896 national convention the Republicans had adopted a bristling platform calling for Cuban independence and proclaiming a new American imperialism. But the notion, long held by historians, that McKinley was swept along against his better judgment by popular opinion and by a Republican war faction led by Theodore Roosevelt, Henry Cabot Lodge, and other aggressive advocates of a "large policy" is not true. McKinley was very much his own man. He was a skilled politician and a canny, if undramatic, president. He would not proceed until he sensed a broad national consensus for war. In particular, he was sensitive to business interests fearful of disruption to an economy that was just recovering from a depression.

The Road to War. On September 18, 1897, the American minister in Madrid asked the Spanish government "whether the time has not arrived when Spain . . . will put a stop to this destructive war." If Spain could not assure an "early and certain peace," the United States would take whatever steps it "should deem necessary to procure this result." At first the Spanish response sparked some hope. The conservative regime fell, and a liberal government, upon taking office in October 1897, moderated its Cuban policy. Spain recalled Weyler, limited reconcentration, and adopted an autonomy plan that would grant Cuba a degree of self-rule but not independence. Madrid's incapacity soon became clear, however. In January 1898, Spanish loyalists in Havana rioted against the offer of autonomy. The Cuban rebels, encouraged by the prospect of American intervention, demanded full independence.

William Randolph Hearst: Jingo

William Randolph Hearst, born in San Francisco on April 29, 1863, was no Horatio Alger hero. His father, George Hearst, had struck it rich in Nevada's Comstock lode, and Willie grew up in the lap of luxury: grand houses, trips to Europe, private tutors, Harvard (class of 1886). His mother, Phoebe, doted on him, at once indulging and smothering her only child. From these unpromising beginnings sprang a strappingly handsome young man of remarkable contradictions, beginning with his voice, which was incongruously thin and high-pitched. Hearst was painfully shy but simultaneously hell-bent on mischief; his pranks at Harvard (which finally got him expelled) were legendary. He was outwardly diffident but had to dominate everyone around him. He was sentimental and generous but also without scruples. When he wanted something, he really wanted it, and he was known late into his life to throw tantrums when he was denied. All this would be of no historical moment—doubtless there were others like him among the progeny of the new millionaires—except for one thing: Hearst did not end up a dissipated alcoholic or, as it was known to happen, even a quietly exemplary citizen. No, Hearst became a great newspaperman and, driven by his inner demons, cut a swath through American history.

His father happened to own the *San Francisco Examiner*, a money-loser that served as the elder Hearst's political organ. At Harvard the son took to reading the *Examiner* and decided that he wanted to run it. His inspiration was Joseph Pulitzer, who had a few years earlier taken over the moribund *New York World* and transformed it into a hugely successful daily. While still a junior, Hearst wrote a remarkable letter to his father outlining his plans for the paper, which would be, like the *World*, "of that class which appeals to the people and which depends for its success upon enterprise, energy and a certain startling originality and not upon the wisdom of its political opinions or the lofty style of its editorials." The elder Hearst was unimpressed. He was thinking about unloading the paper, not pouring more money into it. Supposing it became a great success, he asked the business manager, how much might it make? Maybe $100,000 a year, came the answer. "Hell!" snorted Hearst. "That ain't no money." But the son wasn't interested in the money; he was interested in the *circulation* and the delight he would take from orchestrating the emotions—and maybe even the actions—of thousands upon thousands of readers.

In early 1887 the young Hearst, not yet twenty-four, finally got his wish and, on taking command, immediately pronounced the sleepy *Examiner* "Monarch of the Dailies." It would be "THE LARGEST, BRIGHTEST AND BEST NEWSPAPER ON THE PACIFIC COAST," providing readers with the best news and "THE LATEST AND MOST ORIGINAL SENSATIONS." Sensation was what Hearst was after, copy that would arouse, in his editor's words, "the gee-whiz emotion." For example: Were any grizzly bears left in California? Hearst dispatched an intrepid newsman to the Tehachapi Mountains, where after three months of arduous trapping he caught a grizzly. The beast was chained in a beer wagon, paraded with great fanfare around San Francisco, and given a home in Golden Gate Park. Naturally, it was named Monarch. All this the *Examiner* reported in exhaustive detail, building suspense as the search progressed and ending triumphantly with the carnival display of the unfortunate bear. There was much more of the same: rescues, murders, scandal, sob stories, anything that might give readers the "gee-whiz emotion." The other string in Hearst's bow was that he became a champion of "the people." The *Examiner* embarked on a series of noisy crusades—against the water trust, and got rates cut by 15 percent; against a city charter crafted by venal politicos and their business cronies, and got it defeated; and, on many fronts, against the rapacious Southern Pacific Railroad.

By the early 1890s the *Examiner's* circulation was soaring and Hearst was making money. Looking around for greener fields, his eye fixed on New York City. The *Journal* was for sale, and Hearst got it cheaply. It was an anemic paper, close to folding, but Hearst didn't care. He intended to transform it, pouring money in as he had with the *Examiner* and applying everything he had learned in San Francisco. He was going to war against Pulitzer's *New York World*.

When Hearst took over the *Journal* in October 1895, the Cuban insurrection had already begun. Until then Hearst had shown no interest in foreign affairs,

William Randolph Hearst

but he genuinely felt for the underdog Cubans and, more to the point, saw in their cause just what he needed to drive his circulation war against Pulitzer. Not much actual news could be gotten out of Cuba, for the sporadic fighting took place in the remote interior, beyond the reach of Hearst's correspondents in Havana. It did not matter. Rebel claims were good enough for Hearst, and a drumbeat of superheated articles began to appear about mostly nonexistent battles and about Spanish atrocities. When General Valeriano Weyler took command, the *Journal* immediately dubbed him the "Butcher":

> Weyler the brute, the devastator of haciendas, the destroyer of families and the outrager of women. . . . Pitiless, cold, an exterminator of men . . . inventing tortures and infamies of bloody debauchery. . . .

Weyler's reconcentration program soon put meat into the *Journal's* wild charges and American public opinion began to harden against the Spanish.

The *Journal* was stridently for war. Hearst's jingoism sounded very much like his old crusade again the San Francisco water trust: it was the people versus the interests all over again, the freedom-loving masses against the peace-at-any-price plutocrats. President McKinley was Wall Street's puppet, with the nefarious Senator Hanna pulling the strings. When the *Maine* went down, the *Journal* was ablaze with fiery headlines charging Spanish treachery. That week circulation

passed a million. Impatient for action, Hearst found ammunition even in the suicide of poor Mrs. Mary Wayt:

GRIEVED OVER OUR DELAY

"The Government May Live in
Dishonor," Said She,
"I Cannot."

The next day, April 19, the Senate passed the war resolution, and hostilities commenced. The news from Manila Bay got this screaming headline: "VICTORY . . . Complete! . . . Glorious! . . . THE MAINE IS AVENGED." A few days later, the front page asked readers: "HOW DO YOU LIKE THE JOURNAL'S WAR?"

Was it true? Had Hearst caused the war? For many years historians thought so. Now, with a better understanding of McKinley's administration, they are more inclined to stress the country's endangered strategic interests. Yet there is no denying Hearst's contribution. The war hysteria he nurtured was like a ticking bomb, forcing the president's hand because, as New York's Senator Platt noted, McKinley knew "that the people of the United States will not tolerate much longer the war in Cuba." There were also longer-term consequences. For one, public opinion became a weightier factor in the conduct of American foreign policy: whether democracy and diplomacy are compatible has been debated ever since Hearst's time. Second, Hearst introduced and never let go of a superpatriotism—"Americanism," he called it—that became a permanent, if volatile, element of the nation's political debate.

As for the war with Spain, Hearst had a grand time of it. He hired a boat, took a crew of newsmen down to Cuba, came under fire at El Caney, wrote some creditable dispatches when his star reporter was wounded, rounded up Spanish survivors of the Santiago naval battle, and returned to New York feeling that the world was his oyster.

At that time Hearst was thirty-five, with another fifty-three years to live. The news business, ultimately a huge empire, remained the core of his being. But he also entered New York politics in a quixotic quest for the presidency. He plunged into Hollywood moviemaking and formed a permanent liason with one of his creations, the movie star Marion Davies. He built a castle at San Simeon and entertained extravagantly the rich and famous. All the while he became more enigmatic, more dictatorial, more alone.

In the end Hearst gained immortality in an utterly modern way: he became the inspiration for Orson Welles's great movie *Citizen Kane* (1941). Ordinarily, we do not look to the movies for historical insight, but Welles captured something in Hearst. The plot turns on Kane's dying word, *rosebud*, which proves to be just the name of a sled remembered from his childhood.

On February 9, 1898, the *New York Journal* published a private letter of Dupuy de Lôme, the Spanish minister to the United States. De Lôme called President McKinley "weak" and "a bidder for the admiration of the crowd." Worse, he suggested that the Spanish government was not taking the American demands for reform seriously. De Lôme immediately resigned, but the damage had been done.

A week later the U.S. battleship *Maine* blew up and sank in Havana harbor, with the loss of 260 seamen. "Whole Country Thrills with the War Fever," proclaimed Hearst's *New York Journal*. From that moment onward popular passions against Spain became a major factor in the march toward war.

But McKinley kept his head. He assumed that the sinking had been accidental: What motive could the Spanish have had for attacking the *Maine*? A naval board of inquiry, however, submitted a more damaging report. Disagreeing with a separate Spanish inquiry, the American board concluded that the sinking had been caused by a mine, not, as seems more likely, by an accidental explosion inside the *Maine*. No evidence linked the Spanish to the sinking, but they had failed to protect the American vessel from attack.

This was damning evidence that Spanish control over Cuba had broken down, and it was reinforced by a memorable speech by Senator Redfield Proctor of Vermont after a visit to Cuba. This anti-imperialist senior Republican's account of the devastation in the Cuban countryside made a deep impression and led even the skeptical to conclude that Spain had lost the right to rule Cuba.

McKinley had no stomach for the martial spirit engulfing the country. He was not swept along by the calls for blood to avenge the sinking of the *Maine*. But he did have to attend to an aroused public opinion. Hesitant business leaders also became impatient for the dispute to end. War was preferable to the unresolved Cuban crisis. On March 27, McKinley cabled to Madrid what was in effect an ultimatum: an immediate armistice for six months, abandonment of the practice of reconcentration, and, with the United States as mediator, peace negotiations with the rebels. A telegram the next day added that only Cuban independence would be regarded as a satisfactory outcome to the negotiations.

In response, Spain made a series of desperate concessions, climaxed on April 9 by a unilateral declaration of an armistice whose duration would be at the discretion of the Spanish military. But it rejected American mediation as well as the demand for an independent Cuba. There had never been any chance that the proud Spanish would accept that final humiliation.

On April 11, McKinley sent a message to Congress asking for authority to intervene to end the fighting in Cuba. His motives were as he described them: "In the name of humanity, in the name of civilization, in behalf of endangered American interests which give us the right and the duty to speak and to act, the war in Cuba must stop." The war hawks in Congress—a mixture of Republican jingoists and western Democrats who sympathized with the cause of Cuban independence—were impatient with McKinley's cautious progress. But the president did not lose control of things. On the one crucial difference he had with the war hawks, McKinley prevailed. He beat back their effort to recognize the rebel republican government, which would have greatly reduced the administration's freedom of action in dealing with Spain.

"Remember the Maine!*"*

In late January 1898 the *Maine* entered Havana harbor on a courtesy call. On the evening of February 15 a mysterious blast sent the U.S. battleship to the bottom. This dramatic lithograph conveys something of the impact of that event on American public opinion. Although no evidence ever linked the Spanish authorities to the explosion, the sinking of the *Maine* fed the emotional fires that prepared the nation for war with Spain.

Added to the resolutions empowering the president to employ American forces in Cuba was an amendment by Senator Henry M. Teller of Colorado disclaiming any intention by the United States to use intervention as a pretext for taking possession of Cuba. Teller wanted to make it impossible for European governments to say that "when we go out to make battle for the liberty and freedom of Cuban patriots, that we are doing it for the purpose of aggrandizement for ourselves or the increasing of our territorial holdings." This had to be made clear with regard to Cuba, "whatever," Senator Teller added, "we may do as to some other islands."

Did McKinley have in mind "some other islands"? Was this really a war of aggression secretly motivated by a desire to seize strategic territory from Spain? In a strict sense, almost certainly no. It was not *because* of expansionist ambitions that McKinley forced Spain into a corner. On the other hand, once war came, he saw it as an opportunity to be exploited. As he wrote privately after hostilities began: "While we are conducting war and until its conclusion, we must keep all we get; when the war is over we must keep what we want." Precisely what would be forthcoming, of course, would depend on the fortunes of battle.

The Spoils of War

Hostilities formally began when Spain declared war on April 24, 1898. The day before, President McKinley had called for 125,000 volunteers. Across the country regiments began to form up. Theodore Roosevelt immediately resigned as assistant secretary of the navy, ordered a fancy uniform, and was commissioned lieutenant colonel in a volunteer cavalry regiment that became famous as the Rough Riders. Raw recruits poured into makeshift bases around Tampa, Florida. Confusion reigned. Tropical uniforms did not arrive; the food was bad, the sanitation worse; and rifles were in short supply. No provision had been made for getting the troops to Cuba; the government hastily began to collect a miscellaneous fleet of yachts, lake steamers, and commercial boats. Fortunately, the small regular army was a disciplined, highly professional force, and its seasoned 28,000 troops provided a nucleus for the 200,000 civilians who had to be turned into soldiers inside of a few weeks.

The navy was in better shape and was, as it turned out, the key to the outcome of the war. So outclassed were the Spanish that the Atlantic fleet admiral, Pascual Cervera, expected that his navy would "like Don

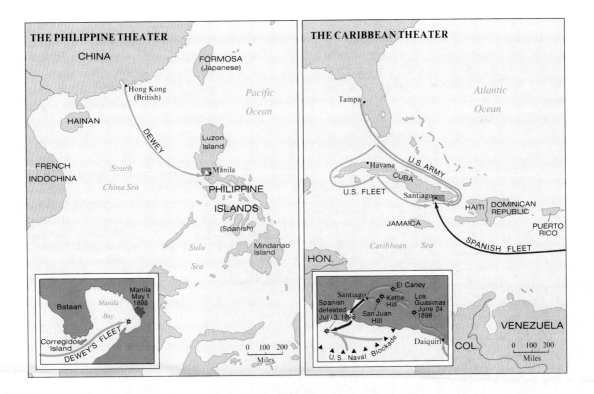

MAP 22.1

The Spanish-American War

The swift American victory in the Spanish-American War resulted from overwhelming naval superiority. Dewey's destruction of the Spanish fleet in Manila harbor doomed the Spaniards in the Philippines. In Cuba, American ground forces won a hard victory on San Juan Hill, for they were ill equipped and poorly supplied. With the United States in control of the seas, the Spaniards saw no choice but to give up the battle for Cuba.

Quixote go out to fight windmills and come back with a broken head." Cervera had nothing to match the U.S. Navy's seven battleships and armored cruisers, and the ships he had were undermanned and ill prepared for battle.

On April 23, acting on plans already drawn up, Commodore George Dewey's small Pacific fleet set sail from Hong Kong for the Philippines. Here, at this Spanish possession in the far Pacific, not in Cuba, the decisive engagement of the war took place. On May 1 the American ships cornered the Spanish fleet in Manila Bay and destroyed it (see Map 22.1). The victory produced euphoria in the United States. Immediately, part of the army being trained for the Cuban campaign was diverted to the Philippines. Manila, the Philippine capital, fell on August 13, 1898.

With Dewey's naval victory, American strategic thinking clicked into place. "We hold the other side of the Pacific and the value to this country is almost beyond imagination," declared Senator Lodge. "We must on no account let the [Philippine] Islands go." President McKinley agreed, and so did his key advisers. An anchor in the western Pacific had long been coveted by naval strategists. At this time, too, the Great Powers were carving up China into spheres of influence. If American commerce wanted a place in that glittering market, the power of the United States would have to be projected into Asia. "With a strong foothold in the Philippine Islands, we can and will take a large slice of the commerce of Asia," Senator Mark Hanna asserted. "That is what we want . . . and it is better to strike while the iron is hot."

Once the decision for a Philippine base had been made, other decisions followed almost automatically. The question of Hawaii was quickly resolved. In 1897 McKinley had reintroduced an annexation proposal in Congress, but it had stalled. In July 1898 Congress pushed Hawaiian annexation through by joint resolution. Hawaii had suddenly acquired a crucial strategic value: it was a halfway station on the way to the Philippines. The navy pressed for a coaling base in the central Pacific; that meant Guam, a Spanish island in the Marianas. There was also a need for a strategically located base in the Caribbean; that meant Puerto Rico. By July, before the assault on Cuba, the full scope of McKinley's war aims had crystallized. There was no question that he had the people behind him. In the wake of Dewey's victory, enthusiasm for colonial annexations swept the country and, as one close reader of the nation's press reported, was "getting so strong it will mean the political death of any man to oppose it pretty soon."

The campaign in Cuba (see Map 22.1) was something of an anticlimax. The Spanish fleet was bottled up in Santiago harbor, and the city itself became the strategic key to the military campaign. Half trained and ill equipped, the American forces moving on Santiago might have been checked by a determined opponent, but the Spaniards lacked the heart for battle. They would fight to maintain their honor, but they had no stomach for a real war against the Americans.

The main battle, on July 1, occurred near Santiago on the heights commanded by San Juan Hill. Roosevelt's dismounted Rough Riders (there had been no room for horses on the transports) seized Kettle Hill.

The Battle of San Juan Hill

On July 1, 1898, the key battle for Cuba took place on heights overlooking Santiago. African-American troops bore the brunt of the fighting. Although generally overlooked, the black role in the San Juan battle is done justice in this contemporary lithograph, without the demeaning stereotypes by which blacks were normally depicted in an age of intensifying racism. Even so, the racial hierarchy is maintained. The blacks are the foot soldiers; their officers are white.

George W. Prioleau

Black Soldiers in a White Man's War

The chaplain of the Ninth Cavalry regiment expresses his bitterness toward the racism experienced by black troopers in the South on their way to battle in Cuba.

Hon. H. C. Smith
Editor, Gazette

Dear Sir:

The Ninth Cavalry left Chickamauga on the 30th of April for Tampa, Fla. We arrived here (nine miles from Tampa) on May 3. From this port the army will sail for Cuba. We have in this camp here and at Tampa between 7,000 and 8,000 soldiers, artillery, one regiment of cavalry (the famous fighting Ninth) and the Twenty-fourth and Twenty-fifth infantries. The Ninth Cavalry's bravery and their skillfulness with weapons of war . . . is well known by all who have read the history of the last Indian war. . . .

Yesterday, May 12, the Ninth was ordered to be ready to embark at a moment's notice for Cuba. . . . These men are anxious to go. The country will then hear and know of the bravery of these sable sons of Ham.

The American Negro is always ready and willing to take up arms, to fight and to lay down his life in defense of his country's flag and honor. All the way from northwest Nebraska this regiment was greeted with cheers and hurrahs. At places where we stopped the people assembled by the thousands. While the Ninth Cavalry band would play some national air the people would raise their hats, men, women and children would wave their handkerchiefs, and the heavens would resound with their hearty cheers. The white hand shaking the black hand. The hearty "goodbyes," "God bless you," and other expressions aroused the patriotism of our boys. . . . These demonstrations, so enthusiastically given, greeted us all the way until we reached Nashville. At this point we arrived about 12:30 A.M. There were about 6,000 colored people there to greet us (very few white people) but not a man was allowed by the railroad officials to approach the cars. From there until we reached Chattanooga there was not a cheer given us, the people living in gross ignorance, rags and dirt. Both white and colored seemed amazed; they looked at us in wonder. Don't think they have intelligence enough to know that Andrew Jackson is dead. . . .

The prejudice against the Negro soldier and the Negro was great, but it was of heavenly origin to what it is in this part of Florida, and I suppose that what is true here is true in other parts of the state. Here, the Negro is not allowed to purchase over the same counter in some stores that the white man purchases over. The southerners have made their laws and the Negroes know and obey them. They never stop to ask a white man a question. He (Negro) never thinks of disobeying. You talk about freedom, liberty, etc. Why sir, the Negro of this country is a freeman and yet a slave. Talk about fighting and freeing poor Cuba and of Spain's brutality; of Cuba's murdered thousands, and starving reconcentradoes. Is America any better than Spain? Has she not subjects in her very midst who are murdered daily without a trial of judge or jury? Has she not subjects in her own borders whose children are half-fed and half-clothed, because their father's skin is black. . . . Yet the Negro is loyal to his country's flag. . . .

The four Negro regiments are going to help free Cuba, and they will return to their homes, some then mustered out and begin again to fight the battle of American prejudice. . . .

Yours truly,
Geo. W. Prioleau
Chaplain, Ninth Cavalry

Source: Cleveland *Gazette* (May 13, 1898), reprinted in Willard B. Gatewood, *"Smoked Yankees" and the Struggle for Empire, 1898–1902* (Urbana: University of Illinois Press, 1971), 27–29.

Then the frontal assault against the San Juan heights began. Four black regiments took the brunt of the fighting (see American Voices, above). White observers grudgingly credited much of the victory to the "superb gallantry" of the black soldiers. In fact, it was not quite a victory. The Spaniards, driven from their forward positions, retreated to a well-fortified second line. The Americans had suffered heavy casualties and were exhausted by heat and illness. It was questionable whether they could have mounted a second assault. They were spared that test, however, by the Spanish. On July 3, in a last futile gesture, Cervera's fleet in Santiago harbor made a suicidal daylight attempt to run the American blockade and was destroyed. A few days later, convinced that Santiago could not be saved, the Spanish forces agreed to surrender.

Three weeks later, Spain sued for peace. The two nations signed an armistice in which Spain agreed to give up Cuba and cede Puerto Rico and Guam to the United States. American forces would occupy Manila pending a peace treaty that would decide the fate of the Philippines.

The Imperial Experiment

The big question was the Philippines. This was an archipelago of over 7,000 islands populated—as William R. Day, McKinley's secretary of state, put it with the characteristic racism of that era—by "eight or nine millions of absolutely ignorant and many degraded people." Not even the most avid American expansionists had advocated colonial rule over such a population: that was European-style imperialism, not what Mahan and his followers had in mind. Both Mahan and Lodge initially advocated keeping only Manila as a western Pacific base. It gradually became clear, however, that Manila was not defensible without controlling the whole of Luzon, the large island on which the city is located.

McKinley and his advisers surveyed the options. One possibility was to return most of the islands to Spain, but the reputed evils of Spanish rule made that a "cowardly and dishonorable" solution. Another possibility was to partition the Philippines with one or more of the Great Powers. There would have been no dearth of takers, particularly Germany, whose ships were prowling the nearby waters. But as McKinley observed, to turn over valuable territory to "our commercial rivals in the Orient—that would have been bad business and discreditable."

Most plausible was the option of granting the Philippines independence. As in Cuba, Spanish rule had already stirred up a rebellion, led by the fiery patriot Emilio Aguinaldo. It would have been feasible to make an arrangement like the one being negotiated with the Cubans over Guantanamo Bay: the lease of a naval base to the Americans as the price for freedom. But after some hesitation McKinley was persuaded that "we could not leave [the Filipinos] to themselves—they were unfit for self-rule—and they would soon have anarchy and misrule over there worse than Spain's was."

In October 1898, while the peace negotiations were in progress, McKinley made a two-week speaking tour of the Midwest to get a reading on public opinion. What he heard from the crowds confirmed his own belief that the United States would have to take the entire archipelago. On October 26 he cabled instructions to that effect to the American delegation in Paris. He had concluded that the United States "cannot let go."

As for the Spaniards, they had little choice against what they considered "the immoderate demands of a conquerer." In the Treaty of Paris they ceded the Philippines to the United States for a payment of $20 million. The treaty encountered harder going at home and was ratified by the Senate (requiring a two-thirds majority) on February 6, 1899, with only a single vote to spare.

The Anti-Imperialists. The narrowness of the administration's victory signaled the revival of an antiexpansionist tradition that had been mostly silenced by the patriotic passions of a nation at war. In the Senate opponents of the treaty invoked the country's republican principles. Imperial expansion, argued the conservative Republican George F. Hoar, meant accepting "the fundamental idea [of the European imperial powers] that the people of immense areas of territory can be held as subjects, never to become citizens." Under the Constitution, "no power is given to the Federal Government to acquire territory to be held and governed permanently as colonies" or "to conquer alien people and hold them in subjugation." And making 8 million Filipinos eligible for citizenship—be it noted, only the prospect of an annexed Philippines had fired real opposition to the treaty—was equally unpalatable to the anti-imperialists, who were no more champions of "these savage people" than were the expansionists who denigrated the self-governing capacity of the Filipinos.

Leading citizens enlisted in the anti-imperialist cause, including the steelmaker Andrew Carnegie, who offered a check for $20 million to purchase the independence of the Philippines; the labor leader Samuel Gompers, who feared the competition of cheap Filipino labor; and Jane Addams, who believed that women should stand for peace. The key group, however, was a social elite of old-line Mugwump reformers such as Carl Schurz, Charles Eliot Norton, and Charles Francis Adams. In November 1899 Boston Mugwumps formed the first Anti-Imperialist League, from which blossomed a national movement over the next year, with chapters in major cities across the country, 30,000 members, and, so they claimed, half a million contributors.

Skillful as they were at publicizing their cause, the anti-imperialists never managed to build a truly popular movement. They were an ill-assorted lot, divided in many ways and, within the Mugwump core, lacking the common touch needed to attract mass support. Nor was it easy to translate anti-imperialism into a viable political cause because the Democrats, once the treaty had been adopted, waffled over the issue. The Democratic standard-bearer, William Jennings Bryan, although an outspoken anti-imperialist, provided confused leadership—he had confounded his friends by favoring ratification of the treaty—and afterward hesitated to stake his party's future on a crusade against a national policy he privately believed to be irreversible. Still, if it was an accomplished fact, Philippine annexation lost the moral high ground because of the remonstrations of the anti-imperialists and the awful events that began to unfold in the Philippines.

War in the Philippines. Two days before the Senate ratified the treaty, on February 4, 1899, fighting broke out between American and Filipino patrols on the edge of Manila. Confronted by the prospect of American annexation, Aguinaldo asserted his nation's independence and turned his guns on the occupying American forces.

The ensuing conflict far exceeded in ferocity the war that had just been concluded with Spain. Fighting tenacious guerrillas, the U.S. Army resorted to the same tactics of reconcentration used by the Spaniards in Cuba, which included moving people into towns, carrying out indiscriminate attacks beyond the perimeters, and burning crops and villages (see American Voices, pages 694 and 695).

Atrocities became commonplace on both sides. The American forces specialized in the "water cure"—forcing water into a person's stomach and then pounding it out—to make captured guerrillas talk. In more than three years of warfare 4,200 Americans and many thousands of Filipinos died. The fighting ended in 1902, and Judge William Howard Taft, who had been appointed governor in 1901, set up a civilian government. He intended to make the Philippines a model of American road building and sanitary engineering.

McKinley's convincing victory over William Jennings Bryan in the 1900 election, although by no means a referendum on American expansionism, at least suggested popular satisfaction with America's overseas adventure. Yet a strong undercurrent of misgivings was evident. Americans had not anticipated the brutal methods needed to subdue the Filipino guerrillas. "We are destroying these islanders by the thousands, their villages and cities," protested the philosopher William James. "No life shall you have, we say, except as a gift from our philanthropy after your unconditional surrender to our will. . . . Could there be any more damning indictment of that whole bloated ideal termed 'modern civilization'?" And when the fighting ended, it was not apparent just what the United States had achieved. The

Emilio Aguinaldo

At the start of the war with Spain, U.S. military leaders brought the Filipino patriot Aguinaldo back from Singapore because they thought he would stir up a popular uprising that would help defeat the Spaniards. Aguinaldo came because he thought the Americans favored an independent Philippines. These differing intentions—it has remained a matter of dispute what assurances Aguinaldo received—were the root cause of the Filipino insurrection that proved far costlier in American and Filipino lives than the war with Spain that had preceded it.

Fighting the Filipinos

The United States went to war against Spain in 1898 partly out of sympathy with the Cuban struggle for independence. Yet the United States found it necessary to use the same brutal tactics to put down the Filipino struggle for independence that the Spaniards had used against the Cubans. Here the Twentieth Kansas Volunteers march through the burning village of Caloocan.

Major General Arthur MacArthur

Subduing the Filipinos—the Ideal

In 1902 MacArthur, the commanding general of U.S. forces in the Philippines, appeared before a Senate committee investigating conditions there. In his presentation he expressed a widely held view of the necessity—and desirability—of American rule.

At the time I returned to Manila [May 1900] to assume the supreme command it seemed to me that we had been committed to a position by process of spontaneous evolution. . . . [O]ur permanent occupation of the islands was simply one of the necessary consequences in logical sequence of our great prosperity. . . . Our conception of right, justice, freedom, and personal liberty was the precious fruit of centuries of strife; that we had inherited much in these respects from our ancestors, and in our own behalf have added much to the happiness of the world, and as beneficiaries of the past and as the instruments of future progressive social development we must regard ourselves simply as the custodians of imperishable ideas held in trust for the general benefit of mankind. In other words, I felt that we had attained a moral and intellectual height from which we were bound to proclaim to all as the occasion arose the true message of humanity as embodied in the principles of our own institutions. . . .

To my mind the archipelago is a fertile soil upon which to plant republicanism. . . . We are planting the best traditions, the best characteristics of Americanism in such a way that they never can be removed from that soil. That in itself seems to me a most inspiring thought. It encouraged me during all my efforts in those islands, even when conditions seemed most disappointing, when the people themselves, not appreciating precisely what the remote consequences of our efforts were going to be, mistrusted us; but that fact was always before me—that going down deep into that fertile soil were the imperishable ideas of Americanism.

Second Thoughts about American Empire

After the shouting was over and the United States had its empire, doubts began to creep in, as is evident in this *Puck* cover in celebration of July 4, 1904. There is the American eagle in all its glory, but with wings spreading far out to the Philippines in one direction and to Puerto Rico in the other, grumbling: "Gee, but this is an awful stretch!"

adventure, wrote Roosevelt's attorney general, "has cost us a great deal of money; and any benefits which have resulted from it to this country are, as yet, imperceptible to the naked eye."

There were, moreover, disturbing constitutional issues that needed to be resolved. Did the Constitution extend to the acquired territories? Did their inhabitants automatically become citizens? In 1901 the Supreme Court ruled negatively on both questions; these were matters for Congress to decide. The special commission appointed by McKinley recommended ultimate independence after an indefinite period of U.S. rule, during which time the Filipinos would be prepared for self-government. In 1916 the passage of the Jones Act formally committed the United States to granting Philippine independence but set no date.

The ugly business in the Philippines rubbed off some of the moralizing gloss but left undeflected the global aspirations driving the United States. In a few years the United States had acquired the makings of a strategic overseas empire: Hawaii, Puerto Rico, Guam, the Philippines, and finally, in 1900, several of the Samoan islands that had been jointly administered with Germany and Britain. The United States, the legal scholar John Bassett Moore remarked in 1899, had moved "from a position of comparative freedom from entanglements into a position of what is commonly called a world power."

Robert P. Hughes and Richard T. O'Brien

Subduing the Filipinos—the Realities

Brigadier General Hughes offered the Senate Committee on the Philippines a different picture of the implanting of American ideals in Filipino soil.

Sen. Rawlins . . . [In] burning towns, what would you do? Would the entire town be destroyed by fire or would only offending portions of the town be burned?

Gen. Hughes: I do not know that we have ever had a case of burning what you would call a town in this country, but probably a barrio or a sitio; probably half a dozen houses, native shacks, where the insurrectos would go in and be concealed, and if they caught a detachment passing they would kill some of them.

Sen. Rawlins: What did I understand you to say would be the consequences of that?

Gen. Hughes: They usually burned the village.

Sen. Rawlins: All the houses in the village?

Gen. Hughes: Yes, every one of them.

Sen. Rawlins: What would become of the inhabitants?

Gen. Hughes: That was their lookout.
. . .

Sen. Rawlins: If these shacks were of no consequence what was the utility of their destruction?

Gen. Hughes: The destruction was as a punishment. They permitted these people to come in there and conceal themselves and they gave no sign. It is always—

Sen. Rawlins: The punishment in that case would fall, not upon the men, who could go elsewhere, but mainly upon the women and little children.

Gen. Hughes: The women and children are part of the family, and where you wish to inflict punishment you can punish the man probably worse in that way than in any other.

Sen. Rawlins: But is that within the ordinary rules of civilized warfare? . . .

Gen. Hughes: These people are not civilized.

Richard T. O'Brien, of M Company, 26th Infantry Volunteers, U.S. Army, gave this account to the Senate Committee.

[How] the order started and who gave it I don't know, but the town was fired on. I saw an old fellow come to the door, and he looked out: he got a shot in the abdomen and fell to his knees and turned around and died. . . .

After that two old men came out, hand in hand. I should think they were over 50 years old, probably between 50 and 70 years old. They had a white flag. They were shot down. At the other end of the town we heard screams, and there was a woman there; she was burned up, and in her arms was a baby, and on the floor was another child. The baby was at her breast, the one in her arms, and this child on the floor was, I should judge, about 3 years of age. They were burned. Whether she was demoralized or driven insane I don't know. She stayed in the house.

Source: U.S. Senate, Committee on the Philippines, *Hearings*, 57th Congress, 1st Session (1902).

Onto the World Stage

From the standpoint of Europeans, the flexing of America's muscles against Spain caused a certain amount of consternation. The assault on an ancient, if decayed, European state seemed to many government leaders the work of a country that was, in the words of the French envoy to Washington, "ignorant, brutal, and quite capable of destroying the complicated European structure." At the instigation of Kaiser Wilhelm II of Germany, the major powers of Europe had tried before war broke out to intercede on Spain's behalf—but only tentatively, because no one was looking for trouble with the Americans. President McKinley had listened politely to the representations of their envoys on April 6, 1898, and had then, dismissively, proceeded with his war.

The decisive outcome confirmed what the Europeans already suspected. After Dewey's naval victory the semiofficial French paper *Le Temps* observed that "what passes before our eyes is the appearance of a new power of the first order." And in a long editorial the London *Times* concluded: "This war must . . . effect a profound change in the whole attitude and policy of the United States. In the future America will play a part in the general affairs of the world such as she has never played before."

A Power among Powers

The politician who most ardently agreed with the London *Times*'s vision of America's future was the man who, with the assassination of William McKinley, became president on September 14, 1901, Theodore Roosevelt. As we have seen, Roosevelt had needed to feel his way on the domestic front, only gradually formulating his progressive program. Roosevelt harbored no such uncertainty about foreign affairs. He was an avid student of the subject, widely traveled abroad and acquainted with many of the European leaders. He had no doubt about how the United States should act now that it was a Great Power.

It was important, first of all, to uphold the country's honor in the community of nations. "I am not hostile to any European power in the abstract," Roosevelt once wrote. "I am simply American first and last, and therefore hostile to any power which wrongs us." Nor should the country ever shrink from righteous battle. "All the great masterful races have been fighting races," Roosevelt declared. Nothing would be worse for the United States, already too commercial for his aristocratic taste, than "slothful and ignoble peace." But when he spoke of war, Roosevelt had in mind actions by the "civilized" nations against "backward peoples" (such as the Filipinos, whose struggle for freedom was being subdued when he entered the White House). Roosevelt felt "it incumbent on all civilized and orderly powers to insist on the proper policing of the world." That was why he sympathized with European imperialism and how he justified American dominance over the Caribbean states.

As for the "civilized and orderly" policemen of the world, however, the worst thing that could happen was for them to fall to fighting among themselves. Roosevelt had an acute sense of the fragility of the world balance of power and was prescient about the chances—in this he was truly exceptional among Americans—of a catastrophic world war. He believed in an American responsibility for helping to maintain the balance of power and recognized that conducting foreign policy to that end would be his most demanding task.

Anglo-American Amity. After the Spanish-American War the European powers had been uncertain about how to deal with the victor. Germany toyed briefly with the notion of an American alliance, but only Great Britain had a clear view of what it wanted from the United States. In the late nineteenth century Britain's position in Europe had steadily worsened. It was being challenged industrially and militarily by a unified Germany. Clashing expansionist ambitions in North Africa and across Asia soured Britain's relations with France

and Russia. And there was general European hostility toward British imperial policy in South Africa, a policy that resulted in the Boer War against the independent-minded Dutch settlers at the end of the 1890s. In its growing isolation Britain turned to the United States. This explains why Britain had bowed to American demands in the Venezuela dispute of 1895. From that time onward, after a century of cool relations (or worse) with its former colonies, Britain strove consistently for a *rapprochement* (literally, a "coming together") with the United States.

In the Hay-Pauncefote Agreement of 1901 Britain gave up its treaty rights to joint participation in any Central American canal project, clearing the way for a canal exclusively under U.S. control. And two years later the last of the vexing U.S.–Canadian border disputes, this one involving British Columbia and Alaska, was settled, again to American satisfaction. The lone British member of the U.S.–Canadian tribunal cast the deciding vote awarding to the United States the Pacific inlets and ports that provided the only convenient access to the Klondike goldfields of the Canadian Yukon.

No formal alliance was forthcoming, but Anglo-American friendship had been placed on such a firm basis that, beginning in 1901, the British admiralty designed its war plans on the assumption of a friendly U.S. Navy. The assumption was that America was "a kindred state with whom we shall never have a parricidal war." Roosevelt heartily agreed: "England and the United States, beyond any other two powers, should be friendly." In his unflagging efforts to maintain a global balance of power, the cornerstone of Roosevelt's policy was the British relationship.

The Big Stick. Among nations, however, what counted was strength, not merely goodwill. Roosevelt wanted "to make all foreign powers understand that when we have adopted a line of policy we have adopted it definitely, and with the intention of backing it up with deeds as well as words." In Roosevelt's famous words: "Speak softly and carry a big stick." By a "big stick" he meant above all naval power.

Under Roosevelt, the battleship program went on apace. By 1904 the U.S. Navy stood fifth in the world, and by 1907 it was second. Roosevelt was a friend of Captain Mahan and a close student of his geopolitical writings. Mahan's program called for a big navy and strategic bases and, as a final step, a canal across Central America. Indeed, the Spanish-American War had demonstrated that strategic need in the most graphic way: the entire country had waited breathlessly as the battleship *Oregon* had sped for sixty days from the Pacific around the tip of South America to join the final action against the Spanish fleet in Cuba.

The Panama Canal. A canal was at the top of Roosevelt's agenda. With the surrender by Britain of its treaty right to a joint canal enterprise in 1901, Roosevelt proceeded to more troublesome matters. For $40 million, the United States purchased from the New Panama Canal Company the assets of de Lesseps's earlier project. Panama was a province of Colombia, so the Roosevelt administration entered into negotiations with Colombia to lease the strip of land through which the canal would run. The Colombian legislature voted down the proposed treaty, partly because the company's rights would soon expire and the sale to the United States could then be negotiated on terms more favorable to Colombia. Furious over what seemed to him a breach of faith, Roosevelt contemplated outright seizure of Panama but settled on a more devious solution.

The key intermediary in the sale of the de Lesseps assets, an engineer named Philippe Bunau-Varilla, let Roosevelt know that an independence movement was brewing in Panama. The United States in turn informed Bunau-Varilla that American ships were steaming toward Panama. The idea was that the Americans would provide cover for the expected uprising. There was a mix-up when the cruiser *Nashville* arrived at Colon, however, and the American commander failed to prevent 400 Colombian troops from disembarking at that small Atlantic port on November 3. Using their wits, the conspirators managed to keep those troops from proceeding to Panama City, and the bloodless revolution against Colombian rule went off on schedule. On November 7 the United States recognized Panama. Less than two weeks later, with Bunau-Varilla serving as the representative of the new republic, Panama signed a treaty that granted the United States a perpetually re-

The Panama Canal
The Canal Zone was acquired through devious means from which Americans could take little pride (and which led in 1978 to the Senate's decision to restore the property to Panama). But the building of the Panama Canal itself was a triumph of American ingenuity and drive. Dr. William C. Gorgas cleaned out the malarial mosquitoes that had earlier stymied the French. Under Colonel George W. Goethals, the U.S. Army overcame formidable obstacles in a mighty feat of engineering. This photograph shows the massive effort under way in December 1904 to excavate the Culebra Cut so that oceangoing ships would be able to pass through.

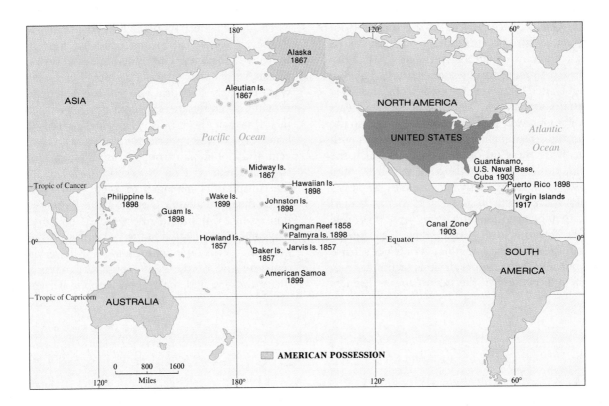

MAP 22.2

The American Empire

In 1890 Alfred T. Mahan wrote that the United States should regard the oceans as "a great highway" across which America would carry on world trade. That was precisely what resulted from the empire the United States acquired after the Spanish-American War. The Caribbean possessions, the strategically located Pacific islands, and, in 1903, the Panama Canal Zone gave the United States commercial and naval access to a wider world.

newable lease on a canal zone. These machinations were a dirty business, but they got Roosevelt what he wanted.

Roosevelt never regretted the victimization of Colombia, although the United States, as a kind of conscience money, paid Colombia $25 million in 1922. Building the canal was one of the heroic engineering feats of the century, involving a swamp-clearing project to rid the area of malaria and yellow fever, the construction of a series of great locks, and the excavation of 240 million cubic yards of earth. It took the U.S. Army Corps of Engineers eight years to finish the huge project. When it opened in 1914, the Panama Canal gave the United States a commanding commercial and strategic position in the Western Hemisphere (see Map 22.2).

Policeman of the Caribbean. Next came the task of making the Caribbean basin secure. The countries there, said Secretary of State Elihu Root, had been placed "in the front yard of the United States" by the

Panama Canal. Therefore, as Roosevelt put it, they had to "behave themselves."

In the case of Cuba, this was readily managed in the settlement that followed the Spanish-American War. Before the United States withdrew from Cuba in 1902, it reorganized Cuban finances and concluded a swamp-clearing program that eliminated yellow fever, a disease that had ravaged Cuba for many years (and had killed probably 4,000 of the occupying U.S. troops). As a condition for gaining independence, Cuba was required to include in its constitution a proviso called the Platt amendment, which gave the United States the right to intervene if Cuban independence was threatened or if Cuba failed to maintain internal order. Cuba also granted the United States a lease on Guantanamo Bay, where the U.S. Navy built a large base.

Roosevelt believed that instability in the Caribbean invited the intervention of European powers. For example, Britain and Germany blockaded Venezuela in 1902–1903 for failing to meet its debt payments. In

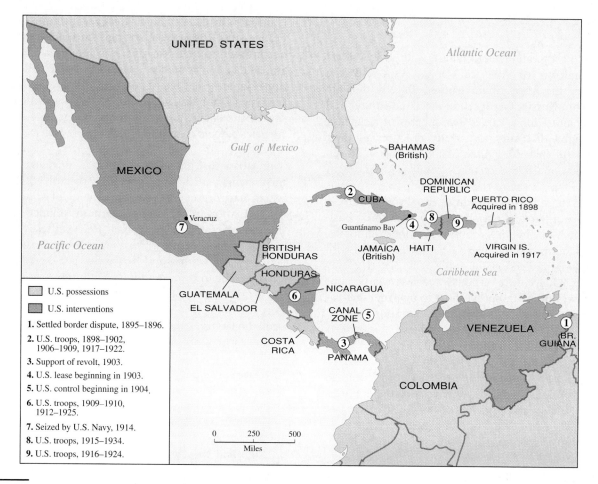

MAP 22.3

Policeman of the Caribbean

After the Spanish-American War the United States vigorously asserted its interest in the affairs of its neighbors to the south. As the record of interventions shows, the United States truly became the "policeman" of the Caribbean.

1904 Roosevelt announced that the United States would act as "policeman" of the region, stepping in "however reluctantly, in flagrant cases . . . of wrong doing or impotence."

This policy became known as the Roosevelt Corollary to the Monroe Doctrine. It transformed what had been a broad principle of opposition to European expansionist ambitions in Latin America into an unrestricted American right to regulate Caribbean affairs. The Roosevelt Corollary was not a treaty with other states; it was a unilateral declaration sanctioned only by American power and national interest.

Under the Roosevelt Corollary the United States intervened regularly in the internal affairs of Caribbean states. In 1905 American authorities took over the customs and debt management of the Dominican Republic; similar financial supervision was imposed on Nicaragua

in 1911 and Haiti in 1916. When internal order broke down, the United States did not hesitate to send in the Marines. Cuba was occupied in 1906, Nicaragua in 1909, and Haiti and the Dominican Republic in later years (see Map. 22.3).

Roosevelt's thinking was primarily strategic; his successor, William Howard Taft, took a more commercial view. American investments in the Caribbean region had grown dramatically after 1900. The United Fruit Company owned about 160,000 acres in Central America by 1913, and U.S. investments in Cuban sugar plantations quadrupled in fifteen years. Taft quickly intervened when disorder threatened American property. But he also regarded business investment as a force for stability in underdeveloped areas. Taft spoke for Dollar Diplomacy—the aggressive coupling of American diplomatic and economic interests abroad.

The Open Door

In the Far East, commercial interests had always stood at the forefront of American policy, especially the prospect of the huge China market. But by the late 1890s Japan, Russia, Germany, France, and Britain had all moved into China, carved out spheres of influence, and instituted discriminatory trade practices in their zones. Fearful that the United States was being frozen out of China, in 1899 Secretary of State John Hay sent an "Open Door" note to the occupying powers: he was attempting to establish the right of equal trade access—an Open Door—for all nations that wanted to do business in China. Even with its control over the Philippines, the United States was in a weak position compared with the occupying powers on the scene. The best that Hay was able to achieve were responses that were ambiguous and highly conditional, but he chose to interpret them as an acceptance of the American Open Door position.

When a secret society of Chinese nationalists launched the Boxer Rebellion in 1900, the United States sent 5,000 troops from the Philippines and joined the multinational campaign to raise the siege of the foreign legations in Peking (Beijing). America took the opportunity to assert a second principle of the Open Door: that China would be preserved as a "territorial and administrative entity." As long as the legal fiction of an independent China survived, so would American claims to equal access to the China market.

With a network of bases stretching across the Pacific, American power could now be projected into Asia. But here the United States faced formidable rivals. The European powers had acceded to American claims to preeminence in the Caribbean, including the Roosevelt Corollary. In the Far East, however, Britain, Germany, France, and Russia were strongly entrenched and were not inclined to defer to American interests. The United States also confronted a strategically placed Asian nation—Japan—that had its own vital interests. Although the Open Door was important to Roosevelt, he quickly saw in the Pacific a more intricate game that called on America to help maintain a balance of power.

The Japanese Challenge. Japan had unveiled its military strength in the Sino-Japanese War of 1894–1895, which had begun the dismemberment of China. With the formation of the Anglo-Japanese Alliance in 1902, the strategic advantage in East Asia shifted to Japan, emboldening it to confront Russia over their rival claims in Manchuria and Korea. In 1904, provoked by Russian demands for a military withdrawal from northern Korea, Japan suddenly attacked the tsar's fleet at Port Arthur, Russia's leased port in China. In a series of brilliant victories the Japanese demolished the Russian military forces in Asia. Roosevelt, eager to restore some semblance of a balance of power, mediated a settlement of the Russo-Japanese War at Portsmouth, New Hampshire, in 1905. Japan emerged as the predominant power in East Asia.

Dismissive of other Asian nations, Roosevelt admired the Japanese—"a wonderful and civilized people . . . entitled to stand in absolute equality with all the other peoples of the civilized world." He conceded that Japan had "a paramount interest in what surrounds the Yellow Sea, just as the United States has a paramount interest in what surrounds the Caribbean." But American strategic and commercial interests in the Pacific had to be accommodated. In exchange for Japanese accep-

The Japanese in California

The Japanese who flocked into California from 1890 onward made a mighty contribution to the state's agriculture, and through tireless labor many of them became independent and highly productive farmers. But the prejudice against them was unrelenting, and when San Francisco's school board sought to segregate Japanese children in 1906, an international incident occurred. President Roosevelt got the segregation order rescinded, and Japan voluntarily agreed to limit emigration to the United States. Despite this so-called gentlemen's agreement, a festering wound had been opened in the relations between the two countries.

tance of American sovereignty over the Philippines, the United States approved of Japan's protectorate over Korea in 1905 and raised no objection when that became full sovereignty six years later. However, a surge of anti-Asian feeling in California complicated Roosevelt's efforts. In 1906 San Francisco's school board placed all Asian students in a segregated school, infuriating Japan. The "gentlemen's agreement" of 1907, in which Japan agreed to restrict immigration to the United States, smoothed matters over, but the periodic resurgence of racism in California led to continuing tensions with the Japanese.

Roosevelt meanwhile moved to balance Japan's military power by increasing American naval strength in the Pacific. American battleships visited Japan in 1908 and then made a global tour in an impressive display of sea power. Late that year, near the end of his administration, Roosevelt achieved a formal accommodation with Japan. The Root-Takahira Agreement confirmed the status quo in the Pacific as well as the principles of free oceanic commerce and equal trade opportunity in China.

However, William Howard Taft entered the White House in 1909 convinced that the United States had been shortchanged. An exponent of Dollar Diplomacy, Taft pressed for a larger role for American bankers and investors in the Far East, especially in railroad construction going on in China. Taft hoped that American capital would counterbalance Japanese power and pave the way for increased commercial opportunities. When the Chinese Revolution of 1911 toppled the ruling Manchu dynasty, Taft supported the Chinese Nationalists as a counterforce to the Japanese. The United States thus entered a long-term rivalry with Japan that would end in war thirty years later.

The triumphant thrust across the Pacific lost some of its luster. The United States had become embroiled in a distant struggle that promised many future liabilities but little of the fabulous profits that had lured Americans to Asia. It was a chastening experience for an emerging world power.

Woodrow Wilson and Mexico

When Woodrow Wilson became president in 1913, he was bent on reform in American foreign policy no less than in domestic politics. Taft's Dollar Diplomacy seemed to Wilson to be an extension abroad of the arrogant business practices that he and other progressives were trying to curb at home. Wilson did not really differ with his predecessors on the importance of economic development overseas. He applauded the "tides of commerce" that would arise from the Panama Canal. But he opposed a commercial diplomacy that bullied weaker

countries into inequitable financial relationships and gave undue advantage to American business. It seemed to Wilson "a very perilous thing to determine the foreign policy of a nation in terms of material interest."

Within two weeks of taking office Wilson demonstrated what he had in mind. American banks had joined an international consortium to provide a loan to China. When the investment banker J. P. Morgan sought his approval, Wilson refused on the grounds that the terms of the loan threatened the independence of the Chinese government. The plan "was obnoxious to the principles upon which the government of our people rests."

The United States, Wilson insisted, should conduct its foreign policy in conformity with its democratic principles. He intended to foster the "development of constitutional liberty in the world" and above all to extend it to the nation's neighbors in Latin America. In a major policy speech in October 1913 he promised those nations that the United States would "never again seek one additional foot of territory by conquest." The president said he would strive to advance "human rights, national integrity, and opportunity" in Latin America. To do otherwise would make "ourselves untrue to our own traditions." Guided by such a moral policy, future generations would arrive at "those great heights where there shines unobstructed the light of the justice of God."

The Mexican Intervention. Mexico became the primary object of Wilson's ministrations. A cycle of revolutions had begun there in 1910. The long dictatorship of Porfirio Diaz was overthrown by Francisco Madero, who spoke much as Wilson did about liberty and constitutionalism. But before Madero could get very far with his reforms, he was deposed and murdered in February 1913 by one of his generals, Victoriano Huerta. Other powers quickly recognized Huerta's provisional government, but the United States had not acted when Wilson entered the White House the next month.

Wilson abhorred Huerta; he called his coup a "usurpation" and Huerta a murderer. Wilson pledged "to force him out." The United States denied recognition to Huerta's government, although that act contradicted America's long-standing tradition of granting quick recognition to new governments. Wilson also subjected Mexico to other pressures, including the threatened use of force. By intervening in this way, Wilson insisted, "we act in the interest of Mexico alone. . . . We are seeking to counsel Mexico for its own good." Wilson meant that he intended to put the Mexican Revolution back on the constitutional path started by Madero. Wilson was not deterred by the fact that American business interests, with enormous investments in Mexico, favored Huerta. On the contrary, that seemed to make him more determined to get Huerta out.

Carranza

Venustiano Carranza (1859–1920), the son of a landowner, was a provincial political figure who turned revolutionary when the dictator Diaz intervened in his election for the governorship of his native state of Coahuila in 1910. Carranza was crucial in bringing the Mexican Revolution to fruition, but he proved to be only a transitional figure because, as an old-fashioned liberal, he opposed the statist direction the revolution took. Before his term as first elected president ended in 1920, he was overthrown and killed in an ambush.

The emergence of armed opposition to Huerta in northern Mexico under Venustiano Carranza strengthened Wilson's hand. Carranza's Constitutionalist movement, as it became known, gave Wilson some grounds for denying recognition to Huerta, whose government did not fully control the country. More important, Carranza signified to Wilson the vitality of the reformist politics that he wanted to foster in Mexico.

But the Constitutionalists were ardent nationalists. They had no desire for American intervention in Mexican affairs. Carranza angrily rebuffed Wilson's efforts to bring about elections through a compromise between the rebels and the Mexican government. He also vowed to resist by force any intrusion of U.S. troops in his country. All he wanted from Wilson, Carranza asserted, was recognition of the Constitutionalists' belligerent status so that they could purchase arms in the United States. In exchange for vague promises to respect property rights and "fair" foreign concessions, Carranza finally got his way in 1914. American weapons began to flow to his troops.

The American contribution to the Constitutionalists' cause went well beyond selling them arms. For one thing, Wilson isolated Huerta diplomatically. Huerta's crucial support came from the British, who wanted to ensure a steady flow of Mexican oil for their fleet. Under intense pressure from Washington, the British withdrew recognition from Huerta in late 1913. In return, the United States became the guarantor of British property interests in Mexico.

When it became clear that neither the loss of British support nor the supplying of Carranza would turn the tide against Huerta, the United States threw its own forces into the game. Using the pretext of a minor insult to the U.S. Navy at Tampico, Wilson ordered the occupation of the major port of Veracruz on April 21, 1914. This action cost 19 American and 126 Mexican lives. At that point the Huerta regime began to crumble. Carranza nevertheless condemned the United States for intervening, and his forces came close to engaging the Americans. When he entered Mexico City in triumph in August 1914, Carranza had some cause to thank the Yankees. But if any sense of gratitude existed, it was overshadowed by the anti-Americanism inspired by Wilson's insensitivity to Mexican pride and revolutionary zeal.

This sad chapter in Mexican-American relations had a chastening effect on Wilson. It revealed to him the difficulties of acting on, or even living up to, well-meant ideals amid the confusion of war, revolution, and clashing national interests. Indeed, there were even more egregious examples on which he might have drawn: despite his anti-imperialist pronouncements, Wilson acted just as his predecessors had by sending in the U.S. Marines when law and order broke down in Haiti in 1915 and in the Dominican Republic in 1916.

The Gathering Storm in Europe

In the meantime, Europe had begun to drift toward a great world war. There were two main sources of tension. One derived from the deadly rivalry between Germany, the new military and economic superpower of Europe, and the European states threatened by its might—above all France, which had been humiliated in the Franco-Prussian War of 1870 and forced to cede the Alsace-Lorraine provinces to Germany. The second danger zone was the Balkans, where the Ottoman Empire was disintegrating and where, in the midst of explosive ethnic rivalries, Austria-Hungary and Russia were maneuvering for dominance. On the basis of these conflicts an alliance system had emerged, with Germany, Austria-Hungary, and Italy (the Triple Alliance) on one side and France and Russia (the Dual Alliance) on the other.

The tensions in Europe were, to some degree, released by European imperial adventures, especially by France in Africa and by Russia in Asia. These activities placed France and Russia in opposition to imperial Britain, effectively excluding Britain from the European alliance system. Fearful of Germany, however, Britain in 1904 composed its differences with France, and the two countries reached a friendly understanding, or *entente*. When Britain came to a similar understanding with Russia in 1907, the basis was laid for the Triple Entente. A deadly confrontation between two great European power blocs became possible.

In these European quarrels Americans had no obvious stake or any inclination, in the words of a cautionary Senate resolution, "to depart from the traditional American foreign policy which forbids participation . . . [in] political questions which are entirely European in scope." But on becoming president, Theodore Roosevelt had taken a lively interest in European affairs, and he was eager, as the head of a Great Power, to make a contribution to the cause of peace there. In 1905 he got his chance.

The Anglo-French entente of the previous year had been based partly on an agreement arranging spheres of influence in North Africa: the Sudan was conceded to Britain, and Morocco to France. Now Germany suddenly challenged France over Morocco. It was a disastrous move, contravening Germany's self-interest in keeping France's attention diverted from Europe by its colonial involvements overseas. Instead, the Morocco issue brought France into conflict with Germany and produced a great European crisis. Kaiser Wilhelm turned to Roosevelt for help. Finding in an obscure commercial treaty with Morocco the basis for American involvement, Roosevelt persuaded France to participate in an international conference, which was held in January 1906 at Algeciras, Spain. With U.S. diplomats playing a key role, the crisis was defused: Germany got a few token concessions, but France's dominance over Morocco was sustained.

Algeciras marked, in actuality, an ominous turning point in which the power blocs that would become locked in battle in 1914 first squared off against one another. But at the time it looked like a diplomatic triumph, and Roosevelt's secretary of state, Elihu Root, boasted of America's success in "preserv[ing] world peace because of the power of our detachment."

Root's words prefigured how the United States would define its role among the Great Powers: it would be the apostle of peace, distinguished by its "detachment," its lack of selfish interests in European affairs. But opposing this internationalist impulse was the tenacious grip of America's traditional isolationism.

The Peace Movement. Enthusiasm ran high in America for the international peace movement that had been launched by the Hague Peace Conference of 1899. The Permanent Court of Arbitration that had been created by the Hague conference offered new hope for the peaceful settlement of international disputes. Both the Roosevelt and the Taft administrations negotiated arbitration treaties with other countries that pledged to submit their disputes to the Hague Court, only to see the treaties emasculated by a Senate unwilling to permit the nation's sovereignty to be compromised in any significant way. Nor was there any sequel to Roosevelt's initiative at Algeciras. It had been coolly received in the Senate and by the nation's press. Roosevelt's successor, William Howard Taft, was not inclined to transgress the doctrine of nonentanglement.

When Woodrow Wilson became president, he chose William Jennings Bryan to be his secretary of state. Bryan was a great apostle of world peace and devoted himself to negotiating a series of "cooling off" treaties with other countries—so called because the parties agreed to wait for one year while the disputed issues were submitted to a conciliation process. These bilateral agreements were admirable, but they were irrelevant to the explosive power politics of Europe. As tensions there reached the breaking point in 1914, the United States remained effectively on the sidelines.

Yet at Algeciras Roosevelt had rightly seen what the future would demand of America. So did the French writer Andre Tardieu, who remarked in 1908:

> The United States is . . . a world power. . . . Its power creates for it . . . a duty—to pronounce upon all those questions that hitherto have been arranged by agreement only among European powers. These powers themselves, at critical times, turn toward the United States, anxious to know its opinion. . . . The United States intervenes thus in the affairs of the universe. . . . It is seated at the table where the great game is played, and it cannot leave it.

Summary

In 1877 the United States was, by any economic or population measure, already a great power. But America's orientation was inward-looking. The lax conduct of its foreign policy—and the neglect of its naval power—reflected the absence of significant overseas concerns. America's rapid economic development, however, began to force the country to look outward, in particular because of the felt need for outlets for its surplus products. By the early 1890s a new strategic outlook had taken hold, best expressed in the writings of Alfred T. Mahan, that called for a battleship navy, an interoceanic canal, and overseas bases from which American naval power could be projected to ensure access to markets in Latin America and Asia. Accompanying this new expansionism were legitimating ideas drawn from Social Darwinism, Anglo-Saxon racism, and America's earlier tradition of Manifest Destiny.

With the Spanish-American War, an opportunity for acting on these imperialist impulses presented itself. On the one hand, America's traditional antiexpansionism was briefly silenced; on the other hand, swift victory enabled the United States to seize from Spain the key possessions it wanted. In taking the Philippines, however, the United States overstepped the bounds of the kind of colonialism palatable to the country—overseas bases, not the rule of alien populations. The result was a resurgence of anti-imperialist sentiment that was deepened by Filipino resistance to annexation. Even so, the McKinley administration realized the strategic goals it had set, and the United States entered the twentieth century poised to fulfill its destiny as a Great Power.

In Europe the immediate consequences were few. Only in its *rapprochement* with Britain and in Roosevelt's involvement in the Moroccan crisis did the United States begin to depart from its traditional policy of avoiding European entanglements. Regarding its regional interests in the Caribbean and Asia, however, the United States moved much more decisively, building the Panama Canal, asserting its dominance over the nearby states, and pressing for the Open Door in China. When Woodrow Wilson became president, he tried to bring the conduct of America's foreign policy into closer conformity with the nation's political ideals, only to have the limitations of that departure driven home by his intervention in the Mexican Revolution. That lesson, however, did not stay Wilson's hand when a great world war engulfed Europe in 1914.

TIMELINE

1875	Treaty brings Hawaii within U.S. orbit
1876	United States achieves favorable balance of trade
1881	Secretary of State James G. Blaine inaugurates Pan-Americanism
1889	Conflict with Germany in Samoa President Harrison begins rebuilding U.S. Navy
1890	Alfred Thayer Mahan publishes *The Influence of Seapower upon History*
1893	Annexation of Hawaii fails Frederick Jackson Turner's "The Significance of the Frontier in American History" Panic of 1893 ushers in economic depression (until 1897)
1894	Sino-Japanese War begins breakup of China into spheres of influence
1895	Venezuela crisis Cuban civil war
1898	Outbreak of Spanish-American War Hawaii annexed Anti-imperialist movement launched
1899	Treaty of Paris Guerrilla war in the Philippines Open Door policy in China
1901	Theodore Roosevelt becomes president; diplomacy of the "big stick" Hay-Pauncefote Agreement
1902	U.S. withdraws from Cuba; Platt amendment gives U.S. right of intervention
1903	U.S. recognizes Panama and receives grant of Canal Zone
1904	Roosevelt Corollary
1905	U.S. mediates Franco-German crisis over Morocco at Algeciras
1907	Gentlemen's Agreement with Japan
1908	Root-Takahira Agreement
1909	Taft becomes president; Dollar Diplomacy
1913	Wilson asserts new principles for American diplomacy Intervention in the Mexican Revolution
1914	Panama Canal opens World War I begins

★   ★   ★

BIBLIOGRAPHY

Two useful surveys of late nineteenth-century diplomatic history are Foster R. Dulles, *Prelude to World Power, 1865–1900* (1965), and Charles S. Campbell, *The Transformation of American Foreign Relations, 1865–1900* (1976). Invaluable as an historiographical guide is Robert L. Beisner, *From the Old Diplomacy to the New, 1865–1900* (2d ed., 1986).

The Roots of Expansionism

Standard works on the preexpansionist era are David M. Pletcher, *The Awkward Years: American Foreign Relations under Garfield and Arthur* (1963), and Milton Plesur, *America's Outward Thrust: Approaches to American Foreign Affairs, 1865–1890* (1971). Walter LaFeber's highly influential *The New Empire, 1860–1898* (1963) places economic interest—especially the need for overseas markets—at the center of scholarly debate over the sources of American expansionism. On American business overseas the definitive work is Myra Wilkins, *The Emergence of the Multinational Enterprise: American Business Abroad from the Colonial Era to 1914* (1970). Other important books dealing with aspects of American expansionism are David Healy, *U.S. Expansionism: The Imperialist Urge in the 1890s* (1970); Robert Seager, *Alfred Thayer Mahan* (1977); Michael Hunt, *Ideology and U.S. Foreign Policy* ((1987); and Kenneth J. Hagan, *This People's Navy: The Making of American Seapower* (1991).

An American Empire

On the war with Spain, see John Offner, *An Unwanted War: The Diplomacy of the United States and Spain over Cuba, 1895–1898* (1988); David S. Trask, *The War with Spain in 1898* (1981); Frank Freidel, *A Splendid Little War* (1958); and Lewis Gould, *The Spanish-American War and President McKinley* (1982), which emphasizes McKinley's strong leadership. Ernest R. May, *Imperial Democracy: The Emergence of America as a Great Power* (1961), exemplifies the earlier view that McKinley was a weak figure who was driven to war by jingoistic pressures. On the Philippines, see Richard E. Welch, *Response to Imperialism: The United States and the Philippine-American War, 1898–1903* (1979), and, for the subsequent history, Peter Stanley, *A Nation in the Making: The Philippines and the United States, 1899–1921* (1974). Robert L. Beisner, *Twelve against Empire: The Anti-Imperialists, 1898–1900* (1968) remains the best book on that subject.

Onto the World Stage

On the European context a useful introduction can be found in the early chapters of Felix Gilbert, *The End of the European Era, 1890 to the Present* (4th ed., 1991). For a stimulating interpretation see L. C. B. Seaman, *From Vienna to Versailles* (1955). On American relations with Britain the standard work is Bradford Perkins, *The Great Rapprochement: England and the United States, 1895–1914* (1968). On Roosevelt's diplomacy the starting point remains Howard K. Beale, *Theodore Roosevelt and the Rise of America to World Power (1956)*. There are keen insights into the diplomatic views of both Roosevelt and Wilson in John Milton Cooper, *The Warrior and the Priest* (1983). On the thrust into the Caribbean, see Walter LaFeber, *The Panama Canal* (1979); Richard Lael, *Arrogant Diplomacy: U.S. Policy toward Colombia, 1903–1922* (1987); David Healy, *Drive to Hegemony: The United States in the Caribbean, 1898–1917* (1888); and Thomas D. Schoonover, *The United States in Central America, 1860–1911* (1991). America's Asian involvements are treated in Thomas J. McCormick, *China Market: America's Quest for Informal Empire, 1893–1901* (1967); Michael H. Hunt, *The Making of a Special Relationship: The United States and China to 1914* (1983); and Akira Iriye, *Pacific Estrangement: Japanese and American Expansion, 1897–1911* (1972). On the Mexican involvement see John S. D. Eisenhower, *Intervention! The United States and the Mexican Revolution* (1993). There is a lively and critical analysis of Wilson's misguided policies in Robert E. Quirk, *An Affair of Honor: Woodrow Wilson and the Occupation of Veracruz* (1962). The revolution as experienced by the Mexicans is brilliantly depicted in John Womack, *Zapata and the Mexican Revolution* (1968).

The Modern State and Society

1914–1945

By 1914 industrialization, economic expansion abroad, and the growth of a vibrant urban culture had laid the foundations for a distinctly *modern* American society. By 1945, after having fought two world wars and weathering a dozen years of economic depression, the edifice of the new society was largely complete.

First, an essential building block of modern American society was a strong national state. This state came late and haltingly to America compared with the industrialized countries in Western Europe. Wary of a permanent concentration of government power in Washington, policy makers quickly dismantled the centralized wartime bureaucracies in 1919. During the 1920s the Harding and Coolidge administrations embraced a philosophy of business-government partnership, believing that unrestricted corporate capitalism would provide for the welfare of the American people. It took the Great Depression, with its uncounted business failures and unprecedented levels of unemployment, to overthrow that long-cherished idea. Franklin D. Roosevelt's New Deal dramatically expanded federal responsibility for the economy and the welfare of ordinary citizens. An even greater expansion of the state resulted from the massive mobilization necessitated by America's entry into World War II. Unlike the experience after World War I, the new state apparatus remained in place when the war ended.

The second defining feature of modern American society was established when the United States was slowly and somewhat reluctantly drawn into the position of world leadership that it still occupies. In 1918 American troops helped provide the margin of victory for the Allies in World War I, and President Wilson helped shape the treaties that ended the war. The United States was not prepared to embrace Wilson's internationalist vision and refused to join the League of Nations, but America's dominant economic position guaranteed an active role in world affairs in the 1920s and 1930s. The globalization of America accelerated in 1941, when the nation threw all its energies into defeating Germany and Japan. The United States became the leader of the alliance that fought those nations and emerged as the dominant world power.

The third characteristic of modern America was the strength of its domestic economy. In the period between the two world wars the American industrial economy was the most productive in the world. American businesses successfully competed in world markets, and American financial institutions played the leading role in international economic affairs. Large-scale corporate organizations replaced smaller family-run businesses. The automobile industry symbolized the ascendancy of mass-production techniques. Many workers shared in the general prosperity but also bore the brunt of economic downturns. These economic uncertainties fueled the dramatic growth of the labor movement in the 1930s.

The fourth step toward modernity was taken when American society was transformed by the great wave of European immigration and the movement from farms to cities. The growth of metropolitan areas gave the nation an increasingly urban tone, and geographical mobility broke down regional differences. Many old-stock white Americans viewed these processes with alarm; in 1924 nativists succeeded in all but eliminating immigration except from within the Western Hemisphere. But internal migration continued to change the face of America as African-Americans moved north to take factory jobs and Dust Bowl farmers moved to the Far West to find better lives.

The fifth defining feature of modern America was the emergence of a mass culture. Americans were drawn into a web of interlocking cultural experiences. Advertising and the new entertainment media—the movies, radio, and magazines—disseminated the values of consumerism. Not even the Great Depression could divert Americans from their desire for leisure, self-fulfillment, and consumer goods. The emphasis on consumption and a quest for a rising standard of living would define the American experience for the rest of the twentieth century.

Despite the forces combining to centralize power and nationalize American culture, modern America has been marked by diversity. The lives of ordinary Americans have been shaped by whether they live in cities or rural areas and whether they are white or nonwhite, male or female, rich or poor, young or old. Describing the centralizing tendencies in modern American life while connecting them to the ongoing diversity of social experience offers clues to the complexity of America's history in the 1914–1945 period and beyond.

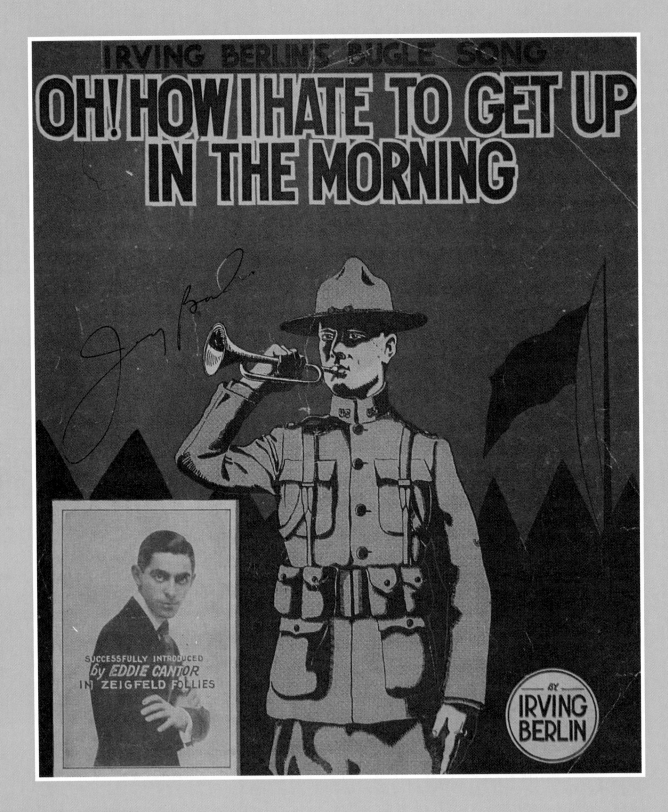

America and the War Effort

Irving Berlin's 1918 sheet music captured the ambivalence surrounding American participation in World War I: soldiers were proud to serve, but it was still hard to get up in the morning.

CHAPTER 23

War and the American State

1914–1920

★　　　★　　　★

"It would be the irony of fate if my administration had to deal chiefly with foreign affairs," Woodrow Wilson told a friend early in his first term. But the United States was no longer just a regional power—it was seated at the table of the "great game" of international politics. When war broke out in Europe in August 1914, Wilson had to play his hand. For more than two years he tried to be an honest broker for the two sides. Only when Germany's resumption of unrestricted submarine attacks threatened American lives and shipping did he reluctantly ask Congress for a declaration of war.

The American decision to enter the conflict in 1917 confirmed one of the most important shifts of power in the twentieth century. The pre–World War I world had been dominated by Europe; the postwar world was increasingly dominated by the United States. America would have emerged as the principal world power eventually because of its economic strength, but World War I hastened the process. The historian Akira Iriye calls this broad transformation the "globalization" of America— how the United States increasingly became "involved in security, economic, and cultural affairs in all parts of the world." This process, which is usually thought to begin with World War II and its aftermath, actually started in 1917.

Once the war was under way, Wilson led the country with the same idealism he had brought to domestic concerns during the Progressive Era (see Chapter 21). In the first major U.S. intervention in Great Power politics, Wilson aimed for a new international order based on democratic ideals.

Despite Wilson's rhetoric, the United States was not ready to wage a modern war in 1917. New federal bureaucracies had to be created to coordinate the efforts of business, labor, and agriculture, a process that hastened the emergence of a national administrative state. War

meant new opportunities for women and for blacks and other ethnic minorities. It also meant new divisions among Americans and new hatreds, first of Germans and Austrians and then of "Bolshevik" Reds. When the war ended, the United States was forced to confront the deep class, racial, and ethnic divisions that had surfaced during wartime mobilization.

The Great War, 1914–1918

When war erupted in August 1914, most Americans saw no reason to get involved in a struggle among Europe's imperialistic powers. No vital American interests were at stake; indeed the United States had good relationships with both sides. But a combination of factors—economic interests, violations of neutral rights, cultural ties with Great Britain and France, and German miscalculations—drew the United States into the war on the Allied side in 1917.

War in Europe

Almost from the moment France, Russia, and Britain formed the Triple Entente in 1907 to counter the Triple Alliance of Germany, Austria-Hungary, and Italy (see Chapter 22), European leaders began to prepare for what they saw as an inevitable conflict. The spark that ignited war came in Europe's perennial tinderbox, the Balkans. Most of the Balkans, including Bosnia, Herze-

govina, and Serbia, had been part of the Turkish Ottoman Empire since the sixteenth century. As the Ottoman Empire slowly disintegrated during the nineteenth century, Austria-Hungary and Russia competed for power and influence in the Balkans. Austria's seizure of the provinces of Bosnia and Herzegovina in 1908 enraged Russia and its client, the independent state of Serbia, which had hoped to form a greater South Slavic state. Serbian terrorists recruited Bosnians to agitate against Austrian rule, and on June 28, 1914, one of them assassinated Franz Ferdinand, the heir to the Austro-Hungarian throne, and his wife in the Bosnian town of Sarajevo.

After the assassination the complex European system of alliances that had for years maintained a fragile peace pulled all the major powers into war. Austria-Hungary blamed Serbia for the assassination and demanded concessions. The Serbs did meet most of the demands and asked for arbitration of the rest. However, this was not enough for Austria, which, assured of support from Germany, declared war on Serbia on July 28. Russia, which had a secret treaty with Serbia, began preparations for war. Germany in turn declared war on Russia and Russia's ally, France. Acting on its Schlieffen Plan, which was designed to eliminate one enemy at a time (that is, overrun France before Russia could mobilize), Germany invaded neutral Belgium as a prelude to conquering France. The brutality of the invasion and Britain's commitment to Belgian neutrality prompted Great Britain to declare war on Germany on August 4. Two days later Russia and Austria-Hungary formally entered the conflict.

The Landscape of War
World War I devastated the countryside: this was the battleground at Ypres in 1915. The carnage of trench warfare also scarred the soldiers who served in these surreal settings, causing the "gas neurosis," "burial-alive neurosis," and "soldiers' heart"—all symptoms of shell shock.

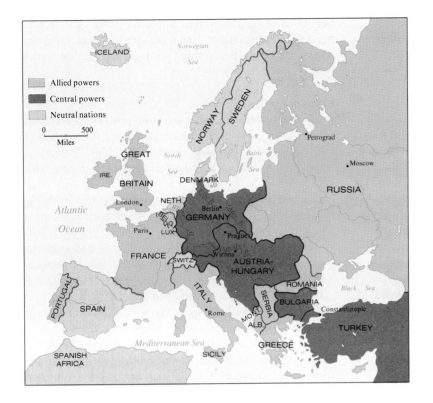

MAP 23.1

Europe at the Start of World War I
In early August 1914 a complex set of interlocking alliances drew the major European powers into war. At first the United States avoided the conflict. Not until April 1917 did America enter the war on the Allied side.

The combatants were thus divided into two rival blocs. The Allied Powers consisted of Great Britain, France, Japan, Russia, and in 1915 Italy. They were pitted against the Central Powers: Germany, Austria-Hungary, and Turkey, joined by Bulgaria in 1915 (see Map 23.1). Because of the alliance system, the conflict spread to parts of the world far beyond Europe, making this a truly global war. The Austrians and Germans faced the Russians on the Eastern Front; Turkey squared off against Russian and British troops in the Middle East and Mesopotamia; and the British, French, and Japanese seized German territories in Africa, China, and the South Pacific. The worldwide scope of the conflict and the huge casualties resulting from campaigns such as Gallipoli in the Dardanelles caused it to be known as the Great War, or later, World War I. It was also the first modern war in which extensive harm was done to civilian populations.

Military Technology. Since the American Civil War and the Franco-Prussian War in 1870, massive industrialization and an escalating arms race among the Great Powers had transformed the technology of war. Every soldier in World War I carried a long-range, high-velocity rifle that could hit a target at 1,000 yards, a vast improvement over the 300-yard range of the rifle-musket used in the American Civil War. Significantly, the mass production of rifles in Europe relied on the adoption of technology developed in Connecticut factories. Another innovation, the machine gun, also had American roots. Its Maine-born inventor, Hiram Maxim, had moved to

Great Britain in the 1880s, heeding a friend's advice: "If you want to make your fortune, invent something which will allow those fool Europeans to kill each other more quickly."

The concentrated fire of rifles and machine guns gave a tremendous advantage to troops in defensive positions. For four bloody years, between 1914 and 1918, the Allies and the Central Powers faced each other on the Western Front, a narrow swath of territory in Belgium and northern France crisscrossed by 25,000 miles of heavily fortified trenches, enough to circle the globe. (Barbed wire, invented to fence the western range, became a devastating weapon of war when coiled above the trenches.) Trench warfare produced unprecedented numbers of casualties. If one side tried to break the stalemate by venturing into the "no-man's-land" between the trenches, its soldiers were mowed down by artillery fire or poison gas, first used by the Germans at Ypres in April 1915. Between February and December 1916 the French suffered 550,000 casualties and the Germans 450,000 as Germany tried to break through the French lines at Verdun. The front did not move.

Military strategists struggled to find ways to break the stalemate on the Western Front. Tanks, first used in the Battle of the Somme in the fall of 1916, proved effective against the machine gun and could crash through the barbed wire protecting enemy trenches, but they did not play the decisive military role that they would in World War II. Neither did airplanes, despite the dramatic advances in aviation since the Wright brothers' 12-second, 120-foot flight at Kitty Hawk,

North Carolina, in 1903. The technology of aerial bombardment was still primitive, so airplanes mainly flew photographic reconnaissance missions.

The Perils of Neutrality

Two weeks after the outbreak of war in Europe President Wilson made the American position clear. In a message widely printed in the newspapers the president called on Americans to be "neutral in fact as well as in name, impartial in thought as well as in action." Wilson wanted to keep out of war partly in order to play a larger, not a smaller, role in world affairs. The child of a Presbyterian minister, Wilson approached foreign affairs with missionary zeal. He never doubted the superiority of the Christian values he had learned as a boy or questioned the chauvinistic belief that the United States was better than the rest of the world. Only if he kept America aloof from the European quarrel, Wilson reasoned, could he impartially arbitrate—and influence—its ultimate settlement.

The nation's divided loyalties also influenced Wilson's policy. Many Americans, including Wilson, felt deep cultural ties to the Allies, especially Britain and France, yet most Catholic Irish-Americans resented the centuries-long British occupation of their home country and the cancellation of Home Rule in 1914. Also 10 million immigrants had come from Germany and Austria-Hungary, and German-Americans made up one of the largest and best established ethnic groups in the United States. Many aspects of German culture, including classical music and Germany's university system, were widely admired. It would not have been easy for Wilson to rally Americans to the Allied side in 1914.

Many Americans had no sympathy for either side. Pacifist sentiment was diffuse but broad, rooted in isolationism as well as disillusionment with America's experience in the Spanish-American War. Progressive Republicans such as Senators Robert La Follette of Wisconsin and George Norris of Nebraska vehemently opposed American participation in the European conflict. Progressive Democrats, including Secretary of State Williams Jennings Bryan, and many western and southern progressives, felt the same. Practically the entire political left, led principally by Eugene Debs and the Socialist party, condemned the war as imperialism, whereas African-American leaders such as A. Philip Randolph identified it as a conflict of the white race only. Newly formed antiwar groups, among them the American Union against Militarism and the Women's Peace Party, both founded in 1915, also mobilized popular opposition. The feminists Jane Addams and Crystal Eastman spoke out against war as an instrument of national policy. Prominent industrialists, notably Andrew Carnegie and Henry Ford, bankrolled antiwar activi-

ties. Ford spent almost half a million dollars in December 1915 to send more than a hundred men and women to Europe on a "peace ship" to negotiate an end to the war.

Conflict on the High Seas. With no stake in the territorial struggles among the European powers, the United States might well have remained neutral if the conflict had not spread to a new theater—the high seas. Here the United States initially had as many arguments with Britain as with Germany. The most troublesome issue concerned freedom of the seas and neutrality rights—the freedom to trade with nations on both sides of a conflict.

By the end of August 1914 the British had imposed a naval blockade on the Central Powers. The Allies were hoping to cut off military supplies and starve the German people into submission, but their actions also prevented neutral nations such as the United States from trading with Germany and its allies. The United States chafed at this infringement of its neutrality rights but chose to do little besides complain, largely because the spectacular increase in trade with the Allies more than made up for the lost trade with the Central Powers. American trade with Britain and France grew from $824 million in 1914 to $3.2 billion in 1916, and by 1917 U.S. bankers had lent the Allies $2.5 billion. In contrast, American trade with and loans to Germany in 1917 totaled only $29 million and $27 million, respectively.

To challenge British control of the seas, the German navy launched a devastating new weapon, the U-boat, short for *Unterseeboot* (undersea boat, or submarine). In February 1915, Germany announced a naval blockade of Great Britain: German submarines would attack any ship transporting military supplies to the British Isles. Traditional rules of naval warfare required submarine commanders to warn and search a ship before sinking it. If a submarine surfaced to do this, however, it would lose its greatest advantage—surprise—and leave itself vulnerable to attack.

Although the Germans sank an American merchant ship without warning on May 1, 1915, it was the sinking of a British luxury liner, the *Lusitania*, off the Irish coast six days later that brought the United States to the brink of war. When the *Lusitania* went down, 1,198 people died, including 128 Americans. The passenger ship, although unarmed, was carrying thousands of cases of ammunition, and an advertisement in a New York newspaper had warned passengers about the risk of attack. Newspapers called the loss of innocent civilian lives "mass murder," and the former president Theodore Roosevelt characterized the attack as "an act of piracy." The National Security League, one of the leading voices in the "preparedness" campaign, intensified its calls for increased appropriations for the armed forces and a system of universal military training.

Wilson sent a series of strongly worded notes to Germany to protest this assault on the freedom of non-belligerents to travel on the high seas, although he did not ban Americans from traveling on the ships of Germany's enemies. The *Lusitania* crisis divided Wilson's government into pro- and anti-British factions. Secretary of State William Jennings Bryan resigned in protest, unable to support Wilson's harsh criticism of Germany's violation of neutrality rights while the president remained silent about Britain's violation of American rights with its blockade.

After the sinking of the *Lusitania*, Wilson had confided to a cabinet member, "I wish with all my heart I saw a way to carry out the double wish of our people, to maintain a firm front in respect of what we demand of Germany and yet do nothing that might by any possibility involved us in war." The crisis continued until September 1915, when Germany announced that submarine commanders would not attack passenger ships without warning. (Eight months later the Germans halted, at least temporarily, attacks on merchant shipping.) For the Germans the danger of drawing the United States into the war far offset the benefits of attacking British ships. A temporary lull set into the naval war.

Throughout 1915 and 1916, Wilson tried at several points to mediate an end to the European conflict through his aide, Colonel Edward House. But House concluded that neither side was interested in serious peace negotiations. Worsening tensions with Germany in turn caused Wilson to rethink his earlier opposition to preparedness. In the fall of 1915 he decided that a half-billion dollar buildup of the army and navy was prudent and desirable, and by 1916 rearmament was well under way.

The 1916 Election. The election of 1916 did not serve as a referendum on the American stance toward the war. The Republican party passed over the prowar belligerence represented by Theodore Roosevelt in favor of Supreme Court Justice Charles Evans Hughes, a former governor of New York. The Democrats renominated Woodrow Wilson, whose campaign emphasized the progressive reform record he had accomplished during his first term (see Chapter 21). The Democrats also picked up votes with their widely circulated campaign slogan, "He kept us out of war." They won a narrow victory over a Republican party reunited after its 1912 split. Despite getting 3 million more votes than he had in 1912, Wilson defeated Hughes by only about 600,000 votes and by 277 to 254 in the electoral college. That slender margin limited Wilson's options in mobilizing the nation for war and planning the postwar peace.

Toward War. The events of early 1917 diminished Wilson's hopes of staying out of the conflict. On January 31 Germany announced the resumption of unrestricted submarine attacks, a decision dictated by the impasse of the land war. Although the Germans knew that this would almost certainly bring the United States into the war, the German general staff assured the government that its submarines could paralyze Allied shipping before the Americans joined the fighting. In response, Wilson broke off diplomatic relations with Germany on February 3.

The release of the "Zimmermann telegram" in late February 1917 also moved the country closer to war. Newspapers published an intercepted communication from Germany's foreign secretary, Arthur Zimmermann, to the German minister in Mexico City, which contained conclusive evidence of German interference in Mexican affairs. In a direct challenge to the Monroe Doctrine, Zimmermann urged Mexico to join the Central Powers in the war. In return, Germany promised to help Mexico recover "the lost territory of Texas, New

The 1916 Campaign
This campaign van sponsored by the Women's Bureau of the Democratic National Committee linked Woodrow Wilson to the themes of progressivism, prosperity, and preparedness. Note the variation on the popular slogan, "Who keeps us out of war?"

Mexico, and Arizona." When the telegram was made public on February 27, this threat to the territorial integrity of the United States jolted both Congressional and public opinion, especially in the West, where support for the war had lagged. Combined with the resumption of unrestricted submarine warfare, the telegram further inflamed anti-German sentiment.

Although the likelihood of Mexico reconquering the border states was slim, the highly volatile situation there (see Chapter 22) continued to concern American policy makers. In the final stages of the Mexican Revolution, the Constitutionalist movement led by Venustiano Carranza consolidated its power against the rebel Pancho Villa. When the United States stopped giving aid to Villa to concentrate its support behind Carranza, Villa orchestrated retaliatory raids along the border, killing sixteen U.S. citizens in January 1916 and razing the town of Columbus, New Mexico, in March. As the Mexican civil war threatened to spill over the Rio Grande into the United States, Wilson sent troops led by General John J. Pershing into Mexico to capture the elusive Villa; soon Pershing's forces resembled an army of occupation rather than troops on a punitive expedition. Strongly supported by Mexican public opinion, Carranza demanded that Pershing withdraw immediately. The two governments backed off, and U.S. troops began to leave early in 1917. The Carranza government received official recognition from Washington on March 13, 1917, less than a month before the United States entered World War I.

Declaring War. Throughout March, U-boats attacked American shipping without warning, sinking three ships on March 18 alone. On April 2, 1917, after consulting his cabinet, Wilson appeared before a special session of Congress to ask for a declaration of war. "It is a fearful thing to lead this great peaceful people into war," Wilson declared. He shared the fears of many Americans who dreaded entering a conflict that had already proved so costly—millions of Europeans killed, their landscapes and social structures destroyed. America had no selfish aims: "We desire no conquest, no dominion. We seek no indemnities for ourselves, no material compensation for the sacrifices we shall freely make. We are but one of the champions of the rights of mankind." In a memorable phrase that was intended to ennoble America's role, he decided that "the world must be made safe for democracy."

Four days later, on April 6, 1917, the United States declared war on Germany. Reflecting the divided feelings of the country as a whole, the vote was far from unanimous. Six senators and fifty members of the House voted against the action, including Representative Jeannette Rankin of Montana, the first woman elected to Congress. "I want to stand by my country," she declared, "but I cannot vote for war."

The First Woman in Congress
In 1916, Jeannette Rankin, a former suffrage organizer, became the first woman elected to Congress. Her vote against U.S. entry into World War I cost her a chance for election to the Senate in 1918. In 1940 Rankin again won election to Congress from Montana. True to her lifelong pacifism, she cast the only vote against American entry into World War II.

Over There

To native-born Americans, Europe seemed a great distance away, literally "over there," as the lyrics of George M. Cohan's popular song described it. After the declaration of war many citizens were surprised to learn that the United States planned to send troops to Europe; they had assumed that the nation's participation could be limited to military and economic aid.

In May 1917 General John J. Pershing, recently returned from the unsuccessful pursuit of Pancho Villa in Mexico, traveled to London and Paris to determine how America could best support the war effort. The answer was clear: as Marshal Joseph Joffre of France put it, "Men, men, and more men." The problem was that the United States had never maintained a large standing army in peacetime. Only about 200,000 soldiers, mostly lifetime volunteers, were on active duty in early 1917. To field a large enough fighting force to enter a global war, the government turned to conscription.

Conscription. The passage of the Selective Service Act in May 1917 demonstrated the increasing impact of the state on ordinary citizens. Unlike the resistance to the draft during the Civil War, no major riots occurred. The

selective service system worked in part because it combined central direction from Washington with local administration and civilian control and thus did not tread on the tradition of individual freedom and local autonomy. Draft registration also demonstrated the potential bureaucratic capacity of the American state. On a single day, June 5, 1917, more than 9.5 million men between the ages of twenty-one and thirty were processed for military service in their local voting precincts.

Although compliance was not universal, most male citizens went along with the draft's premise of service (a key progressive word) as a responsibility of modern citizenship. By the end of the war almost 4 million men, plus a few thousand female navy clerks and army nurses, were in uniform. Nearly 3 million men were inducted through a draft lottery; the rest volunteered. Over 300,000 men evaded the draft (they were called "slackers"), and another 4,000 were classified as conscientious objectors.

Wilson chose General Pershing to head the American Expeditionary Force (AEF), but the newly raised army did not have an immediate impact on the fighting. The new recruits had to be trained and outfitted and then wait for one of the few available transport ships to take them across the submarine-infested Atlantic. By June 1917 only 15,000 AEF troops had arrived in France.

At first the main American contribution was to secure the safety of the seas. When the United States entered the war, German submarines were sinking Allied ships at a rate of about 900,000 tons a month. The U-boats had hampered America's ability to send supplies and munitions to the Allies and threatened the transport of American troops to the European front. Adopting a plan that aimed for safety in numbers, the government began sending armed convoys across the Atlantic. The plan worked: no American soldiers were killed on the way to Europe. Allied shipping losses were cut to 400,000 tons a month by late 1917 and to 200,000 tons by April 1918.

Meanwhile, trench warfare continued its deadly grind on the Western Front. Allied commanders pleaded for American reinforcements for their units, but Pershing was reluctant to put his independent fighting unit under foreign commanders. Because the AEF was not ready as a fighting force until May 1918, the brunt of the fighting continued to fall on the French and British.

The Russian Revolution and the Collapse of the Eastern Front. On the Eastern Front the strain of fighting the Germans had exposed the weaknesses of the Russian government of Tsar Nicholas II, and a general mutiny of the troops led to the overthrow of the monarchy in March 1917. The new provisional government headed by Prince George Lvov and the socialist Alexander Kerensky, which Woodrow Wilson supported, promised democratic reforms but insisted on continuing the war. Russian workers and peasants were sick of the seemingly endless food shortages at home, sick of the horrendous casualties at the front. Conditions were ripe for a second, more sweeping, revolution.

The communist theorist and political activist Vladimir Ilych Lenin, who had been living in exile in Switzerland when the March revolution took place, saw his chance. Lenin was a follower of German political philosopher Karl Marx and anticipated that a period of "dictatorship of the proletariat" (workers) would be necessary to root out capitalism before an ideal, classless society could emerge. The Germans, hoping to promote internal strife in Russia, cannily arranged Lenin's safe passage home in a sealed railroad car. Lenin and a group of Bolshevik revolutionaries arrived in Petrograd (later renamed Leningrad and now St. Petersburg) in April 1917 and began to agitate against the provisional government. On November 6 Lenin directed a Bolshevik-led coup and quickly consolidated his control by promising "peace, land, and bread" to the long-suffering masses.

Call to Arms
To build popular support for the war effort, the government called on artists such as Howard Chandler Christy, Charles Dana Gibson, and James Montgomery Flagg. This 1917 recruiting poster by Flagg was adapted from a June 1916 cover of *Leslie's Illustrated Weekly Newspaper*. The model was the artist.

The new Bolshevik government kept the first part of its promise: Russia agreed to a cease-fire with Germany and Austria-Hungary on December 15, 1917, and signed the Treaty of Brest-Litovsk on March 3, 1918. In return for an end to hostilities, the Bolsheviks surrendered about one-third of Russia's territories, including Russian Poland, Ukraine, the Baltic provinces, and Finland. Yet instead of peace the Russian people got three more years of a devastating civil war.

Allied Victory in the West. The civil war in the new Soviet state would command the Allies' attention only after the armistice. Once hostilities with Russia ended, Germany used its full fighting force to break the stalemate on the Western Front. On March 21, 1918, the Germans launched a major offensive. By May the German army had advanced to the Marne River, within 50 miles of Paris, and attempted to subdue the city by bombardments. Allied leaders intensified their calls for American troops, and Pershing, who was under orders to keep the AEF a separate fighting unit, relented a bit to help the Allies bolster their defenses. About 60,000 American soldiers helped the French repel the Germans in the battles of Château-Thierry and Belleau Wood in May and June. During the fighting, the AEF encountered firsthand the terrible effects of poison gas (see American Voices, page 717).

American reinforcements soon began to arrive in large numbers. Fresh troops flooded the ports of Liverpool in Britain and Brest and Saint Nazaire in France— 245,000 in May 1918, 278,000 more in June, and an additional 306,000 in July. From there they worked their way slowly to the front along the clogged French transportation system. The Allied force, augmented by 85,000 American troops, brought the German offensive to a halt in mid-July. At that point a million American troops were in France, and the counteroffensive began. On July 18 the Allies, with 270,000 American troops, began a successful campaign to drive the Germans back from the Marne. Approximately 100,000 American soldiers helped the British push the Germans north of the Somme River (see Map 23.2).

In mid-September 1918 General Pershing, leading 500,000 American and 100,000 French soldiers, launched an offensive to close a hole in the Allied lines at Saint-Mihiel. After four days of heavy shelling of their positions, the Germans, who had already been preparing to evacuate the area, retreated. On September 26 Pershing launched the last major assault of the war, which pitted over a million American soldiers against vastly outnumbered and exhausted German troops. The Meuse-Argonne campaign, the main American military contribution to the fighting, allowed Pershing to confront the Germans frontally, rather than getting locked in a defensive war of attrition. This successful maneuver pushed the enemy back across the Selle River near Verdun and broke the German defenses at a cost of over 26,000 American lives.

The flood of American troops and supplies during the last six months of the war helped provide the Allied margin of victory. In many ways this contribution was emblematic of the shift in international power as Euro-

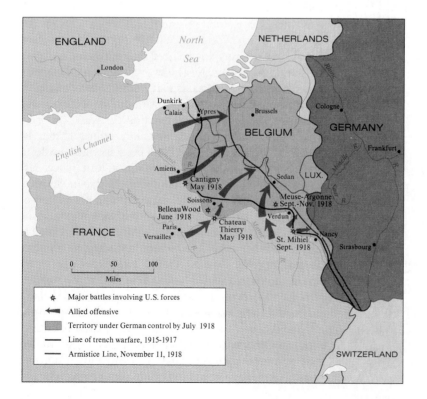

MAP 23.2

U.S. Participation on the Western Front, 1918

When American troops reached the European front in significant numbers in 1918, the Allied and Central powers had been grinding each other down in a war of attrition for almost four years. The influx of American troops and supplies broke the stalemate. Successful offensive maneuvers by the American Expeditionary Force included Belleau Wood, Château-Thierry, and the Meuse-Argonne campaign.

Frederick Pottle

Mustard Gas

Frederick Pottle volunteered for service as an enlisted man in the Medical Corps. He describes here the effects of mustard gas during the battles of Belleau Wood and Château-Thierry in June 1918.

Indeed, those dreadful mustard-gas cases were probably the most painful we had to witness in all our service. As a matter of fact, the majority were in much less serious plight than the wounded men. Mustard gas (it has nothing to with mustard) is a heavy liquid, which, though fairly volatile, will remain for some time clinging to grass and undergrowth, and will burn any flesh with which it comes in contact. It is especially adapted for use by a retreating army. By soaking down with mustard gas the area through which the pursuing American troops had to advance, the Germans made sure that a large number of the advancing force would be incapacitated. The soldier's clothing soon becomes im-

pregnated with the stuff as he brushes through the undergrowth, and the burns develop through the help of moisture. Those parts of the body subject to excessive perspiration are especially affected. The burns are extremely painful, but in general not fatal unless the gas has been inhaled, or (as with other surface burns) a third or more of the total skin area has been affected. A bad feature of mustard gas, however, is that it almost invariably produces temporary, but complete, blindness. Nothing demoralizes a man so much as the fear of losing his sight, and telling him that he will see again in a day or two generally fails to reassure him. The gas cases began to arrive at Juilly as early as June 12. Since most of them were immediately evacuable, we made temporary wards for them in the great cloisters which ran around two sides of the court in front of Wards F and G—the children's dormitories. By the sixteenth there were nearly seven hundred gassed men there, just out of the glare

of the sunny court, lying fully dressed on blanket-covered cots, some of them badly gassed in the lungs and fighting horribly for breath, which could be a little prolonged by giving them oxygen; nearly all blinded, many delirious, all crying, moaning, tossing about. For most of the patients there was nothing to do but renew frequently the wet dressings which relieved somewhat the smart of the burns, and to try to restore their lost morale. For those who had been gassed worst, nothing effectual could be done. They were spared much by being in general delirious, but it required the constant attention of several orderlies to keep some of them in bed. Later on, the hospital service was so organized that the gas cases were handled by special gas hospitals. After we left Juilly we almost never received gas victims unless they were also wounded.

Source: Frederick A. Pottle, *Stretchers: The Story of a Hospital Unit on the Western Front* (New Haven: Yale University Press, 1929), 117–118.

---

pean diplomatic and economic dominance declined and the United States emerged as a world leader. World War I ended on November 11, 1918, when German and Allied representatives signed an armistice in the railway car of Marshal Ferdinand Foch of France.

The American Fighting Force

About 2 million American soldiers were in France when the war ended. Two-thirds of them had seen at least brief action on the Western Front, but most American "doughboys" had escaped the horrors of sustained trench warfare that had sapped the morale of Allied and German troops. (The origin of the nickname "doughboy" is unclear, but may involve the buttons on the uniforms of American infantrymen, which resembled dumplings made of dough.) During the eighteen months in which the United States fought, 50,585 American servicemen were killed in action. Another 60,000 died from other causes, mainly the influenza epidemic that

swept the world in 1918–1919. These casualties were minimal compared with the 8 million soldiers lost by the Allies and the Central Powers. The French lost far more soldiers in the siege of Verdun than the United States did in the entire war.

Although individual bravery was increasingly anachronistic in modern warfare, the war generated its share of American heroes. Sergeant Alvin York single-handedly killed 25 Germans and took 132 prisoners at the battle of Châtel-Chéhéry in the Meuse-Argonne campaign. Although air power played only a minor role in the conduct of the war, it captivated the popular imagination. One of America's best known aces was the former professional race car driver Eddie Rickenbacker (see American Lives, pages 718–719). The aerial exploits of daredevil pilots, often fighting in single combat like medieval knights, provided a thrill that contrasted with the monotony of trench warfare. The popular fascination with York and Rickenbacker suggests a deep-seated need to anoint heroes in what had become an increasingly depersonalized and mechanized pursuit of war.

Summary

The outbreak of the Great War in 1914 posed a great challenge to American diplomacy. For more than two years President Wilson kept the nation out of war, attempting to use American power and prestige to mediate between the two sides. The United States finally entered the war in 1917 because of violations of its neutral rights at sea but, more broadly, because the country's foreign policy reflected the same moral concerns that animated the domestic reform movement. On April 6, 1917, Congress declared war on Germany.

American participation in the war was brief but decisive. Two million freshly recruited "doughboys" helped to turn the tide for the Allies on the Western Front in 1918. Flush with victory, Wilson sought to bring about a peace that would reflect his vision of a new world order. Yet the Versailles treaty only partially reflected the president's hopes for freedom of the seas, peaceful economic expansion, and national self-determination. His postwar plans suffered a worse blow when the Senate refused to ratify the treaty, which included American participation in the League of Nations.

As the Wilson administration put the nation on a war footing, progressive reform energies were largely diverted to the war effort. An army had to be created almost from scratch, American agriculture and manufacturing had to be federally coordinated to produce for the Allies as well as the home market, and American workers had to be recruited for war work and kept on the job. All this absorbed the energies of a new group of professional experts turned government bureaucrats. World War I thus helped create the tools of the modern bureaucratic state, which (though laid aside temporarily at the war's end) would be taken up again during the nation's worst peacetime crisis, the Great Depression.

The government tried to mobilize the minds of the American people as well but succeeded mainly in inflaming passions. Certain groups, such as woman suffragists, found success during the war. But others became targets of repression, including blacks who migrated to northern cities, labor activists, and socialists and other radicals who criticized the government. Domestic tensions erupted in race riots in many northern cities, widespread labor strikes in 1919, and in the Red Scare of 1919–1920.

TIMELINE

1914	Outbreak of war in Europe
	United States declares neutrality
1915	German submarine sinks *Lusitania*
1916	Wilson reelected
	Pershing's expedition to Mexico
1917	U.S. enters World War I
	Revenue Act passed
	Selective Service Act passed
	War Industries Board established
	Suffrage militancy
	East St. Louis race riot
	Espionage Act
	Bolshevik Revolution
	Committee on Public Information
1918	Wilson proposes Fourteen Points
	Meuse-Argonne campaign
	Eugene Debs imprisoned under Sedition Act
	Armistice ends war
	U.S. troops intervene in Soviet Union
1919	Treaty of Versailles
	Chicago race riot
	Steel strike
	Red Scare and Palmer raids; *Schenck v. United States*
	American Legion founded
	League of Nations defeated in Senate
	Eighteenth Amendment (Prohibition)
	War Industries Board disbanded
1920	Nineteenth Amendment (woman suffrage)
	"Soviet Ark" sails
1924	Woodrow Wilson dies

★   ★   ★

BIBLIOGRAPHY

Ronald Schaffer, *America in the Great War: The Rise of the War Welfare State* (1991), and David M. Kennedy, *Over Here: The First World War and American Society* (1980), provide comprehensive overviews of the period. On the links between the Progressive Era and the war, see Neil A. Wynn, *From Progressivism to Prosperity: World War I and American Society* (1986); John A. Thompson, *Reformers and War* (1987); and Robert M. Crunden, *Ministers of Reform: The Progressives' Achievement in American Civilization, 1889–1920* (1982). Ellis W. Hawley, *The Great War and the Search for a Modern Order, 1917–1933* (1979), stresses the continuities between the war years and the 1920s.

The Great War

On America's entry into World War I, see John Coogan, *The End to Neutrality* (1981); Ross Gregory, *The Origins of American Intervention in the First World War* (1971); and Thomas A. Bailey and Paul Ryan, *The Lusitania Disaster* (1975). Recent studies of Wilson include August Hecksher, *Woodrow Wilson* (1991); Kendrick Clements, *The Presidency of Woodrow Wilson* (1992); Robert Ferrell, *Woodrow Wilson and World War I* (1985); John Milton Cooper, Jr., *The Warrior and the Priest: Woodrow Wilson and Theodore Roosevelt* (1983); and Edwin Weinstein, *Woodrow Wilson: A Medical and Psychological Biography* (1981).

For American participation in the war, Russell Weigley, *The American Way of War* (1973), and Edward M. Coffman, *The War to End All Wars* (1968), provide useful introductions. They can be supplemented by Laurence Stallings, *The Doughboys: The Story of the AEF, 1917–1918* (1963), and A. E. Barbeau and Florette Henri, *The Unknown Soldiers: Black Troops in World War I* (1974). John Whiteclay Chambers II, *To Raise an Army* (1987), covers the draft. Allan Brandt, *No Magic Bullet* (1985), discusses anti–venereal disease campaigns. Paul Chapman, *Schools as Sorters* (1988), describes the intelligence-testing movement. Material on Eddie Rickenbacker and other wartime aces can be found in his *Fighting the Flying Circus* (1919) and his autobiography, *Edward Rickenbacker* (1967).

Mobilizing the Home Front

Robert D. Cuff, *The War Industries Board: Business-Government Relations during World War I* (1973), provides an excellent case study of mobilization for war. See also Stephen Skowronek, *Building a New American State: The Expansion of National Administrative Capacities, 1877–1920* (1982), and W. Elliot Brownlee, *Federal Taxation in America* (1996). Valerie Jean Conner, *The National War Labor Board* (1983), covers federal policies toward labor. Jordan Schwarz, *The Speculator* (1981), is a biography of Bernard Baruch.

Maurine Greenwald, *Women, War, and Work* (1980), and Barbara Steinson, *American Women's Activism in World War I* (1982), provide good overviews of women's wartime experiences. Anne F. Scott and Andrew Scott, *One Half the People* (1975); Eleanor Flexner, *Century of Struggle* (1959); and Christine A. Lunardini, *From Equal Suffrage to Equal Rights: Alice Paul and the National Woman's Party, 1910–1928* (1986), cover the final stages of the woman suffrage campaign. On the peace movement, see C. Roland Marchand, *The American Peace Movement and Social Reform, 1898–1918* (1973); Charles Chatfield, *For Peace and Justice: Pacifism in America, 1914–1941* (1971); and Charles DeBenedetti, *Origins of the Modern Peace Movement* (1978). Allen F. Davis, *American Heroine* (1974), is a biography of Jane Addams.

Efforts to promote national unity are covered in Stephen Vaughan, *Holding Fast the Inner Lines: Democracy, Nationalism, and the CPI* (1980); William J. Breen, *Uncle Sam at Home* (1984); and Paul L. Murphy, *World War I and the Origins of Civil Liberties* (1979). On free speech, see Richard Polenberg, *Fighting Faiths: The Abrams Case, the Supreme Court, and Free Speech* (1987), as well as Zechariah Chaffee, Jr., *Free Speech in the United States* (1941). For the experiences of Mexican-Americans, see Rodolfo Acuna, *Occupied America* (1980), and Wayne Cornelius, *Building the Cactus Curtain: Mexican Migration and U.S. Responses from Wilson to Carter* (1980).

An Unsettled Peace

On Wilson's diplomacy, see Thomas Knock, *To End All Wars: Woodrow Wilson and the Quest for a New World Order* (1992); Lloyd Ambrosius, *Woodrow Wilson and the American Diplomatic Tradition* (1987); Arthur Walworth, *Wilson and the Peacemakers* (1986); and N. Gordon Levin, Jr., *Woodrow Wilson and World Politics* (1968). For more on Versailles and the League of Nations, see Thomas Bailey, *Woodrow Wilson and the Great Betrayal* (1945); Ralph A. Stone, *The Irreconcilables: The Fight against the League of Nations* (1970); and Arno J. Mayer, *Politics and Diplomacy of Peacemaking: Containment and Counter Revolution at Versailles* (1967). See also William Widenor, *Henry Cabot Lodge and the Search for an American Foreign Policy* (1980). Anglo-American responses to revolution between 1913 and 1923 are covered in Lloyd C. Gardner, *Safe for Democracy* (1984). On American intervention in Russia, see George F. Kennan, *The Decision to Intervene* (1958); John L. Gaddis, *Russia, The Soviet Union, and the United States* (1978); and Peter Filene, *Americans and the Soviet Experiment, 1917–1933* (1967). Ronald Steel's fine biography, *Walter Lippmann and the American Century* (1980), offers another view of the Versailles conference.

Robert K. Murray, *The Red Scare* (1955), summarizes the antiradicalism of the postwar period. See also John Higham, *Strangers in the Land* (1955); Burl Noggle, *Into the Twenties* (1974); and William D. Miller, *Pretty Bubbles in the Air: America in 1919* (1991). David Brody, *Labor in Crisis* (1965), describes the steel strike of 1919; for a more general overview, see David Montgomery, *The Fall of the House of Labor: The Workplace, the State, and American Labor Activism, 1865–1925* (1987). On race relations, see Joe William Trotter, Jr., ed., *The Great Migration in Historical Perspective* (1991); James R. Grossman, *Land of Hope: Chicago, Black Southerners, and the Great Migration* (1989); William M. Tuttle, Jr., *Race Riot: Chicago in the Red Summer of 1919* (1970); Robert V. Haynes, *A Night of Violence: The Houston Riot of 1917* (1976); and Elliot M. Rudwick, *Race Riot at East St. Louis, July 2, 1917* (1964). For an introduction to the Sacco and Vanzetti case, see Louis Joughin and Edmund Morgan, *The Legacy of Sacco and Vanzetti* (1948), and Roberta Strauss Feuerlicht, *Justice Crucified* (1977).

Advertising Modernity

Artist Maxfield Parrish's calendars for General Electric,
such as this 1920 "Prometheus" for Mazda lamps, gave him
widespread visibility and indicate the power of modern
advertising.

Modern Times

The 1920s

★ ★ ★

In 1924 the sociologists Robert Lynd and Helen Merrell Lynd arrived in Muncie, Indiana, to study the life of a small American city. They observed how the citizens of Middletown (the fictional name they gave the city, which they chose for its middle-of-the-road quality) made a living, maintained a home, educated their young, practiced religion, organized community activities, and spent their leisure time. As the Lynds' fieldwork proceeded, they were struck by how much had changed over the past thirty-five years—the actual lifetime of a middle-aged Middletown resident—and decided to contrast the Muncie of the 1890s with the Muncie of the 1920s. When *Middletown* was published in 1929, this "study in modern American culture" became an unexpected best seller.

Many of the characteristics of modern America were in place by the end of World War I. Participation in the war had made the United States a major player in the world economy; the foundations of large-scale corporate enterprise and a modern state were firmly established. The 1920s, however, rather than World War I, were the watershed in the development of a mass national culture. The Protestant work ethic and the old values of self-denial and frugality began to give way to a fascination with consumption, leisure, and self-realization that is the essence of modern times. In economic organization, political outlook, and cultural values, the 1920s have more in common with the United States today than with the industrializing America of the late nineteenth century.

The prosperity and economic innovations of the 1920s gave the United States the highest standard of living in the world, although not every American benefited from the new way of life. Most farmers, urban blacks, and recent immigrants could not afford many of the new mass-produced consumer goods; instead, they sampled them selectively, adapting them to their traditional

life-styles. Other Americans found that the convenience of consumer goods and the new emphasis on materialism conflicted with religious and cultural mandates to work hard and live frugally. But despite ambivalence toward these changes, the patterns of consumption and leisure that appeared during the "new era" of the 1920s quickly became part of American life.

The Business-Government Partnership of the 1920s

The business-government partnership accelerated by World War I continued to expand on an informal basis throughout the 1920s. The success of the economy from 1922 to 1929 seemed to confirm its ability to regulate itself with minimal government intervention. Gone, or at least submerged, was the reform impulse of the Progressive Era. Business leaders were no longer villains but respected public figures. President Warren Harding captured the prevailing political mood when he offered the American public "not heroics but healing, not nostrums but normalcy."

The Economy

America's transition from a wartime to a peacetime economy was not smooth. In the immediate postwar years the worst problem was runaway inflation. Prices jumped by a third in 1919, accompanied by feverish economic activity. The postwar boom was less an indication of solid economic growth than a reflection of

consumers' desire to buy before prices went higher. In an attempt to decrease the postwar federal debt ($20 billion in 1920), the Wilson administration sharply reduced federal expenditures to stop the inflationary spiral. The Federal Reserve System tightened credit because its expansive money policies had encouraged people to borrow and spend and thus had pushed prices even higher. The new policy resulted in a recession, demonstrating that the government had much to learn about achieving economic stability.

The recession of 1920–1921 was the sharpest short-term downturn the United States had ever faced. Unemployment reached 10 percent. Foreign trade dropped by almost half, from $13.5 billion in 1920 to less than $7 billion in 1921, as European nations resumed production after the disruptions of war. Prices fell so dramatically—more than 20 percent—that much of the inflation of World War I was wiped out. The recession lasted only a short time. By 1922 the economy had started to recover, and the recovery continued, interrupted only by brief, mild downturns, until 1929. Unemployment hovered around 3 or 4 percent, and inflation was negligible. Between 1922 and 1929 the gross national product grew from $74.1 billion to $103.1 billion, approximately 40 percent. Per capita income rose from $641 in 1921 to $847 in 1929. Soon the federal government was recording a budget surplus. This economic expansion provided the backdrop for the partnership between business and government that flourished in the 1920s.

An abundance of new consumer products, particularly the automobile, stimulated recovery and prosperity in the 1920s. Manufacturing output expanded 64 percent, with industries churning out automobiles, appliances, chemicals, electricity, radios, aircraft, and movies. Behind the growth lay new management and

The Assembly Line
The success of the automobile industry contributed significantly to the prosperity of the 1920s, and mass production made automobiles affordable for ordinary citizens, not just the well-to-do. This photograph suggests the aptness of the phrase "rolling off the assembly line." By 1929 there were more than 23 million cars on the road.

mass-production techniques, which resulted in a 40 percent increase in workers' productivity. The value of new construction increased from $6 billion in 1921 to $12 billion in 1927. The demand for goods and services kept unemployment low in most industries throughout the 1920s, but the expanded demand was not strong enough to produce inflation.

One sector of the economy that never fully recovered from the 1920 recession was agriculture. During the inflationary period 1914–1920 farmers had borrowed heavily to finance mortgages and buy farm equipment as they expanded wartime production in response to government incentives, increased demand, and rising prices. When the war ended and European countries resumed agricultural production, the world market was glutted. The price of wheat dropped 40 percent as the government withdrew wartime price supports. Corn prices fell 32 percent and hog prices 50 percent, causing farm income to plunge.

Since American farmers produced mainly for the world market, one key to agricultural recovery was to prevent worldwide surpluses from further depressing domestic prices. Farmers turned to the political system for help. The McNary-Haugen bill, a far-reaching attempt to create permanent federal price supports for agricultural products, used the idea of a "fair exchange value" to guarantee that farmers would recover their production costs no matter what the price was on the world market. A 1924 bill restricting that principle to grain failed in Congress, where the eastern business wing of the Republican party and President Coolidge opposed it as special-interest legislation for agriculture. When midwestern supporters of the bill added cotton, rice, and tobacco to win southern farm support, the measure passed, only to be vetoed by Coolidge in 1927 and again in 1928. The farmers' share of the national income plummeted from 16 percent in 1919 to 8.8 percent at the end of the 1920s.

Besides agriculture, certain "sick industries," such as coal and textiles, missed out on the prosperity of the 1920s. These industries had expanded in response to World War I demands only to face overcapacity or unprofitability and grew sluggishly, if at all, in the 1920s. This underside of economic life foreshadowed the depression of the 1930s.

The Republican Ascendancy

Except for two terms under Woodrow Wilson, the national government had been controlled by the Republican party since 1896. With Wilson's progressive coalition floundering in 1918, the Republicans were in a position to regain the presidency in the upcoming election. In 1920 the Democrats passed over the ailing Wilson in favor of Governor James M. Cox of Ohio, with Assistant Secre-

tary of the Navy Franklin D. Roosevelt as the candidate for vice-president. The Democratic platform called for ratification of U.S. participation in the League of Nations and a continuation of Wilsonian progressivism whereas the Republicans, led by Warren G. Harding and Calvin Coolidge, promised a return to "normalcy," which meant a strong probusiness stance and conservative cultural values. Harding and Coolidge won in a landslide, marking the beginning of a new Republican era that would last until 1932.

Hardly a towering national figure, Harding had built an uninspiring record in Ohio politics before winning election to the U.S. Senate in 1914. With a Republican victory almost a certainty in 1920, party leaders wanted a candidate they could dominate. Genial, loyal, and mediocre, "Uncle Warren" filled the bill.

Harding knew his limitations and tried to assemble a strong cabinet to help him guide the government. Charles Evans Hughes, a former presidential candidate and Supreme Court justice, headed the State Department. As secretary of agriculture, Henry C. Wallace set up conferences between farmers and government agencies such as the Bureau of Agricultural Economics. The financier Andrew W. Mellon ran the Treasury Department, engineering a massive tax cut to reduce the federal surplus. Most of the benefits went to the wealthy, fulfilling Mellon's goal of freeing money for private investment and undercutting the progressive Revenue Acts of 1916, 1917, and 1918.

By far the most active member of the Harding administration was Secretary of Commerce Herbert Hoover, who had successfully headed the Food Administration during the war. Hoover embodied the business-government cooperation of the 1920s, continuing the pattern of state building that had begun during World War I. Unlike Mellon, who wanted to minimize government intervention, Hoover supported expansion of the federal government in what he called the spirit of "associationalism." Voluntary cooperation in the public interest, Hoover maintained, would stabilize prices and assure economic stability in volatile sectors of the economy such as agriculture, construction, and mining. He used persuasion, educational conferences, and fact-finding commissions to accomplish his goals.

Hoover actively promoted trade associations as the key to "associated individualism." There were about 2,000 of these instruments of voluntary cooperation, representing almost every major industry and commodity. Trade associations were supposed to give stability to the economy through conferences, conventions, publicity, lobbying, and trade practice controls. Trade associations used statistics gathered by the Commerce Department and by private groups such as the National Bureau of Economic Research in corporate planning, allocating investments, and controlling markets. Trade conferences organized by the Commerce Department provided a

forum for the exchange of information. The Republican-dominated Federal Trade Commission ignored antitrust laws that forbade such anticompetitive practices. In this it followed the lead of the Supreme Court, which in 1920 had dismissed the long-pending antitrust case against the United States Steel Corporation, ruling that largeness in business was not against the law as long as some competition remained.

Unfortunately, not all of Harding's appointees were as capable as Hoover. Harding was an honest man, but some of his political associates had low ethical standards. When Harding died suddenly in San Francisco in August 1923, evidence of widespread fraud and corruption in his administration had just started to come to light. Charles Forbes, the director of the newly established (1921) Veterans Administration, appeared to be an efficient administrator, until evidence surfaced that he had stolen or squandered $250 million in federal funds. An even more damaging scandal concerned the government's secret leasing of oil reserves in Teapot Dome, Wyoming, and Elk Hills, California, to private companies without competitive bidding. Secretary of the Interior Albert Fall eventually was convicted of taking $300,000 in bribes and became the first cabinet officer in American history to serve a prison sentence.

After Harding's death Vice-President Calvin Coolidge moved into the White House. In contrast to Harding's political cronyism and outgoing style, Coolidge personified Vermont rectitude. As vice-president "Silent Cal" often sat through official functions without uttering a word. A dinner partner once challenged him by saying, "Mr. Coolidge, I've made a rather sizable bet with my friends that I can get you to speak three words this evening." Responded Coolidge icily, "You lose." Like Harding, Coolidge backed business and believed in limited government; he was said to perform all his presidential duties in four hours a day. Coolidge's image of unimpeachable morality reassured voters in the wake of the Harding scandals, and he soon announced that he would run for president in 1924.

The 1924 Election. The Democratic party found it difficult to mount an effective challenge to its more popular and better-financed rival, whose strength came chiefly from the native-born Protestant middle class, augmented by small businesspeople, skilled workers, farmers, northern black voters, and wealthy industrialists. Democrats drew their support mainly from the South and from northern urban political machines such as Tammany Hall in New York, but the interests of those two constituencies often collided. Until the Democrats could build an effective national organization to rival that of the Republicans, they would remain a minority party.

When the Democrats gathered that year in the sweltering July heat of New York City, they were more divided than usual. Their convention, the first to be broadcast live on national radio, lasted seventeen days, prompting the humorist Will Rogers to say, "This thing has got to come to an end. New York invited you people here as guests, not to live." The convention became hopelessly deadlocked between Governor Alfred E. Smith of New York, who had the support of northern urban politicians, and William G. McAdoo of California, Wilson's secretary of the treasury (and son-in-law), the western and southern choice. After 103 ballots the delegates compromised on John W. Davis, a Wall Street lawyer who had served as a West Virginia congressman and an ambassador to Great Britain. To attract rural voters the Democrats chose as their vice-presidential candidate Governor Charles W. Bryan of Nebraska, the brother of William Jennings Bryan.

The 1924 campaign also featured a third-party challenge by Senator Robert M. La Follette of Wisconsin, who ran on the Progressive party ticket. His candidacy mobilized reformers and labor leaders as well as disgruntled farmers. The Progressive party platform called for nationalization of railroads, public ownership of utilities, and the right of Congress to overrule Supreme Court decisions. It also favored the election of the president directly by the voters rather than by the electoral college.

The Republicans won an impressive victory, with Coolidge receiving 15.7 million popular votes to 8.4 million for Davis and winning decisively in the electoral college. Despite La Follette's vigorous campaign, he could not draw many midwestern farm leaders away from the Republican party; his labor support also proved soft. La Follette got almost 5 million popular votes, but carried only Wisconsin in the electoral college.

Perhaps the most significant aspect of the 1924 election was the low voter turnout. Only 52 percent of the electorate voted, compared with the more than 70

Leisure and Politics
Calvin Coolidge was from Vermont but that did not keep Wisconsin boosters from using his campaign slogan to promote tourism in their state.

Women Write the Children's Bureau

The Children's Bureau in the Department of Labor was in charge of administering the Sheppard-Towner Act from 1921 to 1929. In addition to setting up clinics and providing prenatal care, the staff answered letters from anxious mothers, such as the two excerpted here.

Dear Doctor Sherbon:
You can not imagine how much I have enjoyed the Course. As soon as I received it I lay down and never stopped until I read it through. It is splendid, and if every woman could follow each lesson to the letter there would be less suffering. But how are we going to convince our families that such care is necessary? Of course the children can be taught these things, but the husbands and our mothers think it is foolishness to take such care of ourselves.

Do you think it proper to explain to children where they come from and the science of life? I have told my stepson, age 18, all of these things and how he should take care of himself, and also how he should treat girls and how much suffering there was to childbirth, and I was very much criticized by some of the family.

I must close. I am taking up your valuable time and am losing much time of my own. Thank you for all the help and the good you are doing, not only for myself but others.

Dear Madam:
I took your correspondence course last winter and enjoyed it very much although I have been a mother three times and expect to be again as [I] am pregnant three months now. Maybe you have something for me or that might help me in some way, so [I] thot that I would drop you a line.

We are a poor family and live in western Kansas and [are] heavily in debt, so this ordeal is hard for me at present. But what I would like to ask you is if a poor mother can get any county or state aid. My teeth are badly in need of dental work, and [I have] no money to pay the bill and the doctor bill worries me too. The doctor we have gone to is so high I don't see how we can afford it. We owe $125 in doctor bills in another county . . . and I dread any more until back ones are paid.

Isn't there a law in Kansas that unless a confinement case is obstetrical the limit charge is $15 and if obstetrical the limit is $25? He says he charges $25 for a confinement case and $1.00 mileage which would make a total of $37 for us for doctor bill, besides a nurse or lady to nurse and do the work too. But if you know anything about such things you know that mother and babe are sadly neglected if the nurse has all the house work to do too. . . .

Does the county doctor tend to such cases and look to the community for his money? It looks like we ought to be able to do and care for such things without asking for help, but you know there are just lots and lots of mothers in my fix that just drag along and worry because they have no way of buying the most needy things at such a time and are too proud to find out if there is any way to get help. My husband thinks it's awful to get help in any way besides paying for it, but when I know he is not financially able to help, I don't see why I should suffer if there is any way to help me, as any mother or doctor knows at that time a mother needs the best of care in every way. And it's because I have always had to work too soon after childbirth that I am broken down now.

I will see what I hear from you before going into details any more. Hoping you will not think it too trifling a matter to interest you and will answer me as soon as possible. Yours truly.

Source: Molly Ladd-Taylor, *Raising a Baby the Government Way: Mothers' Letters to the Children's Bureau, 1915–1932* (New Brunswick: Rutgers University Press, 1986), 131–132, 136–138.

---

percent who had voted in presidential elections in the late nineteenth century. The nation's newly enfranchised women were not to blame, however: the long-term drop in voting by men, not apathy among women, was responsible for the decline.

Women in Politics. Instead of resting after their suffrage victory, women increased their political activism in the 1920s. Partisan women tried to break into party politics, but the Democrats and Republicans granted them only token positions on party committees. For women, political officeholding remained a "widow's game": about two-thirds of the women in Congress had been appointed to finish their late husbands' terms.

Women were more influential as lobbyists. The Women's Joint Congressional Committee, a Washington-based coalition of ten major women's organizations including the newly formed League of Women Voters and the National Consumers' League, lobbied for reform legislation. Its major accomplishment was the passage in 1921 of the Sheppard-Towner Federal Maternity and Infancy Act, the nation's first federally funded health care program. In an attempt to reduce the high rate of death associated with childbirth, Congress appropriated $1.25 million for well-baby clinics, educational programs, and visiting-nurse projects. Isolated rural women were especially grateful for this government aid, and eagerly sought information from government agencies like the Children's Bureau, which administered the program (see American Voices, above).

The Sheppard-Towner bill passed because politicians feared that if it didn't, women would vote them out of office. As one supporter noted, "If the members could have voted in the cloak room, it would have been killed." However, by the late 1920s politicians realized that women did not vote as a bloc. And other powerful lobbying groups, such as the American Medical Association, strenuously objected to the state being involved in health care at all. In 1929, Congress cut off appropriations for the program.

At mid-decade the Republicans were in an enviable position. The scandals of the Harding years were behind them, and the economy continued to be strong, supporting their policy of placing the responsibility for the national well-being in the hands of corporate capitalism. The informal business-government partnership worked—or so it seemed—until the depression.

Corporate Capitalism

The 1920s saw the triumph of the management revolution that had been reshaping American business since the late nineteenth century (see Chapter 19). Large-scale

River Rouge
Industrial photographers in the 1920s celebrated the power and raw beauty of industrial technology. Charles Sheeler's 1927 photograph shows Ford's River Rouge plant outside Detroit. But where are the workers?

corporate organizations with bureaucratic structures of authority replaced family-run businesses. Ownership was divorced from the control of daily operations, and what the eighteenth-century economist Adam Smith had called the "invisible hand" of market forces gave way to the visible hand of management. But business leaders, indeed most American citizens, remained leery of direct state intervention into the economy.

There were more mergers in the 1920s—368 in 1924 and 1,245 in 1929—than at any time since the heyday of combinations in the 1880s and 1890s. The largest number occurred in rapidly growing industries such as chemicals, electrical appliances and machinery, and automobiles. By 1930 the 200 largest corporations controlled almost half the nonbanking corporate wealth in the United States. It was rare for one corporation to monopolize an entire industry; instead, oligopolies, in which a few large producers controlled an industry, became the norm, such as in auto manufacturing, oil refining, and steelmaking.

By 1920 many industries, especially in manufacturing, had modern organizational structures. The multi-unit enterprise coordinated production and distribution through divisions organized by functions, such as sales, operations, and investment. Alfred P. Sloan, Jr., an engineer and midlevel manager at General Motors in the 1920s, refined this structure by relieving top management of the day-to-day control of production. This shift in responsibility freed management to concentrate on long-range planning while autonomous, integrated divisions met short-range production goals. General Motors' innovative structure set the pattern for large companies in the 1920s and 1930s.

Corporations greatly increased their commitment to research and development, using current earnings to create future profits. Corporate mergers were a major source of capital for this purpose. By 1927 more than a thousand corporations had set up independent research programs, among them Bell Laboratories, the research arm of the American Telephone and Telegraph Company, which was formally incorporated in 1925.

These huge modern corporate structures called for a new breed of man: the professional manager. (Women found few opportunities in the corporate hierarchy until the 1970s.) Increasingly, corporations relied on graduate schools of business, such as Wharton and Harvard, to produce managers, consultants, and executives, many of whom had engineering training. In the 1920s the chief executives at General Motors, General Electric, Singer, Du Pont, and Goodyear had all been engineering classmates at the Massachusetts Institute of Technology.

The nation's financial institutions expanded and consolidated along with its corporations. Total bank assets rose from almost $48 billion in 1919 to $72 billion in 1929, largely because of rising deposits in savings in-

stitutions and business and loan associations, along with life insurance policies and annuities. Mergers between Wall Street banks enhanced the role of New York as the financial center of the United States and the world. In 1929 almost half the nation's banking resources were controlled by 1 percent, or 250, of American banks.

Business leaders enjoyed enormous popularity and respect in the 1920s, their reputations often surpassing those of the era's lackluster politicians. Many politicians and commentators drew parallels between religious activity and business leadership. President Coolidge solemnly declared, "The man who builds a factory builds a temple. The man who works there worships there." The secularization of religion and the glorification of business reached a new height in a book called *The Man Nobody Knows* (1924) by the advertising executive Bruce Barton. The man of the title was Jesus Christ, whom Barton portrayed as the founder of modern business, writing that Christ "picked up twelve men from the bottom ranks of business and forged them into an organization that conquered the world." Barton's parable was an instant best seller.

The most respected businessman of the decade was Henry Ford, whose rise from poor farm boy to corporate giant symbolized the values of rural society and American individualism in a rapidly changing world. Ford's factories, especially the River Rouge plant in suburban Detroit, represented the triumph of mass production. Ironically, this American capitalist hero achieved great popularity in the Soviet Union. At a time when the United States and the Soviet Union had no formal diplomatic relations, Ford sold the Russians 25,000 tractors between 1920 and 1926.

Labor and Welfare Capitalism

Workers shared in the prosperity of the 1920s, although labor lagged behind business in reaping the benefits of technology. Business supported higher wages as a way to increase workers' buying power. With a shorter workweek (five full days and a half day on Saturday), many workers had more leisure time; large firms such as International Harvester offered employees two weeks of paid vacation a year. But scientific management techniques, first put forth in 1895 by Frederick W. Taylor but only widely implemented in the 1920s, reduced labor's control over the work environment.

Decisions from an extremely probusiness Supreme Court led by Chief Justice William Howard Taft also affected workers adversely. For example, in the 1925 *Coronado Coal Company v. United Mine Workers* the Court ruled that a striking union could be prosecuted for restraint of trade. It also struck down federal legislation regulating child labor in *Bailey v. Drexel Furniture*

Company (1922) and the minimum wage for women workers in the District of Columbia in *Adkins v. Children's Hospital* (1923).

The 1920s was also the heyday of "welfare capitalism," a system of labor relations that stressed management's responsibility for the well-being of its employees. Though tinged with paternalism, this system provided benefits to workers at a time when unemployment compensation and old-age pensions did not exist. Employee security was not, however, the primary concern of those corporate programs, which were established mainly to deter the formation of unions.

Welfare capitalism took several forms. Workers could increase their stake in the company by buying stock below the market price, though only a small minority could actually afford to do so. Some firms subsidized mortgages or contributed to employees' savings funds; others set up insurance and pension plans. Many adopted programs for consultation between management and elected representatives of the workers. These employee representation schemes, another device to avert unionization, were called the American Plan in order to establish the idea that unions were un-American. Management's long-term goals included control over the workplace, an open (nonunion) shop, and worker loyalty.

However, the system had serious disadvantages for workers, including a lack of protection against unemployment. Furthermore, welfare capitalism appeared primarily in the largest, most prosperous firms, such as General Electric and U.S. Steel, and reached only a minority of workers. Corporate profits often dictated the nature of the programs. The Proctor & Gamble Company guaranteed forty-eight weeks of employment a year to its soap-manufacturing workers because of the steady demand for soap, but workers in another division who processed vegetable oils, which were subject to sales fluctuations, received no such guarantee.

Welfare capitalism represented a form of labor relations that was squarely in keeping with the values of the 1920s. It placed the responsibility for economic welfare in the private sector rather than the public sector, avoiding the possibility of government interference in the workplace on the side of labor. It also satisfied management's desire to reverse the tide of unionization: union membership dropped from 5.1 million in 1920 to 3.6 million in 1929, about 10 percent of the nonagricultural work force. The number of strikes also fell dramatically from the level in 1919. Welfare capitalism seemed to represent the wave of the future in industrial relations.

Economic Expansion Abroad

As the domestic economy expanded, so did the nation's international position. During the 1920s the United States was the most productive country in the world,

with an enormous capacity to compete in foreign markets. Underlying this increase in international activity was a growing demand from abroad for American consumer products such as radios, telephones, automobiles, and sewing machines. The demand for U.S. capital was just as important. America's emergence as the world's largest creditor nation, a reversal of its pre–World War I status as a debtor nation, represented a dramatic shift of power in world capital markets. American investment abroad more than doubled between 1919 and 1930: by the end of the 1920s American corporations had invested $15.2 billion in foreign countries. This American capital sustained the international economic system in the 1920s.

Manufacturers led the way in foreign investment. Electric companies, including General Electric, built new plants in Latin America, China, Japan, and Australia. Ford had major facilities throughout the British Empire, and General Motors took over established automakers such as Vauxhall in England and Opel in Germany. The International Telephone and Telegraph Corporation, founded in 1920, employed 95,000 workers outside the country, more than did any other U.S. company.

Other American companies invested internationally during the 1920s to take advantage of lower production costs or procure raw materials and supplies, concentrating mainly on Latin America. The three major American meat packers—Swift, Armour, and Wilson—built plants in Argentina to capitalize on its low livestock prices. Fruit growers such as the United Fruit Company established plantations in Costa Rica, Honduras, and Guatemala. American capital ran sugar plantations in Cuba and rubber plantations in the Philippines, Sumatra, and Malaya.

American companies also invested heavily in mining and oil, especially in South America and Canada. The Anaconda Copper Corporation owned Chile's largest copper mine. Standard Oil of New Jersey led American oil companies in acquiring oil reserves in Mexico and Venezuela. (American involvement in the oil-rich Persian Gulf became significant only after World War II.)

American banks supported U.S. enterprises abroad, especially in Europe. European countries, particularly Germany, needed private American capital to finance economic recovery after World War I. Germany had to rebuild its economy and pay reparations to the Allies; Britain and France had to repay wartime loans. As late as 1930 the Allies still owed the United States $4.3 billion. American political leaders, responding to voters' disenchantment with the cost of the nation's participation in the war, rigidly demanded payment. Referring to the European nations, President Coolidge scoffed, "They hired the money, didn't they?"

European countries had trouble repaying their debts because the United States maintained high protective tariffs to keep foreign-made goods out. The Fordney-McCumber Tariff of 1922 followed the long-standing Republican policy of protectionism, and the Hawley-Smoot Tariff of 1930 took economic nationalism even further. American manufacturers favored those high tariffs because they feared that foreign competition would reduce their profits. But the difficulty of selling goods in the United States made it harder for European nations to pay off their debts in dollars.

Concerned about debt repayment, the American banking community and many U.S. corporations with European investments opposed excessively high tariffs and urged modification of the debt structure. They recognized that a rapidly recovering Europe and a freer trade environment would help American business, whereas a weak European economy might undermine long-term loans and investments.

In 1924, at the prodding of the United States, France, Great Britain, and Germany joined with the United States in a plan to improve and promote European financial stability. The Dawes Plan, named for Charles G. Dawes, a Chicago banker who negotiated the agreement, offered substantial loans to Germany and a reduction in the amount of reparations owed to the Allies. But the Dawes Plan did not provide a permanent solution. The international economic system, which depended on the flow of American capital to Germany, reparations payments from Germany to the Allies, and the repayment of debts to the United States, was inherently unstable. If the flow of capital from the United States slowed or stopped, the world financial structure could collapse.

Foreign Policy in the 1920s

Foreign affairs in the interwar period are often viewed through the lens of isolationism, the view that the United States, disillusioned after World War I, willfully retreated from involvement in world affairs. But the term *isolationism* masks the active role that the United States played in world affairs both before and after the Great War. *Globalization* is a more accurate term. Economic expansion into new markets was a major component of the prosperity of the 1920s, and the United States ardently sought a peaceful and stable world order to facilitate American investments in Latin American, European, and Pacific Rim markets. This expansion abroad, which was a continuation of Taft's policy of Dollar Diplomacy (see Chapter 22), was warmly abetted by the appropriate branches of the federal government, such as the State and Commerce departments.

In the 1920s the United States continued its quest for peaceful ways to dominate the Western Hemisphere economically and diplomatically but retreated slightly from military intervention in Latin America. The United States withdrew troops from the Dominican Republic in 1924 but maintained military forces in Nicaragua almost continuously from 1912 to 1933. American

troops also occupied Haiti from 1915 to 1934. Relations with Mexico remained tense as a legacy of U.S. intervention during the Mexican Revolution.

There was little popular or political support, however, for entangling diplomatic commitments to allies, European or otherwise. The United States never joined the League of Nations or the Court of International Justice (the World Court). International cooperation had to come through other forums.

The Washington Conference and the Kellogg-Briand Pact. The 1921 Washington Naval Arms Conference represented a milestone in the history of disarmament and the fulfillment of one of Woodrow Wilson's goals. By placing limits on naval expansion, policy makers hoped to encourage stability in areas such as the Far East and protect the fragile postwar world economy from excessive spending on arms. A hidden agenda was to contain Japan, whose expansionist tendencies were already seen as threatening two decades before the outbreak of World War II.

Led by Secretary of State Charles Evans Hughes, the three leading naval powers—Britain, the United States, and Japan—joined other countries in agreeing to halt construction of large battleships for ten years and maintain current tonnage among Britain, the United States, Japan, Italy, and France at a ratio of 5:5:3:1.75:1.75. (This maintained parity among the big three, since the Japanese fleet operated only in the Pacific.) The conferees even agreed to scrap some existing warships, leading one commentator to exclaim that in a thirty-five-minute speech the secretary of state had sunk "more ships than all the admirals of the world have sunk in a cycle of centuries." Not until the 1980s would the world see another such concerted effort to disarm.

In a similar spirit of international cooperation, the 1928 Kellogg-Briand Peace Pact condemned militarism as a tool for advancing national interests. In 1927 the French foreign minister, Aristide Briand, had asked the United States to sign an agreement guaranteeing France's territorial integrity and outlawing war between France and the United States. Instead, Coolidge's secretary of state, Frank Kellogg, proposed a broader treaty in which participating countries would agree to "condemn recourse to war for the solution of international controversies, and renounce it as an instrument of national policy." Fifteen nations signed the pact in Paris in 1928, with forty-eight more approving it later. The Kellogg-Briand Pact was enthusiastically supported by U.S. peace groups such as the Women's International League for Peace and Freedom and the Conference on the Cause and Cure of War, and the U.S. Senate ratified it 85 to 1. Yet critics claimed that it was nothing more than an "international kiss": lacking enforcement machinery, it was only as effective as its signers made it. For many who abhorred war, however, the pact's broad moral statement was an important contribution to the maintenance of peace.

In the end, fervent hopes and pious declarations were no cure for the massive economic, political, and territorial problems that World War I had left behind. The United States vacillated, as it would in the 1930s, between wanting to play a larger role in world events and fearing that treaties and responsibilities would limit its ability to act unilaterally. Rather than criticize the diplomatic efforts of the 1920s as naive or misguided, it is better to see them as honest but ultimately inadequate efforts to find a will to peace.

A New National Culture

The 1920s represented an important watershed in the development of a mass national culture. A new emphasis on leisure, consumption, and amusement characterized the modern era, although its benefits were more accessible to the white middle class than to minorities and other disadvantaged groups. Automobiles, paved roads, the parcel post service, movies, radios, telephones, mass-circulation magazines, brand names, and chain stores linked Americans in mill towns in the southern Piedmont, rural outposts on the Oklahoma plains, western mining settlements, and ethnic enclaves on the coasts in an expanding web of national experience. In fact, with the exportation of automobiles, radios, and movies to consumers throughout the world, one can even begin to speak of the globalization of the American experience.

Consumption and Advertising

In homes across the country in the 1920s Americans sat down to a breakfast of Kellogg's corn flakes with toast prepared in a General Electric toaster. They got into a Ford Model T to go about their business, perhaps shopping at one of the chain stores, such as Safeway and A & P, which had sprung up across the country. In the evening the family gathered to listen to radio programs such as "Great Moments in History" and "True Story" or read the latest issue of the *Saturday Evening Post*, *Reader's Digest*, or *Collier's*. On weekends they might hop in the car to see the latest Charlie Chaplin film at the local movie theater. Millions of Americans now shared the same daily experiences.

The 1920s was a critical decade in the development of the American consumer society. Although not every family participated in the new life-style, consumption became a cultural ideal for most of the middle class, often providing the criterion for judging self-worth that was once supplied by character, religion, and social standing. Spending money on more and better possessions became a form of self-fulfillment, a gratification of personal needs.

Yet participation in commercial mass culture did not necessarily mean a total conversion to American middle-class values. Buying a Victrola or a radio on credit and listening to the opera singer Enrico Caruso could have been a way for Italian immigrants to keep their culture alive. Nor was owning a car simply a symbol of consumption. "I had bought a jalopy in 1924, and it didn't change me," remembered one Communist party activist. "It just made it easier for me to function." The historian Lizabeth Cohen concluded that "Chicago's ethnic workers were not transformed into more Americanized, middle-class people by the objects they consumed. Buying an electric vacuum cleaner did not turn Josef Dobrowolski into *True Story's* Jim Smith."

The unequal distribution of income limited some consumers' ability to buy the enticing new products. At the height of prosperity in the 1920s, about 65 percent of America's families had an income less than $2,000 a year, which barely supported a decent living standard. The average family income in the bottom 40 percent of the population was $725. Of that amount, a family spent about $290 a year for food, $190 for housing, and $110 for clothing, leaving only $135 for everything else, including medical expenses and emergencies.

Retailers and automobile manufacturers addressed this situation by selling on the installment plan. In those days "buy now, pay later" was a revolutionary concept. Before World War I most urban families paid cash for everything except a house, but in the 1920s the automobile became such an object of desire that consumers put aside their fears of buying on time. In 1927 two-thirds of the cars in the United States were being paid off on the installment plan. Once people saw how easy it was to finance a car, they bought radios, refrigerators, and sewing machines on credit. "A dollar down and a dollar forever," a cynic remarked. But by 1929, banks, finance companies, credit unions, and other institutions were lending consumers over $7 billion a year and consumer lending was the tenth largest business in the United States.

Many of the new products were electric appliances, for which consumers spent about $667 million in 1927. By 1930, 85 percent of American nonfarm households had electricity to run their favorite gadgets. Irons and vacuum cleaners were the most popular appliances, followed by phonographs, sewing machines, and washing machines. Radios, whose production increased twenty-five-fold in the 1920s, sold for around $75. One of the most expensive items was a refrigerator, which cost $900 at the beginning of the decade. Improvements in the technology quickly brought the price down to $180, but many families still had to make do with an old-fashioned icebox.

Because much of the new technology was concentrated in the home, it had a dramatic impact on women's lives. Domestic chores became less arduous: it was far easier to plug in an electric iron than to heat an iron on the stove, and it was quicker and easier to use a vacuum cleaner than a broom and a rug beater. Paradoxically, however, the time women spent on housework did not decline. More middle-class women began to do their own housework and laundry as electric servants replaced human ones. Technology also raised standards of cleanliness so that a man could wear a clean shirt every day instead of just on Sunday, and a house could be vacuumed daily rather than swept weekly.

Advertising became a big business in the 1920s. In 1929 advertisers spent an average of $15 annually on every man, woman, and child in the United States—a total of $2.6 billion—to entice them to buy automobiles, cigarettes, radios, and refrigerators. That year the advertising industry, which the historian Roland Marchand called the "town criers" of modernity, accounted for 3 percent of the gross national product, comparable to its share after World War II.

The Flapper
The flapper phenomenon was not limited to Anglos. This 1921 photograph of a young Mexican-American woman shows how American fads and fashions reached into Hispanic communities across the country.

Portrait of Ettie
This 1923 painting by New York artist Florine Stettheimer of her sister Ettie suggests the personal flamboyance and languid style associated with modern women in the 1920s. No wonder their mothers and grandmothers were shocked. (Columbia University in the City of New York)

Few of the new consumer products could be considered necessities, so advertisements appealed to people's social aspirations by projecting images of successful, elegant, sophisticated people who smoked a certain brand of cigarettes or drove a recognizable make of car. Ad writers also sold products by preying on people's insecurities, coming up with a variety of socially unacceptable diseases, including "sneaker smell," "paralyzed pores," "office hips," "ashtray breath," and the dreaded "BO" (body odor). After the term *halitosis* was discovered in a British medical journal, many consumers rushed out to buy Listerine mouthwash. Yet American consumers were not passive victims of advertisers who manipulated their every whim. America gloried in its role as the world's first mass-consumption economy.

Many of these cultural images came together in the flapper, the media version of the emancipated woman of the 1920s. With her slim, boyish figure, bobbed hair, short skirt, and rolled-down silk stockings, the flapper symbolized the personal freedom trumpeted by movies, advertisements, and other elements of the emerging mass culture. Neither maternal nor wifely, the flapper wore makeup (previously assumed to be a sign of sexual availability in lower-class women) and lit up cigarettes in public, a shocking affront to ladylike decency. Like so many cultural icons, the flapper represented only a tiny minority of women. Yet the image mass-marketed the belief in women's postsuffrage emancipation.

The Automobile Culture

As the predominant symbol of the 1920s, the automobile typified the new consumer-based economy. "Why on earth do you need to study what's changing this country?" a Muncie, Indiana, resident asked the sociologists Robert and Helen Lynd, who were studying American culture and values. "I can tell you what's happening in just four letters: A-U-T-O!" Another Middletowner volunteered, "We'd rather do without clothes than give up the car."

The showpiece of modern capitalism and the ultimate consumer toy, the automobile revolutionized the ways Americans spent their money and leisure time. The isolation of rural life broke down in the wake of the automobile. New phrases such as "filling station" (or, as they were known west of the Rockies, "service stations") entered the nation's vocabulary. The automobile even affected crime, providing gangsters with a "getaway car" and the possibility of "taking someone for a ride." Cars touched so many aspects of American life that the word *automobility* was coined to describe their impact on production methods, the landscape, and American values.

The automobile stimulated the prosperity of the 1920s. Before the introduction of the moving assembly line in 1913, it took Ford workers twelve and a half hours to assemble an auto; it took only ninety-three minutes on an assembly line. In 1927 Ford produced a car every twenty-four seconds. Car sales climbed from 1.5 million in 1921 to 5 million in 1929, when Americans spent $2.58 billion on new and used cars. By the late 1920s a new Ford Model T, which cost $1,000 in 1908, sold for only $295 (at a time when an industrial worker earned about $5 a day). Lower cost and installment buying increased yearly car registrations from 8.5 million in 1920 to 23 million in 1929. By the end of the decade Americans owned about 80 percent of the world's automobiles, an average of one car for every five people.

The growth of the auto industry had a ripple effect on the American economy. In 1929, 3.7 million workers directly or indirectly owed their jobs to the automobile. Auto production stimulated the steel, petroleum, chemical, rubber, and glass industries. Total U.S. demand for oil, mainly in the form of gasoline, multiplied two and a half times between 1919 and 1929, and domestic oil production expanded to meet the need. (The United

The Dust Bowl

Sand and dust everywhere, and not a drop of water—that was how many midwesterners experienced the worst drought in U.S. climatological history. This 1934 painting by Alexandre Hogue captures the bleakness of the drought-stricken landscape. (Alexandre Hogue. *Drought-Stricken Area* 1939. Oil on canvas. 30″ × 42¼″. Dallas Museum of Art, Dallas Art Association Purchase, 1945)

CHAPTER 25

The Great Depression

★　　　★　　　★

Flappers and movie stars in the 1920s, breadlines and hoboes in the 1930s: were the 1920s just "one long party" after which "everyone had a hangover—known as the depression—in the morning"? Did the country really go from unprecedented prosperity to the poorhouse overnight?

Obviously, the contrast between the flush times of the 1920s and the hard times of the 1930s has been too starkly drawn. The vaunted prosperity of the 1920s was never as widespread or as deeply rooted as many believed at the time. Although America's mass-consumption economy was the envy of the world, many people lived on its margins. Nor was every American devastated by the depression. Those with a secure job or a fixed income survived the economic downturn in relatively good shape, and some people even managed to get rich. But few could escape contact with the depression's wide-ranging effects on social, political, and cultural developments.

Almost all our impressions of the 1930s are black and white, in part because widely distributed photographs taken by Farm Security Administration photographers etched this stark visual image of depression America on the popular consciousness. Not every event of the 1930s should be viewed through the lens of the depression, but more than any other factor, it provides the unifying theme for the decade.

The Coming of the Great Depression

Booms and busts are a permanent feature of the business cycle in capitalist economies. Since the beginning of the Industrial Revolution early in the nineteenth century the United States had experienced recessions or panics at

least every twenty years. The most recent downturn had been the postwar recession of 1920–1921. But no slump was as severe or lasted as long as the Great Depression.

The Causes of the Depression

The Great Depression began slowly and almost imperceptibly. After 1927, consumer spending declined and housing construction slowed. Inventories piled up, and in 1928 and 1929 manufacturers began to cut back production and lay off workers. Reduced incomes and buying power reinforced the downturn. By the summer of 1929 the economy was clearly in a recession, although not as severe a downturn as the one that had begun in 1920.

Stock Market Speculation and the Great Crash. Among the causes of the Great Depression, a flawed stock market was an important but not the dominant influence. By 1929 the market had become the symbol of the nation's prosperity and an icon of American business culture. The financier John J. Raskob captured this attitude in a *Ladies' Home Journal* article, "Everyone Ought to Be Rich." Invest $15 a month in sound common stocks, Raskob advised, and in twenty years the investment will grow to $80,000. Not everyone was playing the stock market, however. About 4 million Americans owned stock in 1929, representing about 10 percent of the nation's households. Only 1.5 million had portfolios large enough to require the services of a stockbroker.

Stock prices had been rising steadily since 1921, but in 1928 and 1929 they surged forward, with the average price of stocks rising over 40 percent. All this economic activity was essentially unregulated. Margin buying in particular proceeded at a feverish pace as stockbrokers permitted many of their customers to borrow up to 75

percent of the purchase price of stocks. That easy credit lured more speculators and less creditworthy investors into the market. The Federal Reserve Board warned member banks not to lend money for stock speculation—if prices dropped, many investors would not be able to pay their debts—but no one listened. As long as prices continued to soar, everyone felt like a winner. A noted economist proclaimed in mid-October 1929 that "stock prices have reached what looks like a permanently high plateau."

The stock market had been sliding since early September, but people ignored the warning. On "Black Tuesday"—October 29, 1929—the bubble burst. More than 16 million shares changed hands in frantic trading. Overextended investors, suddenly finding themselves heavily in debt, began to sell their stocks, leading others to follow suit to protect their investments. That set off waves of panic selling, and many stocks found no buyers. Practically overnight, stock values fell from a peak of $87 billion (at least on paper) to $55 billion. The precipitate decline of stock prices became known as the Great Crash.

The impact of Black Tuesday was felt far beyond the trading floors of Wall Street. Speculators who had borrowed from banks to buy their stocks could not repay the loans because they could not sell the stock. These defaults in turn caused bank failures. Since bank deposits were uninsured before the 1930s, a bank failure meant that all the depositors' money was lost. This was a tremendous shock to the middle class, many of whom lost their life savings and had no other resources to cope with the crisis.

The stock market crash intensified the course of the Great Depression in several ways. Besides wiping out the savings of thousands of Americans, it hurt commercial banks that had invested heavily in corporate stocks. Less tangibly, it destroyed the optimism of people who

Wall Street, October 1929
When the stock market collapsed, Julius Rosenwald, the chairman of Sears, Roebuck and Company, offered to guarantee the accounts of Sears employees who had bought stock on margin. The comedian Eddie Cantor jokingly asked for a job as a Sears office boy.

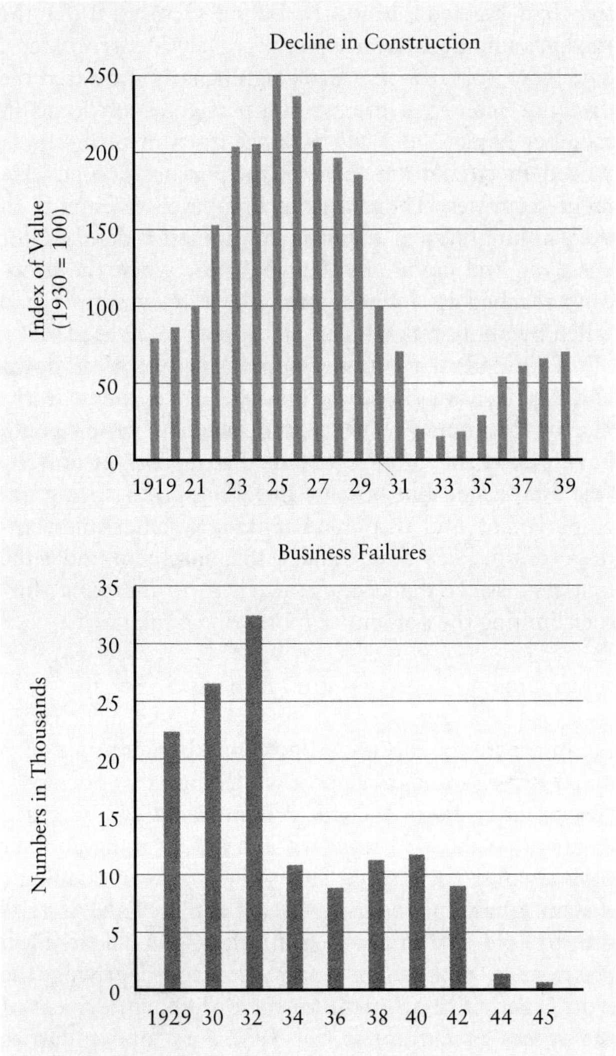

Decline in Construction

Business Failures

FIGURE 25.1

Statistics of the Depression

The top graph shows the decline in construction, as reflected in the value of new building permits; the bottom graph gives the numbers of business failures.

Source: Historical Statistics of the United States, Colonial Times to 1970 (Washington, D.C.: U.S. Government Printing Office, 1975), 626, 912.

had regarded the stock market as the crowning symbol of American prosperity, causing a crisis of confidence that prolonged the depression.

However, the stock market crash and its immediate consequences cannot account for the severity and the length of the Great Depression, especially the deep plunge between 1931 and 1933. The drag of "sick" industries, the growing inequality of wealth, the unstable international financial situation, and the flawed monetary policies of the Federal Reserve System all contributed to the prolonged decline (see Figure 25.1).

Structural Weaknesses. The crash exposed long-standing weaknesses in the American economy. Agriculture was in the worst shape; farmers had never recovered from the recession of 1920–1921. They faced high fixed costs for equipment and mortgages incurred during the inflationary war years. At the same time, prices fell because of overproduction and the resulting surpluses, forcing farmers to default on mortgage payments and risk foreclosure. In 1929 the yearly income of a farmer averaged only $273, compared with $750 in other occupations. Because farmers accounted for about a fourth of the nation's gainfully employed workers in 1929, their difficulties weakened the general economic structure.

Certain basic industries also had economic troubles during the prosperous 1920s, many of them dating back to World War I or the depression of 1920–1921. The textile industry, for example, had steadily declined after the war. Textile firms abandoned New England for cheaper labor markets in the South but continued to suffer from decreased demand and excess capacity. The railroad industry was hit by shrinking passenger revenues, stagnant freight levels, and inefficient management. In addition, the railroads faced stiff competition from truck transportation on publicly subsidized roads.

Mining and lumbering, which had expanded in response to wartime demands, produced too much during peacetime. Coal mining especially was battered by overexpansion, technological obsolescence, and a legacy of bitter labor struggles. New energy sources, including hydroelectric power, fuel oil, and natural gas, were competing with coal. As secretary of commerce, Herbert Hoover had plans to help those ailing industries, but the trade associations that he promoted were ineffectual.

Unequal Distribution of Wealth. The country's unequal distribution of wealth also contributed to the severity of the depression. During the 1920s the share of national income going to families in the upper- and middle-income brackets increased. The tax policies of Secretary of the Treasury Andrew Mellon contributed to that concentration of wealth by lowering personal income tax rates, eliminating the wartime excess-profits tax, and increasing deductions that favored affluent individuals and corporations. In 1929, the lowest 40 percent of the population received only 12.5 percent of aggregate family personal income whereas the top 5 percent received 30 percent. Once the depression began, not enough people could afford to spend the amounts of money necessary to revive the economy.

The Worldwide Depression. The economic problems of the United States had an impact on the rest of the world, and vice versa. The international economic system had been out of kilter since World War I. It could function only as long as American banks exported enough capital to allow European countries to repay their debts and

continue to buy American manufactured goods and agricultural products. By the late 1920s European economies were staggering under the weight of large debts and trade imbalances with the United States, which undercut the recovery that had looked possible earlier in the decade. By 1931 most European economies had collapsed.

In an interdependent world the downturn of the American economy had enormous repercussions. In 1929 the United States had produced over 40 percent of the world's manufactured goods, twice as much as Great Britain and Germany combined; it held 50 percent of the world's gold reserve and accounted for 16 percent of international trade. When American companies cut back production, they also cut back their purchases of raw materials and supplies abroad, and this devastated many foreign economies. American financiers sharply reduced foreign investment and consumers bought fewer European goods, making debt repayment even more difficult and straining the gold standard, the foundation of interwar multilateralism. As economic conditions worsened on the Continent, European demand for American exports fell drastically. When the Hawley-Smoot Tariff of 1930 raised rates to all-time highs, foreign governments retaliated by imposing their own trade restrictions. That further limited the market for American goods, especially agricultural products, and deepened the worldwide depression.

The Deepening Economic Crisis

The Great Depression became self-perpetuating. The more the American economy contracted, the longer people expected the depression to last, and the longer they expected it to last, the more afraid they were to spend or invest their money (if they had any), which was exactly what was needed to stimulate economic recovery. The economy showed some improvement in the summer of 1931 when low prices encouraged consumption, but plunged again late in the fall.

At that point the chronically depressed agricultural sector put pressure on the commercial banking system, worsening the economic contraction. The nation's banks had already been weakened by the stock market crash. When agricultural prices and incomes fell more steeply than usual in 1930, many farmers went into bankruptcy. Rural banks failed in alarming numbers—particularly in the cotton belt—after the harvest of 1930. By November and December so many rural banks had defaulted on their obligations that urban banks also began to fail. The wave of bank failures frightened depositors into withdrawing their savings, further deepening the crisis.

Flawed Monetary Policy. A change in the nation's monetary policy in 1931 added to the banking problems. In the first phase of the depression the Federal Reserve Sys-

tem had reacted cautiously, but in October 1931 the system's managers took several gravely incorrect steps. The New York Reserve Bank significantly increased the discount rate—the interest rate it charged on loans to member banks—and cut back the amount of money it placed in circulation through its purchase of government securities. Those actions hampered the ability of the banking system to meet the domestic demand for currency and credit. By March 1933, when the economy reached its lowest point, the money supply had fallen by about a third from its August 1929 level.

The inadequate money supply forced prices down and deprived businesses of funds for investment. In the face of that money shortage, the American people could have pulled the country out of the depression only by spending faster. But because of falling prices, rising unemployment, and a troubled banking system, Americans preferred to keep their dollars, stashing them under the mattress rather than depositing them in the bank, further limiting the amount of money in circulation.

International Repercussions. Adherence to the gold standard had long been the most sacrosanct principle in the international business community because gold provided a fixed standard against which the value of currencies could be pegged. Great Britain unilaterally decided to abandon the gold standard in 1931, striking another blow against the already shaky international economic system. Currencies no longer had a definite value in relation to gold—and thus to each other—but "floated" in accordance with supply and demand, depriving the world market of a system for the orderly adjustment of the values of currencies. By 1932 forty-one countries had followed Britain's example, and fear spread in Europe that despite Herbert Hoover's unwavering support for the gold standard the United States would follow suit. Consequently, holders of dollars abroad began to demand gold, and gold flowed out of the United States. The Federal Reserve's decision in October 1931 to drive up short-term interest rates successfully attracted gold holders to U.S. investments, temporarily saving the gold standard.

President Hoover later blamed the severity of the depression in the United States on the international economic situation. No other major trading nation was hit as hard as the United States. Although domestic factors far outweighed international ones in causing America's protracted decline, Hoover had a point. During the depression no country stepped forward to provide leadership and stability in the world market as Britain had done before World War I. Instead, nations raised tariff barriers and imposed exchange controls to hoard precious gold, dollars, and pounds sterling in a fit of economic nationalism that prolonged the depression. By 1933 the world economy was showing signs of recovery, although progress remained uneven.

The Downward Spiral. Herbert Hoover personally chose the term *depression* to describe America's post-1929 economic downturn, feeling that that term sounded less ominous than *panic* or *crisis*. Whatever one calls the condition of the American economy from 1929 to 1932, the statistics paint a stark picture. From the height of the prosperity before the stock market crash in 1929 to the depths of the depression in 1932–1933 the gross national product was cut almost in half, declining from $103.1 billion to $58 billion in 1932. Consumption expenditures dropped by 18 percent, construction fell by 78 percent, private investment plummeted by 88 percent, and farm income, already low, was more than cut in half. In this period, 9,000 banks went bankrupt or closed their doors, and 100,000 businesses failed. The consumer price index declined by 25 percent, and corporate profits fell from $10 billion to $1 billion.

Most tellingly, unemployment rose from 3.2 percent to 24.9 percent, affecting approximately 12 million workers (see Figure 25.2). Statistical measures at that time were fairly crude, and unemployment was probably even higher. At least one in four workers was out of a job. Even those who had jobs faced wage cutbacks or the possibility of being laid off. Their stories put a human face on the almost incomprehensible dimensions of this economic downturn.

Employment Agency (detail)
Isaac Soyer's 1937 painting captures the resignation and despair of Americans searching for a job, any job, in the midst of the Great Depression. (Whitney Museum of American Art)

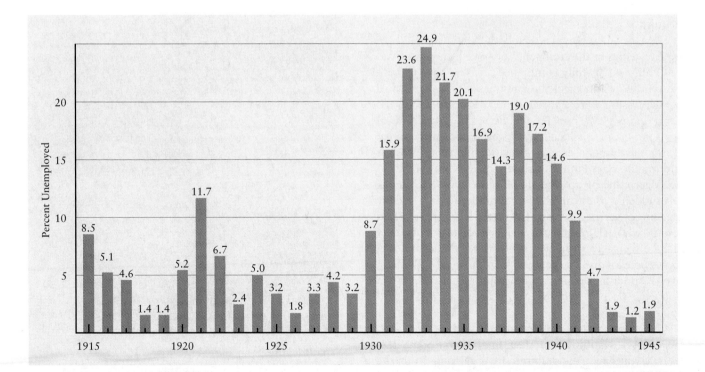

FIGURE 25.2

Unemployment, 1915–1945
As this graph shows, the historically low unemployment levels of the 1920s began to rise in 1930. By 1933 one in four American workers was out of a job.

Hard Times

"We didn't go hungry, but we lived lean." That statement sums up the experiences of many American families during the Great Depression. The vast majority were neither very rich nor very poor. For most the depression did not mean losing thousands of dollars in the stock market or pulling children out of boarding school; nor did it mean going on relief or living in a shantytown. In a typical family in the 1930s, the husband still had a job and the wife was still a homemaker. Life was not easy, but it usually consisted of "making do" rather than suffering stark deprivation.

The Invisible Scar

"You could feel the depression deepen," recalled the writer Caroline Bird, "but you could not look out the window and see it." Many people never saw a breadline or a man selling apples on the corner. The depression caused a private kind of despair that often simmered behind closed doors. "I've lived in cities for many months broke, without help, too timid to get in breadlines," the writer Meridel LeSueur remembered. "I've known many women to live like this until they simply faint on the street from privations, without saying a word to anyone. A woman will shut herself up in a room until it is taken away from her, and eat a cracker a day and be as quiet as a mouse."

"Mass unemployment is both a statistic and an empty feeling in the stomach," observed the writer Cabell Phillips. "To fully comprehend it, you have to both see the figures and feel the emptiness." The victims of the depression were a varied group. The depression did not create poverty; it merely publicized the conditions of the poor. People who had always been poor were joined by the newly poor. Those formerly solid working-class and middle-class families strongly believed in the Horatio Alger ethic of upward mobility through hard work but suddenly found themselves floundering in a society that no longer had a place for them. They were proud people who felt humiliated by their plight, and many blamed themselves for their misfortune. "What is going to become of us?" asked an Arizona man. "I've lost twelve and a half pounds this last month, just thinking. You can't sleep, you know. You wake up at 2 A.M. and you lie and think."

Hard times were distressing for old people, who faced total destitution in their final years. Some lost their savings in bank failures. In a cartoon from the 1930s a squirrel asks a man on a park bench why he did not save for a rainy day. "I did," the man replies listlessly. Children, by contrast, often escaped the sense of bitterness and failure that gripped their elders; some

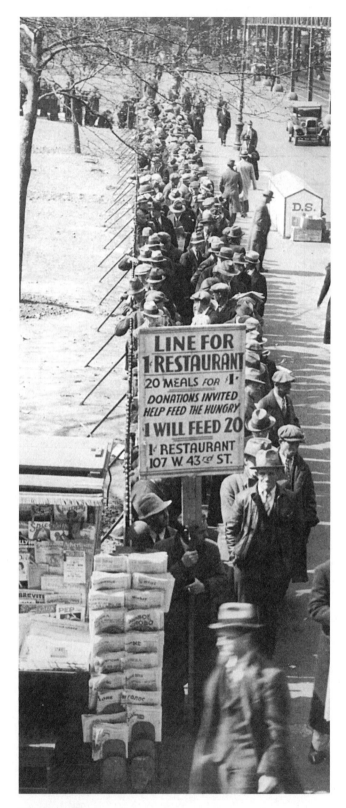

The Breadline
Some of the most vivid images from the depression were breadlines and men selling apples on street corners. Note that all the people in this breadline are men. Women rarely appeared in breadlines, often preferring to endure private deprivation rather than violate standards of respectable behavior.

youngsters thought it was fun to stand in a soup line. Yet hard times made children grow up fast.

Downward mobility was especially hard for middle-class Americans. An unemployed man in Pittsburgh told the journalist Lorena Hickok, "Lady, you just can't know what it's like to have to move your family out of the nice house you had in the suburbs, part paid for, down into an apartment, down into another apartment, smaller and in a worse neighborhood, down, down, down, until finally you end up in the slums." Before a laid-off chauffeur started a relief construction job, he spent the day watching how the other men handled their picks and shovels so he could "get the hang of it and not feel so awkward." A wife broke into tears when her husband, a white-collar worker, put on his first pair of overalls to go to work.

The key to surviving the depression was to maintain one's self-respect. One man spent two years painting his father's house (in fact, he painted it twice). Keeping up appearances, keeping life as close to normal as possible, was an essential strategy. Camaraderie and cooperation helped many families and communities survive as people found that they were all in the same boat. When a driver "accidentally" dumped a load of oranges or coal off the back of his truck, he was contributing to the welfare of the neighborhood. Hoboes developed an elaborate system of sidewalk chalk marks to tell one another at which back doors they could get a meal, an old coat, or some spare change.

After their savings and credit had been exhausted, many families faced the humiliation of going on relief. Seeking aid from state or local governments hurt people's pride and disrupted the traditional pattern of turning to relatives, neighbors, churches, and mutual-aid societies in times of need. A young caseworker tearfully remembered her embarrassment when investigating the homes of these proud people:

> The father was a railroad man who had lost his job. I was told by my supervisor that I really had to see the poverty. If the family needed clothing, I was to investigate how much clothing they had at hand. So I looked into this man's closet . . . he was a tall, gray-haired man, though not terribly old. He let me look into the closet—he was so insulted. . . . He said, "Why are you doing this?" I remember his feeling of humiliation . . . this terrible humiliation. He said, "I really haven't anything to hide, but if you really must look into it. . . ." I could see he was very proud. He was so deeply humiliated. And I was, too.

Even if families survived the demeaning process of being certified for state or local relief, the amount was a pittance. In New York State, for example, where benefits were among the highest in the nation, a family received only $2.39 a week.

Such hardships left deep wounds—the "invisible scar" described by Caroline Bird. One elderly civil servant bought a plot of land outside Washington so that if the depression recurred, she would have the means to live. The labor organizer Larry Van Dusen described another common reaction: "The depression left a legacy of fear, but also a desire for acquisition—property, security. I now have twenty times more shirts than I need, because all during that time, shirts were something I never had." Virginia Durr, a white civil rights activist from Alabama, concurred: "The great majority reacted by thinking money is the most important thing in the world. Get yours. And get it for your children. Nothing else matters. Not having that stark terror come at you again." For many Americans that was the Great Depression: "that stark terror" of losing control over their lives.

Families Face the Great Depression

Sociologists who studied family life during the 1930s found that the depression usually intensified existing behavior. For example, if a family had been stable and cohesive before the depression, it pulled together to overcome the new obstacles. However, if a family had shown signs of disintegration, the depression made the situation worse. On the whole, researchers thought that far more families hung together than broke apart.

In many ways the depression disrupted women's lives less than men's. Millions of men lost their jobs, but few of the nation's 28 million homemakers lost that position in the home. In fact, women's domestic role took on greater importance.

Men and women experienced the Great Depression differently, partly because of the traditional gender roles that governed male and female behavior in the 1930s. Men had been trained from childhood to be breadwinners and considered themselves failures if they could no longer support their families. Women, however, felt their self-importance increase as they struggled to keep their families afloat. The sociologists Robert and Helen Lynd noticed this phenomenon in their follow-up study of Middletown (Muncie, Indiana), published in 1937:

> The men, cut adrift from their usual routine, lost much of their sense of time and dawdled helplessly and dully about the streets; while in the homes the women's world remained largely intact and the round of cooking, housecleaning, and mending became if anything more absorbing.

Even if a wife took a job when her husband lost his, she retained almost total responsibility for housework and child care.

Women made many contributions to family survival during the depression years. With the national median

annual income at $1,160, a typical married woman had $20 to $25 a week to feed, clothe, and provide shelter for her family. Deflation had lowered the cost of living so that milk sold for 10 cents a quart, bread for 7 cents a loaf, and butter for 23 cents a pound. Yet housewives still had to watch every penny. Two friends who often bought hamburger together split 2 pounds for 25 cents and took turns keeping the extra penny. Eleanor Roosevelt described the effects of the depression on these women's lives: "It means endless little economies and constant anxiety for fear of some catastrophe such as accident or illness which may completely swamp the family budget." The line between making do and doing without was often thin.

Despite the hard times, Americans maintained a fairly high level of consumption. Continuing the pattern of the 1920s, households in the middle-income range, the 50.2 percent of American families with an income of $500 to $1,500 in 1935, did much of the buying. Several factors enabled those families more or less to maintain their former standard of living despite pay cuts or unemployment. Deflation lowered the cost of living almost 20 percent between 1929 and 1935, and families spent their reduced income differently. For example, telephone use and clothing sales dropped sharply, but people had a harder time giving up cigarettes, movies, radio, and newspapers, once considered luxuries but now regarded as necessities. The automobile proved to be one of the most depression-proof items in the family budget. Sales of new cars dropped, but gasoline sales were stable, suggesting that people bought used cars or kept their old models running longer.

Some families maintained their life-styles in the 1930s through "deficit living"—that is, using installment payments and credit to stretch their income. This strategy added about 10 percent to a family income under $500 and 2 to 5 percent to a family income in the range of $500 to $1,500. By 1936 consumer credit in the United States had increased by 20 percent over 1929 levels. A Middletown resident summed up the prevailing attitude toward installment buying: "Most of the families I know are after the same things today that they were after before the Depression, and they'll get them in the same way—on credit."

To maintain their families' life-styles, housewives substituted their own labor for goods and services they had formerly purchased. Women sewed their own clothes and canned fruits and vegetables. They practiced small economies such as buying day-old bread and heating several dishes in the oven at once to save fuel. Women who had employed servants did their own housework. Those economies helped pay for cars and movies, which could not be manufactured at home. Women generally accepted their new work stoically. "We had no choice," remembered one housewife. "We just did what had to be done one day at a time."

Demographic Trends

The depression directly affected demographic trends in the 1930s. The marriage rate fell from 10.14 per thousand persons in 1929 to 7.87 in 1932. The divorce rate dropped as well because people could not afford the legal expenses of dissolving failed unions. Although marriage and divorce rates rebounded after 1933, postponement of marriage sometimes became permanent. Elsa Ponselle, a Chicago schoolteacher who later became the principal of one of that city's largest elementary schools, recalled her experience:

> Do you realize how many people in my generation are not married? . . . It wasn't that we didn't have a chance. I was going with someone when the Depression hit. We probably would have gotten married. He was a commercial artist and had been doing very well. . . . Suddenly he was laid off. It hit him like a ton of bricks. And he just disappeared.

The birth rate was the demographic factor most affected by the depression. The birth rate had fallen steadily since 1800, but from 1930 to 1933 it dropped from 21.3 live births per thousand population to 18.4, a 14 percent decrease. The 1933 level, if maintained, would have led to a population decline. The overriding concern was whether a couple could afford to raise a child. The birth rate rose slightly after 1934, but by the end of the decade it had reached only 18.8. In contrast, at the height of the baby boom following World War II, the birth rate was 25 per thousand population.

Birth Control. The extensive limitation of births during the Great Depression would not have been possible without access to effective contraception. The production of diaphragms and condoms was one business that thrived in the 1930s. Abortion remained illegal, but the number of women who had the procedure increased. Because many abortionists operated under unsafe or unsanitary conditions, between 8,000 and 10,000 women died each year from those illegal operations.

The 1930s marked a significant stage in the long history of the birth control movement in America. In 1936 a federal court decision in the case of *United States v. One Package of Japanese Pessaries* struck down all federal restrictions on the dissemination of contraceptive information. Doctors now had wide discretion in prescribing birth control for married couples, which became legal in all states except Massachusetts and Connecticut. Public support for contraception also increased: in a 1936 Gallup poll 63 percent of those interviewed favored making birth control information more widely available.

Margaret Sanger played a major role in encouraging popular acceptance of birth control. She had started her career as a public health nurse in the slums of New York

in the 1910s. Anxious immigrant women continually asked Sanger to tell them the "secret" of how to avoid having more babies. When a patient who had been referred to her died after a botched abortion, Sanger dedicated her life to expanding access to birth control. At first she joined forces with socialist movements aimed at the working class. In the 1920s and 1930s, however, she appealed to the middle class for support, identifying this segment of the population as the key to the movement's success. Sanger also courted the medical profession, pioneering the establishment of birth control clinics staffed by doctors and winning the American Medical Association's endorsement of contraception in 1937. Birth control became less a feminist demand and more a medical issue.

Contraception had long been a private decision between individuals. Its public acceptance increased greatly during the 1930s because of the widespread desire to limit family size for economic reasons. In 1942 the American Birth Control League, which Sanger had founded in 1921, became Planned Parenthood, an organization that remains active today.

Women on the Job

One way for families to make ends meet in the 1930s was to send an additional member of the household to work. At the turn of the century that additional family worker probably would have been a child or a young unmarried adult; in the 1930s it was increasingly a married woman. Instead of expelling women from the work force, the depression solidified their position in it: the 1940 census reported almost 11 million women in the work force, approximately a fourth of the nation's workers and a small increase over 1930. The number of married women employed outside the home rose 50 percent.

Working women, especially married ones, encountered sharp resentment and outright discrimination when they entered the depression workplace. After calculating that the number of employed women roughly equaled the 1939 unemployment total, the editor Norman Cousins suggested this tongue-in-cheek remedy: "Simply fire the women, who shouldn't be working anyway, and hire the men. Presto! No unemployment. No relief rolls. No depression." A 1936 Gallup poll asked whether wives should work when their husbands had jobs, and 82 percent of the people interviewed said no. From 1932 to 1937 the federal government would not allow a husband and wife to hold government jobs at the same time. Many states adopted laws that prohibited married women from working. Such laws were especially widespread in the field of education, yet the proportion of married female schoolteachers rose from 17.9 percent in 1930 to 24.6 percent in 1940.

The attempt to make women scapegoats for the depression rested on shaky moral and economic grounds. Most women worked because they had to. A sizable minority were the sole support of their families, because their husbands had left home or lost their jobs. Single, divorced, deserted, or widowed women had no husbands to support them. Moreover, women rarely took jobs away from men. "Few of the people who oppose married women's employment," observed one feminist in 1940, "seem to realize that a coal miner or steel worker cannot very well fill the jobs of nursemaids, cleaning women, or the factory and clerical jobs now filled by women." Custom, rather than law or economics, made crossovers rare.

The division of the work force by gender gave women a small edge during the depression. Many fields with large numbers of female employees, including clerical, sales, and service and trade occupations, suffered less from economic contraction than did the steel industry, mining, and manufacturing, which employed men almost exclusively. As a result, unemployment rates for women, although extremely high, were somewhat lower than those for men. This small bonus came at a high price, however. The jobs women held reinforced the traditional stereotypes of female work. When the depression ended, women found themselves even more concentrated in low-paying dead-end jobs than when it began.

This gender advantage also benefited white women at the expense of minority group women. To make ends meet, white women willingly took jobs usually held by blacks or minority workers—entering domestic service, for example—and employers were quick to act on their preference for a white work force. White men also took jobs previously held by minority group males.

During the Great Depression there were few feminist demands for equal rights at home or on the job. On an individual basis, women's self-esteem probably rose because of their importance to family survival. Most men and women, however, continued to believe that the two sexes should have fundamentally different roles and responsibilities and that a woman's life cycle should be shaped by marriage and her husband's career. The substantial contributions made by women in the 1930s actually reinforced their overall identification with the home, laying the foundation for the so-called feminine mystique of the 1950s.

Hard Times for Youth

The depression hit the nation's 21 million young people especially hard. Although children only dimly glimpsed the sacrifices made in the 1930s, adolescents knew that making do usually meant doing without. The writer Maxine Davis, who traveled 10,000 miles in 1936 to in-

terview the nation's youth, described them as "runners, delayed at the gun." She added, "The depression years have left us with a generation robbed of time and opportunity just as the Great War left the world its heritage of a lost generation." Studies of social mobility confirm that the young men who entered their twenties during the depression era had less successful careers than did those before or since. About 250,000 young people became so demoralized that they took to the road as hoboes and "sisters of the road," as female tramps were called.

Because job prospects were so dim, some young people chose to stay in school longer. Public schools were free and were warm in the winter. In 1930 less than half the nation's youth attended high school, compared with three-fourths in 1940, at the end of the depression. This was partly due to increased attendance by boys, who had traditionally dropped out of school to work at an earlier age than did girls.

College, however, remained the privilege of a distinct minority. About 1.2 million young people, or 7.5 percent of the population between eighteen and twenty-four, attended college in the 1930s, 40 percent of them women. After 1935 college became a little more affordable because of the National Youth Administration (NYA), which gave part-time employment to more than 2 million college and high school students. This government agency also provided work for 2.6 million out-of-school youths.

College students worked hard in the 1930s; financial sacrifices encouraged seriousness of purpose. The influence of fraternities and sororities declined during the depression, and many students became involved in political movements. Fueled by disillusionment with World War I, thousands took the "Oxford Pledge" never to support a war in which the United States might be involved. In 1936 the Student Strike against War drew support from several hundred thousand students across the country.

Because young people spent more time in school, participating in organized athletics and extracurricular activities, adolescence became increasingly institutionalized in the 1930s, and teenagers developed their own values and patterns of behavior. Peers, rather than parents, influenced their values and tastes. Magazines and movies promoted a youth culture that was closely tied to an ethos of consumption. Teenagers throughout the country read the same comics, wore the same style clothes, and saw the same movies. They also experimented with necking, petting, and dating rituals that shocked their elders. The youth culture became a distinct feature of modern times.

Popular Culture

Popular culture played an important role in pulling the United States through the trauma of the depression. As the novelist Josephine Herbst observed, there was "an almost universal liveliness that countervailed universal suffering." The mass culture that grew so dramatically in the 1920s flourished in the decade that followed.

Movies. The most popular form of entertainment in the 1930s was the movies. More than 60 percent of Americans saw at least one movie a week, with weekly attendance ranging from 60 million to 75 million. In the 5,000 films made during the depression decade, moviegoers were transported to a world where hard times were practically unknown. Yet movies offered more than escapism. Hollywood in the 1930s, observed the film historian Robert Sklar, "directed its enormous powers of persuasion to preserving the basic moral, social and economic tenets of traditional American culture."

World Premiere
Margaret Mitchell's 1936 novel, *Gone with the Wind*, broke all sales records in the 1930s. When it was made into a 1939 movie starring Clark Gable and Vivien Leigh, more than 12,000 fans gathered in Atlanta for the film's premiere at Loew's Grand Theater, which had been transformed into a southern mansion for the event.

Movies remained a big business in the 1930s, but the industry was not depression-proof. Although theaters lowered admission prices from 30 cents to 20, attendance dropped in the early 1930s, and by 1933 one-third of the nation's movie theaters were dark. Many of the major studios, dependent on Wall Street financing, were hurting. Not until 1934 did the industry begin to revive.

In many ways films in the 1930s reflected the progress of the depression. In the grim early years gangster films were especially popular. Two of the most successful were *Little Caesar* (1930), starring Edward G. Robinson, and *The Public Enemy* (1931), in which James Cagney shoved a grapefruit in Mae Clark's face. Those movies were replaced by extravagant Busby Berkeley musicals such as *Gold Diggers of 1933*, suggesting an upswing in the public mood. The Marx brothers kept people laughing with irreverent classics such as *Animal Crackers* (1930) and *Duck Soup* (1933).

The Grapes of Wrath
John Steinbeck's best-selling 1939 novel became one of 1940's top movies, one of the few Hollywood films that tackled contemporary social problems. Ma Joad, played by Jane Darwell, expressed the central message: "We're the people that live. They ain't gonna wipe us out. Why, we're the people—we go on."

Dancing Cheek to Cheek
During the Great Depression, Americans turned to inexpensive recreational activities such as listening to the radio and going to the movies. One of the most popular attractions in Hollywood movies was the dance team of Fred Astaire and Ginger Rogers, who starred together in ten movies.

Mae West titillated audiences with lines such as "It's not the men in my life, but the life in my men that counts" and "I used to be Snow White, but I drifted."

For some moviegoers Mae West's sexual innuendos went too far. To win back customers Hollywood made a highly publicized commitment to upholding ideals of decency and good taste. The Production Code Administration, headed by Joseph Breen, represented Hollywood's effort at self-censorship, an attempt to correct the perceived excesses of early talkies. Fearing a boycott from religious groups such as the Catholic Legion of Decency, studios in 1934 agreed to banish explicit sex, immorality, and violence from the screen. The new standards were so strict that censors barely permitted Rhett Butler to utter the famous last line of *Gone with the Wind*: "Frankly, my dear, I don't give a damn." Critics charged that movies were cutting themselves off from reality, but the repressive standards held sway until the 1950s.

In part because of the Production Code, movies made after 1934 had a different feel compared with those made before that year. Sophisticated, fast-paced "screwball comedies" such as *It Happened One Night*, which swept the Oscars in 1934, epitomized Hollywood's new direction. Walt Disney emerged as a cultural mythmaker during the depression, producing 198 cartoons and classics such as *Snow White and the Seven Dwarfs* (1937), the first feature-length animated film. The 1940 Hollywood adaptation of John Steinbeck's novel *The Grapes of Wrath* was one of the few popular

films to depict the depression in a serious, realistic manner. Even the newsreels downplayed the depression in favor of heroes and heroines from the worlds of sports, entertainment, and popular culture.

At the height of the depression, movies continued to influence consumers. One of the decade's top box-office stars was a curly-headed little girl named Shirley Temple, who made twenty-one films by 1941. Shirley Temple dolls, books, and clothes flooded the market. Similarly, because of the popularity of glamorous blondes such as Jean Harlow, Carole Lombard, and Mae West, sales of peroxide hair rinse skyrocketed. Undershirt sales fell drastically after Clark Gable, a leading sex symbol of the 1930s, took off his shirt in *It Happened One Night* and revealed his bare chest.

Headline History. People relied on newspapers and newsreels for quick coverage of world events. The kidnapping of the twenty-month-old son of Charles and Anne Morrow Lindbergh in 1932 instantly became a national news story. Seventy-five days later the child's body was found in the woods near the Lindbergh home in New Jersey. "BABY DEAD" ran the headlines, and

everyone knew what the two words meant. Other leading news events of the depression years included the birth of the Dionne quintuplets in Canada in 1934; the gunning down of John Dillinger, "Public Enemy Number One," by the FBI in 1934; Jesse Owens's four gold medals at the 1936 Berlin Olympics; the abdication in 1936 of King Edward VIII of Great Britain to marry "the woman I love," an American divorcée named Wallis Warfield Simpson; the disappearance of the aviator Amelia Earhart on a round-the-world flight in 1937; and the fiery crash of the *Hindenburg*, a German dirigible, at Lakehurst, New Jersey, in 1937.

Radio Days. Radio occupied an increasingly large place in popular culture during the 1930s (see Map 25.1). At the beginning of the decade about 13 million households had a radio set; by the end, 27.5 million owned one. Listeners tuned in to daytime serials such as "Ma Perkins" or picked up useful household hints on the "The Betty Crocker Hour." Variety shows featured Jack Benny, George Burns and Gracie Allen, and the ventriloquist Edgar Bergen and his impudent dummy Charlie McCarthy. Millions of listeners followed the adventures

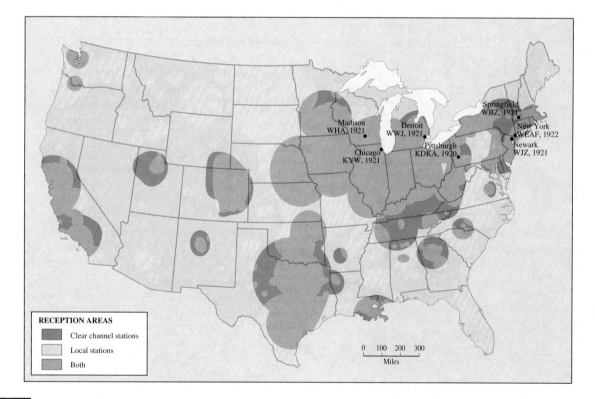

MAP 25.1

The Spread of Radio

In 1938 more than 26 million American households, or about three-quarters of the population, had a radio. Four national networks dominated the field, broadcasting news and entertainment across the country. Powerful clear-channel stations reached listeners hundreds of miles distant. By 1939 only a few sparsely populated areas were beyond radio's reach.

of the Lone Ranger ("Hi-Ho Silver"), Superman, the Shadow, and Dick Tracy.

Radio also brought music to depression-era audiences. Classical music devotees could listen to live Saturday afternoon performances of New York's Metropolitan Opera (begun in 1931 and still being broadcast) or the NBC Symphony Orchestra under the baton of Arturo Toscanini. On the lighter side people loved the new Big Band "swing" music of Benny Goodman, Duke Ellington, and Tommy Dorsey, an outgrowth of the jazz craze of the 1920s, and Cole Porter songs such as "Begin the Beguine" and "Night and Day" from Broadway shows. Radio increased the consumer market for 78-r.p.m. phonograph records of classical music, swing, and Broadway show tunes.

The depression also encouraged a return to traditional values. Attendance at religious services rose. The home once again became a center of leisure activity, with an evening by the radio providing a cheap form of family entertainment. Reading aloud from books borrowed from the public library was another affordable diversion. "Talking was the Great Depression pastime," recalled the columnist Russell Baker. "Unlike the movies, talk was free."

The Social Fabric of Depression America

Much writing about the 1930s has focused on white working-class or middle-class families that were caught in a spiral of downward social mobility. For such groups as African-Americans, farmers, and Mexican-Americans, times had always been hard and during the 1930s they got much harder. As the poet Langston Hughes noted, "The depression brought everybody down a peg or two. And the Negroes had but few pegs to fall."

Blacks and the Depression

Discrimination and limited opportunities had always been part of the lives of African-Americans, who thus viewed the depression differently than most whites did. Black people did not blame themselves for their misfortunes. "It didn't mean too much to him, the Great American Depression, as you call it," one man remarked. "There was no such thing. The best he could be is a janitor or a porter or shoeshine boy. It only became official when it hit the white man." The novelist and poet Maya Angelou, who grew up in Stamps, Arkansas, recalled, "The country had been in the throes of the Depression for two years before the Negroes in Stamps knew it. I think that everyone thought the Depression, like everything else, was for the white folks."

Despite the black migration to northern cities that had begun before World War I, as late as 1940 more than 75 percent of African-Americans still lived in the South. Nearly all the farmers who were black lived in the South, their condition scarcely better than it had been at the end of Reconstruction. Only 20 percent of black farmers owned their own land; the rest toiled at the bottom of the exploitative southern agricultural system, working as tenant farmers, farmhands, and sharecroppers. African-Americans rarely earned more than $200 a year. The earnings of black women cotton pickers in one Louisiana parish averaged only $41.67 a year.

Throughout the 1920s southern agriculture had suffered from falling prices and overproduction. During the depression an already desperate situation got worse. Some black farmers tried to protect themselves by joining the Southern Tenant Farmers Union (STFU), which was founded in 1934. The STFU was one of the few southern groups that welcomed both blacks and whites. "The same chain that holds you holds my people, too," an elderly black farmer reminded whites on the organizing committee. "If we're chained together on the outside we ought to stay chained together in the union." Landowners, however, had a stake in keeping black and white sharecroppers from organizing, and they countered the union's efforts with repression and harassment. In the end the STFU could do little to reform an agricultural system dependent on a single crop—cotton.

The Scottsboro Case. The Scottsboro case epitomized the harsh social and political discrimination that almost all blacks faced in the South in the 1930s. On March 25, 1931, a freight train pulled into Scottsboro, Alabama, carrying a number of hoboes and transients who had caught a free ride. Acting on a tip from the conductor, sheriff's deputies arrested nine black men for fighting with some of the white hoboes.

Suddenly, two white women wearing men's clothing stepped off the boxcar and claimed they had been raped by the nine blacks. The officers accepted without question the accusations of the women, Victoria Price and Ruby Bates, and barely restrained an angry white mob from lynching the accused men on the spot. Two weeks later juries composed entirely of white men found the nine defendants guilty of rape and sentenced eight of them to death. (One defendant escaped the death penalty because he was a minor.) The U.S. Supreme Court overturned the sentences in 1932 and ordered new trials because the defendants had been denied adequate legal counsel.

The youth of the Scottsboro defendants, their hasty trials, and the harsh sentences stirred public protest. The International Labor Defense (ILD), a labor organization closely tied to the Communist party, took over the defense of the so-called Scottsboro boys. The Communist party had targeted the struggle against racism as

The Lynch Mob and Silent Witness
The threat of lynching remained a terrifying part of life for African-Americans in the 1930s, and not just in the South. The photograph on the top shows two young blacks who were lynched by an Indiana mob in 1930. Each day that a person was lynched, the NAACP hung a banner (bottom) outside the window of its New York office. NAACP appeals for federal antilynching legislation received little support from politicians, however.

a priority in the early 1930s but was making little headway. "It's bad enough being black, why be red?" was a common reaction. White southerners resented the interference of those radicals as well as the fact that almost all those involved in the Scottsboro defense were northerners and Jews. In the words of a local solicitor, "Alabama justice cannot be bought and sold with Jew money from New York."

The case was complicated by the southern myth of the inviolate honor and chastity of white womanhood. The stories of the two women contained many inconsistencies, and Ruby Bates later recanted. However, in the South, when a white woman claimed to have been raped by a black man, she was taken at her word. As a court observer remarked, Victoria Price "might be a fallen woman, but by God she is a white woman."

The case dragged on through the courts for the next decade. In new trials held in 1936 and 1937 five of the defendants were convicted and sentenced to long prison terms. The charges against the other four were dropped in 1937. Four of the convicted men were paroled in 1944. The fifth escaped to Michigan, whose governor refused to return him to Alabama.

The Scottsboro case received wide coverage in black communities across the country. Along with the increase in lynching in the early 1930s (twenty blacks were lynched in 1930, twenty-four in 1933), it provided black Americans with a strong incentive to head for northern and midwestern cities. However, the lure of the North was offset by the lack of economic opportunities caused by the depression. About 400,000 black men and women left the South during the 1930s, only about half the number that had departed in the 1920s. Nevertheless, by 1935 eleven cities had more than 100,000 African-Americans. Two of the most popular destinations were the South Side of Chicago and Harlem in New York City.

Harlem in the 1930s In the late nineteenth century Harlem had been a neighborhood of wealthy white families—New York's first suburb—and as late as 1900, blacks made up only a small minority of its population. Then around 1910 the great migration from the South began, a process accelerated by World War I. As blacks moved into Harlem, second-generation Italians and Jews began to move out.

Harlem reached the height of its fame in the 1920s, when it became a mecca for both whites and blacks (see Chapter 24). Adventurous New Yorkers associated Harlem with the Cotton Club and other glittering jazz palaces that catered to white audiences. (Although the clubs featured black performers, they were white-only establishments from which black patrons were excluded.) During the 1920s the black population of New York City increased by about 115 percent, straining Harlem's housing facilities and community services.

The Cotton Club

The Cotton Club, "the aristocrat of Harlem" at Lenox Avenue and 142nd Street, was home to performers such as Duke Ellington, Ethel Waters, and Cab Calloway. Even though blacks provided the floor show and were hired as waiters and busboys at this swinging nightclub, they were not admitted as customers unless they were light-skinned enough to pass for white.

This once-prosperous middle-class community was on the way to becoming a slum.

The depression aggravated the situation. Residential segregation kept blacks from moving elsewhere. African-Americans paid excessive rents to unscrupulous owners who allowed their buildings to deteriorate. Crowded living conditions caused disease and death rates to climb; tuberculosis became a leading cause of death in Harlem. At the height of the depression shelters and soup kitchens staffed by the Divine Peace Mission, under the leadership of the charismatic black religious leader Father Divine, provided 3,000 meals a day for Harlem's destitute. Unemployment rose to 50 percent—twice the national rate—as whites clamored for jobs traditionally held by blacks—waiters, domestic servants, elevator operators, and garbage collectors.

In March 1935 Harlem exploded in the nation's only major race riot of the decade. Its residents were angry about the lack of jobs, a slowdown in relief, and the economic exploitation of the black community. Although entirely dependent on black trade, white-owned stores would not employ blacks. The arrest of a teenage black shoplifter, followed by rumors that he had been severely beaten by white police officers, triggered the riot. False reports of his death fueled the panic, and the city mobilized 500 police officers. Four blacks were killed, and property damage totaled $2 million.

However, the picture was not totally bleak for African-Americans in the 1930s. The New Deal would channel significant amounts of relief money toward blacks outside the South, partly in response to the 1935 riot but mainly in return for growing black allegiance to the Democratic party (see Chapter 26). The National Association for the Advancement of Colored People continued to publicly challenge the status quo of race relations. Although calls for racial justice went largely unheeded during the depression, World War II and its aftermath would provide better opportunities for the struggle for black equality.

Dust Bowl Migrations

Distressed conditions in agriculture had been one of the causes of the Great Depression. In the 1930s things only got worse, especially for farmers on the Great Plains. The decade became known as the "Dirty Thirties" because of the dust storms that blighted the land. The worst drought in the country's history began in 1930 and lasted until 1941. Throughout the decade the three words most often uttered by farmers were "if it rains."

Farmers who moved onto the semiarid Great Plains after the 1870s had always risked the ravages of drought (see Chapter 17). Even in wet years the average rainfall was 20 inches or less—barely enough to raise grain crops. But low rainfall alone did not create the Dust Bowl. National and international market forces, such as the demand for wheat during World War I, caused farmers to push the farming frontier beyond its natural limits by working increasingly marginal land to capture a profit. After that land had been stripped of its natural vegetation, the delicate ecological balance of the plains was destroyed. Nothing remained to hold the soil when the rains dried up and the winds came.

Dust became a plague of everyday life throughout the Great Plains but especially in Oklahoma, Texas, New Mexico, Colorado, Arkansas, and Kansas (see Map 25.2). When the clouds of dust rolled in, streetlights blinked on as if night had fallen. Dust seeped into houses and "blackened the pillow around one's head, the dinner plates on the table, the bread dough on the back of the stove" (see American Voices, page 785). The dust storms were not confined to the plains. In May 1934 the wind took dust clouds to Chicago, where filth fell like snow, dumping the equivalent of 4 pounds of debris per person on the city. Several days later the same clouds blackened the skies and dirtied the streets of Buffalo, Boston, New York, and Washington. That winter red snow fell on New England.

This ecological disaster caused a mass exodus from the land. Their crops ruined, their lands barren and dry, their homes foreclosed for debts they could not pay, thousands of farm families loaded their belongings into

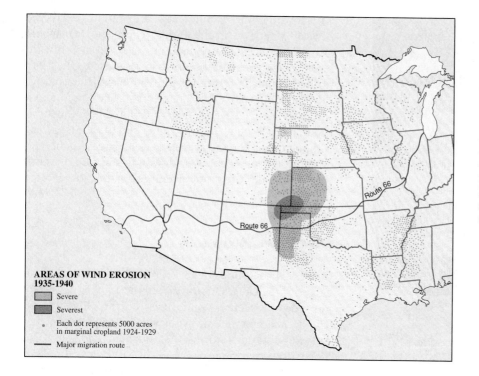

MAP 25.2

The Dust Bowl

A U.S. Weather Bureau scientist called the drought of the 1930s "the worst in the climatological history of the country." Conditions were especially severe in the southern plains, where the dramatic increases in farming on marginal land had strained production before the drought struck. Many farm families saw no choice but to follow Route 66, the highway that went west through Missouri, Oklahoma, and north Texas to California, the promised land.

beat-up Fords and headed west along Route 66 to the promised land of California. The migrants were called "Okies" whether or not they were from Oklahoma. John Steinbeck's novel *The Grapes of Wrath* (1939) immortalized their journey. In the novel the Joads abandon their land not only because of drought but also as a result of the economic forces changing American agriculture. Large-scale commercialized farming had spread to the plains, where family farmers still used draft animals. After the bank forecloses on the Joads' farm, a gasoline-engine tractor, the symbol of mechanized farming, plows under their crops and demolishes their house.

Although a powerful work of fiction, the story of the Joads' struggle does not convey the diversity of the westward migration, which was both a response to hard times and part of the larger migration out of the nation's agricultural heartland that had begun around World War I and continued through the 1970s. Not all Okies were destitute dirt farmers; perhaps one in six was a professional, a business proprietor, or a white-collar worker. Many were participating in chain migrations, that is, following family members or friends to a specific place. For most the drive west was fairly easy: Route 66 was a paved two-lane road, and in a decent car it took three to four days to make it from Oklahoma or Texas to California.

Before the 1930s, California had already undergone changes that had created a type of agriculture different from that practiced by southwestern and midwestern farmers. Agriculture in California was large-scale, intensive, and diversified. The state's wealth came primarily from specialty crops whose staggered harvests

required a great deal of transient labor for short picking seasons. The steady supply of cheap migrant labor provided by Chinese, Mexicans, Okies, and, briefly, East Indians made such farming economically feasible. Carey McWilliams, whose nonfiction *Factories in the Field* (1939) focused national attention on migrant workers, noted that California agriculture was basically industrial in nature:

> Ownership is represented not by physical possession of the land, but by ownership of corporate stock; farm labor, no longer pastoral in character, punches a time clock, works at piece or hourly wage rates, and lives in a shack or company barracks, and lacks all contact with the real owners of the farm factory on which it is employed.

Encouraged by handbills promising good jobs in California, at least 350,000 southwesterners headed west in the 1930s. Some went to metropolitan areas, but about half settled in rural areas. White, native-born Americans had made up about 20 percent of the migratory farm labor force before the depression, but their proportion increased to more than 85 percent in the late 1930s. Since growers needed only 175,000 workers at the peak of the picking season, this surplus assured them a cheap supply of labor, usually docile and willing to work at any price. That price was incredibly low in the 1930s. The average yearly family income of migrant farm workers in California ranged from $350 to $450, less than a third of the subsistence level. Yet what they earned in California was more than what they had left behind.

Ann Marie Low

A Dust Bowl Diary

Born in 1912, Ann Marie Low kept diaries from 1927 to 1937, which describe the devastation wracked by drought and the depression on her family's farm in the Badlands of southeastern North Dakota. They record both a young woman's coming of age and the harshness of life on the farm in the Dust Bowl.

April 25, 1934, Wednesday

Last weekend was the worst dust storm we ever had. We've been having quite a bit of blowing dirt every year since the drouth started, not only here, but all over the Great Plains. Many days this spring the air is just full of dirt coming, literally, for hundreds of miles. It sifts into everything. After we wash the dishes and put then away, so much dust sifts into the cupboards we must wash them again before the next meal. Clothes in the closet are covered with dust.

Last weekend no one was taking an automobile out for fear of ruining the motor. I rode Roany to Frank's place to return a gear. To find my way I had to ride right beside the fence, scarcely able to see from one fence post to the next.

Newspapers say the deaths of many babies and old people are attributed to breathing in so much dirt.

May 21, 1934, Monday

Ethel has been having stomach trou-ble. Dad has been taking her to doctors though suspecting her trouble is the fact that she often goes on a diet that may affect her health. The local doctor said he thought it might be chronic appendicitis, so Mama took Ethel by train to Valley City last week to have a surgeon there remove her appendix.

Saturday Dad, Bud, and I planted an acre of potatoes. There was so much dirt in the air I couldn't see Bud only a few feet in front of me. Even the air in the house was just a haze. In the evening the wind died down, and Cap came to take me to the movie. We joked about how hard it is to get cleaned up enough to go anywhere. . . .

May 30, 1934, Wednesday

Ethel got along fine, so Mama left her at the hospital and came to Jamestown by train Friday. Dad took us both home.

The mess was incredible! Dirt had blown into the house all week and lay inches deep on everything. Every towel and curtain was just black. There wasn't a clean dish or cooking utensil. . . . It took until 10 o'clock to wash all the dirty dishes. That's not wiping them—just washing them. The cupboards had to be washed out to have a clean place to put them.

Saturday was a busy day. Before starting breakfast I had to sweep and wash all the dirt off the kitchen and dining room floors, wash the stove, pancake griddle, and dining room table and chairs. There was cooking, baking, and churning to be done for those hungry men. Dad is 6 feet 4 inches tall, with a big frame. Bud is 6 feet 3 inches and almost as big-boned as Dad. We say feeding them is like filling a silo.

Mama couldn't make bread until I carried water to wash the bread mixer. I couldn't churn until the churn was washed and scalded. We just couldn't do anything until something was washed first. Every room had to have dirt almost shoveled out of it before we could wash floors and furniture.

We had no time to wash clothes, but it was necessary. I had to wash out the boiler, wash tubs, and the washing machine before we could use them. Then every towel, curtain, piece of bedding, and garment had to be taken outdoors to have as much dust as possible shaken out before washing. The cistern is dry, so I had to carry all the water we needed from the well.

That evening Cap came to take me to the movie, as usual. Ixnay. I'm sorry I snapped at Cap. It isn't his fault, or anyone's fault, but I was tired and cross. Life in what the newspapers call "the Dust Bowl" is becoming a gritty nightmare.

Source: Ann Marie Low, *Dust Bowl Diary* (Lincoln: University of Nebraska Press, 1984), 95, 96–98.

Those migrants had a lasting impact on California culture. At first they met outright hostility from old-time Californians, a demoralizing experience for white, native-born Protestants who were ashamed of the negative "Okie" stereotype. But they stayed, filling important roles in the expanding California economy. Soon communities in the San Joaquin Valley—Bakersfield, Fresno, Merced, Modesto, Stockton—took on a distinctly Okie cast, identifiable by southern-influenced evangelical religion and the growing popularity of country music.

Mexican-American Communities

The Mexican-American experience in the West differed from that of Dust Bowl refugees. In the depths of the depression, with American fears about competition from foreign workers at a peak, perhaps a third of the Mexican-American population, primarily immigrants, returned to Mexico. A formal deportation policy instituted by the U.S. government was partly responsible for the exodus, but many more Mexicans left "voluntarily" when work ran out and local relief agencies refused to

extend assistance to them. Pervasive racism and the proximity of Mexico made Mexicans the only immigrants targeted for deportation during the depression.

The deportation of Mexican-Americans was not a response to the arrival of migrants from the Dust Bowl. The largest number of deportations occurred during the Hoover administration, well before the Dust Bowl exodus reached its peak. Most occurred in California and Texas, but Indiana, Illinois, Michigan, and Colorado also repatriated unwanted workers. In 1932, a one-way train ticket cost the equivalent of a week's relief allotment, and officials in many southwestern communities realized that it was cheaper to send migrant workers back to Mexico than to support them during the winter, when there were no crops to pick.

In 1930 Los Angeles was home to 150,000 Mexican-Americans, making it the largest Mexican city outside Mexico. Mexican-Americans spilled out of the downtown area known as "Sonoratown" into neighborhoods or *colonias* in Belvedere and East Los Angeles, where mutual-aid societies, Spanish-language newspapers, and the Catholic Church fostered a sense of community. But Los Angeles lost approximately one-third of its Mexican population during the repatriation drives of the 1930s, which caused profound social dislocations. Although the free trip home at government expense was the source of some *chistes* (jokes), it also caused family separations, disruptions of education for children who were pulled out of school, and extreme financial hardships during the worst years of the depression. And for those who remained in America, repatriation was an unmistakable reminder of the fragility of their status in the United States.

Mexican migration to the United States—legal and illegal—increased steadily throughout the twentieth century, except during the Great Depression and for short periods after the two world wars. The first *bracero* (day laborer) program promoting Mexican immigration had been established during World War I to meet labor shortages. (*Bracero* comes from *brazo*, which means "arm" in Spanish; *braceros* are hired hands, those who work with their arms.) The importation of cheap Mexican labor continued throughout the 1920s. After being deported during the depression, Mexican workers were coaxed back again when World War II caused another labor shortage. The influx of Spanish-speaking migrants with their own culture helped shape the patterns of life and work in the Southwest and the West.

The experiences of his family members as migrant workers during the 1930s influenced a Mexican-American named César Chávez to become one of the twentieth century's most influential labor organizers. Chávez was a child of ten in 1934, when his father lost the family farm, located near Yuma, Arizona. The Chávez family joined the army of migrant workers that followed the crops in California. They experienced continual discrimination, even in restaurants, where signs

proclaimed "White Trade Only." César's father became involved in several bitter labor struggles in the Imperial Valley in the mid-1930s. In 1933 thirty-seven major agricultural strikes occurred in California, including one in the San Joaquin Valley that mobilized 18,000 cotton pickers, the largest agricultural strike to date. All the strikes failed, but they gave the young Chávez a background in labor organizing, which he used to found a national farm workers' union in 1962.

Not all Mexican-Americans were migrant farm workers. A significant number lived in urban areas and held industrial jobs, especially in steel mills, meat-packing plants, and refineries, where they established a vibrant tradition of labor activism. Mexican-American smelter and refinery workers joined the International Union of Mine, Mill and Smelter Workers (known colloquially as "Mine-Mill") in large numbers and became key leaders. Bert Corona launched his career as a labor organizer with the International Longshoremen's and Warehousemen's Union in Los Angeles (see American Lives, pages 788–789). Labor activism was not limited to men. Mexican-American women made up 75 percent of the dressmakers who toiled in Los Angeles's sweatshops, many for less than $5 a week. In 1933 Rose Pesotta, a Polish immigrant labor organizer for the International Ladies' Garment Workers Union (ILGWU), used bilingual appeals to lead a four-week strike of the garment workers in which Mexican-American women were the most active participants.

Migrant Labor in California
Mexican-American workers had faced deportation in the early years of the depression, but their cheap agricultural labor was too essential to growers to make the exile permanent. Here a Chicano worker hauls peppers.

Mexican-American Poverty in Texas
In 1937 Antonia and Pablo Martinez lived in a one-room house in San Antonio, Texas, with his parents and older brother. If either Pablo or Antonia was employed in 1937, it was probably in San Antonio's pecan-shelling industry, which depended heavily on the cheap labor of Mexican-Americans.

In California, Mexican-Americans also found employment in fruit and vegetable processing plants, especially young single women who preferred the higher wages of cannery work to domestic service, needlework, and farm labor. Corporate giants such as Del Monte (California Packing Corporation, or Cal Pak) and Libby, McNeill, and Libby dominated California's food-processing industry. In those plants Mexican-American women earned around $2.50 a day, while their male counterparts earned $3.50 to $4.50. So pervasive was the "cannery culture" that workers could say, "We met in spinach, fell in love in peaches, and married in tomatoes," and their friends would know they were referring to the harvests of March, August, and October. In 1939 labor unions came to the canneries in the form of the United Cannery, Agricultural, Packing, and Allied Workers of America (UCAPAWA), an unusually democratic union in which women, who formed a majority of the rank-and-file workers, played a leading role.

This activism of the 1930s, in the fields and in the factories, demonstrated how the second generation of Mexican immigrants, born in the United States, increasing turned its orientation toward issues of political and economic justice in the United States, rather than retaining primary allegiance to Mexico. According to historian George Sanchez, they were creating "their own version of Americanism without abandoning Mexican culture." Joining American labor unions and becoming more involved in American politics were important steps in creating a Mexican-American ethnic identity.

Herbert Hoover and the Great Depression

During the presidential campaign of 1928 Herbert Hoover predicted that "the poorhouse is vanishing from among us" and stated that America was "nearer to the final triumph over poverty than ever before in the history of any land." Once elected, Hoover planned to preside over an era of Republican prosperity and governmental restraint. Even after the stock market crash in 1929, he stubbornly insisted that the downturn was only temporary. He greeted a business delegation in June 1930 with these words: "Gentlemen, you have come sixty days too late. The Depression is over." In 1931 and 1932, as the country hit rock bottom, Hoover finally acted, but by then it was too little, too late.

The Republican Response

In 1932 the journalist William Allen White wrote an article about the outgoing president entitled "Herbert Hoover—The Last of the Old Presidents, or the First of the New?" White concluded that Hoover had been a little of both, as have historians ever since. Hoover's early efforts to fight the depression are now seen as predecessors of many New Deal programs, and his reputation among historians has risen steadily over the years. Hoover, who lived until 1964, offered a simple explanation for the improvement in his historical stature, telling Chief Justice Earl Warren of the Supreme Court that he had simply managed "to outlive the bastards."

Hoover's approach to the Great Depression was shaped by his priorities as secretary of commerce: he turned to the business community for leadership in overcoming the economic downturn. Hoover asked business to maintain wages voluntarily, keep up production, and work with the government to build confidence in the system.

Fiscal Policy. Hoover did not rely solely on public pronouncements, but also used public funds and federal action to encourage recovery. Soon after the stock market crash he cut federal taxes and called on state and local governments to increase capital spending in the "energetic yet prudent pursuit" of public construction. The 1929 Agricultural Marketing Act gave the federal government its largest role to date in a program of agricultural stabilization and farm relief. In 1930 and the first half of 1931 Hoover raised the federal public-works budget to $423 million, a dramatic increase in an area not traditionally seen as the federal government's responsibility. Hoover also eased the international crisis by declaring, early in the summer of 1931, a moratorium on the payment of Allied debts and reparations.

Bert Corona and the Mexican-American Generation

Bert Corona always considered himself a child of the revolution—the Mexican Revolution. His father, Noe Corona, had crossed the border from Mexico to the United States around 1915 or 1916, seeking safety after being wounded while fighting in Pancho Villa's army. Settling temporarily in El Paso, he married Margarita Escápite Salayandia, and they had four children, including Humberto (his Anglo teachers later Americanized his name to Bert), who was born in 1918.

The border is an apt metaphor for Mexican-American life, capturing the fluidity of crossing back and forth between two countries and two cultures. Bert's family returned to Mexico in 1922, where two years later Noe Corona was assassinated by unknown assailants, presumably political enemies. This loss had a profound effect on Noe's six-year-old son: "The Revolution, my father's role in it, and his martyrdom symbolized the struggle for social justice. This would be the same struggle I would later pursue."

The Corona family resettled in El Paso, where Bert's mother secured a job at the Mexican customs house on the El Paso–Ciudad Juarez border and his grandmother, a doctor, pursued her practice of medicine and midwifery. Being raised by these two women provided Bert with strong female role models. The El Paso school system provided a searing introduction to the discrimination against and unequal treatment of Mexican immigrants in the Southwest. Corona's segregated "Mexican" school in the barrio, geared primarily toward vocational education, was far inferior to white schools. Although he attended an integrated high school with a good academic reputation, racism and discrimination remained very much part of his education, both in daily encounters with his Anglo teachers and classmates and in the general lack of respect for Mexican history and culture in the curriculum. His grandmother said tartly, "Well, you have to understand that the United States writes its history to its own convenience. It always has, and these people always will."

When Bert graduated from high school in 1934 at age sixteen, it was the height of the Great Depression, and El Paso was hard hit. Fortunately, his mother kept her job at the Juarez customs house, but hard times forced many Mexicans to leave. El Paso was a major border crossing for *los repatriados* as they fled the depression and the threat of deportation, but Mexicans were not the only group on the move. The Corona backyard faced the train tracks, and Bert vividly remembered the thousands of Dust Bowl migrants traveling through El Paso on their way west. A hundred-car freight train could carry a thousand Dust Bowlers, and there were three trains in the morning and three in the evening: "It was like the population of a small town coming in every day."

After working for two years in El Paso, Bert headed to the University of Southern California, where he hoped to play basketball and continue his education on an athletic scholarship. But an injury cut short his sports career, and he soon found new interests that took him away from his studies, although he later regretted not getting a college degree. What could possibly have taken precedence over his family's strong belief in education? Participating in the revitalized labor movement and fostering Mexican-American political consciousness, the two causes that shaped the rest of Corona's life.

The Congress of Industrial Organization, or CIO (see Chapter 26), became his vehicle for labor activism: "I had a sense of the historical importance of the CIO, and I viewed the CIO as a movement whose time had come. Nothing could stop it, and—for a time—nothing did." In the 1930s many labor activists focused on organizing Mexican-American migrant workers in the fields, but Corona concentrated on recruiting Los Angeles industrial workers into the newly constituted International Longshoremen's and Warehousemen's Union (ILWU). His organizing was not restricted to Mexican workers, however. Like the CIO, he wanted the entire

Bert Corona addresses a press conference at the National Chicano Political Caucus in 1972.

working class to join unions to work for social change in the workplace and in society as a whole. While organizing at an aviation plant in 1941 he met his future wife, Blanche Taff. The daughter of Polish Jewish immigrants, she shared his commitment to progressive social change. Their marriage fit right into the interracial and interethnic culture of the CIO. So great was their commitment to organized labor that they gave up their honeymoon to participate in a major CIO organizing drive.

In addition to labor organizing, Bert Corona felt a deep commitment to the political mobilization of Spanish-speaking peoples throughout the United States. In 1939 he joined El Congreso Nacional del Pueblo de Habla Español (the National Congress of Spanish-Speaking Peoples), a militant organization founded to fight for the rights of Mexican-Americans and other Latinos as part of the larger struggle against racial and class oppression. There he worked with noted activists such as Luisa Moreno, a Guatemalan-born CIO organizer who had been active in the cannery industry, and

Josefina Fierro, a radical young Mexican-American married to the screenwriter John Bright, who was part of Hollywood's leftist community. Their activist agenda was far to the left of organizations such as the League of United Latin American Citizens (LULAC), founded in 1929, which focused on discrimination and civil rights from a distinctly middle-class perspective.

After serving in the armed forces during World War II, Corona continued to be a labor and community activist. In the 1960s he became involved in the Mexican-American Political Association, or MAPA (see Chapter 30), which mobilized Latino political power to force the Kennedy and Johnson administrations to do more for those constituencies. Since then he has been involved in community organizing, especially of undocumented Mexican workers entering the United States.

Bert Corona exemplifies what the historian Mario Garcia has called the "Mexican-American Generation." These men and women, who were born and raised in the United States, came of political age between the 1930s and the 1950s. They filled the leadership vacuum created when *los repatriados*, mainly older and Mexican-born, returned permanently to that country in the 1930s. Even before terms such as *Mexican-American*, *Hispanic*, and *Latino* were widely used, this generation had the "double consciousness" that W. E. B. DuBois described in African-Americans: a sense of being both *mexicanos* and American citizens. Many members of the Mexican-American Generation shared Corona's commitment to organizing for social change—in their communities, on the job, and in the wider political arena. Tracing their political activism over the years provides a window on the changing character of Mexican-American communities in the United States.

Since the 1930s Bert Corona has seen a dramatic expansion of Latino empowerment, but he remains modest about his role in this story. "It's hard for me to think how I would like to be remembered by history," he told Mario Garcia as they collaborated on a book about his life. "I never planned my life. It just happened the way it did. . . . If my life has meant anything, I would say that it shows that you can organize workers and poor people if you work hard, are persistent, remain optimistic, and reach out to involve as many people as possible. . . . But my life is not over yet, and I continue *la lucha*, the struggle." For Bert Corona that commitment to *la lucha* had its roots in his Mexican heritage, but it first began to flower during the turbulent 1930s.

The federal government's efforts to stimulate business activity were moderately effective, but the depression continued.

By 1931 more drastic action was required, but Hoover faced a cruel dilemma that had been created by the Federal Reserve's contraction of the money supply. If he embraced deficit financing and encouraged recovery through increased government spending, interest rates would remain high, since the federal government would be competing for borrowed capital with corporations and private investors. Hoover decided that significantly higher interest rates posed the greater danger to recovery, so in December 1931 he asked Congress for a 33 percent tax increase to balance the budget. The Revenue Act of 1932 represented the largest peacetime tax increase in the nation's history. Like monetary restriction, higher taxes choked both consumption and investment and contributed significantly to the severity of the Great Depression.

Not all the steps taken by the Hoover administration were so ill conceived. The president pushed Congress to create a system of government home-loan banks in 1932. He also supported the Glass-Steagall Banking Act of 1932, which made government securities available to guarantee Federal Reserve notes and thus counter credit contractions caused by withdrawals of gold. This step temporarily propped up the ailing banking system. The federal government under Hoover also spent $700 million—an unprecedented sum for the time—on public works.

However, Hoover remained adamant in his refusal to consider any plan for direct federal relief for unemployed Americans. Throughout his career he had believed that private organized charities were sufficient to meet social welfare needs. During World War I Hoover had headed the Commission for Relief of Belgium, a private group that distributed 5 million tons of food to relieve the suffering of Europe's civilian population. In 1927 he coordinated a rescue and cleanup operation after a devastating Mississippi River flood left 16.5 million acres of land under water in seven states. This effort involved private charities, including the Red Cross and the Rockefeller Foundation, as well as government agencies such as the U.S. Public Health Service and the National Guard. The success of these and other predominantly voluntary responses to public emergencies confirmed Hoover's belief that private charity, not federal aid, was the "American way." But charities and state and local relief agencies were unable to meet the growing needs of the unemployed.

The Reconstruction Finance Corporation. The centerpiece of Hoover's new initiative to combat the depression was the Reconstruction Finance Corporation (RFC), which Congress approved in January 1932. Modeled on the War Finance Corporation of World War I and developed in collaboration with the business and banking communities, the RFC was the first federal institution created to intervene directly in the economy during peacetime. It was designed to alleviate the credit crunch for business by providing federal loans to railroads, financial institutions, banks, and insurance companies in a strategy that has been called *pump priming*. Money lent at the top of the economic structure stimulates production, which in turn creates new jobs and increases consumer spending. Benefits thus "trickle down" to the rest of the economy.

Congress allocated $500 million for the RFC, but the agency's cautiousness in lending money limited its influence. In July 1932 Congress doubled that amount and authorized loans to the states for relief and public works. Once again the RFC acted far too cautiously, lending only $30 million by the end of 1932. It allocated and spent only 20 percent of the $1.5 billion appropriated for public works projects.

The RFC was a watershed in American political history and the rise of the state. When voluntary cooperation failed, the president turned to federal action to stimulate the economy. Yet Hoover's break with the past had clear limits. In many ways his support of the RFC was just another attempt to encourage business confidence. Compared with previous presidents, Hoover responded to the national emergency on an unprecedented scale. But the nation's needs during the Great Depression were also unprecedented, and federal programs failed to meet them.

Rising Discontent

As the depression deepened, many citizens came to hate Herbert Hoover. Once the symbol of business prosperity, he became the scapegoat for the depression. His declarations that nobody was starving and that hoboes were better fed than ever before seemed cruel and insensitive. His apparent willingness to bail out business and banks while leaving individuals to fend for themselves added to his reputation for coldheartedness (see American Voices, page 791). New terms entered the vocabulary: *Hoovervilles* (shantytowns where people lived in packing crates and other makeshift shelters), *Hoover flags* (empty pockets turned inside out), and *Hoover blankets* (newspapers). The columnist Russell Baker remembered his aunt's exaggerated recital of Hoover's offenses:

> People were starving because of Herbert Hoover. My mother was out of work because of Herbert Hoover. Men were killing themselves because of Herbert Hoover, and their fatherless children were being packed away to orphanages . . . because of Herbert Hoover.

Signs of rising discontent and rebellion began to emerge

The Despair of the Unemployed

In 1931 an unemployed tool and dye designer wrote to the director of the President's Organization for Unemployment Relief (POUR), but his letter drew only this penciled response: "no use answering."

Detroit, Mich.
September 29, 1931

Mr. Walter Gifford
Dear Sir:

You and Pres. Hoover shows at times about the same degree of intelligence as Andy [of the "Amos & Andy" radio show] does. The other night Andy was going to send a fellow a letter to find out his address.

You have told us to spend to end the slump, but you did not tell us what to use for money, after being out of work for two years you tell us this, Pres. Hoover on the other hand tells the working man to build homes, and in face of the fact nearly every working man has had his home taken off him, "some more intelligence." This is a radical letter but the time is here to be radical. when an average of two a day has to take their own life right in the City of Detroit because they can not see their way out. right in the city where one of the worlds riches men lives who made last year 259 000 000 dollars. where hundreds of peoples are starving to death. . . . Mr. Gifford why not come clean . . . remember you have the all seeing eye of God over you. Tell us the reason of the depression is the greed of Bankers and Industrialist who are taking too great of amount of profits . . . . The other day our Pres. Hoover came to Detroit and kidded the soldier boys out of their bonus. Pres Hoover a millionaire worth about 12 000 000 dollars drawing a salary of 75 000 per year from the government asking some boys to forgo their bonus some of them have not 12 dollars of their own "Some more nerve."

Am I right when I say you and he shows the same degree of intelligence as Andy.

J. B.

Source: Quoted in Robert S. McElvaine, *Down & Out in the Great Depression* (Chapel Hill: University of North Carolina Press, 1983), 46–47.

as the country entered the fourth year of the depression. Farmers were among the most vocal groups, banding together to harass the bank agents and government officers who enforced evictions and farm foreclosures and to protest the low prices they received for their crops. Midwestern farmers had watched the price of wheat fall from $3 a bushel in 1920 to barely 30 cents in 1932. Now they formed the Farm Holiday Association under the charismatic leadership of Milo Reno, the sixty-four-year-old former president of the Iowa Farmers' Union. Farmers barricaded local roads and dumped milk, vegetables, and other farm produce because the prices they would fetch on the market would not cover the farmers' costs. Nothing better captured the cruel irony of underconsumption and maldistribution than farmers dumping food at a time when thousands of people were hungry.

Hoovervilles

By 1930 shantytowns had sprung up in most of the nation's cities. In New York City squatters camped out along the Hudson River railroad tracks, built makeshift homes in Central Park, or lived in the city dump. This scene from the old reservoir in Central Park looks east toward the fancy apartment buildings of Fifth Avenue and the Metropolitan Museum of Art, at left.

Protest was not confined to rural America. Bitter labor strikes occurred in the depths of the depression despite the threat that strikers would lose their jobs. In Harlan County, Kentucky, miners struck in 1931 over a 10 percent wage cut, only to see their union crushed by the mine owners and the National Guard. At Ford's River Rouge factory outside Detroit in 1932 a demonstration provoked violence from police and Ford security forces; three demonstrators were killed, and fifty were seriously injured. Some 40,000 people viewed the coffins under a banner charging that "Ford Gave Bullets for Bread."

In 1931 and 1932 violence broke out in the nation's cities. Groups of unemployed citizens battled local authorities over inadequate relief; people staged rent riots and hunger marches. Fearing the consequences of trying to stop this civil disorder, Mayor Anton J. Cermak of Chicago challenged a Congressional committee to send relief or troops.

Some of these urban actions were organized by the Communist party as a challenge to the American capitalist system. For example, the Communist party helped organize "unemployment councils" that agitated for jobs and food and coordinated a hunger march on Washington, D.C., in 1931. The marches were well attended and often got results from local and federal authorities, but they did not necessarily win converts to communism. In the early 1930s the Communist party was still a tiny organization with only 12,000 members.

It was not radicals but veterans who staged the most publicized—and tragic—protest. In the summer of 1932 the "Bonus Army," a ragtag group of about 15,000 unemployed World War I veterans, hitchhiked to Washington to demand that their bonuses, originally scheduled for distribution in 1945, be paid immediately. While they unsuccessfully lobbied Congress, members of the "Bonus Expeditionary Force" (parodying the wartime American Expeditionary Force) camped out in the capital, a visible reminder of the plight of the unemployed. "We were heroes in 1917, but we're bums now," one veteran remarked bitterly. When the marchers refused to leave their Anacostia Flats camp, Hoover called out riot troops led by General Douglas MacArthur, assisted by Majors Dwight D. Eisenhower and George S. Patton, to clear the area. MacArthur's forces burned the encampment to the ground, and in the fight that followed more than a hundred marchers were injured. Newsreel footage captured the deeply disturbing spectacle of the U.S. Army firing on American citizens, and Hoover's popularity plunged even further.

The 1932 Election

Despite evidence of discontent, the nation was not in a revolutionary mood as it approached the 1932 election. Despair and apathy, not anger, characterized the feelings of most citizens. The Republicans, who could find no credible way to dump an incumbent president, unenthusiastically renominated Hoover. The Democrats turned to Governor Franklin Delano Roosevelt of New York, who capitalized on that state's innovative relief and unemployment programs to win the nomination.

Roosevelt's route to the presidential nomination began on a Hudson River estate north of New York City. Born into a wealthy family in 1882, he attended the Groton School, Harvard, and Columbia Law School. Roosevelt gave up his law career in 1910 for a seat in New York's state legislature. He served as assistant secretary of the navy in the Wilson administration, and that earned him the vice-presidential nomination on the losing Democratic ticket in 1920. Except for his allegiance to Democratic rather than Republican party ideology, he consciously modeled his career on that of his distant cousin Theodore Roosevelt, whose niece Eleanor he married in 1905.

Franklin Roosevelt was sidetracked from his path to the White House in 1921 by an attack of polio that left both his legs paralyzed for the rest of his life. Roosevelt fought back from his infirmity, emerging from the ordeal a stronger, more resilient man. "If you had spent two years in bed trying to wiggle your toe, after that anything would seem easy," he said. Eleanor Roosevelt strongly supported her husband's return to public life, serving as his stand-in during the 1920s. She and Louis Howe, Roosevelt's devoted political aide, masterminded his reentry into Democratic politics. Roosevelt won the New York governorship in 1928 and the Democratic presidential nomination in 1932.

The Bonus Army
These children were camped out in the summer of 1932 on the Anacostia Flats of Washington, D.C., while their fathers lobbied Congress for early payment of World War I bonuses. Congress said no, and the U.S. Army violently disbanded the veterans' encampment.

The 1932 campaign foreshadowed little of the New Deal. Roosevelt hinted at new approaches to the depression but stated his goals in vague terms: "The country needs and, unless I mistake its temper, the country demands bold, persistent experimentation." Roosevelt won easily, receiving 22.8 million votes to Hoover's 15.7 million. Despite the economic collapse, Americans remained firmly committed to the two-party system. The Socialist party candidate, Norman Thomas, got fewer than a million votes. The Communist party drew only 100,000 votes for its candidate, party leader William Z. Foster (see Map 25.3).

The 1932 election marked a turning point in American politics: the emergence of a Democratic coalition that would dominate political life for the next four decades. In 1932 Roosevelt won with the support of the Solid South, which returned to the Democratic fold after defecting in 1928 because of Al Smith's religion and views on Prohibition. Roosevelt also drew substantial support in the West. An increasingly large urban vote continued a trend that was first noticed in the 1928 election, when the Democrats successfully appealed to recent immigrants and eth-nic groups in the cities. However, Roosevelt's election was hardly a mandate to reshape American political and economic institutions. Many people voted as much against Hoover as for Roosevelt.

The Interregnum. Having spoken, the voters had to wait until March 1933 before Roosevelt could put his ideas into action. (The interval between election and inauguration was shortened so that it ended on January 20 by the Twentieth Amendment in 1933.) In the worst winter of the depression Americans could do little but hope that things would get better. According to the most conservative estimates, unemployment stood at 20 to 25 percent. The rate was as high as 50 percent in Cleveland, 60 percent in Akron, and 80 percent in Toledo—cities dependent on manufacturing jobs in industries that had basically shut down. The nation's banking system was so close to collapse that many state governors temporarily closed banks to avoid further panic.

By the winter of 1932–1933 the depression had totally overwhelmed public welfare institutions. Private charity and local public relief, whose expenditures had risen dramatically, still reached only a fraction of the needy. Hunger haunted cities and rural areas alike. When a teacher tried to send a coal miner's daughter home from school because she was weak from hunger, the girl replied, "It won't do any good . . . because this is sister's day to eat." In New York City, hospitals reported ninety-five deaths from starvation. This was the America that Roosevelt inherited when he took the oath of office on March 4, 1933.

MAP 25.3

The Election of 1932

Franklin Roosevelt's convincing electoral victory over Herbert Hoover in 1932 resulted from a political realignment and dissatisfaction with the incumbent president. Even in the midst of the gravest crisis capitalism had ever faced, candidates of the Communist and Socialist parties received fewer than 1 million votes out of almost 40 million cast.

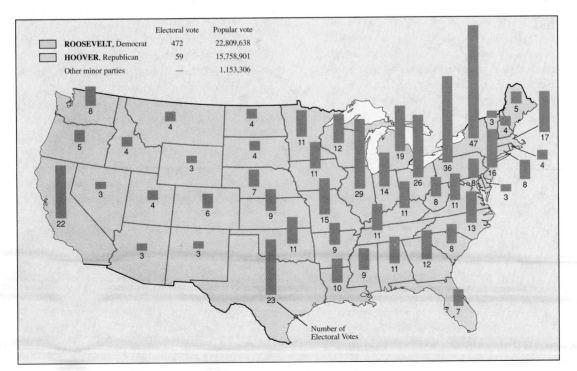

	Electoral vote	Popular vote
ROOSEVELT, Democrat	472	22,809,638
HOOVER, Republican	59	15,758,901
Other minor parties	—	1,153,306

Number of Electoral Votes

Summary

The economic prosperity of the 1920s rested on shaky ground. After the stock market crash of 1929 the economy entered a downward spiral that did not bottom out until 1932–1933. In addition to the collapse of the stock market, the main causes of the depression were underconsumption, an unstable international financial situation, a legacy of "sick industries" and agricultural distress from the 1920s, and the flawed monetary policies of the Federal Reserve System. At first Hoover did not want to intervene in the economy because of his reliance on private charities and his adamant stance on maintaining a balanced budget. Then in 1932 the Hoover administration authorized the first direct federal intervention in the economy during peacetime, the Reconstruction Finance Corporation, to win business and public confidence. Though unprecedented, such measures did not end the Great Depression.

The Great Depression left an "invisible scar" on many people who lived through the 1930s, especially white middle-class Americans. Those who wanted to work blamed themselves if they could not find a job. The impact of the depression was especially catastrophic for African-Americans, Mexican-Americans, and other minorities, for whom times had always been hard. And for farmers in the Midwest things got even worse than they had been in the 1920s. Misguided agricultural practices and drought created the Dust Bowl, forcing many farmers off their land.

Despite the devastating impact of the depression, many aspects of American life and culture continued to conform to traditional patterns. Families pulled together, with women taking on expanded roles—and often new jobs—to help support their households. Young people stayed in school longer. Families sought relief in popular culture, especially movies and radio programs. In 1932 the nation turned to Franklin D. Roosevelt and the Democrats.

TIMELINE

1929	Stock market crash Agricultural Marketing Act
1930	Midwestern drought begins Hawley-Smoot Tariff
1931	Scottsboro case Great Britain abandons gold standard Hoover declares moratorium on Allied war debts Miners strike in Harlan County, Kentucky
1932	Reconstruction Finance Corporation Bonus Army Lindbergh kidnapping Revenue Act of 1933 Height of deportation of Mexican migrant workers Farm Holiday Association founded Strike at Ford's River Rouge plant in Michigan Communist-led hunger marches
1933	Unemployment rises to highest level Franklin Delano Roosevelt becomes president Birth rate drops to lowest level
1934	Southern Tenant Farmers Union founded *It Happened One Night* sweeps Oscars
1935	National Youth Administration Harlem race riot
1936	Student Strike against War Margaret Mitchell's *Gone with the Wind* Jesse Owens wins four gold medals at Berlin Olympics Birth control legalized
1937	*Hindenburg* crash Amelia Earhart disappears
1939	John Steinbeck's *Grapes of Wrath*

★   ★   ★

BIBLIOGRAPHY

Useful overviews of the Great Depression are T. H. Watkins, *The Great Depression: America in the 1930s* (1993); John A. Garraty, *The Great Depression* (1987); and Robert S. McElvaine, *The Great Depression, 1929–1941* (1984).

The Coming of the Great Depression

Historians and economists continue to debate the causes of the Great Depression. See John Kenneth Galbraith, *The Great Crash* (1954); Milton Friedman and Anna Schwartz, *The Great Contraction, 1929–1933* (1965); Charles Kindelberger, *The World in Depression* (1974); Peter Temin, *Did Monetary Forces Cause the Great Depression?* (1976); and Michael Bernstein, *The Great Depression: Delayed Recovery and Economic Change in America, 1929–1939* (1988). Irving Bernstein, *The Lean Years* (1960), offers a compelling portrait of hard times during the Hoover years.

Hard Times

A wealth of material brings the voices of the 1930s to life. The Federal Writers' Project, *These Are Our Lives* (1939); Tom Terrill and Jerrold Hirsch, eds., *Such as Us: Southern Voices of the Thirties* (1978); and Ann Banks, ed., *First-Person America* (1980), all draw on oral histories collected by the Works Progress Administration during the 1930s. See also Richard Lowitt and Maurine Beasley, eds., *One-Third of a Nation: Lorena Hickock Reports the Great Depression* (1981), and Robert S. McElvaine, ed., *Down & Out in the Great Depression* (1983), for firsthand accounts. Evocative secondary sources include Studs Terkel, *Hard Times: An Oral History of the Great Depression* (1970), and Caroline Bird, *The Invisible Scar* (1966).

Descriptions of family life in the 1930s include Robert and Helen Lynd, *Middletown in Transition* (1937); Mirra Komarovsky, *The Unemployed Man and His Family* (1940); and Roger Angell, *The Family Encounters the Depression* (1936). Russell Baker's autobiography, *Growing Up* (1982), provides an often humorous description of family life in the 1930s. Glen H. Elder, Jr., *Children of the Great Depression* (1974), and John A. Clausen, *American Lives: Looking Back at the Children of the Great Depression* (1993), look at the long-term effects. For more on youth, see Maxine Davis, *The Lost Generation* (1936); Eileen Eagan, *Class, Culture, and the Classroom* (1981); Beth L. Bailey, *From Front Porch to Back Seat* (1988); and John Modell, *Into One's Own: From Youth to Adulthood, 1920–1975* (1989).

Frederick Lewis Allen, *Since Yesterday* (1939), provides an impressionistic overview of popular culture in the 1930s. Specific studies of movies and Hollywood include Robert Sklar, *Movie-Made America* (2d ed., 1987); Andrew Bergman, *We're in the Money* (1971); Molly Haskell, *From Reverence to Rape: The Treatment of Women in the Movies* (2d ed., 1987); and Thomas Schatz, *The Genius of the System: Hollywood Film Making in the Studio Era* (1988).

Material on women in the 1930s can be found in Susan Ware, *Holding Their Own* (1982); Winifred Wandersee, *Women's Work and Family Values, 1920–1940* (1981); and Lois Scharf, *To Work and to Wed* (1981). For the special dimensions of white rural women's lives, see Margaret Hagood,

Mothers of the South (1939). Jeane Westin, *Making Do: How Women Survived the '30s* (1976), is a lively account drawn from interviews. The birth control movement is surveyed in Linda Gordon, *Woman's Body, Woman's Right* (2d ed., 1990); James Reed, *From Private Vice to Public Virtue* (1978); Estelle Freedman and John D'Emilio, *Intimate Matters: A History of Sexuality in America* (1988); and Ellen Chesler, *Woman of Valor: Margaret Sanger and the Birth Control Movement in America* (1992).

The Social Fabric of Depression America

Developments in the black community during the 1930s are covered in Cheryl Lyn Greenberg, *"Or Does It Explode?": Harlem in the Great Depression* (1991); Gilbert Osofsky, *Harlem: The Making of a Ghetto* (1966); Gunnar Myrdal, *An American Dilemma* (1944); David Lewis, *When Harlem Was in Vogue* (1981); Jervis Anderson, *This Was Harlem, 1900–1950* (1982); and Robert Weisbrot, *Father Divine and the Struggle for Racial Equality* (1983). James Goodman, *Stories of Scottsboro* (1994), and Dan T. Carter, *Scottsboro* (1969), cover that case. Donald Grubbs, *Cry from Cotton* (1971), tells the story of the Southern Tenant Farmers Union. Robin D. G. Kelley, *Hammer and Hoe* (1990), is an excellent account of Alabama communists during the Great Depression. Donald Worster, *Dust Bowl* (1979), evokes the plains during the "Dirty Thirties," as does Ann Marie Low's memoir, *Dust Bowl Diary* (1984). James N. Gregory, *American Exodus: The Dust Bowl Migration and Okie Culture in California* (1989), treats the experiences of migrants and their impact on California culture and the economy.

On the experiences of Mexican-Americans during the 1930s, see Mario T. Garcia, *Mexican Americans: Leadership, Ideology, and Identity, 1930–1960* (1989) and *Memories of Chicano History: The Life and Narrative of Bert Corona* (1994). George J. Sanchez, *Becoming Mexican American* (1993), examines Chicano Los Angeles from 1900 to 1945. See also Carey McWilliams, *North from Mexico: The Spanish-Speaking People of the United States* (1948), and Richard A. Garcia, *The Rise of the Mexican-American Middle Class* (1990). For Mexican-American women's lives, see Vicki Ruiz, *Cannery Women, Cannery Lives: Mexican Women, Unionization, and the California Food Processing Industry, 1930–1950* (1987), and Patricia Zavella, *Women's Work and Chicano Families* (1987).

Herbert Hoover and the Great Depression

Hoover's response to the depression is chronicled in Alfred Romasco, *The Poverty of Abundance* (1965), and Jordan Schwartz, *The Interregnum of Despair* (1970). See also David Burner, *Herbert Hoover* (1978); Joan Hoff Wilson, *Herbert Hoover: Forgotten Progressive* (1975); and William Barber, *Herbert Hoover, the Economists, and American Economic Policy, 1921–1933* (1986). Eliot Rosen, *Hoover, Roosevelt, and the Brain Trust* (1977), treats the transition between the two administrations, as does Frank Freidel, *Launching the New Deal* (1973). On the 1932 election and the beginnings of the New Deal coalition, see David Burner, *The Politics of Provincialism* (1967); Samuel Lubell, *The Future of American Politics* (1952); and John Allswang, *The New Deal in American Politics* (1978).

New Deal Art

This 1937 poster designed by Lester Beall for the Rural
Electrification Administration celebrated the power of radio,
one of the most potent cultural forces of the 1930s.

CHAPTER 26

The New Deal
1933–1939

★　　　★　　　★

In his bold inaugural address on March 4, 1933, President Franklin Delano Roosevelt declared, "The only thing we have to fear is fear itself." That memorable phrase rallied a nation that had already endured almost four years of the worst economic contraction in its history, with no end in sight.

With his demeanor grim and purposeful, Roosevelt preached his first inaugural address like a sermon. He spoke of the economic and social problems that the nation faced and their possible solutions only in the most general terms. Promising "a leadership of frankness and vigor," Roosevelt issued ringing declarations of his vision of governmental activism: "This Nation asks for action, and action now." Roosevelt repeatedly compared combating the depression to fighting a war. The most explicit parallel was his willingness to ask Congress for "broad Executive power to wage a war against the emergency, as great as the power that would be given to me if we were in fact invaded by a foreign foe." This conception of presidential leadership was well suited to Roosevelt's self-confident personality and pragmatic political style.

In the end, however, Roosevelt intended not to scare the American people but to reassure them. The democratic system was basically sound, he told them, and hard times could be overcome, but only if a dispirited nation chose not to wallow in lethargy. On that cold March day in 1933 Roosevelt urged his fellow citizens to return to the values of hard work, cooperation, and sacrifice that had made the country great. Roosevelt's restoration of hope and confidence was perhaps his greatest contribution to American life during the Great Depression.

The New Deal Takes Over, 1933–1935

When Roosevelt first used the term *New Deal* in his acceptance speech at the Democratic National Convention in 1932, he did not realize that he had named his era. Plucked from deep in the speech by the newspaper cartoonist Rollin Kirby, the term came to stand for the Roosevelt administration's response to the depression. The federal government dominated political and economic life so thoroughly during the 1930s that the term *New Deal* is often used as a synonym for that decade.

The Roosevelt Style of Leadership

Every president since the 1930s has lived in the shadow of FDR. Few of his successors have matched his raw political talent; none have had to face and surmount the twin crises of depression and war. "I have no expectation of making a hit every time I come to bat," Roosevelt disarmingly told his critics. "What I seek is the highest possible batting average." Roosevelt parlayed

FDR
President Franklin Delano Roosevelt was a consummate politician who loved the adulation of a crowd. He consciously adopted a cheerful mien to keep people from feeling sorry for him because of his infirmity, knowing that he could not be a successful politician if the public pitied him.

that experimental tone into a highly effective political and governmental style.

The New Deal represented many things to many people, but one unifying factor was the personality of its master architect, Franklin Delano Roosevelt. The New Deal was "a very personal enterprise." Roosevelt, a superb and pragmatic politician, crafted his administration's program in response to shifting political and economic conditions instead of following a set ideology or plan. He experimented with an idea, and if it did not work, he tried another. Roosevelt juggled advice in the same way. Senator Huey Long of Louisiana complained, "When I talk to him, he says 'Fine! Fine! Fine!' But Joe Robinson [the Senate majority leader] goes to see him the next day and again he says 'Fine! Fine! Fine!' Maybe he says 'Fine!' to everybody."

President Roosevelt established an unusually close rapport with the American people. "Mr. Roosevelt is the only man we ever had in the White House who would understand that my boss is a son of a bitch," remarked one worker. Many ordinary citizens credited him with the positive changes in their lives, saying, "He gave me a job" or "He saved my home." Roosevelt's masterful use of the new medium of radio, typified by the sixteen "fireside chats" he broadcast during his first two terms, fostered this personal identification. More than 450,000 letters poured into the White House in the week after the inauguration, and an average of 5,000 to 8,000 arrived weekly for the rest of the decade. One person had handled public correspondence during the Hoover administration, but it took a staff of fifty under Roosevelt. Roosevelt also became the first president to hire a press secretary.

Franklin Roosevelt continued the expansion of presidential power begun in the administrations of Theodore Roosevelt and Woodrow Wilson. From the beginning Roosevelt centralized decision making in the White House and dramatically expanded the role of the executive branch in initiating policy. For policy formulation he turned to his talented cabinet, which included Interior Secretary Harold Ickes, Frances Perkins at Labor, Henry A. Wallace at Agriculture, and an old friend, Henry Morgenthau, Jr., as secretary of the treasury. During the interregnum he relied so heavily on the advice of the Columbia University professors Raymond Moley, Rexford Tugwell, and Adolph A. Berle, Jr., that the press dubbed them the "Brains Trust."

When searching for new ideas and fresh faces, Roosevelt was just as likely to turn to advisers and administrators scattered throughout the New Deal bureaucracy. Eager young people flocked to Washington to join the New Deal—"men with long hair and women with short hair," wags quipped. Lawyers in their mid-twenties fresh out of Harvard found themselves drafting legislation or being called to the White House for strategy sessions with the president. Paul Freund, a Harvard Law

School professor who worked in the Reconstruction Finance Corporation and the Department of Justice, remembered, "It was a glorious time for obscure people." Many young New Dealers who went on to distinguished careers in government or public service later recalled that nothing could match the excitement of the early New Deal.

The Hundred Days

The first problem that the new president confronted was the banking crisis. Since the stock market crash about 9 million people had lost their savings, a total of $2.5 billion. On the eve of his inauguration thirty-eight states had closed their banks, and banks operated on a restricted basis in the rest. The collapse of the banking system, far more than the stock market crash, brought the depression home to the middle class.

On March 5, the day after his inauguration, the president declared a national "bank holiday" (a euphemism for closing all the banks) and called Congress into special session. On March 9 Congress passed Roosevelt's proposed emergency banking bill, which permitted banks to reopen beginning on March 13, but only if a Treasury Department inspection showed that they had sufficient cash reserves. The House approved the plan after only thirty-eight minutes of debate.

Emergency Banking Act. The Emergency Banking Act, which Roosevelt developed in consultation with banking leaders, was a conservative document that could have been proposed by Herbert Hoover. The difference was the public's reaction. On the Sunday evening before the banks reopened Roosevelt made his first "fireside chat" to a radio audience estimated at 60 million. In

The CCC

The Civilian Conservation Corps (CCC) was one of the most popular New Deal programs. Over ten years, it enrolled 2.75 million young Americans who worked for $1 a day on projects such as soil conservation, disaster relief, reforestation, and flood control. The CCC was limited to men, although a few camps employed out-of-work young women.

simple terms he reassured the people that the banks were now safe, and Americans believed him. When the banks reopened on Monday morning, deposits exceeded withdrawals. "Capitalism was saved in eight days," observed Raymond Moley, who had served as Roosevelt's speechwriter in the 1932 campaign. The banking bill did its job: more than 4,000 banks failed in 1933 (the vast majority in the months before the law took effect), but only 61 closed their doors in 1934 (see Table 26.1).

The Banking Act was the first of fifteen pieces of major legislation enacted by Congress in the opening months of the Roosevelt administration. This legislative session, which came to be called the "Hundred Days," remains one of the most productive ever. Congress created the Home Owners Loan Corporation to refinance home mortgages threatened by foreclosure; fully 20 percent of the nation's homeowners took advantage of it. A second banking law, the Glass-Steagall Act, curbed speculation by separating investment banking from commercial banking. The Glass-Steagall Act also created the Federal Deposit Insurance Corporation (FDIC), which insured bank deposits up to $2,500. The Civilian Conservation Corps (CCC) sent 250,000 young men to live in camps where they did reforestation and conservation work. The Tennessee Valley Authority (TVA) received legislative approval for its innovative plan of govern-

TABLE 26.1

American Banks and Bank Failures, 1920–1940

Year	Total Number of Banks	Total Assets ($ billion)	Bank Failures
1920	30,909	53.1	168
1929	25,568	72.3	659
1931	22,242	70.1	2,294
1933	14,771	51.4	4,004
1934	15,913	55.9	61
1940	15,076	79.7	48

Source: Historical Statistics of the United States: Colonial Times to 1970 (Washington, D.C.: U.S. Government Printing Office, 1975), 1019, 1038–1039.

ment-sponsored regional development and public energy. The price of electricity in the seven-state Tennessee Valley area soon dropped from 10 cents a kilowatt-hour to 3 cents. And in a move that lifted public spirits immeasurably, Roosevelt legalized beer in April. Full repeal of Prohibition came eight months later, in December 1933.

The Agricultural Adjustment Act. The Roosevelt administration targeted three pressing problems: agricultural overproduction, business failures, and unemployment. Roosevelt considered a farm bill "the key to recovery." The Agricultural Adjustment Act (AAA) was developed by Secretary of Agriculture Henry A. Wallace, Assistant Secretary Rexford Tugwell, and the agricultural economist M. L. Wilson in close collaboration with the leaders of major farmers' organizations. A domestic allotment system for seven major commodities (wheat, cotton, corn, hogs, rice, tobacco, and dairy products) gave cash subsidies to farmers who cut production; those benefits were financed by a tax on processing (such as the milling of wheat), which was passed on to consumers. New Deal planners hoped prices would rise in response to the federally subsidized scarcity and thus spur a more general recovery. The AAA firmly established the practice of paying federal subsidies to farmers, a tradition that continues to the present day.

The AAA stabilized the agricultural situation, but its benefits were distributed unevenly. The subsidies for reducing production went primarily to the owners of large and medium-size farms, who often cut production by reducing the acreage of their renters and sharecroppers but continuing to farm their own land. In the South that strategy had a racial component, because many sharecroppers were black whereas the landowners and government administrators were white. As many as 200,000 black tenant farmers were displaced from their land by the AAA. Thus New Deal agricultural policies fostered the migration of marginal farmers in the South and Midwest to northern cities and California and consolidated the economic and political clout of larger landholders.

NRA. The New Deal attacked the problem of economic recovery with the National Industrial Recovery Act, which created the National Recovery Administration (NRA). This agency drew on the World War I experience of Bernard Baruch's War Industries Board and continued the reliance on trade associations of the Coolidge and Hoover administrations. The NRA set up a system of industrial self-government to handle the problems of overproduction, cutthroat competition, and price instability. To achieve its objectives, it established codes of fair competition tailored to prevent the specific practices in each industry that had forced prices downward. The codes set prices and established maximum production quotas, sim-

ilar to what the AAA did for farm products. In effect, those legally enforceable agreements suspended the antitrust laws. Each code also contained provisions covering working conditions. For example, the codes established minimum wages and maximum hours and outlawed child labor completely. One of the most far-reaching provisions, Section 7(a), guaranteed workers the right to organize and bargain collectively "through representatives of their own choosing," and this dramatically spurred the growth of the labor movement.

General Hugh Johnson, a colorful if erratic administrator, headed the NRA. He supervised negotiations for more than 600 NRA codes, ranging from large industries such as coal, cotton, and steel to dog food, costume jewelry, and even burlesque theaters. The negotiating process theoretically took into account equal input from management, labor, and consumers, but business trade associations basically set the terms. Because large companies dominated the trade associations, the code-drafting process further solidified the power of large businesses at the expense of smaller enterprises. Labor had little input, and consumer interests had almost none. An extensive public relations campaign, complete with plugs in Hollywood films such as *Gold Diggers of 1933* and stickers with the NRA slogan, "We Do Our Part," was used to sell the program to skeptical consumers and businesspeople.

Unemployment. The early New Deal also addressed the critical problem of unemployment. The total exhaustion of private and local sources of charity made some form of federal relief essential in the fourth year of the depression, and Roosevelt moved reluctantly toward federal responsibility for the unemployed. The Federal Emergency Relief Administration (FERA), set up in May 1933 under the direction of Harry Hopkins, a New York social worker, offered federal money to the states for relief programs. It was designed to keep people from starving until other recovery measures took hold. Hopkins distributed $5 million in his first two hours in office. When told that some of the projects he had authorized might not be sound in the long run, Hopkins replied, "People don't eat in the long run—they eat every day." During its two-year existence FERA spent $1 billion.

Roosevelt always maintained a strong distaste for the dole. Wherever possible, his administration promoted work relief over cash subsidies; it also consistently favored relief jobs that did not compete directly with the private sector. The Public Works Administration (PWA), under Secretary of the Interior Harold L. Ickes, received a $3.3 billion appropriation in 1933 for a major public-works program. However, Ickes's cautiousness in starting up projects limited the PWA's effectiveness in spurring recovery and providing jobs. In November 1933 Roosevelt assigned $400 million in

PWA funds to a new agency, the Civil Works Administration (CWA), headed by Harry Hopkins. Within thirty days the CWA put 2.6 million men and women to work; at its peak in January 1934 it employed 4 million. CWA workers received $15 a week for jobs such as repairing bridges, building highways, constructing public buildings, and setting up community projects. The CWA, regarded as a stopgap measure to get the country through the winter of 1933–1934, lapsed the next spring after spending all its funds.

Many of these early emergency measures were deliberately inflationary; that is, they were designed to trigger price rises that were thought necessary to stimulate recovery and halt the steep deflation. Another element of this strategy was Roosevelt's executive order on April 18, 1933, to abandon the gold standard and let gold rise in value like any other commodity. As the price of gold rose, so too would agricultural prices, a key to general recovery. The budget director, Lew Douglas, warned that abandoning the gold standard would lead to "the end of Western civilization." That did not happen, but neither did this action have much of an impact on the domestic economy. Its main significance lay in the adoption of a flexible currency system. The Federal Reserve System could now manipulate the value of the dollar in accordance to economic conditions rather than tying the value of the dollar to a fixed standard. This represented an important shift in control over the economy to the public sector.

"Gulliver's Travels"

So many new agencies flooded out of Washington in the 1930s that one almost needed a scorecard to keep them straight. Here a July 1935 *Vanity Fair* cartoon by William Gropper substitutes Uncle Sam for Captain Lemuel Gulliver, tied to the ground by Lilliputians in a parody of Jonathan Swift's *Gulliver's Travels*.

When an exhausted Congress recessed in June 1933, much had been accomplished. Rarely had a president so dominated a legislative session. A mass of "alphabet agencies," as the New Deal programs came to be known, flowed from Washington. They gave the impression of action, but despite a slight economic upturn, they had not turned the economy around.

Nevertheless, Americans saw a ray of hope. In April 1933, at the height of the excitement over the Hundred Days, Walt Disney released a cartoon film called *The Three Little Pigs*. Echoing FDR's assertion that they had nothing to fear but fear itself, many people hummed the film's theme song, "Who's Afraid of the Big Bad Wolf?" as they started down the road toward renewed confidence.

Consolidating the Hundred Days

If the measures taken during the Hundred Days had cured the Great Depression, the rest of the New Deal probably would not have occurred. When the depression stubbornly persisted, FDR and Congress turned to more far-reaching structural reform to replace the emergency recovery measures of 1933. Reforming business practices would be one way to prevent future depressions.

Reforming Wall Street. One obvious target was Wall Street, where insider trading, fraud, and other abuses had contributed to the 1929 crash. In 1934 Congress established the Securities and Exchange Commission (SEC) to regulate the stock market. The commission had the power to regulate the purchase of stocks on credit, or margin buying, and to restrict speculation by those with inside information on corporate plans. The Public Utilities Holding Company Act of 1935 limited the widespread practice of pyramiding holding companies on top of utilities for the sole purpose of issuing stock and inflating profits.

The banking system also came under scrutiny. The Banking Act of 1935 represented a significant consolidation of federal control over the nation's banks. The law authorized the president to appoint a new Board of Governors of the Federal Reserve System. This reorganization placed control of interest rates and other money market policies at the federal level rather than with regional banks. By requiring all large state banks to join the Federal Reserve System by 1942 as a condition for using the federal deposit insurance system, the law further encouraged centralization of the nation's banking system.

Roosevelt was not hostile toward business. He heartily accepted the capitalist system but realized that modern industrial life required more direct federal control to limit some of capitalism's excesses. "To preserve we had to reform," Roosevelt commented succinctly.

Even though he styled himself as the savior of capitalism, he provoked strong hostility from many well-to-do Americans. To the wealthy, Roosevelt became simply "That Man," a traitor to his class. Business leaders and conservative Democrats formed the Liberty League in 1934 to lobby against the New Deal and its "reckless spending" and "socialist" reforms.

The conservative majority on the Supreme Court also disagreed with the direction of the New Deal. On "Black Monday," May 27, 1935, the Supreme Court struck down the NRA, Roosevelt's business recovery plan. In the case of *Schechter v. United States*, the court unanimously ruled that the National Industrial Recovery Act represented an unconstitutional delegation of legislative power to the executive. The so-called sick-chicken case concerned a Brooklyn, New York, firm convicted of violating NRA codes by selling diseased poultry. In its decision the Court also ruled that the NRA was regulating commerce *within* an individual state and that the Constitution limited federal regulation to *interstate* commerce. Roosevelt publicly protested that the Court's narrow interpretation would return the Constitution "to the horse-and-buggy definition of interstate commerce" but could only watch helplessly as the Court threatened to invalidate the entire New Deal.

Challenges from the Left

Other citizens thought the New Deal had not gone far enough. Francis Townsend, a Long Beach, California, doctor, spoke for the nation's elderly. Many Americans feared poverty in old age because few had pension plans and many had lost their life savings in bank failures. In 1933 Townsend proposed an Old Age Revolving Pension Plan, which would give $200 a month (a considerable sum at the time) to citizens over the age of sixty. To receive payments, people would have to retire from their jobs, thereby opening their positions to others, and agree to spend the money within a month. Townsend Clubs soon sprang up across the country, particularly in the Far West.

Father Charles Coughlin also challenged Roosevelt's leadership and attracted a large following, especially in the Midwest. Coughlin, a parish priest in the Detroit suburb of Royal Oak, had turned to the radio in the mid-1920s to enlarge his pastorate. In 1933 about 40 million Americans listened regularly to the "Radio Priest." In many Roman Catholic neighborhoods Coughlin's sermons could be heard blaring from open windows during the summer. At first Coughlin supported the New Deal, but he soon broke with Roosevelt over the president's refusal to support nationalization of the banking system and expansion of the money supply. In 1935 Coughlin

organized the National Union for Social Justice to promote his views as an alternative to "Franklin Double-Crossing Roosevelt." Being both Canadian-born and a Catholic priest, Coughlin could not run for president, but his rapidly growing constituency threatened to become a factor in the 1936 election.

The most direct threat to Roosevelt came from Senator Huey Long. In a single term as governor of Louisiana the flamboyant Long had achieved stunning popularity. Voters applauded his attacks on big business as he lowered their utility bills and increased the share of taxes paid by corporations. And Long's ambitious program of public works, which included the construction of new highways, bridges, hospitals, and schools, benefited all Louisianans and created many jobs. But Long's accomplishments came at a price: to push through his reforms he seized almost dictatorial control of the state government. He maintained control over Louisiana's political machine even after his election to the U.S. Senate in 1930. Long supported Roosevelt in 1932 but made no secret of his own presidential ambitions.

In 1934 Senator Long broke with the New Deal, arguing that its programs did not go far enough. Like Coughlin, he established his own national movement, the Share Our Wealth Society, which had over 4 million

The Kingfish
Huey Long, the Louisiana governor and senator, was one of the most controversial figures in American political history. He took his nickname "Kingfish" from a character in the popular radio show "Amos 'n' Andy." Long inspired one of the most powerful political novels of all time, Robert Penn Warren's *All the King's Men*, which won a Pulitzer Prize in 1946.

followers in 1935. Long argued that the unequal distribution of wealth in the United States was the fundamental cause of the depression. Long's solution was to tax 100 percent of all incomes over $1 million and all inheritances over $5 million and distribute the money to the rest of the population. Every family would be guaranteed about $2,000 annually, he predicted. Long's rapid rise in popularity suggested the potential depth of public dissatisfaction with the Roosevelt administration. The president's strategists feared that Long might join forces with Coughlin and Townsend to form a third party, enabling the Republicans to win the 1936 election.

The Second New Deal, 1935–1938

By 1935 Roosevelt had abandoned his hope of building a classless coalition of rich and poor, workers and farmers, and rural and urban dwellers. Pushed from the left to do more and bitterly criticized by the right for what he had already done, the president had no choice but to abandon the middle ground. For both political and ideological reasons, and with an eye fixed firmly on the 1936 election, Roosevelt moved dramatically to the left. Historians use the term *Second New Deal* to describe the outpouring of legislation that followed.

Legislative Accomplishments

The first beneficiary of Roosevelt's change of direction was the labor movement. The rising number of strikes in 1934, about 1,800 involving a total of 1.5 million workers, reflected the dramatic growth of rank-and-file militancy. After the Supreme Court declared the NRA unconstitutional in 1935, labor demanded legislation that would protect its rights to organize and bargain collectively. Senator Robert F. Wagner of New York, one of labor's staunchest supporters in Congress, had introduced legislation to strengthen and make permanent the protections guaranteed by Section 7(a) of the NIRA even before the Supreme Court decision. Only when Congress was on the verge of passing Wagner's bill did Roosevelt reluctantly support the legislation, signing the National Labor Relations Act, also known as the Wagner Act, on July 5, 1935.

The Wagner Act placed the weight of the federal government on labor's side in the struggle to organize. Most important, it upheld the right of industrial workers to join a union. (The Wagner Act did not cover farm workers' unions.) The law also outlawed many unfair labor practices employers used to squelch unions, such

General Strike, San Francisco, 1934
San Francisco's general strike began with the longshoremen and soon spread to almost every union member (and some middle-class supporters as well) in the city. This striker has been shot in the head during an altercation with police. On July 19, union leaders voted to accept government arbitration, and the strike ended.

as spying on workers, requiring yellow-dog contracts (in which workers had to agree not to join a union in order to be hired), and firing or blacklisting workers because of their union activities. The act established the nonpartisan National Labor Relations Board (NLRB) to protect workers from employer coercion, supervise representation elections, and enforce the guarantee of collective bargaining. If a union won a majority of the votes in a secret election, usually conducted by the NLRB, it was entitled to recognition as the sole bargaining agent for all the employees in a factory or other appropriate bargaining unit. The NLRB had the authority to force employers to comply.

Social Security. The Social Security Act signed by Roosevelt on August 14, 1935, was the second major piece of legislation in this phase of the New Deal. The law was a response to the political mobilization of the na-

tion's elderly through the Townsend and Long movements. It also reflected the prodding of social reformers such as Grace Abbott, head of the Children's Bureau, and Secretary of Labor Frances Perkins. The Social Security Act provided pensions for most workers in the private sector, although agricultural workers and domestics were not initially covered. The pensions were paid out of a federal-state pension fund to which both employers and employees contributed. Roosevelt's advisers decided to fund the program with payroll deductions rather than general tax revenues to insulate it from political attack. The act also established a joint federal-state system of unemployment compensation funded by an unemployment tax on employers and employees.

The Social Security Act was a milestone in the creation of the modern welfare state. With this law, the United States joined industrialized countries such as Great Britain and Germany in providing old-age pensions and unemployment compensation to its citizens. (The Roosevelt administration chose not to push for national health insurance even though most other industrialized nations offered such protection.) The law also mandated categorical assistance, such as aid to the blind, deaf, and disabled and to dependent children. Those recipients were the so-called deserving poor, people who could not support themselves through no fault of their own. The categorical assistance programs, which formed a small part of the New Deal, gradually expanded over the years until they were integral parts of the American welfare system.

The WPA. Roosevelt was never enthusiastic about large expenditures for social welfare programs. As he said in January 1935, the government "must and shall quit this business of relief." But 10 million Americans were still out of work in the sixth year of the depression, a pressing political and moral issue for FDR and the Democrats. The Works Progress Administration (WPA), the main federal relief agency for the rest of the depression, addressed the needs of the unemployed. Harry Hopkins, who had run the Federal Emergency Relief Administration from 1933 to 1935, took command of the new agency. Whereas the FERA had supplied grants to the states for relief programs, the WPA put relief workers on the federal payroll. Between 1935 and 1943 the WPA employed 8.5 million Americans and spent $10.5 billion. The agency constructed 651,087 miles of roads, 125,110 public buildings, 8,192 parks, and 853 airports and built or repaired 124,087 bridges.

The WPA, although an extravagant operation by the standards of the 1930s (it inspired nicknames such as "We Putter Around" and "We Poke Along"), never reached more than a third of the nation's unemployed. Its average wage of $55 a month, well below the gov-

Posters of the WPA
During its eight-year existence the WPA produced 2 million posters from 35,000 designs. WPA posters such as this one designed for the National Park Service to support wildlife conservation show the vitality of American graphic design in the 1930s.

ernment-defined subsistence level of $100 a month, enabled workers to eke out a bare living. The government cut back the program severely in 1941 and ended it in 1943, when the WPA was no longer needed in the full-employment economy resulting from World War II.

The Revenue Act of 1935 showed Roosevelt's willingness to push for reforms that were considered too controversial earlier in his presidency. Much of the business community had already turned violently against Roosevelt in reaction to the NRA, the Social Security Act, the Wagner Act, and the Public Utilities Holding Companies Act. In 1935 he further antagonized the wealthy by proposing a tax reform bill that included federal inheritance and gift taxes, higher personal income tax rates in the top brackets, and increased corporate taxes. Conservatives quickly labeled this an attempt to "soak the rich." Roosevelt, seeking to defuse the popularity of Huey Long's Share Our Wealth plan, was just as interested in the political mileage of the tax bill as in its actual results. The final version of the bill increased federal revenues by only $250 million a year (Table 26.2).

TABLE 26.2

Major New Deal Legislation

Agriculture

1933 Agricultural Adjustment Act (AAA)

1935 Resettlement Administration (RA)
      Rural Electrification Administration

1937 Farm Security Administration (FSA)

1938 Second Agricultural Adjustment Act

Business and Industry

1933 Emergency Banking Act
      Glass-Steagall Act
        (FDIC)
      National Industrial Recovery Act (NIRA)

1934 Securities and Exchange Commission (SEC)
      Public Utilities Holding Company Act

1935 Banking Act of 1935
      Revenue Act (wealth tax)

Conservation and the Environment

1933 Tennessee Valley Authority (TVA)
      Civilian Conservation Corps (CCC)

1936 Soil Conservation and Domestic Allotment Act

Labor and Social Welfare

1933 Section 7(a) of NIRA

1935 Wagner Act
      National Labor Relations Board (NLRB)
      Social Security Act

1937 National Housing Act

1938 Fair Labor Standards Act (FLSA)

Relief

1933 Federal Emergency Relief Administration (FERA)
      Civil Works Administration (CWA)
      Public Works Administration (PWA)

1935 Works Progress Administration (WPA)
      National Youth Administration (NYA)

The 1936 Election

As the 1936 election approached, the broad range of New Deal programs brought new voters into the Democratic coalition. Many had been personally helped by federal programs; others benefited because their interests had found new support in the expanded functions of the government. Roosevelt could count on a potent urban-based coalition of workers, organized labor, northern blacks, white ethnic groups, Catholics, Jews, liberals, intellectuals, progressive Republicans, and middle-class families concerned about old-age dependence and unemployment. The Democrats also held on, though with some difficulty, to their traditional strength among white southerners.

The Republicans realized that they could not compete directly with Roosevelt's popularity and the potent New Deal coalition. To run against Roosevelt, they chose the progressive governor of Kansas, Alfred M. Landon, who accepted the general precepts of the New Deal. But Landon and the Republicans stridently criticized the inefficiency and expense of many New Deal programs and accused FDR of harboring dictatorial ambitions.

Roosevelt's victory in 1936 was one of the biggest landslides in American history. The assassination of Huey Long in September 1935 had deflated the threat of a serious third party challenge; the candidate of the combined Long-Townsend-Coughlin camp, Congressman William Lemke of North Dakota, garnered fewer than 900,000 votes (1.9 percent) for the Union party ticket. Roosevelt received 60.8 percent of the popular vote and carried every state except Maine and Vermont; Landon received 36.5 percent. Landon fought such an uphill battle that the columnist Dorothy Thompson quipped, "If Landon had given one more speech, Roosevelt would have carried Canada." The New Deal was at high tide.

Stalemate

"I see one-third of a nation ill-housed, ill-clad, ill-nourished," the president declared in his second inaugural address in January 1937. Roosevelt's appraisal suggested that he was considering further expansion of the welfare state that had begun to form late in his first term. However, retrenchment, controversy, and stalemate, not further reform, marked the second term.

The Supreme Court Fight. Only two weeks after his inauguration Roosevelt stunned Congress and the nation by asking for fundamental changes in the structure of the Supreme Court, believing that a grave constitutional crisis called for drastic judicial reorganization. After the Supreme Court found the NRA unconstitutional in the *Schechter* decision, in the early months of 1936 it struck down the Agricultural Adjustment Act, the Guffey-Snyder Coal Conservation Act, and New York State's minimum wage law. With the Wagner Act, the TVA, and Social Security coming up on appeal, the future of New Deal reform legislation appeared in doubt.

In response, Roosevelt proposed adding one new justice to the Court for each currently sitting justice over the age of seventy. That scheme, which Roosevelt tried

to pass off as a way to reduce the workload of the elderly justices, would have increased the number of justices from nine to fifteen. Roosevelt's opponents quickly accused him of trying to "pack" the Court with justices favorable to the New Deal. The president's proposal was also regarded as an assault on the principle of separation of powers. The issue became moot when the Supreme Court, in what journalists tagged "a switch in time that saved nine," upheld several key pieces of New Deal legislation, including the Social Security Act, Washington State's minimum wage law, and the Wagner Act.

Charitably, one could say that Roosevelt had lost a skirmish but won the war. In the spring of 1937 one conservative justice, Willis Van Devanter, resigned. Other resignations soon followed. Within four years Roosevelt reshaped the Supreme Court to suit his liberal philosophy with seven new appointments, including Hugo Black, Felix Frankfurter, Stanley F. Reed, and William O. Douglas. Yet his handling of this issue was a costly blunder at a time when he was vulnerable to the lame-duck syndrome that often afflicts second-term administrations. No one yet suspected that FDR would break with tradition by seeking a third term.

Congressional conservatives had long opposed the direction of the New Deal, but the Court-packing episode galvanized the conservatives by demonstrating that Roosevelt was no longer politically invincible. Throughout Roosevelt's second term a conservative coalition in Congress, composed mainly of southern Democrats and Republicans from rural areas, blocked or impeded social legislation. Two pieces of reform legislation that did win passage were the National Housing Act of 1937, which mandated the construction of low-cost public housing, and the Fair Labor Standards Act of 1938, which made permanent the minimum wage, maximum hours, and anti–child labor provisions in the NRA codes.

Roosevelt's attempts to reorganize the executive branch met a different fate. In both 1937 and 1938 Congress refused to consider a plan that would have consolidated all independent agencies into cabinet-rank departments, extended the civil service system, and created the new position of auditor general. Conservatives effectively played on lawmakers' fears that centralized executive management would dramatically reduce Congressional power. Opponents also linked Roosevelt's attempt to reorganize the executive branch to popular fears of fascism and dictatorship abroad, fears fanned especially by Hitler's rise to power in Germany. Roosevelt settled for a weak bill in 1939 that allowed him to create the Executive Office of the President and name six administrative assistants to the White House staff. The White House also took control of the all-important budget process by moving the Bureau of the Budget to the Executive Office from its old home in the Treasury Department.

The Roosevelt Recession. The "Roosevelt recession" of 1937–1938 dealt the most devastating blow to the president's political standing in the second term. Until that point the economy had made steady progress. From 1933 to 1937 the gross national product grew at a yearly rate of about 10 percent, and industrial output finally reached 1929 levels in 1937, as did real income. Unemployment declined from 25 percent to 14 percent, which meant that almost half the people without a job in 1933 had found one by 1937. Many Americans agreed with Senator James F. Byrnes of South Carolina that "the emergency has passed."

The steady improvement cheered Roosevelt. Basically a fiscal conservative, he had never overcome his dislike of large federal expenditures for relief. Accordingly, Roosevelt slashed the federal budget in 1937. Congress cut the WPA's funding in half between January and August, causing layoffs for about 1.5 million workers. Moreover, the $2 billion withheld from workers' paychecks to initiate the new Social Security System further reduced purchasing power. Finally, the Federal Reserve, fearing inflation, tightened credit. The stock market promptly collapsed, and unemployment soared to 19 percent, which translated into more than 10 million workers without jobs. Roosevelt found himself in the same situation that had confounded Hoover. Having taken credit for the recovery between 1933 and 1937, he had to take the blame for the recession.

Roosevelt shifted gears and spent his way out of the downturn. Large WPA appropriations and a resumption of public-works projects poured enough money into the economy to lift it out of the recession by early 1938. Roosevelt and his economic advisers were groping toward the general theories advanced by John Maynard Keynes, a British economist. Keynes proposed that governments use deficit spending to stimulate the economy when private spending proved insufficient. But Keynes's theories would not be conclusively proved until a dramatic increase in federal defense spending for World War II finally ended the Great Depression.

As the 1938 election approached, Roosevelt decided to "purge" some of his most conservative opponents from the Democratic party. In the spring primaries he campaigned against members of his own party who had blocked legislation in Congress and who had generally been hostile or unsympathetic to New Deal initiatives. The purge failed abysmally and widened the liberal-conservative rift in the Democratic party. In the general election Republicans capitalized on the "Roosevelt recession" and the Court-packing backlash to pick up 8 seats in the Senate and 81 in the House. The Republicans also gained 13 governorships.

By 1938 the New Deal had basically run out of steam. For six years Roosevelt had inspired confidence that hard times could be overcome. He showed himself to be a superb politician, successfully balancing de-

mands for more government programs with his own assessment of what was politically feasible. Throughout the New Deal, however, the president always demonstrated clear limits on how far he was willing to go. His instincts were basically conservative, not revolutionary; he saved the capitalist economic system by reforming it. This new activism was a major step beyond the informal and one-sided business-government partnership of the previous decade, but only because the emergency of the depression pushed Roosevelt in that direction. Under normal circumstances, he would have served out his second term, and a new president would have been elected in 1940. Roosevelt won a third term (and eventually a fourth) primarily because the outbreak of World War II in Europe in 1939 made Americans reluctant to risk a change in leadership during such perilous times.

The New Deal's Impact on Society

The New Deal was "somehow more than the sum of its parts." To understand its impact on society, one must look beyond the federal programs that came out of Washington and consider broader changes in political and social life. The New Deal set in motion dramatic growth in the federal bureaucracy. The Roosevelt administration opened unprecedented opportunities for women, blacks, and labor in public life. Its programs and priorities had an enormous impact on the public landscape, and it laid the groundwork for the welfare system that lasted until the 1990s.

Bureaucratic Growth

The New Deal accelerated the expansion of the federal bureaucracy that had been under way since the turn of the century. The number of civilian government employees increased 80 percent in a decade, exceeding a million in 1940. The number of federal employees who worked in Washington grew at an even faster rate, doubling between 1929 and 1940. Power was increasingly centered in the nation's capital, not in the states. In 1939 a British observer summed up the new orientation: "Just as in 1929 the whole country was 'Wall Street conscious,' now it is 'Washington conscious.'"

The new bureaucrats administered federal budgets of unprecedented size. In 1930 the Hoover administration had spent $3.1 billion and had run a surplus of almost $1 billion. With the increase in federal programs to fight the depression, federal expenditures grew steadily to $4.8 billion in 1932, $6.5 billion in 1934, and $7.6 billion in 1936. In 1939, the last year before war mobilization affected the federal budget, expenditures reached $9.4 billion. Government spending outstripped

receipts throughout this period, producing yearly deficits of about $3 billion. Roosevelt had come close to balancing the budget in 1938 but had triggered a major recession. The deficit climbed toward $3 billion again the following year.

The beginnings of big government and bureaucracy are often associated with the Roosevelt years, but many of the problems commonly ascribed to the New Deal belong to later eras. The real step toward expanded government spending came during World War II, not the depression. Federal outlays routinely surpassed $95 billion in the 1940s, and deficits grew to $50 billion. Although the deficit declined in the postwar era, government expenditures never returned to pre–World War II levels.

Women and the New Deal

In the experimental climate of the New Deal unprecedented numbers of women were offered positions in the Roosevelt administration, both as policy makers and as middle-level bureaucrats. Frances Perkins served as secretary of labor throughout all four terms, the first woman named to a cabinet post (see American Lives, pages 808–809). Molly Dewson, a social reformer turned politician, headed the Women's Division of the Democratic National Committee, where she pushed an issue-oriented program that supported New Deal reforms. Roosevelt's appointments of women included the first female director of the mint, the head of a major WPA division, and a judge on the circuit court of appeals. Many of those women were close friends as well as professional colleagues and cooperated in an informal network to advance feminist and reform causes.

Eleanor Roosevelt exemplified the growing prominence of women in public life. In the 1920s she had worked closely with other reformers to increase women's power in political parties, labor unions, and education, an invaluable apprenticeship for her White House years. Franklin and Eleanor's marriage represented one of the most successful political partnerships of all time. He was the pragmatic politician, always aware of what could be done; she was the idealist, the gadfly, always pushing him—and the New Deal—to do more. Eleanor Roosevelt observed in her autobiography,

> He might have been happier with a wife who was completely uncritical. That I was never able to be, and he had to find it in other people. Nevertheless, I think I sometimes acted as a spur, even though the spurring was not always wanted or welcome. I was one of those who served his purposes.

Eleanor Roosevelt underestimated her influence. She served as the conscience of the New Deal.

Frances Perkins:
New Deal Reformer

How should the first woman to serve in the cabinet be addressed? the press wanted to know. "Miss Perkins," came her no-nonsense reply. But the press said "Mr. Secretary" to the secretary of state; how was it to address a woman who was the secretary of labor? After consultation with Speaker of the House Henry Rainey and *Robert's Rules of Order*, the verdict came down: Frances Perkins was to be addressed as "Madam Secretary." As usual, the first woman in the cabinet took the attention to her sex in stride. She kept a deliberately low profile, wearing conservative black dresses, always accessorized with a distinctive tricorne hat. When asked later if being a woman had ever been a handicap, she replied matter-of-factly, "Only in climbing trees."

Frances Perkins's career shows the continuity between Progressive Era activism and New Deal reform. Born in 1880 in Massachusetts, Perkins took advantage of the new opportunities for higher education for women to graduate from Mount Holyoke College in 1902. She then worked in the settlement house movement, in the woman suffrage campaign, and with reform groups trying to pass a bill establishing a fifty-four-hour workweek for New York women and children. Her service on the commission set up to investigate New York factory conditions in the wake of the 1911 Triangle Shirtwaist fire, which killed 146 female garment workers, confirmed her commitment to legislative solutions for social problems. "I'd much rather get a law passed than organize a union," she later said. That orientation shaped her priorities as secretary of labor.

In 1913, at the age of thirty-three, Perkins married Paul C. Wilson, an economist and reformer. She kept her given name and continued to work after her daughter, Susanna, was born in 1916. As she later recalled, "I suppose I had been somewhat touched by feminist ideas and that was one of the reasons I kept my maiden name. My whole generation was, I suppose, the first generation that openly and actively asserted—at least some of us did—the separateness of women and their personal independence in the family relationship." In 1918 her husband became seriously ill and then spent the rest of his life in and out of mental institutions. Out of necessity, Perkins became the family breadwinner.

Perkins moved into government service in 1918 when the newly elected governor, Alfred E. Smith, whom she had met during the Triangle investigation, appointed her to the New York State Industrial Commission. Smith appointed Perkins to the State Industrial Board in 1922 and made her its chairperson in 1926. In 1928 she became New York's industrial commissioner under Smith and then Franklin D. Roosevelt, who replaced Smith as governor that year. Those positions made Perkins one of the highest-ranked women in state government in the immediate postsuffrage period.

When Franklin Roosevelt ran for president in 1932, talk began to circulate that Perkins might be offered a spot in the cabinet, a rumor that she dismissed as a "pipe dream." But to politicians such as Molly Dewson, whose background in social welfare paralleled that of Perkins, Roosevelt's election offered an unprecedented opportunity for women to serve at the national level. Dewson set about convincing Roosevelt of the wisdom of choosing Perkins and overcoming Perkins's own doubts. Perkins was reluctant to leave New York and a job she loved and feared the effect of unwanted publicity on her husband and teenage daughter; the job also would cause financial hardship. Molly Dewson blithely dismissed all those objections, emphasizing the importance of the appointment to the nation's women. "After all, you owe it to the women," Dewson argued repeatedly. "You probably will have this chance and you must step forward to do it." At other times Dewson's pressure was less subtle: "Don't be such a baby. Frances, you do the right thing. I'll murder you if you don't!"

Duty to her sex finally carried the day. As Perkins later explained to the suffrage leader Carrie Chapman Catt, "The overwhelming argument and thought which made me do it in the end in spite of personal difficulties was the realization that the door might not be opened to a woman again for a long, long time, and that I had a kind of duty to other women to walk in and sit down on the chair that was offered, and so establish the right of

others long hence and far-distant in geography to sit in the high seats." Franklin Roosevelt announced Perkins's appointment on February 28, and she was sworn in five days later. Among the members of Roosevelt's original cabinet, only Perkins and Secretary of the Interior Harold Ickes served for all four terms.

As secretary of labor, Perkins took as her mandate the promotion of the general welfare of American workers rather than specific advocacy of the interests of organized labor. She built the Department of Labor into a smoothly functioning bureaucracy and attracted many talented men and women to Washington. She played an especially important role in drafting the 1935 Social Security Act and the 1938 Fair Labor Standards Act. She did not ignore the labor movement, however, and after a period of initial doubt labor leaders realized that Madam Secretary was an important ally in the turbulent era of union mobilization in the 1930s.

An important key to Perkins's success was her personal rapport with Franklin Roosevelt, who, unlike many male politicians, felt comfortable working with strong-minded women. (He, of course, was married to one and met many of the talented women he brought into the New Deal administration through Eleanor.) Perkins called Roosevelt the most complicated human being she had ever met but emphatically asserted that he had never let her down. In 1946 she published *The Roosevelt I Knew*, an autobiographical account of her participation in the New Deal that many believe offers the most perceptive account of the elusive Roosevelt personality.

After Roosevelt's death, Perkins served on the Civil Service Commission under President Harry Truman. When the Republicans regained power in 1952, she left government service for a fulfilling career as a lecturer, maintaining an affiliation with the Cornell School of Industrial and Labor Relations. Perkins died in 1965. Her role in laying the foundation of the modern welfare state was her greatest legacy, but just as important was her demonstration of the contributions that public-spirited women could make to politics and government.

Secretary of Labor
Frances Perkins being greeted by workers at the Carnegie Steel Company in Pittsburgh.

Although Franklin Roosevelt's expansion of the personalized presidency had roots in the administrations of Theodore Roosevelt and Woodrow Wilson, the nation had never seen a first lady like Eleanor Roosevelt. She held press conferences for women journalists, wrote a popular syndicated column called "My Day," and traveled extensively throughout the country. Some people wondered why the first lady did not stay home at the White House like a good wife, but in a Gallup poll in January 1939, 67 percent approved of her conduct, a higher approval rating than the president's at that time. In 1938 *Life* magazine hailed her as the greatest American woman alive.

Without the vocal support of prominent women such as Eleanor Roosevelt, Molly Dewson, and the rest of the female political network, women's needs during the depression might have been overlooked. Grave flaws still marred the treatment of women in New Deal programs. For example, a fourth of the NRA codes set a lower minimum wage for women than for men performing the same jobs. New Deal agencies such as the Civil Works Administration and the Public Works Administration gave jobs almost exclusively to men, mainly because construction work was considered unsuitable for women; only 7 percent of CWA workers were female. The Social Security and Fair Labor Standards acts did not cover major areas of customarily female employment, such as domestic service. The CCC excluded women entirely, leaving critics to ask, Where is the "she-she-she"?

Eleanor Roosevelt and Civil Rights
One of Eleanor Roosevelt's greatest legacies was her commitment to civil rights. For example, she publicly resigned from the Daughters of the American Revolution (DAR) in 1939 when the group refused to let the black operatic singer Marian Anderson perform at Constitution Hall. Roosevelt developed an especially close working relationship with Mary McLeod Bethune of the National Youth Administration, shown here at a conference on black youth in 1939.

Women fared somewhat better under the Works Progress Administration. At the WPA's peak, 405,000 women were on its rolls. The Women's and Professional Projects Division of the WPA, headed by Ellen Sullivan Woodward, a Mississippi social worker, created hundreds of programs to put women to work. Still, at a time when women accounted for about 23 percent of the labor force, they constituted only 14 to 19 percent of WPA workers. For the most part, progress for women did not come from specific attempts to single them out as a group but occurred as part of a broader effort to improve the economic security of all Americans.

Blacks and the New Deal

There were striking parallels between the situation of blacks and women. African-Americans benefited more from the general social and economic programs of the New Deal than from any concerted commitment to civil rights. For black women, race proved more important than gender in determining treatment from the New Deal.

Mary McLeod Bethune, an educator who ran the Office of Minority Affairs of the National Youth Administration, headed the "black cabinet." This informal network worked for fairer treatment of blacks by New Deal agencies in the same way that the women's network advocated feminist causes. Both groups benefited greatly from the support of Eleanor Roosevelt. The first lady's promotion of equal treatment for blacks in the New Deal ranks as one of her greatest legacies.

The vast majority of the American people did not regard civil rights as a legitimate area for federal intervention in the 1930s. The New Deal provided little specific aid for blacks, for whom hard times were a permanent feature that the depression only made worse. Many New Deal programs reflected prevailing racist attitudes. CCC camps segregated blacks, and many NRA codes did not protect black workers. Most tellingly, Franklin Roosevelt repeatedly refused to support legislation making lynching a federal crime, claiming that it would antagonize southern members of Congress whose support he needed to pass New Deal measures.

Nevertheless blacks did receive enormous benefits from New Deal relief programs directed toward poor Americans, regardless of race or ethnic background. Public works projects channeled funds into black communities. Blacks made up about 18 percent of the WPA's recipients although they constituted only 10 percent of the population (see American Voices, page 811). The Resettlement Administration, established in 1935 to help small farmers buy land and aid in the resettlement of sharecroppers and tenant farmers onto more productive land, fought for the rights of black tenant farmers in the South—that is, until angry southerners in Congress cut its appropriations drastically. Still, many

Nora Mair

The Great Depression in Harlem

Nora Mair and her husband, Jack, both Jamaican immigrants, lived in Harlem throughout the 1930s. She worked in a linen shop on Madison Avenue, and he struggled to find employment of any kind. Like many other Americans, black and white, the WPA was their salvation.

We were poor. We didn't pretend. But our gas bill was always paid. Our rent bill was always paid. And we always knew where our next meal was coming from. We shopped on Eighth Avenue. We had everything there. We moved out of West Harlem to 100th Street and Madison Avenue in 1933 because the rent was less than half of what we were paying in West Harlem. We were paying thirty-two dollars a month for a five-room apartment. In Harlem, we would have paid sixty-five dollars, and we had a lovely landlord who painted our house every year. It was a lovely neighborhood—a potpourri of many nationalities. . . .

My husband worked in the day and went to school nights. He graduated from Mechanical Institute in 1928,

and right after that the Depression came, and he couldn't get work in his profession. In the meantime he drove a cab. It was no living at all as a taxi driver. I've known him to work around the clock and only make a dollar and a half.

He would come in in the morning and eat his dinner for his breakfast and then go to bed. I've known him to be so cold, because in those days the cabs only had three doors, that he'd come in and all he would take off was his hat, his shoes, and his overcoat and then into the bed until he was warm. Those things I did resent, because he had more to offer. He met so many people on the cab line—people he knew from Jamaica. He met professors who were driving cabs and couldn't get a job. First it was color. Then it was color and Depression.

There was nothing my husband did not do to make a living. He did not want welfare, and he wanted to be independent. But he couldn't get work as a draftsman. Once, while he was driving a cab, he saw an ad in the paper for a draftsman. He went downtown to

this office, and there was the receptionist. She didn't even look up. She waved him around the back, so he thought to himself, "She didn't ask what I wanted. She just motioned me to the back of the building. What kind of office could be back there?"

When he got back there, a white man with a pail and a mop said to him, "There is the pail and the mop."

"Pail and the mop for what?"

And said Mr. White Man, "Well, that's what you're here for, isn't it? A porter's job?"

Well, I won't tell you what my husband said when he came home, because he came home frothing at the mouth, and told me what he told him.

When the WPA came in, that was the first time he got to work in his profession. He worked on theaters, schools. They did everything, and it meant a lot that he was finally able to work in his field.

Source: Jeff Kisseloff, *You Must Remember This: An Oral History of Manhattan from the 1890s to World War II* (New York: Schocken, 1989), 326–327, 328.

blacks reasoned that the tangible aid coming from Washington outweighed the discrimination that marred many federal programs.

Help from the WPA and other New Deal programs and a belief that the White House—at least Eleanor Roosevelt—cared about their plight caused a dramatic change in blacks' voting behavior. Since the Civil War blacks had voted Republican, a loyalty resulting from Abraham Lincoln's freeing of the slaves. As late as 1932 black voters in northern cities overwhelmingly supported Republican candidates.

Then, in less than four years, blacks turned Lincoln's portrait to the wall and substituted that of Franklin Roosevelt. Because of the harshness of the depression, national politics assumed a new relevance for black Americans outside the South, who gave Roosevelt 71 percent of their votes in 1936. In Harlem, where relief dollars increased dramatically in the wake of the

1935 riot (see Chapter 25), the support was an extraordinary 81.3 percent. Black voters have remained overwhelmingly Democratic ever since.

The Rise of Organized Labor

During the 1930s, labor relations became a legitimate arena for federal action and intervention, and organized labor claimed a place in national political life. Labor's dramatic growth in the 1930s was one of the most important social and economic changes of the decade, an enormous contrast to its demoralized state at the end of the 1920s.

Several factors encouraged the growth of the labor movement: the inadequacy of welfare capitalism in the face of the depression, New Deal legislation such as the Wagner Act, the rise of the Congress of Industrial Orga-

nizations (CIO), and the growing militancy of rank-and-file workers. By the end of the decade the number of unionized workers had tripled to almost 9 million, covering 23 percent of the nonfarm work force. Union strength grew rapidly in manufacturing, transportation, and mining. Organized labor not only won the battle for union recognition but also for higher wages, seniority systems, and grievance procedures. Labor greatly expanded its political involvement as well.

The CIO served as the cutting edge of the union movement by promoting industrial unionism, that is, organizing all the workers in an industry, both skilled and unskilled, into one union. John L. Lewis, the leader of the United Mine Workers and a founder of the CIO, was the leading exponent of industrial unionism. His philosophy put him at odds with the American Federation of Labor (AFL), which favored organizing workers on a craft-by-craft basis. Lewis began to detach himself from the AFL in 1935, and the break was complete by 1938. Although the CIO generated much of the excitement on the labor front in the 1930s, the AFL gained more than a million new members between 1935 and 1940.

Organize

The Steelworkers' Organizing Committee was one of the most vital labor organizations contributing to the rise of the CIO. Note that the artist Ben Shahn chose a male figure to represent the American labor movement in this poster from the late 1930s. Such iconography reinforced the notion that the typical worker was male, despite the large number of women who joined the CIO.

The CIO scored its first major victory in the automobile industry. On December 31, 1936, General Motors workers in Flint, Michigan, staged a sit-down strike, vowing to stay at their machines until management agreed to bargain collectively. The workers lived in the factories and machine shops for forty-four days before General Motors recognized the United Automobile Workers (UAW). The CIO soon won another major victory at the U.S. Steel Corporation. Despite a long history of bitter opposition to unionization (as demonstrated in the 1919 steel strike), "Big Steel" capitulated without a fight and recognized the Steel Workers Organizing Committee (SWOC) on March 2, 1937.

The victory in the steel industry was not complete, however. A group of companies known as "Little Steel" chose not to follow the lead of U.S. Steel in making peace with the CIO, and steelworkers struck the Republic Steel Corporation plant in South Chicago. On Memorial Day, May 31, 1937, strikers and their families gathered for a holiday picnic and rally outside the plant's gates. Tension mounted, rocks were thrown, and the police fired on the crowd, killing ten protesters. All were shot in the back. A newsreel photographer recorded the scene, but Paramount Pictures considered the film of the "Memorial Day Massacre" too inflammatory for distribution. The road to recognition for labor, even with New Deal protections, was still long and violent. Workers in Little Steel did not win union recognition until 1941.

The 1930s were one of the most active periods of labor solidarity in American history. The sit-down tactic spread rapidly. In March 1937, 167,210 workers staged 170 sit-down strikes. Labor unions called for nearly 5,000 strikes that year and won favorable terms in 80 percent of them. Yet large numbers of middle-class Americans felt alienated by sit-down strikes, which they considered attacks on private property. The Supreme Court agreed and in 1939 upheld a law that banned the practice.

The CIO attracted new groups to the union movement. Mexican-Americans and blacks, for example, found the CIO's commitment to racial justice a strong contrast to the AFL's long-established patterns of exclusion and segregation. About 800,000 women workers also found a limited welcome in the CIO. Women participated in major CIO strikes and served as union organizers, especially in textile organizing drives in the South. Few blacks, Mexican-Americans, or women held leadership positions, however.

Women found other ways to participate in the labor movement. During the Flint sit-down strike in 1937 the Women's Emergency Brigade, a group of wives, sisters, and girlfriends of striking workers, supplied food and first aid. Wearing distinctive red berets and armbands, they picketed, demonstrated, and occasionally resorted to tactics such as breaking windows to dissipate the tear

The Sit-Down Strike

These members of the United Auto Workers helped pioneer the sit-down tactic at a General Motors plant in Flint, Michigan, in 1937. In their forty-four-day siege, the workers made use of the car seats awaiting final assembly in GM cars while they passed the time. To avoid any taint of immorality, union leaders asked all women workers in the Flint plant to leave once the sit-down strike began, and the women complied.

gas used against the strikers (see American Voices, page 814). After the strike, however, UAW leaders politely but firmly told the women to go back home where they supposedly belonged.

Labor's new vitality spilled over into political action. The AFL had always stood aloof from partisan politics, but the CIO quickly allied itself with the Democratic party. Through Labor's Nonpartisan League, the CIO gave $770,000 to Democratic campaigns in 1936. Labor also provided one of the few solid lobbies behind Roosevelt's plan to reorganize the Supreme Court. In the 1940s the CIO's Political Action Committee became a major contributor to the Democratic war chest.

Despite the breakthroughs of the New Deal, the labor movement never developed into as dominant a force in American life as had seemed possible in the heyday of the late 1930s. Roosevelt never made the growth of the labor movement a high priority, and many workers remained indifferent or even hostile to unionization.

Although the Wagner Act guaranteed unions a permanent place in American industrial relations, it did not revolutionize working conditions. The important gain of collective bargaining did not redistribute power in American industry; it merely granted labor a measure of legitimacy. Management even found that unions could be a useful buffer against rank-and-file militancy. New Deal social welfare programs also diffused some of the pre-1937 radical spirit by channeling economic benefits to workers whether they belonged to unions or not. In the 1940s the labor movement entered a period of consolidation and then stagnation that continued for several decades.

New Deal Murals

The social realist painter William Gropper portrayed the contributions of labor to modern industry in the heroic, dynamic style that was typical of public art during the depression. This mural, *Construction of a Dam*, was commissioned in 1937 for the Department of the Interior Building in Washington, D.C.

AMERICAN VOICES

Genora Johnson Dollinger

Labor Militancy

During the Flint, Michigan, sit-down strike Genora Johnson Dollinger, the wife of a General Motors striker and the mother of two small children, organized the Women's Emergency Brigade. Women like Dollinger played a major role in the Flint victory.

I was twenty-three years old on December 30, 1936, when the strike started. It lasted forty-four days, a very dramatic forty-four days, until February 11, 1937.

It was New Year's Eve when I realized women had to organize and join in the fight. I was on the picket lines when the men's wives came down. They didn't know why their husbands were sitting inside the plant. Living in a company town, you see, they got only company propaganda through the press and radio. So when they came down on New Year's Eve, many were threatening to divorce their striking husbands if they didn't quit and get back to work to bring home a paycheck.

I knew then that union women must organize on their own in order to talk with these wives. . . .

This was an independent move. It was not under the direction of the union or its administrators—I just talked it over with a few women—the active ones—and told them this is what we had to do.

Women might, after all, be called upon to give their lives. That was exactly the appeal I made while we were forming the brigade—I told the women, "Don't sign up for this unless you are prepared. If you are prone to hysteria or anything like that you'd only be in our way." I told them they'd be linking arms and withstanding the onslaughts of the police and if one of our sisters went down shot in cold blood there'd be no time for hysteria.

Around 500 women answered that call. We bought red berets and made arm bands with the white letters "EB" for Emergency Brigade. It was a kind of military uniform, yes, but it was mainly identification. We wore them all the time so we'd know who to call on to give help in an emergency. I had five lieutenants—three were factory women. I chose them because they could be called out of bed at any hour, if necessary, or sleep on a cot at the union hall. Mothers with children couldn't answer calls like that—although they did sign up for the brigade. Even a few grandmothers became brigadiers and, I remember, one young girl only sixteen.

We had no communication system to speak of. Very few people had telephones so we had to call one woman who was responsible for getting the messages through to many others.

We organized a first aid station and child care center—the women who had small children to tend and couldn't join the EB took care of these jobs.

Listen, I met some of the finest women I have ever come across in my life. When the occasion demands it of a woman and once she understands that she's standing in defense of her family—well, God, *don't fool around with that woman then*. . . .

It's a measure of the strength of those women of the Red Berets that they could perform so courageously in an atmosphere that was often hostile to them. We organized on our own without the benefit of professional leadership, and yet, we played a role, second to none, in the birth of a union and in changing working families' lives forever.

Source: Genora Johnson Dollinger, quoted in Jeane Westin, *Making Do* (Chicago: Follett Publishing, 1976), 223, 225–226, 229.

Other New Deal Constituencies

The growth of the federal government in the 1930s increased the potential impact of its decisions (and spending) on various constituencies. The New Deal considered a broader spectrum of the population worthy of inclusion in the political process, especially if people organized themselves into pressure groups. Politicians recognized the importance of satisfying the concerns of certain blocs of voters to cement their allegiance to the Democratic party. As a result, women, blacks, and labor received more attention from the federal government and gained greater visibility in public life than ever before.

The same was true of Mexican-Americans. The election of Franklin Roosevelt had an immediate effect on Mexican-American communities demoralized by the depression and the deportations of the Hoover years. Mexican-Americans in cities such as Los Angeles and El Paso found it easier to qualify for relief under New Deal guidelines, plus there was more relief to go around. Even though New Deal guidelines prohibited discrimination based on legal status, the new climate encouraged a marked rise in requests for naturalization papers, the first step toward citizenship. Inspired by New Deal rhetoric about economic recovery and social progress through cooperation, Mexican-Americans increasingly identified their future with the United States, not Mexico. This shift was especially evident among members of Bert Corona's "Mexican-American generation"—the American-born children of Mexican immigrants who

filled the leadership vacuum created by the deportations in the early 1930s (see Chapter 25).

Many Mexican-Americans felt a personal connection to President Roosevelt. They warmly applauded his Good Neighbor Policy towards Latin America, whose emphasis on economic cooperation instead of military intervention was seen as a great step forward in hemispheric relations. Mexican-Americans also supported and benefited from the New Deal's labor policies, such as Section 7(a) of the NIRA and the Wagner Labor Relations Act, which fostered an upsurge in labor organizing. For many Mexican-Americans, joining the CIO was an important step in becoming an American.

Participating in the political system increasingly became a part of Mexican-American life. Los Angeles activist Beatrice Griffith noted, "Franklin D. Roosevelt's name was the spark that started thousands of Spanish-speaking persons to the polls." The CIO urged its members to support the Democratic party and the New Deal in local and national elections. In 1939 El Congreso Nacional del Pueblo de Habla Español, the first national civil rights conference for Spanish-speaking peoples, called on its members to become American citizens and vote. The New Deal made it clear that it welcomed the votes of Mexican-Americans and considered them to be an important part of the New Deal coalition. This politicalization was well under way before World War II, and it provided additional spurs to political activism.

But what about groups that were not politically mobilized or that were not recognized as key components of the New Deal coalition? The New Deal's impact on those groups and communities often depended on whether they had sympathetic government administrators in Washington to promote their interests.

Native Americans were one of the nation's most disadvantaged and powerless minorities. Annual individual income in 1934 was only $48, and the unemployment rate was three times the national average. Concerned New Deal administrators such as Secretary of the Interior Harold Ickes and Commissioner of the Bureau of Indian Affairs John Collier tried to correct some of those inequities. The Indian Section of the Civilian Conservation Corps brought needed money and projects to reservations throughout the West, and Indians also received benefits from FERA and CWA work relief projects.

Of far greater significance was the Indian Reorganization Act of 1934, sometimes called the "Indian New Deal." That law reversed the Dawes Severalty Act of 1887 by promoting more extensive self-government through tribal councils and constitutions. The government also reversed the direction of federal Indian policy by abandoning attempts to force native Americans to assimilate into American society in favor of a commitment to cultural pluralism. The New Deal pledged to help preserve Indian languages, arts, and traditions and other aspects of the tribal heritage. The problems of native Americans were so severe, however, that these changes in federal policy produced only marginal results.

The New Deal and the Land

Concern with the land was one of the dominant motifs of the New Deal, and the shaping of the public landscape is among its most visible legacies. Roosevelt brought to the presidency a love of forestry and a conservation ethic nurtured from childhood on his Hudson River estate. New Deal administrators such as Interior Secretary Harold Ickes were avid conservationists. The expansion of federal responsibilities in the 1930s, especially the need to put the unemployed to work on public projects, created a climate conducive to action, as did public concern that was heightened by dramatic images of the drought and devastation of the Dust Bowl. The resulting national resources policy stressed scientific management of the land, conservation instead of commercial development, and the aggressive use of public authority to safeguard both privately and publicly held land.

The most extensive New Deal environmental undertaking was the Tennessee Valley Authority (see Map 26.1). The need for dams to control flooding and erosion in the Tennessee River Basin, a seven-state area with some of the country's heaviest rainfall, had been recognized since World War I. During the 1920s progressives led by Senator George Norris of Nebraska pushed for a public corporation to control flooding and to create a cheap source of electric power on the Tennessee River, but utility companies blocked the project. In 1933 the Tennessee Valley Authority won approval to develop the region's resources under public control. The TVA was the ultimate watershed demonstration area, with its integrated plans for flood control, reforestation, and agricultural and industrial development, including a chemical fertilizer plant. Its hydroelectric grid provided cheap electric power for the valley's residents. The TVA was admired worldwide, becoming one of the most popular destinations for visitors to the United States.

The Dust Bowl helped focus attention on land management and ecological balance. Agents from the Soil Conservation Service in the Department of Agriculture taught farmers the proper technique for tilling hillsides. (Quipped the journalist Alistair Cooke, the New Deal's conception of the common man was someone who could "take up contour plowing late in life.") Government agronomists also tried to remove marginal land from cultivation and prevent soil erosion through better agricultural practices. One of their most widely publicized programs was the creation of the Shelterbelts, which involved planting a line of 220 million trees running roughly along the 99th meridian from Abilene,

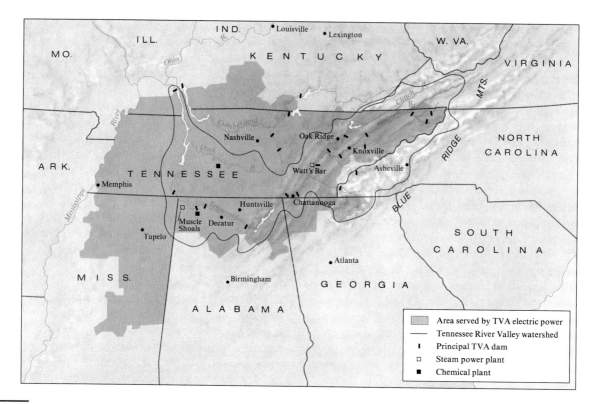

MAP 26.1

The Tennessee Valley Authority

The Tennessee Valley Authority was one of the New Deal's most far-reaching environmental projects. Between 1933 and 1952 the TVA built twenty dams and improved five others. The cheap hydroelectic power generated by the dams brought electricity to hundreds of thousands of local residents.

Texas, to the Canadian border. Planted as a windbreak, the trees also prevented soil erosion. The Shelterbelt program was a personal favorite of Franklin Roosevelt's.

Sometimes political reality dictated specific legislation affecting the environment, such as the Soil Conservation and Domestic Allotment Act of 1936. This legislation filled the void created when the Supreme Court ruled the Agricultural Adjustment Act unconstitutional in January of that year. Under the new act, farmers received payments for cutting the commercial production of crops such as wheat and cotton, which depleted the soil, and planting instead soil-building grasses and legumes such as clover and soybeans. Wheat and cotton were in fact major surplus commodities, and the law provided a way to cut production as well as encourage soil conservation. The Agricultural Adjustment Act of 1938 continued the policy of price supports and payments to farmers to limit production and established soil conservation as a permanent program.

Another priority of the Roosevelt administration was helping rural Americans stay on the land. The Rural Electrification Administration, established in 1935, which brought power to farms, was part of this attempt to im-

prove the quality of rural life (see New Technology, page 817). The New Deal also encouraged urban dwellers to return to rural areas. This "back to the land" motif animated many New Deal projects, especially those planned by the Resettlement Administration under the direction of Rexford Tugwell. Some of the best known examples were planned cooperative communities in rural areas, such as Arthurdale in West Virginia, and the "Greenbelt" residential towns outside Washington, D.C., Cincinnati, and Milwaukee.

Although the TVA, Shelterbelts, and Greenbelt towns were primarily environmental programs, they also put large numbers of the unemployed to work. The Civilian Conservation Corps, the so-called Tree Army, planted some 2 billion trees by 1941, a dozen for every American citizen at the time. Not only was this sound conservation, but it gave the 2.5 million CCC workers a job to do. Similarly, many WPA projects helped achieve conservation and recreational goals.

New Deal construction projects affecting the natural environment are all around us, artifacts from the depression era. CCC and WPA workers built the Blue Ridge Highway, the consummate parkway of the 1930s, con-

Rural Electrification

In 1935 fewer than one-tenth of the nation's 6.8 million farms had electricity. For millions of farm families that stark fact meant a life of unremitting toil made even harsher by the lack of simple conveniences. Farm families used an average of 200 gallons of water a day. Any chore requiring water—and most did—meant pumping the water from a distant well and carrying it to the house or barn in a pair of buckets that weighed as much as 60 pounds. Water had to be heated on a woodstove that required constant tending. Meeting a family's yearly water needs took sixty-three eight-hour days and involved carrying water a distance of 1,750 miles.

Rural women suffered especially from the lack of electricity. Canning, a necessity before refrigeration, kept women standing over steaming vats of fruit or vegetables, often in the worst summer heat, before the freshly harvested produce spoiled. Wash day, traditionally Monday, called for three large zinc washtubs for washing, rinsing, and bleaching. A week's wash consisted of four to eight loads, each requiring three washtubs of clean water hauled from the well. Few rural households could afford commercial soap, so women used lye, which barely got ground-in dirt out of soiled clothes and was very harsh on hands.

If farm women dreaded Monday, they hated Tuesday even more. Tuesday meant ironing, another all-day job. The iron, a 6- or 7-pound wedge of metal, had to be heated on the stove, and because it did not retain heat for more than a few minutes, it took several irons to do a shirt. The women in Texas's hill country called them "sad irons."

A day that began in darkness and was given over to twelve hours of backbreaking toil brought few comforts in the evening. Reading by kerosene lamps strained the eyes. Children's eyes might be strong enough to read in the semidarkness, but few older people could read without squinting. The absence of electricity also meant no radios, which meant no contact with the outside world, no amusement to brighten the darkness.

Studies showed that farmers would find many uses for electricity and would make good customers, but power companies balked at the prospect of electrifying the countryside, claiming that it was not economically feasible to run lines to individual farms. In 1935 the federal government made a commitment to bring power to rural America. The Rural Electrification Administration, an independent agency, promoted the formation of nonprofit farm cooperatives to bring electricity to their regions. For a $5 down payment local farmers could join an association and become eligible for low-interest federal loans covering the cost of installing

"Blue Monday"
Laundry was one of women's hardest household chores. Although this woman did not have to haul water from an outdoor well, she still had to pump it by hand in order to do the wash because her home lacked electricity. She also had to wring out the wet clothes manually, another arduous task.

power lines. Each household was committed to a monthly minimum usage, usually about $3, but as usage increased, the rates came down. By 1940, 40 percent of the nation's farms had electricity; in 1950, the rate reached 90 percent.

Electricity brought relief from the drudgery and isolation of farm life. An electric milking machine saved hours of manual labor, most of it previously done before dawn by the faint glow of a kerosene lamp, so farmers could devote the daylight hours to outdoor chores. An electric water pump lightened many chores, especially hauling water. Electric irons, vacuum cleaners, and washing machines eased women's burdens.

People's responses to rural electrification were poignant. A small child told his mother, "I didn't realize how dark our house was until we got electric lights." One farm woman remembered, "I just turned on the light and kept looking at Paw. It was the first time I'd ever really seen him after dark." Another family, caught unaware by the timing of the hookup, saw its house from a distance and thought it must be on fire. Schoolteachers noticed that children did better at school when they had light to do homework by. Along with the automobile, electricity probably did more than any other technological innovation to break down the barriers between urban and rural life in twentieth-century America.

necting the Shenandoah National Park in Virginia with the Great Smoky Mountain National Park in North Carolina. Government workers built the San Francisco Zoo, Berkeley's Tilden Park, and the canals of San Antonio; the CCC helped complete the East Coast's Appalachian Trail and the West Coast's Pacific Crest Trail through the Sierras. In state parks across the country, cabins, shelters, picnic areas, lodges, and observation towers were built in a style that has been called "government rustic." All those projects shared the New Deal ethos of leisure and recreation coexisting with nature.

What was the long-term impact of the New Deal on land use and conservation? On the Great Plains, probably not very much. Without proper care, many of the Shelterbelts deteriorated, and dust storms struck again in the 1950s. When the CCC and WPA lost their funding in the early 1940s, maintenance work lapsed. But many of the facilities they built still exist today, relics of the conservation ethic and the need to put citizens to work.

Although the New Deal was ahead of its time in its attention to conservation, its legacy to later environmental movements is mixed. Many of the tactics of New Deal projects—damming rivers, blasting fire roads, altering the natural landscape with buildings and shelters—would now be considered too intrusive. The TVA came under attack in the 1970s for its long-standing practice of strip mining and the pollution caused by its power plants and chemical factories. Because of environmental concerns, a project as massive as the TVA probably could never be built today, an ironic conclusion to what was hailed at the time as an enlightened use of government power for the public good.

The Legacies of the New Deal

The New Deal set in motion far-reaching changes, notably the growth of a modern state of significant size. For the first time people experienced the federal government as a concrete part of everyday life. During the 1930s more than a third of the population received direct government assistance from new federal programs such as Social Security, farm loans, relief, and mortgage guarantees. Furthermore, the government made a commitment to intervene in the economy when private instruments of power could not guarantee economic stability. New legislation regulated the stock market, reformed the Federal Reserve System by placing more power in the hands of Washington policy makers, and brought many practices of modern corporate life under federal regulation. The New Deal thus continued and accelerated the pattern begun during the Progressive Era of using federal regulation to bring order and regularity to economic life.

The New Deal also laid the foundations of America's welfare state, that is, the federal government's ac-

The New York World's Fair
The theme of the 1939 World's Fair was "Building the World of Tomorrow." After grimly struggling for a decade to overcome hard times, many Americans were ready to embrace a rosy future of social harmony, interdependence, and material progress. Joseph Binder's prize-winning poster featured the Trylon and the Perisphere, the fair's instantly recognizable symbols.

ceptance of primary responsibility for the individual and collective welfare of the people. Although the New Deal offered more benefits to American citizens than they had ever received before, its safety net had many holes, especially in comparison with the far more extensive welfare systems in Western Europe. The greatest defect of the emerging welfare system was its failure to reach a significant minority of American workers. For example, the Social Security program excluded domestic workers and farm workers for many years. And since state governments administered the programs, benefits varied widely, with southern states consistently providing the lowest amounts. Not until the Great Society programs of President Lyndon Johnson in the 1960s did social welfare programs reach significant numbers of America's poor.

To its credit, the New Deal recognized that poverty was a structural economic problem, not a matter of personal failure. New Deal reformers assumed that once the depression was over, full employment and an active economy would take care of welfare needs, and poverty would wither away. It did not. When later administrations confronted the persistence of inequality and unemployment, they grafted welfare programs onto the jerry-built system left over from the New Deal. Thus the American welfare system would always be marked by its birth during the crisis atmosphere of the Great Depression.

New Deal Coalition. Even if the early welfare system had some serious flaws, it was brilliant politics. The Democratic party courted the allegiance of citizens who benefited from New Deal programs. Organized labor aligned itself with the administration that had made it a legitimate force in modern industrial life. Blacks voted Democratic in direct relation to the economic benefits that poured into their communities. The Women's Division of the Democratic National Committee mobilized 80,000 women at the grass-roots level who supported what the New Deal had done for their communities. The unemployed also looked kindly on the Roosevelt administration. According to one of the earliest Gallup polls, 84 percent of those on relief voted the Democratic ticket in 1936.

The Democratic party did not attract only the down-and-out. Roosevelt's magnetic personality and the dispersal of New Deal benefits to families throughout the social structure brought middle-class voters, many of them first- or second-generation immigrants, into the Democratic fold. The New Deal thus completed the transformation that had begun in the 1920s toward a Democratic party that reflected the interests of ethnic groups, city dwellers, organized labor, blacks, and a broad cross-section of the middle class. Those voters provided the backbone of the Democratic coalition for decades to come.

Yet even in the 1930s the New Deal coalition contained potentially fatal contradictions, mainly involving the issue of race. Because Roosevelt depended on the support of southern white Democrats to pass New Deal legislation, he was unwilling to challenge the economic and political marginalization of blacks in the South. At the same time, New Deal programs were changing the face of southern agriculture by undermining the sharecropping tenant system and encouraging the migration of southern blacks to northern and western cities. Outside the South blacks were not prevented from voting, thus guaranteeing that civil rights would enter the national agenda. The resulting fissures would eventually weaken the coalition that had seemed so invincible at the height of Roosevelt's power.

Culture and Commitment

Many American artists redefined their relationship to society in response to the depression. Never had there been a decade, noted the critic Malcolm Cowley in 1939, "when literary events followed so closely on the flying coat-tails of social events." Political engagement replaced the personal alienation of the 1920s as world events such as the rise of fascism demanded intellectuals' energy. For the first time American culture was considered a valid subject for serious artistic creativity—previously, artists had felt compelled to draw on European models and themes. Although not all art in the decade was federally funded, the New Deal helped foster creative expression through its wide-ranging and controversial experiment in federal patronage of the arts.

New Deal Culture

The depression had dried up traditional sources of private patronage, and creative artists, like most Americans, had nowhere to turn except Washington. The WPA project known as "Federal One" put unemployed artists, actors, and writers to work. Federal One's spirit and purpose extended far beyond relief. New Deal administrators wanted to redefine the relationship between artists and the community so that art would no longer be the province only of the elite. "Art for the millions" became a popular New Deal slogan.

The Federal Art Project (FAP) gave work to many of the twentieth century's leading painters, muralists, and sculptors at a point in their careers when the lack of private patronage might have prevented them from continuing their artistic production. Jackson Pollock, Alice Neel, Willem de Kooning, and Louise Nevelson all received support. Under the direction of Holger Cahill, an expert on American folk art, the FAP commissioned murals for public buildings and post offices across the country. Huge WPA murals covered the walls and ceilings of terminals at the newly constructed La Guardia Airport in New York. As artistic tastes changed in the 1940s and 1950s, most of La Guardia's murals were painted over, but those at its Marine Air Terminal have been restored to their original splendor.

Under the direction of Nicholas Sokoloff, the conductor of the Cleveland Symphony Orchestra, the Federal Music Project employed 15,000 musicians. Government-sponsored orchestras toured the country, presenting free concerts of classical and popular music. Like many New Deal programs, the Music Project emphasized American themes. The composer Aaron Copland wrote his *Billy the Kid* (1938) and *Rodeo* (1942) ballets for the WPA, compositions he based on western folk motifs. The distinctive "American" sound and ath-

Relief Blues
Between 1934 and 1939 an Italian immigrant, O. Louis Guglielmi, found work on the Federal Art Project of the WPA, to which he submitted this painting in 1938. Entitled *Relief Blues*, it represents the social concern and urban realism prominent in American painting during the 1930s. The starkness of the room and its occupants is intensified by the bright red slippers, the pink rose on the floor, and the red lipstick and nail polish of the woman on the left.

letic dance style of these works made them immensely appealing to audiences. The musicologist Charles Seeger and his wife, the composer Ruth Crawford Seeger, cataloged hundreds of American folk songs.

The former journalist Henry Alsberg headed the Federal Writers' Project (FWP), which employed about 5,000 writers at its height (see American Voices, page 821). Young FWP writers who later achieved fame include Saul Bellow, Ralph Ellison, Tillie Olsen, and John Cheever. The black folklorist and novelist Zora Neale Hurston finished three novels while on the Florida FWP, among them *Their Eyes Were Watching God* (1937). Richard Wright won the 1938 *Story* magazine prize for the best tale by a WPA writer and used his spare time to complete *Native Son* (1940).

The FWP produced more than a thousand publications. It collected oral histories of Americans in many walks of life, including a set of 2,000 narratives of former slaves. Its most ambitious project was a set of state guidebooks. Fifty-one state and territorial guides, city guides, and twenty regional guides, including *U.S. One: Maine to Florida*, were published, mostly by commercial presses. Combining tourism, folklore, and history, the guides reflected the resurgence of interest in everything American. They became widely popular, but the choice of subjects sometimes annoyed politicians and state boosters. For example, the 675-page guide to Massachusetts devoted only fourteen lines to the Boston Tea Party and five to the Boston Massacre but allotted thirty-one to the Sacco-Vanzetti case.

Of all the federal creative programs the Federal Theatre Project (FTP) was the most ambitious. American drama thrived in the 1930s, the only time that the United States has had a federally supported national theater. Under the gifted direction of Hallie Flanagan, former head of Vassar College's Experimental Theater, the Theatre Project reached an audience of 25 million to 30 million in the four years of its existence. Talented directors, playwrights, and actors, including Orson Welles, John Huston, and Arthur Miller, offered their talents and services.

The Theatre Project's most successful productions included T. S. Eliot's *Murder in the Cathedral*, Mark Blitzstein's *The Cradle Will Rock*, Shakespeare's *Macbeth* with an all-black cast in a Haitian voodoo setting, and the *Swing Mikado*, a jazz rendition of the Gilbert and Sullivan operetta. Sinclair Lewis's antifascist *It Can't Happen Here* opened simultaneously in eighteen cities across the country, including productions in Spanish and Yiddish. Also popular were miniplays called "Living Newspapers," among them *Triple A Plowed Under*, about farm problems, and *Power*, which dealt with public ownership of utilities.

The theater was one of the most politically committed fields of American creative life in the 1930s. However, Congress was unwilling to appropriate federal funds for what it saw as left-leaning productions, and the FTP was terminated in 1939. Federal One limped along under federal-state sponsorship until 1943, when wartime priorities dealt it a final blow.

Anzia Yezierska

Artists on Relief

Anzia Yezierska's powerful descriptions of immigrant life, particularly *Hungry Hearts* (1920) and *Bread Givers* (1925), brought her fame and a Hollywood movie contract in the 1920s, but she found herself penniless once the depression hit. The Federal Writers' Project was her salvation.

FOUR BILLION DOLLARS FOR JOBS . . . One after another picked up the newspaper, disbelieving. Perhaps because they had fought so hard for it they were stunned. It was too good to be true. And when they were finally convinced that their dream was about to be realized, the discussion became a joyous shouting celebration.

A new world was being born. A world where artists were no longer outcasts, hangers-on of the rich, but backed by the government, encouraged to produce their best work.

The President said so.

People who no longer hoped or believed in anything but the end of the world began to hope and believe again.

In the weeks that followed, radios boomed with it. Everywhere—at grocers, cigar stores, lunch counters, in the streets—people were discussing the President's plan to end unemployment. Every day we read announcements in the newspapers of the prominent men and women appointed by the President to direct the various departments of W.P.A.

One morning as I was in the kitchen of my rooming house fixing breakfast, the radio broadcast a special news item about W.P.A.: a headquarters had just been set up for the new Writers' Project. I hurried to the address, eager to work. Ever since I had marched with the unemployed I was full of ideas for stories. All I needed to begin writing again was the security of a W.P.A. wage to get my typewriter out of the pawnshop. . . .

Each morning I walked to the Project as lighthearted as if I were going to a party. The huge, barracks-like Writers' Hall roared with laughter and greetings of hundreds of voices. As we signed in, we stopped to smoke, make dates for lunch and exchange gossip. Our grapevine buzzed with budding love affairs, tales of salary raises, whispers of favoritism, the political maneuvers of the big shots, and the way Barnes told off Somervell over the phone. There was a hectic camaraderie among us, although we were as ill-assorted as a crowd on a subway express—spinster poetesses, pulp specialists, youngsters with school-magazine experience, veteran newspaper men, art-for-art's-sake literati, and the clerks and typists who worked with us—people of all ages, all nationalities, all degrees of education, tossed together in a strange fellowship of necessity. . . .

"Thank God for the depression!" a tall, gaunt man spouted. "The depression fathered W.P.A.!" His tattered coat hung loose on his shrunken body. A safety pin fastened the frayed collar of his shirt. Unaware of his rags, his ghastly appearance, he fixed his eyes on me. "Roosevelt will go down to posterity as the savior of art in America."

"The savior of art!" I laughed. "At the bargain price of $23.86 per artist."

Source: Anzia Yezierska, *Red Ribbon on a White Horse* (New York: Charles Scribner's Sons, 1950; reprint, New York: Persea Books, 1981), 150, 156, 165.

The Documentary Impulse

The WPA arts projects were influenced by a broad artistic trend called the *documentary impulse*. Combining social relevance with distinctively American themes, this approach characterized artistic expression in the 1930s. The documentary, probably the decade's most distinctive genre, influenced practically every aspect of American culture: literature, photography, art, music, film, dance, theater, and radio.

The documentary impulse involved the communication of real life, the presentation of actual facts and events in a way that aroused the interest and emotions of the audience. Emphasizing observation and narration without relying on overembellished prose for impact, this technique exalted the ordinary, finding beauty and emotion in subjects not usually considered the province of art. It tried to make you, the audience, experience the subject as if you were actually on the scene.

The documentary impulse is evident in John Steinbeck's fiction (see Chapter 25) and John Dos Passos's *U.S.A.* trilogy, which used actual newspaper clippings, dispatches, and headlines in its fictional story. The *March of Time* newsreels, which movie audiences saw before the feature film, presented the news of the world for the pretelevision age, as did the standard opening of radio news broadcasts, "We now take you to. . . ." The filmmaker Pare Lorentz commissioned the composer Virgil Thompson to create music that set the mood for documentary movies such as *The Plow That Broke the Plains* (1936) and *The River* (1936). The new photojournalism magazines, including *Life* and *Look*, founded in 1936

and 1937, respectively, reflected this documentary approach. So did many creative works of the New Deal, from the "Living Newspapers" of the Federal Theatre Project to the American Guide series and oral history interviews prepared by the FWP. The New Deal actually institutionalized the documentary impulse by sending investigators such as the journalist Lorena Hickok and the writer Martha Gellhorn into the field to report on the conditions of people on relief.

The camera was the prime instrument of the documentary impulse. The use of cameras to document social conditions dated back to the probing work of Jacob Riis and Lewis Hine at the turn of the century. When the nation entered another period of intense social and economic questioning in the 1930s, photographers revived and updated this technique. With their haunting images of sharecroppers, Dust Bowl migrants, and the urban homeless, the photographers Dorothea Lange, Walker Evans, and Margaret Bourke-White permanently shaped the image of the Great Depression.

Life
Margaret Bourke-White's photograph of the Fort Peck Dam, with the two human figures in the foreground establishing its scale, graced the inaugural cover of *Life* magazine in 1936. Fort Peck was part of a series of dams the WPA was constructing in the Columbia River Basin for flood control. *Life*'s first issue also contained a photo essay about the town nearest to the Fort Peck Dam, which was named, appropriately, New Deal, Montana.

The federal government played a leading role in compiling the photographic record of the 1930s. In 1935 Roy Stryker, a Columbia economics instructor who had been a teaching assistant under Brains Trust member Rexford Tugwell, took charge of the Historical Section of the Resettlement Administration, with a mandate to document and photograph the American scene for the government. Stryker gathered a talented group of photographers for this massive task, including Evans, Lange, Ben Shahn, Arthur Rothstein, and Marion Post Wolcott. The government hired those photographers solely for their professional skills, not to provide relief, as was done with Federal One's projects. The photographs collected by the Historical Section, which in 1937 became part of the newly created Farm Security Administration (FSA), rank as the best visual representation of life in the United States during the depression decade.

Intellectuals and the Popular Front

In the mid-1930s the rise of fascism in Europe and the Far East called for new forms of political engagement by writers and other intellectuals. Many literary figures participated in a broad leftist movement dedicated to stopping the spread of fascism. The Communist party played a leading role in rallying intellectuals against the fascist threat.

The period from 1935 to 1939 marked the Communist party's greatest appeal in America. Marxism, having predicted the collapse of capitalism, provided an alternative vision of social and economic organization. Communists were scattered throughout all walks of life in the 1930s: working-class activists, intellectuals, housewives, union organizers, farmers, blacks, and even a few New Deal administrators. No longer a small sectarian group, party membership peaked at about a hundred thousand.

The Communist party exerted an especially powerful influence on American writers in the 1930s. Some intellectuals joined the party; many more did not join, but considered themselves "fellow travelers." They sympathized with the party's objectives, wrote for the *Daily Worker* and other party newspapers, and associated with organizations sponsored by the party. The author Mary McCarthy recalled the fascination the party held for her and other intellectuals: "For me, the Communist Party was *the* party, and even though I did not join it, I prided myself on knowing that it was the pinnacle."

The Rise of Fascism in Europe. The courting of intellectuals was part of an important shift in the Communist party's tactics in response to the rise of fascism. Benito Mussolini had established the first fascist regime in Italy in 1922, but fascism did not become a world-

wide threat until Adolf Hitler and the National Socialist party took power in Germany in 1933 and began a program of massive rearmament and expansion of the German state (see Chapter 27).

Fearful of a world war set in motion by fascist aggression, the Soviet Union attempted to mobilize support in democratic countries. In Europe and the United States communist parties called for a "popular front" and welcomed the cooperation of any group concerned about the threat of fascism to civil rights, organized labor, and world peace. As part of the popular front, the American Communist party adopted the slogan "Communism is 20th Century Americanism" and worked for Roosevelt's reelection in 1936; Eleanor Roosevelt, whom communists once depicted as a slave of the ruling class, was now lauded for her humanitarianism. This alliance with American liberal groups at mid-decade represented the height of the party's influence in the United States.

The Spanish Civil War. The popular-front strategy became even more urgent with the outbreak of the Spanish Civil War in 1936. Army forces led by Generalissimo Francisco Franco led a rebellion against the elected republican coalition government. Franco received strong support from the fascist regimes in Germany and Italy, while only the Soviet Union and Mexico backed the Spanish government forces, called the Loyalists. The governments of the United States, Great Britain, and France sympathized with the Loyalists but stayed neutral. In the United States strict neutrality legislation in 1935, 1936, and 1937 forbade arms shipments to either side. Because Franco was receiving substantial military aid from Germany and Italy, the neutrality policy doomed the Loyalists.

Most American activists and intellectuals, overcoming their distaste for war, expressed shock at the policy of nonintervention. The Spanish Civil War became the most vital issue of their generation. "People of my sort," observed the writer Malcolm Cowley, "were more deeply stirred by the Spanish Civil War than by any other international event since the World War and the Russian Revolution." Ernest Hemingway immortalized the conflict in his novel *For Whom the Bell Tolls* (1940).

Approximately 3,200 American men and women volunteered to fight on the Loyalist side. Calling themselves the Abraham Lincoln Brigade, they formed part of an international force of soldiers, ambulance drivers, and support personnel. Years later survivors recalled the struggle as the "good fight." Despite assistance from the Soviet Union, the Loyalists were outnumbered and inadequately supplied. In March 1939 the Spanish republic fell to Franco's forces. More than half the American volunteers died in the carnage, which claimed over 700,000 lives altogether.

Although American intellectuals applauded the Soviet Union's active support of the Spanish Loyalists, many literary figures began to feel uncomfortable in leftist circles. The communists remained suspicious of intellectuals, many of whom were too independent to submit to party discipline. A number of writers found it increasingly difficult to satisfy both their artistic urges and the party's demand for fiction that reflected working-class concerns. They were also deeply distressed by mounting evidence of the Soviet leader Joseph Stalin's widespread political repression.

The Nazi-Soviet Pact. The final blow to the popular front came in August 1939, when the Soviet Union, eager to avoid war, signed a nonaggression pact with Nazi Germany. Stalin's willingness to deal with Hitler devastated many supporters of the popular front. Diehard party members loyally accepted Stalin's about-face, but others left the party in disgust. The heyday of American communism ended abruptly.

With the signing of the Nazi-Soviet pact, the world again stood on the brink of war. Although many Americans considered themselves isolationists and hoped the United States would remain aloof from the coming European conflict, they began to realize that the nation faced a greater enemy than the economic problems that had gripped it for the past decade. Barely twenty years after the "war to end all wars," the United States prepared once again to enter a worldwide struggle for the survival of democracy.

The Spanish Civil War
American volunteers who fought on the Loyalist side against Franco in the Spanish Civil War associated their fight against fascism with the figure of Abraham Lincoln, symbol of democracy and human rights. In a similar spirit, the American machine gun detachment of the Abraham Lincoln Brigade called itself the Tom Mooney Company in honor of the World War I labor activist imprisoned for his alleged role in planting a bomb during a preparedness parade in 1916.

Summary

The New Deal offered a broad-based program of political and economic reform, but its programs were hardly revolutionary. President Hoover had taken the first steps toward involving the federal government more actively in economic life, a trend that Roosevelt continued and expanded. The New Deal never cured the depression, but it restored confidence that Americans could overcome hard times. And it provided a measure of economic security against the worst depression in American history by relieving many of its tragic effects.

The New Deal dramatically expanded the size and power of the federal government, continuing a trend that had begun in the late nineteenth and early twentieth centuries. Decisions made in Washington touched millions of individual lives. The New Deal provided new opportunities and a larger role in public life for blacks, women, and the labor movement. In politics the Democratic coalition of white southerners and the urban working class that had begun to emerge in the 1920s reached a climax in the landslide victory of 1936. By 1938, however, the New Deal had run out of steam and hard times were far from over.

The collapse of the economy encouraged a reassertion of American values in literature and the arts. This artistic flowering was partly supported by a unique experiment in government patronage of the arts through the WPA. Many writers blended artistic concerns with intense political commitment. This activism culminated in the popular front, an alliance of liberals and Communists who joined together to oppose the spread of fascism, especially in the Spanish Civil War. This brief period of cooperation ended in 1939 when the Soviet Union signed an agreement with Nazi Germany, bringing the world to the brink of war again.

TIMELINE

1933	Banking crisis
	FDR's first fireside chat
	Emergency Banking Act
	Glass-Steagall Act establishes FDIC
	Agricultural Adjustment Act
	National Industrial Recovery Act
	Tennessee Valley Authority
	United States abandons gold standard
	Townsend Clubs
1934	Securities and Exchange Commission
	Indian Reorganization Act
1935	Supreme Court finds NRA unconstitutional
	National Union for Social Justice (Father Charles Coughlin)
	Resettlement Administration
	National Labor Relations (Wagner) Act
	Social Security Act
	Works Progress Administration
	Huey Long assassinated
	CIO formed
1935–1939	Communist party at height of influence
1936	Supreme Court finds Agricultural Adjustment Act unconstitutional
	Black cabinet
	Roosevelt reelected
	The Plow That Broke the Plains and *The River*
	Life magazine founded
1936–1939	Spanish Civil War
1937	Sit-down strikes
	Memorial Day Massacre
	Supreme Court reorganization fails
	National Housing Act
1937–1938	"Roosevelt recession"
1938	Aaron Copland, *Billy the Kid*
	Fair Labor Standards Act
1939	Federal Theatre Project terminated
	Nazi-Soviet pact

★   ★   ★

BIBLIOGRAPHY

Comprehensive introductions to the New Deal include Robert S. McElvaine, *The Great Depression* (1984); William E. Leuchtenburg, *Franklin D. Roosevelt and the New Deal* (1963); Barry Karl, *The Uneasy State* (1983); John A. Garraty, *The Great Depression* (1987); Roger Biles, *A New Deal for the American People* (1991); and Harvard Sitkoff, ed., *Fifty Years Later: The New Deal Evaluated* (1985).

The New Deal Takes Over

The New Deal has inspired a voluminous bibliography. Frank Freidel, *Launching the New Deal* (1973), covers the first hundred days in detail. Monographs include Bernard Bellush, *The Failure of the NRA* (1975); Thomas K. McCraw, *TVA and the Power Fight* (1970); John Salmond, *The Civilian Conservation Corps* (1967); Roy Lubove, *The Struggle for Social Security* (1968); Susan Kennedy, *The Banking Crisis of 1933* (1973); Michael Parrish, *Securities Regulation and the New Deal* (1970); Mark Leff, *The Limits of Symbolic Reform: The New Deal and Taxation, 1933–1939* (1984); James Olson, *Saving Capitalism: The Reconstruction Finance Corporation and the New Deal, 1933–1940* (1988); and Bonnie Fox Schwartz, *The Civilian Works Administration, 1933–1934* (1984). Ellis Hawley, *The New Deal and the Problem of Monopoly* (1966), provides a stimulating account of economic policy. Agricultural developments are covered in Theodore Saloutos, *The American Farmer and the New Deal* (1982); Paul Mertz, *The New Deal and Southern Rural Poverty* (1978); and Sidney Baldwin, *Poverty and Politics: The Rise and Decline of the Farm Security Administration* (1968). Greg Mitchell, *The Campaign of the Century* (1992), describes Upton Sinclair's campaign for the California governorship, and Alan Brinkley, *Voices of Protest* (1982), covers the Coughlin and Long movements. See also Leo Ribuffo, *The Old Christian Right: The Protestant Far Right from the Great Depression to the Cold War* (1983).

Roosevelt's second term has drawn far less attention than has the 1933–1936 period. James MacGregor Burns, *Roosevelt: The Lion and the Fox* (1956), provides an overview, as does Barry Karl, *The Uneasy State* (1983). Alan Brinkley, *The End of Reform* (1995), discusses the New Deal and liberalism between 1937 and 1945. The growing opposition to the New Deal is treated in James T. Patterson, *Congressional Conservatism and the New Deal* (1967); Richard Polenberg, *Reorganizing Roosevelt's Government* (1966); and Barry Karl, *Executive Reorganization and Reform in the New Deal* (1963).

The New Deal's Impact on Society

Katie Louchheim, ed., *The Making of the New Deal: The Insiders Speak* (1983), provides an engaging introduction to some of the men and women who shaped the New Deal. See also Peter Irons, *New Deal Lawyers* (1982). On women in the New Deal, see Susan Ware, *Beyond Suffrage* (1981). Blanche Cook, *Eleanor Roosevelt* (1991), takes the story to 1933; see also Lois Scharf, *Eleanor Roosevelt* (1987). George Martin, *Madam Secretary* (1976), covers the career of Frances Perkins. Also of interest is Perkins's memoir, *The Roosevelt I Knew* (1946).

On minorities and the New Deal, see Harvard Sitkoff, *A New Deal for Blacks* (1978); John B. Kirby, *Black Americans in the Roosevelt Era: Liberalism and Race* (1980); Robert Zangrando, *The NAACP Crusade against Lynching, 1909–1950* (1980); and Nancy J. Weiss, *Farewell to the Party of Lincoln* (1983). George J. Sanchez, *Becoming Mexican American: Ethnicity, Culture and Identity in Chicano Los Angeles, 1900–1945* (1993), describes the politicization of Mexican Americans in the 1930s.

Irving Bernstein, *The Turbulent Years* (1970) and *A Caring Society: The New Deal, the Worker, and the Great Depression* (1985), chronicle the story of the labor movement through 1941 in compelling detail. Additional studies include Peter Friedlander, *The Emergence of a UAW Local* (1975); Sidney Fine, *Sit-Down: The General Motors Strike of 1936–1937* (1969); David Brody, *Workers in Industrializing America* (1980); Ronald Schatz, *The Electrical Workers* (1983); Bruce Nelson, *Workers on the Waterfront* (1988); and Lizabeth Cohen, *Making a New Deal: Industrial Workers in Chicago, 1919–1939* (1990). Steven Fraser, *Labor Will Rule* (1991), is a fine biography of Sidney Hillman.

On Indian policy, see Donald Parman, *Navajoes and the New Deal* (1976); Laurence Hauptman, *The Iroquois and the New Deal* (1981); and Laurence C. Kelly, *The Assault on Assimilation: John Collier and the Origins of Indian Policy Reform* (1983). For material on rural electrification, see D. Clayton Brown, *Electricity for Rural America* (1980), and Marquis Childs, *The Farmer Takes a Hand* (1952).

The creation of the New Deal's welfare system is treated in James T. Patterson, *America's Struggle against Poverty* (1981), which carries the story through 1980. Linda Gordon, *Pitied but Not Entitled* (1994), looks at single mothers and the history of welfare. See also Michael Katz, *In the Shadow of the Poorhouse: A Social History of Welfare in America* (1986). For the enduring impact of Franklin Roosevelt on the political system, see William Leuchtenburg, *In the Shadow of FDR* (1983).

Culture and Commitment

The various New Deal programs have found historians in Jerry Mangione, *The Dream and the Deal: The Federal Writers' Project, 1935–1943* (1972); Monty Penkower, *The Federal Writers' Project* (1977); Richard McKinzie, *The New Deal for Artists* (1973); and Jane DeHart Mathews, *The Federal Theater, 1935–1939* (1967). Marlene Park and Gerald Markowitz, *Democratic Vistas* (1984), surveys New Deal murals and art. General studies of cultural expression include William Stott, *Documentary Expression and Thirties America* (1973), and Richard Pells, *Radical Visions and American Dreams* (1973). See also Karen Becker Ohrn, *Dorothea Lange and the Documentary Tradition* (1980), and F. Jack Hurley, *Portrait of a Decade: Roy Stryker and the Development of Documentary Photography in the Thirties* (1972).

Daniel Aaron, *Writers on the Left* (1961), provides an overview of literary currents in the decade. Material on the relationship between intellectuals and the Communist party can be found in Harvey Klehr, *The Heyday of American Communism* (1984). Warren Susman provides a provocative analysis of culture and commitment in the 1930s in *Culture as History* (1984). Peter Carroll, *The Odyssey of the Abraham Lincoln Brigade* (1994), tells the story of Americans in the Spanish Civil War.

Don't Let That Shadow Touch Them

Buy WAR BONDS

Mobilizing the Hearts and Minds of America

This poster used the sinister threat of fascism to American family life to whip up support for the war effort. (Courtesy of the War Memorial Museum of Virginia)

CHAPTER 27

The World at War

1939–1945

★ ★ ★

On a Sunday night in October 1938 the actor Orson Welles's "Mercury Theater of the Air" broadcast a modern version of *The War of the Worlds* (1898) by the British writer H. G. Wells. The fictional news bulletins, interspersed with simulated on-the-spot reports, convinced many people that Martians had landed near Princeton, New Jersey, and were invading the countryside. Even though the broadcast included four announcements that the radio program was a dramatization, some people fled their homes. No one doubted the power of radio anymore.

The reason that so many people believed in that fictional invasion might have been that in September of 1938 radio programs had been interrupted repeatedly by ominous news bulletins about a possible European war. Even the September 30 reports of the Munich agreement among Britain, France, and Germany, which put off the threat of immediate war, did not ease people's fears.

In the late 1930s popular culture reflected America's involvement in international events. The coming of World War II would intensify that involvement. When radios announced on December 7, 1941, that the Japanese had attacked Pearl Harbor, Americans realized that this news flash was not a hoax.

World War II ranks with the New Deal as a crucial period of political and economic change in America. Mobilization pumped money and confidence into the economy, ending the Great Depression. The task of fighting a global war increased the government's influence on people's lives and caused dramatic social changes on the home front. But the most far-reaching impact was international as the United States accepted a leading, and continuing, role in world affairs. However, within wartime strategies lay the seeds of the Cold War that would follow.

The Road to War

The rise of fascism in Europe and Asia in the 1930s threatened the fragile peace that had prevailed since the end of World War I. Established by the Versailles treaty, the League of Nations, which the United States never joined, proved too weak to deal with threats to world peace. Roosevelt foresaw the possibility of America's participation in another European war but bowed to the isolationist sentiment that was predominant in the country. By 1939, however, he was leading the nation toward war.

Depression Diplomacy

During the early years of the New Deal, America's involvement in international affairs, especially in Europe, remained limited. Roosevelt put the national interest first, reasoning that only when the United States regained a stable economy could it be an effective international leader. His message to the 1933 London Economic Conference stated that the United States would not participate in plans to stabilize world currencies and effectively killed any hope of common action. One of Roosevelt's few diplomatic initiatives in the early days of the New Deal was formal recognition of the Soviet Union in November 1933.

The Good Neighbor Policy. During his first term Roosevelt and Secretary of State Cordell Hull worked to consolidate American influence in the Western Hemisphere through a network of trade, economic, and cultural agreements with the Latin American countries. That diplomatic strategy, which combined political and economic goals, became known as the Good Neighbor Policy. At its core was Roosevelt and Hull's recognition that the friendship of Latin American countries was essential to the security of the United States and that to win that trust the United States had to develop more equal partnerships with its neighbors.

To that end, the United States voluntarily renounced the use of military force and armed intervention in the Western Hemisphere. At the Pan-American Conference in Montevideo, Uruguay, in December 1933 Hull proclaimed that "no state has the right to intervene in the internal or external affairs of another." In 1934 Congress repealed the Platt Amendment, a relic of the Spanish-American War, which had asserted the United States's right to intervene in Cuba's internal affairs. The U.S. Navy kept (and still keeps) a major base at Cuba's Guantanamo Bay, a symbol of the American presence.

Debates over Isolationism. Although most Americans wanted to avoid foreign entanglements in the early to mid-1930s, Roosevelt disagreed. An internationalist at heart, he wanted the United States to play a prominent role in an international economic and political system that would foster the long-term prosperity necessary for a lasting peace. But FDR was hampered in that wish by isolationism in both Congress and the nation.

Isolationism had been building throughout the 1920s, a product of disillusionment with American participation in World War I. In 1934 Gerald P. Nye, a Republican senator from North Dakota, began a Congressional investigation into the profits of munitions makers during World War I and then widened the investigation to determine the influence of economic interests on America's decision to declare war. Nye's committee concluded that war profiteers, whom it called "merchants of death," had maneuvered the nation into the war for financial gain.

Most of the committee's charges were dubious or simplistic, but they gave momentum to the isolationist movement. In late 1934 Roosevelt revived a proposal that had been supported by the Republican administrations of the 1920s for the United States to join the World Court, a mild internationalist gesture of symbolic rather than real importance. The Senate rejected it.

The Neutrality Act of 1935 pushed the United States farther along an isolationist course. Explicitly designed to prevent a recurrence of the events that had pulled the United States into World War I, the act imposed an embargo on trading arms with countries at war and declared that American citizens traveled on the ships of belligerent nations at their own risk.

In 1936 Congress expanded the Neutrality Act to ban loans to belligerents, and in 1937 it adopted a "cash and carry" provision: if a country at war wanted to purchase nonmilitary goods from the United States, it had to pay for them in cash and pick them up in its own ships. The goal was to protect American commercial ships from attack. Roosevelt did not like that system because it gave him no discretion to decide whether some belligerents, such as the Spanish Loyalists, deserved American support. But he realized how strong the isolationist spirit was and accepted the verdict of Congress. The neutrality policy would soon be put to the test.

Aggression and Appeasement

World War II had its roots in the settlement of World War I (see Chapter 23). Germany deeply resented the international order laid down by the Treaty of Versailles, while other nations, notably Japan and Italy, revived their dreams of an overseas empire. The League of Nations, the collective security system established at Versailles, proved unable to stop aggression. After 1931 force was used by those who wanted to upset the status quo but never by those who wanted to maintain it.

The first challenge came from Japan. In 1930 that country was controlled by an aggressive and militaristic regime with designs on dominating the Pacific Basin in what would later be known as the Greater East Asia Co-Prosperity Sphere. To become an imperial and industrial power, Japan needed raw materials and markets for its goods. In 1931, desiring a buffer against its enemy, the Soviet Union, Japan occupied Manchuria, the northernmost province of China. China appealed to the League of Nations, which ruled against Japan, but imposed no sanctions and took no action. Japan simply served the required one-year notice of withdrawal from the League. In 1937 Japan launched a full-scale invasion of China, and the League was again helpless to stop the aggression.

Japan's defiance of the League encouraged a dictator half a world away: Italy's Benito Mussolini, who had come to power in 1922 and introduced a fascist system. Fascism in Italy and, later, in Germany rested on an ideology of state control of economic affairs, the subordination of individual rights to the "collectivity," and suppression of the labor movement and the left. Above all, it called for a strong dictatorial leader. Parliamentary government and democratic guarantees were superseded by what Mussolini called, far too benevolently, a "dictatorship of the State over many classes cooperating."

Mussolini had long been unhappy with the Versailles treaty, which had not awarded Italy any former German or Turkish colonies. Also, the Italians had never forgotten their stinging defeat by Abyssinia (modern Ethiopia) in 1896, the first time Africans had successfully defended themselves against white imperialists. In 1935 Italy invaded Ethiopia, one of the few independent countries left in Africa. The Ethiopian emperor, Haile Selassie, appealed to the League of Nations, which condemned the invasion as aggression and this time imposed sanctions. However, the member nations could not agree to impose an oil embargo, so the League's actions had little effect. By 1936 Italian subjugation of Ethiopia was complete.

Not Italy but Germany presented the gravest threat to the world order in the 1930s. The Weimar Republic of the 1920s was fundamentally unstable, saddled with huge reparations payments and a guilt clause for World War I that inflamed nationalist passions. Runaway inflation, fear of communism, labor unrest, and rising unemployment were conditions that Adolf Hitler and his National Socialist (Nazi) party skillfully exploited. On January 20, 1933, Hitler became chancellor of Germany, and the *Reichstag* (legislature) soon gave him dictatorial powers. Hitler took the title of *Führer* ("leader"), proclaimed the Third Reich, and outlawed other political parties.

Hitler's goal was nothing short of world domination, as he made clear in his book *Mein Kampf* (*My*

Hitler
Adolf Hitler seized power in Germany in 1933 and embarked on a plan for world domination. Here he delivers an impassioned address to followers at a 1939 rally. Note the swastika—the Nazi symbol—prominently displayed on the *Führer*'s sleeve and pocket.

Struggle). He would seek to overturn the territorial settlements of the Versailles treaty, "restore" all the Germans of Central and Eastern Europe to a single greater German fatherland, and annex large areas of Eastern Europe to provide *Lebensraum*, or "living space," for Germans. "Inferior races" such as Jews, Gypsies, and Slavs and "undesirables" such as homosexuals and the mentally impaired would have to make way for the "master race." Hitler opened a campaign of persecution against the Jews, including the racial laws of 1933, which forbade marriages between Jews and non-Jews. The first concentration camp was established at Dachau in that year.

Hitler's strategy for gaining territory was to provoke a series of crises that gave Britain and France no alternative but to let him have his way. Germany withdrew from the League of Nations in 1933, and two years later Hitler announced that he planned to rearm Germany in violation of the Versailles treaty. No one stopped him. In 1936 Germany reoccupied the Rhineland, which had been declared a demilitarized zone under the treaty; once again France and Britain took no action. Later that year Hitler and Mussolini joined forces in the Rome-Berlin Axis, a political and military alliance. After the Spanish Civil War broke out in 1936, Germany and Italy armed the Spanish fascists (see Chapter 26).

To fulfill his global strategy, Hitler needed an Asian ally. The obvious choice was Japan. On November 26, 1936, Japan entered into the Anti-Comintern Pact with Germany. The announced purpose was to oppose communism, but the pact was really a military alliance between Japan and the Axis, which was formalized in 1940.

The Failure of Appeasement. Persecution of the Jews and other minorities escalated in Germany, and Hitler's ambitions grew. In 1938 he sent troops to annex Austria, proclaiming an *Anschluss* (union) between Germany and Austria. France and Britain hoped he would go no further, but the German dictator was scheming to seize part of Czechoslovakia, the keystone of Central Europe. Because Czechoslovakia had an alliance with France, war seemed imminent. At the Munich Conference in September 1938 Prime Minister Neville Chamberlain of Britain and Prime Minister Edouard Daladier of France capitulated, agreeing to let Germany annex the Sudetenland, the German-speaking border areas of Czechoslovakia, in return for Hitler's pledge to seek no more territory.

Within six months Hitler's forces overran the rest of Czechoslovakia and threatened to march into Poland, exposing the folly of Chamberlain's pronouncement that the Munich agreement had guaranteed "peace with honor . . . peace for our time." Britain and France realized that their policy of appeasement had been disastrous, and they prepared to take a stand, each relying on its own defenses—Britain on its island isolation and France on the massive fortification of the Maginot Line on its eastern borders. In August 1939 Hitler shocked the world by signing a nonaggression pact with the Soviet Union, allowing Germany to avoid waging war on two fronts. German troops attacked Poland on September 1, 1939, and two days later Britain and France declared war on Germany. World War II had begun.

American Neutrality, 1939–1941

Because it had become a major world power, whatever the United States did would affect the course of the European conflict. Two days after the war started the United States officially declared neutrality. Roosevelt made no secret of his sympathies, however. He pointedly rephrased Woodrow Wilson's declaration of 1914: "This nation will remain a neutral nation, but I cannot ask that every American remain neutral in thought as well." The overwhelming majority of Americans supported the Allies (Britain and France) over the Nazis—84 percent to 2 percent, with 14 percent neutral, according to a 1939 poll—but most Americans did not want to be drawn into another world war.

So began what *Time* magazine would later call America's "thousand-step road to war." After a bitter battle in Congress Roosevelt won a modification of the neutrality laws in November 1939. The Allies could now buy weapons from the United States, but only on the same cash and carry basis established for nonmilitary goods by the 1937 Neutrality Act. To avoid a repetition of the conflicts that drew the United States into World War I, Congress authorized the president to restrict American citizens and ships from entering combat zones and to prevent American merchant ships from carrying cargo to combatants' ports.

After the German conquest of Poland in September 1939, a false calm settled over Europe. This "phony war" lulled many Americans into believing that arming the Allies would be enough to defeat Germany. Hitler soon shattered their complacency. In a few hours on April 9, 1940, Nazi tanks overran Denmark. Norway fell to the Nazi *Blitzkrieg* ("lightning war") next, and the Netherlands, Belgium, and Luxembourg soon followed. Then the Germans stormed into France from the north, bypassing the Maginot Line and making short work of the combined British and French troops. On June 22,

America First
In rallies, radio broadcasts, newspaper advertisements, and even bumper stickers (such as the one pictured here), the America First Committee expressed its opposition to U.S. entry into World War II. This bumper sticker was more likely to have been seen in the Midwest, where the movement was strongest, than in the South. And it would likely have been removed after Pearl Harbor, when the America First Committee pledged full support to the war effort.

1940, France fell. Only Britain stood between the United States and Hitler's plans for world domination.

Intervention Gains. During the summer and fall of 1940 German planes bombarded Britain mercilessly in the Battle of Britain, destroying the myth of its island invincibility. In America the debate between interventionists and isolationists continued. The journalist William Allen White and his Committee to Defend America by Aiding the Allies led the interventionists. Isolationists, including the aviator Charles Lindbergh, Senator Gerald Nye, and the former National Recovery Administrator Hugh Johnson, formed the America First Committee in 1940 to keep the nation out of the war. The Chicago *Tribune*, the Hearst newspapers, and other conservative publications, especially in the Midwest, supported the isolationist cause.

Despite the efforts of the America Firsters, in 1940 the United States moved closer to involvement. Roosevelt began putting the economy and the government on a defense footing by creating the National Defense Advisory Commission and the Council of National Defense in May 1940. In June of that election year he brought two prominent Republicans, Henry Stimson and Frank Knox, into his cabinet as secretaries of war and the navy, respectively, to give a bipartisan character to the war preparations. During the summer the president traded fifty World War I destroyers to Great Britain for the right to build military bases on British possessions in the Atlantic, circumventing the 1939 neutrality legislation through an executive order. In October a bipartisan majority in Congress approved a large increase in defense spending and instituted the first peacetime draft registration and conscription in American history. Another draft law, which came up in August 1941, lengthening draftees' service from one year to two and a half years, passed by a single vote.

The 1940 Election. While the Nazi *Blitzkrieg* raged in Europe, the United States prepared for the 1940 election. Would Roosevelt seek an unprecedented third term? He had not designated a successor, and the war in Europe convinced him that he should run. He submitted to a "draft" at the Democratic National Convention. Although the delegates acclaimed Roosevelt's renomination, they balked at his choice for vice-president, liberal Secretary of Agriculture Henry A. Wallace, to replace John Nance Garner of Texas, a conservative who had long since broken with the New Deal. Wallace's nomination went through only after Eleanor Roosevelt flew to the convention in Chicago and asked the delegates to put politics aside in a national crisis.

The Republicans nominated a political newcomer, Wendell Willkie of Indiana, a lawyer and the president of the Commonwealth and Southern Electric Utilities Company. Willkie, a former Democrat, supported many of the New Deal's domestic and international policies, including Roosevelt's trade of destroyers for military bases. Trying to compete against the charismatic Roosevelt, Willkie portrayed himself as a man of the people, provoking crusty Secretary of the Interior Harold Ickes to call him "a simple barefoot Wall Street lawyer." The platforms of the two parties differed only slightly. Both pledged aid to the Allies but stopped short of calling for American participation in the war.

Initially Willkie conducted his campaign in a bipartisan spirit, but as the election approached, Republican leaders pressured him to go on the offensive. Charging that Roosevelt was leading the country into war, Willkie promised that he would not send "one American boy into the shambles of another war." Roosevelt's reply on October 28, 1940, probably clinched his victory: "I have said this before, but I shall say it again and again and again: Your boys are not going to be sent into foreign wars." (Of course, if the United States was attacked, it would no longer be a foreign war.) Willkie's spirited campaign resulted in a closer election than those of 1932 and 1936, but Roosevelt and the vital Democratic coalition won 55 percent of the popular vote and a more lopsided victory in the electoral college.

Lend-Lease. With the election behind him Roosevelt was in a better position to persuade the American people to increase aid to Britain, which had been at war for eighteen months. In Roosevelt's view the survival of Britain was the key to American security, so anything that helped that country's defense was crucial to the United States. American sympathy for the British was on the rise as scenes of destruction from the nightly German bombings appeared in the newspapers, on the radio, and in newsreels. German submarines were sinking British ships faster than they could be replaced. When Britain could no longer afford to pay cash for arms, Roosevelt decided to "eliminate the dollar sign."

At a press conference in early December 1940 Roosevelt used the analogy of lending a neighbor a garden hose to put out a fire to explain what later became known as lend-lease: "I don't say to him, . . . 'Neighbor, my garden hose cost me $15; you have to pay me $15 for it.' . . . I don't want $15—I want my garden hose back after the fire is over." In a fireside chat at the end of that month Roosevelt reinforced the idea that supplying arms to Britain would not bring the United States closer to war but would enable the nation to serve as "the great arsenal of democracy." In his State of the Union address to Congress in January 1941 Roosevelt connected lend-lease to the defense of democracy at home as well as in Europe. He presented what he called "four essential human freedoms . . . everywhere in the world," his counterparts to Wilson's Fourteen Points of 1918, as reasons for American intervention and as goals for an international postwar society (see Chapter 23). The

Four Freedoms were freedom of speech and expression, freedom of worship, freedom from want, and freedom from fear. Although Roosevelt avoided stating explicitly that America had to enter the war to protect those freedoms, he intended them to be justifications for exactly that occurrence, which he regarded as inevitable.

The United States virtually entered the war when Congress passed the Lend-Lease Act in March 1941. To administer the program, Roosevelt turned to the former relief administrator Harry Hopkins, who became one of his most trusted advisers during the war years. The legislation authorized the president to "lease, lend, or otherwise dispose of" arms and other equipment to any country whose defense was considered vital to the security of the United States. After Germany invaded the Soviet Union in June 1941 (an abandonment of the Nazi-Soviet pact of two years earlier), the United States extended lend-lease to the Soviet Union, which became part of the Allied coalition.

The Atlantic Charter. Roosevelt's determination to aid Britain was reinforced by the rapport he was developing with the British prime minister, Winston Churchill. The two leaders had formed a friendly working relationship while corresponding over aid to Britain but had not met. In August 1941 Roosevelt and Churchill conferred secretly aboard a battleship off the Newfoundland coast to discuss goals and military strategy. Their joint press release, which became known as the Atlantic Charter, provided the ideological foundation of the western cause and of the peace to follow, even before the Japanese attack on Pearl Harbor. The Charter was not an official document, but like Roosevelt's Four Freedoms, it had many similarities to Wilson's Fourteen Points. It called for postwar economic collaboration and guarantees of political stability to ensure that "all men in all the lands may live out their lives in freedom from fear and want." The Charter also supported free trade and the principle of collective security and condemned territorial gains achieved as the spoils of victory.

As in World War I, when Americans started supplying the Allies, Germany attacked American and Allied ships. By September 1941 Nazi submarines and American vessels were fighting an undeclared naval war in the Atlantic, unknown to the American public. In October, Congress authorized the arming of merchant vessels. However, without an actual enemy attack, Roosevelt still hesitated to ask Congress for a declaration of war.

The Attack on Pearl Harbor

The final provocation came not from Germany but from Japan. Tensions between Japan and the United States had been building throughout the 1930s. Japanese military advances in China had upset the balance of

political and economic power in the Pacific, where the United States had long enjoyed the economic benefits of the Open Door policy, especially access to the raw materials and large markets of China (see Chapter 22). After the Japanese invasion of China in 1937, Roosevelt denounced "the present reign of terror and international lawlessness," suggesting that aggressors such as Japan be "quarantined" by peace-loving nations. But he deliberately left the meaning of *quarantine* vague, a political necessity because isolationism was still strong in the land. Despite this, initial public reaction to the speech was strongly favorable, even among some isolationists, though the Hearst newspapers denounced it vigorously.

Even when directly provoked, the United States avoided taking a stand. During the brutal sack of Nanking in 1937 the Japanese sank an American gunboat, the *Panay*, in the Yangtze River. The United States allowed Japan to apologize and accepted more than $2 million in damages, and the incident was quickly smoothed over.

Japan's intentions soon became more expansionist. In 1940 Japan signed the Tri-Partite Pact with Germany and Italy. In the fall of 1941 Japanese troops occupied the northern part of French Indochina. The United States retaliated by effectively cutting off trade with Japan, including vital oil shipments that accounted for almost 80 percent of Japanese consumption. (At that time the United States was producing two-thirds of the world's oil.) Before its supplies ran down, Japan had to decide whether to go to war or accept American demands that it cease its expansionism in Asia. In July 1941 Japanese troops occupied the rest of Indochina; Roosevelt froze Japanese assets in the United States and instituted an embargo on trade with Japan.

In September 1941 the government of Prime Minister Hideki Tojo began secret preparations for war against the United States. Talks between the two nations continued without progress. By November American military intelligence knew that Japan was planning an attack but did not know where it would come. In fact, Japan had decided to mount simultaneous surprise attacks on all the principal British and U.S. naval bases in the western Pacific. Early on Sunday morning, December 7, 1941, Japanese bombers attacked Pearl Harbor, killing more than 2,400 Americans. Eight battleships, three cruisers, three destroyers, and almost two hundred airplanes were destroyed or heavily damaged. Luckily there were no aircraft carriers in port at the time—those vessels would be far more important in the war to come. The Japanese also failed to destroy Pearl Harbor's ship repair facilities and oil reserves, which would have stranded the navy in Hawaii until oil shipments arrived from the West Coast, thousands of miles away. From a military standpoint the Japanese attack was something of a failure.

Pearl Harbor

The U.S. destroyer Shaw *exploded into flames after receiving a direct hit during the surprise Japanese attack on Pearl Harbor on December 7, 1941. It was early Sunday morning, and many of the servicemen were still asleep. More than 2,400 Americans were killed; the Japanese suffered only light losses.*

The attack also failed in its aim to demoralize the United States. Instead, Pearl Harbor united the American people in anger and a determination to fight. Pearl Harbor Day is etched in the memories of millions of Americans who remember precisely what they were doing when they heard about the attack. The next day Roosevelt went before Congress and, calling December 7 "a date which will live in infamy," asked for a declaration of war against Japan. The Senate unanimously voted for war, and the House concurred by a vote of 388 to 1. The lone dissenter was Jeannette Rankin of Montana, who had also opposed American entry into World War I. Three days later Germany and Italy declared war on the United States, and the United States in turn declared war on those nations.

Mobilizing for Victory

The task of fighting a global war accelerated the growing influence of the state on all aspects of American life. Coordinating the changeover from civilian to war production, raising an army, and assembling the necessary work force taxed government agencies to the limit. Mobilization on such a scale demanded cooperation between business executives and political leaders in Washington, solidifying a partnership that had been growing since World War I. But the most dramatic expansion of power occurred at the presidential level when Congress passed the War Powers Act of December 18, 1941, giving Roosevelt unprecedented authority over all aspects of the conduct of the war.

Defense Mobilization

Defense mobilization did more than just end the Great Depression: it caused the economy to more than double. In 1940 the gross national product was at $99.7 billion; it reached $211 billion by the end of the war (see Figure 27.1). After-tax profits of American business companies rose from $6.4 billion in 1940 to $10.8 billion in 1944. Agricultural output grew by a third.

During the war the federal government spent $186 billion on war production, sometimes as much as $250 million a day. The peak of mobilization occurred in late 1943, when two-thirds of the economy was directly involved in the war effort, as opposed to only one-quarter in World War I. By 1945 the United States had turned out 86,000 tanks, 296,000 airplanes, 15 million rifles and machine guns, 64,000 landing craft, and 6,500 ships. Mobilization on this gigantic scale gave a tremendous boost to the economy and, after years of depression, restored faith in the capitalist system.

In this period the federal bureaucracy grew far more than it had during the eight years of the New Deal. The number of civilians employed by the government increased almost fourfold, to 3.8 million. The government gave the civil service exam two or three times a day at the height of wartime hiring. The federal budget of $95.2 billion in 1945 was ten times that of 1939. The national debt grew sixfold, topping out at $258.6 billion in 1945. Along with huge federal budgets came greater acceptance of Keynesian economics, that is, the use of fiscal policy to stimulate economic growth.

Financing the War. Taxes paid about half the cost of the war, compared with 30 percent of the cost of World War

FIGURE 27.1

Government Spending as Percent of GNP

Government defense spending was a minuscule percent of the gross national product in the 1930s, but ballooned during World War II and rose again during the Korean War. Nondefense government spending did not display as wild fluctuations, just a steady, upward trend.

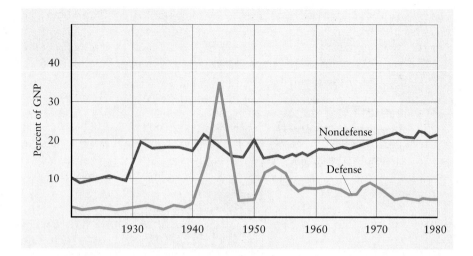

I. The Revenue Act of 1942 continued the income tax reform that had begun during World War I by reaching beyond wealthy individuals and corporations to average citizens. The number of people paying income tax increased from 3.9 million in 1939 to 42.6 million in 1945; tax collections rose from $2.2 billion to $35.1 billion, facilitated by the payroll deductions and tax withholding instituted in 1943. This mass-based tax system, a revolutionary change in the financing of the modern state, was sold to the taxpayers as a way to express their patriotism. War bond drives gave people an opportunity to put their savings at the disposal of the government by buying long-term Treasury bonds, which financed the remaining cost of the war. War bonds had the additional benefit of withdrawing money from circulation, which helped hold down inflation.

Like Woodrow Wilson during World War I, Roosevelt turned to business leaders to run the war economy. Defense preparations had been under way since 1940; 25 percent of the economy was already devoted to war production before Pearl Harbor. In January 1941 Roosevelt established the Office of Production Management under William Knudsen, the president of General Motors. After the Japanese attack Roosevelt disbanded that agency and replaced it with the War Production Board (WPB), headed by Donald Nelson, a former Sears, Roebuck executive.

The WPB awarded defense contracts, evaluated military and civilian requests for scarce resources, and oversaw the conversion of industries to military production. The last Ford rolled off the assembly line in 1942 as automobile plants were converted to bomber production. Business leaders, who had opposed the New Deal and still had the depression on their minds, were reluctant to invest in plant expansion or new production. As a spur, the government granted generous tax write-offs for plant construction. It also approved contracts with cost-plus provisions that guaranteed profits and promised that industries could keep the new factories after the war.

In the interest of efficiency and maximum production, the WPB found it easier to deal with major corporations than with small businesses. The fifty-six largest corporations got three-fourths of the war contracts, with a third going to the top ten. This system of allocating contracts, along with the suspension of antitrust prosecution during the war, hastened the trend toward large corporate structures. In 1940 the hundred largest companies manufactured 30 percent of the nation's industrial output; in 1945 their share was 70 percent. Those corporations formed the core of the military-industrial complex of the postwar years (see Chapters 28 and 29).

The Office of Price Administration and Civilian Supply (OPA) supervised the domestic economy, allocating resources and trying to keep inflation down. By February 1942 retail prices were rising 2 percent a month. In April the OPA froze most prices and rents at their March 1942 levels. When loopholes, especially regarding food prices, undermined that effort, Congress passed the Anti-Inflation Act, which stabilized prices, wages, and salaries. The consumer price index rose 28.3 percent between 1940 and 1945, but most of the inflation occurred before 1943.

Roosevelt remained unsatisfied with the mobilization effort; there were too many government agencies, and their actions often overlapped. In October 1942 he persuaded Justice James F. Byrnes to resign from the Supreme Court to head the Office of Economic Stabilization and, after 1943, the Office of War Mobilization. Byrnes soon became the second most powerful person in the administration and finally brought order to production goals for civilian and military needs. The results were remarkable.

Shipbuilding showed that American productive capacity was at full strength. By 1941 the German navy had crippled transatlantic transport, sinking about 12 million tons of mostly U.S.-built Allied shipping in the North Atlantic. Producing replacement vessels became a high priority. By turning out clunky but easy-to-build

Liberty ships, the United States produced 19 million tons of merchant shipping by 1943, up from 1 million tons two years earlier.

Henry J. Kaiser, a West Coast shipbuilder, performed shipyard production miracles. Using the mass-production techniques of the automobile industry, Kaiser cut the time needed to build a transport ship from 300 days to 17. He motivated workers through high pay and fringe benefits, including one of the country's first prepaid medical programs (see American Lives, pages 836–837). Kaiser's name became synonymous with getting things done fast. Although not all industries could boast of freedom from snafus (an acronym coined during the war from the expression "situation *n*ormal, *a*ll *f*ouled *up*"), business and government compiled an impressive record. As in World War I, industry played a significant role in the military victory.

Mobilizing the American Fighting Force

Going to war meant mobilizing human resources on both the battlefield and the home front. Under the chief of staff, George C. Marshall, the army grew from 200,000 soldiers in 1939 to over 8 million in 1945. By the end of World War II the U.S. armed forces numbered more than 15 million men and women. The army, including those who served in the Army Air Force, enlisted the most, but almost 4 million served in the navy, 600,000 in the marines, and 240,000 in the coast guard.

Draft boards registered about 31 million men between the ages of eighteen and forty-four and ordered physical examinations for about a sixth of the male population. More than half the men failed to meet the physical standards, with defective teeth and poor vision causing the greatest number of rejections.

The military also tried to screen out homosexuals, but its attempts were ineffectual. Once in the services, homosexuals found opportunities to participate in a gay subculture more extensive than that in civilian life.

Class distinctions and racial discrimination prevailed in the armed forces, mainly directed against the approximately 700,000 blacks in uniform. African-Americans served in all branches of the armed forces but were assigned the most menial duties; a great number served as messmen on navy ships, for example. The army even segregated black and white blood banks, a practice without scientific merit. The National Association for the Advancement of Colored People (NAACP) and other civil rights groups chided the government with reminders such as "A Jim Crow army cannot fight for a free world," but the military continued to segregate African-Americans. In contrast, Mexican-Americans were never officially segregated. Unlike blacks, they were welcomed into combat units, and seventeen Mexican-Americans won the Congressional Medal of Honor.

Women in Military Service. About 350,000 American women, both black and white, enlisted in the armed services and achieved a permanent status in the military. There were about 140,000 WAC (Women's Army Corps), 100,000 naval WAVES (Women Appointed for Volunteer Emergency Service), 23,000 members of the Marine Corps Women's Reserve, and 13,000 SPARs (for *Semper Paratus*, or *Always Ready*, the coast guard's motto) in the coast guard. In addition, about 1,000 WASPs (Women's Airforce Service Pilots) ferried planes and supplies in noncombat areas. A third of the nation's registered nurses volunteered for military duty: about 60,000 served in the army and 14,000 in the navy.

The armed forces limited the types of duty assigned to women, as it did with blacks. Women were barred from combat, although nurses and medical personnel sometimes served close to the front lines, risking capture or death. Most jobs reflected stereotypes of women's roles in civilian life—clerical work, communications, and health care. The widely distributed pinups of Betty Grable in a bathing suit, Rita Hayworth in a flimsy nightgown, and, for the black soldiers, the singer Lena Horne were probably closer to the average GI's view of women than a WAC or a WAVE was.

Join the Marines
Government ads pitched patriotic appeals to join the military, and women quickly enlisted. As this poster makes clear, however, one of women's main functions was to free up men so that they could go to the front. (Courtesy of the War Memorial Museum of Virginia)

Henry J. Kaiser: World War II's "Miracle Man"

Henry Kaiser was a workaholic. He hated being alone and hated taking vacations. He worked twenty-hour days and expected his top managers to do the same. If ordinary mortals were trying to sleep in California, he made a long-distance call to an associate in another time zone. "Whenever he had a new idea—and he commonly had a score or so daily—he reached for the telephone," noted his biographer, Mark Foster. As early as 1942 his company was running up then-extravagant phone bills of $250,000 a year.

Kaiser was one of the most widely known figures of the 1940s, a genuine folk hero to many for his ability to get things done but an example of an entrepreneur totally dependent on costly federal boondoggles to his critics. After shipyard triumphs such as building an entire Liberty ship in four days, fifteen hours, and twenty-six minutes in November 1942, the press dubbed him the "Miracle Man." Franklin Roosevelt seriously considered the industrialist for the vice-presidential slot on the 1944 Democratic ticket.

Kaiser's career and the rise of the modern American West went hand in hand. Born in upstate New York in 1882 to German immigrant parents, he left school at thirteen to make his way in the world. In 1906 he headed west to Spokane, Washington, to try to establish himself in business so that he could marry his fiancée; in 1921 he and his family settled permanently in Oakland, California. From 1914 to 1931 Kaiser's contracting business built roads, trying to keep up with the West's insatiable demand for highways for the new automobiles rolling off the assembly lines in Detroit. In the 1930s Kaiser was part of a six-company partnership that successfully bid for massive engineering projects such as building the Hoover and Grand Coulee dams, federally funded public-works projects that permanently changed the western landscape. In the 1930s he also lobbied extensively in Washington, developing contacts with New Deal bureaucrats that would prove invaluable during the war years.

Moved largely by wartime opportunities, Kaiser left construction to launch a career as an industrialist. He made his first big splash—literally—building Liberty ships faster and better than anyone else. But before he could build ships he had to build shipyards. Drawing on the availability of vacant tracts of waterfront unavailable to older shipyards in the East, he constructed work spaces large enough to accommodate the assembly of prefabricated ship components. Kaiser's Richmond, California, shipyards were designed like a city grid, complete with numbered and lettered streets. "It was a city without houses," remembered one worker, "but the traffic was heavy. Cranes, trucks, trains noised by." Recalled a recent migrant from a small Iowa town, "It was such a huge place, something I had never been in. People from all walks of life, all coming and going and working, and the noise. The whole atmosphere was overwhelming to me."

Although Kaiser did not invent the subassembly technique, he was the most successful at applying mass production to shipbuilding. Previously, most jobs in shipbuilding had been skilled or semiskilled, requiring apprenticeship and training far too lengthy for the wartime emergency. To train new workers more quickly, the work process was broken down into small, specialized tasks, in effect deskilling what had previously been a craft. As Kaiser put it, "production is not labor anymore, but a process."

The Kaiser shipyards were known as much for their corporate welfare programs as for their bureaucratized work climate. Kaiser offered his workers innovations such as day care, financial and job counseling, subsidized housing, and especially health care, his most significant long-term contribution. The Kaiser Permanente Medical Care Program was founded in 1942, an outgrowth of prepaid health care plans first tried on remote federal construction projects in the 1930s. This health care system, what is now called a health maintenance organization (HMO), was available to Kaiser workers

for the nominal paycheck deduction of 50 cents a week. Almost 90 percent of his workers exercised that option. Kaiser provided health care for both philanthropic and business reasons. The initial investment was quickly repaid in the form of healthier workers, lower absenteeism, and greater productivity. As a Permanente executive explained, "To the private physician, a sick person is an asset. To Permanente, a sick person is a liability. We'd go bankrupt if we didn't keep most of our members and their families well most of the time."

Whereas many business executives faced the postwar period with cautious trepidation, Kaiser looked forward to peacetime reconversion with the boundless optimism of a farsighted entrepreneur. He was especially excited about opportunities for industrial expansion in the West. Between 1944 and 1946 he identified opportunities in areas such as steel, magnesium, and aluminum as well as foreseeing a demand for mass-produced suburban tract housing. In the 1950s he headed a multinational corporate empire that included dozens of companies with assets close to $1 billion.

To many Americans Henry Kaiser was a twentieth-century incarnation of Horatio Alger, even though he was a portly sixty years old in 1942, when he launched the Richmond shipyards. In terms of managerial style, he was more an old-style "seat-of-the-pants" entrepreneur than a modern corporate bureaucrat. He was a maverick, challenging traditional ways of doing business at every stage of his career. He was a visionary in the role that he saw for an industrial West, a dream which was amply fulfilled in the postwar era. But he was also lucky, his success being the product of a highly favorable set of economic conditions both in the West and globally during World War II and its aftermath. After his death in 1967 his industrial empire largely disappeared, but Kaiser Permanente lives on, one of the country's largest and most successful health maintenance organizations.

The Miracle Man
In November 1942, Henry Kaiser uses an 81-piece, 14-foot-long model of the 10,400-ton Liberty freighter to show shipowners and navy representatives how it was built in the amazing time of 4 days, 15 hours, and 25 minutes.

The WACS Overseas
Not all military women were relegated to stateside duty. These eager WACS, members of the first Women's Army Corps unit to go overseas, have just arrived in North Africa in 1943 to begin their assignments.

Women and the War Effort

When millions of citizens entered military service, a huge hole opened in the American work force. The backlog of depression-era unemployment quickly disappeared, and the United States faced a critical labor shortage. The nation's defense industries provided jobs for about 7 million new workers, including great numbers of women and blacks who were given employment opportunities for the first time.

Government planners "discovered" women while looking for workers to fill the jobs vacated by departing servicemen. The recruiting campaign drew on patriotism. One poster urged, "Longing won't bring him back sooner . . . GET A WAR JOB!" Recruiters promised that women would take to riveting machines and drill presses "as easily as to electric cake-mixers and vacuum cleaners." The artist Norman Rockwell supported the campaign by creating his famous "Rosie the Riveter" cover for the *Saturday Evening Post.*

Although the government directed its propaganda at housewives, women who were already employed gladly abandoned low-paying "women's" jobs as domestic servants or file clerks for higher-paying jobs in defense factories. Suddenly the nation's factories were full of women working as riveters, welders, blast furnace cleaners, and drill press operators (see American Voices, page 839). Women made up 36 percent of the labor force in 1945 compared with 24 percent at the beginning of the war.

Government planners and employers regarded women as just filling in while the men were away. Employers rarely offered day care or flexible hours, and government child care programs set up by the 1940 Lanham Act reached only 10 percent of those who needed them. Because women were responsible for home care as well as their jobs, they had a higher absentee rate than did men. Often, the only way to get shopping done or take a child to the doctor was to skip work. Women war workers also faced discrimination on the job. In shipyards women with the most seniority and responsibility earned $6.95 a day, whereas the top men made as much as $22.

When the men came home from war and the plants returned to peacetime operations, Rosie the Riveter was out of a job. However, many women refused to put on an apron and stay home. Women's participation in the labor force dropped temporarily when the war ended but rebounded steadily for the rest of the 1940s, especially among married women.

Wartime Workers
The photographer Dorothea Lange captured these shipyard construction workers coming off their shift at a factory in Richmond, California, in 1942. Note the large number of women workers and the presence of minority workers. Several of the workers prominently display their union buttons. (Courtesy of the Dorothea Lange Collection. The City of Oakland. The Oakland Museum, 1982)

Fanny Christina Hill

"Rosie the Riveter"

Like many black women, Fanny Christina Hill had been trapped in domestic service until she got a job at North American Aircraft. After quitting near war's end to have a child, she returned to North American Aircraft, where she worked from 1946 until her retirement in 1980—one of the few wartime women who got their jobs back.

I don't remember what day of the week it was, but I guess I must have started out pretty early that morning. When I went there, the man didn't hire me. They had a school down here on Figueroa and he told me to go to the school. I went down and it was almost four o'clock and they told me they'd hire me. You had to fill out a form. They didn't bother too much about your experience because they knew you didn't have any experience in aircraft. Then they give you some kind of little test where you put the pegs in the right hole.

There were other people in there, kinda mixed. I assume it was more women than men. Most of the men was gone, and they weren't hiring too many men unless they had a good excuse. Most of the women was in my bracket, five or six years younger or

older. I was twenty-four. There was a black girl that hired in with me. I went to work the next day, sixty cents an hour. . . .

I was a good student, if I do say so myself. But I have found out through life, sometimes even if you're good, you just don't get the breaks if the color's not right. I could see where they made a difference in placing you in certain jobs. They had fifteen or twenty departments, but all the Negroes went to Department 17 because there was nothing but shooting and bucking rivets. You stood on one side of the panel and your partner stood on this side, and he would shoot the rivets with a gun and you'd buck them with the bar. That was about the size of it. I just didn't like it. I didn't think I could stay there with all this shooting and a'bucking and a'jumping and a'bumping. I stayed in it about two or three weeks and then I just decided I did *not* like that. I went and told my foreman and he didn't do anything about it, so I decided I'd leave.

While I was standing out on the railroad track, I ran into somebody else out there fussing also. I went over to the union and they told me what to do. I went back inside and they sent me to another department where you did bench work and I liked that much bet-

ter. You had a little small jig that you would work on and you just drilled out holes. Sometimes you would rout them or you would scribe them and then you'd cut them with a cutters.

I must have stayed there nearly a year, and then they put me over in another department, "Plastics." It was the tail section of the B-Bomber, the Billy Mitchell Bomber. I put a little part in the gun sight. You had a little ratchet set and you would screw it in there. Then I cleaned the top of the glass off and put a piece of paper over it to seal it off to go to the next section. I worked over there until the end of the war. Well, not quite the end, because I got pregnant, and while I was off having the baby the war was over. . . .

It made me live better. I really did. We always say that Lincoln took the bale off of the Negroes. I think there is a statue up there in Washington, D.C., where he's lifting something off the Negro. Well, my sister always said— that's why you can't interview her because she's so radical—"Hitler was the one that got us out of the white folks' kitchen."

Source: Sherna Berger Gluck, *Rosie the Riveter Revisited: Women, the War, and Social Change* (Boston: Twayne, 1987), 37–38, 42.

Organized Labor

The labor movement also seized opportunities during the wartime mobilization effort. No dramatic changes occurred, but the war confirmed the industrial breakthroughs of the 1930s. By the end of the war almost 15 million workers—a third of the nonagricultural labor force, up from 9 million at the end of the previous decade—belonged to unions.

Organized labor responded to the war with an initial burst of patriotic unity. On December 23, 1941, representatives of major unions made a "no strike" pledge—although nonbinding—for the duration of the war. In January 1942 Roosevelt set up the National War

Labor Board (NWLB), composed of representatives of labor, management, and the public. The board established wages, hours, and working conditions and had the authority to order government seizure of plants that did not comply. Forty plants were seized during the war.

During its tenure the NWLB handled 17,650 disputes affecting 12 million workers. It faced two controversial issues: union membership and wage increases. Union organizers favored either the union shop or the closed shop, but management preferred the open shop. (In a union shop the employees must belong to a certain union or join it within a specified period. In a closed shop the employer may hire only workers who are already members of a union. In an open shop the com-

pany usually employs only nonunion workers.) As a compromise, the NWLB imposed the principle of maintenance of membership. Workers did not have to join a union, but those already in a union had to maintain their membership during the life of the contract.

Agitation for wage increases caused a more serious disagreement. In contrast to the deflation of the depression, inflation pushed prices up throughout the war. Because management wanted to keep production (and profits) running smoothly, it was willing to pay higher wages. However, such raises would conflict with the OPA policy of keeping inflation as low as possible. In 1942 the NWLB established the "Little Steel Formula," which granted a 15 percent wage increase to match the increase in the cost of living since January 1, 1941. Although the NWLB froze hourly wages in principle, it allowed them to rise another 24 percent by 1945. Actually, incomes rose as much as 70 percent because workers earned overtime pay, which was not covered by wage ceilings. The tremendous increase in output during World War II occurred largely because people worked overtime.

Although incomes were higher than anyone could have dreamed of during the depression, many union members felt cheated as they watched corporate profits soar while their wages remained frozen. The high point of dissatisfaction came in 1943. First a nationwide railroad strike was narrowly averted, and then John L. Lewis led more than half a million United Mine Workers out on strike, demanding wages higher than the Little Steel Formula allowed. Lewis won concessions but alienated Congress and, because he had defied the government, became one of the most disliked public figures of the 1940s.

Congress countered Lewis's action by overriding Roosevelt's veto of the Smith-Connally Labor Act of 1943, which required a thirty-day cooling-off period before a strike and prohibited strikes in defense industries entirely. Nevertheless, about 15,000 strikes occurred during the war. Less than one-tenth of a percent of working hours were lost to strikes, but the public perceived the disruptions as far more extensive. Labor unions won acceptance during the war years but also provoked hostility.

Rising Winds of Change for African-Americans

A new mood of militancy appeared among the nation's minorities during wartime. World War II disrupted a number of traditional patterns, and many barriers to racial equality tottered or fell. "A wind is rising throughout the world of free men everywhere," Eleanor Roosevelt wrote during the war, "and they will not be kept in bondage." Black leaders pointed out parallels between anti-Semitism in Germany and racial discrimination in America. Civil rights leaders pledged themselves to a "Double V" campaign: victory over Nazism abroad and over racism and inequality at home.

Even before Pearl Harbor there was evidence that the war might encourage greater black activism. In 1940 only 240 of the nation's 100,000 aircraft workers were black, and most of them were janitors. Black leaders demanded that the government require defense contractors to integrate their work forces. When the government took no action, A. Philip Randolph, head of the Brotherhood of Sleeping Car Porters, a black union, announced plans for a "March on Washington" in the summer of 1941. Roosevelt was not a strong supporter of civil rights, but he feared the embarrassment of a massive public protest. Even more, he worried about a disruption of war preparations. The president agreed to take action, and Randolph canceled the march.

In June 1941 Roosevelt issued Executive Order 8802, declaring it to be the policy of the United States "that there shall be no discrimination in the employment of workers in defense industries or government because of race, creed, color, or national origin." To oversee the policy, he established the Fair Employment Practices Committee (FEPC) in the Office of Production Management.

This federal commitment to minority employment rights was unprecedented but limited in scope. For instance, it did not affect segregation in the armed forces. Moreover, the FEPC, which could not require compliance with its orders, often found that the needs of defense production took precedence over fair employment practices. The FEPC received more than 8,000 complaints, of which it resolved about a third. Blacks made up 8 percent of defense workers in 1944, probably due more to the labor shortage than to FEPC prodding. Another beneficial federal action was the National War Labor Board's decision to ban racial wage differentials, the first time that they had been prohibited by federal law.

Encouraged by the ideological climate of the war years, civil rights organizations increased their membership. The NAACP grew ninefold to 450,000 in 1945. In 1942 James Farmer helped found the Congress of Racial Equality (CORE). Unlike the NAACP, which favored lobbying and legal strategies, CORE used tactics such as demonstrations and sit-ins. In 1944 CORE forced several restaurants in Washington, D.C., to serve blacks after picketing them with signs that read "Are You for Hitler's Way or the American Way? Make Up Your Mind."

An awareness of civil rights was heightened in other ways as well. The Swedish sociologist Gunnar Myrdal wrote a monumental study of race relations, *An American Dilemma: The Negro Problem and Modern Democracy* (1944), focusing many white Americans' attention on the issue for the first time. In 1944 the Supreme

Court ruled in *Smith v. Allwright* that Texas's all-white primary election, a device commonly used to disfranchise blacks in southern states, was unconstitutional. After the Court's decision Congressman Wright Patman of Texas vowed that blacks in his district would vote "over my dead body." Soon, however, in his reelection campaigns Patman was courting black voters at church picnics and other social events. These wartime developments laid the groundwork for the civil rights revolution of the 1950s and 1960s.

Politics in Wartime

At a press conference late in 1943 Roosevelt playfully announced that "Dr. Win the War" had replaced "Dr. New Deal." During the 1940s Roosevelt rarely pressed for social and economic change, thus placating the conservative members of Congress whose bipartisan support he needed to conduct the war. With little protest, he agreed to drop several popular New Deal programs, which were less necessary once war mobilization brought full employment. In 1942 the Civilian Conservation Corps was dismantled, followed in 1943 by the National Youth Administration and the Works Progress Administration. Severe budget cuts crippled the Farm Security Administration, which had represented the interests of poor farmers. The speed with which the government terminated those agencies suggested that they had been more a response to the crisis of the depression than a commitment to promoting the general welfare through federal programs. Programs such as Social Security were left untouched, however.

The war years brought a significant decline in the reform spirit that had flourished in Washington during the 1930s. Few public figures talked about using the war to bring about social change, as they had in World War I. (One exception was reform of the tax system.) Business executives replaced the reformers and social activists who had staffed New Deal relief agencies in the 1930s. Those executives became known as "dollar-a-year men" because they volunteered for government service while remaining on the corporate payroll.

Roosevelt had hoped politics could be shelved for the duration of the war, but that proved unreasonable. The Republicans picked up seats in both houses of Congress and increased their share of state governorships in the 1942 election. Those gains reflected the tendency of the party out of power to improve its position in off-year elections. The Republicans also benefited from a low voter turnout. Relocations caused by enlistment and residency requirements, which temporarily disfranchised newcomers, contributed to the low turnout.

Roosevelt himself did not give up politics. After concluding that continuation of the war made a fourth term necessary, he went on a mild offensive to attract Democratic voters. In his State of the Union address in 1944, the president called for a second Bill of Rights. As the basis of postwar prosperity, he pledged rights such as jobs, adequate food and clothing, a decent home, medical care, and education.

The president's sweeping commitment remained largely rhetorical. Congressional support for this vast extension of the welfare state did not exist in 1944. It was possible, however, to win some of those rights for a special group of American citizens: veterans. The Servicemen's Readjustment Act, known as the GI Bill of Rights, passed in 1944, provided education, job training, medical care, pensions, and mortgage loans for men and women who had served in the armed forces during the war.

The Election of 1944. "I am an old campaigner and I love a good fight," Roosevelt had said during the 1940 election. He approached the 1944 campaign with the same verve, but the years had taken their toll. Concern about Roosevelt's health and the need for a successor prompted the Democrats to drop Vice-President Henry Wallace, whose outspoken support for labor, civil rights, and domestic reform was too extreme for many party leaders. In Wallace's place they chose Senator Harry S. Truman of Missouri.

Truman, a World War I veteran and Kansas City haberdasher whose business had failed in the 1920–1921 recession, found success in politics. Sponsored by Thomas Pendergast, the Democratic boss in Kansas City, he was elected to the Senate in 1934 and again in 1940. Truman became known for heading a Senate investigation of gov-

for full employment after the war
REGISTER to VOTE
CIO POLITICAL ACTION COMMITTEE

Labor and Politics
The CIO's Political Action Committee was formed to harness the political power of new recruits for labor's postwar agenda, especially full employment. Ben Shahn's vivid 1944 poster reinforced the CIO's commitment to racial equality. (Ben Shahn, "For Full Employment after the War Register Vote," 1944, Collection of the Museum of Modern Art)

ernment waste and inefficiency in defense contracts during the war.

The Republicans nominated Governor Thomas E. Dewey of New York. Only forty-two years old, Dewey had won fame fighting organized crime as a U.S. attorney. He accepted the broad outlines of the welfare state and belonged to the internationalist wing of the Republican party. The 1944 election was the closest since 1916 as Roosevelt received 53.5 percent of the popular vote. The Democrats lost ground among farmers, but most ethnic groups remained solidly Democratic. Roosevelt got his customary support from the South, augmented by the overwhelming allegiance of members of the armed forces, who voted by absentee ballot. His margin of victory came from the cities. In urban areas with more than 100,000 people the president drew 60 percent of the vote.

Roosevelt also received strong support from organized labor. Under the prodding of CIO leaders Sidney Hillman and Philip Murray, labor contributed more than $1.5 million, or about 30 percent of the Democratic party's election funds. The CIO's Political Action Committee canvassed door to door and conducted voter registration campaigns. Organized labor continued to play a significant role in the Democratic party after the war.

Life on the Home Front

In contrast to World War I, once Congress declared war, there was almost no domestic opposition to the nation's role in World War II. Americans fought for their way of life and to preserve democracy against Nazi and Japanese totalitarianism. Because the enemies seemed so evil and America's will to win was so strong, many remember it as the "good war." By the spring of 1945 soldiers who had finished their military duty, which averaged sixteen months, were beginning to return home. Fighting had been a dirty, bloody job, a far cry from their visions of saving democracy and stopping fascism. Dreams of marriage, a house in the suburbs, and a new car sustained many soldiers through the horror and tedium of the war. In 1947 veterans and their families made up a fourth of the American population.

"For the Duration"

Although the United States did not suffer the physical devastation that ravaged much of Europe and the Pacific, the war affected the lives of those who stayed behind. Every time relatives of a loved one overseas saw the Western Union boy on his bicycle, they were afraid it meant a telegram from the War Department telling them that their son, husband, or father would not be

coming home. Other Americans tolerated small deprivations daily. "Don't you know there's a war on?" became the standard reply to any request that could not be fulfilled. People accepted the fact that their lives would be different "for the duration."

Just like the soldiers in uniform, people on the home front had a job to do. They worked on civilian defense committees, donated blood, collected old newspapers and scrap material, and served on local rationing and draft boards. About 20 million home "Victory gardens" produced 40 percent of the vegetables grown in the United States. Advertising campaigns displaying the popular "V for Victory" slogan stressed patriotism. All seven war bond drives were oversubscribed.

However, many Americans remember the war years as a time of returning prosperity. Unemployment disappeared, and per capita income rose from $691 in 1939 to $1,515 in 1945. Despite geographical dislocations and shortages of many items, about 70 percent of Americans admitted midway through the war that they had personally experienced "no real sacrifices." A Red Cross worker put it bluntly: "The war was fun for America. I'm not talking about the poor souls who lost sons and daughters. But for the rest of us, the war was a hell of a good time."

During the war years demographic patterns rebounded from their depression-induced declines. Young

Wartime Prosperity
War mobilization brought prosperity to many American households. This photograph, taken in 1942, shows the Hall family of Sheffield, Alabama, in their comfortable home, part of a defense housing project connected with the TVA. The picture looks posed, but the new levels of consumption and affluence it represented were true for many Americans like the Halls.

people could afford to marry, and the imminent departure of men for military service induced many couples to take that step sooner rather than later. Not all those marriages survived the strain of separation or wartime relocation, and the divorce rate also rose. The birth rate went up, with many babies being conceived before their fathers went off to war. In effect, the wartime birth patterns marked the beginning of the "baby boom" that characterized American culture in the postwar period.

Popular Culture. Popular culture, especially the movies, reinforced the connections between the home front and the troops serving overseas. Hollywood escaped the restrictions and cutbacks that affected other industries, in part because studio heads argued that movies built morale. Many Hollywood directors lent their services to the military. Director Frank Capra's "Why We Fight" films, a documentary series produced for the War Department, explained war aims to new soldiers and sailors. John Huston provided an intense portrayal of men in combat in his documentary *The Battle of San Pietro* (1944).

Average weekly movie attendance soared to over 100 million during the war. Demand was so high that many theaters operated around the clock to accommodate defense workers on the swing and night shifts. Many movies had patriotic themes, and films such as *Wake Island* (1942) and *Thirty Seconds over Tokyo* (1945) portrayed life in the armed services. Other movies, such as Frank Capra's *Meet John Doe* (1943) and Alfred Hitchcock's *Lifeboat* (1944), depicted the danger of fascism at home and abroad. Dramas about the struggle on the home front were also popular. In the box-office hit *Since You Went Away* (1943) Claudette Colbert took a war job after her husband left to fight, and the Oscar-winning Greer Garson played a courageous British housewife in *Mrs. Miniver* (1942). Newsreels accompanying feature films kept the public up to date on the war, as did on-the-spot radio broadcasts by commentators such as Edward R. Murrow. Thus popular culture reflected America's new international responsibilities at the same time that it built up morale on the home front.

War correspondents such as John Hersey and Ernie Pyle (who was killed in a foxhole on Ie Shima by a Japanese bullet) reported on the GIs (short for "government issue") for readers back home. Reporters often portrayed the GIs as ordinary boys doing their patriotic duty. "When you looked into the eyes of those boys, you did not feel sorry for the Japs: you felt sorry for the boys," John Hersey wrote of the marines in Guadalcanal in 1944. Another marine who fought at Guadalcanal remembered it as a matter of simple survival: "The only way you could get it over with was to kill them off before they killed you. The war I knew was totally savage."

Entertaining the Troops
The original Stage Door Canteen opened in the basement of a Broadway theater in 1942. It provided servicemen with coffee, doughnuts, and big-time entertainment volunteered by Broadway and Hollywood stars. The canteen's popular weekly radio show was the inspiration for the 1943 movie *Stage Door Canteen*.

Throughout the war the Japanese were hated far more than the Germans were. Whereas Americans often differentiated between evil Nazi leaders and ordinary "good Germans" forced to go along with Nazi excesses, they lumped all Japanese together. Racial epithets like "slant eyes" and "yellow monkeys" were widely used in conversation, and even respected magazines such as *Time*, *Life*, and *Newsweek* routinely referred to the enemy as "Japs." Between American attitudes toward Japan and Nazi atrocities against Jews, racism was a constant undercurrent of World War II.

Rationing. During the war almost anything that Americans ate, wore, or used was subject to rationing or regulation. Rubber became the first scarce item. The Japanese conquest of Malaya and the Netherlands East Indies cut off 97 percent of America's imports of natural rubber, an essential raw material for war production. An entire new industry in synthetic rubber was born, and by late 1944 the United States was producing 762,000 tons of it a year, mostly for the war effort.

Meanwhile, to conserve rubber, the government restricted the sale of tires, a hard sacrifice for the nation's 30 million car owners, many of whom put their autos up on blocks for the duration. If people walked instead of drove, they wore out their shoes. In 1944 shoes were rationed to two pairs per person a year, barely half the average number that people bought before the war.

The government also rationed gasoline and fuel oil. Shortages of fuel oil forced schools and restaurants to shorten their hours, and home thermostats were lowered to 65 degrees. Gasoline rationing, introduced in December 1942, represented both a response to depleted domestic gasoline supplies and an attempt to save wear on precious rubber tires. To further discourage gasoline consumption, Congress imposed a nationwide speed limit of 35 miles per hour; highway death rates dropped dramatically.

People found it harder to cut back on sugar. When sugar disappeared from grocery shelves, the government rationed it at a rate of 8 to 12 ounces per person a week. However, the manufacturers of products such as Coca-Cola and Wrigley's chewing gum received unlimited quantities of sugar by convincing the government that their products helped the morale of the men and women in the armed forces.

By 1943 the amount of meat, butter, and other foods Americans could buy was regulated by a complicated system of rationing points and coupons. Most people cooperated with the restrictions, but almost a fourth occasionally bought items on the black market, especially meat, gasoline, and cigarettes.

Shortages of other consumer products also hit the home front. People finally had enough money to buy refrigerators, cars, and radios, but the components of those items—including rubber, copper, and steel—were earmarked for war production. To placate consumers, many companies ran advertisements promising delayed gratification. After the war, they told the public, you can buy that new house and fill it with all the appliances you want.

But some purchases could not wait. Among the most sought-after items on the black market were women's stockings. In the 1930s women had worn silk stockings, but when the war with Japan cut off imports of silk, they switched to nylon. Unfortunately, nylon was essential to war production: thirty-six pairs of nylons equaled one parachute. In a dramatic fashion change (and one associated with the image of Rosie the Riveter) many women began wearing slacks in public. The strict rationing of food and other items eased in the summer of 1944, when victory appeared on the horizon.

Migration and Family Life. The war not only affected what people ate, drank, and wore, it affected where they lived. People moved from one part of the country to another in unprecedented numbers. When men vol-

unteered for or were drafted into the armed services, their families often followed them to training bases or points of debarkation. The lure of high-paying defense jobs encouraged others to move. About 15 million Americans changed residence during the war years, half of them by moving to another state. The pace of urbanization increased, but this movement was not simply an exodus from rural to urban areas. About 5.4 million people left farms, but 2.5 million moved onto them. The greatest number of people went west.

The federal government supported the growth of industry in the West. The western states not only served as staging areas for the war in the Pacific, they also had room for the new ship- and airplane-building industries. Their remote regions (for instance, Hanford, Washington, and Los Alamos, New Mexico) were ideal places to conduct top-secret research.

As a center of defense production California was affected by wartime migration more than any other state was. "The Second Gold Rush Hits the West," headlined the *San Francisco Chronicle* in 1943. During the war one-tenth of all federal dollars went to California, and the state turned out one-sixth of total war production. California welcomed nearly 3 million new residents during the war, a 53 percent growth in population. They went where the defense jobs were—to Los Angeles, San Diego, and the San Francisco Bay Area. Some towns grew practically overnight. Just two years after the Kaiser Corporation opened a shipyard in Richmond, the population quadrupled.

Migration and relocation often caused strains. Many towns with defense industries had scarce housing and inadequate public transportation; conflicts over public space and recreation erupted between old-timers and newcomers. Of special concern were the young people the war had set adrift from traditional community restraints. Newspapers were filled with stories of "latchkey" children who stayed home alone while their mothers worked in defense plants. Adolescents were even more of a problem. Teenage girls who hung around army bases looking for a good time were known as "victory girls." In 1942 and 1943 juvenile delinquency seemed to be reaching epidemic proportions.

Spurred by the new economic opportunities in defense and factory work, blacks migrated from the South in increasing numbers after the temporary slowdown of the depression. More than a million African-Americans moved to defense centers in California, Illinois, Michigan, Ohio, and Pennsylvania. Their need for jobs and housing led to racial conflict in several cities.

Some of the worst racial violence took place in Detroit, the new home of a large number of southern migrants, both black and white. Competition for scarce housing caused many of the disputes. Early in 1942 black families encountered resistance and intimidation when they tried to move into the Sojourner Truth hous-

ing project in the Polish community of Hamtramck. Similar tensions erupted into violence in June 1943, when a major race riot in Detroit left thirty-four people dead, including twenty-five blacks. Racial conflicts broke out in forty-seven cities across the country during 1943.

Racial violence was not confined to African-Americans. In Los Angeles male Latino teenagers organized *pachuco* (youth) gangs, dressing in broad-brimmed felt hats, pegged trousers, and clunky shoes; wearing long slicked-down hair; and carrying pocket knives on gold chains. The young women that they hung out with favored long coats, *huarache* sandals, and pompadour hairdos. Although "zoot suits" were most popular among Latinos, that style was also taken up by blacks and by a few white working-class teenagers in Los Angeles, Detroit, New York, and Philadelphia as a symbol of alienation and self-assertion. To adults and many Anglos, however, the zoot suit came to symbolize wartime juvenile delinquency.

In Los Angeles white hostility toward Mexican-Americans had been smoldering for some time, and zoot suiters became the targets. In July 1943 rumors that a *pachuco* gang had beaten a white sailor set off a four-day riot, during which white servicemen entered Mexican-American neighborhoods and attacked zoot suiters, tak-

Zoot Suits

Zoot suits gained wide popularity among young Americans during the war. In 1943 this well-dressed teenager greased his hair in a ducktail and wore a loosely cut coat with padded shoulders ("fingertips") that reached midthigh, baggy pleated pants cut tight ("pegged") around the ankles, and a long gold watch chain.

ing special pleasure in slashing the pegged pants of their victims. The attacks occurred in full view of white police officers, who did nothing to stop the violence.

Japanese Relocation

Although racial confrontations and zoot suit riots recalled the widespread racial tensions of World War I, the mood on the home front was generally calm in the 1940s. German culture and German-Americans did not come under suspicion, nor did Italian-Americans. Leftists and communists faced little domestic repression, mainly because after Pearl Harbor the Soviet Union became an ally of the United States. There was one glaring exception to this record of tolerance: the internment of Japanese-Americans on the West Coast. The prejudice and hysteria directed at Japanese-Americans are a reminder of the fragility of civil liberties in wartime.

Immediately after Pearl Harbor the West Coast remained calm. Then, partly as a reflection of the region's vulnerability to attack but also because of inflammatory rhetoric in the Hearst newspapers, coastal residents began to demand protection against supposed Japanese spies. California had a long history of antagonism toward both Japanese and Chinese immigrants (see Chapters 17 and 22). The Japanese-Americans, who clustered together in highly visible communities, were a small, politically impotent minority, numbering only about 112,100 in the three coastal states. Unlike German- and Italian-Americans, the Japanese stood out. "A Jap's a Jap," General John DeWitt stated. "It makes no difference whether he is an American citizen or not."

Mounting fears on the West Coast brought a far-reaching decision from Washington in early 1942, when Roosevelt approved a War Department plan to intern Japanese-Americans in relocation camps for the rest of the war. In March 1942 Milton Eisenhower, a career civil servant and the brother of General Dwight D. Eisenhower, took over the War Relocation Authority, a civilian agency created to carry out that policy. Despite the lack of evidence of disloyalty or sedition—no Japanese-American was ever charged with espionage—few public leaders opposed the plan. The Supreme Court upheld its constitutionality as a legitimate exercise of power during wartime in *Hirabayashi v. United States* (1943) and *Korematsu v. United States* (1944).

The relocation announcement shocked Japanese-Americans, more than two-thirds of whom were native-born American citizens. (They were the *Niseis*, the children of the foreign-born *Isseis*.) The government gave families only a few days to dispose of their belongings and prepare for relocation. Businesses that took a lifetime to build were liquidated overnight, and speculators snapped up Japanese real estate for a fraction of its value. A Japanese-American music teacher got only $30 for her

Japanese Internment
A Japanese-American family arrives at its new "home" in Heart Mountain, Wyoming, after being relocated from the West Coast military zone. The average internee spent 900 days—more than two and a half years—confined behind the barbed wire, which is not visible in this picture.

treasured piano. Another woman, rather than accept $17.50 from a secondhand dealer for her family's heirloom porcelain, broke every piece of it. The government later estimated that the total financial loss to Japanese-Americans was $400 million, but Congress appropriated only $38 million in compensation after the war. Partial restitution came decades later, in 1988, when Congress voted to issue a public apology and give $20,000 in cash to each of the 60,000 surviving internees.

Relocation took place in two stages. First the government sent Japanese-Americans to temporary assembly centers such as the Santa Anita racetrack in Los Angeles, where they lived in stables that horses had occupied a few days earlier. Then they were moved to ten permanent camps away from the coast. Those internment camps in California, Arizona, Utah, Colorado, Wyoming, Idaho, and Arkansas "were in places where nobody had lived before and no one has lived since," a historian commented (see Map 27.1). Milton Eisenhower had hoped the relocation camps would resemble the CCC youth camps of the New Deal, but the barbed wire and enforced communal living mocked his hopes. Although sometimes compared to Nazi concentration camps, the relocation centers more closely resembled Indian reservations (see American Voices, page 847).

All ten camps were in hot, dusty places, and their communal bathroom and dining facilities made family life nearly impossible. Eight people often lived in a space measuring 25 by 20 feet. No one had any privacy; boredom was a major problem. Generational differences between the Issei, with an average age of fifty-five, and the Nisei, with an average age of seventeen, added to the tensions.

Almost every Japanese-American in California, Oregon, and Washington was involuntarily detained for some period during World War II. Ironically, the Japanese-Americans who made up one-third of the population of Hawaii and presumably posed a greater threat because of their numbers and proximity to Japan were not affected.

They were less vulnerable to detention because of the islands' multiracial heritage. The Japanese also provided much of the unskilled labor on the islands, and the Hawaiian economy could not function without them.

Cracks soon appeared in the relocation policy. Japanese-Americans had played an important role in California agriculture, and even with stepped-up recruitment of Mexican-Americans through the *bracero* program, the labor shortage in farming led the government to furlough seasonal Japanese-American agricultural workers from the camps as early as 1942. In addition, about 4,300 young people who had been in college when the relocation order came through were allowed to stay in school if they transferred out of the

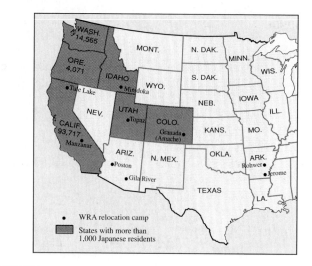

MAP 27.1

WRA Relocation Camps
In 1942 the government ordered 112,000 Japanese-Americans living on the West Coast into internment camps in the nation's interior because of their supposed threat to public safety. Some of the camps were as far away as Arkansas.

Peter Ota

The Insult and Injury of Internment

Peter Ota's father had come from Okinawa in 1904 and had built up a successful fruit and vegetable business in the Los Angeles area. Here the son, a Nisei, remembers his family's internment during World War II. When Peter reached draft age, he was inducted into the army, even though his father and sister remained in the relocation camp for the rest of the war.

It was just my sister and myself. I was fifteen, she was twelve. In April, 1942, we were evacuated to Santa Anita. At the time we didn't know where we were going, how long we'd be gone. We didn't know what to take. A toothbrush, toilet supplies, some clothes. Only what you could carry. We left with a caravan.

Santa Anita is a race track. The horse stables were converted into living quarters. My sister and I were fortunate enough to stay in a barracks. The people in the stables had to live with the stench. Everything was communal. We had absolutely no privacy. When you went to the toilet, it was communal. It was very embarrassing for women, especially. . . .

We had orders to leave Santa Anita in September of 1942. We had no idea where we were going. Just before we left, my father joined us. . . . I can still picture it to this day; to come in like cattle or sheep being herded in the back of a pickup truck bed. We were near the gate and saw him come in. He saw us. It was a sad, happy moment, because we'd been separated for a year.

He never really expressed what his true inner feelings were. It just amazes me. He was never vindictive about it, never showed any anger. I can't understand that. A man who had worked so hard for what he had and lost it overnight. There is a very strong word in Japanese, *gaman*. It means to persevere. Old people instilled this into the second generation: you persevere. Take what's coming, don't react.

He had been a very outgoing person. Enthusiastic. I was very, very impressed with how he ran things and worked with people. When I saw him at Santa Anita, he was a different person.

We were out on a train, three of us and many trains of others. It was crowded. The shades were drawn. During the ride we were wondering, what are they going to do to us? We Niseis [first-generation Japanese-Americans] had enough confidence in our government that it wouldn't do anything drastic. My father had put all his faith in this country. This was his land.

Oh, it took days. We arrived in Amache, Colorado. That was an experience in itself. We were right near the Kansas border. It's a desolate, flat, barren area. The barracks was all there was. There were no trees, no kind of landscaping. It was like a prison camp. Coming from our environment, it was just devastating. . . .

When I think back to my mother and father, what they went through quietly, it's hard to explain. [Cries.] I think of my father without ever coming up with an angry word. After all those years, having worked his whole life to build a dream—an American dream, mind you—having it all taken away, and not one vindictive word. His business was worth more than a hundred thousand. He sold it for five. When he came out of camp, with what little money he had, he put a down payment on an apartment building. It was right in the middle of skid row, an old rooming house. . . . He died a very broken man.

Source: Studs Terkel, *"The Good War": An Oral History of World War Two* (New York: Pantheon, 1984), 29–30, 32–33.

West Coast military zone. Another route out of the camps was enlistment in the armed services. The 442d Infantry Combat Team, a segregated unit serving in Europe and composed entirely of Nisei volunteers, was the most decorated unit in the armed forces.

Most Japanese-Americans accepted relocation stoically. "*Shikata gu nai*," they said—it can't be helped, hardship must be borne. Many Japanese-Americans of the third generation, called the *Sansei*, some of whom were born in the internment camps, and the fourth generation, the *Yonsei*, think their elders should have protested more strongly. With each generation the memory of internment grows dimmer, but this shameful episode has been burned into the national conscience.

Fighting and Winning the War

World War II, noted the military historian John Keegan, was "the largest single event in human history." Fought on six continents at a cost of 50 million lives, it was far more global than World War I. At least 405,000 Americans were killed and 671,000 were wounded in the fighting, representing less than half of 1 percent of the U.S. population. In contrast, the Soviets counted as many as 21 million military and civilian dead during the war, about 8 percent of their people. Dropping the atomic bomb on Hiroshima and Nagasaki in 1945 was the final stage in this most destructive of human conflicts.

Wartime Aims and Strategies

The Allied coalition was composed of Great Britain, the United States, and the Soviet Union, with other nations, notably China and France, playing lesser roles. Franklin Roosevelt, Britain's Winston Churchill, and Joseph Stalin, the premier of the Soviet Union, took the lead in setting overall strategy. The Atlantic Charter, drafted aboard ship during the Churchill-Roosevelt rendezvous off the Newfoundland coast in August 1941, formed the basis of the Allies' vision of the postwar international order. However, Stalin was not part of that agreement, and that would cause later disagreements over its goals.

As far back as the lend-lease negotiations of early 1941, Churchill and Roosevelt had agreed that defeating Germany would be the first military priority because of that country's huge armies, massive industrial capacity, and mastery of technology. Roosevelt's unswerving commitment to Britain's survival provided the basis for a strong, if not always smooth, relationship with Churchill. (Roosevelt's aide Harry Hopkins described his role as that of a "catalytic agent between two prima donnas.") Stalin, however, was something of a mystery. He and Roosevelt did not meet until late in 1943. Although the United States and Great Britain disagreed on issues such as the postwar fate of colonial empires, the potential for conflict with the Soviet Union was far greater.

One way to wear down the Germans was to open a second front on the European continent, preferably in France. The Russians strongly argued for this strategy because it would draw German troops away from Russian soil. The issue came up so many times that the Soviet foreign minister, Vyacheslav Molotov, was said to know only four English words: *yes, no,* and *second front.*

Roosevelt assured Stalin informally that such a front would be opened in 1942. However, the time needed to raise American war production to full capacity and British opposition caused a two-year delay. As a result, for most of the war the Soviet Union bore the brunt of the land battle against Germany. Roosevelt and Churchill's unfulfilled pledges angered Stalin, who was already suspicious about American and British intentions. That mistrust and bitterness carried over into the postwar world in the Cold War that followed.

At various points during the war the three leaders of the Grand Alliance held a series of meetings to discuss military strategy and plan the postwar peace. In January 1943 Roosevelt and Churchill met in Casablanca, Morocco; Stalin did not attend because the Battle of Stalingrad had reached a crucial point. The main outcome of the conference was the Allied demand for unconditional surrender of the Axis powers as a condition for peace. In November 1943 Roosevelt, Churchill, and the Chinese leader Jiang Jeishi (Chiang Kai-Shek) met in Cairo to discuss military operations in the Pacific theater, a conference designed to keep China in the war. To Roosevelt's dismay, Jiang seemed more interested in fighting the communist revolution in his country (see Chapter 28) than in mobilizing the Chinese people to expel the Japanese invaders.

Traveling directly from Cairo to Teheran, Iran, Roosevelt finally met Stalin late in November 1943. At the Teheran Conference Roosevelt and Churchill agreed to Stalin's demand for a second front within six months. In return, Stalin promised to join the fight against Japan after the war in Europe ended, a promise he kept. The three leaders also issued the Teheran Declaration, in which they welcomed the cooperation of all nations in the war and invited them to join the Big Three in a "world family of democratic nations."

At Teheran Churchill and Roosevelt also agreed tacitly to Stalin's demand that Poland's borders be redrawn to give the Soviet Union more territory. But the three leaders disagreed sharply about who should control the rest of Poland and the other Eastern European states. Roosevelt expressed confidence that the personal rapport he had developed with Stalin would aid postwar relations among the superpowers, but Stalin's territorial ambitions in Eastern Europe foreshadowed later divisions.

The War in Europe

During the first six months of 1942 the military news was so bad that it threatened to swamp the Grand Alliance. The Allies suffered severe defeats throughout Europe and on the Atlantic. German armies pushed deeper into Soviet territory, reaching the outskirts of Moscow and Leningrad, and simultaneously started an offensive in North Africa aimed at seizing the Suez Canal. At sea German submarines were crippling American convoys carrying supplies to Europe. Since the United States was the main supplier of oil to the Allies, those attacks struck at the heart of the war effort, which was increasingly dependent on petroleum-based military equipment such as tanks and airplanes.

The major turning point of the war in Europe occurred in the winter of 1942–1943, when the Soviets halted the German advance in the Battle of Stalingrad. The Germans had taken most of the city in over 140 days of sometimes house-to-house fighting, when the Soviets counterattacked. The Germans lost 330,000 soldiers and twenty-two divisions; Russian casualties were also huge. Now came the task of pushing the Germans all the way back through Eastern Europe. By October 1943 Soviet armies stood on the east bank of the Dnieper River, ready to push through the Ukraine into Romania. By mid-1944 those forces had driven the German army out of the Soviet Union.

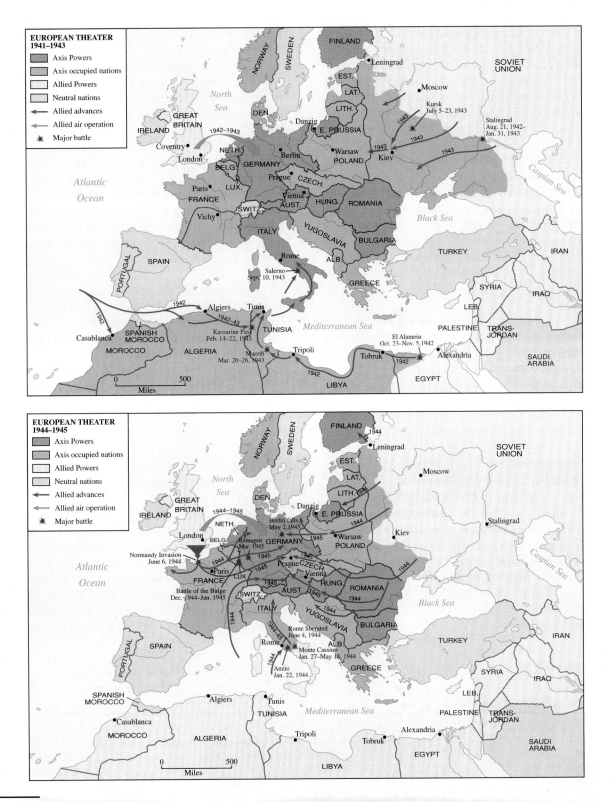

MAP 27.2

War in Europe

a. 1941–1943 Hitler's Germany reached its greatest extent in 1942, when Nazi forces stalled at Leningrad and Stalingrad. The tide of battle turned in the fall, when the Soviet army launched a massive counterattack at Stalingrad and Allied forces began to drive the Germans from North Africa. In 1943 the Allies invaded Sicily and the Italian mainland.

b. 1944–1945 On June 6, 1944 (D-Day), the Allies finally invaded France. It would take almost a year for the Allied forces to close in on Berlin—the Soviets from the east and the Americans, British, and French from the west. Germany surrendered on May 8, 1945.

At the same time, the Allies launched a major offensive in North Africa, Churchill's substitute for a second front in France. Between November 1942 and May 1943 Allied troops under the leadership of Generals Dwight D. Eisenhower and George S. Patton (both protégés of George C. Marshall) defeated Germany's crack Afrika Korps led by General Erwin Rommel.

From Africa the Allied command followed Churchill's strategy of attacking the Axis through what he called its "soft underbelly": Sicily and the Italian penisula. In July 1943 the fascist regime of Benito Mussolini fell, and the new government joined the Allies. The Allies invaded Italy the following fall. Despite help from Italian partisans, the mountainous terrain and heavy resistance from German troops kept them from entering Rome until June 1944 (see Map 27.2). The last German forces in Italy did not surrender until May 1945.

D-Day. The long-awaited invasion of France came on D-Day, June 6, 1944. That morning, after an agonizing delay caused by bad weather, the largest armada ever assembled moved across the English Channel. The beaches of Normandy where the Allies landed—Utah, Omaha, Juno, Gold, and Sword—soon became household words in the United States. Under the command of General Dwight Eisenhower, more than 1.5 million American, British, and Canadian soldiers crossed the Channel over the next few days. In August Allied troops helped liberate Paris, and by September they had driven the Germans out of most of France and Belgium.

In the autumn of 1944 the German military situation looked hopeless. All that year, long-range Allied bombers had made daring daylight raids, damaging Nazi military and industrial installations and pulverizing cities such as Cologne, Dresden, and Berlin, the German capital. The air campaign killed 305,000 people and wounded 780,000, both soldiers and civilians. No one was safe from attack.

Victory in Europe. The Germans were not ready to give up. In December 1944 German forces in Belgium mounted an attack that began the Battle of the Bulge, so called because it made a dent in the Allied defenses. After ten days of heavy fighting in what was to be the final German offensive of the war, the Allies regained their momentum and pushed the Germans back across the Rhine River. Their goal was to take Berlin, the German capital. American and British troops led the drive from the west, and Soviet troops advanced from the east through Poland, getting their first. On April 30, with much of Berlin in rubble from Allied bombing, Hitler committed suicide in his bunker. Germany surrendered on May 8, 1945, which became known as V-E (Victory in Europe) Day.

The Holocaust. When Allied troops advanced into Germany in the spring of 1945, they came face to face with Hitler's "final solution of the Jewish question": the extermination camps where 6 million Jews had been put to death along with another 6 million Poles, Slavs, Gypsies, homosexuals, and other "undesirables." Photographs from Nazi death camps at Buchenwald, Dachau, and Auschwitz, of bodies stacked like cordwood and survivors so emaciated that they were barely alive, horrified the American public and the rest of the world. But it is inaccurate to claim that no one knew about the camps before the German surrender. The Roosevelt administration had reliable information about the death camps as early as November 1942.

The lack of response by the U.S. government to the systematic near annihilation of European Jewry ranks as one of the gravest failures of the Roosevelt administration. So few Jews got out because the United States and the rest of the world would not take them in. State Department policies allowed only 21,000 refugees to enter this country during the war. The War Refugee Board, established in 1944 with little support from the

Hitting the Beach at Normandy
These American reinforcements landed on the beach at Normandy two weeks after D-Day, June 6, 1944. More than a million Allied troops came ashore during the next month. The Allies liberated Paris in August and pushed the retreating Nazi forces behind the German border by September.

The Living Dead
When Allied troops advanced into Germany in the spring of 1945, they came face to face with what had long been rumored—concentration camps, Adolf Hitler's "final solution of the Jewish question." Margaret Bourke-White was one of the first photographers on the scene. This haunting image from the Buchenwald death camp appeared in *Life* magazine.

Roosevelt administration, eventually helped save about 200,000 Jews. Several factors combined to inhibit U.S. action: anti-Semitism; fear of economic competition from a flood of refugees in a country just recovering from the depression; the failure of the media to grasp the magnitude of the story and publicize it accordingly; and the failure of religious leaders, Jews and non-Jews alike, to speak out.

In justifying the American course of action, Roosevelt claimed that winning the war would be the strongest contribution America could make to liberating the camps. But it is hard to escape the conclusion that the United States could have done much more to lessen the Holocaust's terrible human toll.

The War in the Pacific

After the victory in Europe the Allies still had to defeat Japan. American forces bore the brunt of the fighting in the Pacific, just as the Russians had done in the land war in Europe.

At the beginning of 1942 the news from the Pacific was uniformly grim. In the wake of Pearl Harbor, Japan had scored quickly with seaborne invasions of Hong Kong, Wake Island, and Guam. Japanese forces conquered much of Burma, Malaya, and the Philippines as well as the Solomon Islands and threatened Australia and India (see American Voices, page 852). Japan

achieved this huge territorial expansion in only three months. One of the few boosts for American morale came on April 18, 1942, when Colonel James H. Doolittle led sixteen American bombers on the first air raid on Tokyo, but the attack had little military value.

The more significant battles were far to the south. On May 7–8, 1942, in the Battle of the Coral Sea near southern New Guinea, American naval forces halted the Japanese offensive against Australia. Then, in June, at the island of Midway, the Americans inflicted crucial damage on the Japanese fleet. For the first time a major sea battle was waged—and decided—primarily by planes launched from aircraft carriers that never came within sight of each other. Submarines also played an important role in the naval battles, but the human cost was high: 22 percent of American submariners lost their lives during the war, the highest death rate in any branch of the armed services.

After the Battle of Midway the American military command, under General Douglas MacArthur and Admiral Chester W. Nimitz, took the offensive in the Pacific. For the next eighteen months American forces advanced arduously from one island to the next, win-

A New Type of Naval Warfare
The battles of Coral Sea and Midway in 1942 marked a revolution in naval warfare. For the first time, major sea battles were waged—and decided—primarily by planes launched from aircraft carriers. This panorama shows the vastness of these naval encounters.

Anton Bilek

The War in the Pacific

Anton Bilek was taken prisoner when the Japanese overran the Bataan peninsula of the Philippines in April 1942. He describes the infamous "Bataan Death March" and its aftermath.

The next morning, we got orders to get rid of all our arms and wait for the Japanese to come. General King had surrendered Bataan. They came in. First thing they did, they lined us up and started searchin' us. Anybody that had a ring or a wristwatch or a pair of gold-rimmed spectacles, they took 'em. Glasses they'd throw on the floor and break 'em and put the gold rims in their pockets. If you had a ring, you handed it over. If you couldn't get it off, the guy'd put the bayonet right up against your neck. Fortunately I never wore a ring. I couldn't afford one.

They moved us about on the road. Here was a big stream of Americans and Filipinos marchin' by. They told us to get in the back of this column. This was the start of the Death March. (A long, deep sigh.) That was a sixty-mile walk. Here we were, three, four months on half-rations, less. The men were already thin, in shock. Undernourished, full of malaria. Dysentery is beginning to spread. This is even before the surrender. We had two hospitals chuck-full

of men. Bataan peninsula was the worst malaria-infected province of the Philippines.

The Japanese emptied out the hospitals. Anybody that could walk, they forced 'em into line. You found all kinda bodies along the road. Some of 'em bloated, some had just been killed. If you fell out to the side, you were either shot by the guards or you were bayoneted and left there. We lost somewhere between six hundred and seven hundred Americans in the four days of the march. The Filipinos lost close to ten thousand. At San Fernando, we were stuffed into boxcars and taken about thirty-five miles further north. The cars were closed, you couldn't get air. In the hot sun, the temperature got up there. You couldn't fall down because you were held up by the guys stacked around you. You had a lot of guys blow their top, start screamin'. From there, they marched us another seven, eight miles to Camp O'Donnell, which was built hurriedly for the Philippine army. It was built like the huts were built, of native bamboo and *nipa* and grass. There must've been about nine thousand of us and about fifty thousand Filipinos. Americans in one camp, Filipinos in the other. We had to leave after a month and a half.

The monsoon season was starting. A hurricane blew down two of the barracks. Eighty men were killed. Just crushed.

I went blind, momentarily. It scared the hell out of me. I was at the hospital for about two weeks, and the doctor, an American, said, "There's nothing I can do with you. Rest is the only thing. Eat all the rice you can get. That's your only medicine." That's the one thing that pulled me through. He said, "You won't have to go on details." The Japanese were comin' in and they'd take two, three hundred and start 'em repairing a bridge that was blown up. We were losin' a lot of men there. They couldn't work any more. They were dyin'. . . .

I'm back home. It's all over with. I'd like to forget it. I had nothin' against the Japanese. But I don't drive a Toyota or own a Sony. . . . A lotta friends I lost. We had 185 men in our squadron when the war started. Three and a half years later, when we were liberated from a prison camp in Japan, we were 39 left. It's them I think about. Men I played ball with, men I worked with, men I associated with. I miss 'em.

Source: Studs Terkel, *"The Good War": An Oral History of World War Two* (New York: Pantheon, 1984), 85, 90–91, 95–96.

ning major victories at Tulagi and Guadalcanal in the Solomon Islands and at Tarawa and Makin in the Gilberts. They reached the Marshall Islands in early 1944. In October 1944 the reconquest of the Philippines began with a victory in the Battle of Leyte Gulf, a massive naval encounter in which the Japanese lost practically their entire fleet while the Americans suffered only minimal losses (see Map 27.3).

By early 1945 victory over Japan was in sight. The campaign in the Pacific moved slowly toward an anticipated massive and costly invasion of Japan. For a successful assault on the main Japanese island, the Americans needed to capture Iwo Jima and Okinawa. Airstrips there would put U.S. planes within striking distance of Tokyo. American marines won the battles for Iwo Jima (Febru-

ary 1–March 20, 1945) and Okinawa (April 1–June 10) in some of the fiercest fighting of the war. At Iwo Jima the marines sustained more than 20,000 casualties, including 6,000 dead; at Okinawa the toll reached 7,600 dead and 32,000 wounded. The closer U.S. forces got to the Japanese home islands, the more fiercely the Japanese fought. Almost all of the 21,000 Japanese on Iwo Jima died.

By mid-1945 Japan's army, navy, and air force had suffered devastating losses. American bombing of the mainland had killed about 330,000 civilians and crippled the Japanese economy, which had difficulty functioning once oil imports were cut off and in any case could not match American war production. In a last-ditch effort to stem the tide, Japanese pilots began suicidal *kamikaze* missions, crashing their planes and boats

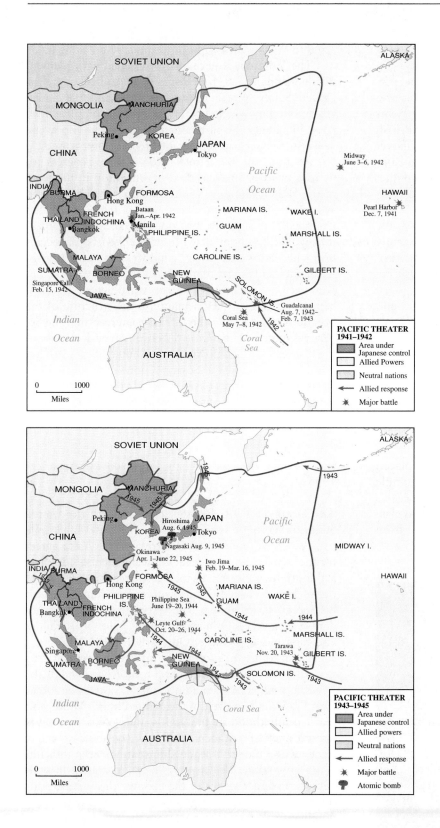

MAP 27.3

War in the Pacific

a. 1941–1942 After the attack on Pearl Harbor in December 1941 the Japanese rapidly extended their domination in the Pacific. The Japanese flag soon flew as far east as the Marshall and Gilbert islands and as far south as the Solomon Islands and parts of New Guinea. Japan also controlled the Philippines, much of Southeast Asia, and parts of China, including Hong Kong. American naval victories at the Coral Sea and Midway stopped further Japanese expansion.

b. 1943–1945 Allied forces retook the islands in the Central Pacific in 1943 and 1944 and the Philippines early in 1945. The capture of Iwo Jima and Okinawa put U.S. bombers in position to attack Japan itself. The Japanese offered to surrender on August 10, after the United States dropped atomic bombs on Hiroshima and Nagasaki.

into American ships. This desperate action, combined with the Japanese military leadership's refusal to surrender, suggested that Japan would keep up the fight despite overwhelming losses. American military commanders grimly predicted millions of casualties in the upcoming invasion.

Planning the Postwar World

In February 1945 Roosevelt, Churchill, and Stalin held what would be their last conference at Yalta, a Black Sea resort. Victory in Europe and the Pacific was in sight, but no agreement had been reached on the peace

to come. Roosevelt remained focused on maintaining Allied unity, the key to postwar peace and stability.

The commitment of the Allies to national self-determination as expressed in the Atlantic Charter presented the three leaders with their thorniest problems during the war and afterward. The fate of British colonies such as India, where an independence movement had already begun, caused friction between Roosevelt and Churchill. A more serious source of conflict was Stalin's desire for a band of Soviet-controlled satellite states to protect his western border.

Stalin had become increasingly inflexible on the issue of Eastern Europe, insisting that he needed friendly (that is, Soviet-dominated) governments there to provide a buffer for Soviet national security. Roosevelt acknowledged the legitimacy of that demand but hoped for democratically elected governments in Poland and the neighboring countries. Unfortunately, the two goals proved mutually exclusive.

At Yalta, Roosevelt and Churchill agreed in principle to the idea of a Soviet sphere of influence in Eastern Europe but left its dimensions deliberately vague. Furthermore, Roosevelt failed to inform the American public of the concessions he had made to maintain the increasingly fragile wartime alliance. In return, Stalin pledged to hold "free and unfettered elections" at an unspecified time. (Those elections never took place.) The compromise reached at Yalta was open to multiple interpretations. Admiral William D. Leahy, Roosevelt's chief military aide, described the agreement as "so elastic that the Russians can stretch it all the way from Yalta to Washington without technically breaking it."

The Yalta conference also proceeded with plans to divide Germany into four zones to be controlled by the United States, Great Britain, France, and the Soviet Union. Berlin, which lay in the middle of the Soviet zone, would also be partitioned among the four powers. The issue of German reparations remained unsettled.

At Yalta the Big Three made further progress toward a postwar international organization in the form of the United Nations. Roosevelt, determined to avoid Woodrow Wilson's mistakes, had already cultivated Congressional support; realizing that such an organization would be impotent without the Soviets' participation, he cultivated their support as well. British, American, and Soviet representatives had already met at Dumbarton Oaks, an estate in Washington, D.C., in September 1944 to begin planning the structure of the organization. At Yalta the Big Three agreed that the Security Council of the United Nations would consist of the five major Allied powers—the United States, Britain, France, China, and the Soviet Union—plus six nations elected on a rotating basis. They also decided that the permanent members of the Security Council should have veto power over decisions of the General Assembly, in which all nations would be represented. Roosevelt, Churchill, and Stalin announced that the United Nations would convene in San Francisco on April 25, 1945.

The Death of FDR. Roosevelt returned to the United States in February, visibly exhausted by his 14,000-mile trip. When he reported to Congress on the Yalta agreements, he made an unusual acknowledgment of his physical infirmity. Referring to the heavy steel braces he wore on his legs, he asked Congress to excuse him if he gave his speech sitting down. The sixty-three-year-old president was a very sick man, suffering from heart failure and high blood pressure. On April 12, 1945, during a short visit to his vacation home in Warm Springs, Georgia, Roosevelt suffered a cerebral hemorrhage and died.

Many Americans could not imagine any leader other than Franklin Roosevelt in the White House. Those who reached adulthood in the 1930s and 1940s had never known another president. Perhaps Roosevelt's greatest legacy was a model of leadership that has been difficult, if not impossible, for later presidents to match. In both depression and war he led the country through perilous times. As a global strategist he grasped America's predominant role and helped educate the country to accept its new international responsibilities.

V-E Day came less than a month after Roosevelt died and Harry Truman succeeded to the presidency. The war in the Pacific ended after Truman ordered the dropping of atomic bombs on two Japanese cities, Hiroshima on August 6 and Nagasaki on August 9. Many later questioned why the United States did not warn

The Big Three at Yalta
With victory in Europe at hand, Roosevelt journeyed to Yalta, on the Black Sea, in 1945, to meet one last time with Churchill and Stalin. It was here that they discussed the problems of peace settlements. The Yalta agreement mirrored a new balance of power and set the stage for the Cold War.

Hiroshima
This was all that remained of Hiroshima's Museum of Science and Industry on August 6, 1945. The shell of the building later became the center of a memorial to those who died in the atomic blast.

Japan about the attack or choose a noncivilian target; the rationale for dropping the second bomb was even less clear. At the time, however, the belief that Japan's military leaders would never surrender unless their country was utterly devastated convinced policy makers that they had to deploy the new weapon. The atomic bombs killed 100,000 people at Hiroshima and 60,000 at Nagasaki. Tens of thousands more died slowly of radiation poisoning. Japan offered to surrender on August 10 and signed a formal treaty of surrender on September 2, 1945. World War II had ended, but a new atomic age of insecurity had begun.

The Onset of the Atomic Age

The development of the atomic bomb was closely linked to wartime military strategy. In December 1938 German scientists had discovered that the nuclei of atoms could be split into smaller particles, a process called fission. With materials prepared from uranium, a chain reaction of nuclear fission would release tremendous amounts of energy. American scientists, including Enrico Fermi and Leo Szilard, many of them refugees from fascist Italy and Nazi Germany, produced the first controlled chain reaction on December 2, 1942, at the University of Chicago.

Scientists soon began working frantically to harness nuclear reactions for military purposes. Their goal was the development of an atomic bomb for use against Germany or, later, Japan. The secret research, called the Manhattan Project, cost $2 billion, employed 120,000 people, and involved the construction of thirty-seven

installations in nineteen states under the direction of General Leslie R. Groves of the U.S. Army Corps of Engineers. In the final stages a team consisting of most of the country's top physicists assembled the bomb at an isolated desert site in Los Alamos, New Mexico. All this was hidden from Congress, the American people, and even Vice-President Truman. The secrecy and scope of this alliance between science and government constitute a dramatic example of how much the power of the state grew during wartime.

Roosevelt had followed the bomb's progress closely. He and his advisers had planned to deploy the bomb to end the war without the dreadful number of American casualties that would have resulted from an invasion of Japan. At the same time, policy makers hoped that the possession of such a powerful weapon—the "master card," in the words of Secretary of War Henry Stimson—might enhance American power in the postwar world. Instead, the new weapon became the first step in a deadly arms race between the United States and the Soviet Union.

Until the last moment the scientists did not know if the atomic bomb would work. On July 16, 1945, near Alamogordo, New Mexico, they watched in wonder as the test bomb exploded in a huge mushroom cloud. President Truman received news of the successful detonation in Potsdam, near Berlin, where he was about to meet with Churchill and Stalin in the final wartime conference about the shape of postwar Europe (see Chapter 28). Truman, who had not known about the bomb before he became president, was ecstatic about its potential. After the bombing of Hiroshima he told aides, "This is the greatest thing in history." Others were not so sure. J. Robert Oppenheimer, one of the leading scientists on the Manhattan Project, watched the test early on that July morning in the New Mexico desert. Overwhelmed by its frightening power, he recalled the words from the *Bhagavad Gita*, a Hindu sacred text: "I am become Death, Destroyer of Worlds."

Franklin Roosevelt's death and the dropping of the atomic bomb came at a critical juncture in world affairs. Many issues had been left deliberately unresolved in the hopes of keeping the wartime alliance intact to guide the transition to peace. But as the war ended, issues such as the fate of Poland and Germany demanded action. The resulting compromises, not all of which were fully reported to the American people, tended to promote spheres of influence as the new basis of international power instead of the ideals of national self-determination and economic cooperation laid out in the Atlantic Charter. Once the common enemies had been defeated, the wartime alliance became strained and then began to split apart in ways so fundamental that it is unlikely that Roosevelt could have kept it together if he had lived. Perhaps the greatest legacy of World War II was the Cold War that followed.

Summary

With the rise of fascism and totalitarianism in Germany, Italy, and Japan, the international situation deteriorated rapidly throughout the 1930s, and the world was at war by 1939. Although most Americans clung to strong isolationist sentiment, President Roosevelt began mobilizing public opinion for intervention and converting the economy to war production. The Japanese attack on Pearl Harbor on December 7, 1941, brought the nation into World War II.

Defense mobilization ended the Great Depression and caused the economy to more than double. As with World War I, mobilization led to a dramatic expansion of the state. On the home front, the war resulted in rationing and shortages of many items but no serious hardships. Geographical mobility increased as labor shortages opened job opportunities for women, blacks, and Mexican-Americans. The labor movement surged, and the ideological climate of fighting Nazism aided the cause of civil rights. However, Japanese-Americans on the West Coast suffered a devastating denial of civil liberties when the government moved them into internment camps.

World War II was a global war, consisting of massive military campaigns in both Europe and the Pacific. The war news was bleak at first, but by 1943 the Allies had started to move toward victory, first in Europe and then in the Pacific. Soviet forces bore the brunt of the fighting in the European theater, while American forces primarily orchestrated the war effort in the Pacific. More than 15 million American men and women served in the armed forces, and at least 405,000 lost their lives.

While the Allied forces mobilized to defeat Germany and Japan, Roosevelt attempted to maintain harmony among the United States, Great Britain, and the Soviet Union. Many of the disagreements over wartime diplomacy would become major problems in the postwar world, especially the fate of Eastern Europe and the intentions of the Soviet Union. Of all the major powers that fought in World War II, only the United States emerged physically unharmed. And at the end of the war, only the United States had a powerful new weapon, the atomic bomb.

TIMELINE

1934	Platt Amendment repealed
1935	Italy invades Ethiopia
1935–1937	Neutrality Acts
1936	Rome-Berlin Axis established Japan joins Anti-Comintern Pact
1937	Japan invades China
1938	Munich agreement *War of the Worlds* broadcast
1939	Nazi-Soviet pact World War II breaks out in Europe
1940	Conscription reinstated America First movement
1941	Roosevelt's third term begins Roosevelt promulgates Four Freedoms Hitler invades Soviet Union Lend-Lease Act passed Fair Employment Practices Commission Atlantic Charter Japanese attack Pearl Harbor
1942	Battles of Coral Sea and Midway halt Japanese advance in the Pacific Women recruited for war industries Japanese relocation Revenue Act of 1942
1942–1945	Rationing
1943	Race riots in Detroit and Los Angeles Fascism falls in Italy Teheran Conference
1944	Gunnar Myrdal, *An American Dilemma* D-Day Reconquest of Philippines GI Bill of Rights
1945	Roosevelt's fourth term begins Germany surrenders Battles of Iwo Jima and Okinawa Yalta Conference Harry S. Truman becomes president after Roosevelt's death United Nations convenes Atomic bombs dropped on Hiroshima and Nagasaki Japan surrenders

★   ★   ★

BIBLIOGRAPHY

John Morton Blum, *V Was for Victory* (1976), and William O'Neill, *A Democracy at War* (1993), offer good introductions to American politics and culture during the war years. A provocative oral history of the war is Studs Terkel, *"The Good War": An Oral History of World War Two* (1984). John Keegan, *The Second World War* (1990), offers the best one-volume account of the battlefront aspects.

The Road to War

Depression and wartime diplomacy are covered in Robert Dallek, *Franklin D. Roosevelt and American Foreign Policy, 1932–1945* (1979), and Akira Iriye, *The Globalizing of America, 1913–1945* (1993). On American isolationism see Wayne Cole, *Roosevelt and the Isolationists, 1932–1945* (1983). Warren T. Kimball, *The Most Unsordid Act* (1969), describes the lend-lease controversy of 1939–1941, whereas *The Juggler: Franklin Roosevelt as Wartime Statesman* (1991), provides an overview of Roosevelt's leadership. Roberta Wohlstetter, *Pearl Harbor* (1962); Herbert Feis, *The Road to Pearl Harbor* (1950); and Gordon W. Prange, *At Dawn We Slept* (1981), describe the events that led to American entry.

Mobilizing for Victory

George Flynn, *The Mess in Washington* (1979), and Harold G. Vatter, *The U.S. Economy in World War II* (1985), discuss America's economic mobilization. David Brinkley, *Washington Goes to War* (1988), offers an engaging journalistic perspective. Mark S. Foster, *Henry J. Kaiser: Builder in the Modern American West* (1989), is a comprehensive biography. Alan Winkler, *The Politics of Propaganda* (1978), covers the Office of War Information. On labor's role during war, see George Lipsitz, *Rainbow at Midnight: Labor and Culture in the 1940s* (1994); Nelson Lichtenstein, *Labor's War at Home: The CIO in World War II* (1982); and Paul Koistinen, *The Hammer and the Sword: Labor, the Military, and Industrial Mobilization, 1920–1945* (1979). For more on politics in wartime, see James McGregor Burns, *Roosevelt: The Soldier of Freedom* (1970), and Alan Brinkley, *The End of Reform* (1995).

Women's roles in wartime are covered by Susan Hartmann, *The Home Front and Beyond* (1982); Karen Anderson, *Wartime Women* (1980); D'Ann Campbell, *Women at War with America* (1984); Ruth Milkman, *Gender at Work* (1987); and Sherna B. Gluck, *Rosie the Riveter Revisited: Women, the War, and Social Change* (1987). Judy Barrett Litoff and David C. Smith, *We're in This War, Too* (1994), includes letters from American women in uniform.

Life on the Home Front

William M. Tuttle, Jr., *"Daddy's Gone to War"* (1993), describes World War II from the perspective of the nation's children. Alan Clive, *State of War* (1979), provides a case study of Michigan during the war; Marilynn S. Johnson, *The Second Gold Rush* (1993), describes Oakland and the East Bay. See also Gerald D. Nash, *The American West Transformed: The Impact of the Second World War* (1985), and Marc Scott Miller, *The Irony of Victory: World War II and Lowell, Massa-*

chusetts (1988). Clayton R. Koppes and Gregory D. Black, *Hollywood Goes to War* (1987), covers the film industry. The experience of black Americans is treated in Albert Russell Buchanan, *Black Americans in World War II* (1977), and Neil Wynn, *The Afro-American and the Second World War* (1975). On racial tensions, see Dominic Capeci, Jr., *Race Relations in Wartime Detroit* (1984), and Mauricio Mazan, *The Zoot Suit Riots* (1984). August Meier and Elliott Rudwick, *CORE* (1973), describes the founding of an important civil rights organization. Richard Dalfiume, *Desegregation of the U.S. Armed Forces* (1969), covers black soldiers in the military. Alan Berube, *Coming Out under Fire* (1990), is an oral history of gay men and lesbians in the military; see also John D'Emilio, *Sexual Politics, Sexual Communities* (1983), for the impact of the war on gay Americans. Maurice Isserman, *Which Side Were You On?* (1982), analyzes the American Communist party during the war. Two compelling accounts of Japanese relocation are Audre Girdner and Anne Loftus, *The Great Betrayal* (1969), and Roger Daniels, *Prisoners without Trial: Japanese-Americans in World War II* (1993). See also Peter Irons, *Justice at War: The Story of the Japanese-American Internment Cases* (1983). Valerie Matsumoto, *Farming the Home Place* (1993), describes a Japanese-American community in California from 1919 to 1982.

Fighting and Winning the War

Extensive material chronicles the American military experience during World War II. Albert Russell Buchanan, *The United States and World War II* (1962), and Russell F. Weigley, *The American Way of War* (1973), provide overviews; Ronald Schaffer, *Wings of Judgement: American Bombing in World War II* (1985), and Bradley F. Smith, *The Shadow Warriors: OSS and the Origins of the CIA* (1983), are more specialized. Cornelius Ryan, *The Last Battle* (1966); John Toland, *The Last Hundred Days* (1966); and Stephen Ambrose, *D-Day, June 6, 1944* (1994) describe the end of the fighting in Europe. David S. Wyman, *The Abandonment of the Jews* (1984), devastatingly describes the lack of American response to the Holocaust from 1941 to 1945. On the Far East, see John W. Dower, *War without Mercy: Race and Power in the Pacific War* (1986); Ronald H. Spector, *Eagle against the Sun: The American War with Japan* (1984); and John Toland, *Rising Sun: The Decline and Fall of the Japanese Empire* (1970).

American diplomacy and the strategy of the Grand Alliance are surveyed in Robert Dallek, *Franklin D. Roosevelt and American Foreign Policy, 1932–1945* (1979), and Lloyd Gardner, *Spheres of Influence* (1993). The relationship between the wartime conferences and the onset of the Cold War are treated in Walter LaFeber, *America, Russia, and the Cold War* (7th ed., 1993), and Stephen Ambrose, *Rise to Globalism* (7th ed., 1993). Richard Rhodes, *The Making of the Atomic Bomb* (1987); McGeorge Bundy, *Danger and Survival* (1988); and Martin Sherwin, *A World Destroyed* (1975), provide compelling accounts of the development of the bomb. See also Gar Alperowitz, *The Decision to Use the Atomic Bomb* (1995); Ronald Takaki, *Hiroshima: Why America Dropped the Atomic Bomb* (1995); and Gregg Herken, *The Winning Weapon* (1980). John Hersey, *Hiroshima* (2d ed., 1985), on the aftermath of the bombing, retains its power fifty years after its original publication.

America and the World

1945 to the Present

THEMATIC TIMELINE

	Diplomacy	Government	Economy	Society	Culture
	The Cold War Era—and After	**Redefining the Role of the State**	**Rise and Fall of U.S. Economic Dominance**	**Social Movements and Demographic Diversity**	**A Consumer Society**
1945	Truman Doctrine (1947) Marshall Plan (1948) NATO founded (1949)	Truman's Fair Deal liberalism Taft-Hartley Act (1947)	Bretton Woods system established: World Bank, IMF, GATT	Migration to cities accelerates Armed forces desegregated	End of wartime rationing Rise of television
1950	Permanent mobilization: NSC-68 (1950) Korean War (1950–53)	Eisenhower's modern Republicanism Warren Court activism	Rise of military-industrial complex Service sector expands	*Brown v. Board of Education* (1954) Montgomery bus boycott	Growth of suburbia Baby boom
1960	Cuban missile crisis (1962) Test ban treaty (1963) Vietnam War escalates (1965)	High tide of liberalism: Great Society, War on Poverty Nixon ushers in conservative era	Kennedy-Johnson tax cut, military expenditures fuel economic growth	Student activism Civil Rights Act; Voting Rights Act Revival of feminism	Shopping malls spread Baby boomers swell college enrollment Youth counterculture
1970	Nixon visits China (1972) SALT initiates détente (1972) Paris Peace Accords (1973)	Watergate scandal; Nixon resigns (1974) Deregulation begins under Ford and Carter	Arab oil embargo (1973–74); inflation surges Deindustrialization Income stagnation	*Roe v. Wade* (1973) Televangelists mobilize evangelical Protestants New Right urges conservative agenda	First Earth Day (1970) Gasoline shortages Apple introduces first personal computer (1977)
1980	Reagan arms buildup INF treaty (1988) Berlin Wall falls	Reagan Revolution Supreme Court conservatism	Reaganomics Budget and trade deficits soar Savings and loan bailout	New Hispanic and Asian immigration	MTV debuts AIDS epidemic
1990	War in the Persian Gulf U.S.S.R. disintegrates; end of the Cold War U.S. peacekeeping forces in Bosnia	Democratic party adopts "moderate" policies Republican Congress shifts federal government tasks to states	Corporate downsizing NAFTA (1993)	Third wave of feminism	Health care crisis Information super-highway

In 1945 the United States entered an era of unprecedented international power and influence. Unlike the period after World War I, American leaders did not avoid international commitments; instead they aggressively pursued U.S. interests abroad, vowing to contain communism around the globe. The consequences of that struggle profoundly influenced the nation's domestic economy, political affairs, and social and cultural trends for the next half century.

First, and most important, the United States took a leading, or hegemonic, role in global diplomatic and military affairs. When the Soviet Union challenged America's vision of postwar Europe, the Truman administration responded by crafting the policies and alliances that came to define the Cold War. That bipolar struggle lasted for more than forty years, spawned two long "hot" wars in Korea and Vietnam, and fueled a terrifying and debilitating nuclear arms race. Although the policy of détente pursued by Richard Nixon and later presidents helped ease tensions, the cold war mentality prevailed until the final collapse and disintegration of the Soviet Union in 1991.

Second, the nation's global commitments had dramatic consequences for American government. Until the national consensus fractured over the Vietnam War, liberals and conservatives agreed on keeping the country in a state of permanent mobilization and maintaining a large and well-equipped military establishment. And all administrations, Republican and Democratic, were willing to intervene in the economy when private initiatives could not maintain steady growth. But liberals also pushed for a larger role for the federal government in the area of social welfare. Under Truman, John F. Kennedy, and especially Lyndon Johnson, the government went beyond the New Deal to erect an extensive structure of federal social programs. In recent years, especially during the presidency of Ronald Reagan in the 1980s and the Republican control of Congress in the mid-1990s, conservatives began to cut back on many of the major programs and tried to delegate federal powers to the states.

Third, thanks to the growth of a military-industrial complex of enormous size and the expansion of consumer culture, the quarter century after 1945 represented the heyday of American capitalism. Economic dominance abroad translated into unparalleled affluence at home. In the early 1970s competition from other countries began to challenge America's economic supremacy. Today, the United States remains the world's largest economy, but increased foreign competition and slow productivity growth since the 1970s have meant declining real wages and stagnant family incomes for most American workers.

Fourth, the victory over fascism in World War II led to renewed calls for America to make good on its promise of liberty and equality for all. In great waves of protests in the 1950s and 1960s African-Americans and then women, Latinos, and other groups challenged the political domination of elite white men. The resulting reforms brought concrete gains for many Americans, but since the late 1970s, conservatives have challenged these initiatives, slowing the progress toward social equality.

Fifth, American economic power in the postwar era accelerated the development of a consumer society. As millions of Americans migrated to new suburban developments after World War II, growing baby-boom families provided an expanded market for household products of all types. Among the most significant were new technological devices—television, video recorders, personal computers—that helped break down the isolation of suburban and rural living. Beginning in the 1960s, however, some people began to question the American obsession with material consumption and the environmental degradation that it caused.

Americans today are living in an increasingly interwoven network of national and international forces. Outside events shape ordinary lives in ways that were inconceivable a century ago. As the cold war era fades into history, the United States remains the sole military superpower, but it shares economic leadership in the new interdependent global system. Will international cooperation replace cold war patterns of confrontation, or will the United States pull back from its global commitments? In tackling domestic problems, will policy makers continue to roll back federal involvement in social and environmental concerns, or will they ultimately seek new solutions? The next chapter of America's history remains to be written.

Danger and Survival

With its first successful test of a hydrogen bomb in 1952,
the United States entered the nuclear age.

CHAPTER 28

Cold War America

1945–1960

★ ★ ★

W hen Harry Truman arrived at the White House on April 12, 1945, after learning of Roosevelt's death, he asked the president's widow, "Is there anything I can do for you?" Eleanor Roosevelt responded with another question, "Is there anything we can do for you? For you are the one in trouble now."

Truman inherited the presidency at one of the most perilous times in modern American history. World War II had catapulted the United States into a position of international leadership, and America emerged from the war as the most powerful country in the world. Of all the former combatants, only the Soviet Union represented an obstacle to American hegemony, or dominance, in global affairs. As the Truman administration set out to create conditions that would maintain American supremacy, Soviet leaders sought to protect their country's interests. Soon the two superpowers were locked in a Cold War that took economic, political, and military forms but did not entail a direct Soviet-American confrontation on the battlefield. The Cold War continued in the 1950s under the Republican presidency of Dwight Eisenhower, who modified some of Truman's initiatives but did little to ease overall tensions. For better or worse, the United States had become a permanent and preeminent force in the international arena.

The Soviet-American conflict of the postwar years had important domestic repercussions. The Cold War boosted military expenditures and fueled a growing arms race with damaging physical and psychological consequences. Moreover, the Cold War fostered a climate of fear and suspicion about internal subversion and a hunt for "subversives" in government, education, and the media. But the economic benefits of internationalism also gave rise to a period of unprecedented affluence and prosperity. That affluence gave the United States the highest standard of living in the world (see

industrial heartland in its zone as part of the larger goal of reviving the European economy. The Soviet Union also began to develop the industrial capacities of its zone. Plans to reunify the country stalled as the United States and the Soviet Union worried that a reunified German state would fall into the other's sphere. The economic base was thus laid for what eventually became the political division into East and West Germany.

In both Germany and Eastern Europe the Americans and Soviets based their actions on different understandings of the past. Stalin was determined to prevent the rebuilding and rearming of Russia's traditional foe, Germany, and for further protection insisted on a security zone of friendly governments in Eastern Europe. Accordingly, between 1945 and 1947 the Soviets repressed democratic parties and installed puppet governments in Poland, Hungary, Rumania, and Bulgaria. Truman, recalling Britain's disastrous appeasement of Hitler in 1938, decided that the United States had to take a hard line against Soviet expansion and stand up to the Soviet dictator. "There isn't any difference in totalitarian states," he said, "Nazi, Communist, or Fascist." Increasingly, Truman and his advisers used the phrase *Red Fascism* to describe the Soviet threat.

The former British prime minister Winston Churchill articulated the deepening pessimism about the Soviet Union shared by American diplomats in 1946. Out of power and eager to establish a platform for his views, Churchill accepted an invitation from President Truman to deliver a major policy address in March 1946 in Fulton, Missouri. Churchill had gone along with plans for a Soviet sphere of influence in Eastern Europe at Yalta but had developed second thoughts, warning ominously about the "expansive tendencies" of the Soviet Union: "From Stettin in the Baltic to Trieste in the Adriatic, an Iron Curtain has descended across the Continent." If the West hoped to preserve peace and freedom in the face of the Soviet challenge, Churchill declared, it must remember that "there is nothing they [the Soviets] admire so much as strength, and there is nothing for which they have less respect than for weakness, especially military weakness."

Churchill's widely publicized Iron Curtain speech helped convince many Americans that the Soviet Union posed a serious threat to national security. That shift represented a return to the American hostility toward Bolshevism first articulated by Woodrow Wilson after the 1917 revolution, a distrust that had delayed diplomatic recognition of the Soviet Union until 1933. The wartime collaboration necessitated by the common fight against fascism receded quickly from memory.

Hopes of international cooperation in the control of atomic weapons also faded. Although U.S. leaders were willing to consider international control in the long run, they did not want to give up their advantage. In the Baruch Plan submitted to the United Nations in 1946, the United States proposed a system of international control that relied on mandatory inspection and supervision but preserved the American nuclear monopoly. The Soviets rejected the plan categorically and worked assiduously to complete their own bomb. The Truman administration pursued its own plans to develop nuclear energy and weapons further. The failure of the Baruch Plan thus signaled the beginning of a frenzied nuclear arms race between the two superpowers.

From the Truman Doctrine to NATO, 1947–1949

By 1947 a new American policy—*containment*—was taking shape. Although its precepts were agreed on in Washington policy-making circles, containment is usually associated with George F. Kennan, an intense, scholarly diplomat who had devoted his career to studying the Soviet Union (see American Lives, pages 866–867). Kennan first articulated containment's basic premises in February 1946 in an 8,000-word cable from his post at the U.S. Embassy in Moscow to his superiors in Washington, where it was widely circulated. He expanded on those ideas in an influential article in the journal *Foreign Affairs* in July 1947. According to Kennan, who was identified only as "X," the Soviets were moving "inexorably along the prescribed path, like a persistent toy automobile wound up and headed in a given direction, stopping only when it meets unanswerable force." To stop this expansionism, Kennan argued, it was necessary to pursue a policy of "firm containment, designed to confront the Russians with unalterable counterforce at every point where they show signs of encroaching upon the interests of a peaceful and stable world."

Kennan's initial formulation recommended economic and diplomatic means to enforce containment, but the policy soon took on a military cast. In one version or another containment defined the foreign policy of every subsequent administration, both Democratic and Republican, well into the 1980s. It ultimately served at least three purposes. By identifying an evil, expansionist enemy, the containment doctrine provided a rallying cry for Americans to unite behind the president in fighting the Soviet threat; it justified the creation of a vast peacetime military machine; and it obscured other objectives of American foreign policy in the economic arena and the Third World. Kennan later denounced the militarization of containment and the vilification of the Soviet Union, charging that such policies and beliefs had undercut attempts at diplomacy.

The emerging containment policy crystallized in 1947 over the situation in Greece. Local communist-inspired guerrillas, whom American advisers mistakenly believed were controlled by Moscow, had fought for control of Greece since the end of 1944. After elections

installed the royalist Popular party in the spring of 1946, several thousand communist guerrillas launched a full-scale civil war against the government and the British occupation authorities. In February 1947 the British informed Truman that they could no longer afford to assist the Greek anticommunists. Fearing a communist takeover in Greece, U.S. policy makers worried that growing Soviet influence there would pose a threat to American and European interests in the eastern Mediterranean and the Middle East, especially in strategically located Turkey and the oil-rich state of Iran.

To counter those threats the president announced what became known as the Truman Doctrine. In a speech to Congress on March 12 he requested large-scale military and economic assistance to Greece and Turkey and called for all Americans "to support free peoples who are resisting attempted subjugation by armed minorities or by outside pressures." To win popular support for the global fight against communism, and to squeeze money out of a stingy Congress, the president followed the advice of Republican Senator Arthur Vandenberg to "scare hell" out of the country. If Greece fell to communism, Truman warned, "the effect upon its neighbor, Turkey, would be immediate and serious. Confusion and disorder might well spread throughout the entire Middle East." This notion of communist contagion was an early version of what Dwight Eisenhower would later call the "domino theory." Not just Greece but freedom itself was at issue, Truman declared: "If we falter in our leadership, we may endanger the peace of the world—and we shall surely endanger the welfare of our own nation."

Despite the open-endedness of this military commitment, Congress quickly approved Truman's request for $300 million in aid to Greece and $100 million for Turkey. The appropriation reversed the postwar policy of sharp cuts in foreign spending and marked a new level of commitment to the emerging Cold War. Truman's skillful manipulation of public opinion helped build a base of bipartisan support in Congress that gave him a greater role in determining future foreign policy.

The Truman administration also worked with Congress to pass the National Security Act, which was designed to streamline defense operations. Signed in July 1947, the act created three new bodies: a single Department of Defense to replace the previous Departments of War and the Navy; the National Security Council, an advisory body charged with helping the president set defense and military priorities; and the Central Intelligence Agency, a national intelligence-gathering operation that replaced the wartime Office of Strategic Services. The Atomic Energy Commission, established in 1946 under the executive branch, worked with the new agencies in the development of atomic energy and weapons. The establishment of these new bureaucratic structures marked the emergence of the *national security state*, a collection of powerful and highly secretive operations in the executive branch. Such structures accelerated the shift of policy-making initiative to the White House.

The Marshall Plan. During this period Secretary of State George Marshall, who had been army chief of staff under Roosevelt, proposed a plan to provide economic as well as military aid to Europe. European economies had been devastated by the war, and conditions worsened in the terrible winter of 1947. Only with a massive influx of outside capital could Europeans begin the process of rebuilding and revitalization. Speaking at Harvard University's commencement in June 1947, Marshall urged the nations of Europe to work out a comprehensive recovery program and then ask the United States for aid. "Any government that is willing to assist in the task of recovery," he promised, "will find full cooperation . . . on the part of the United States government." In Truman's words, the Marshall Plan was "the other half of the walnut" (the first half being the aggressive containment policy of the Truman Doctrine). By bolstering European economies devastated by the war, Marshall and Truman believed, the United States could forestall economic dislocation that would give rise to communism.

The Marshall Plan in Action
Between 1948 and 1951 the European Recovery Program, popularly known as the Marshall Plan after Secretary of State George C. Marshall, contributed over $13 billion toward its objective of "restoring the confidence of the European people in the economic future of their own countries and of Europe as a whole." Here a sign prominently announces that Berlin is being rebuilt with help from the Marshall Plan.

The Wise Men: Architects of Containment

They were, as their biographers Walter Isaacson and Evan Thomas tallied it up, two bankers (W. Averell Harriman, Robert Lovett), two lawyers (Dean Acheson, John McCloy), and two diplomats (Charles Bohlen, George Kennan). Those six friends were among the main architects of the containment policy that dominated American foreign relations from the 1940s through at least the 1960s. Individually their names are not that well known, but collectively they had an enormous impact on postwar developments. In 1965, the presidential aide McGeorge Bundy dubbed these senior statesmen "the wise men," and the name stuck.

At first glance the social profile of the six men, all born between 1893 and 1904, suggests that the foreign policy elite was synonymous with the rich and the powerful in the United States. W. Averell Harriman was the son of the founder of the Union Pacific Railroad, and Robert Lovett's father was the elder Harriman's second in command. Dean Acheson was the son of the Episcopal bishop of Connecticut, and Charles Bohlen was descended from the first American ambassador to France. But the establishment was more of a meritocracy than a closed club: John McCloy came from a poor family in Philadelphia, and George Kennan was an outsider from Milwaukee. Access to education at the elite eastern institutions that trained generations of leaders—prep schools such as Groton and St. Paul's and universities such as Harvard, Yale, and Princeton—was crucial to membership. Averell Harriman taught Dean Acheson to row crew at Groton, they went to Yale together, and their lives remained linked until they died.

After graduation from college, these privileged young men embarked on careers, mainly on Wall Street or in Washington. Charles Bohlen went into the foreign service and became a specialist on Soviet affairs; he was assigned to the first U.S. mission to that country in 1934. George Kennan was also a foreign service officer in Moscow in the 1930s. Dean Acheson spent most of the 1920s and 1930s in private legal practice, as did John McCloy; W. Averell Harriman devoted his attention to business, and Robert Lovett worked with the banking firm of Brown Brothers, which merged with the Harriman empire in 1931.

A common thread among the six lives in the 1920s and 1930s was extensive contact with European affairs, including familiarity with the Soviet Union. The result was a collective internationalism that stood in stark contrast to the isolationism of the 1930s. Not surprisingly, all six ended up in Washington during World War II, a period when their personal and professional relationships coalesced. McCloy and Lovett served as assistant secretaries of war, where they were known as "the Heavenly Twins"; Harriman was ambassador to the Soviet Union, where one of his advisors was George Kennan; Acheson became assistant secretary of state for economic affairs; and Bohlen served as the State Department's chief translator and expert on Soviet affairs, accompanying Roosevelt to Teheran and Yalta.

When the war ended, the six men all joined the Truman administration and embarked on seven years of extraordinary power and influence at one of the most critical moments in modern American history: the onset of the Cold War and the formulation of the policy of containment of the Soviet Union through diplomacy and force. Although containment is associated with George Kennan, its underlying assumptions were shared by all six. They fervently believed that the United States had a moral destiny to provide world leadership in the struggle against communism. The Truman Doctrine and the Marshall Plan epitomized the sweeping commitments they were willing to undertake to promote that world view.

The policy-making process in the Truman administration was fairly intimate and decentralized and hence was amenable to the kind of behind-the-scenes power these members of the establishment thrived on. Acheson was the most influential member of the group, serving as undersecretary of state from 1945 to 1947 and then secretary of state from 1949 to 1953. Charles Bohlen was his special assistant until Bohlen was named minister to France in 1949. George Kennan also served in various capacities in the State Department before being named ambassador to the Soviet Union in 1951. Harri-

man joined the cabinet as secretary of commerce and then became a special assistant to the president, where he played a key role in setting the strategy for the conduct of the Korean War. McCloy served as president of the World Bank and became a vigorous proponent of the Marshall Plan; in 1949 Truman named him U.S. high commissioner for Germany.

These six men wielded power individually, but their impact was enhanced by how they functioned as a group. They had much in common, especially their belief in the cold war ideology of containment. Just as important was their commitment to public service: remarkably free of personal ambition, they saw themselves as public servants who stood above the fray of partisan politics. However, their pattern of alternating between government service and lucrative positions on Wall Street suggests that they had no trouble reconciling public service with private gain.

Dwight Eisenhower's election sent most of the wise men into temporary retirement from public service, but the election of John Kennedy in 1960 called them in from what their biographers called "the wilderness years." Now generally in their fifties and sixties, this older generation served the young president in a variety of capacities: Bohlen and Kennan as ambassadors to France and Yugoslavia, respectively; Harriman as assistant secretary of state for Far Eastern affairs; amd McCloy, Lovett, and Acheson as advisers. Their service demonstrates the continuity of the postwar foreign policy elite from World War II through the 1960s.

After Kennedy's assassination Lyndon Johnson continued to seek their counsel, especially as the Vietnam War escalated. But these six men, who had so forcefully supported standing up to communism in the 1940s and 1950s, began to doubt the American commitment in Southeast Asia. One by one they dropped their support for the war, and some, such as Kennan, who had become a professor at Princeton's Institute for Advanced Study, criticized it publicly. At a March 1968 meeting of the wise men, even Dean Acheson, the epitome of the establishment, told Johnson that the United States had to get out of Vietnam. The defection of the foreign policy elite, those who had framed the Cold War, played a major role in Johnson's decision to begin negotiations to end the war.

The wise men proved to be a hardy bunch, with Harriman, Lovett, and McCloy living into their nineties. They shared the experience of shaping America's cold war policy and overseeing the dramatic expansion of American power and influence in the 1950s and 1960s. But of those who had been "present at the creation" (the title of Acheson's memoirs), only George Kennan was still alive to see the end of the Cold War and the dissolution of the Soviet Union. These events would no doubt have astounded and pleased the "wise men" who had so tirelessly served their country in the postwar years.

President Truman (far left) confers with Secretary of State Robert Lovett and State Department aides George Kennan and Charles Bohlen (from left to right). In the photo on the right Averell Harriman (left) and President Harry Truman (right) greet Secretary of State Dean Acheson on his return from a NATO conference in 1952. McCloy is not shown.

American economic self-interest was also a contributing factor—the legislation required that foreign aid dollars be spent on U.S. goods and services. Moreover, a revitalized Europe centered on a strong West German economy would provide a better market for U.S. goods, and a European common market could serve as a model for economic cooperation.

Within Congress, however, there was significant opposition to Truman's pledge of economic aid to European economies. Republicans called the Marshall Plan a huge "international W.P.A.," a "European T.V.A.," and a "bold Socialist blue-print," none of which was meant as a compliment. As the bill came up for a vote in 1948, an election year, Republicans were reluctant to give the Democratic president a major foreign policy triumph. But not all Republicans were opposed. Senator Arthur Vandenberg, the Republican isolationist turned internationalist who chaired the Senate Foreign Relations Committee, supported the Marshall Plan, just as he had favored the appropriations for Greece and Turkey under the Truman Doctrine.

In the midst of this Congressional stalemate came the communist coup in Czechoslovakia. Czechoslovakia had been one of the few Eastern European countries to hold free elections after the war. The Communists won 38 percent of the vote in May 1946, necessitating a coalition government; neither President Eduard Beneš nor Foreign Minister Jan Masaryk, both greatly admired in the West, were Communists. By early 1948 the fragile coalition had faltered, and the Communists took control in a coup on February 25, 1948. Two weeks later the Communist leadership assassinated Masaryk, an event that Truman said "sent a shock throughout the civilized world." A stark reminder of the menace of Soviet expansion in Europe, the coup served to rally Congressional support for the Marshall Plan. Congress voted overwhelmingly to approve funds for the program in March 1948. Like most other foreign policy initiatives of the 1940s and 1950s, the Marshall Plan won bipartisan support despite the opposition of an isolationist wing of the Republican party.

The historian Thomas J. McCormick calls the Marshall Plan "arguably the most innovative piece of foreign policy in American history." Over the next four years the United States contributed nearly $13 billion to a highly successful recovery effort. Western European economies revived and industrial production increased 64 percent, opening new areas for international trade. The Marshall Plan did not specifically exclude Eastern Europe or the Soviet Union, but it required that all participating nations exchange economic information and work toward the elimination of tariffs and other trade barriers. Soviet leaders denounced those conditions as attempts to draw Eastern Europe into the American orbit and forbade their satellite states of Czechoslovakia, Poland, and Hungary to participate.

The Berlin Airlift. The Marshall Plan accelerated American and European efforts to rebuild and reunify the West German economy. After agreeing to fuse their zones of occupation, the United States, France, and Britain initiated a currency reform program in West Berlin in June

The Berlin Airlift

For 321 days American planes like this DC-6 flew 272,000 missions to bring food and other supplies to Berlin after the Soviet Union had blocked all surface routes into the former German capital. The blockade was finally lifted on May 12, 1949, after the Soviets conceded that it had been a failure.

MAP 28.1

Cold War Europe, 1955

In 1949 the United States sponsored the creation of the North Atlantic Treaty Organization, an alliance of ten European nations, the United States, and Canada. West Germany was formally admitted to NATO in May 1955. A few days later the Soviet Union and seven other communist nations established a rival alliance, the Warsaw Pact.

1948. The economic revitalization of Berlin, located deep within the Soviet zone of occupation, alarmed Soviet policy makers, who feared a resurgent Germany aligned with the West. To forestall that development, the Soviet Union imposed a blockade on all highway, rail, and river traffic to West Berlin that June. In that tense situation Truman responded with an airlift. For nearly a year American and British pilots, who had been dropping bombs on Berlin only four years earlier, flew in 2.5 million tons of food and fuel, nearly a ton for each Berlin resident. On May 12, 1949, Stalin lifted the blockade, which by then had made West Berlin a symbol of resistance to communism.

NATO. The coup in Czechoslovakia and the Berlin crisis convinced U.S. policy makers of the need for a collective security pact. In April 1949, for the first time since the American Revolution, the United States entered into a peacetime military alliance, joining with Western Europe and Canada to create the North Atlantic Treaty Organization (NATO). To back up America's new stance Truman asked Congress for $1.3 billion in military assistance to NATO and authorized the basing of four U.S. army divisions in Western Europe. Under the NATO pact the United States, Britain, France, Italy, Belgium, the Netherlands, Luxembourg, Denmark, Norway, Portugal, Iceland, and Canada agreed that "an armed attack against one or more of them in Europe or North America shall be considered an attack against them all." In May 1949 those nations also agreed to the creation of the Federal Republic of Germany (West Ger-

many). All assumed that it would join NATO, which it did in 1955 (see Map 28.1).

Distressed by the aggressive American effort to promote a new European economic and political order and the deployment of substantial numbers of American troops in Western Europe, the Soviet Union tightened its grip on Eastern Europe in October 1949 by creating a separate government for East Germany, which became the German Democratic Republic. The Soviets also sponsored an economic association, the Council for Mutual Economic Assistance, or COMECON (1949), and a military alliance for Eastern Europe, the Warsaw Pact (1955). The postwar division of Europe was nearly complete.

The "Fall" of China

As mutual suspicion between the United States and the Soviet Union deepened, cold war doctrines influenced the American stance toward Asia as well. American policy there was based on Asia's importance in the world economy as much as on the desire to contain communism. Initially American postwar economic plans for the region centered on a revitalized China, but political instability there prompted the Truman administration to focus instead on developing the Japanese economy. After dismantling Japan's military forces and weaponry, American occupation forces under General Douglas MacArthur supervised the country's reconstruction as a bulwark of Asian capitalism. MacArthur drafted a dem-

ocratic constitution, directed the rebuilding of the economy, and paved the way for the restoration of Japanese sovereignty in 1951.

In China the situation was more precarious. A civil war had been raging in that populous country since the 1930s. Communist forces led by Mao Zedong (Mao Tse-tung) and Zhou Enlai (Chou En-lai) contended for power with conservative Nationalist forces under Jiang Jieshi (Chiang Kai-shek). Jiang had strong connections with the Chinese business community and the West. His wealthy wife had been educated at Wellesley College in Massachusetts and had influential American friends. In contrast, Mao was the son of struggling peasants, a tough, uncompromising leader who inspired loyalty in his associates. Mao won the devotion of China's overtaxed, land-hungry peasants, whom Jiang had alienated with the widespread corruption of his regime and his suppression of agrarian reform. The communists also won support for their resistance against the Japanese forces occupying their country. By 1944 Mao's forces were gaining the upper hand.

Although dissatisfied with the Jiang regime, the Truman administration saw no good alternative to Mao and resigned itself to working with the Nationalists. Between 1945 and 1949 the United States provided more than $2 billion to Jiang's forces, but to no avail. In 1947 General Albert Wedemeyer, who had tried to work with Jiang, reported to President Truman that "until drastic political and economic reforms" were undertaken by the "corrupt, reactionary, and inefficient Chinese National government, United States aid cannot accomplish its purpose." When those reforms did not occur, the Truman administration cut off aid to the Nationalists in August 1949, sealing their fate. The People's Republic of China was formally established on October 1, 1949, and what was left of Jiang's government fled to the island of Formosa (Taiwan).

Many Americans viewed Mao's success as a defeat for the United States. The Republican statesman John Foster Dulles, who would become secretary of state under Eisenhower, called the communist victory in China "the worst defeat the United States has suffered in its history." A pro-Nationalist "China lobby" supported by Senators Karl Mundt of South Dakota, William S. Knowland of California, and other Republicans protested that the State Department under the leadership of Truman's newly appointed secretary of state, Dean Acheson, was responsible for the "loss of China." The publisher Henry R. Luce, born in China to missionary parents, spread those accusations through his magazines, including *Time* and *Life*.

As a result of pressure from the China lobby, most of the State Department's experts on the Far East were forced to resign for supposedly having been too sympathetic to the Chinese communists. The loss of those experts created a critical knowledge gap that would handicap the United States for decades in dealing with Vietnam and other Asian trouble spots. The United States refused to recognize what it called "Red China," instead giving diplomatic recognition to the Nationalists in Taiwan. The United States also used its influence to block China's admission to the United Nations. For almost twenty years afterward, U.S. administrations treated mainland China, the world's most populous country, as a diplomatic nonentity.

Containment Militarized: NSC-68

September 1949 brought another shock: American military intelligence detected a rise in radioactivity in the atmosphere, proof that the Soviet Union had set off an atomic bomb. The American atomic monopoly, which some military and political advisers had argued would last for decades, had ended in just four years. In combination with the communist takeover in China, Russian possession of the bomb made the world look even more threatening.

The end of the American atomic monopoly forced a major reassessment of the nation's foreign policy. To devise a new diplomatic and military blueprint, Truman turned to the National Security Council (NSC). In April 1950 the NSC delivered its report, known as NSC-68, to the president. Using alarmist rhetoric and exaggerated assessments of Soviet capabilities, the document reflected the bleak assumptions that American policy makers held about the Soviet Union: "It is quite clear from Soviet theory and practice that the Kremlin seeks to bring the free world under its dominion by the methods of the cold war." Because the Soviet Union had the military power to "back up infiltration with intimidation," policy makers predicted an "indefinite period of tension and danger." In the immediate postwar period, Kennan's formulation of containment emphasized economic aid and diplomatic pressure to counter Soviet expansionism, but policy makers became increasingly dependent on military force. The new stance thus pointed to far greater militarization of the Cold War.

NSC-68 made several specific recommendations. It favored the development of a hydrogen bomb, an advanced weapon that was a thousand times more destructive than the atomic bombs that had destroyed Hiroshima and Nagasaki. (The United States exploded its first hydrogen bomb in November 1952; the Soviet Union followed suit in 1953.) It supported increases in U.S. conventional forces and a strong system of alliances. Most important, it called for an increase in taxes to finance "a bold and massive program of rebuilding the West's defensive potential to surpass that of the Soviet world." NSC-68 envisioned defense budgets totaling up to 20 percent of the gross national product, four times their level at that time (see Figures 29.1 and

ter 31), a
and Ne
Overall
1950, ro
billion in
though r
Korean V
lion ann
policy ha
more cos

Harry

Harry S.
presiden
of Roose
popular
ance and
generatio
kitchen,"
The majo
sion to a
filtration
played a
coalition
advance
Deal" w
for the n

The Cl

Truman
dent for
tember 1
surrende
ership b
plan for
a period
shaped t
terms of
"useful a
oly, good
from the
cation."
called his
Whe
comed h
cent, ac
populari
such as
guage. V
Truman
economy

curity system was extended to cover 10 million new workers, and benefits were raised by 75 percent. The National Housing Act of 1949 called for the construction of 810,000 units of low-income housing, although only half that number was actually built under the program.

Truman's record on civil rights illustrates the opportunities and obstacles facing proponents of the Fair Deal. Although civil rights issues had long preoccupied the country, they took on a new urgency in the 1940s. The callous treatment of black soldiers during World War II and the lynching of more than forty black men after the war—many of them veterans—sparked widespread black anger. At the same time, black expectations had been raised by wartime opportunities and by symbolic victories such as Jackie Robinson's joining the Brooklyn Dodgers in 1947, breaking the color line in major league baseball. Truman's sympathies for civil rights were reinforced by the realization that black voters were playing an increasingly large role in the Democratic party as they migrated from the South, where they were effectively disfranchised, to northern cities. Finally, Truman was sensitive to the world's view of America's treatment of blacks, especially since the Soviet Union often compared segregation of southern blacks with the Nazis' treatment of Jews.

Lacking a popular mandate on the civil rights issue, Truman resorted to a variety of means to advance the cause. In 1946 he appointed a National Civil Rights Commission; its 1947 report, *To Secure These Rights*, called for an expanded federal role in civil rights that foreshadowed much of the legislation of the 1960s. He ordered the Justice Department to prepare an *amicus curiae* ("friend of the court") brief in the Supreme Court case of *Shelley v. Kraemer* (1948), which struck down as unconstitutional restrictive covenants that enforced residential segregation by barring home buyers on the basis of race or religion. In the same year, Truman signed an executive order desegregating the armed forces. With the outbreak of the Korean War, conditions for black soldiers improved compared with the discrimination that they had faced in World War II. During the rapid mobilization, demands for quick processing of draftees outweighed customary practices such as keeping black and white draftees separate, thus speeding up integration. The Truman administration also proposed a federal antilynching law, federal protection of voting rights (such as an end to poll taxes), and a permanent federal agency to guarantee equal employment opportunities. A filibuster by southern conservatives, however, blocked such legislation in Congress.

Interest groups successfully opposed other key items on the Fair Deal agenda. The American Medical Association quashed a labor-backed movement for national health insurance by denouncing it as the first step toward "socialized medicine." Catholics successfully opposed legislation for aid to education because it did not include subsidies for parochial schools. Farmers refused to join labor in supporting the repeal of Taft-Hartley. In general, the Truman administration failed to mobilize popular and Congressional support for dramatically enlarged federal responsibilities in the economic and social spheres.

Two other factors further limited the Fair Deal's chances for legislative success. One was the outbreak of the Korean War in 1950, which diverted national attention to foreign affairs. The other was the nation's growing fear of internal subversion. The anticommunist crusade was only one manifestation of the way the Cold War was increasingly permeating all facets of American life. Truman's administration played a major role in heightening those domestic tensions.

The Great Fear

As American relations with the Soviet Union deteriorated in the late 1940s and early 1950s, fear of communism fueled a widespread campaign of domestic repression. Americans often call this phenomenon "McCarthyism," after Senator Joseph R. McCarthy of Wisconsin, the decade's most vocal anticommunist. But this "Great Fear" involved more than the work of just one man. It built on the distrust of radicals and foreigners that had manifested itself in the 1850s and in the Red Scare after World War I. Worsening cold war tensions intersected with those deep-seated anxieties and partisan politics to spawn an obsessive concern with internal subversion. Republicans used accusations of communist subversion to discredit the Truman administration, while Truman responded with a government loyalty crusade to protect himself against charges that he was "soft on communism." Ultimately, few Communists were found in positions of power; far more Americans became innocent victims of false accusations and innuendos. The postwar red scare was particularly devastating to the political left, where accusations of guilt by association affected progressives of all stripes.

HUAC. The roots of postwar anticommunism date back to the late 1930s, when liberals and Communists had cooperated in a "popular front" against fascism and often joined together to support New Deal social programs. In 1938 Congressman Martin Dies of Texas and other conservatives launched the House Committee on Un-American Activities (HUAC) to investigate alleged fascist and communist subversion. In the early 1940s HUAC focused almost exclusively on the latter, probing left-wing activity in labor unions and New Deal agencies. During America's wartime alliance with the Soviet Union, HUAC's visibility declined, but it reemerged after the war as Americans grew concerned over Russian expansionism in Eastern Europe. Revelations in

Mark Goodson

Red Hunting on the Quiz Shows, or What's My Party Line?

Active in the television industry from its earliest days, Mark Goodson is a highly successful producer whose game shows have included "What's My Line?" "To Tell the Truth," "Password," and "Family Feud." In this interview Goodson recalls his experience in the industry in the early 1950s, when rampant anticommunism plagued the entertainment business.

I'm not sure when it began, but I believe it was early 1950. At that point I had no connection with the blacklisting that was going on, although I heard about it in the motion picture business and heard rumors about things that had happened on other shows, like *The Aldrich Family*. . . .

Soon afterwards, CBS installed a clearance division. There wasn't any discussion. We would just get the word—"drop that person"—and that was supposed to be it. Whenever I booked a guest or a panelist on *What's My Line?* or *I've Got a Secret*, one of our assistants would phone up and say, "We're going to use so-and-so." We'd either get the okay, or they'd call back and say, "Not clear," or "Sorry, we can't use them." Even advertising agencies—big ones, like Young & Ru-

bicam and BBD&O—had their own clearance departments. They would never come out and say it. They would just write off somebody by saying, "He's a bad actor." You were never supposed to tell the person what it was about; you'd just unbook them. They never admitted there was a blacklist. It just wasn't done. . . .

Anna Lee was an English actress on a later show of ours called *It's News to Me*. The sponsor was Sanka Coffee, a product of General Foods. The advertising agency was Young & Rubicam. One day, I received a call telling me we had to drop one of our panelists, Anna Lee, immediately. They said she was a radical, that she wrote a column for the *Daily Worker*. They couldn't allow that kind of stuff on the air. They claimed they were getting all kinds of mail. It seemed incongruous to me that this little English girl, someone who seemed very conservative, would be writing for a Communist newspaper. It just didn't sound right.

I took her out to lunch. After a little social conversation, I asked her about her politics. She told me that she wasn't political, except she voted Conservative in England. Her husband was a Republican from Texas.

I went back to the agency and said, "You guys are really off your rocker. Anna Lee is nothing close to a liberal." They told me, "Oh, you're right. We checked on that. It's a different Anna Lee who writes for the *Daily Worker*." I remember being relieved and saying, "Well, that's good. You just made a mistake. Now we can forget this." But that wasn't the case. They told me, "We've still got to get rid of her, because the illusion is just as good as the reality. If our client continues to get the mail, no one is going to believe him when he says there's a second Anna Lee." At that point I lost it. I told them their demand was outrageous. They could cancel the show if they wanted to, but I would not drop somebody whose only crime was sharing a name. When I got back to my office, there was a phone call waiting for me. It was from a friend of mine at the agency. He said, "If I were you, I would not lose my temper like that. If you want to argue, do it quietly. After you left, somebody said, 'Is Goodson a pinko?'"

Source: Griffin Fariello, *Red Scare* (New York: Norton, 1995), 320–324.

1946 of a Soviet spy ring operating in Canada and the United States accentuated American fears of Soviet subversion.

In 1947 HUAC helped launch the postwar red scare by holding widely publicized hearings on communist infiltration of the film industry. A group of writers and directors, soon dubbed the "Hollywood Ten," went to jail for contempt of Congress when they cited the Fifth Amendment in refusing to testify about their past associations. Soon afterward ex-FBI agents in Hollywood circulated a list of actors, directors, and writers whose names had been mentioned in the HUAC investigation or whose associates and friends had been described as

politically dubious. Industry executives denied the existence of a blacklist, but for ten years hundreds of people were shut out of work in the entertainment industry (see American Voices, above). The Weavers, a popular folk-singing group, were blacklisted, and politically active actors such as Zero Mostel and John Garfield had difficulty finding work. One day the actress Jean Muir headlined the popular radio show "The Aldrich Family"; the next she was out of a job—fired, the network said, not because she was a Communist but because gossip about her had made her too "controversial."

Anticommunism also emerged as a divisive force in the labor movement. In the 1930s Communists had been

The Red Scare and the Media

After HUAC's 1947 investigation of the film industry, television and radio sponsors became wary of possible communist subversion on the airwaves. In 1950 three ex-FBI agents employed by a private consulting firm produced *Red Channels*, a booklet identifying 151 allegedly subversive entertainers. It was widely circulated among producers and was one of the key tools of the cultural Cold War.

very active in labor organizing, and their contributions had been welcomed, if not openly acknowledged. But as conservatives charged that Soviet-led Communists were taking over American unions, the labor movement reversed itself and purged Communists in the late 1940s. The Taft-Hartley Act fueled this campaign by requiring labor leaders to take oaths swearing they were not Communists before their unions could participate in federally supervised elections. The CIO's president, Phillip Murray, subsequently denounced Communist sympathizers as "skulking cowards . . . apostles of hate." Eleven unions that refused to oust their communist or communist-sympathizing leaders were expelled from the CIO.

The Truman administration inflamed the hysteria by issuing an executive order in March 1947 initiating a comprehensive investigation into the loyalty of all federal employees. More than 6 million individuals were subjected to security checks, 14,000 underwent inten-

sive FBI investigation, and 2,000 were dismissed. The case of Dorothy Bailey, a forty-one-year-old graduate of Bryn Mawr College and the University of Minnesota, was typical. Bailey lost her job with the U.S. Employment Service, where she had worked for fourteen years, because an unidentified informer claimed she was a Communist and associated with known Communists. Denying the charge, she was brought before the District of Columbia regional loyalty board, which introduced no evidence against her and called no witnesses to support its case. She was fired anyway.

Following Washington's lead, many state and local governments, universities, political organizations, churches, and businesses undertook their own antisubversion campaigns. All 11,000 faculty members at the University of California were required to take a loyalty oath; UCLA alone fired 157 who refused to do so. Many Catholic organizations became hotbeds of anticommunism, urging their members to combat "enemies" within the church. Because of the Communist party's historic defense of racial equality, civil rights organizations such as the NAACP and the National Urban League were attacked as communist-front groups; they subsequently purged their left-wing members. Some postwar liberals, such as Henry Wallace and his followers in the Progressive party, continued to seek cooperation with the Soviet Union and defended the participation of Communists in their organizations. But many other liberals, most notably those in Americans for Democratic Action, founded in 1947, shunned potential left-wing allies and embraced a strident anticommunism.

The anticommunist crusade intensified in 1948 when HUAC began an investigation of Alger Hiss, a former New Deal State Department official who had accompanied Franklin Roosevelt to Yalta. The case against Hiss rested on the testimony of the former Communist Whittaker Chambers, a senior editor at *Time*. Chambers claimed that Hiss was a member of a secret communist cell in the government and had passed him classified documents in the 1930s. Hiss categorically denied the allegations and denied even knowing Chambers. Republican Congressman Richard M. Nixon of California orchestrated the HUAC investigation, an event that brought him national recognition and boosted his political career. The Hiss investigation culminated in the dramatic release of the so-called Pumpkin Papers, microfilm that Chambers had hidden in a pumpkin patch on his Maryland farm. (When this supposedly incriminating cache was declassified, it was found to contain only Navy Department documents on life rafts and fire extinguishers.) Because the statute of limitations on espionage had expired by 1949, Hiss was charged instead with perjury for lying about his communist affiliations and acquaintance with Chambers. The first trial resulted in a hung jury; the second, in early 1950, found Hiss guilty and sentenced him to five years in federal prison. The

tisan, anc
crusade a
sive camp
ticket.

The I
nating Ha
discredite
dency, Tr
above 32
percent. I
dealt the
series of
officials i
schemes (
Washingto
to Goverr
the suppo
sevelt and
voters wh
ocrats no
abama fo

Throu
cated Nev
ary eloqu
speeches
get maxir
hower pla
he attacke
"Korea, (
pledge tha
and end t
quipped,

The c
the revela
cret "slush
contempla
adroitly u
ers' symp
paign fun
mink coat
ported ca
struction
"respectal
accepting
named Cl
declared
embarrass
viewers fl
and phone
can leader
The "Che
use the po

Eisen
carrying a
southern
not fare q
control of

conviction of Hiss increased paranoia about a communist conspiracy in the federal government, but after 1950 HUAC's role would be overshadowed by a new investigating committee led by Joseph McCarthy in the Senate.

The Rise and Fall of McCarthy. In February 1950 Senator Joseph McCarthy of Wisconsin delivered a bombshell during a speech in Wheeling, West Virginia: "I have here in my hand a list of the names of 205 men that were known to the Secretary of State as being members of the Communist Party and who nevertheless are still working and shaping the policy of the State Department." McCarthy never revealed the names on his list and later lowered the number to 81 and then to 57. The public was so responsive to his charges that those inconsistencies failed to dent his credibility. For the next four years McCarthy became the central figure in the virulent campaign of anticommunism that consumed the country.

A Marine Air Corps veteran who had won a Senate seat in the 1946 Republican landslide, McCarthy soon discovered that anticommunist rhetoric could boost his political fortunes. Like other Republicans in the late 1940s, he leveled accusations of communist subversion in the government to embarrass Truman and the Democrats. McCarthy's political genius lay in his ability to make his name synonymous with the cause of uncovering subversives in government. Politicians who attacked him exposed themselves to charges of being "soft" on communism, the kiss of death in the postwar political climate. And McCarthy did not hesitate to charge that his critics were themselves part of "this conspiracy so immense." At first his supporters were more visible than his detractors; for example, Democratic Congressman John F. Kennedy of Massachusetts thought "McCarthy may have something." But President Truman called McCarthy's charges "slander, lies, character assassination," although he could do nothing to curb them. When Republican Dwight D. Eisenhower was elected president in 1952, he did not publicly challenge his party's most outspoken senator.

A series of national and international events allowed McCarthy to retain credibility despite his failure to identify a single Communist in the government. The trial and conviction of Alger Hiss in 1950 set the stage for McCarthy's allegations. The Korean War broke out soon afterward, embroiling the United States in a frustrating fight against communism in a faraway land. And in a sensational case in 1951 Julius and Ethel Rosenberg were convicted of passing atomic secrets to the Soviet Union. After a highly controversial trial they were executed in 1953. (Recently released documents from Project Verona, a top-secret intelligence mission during World War II, provide strong evidence of the Rosenbergs' guilt.) Throughout this period McCarthy lashed out against alleged Communists in the State Department and other branches of the government, allegations that he aired before the Senate Permanent Investigating Committee in 1953–1954.

McCarthy overreached himself in early 1954 by launching an investigation into possible subversion in the U.S. Army. The lengthy televised hearings brought McCarthy's smear tactics and leering innuendos into the nation's living rooms, and support for him declined. The passing of the Korean War and the death of Stalin in 1953 also undercut public interest in McCarthy's red-hunting campaign. In December 1954 the Senate voted 67 to 22 to censure McCarthy for unbecoming conduct. He died three years later at the age of forty-eight, his name forever attached to a period of political repression of which he was only the most flagrant manifestation.

The Army-McCarthy Hearings
These 1954 hearings contributed to the downfall of Senator Joseph McCarthy by showing his reckless accusations, bullying tactics, and sneering innuendos to the huge television audience that tuned in each day. Some of the most heated exchanges took place between McCarthy (right) and Joseph Welch (seated, left), the lawyer representing the army. When an exasperated Welch asked, "Have you no decency left, sir?" McCarthy merely shrugged. But the audience broke into applause because someone had finally had the courage to stand up to the senator from Wisconsin.

"Moa

The 1952
stalemate
elected pɪ
to end th
lasted lon
call "mo
proach th
tling, of
predecess
1980s an
licans we
social anɑ
the scope
governing
and confɪ
continueɑ
panding t
Korean W

The Sol

The Rep
largely Pɪ
only a th
publicans
who coulɑ
lican leaɑ
Eisenhow

    Eisen
political

The Military-Industrial Complex
This nuclear reactor in Hanford, Washington, was one of dozens of new weapons-related facilities that had sprung up in the southern and western regions of the United States in the 1940s and 1950s. Even though local residents profited from new employment opportunities generated by the plants, the environmental and health dangers posed by the nuclear industry became a growing source of concern.

ism, and the federal government became increasingly intertwined in the postwar period. According to the National Science Foundation, federal money underwrote 90 percent of the cost of research on aviation and space, 65 percent of that on electricity and electronics, 42 percent of that on scientific instruments, and 24 percent of that on automobiles. With the government footing part of the bill, corporations transformed new ideas into useful products with unprecedented speed. After the Pentagon backed IBM's investment in integrated circuits in the 1960s, those new devices, which were crucial to the computer revolution, were in commercial production within three years (see New Technology, page 898).

The growth of this military-industrial establishment reflected a dramatic shift in national priorities. Military spending took up a greater percentage of national income as measured by the GNP. Between 1900 and 1930, except for the two years that the United States fought in World War I, the country spent less than 1 percent of GNP for military purposes. In the early 1960s the figure was close to 10 percent.

The defense buildup created jobs, and lots of them (see Map 29.1). Taking into account the multiplier effect, which measures the indirect benefits of such employment (the additional jobs created to serve and support defense workers), perhaps one worker in seven nationally owed his or her job to the military-industrial complex in the 1960s. In the South and West, where much of the new military activity was concentrated, dependence on federal defense spending was even greater.

That increased spending put money in the pockets of the millions of people working in defense-related industries but also limited the resources available for domestic social needs. Critics of military spending calculated the trade-offs: the cost of a nuclear aircraft carrier and support ships equaled that of a subway system for Washington, D.C.; and the money spent on one Huey helicopter matched that required for sixty-six units of low-income housing.

Military mobilization also affected Americans in a personal way—for the first time in the nation's history there was a peacetime draft. In the past the armed forces had shrunk to a skeleton volunteer force at the end of each war or foreign engagement. But when World War II ended, the draft was kept in place to meet the military commitments associated with the Cold War: occupation forces in defeated Axis countries, missile deployment operations in Europe, and counterinsurgency forces in the Third World. Suddenly every neighborhood seemed to have a boy in the armed forces; many people made military service a career.

Corporate Strategies

The Cold War and the growth of the state brought major changes to American life, hastening the concentration of power in ever larger economic and political structures. Successful corporate managers adopted flexible strategies to take advantage of the postwar economic climate. They tapped federal money for research and development, diversified their range of products, expanded their multinational operations, and improved their ability to plan.

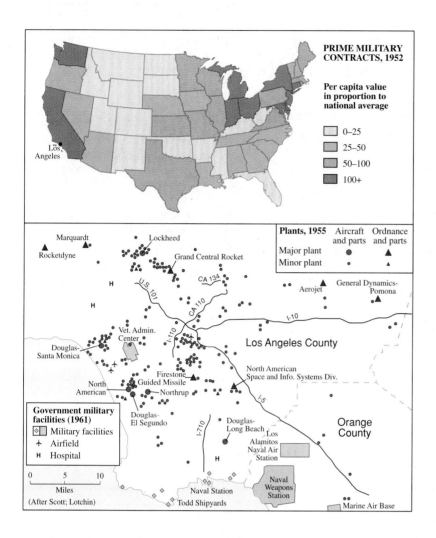

PRIME MILITARY
CONTRACTS, 1952

Per capita value
in proportion to
national average

0–25
25–50
50–100
100+

Plants, 1955 — Aircraft and parts / Ordnance and parts

Major plant
Minor plant

Government military
facilities (1961)
Military facilities
Airfield
Hospital

Marquardt
Rocketdyne
Lockheed
Grand Central Rocket
Aerojet
General Dynamics-Pomona
Vet. Admin. Center
Douglas-Santa Monica
Firestone Guided Missile
North American
Northrup
Douglas-El Segundo
Douglas-Long Beach
Los Alamitos Naval Air Station
Naval Station
Todd Shipyards
Naval Weapons Station
Marine Air Base
North American Space and Info. Systems Div.

Los Angeles County
Orange County

U.S. 101 · CA 134 · CA 110 · I-110 · I-10 · I-5 · I-710

0   5   10
Miles
(After Scott; Lotchin)

MAP 29.1

*The Military-Industrial Complex
in Los Angeles*

The development and expansion of military
facilities and defense contracting during the
Cold War helped boost the populations and
economies of Los Angeles and other Sun Belt
cities and made the economies of some states
highly dependent on defense expenditures.

The predominant thrust of modern corporate life after 1945 continued to be consolidation of economic and financial resources by oligopolies, a few large producers who controlled the national and, increasingly, the world market. In 1970 the top four U.S. firms produced 91 percent of the motor vehicles sold in the domestic market; the top four in tires produced 72 percent, in cigarettes 84 percent, and in detergents 70 percent. Despite laws restricting branch banking to a single state, in 1970 the four largest banks held 16 percent of the nation's banking assets; the top fifty banks held 48 percent.

Diversification was the most important corporate strategy in the postwar era. The classic corporation of the early twentieth century had produced a single line of products; its growth had depended on the vertical integration of related firms (see Chapter 18). After World War II the most successful firms invested heavily in research and development, produced new product lines, and moved into new markets. Because the largest corporations could afford research laboratories, they diversified more easily. CBS, for example, hired the Hungarian inventor Peter Goldmark, who perfected color television during the 1940s, long-playing records in the 1950s, and a video recording system in the 1960s. As the head of CBS Laboratories, Goldmark patented more than a hundred new devices.

Postwar managers also diversified through mergers and acquisitions, creating larger firms called *conglomerates*. By combining companies in unrelated industries, conglomerates offered protection from instability in any single market, making them more effective international competitors. International Telephone and Telegraph became a diversified conglomerate by acquiring Continental Baking, Sheraton Hotels, Avis Rent-a-Car, Levitt and Sons home builders, and Hartford Fire Insurance. Ling-Temco-Vought, another conglomerate, simultaneously produced steel, built ships, developed real estate, and brought cattle to market. These and other corporate acquisitions resulted in the nation's third great merger wave (the first two had taken place in the 1890s and the 1920s), which reached its peak in the 1960s. In 1947 the largest 200 corporations accounted for 30 percent of all value added by manufacturing, but in 1972 the largest 200, by then heavily diversified, accounted for 43 percent of the value added.

The Computer Revolution

The first modern computers—information-processing machines capable of storing and manipulating data according to specified programs—appeared in the 1940s. During World War II engineers and mathematicians at the University of Pennsylvania developed a general-purpose, programmable electronic calculator called ENIAC (Electronic Numerical Integrator and Computer), which could add 5,000 ten-digit decimal numbers in one second. It stood 8 feet tall, measured 80 feet long, and weighed 30 tons; it used 18,000 vacuum tubes for computations. When it performed complex mathematical computations, one scientist noted, ENIAC sounded "like a roomful of ladies knitting." Although ENIAC lacked a central memory and could not store a program, it was the bridge to the modern computer revolution.

Six computers were under construction by 1947, including UNIVAC (Universal Automatic Computer), the first commercial computer system. To the general public in the 1950 the word *UNIVAC* was synonymous with computers. UNIVAC was basically a data-processing system that could be tailored to an individual customer's needs. In 1951 the U.S. Census Bureau bought the first UNIVAC. Soon CBS-TV signed on, using a UNIVAC to predict the outcome of the 1952 presidential election. At 9 P.M., after only the East Coast polls had closed and with only 7 percent of the votes counted, UNIVAC predicted that Dwight D. Eisenhower would sweep the election with 438 electoral votes. CBS programmers and network executives, who had expected a closer election, got jittery and altered the program to give Eisenhower a far narrower margin. When the final tally gave him 442 electoral votes, only 4 votes off the original projection, the commentator Edward R. Murrow observed, "The trouble with machines is people."

Computers are essentially collections of switches, and programs tell the machine which switches to turn on and off. The puzzle that early computer scientists had to solve was how to increase the speed of this basic operation while lowering the cost. The first generation of computers needed vacuum tubes for computation power and used punched cards for writing programs and analyzing data. Computers such as ENIAC were room-sized machines, and programming them could take several days because the programmers had to manually set thousands of switches in the on or off position. The vacuum tubes were the weakest part of early computers; a burnout of

This early computer–data-processing center featured an IBM 704 computer.

just a few tubes could shut down the entire system. Furthermore, the tubes gave off enormous amounts of heat, necessitating noisy and cumbersome air-conditioning units wherever computers operated. After a critical signal relay stopped one early program, scientists finally located the problem—a dead moth trapped in the apparatus, the origin of the term *debugging*.

The 1948 invention of the transistor, a development that revolutionized computers and the whole field of electronics, made the second generation of computers possible. Transistors, like vacuum tubes, served as on-off switches but did not generate heat, burn out, or consume vast quantities of energy. They also were inexpensive to manufacture. The invention of integrated circuits (IC) in 1959 ushered in the third computer generation, characterized by greater sophistication in miniaturization, which meant that the number of transistors that could be installed on a silicon chip increased dramatically, with a corresponding increase in computational power. The fourth computer generation arrived in 1971 with the development of the microprocessor, which placed the entire central processing unit (CPU) of a computer on a single silicon chip (about the size of the letter "O" on this page).

Miniaturization progressed so rapidly that by the mid-1970s a $1 chip provided as much processing power as had the ENIAC of 30 years earlier. Computers and computer technology have become so much a part of modern life that it is hard to remember how recent the origins of this technological revolution are.

The development of giant corporations was also based on the penetration of foreign markets. American products were considered the best in the world and were widely sought after abroad. International strategies enabled American business to enter new regions when domestic markets became saturated or when American recessions cut into sales. During the 1950s U.S. exports nearly doubled, giving the nation a trade surplus of close to $5 billion in 1960.

In their effort to direct large organizations through the uncertainties of the postwar economy, managers placed more emphasis on planning. Increasingly, companies recruited top executives who had business-school training, the ability to manage information, and skills in corporate planning, marketing, and investment. To plan and coordinate effectively, corporate managers had to work more closely with their counterparts in other corporations, large banks, investment firms, law firms, economic research organizations, the federal government, and even the World Bank and the IMF.

The Changing World of Work

Since the late nineteenth century the proportion of Americans employed in the service sector—as professionals, clerical workers, civil servants, and other service workers—had grown steadily. Industrial mobilization during World War II temporarily halted this trend, but it resumed with a vengeance in the postwar era. By 1960 employees in the service sector accounted for more than 60 percent of the labor force. Soon the panelists on the quiz show "What's My Line?" learned to ask mystery guests, "Do you deal in services?"

The New Managerial Class. One of the fastest-growing groups consisted of salaried office workers. From 1947 to 1957 that occupational group increased by 61 percent, whereas the number of factory workers decreased by 4 percent. Growing corporate bureaucracies and increased access to a college education through the GI Bill helped expand the white-collar ranks. Young, predominantly male college graduates used their skills to advance more quickly and at an earlier age than was the case in previous generations.

Such advancement usually led them through the giant bureaucratic structures—big business, government agencies, universities, and the military—that have dominated life in the second half of the twentieth century. As young managers and professionals advanced in their careers, they changed jobs frequently. In the 1950s Atlas Van Lines estimated that corporate managers moved an average of fourteen times—once every two and a half years—during their careers. Perpetually mobile IBM managers joked that the company's initials stood for "I've Been Moved."

Climbing the corporate ladder rewarded men who could get along in a variety of situations. Corporate managers worked hard, sometimes with the assistance of the resident corporate psychologist, to be "well adjusted." Their philosophy was "Evade, don't confront." In *The Lonely Crowd* (1950) the sociologist David Reisman contrasted the stern, formal small business and professional types of earlier years with the corporate managers of the postwar world. He concluded that the new professionals were "other-directed," more concerned about their relations with associates than about adherence to fundamental principles. Critics worried that the conformity of marching off each day in gray flannel suits to work at interchangeable middle-management jobs in huge corporations was stifling men's creativity. The sociologist William Whyte painted a somber picture of "organization men" who left the home "spiritually as well as physically to take the vows of organization life."

Organization Men (and a Few Women)
What happened when the 5:57 discharged commuters in Park Forest, Illinois, a suburb of Chicago? This was the subject of William H. Whyte's *The Organization Man* (1956). Were these hordes of commuters thinking about their stressful day at the office or the martini waiting for them when they walked in the door of their suburban home?

The Trappings of Suburbia
With a ranch house, three cars in the driveway, and a rotary
lawn mower, this homeowner in Baton Rouge, Louisiana,
embodied the middle-class suburban life-style.

the former shipbuilding magnate Henry Kaiser moved
into housing construction in the postwar era, building
subdivisions in and around Los Angeles and San Francisco. Dozens of other developers followed suit, hastening the exodus from the farm and the central city.

Many families financed their homes with mortgages
from the Federal Housing Administration and the Veterans Administration. Before World War II, banks, primarily the savings and loan industry that served this
fairly stable market, usually demanded a 50 percent
down payment and granted no more than ten years to

pay back the balance. After the war the Federal Housing
Administration required only a 5 to 10 percent down
payment and gave homeowners up to thirty-year mortgages at the modest rate of 2 to 3 percent. The Veterans
Administration was even more lenient, requiring only a
token one dollar down payment from qualified veterans.
In 1955 those two agencies wrote 41 percent of all non-
farm mortgages. Such lending demonstrated the quiet
yet revolutionary way in which the federal government
was entering and influencing daily life.

The new suburban homes—and much of the savings and loan and Veterans Administration money—
were reserved almost exclusively for whites. Levittown
homeowners had to sign a covenant prohibiting occupation "by members of other than the Caucasian
Race"; Levitt did not sell houses directly to blacks until
1960. Even then the company carefully screened black
families and made sure that no two black families lived
next door to each other. Other communities adopted
similar covenants to exclude Jews or Asians. In *Shelley
v. Kraemer* (1948) the Supreme Court ruled that restrictive covenants were illegal, but the custom prevailed informally until the civil rights laws of the 1960s banned
private discrimination.

Even though suburbia was often portrayed as a homogeneous, even bland, environment, there were strong
cultural and class variations between suburbs. Older,
wealthy suburbs already occupied the most pleasant locations, including the hills north and west of Los Angeles, Chicago's North Shore, and the heights well to the
east of Cleveland's industrial Cuyahoga Flats. When
less affluent firefighters, plasterers, machine-tool makers, and sales clerks moved to the suburbs, they were far
more likely to move to a modest Levittown than to an
upper-middle-class suburb such as Winnetka, Illinois, or

The Suburban Boom
Hundreds of thousands of World War II
veterans took advantage of low-interest
loans under the G.I. Bill to purchase
new homes in suburban subdivisions
like this one in Los Angeles's San Fernando Valley. (Huntington Library, San
Marino, California, Whittington Collection)

Shaker Heights, Ohio. Blacks shut out of white suburbs established their own communities, such as Lincoln Heights outside Cincinnati, Robbins on the edge of Chicago, and Kinloch near St. Louis. In well-equipped living quarters at bargain prices, working-class and black families could share in the ultimate postwar suburban dream of giving "every kid an opportunity to grow up with grass stains on his pants."

Cars and Highways. Automobiles and highways were essential to this dramatic suburban growth. Suburbanites needed cars to get to work and to take their children to school and piano lessons. About 90 percent of suburban families owned cars, and 20 percent had more than one. In 1945 Americans owned 25 million cars; by 1965 the number had tripled to 75 million.

The car culture that emerged in the 1920s expanded dramatically during the 1950s, with cars becoming symbols of status and success. With gas plentiful and cheap at 15 cents a gallon, no one cared about fuel efficiency (8 miles to the gallon for the biggest gas guzzlers!). American cars became heavier and bigger, creating a disparity in size compared with Japanese or European models that still remains, despite the downsizing of American vehicles since the 1970s.

More cars required more highways, which were funded largely by the federal government. In 1947 Congress authorized the construction of 37,000 miles of highways; the National Interstate and Defense Highway Act of 1956 increased this commitment by another 42,500 miles. One of the largest civil engineering projects in world history, the new roads would be at least four lanes wide and would link the entire country in an integrated interstate system. Gas taxes and user fees for commercial vehicles provided the funding. Congressional supporters justified highway building on the grounds of civil defense at a time of growing anxiety about the Soviet nuclear threat (highways ostensibly would be used as evacuation routes). But its real purpose was to provide a transportation infrastructure for the diffuse pattern of urban and suburban development that characterized the postwar era.

The interstate system changed both the cities and the countryside. It rerouted traffic through rural areas, by-passing old main roads such as Route 1 on the eastern seaboard and the cross-country Route 66, and created new communities of gas stations, fast-food outlets, and motels at anonymous cloverleaf exchanges. In urban areas new highways cut wide swaths through old neighborhoods. Cities were soon plagued by the problems that cars brought to modern life: air pollution and traffic jams. Critics now complained about "autosclerosis," a hardening of the urban arteries.

The federally constructed highways also siphoned funding away from mass transit. Los Angeles, a city now largely dependent on freeways, had a viable mass transit system as late as the 1940s. The Highway Trust Fund set up in 1956 specifically prohibited the use of the fees it collected to promote urban mass transit. By 1960 two-thirds of Americans drove to work each day. The percentage was even higher—between 80 and 95 percent—in Los Angeles, Albuquerque, and Phoenix.

Highway construction had far-reaching effects on patterns of consumption and shopping. Instead of taking a train into the city or walking to a corner grocery store, people hopped into their cars and drove to suburban shopping malls and supermarkets. Although the first mall had appeared in the 1920s, there were only 8 in 1945; by 1960 the number had mushroomed to almost 4,000. When a 110-store complex at Roosevelt Field on suburban Long Island opened in 1956, it was conveniently situated at an expressway exit and had parking for 11,000 cars. Downtown retail areas and department stores soon declined.

Highways and suburbs also lured corporate business and manufacturing away from the cities. In the early 1950s Stanford University in Palo Alto, California, built one of the nation's first *industrial parks*, a suburban, campuslike facility for light manufacturing. Exploiting its ties with university researchers, Stanford Industrial Park attracted cold war defense contractors such as General Electric, Lockheed, and Hewlett-Packard. Those firms soon formed the nucleus of an electronic and high-tech region known as Silicon Valley. On the East Coast, a similar high-tech boom occurred outside Boston along Route 128, led by firms such as Polaroid and the Digital Equipment and Wang computer manufacturers. In the Midwest the number of factories in suburban Chicago doubled between 1947 and 1954, and suburban Detroit had a 220 percent increase.

The U.S. government's financing of highways and home building after World War II helped fuel a suburban explosion that was unique to North America. In war-ravaged European cities postwar housing construction was centered in high-density city neighborhoods or along mass transit lines. Not until the 1960s and 1970s would Europeans experiment with low-density suburban housing, and their central cities never declined as precipitously as American cities did.

State and Local Government. The burgeoning population of metropolitan areas posed new challenges for state and local governments. Those government bureaucracies experienced rapid growth in the postwar period, requiring ever larger budgets (see Figure 29.4). State and local expenditures totaled $14 billion in 1946; in 1970 they rose to almost $150 billion. Employment climbed correspondingly. In 1970 roughly one in seven Americans in the labor force worked for a government bureaucracy, another example of the growth of the state.

West Side Story

In 1961 United Artists released the movie version of Leonard Bernstein's 1957 Broadway hit, *West Side Story*. The plot recast Shakespeare's *Romeo and Juliet* in a Puerto Rican neighborhood on New York's West Side in the 1950s. Confrontations between members of youth gangs and adult figures of authority, as pictured here in a still from the movie, were set to highly stylized song and dance routines.

came after 1965 with the establishment of a Havana-to-Miami airlift under an agreement between the Johnson administration and the Castro regime. The Cuban refugee community grew so quickly that it turned Miami into a cosmopolitan, bilingual city almost overnight. Unlike most new migrants to urban America, Miami's Cubans quickly prospered, in large part because they had arrived with more resources. They differed from most other Latino immigrants in that they were predominantly middle class and politically conservative.

Internal Migration. Internal migration also brought large numbers of people to the cities, especially African-Americans, continuing a trend that had begun during World War I (see Chapter 23). Black migration was hastened by the transformation of southern agriculture. New Deal agricultural policies and the development of synthetic fibers such as rayon and Dacron after World War II caused cotton acreage in the South to decline from 43 million acres in 1929 to less than 15 million in 1959. In addition, the ongoing mechanization of agriculture reduced the demand for farm labor. The mechanical cotton picker, introduced in 1944, further eroded the sharecropper system; it could pick 1,000 pounds an hour compared with the 20 pounds picked by an experienced hand. As a result of these changes, the southern farm population fell from 16.2 million in 1930 to 5.9 million in 1960. Although both whites and blacks left the land, the starkest decline was among black farmers. By 1990 there would be only 69,000 black farmers in the entire nation, just 1.5 percent of the country's farmers.

Where did they go? Some of the migrants settled in southern cities, where they obtained industrial jobs. White southerners from Appalachia moved north to

"hillbilly" ghettos such as Cincinnati's Over the Rhine neighborhood and Chicago's Uptown. In the most dramatic population shift as many as 3 million blacks headed to Chicago, New York, Washington, Detroit, Los Angeles, and other cities between 1940 and 1960. Certain sections of Chicago seemed like the Mississippi Delta transplanted, so pervasive were the migrants. By 1960 about half the nation's black population was living outside the South, compared with only 23 percent before World War II.

Indian Relocation. In western cities, an influx of native Americans also contributed to the rise in the nonwhite urban population. Seeking to end federal involvement in Indian affairs, Congress passed a resolution in 1953 authorizing a program to terminate the legal standing of native tribes and move their members off reservations. The program reflected a cold war preoccupation with conformity and assimilation and enjoyed strong support from mining, timber, and agricultual interests that wanted to open those lands for private development. The Bureau of Indian Affairs encouraged voluntary migration to urban areas by subsidizing moving costs and establishing relocation centers in San Francisco, Denver, Chicago, and other cities. The relocation program proved problematic, as many Indians found it difficult to adjust to an urban environment and culture. Although the policy of forced termination was halted in 1958, some 60,000 Indians had moved to the cities by 1960. Despite the program's stated goal of assimilation, most native American migrants settled together in poor urban neighborhoods alongside other nonwhite groups.

American cities thus saw their nonwhite populations swell at the same time that whites were flocking to the suburbs. From 1950 to 1960 the nation's twelve

Claude Brown

Harlem: Dream and Reality

Claude Brown's *Manchild in the Promised Land* (1965) graphically described the conditions that awaited blacks when they journeyed to the "promised land" of Harlem in the postwar period. Brown dedicated the book to Eleanor Roosevelt, a benefactor of the Wiltwyck School for Boys, which helped troubled youths like Claude Brown break out of the ghetto.

Everybody I knew in Harlem seemed to have some kind of dream. I didn't have any dreams, not really. I didn't have any dreams for hitting the number. I didn't have any dreams for getting a big car or a fine wardrobe. I bought expensive clothes because it was a fad. It was the thing to do, just to show that you had money. I wanted to be a part of what was going on, and this was what was going on.

I didn't have any dreams of becoming anything. All I knew for certain was that I had my fears. I suppose just about everybody else knew the same thing. They had their dreams, though, and I guess that's what they had over me. As time went by, I was sorry for the people whose dreams were never realized.

When Butch was alive, sometimes I would go uptown to see him. He'd be sick. He'd be really messed up. I'd give him some drugs, and then he'd be more messed up than before. He wouldn't be sick, but I couldn't talk to him, I couldn't reach him. He'd be just sitting on a stoop nodding. Sometimes he'd be slobbering over himself.

I used to remember Butch's dream. Around 1950, he used to dream of becoming the best thief in Harlem. It wasn't a big dream. To him, it was a big dream, but I don't suppose too many people would have seen it as that. Still, I felt sorry for him because it was his dream. I suppose the first time he put the spike in his arm every dream he'd ever had was thrown out the window. Sometimes I wanted to shout at him or snatch him by the throat and say, "Butch, what about your dream?" But there were so many dreams that were lost for a little bit of duji [heroin]. . . .

I used to feel that I belonged on the Harlem streets and that, regardless of what I did, nobody had any business to take me off the streets.

I remember when I ran away from shelters, places that they sent me to, here in the city. I never ran away with the thought in mind of coming home. I always ran away to get back to the streets. I always thought of Harlem as home, but I never thought of Harlem as being in the house. To me, home was the streets. I suppose there were many people who felt that. If home was so miserable, the street was the place to be. I wonder if mine was really so miserable, or if it was that there was so much happening out in the street that it made home seem such a dull and dismal place.

When I was very young—about five years old, maybe younger—I would always be sitting out on the stoop. I remember Mama telling me and Carole to sit on the stoop and not to move away from in front of the door. Even when it was time to go up and Carole would be pulling on me to come upstairs and eat, I never wanted to go, because there was so much out there in that street.

You might see somebody get cut or killed. I could go out in the street for an afternoon, and I would see so much that, when I came in the house, I'd be talking and talking for what seemed like hours. Dad would say, "Boy, why don't you stop that lyin'? You know you didn't see all that. You know you didn't see nobody do that." But I knew I had.

Source: Claude Brown, *Manchild in the Promised Land* (New York: Macmillan, 1965), 427–429.

---

largest cities lost 3.6 million whites while gaining 4.5 million nonwhites. This trend continued in the 1960s as urban decay and racial fears accelerated white flight to the suburbs.

Urban Neighborhoods, Urban Poverty

By the time that blacks, native Americans, and Latinos moved into the inner cities, urban America was in poor shape. Housing continued to be a crucial problem. City planners, politicians, and real-estate developers responded to that dilemma with *urban renewal* programs, razing blighted city neighborhoods to make way for modern construction projects. Local residents were rarely consulted about whether they wanted their neighborhoods "renewed." Urban renewal often produced grim high-rise housing projects that destroyed feelings of neighborhood pride and created anonymous open areas that were vulnerable to crime. Between 1949 and 1967 urban renewal demolished almost 400,000 buildings and displaced 1.4 million people.

Urban renewal projects often benefited the wealthy at the expense of the poor. Many downtown "revitalization" projects replaced established racial-ethnic neighborhoods with expensive rental housing or office buildings where suburban commuters worked. Boston's West End, a poor but flourishing Italian community, was

The Dreary Deadlock of Public Housing

As federal funding for public housing dwindled in the early 1950s, some local housing authorities economized by building acres of grim high-rise housing projects that destroyed old neighborhoods and created vacant spaces that proved vulnerable to street crime.

razed by a private developer between 1958 and 1960 to build Charles River Park, an apartment complex whose rents were far too steep for the old residents. In San Francisco some 4,000 residents of the Western Addition, a predominantly black neighborhood, were displaced under an urban renewal program that built luxury housing, a shopping center, and an express boulevard. In both cities residents were forced into less desirable parts of the city, cut off from the vitality of their former neighborhoods. The 575,000 units of public housing built nationwide by 1964 came nowhere close to satisfying the need for affordable urban housing.

Postwar cities were increasingly becoming a place of last resort for the nation's poor. Unlike earlier immigrants, for whom cities were gateways to social and economic betterment, inner-city residents in the postwar period faced diminishing hopes for improvement (see American Voices, page 909). Lured by the promise of plentiful jobs, migrants found that many of those opportunities had relocated to the suburban fringe. Steady employment was out of reach for those who needed it most.

The poor were also trapped in the cities because of racism. Migrants to the city, especially blacks, faced racial hostility and institutional barriers to mobility. Two separate Americas were emerging: a white society in suburbs and peripheral areas, and an inner city populated by blacks, Latinos, and other disadvantaged groups.

Black Activism in the South

In the South black Americans faced not only urban poverty but legal segregation as well. In most southern states in the 1950s it was illegal for whites and blacks to eat in the same rooms in restaurants and luncheonettes,

use the same waiting rooms and toilet facilities at bus and train stations, or ride in the same taxis. All forms of public transportation were rigidly segregated by custom or by law. Even drinking fountains were labeled "White" and "Colored."

Beginning with World War II, the National Association for the Advancement of Colored People (NAACP) redoubled its efforts to combat segregation (see Chapter 27). Throughout the 1940s NAACP lawyers Thurgood Marshall and William Hastie litigated a series of test cases challenging segregation in housing, transportation, and other areas.

Brown v. Board of Education. In 1954 the Supreme Court handed down one of its most far-reaching decisions in a group of challenges to school segregation, consolidated as *Brown v. Board of Education of Topeka, Kansas.* The NAACP had filed the Topeka case on behalf of Linda Brown, a black student who attended a segregated school several miles from her home rather than the nearby white elementary school. The NAACP's chief counsel, Thurgood Marshall, argued that the legal segregation mandated by the Topeka Board of Education was inherently unconstitutional because it stigmatized an entire race and thereby denied it the "equal protection of the laws" guaranteed by the Fourteenth Amendment. In a unanimous decision announced on May 17, 1954, the Supreme Court agreed, overturning the "separate but equal" doctrine of *Plessy v. Ferguson* (see Chapter 19). Speaking for the Court, Chief Justice Earl Warren ruled:

> To separate Negro children . . . solely because of their race generates a feeling of inferiority as to their status in the community that may affect their hearts and minds in a way unlikely ever to be undone. . . . We

conclude that in the field of public education the doctrine of "separate but equal" has no place. Separate educational facilities are inherently unequal. . . . Any language in *Plessy v. Ferguson* contrary to these findings is rejected.

In response to NAACP suits over the next several years, the Supreme Court used the *Brown* precedent to overturn segregation in city parks, public beaches and golf courses, all forms of interstate and intrastate transportation, and public housing. Meanwhile, progress in desegregating schools was frustratingly slow. In a 1955 decision implementing the Topeka decision known as *Brown II*, the Court declared simply that integration should proceed "with all deliberate speed." Many critics would later note that the deliberation was far more evident than the speed.

When it became clear that the Court was not going to back down on civil rights, white resistance solidified. In 1956, 101 members of Congress signed a Southern Manifesto denouncing the *Brown* decision as "a clear abuse of judicial power" and encouraging their constituents to defy it. In that year 500,000 southerners joined White Citizens' Councils dedicated to blocking school integration and other civil rights measures. Some whites revived the old tactics of violence and intimidation, swelling the ranks of the Ku Klux Klan to levels not seen since the 1920s.

So far Eisenhower had accepted the *Brown* decision as the law of the land but had not committed federal power to enforcing it. A crisis in Little Rock, Arkansas, finally forced him to intervene, although reluctantly, on the side of desegregation. In September 1957 nine black students attempted to enroll at the all-white Central High School after the local school board won a court order to implement a desegregation plan. Governor Orval Faubus called out the National Guard to bar them, despite the court order. Then the mob took over. Every day a white crowd taunted the poised but obviously terrified black students with chants such as "Go back to the jungle." As the vicious scenes were replayed on television night after night, Eisenhower reluctantly decided to act. He sent 1,000 federal troops to Little Rock and nationalized 10,000 members of the Arkansas National Guard, ordering them to protect the students. Eisenhower thus became the first president since Reconstruction to use federal troops to enforce the rights of blacks.

The *Brown* decision had shown that the NAACP's strategy of judicial challenge could bring fundamental change, but the magnitude of white resistance to integration had also made it clear that winning in court was not enough. A new strategy was needed to challenge the pervasive racism and segregation that persisted in practice if not in law. Sparked by one tiny but monumental act of defiance, southern black leaders embraced nonviolent protest.

Integration at Little Rock
Angry crowds taunted the nine black students who tried to register in 1957 at the previously all-white Central High School in Little Rock, Arkansas, with chants such as "Two-four-six-eight, we ain't gonna integrate." The court-ordered integration proceeded only after President Eisenhower reluctantly nationalized the Arkansas National Guard.

The Montgomery Bus Boycott. On December 1, 1955, Rosa Parks, a seamstress and a member of the NAACP in Montgomery, Alabama, refused to give up her seat on a city bus to a white man. She was promptly arrested and charged with violating a local segregation ordinance. "I felt it was just something I had to do," Parks stated. Although Parks was hardly the first black southerner to challenge Jim Crow laws, her upstanding social reputation and political connections soon made her case a cause célèbre in the black community.

As the local black community met to discuss the proper response, it turned to the Reverend Martin Luther King, Jr., who had become the pastor at Montgomery's Dexter Street Baptist Church the year before. The son of a prominent black minister in Atlanta, King had received a B.A. from Morehouse College and a Ph.D. in theology from Boston University. King later embraced the teachings of Mahatma Gandhi, who had organized the brilliant campaigns of passive resistance that had led to India's independence from Britain in 1947. After Parks's arrest, King endorsed a plan by a local black women's organization to boycott Montgomery's bus system until it was integrated.

For the next 381 days a united black community formed car pools or walked to work. The bus company neared bankruptcy, and downtown stores complained about the loss of business. But not until the Supreme Court ruled in November 1956 that bus segregation was unconstitutional did the city of Montgomery finally comply. "My feets is tired, but my soul is rested," said one woman boycotter.

The Montgomery bus boycott catapulted King to national prominence. In 1957, with the Reverend Ralph Abernathy and other southern black clergy, he founded the Southern Christian Leadership Conference (SCLC), based in Atlanta. The black church had long been the center of African-American social and cultural life. Now it lent its moral and organizational strength, as well as the voices of its most inspirational preachers, to the civil rights movement. Black churchwomen were one of the movement's strongest constituencies, transferring the skills that they had honed through years of church work to the fight for racial change. The SCLC joined the NAACP as one of the main advocacy groups for racial justice. Even though these groups achieved only limited victories in the 1950s, they laid the organizational groundwork for the dynamic civil rights movement that would emerge in the 1960s.

American Society during the Baby Boom

While black southerners confronted racial prejudice and violence, the lives of most white Americans during those years were more sedate. For much of the white middle class, the postwar era was a period of tranquillity as Americans turned inward to home and family. Couples flocked to the new suburban developments, where they had more children per family than at any time since 1920. They raised their families in a climate of affluence that spawned a pervasive culture of consumption and conformity.

Consumer Culture

As we have seen, prosperity and affluence were a reality for many Americans in the postwar years. In some respects the consumer culture of the 1950s seemed like a return to the 1920s—an overabundance of new gadgets and appliances, the expansion of consumer credit and advertising, more leisure time, the growing importance of the automobile, and the development of new types of mass media—yet there was a significant difference. The postwar economy was far better balanced than that of the 1920s; there was no depressed agricultural sector to detract from the general prosperity. By the 1950s consumption had become a hallmark of middle-class culture. Because of rising incomes, even blue-collar families had discretionary income to spend on consumer goods.

As in the 1920s, though, prosperity was helped along by a dramatic increase in consumer credit, which enabled families to stretch their incomes. Between 1946 and 1958 short-term consumer credit rose from $8.4

billion to almost $45 billion, much of it in the form of car loans. The Diners Club credit card, introduced in 1950 and followed by the American Express card and Bank Americard in 1959, was initially geared toward the business traveler. But by the 1970s the ubiquitous plastic credit cards had revolutionized personal and family finances.

Advertising. With the greater availability of credit, product makers sought to stimulate consumer demand through more aggressive advertising. In 1951 businesses spent more on advertising ($6.5 billion) than taxpayers did on primary and secondary education ($5 billion); advertising expenditures topped $10 billion in 1960. The 1950s gave Americans the Marlboro man; M&M's that melt in your mouth, not in your hand; the Hathaway eye patch; Wonder Bread to build strong bodies in twelve ways; and the "does she or doesn't she?" Clairol woman. Motivational research delved into the subconscious to suggest how the messages should be pitched.

Landmark for Hungry Americans
Conveniently located on major highways and in shopping centers, Howard Johnson's Motor Lodges and Restaurants (colloquially referred to as HoJos) were instantly recognizable by their bright orange roofs. Like the McDonald's Golden Arches, those roofs became familiar roadside beacons for travelers and suburbanites alike.

The ads of the period reflected an uncritical view of American life that suggested falsely that all Americans were white and middle class, all women were homemakers, and all families were nuclear and intact.

Automobiles continued to be the most heavily advertised item in the 1950s, but advertising also promoted a variety of new consumer appliances to fill the suburban home. Many appliances had been unavailable during the war; others were new to the postwar market. In 1946 automatic washing machines replaced the old machines with hand-cranked wringers, and electric dryers also came on the market that year. In 1955, 1.2 million dryers were sold, twice the 1953 total, and commercial laundries across the country struggled to stay in business. Another new item on the market was the home freezer, which enabled families to eat seasonal foods, such as fruits and vegetables, all year and encouraged the dramatic growth of the frozen-food industry. Partly because of the purchase of electrical gadgets for the home, consumer use of electricity doubled during the 1950s.

Leisure Time. Consumers had more free time in which to spend their money than ever before. In 1960 the average worker put in a five-day week, with eight paid holidays a year (double the 1946 standard) plus a paid two-week vacation. The travel industry grew rapidly during the 1950s, with Americans devoting a seventh of the GNP to spending on leisure and entertainment. Americans took to the interstate highway system by the millions, encouraging the dramatic growth of motel chains, roadside restaurants, and fast-food eateries. (The first McDonald's restaurant opened in 1954 in San Bernardino, California; the Holiday Inn motel chain started in Memphis in 1952.) Among the most popular destinations were national and state parks and Disneyland, which opened in Anaheim, California, in 1955. Aided by the strong U.S. dollar and the introduction of jet air travel in 1958, families flooded Europe each summer, earning the unflattering epithet of "ugly Americans" because they expected things to be just like home.

Television

Americans also engaged in new leisure activities at home, television watching being the most popular. TV's leap to cultural prominence was swift and overpowering. There were only ten broadcasting stations in the country and a meager 7,000 sets in American homes in 1947. But in 1948 the CBS and NBC radio networks began offering regular programming on television. Just two years later Americans had purchased 7.3 million TV sets. By 1960, 87 percent of American families had at least one television set.

Television developed as a government-controlled or subsidized service in other countries, but in the United States it emerged as private enterprise geared toward entertainment. Although stations were licensed by the Federal Communications Commission after 1941, television, like radio, depended entirely on advertising and corporate sponsorship for profits. Soon television supplanted radio as the chief diffuser of popular culture. Movies, too, lost the cultural predominance they had enjoyed from the 1920s through the 1940s. Movie attendance shrank throughout the postwar period, and studios increasingly relied on overseas distribution of American films to earn a profit.

At first television brought people together at a neighbor's home or perhaps in a local tavern to watch the World Series or a political convention, but soon it had the opposite effect, isolating and atomizing leisure in the private home. Television fostered a mass national culture far more completely than radio had in the 1920s. Its national network programming promoted homogeneity and reduced regional and ethnic differences (the first live nationwide broadcast, the signing of the peace treaty ending the American military occupation of Japan, occurred in 1951). Viewers had only three or four channels to choose from; public television did not begin until 1967, and cable was a phenomenon of the 1980s.

Television encouraged the consumerism and advertising that have characterized mass culture since the 1920s. As in the golden era of radio in the 1920s and 1930s, corporations produced and sponsored major television shows such as the "Texaco Star Theater" with Milton Berle, the "Camel News Caravan" with John Cameron Swayze, and the "General Electric Theater" hosted by Ronald Reagan. New items entered the home, such as frozen TV dinners of turkey, peas, and mashed potatoes, first introduced in 1954. Now a family could eat a meal in front of the television without having to talk. *TV Guide*, founded in television's breakthrough year of 1948, became the most successful new periodical of the 1950s. Television even affected city services. In 1954 the Toledo water commissioner wondered why water consumption rose dramatically during certain three-minute periods. The answer? All across Toledo, TV watchers flushed their toilets during commercials.

What Americans saw on television, besides the omnipresent commercials, was an overwhelmingly white, Anglo-Saxon world of nuclear families, suburban homes, and middle-class life. A typical show was "Father Knows Best," starring Robert Young and Jane Wyatt. Father left home each morning wearing a suit and carrying a briefcase. Mother was a full-time housewife, always available to and actively interested in her three children but also prone to stereotypical feminine behavior such as bad driving and bursting into tears. The children engaged in amusing antics and harmless rebellion, but family conflicts were invariably resolved. Shows such as "The Honeymooners," starring Jackie Gleason as a Brooklyn bus

"The Honeymooners"
Sewer worker Ed Norton (left, played by Art Carney) and bus
driver Ralph Kramden (Jackie Gleason) joust in an episode
from the popular television series "The Honeymooners."
When Alice Kramden (played by Audrey Meadows) tried to
get a word in edgewise, Ralph's reply was likely to be, "One
of these days, Alice, one of these days, pow! Right in the
kisser!"

driver, and "Life of Reilly," a situation comedy featuring
a California aircraft worker, were rare in their treatment
of working-class lives. Nonwhite characters appeared
mainly as servants, such as Jack Benny's Rochester.

Probably the most popular situation comedy of the
1950s was "I Love Lucy," which revolved around the
adventures of a wacky housewife and her Cuban-born
bandleader husband, portrayed by Lucille Ball and Desi
Arnaz. Because they were married in real life as well as
on television, the show even incorporated Lucy's pregnancy into the story line. Twice as many Americans—
44 million, the figure courtesy of the new sampling firm
of A. C. Nielsen—watched the 1956 show where Lucy
had her baby as watched the inauguration of President
Dwight Eisenhower the next day. The couple later divorced, but off screen.

The types of television programs developed in the
1950s built on older entertainment genres but also pioneered new ones. Taking over a popular radio and movie
category, television offered some thirty westerns by 1959,
including "Gunsmoke," "Wagon Train," and "Bonanza,"
the first color show. National television coverage made
professional sports big-time entertainment and big business—far exceeding the potential of radio. Programming
geared to children, such as Walt Disney's "Mickey
Mouse Club," "Howdy Doody," and "Captain Kanga-

roo," created the first generation of children to grow up
glued to the tube. The appeal of popular quiz shows such
as "Twenty-One" and "The $64,000 Question" was not
diminished even when it was revealed in 1959 that con-
testants had received the questions in advance. Although
the new medium did offer some serious programming,
notably live theater and documentaries, Federal Communications Commissioner Newton Minow concluded in
1963 that television was "a vast wasteland." Its reassuring images of family life and postwar society, however,
dovetailed with the social expectations of many American families.

The Baby Boom

The dislocations of the depression and war years made
both men and women yearn for material and psychological security and a return to traditional values. A
popular 1945 song was called "Gotta Make Up for Lost
Time," and Americans did just that. The postwar generation approached life with an optimism and confidence
notably absent from the depression generation of the
1930s. The GI Bill and other federal programs aided
their quest for unprecedented levels of material security,
as did the general prosperity of the postwar era. As
usual, those options were far more available to the
white middle class than to minorities.

Such individual life choices were taking place
against the backdrop of the Cold War. The historian
Elaine Tyler May used the formulation "cold war, warm
hearth" to capture how home and family seemed to
offer a secure, private retreat from the Cold War and
the atomic age. As Richard Nixon argued in the kitchen
debate with Nikita Khrushchev, stable suburban families would provide a bulwark against the Soviet threat.

Two things were noteworthy about the men and
women who formed families between 1940 and 1960.
First, their marriages were remarkably stable. Not until
the mid-1960s did the divorce rate begin to rise sharply.
Second, they were intent on having children. Everyone
expected to have two or more children—it was part of
adulthood, almost a citizen's responsibility. After a century and a half of declining family size, the birth rate
shot up: more babies were born between 1948 and
1953 than were born in the previous thirty years (see
Figure 29.5). As a result, the American population rose
dramatically from 140 million in 1945 to 179 million in
1960 and to 203 million in 1970.

There are several reasons for this twenty-year upsurge that demographers call the *baby boom*. Because a
sustained rise in the birth rate did not occur in all the
countries affected by World War II, it was not simply a
response to the losses of war. More important was the
drop in the marriage age, a trend that had begun during
the war. The average age at marriage fell to twenty-two

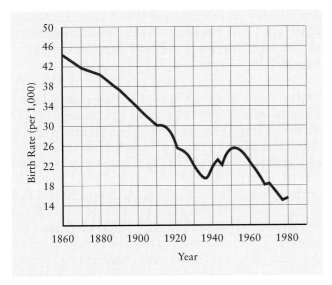

FIGURE 29.5

The Declining American Birth Rate, 1860–1980
When birth rates are viewed over more than a century, the postwar baby boom was clearly an aberration.

for men and twenty for women; in 1951 a third of all women were married by age nineteen. The drop in the marriage age resulted in a surge of young married couples who produced a bumper crop of children.

Even though younger couples were having babies earlier, they were not necessarily having huge numbers of children. Women who came of age in the 1930s had an average of 2.4 children; their counterparts in the 1950s averaged 3.2 children. What made the baby boom happen was that everyone was having children at the same time. This explosion in fertility peaked in 1957 and remained at a high level until the early 1960s. Since the 1960s the birth rate has generally declined, returning to earlier long-term patterns. The postwar baby boom was thus a departure from the norm.

Increased Life Expectancy. A declining death rate also contributed to population growth. Life expectancy at birth had improved steadily over the first half of the twentieth century, from forty-seven years in 1900 to sixty-three years in 1940. Continued improvements in diet, public health, and medical practices further lengthened the life span to seventy-one years in 1970. So did "miracle drugs" such as penicillin (introduced in 1943), streptomycin (1945), and cortisone (1946). When Dr. Jonas Salk perfected a polio vaccine in 1954, he became a national hero. The free distribution of Salk's vaccine in the nation's schools, followed in 1961 by Dr. Albert Sabin's oral polio vaccine, demonstrated the potential of government-sponsored public health programs. The conquest of polio made the children of the 1950s one of the healthiest generations ever.

"Scientific" Child-Rearing. To rear all those baby-boom children and keep them healthy, middle-class parents increasingly relied on the advice of experts. Dr. Benjamin Spock's best-selling *Baby and Child Care* sold a million copies a year after its publication in 1946. Spock urged mothers to abandon the rigid feeding and baby care schedules of an earlier generation. New mothers found Spock's commonsense approach liberating, but it did not totally soothe their insecurities. If mothers were too protective of their children, Spock and others argued, they might hamper their adjustment to a normal adult life. Mothers who wanted to work outside the home felt guilty because Spock recommended that they be constantly available to respond to their children's needs.

The baby boom had a broad and immediate impact on American society. The consumer needs of all those babies fueled the economy as families bought food, diapers, toys, and clothing for their expanding broods. Family spending on consumer goods joined federal expenditures on national security in fueling the unparalleled prosperity and economic growth of the 1950s and 1960s.

The baby boom also prompted a major expansion of the nation's educational system. The new middle class, America's first college-educated generation, placed a high value on education. Suburban parents approved 90 percent of proposed school bond issues during the 1950s. By 1970 school expenditures accounted for 7.2 percent of the gross national product, double the 1950 level.

Polio Pioneers
These Provo, Utah, children each received a "Polio Pioneer" souvenir button for participating in the trial of the Salk vaccine in 1954. Dr. Jonas Salk's announcement the next year that the vaccine was safe and effective made him a national hero.

The postwar baby boom would have a continuing impact on America for many decades. In the 1960s the baby-boom generation swelled college enrollments and, not coincidentally, the ranks of student protesters. By the 1970s, when the baby-boom generation entered the workplace, it had to compete for a limited number of jobs in what had become a stagnant economy. The delayed marriages and later childbearing of the career-oriented baby boomers temporarily caused the birth rate to rise again in the 1980s. And in the 1990s the aging of that group prompted widespread concerns about the future viability of old-age assistance programs such as Social Security and Medicare. The decisions made by many couples in the immediate postwar period to have large families will continue to affect American life well into the twenty-first century.

Contradictions in Women's Lives

"The suburban housewife was the dream image of the young American woman," the feminist Betty Friedan has said of the 1950s. "She was healthy, beautiful, educated, concerned only about her husband, her children, and her home." Friedan gave up a psychology fellowship and a career as a journalist to marry, move to the suburbs, and raise three children. "Determined that I

Home Life: One Reality
This young mother in New Rochelle, a suburb of New York City, was photographed in 1955. Her frenzied situation hints at why 24,000 American women responded to a 1960 *Redbook* magazine article entitled "Why Young Mothers Feel Trapped."

find the feminine fulfillment that eluded my mother . . . I lived the life of a suburban housewife that was everyone's dream at the time," she said (see American Voices, page 917).

The Feminine Mystique. The 1950s were characterized by a pervasive, indeed pernicious, insistence that a woman's place was in the home. There was nothing new about this idea. What Betty Friedan called the "feminine mystique" of the 1950s—that "the highest value and the only commitment for women is the fulfillment of their own femininity"—bore remarkable similarities to the nineteenth-century's cult of true womanhood. But women's lives had changed dramatically since the nineteenth century because of increased access to education and jobs, a declining birth rate, and the greater availability of consumer goods and services. It was much harder to persuade women to stay at home in the 1950s than it had been in the 1850s. In fact, the shrillness with which the message of domesticity was proclaimed represented a reaction to how far women had already strayed from total identification with the home.

The updated version of the cult of domesticity drew on new elements of twentieth-century science and culture, even Freudian psychology, to give it more force. Psychologists equated motherhood with "normal" female sex role identification and berated mothers who worked outside the home. Television, popular music, films, and advertising reinforced that notion by depicting career women as social and sexual misfits. The postwar consumer culture also emphasized women's domestic role as purchasing agent for home and family. "Love is said in many ways," ran an ad for toilet paper. Another asked, "Can a woman ever feel right cooking on a dirty range?"

Although the feminine mystique held cultural sway in the postwar period, not all housewives were as unhappy or as neurotic as Friedan later implied in her 1963 best seller, *The Feminine Mystique*. Many working-class women embraced their new roles as housewives; unlike their mothers and unmarried sisters, they were not compelled to take low-paid employment outside the home. Middle-class wives found constructive outlets for their energy in groups such as the League of Women Voters, the PTA, and the Junior League. As in earlier periods, some women used the rhetoric of domesticity and maternalism to justify political activism, which in this period involved issues of community improvement, racial integration, and nuclear disarmament.

More fundamentally, not all American families could, or did, live by the norms of suburban domesticity. Such ideals were out of reach or totally irrelevant to many racial minorities, inner-city residents, recent immigrants, rural Americans, and homosexuals. Once again there was a significant gap between popular culture and the reality of American lives.

Joy Wilner

A Fifties Housewife

Like millions of middle-class women in the 1950s, Joy Wilner married an ambitious young professional and had children in quick succession. In this passage she recounts the joys and frustrations of her early years of marriage and motherhood and her struggle to accommodate herself to what Betty Friedan has termed the *feminine mystique*.

I felt totally fulfilled, totally happy. We were the perfect couple—Ted was supportive of me and I was supportive of him and we never argued. Well, we didn't know how. We'd had no experience with conflict. Everything was fine. I had my next child sixteen months after the first. The second child was neither exactly planned nor unplanned. I didn't really intend to get pregnant again, but on the other hand, we weren't using birth control because, after all, we already had *one*. . . .

After the second baby, that was the first time I can remember conflict, feelings of being trapped, wondering what I was doing with my life. These weren't very distinct feelings, not like I wonder if this is the right man for me. Just uncomfortable feelings. At some point I expressed some of these feelings, in a very tentative way, to Ted and he said, "Well, if you feel that way, maybe we should get a divorce." I was terrified. The idea of divorce was inconceivable. I never mentioned the subject again.

At the same time, I got such pleasure, real physiological pleasure, from my children—from playing with them, feeding them, watching them develop. Then we moved and Ted went into general practice, and at about the same time I had another child. I became his secretary, his nurse, and I was also handling the children, keeping them out of his hair. And of course, we were also establishing our identity as the doctor and his wife, so there was a lot of socializing. It was a busy time.

What amazes me now is that it never occurred to me not to do this. His career was just my life. There came a time when I felt I didn't have the strength for all this and I started breaking down. I can remember going into the shower and screaming—in the shower so that no one could hear me. Even then I didn't have conscious thoughts of "I hate this life"—I didn't think there was anything objectively wrong with the way I was living, just that I couldn't take it any more.

Source: Brett Harvey, ed., *The Fifties: An Oral History* (New York: HarperCollins, 1993), 103–104.

Women at Work. Another contradictory aspect of postwar culture was that at the height of the feminine mystique more than one-third of American women held jobs outside the home. As the service sector expanded, there was a steady demand for workers in fields traditionally filled by women. The economist Eli Ginzberg called the dramatic rise in the number and kind of women who worked for pay outside the home "the single most outstanding phenomenon of our century."

The increase in the number of working women coincided with another change of equal significance—the dramatic rise in the number of older, married middle-class women who took jobs. At the turn of the century the typical female worker was a young recent immigrant who worked only until she married. By mid-century the typical woman worker was in her forties, married, and had children in school. In 1940 only 15 percent of wives worked; that proportion had doubled by 1960 and reached 40 percent by 1970.

Many women entered the paid labor force to supplement the family income and keep pace with rising standards of living. The wages that many men earned even in the prosperous 1950s and 1960s could not pay for all the necessities of middle-class life: cars, houses, vacations, and a college education for the children. Poorer households needed more than one wage earner just to get by.

How could the society of the 1950s so steadfastly uphold the domestic ideal while an increasing number of wives and mothers took jobs? In many ways the dramatic increase was kept invisible by the women themselves. Fearing public disapproval of their decisions, such women usually justified their work in individual or family-oriented terms: "Of course I believe a woman's place is at home, but I took this job to save for college for our children." Moreover, when women took jobs outside the home, they still bore full responsibility for child care and household management, and this allowed families and society to avoid facing the implications of women's new roles. As one overburdened woman noted, she now had "two full-time jobs instead of just one—underpaid clerical worker and unpaid housekeeper."

Women unionists, particularly those in the female-dominated service occupations, sought to ease this double burden by pushing for part-time schedules, employer-sponsored child care, and paid maternity leave. They

were partly successful in securing their demands in fields such as nursing, where women's labor was in heavy demand. They did not, however, challenge the sexual division of the work force or question the belief that women should shoulder the bulk of domestic responsibilities. The absence of an active feminist movement in the 1940s and 1950s left most women to cope on their own.

Youth Culture

In 1956, only partly in jest, the CBS radio commentator Eric Sevareid questioned "whether the teenagers will take over the United States lock, stock, living room, and garage." Sevareid captured the sense of shock and anxiety felt by many Americans whose children were rebelling against the safe and insulated suburban world that their parents had worked so hard to create. The centrality of youth culture to modern times, a trend first noticed in the 1920s, had its roots in the democratization of education, the growth of peer culture, and the growing consumer independence of teenagers in an age of affluence. Like so much else in the 1950s, the youth culture came down to having money.

Market research convinced advertisers of the existence of a distinct teen market in the 1950s. A 1951 *Newsweek* story noted with awe that the $3 weekly spending money of the average teen was enough to buy 190 million candy bars, 130 million soft drinks, and 230 million sticks of gum. In 1956 advertisers projected an adolescent market of $9 billion for items such as transistor radios (first introduced in 1952), 45-rpm records, clothing, and fads such as Silly Putty (1950) and Hula Hoops (1958). Increasingly, advertisers targeted the young, both to capture their spending money and to exploit their influence on family spending patterns. Note the changing slogans for Pepsi-Cola: "Twice as much for a nickel" (1935), "Be sociable—have a Pepsi" (1948), "Now it's Pepsi for those who think young" (1960), and finally "the Pepsi Generation" (1965).

Hollywood movies played a large role in fostering and legitimizing a separate teenage culture. At a time when general movie attendance was declining because of competition from television, young people made up the largest audience for motion pictures. Soon Hollywood studios catered to this market with films such as *The Wild One* (1951), starring Marlon Brando, and *Rebel without a Cause* (1955), starring James Dean, Natalie Wood, and Sal Mineo. "What are you rebelling against?" a waitress asks Brando in *The Wild One*. "Whattaya got?" he replies.

What really defined this generation, however, was its music. Rejecting the rigid boundaries of earlier American popular music, teenagers in the 1950s discovered rock 'n' roll, an amalgam of white country and western music and the black urban music known as

rhythm and blues. The Cleveland disc jockey Alan Freed played a major role in introducing white America to the new African-American sound by playing rhythm and blues records on white radio stations beginning in 1954. Young white performers such as Bill Haley, Elvis Presley, and Buddy Holly incorporated this sound into their own music and capitalized on the new market (see American Lives, pages 920–921). Between 1953 and 1959 record sales increased from $213 million to $603 million, with rock 'n' roll as the driving force.

Many white adults were appalled. They saw in rock 'n' roll music, teen movies, and magazines such as *Mad* (introduced in 1952) an invitation to race mixing, rebellion, and disorder. The media featured hundreds of stories on problem teens, and in 1955 a Senate subcommittee headed by Estes Kefauver conducted a high-profile investigation of juvenile delinquency and its origins in the popular media. Denunciations of the new youth culture, however, only increased its popularity.

Cultural Dissenters

The youth rebellion was only one aspect of a broader undercurrent of discontent with the conformist culture of the 1950s. Postwar artists, jazz musicians, and writers also expressed their alienation from mainstream society through intensely personal, introspective art forms. In New York, Jackson Pollock and other painters rejected the social realism of the 1930s for an unconventional style that became known as abstract expressionism. Swirling and splattering paint onto giant canvases, Pollock emphasized self-expression in the act of painting and captured the chaotic atmosphere of the nuclear age.

A similar trend characterized jazz, where black musicians developed a hard-driving improvisational style known as bebop. Whether the "hot" bebop of saxophonist Charlie Parker in the 1940s or the more subdued "cool" West Coast sound of the trumpeter Miles Davis in the 1950s, postwar jazz was cerebral, intimate, and individualistic. As such, it stood in stark contrast to the commercialized, dance-oriented "swing" bands of the 1930s and 1940s.

Black jazz musicians found eager fans not only in the African-American community but among young white *beats*. Centered in New York and San Francisco, the beats were a group of writers and poets who disdained the middle-class conformity and suburban materialism of the 1950s. In his poem "Howl" (1956), which became a manifesto of the beat generation, Allen Ginsberg lamented: "I saw the best minds of my generation destroyed by madness, starving hysterical naked, dragging themselves through the angry streets at dawn looking for an angry fix. . . ." In works such as Jack Kerouac's novel *On the Road* (1957) the beats glorified spontaneity, sexual adventurism, drug use, and spirituality. Like other

Abstract Expressionism
One of the leading artists of the abstract expressionist school, Jackson Pollock became famous for his technique of dripping and splattering paint on large canvases with long sticks instead of brushes. Like his other works, *Autumn Rhythm* (1950) highlights Pollock's highly personal abstract style. (The Metropolitan Museum of Art, George Hearn Fund, 1957)

members of the postwar generation, the beats were apolitical; their rebellion was strictly cultural. In the 1960s, however, the beats would inspire a new generation of young rebels who championed both political and cultural change.

The Fifties: The Way We Were?

Like the 1920s, the 1950s are defined almost entirely in cultural terms. But once again an emphasis on affluence, popular culture, and consumption is too superficial to describe such a complex period of economic and social transformation. The popularized view of the "happy days" of the 1950s reflects only a tenuous rendering of reality.

For many Americans the 1950s represent the norm of American society. Families were portrayed as close-knit and intact; children were happy; the economy was growing; and despite the fear of nuclear annihilation, Americans were confident that theirs was the strongest country, both economically and morally, in the world. Changes in American family, political, and social life since 1960 are often seen as declines from this ideal.

But perhaps the fifties were an aberration, not the norm—the result of a unique combination of circumstances that could not be sustained on a permanent basis. The postwar baby boom was certainly an aberration in a 200-year trend toward smaller families. The stability of marriages in the 1940s and 1950s was also atypical in light of the liberalization of social mores in the 1920s and 1930s and the increasing divorce rates after the mid-1960s. Scarred by memories of depression and World War II–era dislocations and scared by the ambiguities of living in the atomic age, the postwar generation embraced family life with a vengeance. Their children, growing up in a more economically and psychologically secure environment, rebelled against this traditional orientation. When social conditions changed in the 1960s, the profamily orientation gave way to a more individualistic ethos that characterized the rest of the century.

Perhaps the greatest aberration, and the reason why our view of the 1950s as the norm is so misleading, is that the postwar affluence was based on international economic conditions that could not continue indefinitely. When the war-devastated economies of Japan and West Germany were rebuilt, those countries took advantage of new technology to compete with and eventually challenge American economic supremacy in one industry after another: steel, rubber, automobiles, electronics, footwear, and textiles. So too did emerging industrial centers in the Pacific Rim such as South Korea, Hong Kong, and Singapore. If we regard the economic dominance of the 1950s as the norm, any decline will appear to be a disturbing loss of American power and economic strength rather than a return to a more balanced state of economic affairs.

The stereotypes of the 1950s are misleading, if not downright false, in other ways too. The picture painted in popular culture of boundless affluence hides, indeed makes invisible, those who did not share equally in the postwar American dream. Many people—displaced factory workers, destitute old people, female heads of households, blacks, and Latinos—watched the affluent society from the outside and wondered why they were not permitted to share in its bounty. Not until the publication of Michael Harrington's *The Other America* in 1962 did Americans begin to realize that in the richest country in the world more than a quarter of the population was poor.

The contrast between suburban affluence and the "other America," between the lure of the city for the poor and minorities and the grim reality of its segregated existence, and between a heightened emphasis on domesticity and widening opportunities for women, would spawn protest and change in the turbulent 1960s. Amid the booming prosperity of the late 1940s and 1950s, however, these fundamental social and economic contradictions were barely noticed.

Elvis Presley: Teen Idol of the 1950s

When Elvis Presley performed on the "Ed Sullivan Show" in 1956, the television cameras zoomed in on his head and shoulders. The close-ups were inspired not by the young singer's good looks but by a deliberate attempt to conceal his lower body. After several scandalous TV appearances earlier that season, CBS decided that Presley's sexually suggestive bumping and grinding were unsuitable for family viewing.

Despite the censorship, Presley's performance was an unprecedented success, claiming over 80 percent of the television audience. His records sold 10 million copies that year alone and would account for a quarter of RCA's record sales over the next decade. More than any other recording artist of the 1950s Presley popularized the new hybrid music known as rock 'n' roll.

Born in East Tupelo, Mississippi, in 1935, Elvis Aron Presley grew up in a white working-class family that keenly felt the hardships of the depression. Like many poor southerners, the Presleys moved frequently in search of work as laborers and mill hands. When Elvis was thirteen, his father found a job at a paint factory in Memphis, and the Presleys settled in one of that city's new public housing projects.

Elvis's earliest exposure to music came through gospel singing at the Pentecostal First Assembly of God church, where his uncle was pastor. Later, when his family lived in or adjacent to the black districts of Tupelo and Memphis (as the South's poorest whites often did), Elvis gravitated toward local churches, bars, and clubs where he gained a lifelong love of blues, gospel, and other black music.

Local radio was an equally powerful force in his musical education. In the late 1940s, commercial radio offered a diverse selection of musical programming, catering to the growing audience of rural migrants who had been moving to southern cities since World War II. Although there had always been significant cross-fertilization between black and white musical styles, industry promoters maintained artificially distinct genres of "hillbilly" and "race" music. After World War II those derogatory labels gave way to the more respectable terms *country and western* and *rhythm and blues*, but the programming remained rigidly segregated.

Young white southerners such as Presley, however, listened to both types of programs. They admired the traditional vocal styles and guitar picking that they heard on the "Grand Ole Opry" and other country shows but also developed a keen appreciation for the blues progressions and driving rhythms of black music. White youngsters' growing fascination with rhythm and blues was not generally acknowledged and was considered somewhat scandalous. But a small group of disc jockeys and record promoters realized the potential of the new market. As the Memphis record producer Sam Phillips once said, "If I could find a white man who had the Negro sound and the Negro feel, I could make a billion dollars."

Phillips found that man in Elvis Presley. In 1953 the nineteen-year-old Presley was working as a truck driver and occasionally stopped by Phillips's Sun Studios to make sample recordings for his friends and family. Phillips remembered his unusual vocal style and later asked him to cut a record with a local band. The result was an eclectic mix of musical styles: a white version of a black blues song, "That's All Right," on one side and a black-influenced interpretation of a bluegrass number, "Blue Moon of Kentucky," on the other. The record was an overnight local sensation and launched Presley into a national recording career the following year. Over the next decade he produced dozens of hits for RCA, including "Hound Dog," "Heartbreak Hotel," "Jailhouse Rock," and "Blue Suede Shoes."

Presley's success was based not only on his music but on his stage presence and his relationship with the audience. With his slicked-back hair, long sideburns, and tight pants, Presley cultivated a lower-class "greaser" look that proved immensely popular with teenage fans. His quivering legs, gyrating pelvis, and playful sneer drove young female fans wild; they frequently mobbed the stage, grabbing at his clothes for souvenirs. Many

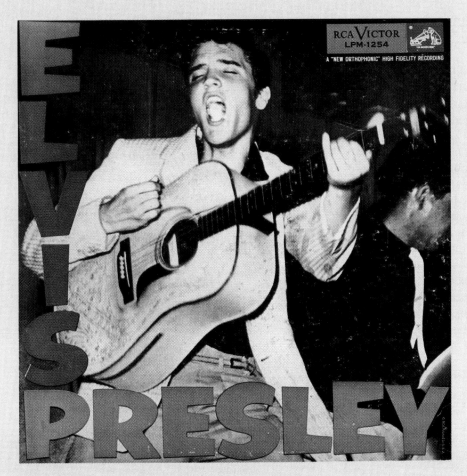

Elvis Presley
The young Elvis Presley (shown here on the cover of his first album in 1956) embodied cultural rebellion against the conservatism and triviality of adult life in the 1950s.

adults, however, condemned such antics, associating them with juvenile delinquency, sexual immorality, and "race mixing." After his first television appearance, a critic described Presley's performance as "suggestive and vulgar, tinged with the kind of animalism that should be confined to dives and bordellos," and another called it "a strip-tease with clothes on." For many adults rock 'n' roll was an invitation to rebellion.

African-Americans found Presley's success and notoriety somewhat ironic. Black musicians such as Chuck Berry had been performing such music for years but with little commercial success among white audiences. To many, the appropriation of black rhythm and blues by white artists was out-and-out theft. In the long run, however, the popularity of rock 'n' roll introduced black performers such as Little Richard, Fats Domino, and James Brown to white as well as black audiences.

Presley's musical popularity declined with his induction into the army in 1958 (the long arm of the state reached even the most popular stars). Afterward he headed for Hollywood, acting and singing in dozens of mostly mediocre teen-oriented movies. He enjoyed a comeback starting in 1968, but his career was hampered by personal problems. In 1977 he died of an accidental drug overdose. Since then he has become a cult figure, spawning hundreds of books and articles and a spate of Elvis impersonators. Graceland, his garish home in Memphis, attracts more visitors per year than does George Washington's estate at Mount Vernon.

Summary

Postwar affluence rested on several foundations, especially the global hegemony of the United States in the immediate postwar period. Federal intervention in the economy, especially in the form of defense spending, fueled prosperity, as did spending for consumer goods. Consumer spending played an especially important role in the reconversion to a peacetime economy. New corporate investment strategies helped expand U.S. influence abroad, and technological change stimulated productivity in both agriculture and industry. These developments influenced the workplace, eliminating jobs in manufacturing and accelerating the growth of the service sector. Organized labor benefited from the postwar economic boom in the form of rising wages and benefits but could not maintain its earlier organizing momentum.

Much of the new economic activity in the postwar period was concentrated in the southern and western states and in the suburban periphery. Cold war defense spending boosted the economies and populations of California, Texas, Florida, and other emerging Sun Belt states. Federal home loan programs and highway construction spurred rapid suburban development, siphoning jobs and white middle-class residents out of the central cities. Blacks, Latinos, native Americans, and other low-income groups largely remained trapped in declining inner-city areas amid growing unemployment, rising crime, and deteriorating housing and education. In the South early civil rights campaigns challenged racial inequality and laid the organizational groundwork for the larger movement that followed in the 1960s. But elsewhere Americans remained mostly quiescent during those years.

After years of depression and war-induced insecurity, Americans turned inward toward home and family. Postwar couples married young, had several children, and—if they were white and middle class—raised them in a climate of suburban affluence. The profamily orientation of the 1950s celebrated social conformity and traditional gender roles, even though millions of women entered the work force. Their children also departed from traditional roles as they embraced a rebellious youth culture of rock 'n' roll music, teen movies, and other consumer phenomena aimed at a youth market.

Jazz musicians, abstract expressionist painters, and beat poets and writers also rebelled against conformity, but their dissent was cultural, not political, in nature. Many of the smoldering contradictions of the postwar period—an unequally shared affluence, institutionalized racism that limited opportunities for nonwhite Americans, and tensions in women's lives—soon surfaced in the social protest movements of the 1960s.

TIMELINE

1944	Bretton Woods economic conference World Bank and International Monetary Fund (IMF) founded Mechanical cotton picker introduced
1946	Dr. Benjamin Spock, *Baby and Child Care*
1947	Levittown, New York, built General Agreement on Tariffs and Trade (GATT) UNIVAC computer developed
1948	CBS and NBC begin regular television programming
1953–1958	Operation Wetback and Indian termination programs
1954	Polio vaccine developed by Dr. Jonas Salk *Brown v. Board of Education of Topeka, Kansas* First McDonald's opens
1955	AFL and CIO reunited Montgomery bus boycott Disneyland opens in Anaheim, California
1956	Interstate Highway Act Elvis Presley popularizes rock 'n' roll via television
1957	Peak of postwar baby boom Eisenhower sends federal troops to protect black students during school desegregation battle in Little Rock, Arkansas Southern Christian Leadership Conference (SCLC) founded
1958	Brooklyn Dodgers move to Los Angeles
1959	Nixon and Khrushchev's "kitchen debate"
1963	California replaces New York as most populous state
1965	Immigration Act abolishes national quota system

★   ★   ★

BIBLIOGRAPHY

General introductions to postwar society include Paul Boyer, *Promises to Keep* (1995); William Chafe, *The Unfinished Journey* (3d ed., 1995); John Diggins, *The Proud Decades* (1988); and David Halberstam, *The Fifties* (1993).

Technology and Economic Change

For overviews on the economic changes of the postwar period, see W. Elliot Brownlee, *Dynamics of Ascent* (1979); David P. Calleo, *The Imperious Economy* (1982); and Harold G. Vatter, *The U.S. Economy in the 1950s* (1963). Robert Kuttner, *The End of Laissez-Faire* (1991), provides ample background on the Bretton Woods system. Herman P. Miller, *Rich Man, Poor Man* (1971), and Gabriel Kolko, *Wealth and Power in America* (1962), discuss inequality in income distribution. Michael Harrington, *The Other America* (1962), documents the persistence of poverty in the postwar era, as does Harry M. Caudill, *Night Comes to the Cumberlands* (1963).

John L. Shover, *First Majority—Last Minority* (1976), analyzes the transformation of rural life in America. David Brody, *Workers in Industrial America* (1980); James R. Green, *The World of the Worker* (1980); and Robert Zeiger, *American Workers, American Unions, 1920–1985* (1986), provide overviews of labor in the twentieth century. On the impact of technology and automation, see Elting E. Morison, *From Know-How to Nowhere* (1974), and David F. Noble, *Forces of Production* (1984). The most influential study of the new middle class remains David Reisman et al., *The Lonely Crowd* (1950). William H. Whyte, *The Organization Man* (1956), provides a similar perspective. See also the work of C. Wright Mills, especially *White Collar* (1951) and *The Power Elite* (1956).

Alfred D. Chandler, *The Visible Hand* (1977), is the definitive history of American corporate structure and strategy. Myra Wilkin, *The Maturing of Multinational Enterprise* (1974), and Richard J. Barnet and Ronald E. Muller, *Global Reach* (1974), describe American business abroad. See also Robert Sobel, *The Age of Giant Corporations* (1972), and the early sections of Barry Bluestein and Bennett Harrison, *The Deindustrialization of America* (1982).

A Suburban Society

The best overviews of urbanization in the South and West are Carl Abbott, *The New Urban America* (1981), and Richard Bernard and Bradley Rice, eds., *Sunbelt Cities* (1983). Kenneth Jackson, *Crabgrass Frontier* (1985), provides an overview of suburban development, which can be supplemented by Jon C. Teaford, *City and Suburb* (1979); Robert Fishman, *Bourgeois Utopias* (1987); and Zane Miller, *Suburb* (1981). Herbert Gans, *The Levittowners* (1967), and Bennett M. Berger, *Working-Class Suburb* (1960), are sociological studies of suburbia written by contemporaries.

The Other America

Reed Ueda, *Postwar Immigrant America* (1994), and David Reimers, *Still the Open Door* (1985), examine new trends in immigration since 1945. Nicholas Lemann examines postwar black migration in *The Promised Land* (1991), and Jacqueline Jones compares black and white urban migrants in *The Dispossessed* (1992). Donald Fixico, *Termination and Relocation* (1986), looks at federal Indian policy from 1945 to 1970.

Jon C. Teaford, *Rough Road to Renaissance* (1990); John Mollenkopf, *The Contested City* (1983); and Kenneth Fox, *Metropolitan America* (1985), offer the most complete accounts of postwar urban development. Herbert Gans, *The Urban Villagers* (1962), tells the story of a Boston Italian community displaced by urban renewal.

Richard Kluger, *Simple Justice* (1975), and Mark Tushnet, *The NAACP's Legal Strategy against Segregated Education* (1987), analyze the *Brown* decision and its context, whereas Anthony Lewis, *Portrait of a Decade* (1964), covers southern reaction to the decision. Martin Luther King, Jr., recounts his experience in the Montgomery bus boycott in *Stride toward Freedom* (1958); and Taylor Branch, *Parting the Waters: America in the King Years, 1954–1963* (1988), provides a good account of King's early years.

American Society during the Baby Boom

Books that highlight the social and cultural history of the 1950s include Elaine Tyler May, *Homeward Bound* (1988); Lary May, ed., *Recasting America* (1989); Douglas T. Miller and Marion Nowak, *The Fifties* (1977); and Stephen Whitfield, *The Culture of the Cold War* (1991).

On popular culture, George Lipsitz, *Time Passages* (1991), surveys postwar television, music, film, and popular culture, and his *Rainbow at Midnight* (2d ed., 1994) looks at working-class culture and rock 'n' roll. Eric Barnouw, *Tube of Plenty* (2d. ed., 1982), chronicles the impact of television. Other treatments of the mass media include James L. Baughman, *The Republic of Mass Culture* (1992); Peter Biskind, *Seeing Is Believing* (1983); and Nora Sayre, *Running Time* (1982). Vance Packard's influential unmasking of the advertising industry, *The Hidden Persuaders* (1957), can be supplemented by Stephen Fox, *The Mirror Makers* (1984).

Richard Easterlin, *American Baby Boom in Historical Perspective* (1962) and *Birth and Future* (1980), analyze the demographic changes. Jane S. Smith, *Patenting the Sun* (1990), looks at Salk's development of the polio vaccine. Diane Ravitch describes education from 1945 to 1980 in *The Troubled Crusade* (1983).

Elaine May's *Homeward Bound* is the classic introduction to postwar family life, providing a historical corollary to Betty Friedan's *Feminine Mystique* (1963). Recent revisionist work challenging this view can be found in Joanne Meyerowitz, ed., *Not June Cleaver* (1994). William H. Chafe, *The American Woman* (1972), and Alice Kessler-Harris, *Out to Work* (1982), survey women's role in the work force.

Youth culture is the subject of William Graeber's *Coming of Age in Buffalo* (1990). James Gilbert, *A Cycle of Outrage* (1986), looks at juvenile delinquency in the 1950s. Peter Guralnick, *Last Train to Memphis* (1994), is the definitive biography of Elvis Presley's early years. Discussions of cultural dissent in the 1950s can be found in Serge Guibaut, *How New York Stole the Idea of Modern Art* (1983); Bruce Cook, *The Beat Generation* (1971); and Dan Wakefield, *New York in the Fifties* (1992).

La Huelga

Long live the cause, long live the strike, proclaimed Paul
Davis's poster for a 1968 Carnegie Hall benefit for César
Chávez's farm workers' union.

The Ascent of Liberalism

1960–1970

★   ★   ★

In his 1961 inaugural address President John Fitzgerald Kennedy challenged a "new generation of Americans" to take responsibility for the future: "Ask not what your country can do for you, ask what you can do for your country." Over the next decade many young Americans responded to that sense of mission. As a civil rights volunteer explained in 1964, "I want to do my part. There's a moral wave building among today's youth, and I intend to catch it."

Ironically, the roots of 1960s activism lay in the tranquil America of the 1950s. The postwar affluence of the middle class produced a self-assured generation of young whites who were optimistic about their ability to cure the nation's social ills. For young African-Americans the affluence of the white middle class was a stark reminder of racial inequality. In the 1960s that same baby-boom generation swelled college enrollments, providing recruits for the civil rights campaign and other student movements. Among women, increased access to education and greater participation in the work force in the postwar era sparked a revival of feminism. Finally, the lofty cold war rhetoric of international freedom and democracy prompted many to press for economic and racial justice at home.

The civil rights movement was the earliest and most influential protest movement in this period. The antisegregation campaign waged by black southerners in the 1950s grew into a nationwide civil rights movement, taking on controversial issues such as voting rights, economic inequality, and community control. The tactics it pioneered—legislative and judicial challenges, nonviolent direct action, and mobilization of public opinion—were soon adopted by women, Mexican-Americans, native Americans, and other groups to press their demands.

The sense of optimism and activism that characterized the social movements of the 1960s also pervaded politics. Drawing on a new generation of academic and corporate leaders, the administrations of John F. Ken-

nedy and—to a much greater extent—Lyndon B. Johnson acted on an abiding faith in the positive influence of government and tried to use federal power to ensure the public welfare at home and protect American interests abroad. This political orientation—known as liberalism—was a continuation of Franklin Roosevelt's New Deal but went beyond it. Under the Great Society, a burst of social legislation in 1964–1965, which marked the high tide of postwar liberalism, the Johnson administration expanded federal activism in areas such as health care, education, and civil rights. Through those programs and other social welfare measures, liberals sought to spread the abundance of a consumer society to greater numbers of people. In essence, they attempted to use the fiscal powers of the state to redress the imbalances of the private economy without directly challenging capitalism.

Liberals also pursued an activist stance abroad. The Kennedy and Johnson administrations sought to protect American political and economic interests in the international arena and took aggressive action against communist influence in Europe, the Caribbean, Vietnam (see Chapter 31), and elsewhere. The growing financial and political costs of that ambitious agenda, however, hampered the further progress of domestic programs and revealed ominous cracks in the postwar liberal consensus.

The Kennedy Magnetism
John Kennedy, the Democratic candidate for president in 1960, used his youth and personality to attract voters. Here the Massachusetts senator draws an enthusiastic crowd on a campaign stop in Elgin, Illinois.

John Kennedy and the Politics of Expectation

Franklin Roosevelt's activist administration had heightened expectations for presidential leadership, and the expansion of presidential power had continued under Truman and Eisenhower. In the 1960s, when American power and resources seemed limitless, many citizens looked to Washington for solutions to international, national, and local problems. Few presidents came to Washington more primed for action than John Kennedy. His "New Frontier" promised to get America moving again through vigorous governmental activism at home and abroad. The British journalist Henry Fairlie referred to this activist impulse as the "politics of expectation." But the legislative achievements of Kennedy's New Frontier, particularly in domestic affairs, were modest.

The New Politics and the 1960 Campaign

The Republicans would have been happy to renominate Dwight D. Eisenhower for president in 1960 but were prevented from doing so by the Twenty-second Amendment. Passed in 1951 by a Republican-controlled Congress to prevent a repetition of Franklin Roosevelt's four-term presidency, the amendment limited future presidents to two full terms.

The Republicans turned to Vice-President Richard M. Nixon, who, like a good 1950s junior executive, had patiently waited for his turn at the top. Nixon campaigned for an updated version of Eisenhower's policies but was hampered by lukewarm support from Eisenhower. Asked whether Nixon had helped make any major policy decisions in his administration, Eisenhower replied, "If you give me a week I might think of one."

In the Democratic primaries, which took on new importance in the television era, Senator John Fitzgerald Kennedy of Massachusetts defeated Senator Hubert Horatio Humphrey of Minnesota. The Senate majority leader, Lyndon Johnson of Texas, who also sought the nomination but did not participate in the primary race, joined the ticket as the vice-presidential nominee. Kennedy, an alumnus of Harvard and a World War II hero, had inherited his love of politics from his grandfathers, both of whom had been colorful Irish-Catholic politicians in Boston. His wealthy father, Joseph P. Kennedy, had headed the Securities and Exchange Commission and served as ambassador to Great Britain under Roosevelt. First elected to Congress in 1946, John Kennedy moved to the Senate in 1952. Ambitious and hard-driven, Kennedy launched his New Frontier campaign in 1960 with a platform calling for civil rights legislation, health care for the elderly, aid to education, urban renewal, expanded military and space programs, and containment of communism abroad. With the country in the

middle of a recession that had pushed unemployment to a postwar high, Kennedy vowed to "get America moving again."

Kennedy's main liabilities were his Catholicism and his youth. At forty-three he was poised to become the youngest man ever elected to the presidency and the nation's first Catholic chief executive. The first Catholic nominee since Al Smith in 1928, Kennedy dealt with the issue of religion directly. In a September address to a group of Protestant ministers in Houston he affirmed his belief in the separation of church and state and declared his political independence from the Vatican. He also handled the youth question skillfully.

Turning his youth into a powerful campaign asset, Kennedy practiced what came to be called the "new politics"—an approach that emphasized youthful charisma, style, and personality rather than issues and platforms. Using the power of the media (particularly television) to reach voters directly, practitioners of the new politics relied on professional media consultants, political pollsters, and mass fund-raising. Kennedy's youth, attractiveness, and charm made for a superb television image. His family's wealth and the contributions he raised from

sources outside traditional party networks paid for his expensive campaign. His mastery of the media enabled him to appeal to voters directly rather than only through the Democratic party.

A series of four televised debates between the two principal candidates, a major innovation of the 1960 campaign, showed how important that medium was becoming to political life. Nixon, far less photogenic than Kennedy and recovering from a minor illness, looked sallow and unshaven under the intense studio lights. Kennedy, in contrast, looked vigorous, cool, and self-confident on screen and dispelled voters' fears that he was not as well prepared for the presidency as the current vice-president was. Polls showed that television did sway political perceptions: voters who listened to the first debate on the radio concluded that Nixon had won, whereas TV viewers judged in Kennedy's favor.

Despite the ground Kennedy picked up in the debates, he won only the narrowest of victories, receiving 49.7 percent of the popular vote to Nixon's 49.5 percent (see Map 30.1). Kennedy had successfully appealed to the diverse elements of the Democratic coalition, attracting large numbers of Catholic and black voters and a sig-

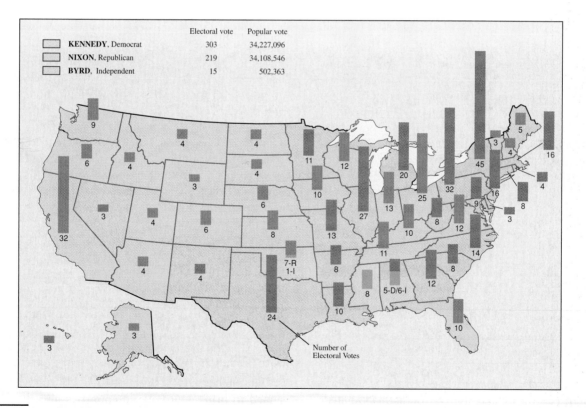

MAP 30.1

The Election of 1960

The Kennedy-Nixon contest was the closest since 1884. Kennedy won twelve states, including Illinois, by less than 2 percent of the two-party vote tally; he lost six others, including California, by a similarly small margin. Fifteen electors cast their votes for the Independent Democrat, Harry F. Byrd. Despite his razor-thin margin of victory, Kennedy won 303 electoral votes, the same number Truman had won in 1948, showing that the electoral college vote can be a misleading indicator of popular support.

nificant sector of the middle class; the vice-presidential nominee, Lyndon Johnson, brought in southern white Democrats. Yet only 120,000 votes separated the two candidates, and the shift of a few thousand votes in key states such as Illinois (where there were confirmed cases of voting fraud) would have reversed the outcome. The electoral results hardly gave Kennedy a mandate for sweeping change, and the Republicans, though still in the minority in Congress, gained 21 seats in the House.

Kennedy's activist bent attracted unusually talented and ambitious people—"the best and the brightest" as the journalist David Halberstam called them. A host of corporate and academic leaders flocked to join the new administration, which was christened "Camelot" by the admiring media after the recently opened Broadway musical about King Arthur. Robert S. McNamara, the former president of the Ford Motor Company, came on board as secretary of defense and introduced modern management techniques to that department. The Republican banker C. Douglas Dillon brought a corporate manager's desire for expanded markets and stable economic growth to the Department of the Treasury. The national security adviser McGeorge Bundy, the State Department planner Walt Rostow, and other trusted advisers came from Harvard, MIT, and other leading universities to join the Kennedy foreign policy team.

Reflecting the all-male Ivy League world in which Kennedy traveled, the administration was overwhelmingly male. He appointed fewer women to federal positions than had Eisenhower or Truman and made only a token attempt to address women's issues with the establishment of the Presidential Commission on the Status of Women in 1961. Subsequent allegations of Kennedy's womanizing and philandering also hurt his reputation in this area.

Activism Abroad

Kennedy's inaugural address was devoted almost entirely to foreign affairs, reflecting the priorities of his presidency: "Let every nation know, whether it wishes us well or ill, that we shall pay any price, bear any burden, meet any hardship, support any friend, oppose any foe to assure the survival and success of liberty." A resolute cold warrior whose family had supported the red-hunting campaign of Senator Joseph McCarthy, Kennedy took a hard line against communist expansionism. He therefore set out to reverse the fiscal conservatism that had limited military growth under the Eisenhower administration, bringing defense spending to its highest level (as a percentage of total federal expenditures) in the cold war era.

The Military Buildup. During the 1960 presidential campaign Kennedy charged that the Eisenhower administration had permitted the Soviet Union to develop superior nuclear capabilities. Once in office, however, he found that no "missile gap" existed. In fact, Eisenhower had built up the American nuclear arsenal at the expense of conventional weapons. In his first national security message to Congress, Kennedy proposed a new policy of *flexible response*, stating that the nation must be prepared "to deter all wars, general or limited, nuclear or conventional, large or small." Congress quickly granted Kennedy's military requests, boosting the number of combat-ready army divisions from eleven to sixteen and authorizing the construction of ten Polaris nuclear submarines and other warships. The result was a major expansion of the military-industrial complex as thousands of workers were recruited to build more weapons systems and military equipment.

Those measures were designed to deter nuclear or conventional attacks by the Soviet Union. But what about the new kind of warfare, the wars of national liberation that had broken out in many Third World countries when their inhabitants sought to overthrow colonial rulers or unpopular dictatorships? In early 1961 the Soviet premier, Nikita Khrushchev, proclaimed that conflicts in Vietnam, Cuba, and other countries were "wars of national liberation," worthy of Soviet support. To counter that threat, Kennedy adopted the new military doctrine of *counterinsurgency*. U.S. Army Special Forces, called the Green Berets for their distinctive headgear, received intensive training in repelling the random, small-scale attacks typical of guerrilla warfare. Vietnam soon provided a testing ground for counterinsurgency techniques (see Chapter 31).

The Peace Corps and Foreign Aid. The idealism and commitment to public service that characterized the New Frontier were perhaps most evident in the newly established Peace Corps, headed by Kennedy's brother-in-law, Sargent Shriver. The idea, Kennedy explained on March 1, 1961, was to create "a pool of trained American men and women" to be sent "overseas by the United States government or through private organizations and institutions to help foreign countries meet their urgent needs for skilled manpower." Thousands of young Americans, many of them recent college graduates, responded to the call, agreeing to devote two or more years to teaching English to Filipino schoolchildren or helping African villagers obtain adequate supplies of water. Embodying the idealism of the early 1960s, the Peace Corps was also a cold war weapon designed to bring Third World countries into the American orbit and away from communist influence.

Kennedy also tried to reinforce American ties to developing countries through programs of economic aid. The State Department's Agency for International Development coordinated foreign aid for the Third World, and its Food for Peace program distributed surplus agricultural products to developing nations. In March 1961 the

The Peace Corps
The Peace Corps, a New Frontier program initiated in 1961, attracted thousands of idealistic young Americans, including this New York woman who volunteered at a hospital in Rio de Janeiro, Brazil.

president proposed "a ten-year plan for the Americas" called the Alliance for Progress, a $20 billion partnership between the United States and the republics of Latin America. Designed to reduce the appeal of communism, the Alliance provided funds for food, education, medicine, and other services but did little to enhance economic growth or improve social conditions in Latin America during the 1960s.

Kennedy often turned to a small circle of personal aides for foreign policy advice rather than relying on the Pentagon and the State Department. Taking the institutional changes of the 1947 National Security Act a step further, he enhanced the authority of the National Security Council by moving its chief into the White House. That shift further concentrated foreign policy initiative in the executive office.

The Bay of Pigs Invasion. The nation's strengthened military arsenal and streamlined security apparatus failed to bring Kennedy the diplomatic success that he had anticipated. In April 1961 Kennedy undertook his first major foreign policy initiative—an effort to overthrow the new Soviet-supported regime in Cuba.

Although the United States had renounced its right to intervene in Cuba's internal affairs in 1934 (see Chapter 27), it retained a base at Guantánamo Bay and nearly total economic and political dominance of the island. In

1956 American companies owned 80 percent of Cuba's utilities, 90 percent of its mining operations, and 40 percent of its sugar plantations. On New Year's Day in 1959 Fidel Castro overthrew the corrupt and unpopular dictatorship of Fulgencio Batista and called for a revolution to reshape Cuban society. At first Castro was willing to deal with the United States on friendly terms, but as he instituted agrarian reforms that affected American interests and nationalized American-owned banks and industries, relations with Washington deteriorated. By early 1961 the United States had declared an embargo on all exports to Cuba, cut back on imports of Cuban sugar, and broken off diplomatic relations with Castro's regime. Isolated by the United States, Cuba turned increasingly toward the Soviet Union for economic and military support.

Concerned about Castro's growing friendliness with the Soviets, in early 1961 Kennedy used plans originally drawn up by the Eisenhower administration to dispatch Cuban exiles to foment an anti-Castro uprising. The invaders had been trained by the Central Intelligence Agency (CIA) but were ill prepared for their task and had little popular support on the island. After landing at Cuba's Bay of Pigs on April 17, the tiny force of 1,400 men was crushed by Castro's troops. Symptomatic of the inept CIA planning, pilots taking off from Nicaragua to provide air cover for the landing forces forgot to set their watches ahead to Cuban time and arrived at the beach an hour late. The anticipated rebellion never occurred.

The Bay of Pigs invasion was an embarrassing failure and cast doubts on Kennedy's activist approach to international affairs. It also adversely affected U.S.-Soviet relations. Khrushchev interpreted the invasion as evidence that American troops would launch an offensive against Cuba in the future and responded by stepping up military aid to Castro.

The Berlin Wall. The growing mistrust between Kennedy and Khrushchev intensified during a June 1961 summit meeting of the United States and the Soviet Union. Weakened by the botched Cuban invasion, Kennedy met with Khrushchev to discuss a nuclear test ban treaty, the civil war in Laos, and the status of Berlin. At the meeting both men were combative, especially about Berlin, which was located squarely in the middle of East Germany but had remained divided into eastern and western sectors. Khrushchev wanted it declared a "free city," which would mean the withdrawal of both Soviet and western occupation forces, but he did not get his way.

Just days after the meeting, Khrushchev heightened international tensions by deploying soldiers to sever East Berlin from the western sector of the city. Determined to confront the Soviets publicly, Kennedy declared in a televised speech on July 25 that Berlin was the "great testing

The Berlin Wall
A West Berlin resident walks alongside a section of the Berlin wall in 1962, a year after its construction. Note the numerous loudspeakers, which the East Germans used to broadcast propaganda over the barricade that divided the city.

place of Western courage and will." He announced that he would ask Congress for large increases in military spending, a massive fallout shelter program, and the authority to mobilize the National Guard, call up the reserves, and extend military enlistments in response to the crisis. With Congressional approval, Kennedy added 300,000 troops to the armed forces and dispatched 40,000 of them to Europe. Undeterred, the Soviets supervised East German construction of the Berlin wall in mid-August to stop the exodus of East Germans to the West; East German guards then began policing the border, with instructions to shoot to kill those trying to escape. Transforming the Berlin wall into a propaganda weapon, Kennedy later visited the city and—standing beside the wall—invoked the solidarity of the free world by declaring *"Ich bin ein Berliner"* ("I am a Berliner"). Until it was dismantled in 1989, the Berlin wall was the supreme symbol of the Cold War.

The Cuban Missile Crisis. The climactic confrontation of the Cold War came in October 1962. After the failed Bay of Pigs invasion, the Kennedy administration increased economic pressure against Cuba and resumed its covert efforts to overthrow the Castro regime (see Map 30.2). Under the code name Operation Mongoose, the CIA attempted to disrupt Cuban trade, supported raids against the island from Florida, and plotted to assassinate Castro. In response to those hostile actions and fearing another U.S. invasion, the Soviets stepped up military aid to Cuba, including the installation of defensive missiles. In early October, American U-2 reconnaissance aircraft photographed Soviet-built bases for intermediate-range ballistic missiles (IRBMs), which could reach U.S. targets as far as 2,200 miles away. At

least some of those nuclear weapons had already been installed, and more were on the way from the Soviet Union. Moreover, the Soviet military commanders in Cuba might have been authorized to use them in the event of an American invasion.

Rather than work through State Department or diplomatic channels, Kennedy confronted the Soviet Union publicly in a somber televised address on Monday, October 22. Displaying the reconnaissance photos as evidence, he announced that the United States would use its newly enlarged navy to impose a "quarantine on all offensive military equipment" intended for Cuba. As the United States and the Soviet Union went on full military alert, people around the world believed that this long-dreaded direct confrontation between the two superpowers would end in nuclear war. Americans living in cities within range of the missiles restocked their bomb shelters and calculated the fastest routes out of town. When Khrushchev denounced the quarantine, tensions mounted higher.

While the world held its breath, the Russian ships halted their voyage. Khrushchev wrote to Kennedy that if the United States agreed not to invade Cuba, the Soviets would remove the missiles. In a second letter Khrushchev demanded the removal of American missiles in Turkey as a condition for resolving the crisis. On his brother Robert's advice, the president publicly agreed to the terms of the first letter but ignored the second one. (He later secretly agreed to remove the missiles from Turkey.) On the following Sunday, after the most harrowing week of the nuclear age, Kennedy and Khrushchev both announced concessions: Kennedy pledged not to invade Cuba, and Khrushchev promised to dismantle the missile bases. "We're eyeball to eyeball," Secretary of State Rusk observed, "and I think the other fellow just blinked."

Although the risk of nuclear war was greater during the Cuban missile crisis than it was at any other time in the postwar period, it led to a slight thaw in U.S.-Soviet relations. In the words of the national security adviser McGeorge Bundy, "having come so close to the edge, the leaders of the two governments have since taken care to keep away from the cliff." Sobered by the Cuban missile crisis and the close brush with nuclear war, Kennedy began to seek ways to reduce international tensions. He turned away from the cold war rhetoric that had characterized his campaign and the first two years of his presidency and began to strive for peaceful coexistence. In a notable speech at American University in June 1963, he stressed the need to "make the world safe for diversity." Russians and Americans alike, he observed, "inhabit this small planet. We all breathe the same air. We all cherish our children's future. And we are all mortal." Soviet leaders, also chastened by the confrontation over Cuba, were willing to talk. In August 1963 the three nuclear powers—the United States, the Soviet Union, and Great Britain—agreed to ban the testing of nuclear weapons in the atmosphere, in space, and underwater. Underground

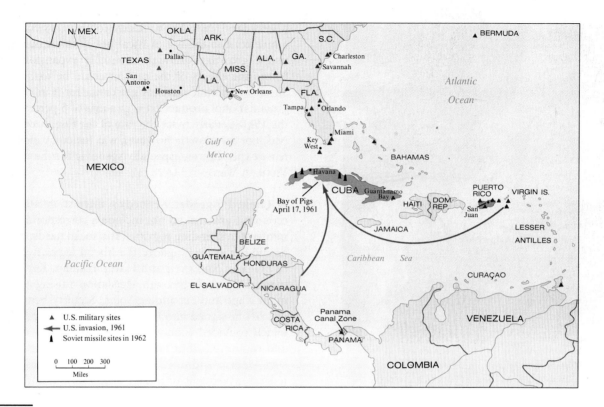

MAP 30.2

The United States and Cuba, 1961–1962

Fidel Castro's takeover in Cuba in 1959 brought cold war tensions to the Caribbean. In 1961 the United States tried unsuccessfully to overthrow Castro's regime by supporting the invasion of Cuban exiles launched from Nicaragua. In 1962 a major confrontation with the Soviet Union occurred over Soviet missile sites in Cuba. The Soviets removed the missiles after President Kennedy ordered a naval blockade of the island, which lies just 90 miles south of Florida.

testing, however, was allowed to continue. The partial test ban treaty was approved by the Senate in the fall of 1963. The new emphasis on peaceful coexistence and mutual accommodation also led to the establishment of a Washington-Moscow telecommunications "hot line" in 1963 so that leaders could contact each other quickly during potential crises.

But no matter how often American leaders talked about opening channels of communication with the Soviets, the obsession with the Soviet military threat to American security remained a cornerstone of U.S. policy. Nor did Soviet leaders moderate their concern over the threat that they believed the United States posed to the survival of the U.S.S.R. The Cold War—and the escalating arms race that accompanied it—would continue for another twenty-five years.

Kennedy's Thousand Days

The expansive vision of presidential leadership that Kennedy and his advisers brought to the White House

worked less well at home than it did abroad. Kennedy, hampered by the lack of a popular mandate in the 1960 election, could not mobilize public support for the domestic agenda of the New Frontier. A conservative coalition of southern Democrats and western and midwestern Republicans effectively stalled most liberal initiatives. More important, Kennedy was not nearly as impassioned about domestic reform as he was about foreign policy.

One domestic program that won both popular and Congressional support was increased funding for space exploration. In response to the Soviet launching of *Sputnik* in 1957, the United States had established the National Aeronautics and Space Administration (NASA), which began the Mercury space program in 1958. On May 5, 1961, just three months after Kennedy took office, Alan Shepard became the first American in space; on February 2, 1962, John Glenn became the first American to orbit the earth. (The Soviet cosmonaut Yuri Gagarin earned the distinction of being the first person in space when he made a 108-hour flight in April 1961.) At the height of American fascination with space, Kennedy proposed in 1961 that "this nation should commit

Project Mercury
Astronaut John Glenn was the first American to orbit the earth as part of the Mercury space program in 1962.

itself to achieving the goal, before this decade is out, of landing a man on the moon and returning him safely to earth." To support this mission (accomplished in 1969), he greatly increased NASA's budget.

Economic Policy. Kennedy's most striking domestic achievement was his use of modern economics to shape fiscal policy. Initially Kennedy had shared the belief of Eisenhower and many business leaders that the federal government could best contribute to economic growth by reducing the national debt and balancing the budget. However, at the urging of Walter Heller, chairman of the Council of Economic Advisers, Kennedy decided on a different course. Rather than increase federal spending to stimulate the economy, he proposed a reduction in the income tax paid by businesses and the public. A tax cut, he argued, would leave more money in the hands of taxpayers, who would then buy more, thus creating more jobs. For a time federal expenditures would exceed federal income, but after a year or two the expanding economy would raise American incomes and generate higher tax revenues.

Congress predictably balked at this unorthodox proposal. Although the federal government had practiced Keynesian economics during the depression of the 1930s, the purposeful use of deficits in a relatively healthy economy was highly controversial. The measure initially died in Congress, but Lyndon Johnson pressed for it after Kennedy's assassination and signed it into law

in February 1964. The Kennedy-Johnson tax cut marked a milestone in the use of fiscal policy to encourage economic growth. Although economic expansion started before the effects of the tax cut could be felt, Kennedy and his economic advisers got credit for it anyway. The gross national product grew at a rate of 5 percent during the 1960s, nearly twice the rate of the Eisenhower years. Much of the growth, however, was fueled by massive defense expenditures, especially spending for the escalating Vietnam War.

A Limited Agenda. Kennedy's interest in stimulating economic growth did not include a corresponding commitment to spending for domestic social needs, although he did not entirely ignore the liberal legislative agenda of Franklin Roosevelt and Harry Truman. Kennedy did manage to push through legislation raising the minimum wage and expanding Social Security benefits, and in 1961 he signed into law the Area Redevelopment Act, which provided economic aid for depressed industrial and rural areas. But on some of his most important issues—federal aid to education, wilderness preservation, federal investment in mass transportation, and medical insurance for the elderly—he ran into determined Congressional opposition from both Republicans and dissenters in his own party.

Discord within the Democratic coalition was particularly evident in the case of aid to education. Most northern Democrats favored such aid but disagreed about important details. Civil rights advocates insisted that federal school aid go only to desegregated schools, while Catholics insisted that federal assistance be extended to parochial systems. Kennedy persuaded most black leaders to accept a school aid plan that ignored existing segregation, but he told southern whites that federal aid would not be guaranteed to segregated schools in the future. Because he was a Catholic, however, Kennedy feared angering non-Catholics by proposing a bill that permitted aid to parochial schools. In the absence of a bill acceptable to all those groups, the education proposal died in committee.

The Warren Court. Some of the most controversial policies of the early 1960s came not from the Kennedy administration but from the Supreme Court. Unlike the New Deal years, when the Court played an obstructionist role, in the postwar period it often acted as a catalyst for sweeping social change. Much of this judicial activism was linked to Earl Warren, the chief justice from 1953 to 1969.

The decisions of the Warren Court arguably had a greater impact on American society than did anything proposed by the president or Congress. The most important decision of the Court, *Brown v. Board of Education*, requiring the desegregation of public schools, had been handed down in 1954 during the Eisenhower

administration (see Chapter 29). In the 1960s the Court made landmark decisions in the area of defendants' rights. In *Gideon v. Wainwright* (1963), *Escobedo v. Illinois* (1964), and *Miranda v. Arizona* (1966) the Supreme Court greatly expanded the rights of people accused of crimes. Tackling the issue of the reapportionment of state legislatures in *Baker v. Carr* (1962) and *Reynolds v. Sims* (1964), the Court put forth the doctrine of "one person, one vote," which substantially increased the representation of both suburban and urban areas, with their concentrations of black and Spanish-speaking residents, at the expense of rural regions. Perhaps the most controversial decision was *Engel v. Vitale* (1962), which banned organized prayer in public schools as a violation of the First Amendment's injunction that "Congress shall make no law respecting an establishment of religion."

President Kennedy, like President Eisenhower before him, pledged to uphold these decisions even when he disagreed with their scope or content. But in allowing the Court to take the lead on such issues, Kennedy surrendered critical opportunities to exercise presidential leadership.

The Kennedy Assassination. Although the first two years of Kennedy's presidency had been plagued by foreign policy crises and domestic inaction, many political observers believed the tide was turning in 1963. But just as Kennedy was maturing as a national leader, tragedy struck. On November 22, 1963, Kennedy went to Texas, a state he needed to win for reelection in 1964, to heal divisions in the party organization there. As he and his wife, Jacqueline, rode in an open car past the Texas School Book Depository in Dallas, he was shot. Kennedy died a half hour later. (Whether the accused killer Lee Harvey Oswald, a twenty-four-year-old loner who had spent three years in the Soviet Union, was the sole gunman became a matter of considerable controversy.) Before *Air Force One* left Dallas to take the president's body back to Washington, a grim-faced Lyndon Johnson was sworn in as president. Kennedy's stunned widow, still wearing her bloodstained pink suit, looked on.

By 1 P.M. Dallas time, just thirty minutes after the shooting, 68 percent of adults in the United States, about 75 million people, knew that Kennedy had been shot. By late afternoon, the proportion had risen to 99.8 percent, showing how the mass media could reach virtually every person in the nation within a few hours. As on Pearl Harbor Day in 1941, people never forgot what they were doing when they heard that Kennedy had been shot. Many ordinary Americans were deeply shocked by the assassination, reflecting their personal identification with the occupants of the White House.

The Kennedy assassination set off a national wave of self-examination. Americans debated whether the murder of the president had been an isolated act or an expression of a tragic flaw in the democratic system. The argument

Burying a President
A grief-stricken Jacqueline Kennedy walked behind her slain husband's casket at his 1963 funeral. To her left is brother-in-law Robert Kennedy, who would be assassinated five years later.

that there was something wrong with the nation gained credence two days after the assassination, when Jack Ruby, a nightclub owner, gunned down Lee Harvey Oswald in the basement of Dallas's police headquarters. Since the television networks were covering Oswald's transfer to another jail, the shooting was broadcast live across the nation. Chief Justice Earl Warren warned ominously about the "forces of hatred and malevolence" that made such acts possible, and newspapers and magazines asked, "What sort of nation are we?"

Kennedy's image of buoyant youth, the trauma of his assassination, and the collective sense that Americans had been robbed of a promising leader contributed to a powerful mystique. Only forty-six at the time of his death, he was the first president born in the twentieth century. The Kennedy mythologizing process had begun even before his tragic death. In June 1963 about 59 percent of the people surveyed claimed to have voted for Kennedy, a big jump over the 49.7 percent who actually had; after the assassination, that figure rose to 65 percent. A British journalist called it "a posthumous landslide."

The Kennedy mystique has overshadowed what most historians agree was at best a mixed record. Kennedy exercised bold presidential leadership in foreign policy, but his flexible response program and his initiatives in Cuba and Berlin marked the height of superpower confrontation during the Cold War. His enthusiasm for fighting communism abroad, however, had no domestic equivalent. Kennedy's proposals for educational aid, medical insurance, and other liberal reforms stalled, and his tax-cut bill languished in Congress until after his death. But perhaps his greatest failing was his reluctance to act on civil rights, which would become the most important domestic issue of the 1960s.

The Civil Rights Movement

Encouraged by *Brown v. Board of Education* and other favorable civil rights decisions, black southerners had stepped up their efforts to dismantle legal segregation in the late 1950s. The Montgomery bus boycotters, Martin Luther King, Jr., and the Southern Christian Leadership Conference (SCLC) developed a strategy of nonviolent direct action that was adopted and expanded by a younger generation of activists in the early 1960s. Those young people, primarily black college students, successfully challenged segregation through more assertive tactics such as sit-ins, freedom rides, and voter registration campaigns.

Sit-Ins and Freedom Rides

A new phase of the movement began in Greensboro, North Carolina, on February 1, 1960, when four black students from North Carolina Agricultural and Technical College—Ezell Blair, Jr., Franklin McCain, Joseph McNeill, and David Richmond—took seats at the "whites only" lunch counter of a local Woolworth's, determined to "sit in" until they were served. When Blair ordered something to eat, "The waitress looked at me as if I were from outer space." The target of their protest demonstrated the capricious nature of southern segregation laws. Blacks could buy toothpaste, underwear, and magazines alongside whites at Woolworth's, but not a sandwich or a cup of coffee.

Although Blair and his fellow protesters were arrested, the sit-in tactic worked and quickly spread to other southern cities. A few months later Ella Baker, an SCLC administrator and a lifelong activist, helped organize the Student Non-Violent Coordinating Committee (SNCC, pronounced "snick") to facilitate the student sit-ins (see American Lives, pages 936–937). By the end of the year, about 50,000 people had participated in sit-ins or other demonstrations, and 3,600 of them had been jailed, usually for disturbing the peace. White store owners quickly realized that they would lose business if the disruptions continued. Black activists and a number of white supporters were thus able to desegregate lunch counters in 126 cities throughout the South.

The success of SNCC's unorthodox tactics encouraged the Congress of Racial Equality (CORE), an interracial group founded in 1942, to adopt a more confrontational strategy. In 1961 CORE's executive director, James Farmer, organized a series of *freedom rides* on interstate bus lines throughout the South. Farmer targeted buses, waiting rooms, toilets, and terminal restaurants to call attention to the continuing segregation of public transportation despite the Supreme Court rulings. Activists, mostly young, both black and white, signed on for the potentially dangerous trips. In Anniston, Alabama,

Racial Violence in Montgomery
The lunch counter sit-ins organized by black students often provoked violence among hostile whites. Here a man swings a baseball bat at a black shopper on a Montgomery, Alabama, street corner the day after an unsuccessful sit-in in 1960.

Racial Violence in Birmingham
When thousands of blacks marched to downtown Birmingham, Alabama, to protest racial segregation in April 1963, they were met with fire hoses and attack dogs unleashed by Police Chief "Bull" Connor. The violence, which was televised on the national evening news, shocked many Americans and helped build sympathy for the civil rights movement among northern whites.

club-wielding Ku Klux Klansmen attacked one of the buses with stones and set it on fire. The freedom riders escaped only moments before the bus exploded. Other riders were brutally beaten in Montgomery and Birmingham, but Alabama's governor, John Patterson, refused to intervene, saying, "I cannot guarantee protection for this bunch of rabble rousers."

Although the Kennedy administration generally opposed the freedom riders' activities, scenes of the beatings and the bus burning on the nightly news prompted Attorney General Robert Kennedy to send in federal marshals to restore order. He also prodded the Interstate Commerce Commission to tighten regulations against segregation on interstate vehicles and in terminal facilities. Faced with potential Justice Department intervention against those who defied the Interstate Commerce Commission rules, most southern communities quietly acceded to the changes. CORE meanwhile learned the lesson that nonviolent protest could succeed if it provoked vicious white resistance and generated publicity. Only when forced to, it appeared, would the federal authorities act.

White southerners also staged violent attacks against blacks who registered to vote. In 1962–1963, when SNCC and CORE began conducting voter registration drives in the South, blacks who tried to register faced pressure, economic intimidation, and physical violence. For example, when Fannie Lou Hamer participated in a SNCC voter registration campaign in 1962, she was evicted from the farm where she had sharecropped for eighteen years. The FBI agents sent to the South, supposedly to protect the voting rights activists, usually sided with the white authorities and occasionally the Ku Klux Klan or did nothing.

JFK and Civil Rights

With the exception of protecting the freedom riders, the Kennedy administration lent little support to the growing civil rights movement. Behind the scenes Kennedy even authorized clandestine FBI surveillance of Martin Luther King, Jr., and a subsequent smear campaign against him. Kennedy seemed to view civil rights protests as irritating political embarrassments that distracted him from more important domestic and international issues.

Political realities, especially tensions within the Democratic coalition, also dampened Kennedy's enthusiasm for civil rights. On the one hand, Kennedy needed the votes of southern Democrats to get his programs through Congress and did not want to alienate them by embracing civil rights. For the same reason, he appointed a number of white supremacist judges to southern benches. On the other hand, blacks had given him strong support in the 1960 election, and Kennedy needed to keep them in the coalition. Thus he reached out to black constituencies with actions such as appointing former National Association for the Advancement of Colored People (NAACP) lawyer Thurgood Marshall to the U.S. Circuit Court of Appeals. But as the civil rights movement became more active and confrontational, Kennedy could not maintain that delicate balancing act.

Events came to a head in 1963 in Birmingham, Alabama, when Martin Luther King, Jr., and the Reverend Fred Shuttlesworth called for a protest against conditions in what King called "the most segregated city in the United States." In April thousands of black demonstrators marched downtown to picket Birmingham's department stores. They were met by Eugene ("Bull") Connor, the city's commissioner of public safety, who used

Ella Baker: Civil Rights Mentor

"Who the hell is this old lady here?" asked more than one impudent and unknowing newcomer to the offices of the Student Non-Violent Coordinating Committee (SNCC) in Atlanta. Regal, matronly, conservatively dressed in a business suit, and always referred to as "Miss Baker," fifty-seven-year-old Ella Baker stood out from the black and white college students who flocked to SNCC in the early 1960s. But once activists watched her in action, few doubted that she belonged. As the veteran SNCC activist John Lewis recalled, "She was much older in terms of age, but I think in terms of ideas and philosophy and commitment she was one of the youngest persons in the movement."

When Baker used her position as the executive secretary of the Southern Christian Leadership Conference (SCLC) to act as the midwife for the birth of SNCC in 1960, she already had years of experience as an organizer and facilitator of social change, almost all of it be-

hind the scenes. As she recalled, "You didn't see me on television, you didn't see news stories about me. The kind of role that I tried to play was to pick up pieces or put together pieces out of which I hoped organization might come. My theory is, strong people don't need strong leaders." Ella Baker recognized the large and often unheralded roles that women played in the emergence of the civil rights movement: "the movement of the Fifties and the Sixties was carried largely by women, since it came out of church groups. . . . The number of women who carried the movement is much larger than that of the men." Her life is a prime example.

Ella Baker was born in Norfolk, Virginia, in 1903 and grew up in rural North Carolina on land that her grandparents had originally farmed as slaves. She drew enormous strength from her family, with her mother's community and church work providing a model for her own later activism. Reflecting the importance placed on

Ella Baker
Baker was a woman of action with a lifelong commitment to social change.

education by black families, especially for daughters who would have to work even if they married, Baker was sent to Shaw College in Raleigh, North Carolina. Soon after graduating in 1927, she headed north to Harlem, arriving just as the Great Depression was drying up opportunities in the promised land of the North. Instead of going to graduate school in sociology as she had hoped, she worked as a journalist, did some political organizing, and was involved in Works Progress Administration consumer projects. She also was married briefly, and unhappily, to a black minister. In the 1940s she traveled around the country as a field organizer for the National Association for the Advancement of Colored People (NAACP) but quit that job when she took on the responsibility of raising a seven-year-old niece. Throughout her career, Baker rarely held a regular job. "How did I make a living? I haven't. I have eked out existence."

When the SCLC was established in 1957 in the wake of the successful Montgomery bus boycott, Baker was recruited "temporarily" to be its executive secretary. She ended up staying two and a half years. Her organizational skills were very important to the developing movement, but she found herself increasingly restive under King's cautious leadership. In addition, she realized, not for the first time, that her lack of deference to male leadership, outspoken manner, and willingness to talk back made black men uncomfortable. She had an especially hard time working with King, who held very traditional ideas about gender roles.

When the student sit-ins erupted spontaneously in early 1960, Baker watched that development with interest and excitement. She persuaded the SCLC to put up $800 toward a conference of student leaders to be held on the campus of her alma mater in Raleigh in April 1960. More than 300 young people attended, a huge outpouring. At the convention Baker encouraged student leaders to chart an independent role, not just to become the "youth wings" of established groups such as the SCLC, the NAACP, and CORE. She did not come right out and say "Don't let Martin Luther King tell you what to do," Julian Bond remembered, but that was clearly what she meant. The students followed her advice, and SNCC remained independent from existing civil rights organizations. Baker's faith in the students was totally in keeping with her lifelong commitment to grass-roots, "group-centered leadership." Probably her greatest dissatisfaction with the SCLC was the way that it revolved so completely around Martin Luther King's leadership.

During the turbulent 1960s Baker offered her organizational skills and material support to SNCC. She never intervened directly in the internal struggles and endless discussions that characterized the group, choosing instead to serve as a facilitator for group consensus and action. She provided not just a bridge across generations but a powerful role model of political engagement and activism. This model was especially important to women, both black and white, who drew the lesson that women could be just as effective as men in the roles of organizer and participant. The nonhierarchical structure of SNCC, with its emphasis on local leadership and individual initiative, provided an egalitarian climate far more conducive to the utilization of female talent than was American society at large. For some women, especially the white volunteers, their experience in SNCC laid the groundwork for the emergence of the women's movement later in the decade.

Voter registration had always been a top priority for SNCC, and in 1964 Baker got involved in an attempt to wrest political power from the regular Democratic party, which remained rigidly all white in the South. Denied access to the right to vote, SNCC organized an alternative political party—the Mississippi Freedom Democratic party (MFDP). Fannie Lou Hamer became the movement's most visible public orator, but Baker played a crucial behind-the-scenes role. Testifying before the credentials committee at the Democratic convention in Atlantic City that summer, Hamer and Baker led the unsuccessful effort to unseat the all-white Mississippi delegation in favor of the MFDP. When President Johnson and the Democratic leadership offered the MFDP token representation in the delegation, the MFDP rejected that compromise as an insult. Baker was not bitter or discouraged by this outcome or the many other setbacks she faced in her career: "I keep going because I don't see the productive value of being bitter. What else *do* you do?"

Ella Baker continued her lifelong commitment to participatory democracy and social change long after SNCC had lost its place on the cutting edge on the civil rights movement. She died in 1986 on her eighty-third birthday. At her memorial service, the civil rights activist Bernice Johnson Reagon, the founder of the singing group Sweet Honey in the Rock, led the assembled friends in a favorite song that captured the determination and spirituality that shaped Ella Baker's lifelong activism: "Guide my feet while I run this race . . . for I don't want to run this race in vain."

snarling dogs, electric cattle prods, and high-pressure fire hoses to break up the crowd; the hoses were so powerful that they ripped bark from trees and tore bricks from buildings. Television cameras captured the entire scene. "The civil rights movement should thank God for Bull Connor," President Kennedy noted. "He's helped it as much as Abraham Lincoln."

Realizing that he could no longer straddle the issue, Kennedy decided to step up the federal role in civil rights. On June 11, 1963, he went on television to promise major civil rights legislation banning discrimination in public accommodations and empowering the Justice Department to seek desegregation on its own authority. Black leaders hailed the speech as a "Second Emancipation Proclamation," but for one person Kennedy's speech came too late. That night, Medgar Evers, the president of the Mississippi NAACP, was shot in the back and killed in his driveway in Jackson. The martyrdom of Evers became a spur to further action.

The March on Washington

To rouse the conscience of the country at large and then to marshal support for Kennedy's bill, civil rights leaders turned to a tactic that A. Phillip Randolph had first suggested in 1941: a massive march on Washington. Martin Luther King, Jr., of the SCLC, Roy Wilkins of the NAACP, Whitney Young of the National Urban League, and the black socialist Bayard Rustin were the principal organizers. They drew support from a broad coalition, including the National Council of Churches, the National Conference of Catholics for Interracial Justice, the American Jewish Congress, and the AFL–CIO's Industrial Union Department.

On August 28, 1963, about 250,000 black and white demonstrators—the largest demonstration up to that time—gathered at the Lincoln Memorial. Speakers and performers alternately uplifted, challenged, and entertained the crowd. The march culminated in a memorable speech that Martin Luther King delivered, indeed preached, in the evangelical style of the black church:

> I have a dream that one day on the red hills of Georgia the sons of former slaves and the sons of former slaveowners will be able to sit down together at the table of brotherhood. I have a dream that one day even the state of Mississippi, a desert state sweltering with the heat of injustice and oppression, will be transformed into an oasis of freedom and justice. I have a dream that my four little children will one day live in a nation where they will not be judged by the color of their skin but by the content of their character.

He ended with an invocation from an old Negro spiritual: "Free at last! Free at last! Thank God almighty, we are free at last!"

Martin Luther King, Jr.
The Reverend Martin Luther King, Jr. (1929–1968), was one of the most eloquent advocates of the black cause in the 1950s and 1960s. For many people, his speech at the 1963 March on Washington was the high point of the event.

King's eloquence and the sight of blacks and whites marching solemnly together did more than any other event to make the civil rights movement acceptable to white Americans. The March on Washington seemed to justify the liberal faith that blacks and whites could work together to promote racial harmony, and it marked the climax of the nonviolent phase of the civil rights movement. It also confirmed King's position, especially in the white liberal community, as the leading speaker for the black cause. Winning the Nobel Peace Prize in 1964 enhanced his stature.

Despite the impact of the march on public opinion, few Congressional votes were changed by the event. Southern senators continued to block Kennedy's legislation by threatening a filibuster. Even more troubling was a new outbreak of violence by white extremists, determined to oppose equality for blacks at all costs. In September a Baptist church in Birmingham was bombed, and four black girls attending Sunday school were killed. Only two months after the Birmingham bombing, President Kennedy was assassinated in Dallas.

Fannie Lou Hamer

Registering to Vote in Mississippi

Fannie Lou Hamer was the youngest of twenty children born to a sharecropping family in Montgomery County, Mississippi. When she tried to register to vote in 1962, she lost her job as a timekeeper on a cotton plantation. In 1964 she led the challenge of the Mississippi Freedom Democratic party to the all-white party regulars in that state.

So then that was in 1962 when the civil rights workers came into this county. Now I didn't know anything about voter registration or nothin' like that, 'cause people had never been told that they could register to vote. . . . So they had a rally. I had gone to church that Sunday, and the minister announced that they were gon' have a mass meeting that Monday night. Well, I didn't know what a mass meeting was, and I was just curious to go to a mass meeting. So I did . . . and they was talkin' about how blacks had a right to register and how they had a right to vote. . . . Just listenin' at 'em, I could just see myself

votin' people outa office that I know was wrong and didn't do nothin' to help the poor. I said, you know, that's sumpin' I really wanna be involved in, and finally at the end of that rally, I had made up my mind that I was gonna come out here when they said you could go down that Friday [August 31, 1962] to try to register. . . .

He [the registrar] brought a big old book out there, and he gave me the sixteenth section of the Constitution of Mississippi, and that was dealing with de facto laws, and I didn't know nothin' about no de facto laws, didn't know nothin' about any of 'em. I could copy it like it was in the book . . . but after I got through copying it, he told me to give a reasonable interpretation and tell the meaning of that section that I had copied. Well, I flunked out. . . .

Monday, the fourth of December, I went back to Indianola to the circuit clerk's office and I told him who I was and I was there to take that literacy test again.

I said, "Now, you cain't have me fired 'cause I'm already fired, and I won't have to move now, because I'm not livin' in no white man's house." I said, "I'll be here every thirty days until I become a registered voter."

I passed that second test, but it made us become like criminals. We would have to have our lights out before dark. It was cars passing that house all times of the night, driving real slow with guns, and pickups with white mens in it, and they'd pass that house just as slow as they could pass it . . . three guns lined up in the back. . . . Pap couldn't get nothin' to do. . . .

So I started teachin' citizenship class, and I became the supervisor of the citizenship class in this county. So I moved around the county to do citizenship education and later on I become a field secretary for SNCC.

Source: Howell Raines, *My Soul Is Rested* (New York: Putnam, 1977), 249–250, 252.

Landmark Legislation

Lyndon Johnson promptly turned the passage of civil rights legislation into a memorial to his slain predecessor, a slightly ironic twist in light of Kennedy's lukewarm support for the cause. As a southerner, Johnson was eager to prove to the nation and to Kennedy's skeptical staff that he was a true liberal and a champion of racial equality. The Civil Rights Act, passed in June 1964 after a two-and-a-half-month filibuster by southern senators, was a landmark in the history of American race relations and one of the greatest achievements of the 1960s. Its keystone, Title VII, outlawed discrimination in employment on the basis of race, religion, national origin, or sex. Another section barred discrimination in public accommodations. The law gave integrationists two powerful new weapons: they could ask the U.S. attorney general to withhold federal funds from any government-run program that was not desegregated, and they could appeal

discrimination in public accommodations and employment to the Equal Employment Opportunity Commission, which Kennedy had established soon after taking office. The Civil Rights Act resulted in the desegregation of public facilities throughout the South, including many public schools, but obstacles to black voting rights persisted.

Freedom Summer. In 1964, with the Civil Rights Act on the brink of passage, black organizations and churches mounted a major civil rights campaign in Mississippi known as Freedom Summer. Drawing on several thousand volunteers from across the country, including many idealistic white college students, Freedom Summer workers established freedom schools for black children, conducted a major voter registration drive, and organized the Mississippi Freedom Democratic party, a political alternative to the all-white Mississippi Democratic organization (see American Voices, above). White

Andy Warhol on Race Relations

The artist Andy Warhol (1928–1987) is usually associated with pop-art spoofs of consumer culture, such as paintings of Campbell's soup cans and Brillo pads, along with magnetic images of popular icons such as Marilyn Monroe and Elizabeth Taylor. Yet he also treated political subjects, as in this provocative 1963 painting, *Red Race Riot*, depicting violence at a civil rights demonstration.

southerners reacted swiftly and violently to those efforts. In June, James Chaney, a CORE volunteer from Mississippi; Andrew Goodman, a student from New York; and Michael Schwerner, a New York social worker, disappeared from Philadelphia, Mississippi, and were presumed murdered. As public demand for an investigation grew, Rita Schwerner, Michael's wife, noted, "We all know that this search . . . is because Andrew Goodman and my husband are white. If only Chaney was involved, nothing would have been done." Six weeks later the FBI discovered the three bodies inside a newly constructed dam five miles away. Goodman and Schwerner had been killed by a single bullet each,

whereas Chaney had been brutally beaten with a chain and shot several times. An investigation later determined that members of the Ku Klux Klan had committed the crime. During Freedom Summer, fifteen civil rights workers were murdered; only about 1,200 black voters were registered.

The Voting Rights Act of 1965. The need for federal action to support voting rights became even clearer in 1965. In February sheriff's deputies in Marion, Alabama, killed Jimmy Lee Jackson, a black voting rights advocate, during a voter registration march. In protest, Martin Luther King and other black leaders called for a massive march on Sunday, March 7, from nearby Selma to the state capital, Montgomery, 54 miles away. Governor George Wallace banned the march, disingenuously citing concern for public safety. As soon as the marchers left Selma, mounted state troopers attacked them in broad daylight with tear gas and clubs. The scene was shown on national television later that night; ironically, ABC broke into *Judgment at Nuremberg*, a film about the Nazi war crimes trials, to show police officers attacking American citizens on the Pettus Bridge.

Lyndon Johnson called Bloody Sunday "an American tragedy" and redoubled his efforts to get Congress to pass his pending voting rights legislation. In a televised speech to a joint session of Congress on March 15 Johnson asserted, "It is wrong—deadly wrong, to deny any of your fellow Americans the right to vote in this country." Then, dramatically and repeatedly, Johnson invoked the best-known slogan of the civil rights movement, "We shall overcome." Watching the speech on television, Martin Luther King was moved to tears.

On August 6 Congress passed the Voting Rights Act of 1965, the second legislative landmark of the civil rights movement. The act suspended the literacy tests and other measures that most southern states had used to prevent blacks from registering to vote. It also authorized the attorney general to send federal examiners to register voters in any county where less than 50 percent of the voting-age population was registered, placing the entire registration and voting process under federal control. Together with the adoption in 1964 of the Twenty-fourth Amendment to the Constitution, which outlawed the federal poll tax, and successful legal challenges to state and local poll taxes, the Voting Rights Act allowed millions of blacks to register and vote for the first time. Congress reauthorized the Voting Rights Act in 1970, 1975, and 1982.

The results in the South were stunning. In 1960 only 20 percent of eligible blacks were registered; in 1964 the figure had risen to 39 percent, and in 1971 to 62 percent (see Map 30.3). As Hartman Turnbow, a Mississippi farmer who had risked his life to register in 1964, later declared, "It won't never go back where it was."

Registering to Vote

Once black citizens could register to vote, they changed the nature of southern politics, opening new channels of political participation and electoral success. In 1989 there were over 4,440 elected black officials in the South, including 578 in Mississippi alone, a dramatic change in the twenty-five years since the passage of the Voting Rights Act of 1965.

Lyndon Johnson and the Great Society

After building a reputation as a crusader for civil rights and an activist in the Kennedy tradition, Johnson went on to win the 1964 presidential election less than a year after assuming office. His landslide victory far exceeded Kennedy's meager mandate in 1960. Johnson then used his astonishing energy and genius for compromise to bring to fruition many of Kennedy's stalled programs and more than a few of his own. Those legislative accomplishments are referred to as the Great Society, Johnson's own phrase to describe his commitment to ending poverty and racial injustice. It was the Great Society, not the much less ambitious New Frontier, that fulfilled and in some cases surpassed the New Deal liberal agenda of the 1930s.

The Great Coalition Builder

Lyndon Baines Johnson brought to the presidency far more legislative experience than had any other modern president, and he used his talent to great effect. Born in the central Texas hill country in 1908, Johnson had served in government since 1932 as a Congressional aide, New Deal administrator, congressman, senator, Senate majority leader, and finally vice-president.

A man of singular force, he often got his way by using what the journalists Rowland Evans and Robert Novak called the "Johnson treatment." Approaching an unsuspecting colleague, he moved "in close, his face

MAP 30.3

Black Voter Registration in the South

After passage of the Voting Rights Act of 1965, black registration in the South increased dramatically. The bars show the number of blacks registered in 1964, before the act was passed, and 1975, after it had been in effect for ten years. States in the Deep South, such as Mississippi, Alabama, and Georgia, had the biggest rises.

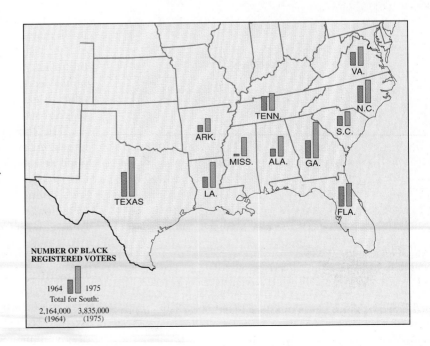

NUMBER OF BLACK
REGISTERED VOTERS

1964   1975
Total for South:
2,164,000   3,835,000
(1964)   (1975)

a scant millimeter from his target, his eyes widening and narrowing, his eyebrows rising and falling. From his pockets poured clippings, memos, statistics. Mimicry, humor, and the genius of analogy made the Treatment an almost hypnotic experience." Johnson invariably left his targets overwhelmed and bruised—and willing to go along with his requests. In his first year as president he used his powers of persuasion to push through the Civil Rights Act and the Kennedy-Johnson tax cut. His major legislative achievements, however, came after his election in 1964.

If 1964 was a year of liberal triumph in Congress, it was a year of conservative retrenchment in the Republican party. The Republican nominee for president in 1964 was Senator Barry Goldwater of Arizona. Goldwater, who was determined to offer "a choice, not an echo," campaigned against the expansion of federal power in areas such as the economy and civil rights. Goldwater's crisp speeches rejected Republican efforts to build a moderate coalition. "Extremism in the defense of liberty is no vice," he stated in his acceptance speech at the Republican convention. "Moderation in the pursuit of justice is no virtue." On foreign affairs Goldwater was an aggressive anticommunist who once joked about "lobbing [a nuclear bomb] into the men's room of the Kremlin."

The 1964 Campaign
Barry Goldwater's 1964 Republican campaign produced some very creative political memorabilia, such as bumper stickers that proclaimed "AuH_2O" (the symbols for gold and water) and this gold elephant wearing glasses like the candidate's.

President Johnson easily won the Democratic nomination. Reaffirming his commitment to the party's liberal agenda, but putting some distance between himself and the Kennedy clan, Johnson passed over Robert F. Kennedy for vice-president in favor of Senator Hubert H. Humphrey of Minnesota, who in 1948 had introduced a controversial civil rights plank that had split the party (see Chapter 28). An attempt by the avowed segregationist George C. Wallace, governor of Alabama, to exploit a white backlash against civil rights showed early strength but then fizzled. Ironically, given his later ordeal in Vietnam, Johnson presented himself as the peace candidate. Using a frightening TV commercial showing a billowing mushroom cloud, Johnson forces exploited public fears about Goldwater's bellicose foreign policy. (The ad was pulled two days later in response to public outcries against fear mongering.)

The Johnson-Humphrey ticket won by one of the largest margins in history, receiving 61.1 percent of the popular vote. This surpassed even the 1936 landslide of that great coalition builder Franklin D. Roosevelt, Johnson's political idol and mentor. And Johnson's coattails were long; his sweeping victory brought Democratic gains in both Congress and the state legislatures.

Enacting the Liberal Agenda

Like most New Deal liberals, Johnson held an expansive view of presidential leadership and the positive role of government. The 1964 election gave him the popular

The "Johnson Treatment"
Lyndon B. Johnson, a shrewd and adroit politician, learned many of his legislative skills while serving as majority leader of the Senate from 1953 to 1960. Here he zeroes in on Senator Theodore Francis Green of Rhode Island. After assuming the presidency Johnson remarked, "They say Jack Kennedy had style, but I'm the one who's got the bills passed."

TABLE 30.1

Major Great Society Legislation

Civil Rights

1964	Twenty-fourth Amendment	Outlawed poll tax in federal elections
	Civil Rights Act	Banned discrimination in employment and public accommodations on the basis of race, religion, sex, or national origin
1965	Voting Rights Act	Outlawed literacy tests for voting; provided federal supervision of registration in historically low-registration areas

Social Welfare

1964	Economic Opportunity Act	Created Office of Economic Opportunity (OEO) to administer War on Poverty programs such as Head Start, Job Corps, and Volunteers in Service to America (VISTA)
1965	Medical Care Act	Provided medical care for poor (Medicaid) and elderly (Medicare)
1966	Minimum Wage Act	Raised hourly minimum wage from $1.25 to $1.40 and expanded coverage to new groups

Education

1965	Elementary and Secondary Education Act	Granted federal aid for education of poor children
	National Endowment for the Arts and Humanities	Provided federal funding and support for artists and scholars
	Higher Education Act	Provided federal scholarships for post-secondary education

Housing and Urban Development

1964	Urban Mass Transportation Act	Provided federal aid to urban mass transit
	Omnibus Housing Act	Provided federal funds for public housing and rent subsidies for low-income families
1965	Housing and Urban Development Act	Created Department of Housing and Urban Development (HUD)
1966	Metropolitan Area Redevelopment and Demonstration Cities acts	Designated 150 "model cities" for combined programs of public housing, social services, and job training

Environment

| 1964 | Wilderness Preservation Act | Designated 9.1 million acres of federal lands as "wilderness areas," barring future roads, buildings, or commercial use |
| 1965 | Air and Water Quality acts | Set tougher air quality standards; required states to enforce water quality standards for interstate waters |

Miscellaneous

1964	Tax Reduction Act	Reduced personal and corporate income tax rates
1965	Immigration Act	Abandoned national quotas of 1924 law, allowing more non-European immigration
	Appalachian Regional Development Act	Provided federal funding for roads, health clinics, and other public works projects in economically depressed regions

mandate and, more important, the filibuster-proof Senate majority that he needed to push his programs forward. "Hurry boys, hurry," he urged his staff. "Get that legislation up to the Hill and out. Eighteen months from now ol' Landslide Lyndon will be Lame-Duck Lyndon." Under Johnson's Great Society, including a multifaceted War on Poverty program, the Eighty-ninth Congress en-

acted more social reform measures than any session had since Roosevelt's first term, offering legislation for every important element of the Democratic coalition (see Table 30.1).

One of Johnson's first big successes was breaking the Congressional deadlock on aid to education. Passed in April 1965, the Elementary and Secondary Education

Act authorized $1 billion in federal funds to benefit impoverished children. By dispensing aid to schools on the basis of the number of needy children in attendance, the act sidestepped the religious issue by granting funds to public and parochial schools alike. In practice, the compromise measure spread funding to a broad spectrum of schools, and the results did not necessarily benefit poor children. Undeterred by such flaws, Johnson pressed for further educational subsidies. Six months later he signed the Higher Education Act, providing the first federal scholarships for college students.

The Eighty-ninth Congress also gave Johnson enough votes to enact the federal health insurance legislation first proposed by Truman. Realizing that it could no longer block some form of federal health insurance, the American Medical Association proposed that federal funds be used to pay doctors as well as hospitals. The result was two new programs: Medicare, a health plan for the elderly funded by a surcharge on Social Security payroll taxes, and Medicaid, a plan for the poor paid for by general tax revenues. Because Congress did not impose a cap on medical expenses, which the medical industry opposed, federal expenditures for the two programs quickly escalated. Once again, by seeking legislative compromises that pleased multiple constituencies, the Johnson administration created expansive and economically unwieldy programs.

Administration programs did not aid only the poor—the middle class benefited, too. Federal urban renewal and home mortgage assistance helped those who could afford to live in single-family homes or modern apartments. Medicare assistance went to every elderly person covered by Social Security, regardless of need. Much of the federal aid to education benefited the children of the middle class. In addition, Johnson successfully pressed for environmental measures that benefited American society as a whole: the expansion of the national park system, improvement of air and water quality, increased land-use planning, and, at the insistence of his wife, Lady Bird Johnson, the Highway Beautification Act of 1965. That year also saw the creation of the National Endowment for the Arts, which supported the performing and creative arts, and the National Endowment for the Humanities, which funded efforts to understand and interpret the nation's cultural and historical heritage. Reaching out to new ethnic constituencies, Johnson signed the Immigration Act of 1965, which abandoned the quota system of the 1920s that had favored European immigrants (see Chapter 24), and replaced it with more uniform hemispheric restrictions. This combination of legislative initiatives helped unite a diverse array of Democratic constituencies and reflected the liberal belief that federal activism could ensure the public welfare and promote fairness. But it involved legislative compromises as well, compromises that ultimately limited the effectiveness of certain programs.

The War on Poverty

Johnson always insisted that the top priority of his Great Society was to put "an end to poverty in our time." The problem of poverty was very real. Poor people made up about a fourth of the American population; three-fourths of the poor were white. The poor in the United States consisted of isolated farmers and miners in Appalachia, blacks and Puerto Ricans in urban ghettos, Mexican-Americans in migrant labor camps and urban barrios, native Americans on reservations, women raising families on their own, and the abandoned and destitute elderly. As Michael Harrington had pointed out in his influential 1962 book, *The Other America*, the poor were everywhere, but their poverty was curiously invisible in an affluent suburban society. Modern technology had "made a longer, healthier, better life possible," Harrington observed, yet it left the poor "on the margin": "They watch the movies and read the magazines of affluent America, and these teach them that they are internal exiles."

New Deal social welfare programs had failed to reach these people. Because unemployment insurance ran out after a few months, it did not provide protection against extended joblessness. Social Security and other social insurance programs provided benefits to workers who paid for them through special taxes, but not all workers were covered. Social welfare programs such as Old Age Assistance, Aid to Dependent Children, and Aid to the Blind had strict restrictions regarding eligibility.

Responding to Harrington and other advocates for the poor, the Johnson administration tried to reduce poverty by expanding long-established social insurance, welfare, and public works programs. It broadened Social Security to include waiters and waitresses, domestic servants, farm workers, and hospital employees. Social welfare expenditures increased rapidly, especially for Aid to Families with Dependent Children (AFDC), as did public housing and rent subsidy programs. Food Stamps, begun in 1964 largely to stabilize farm prices, grew into a major program of assistance to low-income families. The Appalachian Regional Development Act of 1965 provided federal funding for local roads, health clinics, and other public works projects in that poverty-stricken region. As in the New Deal, the social welfare system continued to develop in a piecemeal fashion, with no overall coordination.

The Office of Economic Opportunity (OEO), established by the omnibus Economic Opportunity Act of 1964, became the Great Society's showcase in the War on Poverty. Built around the twin strategies of equal opportunity and community action, OEO programs were so numerous and diverse that they recalled the alphabet agencies of the New Deal. Officials at the OEO quickly realized that identifying poverty was one thing; drafting and implementing programs to address it was quite an-

Project Head Start
This day care center in Chicago's Woodlawn neighborhood was one of the early pilot projects of the Head Start program, one of the most acclaimed programs of LBJ's War on Poverty.

other. Sargent Shriver, who came from the Peace Corps to head the new agency, admitted, "It's like we went down to Cape Kennedy [the NASA space center in Florida] and launched a half dozen rockets at once."

Coordinated by the OEO, the War on Poverty produced some of the most innovative measures of the Johnson administration. Head Start provided free nursery schools to prepare disadvantaged preschoolers for kindergarten. The Job Corps and the Neighborhood Youth Corps provided jobs and vocational training for young people. Upward Bound gave low-income teenagers the skills and motivation to go to college. Volunteers in Service to America (VISTA), modeled on the Peace Corps, promoted community service among youths in impoverished rural and urban areas. The Community Action Program encouraged the poor to demand "maximum feasible participation" in decisions that affected them. Community Action organizers worked closely with 2,000 lawyers employed by the Legal Services Program to provide the poor with free legal aid.

The OEO quickly drew criticism, however. Some of the more militant VISTA and Community Action Program agents encouraged poor people to demand public services long withheld by unresponsive local governments. Community organizers on the government payroll in Syracuse, New York, for example, formed tenants' rights groups to protest conditions in public housing, conducted voter registration drives to unseat unpopular elected representatives, and even used public funds to bail out activists arrested for protesting at local welfare offices. Legal Services lawyers challenged welfare and housing administrations in class-action suits. Needless to say, such activism upset entrenched urban political machines, including many run by Democrats. Mayors such as Sam Yorty of Los Angeles and Richard J. Daley of Chicago vigorously resisted OEO guidelines for including poor people in program planning and administration. Responding to this Democratic opposition, the Johnson administration gradually phased out the Community Action Program and channeled spending for housing, social services, and other urban poverty programs through local municipal governments under the Metropolitan Area and Demonstration Cities acts of 1966.

The Johnson administration put issues of poverty, justice, and access at the center of national political life, but the mixed results suggest the difficulties of promoting fundamental political and economic change through federal initiatives. The effectiveness of the War on Poverty is hard to measure. The statistical decline of poverty in the 1960s suggests that those programs were successful; the proportion of Americans living below the poverty line dropped from 20 percent in 1963 to 13 percent in 1968 (see Figure 30.1). Economic advancement of African-Americans was even more marked. In the 1960s the black poverty rate was cut in half, and millions of blacks moved into the middle class, some through federal jobs in antipoverty programs. But critics charged that the reduction in the poverty rate was due to the decade's booming economy—fueled by the growing war in Vietnam—not to the War on Poverty. Moreover, while the overall standard of living increased, the uneven distribution of

FIGURE 30.1

Americans in Poverty, 1960–1992
During the 1960s, the poverty rate among American families dropped from 20 percent to 13 percent, suggesting that the War on Poverty was bringing more Americans into the economic mainstream. Critics charged, however, that it was economic growth spurred by the Vietnam War that accounted for the decrease.

wealth persisted. The poor were better off in an absolute sense, but they remained as far behind the middle class as ever. The liberals' commitment to corporate capitalism ultimately limited their ability to redistribute wealth.

Cracks in the New Deal Coalition

The Great Society represented the culmination of the liberal social agenda first advanced during the Great Depression. But the implementation of that agenda, which relied on the government to address social and economic problems, revealed deep contradictions in the New Deal coalition. That coalition was inherently unstable, torn among its diverse constituencies and their conflicting priorities. Those contradictions had been lurking in political life since Roosevelt and Truman had begun to expand the power of the federal government, but they surfaced forcefully in the climate fostered by the politics of expectation.

In the 1960s, Kennedy's articulation of the aspirations of many Americans and Johnson's genius for translating those social visions into concrete legislative programs set in motion a remarkable expansion of federal power. Kennedy and Johnson gathered an extraordinarily diverse set of groups into the New Deal coalition—middle-class and poor; white and nonwhite; Protestant, Jewish, and Catholic; urban and rural. As the functions and responsibilities of the government grew, so did demands for further action from that widening cast of politically organized constituencies.

For a brief period between 1964 and 1966 the coalition held together. But inevitably the claims of certain groups—such as the demand of blacks for civil rights and that of the urban poor for increased political power—conflicted with the interests of other Democratic supporters, such as white southerners and northern political bosses who wanted to maintain the status quo. In the end the New Deal coalition, which had fostered a vast expansion of federal power, could not sustain a consensus on the purposes of government activism.

Democrats were also plagued by public disillusionment over the shortcomings of their reforms. In the early 1960s the lofty rhetoric of the New Frontier and the Great Society raised unprecedented expectations for social change. But competition for federal largesse was keen, and the shortage of funds for programs such as the War on Poverty left many promises unfulfilled. This was especially true after 1965, when the escalation of the Vietnam War siphoned funding away from domestic programs. In 1966 the government spent $22 billion on the Vietnam War and only $1.2 billion on the War on Poverty. Ultimately, as Martin Luther King put it, the Great Society was "shot down on the battlefields of Vietnam."

The Continuing Struggle for Civil Rights

Just as the Great Society was plagued by internal divisions and external opposition, so too was the evolving civil rights movement. As the struggle moved outside the South and took on the more stubborn problems of entrenched poverty and racism, black frustration and anger fueled a new racial militance. The rhetoric and tactics of the emerging black power movement shattered the existing civil rights coalition and galvanized white opposition.

Rising Militance

Once the system of legal, or de jure, segregation had fallen, the civil rights movement turned to the more difficult task of eliminating the de facto segregation, enforced by custom, that made blacks second-class citizens throughout the nation. Racial discrimination was less flagrant outside the South, but it was real and pervasive, especially in education, housing, and employment. Although the *Brown* decision outlawed separate schools, it did nothing to change educational systems in areas where schools were all-black or all-white because of residential segregation. In the 1960s, for example, 90 percent of Chicago's black students attended predominantly black schools. Not until 1973 did federal judges begin to extend the desegregation that had begun in the South two decades earlier to schools in the rest of the country.

As civil rights leaders took on the new target of northern racism, the movement fractured along generational lines. Students who had risked assault to sit in at lunch counters or to register to vote grew impatient with the gradualism of their elders. Many of the young freedom riders who had spent months in harsh southern jails found little relevance in Martin Luther King's commitment to nonviolence. Between 1963 and 1965 those activists repudiated the legalistic, nonviolent approach epitomized by the March on Washington and urged blacks to take control of their communities through more radical and, if necessary, violent means.

Black Separatism. Some younger black activists, eager for confrontation and faster change, questioned the goal of integration into white society. Espoused by earlier black leaders such as Marcus Garvey in the 1920s (see Chapter 24), black separatism was revived in the 1960s by the Nation of Islam, popularly known as the Black Muslims. The Nation of Islam had begun as a small sect in the 1930s, but by the 1960s it had more than 10,000 members and many more sympathizers. The Black Muslims proselytized very effectively in pris-

ons, urging black inmates to take charge of their lives by adopting a strict code of personal behavior, including the Muslim ban on the use of drugs, alcohol, and tobacco. The Nation of Islam's ideology was extremely hostile to whites, whom its leader Elijah Muhammad called "blue-eyed devils." Forcefully promoting black nationalism, the group stressed black pride, unity, and self-help.

The Black Muslims' most charismatic figure was Malcolm X. Born Malcolm Little in 1925, he converted to the Nation of Islam while serving time in prison for attempted burglary. Taking the name Malcolm X, he portrayed his transformation from street hustler to minister of Islam as evidence of the redemptive powers of the Black Muslim faith. A brilliant debater and a spellbinding speaker, Malcolm X preached a philosophy quite different from Martin Luther King's. Malcolm advocated militant protest and separatism, although he condoned the use of violence only for self-defense and self-assertion. He was hostile to the traditional civil rights organizations, caustically referring to the 1963 march as the "Farce on Washington" and mocking the "angry revolutionists all harmonizing 'We Shall Overcome . . . Suum Day' while tripping and swinging along arm-in-arm with the very people they were supposed to be angrily revolting against."

In 1964, after a power struggle with Elijah Muhammed, Malcolm X broke with the Nation of Islam. He then made a pilgrimage to Mecca, the holiest site of traditional Islam, and toured Africa, where he embraced the liberation struggles of all colonized peoples. After his return to the United States, he founded the Organization of Afro-American Unity to promote this internationalist vision and moved away from antiwhite rhetoric. On February 21, 1965, Malcolm X was assassinated while giving a speech at the Audubon Ballroom in Harlem. Three Black Muslims were later convicted for the murder. His autobiography, ghostwritten by Alex Haley and published soon after Malcolm's death, became one of the decade's most influential books.

Black Power. Malcolm X's call for black cultural and political independence appealed to young black activists in SNCC and CORE, but many balked at the idea of converting to Islam, preferring a secular black nationalist movement. Soon many of these activists were embracing *black power*, a more aggressive call for black self-reliance and racial pride. As a result of this growing militancy, most civil rights organizations went through a major identity crisis. CORE's decision to bar whites from leadership positions in 1965 was a clear indication of those tensions. The next year, the SNCC leader Stokely Carmichael christened a new era in the black struggle: "The only way we gonna stop them white men from whoopin' us is to take over. We been saying freedom for

Malcolm X (1925–1965)
Charismatic, controversial, and caustic, Malcolm X rarely minced words. "Yes, I'm an extremist," he told the writer Alex Haley. "The black race here in North America is in extremely bad condition. You show me a black man who isn't an extremist and I'll show you one who needs psychiatric attention!" Director Spike Lee's 1992 film, *Malcolm X*, reignited old controversies and started some of its own.

six years and we ain't got nothin'. What we gonna start saying is Black Power!" Carmichael's words marked a public avowal of black power, but his pronouncement merely confirmed the militant forces already present in SNCC and other civil rights groups. In fact, by 1966 most whites had been effectively ejected from the civil rights movement. Focusing on community control and black self-determination, SNCC and other groups admonished whites to go home and work against racism in their own backyards.

In the same year Huey Newton and Bobby Seale, two college students in Oakland, California, founded the Black Panthers as a militant self-defense organization to protect local blacks from police violence. The Panthers' influence quickly spread to other cities, where they undertook a wide range of community organizing projects, including a number of interracial efforts. But the Panthers' affinity for Third World revolutionary movements and armed struggle became their most publicized attribute.

Only three years after Martin Luther King's "I Have a Dream" speech, radical black power activists proposed a new agenda: not nonviolence but armed self-defense, not integration but separatism, not working within the system but preparing for revolution. Among the most significant legacies of black power was the assertion of racial pride. Many young blacks insisted on the term *Afro-American* rather than *Negro*, a term they found demeaning because of its historical association with slav-

ery and racism. Rejecting white tastes and standards, blacks wore African clothing and Afro hairstyles and helped awaken interest in black history, art, and literature. By the 1970s many colleges and universities were offering programs in black studies.

The new black assertiveness alarmed many white Americans. They had been willing to go along with the moderate reforms of the 1950s and early 1960s but became wary when blacks started demanding immediate access to higher-paying jobs, housing in white neighborhoods, integrated schools, and increased political power. In 1966, 84 percent of all whites thought blacks were demanding too much change, up from 34 percent five years earlier.

Summer in the City

A major reason for the erosion of white support was a wave of riots that struck the nation's cities. Every summer from 1964 to 1968 images of defiant black youths and burning buildings filled the nightly news. The rapid growth of de facto segregation in metropolitan areas provided the backdrop for the riots. Without the education

Watts in Flames
The nation's worst racial disturbance since the Detroit race riot of 1943 began in the Watts section of Los Angeles on August 11, 1965. An altercation broke out when white police officers stopped two blacks for a minor traffic violation. Thirty-four persons died in the Watts riot.

and skills needed for most city jobs, successive generations of blacks moving out of the rural South were unable to find employment that paid an adequate wage. Many were unemployed. Moreover, they were angry with white landlords who owned the substandard housing that they were forced to live in, white shopkeepers who earned money from black trade but would not hire black clerks or salespeople, and all-white unions—especially in the construction industry—that controlled access to skilled jobs. Most critically, many blacks came to resent the police, whose violent presence in black neighborhoods made them seem like "an occupying army." Stimulated by the successes of southern blacks who had challenged whites and gotten results, young urban blacks expressed their grievances through their own brand of "direct action."

The first "long hot summer" began in July 1964 in New York City, when police shot a young black criminal suspect in Harlem. Angry youths looted and rioted for a week. The volatile issue of police brutality would set off riots in a number of cities over the next four years. In August 1965 the arrest of a young black motorist in the Watts section of Los Angeles sparked six days of rioting that left thirty-four blacks dead. Ironically, Watts erupted only five days after President Johnson hailed the passage of the Voting Rights Act of 1965 as the next great step toward racial equality. For many young urban blacks the legal gains of the civil rights movement were irrelevant to their daily experience of poverty and economic exploitation. Instead of singing "We shall overcome," Watts rioters shouted "Burn, baby, burn."

The riots of 1967 were the most serious of all (see Map 30.4). Rioting began in several southern cities in the spring, spread to other cities in June, and engulfed twenty-two cities in July and August. The most devastating outbreaks occurred in Newark and Detroit. Forty-three people were killed in Detroit alone, nearly all of them black, and $50 million of property was destroyed. Federal paratroopers, some just back from service in Vietnam, were sent in to restore order, and Mayor Jerome Cavanaugh compared the city to war-ravaged Berlin in 1945. As in most of the riots, the arson and looting were directed at white-owned stores and property, but there was little physical violence against white people. Almost all the reported sniping turned out to involve wild shooting by the police.

The riots finally provoked a response from the federal government. On July 29, 1967, President Johnson appointed a special commission under Governor Otto Kerner of Illinois to investigate the reasons for the rioting. The final report of the National Advisory Commission on Civil Disorders, released in March 1968, detailed the continuing inequality and racism of urban life. It also issued a warning: "Our nation is moving toward two societies, one black, one white—separate and unequal. . . .

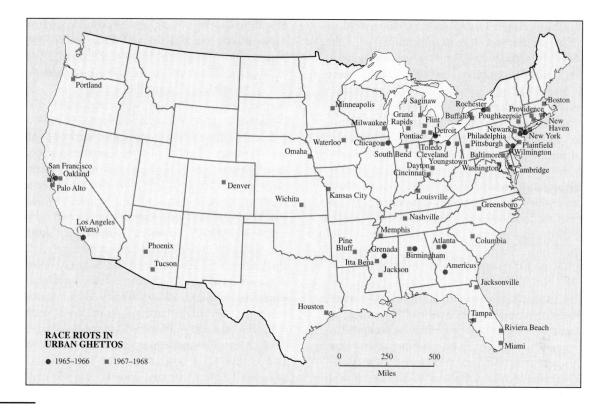

MAP 30.4

Racial Unrest in America's Cities, 1965–1968
American cities suffered through four "long hot summers" of rioting in the mid-1960s. In 1967, the worst year, riots broke out across the United States, including the South and West. Major riots usually did not occur in the same city two years in a row.

What white Americans have never fully understood—but what the Negro can never forget—is that white society is deeply implicated in the ghetto. White institutions created it, white institutions maintain it, and white society condones it."

The Assassination of Martin Luther King, Jr. Barely a month after the Commission on Civil Disorders released its report, Martin Luther King was assassinated in Memphis, Tennessee, where he had gone to support a strike by predominantly black sanitation workers. On April 4, 1968, he was shot by James Earl Ray, a white ex-convict whose motive was unknown. King's death set off an explosion of urban rioting. Major violence broke out in more than a hundred cities. As violence and looting engulfed most of Chicago's West Side, Mayor Richard J. Daley ordered police to "shoot to kill" suspected arsonists. In Washington, National Guard troops with machine guns protected the Capitol; on television, it was framed by the fires from neighboring ghettos.

With King's assassination the civil rights movement lost the black leader best able to stir the conscience of white America. At the time of his death, King was only

thirty-nine years old. During the last years of his life he had moved toward a more comprehensive view of the structural problems of poverty and racism faced by blacks in contemporary America. In 1966 he had confronted the issue of residential segregation in a losing campaign for open housing in Chicago. He also spoke out eloquently against the Vietnam War. In 1968 he was planning a poor people's campaign to raise issues of economic injustice and inequality. How successful King would have been in those endeavors will never be known, but his death marked the passing of an important national leader and was symptomatic of the troubled course of the civil rights movement.

The Legacy of the Civil Rights Movement. The 1950s and 1960s brought permanent, indeed revolutionary, changes in American race relations. Jim Crow segregation was overturned in less than a decade, and federal legislation ensured protection of black Americans' basic civil rights. The enfranchisement of blacks in southern states ended political control there by a lily-white Democratic party and allowed black candidates to enter the political arena. White candidates who had once been ardent

segregationists now courted the black vote. In time Martin Luther King's greatness was recognized even in the South; in 1986 his birthday became a national holiday.

However, much remained undone. The more entrenched forms of segregation and discrimination persisted despite the legal reforms of the 1960s. African-Americans, particularly those in the central cities, continued to make up a disproportionate number of the poor, unemployed, and undereducated. As the civil rights movement gradually disintegrated, its agenda remained unfinished. Nevertheless, it continued to inspire many outside the black community, including Mexican-Americans, native Americans, and women.

The Spreading Demand for Equal Rights

Following the example set by the civil rights movement, Mexican-Americans and native Americans organized to press their claims. Although both groups had long histories of organizing for equal rights, the black civil rights movement provided a fresh and innovative model for social change, particularly among the young. As a civil rights worker observed, "What started out as an identify crisis for Negroes turned out to be an identity crisis for the nation."

Mexican-American Activism. Although Mexican-Americans had been actively working for civil rights since the 1930s (see Chapter 25), the emphasis had been on labor organizing, veterans' rights, and community affairs. Until 1960 few Spanish-speaking Americans had participated in electoral politics. Poverty, an uncertain legal status, and language barriers made political mobiliza-tion difficult. That situation began to change when the Mexican-American Political Association (MAPA) mobilized support for Kennedy in 1960, probably providing his margin of victory in the closely contested states of Texas, New Mexico, and Illinois. In return, Kennedy appointed several Mexican-American leaders to posts in Washington. Over the next four years, MAPA and other political organizations successfully worked to elect Mexican-American candidates to Congress, including Edward Roybal of California and Henry González and Elizo de la Garza of Texas in the House, and Joseph Montoya of New Mexico in the Senate.

Younger Mexican-Americans quickly grew impatient with MAPA, however. More radical and more inclined to celebrate cultural achievements and traditions, the younger leaders pursued increasingly diverse goals. The barrios of Los Angeles and other western cities produced the militant Brown Berets, who modeled themselves on the Black Panthers (who wore black berets). Rejecting the assimilationist approach of their elders, 1,500 Mexican-American students met in Denver in 1969 to hammer out a new nationalist political and cultural agenda. They proclaimed a new term, *Chicano*, to replace *Mexican-American* and subsequently organized a political party, La Raza Unida ("The United Race"), to promote Mexican-American interests and candidates. Chicano students in California and other southwestern states also staged demonstrations and boycotts to press for bilingual education, the hiring of more Chicano teachers, and the creation of programs in Chicano studies. By the 1970s there were dozens of those programs in universities throughout the region.

Chicano strategists also pursued economic objectives. Working in the fields around Delano, California,

César Chávez

Mexican-American labor leader César Chávez addresses a rally in Guadalupe, California. Chávez won national attention in 1965 during a strike of migrant farm workers, most of them Mexican-Americans, against California grape growers. Drawing on tactics from the civil rights movement, Chávez called for nonviolent action and effectively mobilized support by persuading white liberals to boycott nonunion table grapes.

the labor leader César Chávez organized the United Farm Workers (UFW), the first union to represent migrant workers successfully. A 1965 grape pickers' strike and a nationwide boycott of table grapes brought Chávez and his union national publicity. They won the support of the AFL–CIO and Senator Robert F. Kennedy of New York, and Chávez was soon receiving almost as much media attention as was Martin Luther King, Jr. Protesting employer harassment of the UFW and subsequent outbreaks of violence in the fields, Chávez undertook a twenty-five-day fast in 1968. Victory came in 1970, when California grape growers signed contracts recognizing the UFW.

Asserting Rights for Native Americans. American Indians also found a model in the civil rights movement. Native Americans, who numbered nearly 800,000 in the 1960s, were an exceedingly diverse group, divided by language, tribal history, region, and degree of integration into mainstream American life. Moreover, the termination policy that had begun in the 1950s (see Chapter 29) had accelerated the breakdown of tribal life and the dispersal of native American populations. But native Americans also shared certain things, such as an unemployment rate ten times the national average, the worst poverty, the most inadequate housing, the highest disease rates, and the least access to education of any group in the United States.

As early as World War II, the National Council of American Indians had lobbied for the improvement of those conditions, but now some Indian groups became more assertive. In 1961 representatives of sixty-seven tribes issued a Declaration of Indian Purpose that foreshadowed much of the later civil rights activism. During the War on Poverty, Indian groups successfully lobbied the Johnson administration to channel antipoverty funds into their communities. Paralleling the growing militancy in the black civil rights movement, younger native Americans challenged the accommodationist approach of their elders. Like blacks and Mexican-Americans, they proposed a new name for themselves—*native Americans*—and organized protests and demonstrations to build support for their cause. In 1968 several Chipewyan from Minnesota organized the militant American Indian Movement (AIM), which drew its strength from the third of the native American population that lived in "red ghettos" in cities throughout the West.

AIM consciously modeled itself on the black power movement, and for a few years its tactics attracted considerable public attention. In November 1969 AIM seized the deserted federal penitentiary on Alcatraz Island in San Francisco Bay, offering the government $24 worth of trinkets to pay for it. (This was supposedly what the Dutch had paid the native inhabitants for Manhattan Island in 1626.) The occupation of Alcatraz lasted until the summer of 1971. In November 1972 a thousand protesters occupied the headquarters of the Federal Bureau of Indian Affairs in Washington, D.C., which was to many native Americans a hated symbol of the inconsistent federal policy on tribal welfare (see American Voices, page 952).

In February 1973, 200 Sioux organized by AIM leaders began an occupation of the tiny village of Wounded Knee, South Dakota, the site of the army massacre of the Sioux in 1890 (see Chapter 17). They were protesting the light sentences given to a group of white men convicted of killing a Sioux in 1972. The protesters took eleven hostages and occupied several buildings to dramatize their cause. But when a gun battle with the FBI left one protester dead and another wounded, the seventy-one-day siege collapsed. These militant confrontations captured media attention but alienated many white onlookers. In general, however, the new native American activism helped spur government action on tribal issues (see Chapter 32).

Wounded Knee Revisited
In 1973 members of the American Indian Movement staged a seventy-one-day protest at Wounded Knee, South Dakota, the site of the 1890 massacre of 200 Sioux by U.S. soldiers. The takeover was sparked by the murder of a local Sioux by a group of whites but quickly expanded to include demands for basic reforms in federal Indian policy and tribal governance.

Mary Crow Dog

The Trail of Broken Treaties

In November 1972 nineteen-year-old Mary Crow Dog and several hundred other Sioux from the Rosebud and Pine Ridge reservations in South Dakota traveled to Washington, D.C. Their group was one of several caravans participating in a protest known as the Trail of Broken Treaties, which ended in a six-day occupation of the Bureau of Indian Affairs headquarters.

When we arrived in Washington we got lost. We had been promised food and accommodation, but due to government pressure many church groups which had offered to put us up and feed us got scared and backed off. . . .

Somebody suggested, "Let's all go to the BIA." It seemed the natural thing to do, to go to the Bureau of Indian Affairs building on Constitution Avenue. They would have to put us up. It was "our" building after all. Besides, that was what we had come for, to complain about the treatment the bureau was dishing out to us. . . . Next thing I knew we were in it. We spilled into the build-

ing like a great avalanche. Some people put up a tipi on the front lawn. . . . The building finally belonged to us and we lost no time turning it into a tribal village. . . .

We pushed the police and guards out of the building. Some did not wait to be pushed but jumped out of the ground-floor windows like so many frogs. We had formulated twenty Indian demands. These were all rejected by the few bureaucrats sent to negotiate with us. . . . Soon we listened to other voices as the occupation turned into a siege. I heard somebody yelling, "The pigs are here." I could see from the window that it was true. The whole building was surrounded by helmeted police armed with all kinds of guns. A fight broke out between the police and our security. Some of our young men got hit over the head with police clubs and we saw the blood streaming down their faces. . . .

We barricaded all doors and the lowest windows with document boxes, Xerox machines, tables, file cabinets,

anything we could lay our hands on. . . .

From then on, every morning we were given a court order to get out by six P.M. Come six o'clock and we would be standing there ready to join battle. I think many brothers and sisters were prepared to die right on the steps of the BIA building. . . .

In the end a compromise was reached. The government said. . . they would appoint two high administration officials to seriously consider our twenty demands. Our expenses to get home would be paid. Nobody would be prosecuted. Of course, our twenty points were never gone into afterward. From the practical point of view, nothing had been achieved. . . . But morally it had been a great victory. We had faced White America collectively, not as individual tribes. We had stood up to the government and gone through our baptism of fire. We had not run.

Source: Mary Crow Dog, Lakota Woman (New York: Grove Weidenfeld, 1990), 84–85,88–91.

Identity Politics. Civil rights, once seen as a movement exclusively for the rights of black people, also sparked a new awareness among some predominantly white groups. Americans of Polish, Italian, Greek, and Slavic descent, most of them working-class and Catholic, proudly embraced a new ethnic identity modeled on black pride. George Wiley organized poor people, mostly women on welfare, into the National Welfare Rights Organization. Calling welfare a right, not a privilege, activists staged sit-ins at government offices to demand better treatment and higher benefits.

Homosexual men and women also banded together to protest legal and social oppression based on sexual orientation. Moving beyond an older legalistic approach to homosexual rights, the gay liberation movement was born in 1969 with the "Stonewall riot" in New York City, in which patrons of a gay bar in Greenwich Village fought back against police harassment. The assertion of

gay pride that followed the Stonewall incident drew heavily on the language and tactics of the civil rights movement. Activists took the new name of gay rather than homosexual; founded advocacy groups, newspapers, and political organizations to challenge discrimination and prejudice; and provided emotional support for those who "came out" by publicly affirming their homosexual identity. Models for increased political activism based on heightened group identity represented one of the most significant legacies of the African-American struggle to the rest of American society.

The Revival of Feminism

The black civil rights movement also helped reactivate feminism, a movement that had been languishing since the 1920s. Just as the abolition movement had been the

training ground for an earlier generation of women's rights advocates in the nineteenth century, young feminists in the 1960s were inspired and influenced by the black struggle. But the revival of feminism also grew out of postwar social and demographic changes that affected younger and older women alike.

Women's Changing Lives. In the 1960s more women were attending college and working outside the home than ever before. At the same time, married women were having fewer children and were more likely to get a divorce. The most sweeping change was the dramatic rise in women's participation in the work force. In 1950 almost one-third of women were employed, and one-quarter of those workers were married. By 1970, 42.6 percent of women were working, and four out of ten working women were married (see Figure 30.2). Especially significant was the growth in the number of working women with preschool children—up from 12 percent in 1950 to 30 percent in 1970. In the postwar consumer society working mothers were becoming both socially accepted and economically necessary.

Women also benefited from increased access to education. Immediately after World War II the percentage of women college students declined: the GI Bill gave men a temporary advantage in access to higher education, and many college women dropped out to marry and raise families at the height of the baby boom. By 1960, however, the percentage of women students had climbed to 35 percent, and in 1970 it reached 41 percent.

The meaning of marriage was changing, too. The baby boom turned out to be only a temporary interruption of the century-long decline in the birth rate. The introduction of the birth control pill, first marketed in 1960, and the intrauterine device (IUD) helped women control their fertility. Women had fewer children and, because of increased life expectancy (75 years in 1970, up from 54 years in 1920), devoted fewer years to raising children. At the same time, the divorce rate, which

had risen slowly throughout the twentieth century, grew precipitously as the states liberalized divorce laws. It doubled from 15 per thousand marriages in 1960 to 32 per thousand in 1975. Women could no longer assume that their marriages would last until "death do us part."

As a result of these changes, traditional gender expectations were dramatically undercut. American women's lives now usually included work and marriage, often child-rearing and a career, and possibly bringing up children as a single parent after a divorce. Those changing social realities created a major constituency for the emerging women's movement of the 1960s.

Paths to Feminism. Two distinct movements helped stimulate the revival of feminism during those years. The women's rights branch, led by the National Organization for Women (NOW), consisted of older, politically active professional women who sought change by working through the political system. The women's liberation branch, by contrast, attracted primarily younger women, especially recent college graduates who had been active in civil rights and the protests against the Vietnam War. Their vision of feminism was more radical and confrontational. Mirroring the separatism of black power advocates, they were initially somewhat hostile to men.

In 1961 John Kennedy established a Presidential Commission on the Status of Women, an attempt to counter criticism of his administration's poor record on women's issues. Eleanor Roosevelt served as honorary head of the commission. The group's 1963 report documented the employment and educational discrimination faced by women, but its impact extended beyond its rather conservative recommendations. Most important, the presidential commission and the state commissions that were its offshoots set up a rudimentary nationwide network of women in public life who were concerned about feminist issues.

Another spark that ignited the revival of feminism was Betty Friedan's best-selling book, *The Feminine Mys-*

FIGURE 30.2

Women in the Labor Force, 1800–1994

Over the past two centuries women have steadily increased their participation in the labor force. Paid employment outside the home has become part of the life cycle of most women.

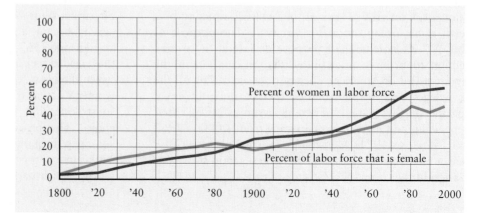

tique, published in 1963. That book, a pointed indictment of women's suburban domesticity, grew out of Friedan's experiences as a housewife in the 1950s. Friedan called it "the problem that has no name":

> As she made the beds, shopped for groceries, matched slipcover material, ate peanut butter sandwiches with her children, chauffeured Cub Scouts and Brownies, lay beside her husband at night—she was afraid to ask even of herself the silent question—"Is this all?"

Women responded enthusiastically to Friedan's story, especially white, college-educated, middle-class women whose backgrounds resembled the author's. Friedan's book sold 3 million copies, and many more women read excerpts in major women's magazines. *The Feminine Mystique* gave women a vocabulary for their dissatisfaction and introduced many of them to the powerful ideas of modern feminism—women's self-realization through employment, continuing education, and other activities outside the home.

Legislating Women's Rights. Like so many constituencies in postwar America, women's rights activists looked to the federal government for action. In 1963, as recommended by the Presidential Commission on the Status of Women, Congress passed the Equal Pay Act, which directed that men and women be paid the same wages for doing the same job. Even more important was the Civil Rights Act of 1964, which had as great an impact on women as it did on blacks and other minorities. The key provision, Title VII, barred discrimination in employment on the basis of race, color, religion, national origin, or sex. The category of sex was added by a conservative representative who hoped to make the bill so controversial that it would be killed. His strategy backfired. Title VII eventually became a powerful tool in the fight against sex discrimination. Initially, however, the Equal Employment Opportunity Commission avoided implementing it.

Dissatisfied with the commission's reluctance to defend women's rights, Friedan and others founded the National Organization for Women in 1966. NOW, modeling itself on groups such as the NAACP, aimed to be a civil rights organization for women. "The purpose of NOW," its statement of purpose declared, "is to take action to bring women into full participation in the mainstream of American society now, exercising all the privileges and responsibilities thereof in truly equal partnership with men." Friedan served as NOW's first president, and its membership grew from 1,000 in 1967 to 15,000 in 1971. Men made up a fourth of NOW's early membership. It is still the largest feminist organization in the United States.

Women's Liberation. Women's liberationists came to feminism by a different path. White women had made up about half the students who went south with SNCC in the 1964 Freedom Summer project. While in Mississippi, they received conflicting messages. College women developed self-confidence and organizational skills and found role models in the black women and older southern white women who were prominent in the civil rights movement, such as Ella Baker, Anne Braden, and Virginia Foster Durr. Yet women volunteers also found that they were expected to do all the cleaning and cooking at the Freedom Houses where SNCC volunteers lived. "We didn't come down here to work as a maid this summer," one complained.

Intensely committed to black civil rights and lacking a feminist vocabulary to express their concerns, Freedom Summer volunteers raised their objections only tentatively. When they did, they compared women's position to that of blacks. "Assumptions of male superiority are as widespread and deeply rooted and every bit as crippling to the woman as the assumptions of white superiority are to the Negro," they argued. Both black and white men in the movement laughed off those attempts to raise feminist issues. Stokely Carmichael made one of the most notorious retorts: "The only position for women in SNCC is prone."

After 1965 black power militancy made white women unwelcome in the civil rights movement. But when they transferred their energies to the student and antiwar groups that were emerging in that period (see Chapter 31), they found that New Left groups were equally male-dominated and unsupportive. Once again women were expected to take notes or serve coffee while men monopolized the leadership roles. As the antiwar movement adopted draft resistance as its central strategy, women found themselves treated primarily as sex objects. "Girls say yes to guys who say no" was a popular slogan. Women who tried to raise feminist issues at conventions were shouted off the platform with jeers such as "Move on, little girl, we have more important issues to talk about here than women's liberation." The "little girl" who received that taunt was Shulamith Firestone, whose subsequent book, *The Dialectic of Sex* (1971), became an early text of the women's movement.

Around 1967 groups of radical women realized that they needed their own movement. The contradiction between the New Left's commitment to egalitarianism and women's actual treatment by male leaders had become so striking that women felt that they had no other choice. This process occurred independently in five or six cities, including Chicago, San Francisco, and New York. In contrast to women's rights groups such as NOW, which had traditional organizational structures

Feminism on the March
The visibility of the feminist movement reached a new peak in 1970 when thousands of women in New York and other cities around the country marched to celebrate the fiftieth anniversary of women's suffrage. (© Bettye Lane)

and dues-paying members, radical women participated in loose collectives with shifting memberships that often lacked any coordinating structure.

The women's liberation movement (or "women's lib," as it was dubbed by the somewhat hostile media) went public when it staged a protest at the 1968 Miss America pageant. The demonstration included a "freedom trash can" into which women were encouraged to throw false eyelashes, hair curlers, brassieres, and girdles—all considered symbols of female oppression. The media quickly labeled the radical feminists "bra burners." The derisive name stuck, although no brassieres were actually burned.

A technique with a more lasting impact was *consciousness raising*—group sessions in which women shared their experiences of being female. Swapping stories about being passed over for promotion, needing a husband's signature on a credit card application, and enduring the humiliation of whistles and leers while walking down the street helped participants realize that their individual problems were part of a wider pattern of oppression. The slogan "The personal is political" became a rallying cry of the early radical feminists.

The High Tide of Feminism. Before 1969 most women learned about the feminist movement through word of mouth. After that time, media attention brought women's issues to a much broader audience than could have been reached by NOW or the women's liberation collectives. A flood of new converts broke down the barriers between the two branches of the movement. Feminism's

potential as a mass movement was demonstrated on August 26, 1970, when thousands of women throughout the country marched to celebrate the fiftieth anniversary of the Nineteenth Amendment. The feminist movement as a whole, however, remained largely white and middle-class.

The distinction between women's rights and women's liberation also began to blur because of a growing convergence of interests. Radical women learned that key feminist goals—child care, equal pay, abortion rights—could best be achieved in the political arena. At the same time, more traditional political activists developed a broader view of women's oppression, including tentative support for divisive issues such as abortion and lesbian rights. Feminists were beginning to think of themselves as part of a broad, growing, and increasingly influential social movement.

The rebirth of feminism in the 1960s laid the foundation for more vigorous activism among women in the 1970s (see Chapter 32). Not until then would the movement grapple with the fact that perhaps as many issues divided women—race, class, age, sexual preference—as unified them.

Summary

The contradictions of postwar affluence gave rise to new social and political activism in the early 1960s. As Americans looked to Washington for solutions to the nation's social and economic ills, the Democrats offered a diverse array of federal programs designed to appeal to a broad range of constituencies. John F. Kennedy first set the agenda for this politics of expectation in his 1960 presidential bid, but the domestic accomplishments of his New Frontier were limited. Kennedy's activism was more evident in foreign policy, where he remained a resolute cold warrior. A potential nuclear confrontation during the Cuban missile crisis, however, resulted in a more accommodating approach toward the Soviet Union after 1962. As Kennedy worked to remake the New Frontier for a second term, an assassin's bullet ended his life in November 1963.

On the social front, the most significant expression of 1960s activism was the civil rights movement. Led by established religious figures such as Martin Luther King, Jr., and energized by a younger generation of black college students, the movement won major legislative victories, including the passage of the Civil Rights and Voting Rights acts of 1964–1965. Through those measures the nation ended legal segregation, outlawed racial discrimination, and expanded black voting rights and political power.

On the national level, Lyndon Johnson played a critical role in pushing civil rights legislation through Congress. Moreover, Johnson used his formidable political skills to usher in the most ambitious legislative reform program since the New Deal. Under his Great Society, Congress funded an array of new programs in education, medical care, social welfare, housing, transportation, and environmental protection. But even though the Great Society raised hopes, it could not always deliver on its promises. Increasing military expenditures for the escalating Vietnam conflict limited federal funds for domestic programs. And as federal functions and responsibilities grew, it became increasingly difficult to accommodate the diverse and often competing constituencies in the Democratic coalition. By the late 1960s the liberal consensus had broken down.

The civil rights movement also began to disintegrate during this period. Rising militancy and racial strife divided the movement and fueled white opposition to change. At the same time, however, the new black power movement encouraged racial pride and assertiveness, serving as a model for other minority groups and women in their struggles for equality.

TIMELINE

1960	Greensboro, North Carolina, sit-ins Birth control pill becomes available John F. Kennedy elected president
1961	Presidential Commission on the Status of Women established Peace Corps established Freedom rides Bay of Pigs invasion Berlin wall erected
1962	Michael Harrington, The *Other America*, describes the persistence of poverty John Glenn orbits the earth Cuban missile crisis
1963	Betty Friedan, *The Feminine Mystique* Civil rights protest in Birmingham, Alabama Equal Pay Act March on Washington Test ban treaty John F. Kennedy assassinated; Lyndon B. Johnson assumes presidency
1964	Tax Reduction Act Freedom Summer Civil Rights Act Economic Opportunity Act inaugurates War on Poverty Johnson elected president Wilderness Preservation Act
1965	Malcolm X assassinated Civil rights march from Selma to Montgomery, Alabama Voting Rights Act Medicare and Medicaid Elementary and Secondary Education Act Immigration Act Air and Water Quality acts
1966	National Organization for Women (NOW) founded Stokely Carmichael proclaims black power
1967	Height of race riots in northern cities
1968	Martin Luther King, Jr., assassinated Women's liberation movement emerges
1969	American Indian Movement seizes Alcatraz Stonewall riot leads to gay liberation movement United States lands first astronauts on the moon

★   ★   ★

BIBLIOGRAPHY

There are a growing number of survey works on the 1960s; among the best are David Steigerwald, *The Sixties and the End of Modern America* (1995); David Farber, *The Age of Great Dreams: America in the 1960s* (1994); and Allen J. Matusow, *The Unraveling of America* (1984).

The Politics of Expectation

The literature on the Kennedy years is voluminous. Among the best general accounts are Richard Reeves, *President Kennedy: Profile of Power* (1993); James Giglio, *The Presidency of JFK* (1991); David Burner, *JFK and a New Generation* (1988); and Jim F. Heath, *Decade of Disillusionment: The Kennedy-Johnson Years* (1975). Critical views appear in David Halberstam, *The Best and the Brightest* (1972); Henry Fairlie, *The Kennedy Promise: The Politics of Expectation* (1973); and Garry Wills, *The Kennedy Imprisonment* (1980).

On foreign policy in the Kennedy years, see Michael Beschloss, *The Crisis Years: Kennedy and Khrushchev, 1960–1963* (1990); Thomas Paterson, *Kennedy's Quest for Victory* (1989); and Richard Walton, *Cold War and Counterrevolution* (1972). Robert Kennedy, *Thirteen Days* (1969), provides a participant's account of the Cuban missile crisis, which can be supplemented by James Nathan, *The Cuban Missile Crisis Revisited* (1992); Raymond Garthoff, *Reflections on the Cuban Missile Crisis* (1989); and Thomas Paterson, *Contesting Castro* (1994). On the Warren Court, see Bernard Schwartz, *Super Chief: Earl Warren and the Supreme Court* (1983). Earl Warren was the chief author of the Warren Report (1964) investigating the Kennedy assassination. More recently, Gerald Posner, *Case Closed* (1993), provides the most definitive treatment of that event.

The Civil Rights Movement

Robert Weisbrot, *Freedom Bound* (1990); Harvard Sitkoff, *The Struggle for Black Equality* (2nd ed., 1993); and Clayborne Carson, et al., *The Eyes on the Prize Civil Rights Reader* (1991), offer comprehensive overviews. Histories of the major civil rights organizations include Carson's study of SNCC, *In Struggle* (1981), and August Meier and Elliot Rudwick, *CORE* (1973). Mary Aickin Rothschild, *A Case of Black and White* (1982), and Doug McAdam, *Freedom Summer* (1988), describe the experiences of northern volunteers during Freedom Summer. Two fine oral histories of the civil rights movement are Howell Raines, *My Soul Is Rested* (1977), and Henry Hampton and Steve Fayer, *Voices of Freedom* (1990).

Local accounts of grass-roots organizing include William H. Chafe's superb study of Greensboro, North Carolina, *Civilities and Civil Rights* (1980), and two recent studies of Mississippi, John Dittmer, *Local People* (1994), and Charles M. Payne, *I've Got the Light of Freedom* (1995). The role of women in the civil rights movement is examined in Vicki L. Crawford et al., *Women in the Civil Rights Movement: Trailblazers and Torchbearers, 1941–1965* (1990).

The material on Martin Luther King, Jr., is extensive and continues to grow. King told his own story in *Why We Can't Wait* (1964). His biographers include David Garrow, *Bearing the Cross* (1986); Taylor Branch, *Parting the Waters* (1988); Stephen Oates, *Let the Trumpet Sound* (1982); and David Lewis, *King* (1970).

Lyndon Johnson and the Great Society

Lyndon Johnson's account of his presidency can be found in *The Vantage Point* (1971). Doris Kearns, *Lyndon Johnson and the American Dream* (1976), and Merle Miller, *Lyndon: An Oral Biography* (1980), are based on extensive conversations with LBJ. Rowland Evans and Robert D. Novak offer a vigorous portrait in *Lyndon B. Johnson: The Exercise of Power* (1966). Robert A. Caro focuses on Johnson's early career in *The Path to Power* (1982) and *Means of Ascent* (1989), as does Robert Dallek in *Lone Star Rising* (1991).

Michael Harrington called attention to poverty in *The Other America* (1962) and later critiqued the War on Poverty in *The New American Poverty* (1984). Charles Murray's conservative viewpoint in *Losing Ground: American Social Policy, 1950–1980* (1983) can be balanced by Michael Katz's liberal perspective in *The Undeserving Poor* (1989).

The Continuing Struggle for Civil Rights

Major texts of the black power movement include Stokely Carmichael and Charles Hamilton, *Black Power* (1967); James Baldwin, *The Fire Next Time* (1963); and Eldridge Cleaver, *Soul on Ice* (1968). *The Autobiography of Malcolm X* (cowritten with Alex Haley) has become a black literary classic. Hugh Pearson, *The Shadow of the Panther* (1994), looks at Huey Newton and the Black Panthers, as does the former Black Panther Elaine Brown, *A Taste of Power* (1992).

Report of the National Advisory Commission on Civil Disorders (1968) analyzes the decade's major race riots. See also Joe R. Feagin and Harlan Hahn, *Ghetto Revolts* (1973), and Robert Fogelson, *Violence as Protest* (1971). Sidney Fine's book on the Detroit riot, *Violence in the Model City* (1989), provides the most thorough historical treatment of race rioting in this period.

Carlos Muñoz, Jr., *Youth, Identity and Power: The Chicano Movement* (1989), and Juan Gomez-Quiñones, *Chicano Politics* (1990), examine the rise of the Chicano movement in the 1960s. Peter Matthiessen, *In the Spirit of Crazy Horse* (1983), chronicles the American Indian Movement's ongoing conflict with the FBI and the federal government. See also Stan Steiner, *The New Indians* (1968); Helen Hertzberg, *The Search for an American Indian Movement* (1971); and Wilcomb Washburn, *Red Man's Land, White Man's Law* (1971). John D'Emilio, *Sexual Politics, Sexual Communities* (1983), describes the emergence of gay identity between 1940 and 1970, while Martin Duberman, *Stonewall* (1993), looks at the birth of the gay movement in the late 1960s.

Jo Freeman, *The Politics of Women's Liberation* (1975); Barbara Deckard, *The Women's Movement* (1975); and Judith Hole and Ellen Levine, *The Rebirth of Feminism* (1971), chronicle the revival of feminism in the 1960s and 1970s. Sara Evans, *Personal Politics* (1979), traces the roots of feminism in the civil rights movement and the New Left, and Alice Echols, *Daring to Be Bad* (1989), examines radical feminism from 1967 to 1975. General histories of women's activism in the 1960s include Cynthia Harrison, *On Account of Sex: The Politics of Women's Issues, 1945–1968* (1988); Leila J. Rupp and Verta Taylor, *Survival in the Doldrums: The American Women's Rights Movement* (1987); and Susan M. Hartmann, *From Margin to Mainstream: American Women and Politics since 1960* (1989).

Jungle Warfare

Guerrilla warfare in Vietnam was characterized by frequent
skirmishes and casualties, but large battles were rare. Enemy
lines were unclear in the heavy jungle underbrush, and
territory conquered one day was often lost the next. For
many soldiers, waging war under such conditions was
frustrating and demoralizing.

The Vietnam Experience
1961–1975

★   ★   ★

Just as the civil rights movement revealed the short-comings of American domestic life in the 1960s, the Vietnam War challenged the fundamental assumptions of the nation's foreign policy. Since the late 1940s American policy makers—Democratic and Republican alike—had agreed on the need to maintain American military and economic superiority and contain communism around the globe. This cold war policy led to numerous military and diplomatic conflicts between the United States and the Soviet Union, including a three-year war in Korea. Whereas some Americans questioned the policy of global containment, most U.S. policy makers were convinced that aggressive action against communism was imperative, particularly in the developing nations of the Third World. The future of democracy and the credibility of American power in the postwar world appeared to be at stake.

The struggle over Vietnam called those assumptions into question. Like many new nations in the postcolonial world, Vietnam was characterized by a volatile mix of nationalist sentiments, religious and cultural conflicts, economic needs, and political turmoil. The rise of communism in Vietnam was only one phase of that nation's larger struggle against colonialism, which eventually resulted in a bloody civil war. But American policy makers viewed these events through the lens of the Cold War, interpreting them as communist-inspired moves toward global domination. Their failure to understand the complexity of Vietnam's internal conflicts led to a long and ultimately disastrous war.

Spanning nearly thirty years, the Vietnam conflict occupied American administrations from Truman to Ford. U.S. troops fought in Vietnam for more than eleven years—from 1961 to 1973—making it the nation's longest war. Moreover, as the country's first major military defeat, the war shook American confidence and damaged the international credibility it was supposed to

uphold. The war also took its toll at home. While defense spending temporarily boosted the economy, it fueled inflation and diverted resources from domestic uses. As the war dragged on, a growing number of citizens came to oppose U.S. involvement as antiwar sentiments spread across college campuses to the nation's streets, living rooms, and halls of state. Not since the Civil War had the nation been so deeply and bitterly divided. Debates about the meaning and lessons of the war still resonate in American life.

Into the Quagmire, 1945–1968

Although most Americans first learned about the Vietnam War in the mid-1960s, the roots of U.S. involvement date back to the Truman administration. At the end of World War II the political instability produced by the decolonization of Southeast Asia became a source of concern for policy makers wary of communist infiltration. The Eisenhower and Kennedy administrations gradually increased economic and military aid to South Vietnam, laying the groundwork for a major escalation of U.S. involvement under Lyndon Johnson.

The Roots of American Involvement

Vietnam had been part of the French colony of Indochina (along with Laos and Cambodia) since the late nineteenth century but was occupied by Japan during World War II. Native resistance to the Japanese was led by Ho Chi Minh and the Vietnam Independence League, the Vietminh. A former schoolteacher and maritime worker, Ho Chi Minh had embraced communism in 1920 and later lived in Moscow. First and foremost, however, Ho and the Vietminh were nationalists who wanted to end foreign rule in Vietnam. During World War II the Vietminh resisted the Japanese occupation, working with the U.S. Office of Strategic Services to conduct espionage missions and rescue downed American pilots.

The Japanese surrender in 1945 created a political vacuum and an opportunity for Vietnamese independence. With words drawn from the American Declaration of Independence, Ho proclaimed an independent republic of Vietnam that September. Hoping to maintain its overseas empire, France rejected his claim and reasserted control over the country, granting it only a token measure of freedom. Tensions between the French and the Vietminh escalated, and in December 1946 a French warship bombarded Haiphong, killing 6,000 Vietnamese civilians. Ho and the military strategist Vo Nguyen Giap then launched counterattacks to drive out the French. Thus began the first phase of the conflict, an eight-year struggle that the Vietminh called the Anti-French War of

Resistance. Appealing to American anticolonial sentiment, Ho called on President Truman to support the struggle for Vietnamese independence. Truman, however, ignored those appeals and offered covert support to the French in hopes of stabilizing a politically chaotic region and rebuilding the French economy. While proclaiming official neutrality in the conflict, the United States made $160 million available to the French for use in Indochina in 1946 and subsequently allowed them to use Marshall Plan funds for military operations there.

By the end of the decade cold war developments and objectives prompted the United States to take a stronger and more public stand on behalf of the French. After the Chinese revolution of 1949, the United States was concerned that China—along with the Soviet Union—might actively support Asian anticolonial struggles and that newly independent countries would align themselves with the communists. At the same time, Republican charges that the Democrats had "lost China" influenced Truman to take a firmer stand against perceived communist aggression in both Korea and Vietnam. Truman also wanted to maintain good relations with France, whose support was crucial to the success of the new NATO alliance. Finally, Indochina played a strategic role in Secretary of State Dean Acheson's plans for an integrated Pacific Rim regional economy centered on a reindustrialized Japan. Envisioning Indochina as a supplier of cheap raw materials and a profitable market for Japanese goods and services, American policy makers insisted that it remain a part of the capitalist free-market system.

For all these reasons, when the Soviet Union and the new Chinese leaders recognized Ho's government early in 1950, the United States—along with Great Britain—recognized the noncommunist government of Bao Dai that had been installed by the French the previous year. After the outbreak of the Korean War, Truman also decided to send supplies to French troops stationed in Vietnam to deter a possible communist invasion there. Military support continued under the Eisenhower administration. By mid-1954 the United States had sent more than $2 billion worth of military supplies to the French in Vietnam, plus another $703 million in technical and economic assistance, shouldering nearly 80 percent of the cost of the war. President Eisenhower argued that such aid was essential in preventing what he called the domino effect: "You have a row of dominoes set up, you knock over the first one, and what will happen to the last one is the certainty that it will go over very quickly." The loss of South Vietnam, Eisenhower asserted in April 1954, "would have grave consequences for us and for freedom."

Dienbienphu and the Geneva Accords. Despite these joint French-American efforts, the Vietminh forces gained strength in northern Vietnam. In the spring of 1954 the

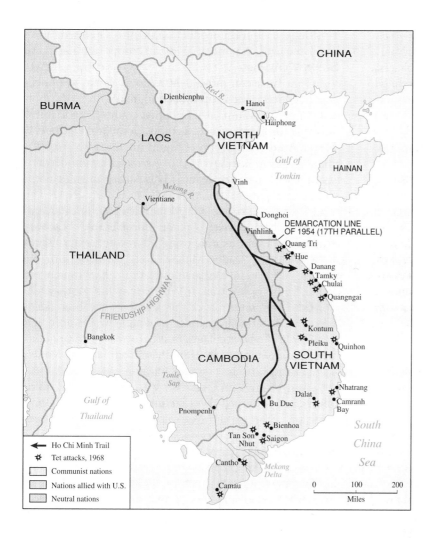

MAP 31.1

The Vietnam War, 1954–1975

The Vietnam War was a guerrilla war, fought in skirmishes and inconclusive encounters rather than decisive battles. Supporters of the National Liberation Front filtered into South Vietnam along the Ho Chi Minh Trail, which wound through Laos and Cambodia. In January 1968 Vietcong forces launched the Tet offensive, a surprise attack on several South Vietnamese cities and provincial centers shown at left. American vulnerability to these attacks served to undermine U.S. credibility and fueled opposition to the war.

French made a last stand at the isolated administrative fortress of Dienbienphu, where the Vietminh surrounded them. France asked the United States to launch air strikes from nearby carriers to break the siege. Several members of the Joint Chiefs of Staff urged Eisenhower to take action (including the possible use of nuclear weapons), but Congressional opposition at home and Britain's refusal to join a pro-French coalition convinced him to abstain from direct military intervention. Dienbienphu fell in May after a fifty-six-day siege.

The dramatic turn of events at Dienbienphu enhanced the negotiating position of the Vietminh at a conference in Geneva sponsored by Britain and the Soviet Union to discuss problems in the Far East. The resulting 1954 Geneva Accords temporarily partitioned Vietnam at the 17th parallel (see Map 31.1), committed France to withdraw its forces north of that line within ten months, and forbade both North and South Vietnam to enter into a military alliance with an outside power. A final declaration provided that the two partitioned sectors would hold free elections within two years to choose a unified government for the entire nation. Eight of the nine national delegations in atten-

dance signed the agreements, including China and the Vietminh, both of which were confident that Ho would win the elections of 1956. The United States refused to sign the Geneva Accords but issued a separate protocol acknowledging the agreements and promising to "refrain from the threat or use of force to disturb them."

The Creation of South Vietnam. Eisenhower had no intention of allowing a communist electoral victory in Vietnam and wanted to establish a permanent South Vietnamese state. With the help of CIA military operatives, the Eisenhower administration had made sure that a pro-American government took power in South Vietnam in June 1954, just before the accords were signed. Ngo Dinh Diem, an anticommunist Roman Catholic who had spent the previous eight years in the United States, returned to Vietnam and was installed as the premier of the French-backed South Vietnamese government under Emperor Bao Dai. The next year Diem disposed of Bao Dai through a national referendum establishing Diem as the president of an independent South Vietnam. In a rigged election—in which his ballots were printed on red paper, a Vietnamese symbol

of good luck, whereas Bao Dai's were green, which stood for misfortune—Diem won an unlikely 98.2 percent of the vote. With the support of the United States, he then called off the reunification elections scheduled for 1956, mainly because he realized that the popular Ho Chi Minh would win easily in both the north and the south. Diem's was just one in a long line of U.S.-backed governments that failed to win the allegiance of the Vietnamese population.

From the perspective of the Vietnamese, the Geneva Accords marked only a brief interlude between two wars, one to end French colonial control and a second to reunify Vietnam. In March 1956 the last French soldiers left Saigon, and the United States replaced France as the dominant foreign power in South Vietnam. American policy makers now asserted that a noncommunist South Vietnam was vital to the security interests of the United States, and they charted American policy accordingly.

In reality, Vietnam was too small to play a significant role in the international balance of power; its communism was regional and intensely nationalistic, not expansionist. Nevertheless, Eisenhower and subsequent U.S. presidents continued to see South Vietnam as vital to American security. Between 1955 and 1961 the Eisenhower administration sent Diem an average of $200 million a year in aid, mostly military. In addition, approximately 675 American military advisers were stationed in Saigon, the capital of South Vietnam. Having stepped up U.S. involvement considerably, Eisenhower left office, passing the Vietnam situation to his successor, John F. Kennedy.

The Kennedy Years

President Kennedy saw Vietnam as an ideal laboratory to try out the counterinsurgency techniques that were the centerpiece of his military policy (see Chapter 30). But he first had to prop up the faltering regime of Ngo Dinh Diem, who remained highly unpopular because of his administration's corruption and ruthless brutality, aloofness from the peasantry, and greedy land policy. The Diem regime also faced a growing military threat after December 1960, when the North Vietnamese Communist party organized most of Diem's opponents in South Vietnam into a revolutionary movement known as the National Liberation Front (NLF). To shore up Diem's administration, Kennedy increased the number of American military "advisers" (an elastic term that included helicopter units, special forces, minesweeping details, and reconnaissance pilots) to more than 16,000 by November 1963. As part of the counterinsurgency strategy he also sent economic development specialists to win the "hearts and minds" of Vietnamese peasants away from the insurgents while at the same time in-

creasing agricultural production. Kennedy refused, however, to send American combat troops to assist the South Vietnamese.

The American aid did little good. Diem's political inexperience and corruption, combined with his Catholicism in a predominantly Buddhist country, made it impossible for him to create a stable, popular government. He enjoyed much more support in faraway America than he did in his native land. As the situation deteriorated, Diem consistently misled his American allies about South Vietnamese military and social progress. The NLF's guerrilla forces—called the Vietcong by Diem and his American advisers—made considerable headway against the Diem regime, using the revolutionary tactics of the Chinese leader Mao Zedong to blend into the South Vietnamese civilian population "like fish in the water." But opposition to Diem was far more widespread. Large segments of the peasantry had been alienated by his strategic hamlet program, which uprooted families and whole villages into barbed wire compounds in a vain attempt to separate them from Ho Chi Minh's sympathizers.

Anti-Diem sentiment also was strong among Buddhists, who charged the government with religious persecution. Starting in May 1963, militant Buddhists staged a dramatic series of demonstrations against Diem, including several self-immolations that were recorded by American television crews. Diem's regime retaliated with raids on temples and mass arrests of Buddhist priests in August, prompting more antigovernment demonstrations.

Kennedy decided that Diem had to be removed. Ambassador Henry Cabot Lodge, Jr., let it be known in Saigon that the United States would support a military coup that had "a good chance of succeeding." On November 1, 1963, Diem was driven from office and assassinated by a faction of the South Vietnamese army. America's role in the coup reinforced the links between the United States and the new regime in South Vietnam, making the prospect of withdrawal from the region less acceptable to U.S. policy makers.

Less than a month later Kennedy himself was assassinated. Although historians continue to debate whether Kennedy would have withdrawn American forces from Vietnam if he had lived, the actions of his administration clearly accelerated U.S. involvement. When Lyndon Johnson took his place as president, he retained many of Kennedy's foreign policy advisers and quickly declared his intention to maintain support for South Vietnam. "I am not going to be the President who saw Southeast Asia go the way China went," Johnson asserted weeks after taking office. A new phase in the Americanization of the war was about to begin. When Johnson assumed the presidency, there were 16,000 American troops in Vietnam; when he left office in January 1969, there were more than 500,000.

Escalation

The removal of Diem did not lead to improvements in the efficiency or popularity of the Saigon government. Various military governments, most notably a coalition headed by General Nguyen Khanh, tried to build popular support, but with little success. American policy makers realized that the Eisenhower-Kennedy policy of sending military advisers and supplies could no longer save the situation. But Johnson would need at least tacit Congressional support, perhaps even a declaration of war, to commit U.S. forces to an offensive strategy. Originally Johnson had wanted to wait until after the 1964 election to place this controversial request before Congress, but events gave him an opportunity to win authorization sooner.

The Gulf of Tonkin Resolution. During the summer of 1964 American naval forces conducted surveillance missions off the North Vietnamese coast to aid South Vietnamese amphibious attacks on the area. The North Vietnamese resisted the attacks, and President Johnson told the nation that on August 2 and 4 North Vietnamese torpedo boats had fired on American destroyers in international waters in the Gulf of Tonkin. At Johnson's request, Congress authorized him to "take all necessary measures to repel any armed attack against the forces of the United States and to prevent further aggression." On August 7 the Gulf of Tonkin resolution passed 88 to 2 in the Senate and 416 to 0 in the House. Only Senators Wayne Morse of Oregon and Ernest Gruening of Alaska opposed it as a "predated declaration of war" that further increased the president's ability to carry out foreign policy without consulting Congress (both subsequently lost their bids for reelection).

Many questions were later raised about the resolution. A draft had been ready for several months, awaiting just such an incident. The evidence of a North Vietnamese attack was particularly sketchy in the case of the second incident. In the middle of heavy wind, rain, and fog, the U.S.S. *Maddox* and *C. Turner Joy* had reported that they were under attack by torpedoes and had begun firing at targets that they saw on their radar screens. Naval aircraft called in to support the destroyers saw no enemy boats but fired missiles as instructed. Soon afterward Captain John J. Herrick, commander of the *Maddox*, contacted Washington and expressed doubt that an attack had occurred, attributing the phenomenon to faulty radar caused by bad weather. As the president admitted soon afterward, "For all I know, our navy was shooting at whales out there." But this unverified attack got Johnson what he wanted—a sweeping mandate to conduct Vietnam operations as he saw fit. It was the only formal approval of American intervention in Vietnam ever granted by Congress. Johnson's outspokenness on the Gulf of Tonkin incident also served to undercut claims by the Republican presidential contender, Barry Goldwater, that Johnson was unwilling to take a firm stand against communist aggression in Vietnam.

During the 1964 presidential campaign (see Chapter 30) Johnson declared, "We are not going to send American boys nine or ten thousand miles away from home to do what Asian boys ought to be doing for themselves." Yet plans were already being drawn up for a possible escalation of American efforts. Johnson's secretary of defense, Robert McNamara, and other top advisers argued that only a rapid, full-scale deployment of U.S. forces could prevent the imminent defeat of the South Vietnamese government and lay the groundwork for an eventual victory over the communists. With Congressional support assured and the 1964 election safely over, the Johnson administration began the fateful move toward the total Americanization of the war. The escalation, which was accomplished during the first several months of 1965, took two forms: the initiation of direct bombing campaigns against North Vietnam and the deployment of ground troops.

Operation Rolling Thunder. The first phase of escalation was Operation Rolling Thunder, a protracted campaign of bombing attacks against North Vietnam that was launched on March 2, 1965. Retaliatory air strikes against North Vietnamese targets had already been undertaken in February; what was significant about the new plans was that the bombing was not linked to a specific act of provocation but was an open-ended policy. Such bombing raids, the national security adviser McGeorge Bundy reasoned, would cripple the North Vietnamese economy and force the communists to the bargaining table. A special target was the Ho Chi Minh Trail, an elaborate network of paths, bridges, and shelters that stretched from North Vietnam through Cambodia and Laos into South Vietnam (see Map 31.1). By 1967 some 20,000 Vietnamese soldiers moved southward along that route each month, along with the military hardware and other resources necessary to supply them.

Between 1965 and 1968 Operation Rolling Thunder (named for a Protestant hymn) dropped a million tons of bombs on North Vietnam, 800 tons a day for three and a half years. Each B-52 bombing sortie cost $30,000; by early 1966 the direct costs of the air war exceeded $1.7 billion. From 1965 to 1973 the United States dropped three times as many bombs on North Vietnam, a country roughly the size of Texas, as had fallen on Europe, Asia, and Africa during World War II. The several hundred captured pilots downed in the raids then became pawns in negotiations with the North Vietnamese over the fate of prisoners of war.

To the amazement of American advisers, the bombing had little effect on the ability of the Vietnamese to wage war. The flow of troops and supplies to the south continued unabated as the North Vietnamese quickly

Aerial Bombing in Vietnam
The bombs dropped by U.S. forces in an attempt to root out Vietcong sympathizers inflicted heavy damage on the countryside and caused many civilian deaths. B-52s dropped most of the bombs.

rebuilt roads and bridges, moved munitions plants underground, and constructed a network of tunnels and shelters. Instead of destroying enemy morale and bringing the North Vietnamese to the bargaining table, Operation Rolling Thunder intensified their nationalism and will to fight. The bombing continued nevertheless.

The Arrival of U.S. Ground Troops. A week after the launching of Operation Rolling Thunder, the United States made its first official assignment of ground troops to combat duty in South Vietnam. On March 8 the first U.S. Marines waded ashore at Danang, South Vietnam's second largest city, to protect the nearby American air base—the launching site for Operation Rolling Thunder sorties. Soon they were patrolling the countryside and skirmishing with the enemy. Beginning in the summer of 1965, combat operations shifted from a defensive stance to a search-and-destroy mission designed to uncover

and kill Vietcong forces. Fearing Congressional opposition to this expanded military commitment, the Johnson administration did not reveal that a major change in policy had occurred.

Over the next three years the number of American troops in Vietnam grew dramatically. Although in 1965 U.S. troops were accompanied by military forces from Australia, New Zealand, and South Korea, the war increasingly became an American struggle, fought for American aims. More than 75,000 soldiers were fighting there in June 1965, and 189,000 by the end of that year. In 1966 more than 380,000 American soldiers were stationed in Vietnam; there were 485,000 in 1967; and 536,000 in 1968 (see Figure 31.1). The increasing demands of General William Westmoreland, commander of the U.S. forces in Vietnam, confirmed a prediction made by the presidential adviser George Ball in 1961. Ball had warned President Kennedy that if Amer-

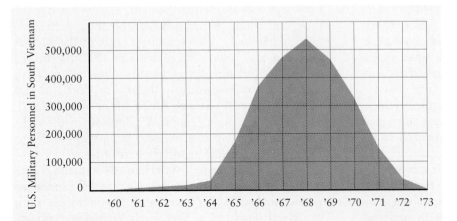

FIGURE 31.1

U.S. Troops in Vietnam, 1960–1973
When Lyndon Johnson escalated the Vietnam War, troop levels rose from 23,300 in December 1964 to 184,300 a year later. Troop levels eventually peaked to more than 543,000 personnel. Under Richard Nixon's Vietnamization program, beginning in the summer of 1969 levels drastically declined; the last U.S. military forces left South Vietnam on March 29, 1973.

ican ground troops were committed to Vietnam, there would be 300,000 on the ground within five years. Kennedy had laughed and said, "George, you're crazier than hell." But as Kennedy observed before his death, requests for troops were like having a drink: "The effect wears off, and you have to take another."

The massive commitment of troops and air power after 1965 threatened to destroy Vietnam's countryside and fragile resources. Taking to the extreme Johnson's call "to leave the footprints of America in Vietnam," the campaign of extensive defoliation and military bombardment made it difficult for peasants to practice the agriculture that provided the economic and cultural base of Vietnamese society. After one devastating but not unusual engagement the commanding U.S. officer claimed, using the logic of the time, "It became necessary to destroy the town in order to save it." Graffiti on a plane that dropped defoliants read, "Only you can prevent forests." (In later years chemicals such as Agent Orange were found to have highly toxic effects on humans and the environment.) The devastation was not limited to North Vietnam. South Vietnam, America's ally, suffered major damage and absorbed more than twice the total bomb tonnage dropped on the north. In Saigon and other South Vietnamese cities the influx of American soldiers and dollars distorted the local economy, leading to corruption and prostitution and setting off uncontrollable inflation and black market activities.

Why did the dramatically increased American presence in Vietnam from 1965 on fail to turn the tide of the war? Certain advisers, such as former Lieutenant Colonel John Paul Vann, argued that military intervention would do little unless it was accompanied by reform of the Saigon government and increased efforts at building popular support in the countryside. Throughout the war, however, most South Vietnamese remained distrustful of and disaffected from the brutal and corrupt Saigon government. Other critics claimed that the war was lost because the United States never committed its full military might to total victory, although what total victory would have entailed remains in dispute. It is true, however, that military strategy was inextricably tied to political considerations. For domestic reasons, policy makers often searched for the elusive "middle ground" between an all-out invasion (and the possibility of sparking a nuclear exchange between the superpowers) and the politically unacceptable alternative of disengagement. Hoping to win a war of attrition, the Johnson administration assumed that American superiority in personnel and weaponry would ultimately triumph. But this limited commitment was never enough to ensure victory, however defined.

The determination of the Vietnamese was also a major factor. In the 1940s Ho Chi Minh had told his French imperialist foes, "You can kill ten of my men for every one I kill of yours, but even at those odds, you will lose and I will win." That same statement held true twenty years later against the Americans. The Vietcong were prepared to accept limitless casualties and to fight for as many years as necessary. North Vietnamese strategists astutely realized that the war did not have to be won on the battlefield, accurately predicting that American public opinion would not tolerate an extended war of attrition. Time was on the Vietcong's side, although at an enormous cost to both Vietnam and the United States.

Vietnam from the Perspective of Americans Who Fought the War

Volunteers and Recruits. Approximately 2.8 million Americans served in Vietnam. With an average age of only nineteen, this was one of the youngest fighting forces in U.S. history. Whereas most of those servicemen and -women were too young to vote or drink (the voting age was twenty-one until the passage of the Twenty-sixth Amendment in 1971), they were old enough to fight . . . and die. They served for a variety of reasons. Some were volunteers, including some 7,000 women enlistees who joined out of a sense of patriotic duty or because they had few options at home and wanted to "see the world."

But many others served because they were drafted. Until the country shifted to an all-volunteer force in 1973, the draft stood as a concrete reminder of the government's impact on the lives of ordinary Americans. As troop needs increased, the draft reached deeper into the male population. The casualty figures reflected the increasing role of draftees in Vietnam. In 1965 draftees accounted for 16 percent of total battle deaths; that figure rose to 34 percent in 1967. By 1969, 62 percent of army deaths involved draftees. Blacks were drafted and died roughly in the same proportion to their share of the draft-age population (about 12 to 13 percent), although black casualty rates were significantly higher in the early 1960s. Even more than in other recent wars, sons of the poor and the working class shouldered a disproportionate amount of the fighting, forming an estimated 80 percent of the enlisted ranks. Young men from more affluent backgrounds were more likely to avoid combat through student deferments, medical exemptions, and appointments to National Guard and reserve units—alternatives that made Johnson's Vietnam policy more palatable to the middle class.

Life in "Nam." Many draftees and enlistees initially shared cold war assumptions about the need to fight communism and believed in the superiority of the American military. However, the Vietnam experience quickly challenged simple notions of patriotism and the inevitability

AMERICAN VOICES

Ron Kovic

A Vietnam Veteran Remembers

Born on the Fourth of July in 1946, Ron Kovic wanted to be an American hero. He enlisted in the marines and was sent to Vietnam. Kovic came home in a wheelchair and, after a long period of recovery, joined the antiwar movement.

I had been shot. The war had finally caught up with my body. I felt good inside. Finally the war was with me and I had been shot by the enemy. I was getting out of the war and I was going to be a hero. I kept firing my rifle into the tree line and boldly, with my new wound, moved closer to the village, daring them to hit me again. For a moment I felt like running back to the rear with my new million-dollar wound but I decided to keep fighting in the open. A great surge of strength went through me as I yelled for the other men to come out from the trees and join me. I was limping now and the foot was beginning to hurt so much, I finally lay down in almost a kneeling position, still firing into the village, still unable to see anyone. I seemed to be the only one left firing a rifle. Someone came up from behind me, took off my boot and began to bandage my foot. The whole thing

Ron Kovic

was incredibly stupid, we were sitting ducks, but he bandaged my foot and then he took off back into the tree line.

For a few seconds it was silent. I lay down prone and waited for the next bullet to hit me. It was only a matter of time, I thought. I wasn't retreating, I wasn't going back, I was lying right there and blasting everything I had into the pagoda. The rifle was full of sand and it was jamming. I had to pull the bolt back now each time trying to get a

round into the chamber. It was impossible and I started to get up and a loud crack went off next to my right ear as a thirty-caliber slug tore through my right shoulder, blasted through my lung, and smashed my spinal cord to pieces.

I felt that everything from my chest down was completely gone. I waited to die. I threw my hand back and felt my legs still there. I couldn't feel them but they were still there. I was still alive. And for some reason I started believing, I started believing I might not die, I might make it out of there and live and feel and go back home again. I could hardly breathe and was taking short little sucks with the one lung I had left. The blood was rolling off my flak jacket from the hole in my shoulder and I couldn't feel the pain in my foot anymore, I couldn't even feel my body. I was frightened to death. I didn't think about praying, all I could feel was cheated.

All I could feel was the worthlessness of dying right here in this place at this moment for nothing.

Source: Ron Kovic, *Born on the Fourth of July* (New York: McGraw-Hill, 1976), 221–222.

---

of American victory (see American Voices, above). The first thing new soldiers noticed when they got off the plane was the stench of death, napalm, and human waste in this torrid jungle country. Sometimes they had to sprint from the plane to the safety of the base buildings because of mortar attacks, a sign of the boldness with which enemy forces operated throughout the country.

Unlike World War II soldiers, who served "for the duration," Vietnam soldiers had a one-year tour of duty. For many it was simply a matter of getting through 365 days. For the first ninety days or so they were "cherries," slang for virgins. Once they neared the end of the tour, soldiers might carry a "short-timer's stick" notched for the remaining days left; as each day passed, they would cut off another notch until only a small stub remained. Some soldiers even longed for "million-dollar wounds"—

serious but nonfatal injuries that would result in permanent removal from the battlefield. "Grunts" (ordinary infantrymen) and "bloods" (the name that black draftees called themselves) were a superstitious lot and were always afraid of being "wasted" (killed) with only a few days to go. Some soldiers deliberately avoided making close friends in case their buddies caught a grenade or triggered a booby trap on a routine patrol.

In "Nam" (soldiers' shorthand for Vietnam) days passed in boring menial work punctuated by flashes of intense fighting. "Most of the time, nothing happened," a soldier recalled, "but when something did, it happened instantaneously and without warning." The pressure of waging war in those conditions drove many soldiers to seek escape in alcohol or cheap and readily available drugs.

The fighting had a surreal quality. Combat often intensified at night, with incoming and outgoing firepower lighting up the sky while soldiers huddled sleeplessly on watch. There were rarely large-scale battles, only skirmishes; no front lines or conquering of territory, just operations during the day in areas that reverted to Vietcong control at night. Although whole units might be ambushed, casualties typically came in twos and threes. A former marine captain recalled:

> You never knew who was the enemy and who was the friend. They all looked alike. They all dressed alike. They were all Vietnamese. Some of them were Vietcong. Here's a woman of twenty-two or twenty-three. She is pregnant, and she tells an interrogator that her husband works in Danang and isn't a Vietcong. But she watches your men walk down a trail and get killed or wounded by a booby trap. She knows the booby trap is there, but she doesn't warn them. Maybe she planted it herself.

He concluded graphically, "It wasn't like the San Francisco Forty-Niners on one side of the field and the Cincinnati Bengals on the other. The enemy was all around you."

Because territorial gains were often temporary and illusory, American success was measured in gruesome "body counts"—the number of enemy soldiers killed—and "kill ratios"—the ratio between enemy losses and U.S. casualties. "If it's dead and Vietnamese, it's VC [Vietcong]" was the rule of thumb in the bush. Casualty figures were often deliberately inflated. As a twenty-four-year-old army captain recalled, "I went out and killed one VC and liberated a prisoner. Next day the major called me in and told me that I'd killed fourteen VC and liberated six prisoners. You want to see the medal?"

Racism was a fact of everyday life in Vietnam. It was difficult to differentiate between friendly South Vietnamese and Vietcong sympathizers, and many soldiers lumped them together as "gooks." A draftee noted of his indoctrination, "The only thing they told us about the Vietcong was they were gooks. They were to be killed. Nobody sits around and gives you their historical and cultural background. They're the enemy. Kill, kill, kill."

Fighting and surviving in such conditions took its toll. "War is not killing," one soldier recalled. "Killing is the easiest part of the whole thing. Sweating twenty-four hours a day, seeing guys drop all around you of heatstroke, not having food, not having water, sleeping only three hours a night for weeks at a time, that's what war is. Survival." Another veteran echoed that sentiment: "The hardest thing to come to grips with was the fact that making it through Vietnam—surviving—is probably the only worthwhile part of the experience. It wasn't going over there and saving the world from communism or defending the country." Such cynicism and bitterness were common.

Women who served in Vietnam shared many of these experiences. As WACs, nurses, and civilian service workers with organizations such as the USO, women volunteers witnessed massive doses of death and mutilation, mainly inflicted on soldiers barely out of their teens. They tried not to get caught up in it emotionally, but as a navy nurse recalled, "It's pretty damn hard not getting involved when you see a nineteen- or twenty-year-old blond kid from the Midwest or California or the East Coast screaming and dying. A piece of my heart would go with each."

The Consensus Begins to Unravel

During the Kennedy and early Johnson years there was a broad consensus for the administration's conduct of foreign affairs, as there had been generally throughout the cold war period. Both Democrats and Republicans supported Johnson's escalation of the war, and public opinion polls showed strong popular support for his policies in 1965–1966. But in the late 1960s public opinion began to turn against the war. In July 1967 a Gallup poll revealed that for the first time, a majority of Americans disapproved of Johnson's Vietnam policy and believed that the war had reached a stalemate.

The Television War. Television had much to do with shaping American attitudes toward the war. Vietnam was the first war in which television brought the fight-

A Televised War

This harrowing scene from Saigon during the Tet offensive in 1968 was broadcast on U.S. network news. The NBC bureau chief described the film in a terse telex message: "A VC OFFICER WAS CAPTURED. THE TROOPS BEAT HIM. THEY BRING HIM TO [Brigadier General Nguyen Ngoc] LOAN WHO IS HEAD OF SOUTH VIETNAMESE NATIONAL POLICE. LOAN PULLS OUT HIS PISTOL, FIRES AT THE HEAD OF THE VC, THE VC FALLS, ZOOM ON HIS HEAD, BLOOD SPRAYING OUT. IF HE HAS IT ALL ITS STARTLING STUFF."

ing directly into the nation's living rooms. The escalation in Vietnam came just two years after the expansion of the nightly network news broadcast from fifteen minutes to half an hour in 1963. By 1967 CBS and NBC were spending $5 million a year to cover the war from their expanded Saigon bureaus. This investment guaranteed that Vietnam appeared on the news every night. Reporters soon learned that combat footage—what they called "shooting bloody"—had a better chance of airing than did reports about social reform or political developments. Every night Americans saw U.S. soldiers advancing steadily in the countryside and heard about staggering Vietcong losses and minimal U.S. casualties.

Growing Doubts. Despite the glowing reports that were fed to the American public about the progress of the war, by 1967 many administration officials had privately reached more pessimistic conclusions. Secretary of Defense Robert McNamara, one of the architects of the war, expressed opposition to the expansion of the air war and sent a memo to the president in November arguing that continued escalation "would be dangerous, costly in lives, and unsatisfactory to the American people." A few weeks later McNamara left the Defense Department for the World Bank. "I do not know," he later wrote, "whether I quit or was fired." McNamara's doubts were confirmed by Pentagon analysts who estimated that the Vietcong, with only minimal assistance from other communist powers, could marshal 200,000 guerrillas a year indefinitely.

Despite that prognosis, President Johnson continued to insist that victory in Vietnam was vital to U.S. national security and prestige. Journalists, especially those who had spent time in Vietnam, soon commented that the Johnson administration suffered from a "credibility gap." The administration, they charged, was concealing important and discouraging information about the progress of the war. Television coverage of hearings by the Senate Foreign Relations Committee in February 1966 (chaired by J. William Fulbright, an outspoken critic of the war) also raised questions about the administration's Vietnam policies.

Economic events also put Johnson and his advisers on the defensive. In 1966 the federal deficit was $9.8 billion. It jumped to $23 billion in 1967, with the Vietnam War costing the taxpayers $27 billion that year. Although the war was consuming only 3 percent of the gross national product, compared with 42 percent at the height of World War II and 12 percent during the Korean War, its costs became more evident as the growing federal deficit nudged the inflation rate upward. But only in the summer of 1967 did Johnson ask for a 10 percent surcharge on individual and corporate income, which Congress delayed approving until 1968. By then the inflationary spiral that would plague the American economy throughout the 1970s was already well under way.

The Early Antiwar Movement. Another major problem facing the Johnson administration was the growing strength and visibility of the antiwar movement. As in every American military conflict, a small group of dissenters opposed the war from the beginning, including pacifist organizations such as the War Resisters League and the Women's International League for Peace and Freedom and religious groups such as the Fellowship for Reconciliation and the Quakers. Those groups were joined by a new generation of peace activists that had emerged in the 1950s to protest atmospheric nuclear testing. Concern over fallout and traces of radioactive strontium 90 in milk led to the founding of groups such as SANE (the National Committee for a Sane Nuclear Policy), Physicians for Social Responsibility, and Women Strike for Peace. Those activists opposed the escalating arms race in general and atmospheric testing in particular and lobbied successfully for the 1963 nuclear test ban treaty between the United States and the Soviet Union.

Between 1963 and 1965, as the American presence in Vietnam grew, peace activists in both older and newer organizations staged periodic protests, vigils, and petitioning and letter-writing campaigns against U.S. involvement in the war. After the escalation of combat in the spring of 1965, various antiwar coalitions organized several mass demonstrations in Washington that brought out 20,000

Women March for Peace, 1962
Members of the Women's Strike for Peace set up picket lines at the Capitol in December 1962 to urge an end to atmospheric testing of nuclear weapons by the United States and the Soviet Union. Such protest groups were forerunners of the broader movement that opposed the Vietnam War after 1965.

to 30,000 people. Pacifist and religious groups were joined by growing numbers of students, housewives, politicians, artists, and other Americans opposed to the war. Although they were a diverse lot, the participants shared a common skepticism about the means and aims of U.S. policy. Critics of intervention argued that the war was morally wrong and antithetical to American ideals; that the goal of an independent, anticommunist South Vietnam was unattainable; and that American military involvement would not help the Vietnamese people.

Norman Morrison provides an example of how strongly some Americans felt about Vietnam. In November 1965 Morrison, a thirty-two-year-old Quaker activist, married and the father of an eighteen-month-old daughter, set himself on fire and burned to death near the gates of the Pentagon, 40 yards from Defense Secretary McNamara's office. He undertook this protest against the immorality of the war after reading an account by a French priest who had despaired at seeing his Vietnamese parishioners burned by napalm (a lethal incendiary substance) during a bombing attack. Like the priest, Morrison was anguished about his inability to stop the carnage. To his wife of ten years he left this note: "Know that I love thee but must act for the children of the priest's village."

Morrison's suicide shocked the nation. Even McNamara later admitted that he was horrified by this "outcry against the killing that was destroying the lives of so many Vietnamese and American youth." Three weeks later an estimated 30,000 antiwar protesters converged on the White House, including a large contingent of college students. Over the next few years student protesters flocked to the antiwar movement in great numbers, increasing its visibility and political clout. The fervor of this new generation drove not only the antiwar movement but a youthful rebellion that challenged authority on nearly every front.

The Challenge of Youth, 1962–1970

"There is everywhere protest, reevaluation, attack on the Establishment," the social critic Paul Goodman asserted at the end of the 1960s. The novelist Norman Mailer agreed: "We're in a time that's divorced from the past. . . . There's utterly no tradition anymore." The sources of this youthful rebellion lay in the political and social developments of the postwar era, particularly the early 1960s. The idealism of Kennedy's New Frontier raised students' expectations of what they and their society could accomplish. The civil rights movement ignited the challenge to established institutions, teaching college students protest tactics such as marches, sit-ins, and mass confrontations.

Finally, the escalation of the Vietnam War in 1965 offered a compelling political cause to rally around, especially as the draft affected more college-age men. Vietnam would become the defining political issue of their generation.

Student Activism

The 1960s witnessed the first active student movement since the 1930s. But whereas most of that depression-scarred generation had been unable to afford higher education, its children—the baby boomers—flocked to colleges and universities in the postwar period. In addition, many soldiers who had served in World War II and the Korean War used the benefits of the GI Bill to finance higher education that otherwise would have been out of their reach. Those veterans, many of them from working-class backgrounds, later sent their children to college as well. In 1940 only 15 percent of all youth between the ages of eighteen and twenty-one attended college; in 1963 the proportion had reached almost 50 percent.

In the 1950s most students accepted the practical career-oriented values of their society. Engineering and business administration (for men) and home economics and teaching (for women) were the most popular courses of study, and students took little part in politics. Some critics suggested that students, responding to the repressive atmosphere of McCarthyism, had become a "silent generation." Even so, many young people felt dissatisfied in the 1950s. The youthful rebellion evident in rock 'n' roll and portrayed in Hollywood films such as *Rebel without a Cause* (see Chapter 29) was one expression of this dissatisfaction. J. D. Salinger's best-selling novel *The Catcher in the Rye* (1951) offered a more explicit critique of the materialism of postwar American society. With a dawning awareness of the existence of poverty and the ever present threat of nuclear war, the novel's teenage protagonist gradually sheds his naiveté and quietly rejects the middle-class pretensions of his family, neighbors, and schoolmates. The book is a withering attack on the hypocrisy of a society that insists that all is well because the economy is booming—a notion that found wide acceptance among youths in the 1960s.

Early Stirrings. Youth rebellion took a distinctly political form in the early 1960s. In June 1962 forty students from Big Ten and Ivy League universities met at a United Auto Workers conference center in Port Huron, Michigan, to found Students for a Democratic Society (SDS). Their manifesto, written by Tom Hayden, a University of Michigan student, drew heavily on the writings of the radical Columbia University sociologist C. Wright Mills. The Port Huron Statement expressed hostility toward bureaucracy, rejected cold war ideology (including

but not limited to the Vietnam conflict), emphasized participatory politics, and designated students as the major force for change in society. SDSers referred to their movement as the "New Left" to distinguish themselves from the "Old Left"—communists, socialists, and other left-wing sectarians of the 1930s and 1940s. Consciously adopting the activist tactics pioneered by the civil rights movement, SDS devoted much of its early attention to grass-roots organizing in cities and on college campuses.

The first student protests broke out at the University of California at Berkeley. In the fall of 1964 the university administration banned political activity near the Telegraph Avenue entrance to the campus, where student groups had traditionally distributed leaflets and recruited volunteers. In response, all the major student organizations, from SDS to the conservative Youth for Goldwater, formed a coalition to protest what they considered to be an abridgment of free speech. The Free Speech Movement organized a sit-in at the main administration building and persuaded the university to drop the ban.

The Free Speech Movement owed a strong debt to the civil rights movement. Berkeley had sent more volunteers to Freedom Summer in Mississippi in 1964 than had any other campus, and the students had been radi-

Free Speech at Berkeley, 1964
Students at the University of California's Berkeley campus protested the administration's decision to ban political activity in the school plaza. Free speech demonstrators, many of them active in the civil rights movement, relied on the tactics and arguments that they learned in that struggle.

calized by the experience. The student leader Mario Savio spoke for many of them:

> Last summer I went to Mississippi to join the struggle there for civil rights. This fall I am engaged in another phase of the same struggle, this time in Berkeley. The two battlefields may seem quite different to some observers, but this is not the case. The same rights are at stake in both places—the right to participate as citizens in a democratic society and to struggle against the same enemy. In Mississippi an autocratic and powerful minority rules, through organized violence, to suppress the vast, virtually powerless majority. In California, the privileged minority manipulates the university bureaucracy to suppress the students' political expression.

On a deeper level Berkeley students were challenging the university because it had grown too big, too impersonal, and too insulated from the major social issues of the day. The largest universities, like the largest corporations, had grown the fastest in the postwar era. In 1940 only two campuses had as many as 20,000 students; in 1969 thirty-nine were at least that large. Many students felt that they were treated brusquely and impersonally in those "multiversities." Emboldened by the Berkeley experience, students at institutions across the country were soon protesting everything from dress codes to course requirements, tenure decisions, and academic grading systems.

Students also protested the universities' complicity in the problems of the ghettos that surrounded many urban campuses. Columbia, for example, was a major property owner in Harlem, which borders its campus. In 1968 Columbia announced plans to build a new gymnasium, displacing local stores and housing. Chanting "Gym Crow must go," students tore down the fence at the construction site and took over several university buildings, including the office of the president, Grayson Kirk. (Photographs of protesters sampling Kirk's cigars and sherry did little to build public support.) At Berkeley, students and administrators clashed in 1969 over a parcel of vacant land near the campus that a coalition of students and residents had turned into a "People's Park." When the university asserted its right to the land, a violent confrontation broke out and an onlooker was killed. At both Columbia and Berkeley the administration decided to use city police officers to break up the demonstrations; the brutality of the police radicalized many more students than had originally supported the protests. As campus disturbances spread, more and more university buildings were blocked, occupied, or picketed, and classes were frequently dismissed or canceled.

Although black students participated in many of the protests, student movements increasingly split along racial lines, reflecting the separatism that characterized the civil rights movement in the mid-1960s. Whereas white students focused increasingly on the antiwar

movement, black students inspired by the black power movement demanded courses in African-American history and culture. University administrators were open to such demands as a way to ease campus unrest, and many universities established Afro-American or black studies departments in the late 1960s and early 1970s. By including the study of black society and culture in the curriculum and acknowledging race as a key factor in American life, those new courses and programs had an enduring impact on the way American history was taught and written. Black protesters also won university support for separate dormitories and cultural centers to provide a sense of community for blacks on predominantly white campuses.

The Antiwar Movement. But no issue provoked more impassioned and sustained protest than the Vietnam War. When President Johnson dramatically escalated the war in March 1965, faculty members and student activists at the University of Michigan organized a teach-in against the war. In marathon sessions they debated the political, diplomatic, and moral aspects of U.S. involvement in Vietnam. Teach-ins quickly spread to other universities as students turned their attention to antiwar protests.

A strong spur to activism was a change in the Selective Service System. In the past, young men could use deferments for college, graduate school, teaching, and parenthood to avoid the draft until they reached the cutoff age of twenty-six. Over the course of the war the government issued more than 8 million deferments, a disproportionate number of which went to wealthy whites. In response to criticism of the class and racial bias inherent in the system, the Selective Service gradually phased out deferments. In January 1966 automatic student deferments were abolished.

Young men's options were limited. Some enlisted in the National Guard or the reserves to avoid being sent to Vietnam. Some reluctant draftees sought sympathetic doctors to give them medical or psychiatric excuses or to help them fail the induction physical. Others filed for conscientious objector status, fulfilling their military commitment through alternative service in the United States or noncombatant duty in Vietnam. Several thousand ignored the induction notice entirely, risking prosecution for draft evasion, while others left the country (Canada and Sweden were the most popular destinations). The Resistance, started at Berkeley and Stanford and widely recognized by its omega symbol, provided support to draft resisters. Opponents of the war burned their draft cards in public acts of civil disobedience, closed down induction centers with mass protests, and on a few occasions broke into Selective Service offices to destroy or mutilate files.

As antiwar and draft protests multiplied, students realized that their universities were deeply implicated in the war effort. In some cases as much as 60 percent of a university's research budget came from government contracts, especially from the Defense Department. Protesters blocked campus recruitment by the Dow Chemical Company because it produced napalm and Agent Orange. Arguing that universities should not train students for war, protesters demanded that the Reserve Officer Training Corps (ROTC) be removed from campus. The ROTC was one of the main targets of student protests at Columbia in 1968 and Harvard in 1969.

Mass demonstrations against the war consumed much of the energy of the student movement in the late 1960s as students became part of the much larger antiwar movement of peace activists, housewives, religious leaders, and a few elected officials. Nationwide student strikes, mass demonstrations in Washington, D.C., and other organized protests became commonplace after 1967. More than 100,000 antiwar demonstrators marched on Washington in October 1967 as part of "Stop the Draft Week." The event culminated in a "siege of the Pentagon" in which protesters clashed with police and federal marshals, resulting in hundreds of arrests and several beatings of demonstrators. Lyndon Johnson, who had earlier dismissed antiwar protesters as "nervous Nellies," rebellious children, or communist dupes, now faced large-scale public opposition to his policies. The administration thus waged a two-front offensive: a military operation in Vietnam and a war for public opinion at home.

The Rise of the Counterculture

Antiwar sentiment and protest accelerated the erosion of confidence in established American institutions and values. But while the New Left took to the streets in protest, a growing number of young Americans chose to undertake their own revolution against the "respectable" standards of middle-class society. Building on the sense of personal alienation and cultural rebellion articulated by the beat generation in the 1950s, youths in the 1960s pioneered new forms of cultural expression. Dubbed the *counterculture* because it challenged so many established values, the movement encouraged personal liberation through new musical and clothing styles, spiritual exploration, and experimentation with sex and drugs.

The impact of the counterculture was readily evident even to the uninitiated. In an amazingly short period of time young people's clothing and hairstyles changed radically. At Berkeley's free speech demonstrations in 1964, young men wore coats and ties and women wore skirts and sweaters. At antiwar protests just three or four years later, youths defiantly dressed in unisex ragged blue jeans, tie-dyed T-shirts, beads, and army fatigues. Unorthodox clothes and long, unkempt hair identified a new phenomenon of American youth culture, the *hippie*.

Flower Children
Yale law professor Charles A. Reich celebrated the new freedom of youth in his best-selling book *The Greening of America* (1970). Reich described a new consciousness that had "emerged out of the wasteland of the Corporate State, like flowers pushing up through the concrete pavement." Counterculture hippies were also called flower children.

The uncomprehending older generation often had a simple response: "Get a haircut."

Popular Music. Throughout the 1960s popular music mirrored changing political moods. The folksinger Pete Seeger set the tone for the era's political idealism with songs such as the antiwar ballad "Where Have All the Flowers Gone?" Another folksinger, Joan Baez, gained national prominence for "We Shall Overcome" and other folk and political anthems that she performed at protest rallies in the mid-1960s. In 1963, the year of the Birmingham demonstrations and President Kennedy's assassination, Bob Dylan's "Blowin' in the Wind" reflected the impatience of people whose faith in liberalism was wearing thin.

Early in 1964 the Beatles, four working-class youths from Liverpool, England, burst onto the American scene. As Elvis Presley had eight years earlier, they thrust their way into the national consciousness through a series of television appearances on "The Ed Sullivan Show." The Beatles' music, by turns lyrical and driving, was phenomenally successful, spawning a commercial and cultural phenomenon called Beatlemania. The more rebellious, angrier music of other British groups, notably the Rolling Stones, found a broad American audience shortly afterward.

The Drug Culture. Drugs were almost as important as rock music in the youth culture of the 1960s. Drugs were hardly new to the American scene: many jazz musicians from the 1920s on had used heroin and cocaine, and the

beats had experimented with mind-altering drugs in San Francisco and New York. Now widespread recreational use of drugs extended beyond artistic and jazz circles.

Marijuana was the preferred drug among college students, but stronger drugs also gained popularity. The hallucinogen lysergic acid diethylamide, popularly known as LSD or "acid," was one of the most potent. It was popularized in California by the writer Ken Kesey and his eccentric followers, the Merry Pranksters, who conducted "acid tests" (public "happenings" where tabs of LSD were distributed) in 1965 and 1966. San Francisco bands such as the Grateful Dead and the Jefferson Airplane, the Seattle-born guitarist Jimi Hendrix, and Britain's Pink Floyd developed a style of music known as "acid rock," characterized by long, heavily amplified guitar solos and psychedelic effects. The Beatles, whose early songs had simply stated "I Want to Hold Your Hand" and "Please, Please Me," later recorded tunes such as "Lucy in the Sky with Diamonds" (1967), whose "tangerine trees and marmalade skies" celebrated the new drug-induced consciousness.

For a brief time adherents of the counterculture believed that a new age was dawning. "The closest Western Civilization has come to uniting since the Congress of Vienna in 1815 was the week the *Sgt. Pepper* album was released," gushed a rock critic about the Beatles' 1967 release. Others pointed to the "age of Aquarius"

Sgt. Pepper's Lonely Hearts Club Band
The colorful collage on the cover of this 1967 Beatles album allowed fans to debate (occasionally under the influence of marijuana or LSD) the symbolism of those depicted. Can you identify Mae West, Karl Marx, Bob Dylan, Albert Einstein, Lenny Bruce, and Marilyn Monroe, as well as the "Fab Four" in their various disguises? (©Apple Corps Ltd.)

proclaimed in the 1968 Broadway rock musical *Hair*. In 1967 the "world's first Human Be-In" drew 20,000 people to Golden Gate Park in San Francisco. The beat poet Allen Ginsberg "purified" the site with a Buddhist ritual, political activists embraced "drug freaks," and the LSD advocate Timothy Leary, a former Harvard psychology instructor, urged the gathering to "turn on to the scene, tune in to what is happening, and drop out." In the summer of 1967—dubbed the "Summer of Love"—San Francisco's Haight-Ashbury, New York's East Village, and Chicago's Uptown neighborhoods were crowded with young people as well as swarms of reporters and busloads of tourists who gawked at the so-called flower children. Faith in instant love and peace quickly turned sour, however, as dropouts, drifters, and teenage runaways tried to cope with bad drug trips, venereal disease, loneliness, and violence. In 1967 seventeen murders and more than a hundred rapes were reported in Haight-Ashbury alone.

Meanwhile, the appeal of rock music and drugs continued to spread. In August 1969 400,000 young people journeyed to Bethel, New York, to attend the three-day Woodstock Music and Art Fair. Despite torrential rain and numerous drug overdoses, the festival was heralded as the birth of the "Woodstock nation" as participants "got high" on music, drugs, and sex. A few months later, however, an outdoor concert by the Rolling Stones at Altamont Speedway near San Francisco degenerated into a near riot, leaving four dead and hundreds injured.

Rejecting both the mainstream culture and the growing anarchy of the counterculture, some young people headed for rural communes. Communes were located in isolated areas such as the mountains between Santa Cruz and San Francisco, the wide-open spaces of New Mexico, and the pastoral solitude of Vermont, away from the watchful eye of mainstream America (and local drug enforcement agents). Following in the tradition of earlier American utopian communities, communes provided economic and sexual alternatives to nuclear families. They also promised a return to the land as members banded together to grow their own food, bake their own bread, and reject the materialism and commercialism of American life in an attempt at self-sufficiency. But the communes of the 1960s did not just look backward. Their advocacy of organic farming—growing food without chemicals or pesticides—anticipated and influenced the environmental concerns that would emerge in the 1970s and 1980s (see Chapter 32).

Although the counterculture and the New Left were different movements, the distinction was sometimes blurred. Many antiwar protesters adopted hippie clothing, experimented with drugs, and embraced the more politically oriented rock music. While most flower children professed to be politically apathetic, their antiauthoritarianism seemed threatening to many adults. Furthermore, groups such as the Youth International Party, or "Yippies," led by Abbie Hoffman and Jerry Rubin, combined political and cultural rebellion to attract media attention. During the October 1967 March on Washington the Yippies dressed like witches and attempted to levitate the Pentagon as a way to end the war. To many adult observers the antiwar movement and the counterculture had become indistinguishable.

The Long Road Home, 1968–1975

In 1968, as Lyndon Johnson planned his reelection campaign, Vietnam had become the central domestic and foreign policy issue, eclipsing the struggle for civil rights. Antiwar protests and America's vulnerability on the battlefield—as evidenced by the Tet offensive of January–February 1968—had begun to erode public support for the war. Vietnam also cast a shadow over domestic events as antiwar protests divided and disrupted the Democratic National Convention in Chicago that summer. The Chicago riot, along with two major political assassinations that year, shocked the nation and ushered in a new conservatism represented by the Republican presidency of Richard Nixon. But like his predecessors, Nixon found it difficult to extricate the United States from Vietnam, and American troops fought for nearly five more years.

While the Johnson administration insisted that there was "light at the end of the tunnel" in late 1967, the reality was otherwise. American casualty rates continued to rise, North Vietnamese and Vietcong forces fought on, and the South Vietnamese government enjoyed little popular support. Since the assassination of Diem in 1963 South Vietnam had undergone a confusing series of coups and countercoups by various factions of the military. In June 1965 Generals Nguyen Van Thieu and Nguyen Cao Ky took power in a military coup. After widespread Buddhist uprisings against the new regime in the spring of 1966, the Johnson administration pressured the South Vietnamese government to adopt democratic reforms, including a new constitution and popular elections. With American help Thieu was elected president of South Vietnam in September 1967. Thieu's regime, the Johnson administration hoped, would broaden its support at home, legitimize the South Vietnamese government in the eyes of the American public, and advance the military struggle against the communists.

1968: A Year of Shocks

The Tet Offensive. Those hopes were quickly shattered on January 30, 1968, when the Vietcong unleashed a

Steve Lerner

The Siege of Chicago

Steve Lerner published this account of the altercation between protesters and the Chicago police during the Democratic National Convention in August 1968 in the *Village Voice*. The scene is Lincoln Park on Chicago's North Side, where many of the protesters congregated.

Around midnight on Tuesday some four hundred clergy, concerned local citizens, and other respectable gentry joined the Yippies, members of Students for a Democratic Society, and the National Mobilization Committee to fight for the privilege of remaining in the park. Sporting armbands decorated with a black cross and chanting pacifist hymns, the men of God exhorted their radical congregation to lay down their bricks and join in a nonviolent vigil. . . .

During the half-hour interlude between the arrival of the clergy and the police attack, a fascinating debate over the relative merits of strict nonviolence versus armed self-defense raged between the clergy and the militants. While the clergy was reminded that their members were "over thirty, the opiate of the people, and totally irrelevant," the younger generation was warned that "by calling the police pigs and fighting with them you become as bad as they are." Although the conflict was never resolved, everyone more or less decided to do his own thing. By then the demonstrators, some eight hundred strong, began to feel the phalanx of police which encircled the park moving in; even the most militant forgot his quibbles with "the liberal-religious sellout" and began to huddle together around the cross.

When the police announced that the demonstrators had five minutes to move out before the park was cleared, everyone went into his individual kind of panic. One boy sitting near me unwrapped a cheese sandwich and began to stuff it into his face without bothering to chew. A girl standing at the periphery of the circle who had been alone all evening walked up to a helmeted boy with a mustache and ground herself into him. People all over the park were shyly introducing themselves to each other as if they didn't want to die alone. "My name is Mike Stevenson from Detroit; what got you into this?" I heard someone asking behind me. Others became increasingly involved in the details of survival: rubbing Vaseline on their face to keep the Mace from burning their skin, buttoning their jackets, wetting their handkerchief and tying it over their nose and mouth. "If it's gas, remember, breathe through your mouth, don't run, don't pant, and . . . don't rub your eyes," someone thoughtfully announced over the speaker. A boy in the center of the circle got up, stepped over his seated friends, and made his way toward the woods. "Don't leave now," several voices called in panic. The boy explained that he was just going to take a leak.

It happened all in an instant. The night which had been filled with darkness and whispers exploded in a fiery scream. Huge tear-gas canisters came crashing through the branches, snapping them, and bursting in the center of the gathering. From where I lay, groveling in the grass, I could see ministers retreating with the cross, carrying it like a fallen comrade. Another volley shook me to my feet. Gas was everywhere. People were running, screaming, tearing through the trees. Something hit the tree next to me, I was on the ground again, someone was pulling me to my feet, two boys were lifting a big branch off a girl who lay squirming hysterically. I couldn't see. Someone grabbed onto me and asked me to lead them out of the park. We walked along, hands outstretched, bumping into people and trees, tears streaming from our eyes and mucus smeared across our faces. I flashed First World War doughboys caught in no-man's-land during a mustard gas attack. I felt sure I was going to die. I heard others choking around me. And then everything cleared.

Source: Steve Lerner account from the *Village Voice*, excerpted in Norman Mailer, *Miami and the Siege of Chicago: An Informal History of the Republican and Democratic Conventions of 1968* (New York: New American Library, 1968), 151–152.

Hilton Hotel where most of the delegates were staying.

While protesters chanted "The whole world is watching!" the television networks ran film of the riot during the nominating speeches. In one memorable moment, Senator Abraham Ribicoff of Connecticut interrupted his nominating speech for Senator McGovern to interject, "With George McGovern we wouldn't have Gestapo tactics on the streets of Chicago." The cameras panned to Mayor Daley, livid with rage and clearly mouthing obscenities.

Television coverage of the riots was hardly excessive—about 32 minutes on CBS and less than 14 minutes on NBC—but it cemented an impression of the Democrats as the party of disorder. The Democrats dispiritedly gave the nomination to Hubert H. Humphrey, who chose Senator Edmund S. Muskie of Maine as his running mate. The convention approved a middle-of-the-road platform that endorsed Johnson's policy of continuing the fighting in Vietnam while exploring diplomatic means to end the conflict.

Chicago, 1968
On August 28 thousands of antiwar demonstrators gathered outside the Conrad Hilton Hotel in downtown Chicago, site of the Democratic National Convention. When Mayor Richard Daley ordered the Chicago police to disperse the crowd, a violent melee ensued in which hundreds were injured.

Political Backlash

An enduring result of the Democratic convention was the beginning of a backlash against protest. The general public did not differentiate between the antics of the small group of Yippies and the more serious actions of a far greater number of antiwar activists who were trying to work within the system. Polls showed overwhelming support for Mayor Daley and the police.

A Changing Mood. The New Left began to falter after 1968. Discredited by the events in Chicago, SDS members found themselves unable to agree on basic goals and tactics. Moreover, SDS and other antiwar groups fell victim to police harassment and FBI and CIA counterintelligence campaigns that infiltrated and disrupted radical political organizations. After 1968 the New Left splintered into factions, its energy spent. One radical faction broke off from SDS to form the Weathermen (taking the name from a Bob Dylan song). A tiny band of self-styled revolutionaries, the Weathermen and their imitators embraced violence and conducted dozens of terrorist bombings, including the destruction of the Army Math building at the University of Wisconsin at Madison in August 1970. The FBI quickly targeted those groups, and many of their members were forced to go underground to avoid arrest. The violent activities of the Weathermen and other extremist groups alienated many young people from the New Left, but broad-based antiwar protests continued until 1971.

Among the general public, the turmoil surrounding the New Left and the antiwar movement strengthened support for proponents of "law and order," which became the conservative catchphrase of the next several years. Many Americans, though opposed to the war, were fed up with protest and dissent. Governor George C. Wallace of Alabama, a third-party candidate, skillfully exploited the public's growing hostility by making student protests and urban riots his chief campaign issues. Articulating the resentments of many working-class whites, he delivered a populist message that combined attacks on liberal intellectuals and government elites with

Hard Hats
Many construction workers (and the unions they belonged to) were vocal supporters of the Vietnam War. Sometimes hard hats clashed with long-haired protesters during antiwar marches and sidewalk demonstrations.

strident denunciations of school desegregation and forced busing.

Richard Nixon, even more than George Wallace, tapped the growing conservative mood of the electorate. After his unsuccessful presidential campaign in 1960 and his loss in the California gubernatorial race in 1962, Nixon engineered an amazing political comeback. In 1968 the "new" Nixon easily beat back primary challenges by three governors—Ronald Reagan of California, George Romney of Michigan, and Nelson Rockefeller of New York—to win the Republican nomination. He chose Maryland's governor, Spiro Agnew, as his running mate to attract southern voters who opposed Democratic civil rights legislation, especially potential Wallace supporters. In what his campaign adviser Kevin Phillips called the "southern strategy," Nixon hoped to make impressive inroads in the once solidly Democratic South. He also used traditional populist appeals, pledging to represent the "quiet voice" of the "great majority of Americans, the forgotten Americans, the nonshouters, the nondemonstrators." He em-

phatically declared, "The first civil right of every American is to be free from domestic violence."

Despite the Democratic debacle in Chicago, the election was close. Humphrey rallied in the last weeks of the campaign by gingerly disassociating himself from Johnson's war policies. Furthermore, in a televised address on October 31 President Johnson announced a complete halt of the bombing of North Vietnam. Nixon countered by intimating that he had his own plan for ending the war (although in reality no such plan existed). Nixon received 43.4 percent of the vote to Humphrey's 42.7 percent, defeating him by a scant 510,000 votes out of the 73 million cast (see Map 31.2). Wallace finished with 13.5 percent of the popular vote, becoming the most successful third-party candidate since the Progressive party's Robert M. La Follette in 1924. Nixon owed his election largely to the split in the Democratic coalition, but the success of the southern strategy hinted at the future emergence of a new Republican majority. In the meantime, however, the Democrats retained a majority in both houses of Congress.

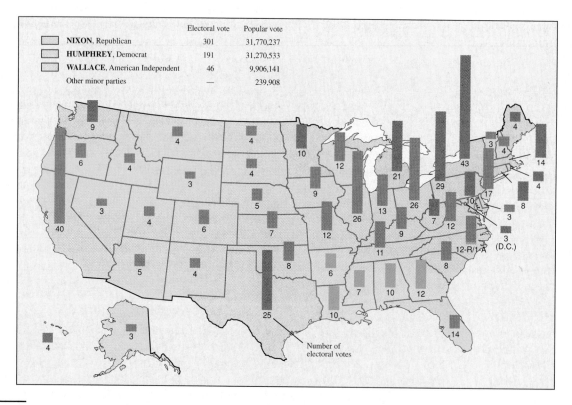

MAP 31.2

The Election of 1968
As late as mid-September the third-party candidate George C. Wallace of Alabama had the support of 21 percent of the voters. But in November he received only 13.5 percent of the vote, winning five states and showing that the South was no longer solidly Democratic. The Republican Richard M. Nixon defeated Hubert H. Humphrey with only 43.4 percent of the popular vote.

The "Silent Majority." The closeness of the 1968 election suggested how polarized American society had become over the Vietnam War and other events of the 1960s. Nixon appealed to what came to be known as the *silent majority*—the average, hardworking, nonprotesting (and generally white) American. According to the social scientists Ben J. Wattenberg and Richard Scammon in their influential book *The Real Majority* (1970), the typical American was a white forty-seven-year-old machinist's wife from Dayton, Ohio, and this was what she was concerned about:

> To know that the lady in Dayton is afraid to walk the streets alone at night, to know that she has a mixed view about blacks and civil rights because before moving to the suburbs she lived in a neighborhood that became all black, to know that her brother-in-law is a policeman, to know that she does not have the money to move if her new neighborhood deteriorates, to know that she is deeply distressed that her son is going to a community junior college where LSD was found on campus—to know all this is the beginning of contemporary political wisdom.

Although political appeals after 1968 suggested a growing consensus among voters who were (in the words of Wattenberg and Scammon) "unblack, unpoor, and unyoung," protest and controversy would remain part of the political process until the divisive issue of the Vietnam War was resolved.

Nixon's War

Vietnam, long Lyndon Johnson's war, now became Richard Nixon's; 15,000 Americans would lose their lives in that conflict during Nixon's presidency. Yet Nixon operated in a political climate that differed fundamentally from that of Johnson (see Chapter 32 for Nixon's domestic agenda). Initially Nixon sought to end the war by expanding its scope as a means of pressuring the North Vietnamese to negotiate. But Nixon and his national security adviser, Henry Kissinger, soon realized that the public would not support major sacrifices to win the war and searched for another way out. A new plan to reduce American troop involvement called Vietnamization delegated most of the ground fighting to South Vietnamese troops, but it would take six more years to end U.S. involvement.

Shortly after Nixon took office, he sent a letter to Hanoi proposing mutual withdrawals of American and North Vietnamese forces. In March 1969, to convince Hanoi that the United States meant business, Nixon ordered secret bombing raids on neutral Cambodia, through which the North Vietnamese transported supplies and reinforcements. To keep Congress and the public ignorant about those sorties, the air force officials in charge of the bombings fed accurate information about the raids into one Defense Department computer while placing data omitting the Cambodian targets into another. The faulty projections from the second computer were the ones given to Congress. The secret war culminated in an April 30, 1970, "incursion" by American ground forces into Cambodia to destroy enemy troop havens there. Over the next three months the Americans captured 2,000 enemy troops and destroyed 8,000 bunkers, temporarily disrupting North Vietnamese supply lines. But the invasion proved to be only a short-term setback for North Vietnam and produced a diplomatic stalemate as the North Vietnamese and the Vietcong continued to boycott the Paris peace talks. Most critically, the American invasion of Cambodia—along with the ongoing North Vietnamese intervention there—served to destabilize that country, allowing for a takeover by the ruthless Khmer Rouge in the late 1970s.

The administration's failure to end the war through intensified bombing campaigns persuaded Nixon and Kissinger to pursue Vietnamization. On June 8, 1969, Nixon announced that 25,000 American troops would be withdrawn by August and replaced by South Vietnamese forces. The troop withdrawals helped persuade the North Vietnamese to begin secret negotiations with Kissinger that August, but the diplomatic stalemate continued. Nixon, meanwhile, stepped up attacks against North Vietnamese and Vietcong targets, hoping to pressure Hanoi to negotiate while strengthening Thieu's faltering South Vietnamese government as Vietnamization went into effect. When Nixon took office, more than 543,000 American soldiers were serving in Vietnam; by the end of 1970 there were 334,000, and two years later there were 24,200. American casualties and the political liabilities that they generated fell correspondingly. But the slaughter in Vietnam continued. As the U.S. ambassador to Vietnam, Ellsworth Bunker, noted cynically, it was just a matter of changing "the color of the bodies."

The War at Home. As with Lyndon Johnson, who by 1968 had become so unpopular that his appearance caused protests everywhere except on military bases, antiwar demonstrators denounced Richard Nixon and his Vietnamization policy. On October 15, 1969, millions of people in cities across the country joined a one-day "moratorium" to protest the war. A month later, more than a quarter of a million people mobilized in Washington to call for an end to the fighting, the largest antiwar demonstration to date.

To discredit his critics Nixon denounced student demonstrators as "bums" and stated that "North Vietnam cannot defeat or humiliate the United States. Only Americans can do that." Vice-President Spiro Agnew attacked dissenters as "ideological eunuchs" and "natter-

Kent State

The shootings by National Guardsmen of four students at Kent State University in Ohio on May 4, 1970, set off campus demonstrations and protests across the country. The protester shown here holds a placard memorializing the slain students as well as the two black students killed soon afterward at Jackson State College in Mississippi. The president of Columbia University called May 1970 "the most disastrous month . . . in the history of American higher education."

ing nabobs of negativism." Nixon staunchly insisted that he would not be swayed by the mounting protests against the war. During the November 1969 march on Washington the president barricaded himself in the White House and watched football on television.

The most extensive outbreak of student unrest came in the spring of 1970, after the invasion of Cambodia, when antiwar leaders organized a national student strike. At Kent State University outside Cleveland, panicky National Guardsmen fired into a crowd of students at a noontime antiwar rally on May 4. Four people were killed, and eleven were wounded. Only two of those killed, Jeffrey Miller and Alison Krause, had been at the demonstration; William Shroeder and Sandra Scheur were passing by on their way to class. Soon afterward National Guardsmen shot and killed two black women students while storming a dormitory at Jackson State College in Mississippi. More than 450 colleges closed down on strike, and 80 percent of all American college campuses experienced some kind of protest. In June 1970, immediately after the Kent State slayings, a Gallup poll reported that campus unrest was the main issue troubling Americans.

At the same time, however, dissatisfaction with the war continued to spread. Congressional opposition, which had been growing since Fulbright's Foreign Relations Committee hearings in 1966, intensified with the invasion of Cambodia. In June 1970 the Senate expressed its disapproval by voting to repeal the Gulf of Tonkin resolution authorizing U.S. military action and by passing the Church-Cooper amendment, which cut off all funding for operations in Cambodia by the end of the month. Even American troops in Vietnam showed mounting opposition to their mission. From 1969 to 1971 the number of troops refusing combat orders steadily increased, and thousands of U.S. soldiers deserted. The majority fought on, but many sewed peace symbols onto their uniforms. A number of overbearing junior officers were "fragged," that is, killed or wounded by fragmentation grenades thrown by their own soldiers. At home a group called Vietnam Veterans against the War turned in their combat medals at mass demonstrations at the U.S. Capitol.

My Lai. In 1971 Americans were again confronted with the sheer brutality of the Vietnamese conflict when Lieutenant William L. Calley was court-martialed for atrocities committed in the Vietnamese village of My Lai. In March 1968 Calley had commanded a platoon on a routine search-and-destroy mission. Retaliating for casualties sustained by their buddies in an earlier engagement, the soldiers apparently murdered 350 Vietnamese villagers. The incident came to light because one member of the platoon refused to go along with a military cover-up; the investigative reporter Seymour Hersh of the *New York Times* broke the story. In the court-martial proceedings, a jury of six soldiers who had served in Vietnam sentenced Calley to life imprisonment for his part in the massacre. Yet George Wallace and some Congressional conservatives called Calley a hero rather than a villain, and after President Nixon's intervention, his sentence was reduced, and he was paroled in 1974.

Despite the controversy surrounding the Kent State shootings and the My Lai massacre, antiwar activism declined in the early 1970s. After a final outbreak of protest and violence following Kent State, the universities stayed relatively calm. Student strikes in the spring of 1971 and 1972, while large in numbers, never approached the emotional intensity of earlier demonstrations. Nixon's promises to continue troop withdrawals, end the draft, and institute an all-volunteer army by 1973 deprived the antiwar movement of important organizing issues, particularly on college campuses. In the early 1970s many student activists refocused their energies on causes such as feminism and environmentalism whereas others simply "burned out."

Détente. At the same time that Nixon was prosecuting the war in Vietnam, ostensibly to halt the spread of communism, he was formulating a new policy toward the Soviet Union and China. Known as *détente* (the French word for a relaxation of tensions), Nixon's policy called for peaceful coexistence with those two communist powers and sought to link those overtures of friendship with his own plan to end the Vietnam War. In befriending China and the Soviet Union, Nixon encouraged them to reduce military aid to the North Vietnamese, thus pressuring them to the negotiating table. As a lifelong anticommunist crusader, Nixon had greater political maneuverability to reach out to the two communist superpowers than a Democratic president would have had. After all, no one could accuse Richard Nixon of being soft on communism. Henry Kissinger influenced the president's thinking in this direction.

Since the Chinese revolution of 1949 the United States had refused to recognize the government of the People's Republic of China, instead giving unconditional support to the Nationalist Chinese government in Taiwan. Nixon moved away from that policy, reasoning that the United States could exploit the growing rift between the People's Republic of China and the Soviet Union. He sent Kissinger on a secret mission to Beijing in the summer of 1971 and in July told a startled world that he would visit the People's Republic in the near future. He did so in February 1972, walking along the Great Wall and toasting Chinese leaders in Beijing. Nixon's visit set the stage for the formal establishment of diplomatic relations, which took place in 1979.

In a similar spirit of détente Nixon journeyed to Moscow in May 1972 to sign SALT I, a treaty resulting from Strategic Arms Limitations Talks between the United States and the Soviet Union. Although Nixon boasted that the SALT agreement was a dramatic step toward stopping the arms race, the accords only limited the production and deployment of intercontinental ballistic missiles (ICBMs) and antiballistic missile systems (ABMs). They left untouched newer and equally destructive weapons systems such as multiple independently targetable reentry vehicles (MIRVs), which enabled a single missile to carry up to fourteen separate warheads. Yet the treaty was also an acknowledgment that the United States could no longer afford the massive military spending that would have been necessary to regain the nuclear and military superiority of the immediate postwar years. By the early 1970s factors such as inflation, the decline in American hegemony over the world system, and domestic dissent were limiting and reshaping American options in international relations. Most critically, Nixon hoped that a rapprochement with the Soviets would help resolve the prolonged crisis in Vietnam.

American Withdrawal from Vietnam. The Paris peace talks had been in a stalemate since 1968, hamstrung by the conflicting demands of North Vietnam, South Vietnam, and the United States. In the meantime, Vietnamization continued and American casualties decreased, but the South Vietnamese military was unable to fill the vacuum. In March 1971 the South Vietnamese suffered a major defeat after launching an attack against North Vietnamese supply routes along the Ho Chi Minh Trail in Laos. The South Vietnamese forces were quickly repelled and sustained heavy casualties. Later that year, as American troops withdrew from the region, communist forces stepped up their attacks on Laos, Cambodia, and South Vietnam. The next spring North Vietnamese forces launched a major new offensive, attacking South Vietnamese targets south of the demilitarized zone, in Binh Long province and in the Central Highlands (see American Lives, pages 982–983). As the fighting intensified, Nixon ordered B-52 bombing raids against North Vietnam in April and the mining of all North Vietnamese ports a month later.

Increased combat activity in the spring of 1972 and growing political pressure on the Nixon administration helped revive the Paris peace negotiations. With the fall presidential elections looming, Nixon hoped to undercut his antiwar critics by making concessions to the North Vietnamese. That October Henry Kissinger and the North Vietnamese negotiator Le Duc Tho reached a cease-fire agreement calling for the withdrawal of the remaining U.S. troops, the return of all American prisoners of war, and the continued presence of North Vietnamese troops in South Vietnam (a major sticking point in earlier negotiations). Nixon and Kissinger also promised the North Vietnamese substantial aid for postwar reconstruction. On the eve of the 1972 presidential election Kissinger announced that "peace is at hand," and Nixon returned to the White House with a resounding electoral victory (see Chapter 32).

The peace initiative, however, soon stalled when the South Vietnamese rejected the provision concerning North Vietnamese troop positions. With negotiations deadlocked, Nixon stepped up military action again. For the benefit of President Thieu, home-front hawks, and the Third World in general, he initiated the "Christmas bombings," a final destructive demonstration of American military strength. From December 17 to December 30, 1972, American planes subjected North Vietnamese civilian and military targets in Hanoi and Haiphong to the most devastating bombing of the war. Finally, on January 27, 1973, a cease-fire was signed in Paris by representatives of the United States, North and South Vietnam, and the Vietcong; it differed little from the proposal of the previous October. The Paris Peace Accords

John Paul Vann: Dissident Patriot

The divisions caused by the Vietnam War haunted Arlington National Cemetery on June 16, 1972, when 300 mourners assembled for the funeral of John Paul Vann. "The soldier of the war in Vietnam," Vann had been killed in a helicopter crash in the Central Highlands the week before. Politicians and military leaders closely associated with the war effort were very much in evidence—General William Westmoreland, CIA Director William Colby, the conservative journalist Joseph Alsop, and Secretary of State William Rogers. But so were Daniel Ellsberg, a former Pentagon official who had publicly turned against the war, and Senator Edward Kennedy, another war opponent who had shared Vann's concern about the plight of Vietnamese refugees. In a time of intense polarization over a war that was still going on, this assemblage of "hawks" and "doves" was highly unusual.

Vann's family also showed the rifts over Vietnam that day. His wife of twenty-six years, Mary Jane, had requested two pieces of music: the upbeat "Colonel Bogie March" from the film *The Bridge on the River Kwai,* one of her husband's favorites, and the haunting antiwar ballad "Where Have All the Flowers Gone?" to express her opposition to the war. One of Vann's sons, twenty-one-year-old Jesse, hated the war so profoundly that he tore his draft card in two at the funeral, placing half of it on his father's casket. He planned to give the other half to President Richard Nixon at the White House ceremony after the funeral, where his father would be presented posthumously with the Presidential Medal of Freedom. Only at the last moment was Jesse talked out of his act of defiance, agreeing that this was, after all, his father's day, and that his father had believed in the war in Vietnam.

Also at the funeral was *New York Times* reporter Neil Sheehan, who decided at that moment to write a biography of Vann, which he published sixteen years later, *A Bright and Shining Lie.* Sheehan, along with David Halberstam and other reporters, had fallen under Vann's spell during his first tour of duty in Vietnam in 1963, when Vann seemed to be the only American offi-

cial who was willing to admit that the war was not going well. Sheehan had continued to rely on Vann's outspoken assessments for the rest of the war. "In this war without heroes, this man had been the one compelling figure," Sheehan concluded. "By an obsession, by an unyielding dedication to the war, he had come to personify the American endeavor in Vietnam."

John Paul Vann was an enormously complicated person—a born leader, a visionary, a man who knew no physical fear, but most of all a true believer in America's mission to share democracy with countries "less fortunate" than ours. His early years were shaped by poverty and lack of opportunity. Born in 1924 to a working-class family in Norfolk, Virginia, he grew up poor during the Great Depression. A colleague later remembered him as a "cocky little red-necked guy with a rural Virginia twang." World War II offered a ticket out; when Vann turned eighteen in 1943, he enlisted and made the army his career. He served with distinction in the Korean War and then took assignments in West Germany and the United States. But in 1959 his service record was stained by accusations of the statutory rape of a fifteen-year-old girl. Even though the army eventually dropped the charges, the scandal effectively prevented him from moving up in the military bureaucracy. Neil Sheehan later concluded that Vann's "moral heroism" in speaking out against the conduct of the war to the seeming detriment of his career was rooted in his awareness that he had nothing to lose, although reporters did not know the full story at the time.

In 1963 the thirty-nine-year-old Lieutenant Colonel Vann was sent to Vietnam, where he served as a senior adviser to a South Vietnamese infantry division in the Mekong Delta. At the battle of Ap Bac he watched his South Vietnamese counterpart purposely refuse to fight the battle the way it had been planned and let the enemy escape. In a moment of epiphany Vann realized that the rosy reports being fed to Saigon and Washington were false, that Saigon suffered from "an institutionalized unwillingness to fight." After unsuccessful attempts to enlighten his superiors, he leaked his meticulously docu-

Planning Strategy
Lieutenant Colonel John P. Vann (left) shown during his tour of duty in Vietnam in 1963 discussing a tactical decision.

mented assessments to reporters such as Halberstam and Sheehan. His candor won him few friends in the military, and at the end of his tour of duty he was reassigned to the Pentagon. He tried to alert the Joint Chiefs of Staff that the war was not being won, but at the last moment the scheduled briefing was canceled, in large part because the Joint Chiefs did not want to hear his version of the problem. Vann resigned from the army soon afterward.

Less than two years later, in 1965, Vann was back in Vietnam just as the major escalation of the war was getting under way. Except for brief trips home, he stayed there until his death. His first position was as a civilian pacification representative for the Agency for International Development, working to win over the peasants to the South Vietnamese side rather than the National Liberation Front. His honesty and unmatched familiarity with conditions in the countryside led him to conclude that the communists were doing a far better job at appealing to the local population than was the corrupt Saigon government: as he wrote to a friend in 1965, "If I were a lad of eighteen faced with the same choice—whether to support the GVN [Government of Vietnam] or the NLF—and a member of a rural community, I would surely choose the NLF." His concern for winning over the local peasantry made him an outspoken opponent of the heavy bombing inflicted on the Vietnamese countryside to roust Vietcong sympathizers. He also strongly criticized General Westmoreland's strategy of sending in more American troops to wear down the Vietcong in a war of attrition, arguing that this would be useless without major reforms in the Saigon government.

Despite his role as a gadfly and even though he was now a civilian, Vann assumed more and more responsibility in the day-to-day conduct of the war. In 1971 he was given authority over all the U.S. military forces in the Central Highlands, the equivalent of the position of major general. But by then, according to Sheehan, Vann had "lost his compass." He was no longer able to assess realistically the ability or will of the South Vietnamese to fight without American aid. He continued to insist that the war could be won through pacification and reform in Saigon despite evidence of growing Vietcong strength. When his helicopter went down at Kontum in 1972, he had almost single-handedly saved the Central Highlands from a North Vietnamese offensive. Within six months the United States formally ended its involvement. Two years later Vietnam was reunited under communist rule.

John Paul Vann never wavered in his belief that in Vietnam America's cause was just and its intentions good. He had no quarrel with the war itself, just with the way it was fought. Vann thought he knew the answers, but Saigon and Washington chose not to listen. His life and death serve as a reminder of the complexities of the Vietnam experience: Could it ever really have been "won," and what would "winning" have meant? Neil Sheehan is convinced that Vann "died believing he had won his war."

Hanoi Devastated
The North Vietnamese capital, Hanoi, sustained heavy damage from bombing raids by American B-52s. The most devastating raids occurred during the "Christmas bombings" in December 1972, just weeks before the Paris Peace Accords were signed.

failed to deliver Nixon's often-repeated promise of "peace with honor." Basically, they mandated the unilateral withdrawal of American troops in exchange for the return of American prisoners of war held in North Vietnam. For most Americans that amount of face-saving was enough.

But the 1973 accords did not resolve Vietnam's civil war. Without massive U.S. military and economic aid and with North Vietnamese guerrillas operating freely throughout the countryside, it was only a matter of time before the South Vietnamese government of General Nguyen Van Thieu fell to the more disciplined and popular communist forces. In March 1975 North Vietnamese forces launched a final offensive. Horrified American viewers watched on television as South Vietnamese officials and soldiers struggled with American embassy personnel for space on the last helicopters that flew out of Saigon before North Vietnamese troops entered the city. On April 29, 1975, Vietnam was reunited; Saigon was renamed Ho Chi Minh City in honor of the communist leader, who had died in 1969.

The Legacy of Vietnam

The Vietnam War exacted an enormous cost from America in human terms. Some 58,000 U.S. troops died, and

another 300,000 were wounded. Even those who came back unharmed returned to a sometimes hostile or indifferent reception. Coming home alone, with no deprogramming or counseling, most Vietnam veterans found the transition abrupt and disorienting. Once back, they felt embarrassed when they dove under a table at the sound of firecrackers on the Fourth of July or froze when a plane flew overhead. Mainly the Vietnam experience was ignored. As one vet recalled, "Bringing up the Nam was like farting at the dinner table. Everybody looks away embarrassed and acts like nothing happened. Well, pardon me." The psychological tensions of serving in Vietnam and the abrupt transition back to America sowed the seeds of what is now recognized as posttraumatic stress disorder—recurring physical and psychological problems, often leading to higher than average rates of divorce, unemployment, and suicide. Only in the 1980s did America begin to make its peace with those who had served in the nation's most unpopular war.

In Southeast Asia the damage was far greater. The war claimed an estimated 1.5 million Vietnamese lives and devastated the country's physical and economic infrastructure. Neighboring Laos and Cambodia also suffered, particularly Cambodia, where chaotic conditions led to a political takeover by the deadly Khmer Rouge. From 1975 to 1979 the Khmer Rouge Communists killed an estimated 2 million Cambodians (25 percent of the

population) in a brutal "relocation" campaign. All told, the war produced nearly 10 million Southeast Asian refugees, many of whom immigrated to the United States. Among the refugees were thousands of Amerasians, the offspring of American soldiers and Vietnamese women. Spurned by their fathers and most Vietnamese, more than 30,000 Amerasians immigrated to the United States in the 1990s.

The defeat in Vietnam prompted Americans to think differently about foreign affairs and acknowledge the limits of U.S. power abroad. The United States became less willing to plunge into overseas military commitments, a controversial development that conservatives dubbed the "Vietnam syndrome." In 1973 Congress declared its hostility to undeclared wars like those in Vietnam and Korea by passing the War Powers Act, which required the president to report any use of military force within forty-eight hours and directed that hostilities cease within sixty days unless Congress declared war. When

Congress did agree to foreign intervention, as in the Persian Gulf War of 1990–1991, American leaders would insist on obtainable military objectives and careful handling of the media—elements that had often been lacking in Vietnam. Any future foreign entanglement would be evaluated in terms of its potential for becoming "another Vietnam."

The Vietnam War also affected American economic and social affairs. At a total price of over $150 billion, the war siphoned economic resources from domestic needs, added to the deficit, and fueled inflation (see Chapter 32). Lyndon Johnson's Great Society programs had been pared down accordingly, and domestic reform efforts slowed thereafter. Moreover, the war critically shattered the liberal consensus that had supported the Democratic coalition. The discrediting of liberalism, increased cynicism about government, and the growing social turmoil that accompanied the war paved the way for a resurgence of the Republican party.

The Vietnam Veterans' Memorial

Conceived and funded by a small group of veterans, the Vietnam Veterans' Memorial was dedicated in Washington, D.C., in November 1982. The memorial, designed by a Yale architecture student, Maya Ling Lin, consists of two walls of black granite inscribed with the names of 58,183 men and women who died in the war. The wall of names has tremendous emotional impact on viewers and has become one of the most popular tourist destinations in the nation's capital.

Summary

America's involvement in Vietnam lasted nearly thirty years, growing incrementally from one administration to the next. Under Truman and Eisenhower the United States threw its support behind the French and, later, the South Vietnamese government in an effort to contain the communist threat in Asia. Kennedy continued that commitment and increased the number of U.S. military advisers in South Vietnam. But it was under Lyndon Johnson that the war escalated from an ostensibly defensive action to an offensive combat mission. Between 1965 and 1968 sustained bombing attacks on North Vietnam were accompanied by ever larger infusions of U.S. ground troops. But the Tet offensive of January 1968 shook American confidence and marked the beginning of U.S. efforts to disengage from the conflict. Richard Nixon spent another five years trying to end the war, promising Americans "peace with honor." Under his program of Vietnamization, Nixon gradually withdrew U.S. troops while secretly bombing and later invading Cambodia. The final withdrawal of American troops took place in 1973 under the terms of the Paris Peace Accords. The war marked a turning point in U.S. foreign relations, revealing the limitations of American military power in a complex postwar world.

The war also had serious consequences at home as Americans turned against each other in bitter conflict. Beginning with a small number of pacifist, religious, and antinuclear protesters in the early 1960s, the antiwar movement burgeoned after the escalation of the conflict in 1965. The military draft in particular sparked a broad-based antiwar movement among college students and other young people, who staged a series of mass protests between 1967 and 1971. The spirit of rebellion was not limited to the antiwar movement. The New Left challenged university policies and corporate dominance of society, while the more apolitical counterculture preached personal liberation through sex, drugs, music, and spirituality.

The domestic struggle over the war and other issues divided the Democratic party, resulting in a riotous Democratic National Convention in the summer of 1968. The assassinations of Martin Luther King, Jr., and Robert Kennedy and a series of urban riots that year further shocked the nation and fueled a growing public desire for law and order. Even though antiwar protests continued into the early 1970s, a new mood of conservatism took hold in the country, contributing to the resurgence of the Republican party.

TIMELINE

1946	War begins between French and Vietminh
1950	China and Soviet Union recognize Ho Chi Minh's government
	U.S. recognizes French-backed government of Bao Dai and begins sending military aid to Vietnam
1954	French defeat at Dienbienphu
	Ngo Dinh Diem takes power in South Vietnam
	Geneva Accords
1960	Founding of National Liberation Front in South Vietnam
1962	Students for a Democratic Society (SDS) founded
1963	Coup ousts Ngo Dinh Diem in Vietnam
1964	Free Speech Movement at Berkeley
	Gulf of Tonkin resolution
1965	First U.S. combat troops arrive in Vietnam
	Operation Rolling Thunder
1967	Hippie counterculture's Summer of Love
1968	Tet offensive
	Martin Luther King, Jr., assassinated
	Peace talks open in Paris
	Robert F. Kennedy assassinated
	Riot at Democratic National Convention in Chicago
1969	Vietnam moratorium
	Woodstock festival
1970	Nixon orders invasion of Cambodia; renewed antiwar protests
	Kent State and Jackson State killings
	Gulf of Tonkin resolution repealed
1972	Nixon visits People's Republic of China
	SALT I Treaty with Soviet Union
	Christmas bombings
1973	Paris Peace Accords
	War Powers Act
1975	Fall of Saigon

★   ★   ★

BIBLIOGRAPHY

Among the best general accounts of the Vietnam War are George Herring, *America's Longest War* (2d ed., 1986); Stanley Karnow, *Vietnam: A History* (rev. ed., 1991); and Marilyn Young, *The Vietnam Wars, 1945–1990* (1991). Guenter Lewy offers a controversial defense of American involvement in *America in Vietnam* (1978).

Into the Quagmire

The origins of American involvement in Vietnam are covered in Loren Baritz, *Backfire: A History of How American Culture Led Us into Vietnam* (1985); Larry Berman, *Planning a Tragedy* (1982) and *Lyndon Johnson's War* (1989); Lloyd Gardner, *Approaching Vietnam* (1988); Conrad Gibbons, *The U.S. Government and the Vietnam War* (1986–1989); David Halberstam, *The Best and the Brightest* (1972) and *The Making of a Quagmire* (rev. ed., 1987); Gary Hess, *The United States' Emergence as a Southeast Asian Power, 1940–1950* (1987); and Brian Van-DeMark, *Into the Quagmire* (1991). A fascinating insight into Vietnam policy making in the 1960s can be found in Neil Sheehan, *The Pentagon Papers* (1971). Secretary of Defense Robert McNamara offers an insider's view and belated apologia in *In Retrospect* (1995). James C. Thompson, *Rolling Thunder* (1980), and John Galloway, *The Gulf of Tonkin Resolution* (1970), cover specific topics. Eric Bergerud, *Dynamics of Defeat* (1991), examines the military aspects of the war, and Daniel Hallin, *The Uncensored War* (1986), and Clarence R. Wyatt, *Paper Soldiers* (1993), look at the role of the media. Frances FitzGerald, *Fire in the Lake* (1972), discusses the war in the context of South Vietnamese society.

For a sense of what the war felt like to the soldiers who fought it, see Mark Baker, *Nam* (1982); Philip Caputo, *Rumor of War* (1977); Gloria Emerson, *Winners and Losers* (1976); Michael Herr, *Dispatches* (1977); Tim O'Brien, *If I Die in a Combat Zone* (1973); and Ron Kovic, *Born on the Fourth of July* (1976). Wallace Terry, *Bloods* (1984), surveys the experiences of black veterans, and Keith Walker, *A Piece of My Heart* (1985), introduces the often forgotten stories of the women who served in Vietnam. Lawrence Baskir and William A. Strauss, *Chance and Circumstance: The Draft, the War, and the Vietnam Generation* (1978), explains who was drafted and why. Christian G. Appy offers a class analysis of the Vietnam experience in *Working-Class War* (1993). Neil Sheehan surveys the entire Vietnam experience through the life of the career soldier John Paul Vann in *A Bright and Shining Lie* (1988).

The Challenge of Youth

The student activism of the 1960s has drawn its share of scholarly chroniclers. See Kenneth Keniston, *The Uncommitted* (1965) and *Young Radicals* (1969); Daniel Bell and Irving Kristol, *Confrontation* (1969); Nathan Glazer, *Remembering the Answers* (1970); and Philip Slater, *The Pursuit of Loneliness* (1970). On student revolt, see W. J. Rorabaugh, *Berkeley at War* (1989); Seymour Lipset and Sheldon Wolin, eds., *The Berkeley Student Revolt* (1965); Jerry Avorn, *Up against the Ivy Wall* (1968); Kirkpatrick Sale, *SDS* (1973); Wini Breines, *Community and Organization in the New Left, 1962–1968*

(1982); and James Miller, *Democracy Is in the Streets* (1987). Terry Anderson, *The Movement and the Sixties* (1994), and Irwin Unger, *The Movement: A History of the American New Left* (1974), provide general accounts of 1960s activism. Todd Gitlin, *The Whole World Is Watching* (1980), discusses the impact of the mass media on the New Left.

The definitive book on the antiwar movement is Charles DeBenedetti, with Charles Chatfield, *An American Ordeal* (1990). Nancy Zaroulis and Gerald Sullivan, *Who Spoke Up: American Protest against the War in Vietnam, 1963–1975* (1984), examines the role of the New Left in the antiwar movement, while Melvin Small and William D. Hoover, eds., *Give Peace a Chance: Exploring the Vietnam Antiwar Movement* (1992), is an anthology of recent work.

Morris Dickstein, *Gates of Eden* (1977), is an excellent account of cultural developments in the 1960s. Todd Gitlin, *The Sixties: Years of Hope, Days of Rage* (1987), also treats the counterculture extensively. Other sources include Theodore Roszak, *The Making of a Counter-Culture* (1969), and Charles Reich, *The Greening of America* (1970). Gerald Howard, ed., *The Sixties* (1982), is a good anthology of the decade's art, politics, and culture. Philip Norman, *Shout! The Beatles in Their Generation* (1981), and Jon Weiner, *Come Together: John Lennon in His Times* (1984), cover developments in popular music. Tom Wolfe, *Electric Kool-Aid Acid Test* (1965), describes the antics of Ken Kesey and his Merry Pranksters. Joan Didion, *Slouching toward Bethlehem* (1968) and *The White Album* (1979), explores the darker side of the hippie phenomenon.

The Long Road Home

The Tet offensive is the subject of Don Oberdoffer, *Tet! The Turning Point in the Vietnam War* (1971), whereas the domestic events of 1968 are covered in David Caute, *The Year of the Barricades* (1968); David Farber, *Chicago '68* (1988); and Lewis Chester, Godfrey Hodgson, and Bruce Page, *An American Melodrama* (1970). Norman Mailer provides a contemporary view of the conventions in *Miami and the Siege of Chicago* (1968). Dan Carter, *The Politics of Rage* (1996), examines the political career of George Wallace, while Kevin Phillips, *The Emerging Republican Majority* (1969), and Richard Scammon and Ben J. Wattenberg, *The Real Majority* (1970), describe the voters Richard Nixon tried to reach. Theodore H. White, *The Making of the President—1968* (1969), covers the divisive election of 1968.

Robert S. Litwak, *Détente and the Nixon Doctrine* (1984); Seymour Hersh, *The Price of Power* (1983); and Tad Szulc, *The Illusion of Peace* (1978), are overviews of Nixon's foreign policy. On his Vietnam policy see the general works on Vietnam listed above as well as the highly critical study by William Shawcross, *Sideshow: Kissinger, Nixon, and the Destruction of Cambodia* (1979). An account of the My Lai massacre can be found in Seymour Hersh, *Cover-Up* (1972). Frank Snepp, *Decent Interval* (1977), examines the Paris peace process. Robert Jay Lifton, *Home from the War* (1973); Paul Starr, *The Discarded Army* (1973); and Lawrence Baskir and William A. Strauss, *Chance and Circumstance*, discuss the problems of returning Vietnam veterans.

Our Fragile Environment

NASA photographs from space captured both the beauty and
the fragility of the earth.

The Lean Years

1969–1980

★　　　★　　　★

As the Vietnam War ended, Americans turned inward to attend to their own needs and interests, just as they had done in the years after World Wars I and II. But the 1970s, unlike the 1920s and 1950s, were not a time of post-war prosperity and optimism. To many Americans the withdrawal from Vietnam represented an ignominious defeat that underscored the diminished role of U.S. power in the international arena. Growing economic problems in the early 1970s—rising oil prices, runaway inflation, declining productivity, and stagnating incomes—compounded that sense of disillusionment. In the mid-1970s industrial competition abroad, together with the newly asserted independence of the oil-producing Arab nations, produced a severe economic crisis at home. As the dollar plummeted on the world market and the trade deficit soared, the overwhelming economic superiority of the United States came to an end.

Americans also grew disenchanted with political leadership in the 1970s as one public official after another resigned for misconduct, including President Richard Nixon. The Watergate scandal became the defining experience of the decade, a symbol of the growing cynicism and waning confidence that pervaded the nation in the 1970s. In the wake of Watergate, the lackluster administrations of Gerald Ford and Jimmy Carter failed to provide the leadership necessary to cope with the economic and international insecurities that beset the nation. This failure of political leadership contributed to Americans' growing skepticism about government and its capacity to improve people's lives.

But the 1970s was a paradoxical decade: in the midst of growing disaffection and conservatism there was also an ongoing commitment to social change. Some of the social movements of the 1960s, such as feminism and environmentalism, had their greatest impact in the 1970s. As former student radicals moved into the political mainstream, they took their struggles from the

eran Jesse Jackson replaced Mayor Richard Daley of Chicago as head of the Illinois delegation.

McGovern's campaign against Nixon was an unrelieved disaster. Surprised to learn that his running mate, Senator Thomas F. Eagleton of Missouri, had undergone electroshock therapy for depression some years earlier, McGovern first supported him "1,000 percent" and then abruptly insisted that he quit the ticket. Sargent Shriver, the former head of the Peace Corps and the Office of Economic Opportunity, joined the ticket, but McGovern's waffling over Eagleton made him appear weak and indecisive. Moreover, he was far too liberal for many traditional Democrats, who rejected his ill-defined proposals for welfare reform, did not rally around his calls for unilateral withdrawal from Vietnam, and ignored his charges that the Nixon administration had corruptly abused its power.

Nixon's campaign took full advantage of McGovern's weaknesses. Although the president had failed to end the war, his Vietnamization policy had reduced weekly American combat deaths from 300 in 1968 to almost none in 1972. Henry Kissinger's premature declaration that "peace is at hand" raised hopes for a negotiated settlement (see Chapter 31). Those initiatives robbed the Democrats of their greatest appeal—their antiwar stance. In addition, the improving economy helped the Republicans.

Nixon won handily, receiving nearly 61 percent of the popular vote and carrying every state except Massachusetts and the District of Columbia. McGovern's showing pointed to a significant erosion of the traditional Democratic coalition: he received only 18 percent of the southern white Protestant vote and 38 percent of the big-city Catholic vote. Only blacks, Jews, and low-income voters remained loyal. Yet Nixon failed to kindle strong Republican loyalty in the electorate. Only 55.7 percent of eligible voters bothered to go to the polls, and the Democrats maintained control of both houses of Congress.

Watergate

Watergate, the great constitutional crisis of the early 1970s, was a direct result of Nixon's ruthless political tactics, his secretive style of governing (as in the bombing of Cambodia), and his obsession with the anti–Vietnam War movement. Many Americans saw Watergate as consisting of only the evil deeds of one person (Richard Nixon) and one unlawful act (the obstruction of justice after the break-in). But Watergate was not an isolated incident; it was part of a broad pattern of illegality and misuse of power that flourished in the crisis atmosphere of the Vietnam War.

The new administration began to stretch the boundaries of the law under the guise of national security just four months into Nixon's first term. In the spring of 1969, after the New York Times reported the secret bombing of Cambodia, the White House asked the FBI to find out who had leaked the story. Without seeking a warrant, the FBI illegally tapped the phone conversations of several journalists and low-level staffers on the National Security Council. The source of the leak was never found, but the precedent for warrantless surveillance had been set.

Over the next several years the Nixon administration would repeatedly invoke supposed domestic threats to national security to justify its actions. In 1970 the White House asked Tom Huston, a former army intelligence officer, to draw up an extensive plan for secret domestic counterintelligence—opening mail, tapping phones, and arranging break-ins—to discredit the antiwar movement. President Nixon approved the scheme, which involved coordinated efforts by the FBI, CIA, and Justice Department. The FBI's director, J. Edgar Hoover, however, refused to cooperate with other government agencies in activities that he interpreted as being exclusively within the domain of the FBI.

The Pentagon Papers. Nixon's obsession with the antiwar movement grew in June 1971, when Daniel Ellsberg, a former Defense Department analyst who had become disillusioned with the war, leaked the so-called Pentagon Papers to the New York Times. The Pentagon Papers was a classified study (with accompanying documents) commissioned by Secretary of Defense Robert McNamara in 1967 and completed eighteen months later. The report detailed so many American blunders and misjudgments that McNamara had commented on first reading it, "You know, they could hang people for what is in there." In a subsequent court challenge the Nixon administration attempted to block publication of the Pentagon Papers. In an effort to discredit Ellsberg, White House underlings broke into his psychiatrist's office to look for damaging information. The burglars failed to turn up anything embarrassing on Ellsberg, and the judge dismissed the pending case against him when the break-in was revealed.

In preparation for the 1972 campaign, the White House had established a clandestine intelligence group led by the former CIA agents G. Gordon Liddy and Howard Hunt. Known as the "plumbers" because they were supposed to plug leaks of government information, they relied on tactics such as using the Internal Revenue Service and other agencies to harass opponents of the administration named on an "enemies list" drawn up by the presidential counsel John Dean. A major target of the plumbers was the Democratic party, whose front-runner, Senator Edmund Muskie of Maine, was the object of several "dirty tricks" during the primaries. For example, New Hampshire voters were awakened in the middle of the night by callers from the "Harlem for Muskie" com-

mittee, and posters appeared in Florida saying "Help Muskie in Busing More Children Now." Most damaging was a letter to a New Hampshire newspaper forged by one of Nixon's campaign aides accusing Muskie of ethnic insensitivity. Together those "dirty tricks" derailed Muskie's primary campaign.

These secret and highly questionable activities were financed by massive illegal fund-raising efforts by the Committee to Re-Elect the President (known as CREEP), which was headed by Attorney General John Mitchell. In soliciting funds from major corporations, Nixon fundraisers used high-pressure tactics that included implied threats of federal tax audits and other punitive measures for companies that failed to contribute. CREEP subsequently raised over $20 million, a portion of which was used to finance various dirty tricks, including the break-in that led to the Watergate scandal.

The Break-in. Early in the morning of June 17, 1972, an alert security guard noticed something amiss at the door to the headquarters of the Democratic National Committee at the Watergate apartment complex in Washington. Five men carrying cameras, wiretapping equipment, and a large amount of cash were arrested; two accomplices were apprehended soon afterward. Two of the accused men had worked as security consultants in the White House, and a third had held a responsible position in CREEP; the remaining four, all from Miami, had been involved in CIA-linked anti-Castro activities. Nixon's press secretary, Ronald Ziegler, promptly dismissed the break-in as a "third-rate burglary attempt." Nixon claimed that the White House counsel John Dean had conducted a full investigation of the incident (no such investigation ever took place) and stated categorically that "no one on the White House staff, no one in this administration, presently employed, was involved in this very bizarre incident." The cover-up had begun.

Subsequent investigations revealed that six days after the break-in the president had ordered his chief of staff, H. R. Haldeman, to instruct the CIA to tell the FBI not to probe too deeply into connections between the White House and the burglars. That action constituted obstruction of justice. Nixon apparently feared that the Watergate burglary would lead to an investigation of the dubious fund-raising methods and political sabotage practiced by his reelection committee.

Trial and Investigations. The Watergate burglars were convicted in January 1973. With Nixon's approval, John Dean tried to buy their continued silence with $400,000 in hush money and hints of presidential pardons. However, prodded by the presiding judge, John Sirica, one of the convicted burglars began to talk. Two tenacious investigative reporters at the *Washington Post,* Carl Bernstein and Bob Woodward, kept the story alive, exposing the attempted cover-up and tracing it

back to the White House. In February the Senate voted 77 to 0 to establish a select committee to investigate the scandal. Dean started to get nervous, and in March 1973 he warned Nixon, referring to the cover-up, that "there is a cancer within, close to the presidency, that is growing." In April Nixon accepted the resignations of Haldeman, Assistant Secretary of Commerce Jeb Stuart Magruder, and chief domestic adviser John Ehrlichman, all of whom had been implicated in the cover-up. He also fired Dean, who had agreed to testify in the case in exchange for immunity from prosecution.

In May the Senate Watergate committee, chaired by Senator Sam Ervin of North Carolina, began a summer of nationally televised hearings. On June 14 Magruder testified before the committee, confessing his guilt and implicating Attorney General John Mitchell, Dean, and others in the Watergate affair (see American Voices, page 994). In five days of riveting testimony in late June, Dean implicated Nixon in the cover-up. Even more startling testimony from the aide Alexander Butterfield revealed that Nixon had a secret taping system in the Oval Office. "I was hoping you fellows wouldn't ask me about that," Butterfield sheepishly told the committee. Until the existence of the tapes was disclosed, it had been Dean's word against Nixon's; now it appeared possible to find out what had actually been said.

The president steadfastly "stonewalled," citing executive privilege and national security as his reasons for

Watergate Hearings
Some of the most damaging testimony against President Richard Nixon came from the former White House counsel John Dean, shown testifying before the Senate Watergate Committee in June 1973. Revelations from a secret taping system in the Oval Office later confirmed Dean's nearly total recall of conversations he had had with the president.

Jeb Stuart Magruder

The Watergate Hearings

Jeb Stuart Magruder was assistant secretary of commerce in the Nixon administration and a key member of the Committee to Re-Elect the President. After his role in the Watergate scandal came to light in April 1973, he was forced to resign. On June 14, 1973, he testified before the Senate investigating committee on Watergate about his role in the cover-up.

Senator Howard Baker: Was there any question in your mind that the plan [to break in to the Democratic National Committee headquarters in Miami] was agreed to by Mr. Mitchell?

Jeb Stuart Magruder: No, sir, there was no doubt. But it was a reluctant decision. . . . We knew it was illegal, probably inappropriate. We didn't think that much would come of it. . . .

Q. I still can't quite come to grips with why you all had an expressed reservation about this and you still went ahead with it.

A. . . . I had worked for some two years, three years, really in the White House and at that time, I was mainly engaged in the activities trying to generate some support for the President. During that time, we had worked primarily relating to the war situation and worked with antiwar groups.

Now I had gone to college, as an example, under—and had a course in ethics as an example under William Sloane Coffin, whom I respect greatly. I have great regard for him. He was quoted the other day as saying, well, I guess Mr. Magruder failed my course in ethics. And I think he is correct.

During this whole time . . . we saw continuing violations of the law done by men like William Sloane Coffin. He tells me my ethics are bad. Yet he was indicted for criminal charges. He recommended on the Washington Monument grounds that students burn their draft cards and that we have mass demonstrations, shut down the city of Washington.

Now, here are ethical, legitimate people whom I respected. I respect Mr. Coffin tremendously. He was a very close friend of mine. I saw people I was very close to breaking the law without any regard for any other person's pattern of behavior or belief.

So consequently, when these subjects came up although I was aware they were illegal we had become somewhat inured to using some activities that would help us in accomplishing what we thought was a cause, a legitimate cause. . . . that is basically, I think, the reason why that decision was made, because of that atmosphere that had occurred and to all of us who had worked in the White House, there was that feeling of resentment and of frustration at being unable to deal with issues on a legal basis.

Source: Gerald Gold and the staff of the *New York Times*, eds., *The Watergate Hearings: Break-in and Cover-up* (New York: Bantam Books, 1974), 257–259.

refusing to release the tapes. Archibald Cox, a special prosecutor appointed by Nixon to investigate the Watergate case, petitioned a lower federal court to order the president to hand over the tapes. The court issued the order in October, but Nixon again refused to comply. When Cox continued to insist that the president hand over the original tapes, Nixon ordered Attorney General Elliott Richardson to fire Cox. Richardson refused and resigned, as did Assistant Attorney General William Ruckelshaus. Solicitor General Robert Bork, third in command in the Justice Department, carried out the orders, but this "Saturday Night Massacre" sparked public outrage and renewed demands for release of the tapes.

After additional federal subpoenas the following spring, Nixon released heavily edited transcripts of the tapes, whose most frequent words seemed to be *expletive deleted*, a phrase necessitated by the extensive profanity on the tapes. Senate Republican leader Hugh Scott called the edited transcripts "deplorable, disgusting, shabby,

immoral." Most suspicious was an eighteen-minute gap in the tape of a crucial meeting of Nixon, Haldeman, and Ehrlichman on June 20, 1972, three days after the break-in.

The Final Days. The Watergate affair moved into its final phase in the summer of 1974, when a committee of the House of Representatives convened impeachment hearings. On July 30 seven Republicans joined the Democratic majority to vote three articles of impeachment against Richard Nixon: obstruction of justice, abuse of power, and acting in a way that subverted the Constitution. Two days later the Supreme Court ruled unanimously that Nixon had no right to claim executive privilege as a justification for refusing to turn over the additional tapes requested by the second special prosecutor. Under duress, on August 5 Nixon released the unexpurgated tapes, which contained shocking evidence (the so-called smoking gun) that he had ordered the cover-up as early as six days after the break-in. In effect,

Nixon Resigns
On August 9, 1974, Richard M. Nixon became the first
American president to resign. He is shown here minutes after
turning over the presidency to Gerald R. Ford. Nixon retired
to his home in San Clemente, California, refusing to admit
guilt for what had happened.

the president had been lying to the American people
since that time. A delegation of the most senior members of Congress, led by Senator Barry Goldwater, informed the president that no more than fifteen senators
still supported him. Facing certain conviction in a Senate trial, on August 9, 1974, Nixon became the first
U.S. president to resign.

The next day Vice-President Gerald Ford was sworn
in as president. In 1973 Ford, a former Michigan congressman and house minority leader, had replaced Spiro
Agnew, who had been forced to resign after being indicted
for accepting kickbacks on construction contracts while
serving as governor of Maryland and vice-president. The
transfer of power from Nixon to Ford went remarkably
smoothly. A month later, however, Ford stunned the
nation by granting a "full, free, and absolute" pardon of
Nixon "for all offenses he had committed or might have
committed during his presidency." Ford took that action,
he said, to spare the country the agony of rehashing
Watergate.

The Aftermath. In the aftermath of Watergate twenty-
five members of the Nixon administration went to
prison, including Nixon's closest advisers, H. R. Haldeman, John Ehrlichman, and John Mitchell. Nixon retired to his estate in San Clemente, California. Although
named as an "unindicted co-conspirator," he refused to
admit guilt for what had happened, conceding only that
Watergate represented an error of judgment.

In response to the abuses of the Nixon administration, Congress adopted several reforms to contain the
power of what the historian Arthur M. Schlesinger, Jr.,
called "the imperial presidency." The 1974 Congressional Budget and Impoundment Control Act restricted
the president's authority to impound federal funds (that
is, refuse to spend money appropriated by Congress for
programs opposed by the White House). A strengthened
Freedom of Information Act in 1974 gave citizens greater
access to files that federal government agencies had
amassed on them. Finally, the Fair Campaign Practices
Act of 1974 limited campaign contributions and provided for stricter accountability and public financing of
presidential campaigns. Ironically, while the campaign
law curbed some abuses, it created new ones. Because it
allowed an unlimited number of political action committees (PACs) to donate up to $5,000 per candidate, corpo-
rations and lobbying groups found that they could
increase their influence through multiple donations. By
the end of the decade there were close to 3,000 PACs,
which together played an increasingly pivotal—and some
would argue unethical—role in national elections.

Perhaps the most significant legacy of Watergate was
the wave of cynicism that swept the country in its wake.
Beginning with Lyndon Johnson's "credibility gap" in
the Vietnam War, public distrust of government had accelerated with the disclosure of Nixon's secret bombing
of Cambodia and the illegal surveillance and harassment
of antiwar protesters and other political opponents. The
saga of Watergate seemed to confirm the suspicions of
many Americans that politicians were hopelessly corrupt
and that the federal government was out of control.
Tragically, that cynicism would pervade Americans'
thinking about politics for the foreseeable future.

Lowered Expectations
and New Challenges

The political disillusionment of Americans was compounded by economic difficulties. After twenty-five
years of world leadership, the economic dominance of
the United States had begun to fade. Growing international demands for natural resources, particularly oil,
and unstable access to foreign supplies wreaked havoc
with the domestic economy. At the same time, foreign

competitors were successfully expanding their share of the world market, edging out American-made products. The result was a sharp downturn in the economy that marked the end of America's overwhelming economic superiority in the postwar era.

The Hydrocarbon Age

"Without oil," Interior Secretary Harold Ickes had noted back in 1933, "American civilization as we know it could not exist." That continues to be true today, when not only the United States but the entire modern world lives in a hydrocarbon age, dependent on petroleum and its by-products. In the twentieth century oil supplanted coal as the main energy source for the industrial world because it was cheaper, cleaner, and more abundant (see Figure 32.1). Between 1949 and 1972, world energy consumption more than tripled, and the demand for oil increased more than five and a half times. Access to oil, especially at the low prices that prevailed in the 1950s and 1960s, fostered rapid economic growth and rising standards of living in most of the world, especially in the United States.

Until well into the twentieth century the United States was the world's leading producer and consumer of oil. During World War II America still produced two-thirds of the world's oil, but its share fell to only 22 percent in 1972, even though domestic production continued to rise. By the late 1960s the United States was buying more and more oil on the world market to keep up with shrinking domestic reserves and growing de-

mand. Daily imports rose from 3.2 million barrels in 1970 to 6.2 million by the summer of 1973.

America imported oil primarily from the Middle East, where production increased a stupendous 1,500 percent in the twenty-five years after World War II. For decades European and American oil companies had dominated petroleum exploration and production in that region, reaping enormous profits. But with the rise of nationalism and the decline of colonialism in the postwar era, Persian Gulf nations sought to increase their control of the industry. In 1960 oil-producing countries in the Third World formed OPEC (the Organization of Petroleum Exporting Countries) in an attempt to exercise more control over the world oil market. Five of the founding countries—the Middle Eastern states of Saudi Arabia, Kuwait, Iran, and Iraq, plus Venezuela—were the source of more than 80 percent of the world's crude oil exports. In 1960 the oil industry was in the middle of a twenty-year period of surplus capacity, and prices stayed low. In the early 1970s, however, the balance shifted. Several trends—a sharp increase in worldwide demand, the end of excess capacity, political instability in the Middle East, the shift of the United States from a net exporter to a net importer of oil—came together to set the stage for what would soon be OPEC's "golden age."

The year 1973 was the turning point. Between 1973 and 1975 OPEC deliberately raised the price of a barrel of oil from $3 to $12. At the end of the decade the price peaked at $34 a barrel. Because the United States depended heavily on Middle Eastern oil, the price rise set off furious inflation.

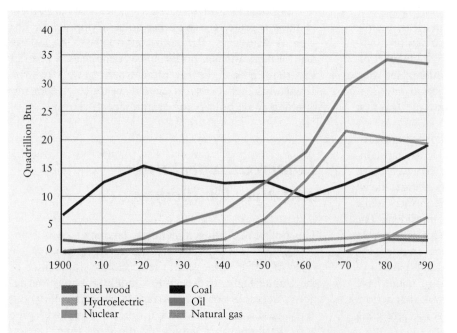

FIGURE 32.1

U.S. Energy Consumption, 1900–1990

Coal was the nation's primary source of energy until the 1950s, when oil and natural gas became the dominant fuels. The use of nuclear and hydroelectric power also rose substantially in the postwar era. Since the late 1970s fuel-efficient automobiles and conservation measures have reduced total energy use.

Fuel wood   Coal
Hydroelectric   Oil
Nuclear   Natural gas

No Gas
During the energy crisis of 1973–1974 American motorists faced widespread gasoline shortages for the first time since World War II. Although gas was not rationed, gas stations were closed on Sundays, air travel was cut by 10 percent, and a national speed limit of 55 miles per hour was imposed.

Also in 1973 OPEC instituted an oil embargo, demonstrating that oil could be used as a weapon in global politics. The embargo was a reponse to international actions surrounding a surprise invasion of Israel by Egyptian and Syrian forces on October 6, 1973 (which was Yom Kippur, the holiest day in Judaism). At first American policy makers held back on supporting Israel for fear of jeopardizing relations with the oil-producing countries, which favored the invaders. But the initial attack was so devastating that the United States reversed its stand and quickly sent supplies and military equipment that enabled the Israelis to regain most of their lost territory in a few weeks. A cease-fire soon ended the fighting, but the international repercussions were just beginning. In retaliation against the United States, Western Europe, and Japan, all of which had aided Israel in the Yom Kippur War, OPEC halted all exports to those countries. The embargo lasted until 1974.

The United States scrambled to meet its domestic energy needs. Americans were forced to curtail their driving or spend long hours in line at the pumps; gas prices climbed 40 percent in a matter of months. A national speed limit of 55 miles per hour was instituted to conserve fuel. Drivers wanted to buy more fuel-efficient cars, but the U.S. automobile industry had little to offer except "gas-guzzlers" that had been built to run on cheap gasoline. Soon the domestic auto industry was in a slump as Americans bought cheaper, more fuel-efficient foreign cars, primarily those manufactured in Japan and West Germany. Since the United States owed much of its twentieth-century prosperity to the automobile (one in six jobs was tied directly or indirectly to that industry in the 1970s), this downturn had profound implications for the American economy.

The energy crisis was an enormous shock to the American psyche. Suddenly Americans felt like hostages to economic forces beyond their control. As OPEC's oil ministers set higher oil prices at their annual meetings, they seemed to be able to determine whether western economies grew or stagnated. Despite extensive public education about energy conservation and a second gas shortage in 1979 caused by the Iranian revolution, Americans could not wean themselves from foreign oil. In 1970 the United States imported $4 billion of foreign oil; the figure would grow to $90 billion by 1980. Inflation caused only part of the rise. Americans used even more foreign oil after the energy crisis than they had before, a testimony to the enormous thirst of modern industrial and consumer societies for petroleum.

Economic Troubles

While the energy crisis dealt a swift blow to the U.S. economy, other long-term economic developments were equally troubling. The high cost of the Vietnam War and the Great Society, coupled with relatively low tax increases, resulted in a steadily growing federal deficit. In the industrial sector growing competition from the reviving economies of West Germany and Japan reduced demand for American goods worldwide. In 1955 American-made goods accounted for 32 percent of all imports by major capitalist countries; by 1970 U.S. products accounted for only 18 percent of the total, and that proportion continued to decline in the 1970s. In 1971 the dollar fell to its lowest level on the world market since 1949, and the United States posted its first trade deficit in almost a century.

That year Nixon took several bold steps to stem the decline in currency and trade—and to avoid a recession before the 1972 election. Most important, he suspended the Bretton Woods system that had been set up at the United Nations monetary conference in 1944 (see Chapter 29). The dollar now fluctuated in relation to the

price of an ounce of gold, which increased from its former set price of $35 to as much as $800 on the international market during the 1970s. The abandonment of Bretton Woods, one of the pillars of the postwar economic order, was designed to encourage foreign trade by effectively devaluing the dollar, and it represented a frank acknowledgment that America's currency was no longer the world's strongest. Nixon also instituted wage and price controls to curb inflation and offered a "full employment" budget for 1972, including $11 billion in deficit spending to boost the sluggish economy.

Such measures temporarily improved the economic picture, but the general decline persisted. Overall economic growth as measured by the gross national product (GNP) averaged 4.1 percent per year in the 1960s but only 2.9 percent in the 1970s. Tellingly, all the real growth occurred before 1973, the year the OPEC oil embargo began. By 1980 nine Western European countries had surpassed the United States in per capita GNP. Since 1973 most American workers have seen their real incomes drop and have maintained their family income levels only by working longer hours or having additional family members join the paid work force.

These economic changes produced a noticeable decline in most Americans' standard of living. Discretionary income per worker dropped 18 percent between 1973 and the early 1980s. At the same time, galloping inflation forced consumer prices upward, reaching "double-digit" peaks of around 10 percent in 1974 and over 13 percent in 1980 (see Figure 32.2). Housing prices rose even more rapidly; the average cost of a single-family home more than doubled in the 1970s. To combat inflation, the Federal Reserve Board raised interest rates to as much as 20 percent in the late 1970s, making home loans and home ownership inaccessible to wider segments of the working class and middle class, including many baby boomers who were entering adulthood.

Those young adults also faced a constricted job market in the late 1970s as a record number of baby-boom job seekers competed for a limited number of positions. Unemployment peaked at around 9 percent in 1975, declined briefly, and then edged upward again, hovering at around 6 to 7 percent in the late 1970s. The devastating combination of inflation and unemployment—known as *stagflation*—was resistant to traditional government remedies such as deficit spending and tax reduction and bedeviled presidential administrations from Nixon to Reagan.

Deindustrialization. American economic woes were most acute in the industrial sector, which entered a prolonged period of decline. The economists Barry Bluestone and Bennett Harrison estimate that the United States lost between 32 million and 38 million jobs in the 1970s as a direct result of *deindustrialization*, "the widespread, systematic disinvestment in the nation's productive capacity." Investors who had formerly bought stock in basic U.S. industries now speculated on the stock market, or put their money into mergers and acquisitions, or invested in foreign companies. U.S. firms relocated overseas partly to take advantage of cheaper labor and production costs and partly because federal tax law permitted corporations to deduct foreign expenses from their domestic profits. By the end of the 1970s the hundred largest multinational corporations and banks were earning more than a third of their overall profits abroad. For some corporations the proportion was much higher: in 1979, 94 percent of Ford's profits came from overseas operations, as did 83 percent of the profits earned by the banking giant Citicorp in 1977.

The most dramatic consequences of deindustrialization occurred in the older northeastern and midwestern industrial regions that came to be known as the Rust Belt. Nightly newscasts were full of stories of the clos-

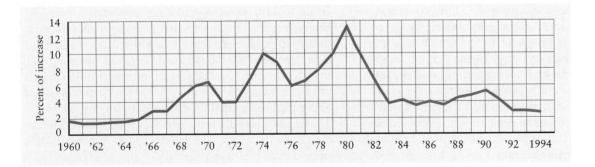

FIGURE 32.2

The Consumer Price Index, 1960–1994
The annual inflation rate peaked in 1980, the last year of Carter's presidency.

Source: U.S. Statistical Abstract, 1995.

ings of unprofitable plants. The dominant images of American industry in the mid-twentieth century—huge factories such as Ford's River Rouge outside Detroit; the General Electric plant in Lynn, Massachusetts; and the U.S. Steel compound in Gary, Indiana—were becoming relics of a past stage of industrial development. In some cases, such as the steel industry, older plants became unprofitable because U.S. firms had failed to invest sufficiently in research and development and were outflanked by foreign competitors.

When a community's major employer closed up shop and left town, the effect was devastating. In 1977 the Lykes Corporation shut down the Campbell Works of the Youngstown Sheet and Tube Company, laying off 4,100 Ohio steelworkers. Two years later the community was still reeling. A third of the displaced workers, too old to retrain for new positions, had been forced to take early retirement at half their previous salaries. Ten percent had moved, many of them to nonunion jobs in the Sun Belt. Another 15 percent were still looking for work, their unemployment compensation long since exhausted. Among the 40 percent who were the "success stories" (those who had found other jobs), many had taken huge wage cuts. A former rigger, for instance, was selling women's shoes for $2.37 an hour. *Fortune* magazine tried to make Youngstown's story upbeat, titling it "Youngstown Bounces Back," but the economic reality belied its cheerful conclusions. The caption of a photograph of an unemployed steelworker sitting at a piano read, "Crane operator Ozie Williams, thirty-two, has a lot of time to practice his music." The impact of such plant closings rippled through communities across America's heartland. Very few have "bounced back," and the number of industrial ghost towns has continued to grow.

Challenges for Labor. The changing economic conditions that fostered foreign investment and plant closings posed critical problems for the labor movement. In labor's heyday during the 1940s and 1950s American managers had often cooperated with unions; with profits high, there was room for accommodation. But as foreign competition cut into American corporate profits in the 1970s, industry was less willing to treat labor as a partner in making economic decisions. Union leaders might learn about a plant closing on the news at the same time that ordinary workers and the general public did. Union leaders shifted their priorities to holding on to gains they had already won.

Under such conditions, the power of organized labor declined. In the 1970s union membership dropped from 28 percent to 23 percent of the work firce. Labor's bargaining position was increasingly vulnerable in the face of multinational conglomerates with vast international resources and mobility. Some employers facing strikes or labor problems simply closed down their domestic operations and turned to a cheaper, more compliant work force abroad. In a competitive global environment labor's prospects for regaining its earlier strength were dim.

Social Gridlock: Reform and Reaction in the 1970s

The journalist Tom Wolfe labeled the 1970s the "Me Decade" because of its widespread obsession with lifestyles and personal well-being. The historian Christopher Lasch referred derisively to its "culture of narcissism." Yet those labels hardly do justice to a decade in which environmentalism, feminism, lesbian and gay rights, and other social movements blossomed. Furthermore, such characterizations neglect the growing social conservatism that was in part a response to such movements. In fact, all these trends coexisted in a pattern of shifting crosscurrents that made the 1970s a complex and transitional decade.

Turning Inward

The youth culture of the 1960s had revolutionized lifestyles and cultural expression, but after 1970 its spirit was absorbed and marketed by the larger consumer culture. The crowds at Woodstock and other rock festivals had revealed the size of the youth market, and corporate entrepreneurs rushed to cash in. Symbols of cultural defiance were thus co-opted and homogenized by the mass culture. The ragged bell-bottoms of the 1960s became the expensive designer jeans of the 1970s. The unkempt hair and beards of male hippies emboldened some middle-aged executives to sport mustaches or allow their hair to cover their ears. The "Afro" hairstyle, once worn only by radical black activists, influenced blacks and whites of both sexes to let their hair go natural. Health foods soon became a multi-million-dollar business, packaged and sold in the consumer marketplace. Once paragons of the underground press, the *Village Voice* and *Rolling Stone* became respected voices of American journalism. The alternative styles of the 1960s thus filtered into the dominant culture.

As the baby-boom generation moved off college campuses and into the work force, public attention focused on the "selling out" of 1960s radicals. The media reveled in stories about the former Yippie leader Jerry Rubin, who became a Wall Street stockbroker, and the former Black Panther Eldridge Cleaver, who became a clothing designer and a born-again Christian. Leaving the counterculture behind, baby boomers settled down to pursue careers and material wealth.

Lois Marie Gibbs: Environmental Activist

In 1978 Lois Gibbs was a twenty-seven-year-old housewife in Niagara Falls, New York. A chemical worker's wife and the mother of two children, Gibbs spent her days cooking, shopping, and cleaning the family's modest three-bedroom home. Two years later Gibbs was a nationally known figure. As the leader of the fight against toxic waste at the Love Canal, she organized hundreds of local families, squared off with the governor of New York State, testified before Congress, appeared on national television, and was recognized by President Jimmy Carter for her efforts. She was, as she liked to put it, "the housewife who went to Washington."

Born in Grand Island, New York, in 1951, Lois Conn was one of six children in a typical blue-collar family in the industrial region surrounding Buffalo. After graduating from high school in 1969, she worked as a nurse's aide at a convalescent home and married Harry Gibbs, a worker at a local chemical plant. After the birth of their first child they purchased a home in a quiet, tree-lined neighborhood. Lois quit her job to stay at home and gave birth to a daughter in 1975. With no inkling of what lay beneath them, the Gibbses finished their basement, tended their garden, and enjoyed a peaceful suburban existence.

The first sign of trouble came in 1977, when the Gibbses' son, Michael, entered kindergarten at the neighborhood school. Within three months, he developed epilepsy and soon contracted asthma and chronic urinary and ear infections. The following spring Gibbs read newspaper reports about toxic chemicals buried beneath the school and tried to have her son transferred. When school officials rejected her request, insisting that the school was safe, Gibbs launched a petition drive to have the school closed.

At first Gibbs was reticent about approaching her neighbors, afraid of having doors slammed in her face. But what she found surprised her; not only were people interested and concerned about the dangers of chemicals, many of them had health problems of their own, including respiratory ailments, cancer, miscarriages, and birth defects. "The more I heard, the more frightened I became," said Gibbs. "The entire community seemed to be sick."

Gibbs set out to educate herself about the area's history. Consulting local newspaper files, she learned about Love Canal, a six-mile-long canal project developed by William T. Love in the 1890s to connect the upper and lower branches of the Niagara River. Construction had been under way when the depression of 1893 doomed the project, leaving a partially dug trench. The land later became a dump site used mainly by the Hooker Chemical Corporation, which disposed of 22,000 tons of chemical wastes there between 1942 and 1953. (Health officials eventually identified over 200 different compounds at the site, including highly toxic substances such as dioxin—used in the herbicide Agent Orange—toluene, and benzene.) After filling and covering over the site in 1953, Hooker sold the land to the Board of Education for one dollar, stipulating that the company not be held responsible for any future injury or death. Housing subdivisions soon sprung up around the site, and a new elementary school near the corner of the canal opened in 1955.

By the time Gibbs began meeting with her neighbors in 1978, rusted metal drums were surfacing in backyards, chemical sludge was seeping into basements, and residents were complaining about dead trees, burned feet, and a recurring stench. In June of that year the New York State Health Department began collecting air, soil, and blood samples from households closest to the canal. After finding abnormally high rates of birth defects and miscarriages, the health department issued an order on August 2 for reconstruction of the canal site and recommended the evacuation of all pregnant women and children under age two. Soon afterward concerned residents established the Love Canal Homeowners Association (LCHA) to fight for permanent relocation of Love Canal families and elected Lois Gibbs as its president. Under pressure from Gibbs and the LCHA, New York's governor, Hugh Carey, agreed a few days later to relocate the 239 families closest to the canal, purchasing their homes at the replacement value.

While Gibbs and the LCHA applauded Carey's action, they worried about the other 810 families remaining in the neighborhood, many of whose homes also

Lois Gibbs
A 27-year-old housewife in Niagara Falls, New York, Lois Gibbs became leader of a campaign against toxic waste in her neighborhood in 1978. As president of the Love Canal Homeowners Association, Gibbs fought successfully for the permanent relocation of more than 1,000 Love Canal families.

showed dangerous levels of chemicals. Gibbs appealed to federal and local officials for further action but encountered repeated delays, denials, and rebuffs. The mayor of Niagara Falls denounced Gibbs's efforts, claiming that the adverse publicity would destroy the city's tourist industry. Meanwhile, the state health department refused to relocate more families until it could complete further studies. At one point in 1979 the department claimed to have lost the residents' health records and instructed them to start the lengthy documentation process all over again.

Faced with bureaucratic inertia, Gibbs sought out sympathetic scientists to help the residents conduct their own studies. Their most important finding came from a neighborhood survey showing that health problems clustered around swales—underground drainage ditches that led away from the canal—thus suggesting more widespread contamination. The LCHA promptly released the findings to the media. Gibbs got publicity in other ways as well: she appeared on talk shows, organized picketing at the canal construction site, and was arrested for blocking truck traffic. When state officials

still failed to take action, Gibbs led a group of citizens to the state capital, in Albany, bearing cardboard coffins symbolizing Love Canal victims. Throughout the Love Canal crisis Gibbs made frequent trips to Albany and Washington to negotiate with state officials, the governor's office, Senator Daniel Patrick Moynihan, and other federal representatives.

Gibbs's new activities caused tension in her marriage. "My husband was getting upset with me," she recalled, "I was never home . . . dinner was never on time." Like other housewives involved in the crisis, Gibbs gained a new independence through her activities outside the home. She and her husband divorced in 1980.

In May of that year events at Love Canal came to a head when the U.S. Environmental Protection Agency (EPA) released a study showing abnormally high levels of chromosome breakage in Love Canal residents (suggesting increased risks of cancer, miscarriage, and birth defects). In an act of desperation Gibbs and two other housewives took two EPA officials hostage in the LCHA office while hundreds of angry residents surrounded the building, demanding federal relocation of Love Canal families. Coming in the middle of the Iranian hostage crisis, the women's ploy brought national media coverage but also a threat of reprisal from the FBI. To avoid violence Gibbs released the officials, but she also demanded a response from President Jimmy Carter within forty-eight hours. Two days later, on May 21, Carter declared a health emergency at Love Canal, authorizing the temporary relocation of the remaining 810 families. Later that year he signed a bill permitting the permanent relocation of those families and the purchase of their homes; he also signed a bill establishing a "Superfund" to clean up Love Canal and thousands of other toxic waste sites identified by the EPA.

Using part of the $30,000 that the state paid for her home, Gibbs and her children moved to Washington, D.C., in 1981. There she founded the Citizens Clearinghouse for Hazardous Waste, a consulting group for grass-roots organizations working on problems related to pesticides, solid waste, asbestos, and other toxic substances. She married a toxicologist, gave birth to two more children, and has continued to work as the director of the Citizens Clearinghouse to the present day.

One of the communities the Citizens Clearinghouse will be watching is Love Canal. In 1990 the EPA declared Love Canal habitable again after a 12-year, $250 million cleanup. The elementary school and the 239 houses closest to the canal were demolished, but 236 other homes were rehabilitated and sold at discount prices to eager buyers. Public officials insist that the new containment system has safely and permanently sealed off the dump. Lois Gibbs is not so sure.

Environmental Legislation. Citizens' concerns over nuclear power, chemical contamination, pesticide poisoning, and other environmental issues created bipartisan support for a spate of federal legislation in the late 1960s and 1970s. In 1969 Congress passed the National Environmental Policy Act, requiring the developers of public projects to file an environmental impact statement (EIS) to assess the consequences of changing use patterns on a particular ecosystem. The EIS soon became a useful tool for citizens' groups trying to block unwanted development by private industry or government. The next year Nixon established the Environmental Protection Agency and signed the Clean Air Act, which toughened standards for auto emissions to reduce smog and air pollution. Following the lead of several state governments, Congress banned the use of DDT in 1972. Wildlife protection provided by the Endangered Animals Act of 1964 was expanded under the Endangered Species Act (1973), granting species such as snail darters and spotted owls protected status, which had to be balanced against human concerns regarding employment, development, and recreation. In 1980 Jimmy Carter signed a bill creating a $1.6 billion "Superfund" to clean up chemical pollution sites and, through an executive order in 1978, set aside 56 million acres in Alaska as national park and forest lands. Environmental protection thus joined social welfare, defense, and national security as areas for federal intervention in the postwar era.

The Consumer Movement

Paralleling the rise of environmentalism was a growing consumer protection movement that sought to eliminate harmful products and curb dangerous practices by American corporations. The consumer movement had its origins in the Progressive Era with the founding of government agencies such as the Food and Drug Administration (see Chapter 21). After decades of inertia the consumer movement reemerged in the 1960s under the leadership of Ralph Nader, a young Harvard-educated lawyer who took on U.S. automakers over unsafe and wasteful design practices. In his book *Unsafe at Any Speed* (1965) Nader attacked General Motors for putting flashy style ahead of safe handling and fuel economy in its design of the Chevrolet Corvair.

Nader later won a lawsuit against General Motors and used the proceeds to launch a Washington-based consumer protection organization in 1969. Staffed by a handful of lawyers and hundreds of student volunteers known as "Nader's raiders," the organization gave rise to the Public Interest Research Group, a national network of consumer groups that focused on issues ranging from product safety to consumer fraud and environmental pollution. Nader's organization pioneered legal tactics such as the class-action suit (which allowed people with common grievances to sue as a group) and became a model for dozens of other groups that emerged in the 1970s and afterward to combat the health hazards of smoking, unethical insurance and credit practices, and other consumer problems. The establishment of the federal Consumer Products Safety Commission in 1972 reflected the growing importance of consumer protection in American life.

The Women's Movement

Along with environmentalism, feminism proved to be the most enduring movement of the 1960s. In the early 1970s, the women's movement scored significant victories, including increased educational opportunities, a growing network of women-oriented services and organizations, and increased access to abortion.

Women's opportunities expanded dramatically in the area of higher education. Formerly all-male bastions, including Yale, Princeton, and the U.S. Military Academy, admitted women undergraduates for the first time; women's colleges such as Vassar and Sarah Lawrence admitted men. Under pressure from female students and faculty members, hundreds of colleges started women's studies programs, and the proportion of women in most graduate and professional schools rose markedly. With the passage of Title IX of the Educational Amendments Act of 1972, Congress broadened the 1964 Civil Rights Act to include educational institutions, prohibiting colleges and universities that received federal funds from discriminating on the basis of sex. By requiring schools to fund sports programs for women at a level comparable to that for men, Title IX increased women's access to sports and athletic competition.

The women's movement grew more sophisticated, generating an array of women-oriented services and organizations. Rape crisis centers, battered women's shelters, and feminist health collectives proliferated in cities across the country. *Our Bodies Ourselves*, a women's health manual published by a group of Boston women in 1973, quickly became a best seller. Women's bookstores catered to a feminist clientele with an assortment of new women's newspapers, books, and academic journals. In 1972 Gloria Steinem and other journalists founded *Ms.* magazine, the first consumer magazine aimed at a feminist audience. Several new national women's organizations emerged in the early 1970s, and many of the established groups continued to grow. By 1977 the National Organization for Women (NOW) had 65,000 members.

Women and Politics. Women were also increasingly visible in politics and public life. The National Women's Political Caucus, founded in 1971, actively promoted the election of women to public office. Bella Abzug, Elizabeth

Holtzman, Shirley Chisholm, Patricia Schroeder, and Geraldine Ferraro served in Congress; Ella Grasso won election as Connecticut's governor in 1974, and Dixie Lee Ray as Washington's in 1976. Twenty thousand women came to Houston in November 1977 for the first National Women's Conference, part of the observance of the United Nations' International Women's Year. Their "National Plan of Action" represented a hard-won consensus on topics ranging from violence against women to homemakers' rights, the needs of older women, health, and, most controversially, abortion rights and other reproductive issues.

Women's political mobilization resulted in significant legislative and administrative gains. In addition to Title IX, Congress passed the Equal Credit Opportunity Act of 1974, which made it possible for women to get credit, including charge cards and mortgages, in their own names and on the basis of their own (not their husbands') incomes. Congress also authorized child care deductions for working parents and employment benefits for married female federal employees. Under the Carter administration women received a record number of federal appointments, including three cabinet-level positions.

The Expanding Women's Movement
By the late 1970s the feminist movement had broadened its base, attracting women of all ages and backgrounds, such as this delegate to the 1977 National Women's Conference in Houston, Texas. As the slogan on her hat implies, though, the women's movement was already on the defensive against right-wing claims that the feminist movement was undermining traditional values. (© Bettye Lane)

Abortion Rights. The Supreme Court also advanced the cause of women's rights, although not always along the lines favored by the women's movement. In several rulings the Court read a right of privacy into the Ninth and Fourteenth amendments' concept of personal liberty to give women more control over their reproductive lives. In 1965 the case of *Griswold v. Connecticut* had overturned state laws against the sale of contraceptive devices to married adults; in 1972 *Baird v. Eisenstadt* extended this protection to single persons. In 1973 *Roe v. Wade* struck down Texas and Georgia statutes that allowed abortions only if the mother's life was in danger. According to this 7–2 decision, states could no longer outlaw abortions performed during the first trimester, or three months, of pregnancy. Rather than addressing the issue in feminist terms, such as women's right to control their own bodies, the justices interpreted abortion as a medical issue, basing their decision on the confidentiality of the doctor-patient relationship as well as the individual's right to privacy.

Roe v. Wade nationalized the liberalization of state abortion laws that had begun in New York in 1970 but also fueled the development of a powerful antiabortion movement. Believing that the rights of a fetus take precedence over a woman's right to choose whether to terminate a pregnancy, abortion opponents attempted to circumvent and overturn the *Roe v. Wade* decision. In 1976 Representative Henry Hyde of Illinois sponsored an amendment to deny Medicaid funds for abortions for poor women. Passed over a presidential veto, the amendment was upheld by the Supreme Court in 1980. The Hyde Amendment was one of the opening rounds in a protracted legislative and judicial campaign to chip away at the *Roe* decision.

The Equal Rights Amendment. In the 1970s the women's movement increasingly united around the proposed Equal Rights Amendment (ERA) to the Constitution, which stated in its entirety, "Equality of rights under the law shall not be denied or abridged by the United States or any State on the basis of sex." The ERA, first introduced in Congress in 1923 by the National Woman's Party, was dusted off by modern feminists. In 1970 the measure passed the House but died in the Senate. In the 1971–1972 session it passed both houses and was submitted to the states for ratification. Thirty-four states quickly passed the ERA between 1972 and the end of 1974, but then the momentum stopped (see Map 32.1). Only Indiana ratified after that point, leaving the amendment three states short of the necessary three-fourths majority. Most of the nonratifying states were in the South and the West; Illinois also held out despite spirited campaigns there by ERA supporters. Congress extended the deadline for ratification until June 30, 1982, but the Equal Rights Amendment still fell short.

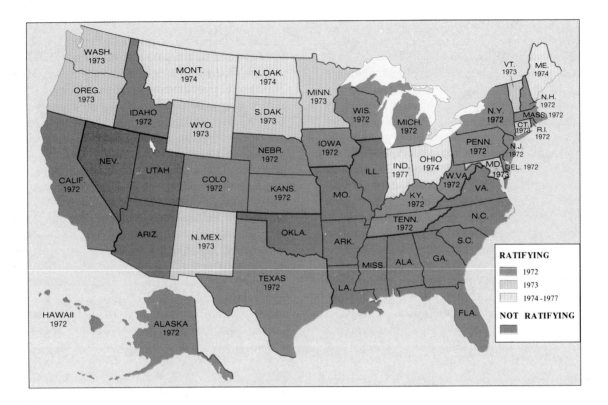

MAP 32.1

States Ratifying the Equal Rights Amendment
The Equal Rights Amendment quickly won support in 1972 and 1973 but then
stalled. ERAmerica, a coalition of women's groups formed in 1976, lobbied extensively, particularly in Florida, North Carolina, and Illinois, but failed to sway the
conservative legislatures in those states. Efforts to revive the ERA in the 1980s were
unsuccessful.

Stalemate. The fate of the ERA and the battle over
abortion rights show that by the mid-1970s the momentum of the women's movement was beginning to slow.
The feminist movement was becoming increasingly divided over issues of race, class, age, and sexual orientation. For many nonwhite and working-class women
the movement seemed to represent the interests of self-
seeking white career women. The ERA, for example,
promised to open certain high-paying occupations to individual women but also would eliminate protective
legislation considered essential by many women workers. At the same time the women's movement faced
growing social conservatism among Americans generally. Although 63 percent of the women polled in 1975
said that they favored "efforts to strengthen and change
women's status in society," a growing minority of men
and women expressed concern over what seemed to be
revolutionary changes in women's traditional roles. Especially disturbing to many conservatives were attitudes
that seemed to denigrate women who chose to be full-
time housewives.

Phyllis Schlafly, long active in conservative causes—
she had written *A Choice, Not an Echo*, a best seller ex-
tolling Barry Goldwater, in 1963—led the antifeminist
backlash. Despite her law degree and active career while
raising five children, Schlafly advocated traditional roles
for women. As she told audiences, "A man's first significant purchase is a diamond for his bride, and the major
financial investment of his life is a home for her to live
in." She baited feminists by opening her speeches with
"I'd like to thank my husband for letting me be here
tonight."

Schlafly's STOP ERA organization claimed that the
amendment would create an unnatural "unisex society,"
permit women to be drafted, legalize homosexual marriages, and prohibit separate toilets for men and women.
(Feminists argued that those charges were groundless.)
Grass-roots networks mobilized conservative women,
who then showed up at statehouses with home-baked
bread and apple pies, symbols of their traditional domestic roles. The message that women would lose more
than they would gain if the ERA passed found favor

among many men and women, especially those troubled by the rapid pace of social change.

Although the feminist movement was on the defensive by the mid-1970s, women's lives showed no signs of returning to the patterns of the 1950s. Pervasive changes in women's employment and family lives that had begun in earlier decades accelerated in the 1970s. Because of increasing economic pressures, the proportion of women in the paid work force continued to rise, from 44 percent in 1970 to 51 percent in 1980. With easier access to birth control, many women enjoyed greater sexual freedom before, during, and after marriage (although they also became more vulnerable to male sexual pressures). With a growing number of career options available to women, particularly educated white women, many stayed single or delayed marriage and child-rearing. The birth rate thus continued its postwar decline, reaching an all-time low in the mid-1970s (see Figure 29.5). At the same time, the divorce rate rose 82 percent in the 1970s as more men and women elected to leave unhappy marriages.

Although such changes brought increased autonomy for many women, they also caused new hardships, particularly in poor and working-class families. Divorce left many women with low-paying jobs and inadequate child care. More tolerant attitudes toward premarital sex, along with other social and economic factors, contributed to rising teenage pregnancy rates. In the 1970s teenage mothers—most of them poor and ill educated—gave birth to one of every six children. Rising divorce and adolescent pregnancy rates produced a sharp rise in the number of female-headed families, which in turn resulted in a "feminization" of poverty. In 1980 women accounted for 66 percent of the nation's adults living below the poverty line. Such developments made many Americans uneasy and fueled a growing wave of social reaction.

Gays and Lesbians

Like the women's movement, the gay liberation movement of the 1960s achieved greater visibility in the 1970s. Thousands of gay men and lesbians "came out" in those years, publicly proclaiming their sexual orientation. Growing gay communities in New York's Greenwich Village, San Francisco's Castro, and other urban enclaves gave rise to hundreds of new gay and lesbian clubs, churches, businesses, and political organizations. In 1973 the National Gay Task Force launched a campaign to have gay men and lesbians included as a protected group under civil rights laws covering employment and housing. Such efforts were most successful on the local level; during the 1970s Detroit, Boston, Los Angeles, Miami, San Francisco, and other cities passed laws barring discrimination on the basis of sexual preference.

Like abortion, the ERA, and other controversial social issues, gay rights came under attack from conservatives who believed that such protection would encourage immoral behavior. When the Miami city council passed a measure banning discrimination against gay men and lesbians in 1977, the singer Anita Bryant led a campaign to repeal the law by popular referendum. Later that year voters overturned the measure by a two-to-one majority, prompting similar anti–gay rights campaigns around the country.

Racial Minorities

Although the civil rights movement was in disarray by the late 1960s, minority group protests produced new policies that led to limited social and economic gains for those groups in the 1970s. Native Americans saw some of the most significant changes as their protests resulted in federal action under the Nixon administration. In 1971 the Alaska Native Land Claims Act restored 40 million acres and paid $960 million in compensation to Eskimos, Aleuts, and other native peoples. Smaller settlements were made with tribes in Maine, New Mexico, South Dakota, and Washington State. Most important, the federal government abandoned the tribal termination program that it had begun in the 1950s (see Chapter 29). Under the Indian Self-Determination Act of 1974, Congress restored the legal status of tribes as governing entities and gave them authority over federal programs on reservations (see Map 32.2).

Busing. The court-mandated busing of children to achieve school integration proved to be the most disruptive social issue of the 1970s. After its 1954 ruling in *Brown v. Board of Education of Topeka*, the Supreme Court had called for desegregation "with all deliberate speed" (see Chapter 29), but progress was limited before 1970. In the 1970s, however, the courts and the Justice Department pushed for more action, beginning in the South, which grudgingly complied, and then in the rest of the country. In 1971 the Supreme Court upheld a federal judge's order requiring the Charlotte-Mecklenburg, North Carolina, school system to transport students from their neighborhoods to more distant schools to integrate the citywide school system. The following year the Supreme Court upheld a lower court decision in Colorado that mandated the use of busing in northern and western states as well. In *Milliken v. Bradley* (1974) the Court narrowly rejected a proposal to combine the schools of a city and its suburbs to achieve racial balance but specified that cities, with their deeply ingrained patterns of residential segregation, had to use busing within municipal boundaries to integrate their classrooms. The decision sparked both class- and race-based resentments; many white working-class city dwellers objected to busing not

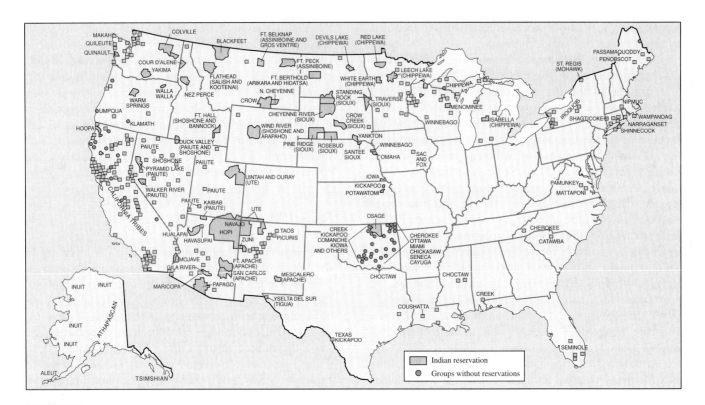

MAP 32.2

American Indian Reservations

Although native Americans have been able to preserve small enclaves in the northeastern states, most Indian reservations are in the West. Beginning in the 1970s, various nations filed land claims against federal and state governments.

only because they opposed racial integration but because such schemes had been devised by affluent suburbanites whose school districts were unaffected by the plans.

The most violent opposition occurred in Boston in 1974–1975. The strongly Irish-Catholic working-class neighborhood of South Boston responded to the arrival of black students from the Roxbury section with mob scenes reminiscent of Little Rock in 1957 (see American Voices, page 1009). Armed riot police were needed to keep South Boston High School open. Many white parents in Boston and other cities threatened by court-ordered busing transferred their children to private schools; the resulting "white flight" increased the racial imbalance that busing was intended to solve. Some black

An Antibusing Confrontation in Boston

Tensions over court-ordered busing ran high in Boston in 1976. When a black lawyer tried to cross the city hall plaza during an antibusing demonstration, he became another victim of Boston's climate of racial hatred and violence. This photograph by Stanley Forman for the *Boston Herald American*, showing protesters trying to impale the man with a flagstaff, won a Pulitzer Prize.

Phyllis Ellison

Busing in Boston

Nowhere in the North was busing more divisive than in Boston in 1974–1975. Phyllis Ellison was one of fifty-six black students from the predominantly black neighborhoods of Columbia Point and Roxbury assigned to South Boston High School. Here she describes incidents from her sophomore year, including the day that a white student was stabbed by a black student during a melee at the school. The student's wound was not fatal, but the incident led to heightened resistance and recriminations.

I remember my first day going on the bus to South Boston High School. I wasn't afraid because I felt important. I didn't know what to expect, what was waiting for me up the hill. We had police escorts. I think there was three motorcycle cops and then two police cruisers in front of the bus, and so I felt really important at that time, not knowing what was on the other side of the hill.

Well, when we started up the hill you could hear people saying, "Niggers go home." There were signs, they had made a sign saying, "Black people stay out. We don't want any niggers in our

school." And there were people on the corners holding bananas like we were apes, monkeys. "Monkeys get out, get them out of our neighborhood. We don't want you in our schools.". . .

You can't imagine how tense it was inside the classroom. A teacher was almost afraid to say the wrong thing, because they knew that that would excite the whole class, a disturbance in the classroom. The black students sat on one side of the classes. The white students sat on the other side of the classes. . . . In the lunchrooms . . . [it] was the same thing. . . . So really, it was separate, I mean, we attended the same school, but we really never did anything together. . . .

I remember the day Michael Faith got stabbed vividly, because I was in the principal's office and all of a sudden you heard a lot of commotion and you heard kids screaming and yelling and saying, "He's dead, he's dead. That black nigger killed him. He's dead, he's dead." And then the principal running out of the office. There was a lot of commotion and screaming, yelling, hollering, "Get the niggers at Southie." I was really afraid. And the principal came back into the office and said, Call

the ambulance and tell all the black students that were in the office to stay there. A police officer was in there and they were trying to get the white students out of the building, because they had just gone on a rampage and they were just going to hurt the first black student that they saw. . . . The black students were locked in their rooms and all the white students were let go out of their classrooms. I remember us going into a room, and outside you just saw a crowd of people, I mean, just so many people, I can't even count. . . . I remember the police cars coming up the street, attempting to, and people turning over the police cars, and I was just amazed that they could do something like that. The police tried to get horses up. They wouldn't let the horses get up. They stoned the horses. They stoned the cars. And I thought that day that we would never get out of South Boston High School. . . .

Source: Henry Hampton and Steve Fayer, Voices of Freedom: An Oral History of the Civil Rights Movement from the 1950s through the 1980s (New York: Bantam, 1990), 600, 610, 612–613.

parents also came to oppose busing, calling instead for more funding and greater efforts to improve schools in predominantly black neighborhoods. By the late 1970s federal courts were backing away from their earlier insistence on busing to achieve racial balance.

Affirmative Action. Almost as divisive as busing was the implementation of *affirmative action*—procedures designed to redress historical patterns of race and sex discrimination in employment and education. First put forward by Lyndon Johnson's Department of Labor in 1968, affirmative action was refined by a series of Supreme Court and lower court rulings that identified acceptable procedures, including hiring and enrollment goals, special recruitment and training programs, and *set-asides* (specially reserved slots) for women and minority

students, employees, and contractors on government-subsidized construction projects.

Affirmative action programs helped expand opportunities for blacks and Latinos during those years. Among black Americans, access to higher education increased significantly; the number of black students enrolled in colleges and universities doubled between 1970 and 1977 to 1.1 million, or 9.3 percent of the total student enrollment. A small but growing number of black graduates moved into white-collar professions in corporations, banks, universities, and law firms. Others found new opportunities in civil service occupations such as law enforcement and firefighting or entered apprenticeships in the skilled construction trades. Latinos experienced similar gains in education and "token" advances in the professions and skilled trades. On the

whole, however, both groups experienced only marginal economic improvement as poor and working-class non-whites bore the brunt of job loss and unemployment in the 1970s.

Nevertheless, many whites, who were also feeling the economic pinch, came to resent affirmative action programs as infringements on their rights. A growing number of white men soon raised the cry of "reverse discrimination," claiming that they had been passed over in favor of less qualified minority group members or women. In 1978 a white man named Allan Bakke sued the University of California Medical School at Davis for rejecting him while admitting minority candidates with lesser qualifications. The Supreme Court ruling in *Bakke v. University of California* was inconclusive: by a 5 to 4 margin the Court proclaimed that the medical school's strict quota—setting aside 16 out of 100 places for "disadvantaged students"—was illegal and ordered Bakke admitted. At the same time, also by a 5 to 4 margin, it ruled that racial factors could properly be considered in making hiring and admission decisions, thus upholding the principle of affirmative action. But the *Bakke* decision was clearly a setback for the proponents of affirmative action, and it set the stage for subsequent efforts to eliminate those programs in the 1990s.

The Politics of Resentment

The often vociferous public opposition to busing, affirmative action, gay rights ordinances, and the Equal Rights Amendment, along with the rapidly growing antiabortion movement, constituted a broad backlash against the social changes of the previous decade. More important, the new conservatism was a product of economic changes in the 1970s that left many working-class and middle-class Americans with lower incomes, rising prices, and higher taxes. Richard Nixon had successfully appealed to those "ordinary Americans" back in 1968; the political power of this appeal grew even stronger with the economic crises of the early 1970s. Such pressures fueled what the conservative writer Alan Crawford has termed the "politics of resentment"—a grass-roots revolt against "special-interest groups" (women, minorities, gays, and so on) and growing expenditures on social welfare. Such groups and programs, conservatives believed, robbed other Americans of educational and employment opportunities and created a fiscal burden on the working and middle classes.

Although the politics of resentment most often centered on socioeconomic issues, it also took the form of local taxpayers' revolts. In 1978 California voters passed Proposition 13, a measure that reduced property taxes and eventually undercut local governments' ability to maintain schools and other public services. Promising tax relief to middle-class homeowners and reduced funding for busing and other programs benefiting the urban

poor, Proposition 13 became the model for similar tax-cutting measures around the country in the late 1970s and 1980s.

Evangelical Religion. The rising popularity of evangelical religion also fueled the conservative resurgence of the 1970s. Fundamentalist, holiness, and Pentecostal sects that fostered a "born-again" experience had been growing steadily since World War II under the leadership of charismatic preachers such as Billy Graham, who used the media, especially television, to spread the gospel. Soon evangelical groups set up their own school systems, newspapers, and broadcasting networks. A new breed of *televangelists*, such as Jerry Falwell, built vast electronic ministries through religious programs aired on the new Christian Broadcasting Network founded by the Virginia preacher Pat Robertson.

In the 1970s, when membership in the liberal mainstream Protestant churches declined, evangelical denominations showed energetic growth. According to a Gallup poll conducted in 1976, some 50 million Americans, about a quarter of the population, were affiliated with evangelical churches. President Jimmy Carter proudly proclaimed the influence of Jesus Christ in his life, as did the singers Pat Boone and Johnny Cash, the former Watergate convicts Jeb Magruder and Charles Colson, and the black power activist Eldridge Cleaver.

The New Right. During the 1970s evangelicals spoke out on a broad range of social and cultural issues, denouncing abortion, busing, sex education, pornography, feminism, and gay rights. Concerned with the same economic issues that engaged other conservatives, the Christian right added a strong dimension of moral indignation, particularly over issues of family life and sexuality. In 1979 Jerry Falwell founded the Moral Majority, a Christian political organization that promoted "family values"—traditional gender roles, heterosexuality, family cohesion—and staunch anticommunism. The extensive media and fund-raising networks of the Christian right became the organizational base for the larger conservative movement known as the New Right. Using computerized mass mailing campaigns that targeted evangelical constituencies, New Right political groups such as the National Conservative Political Action Committee and the American Conservative Union mobilized thousands of followers and millions of dollars to support conservative candidates and causes.

During the 1970s conservatives were most active at the local level, building a national movement from the ground up that would help to elect Ronald Reagan in 1980. Environmentalists and other liberal activists shared this grass-roots approach but were less effective in using modern technological tools to sustain a mass following. Among both liberals and conservatives the dynamism of local organizing developed in the absence of effective political leadership on the national level.

Post-Watergate Politics: Failed Leadership

In the wake of Watergate many citizens became cynical about the federal government and politicians in general. "Don't vote. It only encourages them" read one bumper sticker for the 1976 presidential campaign. "The lesser of two evils is still evil" proclaimed another. Political leaders proved unable to deal with the rising inflation, stagnant growth, and declining productivity that plagued the U.S. economy in the 1970s. The fall of Saigon in 1975 reminded Americans of the failure of the nation's Vietnam policy. The world was changing, and Americans had to grapple with the unsettling idea that perhaps the United States was no longer the all-powerful country it had been for much of the postwar era. As Americans approached the 1980 election, this growing sense of impotence erupted in fury over the Iranian hostage crisis.

Ford's Caretaker Presidency

Gerald Ford, who had become vice-president after Spiro Agnew's resignation, was unable to establish his legitimacy as president during the two years he held the office. His pardon of Nixon a month after becoming president hurt his credibility as a political leader. Moreover, Ford was a less activist executive than Nixon, preferring a more conservative laissez-faire approach that emphasized voluntary action by the private sector. Ford's hostility to federal initiatives often put him at odds with the Democrats, who, in the wake of Watergate, increased their majorities in both houses of Congress in the 1974 elections.

Ford's biggest problem as president was the economy, which was reeling from inflation set in motion by the Vietnam War and worsened by rising OPEC prices and the growing trade deficit. The 1974 inflation rate soared to almost 12 percent. In an attempt to curtail prices, the Federal Reserve Board tightened the money supply and drove up interest rates. Ford's voluntary program to "Whip Inflation Now," complete with much-mocked "WIN" buttons, was ineffective. The following year the economy entered its deepest downturn since the Great Depression. Production declined more than 10 percent, and nearly 9 percent of the work force was unemployed. The 1975 recession temporarily reduced inflation to less than 5 percent, but the rate soon rose again. Many of these economic problems were beyond the president's control, but Ford's failure to take more vigorous action made him appear timid and ineffective.

In foreign policy Ford was equally lacking in presidential leadership. He maintained Nixon's initiatives toward détente by asking Henry Kissinger to stay on as secretary of state, a position he had held since 1973. Ford met with Soviet leaders at Vladivostok to begin hammering out the details of a hoped-for SALT II (Strategic Arms Limitation Talks) agreement, but there was little concrete progress made on arms control. Ford and Kissinger also continued Nixon's policy of increasing American support for the shah of Iran, failing to notice that the shah's policy of rapid modernization was provoking bitter opposition and antiwestern sentiment among Iran's growing Muslim fundamentalist population.

After the abuses of the Nixon era, Ford's personal style and candor were refreshing, but he failed to convey the assurance and competence needed in a time of mounting economic and international problems. "Gerald Ford is an awfully nice man who isn't up to the presidency," *The New Republic* concluded, and the voters agreed.

Jimmy Carter: The Outsider as President

Only in the skewed political atmosphere of post-Watergate America could the Democrats have chosen their 1976 nominee, James E. Carter, Jr. "Jimmy Who?" the media scoffed at first about this engineer and former entrepreneur in agricultural commodities from Plains, Georgia, popularly portrayed as a peanut farmer. But they soon changed their tune as Carter won key primaries, giving his candidacy momentum and credibility. Carter played up his role as a Washington outsider (his previous political experience had been as governor of Georgia and before that as a state senator) and pledged to restore morality to government. "I will never lie to you," he piously told voters.

The 1976 presidential campaign was one of the blandest in years. On the Republican side President Ford staved off a conservative challenge from Governor Ronald Reagan of California; then he dumped his moderate vice-president, Nelson Rockefeller, in favor of the more conservative Senator Robert J. Dole of Kansas. Carter chose as his running mate Senator Walter F. Mondale of Minnesota, who had ties to the traditional Democratic constituencies of labor, liberals, blacks, and big-city machines. Avoiding issues and controversy, Carter won the election with 50 percent of the popular vote to Ford's 48 percent.

Carter immediately tried to set a different tone for his administration. On Inauguration Day he renounced formal wear in favor of a business suit; instead of riding in a limousine, he and his wife, Rosalynn, walked from the Capitol to the White House. Throughout his term he relied heavily on symbolic gestures—dressing in an informal cardigan sweater for fireside chats to the nation, carrying his own luggage on and off planes, holding town meetings, and staying in the homes of ordinary citizens. Carter's homespun approach soon wore thin as people looked for substance behind the symbols. "If the Carter administration were a television show," the columnist Russell Baker quipped, "it would have been canceled months ago."

Domestic Leadership. Part preacher, part technocrat (he had served on a nuclear submarine in the early 1950s), Carter failed to develop an effective style of domestic leadership, a task made more difficult by the post-Watergate climate of skepticism and apathy. His campaign as an outsider had distanced him from traditional sources of power in Washington, and he did little to heal the breach. Well into the term Carter's chief domestic aide, Hamilton Jordan, had never introduced himself to Thomas ("Tip") O'Neill, the Speaker of the House of Representatives and the most powerful Democrat on Capitol Hill. Shying away from established Democratic leaders, Carter turned to advisers and friends who had worked with him in Georgia, none of whom had national experience. When his budget director, Bert Lance, was questioned about financial irregularities at his Atlanta bank, the case undercut Carter's pledges to restore integrity and morality to the government.

Inflation was Carter's major domestic challenge. When he took office, the nation was still recovering from the severe 1975–1976 recession. To speed the recovery Carter called for increased government spending and lower taxes. When those actions provoked renewed inflation, he reversed himself, calling for spending cuts and a delay in the tax reductions. This zigzag fiscal policy eroded both business and consumer confidence. Unemployment hovered between 6 and 7 percent, and inflation rose from 6.5 percent in 1977 to 13.4 percent in 1980. As the Federal Reserve Board raised rates to counter inflation, interest rates briefly topped 20 percent in 1980, a historic high. A deep recession finally broke the inflationary spiral in 1982, a year after Carter left office.

The domestic initiatives of the Carter administration expanded the federal bureaucracy in some cases while limiting its reach in others. Carter created the separate cabinet-level departments of energy and education and approved new environmental protection measures such as the Superfund and new park and forest lands in Alaska. But continuing a trend begun by President Nixon, Carter also tried to reduce the scope of federal activities. He reformed the civil service system to streamline the federal bureaucracy and presided over the deregulation of the airline, trucking, and railroad industries. With deregulation, federal price controls on passenger fares and freight charges were eliminated in the belief that free market competition would encourage lower prices. Prices often did drop, but the resulting cutthroat competition drove many firms out of business and encouraged corporate consolidation. Carter also unsuccessfully supported gradual decontrol of oil and natural gas prices as a spur to domestic production and conservation.

Overall, however, Carter's attempt to provide leadership during the energy crisis failed. He called efforts for energy conservation "the moral equivalent of war" (borrowing a phrase from the nineteenth-century philosopher William James). The media, unable to find the specifics, reduced the phrase to "MEOW." In early 1979 a revolution in Iran spurred higher oil prices, and gas lines again reminded Americans of their dependence on foreign oil. That summer Carter's approval rating dropped to 26 percent, lower than Richard Nixon's at the height of the Watergate scandal.

Foreign Policy and Diplomacy. Jimmy Carter's commitment to human rights was the centerpiece of his new direction in foreign affairs. He criticized the suppression of dissent in the Soviet Union—especially as it affected the right of Jewish citizens to emigrate—and withdrew economic and military aid from Argentina, Uruguay, Ethiopia, and other noncommunist countries that violated human rights. He also established an Office of Human Rights within the State Department. But he could not change the internal policies of longtime U.S. allies and serious human rights violators such as the Philippines, South Korea, and South Africa. He did, however, raise the profile of human rights as a moral issue, one that future administrations would have to address.

In Latin America, Carter's most important contribution was the resolution of the lingering dispute over control of the Panama Canal. In a treaty signed on September 7, 1977, the United States agreed to turn over control of the canal to Panama on December 31, 1999. In return, the United States retained the right to send its ships through the canal in case of war, even though the canal itself would be declared neutral territory. Despite conservatives' outcry that the United States was giving away more than it got, the Senate narrowly approved the treaty.

President Carter achieved his most stunning success in the Middle East. Relations between Egypt and Israel had remained tense since the 1973 Yom Kippur War. In November 1975 Israel's prime minister, Menachem Begin, moved to break the ice by inviting the Egyptian president, Anwar Sadat, to Israel to discuss the possibility of peace. Sadat came in 1977, but the talks stalled. President Carter broke the stalemate in 1978 by inviting Begin and Sadat to Camp David, the presidential retreat in the Maryland mountains. Two weeks of discussions and Carter's promise of significant additional foreign aid to Egypt persuaded Sadat and Begin to agree on a "framework for peace." The framework included Israel's return of the Sinai peninsula, which it had occupied since 1967; the transfer of Sinai territory took place from 1979 to 1982.

Carter had campaigned to free the United States from its "inordinate fear of Communism," but relations with the Soviet Union soon became tense, largely because of problems surrounding the SALT II arms limitation talks. By the time Carter met the Soviet leader Leonid Brezhnev in Vienna in July 1979 to sign the accords, the president had ordered the construction of a new category of ballistic missiles (Pershing II) and the Soviets had gone ahead with new SS-20 missiles. The SALT II treaty of 1979, which did not cover the new

A Framework for Peace
President Jimmy Carter's greatest foreign policy achievement was the personal diplomacy that he exerted to persuade President Anwar Sadat of Egypt (left) and Prime Minister Menachem Begin of Israel (right) to sign a peace treaty in 1978.

systems, was therefore behind the current technology and could do little to stop the escalating arms race.

In December 1979 hopes for Senate ratification of the arms control treaty were dashed by the Soviet Union's invasion of Afghanistan. Carter called this the most serious threat to world peace since World War II, largely because he feared that the Soviet move was a strategic step toward the rich Middle Eastern oil supplies. In retaliation, the United States curtailed grain sales to the U.S.S.R. and boycotted the 1980 summer Olympic games in Moscow. (The Soviets returned the gesture by boycotting the 1984 summer games in Los Angeles.) When Carter left office in 1981, relations with the Soviet Union were worse than they had been when he came in.

The Iranian Hostage Crisis. The most serious foreign policy problem of the Carter administration occurred in Iran. Ever since the CIA had helped install Muhammad Reza Pahlavi on the throne in 1953, the United States had counted on his regime to be a faithful ally in the troubled Middle East. The shah was a major customer for American arms, using "petrodollars" from the sale of oil to the United States to purchase close to $20 billion worth of weapons between 1972 and 1979. President Carter had visited Iran in late 1977 and declared it "an island of stability in one of the more troubled areas of the world." With this personal endorsement, the human rights advocate Carter overlooked the repressive

tactics of Iran's CIA-trained secret police, SAVAK. For the Carter administration, as it was for the previous cold war policy makers, access to oil reserves and support for the shah's consistently anticommunist stance outweighed all other considerations.

Early in 1979 a revolution led by a fundamentalist Muslim leader, the Ayatollah Ruhollah Khomeini, overthrew the shah's government and drove him into exile. The United States had ignored warning signals that the shah's efforts to westernize Iran had offended fundamentalist Islamic leaders; the CIA had also downplayed the extent to which hatred of the United States had helped coalesce opposition to the shah. Once the mullahs (religious leaders) were in power, the United States was unsure how to deal with the new Iranian officials, who denounced the Soviet Union and the United States with equal ferocity.

In late October 1979 the Carter administration made a controversial decision to admit the deposed shah, who was suffering from incurable cancer, into the United States for medical treatment. Iran's new leaders had warned that such an action would provoke retaliation, but Henry Kissinger and other foreign policy leaders argued that the United States owed it to the shah both for humanitarian reasons and in return for his years of support for American policy. In response, on November 4, 1979, fundamentalist Muslim students under Khomeini's direction seized the U.S. embassy in Teheran, taking American hostages in a flagrant violation of the principle of diplomatic immunity. After the release of nineteen hostages, primarily women, black marines, and those

American Hostages in Iran
Images of blindfolded, handcuffed American hostages seized by Iranian militants at the American embassy in Teheran in November 1979 shocked the nation and created a foreign policy crisis that eventually cost Jimmy Carter the presidency.

with serious illnesses, fifty-two remained in captivity. The hostage takers demanded that the shah be returned to Iran for trial and punishment, but the United States refused. President Carter suspended arms sales to Iran, froze Iranian assets in American banks, and threatened to deport Iranian students in the United States, but no more hostages were released.

For the next fourteen months the Iranian hostage crisis paralyzed the presidency of Jimmy Carter. Night after night humiliating pictures of blindfolded hostages appeared on television newscasts. (Media-conscious Iranian students printed their anti-American placards in English.) The late-night television news program "Nightline," featuring the journalist Ted Koppel, originated as "America Held Hostage," a nightly update on the news from Iran that provided an unexpected way for ABC to compete with Johnny Carson's "Tonight Show."

The extensive media coverage and Carter's insistence that the safe return of the hostages was his top priority enhanced their value to their captors. But amid mounting calls for strong American action Carter could do little to win their release until the Iranian government was willing to negotiate. An attempt to mount a military rescue of the hostages failed miserably in April 1980, six months into the crisis, because of helicopter equipment failures in the desert. Secretary of State Cyrus Vance, who had not been informed about the rescue attempt, resigned in protest, claiming that it had further endangered the lives of the hostages. The abortive rescue mission reinforced the view of Carter as bumbling and ineffective.

The White House took on an embattled tone. President Carter decided not to campaign in the presidential primary elections that were under way in 1980, claiming that he wanted to devote all his energy to the safe return of the hostages. This "above politics" stance helped Carter beat back a challenge from Senator Edward Kennedy of Massachusetts for the Democratic nomination but worked against him during the general presidential campaign.

The Election of 1980

With Carter embroiled in the hostage crisis, the Republicans gained momentum and nominated a former California governor, Ronald Reagan. Born in Tampico, Illinois, Reagan won a modest reputation as a Hollywood actor in the late 1930s and early 1940s. After World War II he served as president of the Screen Actors Guild and was deeply affected by the anticommunist crusade in Hollywood. He testified before the House Un-American Activities Committee in 1947 and cooperated with studio owners and the FBI in blacklisting alleged Communists from the film industry. His political philosophy shifted from New Deal Democrat to conservative Republican, and in 1954 he began to work as a corporate spokesman on television for General Electric. After endorsing Barry Goldwater in 1964, Reagan decided to enter politics. Following his two terms as governor of California from 1967 to 1975, Reagan made a bid for the presidency but lost the nomination to Gerald Ford. During the 1980 primaries he handily dispatched his opponents, including former U.N. ambassador and CIA director George Bush, whom he then chose as his running mate.

In the final months of the campaign, Carter took on an embattled and defensive tone while Reagan remained upbeat and decisive. Reagan continually harped on the hostage stalemate, calling the Iranians "barbarians" and "common criminals" and hinting that he would take strong action to win the hostages' return. More important, Reagan effectively appealed to the politics of resentment that flourished during the lean years of the 1970s. In a televised debate between the candidates, Reagan emphasized the economic plight of working- and middle-class Americans when he posed the rhetorical question, "Are you better off today than you were four years ago?" Battered by inflation, unemployment, and income stagnation, many viewers answered no.

In the general election in November, Reagan and Bush won handily with 51 percent of the popular vote to Carter's 41 percent (see Map 32.3). The Republican landslide also gave that party control of the Senate for the first time since 1954, although the Democrats maintained their hold on the House. Voter turnout, however, was at its lowest level since the 1920s; only 53 percent of those eligible went to the polls, and many poor and working-class voters stayed away. Nevertheless, the election confirmed the growing power of the Republican party since Richard Nixon's victory in 1968, and Reagan's more hard-line conservatism helped push the party to the right.

One key to the Republican resurgence of the 1970s was money. As the party of the wealthy and the business community, Republicans had access to financial resources that far exceeded those available to the Democrats, whose main support had traditionally come from organized labor. The political action committees that had proliferated under the Fair Campaign Practices Act of 1974 collected large sums for both parties, but particularly for the Republicans. The GOP's financial superiority enabled it to make sophisticated and effective use of television and direct mail to reach voters directly.

Another key was a realignment of the electorate. The core of the Republican party that elected Ronald Reagan remained the upper-middle-class white Protestant voters who supported balanced budgets, disliked government activism, feared crime and communism, and believed in a strong national defense. Those values had been the essence of postwar conservatism. Now new groups gravitated toward the Republican vision, often for reasons of economic self-interest: southern whites disaffected by big government and black civil

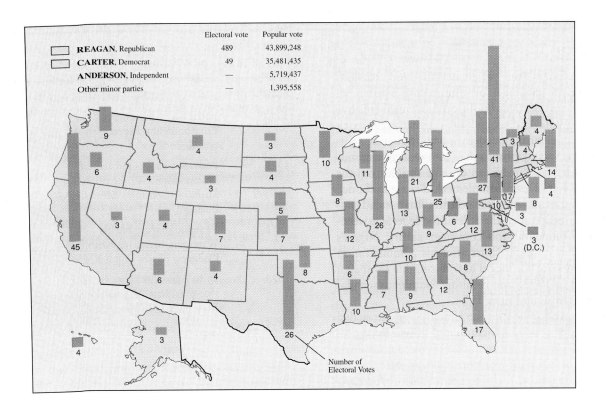

MAP 32.3

The Election of 1980

Ronald Reagan defeated the Democratic incumbent, Jimmy Carter, winning all but five states and the District of Columbia. Winning 51 percent of the popular vote, Reagan cut deeply into the traditional Democratic coalition by wooing many southern whites, urban ethnics, and blue-collar workers. Republicans also won control of the Senate for the first time since 1954.

rights gains; urban ethnics who had moved to the suburbs; blue-collar workers, especially Catholics; young voters who identified themselves as conservatives; and voters in the West, a region traditionally more conservative than the East and the Midwest. With the wooing of these "Reagan Democrats," the Republican party made deep inroads into Democratic territory, eroding that party's traditional coalition of southerners, blacks, laborers, and urban ethnics.

Perhaps the most significant constituency energizing the Republican party was the New Right, whose emphasis on traditional values and fundamentalist Christian morality dovetailed well with conservative Republican ideology. In 1980 its concerns formed the basis for the party's platform, which called for a constitutional ban on abortion, voluntary prayer in the public schools, and a mandatory death penalty for certain crimes. The Republican party also demanded an end to court-mandated busing and, for the first time in forty years, opposed the Equal Rights Amendment. A key factor in the 1980 election, the emergence of the New Right contributed to the conservative rebirth of the Republican party under Ronald Reagan.

At the exact moment when Carter turned over the presidency to Reagan on January 20, 1981, the Iranian government released the American hostages after 444 days of captivity. The hostages returned home to an ecstatic patriotic welcome, a reflection of American frustration over their long ordeal. While most Americans continued to maintain that "We're Number One," the hostage crisis in Iran came to symbolize the loss of America's power to control world affairs. Its psychological impact was magnified because it came at the end of the decade that had witnessed Watergate, the American defeat in Vietnam, and the OPEC embargo. To a great extent this decline in influence was magnified by the unusual predominance the United States had enjoyed after World War II, an advantage that could not realistically have been expected to last forever. The return to economic and political power of Japan and Western Europe, the control of vital oil resources by Middle Eastern countries, and the industrialization of some Third World nations had widened the cast of international actors. Still, many Americans were unable to accept anything less than the economic and political supremacy of the postwar years. Ronald Reagan rode their frustrations to victory in 1980.

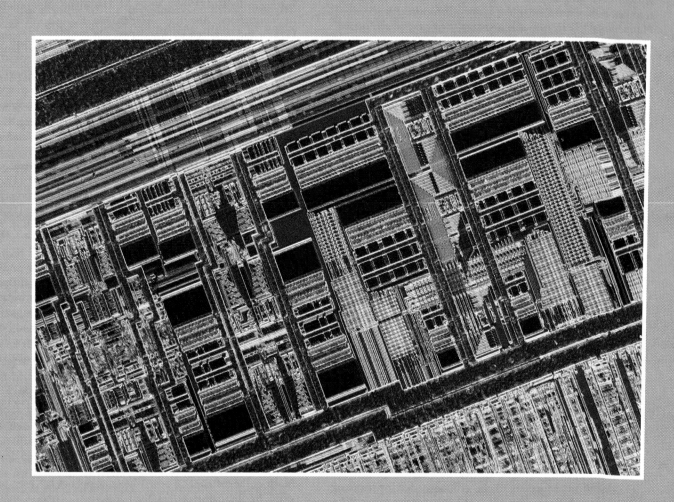

The Soul of the Machine

This magnification of a Pentium computer chip could almost be mistaken for an aerial view of a small town surrounded by well-tended parks and gardens.

CHAPTER 33

A New Domestic and World Order

1981 to the Present

★　　　★　　　★

In the 1920s Americans were drawn into a national web of shared experience. In the 1980s and 1990s globalization linked Americans with the rest of the world. Political choices made in Washington had international economic implications. But decisions made in Tokyo, Beijing, Bonn, and Brussels were becoming just as important, affecting the kinds of consumer products Americans could buy, interest rates, and even whether American workers kept their jobs. As the "old world order"—U.S. economic dominance and cold war rivalry—came to an end in the 1980s and 1990s, America began to share power and influence with other nations in an interconnected global economy.

Paradoxically, with the collapse of the Soviet Union in 1991, the United States achieved military dominance as the world's only remaining superpower. For forty-five years the Cold War had shaped American foreign and domestic policy. The "new world order" that would replace the old political relationships among nations was still emerging, but it was clear that the international community continued to seek American leadership on issues of peace and war.

As the United States struggled to redefine its role in the world, a crucial debate raged at home over the role of the state. The rise of the state, one of the most important developments in twentieth-century American history, was slowed and even partially reversed by Ronald Reagan's election in 1980 and the election of a Republican Congress in 1994. New Deal liberalism and an activist federal government were in retreat. In his 1996 State of the Union address, President Clinton acknowledged this new domestic order by declaring, "The era of big government is over." As the United States approached a new century in which the economic challenges of global competition would replace the military challenges of the Cold War, Americans were asking basic questions about the role of government in national life.

The Reagan Presidency, 1981–1989

Ronald Reagan's overwhelming victory in the 1980 election reflected the new electoral clout of the Sun Belt, a region traditionally more conservative than the Northeast or Midwest (see Map 33.1). Reagan seized the chance to redefine the nation's priorities. Since the New Deal programs of the 1930s, Americans had generally assumed that the nation's social and economic problems could best be solved by federal action. The election of Ronald Reagan called into question almost half a century of activism. "Government is not the solution to our problem," he declared. "Government is the problem." During his tenure in office only the defense budget continued to grow dramatically as part of a massive military buildup.

The Reagan Style

When the sixty-nine-year-old Ronald Wilson Reagan took office in January 1981, he was the oldest man ever to serve as president. (He was actually six years older than John F. Kennedy would have been if Kennedy had lived.) He showed his remarkable physical stamina just months into office when he survived an assassination attempt outside a Washington, D.C., hotel. Just as robust was his personal popularity, which remained comparatively high throughout his two terms. He became known as the "Great Communicator" because of his ability to establish a rapport with the American people through the medium of television.

During his long acting career and eight years as governor of California, Reagan had developed a somewhat removed leadership style. Once, when asked what kind of governor he would be, he replied, "I don't know, I've never played a governor." Many observers found him better at generalizations and encouragement than at details: "We have a great task ahead of us," Reagan would say, but he would never state what that task was. Recalled Donald Regan, who was named secretary of the Treasury after one brief phone conversation, "From the first day to the last at Treasury, I was flying by the seat of my pants. The President never told me . . . what he wanted to accomplish in the field of economics."

To maintain his hands-off style of governing, Reagan depended on the support and advice of his ap-

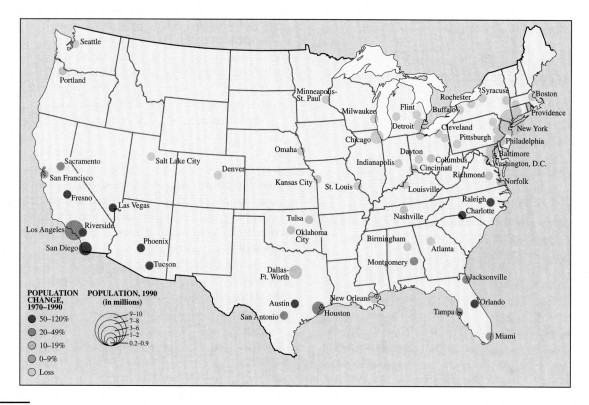

MAP 33.1

The Growth of the Sun Belt, 1970–1990

The Sun Belt states of the South and the West were key to the Republican resurgence in the 1980s. Whereas older industrial cities such as New York, Chicago, Philadelphia, and Detroit lost population, newer metropolises—Phoenix, Houston, and San Diego—grew spectacularly.

The Great Communicator
Ronald Reagan felt totally at home in front of the camera, trading stories and one-liners with audiences and the press. Commentator Gary Wills observed, "Reagan runs continuously in everyone's home movies of the mind. . . . He is, in the strictest sense, what Hollywood promoters used to call 'fabulous'."

pointees. Among his closest advisers were Chief of Staff James Baker, presidential counselors Edwin Meese and Michael Deaver, and Regan, who became chief of staff in 1985 when Baker moved to the Treasury. Reagan also relied heavily on his wife, Nancy, who was fiercely protective of both his image and his schedule, even to the point of consulting an astrologer before planning major White House events.

Reaganomics

Reagan and his economic team's first priority was to reshape the nation's fiscal and tax policies. The term *Reaganomics* came to stand for the tax cuts and domestic budget reductions enacted in 1981 and 1982 and the controversial *supply-side* economic theory that lay behind them. According to this theory, high taxes siphoned capital that would otherwise be invested to stimulate economic growth. Tax cuts would give businesses and individuals more money to invest, investments would cause the economy to expand, and total

tax revenues would be greater—despite the lower tax rates. Government expenditures would be trimmed by shrinking government benefits, especially entitlement programs such as welfare that had begun during the New Deal. And the federal budget deficit would go down. That, at least, was the theory. Critics charged that conservative Republicans deliberately cut taxes to force reductions in federal funding for the social programs that they abhorred.

The first part of this economic policy—tax cuts—was enacted in the Economic Recovery Tax Act of 1981, arguably the most significant legislation of the Reagan years. Based on a proposal by Senator William Roth of Delaware and Representative Jack Kemp of New York, this across-the-board tax cut reduced basic personal income tax rates 25 percent over three years. It also introduced the indexation of tax brackets, which kept tax rates constant when incomes rose solely because of inflation. According to the budget director, David Stockman, the tax cut was supposed to be linked with large cutbacks in expenditures, especially in human services. Congressional resistance kept programs such as Social Security and Medicare intact, but more than half of Reagan's proposed cuts were enacted, including cuts in Food Stamps, unemployment compensation, and welfare programs such as Aid to Families with Dependent Children (AFDC).

All the money saved—and far more—was plowed into a $1.2 trillion, five-year defense buildup orchestrated by the president and Defense Secretary Caspar Weinberger. This huge increase fulfilled Reagan's campaign pledge to "make America Number One again" militarily. The B-1 bomber, which Carter had canceled, was resurrected, and the development of a new missile system, the MX, was begun. Reagan's most ambitious, and controversial, weapons plan was the 1983 Strategic Defense Initiative (SDI), popularly known as "Star Wars" from the movie of that name. SDI would be a satellite and laser shield to detect and intercept incoming missiles. Reagan supporters claimed that SDI would render nuclear war obsolete, but scientists doubted its feasibility.

Another basic tenet of Reaganomics was that many federal regulations were unnecessary and impeded productivity because of the high cost of compliance. Thus, the administration moved to abolish or reduce federal regulations affecting the workplace, health care, consumer protection, and the environment. Much of the responsibility, and the cost, of those activities was transferred to the states.

Meanwhile, the Federal Reserve Board used monetary policy to combat inflation, which had been high since the mid–1970s. By raising the interest rate for corporate borrowers, the Federal Reserve reduced inflation from 12.4 percent in 1980 to 4 percent in 1982. But tightening the money supply in that way also reduced business investment, contributing to a relatively brief

but severe recession in 1981–1982. The economy began growing again early in 1983. For the rest of the decade inflation stayed low, aided by a worldwide drop in energy costs, and the Reagan administration presided over the longest peacetime economic expansion in American history. But this economic growth in the 1980s was unexceptional, with the gross national product growing at about 2.5 percent a year (below the average of 2.8 percent in the 1970s) and productivity growth averaging only a little over 1 percent a year.

If all had gone according to the administration's plan, the budget should have been balanced by 1984, but that did not happen. Supply-side economics did not work as advertised, and the promised increased revenue from economic growth fell far short of expectations. Furthermore, despite what seemed like wrenching cuts in federal programs, the drop in revenues from the tax cuts was far steeper than the amount pruned from the budget, mainly because of the military buildup. Federal deficits began to balloon alarmingly.

Foreign Relations

Détente had collapsed late in the Carter administration after the Soviet Union's invasion of Afghanistan. Reagan entered the presidency with a confrontational approach toward the Soviet Union, including a strong commitment to stopping communist expansion in developing nations. Giving voice to the beliefs of Republican hard-liners, Reagan articulated some of the harshest anti-Soviet rhetoric since the 1950s, calling the Soviet Union an "evil empire."

The administration reserved its most concerted attention for Central America. Halting what was seen as the spread of communism in that region became practically an obsession. In El Salvador it supported a repressive right-wing regime that was fighting against leftists. In 1983 Reagan ordered U.S. Marines to invade the tiny Caribbean island of Grenada, claiming that its Cuban-supported communist regime posed a threat to other states in the region.

Reagan's top priority, however, was to overthrow the Sandinista government in Nicaragua. The Sandinistas were former guerrillas who had overthrown the right-wing regime of President Anastasio Somoza in 1979. They were leftists but not communists, although they were friendly with Marxist leaders such as Cuba's Fidel Castro. In 1981 the United States suspended aid to Nicaragua, charging that the Sandinista government, along with Cuba and the Soviet Union, was supplying arms to the rebels in El Salvador, a charge that the Sandinistas denied. At the same time, the CIA began to provide extensive covert support to Nicaragua's opposition forces, known as the "Contras," or counterrevolutionaries. Reagan called the Contras "freedom fighters," but Congress was not convinced. In 1984 it passed the Boland Amendment, banning the CIA or any other intelligence agency from providing military support to the Contras. Thus began a tug of war between Congress and the Reagan administration that would produce the greatest crisis of Reagan's presidency.

Reagan's Second Term

The 1984 Election. In 1984 the Democrats nominated Walter Mondale, Carter's vice-president and a former Minnesota senator, to run against Ronald Reagan. A protégé of Hubert Humphrey with strong ties to labor unions, minority groups, and party leaders, Mondale epitomized the New Deal coalition. He appealed to many women voters by selecting Representative Geraldine Ferraro of New York as his running mate, the first woman on a major party ticket. Reagan campaigned on the theme "It's Morning in America," suggesting that a new day of prosperity and pride was dawning. Voters gave him a landslide victory in which he carried the entire country except Minnesota and the District of Columbia. He did especially well among young (eighteen- to twenty-one-year-old) voters, receiving 62 percent of their support.

After a string of administrations that had ended in discord (Johnson and Vietnam), disgrace (Nixon and Watergate), or frustration (Carter and Iran), many Americans responded warmly to Reagan's confident leadership. Reagan was a convincing performer, and voters believed him when he said he could solve the nation's problems. Reagan's enormous personal popularity recalled that of Dwight Eisenhower in the 1950s. Also like Eisenhower,

A First for the Nation
Geraldine Ferraro, Walter Mondale's running mate in 1984, was the first woman nominated by a major party to its national ticket. Despite her presence, a majority of women voted for Reagan in the 1984 Republican landslide.

his coattails were short: Democrats maintained control of the House and picked up two seats in the Senate; they would regain control of the Senate in 1986.

The Iran-Contra Affair. Reagan's second term was marred by a major scandal in 1986. A Beirut, Lebanon, newspaper broke the story that the administration had negotiated an arms-for-hostages deal with the revolutionary government of Iran, the same government Reagan had denounced during the 1980 hostage crisis. At the instigation of the CIA's director, William Casey, and the national security adviser, Robert McFarlane, the United States had secretly sold arms to Iran, which was locked in a costly and lengthy war with neighboring Iraq. The intent was to gain Iran's help in freeing American hostages held by pro-Iranian forces in Lebanon. (Only one hostage was released.) These arm sales generated large profits, some of which, in the most controversial aspect of what became known as the Iran-Contra affair, were diverted as military aid for the Contras in Nicaragua. The diversion was both illegal (contravening the Boland Amendment) and unconstitutional (bypassing the sole right of Congress to appropriate funds).

The arms-for-hostages deal had been discussed at the highest levels of government, but the diversion of funds to the Contras seems to have been the brainstorm of Marine Lieutenant Colonel Oliver North, who was on assignment to the National Security Council. After the American press picked up the story, North shredded hundreds of documents but missed a key memo that linked the White House to the plan. Congress investigated the mounting scandal in 1986 and 1987, but White House officials testifed that the president knew nothing about the diversion. Ronald Reagan's defense remained simple and consistent: "I don't remember."

The full story of the illegal arms operation may never be known. The scandal bore many similarities to Watergate, including the possibility that the president had acted illegally, but this time there were no significant calls for impeachment. Early in Reagan's administration, Representative Patricia Schroeder of Colorado, one of his harshest critics in Congress, had coined the phrase "Teflon presidency" to describe Reagan—bad news didn't stick; it just rolled off. Reagan weathered "Iran-Contragate," but the scandal did weaken his presidency.

The Return of Détente. His authority diminished by scandal and facing a Congress once again controlled by Democrats, Reagan proposed no bold initiatives in domestic policy in his last two years in office. Surprisingly for a man who had instigated a massive arms buildup to halt the spread of communism and had refused to meet with Soviet leaders, the greatest success of Reagan's second term was a reduction in tensions with the Soviet Union.

This shift was facilitated by the ascent to power in 1985 of Mikhail Gorbachev. In that year, Gorbachev and Reagan met in Geneva at the first superpower summit meeting since 1979. They met again the following year in Reykjavik, Iceland. In December 1987 Reagan and Gorbachev agreed at a Washington summit to eliminate all intermediate-range missiles based in Europe, the first time an existing category of weapons had been scrapped, and the most significant postwar disarmament decision since the 1972 SALT I agreement. Although a fourth summit in Moscow in April 1988 produced no further cuts in nuclear arms, the sight of the two first families attending the Bolshoi Ballet together and strolling amiably in Red Square demonstrated the new cordial relationship between the former rivals. (The incongruity of consummate cold warrior Ronald Reagan in Red Square was on a par with the sight of Richard Nixon strolling along the Great Wall of China in 1972.) When the Soviets announced soon afterward that they were withdrawing from Afghanistan, prospects for cooperation appeared to be even brighter.

Reagan Legacies

Reagan came into the presidency promising to dismantle an intrusive federal bureaucracy, reduce federal entitlement programs, give free-market forces greater scope in the economy, and stand up to the Soviet menace. Whereas he made significant progress toward some of his goals, overall the so-called Reagan Revolution proved to be more of a "Reagan revision." Reagan reordered the priorities of the national government but failed to reduce its size or scope. When he left office, government functions remained much as he had found them. Although spending for most poverty programs had been cut, Social Security and other entitlement programs remained untouched. But the spending cuts and Reagan's antigovernment rhetoric had changed the terms of political debate and laid the foundation for the Republican landslide in 1994.

One of Reagan's most significant legacies was his conservative judicial appointments, the area where the New Right had the greatest impact on his administration. In 1981 Reagan nominated Sandra Day O'Connor to the Supreme Court, the first woman ever to serve; he later appointed two other justices, Antonin Scalia and Anthony Kennedy, who were far more conservative than the moderate O'Connor. Justice William Rehnquist, a noted conservative who had been appointed by Nixon, was elevated to chief justice in 1986. The former Supreme Court justice William Brennan used to tell his clerks, "Five votes can do anything around here," and under Rehnquist's leadership the Court, often by a 5–4 margin, chipped away at the Warren Court's legacy in areas such as individual liberties, affirmative action, and the rights of criminal defendants.

Another Barrier Falls

In 1981 Sandra Day O'Connor (shown here with Chief Justice Warren Burger) became the first woman appointed to the Supreme Court. In 1993 she was joined by Ruth Bader Ginsburg.

Ironically, for a president who had promised to balance the budget by 1984, Reagan's most enduring legacy was the national debt, which tripled during his two terms from the combined effects of vastly increased military spending, substantial tax reductions for high-income taxpayers, and Congress's refusal to approve the deep cuts in domestic programs that Reagan requested (see Figure 33.1). There had been federal deficits before, but never on this scale. In 1989 the national debt stood at $2.8 trillion, more than $11,000 for every American citizen. Interest payments on the borrowed money, $216 billion per year by 1988, were the fastest-growing item in the federal budget.

Trade with other nations was also running at an annual deficit that reached $171 billion in 1987. Exports had been falling since the 1970s as American products encountered increasing competition in world markets. The high exchange rate for dollars in the early 1980s made U.S. goods more expensive for foreign buyers whereas imports became more affordable for Americans. The budget and trade deficits contributed to a major shift in 1985: for the first time since 1915 the United States was a debtor, not a creditor, nation. Since then, with phenomenal speed, the United States has accumulated the world's largest foreign debt.

It was difficult for the political system to address the annual budget deficits and their ramifications. Members of Congress were unwilling to cut programs that their

FIGURE 33.1

The Escalating Federal Debt, 1939–1994

The federal debt, which soared during World War II, remained fairly stable until the huge annual deficits of the 1980s. Deficits still remained high in the 1990s but political pressure to balance the budget promised reductions in the national debt.

Source: U.S. Statistical Abstract, 1995.

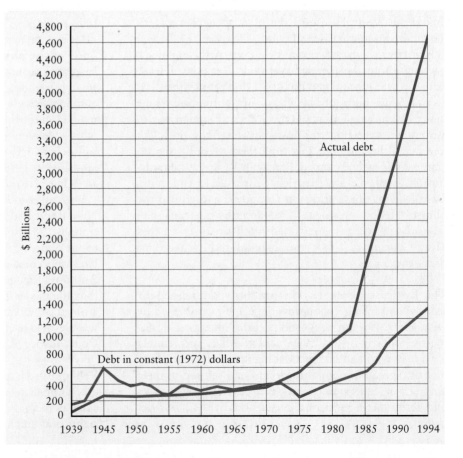

constituents depended on for services or jobs, and few were willing to recommend new taxes. In 1985 Congress passed the Gramm-Rudman Balanced Budget and Emergency Deficit Reduction Control Act, which was intended to achieve a balanced budget by 1991 by mandating specific cuts that would be instituted automatically if deficit reduction targets were not met. (The cuts were never implemented.) The annual deficit peaked at $221 billion in 1986 and then dropped slightly before leveling off, but the damage had been done. The national debt, along with the interest needed to service it, will continue to be a drag on the nation's economy and social fabric well into the twenty-first century.

The Bush Presidency and the End of the Cold War, 1989–1993

George Herbert Walker Bush had been a loyal vice-president, but he did not share all of Reagan's conservative views. In fact, many Americans wondered if he had any ideology at all. The debt inherited from the Reagan years, along with Bush's preference for foreign affairs, kept him from articulating a clear domestic agenda. The end of the Cold War removed the Soviet Union as a credible threat, but new post–cold war challenges quickly appeared. During the Persian Gulf crisis in 1990 Bush called for a "new world order . . . in which nations recognize the shared responsibility for freedom and injustice." As events abroad progressed dramatically, especially the collapse of the Soviet Union in 1991, the United States grappled with the implications of this new world order.

The Bush Administration

The 1988 Election. Bush won the Republican nomination by beating back challenges from the Senate minority leader Robert Dole, the television evangelist Pat Robertson, and the tax-cutting representative Jack Kemp. He chose a young conservative Indiana senator, Dan Quayle, for vice-president. Even many Republicans questioned Quayle's qualifications to assume the duties of the president, while Democrats, noting his hawkish views on defense, charged him with hypocrisy for having avoided service in Vietnam by joining the Indiana National Guard.

The Democratic primaries became a contest between Governor Michael Dukakis of Massachusetts and the charismatic civil rights leader Jesse Jackson, whose populist Rainbow Coalition embraced the diversity of Democratic constituencies. Dukakis, a somewhat bland figure known for a technocratic approach to state government, won the nomination. For his vice-president, he passed over Jackson in favor of Senator Lloyd Bentsen of Texas.

The 1988 campaign had a harsh cast to it, with negative commercials and brief televised *sound bites* replacing discussion of the issues. The sound bite "Read My Lips: No New Taxes" from Bush's acceptance speech at the Republican convention became that party's campaign mantra. A television ad criticizing Massachusetts' prison furlough program pandered to racist fears by including a mug shot of Willie Horton, a black convicted murderer who had committed another murder while on parole. Forced on the defensive, Dukakis failed to mount an effective campaign. Bush carried thirty-eight states, winning the popular vote 53.4 percent to 45.6 percent. Only 50 percent of eligible voters went to the polls.

Domestic and Economic Policy. In his campaign Bush had promised to preside over a "kinder, gentler administration" and, without giving specifics, announced his intention to go down in history as the education and environment president. He made good on the first part by convening the meeting of state governors that launched the Goals 2000 initiative to write national standards for public schools. His environmental policy was less substantial. Bush's appointments to the Environmental Protection Agency, such as William Ruckelshaus as its head, were more moderate than the conservative ideologues named by Reagan, but Bush only reluctantly attended the 1992 Earth Summit in Rio de Janeiro to sign the treaty on global warming.

For the most part Bush's domestic policy was devoted to coping with the failures and the shortcomings of his predecessor's economic policies, especially the budget deficit. In his 1990 message to Congress, the budget director, Richard Darman, compared the federal budget to the Cookie Monster on "Sesame Street" because of its "excessive tendencies towards consumption." The 1985 Gramm-Rudman Act had mandated automatic cuts if budget targets were not met in 1991. Facing the prospect of a halt to nonessential government services and layoffs of thousands of government employees, Congress struggled to produce a deficit-reduction plan. The resulting bipartisan compromise combined cuts in spending with increased taxes and fees in recognition of the fact that the supply-side theory that lower taxes would produce higher revenues had not worked. Bush had been forced by inevitable circumstances to break his "no new taxes" campaign promise. Bush's acceptance of the quantitatively largest tax increase in history earned him the undying enmity of Republican conservatives, who saw it as a betrayal of Reaganomics, and would dramatically hurt his chances for reelection in 1992.

The federal government can run up deficits, but state and local governments cannot. Under Reagan's

new federalism, states and localities had been forced to take over some federal programs entirely and cope with cuts in federal grants for many other programs, including housing, education, transportation, public works, and social services. Federal-state programs such as Medicaid, whose costs soared in the 1970s and 1980s as a result of inflation and higher demand, accounted for increasingly large parts of state budgets, as did spending for welfare, education, and prisons. State and local governments could balance their budgets only by finding new sources of revenue (thus risking taxpayer revolts) or by reducing spending and services. Fiscal conditions were especially bad in the Northeast, but California and several midwestern states also faced severe shortfalls.

A recession that began in 1990 further eroded state and local tax revenues. Poverty increased sharply, and incomes declined. In 1991 unemployment approached 7 percent nationwide; state and local governments laid off workers to save money even as they faced greater demands for social services and unemployment compensation. Industrial and white-collar layoffs spread, and in many American families someone had already lost a job or feared that it might happen soon. Recovery was slowed by the massive federal debt, overburdened state and local governments, and decreasing consumer confidence.

The Savings and Loan Crisis. Yet another drag on the economy was the collapse of the savings and loan industry. The scandal had its roots in decisions made during the Reagan administration, but its full impact was felt only after Bush took office.

Savings and loan associations (S & L's), also called "thrifts," invested depositors' savings in home mortgages. Since 1934 deposits in S & L's had been insured by the Federal Savings and Loan Insurance Corporation (FSLIC). After S & L's complained in 1982 that high inflation and soaring interest rates were reducing their profits, Reagan's deregulation program permitted them to invest in commercial real estate and businesses. Such investments were more risky than home mortgages, and lack of supervision from Washington encouraged many speculative deals and some fraudulent ones.

The real-estate market had boomed for most of the 1980s, and so the loans and investments were profitable. But when construction and the oil boom in the Southwest slowed and the stock market tumbled sharply in 1987, savings and loan associations' losses mounted, and the value of their assets plummeted. Some S & L's were taken over by commercial banks, but many simply went bankrupt, forcing the federal government to make good its guarantee to depositors. To recoup some of the massive losses, the Bush administration set up a temporary agency in 1989 to sell the remaining assets, primarily defaulted real estate. It took the Resolution Trust Corporation six years to clear up the mess, at a total cost to American taxpayers of $150 billion.

Supreme Court Conservatism. During the Bush administration the Supreme Court continued to move away from liberal activism toward a more conservative stance. The shift was felt especially in regard to the issue of abortion. The 1989 *Webster v. Reproductive Health Services* decision permitted states to restrict abortion, and the next year, in *Rust v. Sullivan*, the Court upheld a federal regulation that barred personnel at federally funded health clinics from discussing abortion with their clients. In 1992, in *Planned Parenthood v. Casey*, a 5–4 decision upheld a Pennsylvania law mandating a twenty-four-hour waiting period and informed consent before an abortion could be performed. Yet the Court also reaffirmed what it called the "essential holding" of *Roe v. Wade*: women have a constitutional right to abortion.

In 1990 David Souter, a little known federal judge from New Hampshire who appealed to Bush because he had not taken a stand on abortion, easily won confirmation to the Supreme Court. But the next year a major controversy erupted over Bush's nomination of Clarence Thomas, a black conservative with little judicial experi-

A Woman of Conscience
Accusations by University of Oklahoma professor Anita Hill that Supreme Court nominee Clarence Thomas had sexually harassed her sparked fierce political debate. Many felt that if there had been more women in the Senate, Professor Hill's charges would have been treated more seriously. In fact, women's representation did increase after the 1992 election to six women in the Senate and forty-seven in the House of Representatives.

ence. Just as Thomas's confirmation hearings were drawing to a close, his former colleague Anita Hill testified publicly to what she had earlier told Senate investigators: Thomas had sexually harassed her at the Department of Education and the Equal Employment Opportunity Commission in the early 1980s. After widely watched (and widely debated) televised testimony by both Thomas and Hill before the all-male Senate Judiciary Committee, the Senate confirmed Thomas by a narrow margin. In the wake of the hearings, national polls confirmed the pervasiveness of sexual harassment on the job: four out of ten women said that they had been the object of unwanted sexual advances from men at work. Politically minded women vowed to increase their representation in Congress in the 1992 election.

The Collapse of Communism

For years American policy makers had warned about the "domino" effect of countries falling to communism. Now the domino effect was unexpectedly working in the opposite direction. In 1989 the grip of communism on Eastern Europe loosened and then let go completely in a series of mostly nonviolent "velvet revolutions." Soon the Soviet Union itself succumbed to the forces of change.

The background for those dramatic upheavals lay in the changes set in motion by the Soviet president Mikhail Gorbachev after 1985. His policies of *glasnost* (openness) and *perestroika* (economic restructuring) signaled a willingness to tolerate significant changes in the Soviet bloc and in Soviet relationships with the rest of the world. Gorbachev established a strong personal rapport with both Reagan and Bush and raised enormous expectations worldwide about the possibilities of change in the U.S.S.R. But the Soviet leader, who was always more popular outside his country than at home, found it was easier to call for the dismantling of the old system than to build something new. In addition, the desire of a number of Soviet republics to apply the lessons of Eastern Europe and gain independence threatened the very existence of the country.

On August 19, 1991, while Gorbachev was vacationing at his summer home in the Crimea, officials in his own government tried to oust him. The precipitating factor was the imminent signing of the Union Treaty, which would have given limited autonomy to the fifteen Soviet republics and increased power to the republics' recently elected leaders. The plotters—officials of the Communist party, bureaucrats and overlords of the central economy, and leaders of the internal police force and KGB—stood to lose the most from decentralization. But by August 21, the coup had failed and the grip of the Communist party over the Soviet Union was bro-

Gorbachev and Bush
The leaders of the two superpowers, shown here at a press conference during the Malta summit in December 1989, developed a warm personal relationship. Some critics later felt that Bush delayed reacting to changes in the Soviet Union out of loyalty to his friend.

ken. The Baltic republics of Latvia, Estonia, and Lithuania declared their independence and soon gained diplomatic recognition from the United States and the rest of the world. In December the Union of Soviet Socialist Republics formally dissolved itself to make way for the eleven-member Commonwealth of Independent States (CIS). The charismatic reform leader Boris Yeltsin remained as president of the largest and most populous republic, Russia; Gorbachev was out of a job.

In 1956 Nikita Khruschev had told the United States, "We will bury you," but now the tombstone read, "The Soviet Union, 1917–1991." For more than forty years the United States had been locked in an ideological battle with its archenemy, the Soviet Union. American citizens had endured secret radiation experiments, fear of nuclear annihilation, and anticommunist witch-hunts. During the Cold War the United States spent some *$4 trillion* on nuclear weapons alone. Republicans claimed that Reagan's military buildup had caused the Soviet Union to collapse, but George Kennan—the only original architect of containment still alive—disagreed, dismissing such claims as "intrinsically silly": "Nobody—no country, no party, no person—'won' the cold war. . . . That the conflict should now be formally ended is a fit occasion for satisfaction but also for sober re-examination of the part we took in its origin and long continuation." As Kennan concluded, both sides paid a heavy price.

The director of the Central Intelligence Agency summed up the dilemma of forging a post–cold war policy: "We have slain a large dragon, but we live now

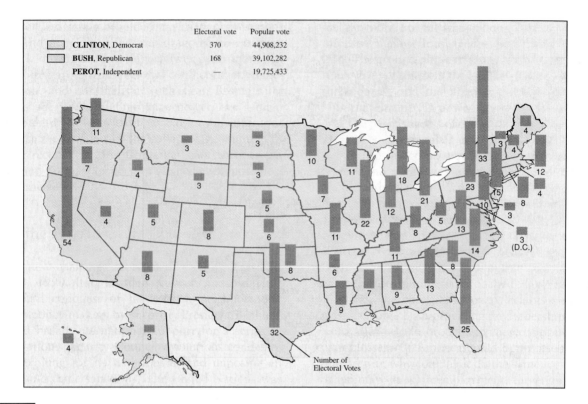

MAP 33.3

The Election of 1992

The first national election since the end of the Cold War was dominated by concern over the economy. The first-ever all-southerner Democratic ticket of Bill Clinton and Al Gore won broad support across the country, cutting into Republican strongholds in the South and West. The independent candidate, H. Ross Perot, won no electoral votes but polled an impressive 19 percent of the popular vote.

highest for an independent candidate since Theodore Roosevelt in 1912. The Democrats retained control of both houses of Congress, ending twelve years of divided government. But the narrowness of Clinton's victory and the public's perception that he did not really stand for anything did not augur well for his ability to lead the country.

An Age of Anxiety

Opinion polls in the early 1990s showed that Americans were deeply worried about the future—their own and their childrens'. Concerns about the economy topped the list; the economist Paul Krugman called the 1980s and 1990s "the age of diminished expectations." But the uncertainties involved more than the economy. Just as in the 1970s, Americans turned inward toward their own needs and interests, despite the globalization of so many aspects of modern American life.

The New Economic Order

The slow growth in productivity and the growing inequality in income distribution have been the two most salient economic trends of the past two decades. From the late nineteenth century through World War II productivity grew at an average of about 1.8 percent per year, enough to double living standards every forty years. From 1945 until 1973 productivity grew 2.8 percent annually, allowing the standard of living to double in one generation. Since 1973, however, productivity has increased less than 1 percent annually, barely enough to double the standard of living in eighty years. (Productivity began to rise a little more sharply around 1992, but it is too early to tell if this represents a long-term trend.)

Along with slowed productivity went stagnating real income (see Figure 33.2). Adjusted for inflation, the wages of the typical, or median, family basically stayed the same. In 1991 the typical family's real income was only 5 percent higher than it had been in 1973, and that increase was achieved mainly because Americans were

working more hours and because multiple members of a household were employed.

At the same time that wage stagnation was squeezing the middle class, economic inequality increased—the rich got richer, the poor got poorer, and the middle class shrank. Instead of the broadly based prosperity of the postwar years, statistics from the Congressional Budget Office showed that the richest *1 percent* of American families reaped most of the gains of Reaganomics in the 1980s. Economists debated the causes for the shift, with some stressing reduced tax rates for the wealthy and others pointing to factors such as higher returns on capital gains and the explosion of executive pay. But the trend was clear—the first significant widening of the gap since the 1920s—and it accelerated in the 1990s. In 1996 the United States was the most economically stratified industrial nation in the world.

In contrast to earlier generations, who had aspired to doing better financially than their parents, many young adults wondered if they would ever achieve even a modest middle-class life-style. This opportunity gap of potential downward mobility seemed especially acute for the 75 million Americans born between 1961 and 1981. Said an insurance administrator from Alabama born in 1965, "I think the next generation will have smaller houses, smaller cars. I cannot outdo my parents and I

don't think I'll ever be able to. We struggle to make ends meet and we're a two-income household. It shouldn't be like that."

These diminished expectations were related in part to the jobs that were available in the 1990s. Lifetime careers with a single employer were increasingly rare. More typically, the average worker could expect to make several job or career shifts over the course of her or his working life. Confirming a long-term pattern, the number of minimum wage service jobs continued to grow, while the number of union-protected manufacturing jobs kept shrinking. The discount retailer Wal-Mart is now the second largest employer in the country after General Motors.

Much of the job growth has occurred in the *contingent* work force, which includes temporary and part-time workers as well as consultants and freelancers. In 1994 more than one-fifth of the work force, almost 25 million workers, had part-time or temporary jobs. (These positions are sometimes referred to as "McJobs," a reference to jobs at fast-food outlets like McDonalds.) Contingent workers are paid far less than are full-time employees, rarely belong to unions, and often do not get job-related benefits such as health insurance, sick leave, and a paid vacation.

The farming out of work to contingent workers was related to another major employment trend of the 1980s and 1990s: *downsizing*, in which companies deliberately shed permanent workers to cut wage costs and increase profits. In the 1970s most layoffs had involved industrial and manufacturing jobs, especially in the Rust Belt (see Chapter 32), but in the 1980s and 1990s downsizing spread to middle management. For example, from 1980 to 1995 IBM shrank its work force from 400,000 to 220,000, a 45 percent decrease. Governments also scaled back, eliminating 454,000 public service jobs between 1979 and 1993. Unlike jobs lost during recessions, those jobs did not come back when the economy picked up after 1992.

The human costs of downsizing were often devastating. When John Thomas, a fifty-nine-year-old AT&T employee who had spent forty years with the company was told that his job was "not going forward," he reacted this way: "I've had to downsize people myself, and now it's happening to me. It's not pleasant. I tried to accept it with class, but I went through a lot of emotions—sadness, worry, concern. Now I have a headache." When a fifteen-person department at Chemical Bank was downsized to one worker, she sobbed for her missing co-workers and wondered why she had been spared. Since the economy continues to generate new jobs, most laid-off workers eventually find work, but often at a large pay cut in addition to their emotional scars. The few federal job retraining programs reach only a minority of displaced workers.

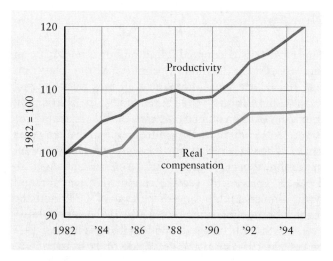

FIGURE 33.2

Productivity and Wages, 1982–1995
Usually as productivity increases, so does labor's share of national income. In the 1990s, however, workers failed to reap the rewards of the increased productivity shown here. Labor's relative loss in real compensation in turn contributed to a rise in corporate profits.

Women, Work, and Families. These economic trends put even more pressure on women to seek paid employment outside the home. In 1994, 58.8 percent of women were in the labor force (up from 38 percent in 1962), compared with 75.1 percent of men. The traditional nuclear family of employed father, homemaker wife, and children was found in less than 15 percent of U.S. households. Married working women and single or divorced working women with children continued to bear the major share of household and child care responsibilities. For working parents with children, family schedules were often as intricate as time-motion studies.

While the media often focused on the breakthroughs made by women near the top of the corporate ladder, one of every five working women still held a clerical or secretarial job, the same proportion as in 1950. Women's pay lagged behind men's, with the gap even wider for black and Latino women. Yet women continued to make inroads in male-dominated fields. Among all workers under age thirty-five, women accounted for one in three doctors, four in ten mail carriers, and a majority of purchasing agents.

Other Corporate Strategies. Another major cause of diminished economic expectations in the 1980s and 1990s was the widespread fear that American corporations were no longer competitive in the global marketplace. Americans viewed with increasing alarm the economic success of Germany and Japan, the growing U.S. trade deficit, and the infusion of foreign investment money into the United States.

In an increasingly global economy American corporations tried to respond to rapidly changing market conditions by offering innovative products and services at competitive prices. Using a term popularized by Michael Hammer and James Champy, management consultants advised businesses to "reengineer the corporation," that is, rethink their work processes. Very often the models were corporations in Japan and Germany.

Some American companies did manage to reinvent themselves. In 1980–1981 the Ford Motor Company had lost $2.5 billion despite laying off 150,000 workers. This desperate situation led management to rethink its corporate vision. Instead of the old "us versus them" mentality, Ford tried to implement more of a partnership between management and the rank and file. It also shifted its focus away from maximum output to quality and consumer satisfaction, in effect making assembly-line workers more involved in the company and its products by giving them more responsibility. The popular Ford Taurus, introduced in 1986, typified the new focus on quality.

Labor Movement Responses. At first United Auto Workers (UAW) leaders were dubious about Ford's plans, especially when the company would not rule out future layoffs. But afraid that Ford might go bankrupt, in 1982 the UAW agreed to freeze wages and benefits, delay cost-of-living increases, and stop local strikes. Said the president of the UAW local at Ford's South Chicago plant, "I think we both realized over a period of time that we were in the same boat. When the boat sinks, we all drown. . . . It's a survival thing."

In the 1980s and 1990s the labor movement remained on the defensive, hurt by job losses to other countries, downsizing, fears of further layoffs, government hostility, worker indifference, and its inability to unionize unskilled and low-paid workers. Although union membership was now one-third female and one-fifth black, union leadership remained overwhelmingly white and male. The number of union members declined from 20 million in 1978 to 16.6 million in 1993, representing only 15.8 percent of the labor force. The Reagan administration took a tough antiunion stance from the start, breaking a nationwide strike by air traffic controllers in 1981 and destroying their union. Reagan's action signaled to the business community that it was acceptable to be antiunion, and there were sharp labor confrontations at Eastern Airlines, Greyhound, Phelps Dodge, Ravenswood Aluminum, Caterpillar, and Pittston Coal. In the mid-1990s new union leadership, a wave of union mergers, and an increased emphasis on reaching new members raised hopes that organized labor would reverse its decline.

The Strains of an Increasingly Pluralistic Society

The 1990 census counted 246.9 million Americans, an increase of over 22 million people since the 1980 census. By far the most dramatic shift was the changing racial composition of the United States. In 1990 one in four Americans claimed African, Asian, Hispanic, or American Indian ancestry, up from one in five ten years earlier. The main reason for the shift was increased immigration, especially from Latin America and Asia. In 1994, 8.7 percent of the U.S. population was foreign-born, almost double the 4.8 percent of 1970 and the highest proportion since World War II. This level, however, was still far below its modern historic high of 14.7 percent in 1910 after the great tide of early twentieth-century immigration.

In the 1980s over 7 million immigrants entered the country, accounting for more than a third of the population growth in that decade. LAX and JFK, the Los Angeles and New York international airports, were the main points of entry, replacing Ellis Island, which, after decades of abandonment and decay, was turned into a museum and tourist attraction. The first major immigration legislation since 1965, the 1986 Immigration Reform and Control Act (Simpson-Mazzoli Act), attempted to establish a fair entry process. It also granted legal status to some ille-

gal aliens, primarily Mexicans and other Latinos, who had entered the United States before 1982. Revisions to the law in 1990 expanded the quota of immigrants to 700,000 per year and gave priority to skilled workers and relatives of current residents.

Hispanic Immigration. Much of the new immigration came from Latin America and the Caribbean. In 1950 there were 4 million Hispanics in this country; in 1990 the number was 22.4 million. The terms *Hispanic* and *Latino*, which include Spanish-speaking people from Mexico, Cuba, Puerto Rico, El Salvador, and other Latin American countries, represent a variety of distinctive heritages. Hispanics are the second largest minority group after blacks and the second fastest growing after Asians. Western states such as California, Texas, and New Mexico, which border on Mexico, originally contained the most immigrants, but in the postwar period new arrivals from Puerto Rico and Central and South America increasingly settled on the East Coast. Latinos now live in urban areas throughout the country, making up one-tenth of the populations of Florida and New York, for example (see Map 33.4).

Asian-Americans. Asia was the other major source of immigrants. This migration, which increased almost 108 percent from 1980 to 1990, consisted mainly of Chinese, Filipinos, Vietnamese, Laotians, Cambodians, Koreans, Pakistanis, and Asian Indians. California had more Asian-Americans, almost 10 percent of the population, than did any other state. Chinese-Americans are still the dominant Asian group in the United States, followed by Filipinos (see Map 33.5).

Some of this immigration was traceable to upheavals in Southeast Asia. More than 700,000 Indochinese refugees entered the country in the decade after American involvement in Vietnam ended in 1975. The first arrivals were highly educated people, who, after a few years, generally achieved economic success. Many of the later refugees came with less education and fewer skills and struggled for a foothold in new Indochinese neighborhoods that developed in Arlington, Virginia; Lowell, Massachusetts; and elsewhere. When the Cambodian population in that former textile town of Lowell increased from 3,500 in 1985 to 20,000 just three years later, local resources were strained, and the school system struggled to find bilingual teachers fluent in Khmer, the Cambodian language.

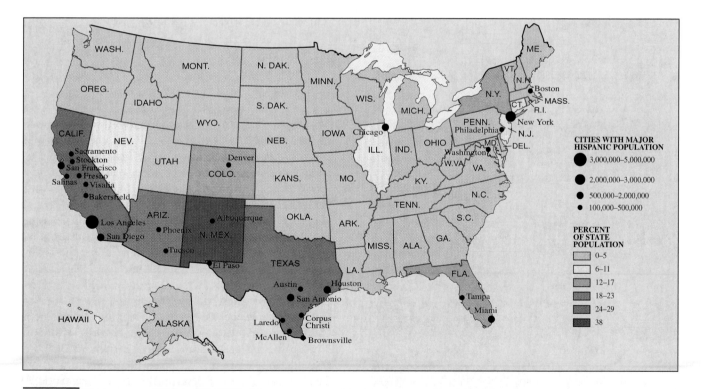

MAP 33.4

Hispanic-American Population, 1990

The Hispanic population of the United States is concentrated in California, New York, Texas, Florida, and Illinois, mainly in their urban areas. Demographers predict that Hispanic-Americans will overtake African-Americans as the largest minority group early in the twenty-first century and that by the year 2050 only about half the U.S. population will be comprised of non-Hispanic whites.

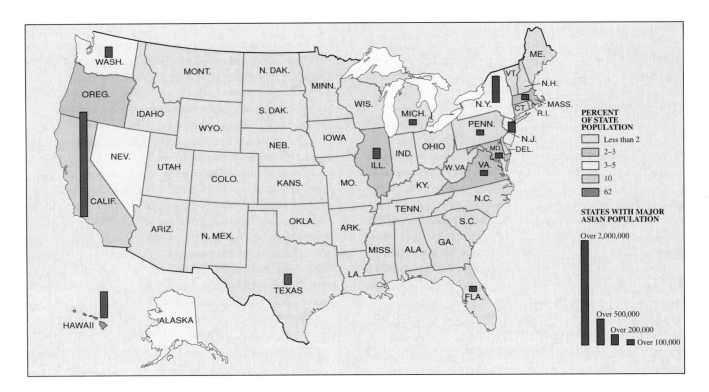

MAP 33.5

Asian-American Population, 1990

In 1990 Asian-Americans made up just under 3 percent of the total U.S. population. Asian population is concentrated on the East and West coasts, especially in California, and in major cities.

New Immigrants

In the 1980s many Korean immigrants got their start by opening small grocery stores in urban neighborhoods. Their success sometimes led to conflict with other racial groups, such as blacks and Hispanics, who were often their customers as well as competitors.

Asian-Americans were often referred to as a "model minority" because of their educational and professional success. Yet this label, which most Asian-Americans see as an unwelcome ethnic stereotype, masked their enormous diversity. Koreans, Laotians, and Chinese did not share a common language or customs, but they were all subjected to racial slurs and blatant discrimination. Informal quotas, especially in college admissions, recalled similar expressions of anti-Semitism as late as the 1950s.

Ethnic Diversity. The new immigration affected the social, economic, and cultural landscape of the country. Thriving ethnic enclaves were one example: Little Saigon in Orange County, California; Little Havana in Miami; Koreatown in Los Angeles. Tens of thousands of Soviet Jews fleeing religious and political persecution in the 1980s created Little Odessa in Brooklyn, New York. At least 300 periodicals served immigrant readers: *Nguoi Viet* in California, *La Voz de Houston* in Texas, and *Korea Times* in Queens, New York. Koreans purchased and revitalized corner grocery stores in New York City, Los Angeles, and Washington, D.C. People from the Indian subcontinent managed small hotel chains in California, and Vietnamese dominated the shrimp industry in

Texas. But demographers noted another pattern in major metropolitan areas with heavy immigration: for every immigrant who moved in, a native-born (usually white) person left.

Anti-Immigrant Sentiment. Immigrants have been the focus of hostility at many points in America's history. In the 1840s fears of Catholic Irish and German immigrants sparked violence and urban riots. At the turn of the century nativists decried the impact of immigrants from southern and Eastern Europe on Anglo-Saxon culture and in 1925 secured the passage of legislation severely restricting immigration from those areas. Anti-immigrant sentiment has always surged in times of unsettling economic or cultural change. Similar patterns were at play in the 1980s and 1990s, when increased immigration caused an agitated debate over access to jobs, education, and social services.

Economists generally believe that immigrants give more than they take, providing a fresh source of predominantly youthful and highly motivated workers who take jobs that are not wanted by other people or move into new jobs in the growing service sector. But many American-born workers still feared that immigrants would adversely affect their job prospects in a time of diminished economic opportunity. Immigrants, both legal and illegal, provided inviting targets when budgetary crises on the state and local levels mandated cutbacks. Polls showed strong public support for denying government assistance to all immigrants, regardless of their legal status, on the unfounded assumption that immigrants were lured here by generous public services.

These tensions came to a head in California, which had absorbed far more immigrants in the 1980s than any other state had. That state grew by 6.1 million, with more than a third of the growth coming from foreign immigration. Although California's overall growth has slowed since 1990, immigration has not. In 1994 California voters overwhelmingly approved a ballot initiative provocatively called "Save Our State," also known as Proposition 187. This initiative barred undocumented aliens from public schools, nonemergency care at public health clinics, and all other state social services. It also required law enforcement officers, school administrators, and social workers to report suspected illegal immigrants to the federal Immigration and Naturalization Service. While the constitutionality of the ballot referendum was immediately challenged, anti-immigrant feeling spread to other parts of the country and would be a hotly debated issue in the 1996 election.

The Plight of Urban America. One by-product of this increased immigration was that black Americans constituted a comparatively smaller percentage of the minority population in 1990 than they had earlier in the century. (Black immigration from the Caribbean and Africa has been too small to affect this trend.) Demographers predict that Latinos will outnumber blacks early in the twenty-first century. Blacks and recent immigrants sometimes found themselves competing for the same jobs. Both African-Americans and new immigrants often lived in urban areas, but rarely in the same neighborhoods as a result of prevailing patterns of ethnic and racial segregation.

The cities where most new immigrants settled in the 1990s were often in dire shape. Urban renewal projects had demolished dilapidated but still livable housing and replaced it with civic complexes and shiny office projects. Government inaction also contributed to the deterioration of the inner cities. Federal attention to urban areas peaked between 1964 and 1972; since then, inner-city problems have largely been left to the cash-strapped cities to solve.

Joblessness became a way of life for inner-city residents, two-parent households were scarce, and social contacts outside the neighborhood were rare. At the heart of the problem was the inability to find productive work. Urban unemployment rates rose as high as 60 percent, in part for demographic reasons: inner cities had a far larger proportion of young people than did the general population as a result of a higher birth rate and a younger age of childbearing. Cities had too few entry-level jobs, and most of the inner cities' unemployed lacked the training necessary for better-paying jobs.

In the 1980s the historical tide of black migration to the cities that had begun before World War I started to recede. Southern blacks who learned about the poor job prospects were less likely to seek new lives in urban areas; quite the contrary, anyone who could was leaving the inner cities, usually for a more stable neighborhood or the suburbs. In Los Angeles, as Asians and Latinos moved in, blacks moved out, usually to neighboring counties such as Riverside, San Bernardino, and Ventura. Some blacks even made a reverse migration back to the South. Compared with the crime-ridden and dilapidated housing projects in Chicago or South-Central Los Angeles, the post–civil rights South seemed attractive. Atlanta was one of the most popular destinations.

In April 1992 the frustration and anger of impoverished urban Americans erupted in five days of riots in Los Angeles, the worst civil disorders since the 1960s. The violence took sixty lives and caused $850 million in damage. The rioting was set off by the acquittal on all but one charge of four white Los Angeles police officers accused of using excessive force while arresting a black motorist, Rodney King, on March 3, 1991. The predominantly white Simi Valley jury was not swayed by a graphic eighty-one-second amateur video of the arrest that showed the officers kicking, clubbing, and beating King. The video, which was shown repeatedly on television, brought renewed attention to the issue of police brutality and the harassment of minorities. Three of the officers were later convicted on federal charges of violating King's civil rights.

To Live and Die in L.A.
The images from South-Central Los Angeles in the wake of the 1992 riots looked eerily similar to those from Watts in 1965. The underlying causes were similar as well—police brutality, racism, and frustration about lack of jobs and opportunity.

The Los Angeles riots exposed the cleavages in urban neighborhoods. Many blacks trapped in the nation's inner cities resented recent immigrants who were struggling to get ahead and often succeeding. As a result some blacks targeted Korean-owned stores for arson and looting. Latinos also felt frustrated about high unemployment and crowded housing conditions. According to the Los Angeles Police Department, Latinos accounted for more than half of those arrested and a third of those killed during the rioting. The riots were not just a case of black rage at white injustice; they also contained a strong class element as people reacted against the failure of the American system to address the needs of all poor people, not just blacks (see American Voices, page 1037).

Affirmative Action. From the beginning of affirmative action in 1965 many white men had protested that it was unfair and discriminatory. Some, like Allen Bakke, even took their cases to court (see Chapter 32). But affirmative action remained official government policy until the 1990s, when arguments over minority and immigrant rights as well as the shrinking economy and white resentment fueled a renewed debate on the issue. Affirmative action had become more than a black-white or women's issue, pitting racial and ethnic groups against each other in a kind of three-dimensional game of chess in which, for example, gains for blacks and Hispanics came at the expense of Asian-Americans.

The impact of affirmative action was most evident in college admissions. The University of California system had undertaken one of the most far-reaching plans. As late as 1984 whites had made up about two-thirds of the undergraduate student body. In 1994, as a result of the implementation of affirmative action, students at the Berkeley campus were 39 percent Asian, 32 percent white, 14 percent Latino, 6 percent black, and 1 percent native American, with 8 percent of students not identifying their race. In 1995, under pressure from the Republican governor, Pete Wilson, the Regents of the University of California reexamined their preference-based system. Despite opposition from the university's president and many faculty members, who warned that repeal would lead to precipitous drops in the numbers of black and Latino freshmen, the Regents narrowly voted to scrap the twenty-year-old policy.

Criticism of affirmative action came from many sources. Some conservative blacks felt it merely reinforced white prejudices that the only way minorities could get ahead was through preferential treatment. Others argued that affirmative action did little to help the truly disadvantaged, offering opportunities instead to those who would probably have been able to get ahead without it. In a time of anxiety about jobs and the economy in general, affirmative action became a scapegoat for many who were not succeeding economically, especially the white men who had borne the brunt of layoffs in the 1980s and 1990s. The 1994 elections transformed the goal of abolishing affirmative action into a mainstream political issue, and a 1995 Supreme Court decision casting doubts on federal programs that gave preference based on race will probably increase the momentum of the opponents of affirmative action.

Culture Wars. One reason affirmative action became a political issue in the 1990s was that many people saw it as part of an ideology that threatened core American values. Lumping affirmative action together with *multiculturalism*—the attempt to represent the diversity of American society and its peoples—critics feared that all this counting by race, gender, sexual preference, and age would lead to a "balkanization" of American society. Attempts to revise American history textbooks along multicultural lines were especially contentious, as were efforts by universities such as Stanford to revise college curricula to include the study of non-European cultures.

Culture wars broke out on other fronts as well. Conservatives in Congress led an effort to eliminate federal funding for the arts, humanities, and public television, arguing that the federal government should not be in the business of supporting works that many found offensive or antithetical to traditional American values. The National Endowments for the Arts and the Humanities survived, but with drastically reduced budgets. Conservatives found another tempting target in the

Rubén Martínez

L.A. Journal

Rubén Martínez, born to Mexican and Salvadoran parents and raised in Los Angeles, describes himself as a member of the generation "that arrived too late for Che Guevara and too early for the fall of the Berlin Wall." In this excerpt he compares daily life in Los Angeles with San Salvador's state of siege.

June 1991

Was that a shotgun? In answer, a series of pops . . . a small automatic? I crouch by the window, look into the hazy balmy night. Mute buildings. Now, from afar, another sound begins, like the whine of a mosquito in the darkness of a stifling room in the tropics. The whine becomes a roar that rattles the windows. A shaft of light pours down from the sky. Sirens shriek in the distance. They come closer . . . closer: patrol cars race up the avenue.

I am not in San Salvador, I tell myself. Those are not soldiers down there, bursting through doors to ransack the apartments of high school kids who participated in a protest march . . . Y is okay, she works for a human rights organization in Los Angeles, she's not FMLN in San Salvador anymore, this is Los Angeles, not San Salvador, this is 1991, not 1979, this is gang strife, not civil war. I don't believe myself. Images past and present merge: It is 1979 and

1991 and San Salvador and Los Angeles and gang strife and civil war all at once.

When the helicopters thud-thud-thud-thud fades away, I light a cigarette. Did the bullets find their mark in a rival gangster, a three-year-old's skull? I wait for the ambulance's siren, but the neighborhood remains quiet. The bullets found nothing but the night, as though the night itself were both target and victim of the desperate rage that led the finger to pull on the trigger.

I return to my post next to the computer, in my Echo Park apartment (my latest stop in search of a home) whose living room holds my altar. Amidst votive candles and before a crucifix, I've gathered together objects from the living and the dead: a wallet-sized photo of Y, her stare questioning me across the distance of our latest—and final?—separation; on a cassette sleeve, a photo of Mexico City kids who look like a cross between Irish idealists U2 and the street toughs of *Los Olvidados*; a black-and-white snapshot of a graffiti artist cradling his brutally scarred arm, result of an evening when the bullets did find their mark; a brittle, yellowed leaf from Palm Sunday at La Placita, where Father Luis Olivares showered the thousands of Mexicanos and Centro-americanos surrounding

him with holy water; the embossed card that says that one Fidel Castro Ruz, *Presidente del Consejo de Estado y del Gobierno de la República de Cuba*, requests my presence at a reception; a rather ugly postcard entitled "La Frontera, Tijuana, BC," that shows an antiseptic-clean highway on one side and a labyrinth of dusty paths on the other . . . shards of my identity. . . .

This jumble of objects is as close as I get to "home." As close as I get, because my home is L.A. and L.A. is an anti-home; that's why I've left it so many times, and returned just as many. . . .

I turn off the overhead light so that the candle flame transforms the shadow of the crucifix on the wall into a pair of wavering, reaching arms. I gaze upon the photos of my late grandparents. This is my history, I tell myself. "This is my home," I whisper, looking out through the window again at the avenues of Echo Park, which are now as deserted and tense as any in San Salvador during a state of siege. . . .

Source: Rubén Martínez, *The Other Side: Fault Lines, Guerrilla Saints, and the True Heart of Rock 'n' Roll* (Verso: London and New York, 1992), 165–166.

---

speech codes adopted by some colleges to ban racist or sexist comments from everyday language. Whether someone's words were "p.c." (politically correct) became a red flag, with the implication that somehow it had become impossible to say anything without offending someone.

Backlash against Feminism. The women's movement also became a target of conservative critics, who charged that feminist demands had gone too far. In the widely read *Backlash: The Undeclared War on American Women* (1991), the journalist Susan Faludi described a powerful backlash against the gains American women had won in the 1960s and 1970s. Spearheaded by New Right leaders and organizations such as Concerned

Women for America, the backlash was aided by television, newspapers, and even women's magazines. The media held the women's movement responsible for every ill afflicting modern women—from infertility to eating disorders to rising divorce rates to the "man shortage." Too much freedom had caused women unhappiness was the antifeminist message of the 1980s and 1990s. Feminists such as Faludi replied that women were unhappy precisely because they had not yet achieved equality. And despite the conservative attacks, polls showed strong support for many items on the feminist agenda, such as pay equity, increased access to jobs, reproductive rights, and more equitable sharing of household and child care responsibilities.

Backlash

The 1987 movie *Fatal Attraction* typified Hollywood's nega-tive portrayal of independent women in that decade. The plot centers on a homicidal single career woman (played by Glenn Close) who nearly destroys a happily married man (Michael Douglas) after a casual affair. The original screenplay had Close's character slit her throat over her unrequited love, but in the final version she is killed by Douglas's wife. According to the journalist Susan Faludi, the message is clear: "The best single woman is a dead one."

Feminism also exhibited racial and generational fault lines. Despite the attempts of prominent feminist organi-zations such as the National Organization for Women (NOW) to focus on differences among women, African-Americans and other women of color often resented being tokens in a predominantly white movement. Many young women felt that the movement had become too obsessed with women as passive victims (of date rape, discrimination, sexual harrassment, the media's beauty myth, and so forth) rather than offering women models of empowerment. But other young women, influenced by women's studies programs and the explosion of femi-nist scholarship, forged a third wave of feminism in the 1990s (see American Voices, page 1039).

The deep national divide over abortion showed how one of the main issues associated with feminism contin-ued to polarize the country. The increase in harassment and violence by abortion opponents was one of the most chilling manifestations of the antifeminism of the 1980s and 1990s. In 1994 four workers were killed, including two receptionists at Boston clinics. Although only a fraction of antiabortion activists supported such ex-treme acts, disruptive confrontational tactics made it more dangerous to receive what was still a woman's legal right to an abortion. In May 1994 Congress passed the Freedom of Access to Clinic Entrances Act (FACE), which provided federal fines and prison terms for those who used physical obstruction or intimidation to inter-fere with access to reproductive health services.

Gay Rights. The issue of sexual preference, especially the introduction of educational programs teaching toler-ance for gays, also became part of the fractured national debate about multiculturalism. As more gays "came out of the closet," activists gained more political clout in their campaign for gay rights. In more than a hundred communities across the country, civil rights legislation protected gays from discrimination in public housing, education, real estate, public accommodations, and em-ployment. Certain cities, including New York City, Washington, D.C., and San Francisco, allowed same-sex couples to register as domestic partners.

To conservatives, especially the Christian Right and its sympathizers in Congress, a gay life-style was an af-front to traditional family values. Pat Robertson, Jesse Helms, and others denounced civil rights protections for gays as undeserved "special rights." Such tactics helped antigay forces win a 1992 Colorado referendum to add a state constitutional amendment barring local jurisdic-tions from passing laws protecting gays and lesbians from discrimination. The Colorado provision was over-turned by the U.S. Supreme Court in 1996, but this had no effect on the rising incidence of antigay harassment and violence. Twenty-five years after Stonewall gay peo-ple were more visible in American society but were not universally accepted.

The AIDS Epidemic. One of the largest challenges that the gay community has faced is AIDS, although it is grossly inaccurate to see this solely as a gay issue. Ac-quired immune deficiency syndrome (AIDS) was first recognized in 1981, and its cause was soon identified as the human immunodeficiency virus (HIV). (HIV is transmitted through the exchange of infected body flu-ids such as semen and blood.) Initially, little organized action or government funding was directed toward AIDS research or treatment, and critics charged that this reflected society's antipathy toward gay men, who were the disease's earliest victims. AIDS began to gain public attention only when it became clear that heterosexuals, such as hemophiliacs who received the virus through blood transfusions, were affected as well. The 1985 death from AIDS of the film star Rock Hudson, who had hidden his sexual orientation to maintain his Holly-wood career, finally broke through the barrier of public apathy. Another galvanizing moment was the 1991 an-nouncement by the basketball great Earvin ("Magic") Johnson that he was HIV-positive.

As early as the mid-1980s AIDS cases began to in-crease among heterosexuals, especially intravenous drug addicts and their sexual partners, as well as bisexuals. Women now constitute the group with the fastest grow-ing incidence of HIV infection. The new female faces of the AIDS epidemic were represented at the 1992 na-tional party conventions by Elizabeth Glaser and Mary Fisher. Glaser told the assembled Democrats how she

Laurie Ouellette

A Third-Wave Feminist

Laurie Ouellette, born in 1966 and educated at the University of Minnesota, represents the generation of women who benefited from the changes set in motion by the revival of feminism but are confused about what feminism means. She calls on the movement to broaden its vision.

As a member of the first generation of women to benefit from the gains of the '70s women's movement without participating in its struggles, I grew up on the sidelines of feminism—too young to take part in those moments, debates, and events that would define the women's movement but old enough to experience firsthand the societal changes it had wrought.

Ironically, it is due to the modest success of feminism that many young women like myself were raised with an illusion of equality. Like most women my age, I never really thought much about feminism while I was growing up. Looking back, though, I believe it has always influenced me. Growing up with divorced parents, especially a father who was ambivalent about parental responsibilities, probably has much to do with this fact. I was only five when my parents separated in 1971, and I couldn't possibly have imagined or understood the ERA marches or the triumphal result of *Roe v. Wade* that would make history in just a few short years. Certainly I couldn't have defined the word *feminism*. Still, watching my mother strug-

gle emotionally and financially as a single parent made the concept of gender injustice painfully clear. . . .

It was at the University of Minnesota that I first took an interest in feminist classics like *The Feminine Mystique, Sisterhood Is Powerful*, and *Sexual Politics*. They expressed the anger of an earlier generation that simultaneously captivated me and excluded me. Reading them so long after the excitement of their publication made my own consciousness-raising seem anticlimactic. Like many of my white middle-class friends, I believed that we wouldn't have to worry about issues like discrimination, oppression, and getting stuck in the housewife role. We wondered why we should join forces with a battle for women's equality that the media repeatedly declared was already "won."

My experiences after college made me think again about feminism. A public television internship where I was expected to perform menial secretarial tasks while my male (and, I might add, less experienced) co-interns worked on interesting and challenging projects shocked me into realizing the difficulties facing women in the workplace. Likewise, living in an inner-city neighborhood and being involved in community issues there showed me the dire need for feminism in the lives of the poor women, elderly women, and women of color who were my neighbors. Watching these women, many of them single mothers, struggle daily to find shelter, child care, and food made me

realize that they had not been touched at all by the women's movement gains of the '70s. . . .

My 24-year-old sister stands out as an example of other routes that feminism must move toward. Whereas I have focused my energies on attending graduate school and working toward a professional career, she has chosen to forfeit similar plans, for now, in favor of marrying young, moving to the country, and raising a family. Does she signify a regression into the homemaker role of the 1950s? On the contrary. For her, issues such as getting midwifery legalized and insured, providing information about breast-feeding to rural mothers, countering the male-dominated medical establishment by using and recommending natural and alternative healing methods, and raising her own daughter with positive gender esteem are central to a feminist agenda.

Only by recognizing and helping to provide choices—both lifestyle and reproductive—for women of all races, economic levels, and ages, as well as supporting all women in their struggles to make those choices, will the women of my generation, the first to be raised in the shadow of feminism and witness its successes and failures, be able to build a successful third wave of the feminist movement.

Source: Laurie Ouellette, "Our Turn Now: Reflections of a 26-Year-Old Feminist," *Utne Reader* (July-August, 1992), 118–120.

had contracted the virus through a tainted blood transfusion and then unknowingly passed it on to her nursing infant and a later child. Mary Fisher, the daughter of a prominent conservative fund-raiser, told the Republicans how she learned from a blood test that she had contracted the virus from her former husband. "If you believe you are safe, you are at risk," said Fisher.

Some people have lived for years symptom-free while being HIV-positive, but no cure or vaccine is in

sight. The barriers to further research and effective prevention are as much political and bureaucratic as medical. Many nonurban Americans see the AIDS epidemic as another expression of big-city decay. Federal red tape and prohibitive expense have limited the distribution of drugs such as AZT that delay the onset and reduce the severity of the symptoms despite the dramatic protests of the advocacy group ACT-UP (AIDS Coalition to Unleash Power). More Americans have died of AIDS than

ACT UP

This poster *Untitled* (1989) by artist Keith Haring for the group ACT UP (AIDS Coalition to Unleash Power) was used to mobilize public action against the deadly disease, which would later claim Haring's life.

were killed in the Korean and Vietnam wars combined, and in 1995 AIDS was the leading cause of death among all Americans aged twenty-five to forty-four. The toll, in the United States and throughout the world, continues to rise.

Popular Culture and Popular Technology

Image was everything in the 1980s and 1990s, or so commentators said, pointing to the rock stars Michael Jackson and Madonna and even to President Reagan. One strong influence was MTV, which premiered in 1981. With its creative choreography, flashy colors, and rapid cuts, it seemed a perfect fit to the short attention span of a TV generation raised on shows such as "Sesame Street." The MTV style soon showed up in mainstream advertising, network television shows such as "Miami Vice," and even political campaigns. The national newspaper *USA Today*, which debuted in 1982, adapted the style, featuring eye-catching graphics, color photographs, and short, easy-to-read articles. Soon more staid newspapers followed suit.

New technology, especially satellite transmission and live "minicam" broadcasting, reshaped the television industry. Also new was the increased availability of cable channels. In the 1950s Americans had only three networks to choose from; public television did not debut until 1967. By the end of the 1980s upstarts such as Ted Turner's all-news CNN (Cable News Network), ESPN's all-sports channel, and the Fox network were challenging the major networks for viewers and profits. Media, communications, and entertainment were big business, increasingly drawn into global financial networks, markets, and mergers.

Technology also entered and reshaped the home. The 1980s saw the introduction of videocassette recorders

(VCRs), compact disc players, cellular phones, and inexpensive fax (facsimile) machines. In 1993 more than three-quarters of American households had a VCR. At first Hollywood feared decreasing box office admissions, but it soon found that VCRs created a large new market for recent films, as well as for vintage movies. Video was everywhere—stores, elevators, airplanes, tennis courts, operating rooms. With the introduction of camcorders, the family photo album could be supplemented by a video of a high school graduation, a marriage, or a birth.

But it was the personal computer that truly revolutionized the home and the office. The big breakthrough came from the upstart Apple Computer Company. Two young hobbyists, Steve Jobs and Steve Wozniak, operating from a bedroom and garage in Palo Alto, California, built the first easy-to-use, small, inexpensive computer. In 1977 they offered their Apple II personal computer for only $1,195, and it was a runaway success. Belatedly, other companies scrambled to get into the market. IBM, a leader in producing tabulating machines and mainframe computers for business and government, offered its first personal computer in the summer of 1981. Software companies such as Microsoft and Lotus grew rapidly by providing operating systems and other software for this expanding market (see American Lives, pages 1042–1043). In January 1983 *Time* magazine broke with fifty-five years of tradition by naming the personal computer its "machine of the year." In 1995, 37 percent of American households had at least one personal computer.

The impact of the personal computer on business was nearly universal. More than any other technological advance, the computer created the modern electronic office. Even the smallest business could keep all its records, do all its correspondence and billing, and run its own direct-mail advertising campaigns on a single desktop machine. The very concept of the office was changing as a new class of *telecommuters* were able to work at home via computer, electronic mail, and fax machine.

Over the next decades the world's telecommunications systems will be rebuilt with hair-thin fiber-optic strands with a far greater *bandwidth* (information-carrying capacity) than copper wire. Fiber-optic cables, microwave relays, and satellites can transmit massive quantities of information to and from almost any place on earth and even from space. The term *information superhighway* refers to this vast expansion of communications technology.

The Internet is the aspect of the information superhighway that has reached the most people so far—an estimated 35 million in 160 countries in 1995. The Internet had cold war roots, originating in a 1969 effort by the Pentagon to create a communications network that could survive a nuclear war. The Pentagon gave up control of the Internet in 1984, and the subsequent rapid

spread of personal computers, modems, and networked computing made the Internet attractive (some would say addictive) to average citizens and commercial enterprises. Welcome to *cyberspace*, that place behind the computer screen you can't see, but you know is there.

At first the Internet was used mainly by scientists and other professionals to communicate with their peers through electronic mail (*E-mail*), but the arrival of the World Wide Web in 1991 enhanced its commercial possibilities. The Web allowed companies, organizations, political campaigns, and even the White House to create their own "home pages" of visual and textual information for consumers to click on to at their discretion. Businesses and entrepreneurs began to use home pages to sell their products and services, leading critics to fear that the Net would turn into one big shopping mall. But many people think that cyberspace will be one of the driving forces for economic growth in the twenty-first century.

The implications of this almost instantaneous access to information are staggering. On January 5, 1995, the Library of Congress unveiled "Thomas" (named for Thomas Jefferson), an on-line service providing access to legislation, committee reports, and other Congressional documents. During the first four days of its operation 28,000 individuals and 2,500 organizations used Thomas to download more than 175,000 documents. More citizens had accessed Thomas in a day than normally used the Library of Congress in a week.

Whereas this access was touted as making information democratically available to all American citizens, it really was available only to those who had access to the current technology or who could pay the monthly fees to be wired. In many ways, who is going to get on the information superhighway and who is going to be left by the wayside is one of the most troubling issues for the next century. It has been called "information apartheid" or "electronic redlining," a term derived from the banking practice of refusing loans to people in low-income areas.

The gap between information haves and have-nots is wide and getting wider. In 1995 only 10 percent of American households (generally those with incomes above $50,000) had the computers, modems, telephone connections, and gateway software necessary to participate in this revolution. According to a 1993 Census Bureau study, the gap was racial as well as economic: 37.5 percent of whites had computers at home, work, or school, compared with 25 percent of blacks and 22 percent of Hispanics.

The futurists Alvin and Heidi Toffler use the term Third Wave to describe how these new computing and telecommunications technologies will transform the global economy as dramatically as did the first wave (the agricultural revolution) and the second (the Industrial Revolution). If the wave of the future is indeed informa-

tion, those who are highly educated and computer-literate will have the advantage. Those who are not, for reasons of class, race, or location, will find themselves even more disadvantaged as they compete in the twenty-first-century workplace.

Restructuring the Domestic Order: Public Life since 1993

The strong showing of the independent candidate Ross Perot in the 1992 presidential election reflected widespread popular dissatisfaction with the American political system. Like using a remote control device, Americans were clicking off politics as usual. After sixty years of supporting federal activism to combat social ills, the Democratic party found that its core ideology was out of step with a country more concerned with cutting taxes, scaling back government, and balancing the budget. As Democrats abandoned many of their long-held liberal beliefs, the Republican party moved even farther to the right. Looming over all their political debates was the federal deficit.

The Clinton Administration

As William Jefferson Clinton was sworn into office in January 1993, hopes were high that the Democratic Congress and Democratic president would cooperate to pass legislation long stalled by partisan disputes. The first signs were promising. Congress passed the Family and Medical Leave Act in February 1993, providing workers with up to twelve weeks of unpaid leave to tend to a newborn or adopted child or a family medical emergency. President Bush had twice vetoed similar bills. In May, Congress passed the so-called motor-voter bill, which required states to allow citizens to register to vote when they applied for or renewed a driver's license. But Clinton got sidetracked when he tried to implement his campaign promise to lift the ban on gays serving in the armed forces. His compromise policy of "don't ask, don't tell, don't pursue" satisfied no one, and the bungled handling of this emotionally charged issue called into question his willingness to stand firm on issues of principle.

By the time Clinton took office the economy had pulled out of the 1990 recession. He then focused "like a laser" on economic issues, which included crafting trade policies to open foreign markets to U.S. goods. In December 1992 President Bush had signed the North American Free Trade Agreement (NAFTA), an agreement among the United States, Canada, and Mexico to create a free-trade zone covering all of North America, the

AMERICAN LIVES

Bill Gates:
Microsoft's Leader in the
Computer Revolution

In the eleventh grade Bill Gates told a friend that he would be a millionaire by the time he was thirty. When Gates went to Harvard two years later, he revised it downward to twenty-five. He was being far too modest. At the age of thirty-one Bill Gates became the youngest self-made billionaire ever. In 1992 *Forbes* magazine named him the richest person in America. What was the source of all this wealth? Microsoft, whose software runs on eight of every ten personal computers in the world. Microsoft is the most successful start-up company in the history of American business.

William Henry Gates III (always called Trey by his family) was born into a wealthy Seattle family in 1955. His father, William Gates, Jr., is a successful corporate lawyer and former president of the Washington State Bar Association; his mother, Mary, was a prominent United Way volunteer who also served as a regent of the

University of Washington. Gates attended the exclusive Lakeside School, which was one of the first in the country to offer students computer access through a time-sharing arrangement paid for by the school's mothers' club. The eighth-grader was hooked. Another Lakeside classmate and computer whiz was the tenth-grader Paul Allen, who joined Gates to found a company called Traf-O-Data that counted vehicles at busy intersections by using a rudimentary computer device. In 1975 these two former classmates founded Microsoft. Allen was twenty-one, and Gates, who would soon drop out of Harvard, all of nineteen.

Actually Gates looked even younger. When Miriam Lubow became Microsoft's office manager in 1977, she was appalled when some "kid" whipped by her desk into the office of "Mr. Gates" and began playing with the computer terminal. That kid was Bill Gates. But looks

Microsoft Employees, 1978
This group portrait shows eleven of Microsoft's thirteen employees as the company was about to relocate from Albuquerque to Seattle. Bill Gates is in front row, far left; Paul Allen is in front row, far right.

can be deceiving, as competitors have found out whenever they do business with this formidable entrepreneur.

In certain ways Gates and Allen were classic hackers—nerdy, mathematically inclined, and fascinated by the possibilities for computation (and mischief) that early computers provided. But most hackers saw computers as a hobby or a game. Back then the thought of owning one's own computer seemed as far-fetched as owning a nuclear submarine. But right from the start Gates and Allen saw commercial possibilities in the new field, long before the personal computer revolution of the 1980s. They anticipated that there would be money to be made writing, but especially marketing, software for the new machines. Microsoft's domination has resulted less from developing innovative new products than from anticipating trends in the industry, getting products quickly into the market, and then using its market share to bludgeon the competition. The phenomenal success of products such as MS-DOS and Windows was due as much to Microsoft's relentless marketing barrage as to any inherent technological superiority of its products.

In the early days Microsoft was more like a college dorm than a business. The "Microkids" were barely out of their teens, and some were still in high school. Nobody kept regular hours, and they existed on junk food, rock music, and free Coke (a tradition that Microsoft still maintains). A married employee was an oddity, and almost all the programmers were men. Gates's competitive and confrontational managerial style set the tone: "That's the stupidest thing I ever heard" was a frequently heard comment. But the Microkids thrived under the pressure. As Gates later said, "It's a lot of fun to work with very smart people in a competitive environment."

Gates literally could not sit still, and the Seattle-based Microsoft continued to grow at a fantastic rate. Gates had once thought it might employ 20 people; by 1982, Microsoft had 200 employees and sales of $32 million. In 1985, when the company went public, Gates, Allen (who had left the company in 1983 after a bout with Hodgkin's disease), and many Microsoft employees became overnight millionaires. Allen later cashed in some of his stock to buy the Portland Trailblazers.

Bill Gates does not act like a person with a net worth of approximately $10 billion. He flies coach rather than first class, hates limousines, and is somewhat casual about his appearance. He personally responds to hundreds of E-mail messages a day. He works incredibly long hours and expects his employees to do the same.

However, only billionaires can afford to spend $40 million on a house such as the one that Gates is building on Lake Washington outside Seattle for himself and his wife, Microsoft product manager Melinda French, whom he married on New Year's Day, 1994. The house is a series of interconnected pavilions set deep into a hillside, with its own salmon estuary, a twenty-car subterranean garage, a trampoline room, and video "walls" in every room to display changing electronic images of art (for which Gates has bought the rights from major museums) to suit the mood. "Working for Bill, you design for change," said the architect. That sums up Gates's approach to business as well.

The next step for Gates and Microsoft is onto the information superhighway. The personal computers that he had the vision to see as being part of daily life are evolving into a new kind of machine: a communications device that connects people to the Internet and beyond. Gates wants Microsoft to be part of that connection. Competitors such as Lotus, Sun Microsystems, Novell, and Apple complain that Microsoft has gotten too big, and the Justice Department and the Federal Trade Commission closely monitor its corporate acquisitions. But Gates disputes the notion that he exercises monopoly power over the industry. Why should he be penalized for being the best in a highly competitive market? Gates responds to the "Bill-bashers." Microsoft products are just delivering on the company motto, "We Set the Standard."

When Gates was asked the reasons for his success, he replied (by electronic mail, of course), "Besides a lot of luck, a high energy level and perhaps some IQ I think having an ability to deal with things at a very detailed level and a very broad level and synthesize between them is probably the thing that helps me the most. This allows someone to take deep technical understanding and figure out a business strategy that fits together with it." Friends note his "extraordinary bandwidth," that is, the amount of information he can absorb, but it is his insights into business rather than technology that set Gates apart. His entrepreneurial streak would have made Henry Ford or John D. Rockefeller proud, but Gates keenly worries about being left behind in the next stage of the computer revolution: "It's a little scary that as computer technology has moved ahead there's never been a leader from one era who was also a leader in the next." He takes this as a warning and a challenge: "But I want to defy historical tradition."

"Software is cool," Gates told CNN's Larry King to explain the hoopla surrounding the release of Microsoft's Windows 95. To the computer crowd, cool is the opposite of random, which means out of it, wrong, or inane. No one, especially not his competitors, has ever accused Bill Gates of being random.

Clinton/Gore

Baby boomers Bill Clinton and Al Gore billed themselves as representing a "new generation of leadership." Born in 1946 and 1948 respectively, they came of age in the turbulent 1960s. Vietnam, not World War II or Korea, was the war that defined their generation.

largest such zone in the world. NAFTA was strongly supported by the business community but bitterly opposed by labor unions worried about losing jobs to lower-paid Mexican workers and by environmentalists concerned about weak enforcement of antipollution laws south of the border. In what was seen as a major defeat for labor, a coalition of free-trade Democrats and Republicans narrowly passed NAFTA in November 1993.

Less controversial were the new provisions of the General Agreement on Tariffs and Trade (GATT), the treaty governing most international trade, which was part of the Bretton Woods system created by the major economic powers at the end of World War II. This new round of revisions, the eighth since the 1940s, cut tariffs on many manufactured products and for the first time established regulations protecting intellectual property such as patents, copyrights, and trademarks for software, entertainment, and pharmaceuticals. The U.S. Senate ratified the treaty in December 1994.

With the recession over, crime replaced the economy as a major concern among voters. In 1993 Congress passed the Brady Handgun Violence Prevention Act, named for James Brady, the White House press secretary who was crippled in the 1981 attempted assassination of President Reagan. A much more wide-ranging piece of legislation was the 1994 Omnibus Violent Crime Control and Prevention Act, which authorized $30.2 billion for stepped-up law enforcement, crime prevention, and prison construction and administration; it also expanded the death penalty to cover more than fifty federal crimes and banned the sale and possession of certain kinds of assault weapons.

Health Care. The issue on which Clinton staked his political fortunes was health care. The United States was spending more on health care than any other country in the world: $750 billion in 1991, up 11 percent from the year before. Yet it remained the only major industrialized country not to provide national health insurance, in part because of Roosevelt's decision not to push for a federal health care program in the 1930s. Spiraling medical costs (double the rate of inflation since 1970), rising premiums, and the large number of Americans without health insurance (one-sixth of the population in 1990) had brought the health care system to a crisis.

Despite his slender electoral mandate, the new president felt that his campaign promise to guarantee universal health insurance was finally within reach. He chose his wife, Hillary Rodham Clinton, to head the task force drafting the legislation, a controversial move since no first lady had ever played such a formal role in policy making. The Clinton proposal adopted the idea of *managed competition*: market forces, not the government, would control health care costs and expand access.

It took 1,300 pages to explain all the details when the legislation was submitted to Congress, a symptom of how this complex issue would defy an easy political resolution. Special-interest groups, including the well-financed

A Forceful and Controversial First Lady

Drawing inspiration from Eleanor Roosevelt, Hillary Rodham Clinton hoped the country would be ready for a first lady who could play a role in shaping policy. It wasn't. Throughout her husband's administration, she was subjected to intense criticism for everything from her role in health care reform to the Whitewater land deal to her frequently changing hairstyle.

pharmaceutical and insurance industries, began picking the plan apart. Small business owners argued that the requirement that all but the tiniest firms provide health insurance for their employees would bankrupt them or force them to lay off workers. During the campaign many Americans had expressed support for health care reform, but many began to fear what the changes might bring. In August 1994 the Senate failed to act on the plan, and by September Congressional leaders admitted that health reform was dead.

While the political system dithered, private market forces were already transforming the nation's medical system, replacing the traditional "fee for service" system with managed care plans that limited consumers' choice of doctors and treatments to cut costs. Medical care had become the domain of Wall Street and big business, and growing numbers of Americans had joined health maintenance organizations or looser "preferred provider" networks. While managed care succeeded in curbing the cost of health care premiums, private sector initiatives did nothing to help the unemployed and workers without health insurance, whose numbers continued to grow. An estimated 43.4 million Americans had no health insurance in 1995, almost 20 percent of the population under the age of sixty-five.

Post–Cold War Foreign Policy. One reason why health care reform failed was that President Clinton never devoted his full attention to building a consensus for the plan and shepherding it through Congress. In October 1993, for example, just after Clinton had announced the plan, twelve American soldiers were killed on a United Nations peacekeeping mission in Somalia. Then Clinton had to turn his attention to divisive issues such as the closely contested NAFTA vote, Haiti, and the worsening situation in Bosnia. This patchwork approach to foreign policy added to the perception of Clinton as vacillating, indecisive, and lacking a central vision. Not until 1996 did Clinton's foreign policy team begin to articulate a clear policy on when the United States should intervene in crises overseas.

In the former Soviet Union the increasing unpopularity of the Russian president Boris Yeltsin's efforts to bring about market reforms made American leaders less optimistic about the emergence of democracy within that country. Yeltsin's harsh repression of dissent in the breakaway region of Chechnya strained the already difficult relationship with the United States. In elections held in 1996 Yeltsin struggled to defeat his communist opponent, Gennadi Zyuganov.

Nothing seemed more intractable than the problems engulfing the former state of Yugoslavia, which typified the localized conflicts based on ethnicity, religion, and nationality that replaced the superpower conflicts of the cold war era. In what military analysts call "postmodern" or "future" wars, there is no distinction between armies and people—anybody who gets in the way gets killed. Unlike the Persian Gulf War, these conflicts do not rely on highly sophisticated technology and massive armies, but that does not keep them from being incredibly destructive.

The roots of the Bosnian conflict go back at least as far as the outbreak of World War I, but the immediate backdrop was the breakup of the state of Yugoslavia in 1991 into five independent states in the wake of the collapse of communism in Eastern Europe. Croatia and Slovenia secured their independence from the rump Yugoslavia government in brief, though intense, civil wars. Bosnia was not so lucky. The province of Bosnia and Herzegovina declared its independence in 1992, and its government, made up largely of Muslims and committed to a multiethnic (Serb, Croat, and Muslim) state, was quickly recognized by the United Nations. Bosnian Serbs, supported financially and militarily by Yugoslavia, formed their own breakaway state. They began a siege of the Bosnian capital, Sarajevo, site of the 1984 Winter Olympics, and launched a campaign of "ethnic cleansing" in the countryside. Bosnian Muslims and Croats were driven from their homes, put in concentration camps, or shot to death in mass executions. More than 250,000 people were killed or reported missing after war broke out in April 1992.

After three years of unsuccessful efforts by the European powers to stop the carnage, it was clear that the

Clinton in Bosnia
In his role as commander in chief, President Clinton visited Bosnia in January 1996 to show his support for the peacekeeping mission. Here he salutes American troops in the Bosnian town of Tuzla.

United States still had a critical role to play in guaranteeing European security. In November 1995 President Clinton and Secretary of State Warren Christopher facilitated a peace accord that ended the war, at least temporarily. Only the power of the United States commanded the respect of the three warring factions, and so the United States sent troops to Bosnia as part of a NATO-led force to implement the peace. As the world's only superpower, the United States was compelled to exercise its leadership—backed up by military force—to end the worst conflict in Europe since World War II.

At the same time, the end of cold war superpower rivalry presented unexpected opportunities to resolve other long-standing regional, ethnic, and religious conflicts. In Haiti, the threat of a U.S. invasion in October 1993 led to the restoration of the exiled president, Jean-Bertrand Aristide, who had been ousted by a military coup in 1991. In South Africa, the end of the fifty-year policy of racial separation was capped by the election of Nelson Mandela, who had spent twenty-seven years in prison for challenging apartheid, as the country's first black president in May 1994. With President Clinton proudly looking on, Israeli Prime Minister Yitzhak Rabin and Yasir Arafat, chairman of the Palestine Liberation Organization, signed an agreement in May 1994 allowing limited Palestinian self-rule in the Gaza Strip and Jericho. And in a move that was seen as a symbolic end to the American experience in Vietnam, the United States established diplomatic relations with Hanoi in July 1995, two decades after the fall of Saigon.

With the end of the Cold War, many citizens had hoped for a *peace dividend*, redirecting money from defense to domestic programs. But America's global responsibilities had not declined. Defense spending stayed near its cold war levels even in the Clinton administration. Despite closing up to 130 military bases around the country and making cutbacks in research and development for new weapons systems, the post–cold war defense budget averaged $280 billion, compared with the cold war average of $304 billion (in 1996 dollars). This small peace dividend was swallowed up by the huge deficit.

"The Era of Big Government Is Over"

The 1994 midterm election produced one of the most significant sea changes in recent political history, the culmination of the shift that had begun with Ronald Reagan's election in 1980. Republicans gained 52 seats in the House, giving them control for the first time in forty years; they also retook the Senate for the first time since 1986. The centerpiece of the new Republican majority in the House was the Contract with America, a list of legislation that Newt Gingrich of Georgia, the new Speaker, promised would be voted on in the first 100 days of the session. The key elements of the contract were constitutional amendments to balance the budget and set term limits for Congressional office, $245 billion in tax cuts for individuals and incentives for small businesses, cuts in welfare and other entitlement programs, anticrime initiatives, and cutbacks in federal regulations. Addressing the Republican Congress in his State of the Union message in January 1996, President Clinton acknowledged that "the era of big government is over."

Republicans in Congress

House Speaker Newt Gingrich, shown here in front of the Capitol in 1994, announces the Contract with America, which 73 freshmen Republican candidates rode to victory in the November election. The House's 236-member Republican majority passed many of the contract's planks in 1995, but most either failed to win passage in the Senate or were vetoed by President Clinton. By 1996 the Republican revolution had stalled on Capitol Hill.

Balancing the Budget. The Republicans' commitment to tax cuts *and* a balanced budget by the year 2002 led them to propose much deeper cuts than most Americans would accept. A glance at the major components of the federal budget suggests the difficulty of balancing the budget while also cutting taxes. The budget is divided into five roughly equal parts: interest on the debt; defense; health care costs (Medicare and Medicaid); Social Security; and discretionary spending, that is, everything else. Interest on the debt must be paid. Defense spending in the post–cold war world has declined only slightly. That leaves Medicare and Medicaid, Social Security, and everything else. Since Social Security was considered untouchable, Congress looked for savings in health care and discretionary spending.

Despite the failure of Clinton's health reform bill, by 1995 everyone agreed that it was essential to bring health care costs under control. Medicare, signed into law by President Johnson in 1965, had cost almost $160 billion in 1994, almost 10 percent of the entire federal budget. As new medical technologies proliferated and the number of elderly people increased, expenses were rising at a rate of 10 percent a year. In the fall of 1995 Congress passed a budget cutting $270 billion from projected spending on Medicare and $170 billion from Medicaid over seven years. Other savings came from cuts in various discretionary programs, including education and the environment. Clinton accepted Congress' resolve to balance the budget in seven years, but, vowing to protect the nation from an "extremist" Congress, he vetoed the budget itself. Unfunded departments of the government were forced to shut down twice, and polls showed that a majority of Americans held Congress, not the president, responsible. The budget that Clinton finally signed in April 1996 left Medicare and Social Security intact, though it did meet the Republicans' goal of cutting $23 billion in discretionary spending.

Welfare Reform. Since the Reagan Era, the old argument that the federal government has an obligation to the poor has been supplanted by rhetoric about cost-effectiveness, incentives, personal responsibility, and turning programs over to the states. Although Clinton had promised in the 1992 campaign to "end welfare as we know it," serious debate on the issue did not begin until the Republicans took over Congress in 1995. Welfare, a joint federal-state program, represented a fairly small part of the budget, but to Republicans it had become the prime example of misguided government priorities. The benefits of the main welfare program, AFDC, were far from generous: the average annual welfare payment to families (including Food Stamps) was $7,740, well below the 1995 poverty line of $12,188. In the 1990s both Democratic and Republican statehouses had adopted various financial incentives to try to change welfare beneficiaries' behavior, including setting time limits, imposing work requirements, and denying benefits for additional children born to women on AFDC. After vetoing two earlier versions, in August 1996 President Clinton signed a historic overhaul of the welfare system that ended the federal guarantee of cash assistance to poor children by abolishing AFDC, required most adult recipients to find work within two years, set a five-year limit on payments to any family, and gave states wide discretion in running their welfare programs.

The 1996 Election

The Republican takeover of Congress had one unintended consequence—it unified the usually fractious Democrats behind Bill Clinton. Unopposed in the primaries, Clinton was able to burnish his image as a moderate "New Democrat." His political fortunes were aided by the strong performance of the economy and the unpopularity of the Republican Congress since the government shutdowns.

In the Republican primaries, voters flirted with conservative commentator Pat Buchanan and magazine publisher Steve Forbes before settling on Senate Majority Leader Bob Dole of Kansas as their presidential candidate. Dole was acceptable to both conservative and moderate wings of the party, though his detached campaign style failed to generate much enthusiasm. He made a 15 percent across-the-board tax cut the centerpiece of his campaign, selecting former representative Jack Kemp, a leading proponent of supply-side economics, as his running-mate. Dole and Kemp promised to cut taxes *and* balance the budget by 2002, but their failure to specify what programs they would cut to achieve those goals undermined the credibility of the plan.

Americans seemed to have made up their minds early about the candidates, which made for a rather desultory campaign. Clinton emphasized his success in reducing the budget deficit, raising the minimum wage to $5.15, and reforming welfare, and he took credit for the 10 million new jobs created during his administration. In November, Clinton became the first Democratic president since Franklin Roosevelt to win reelection (see Map 33.6). Voter turnout was the lowest since Calvin Coolidge won in 1924. Despite fears of Democratic coattails, Republicans retained control of the House of Representatives and increased their majority in the Senate; they also maintained control of the majority of statehouses. Among the record number of initiatives on state ballots the most significant to win was California's Proposition 209, which sought to abolish affirmative action in government hiring, contracts, and public college admissions. In general, however, the main lesson of the election was voters' endorsement of the status quo

Summary

Ronald Reagan's administration advocated a smaller role for the federal government in domestic programs and the restoration of American prestige abroad through a massive military buildup. The term *Reaganomics* stood for tax cuts and budget reductions enacted in 1981 and 1982. Reagan's economic policies, notably deregulation and tax cuts, added to the concentration of wealth in the 1980s. Reagan remained enormously popular throughout his two terms but left large budget deficits to his successor, Vice-President George Bush.

The most dramatic change during the Bush administration was the end of the Cold War, which had been the guiding principle of American foreign policy since the end of World War II. The dramatic collapse of communism in the Soviet Union in 1991 further complicated the old truisms. The post–cold war future seemed to promise a fragile world peace that would be vulnerable to regional and ethnic conflicts but in which the United States, as the world's only remaining superpower, would still play the dominant leadership role. The United States also played a leading role in an increasingly global economy but no longer dominated the world economy as it had done during the *Pax Americana* of the immediate postwar world.

American society in the 1980s and 1990s continued to turn inward to address its own needs. Increased immigration, notably from Asia and Latin America, changed the demographic balance of many areas, especially the cities, and the strains of an increasingly diverse society were reflected in debates over affirmative action and multiculturalism. Slow productivity growth, wage stagnation, and growing inequality in income were the major domestic economic trends. Meanwhile, American businesses struggled to compete in an increasingly competitive global marketplace. The information superhighway and cyberspace pointed to a high-tech future.

Soon after the Democrats regained the White House with the election of Bill Clinton in 1992, the Republican landslide of 1994 reshaped politics dramatically by emphasizing a balanced budget, tax cuts, and shrinking the federal government by turning programs over to the states. In January 1996 even President Clinton admitted, "The era of big government is over." In August he signed a welfare reform bill that ended the federal guarantee of cash assistance to the poor. Clinton won reelection to a second term, but continued Republican control of Congress suggested that the long-term trend of federal activism had been reversed.

TIMELINE

1981	Economic Recovery Tax Act Sandra Day O'Connor nominated to Supreme Court MTV premieres Beginning of AIDS epidemic
1982	Recession
1983	Star Wars proposed
1984	Geraldine Ferraro becomes first woman on major party ticket
1985	Gramm-Rudman Balanced Budget Act United States becomes a debtor nation Mikhail Gorbachev takes power in U.S.S.R
1986	Iran-Contra affair Simpson-Mazzoli Immigration Act
1987	Montreal environmental protocol Stock market collapse
1988	George Bush elected president
1989	Savings and loan crisis Political revolutions in Eastern Europe *Webster v. Reproductive Health Services*
1990–1991	Persian Gulf crisis
1990–1992	Recession
1991	Dissolution of Soviet Union ends Cold War Clarence Thomas–Anita Hill hearings
1992	Los Angeles riots Earth Summit at Rio de Janeiro Bill Clinton elected president
1993	Family and Medical Leave Act NAFTA ratified
1994	Omnibus Violent Crime Control and Prevention Act Health care reform fails Republicans gain control of Congress
1995	Congress passes parts of the Contract with America United States establishes diplomatic relations with Vietnam University of California votes to end affirmative action plan Twenty-fifth anniversary of Earth Day U.S. troops enforce peace in Bosnia
1996	Personal Responsibility and Work Opportunity Act (welfare reform) Bill Clinton reelected president

★   ★   ★

BIBLIOGRAPHY

Few historians have turned their attention to the period after 1980, leaving the field to journalists, economists, and political scientists. The Bureau of the Census offers a fine introduction to the period in its *Statistical Abstract of the United States* (114th ed., 1994). Essays on important issues are available in the *Congressional Quarterly Researcher*. Indexes to newspapers and periodicals point toward stories on major events.

The Reagan Presidency

Haynes Johnson, *Sleepwalking through History* (1991), provides an excellent overview of America in the Reagan years. See also Robert Dallek, *Ronald Reagan: The Politics of Symbolism* (1982); Michael Rogin, *Ronald Reagan: The Movie* (1987); and Lou Cannon, *President Reagan: A Role of a Lifetime* (1991). Nancy Reagan presents her interpretation of the Reagan years in *My Turn* (1989), and the speechwriter Peggy Noonan offers an insider's view in *What I Saw at the Revolution* (1990).

On Reaganomics, George Gilder's *Wealth and Poverty* (1981) represents the views held by many in the Reagan administration, but David Stockman's memoir, *The Triumph of Politics* (1986), is more revealing. See also Benjamin Friedman, *Day of Reckoning: The Consequences of American Economic Policy under Reagan and After* (1988).

For foreign policy, Stephen Ambrose, *Rise to Globalism* (7th ed., 1993), provides a comprehensive overview of the Reagan and Bush years. The Iran-Contra scandal is covered in Jane Hunter et al., *The Iran-Contra Connection* (1987). Good introductions to the United States and Central and South America include Walter LaFeber, *Inevitable Revolutions* (1984); Abraham F. Lowenthal, *Partners in Conflict: The United States and Latin America* (1987); and Kenneth Coleman and George C. Herring, eds., *The Central America Crisis* (1985).

The Bush Presidency and the End of the Cold War

On the Bush administration, see James A. Baker, *The Politics of Diplomacy* (1995); Barbara Bush, *Barbara Bush: A Memoir* (1994); and Stephen R. Graubard, *Mr. Bush's War: Adventures in the Politics of Illusion* (1992). On politics, see E. J. Dionne, *Why Americans Hate Politics* (1992); William Greider, *Who Will Tell the People?* (1992); and Kevin Phillips, *The Politics of Rich and Poor: Wealth and the American Electorate in the Reagan Aftermath* (1990).

The emergence of a new world order has provoked commentary from economists, journalists, and historians, including Paul Kennedy, *The Rise and Fall of the Great Powers* (1987); Joseph Nye, *Bound to Lead: The Changing Nature of American Power* (1990); Robert Kuttner, *The End of Laissez Faire: National Purpose and the Global Economy after the Cold War* (1991); and Henry R. Nau, *The Myth of America's Decline: Leading the World Economy into the 1990s* (1990). Bernard Gwertzman and Michael T. Kaufman, eds., *The Collapse of Communism* (1990), reviews the events of 1989 through articles published in the *New York Times*. See also Michael Beschloss and Strobe Talbott, *At the Highest Levels: The Inside Story of the End of the Cold War* (1994). H. Norman Schwartzkopf's autobiography, *It Doesn't Take a Hero* (1992), recounts the Gulf War, as does former chairman of the Joint Chiefs of Staff Colin Powell in *My American Journey* (1995).

An Age of Anxiety

Paul Krugman provides an overview of economic trends since the 1970s in *Peddling Prosperity: Economic Sense and Nonsense in the Age of Diminished Expectations* (1994); Jeffrey Madrick, *The End of Affluence* (1995), makes similar points. For overviews of U.S. competitiveness in the global marketplace, see Hedrick Smith, *Rethinking America* (1995); Lester Thurow, *Head to Head: The Coming Economic Battle among Japan, Europe, and America* (1992); and Robert B. Reich, *The Work of Nations: Preparing Ourselves for 21st Century Capitalism* (1991). Books that address the growing inequality in American life include William J. Wilson, *The Truly Disadvantaged* (1987); Michael Katz, *The Undeserving Poor: From the War on Poverty to the War on Welfare* (1989); Nicholas Lemann, *The Promised Land* (1989); and Linda Gordon, *Pitied but Not Entitled: Single Mothers and the History of Welfare* (1994).

On the problems of women, work, and families, see Hilda Scott, *Working Your Way to the Bottom: The Feminization of Poverty* (1985); Arlie Hochschild, *The Second Shift: Working Parents and the Revolution at Home* (1989); and Juliet Schor, *The Overworked American* (1991). For feminism and its critics, see Susan Faludi, *Backlash: The Undeclared War on American Women* (1991). Toni Morrison, ed., *Race-ing Justice, En-gendering Power* (1992), covers the Clarence Thomas-Anita Hill hearings.

David Reimers, *Still the Golden Door* (2d ed., 1992), covers immigration policy in the postwar period. Linda Chavez, *Out of the Barrio* (1991), discusses Hispanic assimilation, while Ronald Takaki, *Strangers from a Different Shore* (1989), covers Asian-Americans. Also of interest is Julian Simon, *The Economic Consequences of Immigration* (1989).

Randy Shilts, *And the Band Played On: Politics, People, and the AIDS Epidemic* (1987), is a controversial critique of inaction in the early years of the AIDS epidemic. See also Elinor Burkett, *The Gravest Show on Earth: America in the Age of AIDS* (1995). Allan Bloom, *The Closing of the American Mind* (1987), and E. D. Hirsch, Jr., *Cultural Literacy* (1988), deal with issues of curriculum, learning, and literacy. For differing views on affirmative action, see Stephen L. Carter, *Reflections of an Affirmative Action Baby* (1991), and Gertrude Ezorsky, *Racism and Justice: The Case for Affirmative Action* (1991). For the story of Bill Gates and Microsoft, see Steven Manes, *Gates: How Microsoft's Mogul Reinvented an Industry—and Made Himself the Richest Man in America* (1993); James Wallace, *Hard Drive* (1992); and Gates's own *The Road Ahead* (1995).

Restructuring the Domestic Order

For an excellent overview of Clinton's first year, see Elizabeth Drew, *Finding His Voice* (1994). Other sources include Bob Woodward, *The Agenda* (1994); Roger Morris, *Promises of Change* (1996); and Richard Cohen, *Changing the Guard* (1993). On the Republican agenda, see Newt Gingrich, *To Renew America* (1995).

Gregg Easterbrook provides a general overview of the environment in *A Moment on the Earth* (1995). Al Gore, *Earth in the Balance* (1992), reports on how well or poorly the world is doing on environmental awareness. Daniel Yergin, *The Prize* (1991), chronicles how oil dominates modern life, with both economic and environmental consequences.

The Declaration of Independence

★   ★   ★

The Unanimous Declaration of the Thirteen United States of America

When in the Course of human events, it becomes necessary for one people to dissolve the political bands which have connected them with another, and to assume among the Powers of the earth, the separate and equal station to which the Laws of Nature and of Nature's God entitle them, a decent respect to the opinions of mankind requires that they should declare the causes which impel them to the separation.

We hold these truths to be self-evident, that all men are created equal, that they are endowed by their Creator with certain unalienable rights, that among these are Life, Liberty, and the pursuit of Happiness. That to secure these rights, Governments are instituted among Men, deriving their just powers from the consent of the governed. That whenever any Form of Government becomes destructive of these ends, it is the Right of the People to alter or to abolish it, and to institute new Government, laying its foundation on such principles and organizing its powers in such form, as to them shall seem most likely to effect their Safety and Happiness. Prudence, indeed, will dictate that Governments long established should not be changed for light and transient causes; and accordingly all experience hath shown, that mankind are more disposed to suffer, while evils are sufferable, than to right themselves by abolishing the forms to which they are accustomed. But when a long train of abuses and usurpations, pursuing invariably the same Object evinces a design to reduce them under absolute Despotism, it is their right, it is their duty, to throw off such Government, and to provide new Guards for their future security.—Such has been the patient sufferance of these Colonies; and such is now the necessity which constrains them to alter their former Systems of Government. The history of the present King of Great Britain is a history of repeated injuries and usurpations, all having in direct object the estab-lishment of an absolute Tyranny over these States. To prove this, let Facts be submitted to a candid world.

He has refused his Assent to Laws, the most wholesome and necessary for the public good.

He has forbidden his Governors to pass Laws of immediate and pressing importance, unless suspended in their operation till his Assent should be obtained; and, when so suspended, he has utterly neglected to attend to them.

He has refused to pass other Laws for the accommodation of large districts of people, unless those people would relinquish the right of Representation in the Legislature, a right inestimable to them and formidable to tyrants only.

He has called together legislative bodies at places unusual, uncomfortable, and distant from the depository of their public Records, for the sole purpose of fatiguing them into compliance with his measures.

He has dissolved Representative Houses repeatedly, for opposing with manly firmness his invasions on the rights of the people.

He has refused for a long time, after such dissolutions, to cause others to be elected; whereby the Legislative powers, incapable of Annihilation, have returned to the People at large for their exercise; the State remaining in the mean time exposed to all the dangers of invasion from without and convulsions within.

He has endeavoured to prevent the population of these States; for that purpose obstructing the Laws of Naturalization of Foreigners; refusing to pass others to encourage their migrations hither, and raising the conditions of new Appropriations of Lands.

He has obstructed the Administration of Justice, by refusing his Assent to Laws for establishing Judiciary powers.

He has made Judges dependent on his Will alone, for the tenure of their offices, and the amount and payment of their salaries.

He has erected a multitude of New Offices, and sent hither swarms of Officers to harass our People, and eat out their substance.

He has kept among us, in times of peace, Standing Armies without the Consent of our legislature.

He has combined with others to subject us to a jurisdiction foreign to our constitution, and unacknowledged by our laws; giving his Assent to their Acts of pretended Legislation:

For quartering large bodies of armed troops among us:

For protecting them, by a mock Trial, from Punishment for any Murders which they should commit on the Inhabitants of these States:

For cutting off our Trade with all parts of the world:

For imposing taxes on us without our Consent:

For depriving us of many cases, of the benefits of Trial by jury:

For transporting us beyond Seas to be tried for pretended offences:

For abolishing the free System of English Laws in a neighbouring Province, establishing therein an Arbitrary government, and enlarging its Boundaries so as to render it at once an example and fit instrument for introducing the same absolute rule into these Colonies;

For taking away our Charters, abolishing our most valuable Laws, and altering fundamentally the Forms of our Governments:

For suspending our own Legislatures, and declaring themselves invested with Power to legislate for us in all cases whatsoever.

He has abdicated Government here, by declaring us out of his Protection and waging War against us.

He has plundered our seas, ravaged our Coasts, burnt our towns, and destroyed the lives of our people.

He is at this time transporting large armies of foreign mercenaries to compleat the works of death, desolation, and tyranny, already begun with circumstances of Cruelty & perfidy scarcely parallelled in the most barbarous ages, and totally unworthy the Head of a civilized nation.

He has constrained our fellow Citizens taken Captive on the high Seas to bear Arms against their Country, to become the executioners of their friends and Brethren, or to fall themselves by their Hands.

He has excited domestic insurrections amongst us, and has endeavoured to bring on the inhabitants of our frontiers, the merciless Indian Savages, whose known rule of warfare, is an undistinguished destruction of all ages, sexes, and conditions.

In every stage of these Oppressions We have Petitioned for Redress in the most humble terms: Our repeated Petitions have been answered only by repeated injury. A Prince, whose character is thus marked by every act which may define a Tyrant, is unfit to be the ruler of a free people.

Nor have We been wanting in attention to our British brethren. We have warned them from time to time of attempts by their legislature to extend an unwarrantable jurisdiction over us. We have reminded them of the circumstances of our emigration and settlement here. We have appealed to their native justice and magnanimity, and we have conjured them by the ties of our common kindred to disavow these usurpations, which, would inevitably interrupt our connections and correspondence. They too have been deaf to the voice of justice and of consanguinity. We must, therefore, acquiesce in the necessity, which denounces our Separation, and hold them, as we hold the rest of mankind, Enemies in War, in Peace Friends.

We, therefore, the Representatives of the United States of America, in General Congress, Assembled, appealing to the Supreme Judge of the world for the rectitude of our intentions, do, in the Name, and by Authority of the good People of these Colonies, solemnly publish and declare, That these United Colonies are, and of Right ought to be FREE AND INDEPENDENT STATES; that they are Absolved from all Allegiance to the British Crown, and that all political connection between them and the State of Great Britain, is and ought to be totally dissolved; and that as Free and Independent States, they have full Power to levy War, conclude Peace, contract Alliances, establish Commerce, and to do all other Acts and Things which Independent States may of right do. And for the support of this Declaration, with a firm reliance on the Protection of Divine Providence, we mutually pledge to each other our Lives, our Fortunes, and our sacred Honor.

John Hancock

Button Gwinnett	George Wythe	James Wilson	Josiah Bartlett
Lyman Hall	Richard Henry Lee	Geo. Ross	Wm. Whipple
Geo. Walton	Th. Jefferson	Caesar Rodney	Saml. Adams
Wm. Hooper	Benja. Harrison	Geo. Read	John Adams
Joseph Hewes	Thos. Nelson, Jr.	Thos. M'Kean	Robt. Treat Paine
John Penn	Francis Lightfoot Lee	Wm. Floyd	Elbridge Gerry
Edward Rutledge	Carter Braxton	Phil. Livingston	Step. Hopkins
Thos. Heyward, Junr.	Robt. Morris	Frans. Lewis	William Ellery
Thomas Lynch, Junr.	Benjamin Rush	Lewis Morris	Roger Sherman
Arthur Middleton	Benja. Franklin	Richd. Stockton	Sam'el Hunington
Samuel Chase	John Morton	Jno. Witherspoon	Wm. Williams
Wm. Paca	Geo. Clymer	Fras. Hopkinson	Oliver Wolcott
Thos. Stone	Jas. Smith	John Hart	Matthew Thornton
Charles Carroll of Carrollton	Geo. Taylor	Abra. Clark	

The Articles of Confederation and Perpetual Union

★   ★   ★

BETWEEN THE STATES OF NEW HAMPSHIRE, MASSACHU-
SETTS BAY, RHODE ISLAND AND PROVIDENCE PLANTA-
TIONS, CONNECTICUT, NEW YORK, NEW JERSEY, PENN-
SYLVANIA, DELAWARE, MARYLAND, VIRGINIA, NORTH
CAROLINA, SOUTH CAROLINA, GEORGIA.*

Article 1.

The stile of this confederacy shall be "The United States of
America."

Article 2.

Each State retains its sovereignty, freedom and independence,
and every power, jurisdiction, and right, which is not by this
confederation expressly delegated to the United States, in
Congress assembled.

Article 3.

The said states hereby severally enter into a firm league of
friendship with each other for their common defence, the security of their liberties and their mutual and general welfare;
binding themselves to assist each other against all force offered to, or attacks made upon them, or any of them, on account of religion, sovereignty, trade, or any other pretence
whatever.

*This copy of the final draft of the Articles of Confederation is taken from
the *Journals*, 9:907–925, November 15, 1777.

Article 4.

The better to secure and perpetuate mutual friendship and intercourse among the people of the different states in this
union, the free inhabitants of each of these states, paupers,
vagabonds, and fugitives from justice excepted, shall be entitled to all privileges and immunities of free citizens in the several states; and the people of each State shall have free ingress
and regress to and from any other State, and shall enjoy
therein all the privileges of trade and commerce, subject to the
same duties, impositions, and restrictions, as the inhabitants
thereof respectively; provided, that such restrictions shall not
extend so far as to prevent the removal of property, imported
into any State, to any other State of which the owner is an inhabitant; provided also, that no imposition, duties, or restriction, shall be laid by any State on the property of the United
States, or either of them.

If any person guilty of, or charged with treason, felony, or
other high misdemeanor in any State, shall flee from justice
and be found in any of the United States, he shall, upon demand of the governor or executive power of the State from
which he fled, be delivered up and removed to the State having
jurisdiction of his offence.

Full faith and credit shall be given in each of these states
to the records, acts, and judicial proceedings of the courts and
magistrates of every other State.

Article 5.

For the more convenient management of the general interests
of the United States, delegates shall be annually appointed, in
such manner as the legislature of each State shall direct, to
meet in Congress, on the 1st Monday in November in every

year, with a power reserved to each State to recal its delegates, or any of them, at any time within the year, and to send others in their stead for the remainder of the year.

No State shall be represented in Congress by less than two, nor by more than seven members; and no person shall be capable of being a delegate for more than three years in any term of six years; nor shall any person, being a delegate, be capable of holding any office under the United States, for which he, or any other for his benefit, receives any salary, fees, or emolument of any kind.

Each State shall maintain its own delegates in a meeting of the states, and while they act as members of the committee of the states.

In determining questions in the United States, in Congress assembled, each State shall have one vote.

Freedom of speech and debate in Congress shall not be impeached or questioned in any court or place out of Congress: and the members of Congress shall be protected in their persons from arrests and imprisonments, during the time of their going to and from, and attendance on Congress, *except for treason*, felony, or breach of the peace.

Article 6.

No State, without the consent of the United States, in Congress assembled, shall send any embassy to, or receive any embassy from, or enter into any conference, agreement, alliance, or treaty with any king, prince, or state; nor shall any person, holding any office of profit or trust under the United States, or any of them, accept of any present, emolument, office or title, of any kind whatever, from any king, prince, or foreign state; nor shall the United States, in Congress assembled, or any of them, grant any title of nobility.

No two or more states shall enter into any treaty, confederation, or alliance, whatever, between them, without the consent of the United States, in Congress assembled, specifying accurately the purposes for which the same is to be entered into, and how long it shall continue.

No state shall lay any imposts or duties which may interfere with any stipulations in treaties entered into by the United States, in Congress assembled, with any king, prince, or state, in pursuance of any treaties already proposed by Congress to the courts of France and Spain.

No vessels of war shall be kept up in time of peace by any State, except such number only as shall be deemed necessary by the United States, in Congress assembled, for the defence of such State or its trade; nor shall any body of forces be kept up by any State, in time of peace, except such number only as, in the judgment of the United States, in Congress assembled, shall be deemed requisite to garrison the forts necessary for the defence of such State; but every State shall always keep up a well regulated and disciplined militia, sufficiently armed and accoutred, and shall provide, and constantly have ready for use, in public stores, a due number of field pieces and tents, and a proper quantity of arms, ammunition and camp equipage.

No State shall engage in any war without the consent of the United States, in Congress assembled, unless such State be actually invaded by enemies, or shall have received certain advice of a resolution being formed by some nation of Indians to invade such State, and the danger is so imminent as not to admit of a delay till the United States, in Congress assembled, can be consulted; nor shall any State grant commissions to any ships or vessels of war, nor letters of marque or reprisal, except it be after a declaration of war by the United States, in Congress assembled, and then only against the kingdom or state, and the subjects thereof, against which war has been so declared, and under such regulations as shall be established by the United States, in Congress assembled, unless such State be infested by pirates, in which case vessels of war may be fitted out for that occasion, and kept so long as the danger shall continue, or until the United States, in Congress assembled, shall determine otherwise.

Article 7.

When land forces are raised by any State for the common defence, all officers of or under the rank of colonel, shall be appointed by the legislature of each State respectively, by whom such forces shall be raised, or in such manner as such State shall direct; and all vacancies shall be filled up by the State which first made the appointment.

Article 8.

All charges of war and all other expences, that shall be incurred for the common defence or general welfare, and allowed by the United States, in Congress assembled, shall be defrayed out of a common treasury, which shall be supplied by the several states, in proportion to the value of all land within each State, granted to or surveyed for any person, as such land and the buildings and improvements thereon shall be estimated according to such mode as the United States, in Congress assembled, shall, from time to time, direct and appoint.

The taxes for paying that proportion shall be laid and levied by the authority and direction of the legislatures of the several states, within the time agreed upon by the United States, in Congress assembled.

Article 9.

The United States, in Congress assembled, shall have the sole and exclusive right and power of determining on peace and war, except in the cases mentioned in the 6th article; of sending and receiving ambassadors; entering into treaties and alliances, provided that no treaty of commerce shall be made, whereby the legislative power of the respective states shall be restrained from imposing such imposts and duties on foreigners as their own people are subjected to, or from prohibiting the exportation or importation of any species of goods or commodities whatsoever; of establishing rules for deciding, in all cases, what captures on land or water shall be legal, and in what manner prizes, taken by land or naval forces in the ser-

vice of the United States, shall be divided or appropriated; of granting letters of marque and reprisal in times of peace; appointing courts for the trial of piracies and felonies committed on the high seas, and establishing courts for receiving and determining, finally, appeals in all cases of captures; provided, that no member of Congress shall be appointed a judge of any of the said courts.

The United States, in Congress assembled, shall also be the last resort on appeal in all disputes and differences now subsisting, or that hereafter may arise between two or more states concerning boundary, jurisdiction or any other cause whatever; which authority shall always be exercised in the manner following: whenever the legislative or executive authority, or lawful agent of any State, in controversy with another, shall present a petition to Congress, stating the matter in question, and praying for a hearing, notice thereof shall be given, by order of Congress, to the legislative or executive authority of the other State in controversy, and a day assigned for the appearance of the parties by their lawful agents, who shall then be directed to appoint, by joint consent, commissioners or judges to constitute a court for hearing and determining the matter in question; but, if they cannot agree, Congress shall name three persons out of each of the United States, and from the list of such persons each party shall alternately strike out one, the petitioners beginning, until the number shall be reduced to thirteen; and from that number not less than seven, nor more than nine names, as Congress shall direct, shall, in the presence of Congress, be drawn out by lot; and the persons whose names shall be so drawn, or any five of them, shall be commissioners or judges to hear and finally determine the controversy, so always as a major part of the judges who shall hear the cause shall agree in the determination; and if either party shall neglect to attend at the day appointed, without shewing reasons which Congress shall judge sufficient, or, being present, shall refuse to strike, the Congress shall proceed to nominate three persons out of each State, and the secretary of Congress shall strike in behalf of such party absent or refusing; and the judgment and sentence of the court to be appointed, in the manner before prescribed, shall be final and conclusive; and if any of the parties shall refuse to submit to the authority of such court, or to appear or defend their claim or cause, the court shall nevertheless proceed to pronounce sentence or judgment, which shall, in like manner, be final and decisive, the judgment or sentence and other proceedings begin, in either case, transmitted to Congress, and lodged among the acts of Congress for the security of the parties concerned: provided, that every commissioner, before he sits in judgment, shall take an oath, to be administered by one of the judges of the supreme or superior court of the State where the cause shall be tried, "well and truly to hear and determine the matter in question, according to the best of his judgment, without favour, affection, or hope of reward:" provided, also, that no State shall be deprived of territory for the benefit of the United States.

All controversies concerning the private right of soil, claimed under different grants of two or more states, whose jurisdictions, as they may respect such lands and the states which passed such grants, are adjusted, the said grants, or either of them, being at the same time claimed to have originated antecedent to such settlement of jurisdiction, shall, on the petition of either party to the Congress of the United States, be finally determined, as near as may be, in the same manner as is before prescribed for deciding disputes respecting territorial jurisdiction between different states.

The United States, in Congress assembled, shall also have the sole and exclusive right and power of regulating the alloy and value of coin struck by their own authority, or by that of the respective states; fixing the standard of weights and measures throughout the United States; regulating the trade and managing all affairs with the Indians not members of any of the states; provided that the legislative right of any State within its own limits be not infringed or violated; establishing and regulating post offices from one State to another throughout all the United States, and exacting such postage on the papers passing through the same as may be requisite to defray the expences of the said office; appointing all officers of the land forces in the service of the United States, excepting regimental officers; appointing all the officers of the naval forces, and commissioning all officers whatever in the service of the United States; making rules for the government and regulation of the said land and naval forces, and directing their operations.

The United States, in Congress assembled, shall have authority to appoint a committee to sit in the recess of Congress, to be denominated "a Committee of the States," and to consist of one delegate from each State, and to appoint such other committees and civil officers as may be necessary for managing the general affairs of the United States, under their direction; to appoint one of their number to preside; provided that no person be allowed to serve in the office of president more than one year in any term of three years; to ascertain the necessary sums of money to be raised for the service of the United States, and to appropriate and apply the same for defraying the public expences; to borrow money or emit bills on the credit of the United States, transmitting, every half year, to the respective states, an account of the sums of money so borrowed or emitted; to build and equip a navy; to agree upon the number of land forces, and to make requisitions from each State for its quota, in proportion to the number of white inhabitants in such State; which requisitions shall be binding; and thereupon, the legislature of each State shall appoint the regimental officers, raise the men, and cloathe, arm, and equip them in a soldier-like manner, at the expence of the United States; and the officers and men so cloathed, armed, and equipped, shall march to the place appointed and within the time agreed on by the United States, in Congress assembled; but if the United States, in Congress assembled, shall, on consideration of circumstances, judge proper that any State should not raise men, or should raise a smaller number than its quota, and that any other State should raise a greater number of men than the quota thereof, such extra number shall be raised, officered, cloathed, armed, and equipped in the same manner as the quota of such State, unless the legislature of such State shall judge that such extra number cannot be safely spared out of the same, in which case they shall raise, officer, cloathe, arm, and equip as many of such extra number as they judge can be safely spared. And the officers and men so cloathed, armed, and equipped, shall march to the place appointed and within the time agreed on by the United States, in Congress assembled.

The United States, in Congress assembled, shall never engage in a war, nor grant letters of marque and reprisal in time of peace, nor enter into any treaties or alliances, nor coin money, nor regulate the value thereof, nor ascertain the sums and expences necessary for the defence and welfare of the United States, or any of them: nor emit bills, nor borrow money on the credit of the United States, nor appropriate money, nor agree upon the number of vessels of war to be built or purchased, or the number of land or sea forces to be raised, nor appoint a commander in chief of the army or navy, unless nine states assent to the same; nor shall a question on any other point, except for adjourning from day to day, be determined, unless by the votes of a majority of the United States, in Congress assembled.

The Congress of the United States shall have power to adjourn to any time within the year, and to any place within the United States, so that no period of adjournment be for a longer duration than the space of six months, and shall publish the journal of their proceedings monthly, except such parts thereof, relating to treaties, alliances or military operations, as, in their judgment, require secrecy; and the yeas and nays of the delegates of each State on any question shall be entered on the journal, when it is desired by any delegate; and the delegates of a State, or any of them, at his, or their request, shall be furnished with a transcript of the said journal, except such parts as are above excepted, to lay before the legislatures of the several states.

Article 10.

The committee of the states, or any nine of them, shall be authorized to execute, in the recess of Congress, such of the powers of Congress as the United States, in Congress assembled, by the consent of nine states, shall, from time to time, think expedient to vest them with; provided, that no power be delegated to the said committee, for the exercise of which, by the articles of confederation, the voice of nine states, in the Congress of the United States assembled, is requisite.

Article 11.

Canada acceding to this confederation, and joining in the measures of the United States, shall be admitted into and entitled to all the advantages of this union; but no other colony shall be admitted into the same, unless such admission be agreed to by nine states.

Article 12.

All bills of credit emitted, monies borrowed and debts contracted by, or under the authority of Congress before the assembling of the United States, in pursuance of the present confederation, shall be deemed and considered as a charge against the United States, for payment and satisfaction whereof the said United States and the public faith are hereby solemnly pledged.

Article 13.

Every State shall abide by the determinations of the United States, in Congress assembled, on all questions which, by this confederation, are submitted to them. And the articles of this confederation shall be inviolably observed by every State, and the union shall be perpetual; nor shall any alteration at any time hereafter be made in any of them, unless such alteration be agreed to in a Congress of the United States, and be afterwards confirmed by the legislatures of every State.

These articles shall be proposed to the legislatures of all the United States, to be considered, and if approved of by them, they are advised to authorize their delegates to ratify the same in the Congress of the United States; which being done, the same shall become conclusive.

The Constitution of the United States of America

★　　★　　★

We the People of the United States, in Order to form a more perfect Union, establish Justice, insure domestic Tranquility, provide for the common defence, promote the general Welfare, and secure the Blessings of Liberty to ourselves and our Posterity, do ordain and establish this Constitution for the United States of America.

Article I

Section 1 All legislative Powers herein granted shall be vested in a Congress of the United States, which shall consist of a Senate and a House of Representatives.

Section 2 The House of Representatives shall be composed of Members chosen every second Year by the People of the several States, and the Electors in each State shall have the Qualifications requisite for Electors of the most numerous Branch of the State Legislature.

No Person shall be a Representative who shall not have attained to the Age of twenty-five Years, and been seven Years a Citizen of the United States, and who shall not, when elected, be an Inhabitant of that State in which he shall be chosen.

Representatives and direct Taxes shall be apportioned among the several States which may be included within this Union, according to their respective Numbers, *which shall be determined by adding to the whole Number of free Persons, including those bound to Service for a Term of Years, and excluding Indians not taxed, three fifths of all other Persons.** The actual Enumeration shall be made within three Years after the first Meeting of the Congress of the United States, and within every subsequent Term of ten Years, in such Manner as they shall by Law direct. The Number of Representatives shall not exceed one for every thirty Thousand, but each State shall have at Least one Representative; and *until such enumeration shall be made, the State of New Hampshire shall be entitled to chuse three, Massachusetts eight, Rhode Island and Providence Plantations one, Connecticut five, New-York six, New Jersey four, Pennsylvania eight, Delaware one, Maryland six, Virginia ten, North Carolina five, South Carolina five, and Georgia three.*

When vacancies happen in the Representation from any State, the Executive Authority thereof shall issue Writs of Election to fill such Vacancies.

The House of Representatives shall chuse their Speaker and other Officers; and shall have the sole Power of Impeachment.

Section 3 The Senate of the United States shall be composed of two Senators from each State, *chosen by the Legislature thereof,*[†] for six Years; and each Senator shall have one Vote.

Immediately after they shall be assembled in Consequence of the first Election, they shall be divided as equally as may be into three Classes. The Seats of the Senators of the first Class shall be vacated at the Expiration of the second Year, of the second Class at the Expiration of the fourth Year, and of the third Class at the Expiration of the sixth Year, so that one-third may be chosen every second Year; and if Vacancies happen by Resignation, or otherwise, during the Recess of the Legislature of any State, the Executive thereof may make temporary Appointments until the next Meeting of the Legislature, which shall then fill such Vacancies.[‡]

No person shall be a Senator who shall not have attained to the Age of thirty Years, and been nine Years a Citizen of the United States, and who shall not, when elected, be an Inhabitant of that State for which he shall be chosen.

The Vice President of the United States shall be President of the Senate, but shall have no Vote, unless they be equally divided.

Note: The Constitution became effective March 4, 1789. Provisions in italics have been changed by constitutional amendment.

*Changed by Section 2 of the Fourteenth Amendment.

[†]Changed by Section 1 of the Seventeenth Amendment.

[‡]Changed by Clause 2 of the Seventeenth Amendment.

The Senate shall chuse their other Officers, and also a President pro tempore, in the absence of the Vice President, or when he shall exercise the Office of President of the United States.

The Senate shall have the sole Power to try all Impeachments. When sitting for that Purpose, they shall be on Oath or Affirmation. When the President of the United States is tried, the Chief Justice shall preside: And no Person shall be convicted without the Concurrence of two thirds of the Members present.

Judgment in Cases of Impeachment shall not extend further than to removal from Office, and disqualification to hold and enjoy any Office of honor, Trust or Profit under the United States: but the Party convicted shall nevertheless be liable and subject to Indictment, Trial, Judgment and Punishment, according to Law.

Section 4 The Times, Places and Manner of holding Elections for Senators and Representatives, shall be prescribed in each State by the Legislature thereof; but the Congress may at any time by Law make or alter such Regulations, except as to the Places of Chusing Senators.

The Congress shall assemble at least once in every Year, and such Meeting *shall be on the first Monday in December, unless they shall by Law appoint a different Day.**

Section 5 Each House shall be the Judge of the Elections, Returns and Qualifications of its own Members, and a Majority of each shall constitute a Quorum to do Business; but a smaller number may adjourn from day to day, and may be authorized to compel the Attendance of absent Members, in such Manner, and under such Penalties, as each House may provide.

Each House may determine the Rules of its Proceedings, punish its Members for disorderly Behavior, and, with the Concurrence of two thirds, expel a Member.

Each House shall keep a Journal of its Proceedings, and from time to time publish the same, excepting such Parts as may in their Judgment require Secrecy; and the Yeas and Nays of the Members of either House on any question shall, at the Desire of one-fifth of those Present, be entered on the Journal.

Neither House, during the Session of Congress, shall, without the Consent of the other, adjourn for more than three days, nor to any other Place than that in which the two Houses shall be sitting.

Section 6 The Senators and Representatives shall receive a Compensation for their Services, to be ascertained by Law, and paid out of the Treasury of the United States. They shall in all Cases, except Treason, Felony and Breach of the Peace, be privileged from Arrest during their Attendance at the Session of their respective Houses, and in going to and returning from the same; and for any Speech or Debate in either House, they shall not be questioned in any other Place.

No Senator or Representative shall, during the Time for which he was elected, be appointed to any civil Office under the Authority of the United States, which shall have been created, or the Emoluments whereof shall have been increased, during such time; and no Person holding any Office under the

United States, shall be a Member of either House during his Continuance in Office.

Section 7 All Bills for raising Revenue shall originate in the House of Representatives; but the Senate may propose or concur with Amendments as on other Bills.

Every Bill which shall have passed the House of Representatives and the Senate, shall, before it becomes a Law, be presented to the President of the United States; If he approve he shall sign it, but if not he shall return it, with his Objections to that House in which it shall have originated, who shall enter the Objections at large on their Journal, and proceed to reconsider it. If after such Reconsideration two thirds of that House shall agree to pass the Bill, it shall be sent, together with the Objections, to the other House, by which it shall likewise be reconsidered, and if approved by two thirds of that House, it shall become a Law. But in all such Cases the Votes of both Houses shall be determined by Yeas and Nays, and the Names of the Persons voting for and against the Bill shall be entered on the Journal of each House respectively. If any Bill shall not be returned by the President within ten Days (Sundays excepted) after it shall have been presented to him, the Same shall be a Law, in like Manner as if he had signed it, unless the Congress by their Adjournment prevent its Return, in which Case it shall not be a Law.

Every Order, Resolution, or Vote to which the Concurrence of the Senate and the House of Representatives may be necessary (except on a question of Adjournment) shall be presented to the President of the United States; and before the Same shall take Effect, shall be approved by him, or being disapproved by him, shall be repassed by two thirds of the Senate and House of Representatives, according to the Rules and Limitations prescribed in the Case of a Bill.

Section 8 The Congress shall have Power To lay and collect Taxes, Duties, Imposts and Excises, to pay the Debts and provide for the common Defence and general Welfare of the United States; but all Duties, Imposts and Excises shall be uniform throughout the United States;

To borrow money on the credit of the United States;

To regulate Commerce with foreign Nations, and among the several States, and with the Indian Tribes;

To establish an uniform Rule of Naturalization, and uniform Laws on the subject of Bankruptcies throughout the United States;

To coin Money, regulate the Value thereof, and of foreign Coin, and fix the Standard of Weights and Measures;

To provide for the Punishment of counterfeiting the Securities and current Coin of the United States;

To establish Post Offices and post Roads;

To promote the Progress of Science and useful Arts, by securing for limited Times to Authors and Inventors the exclusive Right to their respective Writings and Discoveries;

To constitute Tribunals inferior to the supreme Court;

To define and punish Piracies and Felonies committed on the high Seas, and Offenses against the Law of Nations;

To declare War, grant Letters of Marque and Reprisal, and make Rules concerning Captures on Land and Water;

To raise and support Armies, but no Appropriation of Money to that Use shall be for a longer Term than two Years;

To provide and maintain a Navy;

---

*Changed by Section 2 of the Twentieth Amendment.

To make Rules for the Government and Regulation of the land and naval Forces;

To provide for calling forth the Militia to execute the Laws of the Union, suppress Insurrections and repel Invasions;

To provide for organizing, arming, and disciplining the Militia, and for governing such Part of them as may be employed in the Service of the United States, reserving to the States respectively, the Appointment of the Officers, and the Authority of training the Militia according to the discipline prescribed by Congress;

To exercise exclusive Legislation in all Cases whatsoever, over such District (not exceeding ten Miles square) as may, by Cession of particular States, and the acceptance of Congress, become the Seat of Government of the United States, and to exercise like Authority over all Places purchased by the Consent of the Legislature of the State in which the Same shall be, for the Erection of Forts, Magazines, Arsenals, dock-Yards, and other needful Buildings;—And

To make all Laws which shall be necessary and proper for carrying into Execution the foregoing Powers, and all other Powers vested by this Constitution in the Government of the United States, or in any Department or Officer thereof.

Section 9 *The Migration or Importation of such Persons as any of the States now existing shall think proper to admit, shall not be prohibited by the Congress prior to the Year one thousand eight hundred and eight but a tax or duty may be imposed on such Importation, not exceeding ten dollars for each Person.*

The privilege of the Writ of Habeas Corpus shall not be suspended, unless when in Cases of Rebellion or Invasion the public Safety may require it.

No Bill of Attainder or ex post facto Law shall be passed.

No capitation, or other direct, Tax shall be laid, unless in Proportion to the Census or Enumeration herein before directed to be taken.*

No Tax or Duty shall be laid on Articles exported from any State.

No Preference shall be given by any Regulation of Commerce or Revenue to the Ports of one State over those of another: nor shall Vessels bound to, or from, one State, be obliged to enter, clear, or pay Duties in another.

No Money shall be drawn from the Treasury, but in Consequence of Appropriations made by law; and a regular Statement and Account of the Receipts and Expenditures of all public Money shall be published from time to time.

No Title of Nobility shall be granted by the United States: And no Person holding any Office of Profit or Trust under them, shall, without the Consent of the Congress, accept of any present, Emolument, Office, or Title, of any kind whatever, from any King, Prince, or foreign State.

Section 10 No State shall enter into any Treaty, Alliance, or Confederation; grant Letters of Marque and Reprisal; coin Money; emit Bills of Credit; make any Thing but gold and silver Coin a Tender in Payment of Debts; pass any Bill of Attainder, ex post facto Law, or Law impairing the Obligation of Contracts, or grant any Title of Nobility.

No State shall, without the Consent of the Congress, lay any Imposts or Duties on Imports or Exports, except what may be absolutely necessary for executing its inspection Laws: and the net Produce of all Duties and Imposts, laid by any State on Imports or Exports, shall be for the Use of the Treasury of the United States; and all such Laws shall be subject to the Revision and Control of the Congress.

No State shall, without the Consent of the Congress, lay any duty of Tonnage, keep Troops, or Ships of War in time of Peace, enter into any Agreement or Compact with another State, or with a foreign Power, or engage in War, unless actually invaded, or in such imminent Danger as will not admit of delay.

Article II

Section 1 The executive Power shall be vested in a President of the United States of America. He shall hold his Office during the Term of four Years, and, together with the Vice President, chosen for the same Term, be elected, as follows:

Each State shall appoint, in such Manner as the Legislature thereof may direct, a Number of Electors, equal to the whole Number of Senators and Representatives to which the State may be entitled in the Congress; but no Senator or Representative, or Person holding an Office of Trust or Profit under the United States, shall be appointed an Elector.

The Electors shall meet in their respective States, and vote by Ballot for two Persons, of whom one at least shall not be an Inhabitant of the same State with themselves. And they shall make a List of all the Persons voted for, and of the Number of Votes for each; which List they shall sign and certify, and transmit sealed to the Seat of the Government of the United States, directed to the President of the Senate. The President of the Senate shall, in the Presence of the Senate and House of Representatives, open all the Certificates, and the Votes shall then be counted. The Person having the greatest Number of Votes shall be the President, if such Number be a Majority of the whole Number of Electors appointed; and if there be more than one who have such Majority, and have an equal Number of Votes, then the House of Representatives shall immediately chuse by Ballot one of them for President; and if no Person have a Majority, then from the five highest on the List the said House shall in like Manner chuse the President. But in chusing the President, the Votes shall be taken by States, the Representation from each State having one Vote; a quorum for this Purpose shall consist of a Member or Members from two thirds of the States, and a Majority of all the States shall be necessary to a Choice. In every Case, after the Choice of the President, the Person having the greatest Number of Votes of the Electors shall be the Vice President. But if there should remain two or more who have equal Votes, the Senate shall chuse from them by Ballot the Vice President. *

The Congress may determine the Time of chusing the Electors, and the Day on which they shall give their Votes; which Day shall be the same throughout the United States.

No Person except a natural born Citizen, or a Citizen of the United States, at the time of the Adoption of this Constitution, shall be eligible to the Office of President; neither shall any Person be eligible to that Office who shall not have at-

---

*Changed by the Sixteenth Amendment.

*Superseded by the Twelfth Amendment.

tained to the Age of thirty five Years, and been fourteen Years a Resident within the United States.

In Case of the Removal of the President from Office, or of his Death, Resignation, or Inability to discharge the Powers and Duties of the said Office, the same shall devolve on the Vice President, *and the Congress may by Law provide for the Case of Removal, Death, Resignation, or Inability, both of the President and Vice President, declaring what Officer shall then act as President, and such Officer shall act accordingly, until the Disability be removed, or a President shall be elected.**

The President shall, at stated Times, receive for his Services a Compensation, which shall neither be increased nor diminished during the Period for which he shall have been elected, and he shall not receive within that Period any other Emolument from the United States, or any of them.

Before he enter on the Execution of his Office, he shall take the following Oath or Affirmation:—"I do solemnly swear (or affirm) that I will faithfully execute the Office of President of the United States, and will to the best of my Ability, preserve, protect and defend the Constitution of the United States."

Section 2 The President shall be Commander in Chief of the Army and Navy of the United States, and of the Militia of the several States, when called into the actual Service of the United States; he may require the Opinion, in writing, of the principal Officer in each of the executive Departments, upon any Subject relating to the Duties of their respective Offices, and he shall have Power to Grant Reprieves and Pardons for Offences against the United States, except in Cases of Impeachment.

He shall have Power, by and with the Advice and Consent of the Senate, to make Treaties, provided two thirds of the Senators present concur; and he shall nominate, and by and with the Advice and Consent of the Senate, shall appoint Ambassadors, other public Ministers and Consuls, Judges of the supreme Court, and all other Officers of the United States, whose Appointments are not herein otherwise provided for, and which shall be established by Law: but the Congress may by Law vest the Appointment of such inferior Officers, as they think proper, in the President alone, in the Courts of Law, or in the Heads of Departments.

The President shall have Power to fill up all Vacancies that may happen during the Recess of the Senate, by granting Commissions which shall expire at the End of their next Session.

Section 3 He shall from time to time give to the Congress Information of the State of the Union, and recommend to their Consideration such Measures as he shall judge necessary and expedient; he may, on extraordinary Occasions, convene both Houses, or either of them, and in Case of Disagreement between them, with Respect to the Time of Adjournment, he may adjourn them to such Time as he shall think proper; he shall receive Ambassadors and other public Ministers; he shall take Care that the Laws be faithfully executed, and shall Commission all the Officers of the United States.

Section 4 The President, Vice President and all civil Officers of the United States, shall be removed from Office on Impeachment for, and Conviction of, Treason, Bribery, or other high Crimes and Misdemeanors.

Article III

Section 1 The judicial Power of the United States, shall be vested in one supreme Court, and in such inferior Courts as the Congress may from time to time ordain and establish. The Judges, both of the supreme and inferior Courts, shall hold their Offices during good Behaviour, and shall, at stated Times, receive for their Services a Compensation, which shall not be diminished during their Continuance in Office.

Section 2 The judicial Power shall extend to all Cases, in Law and Equity, arising under this Constitution, the Laws of the United States, and Treaties made, or which shall be made, under their Authority;—to all Cases affecting Ambassadors, other public Ministers and Consuls;—to all Cases of admiralty and maritime Jurisdiction;—to Controversies to which the United States shall be a Party;—to Controversies between two or more States;—*between a State and Citizens of another State;**—between Citizens of different States;—between Citizens of the same State claiming Lands under Grants of different States, and between a State, or the Citizens thereof, and foreign States, Citizens or Subjects.

In all Cases affecting Ambassadors, other public Ministers and Consuls, and those in which a State shall be Party, the supreme Court shall have original Jurisdiction. In all the other Cases before mentioned, the supreme Court shall have appellate Jurisdiction, both as to Law and Fact, with such Exceptions, and under such Regulations as the Congress shall make.

The trial of all Crimes, except in Cases of Impeachment, shall be by Jury; and such Trial shall be held in the State where said Crimes shall have been committed; but when not committed within any State, the Trial shall be at such Place or Places as the Congress may by Law have directed.

Section 3 Treason against the United States, shall consist only in levying War against them, or in adhering to their Enemies, giving them Aid and Comfort. No Person shall be convicted of Treason unless on the Testimony of two Witnesses to the same overt Act, or on Confession in open Court.

The Congress shall have Power to declare the Punishment of Treason, but no Attainder of Treason shall work Corruption of Blood, or Forefeiture except during the Life of the Person attainted.

Article IV

Section 1 Full Faith and Credit shall be given in each State to the public Acts, Records, and judicial Proceedings of every other State. And the Congress may by general Laws prescribe the Manner in which such Acts, Records, and Proceedings shall be proved, and the Effect thereof.

Section 2 The Citizens of each State shall be entitled to all Privileges and Immunities of Citizens in the several States.

A Person charged in any State with Treason, Felony, or other Crime, who shall flee from Justice, and be found in another State, shall on demand of the executive Authority of the State from which he fled, be delivered up, to be removed to the State having Jurisdiction of the Crime.

No Person held to Service or Labour in one State, under the Laws thereof, escaping into another, shall, in Consequence of any Law or Regulation therein, be discharged from such Service or Labour, but shall be delivered up on Claim of the Party to whom such Service or Labour may be due.*

Section 3 New States may be admitted by the Congress into this Union; but no new State shall be formed or erected within the Jurisdiction of any other State; nor any State be formed by the Junction of two or more States, or parts of States, without the Consent of the Legislatures of the States concerned as well as of the Congress.

The Congress shall have Power to dispose of and make all needful Rules and Regulations respecting the Territory or other Property belonging to the United States; and nothing in this Constitution shall be so construed as to Prejudice any Claims of the United States, or of any particular State.

Section 4 The United States shall guarantee to every State in this Union a Republican Form of Government, and shall protect each of them against Invasion; and on Application of the Legislature, or of the Executive (when the Legislature cannot be convened) against domestic Violence.

Article V

The Congress, whenever two thirds of both Houses shall deem it necessary, shall propose Amendments to this Constitution, or, on the Application of the Legislatures of two thirds of the several States, shall call a Convention for proposing Amendments, which, in either Case, shall be valid to all Intents and Purposes, as Part of this Constitution, when ratified by the Legislatures of three fourths of the several States, or by Conventions in three fourths thereof, as the one or the other Mode of Ratification may be proposed by the Congress; Provided that no Amendment which may be made prior to the Year One thousand eight hundred and eight shall in any Manner affect the first and fourth Clauses in the Ninth Section of the first Article; and that no State, without its Consent, shall be deprived of its equal Suffrage in the Senate.

Article VI

All Debts contracted and Engagements entered into, before the Adoption of this Constitution, shall be as valid against the United States under this Constitution, as under the Confederation.

This Constitution, and the Laws of the United States which shall be made in Pursuance thereof; and all Treaties made, or which shall be made, under the Authority of the United States, shall be the supreme Law of the Land; and the Judges in every State shall be bound thereby, any Thing in the Constitution or Laws of any State to the Contrary notwithstanding.

The Senators and Representatives before mentioned, and the Members of the several State Legislatures, and all executive and judicial Officers, both of the United States and of the several States, shall be bound by Oath or Affirmation, to support this Constitution; but no religious Test shall ever be required as a Qualification to any Office or public Trust under the United States.

Article VII

The Ratification of the Conventions of nine States shall be sufficient for the Establishment of this Constitution between the States so ratifying the Same.

Done in Convention by the Unanimous Consent of the States present the Seventeenth Day of September in the Year of our Lord one thousand seven hundred and Eighty seven and of the Independence of the United States of America the Twelfth. In Witness whereof We have hereunto subscribed our Names.

---

*Superseded by the Twelfth Amendment.

Go. Washington
President and deputy from Virginia

New Hampshire
John Langdon
Nicholas Gilman

Massachusetts
Nathaniel Gorham
Rufus King

Connecticut
Wm. Saml. Johnson
Roger Sherman

New York
Alexander Hamilton

New Jersey
Wil. Livingston
David Brearley
Wm. Paterson
Jona. Dayton

Pennsylvania
B. Franklin
Thomas Mifflin
Robt. Morris
Geo. Clymer
Thos. FitzSimons
Jared Ingersoll
James Wilson
Gouv. Morris

Delaware
Geo. Read
Gunning Bedford jun
John Dickenson
Richard Bassett
Jaco. Broom

Maryland
James McHenry
Dan. of St. Thos. Jenifer
Danl. Carroll

Virginia
John Blair
James Madison, Jr.

North Carolina
Wm. Blount
Richd. Dobbs Spaight
Hu Williamson

South Carolina
J. Rutledge
Charles Cotesworth Pickney
Pierce Butler

Georgia
William Few
Abr. Baldwin

Amendments to the Constitution

★   ★   ★

Amendment I [1791]*

Congress shall make no law respecting an establishment of religion, or prohibiting the free exercise thereof; or abridging the freedom of speech, or of the press; or the right of the people peaceably to assemble, and to petition the Government for a redress of grievances.

Amendment II [1791]

A well regulated Militia, being necessary to the security of a free State, the right of the people to keep and bear Arms shall not be infringed.

Amendment III [1791]

No Soldier shall, in time of peace, be quartered in any house, without the consent of the Owner, nor in time of war, but in a manner to be prescribed by law.

Amendment IV [1791]

The right of the people to be secure in their persons, houses, papers, and effects, against unreasonable searches and seizures, shall not be violated, and no Warrants shall issue, but upon probable cause, supported by Oath or affirmation, and particularly describing the place to be searched, and the persons or things to be seized.

Amendment V [1791]

No person shall be held to answer for a capital or otherwise infamous crime, unless on a presentment or indictment of a Grand Jury, except in cases arising in the land or naval forces, or in the Militia, when in actual service in time of War or public danger; nor shall any person be subject for the same offence to be twice put in jeopardy of life or limb; nor shall be compelled in any criminal case to be a witness against himself, nor be deprived of life, liberty, or property, without due process of law; nor shall private property be taken for public use, without just compensation.

Amendment VI [1791]

In all criminal prosecutions, the accused shall enjoy the right to a speedy and public trial, by an impartial jury of the State and district wherein the crime shall have been committed, which district shall have been previously ascertained by law, and to be informed of the nature and cause of the accusation; to be confronted with the witnesses against him; to have compulsory process for obtaining witnesses in his favor, and to have the Assistance of Counsel for his defence.

Amendment VII [1791]

In suits at common law, where the value in controversy shall exceed twenty dollars, the right of trail by jury shall be preserved, and no fact tried by a jury, shall be otherwise reexamined in any Court of the United States, than according to the Rules of the common law.

Amendment VIII [1791]

Excessive bail shall not be required, nor excessive fines imposed, nor cruel and unusual punishments inflicted.

Amendment IX [1791]

The enumeration in the Constitution, of certain rights, shall not be construed to deny or disparage others retained by the people.

*The dates in brackets indicate when the amendments were ratified.

Amendment X [1791]

The powers not delegated to the United States by the Constitution, nor prohibited by it to the States, are reserved to the States respectively, or to the people.

Amendment XI [1798]

The Judicial power of the United States shall not be construed to extend to any suit in law or equity, commenced or prosecuted against one of the United States by Citizens of another State, or by Citizens or subjects of any foreign state.

Amendment XII [1804]

The Electors shall meet in their respective States and vote by ballot for President and Vice-President, one of whom, at least, shall not be an inhabitant of the same State with themselves; they shall name in their ballots the person voted for as President, and in distinct ballots the person voted for as Vice-President, and they shall make distinct lists of all persons voted for as President, and of all persons voted for as Vice-President, and of the number of votes for each, which lists they shall sign and certify, and transmit sealed to the seat of the government of the United States, directed to the President of the Senate;—the President of the Senate shall, in the presence of the Senate and House of Representatives, open all the certificates and the votes shall then be counted;—The person having the greatest number of votes for President, shall be the President, if such number be a majority of the whole number of Electors appointed; and if no person have such majority, then from the persons having the highest numbers not exceeding three on the list of those voted for as President, the House of Representatives shall choose immediately, by ballot, the President. But in choosing the President, the votes shall be taken by States, the representation from each State having one vote; a quorum for this purpose shall consist of a member or members from two-thirds of the States, and a majority of all the States shall be necessary to a choice. And if the House of Representatives shall not choose a President whenever the right of choice shall devolve upon them, before *the fourth day of March* next following, then the Vice-President shall act as President, as in the case of the death or other constitutional disability of the President.*—The person having the greatest number of votes as Vice-President, shall be the Vice-President, if such number be a majority of the whole number of Electors appointed, and if no person have a majority, then from the two highest numbers on the list, the Senate shall choose the Vice-President; a quorum for the purpose shall consist of two-thirds of the whole number of Senators, and a majority of the whole number shall be necessary to a choice. But no person constitutionally ineligible to the office of President shall be eligible to that of Vice-President of the United States.

Amendment XIII [1865]

Section 1 Neither slavery nor involuntary servitude, except as a punishment for crime whereof the party shall have been duly convicted, shall exist within the United States, or any place subject to their jurisdiction.

Section 2 Congress shall have power to enforce this article by appropriate legislation.

Amendment XIV [1868]

Section 1 All persons born or naturalized in the United States, and subject to the jurisdiction thereof, are citizens of the United States and of the State wherein they reside. No State shall make or enforce any law which shall abridge the privileges or immunities of citizens of the United States; nor shall any State deprive any person of life, liberty, or property, without due process of law; nor deny to any person within its jurisdiction the equal protection of the laws.

Section 2 Representatives shall be apportioned among the several States according to their respective numbers, counting the whole number of persons in each State, excluding Indians not taxed. But when the right to vote at any election for the choice of electors for President and Vice-President of the United States, Representatives in Congress, the Executive and Judicial officers of a State, or the members of the Legislature thereof, is denied to any of the male inhabitants of such State, being twenty-one years of age, and citizens of the United States, or in any way abridged, except for participation in rebellion, or other crime, the basis of representation therein shall be reduced in the proportion which the number of such male citizens shall bear to the whole number of male citizens twenty-one years of age in such State.

Section 3 No person shall be a Senator or Representative in Congress, or elector of President and Vice-President, or hold any office, civil or military, under the United States, or under any State, who, having previously taken an oath, as a member of Congress, or as an officer of the United States, or as a member of any State legislature, or as an executive or judicial officer of any State, to support the Constitution of the United States, shall have engaged in insurrection or rebellion against the same, or given aid or comfort to the enemies thereof. Congress may by a vote of two-thirds of each house, remove such disability.

Section 4 The validity of the public debt of the United States, authorized by law, including debts incurred for payment of pensions and bounties for services in suppressing insurrection or rebellion, shall not be questioned. But neither the United States nor any State shall assume or pay any debt or obligation incurred in aid of insurrection or rebellion against the United States, or any claim for the loss or emancipation of any slave; but all such debts, obligations and claims shall be held illegal and void.

Section 5 The Congress shall have power to enforce, by appropriate legislation, the provisions of this article.

Amendment XV [1870]

Section 1 The right of citizens of the United States to vote shall not be denied or abridged by the United States or by any State on account of race, color, or previous condition of servitude—

---

*Superseded by Section 3 of the Twentieth Amendment.

Section 2 The Congress shall have power to enforce this article by appropriate legislation.

Amendment XVI [1913]

The Congress shall have power to lay and collect taxes on incomes, from whatever source derived, without apportionment among the several States, and without regard to any census or enumeration.

Amendment XVII [1913]

The Senate of the United States shall be composed of two Senators from each State, elected by the people thereof, for six years; and each Senator shall have one vote. The electors in each State shall have the qualifications requisite for electors of the most numerous branch of the State legislatures.

When vacancies happen in the representation of any State in the Senate, the executive authority of such State shall issue writs of election to fill such vacancies: *Provided*, That the legislature of any State may empower the executive thereof to make temporary appointments until the people fill the vacancies by election as the legislature may direct.

This amendment shall not be so construed as to affect the election or term of any Senator chosen before it becomes valid as part of the Constitution.

Amendment XVIII [1919]

Section 1 After one year from the ratification of this article the manufacture, sale, or transportation of intoxicating liquors within, the importation thereof into, or the exportation thereof from the United States and all territory subject to the jurisdiction hereof for beverage purposes hereby prohibited.

Section 2 The Congress and the several States shall have concurrent power to enforce this article by appropriate legislation.

Section 3 This article shall be inoperative unless it shall have been ratified as an amendment to the Constitution by the legislatures of the several States, as provided by the Constitution, within seven years from the date of submission hereof to the States by the Congress.*

Amendment XIX [1920]

The right of citizens of the United States to vote shall not be denied or abridged by the United States or by any State on account of sex.

Congress shall have power to enforce this article by appropriate legislation.

Amendment XX [1933]

Section 1 The terms of the President and Vice-President shall end at noon on the 20th day of January, and the terms of Senators and Representatives at noon on the 3d day of January,

of the years in which such terms would have ended if this article had not been ratified; and the terms of their successors shall then begin.

Section 2 The Congress shall assemble at least once in every year, and such meeting shall begin at noon on the 3d day of January, unless they shall by law appoint a different day.

Section 3 If, at the time fixed for the beginning of the term of the President, the President elect shall have died, the Vice-President elect shall become President. If a President shall not have been chosen before the time fixed for the beginning of his term, or if the President elect shall have failed to qualify, then the Vice-President elect shall act as President until a President shall have qualified; and the Congress may by law provide for the case wherein neither a President elect nor a Vice-President elect shall have qualified, declaring who shall then act as President, or the manner in which one who is to act shall be selected, and such person shall act accordingly until a President or Vice-President shall have qualified.

Section 4 The Congress may by law provide for the case of the death of any of the persons from whom the House of Representatives may choose a President whenever the right of choice shall have devolved upon them, and for the case of the death of any of the persons from whom the Senate may choose a Vice-President whenever the right of choice shall have devolved upon them.

Section 5 Sections 1 and 2 shall take effect on the 15th day of October following the ratification of this article.

Section 6 This article shall be inoperative unless it shall have been ratified as an amendment to the Constitution by the legislatures of three-fourths of the several States within seven years from the date of its submission.

Amendment XXI [1933]

Section 1 The eighteenth article of amendment to the Constitution of the United States is hereby repealed.

Section 2 The transportation or importation into any State, Territory, or possession of the United States for delivery or use therein of intoxicating liquors, in violation of the laws thereof, is hereby prohibited.

Section 3 This article shall be inoperative unless it shall have been ratified as an amendment to the Constitution by conventions in the several States, as provided in the Constitution, within seven years from the date of submission hereof to the States by the Congress.

Amendment XXII [1951]

Section 1 No person shall be elected to the office of President more than twice, and no person who has held the office of President, or acted as President, for more than two years of a term to which some other person was elected President shall be elected to the office of the President more than once. But this Article shall not apply to any person holding the office of

*Repealed by Section 1 of the Twenty-First Amendment

President when this Article was proposed by the Congress, and shall not prevent any person who may be holding the office of President, or acting as President, during the term within which this Article becomes operative from holding the office of the President or acting as President during the remainder of such term.

Section 2 This article shall be inoperative unless it shall have been ratified as an amendment to the Constitution by the legislatures of three-fourths of the several States within seven years from the date of its submission to the States by the Congress.

Amendment XXIII [1961]

Section 1 The District constituting the seat of Government of the United States shall appoint in such manner as the Congress may direct:

A number of electors of President and Vice-President equal to the whole number of Senators and Representatives in Congress to which the District would be entitled if it were a State, but in no event more than the least populous State; they shall be in addition to those appointed by the States, but they shall be considered, for the purposes of the election of President and Vice-President, to be electors appointed by a State; and they shall meet in the District and perform such duties as provided by the twelfth article of amendment.

Section 2 The Congress shall have power to enforce this article by appropriate legislation.

Amendment XXIV [1964]

Section 1 The right of citizens of the United States to vote in any primary or other election for President or Vice-President, for electors for President or Vice-President, or for Senator or Representative in Congress, shall not be denied or abridged by the United States or any State by reason of failure to pay any poll tax or other tax.

Section 2 The Congress shall have power to enforce this article by appropriate legislation.

Amendment XXV [1967]

Section 1 In case of the removal of the President from office or of his death or resignation, the Vice-President shall become President.

Section 2 Whenever there is a vacancy in the office of the Vice-President, the President shall nominate a Vice-President who shall take office upon confirmation by a majority vote of both houses of Congress.

Section 3 Whenever the President transmits to the President pro tempore of the Senate and the Speaker of the House of Representatives his written declaration that he is unable to discharge the powers and duties of his office, and until he transmits to them a written declaration to the contrary, such powers and duties shall be discharged by the Vice-President as Acting President.

Section 4 Whenever the Vice-President and a majority of either the principal officers of the executive departments or of such other body as Congress may by law provide, transmit to the President pro tempore of the Senate and the Speaker of the House of Representatives their written declaration that the President is unable to discharge the powers and duties of his office, the Vice-President shall immediately assume the powers and duties of the office as Acting President.

Thereafter, when the President transmits to the President pro tempore of the Senate and the Speaker of the House of Representatives his written declaration that no inability exists, he shall resume the powers and duties of his office unless the Vice-President and a majority of either the principal officers of the executive department or of such other body as Congress may by law provide, transmit within four days to the President pro tempore of the Senate and the Speaker of the House of Representatives their written declaration that the President is unable to discharge the powers and duties of his office. Thereupon Congress shall decide the issue, assembling within forty-eight hours for that purpose if not in session. If the Congress, within twenty-one days after receipt of the latter written declaration, or, if Congress is not in session, within twenty-one days after Congress is required to assemble, determines by two-thirds vote of both Houses that the President is unable to discharge the powers and duties of his office, the Vice-President shall continue to discharge the same as Acting President; otherwise, the President shall resume the powers and duties of his office.

Amendment XXVI [1971]

Section 1 The right of citizens of the United States, who are eighteen years of age or older, to vote shall not be denied or abridged by the United States or by any state on account of age.

Section 2 The Congress shall have power to enforce this article by appropriate legislation.

Amendment XXVII [1992]

No law varying the compensation for services of the Senators and Representatives, shall take effect, until an election of Representatives shall have intervened.

The American Nation

★ ★ ★

Admission of States into the Union

State	Date of Admission	State	Date of Admission	State	Date of Admission
1. Delaware	December 7, 1787	18. Louisiana	April 30, 1812	35. West Virginia	June 20, 1863
2. Pennsylvania	December 12, 1787	19. Indiana	December 11, 1816	36. Nevada	October 31, 1864
3. New Jersey	December 18, 1787	20. Mississippi	December 10, 1817	37. Nebraska	March 1, 1867
4. Georgia	January 2, 1788	21. Illinois	December 3, 1818	38. Colorado	August 1, 1876
5. Connecticut	January 9, 1788	22. Alabama	December 14, 1819	39. North Dakota	November 2, 1889
6. Massachusetts	February 6, 1788	23. Maine	March 15, 1820	40. South Dakota	November 2, 1889
7. Maryland	April 28, 1788	24. Missouri	August 10, 1821	41. Montana	November 8, 1889
8. South Carolina	May 23, 1788	25. Arkansas	June 15, 1836	42. Washington	November 11, 1889
9. New Hampshire	June 21, 1788	26. Michigan	January 26, 1837	43. Idaho	July 3, 1890
10. Virginia	June 25, 1788	27. Florida	March 3, 1845	44. Wyoming	July 10, 1890
11. New York	July 26, 1788	28. Texas	December 29, 1845	45. Utah	January 4, 1896
12. North Carolina	November 21, 1789	29. Iowa	December 28, 1846	46. Oklahoma	November 16, 1907
13. Rhode Island	May 29, 1790	30. Wisconsin	May 29, 1848	47. New Mexico	January 6, 1912
14. Vermont	March 4, 1791	31. California	September 9, 1850	48. Arizona	February 14, 1912
15. Kentucky	June 1, 1792	32. Minnesota	May 11, 1858	49. Alaska	January 3, 1959
16. Tennessee	June 1, 1796	33. Oregon	February 14, 1859	50. Hawaii	August 21, 1959
17. Ohio	March 1, 1803	34. Kansas	January 29, 1861		

Territorial Expansion

Territory	Date Acquired	Square Miles	How Acquired
Original states and territories	1783	888,685	Treaty of Paris
Louisiana Purchase	1803	827,192	Purchased from France
Florida	1819	72,003	Adams-Onís Treaty
Texas	1845	390,143	Annexation of independent country
Oregon	1846	285,580	Oregon Boundary Treaty
Mexican cession	1848	529,017	Treaty of Guadalupe Hidalgo
Gadsden Purchase	1853	29,640	Purchased from Mexico
Midway Islands	1867	2	Annexation of uninhabited islands
Alaska	1867	589,757	Purchased from Russia
Hawaii	1898	6,450	Annexation of independent country
Wake Island	1898	3	Annexation of uninhabited island
Puerto Rico	1899	3,435	Treaty of Paris
Guam	1899	212	Treaty of Paris
The Philippines	1899–1946	115,600	Treaty of Paris; granted independence
American Samoa	1900	76	Treaty with Germany and Great Britain
Panama Canal Zone	1904–1978	553	Hay–Bunau-Varilla Treaty
U.S. Virgin Islands	1917	133	Purchased from Denmark
Trust Territory of the Pacific Islands*	1947	717	United Nations Trusteeship

*A number of these islands have recently been granted independence: Federated States of Micronesia, 1990; Marshall Islands, 1991; Palau, 1994.

Presidential Elections

Year	Candidates	Parties	Percent of Popular Vote	Electoral Vote	Percent Voter Participation
1789	**George Washington**	No party designations	*	69	
	John Adams†			34	
	Other candidates			35	
1792	**George Washington**	No party designations		132	
	John Adams			77	
	George Clinton			50	
	Other candidates			5	
1796	**John Adams**	Federalist		71	
	Thomas Jefferson	Democratic-Republican		68	
	Thomas Pinckney	Federalist		59	
	Aaron Burr	Democratic-Republican		30	
	Other candidates			48	
1800	**Thomas Jefferson**	Democratic-Republican		73	
	Aaron Burr	Democratic-Republican		73	
	John Adams	Federalist		65	
	Charles C. Pinckney	Federalist		64	
	John Jay	Federalist		1	
1804	**Thomas Jefferson**	Democratic-Republican		162	
	Charles C. Pinckney	Federalist		14	
1808	**James Madison**	Democratic-Republican		122	
	Charles C. Pinckney	Federalist		47	
	George Clinton	Democratic-Republican		6	
1812	**James Madison**	Democratic-Republican		128	
	DeWitt Clinton	Federalist		89	
1816	**James Monroe**	Democratic-Republican		183	
	Rufus King	Federalist		34	
1820	**James Monroe**	Democratic-Republican		231	
	John Quincy Adams	Independent Republican		1	
1824	**John Quincy Adams**	Democratic-Republican	30.5	84	26.9
	Andrew Jackson	Democratic-Republican	43.1	99	
	Henry Clay	Democratic-Republican	13.2	37	
	William H. Crawford	Democratic-Republican	13.1	41	
1828	**Andrew Jackson**	Democratic	56.0	178	57.6
	John Quincy Adams	National Republican	44.0	83	
1832	**Andrew Jackson**	Democratic	54.5	219	55.4
	Henry Clay	National Republican	37.5	49	
	William Wirt	Anti-Masonic	8.0	7	
	John Floyd	Democratic	‡	11	
1836	**Martin Van Buren**	Democratic	50.9	170	57.8
	William H. Harrison	Whig		73	
	Hugh L. White	Whig		26	
	Daniel Webster	Whig	49.1	14	
	W. P. Mangum	Whig		11	
1840	**William H. Harrison**	Whig	53.1	234	80.2
	Martin Van Buren	Democratic	46.9	60	

*Prior to 1824, most presidential electors were chosen by state legislators rather than by popular vote.
†Before the Twelfth Amendment was passed in 1804, the electoral college voted for two presidential candidates; the runner-up became vice-president.
‡Percentages below 2.5 percent have been omitted. Hence the percentage of popular vote might not total 100 percent.

Year	Candidates	Parties	Percent of Popular Vote	Electoral Vote	Percent Voter Participation
1844	**James K. Polk**	Democratic	49.6	170	78.9
	Henry Clay	Whig	48.1	105	
	James G. Birney	Liberty	2.3		
1848	**Zachary Taylor**	Whig	47.4	163	72.7
	Lewis Cass	Democratic	42.5	127	
	Martin Van Buren	Free Soil	10.1		
1852	**Franklin Pierce**	Democratic	50.9	254	69.6
	Winfield Scott	Whig	44.1	42	
	John P. Hale	Free Soil	5.0		
1856	**James Buchanan**	Democratic	45.3	174	78.9
	John C. Frémont	Republican	33.1	114	
	Millard Fillmore	American	21.6	8	
1860	**Abraham Lincoln**	Republican	39.8	180	81.2
	Stephen A. Douglas	Democratic	29.5	12	
	John C. Breckinridge	Democratic	18.1	72	
	John Bell	Constitutional Union	12.6	39	
1864	**Abraham Lincoln**	Republican	55.0	212	73.8
	George B. McClellan	Democratic	45.0	21	
1868	**Ulysses S. Grant**	Republican	52.7	214	78.1
	Horatio Seymour	Democratic	47.3	80	
1872	**Ulysses S. Grant**	Republican	55.6	286	71.3
	Horace Greeley	Democratic	43.9		
1876	**Rutherford B. Hayes**	Republican	48.0	185	81.8
	Samuel J. Tilden	Democratic	51.0	184	
1880	**James A. Garfield**	Republican	48.5	214	79.4
	Winfield S. Hancock	Democratic	48.1	155	
	James B. Weaver	Greenback-Labor	3.4		
1884	**Grover Cleveland**	Democratic	48.5	219	77.5
	James G. Blaine	Republican	48.2	182	
1888	**Benjamin Harrison**	Republican	47.9	233	79.3
	Grover Cleveland	Democratic	48.6	168	
1892	**Grover Cleveland**	Democratic	46.1	277	74.7
	Benjamin Harrison	Republican	43.0	145	
	James B. Weaver	People's	8.5	22	
1896	**William McKinley**	Republican	51.1	271	79.3
	William J. Bryan	Democratic	47.7	176	
1900	**William McKinley**	Republican	51.7	292	73.2
	William J. Bryan	Democratic; Populist	45.5	155	
1904	**Theodore Roosevelt**	Republican	57.4	336	65.2
	Alton B. Parker	Democratic	37.6	140	
	Eugene V. Debs	Socialist	3.0		
1908	**William H. Taft**	Republican	51.6	321	65.4
	William J. Bryan	Democratic	43.1	162	
	Eugene V. Debs	Socialist	2.8		
1912	**Woodrow Wilson**	Democratic	41.9	435	58.8
	Theodore Roosevelt	Progressive	27.4	88	
	William H. Taft	Republican	23.2	8	
	Eugene V. Debs	Socialist	6.0		

Year	Candidates	Parties	Percent of Popular Vote	Electoral Vote	Percent Voter Participation
1916	**Woodrow Wilson**	Democratic	49.4	277	61.6
	Charles E. Hughes	Republican	46.2	254	
	A. L. Benson	Socialist	3.2		
1920	**Warren G. Harding**	Republican	60.4	404	49.2
	James M. Cox	Democratic	34.2	127	
	Eugene V. Debs	Socialist	3.4		
1924	**Calvin Coolidge**	Republican	54.0	382	48.9
	John W. Davis	Democratic	28.8	136	
	Robert M. LaFollette	Progressive	16.6	13	
1928	**Herbert C. Hoover**	Republican	58.2	444	56.9
	Alfred E. Smith	Democratic	40.9	87	
1932	**Franklin D. Roosevelt**	Democratic	57.4	472	56.9
	Herbert C. Hoover	Republican	39.7	59	
1936	**Franklin D. Roosevelt**	Democratic	60.8	523	61.0
	Alfred M. Landon	Republican	36.5	8	
1940	**Franklin D. Roosevelt**	Democratic	54.8	449	62.5
	Wendell L. Willkie	Republican	44.8	82	
1944	**Franklin D. Roosevelt**	Democratic	53.5	432	55.9
	Thomas E. Dewey	Republican	46.0	99	
1948	**Harry S. Truman**	Democratic	49.6	303	53.0
	Thomas E. Dewey	Republican	45.1	189	
1952	**Dwight D. Eisenhower**	Republican	55.1	442	63.3
	Adlai E. Stevenson	Democratic	44.4	89	
1956	**Dwight D. Eisenhower**	Republican	57.6	457	60.6
	Adlai E. Stevenson	Democratic	42.1	73	
1960	**John F. Kennedy**	Democratic	49.7	303	64.0
	Richard M. Nixon	Republican	49.5	219	
1964	**Lyndon B. Johnson**	Democratic	61.1	486	61.7
	Barry M. Goldwater	Republican	38.5	52	
1968	**Richard M. Nixon**	Republican	43.4	301	60.6
	Hubert H. Humphrey	Democratic	42.7	191	
	George C. Wallace	American Independent	13.5	46	
1972	**Richard M. Nixon**	Republican	60.7	520	55.5
	George S. McGovern	Democratic	37.5	17	
1976	**Jimmy Carter**	Democratic	50.1	297	54.3
	Gerald R. Ford	Republican	48.0	240	
1980	**Ronald W. Reagan**	Republican	50.7	489	53.0
	Jimmy Carter	Democratic	41.0	49	
	John B. Anderson	Independent	6.6	0	
1984	**Ronald W. Reagan**	Republican	58.4	525	52.9
	Walter F. Mondale	Democratic	41.6	13	
1988	**George H. W. Bush**	Republican	53.4	426	50.3
	Michael Dukakis	Democratic	45.6	111*	
1992	**Bill Clinton**	Democratic	43.7	370	55.1
	George H. W. Bush	Republican	38.0	168	
	H. Ross Perot	Independent	19.0	0	
1996	**Bill Clinton**	Democratic	49†	379	49.0†
	Robert J. Dole	Republican	41†	159	
	H. Ross Perot	Reform	8†	0	

*One Dukakis elector cast a vote for Lloyd Bentsen.
†Preliminary figure.

Supreme Court Justices

Name	Terms of Service	Appointed by	Name	Terms of Service	Appointed by
John Jay*, N.Y.	1789–1795	Washington	Joseph McKenna, Cal.	1898–1925	McKinley
James Wilson, Pa.	1789–1798	Washington	Oliver W. Holmes, Mass.	1902–1932	T. Roosevelt
John Rutledge, S.C.	1790–1791	Washington	William R. Day, Ohio	1903–1922	T. Roosevelt
William Cushing, Mass.	1790–1810	Washington	William H. Moody, Mass.	1906–1910	T. Roosevelt
John Blair, Va.	1790–1796	Washington	Horace H. Lurton, Tenn.	1910–1914	Taft
James Iredell, N.C.	1790–1799	Washington	Charles E. Hughes, N.Y.	1910–1916	Taft
Thomas Johnson, Md.	1792–1793	Washington	**Edward D. White**, La.	1910–1921	Taft
William Paterson, N.J.	1793–1806	Washington	Willis Van Devanter, Wy.	1911–1937	Taft
John Rutledge, S.C.	1795	Washington	Joseph R. Lamar, Ga.	1911–1916	Taft
Samuel Chase, Md.	1796–1811	Washington	Mahlon Pitney, N.J.	1912–1922	Taft
Oliver Ellsworth, Conn.	1796–1800	Washington	James C. McReynolds, Tenn.	1914–1941	Wilson
Bushrod Washington, Va.	1799–1829	J. Adams	Louis D. Brandeis, Mass.	1916–1939	Wilson
Alfred Moore, N.C.	1800–1804	J. Adams	John H. Clarke, Ohio	1916–1922	Wilson
John Marshall, Va.	1801–1835	J. Adams	**William H. Taft**, Conn.	1921–1930	Harding
William Johnson, S.C.	1804–1834	Jefferson	George Sutherland, Utah	1922–1938	Harding
Brockholst Livingston, N.Y.	1807–1823	Jefferson	Pierce Butler, Minn.	1923–1939	Harding
Thomas Todd, Ky.	1807–1826	Jefferson	Edward T. Sanford, Tenn.	1923–1930	Harding
Gabriel Duvall, Md.	1811–1835	Madison	Harlan F. Stone, N.Y.	1925–1941	Coolidge
Joseph Story, Mass.	1812–1845	Madison	**Charles E. Hughes**, N.Y.	1930–1941	Hoover
Smith Thompson, N.Y.	1823–1843	Monroe	Owen J. Roberts, Penn.	1930–1945	Hoover
Robert Trimble, Ky.	1826–1828	J. Q. Adams	Benjamin N. Cardozo, N.Y.	1932–1938	Hoover
John McLean, Ohio	1830–1861	Jackson	Hugo L. Black, Ala.	1937–1971	F. Roosevelt
Henry Baldwin, Pa.	1830–1844	Jackson	Stanley F. Reed, Ky.	1938–1957	F. Roosevelt
James M. Wayne, Ga.	1835–1867	Jackson	Felix Frankfurter, Mass.	1939–1962	F. Roosevelt
Roger B. Taney, Md.	1836–1864	Jackson	William O. Douglas, Conn.	1939–1975	F. Roosevelt
Philip P. Barbour, Va.	1836–1841	Jackson	Frank Murphy, Mich.	1940–1949	F. Roosevelt
John Cartron, Tenn.	1837–1865	Van Buren	**Harlan F. Stone**, N.Y.	1941–1946	F. Roosevelt
John McKinley, Ala.	1838–1852	Van Buren	James F. Byrnes, S.C.	1941–1942	F. Roosevelt
Peter V. Daniel, Va.	1842–1860	Van Buren	Robert H. Jackson, N.Y.	1941–1954	F. Roosevelt
Samuel Nelson, N.Y.	1845–1872	Tyler	Wiley B. Rutledge, Iowa	1943–1949	F. Roosevelt
Levi Woodbury, N.H.	1845–1851	Polk	Harold H. Burton, Ohio	1945–1958	Truman
Robert C. Grier, Pa.	1846–1870	Polk	**Frederick M. Vinson**, Ky.	1946–1953	Truman
Benjamin R. Curtis, Mass.	1851–1857	Fillmore	Tom C. Clark, Texas	1949–1967	Truman
John A. Campbell, Ala.	1853–1861	Pierce	Sherman Minton, Ind.	1949–1956	Truman
Nathan Clifford, Me.	1858–1881	Buchanan	**Earl Warren**, Cal.	1953–1969	Eisenhower
Noah H. Swayne, Ohio	1862–1881	Lincoln	John Marshall Harlan, N.Y.	1955–1971	Eisenhower
Samuel F. Miller, Iowa	1862–1890	Lincoln	William J. Brennan, Jr., N.J.	1956–1990	Eisenhower
David Davis, Ill.	1862–1877	Lincoln	Charles E. Whittaker, Mo.	1957–1962	Eisenhower
Stephen J. Field, Cal.	1863–1897	Lincoln	Potter Stewart, Ohio	1958–1981	Eisenhower
Salmon P. Chase, Ohio	1864–1873	Lincoln	Bryon R. White, Colo.	1962–1993	Kennedy
William Strong, Pa.	1870–1880	Grant	Arthur J. Goldberg, Ill.	1962–1965	Kennedy
Joseph P. Bradley, N.J.	1870–1892	Grant	Abe Fortas, Tenn.	1965–1969	Johnson
Ward Hunt, N.Y.	1873–1882	Grant	Thurgood Marshall, Md.	1967–1991	Johnson
Morrison R. Waite, Ohio	1874–1888	Grant	**Warren E. Burger**, Minn.	1969–1986	Nixon
John M. Harlan, Ky.	1877–1911	Hayes	Harry A. Blackmun, Minn.	1970–	Nixon
William B. Woods, Ga.	1881–1887	Hayes	Lewis F. Powell, Jr., Va.	1971–1987	Nixon
Stanley Matthews, Ohio	1881–1889	Garfield	William H. Rehnquist, Ariz.	1971–1986	Nixon
Horace Gray, Mass.	1882–1902	Arthur	John Paul Stevens, Ill.	1975–	Ford
Samuel Blatchford, N.Y.	1882–1893	Arthur	Sandra Day O'Connor, Ariz.	1981–	Reagan
Lucius Q. C. Lamar, Miss.	1888–1893	Cleveland	**William H. Rehnquist**, Ariz.	1986–	Reagan
Melville W. Fuller, Ill.	1888–1910	Cleveland	Antonin Scalia, Va.	1986–	Reagan
David J. Brewer, Kan.	1890–1910	B. Harrison	Anthony M. Kennedy, Cal.	1988–	Reagan
Henry B. Brown, Mich.	1891–1906	B. Harrison	David H. Souter, N.H.	1990	Bush
George Shiras, Jr., Pa.	1892–1903	B. Harrison	Clarence Thomas, Ga.	1991–	Bush
Howell E. Jackson, Tenn.	1893–1895	B. Harrison	Ruth Bader Ginsburg, N.Y.	1993–	Clinton
Edward D. White, La.	1894–1910	Cleveland	Stephen G. Breyer, Mass.	1994–	Clinton
Rufus W. Peckham, N.Y.	1896–1909	Cleveland			

*Chief Justices are printed in bold type.

The American People:
A Demographic Survey

★ ★ ★

A Demographic Profile of the American People

Year	Life Expectancy from Birth		Average Age at First Marriage		Number of Children Under 5 (per 1,000 Women Aged 20–44)	Percent of Women in Paid Employment	Percent of Paid Workers Who Are Female
	White	Black	Male	Female			
1820					1,295	6.2%	7.3%
1830					1,145	6.4	7.4
1840					1,085	8.4	9.6
1850					923	10.1	10.8
1860					929	9.7	10.2
1870					839	13.7	14.8
1880					822	14.7	15.2
1890			26.1	22.0	716	18.2	17.0
1900	47.6	33.0	25.9	21.9	688	21.2	18.1
1910	50.3	35.6	25.1	21.6	643	24.8	20.0
1920	54.9	45.3	24.6	21.2	604	23.9	20.4
1930	61.4	48.1	24.3	21.3	511	24.4	21.9
1940	64.2	53.1	24.3	21.5	429	25.4	24.6
1950	69.1	60.8	22.8	20.3	589	29.1	27.8
1960	70.6	63.6	22.8	20.3	737	34.8	32.3
1970	71.7	65.3	22.5	20.6	530	43.3	38.0
1980	74.4	68.1	24.7	22.0	440	51.5	42.6
1990	76.2	71.4	26.1	23.9	377	57.4	45.2

Source: Historical Statistics of the United States, Colonial Times to 1970 (1975); Statistical Abstract of the United States, 1991.

American Population

Year	Population	Percent Increase	Year	Population	Percent Increase
1610	350	—	1810	7,239,881	36.4
1620	2,300	557.1	1820	9,638,453	33.1
1630	4,600	100.0	1830	12,866,020	33.5
1640	26,600	478.3	1840	17,069,453	32.7
1650	50,400	90.8	1850	23,191,876	35.9
1660	75,100	49.0	1860	31,443,321	35.6
1670	111,900	49.0	1870	39,818,449	26.6
1680	151,500	35.4	1880	50,155,783	26.0
1690	210,400	38.9	1890	62,947,714	25.5
1700	250,900	19.2	1900	75,994,575	20.7
1710	331,700	32.2	1910	91,972,266	21.0
1720	466,200	40.5	1920	105,710,620	14.9
1730	629,400	35.0	1930	122,775,046	16.1
1740	905,600	43.9	1940	131,669,275	7.2
1750	1,170,800	29.3	1950	150,697,361	14.5
1760	1,593,600	36.1	1960	179,323,175	19.0
1770	2,148,100	34.8	1970	203,235,298	13.3
1780	2,780,400	29.4	1980	226,545,805	11.5
1790	3,929,214	41.3	1990	248,709,873	9.8
1800	5,308,483	35.1	1993	259,383,000	4.3

Note: These figures largely ignore the native American population. Census takers never made any effort to count the native American population that lived outside their political jurisdictions and compiled only casual and incomplete enumerations of those living within their jurisdictions until 1890. In that year the federal government attempted a full count of the Indian population: the Census found 125,719 Indians in 1890, compared with only 12,543 in 1870 and 33,985 in 1880.
Source: Historical Statistics of the United States, Colonial Times to 1970 (1975); Statistical Abstract of the United States, 1995.

White/Nonwhite Population

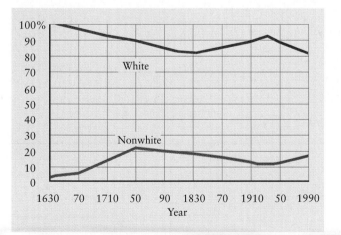

Urban/Rural Population

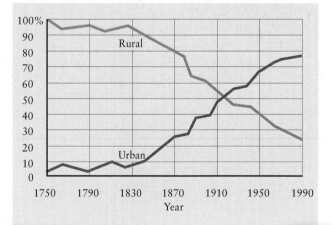

The Ten Largest Cities by Population, 1700–1990

		City	Population				City	Population
1700	1.	Boston	6,700		1910	1.	New York	4,766,883
	2.	New York	4,937*			2.	Chicago	2,185,283
	3.	Philadelphia	4,400†			3.	Philadelphia	1,549,008
						4.	St. Louis	687,029
1790	1.	Philadelphia	42,520			5.	Boston	670,585
	2.	New York	33,131			6.	Cleveland	560,663
	3.	Boston	18,038			7.	Baltimore	558,485
	4.	Charleston, S.C.	16,359			8.	Pittsburgh	533,905
	5.	Baltimore	13,503			9.	Detroit	465,766
	6.	Salem, Mass.	7,921			10.	Buffalo	423,715
	7.	Newport, R.I.	6,716					
	8.	Providence, R.I.	6,380		1930	1.	New York	6,930,446
	9.	Marblehead, Mass.	5,661			2.	Chicago	3,376,438
	10.	Portsmouth, N.H.	4,720			3.	Philadelphia	1,950,961
						4.	Detroit	1,568,662
1830	1.	New York	197,112			5.	Los Angeles	1,238,048
	2.	Philadelphia	161,410			6.	Cleveland	900,429
	3.	Baltimore	80,620			7.	St. Louis	821,960
	4.	Boston	61,392			8.	Baltimore	804,874
	5.	Charleston, S.C.	30,289			9.	Boston	781,188
	6.	New Orleans	29,737			10.	Pittsburgh	669,817
	7.	Cincinnati	24,831					
	8.	Albany, N.Y.	24,209		1950	1.	New York	7,891,957
	9.	Brooklyn, N.Y.	20,535			2.	Chicago	3,620,962
	10.	Washington, D.C.	18,826			3.	Philadelphia	2,071,605
						4.	Los Angeles	1,970,358
1850	1.	New York	515,547			5.	Detroit	1,849,568
	2.	Philadelphia	340,045			6.	Baltimore	949,708
	3.	Baltimore	169,054			7.	Cleveland	914,808
	4.	Boston	136,881			8.	St. Louis	856,796
	5.	New Orleans	116,375			9.	Washington, D.C.	802,178
	6.	Cincinnati	115,435			10.	Boston	801,444
	7.	Brooklyn, N.Y.	96,838					
	8.	St. Louis	77,860		1970	1.	New York	7,895,563
	9.	Albany, N.Y.	50,763			2.	Chicago	3,369,357
	10.	Pittsburgh	46,601			3.	Los Angeles	2,811,801
						4.	Philadelphia	1,949,996
1870	1.	New York	942,292			5.	Detroit	1,514,063
	2.	Philadelphia	674,022			6.	Houston	1,233,535
	3.	Brooklyn, N.Y.	419,921†			7.	Baltimore	905,787
	4.	St. Louis	310,864			8.	Dallas	844,401
	5.	Chicago	298,977			9.	Washington, D.C.	756,668
	6.	Baltimore	267,354			10.	Cleveland	750,879
	7.	Boston	250,526					
	8.	Cincinnati	216,239		1990	1.	New York	7,322,564
	9.	New Orleans	191,418			2.	Los Angeles	3,485,398
	10.	San Francisco	149,473			3.	Chicago	2,783,726
						4.	Houston	1,630,553
						5.	Philadelphia	1,585,577
						6.	San Diego	1,110,549
						7.	Detroit	1,027,974
						8.	Dallas	1,006,877
						9.	Phoenix	983,403
						10.	San Antonio	935,933

*Figure from a census taken in 1698.
†Philadelphia figures include suburbs.
‡Annexed to New York in 1898.
Source: U.S. Census data.

Foreign Origins of the American People

Immigration by Decade

Year	Number	Percent of Total Population	Year	Number	Percent of Total Population
1821–1830	151,824	1.6	1921–1930	4,107,209	3.9
1831–1840	599,125	4.6	1931–1940	528,431	0.4
1841–1850	1,713,251	10.0	1941–1950	1,035,039	0.7
1851–1860	2,598,214	11.2	1951–1960	2,515,479	1.6
1861–1870	2,314,824	7.4	1961–1970	3,321,677	1.8
1871–1880	2,812,191	7.1	1971–1980	4,493,000	2.2
1881–1890	5,246,613	10.5	1981–1990	7,338,000	3.0
1891–1900	3,687,546	5.8	1991–1993	3,705,000	1.4
1901–1910	8,795,386	11.6	Total	27,043,835	
1911–1920	5,735,811	6.2			
Total	33,654,785		1821–1993 Grand Total	60,698,620	

Source: U.S. Bureau of the Census, *Historical Statistics of the United States, Colonial Times to 1970* (1975), Part I, pp. 105–106; *Statistical Abstract of the United States*, 1995.

Regional Origins

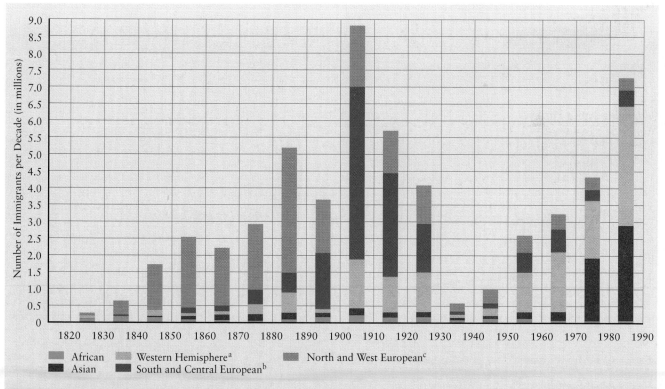

^a Canada and all countries in South America and Central America.

^b Italy, Spain, Portugal, Greece, Germany (Austria included, 1938–1945), Poland, Czechoslovakia (since 1920), Yogoslavia (since 1920), Hungary (since 1861), Austria (since 1861, except 1938–1945), former U.S.S.R. (excludes Asian U.S.S.R. between 1931 and 1963), Latvia, Estonia, Lithuania, Finland, Romania, Bulgaria, Turkey (in Europe), and other European countries not classified elsewhere.

^c Great Britain, Ireland, Norway, Sweden, Denmark, Iceland, Netherlands, Belgium, Luxembourg, Switzerland, France.

Source: Stephan Thernstrom, ed., *Harvard Encyclopedia of American Ethnic Groups* (1980), p. 480; and U.S. Bureau of the Census, *Statistical Abstract of the United States*, 1991.

The Labor Force

(thousands of workers)						
Year	Agriculture	Mining	Manufacturing	Construction	Trade	Other	Total
1810	1,950	11	75	—	—	294	2,330
1840	3,570	32	500	290	350	918	5,660
1850	4,520	102	1,200	410	530	1,488	8,250
1860	5,880	176	1,530	520	890	2,114	11,110
1870	6,790	180	2,470	780	1,310	1,400	12,930
1880	8,920	280	3,290	900	1,930	2,070	17,390
1890	9,960	440	4,390	1,510	2,960	4,060	23,320
1900	11,680	637	5,895	1,665	3,970	5,223	29,070
1910	11,770	1,068	8,332	1,949	5,320	9,041	37,480
1920	10,790	1,180	11,190	1,233	5,845	11,372	41,610
1930	10,560	1,009	9,884	1,988	8,122	17,267	48,830
1940	9,575	925	11,309	1,876	9,328	23,277	56,290
1950	7,870	901	15,648	3,029	12,152	25,870	65,470
1960	5,970	709	17,145	3,640	14,051	32,545	74,060
1970	3,463	516	20,746	4,818	15,008	34,127	78,678
1980	3,364	979	21,942	6,215	20,191	46,612	99,303
1990	3,186	730	21,184	7,696	24,269	60,849	117,914
1994	3,409	669	20,157	7,493	25,699	65,633	123,060

Source: Historical Statistics of the United States, Colonial Times to 1970 (1975), 139; Statistical Abstract of the United States, 1995, Table 653.

Changing Labor Patterns

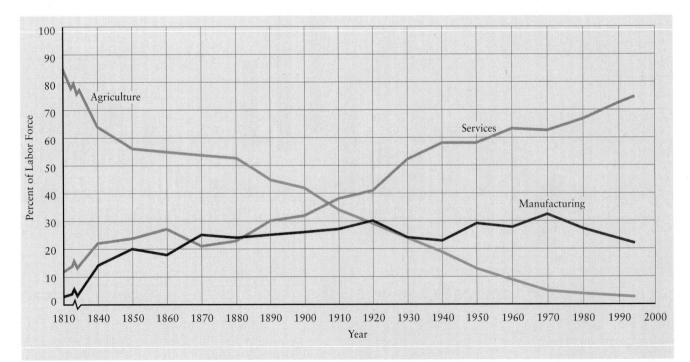

The Aging of the U.S. Population

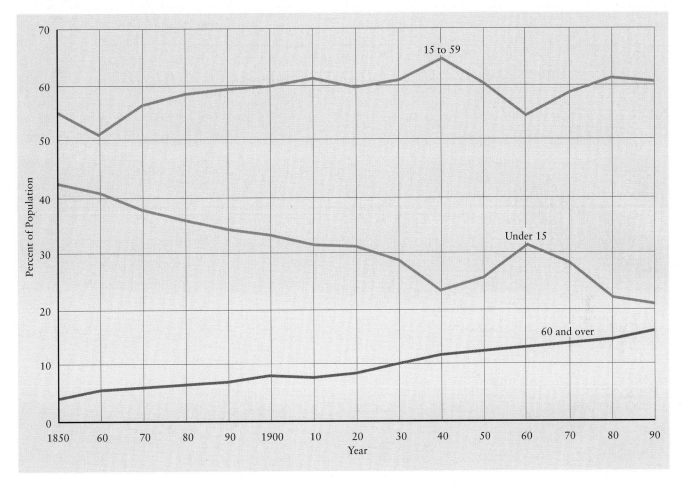

The American Government and Economy

★　　　　　★　　　　　★

The Growth of the Federal Government

Year	Employees (millions)		Receipts and Outlays ($ millions)	
	Civilian	Military	Receipts	Outlays
1900	0.23	0.12	567	521
1910	0.38	0.13	676	694
1920	0.65	0.34	6,649	6,358
1930	0.61	0.25	4,058	3,320
1940	1.04	0.45	6,900	9,600
1950	1.96	1.46	40,900	43,100
1960	2.38	2.47	92,500	92,200
1970	3.00	3.06	193,700	196,600
1980	2.99	2.05	517,112	590,920
1990	3.23	2.04	1,031,321	1,252,705
1993	3.04	1.70	1,153,535	1,408,675

Source: Statistical Profile of the United States, 1900–1980; Statistical Abstract of the United States, 1995.

Gross National Product, 1840–1990

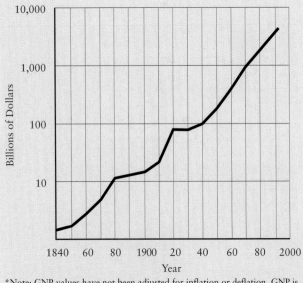

*Note: GNP values have not been adjusted for inflation or deflation. GNP is plotted here on a logarithmic scale.
Source: Statistical Abstract of the United States, 1995.*

GNP per Capita, 1840–1990

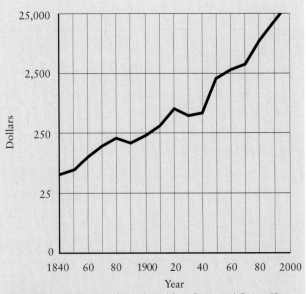

Note: GNP values have not been adjusted for inflation or deflation. The GNP is plotted here on a logarithmic scale.

Consumer Price Index and Conversion Table

This index estimates how consumer prices changed on the average over ten-year intervals. Such estimates are highly uncertain, particularly when they are used to make comparisons over long periods of time. This is partly because it is extremely difficult to measure how the typical mix of goods (each with its own price) purchased by consumers changes over time.

To convert £ (pounds Sterling, until 1770) or $ (U.S. dollars, beginning in 1780) from any date in the past to the equivalent in 1990 dollars, multiply the historical price by the appropriate number in this column. For example, £10 Sterling in 1730 would equal about $867 in 1990. (£10 × 86.7 = $867); or $10 in 1870 would equal about $99 in 1990 ($10 × 9.9 = $99).

Year	Price Index (1860 = 100)	Conversion Multiplier
1700	130	53.3
1710	100	69.3
1720	76	91.3
1730	80	86.7
1740	66	105.1
1750	84	82.6
1760	96	72.3
1770	100	69.3
1780	165	9.5
1790	148	10.6
1800	151	10.4
1810	148	10.6
1820	141	11.1
1830	111	14.1
1840	104	15.1
1850	94	16.6
1860	100	15.6
1870	157	9.9
1880	123	12.7
1890	109	14.3
1900	101	15.5
1910	114	13.7
1920	240	6.5
1930	200	7.8
1940	168	9.3
1950	288	5.4
1960	354	4.4
1970	464	3.4
1980	985	1.6
1990	1563	1.0

Source: Adapted from John J. McCusker, "How Much Is That in Real Money? A Historical Price Index for Use as a Deflator of Money Value in the Economy of the United States," *Proceedings of the American Antiquarian Society*, Vol. 101, pt. 2, (1991), 297–390.

Illustration Credits

★ ★ ★

Chapter 1   **P. 2:** Oronoz.   **P. 4:** Dumbarton Oaks Research Library and Collections, Washington, D.C.   **P. 5:** Robert Knight/Leo de Wys.   **P. 6:** Ohio Historical Society.   **P. 8:** Library of Congress. **P. 9:** Amerind Foundation, Dragoon, AZ. Photo by Robin Stancliff. **P. 12:** Musée Condé/Giraudon/Art Resource.   **P. 13:** J. Bourdichon. *Les quatres etats de la societé: le travail,* 15th century. Giraudon/Art Resource, NY.   **P. 15:** Mathias Grünwald, *Isenheim Altar Piece* (central panel), early 16th c., Musée Unterlinden, Colmar/Giraudon/Art Resource.   **P. 16:** *Pepper Harvesting in Malabar,* 14th c. French ms. illus. Bibliothèque Nationale, Paris.   **P. 17** (top): Ergun Çagutay: Istanbul (From *Sahinsahname,* Vol. I, Universite Kutuphanesi, Instanbul).   **P. 17** (bottom): Piero della Francesca, *The Ideal City,* 15th c. Scala/Art Resource.   **P. 23:** Corbis-Bettmann.   **P. 25:** *Don Luis de Velasco Murdering the Jesuits,* 1571. Courtesy of the John Carter Brown Library at Brown University.   **P. 29:** Cornelius de Zeeuw. *Pierre de Moucheron and His Family,* n.d. Rijksmuseum, Amsterdam. **P. 31:** *Sir Walter Raleigh and His Son,* unknown artist, 1602. By Courtesy of the National Portrait Gallery, London.   **P. 32:** *Elizabeth I* (Armada Portrait). Anonymous. Private collection. Bridgeman Art Library, London.

Chapter 2   **P. 36:** Ashmolean Museum, Oxford.   **P. 41:** Nettie Lee Benson Latin American Collection, University of Texas at Austin, General Libraries.   **P. 44:** John White, *Indians Fishing,* British Museum.   **P. 46:** Collection of the Maryland Historical Society, Baltimore.   **P. 49:** Colonial Williamsburg Foundation.   **P. 51:** Collection of the Maryland Historical Society, Baltimore.   **P. 53:** Paul Rocheleau.   **P. 54:** Courtesy of the American Antiquarian Society.   **P. 56** (top and center): Courtesy Essex Institute, Salem, MA.   **P. 56** (bottom): Courtesy of the Pilgrim Society, Plymouth, MA.   **P. 59:** Courtesy of the American Antiquarian Society.   **P. 61:** Anon. *Elizabeth Freake & Baby* c. 1671–74. 17th-c. Worcester Art Museum, Worcester, MA. Gift of Mr. and Mrs. Albert W. Rice.   **P. 63:** Shelburne Museum, Shelburne, VT. Photograph by Ken Burris.   **P. 65:** *Pocahantas, Daughter of Powhatan Chief.* Unidentified artist, after 1616. National Portrait Gallery, Smithsonian Institution/Art Resource, NY.

Chapter 3   **P. 68:** *Bristol Docks and Quay* (detail), early 18th c., City of Bristol Museum and Art Gallery/Bridgeman Art Library, London.   **P. 70:** Mansell Collection.   **P. 74:** *James II,* by Godfrey Kneller, late 17th c. Courtesy of the National Portrait Gallery, London.   **P. 75:** New York State Historical Association, Cooperstown. **P. 79:** Benin Bronze Plaque: *Mounted King and Attendants,* c. 1550–1680. The Metropolitan Museum of Art, NY. The Michael C. Rockefeller Memorial Collection.   **P. 82:** The Library Company of Philadelphia.   **P. 84** (left): National Maritime Museum, London. **P. 84** (right): Library of Congress.   **P. 87:** Colonial Williamsburg Foundation.   **P. 88:** Courtesy, Georgia Department of Archives and History, Atlanta.   **P. 89:** Abby Aldrich Rockefeller Folk Art Center, Williamsburg, VA.   **P. 90:** Thomas Coram, *View of Mulberry Plantation (slave quarters).* Gibbes Museum of Art/CAA Collection, Charleston.   **P. 91:** Maryland Historical Society, Baltimore.   **P. 97:** National Trust Photographic Library/John Hammond.

Chapter 4   **P. 102:** Colonial Williamsburg Foundation.   **P. 104:** Anon (American), *The Cheney Family,* c. 1795, National Gallery of Art, Washington. Gift of Edgar William and Bernice Chrysler Garbisch.   **P. 105:** The Connecticut Historical Society, Hartford. **P. 106:** *Lady Undressing for a Bath.* Attributed to Gerardus Duyckinck, c.1730–40. National Gallery of Art, Washington. Gift of Edgar William and Bernice Chrysler Garbisch.   **P. 112:** Courtesy, Museum of Fine Arts, Boston. Bequest of Maxim Karolik.   **P. 114:** Philadelphia Museum of Art, from the Clarence W. Brazer Collection. **P. 117:** John Steper and Henry Dawkins, *A Southeast Prospect of the Pennsylvania Hospital,* c. 1761. The Library Company of Philadelphia.   **P. 127:** Joseph Badger, *Rev. Jonathan Edwards,* 1720. Yale University Art Gallery. Bequest of Eugene Phelps Edwards, 1938. **P. 128:** Stock Montage, Inc.   **P. 129:** Private Collection.   **P. 132:** *View from Bushango Tavern, 5 Miles from York Town on the Baltimore Road,* July 1788, *Columbian Magazine.* Collection of The New-York Historical Society.

Chapter 5   **P. 136:** Ralph Earl, *Occupation of Concord by the British,* (detail), n.d. Photograph Courtesy Concord Antiquarian Museum, Concord, MA.   **P. 141:** Courtesy, American Antiquarian Society.   **P. 143:** Print Collection. Miriam and Ira D. Wallach Division of Art, Prints and Photographs. The New York Public Library. Astor, Lenox and Tilden Foundations.   **P. 144:** Courtesy of the John Carter Brown Library at Brown University, Providence, RI.   **P. 147:** John Singleton Copley, *Samuel Adams,* c. 1772. Courtesy, Museum of Fine Arts, Boston. Deposited by the City of Boston.   **P. 148:** Anon, *Patrick Henry,* n.d., Shelburne Museum, Shelburne, VT. Photograph by Ken Burris.   **P. 149:** Courtesy of the Essex Institute, Salem, MA. **P. 155:** Print Collection. Miriam and Ira D. Wallach Division of Art, Prints and Photographs. The New York Public Library. Astor, Lenox and Tilden Foundations.   **P. 157:** Courtesy of the John Carter Brown Library at Brown University, Providence, RI.   **P. 158:** Joseph Cole, *George Hewes,* 1835. Courtesy of The Bostonian Society/Old State House.   **P. 159:** Library of Congress.   **P. 161:** *William Pitt* from (book) *Aubenteuil, Essais Historiques et Politiques sur la Revolution*

Chapter 11   P. 326: Robert Cruikshank, *President's Levee or All Creation Going to the White House,* n.d., © by the White House Historical Association, Washington, D.C. Photograph by the National Geographic Society.   **P. 330:** Philip Haas, *John Quincy Adams,* (daguerreotype), c. 1843, The Metropolitan Museum of Art, Gift of I. N. Phelps Stokes, Edward S. Hawes, Alice Mary Hawes, Marion Augusta Hawes, 1937.   **P. 332:** Collection of The New-York Historical Society.   **P. 334:** Library of Congress.   **P. 335:** S. Bernard, *View along the East Battery, Charleston,* Oil on canvas, c. 1831 23½ × 35¼ in, Yale University Art Gallery, Mabel Brady Garvan Collection #1932.282   **P. 336:** The Gibbes Museum of Art Carolina Art Association, Charleston, SC.   **P. 337:** George Catlin, *muk a tah mish o kah kaik, the Black Hawk,* mid 19th c., watercolor on paper. Courtesy of the Thomas Gilcrease Institute of American History and Art, Tulsa, OK.   **P. 341:** Archives Division, Texas State Library.   **P. 345:** General Research Division, The New York Public Library, Astor, Lenox and Tilden Foundations.   **P. 347:** From *The Union,* 1835. Courtesy The New York Public Library.   **Pp. 348, 351 and 352:** Collection of The New-York Historical Society.

Chapter 12   P. 356: C.C.A. Christensen, *The Handcart Pioneers,* 1900. Courtesy Museum of Church History and Art, Salt Lake City, UT.   **P. 360 (left and right):** Corbis-Bettmann.   **P. 360 (center):** The American Antiquarian Society, Worcester, MA.   **P. 361:** Culver Pictures.   **P. 364:** Joshua H. Bussell, *The Shaker Community at Poland Hill, Maine,* c. 1850, Collection of the United Society of Shakers, Sabbathday Lake, ME.   **P. 367:** Culver Pictures.   **P. 369 (left and center):** Library of Congress.   **P. 369 (right):** Collection of Rhoda Jenkins and John Barney, Greenwich, CT.   **P. 371:** Courtesy Trenton State Hospital.   **P. 372:** Corbis-Bettmann.   **P. 375:** Unknown, *William Lloyd Garrison,* (daguerreotype), 19th c., The Metropolitan Museum of Art, Gift of I. N. Stokes, Edward S. Hawes, Alice Mary Hawes, Marion Augusta Hawes, 1937.

Chapter 13   P. 382: William Aiken Walker, *Plantation Economy in the Old South,* (detail), c. 1876, The Warner Collection of Gulf States Paper Corporation, Tuscaloosa, AL.   **P. 385:** Franz Holzlhuber, *Sugarcane Harvest in Louisiana & Texas,* c. 1856–60, Collection of Glenbow Museum, Calgary, Alberta, Canada.   **P. 389 (top):** Eyre Crowe, *Richmond Slave Market Auction,* n.d., The Collection of Jay P. Altmayer.   **P. 389 (bottom):** John Antrobus, *Plantation Burial,* c. 1860, The Historic New Orleans Collection.   **P. 391:** Sophia Smith Collection, Smith College, MA.   **P. 394:** Culver Pictures.   **P. 395:** Charles Blauvelt, *A German Immigrant Inquiring His Way,* c. 1855. North Carolina, Museum of Art, Raleigh. Purchased with funds from the State of North Carolina.   **P. 397:** Library of Congress.   **P. 398 (top):** Engraving by W. W. Wilson, *Constructing a Balloon Frame House,* c. 1855, The Metropolitan Museum of Art, Harris Brisbane Dick Fund, 1934.   **P. 398 (bottom):** Culver Pictures.   **P. 399:** Currier and Ives, *Home Sweet Home,* c. 1869, Museum of the City of New York. The Harry T. Peters Collection.   **P. 400:** Stowe-Day Foundation, Hartford, CT.   **P. 406:** The Pat Hathaway Collection of California Views.   **P. 411:** From the Collection of the Dallas Historical Society.

Chapter 14   P. 414: John Steuart Curry, *John Brown Mural,* in the Kansas State Capitol, 1941, Kansas Historical Society. Photo as published in *"The Story of America"* © National Geographic Society, 1984.   **P. 419 (top):** Courtesy the Amon Carter Museum, Fort Worth, TX.   **P. 419 (bottom):** Samuel Chamberlain, *Street Fighting in the Calle de Iturbide,* 1855–61, The West Point Museum, United States Military Academy. From *The Old West: The Mexican War.* Photo by Paulus Leeser © 1978 Time/Life Books, Inc.   **P. 424:** The Historical Society of Pennsylvania, Philadelphia.   **P. 427:** California State Library, Sacramento. Daguerreotype Collection.   **P. 430 (top):** Culver Pictures.   **P. 430 (bottom):** Corbis-Bettmann.   **P. 432:** Chicago Historical Society.   **P. 433:** Corbis-Bettmann.   **P. 437:** The Kansas

State Historical Society, Topeka.   **P. 439:** Library of Congress.   **P. 440:** Missouri Historical Society, St. Louis.   **P. 443:** The Lincoln Museum, Fort Wayne, Indiana, a part of the Lincoln National Corporation.   **P. 444:** National Portrait Gallery, Washington, D.C./Art Resource.   **P. 445:** The Ohio Historical Society, Columbus.   **P. 446:** National Park Service, Harper's Ferry.

Chapter 15   P. 448: The Seventh Regiment Fund, Inc., (detail), New York City   **P. 454:** Virginia State Library and Archives, Richmond.   **P. 455:** CBH Jackson Collection, Smithsonian Institution. From *Echoes of Glory: Arms and Equipment of the Union.* Photograph by Larry Sherer © 1991 Time-Life Books Inc.   **P. 457:** Culver Pictures.   **P. 460:** Massachusetts Commandery Military Order of the Loyal Legion and the US Army Military History Institute.   **Pp. 461 and 464:** Library of Congress.   **P. 466:** From *The Civil War: Twenty Million Yankees.* Photograph by Larry Sherer © 1985 Time/Life Books, Inc. Courtesy of the United States Senate Collection.   **Pp. 471, 473 and 478:** Library of Congress.   **P. 479:** L.M.D. Guillaume, *The Surrender of General Lee to General Grant, April 9, 1865,* Appomatox Court House National Historical Park.   **P. 480:** National Archives (Mathew Brady Collection).

Chapter 16   P. 484: Chicago Historical Society.   **Pp. 486 and 488:** Library of Congress.   **P. 489:** Chicago Historical Society.   **P. 491:** Collection of The New-York Historical Society.   **P. 493:** Library of Congress.   **P. 496:** Collection of Mrs. Nancy W. Livingston and Mrs. Elizabeth Livingston Jaeger. Photograph Courtesy of the Los Angeles County Museum of Art.   **P. 497:** Corbis-Bettmann.   **P. 499:** Library of Congress.   **P. 500:** From *Harper's Weekly,* June 23, 1866, Courtesy of the Newberry Library, Chicago.   **P. 501:** Rutherford B. Hayes Presidential Center, Spiegel Grove, Freemont, OH.   **P. 504:** Collection Tennessee State Museum. Photo by Karina McDaniel. Courtesy Tennessee State Library & Archives, Nashville, TN.   **P. 507:** Brown Brothers.   **P. 510:** Historical Pictures/Stock Montage, Inc.   **P. 513:** *Frank Leslie's Illustrated Newspaper,* Sept. 23, 1876. Courtesy of the Newberry Library, Chicago.

Chapter 17   P. 518: Courtesy of the New-York Historical Society, Bella C. Landauer Collection.   **P. 521:** America Hurrah, New York City.   **P. 523:** North Wind Pictures.   **P. 524:** Culver Pictures.   **P. 525:** Buffalo Bill Historical Center, Cody, WY. Gift of the Coe Foundation.   **P. 526:** Culver Pictures.   **P. 527:** The Kansas State Historical Society, Topeka.   **P. 529:** Library of Congress.   **P. 532:** Archives & Manuscript Division of the Oklahoma Historical Society.   **P. 533:** Smithsonian Institution, Photo no. 3200-b-8 (National Anthropological Archives)   **P. 536:** The Huntington Library, San Marino, CA.   **P. 538:** Courtesy of the Thomas Gilcrease Institute of American History and Art, Tulsa, OK.   **P. 540:** Bancroft Library, University of California, Berkeley.   **P. 541:** William Hahn, *Market Scene, Sansome Street,* 1872, Oil on canvas, 60 in. × 96 in., Crocker Collection, Crocker Art Museum, Sacramento, CA.   **P. 543:** Yosemite National Park Research Library, Yosemite National Park, CA.   **P. 545:** Denver Public Library, Western History Division. Photo by Charles Redmond.

Chapter 18   P. 550: Chicago Historical Society.   **P. 553:** Historical Pictures/Stock Montage, Inc.   **Pp. 555 and 558:** Culver Pictures.   **P. 562:** National Museum of American History, Smithsonian Institution.   **P. 564:** *Harper's Weekly,* vol. 31, 1887, pp. 158–159, Courtesy of the Newberry Library, Chicago.   **P. 567 (top):** Thomas Anshutz, *The Ironworkers Noontime,* 1880. The Fine Arts Museums of San Francisco, Gift of Mr. and Mrs. John D. Rockefeller 3rd, 1979.7.4.   **P. 567 (bottom):** International Museum of Photography at George Eastman House, Rochester, NY.   **P. 569:** Corbis-Bettmann.   **P. 571:** Library of Congress.   **P. 572:** Corbis-Bettmann.   **P. 575:** Library of Congress.   **P. 578:** The George Meany Memorial Archives. Negative # 91   **P. 579:** The Newberry Library.

Chapter 19   **P. 584:** Museum of American Political Life, University of Hartford, West Hartford, CT. Photo: Sally Andersen-Bruce. **P. 586:** Culver Pictures. **P. 589:** Brown Brothers. **P. 591:** Museum of American Political Life, University of Hartford, West Hartford, CT. Photo: Sally Andersen-Bruce. **P. 593:** From the collection of the Newport Historical Society, Newport, RI (P292). **P. 594:** The Kansas State Historical Society, Topeka. **P. 596:** Courtesy Northwestern University Archives/Photograph by Alexander Hesler. **P. 597:** Brown Brothers. **P. 598:** The Kansas State Historical Society, Topeka. **P. 601:** Culver Pictures. **P. 602:** Collection of the New-York Historical Society. **P. 604:** Museum of American Political Life, University of Hartford, West Hartford, CT. Photo: Steven Laschever. **P. 608:** Library of Congress. **P. 610:** General Research Division, New York Public Library, Astor, Lenox and Tilden Foundations.

Chapter 20   **P. 614:** Theodore Groll, *Washington Street, Indianapolis at Dusk*, 1892–1895, Indianapolis Museum of Art, Gift of a Couple of Old Hoosiers. **P. 619** (top): Corbis-Bettmann. **P. 619** (bottom): Andrew Smith Gallery/KEA. **P. 620:** Museum of the City of New York, Gift of Louis Stearns, 1889–1914. **P. 624:** Andrew Smith Gallery/KEA. **P. 625:** New York Public Library, Astor, Lenox, and Tilden Foundations. **P. 628:** Culver Pictures. **P. 629:** W. Louis Sonntag, Jr., *The Bowery at Night*, 1895, Museum of the City of New York, Gift of Mrs. William B. Miles. **P. 631:** Archives of Industrial Society, University Library System, University of Pittsburgh. **P. 632:** Local History and Genealogy Division, New York Public Library, Astor, Lenox and Tilden Foundations. **P. 634:** Culver Pictures. **P. 635** (top): Historical Pictures/Stock Montage, Inc. **P. 635** (bottom): Brown Brothers. **P. 637:** The Preservation Society of Newport County, Newport, RI. **P. 639:** Courtesy of the Cincinnati Historical Society. **P. 640:** Museum of the City of New York, Byron Collection. **P. 641:** John Singer Sargent, *Mr. and Mrs. Isaac Newton Phelps Stokes*, 1897. Oil on canvas, 84¼″ × 39¾″. The Metropolitan Museum of Art, New York. Bequest of Edith Minturn Phelps Stokes (Mrs. I.N.), 1938 (38.104).

Chapter 21   **P. 646:** George Wesley Bellows, *Cliff Dwellers*, 1913. Oil on canvas. 39½″ × 41½″. Los Angeles County Museum of Art, Los Angeles County Fund. **P. 650** (left): Ida M. Tarbell Collection, Reis Library, Allegheny College, Meadville, PA. **P. 650** (right): Culver Pictures. **P. 652:** State Historical Society of Wisconsin, Madison. **P. 653:** Courtesy NAACP National Headquarters. **P. 654:** Schlesinger Library, Radcliffe College, Cambridge, MA. **P. 656:** Chicago Historical Society. **P. 657:** Brown Brothers. **P. 658:** Corbis-Bettmann. **P. 659:** Brown Brothers. **P. 666:** Library of Congress. **P. 667:** Edward Steichen, *J. Pierpont Morgan*, 1903, Plate V from the boxed edition deluxe of the Steichen supplement to *Camera Work*, April 1906. Published simultaneously with XIV April 1906. Gravure, 8⅛ in. × 6¼ in. Collection, The Museum of Modern Art, New York. Gift of A. Conger Goodyear. **P. 668:** Library of Congress. **P. 671:** Woodrow Wilson-Democratic Nominee For President, *Harper's Weekly*, 7/13/12, Courtesy the Newberry Library, Chicago.

Chapter 22   **P. 676:** James G. Tyler, *Battle of Santiago de Cuba*, 1898, Courtesy Franklin D. Roosevelt Library (#CT79-66(2)). **P. 679:** Hawaii State Archives. **P. 680:** Courtesy of the New-York Historical Society, Bella C. Landauer Collection. **P. 682:** Culver Pictures. **P. 683:** U.S. Naval Historical Center, Washington, D.C. **P. 687:** Archive Photos. **P. 688:** *Destruction of the U.S. Battleship Maine in Havana Harbor, Feb. 15, 1898*. Kurz & Allison Chromolith, Chicago Historical Society. **P. 690:** Library of Congress. **P. 693** (top): National Archives. **P. 693** (bottom): G.W. Peters in *Harper's Weekly*, April 22, 1899, Courtesy of the Newberry Library, Chicago. **P. 694:** Joseph Keppler, Jr., *His 126th Birthday–Gee, but this is an awful stretch!*, from *Puck*, June 29, 1904, Courtesy of the Newberry Library, Chicago. **P. 697:** UPI/Corbis-Bettmann. **P. 700:** The Pat Hathaway Collection of California Views. **P. 702:** Aultman Collection, El Paso Public Library.

Chapter 23   **P. 708:** The Lester Levy Collection of Sheet Music. Milton S. Eisenhower Library. The Johns Hopkins University, Baltimore, MD. *Oh, How I Hate to Get Up in the Morning* © 1918 by Irving Berlin; © renewed 1945 by Irving Berlin; © assigned to Trustees of God Bless America Fund **P. 710:** Imperial War Museum, London. **P. 713:** Corbis-Bettmann. **P. 714:** UPI/Corbis-Bettmann. **P. 715:** Library of Congress. **P. 719:** Corbis-Bettmann. **Pp. 720 and 721:** UPI/Corbis-Bettmann. **P. 724:** National Archives, photo by M. Rudolph Vetter. **P. 725:** Schlesinger Library, Radcliffe College, Cambridge, MA. **P. 727:** Library of Congress. **P. 728:** Historical Pictures/Stock Montage, Inc. **P. 730:** William Orpen, *The Signing of the Peace in the Hall of Mirrors, Versailles, June 1919*, Imperial War Museum, London. **P. 732**(all): Chicago Historical Society, photo by Jun Fujita. **P. 735:** Ben Shahn. *Bartolomeo Vanzetti and Nicola Sacco*, from the Sacco-Vanzetti series of twenty-three paintings (1931–32). Tempera on paper over composition board, 10½″ × 14½″ (26.7 cm x 36.8 cm). The Museum of Modern Art, New York. Gift of Abby Aldrich Rockefeller. Photograph © 1996 The Museum of Modern Art, New York.

Chapter 24   **P. 738:** Mazda, General Electric, Courtesy Dartmouth College, Baker Library, Hanover, NH. Photo: © 1992 Jeffrey Nintzel. All rights reserved. **P. 740:** Brown Brothers. **P. 742:** Museum of American Political Life, University of Hartford, West Hartford, CT. Photo: Steven Laschever. **P. 744:** Charles Sheeler, *Untitled (River Rouge Plant)*, 1927, University Art Museum, University of New Mexico, Albuquerque. Gift of Eleanor and Van Deren Coke. **P. 748:** *Portrait of Luisa Ronstadt Espinel*, c. 1921, Arizona Historical Society Library. Gift of Edward Ronstadt, Mexican Heritage Project. **P. 749:** Florine Stettheimer, *Portrait of My Sister Ettie*, 1923. Columbia University in the City of New York, Gift of the Estate of Ettie Stettheimer, 1967. Photo: Gregory W. Schmitz, NYC. **P. 750:** Corbis-Bettmann. **P. 751:** Globe Photos. **P. 752:** Photofest. **P. 753:** Courtesy Christopher Casler. **P. 754:** Kansas City Museum, Kansas City, Missouri. **P. 755:** George Bellows, *Dempsey and Firpo*, 1924, Oil on canvas, 51 in. × 63¼ in., Whitney Museum of American Art, New York City. Purchased with funds from Gertrude Vanderbilt. Whitney 31.95. Photo by Geoffrey Clements. **P. 760:** W.A. Swift Collection, Archives & Special Collections, A.M. Bracken Library, Ball State University, Muncie, IN. **P. 761:** John Sloan, *The Lafayette*, 1928, Oil on canvas, 30½ × 36¼ in., The Metropolitan Museum of Art, New York. Gift of Friends of John Sloan, 1928 (28.18). **P. 763:** Henry Lee Moon Library and Civil Rights Archive, NAACP, Washington, D.C.

Chapter 25   **P. 768:** Alexandre Hogue. *Drought-Stricken Area*, 1934. Oil on canvas. 30″ × 42¼″. Dallas Museum of Art, Dallas Art Association Purchase, 1945.6. **P. 770:** UPI/Corbis-Bettmann. **P. 773:** Isaac Soyer, *Employment Agency*. 1937. Oil on canvas, 34¼″ × 45″. Whitney Museum of American Art, New York. Purchase 37.44. Photograph by Geoffrey Clements. **P. 774:** Franklin D. Roosevelt Library, Hyde Park, NY. **P. 778:** UPI/Corbis-Bettmann. **P. 779** (both): Courtesy of Steve Schapiro. **P. 780:** Corbis-Bettmann. **P. 782** (top): UPI/Corbis-Bettmann. **P. 782** (bottom): Schomburg Center for Research in Black Culture, The New York Public Library. Astor, Lenox, and Tilden Foundations. **P. 783:** UPI/Corbis-Bettmann. **P. 786:** Library of Congress. **P. 787:** University of Texas, The Institute of Texan Cultures, *San Antonio Light* Collection. **P. 789:** Courtesy Bert Corona. **P. 791:** Corbis-Bettmann.

Chapter 26   **P. 796:** Mitchell Wolfson, Jr. Collection, The Wolfsonian, Miami Beach, Florida and Genoa, Italy. **P. 798:** AP/World Wide Photos. **P. 799:** Library of Congress. **P. 801:** Courtesy *Vanity Fair* © 1935 (renewed 1963) by The Condé Nast Publications, Inc. **Pp. 802 and 803:** UPI/Corbis-Bettmann. **P. 804:** Library of Con-

Copyright Notices

Chapter 2 **P. 40:** G. P. Hammond and Agapito Rey, *Don Juan de Oñate, Colonizer of New Mexico, 1595–1628.* Copyright 1953 University of New Mexico Press. Reprinted by permission.

Chapter 4 **P. 113:** Reprinted by permission of the publishers from *Journey to Pennsylvania* by Gottlieb Mittelberger, edited and translated by Oscar Handlin and John Clive, Cambridge, Mass.:Harvard University Press, Copyright © 1960 by the President and Fellows of Harvard College.

Chapter 5 **P. 150:** Reprinted from *The Letterbook of Eliza Lucas Pinckney, 1739–1762*, ed. Elise Pinckney and Marvin R. Zahniser. Courtesy of the South Carolina Historical Society.

Chapter 7 **P. 199:** Jackson Turner Main, "Government by the People: The American Revolution and the Democratization of the Legislatures," *William and Mary Quarterly*, 3d Ser., 23 (1966). Reprinted by permission of the Institute of Early American History and Culture.

Chapter 8 **Pp. 243, 257; Chapter 9 P. 279:** Excerpts from *Sources of the American Social Tradition*, edited by David J. Rothman and Sheila M. Rothman. Copyright © 1975 by David J. Rothman. Reprinted by permission of BasicBooks, a division of HarperCollins Publishers, Inc.

Chapter 13 **P. 387:** C. Vann Woodward, *Mary Chesnut's Civil War*. Copyright © 1981 by Yale University Press. Reprinted by permission of Yale University Press.

Chapter 14 **P. 418:** Joseph E. Chance, ed., *The Mexican War Journal of Captain Frank Smith*. Reprinted by permission of University Press of Mississippi.

Chapter 15 **P. 453:** "Figure: Economies, North and South, 1860" from *The Reinterpretation of American Economic History* by Robert W. Fogel and Stanley L. Engerman. Copyright © 1971 by Harper & Row Publishers, Inc. Reprinted by permission of HarperCollins Publishers, Inc. **P. 468:** Excerpts from W. Maury Darst, "The Vicksburg Diary of Mrs. Alfred Ingraham," reprinted courtesy *Journal of Mississippi History*. **P.475:** From *All for the Union* by Robert Hunt Rhodes. Copyright © 1991 by Robert Hunt Rhodes. Reprinted by permission of Crown Publishers, Inc.

Chapter 17 **P. 528:** H. Arnold Barton, ed. *Letters from the Promised Land*. Copyright © 1975 by the University of Minnesota Press. Reprinted by permission of the University of Minnesota Press. **P. 534:** Reprinted from *Black Elk Speaks*, by John G. Neihardt, by permission of the University of Nebraska Press. Copyright 1932, 1959, 1972, by John Neihardt. Copyright © 1961 by the John G. Neihardt Trust. **P. 547:** Table from *The Nation Transformed* by Sigmund Diamond, ed. Copyright © 1963 by Sigmund Diamond. Reprinted by permission of George Braziller, Inc.

Chapter 18 **P. 565:** Table: "Comparison of South and Non-South Value-Added per Worker, 1910" from *Old South, New South: Revolutions in the Southern Economy Since the Civil War* by Gavin Wright. Copyright © 1987 by BasicBooks, Inc. Reprinted by permission of Basic Books, a division of HarperCollins Publishers, Inc.

Chapter 21 **P. 651:** Reprinted with the permission of Scribner, an imprint of Simon & Schuster from *Bare Hands and Stone Walls* by Charles Edward Russell. Copyright 1933 Charles Edward Russell; copyright renewed © 1961 Charles Edward Russell. **P. 660:** Joan Morrison and Charlotte Fox Zabusky, eds., *American Mosaic: The Immigrant Experience in the Words of Those Who Lived It*. Copyright © 1980, Joan Morrison and Charlotte Fox Zabusky. Currently available from the University of Pittsburgh Press.

Chapter 22 **P. 691:** Reprinted by permission of the University of Arkansas Press from *"Smoked Yankees"* by Willard B. Gatewood © 1987.

Chapter 23 **P. 717:** Frederick A. Pottle, *Stretchers: The Story of a Hospital Unit on the Western Front*. Copyright (1929) by Yale University Press. Reprinted by permission.

Chapter 24 **P. 759:** Reprinted with the permission of Simon & Schuster from *The Aspirin Age* by Isabel Leighton. Copyright © 1949 by Simon & Schuster. Copyright renewed 1976 by Simon & Schuster.

Chapter 25 **P. 785:** Reprinted from *Dust Bowl Diary*, by Ann Marie Low, by permission of the University of Nebraska Press. Copyright 1984 by the University of Nebraska Press. **P. 791:** Robert S. McElvaine, ed., *Down and Out in the Great Depression: Letters from the Forgotten Man*. Copyright © 1983 by the University of North Carolina Press. Reprinted by permission of the publisher.

Chapter 26 **P. 811:** Excerpts from *You Must Remember This, An Oral History of Manhattan from the 1890's to World War II*, copyright © 1989 by Jeff Kisseloff, reprinted by permission of Harcourt Brace & Company. **P. 814:** From *Making Do: How Women Survived the 30's* by Jeane Westin. Copyright ©1976 Jeane Westin. All rights reserved. **P. 821:** Selections from *Red Ribbons on a White Horse* by Anzia Yezierska, copyright © 1950 by Anzia Yezierska, renewed 1978 by Louise Levitas Henriksen. Reprinted by permission of Persea Books, Inc.

Chapter 27 **P. 839:** Excerpted with permission of Twayne Publishers, an imprint of Simon & Schuster Macmillan, from *Rosie the Riveter Revisited: Women, the War, and Social Change* by Sherna Berger Gluck. Copyright © 1987 by Sherna Berger Gluck. **Pp. 847, 852:** From *The Good War* by Studs Terkel. Copyright © 1984 by Studs Terkel. Reprinted by permission of Pantheon Books, a division of Random House, Inc.

Chapter 28 **P. 879:** From *Red Scare: Memories of the American Inquisition, An Oral History* by Griffin Fariello. Copyright © 1995 by Griffin Fariello. Reprinted by permission of W. W. Norton & Company, Inc. **P. 889:** From *Facing the Danger* by Sam Totten and Martha Wescoat Totten, © 1984, The Crossing Press.

Chapter 29 **P. 909:** Reprinted with the permission of Simon & Schuster from *Manchild in the Promised Land* by Claude Brown. Copyright © 1965 by Claude Brown. **P. 917:** Selected excerpts from *The Fifties: A Women's Oral History* by Brett Harvey. Copyright © 1993 by Brett Harvey. Reprinted by permission of HarperCollins Publishers, Inc.

Chapter 30 **P. 939:** Reprinted by permission of The Putnam Publishing Group from *My Soul Is Rested* by Howell Raines. Copyright © 1977 by Howell Raines. **P. 952:** Reprinted by permission of Grove Atlantic, Inc.

Chapter 31 **P. 964:** Figure from George Donelson Moss, *Vietnam: An American Ordeal*, 2d ed., © 1994 p. 415. Adapted by permission of Prentice Hall, Upper Saddle River, New Jersey. **P. 976:** Reprinted by permission of Stephen D. Lerner.

Chapter 32 **P. 1009:** From *Voices of Freedom* by Henry Hampton and Steve Fayer. Copyright © 1990 by Blackside, Inc. Used by permission of Bantam Books, a division of Bantam Doubleday Dell Publishing Group, Inc.

Index

Political divisions as of September 1996